D1615531

TRADE MARKS
AND
TRADE NAMES

AUSTRALIA
Law Book Co—Sydney

CANADA
Carswell—Toronto

HONG KONG
Sweet & Maxwell Asia

NEW ZEALAND
Brookers—Wellington

SINGAPORE and **MALAYSIA**
Sweet & Maxwell Asia
Singapore and Kuala Lumpur

KERLY'S

LAW OF

TRADE MARKS

AND TRADE NAMES

FOURTEENTH EDITION

By

DAVID KITCHIN
One of Her Majesty's Counsel, 8 New Square

DAVID LLEWELYN
Solicitor, Partner, White & Case, London

JAMES MELLOR
Barrister, 8 New Square

RICHARD MEADE
Barrister, 8 New Square

THOMAS MOODY-STUART
Barrister, 8 New Square

DAVID KEELING
Member, Second Board of Appeal, OHIM

Consulting Editor

The Rt. Hon. Sir Robin Jacob

LONDON
SWEET & MAXWELL
2005

First Edition	(1894) By D. M. Kerly
Second Edition	(1901) By D. M. Kerly
Third Edition	(1908) By D. M. Kerly
Fourth Edition	(1913) By F. G. Underhay
Fifth Edition	(1923) By F. G. Underhay
Sixth Edition	(1927) By F. G. Underhay
Seventh Edition	(1951) By R. G. Loyd and F. E. Bray
Eighth Edition	(1960) By R. G. Loyd
Ninth Edition	(1966) By T. A. Blanco White
Tenth Edition	(1972) By T. A. Blanco White and Robin Jacob
Eleventh Edition	(1983) By T. A. Blanco White and Robin Jacob
Twelth Edition	(1986) By T. A. Blanco White and Robin Jacob
Thirteenth Edition	(2001) By D. Kitchin, D. Llewelyn, J. Mellor, R. Meade and T. Moody-Stuart
Fourteenth Edition	(2005) By D. Kitchin, D. Llewelyn, J. Mellor, R. Meade and T. Moody-Stuart and D. Keeling

Published in 2005 by
Sweet & Maxwell Limited of
100 Avenue Road
London NW3 3PF

Typeset by LBJ Typesetting Ltd of Kingsclere
Printed and Bound in Great Britain
by William Clowes Ltd, Beccles, Suffolk

No natural forests were destroyed
to make this product, only farmed
timber was used and replanted.

ISBN 0421—86080—4

A CIP catalogue record for this book
is available from the British Library.

FOREWORD

Just 111 years after its first publication in 1894, it is a pleasure to welcome this new, fourteenth and much revised edition of one of the classic textbooks of English law. *Kerly* has been for generations a mainstay of trade mark practitioners, and as a classic it combines the best of the old and the new. In particular, it is now not only a book on English law, but a book on European law.

The Trade Marks Act 1994, and the corresponding legislation in the other 24 Member States of the European Union, are in large part designed to implement the European Trade Marks Directive, and the legislation has to be understood in the light of that Directive. Although entitled the First Council Directive to approximate the laws of the Member States relating to trade marks, it is by no means merely a first step in the harmonisation of trade mark law; on the contrary, it provides rather complete harmonisation of the laws of the Member States on many of the basic features of trade mark law. Thus it lays down, among other things, the essential provisions governing the nature of a trade mark; the grounds for refusal or invalidity; the rights conferred by a trade mark; and the conditions governing the exhaustion of rights.

Courts and practitioners will therefore take an approach to the UK legislation which differs from their traditional approach and reflects the European source of the legislation. Often, indeed, as the courts have increasingly recognised, it is best to go straight to the Directive, rather than to the implementing provisions which are, at best, only a reflection of the original.

Alongside the Directive, the Community Trade Mark Regulation, whose terms often mirror those of the Directive, provides for a Community trade mark effective throughout the European Union. Decisions under the Regulation are taken by the Community Trade Mark Office ("OHIM") in Alicante, with appeal from the Boards of Appeal there to the European Court of First Instance and in the last resort to the European Court of Justice; but issues under the Regulation may also come before national courts.

The Directive and the Regulation are broadly framed, and will often call for interpretation—where necessary, by way of a reference from the national court to the Court of Justice. Under Article 234 (formerly 177) of the EC Treaty, wherever a decision on a question of Community law is necessary to enable it to give judgment, any national court may, and a court of last instance must, refer the question to the Court of Justice, whose case-law is binding on national courts.

The Court applies principles of interpretation which may differ from those of national law and from those traditionally applied by English courts. It will have regard to the purposes of the legislation, to the preamble (which may be lost sight of when the substantive provisions are transposed into national legislation) and to the context—including various international instruments. It may also have regard if necessary to the different language versions of the Community texts: although that technique of interpretation seems increasingly implausible as more languages—currently 20—are deemed to be equally authentic.

As national courts have recognised, the Court of Justice is best placed to resolve points of principle in the interpretation of Community texts. Moreover its rulings, since they are binding on all national courts, will have the effect of maintaining the unity of the law.

Already the Court has ruled on numerous fundamental aspects of the Community legislation. Full account is given in this book of the Court's case-law—rightly, in view of its binding character; and the authors are willing to examine the implications of the case-law and how it might develop.

Some aspects of the case-law have been criticised—not least by English practitioners, and occasionally even by English judges. This is hardly surprising (have the decisions of any court on any important topic ever escaped criticism?), and I do not seek here to defend the case-law "globally"—although I must record that in many encounters with practitioners and judges across Europe, I have found a high level of appreciation for the main lines of the case-law.

This book reflects a steep learning curve in trade mark law and practice, even since the last edition in 2001.

National courts and practitioners are still adjusting to the European dimension, and recognising that past practice of national systems may have to be reconsidered. For their part, the European Court of Justice and the Court of First Instance are still confronting new issues of trade mark law, and are still learning from experience of, and reaction to, issues already handled. It is right to recognise, as does Chapter 1, that since the last edition of this work there has been substantial progress in resolving many of the moot points in the regime, but that there remain areas where criticism is both justified and necessary.

This edition also has benefited from much revision: fundamental issues have been rethought and the presentation is restructured. Reflecting more fully, as it now does, the European sources of trade mark law, while raising questions where appropriate about the direction of that law, this book will be an invaluable source for judges and practitioners not only in the United Kingdom but throughout the European Union.

Francis G. Jacobs
Advocate General
Court of Justice of the European Communities

PREFACE

Kerly is now 111 years' old. Until the advent of the new EU law of trade marks in 1994, 99 years on from the first edition, not a lot really happened in UK trade mark law. There had been a few Acts, liberalising the law here and there (*e.g.* as to licensing and as to the kind of mark which could be registered) but the law was basically the same—one could still refer to and rely on old cases for many aspects. Trade mark litigation involving any issue of law was rare—people knew where they were without having to ask a judge. Since the war (I haven't counted them) I do not suppose there were more than 10 cases which went to the House of Lords.

The Directive of 1989 and its subsequent implementation changed all that. Trade mark law has become much more complicated, and, I am afraid to say, much more uncertain. Although it has never been possible to say exactly what a trade mark is or what it is for, it was possible to approximate towards it. Einstein once said that physics consisted of a series of approximations towards the truth. The same was somewhat true of the legal meaning of trade mark which developed under the old law—it became more precise without every actually achieving precision. Now we have moved back a lot, as the splendid discussion in Chapter 2 shows.

As I observed in an earlier Preface, the Directive seems to have been written on the basis that there were no lessons to be learned from history. All the experience of trade mark problems learned in the Member States over the previous 100 years or so was ignored. So the Court of Justice had to start from scratch—using a document which did not itself provide clear answers to any of the well-known problems (*e.g.* fundamentally, must a defendant be using the mark complained of as a trade mark, what is meant by "distinctive", what amounts to use and so on). The mass of cases in the last 11 years (by way of reference and appeal from OHIM) proves the uncertainty of the Directive itself. But it also shows the Court itself has no clear views of trade mark law—look for instance at the *Chiemsee, Baby Dry, Doublemint* and *Sat.2* series of cases discussed in Chapter 8.

Unfortunately, despite all the cases the clear impression one has is that things are less certain now then before. All too often the rulings of the ECJ in this area of law (I find the contrast, with, *e.g.* VAT where the rulings are pretty clear, remarkable) are not sufficiently precise for the needs of industry. A trade mark is a guarantee of origin? Yes but infringed if used on imports unless there is express permission; yes, but infringed if a notice of intention to parallel import from within the EU is given in time? And how can a mere colour ever really alone guarantee origin? What is the point of protecting a part of an advertising slogan? And is that really a guarantee of origin?

I do not know the reasons for the less-than-perfect guidance coming from the ECJ. Part of it is undoubtedly the fact that the Judges are not trade mark specialists and trade mark law is unexpectedly full of pitfalls, inherent ambiguities and complex concepts. Part of it may be that it is very difficult without experience to take a holistic approach (for instance what counts as use for infringement should be the same as that which counts as use for the purpose of validity). Whatever the reason, the authors of a textbook on the subject are faced with a mass of cases, parts of which are inconsistent with others. The authors have to strive to set out that which is reasonably certain, discuss the problems and identify uncertainties and give sound opinion where that is possible. These authors have done that to a remarkable degree. This is a thoughtful edition of *Kerly*.

What has become even clearer is that the UK legislation has not been a helpful way of implementing the Directive. I remain at a loss to understand why, when a Directive is specific (as it is here) our legislators even begin to think it a useful exercise to try to re-write it or renumber it. *Kerly* has criticised this—and it is becoming customary in the courts to ignore the bits of the UK Act which are supposed to implement the Directive. One just goes straight to the Directive. In that connection I remain baffled by the recent amendment to the Act which is supposed to bring it in line with the interpretation of Art.5(2) of the Directive in *Adidas/Fitness World.* Whatever was the point? The language of our Act before amendment tracked the Directive—so our courts would follow the interpretation given by the ECJ anyway. If every time the ECJ interpreted a Directive we adjusted our implementing legislation (whether by Act of Parliament or Regulation under s.2 of the European Communities Act 1972) we would all go mad. And what if the ECJ changes its mind or qualifies its interpretation?It would be helpful if those responsible for UK trade mark legislation read *Kerly* and focussed on what really matters.

This is also a more rounded edition than last time. For however good its discussion of substantive law may be, a practical textbook must also explain how the system(s) implementing the law actually work—law does not exist in a vacuum, it depends on procedure for life. That is particularly true of a commercial subject such as trade mark law. *Kerly* recognises this—and so this edition not only has an explanation of procedure before the English courts, but also, for the first time, a valuable explanation of how things work in OHIM. The addition of David Keeling to the team of editors to deal with this was a masterful idea.You need someone who knows how a system works to write about it—no-one can understand legal procedure by reading rules, just as no-one could understand chess by simply understanding the rules—to understand that a knight moves 2,1 is not to understand what a knight does. David Keeling's contribution has made *Kerly* a more valuable book indeed.

Finally it will be noted that I am described as "Consulting Editor".No-one should assume that I have put any actual work into this edition—I am not entitled to any of the credit due to the masterful work of the actual authors. I am just proud to be associated with it.

Robin Jacob
Royal Courts of Justice
August 2005

CONTENTS

APPENDICES

TABLE OF CASES

TABLE OF STATUTES

TABLE OF STATUTORY INSTRUMENTS

TABLE OF EUROPEAN LEGISLATION

TABLE OF INTERNATIONAL CONVENTIONS
AND TREATIES

PART 1

CHAPTER 1

INTRODUCTION

It is now more than 10 years since the Trade Marks Act 1994 ("the Act") came into force and nearly 10 years since the Office for the Harmonisation of the Internal Market ("OHIM") opened its doors for receipt of applications for a Community Trade Mark under Council Regulation 40/94 ("the Regulation"). The last edition of this work described the fundamental changes in registered trade mark law in the United Kingdom wrought by the Act and the Regulation and anticipated how some of the myriad of issues raised by the new system might be resolved. This edition explains, and where appropriate criticises, how certain of those issues have been clarified either by the courts in this country or at European level by the European Court of Justice ("ECJ"), Court of First Instance ("CFI") or OHIM Boards of Appeal.

The principal basis for the Act is the 1988Council Directive relating to trade marks ("the Trade Marks Directive") and it is to the wording of the provisions of that Trade Marks Directive that the English courts have paid attention where those words have been interpreted or changed in those of the Act (or indeed even where they are the same but with different numbering, "to make this judgment more intelligible to a reader in another EU country", *per* Jacob L.J. in *Reed Executive v Reed Business Information*).[1]

1. The origins of the Trade Marks Directive

The Trade Marks Directive is "The First Council Directive of 21 December 1988 to approximate the laws of the Member States relating to trade marks"; "The First" indicating that approximation is not complete (although as time passes it is becoming increasingly unlikely that further approximation will be effected through additional directives on the subject.) The third recital to the Directive says:

> "… it does not appear to be necessary at present to undertake full-scale approximation of the trade marks laws of the Member States and it will be sufficient if approximation is limited to those national provisions of law which most directly affect the functioning of the internal market".

The first proposal for "a first Council Directive to approximate the law of the Member States relating to trade marks" was published in November 1980.[2] It coincided with a proposal for the Community Trade Mark. The proposed Directive was seen as a necessary step to pave the way for the establishment of a Community Trade Mark system. The proposal was submitted to the Economic and Social Committee for its opinion[3] which resulted in a revised proposal being

1–001

1–002

1–003

1–004

---

[1] [2004] R.P.C. 767, CA, at para.19.
[2] see the Explanatory Memorandum, COM (80) 635 final, and the first draft of the Directive, December 31, 1980: [1980] O.J. C 351/1.
[3] [1981] O.J. C 310/22.

submitted to the Council in December 1985.[4] This revised text was submitted to the Working Group and a new text was published in December 1987.

The Council approved the new text[5] in June 1988, the advice of the Economic and Social Committee was received in October 1988, the European Parliament gave its opinion in December 1988;[6] and the Trade Marks Directive was finally adopted by the Council on December 21, 1988.[7]

2. Statutory interpretation

1–005 At the meeting of the Council at which the Directive was adopted, certain statements were made by the Council and the Commission which were entered into the Minutes of the Council. The Minutes have subsequently become available and are accessible on the website of OHIM. Although of historical interest, it is clear that the Minutes (which consist of various comments on a number of the Articles in the Directive) are of no legal significance and cannot be used for the purpose of interpreting legislation as no reference is made to them in the wording of the Directive.[8]

1–006 Quite apart from matters European, the standard rules in *Pepper (Inspector of Taxes) v Hart*[9] apply to the Parliamentary debates during passage of the Trade Marks Bill. It should be noted that the rule in *Pepper (Inspector of Taxes) v Hart* operates by way of an exception to the general rule that excludes reference to Parliamentary material as an aid to statutory construction. Reference is permitted under *Pepper (Inspector of Taxes) v Hart* if: (1) legislation was ambiguous or obscure or led to absurdity; (2) the material relied upon consisted of one or more statements by a Minister or other promoter of the Bill together, if necessary, with such other Parliamentary material that is necessary to understand such statements and their effect; and (3) the statements relied upon were clear.

1–007 However, the Parliamentary debates on the Bill do not provide much fruit to aid interpretation of provisions in Part I of the Act, for the simple reason that the Government resisted and secured the defeat or withdrawal of all amendments which altered wording derived from the Trade Marks Directive, by saying that they were obliged to implement the Directive. Thus:

> "in the case of a provision intended to implement a Directive I cannot think that the Pepper principle can apply. The intention of Parliament is to implement whatever the Directive means. Views expressed in Parliament about the meaning, even by a Minister, cannot assist in resolving any ambiguity which stems from the Directive itself. Neither the courts of any other country whose trade mark laws are supposed to implement the Directive, or the European Court of Justice in interpreting it, would refer to what a British Minister said in Parliament in the course of implementation here. It would be irrelevant. What matters is the language of the Directive",

per Jacob J. (as he then was) in the "Treat" case.[10] For that reason, judges have preferred to take the wording of the Trade Marks Directive rather than the form of its implementation in the Act where different.

---

[4] [1985] O.J. C 251/4.
[5] In EU parlance "adopted a common position".
[6] [1988] O.J. C 309.
[7] [1989] O.J. L 40/1. See App.7.
[8] *R. v Immigration Appeal Tribunal Ex p. Antonissen* [1991] 2 C.M.L.R. 373, ECJ.
[9] [1993] A.C. 593.
[10] [1996] R.P.C. 281 at 292. Of course, were the issue the interpretation of the words of the Act, due

Indeed, even where the provisions of the Act are not derived from the Trade Marks Directive, such as the criminal provisions contained in s.92, they too must be interpreted as far as possible to give effect to the Directive.[11]

3. Community trade mark

The 1993 Council Regulation introducing the Community Trade Mark (CTM) has meant that since April 1996 it has been possible to obtain a registered trade mark with effect in the United Kingdom by two different routes. The first is the traditional route to the Trade Marks Registry in Newport[12] (which may be made via Geneva—see below); the second is via an application to OHIM in Alicante, Spain. If satisfied that the mark complies with the conditions for registrability set out in the Regulation, OHIM grants an EU-wide right with effect in the United Kingdom as well as all other 24 Member States. Thus, the two systems run in parallel and are connected intimately. Details of the procedural aspects of the CTM system, including the consequences of the enlargement of the EU in May 2004, are set out in Ch.6 and substantive issues concerning CTMs are dealt with in Chs 2, 8, 9, 10 12, 13, 14 and 17. Where they occur, differences in the approaches to particular issues taken in the UK and in OHIM or the CFI are explained and commented upon.

1–008

4. Madrid Protocol

A registered trade mark with effect in the United Kingdom and in the EU may be also obtained via the mechanism provided in the Madrid Protocol.[13] Under the Protocol an applicant for a so-called "international registration" must file through the national trade marks office or OHIM in which a base national or CTM application or registration has been made. That office then transmits the application to WIPO in Geneva and thereafter the mark is sent to and treated by the individual national offices specified as if it is a normal domestic application. Effectively, the Protocol provides a means of obtaining registrations in a large number of signatory countries at less cost and inconvenience than if applications were filed in each country separately. The details (including those introduced by the link between the Protocol and the CTM system) are set out in Ch.7.

1–009

5. Paris Convention

For the first time, the 1994 Act provides specific protection for "well-known marks" within the meaning of Article 6*bis* of the Paris Convention. The protection conferred is independent of the rights conferred by registration and applies to marks falling within Art.6*bis* regardless of whether they are registered in the United Kingdom or not. Other provisions specifically implementing parts of the Paris Convention include the injunctive remedy, based on Art.6*septies*, for a proprietor of a mark against unauthorised use in the United Kingdom by his agent. Although little used to date, the details of how the Act gives effect to certain provisions of the Paris Convention are set out in the relevant sections of this work.

1–010

---

to ambiguity, and the Directive left details to Member States, *Pepper v Hart* would apply to Ministerial statements: *South Central Trains v Christopher Rodway* [2005] EWCA Civ 443 at para.36.

[11] *per* Lord Nicholls of Birkenhead in *R. v Johnstone* [2003] F.S.R. 748, H.L. at para.29.

[12] Or through the branch offices.

[13] This is a Protocol to the Madrid Agreement 1891, which in turn is a specialised agreement under the Paris Convention 1883. The UK is not a party to the Madrid Agreement.

6. Old authorities

1–011   Whilst it is true that the Act (together with the Trade Marks Directive) provides a fresh start for the law of registered trade marks in the United Kingdom, "many of the basic concepts in the Directive appear to be the same as, or closely similar to, those which have informed the previous domestic law."[14] Every system for the registration of trade marks has to deal with the underlying concepts forming the foundation of such a system: concepts such as distinctiveness (see Ch.8); what is required for registration (see Chs 5, 6, 8 and 9); descriptiveness and what degree will prevent registration (see the critical analysis of the case-law in Ch.8); similarity between a registered mark and an allegedly infringing sign (see Ch.14). What a coherent trade mark system has to do when dealing with these (and other) concepts is to decide where the line is drawn: for example, what degree of distinctiveness or descriptiveness or similarity or confusion/risk of confusion is required (see Chs 8, 9 and 14 on the related analyses in registration and infringement cases)? It is in these areas, as well as many others, that reference to cases decided under previous Acts may be of some, limited, assistance, although obviously the extent of assistance given by such old cases is reduced as the *corpus* of cases decided under the new law increases in bulk (as is noted in Ch.8, on the Art.3(1)/Art.7(1) absolute grounds for refusal "a small mountain" has accumulated since the last edition). But, in all cases except those relating to remedies and procedural matters generally (as to which see Ch.19, which cites many old authorities), it will always be assistance only: it should not be forgotten at any point that the system is fundamentally different to that which went before and frequently demands a fresh look.

1–012   On the other hand, the forensic nature of the legal process in the United Kingdom requires a deep analysis of both the purpose and coherence of the system (see, for example, the discussion in Ch.2 of the meaning of "capable of distinguishing" and in Ch.14 on whether trade mark use is required for infringement). It is the words of the Act (and behind it the TM Directive) which must be interpreted and applied: as was noted by Laddie J. in *Wagamama*[15] if a fundamental change is intended it should be made clear, in extent and scope. The law remains a law of registered trade marks, it is not a law governing unfair competition and in applying and interpreting the provisions of the Act (and the TM Directive and the CTM Regulation, when relevant) the practitioner must always bear this in mind.

1–013   On the other hand, it cannot be ignored also that there remain around the Member States, and indeed between OHIM and trade mark offices in the Member States, not insignificant differences in approach to many issues and again these are commented upon where appropriate (see, for example, the explanation in Ch.8 of the German attitude to the registration as trade marks of the shapes of bottles; and in Chs 6 and 8 on the interpretation of "bad faith"). Notwithstanding these differences, it is fair to say that since the last edition of this work there has been substantial progress to resolving many of the moot points in the regime, although there remain areas where criticism is both justified and necessary (such as the weak judgments of the CFI commented upon in Ch.8.)

---

[14] *per* Lord Walker of Gestingthorpe in *R. v Johnstone* [2003] F.S.R. 748, H.L. at para.63.
[15] See para.9–045.

7. **Common law**

Other aspects of the legal treatment of unfair trading have changed in the years since the last edition and developments in areas such as passing off and trade libel are described and commented upon in Chs 15 and 18. In addition, to a large extent the chapters on passing off and trade libel have been re-written in a more modern format. **1–014**

8. **Procedure**

In recent years there has been a marked shift in the attitude of the courts away from the use of the interim injunction as the main tool for curtailing alleged trade mark infringements or passing off. This has been coupled with a streamlining of procedure and more pro-active judicial involvement to ensure a shortening of the time taken to litigate intellectual property disputes. In addition, the Civil Procedure Rules (CPRs) have now been in effect for more than six years, with the overriding objective of "enabling the courts to deal with cases justly".[16] The CPRs and their underlying objective have had significant impact on both High Court and Appointed Person proceedings involving trade marks and on proceedings in the Registry. They have moved procedure in the English courts in the direction of the civil law tradition, at least to the extent of making judges the managers of litigation through its various stages. **1–015**

Where relevant, the impact of these changes in procedure is identified and commented upon (particularly in Ch.9).

---

[16] CPR r.1.1.

CHAPTER 2

A "TRADE MARK" IN EU TRADE MARK LAW

INTRODUCTION

2–001 This Chapter deals with the meaning of the expression "trade mark". Any reader who is wondering why it is necessary to devote a whole chapter to this simple expression will, we hope, find the answer below. This Chapter is divided into the following sections:

1. The essential function of a trade mark
2. How to define a trade mark?
3. Does EU law define "trade mark"?
4. "Sign"
5. Graphical Representation
6. "Capable of Distinguishing" and "unravelling the skein"
7. "In relation to goods or services" & retail services
8. Annex: the derivation of the relevant provisions

2–002 The previous title of this Chapter ("The Definition of a Trade Mark") was prompted by the fact that s.1(1) of the Trade Marks Act 1994 contains what appears to be a definition of "trade mark" for the purposes of UK trade mark law. As we explain below, neither the TM Directive nor the CTM Regulation contains a definition of "trade mark". The nearest they come to a definition is an Article which sets out the signs of which a trade mark may consist. The UK "definition" is nothing more than the product of unnecessary fiddling with the provisions of a directive, serving only to alter or obscure the meaning of the original provision. For those who are interested, these considerations assist in "unravelling the skein" formed by Arts 2 and 3(1)(a)–(d) of the TM Directive (Arts 4 and 7(1)(a)–(d) of the CTM Regulation).

1. The essential function of a trade mark

2–003 A trade mark is (or should be) a badge of origin. In other words it indicates the source or the trade origin of the goods or services in respect of which it is used. A trade mark may do other things as well, but it must act as a badge of origin.

2–004 This fundamental concept is stated, in a rather backhanded way, in the tenth recital to the TM Directive: "Whereas the protection afforded by the registered trade mark, the function of which is in particular to guarantee the trade mark as an indication of origin …" Equivalent wording is found in the seventh recital to the CTM Regulation.

2–005 The ECJ expresses this concept as the "essential function" of a trade mark. This notion was developed in the context of the free movement of goods[1] years before the TM Directive. In its decisions concerning the TM Directive and CTM

---

[1] See further in Ch.16 Limitations of Enforcement and Exploitation.

Regulation, the ECJ has emphasised from time to time the role of the "essential function" as underlying many aspects of EU trade mark law. For example, in *Sieckmann*:[2]

> "It is also clear from the Court's case-law that the essential function of a trade mark is to guarantee the identity of the origin of the marked product or service to the consumer or end-user by enabling him, without any possibility of confusion, to distinguish that product or service from others which have another origin and that, for the trade mark to be able to fulfil its essential role in the system of undistorted competition which the EC Treaty seeks to establish, it must offer a guarantee that all the goods or services bearing it have been manufactured or supplied under the control of a single undertaking which is responsible for their quality (see, in particular, Case C–349/95 *Loendersloot* [1997] E.C.R. I-6227, paras 22 and 24; Case C–39/97 *Canon* [1998] E.C.R. I-5507, para.28, and *Philips*, para.30)."

OTHER FUNCTIONS OF A TRADE MARK

Provided a trade mark performs its "essential function" of indicating origin, it is perfectly permissible for a trade mark to carry out other functions as well. These "other functions" have been variously described, but include at least, the quality function and the advertising function as well as, in some cases, a descriptive function. To explain a little further: the quality function of a trade mark is that the trade mark offers a guarantee to the consumer that the quality of the goods or services will be that to which the consumer has become accustomed. The "advertising" function relates to the "cachet" or "aura" which the consumer associates with the mark, usually as the result of the way the proprietor has used and promoted the mark and its goods or services. As for the descriptive function, it is important not to misunderstand it. Wholly descriptive marks are not registrable. However, some of the most powerful trade marks are those which indicate origin but also contain an allusion to some characteristic of the goods or services. **2–006**

Whether, and to what extent, any particular trade mark does perform other functions depends on the particular circumstances: the mark itself, the market in which it is used, the way in which the proprietor uses and promotes the mark and hence, the reputation attaching to the mark and so on.

Each of these functions of a trade mark may change. The assignment of a trade mark to a new proprietor results in a change of origin, although the consumer may or may not be aware of the change. It is open to the trade mark proprietor to change the quality of the goods or services supplied under the mark and/or to change the "cachet" or "aura" attaching to the mark by a change in advertising. Such changes are not without risk. So far as the registration is concerned, the ultimate risk is that the mark becomes deceptive and liable to revocation.[3] **2–007**

THE IMPORTANCE OF THE "ESSENTIAL FUNCTION"

The "essential function" of a trade mark is a concept which deserves to be kept in mind in all issues which concern a registered trade mark—whether an application **2–008**

---

[2] Case C–273/00 *Sieckmann* [2002].E.C.R. I-11737; [2003] Ch.487; [2003] E.T.M.R. 37; [2003] R.P.C. 38, para.35, ECJ.

[3] Consider the case of *Elizabeth Emanuel*, O-017–04, January 16, 2004, Decision of the Appointed Person (David Kitchin Q.C.), which has resulted in a reference to the ECJ. See further in Ch.10 under s.46(1)(d).

satisfies the definition of "trade mark", on the key issue of distinctive character, on infringement, the defences thereto and on issues of genuine use. The "essential function" of a trade mark underlies the whole of the EU law relating to registered trade marks.

2. How to define a trade mark?

2–009 In the developed world, we encounter a vast number of trade marks. We react to them instinctively: in other words, a proper trade mark performs its function without us having to consciously think—that's a trade mark, let alone—that's a trade mark of company X or firm Y or the individual trader Z.[4] You know a trade mark when you see one, but it is much more difficult to describe precisely its attributes or to explain precisely why something else does not have the ability to function as a trade mark.

2–010 Speaking in general terms, we can define a trade mark as being a sign which distinguishes[5] particular goods or services of one undertaking from the goods or services of other undertakings. That is easy enough, but things start to get more complicated when you want to create a registration system. Any registration system is going to be an imperfect way of capturing all the attributes of trade marks which operate in the market.[6] The best that can be achieved is to have a registration system which records the most concrete attributes of each trade mark. The trouble is that you then need to devise a set of rules or definitions under which these attributes are going to be recorded. And these rules also have to take account of other consequences of a registration system, for example: a trader may well want to achieve registration of a trade mark before he starts to use it.[7] Hence, if you want to define "trade mark" for the purposes of a registration system, the definition has to deal with two aims: capturing the attributes of a trade mark but in a way which is sufficiently concrete or certain so that these attributes can be presented in a register.

2–011 As explained in the next section, we believe that when the UK legislature implemented the TM Directive into UK law it incorrectly thought that the directive defined "trade mark". In fact, the attributes of a "trade mark" in EU trade mark law have to be gathered from various sources, some explicit and some implicit.

3. Does EU law define "trade mark"?

2–012 Article 2 of the TM Directive was entitled "Signs of which a trade mark may consist" and provided:

> "A trade mark may consist of any sign capable of being represented graphically, particularly words, including personal names, designs, letters, numerals, the shape of goods or of their packaging, provided that such signs are

---

[4] Unless, in the case of the individual trader, the surname is the trader's trade mark, *e.g.* Randalls the butchers. For the difficulties created by surnames as registered trade marks see Ch.8 and the ECJ judgment in *Nichols*.

[5] *i.e.* the trade mark must actually distinguish. This may seem a rather obvious point, but it is necessary to keep it in mind when we come to s.1 of the Act.

[6] For example, our existing systems do not record whether a trade mark has a reputation in the market, or how substantial that reputation may be.

[7] This is reflected in Art.15(3) of TRIPS: "actual use of a trademark shall not be a condition for filing an application for registration."

capable of distinguishing the goods or services of one undertaking from those of other undertakings."

Article 4 of the CTM Regulation contains essentially the same provision.

In the Annex to this Chapter we have set out the drafting history of Articles 2 and 3(1) of the TM Directive in conjunction with Articles 4 and 7(1) of the CTM Regulation. Although the drafting history reflects the legal and political issues which were being debated over time, we suggest that the purposes of Art.2 were tolerably clear by the time the TM Directive was adopted. **2–014**

The first level of harmonisation required by the TM Directive was designed to pave the way for the introduction of the CTM system. Evidently the existing laws of Member States varied as to the types of sign which could be registered as trade marks. Hence, it was necessary to specify the types of sign which could be registered as trade marks, so that all Member States appreciated that any old limitations on types of sign no longer applied. In fact, no limit on the types of sign was imposed, provided the sign in question met the other requirements. The examples given were thought to reflect what businesses actually used as trade marks, and the removal of limitations was designed to encourage application for Community trade marks. This then, was the primary purpose of Art.2. **2–015**

A further important purpose of Art.2 was that it was to reflect the basic function of a trade mark. Right from the start, what became Art.2[8] was said to be "geared particularly to the question whether the relevant sign is capable of performing the basic function of a trade mark. That function, in economic and legal terms, is to indicate the origin of goods or services and to distinguish them from those of other undertakings." **2–016**

Accordingly, Article 2 of the TM Directive did not define "trade mark", it was telling Member States about the signs of which a trade mark may consist. Article 2 did lay down certain requirements for a "trade mark". Not surprisingly, they relate to what a trade mark is supposed to do but they are directed, at least in part, to the operation of a registration system (graphical representation). Article 2 reflected the basic function of a trade mark but did not express it directly. **2–017**

Were Member States given an option in Article 2?

The use of the word "may" in a directive is usually an indication to Member States that they have the option whether to implement the provision in question or to what extent. In the context of Art.2, we doubt very much that Member States were being given any option at all. The better view is that the word "may" was used in the sense of the title of the Article, to indicate to Member States an open-ended notion of the signs which could be presented for registration, provided they met the stated requirements **2–018**

UK implementation

Article 2 of the TM Directive was implemented by the UK in s.1 of the 1994 Act. **2–019**

"**Section 1**—(1) In this Act a "trade mark" means any sign capable of being

---

[8] At this point, what became Art.2 was to be found in the proposal for the Community trade mark, where the proposed Article "Signs of which a Community trade mark may consist" ended with these words: "any other signs which are capable of distinguishing the goods or services of one undertaking from those of other undertakings." It was this expression which was geared to the basic function of a trade mark.

represented graphically which is capable of distinguishing goods or services of one undertaking from those of other undertakings.

A trade mark may, in particular, consist of words (including personal names), designs, letters, numerals or the shape of goods or their packaging.

(2) References in this Act to a trade mark include, unless the context otherwise requires, references to a collective mark (see section 49) or certification mark (see section 50)."

2–020   The Trade Marks Act 1994 starts with what appears to be a fundamental definition of "trade mark", which applies to every type of mark. This chapter is concerned with signs or marks of individual undertakings. Collective and certification marks perform a somewhat different function and are dealt with in Ch.12.

2–021   In fact, s.1(1) chopped Art.2 into two parts. The UK draftsman correctly understood that the examples of "sign" were not exhaustive. Having carved that notion out, the draftsman then tried to make the remainder into a definition of "trade mark": "In this Act a trade mark means…" In terms of EU law, the alteration in structure and content is of no consequence because s.1(1) has to be interpreted so as to conform with Art.2 of the directive. In practice, the alteration has not helped. As we have explained above, we do not believe that Article 2 of the TM Directive defines "trade mark". We return to the consequences of this point in section 6 below, where we discuss further the interpretation of Art.2 and in particular the expression "capable of distinguishing". The fact that Art.2 does not define "trade mark" does not prevent it from laying down certain requirements with which a sign must conform if it is to avoid the absolute ground for refusal set out in Article 3(1)(a) of the TM Directive (Article 7(1)(a) of the CTM Regulation), implemented in s.3(1)(a) of the Act. Accordingly, we turn to the requirements which are expressed in Art.2.

2–022   Article 2 contains three basic requirements.[9] To qualify as a trade mark, the candidate must be (1) a sign which (2) is capable of being represented graphically and which (3) is capable of distinguishing the goods or services of one undertaking from those of other undertakings. Subsumed is a fourth requirement: that the sign must be used *in relation to* the goods or services defined in the specification. For most trade marks, this requirement is so obviously satisfied that it deserves no attention. However, this is where the issue over "retail services" arises, discussed in section 7 below.

2–023   The three basic requirements will be discussed in turn. The first two are closely related—the sign is what is used or proposed to be used in practice and the graphical representation of it is that which appears on the register and will constitute the registered trade mark. The third requirement introduces the key issue of distinctiveness, which is discussed more fully in the context of the absolute grounds for refusal of a mark—see Ch.8.

2–024   Conventional trade marks (*i.e.* word and figurative marks) will normally have no trouble meeting the first two requirements in s.1(1). It will be seen that issues tend to arise for the more unconventional candidates: not merely signs comprising smells, sounds or colour but any candidate comprising matter which is not normally taken to carry trade mark significance.

---

[9] See para.23 of Case C–104/01 *Libertel* [2003] E.C.R. I-3793; [2004] Ch.83; [2004] F.S.R. 4; [2003] E.T.M.R. 63, ECJ, where the ECJ stated these three requirements in relation to a colour mark. The same must apply to all applications.

4. Sign

The word "sign" is used in the 1994 Act, TM Directive and CTM Regulation as a general term to include all candidates which may constitute a "trade mark" and all candidates for allegations of infringement.[10]   **2–025**

Section 1(1) includes a list of examples of what types of sign are included. The list is obviously not exhaustive. The implementation of the TM Directive gave rise to debate about the types of mark which became registrable for the first time. "Sign" is an expression wide enough to include a wide range of unusual marks, such as marks consisting of a single colour, a smell, a sound or a moving image. In the previous edition, we suggested that the use of the word "sign" makes the definition of "trade mark" flexible and open-ended, subject to the other requirements, but that a "sign" had to signify something or convey a message about the relevant goods or services so that a mere decoration would not qualify as a sign. For the moment we can leave on one side the question as to whether the sign conveys the right message (*i.e.* indicating origin) because that question arises under the absolute grounds in s.3(1). However, subsequent case law has demonstrated that the requirement that the candidate for registration is a "sign" can be important, particularly for the more unconventional trade marks.   **2–026**

In *Libertel* the application was for the colour orange for certain telecommunications goods and services. The reproduction of the mark comprised an orange rectangle, and was accompanied by a description "orange", without reference to any colour code. Leaving aside problems concerned with the graphical representation (discussed below), for the ECJ the first point was whether the application constituted a sign:[11]   **2–027**

> "…it must be pointed out that a colour *per se* cannot be presumed to constitute a sign. Normally a colour is a simple property of things. Yet it may constitute a sign. That depends on the context in which the colour is used. None the less, a colour *per se* is capable, in relation to a product or service, of constituting a sign."

In *Heidelberger Bauchemie*[12] the application was for registration of the colours blue and yellow as a trade mark for various products used in the building trade including adhesives, paints, lubricants and insulating materials. The "reproduction of the mark" comprised a rectangular piece of paper, the upper part blue and the lower part yellow, and was accompanied by the following description: "The trade mark applied for consists of the applicant's corporate colours which are used in every conceivable form, in particular on packaging and labels."   **2–028**

Against that background, the ECJ expanded on *Libertel*, as follows:

> "For the purposes of the application of Article 2 of the Directive, it is necessary to establish that in the context in which they are used colours or combinations of colours which it is sought to register in fact represent a sign. The purpose of that requirement is in particular to prevent the abuse of trademark law in order to obtain an unfair competitive advantage."

Prompted perhaps by the overt claim to use "in every conceivable way" of a colour combination without any spatial delimitation, it appears that the ECJ found   **2–029**

---

[10] The 1994 Act, s.10, uses the neutral word "sign" (as opposed to "trade mark", used in s.9) to describe what infringes a registered trade mark. S.11 uses both "sign" and "indication" in defining some of the defences to infringement.

[11] Case C–104/01 [2003] E.C.R. I-3793; [2004] Ch.83; [2004] F.S.R. 4; [2003] E.T.M.R. 63, ECJ.

[12] Case C–49/02 [2004] E.T.M.R. 99, ECJ.

the Heidelberger application verging on an abuse of the harmonised trade mark registration system, and questioned whether the application constituted a sign at all.

2–030   It remains to be seen whether the ECJ will develop the requirement of "sign" for the purpose of preventing abuse of trademark law. It also remains to be seen what the ECJ meant when they referred in these two cases to "the context" in which colours or combinations of colours are used. There are two possibilities here. The first is that the context is that defined by the scope of the application itself—the trade mark registry or tribunal must ask itself: looking at the context defined by this application, does the application in fact constitute a sign? The second and more interesting possibility is that the ECJ had in mind a process of inquiry by the registry of the applicant: please show us how this mark is going to be used or has been used, so that we can satisfy ourselves it constitutes a sign. Unfortunately, the ECJ is much more likely to have had the first possibility in mind. The second would be unworkable in practice—any examples the applicant put forward could not limit the scope of the application—although if such a process of inquiry were routine, it might eliminate at an early stage applications which are not trade marks at all.

2–031   The current system can be said to be loaded in favour of the applicant in the sense that the process of isolating what is being claimed for registration robs the "sign" of the context in which it is normally used or proposed to be used. The process of isolation can mean that a sign which is in practice below the borderline of distinctiveness achieves registration. By contrast if such a sign were seen in the actual context in which it was used or proposed to be used, it would be immediately apparent the sign possessed insufficient or no distinctive character at all. It may be said that these considerations are a bit philosophical, but the difference between considering the sign in its likely context as opposed to taking the application purely as it stands could explain the apparent difference between the UK and OHIM on the minimum degree of distinctive character required to overcome an Art.3(1)(b)/Art.7(1)(b) objection.[13]

5. Graphical representation

2–032   In order to be the subject of a valid application or registration, the sign must be "capable of being represented graphically". The capability must be realised on the application form.[14] The basic requirements are now clear. The function of the graphical representation is to enable the sign in question to be represented visually, so that it can be precisely identified.[15] The graphical representation itself must be: clear, precise, self-contained, easily accessible, intelligible, durable, unequivocal and objective.[16]

---

[13] This is discussed further in Ch.8.
[14] Until the applicant files a graphic representation which is acceptable, the UK Registry treats the application as incomplete, with the result that the application is not afforded a filing date until it is complete: see *Ty Nant Spring Water Ltd's Application* [1999] E.T.M.R. 981 (Appointed Person, G. Hobbs Q.C.). The Registry issues a "filing deficiency notice" under r.11, which gives the applicant a non-extendible period of two months within which to present an acceptable representation. See the UK Registry Work Manual, Ch.3, para.4.3.
[15] Case C–273/00 *Sieckmann* [2002].E.C.R. I-11737; [2003] Ch.487; [2003] E.T.M.R. 37; [2003] R.P.C. 38, para.46, ECJ.
[16] *Sieckmann*, paras 47–55.

SELECTING THE GRAPHIC REPRESENTATION

The selection of the graphic representation is an important step for any applicant **2–033** because the trade mark is defined by the graphic representation which is filed on or with the application form. The graphic representation provides or should provide a fixed point of reference showing what the mark is. During the application process, the ability to amend the graphic representation is extremely limited, since it is only possible to correct errors of wording or copying or obvious mistakes and even those corrections must not substantially affect the identity of the trade mark.

Almost every applicant has some degree of manoeuvre when selecting the **2–034** graphic representation. Even conventional word marks are likely to be used or proposed to be used in a particular script and/or in conjunction with other distinctive matter. In such a case, the applicant may have to choose between representing his sign (1) with all accompanying distinctive matter; (2) as the word in the particular script; or (3) as the word in any script. In making the choice, the applicant has to consider the particular circumstances of his sign and balance the desire to secure wider rights for his sign against the risk that the graphic representation he selects may increase the force of any absolute or relative grounds for refusal. At least for conventional marks, this type of selection process is not new, being a familiar process in the UK under the 1938 Act.

Even within the confines of ECJ jurisprudence, there may be more than one **2–035** way in which to represent the sign graphically, particularly for unconventional marks. On the one hand, the scope of the rights obtained through registration of one form of graphic representation may be wider because the sign is defined in a less precise manner than is dictated by another form of graphic representation. On the other hand, the applicant will be concerned to ensure that his choice of representation is acceptable to the Registry, not least so that he maintains the priority of his filing date. The general scheme of the 1994 Act is that rights are secured by the first to file, rather than the first to use (which was broadly the position under the 1938 Act). In practice, wealthy traders can avoid any dilemma by filing a number of applications, each one featuring a more ambitious graphic representation.[17] In that way, the trader avoids any priority concerns but at the same time presses the boundaries of graphic representation so as to secure the widest possible protection for the signs he considers to be distinctive of his goods or services. For less wealthy traders, it may be important to get the graphic representation right first time.

PERMISSIBLE VARIATION

The requirements that the sign must be "precisely identified" and the graphical **2–036** representation must be "precise" and "unequivocal" are capable of being taken too far. The underlying policy reasons do not require every mark on the register to be defined with absolute precision. The degree of precision required must depend on the mark itself and its distinctive character. For any mark, there is a degree of permissible variation in its graphical representation. Consider a word-only registration. The graphical representation is the word in capitals in plain

---

[17] One would think they might not want to signal their intentions so clearly, but experience indicates they do not really care (cf. in a slightly different context, the hundreds of dishwasher tablet applications).

type. Such a registration covers the word in a very wide range of typefaces. The variation in presentation is permissible because the distinctive character of the mark resides in the word itself and that does not change. A different type of permissible variation is seen in hologram or "movement" marks—see below. There are other marks where the degree of permissible variation is going to be very small indeed if not practically non-existent. It may well prove easier to justify permissible variation where the variation occurs in the actual use made of the mark, so that it can be seen and/or proved that the public see the same mark.[18] In many cases, this notion of permissible variation has to be expressed in a series of marks[19], but, we suggest, not invariably.

2–037   Under the open-ended definition contained in s.1(1) of the 1994 Act, it is possible to characterise as a "sign" virtually any feature used in trade. The more unconventional the feature or sign, the greater the problems for the applicant in meeting the requirements of graphic representation and distinctiveness. The remainder of this discussion is largely directed at the sorts of problems which arise for unconventional signs.

REASONS FOR THIS REQUIREMENT

2–038   This requirement arises from important practical considerations concerned with certainty. First, the relevant trade mark office must know with certainty what is comprised in the sign in question, so that it can maintain an accessible Register of Trade Marks and fulfil its functions of examination and publication of applications. Secondly, and of greater importance, other traders must be able to ascertain with certainty exactly what their competitors (actual or potential) have registered or have applied to register.

2–039   In the UK, these considerations have been explained as follows:

"It is … essential for traders to be able to identify with clarity what the registered trade mark is…. This is a fundamental aspect of the law and it is for this reason that the graphical representation, being the means by which the trade mark is defined, must be adequate to enable the public to determine precisely what the sign is that is the subject of the registration."[20]

"The degree of precision with which the sign is represented must be sufficient to permit full and effective implementation of the provisions of the Act relating to absolute unregistrability (section 3), relative unregistrability (section 5), infringement (section 10) and public inspection of the Register (section 63). These provisions call for a fixed point of reference: a graphic representation in which the identity of the relevant sign is clearly and unambiguously recorded. There may be more than one way of representing a sign graphically with that degree of precision. It seems clear that a sign (such as a sound or aroma) can be taken to have been represented graphically with the required degree of precision when figuratively represented, even though in-

---

[18] A concrete example will help. Consider the way Adidas use their three-stripe mark on, say, tracksuit trousers. They vary the position and relative length of the stripes, yet it is reasonable to assume that the public see the same mark.

[19] See s.41 and r.21.

[20] Simon Thorley Q.C. as the Appointed Person in *Swizzels Matlow Ltd's Application (No.2)* [2000] E.T.M.R. 58.

terpretation or analysis may then be required in order to detect or demonstrate use of it."[21]

GUIDANCE FROM THE ECJ

Those UK decisions must now be read in the light of the more recent judgments of the ECJ. The overall approach of the ECJ is very similar indeed, but more restrictive for the most unconventional marks (such as a sound or aroma).   **2–040**

There are now four ECJ judgments which have dealt with the requirement of graphical representation. The function of the graphical representation is to enable the sign to be represented visually, particularly by means of images, lines or characters, so that it can be precisely identified.[22] In order to fulfil its function, the graphical representation of any sign put forward for registration must be: clear, precise, self-contained, easily accessible, intelligible, durable, unequivocal and objective.[23]   **2–041**

Different aspects of these requirements come to the fore, depending on the type of sign under examination and the attempt at graphical representation. We examine the categories of unconventional signs in turn.

SMELLS/OLFACTORY SIGNS

In *Sieckmann*, the application was to register an olfactory mark comprising "the pure chemical substance methyl cinnamate (= cinnamic acid methyl ester)" and the structural formula was provided: C6H5-CH = CHCOOCH3. In addition, Mr Sieckmann gave details where one could obtain the chemical, he submitted with his application an odour sample of the sign in a container and stated that the scent was usually described as 'balsamically fruity with a slight hint of cinnamon'.   **2–042**

The ECJ answered the various questions referred to it in the following way. First, it stated that a trade mark may consist of a sign which is not in itself capable of being perceived visually, provided that it can be represented graphically. Second, so far as the graphic representation is concerned, it laid down the requirements that it must be clear, precise, self-contained, easily accessible, intelligible, durable and objective. Third, the ECJ stated that, in respect of an olfactory sign, the requirements of graphic representability are not satisfied by a chemical formula, by a description in written words, by the deposit of an odour sample or by a combination of those elements. A chemical formula is not sufficient because few people would recognise from the formula the odour in question: hence, the chemical formula would not be sufficiently intelligible. A further point was that the formula does not represent the odour, but the substance itself. A description in written words is not sufficient because it is not sufficiently clear, precise and objective. The deposit of an odour sample does not constitute a graphic representation. Furthermore, an odour sample is not sufficiently stable or durable. None of those options, whether individually or in combination would be, in the opinion of the ECJ, sufficiently clear and precise.   **2–043**

In the light of those emphatic statements, one may ask: how else can one attempt to provide a satisfactory graphic representation of an olfactory mark? There   **2–044**

---

[21] Geoffrey Hobbs Q.C. as the Appointed Person in *Ty Nant Spring Water Ltd's Trade Mark Application* [2000] R.P.C. 55.

[22] Case C–273/00 *Sieckmann* [2002].E.C.R. I-11737; [2003] Ch.487; [2003] E.T.M.R. 37; [2003] R.P.C. 38, para.46, ECJ.

[23] *Sieckmann*, paras 47–55.

are some possibilities which Mr Sieckmann did not put forward, such as defining the odour by reference to accepted standards of classification for odorants such as *Zwaardemaker* (1985) with 30 sub-classes or *Linnaeus* (1756) with seven classes, but it is very difficult to find any alternative which would satisfy the requirements laid down by the ECJ.[24] The practical effect of the *Sieckmann* judgment is probably that it is impossible to obtain a valid registration of an olfactory mark[25] unless or until the requirements for recording the "sign" in question are changed to allow representations other than purely graphic or descriptions in words.[26]

Taste marks

2–045   For obvious reasons, taste marks fall to be treated in the same way as smell marks. An application for "The taste of artificial strawberry flavour" as a gustatory trade mark for pharmaceutical preparations was refused. In the event, the OHIM Board of Appeal did not find it necessary to rule on the inadequacy of the graphical representation, but indicated, correctly, that the logic of *Sieckmann* had to apply to gustatory marks.[27]

Sound marks

2–046   In *Shield Mark*,[28] a variety of marks had been registered with two themes: one being a cock crow and the other being the first nine notes of Beethoven's Für Elise. Each registration varied in the description of the mark. For example, the "cockcrow" marks were described variously as: Sound mark: a cock crow; the denomination Kukelekuuuuu (an onomatopoeia suggesting, in Dutch, a cockcrow); and Sound mark, the trade mark consists of an onomatopoeia imitating a cockcrow. The Für Elise marks were described in virtually every conceivable combination: the sequence of musical notes E, D#, E, D#, E, B, D, C, A; the reproduction of the melody formed by the sequence of notes as described; the reproduction of the melody as played on a piano; the notes on a musical stave; and "the first nine notes of Für Elise".

2–047   The reference to the ECJ arose in the counterclaim to invalidate the marks in the course of infringement proceedings, which had all the characteristics of a manufactured test case. The ECJ (1) re-affirmed the general requirements set out in *Sieckmann* for a graphic representation, (2) re-affirmed the general principle that the question whether any particular graphic representation was sufficient was a matter for the national court to determine but (3) nevertheless felt able to provide guidance as to the circumstances in which representation of sound marks by musical notes or written language could be sufficient.

---

[24] Another applicant attempted to represent a fragrance graphically using what appeared to be some sort of print-out from a HPLC analysis, together with a written description "Une note verte gazon, hespéridée (bergamote, citron), florale (fleur d'oranger, jacinthe) rosée, musquée". Not surprisingly, this was rejected as inadequate both by the examiner and the OHIM BoA: R–186/2000–4 [2005] E.T.M.R. 42.

[25] The decisions of the OHIM Boards of Appeal accepting written descriptions as sufficient graphic representations ("the smell of fresh cut grass" for tennis balls *Venootschap Onder Firma Senta Aromatic Marketing's Application* [1999] E.T.M.R. 429, OHIM BoA R 156/1998/2) and "the scent of raspberries" in respect of fuels, particularly diesel *Myles Ltd's Application* R–711/1999–3 OHIM BoA) have clearly been overruled by *Sieckmann*.

[26] In America, apparently, written descriptions are acceptable, *e.g.* "The mark is a high impact, fresh, floral fragrance reminiscent of Plumeria blossoms" registered for sewing thread and embroidery yarn.

[27] R–120/2001–2, August 4, 2003.

[28] Case C–283/01 [2004] Ch. 97; [2004] R.P.C. 17; [2004] E.T.M.R. 33, ECJ.

Describing a sound in written language will not automatically fail to qualify, **2–048**
but the ECJ made it clear that the written descriptions at issue (the first nine notes
of Für Elise, a cockcrow) were not sufficiently clear or precise and did not make
it possible to determine the scope of the protection sought.[29]

A simple onomatopoeia cannot, by itself, satisfy the requirements for two **2–049**
reasons. If the sound sign is represented graphically by a simple onomatopoeia, it
is unclear whether the sign is the onomatopoeia itself, as pronounced, or the
actual sound or noise of which the onomatopoeia is the phonetic imitation. Even
where it is made clear that the sign is the onomatopoeia as pronounced, it is likely
to lack the required clarity or precision not least because an onomatopoeia may
be perceived differently, depending on the individual, or from one Member State
to another (the Dutch onomatopoeia for a cockcrow being a good example).[30]

So far as musical notes are concerned, a mere sequence of notes (such as E, **2–050**
D#, E, D#, E, B, D, C, A) does not make it possible to determine the pitch or the
duration of the notes, which are essential parameters of the melody sought to be
represented, and hence fail to meet the requirements of being clear, precise or
self-contained. If one adds a stave (which will include accidentals—sharp, flat or
natural), clef (to indicate pitch), musical notes and rests (which indicate the
values, *e.g.* minim, crotchet, quaver etc.), then the graphic representation will
meet the requirements of being clear, precise, self-contained, easily accessible,
intelligible, durable and objective.[31]

Where one draws the line is arbitrary. The ECJ appeared to accept this, recog- **2–051**
nising that even if such a representation was not immediately intelligible, it was
sufficiently easily intelligible to enable the competent authorities, traders and
public to know precisely what the sign was.[32]

The ECJ has set the requirements that the graphical representation be clear,
precise and self-contained at a reasonably high level and higher than in the United
States.[33]

The ECJ did not consider all ways in which a sound can be represented. MGM **2–052**
attempted to register their "roar of a lion" using the combination of a spectrogram and the description: "The trade mark is constituted by the sound produced
by the roar of a lion and is represented by the spectrogram abovementioned." The
applicant argued that a spectrogram was no worse than musical notation: the
average consumer being unable to read or immediately understand them equally.
Although the MGM spectrogram was rejected as being inadequate, the OHIM
Board of Appeal[34] reached the conclusions *obiter* that (1) in terms of precision
and accuracy, a sonogram[35] is superior to musical notation since it conveys more
nuances, including sound characteristics and (2) the fact that a certain amount of
training and experience was required before a person could read sonograms so as

---

[29] Case C–283/01 *Shield Mark* [2004] Ch. 97; [2004] R.P.C. 17; [2004] E.T.M.R. 33, ECJ, para.59.
[30] Case C–283/01 *Shield Mark* [2004] Ch. 97; [2004] R.P.C. 17; [2004] E.T.M.R. 33, para.60, ECJ.
[31] Case C–283/01 *Shield Mark* [2004] Ch. 97; [2004] R.P.C. 17; [2004] E.T.M.R. 33, paras 61–2, ECJ.
[32] Case C–283/01 *Shield Mark* [2004] Ch. 97; [2004] R.P.C. 17; [2004] E.T.M.R. 33, para.63, ECJ.
[33] An example from America is the mark "Clop, clop, clop, moo" for restaurant services. A CTM application for the sound mark "click" was rejected because the representation was insufficiently clear and precise: Case R–1/1998–2, OHIM BoA, noted as *Qlicksmart Pty Ltd's Application* [1999] E.T.M.R. 335, a decision in line with the later ECJ guidance.
[34] R–781/1999–4, August 25, 2003, corrected on September 29, 2003 [2004] E.T.M.R. 34.
[35] The decision explains the differences between various types of diagrams—oscillogram, spectrum, spectrogram and sonogram). The advantage of a spectrogram is that it is a three-dimensional depiction of the distribution of the signal's frequency content *i.e.* relative volume, indicated by

to be able to perceive the noise or sound depicted was no different to the situation as regards musical notation. This decision came between the A-G's Opinion and the Judgment in *Shield Mark* and it remains to be seen whether a full sonogram will satisfy OHIM. Debating the adequacy of musical notation and sonograms is rather quaint when one takes into account that most registrations are accessed electronically and it would be very easy to include recordings of sound marks (*e.g.* in a .wav file). However, unless or until other forms of representation are permitted, applicants will have to use the existing tools to define their sound as precisely as possible.

2–053   One cannot help feeling that the ECJ might have got a little overzealous when laying down the requirements for graphical representation. The real reason why signs such as those in issue in *Sieckmann* and *Shield Mark* are not registrable is because they lack distinctive character in the absence of prolonged use and education of the public. For those signs where distinctive character can be proved[36], the requirement for graphical representation ought not to bar registration.

COLOURS

2–054   In the context of colour marks, it helps to recognise at the outset that there are two issues which have to be considered: the first concerns how one defines the colour(s); the second, entirely separate, issue concerns spatial delimitation of the sign. The first issue arises for all colour marks. Whether the second issue arises at all depends on the graphical representation of the sign. For the purposes of discussion, it is convenient to use three broad categories: (1) a colour (or combination) used to form a figurative mark (*e.g.* a red triangle or an orange square of particular size); (2) a sign comprising the shape of goods in a particular colour or colour combination (*e.g.* the body of a drill in one colour, and the handle in another) and (3) those signs where the representation is simply a block of one colour or a combination of colours. Unless the particular shape is put forward simply as an example, signs in the first two categories are properly spatially limited and usually, no special issue on graphical representation arises. This discussion is about signs where the actual form of the sign is unclear. If the representation of the sign is simply a block of one colour or a combination of colours then, in the absence of clear indications to the contrary, it should be assumed that the application is for that colour without any spatial delimitation. Most applicants for such signs decline to specify just how vague their sign really is and it is important to understand what is being claimed.

SINGLE COLOURS

2–055   Once the ECJ had stated the general requirements for a graphic representation in *Sieckmann*, it was not difficult to predict how an application for a single colour would fare. In fact, the ECJ has now dealt with three cases involving colour marks *Libertel*,[37] *Heidelberger Bauchemie*[38] and *KWS Saat*.[39] As mentioned above, in *Libertel* the application was for the colour orange for certain telecom-

---

blackening) versus frequency (vertical axis) and time (horizontal axis). A sound spectrogram is called a sonogram.

[36] For example, MGM claim to have used their "roar of a lion" mark for films since 1928.

[37] Case C–104/01 [2003] E.C.R. I-3793; [2004] Ch. 83; [2004] F.S.R. 4; [2003] E.T.M.R. 63.

[38] Case C–49/02 [2004] E.T.M.R. 99, ECJ.

[39] Case C–447/02, October 21, 2004, ECJ

munications goods and services. The reproduction of the mark comprised an orange rectangle, and was accompanied by a description "orange", without reference to any colour code. In an important judgment on a number of issues, the ECJ did not really get to grips with the problem of spatial delimitation, merely questioning as a preliminary point and in a single short paragraph, whether a single colour, without any spatial delimitation, constituted a sign (see above). On graphical representation, the ECJ concentrated on the first issue we mentioned above—how to specify the colour. They did this by repeating the *Sieckmann* criteria and went on to discuss how those applied to signs comprising colour(s) *per se*:[40]

> a mere sample of a colour (particularly on paper) is unlikely to be sufficiently durable;
>
> a written description of a colour may suffice, but it depends on the circumstances and the description. Designating a colour using an internationally recognised identification code will constitute a graphic representation, being precise and stable;
>
> a combination of a sample of the colour with a written description may suffice provided it meets the general criteria—clear, precise, self-contained, easily accessible, intelligible and objective.

In the light of *Libertel*, the UK Registry Work Manual indicates that marks **2–056** consisting of colour alone will be considered to be graphically represented if filed in the form of a written description (*e.g.* dark blue) with the relevant code from an internationally recognised colour identification system (such as Pantone, RAL or Focoltone).[41] Standing on its own, this indication is incomplete because it fails to include any consideration of spatial delimitation of the colour.

In *KWS Saat*,[42] the application was also for the single colour orange essentially for seeds but also treatment installations for seeds, consultancy services and agricultural, horticultural and forestry products generally. The application was rejected on distinctiveness grounds. The inadequacy of the graphical representation was passed over. The case seems to have been conducted on the unstated assumption that the colour would cover all the products. One can understand seeds being coloured orange, but what about seed packets, the other products and the services. The graphical representation left it entirely unclear as to the form or forms in which the colour would appear. Again, the problem of spatial delimitation was missed.

COLOUR COMBINATIONS

In *Heidelberger Bauchemie*,[43] the ECJ got slightly more to grips with the issue of **2–057** spatial delimitation, probably because the facts of the case highlighted the issue more clearly. As mentioned above, the application was for registration of the colours blue and yellow as a trade mark for various products used in the building trade including adhesives, paints, lubricants and insulating materials. The "reproduction of the mark" comprised a rectangular piece of paper, the upper part blue and the lower part yellow, and was accompanied by the following description:

---

[40] *Libertel*, paras 30–37.
[41] Ch.6, para.16.1.1, accessible on the website at *www.patent.gov.uk/tm/reference/workman/chapt6/sec16.pdf*. At the time of writing, the latest version was dated July 2004, but sections are updated from time-to-time.
[42] Case C–447/02, October 21, 2004, ECJ.
[43] Case C–49/02 [2004] E.T.M.R. 99, ECJ.

2–058   "The trade mark applied for consists of the applicant's corporate colours which are used in every conceivable form, in particular on packaging and labels."

2–059   Apart from the issue whether the application was for a "sign" at all (see above), the ECJ held that the graphical representation lacked the necessary qualities of precision and uniformity, since it allowed numerous different combinations. It held that "a graphic representation consisting of two or more colours, designated in the abstract and without contours, must be systematically arranged by associating the colours concerned in a predetermined and uniform way." However, associating the colours in a predetermined and uniform way is only half the problem. Surely of greater importance was the lack of any form or spatial delimitation of the "sign" itself. One could specify that the upper half of the sign was blue and the lower half yellow, but that would tell you nothing about the form of the sign: it could be a circle, a square, an ill-defined blob or it could cover the entirety of the packaging or label, but what about insulating materials, what about services, what about use on invoices? The same issues (about the form of the sign) applied to the *Libertel* application. Perhaps the issue was not really grasped there because it was easier to make the implicit assumption that the orange colour was going to cover all the telecommunications goods, but one wonders whether this could be a valid assumption. In addition, how was the orange going to be used in relation to services?

Considerations of this nature illustrate just how objectionable applications for colour(s) are when there is no attempt to indicate the form which the colour will take.

THREE-DIMENSIONAL SHAPES

2–060   Less extreme issues arise in relation to signs which comprise a three-dimensional shape. There are three particular issues to which we draw attention:

First, most applications contain a picture or line-drawing which shows the three-dimensional shape in question. If the picture or line-drawing is obscure, then the relevant registry should insist on a representation which is precise and clear.

2–061   Second, in certain jurisdictions it was unclear under the previous law whether a registration for a three-dimensional shape was permissible. Hence, there are a number of (pre-existing) registrations containing two-dimensional line drawings masquerading as three-dimensional marks (the three-headed shaver marks considered in the *Philips* cases are good examples). Now the applicant is normally obliged to specify whether the application is for a three-dimensional mark.

2–062   Third, any application for a three-dimensional shape which does not contain a picture or line drawing must be viewed with great suspicion. Any attempt to define a three-dimensional mark in a written description alone will almost certainly not provide a sufficiently clear or precise representation of the mark. This is a general topic to which we now turn.

MARKS INVOLVING MOVEMENT, HOLOGRAMS

2–063   There is no reason in principle why a hologram or a mark showing movement cannot perform the function of a trade mark. The UK Registry seems to accept that such marks can meet the *Sieckmann* criteria.[44] Normally, the graphical representation of a hologram mark will be required to show each of various views depicted in the hologram, so that all the material features of the mark can be discerned. Likewise, movement marks can be represented by a series of still images, provided it is made clear that the mark is a moving image, what the image depicts, how many images are involved, their order and the fact that there is a single sequence of movement.[45]

FURTHER POINTS

In 1998, when the requirements for graphic representation were still in the early stages of development, the UK Trade Mark Registry defined three criteria, which were approved as "highly relevant considerations".[46] To an extent they have been overtaken by the ECJ judgments and this is no doubt the reason why these criteria no longer appear in the Registry Work Manual. We believe they are still worth consideration, because they help to highlight some considerations which are not dealt with in the ECJ judgments.   **2–064**

"In the Registrar's view, a sign is graphically represented when:

(a) it is possible to determine from the graphical representation precisely what the sign is that the applicant uses or proposes to use without the need for supporting samples etc;

(b) the graphical representation can stand in place of the sign used or proposed to be used by the applicant because it represents that sign and no other;

(c) it is reasonably practicable for persons inspecting the register, or reading the Trade Marks Journal, to understand from the graphical representation what the trade mark is."

The first criterion confirms that the sign is defined by the graphic representation on the form of application. Provided that the observer has first been equipped with any skills necessary to interpret the graphic representation (as to which, see below at para.2–068), the representation should stand on its own to identify the trade mark. It is not permissible to refer to extraneous matter, either explicitly or implicitly. The idea of an implicit reference may seem odd, but an applicant may, deliberately or otherwise, choose to file a graphic representation which does not precisely define the sign he actually uses.[47] It is a natural tendency for anyone looking at a graphic representation to try to understand and make sense of it. Unconsciously, the observer may be filling in the gaps by drawing on his knowledge of the sign which the trader actually uses in practice. This must be resisted. Any prior knowledge of the way in which a sign may be used in practice must be put out of mind when examining the graphic representation.[48]   **2–065**

The second criterion refers to the degree of precision with which the trade mark should represent the sign which the applicant either uses or proposes to use   **2–066**

---

[44] See the UK Registry Work Manual, Ch.6, para.16.5.

[45] See the attempt by Lamborghini to register a movement mark comprising upward swivelling car doors, R–772/2002–1 [2005] E.T.M.R. 43. The application was rejected under Arts 7(1)(b) and 7(1)(e)(ii).

[46] By Simon Thorley Q.C. as the Appointed Person in *Swizzels Matlow Ltd's Application (No.2)* [2000] E.T.M.R. 58.

[47] See, *e.g.* the written description in *Swizzels Matlow Ltd's Application (No.2)* [2000] E.T.M.R. 58: "The trade mark consists of a circular compressed tablet bearing a raised heart outline on both flat surfaces and containing within the heart outline on one side any of several different words or phrases.", which some will recognise as a description of "Lovehearts".

[48] PAC 2/00 said "The representation put forward should not assume that the reader has prior

in trade. Obviously the ECJ has dealt with this point in some detail. The sign which is either used or proposed to be used in trade must obviously be the guide, together with the public perception, actual or anticipated, of the sign. It is suggested that the representation should be a faithful one, particularly if the sign has not yet been used. If the sign has been used and the applicant wishes to register a less than faithful representation of it, there must be a heavy onus on him to justify that his alternative representation should be registered.[49] Of course, lack of precision in the representation which is sought to be registered may create greater problems for the applicant in showing that the representation possesses sufficient distinctive character to warrant registration. In exceptional circumstances, it may be possible to justify an alternative representation by showing that it coincides with the public perception of the trade mark.

2–067   The third criterion is concerned with the ease with which the graphic representation can be understood. The standard has been more or less set by the ECJ in *Shield Mark*,[50] although there can be no uniform standard. It must be a question of degree depending largely on the type of mark involved. However, it is suggested that once the observer has been equipped with the necessary interpretative skills, understanding what the mark comprises should be an immediate[51] consequence. If undue effort is required to understand the graphic representation, or if the observer is left in a state of uncertainty, it is likely to be an indication that the representation as filed does not adequately represent the sign which lies behind the application. More effort is likely to be required to understand representations of less conventional types of mark.

HOW MUCH INTERPRETATION IS PERMISSIBLE

2–068   It is obvious that understanding what a trade mark is should be easy. After all, for a trade mark to carry out its function in the market, recognition of it by the relevant public has to be almost instantaneous. It is suggested that the notional observer cannot be expected to have anything more than familiarity with everyday skills and modes of expression. Here we draw together the considerations which apply to various types of mark.

(1) Signs which contain words, designs, letters or numerals are considered conventional. The only skills required to understand the graphic representation of such marks are a familiarity with our alphabet, our systems of numerals and a degree of literacy, all of which are taken for granted. By contrast, the average consumer is not taken to understand marks in, say, Arabic or Cyrillic[52] unless possibly and exceptionally, the marks are used and only used in a section of the population which does understand them.

(2) The same skills are required to understand a written description of a sign. However, written descriptions alone raise particular problems which are considered below.

(3) Three-dimensional signs (shapes, etc.) are normally expected to be graphi-

---

knowledge of the actual sign used by the applicant", but if the reader does have prior knowledge, it must be put out of mind.

[49] PAC 2/00 said: "Attempts to define signs more broadly in terms of perceived infringement rights inevitably lead to ambiguity and rejection."

[50] Case C–283/01 [2004] Ch. 97; [2004] R.P.C. 17; [2004] E.T.M.R. 33, para.59, ECJ

[51] PAC 2/00 said this: "Any colour standards, musical notation or scientific measurements put forward to represent marks must be precise and (a) make it reasonably practical for users of the system to be able to obtain a clear understanding of the mark, and (b) be able to accurately compare the sign the applicant uses or proposes to use with other similar signs."

[52] See, *e.g.* the observations of Jacob J. in *Smirnov*, April 7, 2003.

cally represented by a line drawing or photograph. Line drawings are likely to be easier to understand, being clearer and more precise than photographs.

(4) A sound mark may be graphically represented in conventional musical notation: notes on a stave.[53] As we commented above, in *Shield Mark*, the ECJ proceeded on the basis that the notional observer can understand musical notation, even though only a musician may be able to understand the representation immediately, whereas others less familiar with musical notation may either require some help or more time to work out what the sound is. Onomatopoeias are generally more accessible to the public, but insufficiently precise for the ECJ. It remains to be seen whether sonograms are approved as acceptable.

(5) So far as colour marks are concerned, the colour(s) must be defined by reference to well-known colour standards. Attempts to define colours by reference to anything more complicated than a well-known colour standard are likely to be rejected.[54] For example, a mark defined as "a blue bottle of optical characteristics such that if the wall thickness is 3 mm the bottle has, in air, a dominant wavelength of 472 to 474 nanometres, a purity of 44 to 48%, an optical brightness of 28 to 32%." required the use of a spectrophotometer to translate those optical characteristics into the colour known as cobalt blue or to test any other colour to see if it fell within the definition. The precision in the definition served to veil the identity of the sign.[55]

(6) The same point applies to marks consisting of an aroma or a taste: precision could be achieved using gas or high performance liquid chromatography, but it would conceal the identity of the sign. At the moment there does not seem to be any practical way in which a smell or taste mark can be adequately graphically represented.

DESCRIPTIONS IN WORDS ALONE

A graphic representation which consists only of a description in words requires very careful scrutiny. Pre-*Sieckmann*, a description in words alone sometimes proved acceptable at OHIM: perhaps the best example was the sign consisting of "the smell of fresh cut grass" for tennis balls.[56] The UK approach was stricter, it being observed that it is unlikely that a mere description of a three-dimensional article would, in practice, ever be sufficiently precise to meet the needs of the Act.[57] Post-*Sieckmann*, it is very difficult to see how a written description alone can ever be acceptable. The following (pre-*Sieckmann*) examples demonstrate why:

2–069

(1) A sign described as "a chewy sweet on a stick" was held to be incapable of being represented graphically.[58]

(2) The application for a three-dimensional mark contained the following representation: "the trade mark consists of a circular compressed tablet

[53] Case C–283/01 *Shield Mark* [2004] Ch. 97; [2004] R.P.C. 17; [2004] E.T.M.R. 33, para.59, ECJ. See para.2–050.

[54] Further guidelines on colours are contained in PAC 2/00.

[55] *Ty Nant Spring Water Ltd's Trade Mark Application* [2000] R.P.C. 55 (Appointed Person).

[56] See para.2–044 and the notes therein.

[57] By the Appointed Person, Simon Thorley Q.C., in *Swizzels Matlow Ltd's Application (No.2)* [2000] E.T.M.R. 58 ("Lovehearts"). Prompted by that observation, PAC 2/00 stated: "The Registrar will normally refuse to accord a filing date to applications describing three-dimensional marks in words until a pictorial representation of the shape is filed."

[58] *Swizzels Matlow Ltd's Application (No.1)* [1998] R.P.C. 244, Regy.

bearing a raised heart outline on both flat surfaces and containing within the heart outline on one side any of several different words or phrases." That description was held to be inadequate to constitute a graphical representation.[59] It was also said that "the description pre-supposes a knowledge on the part of the trader of the Lovehearts product as sold over the years and as is shown in [the] declaration. This cannot be a correct approach."

(3) The graphic representation was a hologram. The applicant admitted that it was "very unlikely that a relatively low number of photographic views would suffice for a complete description of the mark". Accordingly, the mark was not graphically represented and the application rejected under s.3(1)(a) of the 1994 Act.[60]

(4) "The marks consist of a set of forty nine coloured lottery balls, each marked with a number... nine white balls... ten blue balls... ten pink balls ..." etc. The application was rejected under s.3(1)(a).[61]

2–070   Examples from OHIM are:

(a) A sign described as "the vacuum packing of an article of clothing in an envelope of plastic" was held by the Second Board of Appeal at OHIM not to convey a clear and precise appearance of the mark itself. The description could not be considered to be a *reproduction* of the mark[62] (emphasis added).

(b) The applicant specified the type of mark as a colour mark and stated that the mark consisted of the colour "orange". Objection was taken that this description was too vague, since the wide generic term "orange" encompassed a wide range of different colour shades, from dark to light and from yellowish to reddish orange.[63]

(c) By contrast, an application for the colour mark LIGHT GREEN included a specimen of the precise colour claimed together with the following description "the colour light-green itself in the specific hue as is shown on the enclosed specimen of the colour". This was an acceptable graphic representation, although the application was refused on other grounds.[64]

CONSEQUENCE OF DEFICIENCY IN GRAPHIC REPRESENTATION

2–071   If it is concluded that the graphic representation is inadequate, it does not follow that the application concerns a sign which is not "capable of being represented graphically". An applicant may then be given an opportunity to file a proper graphic representation, which he must do within two months.[65] The consequence is a loss of priority,[66] because an application is only accorded a filing date once

[59] *Swizzels Matlow Ltd's Application (No.2)* [2000] E.T.M.R. 58. Simon Thorley Q.C. as the Appointed Person.

[60] *Checkpoint Security Services Ltd's Application*, June 7, 1999, Regy.

[61] *Camelot Group Plc's Application* SRIS O/125/99, April 8, 1999, Regy. "The description filed gives rise to an infinite variety of marks."

[62] *Antoni and Alison's Application* [1998] E.T.M.R. 460, OHIM BoA.

[63] *Orange Ltd's Application* [1998] E.T.M.R. 337, OHIM BoA.

[64] *Wm Wrigley Jr Company's Application* [1999] E.T.M.R. 214, OHIM BoA.

[65] Trade Mark Rules, r.11, which gives a period of two months to remedy any deficiencies. For CTM applications, the Implementing Regulation, r.9(2) is to the same effect.

[66] See *Robert McBride's Application* [2003] R.P.C. 19, p.343, (Geoffrey Hobbs Q.C. as the Appointed Person)—filing date given only when the applicant resolved uncertainty over colours by supplying pantone references.

everything required is furnished by the applicant either to the United Kingdom Registry[67] or to OHIM.[68]

6. Capable of distinguishing the goods or services of one undertaking from those of other undertakings—unravelling the skein[69]

SUMMARY

As in the previous edition, we start this section with a summary of the position   **2–072**
for those who do not want or need the detail. The true interpretation of this expression "capable of distinguishing" remains undecided, although we suggest the answer is reasonably clear. For the most part, in the everyday application of the absolute grounds for refusal in Arts 3(1)(b)–(d) of the TM Directive (Arts 7(1)(b)–(d) of the CTM Regulation) any puzzle over the interpretation of "capable of distinguishing" is bypassed. Accordingly, one might ask: why bother with this puzzle?

There are good reasons to do so. It would be preferable if the provisions which   **2–073**
concern distinctive character (in Arts 2, 3(1)(b)–(d) and 3(3) of the TM Directive, equivalent to Arts 4, 7(1)(b)–(d) and 7(3) of the CTM Regulation) could be interpreted as a coherent whole. Indeed, a coherent interpretation of the whole might inform our understanding of the individual parts—(1)(b) and (c) in particular. Distinctive character is the skein which runs through the groups of provisions in both the TM Directive and the CTM Regulation. Unravelling the skein ought to result in a coherent interpretation. There are two competing theories which seek to unravel the skein and present a coherent interpretation.

One theory, which we will call the German theory, relies on the introduction to   **2–074**
the debate and use of concepts of *abstract* and *concrete* distinctiveness, well-known, apparently, to German trade mark lawyers but unknown to everyone else. This theory (which is explained in greater detail below) says that Arts 3(1)(b)–(d) and 3(3) are concerned with *concrete* distinctiveness: the ability of the trade mark to distinguish the particular goods or services for which it is registered. On the other hand, Art.2 and the expression "capable of distinguishing" are concerned with *abstract* distinctiveness: the ability of the trade mark to distinguish in the abstract, without reference to any particular goods or services. The advantage of this theory is that it does achieve a measure of coherence. The disadvantage is that there is not the slightest hint of it anywhere unless you already know of the underlying concepts, and in fact, this theory is inconsistent with the *travaux preparatoires*.

Underpinning a second theory is the essential function of a trade mark—not a   **2–075**
bad place to start. What could be less surprising than the realisation that the basic requirements of a "trade mark" include reference to the "essential function" of a trade mark? The expression "capable of distinguishing" reflects and encapsulates

---

[67] 1994 Act, s.33(1).

[68] Implementing Regulation, r.9(1).

[69] A-G Jacobs used this expression in BABY-DRY when he first discussed this issue. The "skein" is "distinctive character" which runs through Arts 2, 3(1)(a)–(d) and 3(3) of the Directive and, likewise, through Arts 4, 7(1)(a)–(d) and 7(3) of the CTM Regulation. See [2001] E.C.R. I-6251; [2002] Ch. 82; [2002] R.P.C. 17.

that essential function. Hence, when it is used, a trade mark must be capable of distinguishing the goods and services of one undertaking from those of other undertakings. "Capable of distinguishing" means "able to distinguish" or "serves to distinguish".

2–076   In the remainder of this section, we discuss the various indications which can be said to support one theory or the other. In summary, we believe the second theory is correct and is to be preferred. Furthermore, if this puzzle had been tackled at an earlier stage, we might have avoided some of the problems which have been encountered over the proper interpretation of Arts 3(1)(b) & (c) of the Directive (Arts 7(1)(b) & (c) of the CTM Regulation). These further considerations are discussed in Ch.8.

INTERPRETATION IN MORE DETAIL

2–077   As mentioned above, as far as we are aware, there are two theories which attempt to make logical sense of Arts 3(1)(a)–(d), 3(3) when read in conjunction with Art.2. The two theories overlap to a considerable degree, but part company when it comes to the expression "capable of distinguishing" in Art.2. It is necessary to explain the competing theories in a little more detail.

THE GERMAN THEORY[70]

2–078   The German theory runs as follows. In the TM Directive (and the same reasoning applies to the identical provisions in the CTM Regulation) it is necessary to start at the end with Art.3(3) (the proviso in s.3(1)). This provision makes it clear that the grounds in Arts 3(1)(b), (c) and/or (d) may be overcome "if, before the date of application for registration and following the use which has been made of it [the trade mark], it has acquired a distinctive character". This imposes a positive requirement for a distinctive character acquired through use or by nurture.

2–079   The next step is to move to Arts 3(1)(b), (c) & (d). It is clear, and the ECJ has confirmed, that (1) there is considerable overlap between these three provisions (2) the grounds in Arts 3(1)(c) & (d) are effectively subsets of Art.3(1)(b), dealing with particular situations where a mark will not have any distinctive character. Logic dictates that these provisions impose a positive requirement that the trade mark must possess a distinctive character. If one only takes use into account under Art.3(3), then these grounds examine the qualities of the trade mark in the absence of use. Hence these provisions impose a positive requirement that the trade mark possesses a distinctive character by nature, absent consideration of any use.

2–080   The third and final step is back to the beginning—Art.3(1)(a) and its incorporation of the definition in Art.2. Article 2 starts by setting out the signs of which a trade mark may consist, but ends with the important proviso "provided that such signs are capable of distinguishing the goods or services of one undertaking from those of other undertakings", wording which also appears in Recital 7.

2–081   It is at this point that the German theory introduces the concepts of *abstract* and *concrete* distinctiveness. The theory is that Arts 3(1)(b),(c), (d) and 3(3) are

---

[70] We use this shorthand only because the theory utilises concepts from German trade mark law. A more detailed explanation of this theory can be found in the article by David Keeling "About Kinetic watches, easy banking and nappies that keep a baby dry" [2003] I.P.Q. No.2, p.131 at pp.133–136. Since David Keeling supports the German theory, it will be understood that the views in this Chapter do not represent his.

dealing with *concrete* distinctiveness—that is, the ability to distinguish the particular goods or services the subject of the application or registration of one undertaking from those of other undertakings. By contrast, Art.2 is dealing with *abstract* distinctiveness—that is, the ability to distinguish in the abstract, without regard to any particular goods or services.

Once it has been stated, this theory has a certain attractiveness to those wishing to make these provisions fit a logical structure and it has a number of adherents.[71]

A SECOND THEORY

A second theory attempts to make sense of (1) the purpose of Art.2, (2) the language used and (3) its relationship with Art.3.

2–082

A proper understanding of the purpose of Art.2 starts with Recital 7:

2–083

"Whereas attainment of the objectives at which this approximation of laws is aiming requires that the conditions for obtaining and continuing to hold a registered trade mark are, in general, identical in all Member States; whereas, to this end, it is necessary to list examples of signs which may constitute a trade mark, provided that such signs are capable of distinguishing the goods or services of one undertaking from those of other undertakings;"

This wording makes it clear[72] that the first purpose of Art.2 was to provide a list for all Member States of the types of signs which may constitute a trade mark. The second purpose of Art.2 was to introduce and/or emphasise the essential function of a trade mark: to distinguish the goods or services of one undertaking from those of other undertakings. Bearing in mind that Art.2 is the closest the Directive gets to define what a trade mark is, it seems unlikely that the proviso in Art.2 was intended to refer to the obscure concept of *abstract* distinctiveness. It seems much more likely that the requirement that the sign must be "capable of distinguishing etc." is a reference to the essential function of a trade mark.

2–084

To this end, the language used ("capable of distinguishing") can be interpreted entirely consistently with the essential function of a trade mark and with the provisions in Art.3. The expression "capable of distinguishing" takes account of the fact that marks may not have been used before an application is filed, but contemplates what must occur when the mark is used. When a mark is put to use, it must distinguish the goods and services of one undertaking from those of other undertakings. Hence "capable of" means "able to", in the sense of "if used, it distinguishes..." This is what trade mark do (or are supposed to do).

2–085

This interpretation ensures that Art.2 is consistent with Art.3. A sign which is capable of distinguishing must have distinctive character, yet the actual examination of whether a trade mark has distinctive character is left to Art.3, where the mark is examined absent use under Arts 3(1)(b)–(d), and taking use into account under Art.3(3).

2–086

THE CYNIC'S THEORY

There is yet another, more cynical theory which does not attempt to make these provisions fit together. In effect, it says (1) Arts 3(1)(b)–(d) are derived from the Paris Convention; (2) the "capable of distinguishing" requirement in Art.2, plus Art.3(3) were unnecessarily grafted on top; (3) it cannot be assumed that EU

2–087

---

[71] See, in David Keeling's article, the references in nn.7 and 8, [2003] I.P.Q. 131 at 134–5.
[72] And it is further emphasised by consideration of the *travaux preparatoires*. See section 8, below.

legislation of this type is drafted with strict logic in mind, since there are political pressures (reflected in the Minutes of the Council) caused by particular Member States trying to influence the drafting; and accordingly (4) there is little point in striving to find a logical, internally consistent interpretation of these provisions. We believe this is too defeatist.

THE PARIS CONVENTION AND TRIPS

2–088   The drafting history of these provisions in the TM Directive is out in the Annex to this Chapter—see section 8. The wording used in Arts 3(1)(b), (c) and (d) derives from Art.6*quinquies* B.2 of the Paris Convention. The Paris Convention contains no equivalent to Art.3(3), Art.3(1)(a) or Art.2. The simpler formula used in the Paris Convention appears to impose the implicit requirement that a trade mark must possess distinctive character to be registrable. This is made more explicit in Art.15(1) of TRIPS which provides: "where signs are not inherently capable of distinguishing the relevant goods or services, Members may make registrability depend on distinctiveness acquired through use." One should also note recital 12 to the TM Directive, which states in part "whereas it is necessary that the provisions of this Directive are entirely consistent with those of the Paris Convention". Whilst this is an important consideration, it rather begs the question of whether, by grafting additional provisions on top of the formula adopted from the Paris Convention, the meaning of the original provisions has been altered. Clearly this recital is a strong indication that we should strive to find that it has not. Article 15(1) of TRIPS adopts the same expression "capable of distinguishing": "Any sign, or combination of signs, capable of distinguishing the goods or services of one undertaking from those of other undertakings, shall be capable of constituting a trademark."

PROBLEMS WITH THE GERMAN THEORY

2–089   There are a number of problems with the German theory:

First, there is no hint of this theory in any of the *travaux preparatoires*. In fact, the German theory is inconsistent with the *travaux preparatoires*.

Second, there is no hint of this theory even in inadmissible aids to construction such as the Minutes of the Meeting of the Council at which the TM Directive was adopted.[73]

Third, one might ask: how were we supposed to know that "capable of distinguishing" is to be interpreted in accordance with some concepts in German law? Furthermore: why German law over any of the other pre-Directive laws of Member States: after all, UK law previously used the very expression "capable of distinguishing".

Fourth, it does not make much sense to divorce a trade mark from the goods or services the subject of the application or registration. After all, Article 1 defines the scope of the Directive in these terms: "This Directive shall apply to every trade mark in respect of goods or services which is the subject of registration or of an application in a Member State."

Fifth, there is no particular reason why there has to be a difference between the standards of distinctiveness in Arts 2 and 3. One would have thought that one standard of distinctiveness was preferable.

Sixth, what is the point of "abstract distinctiveness"? There appears to be

[73] See, in the previous edition, para.1–05.

none. Any "sign" which fails the test of "abstract distinctiveness" will automatically fail the test for "concrete distinctiveness". Passing the first hurdle says nothing about whether the sign will pass the second.

Seventh, the German theory is probably inconsistent with TRIPS.

Accordingly, the best that can be said is that this theory has the benefit of convenience, in that it provides *a* solution to the apparent conundrum of Arts 2 and 3(1) & (3) of the Directive or Arts 4, 7(1) & (3) of the CTM Regulation.

GUIDANCE FROM THE ECJ

When one turns to the jurisprudence of the ECJ, the indications as to which theory is correct are somewhat contradictory. It may be recalled that the reference to the ECJ in *Philips* might have been an opportunity to sort out this puzzle, but both A-G Colomer and the Court answered the first question without doing so.[74] The Court did confirm that "[the] essential function of the trade mark is also clear from the wording and the structure of the various provisions of the Directive concerning the grounds for refusal of registration" but did not link the essential function directly to Art.2 until later (see below). In BABY-DRY, A-G Jacobs referred to the fact that "Unravelling the skein formed by Articles 4 and 7(1)(a) to (d) of the Trade Mark Regulation (or Articles 2 and 3(1)(a) to (d) of the Trade Marks Directive, which are essentially the same) is not an obviously easy matter." He rather ducked the issue, suggesting that "too great a degree of coherence or unification need not be sought but rather that, at least in the context of the present case, the various provisions should be interpreted each within its own sphere."[75]

2–090

SUPPORT FOR THE SECOND THEORY

We can start with *Merz & Krell* in which the ECJ stated:

2–091

> [the] "essential function of trade marks has been incorporated by the Community legislature into Article 2 of the Directive...".[76]

The same point was made in *Arsenal*[77], and in *Björnekulla*:[78]

2–092

> "21. That essential function of trade marks has been incorporated by the Community legislature into Article 2 of the Directive, which provides that signs which are capable of being represented graphically may only constitute a trade mark if they are capable of distinguishing the goods or services of one undertaking from those of other undertakings (*Merz & Krell*, paragraph 23).
>
> 22. That condition is given effect to in, inter alia, Articles 3 and 12 of the Directive. While Article 3 specifies the circumstances in which a trade mark is incapable, *ab initio*, of fulfilling its function as an indication of origin, Article 12(2)(a) addresses the situation where the trade mark is no longer capable of fulfilling that function."

---

[74] Case C–299/99 *Philips Electronics NV v Remington Consumer Products Ltd* [2003] R.P.C. 2 (A-G, see paras 43–45) and [2003] Ch.159 (ECJ, paras 29–40).

[75] Case C–383/99 P *Procter & Gamble v OHIM* [2002] R.P.C. 17, p.349, see paras 61 and 67.

[76] Case C–517/99 *Merz & Krell* [2001] E.C.R. I-6959; [2002] E.T.M.R. 21, para.23.

[77] Case C–206/01 *Arsenal Football Club v Reed* [2002] E.C.R. I-10273; [2003] Ch. 454; [2003] R.P.C. 9, para.49.

[78] Case C–371/02 *Björnekulla Fruktindustrier AB v Procordia Food AB* [2004] R.P.C. 45; [2004] E.T.M.R. 69, paras 21–22.

2–093   More recently the same point has been made in *Nichols*:[79]

"Article 2 of Directive 89/104 contains a list, described as a list of examples in the seventh recital in the preamble to that directive, of signs which may constitute a trade mark, provided that such signs are capable of distinguishing the goods or services of one undertaking from those of other undertakings, that is to say to fulfil the trade marks function as an indicator of origin."

and reiterated in *Budweiser*:[80]

"Thus, like Article 2 of Directive 89/104, Article 15 of the TRIPs Agreement lays down a guarantee of origin which is the essential function of a trade mark."

Finally, in *HAVE A BREAK*, the ECJ stated:[81]

"...it should be pointed out that, under Article 2 of the directive, a mark has distinctive character when it is capable of distinguishing the goods or services of one undertaking from those of other undertakings."

2–094   These *dicta* do not admit of any concept of mere *abstract* distinctiveness in Art.2, nor is it possible to speak of the essential function of a trade mark in the abstract or without reference to the particular goods or services in respect of which the trade mark is registered or used. Accordingly, we suggest these *dicta* support the second theory.

CONTRARY INDICATIONS

2–095   There are, however, some contrary indications in ECJ judgments interspersed among those referred to above. In POSTKANTOOR,[82] para.80, the ECJ seemed to be edging towards acceptance of the German theory, stating:

"As a preliminary point, it is appropriate to observe, first, that the purpose of Art.2 of the Directive is to define the types of signs of which a trade mark may consist (Case C–273/00 *Sieckmann* [2002] E.C.R. I-11737, para.[43]), irrespective of the goods or services for which protection might be sought (see to that effect *Sieckmann*, paras [43] to [55], Libertel, paras [22] to [42], and Case C–283/01 *Shield Mark* [2003] E.C.R. I-0000, paras [34] to [41]). It provides that a trade mark may consist inter alia of words and letters, provided that they are capable of distinguishing the goods or services of one undertaking from those of other undertakings." (emphasis added)

2–096   More recently, in his Opinion in SAT.2, A-G Jacobs referred to the provisions in Arts 4 and 7(1)(b) of the CTM Regulation and posed the question: "Is this mere repetition or do the concepts differ?". He considered that, in the light of Art.7(3):

"it seems sensible to assume that Articles 4 and 7(1)(a) refer to a general, absolute, abstract capacity to distinguish products of different origins, whereas Article 7(1)(b) is intended to connote distinctiveness in relation to the class of product in question."[83]

2–097   The ECJ did not discuss the point and, despite his generally good track record

---

[79] Case C–404/02 *Nichols plc v Registrar of Trade Marks* [2005] R.P.C. 12, p.243, para.22.
[80] Case C–245/02 *Anheuser-Busch Inc v Budĕjovický Budvar, národní podnik* [2005] E.T.M.R. 27, para.69, ECJ.
[81] Case C–353/03 *Société des produits Nestlé SA v Mars UK Ltd*, July 7,2005, ECJ.
[82] Case C–363/99 [2004] E.T.M.R. 57.
[83] See paras 15 and 16 of his Opinion, Case C–329/02 [2004] E.T.M.R. 80.

in trade mark cases, it does not appear that A-G Jacobs considered the second theory.

Shortly afterwards, in *3-D Tablets for dishwashers*,[84] the ECJ stated:

"the fact that a sign is, in general, capable of constituting a trade mark within the meaning of Article 4 of [the CTM Regulation] does not mean that the sign necessarily has distinctive character for the purposes of Article 7(1)(b).. in relation to a specific product or service." Although the ECJ was not considering the specific point, that statement is consistent with the German theory, but not necessarily inconsistent with the second, because the assessment of distinctive character obviously must take place under Article 7(1)/ Article 3(1).

When one starts to examine the support for the proposition stated in POST-KANTOOR, there is precious little to it.   **2–098**

First, this observation was evidently *obiter* because in the next paragraph, the ECJ also stated that "…an interpretation of Art.2 of the Directive appears not to be useful for the purposes of deciding the present case."

Second, when one looks at the relevant paragraphs of *Sieckmann*, *Libertel* and *Shield Mark*, cited in support of the proposition that the examination under Art.2 is "irrespective of the goods or services for which protection might be sought", one finds that all those passages are concerned with graphical representation. None of them is concerned with or contains any discussion about the interpretation of "capable of distinguishing".

Third, this observation does not appear to derive from anything in the Opinion of A-G Colomer. In paras 39–41 of his Opinion he referred, obliquely, to the possibility that the examination under Art.2 "may be somewhat abstract in nature", but made his views plain that he could see no point in having more than one standard for distinctiveness or making any assessment in the abstract.

On balance, we suggest that both logic (as explained above and as expressed in the first group of *dicta* from the ECJ) and the origins of Art.2 (as shown in the *travaux preparatoires*) provide strong support for the second theory. Article 2 of the Directive does introduce and encapsulate the essential function of a trade mark. By contrast, the German theory conveniently provides its own logic (of *abstract* and *concrete* distinctiveness), is inconsistent with the origins of Art.2 and does not, in fact, provide a satisfactory interpretation.   **2–099**

7. "in relation to goods or services"

For most applications, no issue arises over the goods or services in respect of which the mark has been applied for. The principal reason is because the choice of goods or services is for the applicant, and the relevant registry rarely has any reason to question that choice. At the moment, over-broad specifications are almost invariably left to revocation proceedings. There are two particular issues which can arise and both concern retailing. The first is a short one, whether or the extent to which the trading name of a shop is being used in relation to the goods on sale in it. The second is the well-known issue over whether registrations can be obtained for "retail services", which has now reached the ECJ.   **2–100**

---

[84] Joined Cases C–468/01P to C–472/01P *Procter & Gamble Co v OHIM* [2004] E.T.M.R. 88, para.30.

Name of a business used in relation to goods

2–101   Whether a business name is being used in relation to goods sold by that business depends on the facts. If the business is the source of particular goods, the answer is obvious. So far as retail outlets are concerned, if the trade mark which appears on the goods is the same as the name of the business, then no issue arises. If the goods bear no trade mark the average consumer is likely to perceive the name of the business as the indicator of trade source of those goods, although the trade connection may be weak if the goods are standard items. If, however, the goods bear the trade marks of third parties, it is unlikely that the name of the business or shop is being used in relation to those particular goods.[85] The average consumer would say that the mark actually on the goods is the trade mark, and the name of the shop or business is just that.

Retail Services

2–102   For some years after the introduction of the 1994 Act and the CTM system, both the United Kingdom Registry and OHIM operated a policy of rejecting applications in so far as they covered "retail services" and the like,[86] such as mail order services and the Internet equivalent of "electronic trading in goods". The OHIM Examination Guidelines simply stated that the "activity of retail trading in goods is not as such a service".[87] The United Kingdom Registry took a similar line, but provided more reasoning in the Work Manual[88] as to how this objection arose. The objection was taken under s.3(1)(a) on the basis that it is implicit in s.1(1) that the undertakings are trading in goods or services. Therefore, it was said "marks in respect of such services provided by retailers which are merely ancillary to trading in goods would not appear to be registrable under the 1994 Act because such services cannot either constitute a business in the provision of services or be services in respect of which a trade mark may be registered."

2–103   In the context of s.1(1), this reasoning appeared artificial and overly reminiscent of the position under the 1938 Act.[89] It seems reasonable to assume that for many years, members of the public have thought or would think (if asked) that they were being provided with a distinct service in some large department stores or specialist retailers, over and above simply being provided with goods available for purchase. However luxurious the additional service may be, it is true to say it can only be ancillary to the trade in the goods themselves.

Policy considerations

2–104   There is no express basis for an objection to registrations for "retail services" in the 1994 Act, the TM Directive or the CTM Regulation, and it would be very difficult to formulate an objection to exclude registration for these ancillary "looking after customers" services. The objection appeared to be based on policy

---

[85] See the remarks of Jacob J. in *Crate & Barrel*, where he did not actually decide the point but made his views plain: *Euromarket Designs Inc v Peters* [2001] F.S.R. 20, p.288, see para.56.

[86] Just as test cases were brought under the 1938 Act *Boots Co, Re; sub nom. Dee Corp* [1990] R.P.C. 159, CA), test cases were brought under the 1994 Act. These eventually caused the UK Registry to change its practice on "retail services". See PAC 13/00, September 27, 2000.

[87] OHIM Examination Guidelines 4.3(j).

[88] The old version of Ch.6, paras 2.3.10–12 and 6.5.5.

[89] Established in *Dee's Application* [1990] R.P.C. 159 CA. Of course, the old requirement that the services had to be provided for money or money's worth had to be dropped for the purposes of the 1994 Act.

grounds concerned with administrative burden, despite the fact that there are other trade mark systems which have accommodated registrations for "retail services" and the like without apparent problem. Here, retailers could already obtain registrations covering the goods that they sold. If every retailer was also entitled to protection covering "retail services" provided in selling those goods, the thinking was that this would place a considerable additional and unnecessary burden on trade mark systems. In fact, this problem (if it be a problem) is not confined to applications from retailers. If registrations were permitted for retail services, in theory every trader would be entitled to a registration to cover the services provided in "looking after customers", whatever the trade and whatever the goods or services. Thus, one would expect every applicant to apply automatically to cover the goods or services in which he traded and for ancillary services under the general rubric of "looking after customers".

GIACOMELLI[90]

The prevailing thinking was being challenged in a number of test cases. The first to be decided was an application by Giacomelli Sport SpA for a CTM for the following services: **2–105**

"Bringing together, for the benefit of others, of a variety of goods (excluding transport thereof), enabling customers to conveniently view and purchase those goods".

Due to the importance of the issue, the OHIM Board of Appeal invited the President of OHIM to make comment on the appeal. His principal objection against registrations for retail services was that they would amount to "cover-all" registrations, which would be uncertain in scope, leading to difficulties in classification and in the comparison of marks for the purposes of registration and infringement. He also drew attention to the Joint Statement contained in the Minutes of the Council Meeting at which the CTM Regulation was adopted, which expressed the view that a CTM would not be available for retail services.[91]   **2–106**

The Board of Appeal rejected any reliance on the statement in the Minutes[92] and observed that the President's comments were really concerned with administrative matters and did not impact on the legal position. As to the legal position, the Board observed that "service" was not defined in the CTM Regulation and decided that the concept should be construed widely. The Board then made some observations on the common experience of retailing, observing correctly that the goodwill of a retail business is, by and large, built on the service it provides.[93]   **2–107**

In principle, the Board was prepared to allow a registration for this type of service, but remitted the application to the examiner to allow the applicant to specify the services with greater clarity. The services had to be linked to the goods concerned, in this case "sports goods".   **2–108**

---

[90] [2000] E.T.M.R. 277, Second BoA.

[91] "The Council and the Commission consider that the activity of retail trading in goods is not as such a service for which a Community trade mark may be registered under this Regulation."

[92] Following established ECJ authority in *Antonissen* [1991] E.C.R. I-745, para.18: "...such a declaration cannot be used for the purpose of interpreting a provision of secondary legislation where, as in this case, no reference is made to the content of the declaration in the wording of the provision in question."

[93] There are some web-sites which do nothing except bring together advertisements for goods. They do not even sell the goods, simply taking a commission from the actual seller of the goods. The commission may not even be based on sales of goods, but on hits on the web-site.

This was a sensible decision, reflecting the reality of consumer's experience with retailers. By contrast, the opposing arguments—that retail services are merely ancillary to the trade in goods and benefit only the retailer—look artificial.

The views of the ECJ

2–109   It has taken some time for this issue to reach the ECJ, but it has done so in a reference from the Bundespatentgericht in Germany in *Praktiker Bau-*.[94] The Opinion of A-G Léger is well-reasoned and persuasive. As usual, the ECJ did not adopt all the detail of his reasoning which proceeds through a number of stages. For reasons which are explained elsewhere, A-G Léger's analysis has implications which extend well beyond the discrete issue relating to "retail services".

2–110   A-G Léger starts with first principles: the essential function of a trade mark. This leads him to the view that, in so far as the object of a service mark is to permit consumers to identify the undertaking which provides that service, the registration of a service mark implies that the service in question is identifiable as such. In other words, it is important that the activity in question can be perceived by consumers as constituting the provision of a service. By contrast, if consumers could not perceive the service as such, it would make the scope of the registration indefinable.

2–111   The next stage in the analysis looks to the requirements of the registration system. Paragraphs 49–52 of *Sieckmann* explain why "it must be possible to identify the sign in question in a sure and precise manner in order to permit the competent authorities to meet their regulatory obligations and the holder of the mark and other operators to know exactly the scope of the rights conferred by registration". These requirements are then transposed to the products and services in question. In A-G Léger's opinion[95]:

> "the sign, on the one hand, and the products and services which that sign must be used to designate, on the other, constitute the two indissociable elements of registration which make it possible to determine the rights conferred by each trade mark registered."

2–112   Having reviewed the practices of various national registries and OHIM, A-G Léger recommended:

1. services provided in the context of a retail trade in goods are services in respect of which a trade mark may be registered;
2. that expressions such as "retail trade" or "retail services" are not sufficiently explicit to describe the content of such services;
3. a sufficiently precise description of the services in question will depend on the circumstances, but the further qualification may specify the product or products to which the retail services apply, or indicate the sector of activity concerned (*e.g.* sports clothing sector) or the type of shop (*e.g.* furniture shop). However, a simple reference to services provided in a department store or supermarket[96] is not likely to be sufficiently precise in view of the great diversity of products which may be sold through those types of outlet.

---

[94] Case C–418/02 *Praktiker Bau- und Heimwerkermarkte AG*. Opinion of A-G Léger dated January 13, 2005, Judgment of ECJ, July 7, 2005.

[95] Case C–418/02 *Praktiker Bau- und Heimwerkermarkte AG*, para.63 (of an unofficial translation).

[96] These observations were prompted by views expressed by the President of OHIM in his Communication No.3/01 (issued after the *Giacomelli Sport* decision) to the effect that "retail services of a department store" or "retail services of a supermarket" were sufficient. In fact, the President was of the view that specifying the field of activity, although desirable, was not legally necessary.

The ECJ followed A-G Léger's recommendations but not the detail of his **2–113** reasoning. The judgment has approved the general approach taken by at least the UK TM Registry and OHIM. The principle is obviously not restricted to traditional retailers. It is capable of extension to all modern forms of retailing-mail order, telephone and Internet—provided that the service can be perceived as a distinct service by the consumer. There is no need to confine this principle to retailing—any service which can be perceived as a distinct service by the consumer ought to be capable of being included in a specification of services.

8. Annex

THE DERIVATION OF THE RELEVANT PROVISIONS OF THE TM DIRECTIVE AND CTM REGULATION

As mentioned in the main text, the proposals which led to the TM Directive were **2–114** closely intertwined with proposals which led to the CTM Regulation. Accordingly, it is necessary to track the progress of the relevant provisions chronologically through the various proposals for the TM Directive and the CTM Regulation. Words in italics have been added for clarification. For ease of reference, we start by setting out again the end result, the relevant provisions of the TM Directive:

Recital (7): **2–115**

"Whereas attainment of the objectives at which this approximation of laws is aiming requires that the conditions for obtaining and continuing to hold a registered trade mark are, in general, identical in all Member States; whereas, to this end, it is necessary to list examples of signs which may constitute a trade mark, provided that such signs are capable of distinguishing the goods or services of one undertaking from those of other undertakings; whereas the grounds for refusal or invalidity concerning the trade mark itself, for example, the absence of any distinctive character, ... are to be listed in an exhaustive manner."

Recital (10): **2–116**

"... the function of [the registered trade mark] is in particular to guarantee the trade mark as an indication of origin ...".

Article 2: *Signs of which a trade mark may consist* **2–117**

"A trade mark may consist of any sign capable of being represented graphically, particularly words, including personal names, designs, letters, numerals, the shape of goods or their packaging, provided that such signs are capable of distinguishing the goods or services of one undertaking from those of other undertakings."

Article 3 *Grounds for refusal or invalidity* **2–118**

"1. The following shall not be registered or if registered shall be liable to be declared invalid:

(a) signs which cannot constitute a trade mark;

(b) trade marks which are devoid of any distinctive character;" etc.

PROPOSAL FOR A FIRST COUNCIL DIRECTIVE TO APPROXIMATE THE LAWS
OF THE MEMBER STATES RELATING TO TRADE MARKS[97] — 1980

Extracts from the explanatory memorandum

2–119 "Introduction

Initially it is proposed to approximate those provisions of trade mark law which currently have the strongest and most direct influence on the establishment and functioning of the common market in marked goods. These are the rules governing the scope of the protection afforded to trade marks, use of trade marks, amicable settlement of conflicts and the relative and absolute grounds for the refusal of registration or invalidation of trade marks.

The widely advocated approximation of further major areas of national trade mark law, such as the definition of registrable signs ... can in the Commission's opinion wait until a later Directive.

Another important reason for starting with this limited measure of approximation is the fact that, along with the Directive, a proposal is being submitted to establish a Community trade mark. The proposal for a Regulation seeks the same ends as the Directive but by a different route... The two proposals are complementary and must therefore be looked at and judged together."

2–120 "Article 2: *commentary*

"The absolute grounds for refusing registration listed in paragraphs (1) and (2) are similar to those laid down in Article 6 of the proposal for a Regulation. Reference is therefore made to the commentary on that Article in the Explanatory Memorandum to the Regulation.

The list of absolute grounds for refusal is exhaustive...."

Extracts from the recitals

2–121 [Whereas]

"it does not appear to be necessary at present to undertake full-scale harmonisation of the trade mark laws of Member States. It will be sufficient if approximation is limited to those national provisions of law which most directly affect free movement of goods and services ... It is, further, important not to disregard the solutions and advantages which the Community trade mark system affords to undertakings wishing to acquire trade marks. Under this system, there is no point in requiring the Member States, inter alia, to authorise the registration of additional categories of signs or to recognise service marks... attainment of the objectives at which this approximation of laws is aiming requires that the conditions for obtaining and continuing to hold a trade mark are, in general, identical in all Member States;

The purpose of protection is to guarantee the trade mark's function as an indicator of origin."

Article 2: *text*

2–122 "(1) Trade marks shall be refused registration or shall be invalidated if, on the date of application therefor, they consist of signs which, under the

---

[97] 59 COM(80) 635 final, dated November 19, 1980.

law of the Member State concerned, cannot constitute a trade mark or be held as such by the applicant, or if, on that date, are devoid of distinctive character in a Member State, and in particular:

   (a) those which consist solely of signs or indications which in trade may be requisite for the purpose of showing the kind, quality … etc. or other characteristics of the goods or service, unless those marks have acquired distinctive character in consequence of the use made of them;

   (b) those which consist solely of signs or indications which are customarily used to designate the goods or service in the current language of the trade or in the bona fide and established practices thereof."

PROPOSAL FOR A COUNCIL REGULATION ON COMMUNITY TRADE MARKS — 1980

Section 1: Definition of a Community trade mark,[98] Obtaining a Community Trade Mark

Article 3: commentary

"This provision defines the types of signs of which Community trade marks   **2–123** may consist. It is geared particularly to the question whether the relevant sign is capable of performing the basic function of a trade mark. That function, in economic and legal terms, is to indicate the origin of goods or services and to distinguish them from those of other undertakings.

No type of sign is automatically excluded from registration as a Community trade mark. Article 3 lists the types of signs used most frequently by undertakings to identify their goods or services, but it is not an exhaustive list. It is designed to simplify the adaptation of administrative practices and court judgments to business requirements and to encourage undertakings to apply for Community trade marks.

Depending on the circumstances, therefore, the Trade Marks Office, the national courts or, in the last resort, the Court of Justice will be responsible for determining whether, for example, solid colours or shades of colours, and signs denoting sound, smell or taste may constitute Community trade marks."

Recitals: *short extracts*

"The rights in a Community trade mark are not to be capable of being   **2–124** obtained otherwise than by registration, and registration is to be refused if the trade mark is not distinctive, is unlawful or is not available....

The purpose of protection is to guarantee the trade mark's function as an indicator of origin...".

Article 1: *Community trade marks*

"(1) A trade mark for goods or services which conforms with the condi-   **2–125** tions contained in this regulation and is registered in manner herein provided is hereinafter referred to as a 'Community trade mark'".

---

[98] Contained in the same document as the Proposal for the Directive. 59 COM(80) 635 final, dated November 19, 1980.

Article 3: *Signs of which a Community trade mark may consist*

2–126   "A Community trade mark may consist of words (including surnames), designs, letters, numerals, combinations of colours, the shape of goods or of their packaging, or of any other signs which are capable of distinguishing the goods or services of one undertaking from those of other undertakings."

Article 6: *Absolute grounds for refusal*

2–127   "(1) Trade marks which do not conform to the requirements of Article 3 ... and trade marks which are not distinctive, shall not be registered; in particular the following trade marks shall not be registered:
(a) those which consist solely of signs or indications which in trade may be requisite for the purpose of showing the kind, quality ... etc... or other characteristics of the goods or service;
(b) those which consist solely of signs or indications which are customarily used to designate the goods or service in the current language of the trade or in the bona fide and established practices thereof.
(4) Paragraph 1(a) shall not apply if the trade mark has become distinctive in consequence of the use which has been made of it.

AMENDED PROPOSAL FOR A COUNCIL REGULATION ON THE COMMUNITY TRADE MARK[99] — 1984

Commentary on the Articles

2–128   "Title II: The law relating to trade marks
Section 1: Definition of a Community trade mark, Obtaining a Community trade mark
Articles 3 and 4
The amendments to these two articles are purely a matter of drafting.
Article 6
The wording of paragraph 2(b) was brought into line with that of Article 6 *quinquies* B3 of the Paris Convention...."

Recitals: relevant extracts

2–129   "The rights in a Community trade mark are not to be capable of being obtained otherwise than by registration, and registration is to be refused if the trade mark is not distinctive, is unlawful or is not available....
The purpose of protection is to guarantee the trade mark's function as an indicator of origin ..."

Text—amendments indicated by underlining

2–130   Article 1: Community trade marks
(1) A trade mark for goods or services which conforms with the conditions contained in this regulation and is registered in manner herein provided is hereinafter referred to as a "Community trade mark".

2–131   Article 3: Signs of which a Community trade mark may consist
A Community trade mark may consist of any signs, particularly words, including personal names, designs, letters, numerals, combinations of colours, the shape

[99] COM (84) 470 final, dated July 31, 1984.

of goods or of their packaging, or of any other signs which are capable of distinguishing the goods or services of one undertaking from those of other undertakings.

Article 6 Absolute grounds for refusal   **2–132**

(1) Trade marks which do not conform to the requirements of Article 3 … and trade marks which are not distinctive, shall not be registered; in particular the following trade marks shall not be registered:

(a) those which consist solely of signs or indications which in trade may be requisite for the purpose of showing the kind, quality … etc… or other characteristics of the goods or service;

(b) those which consist solely of signs or indications which are customarily used to designate the goods or service in the current language of the trade or in the bona fide and established practices thereof.

(4) Paragraph 1(a) shall not apply if the trade mark has become distinctive in relation to the goods or services for which registration is requested in consequence of the use which has been made of it."

AMENDED PROPOSAL FOR A FIRST COUNCIL DIRECTIVE TO APPROXIMATE THE LAWS OF THE MEMBER STATES RELATING TO TRADE MARKS[1] — 1985

Article 2: text—amendments indicated by underlining

"(1) Trade marks shall be refused registration or shall be invalidated if,   **2–133** on the date of application therefor, they consist of signs which, under the law of the Member State concerned, cannot constitute a trade mark or be held as such by the applicant, or if, on that date, are devoid of distinctive character in that Member State, and in particular:

(a) those which consist solely of signs or indications which in trade may be requisite for the purpose of showing the kind, quality … etc. or other characteristics of the goods or service, unless those marks have acquired distinctive character in consequence of the use made of them;

(b) those which consist solely of signs or indications which are customarily used to designate the goods or service in the current language of the trade or in the bona fide and established practices thereof.

(4) Paragraph 1(a) shall not apply if the trade mark has become distinctive in relation to the goods or services for which registration is requested in consequence of the use which has been made of it."

Before the Directive was adopted on December 21, 1988, there was an intermediate text of December 15, 1987, which was not published. The changes made between the 1985 Proposal and the TM Directive are apparent.

---

[1] COM (85) 793 final, dated December 17, 1985.

CHAPTER 3

THE REGISTER OF TRADE MARKS AND THE TRADE MARKS BRANCH OF THE PATENT OFFICE

1. The Register

THE REGISTER

3–001   The Register of Trade Marks was established by the Trade Marks Registration Act 1875[1] and it is now continued under s.63 of the Trade Marks Act 1994, which provides that it is to be maintained by the Registrar. In fact, it has been kept on computer for some years now.

RULE-MAKING POWER

3–002   By s.78 of the 1994 Act, the Secretary of State has a broad power to make rules under specific sections of the Act authorising the making of rules, to make rules prescribing things which the Act permits or requires to be prescribed, and "generally for regulating practice and procedure" under the Act.[2]

3–003   Particular instances of the rule-making powers include the making of provisions for filing applications and other documents, for making and filing translations, for service, for rectifying irregularities, and for setting and extending time limits.[3]

The current rules are the Trade Marks Rules 2000, as amended.[4] They are referred to herein, in their amended form, as "the 2000 Rules".

2. The Comptroller or Registrar

CONTROL OF THE REGISTER

3–004   The Register is maintained by the Comptroller-General of Patents, Designs and Trade Marks, who is referred to in the 1994 Act as "the Registrar".[5]

One of the duties of the Comptroller-General is to include in his annual report under s.121 of the Patents Act 1977, a report on the execution of the 1994 Act, including the discharge of his functions under the Madrid Protocol. The report

---

[1] ss.1 and 7.

[2] s.78(1).

[3] s.78(2).

[4] SI 2000/136 as amended by the Trade Marks (Amendment) Rules 2001 (SI 2001/3832) and the Trade Marks (Amendment) Rules 2004 (SI 2004/947). For the current, amended, form of the rules see App.2. The Rules made under the 1938 Act may be found in previous editions of this work.

[5] s.62.

also has to include an account of the money received and paid by him in connection with his execution of the Act.[6]

Exclusion of liability of the Registrar

By s.70 of the 1994 Act, the Registrar is not to be taken to warrant the validity of any registration of a trade mark under the Act or under any treaty to which the United Kingdom is a party, and his liability in relation to connected examinations, examination reports and proceedings consequent on examinations is also excluded.

3–005

It does not seem that the exclusions provided for cover all aspects of the Registrar's duties. For example, they would not appear to exclude liability for a failure to maintain the Register accurately, or to provide accurate information about an application.[7]

3–006

The exclusion of the Registrar's liability extends to his officers.[8]

3. Division of the Register

Under the Trade Marks Act 1938 Act, and since the Trade Marks Act 1919, the Register was divided into two parts, A and B. The distinction, in general terms, was that registration in Part B could be obtained for marks which lacked sufficient distinctiveness to be included in Part A. However, Part B marks conferred more limited rights.

3–007

Under the 1994 Act, this distinction has been abolished. In the transitional provisions of the 1994 Act, it was provided that existing registered marks at the date of commencement should all be transferred to the new Register kept under the 1994 Act without regard to whether they had previously been in Part A or Part B.[9]

3–008

After the passage of the 1994 Act, the old distinction potentially had some continuing significance in relation to acts alleged to infringe under the 1994 Act but which had begun before its commencement and continued thereafter. Under the transitional provisions of the 1994 Act, it is not an infringement to continue use of a mark after commencement if it did not amount to infringement beforehand.[10] Since the test for infringement under the 1938 Act depended to some extent on whether the mark in question was registered in Part A or Part B,[11] it was possible, in relation to acts which had been continuing since before commencement of the 1994 Act, that it would be necessary to consider whether, historically, the mark in question was registered in Part A or Part B. There do not appear to have been any cases in which this possibility arose, however, and now that implementation of the 1994 Act is so long ago that the limitation period has been expired for some years, it probably never will.

3–009

---

[6] s.71.

[7] Of course, the fact that s.70 does not exclude liability does not mean that the Registrar would be liable if such a failure did take place. A person aggrieved by such a failure would still have to prove the existence of a duty of care, negligence and damage in order to bring a successful action.

[8] s.70(3).

[9] Sch.3, para.2(1).

[10] Sch.3, para.4(2). See Ch.14 for a more detailed consideration of the defences available under the transitional provisions.

[11] The law of infringement under the 1938 Act is not considered in any detail in this edition of this work, but is covered in depth in earlier ones.

4. Entries on the Register

INTRODUCTION

3–010   Both registered trade marks and registrable transactions are to be recorded on the Register.

DETAILS OF REGISTERED MARKS TO BE ENTERED ON THE REGISTER

3–011   Details of registered trade marks are required to be entered on the Register by s.63(2)(a) of the 1994 Act, and the matters to be entered in respect of them are stipulated by the 2000 Rules.[12] The matters are:

(1) the effective date of registration (*i.e.* the date of filing of the application for registration);[13]

(2) the actual date of registration (*i.e.* the date of entry in the Register);

(3) the priority date (if any);

(4) the name and address of the proprietor;

(5) the address for service (if any);[14]

(6) any disclaimer or limitation;

(7) any memorandum or statement of the effect of any memorandum relating to a trade mark of which the Registrar has been informed;

(8) the goods or services in respect of which the mark is registered;

(9) where the mark is a collective or certification mark, that fact;

(10) where the mark has been registered pursuant to s.5(5) on the basis of consent of the proprietor of an earlier trade mark or other earlier right, that fact;

(11) where the mark is registered pursuant to a transformation application, the number of the international registration and either (a) the date accorded to the international registration under Article 3(4) of the Madrid Protocol, or (b) the date of recordal of the request for extension to the United Kingdom of the international registration under Article 3 of the Madrid Protocol, as the case may be;

(12) where the mark arises from the conversion of a Community trade mark or an application for a Community trade mark, the number of any other registered trade mark from which the Community trade mark or the application for a Community trade mark claimed seniority and the earliest seniority date.

ENTRY OF REGISTRABLE TRANSACTIONS ON THE REGISTER

3–012   The general requirement for details of registrable transactions to be entered on the Register is contained in s.63(2)(b) of the 1994 Act. In addition, s.25 requires particulars of registrable transactions to be entered on application by a person claiming to be entitled to an interest in or under a registered mark by virtue of a registrable transaction, or any other person claiming to be affected by such a transaction.

---

[12] r.39.

[13] In accordance with s.40(3).

[14] Under r.10, an address for service in the UK is required for many purposes under the Act. In particular, all applicants for registration must provide one.

The types of dealing which are registrable transactions under the Act[15] are as follows: **3–013**

(1) an assignment of a trade mark or any right in it;
(2) the grant of a licence under a trade mark;
(3) the granting of any security interest (whether fixed or floating) over a registered trade mark or any right in or under it;
(4) the making by personal representatives of an assent in relation to a registered trade mark or any right in or under it;
(5) an order of a court or other competent authority transferring a registered mark or any right in or under it.

DETAILS OF REGISTRABLE TRANSACTIONS TO BE ENTERED ON THE REGISTER

The matter to be entered in the Register in respect of a registrable transaction is set out in the 2000 Rules[16] and depends on the nature of the transaction, save that in all cases the date on which the entry was made in the Register must be entered. **3–014**

In relation to assignments, the matters to be entered on the Register are (1) the name and address of the assignee, (2) the date of the assignment, and (3) where the assignment is in respect of any right in the mark, a description of the right assigned. **3–015**

In relation to licences, the matters to be entered on the Register are (1) the name and address of the licensee; (2) where the licence is an exclusive licence, that fact;[17] (3) where the licence is limited, a description of the limitation; and (4) the duration of the licence if the same is or is ascertainable as a definite period.[18] **3–016**

For security interests, the following are to be entered on the Register: (1) the name and address of the grantee; (2) the nature of the interest (whether fixed or floating); (3) the extent of the security and the right in or under the mark secured. **3–017**

In the case of the making by personal representatives of an assent, the following matters are to be entered on the Register: (1) the name and address of the person in whom the mark or any right in or under it vests by virtue of the assent; and (2) the date of the assent. **3–018**

Finally, where the registrable transaction is an order of a court or other competent authority transferring a mark or any right in or under it, the matters to be entered on the Register are: (1) the name and address of the transferee; (2) the date of the order;[19] and (3) where the transfer is in respect of a right in the mark, a description of the right transferred. **3–019**

Trusts and equities are specifically excluded from being entered on the Register, and the Registrar is not affected by any notice of them.[20]

---

[15] s.25(2). Further information about the various types of registrable transaction under the Act, and the consequences of registration and non-registration may be found in Ch.13.

[16] r.40.

[17] Hence if the Register is silent, it seems that it may be taken that the licence is non-exclusive.

[18] It appears that if the licence is not of a definite or definitely ascertainable period, nothing will be entered on the Register, and a person who may be affected by the licence will be unable to find out the likely duration. This is unsatisfactory.

[19] It seems strange that there is no express requirement that the court or other competent authority be named. Usually it will be the Chancery Division of the High Court, but that is not the only possibility.

[20] s.26.

Procedure for giving notice of a registrable transaction

3–020   The following forms are to be used for making an application to register a registrable transaction.[21] For the grant of a licence, Form TM50; for an amendment to, or termination of a licence, Form TM51; for a transaction relating to the grant, amendment or termination of any security interest, or relating to an assent by personal representatives, or an order of a court or competent authority, Form TM24;[22] for an assignment or any other transaction not already mentioned, Form TM16.

3–021   Applications to register assignments must be signed by or on behalf of the parties. Other applications of the types referred to above must be signed by or on behalf of the grantor of the licence or security interest, or be accompanied by sufficient documentary evidence to establish the transaction.[23]

3–022   If a transaction is sought to be registered which has been effected by an instrument chargeable with duty, the application for its registration is subject to the Registrar being satisfied that the instrument has been duly stamped.[24]

Transactions concerning applications for registration

3–023   Section 27(1) of the Act provides that the provisions of ss.22 to 26, which relate to registered trade marks as objects of property, assignments, and registrable transactions, also apply to applications for registration.

However, applications for registration and transactions concerning them are not registered as such. Instead, where an application for registration has been made and is the subject of a transaction which would have been registrable were the mark already registered, notice is given to the Registrar of the details of the transaction.[25]

3–024   The procedure and forms used to apply to give notice to the Registrar of transactions concerning an application for registration are the same as for transactions concerning a registration.[26]

3–025   Where notice has been given to the Registrar of particulars of a transaction concerning an application for registration, and the mark concerned is subsequently registered, the Registrar is to enter the particulars on the Register.[27]

Transitional provisions

3–026   The transitional provisions concerning registration of transactions affecting registered trade marks are contained in Sch.3, para.8 of the 1994 Act. They are almost certainly of no continuing practical effect given the passage of time since the 1994 Act was implemented, and are covered in more detail in the previous edition of this work.

---

[21] r.41(1).
[22] Which is also for use in relation to transactions affecting a designation under the Madrid Protocol.
[23] r.41(2).
[24] r.41(3). See Ch.13. Stamp duty is not in fact now chargeable on most assignments concerning trade marks.
[25] s.27(3).
[26] r.41(1).
[27] r.41(4).

5. Alteration of entries on the Register

RECTIFICATION OR CORRECTION OF THE REGISTER

The powers to amend the Register considered here, which arise under s.64 of the 1994 Act, are distinct from the powers to revoke or invalidate a registered trade mark under ss.46 and 47 of the 1994 Act.[28]   **3–027**

Errors or omissions in the Register may be rectified on the application of "any person having a sufficient interest", except in relation to matters affecting the validity of the registration of a trade mark,[29] and such an application may be made either to the Registrar or to the court. The application must be made to the court if proceedings concerning the trade mark in question are pending in the court, and the Registrar has power to refer the application to the court in any event.[30]   **3–028**

ERRORS AFFECTING VALIDITY

Presumably, errors which could affect the validity of the registration of a trade mark, and which accordingly could not be corrected under s.64(1), would include such matters as mistakes concerning the identity of its proprietor,[31] or the specification of goods, which affected its liability to revocation for non-use.   **3–029**

A question which arises under s.64 is the standard to be applied in determining whether the matter in question is one "affecting the validity" of the registration concerned and hence not capable of being addressed under the section. One reading of the section is that the powers conferred may be exercised unless the matter concerned is such that, if not addressed, the mark would actually be wholly or partially invalid. Another possible meaning is that correction under s.64 may not be performed if the matter is of such a nature and/or degree of seriousness that there is a reasonable prospect of the registration being wholly or partially invalid as a result of it.   **3–030**

It is suggested that the latter meaning is to be preferred. Otherwise, it may be necessary to decide whether and how the validity of the registration concerned would be affected by the correction sought, merely in order to determine the threshold question of whether there is power under the section to deal with the application for correction.   **3–031**

On the other hand, however, if the proviso under s.64(1) is interpreted too broadly, so that an excessively wide range of matters are treated as "affecting the validity" of the mark in question, the effect will be that proprietors are unfairly precluded from making inoffensive corrections. It should be recalled that if s.64 cannot be invoked, the only procedural alternatives are ss.45, 46 and 47, and under those provisions the only possible results which alter the Register are the complete or partial surrender, revocation or invalidity of the mark.   **3–032**

In *Andreas Stihl AG's Application*[32] this question arose because the Registry accidentally advertised the application with a specification of goods which was too narrow. The applicant did not notice until after registration, whereupon it   **3–033**

---

[28] As to which, see Ch.10.
[29] s.64(1) of the Act.
[30] s.64(2).
[31] Rather than just an error in describing the correct person, perhaps by a misspelling or by using a trading name instead of the correct corporate name.
[32] [2001] R.P.C. 12.

sought rectification to change the specification of goods to cover all those for which it had initially applied. The Registry refused on the ground that the amendment sought would extend the scope of the registration, and the applicant appealed. The Appointed Person, who held that the amendment sought was one "affecting validity" and therefore not allowable.[33] The reasoning of the decision was that "affecting validity" should be construed broadly so that the provisions of the 1994 Act relating to examination, advertisement and opposition could not be circumvented. It is of course correct that allowing a broadening of the specification of goods after grant would mean that a part of the monopoly would not have been the subject of opposition, but it is submitted that it does not follow that the amendment is one "affecting validity". The Registry might well be convinced based on the matters it *has* examined that the extended scope would be just as valid as that granted, and in the particular case under consideration there was no reason identified to think that the broader scope might be any less valid. In addition, it is hard to envisage any amendment (beyond the most trivial) which changes the mark or the specification of goods (unless to narrow it) and which is not one "affecting validity" in the very broad sense adopted in the above case. It will always be possible to say that the new form of registration should have been examined, advertised and open for opposition.

3–034   Under the CTM Regulation, the Court of First Instance took a more forgiving attitude in *Signal Communications Ltd v OHIM*[34], where the applicant for the mark TELEEYE accidentally misspelt it as TELEYE in its application form. The legal issue was not the same, since the mark had not been granted, and the question was whether the mark was substantially the same with and without the misspelling. The court held that it was, having regard in particular to the fact that the priority application relied upon showed the mark correctly.

"PERSON HAVING A SUFFICIENT INTEREST"

3–035   There is no definition in the Act of a "person having a sufficient interest", but clearly it would at least include the proprietor or a party to any registrable transaction incorrectly recorded. Most rectification proceedings under the 1938 Act, which could be brought by persons other than the Registrar or proprietor required that the applicant be a "person aggrieved".[35] The requirement was interpreted very broadly, and in general, anyone in the trade concerned had sufficient locus to apply,[36] while anyone alleged to infringe a mark was always a person aggrieved by its registration. The effect of the requirement was therefore to exclude only busybodies or persons with only a fanciful interest.

3–036   It seems likely that a similar standard will be applied under s.64, although since the provision applies only to errors and omissions and not to matters affecting validity, there will plainly be less interest in its use from persons who are concerned that they are to be sued; they will generally apply under ss.46 and 47 instead.

Procedure for seeking rectification or correction

3–037   Rectification or correction under s.64(1) is to be sought on Form TM26(R)

---

[33] The Appointed Person referred to the court the question of whether the Registry had power to try to solve the problem by withdrawing the registration altogether and advertise it afresh.
[34] [2002] E.T.M.R. 38.
[35] See the 1938 Act, ss.32, 26, 27(4), 33 and 37 with Sch.1.
[36] See previous editions of this work for details.

together with a statement of the grounds on which the application is made and any evidence to support those grounds.[37]

Unless the proprietor himself has applied for rectification or correction, the Registrar must send a copy of the application and statement of grounds, and any evidence filed, to the proprietor.[38] The Registrar may, at that time, give directions for the filing of subsequent evidence.[39]   **3–038**

Upon completion of the evidence, the Registrar is to hold a hearing if either of the parties requires it. Having made a decision, notice of it is to be sent to the parties, and the time for appeal runs from the date of sending.[40]   **3–039**

A person (other than the proprietor) who claims to have an interest in an application under s.64 may apply for leave to intervene. Such an application must be made on Form TM27 stating the nature of the applicant's interest. The Registrar may refuse leave, or grant it on such terms and conditions (including an undertaking as to costs) as he thinks fit, and there is power to hold a hearing to determine whether intervention should be allowed.[41] If intervention is allowed, the intervener is thereafter treated as a party for the purposes of the proceedings.[42]   **3–040**

CORRECTIONS DATE BACK

Errors and omissions corrected under s.64(1) and (2) of the 1994 Act are deemed never to have been made,[43] unless the Registrar or court otherwise directs.   **3–041**

Change of name and address

Changes of the name and address of the proprietor or a licensee are permitted under s.64(4), and can be made by the Registrar upon request. A request should be made on Form TM21.[44] Applications to change an address for service are to be made on Form TM33.[45]   **3–042**

REMOVAL OF MATTER WHICH HAS CEASED TO HAVE EFFECT

The Registrar can remove from the Register matter which appears to him to have ceased to have effect.[46] An example might be an expired exclusive licence.   **3–043**

The procedure to be followed is provided for by r.45 of the 2000 Rules. The Registrar may publish his intention to remove the matter, and is obliged to notify his intention to any person whom he considers to be affected by the removal.

Any person wishing to object to the intended removal must file a notice of opposition on Form TM7. A person whom the Registrar considered to be affected and notified accordingly, may file his objections in writing or may request that his objections be heard orally. If there is an objection, r.54 applies, and the Registrar must hold a hearing if requested to do so before making a finding adverse to the person objecting.   **3–044**

---

[37] 2000 Rules, r.34(1).
[38] r.34(2)(a).
[39] r.34(2)(b).
[40] r.34(3) and (4).
[41] r.35(1).
[42] r.35(2).
[43] s.64(3).
[44] 2000 Rules, r.44(1). Curiously, the rule allows changes by the proprietor or a licensee or any person having an interest in or charge on a registered mark which has been registered under r.40, while s.64(4) only allows changes by the proprietor or licensee.
[45] r.44(2).
[46] 1994 Act, s.64(5).

3–045   If there are no objections, the Registrar may remove the matter (and presumably will do so); if there are objections and the Registrar is still of the view that the matter has wholly or partially ceased to have effect, he may remove it, or, if appropriate, part of it.[47]

FALSIFICATION OF THE REGISTER

3–046   It is an offence to cause a false entry to be made on the Register, knowing or believing it to be false. It is also an offence to make anything falsely purporting to be a copy of the Register or to cause such a thing to be tendered in evidence; in either case knowing or having reason to believe in its falsity.[48]

These offences are explained in more detail in Ch.19.

6. Inspection of the Register, and obtaining information

INSPECTION AND PROVISION OF COPIES OF THE REGISTER

3–047   By s.63(3) of the 1994 Act, the Register is to be open to public inspection, and copies of extracts and entries are to be made available. The entry on the Register relating to a registered trade mark may be accessed online at the Trade Mark Registry website.[49]

3–048   Rules 42 and 43 of the 2000 Rules implement the requirements of s.63(3). Under r.42(2) the right of inspection extends to any part of the Register kept otherwise than in documentary form.

The Registrar is required to provide a certified copy or extract, or an uncertified copy or extract of any entry in the Register, as requested on Form TM31R.[50]

REQUESTS FOR INFORMATION AND INSPECTION OF DOCUMENTS

3–049   In addition to rights to inspect the Register and to obtain copies, s.67 of the 1994 Act allows requests for information about applications for registration and registered trade marks to be made. The information which will be made available following such a request depends on whether or not the application for registration of the mark in question has been published.

3–050   Before publication, and in the absence of consent from the applicant for registration, a person seeking information can only obtain inspection of the application, any amendments to it, and any particulars of a registrable transaction which have been provided to the Registrar under r.41 of the 2000 Rules.[51] There is a limited exception where a person seeking information has been told of an application and that proceedings are to be brought against him in respect of it following publication. In that case, he may obtain the same information as if the application had already been published.[52]

3–051   After publication of an application, the general position is that inspection is to be permitted of all documents filed at the Registry in relation to a registered mark

---

[47] rr.45(3) and (4).
[48] ss.94(1) and (2) of the Act.
[49] The website is at *www.patent.gov.uk.*
[50] r.43.
[51] s.67(2) and r.49.
[52] s.67(3).

or application for registration.[53] However, there are a number of exceptions to this rule. The Registrar is not required to allow inspection of any document until after he has finished using it for any procedure to which it is relevant.[54] Further, the right of inspection does not extend to:

(1) any document until 14 days after its filing;
(2) purely internal Registry documents;
(3) documents sent to the Registry for inspection and then returned to the sender;
(4) requests for information under r.48;
(5) documents issued by the Registry which the Registrar considers should be treated as confidential;
(6) any document in relation to which the Registrar issues directions under r.51 that it be treated as confidential.

In addition, the right of inspection is not retrospective. It does not apply to **3–052** documents sent to the Registry before commencement of the Act, or documents sent after commencement but relating to applications under the 1938 Act.[55] It also does not apply to documents which disparage any person in a way likely to damage him.[56] There is no right of appeal from a decision of the Registrar to refuse inspection of 1938 Act documents, or disparaging documents.[57]

CONFIDENTIAL DOCUMENTS

Rule 51 of the 2000 Rules gives the Registrar power to order that any document **3–053** other than a form required by him be treated as confidential. Documents which might contain confidential information could include financial information in agreements required to be registered, or confidential aspects of evidence submitted to the Registry.

In relation to a document filed with the Registry, a request that it, or part of it, **3–054** be treated as confidential must be made when it is filed, or within 14 days thereafter. While the Registrar is considering the request, the document is not open to public inspection.[58]

Once the Registrar has directed that a document be treated as confidential, it is **3–055** not open to public inspection except with the leave of the Registrar.[59] Such a direction may be withdrawn, but prior consultation with the person who sought confidentiality is required unless it is not reasonably practical.[60]

The Registrar may also direct that a document issued by the Registry be treated **3–056** as confidential. If he gives such a direction, the document is not open to public inspection except by his leave.[61] Such instances are likely to be rare, but could include a situation where written reasons for a Registry decision include extracts from confidential evidence filed by the parties.

---

[53] r.50(1).
[54] r.50(2).
[55] rr.40(4)(b) and (c).
[56] r.50(4)(a).
[57] r.50(5). It is hard in any event to see in what sense the Registrar has to make a "decision" in connection with this rule. Other than perhaps in relation to disparaging documents there will be no room for debate as to whether documents should be open for inspection.
[58] r.51(1).
[59] r.51(2).
[60] r.51(3).
[61] r.51(4).

Searches

3–057   It is generally advisable before offering a mark for registration to cause a search to be made through the Register to discover whether any of its essential features have been anticipated in such manner as to be a bar to the application;[62] and it is often necessary or advisable for other purposes. Searches by the public are greatly facilitated by indexes maintained by the Registry and computerised searching facilities which are available.

An effective search against a trade mark will need to take into account both relevant registrations (and applications) for goods and for services.

Caveats

3–058   A party wishing to be informed in case some action is taken in respect of a registered trade mark may file a caveat with the Trade Mark Registry on Form 31C. Matters of which such a party may ask to be informed include the publication of an application, the filing of an opposition, and the receipt of an application to register an assignment. Once such an event takes place, the Registry will inform the person entering the caveat, and it will be removed.

The Trade Marks Journal

3–059   The Patent Office publishes a weekly Trade Marks Journal. It contains details of all trade marks applications accepted that week, registrations, renewals, assignments, licences, other applications which affect the status and scope of registered trade marks as well as news and notices of interest to the trade mark world. It is available online at *www.patent.gov.uk/tm/tmj/index.htm.*

7. Procedural matters concerning the Registry

Agency

3–060   Subject to very limited exceptions, anything required or authorised by the Act to be done by or to a person in connection with the registration of a trade mark, or any procedure relating to a registered trade mark, may be done by an agent.[63]

Requirement for a Hearing before an Adverse Decision

3–061   Rule 53 requires that the Registrar must give a party an opportunity to be heard before taking any decision which is or may be adverse to him.

---

[62] See Ch.9.
[63] s.82 and rr.52 and 53. For further details see Ch.24.

CHAPTER 4

CLASSIFICATION OF GOODS AND SERVICES; MARKS FORMERLY ASSOCIATED

1. The classes

CLASSES

The significance of classification under the Trade Marks Act 1994 is markedly **4–001** different from that under the Trade Marks Act 1938. Under the 1938 Act, the rights conferred by registration were strictly limited to the particular goods (or services) for which the mark was registered.[1] This is no longer so under the 1994 Act, which provides protection in relation to goods or services similar to those for which the mark in question is registered, as well as identical goods or services, provided that a likelihood of confusion on the part of the public can be shown.[2]

This change will no doubt reduce the practical importance of the classification **4–002** of goods and services. In addition, under the 1994 Act, it is now possible to make a single application for a trade mark with a specification of goods and services covering more than one class.[3] As a result, classification is now very largely a matter of administrative convenience.

The scheme of classification used under the 1994 Act now forms Schs 3 and 4 **4–003** to the Rules.[4] Schedule 4 sets out the current version of the classes of the International Classification of Goods and Services drawn up under the Nice Agreement, and applies to all registrations dated after January 1, 2002. Sch.3 sets out the previous version, which continues to apply to all earlier marks, except that upon reclassification under r.46, they also fall under Sch.4.[5] Similar classifications were also used under the 1938 Act. The present version provides for 34 classes of goods and 9 classes of services.

REGISTRATION BY REFERENCE TO THE CLASSIFICATION

There has long been a practice for applicants for registration to seek and the Reg- **4–004** istrar to grant registration for all (or part) of the goods within a particular class by reference to the class, usually with the words "all included in class ..." in the specification of goods. There are many such marks on the Register. Where this

---

[1] 1938 Act, ss.4–6.

[2] s.5(2) in relation to relative grounds for refusal of registration and s.10(2) in relation to infringement, and see Chs 9 and 14.

[3] This was not possible under the 1938 Act and the Rules made under it, which required a separate application for each class: Trade Marks and Service Marks Rules 1986, rr.21(2) and 23.

[4] The Trade Marks Rules 2000, SI 2000/136 as amended. See App.2. The 1994 Act, s.34, provides for classification, and also that any question as to which class goods fall into is to be decided by the Registrar, whose decision is final.

[5] See r.7 of the 2000 Rules as amended.

has been done, and the question arises as to whether any particular goods do or do not fall within the registration, the approach adopted under the 1938 Act was to look to the Registrar's practice at the date of registration,[6] rather than simply construing the words defining the class. The same approach has now been applied under the 1994 Act.[7] However, since the rights conferred by registration now extend beyond the particular goods or services specified, this question may not be of such importance in future, at least in relation to infringement.

4–005   Reference to the class of goods or services in the specification of an application is important for another reason: only certain amendments to an application are permissible, and are set out in s.39 of the 1994 Act. They do not include an amendment to the specification of goods and services. In *Altecnic Ltd's Application*,[8] the question arose whether changing the class of an application was an impermissible amendment under s.39, or whether the Registry could simply, at the invitation of the applicant, reclassify the goods in question under s.34. The situation was somewhat complex because the original application had expressly referred to "all other goods in class 7", but that reference had been deleted from the specification by a (permissible) limiting amendment under s.39; the application had progressed in Class 7 thereafter until the applicant persuaded the Registry to reclassify it in Class 11, to which an opponent had objected. The Court of Appeal held that an application for a trade mark has to be construed as a whole, that classification is not purely a matter of administrative convenience, and that, particularly in the case of an application whose specification refers to the class of goods and/or services, but even potentially where there is no such reference, amending its class is likely to be a substantive amendment, and therefore not permitted under s.39. By treating the issue of one of construction of the application as a whole, it appears that the court left open the possibility that (particularly where there is no reference in the specification to the class) in certain limited circumstances a change of class will be permitted, perhaps if the terms of the specification are so clear that there is no possibility that changing their class will affect the scope.

4–006   There has also been a practice in the past of applicants for registration seeking a specification for an entire class, or for a large range of goods or services in a class. In some cases this was acceptable, although the Rules made under the 1938 Act[9] gave the Registrar a discretion to refuse registration for such broad specifications unless he was satisfied that the breadth was merited by the applicant's actual or intended use. It is likely that a different approach is called for under the 1994 Act, particularly in view of the infringement provisions. A specification covering even a single description of goods may be too broad if there are many different and distinct varieties of such goods and the applicant only trades or intends to trade in some of them.[10] This topic is covered in further detail in Ch.9.

---

[6] *Cal-U-Test* [1967] F.S.R. 39. See also "GE" at first instance, [1969] R.P.C. 418 at 458–459. This issue was not addressed by the Court of Appeal.

[7] *Avnet v Isoact* [1998] F.S.R. 16.

[8] [2002] R.P.C. 34.

[9] Trade Marks and Service Marks Rules 1986, r.21(5).

[10] *Mercury Communications Ltd v Mercury Inter-Active (UK) Ltd* [1995] F.S.R. 850, where it was held that registration for "computer software" would normally be too wide.

2. Conversion

CONVERSION TO THE NEW CLASSIFICATION

Following the passage of the 1994 Act, there remained on the Register a number **4–007**
of marks which were originally registered before the commencement of the 1938
Act, and for which the specification of goods was determined in accordance with
an earlier classification providing for 50 classes of goods.[11] The 1938 Act[12]
contained provisions allowing for the conversion to the new classification, but it
was a voluntary scheme under which a proprietor could seek conversion if he
wanted it, without giving the Registrar or the Board of Trade any power to require
it. The 1994 Act[13] provided for rules to be made compelling the conversion of
registrations under the old classification to the new one.

The provisions for conversion from the pre-1938 classification are no longer **4–008**
relevant and no longer apply, and instead the procedure for such conversion
(which is essentially unchanged) may now be applied to adapt registrations from
the pre-2002 to post-2002 classifications referred to above.[14]

PROCEDURE FOR CONVERSION

If the Registrar intends to convert a mark to the new classification, he must give **4–009**
the proprietor written notice of his proposals. The proprietor then has three
months to make written objections. If he makes no written objections then he
loses the right to object any further and the Registrar will publish the proposals.[15]
If the proprietor does make objections, then the Registrar will consider them, and
thereafter either publish his original proposals, or proposals amended in the light
of the objections. The Registrar's decision about the proposals to be published is
final and not subject to appeal.[16]

Following publication of the Registrar's proposals under r.40, there is an op- **4–010**
portunity to oppose. Any opposition must be filed on Form TM7 within three
months of publication of the proposals. The grounds of opposition must be stated,
and in particular they must set out how the proposed amendments would be contrary to s.65(3).[17] Evidence is admissible for the determination of the opposition,
and the opponent is entitled to a hearing before a decision is made.[18]

If there is no opposition, or following the determination of any opposition **4–011**
which is entered, the Registrar is to enter the amendments decided upon. His decision is final and not subject to appeal.[19]

CONVERSION CANNOT GENERALLY INCREASE SCOPE OF REGISTRATION

Since the old and new classifications do not exactly correspond, there is obvi- **4–012**
ously potential for the scope of a registration to change in the course of

---

[11] The classification was preserved in Sch.3 of the Rules under the 1938 Act
[12] s.36.
[13] s.65 and Sch.3, para.12 of the transitional provisions to the 1994 Act giving the Registrar power
to convert existing registered marks.
[14] At para.4–003.
[15] rr.46(2) and (3).
[16] r.46(4).
[17] r.47(1). As to s.65(3), see para.4–014.
[18] r.47(2).
[19] r.47(3).

conversion. This may in particular be the case where the specification of goods in an old registration is by reference to the classification itself.

4–013   The 1994 Act recognises that it would in general not be right to extend the scope of the proprietor's monopoly as a side-effect of reclassification. On the other hand, a complete bar to extending the scope of registration could make phrasing the new specification of goods unnecessarily complex and result in specifications which were wordy and unclear.

4–014   Accordingly, s.65(3) provides that the power to reclassify shall not be exercised so as to extend the rights conferred by a registration, except where it appears to the Registrar that avoiding such extension "would involve undue complexity" and that any extension would not be substantial and would not adversely affect the rights of any person. This provision allows the Registrar to form his own view of the significance of a reclassification which extends a registration, even in the absence of observations by the proprietor or anyone else who might be affected. It surely also must mean that if reclassification is opposed by a person whose activities do not infringe the existing registration, but would (or might arguably) infringe the registration as proposed to be amended, the reclassification should not take place in that manner. In any event, even if the extension of the proprietor's rights would not affect anyone else, it can only be permitted if it is not substantial.

3. Marks formerly associated

ASSOCIATED TRADE MARKS — THE OLD LAW

4–015   Under s.23 of the 1938 Act, the Registrar had the power to require that marks be associated. The Registrar's power to require association arose if a proprietor held or applied for marks which were identical to one another or closely resembled one another, in respect of the same goods or goods of the same description.[20]

4–016   The effect of association was that the proprietor could only assign the marks together. Assignment separately was not permitted unless the Registrar could be persuaded to dissolve the association, and only had power to do so if the Registrar was satisfied that there was no likelihood of deception or confusion if the associated marks were in use by different persons. This requirement reflected the whole purpose of association, which was to avoid the same or similar marks being used on the same or similar goods by different people.

Association did offer some benefits for proprietors, though: under s.30 of the 1938 Act, use of one associated mark could count as use of the others.

ABOLITION OF ASSOCIATION

4–017   Association of marks has been abolished by the transitional provisions of the 1994 Act, Sch.3, para.2(3).[21] Associations entered on the Register ceased to have effect on commencement.

EFFECT ON MARKS FORMERLY ASSOCIATED

4–018   The result of associations ceasing to have effect is that associated marks may now

---

[20] The same power existed where identical or similar marks were registered or applied for in respect of goods and associated services: Trade Marks Act 1938, s.23(2A).

[21] Save in the case of marks registered as a series under the 1938 Act: Sch.3, para.2(2).

be assigned separately without any procedural hindrance and without any involvement of the Registrar. However, there may still be difficulties following such an assignment if the result is to mislead consumers. There are a numbers of types of assignment which are permitted under the 1994 Act but which would not have been allowed under the 1938 Act because of their tendency to deceive, and the issues which they present are considered in Chs 10 and 13.

CHAPTER 5

NATIONAL REGISTRATION OF TRADE MARKS

1. Preliminary

5–001   The Trade Marks Act 1994 makes provision in respect of the registration of trade marks of various types. First, it makes provision in respect of the national registration of trade marks. This chapter is concerned with the process of registration of such marks.

5–002   Secondly, the 1994 Act makes provision in respect of applications under the Madrid Protocol. This came into effect in the United Kingdom on April 1, 1996[1] and is considered in Ch.6. For the purposes of this chapter it is important to note the following matters. Protection may now be sought in the United Kingdom for an international registration originating in another contracting state. Such an international registration is entitled to become protected in the United Kingdom (and so become a protected international trade mark (UK)) where it satisfies the requirements of a national application for registration. Accordingly, the discussion below of the requirements of a national application is relevant also to an international registration designating the United Kingdom. It is also important to note that an international application may originate in the United Kingdom and be founded on an application for registration of a national mark. On receipt of a notice of opposition filed against an International Registration, the Trade Marks Registry forwards a copy of the notice of opposition to the International Bureau.[2] If the national application is refused or restricted then the Registrar must notify the International Bureau and request that the international registration be cancelled or amended accordingly. It is, however, possible to transform the international application into national applications and hold the original priority date. All these matters and other aspects of the Madrid Protocol are discussed further in Ch.6.

5–003   Finally, the 1994 Act makes provision in respect of Community trade marks. Applications for Community trade marks are dealt with substantively by the Office for the Harmonization of the Internal Market (OHIM) located in Alicante, Spain and accordingly are not discussed further here. However, and as in the case of international registrations, the 1994 Act provides for the transformation of applications for such Community trade marks into applications for national registrations. The Community trade mark system is explained in Ch.6.

5–004   There is a further general matter which should be mentioned at the outset. National applications are prosecuted through the Registry. Here the practice has been amended to reflect the changes recommended in the Reports by Lord Woolf, "Access to Justice". Although the Civil Procedure Rules do not apply directly to Registry proceedings, in general it may be assumed that in so far as the Registrar has a discretion it will be exercised in accordance with the overriding objective

---

[1] The Trade Marks (International Registration) Order 1996, SI 1996/714.
[2] See TPN 2/2001 for general procedural matters concerning notices of opposition filed in respect of international registrations in respect of which protection is sought in the UK.

set out in r.1.1 of the Civil Procedure Rules 1998.[3] This includes, so far as is practicable:

(1) ensuring that the parties are on an equal footing;
(2) saving expense;
(3) dealing with the case in ways which are proportionate;
    (a) to the amount of money involved;
    (b) to the importance of the case;
    (c) to the complexity of the issues; and
    (d) to the financial position of each party;
(4) ensuring that it is dealt with expeditiously and fairly; and
(5) allotting to it an appropriate share of the court's resources, while taking into account the need to allot resources to other cases.

2. Procedure on national application to register

WHO MAY APPLY TO REGISTER A MARK

Any person may apply to register a trade mark provided the statutory requirements of an application are met. These are discussed below. The application will proceed and the mark will duly be registered provided that the mark satisfies the definition of a trade mark and is not objectionable by reason of any of the absolute or relative grounds for refusal.[4] The absolute grounds of refusal are discussed in Ch.8, and the relative grounds for refusal in Ch.9. **5–005**

ESSENTIAL PARTICULARS OF AN APPLICATION

An application for registration of a trade mark is made to the Registrar. Section 32(2) of the 1994 Act requires an application to contain: **5–006**

(1) a request for registration of a trade mark;
(2) the name and address of the applicant; (note that partnerships applying to register a mark may be recorded as a partnership without naming each individual partner. PAN 2/04)
(3) a statement of the goods or services in relation to which it is sought to register the trade mark; and
(4) a representation of the mark.

In addition the application must state that the trade mark is being used, by the applicant or with his consent, in relation to the goods or services specified, or that he has a bona fide intention that it should be so used.[5]

All applications are subject to the payment of the appropriate application and class fees.[6]

---

[3] TPN 1/2000.

[4] The Registrar has no residual power to refuse an application if the statutory requirements of an application are met and the mark is not objectionable by reason of any of the absolute or relative grounds for refusal: *Eurolamb* [1997] R.P.C. 279; *Procter & Gamble (bottle shapes)* [1999] R.P.C. 673 at 675, CA. This is in contrast to the position under the Trade Marks Act 1938. S.17(2) of that Act conferred on the Registrar a discretion to refuse an application for registration even though the requirements for registration were satisfied.

[5] s.32(3).

[6] s.32(4) and r.5(1). The appropriate fees are set out in a schedule published by the Registry and are regularly reviewed. The current schedule is reproduced in App.3. The fees must be paid within two months of the date of notice to the applicant.

General requirements

5–007   The application must be filed on Form TM3.[7] The nature of the mark should be made clear on the application.

The specific requirements for applications for three dimensional marks or claiming colour as an element of a mark and for words shown in a particular graphical form in rr.5(2)–(4) of the Trade Marks Rules 2000 have been removed by the Trade Mark (Amendment) Rules 2004. However, the Registrar has adopted the following practice in relation to marks incorporating or consisting of colour:[8]

(1) It is not necessary to include colour identification codes (*e.g.* pantone numbers) for marks which incorporate colour, but such codes will be recorded if provided. Applicants who provide only a black and white representation will only be accorded a filing date when the colour(s) claimed have been identified.

(2) The Registrar will adopt the following approach when considering whether marks consisting of colour alone have been graphically represented for the purposes of s.1(1):

    a. Colour samples on paper are not durable enough to constitute a graphical representation.

    b. A written description of the colour (*e.g.* "dark blue") accompanied by a code from an internationally recognised colour identification system will be considered acceptable.

    c. Other means of graphical representation will only be accepted if they are presented in a way that is "clear precise, self contained, easily accessible, intelligible, durable and objective."[9]

(3) Where colour is applied to goods or packaging, an appropriate description should be included identifying which areas bear which colours.

Graphical representation must be precise

5–008   The graphical representation must record the identity of the sign clearly and unambiguously.[10]

---

[7] r.5(1).

[8] PAN 3/03.

[9] See the decisions of the ECJ in *Libertel* C–104/01, [2004] F.S.R. 4 and *Sieckmann v Deutsches Patent und Markenamt* C–273/00 [2003] R.P.C. 38.

[10] *Libertel* C–104/01, [2004] F.S.R. 4, *Ty Nant Spring Water's Application* [1999] R.P.C. 392; [2000] R.P.C. 55 (a colour should have been specified by hue and included a graphic example) and the cases there cited; *Creola* [1997] R.P.C. 507 (application must be sufficiently clear and distinct to allow all the essential features to be identified); *Antoni & Allison's Application* [1998] E.T.M.R. 460 (a mere description not conveying the clear and precise appearance of a 3D mark not adequate); *Orange Personal Communications Ltd's Application* [1998] E.T.M.R. 337 (the word "orange" not sufficiently precise); *Robert McBride Ltd's Application* [2003] R.P.C. 19 (on the same point but with reference to the word "yellow" and the effect on the filing date of failing to properly specify a claimed colour); *Swizzels Matlow Ltd's Application* [1999] R.P.C. 879 (unlikely that a mere description of 3D mark would, in practice, ever be sufficiently precise); *Venootschap onder Firma Senta Aromatic Marketing's Application* [1999] E.T.M.R. 429 ("the smell of fresh cut grass", for tennis balls, was sufficiently precise, in fact) cf. *Sieckmann* C–273/00 [2003] R.P.C. 38 (use of chemical formulae not sufficient to identify a smell mark) and *John Lewis of Hungerford Ltd's Application* [2001] R.P.C. 28 ("the smell, aroma or essence of cinnamon" in respect of furniture suffered from the defect that it did not refer to an objective, generally accessible (and presumably permanent) benchmark and so relied on the subjective impression of that aroma); *Shield Mark BV v Joost h.o.d.n. Memex* C–283/01 [2004] R.P.C. 17 ECJ (application register the opening bars of "Für Elise" as sound marks: depiction of the notes making up the sign, or an indication that the sign was the cry of an animal, or an onomatopoeia,

Date of filing

The date of filing is the date upon which documents containing everything **5–009** required by s.32(2) are furnished to the Registrar. If documents are furnished on different days then the date of filing is the last of those days.[11] The filing date is important because, subject to a claim to priority, this is the date from which, once granted, the rights of the proprietor have effect.[12]

CLAIM TO PRIORITY

Where a right to priority is claimed then particulars of the claim should be **5–010** included in the application. The requirements are specified in r.6 of the 2000 Rules. A certificate by the registering or other competent authority of the country of the priority application must be filed within three months of the application.

APPLICATION MAY RELATE TO MORE THAN ONE CLASS

The classification of goods and services is addressed in Ch.4. An application may **5–011** be made for registration of a trade mark in respect of goods and services in more than one class.[13]

Every application must specify the class to which it relates and list the goods or services appropriate to that class, described in such a way as to indicate clearly the nature of those goods and services and allow them to be classified.[14] This aspect of the specification has an important role to play in determining the boundaries of the registration. The scope of the registration will be determined by reference to the specified goods or services and the class. If the application relates to more than one class, then the specification must set out the classes in consecutive numerical order. If the application does not comply with these requirements a notice will be sent to the applicant specifying a period of not less than two months in which the default must be rectified, failing which the application will be treated as abandoned.[15] Where an application covers more than one class then additional fees are payable for each further class.

If the specification contained in the application lists items by reference to a **5–012** class in which they do not fall then the applicant may request that the application be amended to include the appropriate class.[16] But this will only be allowed where it does not offend against s.39(2). Accordingly, amendment will be allowed only in limited circumstances, such as where the specification explicitly lists goods or services which are in a different class and have been included only because of an error of wording or an obvious mistake. Similarly, if there is a contradiction between the whole list of goods or services and the class number then this would likely be regarded as an obvious mistake.[17] However, an application which specifies goods or services that fall within more than one class by reference to only one of those classes cannot be amended to refer to the goods within the classes

---

without more, was not sufficient. However, depiction of notes on a stave with divided into measures and with a clef, rests etc. was sufficient.) see also PAC 2/00.

[11] s.33.

[12] s.9(3) provides that the rights of the proprietor have effect from the date of registration which, in accordance with s.40(3), is the date of filing of the application for registration.

[13] r.8 and Form TM3A.

[14] r.8(2)(a) and (b).

[15] r.8A.

[16] r.8(4).

[17] Practice Amendment Circular (PAC) 2/99.

not specifically identified; the failure to identify the other classes is not an obvious mistake. By way of example, an application register CAREMIX for "valves; valves for use in water circulation; blending valves; and all other goods and services in Class 7" could not be amended to refer to "valves" in Class 11 in that it was not an obvious mistake.[18]

ADDRESS FOR SERVICE

5–013   Every applicant for registration of a trade mark must file an address for service in the United Kingdom.[19] The address for service of an applicant for registration of a trade mark is, on registration, deemed to be the address for service on the registered proprietor, subject to a filing to the contrary.[20] Anything sent to the applicant (or opponent) at his address for service is deemed to have been properly sent. The Registrar may, where no address for service is filed, treat as the address for service of the person concerned his trade or business address in the United Kingdom, if any. Where an address for service is not filed, the Registrar will send the person concerned notice to file an address for service within two months of the date of the notice, and if that person fails to do so the application will be treated as abandoned (or, in the case of an opposition, withdrawn).

USE OR BONA FIDE INTENTION TO USE

5–014   This statement is a requirement of the 1994 Act. To this end the Form TM3 contains the statement "The Trade Mark is being used by the applicant or with his or her consent, in relation to the goods or services stated, or there is a bona fide intention that it will be so used". The applicant must sign the statement. If he fails to do so it will be treated as a deficiency.[21]

5–015   A number of points arise from this requirement. First, it seems that the requirement extends to all the goods and services the subject of the application. Under the 1938 Act it was common to register the mark for goods of the same description as those in relation to which it was actually intended to use the mark.[22]

5–016   Secondly, it is not at all clear what is meant by the words "or that he has a bona fide intention that it should be so used". These words do not appear in the Directive and it seems likely that they are derived from s.26(1) of the 1938 Act. The authorities under the 1938 Act may accordingly provide some assistance. There it was tolerably clear that bona fide meant genuine, judged by commercial stan-

---

[18] *Altecnic Ltd's Application* [2002] R.P.C. 34 CA. See also paras 5–064 and 5–065.

[19] r.10. Any person opposing an application must also file such an address for service.

[20] A filing to the contrary can be made under r.10(1) or r.44(2).

[21] The position may be contrasted with that under the 1938 Act. There it was part of the definition of a trade mark that the mark was used or proposed to be used s.68). Exceptions were provided by s.29 where either a corporation was about to be established and the applicant intended to assign the mark to the corporation or where the application was accompanied by an application for registration of a person as registered user. This created some anomalies. For example it was held not to cover the situation where the applicant had not yet selected his registered users: *Pussy Galore* [1967] R.P.C. 265.

[22] The proviso to s.26 of the 1938 Act stated that, except where the applicant had been permitted under s.12(2) to register an identical or nearly resembling mark in respect of the goods in question or where the tribunal was of the opinion that he might properly be permitted to register such a mark, the tribunal might refuse an application to remove a mark for non-use if it was shown that any proprietor had in fact made bona fide use of the trade mark in relation to goods of the same description or services associated with the goods or goods of the same description. A similar proviso existed in relation to services.

dards, even if carried out for an ulterior motive.[23] It was also a requirement of the 1938 Act, although introduced as part of the definition of a trade mark, that the intention to use be a "definite and present intention".[24]

Thirdly, there is as yet no clear authority as to the consequences of making such a declaration which is not correct. Certainly there is no express sanction provided by the 1994 Act. It seems that it would render the application vulnerable to an attack under s.3(6) as one made in bad faith. This is a subject addressed in Ch.7.[25]

5–017

DEFICIENCIES IN THE APPLICATION

Where an application fails to satisfy the requirements of ss.32(2), (3) or (4) of the 1994 Act or rr.5(1) or 8(2)(a) or 10 of the 2000 Rules, then the Registrar will notify the applicant of the deficiency or, in the case of s.32(4), the failure to make payment.[26] The applicant then has two months from the date of the notice to remedy the deficiency or default.

5–018

If the applicant fails to remedy the deficiency (or make the necessary payment) within the two months of the notice then the application will be deemed never to have been made in the case of a failure under s.32(2) and shall be treated as abandoned in the case of a failure under s.32(3) or (4) or rr.5(1), 8(2) or 10.

5–019

The time limit of two months is not extendible.[27]

TRANSITIONAL ARRANGEMENTS

There are still some applications pending which were made under the 1938 Act. These are provided for in Sch.3 of the 1994 Act. As a general rule all such applications are dealt with under the old law (Sch.3, paras 1 and 10 of the 1994 Act).[28] But that is subject to the following.

5–020

In the case of pending applications for registration not advertised under s.18 of the 1938 Act prior to commencement, the applicant could give notice to the Registrar claiming to have registrability determined in accordance with the 1994 Act (Sch.3, para.11 of the 1994 Act and r.68 of the 2000 Rules). The notice had to be in the prescribed form, accompanied by the appropriate fee and given no later than six months after the date of commencement. Any such notice properly given was irrevocable.

5–021

Where an application for registration made under the 1938 Act has been advertised after commencement, the period within which notice of opposition may be filed is three months from the date of advertisement and that period is not

5–022

---

[23] *Electroluxv Electrix (No.2)* (1954) 71 R.P.C. 23, CA; *Imperial v Philip Morris, "Nerit"* [1982] F.S.R. 72, CA, a ghost mark case; *"Huggars"* [1979] F.S.R. 310, another ghost mark case; *Levi Strauss v Shah* [1985] R.P.C. 371 at 378; *"Concord"* [1987] F.S.R. 209; *"Kodiak"* [1990] F.S.R. 49; *1–800 Flowers* [2000] E.T.M.R. 369.

[24] *Imperial v Philip Morris* [1982] F.S.R. 72.

[25] The courts have not attempted to explain the scope of the provision and it may require a reference to the ECJ: *Road Tech Computer Systems v Unison Software* [1996] F.S.R. 805. In *Gromax Plasticulture v Don & Low Nonwovens* [1999] R.P.C. 367, Lindsay J. considered that it includes dishonesty and also some dealings which fall short of the standards of acceptable commercial behaviour observed by reasonable and experienced men in the particular area being examined; *Demon Ale* [2000] R.P.C. 345 (appointed person); *Sheimer* ("Visa") [2000] R.P.C. 484; [1999] E.T.M.R. 519 (appointed person).

[26] rr.10(6) and 11. See, *e.g. Ty Nant Spring Water Ltd's Application* [2000] R.P.C. 55.

[27] r.68.

[28] In the case of applications being dealt with under the 1938 Act the appointed person accordingly has no power to hear appeals from the Registrar on opposition: *"Tabo"* [2000] R.P.C. 360.

extendible (Sch.3, para.10(2) of the 1994 Act and r.67 of the 2000 Rules). Section 23 of the 1938 Act (relating to associated marks) is to be disregarded in dealing after commencement with old applications for registration (Sch.3, para.10(3) of the 1994 Act).

EXAMINATION OF THE APPLICATION

5–023   Once it has been determined that the application satisfies the basic requirements of the 1994 Act, it proceeds to examination. In particular the Registrar will consider whether the application appears to meet the requirements of s.1, whether any of the absolute grounds of refusal of s.3 apply or whether the application offends against the provisions of s.4 relating to specially protected emblems. In addition, applications which have satisfied the formalities requirements of the Act can be and are entered onto the Optics and Trims database systems. These permit the Registrar to carry out a search of earlier trade marks, as defined in s.6 of the Act, to consider the application for conflict with any such marks and whether any objection should be raised under s.5 of the Act. These objections are discussed further below.

5–024   If it appears to the Registrar that the requirements for registration are not satisfied then the applicant is informed and given an opportunity to make representations or to amend the application.[29] This is done by means of the examination report. If significant objections are raised by the Registry in the examination report, then the applicant has a period of three months to respond, unless a substantive objection on relative grounds is raised, in which case the period is six months.[30] If the applicant fails to respond to this or a subsequent letter then the Registrar will refuse the application.[31] Generally any objections raised in relation to an application will lead to discussion with the Registry as to the possibilities for resolving the objection by, for example, amending the application or filing evidence. These are discussed further below.

Is the mark a trade mark?

5–025   The Registrar must consider whether the mark applied for is a trade mark within the meaning of s.1 of the 1994 Act. Particular consideration is given to shapes, colours, sounds and smells. To satisfy the requirements of s.1, these must be capable of being represented graphically and capable of distinguishing the goods or services of one undertaking from those of other undertakings. Care should be taken in the case of shapes that they do accurately represent the mark sought to be protected. In the case of colours it must be expected that the Registry will take a conservative line in respect of single colours, and much may depend upon the choice of colours and the way they are used.[32] As to sounds and smells, these pose particular problems when it comes to graphical representation and it must also be expected that the Registry will require convincing evidence that they are capable of distinguishing the goods or services of the applicant. (See Ch.2, para.2–008.) The Registry has issued guidance covering applications to register slogans (PAN 2/05) and surnames (PAN 1/05).

---

[29] s.37(3).
[30] PAN 2/03.
[31] s.37(4).
[32] See, *e.g. Ty Nant Spring Water Ltd's Application* [2000] R.P.C. 55; [1999] R.P.C. 392V.

The absolute grounds of refusal

The absolute grounds for refusal are set out in ss.3 and 4 of the 1994 Act. The **5–026**
Registrar will raise these grounds as objections where it appears they are
applicable. Each of the objections raised will be specified and the basis for it
given. To overcome any such objection the applicant should consider lodging evidence of use, restricting the goods or services the subject of the application, limitations and disclaimers and obtaining consents. These are all considered further
below.

The relative grounds of objection

The Registrar must search for conflicting marks to determine if any of the relative **5–027**
grounds of objection specified in s.5 of the 1994 Act appears to be applicable.
This is done using the Optics and Trims systems. The Registrar attempts to search
all classes which contain the same or similar goods or services to those the subject
of the application. If any marks are found which have an earlier filing date or an
earlier priority date, then they will be considered. If the owner of a later filed
mark claims earlier use, then the conflicting rights will usually have to be resolved
by opposition. The Registrar will determine whether the similarity between the
marks and the goods or services is such that there is a likelihood of confusion. If
it is considered that there is then the objection will be raised and the basis for it
given.[33]

The Registry has issued guidance as to how it deals with pending earlier **5–028**
citations.[34] Such earlier citations are earlier trade marks within the meaning of
s.6, subject to their being registered. It appears that such earlier citations will be
dealt with differently depending on whether they arise in *ex parte* proceedings
(examination) or *inter partes* proceedings (opposition or invalidation). The Registry has indicated that unless such pending earlier citation arise in the course of
opposition or invalidation proceedings, they will be dealt with as follows: Where
there are other absolute grounds for refusal the Registry will expect applicants to
overcome them, and if they should fail to do so then refusal will be based upon
them, subject to the caveat that there are other potential grounds for refusal which
may have to be dealt with on appeal. Where there are other relative grounds for
refusal based upon registered trade marks, then again applicants will be expected
to progress matters. However, a request for suspension will be considered. Where
there are no other grounds for refusal then the Registry will suggest suspending
the application, but because suspension is undesirable in the context of examination, objections based upon pending marks will only be maintained by the Registry if they would be clearly fatal to the application should they mature to
registration.[35]

In opposition and invalidation proceedings however, the Registry procedure is **5–029**
that during the review of proceedings following the final round of evidence[36] the
Hearing Officer will consider whether the proceedings are based on any pending

---

[33] Where the only component of the earlier mark which could be regarded as creating a similarity
with a later trade mark is the subject of a disclaimer to any exclusive right, the examiner will not
consider the marks to be similar enough to create a likelihood of confusion following *Paco Holdings v Paco Rabanne Parfums* [2000] R.P.C. 451; PAC 3/00; cf. *"Fountain"* [1999] R.P.C. 490.
[34] PAC 1/99 and TPN3/2004.
[35] PAC 1/99.
[36] Para.(a) TPN 5/2000.

earlier trade marks which are likely to lead to refusal or cancellation of the application or registration. If so, then the Hearing Officer is likely to suggest that proceedings be suspended to await the outcome of the pending earlier trade mark or marks.[37]

5–030   In seeking to overcome any such objection applicants should consider filing evidence of use; restricting the goods or services the subject of the application; honest concurrent use; obtaining consents; removal or limitation of the earlier mark; disclaimers; and division of the application. These are discussed further below. The applicant has a period of three months to respond to objections raised by the Registry in examination reports, unless a substantive objection on relative grounds is raised, in which case the period is six months.[38]

EVIDENCE OF USE

5–031   Where an objection is raised under ss.3 or 5 of the 1994 Act it may be possible to overcome that objection by filing evidence of use. Indeed, in the case of certain objections under s.3, this is specifically contemplated by the Act which provides that an application shall not be refused registration by virtue of ss.3(1)(b), (c) or (d) if, before the application for registration, it has acquired a distinctive character as a result of the use made of it.[39] Evidence of use may also overcome an objection under s.3(3)(b). Such evidence commonly details sales (value and quantity) under the mark on an annual basis, the territory in which sales have occurred, details of advertising and promotion, again on an annual basis, providing illustrative samples and details of how the mark has appeared on the goods or in relation to the services, again providing samples or photographs.

5–032   The extent and duration of use required will vary depending on the nature of the mark objected to. The Registry has given a general indication that it would usually expect a mark, the subject of an objection under s.3(1), to have been used on a reasonable scale for five years. But less use may suffice in cases where the objection is not very strong. Conversely evidence of more use, coupled with trade and possibly survey evidence, may be required where the mark is inherently very descriptive or otherwise lacking a distinctive character.

5–033   It must be remembered that proceedings before the Registrar are proceedings to which the strict rules of evidence apply.[40] Although the Registrar has had a practice of considering informal evidence, such evidence should thereafter be made the subject of a statutory declaration or affidavit because otherwise the task of any appellant tribunal will be made difficult, if not impossible.[41]

5–034   The courts have expressed some scepticism that distinctiveness of some marks can ever be established by evidence of use alone. In the case of highly descriptive

---

[37] TPN 3/2004.

[38] PAN 2/03.

[39] s.3(1), proviso.

[40] *"St Trudo"* [1995] R.P.C. 370; Practice Notice of January 4, 1999 [1999] R.P.C. 294; this supersedes the Practice Direction of July 12, 1995 [1995] R.P.C. 381. In proceedings which began on or after January 31, 1997 evidence is not to be excluded on the basis it is hearsay. The weight to be given to any such evidence is a matter for the Registrar to consider in accordance with the Civil Evidence Act 1995, s.4. See further paras 5–105 and 5–110.

[41] *"Fresh Banking"* [1998] R.P.C. 605.

or laudatory words it will be necessary to show that the public recognise the mark applied for as a trade mark distinctive of the goods or services of the applicant.[42]

RESTRICTION OF THE GOODS OR SERVICES

Restriction of the goods or services the subject of the application is one of the few amendments of an application permissible under the 1994 Act.[43] This may serve to avoid an objection under s.3 or s.5.

5–035

Restriction of the specification can be achieved in a number of ways. Particular goods or services which have given rise to the objection can simply be deleted. But often there is a general description which requires amendment. In such cases restriction can be achieved either by excluding particular goods or services by use of the expression "... but not including ..." or by introducing a limitation such as "... all for ..." or "... all made from ...".

5–036

LIMITATION AND DISCLAIMER

An applicant may voluntarily disclaim any right to the use of any specified element of a trade mark or agree that the rights conferred by the registration shall be subject to a specified or other territorial limitation.[44] Such geographical or other limitations (such as "Milk and cheese, for sale in Northern Ireland") should be expressly identified as limitations under s.13 of the 1994 Act and if included in the application should be entered in Box 11 of the Form TM3. On the other hand, restrictions which define the nature of the goods or services in the application (such as "Milk and cheese, the produce of Northern Ireland") should be included in the specification of goods and services.[45]

5–037

Unlike the position under the 1938 Act, the Registrar has no express power to impose a condition or limitation or to require a disclaimer.[46] If it is considered that the mark is objectionable and no suitable limitation or disclaimer is offered, then on the express wording of the 1994 Act the Registrar has no alternative but to refuse the application. However, the Appointed Person has held that the combined effect of ss.37(3)–(4) and 40(1) of the 1994 Act is to permit the Registrar to direct the applicant to amend the goods and services specified, whether by deletion or limitation, and to stipulate that unless the applicant elects to make that amendment, the application shall be refused.[47]

5–038

Disclaimers provide a useful way of dealing with objections raised by the Registrar or during opposition and where a disclaimer is necessary to preserve the essential validity of the trade mark.[48] But an applicant's offer to disclaim part of his mark will not often assist in overcoming a s.5 objection because the Registry

5–039

---

[42] See *British Sugar v Robertson* [1996] R.P.C. 281 at 286; *Philips v Remington* [1998] R.P.C. 283 (Jacob J.) and [1999] R.P.C. 809, CA.

[43] s.39(1). Amendment of an application is only permitted to a limited degree, see paras 5–064 to 5–066.

[44] s.13.

[45] PAN 6/04.

[46] Conditions are not permitted under the 1994 Act. Any condition entered on the register under the old law ceased to have effect on commencement of the 1994 Act: Sch. 3, para.3(1).

[47] *Nettec Solutions Ltd's Application* [2003] R.P.C. 17.

[48] Under the old law the Registrar might require a disclaimer of, for example, a part of the mark which was descriptive even in the case where the mark was *prima facie* registrable. So, in the case of word marks being variations of ordinary words, he might require a disclaimer of the ordinary word. In the case of devices, he might require a disclaimer of letters or numerals comprised within the device. The assumption behind the requirement of the disclaimer was that no rights could in fact be claimed in the part disclaimed. However, it served to prevent uncertainty

considers that an admission made by the applicant cannot of itself be deemed to affect the scope of protection of the earlier mark.[49]

5–040   Limitations are also a valuable way of overcoming objections raised by the Registrar or under opposition. So, for example, a limitation may be offered where the specification of goods or services is too wide or where, absent a limitation, such as to colour, the mark would not be distinctive. If, however, a proposed limitation substantially affects the identity of the mark applied for, it is viewed as an amendment and is likely to be prohibited by s.39(2) of the 1994 Act.[50]

5–041   Rule 24 of the 2000 Rules provides that where the applicant for registration of a trade mark or the proprietor by notice in writing sent to the Registrar disclaims any right to the exclusive use of any specified element of a trade mark or agrees that the rights conferred by the registration shall be subject to a specified territorial or other limitation, then the Registrar shall make the appropriate entry in the Register and publish the disclaimer or limitation.

It is notable that conditions are not permissible under the 1994 Act.

CONSENTS

5–042   This is a potentially important way of overcoming objections under s.5. It is provided by s.5(5) that nothing in s.5 prevents the registration of a trade mark where the proprietor of the earlier trade mark or other earlier right consents to the registration. So if the applicant obtains the consent of the proprietor of the cited mark to the registration the Registrar cannot maintain the objection. The Registrar has no discretion in this regard.

5–043   This position is in marked contrast to the position under the 1938 Act. There the consent did not remove the statutory objection and the Registrar could only consider the consent as evidence in relation to the issue of the likelihood of confusion.

5–044   An interesting issue may arise if the consent is only provided on condition that the new mark is used in a particular way.[51] The issue might turn on the way the transaction is construed. If the consent itself is conditional, then this would not appear to satisfy the requirements of the Act. On the other hand, if the consent is unconditional but is provided as part of an agreement which includes a term specifying the manner of use then, it is suggested, the provision would be satisfied and, in the event of breach, the earlier proprietor would have to sue for breach of contract.

HONEST CONCURRENT USE

5–045   Section 7 of the 1994 Act provides that where the applicant can establish by evidence that there has been honest concurrent use, then the Registrar shall not refuse the application under s.5 unless the objection is raised in opposition proceedings. Honest concurrent use means such use that would have constituted

---

in the minds of rival traders as to the scope of the registration. Where on the other hand it was obvious that no rights could be claimed in only part of the mark the Registrar would not require a disclaimer. This valuable role of disclaimers appears to have no place under the new law.

[49] PAC 3/00.

[50] *Nestlé SA's Application* [2004] R.P.C. 27: An application to register the shape of a POLO mint was limited during a hearing before the Registry to the size (diameter of hole and other dimensions) and colour of a standard POLO mint. On appeal the application to limit was refused as substantially affecting the identity of the mark.

[51] As in *Peck v Zelcker* ("Polly Peck") [1963] R.P.C. 85.

honest concurrent use under the 1938 Act. What use satisfies this requirement is explained in Ch.8. If the Registrar believes it to be established, then she must allow the application to proceed to publication where the proprietor of the earlier right may or may not oppose. There is no requirement in the 1994 Act that the proprietor of the earlier right be notified of the application, although the advertisement will include an indication of the basis upon which it has been allowed to proceed.

If an application for a trade mark is opposed by the proprietor of an earlier trade mark or earlier right, then honest concurrent use will not of itself overcome the objection under s.5. But the fact that the two marks have been concurrently used without confusion or without the later mark taking unfair advantage of the earlier mark's reputation may be relevant in reaching a conclusion as to the validity of the objection.[52]

5–046

REMOVAL OR LIMITATION, TRANSFER OR SURRENDER OF THE EARLIER MARK

In appropriate circumstances an application can be made to remove or limit the earlier mark. Such proceedings may be brought under s.46 of the 1994 Act to revoke the earlier mark or under s.47 to seek a declaration of invalidity. In general such an application may be made to the Registrar or the court and the procedure and requirements are discussed in detail in Chs 9 and 18.

5–047

It should be noted that if a trade mark is revoked under s.46 then the rights of the proprietor are deemed to have ceased as from the date of the application for revocation unless the court or the Registrar is satisfied that the grounds for revocation existed at an earlier date. Since the merits of an application for registration are considered as at the date of that application, it will be necessary to secure a finding that the mark revoked was invalid as of that date.

5–048

In appropriate cases it may be expected the Registrar will stay an application for registration until such an application for revocation or declaration has been resolved.

5–049

An alternative course is to reach an agreement with the earlier proprietor that he surrenders the earlier mark in respect of the relevant or all of the goods or services for which it is registered under s.45, or that he transfers it to the applicant by assignment under s.24. It is notable that pending applications can be assigned under the 1994 Act.[53]

DIVISION

Division is a useful option where objection is taken to the application on the basis of only some of the goods or services the subject of that application. Rather than holding up or risking refusal of the whole application, an applicant can divide the application into two or more parts.[54] In this way the acceptable part can proceed to publication leaving the applicant to address with the Registrar the goods or services in relation to which objection has been taken.

5–050

Where an application is divided each divisional application will retain the original filing date and is then treated as a separate application. In so far as op-

5–051

---

[52] "React" [1999] R.P.C. 529.
[53] See ss.34 and 37 and Ch.13.
[54] See 1994 Act, s.41; 2000 Rules, r.19 and Form TM12.

position may have been lodged or third party observations made, they will be treated as having been lodged or raised in relation to each divisional application. Of course, in so far as they related to some only of the goods or services of the original application (which is not unlikely in the case of multi-class applications) they may fall away in relation to one or more of the divisional applications. Upon division of an original application any licence or other interest will be deemed to apply in relation to each of the divisional applications.

An applicant for a series of marks may not divide his application into separate applications of each of the marks, at least at the stage of opposition.[55]

EARLIER REGISTRATIONS OF THE APPLICANT

5–052   Sometimes the Registry will accept an application which it would otherwise deem to be *prima facie* objectionable on the basis of a prior registration of the applicant where the marks and the goods or services are either the same or very similar.[56]

ACCEPTANCE OR REFUSAL OF THE APPLICATION

5–053   If the Registrar is duly satisfied that the requirements of the Act are met, then she must accept the application and allow it to proceed to publication (advertisement under the 1938 Act).[57] If she is not then she must refuse the application. If the Registrar is minded to refuse an application then before making her decision she must give the applicant an opportunity to be heard and she must give the applicant at least 14 days notice of the time when he may be heard, unless the applicant consents to shorter notice.[58] The applicant may attend himself or by an agent or may make submissions in writing.

5–054   Where the Registrar makes a decision following a hearing or after considering any submission in writing, then she must send a notice of her decision to the applicant. If the notice does not contain reasons then the applicant can request the Registrar to send him a statement of the reasons for the decision.[59] Such a request must be made within one month of the date on which the notice was sent.[60] If the notice contains reasons then, for the purpose of any appeal, the date of the decision is the date upon which the notice is sent. If it does not, then the date upon which the statement of reasons is sent is deemed to be the date of the decision for the purposes of any appeal against it.[61]

As before, it seems that an *ex parte* decision of the Registrar prior to advertisement would not bind her if opposition is entered.[62]

ONUS BEFORE THE REGISTRAR

5–055   The Registry has taken the view that the overall effect of s.37 of the 1994 Act is that the Registrar is required to make a judgment about whether registration

---

[55] *Dualit Ltd's Trade Mark Applications* [1999] R.P.C. 890; [1999] R.P.C. 304.
[56] Detailed guidelines setting out the approach adopted by the Registrar in relation to such prior registrations can be found in PAC 7/00.
[57] s.37(5); *Procter & Gamble* [1999] R.P.C. 673, CA. There is no residual discretion to refuse to allow the application to proceed.
[58] r.54.
[59] r.62 and Form TM5.
[60] r.62(2).
[61] r. 62.
[62] *"Solibrisa"* (1948) 65 R.P.C. 17 at 23, Regy.

should be allowed, but that there is no overall onus to be discharged, one way or the other.[63]

APPEAL FROM AN EX PARTE DECISION OF THE REGISTRAR

An appeal lies from a decision of the Registrar to refuse an application and such an appeal may be brought either to an appointed person or to the court.[64] Appeals are discussed generally at paras 5–133 to 5–137.

5–056

SECOND APPLICATION FOR THE SAME MARK

Where a mark has already been rejected for registration, a second application to register it, raising essentially the same issues, may properly be rejected on that ground alone.[65] Where however the application is one calling for evidence of distinctiveness of the mark, it by no means follows that a second application will raise the same issues as the first; the further period of use between the dates of the two applications may well so increase the reputation of the mark as to enable the applicant to produce evidence convincing to the Registrar whereas previously she was unable to do so.[66] Indeed the mere fact that the applications concern different dates may be enough to prevent the identity of issue required for an actual estoppel.[67]

5–057

PUBLICATION

When an application has been accepted the Registrar causes it to be published[68] in the Trade Marks Journal. Thereafter third parties may oppose the application and observations may be made to the Registrar in writing.

5–058

The published representation must clearly depict the essential features which are sought to be the subject of the rights granted by the registration. If it does not then the advertisement is a nullity.[69]

OBSERVATIONS

Where an application has been published, any person may at any time before the registration of the trade mark, make observations in writing to the Registrar as to whether the trade mark should be registered. The Registrar will inform the applicant of any such observations.[70] Any person who makes observations does not become a party to the proceedings. This is a new provision, introduced at the

5–059

---

[63] *"Eurolamb"* [1997] R.P.C. 279; *Procter & Gamble (soap tablet shape)* [1998] R.P.C. 710; *Procter & Gamble (bottle shape)* [1999] R.P.C. 673, CA; but note should be taken of s.37(4) which provides that if the applicant fails to satisfy the Registrar that the requirements of the 1994 Act are met, then the Registrar must refuse to accept the application. See also the comments on onus in the course of opposition, in para.5–118.

[64] s.76.

[65] *Massachusetts Saw* (1918) 35 R.P.C. 137. See also *Hunt* (1911) 28 R.P.C. 392, where an opponent waived his right to plead *res judicata* and consented to registration.

[66] Thus the application to register "Daimler" which was successful in 1916 *Daimler* (1916) 33 R.P.C. 337) must have failed if it had been made in 1901: see *Daimler v British Motor Traction* (1901) 18 R.P.C. 465. Indeed, in earlier editions of this work it was suggested to be normal practice, where an application was rejected on the ground of insufficient user to establish distinctiveness, to abandon the application and file a fresh one rather than to attempt to appeal.

[67] *Unilever* [1987] R.P.C. 13 at 20.

[68] s.38(1).

[69] *"Creola"* [1997] R.P.C. 507.

[70] s.38(3).

request of interests consulted by the Government, and is consistent with the practice of the OHIM and that adopted under the Patents Act 1977.[71]

5–060   Such observations could, for example, suggest that a s.3 objection should have been raised or that a third party has an earlier trade mark which raises a s.5 objection. On receipt of such observations they will be considered by the Registrar and she will issue a preliminary opinion to the person who submitted the observations and to the applicant. If the Registrar considers that the application was accepted in error, the applicant will be invited to respond. If, after considering the applicant's response, the Registrar still considers the application was accepted in error, the applicant will be given the opportunity to amend the application, file evidence and, in due course, attend a hearing before the Registrar reaches a final decision that the application should be rejected.

5–061   The Registrar can only reject an application upon the basis of matter raised in observations if it appears to her, having regard to matters coming to her notice since she accepted the application, that it was accepted in error.[72] Accordingly, if the observations only raise matter which has previously been considered then it appears the Registrar cannot reject the application.

The weight to be attached to any observations will depend upon all the circumstances of the case.[73]

5–062   It should be noted that the time for opposition is not suspended whilst observations are being considered.[74] For this reason and that mentioned in the preceding paragraph any potential opponent should be wary of relying on observations rather than filing an opposition.

FURTHER POWER TO REFUSE

5–063   Where an application has been accepted, and there is no opposition or any opposition has failed or been withdrawn, then the Registrar must register the mark (provided the proper fee is paid), unless it appears to her having regard to matters coming to her notice since she accepted the application that it was accepted in error.[75] Accordingly, where new facts come to the attention of the Registrar after acceptance which justify refusal of the application, then the original acceptance can be regarded as an error. The Registrar should give the applicant the opportunity to be heard before deciding that the application should not proceed.

AMENDMENT OF THE APPLICATION

5–064   Amendment of an application is only permitted in limited circumstances under the 1994 Act. An applicant may at any time withdraw his application or restrict the goods or services covered by the application.[76] If the application has been published then the Registrar will publish the withdrawal or restriction.

5–065   In other respects, an application may be amended only by correcting (1) the

---

[71] The provision was so explained by Lord Strathclyde, Minister of State, Department of Trade (Public Bill Committee, Third Sitting, January 19, 1994 at col.81).

[72] s.40(1).

[73] *"Messiah from Scratch"* [2000] R.P.C. 44.

[74] Although if the application is amended there will be an opportunity to oppose the amendment under r.18.

[75] s.40(1) and *"Creola"* [1997] R.P.C. 507. Under the 1938 Act the Board of Trade could also direct the application be refused s.19(1)); no such power lies in the appointed person under the 1994 Act.

[76] s.39(1). This is a valuable tool for overcoming objections and is referred to in para.5–039.

name or address of the applicant; (2) errors of wording or copying; or (3) obvious mistakes; and then only where the correction does not substantially affect the identity of the trade mark or extend the goods or services covered by the application.[77]

A request for an amendment of an application to correct an error or to change **5–066** the name or address of the applicant and, after publication, a request for any amendment must be made on Form TM21.[78] If the application to amend is made under s.39 of the 1994 Act after publication and the amendment would affect the representation of the mark, then the amendment or a statement of the effect of the amendment will be published and thereafter opposition can be lodged by any third party and will be dealt with as a substantive opposition.[79]

Non-completion within the prescribed period

A trade mark cannot be registered unless the prescribed fee is paid in the **5–067** prescribed period.[80] If the fee is not paid then the application is deemed to be withdrawn.

Merger of applications

An applicant for a number of trade marks may apply to have them merged at any **5–068** time before preparations for their publication have been completed by the Office.[81] The application is made on Form TM17. The Registrar will allow merger if the applications are in respect of the same mark, bear the same date of application and are, at the time of the request, in the name of the same person.

After registration an application may also be made by a proprietor for merger **5–069** and, if the registrations to be merged relate to the same mark, merger will be allowed. The application is again made on Form TM17 and must be accompanied by the appropriate fee. Any limitations or disclaimers will apply to the merged mark and if the original applications had different filing dates then the date of the merged registration will be treated as the latest of them. Any particulars of licences or interests in the original registrations will be entered in relation to the merged mark.

Application for a series of marks

An applicant may apply to register a number of marks as a series.[82] The marks **5–070** must all resemble each other as to their material particulars and differ only as to matters which when considered as a separate element of the trade mark would not be regarded as having distinctive character and in the context of the mark as a

---

[77] s.39(2). See, *e.g. Altecnic Ltd's Application* [2002] R.P.C. 34 CA and *Andreas Stihl DG & Co's Application* [2001] R.P.C. 12 (A decision of the appointed person referred to the High Court on a different matter of procedure). Under the 1938 Act the discretion was much wider s.19(1) and r.121). Accordingly any cases under the old law must be treated with caution. Nevertheless the following cases provide interesting illustrations: in *Baker* [1908] 2 Ch. 86 at 109, 25 R.P.C. 513 at 524, the court allowed a correction to be made to the name of the applicants. In *Mann* (1919) 36 R.P.C. 189, Sargant J., on appeal from the Registrar, allowed the applicant to correct an amendment made by a slip on his part in the statement of his trading name. An application to amend the specification of goods in an opposition was refused as widening in *Crowther* (1948) 65 R.P.C. 369, Regy.
[78] 2000 Rules, r.17.
[79] rr.13 and 18.
[80] s.40(2).
[81] s.41 and r.20.
[82] s.41 and r.21.

whole, do not substantially affect the identity of the trade mark.[83] The advantage of such an application is the saving in fees and avoidance of separate applications in each case.

5–071   Under r.21 of the 2000 Rules, the application may be divided into separate applications in respect of one or more of the marks in the series at any time before the preparations for the publication of the series have been completed by the Office (subject to the Registrar being satisfied that the division requested conforms with s.41(2) of the 1994 Act and the payment of the appropriate fees). An application or registration may be amended at any time to delete a mark in the series by request of the applicant or proprietor. If deleted from an application, the application is treated as being withdrawn insofar as it relates to deleted mark.[84] An application for a series may not be divided under r.19, at least at the stage of opposition.[85]

CERTIFICATE OF REGISTRATION

5–072   On registration the Registrar publishes the registration, specifying the date upon which the registration was entered upon the Register and she issues to the applicant a certificate of registration (s.40(4) and r.16).

Registration has effect as of the date of filing,[86] a provision particularly important for the purposes of infringement.

APPLICATIONS TO REGISTER COLLECTIVE MARKS

5–073   An application may be made to register a collective mark under the provisions of s.49 and Sch.1 of the 1994 Act. The substantive topic of collective marks is addressed in Ch.11. Such a mark is used to distinguish the goods or services of members of an association which is the proprietor of the mark from those of other undertakings. The Registry considers that a mark cannot function as a trade mark and as a collective mark in respect of the same goods and services. As a result, if applications are made to register an identical mark (or marks so nearly alike as to constitute essentially the same mark) as both a collective mark and as a trade mark, the Registry will raise an objection to the later of the two applications.[87]

5–074   An application is made for a collective trade mark in the same way as for an ordinary trade mark. The formalities of it are checked as for an ordinary mark and, if they are satisfied, it will be examined.

5–075   Within nine months of the date of the application the applicant must file with the Registrar the regulations governing the use of the mark.[88] These must specify the persons authorised to use the mark, the conditions of membership of the association and, where they exist, the conditions of the use of the mark, including any sanctions against misuse.

5–076   The regulations will be considered by the Registrar and, if she is satisfied that they comply with the requirements, are not contrary to public policy and morality

---

[83] s.41(2) and *Logica's Trade Marks* BLO/068/03. See generally PAN 1/03 for examples of the approach adopted by the Registry.
[84] r.21(3A).
[85] *Dualit Ltd's Trade Mark Applications* [1999] R.P.C. 304; [1999] R.P.C. 980.
[86] s.9(3).
[87] PAC 2/01.
[88] 1994 Act, Sch.1, para.5, and 2000 Rules, r.22.

(and the prescribed fees are paid) she will duly notify the applicant and allow the application to proceed to publication, as in the case of ordinary applications. The application may be opposed and observations filed. If any opposition is dealt with, then the mark will be registered, just as in the case of an ordinary mark, and the regulations made available for inspection by the public.

The regulations associated with a collective mark may be amended.[89] The Registrar may cause the amendments to be published, in which case they may be opposed.

APPLICATIONS TO REGISTER CERTIFICATION TRADE MARKS

An application may be made for a certification mark under the provisions of s.50 and Sch.2 of the 1994 Act. The substantive topic of certification marks is addressed in Ch.11.

5–077

As in the case of a collective mark, an application is made for a certification trade mark in the same way as for an ordinary trade mark. The formalities of it are checked as for an ordinary mark and, if they are satisfied, it will be examined. Again, as with a collective mark the Registry considers that a mark cannot function as a trade mark and as a certification mark in respect of the same goods and services. As a result, if applications are made to register an identical mark (or marks so nearly alike as to constitute essentially the same mark) as both a certification mark and as a trade mark, the Registry will raise an objection to the later of the two applications.[90]

5–078

Within nine months of the date of the application the applicant must file with the Registrar regulations governing the use of the mark.[91] These must indicate who is authorised to use the mark, the characteristics to be certified by the mark, how the certifying body is to test those characteristics and to supervise the use of the mark, the fees (if any) to be paid in connection with the operation of the mark and the procedures for resolving disputes.

5–079

As in the case of a collective mark, the regulations will be considered by the Registrar and, if she is satisfied that they comply with the requirements, are not contrary to public policy and morality, and that the applicant is in a position and competent to certify the goods or services the subject of the application (and the prescribed fees are paid), she will duly notify the applicant and allow the application to proceed to publication. The application may be opposed and observations filed. If any opposition is dealt with, then the mark will be registered, just as in the case of an ordinary mark, and the regulations made available for inspection by the public.

5–080

The regulations associated with a certification mark may be amended.[92] The Registrar may cause the amendments to be published, in which case they may be opposed.

---

[89] Sch.1, para.10 and r.23.
[90] PAC 2/01.
[91] Sch.2, para.6 and r.22.
[92] Sch.2, para.11 and r.23.

IRREGULARITIES AND EXTENSIONS OF TIME

5–081   This topic is addressed generally under the heading of "Opposition to Registration."[93]

3. Opposition to registration

5–082   Once an application has been published any person may, within the prescribed time, give notice to the Registrar of opposition to the registration.

PROCEDURE ON OPPOSITION

5–083   The procedure relating to opposition proceedings is governed by s.38 of the 1994 Act and rr.13–13C of the 2000 Rules as amended by the Trade Marks (Amendment) Rules 2004.[94] The rule is clear in its directions and is reproduced in App.2. In outline the procedure is as follows.

5–084   Within three months of the date of publication of the application, notice of opposition must be sent to the Registrar in the prescribed form (TM7). No extension of this time can be allowed.[95] A copy of the notice will be sent by the Registrar to the applicant. The date upon which the TM7 is sent to the applicant is known as "the notification date". The notice of opposition must include a statement of the grounds of opposition. Where the opposition is based on an earlier registered trade mark, then the notice must include a representation of the earlier trade mark, the classes in respect of which it is registered and the goods and services in respect of which it is registered and upon which the opposition is based. Further, where the registration period for the earlier mark was completed more than five years before the date of publication of the opposed application, the statement of grounds must include a statement detailing whether the earlier mark has been put to genuine use in relation to each of the goods or services on which the opposition is based, and if not, detailing any proper reasons for non-use. This statement in known as "the statement of use".

5–085   Where the opposition is based on a mark in respect of which an application for registration has been made the statement of grounds should include a representation of the mark, the classes in which and the goods and services for which it has been applied and upon which the opposition is based. There is, of course, no need for a statement of use in respect of earlier applications. Where the opposition is made under s.5(4)(a) of the Act, the statement of grounds should include a representation of the mark and a statement of the goods or services in respect of which the protection conferred by the right relied upon is claimed.

5–086   Subject to the "cooling-off period", within three months of the date upon which the Registrar sends to the applicant a copy of the statement, the applicant may file a counter-statement, in conjunction with a notice of the same, on Form TM8.[96]

---

[93] See paras 5–121 to 5–127.
[94] The amended rules came into force on May 5, 2004. For proceedings commenced before that date, see the transitional provisions at rr.20–24 of the Trade Marks (Amendment) Rules 2004.
[95] r.68(3).
[96] The requirements as to the content and presentation of this document are discussed in paras 5–095 to 5–099.

No extension of this time can be allowed (again, subject to the cooling-off period).[97] A copy will be sent by the Registrar to the opponent.

The Rules provide for a cooling-off period at the start of opposition proceed-   **5–087**
ings and when sought by both parties. At any time before the expiry of the three-month period for filing the counter-statement, the Registrar may, on request, grant an extension of twelve months where the request is filed on Form TM9c and with the consent of both the applicant and the opponent.[98] The applicant can bring the cooling off period to an end prior to the end of the twelve month period by filing its Form TM8. In order to bring the cooling off period to an end prior to the end of the twelve month period by filing the opponent must file a Form TM9t. The applicant then has one month to file its TM8, subject to the condition that the applicant will never have less than three months from the notification date in which to file its TM8. The TM8 will be sent by the Registry to the opponent.

The counter-statement should set out which aspects of the grounds of opposi-   **5–088**
tion are admitted and which are denied and any positive grounds relied upon in support of the application. Where a notice and counter-statement are not filed by the applicant within the prescribed period, then he is deemed to have withdrawn his application for registration.[99]

If an opposition (or any part of it) is based on relative grounds under ss.5(1) or   **5–089**
(92) of the 1994 Act then the Registrar will consider the grounds of opposition and the counterstatement and will either provide the parties with a preliminary indication of whether or not she considers that the mark should be registered in respect of the goods and services listed in the application or will inform them that she thinks that it would be inappropriate for such a preliminary indication should be given.[1] The Registrar need not give reasons in the preliminary indication. The date upon which any such preliminary indication is sent to the parties is known as "the indication date".

If the preliminary indication is that the mark should be registered for all the   **5–090**
goods and services listed in the application, then unless the opponent files notice of intention to proceed with the opposition within one month of the indication date, the opposition is deemed to have been withdrawn.[2] Where the preliminary indication is that the mark should be registered for some (but not all) of the goods and services for which it has been applied, then unless the applicant or opponent file notice of intention to proceed within one month of the indication date, or within two months of the indication date the applicant requests amendment of the application so as to remove the goods or services in respect of which the indication was negative, the applicant is deemed to have withdrawn the application in its entirety.[3] Where the preliminary indication is that the mark should be refused for all the goods and services listed in the application, then unless the applicant files notice of intention to proceed with the application within one month of the indication date, the opposition is deemed to have been withdrawn.[4]

All notices of intention to proceed should be filed on Form TM58. If any party   **5–091**
files such a notice, the Registrar will forward it to the other parties. The date upon

---

[97] r.62(3).
[98] r.13A.
[99] r.13A(1).
[1] r.13B.
[2] r.13B(4)(a).
[3] r.13B(4)(b).
[4] r.13B(4)(c).

which that notification is sent is known as "the initiation date", unless the Registrar has notified the parties that a preliminary indication is not going to be given, in which case the initiation date is taken to be the date upon which the TM8 is sent to the opponent by the Registrar.

5–092   Once the initiation date has passed the time periods for the filing evidence begin to run. The opponent files evidence first, within three months of the initiation date. If a statement of use has been filed and is either not admitted or denied by the applicant, the opponent must file evidence supporting the statement of use. He must also send a copy of the evidence to the applicant (evidence is only considered to have been filed when it has been received by the Registrar and sent to all other parties).[5] If no evidence is filed by the opponent then, unless the Registrar otherwise directs, the opposition is deemed to have been withdrawn.[6] The Registrar will usually allow the opposition to continue if the opponent wishes to rely on oral submissions and has based his opposition, at least in part, upon an earlier registration, in which case the Registrar will notify the applicant that of any direction she has made to that effect. Thereafter the applicant must file evidence within three months and again send a copy to the opponent. Any reply evidence, and it must be strictly reply evidence, must be filed by the opponent within three months of the sending to him of the evidence of the applicant and a copy sent to the applicant. No further evidence may be filed except with the leave of the Registrar.[7] Once the evidence is completed the Hearing Officer will carry out a case review and will indicate whether or not he considers that a hearing is necessary for a decision to be reached. If he does not consider that a hearing is necessary he will set a deadline for the parties to request an oral hearing. If a hearing is requested, or if he considers it necessary, the Hearing Officer will then set a date for the hearing. Where two rival applicants file cross-oppositions, it is customary to decide the course of proceedings at a preliminary hearing.

WHO MAY OPPOSE

5–093   Any person may oppose a trade mark application, and opposition may be lodged by joint opponents if this is made clear. In general it appears the objections may be taken by any person.[8] But by way of exception, it appears a s.60 objection (application by an agent or representative) may only be taken by the proprietor of the mark in a Convention country.[9]

GROUNDS OF OPPOSITION

5–094   The grounds of opposition relied on by an opponent are likely to be drawn from the following:

(1) The sign the subject of the application is not a trade mark within the meaning of the 1994 Act because it is not capable of being represented graphically or because it is not capable of distinguishing.

(2) The mark is devoid of any distinctive character such that registration would be contrary to s.3(1)(b).

(3) The mark consists exclusively of descriptive matter prohibited by s.3(1)(c) or (d).

---

[5] r.13C(7).
[6] r.13C(2).
[7] r.13C(6).
[8] See the mandatory words of ss.3, 4 and 5 and s.38(2). *"Wild Child"* [1998] R.P.C. 455.
[9] This includes countries party to the WTO Agreement (TRIPS): SI 1999/1899.

(4) The mark consists exclusively of a shape prohibited by s.3(2).

(5) The mark is of such a nature as to deceive the public (for example as to nature, quality, or geographical origin of the goods or service) or is contrary to public policy or to accepted principles of morality.

(6) Use of the mark is prohibited in the United Kingdom by an enactment or rule of law or by a provision of Community law.

(7) The application was made in bad faith, for example with a false statement as to use or intention to use the mark or because the applicant is not properly entitled to the mark (ss.3(6) and 32).

(8) The mark conflicts with an earlier trade mark and registration would be contrary to s.5(1)–(3).

(9) Use of the mark is liable to be prevented by virtue of a rule of law, such as passing off, or by the proprietor of another earlier right such as copyright, design right or a registered design.

(10) Registration would be contrary to the provisions of ss.56–60 (relating to the Paris Convention).

(11) The mark consists of a specially protected emblem (ss.3(5) and 4).

STATEMENT OF GROUNDS OF OPPOSITION AND COUNTER-STATEMENT: CONTENT AND PRESENTATION

The Registry has emphasised that the statements filed before the Registry must include all of the grounds which the party responsible for the filing intends to pursue and which are to be supported by evidence. Mere recitation of the relevant sections of the 1994 Act (or the provisions of a rule) will not be sufficient. There must be a sufficient degree of particularisation for the other side (and the Registry) to have a clear view of the nature of the dispute and have sufficient detail of, for example, the earlier trade marks or earlier rights and their use, on which the litigant intends to proceed.[10] **5–095**

If a party fails to provide in the statement of case sufficient information as to the nature or extent of the grounds upon which the proceedings rely, then further particulars should be sought or may be required by the Registrar of her own motion.[11] Until the statement of case is in order the proceedings will not be progressed and the subsequent delay may be a factor which will be taken into account in the award of costs. **5–096**

The Registry has issued broad guidelines as how the statements should be set out.[12] In general the person initiating the proceedings should set out the matter in issue, the facts to be relied upon and the relief sought. The facts to be relied upon (as distinct from the evidence that will be adduced to support them) should be set out concisely but fully. Costs need not be claimed specifically, but frequently they are. **5–097**

In the counter-statement the applicant should state which of the allegations in the statement of opposition are denied and why (and if it is intended to put **5–098**

---

[10] TPN 1/2000; reproduced in App.5. This Notice advises of changes in practice effective from April 26, 2000. The changes have been introduced to give effect to the Woolf Recommendations and bring together observations in a number of cases including *"Wild Child"* [1998] R.P.C. 455; *"Coffee mix"* [1998] R.P.C. 717 and *"Demon Ale"* [2000] R.P.C. 345, all decisions of the appointed person. See also *Julian Higgins' Application* [2000] R.P.C. 321; and *Club Europe* [2000] R.P.C. 329 (both decisions of the Vice-Chancellor); *"Geobank"* [1999] R.P.C. 682, Regy.

[11] Under r.57 and as suggested in *"Wild Child"* [1998] R.P.C. 455; see also TPN 1/2000 and PAN 3/04.

[12] We set out below what we perceive to be the essential aspects of the guidance given for the purposes of opposition, but reference should be made to TPN 1/2000 for the whole.

forward an alternative version of events, what that version is); which of the allegations in the statement it is unable to admit or deny (because, for example, it has no knowledge of them) but requires the opponent to prove; which of the allegations in the statement it admits. The Registry has also explained that the purpose of the counter-statement is to narrow down the field of dispute. Whilst in the past counter-statements have sometimes been very sketchy, that is no longer acceptable. If a counter-statement leaves uncertainty about what is in dispute, then it is unacceptable; it must deal specifically with every allegation in the statement. Costs need not be claimed specifically, though they usually are.

5–099   If the presentation of the statement or counter-statement is clearly inadequate the Registrar will refuse to serve it.

Statements should contain a declaration confirming the accuracy and truth of the matters contained in them.[13]

AMENDING GROUNDS OF OPPOSITION

5–100   The Registrar can, before the opposition is determined, give leave to amend a notice of opposition by, for example, the introduction of a further ground of objection.[14] A counter-statement can also be amended, with leave. Under para.22 of TPN 4/2000 the Registry will consider each application to amend on its merits, but will generally favour such applications on the basis that amendment is likely to avoid a multiplicity of proceedings and allow disputes to be resolved promptly and at less cost to the parties.[15] The Registrar does have the power, in an appropriate case, to allow one opponent to be substituted for another.[16]

5–101   On appeal in a registration case, whether before publication or in opposition, there is no statutory restriction on the objections which may be taken.[17] But it is suggested that such an objection could not be taken without leave and that leave would not be given unless the parties would suffer no prejudice, for example because it had already been addressed fully in evidence.[18]

DISCLOSURE

5–102   The Registrar has the powers of an official referee of the Supreme Court in relation to disclosure and the production of documents.[19] In addition, she has the power at any stage of the proceedings to direct that such documents, information or evidence as she shall reasonably require shall be filed.[20]

5–103   The Registrar accordingly has power to order general or specific disclosure.

---

[13] TPN 1/2000, paras 27–29.

[14] This was expressly permitted by the Rules under the 1938 Act r.121). Under the 1994 Act there is no equivalent rule but such amendments are presumably to be treated as irregularities rectifiable with leave under the 2000 Rules, r.66. For an illustration of amendment being allowed where it was considered it would cause no injustice, see *C (Device) Trade Mark* [1998] R.P.C. 439.

[15] In *Lowden v Lowden Guitar Co Limited* [2004] EWHC 2531 (Ch), an appeal to the High Court in an application for revocation for non-use in which the proprietor had failed to file a counter-statement within the time limit prescribed under r.31(2) (now 31(3)) Patten J. held that permission to amend the statement of grounds could not granted without the clock being reset on the time for the service of a counter-statement and a full three month period for the service of the amended counter-statement being allowed.

[16] *Pharmedica's Application* [2000] R.P.C. 536; cf. *Kirkbi AG's Applications* [1999] R.P.C. 733.

[17] Such a restriction was provided by the 1938 Act, ss.17(6) and 18(9).

[18] *Contrast Kenrick and Jefferson* (1909) 26 R.P.C. 641, where leave was refused, with *Brown Shoe* [1959] R.P.C. 641, where it was given, the objection being dismissed as a technicality, the point having been clearly raised in the evidence.

[19] 2000 Rules, r.58.

[20] r.57.

The Registry has, however, indicated that it is unlikely that standard disclosure would ever be ordered but that specific disclosure may be ordered in accordance with the principles set out in the CPR.[21] In particular the Registrar will take into account all the circumstances of the case and the overriding objective described in Part 1 of the CPR.[22] In practice it seems likely that in most cases disclosure will only be ordered if it relates to matters in question in the proceedings and disclosure is necessary to dispose fairly of the proceedings or to reduce costs.[23] The Registry has suggested disclosure would only be ordered after evidence has been filed.[24] But this must now be regarded with some doubt in the light of the more recently stated requirements as to the adequacy of statements of case.[25]

EVIDENCE

General

Evidence is generally filed in the form of statutory declaration or affidavit.[26] But a witness statement verified by a statement of truth[27] may be used as an alternative although the Registrar may give a direction as she thinks fit in any particular case that the evidence must be given by affidavit or statutory declaration instead of or in addition to the witness statement.[28] A mere witness (as opposed to a party to proceedings) cannot withdraw his or her written evidence once it has been filed.[29]   **5–104**

Where a party adduces evidence of a statement made by a person otherwise than while giving oral evidence in proceedings and does not call that person as a witness, then the Registrar may permit the other party to call that person as a witness and cross-examine them on that statement.[30]   **5–105**

Generally the Registrar has the powers of an official referee in relation to the examination of witnesses on oath.[31]

Cross-examination

In addition to these general powers the 2000 Rules do make further specific provision in relation to the giving of evidence. In any case the Registrar has a discretion to take oral evidence in addition to or in lieu of written evidence and she shall, unless she otherwise directs, allow any witness to be cross examined on that evidence.[32] In practice the Registrar requires notice of any wish to have a witness give oral evidence.[33] Cross-examination before the Registrar is relatively infrequent but more common than it was under the old law. The approach taken   **5–106**

---

[21] TPN 1/2000.

[22] See para.5–004.

[23] *Merrell Dow Pharmaceuticals Inc's (Terfenadine) Patent* [1991] R.P.C. 221. The value of the material to be disclosed may be weighed against the burden disclosure would impose: *Mölnlycke v Procter & Gamble (No.3)* [1990] R.P.C. 498. "Fishing discovery" is unlikely to be ordered: *British Leyland Motor Corporation v Wyatt Interpart (No.1)* [1979] F.S.R. 39; TPN 1/2000.

[24] *"Lifesavers"* [1997] R.P.C. 563.

[25] TPN 1/2000.

[26] r.55(1). The formalities for making and subscribing a statutory declaration or affidavit are set out in r.56.

[27] TPN 1/2000.

[28] r.55(3).

[29] *Joe Cool (Manchester) Ltd's Application* [2000] R.P.C. 926.

[30] r.55(5).

[31] r.58.

[32] r.55(2).

[33] Practice Notice of January 4, 1999 [1999] R.P.C. 294.

by the Registry under the 1994 Act is that set out by Ferris J. in *Alliance & Leicester plc's Application*:[34]

> "I do not think that it is possible to give an exhaustive statement of the circumstances in which cross-examination should be allowed. It seems to me that the words of Lord Evershed in *Kiddax*[35] provide the best guide, that is to say:
>
> > 'It is only consistent with the general principles upon which we administer justice here that if a party desires to test the evidence which appears by affidavit or statutory declaration, then *prima facie* and within reason he should be allowed to do so.'
>
> Lord Evershed's ensuing words indicate that he envisaged the qualification 'within reason' as enabling the court to avoid doing something which would be 'gravely oppressive'."

5–107   It is not necessary to show a direct conflict of evidence on a particular point. Notwithstanding the apparent breadth of this test, where there is nothing to be tested in cross examination, or the issues are unimportant, or the request for cross examination disproportionate having regard to the cost, hearing time or availability of witnesses, cross examination is likely to be refused. If a party who has been ordered to attend for cross examination fails to show up then it is for the Hearing Officer to consider what weight, if any, should be given to the untested evidence.

5–108   Where cross-examination does not take place, the Registrar will nevertheless consider and form her own view as to the evidential value of the evidence before her.[36]

Registrar may require evidence

5–109   The Registrar is not required to rely solely on the evidence the parties wish to place before her. At any stage of the proceedings she may direct that such documents, information or evidence as she may reasonable require shall be filed within such period as she may specify.[37]

Hearsay evidence

5–110   In proceedings which began on or after January 31, 1997 hearsay evidence of matters of fact or opinion will not be excluded. But the weight to be given to any such evidence is a matter for the Registrar, in accordance with s.4 of the Civil Evidence Act 1995.[38] The following points are particularly notable. If the formal evidence contains hearsay, it should be filed in sufficient time and it should contain sufficient particulars to enable the other parties to deal with it. If the provision of further particulars of or relating to it is reasonable and practicable, they should be given on request. Under s.4 of the 1995 Act the weight to be given to the evidence is a matter for the Registrar and regard may be had, in particular, to the following:

---

[34] [2002] R.P.C. 29.
[35] *"Kiddax"* [1959] R.P.C. 167.
[36] *" Wild Child"* [1998] R.P.C. 455.
[37] 2000 Rules, r.57. See PAN 3/04 for the approach to this power taken by the Registry.
[38] Practice Notice of January 4, 1999 [1999] R.P.C. 294. In proceedings which began before the January 31, 1997, the Registrar continues to apply the Patent Office Practice Direction of June 20,1995 [1995] R.P.C. 381. See also *"Trudo"* [1995] R.P.C. 370; *Oasis Stores* [1998] R.P.C. 631.

(1) whether it would have been reasonable and practicable for the party by whom the evidence was adduced to have produced the maker of the original statement as a witness;

(2) whether the original statement was made contemporaneously with the occurrence or existence of the matters stated;

(3) whether the evidence involves multiple hearsay;

(4) whether any person involved had any motive to conceal or misrepresent matters;

(5) whether the original statement was an edited account, or was made in collaboration with another or for a particular purpose;

(6) whether the circumstances in which the evidence is adduced as hearsay are such as to suggest an attempt to prevent proper evaluation of its weight.

Importance of evidence

The Registrar is unwilling to regard unsupported assertions as sufficient to sustain an objection under s.5(4) of the 1994 Act.[39] **5–111**

The question of evidence relating to the deceptive resemblance of marks is discussed in Ch.6.

Evidence not in proper form

The Registry has the practice of requiring receipt of formally correct affidavits, statutory declarations or witness statements to trigger subsequent evidence stages. The Registry will not normally accept the receipt of unsigned witness statements or unsworn affidavits or statutory declarations as meeting time deadlines, but exceptionally may do so provided a proper version of the evidence is filed within a specified period.[40] **5–112**

CASE MANAGEMENT, PRE-HEARING REVIEWS AND ALTERNATIVE DISPUTE RESOLUTION (ADR)

At any stage of the proceedings the Registrar may direct that the parties attend at a case management conference where they will have the opportunity to be heard with regard to the conduct of the proceedings.[41] At such a conference the Registrar may give such directions as to the conduct of the hearing as she thinks fit. At least 14 days notice will be given. The purpose of this provision is to allow the Registrar to take a more pro-active role in the conduct of the hearing and to consider such matters as the need to clarify the issues, the degree of complexity of the matter, any related actions between the parties and any wider public interest issues.[42] **5–113**

Similarly, before any hearing the Registrar may direct the parties to attend a pre hearing review at which directions may be given as to the conduct of the **5–114**

---

[39] "*Wild Child*" [1998] R.P.C. 455 at 465. The same ought to be the case for any objection which the Registrar cannot assess for herself, such as an objection under s.5(3) which is supported by a contention that the earlier trade mark is particularly distinctive through use or an objection under s.60. See also under "Onus", at para.5–118.

[40] TPN 1/2000.

[41] 2000 Rules, r.36.

[42] TPN 1/2000. The same Notice mentions that the Office intends issuing questionnaires on a selective basis, prior to the evidence rounds, which should help the parties and the hearing officer to gain a clearer appreciation of the issues.

hearing.[43] Again, at least 14 days notice will be given. This gives the Registrar a similar opportunity to consider making directions in relation to the matters referred to above.

The Registrar may ask the parties whether they have considered ADR and, where appropriate, will provide information about ADR.

STAY OF PROCEEDINGS

5–115 In an appropriate case the Registrar will stay proceedings, for example pending the resolution of High Court proceedings where the same or practically the same questions or issues are being determined.[44]

THE OPPOSITION HEARING

Skeleton arguments

5–116 Hearing officers require parties, particularly those represented by professional practitioners, to supply skeleton arguments, together with authorities, by 2.00pm two working days prior to the hearing.[45]

Presentation

5–117 Upon the completion of the evidence the Registrar will fix a date for the hearing, if requested by any party. At the hearing it is now customary for the opponent to begin, the applicant answers and finally the opponent replies to any new points raised by the applicant. Note that from June 1, 2002 the Registry reduced the formality surrounding *inter partes* hearings; the hearing officer is no longer announced on entry into the Tribunal room and those present are no longer expected to stand when he or she enters.[46]

The Registrar will encourage the parties to hold hearings, case management conferences and pre-hearing reviews using telephone conferencing arrangements and video links, where this can reasonably be achieved and will save costs.[47]

Onus

5–118 There is no overall onus on the applicant in opposition proceedings. Accordingly, where the opponent raises objections under s.5(3) or (4) of the 1994 Act, he must make them out.[48]

Time spent on hearing and cross examination

5–119 It has been indicated that it is generally the intention of the Registrar not to impose

---

[43] r.37.

[44] *Airport Restaurants v Southend-on-Sea Corporation* [1960] 2 All E.R. 888; *Thames Launches v Trinity House Corp (No.1)* [1961] Ch. 197; *Sears v Sears Roebuck* [1993] R.P.C. 385; *"Genius"* [1999] R.P.C. 741. Similarly it may be appropriate to grant a stay pending an appeal where relevant issues of principle are likely to be determined: *Philips Electronics v Remington (No.2)* [1999] E.T.M.R. 835. See also TPN 6/2004 and TPN 3/2004.

[45] TPN 1/2004.

[46] TPN 1/2002: Those whose knees automatically propel them upwards when the Hearing Officer enters are not discouraged from standing, but it is anticipated that this somewhat pavlovian impulse will gradually subside with the passage of time.

[47] TPN 1/2000.

[48] *"Audi-Med"* [1998] R.P.C. 863; *Oasis Stores* [1998] R.P.C. 631. But where an application was accepted on the basis of evidence subsequently shown to be misleading, the applicant ought not to be in a more favourable position in opposition than prior to acceptance and consequently the opposition should be decided on the balance of the evidence and without assuming a burden of proof one way or the other: *Dualit* [1999] R.P.C. 304.

time limits on the length of the hearing or cross-examination, but there remains a discretion to do otherwise.[49]

Presentation of new evidence at the hearing

The practice of introducing new evidence at hearings is to be discouraged and, it must be assumed, such evidence will only rarely be allowed and where it is unlikely to prejudice the other party. Documents may, however, be introduced in cross examination where designed to test the honesty or reliability of a witness.[50]   **5–120**

Hearing in public

Unless the Registrar otherwise directs, the hearing before the Registrar of any dispute between two or more parties relating to any matter in connection with an application for the registration of a mark or a registered mark will be held in public.[51]   **5–121**

The decision

When the Registrar has made a decision on the acceptability of an opposed mark she will send to the applicant and the opponent written notice of it, stating the reasons for her decision.   **5–122**

Where grounds for refusal of registration exist in respect of only some of the goods or services the subject of the application, then refusal of registration shall cover those goods or services only.[52]

Decisions of the Registrar to refuse registration should be based upon grounds of objection which the applicant has been given the opportunity to address in representations to the Registrar, made orally if so desired.[53]

COSTS

General

Under s.68 of the 1994 Act and r.60 of the 2000 Rules the Registrar may, in any proceedings before her, by order award to any party such costs as she may consider reasonable, and direct how and by what parties they are to be paid. In a contested opposition costs usually follow the event. By tradition costs were awarded in accordance with published scales which were not intended to cover all expenses actually incurred. The Registry is now somewhat more likely to order that a more realistic contribution be made, and, more frequently than in the past, to make costs orders as the cause for them arises and to attach a deadline for payment.[54] The current scales are reproduced in App.5.   **5–123**

Security for costs

The Registrar may require any person who is a party to any proceedings before her to give security for costs in relation to those proceedings and she may require   **5–124**

---

[49] TPN 1/2000.
[50] TPN 1/2000.
[51] 2000 Rules, r.59.
[52] Art.13 of the Directive. See also *"Mister Long"* [1998] R.P.C. 401; *"Wild Child"* [1998] R.P.C. 455; *"Naturelle"* [1999] R.P.C. 326; *"QS by S Oliver"* [1999] R.P.C. 520.
[53] *"Xe"* [2000] R.P.C. 405.
[54] TPN 2/2000; reproduced in App.5.

security for the costs of any appeal from her decision.[55] Security can be ordered against the applicant or an opponent.[56] Security will only be awarded on application and not on the Registry's own initiative. The amount of the award is determined on a case-by-case basis and proportionately to the estimated costs likely to be awarded at the conclusion of the proceedings.[57]

Irregularities

5–125   Subject to the specific provisions of r.68 of the 2000 Rules relating to time limits, the Registrar has a general power to allow the rectification of any irregularities in procedure in or before the Office or the Registrar on such terms as she may direct.[58]

5–126   Where there has been an interruption or dislocation in the postal services or an interruption in the normal operation of the Office then, by certification, particular days may be disregarded. So also the Registrar may extend any period for the giving, making or filing of any notice, application or other document where failure to meet that time limit was attributable to a failure or undue delay in the United Kingdom postal services.[59]

Alteration of time limits by the Registrar

5–127   The Registrar has a general power to extend time limits, with certain important exceptions.[60] The exceptions set out in the 2000 Rules (as amended by the Trade Marks (Amendment) Rules 2004) are r.10(6) (failure to file address for service), r.11 (deficiencies in the application), rr.13(1) (time for filing opposition), 13A(1) (time for filing counterstatement), r.23(4) (time for filing opposition), r.25(3) (time for filing opposition), r.29 (delayed renewal) and r.30 (restoration of registration), r.31(3) (time for filing counter-statement and evidence of use or reasons for non-use), r.32(3) (time for filing counter-statement), r.33(6) (time for filing counter-statement) and r.47 (time for filing opposition). In the case of these exceptions there is no power to extend the time limits at all, save in circumstances of procedural irregularity at the fault of the Registry, as prescribed by r.68(7).[61]

5–128   Where the Registrar does have power, then the party seeking an extension should apply for the extension before the time limit has expired. The Registrar may grant such extension and on such terms as she thinks fit. If the request is not made until after the time has expired, then the Registrar may nevertheless grant an extension if she is satisfied with the explanation for the delay in requesting the extension and it appears to her just and equitable so to do.[62]

5–129   It appears that the Registrar has a general discretion save as expressly confined as above. It is for the party in default to satisfy her that, despite the default, the discretion to extend time should be exercised in his favour. All relevant matters

---

[55] s.68 and r.61.
[56] *Sun Microsystems Inc's Application* [2001] R.P.C. 25.
[57] TPN 2/2000.
[58] r.66.
[59] r.67.
[60] r.68.
[61] *OMITEC Trade Mark* (BL O/018/02); *KML Invest AB's Trade Mark Application* [2004] R.P.C. 47. Note that with amendment of the 2000 Rules many of the rule numbers under which time limits are imposed were changed, making decisions under the old rules confusing in some instances.
[62] r.68(4) and (5).

should be taken into account including the explanation for any delay,[63] the public interest in ensuring that valid applications for registration should succeed and valid objections to registrations should be upheld without undue delay and whether refusal is likely to lead to another action between the same parties covering essentially the same subject-matter by way of an application to have the registration declared invalid.[64] But it is to be noted that if the request is not made until after the time has expired then the further requirements set out above must be satisfied.[65]

Where a time period for the filing of evidence is due to begin upon the expiry **5–130** of a period in which another party may file evidence and that other party notifies the Registrar that he does not wish to file any, or any further, evidence, then the Registrar may direct that the time period in which the first-mentioned party may file evidence shall begin on the date specified in the direction.[66]

Where there is an irregularity or prospective irregularity relating to a failure to **5–131** comply with a time limit and which is attributable to an error, default or omission on the part of the Office or Registrar then the Registrar may alter the time or period in question upon such terms as she may direct.[67]

REGULATION OF PROCEDURE

The Registrar has a the power to regulate the procedure before her in such a way **5–132** that she neither creates a substantial jurisdiction where none existed, nor exercises that power in a manner inconsistent with the express provisions conferring jurisdiction upon her.[68]

4. Appeal from the Registrar

THE TRIBUNAL OF APPEAL

An appeal lies from any decision by the Registrar, except as otherwise provided **5–133** by the 2000 Rules. For this purpose "decision" includes any act of the Registrar in the exercise of a discretion vested in her by or under the 1994 Act.[69] Any appeal may be brought to an appointed person or to the court.

Accordingly, an appeal from the refusal by the Registrar to register a trade **5–134** mark otherwise than in opposition may be brought to the court or to the appointed person. So also may an appeal be brought to the court or the appointed person from the decision of the Registrar in an opposition. It also appears that an appeal lies against any other decision by the Registrar in the exercise of her discretion, including any interlocutory decision, subject to the exceptions referred to below.

There are two exceptions where the 2000 Rules expressly provide there shall **5–135**

---

[63] Absent any explanation, an extension is unlikely to be granted: *Ghayasuddin Siddiqui's Application* [2001] E.T.M.R. 38.

[64] *"Liquid Force"* [1999] R.P.C. 429. This potentially marks a softening of the approach adopted in *"SAW"* [1996] R.P.C. 507, a decision under the particular words of r.114 of the 1938 Act to the effect that good reasons must be provided for any extension and the total time allowed should not exceed six months.

[65] *"Genius"* [1999] R.P.C. 741.

[66] 2000 Rules, r.68(6).

[67] r.68(7).

[68] *Pharmedica's Application* [2000] R.P.C. 536; *Langley v North West Water Authority* [1991] 3 All E.R. 610.

[69] s.76.

be no right of appeal. First, a decision of the Registrar under r.46 to publish proposals for such amendment of entries on the register as she considers necessary for the purpose of reclassifying the specification of a registered trade mark is final and not subject to appeal. So also is her decision on the substantive issue under r.47. Secondly, no appeal lies from a decision of the Registrar under r.50(4) not to make any document or part of a document available for public inspection.

Where an appeal is made to the court, there may be further appeals to the Court of Appeal and to the House of Lords, subject in each case to the appropriate leave.

THE NATURE OF THE APPEAL

5–136   An appeal from a decision of the Registrar is to be approached as would an appeal to the Court of Appeal from the High Court. Accordingly it is not a complete rehearing, the decision of the Registrar should not be ignored and it should be affirmed unless it is wrong or unjust because of a serious procedural or other irregularity in the proceedings below.[70]

TIME RUNS FROM THE DECISION

5–137   For the purpose of any appeal, time runs from the decision of the Registrar. When the Registrar has made a decision then she must send a notice of her decision in writing to each of the parties to the proceedings. Subject to the following, the date of her decision is deemed to be the date the notice was sent. If a statement of reasons is not included with the notice, then any party may, within one month of the date on which the notice was sent to him, request the Registrar, on the appropriate form, to send him a statement of reasons for the decision and upon such a request the Registrar will send a statement. The date on which the statement is sent is then deemed to be the date of the Registrar's decision for the purposes of any appeal.[71]

APPEAL TO THE APPOINTED PERSON

5–138   Any appeal may be brought to an appointed person.[72] Notice of Appeal must be sent to the Registrar within 28 days of the date of the Registrar's decision which is the subject of the appeal. The Notice of Appeal should be filed on Form TM55, accompanied by a statement in writing of the appellant's grounds of appeal and his case in support of the appeal.[73] The Registrar will send a copy of the notice and statement to the appointed person and to any other party to the proceedings.[74]

5–139   If the appointed person hears and determines the appeal then his decision is

---

[70] CPR, r.52.11; see generally, *Royal Enfield Trade Marks* [2002] R.P.C. 24, *Tanfern v Cameron-MacDonald* [2000] 2 All E.R. 801, CA and, in relation to appeals against the exercise of a discretion, *G v G* [1985] 2 All E.R. 225 at 229; [1985] 1 W.L.R. 647 at 652, HL; *"Magic Ball"* [2000] R.P.C. 439; *Re Procter and Gamble's Application* [1999] R.P.C. 673 at 677, CA. But if it is not clear that the Registrar has approached the matter in the correct way, then the matter should be considered afresh: *"Open Country"* [1998] R.P.C. 408 at 409; [2000] R.P.C. 477 at 481, CA.
[71] 2000 Rules, r.62.
[72] 1994 Act, ss.76 and 77.
[73] r.63(1).
[74] r.63(2) and (3).

final. There is no further right of appeal. An appeal to the appointed person against a decision by the Registrar involving the exercise of discretion is not a rehearing.[75]

Where an appeal is brought to an appointed person he may refer the appeal to the court if it appears to him that a point of general legal importance is involved or if the Registrar or any party to the proceedings before the Registrar requests that it be so referred.[76] Before referring the appeal the appointed person must give the appellant and any other party an opportunity to make representations as to whether he should adopt that course. One of the factors he will take into account will be that there can be no further appeal from his decision.   **5–140**

The appointed person may remit the matter to the Registrar for further consideration, in an appropriate case.[77] Although the appointed person has in the past remitted a matter to be re-heard on grounds of procedural irregularity in circumstances where an authority not cited in the hearing before the Registrar was relied upon in the decision without allowing the parties to make submissions on that authority[78], such a re-hearing is not automatic. Failure to give a party the opportunity to make submissions on an authority may, not must, amount to a beach of natural justice. If the authority in question was not central to the decision it is unlikely that any prejudice has been suffered by the unsuccessful party and the matter should not be remitted.[79] This can be assessed by the appointed person.   **5–141**

PRACTICE BEFORE THE APPOINTED PERSON

The appointed person has the same powers as the Registrar as to costs, security for costs and evidence. He, like the Registrar, has the powers of an official referee of the Supreme Court.[80]   **5–142**

The statement of the grounds of appeal and the statement of case in support of appeal form an important part of the appeal procedure. They must outline each of the grounds of appeal relied upon and state the case relied upon in support of those grounds. There is an inherent power to amend the documents in an appropriate case.[81]

If the appeal is to be determined by the appointed person and not referred to the court, then he will send out notice of the time and place of the hearing. If all parties inform the Appointed Person that they do not want an oral hearing then the Appointed Person has a discretion to hear and determine the case on the basis of written representations.[82] After the hearing he will send a copy of his decision, with a statement of his reasons, to the Registrar and to each person who was a party to the proceedings before him.   **5–143**

---

[75] See generally para.5–128 and *A.J. and M.A. Levy's T.M.* [1999] R.P.C. 291.

[76] See s.76(3) and, for the relevant procedure, r.64. This power should be used sparingly, otherwise the clear object of the legislation to provide a relatively inexpensive, quick and final resolution of appeals by a specialist tribunal would be defeated: *A.J. and M.A. Levy's T.M. (No. 2)* [1999] R.P.C. 358; *"Academy"* [2000] R.P.C. 35. See also *Jimmy Nicks Application* [1999] E.T.M.R. 445.

[77] *Ty Nant Spring Water Ltd's Application* [2000] R.P.C. 55; *"Xe"* [2000] R.P.C. 405. See also the decision of Richard Arnold Q.C., sitting as the appointed person in *Applied Technologies Manufacturing limited* (O–348-04).

[78] *Silver Spring Mineral Water Co Ltd's Application* [2003] R.P.C. 21 where the Registrar relied on a decision of the High Court handed down after the hearing before him and did not allow the applicant an opportunity to address him on that authority, the appointed person remitted the case to the Registrar to be re-heard.

[79] *Sheridan v Stanley Cole (Wainfleet) Limited* [2003] EWCA Civ 1046; [2004] 4 All E.R. 1181 CA.

[80] s.76(5).

[81] *"Coffeemix"* [1998] R.P.C. 717.

[82] r.65(3).

5–144   The appointed person has an inherent power to regulate the procedure before him in a manner conducive to the just and fair determination of the appeal. The discretionary powers of the appointed person and the High Court are the same[83] and they include a power to hear a representative of the Registrar.[84]

APPEAL TO THE COURT

5–145   The appeal is brought by appeal notice.[85] The notice should set out the grounds of appeal and why the decision appealed against was wrong or unjust.

    The appeal notice must be issued within 28 days of the decision appealed from. Within 21 days of issue the notice of appeal must be served on the Registrar and any respondents and lodged with the clerk or other person in charge of the Chancery List.[86] Thereafter a respondent may file and serve a respondent's notice.[87]

5–146   The court may make any decision which ought to have been made by the Registrar or any further or other order as the case may require or may remit the matter for rehearing and determination.[88]

EVIDENCE ON APPEAL

5–147   On appeal before the court or the appointed person new evidence may be admitted only with leave.[89] The onus is on the party applying for leave to admit the evidence to justify the exercise of discretion in his favour but there are no express limits placed upon the discretion or criteria set for its exercise, save that the discretion should be exercised in accordance with the overriding objective and the concept of proportionality.[90] Relevant factors are likely to include the following[91]:

(1) Whether the evidence could have been filed earlier and, if so, how much earlier.
(2) If it could have been, what explanation for the late filing has been offered to explain the delay.
(3) The nature of the mark.
(4) The nature of the objections to it.
(5) The potential significance of the new evidence.
(6) Whether the other side will be significantly prejudiced by the admission of the evidence in a way which cannot be compensated, for example by an order for costs.

---

[83] *"Academy"* [2000] R.P.C. 35.
[84] *"Corgi"* [1999] R.P.C. 549. See also *"Coffeemix"* [1998] R.P.C. 717: the appointed person has an inherent power to allow amendments to the notice of appeal and supporting documents.
[85] CPR, r.52 and the Practice Direction supplementing Pt 52, which set out all the requirements to be met by the appellant and respondent.
[86] See CPR Pt 63 and the Practice Direction supplementing it, reproduced in Apps 32 and 33.
[87] CPR, r.52.5.
[88] CPR, r.52.10. And see, *e.g. Swiss Miss* [1998] R.P.C. 889, CA.
[89] CPR, r.52.11, previously RSC, Ord.55, r.7(2).
[90] *Du Pont Trade mark* [2004] F.S.R. 15 CA and the judgment of Hale L.J. in *Hertfordhire Investments Ltd v Bubb* [2000] 1 W.L.R. 2318 at 2325D–H. See also *Club Europe* [2000] R.P.C. 329; *Julian Higgins' Application* [2000] R.P.C. 321, both decisions of the Vice-Chancellor; *Hunt Wesson* ("Swiss Miss") [1996] R.P.C. 233. In his judgment in *Swiss Miss* Laddie J. reviews the earlier authorities; *Dualit v Rowlett Catering Appliances* [1999] F.S.R. 865.
[91] *per* Laddie J., in ("Swiss Miss") [1996] R.P.C. 233, at 241–242; although these matters will, in most cases, be the important ones, the Vice-Chancellor has cautioned against any attempt to confine the statutory discretion within a straightjacket: *Club Europe* [2000] R.P.C. 329, at 338. See also *"Wunderkind"* [2002] R.P.C. 45 and *"Mezzacorona"* [2004] R.P.C. 25.

(7) The desirability of avoiding multiplicity of proceedings.

(8) The public interest in not admitting onto the Register invalid marks.

MODIFICATION OF THE APPLICATION ON APPEAL

The opportunity to make amendments to an application is strictly limited by the **5–148** Act and is the subject of earlier discussion. In general an application may be made to amend an application under s.13 of the 1994 Act by disclaimer or limitation or under s.39 by way of restricting the goods or services the subject of the application. It would seem undesirable that this should be raised on appeal if it has not been the subject of consideration by the Registrar.[92] It is suggested that in such circumstances the appointed person and the court have a discretion to allow it to be raised, assuming the statutory requirements are satisfied, although they would be very reluctant to do so, save in a very clear case. The court and the appointed person certainly have a discretion to remit the matter to the Registrar where appropriate.

COSTS ON APPEAL AND FURTHER APPEAL

The appointed person has the power to award to any party such costs as he may **5–149** consider reasonable, and to direct how and by what parties they are to be paid.[93] In the case of oppositions the appointed person usually awards costs in accordance with the scale of costs which applies in Registry proceedings.[94] In the case of unsuccessful appeals to the appointed person against refusals by the Registrar (*ex parte* proceedings), there will normally be no order for costs.[95]

In the High Court costs will be awarded in accordance with the High Court **5–150** practice and will usually follow the event.[96]

The Registrar has indicated that in the case of appeals in "without notice" (*ex parte*) proceedings to the High Court, she would expect costs to be awarded against her should she lose on appeal. So also she should seek costs if successful unless the party paying is likely to suffer some form of hardship or where a significant point of general legal interest is involved.[97]

---

[92] Practical difficulties are also presented in that where the amendment affects the representation of the trade mark or the goods or services the subject of the application, the Registrar is required by the 2000 Rules, r.18 to publish the amendment for opposition purposes. On the other hand, where an application is amended under s.13, the Registrar is required by r.24 to publish the amendment, but it is not then open to opposition.

[93] rr.54 and 59.

[94] See, *e.g.*, *"Wild Child"* [1998] R.P.C. 455; *"Academy"* [2000] R.P.C. 35.

[95] *"AD 2000"* [1997] R.P.C. 168. TPN 2/2000. If a party has acted unreasonably then an order for costs may be sought: *Jaleel (S.M.) & Co Ltd's Application* [2000] R.P.C. 471.

[96] The court must have regard to all the circumstances, including the conduct of the parties and whether a party has succeeded on part of his case, even if he has not been wholly successful. The court will make a summary assessment in cases which have not lasted for more than a day unless there is a good reason not to do so.

[97] TPN 2/2000.

CHAPTER 6

COMMUNITY TRADE MARK PROCEDURE

6–001   The purpose of this Chapter is to address the aspects of procedure specific to the Community trade mark. A Community trade mark ("CTM") is a unitary trade mark providing the same rights and protection, and having equal effect, throughout the European Community.[1] It can only be registered, transferred, revoked or surrendered in respect of the whole Community. Apart from this important "Community-wide" aspect and from procedural matters relating to the administration of the CTM system, much of the law applicable to CTMs is similar to the law governing national trade marks in the United Kingdom and in other EU Member States. The main substantive provisions of Council Regulation (EC) No.40/94 on the Community trade mark[2] ("the CTM Regulation") are largely identical to the corresponding provisions of the TM Directive,[3] which was implemented in the United Kingdom by the 1994 Act. The reader will therefore be cross-referred to the sections in this work addressing the analogous United Kingdom law.

6–002   The CTM Regulation established the Office for Harmonisation in the Internal Market (Trade Marks and Designs) ("OHIM") to administer the CTM Register. OHIM has its seat in Alicante (Spain). This chapter deals first with general provisions relating to the CTM system and the operations of OHIM, then the specific rules governing applications for CTMs, oppositions, registration and renewal of CTMs, dealings with CTMs, the enforcement of CTMs, applications for the cancellation of CTMs, and the conversion of CTMs and CTM applications into applications for national registrations. Finally, the chapter deals with the consequences for the CTM system of the enlargement of the European Union as a result of the accession of 10 new Member States on May 1, 2004.

1. The relevant legislation

6–003   On December 20, 1993, as part of the European Union's drive towards the harmonisation of economic activities in the internal market, the Council of the European Union adopted the CTM Regulation. The Regulation, which is directly applicable, establishes the CTM system and provides a complete code determining who is entitled to apply for a CTM, what marks can be registered and the rights conferred by registration, without need for further national legislation.[4] Following the establishment of the World Trade Organisation the CTM Regula-

---

[1] Although the European Community ("EC") and the European Union ("EU") are technically different concepts, the two terms may both be used to refer to the geographical and political entity which at the time when the CTM system came into operation (April 1, 1996) comprised 15 Member States: Belgium, Denmark, Germany, Greece, Spain, France, Ireland, Italy, Luxembourg, the Netherlands, Austria, Portugal, Finland, Sweden and the United Kingdom. On May 1, 2004, a further 10 countries acceded to the EC and EU: Cyprus, the Czech Republic, Estonia, Hungary, Latvia, Lithuania, Malta, Poland, Slovakia and Slovenia.

[2] O.J. EC 1994 L 11, p.1. The initials "OJ EC" stand for "Official Journal of the European Communities". This was renamed the "Official Journal of the European Union" (O.J. EU) as from February 2003.

[3] Directive 89/104/EEC, O.J. EC 1989 L 40, p.1.

[4] There are nonetheless some matters of detail that need to be dealt with nationally. S.52 of the 1994 Act empowers the Secretary of State to adopt provisions in connection with the operation of

tion was amended by Council Regulation (EC) No.3288/94[5] in order to take account of the provisions of the TRIPs Agreement.[6] Detailed rules governing proceedings in OHIM are laid down in Commission Regulation (EC) No.2868/95 ("the Implementing Regulation").[7] Further procedural rules governing appeals to the OHIM Boards of Appeal are provided by Commission Regulation (EC) No.216/96 ("the Appeals Regulation").[8] The fees payable in respect of CTM proceedings are set out in Commission Regulation (EC) No.2869/95 on the fees payable to OHIM ("the Fees Regulation").[9]

A major overhaul of the CTM Regulation, in the light of experience acquired since the inception of the CTM system, was undertaken by Council Regulation (EC) No.422/2004 of February 19, 2004.[10] The Implementing Regulation, Appeals Regulation and Fees Regulation were, at the time of writing, also in the process of being amended.[11]					**6–004**

2. The basic provisions governing the registration of CTMs

The rules on what types of sign may constitute a CTM are similar to those set out in Article 2 of the TM Directive and given effect in s.1(1) of the 1994 Act. There are two essential rules: the sign must be capable of being represented graphically and be capable of distinguishing the goods or services of one undertaking from those of other undertakings.[12]					**6–005**

Article 7 of the CTM Regulation[13] sets out the absolute grounds for refusal of a CTM, which to a great extent mirror the provisions of Article 3 of the TM Directive and s.3 of the 1994 Act.[14] It is important to bear in mind that the absolute grounds for refusal set out in Art.7(1) prevent registration as a CTM even if the grounds for non-registrability obtain in only part of the Community.[15] This is a logical consequence of the unitary nature of the CTM.					**6–006**

A further point to note is that there is no "bad faith" provision in Art.7 corresponding to s.3(6) of the 1994 Act. Thus no objection based on an application being too broad or on the absence of an intention to use the mark may be raised by the OHIM examiner. As a result the OHIM examiners and Boards of Appeal often have to contend with extremely long lists of goods and services. Each item on the list has to be considered separately. When, for example, a German company called Taurus-Film GmbH & Co applied to register "Cine Action" and "Cine Comedy" as trade marks for a wide range of goods and services, including "production, reproduction, showing and rental of films, videos and other televi-					**6–007**

---

the CTM Regulation. This has been done by the Community Trade Mark Regulations, SI 1996/1908.

[5] O.J. EC 1994 L 349, p.83.

[6] Agreement on Trade Related Aspects of Intellectual Property Rights.

[7] O.J. EC 1995 L 303, p.1.

[8] O.J. EC 1996 L 28, p.11.

[9] O.J. EC 1995 L 303, p.33.

[10] O.J. EU 2004 L 70, p.1.

[11] Commission Regulation (EC) No 2082/2004 amending the Appeals Regulation O.J. EU 2004 L 360, p.8) was adopted on December 6, 2004, and came into force on December 27, 2004. Up-to-date information about the relevant legislation may be found on the OHIM website *www.oami.eu.int*).

[12] See Ch.2.

[13] In the rest of this chapter, references to numbered Articles are references to the CTM Regulation, unless otherwise stated. References to numbered Rules relate to the Implementing Regulation.

[14] See Ch.8.

[15] Art.7(2).

sion programmes" in Class 41, the "broad-brush" approach taken by the examiner (and to a lesser extent, by the Board of Appeal) was rejected by the Court of First Instance.[16] The Court held that the marks must be accepted for services such as "cultural activities, organization and conducting of shows, quizzes and musical events" and "management and exploitation of copyright and industrial property rights for others".[17] The fact that the marks were totally descriptive as regards any activity that the applicant was likely to pursue was not considered relevant. Bad faith may, on the other hand, be relied on as the basis for a declaration of invalidity of a registered CTM on application to OHIM or by way of a counterclaim in infringement proceedings.[18] OHIM does not however interpret bad faith as including the practice of registering a trade mark for goods or services in relation to which there is no intention of use.[19] It has in any event been questioned whether the UK practice is consistent with Article 3(2)(d) of the TM Directive, that being the optional provision on which s.3(6) of the 1994 Act is based.[20]

6–008   The relative grounds for refusal of a CTM are to be found at Art.8. Again, the provisions of the CTM Regulation closely mirror those of the TM Directive (Art.4), and consequently, those of the 1994 Act (s.5). The differences between the relative grounds for refusal in national and CTM applications are addressed in detail in Ch.9. As in the case of absolute grounds, the fundamental principle is that a relative ground existing anywhere in the Community is capable of defeating an application to register a CTM. Relative grounds may not, however, be raised by OHIM on its own motion; they must be invoked by the owner of the relevant right.

3. The structure of OHIM

6–009   OHIM is a legal entity under the laws of each Member State, capable of acquiring and disposing of movable and immovable property and participating in legal proceedings.[21]

6–010   The day-to-day management of OHIM in entrusted to the OHIM President[22], who is appointed by the Council of the European Union acting on a proposal from the Administrative Board of OHIM.[23] The Administrative Board is composed of representatives of the Member States and the Commission.[24] In addition to its participation in the appointment of senior officials of OHIM, the Administrative Board performs a supervisory role.[25] A Budget Committee, composed in the same way as the Administrative Board, is responsible for adopting the OHIM budget and giving a discharge to the President in respect of the implementation of the budget.[26]

6–011   Article 125 establishes five distinct bodies, within OHIM, for the purpose of taking decisions in connection with the registration of trade marks:

---

[16] Cases T–135/99 and T–136/99 *Taurus-Film GmbH & Co v OHIM* ('Cine Action' and 'Cine Comedy') [2001] E.C.R. II-382.

[17] The acceptance of the mark for "cultural activities" seems surprising, unless one assumes that action films and comedies can never amount to culture.

[18] Art.51.

[19] See paras 8–258 *et seq.*

[20] See paras 8–264 *et seq.*

[21] Art.111.

[22] Art.119 confers extensive powers of management on the President.

[23] Art.120.

[24] Art.122.

[25] Art.121.

[26] Arts 133–137.

1. Examiners: responsible, essentially, for decisions on absolute grounds;[27]
2. Opposition Divisions: responsible for decisions on oppositions;[28]
3. Cancellation Divisions: responsible for decisions on applications for revocation or for a declaration of invalidity of a CTM;[29]
4. An Administration of Trade Marks and Designs and Legal Division: responsible for decisions which do not fall within the competence of the above three bodies, in particular decisions in respect of entries in the Register of CTMs;[30]
5. Boards of Appeal: responsible for decisions on appeals against decisions of the above four bodies.[31]

OHIM's original administrative structure corresponded closely to the scheme **6–012** of Art.125. This is no longer true, following an internal reorganisation carried out in 2003. OHIM now has a Trade Marks Department. As regards issues of substantive trade mark law, all the powers conferred on examiners, Opposition Divisions and Cancellation Divisions by the CTM Regulation are exercised within the Trade Marks Department. Decisions on procedural matters are taken within an Administration of Trade Marks and Designs Department, which presumably performs the functions of the Administration of Trade Marks and Designs and Legal Division. The effect of the reorganisation is that the same persons may function as examiners and as members of an Opposition or Cancellation Division. This is perfectly compatible with the CTM Regulation, provided that the terms of Art.132(1) are complied with. This provides, in particular, that two of the three members of an Opposition Division must not have taken part in examining the trade mark application[32] and that members of the Cancellation Divisions may not take part in any proceedings if they have participated in the final decision on the case in the proceedings for registration or in opposition proceedings.

4. Capacity

Article 5, in its original version, contained complex rules concerning nationality **6–013** requirements for the ownership of CTMs. The usefulness of these rules was never apparent, except perhaps to those who believe that the privilege of owning intellectual property should only be extended to foreigners on a basis of strict reciprocity. These rules have in any event been swept away by Regulation No.422/2004. The amended version of Art.5 provides simply that:

> "Any natural or legal person, including authorities established under public law, may be the proprietor of a Community trade mark."

Companies and firms are legal persons if under the law governing them they have the capacity in their own name to have rights and obligations of all kinds, to make contracts or accomplish other legal acts and to sue and be sued.[33]

---

[27] Art.126.

[28] Art.127.

[29] Art.129.

[30] Art.128. The reference to designs in the name of this body was added by Article 104 of Council Regulation (EC) No.6/2002 on Community designs, O.J. EC 2002 L 3, p.1.

[31] Art.130.

[32] The logic of this rule is not self-evident, since participation in the examination of a trade mark application on absolute grounds is not likely to diminish a person's objectivity when he is called upon to examine an opposition against the application based on relative grounds.

[33] Art.3. For a case on the application of this rule, see Case R–195/1998-1 *Nauta Dutilh*. Case numbers beginning with a capital "R" refer to decisions of the OHIM Boards of Appeal.

5. OHIM's language regime

6–015   The language regime established by the CTM Regulation is extremely complex. The reason for this complexity is obvious. When the CTM system began to operate, the European Community had eleven official languages.[34] This number rose to 20 on May 1, 2004.[35] It would be unreasonable to expect OHIM to be staffed exclusively by polyglots capable of processing trade mark applications in 20 languages. Moreover, opposition and cancellation proceedings involve two or more parties; if all parties were allowed to use their own language, translation costs would be prohibitive. The OHIM language rules are an attempt to rationalise Europe's tower of Babel and to create a practical system that takes account of commercial reality and responds to the needs of the parties to OHIM proceedings. The key element in the chosen solution was the decision to adopt English, French, German, Italian and Spanish as the OHIM languages.[36] The decision to grant these languages a special status was due to their being the five most widely spoken languages in Europe. The validity of the language regime was challenged unsuccessfully, on grounds of discrimination, in *Kik v OHIM*.[37]

6–016   Applications for CTMs may be made in any of the official languages of the European Community.[38] The language chosen is known as the language of the application. Each application must stipulate a second language, which must be one of the OHIM languages.[39] If the language of the application is not one of the OHIM languages, OHIM must arrange for the application "as described in Article 26(1)" to be translated into the stipulated second language.[40] If the applicant is the only party to proceedings before OHIM, the language of proceedings will be the language of the application. OHIM may, however, send written communications to the applicant in the second stipulated language if the language of the application is not one of the OHIM languages.[41]

6–017   The practice of the OHIM examiners was to send all written communications in the second language whenever the application was filed in a non-OHIM language. The OHIM Boards of Appeal ruled in several decisions[42] that, while it was legitimate for OHIM to use the second language for letters of objection on absolute grounds, requests for clarification and such like, documents that were in the nature of a decision (*e.g.* a decision rejecting the application on absolute grounds) should be in the language of the application. In *Kik v OHIM* the Court of Justice went much further and held that OHIM must draft all procedural documents in the language of the proceedings. Surprisingly, the Court held that the expression "written communications" in Art.115(4) encompassed only such insubstantial items as covering letters. OHIM is still attempting to grapple with the practical consequences of this ruling—a task that was not made easier by the

---

[34] Danish, Dutch, English, Finnish, French, German, Greek, Italian, Portuguese, Spanish and Swedish.

[35] The new languages are: Czech, Estonian, Hungarian, Latvian, Lithuanian, Maltese, Polish, Slovakian and Slovenian.

[36] Art.115(2).

[37] Case C–361/01P *Kik v OHIM* [2003] E.C.R. I-8283.

[38] Art.115(1).

[39] Art.115(3).

[40] Art.115(3).

[41] Art.115(4).

[42] *e.g.* Case R–314/1999-1 TOP, O.J. OHIM 2/03, p.283, and Case R–387/1999-2 ENERGY PLUS, O.J. OHIM 1/03, p.89.

addition of nine new languages on May 1, 2004. On April 30, 2004, the President of OHIM issued a Communication on the subject.[43]

Notices of opposition or applications for the cancellation of a CTM[44] must be filed in one of the OHIM languages.[45] If the language in which such a notice or application is filed is the language of the contested CTM application (or of the CTM application that led to the registration of the contested CTM) or the second language stipulated in the CTM application, then that language is designated the language of proceedings.[46] If not, the party filing the notice of opposition or application for cancellation must within one month arrange for it to be translated into either the language of the CTM application (if it is an OHIM language) or into the stipulated second language at his own expense.[47] The language chosen is then designated the language of proceedings.[48]

6–018

What this means in practical terms is that the opponent (or the applicant for cancellation) may in certain situations be able to choose the language of proceedings. That will be the case whenever the language of the contested CTM application (or of the CTM application that led to the registration of the contested CTM) is an OHIM language. The opponent or applicant for cancellation will be able to choose that language or the second language stipulated in the CTM application. Where the language of the CTM application is not an OHIM language, any opposition or cancellation proceedings in relation to that application or the ensuing registration will have to be conducted in the second language stipulated in the CTM application.

6–019

In written proceedings before OHIM any party may use any of the OHIM languages (unless the Implementing Regulation provides otherwise).[49] However, if the language used is not the designated language of proceedings, then within one month of the date of submission of the document in question the party must supply a translation thereof into the designated language of proceedings.[50]

6–020

In opposition and cancellation proceedings where the evidence in support of the opposition or the application for cancellation is not filed in the language of proceedings, the opponent or applicant for cancellation must file a translation of the evidence.[51] The OHIM opposition and cancellation divisions tend to apply this rule strictly and refuse to take account of evidence that is not made available in the language of proceedings. That may be unduly harsh. The purpose of the translation requirement is to ensure that the Office and the other parties can understand the evidence. This does not necessarily mean that every page of every document must be translated, especially in the case of voluminous evidence to establish that a trade mark has a reputation.[52] Curiously, a different and more reasonable rule applies to evidence of use which the opponent or the applicant for

6–021

---

[43] Communication No.4/04 of the President of OHIM. Henceforth OHIM will use the language of the application for all correspondence relating to the application (in so far as the applicant remains the only party to the proceedings), unless the applicant expressly indicates that he wishes OHIM to use the second language.

[44] The term "cancellation" is used here as a general term to cover revocations and declarations of invalidity.

[45] Art.115(5).

[46] Art.115(6).

[47] Art.115(6) in conjunction with rr.17(1) and 38(1).

[48] Art.115(6).

[49] r.96(1).

[50] r.96(1).

[51] rr.17(2) and 38(2).

[52] Case R–625/2002-2 MAISON DU CAFÉ.

cancellation is required to produce under Art.43(2) or Art.56(2) respectively. In such cases the Office "may require" the party in question to submit a translation of the evidence.[53]

6–022   There is some controversy about what is or is not a translation. Some Board of Appeal decisions have held that a translation must reproduce the structure and contents of the original document.[54] Others have pointed out that there is no rule prescribing the form and manner in which translations must be presented; therefore, not every word on documents such as registration certificates need be translated if the relevant information has been provided to the Office in the notice of opposition or in other documents.[55]

6–023   Rule 97 of the Implementing Regulation lays down complex rules concerning the use of languages in oral proceedings before OHIM. Oral proceedings being an extreme rarity at OHIM,[56] the reader is referred to the source materials.

6. Representation

6–024   Natural or legal persons domiciled in or having either their principal place of business or a real and effective industrial or commercial establishment in the European Community are entitled to represent themselves in proceedings before OHIM.[57] If they wish, such parties may instead be represented by an employee.[58] The employee of a legal person entitled to be represented in this way may also represent other legal persons economically connected with his employer, even if they themselves have no industrial or commercial establishment within the European Community.[59] Other than in respect of filing an application for a CTM, natural or legal persons not domiciled or having either their principal place of business or a real and effective industrial or commercial establishment in the European Community must be professionally represented before OHIM.[60] Representatives acting before OHIM must file a written notice of authorisation signed by the party who appointed them.[61] It is possible to file authorisations covering more than one application or CTM registration.[62] Any notification or other communication by OHIM to an authorised representative has the same effect as if it had been addressed to the person represented, and vice versa.[63]

6–025   Only the following people may act as professional representatives before OHIM:[64]

(1) legal practitioners qualified in a Member State and having their place of business in the European Community, to the extent that they are entitled to act as representatives in trade mark matters in the Member State in which they are qualified;

---

[53] rr.22(4) and 40(5).
[54] e.g. Case R–296/1999-1 SPORTS EXPERTS, OH OHIM 7–8/2001, p.1549. Another case in which a strict view of the translation requirement was taken is Case R–47/2000-4 KRISS/CHRIS & CRIS (fig.), O.J. OHIM 9/2001, p.1707.
[55] e.g. Case R–746/1999-2 UNIPRESS/UNIPRESS, O.J. OHIM 7–8/2001, p.1455.
[56] An oral hearing was held by the Board of Appeal in Case R–283/1999-3 HOLLYWOOD/HOLLYWOOD, O.J. OHIM 2/02, p.281.
[57] Arts 88(1) and (2).
[58] Art.88(3).
[59] Art.88(3).
[60] Art.88(2).
[61] Art.88(2).
[62] r.76(1).
[63] r.77.
[64] Art.89.

(2) professional representatives whose names appear on a list maintained for that purpose by OHIM.

In order to obtain entry on the list of professional representatives, a representative must be a national of a Member State (unless exempted from this requirement by the President of OHIM), must have his place of business or employment in the European Community and must be entitled to represent natural or legal persons in trade mark matters before the central industrial property office of a Member State.[65] Entry is obtained on receipt of a request, accompanied by a certificate from the central industrial property office of the Member State concerned.[66]

7. Fees

OHIM is in principle supposed to be self-financing. It derives its income from fees charged for the various operations relating to CTMs. The fees are fixed by the Fees Regulation at such a level as to ensure a balanced budget.[67] All fees are in euros. Payment may be made by payment or transfer into a bank account held by OHIM, by delivery or remittance of cheques made payable to OHIM, in cash[68] or by other methods allowed by the OHIM President, in particular by means of deposits in current accounts held with OHIM.[69] The President of OHIM has made use of this option[70] and current accounts have become the standard method of payment for many of the parties to proceedings before OHIM and their representatives.

6–026

The date on which a fee is paid or deemed to be paid can be crucial, *e.g.* for the purpose of obtaining a filing date[71] or for filing a valid opposition,[72] application for cancellation[73] or notice of appeal.[74] Article 8 of the Fees Regulation contains rules as to when payment is deemed to be made. In this respect, there are major advantages in having a current account with OHIM; the rules[75] as to when payment is deemed to be made by current account holders are generous, with the result that they are unlikely to miss a deadline through non-payment of a fee. Even if there are no funds in the account, that does not necessarily mean that payment is not deemed to be made on the due date, because OHIM grants the account holder a 30-day period in which to top up the account.[76]

6–027

The rules concerning other methods of payment are relatively harsh. Where, for example, payment is made by cheque, Article 6(1) of the Fees Regulation requires the cheque to be denominated in euros. In one case, where both parties were Spanish, the opponent paid the opposition fee by means of a cheque drawn on a Spanish bank in pesetas for the equivalent amount (at a time when the peseta

6–028

---

[65] Art.89(2). This provision was amended in 2004. The previous version appeared to conflict with Article 42 of the EC Treaty (freedom of establishment) inasmuch as the representative's capacity to act before a national office had to be established in the Member State in which he had his place of business or employment.

[66] Art.89(3).

[67] Art.139.

[68] Fees Regulation, Art.5(1).

[69] Fees Regulation, Art.5(2).

[70] Decision No.EX-96-1 of the President of OHIM of January 11, 1996 (O.J. OHIM 1996, p.48), as of July 30, 1997 (O.J. OHIM 1996, p.1454).

[71] Art.27.

[72] Art.42(3).

[73] Art.55(2).

[74] Art.59.

[75] Decision No.EX-96-1, Art.7.

[76] Decision No.EX-96-1, Art.8.

was still the official currency of Spain). This was held not to comply with Article 6(1) of the Fees Regulation and the opposition was rejected.[77]

6–029   In principle, the full amount of any fee must be paid within the relevant time limit.[78] OHIM may, however, "overlook any small amount lacking" where this is considered justified.[79] A frequent problem is that payments by means of bank transfer are reduced as a result of bank charges—a matter over which the payer may have little control. In one case the Board of Appeal held that a shortfall of €12.02, in relation to a fee of €975, was small enough to be overlooked, since the amount lacking was only 1.2 per cent of the total.[80]

8. Time limits and the consequences of non-compliance

Rules governing the fixing, expiry and extension of time limits

6–030   The CTM legislation provides in many places for certain operations to be undertaken within a specific time limit. Rules concerning the calculation of time limits, their duration and expiry are laid down in the Implementing Regulation.[81] The consequences of non-compliance with a time limit vary. They are frequently serious and may result in a loss of rights. Articles 78 and 78a make it possible in certain cases to re-establish rights that are lost through non-observance of a time limit. Those involved in proceedings before OHIM are advised none the less to pay close attention to time limits and to endeavour to observe them in all cases.

For the detailed rules on the calculation of time limits, the reader is referred to r.70.

6–031   The legislation makes a basic distinction between time limits whose duration is fixed by OHIM and those whose duration is fixed directly by the legislation. The duration of the former may, under certain conditions laid down in r.71, be extended. No provision is made for the extension of time limits whose duration is fixed directly by the legislation; as a result these are in principle non-extendable.[82]

6–032   When the legislation provides for a time limit to be fixed by OHIM, it may not be shorter than one month, where the party concerned has his domicile or principal place of business or an establishment within the European Community. Otherwise the minimum period is two months. In all cases the maximum duration is six months.[83] Such time limits may be extended if the party concerned requests an extension before the expiry of the original time limit.[84] Where other parties are involved in the proceedings, OHIM may refuse to grant an extension unless the other parties give their agreement.[85]

6–033   If a time limit expires on a day when OHIM is not open for business or when

---

[77] Case R–443/2001-2 GABARRO.
[78] Fees Regulation, Art.9(1).
[79] Fees Regulation, Art.9(2).
[80] Case R–943/2000-4 ROSSO BIANCO, O.J. OHIM 10/02, p.1961.
[81] See rr.70–72.
[82] Case T–232/00 *Chef Revival USA Inc v OHIM* [2002] E.C.R. II-2749, at paras 35 and 43.
[83] r.71(1).
[84] r.71(1).
[85] r.71(2). The English version implies that OHIM cannot extend a time limit without the agreement of the other parties in *inter partes* proceedings; the other language versions show that OHIM is not obliged to impose such a condition.

mail is not being delivered in Alicante (in particular, at the weekend or on a public holiday), it is automatically extended till the next working day.[86]

The legislation generally gives the impression that time limits are of a peremptory nature. However, the Court of First Instance has sometimes suggested that OHIM, in particular at the appeal stage, should not require strict compliance with time limits. The case law is not uniform and it is possible that a more lenient approach is required in *ex parte* proceedings than in *inter partes* proceedings.[87] In the BABY-DRY case[88] the Court of First Instance held that the Board of Appeal must allow the applicant to plead acquired distinctiveness even though the applicant had not raised such an issue when the examiner objected to the mark on the grounds of lack of distinctiveness and invited the applicant to submit observations to overcome the objection within a period of two months. At first sight that appears to be contrary to r.11(3), which states that OHIM must refuse the CTM application if the applicant does not overcome an objection to registration based on absolute grounds within the period specified by OHIM.[89]

6–034

The proceedings at issue in BABY-DRY were *ex parte*. In *Chef Revival USA Inc v OHIM*[90] and *Institut für Lernsysteme GmbH v OHIM* (ILS/ELS)[91] the Court indicated that non-compliance with time limits could not be overlooked so easily in *inter partes* cases.[92] In the last-mentioned case the Court held that additional evidence of use of the opponent's mark which was submitted after the expiry of the period prescribed by the Opposition Division under r.22(1) must be disregarded by the Opposition Division and the Board of Appeal. There is a manifest contradiction between that ruling and the judgment delivered 11 months later in *Henkel KGaA v OHIM* (KLEENCARE/CARCLIN),[93] in which the Court held that an opponent who had submitted some evidence of use of his earlier trade mark within the period prescribed by the Opposition Division must be allowed to submit further evidence before the Board of Appeal, "subject only to Article 74(2)". The latter provision allows OHIM to disregard facts or evidence which are not submitted in due time by the parties concerned. The precise meaning of Art.74(2) is far from clear. OHIM has argued before the Court of First Instance that it does not apply at all when a specific time limit has been set and not observed. OHIM argues that in such cases it has no discretion to admit evidence submitted out of time.[94]

6–035

---

[86] This is the effect of rr.72(1) and (2).

[87] For more information about the distinction between *ex parte* and *inter partes* proceedings at OHIM see paras 6–059 and 6–060.

[88] Case T–163/98 *Procter & Gamble v OHIM* [1999] E.C.R. I-6279.

[89] The Court did not however cite r.11(3) and may not have been aware of its existence.

[90] Case T–232/00 *Chef Revival USA Inc v OHIM* [2002] E.C.R. II-2749.

[91] Case T–388/00 *Institut für Lernsysteme GmbH v OHIM* (ELS/ILS (fig.)) [2002] E.C.R. II-4301, at para.26.

[92] A similar line had been taken by the Boards of Appeal: *e.g.* Case R–562/1999-1 NIDEK (fig.)/NIDER(S), O.J. OHIM 12/2000, p.1787, and Case R–472/2001–1 BIBA/BIBA (fig.), O.J. OHIM 10/02, p.1941.

[93] Case T–308/01 *Henkel KGaA v OHIM* [2003] E.C.R.II–3253. See also Case T–164/02 *Kaul GmbH v Bayer AG*, judgment of November 10, 2004.

[94] *Chef Revival USA Inc v OHIM*, at para.26. The Court expressly refrained from ruling on this point (see para.65 of the judgment). A different position with regard to Art.74(2) was taken by the Board of Appeal in Case R–714/1999-2 SAINCOSA (fig.)/SAINCO (fig), O.J. OHIM 9/2001, p.1687. The facts of that case show that even in *inter partes* cases there are situations in which time limits should not be applied too severely. The opponent, invited to prove that his mark had been put to genuine use, faxed to OHIM a document summarizing the evidence one day before the expiry of the time limit and indicated that the actual evidence, consisting of several hundred

RESTITUTIO IN INTEGRUM: ARTICLE 78

6–036   Article 78 provides that a party to proceedings before OHIM who, in spite of taking all due care required by the circumstances, was unable to observe a time limit "*vis-à-vis* the Office" is entitled in some circumstances to apply to OHIM for the restoration of any right or means of redress lost as a result of the non-compliance. This is known as "*restitutio in integrum*".

6–037   The time limits for claiming Convention priority (Art.29(1)) and for filing an opposition (Art.42(1)) are excluded from this provision. So too are the time limits to which an application for *restitutio in integrum* is subject by virtue of Art.78(2).

6–038   The application must be filed in writing within two months of the removal of the cause of non-compliance with the time limit[95] and in any event within a year of the expiry of the time limit in question.[96] The application is not deemed to have been filed until the corresponding fee is paid.[97] The application must state the grounds upon which it is based and set out the facts upon which it relies.

6–039   Rights restored under this article cannot be relied upon by the applicant for, or proprietor of, a CTM against a third party who, in good faith, has put goods on the market or supplied services under a mark which would otherwise infringe the CTM in the period between the loss of the rights in question and the publication of re-establishment of those rights.[98] Such a third party is entitled to challenge the decision re-establishing the rights in question within two months of the date of publication of the re-establishment.

6–040   OHIM has generally taken a strict view towards applications for *restitutio in integrum*. This approach has been confirmed by the Boards of Appeal, which have insisted that, where a party to proceedings before OHIM employs a professional representative, the relevant standard of care is that which may be expected from a qualified professional.[99] The test of "all due care required by the circumstances" has not been easy to satisfy.[1] The representative must show that he has put in place a working system that makes a loss of rights due to non-observance of a time limit generally excluded.[2] In one case the Board of Appeal held that the non-observance of a time limit must be due to abnormal and unforeseeable difficulties beyond the control of the person concerned.[3] That comes close to applying a *force majeure* test, which may be excessively stringent.

CONTINUATION OF PROCEEDING: ARTICLE 78A

6–041   To attenuate the severity of the conditions governing *restitutio in integrum* Reg.422/2004 introduced an alternative means of overcoming the consequences

---

pages of documents, was being sent by post. Although the documents arrived two days after the expiry of the time limit, the Board of Appeal held—rightly, it is submitted—that the evidence should have been admitted.

[95] One case on the application of this provision has reached the Court of First Instance: see Case T–71/02 *Classen Holding KG v OHIM* (EXPRESSION/BECKETT EXPRESSION) [2004] E.T.M.R. 84, CFI.

[96] A failure to comply with these time limits cannot be the subject of an application for *restitutio in integrum*: Art.78(5).

[97] The fee for *restitutio in integrum* is set at €200.

[98] Art.78(6).

[99] *e.g.* Case R–984/2001-4 THUMB DRIVE.

[1] *e.g.* Case R–60/2001-4 ITWEBCAST, O.J. OHIM 11/02, p.2117.

[2] Case R–728/2001-1 AMICELLI BOX (3-D)/TOBLERONE (3-D), O.J. OHIM 12/02, p.2377.

[3] Case R–410/2000-3 ROMANZA/ROMANA SAMBUCA (fig.), O.J. OHIM 2/03, p.323.

of non-compliance with a time limit. This is described as "continuation of proceedings" and is dealt with in Article 78a of the CTM Regulation.[4]

Any party to proceedings before OHIM who has omitted to observe a time limit *vis-à-vis* OHIM may, upon request, obtain the continuation of proceedings, provided that at the time the request is made the omitted act has been carried out. The request must be presented within two months following the expiry of the unobserved time limit. The request is not deemed to have been filed until the fee for continuation of the proceedings has been paid.[5] **6–042**

Although a continuation of proceedings under Art.78a is much easier to obtain than *restitutio in integrum* under Art.78, the range of time limits that are excluded from this procedure is wider. In addition to the time limits for claiming Convention priority, filing an opposition and applying for *restitutio* itself, Art.78a does not apply to *inter alia* the time limits for obtaining a filing date under Arts 27 and 36(2), claiming exhibition priority under Art.33, requesting renewal of a CTM under Art.47(3), filing appeals to the OHIM Board of Appeal or Court of First Instance under Arts 59 and 63(5) respectively and applying for conversion under Art.108.[6] **6–043**

Article 78a (3) provides that the "department competent to decide on the omitted act shall decide upon the application". Presumably OHIM has no discretion in the matter. If the formal and substantive conditions are satisfied, the application must be granted. **6–044**

9. Evidence

There are various situations in which the parties to proceedings before OHIM may be required to prove facts. For example, a CTM applicant may need to prove that the mark applied for has acquired distinctiveness through use. An opponent may need to prove that his mark has been put to genuine use, or that it has acquired a reputation; or he may need to adduce evidence to substantiate the existence of his earlier right. **6–045**

Under Art.76 the means of giving or obtaining evidence include the following: **6–046**
   (a) hearing the parties;
   (b) requests for information;
   (c) the production of documents and items of evidence;
   (d) hearing witnesses;
   (e) opinions by experts;
   (f) statements in writing sworn or affirmed or having a similar effect under the law of the State in which the statement is drawn up.

Although it is clear from Art.76(f) that evidence in the form of affidavits and similar statements is admissible, OHIM is generally reluctant to give decisive weight to "self-generated" evidence unless it is corroborated in some way. This position has been supported in some decisions of the Boards of Appeal.[7] In other decisions the Boards have pointed out that the legislation does not expressly **6–047**

---

[4] At the time of writing this provision had not yet entered into force. The Commission must determine the date when it enters into force, once the necessary implementing measures have been adopted Reg.422/2004, Art.2(2)).

[5] Art.78a(1). The fee is refundable if the application is not granted Art.78a(5)).

[6] Art.78a(2). The reference to Art.63(5) in this provision is superfluous. The time limit for appealing to the Court of First Instance is not a "time limit vis-à-vis the Office". Therefore neither Art.78 nor Art.78a can apply to it.

[7] *e.g.* Case R–990/2002-1 VELVET/VELVELITH.

sanction the practice of giving relatively little weight to affidavit evidence.[8] It is submitted that the correct view is that OHIM must assess the probative value of any evidence in the light of all the circumstances. One of the factors that may legitimately be taken into account is whether the evidence was generated by the party concerned and whether it is supported by evidence from external sources. This position has been supported by the Court of First Instance.[9]

10. Decisions

6–048   All decisions of OHIM must state, in writing, the reasons on which they are based.[10] Decisions may only be based on reasons or evidence in respect of which the parties concerned have had an opportunity to present their comments.[11]

6–049   The Court of First Instance has sometimes interpreted these requirements in a manner that is questionable. In the LITE case the OHIM examiner refused the mark on the ground that it lacked distinctive character (Art.7(1)(b)). The Board of Appeal confirmed that decision and added that the mark consisted exclusively of signs or indications that might serve in trade to designate the nature of the goods (Art.7(1)(c)). The Court annulled the Board's decision, in so far as it was based on Art.7(1)(c), on the ground that the applicant had not had an opportunity to comment on the applicability of that provision. However, the Court went on to confirm the refusal, under Art.7(1)(b), stating that the mark is "currently a generic, usual or commonly-used name in the sector ... at issue".[12] That reasoning appears to amount to an application of Art.7(1)(d)—a matter on which the applicant was not invited to comment.

6–050   In *Glasverbel v OHIM*[13] the mark applied for was "an adherent design for application to the surface of glass products". The examiner objected on the basis of Art.7(1)(b). The applicant adduced evidence of use in an attempt to show that the mark had acquired distinctiveness within the meaning of Art.7(3). The examiner rejected that plea on the ground that the evidence showed that the applicant's products had always been marketed under a specific word mark and that consumers would therefore distinguish the products on the basis of the word mark rather than the pattern. The Board disagreed with that approach but rejected the plea of acquired distinctiveness on the ground that the evidence adduced by the applicant did not demonstrate use on a sufficiently large scale and in a sufficiently broad part of the European Community. The Court annulled the Board's decision on the ground that the applicant had not had a chance to comment on the Board's reasoning, which was different from that of the examiner. Taken to its logical conclusion, the Court's approach would force the Boards of Appeal to send their draft decisions to the parties for comment. In *Lidl Stiftung & Co KG v OHIM*[14] the Court of First Instance recognised that the Board of Appeal may rule on the sufficiency of evidence provided by a party, without inviting the party to comment on

---

[8] *e.g.* Case R–53/2000-3 CONDOR/CONDOR, O.J. OHIM 4/02, p.781, and Case R–644/2000-4 MARCA FAMILY FASHION (fig.)/MARCO, O.J. OHIM 2/03, p.375.
[9] Case T–303/03 *Lidl Stiftung & Co KG v OHIM*, judgment of June 7, 2005, not yet reported.
[10] Art.73 and r.52(1).
[11] Art.73.
[12] Case T–79/00 *Rewe Zentral AG v OHIM* (LITE) [2002] E.C.R. II-705, at para.33.
[13] Case T–36/01 *Glasverbel v OHIM* [2002] E.C.R. II-3887.
[14] Case T–303/03 *Lidl Stiftung & Co KGO v OHIM*, judgment of June 7, 2005, not yet reported.

the Board's appraisal of the evidence. In *Krüger GmbH & Co KG v OHIM*,[15] the court held that the Board does not have to invite the parties to comment on the final position that it intends to take as regards factual assessments. The conclusion must be that the Court no longer adheres to the position taken in *Glasverbel*.

The Boards of Appeal have themselves sometimes criticised the OHIM examiners for lack of reasoning. In the *Fuji Photo Film Co Ltd* (IX) the Board held that a decision rejecting the trade mark 'IX' as devoid of distinctive character needed more, by way of reasoning, than a reference to a statement in the OHIM Examination Guidelines to the effect that two-letter marks are as a general rule devoid of distinctive character.[16] OHIM changed its practice as a result of that decision. 6–051

According to Art.74(2), OHIM is entitled to diregard facts or evidence which are not submitted in time by the parties concerned. Surprisingly, the Court of First Instance has criticised the Board of Appeal for not taking into account additional observations submitted by an appellant one year after the expiry of the deadline for filing the grounds of appeal and nine days before the Board's decision was signed.[17]

Decisions which are open to appeal must be accompanied by a written communication indicating that any notice of appeal must be filed in writing at the Office within two months of the date of notification of the decision in question.[18] 6–052

OHIM is in principle required to examine the facts of its own motion. Opposition proceedings and cancellation proceedings based on relative grounds for refusal provide the exception to this general rule. In such proceedings, which can only be brought by the proprietor of the earlier right relied on, OHIM is restricted to the facts, evidence and arguments adduced by the parties to the proceedings, and may grant only the relief sought.[19] In cancellation proceedings based on absolute grounds, however, OHIM is free to examine issues and evidence of its own motion. This means, logically, that it may take into account evidence submitted by the parties out of time.[20] 6–053

All decisions of the Opposition Divisions, Cancellation Divisions and Boards of Appeal are made available to the public, in the language of the proceedings,[21] on the OHIM web site. A selection of decisions is published, in the five OHIM languages, in the OHIM Official Journal.[22] 6–054

11. Appeals

Appeals from decisions of examiners, Opposition Divisions, Cancellation Divisions and the Administration of Trade Marks and Designs and Legal Division lie at first instance to the OHIM Boards of Appeal.[23] Decisions which do not terminate proceedings for a party can only be appealed together with the final de- 6–055

---

[15] Case T–273/02 *Krüger GmbH & Co KG v OHIM*, judgment of April 20, 2005, not yet reported.
[16] Case R–4/1998-2 *Fuji Photo Film Co Ltd* ('IX'), O.J. OHIM 10/98, p.1059.
[17] Case T–315/03 *Wilfer v OHIM*, judgment of June 8, 2005, not yet reported.
[18] r.52(2).
[19] Art.74(1). See, however, Case T–308–01 *Henkel KGaA v OHIM* [2003] E.C.R. II–3253, at para.29, as regards the Board of Appeal's duty to examine arguments of its own motion in such cases.
[20] Case R–397/2000-1 PROTEOMICS, O.J. OHIM 7–8/2001, p.1505.
[21] English is the language of the proceedings in approximately two-thirds of the cases.
[22] Provision for the publication of this Official Journal ("OJ OHIM") is made in Art.85(b).
[23] Art.57(1).

cision, unless such a decision itself expressly allows for a separate appeal.[24] Any party to proceedings who is adversely affected by a decision has the right to appeal. All other parties to the proceedings become parties to the appeal as of right.[25]

6–056   Notice of appeal must be filed in writing at OHIM within two months of notification of the decision.[26] The notice of appeal must state the name and address of the appellant (and the name and business address of any appointed legal representative) and identify the contested decision and set out the extent to which amendment or cancellation of the decision is sought.[27] The notice of appeal must be filed in the language of the proceedings in which the decision was taken.[28] It is only deemed to have been filed on payment of the appeal fee (€800).[29] If the appeal fee is paid after expiry of the time limit, the appeal is deemed not to have been filed and the fee is refunded.[30] A written statement setting out the grounds of appeal must be filed within four months of notification of the contested decision.[31]

6–057   The first issue to be considered is whether the appeal is admissible.[32] Rule 49 defines the conditions of admissibility. Certain deficiencies cannot be remedied once the two-month time limit laid down in Art.59 has expired.[33] That applies to the following deficiencies:

- The appeal is filed by a party not entitled to appeal;
- The appeal is directed against a non-appealable decision;
- The notice of appeal is not filed in the relevant language of proceedings;
- The notice of appeal does not identify the contested decision, or does not indicate the extent to which amendment or cancellation of the contested decision is requested.

Similarly, if the grounds of appeal are not filed within four months of notification of the contested decision, that deficiency cannot be remedied subsequently.[34]

6–058   Other deficiencies—such as a failure to indicate properly the appellant's name and address or the name and business address of a representative appointed by the appellant—may be remedied within a time limit specified by the Board of Appeal.[35] Failure to remedy the deficiency within the time limit renders the appeal inadmissible.

6–059   Once the statement of grounds has been filed, the OHIM department which took the contested decision has a period of one month in which to consider whether to rectify the decision if it is found to be admissible and well founded. In the original version of the CTM Regulation this was known as "interlocutory revision" and was available only where the appellant was not opposed by another

---

[24] Art.57(2). For an example of a "non-final" decision that could not be separately appealed, see Case R–53/1999-2 AUTOLEARNING INSIDE/INTEL INSIDE, O.J. OHIM 1/2001, p.125.

[25] Art.58.

[26] The notice of appeal form is available on the OHIM website.

[27] r.48(1).

[28] r.48(2).

[29] Art.59.

[30] r.49(3).

[31] Art.59.

[32] Arts 60(1) and 61(1).

[33] r.49(1).

[34] In *Classen Holding KG v OHIM* the Court of First Instance rejected the argument that the Board of Appeal had infringed the appellant's right to due process by dismissing the appeal as inadmissible because the grounds of appeal were not filed within the time limit.

[35] r.49(2).

party.[36] Such proceedings are generally known as *ex parte* proceedings. Appeals against decisions of examiners and the Administration of Trade Marks and Designs and Legal Division are *ex parte* in this sense. Approximately 6.5 per cent of appeals in such cases have led to the contested decision being rectified by the department that took the contested decision.

Since the reforms of 2004 this possibility of self-rectification—now known **6–060** simply as "revision"—is available also in *inter partes* cases, *i.e.* where the opponent is opposed by another party. However, in such cases the department whose decision is contested (an Opposition Division or Cancellation Division) must notify the other party of its intention to rectify the decision and may only do so if the other party accepts the rectification within a period of two months.[37] This is likely to be a rare event, but may happen, for example, if the decision was based on a procedural or preliminary issue and both parties prefer a decision on the substance.

If the department whose decision is contested does not rectify the decision, it **6–061** must remit the appeal to the Board of Appeal without delay, and without comment as to its merits.[38]

The procedure before the Board of Appeal is relatively simple and informal. In **6–062** practice it is almost exclusively written, though an oral hearing may be held if the Board deems it expedient.[39] The Board may invite the parties to file written observations as often as necessary.[40] The procedural provisions applicable to the department which took the contested decision apply to the appeal proceedings unless otherwise provided.[41] Additional provisions, applicable specifically to the Boards of Appeal, are contained in the Appeals Regulation. This Regulation is surprisingly short and is far from exhaustive. It provides, in particular, that the chairperson of the Board must designate one of the members of the Board as rapporteur. The chairperson may also designate him or herself as rapporteur. The rapporteur is responsible, among other things, for drafting the decision.

Detailed rules governing the content of the decision are contained in r.50(2). If **6–063** the Board decides that the appeal should be allowed, it may either exercise any power within the competence of the department responsible for the contested decision or remit the case to that department for further prosecution.

Under the original version of the CTM Regulation the Board of Appeal was in **6–064** all cases to consist of three members (including the chairperson). The legislation envisaged the existence of a number of Boards, each with its own chairperson. No provision was made for any of the chairpersons, or anyone else, to perform a general managerial role within the Boards. Regulation 422/2004 has introduced a number of structural modifications. The Boards are now endowed with their own President, who exercises "managerial and organisational powers" and chairs the newly created Enlarged Board of Appeal.[42] Although this is not expressly stated, the function of the Enlarged Board is clearly to ensure uniformity in the case law.

---

[36] Art.60, before amendment.

[37] Art.60a.

[38] Arts 60(2) and 60a(4).

[39] Art.75, and Appeals Regulation, Art.9. So far, only one hearing has been held; that was in Case R–283/1999-3 HOLLYWOOD/HOLLYWOOD, O.J. OHIM 2/02, p.281.

[40] Art.61(2). In *inter partes* proceedings, provision is made for the appellant and respondent to file a statement of grounds of appeal, a response, a reply and a rejoinder; Appeals Regulation, Art.8(2).

[41] r.50(1).

[42] Art.131(1), as amended by Reg.422/2004.

Rules governing the composition of the Enlarged Board are laid down in Art.1(a) of the Appeals Regulation.[43] The Enlarged Board (renamed "the Great Board") consists of nine members, including the President of the Boards of Appeal. The Appeals Regulation also lays down rules on the referral of cases to the Enlarged Board,[44] account being taken of the "legal difficulty or the importance of the case or of special circumstances which justify it".[45] Conversely, cases involving no legal or factual difficulty may now be referred to a single member, who must be legally qualified.[46] It seems likely that the great majority of cases will continue to be dealt with by a Board consisting of three members, of whom at least two must be legally qualified.[47]

6–065   Decisions of the Boards of Appeal may be appealed to the Court of First Instance of the European Communities.[48] Such actions may only be brought on the following grounds:

    (1) lack of competence;
    (2) infringement of an essential procedural requirement;
    (3) infringement of the EC Treaty, the CTM Regulation or any rule of law relating to their application;
    (4) misuse of power.[49]

6–066   Such actions must be brought before the Court of Justice within two months of notification of the decision of the Board of Appeal. The Court of First Instance can annul or alter the contested decision. A further appeal, on a point of law only, lies to the Court of Justice.

12. Correction of mistakes

6–067   In an Office that deals with approximately 50,000 trade mark applications a year it is inevitable that some mistakes will occur. The Implementing Regulation contains several provisions allowing for the correction of mistakes. Rule 27 provides that, where the registration of a CTM or the publication of the registration contains "a mistake or error[50] attributable to the Office", OHIM is to correct the error or mistake of its own motion or at the request of the proprietor of the CTM. Rule 14 provides in similar fashion for the correction of mistakes in the publication of a CTM application. In addition, r.53 allows OHIM departments to correct "only linguistic errors, errors of transcription and obvious mistakes".

6–068   Following the reforms of 2004 OHIM now has a general power to cancel erroneous entries in the Register and to revoke erroneous decisions. Article 77a of the CTM Regulation provides that, where OHIM has "made an entry in the Register or taken a decision which contains an obvious procedural error attributable to the Office, it shall ensure that the entry is cancelled or the decision is revoked".

---

[43] As amended by Reg.2082/2004.
[44] Art.130(4).
[45] Art.130(3). The rules are to be found in Art.1(b) of the Appeals Regulation, as amended.
[46] Art.130(2) and (5), as amended by Reg.422/2004. This provision is unlikely to be used much in practice. It has been implemented by Art.1(c) of Reg.216/96, as amended.
[47] Art.130(2).
[48] Art.63, which provides for an appeal to the European Court of Justice. The 13th recital in the preamble to the CTM Regulation makes clear that this jurisdiction is to be exercised at first instance by the Court of First Instance.
[49] Art.63(2). The language of this provision has been borrowed from Art.230 of the EC Treaty.
[50] One wonders what the difference might be between a mistake and an error. The French and Spanish versions likewise use two different terms. The German and Italian versions, on the other hand, use only one.

The OHIM department that made the entry or took the erroneous decision is responsible for cancelling the entry or revoking the decision.[51] It may do so of its own motion or at the request of one of the parties and must in any event consult the parties to the proceedings and any proprietor of rights in the CTM in question that are entered in the Register.[52] Such action may only be taken within six months from the date on which the entry was made in the Register or the erroneous decision was taken.

The new provision is without prejudice to the parties' rights to appeal to the Board of Appeal or to the Court of First Instance, or to the possibilities (described above) for correcting errors in accordance with the Implementing Regulation.[53] **6–069**

13. Communications with OHIM

Rules 79 to 82 provide that written communications with OHIM, including trade mark applications, notices of opposition and such like, may be made by submitting a signed original of the document to OHIM (whether by post, personal delivery or other means), by submitting a signed original by fax,[54] by telex or telegram or by electronic means. **6–070**

Where an application for a CTM is made by fax the required original reproduction of the mark applied for must be submitted directly to OHIM if there is a graphic image in colour or if a device mark[55] might not transmit clearly by fax.[56] If such hard copies are received by OHIM within one month of the fax, the application is deemed to have been filed on the earlier date.[57] Otherwise, the date of receipt is taken to be that on which the hard copies arrive, at least when the reproduction of the mark is necessary for the purpose of obtaining a filing date. OHIM strives to operate a paperless office system, scanning all correspondence (including representations of marks) on receipt. This may have the unfortunate effect that images of device marks get distorted through no fault of the applicant. **6–071**

14. Costs in proceedings before OHIM

The unsuccessful party in opposition proceedings, cancellation proceedings, or appeal proceedings bears the fees incurred by the other party and "all costs".[58] However, where each party succeeds on some and fails on other heads, the OHIM department in question may decide on a different apportionment of costs.[59] A different apportionment may also be made for "reasons of equity".[60] The party who terminates the proceedings by withdrawing the CTM application, opposition, application for cancellation, or appeal, bears the fees and costs incurred by the other **6–072**

---

[51] Art.77a(2).

[52] Art.77a(2).

[53] Art.77a(3).

[54] r.80 uses the expression "telecopier" instead of "fax". In the United States "telecopier" is a registered trade mark belonging to the Xerox Corporation.

[55] Device marks are normally referred to as "figurative marks" in OHIM terminology.

[56] r.80. These rules apply *mutatis mutandis* to applications submitted by telex, telegram or electronic means: rr.81 and 82.

[57] Art.80(1).

[58] Art.81(1).

[59] Art.81(2).

[60] Art.81(2)

party "as stipulated in paras (1) and (2) [of Art.81]".[61] This bizarre wording makes it possible, because of the reference to para.(2), for the adjudicating body to apportion the costs when proceedings are terminated by such a withdrawal.[62] When the CTM applicant restricts the list of goods and services in respect of which registration is sought and the opponent then withdraws the opposition, it may be appropriate to apportion the costs. OHIM has a wide margin of discretion in this respect.[63] A party who contemplates terminating the proceedings by a withdrawal would in any event be well advised to seek an agreement on costs with the other party.

6–073   If a case does not proceed to "judgment", the costs are in the discretion of the relevant OHIM department.[64] OHIM must take note of any settlement on costs reached by the parties to proceedings.

6–074   The Opposition Division, Cancellation Division or Board of Appeal must fix the amount of costs when the costs are limited to the fees paid to OHIM and the costs of representation. In other cases the registry of the Boards of Appeal or a member of staff of the Opposition Division or Cancellation Division must fix the amount to be reimbursed on request.[65] Such a decision is reviewable by the Opposition Division, Cancellation Division or Board of Appeal. The request for review must be filed within one month and is subject to a fee of €100.[66]

6–075   Detailed rules on the recovery of fees and costs are contained in r.94. The only fees that may be recovered are the opposition fee, the fee for an application for cancellation and the appeal fee.[67] The only costs that may be recovered are "costs essential to the proceedings and actually incurred by the successful party".[68] In practice the main costs will relate to representatives' fees. The maximum amounts that may be recovered under this head are fixed by r.94(7)(f). The amounts in question (€250 for opposition proceedings, €400 for cancellation proceedings and €500 for appeal proceedings) will usually be considerably lower than the fees actually charged by the representative, so even the successful party is likely to be out of pocket. Provision is also made for travel and subsistence costs in the event of an oral hearing.

6–076   Costs decisions of OHIM are enforceable throughout the European Community under the rules of civil procedure in the State in which enforcement is to be carried out.[69] The order for such enforcement is appended to the decision and is enforceable without other authority than the verification of the decision by the designated authority in each Member State.[70] A party seeking to enforce such an order should use the usual national channels. Enforcement of such costs orders is

---

[61] Art.81(3).

[62] Joined Cases T–124/02 and T–156/02 *The Sunrider Corp v OHIM*, judgment of April 28, 2004, at para.56.

[63] T–124/02 and T–156/02 *The Sunrider Corp v OHIM* judgment of April 28, 2004, at paras 54 and 60.

[64] Art.81(4).

[65] Art.81(6), as amended by Reg.422/2004.

[66] r.94(4) and Fees Regulation, Art.2, point 30.

[67] r.94(6).

[68] r.94(7).

[69] Art.82.

[70] Governed in the UK by the European Communities (Enforcement of Community Judgments) Order 1972, SI 1972/1590, as amended by SI 1998/1259.

regulated by the courts of the Member States and may only be suspended by a decision of the Court of Justice.[71]

15. The CTM application procedure: from filing to publication

Filing

The application for a CTM can be filed either at OHIM or at "the central industrial property office of a Member State or at the Benelux Trade Mark Office".[72] In the United Kingdom applications may be filed at the Trade Marks Registry of the Patent Office. The national offices are obliged to forward all applications to OHIM within two weeks of filing.[73] The original version of the CTM Regulation provided that, if an application filed nationally did not reach OHIM within one month of being filed, it was deemed to have been withdrawn. This seemed unduly harsh on the applicant, whose rights might be severely impaired through no fault of his own. The Regulation now provides that, if an application filed nationally reaches OHIM more than two months after filing, it is deemed to have been filed on the date on which it reaches OHIM.[74]

6–077

The granting of a filing date

All applications must contain a representation of the trade mark, a list of the goods and services in respect of which the registration is requested (grouped according to the Nice Classification) and a statement of the identity of the applicant setting out his name, address and nationality.[75] It is sufficient to identify natural persons by their family name and given name(s). Legal entities must be identified by their official designation and the law of the State governing them must be set out.[76]

6–078

The date on which the above information is supplied to OHIM becomes the filing date of the application, provided the basic fee for the application is paid within one month.[77] The filing date may be of crucial importance because the general rule in opposition and cancellation proceedings is that the earlier right prevails over the later right.[78]

6–079

If the above conditions for granting a filing date are not satisfied, OHIM notifies the applicant of the deficiencies. If these are remedied within two months of receipt of the notification, the date on which they are remedied becomes the filing date. If the deficiencies are not remedied within two months, the application lapses.[79]

6–080

Fees on application

In addition to the basic fee (currently set at €975) a further fee of €250 is payable for each class exceeding three to which the goods and services applied for

6–081

---

[71] Art.82(4).
[72] Art.25.
[73] Art.25(2).
[74] Art.25(3), as amended by Reg.422/2004.
[75] Art.26, in conjunction with r.1.
[76] Art.26, in conjunction with r.1
[77] Art.27.
[78] See Arts 8, 52 and 53 and TM Directive, Arts 4 and 9.
[79] rr.9(1) and (2).

belong.[80] An applicant who fails to pay the class fees in full is notified by OHIM with a request for payment within a specified period. If payment is not made within the time limit the application is deemed to have been withdrawn with regard to the classes for which the class fees have not been paid in full. In the absence of other criteria to determine which classes are intended to be covered, OHIM takes the classes to have been covered in order of classification.[81]

Representation of the mark

6–082   If an applicant does not wish to claim any special graphic feature, font or colour, the mark should be reproduced in normal script.[82] Such marks are described as "word marks" on the OHIM application form, although that term is not actually used in the legislation. Word marks may be in lower or upper case. The case in which a mark is typed in the application will be followed in publications through to registration.[83] Applications for device marks or marks in fancy script[84] should include a representation of the mark on a separate sheet of paper (no larger than A4) bearing the name and address of the applicant and should be capable of being clearly reproduced in a space 8cm wide by 16cm high.[85] Applications for three-dimensional marks must state this fact, and must depict the mark graphically or photographically, with no more than six different perspectives.[86] An application for a registration in colour should indicate this and must identify the colours making up the mark. The reproduction of the mark should be in the colours claimed.[87]

6–083   If an application is made for a colour *per se*, then OHIM has generally been satisfied with either a code number for the colour (*e.g.* a Pantone ® code) or a graphical reproduction of the colour. An application to register the colour orange using only the word "orange" to describe the mark does not comply with the necessary formalities.[88] The *Libertel* judgment of the European Court of Justice implies that a graphical reproduction by itself may not be sufficient; an internationally recognized code may be required.[89]

6–084   Following the *Libertel* judgment the OHIM President issued a Communication setting out OHIM's position on colour marks.[90] The President pointed out that the problem of deterioration of a colour reproduction over a period of time, which determined the Court's position, does not arise in respect of CTMs because the OHIM Register is, in practice, kept in electronic form. The Communication nevertheless advises applicants for colour marks *per se* to include a reference to an internationally recognised code, if one is available. As regards colour marks *per se* filed before the date of the Communication, including marks already registered, OHIM will allow the addition of a colour code.

---

[80] r.4.
[81] r.9(5).
[82] r.3(1).
[83] r.3(1).
[84] Device marks and marks in fancy script are referred to as figurative marks in OHIM terminology.
[85] r.3(2).
[86] r.3(4).
[87] r.3(5).
[88] Case R–7/1997-3 ORANGE, O.J. OHIM 5/98, p.641; [1998] E.T.M.R. 337.
[89] Case C–104/01 *Libertel Groep BV v Benelux-Merkenbureau* [2003] E.C.R. I-3793.
[90] Communication No. 6/03 of November 10, 2003, O.J. OHIM 1/04, p.89.

PRIORITY AND SENIORITY

Although the concepts of priority and seniority are sometimes confused, there are **6–085** clear differences between them. The term "priority", in the technical sense in which it is used here, refers to the possibility for a trade mark applicant to obtain a filing date earlier than the date on which the application is actually filed, as a result either of Art.4 of the Paris Convention for the Protection of Industrial Property ("Convention priority") or of the Paris Convention on International Exhibitions ("exhibition priority"). Priority, in this sense, applies both to CTMs and to national trade marks. Seniority, on the other hand, is a specific feature of the CTM system whereby the proprietor of a CTM is able to retain whatever rights he enjoyed in a Member State as a result of an earlier registration of an identical trade mark in respect of the same goods and services, even though he surrenders the national trade mark or allows it to lapse.

Priority or seniority can be claimed in relation to CTM applications for marks **6–086** identical to the prior mark and in respect of goods or services identical with or contained within those for which the earlier mark has been applied for, registered or exhibited.[91]

A person who has filed an application for a trade mark in a State party to the **6–087** Paris Convention or the WTO Agreement (or a State which is not party to the Paris Convention or to the WTO Agreement but grants priority rights in respect of CTM applications) obtains a right of priority. This means that if that person, during the next six months, files a CTM application for the same trade mark, his CTM application will obtain the filing date of the first application.[92] The goods or services in respect of which the CTM application is filed must be identical with or contained within those for which the first application was filed.[93] The right to priority arises from any national filing sufficient to establish a filing date, irrespective of the outcome of the application.[94] Thus a United Kingdom application which complied with the requirements of s.32 of the 1994 Act and so was granted a filing date, but was later abandoned, would suffice to provide an earlier priority date. On the other hand, failure to comply with the requirements of s.32(2) of the 1994 Act leads to an application being deemed never to have been made. This would not give rise to a claim to priority. The right to priority is determined by the acquisition of a filing date under national law.

A party wishing to rely on such a claim to priority must make a declaration of **6–088** priority either with his application or within two months of the filing date.[95] Such a declaration must state the file number of the prior application relied on and the applicant must supply a copy of the application certified by the authority to which it was submitted, together with a certificate issued by that authority mentioning the filing date thereof, within three months of the date of receipt of the declara-

---

[91] Art.29(5).
[92] Arts 29(1) and 31, in conjunction with Art.4 of the Paris Convention. If a subsequent application is made for the same mark in respect of the same goods and services, it can only be used to determine priority if the first application has been abandoned or refused without being open to public inspection or being used as the basis for another priority claim at the date of the subsequent application: Art.29(4).
[93] Art.29(1).
[94] Art.29(3).
[95] rr. 6(1) and (2).

tion of priority.[96] Instead of original documents the applicant may submit "accurate photocopies".[97]

6–089   A CTM application that has been granted a filing date is equivalent, in the Member States, to a regular national filing.[98] This means that a CTM application may itself form the basis of a claim for priority in other countries that belong to the Paris Convention or WTO.[99]

6–090   Exhibition priority (which cannot be used to extend the right to priority from an earlier application discussed above)[1] may be claimed by an applicant who has displayed goods or services under the mark applied for at an official or officially recognised international exhibition[2] if the application is filed within six months of the date of first display of the goods or services. The effect of successfully claiming exhibition priority is that the date on which the goods or services were first displayed at the qualifying exhibition becomes the filing date.[3] A party wishing to claim exhibition priority must make a declaration of priority either with his application or within two months of the filing date.[4] Such a declaration must state the name of the exhibition and the date of first display of the goods or services.[5] Within three months of the date of receipt of the declaration of priority, the applicant must file at OHIM a certificate issued at the exhibition by the authority responsible for the protection of industrial property at the exhibition in question. The certificate must state the opening date of the exhibition, confirm that the mark was in fact used for the goods or services claimed by the applicant and, where the first use of the mark was not on the opening day of the exhibition, set out the date of the first use.

6–091   The proprietor of an earlier trade mark registered in a Member State or States who applies for an identical trade mark for registration as a CTM for goods or services which are identical with or contained within those for which the earlier trade mark is registered may claim for the CTM the seniority of the earlier trade mark in the Member State or States in which it was registered.[6] The sole effect of such a claim is that, where the proprietor of the CTM surrenders an earlier national registration or allows it to lapse, he is deemed to continue to have the same rights as he would have had if the earlier trade mark had continued to be registered.[7] The right to claim seniority is lost if the earlier national trade mark is revoked, declared invalid or surrendered prior to the registration of the CTM.[8]

---

[96] r.6(1).
[97] r.6(6) in conjunction with Decision EX-96-3 of the OHIM President (O.J. OHIM 4/96, p.395).
[98] Art.32.
[99] Art.4.A(2) of the Paris Convention.
[1] Art.33(3).
[2] Falling within the terms of the Convention on International Exhibitions signed in Paris on November 22, 1928, as revised. Communication No.1/03 of the President of OHIM concerning exhibition priorities (O.J. OHIM 4/03, p.881) points out that very few exhibitions give rise to a claim of priority and that no such exhibition is scheduled for the foreseeable future.
[3] Art.33(1) in conjunction with Art.31.
[4] r.7.
[5] r.7.
[6] Art.34.
[7] Art.34(2).
[8] Art.34(3).

Seniority can be claimed either by an applicant for a CTM[9] or by the proprietor of a CTM after registration.[10]

The purpose of seniority is to make the CTM system attractive for persons who already own registered trade marks in Member States.[11] As a result of claiming seniority such persons can allow their national registrations to lapse, thus avoiding the expense and inconvenience of renewing those registrations periodically, but are able to retain all the rights they enjoyed in respect of the national registrations, in particular earlier filing dates (hence the name "seniority").   **6–092**

To make a valid seniority claim it is necessary to satisfy the "triple identity rule": the CTM applicant/proprietor must be the same person as the proprietor of the earlier national registration, the trade marks must be identical and the goods and services covered by the CTM must be identical with or contained within those for which the earlier trade mark is registered.   **6–093**

As regards the last requirement, the OHIM practice is to allow the claim to the extent to which the goods and services overlap. Thus, if the earlier mark is registered for "umbrellas, raincoats, shoes and handbags", and the CTM is registered for "raincoats, shirts and shoes", seniority may be claimed as regards raincoats and shoes. OHIM examiners have tended to apply the other two parts of the triple identity rule strictly. The OHIM Boards of Appeal have sometimes taken a more lenient approach. In the *BatMark* case[12] the CTM applicant was not the registered proprietor of the earlier trade marks at the time when the CTM application was field. The earlier trade marks were in the process of being transferred to the applicant but the assignments had not yet been recorded by the registries in the Member States concerned. The Board of Appeal held that actual ownership of the earlier marks was more important than the appearance of ownership and that it was not necessary for all the conditions to be satisfied at the filing date. The Board allowed the seniority claim, observing that the assignments had in the meantime been recorded in the relevant registries. In another case the CTM applied for was THINKPAD (written as one word) and the earlier trade mark was THINK PAD (written as two words). The Board of Appeal held that the trade marks were identical for the purposes of a seniority claim.[13]   **6–094**

For further information about the evidence to be provided on claiming priority or seniority, the reader is referred to Decision No. EX-96-3[14] and Communication No. 3/96[15] of the President of OHIM.   **6–095**

AMENDMENT OF THE APPLICATION

The applicant may at any time withdraw his CTM application or restrict the list of goods and services in respect of which the trade mark is to be registered.[16] In other respects a CTM application may be amended only by correcting the name and address of the applicant, errors of wording or of copying, or obvious mistakes, provided that such correction does not substantially change the trade mark or   **6–096**

---

[9] Art.34 and r.8.
[10] Art.35 and r.28.
[11] See Case R–5/1997-1 *BatMark, Inc* (VICEROY), at para.29.
[12] See Case R–5/1997-1 *BatMark, Inc* (VICEROY), at para.29.
[13] Case R–10/1998-2 THINKPAD.
[14] O.J. OHIM 4/96, p.395.
[15] O.J. OHIM 5/96, p.595.
[16] Art.44(1).

extend the list of goods and services.[17] Rule 13 contains the relevant implementing rules.

6–097   There are thus two principles governing the amendment of the application. First, the list of goods and services may be modified, provided that everything in the amended list is contained within the original list, even though different terminology is used. Second, the trade mark itself must not be substantially changed.

6–098   The extent to which the list of goods and services may be modified is illustrated by the *Financial Interactive, Inc* case.[18] The applicant applied to register the trade mark SOUNDEQUITY for "telecommunications services" in Class 38. It subsequently asked for the specification to be changed to "dissemination by means of computer network of multi-media files containing qualitative information regarding the investment industry, investment advisors, managed investment funds, investment fee programs and related investment matters". The Board of Appeal held that this was a legitimate restriction of the original specification, since the redefined services fell within the term "telecommunications".

6–099   The question as to what constitutes a substantial modification of the trade mark has been dealt with in a number of cases. The leading case is *Signal Communications Ltd. v OHIM*.[19] The applicant applied to register TELEYE for video surveillance systems and the like, but claimed the priority of a US application for TELEEYE. A few months later the applicant informed OHIM that a typographical error had been made and asked for the application to be amended so as to show the mark TELEEYE. The examiner's refusal was confirmed by the Board of Appeal, which noted that TELEEYE was visually, phonetically and conceptually different from TELEYE. The Court of First Instance implied, surprisingly, that these criteria were irrelevant[20] and held that the correction was in no way abusive and did not entail a substantial alteration of the trade mark.[21] The Court was heavily influenced by the fact that the applicant would lose its priority claim if the amendment was not permitted.

6–100   The rationale of Art.44(2) was considered by the Board of Appeal in *The Stroh Brewery Company*,[22] in which the Board ruled that RANIER could not be changed to RAINIER. The Board observed that, once a CTM application was filed, it might form part of a computerised search of CTM applications and that the rights of third parties might be affected if substantial amendments of the mark were permitted. The Board held that Art.44(2) must be strictly applied.[23]

6–101   In *Richardson-Vicks Inc*[24] the applicant filed the highly descriptive word mark NATURAL BEAUTY for cosmetics *inter alia*. The Board refused to allow the mark to be amended by the addition of a distinctive device.

---

[17] Art.44(2).

[18] Case R–517/2001-1 *Financial Interactive, Inc* (SOUNDEQUITY), O.J. OHIM 1/03, p.33. See also Case R–6/2003-3 *Ratiopharm GmbH* (BioGeniX) O.J. OHIM 9/03, p.1657.

[19] Case T–128/99 *Signal Communications Ltd v OHIM* (TELEYE) [2001] E.C.R. II-3273.

[20] At para.52.

[21] At para.50.

[22] Case R–196/1998-2 *The Stroh Brewery Company* (RANIER), O.J. OHIM 10/00, p.1325. A similar approach was taken in Case R–447/1999-2 VALENTINE CLAVEROL, O.J. OHIM 9/02, p.1663.

[23] At para.22.

[24] Case R–40/1998-3 *Richardson-Vicks Inc* (NATURAL BEAUTY), O.J. OHIM 1/99, p.205.

In the BLUE WATER case[25] the Board of Appeal was noticeably more lenient.   **6–102**
The mark was represented on the application form as BLUE WATER/
BLUEWATER. The applicant was allowed to change this to BLUEWATER.

SEARCHES

Once an application has been accorded a filing date OHIM is required to draw up   **6–103**
a search report citing earlier CTMs or CTM applications which might form the
basis of an opposition against the application under Art.8.[26] The original version
of Art.39 also provided for a search of national trade mark registers to be carried
out by the respective national offices, in so far as the Member States had indicated
a willingness to conduct such searches.[27]

The main purpose of the search reports, both Community and national, is to   **6–104**
help the CTM applicant to make an informed decision as to whether the application is worth proceeding with, in view of the likelihood of a successful opposition
being filed. For that reason OHIM is required to transmit the search reports to the
CTM applicant without delay,[28] and after that is done a period of one month must
elapse before the application is published in the Community Trade Marks
Bulletin.[29] This gives the applicant a chance to withdraw the application, before
publication, if the search reports suggest that it is likely to fail on relative grounds.
However, the Community search report serves an additional purpose, for OHIM
is required to inform the proprietors of earlier CTMs cited in the report (and the
applicants for CTMs with an earlier filing date that are cited) that the application
has been published.[30]

At this stage several points may be noted. First, OHIM does not raise relative   **6–105**
grounds of its own motion; the owner of the earlier right must file an opposition if
he wishes to prevent the application from proceeding to registration. Second,
OHIM informs the CTM applicant about earlier rights that might form the basis
of an opposition. Third, in so far as the earlier right is a CTM or CTM application, OHIM also informs the proprietor of the earlier right about the application.
Fourth, the search reports are for information only; the fact that an earlier right is
cited does not mean that an opposition based on it is likely to succeed, and
conversely the non-citation of an earlier right does not mean that it cannot be successfully invoked in opposition proceedings.

The national search reports were widely perceived as being unhelpful. One   **6–106**
problem was the absence of any standard format for these reports. Article 39(7)
of the CTM Regulation (in its original version) required the Commission to
submit a report to the Council of Ministers on the operation of the search system
within five years of the opening of OHIM for the filing of applications. The Commission's report[31] concluded that the system of searches was costly, time-
consuming and burdensome for OHIM, the national offices and the CTM
applicant. Moreover, the system did not provide the applicant with a cost-effective
and valuable tool for monitoring the existence of prior rights. The Commission
therefore proposed to abolish the search system completely.

---

[25] Case R–117/1998-1.
[26] Art.39(1).
[27] Art.39(2), before amendment. France, Germany and Italy do not provide search reports in connection with CTM applications.
[28] Art.39(5). This will eventually become Art.39(6) as a result of Reg.422/2004.
[29] Art.39(6). This will become Art.39(7).
[30] Art.39(6). This will become Art.39(7).
[31] COM (2002) 754 final.

6–107   Abolition of the national search reports encountered opposition in some quarters because the reports (which have to be paid for by OHIM[32]) provide a source of income to the national offices. In the end a compromise was reached. The existing system continues until March 10, 2008.[33] Thereafter the national search reports will be prepared only if the CTM applicant makes a request for them at the time of filing the application and pays a separate search fee.[34] The search reports will be prepared on a standard form drawn up by OHIM, the essential contents of which are to be set out in the Implementing Regulation.[35]

EXAMINATION AS TO ABSOLUTE GROUNDS FOR REFUSAL

6–108   The absolute grounds for refusal of a CTM application are set out in Art.7. The substantive nature of those provisions is addressed in Ch.8. Where the OHIM examiner considers that, under Art.7, the mark applied for may not be registered for any or all of the goods and services specified in the application, the examiner must notify the applicant of the grounds for refusing registration and prescribe a period within which the applicant may withdraw or amend the application or submit observations.[36] If the applicant fails to overcome the objection within the period specified, OHIM must refuse the application in whole or in part.[37]

6–109   Where the trade mark contains an element which is not distinctive, and where the inclusion of that element in the trade mark could give rise to doubts as to the scope of protection of the trade mark, the applicant may be requested to disclaim any exclusive right to that element as a precondition to registration.[38] In practice OHIM makes little or no use of this option, presumably on the ground that the trade mark must in any event be examined as a whole, by virtue of the terms of Art.7(1)(b), (c) and (d), and registration does not confer a monopoly over non-distinctive elements contained in it.[39] Uncertainty about the scope of protection of a registered trade mark is often inevitable.

PUBLICATION

6–110   If the application fulfils all the conditions required for acceptance it will be published in the Community Trade Marks Bulletin no earlier than one month after the search reports have been provided to the applicant.[40] The published application must set out the name and address of the applicant and his legal representative (if applicable), a representation of the mark, indicating whether it is three-dimensional and any colours claimed, a classified list of the goods and services applied for, the filing date, particulars of any claim of priority or seniority, any statement that the mark has become distinctive as a consequence of the use made of it, any disclaimer and an indication of the language of the application and the second language chosen by the applicant.[41]

---

[32] Art.39(4). This will become Art.39(5).
[33] See Art.2(3) of Reg.422/2004.
[34] Art.39(2), as amended.
[35] Art.39(4), as amended.
[36] r.11(1).
[37] r.11(3).
[38] Art.38(2) and r.11(2).
[39] That is confirmed by Art.12 b.
[40] Arts 39(6) and 40(1).
[41] r.12 in conjunction with r.3.

OBSERVATIONS BY THIRD PARTIES

Following publication of the CTM application, any natural or legal person, and **6–111** any group or body representing manufacturers, producers, suppliers of services, traders or consumers is entitled to submit written observations to OHIM as to why the mark should not be registered.[42] Observations by third parties generally relate to the absolute grounds for refusal set out in Art.7. (The relative grounds for refusal[43] only take effect on opposition by the proprietor of the earlier right relied upon). Third parties making observations do not become parties to proceedings before the Office. As such they have no right of appeal if the observations have no effect.[44] Any such observations are sent to the CTM applicant, who is invited to submit comments.[45] This makes it clear that the Office may refuse the application on absolute grounds even after it has been published, in particular as a result of third-party observations.

16. The opposition procedure

In the period of three months following its publication[46] a CTM application may **6–112** be opposed on the relative grounds for refusal laid down in Art.8.[47] Oppositions may only be filed by the proprietors of the earlier rights set out in Art.8 or, in the case of rights under Art.8(1) and (5), their authorised licensees. OHIM cannot raise objections based on relative grounds of its own motion.

An opposition is not treated as duly entered until the opposition fee has been **6–113** paid.[48] The fee (€350) must be paid within the opposition period (*i.e.* the three months following publication of the contested CTM application).[49]

QUALIFYING RIGHTS

The substantive issues concerning relative grounds for refusal are addressed in **6–114** Ch.9. Here it is sufficient to point out that a relative ground existing anywhere in the European Community is sufficient, if invoked by the proprietor of the earlier right, to defeat a CTM application. The following types of earlier right may serve as the basis of an opposition under Art.8: CTMs, trade marks registered in a Member State, trade marks registered at the Benelux Trade Mark Office, trade marks registered under the Madrid Arrangement or Protocol and having effect in a Member State, and applications for the above types of registered trade marks, subject to their proceeding to registration. Oppositions may also be based on unregistered trade marks of "more than mere local significance" in so far as these are protected in a Member State and on trade marks which are well-known in a Member State in the sense in which the words "well known" are used in Art.6*bis* of the Paris Convention.

The opponent's earlier right must obviously exist at the time when the opposi- **6–115** tion is filed. It is not clear whether the opponent can be required to show that it continues to exist after that point, in particular by filing a copy of a renewal cer-

---

[42] Art.41(1).
[43] Art.8.
[44] Art.41(1).
[45] Art.41(2).
[46] Also upon re-publication of an amended application pursuant to Art.44.
[47] Art.42 (1).
[48] Art.42(3).
[49] r.18(1).

tificate if his registration expires at some point in the opposition procedure. Such a requirement has been imposed by the Opposition Divisions but this has been criticised by an OHIM Board of Appeal.[50]

THE NOTICE OF OPPOSITION

6–116   The opposition procedure is governed by rr.15–22. These provisions are complex and, in places, ambiguous. As a result they have occasionally led to conflicting decisions from the OHIM Boards of Appeal. At the time of writing a proposal to amend the Implementing Regulation is under consideration.

6–117   A form for the notice of opposition is available on the OHIM web site. The information that must be contained in the notice of opposition is set out in r.15. Essentially, the notice of opposition must:

(1) Identify the opposed CTM application and specify the goods and services against which the opposition is entered;
(2) Identify the opponent and the earlier right on which the opposition is based, and contain a representation of the trade mark or sign that is protected by the earlier right;
(3) As regards the goods and services in respect of which the earlier right is protected, indicate those goods and services on which the opposition is based;
(4) Explain the grounds on which the opposition is based.

6–118   If the opposition is based on an earlier registered trade mark, the notice of opposition must provide a statement to that effect and identify whether the earlier mark is a CTM or a national registration, identifying the Member State or Member States in which it is registered or, where the earlier mark is the subject of an international registration, an indication of the Member State or Member States to which protection of that earlier mark has been extended.[51] Where available, the notice of opposition should set out the file number or the registration number and the filing date, including the priority date, of the earlier mark.[52]

6–119   Where the opposition is based on an earlier mark which is a well-known mark in a Member State or States within the meaning of Art.8(2)(c) (*i.e.* well-known in the sense in which the term is used in Art.6*bis* of the Paris Convention), it should contain a statement to that effect and set out the Member State or States in which the earlier mark is well-known.[53]

6–120   Where the opposition is based on an earlier mark having a reputation within the meaning of Art.8(5), the notice of opposition must provide a statement to that effect and identify where that earlier mark is registered or applied for.[54]

6–121   Where the opposition is based on an earlier right under Art.8(4) (*i.e.* an unregistered trade mark), the notice of opposition must say so and identify the Member State or States where that earlier right exists.[55]

ADMISSIBILITY

6–122   The Implementing Regulation requires OHIM (in the form of an Opposition

---

[50] Case R–215/2003-1 CHEMSIZE/EMSIZE.

[51] r.15(2)(b)(i).

[52] r.15(2)(b)(ii).

[53] r.15(2)(b)(iii).

[54] r.15(2)(b)(iv). Although this provision refers to marks registered or applied for, Art.8(5) appears to be concerned exclusively with trade marks that have been registered.

[55] r.15(2)(b)(v). This provision is elliptical but it appears to refer to rights that may be invoked under Art.8(4).

Division) to decide first on the admissibility of the opposition. Rule 18(1) defines certain deficiencies which cannot be remedied after the expiry of the opposition period (*i.e.* the three months following publication of the CTM application).[56] This applies where the notice of opposition does not comply with Art.42 or where it does not clearly identify the opposed application or the earlier mark or right on which the opposition is based. The Court of First Instance has held that the earlier mark is properly identified for these purposes if the notice of opposition indicates the registration number and the Member State in which it is registered.[57]

The requirements of Art.42 are as follows: **6–123**

1. The notice of opposition must be filed in writing within the aforesaid three-month period;
2. The opposition fee must be paid within the same period;[58]
3. The notice of opposition must specify the grounds on which it is made.

If the notice of opposition is tainted with any of the above deficiencies, OHIM is obliged to declare it inadmissible, unless the deficiency is remedied before the expiry of the opposition period.[59]

If the notice of opposition does not comply with other provisions of the CTM   **6–124**
Regulation or the Implementing Regulation, r.18(2) requires OHIM to inform the opponent and call upon him to remedy the deficiency within two months. If the deficiency is not remedied within that period, the opposition must be rejected as inadmissible.

The Opposition Divisions have tended to apply these rules strictly and   **6–125**
sometimes with excessive formalism. Oppositions have, for example, been rejected as inadmissible because the opponent failed to tick a particular box on the notice of opposition form. The Boards of Appeal have generally been more liberal.[60]

PARTICULARS IN SUPPORT OF THE OPPOSITION

The opponent may include particulars of the facts, evidence and arguments pre-   **6–126**
sented in support of the opposition, accompanied by the relevant supporting documents, in the notice of opposition.[61] If such particulars are not filed with the notice of opposition, OHIM must request them within a specified period.[62]

If the opposition is based on an earlier registered trade mark which is not a   **6–127**
CTM, the particulars should contain evidence of the registration or filing of that earlier mark, "such as a certificate of registration". If the opposition is based on a well-known mark (as referred to in Art.8(2)(c)) or on a mark having a reputation

---

[56] This time limit cannot be extended: Case T–232/00 *Chef Revival USA, Inc v OHIM* [2002] E.C.R. II-2749, at para.34.

[57] T–186/04 *Spa Monople v OHIM*, judgment of June 15, 2005, not yet reported.

[58] If the fee is paid after the expiry of the opposition period, it must be refunded: r.18(1).

[59] r.18(1).

[60] *e.g.* Case R–200/1998-3 EDITIONAL PLANETA. In that case the opponent did not indicate which paragraph of Art.8 was being invoked. The Opposition Division held that the opponent had failed to specify the grounds on which the opposition was based. The Board of Appeal took the view that the grounds of opposition must be likelihood of confusion under Art. 8(1)(b) since the opponent's mark was clearly not identical to the contested mark. In Case R–165/1998-2 ENIGMA/ENIGMA ITALY (fig.) the Board of Appeal annulled a decision rejecting the opposition as inadmissible because the opponent had ticked the box indicating "identical marks/identical goods or services"; since the marks were not in fact identical it was obvious that the opposition was based on likelihood of confusion.

[61] r.16.

[62] r.20(2).

(as referred to in Art.8(5)), the particulars should contain evidence demonstrating that it is well-known or that it has a reputation. If the opposition is based on of "any other earlier right", particulars and evidence should be provided of the acquisition and scope of protection of that right.[63] Thus, if the opposition is based on an unregistered trade mark or other sign under Art.8(4), the opponent must adduce evidence that under the law of the Member State concerned the right exists and has the necessary scope of protection.[64] OHIM treats questions of national law as issues of fact which the parties must prove by evidence.[65]

6–128   If the opposition is based on a right protected under the law of passing off in the United Kingdom, the opponent would be advised to cite s.5(4) of the 1994 Act and to provide information about the relevant law (*e.g.* extracts from Ch.15 of this book or copies of judgments on the subject). He should also adduce the sort of evidence as regards reputation, misrepresentation and likelihood of damage that would be needed in order to succeed in an action for passing off in the United Kingdom.[66]

6–129   In the case of registered trade marks it is not absolutely essential to produce a copy of a registration certificate in order to substantiate the opponent's earlier right. OHIM accepts copies of extracts from trade mark registers and official databases. Opponents sometimes produce extracts from private databases (*e.g.* the DEMAS database, which appears to enjoy a high status in Germany, being produced by the company that publishes the official Trade Mark Bulletin on behalf of the German Patent Office). The OHIM Boards of Appeal have generally accepted extracts from DEMAS and from databases of similar standing, overruling decisions of Opposition Divisions that rejected documents from unofficial sources.[67]

6–130   Faced with a huge number of oppositions, OHIM has had recourse to standard letters, in particular letters inviting the opponent to produce evidence. The earlier version of these standard letters was considered unsatisfactory by the Boards of Appeal inasmuch as it contained a very general reference to the possibility of filing whatever evidence the opponent thought necessary. Opposition Divisions then rejected the opposition when the opponent failed to produce some specific item of evidence such as a registration certificate or a translation thereof. This was held in some Board of Appeal decisions to be contrary to r.20(2), which could be read as implying that if the Opposition Division determines that a specific item of essential evidence (such as a registration certificate or a translation thereof) has not been submitted by the opponent, it must inform him of the omission and invite him to submit the missing document.[68] A different strain of case law holds, however, that r.20(2) merely requires the Opposition Division to

---

[63] r.16(2).

[64] The burden of proof lies on the opponent in this respect: Case R–503/2000-1 SVENSSON/ SVENSON S.A., O.J. OHIM 3/02, p.521.

[65] Guidelines concerning proceedings before OHIM, Part C, Ch.4, para.5.4 (O.J. OHIM 5/2003, p.1097).

[66] For an example of a successful opposition based on passing off, see Case R–906/2001-1 *Real Time Consultants v Manpower* (Da Vinci device), O.J. OHIM 7–8/02, p.1427.

[67] *e.g.* Decisions in Case R–1071/2000-3 ventcare/CareVent (fig.), Case R–843/2000-3 HEIN (fig.)/ HEINE (fig.), Case R–520/2000-4 VISION/EYE'D VISION. These may be contrasted with the decisions in Case R–1055/2000-1 PIZZERIA REGINA/REGINA (fig.) and Case R–1145/2000-4 MEDITERANEAS (fig.)/MEDITERRANEA.

[68] *e.g.* Case R–65/2000-2 T'KOM/T-COM and R–184/2001-3 SmartGuard/SMARTPASS.

issue a general invitation to the opponent to submit evidence.[69] OHIM has since modified its practice by annexing to the standard letter a schedule explaining precisely what evidence must be filed. The Boards of Appeal have held that the Opposition Division is entitled to reject the opposition where the opponent fails to produce an essential item of evidence specified in the schedule.[70]

Issues concerning the use of languages and the translation of evidence in op-   **6–131**
position proceedings are dealt with above.[71]

COMMENCEMENT OF OPPOSITION PROCEEDINGS (THE "COOLING-OFF" PERIOD)

If the notice of opposition is not rejected as inadmissible, OHIM notifies the   **6–132**
CTM applicant of the opposition and invites him to file observations within a specified period. At this stage OHIM informs the applicant that, unless the application is withdrawn or restricted to goods and services against which the opposition is not directed, the opposition proceedings will be deemed to commence two months later.[72] This is known as the "cooling-off" period. It may be extended at the joint request of the parties.[73]

The purpose of the cooling-off period is to give the parties a chance to reach a   **6–133**
friendly settlement. OHIM may, at any stage, if it thinks fit, invite the parties to make such a settlement.[74] A large proportion of oppositions are in fact settled on a friendly basis. Often the parties find that their respective trade marks can co-exist, provided the goods or services in respect of which they are used are not too close.

If the CTM applicant withdraws the application, or restricts it in the above   **6–134**
sense, within the cooling-off period, OHIM informs the opponent and refunds the opposition fee.[75] If the application is not withdrawn or thus restricted, the CTM applicant must file any observations on the opposition within the period specified by OHIM.[76]

OHIM must invite the parties to opposition proceedings to file observations on   **6–135**
submissions by the other parties or communications from OHIM as often as is necessary.[77]

If the opposition is based on an application to register a trade mark, OHIM   **6–136**
may stay proceedings pending determination of that application.[78] OHIM may

---

[69] *e.g.* Cases R–1145/2000-4, Case R–334/2001-1 EUROFOCUS/FOCUS, O.J. OHIM 7–8/03, p.1425, and R–830/2001–1 SCALA/SCALA. An appeal against the Board's decision in the SCALA/SCALA case was dismissed by an order of the Court of First Instance as "lacking any foundation in law" T–235/02 *Strongline A/S v OHIM*, order of November 17, 2003). The least that one can say is that it is surprising that the Court should have felt entitled to proceed by way of an order, as opposed to a full judgment, in a case that raised fundamental issues of procedural law on which diverging positions had been taken by the Boards of Appeal. The Court's order was, however, based solely on the interpretation of r.17(2). The relevance of r.20(2) was not considered. Moreover, the Court appeared unaware of the substantial case law of the Boards of Appeal in this area.
[70] *e.g.* Case R–362/2003-2 E-ROLL/EROL.
[71] See para.6–017 *et seq.*
[72] r.19(1).
[73] r.19(2).
[74] Art.43(4). This applies also to the Boards of Appeal, since they are part of the Office.
[75] r.19(3).
[76] r.20(1).
[77] Art.43(1).
[78] r.19(2).

also suspend proceedings if there are any other circumstances which make a stay appropriate.[79]

6–137   A CTM applicant is entitled at any time to withdraw the application or to restrict the list of goods and services in respect of which a mark is applied for.[80] If the list of goods and services is restricted while opposition proceedings are pending, OHIM must inform the opponent and invite him to submit observations stating whether the opposition is still maintained and, if so, against which of the remaining goods and services.[81]

PROOF OF USE OF THE EARLIER TRADE MARK

6–138   The CTM applicant is entitled to require the opponent to prove that an earlier trade mark relied upon in the opposition has been put to genuine use in the Community (if a CTM) or in the relevant Member State (if a national trade mark) over the period of five years prior to publication of the application, or that there are proper reasons for non-use.[82] This provision only applies if the mark relied upon has at that date been registered for at least five years.[83] Evidence of use should provide details of the place, time, extent and nature of use of the opposing trade mark for the goods and services in respect of which it is registered and on which the opposition is based.[84] Evidence should, in principle, be confined to the submission of supporting documents and items such as packages, labels, price lists, catalogues, invoices, photographs, newspaper advertisements, affidavits and written statements having similar effect under national law.[85] OHIM may require a translation of the evidence into the language of the proceedings.[86]

6–139   If the opponent fails to provide such proof, the opposition must be rejected.[87] If the opponent only provides proof of use in respect of some of the goods and services for which the mark relied on is registered, then for the purposes of the opposition the mark is treated as being registered only in respect of those goods and services.[88] No provision is made in Art.43(2) as to the effect of providing proof of proper reasons for non-use only in relation to some of the goods and services for which a mark is registered. It is submitted that such partial proof has the same effect as partial proof of use.

6–140   Surprisingly, the legislation does not prescribe any time limit within which the CTM applicant may submit a request for the opponent to prove use of his mark. The Boards of Appeal have held that such a request cannot be made for the first time during the appeal proceedings.[89] In one case the Board held—correctly, it is submitted—that the request should be submitted within the time limit laid down

---

[79] r.20(6).
[80] Art.44(1). See para.6–095 et seq.
[81] r.20(5).
[82] Art.43(2) and (3). The concept of genuine use is discussed in Ch.10, para.10–140 et seq.
[83] Art.43(2).
[84] r.22(2).
[85] r.22(3).
[86] r.22(4).
[87] Art.43(2).
[88] Art.43(2) An OHIM Board of Appeal has held that, where the CTM applicant asserts that the opponent's mark has been used only in relation to part of the goods for which it is registered and the opponent makes no attempt to refute that assertion, the mark must be treated as being registered only in respect of that part of the goods, even though the applicant does not formally request proof of use: Case R–222/1999-2 ENANTONE/ENANTYUM, O.J. OHIM 7–8/01, p.1465.
[89] e.g. Case R–687/1999-3 POP SWATCH/POLWATCH, O.J. OHIM 10/01, p.1855, and Case R–233/2000-1 PetStar/STAR, O.J. OHIM 5/02, p.889.

by the Opposition Division when it notifies the CTM applicant of the opposition and invites him to submit observations.[90]

THE DECISION ON THE OPPOSITION

Once OHIM has given the parties the opportunity to submit observations an Op-   **6–141** position Division will examine and decide on the opposition. If the examination reveals that the trade mark is not registrable in respect of some or all of the goods and services for which the application was made, the CTM application must be refused in respect of those goods and services. Otherwise, the opposition must be rejected.[91]

MULTIPLE OPPOSITIONS

Where a number of oppositions are entered in respect of the same CTM applica-   **6–142** tion, OHIM may deal with them jointly or separately, as it sees fit.[92] If a prelimi- nary examination of one of the oppositions suggests that the CTM application may have to be refused, OHIM may suspend the other opposition proceedings.[93] These are then deemed to have been disposed of without decision, and 50 per cent of the opposition fees must be reimbursed, if the CTM application is ultimately rejected on the basis of the opposition that was not suspended.[94]

A fortiori, if a single opposition is based on more than one earlier right the Op-   **6–143** position Division is entitled to reject the CTM application on the basis of one of the earlier rights; it is not required to rule on whether the opposition should also succeed on the basis of the other earlier rights.[95] Opponents have tried to argue that this is unfair because they may then have to launch separate opposition proceedings in the Member States in which those other earlier rights are registered, if the CTM applicant applies for conversion into national applications under Art.108. The argument is misconceived. It is not the function of OHIM to decide on trade mark conflicts throughout the European Community. Once it is clear that the CTM application cannot proceed to registration, OHIM cannot be expected to pronounce on points that have become moot. That is clear from the provisions on multiple oppositions in r.21.

17. Registration

If no opposition is lodged within the three months following publication of the   **6–144** CTM application, or all oppositions have been rejected, the application will proceed to registration on payment of a registration fee[96] consisting of a basic fee (€1,100) and an additional class fee (€200) for each class exceeding three in re-

---

[90] PetSTAR/STAR (cited in the previous note). However, in Case R–641/1999–3 SIDI (fig.)/SIDE 1 (fig.) the Board annulled a decision of the Opposition Division which had rejected as out of time a request for proof of use submitted seven months after the expiry of the time limit given to the CTM applicant for submitting observations. The position taken by the Board of Appeal in PetStar/STAR has since been followed by the Court of First Instance: see Case T–112/03 *L'Oréal S A v OHIM*, judgment of March 16, 2005, at paras 28–30, not yet reported.

[91] Art.43(5).

[92] r.21(1).

[93] r.21(2).

[94] r.21(4).

[95] This position has been confirmed by the Court of First Instance: see judgment of September 16, 2004, in Case T–342/02 *Metro-Goldwyn-Mayer Lion Corp v OHIM*.

[96] Art.45.

spect of which the mark is to be registered.[97] If the applicant (or his agent) has a current account with OHIM[98] the registration fee is deducted automatically, unless instructions to the contrary are received. The registration fee must be paid within two months of its being requested by OHIM.[99] Failure to pay the fee will result in a notification of the deficiency, after which the applicant is given another two months in which to make the payment on condition that an additional fee is also paid.[1] If the fee is not paid within this second period of two months the application is deemed to have been withdrawn.[2]

6–145   The registration is published in the Community Trade Marks Bulletin.[3] OHIM issues to the proprietor of the trade mark a registration certificate. The particulars that must figure on this certificate are laid down in r.84(2).[4]

18. Division of a CTM application or registration

6–146   A CTM may be applied for and registered in respect of a wide range of goods and services. There may be situations in which the applicant for, or proprietor of, a CTM decides that it is in his best interests to have, instead of a single application or registration covering a range of goods and services, two or more separate applications or registrations, each covering different goods and services. Such a possibility was introduced by Reg.422/2004.

6–147   Article 44a allows the CTM applicant to divide the application by declaring that some of the goods or services included in the original application will be the subject of one or more divisional applications. The goods or services in the divisional application may not overlap with the goods or services which remain in the original application or those which are included in other divisional applications.[5] The declaration of division is subject to a fee.[6] The divisional application preserves the filing date and any priority date and seniority date of the original application.[7]

6–148   A declaration of division is not admissible if it would have the effect of introducing a division among the goods or services against which an opposition has been entered, until the decision of the Opposition Division has become final or the opposition proceedings are terminated otherwise.[8] The Implementing Regulation may also lay down certain periods during which a declaration of division is not admissible.[9]

6–149   Article 48a makes analogous provisions for the division of a CTM registration. Once again there is a rule against introducing a division among goods or services which are the subject of contentious proceedings. Where an application for revocation of the CTM or for a declaration of its invalidity is pending, a declaration of division is not admissible if it would have the effect of introducing a division

---

[97] r.23(1) and Fees Regulation, Art.2.
[98] See para.6–025 *et seq.*
[99] r.23(2).
[1] r.23(3).
[2] Art.45.
[3] r.23(5).
[4] r.24(1).
[5] Art.44a(1).
[6] Art.44a(4).
[7] Art.44a(7).
[8] Art.44a(2)(a).
[9] Art.44a(2)(b).

among the goods or services against which the application is directed, until the decision of the OHIM Cancellation Division has become final or the proceedings are terminated otherwise.[10] Where a counterclaim for revocation or for a declaration of invalidity has been entered in a case before a CTM court, a divisional application is not admissible if it would have the effect of introducing a division among the goods or services against which the counterclaim is directed, until the mention of the CTM court's judgment is recorded in the Register.[11]

19. Renewal

The basic duration of a CTM registration is 10 years from the date of filing of the application. The registration can be renewed for an unlimited number of further 10-year periods.[12] At least six months prior to the expiry of the registration, OHIM must notify the proprietor and all parties with a registered right in the CTM (such as a licensee) of the approaching expiry.[13] Failure by OHIM to provide notification of pending expiry does not affect the expiry[14] of a mark or engender liability on the part of OHIM.[15] **6–150**

The request for renewal of a CTM registration should be submitted during the period of six months ending on the last day of the month in which protection ends. Failing this, the request may be submitted and the renewal fee paid within a further period of six months, on payment of an additional fee.[16] **6–151**

An application for renewal of a CTM registration must state whether renewal is requested for all the goods and services covered by the registration or merely for part of them. In the latter case, the application must indicate those goods and services for which renewal is requested.[17] **6–152**

On application for renewal, a renewal fee must be paid consisting of a basic fee (€2,500) and an additional class fee (€500) for each class exceeding three in respect of which the mark is to be renewed.[18] If a request is submitted or fees paid only in respect of some of the goods and services for which the mark was originally registered, it will be renewed only for those goods and services.[19] If the application does not make clear which class or classes of goods and services are to be covered, OHIM will take the classes into account in order of classification.[20] The renewal of a mark is recorded in the Register.[21] **6–153**

If an application for renewal is filed before the end of the six-month period after expiry of the registration but the other formalities governing renewal set out above are not complied with, OHIM must inform the applicant of the deficiency. If the deficiency is not remedied before the end of the six-month period following expiry of the registration, or if the renewal fee is not paid within that period, OHIM will determine that the registration has expired and will notify the propri- **6–154**

---

[10] Art.48a(2)(a).
[11] Art.44a(2)(b).
[12] Art.46.
[13] Art.47(2) and r.29.
[14] r.29.
[15] Art.47(2).
[16] Art.47(3).
[17] r.30(1).
[18] Art.47(3) and r.30(2).
[19] Art.47(4).
[20] r.30(4).
[21] Art.47(5).

etor, the applicant for renewal and any person recorded in the Register as having rights in the mark to that effect.[22]

6–155   Where the determination of expiry of a mark has become final, OHIM cancels the mark from the Register. The cancellation takes effect from the day after the day on which the registration expired.[23]

20. Alteration of a CTM

6–156   A CTM may not be altered in the register during the period of registration or on renewal.[24] Nevertheless, where the CTM contains the name and address of the proprietor, any alteration of the name or address not substantially affecting the identity of the trade mark as originally registered may be registered at the request of the proprietor.[25] The alteration must be published and third parties whose rights might be affected may challenge the registration of the alteration within a period of three months from publication.[26]

6–157   It is not clear whether the CTM must contain both the name *and* the address of the proprietor in order for Art.48(2) to apply. It would be logical to apply this rule if the mark contains either of those elements, though the wording of Art.48(2) suggests otherwise.

21. Surrender

6–158   A CTM may be surrendered in respect of some or all of the goods and services in respect of which it is registered.[27] To surrender a registered CTM the proprietor must declare his intention to OHIM in writing.[28] Where surrender is declared only for some of the goods and services for which the mark is registered, the declaration must specify the goods and services for which the CTM is surrendered.[29]

6–159   The surrender does not have effect until entered in the Register.[30] In principle, it can only be entered in the Register with the agreement of the proprietor of any registered right in the mark.[31] However, where a licence has been registered, surrender is entered in the Register three months after the date on which the proprietor of the CTM satisfies OHIM that he has informed the licensee of his intention to surrender it.[32]

22. Dealings with CTMs

6–160   The general rule is that a CTM or an application for a CTM[33] is to be dealt with, "as an object of property", in its entirety and for the whole area of the Community in the same way as a national trade mark registered in the Member State in which, according to the Register, the proprietor has his seat or domicile, or

---

[22] r.30(4).
[23] r.30(5).
[24] Art.48(1).
[25] Art.48(2).
[26] Art.48(3).
[27] Art.49.
[28] Art.49(2).
[29] r.36(1)(d).
[30] Art.49(2).
[31] Art.49(3).
[32] r.36(2). The surrender is however entered on the Register forthwith if the CTM proprietor can show that the licensee has consented.
[33] Any reference to a CTM in this section includes an application for a CTM Art.24).

failing that, has an establishment.[34] If two or more joint proprietors are mentioned in the Register, the seat, domicile or place of establishment of the first-named proprietor is decisive.[35] If that person does not have a domicile, seat or place of establishment in a Member State, then this rule is applied in turn to each of the subsequent joint proprietors in the order in which they are mentioned.[36] If none of the proprietors has a seat, domicile or place of establishment in a Member State, then the CTM or application is dealt with in the same way as a Spanish national trade mark (Spain being the Member State in which OHIM is situated).[37] Notwithstanding the general rule, Arts 17 to 24 set out the substantive law and necessary formalities relating to certain specific dealings with CTMs.

ASSIGNMENT OF CTMs

A CTM may be assigned[38] in respect of some or all of the goods or services in respect of which it is registered or applied for[39] but cannot be assigned other than in respect of the entire Community.[40] A CTM may be assigned separately from the undertaking which owns it.[41] With two exceptions assignments of CTMs are void unless made in writing and signed by all parties to the assignment.[42] The first exception is that any transfer of the whole undertaking which is the proprietor of a CTM is deemed to include the transfer of the CTM (except where there is an agreement to the contrary or "circumstances clearly dictate otherwise").[43] The second exception is that assignments made as a result of judgments need not comply with the usual formalities.[44] **6–161**

On request of one of the parties, an assignment is entered in the Register and published.[45] An application for registration of an assignment must contain certain information specified in r.31. **6–162**

If it is clear to OHIM from the assignment documents that as a result of the assignment the CTM is likely to mislead the public concerning the nature, quality or geographical origin of the goods or services in respect of which it is registered, OHIM is precluded from registering the assignment unless the assignee agrees to limit the registration to goods and services in respect of which the trade mark is not misleading.[46] As a general rule the question whether a trade mark is misleading does not depend on the identity of its proprietor. This provision is likely, therefore, to be applied only in exceptional cases—for example, where the assignee has no connection with a geographical location alluded to in the trade mark and there is a real likelihood that consumers would assume otherwise. **6–163**

LICENSING

A CTM may be licensed in respect of some or all of the goods or services for **6–164**

---

[34] Arts 16(1) and 24.
[35] Art.16(3).
[36] Art.16(3).
[37] Art.16(2).
[38] Although the term "assignment" is used here since it is more familiar to English lawyers, the CTM Regulation uses the term "transfer" throughout.
[39] Art.17(1).
[40] Art.1(2).
[41] Art.17(1).
[42] Art.17(3).
[43] Art.17(2).
[44] Art.17(3).
[45] Art.17(5).
[46] Art.17(4).

which it is registered, and in relation to the whole or part of the Community. The licence may be exclusive or non-exclusive. No formalities are prescribed for the grant of a licence.[47]

6–165 The proprietor of a CTM may institute infringement proceedings against a licensee who contravenes any provision in the licence concerning its duration, the form in which the mark is to be used, the scope of the goods and services in respect of which the mark may be used, the territory in which the trade mark may be affixed or the quality of goods or services provided by the licensee.[48]

6–166 The grant or transfer of a licence is entered in the Register and published on request of one of the parties.[49] The registration of licences or other rights can be cancelled or modified on application in writing by one of the persons concerned.[50]

EFFECT *VIS-À-VIS* THIRD PARTIES

6–167 Until an assignment has been registered, the assignee is not entitled to rely on his rights arising from registration of a CTM.[51] Thus an unregistered assignee cannot issue infringement proceedings or rely on the CTM for the purposes of an opposition.

6–168 Any assignment, licence or grant of a right *in rem* concerning a CTM is only effective against third parties after entry in the Register, except that such an act has effect against third parties who have acquired rights in the CTM after the act but who knew of the act at the date when the rights were acquired.[52]

RIGHTS *IN REM* AND LEVY OF EXECUTION

6–169 A CTM may be given as security or be the subject of rights *in rem*.[53] Such rights may be entered in the Register on request.[54]

6–170 A CTM may be levied in execution.[55] International jurisdiction is determined in accordance with art.16.[56]

INSOLVENCY PROCEEDINGS

6–171 The only Member State in which a CTM may be involved in "bankruptcy or like proceedings" is that in which such proceedings are first brought.[57]

23. Community collective marks

6–172 A Community collective mark is a CTM which is described as such when the mark is applied for and is capable of distinguishing the goods or services of the members of the association which is the proprietor of the mark from those of other undertakings.[58] A Community collective mark may be applied for by "associations of manufacturers, producers, suppliers of services or traders which,

---

[47] Art.22(1).
[48] Art.22(2).
[49] Art.22(5).
[50] r.35(1).
[51] CTM Regulation, Art.17(6).
[52] Art.23(1).
[53] Art.19(1).
[54] Art.19(2).
[55] Art.20(1).
[56] Art.20(2). See para.6–159.
[57] Art.21(1).
[58] Art.64(1). On the subject of collective marks in general, see Ch.12.

under the terms of the law governing them, have the capacity in their own name to have rights and obligations of all kinds, to make contracts or accomplish other legal acts and to sue and be sued, as well as legal persons governed by public law".[59]

An applicant for a Community collective mark must submit regulations governing its use, either with the application or within a period of two months.[60] The regulations governing use must specify "the persons authorized to use the mark, the conditions of membership of the association and, where they exist, the conditions of use of the mark, including sanctions".[61]   **6–173**

Community collective marks are subject to the same absolute grounds of refusal as ordinary CTMs, subject to the following differences.   **6–174**

In derogation from Art.7(1)(c), signs or indications which may serve in trade to designate the geographical origin of the goods or services may constitute Community collective marks.[62] Such marks cannot be invoked against a third party who is entitled to use a geographical name or against any third party who uses the sign in question in accordance with honest practices in industrial or commercial matters.[63] Moreover, the regulations governing the use of such a Community collective mark must authorize any person whose goods or services originate in the geographical area concerned to become a member of the association which is the proprietor of the mark.[64]

An application for a Community collective mark must be refused if the regulations governing its use are contrary to public policy or to accepted principles of morality[65] or if the public are liable to be misled as regards the character or the significance of the mark, in particular if it is likely to be taken as something other than a Community collective mark.[66] It is possible to overcome those objections by amending the regulations governing the use of the Community collective mark.[67]   **6–175**

24. Enforcement of CTMs

THE COMMUNITY TRADE MARK COURTS

The rights conferred on the proprietor of a CTM are addressed in detail in Ch.14, and are to a great extent analogous to those of the proprietor of a national trade mark.[68] The rights conferred by a CTM are enforceable before the "Community trade mark courts". Each Member State was required to designate Community trade mark courts ("CTM courts") of first and second instance within three years of the entry into force of the CTM Regulation (which time limit elapsed on March 15, 1997). So long as a Member State has not complied with its obligation to designate CTM courts, jurisdiction lies with those national courts which have juris-   **6–176**

---

[59] Art.64(1).

[60] Art.65 in conjunction with r.43.

[61] Art.65(2). Certain additional requirements are contained in r.43(2).

[62] Art.64(2).

[63] Art.64(2).

[64] Art.65(2).

[65] Art.66(1).

[66] Art.66(2). The provisions of Art.66(1) and (2) are additional to those of Art.7(1)(f) and (g).

[67] Art.66(3).

[68] Art.9 of the CTM Regulation mirrors Art.5 of the Directive, which is implemented in the United Kingdom by s.10 of the 1994 Act.

diction in respect of national trade marks. The High Court in England and Wales and Northern Ireland and the Court of Session in Scotland were designated CTM courts in the United Kingdom by the Community Trade Marks Regulations 1996.[69] As from April 1, 2005, certain county courts in England and Wales are also designated CTM courts. The original version of the Regulations did not distinguish between courts of first and second instance. This omission was corrected by the Community Trade Mark (Designation of Community Trade Mark Courts) Regulations 2005.[70] The CTM courts of second instance are the Court of Appeal in England and Wales and Northern Ireland, and the Court of Session in Scotland. As regards Scotland, the legislation continues to be ambiguous, since it speaks simply of the "Court of Session". Presumably the Court of Session (Outer House) is the CTM court of first instance and the Court of Session (Inner House) is the CTM court of second instance.

6–177 The conditions under which an appeal may be lodged with a CTM court of second instance are to be determined by national law.[71] The ordinary national rules concerning further appeals are applicable in respect of judgments of the CTM courts of second instance.[72]

6–178 The CTM courts have exclusive jurisdiction over CTM infringement actions, including—if permitted under national law—*quia timet* actions[73] and actions for a declaration of non-infringement in respect of CTMs.[74] The CTM courts also have exclusive jurisdiction for counterclaims for revocation or for a declaration of invalidity of a CTM.[75]

JURISDICTIONAL RULES

6–179 The CTM Regulation lays down detailed rules to determine which Member State's CTM courts have jurisdiction in the above actions. The general rule is that proceedings should be brought in the CTM courts of the Member State in which the defendant is domiciled or, if not domiciled in any Member State, has an establishment.[76] If the defendant has neither a domicile nor an establishment in any Member State, proceedings must be brought in the Member State where the claimant is domiciled or, failing that, has an establishment.[77] If none of the above conditions is fulfilled, proceedings must be brought in Spain (*i.e.* the Member State where OHIM has its seat).[78]

6–180 Notwithstanding the above, the CTM courts of a different Member State acquire jurisdiction if the parties conclude a valid jurisdiction agreement under Article 17 of the Brussels Convention.[79] The same applies by virtue of Article 18

---

[69] SI 1996/1908.
[70] SI 2005/440.
[71] Art.101(2).
[72] Art.101(3).
[73] Art.92(a) speaks of "actions in respect of threatened infringement relating to Community trade marks".
[74] Art.92.
[75] Art.92(d).
[76] Art.93(1).
[77] Art.93(2).
[78] Art.93(3).
[79] Art.93(4)(a).

of the Brussels Convention if the defendant enters an appearance before a different CTM court.[80]

A CTM court whose jurisdiction is based on any of the above provisions has jurisdiction in respect of infringing acts committed or threatened within the territory of any of the Member States.[81] Infringement actions may also be brought in the CTM courts of the Member State in which the infringing act has been committed or threatened;[82] in that case, however, the courts have jurisdiction only in respect of acts committed or threatened within the territory of the Member State in question.[83] Thus, if a CTM is being infringed in several Member States its proprietor has a choice: he may sue the infringer in each of those countries in respect of the acts committed in each country or he may claim in respect of all the infringing acts in the country whose CTM courts have jurisdiction on the basis of the domicile or place of establishment of the defendant or claimant (or in the CTM courts of Spain if neither party has a domicile or place of establishment in the European Community). To that extent the CTM Regulation allows forum-shopping. **6–181**

Similar rules apply as regards "provisional and protective measures" (*e.g.* interim injunctions). Where these measures are granted by a CTM court which has "pan-European jurisdiction" under Art.93(1)–(4) they may be enforced in any Member State. A CTM court whose jurisdiction is based on the place of infringement cannot grant provisional and protective measures with extra-territorial effect.[84] **6–182**

Contesting the validity of the claimant's CTM

Article 95(1) states that the CTM courts must treat the CTM as valid, unless its validity is put in issue by the defendant by way of a counterclaim for revocation or for a declaration of invalidity.[85] That statement should not, however, be taken at face value, for reasons that are explained in the following paragraphs. When a counterclaim for revocation or for a declaration of invalidity is pleaded, the CTM proprietor may request the CTM court to stay the proceedings and to fix a time limit within which the defendant must apply to OHIM for revocation of the CTM or for a declaration of its invalidity.[86] If the defendant fails to make such an application within the prescribed period, the proceedings before the CTM court are continued and the counterclaim is deemed to have been withdrawn.[87] **6–183**

It is important to note that when a counterclaim is pleaded by the defendant the CTM court is not obliged to stay proceedings, at the request of the CTM proprietor, and to refer the defendant to OHIM. It may, if it chooses, rule on the counterclaim for revocation or for a declaration of invalidity itself. It must do so if the CTM proprietor does not ask it to stay proceedings and refer the defendant to OHIM under Art.96(7). In these circumstances the CTM court has the power **6–184**

---

[80] Art.93(4)(b). Arts 17 and 18 of the Brussels Convention have now been replaced by Arts 27 and 28 of Reg.44/2001: see below.

[81] Art.94(1).

[82] Art.93(5).

[83] Art.94(2).

[84] Art.99.

[85] Such a counterclaim may not be pleaded in an action for a declaration of non-infringement Art.95(2)).

[86] Art.96(7).

[87] Art.96(7).

to revoke the CTM or declare it invalid. OHIM is then required to mention the judgment of the CTM court in the Register.[88]

6–185   There is an alternative means by which the defendant in infringement proceedings may contest the validity of the claimant's CTM. By virtue of Art.95(3), he may, instead of pleading a counterclaim, raise a defence based on the argument that the CTM could be revoked for non-use or declared invalid on account of an earlier right of the defendant. This would enable the court to dismiss the infringement action without having the CTM deleted from the Register. Strangely, Art.95(3) does not seem to permit the defendant in an infringement action to argue that the CTM could be declared invalid on absolute grounds. In *International Business Machines v Web-Sphere Ltd*[89] the High Court nonetheless allowed the defendant to raise such an argument. It did so on the basis, not of Art.95(3), but of Art.103, which states that:

> "A national court which is dealing with an action relating to a Community trade mark, other than the action referred to in Article 92, shall treat the trade mark as valid."[90]

6–186   Article 103 seems to confer on the CTM courts a broad power to treat a CTM as invalid when trying an infringement action. The breadth of that power is curtailed by Art.95(3), the relevance of which was not addressed in the *Web-Sphere* case. One must in any event regret the lack of clarity of the legislation.

Related actions

6–187   In any action other than an application for a declaration of non-infringement, a CTM court is obliged to stay the proceedings if the validity of the CTM has already been put in issue before another CTM court by way of a counterclaim for revocation or for a declaration of invalidity or where an application for such relief has already been filed at OHIM (see below), unless there are "special grounds for continuing the hearing".[91] The court in question has the power to grant interim relief for the duration of the stay.[92]

6–188   OHIM (acting through a Cancellation Division) is under a similar obligation to stay proceedings in which revocation or a declaration of invalidity of a CTM is sought if the validity of the mark is already in issue before a CTM court.[93] However, each of the parties to the proceedings before the CTM court may apply to that court for a stay of proceedings pending the determination of the OHIM application. If a stay is granted in the CTM court, the OHIM proceedings continue.[94]

The law to be applied by CTM courts

6–189   The CTM courts are required to apply the provisions of the CTM Regulation.[95] In all matters not covered by the Regulation (such as criminal sanctions for misuse

---

[88] Art.96(6) and r.84(3)(o).
[89] [2004] EWHC 529 (Ch).
[90] The other language versions, as well as the context, suggest that this should read "other than the actions [plural] referred to in Article 92".
[91] Art.100(1).
[92] Art.100(3).
[93] Art.100(2).
[94] Art.100(2)
[95] Art.97(1). The provisions of the CTM Regulation are in any event directly applicable by virtue of Art.249 of the EC Treaty.

of CTMs, remedies for unjustified threats and the powers of the customs authorities in respect of importation of infringing goods), a CTM court applies its national law, including its private international law.[96] Unless otherwise provided in the CTM Regulation, it applies the procedural rules governing the same type of action relating to a national trade mark.[97] Where the court finds that the defendant has infringed or threatened to infringe a CTM, it must issue an injunction prohibiting the infringing acts and take whatever measures are available in its national law to secure compliance.[98]

The Community Trade Marks Regulations 1996[99] extended the following sections of the 1994 Act to apply to CTMs: s.21 (groundless threats), ss.89–91 (powers of Customs and Excise in respect of the importation of infringing goods), ss.92, 93 and 97 (criminal offences and forfeiture). Those Regulations also introduced a criminal offence of making false representations that a sign is registered as a CTM or as to the goods or services for which it is registered. **6–190**

Simultaneous and successive actions based on CTMs and national trade marks

Where infringement actions are brought in the courts of different Member States involving the same cause of action and between the same parties, one court seised on the basis of a national trade mark and the other on the basis of a CTM, there would clearly be scope for conflicting decisions if both actions were to proceed to trial concurrently. To obviate that danger Art.105 lays down certain provisions modelled on Articles 21 and 22 of the Brussels Convention. **6–191**

If the two marks in question (*i.e.* the claimant's national trade mark and his CTM) are identical and are registered in respect of identical goods or services, the court not first seised *must* decline jurisdiction of its own motion (unless the jurisdiction of the court first seised is challenged, in which case the court not first seised may instead stay its proceedings pending resolution of the challenge).[1] If the two marks in question are identical and are registered in respect of similar goods or services, or if the marks are similar and are registered in respect of similar or identical goods or services, the court not first seised *may* stay its proceedings.[2] **6–192**

A court hearing an infringement action based on a CTM must dismiss the action if a final judgment on the merits has previously been given on the same cause of action and between the same parties on the basis of an identical national trade mark registered for identical goods or services.[3] Similarly, a court must reject an infringement action based on a national trade mark if final judgment has been given on the same cause of action and between the same parties on the basis of an identical CTM registered for identical goods or services.[4] **6–193**

---

[96] Art 97(2).
[97] Art.97(3).
[98] Art.98(1).
[99] SI 1996/1908.
[1] Art.105(1)(a).
[2] Art.105(1)(b) The word "valid" in Art.105(1)(a) and (b) should read "registered" or "in force": see the comments of Laddie, J., in *Prudential Assurance Company Limited v Prudential Insurance Company of America* [2002] ETMR 1013; IP & T 781, at para.76.
[3] Art.105(2).
[4] Art.105(3).

6–194 The above provisions concerning simultaneous and successive actions do not apply in respect of interim or protective measures.[5]

THE APPLICABILITY OF THE BRUSSELS CONVENTION

6–195 Unless otherwise specified in the CTM Regulation (in particular, in the provisions that have just been examined), the Brussels Convention on Jurisdiction and the Enforcement of Judgments in Civil and Commercial Matters applies to proceedings relating to CTMs and CTM applications, as well as to proceedings relating to simultaneous and successive actions on the basis of CTMs and national trade marks.[6] Since the adoption of the CTM Regulation the Brussels Convention has been replaced by Council Regulation (EC) No.44/2001,[7] the provisions of which are largely the same.

25. The cancellation of CTMs by OHIM

6–196 It is important to bear in mind that the rights of the CTM proprietor are not unassailable. As explained above, the CTM may be revoked or declared invalid by the CTM court as a result of a counterclaim pleaded by the defendant in infringement proceedings. The CTM may also be revoked or declared invalid by OHIM (acting through a Cancellation Division). The substantive grounds on which revocation or a declaration of invalidity may be sought are the same, regardless of whether such relief is requested by way of an application to OHIM or a counterclaim in the CTM court. Those grounds are dealt with in Ch.10.

6–197 *Locus standi* to apply to OHIM for revocation or for a declaration of invalidity on absolute grounds is defined in extremely broad terms. Such an application may be submitted by any natural or legal person or any trade or consumers association which has the capacity to sue in its own name under the law governing it.[8]

6–198 *Locus standi* to apply for a declaration of invalidity on relative grounds is much narrower. Such applications may be made by persons who were entitled to file oppositions against the application for the CTM in question and on the grounds on which an opposition could be based.[9] An application for a declaration of invalidity on relative grounds may, additionally, be filed by the owners of certain rights specified in Art.52(2), namely: any right to a name, personal portrayal, copyright or other industrial property right.[10]

6–199 Applications must be filed in writing with a statement of grounds.[11] The application must identify the registration number of the contested CTM and the name and address of the proprietor and specify the registered goods and services in respect of which revocation or a declaration of invalidity is sought.[12]

6–200 In the case of an application for a declaration of invalidity based on an earlier

---

[5] Art.105(4).
[6] Art.90.
[7] O.J. EC 2001 L 12, p.1. The Brussels Convention continues to apply as regards relations between Denmark and the other Member States.
[8] Art.55(1)(a). For an example of a case in which a CTM was declared invalid on absolute grounds, see joined Cases T–160/02 to T–162/02 *Naipes Heraclio Fournier S.A. v OHIM*, judgment of May 11, 2005, not yet reported.
[9] Arts 55(1)(b) and 52(1).
[10] Arts 55(1)(c) and 52(2).
[11] Art.55(2).
[12] r.37(a).

right that could have been invoked in opposition proceedings, the applicant must provide particulars of the right on which the application is based and, if necessary, particulars showing that the applicant is entitled to adduce the earlier right as a ground for invalidity.[13] In the case of an application based on any of the additional rights that may be invoked under Art.52(2), the applicant must provide particulars of the right on which the application is based and particulars showing that the applicant is the proprietor of an earlier right as defined by Art.52(2) or is entitled, under the national law applicable, to lay claim to that right.[14]

Applications for revocation or for a declaration of invalidity are decided upon by a Cancellation Division of OHIM. The procedure is broadly similar to that laid down for opposition proceedings.[15]   **6–201**

One of the significant differences concerns the rules governing proof of use of an earlier registered trade mark relied on by the applicant for a declaration of invalidity on relative grounds. In opposition proceedings, it will be recalled, the CTM applicant may require the opponent who relies on an earlier trade mark—provided this has been registered for at least five years at the date of publication of the CTM application—to furnish proof that the trade mark has been put to genuine use during the five years preceding that date. The CTM proprietor may impose a similar requirement on the party who invokes an earlier registered trade mark in support of an application for a declaration that the CTM is invalid.[16] In addition, the applicant for the declaration of invalidity will be required to furnish proof that his earlier trade mark has been put to genuine use during the five years preceding the date of the application for a declaration of invalidity, provided the earlier trade mark has at that date been registered for not less than five years.[17] The justification for imposing this twin burden on the cancellation applicant is that he should not be allowed to attack the CTM if his own trade mark was liable to be cancelled for non-use either at the time when opposition proceedings might have been launched or at the time when he applied for cancellation of the CTM.   **6–202**

If examination of an application for a declaration of invalidity reveals that the CTM should not have been registered in respect of some or all of the goods and services for which it was registered, the CTM is declared invalid in respect of those goods and services. If examination of an application for revocation reveals that the CTM should cease to be registered, in respect of some or all of the goods and services for which it was registered, it is revoked in respect of those goods or services. Otherwise, the application is rejected.   **6–203**

The effect of a declaration of invalidity is that the CTM is deemed not to have had, as from the outset, the effects produced by registration, to the extent that it is declared invalid (*i.e.* with regard to the goods and services in respect of which it is found to be invalid).[18] Revocation, on the other hand, has effect as from the date on which the application for revocation was made or the date from which the counterclaim was pleaded.[19]   **6–204**

No application is admissible if an earlier application relating to the same subject matter and cause of action and involving the same parties has been previ-   **6–205**

---

[13] r.37(b)(ii).
[14] r.37(b)(iii).
[15] See rr.37–41.
[16] Art.56(2).
[17] Art.56(2).
[18] Art.54(2).
[19] Art.54(1).

ously adjudicated on in the courts of a Member State and has acquired the authority of a final decision.[20]

26. Conversion

6–206   To the extent that a CTM application is withdrawn, deemed to be withdrawn or refused, or that a CTM ceases to have effect, the applicant for, or proprietor of, the CTM may request that the CTM or the application for a CTM be converted into a national trade mark application (or into a series of national trade mark applications).[21] Conversion cannot occur if:

(1) the rights of the CTM proprietor have been revoked for non-use, unless in the Member State for which conversion has been requested the mark has been put to use which would be considered genuine use under the laws of that Member State;[22] or

(2) grounds for refusal of registration or grounds for revocation or invalidity apply to the CTM application or to the CTM in the Member State in question.[23]

The national trade mark application resulting from conversion enjoys the same filing date and, if applicable, the same priority and seniority as the parent CTM (or CTM application).[24]

6–207   An application for conversion must be filed within a time limit of three months. Time begins to run from whichever of the following dates is applicable:

1. The date of the relevant communication from OHIM, in cases where the CTM application is deemed to be withdrawn;[25]

2. The date on which the CTM application is withdrawn;[26]

3. The date on which the CTM ceases to have effect as a result of its surrender being recorded or the expiry of its registration following a failure to renew it;[27]

4. The date on which the OHIM decision becomes final, in cases where the CTM application is refused by OHIM;[28]

5. The date on which the decision of OHIM or of the CTM court becomes final, in cases in which the CTM ceases to have effect as a result of a decision of OHIM or of a CTM court.[29]

6–208   The mandatory contents of an application for conversion are set out in r.44. In particular, the application must specify the Member State or States in respect of which conversion is requested.

6–209   If an application for conversion does not comply with Art.108(1) (that is to say, the CTM application or CTM is still extant in some way which overlaps with the conversion application) or is not filed within the relevant three-month period, it must be rejected.[30] If the conversion fee prescribed by the Fees Regulation is not paid within the relevant three-month period, the application is deemed not to

---

[20] Art.55(3).
[21] Art.108.
[22] Art.108(2)(a).
[23] Art.108(2)(b).
[24] Art.108(3).
[25] Art.108(4).
[26] Art.108(5).
[27] Art.108(5).
[28] Art.108(6).
[29] Art.108(6)
[30] r.45(1).

have been filed.[31] Where any of the other formal requirements set out above are not met, OHIM must inform the applicant of such deficiencies and ask for them to be remedied within a specified period. If they are not remedied in good time, the application is rejected.[32]

Since the entry into force of Reg.422/2004[33] OHIM must also check whether **6–210** the application for conversion complies with Art.108(2). This means, in particular, that, where a CTM application has been refused, or a CTM declared invalid, on absolute or relative grounds, OHIM must ascertain whether in accordance with the relevant decision—which may be the decision of an OHIM examiner, Opposition Division, Cancellation Division or Board of Appeal, or the decision of a CTM court ruling on a counterclaim for a declaration of invalidity—an absolute or relative obstacle prevents the trade mark from being registered in the Member State or States for which conversion is requested.

Various scenarios can be envisaged. Where, for example, a CTM application is **6–211** rejected in opposition proceedings on account of a conflict with an earlier Benelux trade mark, the application for conversion may proceed as regards Member States other than the Benelux countries. If, however, the earlier right is a CTM, conversion is not available at all since the earlier right is protected throughout the European Community. The same applies *mutatis mutandis* when a CTM is declared invalid on relative grounds by an OHIM Cancellation Division or Board of Appeal or by a CTM court. Where a CTM application is rejected, or a CTM is declared invalid, on absolute grounds, conversion will not be available at all if the objection obtains in all the Member States (for example, in the case of a three-dimensional trade mark or a trade mark for a colour *per se*, unless the party concerned claims acquired distinctiveness as a result of use in the Member State in question). If the objection is based on the meaning of a word mark in a particular language, conversion may be available in respect of Member States in which that language is not widely understood.

It is not clear what happens if conversion is requested after a CTM has been **6–212** revoked on grounds of non-use. According to the wording of Art.108(2)(a), the proprietor of the revoked CTM is entitled to request conversion in so far as the trade mark has been put to use that would be considered to be genuine use under the laws of the Member State in question. However, these laws have been harmonised as a result the TM Directive. The provisions of Article 10 of the Directive, on the user requirement, are *mutatis mutandis* identical to those of Article 15 of the CTM Regulation. It has always been assumed that genuine use in a single Member State is sufficient to prevent revocation of a CTM on grounds of non-use. (That is one of the great attractions of the CTM system.) It is difficult therefore to see how a CTM properly revoked on grounds of non-use can be deemed to have been put to genuine use in any Member State for which conversion is requested.

If the application for conversion complies with the requirements of the CTM **6–213** Regulation and the Implementing Regulation it is transmitted to the central industrial property office of the specified Member State or States.[34] The national

---

[31] r.45(2).

[32] r.45(3).

[33] Point 29 of Art.1 of Reg.422/2004 amended Art.109(3) of the CTM Regulation.

[34] Art.109(3) and r.47. For example, the Patent Office in the case of the United Kingdom.

offices may obtain from OHIM any additional information enabling them to decide on the resulting application for a national trade mark.[35]

6–214   The national offices may not subject the application to "formal requirements of national law which are different from or additional to those provided for" in the CTM Regulation and Implementing Regulation.[36] The national offices may, however, require the applicant to pay the national application fee, file a translation of the request and of the documents accompanying it, indicate an address for service in the State in question and supply a representation of the trade mark in the number of copies specified by the State in question.[37]

27. Enlargement of the European Union

6–215   On May 1, 2004, 10 new Member States[38] acceded to the European Union. Enlargement on such a scale was bound to have major repercussions on the CTM system. These are dealt with in a new Art.142a, which was added to the CTM Regulation by the Act governing the Accession of the new Member States. The new article was subsequently renumbered as Art.159a by Reg.422/2004. The main challenge posed by enlargement was to maintain the unitary character of the CTM without prejudicing pre-existing rights in the new Member States.[39]

AUTOMATIC EXTENSION OF EXISTING CTMs TO THE NEW MEMBER STATES

6–216   As from the date of accession of the new Member States, all CTMs registered or applied for before that date were automatically extended to the territory of those Member States "in order to have equal effect throughout the Community".[40] This extension took place by operation of law, without any administrative formality or fee.[41]

6–217   If a CTM was applied for before the date of accession, it cannot be refused on the basis of any of the absolute grounds for refusal listed in Art.7(1) if these grounds become applicable solely because of the accession of a new Member State.[42] This means, for example, that if a CTM application was filed before May 1, 2004, for a trade mark that is descriptive, misleading or contrary to public policy or morality because of its meaning in one of the nine new languages of the Community, the application cannot be refused on that ground (unless one takes the view that the meaning in the language in question is something that should have been taken into account before enlargement). CTMs applied for before the date of accession may not be declared invalid on absolute grounds if the grounds of invalidity became applicable solely because of the accession of a new Member State.[43] Such rights are said to be "grandfathered".

6–218   CTMs applied for before the date of accession are also protected against invalidation on relative grounds under Art.52 on the basis of an earlier national

---

[35] Art.110(1), following amendment by Reg.422/2004.
[36] Art.110(2).
[37] Art.110(3).
[38] See para.6–001.
[39] Communication No. 5/03 of the President of OHIM of October 16, 2003 (O.J. OHIM 1/2004, p.69).
[40] Art.159a(1).
[41] Communication No.5/03 of the OHIM President, at para.II.1.
[42] Art.159a(2).
[43] Art.159a(4).

right that was registered, applied for, or acquired in a new Member State prior to the date of accession. Exceptionally, opposition proceedings may be entered against CTM applications filed in the six-month period before accession (*i.e.* between November 1, 2003, and April 30, 2004) on the basis of earlier rights acquired in good faith in one of the new Member States before the date of accession.[44] It goes without saying that in determining whether there is an earlier right, any priority dates are taken into account. Thus, to give a simple example, if a CTM application was filed on January 15, 2004, claiming the priority of an Australian application filed on December 12, 2003, an opposition may be entered by the proprietor of a Polish trade mark filed on February 28, 2004, with a priority claim reaching back to November 25, 2003. The period for filing such an opposition is the normal opposition period referred to in Art.42, *i.e.* three months after publication of the CTM application.

Two points must be stressed here. First, the earlier right relied on by the opponent must have been acquired in good faith. Secondly, while the owner of an earlier right normally has a choice between filing an opposition and applying for cancellation at the post-registration stage, the latter option is not available in this type of situation. The owner of an earlier right in one of the new Member States who fails to oppose a CTM application filed between November 1, 2003, and April 30, 2004, using the exceptional provision in Art.159a(3), cannot apply to OHIM for a declaration of invalidity or counterclaim for invalidity in infringement proceedings before a CTM court.[45]   **6–219**

LIMITATIONS ON THE USE OF AUTOMATICALLY EXTENDED CTMs: PUBLIC-INTEREST MATTERS

It is possible that some CTMs filed before the date of accession will consist entirely of terms that are descriptive in one of the languages of the new Member States. Such terms should not of course be the subject of monopoly rights as a result of trade mark protection; they must remain available for use by all. A further problem is that some of the CTMs that are automatically extended to the new Member States may be misleading in one of the languages of the new Member States. Or again they may have obscene connotations in one of these languages.   **6–220**

All such trade marks would have been refused registration under Art.7(1)(c), (f) or (g) if they had been filed after April 30, 2004.

Article 159a does not expressly indicate how these problems are to be dealt with. In fact the solution is to be found in Arts 12(b) and 106(2).   **6–221**

By the terms of Art.12(b) a CTM does not entitle its proprietor to prohibit a third party from using "descriptive" indications in the course of trade. If someone had filed a CTM application for the word BAQRA in respect of meat and dairy products before May 1, 2004, OHIM would doubtless have registered the mark even though it is the Maltese word for "cow". Its proprietor would not, because of Art.12(b), be able to prevent other traders in Malta from using the word to indicate the bovine origin of their products. He would, however, own a valid

---

[44] Art.159a(3).
[45] That is clear from Art.159a(4), second indent.

CTM which he could in principle enforce in those Member States, both old and new, in which the term was not descriptive.[46]

6–222   By the terms of Art.106(2) proceedings may be brought under the civil, administrative or criminal law of a Member State or under provisions of Community law for the purpose of prohibiting the use of a CTM to the extent that the use of a national trade mark may be prohibited under the law of the Member State or under Community law. This should make it possible for action to be taken in the Member State concerned if an automatically extended CTM happens to be deceptive, obscene, blasphemous or otherwise unacceptable on account of its meaning in one of the new Community languages. The validity of the CTM would not however be affected and it could continue to be used and enforced in the other Member States, both old and new.

Limitations on the use of automatically extended CTMs: prior rights

6–223   It is equally possible that some of the automatically extended CTMs will clash with earlier rights that are protected in the new Member States. The owners of these earlier rights are protected by the terms of Arts 106 and 107. Article 159a(5) refers to those provisions expressly and states that the use of a CTM applied for before May 1, 2004, may be prohibited pursuant to Arts 106 and 107 "if the earlier trade mark or other right was registered, applied for or acquired in good faith in the new Member State prior to the date of accession of that State; or, where applicable, has a priority date prior to the date of accession of that State".

6–224   Article 106(1) is a general provision which is intended to protect the owners of earlier rights who, for whatever reason, have not prevented a conflicting trade mark from becoming a CTM by filing an opposition and have not applied for and obtained the cancellation of the CTM. Unless otherwise provided, the CTM Regulation does not affect the right existing under the laws of the Member States to invoke claims for infringement of earlier rights within the meaning of Art.8 or Art.52(2) in relation to the use of a later CTM.[47]

6–225   Article 107 protects earlier rights whose validity is limited to a particular locality. The proprietor of such a right may oppose the use of a later CTM in the territory where his right is protected in so far as the law of the Member State concerned so permits.

6–226   The earlier rights protected under Arts 106(1) and 107 may cease to be protected if the proprietor thereof acquiesces in the use of a later CTM for five years or more.[48]

6–227   The effect of these provisions may be illustrated by way of an example. Suppose that a CTM filed before enlargement conflicts with an earlier trade mark registered in Lithuania. The validity of the CTM is not affected but, on the con-

---

[46] It must none the less be stressed that the existence of Art.12(b) is not a ground for relaxing the application of Art.7(1)(b), (c) and (d). Although the Court of Justice created the impression that that was the case in its BABY-DRY judgment Case C–383/99-P *Procter & Gamble v OHIM* [2001] E.C.R. I-6251), it corrected the error less than two years later in Case C–104/01 *Libertel v Benelux Merkenbureau* [2003] E.C.R. I-3793, which concerned the equivalent provisions of the TM Directive.

[47] Art.106(1).

[48] Art.106(1) in conjunction with Arts 53(2) and 107(2).

trary, is extended to the new Member States, including Lithuania.[49] However, the proprietor of the CTM cannot enforce it against the earlier trade mark in Lithuania.[50] The proprietor of the Lithuanian trade mark may sue for infringement if the CTM proprietor uses the mark in Lithuania.[51] If the proprietor of the Lithuanian trade mark knowingly acquiesces in the use of the CTM for a successive period of five years, he loses the right to bring infringement proceedings.[52] He may, however, continue to use his trade mark in Lithuania.[53]

---

[49] Art.159a(1).
[50] This is not expressly stated in the legislation. It must be inferred from the fact that the proprietor of the earlier mark in the new Member State may treat the use of the CTM as an infringement.
[51] Art.159a(5) in conjunction with Art.106(1).
[52] Art.106(1), second sentence, in conjunction with Art.53(2).
[53] Art.53(3).

CHAPTER 7

THE MADRID SYSTEM

1. International registration of trade marks

THE MADRID AGREEMENT AND PROTOCOL

7–001 The Madrid Agreement concerning the International Registration of Marks ("the Agreement") was signed on April 14, 1891. It provided for trade marks registered in one country to be extended to other countries. The system worked reasonably well in those countries that used it but, as a result of a number of perceived defects, failed to attract many adherents. Major trading nations such as the United States, Canada, Australia, the United Kingdom, Japan and South Korea remained outside the system. In an attempt to make the system attractive to a wider range of countries the Agreement was complemented by a Protocol ("the Protocol"), which was adopted in Madrid on June 27, 1989, and came into force on April 1, 1996. The Agreement and the Protocol together form the "Madrid System", which is administered by the International Bureau of the World Intellectual Property Organization (WIPO) based in Geneva. The countries that have adhered to the Agreement or the Protocol (or both) constitute the "Madrid Union". Rules implementing the Agreement and Protocol have been adopted and are known as the "Common Regulations".[1]

7–002 The United Kingdom ratified the Protocol on April 6, 1995. It is envisaged that all Member States of the European Union will accede to the Protocol.[2] In addition, the European Community itself acceded to the Protocol as from October 1, 2004.[3] This was made possible by Art.14(1)(b) of the Protocol, which permits the accession of an intergovernmental organisation that has a regional Office for the purpose of registering trade marks.

7–003 The Agreement and the Protocol are "independent, parallel treaties with separate, but overlapping, memberships".[4] The relationship between the two instruments is complex but need not be addressed here; since the United Kingdom and the European Community belong only to the Protocol, lawyers based in the United Kingdom need to be familiar with the Protocol rather than the Agreement.

AN OVERVIEW OF THE SYSTEM

7–004 In order to use the system it is necessary to have one of three specified links with a Protocol member country, namely:

---

[1] These are available on the WIPO website.

[2] At the time of writing all the EU Member States except Malta had acceded to the Protocol. As of September 2004 the Madrid Union had 77 members, of whom 67 belonged to the Protocol. The members include the United States, Japan, Korea, Australia, Russia, China and Turkey. Notable absentees are Canada and the countries of Latin America.

[3] Council Decision 2003/793/EC of October 27, 2003 O.J. EC 2003 L 296, p.20).

[4] WIPO Guide to the International Registration of Marks, para.02.16. The Guide may be downloaded from the WIPO website.

— be a national of a Protocol member country; or
— be domiciled in a Protocol member country; or
— have a real and effective industrial or commercial establishment in a Protocol member country.[5]

Such a person (which may of course be a corporation) must hold a trade mark registration, or an application for a registered trade mark, in a Protocol member country with which he has one of those links. This is known as "the basic registration" or "the basic application" and the country in which it exists is known as "the country of origin". The national Office which has registered the trade mark or to which the application has been submitted is known as "the Office of origin". The holder of the basic registration or the basic application files an application for an international registration with the Office of origin, which, after checking that the particulars appearing in the international application correspond to the particulars appearing in the basic registration or basic application, forwards the international application to the International Bureau of WIPO. The international application must relate to the same trade mark as the basic registration or application and must be for the same goods or services (or for goods or services contained within those covered by the basic registration or application). The International Bureau registers the trade mark, awarding it the date on which the international application was received at the Office of origin, provided that it is received by the International Bureau within two months from that date.[6] The International Bureau notifies the international registration to the national trade mark Offices of the countries in which the applicant has requested protection ("the designated countries"). Each Office then examines the trade mark in accordance with its own national law and must inform the International Bureau, within a specific time limit, if the trade mark cannot be protected in that country. Under the Agreement the time limit was 12 months. The Protocol allows Contracting Parties to make a declaration extending the time limit to 18 months and to declare further that a refusal of protection based on an opposition may be issued after the expiry of that period,[7] provided that certain conditions are complied with. In so far as protection is not refused, the trade mark is protected in each designated country, as from the date of the international registration, in the same way as if it had been registered in that country.[8] The holder of the international registration may also ask for protection to be extended to a Protocol country subsequently to the date of the international registration. In that event, the mark will be protected as from the date when the request for extension is recorded by the International Bureau.[9] An international registration is valid for a period of 10 years and may be renewed for further periods of 10 years.[10]

7–005

UNITED KINGDOM AND COMMUNITY LEGISLATION IMPLEMENTING THE PROTOCOL

The provisions of the Protocol were implemented within the United Kingdom by

7–006

---

[5] Protocol, Art.2. In the case of the European Community it is necessary to be a national of an EU Member State or have a domicile or real and effective industrial or commercial establishment in EU territory.

[6] Protocol, Art.3(4). Otherwise the international registration bears the date on which the application was received by the International Bureau.

[7] Protocol, Art.5(2)(b) and (c).

[8] Protocol, Arts 6 and 7.

[9] Protocol, Art.3 *ter* (2).

[10] Protocol, Arts 6 and 7.

way of the Trade Marks (International Registration) Order 1996[11] ("the 1996 Order"), as amended by the Trade Marks (International Registration) (Amendment) Order 2000[12], the Trade Marks (International Registration) (Amendment) Order 2002[13], and the Trade Marks (International Registration) (Amendment) Order 2004.[14]

7–007   The accession of the European Community to the Protocol necessitated some minor adjustments to UK law in order to ensure that international registrations designating the European Community are properly protected in the United Kingdom. Those adjustments were made by the Trade Marks (International Registrations Designating the European Community, etc.) Regulations 2004.[15]

7–008   The Community legislation implementing the Protocol is to be found in:
— Council Regulation (EC) No.1992/2003 amending Regulation No.40/94 on the Community trade mark;[16]
— Commission Regulation (EC) No.782/2004 amending Regulation No.2868/95 implementing Council Regulation (EC) No.40/94;[17]
— Commission Regulation (EC) No.781/2004 amending Regulation No.2869/95 on the fees payable to OHIM.[18]

INTERNATIONAL REGISTRATIONS DESIGNATING THE UNITED KINGDOM

7–009   International trade marks are entitled to protection in the United Kingdom if they would have been registrable under the provisions of the 1994 Act and the Trade Mark Rules if applied for as a national registration in the United Kingdom.[19] If an application for an international registration designates the United Kingdom, or an application is made to extend an international trade mark to the United Kingdom after registration, the International Bureau will notify the Trade Marks Registry.

7–010   The procedure followed by the Registry is essentially the same as in the case of a national application. The matter is, however, complicated by the mandatory time limits contained in Art.5 of the Protocol. If the United Kingdom is unable to grant protection the Registrar must, in principle, send a notice of refusal to the International Bureau within 18 months of receiving the notification of the request for protection. It is possible to notify a refusal resulting from an opposition after the expiry of the 18-month time limit but only if the Registrar has informed the International Bureau, in a specific case, that oppositions may be filed after the expiry of that time limit. It is important to appreciate that the "notice of refusal" referred to in Art.5 of the Protocol is in reality only a provisional refusal, not a final decision. This has now been made clear in the UK legislation: the expression "notice of refusal" in the original version of the 1996 Order has been replaced by "notice of provisional refusal".[20]

7–011   The international mark is examined by the Registrar in the same manner as a

---

[11] SI 1996/714.
[12] SI 2000/138.
[13] SI 2002/692.
[14] SI 2004/948.
[15] SI 2004/2332.
[16] O.J. EU 2003 L 296, p.1.
[17] O.J. EU 2004 L 123, p.88.
[18] O.J. EU 2004 L 123, p.85.
[19] 1996 Order, Art.3.
[20] See SI 2002/692 amending the 1996 Order. The Common Regulations and the Community legislation also speak of notices of provisional refusal.

national application.[21] If the requirements for registration are not met, or are met only in relation to some of the goods or services covered by the international registration, the Registrar issues a notice of provisional refusal to the International Bureau,[22] which immediately provides a copy of the notice to the holder of the international registration. The notice specifies a period within which the holder can make representations.[23] The holder must provide an address for service in the United Kingdom.[24] If no representations are made, the refusal stands. If representations are filed, the International Bureau is notified when a final decision is reached by the Registry.

If the mark appears to be eligible for registration, the application is published by the Registrar. If this event takes place more than 14 months after the date on which the International Bureau notified the request for protection to the United Kingdom, the Registrar must inform the International Bureau of the possibility that oppositions may be filed after the expiry of a period of 18 months from that date.[25] This is to ensure that the terms of Article 5 of the Protocol are complied with. Observations as to whether the mark should be registered may be made in writing to the Registrar by any person. A person filing such observations does not become a party to the proceedings.[26]   **7–012**

Any person may oppose the application within three months of publication.[27] The detailed rules governing opposition proceedings are laid down in Arts 10A, 10B and 10C of the 1996 Order. The procedure is similar to that laid down in the Trade Mark Rules 2000 for normal oppositions. Notice of opposition must be given on Form TM7 and must include a statement of the grounds of opposition and an address for service in the United Kingdom. The Registrar must send a notice of provisional refusal to the International Bureau, stating the grounds on which the opposition is based. The Registrar must send a copy of Form TM7 to the holder of the international registration. The holder then has three months in which to file a counter-statement on Form TM8 (unless a cooling-off period has been granted with the agreement of the holder and the opposing party). Opposition proceedings then continue essentially as in a national application. Section 6A of the 1994 Act and rr.13B, 13C, 14, 36 and 37 of the Trade Mark Rules apply.[28]   **7–013**

Following a final decision in any opposition proceedings, the Registrar notifies the International Bureau. If and to the extent that the opposition fails, the mark proceeds to registration. Otherwise it does not receive protection in the United Kingdom. Trade marks that are protected in the United Kingdom under the Protocol are known as "international trade marks (UK)".[29]   **7–014**

If the United Kingdom was designated as a State in which protection was sought in the original international application, or the application for protection in the United Kingdom was made subsequently but before the registration date of the international registration, then the trade mark is treated as being registered   **7–015**

---

[21] 1996 Order, Art.9.
[22] 1996 Order, Art.9(3).
[23] 1996 Order, Art.9(4).
[24] 1996 Order, Art.9(5).
[25] 1996 Order, Art.11(2).
[26] 1996 Order, Art.10(3).
[27] 1996 Order, Art.10(2).
[28] 1996 Order, Art.10C(2).
[29] 1994 Act, s.53.

under the 1994 Act as of the date of the international registration. If the application for protection in the United Kingdom was made after the registration date of the international registration, the trade mark is treated as registered as of the date on which the request for protection in the United Kingdom was recorded in the International Register.

7–016   The proprietor of an international registration enjoys the same protection as would have been provided if the mark had been filed directly at the relevant national trade mark Office.[30] The proprietor of an international trade mark (UK) is entitled to the rights and remedies set out in ss.9–12 and 14–20 of the Trade Marks Act 1994.[31] The proprietor of the international registration is subject to the threats provisions of s.21 of the 1994 Act.[32] The provisions relating to criminal offences and forfeiture of infringing goods set out in ss.89–93 and 98 of the 1994 Act apply to international trade marks (UK).[33] It is an offence falsely to represent that a mark is protected as an international trade mark (UK).[34]

INTERNATIONAL REGISTRATIONS ORIGINATING IN THE UNITED KINGDOM

7–017   An applicant for a United Kingdom trade mark, or the proprietor of a United Kingdom registration, may apply for international registration of the mark through the Registrar if the applicant is:

(1) a British citizen, British dependant territories citizen, a British overseas citizen, a British subject or a British protected person;

(2) a body or corporation sole incorporated or constituted under the law of any part of the United Kingdom;

(3) a person domiciled in the United Kingdom; or

(4) a person who has a real and effective industrial or commercial establishment in the United Kingdom.[35]

The applicant may be required by the Registrar to provide evidence to establish eligibility on one of the above grounds to apply for international registration.[36]

7–018   The international application must be made on form MM2, which can be obtained from the Patent Office or WIPO.[37] The application should set out the same particulars as those required in a United Kingdom national application or contained in a United Kingdom registration at the time of application.[38] It should set out the goods or services in respect of which protection is claimed, classified according to the Nice Classification. If the application complies with the above requirements the Registrar submits it the International Bureau.

7–019   On receipt, the International Bureau registers the mark applied for. An international registration bears the date on which the international application was received by the Office of origin, provided that the application is received by the International Bureau within a period of two months from that date.[39] Otherwise, the registration is accorded the date of receipt by the International

---

[30] Protocol, Art.4.
[31] 1996 Order, Art.4.
[32] 1996 Order, Art.4(6).
[33] 1996 Order, Arts 16 and 17.
[34] 1996 Order, Art.18.
[35] 1996 Order, Art.22(2).
[36] 1996 Order, Art.22(4).
[37] Patent Office Trade Marks Manual, Ch.10, para.3.3.2.
[38] 1996 Order, Art.22(3).
[39] Protocol, Art.3(4).

Bureau. The International Bureau notifies the national Offices in the designated countries and those Offices then process the application under their national law, notifying the International Bureau if or to the extent that the mark is refused in that country. Unless notification of refusal is given to the International Bureau in accordance with the procedure described above, the mark is protected in each of the designated countries in the same way as if it had been registered nationally.

REVOCATION AND INVALIDITY

An international trade mark (UK) may be revoked or declared invalid in the same way as a national registration.[40] The provisions of ss.46 and 47 of the 1994 Act apply, subject to certain modifications due largely to differences of terminology.[41] The provisions of rr.31–31 B, 32–32 B, 33–33 B and 35–37 apply.[42]   **7–020**

If or to the extent that an international trade mark (UK) is revoked or declared invalid, the Registrar notifies the International Bureau. In the case of a declaration of invalidity the trade mark is deemed (to the extent that it is invalidated) never to have been protected in the United Kingdom. In the case of a revocation it is deemed (to the extent that it is revoked) to have ceased to exist from the date on which the revocation is recorded in the International Register. Moreover, the invalidity or revocation does not affect transactions "past and closed as at the date when the invalidity is recorded in the International Register".[43]   **7–021**

CENTRAL ATTACK, DEPENDENCY AND TRANSFORMATION

During the first five years of its life an international registration is "dependent" on the registration or application in the country of origin.[44] This means that anything that happens to the basic registration or application will have repercussions on the international registration. If the basic application does not proceed to registration in the country of origin, the international registration is cancelled and the mark is denied protection in the other countries designated by the holder of the international registration. The same consequence ensues if the basic registration is extinguished for any reason within five years from the date of the international registration.[45] The same occurs if the basic application is rejected or the basic registration revoked, invalidated or otherwise cancelled after the expiry of that period as a result of any action or proceeding (in particular an opposition) that was commenced within that period.[46]   **7–022**

This means that it is possible to kill the international registration by attacking the basic application or registration in the country of origin. This is known as the principle of "central attack", which was considered to be one of the weaknesses of the Agreement. To palliate the effects of central attack, Art.9*quinquies* of the   **7–023**

---

[40] 1996 Order, Arts 13–15.

[41] For example, references to the form in which the trade mark is registered are construed as references to the form in which the mark is protected and references to the goods or services for which the trade mark is registered are construed as references to the goods or services for which the mark is protected: 1996 Order, Art.13(2).

[42] 1996 Order, Art.13(4) as amended by SI 2000/138 and by SI 2004/948.

[43] 1996 Order, Art.13(5).

[44] Protocol, Art.6(2).

[45] Protocol, Art.6(3).

[46] Protocol, Art.6(3) Where the country of origin is the United Kingdom and the UK application or registration ceases to subsist as a result of any of these events, the Registrar is required to inform the International Bureau and request the cancellation of the international registration: 1996 Order, Art.23.

Protocol introduced the possibility of transforming an international registration into an application for a national registration. Article 9*quinquies* provides that, where an international registration is cancelled following the demise of the basic application or registration in the country of origin, the holder of the international registration may apply for the registration of the same mark with the Office of any of the Contracting Parties in the territory of which the international registration had effect; if the application is filed within three months from the date of cancellation of the international registration and the goods and services specified in the application are covered by the goods and services of the international registration, it is treated as though it had been filed on the date of the international registration (or on the date of recordal of the request for extension of protection, in the case of a request for extension of protection made subsequently to the international registration under Art.3*ter*(2) of the Protocol). If the international registration enjoyed priority, that too is preserved.

7–024   The United Kingdom legislation on transformation is contained in Arts 19 and 20 of the 1996 Order. This provides that, when an international registration designating the United Kingdom is cancelled at the request of the country of origin in respect of some or all of the goods or services for which it was registered, a transformation application may be made (on Form TM3), within the three months following the date of cancellation, for registration in the United Kingdom of a trade mark identical to that cancelled in respect of some or all of the cancelled goods or services, by the person who was the holder of the international registration immediately before its cancellation.

7–025   If the international mark had already become protected in the United Kingdom as a result of completing the examination and opposition procedure before the date of the transformation application, then it is registered as a United Kingdom trade mark.[47] If not, it continues to undergo the examination and opposition procedure, being treated as a national application.[48]

7–026   A trade mark registered pursuant to a transformation application is treated as if it had been registered in the United Kingdom as of the date of the international registration, unless the application to extend protection to the United Kingdom was made after the original international registration, in which case the United Kingdom date of registration is taken to be the date on which the request for extension was recorded by the International Bureau.[49]

EFFECT OF CONCURRENT INTERNATIONAL AND NATIONAL REGISTRATIONS

7–027   Where the same person holds an international registration and an earlier national registration in a territory to which the international registration has been extended, and all the goods and services covered by the national registration are also covered by the international registration, the international registration is deemed to replace the national registration, without prejudice to any rights acquired by virtue of the national registration.[50]

7–028   If a trade mark proprietor owns a United Kingdom registered trade mark that is also a protected international trade mark (UK) and:

(1) all of the goods and services for which the trade mark is registered nationally are covered by the international registration, and

---

[47] 1996 Order, Art.20(1).
[48] See 1996 Order, Art.20(2) and (3).
[49] 1996 Order, Art.19(3).
[50] Protocol, Art.4 *bis*.

(2) the United Kingdom registration has an earlier registration date than the international registration,

then the international trade mark (UK) is treated for the purposes of the 1994 Act as having been registered as of the date of registration of the national mark in respect of all the goods and services shared by the two marks. Further, for the purpose of determining whether the international mark is an earlier trade mark under the 1994 Act, it is treated as having the date of application of the national mark, taking into account any earlier priority date claimed by the national mark. The holder of the international trade mark (UK) may apply on Form TM28 for the international registration to be noted in the national Register against the United Kingdom registered trade mark.[51]

DEALINGS WITH INTERNATIONAL TRADE MARKS

The provisions of the 1994 Act concerning registered trade marks as objects of property apply, with the necessary modifications, to international trade marks (UK).[52] Thus an international trade mark (UK) may be assigned in the same way as a trade mark registered nationally in the United Kingdom. The provisions of the 1994 Act on licensing likewise apply, with the necessary modifications, to international trade marks (UK).[53]   **7–029**

Under the Protocol the International Bureau is required to record in the International Register any change in the ownership of an international registration, in respect of any of the designated countries, at the request of the holder of the registration or of the Office concerned made *ex officio* or at the request of an interested person.[54] The Common Regulations allow for the recording of licences in the International Register.[55]   **7–030**

An assignee or licensee of an international trade mark (UK) should submit a request to the International Bureau for recordal of the transaction in the International Register within six months of the date of the transaction. Failure to submit such a request within that period, or as soon as practical thereafter, will result in loss of entitlement to damages or an account of profits in respect of any infringement of the trade mark between the date of the transaction and its recordal in the International Register.[56]   **7–031**

THE LINK BETWEEN THE PROTOCOL AND THE CTM SYSTEM

As a result of the European Community's accession to the Protocol, the CTM system has, since October 1, 2004, been fully integrated into the international registration system. This has two important consequences: **7–032**

(1) The holder of an international registration originating in a country that belongs to the Protocol (including an EU Member State) may ask for protection to be extended to the European Community and thus obtain a CTM via the international system.

(2) A CTM or an application for a CTM can serve as a basic registration or

---

[51] 1996 Order, Art.7.
[52] 1996 Order, Art.5. The relevant provisions are ss.22–24 and 26 of the 1994 Act. Section 24(2)(b)—concerning assignments with limitations in relation to the use of the trade mark in a particular locality—is expressly excluded.
[53] 1996 Order, Art.7.
[54] Protocol, Art.9. The new owner must, however, be a person who is entitled to file international registrations under Article 2(1) of the Protocol.
[55] Common Regulations, r.20 *bis*.
[56] 1996 Order, Art.6(5).

basic application for the purposes of the Protocol. The CTM proprietor or applicant may apply through OHIM (as the Office of origin) for an international registration and ask for protection to be extended to other Protocol countries.

(a) International registration designating the European Community

7–033   An international registration designating the European Community has the same effect as an application for a CTM. If no refusal is notified in accordance with Arts 5(1) and (2) of the Protocol or if any refusal is withdrawn, the international registration has the same effect as the registration of the mark as a CTM.[57]

7–034   In the United Kingdom an international registration designating the European Community is referred to as an "international trade mark (EC)".[58] The UK legislation has been amended so as to ensure that such a trade mark enjoys the same protection as a CTM.[59]

7–035   The procedure followed by OHIM in the case of an international registration designating the European Community is essentially the same as in the case of an ordinary CTM application, subject to a number of differences in terminology and changes made necessary by the mandatory time limits laid down in Article 5 of the Protocol.

7–036   As in the case of an ordinary CTM application, two languages must be specified. The first language will be the language in which the international application was filed (*i.e.* English, French or Spanish). The holder of the international registration must designate a second language, which must be one of the five OHIM languages.[60]

7–037   OHIM immediately publishes the particulars of the international registration in the CTM Bulletin.[61]

7–038   Examination as to absolute grounds for refusal takes place in the same way as in the case of an ordinary CTM application,[62] except that it occurs after publication of the particulars in the CTM Bulletin, whereas an ordinary application is published only after OHIM has first carried out an *ex officio* examination as to absolute grounds.

7–039   If the examiner considers that the mark is not eligible for registration on absolute grounds, OHIM issues a "notification of provisional refusal".[63] This must state the reasons on which it is based and specify a time limit within which the holder of the international registration may submit observations. If the holder fails to overcome the objection within the time limit, OHIM takes a decision refusing protection in whole or for a part of the goods or services covered by the international registration. This decision is equivalent to a decision refusing a CTM application under Article 38 of the Regulation and is appealable in the same way.[64]

7–040   An international registration designating the European Community is subject

---

[57] Reg.40/94, Art.146.
[58] S.53 of the 1994 Act, as amended by SI 2004/2332, Reg.5.
[59] SI 2004/2332.
[60] Implementing Regulation, rr.112(3) and 126.
[61] Art.147. The OHIM web site describes this as "republication", the initial publication having taken place in the International Bureau's Gazette.
[62] Art.149(2).
[63] r.112(1).
[64] r.112(4).

to opposition in the same way as a published CTM application. A notice of opposition may be filed within a three-month period commencing six months after publication of the particulars of the international registration in the CTM Bulletin.[65] If a notice of opposition is filed before the expiry of the period of six months after publication of the particulars, it is deemed to have been filed on the first day following the expiry of that period.[66] When an opposition is entered, OHIM issues a notice of provisional refusal of protection.[67] The normal rules governing opposition proceedings apply, subject to some minor differences of terminology.[68] Although the relevant legislation is somewhat obscure, it is clear that an Opposition Division must decide whether the opposition is justified or not. If the opposition is justified, a decision refusing protection is taken. This is equivalent to a decision refusing a CTM application.[69] The decision may of course relate to part only of the goods and services covered by the international registration. In so far as the opposition is not justified, the provisional refusal is withdrawn. The normal appeal procedure is applicable, whatever the decision. Once the decision becomes final, OHIM informs the International Bureau either that the mark is protected in the European Community or that protection is refused.[70]

If protection is refused by OHIM or if the designation of the European Community ceases to have effect, the holder of the international registration may ask for the designation of the European Community to be converted either into a national trade mark application under Arts 108 to 110 of the Regulation or into the designation of an EC Member State that belongs to the Protocol or the Agreement.[71] This latter possibility is not expressly foreseen in the Protocol or the Agreement. It is, however, logical and an attempt was made to provide some sort of legal basis for it in a notification attached to the European Community's instrument of accession to the Protocol.[72]   **7–041**

The effects of an international registration designating the European Community may be declared invalid. The application for such a declaration takes the place of an application for revocation or for invalidation under Acts 50, 51 and 52.[73] Once the decision has become final, OHIM notifies the International Bureau accordingly.[74]   **7–042**

(b) International registration based on a CTM or a CTM application

To take advantage of this option the holder of the CTM or the CTM application must: **7–043**

— be a national of an EU Member State; or
— be domiciled in the territory of the EU; or

---

[65] Art.151(2).
[66] r.114(3).
[67] r.115(1).
[68] r.114(2).
[69] r.115(5).
[70] r.115(5).
[71] Art.154.
[72] The notification is appended to Council Decision 2003/793/EC.
[73] Art.153.
[74] r.117.

— have a real and effective industrial or commercial establishment in the territory of the EU.[75]

7–044   The application for an international registration must be filed at OHIM using a special form provided by OHIM.[76] It may be filed in any official language of the European Community but if it is not filed in one of the languages allowed under the Protocol the applicant must indicate a second language from among them.[77] The application will be submitted to the International Bureau in the chosen language. The application is deemed not to have been filed until the required fee has been paid.[78] The fee is currently set at €300.[79] If the application does not contain an indication of the goods and services in the language in which the application is to be submitted to the International Bureau, the applicant must authorise OHIM to provide a translation.[80]

7–045   OHIM carries out the formalities check required by Art.3 of the Protocol. If it detects any deficiencies concerning in particular the indication of the goods and services or the correspondence between the particulars of the international application and the basic application or registration, OHIM invites the applicant to remedy them within a prescribed period.[81] If the applicant fails to comply within that period, OHIM refuses to forward the application to the International Bureau.[82] If the application complies with the above requirements, OHIM must forward it to the International Bureau as soon as possible.[83] Thereafter it is dealt with in the same way as an application submitted through the national Office of a Protocol member country.

7–046   A request for territorial extension made subsequent to the international registration under Article 3*ter*(2) of the Protocol must be filed in the language in which the international application was filed.[84]

---

[75] Protocol, Art.2(1)(ii). The Protocol does not define nationality. It is for each EU Member State to determine which individuals and corporate bodies possess its nationality. As far as the United Kingdom is concerned, it would be logical to apply by analogy the terms of Art.22(2) of the 1996 Order to determine who possesses UK nationality for the purpose of filing an international application through OHIM.

[76] Arts 141(1) and 142(1).

[77] Art.142(2). The languages allowed under the Protocol are English, French and Spanish: Rule 6 of the Common Regulations.

[78] Art.142(5).

[79] Fees Regulation, Art.2, point 31, as amended by Reg.781/2004.

[80] rr.102(4) and 103(3), as amended by Reg.782/2004.

[81] r.103(2).

[82] r.103(4).

[83] Art.142(4) and r.104.

[84] Art.144. Implementing rules concerning subsequent designations are contained in r.105.

CHAPTER 8

ABSOLUTE GROUNDS FOR REFUSAL OF REGISTRATION

INTRODUCTION

This is a long chapter dealing with the disparate topics raised in s.3 of the Trade   **8–001**
Marks Act 1994, Article 3 of the TM Directive and Article 7 of the CTM
Regulation. Whilst the topics raised in ss.3(2)–3(6) of the Act and their European
equivalents are important, we make no apology for the length of the discussion
devoted to the absolute grounds raised in s.3(1) and in particular to the vital
subject of distinctive character.

Since the last edition, a small mountain of case law has accumulated in relation   **8–002**
to the Art.3(1)/Art.7(1) grounds. Whilst there has been some progress, it has been
disappointingly small. Much greater progress could have been and could be made
if greater attention had been and were to be paid to promoting a proper
understanding of distinctive character. Instead there has been much tip-toeing
around the edges, mostly sorting out the interplay between the different grounds.
In those cases where the ECJ has indicated the level of distinctive character
required for registration, the level has been set too low. That of itself gives rise to
concern that the ECJ itself does not fully understand distinctive character,
notwithstanding the fact that their judgments are consistently correct in stating
what distinctive character is. The CFI has less understanding of the concept than
the ECJ. The errors in the CFI judgments are perpetuated by their repeated citation of their own previous decisions, with insufficient attention being paid to
judgments of the ECJ.

STRUCTURE OF THIS CHAPTER

The way the case law has developed has caused us to adopt a different approach   **8–003**
to the Art.3(1)/7(1) grounds. For ease of reference, this chapter is divided into the
following sections, which start at the paragraph numbers indicated:

1. Overview of absolute grounds

8–004 Section 3 of the 1994 Act contains the absolute grounds for refusal of a trade mark. The grounds are absolute by contrast with the relative grounds set out in s.5. The relative grounds are concerned with conflict between the trade mark applied for and individual rights held by other traders. Section 3 operates at a more fundamental level, looking at the nature of the mark itself, its distinctiveness, both inherent and acquired, and tests the mark against various public policy matters.

THE INFLUENCE OF THE TRADE MARKS DIRECTIVE

8–005 One of the recitals to the Trade Marks Directive explains that the absolute grounds of refusal "are to be listed in an exhaustive manner" (even though some are optional) in order to ensure that "the conditions for obtaining and continuing to hold a registered trade mark are, in general, identical in all Member States" so as to achieve the Directive's stated aim of approximation of trade mark laws in Member States.

8–006 The United Kingdom has elected to implement most, but not all, of the optional grounds for refusal contained in the TM Directive. Section 3 manages to provide an exhaustive list of all the absolute grounds for refusal through cross-references to ss.1(1) and 4, and s.4 (as amended) itself cross-refers to ss.57 and 58 of the 1994 Act.

8–007 For the most part, s.3 follows the wording of Article 3 of the TM Directive. Where attempts were made to try to improve the wording, the changes either made no difference (in s.3(1)(a)) or introduced obscurity (in s.3(4)). It is a clear principle of Community law that measures in national law which implement a

Community provision are to be interpreted, so far as possible, in accordance with that provision. To an increasing extent, some United Kingdom judges[1] refer directly to the relevant provision in the TM Directive, not least to make their judgments more intelligible to others in the EU. This is a convenient aid to interpretation, even if it does bypass the actual provision which is in force in the United Kingdom. Similarly, Article 3(1) of the Directive is largely identical to Article 7(1) of the CTM Regulation.

THE GROUNDS ARE APPLICABLE TO ALL REGISTERED TRADE MARKS

On its face, s.3 of the 1994 Act is directed at applications for trade marks under the 1994 Act. In relation to such applications, any of the grounds may be raised by the Registry at the examination stage and/or by a rival trader in opposition proceedings. However, all registered trade marks remain subject to possible scrutiny under the grounds listed in s.3, even those registered long before the 1994 Act came into force. A trade mark may be invalidated under s.47 because it was registered in breach of any of the grounds set out in s.3. In theory, s.3 has effect back to the time when the earliest existing registration was put on the Register.

8–008

THE OBJECTIONS IN OUTLINE

The absolute grounds for refusal fall into two categories. The grounds in s.3(1) of the 1994 Act are concerned with aspects of the key issue of distinctiveness, whereas the remaining subsections are concerned with various policy considerations other than distinctiveness. By way of an overview, the effect of each of the grounds is as follows.

8–009

Section 3(1)(a)—the cross-reference to s.1(1) means a sign must qualify as a "trade mark" before it can be registered. The sign must be represented graphically and must be capable of distinguishing the goods or services in question from those of other undertakings.

8–010

Section 3(1)(b), (c) and (d) are directly concerned with aspects of distinctiveness. This is confirmed by the fact that if one of these grounds is established, it can be overcome under the proviso by showing that the mark has, through use, become distinctive. Although s.3(1)(b) ("devoid of distinctive character") comes first, it has the broadest scope and is the sweeping up provision. Section 3(1)(c) is designed to prevent registration of marks which are descriptive, *i.e.* signs which honest traders may legitimately wish to use. There is considerable overlap with s.3(1)(d) ("customary in the trade"), designed to prevent registration of signs which traders actually use to the extent they have become customary. As shorthand, these three grounds prevent registration of marks which are non-distinctive, descriptive or generic, unless the mark can be shown to have become distinctive through use.

8–011

Section 3(2) is concerned with certain aspects of shapes, but has limited scope. Case law has shown that s.3(1)(b) has a significant role to play in relation to marks comprising the shape of goods or their packaging. The shapes under examination in s.3(2) are not the two-dimensional shapes used in device or logo marks, but three-dimensional shapes and two-dimensional representations of them. There are three separate provisions, each dealing with a particular aspect of the

8–012

---

[1] Lord Justice Jacob, in particular.

distinctiveness of shapes. In essence, these provisions are designed to prevent attempts by traders to monopolise shapes which: (1) are wholly descriptive of the goods themselves or (2) are functional or (3) have "eye appeal". If established, in theory these grounds preclude registration even if the shape in question can in fact be shown to be distinctive of a particular trader's goods. In practice, this is unlikely to occur. If the sign can be proved to have distinctive character, it is an indication that the sign consists of more than exclusively the forbidden shape.

8–013   Section 3(3) is concerned with marks which are deceptive or contrary to public policy.

Section 3(4) is concerned with marks the use of which is prohibited by United Kingdom or Community legislation other than trade mark law.

Section 3(5) cross-refers to s.4, which places restrictions on the registration of marks which comprise or contain "official" signs.

Section 3(6) precludes the registration of a trade mark if or to the extent the application is made in bad faith. This ground appears to provide the only mechanism by which proprietorship can be challenged.

8–014   In some respects, s.3 of the 1994 Act contains a rather disparate list of objections. Some stand on their own, ss.3(5) and 3(6) in particular. Others are the more obvious result of policy considerations and are designed to ensure that, to the extent that trade mark laws in Europe are harmonised, the privilege of registration is secured only for those signs which properly function as trade marks. The legislative intent and therefore the scope of a number of the grounds are not always immediately obvious, although the ECJ has now highlighted the public or general interest underlying many of them. One thing is clear, that it is necessary to construe individual grounds in the context both of s.3/Art.3/Article 7 as a whole and as part of the overall scheme of trade mark protection set out in the 1994 Act, the TM Directive and the CTM Regulation.

RELEVANT BACKGROUND

8–015   Although these grounds are "absolute", this does not mean that the sign in question is considered in a vacuum. Far from it. The tribunal must ensure that it is sufficiently educated about the relevant trade so that it is able properly to assess applicable grounds. This is obvious in the case of s.3(1)(d) of the 1994 Act, but no less important in assessing the grounds in subss.(1)(c), (b), (2) and (3). In the initial stages of examination of an application in the United Kingdom, the Registry has the power to order the provision to it of such further information as it may require.[2] Examiners (both in the UK and at OHIM) frequently refer to material gathered from Internet searches.

APPLICATION OF THE ABSOLUTE GROUNDS

8–016   Apart from s.3(2) of the 1994 Act, whose provisions apply only to shapes of goods, the grounds apply to all types of sign and trade mark and all goods and services. Under each ground for refusal, the same test must be applied whether the sign consists of a shape, words, numerals or one of the more exotic types of sign. Each applicable ground must be applied to the sign or trade mark as a whole. Where necessary the effect of the sign or trade mark must be gauged by considering notional and fair use of it across the entire specification of goods or services.

---

[2] r.57. Note also the use of information gathered from the Internet: PAC 11/00, August 2000.

2. Distinctive character

We start by stating the obvious propositions that: **8–017**

(1) whether a sign possesses distinctive character, inherent or acquired, is a question of fact;

(2) whatever the sign or type of sign, the same amount of distinctive character should be required before the sign is properly registered as a trade mark, whether the distinctive character is inherent or whether it has been acquired through use;

(3) the assessment of inherent distinctive character depends upon the mark itself. This does not mean that the sign or mark is assessed in a vacuum: the trade of the goods or services in question provides the context;

(4) the assessment of distinctive character acquired through use requires an overall assessment of the way in which the mark has been used to ascertain whether the mark has become distinctive.

We propose to deal with acquired distinctive character first, even though it   **8–018**
may seem slightly strange to do so. The reason is because the ECJ had to tackle acquired distinctive character before inherent.

2.1 ACQUIRED DISTINCTIVE CHARACTER—THE PROVISO TO SECTION 3(1), ARTICLE 3(3), ARTICLE 7(3)

The issue of whether a mark has acquired a distinctive character through use   **8–019**
arises only if the mark is subject to an objection under one or more of s.3(1)(b), (c) or (d). It is now clear that this issue requires an overall assessment of the ability of the mark to distinguish in fact. The overall assessment is made taking into account the presumed expectations of the average consumer of the category of products concerned "[who] is deemed to be reasonably well-informed and reasonably observant and circumspect".[3] The "average consumer" test allows a variety of sources of evidence to be taken into account but discourages repetitive evidence.[4]

WINDSURFING CHIEMSEE

In *Windsurfing Chiemsee*,[5] the European Court was asked what was required in   **8–020**
order for a mark to have acquired distinctive character through use. The mark in

---

[3] The quote is from *Lloyd Schuhfabrik Meyer & Co GmbH v Klijsen Handel BV* [1999] E.C.R. I–3819; [2000] F.S.R. 77; [1999] E.T.M.R. 690, ECJ, but the words originate in para.37 of *Gut Springenheide GmbH & Tusky v Oberkreisdirektor des Krieses Steinfurt—Amt fur Lebensmitteluberwachung* [1998] E.C.R. I–4657; [1999] E.T.M.R. 425, a case about whether a statement on a pack of eggs was liable to mislead, contrary to an EC Regulation on marketing standards for eggs. The concept is not unique to European jurisprudence. When considering the analogous question of whether the defendant's use of "Treat" would be seen as a trade mark or as descriptive use, Jacob J. considered what "the average consumer" would think: see *British Sugar* [1996] R.P.C. 281 at 300.

[4] See, *e.g.* the comments of Chadwick L.J. in *Bach Flower Remedies* [2000] R.P.C. 513 at 534: "What is required, in the context of the proviso, is that persons in that class, or at least a significant proportion of persons in that class, identify the words or word in question as distinctive of the origin of the goods." "… in seeking to apply the test, the court is unlikely to be assisted by repetitive evidence from individual consumers, put forward by each party as the embodiment of the average consumer. The task for the court is to inform itself, by evidence, of the matters of which a reasonably well-informed and reasonably observant and circumspect consumer of the products would know; and then, treating itself as competent to evaluate the effect which those matters would have on the mind of such a person with that knowledge, ask this question: would he say that the words or word identify, for him, the goods as originating from a particular undertaking."

[5] Case C–108/97 *Windsurfing Chiemsee Produktions- und Vertriebs GmbH v Boots- und Segelzubehor Walter Huber & Franz Attenberger* [1999] E.C.R. I-2779; [2000] Ch. 523, ECJ.

question was Chiemsee, the name of the largest lake in Bavaria. Although this guidance was given in the context of a mark of geographical significance, it is plain that it is of general application:

"44. The first point to note is that Article 3(3) of the Directive provides that a sign may, through use, acquire a distinctive character which it initially lacked and thus be registered as a trade mark. It is therefore through the use made of it that the sign acquires the distinctive character which is a prerequisite for its registration.

45. Article 3(3) therefore constitutes a major exception to the rule laid down in Articles 3(1)(b), (c) and (d), whereby registration is to be refused in relation to trade marks which are devoid of any distinctive character, descriptive marks, and marks which consist exclusively of indications which have become customary in the current language or in the bona fide and established practices of the trade.

46. Secondly, just as distinctive character is one of the general conditions for registering a trade mark under Article 3(1)(b), distinctive character acquired through use means that the mark must serve to identify the product in respect of which registration is applied for as originating from a particular undertaking, and thus to distinguish that product from goods of other undertakings.

47. It follows that a geographical name may be registered as a trade mark if, following the use which has been made of it, it has come to identify the product in respect of which registration is applied for as originating from a particular undertaking and thus to distinguish that product from goods of other undertakings. Where that is the case, the geographical designation has gained a new significance and its connotation, no longer purely descriptive, justifies its registration as a trade mark.

48. Windsurfing Chiemsee and the Commission are therefore right to assert that Article 3(3) does not permit any differentiation as regards distinctiveness by reference to the perceived importance of keeping the geographical name available for use by other undertakings.

49. In determining whether a mark has acquired distinctive character following the use made of it, the competent authority must make an overall assessment of the evidence that the mark has come to identify the product concerned as originating from a particular undertaking, and thus to distinguish that product from goods of other undertakings.

50. In that connection, regard must be had in particular to the specific nature of the geographical name in question. Indeed, where a geographical name is very well-known, it can acquire distinctive character under Article 3(3) of the Directive only if there has been long-standing and intensive use of the mark by the undertaking applying for registration. A fortiori, where a name is already familiar as an indication of geographical origin in relation to a certain category of goods, an undertaking applying for registration of the name in respect of goods in that category must show that the use of the mark—both long-standing and intensive—is particularly well established.

51. In assessing the distinctive character of a mark in respect of which registration has been applied for, the following may also be taken into account: the market share held by the mark; how intensive, geographically widespread and long-standing use of the mark has been; the amount invested

by the undertaking in promoting the mark; the proportion of the relevant class of persons who, because of the mark, identify goods as originating from a particular undertaking; and statements from chambers of commerce and industry or other trade and professional associations.

52. If, on the basis of those factors, the competent authority finds that the relevant class of persons, or at least a significant proportion thereof, identify goods as originating from a particular undertaking because of the trade mark, it must hold that the requirement for registering the mark laid down in Article 3(3) of the Directive is satisfied. However, the circumstances in which that requirement may be regarded as satisfied cannot be shown to exist solely by reference to general, abstract data such as predetermined percentages.

53. As regards the method to be used to assess the distinctive character of a mark in respect of which registration is applied for, Community law does not preclude the competent authority, where it has particular difficulty in that connection, from having recourse, under the conditions laid down by its own national law, to an opinion poll as guidance for its judgment (see, to that effect, Case C–210/96 *Gut Springenheide and Tusky* [1998] ECR I-4657, paragraph 37)."

The true significance of this rather oblique reference to Gut Springenheide **8–021** emerged later, perhaps most clearly in *Philips*, where the ECJ stated:[6]

"65. ... the distinctive character of a sign consisting of the shape of a product, even that acquired by the use made of it, must be assessed in the light of the presumed expectations of an average consumer of the category of goods or services in question, who is reasonably well-informed and reasonably observant and circumspect (see to that effect, the judgment in Case C–210/96 *Gut Springenheide...*)".

Subsequent cases in which acquired distinctive character has been in issue **8–022** have consistently quoted *Windsurfing Chiemsee*, para.52 and *Philips*, paras 61 and 62.[7] Subsidiary propositions are:

(1) Where it must be shown that a mark has acquired distinctiveness in order to overcome one of the absolute grounds in Art 3(1)/Art 7(1), it must be shown that the mark became distinctive through use before the application was filed: ECOPY, paragraph 36.[8]

(2) In the case of an application for a CTM, acquired distinctive character must be demonstrated in the substantial part of the Community where the relevant absolute ground was established: OPTIONS, paragraph 27.[9]

(3) Distinctive character may be acquired when the mark is used as part of or in conjunction with another mark, but it is for the national court to assess whether the mark applied for identifies the origin of a product or service.[10]

(4) When assessing the acquisition of distinctive character through use, the identification, by the relevant class of persons, of the product or service as

---

[6] [2002] E.C.R. I-5475; [2003] Ch. 159; [2003] R.P.C. 2, ECJ.

[7] See [1999] E.C.R. I-2779; [2000] Ch. 523 and [2002] E.C.R. I-5475; [2003] Ch. 159; [2003] R.P.C. 2, respectively.

[8] Case T–257/01, ECOPY, CFI; [2002] E.C.R. II-5301; [2003] E.T.M.R. 99. Applied in *Audi AG v OHIM* Case T–16/02, TDI, CFI, December 3, 2003; [2004] E.T.M.R. 59.

[9] Case T–91/99, OPTIONS, CFI; [2000] E.T.M.R. 1925; [2004] E.T.M.R. 554. Applied in *Audi AG v OHIM* Case T–16/02, TDI, CFI, December 3, 2003; [2004] E.T.M.R. 59.

[10] Case C–353/03, HAVE A BREAK, ECJ, July 7, 2005.

originating from a given undertaking must be as a result of the use of the mark as a trade mark.[11]

IS "ASSOCIATION" ENOUGH?

8–023   The answer to this question depends on the meaning one gives to "associate", but in general terms the answer is "no". The issue tends to arise in cases where the applicant for the trade mark has enjoyed (due to other intellectual property rights) a period of *de facto* monopoly in the shape of the product or some part of it. As Patten J. has put it, "The difficulty lies in establishing during the monopoly period what more is required, beyond association of the product with the actual manufacturer, for it to achieve trade mark status." The answer is reasonably clear, but perhaps not *acte clair*, with the result that two UK judges have referred this point to the ECJ.[12] The issue tends to arise because of what the ECJ said in Paragraph 65 of *Philips*:[13]

> "In the light of those considerations, the answer to the third question must be that, where a trader has been the only supplier of particular goods to the market, extensive use of a sign which consists of the shape of those goods may be sufficient to give the sign a distinctive character for the purposes of Article 3(3) of the Directive in circumstances where, as a result of that use, a substantial proportion of the relevant class of persons associates that shape with that trader and no other undertaking or believes that goods of that shape come from that trader. However, it is for the national court to verify that the circumstances in which the requirement under that provision is satisfied are shown to exist on the basis of specific and reliable data, that the presumed expectations of an average consumer of the category of goods or services in question, who is reasonably well-informed and reasonably observant and circumspect, are taken into account and that the identification, by the relevant class of persons, of the product as originating from a given undertaking is as a result of the use of the mark as a trade mark." (emphasis added).

8–024   Of course, extensive use of a sign can only be relevant to substantiate a claim to acquired distinctiveness under the proviso to s.3(1)/Art.3(3) of the Directive/ Art.7(3) of the CTM Regulation, as the ECJ pointed out in *Mag Instrument (Shape of Torch)*:[14]

> "In that regard, it must be held that that evidence relates to the perception of the marks in question by consumers at a time when the torches in question had already been on the market for many years and when consumers were thus accustomed to their shape. Moreover, the appellant has itself accepted in its application that that evidence 'could also relate to the fact that the relevant public has associated the shape of the torches with the appellant...by reason in particular of their use in trade'.
>
> In those circumstances, the Court of First Instance was entitled, at paragraph 39 of the contested judgment, to hold, without distorting the evidence sum-

---

[11] Case C–353/03, HAVE A BREAK, ECJ, July 7, 2005, paragraph 26, citing *Philips* Case C–299/99 [2002] E.C.R. I-5475; [2003] Ch.159; [2003] R.P.C. 2, para.64, and see para.8–025.

[12] Jacob J. in VIENNETTA, *Unilever plc's Trade Mark Application* [2002] EWHC 2709; [2003] R.P.C. 35, (although the reference was withdrawn when the case settled) and Patten J. in *Dyson Ltd's Trade Mark Application* [2003] EWHC 1062; [2003] R.P.C. 47.

[13] Case C–299/99, *Philips v Remington* [2002] E.C.R. I-5475; [2003] Ch.159; [2003] R.P.C. 2. Paragraph 65 needs to be read in conjunction with the paragraphs which lead up to it: paras 51, 57-64.

[14] Case C–136/02, *Mag Instrument v OHIM*, ECJ, March 16, 2004 at paras 55-56.

marised at paragraphs 21 and 22 of the contested judgment, that that evidence failed to show that the marks in question had distinctive character within the meaning of Article 7(1)(b) of Regulation No 40/94, and that it was only capable of establishing that those marks could become distinctive in consequence of the use made of them for the purposes of Article 7(3) of that regulation."

We suggest that the ECJ will affirm what it said in *Philips*, para.65.[15] Thus, we propose the following propositions: **8–025**

(1) mere association with a particular manufacturer is not enough;

(2) the use of the sign must establish, in the perception of the average consumer, that the product originates from a particular undertaking;

(3) that perception must result from the use of the sign as a trade mark–in other words, the proprietor must have done something in his use to identify the sign as being a trade mark, and mere extensive use during a period of monopoly, without more, is most unlikely to have achieved this.

2.2 INHERENT DISTINCTIVE CHARACTER

Obviously, distinctive character is the same, whether inherent or acquired. The ECJ has consistently stated and recognised that distinctive character requires the mark to act as an indication of origin. See by way of examples: **8–026**

(1) *Linde*, paras 40 and 47:[16]

"40. For a mark to possess distinctive character within the meaning of that provision it must serve to identify the product in respect of which registration is applied for as originating from a particular undertaking, and thus to distinguish that product from products of other undertakings (see *Philips*, para.35).

47. As paragraph 40 of this judgment makes clear, distinctive character means, for all trade marks, that the mark must be capable of identifying the product as originating from a particular undertaking, and thus distinguishing it from those of other undertakings."

(2) *Libertel*, para.62:[17]

"62. It is settled case-law that the essential function of a trade mark is to guarantee the identity of the origin of the marked goods or service to the consumer or end user by enabling him, without any possibility of confusion, to distinguish the goods or services from others which have another origin (see *Canon*, paragraph 28, and Case C–517/99 *Merz & Krell* [2001] E.C.R. I-6959, paragraph 22). A trade mark must distinguish the goods or services concerned as originating from a particular undertaking. In that connection, regard must be had both to the ordinary use of trade marks as a badge of origin in the sectors concerned and to the perception of the relevant public."

(3) DAS PRINZIP, para.42:[18]

"42. It is also clear from the case-law that the distinctiveness of a trade mark within the meaning of Article 7(1)(b) of Regulation No 40/94 means that the mark in question makes it possible to identify the product for which registration is sought as originating from a

---

[15] Case C–299/99, *Philips v Remington* [2002] E.C.R. I-5475; [2003] Ch.159; [2003] R.P.C. 2. Note how precise the language of the ECJ was in that paragraph.

[16] C–53/01, [2003] E.C.R. I-3161; [2003] R.P.C. 45; [2003] E.T.M.R. 78.

[17] C–104/01, [2003] E.C.R. I-3793; [2003] E.T.M.R. 41.

[18] C–64/02, ECJ, October 21, 2004, [2005] E.T.M.R. 58.

given undertaking and therefore to distinguish the product from those of other undertakings and, therefore, is able to fulfil the essential function of the trade mark (see, to that effect, in particular *Procter & Gamble v OHIM*, paragraph 32, and the case-law there cited, and, in relation to the same provision contained in Article 3(1)(b) of Directive 89/104, *Merz & Krell*, paragraph 37, and *Linde and Others*, paragraph 40, and the case-law there cited)."

8–027   Numerous statements to like effect can be found in other ECJ judgments. What is striking, however, is that the ECJ has not so far provided any elucidation of the concept, apart from one or two asides. For example, in *Mag Instrument*, the Court stated the well settled proposition that, when assessing whether a mark has distinctive character, the assessment must be carried out in relation to the presumed expectations of an average consumer of the goods or services in respect of which registration is sought. Nonetheless, the Court accepted that evidence based on the actual perception of the mark by consumers may provide guidance, and continued:[19]

"However, in order to contribute to the assessment of the distinctiveness of a mark for the purposes of Article 7(1)(b) of Regulation No 40/94, that evidence must show that consumers did not need to become accustomed to the mark through the use made of it, but that it *immediately enabled them to distinguish* the goods or services bearing the mark from the goods or services of competing undertakings." *Mag Instrument* para.50. (emphasis added).

THE CFI

8–028   When dealing with inherent distinctive character under Art.7(1)(b), the judgments of the CFI's present a curious picture. On the one hand, the CFI's record on what is caught or not caught by Art.7(1)(b) is probably no worse than the ECJ (with one or two notable exceptions—*e.g.* NEW BORN BABY).[20] On the other hand, and despite the consistent statements emanating from the ECJ, the CFI has consistently relied upon and repeated its own statements regarding distinctive character which we believe display a fundamental misunderstanding of the concept. Take, for example, the following standard paragraphs which have now appeared in many CFI judgments:

"It should be noted at the outset that, according to case-law, the trade marks covered by Article 7(1)(b) of Regulation No 40/94 are in particular those which, from the point of view of the relevant public, are commonly used in trade for the presentation of the goods or services concerned or in connection with which there exists, at the very least, concrete evidence justifying the conclusion that they are capable of being used in that manner (Joined Cases T–79/01 and T–86/01 *Bosch v OHIM (Kit Pro and Kit Super Pro)* [2002] E.C.R. II-4881, paragraph 19; and Case T–305/02 *Nestlé Waters France v OHIM (Shape of a bottle)* [2003] E.C.R. II-0000, paragraph 28)."

"the signs referred to in that provision [Article 7.1.b] are incapable of performing the essential function of a trade mark, namely that of identifying

[19] C–136/02, ECJ, October 7, 2004.
[20] Case T–140/00 *Zapf Creation v OHIM* [2001] E.C.R. II-2927. Following the Opinion of A.G. Jacobs of February 18, 2004, Zapf Creation withdrew its trade mark application, resulting in the ECJ Order on the appeal, Case C–498/01, Order of December 1, 2004.

the origin of the goods or services, thus enabling the consumer who acquired them to repeat the experience, if it proves to be positive, or to avoid it, if it proves to be negative, on the occasion of a subsequent acquisition (Case T–79/00 *Rewe-Zentral v OHIM (LITE)* [2002] E.C.R. II-705, paragraph 26; *Kit Pro and Kit Super Pro*, paragraph 19; Joined Cases T–324/01 and T–110/02 *Axions and Belce v OHIM (Brown cigar shape and gold ingot shape)* [2003] E.C.R. II-1897, paragraph 29; and *Shape of a bottle*, paragraph 28 [Case T–305/02 *Nestlé Waters France v OHIM (Shape of a bottle)* [2003] E.C.R. II-0000])." *Shape of a white and transparent bottle (Henkel)* Case T–393/02, November 24, 2004, para.30.

As the citations indicate, these propositions have been used by the CFI consistently for over two years. The notion that Art.7(1)(b) is properly characterised by the "commonly used/capable of being commonly used" test has now been corrected by the ECJ: see DAS PRINZIP,[21] para.37. As for the second paragraph, it might be thought that the proposition is unobjectionable because it refers to the essential function of a trade mark and correctly identifies that function as identifying the origin of goods or services. The problem with the second passage is that this essential function is equated with merely the ability to *recognise* the mark on a subsequent occasion. A mark's capacity to trigger recognition means that it is different and may even be eye-catching, but it is no guarantee of inherent distinctive character. The problems inherent in these two paragraphs become apparent when one sees how these concepts are applied: *e.g.* if something is not common (*i.e.* different from what is currently used) then it has distinctive character. See for example, how the CFI stated their conclusions in relation to a sign comprising the shape of a shampoo-type bottle:

8–029

"it appears that the combination of the elements has a truly individual character and cannot be regarded as altogether common to all the products in question. It should be pointed out that the container which it is sought to register possesses certain features which distinguish it from containers for washing and cleaning products commonly used on the market.

That combination thus confers on the bottle in question a particular and unusual appearance which is likely to attract the attention of the relevant public and enable that public, once familiar with the shape of the packaging of the goods in question, to distinguish the goods covered by the registration application from those having a different commercial origin (see, to that effect, Case T–128/01 *Daimler Chrysler v OHIM (Grille)* [2003] ECR II-701, paragraphs 46 and 48; and *Shape of a bottle*, paragraph 41).

Accordingly, since, as stated above, the mark applied for is made up of a combination of elements, in a characteristic presentation, which distinguish it from other shapes available on the market for the products concerned, it must be held that the mark applied for, taken as a whole, possesses the minimum degree of distinctiveness required."

Shape of a white and transparent bottle (Henkel) Case T–393/02, November 24, 2004, paras 40, 42.

This type of reasoning is by no means unique.

2.3 A PROPER UNDERSTANDING OF DISTINCTIVE CHARACTER

The essential function of a trade mark is to distinguish the goods and/or services

8–030

---

[21] C–64/02, ECJ, October 21, 2004, [2005] E.T.M.R. 58.

of one undertaking from those of other undertakings and "distinguish" must be understood in that way.[22] The attribute of a trade mark which gives it the necessary ability to "distinguish" is its distinctive character, but the assessment of distinctive character is really an assessment of whether the sign/trade mark can distinguish in the sense just mentioned.

8–031   Problems arise if "distinguish" is used or understood more loosely. The examples given below demonstrate that "distinguish" can be and has been used to mean different things. First, there is the correct meaning: see the citations from the ECJ judgments set out above.

8–032   Second, "distinguish" can be used in the sense of "different". This meaning often creeps into cases involving the shapes of goods or their packaging, where the applicant frequently argues to this effect: "my mark has (the minimum degree of) distinctive character because it can clearly be distinguished from others in the market." This type of argument is utterly bogus. It amounts to nothing more than saying that "my mark is different". Deployment of this type of argument is a clear sign that the mark does not have distinctive character.

8–033   Third, "distinguish" or "distinctive" is used in the sense of "standing out", likely to attract the attention of the consumer. This is a slight variation on "different", in that the mark is now adjudged to be sufficiently different such that it attracts the attention of the consumer. However, there are many things which will attract the attention of the consumer (bright or garish colours, snazzy graphics, bold claims) which have nothing to do with distinctive character. The usefulness of this concept depends entirely on whether the consumer's attention is attracted in the right 'trade-origin message' manner.

8–034   Fourth, "distinguish" is used in the "recognition" sense. Again, this may be only a slight variant on the above, but it has a greater aura of respectability because it involves the average consumer. Thus, the applicant argues to this effect: "my mark has distinctive character because the average consumer would recognise it, thereby enabling him or her to repeat the purchasing experience if positive or avoid it if negative." The CFI has correctly rejected recognition as being sufficient in some cases, e.g.:

> "49. The fact that consumers may get into the habit of recognising such a product from its get up is not enough to preclude the ground for refusal based on Article 7(1)(b) of the Regulation." Unilever v OHIM.[23]

8–035   The "recognition" argument presupposes (illegitimately) that education of the public through use has already commenced to some unknown degree. If a mark does possess inherent distinctive character, it should convey the trade origin message immediately when first encountered.[24]

8–036   It may be thought that these points about the proper meaning of "distinguish" are or should be obvious. The ECJ has been consistent in its interpretation. In the UK, these points were clearly identified by Laddie J. in Yakult,[25] where the application was to register the shape of a bottle:

> "At all times the Registry has to ask whether the design is distinctive as a badge of origin. The exercise to be undertaken was described by the European Court of Justice in Lloyd Schuhfabrik Meyer & Co GmbH v. Klijsen Handel BV [2000] F.S.R. 77; Case C–342/97, [1999] E.C.R. I-3819:

---

[22] For further detail, see the start of Ch.2.

[23] Case T–194/01.

[24] Mag Instrument, para.50, cited at para.8–027.

[25] Yakult Honsha KK's Trade Mark Application [2001] R.P.C. 39, p.756 at pp.758–9.

"In determining the distinctive character of a mark ... the national court must make an overall assessment of the greater or lesser capacity of the mark to identify the goods or services for which it has been registered as coming from a particular undertaking, and thus to distinguish those goods or services from those of other undertakings ..." (para.22).

9. In my view the same point was made even more succinctly by Lloyd J. in *Dualit Ltd's (Toaster Shapes) Trade Mark Applications* [1999] R.P.C. 890, a case concerning an application to register the shape of an electric toaster as a trade mark:

"... does [the mark] have a meaning denoting the origin of the goods?" (p.897).

10. Where inherent distinctiveness is concerned, the Registry has to find that the mark performs the function of identifying origin even before the public is educated that it is so used for that purpose. Where invented, non-descriptive word marks are concerned, it may be easy to come to such a finding. But where a container is in issue it may well be much more difficult. As [Counsel for the Applicant] rightly conceded, the fact that a container is unusual or attractive does not, per se, mean that it will be taken by the public as an indication of origin. The relevant question is not whether the container would be recognised on being seen a second time, that is to say, whether it is of memorable appearance, but whether by itself its appearance would convey trade mark significance to the average customer. For the purpose of this appeal, I am prepared to accept that the bottle shape which is the subject of these applications is both new and visually distinctive, meaning that it would be recognised as different to other bottles on the market. That does not mean that it is inherently distinctive in a trade mark sense."

However, there are now numerous examples which demonstrate, if proof were **8–037** needed, why a proper understanding of distinctive character is essential. In addition to the general approach of the CFI to Art.7(1)(b) as set out above,[26] a review of appellate decisions on applications to register the shapes of bottles at OHIM provides an indication of the scale of the problem. The tip of the metaphorical iceberg comprises the CFI judgments in *Shape of a bottle (Nestlé Waters France)*[27] and *Shape of a white and transparent bottle (Henkel)*.[28] Beneath the water there lie many OHIM Board of Appeal decisions on applications to register the shapes of bottles and jars. To be fair, more have been rejected[29] under Art.7(1)(b) than accepted and at least the OHIM Boards of Appeal rejected the Nestlé Waters France plastic water bottle[30] and the Henkel white shampoo bottle. However, the ones which the OHIM Boards of Appeal have allowed through cause concern. They were found to possess sufficient inherent distinctive character because the consumer would have the shape of the bottle or jar in question "in the mind as a specific manufacturer's trade mark." The shapes in question were: Granini bottle;[31] a clear glass bottle with a waist and some bobbles;[32] a

---

[26] See paras 8–028 to 8–029.
[27] Case T–305/02, December 3, 2003.
[28] Case T–393/02, November 24, 2004.
[29] For some recent examples, see R–66/2004-1 (Heinz sauce bottle), R–490/2003-2 (Limonadenflasche), R–267/2003-2 (Plastikflaschenform), R–792/2002-1 (Flasche mit Langsrillen).
[30] R–719/2000-4.
[31] R–139/1999-1, August 4, 1999.

feeding bottle;[33] Nescafé jar;[34] the Galliano bottle;[35] the José Cuervo bottle (Bottle with Striations)[36] and a perfume bottle.[37]

8–038   A glance at the bottles and jars in question indicates the muddled thinking. What appears to have happened is that a Board of Appeal recognised that one or more of these bottles or jars had been used for some time and hence reached the conclusion that the public was able to recognise the shape in question. For Art.7(1)(b), they should have considered the position absent use. A further possible influence might have been the attitude, emanating from Germany, that it is now time that the law recognised shapes of bottles as trade marks because by granting protection to three-dimensional trade marks, consumers will then become accustomed to the fact that such marks indicate origin.[38] Such a view puts the cart firmly before the horse. In reality, none of these bottles or jars has inherent distinctive character. In use, they always carry a label bearing the real trade mark for those goods. We do not say that it is impossible for goods to bear more than one trade mark, but the reality is that none of the applicants for these marks use or trust the shape as an indication of origin. They can only acquire distinctive character after many years of use. Most of them can only aspire to recognition on the part of the consumer, which, as pointed out above,[39] is not enough for distinctive character.

2.4 WHAT AMOUNT OF DISTINCTIVE CHARACTER IS REQUIRED?

8–039   Apart from "enough", there is no easy answer to this question. For any given mark it is impossible to state how much distinctive character is required to overcome an Art.3(1)(b)/7(1)(b) objection and, for obvious reasons, no-one can ever give a concrete answer to this question, not even the ECJ. The reasons are fairly obvious. Assessment of distinctive character is not an exact science, it requires a judgement to be made based on all relevant factors. It is the type of multi-factorial assessment which is not susceptible of an appeal unless the assessment displays an error of principle.

8–040   The problem is that, however much that appeals to the CFI and further appeals or references to the ECJ are said only to involve points of law, their decisions nonetheless do contain, on occasion, guidance on what amount of distinctive character is sufficient to overcome these objections, whether the Court intended to give that guidance or whether it is inferred from the decision or the reasoning of the Court.

DECISIONS OF THE ECJ

8–041   There are three decisions of the ECJ which, in our view, set the hurdle too low for the amount of distinctive character required to overcome one of the Art.3(1)/ 7(1) objections. They are BABY-DRY, SAT.2 and DAS PRINZIP. What these

---

[32] R–205/1998-2, November 17, 1999.
[33] R–337/2000-1, December 19, 2000.
[34] R–739/1999-1, February 13, 2001.
[35] R–537/1999-2, March 21, 2001.
[36] R–321/2000-3, April 4, 2001.
[37] R–476/2001-3, August 7, 2001.
[38] See the paper given by the President at the Bundesgerichtshof, Prof. Dr. Eike Ullmann, at the Third European Trade Mark Judges' Symposium held at OHIM in September 2003. His paper is available on the OHIM website as "Ullmann TR EN revised.pdf".
[39] See para.8–034.

judgments have in common is the fact that the ECJ substituted its own assessment of the facts and each one was flawed. The flaws in BABY-DRY are well-known and are discussed in greater detail below under s.3(1)(c).[40] The flaw in SAT.2[41] lies in the introduction in para.44 of the factual proposition that "The frequent use of trade marks consisting of a word and a number in the telecommunications sector indicates that that type of combination [*i.e.* SAT.2] cannot be considered to be devoid, in principle, of distinctive character." Presumably this was a reference to the fact that broadcasters throughout the EU use acronyms comprising three letters together with numbers to indicate their different channels. The three-letter acronyms are distinctive because of extensive use and because they are acronyms and not simple abbreviations of descriptive terms. They form no basis for concluding that SAT.2 possesses inherent distinctive character for a satellite channel. So far as DAS PRINZIP DER BEQUEMLICHKEIT is concerned, for furniture, it is difficult to comprehend how the laudatory expression "The Comfort Principle" for furniture could possibly be said to possess *inherent* distinctive character.[42]

DECISIONS OF THE CFI

We have already mentioned decisions of the CFI where a very low hurdle for distinctive character has led to shapes of bottles passing Art.7(1)(b) objections. Even where the CFI reaches the right result, there are indications that a very low hurdle for distinctive character is set. See, for example: **8–042**

> "Article 7(1)(b) of Regulation No 40/94 requires the examiner and, in appropriate cases, the Board of Appeal, to examine—by an a priori examination and without reference to any actual use of the sign for the purposes of Article 7(3) of Regulation No 40/94—whether there appears to be <u>no possibility</u> that the sign may be capable of distinguishing, in the eyes of the relevant public, the products or services in question from those of a different origin, when that public will be called upon to make its choice in commerce (Case T–87/00 *Bank für Arbeit und Wirtschaft v OHIM (EASYBANK)* [2001] ECR II-1259, paragraph 40)." (emphasis added). Case T–360/03 *Shape of a cheese box (Frischpack)* November 23, 2004, para.29.[43]

"MINIMUM DEGREE OF DISTINCTIVE CHARACTER"

In other judgments on Art.7(1)(b), the CFI has developed the concept that it follows from the wording in Art.3(1)(b)/7(1)(b) that "a minimum degree of distinctive character is sufficient" to overcome those grounds: see EUROCOOL and *Grille*.[44] Despite the fact that this concept has been expressly mentioned in the arguments of the parties in ECJ judgments and in the relevant passages of the CFI judgment under appeal, the ECJ appears to have studiously avoided adopting this concept. The closest the ECJ has got is in *Companyline*. In its reasoned Order dismissing the appeal as unfounded, the ECJ referred to the findings of fact at every stage of the proceedings that the sign at issue was "wholly devoid of   **8–043**

---

[40] See paras 8–083 to 8–099, especially paras 8–091, 8–093, 8–098 and 8–099.
[41] C–329/62, ECJ, September 16, 2004.
[42] C–64/02, ECJ, October 21, 2004, [2005] E.T.M.R. 58. For marks comprising slogans, the context in which the mark is assessed may account for the difference. See para.2–031.
[43] [2005] E.T.M.R. 48.
[44] Case T–34/00, *Eurocool Logistik v OHIM (EUROCOOL)* [2002] E.C.R. II-683, para.39 and Case T–128/01 *DaimlerChrysler v OHIM (Grille)* [2003] E.C.R. II-0000, paras 46 and 48.

distinctive character" and continued: "Logically, therefore, the question as to what level of distinctiveness is required for the threshold of 'minimum degree of distinctiveness' to be crossed no longer arises."[45]

8–044   In one sense, the CFI is obviously right to state that there must be a minimum degree of distinctiveness which overcomes Art.7(1)(b) or 3(1)(b). On the other hand, we believe it is no accident that the ECJ has avoided adopting this concept. The reason why this is a prudent course is because adoption of the concept immediately invites questions (prompted by applicants) designed to find out precisely where this minimum level lies. Not only are these questions impossible to answer properly, but they are probably the wrong question in any event. Indeed, the ECJ has stated (COMPANYLINE, para.20)[46] that there is no obligation when determining whether a mark is objectionable under Art.3(1)(b)/7(1)(b) to rule on the possible dividing line between the concept of lack of distinctiveness and that of minimum distinctiveness. It may also be noted how the "minimum degree of distinctiveness" is re-interpreted into the "minimal" degree of distinctiveness required to overcome Art.7(1)(b).[47]

8–045   It could be said that the CFI reasoning is consistent with the language of Art.7(1)(b)—"devoid of any distinctive character". However, it lacks appreciation of the protective purpose of Art.7(1)(b) (or c or d), or that, before a sign can be said to possess distinctive character, it must take a step up out of the morass of non-distinctive material.

UK DECISIONS

8–046   In the UK, tribunals at various levels have refused to accept that any amount of distinctive character will do but when they have done so, it seems clear that they are putting a gloss (and conscious of it) on the language used in the Act, Directive or Regulation. For example:

> "Despite the fairly strong language of section 3(1)(b), 'devoid of any distinctive character'—and Mr Morcom emphasised the word 'any'—that provision must in my judgment be directed to a visible sign or combination of signs which can by itself readily distinguish one trader's product ... from that of another competing trader. ... An objection on those grounds cannot in my judgment be treated (in the words of Younger J. in the *Standard Woven Fabric* case (1918) 35 R.P.C. 53 at 58) as being on 'grounds which were fanciful and which, in a business sense, were insubstantial'. On the contrary, any objection on those grounds would be a practical and businesslike objection.": *per* Robert Walker L.J. in Procter & Gamble's Trade Mark Application.[48]

8–047   The problem is that the more the CFI uses the concept of the "minimum degree

---

[45] Case C–104/00, *DKV Deutsche Krankenversicherung AG v OHIM* (COMPANYLINE) [2002] E.C.R. I-7561; [2003] E.T.M.R. 20, para.18.
[46] Case C–104/00 [2002] E.C.R. I-7561; [2003] E.T.M.R. 20.
[47] See DAS PRINZIP, para.31. Case C–64/02 ECJ, October 21, 2004, [2005] E.T.M.R. 58.
[48] [1999] R.P.C. 673 at 679 and 680–681. See also (1) *British Sugar v James Robertson & Sons* [1996] R.P.C. 281 at 306, Jacob J. Note that the words "distinctive" and "inherently" appear to have been mistakenly transposed in the report. (2) *Philips v Remington* [1999] R.P.C. 809 at 819, Aldous L.J.

of distinctiveness required", the more likely it is that national courts are persuaded that any extent of distinctive character is sufficient.[49]

THE POTENTIAL PUZZLE

The wording used in Sections/Arts 3(1)(b), (c) & (d) appears, at first sight, to set an absolute and very low requirement for distinctive character: "*devoid* of *any* distinctive character*" and "trade marks which consist *exclusively*" of, essentially non-distinctive signs or indications. Faced with this language, applicants have argued repeatedly that they need only show a scintilla of distinctive character in order to overcome these hurdles and/or that the hurdle is very low.

8–048

Underlying many of the arguments put forward by applicants seeking to overcome Art.7(1)(b)/3(1)(b) grounds is the beguiling notion that there is a sliding scale of distinctiveness from, say, 0 to 100, where 100 is wholly distinctive and 0 is wholly devoid of distinctive character/wholly descriptive/completely generic. The notion of a scale of distinctiveness can be useful to explain how a mark may be distinctive yet also convey a message which is descriptive of the goods or services in question,[50] and also how the message conveyed by a mark may change over time. This notion can be mis-used. Applicants like the concept of a sliding scale because they can argue that a low score of 1, 2, 3, x etc must be sufficient to overcome these absolute grounds. If the tribunal or Court then says, well, a minimum degree of distinctive character is more than x, then the applicant argues his mark is just over that minimum level. This type of argument is essentially bogus and there are two ways to explain why.

8–049

First, this "sliding scale" argument ignores the fact that marks below the borderline set by these absolute grounds suffer from a disability or inertia. In truth, the only way to overcome such disability or inertia is through the correct type of use on a substantial scale so that the public are educated to understand the mark conveys an origin message. The "sliding scale" argument allows the disability or inertia to be ignored, and this is illegitimate.

8–050

Second, if the "sliding scale" notion is adopted, it should be recognised that it works down to a notional point, but then there is a cliff or step. Marks with sufficient inherent distinctive character are able to step up out of the morass of non-distinctive matter.[51]

The further point is that the assessment of distinctive character has to be undertaken through the eyes of the average consumer of the goods or services in question. The average consumer test itself contains a threshold, in this sense: an applicant may be able to show that a small proportion of people do understand his mark to convey an origin message, but that is not sufficient to show that the average consumer would so understand the mark.

8–051

These considerations in fact provide the answer as to why the absolute grounds

8–052

---

[49] See, for example, the CA in HAVE A BREAK [2003] EWCA 1072, para.23, where they stated: "If the mark for which registration is sought is distinctive in the relevant sense to any extent then its registration is not precluded by s.3(1)(b)." (emphasis added, probably the result of the earlier reference to the CFI judgment in *Grille*, see above).

[50] see, *e.g.* Jacob J. in *Philips* and Jacob L.J. in *Bongrain S.A. (Shape of cheese)* [2004] EWCA 1690, CA, December 17, 2004, at para.26. [2005] R.P.C. 14; [2005] E.T.M.R. 47.

[51] That, again, emphasises that there is a borderline that has to be crossed if the mark is to acquire the distinctiveness required to evade s.3(1)(b). The distinctiveness must be sufficient not merely to show that the product is different; it has to go further and demonstrate the trade origin of the product. This borderline cannot of course be defined. Assessing whether a mark has crossed it is a matter of judgment in each case.

are expressed as they are. They do not need to be expressed or interpreted in terms of a minimum level of distinctive character because of the nature of distinctive character. It carries with it its own threshold.

8–053   Many of the problems caused by setting too low a standard for distinctive character could be overcome if the ECJ were to state clearly that the basic requirement for registration of any mark is that it must possess a distinctive character, whether inherent or acquired.

3. Interplay between the grounds in section 3(1) and common principles

INTERPLAY

8–054   The interplay between and the role of the grounds in s.3(1)/Art.3(1)/Art.7(1) have been the subject of many judgments of the ECJ. As regards interplay, the principles were conveniently and succinctly summarised in certain paragraphs in the BAR-X case.[52] For ease of reference, the footnotes in the Judgment are set out in brackets:

"11. The case law of the European Court of Justice confirms that:"

...

(3) each ground for refusal or invalidity operates independently of the others and calls for separate examination (POSTKANTOOR, paras 67 & 85);

(4) the applicability of any one of the specified grounds is sufficient to prevent registration (COMPANYLINE, para 29);

(5) the inapplicability of one ground may coincide with the applicability of another (POSTKANTOOR, para 69);

(6) a mark can accordingly be devoid of any distinctive character for the purposes of Article 3(1)(b) (Section 3(1)(b) of the Act) without also being unduly descriptive for the purposes of Article 3(1)(c) (Section 3(1)(c) of the Act) (POSTKANTOOR, para 70, BIOMILD, para 19);

(7) however, a mark which is unduly descriptive for the purposes of Article 3(1)(c) (Section 3(1)(c) of the Act) is necessarily devoid of distinctive character for the purposes of Article 3(1)(b) (Section 3(1)(b) of the Act) (BIOMILD, para.19);"

COMMON PRINCIPLES

8–055   (A) The relevant attributes of the mark (distinctive character etc.) must be assessed by reference to the goods or services in respect of which registration is sought. (POSTKANTOOR, para.33)

(B) The assessment must be of the mark as a whole.

(C) The assessment must be carried out applying the perception of the average consumer for the goods or services in question.

---

[52] *Electrocoin Automatics Ltd v Coinworld Ltd* [2005] F.S.R. 7, p.79, Geoffrey Hobbs Q.C. sitting as a deputy judge of the High Court, Chancery Division. We have extracted the paragraphs dealing with interplay. Paras (2), (8), (9) and (10) dealt with application, see below. As for point 1, the Judge made the point, correctly, that paras 80 & 81 of the ECJ judgment in POSTKANTOOR was authority for the proposition that " Article 2 s2(1) [sic, sc s1(1)] of the Act) defines the characteristics of 'signs of which a trade mark can consist' irrespective of the goods or services for which protection might be sought." We have questioned whether this interpretation of Art.2 is correct. See the discussion in Ch.2, at paras 2–072 onwards, especially at paras 2–092 to 2–095.

(D) Subject to the context expressed in (A) to (C), the mark is assessed absent use.

(E) Exactly the same criteria apply whatever the nature of the mark. In other words, none of these provisions draws any distinction between different categories of mark, and no category of mark is excluded from consideration. Stricter criteria must not be applied to specific categories of mark.

(F) However, the perception of the average consumer is not necessarily the same for all categories of mark. Hence, for example, it can prove more difficult to establish distinctive character in the case of a three-dimensional mark comprising the shape of the goods or their packaging, than in the case of a word or figurative mark (*Shape of detergent bottle (Henkel)*, para.52).

ASSESSING THE MARK AS A WHOLE

Principles (A) to (C) deserve some further discussion, not least because there are numerous examples of tribunals being found to have committed a reviewable error in their assessment of marks which comprise a combination of elements. For such marks, it is normal and permissible for a tribunal to examine the constituent elements of such a mark, provided that it then goes on to assess the whole. It is only the assessment of the whole which matters, anything else is secondary. Care is required in the way in which the tribunal expresses its findings, and in particular, the way in which it moves from interim findings on individual constituent elements to its principal assessment of the mark as a whole. For example, if the assessment of the whole is based too closely on merely the sum of views concerning constituent elements, a reviewing tribunal may detect an error of law, as the ECJ did in SAT.2, finding that the CFI had based itself on a presumption that elements individually devoid of distinctive character cannot, on being combined, present such a character.[53] The point here is that "each mark must be assessed as a whole" is a corollary of the notion that "The average consumer normally perceives a mark as a whole and does not proceed to analyse its various details."[54] Thus, whilst the tribunal can examine the constituent elements as a step in its analysis, it must then take a step back from the detail, consciously adopt the perception of the average consumer and assess the mark as a whole—a global assessment. As a practical matter, it will usually but not invariably[55] be the case that a mark which comprises merely a combination of elements, each of which is devoid of distinctive character or descriptive, will be found, as a whole, to be devoid of distinctive character, unless the combination itself is more than the sum of its parts.   **8–056**

Not surprisingly, the ECJ has made it clear that the obligation to assess the mark as a whole (particularly where the mark comprises a number of elements)   **8–057**

---

[53] Although the reasoning of the CFI revealed other errors (such as the use of the "commonly used" test—see below), on this point the ECJ was a little over-critical, probably because they thought that SAT.2 possessed inherent distinctive character for a satellite TV channel. See our criticism at para.8–041.

[54] *Sabel v Puma* [1997] E.C.R. I-6191; [1998] R.P.C. 199; [1998] E.T.M.R. 1, para.24, *Lloyd Schuhfabrik* [1999] E.C.R. I-3819; [2000] F.S.R. 77; [1999] E.T.M.R. 690, para.18.

[55] See SAT.2.

applies whether Art.3(1)(b)/7(1)(b) is being considered or 3(1)(c)/7(1)(c).[56] The same must also apply to 3(1)(d)/7(1)(d).

THE ORDER IN WHICH THE GROUNDS ARE APPLIED

8–058   For convenience, we discuss the grounds in s.3(1)/Art.3(1)/Art.7(1) in the order in which they appear in the legislation. In practice, s.3(1)(a) and equivalents have been sidelined, perhaps wrongly as we discuss below. The logical order in which to consider the other grounds in practice is in reverse order, for the following reasons:

> First, as a matter of general interpretation, 3(1)(d)/7(1)(d) and 3(1)(c)/7(1)(c) deal with particular situations whereas each of 3(1)(b) & 7(1)(b) is a general, "sweep-up" provision;
>
> Second, this is how courts and tribunals naturally approach these provisions in practice. The grounds of objection under 3(1)(d)/7(1)(d) and 3(1)(c)/7(1)(c) have more concrete subject-matter than 3(1)(b)/7(1)(b);
>
> Third, a practice of leaving 3(1)(b)/7(1)(b) until last helps to prevent situations where a mark manages to escape (*e.g.* on appeal) an objection under either 3(1)(c)/7(1)(c) or 3(1)(d)/7(1)(d) yet, for procedural reasons, does not face a properly sustainable objection under 3(1)(b)/7(1)(b).[57]
>
> Fourth, again, a practice of leaving a proper examination under 3(1)(b)/7(1)(b) until last is particularly desirable in cases where the mark just manages to escape objections under 3(1)(c)/7(1)(c) or 3(1)(d)/7(1)(d) because they do not comprise descriptive or generic matter *exclusively*. At this point, the tribunal needs to consider, as a separate matter, whether the mark as a whole possesses any or sufficient distinctive character to escape 3(1)(b)/7(1)(b). Although it depends on the facts of each case, in many cases the mark will not. Unfortunately, there are numerous examples of cases where the fact that a mark has escaped a c or d objection is taken as determining that the mark possesses sufficient distinctive character to escape 3(1)(b)/7(1)(b). This is discussed in further detail below.

4. Section 3(1)(a), Article 3(1)(a), Article 7(1)(a)

8–059   "s.3—(1) The following shall not be registered:

(a) signs which do not satisfy the requirements of section 1(1)"

DERIVATION

8–060   Article 3(1)(a) of the TM Directive uses the words "signs which cannot constitute a trade mark". Despite the difference in wording, s.3(1)(a) clearly can be and should be interpreted to have the same meaning as the provision in the Directive. Hence, it is suggested there is no difference in meaning. Either way, a sign which does not qualify as a "trade mark" shall not be registered.

8–061   Section 3(1) of the 1994 Act is concerned with the fundamental issue of distinctiveness—the essential function of a trade mark. Notwithstanding the structure and wording of s.3(1), it is suggested that it sets out a simple and fundamental requirement which any sign must fulfil before it can properly be

---

[56] See the references in SAT.2, para.28 to BIOMILD, paras 40, 41, and POSTKANTOOR, paras 99, 100.

[57] At first sight, BABY-DRY might be considered an example. However, the reasoning of the ECJ in relation to 7(1)(c) would have overcome an objection under 7(1)(b). Whether it should have done so is another matter, discussed at para.8–088.

registered as a trade mark. The requirement is that the sign must possess a distinctive character, inherent or acquired, so that it can carry out the essential function of a trade mark which is to distinguish the goods or services of one undertaking from those of other undertakings. However, the structure and wording of s.3(1) serve to obscure this point in two ways. First, the individual grounds are not mutually exclusive with the result there is much overlap. Secondly, each of the grounds is expressed negatively, the only positive requirements being contained in the proviso, a provision which applies only in limited circumstances, and (via s.3(1)) in s.1(1). These may also be reasons why the interpretation of s.3(1)(a) and (b)/Art.3(1)(a) and (b) has proved to be less than straightforward.

There can be no dispute that s.3(1) contains a positive requirement that, to be **8–062** eligible for registration, a sign must possess a distinctive character, inherent or acquired. The issue is where that positive requirement is to be found in the statutory provisions.

It is clear that if a mark possesses inherent distinctive character, it will avoid **8–063** subss.(1)(b), (c) and (d) of s.3. Accordingly, it is possible to say that those provisions impose a positive requirement for an inherent distinctive character, even though this is normally done purely by reference to s.3(1)(b) and its equivalents.[58] If s.3(1)(b) is the only source of this positive requirement, it is strange that this vital characteristic of any trade mark is left to be implied from negative prohibition(s), particularly when one of the Recitals to the TM Directive draws particular attention to the requirement that a mark is "capable of distinguishing".

In Ch.2, it is suggested that the "capable of distinguishing" requirement in **8–064** s.1(1) imposes the positive requirement for registrability that a trade mark must possess a distinctive character. Section 1(1) and its equivalents say nothing about whether the distinctive character is inherent or acquired. Those provisions do not care, as long as the sign will serve to distinguish when put to use. This may be the reason why s.3(1)(a) and its equivalents are not subject to the proviso/Art.3(2)/Art.7(2) regarding acquired distinctiveness.

There is no clear answer to the puzzle, but we suggest that this interpretation **8–065** makes the best sense of ss.1 and 3/Arts 1 and 3/Arts 4 and 7. Instead of being sidelined, because of the puzzle it created, s.3(1)(a) is possibly the most important absolute ground of all because it carries the overreaching requirement that a sign must serve to distinguish when put to use in relation to the goods or services for which it is registered. The fact that grounds (b), (c) and (d) then examine distinctiveness from other angles is no obstacle to this approach. It just means that on the essential issue of distinctiveness, the Directive and CTM Regulation take a belt-and-braces approach.

It should, perhaps, be emphasised that the assessment of distinctive character **8–066** of most trade marks is a straightforward process. One can see they have a degree of inherent distinctive character which is the foundation for additional distinctive character acquired through use. Most of this discussion is concerned with signs which have problems qualifying as trade marks. There are a number of reasons why it will continue to be necessary to examine these problem signs with care:

(1) the enduring reason: "Wealthy traders are habitually eager to enclose part

---

[58] See, *e.g. Windsurfing* [1999] E.T.M.R. 585, para.46; *Philips v Remington* [1999] R.P.C. 809 at 819.

of the great common of the English language and to exclude the general public of the present day and of the future from access to the enclosure.";[59]

(2) with the open-ended concept of "sign", the enclosure sought is not confined to matters of language but extends to all features of goods or their packaging;

(3) the advent of the (partially) harmonised law of trade marks represented by the 1994 Act and the TM Directive generated the perception that it is easier to secure registration than previously. Early experience of OHIM strongly contributed to this perception, but there are signs that practice at OHIM is becoming more consistent;

(4) the pressure to employ relatively descriptive marks is probably increasing. The consumer is bombarded with marks. In this environment, the trader wants to get his message across quickly, which means that the characteristic of the goods or services which the trader wishes to emphasise is often more or less directly described in a mark. At the same time, the trader must distance his product or service from those of his competitors, so he wishes to prevent others using the same or similar mark, no matter how descriptive it is. This is not something confined to wealthy traders.

(9) a mark that initially lacked the distinctive character required for registration can be or remain registered under Article 3(3) (the provisos to Sections 3(1) and 47(1) of the Act) if it is found to have acquired a distinctive character through use (*Philips*, para.58);

(10) a mark does not have to be universally distinctive in order to be registrable: it is sufficient for it to be distinctive according to the perceptions and recollections of a significant proportion of the relevant class of persons (*Philips*, paras 59–61)."

5. Section 3(1)(b)/Article 3(1)(b), Article 7(1)(b) CTMR: non-distinctive marks

8–067   "s.3—(1) The following shall not be registered:

(b) trade marks which are devoid of any distinctive character"

DERIVATION

8–068   The words used in section 3(1)(b) are identical to those used in Article 3(1)(b) of the TM Directive and Article 7(1)(b) of the CTM Regulation. In fact, the trio of provisions in (b), (c) and (d) derive from Article 6*quinquies* B.2 of the Paris Convention.

COMMENTARY

8–069   This section is short, for two reasons. First, because all the discussion has already been set out above. See ss.2, 3 & 4, and for further explanation, s.6 in Ch.2. Second, in the previous edition we set out numerous examples of the application of s.3(1)(b)/Art.3(1)(b)/7(1)(b) in practice. With the present state of the law, we see no point in doing so in this edition. Applicants seize on decisions which set the lowest possible hurdle for distinctive character. We have highlighted above[60] the decisions of the ECJ which we suggest set the hurdle too low for distinctive-

---

[59] "Perfection": *Joseph Crosfield & Sons' Application* (1909) 26 R.P.C. 837 at 854, CA, *per* Cozens-Hardy M.R.
[60] See paras 8–002 and 8–041.

ness: BABY-DRY, SAT.2 and DAS PRINZIP. We have also drawn attention to the unsatisfactory reasoning in CFI judgments which indicate they set the hurdle too low: NEW BORN BABY and the shapes of bottles cases.[61]

In all of this, one has to feel for those who actually have to apply the absolute grounds, and those at the first appellate level. Whilst there are indications that the standards set by the ECJ and CFI have an effect (see, *e.g.* the shapes of bottles cases at OHIM Board of Appeal level), for the most part it appears that those actually tasked with applying absolute grounds have a good appreciation of what constitutes distinctive character and what does not.[62] They deserve clearer guidance from the higher courts.   **8–070**

5.1 Case law on the various types of mark

Even though exactly the same criteria apply whatever the nature of the mark, the average consumer's perception may (does) differ. The following judgments (principally of the ECJ) on particular types of mark demonstrate the prevailing views as to the average consumer's perception. In App.33, we provide a table listing, in chronological order, the 27 cases on absolute grounds which have so far been resolved at ECJ level, 16 of which were resolved in 2004.   **8–071**

WORD MARKS

ECJ judgments on ordinary word marks tend to be concerned with Art. 3(1)(c)/ Art 7(1)(c) and Art 3(1)(d)/Art.7(1)(d). The views of the ECJ as regards ordinary word marks for the purposes of Art 3(1)(b)/Art 7(1)(b) are usually to be found in judgments dealing with more unconventional marks, which proceed on the basis that the average consumer is accustomed to making assumptions about the origin of products when he or she sees a word mark (which is not descriptive or generic) or, for that matter, a figurative mark. In this regard, the context in which the mark is assessed is all-important. The in-built assumption[63] seems to be that word and figurative marks will be seen by the average consumer in the place on the goods where they normally expect to see a trade mark.   **8–072**

Surnames—Nichols

In *Nichols*,[64] the ECJ stated: **8–073**

> "25. The criteria for assessment of the distinctive character of trade marks constituted by a personal name are therefore the same as those applicable to the other categories of trade mark.
>
> 26. Stricter general criteria of assessment based, for example, on:
> — a predetermined number of persons with the same name, above which that name may be regarded as devoid of distinctive character,
> — the number of undertakings providing products or services of the type covered by the application for registration, or
> — the prevalence or otherwise of the use of surnames in the relevant trade,

cannot be applied to such trade marks.

---

[61] See paras 8–028, 8–029 and 8–037.
[62] See a prime example in WHITENING MULTI-ACTION, OHIM Second BoA, R–118/2003–2, [2004] E.T.M.R. 98.
[63] See para.2–031.
[64] Case C–404/02, September 16, 2004; [2005] R.P.C. 12.

27. The distinctive character of a trade mark, in whatever category, must be the subject of a specific assessment."

The judgment of the ECJ does not provide a great deal of guidance and leaves TM Registries with a difficult judgment.

SLOGANS

8–074   There have been numerous attempts to register slogans as trade marks. Again, the ECJ has emphasised that the criteria for assessment of the distinctive character of slogans are no different to those applicable to other categories of mark.[65] One has to wonder whether concentration on this principle has diverted attention away from the fact that slogans usually suffer from a disability from a trade mark point of view—they are usually laudatory about some aspect or quality of the goods or services, as the CFI noted in MEHR FÜR IHR GELD:[66]

"25. However, registration of a trade mark which consists of signs or indications that are also used as advertising slogans, indications of quality or incitements to purchase the goods or services covered by that mark is not excluded as such by virtue of such use (see, by analogy, *Merz & Krell*, cited above, paragraph 40). A sign which fulfils functions other than that of a trade mark in the traditional sense of the term is only distinctive for the purposes of Article 7(1)(b) of Regulation No 40/94 however if it may be perceived immediately as an indication of the commercial origin of the goods or services in question, so as to enable the relevant public to distinguish, without any possibility of confusion, the goods or services of the owner of the mark from those of a different commercial origin (BEST BUY, cited above, paragraph 21)."

SHAPE MARKS—COMPRISING THE PRODUCT ITSELF OR ITS PACKAGING

8–075   The development of the ECJ's thinking can be traced through the various judgments[67] which have dealt with marks comprising the shape of goods or their packaging.[68] The culmination is in paras 29-32 of Mag Instrument (Shape of torch):[69]

"29. For a trade mark to possess distinctive character for the purposes of Article 7(1)(b) of Regulation No 40/94, it must serve to identify the goods or services in respect of which registration is applied for as originating from a particular undertaking, and thus to distinguish the goods or services from

---

[65] See Case C–64/02 DAS PRINZIP DER BEQUEMLICHKEIT, ECJ, October 21, 2004 at paras 42–44.

[66] Case T–128/02, CFI, June 30, 2004. MEHR FÜR IHR GELD means "More for your money". To similar effect are various CFI cases involving slogans like: REAL PEOPLE, REAL SOLUTIONS (Case T–130/01, [2002] E.C.R. II-5179, [2003] E.T.M.R. 57); BEST BUY (Case T–122/01, CFI, July 3, 2003, [2004] E.T.M.R. 19–actually a case about a figurative mark comprising a label with the words BEST BUY).

[67] Cases C–53/01–55/01, *Linde (Shape of forklift truck, torch, watch)* [2003] E.C.R.I-3161, [2003] R.P.C.45; Case C–218/01, *Henkel (Shape of detergent bottle)* [2004] E.C.R. I-0000; Cases C–456/01, 468/01, 472/01, *Henkel v OHIM, Procter & Gamble v OHIM (Shape of detergent tablets)* [2004] E.C.R. I-0000; [2004] E.T.M.R 87 & 88; Case C–107/03, *Procter & Gamble v OHIM (Shape of waisted soap bar)*, ECJ, September 29, 2004.

[68] The same considerations apply to a design applied to the surface of goods: Case C–445/02 , *Glaverbel (Glass Pattern)*, Order of the ECJ, June 28, 2004. The exception (which proves the rule) is the CFI judgment in Case T–128/01, *DaimlerChrysler v OHIM (Grille)* [2003] E.C.R. II-701, [2003] E.T.M.R. 87, where a figurative mark comprising a drawing of a Jeep grille was held to have sufficient distinctive character to avoid Art.7(1)(b). The decision was based on expert evidence that vehicle grilles are used to identify makes of car.

[69] Case C–136/02, ECJ, October 7, 2004. The references to *Henkel v OHIM* are to C–457/01, one of the shape of detergent tablet cases.

those of other undertakings (see *Henkel v OHIM*, paragraph 34 and the case-law cited there).

30. The criteria for assessing the distinctive character of three-dimensional marks consisting of the shape of the product itself are no different from those applicable to other categories of trade mark. None the less, for the purpose of applying those criteria, the relevant public's perception is not necessarily the same in the case of a three-dimensional mark consisting of the shape of the product itself as it is in the case of a word or figurative mark consisting of a sign which is independent from the appearance of the products it denotes. Average consumers are not in the habit of making assumptions about the origin of products on the basis of their shape or the shape of their packaging in the absence of any graphic or word element and it could therefore prove more difficult to establish distinctiveness in relation to such a three-dimensional mark than in relation to a word or figurative mark (see *Henkel v OHIM*, paragraph 38 and the case-law cited there).

31. In those circumstances, the more closely the shape for which registration is sought resembles the shape most likely to be taken by the product in question, the greater the likelihood of the shape being devoid of any distinctive character for the purposes of Article 7(1)(b) of Regulation No 40/94. Only a mark which departs significantly from the norm or customs of the sector and thereby fulfils its essential function of indicating origin, is not devoid of any distinctive character for the purposes of that provision (see, to that effect, *Henkel v OHIM*, paragraph 39 and the case-law cited there).

32. Therefore, contrary to what the appellant submits, where a three-dimensional mark is constituted by the shape of the product for which registration is sought, the mere fact that that shape is a 'variant' of a common shape of that type of product is not sufficient to establish that the mark is not devoid of any distinctive character for the purposes of Article 7(1)(b) of Regulation No 40/94. It must always be determined whether such a mark permits the average consumer of that product, who is reasonably well informed and reasonably observant and circumspect, to distinguish the product concerned from those of other undertakings without conducting an analytical examination and without paying particular attention."

Although marks comprising the shape of goods or their packaging are usually **8–076** dealt with under Arts 3(1)(b)/7(1)(b), there is nothing which in principle excludes the application of Arts 3(1)(c)/7(1)(c) or 3(1)(d)/7(1)(d). The ECJ emphasised this point in *Linde*.[70]

SINGLE COLOURS AND COLOUR COMBINATIONS

"65. The perception of the relevant public is not necessarily the same in the **8–077** case of a sign consisting of a colour *per se* as it is in the case of a word or figurative mark consisting of a sign that bears no relation to the appearance of the goods it denotes. While the public is accustomed to perceiving word or figurative marks instantly as signs identifying the commercial origin of the goods, the same is not necessarily true where the sign forms part of the look of the goods in respect of which registration of the sign as a trade mark is sought. Consumers are not in the habit of making assumptions about the

---

[70] Case C–53/01, ECJ, April 8, 2003, [2003] E.C.R. I-3161; [2003] R.P.C. 45; [2003] E.T.M.R. 78, see paras 63 to 77, especially para.69.

origin of goods based on their colour or the colour of their packaging, in the absence of any graphic or word element, because as a rule a colour per se is not, in current commercial practice, used as a means of identification. A colour *per se* is not normally inherently capable of distinguishing the goods of a particular undertaking.

66. In the case of a colour *per se*, distinctiveness without any prior use is inconceivable save in exceptional circumstances, and particularly where the number of goods or services for which the mark is claimed is very restricted and the relevant market very specific." *Libertel*[71]

In *Libertel*, the mark comprised the colour orange for telecommunications services.[72] The later judgment of the ECJ in *Heidelberger BauChemie*, dealing with a colour combination of blue and yellow was even stronger:[73]

"37. As regards the question whether, for the purposes of this provision, colours or combinations of colours are capable of distinguishing the goods or services of one undertaking from those of other undertakings, it must be determined whether or not those colours or combinations of colours are capable of conveying precise information, particularly as regards the origin of a product or service.

38. It follows from paragraphs 40, 41 and 65 to 67 of Libertel that, whilst colours are capable of conveying certain associations of ideas, and of arousing feelings, they possess little inherent capacity for communicating specific information, especially since they are commonly and widely used, because of their appeal, in order to advertise and market goods or services, without any specific message.

39. Save in exceptional cases, colours do not initially have a distinctive character, but may be capable of acquiring such character as the result of the use made of them in relation to the goods or services claimed."

FIGURATIVE MARKS

6. Section 3(1)(c)/Article 3(1)(c), Article 7(1)(c) CTMR: descriptive marks

8–078   "s.3—(1) The following shall not be registered:

(c) trade marks which consist exclusively of signs or indications which may serve, in trade, to designate the kind, quality, quantity, intended purpose, value, geographical origin, the time of production of goods or of rendering of services, or other characteristics of goods or services".

DERIVATION

8–079   The wording in subs.(c) is identical to that used in Article 3(1)(c) of the Directive and Article 7(1)(c) of the CTM Regulation. Ultimately, it derives from Article 6*quinquies* B.2 of the Paris Convention.

---

[71] Case C–104/01, ECJ, May 6, 2003, [2003] E.C.R. I-3793; [2004] Ch.83, [2004] F.S.R. 4; [2003] E.T.M.R. 63.
[72] See also Case C–447/02, *KWS Saat (Orange for seeds)*, ECJ, October 21, 2004.
[73] Case C–49/02, ECJ, June 24, 2004.

Purpose

The purpose of this ground of objection is to prevent the registration of signs which are descriptive of the goods or services or some characteristic of them. These descriptive marks are excluded from registration because they consist of signs or indications which honest traders either use or may wish to use without any improper motive.[74]   **8–080**

6.1 Established principles

The ECJ has now considered Art.3(1)(c) and its equivalent Art.7(1)(c) in a number of judgments, namely CHIEMSEE,[75] BABY-DRY,[76] Linde,[77] DOUBLE-MINT,[78] POSTKANTOOR,[79] BIOMILD,[80] and reasoned Orders, namely UNIVERSAL TELEFONBUCH[81] and STREAMSERVE.[82]   **8–081**

The following principles now appear to be clear: **8–082**

(1) Art.3(1)(c)/7(1)(c) are in the public interest, to ensure that descriptive terms may be freely used by all (DOUBLEMINT, para.31; POSTKANTOOR, para.68). Recently, the ECJ has taken to referring to the "general interest" underlying the provisions in 3(1)/7(1), rather than the public interest.[83]

(2) It is not necessary that such descriptive terms are actually in use, it is sufficient that such signs and indications could be used to designate a characteristic of the goods or services (DOUBLEMINT, para.32; POST-KANTOOR, para.97).[84]

(3) Accordingly, a sign must be refused under these provisions if at least one of its possible meanings designates a characteristic of the goods or services concerned (DOUBLEMINT, para.32).

(4) Likewise, it is irrelevant if there are other, more usual signs or indications for designating a particular characteristic of the goods or services. These provisions do not require that the sign or indication under examination should be the only way of designating the characteristic in question (POSTKANTOOR, para.57). It is irrelevant if there are synonyms.

(5) "exclusively" requires a purposive approach.

6.2 BABY-DRY

[85]Getting to the current state of the law has not been straightforward. In particular, the development of the law on Art.3(1)(c)/7(1)(c) in particular, as well as on Art.3(1)(b)/7(1)(b), has not been assisted by the decision of the full Court of the   **8–083**

---

[74] cf. the test applied under the 1938 Act. See "W &G", *Du Cros (W&G) Ltd's Application* [1913] A.C. 624; 30 R.P.C. 660.

[75] Case C–108/97 [1999] E.C.R. I-2779; [2000] Ch. 523; [1999] E.T.M.R. 585.

[76] Case C–383/99 [2001] E.C.R. I-6251; [2002] Ch. 82; [2002] R.P.C. 17.

[77] Case C–53/01 [2003] E.C.R. I-3161; [2003] R.P.C. 45; [2003] E.T.M.R. 78.

[78] Case C–191/01 [2004] R.P.C. 18.

[79] Case C–363/99, ECJ, February 12, 2004, [2004] E.T.M.R. 78.

[80] Case C–265/00 ECJ, February 12, 2004 E.T.M.R. 58.

[81] Case C–326/01, ECJ, February 5, 2004.

[82] Case C–150/02, ECJ, February 5, 2004.

[83] See STREAMSERVE, para.25, Case C–150/02 (in relation to Art.3(1)(c)/7(1)(c)) and SAT.2, para.25, Case C–329/02 [2005] E.T.M.R. 20, (in relation to each of the grounds in Art.7.1, and hence Art.3.1).

[84] Note how use of a mark can make the situation worse: See LINKIN PARK, O–035–05, Appointed Person (R. Arnold Q.C.) February 7, 2005.

[85] Case C–383/99, *Procter and Gamble v OHIM* [2001] E.C.R. I-8251; [2002] Ch. 82; [2002] R.P.C. 17.

ECJ in BABY-DRY. It would be best if we were able simply to forget about BABY-DRY. The judgment on the merits of the appeal is of very little use: parts of it are wrong and the remainder requires substantial qualification either by reference to later ECJ judgments or in respects which the ECJ has yet to tackle. However, we cannot simply forget about BABY-DRY because the ECJ, for understandable reasons, was not willing to admit quickly that it had made a mistake. Accordingly, it is necessary to provide a proper explanation and critique of BABY-DRY.

8–084   Before analysing BABY-DRY, it helps to understand that there are essentially two ways to avoid an objection under Art.3(1)(c)/7(1)(c). (In this regard, we leave aside for later consideration the further route whereby distinctive character acquired in consequence of use means that the objection does "not apply"— Art.3(3)/7(3)):

> First, by demonstrating that the mark as a whole has sufficient inherent distinctive character, notwithstanding the presence in the mark of signs or indications which are objectionable.
>
> Second, by demonstrating that the mark has a material or tangible part to it which does not designate a characteristic of the goods or services. In other words the mark escapes objection because it does not consist *exclusively* of an objectionable sign or indication. This second route overlaps with the first if the non-objectionable portions of the mark (the "extra") serve to confer sufficient inherent distinctive character on the whole. The point is that the "extra" does not have to confer distinctive character to mean that the mark as a whole escapes 3(1)(c)/7(1)(c).

8–085   It may be thought that escaping Art.3(1)(c)/7(1)(c) via the second route and not the first is a pyrrhic victory, because the mark will be caught by an Art.3(1)(b)/7(1)(b) objection: the case of "Cycling IS..." being, perhaps, a slightly unusual example.[86] There, it was more what was absent from the mark which meant that the mark did not consist exclusively (*i.e.* simply and solely) of descriptive matter. It was held that the ellipsis (the three dots) "visibly invites people to add meaning to the words". Hence, the "combination of words does not lack descriptive power, but the description is unfinished." Having escaped the objection under Art.3(1)(c), the mark fell foul of Art.3(1)(b).

8–086   Such an outcome presupposes that both objections have been taken and are still in play, which is not always the case. The appeals in BABY-DRY proceeded only on the Art.7(1)(c) ground and Art.7(1)(b) was not in issue. It is possible that if the Art.7(1)(b) ground had remained in issue, so that the Court had been forced to focus more clearly on "distinctive character", such an objection would have been upheld.

8–087   In the result, the reasoning by which the ECJ decided that the mark escaped Art.7(1)(c) encompassed both routes and this was clearly indicated in its conclusion:

> "44. Word combinations like BABY-DRY cannot therefore be regarded as exhibiting, as a whole, descriptive character; they are lexical inventions bestowing distinctive character on the mark so formed and may not be refused registration under Article 7(1)(c) of Regulation No 40/94."

---

[86] "Cycling IS..." *Trade Mark Application* [2002] R.P.C. 37, p.729. The Appointed Person (G. Hobbs Q.C.). This was one of the first decisions at a higher level in the UK after BABY-DRY, and the Appointed Person was keen to ensure, so far as he was able, that BABY-DRY was not misunderstood.

It is certainly the case that UK tribunals in particular have sought ways to limit the effect of BABY-DRY to Art.3(1)(c)/7(1)(c). For example, in "CYCLING IS…"…, Geoffrey Hobbs Q.C. was at pains to point out[87] that the judgment was only concerned with Art.7(1)(c). and hence that it had little or no effect on the approach to Art.3(1)(b)/7(1)(b). However, one cannot avoid the fact that the way the judgment is worded has a direct effect on Art.3(1)(b)/7(1)(b), notwithstanding the fact that those provisions were not strictly in issue. Following the judgment of the ECJ, the on-going proceedings came before a different Board of Appeal. It is clear from their decision[88] that, left to themselves, they would have found the mark devoid of distinctive character but felt bound by the reasoning of the ECJ (paras 40 and 44 in particular) to find that no objection existed under Art.7(1)(b). The Court of Appeal drew attention to the same point in HAVE A BREAK.[89]

8–088

BABY-DRY

BABY-DRY was the first appeal to be heard by the Court of Justice concerning a Community trade mark. Possibly because of this, the Court comprised 11 Judges (what is now referred to as the Grand Chamber) and they received an Opinion from A.G. Jacobs who, by that time, had established a good track record in trade mark cases. Despite this, when one comes to analyse the findings of the court on the substance of the appeal, there is very little which can be relied upon, substantial parts of the reasoning are wrong, and the remainder requires substantial qualification. If one was being charitable, one might say that the language the Court used was unfortunate and liable to be misunderstood, but in reality, the reasoning went seriously wrong, as will now be explained by reference to the key paragraphs of the judgment.

8–089

In CHIEMSEE (*Windsurfing*), in part of its reasoning, the ECJ had made a slight, perhaps inadvertent, error. Paragraph 25 of the judgment suggests that Art.3(1)(c) applied to descriptive signs or indications "including as collective marks or *as part of* complex or graphic marks". (emphasis added). All subsequent judgments, including BABY-DRY, have avoided this error, applying the word "exclusively".

8–090

THE RETREAT FROM BABY-DRY: (1) THE ROLE OF THE DEFENCES

The ECJ approached the interpretation of Art.7(1)(c) with the defences to infringement (in Art.12 of the CTM Regulation/Art.6 of the Directive) expressly in mind. This approach was contrary to the long-standing notion that honest traders should not have to look to a defence. In subsequent judgments, the ECJ has stated expressly that the existence of defences to infringement should not be taken into account in the interpretation of absolute grounds. To do so would be an abdication of the responsibility to undertake a stringent and full examination, in order to prevent trade marks from being improperly registered.[90]

8–091

(2) perceptible difference/significant departure/variant

In BABY-DRY, the ECJ used various expressions to indicate what it regarded as

8–092

---

[87] "CYCLING IS…" [2002] R.P.C. 37, p.729 at paras 43–44.
[88] R–35/1998-3, Decision of the Third Board of Appeal of July 17, 2002.
[89] [2003] EWCA 1072, CA.
[90] See *Libertel*, paras 58–59. See also Case C–404/02, *Nichols*, paras 32, 33, and Case C–64/02, DAS PRINZIP, para.45.

the disqualifying criteria for the application of Art.7(1)(c) ("the usual way of designating the goods or services" (para.39), "the normal way of referring to the goods" (para.42)) and what would be sufficient to escape those disqualifying criteria ("any perceptible difference" (para.40), a "syntactically unusual juxtaposition" (para.43), "lexical invention"(para.44)).

8–093   In later judgments on both Art.3(1)(c)/7(1)(c) and 3(1)(b)/7(1)(b), the ECJ has qualified these expressions to such an extent that they cannot really be relied upon at all.

> "Thus, a mark consisting of a word composed of elements, each of which is descriptive of characteristics of the goods or services in respect of which registration is sought, is itself descriptive of those characteristics for the purposes of Article 3(1)(c) of the Directive, unless there is a perceptible difference between the word and the mere sum of its parts: that assumes either that, because of the unusual nature of the combination in relation to the goods or services, the word creates an impression which is sufficiently far removed from that produced by the mere combination of meanings lent by the elements of which it is composed, with the result that the word is more than the sum of its parts, or that the word has become part of everyday language and has acquired its own meaning, with the result that it is now independent of its components. In the second case, it is necessary to ascertain whether a word which has acquired its own meaning is not itself descriptive for the purpose of the same provision." POSTKANTOOR, paragraph 100.[91]

> "48. According to the case-law of the Court, for a mark to possess distinctive character within the meaning of Article 3(1)(b), it must serve to identify the product in respect of which registration is applied for as originating from a particular undertaking, and thus to distinguish that product from products of other undertakings (*Linde*, para.40).

> 49. It follows that a simple departure from the norm or customs of the sector is not sufficient to render inapplicable the ground for refusal given in Article 3(1)(b) of the Directive. In contrast, a trade mark which significantly departs from the norm or customs of the sector and thereby fulfils its essential original [sc. origin] function is not devoid of distinctive character." *Shape of detergent bottle (Henkel)*.[92]

8–094   In the passage just quoted, note the importance of the additional element "and thereby fulfils its essential function". There are two points to note:

> First, as Mann J. has pointed out, in this passage the ECJ is not stating a test, such that, for example, a significant departure from the norm means that the mark will fulfil its essential function. Rather, the ECJ is indicating the required result of an assessment if the ground was to be overcome.[93]

> Second (and it is the same point), "thereby" does not mean "therefore".[94]

8–095   See also:

> "In those circumstances, the more closely the shape for which registration is sought resembles the shape most likely to be taken by the product in ques-

[91] Case C–363/99, February 12, 2004. Similarly BIOMILD, Case C–265/00, issued on the same day.
[92] Case C–218/01, February 12, 2004.
[93] *Reckitt Benckiser NV v Robert McBride Ltd* [2004] EWHC 1403, June 11, 2004, para.13.
[94] *Bongrain SA* [2004] EWCA 1690, CA, para.27, where the CA was referring to the almost identical wording in the detergent tablet judgments issued 15 days after *Shape of detergent bottle (Henkel)*.

tion, the greater the likelihood of the shape being devoid of any distinctive character for the purposes of Article 7(1)(b) of Regulation No 40/94. Only a trade mark which departs significantly from the norm or customs of the sector and thereby fulfils its essential function of indicating origin, is not devoid of any distinctive character for the purposes of that provision (see, in relation to the identical provision in Article 3(1)(b) of First Directive 89/104, *Henkel*, paragraph 49" *Shape of waisted soap bar (Procter & Gamble).*[95]

And finally: **8–096**

"...the mere fact that that shape is a 'variant' of a common shape of that type of product is not sufficient to establish that the mark is not devoid of any distinctive character for the purposes of Article 7(1)(b) of Regulation No 40/94. It must always be determined whether such a mark permits the average consumer of that product, who is reasonably well informed and reasonably observant and circumspect, to distinguish the product concerned from those of other undertakings without conducting an analytical examination and without paying particular attention." *Shape of a torch (Mag Instrument)*, para.32.[96]

(3) The significance and impact of the designation

In BABY-DRY, the ECJ indicated that Art.3(1)(c)/7(1)(c) only applied to those   **8–097**
marks which

"may serve in normal usage from a consumer's point of view to designate, either **directly or by reference to one of their essential characteristics**, goods or services such as those in respect of which registration is sought." BABY-DRY, para.39 (emphasis added).

By contrast, in later judgments, the ECJ has emphasised that the freedom to   **8–098**
use such indications applies irrespective of how significant the characteristic may be commercially:

"It is also irrelevant whether the characteristics of the goods or services which may be the subject of the description are commercially essential or merely ancillary. The wording of Article 3(1)(c) of the Directive does not draw any distinction by reference to the characteristics which may be designated by the signs or indications of which the mark consists. In fact, in the light of the public interest underlying the provision, any undertaking must be able freely to use such signs and indications to describe any characteristic whatsoever of its own goods, irrespective of how significant the characteristic may be commercially." POSTKANTOOR, para.102.

The ECJ has also held that, instead of the descriptive designation needing to be   **8–099**
"direct", it is the distinctive meaning of the mark which must make an immediate impact on the average consumer:

"...in order to contribute to the assessment of the distinctiveness of a mark for the purposes of Article 7(1)(b) of Regulation No 40/94, that evidence must show that consumers did not need to become accustomed to the mark through the use made of it, but that it immediately enabled them to distinguish the goods or services bearing the mark from the goods or services of competing undertakings. As the Office rightly argues, Article 7(3)

---

[95] Case C–107/03, September 23, 2004.
[96] Case C–136/02, October 7, 2004.

of Regulation No 40/94 would be redundant if a mark fell to be registered in accordance with Article 7(1)(b) by reason of its having become distinctive in consequence of the use made of it." *Shape of a torch (Mag Instrument)*, para.50.[97]

7. Section 3(1)(d)/Article 3(1)(d), Article 7(1)(d) CTMR: generic marks

8–100   "**s.3**—(1) The following shall not be registered—

(d) trade marks which consist exclusively of signs or indications which have become customary in the current language or in the bona fide and established practices of the trade."

DERIVATION

8–101   The wording of this sub-paragraph is identical to Article 3(1)(d) of the TM Directive and Article 7(1)(d) of the CTM Regulation. These provisions are directed at preventing registration of those signs or indications which honest traders customarily use in trade-signs which are generic.

8–102   The main applicable principles are reasonably well settled. The essence of the objection is that the sign is generic, with the primary focus usually being on the perception of the mark amongst consumers, although the perception in the trade may be important in certain circumstances. Each case will turn on its own facts and evidence. The challenge with these grounds is to compile a sufficiently convincing body of evidence.

8–103   In BRAVO (*Merz & Krell*), the applicant sought to register the laudatory mark BRAVO for writing implements. There are two important passages in the judgment of the ECJ. Paragraphs 21–24 set out the important background considerations to the interpretation of Art.3(1)(d). It will be understood that the same considerations apply by way of general approach to the other provisions as well.

"21. Trade mark rights constitute an essential element in the system of undistorted competition which the Treaty is intended to establish. In such a system, undertakings must be able to attract and retain customers by the quality of their products or services, which is made possible only by distinctive signs allowing them to be identified (see, inter alia, Case C–349/95 *Loendersloot* [1997] ECR I-6227, paragraph 22).

22. From that point of view, the essential function of the trade mark is to guarantee the identity of the origin of the marked goods or service to the consumer or end user by enabling him, without any possibility of confusion, to distinguish the goods or service from others which have another origin (see, inter alia, Case C–39/97 *Canon* [1998] ECR I-5507, paragraph 28).

23. That essential function of trade marks has been incorporated by the Community legislature into Article 2 of the Directive, which provides that signs which are capable of being represented graphically may only constitute a trade mark if they are capable of distinguishing the goods or services of one undertaking from those of other undertakings.

24. Accordingly, signs or indications that are not capable of fulfilling the

---

[97] Case C–136/02, October 7, 2004. See also *Stand up Pouch (Deutsche SiSi-Werke)*, Case T–146/02, January 28, 2004, para.38.

essential function of a trade mark cannot enjoy the protection conferred by registration. As is made clear by the tenth recital in the preamble to the Directive, the purpose of the protection afforded by the registered trade mark is in particular to guarantee that trade mark's function as an indication of origin.

25. Article 3(1)(d) of the Directive must be interpreted in the light of those considerations."

The status of these paragraphs is indicated by the fact that they have been cited **8–104** in a number of later ECJ judgments dealing with other areas of trade mark law which touch on the fundamental issue of what a trade mark is supposed to do and how far the protection provided by a registration should extend.

In a later group of paragraphs, the ECJ focus directly on the interpretation of **8–105** Art.3(1)(d). In these paragraphs the ECJ is essentially saying: apply the words of the provision and do not get sidetracked by other considerations (such as descriptiveness or the fact that the mark is a slogan):

"35. It must first of all be observed that, although there is a clear overlap between the scope of Articles 3(1)(c) and 3(1)(d) of the Directive, marks covered by Article 3(1)(d) are excluded from registration not on the basis that they are descriptive, but on the basis of current usage in trade sectors covering trade in the goods or services for which the marks are sought to be registered.

36. It follows that, in order for Article 3(1)(d) of the Directive to be effective, the scope of the provision in respect of which the Court's interpretation is sought should not be limited solely to trade marks which describe the properties or characteristics of the goods or services covered by them.

37. In that regard it must be pointed out that signs or indications constituting a trade mark which have become customary in the current language or in the bona fide and established practices of the trade to designate the goods or services covered by that mark are not capable of distinguishing the services of one undertaking from those of other undertakings and do not therefore fulfil the essential function of a trade mark—unless the use which has been made of those signs or indications has enabled them to acquire a distinctive character capable of being recognised under Article 3(3) of the Directive.

38. In such a case it is not therefore necessary to consider whether the signs or indications in question are descriptions of the properties or characteristics of the goods or services.

39. It also follows that, where the signs or indications concerned have become customary in the current language or in the bona fide and established practices of the trade to designate the goods or services covered by the mark, it is of little consequence that they are used as advertising slogans, indications of quality or incitements to purchase those goods or services.

40. However, registration of a trade mark which consists of signs or indications that are also used as advertising slogans, indications of quality or incitements to purchase the goods or services covered by that mark is not excluded as such by virtue of such use. It is for the national court to determine in each case whether the signs or indications have become customary in the current language or in the bona fide and established practices of the trade to designate the goods or services covered by that mark.

41. It follows that Article 3(1)(d) of the Directive must be interpreted as

meaning that it subjects refusal to register a trade mark to the sole condition that the signs or indications of which the trade mark is exclusively composed have become customary in the current language or in the bona fide and established practices of the trade to designate the goods or services in respect of which registration of that mark is sought. It is immaterial, when that provision is applied, whether the signs or indications in question describe the properties or characteristics of those goods or services."

8–106   In BSS *Alcon*) the ECJ had to consider the equivalent provision in Article 7(1)(d) of the CTM Regulation in relation to the mark "BSS".[98] The ECJ was able to dispose of the appeal by way of a reasoned Order, since the CFI had correctly applied the principles laid down in *Merz & Krell* (especially paras 35 and 37) and, in reality, the appellant sought to criticise the assessment of the facts by the CFI. The subsidiary points which arose concerned (a) the use of materials published after the date of application and (b) the use of materials published outside the EU.

8–107   The ECJ:

(1) confirmed that the date of filing of the application was the material date (para.40);

(2) adopted the common sense view that it was legitimate to take account of materials published after the relevant date in so far as they "enabled the drawing of conclusions on the situation as it was on that date", citing by analogy its Order in *La Mer Technology*—a case on genuine use (para.41);[99]

(3) again adopted the common sense view that materials published outside the EU could shed light on the issue whether the relevant class of persons (in that case the "scientific community") in the EU regarded the term BSS as customary.

"THE TRADE"

8–108   Article 3(1)(d)/7(1)(d) speak of "customary in the current language or in the bona fide and established practices of the trade" and this potentially raises two issues: first, does it mean "customary in the current language" *of the trade* or generally and second, what is meant by "the trade". Both issues have effectively been answered in a reference to the ECJ concerned with the closely analogous, but not identical provision in s.46(1)(c)/Article 12(2)(a) of the Directive/Article 50(1)(b) of the CTM Regulation, which provide for revocation "if, in consequence of acts or inactivity of the registered proprietor, the trade mark has become the common name in the trade for a product or service in respect of which it is registered".

8–109   In *Bjornekulla*, the mark BOSTONGURKA was alleged to have become the generic name for chopped pickled gherkins. The applicant for revocation relied on market survey evidence from consumers, and the owner of the mark relied on market surveys conducted amongst operators in the trade. The ECJ was essentially asked to interpret "the trade" in the context of Article 12(2)(a) of the Directive.

8–110   Even though this was not a particularly difficult question, the judgment of the

---

[98] Case C–192/03 BSS *Alcon Inc v OHIM*) Order of October 5, 2004. The evidence showed that BSS was an abbreviation for a "balanced salt solution" or "buffered saline solution". The application was in respect of "ophthalmic pharmaceutical preparations; sterile solutions for ophthalmic surgery" which, reading between the lines, was essentially for balanced salt solutions etc.

[99] Case C–259/02, ECJ, [2004] E.C.R. I-1159; [2004] F.S.R. 38. See para.10–045.

ECJ is short and impeccably reasoned. Although largely based on the approach it took in *Merz & Krell*, the ECJ carried that reasoning further, coincidentally shedding some further light on Article 3 of the Directive, so it is worth setting out the relevant paragraphs in full:

> "20. The essential function of the trade mark is to guarantee the identity of the origin of the marked goods or service to the consumer or end user by enabling him, without any possibility of confusion, to distinguish the goods or service from others which have another origin (see, inter alia, Case C–39/97 *Canon* [1998] ECR I-5507, paragraph 28, and Case C–517/99 *Merz & Krell* [2001] ECR I-6959, paragraph 22). For the trade mark to be able to fulfil its essential role in the system of undistorted competition which the EC Treaty seeks to establish, it must offer a guarantee that all the goods or services bearing it have been produced under the control of a single undertaking which is responsible for their quality (*Canon*, paragraph 28).
>
> 21. That essential function of trade marks has been incorporated by the Community legislature into Article 2 of the Directive, which provides that signs which are capable of being represented graphically may only constitute a trade mark if they are capable of distinguishing the goods or services of one undertaking from those of other undertakings (*Merz & Krell*, paragraph 23).
>
> 22. That condition is given effect to in, inter alia, Articles 3 and 12 of the Directive. While Article 3 specifies the circumstances in which a trade mark is incapable, *ab initio*, of fulfilling its function as an indication of origin, Article 12(2)(a) addresses the situation where the trade mark is no longer capable of fulfilling that function.
>
> 23. If the function of the trade mark as an indication of origin is of primary importance to the consumer or end user, it is also relevant to intermediaries who deal with the product commercially. As with consumers or end users, it will tend to influence their conduct in the market.
>
> 24. In general, the perception of consumers or end users will play a decisive role. The whole aim of the commercialisation process is the purchase of the product by those persons and the role of the intermediary consists as much in detecting and anticipating the demand for that product as in increasing or directing it.
>
> 25. Accordingly, the relevant circles comprise principally consumers and end users. However, depending on the features of the product market concerned, the influence of intermediaries on decisions to purchase, and thus their perception of the trade mark, must also be taken into consideration."

The underlying issue is whether the trade mark remains able to carry out its essential function. The primary focus is directed at the point of purchase. Hence, in most cases, the perception of consumers or end users will be important—"play a decisive role". However, it is necessary to examine the features of the product market concerned. The ECJ clearly had in mind that circumstances can vary widely from the self-service environment of the supermarket to situations where the decision to purchase is based on specific advice from someone in the trade. **8–111**

"CURRENT LANGUAGE"

This interpretation of "trade" gives a clear indication as to the proper interpretation of "customary in the current language" (which effectively bypasses the issue of whether this refers to the current language generally or the current language in **8–112**

the trade). It depends on the features of the product or service market concerned. For ordinary consumer items, the current language of consumers will be important. In specialised areas of trade, one would expect the focus to be on the current language in that trade. This approach is confirmed by BSS, where only the specialists in the trade would have automatically understood BSS to stand for balanced salt solution.

THE PUBLIC INTEREST

8–113   The ECJ has made it clear that public interest considerations underlie each of the provisions in Art.3(1)/7(1), although to date, the ECJ has not spelt out the nature of the public interest which underlies Art.3(1)(d)/7(1)(d). It may be thought that it is not particularly difficult to discern the nature of the relevant public interest from what the ECJ has said already: Art.3(1)(d)/7(1)(d) are in the public interest, to ensure that generic terms may be freely used by all. In some respects, this is a stronger public interest than that underlying Art.3(1)(c)/7(1)(c), because such generic terms must actually be in current use, as opposed to being capable of being used in the future. Alternatively, the public interest lies in the fact that marks caught by these provisions are not capable of functioning as trade marks and therefore do not deserve to be protected. Expressing the underlying public interest in these terms serves to emphasise that these provisions set a high hurdle. Not only must the mark consist *exclusively* of generic matter, but the fact of genericism must be established. Bearing in mind the primary role of 3(1)(d)/7(1)(d) are to prevent traders seeking to monopolise terms which are already generic, the fact of genericism can usually be demonstrated. More difficult issues arise when the mark under consideration has been used for some time as a trade mark before application is made or when an existing registration is sought to be revoked as having become generic. In those situations, the precise way in which the underlying public interest is expressed can have a marked influence on how strictly these provisions are applied in practice.

SCOPE

8–114   There is clearly a significant degree of overlap between this provision and s.3(1)(c) of the 1994 Act. However, s.3(1)(d) has a role in excluding from registration signs or indications where the descriptive element is not readily apparent, yet they are signs or indications which a number of traders actually use.

8–115   Some obvious examples of signs or indications which would be precluded from registration by s.3(1)(d) are marks which consisted of stars for hotel services, stars for brandy, a bunch of grapes for wine, a representation of a chef for food or for restaurant services[1] or of a mechanic or spanner for car repair services. TREAT for dessert sauces and syrups[2] was declared invalid under this ground. However, due to the word "exclusively" a mark would not be caught by this ground simply because it included such customary matter, provided the mark contained other distinctive elements.

EVIDENCE

8–116   The evidence necessary to establish this ground may depend upon the tribunal.

---

[1] These examples appear in the Registry Work Manual.
[2] *British Sugar plc v James Robertson & Sons Ltd* [1996] R.P.C. 281, Jacob J.

Certainly OHIM examiners and the United Kingdom Registry will look for evidence from dictionaries and the like to show a mark is customary in the current language of the trade or for evidence of trade usage to show that the mark is customary in the practices of the trade. In MINI CLAW,[3] a single entry from an edition of a dictionary published 30 years ago, which did not appear in subsequent editions or in other dictionaries, was insufficient to establish that the word CLAW was current in the language of the gardening trade. Equally, one reference in trade literature (of the opponent) was insufficient to show the term was customary in established practices in the trade.

In OHIM, the evidential requirements appear to be less strict, at least at the *ex parte* stage. In LIGHT GREEN and YELLOW, this ground was held established apparently on the basis of the general knowledge and experience of the members of the Board of Appeal.[4]   **8–117**

In most cases, if the evidence is insufficient to establish this ground, it may establish an objection under Art.3(1)(c)/7(1)(c).

8. Miscellaneous points

8.1 PRIMARY, SECONDARY AND LIMPING MARKS

Potentially, this is a problem which faces any trader who claims that there is more than one badge of origin for his product or service. The trader has a primary mark which the public see as a badge of origin. However, the trader wishes to establish a secondary mark as an additional badge of origin. Whether he succeeds obviously depends on the facts. The potential problem is avoided if, for example, the secondary mark has an inherent distinctive character of its own,[5] particularly if such a mark joins a group of other secondary marks on a range of products all sold under a recognised house mark. However, the problem faces any trader who adopts as his secondary mark a descriptive or laudatory word, some feature of the goods or their get-up which is seen as decorative or, worse, functional. The problem inherent in the mark itself is then compounded by being used in conjunction with a distinctive mark.   **8–118**

Here, the trader faces a dilemma. He does not want to remove his primary distinctive mark from the product altogether, for fear that the public would then be unable to identify the origin of the product. On the other hand, he must reduce the public's reliance on the primary mark and attempt to increase recognition and hence reliance on the secondary mark or feature of the product. This exercise is very difficult to do on the product itself, but is much easier to achieve in advertising where a campaign emphasises the secondary mark to the public. In time, the advertising may even drop the primary mark, indicating a degree of confidence on the part of the trader in the ability of his secondary mark to distinguish.[6]   **8–119**

Examples where the secondary mark was held not to be registrable are as follows: **8–120**

---

[3] [1999] E.T.M.R. 505 (note), Regy.

[4] For a comment on this decision (and on the decisions of the Swiss Supreme Court in "White/Green Tablets", October 14, 1999 and German Supreme Court and Federal Patent Court in "Yellow/Black", December 10, 1998 and October 25, 1999, respectively), see Johannes/Zurkinden, Gelb/schwarz MarkenR 5/2000 at 153–159.

[5] An example is the combination of the ICI and DULUX marks. The example quoted by Jacob J. in *Philips v Remington* was FORD and FIESTA.

[6] Certain cigarette manufacturers have been adept at this type of advertising.

(1) The primary mark was "Silver Spoon" in a device. The secondary mark was "Treat", registered on evidence of use. Jacob J. said: "Mere evidence of use of a highly descriptive or laudatory word will not suffice, without more, to prove that it is distinctive of one particular trader-is taken by the public as a badge of origin. This is all the more so when the use has been accompanied by what is undoubtedly a distinctive and well-recognised trade mark." (*British Sugar plc v James Robertson & Sons Ltd* [1996] R.P.C. 281.)

(2) The primary marks were "Philips" and "Philishave". The secondary mark was a picture of a three-headed rotary shaver, but was treated as covering the three-dimensional shape as well. The secondary mark was described as "limping" by Jacob J. and as "supporting" by Aldous L.J. The registration of the secondary mark was held invalid, principally because the primary message the mark conveyed was "here is a three headed rotary shaver".[7]

(3) The primary mark was "Dualit". The secondary mark was essentially the shape of the toaster. Registration of the secondary mark was refused, the applicant failing to show that the secondary mark had acquired a distinctive character of its own, through use-perhaps a hard case.[8]

(4) In "7", the OHIM Third Board of Appeal stated that "... where a claimed mark appears together with the name of the supplier for specific products, there is a prima facie presumption that that mark functions as a mere identifier sign." "... a mere identifier sign will not function as a trade mark, but rather as a means of distinguishing the appellant's various products from one another."[9]

8.2 EVIDENCE OF DISTINCTIVENESS

8–121   Gathering a worthwhile body of evidence which proves that a mark is distinctive is not easy. Marks which are distinctive hardly require evidence, and evidence is usually required where there is a perceived problem with distinctiveness. Generally, a combination of evidence is called for and there is a familiar range of options.[10] The greater the perceived difficulty in proving distinctiveness, the further one must explore the range of evidential options.

8–122   The starting point is usually financial evidence of turnover and advertising and promotional expenditure for the goods or services in question, accompanied by examples of how the mark is used in practice. Evidence from third party trade sources can be powerful, but the weight of such evidence often depends upon its perceived independence. Evidence from suppliers or distributors is generally given less weight than evidence from independent trade associations, consumer organisations and competitors. Evidence from trade buyers sheds little light on whether the relevant class of consumers identify the goods or service in question as originating from a particular undertaking because of the trade mark. As Lloyd J. pointed out in *Dualit*, it is the business of trade buyers to know the products of the different manufacturers in the market.[11]

8–123   The ultimate source of evidence is the body of consumers for the goods or ser-

---

[7] *Philips v Remington* [1999] R.P.C. 809; [1999] E.T.M.R. 816. CA.

[8] *Dualit* [1999] R.P.C. 890, Lloyd J.

[9] [2000] E.T.M.R. 14, paras 23 and 22.

[10] The UK Registry Work Manual provides guidance on evidence of use—see Ch.6, Parts 7.1–7.4. Likewise OHIM has issued a practice note on Evidence of Use.

[11] *Dualit* [1999] R.P.C. 890 at 898.

vices in question. Well-conducted opinion polls can be persuasive,[12] but require much thought and care and are often very expensive. The problems which have been experienced in the United Kingdom with the reliability of opinion polls over the years have prompted many to use them solely or primarily as a witness gathering exercise, but the courts are increasingly reluctant to permit repetitious evidence from selected members of the public.[13] Often the most powerful evidence of distinctiveness comes from the successful prosecution of cases in passing off. Even if a passing off case settles before full trial, evidence of true instances of deception will also prove the distinctiveness of the mark.

Gathering worthwhile evidence requires the practitioner to consider the circumstances carefully, to utilise the client's knowledge of the trade and, whilst working within budget, to avoid the most common problems which are seen with evidence of distinctiveness. These problems occur for a variety of reasons: due to lack of communication, lack of knowledge/diligence, budgetary constraints and because the mark is not, in fact, sufficiently distinctive. Sometimes attempts are made to disguise perceived weaknesses in the evidence by shrouding them in obscurity, but this is usually counterproductive because then the tribunal loses confidence in the reliability of such evidence of distinctiveness as exists. **8–124**

Here, we discuss three particular problems which have been the subject of comment in recent cases. They concern: "mere evidence of use"; "evidence of association or recognition"; "evidence in standard form".

MERE EVIDENCE OF USE

There has been a tendency for applicants seeking to demonstrate distinctiveness acquired through use, to rely on financial evidence of turnover and advertising expenditure.[14] This type of financial evidence is a necessary part of any attempt to prove acquired distinctiveness, but it cannot do the job by itself. As Jacob J. has said: **8–125**

> "Mere evidence of use of a highly descriptive or laudatory word will not suffice, without more, to prove that it is distinctive of one particular trader—is taken by the public as a badge of origin. This is all the more so when the use has been accompanied by what is undoubtedly a distinctive and well-recognised trade mark."[15]

and, later in the same judgment:

> "I have already described the evidence used to support the original registration. It was really no more than evidence of use. Now it is all too easy to be beguiled by such evidence. There is an unspoken and illogical

---

[12] The *Philips* case provides an example of differing attitudes to surveys in different Member States. In Sweden, market research appeared to have been accepted uncritically as establishing the picture of the three-headed shaver as distinctive; whereas Jacob J. said "... experience of detailed examination of opinion polls (including questioning of interviewees) conducted for the purpose of litigation in the English courts has shown that such polls may not be reliable. They certainly require detailed scrutiny. For instance, leading and non-leading questions often produce quite different answers. And sometimes it turns out that the public were just guessing at matters which had never, in their ordinary shopping, bothered them at all.": [1998] R.P.C. 283 at 303.

[13] See Morritt and Chadwick L.JJ. in *Bach Flower Remedies* [2000] R.P.C. 513 at 526, paras 35 and at 535.

[14] This tendency may have been encouraged by the standard form of evidence of use which has been part of the Registry Work Manual for some years. The apparent concentration on turnover and advertising expenditure may obscure the fact that what is required is evidence of distinctiveness and not evidence of use.

[15] *British Sugar* [1996] R.P.C. 281 at 286.

assumption that "use equals distinctiveness". The illogicality can be seen from an example: no matter how much use a manufacturer made of the word "Soap" as a purported trade mark for soap the word would not be distinctive of his goods."[16]

8–126   To similar effect, Morritt L.J. in *Bach Flower Remedies*:

"First, use of a mark does not prove that the mark is distinctive. Increased use, of itself, does not do so either. The use and increased use must be in a distinctive sense to have any materiality."[17]

8–127   This is the point. It is necessary to combine evidence of the scale of use provided by financial information with evidence that the use has been so as to distinguish—on the product, in relation to the service, in advertising or promotion. Sometimes the way in which the mark is presented to the public indicates whether the owner really trusts the mark to function as a trade mark.

EVIDENCE OF RECOGNITION OR ASSOCIATION

8–128   This type of evidence comes from third parties. It can be convincing if either the context or other evidence shows that the recognition is of the sign acting as a trade mark—as a badge of origin. Likewise, with evidence of association. More often, the context or other evidence is missing. As Jacob J. observed in *British Sugar*:

"recognition [of the word] does not necessarily mean recognition as a trade mark." and "... recognition is not the same thing as perception as a trade mark—as not only recognising the word but as regarding it, in itself, as denoting the goods of one particular trader."[18]

8–129   Also, the Registrar's hearing officer in *Dualit* said:[19]

"As Jacob J. noted in the *Philips* case, the word 'associates' can have a number of meanings. The word could be used by those that mean 'first come to mind', 'best known one' 'only one I can think of—but there may be others'. None of those meanings amount to recognition of the sign as a trade mark. On the other hand the witness may mean 'that shape tells me it's a Dualit—I'd definitely expect it to be a Dualit and be confused if it wasn't'. That sort of recognition is more likely to support the claim that the sign(s) is regarded as a trade mark."

These are subtle, but important distinctions.

EVIDENCE IN STANDARD FORM

8–130   This vice often features with inadequate evidence of association. Thus, statements are made in essentially standard form by a number of distributors of the applicant's products containing phrases along the lines of: "I associate [the sign in question] with the products of [the applicant]" (the word "exclusively" may be an optional extra) or "I recognise [the sign in question] as being the trade mark of [the applicant]". Although this type of evidence is put in to help, its effect may be worse than neutral for a number of reasons. First, the basic rule that statements

---

[16] At 302.

[17] [2000] R.P.C. 513 at 530.

[18] At 304.

[19] *Dualit Ltd's (Toaster Shapes) Trade Mark Applications* [1999] R.P.C. 304 at 317, Mr Allan James. On appeal, Lloyd J. upheld the decision on somewhat different grounds, but was even more sceptical of the evidence.

should be written in the witnesses' own words has been infringed with the result that it looks as if the words have been put into the mouth of the witness, and they probably have. Secondly, it is quite unclear what the witness means to say, even if he or she did understand the significance of the words put into their statement. Thirdly, even if it is assumed the witness did understand the significance of the words used, the tribunal will assume that the witness could not say anything more favourable.

Again, as the Registrar's hearing officer observed in *Dualit*:[20]　　**8–131**

"Given that this type of application gives rise to relatively subtle questions of perception, it appears to me to be important for the witnesses' evidence to consist of their own words."

8.3 SECONDARY MEANING

In *Windsurfing* the ECJ indicated that the corollary of a mark having acquired a **8–132** distinctive character through use was that the mark "has gained a new significance and its connotation, no longer purely descriptive, justifies its registration as a trade mark."[21] The issue which remains is whether the secondary meaning or new significance must displace the primary non-distinctive meaning, and, to what extent.

These are difficult issues, yet familiar. The same type of issue arises in the law **8–133** of passing off and arose under the old Act. However, the extent to which a descriptive sign must acquire a secondary[22] distinctive meaning in order to satisfy the proviso ought to be different to that required in the law of passing off and is not necessarily the same as was required under the old Act. Of course, it is a question of fact (and therefore of degree) whether a particular sign has acquired sufficient distinctive character to justify registration under the proviso. But stating that principle does not give much guidance as to what "sufficient distinctive character" really means. Already under the 1994 Act there have been a number of cases which mention this issue and unless they are properly understood, they can be misinterpreted. Therefore, in this section we aim to provide some guidance on this issue. The guidance can be stated in these propositions:

(1) It is not necessary for the secondary distinctive meaning to displace entirely the primary descriptive meaning of a sign. However, when the sign is used in relation to the goods or services in question, the average consumer should understand the sign to denote origin.

(2) The extent to which the secondary distinctive meaning must displace the primary descriptive meaning to justify registration as a trade mark should be greater than the minimum required to sustain an action in passing off.

(3) The extent to which the secondary distinctive meaning must displace the primary descriptive meaning to justify registration as a trade mark is a question of degree which will depend upon the degree of descriptiveness of the sign. The more descriptive the sign, the greater the extent to which the primary descriptive meaning must be displaced. The more descriptive a sign is, the greater are the negative (descriptive) qualities of the sign which must be displaced and overcome by positive distinctive qualities. Ultimately, when making this judgment the tribunal is likely to be

---

[20] *Dualit Ltd's (Toaster Shapes) Trade Mark Applications* [1999] R.P.C. 304.
[21] para.47, cited at para.8–020.
[22] In this context, the terms "primary" and "secondary" indicate the sequence in which the meanings were acquired, although they also indicate that the primary descriptive meaning is the default.

influenced by considerations which were familiar under the old Act. To what extent would registration interfere with the rights of honest traders? To what extent does this sign really operate as a trade mark? To what extent is it thought necessary to keep this sign free for others to use?[23]

8–134   Of course, the context is always defined by the relevant goods or services in question. In an entirely different context, the sign may only bear its descriptive meaning, but this does not matter. Laddie J. pointed out in *Jeryl Lynn*[24] that the signs Penguin, Ford and Golf have acquired distinctive character in relation to certain goods, whereas in other contexts, they have retained entirely their descriptive meaning.

8–135   Even in the context of the relevant goods or services, it has long been the case that a trade mark may be both distinctive and also convey something by way of a description of the goods or services. One need only take the example of a mark which contains a skilful and covert allusion to some characteristic of the goods (for example the purpose or their quality). These are often regarded as being the most valuable trade marks, being distinctive yet also having an element of descriptive character in them. The point goes further, as Jacob J. explained in *Philips*:[25]

> "Now it is of course the case that a mark (particularly a word mark) may be both distinctive of a particular manufacturer and yet also convey something by way of a description of the goods—Mr Pumfrey gave "Weldmesh" for welded mesh as an example. The word denotes the welded mesh of a particular manufacturer (See *WELDMESH Trade Mark* [1966] R.P.C. 220) But you can take this argument too far. There are words which are so descriptive that they cannot be trade marks—"soap" for "soap". The difference is one of degree, but important nonetheless. There are degrees of descriptiveness ranging from the skilful but covert allusion to the common word for the goods. On the scale of distinctiveness you come to a point where a word is so descriptive that it is incapable of distinguishing properly, even if it does so partially."

8–136   As for the second proposition, the reason for the suggested distinction on the subject of secondary meaning between the law of passing off and registration of a trade mark is as follows. The principles developed in passing off cases allow a flexible approach to the facts of a particular case. If the case involves a sign with a primary descriptive meaning, the court can effectively alter the extent to which it requires the plaintiff to demonstrate a secondary meaning by balancing the interests of the parties and the public. For example, the plaintiff may have to endure some confusion and small differences may suffice, and a different result may obtain if the court considers that people really are being misled. By contrast, registration of a trade mark confers an exclusive right—a monopoly right. The defences in s.11 only allow a balancing of interests to a very limited extent, and even then the law appears to be reasonably settled that "honest men should not have to look for a defence". In order to justify the exclusive right which covers the wide range of situations which fall within the infringement provisions, it is

---

[23] Compare the various submissions made in *Windsurfing* and the fact that the ECJ sensibly avoided any attempt at evaluating the need to which a sign should be kept free for others.

[24] [1999] F.S.R. 491.

[25] In *Philips v Remington* [1998] R.P.C. 283 at 301, having cited the well-known passage from the judgment of Fletcher Moulton L.J. in *Joseph Crosfield's Application (Perfection Trade Mark)* (1909) 26 R.P.C. 837 at 857.

suggested that the applicant must demonstrate that a secondary distinctive mean-ing has displaced the primary descriptive meaning to a greater extent than may be required for success in passing off. An applicant who fails to make the grade is then left to prove his case in passing off.

On the third proposition, consider the relevant *dicta* from *British Sugar*, where **8–137** the sign was the laudatory term "Treat" for dessert sauces and syrups:

> "A word or words to be really distinctive of a person's goods must generally be incapable of application to the goods of anyone else".[26]

> "It is precisely because a common laudatory word is naturally capable of application to the goods of any trader that one must be careful before concluding that merely its use, however substantial, has displaced its com-mon meaning and has come to denote the mark of a particular trader."[27]

> "Is my finding that to some but not most people "Treat" has some trade mark significance enough? This depends on what is meant by a distinctive character. Neither the Directive nor the Act throw any light on this... . Take a very descriptive or laudatory word. Suppose the proprietor can educate 10% of the public into recognising the word as his trade mark. Can that re-ally be enough to say it has acquired a distinctive character and so enough to let the proprietor lay claim to the word as a trade mark altogether? The character at this stage is partly distinctive but mainly not. I do not think it would be fair to regard the character of the word as distinctive in that state of affairs. But if the matter were the other way round, so that to 90% of people it was taken as a trade mark, then I think it would be fair so to regard it. This all suggests that the question of factual distinctive character is one of degree. The proviso really means 'has the mark acquired a sufficiently distinctive character that the mark has really become a trade mark'. In the case of common or apt descriptive or laudatory words compelling evidence is needed to establish this ... it must be shown in a case of this sort that the mark has really become accepted by a substantial majority of persons as a trade mark—is or is almost a household word."[28]

Jacob J. suggested that even recognition by 60 per cent of the public as a trade **8–138** mark would not satisfy the proviso for such a common laudatory term, although we suspect that elsewhere in Europe such a figure would be considered sufficient. His approach is consistent with the general guidance provided by the ECJ in *Windsurfing*, where the court indicated that the proviso would be satisfied by a mark which was "no longer purely descriptive" (emphasis added). In a case decided after *Windsurfing* (MESSIAH FROM SCRATCH),[29] the appointed person (S. Thorley, Q.C.) correctly observed:

> "... it is not necessary that the secondary meaning should have displaced the primary meaning, it is however necessary that it has gained a sufficient new significance as indicating origin to justify registration so as to leave third parties who wish to use the designation in its descriptive sense to rely upon the defence provided by section 11 of the Act."

---

[26] At 302, citing from the judgment of Lord Russell in *The Shredded Wheat Co Ltd v Kelloggs* (1940) 57 R.P.C. 137 at 145.
[27] At 302.
[28] At 306.
[29] [2000] R.P.C. 44, at para.51

8.4 The geographical extent of acquired distinctiveness required for Article 7(3) CTM Regulation

8–139   Article 7(1) of the CTM Regulation sets out the absolute grounds for refusal of an application for a Community trade mark. Art.7(2) provides that Art.7(1) ("The following shall not be registered:") shall apply notwithstanding that the grounds of non-registrability obtain in only part of the Community. Then Art.7(3) provides for the major exception: Article 7(1)(b)(c) and (d) "shall not apply if the trade mark has become distinctive in relation to the goods or services for which registration is requested in consequence of the use which has been made of it."

8–140   Following Windsurfing, the OHIM Boards of Appeal have stated that two conditions need to be satisfied for a claim of acquired distinctiveness:

> "(1) the trade mark must be used in the Community as a whole or, at least, in a substantial part thereof, in such a way that
>
> (2) a sufficiently large part of the relevant class of persons recognises the sign as a distinctive trade mark at the time the application is filed (see…Windsurfing… para.46)."[30]

8–141   Even before Windsurfing, applicants argued that Art.7(3) was satisfied if they proved acquired distinctiveness in a substantial part of the Community. However, the Court of First Instance has taken a harder line, ruling in OPTIONS that a sign must possess a distinctive character throughout the Community:

> "… in order to be accepted for registration, a sign must possess a distinctive character throughout the Community. That requirement, enabling consumers to distinguish the goods or services of one undertaking from those of other undertakings in accordance with Article 4 [CTMR], is essential for that sign to be able to exercise the function of a Community trade mark in economic life.
>
> The principle of the unitary character of the Community trade mark is expressly applied in Article 7(2) … Article 7(3) … must be read in the light of that principle. On that basis, in order to have the registration of a trade mark accepted under Article 7(3) …, the distinctive character acquired through the use of that trade mark must be demonstrated in the substantial part of the Community where it was devoid of any such character under Article 7(1)(b), (c) and (d)."[31]

8–142   It appears from that passage that the required distinctive character may be inherent, acquired or a combination of the two. For example, if a sign has a descriptive meaning in a particular language, but not in other languages, it will be sufficient for the applicant to prove acquired distinctiveness in those countries where the former language is commonly used, and to rely on inherent distinctiveness in other countries in the Community. What is clear is that distinctive character is required throughout the Community.[32]

8–143   It is not necessary to prove use in every Member State of the Community. Advertising and sale of goods in major Member States may well spill over into other countries, particularly in continental Europe, sufficiently to render the sign distinctive in those other countries even though sales there may be small or non-existent.

---

[30] See *e.g. Ty Nant* [1999] E.T.M.R. 974, para.15, OHIM Third Board of Appeal.
[31] OPTIONS Case T–91/99, Court of First Instance, March 30, 2000, paras 24–27.
[32] This is obviously correct, particularly in view of the observations about the role of Art.7(3) CTM Regulation/ Article 3(3) of the TM Directive in *Windsurfing* (see para.8–020).

8.5 DISCLAIMERS AND LIMITATIONS

A disclaimer serves the same purpose as under the old law—the disclaimed mat-   **8–144**
ter must be left out of account for all purposes.[33] Limitations may be territorial or
related to some aspect of the goods or services, or the use of colour in the mark.
There is some divergence of practice between the Registry and OHIM on
disclaimers and limitations.

Section 13(1) of the 1994 Act appears to contemplate only disclaimers and   **8–145**
limitations which are volunteered by the applicant: "An applicant… may disclaim
etc.". By contrasting this with the position under the 1938 Act where there was
express power[34] to require a disclaimer of, for example, non-distinctive matter,
the Registry has taken the view that it has no power to require an applicant to
make a disclaimer or limitation[35] and can only take a passive role. This is an odd
position to take and can only lead to shadow boxing between applicant and
Registry. It cannot be contrary to s.13 for an examiner to state his view that a
mark cannot be registered without non-distinctive matter being disclaimed. In
practice, the application of disclaimers should be uniform so that traders inspecting the Register are not left in doubt over the scope of registrations.

So far as OHIM is concerned, Article 38(2) of the CTM Regulation provides: **8–146**
"Where the trade mark contains an element which is not distinctive, and
where the inclusion of said element in the trade mark could give rise to
doubts as to the scope of protection for the trade mark, the Office may
request, as a condition for registration of the said trade mark, that the applicant state that he disclaims any exclusive right to such element."

The Examination Guidelines[36] indicate how this provision is to be operated in   **8–147**
practice. Thus, descriptive and other common non-distinctive elements such as
borders and commonplace shapes of containers need not be disclaimed. In reality, the use of disclaimers, both in the UK and at OHIM, under EU trade mark
law appears to be very patchy.

8.6 RELIANCE ON OTHER REGISTRATIONS

When one or more grounds have been raised, applicants frequently argue the   **8–148**
ground cannot apply by relying on other trade marks which have achieved
registration. There are essentially three situations, each raising different
considerations: (1) same or similar mark, same office; (2) same mark, different
offices; (3) similar marks. These are discussed in turn.

The first is where the applicant has existing registration(s) granted by the same   **8–149**
office for the same or similar marks. In those circumstances, the existence of the
other registrations is likely to provide powerful support for the application in
question and to overcome objections.[37]

The second situation arises most often in connection with applications for   **8–150**

---

[33] See CIFUENTES [2005] EWHC 1729.

[34] In s.14.

[35] Work Manual, Ch.6, para.14.

[36] See para.8.13.

[37] In BURST ADVISOR [2000] E.T.M.R. 89 (note), the OHIM BoA was influenced by the fact that
two other very similar applications had been accepted for almost identical goods: BURSTAID
and BURSTWARE. The Examiner's objection under Art.7(1)(b) was overruled because the mark
did not convey a direct and precise indication of the nature or intended purpose of the goods applied for "computer software for use in monitoring the rate of data flow"!

CTMs. The examiner raises one of the absolute grounds of objection, to which the applicant responds by citing its registration for the same mark in one or more countries in the EU. The Examination Guidelines[38] take a sensible approach, suggesting that weight may be given to registrations in countries which are known to operate reasonably rigorous examination of applications, such as the United Kingdom, and this does occur in practice.[39] More often than not, the existence of registrations in other countries is treated as insufficient to overcome the reasoning already expressed, particularly where no information is supplied concerning the circumstances or criteria taken into account which lead to the registrations in question.[40] Even if a national trade mark office has held a mark to be sufficiently distinctive to warrant registration, the Boards of Appeal have stated that the same finding does not necessarily have to be reached by the examiner "who must in each case make his own assessment as to the existence of absolute grounds of refusal."[41] The Boards of Appeal have also pointed out that the CTM system runs in parallel with national systems and is not subordinate or ancillary to them, and that, despite harmonisation, one cannot expect that every trade mark office will invariably take the same view.[42] Where national registrations are relied upon by the Boards of Appeal, it is to support the conclusion already reached. Certainly, other registrations are treated as irrelevant where it appears that the sign has a particular meaning in a foreign language which appears not to have been appreciated when granting the other registrations.

8–151   In the third situation, applicants rely on the state of the register: they cite the existence of registrations for the same type of mark in support of their own application. For example, the objection raised is that the mark is descriptive, contrary to s.3(1)(c). The applicant responds by citing registrations of marks which it believes are as or more descriptive. In these circumstances, the other registrations are rightly regarded as irrelevant. The principal reason is because one has no idea of the circumstances in which the other marks achieved registration—extensive evidence may have been required to achieve registration, alternatively the relevant examiner may have made a mistake.[43]

8–152   In this regard there is a slight divergence in practice between the United

---

[38] See para.8.1.4: "If a trade mark is already registered in many or all the Member States of the Community this will be an indication to the examiner that absolute grounds for refusal are unlikely to exist. Examiners should take particular account of registrations of trade marks under examination systems in Member States which apply standards of absolute grounds of refusal similar to those in the Regulation. In neither case will existing registrations be decisive for the examiner but he will have to take them into account."

[39] "The registration of a trade mark for a particular item of goods [in issue] in a Member State ... particularly under the harmonised trade mark law ... has a certain presumptive effect for the registration procedure of a Community trade mark." Case R–34/1998-3 LASTING PERFORMANCE, July 27, 1998, para.17.

[40] See, e.g. Case R–94/1998-1 OPTIMA, OHIM BoA, where the mark was rejected under the equivalent of s.3(1)(b) and (c) since it means "the very best" in Portugese. The applicant relied on a number of registrations which it had obtained for the mark in Portugal, but it did not explain how those registrations had been achieved.

[41] Case R–34/1998-3 LASTING PERFORMANCE, July 27, 1998, para.17.

[42] See Case R–66/1998-1 COMFORT PLUS [1999] E.T.M.R. 575, para.18, OHIM BoA.

[43] "That follows from the principle of legality, according to which no person may rely, in support of his claim, on an unlawful act committed in favour of another (see, for example, judgment of the Court of Justice in ... *Williams v Court of Auditors* [1985] E.C.R. 2225, para.14 and ... EASI-CASH Case R–96/1998-1, para.17)": Case R–161/1998-1, *100% Pure Goodness*, OHIM First BoA.

Kingdom Registry and OHIM. In the United Kingdom, it is customary to cite Jacob J. in *British Sugar*:[44]

> "It has long been held under the old Act that comparison with other marks on the register is in principle irrelevant when considering a particular mark tendered for registration, see *e.g. MADAME Trade Mark* [1966] R.P.C. 541) and the same must be true under the 1994 Act."

Certain Boards of Appeal have expressed the view that the examiner may be under a duty to consider whether the cases are so similar as to require identical treatment, in particular where the goods or services of the application and the cited registrations are competing.[45] Others have stated that each mark has to be assessed on its own circumstances: any irregularity which might have occurred in relation to some other marks should not be compounded.[46]   **8–153**

RELIANCE ON DECISIONS OF TRIBUNALS/COURTS IN OTHER MEMBER STATES

Decisions of the European Court of Justice and the European Court of First Instance (the court of appeal from the OHIM Boards of Appeal) are binding throughout the EU. Decisions on matters of law of other national tribunals or courts within the EU on equivalent provisions are persuasive but not binding. Laddie J. has stated:[47]   **8–154**

> "It would not be right for an English Court, if it is firmly of a different view, to follow the route adopted by the courts of another Member State simply because the other courts expressed a view first. The scope of European legislation is too important to be decided on a "first past the post" basis."

9. Shapes—section 3(2)

"**s. 3**—(2): A sign shall not be registered as a trade mark if it consists exclusively of—   **8–155**

(a) the shape which results from the nature of the goods themselves,
(b) the shape of goods which is necessary to obtain a technical result, or
(c) the shape which gives substantial value to the goods."

DERIVATION

The wording of paras (a)–(c) of s.3(2) of the 1994 Act is identical to the wording in Article 3(1)(e) of the TM Directive and Article 7(1)(e) of the CTM Regulation. Differently worded provisions, which were similar to provisions in Benelux law, were contained in the earliest drafts of the Directive, but their applicability at that stage depended upon whether shapes could constitute trade marks under the law of the particular Member State. The reference to "sign" was retained, as in Article 3(1)(a) of the TM Directive.   **8–156**

---

[44] *British Sugar* [1996] R.P.C. 281 at 305.
[45] XTRA [1998] E.T.M.R. 562, and FOODSAVER [1999] E.T.M.R. 191 (note).
[46] TELEPAELLA [1998] E.T.M.R. 708 (note), OHIM BoA.
[47] *Wagamama* [1995] F.S.R. 713 at 728. In the "three headed rotary shaver" litigation, there was a divergence of view between the majority in the Swedish Court of Appeal on the one hand and Jacob J. and the English Court of Appeal on the other as to the meaning of "shape necessary to achieve a technical result" in s.3(2)(b). The reference to the ECJ resolved this divergence. See para.8–158.

GENERAL

8–157   Section 1(1) of the 1994 Act confirms that a trade mark may consist of the shape of goods or their packaging. Before these shapes can achieve registration as trade marks, they must not only satisfy the representation and distinctiveness requirements of s.3(1), they must overcome these three prohibitions in s.3(2). Each subsection is concerned with a different (but not necessarily distinct) aspect of shape. Section 3(2) is designed to prevent these shapes being registered trade marks for goods.

THE JUDGMENT OF THE ECJ IN *PHILIPS*

8–158   In *Philips*[48] the ECJ explained the rationale behind these provisions, and the second in particular, as follows:

"78. The rationale of the grounds for refusal of registration laid down in Article 3(1)(e) of the Directive is to prevent trade mark protection from granting its proprietor a monopoly on technical solutions or functional characteristics of a product which a user is likely to seek in the products of competitors. Article 3(1)(e) is thus intended to prevent the protection conferred by the trade mark right from being extended, beyond signs which serve to distinguish a product or service from those offered by competitors, so as to form an obstacle preventing competitors from freely offering for sale products incorporating such technical solutions or functional characteristics in competition with the proprietor of the trade mark.

79. As regards, in particular, signs consisting exclusively of the shape of the product necessary to obtain a technical result, listed in Article 3(1)(e), second indent, of the Directive, that provision is intended to preclude the registration of shapes whose essential characteristics perform a technical function, with the result that the exclusivity inherent in the trade mark right would limit the possibility of competitors supplying a product incorporating such a function or at least limit their freedom of choice in regard to the technical solution they wish to adopt in order to incorporate such a function in their product.

80. As Article 3(1)(e) of the Directive pursues an aim which is in the public interest, namely that a shape whose essential characteristics perform a technical function and were chosen to fulfil that function may be freely used by all, that provision prevents such signs and indications from being reserved to one undertaking alone because they have been registered as trade marks (see, to that effect, *Windsurfing Chiemsee*, paragraph 25).

81. As to the question whether the establishment that there are other shapes which could achieve the same technical result can overcome the ground for refusal or invalidity contained in Article 3(1)(e), second indent, there is nothing in the wording of that provision to allow such a conclusion.

82. In refusing registration of such signs, Article 3(1)(e), second indent, of the Directive reflects the legitimate aim of not allowing individuals to use registration of a mark in order to acquire or perpetuate exclusive rights relating to technical solutions."

---

[48] Case C–299/99, *Philips Electronics N.V. v Remington Consumer Products Ltd* [2002] E.C.R. I-5475; [2003] Ch. 159; [2003] R.P.C. 2, p.14, ECJ (A-G [2001] R.P.C. 38, p.745)

83. Where the essential functional characteristics of the shape of a product are attributable solely to the technical result, Article 3(1)(e), second indent, precludes registration of a sign consisting of that shape, even if that technical result can be achieved by other shapes.

84. In the light of those considerations, the answer to the fourth question must be that Article 3(1)(e), second indent, of the Directive must be interpreted to mean that a sign consisting exclusively of the shape of a product is unregistrable by virtue thereof if it is established that the essential functional features of that shape are attributable only to the technical result. Moreover, the ground for refusal or invalidity of registration imposed by that provision cannot be overcome by establishing that there are other shapes which allow the same technical result to be obtained."

We discuss the detail of paras 79–84, below.[49]

PUBLIC INTEREST

The ECJ has stated repeatedly that each of the various absolute grounds for refusal must be interpreted in the light of the public interest underlying each of them.[50] However, the public interest identified by the ECJ in *Philips* as underlying Art.3(1)(e) requires a little further explanation.   **8–159**

Article 15(1) of TRIPS lays down the essential requirements for a trade mark. It must be capable of distinguishing the goods or services of one undertaking from those of other undertakings. Signatories may require trade marks to be visually perceptible. Article 15(2) of TRIPS goes on to permit signatories to have other grounds for refusal, provided they do not derogate from the provisions of the Paris Convention, the relevant provisions, so far as absolute grounds are concerned, being in Article 6*quinquies* B 2 & 3. One can see the origin of many of the grounds in Article 3 of the TM Directive, but the Paris Convention contains nothing equivalent to Article 3(1)(e) of the TM Directive or 7(1)(e) of the CTM Regulation. Hence, a potential issue was whether these provisions were compatible with the Paris Convention and TRIPS.   **8–160**

In *Philips* the ECJ managed to avoid any incompatibility with TRIPS.[51] It did this by explaining that "Article 3(1)(e) is thus intended to prevent the protection conferred by the trade mark right from being extended, beyond signs which serve to distinguish…". Article 3(1)(e) is thus a belt-and-braces provision. Signs caught are unable or are deemed unable to distinguish. One might say that Art.3(1)(e) (and Article 7(1)(e) of the CTM Regulation) are therefore unnecessary. One might also say that, to be compatible with TRIPS, they have to be unnecessary and, in view of the way the case law has developed under Art.3(1)(b) as regards the shape of goods or packaging, the role of these provisions is very narrow indeed. Nonetheless, each one serves a particular purpose. In the light of the general rationale explained in *Philips*, we can offer more explanation of the public interest underlying each provision. Traders should not be able to obtain the potentially indefinite protection afforded by a trade mark and thereby create an obstacle to competitors because: **8–161**

---

[49] See para.8–183.

[50] See, *e.g. Philips*, para.77, *Windsurfing*, paras 25–27.

[51] It is unclear whether this was intentional or not, but no matter. TRIPS was not referred to by the ECJ or the A.G. and TRIPS only started to be referred to by the ECJ some years after the judgment in *Philips*.

(a) shapes which result from the nature of the goods themselves cannot be considered distinctive and cannot be reserved to one undertaking. Unlike the other two provisions, the first does not involve any other intellectual property right. It seems to be based purely on the policy consideration.

(b) shapes which are necessary to achieve a technical result are protected by other intellectual property rights of limited duration (patents and designs) and absent those rights, competitors should be free to use such shapes.

(c) similarly, shapes which add substantial value to the goods are protected by other intellectual property rights of limited duration (design rights) and absent those rights, competitors should be free to use such shapes.

Relevance of distinctiveness or lack of it

8–162   It is clear that distinctiveness or lack of it has no direct relevance to these grounds. They cannot be overcome by proving that the mark has acquired distinctiveness through use. However, the types of shape prohibited under s.3(2) are, by their nature, very likely to have difficulties in satisfying the distinctiveness requirements of s.3(1), so distinctiveness or lack of it is very likely to be in issue.[52] The Court of First Instance has held that these shape objections are not to be equated with lack of distinctiveness under s.3(1)(b)/Art.7(1)(b) CTM Regulation.[53] However, it is suggested that if a shape can be shown to be distinctive in fact, it is an indication that the shape does not consist exclusively of one of the forbidden shapes.

Approach to these grounds

8–163   Once it has been confirmed that the sign in question does consist of a "shape", there are two issues:

(1) does the shape in question fall into one (or more) of the prohibited categories?

(2) does the sign consist exclusively of that shape?

Sign and shape

8–164   At the outset it is necessary to clarify what sort of signs constitute shapes within these provisions. In the context of goods, "shape" suggests a three-dimensional form, consistent with Article 2 of the TM Directive and Article 4 of the CTM Regulation which both expressly permit a trade mark to consist of "the shape of goods or their packaging". Confusion may arise at the stage where the sign is represented graphically. The graphic representation of the sign is in two-dimensions. But is the sign a three-dimensional shape or a two-dimensional drawing or picture of the shape? The answer to this question ought to be clear from the description of the mark on the application form. Even if it is not, it should make no difference to the application of these provisions, and this was the approach taken in *Philips v Remington*, both by Jacob J.[54] and the ECJ. Indeed, the ECJ

---

[52] In *BP's Application* [1999] E.T.M.R. 282 (oil containers) the OHIM Second Board of Appeal indicated that even if a shape mark consisting of an ordinary container escapes these shape grounds, it will still require a very high degree of distinctiveness in order to be registrable. We suggest this remains correct, notwithstanding what has happened subsequently.

[53] Case T–122/99, "Soap (device)", Court of First Instance, February 16, 2000, [2000] E.C.R. II-265; [2000] E.T.M.R. 580.

[54] See the comments of Jacob J. [1998] R.P.C. 283 at 290.

stated expressly that these provisions apply to "a sign consisting exclusively of the shape of the product or of a graphic representation of that shape...".[55]

For the most part, the "shapes" considered against these provisions will be three-dimensional shapes and two-dimensional representations of them, but not exclusively so. It is possible to conceive of two-dimensional shapes (such as silhouettes), and there are certain types of laminar goods which can be argued to be essentially two-dimensional (such as novelty greetings cards), even though they are in fact three-dimensional. The real distinction is between external or exterior features (*i.e.* three-dimensional shapes and two-dimensional representations of them, including silhouettes) and patterns or designs applied to the surface or interior of goods.[56] Fortunately, it is likely to be evident when a sign comprises the shape of goods or their packaging, as opposed to being a two-dimensional design or pattern.   **8–165**

EXCLUSIVELY

These grounds only apply if the sign consists exclusively of one of the prohibited types of shape. This requirement raises two related issues. First, there is the general issue of what degree of "surplus" or "capricious addition" is required to avoid any one of the grounds in s.3(1)(c),(d) and (b) or 3(2) (see above). Secondly, there are particular considerations applicable to each ground in s.3(2), and these are discussed below.   **8–166**

SHAPES RESULTING FROM THE NATURE OF THE GOODS THEMSELVES

This ground prevents the registration of shapes resulting from the nature of the goods. It is not concerned to prevent registration of marks consisting of the shape of the goods themselves. Indeed, there would be no reason to do so since the shape of distinctively shaped goods can function as a trade mark. So this ground requires consideration of what is meant by "the nature of the goods themselves" and "the shape which results" therefrom.   **8–167**

THE NATURE OF THE GOODS THEMSELVES

The nature of the goods refers to their essential qualities or innate characteristics—this is what Aldous L.J. was referring to in *Philips v Remington (No.1)* when he said it is difficult to envisage such shapes, except those that are produced in nature, such as bananas.[57] Thus, a sign consisting of the shape of a banana for bananas would be a shape which results from the nature of the goods themselves. So too, would a sign consisting of a bunch of bananas for bananas, the shape of an American football for American footballs or the shape of a lemon for lemons.   **8–168**

Thus, when considering the question as to whether a sign is exclusively a shape which results from the nature of the goods, careful consideration needs to   **8–169**

---

[55] *Philips*, end of para.76, [2002] E.C.R. I-5475; [2003] Ch. 159; [2003] R.P.C. 2; [2002] E.T.M.R. 81.

[56] Under similar but not identical provisions in Benelux law, the Benelux Court of Justice held that shapes only cover three-dimensional designs and not two-dimensional patterns such as the Burberry check: Burberrys (December 16, 1991).

[57] [1999] R.P.C. 809 at 820. An OHIM Board of Appeal held that a three-dimensional mark of a bar of soap with longitudinal curved indents in the sides was a shape which resulted from the nature of the goods themselves. This was obviously wrong, as was accepted on appeal to the Court of First Instance: Case T–122/99 "Soap (device)", Court of First Instance, February 16, 2000, [2000] E.C.R. II-265; [2000] E.T.M.R. 580.

be given to the goods in order to determine their nature, and the sign. Consider the following:

> (1) A picture of a lemon as a proposed trade mark for lemons would not be registered because the sign would consist exclusively of a shape which results from the nature of the goods themselves—lemons. Likewise a picture of lemons on the branch, or a silhouette of a lemon.
>
> (2) If the goods were lemon juice, then it is suggested that a picture of a lemon should not fall foul of this particular provision, although other objections would be likely under s.3(1)(b) and (c), subject to proof of distinctive character under the proviso. Likewise if the proposed mark was a yellow plastic container in the shape of a lemon.

WHAT ARE "THE GOODS"?

8–170   Thus far, the analysis is overly simple, because of the specification of goods chosen. Applicants are most unlikely to make life so simple. In *Philips v Remington*, Jacob J. raised the question of how does one define what "the goods" are? He pointed out that if one takes the specification of goods, the result will be partly adventitious. What about the shape of an American football for "balls" and not just American footballs? He considered that one could not go simply by the specification of goods. He suggested that the answer was partly one of degree— one must ask what the goods are as a practical business matter. In the Court of Appeal, Aldous L.J. said that "the goods" refer to any of the goods in respect of which the mark is registered or sought to be registered. Thus, he said, a picture of a banana for fruit would be just as objectionable as for bananas.[58]

8–171   In practice, this "American football" problem will always arise and there are two possible solutions to it. One is to say that (subject to the other provisions in s,3 of the 1994 Act) the applicant can have a registration consisting of the shape of an American football provided the specification expressly excludes American footballs. This solution produces an unsatisfactory and anomalous situation when one considers the position of the honest trader who uses the shape of an American football to promote his American footballs. Potentially he is driven to s.11 to find a defence, because American footballs will undoubtedly be similar to other balls used in sport. The result of this analysis strongly supports what Aldous L.J. decided. It is enough if the shape results from the nature of any of the goods for which registration is sought, subject only to usual *de minimis* considerations.

8–172   Thus this particular provision has a limited scope. It may be summarised as "You cannot register the natural shape of the goods". The natural shape of goods is descriptive of them. These are shapes which traders may legitimately want to use.

8–173   If this analysis is correct, if the goods have been the subject of substantial design input, then there can be no shape which results from the nature of the goods themselves. This explains why Philips' three headed shaver mark did not fall foul of this provision. In *Philips v Remington*, the mark consisted of a picture of a three-headed rotary electric shaver and was registered for "electric shavers". At first instance, Jacob J. held the mark invalid, *inter alia*, as contrary to s.3(2)(b), but not (a) or (c).[59] The Court of Appeal agreed, but for different reasons.[60]

8–174   In view of the overlap between this ground and s.3(1)(c) (and 3(1)(b) and (d)

---

[58] [1998] R.P.C. 283 at 304, and [1999] R.P.C. 809 at 820.
[59] [1998] R.P.C. 283.

for that matter), one might ask why the proviso to s.3(1) does not apply to s.3(2)—if a trader can overcome a s.3(1)(c) objection by proving acquired distinctiveness, why not a s.3(2)(a) ground? The answer probably lies in the fact that the natural shapes of goods are so descriptive—comparable to "lemon" for lemons, that there is no practical possibility that a trader would be able to educate the public to see such a shape as a badge of origin.

Shape necessary to obtain a technical result

This provision has been the subject of protracted examination in the three-headed shaver litigation.   **8–175**

Necessary — Philips No. 1

In *Philips v Remington (No.1)*, the 208 mark in issue consisted of a drawing of the top portion of a three-headed rotary shaver, the heads being arranged in the form of an inverted equilateral triangle. *Philips* proved that other arrangements of three heads produced the same technical result and argued that the shape of the three-headed shaver shown in the mark was not therefore necessary to obtain the technical result. Not surprisingly, this argument failed at every level. The ECJ dismissed it in short order.[61] The mark was invalid under s.3(2)(b).   **8–176**

The argument that a shape is not excluded by this provision if the same or a similar technical result can be achieved by other shapes approaches the problem from the wrong end. The focus of this provision is not on the technical result, but on the shape in question and the technical effect of it. If the shape in question does nothing (in substance) but produce a technical result, then the shape is unregistrable. There may be a variety of shapes which produce the same technical result, but all of them are unregistrable, because honest traders should be able to use all such functional shapes in their products.   **8–177**

Consider an example outside the realm of shavers—the technical result obtained by a corkscrew. The guts of a corkscrew can employ various designs of helical screw. All of them are necessary to achieve the technical result. A sign comprising just the shape of any one of those designs of helical screw should not be registered. However, there is plenty of scope for the designer to make his corkscrew look different to those of other manufacturers, so a sign consisting of the shape of the whole of the corkscrew would not consist exclusively of the prohibited shape. Whether the shape of the whole of the corkscrew was seen as a badge of origin is another matter.   **8–178**

The sub-text is: if the use of such shapes is to be restricted, it is through the law of designs and patents, but not trade marks. The technical result need not be novel or inventive. Indeed, the more commonplace the technical result, the greater the need to prevent registration of the shape or shapes which are necessary to achieve that result.   **8–179**

Again, a shape which is necessary to obtain a technical result is likely also to indicate the intended purpose of the goods, may be customary and/or non-distinctive in any event (cf. s.3(1)(c), (d) and (b), above).   **8–180**

Exclusively — Philips (No.2)

In *Philips (No.2)*, the 452 mark in issue was very slightly different to the 208   **8–181**

---

[60] [1999] R.P.C. 809.
[61] See paras 81–84, at para.8–158.

mark the subject of the first round. The three shaving heads sat within a raised faceplate of clover leaf design rather than the uniform triangular shape. It was proved that this raised faceplate performed the function of stretching the skin and raising the hairs to be shaved. As before, the fact that other shapes of faceplate could perform the same function did not matter, and the mark as a whole was held invalid under s.3(2)(b). The main focus of the case really turned on "exclusively". This issue had been in play in *Philips (No.1)*, in which Jacob J. made the common sense observation: "I do not believe that shapes with trivial embellishments or variants are outside the exclusion from registrability."[62]

PHILIPS NO.2

8–182   In *Philips v Remington (No.2)*[63] Philips argued (placing particular emphasis on the ECJ's use of "solely" or "only") that if the shape included any feature which is non-functional—some form of embellishment—then the prohibition has no effect. As appears from the judgment of Rimer J., the case was greatly over-complicated. As he observed: "...it is important to remember that all that this lit-igation is about is the business end of a piece of electrical equipment whose sole purpose is functional."

8–183   The first problem lay in trying to discern a consistent meaning in paras 78–84 of the judgment of the ECJ.[64] Those paragraphs only read consistently if the word "functional" in the expression "essential functional characteristics" in paras 83 and 84 is treated as included in error, as Rimer J. did. Once that is done, the rele-vant test can be expressed as follows:

(1) In every case it is a question of fact as to whether the shape in issue falls foul of the prohibition.

(2) The shape in issue must be assessed in order to identify its essential characteristics or features.

(3) If those essential characteristics or features are solely attributable to achieving the intended technical result, the prohibition applies. It will make no difference if the shape includes non-essential features which are not so attributable.

(4) The test is an objective one and does not depend upon the subjective inten-tions of the designer of the shape.

(5) Such a conclusion is not prevented by a finding that a different shape can also achieve the same technical result.

8–184   The subtleties of some of these points are illustrated by the facts and argu-ments in the case itself. Philips contended that the clover leaf design of faceplate was not introduced for any technical reason and, apart from the areas immediately surrounding the three cutting heads, performed no technical function at all. By reference to the stages of the test we have set out above, the Judge held:

(2) the clover leaf was not an essential feature of the shape of the mark as a whole. However, the question was whether the whole of the faceplate, of which the clover leaf formed part, was attributable solely to the technical result;

(3) the clover leaf did perform an essential function—of stretching the skin and raising the hairs. The fact that other shapes would achieve the same

---

[62] [1998] R.P.C. 283 at 308.
[63] *Koninklijke Philips N.V. v Remington Consumer Products Ltd* [2005] F.S.R. 17, p.325.
[64] Set out at para.8–158

function was no answer. The prohibition did not require or allow examination of every part of every essential feature. Provided each such feature as a whole performed a technical function, it did not matter that minute elements of it might not contribute. On the facts, the Judge held that the whole of the face plate, including the clover leaf, contributed to the overall technical objective.

Plainly, the analysis of the precise technical function of minute elements of the mark was inappropriate. "exclusively" requires a purposive, common sense approach.

Other examples of the application of this provision demonstrate some of the difficulties: **8–185**

(1) The representation of the mark was this description: "a chewy sweet on a stick". Registration was rightly refused under ss.1(1) and 3(1)(a) of the 1994 Act because the sign was not capable of being represented graphically. However, an objection under s.3(2)(b) was also upheld, on the basis that a stick was an entirely functional characteristic of the goods. This reasoning was wrong because the stick was not exclusively the shape sought to be registered.[65]

(2) Application was made to OHIM and the United Kingdom Registry to register the shape of a bar of soap which had indentations on the longitudinal sides. The applications were refused under s.3(1)(b) and its equivalent mainly because the sign just looked like a bar of soap. The OHIM Board of Appeal also upheld an objection under the equivalent of s.3(2)(b) saying: "the indentation on the longitudinal part functions to allow a better grip of the product. Since it could not conceivably be achieved in any other way, the Board considers that the claimed shape consists of a shape which is necessary to obtain a technical result ..."[66] Although the decision of the Board of Appeal was overturned by the Court of First Instance on various procedural grounds,[67] the conclusion appears correct, but the reasoning is wrong since one could conceive of other shapes of indentation which would achieve the same technical result. The United Kingdom Registry did not take a s.3(2)(b) objection.[68]

(3) The mark comprised a lug for holding and securing a drum leg, consisting of a small cylinder projecting from a larger cylinder with the leg passing through the smaller cylinder. This shape of drum lug was said to be highly distinctive, since most drum lugs were rectangular. An objection under Art.7(1)(e)(ii) was not upheld, on the ground that the same technical result could be obtained with a significantly different shape. As stated, the reasoning is contrary to the Philips ECJ judgment.[69]

(4) The mark comprised the shape of an 8-boss "Lego" brick, in red, registered for "playthings". The OHIM Cancellation Division held that each of the elements of the shape of the mark, and thereby the shape of the mark as a whole, is necessary to obtain a technical result, contrary to Art.7(1)(e)(ii). The fact that the brick was red did not alter the fact that the

---

[65] *Swizzels Matlow Ltd's Application* [1998] R.P.C. 244, Regy.
[66] Case 74/1998-3, OHIM BoA, March 15, 1999, see para.27.
[67] "Soap (device)", Court of First Instance, February 16, 2000, [2000] E.C.R. II-265; [2000] E.T.M.R. 580.
[68] *Procter & Gamble's Trade Mark Application* [1998] R.P.C. 710, Regy. The headnote is incorrect in saying that a s.3(2)(b) objection "was not made out". The objection was not taken, although perhaps it should have been.
[69] R–202/1999-1, December 22, 1999 (before the Judgment of the ECJ in *Philips*).

sign consisted exclusively of the shape of goods which is necessary to obtain a technical result.[70]

(5) The mark comprised a three-dimensional configuration of ribbing applied to the casing of a centrifugal type of pump casing, reminiscent of a shell. The OHIM First Board of Appeal held the mark (whatever it was) had sufficient distinctive character to overcome Art.7(1)(b) and also held that the mark did not result from the nature of the goods themselves nor was necessary to obtain a technical result. The Board appeared to accept that the ribbing was necessary for structural reasons, that other manufacturers of such pumps must remain free to strengthen their pump casings with ribbing which radiates around the circumference of the casing, but held that it was not necessary to use ribbing arranged in precisely the same manner as the ribbing shown in the mark. The reasoning is naive and led to the wrong result.[71]

(6) The mark comprised the head portion of a toothbrush, with bristles of varying length and arranged at opposing slight angles. Even though the toothbrush in issue had a specific technical effect, it did not fall foul of Art.7(1)(e) since there were other technical means of achieving the same end.[72]

(7) The mark comprised a three-dimensional shape of packaging. It was a yoghurt pot with two triangular compartments differing in size (one for topping, one for the yoghurt). It was held that all the essential features of the shape were functional and the mark was refused registration under s.3(2)(b).[73]

SIGNS WHICH CONSIST EXCLUSIVELY OF THE SHAPE WHICH GIVES SUBSTANTIAL VALUE TO THE GOODS

8–186   Of the three provisions, the purpose and scope of this one is the most obscure. The way in the ECJ explained the rationale behind Article 3(1)(e) of the TM Directive in *Philips*[74] did not seem to address substantial value at all, other than in terms of technical solution or functional characteristics. Yet this provision seems to be dealing with something different—the contribution of the shape to the value of the goods. Whether the contribution comes from technical or aesthetic features, again the underlying public interest appears to be as follows: traders should not be able to obtain the potentially indefinite protection afforded by a trade mark and thereby create an obstacle to competitors because shapes which add substantial value to the goods are protected by other intellectual property rights of limited duration and absent those rights, competitors should be free to use such shapes. If this reasoning is correct, it suggests that this provision covers both technical and aesthetic shapes.

8–187   As Jacob J. observed in *Philips*:[75] "Good trade marks add value to goods-that is one of the things they are for. So one must not take this exclusion too literally." The difficulty is in deciding what degree of value contributed by the shape should trigger this provision.

8–188   Jacob J. went on to say: "I think what is meant is an exclusion of shapes which

---

[70] C–107029/1, July 30, 2004.
[71] R–82/1999-1, December 21, 1999.
[72] R–406/2000-3, March 28, 2001.
[73] UK TM Registry O/183/04, a decision of Allan James, June 25, 2004.
[74] See para.78, set out above.
[75] [1998] R.P.C. 283 at 309. With the subsequent approval of the CA, [1999] R.P.C. 809 at 822.

exclusively add some sort of value (design or functional appearance or perhaps something else though I cannot think of anything) to the goods disregarding any value attributable to a trade mark (*i.e.* source identification) function. A question of degree is obviously involved. For instance the Rolls Royce grille adds value to a Rolls Royce. But it does so primarily because it signifies Rolls Royce and not because of its inherent shape." Jacob J. concluded that the shape of the three-headed shaver was recognised as having an engineering function, and for that reason it added substantial value to the goods.

The Court of Appeal disagreed with the approach of Jacob J., saying that the purpose of this provision was to exclude "aesthetic-type shapes", *i.e.* shapes which have eye appeal.[76] The decision whether the value is substantial requires: "a comparison ... between the shape sought to be registered and shapes of equivalent articles. It is only if the shape has, in relative terms, substantial value that it will be excluded from registration." As a matter of general approach, this seems to be sensible and correct. It remains to be seen whether substantial value should be restricted to aesthetic shapes. One might say that technical or functional features are adequately covered already, but it is difficult to see why, if technical features do add substantial value to the goods, they should be left out of account under this provision. **8–189**

In practice, the application of this provision is likely to remain difficult, as is shown by the United Kingdom Registry decision concerning the shape of Dualit toasters.[77] In *Dualit*, the signs were the shape of two models of Dualit toaster. In the UK TM Registry, the hearing officer decided, after much analysis (which itself indicates the difficulties in applying this provision), that the eye appeal of the signs did give substantial value to the goods. He seems to have reached this view largely because the Dualit toaster was hailed as a "design classic" but also on the evidence of pricing. The price of the Dualit toasters was about seven times the price of most domestic toasters. However, the Dualit toasters were of catering quality, and the price was comparable with other catering toasters of similar quality. Apparently, the competitors in this new niche market created by Dualit priced their offerings midway between Dualit and the ordinary domestic toasters. The robustness and longevity of the Dualit toasters contributed to their high cost, and some value had to be attributed to the Dualit mark which appeared on the toasters. There was therefore, evidence of some price premium. The hearing officer decided that price was an important factor but not the sole factor to be taken into account. **8–190**

Some people are prepared to pay extra for good design. The problem is that "good design" can often involve (1) more expensive design input, (2) better quality materials, (3) a more exclusive product (*i.e.* not mass-produced, possibly with some control over retail distribution). The existence of some or all of these factors is likely to lead to a higher price being charged for the product, compared with products which do the same job. This provision appears to require concentration simply on the shape in question, leaving aside the value attributable to the quality of materials or matters of technical or functional design. This is what the hearing officer in *Dualit* was doing. **8–191**

---

[76] At p.822. This does not mean, necessarily, that the shape must be registrable as a design.

[77] *Dualit Limited's (Toaster Shapes) Trade Mark Applications* [1999] R.P.C. 304, Regy. On appeal, Lloyd J. rejected the application under s.3(1)(b) and considered he did not need to deal with the "different and difficult issues" which arose under s.3(2)(c). If it had proved necessary to deal with it, the judge said he would almost certainly have referred the matter to the ECJ for a preliminary ruling.

8–192   Having stripped out factors irrelevant to this provision, one is left with the aspects of design of shape where the designer has room for manoeuvre: does his or her design input to the shape give substantial value to the goods. This issue is to be answered by comparing the shape sought to be registered with shapes of equivalent articles.[78] If the designer has an established reputation,[79] then it is very likely that substantial value would be found. But even if the designer is unknown, "good design" may well be taken to have added substantial value to goods.

OTHER EXAMPLES

8–193   (1) The mark comprised the shape of a glass jar with eight faces (the new Nescafé shape). The shape was held not to give substantial value to the goods.[80]

(2) The mark comprised the shape of a savoury snack, resembling a flower with six non-uniform petals. It is unclear why Art.7(1)(e) was considered, but the OHIM First Board of Appeal found the mark was not prohibited under any of the three limbs of Art.7(1)(e).[81]

10. Public policy, deceptive marks

THE PROVISIONS

8–194   "s.3—(3): A trade mark shall not be registered if it is

(a) contrary to public policy or to accepted principles of morality, or

(b) of such a nature as to deceive the public (for instance as to the nature, quality or geographical origin of the goods or service)."

8–195   Section 3(3) implements two separate grounds of refusal in Articles 3(1)(f) and 3(1)(g) of the TM Directive, corresponding to Articles 7(1)(f) and 7(1)(g) of the CTM Regulation. The same wording is used in all three sets of provisions.

PUBLIC POLICY, ACCEPTED PRINCIPLES OF MORALITY

8–196   Like other absolute grounds, these provisions are directed at the intrinsic qualities of mark itself, and they are not concerned with circumstances relating to the conduct of the applicant.[82] There would appear to be a good deal of overlap between "contrary to public policy" and "contrary to accepted principles of morality", although the latter is invoked far more frequently. Both phrases are deliberately broad. It is suggested that they are designed to prevent registration of marks which would cause offence to a section of the public.[83] Offence may be caused on matters of race, sex, religious beliefs or general matters of taste and

---

[78] Bearing in mind that eye appeal may be a requirement for any article in the relevant market.

[79] For example, it is suggested that a sign which consisted exclusively of the shape of a table or chair by Eileen Grey or Philippe Starck for furniture would not be registrable under this provision. Such a sign could be registrable for services, but the consent of the designer or his or her estate might well be required.

[80] R–739/1999-1, February 13, 2001.

[81] R–467/1999-1, December 15, 1999.

[82] The Court of First Instance so held in relation to an attempt to invoke Art.7(1)(f) in the context of an opposition TUFFTRIDE/NU-TRIDE. The allegation had nothing to do with the mark applied for, NU-TRIDE, and everything to do with bitterness towards a former commercial representative. See Case T–224/01, para.76, [2003] E.C.R. II-1589. Similarly, at OHIM, an allegation that a mark (INTERTOPS) was contrary to public policy was rightly held to be misconceived. The basis for the allegation was that the applicant did not have a licence to conduct gambling in Germany. See the decision of the Fourth Board of Appeal, R–338/2000-4.

[83] OHIM appears to be using this ground to refuse applications for the names of particularly famous

decency. Offence may be caused by words and/or images. It should be remembered that there is a dividing line between offensive marks and trade marks which might be considered by some to be in poor taste—the latter should not fall foul of this provision.

Some useful guidance is given in the UK Trade Mark Registry Work Manual. **8–197** It suggests that marks which encouraged or promoted drugs,[84] counterfeiting,[85] pornography,[86] criminal activity,[87] and the like would be refused under this provision as being contrary to public policy, whereas fairly mild bad language,[88] fairly,[89] or relatively[90] inoffensive expressions and fairly mild slang[91] expressions would not be considered to be contrary to accepted principles of morality.

Likewise the OHIM Guidelines provide: **8–198**

"Words or images which are offensive, such as swear words or racially derogatory images, or which are blasphemous are not acceptable. There is a dividing line between this and trade marks which might be considered in poor taste. The latter do not offend."

In the UK, more specific guidance on the correct approach was given in *Gha-* **8–199** *zilian's Trade Mark Application:*[92]

"The dividing line is to be drawn between offence which amounts only to distaste and offence which would justifiably cause outrage or would be the subject of justifiable censure as being likely significantly to undermine current religious, family or social values. The outrage or censure must be amongst an identifiable section of the public and a higher degree of outrage or censure amongst a small section of the community will no doubt suffice just as lesser outrage or censure amongst a more widespread section of the public will also suffice."

In that case it was also emphasised that s.3(3) was not concerned with political **8–200** correctness but with principles of morality, a different and less readily invoked standard. The test is objective: using the concept of a "right-thinking member of the public", it must be assessed whether the mark in question would cause outrage or censure amongst a relevant section of the public,[93] if, for example, they saw the mark on an advertising poster.[94]

At OHIM, the mark "DICK & FANNY" was held to fall short of being con- **8–201**

---

people: applications refused under Art.7(1)(f) for: BILL CLINTON, FIDEL CASTRO, and JOHANNES PAUL II.

[84] *e.g.* WHITE DOVE (apparently a type of drug) or YOU DON'T NEED WINGS TO FLY.

[85] *e.g.* COPYCAT PERFUMES.

[86] *e.g.* SNUFF MOVIES.

[87] See the preceding footnote.

[88] *e.g.* RAATZ PIZS for beer; KRAP in a device mark. Both accepted. On the other side of the line, BOLOX would be considered contrary to accepted principles of morality in view of bad language. BOLLOX has been refused as a CTM under the equivalent provision of Art.7(1)(f) of the CTM Regulation. Likewise, at OHIM: FUCK of the YEAR.

[89] BREWERS DROOP, accepted.

[90] OLD FARTS; BAD ASS BOYS. Both accepted.

[91] BONK in a device. Accepted.

[92] [2002] R.P.C. 33, p.628, at para.30. A decision of Simon Thorley Q.C. sitting as the Appointed Person, affirming the Registry's refusal of TINY PENIS, but for slightly different reasons.

[93] The approach in TINY PENIS has been applied by the UK TM Registry to refuse JESUS for a range of goods O-210-03, and FOOK for clothing O-133-04. Both affirmed an appeal to the Appointed Person: JESUS (G. Hobbs Q.C.) O-021–05, January 18, 2005; FOOK (D. Kitchin Q.C.) O-182–05, June 23, 2005, notwithstanding the film *"Meet the Fockers"*.

[94] In the UK, the mark FCUK is reasonably well-known, justified as an acronym for French Connection UK yet popular because of the misspelling. The mark has been registered in the UK and at OHIM, although the company wisely abandoned its application for FCUKING. FCUK AT

trary to accepted principles of morality since, of the two meanings, the tasteless and "rather smutty" non-formal English one did not proclaim any opinion, contained no incitement and conveyed no insult.[95]

8–202   At first instance in *Philips v Remington*, Jacob J. invoked the continental concept of *ordre publique*. He expressed the view that this was not aimed at preventing the trade mark system being used to obtain automatic and indefinite extension of the monopoly conferred by a patent, design or copyright.[96]

DECEPTIVE MARKS

8–203   Section 3(3)(b) of the 1994 Act prevents the registration of deceptive marks, a notion familiar in the UK from s.11 of the 1938 Act. The paragraph itself cites some non-exhaustive examples: trade marks which are of such a nature as to deceive the public as to nature, quality or geographical origin of the goods or services. In general, if a mark gives rise to an expectation which will not be fulfilled, then registration will be refused. The expectation (and hence the objection) must be a real one, as opposed to something obscure or fanciful, arising from the mark itself.

8–204   There are two features of this provision to note. First, it is an absolute and not a relative ground for refusal. It is concerned with deceptiveness which is inherent in the mark itself, as opposed to deception caused by the similarity of the mark to another.[97] The latter type of objection arises under the relative grounds in s.5. Likewise, an objection that use of a mark would result in passing off arises under s.5(4)(a) and not under s.3(3)(b). Secondly, the paragraph refers expressly to deception caused by the nature of the mark itself. This does not mean that the mark has to be considered in a vacuum. It must be considered against the goods or services applied for and in the general context of the relevant trade.

PRACTICE

8–205   The practice of the UK TM Registry under the 1938 Act was to consider notional use of the mark across the entire specification of goods or services. If there was any possibility of deception, then an objection was raised under s.11. The practice resulted in a large number of objections and consequent limitations on the specifications of goods. This was so, even where there was no realistic possibility of deception but the specification was too wide.[98] The UK Registry has indicated a change in practice, so that under the 1994 Act an objection will only be raised where, in the examiner's view, there is any real possibility of deception of the public. The thinking is that traders will use marks responsibly: if they do use marks deceptively, they will lose the registration under s.47, they will fall foul of trading standards and will lose customers. By contrast, the Examination Guide-

---

HOME remains pending. Apparent imitators have succeeded in registering CNUT in the UK and at OHIM, as well as WNAK and WNAKER in the UK, all for clothing. One wonders whether these slipped under the radar.

[95] Decision of the Fourth Board of Appeal, R–111/2002-4. The applicant, Dick Lexic Ltd, evidently incline to the single entendre.

[96] [1998] R.P.C. 283 at 309. This point was not considered on appeal.

[97] Relying on *Jardex* [1946] R.P.C. 63, an opponent tried to use s.3(3)(b) against GALAXY for "Preparations for killing weeds and destroying vermin", citing public policy in the risk to children accustomed to eating the chocolate so named. This ground failed, because the mark in itself would not deceive the public. The opposition succeeded under s.5(3): GALAXY, May 19, 2000, Regy.

[98] An example is HARTLEY'S STRAWBERRY JAM for jams or fruit preserves, which previously would have been limited to strawberry jam or fruit preserves consisting primarily of strawberries.

lines[99] issued by OHIM indicate a more rigorous approach, closer to the practice operated under the 1938 Act. In either case, the examiner has to consider the nature of the trade and its customers: does the mark give rise to a real (as opposed to a fanciful) expectation that the goods are made from a particular material, have a particular quality or come from a particular locality? An examiner's initial concerns may be allayed through discussions with the applicant.

SOME EXAMPLES

(1) nature of goods: composition: ORLWOOLA[1] for suits: descriptive if all wool; deceptive if not;   **8–206**

(2) quality of goods: CHINA-THERM[2] for insulated cups made of plastic;

(3) geographical origin of goods: a mark containing the words "Norwegian Sardines"—when there were no such things;[3]

(4) geographical origin of services: a mark comprising a shamrock, but not for services from Ireland.[4]

(5) EU CHAMPIONSHIP IN BUSINESS MANAGEMENT refused at OHIM under Article 7.1(g);

(6) FILET-O-FISH, also refused under Art.7.1(c) and (g), presumably because descriptive if the goods were a filet of fish, deceptive if not. Likewise ONLYGLASS.

(7) LEM BRUSCO, refused under Art.7(1)(g), presumably because would cause deception as regards Lambrusco.

(8) INTERNATIONAL STAR REGISTRY, refused under Art.7(1)(g), as being likely to mislead consumers into believing that the organisation which uses it is an authoritative body empowered to give names to stars.[5] On the other side of the line, THE ECOMMERCE AUTHORITY was held not deceptive but merely laudatory.[6]

(9) TITAN, refused under Art.7(1)(g) and (c), for portable buildings. In German, Danish and Swedish, titan means titanium.[7]

(10) POUDRE LIBRE NATURELLE, cancelled under Art.7(1)(g) as being deceptive for cosmetics which were not powders (and descriptive for those which were).[8] On the other side of the line, METALJACKET for rust-proofing preparations was suggestive and therefore neither deceptive nor descriptive.[9]

Examples of other types of deception which could fall within this provision are: marks which imply official approbation[10] or where a substantial change takes place in the form of trade connection between the user and the goods, so as to render the mark deceptive.[11]

---

[99] Examination Guidelines, para.8.8.

[1] [1910] 1 Ch. 130.

[2] [1980] F.S.R. 21.

[3] *Concord Canning* (1932) 49 R.P.C. 323.

[4] cf. *McGlennon* (1908) 25 R.P.C. 797 and *Grundig* [1968] R.P.C. 89.

[5] Decision of the First Board of Appeal, R–468/1999-1.

[6] Decision of the First Board of Appeal, R–803/2000-1.

[7] Decision of the Third Board of Appeal, R–789/2001-3.

[8] Decision of the First Cancellation Division, September 19, 2000.

[9] Decision of the First Board of Appeal, R–314/2002-1.

[10] *e.g.* ROYAL WORCESTER was refused under the 1938 Act, s.11, not only for possibly suggesting royal patronage, but also because it failed to make it clear that the Worcester being referred to was in the United States.

[11] The 1994 Act contains no equivalent of s.62 of the 1938 Act, but licensing is now much more

OVERCOMING A SECTION 3(3)(B) OBJECTION

8–207   In certain circumstances, an objection under s.3(3)(b) may be overcome: it may be possible to file evidence to show that the mark is not deceptive[12] the applicant may be able to rely on a previous registration for the same goods or services;[13] or, most frequently, the applicant agrees to limit the specification of goods or services, so as to excise those goods or services for which the mark would be deceptive.[14] There were other methods of overcoming deceptiveness objections under s.11 of the 1938 Act which cannot be employed under the 1994 Act, such as conditions of registration (which no longer exist[15]), amendment of the mark itself[16] or variation clauses.

8–208   Often a mark which is more or less descriptive of some goods or services would be deceptive if used in relation to different goods or services. Thus, an application may face objections under ss.3(1)(c) and 3(3)(b) of the 1994 Act from the outset. Alternatively, the objections may arise at different stages. If the principal objection is under s.3(1)(c), the applicant might suggest limiting the goods or services to avoid the descriptiveness objection, with the result that the mark is deceptive in relation to the remaining goods, attracting a s.3(3)(b) objection.[17] In previous editions of this work, it was suggested (under the 1938 Act) that if the objection fails under one head, it will probably fail under both. Whilst that may be true for much of the time, the rule of thumb is probably less applicable under the new provisions. A mark may avoid s.3(1)(c) of the 1994 Act because it is not exclusively an indication designating the kind or quality of the goods, yet have a specification which is wide enough to cause the mark to deceive if used in relation to some goods or services.

11. Illegal marks—section 3(4)

SECTION 3(4)

8–209   "s.3(4): A trade mark shall not be registered if or to the extent that its use is prohibited in the United Kingdom by any enactment or rule of law or by any provision of Community law."

THE CTM REGULATION

8–210   Curiously, there is no provision in Article 7 of the CTM Regulation which corresponds to Article 3(2)(a) of the Directive, although Article 7(1)(j) contains a much more limited prohibition on registration of trade marks which contain or

---

common, so the change in trade connection would have to be substantial to render a mark deceptive. cf. s.46(1)(d) and ELIZABETH EMANUEL—see para.10–027.

[12] For example, METALBOX for boxes other than metal might be considered deceptive. Evidence would show the mark to have acquired a secondary, distinctive and non-deceptive meaning.

[13] The Work Manual suggests that reliance on a previous registration for the same goods or services is conclusive, but one should consider the possibility that the previous registration was accepted in error.

[14] An objection to ARMADILLO for clothing and footwear was overcome by the limitation "none being made from animal skins". Decision of the Fourth Board of Appeal, R–0167/2002-4.

[15] See Sch.3 to the Act, para.3(1).

[16] See s.39(2), which only allows corrections which do not substantially affect the identity of the mark.

[17] e.g. at OHIM, POUDRE LIBRE NATURELLE was refused under Art.7(1)(g), descriptive for cosmetics in the form of powders and deceptive for those which were not. Decision of the First Cancellation Division, September 19, 2000.

consist of geographical indications for wines or spirits for wines or spirits not having that origin. This is dealt with below.

INFLUENCE OF THE TM DIRECTIVE

Article 3(2)(a) of the TM Directive is an optional ground for refusal. It provides **8–211** that a trade mark shall not be registered, etc., where and to the extent that the use of that trade mark may be prohibited pursuant to the provisions of law *other than trade mark law* of the Member State concerned or of Community law. Needless potential confusion would have been avoided if the UK had used the words of the Directive. Nonetheless, when s.3(4) is construed in the light of the TM Directive, it is clear that it can only be referring to matters outside the 1994 Act.

REQUIREMENTS

This is an absolute ground for refusal and, as indicated above, is concerned with **8–212** the trade mark itself. An objection that use of the mark would cause passing off arises under s.5(4)(a) of the 1994 Act and not under this subsection.

For an objection to arise, it is necessary to identify a specific provision in an **8–213** Act of Parliament or Statutory Instrument or in Community legislation or a specific rule of law. Examples are as follows:

(1) use of the Red Cross and other emblems, contrary to s.6 of the Geneva Conventions Act 1957;
(2) use of the Royal Arms, if the use would be contrary to s.92(2) of the Patents Act 1977;
(3) use of the word "Anzac", contrary to the "Anzac" (Restriction on Trade Use of Word) Act 1916.

So far as Community legislation is concerned, increasingly the EU has **8–214** legislated to protect particular designations of origin or characteristics of goods,[18] and one can expect further legislation in the future. Examples are "Champagne", "Cognac", etc. Only persons producing in the appropriate region and/or according to the right method are entitled to use these terms. The Regulation then in force was enforced to prevent the use of "Champagne" in "Elderflower Champagne": see *Taittinger v Allbev Ltd* [1993] F.S.R. 641. Under s.3(4) of the 1994 Act, Allbev would be prevented from registering a mark such as "Thornycroft Elderflower Champagne". Likewise, an application to register the same mark as a CTM would be refused under Article 7(1)(j) of the CTM Regulation. Applications to register DUQUE DE VILLENA and DUQUE DE PENAFIEL were refused under this provision as containing inapplicable protected geographical indications for wines.[19]

12. Specially protected emblems—sections 3(5), 4, 57 and 58

SECTION 3(5)

"s.3(5): A trade mark shall not be registered in the cases specified, or referred **8–215** to, in section 4 of the 1994 Act (specially protected emblems)."

Purpose

Section 4 of the 1994 Act provides differing measures of protection for emblems **8–216**

---

[18] See Ch.10.
[19] Decisions of the Second Board of Appeal, R–1221/2000-2 and R–1222/2000-2.

in the following six classes: first, matters Royal; secondly, the flags of the United Kingdom; thirdly, national emblems of signatories to the Paris Convention; fourthly, emblems of certain international organisations; fifthly, coats of arms; and sixthly, Olympic symbols. The first, second and fifth classes are concerned with domestic protection for the types of emblem originating in a Convention country outside the United Kingdom which may qualify for protection under the Paris Convention.

8–217   Protection for these classes of emblems originates from four sources. First, Article 6*ter* of the Paris Convention (via Article 3(1)(h) of the TM Directive, corresponding to Article 7(1)(h) of the CTM Regulation). Secondly, the optional provisions of Article 3(2) of the TM Directive allow protection to extend beyond Article 6*ter*, citing signs of "high symbolic value, in particular a religious symbol" and "badges, emblems and escutcheons"[20] of public interest.[21] Thirdly, the choices made by the United Kingdom when implementing the optional provisions of the TM Directive.[22] Fourthly, the Olympic Symbol etc. (Protection) Act 1995 which added subs.(5) to s.4.

8–218   Although the extent of protection varies between the classes, the basic object is to prevent trade marks being registered which misrepresent themselves as being "official".

CTM Regulation

8–219   As indicated above, Articles 7(1)(h) and (i) of the CTM Regulation correspond to Articles 3(1)(h) and 3(2)(c) of the TM Directive. At OHIM, Article 7(1)(h) (Art.6*ter* of the Paris Convention) has prevented the registration of a mark which included a ring of 12 stars (cf. the European emblem)[23] and Art.7(1)(i) (badges etc of particular public interest) has prevented the registration of a figurative mark which included the word "euro" and the euro symbol.[24]

MATTERS ROYAL

8–220   In essence, signs which are likely to lead persons to think that Royal patronage or authorisation has been conferred shall not be registered without consent. In fact, the protection is somewhat broader than that, since registration of a mark is prohibited without the consent of Her Majesty or the relevant member of the Royal Family if it contains or consists of any of the following:

(1) any of the Royal arms or any of the principal armorial bearings of the Royal arms or any insignia so nearly resembling them as to be likely to be mistaken for any of them;

(2) a representation of the Royal crown or any of the Royal flags;

(3) a representation of Her Majesty or any member of the Royal family or any colourable imitation thereof; or

(4) words letters or devices likely to lead persons to think that the applicant has or recently has had Royal patronage or authorisation.

---

[20] An escutcheon is a shield displaying a coat of arms.

[21] See Arts 3(2)(b) and (c) of the TM Directive.

[22] Art. 3(2)(b) of the TM Directive is an optional prohibition against trade marks which cover "a sign of high symbolic value, in particular a religious symbol." There is no directly equivalent provision in the 1994 Act, although s.3(3)(a) (public policy/accepted principles of morality) no doubt cover much of the same ground.

[23] Case T–127/02, Court of First Instance, April 21, 2004.

[24] Decision of the Third Board of Appeal, R–190/1999-3.

The Trade Mark Registry has been provided with a list of those considered by the Queen to be members of the Royal Family.[25] Representations of the Royal Arms and the Royal crowns may be found in Registry Work Manual. Persons wishing to apply for consent should contact the Lord Chamberlain at Buckingham Palace.   **8–221**

The position under the 1938 Act

Under the 1938 Act, certain of these matters were dealt with in s.61, and certain other matters were left to the Rules, and in particular r.16. Paragraphs (a) to (d) of s.4(1) are clearly based upon the same paragraphs of r.16. Rule 16 obliged the Registrar to consider whether to refuse to accept an application for a mark which included such matters. Now s.4(1) of the 1994 Act forbids registration unless a relevant consent has been given.   **8–222**

Under the 1938 Act, application was made for the mark *"Queen Diana"* [1991] R.P.C. 395. The Registrar refused the application, purporting to apply r.16. The relevant words of r.16 were substantially identical to those in s.4(1)(d) of the 1994 Act, namely "the use of any words, letters or devices in such a manner as to be likely to lead persons to think that the applicant either has or recently had had Royal patronage or authorisation".   **8–223**

The Board of Trade allowed an appeal and directed that the mark proceed to registration. It was held that r.16 did not apply since there was no Queen Diana and the mark was not likely to indicate Royal patronage. Due to the similarity in the wording of the provisions, it would appear that an application under the 1994 Act for, say, a "King William IV" mark would not fail by reason of s.4(1), even if no consent was obtained. Section 4(1)(d) only militates against a representation without consent of Royal patronage or authorisation which is either current or dates from the recent past. The paragraph avoids any consideration of what may happen in the future, however likely the future events may seem.   **8–224**

Whilst registration may be obtained of "King Charles III" or "King William IV" marks without the appropriate consent from members of the Royal Family and prior to any succession in the monarchy, upon the relevant succession taking place such marks ought to be removed from the Register. Whether the result should be revocation of the mark or a declaration of invalidity and whether any such result may be achieved are matters discussed in Ch.10.   **8–225**

Flags

Section 4(2) of the 1994 Act provides a measure of protection for the Union Jack and the flags of England, Scotland, Wales, Northern Ireland and the Isle of Man. Registration of a trade mark which contains or consists of a representation of any of those flags is prohibited if, in the opinion of the Registrar, use of the trade mark would be misleading or grossly offensive. In addition to this specific prohibition, objections might also arise under s.3(3) and 3(5). Thus, a trade mark which incorporates a representation of the Union Jack could be misleading if it suggests that goods are manufactured in the United Kingdom when they are not.   **8–226**

Article 6ter of the Paris Convention

Section 4(3) prohibits the registration of a trade mark which falls within the cases   **8–227**

---

[25] Currently numbering 38.

mentioned in ss.57 and 58 of the 1994 Act. Those sections implement Article 6*ter* of the Paris Convention, which is concerned with protection for national or state emblems of Convention countries and with emblems of certain international organisations. Registration of trade marks which consist of or contain the protected emblems is prevented in certain circumstances. In this context, a "Convention country" means a country, other than the United Kingdom, which is a party to the Paris Convention.[26]

8–228   Flags of Convention countries receive automatic protection. All other emblems only receive protection if they have been notified in accordance with the procedure specified in s.59. Briefly, the country concerned notifies the United Kingdom that it desires to protect the emblem in question. In the absence of an objection from the United Kingdom, two months after the notification the emblem is regarded as protected under the Paris Convention. The Registrar keeps a list of the protected emblems, which is open to public inspection.[27]

Section 57: national emblems, etc., of Convention countries

8–229   The emblems concerned are flags and, subject to notification, armorial bearings or other state emblems and official signs or hallmarks which indicate control or warranty in relation to goods or services.

8–230   Section 57 provides three levels of protection:

(1) marks containing or consisting of the flag of a Convention country cannot be registered without authorisation of the competent authorities unless it appears to the Registrar that use of the flag in the manner proposed is permitted without such authorisation;

(2) for armorial bearings or any other state emblem protected under the Convention, registration must be refused without authorisation of the competent authorities;

(3) official signs or hallmarks cannot be registered without authorisation of the competent authorities in relation to the same or similar goods or services as those in relation to which they indicate control or warranty.

In each case the protection is extended to anything which, from a heraldic point of view imitates the flag, other state emblem, sign or hallmark.

Section 58: emblems of international organisations

8–231   Subject to the notification procedure, the emblems concerned are armorial bearings, flags or other emblems and abbreviations and names of international intergovernmental organisations of which one or more Convention countries are members. This class of emblems cannot be registered without the authorisation of the organisation concerned unless it appears to the Registrar that the use of the emblem in question does not indicate a connection with the organisation and is not likely to mislead the public as to the existence of a connection. The class is extended to cover anything which, from a heraldic point of view, imitates any such emblem. There is a saving for the rights of any person whose *bona fide* use of their trade mark began before the relevant provisions of the Convention entered into force for the United Kingdom, on January 4, 1962.

---

[26] See s.55(1)(b). For a list of the signatories to the Paris Convention, see the WIPO website at *www.wipo.org.*

[27] Pursuant to s.59(4).

Imitation "from a heraldic point of view"

It would appear that the notion of imitation "from a heraldic point of view" creates wide protection. A practical illustration is provided by an application for a CTM which included a ring of 12 stars—the European emblem. Under Art.6*ter*, the notification relating to the European emblem comprises a precise geometric description containing no less than 149 words. The heraldic description reads "On a field azure a circle of 12 mullets or, their points not touching." The Court of First Instance held that "when making a comparison "from a heraldic point of view", regard must be had to the heraldic description and not to the geometric description, which is by nature much more detailed."[28]   **8–232**

Coats of arms

The combination of s.4(4) of the 1994 Act and r.9 of the Trade Mark Rules 2000 prohibits the registration without consent of a trade mark which consists of or contains any arms to which a person is entitled by virtue of a grant of arms by the Crown or any insignia so nearly resembling such arms as to be likely to be mistaken for them. Consent must be given by or on behalf of the person entitled to the arms. Registration of such a mark does not authorise use of the arms contrary to the laws of arms.   **8–233**

The Registrar of Trade Marks has indicated that he calls upon expert assistance from the Garter King of Arms in the operation of this provision. If a mark is considered to nearly resemble armorial bearings, the relevant bearings have to be identified and a copy sent to the applicant. The unresolved question is from whose point of view the nearly resembling test should be applied, particularly since insignia considered to be very similar to the expert heraldic eye might look rather different to a member of the general public.   **8–234**

Bearing in mind that ss.57 and 58 of the 1994 Act do not offer any protection for arms originating in the United Kingdom, it might be thought that this subsection was supposed to provide equivalent protection. However, subs.4(4) may be contrasted with the provisions of ss.57(4) and 58(3) which extend their protection to any emblem which "from a heraldic point of view" imitates an emblem protected under the Paris Convention. If the intention was to provide the same degree of protection here as United Kingdom arms receive in Convention countries abroad, the intention may not have been fulfilled. In the absence of express provision indicating a specialist test, the "nearly resembling" test here probably ought to be interpreted from the point of view of the general public.   **8–235**

Olympic symbols

The Olympic Symbol etc (Protection) Act 1995 caused the addition of s.4(5) to the 1994 Act.[29] This prevents the registration of a trade mark which consists of or contains a "controlled representation" unless the application is made by the proprietor of the Olympics Association Right or with his consent. Currently, the British Olympic Association is the proprietor of that Right and it has indicated that it will not normally grant consent.   **8–236**

---

[28] Case T–127/02, Court of First Instance, April 21, 2004, affirming the refusal, under Article 7(1)(h) of the CTM Regulation of a figurative mark containing the word element ECA surrounded by a ring of 12 stars.

[29] In force from September 21, 1995.

8–237   "Controlled representation" includes the Olympic Symbol, the Olympic Motto (Citius, Altius, Fortius), the words Olympic(s), Olympian(s) and Olympiad(s) and a representation of something so similar to the Olympic Symbol or the Olympic Motto as to be likely to create in the public mind an association with those items.

8–238   An application filed in 1998 for the word OLYMPIC alone and with the device of an Olympic torch for cooking oils was refused registration under section 3(5) even though the applicant had been using the marks on a significant scale since 1990.[30]

13. Bad faith—section 3(6)

SECTION 3(6)

8–239   Section 3(6): "A trade mark shall not be registered if or to the extent that the application is made in bad faith."

SUMMARY

8–240   Although the evidence is largely apocryphal, it seems clear that this provision has been enforced substantially more vigorously in the UK than in other Member States or at OHIM. There seem to be three principal reasons for this: the first is the lack of a uniform interpretation of "bad faith", which is undoubtedly an autonomous concept of EU law; the second is the existence of s.32(3) of the Act, a home-grown provision, which requires every applicant to state that the mark applied for is being used or that he has a *bona fide* intention to use it; and the third is the wide variation with which Member States implemented the optional provision in the TM Directive.

8–241   It will be seen that there is a substantial amount of agreement across the EU and at OHIM as to what types of conduct constitute bad faith.[31] At the margin, however, there are certain activities which have been found to constitute bad faith in the UK which would be unlikely to be condemned elsewhere. Sooner or later, and preferably sooner, appropriate facts will arise which will require a tribunal to make a reference to the ECJ for an authoritative interpretation of the scope of "bad faith" in EU law.

8–242   There is no definition of "bad faith" in the Act, the Directive or the CTM Regulation. The concept is not unknown in United Kingdom law but continental lawyers are likely to be more familiar with it, since consequences flow from acts done *contra bones mores* or in bad faith in many civilian systems of law.

8–243   The relevant provisions contemplate bad faith extending to the whole or only part of the application.[32] If the whole of an application is made in bad faith, it indicates (though not exclusively) that the applicant has no entitlement to the mark, *i.e.* the applicant is not the true proprietor of the mark. It is worth noting

---

[30] Olympic (SRIS O/081/00), Regy.

[31] The impending prospect of enlargement of the CTM to cover 25 countries resulted in a short comparative case study by OHIM, published on January 31, 2003. It can be found on the OHIM website and is discussed in further detail below.

[32] Not as explicitly as Art.13 of the TM Directive—see G. Hobbs Q.C. as the appointed person in DEMON ALE [2000] R.P.C. 345 at 355.

that this is the only ground of refusal under which issues of proprietorship can be raised.[33]

If the bad faith extends to only part of an application, that indicates (again not exclusively) that the scope of the application is too broad, the prime example being that the specification of goods or services sought is too wide. Those may be the main situations which arise. However, this provision is of the broadest scope. The making of any false statement or representation, even implicit, in connection with an application for a trade mark may be sufficient to fulfil this ground.[34]   **8–244**

There appear to be three main topics for discussion. As usual, these topics are, to varying degrees, inter-related: **8–245**

1. Identification of common ground as to what constitutes bad faith;
2. Has the TM Directive been properly implemented? Strictly, this issue must be examined country by country. So far as the UK is concerned, the issue is whether s.32(3) of the Act is compatible with the TM Directive (and, for that matter, with TRIPS)? So far as other Member States are concerned, the issue is whether partial implementation of Article 3(2)(d) of the TM Directive is permissible?
3. What is the true interpretation of "bad faith": what is the test?

Pending a suitable decision of the ECJ, in this section we give a flavour of the degree of variation in implementation of the TM Directive[35] before setting out how "bad faith" has been interpreted in the UK[36] and at OHIM.[37] Finally, we venture to suggest the type of interpretative guidance the ECJ is likely to give.[38]   **8–246**

DERIVATION

Section 3(6) derives from Article 3(2)(d) of the TM Directive which provided: **8–247**

"Any member state may provide that a trade mark shall not be registered or, if registered, shall be liable to be declared invalid where and to the extent that: the application for registration of the trade mark is made in bad faith by the applicant."

EQUIVALENT PROVISION IN THE CTM REGULATION.

"Bad faith" is not an absolute ground for refusal of an application for a CTM, although the relative grounds prevent a registration in the name of an agent of the proprietor of the mark without consent.[39] Once a CTM registration has been granted, an application can be made to have the registration declared invalid where the applicant was acting in bad faith when he filed the application.[40]   **8–248**

---

[33] An Italian Judge has observed that the purpose of the bad faith provision is there to provide "advanced protection to any party which, even if it has planned to register a trade mark it uses, has not actually done so yet." and also to those situations where the proprietor is still preparing to use his mark, where he has a "legitimate expectation" of protection. See *Benckiser v Henkel* [1999] E.T.M.R. 614 at 637, Court of Naples.

[34] Although, as G. Hobbs, Q.C. (as the appointed person) put it in DEMON ALE [2000] R.P.C. 345 at 356, "I do not think that section 3(6) requires applicants to submit to an open-ended assessment of their commercial morality". The ground is restricted to the application made in bad faith.

[35] See para.8–249.

[36] See paras 8–250 to 8–257.

[37] See paras 8–258 to 8–262.

[38] See paras 8–269, 8–270 and 8–276.

[39] Art.8.3 CTM Regulation.

[40] Art.51.1.(b) CTM Regulation. The application can be made to OHIM or by way of counterclaim in infringement proceedings *i.e.* in any of the Community Trade Mark Courts).

THE POSITION IN VARIOUS MEMBER STATES

8–249   There is a good deal of variation in the implementation across Member States. The UK and some other Member States (*e.g.* Ireland, Greece, Italy) have fully implemented this optional[41] provision in the TM Directive, essentially by using the words in the Directive, so that bad faith is a ground for refusal as well as invalidity. The Benelux has bad faith as a ground for refusal and invalidity, expressed to include two particular situations. In France, the relevant provision appears limited to situations where the registration has been applied for fraudulently with respect to the rights of another person or in violation of a statutory or contractual obligation and even then, the ground may only be invoked by a person who believes he has a right in the mark—he may then claim ownership. There are other countries (*e.g.* Germany and Italy) which have, at national level, essentially the same scheme as under the CTM Regulation. Spain and Portugal only provide for annulment on the grounds of bad faith. Finland, Sweden and Denmark[42] have a provision limited to the situation where the mark applied for is confusingly similar to one already in prior use to the knowledge of the applicant.

HARMONISATION?

The law as it has developed in the UK

8–250   The seminal passage is that of Lindsay J. in *Gromax*:

> "I shall not attempt to define bad faith in this context [sc. of section 3(6)]. Plainly it includes dishonesty and, as I would hold, includes also some dealings which fall short of the standards of acceptable commercial behaviour observed by reasonable and experienced men in the particular area being examined. Parliament has wisely not attempted to explain in detail what is or is not bad faith in this context; how far a dealing must so fall-short in order to amount to bad faith is a matter best left to be adjudged not by some paraphrase by the courts (which leads to the danger of the courts then construing not the Act but the paraphrase) but by reference to the words of the Act and upon a regard to all material surrounding circumstances."[43]

8–251   Having referred to those observations, G. Hobbs Q.C. (as the appointed person) said (in DEMON ALE [2000] R.P.C. 345 at 356):

> "These observations recognised that the expression 'bad faith' has moral overtones which appear to make it possible for an application for registration to be rendered invalid under section 3(6) by behaviour which otherwise involves no breach of any duty, obligation, prohibition or requirement that is legally binding on the applicant. Quite how far the concept of bad faith can or should be taken consistently with its Community origins in Article 3(2)(d) of the Directive is a matter upon which the guidance of the European Court of Justice seems likely to be required; *Road Tech Computer Systems*

---

[41] This provision may be optional because not all countries have trade mark registries which are equipped to examine applications with the rigour of the UK Registry.

[42] Successfully invoked in RED LOBSTER, where the applicant had admitted in a published interview that he was strongly inspired by the American chain of RED LOBSTER. "The Americans do a tremendous job and as they have protected neither the concept nor the name in Scandinavia, I do not see any obstacle to my inspiration." However, the Court did, holding in favour of the Americans. The OHIM Bad Faith Case Study characterises this case as one of bad faith.

[43] *Gromax Plasticulture Ltd v v Don & Low Nonwovens Ltd* [1999] R.P.C. 367, at 379.

Ltd v. Unison Software (UK) Ltd [1996] F.S.R. 805 at 817, 818, per Robert Walker J."

THE FOCUS ON THE "MENTAL ELEMENT"

In the absence of guidance from the ECJ, the Appointed Person (in the guise of Mr Hobbs Q.C.) and now the Court of Appeal have derived guidance from UK case law concerned with the circumstances in which liability is imposed in the UK for acting as an accessory to a breach of trust. At a general level, one can see that reference to the standards imposed in other areas of the law might shed light on "the standards of acceptable commercial behaviour observed by reasonable and experienced men in the particular area being examined." However, this line of inquiry has now created a bit of a mess. An attempt, by the Court of Appeal, to bring various approaches into line does not seem to have worked. In order to explain what the current state of the law is in the UK, it is necessary to explain the focus on the mental element required for a finding of bad faith.

8–252

This process began with this observation in DEMON ALE:[44]

8–253

"… the observations of Lord Nicholls on the subject of dishonesty in *Royal Brunei Airlines Sdn. Bhd. v. Philip Tan* [1995] 2 A.C. 378 (PC) at p389 do seem to me to provide strong support for the view that a finding of bad faith may be fully justified even in a case where the applicant sees nothing wrong in his own behaviour."

The process continued in DAAWAT,[45] where Mr Hobbs Q.C., discussed how the observations of Lord Nicholls in *Royal Brunei Airlines*[46] had been taken further in the opinion of Lord Hutton in *Twinsectra v Yardley*:[47]

8–254

"Whilst in discussing the term 'dishonesty' the courts often draw a distinction between subjective dishonesty and objective dishonesty, there are three possible standards which can be applied to determine whether a person has acted dishonestly. There is a purely subjective standard, whereby a person is only regarded as dishonest if he transgresses his own standard of honesty, even if that standard is contrary to that of reasonable and honest people. This has been termed the 'Robin Hood test' and has been rejected by the courts. As Sir Christopher Slade stated in *Walker v. Stones* [2000] Lloyds Rep PN 864, 877 para.164:

'A person may in some cases act dishonestly, according to the ordinary use of language, even though he genuinely believes that his action is morally justified. The penniless thief, for example, who picks the pocket of the multi-millionaire is dishonest even though he genuinely considers that theft is morally justified as a fair redistribution of wealth and that he is not therefore being dishonest.'

Secondly, there is a purely objective standard whereby a person acts dishonestly if his conduct is dishonest by the ordinary standards of reasonable and honest people, even if he does not realise this.

Thirdly, there is a standard which combines an objective test and a subjective test, and which requires that before there can be a finding of dishonesty

---

[44] [2000] R.P.C. 345.
[45] [2003] R.P.C. 11.
[46] [1995] 2 A.C. 378, HL.
[47] [2002] 2 A.C. 164, HL, at para.27.

it must be established that the defendant's conduct was dishonest by the ordinary standards of reasonable and honest people and that he himself realised that by those standards his conduct was dishonest. I will term this 'the combined test'."

8–255   In DAAWAT,[48] Mr Hobbs questioned whether s.3(6) required the application of this "combined test". He pointed out there were three indications that the "combined test" was not required: first, the passage in *Gromax*; second, when dealing with the analogous situation of cybersquatting, the Court of Appeal in *BT v One in a Million* did not appear to have required a "combined test" to be satisfied and, third, he pointed out that the test applied at OHIM appeared consonant with the approach in *Gromax*, again not requiring conscious dishonesty.

8–256   Subsequently, in CHINAWHITE,[49] the Court of Appeal made a series of somewhat confusing[50] statements in an apparent attempt to present the UK law on "bad faith" as coterminous with the approach at OHIM:

First, all three members of the Court were in agreement that the Lord Hutton's "combined test" for dishonesty applied in the context of s.3(6), having earlier rejected the submission that s.3(6) required dishonesty.

Second, the Court expressly approved the passage quoted above from *Gromax*. Apart from clearly indicating that dishonesty is sufficient but not essential, that passage appears to reflect an objective test, as Mr Hobbs Q.C. observed in DAAWAT.

Third, the Court apparently regarded the "combined test" as consistent with the position at OHIM, based on their review of three OHIM decisions, including BE NATURAL and *Senso di Donna* which, as explained below,[51] appear to suggest (a) that dishonesty is sufficient but not essential and (b) a wholly objective test.

8–257   We return below to discuss the issue of whether the test is objective or whether it is the "combined test". So far as the UK is concerned, the Court of Appeal has clearly held that the "combined test" applies. The remaining problem is to reconcile the adoption of the "combined test" with *Gromax*. This can be done once one realises that references to the "combined test" were simply to the mix of objective and subjective elements, and not to the standard of behaviour required. Hence: "The test is the combined test and the standard must be of acceptable commercial behaviour observed by reasonable and experienced persons in the particular commercial area being examined. I stress "acceptable commercial behaviour" to exclude behaviour that may become prevalent, but which would not on examination be deemed to be acceptable."[52]

DEVELOPMENT OF THE CONCEPT OF "BAD FAITH" AT OHIM

8–258   For understandable reasons, it took a little time before the tribunals at OHIM had to deal with allegations of bad faith. The first decision was *Trillium*,[53] in which the allegation was that the application for "computer software; communications software" had been made in bad faith in so far as the specification extended be-

---

[48] [2003] R.P.C. 11. See paras 86 to 96.
[49] *Harrisons Trade Mark Application* [2004] EWCA 1028; [2005] F.S.R. 10.
[50] See the analysis of the Appointed Person (Richard Arnold Q.C.) in *Robert McBride's Application*, November 22, 2004, paras 28–31.
[51] See para.8–260.
[52] para.33 of the Judgment (Sir William Aldous, Arden and Pill L.JJ. agreeing) [2004] EWCA 1028; [2005] F.S.R. 10.
[53] Case C–000479899/1, *Trillium*, Decision of the First Cancellation Division, March 28, 2000.

yond "telecommunications switching software" (since that was all the applicant did). The allegation failed, whereas in the UK it was likely to have succeeded. The First Cancellation Division took a rather narrow view of "bad faith":

> "Bad faith is a narrow legal concept in the CTMR system. Bad faith is the opposite of good faith, generally implying or involving, but not limited to, actual or constructive fraud, or a design to mislead or deceive another, or any other sinister motive. Conceptually, bad faith can be understood as a 'dishonest intention'. This means that bad faith may be interpreted as unfair practices involving lack of any honest intention on the part of the applicant of the CTM at the time of filing."

The Cancellation Division stated categorically that there was no "intention to use" requirement for a CTM application, a point to which we return below. **8–259**

In later decisions, the scope of bad faith has been widened somewhat. For example in BE NATURAL,[54] the First Cancellation Division repeated the paragraph quoted above and continued: **8–260**

> "Bad faith can be understood either as unfair practices involving lack of good faith on the part of the applicant towards the Office at the time of filing, or unfair practices based on acts infringing a third person's rights. There is bad faith not only in cases where the applicant intentionally submits wrong or misleadingly insufficient information to the Office, but also in circumstances where he intends, through registration, to lay his hands on the trade mark of a third party with whom he had contractual or precontractual relations."

More recently, in DAAWAT,[55] the Cancellation Division had to deal with essentially the same facts as had arisen in the UK and found that the CTM applicant was acting in bad faith at the time of filing "because it knew or, at least, should have known that such filing constituted an unfair practice involving lack of any honest intention vis-à-vis the applicant [for invalidation] because it in fact precluded the latter from expanding its trade mark to Europe without the proprietor's consent." **8–261**

As to the law, the Cancellation Division referred to the OHIM Bad Faith Case Study, and then essentially repeated the two paragraphs quoted above.[56] In view of the concentration in the UK on the mental element, the OHIM Bad Faith Case Study[57] misquotes *Gromax* in a significant respect—characterising that case as saying that bad faith can be considered to mean "dishonesty which would fall short of the standards of acceptable commercial behaviour". **8–262**

IMPLEMENTATION OF THE TM DIRECTIVE

Before discussing the two issues which arise (which may be characterised as over and under-implementation), it may help to highlight three passages in the seventh recital to the TM Directive: **8–263**

> "Whereas attainment of the objectives at which this approximation of laws is aiming requires that the conditions for obtaining and continuing to hold a registered trade mark are, *in general*, identical in all Member States"

---

[54] *Surene Pty Ltd v Multiple Marketing Ltd*, Case C–000053447/1. See also *Senso di Donna* [2001] E.T.M.R. 5, para.17, and *Lancôme* [2001] E.T.M.R. 89.

[55] Case C–000659037/1, June 28, 2004, see para.12.

[56] Case C–000659037/1, June 28, 2004, see para.8, which includes the words quoted in paras 8–258 and 8–260.

[57] *http://oami.eu.int/en/enlargement/pdf/badfaithC53101.pdf.*

"whereas the grounds for refusal or invalidity *concerning the trade mark itself*, ... are to be listed in an exhaustive manner, [even though some are optional];

"whereas Member States will be able to maintain or introduce into their legislation grounds of refusal or invalidity linked to conditions for obtaining and continuing to hold a trade mark for which there is no provision of approximation concerning, for example, the eligibility for the grant of a trade mark, the renewal of the trade mark or rules on fees, or related to the non-compliance with procedural rules."

IS SECTION 32(3) OF THE ACT COMPATIBLE WITH THE TM DIRECTIVE (AND, FOR THAT MATTER, WITH TRIPS)?

8–264   Section 32(3) requires every applicant for a UK trade mark to state "that the trade mark is being used, by the applicant or with his consent, in relation to [the goods and services applied for] or that he has a bona fide intention that it should be so used." This statement has to be confirmed by a statement of truth on the application form (TM3). The first anomaly is that an applicant under the Madrid Agreement is not required to make such a statement, let alone verify it,[58] yet will obtain identical protection.

8–265   The requirement for this statement has enabled the bad faith ground to be invoked against the following (independent of any issue over the true ownership of the mark):

(a) applications containing "overly wide" specifications of goods and/or services;

(b) applications where a doubt is raised over the applicant's intention to use the mark; and

(c) by way of a subset of "intention to use", situations where the mark applied for differs from the mark actually used in the market.[59]

8–266   In the context of s.32(3), the Appointed Person[60] has held that "Insofar as the applicant makes a materially false statement in this regard then I believe the application is made in bad faith.", where the requirement that the false statement be "material" allows all the facts and circumstances to be taken into account.

Thus, the practical effect of s.32(3) is that, in the UK, bad faith encompasses activities which do not constitute bad faith elsewhere in the EU.

8–267   It would appear that no court or tribunal has yet had to grapple with the precise point although two Appointed Persons (Messrs Hobbs and Kitchin) have stated they see no reason to doubt that s.32(3) was compatible with Community law,[61] whereas Neuberger J. has stated[62] it was arguable that the sub-section was not valid at least if it was interpreted as requiring the applicant to verify his intention

---

[58] Art.3(2) of The Trade Marks (International Registration) Order 1996 (as amended) expressly excludes the application of, *inter alia*, ss.32–34.

[59] Compare BETTY'S KITCHEN CORONATION STREET (in use, the two parts of the mark could not be read as a composite whole. Furthermore, there was some "history" O-360-99) with *Robert McBride's Application* (application made for a two-dimensional representation of the goods, actual use was the three-dimensional shape of the goods. The finding of bad faith in the Registry was overturned on appeal by Mr Richard Arnold Q.C. as the Appointed Person, November 22, 2004, O-355-04.)

[60] Mr David Kitchin Q.C. in *Kinder (Ferrero SpA and Soremartee SA v Soldan Holding & Bonbonspezialitäten GmbH* O-279-03, [2004] R.P.C. 29, para.23.

[61] DEMON ALE [2000] R.P.C. 345 (G. Hobbs Q.C.); KINDER O-279–03, [2004] R.P.C. 29, paras 20 and 24), (D. Kitchin Q.C.)

[62] *Knoll AG's Trade Mark* [2003] R.P.C. 10, see para.34.

to use the mark in relation to the full width of the specification of goods or services set out in the application form. It is possible to interpret most of the scope of s.32(3) in a manner compatible with Community law, through the requirement for "material" falsity. Purposive interpretation does not provide the solution where it is clear that the applicant did not have an intention to use the mark at the date of application, even if later on he forms a settled intention to use the mark (or even uses it). The applicant has made a materially false statement. In so far as the effect of s.32(3) results in those circumstances as constituting bad faith, there is a clear and irreconcilable difference between UK law and Community law. Certainly, OHIM has stated in terms that there is no "intention to use" requirement. Since OHIM reflects what may be loosely termed a "continental" approach, it seems likely that most other Member States align with OHIM and have no "intention to use" requirement.

In these circumstances, there are four possibilities: **8–268**

Section 32(3) is invalid, being inconsistent with the TM Directive;

Section 32(3) is valid, and "bad faith" has a wider meaning in the UK than elsewhere in the EU;

Section 32(3) is valid, "bad faith" has a uniform meaning across the EU but wider scope in the UK than elsewhere in the EU;

Section 32(3) is valid, because the true interpretation of bad faith encompasses an implicit requirement of an "intention to use".

Whilst there are powerful reasons in principle which support an "intention to   **8–269** use" requirement, it seems doubtful that the ECJ will impose one through a wide interpretation of "bad faith". Furthermore, it is highly unlikely that the ECJ would not give a uniform interpretation of "bad faith". It is possible, though unsatisfactory, that the ECJ might say that "bad faith" has wider scope in the UK than elsewhere, but this would hardly reflect the spirit of the recital to the effect that conditions for obtaining marks should be the same.

It is also possible that the ECJ could characterise s.32(3) as a provision   **8–270** contemplated by the last part of the seventh recital,[63] and therefore compatible with the Directive. Again, this would be an unsatisfactory result. That last part of the seventh recital appears to be concerned with essentially administrative matters. An applicant who fails to comply with administrative requirements has only himself to blame if the result is refusal of the application. Section 32(3) is materially different to the examples mentioned in the recital—it has a direct effect on the scope of an absolute ground for refusal.

COMPATIBILITY WITH ARTICLE 15(3) OF TRIPS?

The wider question is whether an intention to use requirement is compatible with   **8–271** Article 15(3) of TRIPS, which provides:

"Members may make registrability depend on use. However, actual use of a trademark shall not be a condition for filing an application for registration. An application shall not be refused solely on the ground that intended use has not taken place before the expiry of a period of three years from the date of application."

---

[63] Quoted at para.8–263.

8–272   OHIM has taken the view[64] that an "intention to use" requirement is incompatible with this provision. However, incompatibility depends partly on interpretation. If the requirement means the applicant has to intend to use at some point in the five years after the mark is actually put on the register, it may be compatible. If, as seems currently to be the law in the UK, s.32(3) requires a present and settled intention to use the mark, it is probably incompatible.

At the very least, it would appear that some amendment is required.

WAS PARTIAL IMPLEMENTATION (BY CERTAIN MEMBER STATES) OF ARTICLE 3(2)(D) OF THE TM DIRECTIVE PERMISSIBLE?

8–273   There are probably only two answers to this question and it is not easy to predict what the ECJ will say if the issue comes before it. The argument in favour of partial implementation is that Member States were given an option whether to have "bad faith" as an absolute ground for refusal or invalidity. Since it was entirely permissible for a Member State to have no "bad faith" ground at all, the argument is that it must be permissible to legislate for an absolute ground which encompasses only part of the full scope of "bad faith". The argument against partial implementation requires the TM Directive to be interpreted as presenting Member States with an all or nothing choice: you either have a ground which implements Art.3(2)(d) in full or not at all.

8–274   On this point, the seventh recital to the TM Directive (quoted above) seems to be neutral. Article 3(2)(d) is an optional provision, indicating that it was not considered essential for this first round of harmonisation. However, it seems to be implicit in certain other recitals that the reason for this provision being optional was to accommodate those national trade mark systems which did not have experience of making the type of assessment required. If this is right, then it provides some support for an all or nothing approach—if you have the ability, and you exercise the option, it must be exercised fully. Other factors in favour of such an approach are the overall desirability of having identical conditions for obtaining a trade mark (so far as is possible), and the fact that bad faith is an exception to acquiescence (Article 9 of the TM Directive, s.48 of the Act, Article 53 of the CTM Regulation).

THE MENTAL ELEMENT

8–275   In the UK, the test for bad faith is the combination, laid down by the Court of Appeal in CHINAWHITE,[65] of *Gromax* and the "combined test" from *Twinsectra*, with objective and subjective elements. Properly interpreted, the combination is best expressed as follows:

> Before there can be a finding of bad faith, it must be established that the applicant's conduct in filing the application fell short of the standards of acceptable commercial behaviour observed by reasonable and experienced men in the particular area being examined and that the applicant himself realised that by those standards his conduct fell short.

8–276   In CHINAWHITE,[66] Arden L.J. correctly characterised "bad faith" as "an autonomous concept of European Union law. It remains a mystery as to why EU

---

[64] In its Bad Faith Case Study, January 31, 2003.
[65] [2004] EWCA 1028; [2005] F.S.R. 10.
[66] [2004] EWCA 1028; [2005] F.S.R. 10, at para.40.

law would have any regard at all to the "combined test" in *Twinsectra*. It would be entirely fortuitous if EU law happened to require this "combined test". However, there are a number of indications that the ECJ is most unlikely to advocate a "combined test" for bad faith:

(1) It is unnecessarily complicated. For situations where liability requires dishonesty, one can see the reasons why some subjective element is required. Where one is considering a rather vaguer standard (conduct falling short of acceptable standards), the subjective element is more difficult to apply and to justify. Furthermore, allegations of bad faith may be made many years after the relevant application date.

(2) An objective test would appear to be sufficient. The objective approach in *Gromax* appears to have worked satisfactorily in practice.[67]

(3) OHIM applies an objective test. As the Appointed Person has observed[68] (Mr Richard Arnold Q.C.): "I doubt whether Article 51(1)(b) of the [CTM] Regulation can involve consideration of the applicant's subjective state of mind since (a) evidence in OHIM proceedings is written and there is generally no cross-examination and (b) the applicant will frequently be a body corporate."

(4) It would appear that in most[69] other Member States, an objective test is applied (known or should have known[70]), in line with the general approach in civilian law countries.

(5) The ECJ appears to favour objective criteria (cf. *Ansul*, where the interpretation of "genuine use" appears to be entirely objective, in circumstances where a limited subjective element was a possibility).

In the previous edition of this book,[71] we suggested the test should be "principally objective with a limited subjective element so that evidence from the applicant as to his state of mind at the time may be taken into account". We also suggested that such a test would allow "the issue of bad faith to be decided according to who is entitled, as a matter of legal right, to ownership of the mark, which ought to be the factor of greatest importance" even in circumstances where the applicant believes, honestly yet incorrectly that he was entitled to apply for the mark.

When may the issue arise?

Section 3(6) of the 1994 Act is concerned with the state of affairs which existed **8–277** as at the date of application. The issue of whether the application was made in bad faith can arise in four different ways for a United Kingdom registered trade mark. First, in sufficiently obvious cases, the ground may be raised by the Regis-

---

[67] Contrary to initial expectations, most allegations of bad faith of substance are dealt with in the UK without cross-examination, despite a greater willingness to allow cross-examination if reasons are put forward as to why it is necessary. In other words, most people run the allegations on an objective basis.

[68] *Robert McBride's Application*, November 22, 2004.

[69] For historical reasons, Ireland is likely to continue to be influenced by UK law. As indicated above, the Benelux provision has two specific limbs— Art.4(6)(a) indicates an objective test (knew or should have known), Art.4(6)(b) seems to require knowledge (of use of the mark outside Benelux) plus direct relations with the user of the mark. One can readily see that such knowledge might well be imputed from the circumstances, without an examination of the subjective state of mind of the applicant.

[70] A full comparative study is beyond the (current) scope of this book. For an indication of the situation see the INTA study "Bad Faith Provisions in the European Union and in the EU Candidate Countries", April 8, 2002, which can be found on the OHIM website.

[71] 13th ed., paras 8–215 to 8–216.

try at the examination stage.[72] Secondly, at the opposition stage. Thirdly, in proceedings for a declaration of complete or partial invalidity of a registration under s.47. Fourthly, under s.48(1) (effect of acquiescence).

8–278   As indicated above, in relation to a CTM, bad faith is not a ground for refusal of a CTM application, cannot be raised in opposition proceedings, and the issue can only be raised in proceedings for invalidity under Art.51.1.(b) and to defeat an allegation of acquiescence under Art.53.[73]

8–279   Under ss.47 and 48, the allegation that an application was made in bad faith can be raised in relation to any registered trade mark, whether the application for it was examined under the 1994 Act or under previous legislation. Although not necessarily determinative, the statements made by the applicant to the Registry at the time of application and during the application stage are likely to be relevant to the issue of bad faith. Hence it may be necessary to examine what statements and representations were actually made at the time of application, even under previous Acts.

PLEADING AND PRACTICE

8–280   Before the United Kingdom Registry began to exercise case management, adopting and adapting the principles of the Civil Procedure Rules, bad faith was frequently pleaded[74] only to be abandoned at the hearing, by which time it was clear that there was no evidence to support the allegation. There was a lack of appreciation that an allegation of bad faith is a serious one and, like an allegation of fraud, ought to be properly substantiated in a pleading and pleaded only where there exists *prima facie* evidence justifying the allegation.[75] The introduction of case management in early 2000[76] has meant that unparticularised allegations of bad faith are now unlikely to pass the Registry's initial review of the statement of grounds.

8–281   One might have expected allegations of bad faith to have resulted in a greater recourse to discovery or disclosure of documents and/or cross-examination. However, in practice, where triable issues of bad faith have arisen in oppositions, the vast majority have been decided without any cross-examination.[77] In at least some cases, it is apparent that the need for cross-examination was avoided by the applicant simply failing to respond at all in his evidence to issues of bad faith raised in the opponent's evidence which called for a response. The absence of cross-examination seems to have caused no difficulty in most cases, since the outcome is normally apparent. However, in more complex or finely balanced situations, an allegation of bad faith may fail unless precise allegations have been pleaded in the statement of grounds, spelt out in the written evidence or are put to the applicant in cross examination.

---

[72] See the Registry's Practice Amendment Circular PAC 10/00 concerning "Examination of wide specifications and objections under section 3(6) of the Act".

[73] See further paras 8–258 to 8–262.

[74] Almost as a catch-all, just in case something turned up. There was little adverse consequence.

[75] See, in a different context, the comments of Lightman J. in *Melton Medes Ltd v S.I.B.* [1995] 2 W.L.R. 247 at 256.

[76] See the changes made in the Trade Mark Rules 2000, in force February 17, 2000 and the two "Tribunal Practice Notices" TPN 1/2000 and 2/2000, the first concerned with case management and the second with the bases upon which costs are awarded. With these powers, the Registry is now able to take a tougher line.

[77] Of course, where allegations of bad faith arise in proceedings in the High Court, disclosure and cross-examination are the norm: *e.g. Gromax Plasticulture Ltd v Don & Low Nonwovens Ltd* [1999] R.P.C. 367, Lindsay J., where the allegation failed.

EXAMPLES

Decisions made under s.3(6) of the 1994 Act fall into one of three broad catego-   **8–282**
ries: ownership of the mark, intention to use and width of specification. Examples
in each of these categories will be discussed in turn, since they raise somewhat
different, although sometimes overlapping issues.

Ownership of the Mark

Bad faith established

(1) Some two years after use of the mark commenced in the United Kingdom,   **8–283**
   the sole distributor registered a slightly different form of the mark in his
   own name. The mark had been coined in the USA three years before being used in the United Kingdom. The true owner of the mark succeeded in
   having his name substituted as proprietor (under s.60). But for that provision, a declaration of invalidity would have been made, it being held that
   the application was made in bad faith.[78]

(2) A Spanish applicant applied to register JARVARD for items of clothing.
   In the United Kingdom, the mark was held to be not confusingly similar
   to HARVARD. In proceedings between the same parties in Spain, the applicant had opposed the opponent's application for HARVARD on the
   grounds that it was confusingly similar to JARVARD. The applicant had
   previously applied to register HARVARD for itself in Spain, despite being aware of the opponent's college and of its concern about the possibility of confusion. Bad faith was held to be established, apparently on the
   basis of "making use of another's reputation" and because the applicant
   offered no response to the allegations.[79]

(3) The mark applied for showed a "striking similarity" to marks which had
   been long used by the opponent. The applicant did not deny an allegation
   that he had clearly copied the mark. Application refused.[80]

(4) The opponent acquired a business owned by the applicant. Whilst still
   employed as a manager by the opponent, the applicant applied for two different marks. Oppositions succeeded under s.3(6).CUSTOMER CARE
   (SRIS O/039/99) and PROFINISH/99) both Regy.

(5) The opponent, an Australian company, appointed a United Kingdom distributor who utilised the services of the applicant to warehouse and distribute the product. The applicant also ordered the product direct from the
   opponent. Bad faith was held established, the applicant being "fully
   aware" of the opponent's intention to use the mark in the United Kingdom.
   The applicant failed to offer any response to the prima facie case.[81]

(6) The opponent had an established business in the US under the mark and
   had begun to trade in the United Kingdom. The applicant was a United
   Kingdom customer and had proposed a licence arrangement. The applicant adopted the US mark. When challenged, he sought to register the
   mark in combination with his own name. The combined mark was confusingly similar to the US mark. Bad faith was established: "It is difficult to
   see how a person who applies to register a mark in his own name which
   he has previously recognised as the property of a potential overseas

---

[78] TRAVELPRO [1997] R.P.C. 864, Regy. The registered proprietor made no response to the
   allegations.
[79] *Kundry SA's Application* [1998] E.T.M.R. 178, Regy. Some of the allegations appeared to have
   little to do with bad faith so far as the UK application was concerned.
[80] *Team Lotus* [1999] E.T.M.R. 669, Regy.
[81] BE NATURAL (SRIS O/106/99), Regy.

principal can be said to be acting in accordance with acceptable standards of commercial behaviour."[82]

(7) An independent producer was hired on a freelance basis to produce a radio programme using the broadcaster's resources. Even though the producer instigated the name BLACK MIX, clearly felt he was the prime mover in persuading the broadcaster to make the programme and had a significant role as producer, his role did not carry with it proprietorial rights over the name. The hearing officer decided the issue of proprietorship, as a matter of legal right, against the applicant and held, in consequence, that the application was made in bad faith despite the finding also that he had "a genuine and strongly held belief ... that he was entitled to the mark and could apply for registration."[83]

Bad faith not established

8–284

(1) In the early days of a joint venture, one of the participants, the defendant, registered the mark adopted for the products to be sold by the venture. The defendant later ceased to be the manufacturer, but still maintained some measure of quality control over the products. The plaintiff, originally the distributor in the venture, alleged the application had been made in bad faith. It was held that, at the date of application, the defendant honestly regarded itself as a, indeed, the person launching the product and entitled to apply for registration.[84]

(2) The opponent alleged that the applicant had copied its mark on a visit to a trade show in the USA. The applicant gave an explanation of the derivation of its mark and disputed the opponent's version of a telephone conversation said to be material. Neither party wished to attend a hearing. The allegation of bad faith failed, it being held that the applicant's version of events was more likely.[85]

(3) A racing driver applied to register his nickname "JOS THE BOSS". The allegation of bad faith from the opponent, Hugo Boss Ltd, was that the applicant had deliberately sought to register a trade mark to which he was not entitled. The opponent wholly failed to discharge the onus on it.[86]

(4) The application was for an "A in a star" device mark. The opponent made an overstated claim to a "worldwide reputation" in their mark, which was held to be very similar. The evidence from both sides was said to be "very thin". The allegation of bad faith failed since the opponent failed to discharge the onus on it to establish that their mark was well-known to the point that the applicant must have known it belonged to them, or would have known through some other circumstance, such as a trade connection.[87]

(5) An allegation that the applicant "should have been aware" of the opponent's mark was held, not surprisingly, to be not sufficient to sustain this ground of bad faith.[88]

---

[82] NEW CENTURY (SRIS O/018/00), Regy.

[83] BLACK MIX (SRIS O/048/00), Regy. A case where, subjectively, the applicant really believed the mark was his whereas, objectively, it was held that he could not walk off with the mark. The objective view prevailed.

[84] *Gromax Plasticulture Ltd v Don & Low Nonwovens Ltd* [1999] R.P.C. 367, Lindsay J., who declined to attempt a definition of bad faith, for fear of the tendency of others later to construe the paraphrase rather than the words of the 1994 Act itself.

[85] *Wackers* [1999] R.P.C. 453, Regy.

[86] JOS THE BOSS (SRIS O/170/99), Regy.

[87] "A" (SRIS O/081/99), Regy.

[88] GIVE ME FIVE (SRIS O/133/99), Regy and 7 HEAVEN (SRIS O/023/99), Regy, are just two

No bona fide intention to use the mark

Bad faith established

(1) An apparently dormant company, which offered various services of dubi-   **8–285**
ous legality and was operated by "a trade mark broker", registered a mark
in the United Kingdom and various other European countries in various
classes. The applicant for invalidity had used the mark extensively in the
USA. Whilst the Americans must have suspected their mark had been
hijacked, the issue was whether the registered proprietor had had a *bona
fide* intention to use the mark. This allegation of bad faith succeeded, the
proprietor of the mark failing to respond to the "strong prima facie case"
established in all the circumstances.[89]

(2) The applicant, an antique dealer, applied for a mark for "beer; mineral
waters". There was some evidence of telephone conversations with the
applicant in which he was alleged to have admitted that he made the application to prevent the mark being used on "alcopops", that he had nothing to do with brewing and did not at any stage intend to use the mark in
connection with beer. In his counterstatement, the applicant said he was
thinking of a mineral water not a beer, but filed no evidence. Since the applicant had no trade in beer and no *bona fide* intention to trade in beer, the
statement to the contrary on his application form was held to have been
made in bad faith, leading to the whole of the application being refused.[90]
The decision was confirmed on appeal.[91]

Bad faith not established

(1) The opponent alleged the applicant had no *bona fide* intention to use the   **8–286**
mark applied for in respect of "telephonic and broadcast communication
services via cable, satellite and television" because the applicant had no
licence from the ITC to provide a television broadcasting service. In response, the applicant filed evidence stating it intended to apply for appropriate licences and to commence use once registration of the mark was
achieved. Since the application could be one in a sequence of commercial
steps, the ground of opposition was dismissed.[92]

(2) A few days after an independent producer and a broadcaster parted
company, the producer applied to register BLACK MIX, the name of a
radio programme produced by him on a freelance basis for the broadcaster.
It was said he had no *bona fide* intention to use; alternatively that his
intention was contingent. A lengthy explanation of the producer's steps to
develop a community radio station defeated the attack. Bad faith was
established on the issue of proprietorship (see para.8–283, illustration (7),
above).[93]

Width of specification

Bad faith established

(1) A singer, known professionally as Mickey Dee, was employed as manager   **8–287**

---

examples where the allegation of bad faith should never have been made. Unless there is a clear
intent to ride on the back of an established reputation, the adoption of a mark which is merely
similar is unlikely to warrant an allegation of bad faith.

[89] OXYFRESH (SRIS O/095/99), Regy.
[90] DEMON ALE (SRIS O/072/99), Regy.
[91] Appointed person (G. Hobbs, Q.C.) September 28, 1999. When the basis of the objection was
explained to the applicant, he was not disposed to dispute it. Neither the pleadings nor the evidence had made the point clearly.
[92] YTV (SRIS O/042/99), Regy.
[93] BLACK MIX (SRIS O/048/00), Regy.

and joint licensee of a nightclub, which was relaunched shortly after his recruitment as Mickey Dees. He secured registration of MICKEY DEES (NIGHTCLUB) in respect of "provision of nightclub services; presentation of live music performances". The owner of the nightclub applied for a declaration of invalidity, alleging bad faith. The claim succeeded so far as the provision of nightclub services were concerned, because the proprietor of the mark could not claim to be able to provide the full range of services and because he knew the mark was being used by his employer. It was held that the proprietor of the mark was not entitled to claim ownership of the mark in respect of all the services claimed, but was given the opportunity to restrict his registration to "the provision of singing and musician services by an entertainer".[94]

(2) The application was filed in respect of "on-line services including video on-line magazine service". The opponent claimed that the mark was not being used and the applicant had no intention to use. The hearing officer referred to the Registry's current practice which was that the term "on-line services" was too vague and required clarification. The applicant had ceased trading and offered no evidence to support such a wide-ranging specification of services. It was held the application was filed in bad faith.[95]

(3) In earlier proceedings[96] the opponent applied for revocation for non-use of two marks acquired by the applicant some five years previously. Immediately prior to the revocation proceedings, the opponent had given notice of its interest in adopting the mark, and mentioned that its investigations showed no use of the marks. This correspondence led to the fresh application for the same mark. The applicant gave no instructions about the specification of goods, so its agent, erring on the side of caution, copied the specifications from the earlier registrations. The applicant filed evidence saying they had a particular lollipop product in mind for the mark and indicating the mark would not be applied to other products in their range. It was held that the application was filed in bad faith, for two reasons: the applicant was aware that the opponent wished to use the mark, the application being filed to present another defence and to frustrate the intentions of the opponents; secondly, because it was clear that the applicant had no intention of using the mark on anything other than a lollipop, whereas the application was for a wide range of goods: confectionery, chocolate, biscuits, cakes, etc.[97]

Bad faith not established

8–288   Bad faith was alleged on the basis that there was no intention to use the mark in relation to all or any of the goods applied for. The hearing officer commented that the range of goods applied for was "not overly wide" and the evidence of use since the application showed the intentions had been put into practice. The allegation failed.[98]

Other situations

8–289   In the light of the above, it is suggested that bad faith would be established in the

---

[94] *Mickey Dees (Nightclub) Trade Mark* [1998] R.P.C. 359, Regy.
[95] NEON (SRIS O/020/99), Regy.
[96] Magic Ball (No.1) SRIS O/084/99, Regy, which succeeded in part.
[97] Magic Ball (No. 2) SRIS O/123/99, Regy. On new evidence being admitted on appeal, the finding of bad faith was reversed: S. Thorley, Q.C. as the appointed person, August 1, 2000.
[98] DELICE (SRIS O/162/99), Regy.

following situations which have not yet arisen for decision. Comment is offered in relation to some of these examples:

Attempts to hijack a mark or spoil a competitor's plans

(1) The applicant has no *bona fide* intention to use the trade mark at all, but wishes to prevent a competitor from using the, or a similar, mark; **8–290**

(2) The applicant has no present or fixed intention to use the mark, but wishes to stockpile the mark for use at some indeterminate time in the future;

(3) The applicant becomes aware that someone else plans to use the mark, and files a pre-emptive application with a view to selling it.[99]

The specification of goods or services is too broad

(1) The applicant has used the mark on a limited range of goods for some years. He has no current plans to expand his use beyond the existing range of goods but the specification of goods for which he applies is much wider. **8–291**

(2) The applicant has used the mark on a limited range of goods for some years. He has no current plans to expand his use beyond the existing range of goods but he is advised to apply for a specification of goods of much wider scope, in order to secure the widest infringement rights. He follows the advice.

In this latter example, the applicant might think, having acted on advice from his specialist advisers, that he was safe from an allegation of bad faith. In fact, his position ought to be worse or no better than the applicant in the first example. If such advice were given, the dangers of following the advice should be spelt out. If they are not, then the applicant may ultimately have a claim against his adviser.

(3) The proprietor of the mark secured his registration well before the 1994 Act. When applying, the specification of services was drafted in accordance with the general practice then prevailing so as to cover the services for which the mark was used/intended to be used plus a wide range of services which were possibly of the same description to ensure the broadest possible rights of infringement.

(4) A mark used by a software house for a specialist accounting software package secured a registration for "computer hardware and software".

Some discussion of these two examples is required. Where there is a clear discrepancy between actual use/intended use and the specification applied for, bad faith can be found with relative ease. Often the discrepancy will not be so obvious—the Registry have indicated[1] that they can only raise a s.3(6) objection in extreme cases or where vague or wide terminology is used.[2] The difficulty is in deciding the appropriate level of generality in a specification which gives adequate protection to the trader concerned. Often, the appropriate level of generality can only be decided with knowledge of the trade concerned, but this type of enquiry is not compatible with bad faith. **8–292**

It is likely that a very large number of registrations were made under previous **8–293**

---

[99] cf. *British Telecommunications v One in a Million* [1999] 1 W.L.R. 903, CA., where Internet domain names comprising the names of well-known companies were held to be "instruments of fraud" in the hands of traders in domain names.

[1] Work Manual, Ch.6, s. 9.11.1, but note rule 57 which allows the Registrar to call for such information or documents as he may require—if necessary to justify a wide specification.

[2] See TESCO WE SELL FOR LESS, O-256-04 [2005] R.P.C. 17, Appointed Person, Ruth Annand, where a "wide-claiming" allegation of bad faith failed: see paras 17–27 especially 24.

Acts which have specifications of goods or services which are "too broad" according to the new order of the TM Directive and 1994 Act. With the broader infringement provisions of the 1994 Act, it is suggested that registrations should be confined to specifications of those goods or services in respect of which the mark is actually used. There is now no need or place for a registration to provide any additional penumbra of protection around the actual scope of use/intended use. In many cases, the width of the specification is unlikely to make any practical difference. However, in appropriate cases of conflict between the actual business of one party and a wide registration of another, the solution is likely to be an attempt to restrict the width of the specification with the two-pronged attack of non-use and bad faith. Token use to avoid the charge of non-use may support the allegation of bad faith. If there are difficulties with non-use, then difficult questions may have to be tackled in the allegation of bad faith. The proprietor would argue that he could not possibly be held to have made his application in bad faith because he followed the established practices of the time. This argument could not be met by transposing back in time practices or considerations under the 1994 Act. Ultimately, it may be the case that the degree of harmonisation intended in the Directive was not sufficient to cope with all the problems which might arise in the process of changing from the 1938 Act regime to the new regime.

MARKS INCORPORATING THE NAME OR IMAGE OF A WELL-KNOWN PERSON, WITHOUT THEIR AGREEMENT

8–294   This is the third example put forward by the Registry as a situation where bad faith might be found. Since it can hardly have been the intent of the legislature for this bad faith provision to incorporate a new and distinct right of personality, the wide range of situations covered by this example need careful consideration. It has been indicated that the example was intended only to apply to living persons,[3] but consideration of the possible positions of both living and deceased well-known persons will serve to highlight the difficulties in finding bad faith within this example.

8–295   Some people become well-known to the public because they are the source of products which are sold on an extensive scale and are popular—pop musicians are a prime example. Others, such as sports personalities or entertainers, become famous because of what they do—but what they do does not normally involve the provision of any product or service, other than to the very limited extent of providing entertainment. Generally, therefore, only a relatively small proportion of "famous people" have become so because their name or image indicated the trade origin of products or services. For those that have, one would expect appropriate trade marks to have been registered in the normal way. Where trade mark protection is lacking, such persons may be vulnerable to their trade marks being "hi-jacked" but that is not a problem which is confined to well-known persons and bad faith may be established on the normal principles discussed above.

8–296   In certain disciplines, fame brings opportunities to endorse the products of particular manufacturers. Endorsement of related products by a well-known sports personality is simply a method of promoting the products in question. The name or image of the well-known person does not and is not intended to indicate trade

---

[3] By the Registry's hearing officer in Jane Austen SRIS O/198/99, July 12, 1999.

origin. Far from it. The name or image of the personality is used in conjunction with the trade mark applied to the product. The name or image simply identifies the person.

In certain circumstances, personalities may move beyond endorsement to use their own name or image as the trade mark of products related to what they do. Provided that the public are educated to perceive the name or image as indicating trade origin,[4] then such persons have joined the ranks of trade mark owners. Bad faith may arise on the normal principles discussed above, if a third party hijacks the mark.   **8–297**

Thus far, we have identified some examples where the name or image of well-known persons may indicate trade origin, but no special bad faith rule is required and the normal principles apply. Such persons are the exception rather than the rule. We turn to consider the position of well-known people whose name or image do not, *prima facie*, indicate trade origin.   **8–298**

In this latter situation, the argument presumably is that bad faith arises because the applicant seeks to exploit the name or image without permission, even though the person in question would not be entitled to register his or her own trade mark. That this argument should succeed is by no means clear since it is difficult to see why "taking advantage of someone else's reputation" without permission should constitute bad faith unless the reputation is one of trade origin. If this type of bad faith argument succeeds, it is limited to the right to stop an exploitative registration, but it is beginning to establish some right of personality. The Court of Appeal in Elvis Presley were quite clear that there was no free standing general right to character exploitation enjoyable exclusively by a celebrity. A celebrity could only enjoy rights under the 1938 Act if the critical issue of distinctiveness was established. As to establishing distinctiveness, Simon Brown L.J. said ([1999] R.P.C. 567 at 598):   **8–299**

> "In addressing the critical issue of distinctiveness there should be no a priori assumption that only a celebrity or his successors may ever market (or licence the marketing of) his own character. Monopolies should not be so readily created."

It is suggested that the 1994 Act requires the same approach.

Thus far, we have been considering the position of celebrities either living or recently deceased: persons whose fame may have endured into the period of modern merchandising and/or generated a demand for memorabilia. The use of the name or image of a personality on items of memorabilia is unlikely to be taken as anything other than an indication of the content or character of the goods. Thus, an application for a mark would fail under s.3(1)(c) and/or (b) of the 1994 Act, but not, it is suggested, for bad faith.   **8–300**

The position may be different as regards items of merchandise which feature the name or image of a well-known living person or group. It largely depends on whether the relevant public have been educated to perceive marks used on merchandise as really indicating trade origin. Use on merchandise of the name in a stylised script which is the form of the trade mark on the principal product may be taken as an indication of trade origin, leaving others to manufacture similar items of merchandise which do not use the "official" script.   **8–301**

---

[4] This may be difficult to achieve. As Laddie J. pointed out at first instance in *Elvis Presley* [1997] R.P.C. 543, people can become so well-known that their names then possess very little inherent distinctiveness.

8–302   As regards famous individuals from history, again it is unlikely that the use of their name or image on items of memorabilia or commercial consumer items would be taken as indicating trade origin, without significant education of the public through exclusive use. If the name has come to indicate trade origin, there seems to be no reason why registration should be prevented on the ground of bad faith. The trustees of the Jane Austen Memorial Trust failed to establish bad faith in relation to an application to register the name of the author for soaps and similar items. The allegation was framed largely in terms of some general disentitlement on the applicant's part arising from Jane Austen's fame and literary heritage, but it was held that registration would have no detrimental effect on her literary heritage. Bad faith was not established although the application failed under s.3(1)(b).[5]

---

[5] *Jane Austen* (SRIS O/198/99), Regy. Although bad faith was not in issue, an application to register "Diana, Princess of Wales" for a wide range of goods and services likewise failed under s.3(1)(b): SRIS O/261/00, Regy, July 31, 2000.

CHAPTER 9

RELATIVE GROUNDS FOR REFUSAL OF REGISTRATION

1. Introduction

This chapter is concerned with the grounds for refusal of registration of a mark **9–001** which arise from conflicts with earlier marks. These grounds are accordingly referred to as the relative grounds for refusal. They must be contrasted with and are additional to the absolute grounds for refusal which are provided by ss.1 and 3 of the Trade Marks Act 1994 and which relate to the nature of the mark itself, its distinctiveness and other public policy considerations.

The relative grounds for refusal are essentially set out in ss.5 and 6 of the 1994 **9–002** Act. These sections implement the mandatory provisions and most of the optional provisions of Article 4 of the Trade Marks Directive.[1]

Relative grounds fall into two categories, those based on "earlier trade marks" **9–003** and those based on "earlier rights". Each of these is defined and the subject of discussion below. Earlier trade marks are primarily concerned with earlier registrations and applications, but are not limited to national trade marks. They include Community trade marks, international marks designating the United Kingdom and marks entitled to protection under the Paris Convention or the WTO Agreement, of which the Agreement on Trade Related Aspects of Intellectual Property Rights (TRIPS) is an integral part. Earlier rights, on the other hand, are other private rights, such as passing off and copyright which render the use of the mark liable to be prevented. Special protection is also afforded against the unauthorised acts of agents. In any proceedings each relative ground must be addressed separately.

In this chapter we consider these topics in turn and then the notion of honest **9–004** concurrent use which, despite having no foundation in the TM Directive, is introduced into the 1994 Act. It may be raised before the Registrar, essentially at the examination stage only. It falls away once a mark is the subject of opposition by the proprietor of the earlier trade mark or earlier right.

We also address the relative grounds for refusal of registration which arise **9–005** under the Community trade mark system. The Community Trade Mark Regulation[2] allows a trade mark having effect throughout the Community to be obtained on the basis of an application to the Office for Harmonization in the Internal Market (OHIM). The CTM Regulation broadly follows the same scheme as the TM Directive with regard to the prohibition of the registration of marks which conflict with earlier trade marks or rights. But there are some differences. Importantly, OHIM cannot raise relative grounds of its own motion. In each section of this chapter we explain where the two schemes diverge.

There have been two recent developments in connection with the CTM Regula- **9–006** tion which are of particular importance. First, the Madrid Protocol entered into

---

[1] Directive 89/104.
[2] Council Regulation 40/94, as amended.

force with respect to the European Community on October 1, 2004. The implications of this are discussed in Ch.7.

9–007   Secondly, on May 1, 2004 the Community was enlarged by the accession of 10 new Member States. As from the date of accession a Community trade mark registered or applied for before the date of accession automatically extends to the territory of those new Member States in order to have equal effect throughout the Community.[3] Nevertheless, for the purposes of relative grounds, an exceptional opposition right was established. Where an application for a Community trade mark was filed in the six months prior to the date of accession then earlier trade marks or earlier rights in the new Member States may be relied upon in opposition proceedings, provided they were acquired in good faith.[4]

2. Conflict with earlier trade marks

A. THE OBJECTIONS IN OUTLINE

Introduction

9–008   A mark shall not be registered if it conflicts with an earlier trade mark in three categories of cases. Each of them has its own requirements which are dealt with separately below. But for convenience they may be summarised as follows: first, where the marks and goods or services are identical; secondly, where because there is a similarity of marks and of goods or services there exists a likelihood of confusion of the public; thirdly, where an earlier mark has a reputation and use of the later mark would take unfair advantage of or be detrimental to the distinctive character or repute of the earlier mark.

9–009   It will be noted that in all essential respects these provisions are mirrored in the infringement provisions of s.10 of the 1994 Act. For this reason decisions on each topic are relevant to the other.

Use provisions
The 1994 Act

9–010   The 1994 Act has been amended to require an opponent to an application for the registration of a trade mark and any applicant for a declaration of invalidity who relies upon an earlier trade mark to show that it has been used.[5] This brings the position under the 1994 Act into line with the CTM Regulation.

9–011   In opposition or invalidity proceedings based upon an earlier trade mark the use conditions must be satisfied if the registration procedure for the earlier trade mark was completed five years before the publication of the application in issue (in the case of an opposition) or before the date of the application (in the case of an application for a declaration of invalidity).[6]

9–012   Account will only be taken of goods or services in relation to which the earlier

---

[3] Art.159a (1) of the CTM Regulation, as amended.
[4] Art.159a (3)of the CTM Regulation.
[5] s.6A and s.47 (2A)–(2E) of the 1994 Act, introduced by the Trade Marks (Proof of Use, etc.) Regulations 2004, which came into force on May 5, 2004. They implement Art.11(1) and (2) of the TM Directive. Under the transitional provisions they do not apply to any application for the registration of a trade mark which was published or to any application for a declaration of invalidity which was made before they came into force.
[6] s.6(A)(1) and (2); s.47(2A).

mark has been put to genuine use in the United Kingdom during that five year period, unless there are proper reasons for the non-use.[7] The earlier mark is treated as registered only in respect of those goods or services in respect of which the use conditions are satisfied.[8]

Use includes use in a form differing in elements which do not alter the distinctive character of the mark in the form in which it was registered, and use in the United Kingdom includes affixing the trade mark to goods or to the packaging of goods in the United Kingdom solely for export purposes.[9] **9–013**

Where the earlier trade mark is a Community trade mark then the genuine use must have taken place in the European Community.[10] **9–014**

The Community Trade Mark Regulation

As indicated, the position under the CTM Regulation is essentially the same as that now applying under the 1994 Act.[11] **9–015**

In the case of an opposition or invalidity proceedings the party relying on the earlier trade mark may be required to prove that it has been put to genuine use in the Community (if a Community trade mark) or in the relevant member State (if a national trade mark) over the period of five years prior to the publication of the application (in an opposition) or the date of the application (in proceedings for a declaration of invalidity), or that there are proper reasons for the non-use. Again, the provision only applies if the earlier trade mark has, at that time, been registered for at least five years.[12] **9–016**

B. SECTION 5(1): WHERE THE MARKS AND THE GOODS OR SERVICES ARE IDENTICAL

General

Section 5(1) of the 1994 Act reads: **9–017**

> "A trade mark shall not be registered if it is identical with an earlier trade mark and the goods or services for which the trade mark is applied for are identical with the goods or services for which the earlier trade mark is protected."

This subsection implements the mandatory provisions of Art.4(1)(a) of the TM Directive. For an objection to arise a number of requirements must be satisfied.

Earlier trade mark

First, there must be an earlier trade mark. This is defined in s.6 of the Act and is considered in paras 9–122 to 9–133.[13] **9–018**

---

[7] s.6(A)(3); s.47(2B). As to genuine use, and what may constitute proper reasons for non-use, see the discussion in Ch.10, paras 10–038 to 10–076.
[8] s.6(A)(6); s.47(2E).
[9] s.6(A)(4); s.47(2C). See also the discussion in Ch.10, paras 10–070 to 10–071.
[10] s.6(A)(5); s.47(2D).
[11] CTM Regulation, Arts 43 and 56.
[12] See the discussion in Ch.5, paras 5–082 to 5–092 (opposition), and Ch.10, paras 10–012 to 10–015 (declaration of invalidity).
[13] As is the equivalent provision in the CTM Regulation, Art.8(2).

The trade marks must be identical

9–019   Secondly, the earlier trade mark must be identical to the mark applied for. A sign is identical with a trade mark where it reproduces, without any modification or addition, all the elements constituting the trade mark or where, viewed as a whole, it contains differences so insignificant that they may go unnoticed by the average consumer.[14] The comparison must be between the whole mark applied for and the earlier registered mark.[15]

The goods or services must be identical

9–020   Thirdly, the goods or services the subject of the application must be the same as those the subject of the earlier trade mark.[16] This requires a consideration of the scope of the respective specifications.[17] Although not explicit, it would seem that this provision can only sensibly be interpreted as prohibiting registration where there is an overlap of goods or services.[18]

9–021   If the marks are identical, and any of the goods or services are identical then the prohibition applies.

Position under the Community Trade Mark Regulation

9–022   Article 8(1)(a) of the CTM Regulation provides an objection in the same terms, save that it may only be taken upon opposition and by the proprietor of the earlier trade mark or by a licensee authorised by him,[19] or in invalidity proceedings.[20]

Goods or services for which the earlier trade mark is protected

9–023   The 1994 Act and the corresponding provision of the TM Directive use the word "protected" rather that "registered" in referring to the goods or services the subject of the earlier trade mark.[21] In one sense the goods or services for which such a mark is "protected" extend beyond those in respect of which it is "registered" because of the provisions offering protection in respect of the use of the mark on similar goods or services where there is a likelihood of confusion.

9–024   It is suggested, however, that the words "protected" and "registered" should, at least in the context of earlier registered marks, be regarded as synonymous for the reason that any other interpretation would import into the objection a consideration of the likelihood of confusion and that is something which it is evidently specifically designed to avoid.[22]

9–025   But earlier trade marks also include marks protected under the Paris Conven-

---

[14] *L T J Diffusion v Sadas* ("Arthur et Félicie") [2003] F.S.R. 34 at p.608; *Reed Executive v Reed Business Information* [2004] R.P.C. 40 at p.767, CA; *Compass Publishing v Compass Logistics* [2004] EWHC 520; [2004] R.P.C. 41. See also the discussion in Ch.14, paras 14–051 to 14–054.

[15] Contrast the difficulty identifying the defendant's mark in considering the issue of infringement; see the discussion in Ch.14, paras 14–049 to 14–050.

[16] See the discussion in paras 9–023 to 9–025.

[17] As to the scope of a specification, see the discussion in Ch.14, paras 14–041 to 14–045.

[18] This is the approach taken in OHIM: Opposition Guidelines, March 2004, Part 2, Ch.1.

[19] CTM Regulation, Art.42(1)(a).

[20] CTM Regulation, Art. 52.

[21] TM Directive, Art.4(1)(a). In Art.4(1)(b), which is implemented by s.5(2), the words are "the goods or services covered by the trade marks". The 1994 Act, s.5(2), however, again uses the word "protected" in referring to the goods or services the subject of the earlier trade mark. The CTM Regulation uses the word "protected" in both Art.8(1)(a) and (b). In the CTM Regulation, Art.8(5), the word "registered" is used, and this may have implications on the scope of the provision, as discussed in para.9–096.

[22] See Recital 10 of the TM Directive and Recital 7 of the CTM Regulation.

tion and the TRIPS Agreement as well-known trade marks, and such marks may well not be registered at all. Here it is suggested that the protected goods or services the subject of the earlier mark must, by analogy, be those in respect of which the mark is well-known in the United Kingdom.[23]

C. SECTION 5(2): WHERE THE MARKS AND THE GOODS OR SERVICES ARE IDENTICAL OR SIMILAR AND THERE IS A LIKELIHOOD OF CONFUSION

General

Section 5(2) of the 1994 Act reads: **9–026**

"A trade mark shall not be registered if because—

(a) it is identical with an earlier trade mark and is to be registered for goods or services similar to those for which the earlier trade mark is protected, or

(b) it is similar to an earlier trade mark and is to be registered for goods or services identical with or similar to those for which the earlier trade mark is protected,

there exists a likelihood of confusion on the part of the public, which includes the likelihood of association with the earlier trade mark."

This subsection implements the mandatory provisions of Article 4(1)(b) of the   **9–027** TM Directive. For all practical purposes its wording is identical to the infringement provision of s.10(2) of the 1994 Act. It prohibits the registration of a trade mark which would be likely to cause confusion of the public as a result of its being identical with or similar to an earlier trade mark and because it is to be registered in respect of goods or services the same as or similar to those the subject of the earlier trade mark. As to the use of the word "protected" in this context, reference is invited to the discussion in paras 9–023 to 9–025.

It is apparent from the words of s.10(2) and of Art.4(1)(b), that the likelihood   **9–028** of confusion on the part of the public is fundamental to the objection. This has been confirmed by the European Court of Justice in *Sabel v Puma*[24] where the Court stated, at para.18, that:

"In that connection, it is to be remembered that Article 4(1)(b) of the Directive is designed to apply only if, by reason of the identity or similarity both of the marks and of the goods or services which they designate, 'there exists a likelihood of confusion on the part of the public, which includes the likelihood of association with the earlier trade mark'. It follows from that wording that the concept of the likelihood of association is not an alternative to that of likelihood of confusion, but serves to define its scope. The terms of the provision itself exclude its application where there is no likelihood of confusion on the part of the public."

In the following sections we consider important issues in relation to this provi-   **9–029** sion and, in particular, how the likelihood of confusion is to be assessed and the factors to be taken into account; whether or not there is a threshold requirement that the goods or services be "similar"; the factors to be taken into account in assessing similarity; and finally, the nature of the relevant confusion.

---

[23] See 1994 Act, s.56.
[24] [1997] E.C.R. I-6191; [1998] R.P.C. 199. See also *Canon v MGM* [1998] E.C.R. I-5507; [1997] R.P.C. 117; *Lloyd Schufabrik Meyer v Klijsen Handel* [1999] E.T.M.R. 690; *Marca Mode v Adidas* [2000] E.C.R. I-4861, para.34. In *Marca Mode*, the ECJ rejected the submission of Adidas that, in respect of well-known marks, the likelihood of association is sufficient to justify a prohibition where a likelihood of confusion "cannot be ruled out".

Position under the Community Trade Mark Regulation

9–030   Article 8(1)(b) of the CTM Regulation is in similar terms, save that the objection can only be taken on opposition and by the proprietor of the earlier trade mark or a licensee authorised by him,[25] or in invalidity proceedings.[26]

9–031   The likelihood of confusion on the part of the public must be "in the territory in which the earlier trade mark is protected".[27] Consequently, co-existence of the marks in countries other than those in respect of which the opponent has cited prior registrations is not a factor to be taken into account.[28] An earlier trade mark may be distinctive in the Member State of registration even if it is descriptive in the language of another Member State.[29] Registration of a Community trade mark must be refused even if a relative ground of refusal obtains in only part of the Community.[30] Tourists forming a minority of the relevant public do not represent the average consumer.[31]

Assessment of the likelihood of confusion

(i) *Introduction*

9–032   The words of Article 4 of the TM Directive and s.5(2) of the 1994 Act require that the likelihood of confusion is caused by the identity or similarity of the marks and the goods or services.[32] It is not enough that the likelihood of confusion is caused by some other factors external to the marks, such as associated advertising materials or packaging. In addition these provisions require a likelihood of confusion as to origin, a matter discussed further below.

9–033   The likelihood of confusion is to be assessed globally, taking into account all factors relevant to the marks and goods and services in issue, and this will include any reputation attaching to the earlier trade mark. This has been made clear by the ECJ in *Sabel v Puma*:[33]

> "... Article 4(1)(b) does not apply where there is no likelihood of confusion on the part of the public. In that respect it is clear from the tenth recital in the preamble to the Directive that the appreciation of the likelihood of confusion 'depends on numerous elements and, in particular, on the recognition of the trade mark on the market, of the association which can be made with the used or registered sign, of the degree of similarity between the trade mark and the sign and between the goods or services identified'. The likelihood of confusion must therefore be appreciated globally, taking into account all factors relevant to the circumstances of the case.
>
> That global appreciation of the visual, aural or conceptual similarity of the marks in question, must be based on the overall impression given by the

---

[25] CTM Regulation, Art.42(1)(a).

[26] CTM Regulation, Art.52.

[27] Considered from the perspective of the average consumer in the Member State where the earlier mark is protected. See, *e.g.*: *José Alejandro SL v OHIM, Anheuser Busch intervener* [2004] E.T.M.R. 15 at p.177 (CFI); *Institut für Lernsysteme v OHIM* [2002] E.C.R. II-4301, at para.48 (CFI).

[28] See, *e.g. Icart SA's Application* [2000] E.T.M.R. 180.

[29] *Matratzen Concord v OHIM* [2003] E.C.R. II-4335, (CFI).

[30] *Mulhens v OHIM (ZIRH)* [2004] E.T.M.R. 101 (CFI).

[31] *Alpine Electronics v El Corte Ingles* [2004] E.T.M.R. 49 at p.664 (OHIM BoA).

[32] So also in the case of the CTM Regulation, Art.8(1).

[33] [1997] E.C.R. I-6191; [1998] R.P.C. 199 at paras 22–24. See also *Lloyd Schuhfabrik Meyer* [1999] E.T.M.R. 690, at para.18.

marks, bearing in mind, in particular, their distinctive and dominant components. The wording of Article 4(1)(b) of the Directive— '… there exists a likelihood of confusion on the part of the public …'—shows that the perception of marks in the mind of the average consumer of the type of goods or services in question plays a decisive role in the global appreciation of the likelihood of confusion. The average consumer normally perceives a mark as a whole and does not proceed to analyse its various details.

In that perspective, the more distinctive the earlier mark, the greater will be the likelihood of confusion. It is therefore not impossible that the conceptual similarity resulting from the fact that two marks use images with analogous semantic content may give rise to a likelihood of confusion where the earlier mark has a particularly distinctive character, either per se or because of the reputation it enjoys with the public."

(ii) *General principles*

Sabel v Puma and later cases establish a number of fundamental propositions: **9–034**

(a) A GLOBAL ASSESSMENT

The likelihood of confusion must be appreciated globally, taking into account   **9–035**
all factors relevant to the circumstances of the case.[34]

(b) THE PUBLIC

The matter must be considered through the eyes of the average consumer of   **9–036**
the goods or services in issue.[35] For the purposes of the global appreciation, the average consumer of the category of products concerned is deemed to be reasonably well informed and reasonably observant and circumspect.[36]

(c) THE DEGREE OF SIMILARITY BETWEEN THE MARKS

In order to assess the degree of similarity between the marks concerned, the   **9–037**
national court must determine the degree of visual, aural or conceptual similarity between them and, where appropriate, evaluate the importance to be attached to those different elements taking account of the category of goods or services in question and the circumstances in which they are marketed.[37]

(d) OVERALL IMPRESSION OF THE MARKS IS TO BE CONSIDERED

The global appreciation of the likelihood of confusion must, as regards the vi-   **9–038**
sual, aural or conceptual similarity of the marks in question, be based upon the overall impression created by them, bearing in mind, in particular, their distinctive and dominant components. The perception of marks in the mind of the average consumer of the category of goods or services in question plays a decisive role in the global appreciation of the likelihood of confusion. The average

---

[34] *Sabel v Puma* [1997] E.C.R. I-6191; [1998] R.P.C. 199, at paras 22–24.
[35] *Sabel v Puma*, [1997] E.C.R. I-6191; [1998] R.P.C. 199 at paras 22–24; *Bach Flower Remedies v Healing Herbs* [2000] R.P.C. 513, CA. The position of the trade is also likely to be relevant. If the trade is confused then it is likely the average consumer will be too.
[36] *Lloyd Schuhfabrik Meyer* [1999] E.T.M.R. 690, at paras 26–27; *Gut Springenheide and Tusky* [1998] E.C.R. I-4657, at para.31. This test is consistent with earlier UK law. So, in considering passing off, the courts have rejected confusion by a "moron in a hurry" in favour of ordinary sensible members of the public: *Morning Star v Express Newspapers* [1979] F.S.R. 113; cf. *Newsweek v British Broadcasting Corporation* [1979] R.P.C. 441, CA.
[37] *Lloyd Schuhfabrik Meyer* [1999] E.T.M.R. 690 at para.27.

consumer normally perceives a mark as a whole and does not proceed to analyse its various details.[38]

(e) THE DISTINCTIVE CHARACTER OF THE EARLIER MARK

9–039   The more distinctive the earlier mark, the greater will be the likelihood of confusion. A mark may have a particularly distinctive character either *per se*, or because of the reputation it enjoys with the public.[39]

(f) IMPERFECT RECOLLECTION

9–040   Account is to be taken of the fact that the average consumer only rarely has the chance to make a direct comparison between the different marks but must place his trust in the imperfect recollection of them he has kept in his mind. It should also be borne in mind that the average consumer's level of attention is likely to vary according to the category of goods or service in question.[40]

(g) SIMILARITY OF THE GOODS OR SERVICES

9–041   Appreciation of the likelihood of confusion also depends on the degree of similarity between the goods or services identified.[41]

(h) INTERDEPENDENCE OF THE RELEVANT FACTORS

9–042   Furthermore, a global assessment of the likelihood of confusion implies an interdependence between the various relevant factors. So, a lesser degree of similarity between the goods or services may be offset by a greater similarity between the marks, and vice versa. So also registration of a mark may have to be refused, despite a lesser degree of similarity between the goods or services covered, where the marks are very similar and the earlier mark, in particular on account of its reputation, is highly distinctive.[42]

(i) RELEVANT CONFUSION

9–043   The risk that the public might believe that the goods or services in question come from the same undertaking, or from economically linked undertakings, does constitute a likelihood of confusion within the meaning of the section.[43]

9–044   On the other hand, mere association which the public might make between two marks as a result of their analagous semantic content is not in itself a sufficient ground for concluding there is a likelihood of confusion.[44]

(iii) *Confusion as to origin*

9–045   As indicated above, the sort of confusion required to satisfy this provision is

---

[38] *Sabel v Puma* [1997] E.C.R. I-6191; [1998] R.P.C. 199, at paras 23 and 25. And see generally, paras 9–069 to 9–083.

[39] *Sabel v Puma* [1997] E.C.R. I-6191; [1998] R.P.C. 199, at paras 22–24. And see generally, paras 9–069 to 9–083 .

[40] *Lloyd Schuhfabrik Meyer* [1999] E.T.M.R. 690 at para.26. See, by way of example, *Jean Pierre Koubi v OHIM* [2004] E.T.M.R. 61.

[41] *Sabel v Puma* [1997] E.C.R. I-6191; [1998] R.P.C. 199, at paras 22–24. See the discussion in paras 9–047 to 9–058 as to whether there is a threshold requirement that the goods or services be similar; and in paras 9–059 to 9–068 as to the factors to be considered.

[42] *Sabel v Puma* [1997] E.C.R. I-6191; [1998] R.P.C. 199 in particular at paras 22–24; *Canon v MGM* (ECJ) [1998] E.C.R. I-5507; [1999] R.P.C. 117, in particular at paras 18–28. See, by way of example, *Landre v International Paper* [2001] E.T.M.R. 73 (p.794) OHIM BoA.

[43] *Canon v MGM* (ECJ) [1998] E.C.R. I-5507; [1999] R.P.C. 117, at paras 29–30; *Sabel v Puma* [1997] E.C.R. I-6191; [1998] R.P.C. 199, paras 16–18. See also the discussion in paras 9–045 to 9–046.

[44] *Sabel v Puma* [1997] E.C.R. I-6191; [1998] R.P.C. 199 at para.26. See also the discussion in paras 9–045 to 9–046.

confusion as to origin. It is not enough that on seeing the mark the subject of the application, the earlier mark is "called to mind" if there is no possibility of the customer being under any misapprehension as to the origin of the goods or services. The mere association which the public might make between two trade marks as a result of their analogous semantic content is not in itself a sufficient ground for concluding that there is a likelihood of confusion within the meaning of the provision.[45]

However, confusion as to origin extends beyond simply mistaking the one mark for the other. It also includes cases where the public wrongly believe that the goods or services have their origin in the same enterprise or otherwise make a connection between the proprietors of the sign applied for and those of the earlier mark and confuses them.[46] This connection must be in the nature of an economic link.[47] So if the public believe that the goods or services are under the control and licence of the proprietors of the earlier mark, that would seem to be enough.[48] Similarly it is objectionable if they believe the later mark is a sub-brand.[49]

9–046

(iv) Similar goods or services—a threshold requirement?

The issue

It is now established that the degree of similarity between the relevant goods and services is an important matter which must be taken into account in consider-

9–047

---

[45] *Wagamama v City Centre Restaurants* [1995] F.S.R. 713; *Sabel v Puma* [1997] E.C.R. I-6191; [1998] R.P.C. 199. The ECJ declined to interpret the TM Directive so as to include non-origin association as forbidden by Benelux law and explained in *Henri Jullien BV v Verschuere Norbert (Union, Union Soleure)*, Jurisprudence of Benelux Court of Justice, [1984] E.C.C. 14, p.36; see also *Lucas Bols v Colgate Palmolive (Claeryn and Klarein)* (1976) 7 I.I.C. 420; Jurisprudence of Benelux Court of Justice 1975, p.472. The position is the same under the CTM Regulation: *Oberhauser v Ohim–Petit Liberto (Fifties)* [2002] E.C.R. II 4359.

[46] The ECJ in *Sabel v Puma* [1997] E.C.R. I-6191; [1998] R.P.C. 199, at para.16, referred to the submission that "the likelihood of association may arise in three sets of circumstances: (1) where the public confuses the sign and the mark in question (likelihood of direct confusion); (2) where the public makes a connection between the proprietors of the sign and those of the mark and confuses them (likelihood of indirect confusion or association); (3) where the public considers the sign to be similar to the mark and perception of the sign calls to mind the memory of the mark, although the two are not confused (likelihood of association in the strict sense)." The court considered, at para.18, it was therefore necessary to determine whether the TM Directive, Art.4(1)(b), could apply where there was no likelihood of direct or indirect confusion, but only a likelihood of association in the strict sense. It held: "The terms of the provision itself exclude its application where there is no likelihood of confusion on the part of the public".

[47] *Canon v MGM* (ECJ) [1998] E.C.R. I-5507; [1999] R.P.C. 117, at para.30 of the judgment: "... there may be a likelihood of confusion within the meaning of Article 4(1)(b) of the Directive even where the public perception is that the goods or services have different places of production. By contrast there can be no such likelihood where it does not appear that the public could believe that the goods or services come from the same undertaking or, as the case may be, from economically linked undertakings". For an illustration of the application of this principle, see *HIJ Mannenmode v Nienhaus & Lotz*, a decision of the District Court of Utrecht [1999] E.T.M.R. 730.

[48] This would of course be entirely within the recognised subject-matter of a trade mark, namely as an indication that the goods or services have originated under the control of a single undertaking which is responsible for their quality. It may also be sufficient if the public believe that the goods or services are simply licensed by the proprietor of the earlier trade mark. After all, that is consistent with the Directive, which provides, in Art.10(3), that use of the trade mark with the consent of the proprietor shall be deemed to constitute use by the proprietor. See: *10 Royal Berkshire Polo Club Trade Mark* [2001] R.P.C. 32; *Raleigh International Trade Mark* [2001] R.P.C. 11. So in *Betty's Kitchen Coronation Street Trade Mark* [2000] R.P.C. 825 it was enough that consumer awareness of dual branding would lead to the assumption that there was a link between the goods of the opponent and the makers of the television programme 'Coronation Street'.

[49] *John-Pierre Koubi v OHIM, Fabricas Lucia Antonio Betere intervening* [2004] E.T.M.R. 61 (CFI): "Conforflex" confusingly similar to "Flex"; *Feeling v Comercial Jacinto Parera* [2004] E.T.M.R. 82 OHIM BoA.

ing the likelihood of confusion.[50] But before considering the factors which may be relevant to the assessment of similarity it is necessary to address a preliminary question: Is there a boundary or outer limit to the goods and services which may be considered similar for the purposes of s.5(2) of the Act (Article 4(1)(b) of the Directive; Article 8(1)(b) of the CTM Regulation)?

9–048   If there is no such boundary or threshold then the question to be addressed is simply whether or not there is a likelihood of confusion taking into account the similarity of the marks, the goods or services and all other relevant matters.[51] If there is a boundary or threshold, then there can be no application of s.5(2) if the goods or services are not sufficiently alike as to be "similar" within the meaning of the provision, irrespective of the likelihood of confusion.

The decisions of the European Court of Justice

9–049   This question has been addressed, although not entirely clearly, by the European Court of Justice in *Canon v MGM*.[52] The case concerned an application by MGM to register the mark CANNON in respect of, *inter alia*, films recorded on video tape cassettes (video tape cassettes) and the opposition to it by Canon on the grounds of its earlier trade mark CANON in respect of, *inter alia*, recording and production devices for video tapes (video recorders). The Bundespatentgericht (Federal Patent Court) considered that the goods were not so similar that the average purchaser might form the opinion that they were made by the same enterprise and that accordingly Art.4(1)(b) was not satisfied. On appeal, the Bundesgerichtshof considered that the provision might be satisfied if account could be taken of the reputation attaching to the earlier mark CANON and accordingly referred the following question for a preliminary ruling:[53]

> "May account be taken, when assessing the similarity of the goods or services covered by the two marks, of the distinctive character, in particular the reputation, of the mark with earlier priority ... so that, in particular, likelihood of confusion within the meaning of Article 4(1)(b) of Directive 89/104 must be taken to exist even if the public attributes the goods and/or services to different places of origin?"

9–050   At the hearing argument was directed to the issue of whether the test for assessing the similarity of goods or services was objective (*i.e.* unrelated to the nature of the marks in question), as contended for by MGM and the United Kingdom Government, or whether it was permissible to consider goods or services to be similar in relation to particularly distinctive marks when such goods or services would not be considered similar in relation to other less distinctive marks.[54]

9–051   The court held (at para.24) that the distinctive character of a trade mark, and in particular its reputation, must be taken into account when determining whether the similarity between the goods or services covered by the two marks is sufficient to give rise to the likelihood of confusion. In so finding the court was clearly following the decision in *Sabel* that the likelihood of confusion must be assessed globally taking into account all relevant matters.

9–052   This finding does not, however, directly address the issue of whether or not

---

[50] See paras 9–033 and 9–041.
[51] The appointed person has, at least on occasion, taken this line: see *"Balmoral"* [1999] R.P.C. 297; *"Naturelle"* [1999] R.P.C. 326; *Raleigh International Trade Mark* [2001] R.P.C. 11 (p.202).
[52] [1999] R.P.C. 117.
[53] para.11 of the judgment.
[54] See paras 31–51 of the opinion of the A.G.

there is a threshold test. But in reaching its conclusion the court appears to have considered that there is a threshold and that the question of similarity must itself be assessed globally. In particular it found, at paras 22 and 23:

"22. It is, however, important to stress that, for the purpose of applying Article 4(1)(b), even where a mark is identical to another with a highly distinctive character, it is still necessary to adduce evidence of similarity between the goods or services covered. In contrast to Article 4(4)(a), which expressly refers to the situation in which the goods or services are not similar, Article 4(1)(b) provides that the likelihood of confusion presupposes that the goods or services are identical or similar.

23. In assessing the similarity of the goods or services concerned, as the French and United Kingdom Governments and the Commission have pointed out, all the relevant factors relating to those goods or services themselves should be taken into account. Those factors include, *inter alia*, their nature, their end users and their method of use and whether they are in competition with each other or are complementary."

This conclusion is also consistent with the Opinion of the Advocate General. **9–053** He similarly considered that the degree of recognition of the earlier mark is relevant in deciding whether there is sufficient similarity to give rise to a likelihood of confusion, an approach entirely consistent with *Sabel*. But he also appears to have considered that there is a threshold. Such is apparent from paras 46–50 of his Opinion, which include the following passage:

"I accept that a flexible test of the similarity of goods or services might lead to different interpretations of such similarity in different Member States, a new mark might not be caught by Article 4(1)(b) of the Directive in one Member State simply because it is considered in that State that, despite the reputation of the earlier mark and a likelihood of confusion, the goods or services are not sufficiently similar. In such a case, however, the fact that the earlier trade mark has a reputation may well mean that in that Member State Article 4(4)(a) or Article 5(2) of the Directive (concerning the protection of a mark in relation to dissimilar goods or services) would apply instead."

More recently in *Vedial v OHIM (Hubert)*[55] the Court affirmed the position in **9–054** considering the application of Art.8(1)(b) of the TM Regulation. It held, at para.51:

"For the purposes of applying Article 8(1)(b) of Regulation No. 40/94, the likelihood of confusion presupposes both that the mark applied for and the earlier mark are identical or similar, and that the goods or services covered by the application for registration are identical or similar to those in respect of which the earlier mark is registered. Those conditions are cumulative (see to that effect, on the identical provisions of Article 4(1)(b) of [the TM Directive], Case C–39/97 *Canon* [1998] E.C.R. I-5507, paragraph 22)."

English decisions

The English court considered the question in the *British Sugar* in relation to **9–055** the infringement provisions of s.10(2) of the 1994 Act. Jacob J. expressly rejected the contention that there was a single composite question. He considered that the issue of whether or not the relevant goods or services were similar was a separate

---

[55] Case C–106/03P [2005] E.T.M.R. 23.

question which had to be answered. If the respective goods or services were not similar, then there could be no infringement under s.10(2) of the Act.[56]

9–056   The same approach has since been taken in other infringement cases.[57] In *Intel Corp v Sihra*[58] Patten J. said, at para.12:

> "It is clear that the flexibility inherent in this global approach leaves intact the threshold requirement for a recognisable degree of similarity between the goods and services in question. The distinctiveness and strength of the earlier mark may lessen the degree of similarity required, but it does not eliminate it. The remedy for the proprietor of a distinctive mark which is challenged in respect of non similar goods is to oppose registration under s.5(3)."

The correct general approach

9–057   In the light of these authorities it is submitted the correct general approach may be summarised as follows. Some trade marks are so famous that there will exist a likelihood of confusion even if they are used on wholly dissimilar goods or services. In such a case s.5(2) cannot be invoked. The likelihood of confusion would not be attributable to any similarity between the goods or services in issue. The prohibition requires there to be at least *some* similarity between the goods or services the subject of the earlier mark and those the subject of the application. Furthermore, it must follow that the issue of whether or not particular goods or services bear some similarity must be answered independently of the marks in issue.[59] This is a matter which must be considered from the perspective of the average consumer but will necessarily depend upon objective criteria, which we discuss in the following section.[60]

9–058   It must however be noted that the likelihood of confusion must still be assessed globally and there is an interdependence of the relevant factors. Accordingly, and provided the goods or services bear some similarity, a lesser degree of similarity between the goods or services may be offset by a greater similarity between the marks, and vice versa.

(v) *Similar goods or services—the objective factors to be considered*

9–059   As para.23 of the decision in *Canon* makes clear,[61] all factors relating to the goods or services themselves must be taken into account. These include, *inter alia*, their nature, their end users[62] and their method of use and whether they are in competition with each other or are complementary.

9–060   Hence the following types of factors may be of assistance:

---

[56] [1996] R.P.C. 281 at 294. Jacob J. went rather further and considered that the question of similarity of goods was wholly independent of the particular mark and sign in issue, observing that "if one elides the two questions then a strong mark would get protection for a greater range of goods than a weak mark". This must be regarded as, at best, an incomplete statement of the law in the light of *Canon*.

[57] *Premier Brands v Typhoon* [2000] E.T.M.R. 1071; [2000] F.S.R. 767. *Harding v Smilecare* [2002] F.S.R. 37;

[58] *Intel Corp v Sihra* [2003] EWHC 17 (Ch); [2004] E.T.M.R. 44 at p.595.

[59] An approach apparently followed by the Registry: see *e.g.* "*Zippo*" [1999] R.P.C.173; "*QS by S. Oliver*" [1999] R.P.C. 520.

[60] Thus OHIM approach the issue on the following basis: the products are similar if, supposing identical marks, the public could believe they come from the same or economically linked undertakings: OHIM Opposition Guidelines, March 2004, Part 2 Ch. 2B, para.2.2.3. For such an approach to be consistent it must be assumed that the marks have not been used and that they are only of average inherent distinctiveness.

[61] Cited in para.9–052.

[62] It has been suggested that this is an incorrect translation and should read: "purpose of use".

(1) the uses of the respective goods or services;

(2) the users of the respective goods or services;

(3) the physical nature of the goods or acts of service;

(4) the trade channels through which the goods or services reach the market;

(5) in the case of self-serve consumer items, where in practice they are respectively found or likely to be found in supermarkets and in particular whether they are, or are likely to be, found on the same or different shelves;

(6) the extent to which the respective goods and services are in competition with each other: that inquiry may take into account how those in trade classify goods, for instance whether market research companies, who of course act for industry, put the goods or services in the same or different sectors.[63]

Resolution of the issue may require evidence directed to the position as at the date of the application.[64]

Some illustrations

Some decisions concerning the question of similar goods or services under the TM Directive or the CTM Regulation are set out below. These should be regarded as no more than a guide because circumstances may change and vary from territory to territory.[65] **9–061**

Similar goods or services

"Organic fertilisers" similar goods to "chemicals used in horticulture and forestry" since they have a similar function and are likely to be sold in the same shops.[66] **9–062**

"Wines" similar to "whisky" and "bar services", since people would think that the supplier of one was engaged in the supply of the other.[67]

"Coffee, tea and cocoa" similar to "coffee substitutes" as they are intended for the same use.[68]

"Skin care, sun care and hair care preparations; perfumery, essential oils, soaps" similar to "perfumes; cosmetics; non-medicated toilet preparations; soaps; shampoos; preparations for the hair; dentifrices; anti-perspirants; deodorants for personal use".[69] **9–063**

"Leather goods, leather bags, other leather goods not specifically made for the things they contain, containers and purses" similar to "clothing".[70]

Services offered by beauty salons; solarium services" similar to "business assistance with beauty preparations, sales" and "beauty preparations, perfumery, **9–064**

---

[63] *British Sugar v James Robertson* [1996] R.P.C. 281 at 294–297, elaborating the old judicial test of goods of the same description articulated by Romer J. in *Jellinek* (1946) 63 R.P.C. 59 at 70, approved by the House of Lords in *Daiquiri Rum* [1969] R.P.C. 600 at 620. The same list was cited in the Opinion of A.G. Jacobs in *Canon v MGM* [1998] E.C.R. I-5507, at para.45. For further decisions on the test applied under the 1938 Act, reference is invited to the 12th edition of this work, and supplement, at paras 10–11 to 10–15.

[64] See, *e.g.* "Zippo" [1999] R.P.C. 173; *Raleigh International Trade Mark* [2001] R.P.C. 11 (p.202).

[65] It will be noted that in the case of the CTM Regulation the likelihood of confusion is to be assessed "in the territory where the earlier trade mark is protected": Art.8(1)(b).

[66] *Humic* [1999] E.T.M.R. 26 (OHIM).

[67] "Balmoral" [1999] R.P.C. 297.

[68] *Lutz Quasdorf v Les Sirenes* [1999] E.T.M.R. 152 (OHIM).

[69] "Naturelle" [1999] R.P.C. 326.

[70] "QS by S. Oliver" [1999] R.P.C. 520.

cosmetics dietetic substances" since the goods and services of the conflicting marks could be offered together and be intended for the same public.[71]

9–065   "Consultancy on the organisation and management of commercial and industrial businesses" similar to "assistance to industrial and commercial businesses; consultancy information, research, inquiries or business management" in that they both have the same objective of the provision of specific industrial and commercial knowledge to commercial entities in the determination of their choice of business.[72]

"Buttons, press studs, buckles (clothing accessories), buckles for footwear and garments, eyelets and buttonholes for footwear and garments, patches and rivets for garments" in Class 26 similar to "outer and inner wear, knitwear including boots, shoes and slippers; clothing articles including boots, shoes and slippers; outer and inner garments of fabric and knitwear, including boots shoes and slippers; clothing articles, shoes and hats".[73]

Milk and cheese similar since, in the eyes of the relevant public, they belong to a single product family and may easily be regarded as components of a general range of milk products capable of having a common commercial origin.[74]

9–066   Footwear similar to clothing since they are both worn, have the function of covering and protecting and are often sold in the same outlets.[75]

Goods or services which are not similar

9–067   "Bags, cases and pocket wallets made of leather; umbrellas and parasols" not similar to "cigarette lighters and lighter fuel".[76]

"Sports bags, shopping bags, toilet bags, key bags" not similar to "clothing".[77]

"Electronic devices for attracting and killing insects" not similar to "aromatherapy diffusing apparatus".[78]

9–068   Alcoholic beverages other than beer not similar to coffee.[79]

Financial services to dentists not similar to dental services.[80]

Milk products (Class 29), flour and preparations made from cereals (Class 30) not similar to foodstuff for animals, including non-medicated food additives and food supplements for animals (Class 31).[81]

Pharmaceutical products not similar to medical devices.[82]

(vi) Similar marks—the factors to be considered

9–069   The general principles to be adopted are set out in paras 9–032 to 9–044.

Normal and fair use

9–070   In applying those principles the correct approach is to consider a normal and fair use of the mark the subject of the application and, where the earlier mark is a

---

[71] *Beauty Free Shop* [1999] E.T.M.R. 20 (OHIM).
[72] *Mars* [1999] E.T.M.R. 402 (OHIM).
[73] *Zanella SNC's Application* [2000] E.T.M.R. 69 (OHIM).
[74] *Pedro Diaz v OHIM, Granjas Castello intervening* [2004] E.T.M.R. 42 at p.575 (CFI).
[75] *O'Neill Inc's Application* [2004] E.T.M.R. 50 (OHIM).
[76] *"Zippo"* [1999] R.P.C. 173.
[77] *"QS by S.Oliver"* [1999] R.P.C. 520.
[78] *"Lifesystems"* [2000] R.P.C. 851.
[79] *Casa Girelli's Application* [2002] E.T.M.R. 66 at p.748.
[80] *Harding v Smilecare* [2002] F.S.R. 37 at p.589.
[81] *Lidl Stiftung v Heinz Iberica* [2003] E.T.M.R. 25 at p.312 (OHIM, BoA).
[82] *Innodis PLC's Application* [2004] E.T.M.R. 36 at p.502 (Cour D'Appel De Paris).

registered mark which has not been used, a normal and fair use of that mark too.[83] Where the earlier mark has been used, then, in the absence of argument or evidence to the contrary, the way in which the proprietor has used it can be said, at the very least *prima facie*, to be the paradigm case of its use in a normal and fair manner.[84]

Distinctive character of the earlier mark

As discussed, the tribunal must also consider the distinctive character of the earlier mark. Where the earlier mark has been used and has acquired a more distinctive character it is clear, following *Sabel v Puma*, that this is a matter which must be taken into account as a factor likely to increase the risk of confusion. Under the old law it was sometimes argued that once a mark becomes a household word it is too well-known to be confused with others.[85] This approach seems virtually untenable in the light of *Sabel* and *Canon*, above. But logically it is hard to see why this should be so. The likelihood of confusion is to be determined as a matter of fact. Similar marks may more readily be distinguished when one of them is very well-known.[86] **9–071**

(1) The Picasso estate was the proprietor of the trade mark "Picasso" registered in respect of vehicles. The estate opposed an application to register the trade mark "Picarro" for identical goods. Held, there was no likelihood of confusion because, *inter alia*, from a conceptual point of view the word "Picasso" was particularly well-known to the relevant public as the name of the famous painter and not similar to "Picarro" which, if anything, would be understood as a character in Spanish literature.[87] **9–072**

(2) Application to register the mark "Starix" and a red oval in respect of certain types of equipment in Class 9 and for telecommunications in Class 38 was allowed despite the earlier registration of the mark "Asterix" for similar goods and services. Held, there was no likelihood of confusion because, *inter alia*, the average consumer would more readily associate the earlier mark with the character in the widely known cartoon series.[88]

By contrast, when a mark is very well-known the use of the same mark on rather different goods may be likely to cause confusion. **9–073**

In determining the distinctive character of an earlier registered mark the tribunal must make an overall assessment of the greater or lesser capacity of the mark to identify the goods or services for which it has been registered as coming **9–074**

---

[83] *Smith Hayden* ("Ovax") (1946) 63 R.P.C. 97 at 101; *Berlei v Bali* ("Bali") [1969] R.P.C. 472 HL; these tests have been adopted under the 1994 Act as appropriate in these circumstances: *"Balmoral"* [1999] R.P.C. 297; *"Ener-Cap"* [1999] R.P.C. 362; *"React"* [1999] R.P.C. 529 Regy; and [2000] R.P.C. 285 on appeal to the appointed person.

[84] *Premier Brands v Typhoon* [2000] E.T.M.R. 1071; [2000] F.S.R. 767; *Open Country* [2000] R.P.C. 477, CA.

[85] see, *e.g. Smith Hayden* ("Ovax") (1946) 63 R.P.C. 97 at 102; *Ana Laboratories* (1951) 69 R.P.C. 146.

[86] A point noted by Pumfrey J. in *DaimlerChrysler v Javid Alavi* [2001] R.P.C. 42, at para.80; and again in *Reef Trade Mark* [2001] R.P.C. 19 at para.14, where he suggested that the proposition that there is a greater likelihood of confusion with very distinctive marks is a surprising one, and perhaps only a presumption of fact, since it cannot be a legal issue; A.G. Colomer is also of the same mind: *Arsenal Football Club v Reed* [2003] R.P.C. 9. The proposition was also questioned by Jacob L.J. in *Reed Executive plc v Reed Business Information Ltd* [2004] EWCA Civ 159; [2004] R.P.C. 40, at paras 83–86, although he noted that there was also some truth in the opposite proposition that where a mark is largely descriptive small differences may suffice to avoid confusion.

[87] *Claude Ruiz-Picasso v OHIM (Picasso/Picarro)*, Case T–185/02 [2005] E.T.M.R. 22.

[88] *Les éditions Albert René v OHIM (Starix/Asterix)* [2004] E.T.M.R. 62, (CFI)

from a particular undertaking, and thus to distinguish those goods or services from those of other undertakings.[89]

9–075   In making that assessment, account should be taken, in particular, of the inherent characteristics of the mark, including the fact that it does or does not contain an element descriptive of the goods or services for which it has been registered; the market share held by the mark; how intensive, geographically widespread and long standing use of the mark has been; the amount invested by the undertaking in promoting the mark; the proportion of the relevant section of the public which, because of the mark, identifies the goods or services as originating from a particular undertaking; and statements from chambers of commerce and industry or other trade and professional associations.[90]

9–076   Use of a mark does not prove it is distinctive; the use must be in a distinctive sense to have any materiality.[91] Similarly, the question whether licensed use of a mark can be taken into account depends on whether it has amplified the distinctiveness and reputation of the mark.[92]

Distinctive character of the later mark

9–077   If the reputation attaching to the registered trade mark is relevant in determining the likelihood of confusion, in particular as a factor likely to increase the risk of confusion, then it may be anticipated that an applicant for registration will contend that the reputation attaching to his mark is a factor likely to reduce any risk of confusion.[93] Such an approach has been taken by an OHIM Board of Appeal.[94]

Applicant's intention

9–078   If in fact it is known what use an applicant intends to make of his mark, then that use cannot be excluded. Evidence that an intended use is particularly likely to be confusing is helpful to an opponent, to prevent such use being dismissed as unfair or fanciful.[95]

Deceptive resemblance

9–079   The issue of deceptive resemblance, and the factors to be taken into account in assessing it, has received much attention over the years and it is anticipated the approach developed under the old law will be helpful in considering the issue under the 1994 Act. Reference is invited to Ch.17, where the topic is addressed in detail. For many cases it may be enough to follow the guidance given in *Sabel v Puma* that account should be taken of the visual, aural and conceptual similarity of the marks in question,[96] including the overall impression given by the marks, and bearing in mind, in particular, their respective distinctive and dominant

---

[89] *Windsurfing Chiemsee v Huber and Attenberger* [1999] E.C.R. I-2779, para.49; *Lloyd Schuhfabrik Meyer v Klijsen Handel* [1999] E.T.M.R. 690, at para.22.

[90] *Windsurfing Chiemsee v Huber and Attenberger* [1999] E.C.R. I-2779 at para.51; *Lloyd Schuhfabrik Meyer v Klijsen Handel* [1999] E.T.M.R. 690 at para.23.

[91] *10 Berkshire Polo Club Trade Mark* [2001] R.P.C. 32; *Raleigh International Trade Mark* [2001] R.P.C. 11.

[92] *Raleigh International Trade Mark* [2001] R.P.C. 11.

[93] It may be argued such an approach is consistent with the TM Directive, Art.3(3), which makes special provision with regard to the absolute grounds for refusal of Art.3(1)(b),(c) or (d), where the mark has acquired a distinctive character. cf. *Leroy Merlin v K2*, Case R–66/2001-4 [2003] E.T.M.R. CN3; OHIM BoA.

[94] *Porsche v Intertex Hobby, Boxster/Bosker*, Case R–77/2003-2, decision of May 11, 2004. It is understood this is the subject of appeal.

[95] *"Grundig"* [1968] R.P.C. 89; *"Players"* [1965] R.P.C. 363; *"Woodies"* [1965] R.P.C. 366.

[96] It is not necessary that the marks be similar in each of these respects: *Mystery Drinks v OHIM, Karlsberg Brauerei intervening* (MYSTERY) [2004] E.T.M.R. 18, (CFI).

components.[97] It is not appropriate, however, to concentrate on the similarities to the exclusion of the differences between the marks.[98]

It follows that if the respective marks are similar in respects which are distinctive and origin specific then this will tend to increase the likelihood of confusion.[99] Conversely, if the marks are only similar in respects which are descriptive or origin neutral then this will tend to decrease the likelihood of confusion.[1]

9–080

The public will not generally consider a descriptive element forming part of a complex mark as the distinctive and dominant element of the overall impression created by the mark.[2]

9–080A

The factors relevant to the assessment of the likelihood of confusion are, however, interdependent. Accordingly, even in circumstances where the earlier mark is distinctive only to a small degree there may be a likelihood of confusion if the goods or services are identical and there is a high degree of similarity between the conflicting marks.[3]

9–080B

In the global assessment of the likelihood of confusion, the visual, aural or conceptual aspects of the opposing signs do not always have the same weight. It is appropriate to examine the objective conditions under which the goods may be present on the market.[4] So, for example, it is possible that a mere phonetic similarity between trade marks may create a likelihood of confusion.[5] On the other hand, the degree of phonetic similarity will be of less importance if the goods are marketed in such a way that the relevant public will usually see the trade mark;[6] or if one of the marks has a clear conceptual meaning.[7] All will depend upon the global assessment.

9–080C

Use of a family of marks

Use of a family of marks may support the contention that a mark or particular element of a mark is distinctive. But evidence of entries in the register of trade marks will not be of assistance. Such entries do not necessarily reflect the position in the marketplace or affect the way in which marks are perceived and remembered.[8]

9–081

Disclaimer

Where a trade mark is registered subject to a disclaimer of the right to the

9–082

---

[97] See paras 22–24 of the judgment, cited in para.9–033, of the text; applied in *Premier Brands v Typhoon* [2000] E.T.M.R. 1071; [2000] F.S.R. 767. In England under the old law the famous test for word marks was articulated in *Pianotist* (1906) 23 R.P.C. 774 at 777; see also *Smith Hayden* ("Ovax") (1946) 63 R.P.C. 97.

[98] See, *e.g. Croom's Trade Mark Application* [2005] R.P.C. 2.

[99] See paras 9–071 to 9–076, and see, *e.g. Wagamama v City Centre Restaurants* [1995] F.S.R. 713; *Torremar Trade Mark* [2003] R.P.C. 4.

[1] See, *e.g., The European v The Economist Newspaper* [1998] F.S.R. 283; *Torremar Trade Mark* [2003] R.P.C. 4.

[2] *Alejandro v OHIM (BUDMEN)* Case T–/01[2004] E.T.M.R. 15.

[3] *Mystery Drinks v OHIM—Karlsberg Brauerei intervening (MYSTERY)* [2004] E.T.M.R. 18; [2003] E.C.R. II-43; *Interquell v OHIM; Provimi Intervening* [2004] E.T.M.R. 85, (CFI); see also para.9–042.

[4] *New Look v OHIM (NLSPORT)* Cases T–117/03 to T–119/03, [2005] E.T.M.R. 35.

[5] *Lloyd Schuhfabric Meyer*, at para.28; *Mystery Drinks*, at para.4; *Phillips-Van Heusen v OHIM (BASS)* [2004] E.T.M.R. 60.

[6] See, *e.g. Mulhens v OHIM (ZIRH)* [2004] E.T.M.R. 101 (CFI); *Lidl Stiftung v Kingsley Foods (KINGSLEY/KING LI)*, Case R–508/2003-1, [2005] E.T.M.R. 38 (OHIM BoA).

[7] See, *e.g. El Corte Ingles v OHIM (MUNICOR/MUNDICOLOR)* [2004] E.T.M.R. 103 (CFI).

[8] *The Infamous Nut Co Ltd's Trade Marks* [2003] R.P.C. 7; *Torremar Trade Mark* [2003] R.P.C. 4; *Lifesource International Inc's Application* [2001] E.T.M.R. 106. It follows that where an opponent relies on proprietorship of more than one earlier trade mark, the registrability of the applicant's mark must be considered against each of the earlier trade marks separately: *Ener-Cap Trade Mark* [1999] R.P.C. 362.

exclusive use of a specified element of the registered mark, the rights conferred by registration are restricted accordingly. It follows that an objection based upon an earlier registration cannot succeed where the only resemblance between the marks in issue is an element for which protection has been disclaimed.[9]

Same test for all goods and services

9–083   It has been suggested that the likelihood of confusion should be accepted more readily in cases concerning pharmaceuticals in the light of the potentially serious consequences flowing from confusion. But OHIM takes the view that in many cases no special criteria need to be applied because the intervention of qualified professionals will reduce the likelihood of mistakes.[10]

(vii) *The standard to be applied*

9–084   There is little by way of guidance at present as to how the test is to be applied. It has been said that the risk of confusion must be "genuine and properly substantiated".[11] This approach is akin to that under the 1938 Act, where the issue was whether there was no reasonable likelihood of confusion amongst a substantial number of persons, although that was a gloss which had to be properly and sensibly applied.[12]

9–085   It has been emphasised in relation to the equivalent test for infringement that the question is not whether there will be confusion but whether there is a risk that the average consumer will believe that the services (or goods) are those of or associated with the proprietor of the earlier mark.[13]

(viii) *Point of confusion*

9–086   As under the old law, it is likely that confusion which occurs after the point of sale can be taken into account, provided it arises from the use of the offending trade mark.[14] A trade mark continues to identify origin even after sale.[15]

(ix) *Date of assessment*

9–087   The likelihood of confusion must be assessed as at the date of the application for the mark in issue. It is suggested that subsequent experience may nevertheless be relevant as providing an indication of a tendency to confuse.[16] It may also be proper to take into account events which occur between the date of the applica-

---

[9] *Paco Holdings v Paco Rabanne Parfums* [2000] R.P.C. 451; *Torremar Trade Mark* [2003] R.P.C. 4.

[10] *Choay v Boehringer Ingelheim* [2001] E.T.M.R. 69.

[11] See Opinions of A.G. Jacobs in *Sabel v Puma* [1997] E.C.R. I-6191; [1998] R.P.C. 199, at paras 52 and 55, and in *Marca Mode v Adidas* [2000] E.T.M.R. 561 at para.47 In *Marca Mode* the ECJ concluded (at para.42) that it was not enough that the possibility of confusion "cannot be ruled out". See also *10 Berkshire Polo Club Trade Mark* [2001] R.P.C. 32; *Raleigh International Trade Mark* [2001] R.P.C. 11.

[12] *Smith Hayden* ("Ovax") (1946) 63 R.P.C. 97 at 101; *Berlei v Bali* ("Bali") [1969] R.P.C. 472 at 496, HL, *per* Lord Upjohn. Similarly, and by analogy with the position under the 1938 Act, there may be confusion within the meaning of the TM Directive even though the purchaser is not, in the end, confused. Under the 1938 Act it was established that if persons were likely to wonder whether the goods were made or services provided by an opponent, then the mark applied for was one which was likely to cause confusion because people's minds would be put into a state of doubt or uncertainty: *Hack* (1940) 58 R.P.C. 91 at 102–103.

[13] *Thomson Holidays v Norwegian Cruise Lines* [2003] R.P.C. 32,(CA).

[14] A point particularly relevant to infringement; see *Levi Strauss v Kimbyr Investments* [1994] F.S.R. 335 (High Court of New Zealand); *Levi Strauss v Shah* [1985] R.P.C. 371.

[15] *Arsenal v Reed* [2002] E.C.R. I-10273.

[16] *Helena Rubinstein* [1960] R.P.C. 229.

tion and the date of the final decision if it means that the objection falls away; for example, the specification of goods or services of the earlier mark be limited, the earlier mark may be cancelled or it may be assigned to the applicant.[17]

D. SECTION 5(3): WHERE THE USE OF THE MARK WITHOUT DUE CAUSE WOULD TAKE UNFAIR ADVANTAGE OF OR BE DETRIMENTAL TO THE DISTINCTIVE CHARACTER OR REPUTE OF THE EARLIER MARK

General

Section 5(3) of the Trade Marks Act (as amended by the reg.7 of The Trade marks (Proof of Use etc.) Regulations 2004)[18] provides: **9–088**

"A trade mark which:

is identical with or similar to an earlier trade mark,

shall not be registered if, or to the extent that, the earlier trade mark has a reputation in the United Kingdom (or in the case of a Community trade mark in the European Community) and the use of the later mark would, without due cause, take unfair advantage of, or be detrimental to, the distinctive character or repute of the earlier trade mark."

Section 5(3) implements the mandatory provisions of Art.4(3) and the optional   **9–089** provisions of Art.4(4)(a)[19] of the TM Directive. For all practical purposes its wording is identical to that of the infringement provision of s.10(3) of the 1994 Act.[20]

This subsection provides a ground of prohibition in cases where the trade mark   **9–090** sought to be registered is identical to or similar to an earlier trade mark which has a reputation and where the use of the later mark without due cause would take unfair advantage of, or be detrimental to, the distinctive character or repute of the earlier trade mark. Despite the words of the subsection, the prohibition is not limited to cases where the goods or services are dissimilar, a matter discussed further below.[21] It is clear from Recital 9 to the TM Directive that this provision reflects the option of Member States to provide more extensive protection to those trade marks which have a reputation.

It has been considered that because this provision (or at least its infringement   **9–091** counterpart) represents a significant extension to the protection hitherto afforded to proprietors of registered trade marks in this country and because it does not involve such a significant change to the domestic law of at least some of the other Member States of the Community, significant assistance may be available from the jurisprudence developed elsewhere within the European Community.[22] In particular, regard may usefully be had to the law of unfair competition in Germany and the Benelux law of infringement.[23]

There are two fundamental distinctions between this prohibition and that of   **9–092**

---

[17] *Transpay Trade Mark* [2001] R.P.C. 10.

[18] SI 2004/946; the Regulations came into force on May 5, 2004.

[19] Although it appears that the Act goes a little further in that Art.4(4)(a) only refers to earlier trade marks which are registered for goods or services which are not similar to those the subject of the application. The Act, on the other hand, refers to the goods or services for which the earlier trade mark is protected and so includes, presumably, well-known marks under the Paris Convention—such marks falling within the definition of "earlier trade marks" in s.6.

[20] This was also amended by the Trade Marks (Proof of Use, etc.) Regulations 2004; SI 2004/946.

[21] At paras 9–098 to 9–100.

[22] *Premier Brands v Typhoon* [2000] E.T.M.R. 1071; [2000] F.S.R. 767.

[23] In *Premier Brands* the Judge expressly drew assistance from two authorities of the German Federal Supreme Court. As to the case where the use of a sign takes unfair advantage of a mark

s.5(2). First, s.5(3) does not expressly require any confusion, whether as to origin or otherwise. This is a matter discussed further below.[24]

9–093   Secondly, s.5(3) applies whether the goods or services in issue are similar or not. By contrast it seems that in the case of s.5(2) there is a threshold requirement that the respective goods or services are similar.[25] Frequently these objections are pleaded in the alternative, although in a suitable case a mark could give rise to objections under both subsections.

9–094   The relevant date as of which the requirements of the prohibition are to be considered must be the date of application for the mark in issue.[26]

Position under the Community Trade Mark Regulation

9–095   Article 8(5) of the CTM Regulation is in similar terms to s.5(3) of the 1994 Act: But it applies only upon opposition by the proprietor of an earlier trade mark or a licensee authorised by him.[27] Where the earlier trade mark is a Community trade mark it must have a reputation in the Community. Where the earlier trade mark is a national trade mark it must have a reputation in the Member State concerned. In either case the use without due cause of the mark applied for must take advantage of or be detrimental to the distinctive character or repute of the earlier trade mark.

9–096   There is a basis for contending that this provision of the CTM Regulation only applies in the case of earlier registered marks. In contrast to the provisions of Art.8(1) which refer to the goods or services for which the earlier mark is protected, Art.8(5) refers to the goods or services for which the earlier mark is registered.

Similar trade marks

9–097   The mark the subject of the application and the earlier trade mark must be identical or similar. The condition of similarity requires the existence, in particular, of elements of visual, aural or conceptual similarity.[28] This is a subject discussed in relation to the objection under s.5(2) of the 1994 Act and reference is invited to paras 9–069 to 9–083.

---

with an established goodwill he referred to *Dimple* [1985] G.R.U.R. 550, where the German Federal Supreme Court said: "The courts have repeatedly held that it constitutes an act of unfair competition to associate the quality of one's goods or services with that of prestigious competitive products for the purpose of exploiting the good reputation of a competitor's goods or services in order to enhance one's promotional efforts". As to the case where the use of the sign is detrimental to a well established mark he referred to *Quick* [1959] G.R.U.R. 182 where the German Federal Supreme Court said: "[T]he owner of … a distinctive mark has a legitimate interest in continuing to maintain the position of exclusivity he acquired through large expenditures of time and money and that everything which could impair the originality and distinctive character of his distinctive mark, as well as the advertising effectiveness derived from its uniqueness, is to be avoided … Its basic purpose is not to prevent any form of confusion but to protect an acquired asset against impairment". He also considered that "dilution" was a useful concept to have in mind when considering the application of s.10(3) to a particular set of facts, a view fortified by the fact that Art.5(2) is based upon Benelux law; and that this has been said to occur normally in one of two ways, namely by "blurring" or by "tarnishing". Blurring is explained in *Taittinger v Allbev* [1993] F.S.R. 641 at 678, and an important example of tarnishing is that found in *Lucas Bols v Colgate Palmolive* (Claeryn/Klarein) (1976) 7 I.I.C. 420; Jurisprudence of Netherlands Court of Justice 1975, at 472. For further discussion see "Famous and well known Trade Marks" by Mostert, 1997.

[24] At paras 9–107 to 9–110.
[25] See further the discussion in paras 9–047 to 9–058.
[26] And this is the approach taken by the appointed person: see *Corgi* [1999] R.P.C. 549.
[27] CTM Regulation, Art.42(1)(a).
[28] *Adidas-Salomon v Fitnessworld* [2004] E.T.M.R. 10.

All goods and services

In its original form the subsection closely followed the words of Arts 4(3) and **9–098**
4(4)(a) of the TM Directive. These refer to the registration of a mark in respect of
goods and service which are *not* similar to those the subject of an earlier
registration. However, the question arose as to whether they also apply where the
respective goods and services *are* similar or identical. That question has now
been answered by two decisions of the European Court of Justice.

In *Davidoff v Gofkid*[29] the Court concluded that Arts 4(4)(a) and 5(2) of the **9–099**
Directive are to be interpreted as entitling Member States to provide specific
protection for well-known registered trade marks in cases where a later mark or
sign, which is identical with or similar to the registered mark, is intended to be
used or is used for goods or services identical with or similar to those covered by
the registered mark.

In *Adidas-Salomon v Fitnessworld*[30] the Court confirmed that if a Member **9–100**
State exercises the option provided by Article 5(2) of the TM Directive it *must*
grant protection which is at least as extensive for identical or similar goods or
services as for non-similar goods or services.

These decisions are implemented in the amended subsection.

The earlier trade mark must have a reputation

This is a particular requirement of this prohibition, in contrast to the position **9–101**
under s.5(2) of the 1994 Act. There the earlier mark need not have been used at
all.

The reputation must exist in the United Kingdom or, in the case of a Com- **9–102**
munity trade mark, in the European Community. Reputation is a concept well
understood by our courts and may exist independently of goodwill.[31] Accordingly, in the case of earlier national trade marks, it would seem that the prohibition could apply where the earlier trade mark has a reputation but no goodwill
established by actual use in the United Kingdom.

As to the extent of reputation necessary to support the objection, it appears that **9–103**
the degree of knowledge required must be considered to be reached when the
earlier mark is known by a significant part of the public concerned by the products
or goods covered by the trade mark.[32] It should also be noted that the material
requirements of the objection discussed below must also be satisfied and this is
unlikely to be the case unless the reputation of the earlier trade mark is significant.
It also follows that the stronger the distinctive character and reputation of the
earlier mark, the easier it is to establish detriment to it.[33] It is not required that the

---

[29] [2003] E.T.M.R. 42. The Court declined to follow the Opinion of the A.G., reported at [2002]
E.T.M.R. 99. Instead, the Court accepted the argument that Arts 4(4)(a) and 5(2) of the Directive
could not be given an interpretation which would lead to well-known marks having less protection where a sign is used for identical or similar goods or services than where a sign is used for
non-similar goods or services.

[30] [2004] E.T.M.R 10.

[31] See, for a general discussion of these issues, Ch.14.

[32] *General Motors v Yplon* [1999] All E.R. (EC) 865; [1999] E.T.M.R. 950, at para.24, ECJ. This
also seems to be the approach adopted by the Registry: see *Ruefach Marketing* [1999] E.T.M.R.
412. The reputation must be in the mark relied upon: *CDW Graphic Design Ltd's Trade Mark
Application* [2003] R.P.C. 30.

[33] *Premier Brands v Typhoon* [2000] E.T.M.R. 1071; [2000] F.S.R. 767; *General Motors v Yplon*
[1999] All E.R. (EC) 865; [1999] E.T.M.R. 950, at paras 23–27.

reputation extends throughout the United Kingdom, although it must exist in a substantial part of it.[34]

9–104   It is suggested that the relevant date for consideration of this and the other aspects of the objection is the date of the application in issue. The reputation must exist at that date.

Without due cause would take unfair advantage of or be detrimental to the distinctive character or repute of the earlier trade mark.

9–105   These are the most crucial words of the subsection. They contemplate a number of alternatives.It is sufficient if the use of the later mark in relation to any of the goods or services for which it is to be registered would, without due cause:

(1) take unfair advantage of the distinctive character or repute of the earlier trade mark; or

(2) be detrimental to the distinctive character or repute of the earlier trade mark.

9–106   It is to be noted that these requirements mean that the provision and its infringement counterpart do not have the sweeping effect of preventing the registration or use of a sign which is the same as, or similar to, a registered trade mark with a reputation; nor are they intended to enable the proprietor of a well-known registered trade mark to object as a matter of course to the registration or use of a sign which may remind people of his mark.[35] Moreover, the objection must be properly established on the evidence. Detriment to and unfair advantage of distinctive character or repute must be provable by real, as opposed to theoretical, evidence and cannot be merely assumed from the fact that the earlier mark has a substantial reputation.[36]

(a) Is confusion as to origin necessary?

9–107   It has become clear that confusion as to origin is not an essential requirement of the prohibition, despite some early authority in this country to the contrary.[37]

The European Court of Justice explained in *Sabel v Puma*,[38] at paras 20 and 21:

"Furthermore ... Article 4(3) and (4)(a) and Article 5(2) of the Directive ... permit the proprietor of a trade mark which has a reputation to prohibit the use without due cause of signs identical with or similar to his mark and do not require proof of confusion, even where there is no similarity between the goods in question.

In that respect, it is sufficient to note that, unlike Article 4(1)(b), those

---

[34] *General Motors v Yplon* [1999] All E.R. (EC) 865; [1999] E.T.M.R. 950, at paras 28–29. So, *e.g.* a reputation in a substantial part of England would appear sufficient.

[35] *Premier Brands v Typhoon* [2000] E.T.M.R. 1071; [2000] F.S.R. 767; and see the discussion of the requirements of the provision below.

[36] *Mastercard International v Hitachi Credit* [2005] E.T.M.R. 10; *Quorn Hunt's Application* [2005] E.T.M.R. 11, Regy; and see also Ch.14, para.14–089; OHIM adopts the same approach: unfair advantage or detriment are requirements that need to be positively established; see, *e.g. Ferrero v Kindercare Learning (KINDERCARE/kinder et al)*, Case R–1004/2000, [2005] E.T.M.R. 6, OHIM BoA.

[37] See, for example, *Baywatch v Home Video Channel* [1997] F.S.R. 22; *BASF v CEP*, an unreported decision of Knox J. of October 26, 1995. More recently the High Court took the contrary view: *Premier Brands v Typhoon* [2000] E.T.M.R. 1071; [2000] F.S.R. 767; as did the Registry: *Oasis Stores* [1998] R.P.C. 631; *"Audi-Med"* [1998] R.P.C. 863; and the appointed person: *"Corgi"* [1999] R.P.C. 549.

[38] [1997] E.C.R. I-6191; [1998] R.P.C. 199. It is also of note that the A.G. in his Opinion, at para.48, expressly rejected the argument that found favour in *Baywatch v Home Video Channel* and identified the purpose of the provision as being to protect marks with a reputation.

provisions apply exclusively to marks which have a reputation and on condition that use of the third party's mark without due cause takes unfair advantage of, or is detrimental to, the distinctive character or repute of the trade mark."

Similarly, in *Marca Mode v Adidas*,[39] the Court said, at para.36: **9–108**

"The interpretation is not inconsistent with Article 5(2) of the Directive which establishes, for the benefit of well-known trade marks, a form of protection whose implementation does not require the existence of a likelihood of confusion. That provision applies to situations in which the specific condition of the protection consists of the use of the sign in question without due cause which takes unfair advantage of, or is detrimental to, the distinctive character or repute of the trade mark".

The position has now been confirmed by the decision of the Court in *Adidas-* **9–109**
Salomon v Fitnessworld.[40] There must be a degree of similarity between the mark and the sign such that the relevant section of the public makes a connection or establishes a link between them, even though it does not confuse them. As the Court explained, at paras 29–31:

"The infringements referred to in Art.5(2) of the Directive, where they occur, are the consequence of a certain degree of similarity between the mark and the sign, by virtue of which the relevant section of the public makes a connection between the sign and the mark, that is to say, establishes a link between them even though it does not confuse them (see, to that effect Case C–375/97 *General Motors* [1999] E.C.R. I-5421, para.23).

The existence of such a link must, just like a likelihood of confusion in the context of Art.5(1)(b) of the Directive, be appreciated globally, taking into account all factors relevant to the circumstances of the case (see, in respect of the likelihood of confusion Sabel, para.22, and Marca Mode, para.40).

The answer to Question 2(a) must therefore be that the protection conferred by Art.5(2) of the Directive is not conditional on a finding of a degree of similarity between the mark with a reputation and the sign such that there exists a likelihood of confusion between them on the part of the relevant section of the public. It is sufficient for the degree of similarity between the mark with a reputation and the sign to have the effect that the relevant section of the public establishes a link between the sign and the mark."

If the public views the sign purely as an embellishment then it would not es- **9–110**
tablish the necessary link with the registered mark.[41] Similarly, it is not enough that the earlier trade mark is called to mind.[42] It has been held that the link needs to have an effect on the economic behaviour of the consumer.[43]

(b) *Without due cause*

There is no guidance in the TM Directive as to the limitation introduced by these **9–111**

---

[39] [2000] E.C.R. I-4861. See also: paras 33 and 34 of the Opinion of the A.G. in *Arsenal Football Club* [2002] E.C.R. I-10273; para.47 of the Opinion of the A.G. delivered on July 10, 2003 in Case C–408/01 *Adidas v Fitnessworld*.
[40] [2004] E.T.M.R. 10, at p.129.
[41] *Adidas-Salomon* [2004] E.T.M.R. 10 at paras 38–41.
[42] *Premier Brands v Typhoon* [2000] E.T.M.R. 1071; [2000] F.S.R. 767.
[43] *Electrocoin Automatics v Coinworld* [2004] EWHC 1498 (Ch), at para.102, a decision of Mr Hobbs Q.C. sitting as a deputy High Court judge.

words. They have, however, been carefully considered in the *Premier Brands*[44] case. First, it was emphasised that regard must be had to the purpose of the provision, namely to protect the value and goodwill of trade marks, particularly in cases where they are well-known, from being unfairly taken advantage of or unfairly harmed. It is therefore not enough that the later mark has been innocently adopted. Secondly, the words "being without due cause" have to be read as not merely governing the words "the use of the sign", but also as governing the words "takes unfair advantage of, or is detrimental to". Thirdly, this approach is consistent with the view of the Benelux Court in *Lucas Bols*[45] where, when discussing the meaning of "without justifiable reason" which appeared in a similar context in the Uniform Benelux Trade Mark Act as "without due cause" in s.10(3) of the 1994 Act, the Court said:

> "What this rule requires, as a rule, is that the user (of the mark) is under such a compulsion to use this very mark that he cannot honestly be asked to refrain from doing so regardless of the damages the owner of the mark would suffer from such use, or that the user is entitled to the use of the mark in his own right and does not have to yield this right to that of the owner of the mark …".

9–112   In the same case, the Benelux Court suggested that a "justifiable reason" may be "if the user can assert an older right than that of the [registered proprietor]" but went on that whether the alleged infringer could establish a "justifiable reason" must be "resolved by the trial judge according to the particular facts of each case".

(c) *Unfair advantage*

9–113   This specifically contemplates a benefit accruing to the applicant through the use of the mark applied for. In cases where the public are confused into thinking that there is a commercial connection between the suppliers of the goods or services supplied under the earlier trade mark and the mark the subject of the application, then it is to be anticipated that the prohibition will apply. Such confusion as to origin (origin association) is likely to take unfair advantage of and be damaging to the distinctive nature or reputation of the earlier trade mark.

9–114   The more difficult case is where the earlier trade mark is likely to be brought to mind by the use of the mark the subject of the application, but where members of the public are unlikely to believe there is any economic connection between the suppliers (non-origin association). Simply being reminded of a similar trade mark with a reputation for dissimilar goods does not amount to taking unfair advantage of the repute of the mark.[46] So the use of dictionary words which allude to the nature of the goods and cause non-origin association is unlikely to be regarded as sufficient in itself to result in the application of the prohibition.[47] It is suggested that the position would be different if the applicant has adopted a highly distinctive earlier trade mark and the use of the mark will inevitably result in an advantage accruing to the applicant and where there is no justification for that

---

[44] [2000] E.T.M.R. 1071; [2000] F.S.R. 767.
[45] (1976) 7 I.I.C. 420 at 425.
[46] See paras 9–106 and 9–110.
[47] See, *e.g. Oasis Stores* [1998] R.P.C. 631.

use.[48] It will cover cases where there is clear exploitation and free-riding on the coattails of a famous mark or an attempt to trade upon its reputation.[49]

OHIM adopts the following approach. It considers that unfair advantage is taken when another undertaking exploits the distinctive character or repute of the earlier mark to the benefit of its own marketing efforts. In such a case that undertaking effectively uses the renowned mark as a vehicle for generating consumer interest in its own products. The advantage for that undertaking arises in the substantial saving on investment in publicity and promotion for its own goods, since it is able to "free ride" on that already undertaken by the earlier reputed mark. It is unfair since the reward for the costs of promoting, maintaining and enhancing a particular trade mark should belong to the owner of the earlier trade mark in question.[50]

9–114A

The stronger the earlier mark's distinctive reputation and character the easier it will be to accept that unfair advantage has been taken or detriment has been caused.[51] Further, the closer the similarity between the marks the greater is the risk that unfair advantage will be taken. An identity or a very high degree of similarity is a factor of particular importance in establishing that an unfair advantage will be taken.[52] So also, the greater the proximity between the goods and the circumstances in which they are marketed, the greater the risk that the public in question will make a link between the mark and the sign in question.[53]

9–114B

(1) LIPOSTATIN was refused in respect of, *inter alia*, cosmetics and abrasive and scouring preparations in the light of the earlier registration of LIPOSTAT for anti-cholesterol tablets. The OHIM BoA considered that the use of LIPOSTATIN in relation to cosmetic preparations would make the public think that the goods had comparable medicinal qualities to LIPOSTAT and so would take unfair advantage of the earlier mark, and that its use in relation to abrasive and scouring preparations would damage the quality image of the earlier mark.[54]

(2) BIBA was refused in relation to cosmetics, accessories, leather goods and clothing on the basis it would take unfair advantage of the reputation associated with the earlier mark BIBA registered and used in respect of magazines for young women.[55]

(3) In MAGEFESA the earlier mark contained a distinctive word element and a distinctive device. The whole of the mark was copied by the applicant

---

[48] See *Dimple* [1985] G.R.U.R. 550 and the discussion in *Premier Brands v Typhoon* [2000] E.T.M.R. 1071; [2000] F.S.R. 767.

[49] See para.39 of the Opinion of the A.G. in Case C–408/01 *Adidas v Fitnessworld* delivered on July 10, 2003. He suggests, by way of example, that Rolls Royce would be entitled to prevent a manufacturer of whisky from exploiting the reputation of the Rolls Royce mark in order to promote his brand. See also *Inlima's Application* [2000] R.P.C. 661: use of the applicant's mark would be 'parasitic', unjustly drawing upon the recollection of the opponent's trade mark.

[50] *Mango Sport System v Diknah (Mango)*, Case R–308/2003-1, [2005] E.T.M.R. 5, OHIM BoA; *Hachel v Excelsior Publications (Biba)*, Case R–472/2001-1, February 8, 2002, OHIM BoA; *Ferrero v Kindercare Learning (KINDERCARE/kinder et al)*, Case R–1004/2000, [2005] E.T.M.R. 6, OHIM BoA, at para.26; *COSMOPOLITAN COSMETICS/COSMOPOLITAN*, Case R–552/2004-4, July 26, 2001, OHIM BoA.

[51] *General Motors*, at para.30; *Mango Sport System*, at para.20.

[52] *Mango Sport System*, at para.21; *Ferrero*, at para.27.

[53] *Mango Sport System*, at para.22.

[54] *E.R Squibb v Pharmalife Italia (Lipostatin/Lipostat)* Case R–1007/2000-1, decision of November 30, 2001 OHIM BoA.

[55] *Hachel v Excelsior Publications* (Biba) Case R–472/2001-1, decision of February 8, 2002, OHIM BoA.

for a CTM. The OHIM BoA considered that could not have happened by accident and was clearly intended to take advantage of the earlier mark.[56]

(4) MANGO for protective helmets was refused on the basis that it would take unfair advantage of the reputation attaching to the mark MANGO registered and used in relation to clothing and which was aimed at fashion conscious young women.[57]

(d) *Detrimental to the distinctive character or repute of the earlier trade mark*

9–115 These words encompass two alternatives. It is enough if the use of the mark would, without due cause, be detrimental to the distinctive character or repute of the earlier trade mark. Repute is clear enough, it being a requirement that the earlier trade mark has a reputation. What is not so clear is the meaning of distinctiveness in this context. It could be referring to the inherent distinctiveness of the mark or its distinctiveness arising from both its inherent distinctiveness and its distinctiveness in fact. It is suggested that the latter is the preferable interpretation for otherwise there would be no nexus between the requirement that the earlier trade mark has a reputation and the requirement that the use of the later mark would take unfair advantage of, or be detrimental to, the distinctive character of the earlier mark.

9–116 As before, where there is in fact confusion as to origin, it is suggested that the prohibition must apply.[58] But, as discussed in paras 9–107 to 9–110, it is not limited to such cases and the use of a famous mark by a party other than the proprietor may cause damage through erosion of distinctiveness or association, even in cases where there is no likelihood of origin confusion. This was recognised by the European Court of Justice and the Advocate General in *Sabel v Puma*.[59] So also in *British Sugar* Jacob J. said of the corresponding words in s.10(3) of the 1994 Act:[60]

> "I only note it might cater for the case where the goods were vastly different but the marks the same or similar and the proprietor could show that the repute of his mark was likely to be affected. The sort of circumstances of the Dutch *Claeryn/Klarein* case (mark for gin infringed by identical sounding mark for detergent, damage to the gin mark image) may fall within this kind of infringement, even though they do not fall within section 10(2) because there is no likelihood of confusion as to trade origin."

9–117 *Premier Brands*[61] establishes there are at least two ways in which detriment may be caused despite an absence of confusion as to origin. First, the use of the later mark may erode the distinctiveness of the earlier mark. Erosion of

---

[56] *Magefesa v Industrias Domesticas Inoxidables* (Magefesa) Case R–303/200-2, decision of November 8, 2001, OHIM BoA.

[57] *Mango Sport System v Diknah (Mango)*, Case R–308/2003-1, [2005] E.T.M.R. 5, OHIM BoA.

[58] see, *e.g. Sheimer* [2000] R.P.C. 484; [1999] E.T.M.R. 519, use of the mark VISA on condoms bound to have a detrimental effect on the mark VISA used for credit card services. cf. *Oasis Stores* [1998] R.P.C. 631, use of EVEREADY on condoms unlikely to be confused with EVEREADY for batteries; *DaimlerChrysler v Javed Alavi* [2001] R.P.C. 42, public unlikely to make a connection between MERC branded clothing and Mercedes cars.

[59] See para.9–107.

[60] [1996] R.P.C. 281 at 295. The *Claeryn/Klarein* judgment is reported at (1976) 7 I.I.C. 420.

[61] [2000] E.T.M.R. 1071; [2000] F.S.R. 767.

distinctiveness can be damaging, as observed by Sir Thomas Bingham M.R. in *Taittinger v Allbev*:[62]

> "The first plaintiff's reputation and goodwill in the description Champagne derive not only from the quality of their wine and its glamorous associations, but also from the very singularity and exclusiveness of the description, the absence of qualifying epithets and imitative descriptions. Any product which is not Champagne but which is allowed to describe itself as such must inevitably, in my view, erode the singularity and exclusivity of the description Champagne and so cause the first plaintiffs damage of an insidious but serious kind".

This damage has also been described as dilution, the essence of which is the blurring of the distinctiveness of a mark such that it is no longer capable of arousing immediate association with the goods or services for which it is registered and used.[63]   **9–118**

Secondly, there may be tarnishing, as in *Lucas Bols* where the mark Claeryn for gin was held to be infringed by the use of the sign Klarein for detergent and the court explained:[64]   **9–119**

> "It is ... possible ... that the goods to which [the use of] a similar mark relates, appealed to the sensations of the public in such a way that the attraction and the 'capacity of the mark to stimulate the desire to buy' the kind of goods for which it is registered, are impaired."

OHIM adopts the following approach. First, it has noted that a trade mark works not only as an indication of origin, but also serves as a "communication tool" which must be protected as well.[65] It has explained that the message incorporated into the trade mark, whether it is informative or symbolic may refer to the product's qualities, or indeed to intangible values such as lifestyle, exclusivity, adventure and youth. It may result from the qualities of the product or service for which it is used, but also from its proprietor's reputation or other elements based upon the particular presentation of the product or service or on the exclusivity of sales networks.[66]   **9–119A**

Detrimental effect occurs where the later mark is used for goods or services which provoke a reaction of annoyance or displeasure, whether through their intrinsic nature or because of the unpleasant mental association with the goods for which the earlier mark is reputed.[67] It may also occur when the trade mark applied for is used in an unpleasant, obscene or degrading context, or in a context   **9–119B**

---

[62] [1993] F.S.R. 641 at 678, cited in *Premier Brands*. See also *Parfums Givenchy v Designer Alternatives* [1994] R.P.C. 243, CA; cf. *Harrods v Harrodian School* [1996] R.P.C. 697, CA, where some criticism was made of this approach, but in the context of a claim for passing off which requires damage resulting from a misrepresentation.

[63] See para.37 of the Opinion of the A.G. in Case C–408/01 *Adidas v Fitnessworld*. He explains the concept was first articulated by Schechter 'The rational basis of trade mark protection', Harvard Law Review 1927, p.813 and, by way of example: "if you allow Rolls Royce restaurants and Rolls Royce cafeterias, and Rolls Royce pants, and Rolls Royce candy, in 10 years you will not have the Rolls Royce mark any more".

[64] (1976) 7 I.I.C. 420, and cited in Premier Brands. The court in Premier Brands also referred to *Sheimer* [2000] R.P.C. 484; [1999] E.T.M.R. 519; *American Express v Libra Approved Laboratories*, 10 US PQ 2d 2006, a decision of the New York District Court, and *Mars* (1995) 26 I.I.C. 282, a decision of the German Federal Supreme Court. See also para.38 of the Opinion of the A.G. in Case C–408/01 *Adidas v Fitnessworld*.

[65] *Elleni Holding v Sigla (VIPS)*, Case R–1127/2000-3, [2005] E.T.M.R. 51, BoA, para.40.

[66] *Elleni Holding*, para.41.

[67] *Ferrero v Kindercare Learning (KINDERCARE/kinder et al)*, Case R–1004/2000, [2005] E.T.M.R. 6, OHIM BoA, para.30.

which is not inherently unpleasant but which proves to be incompatible with the earlier trade mark's image.[68] These cases give rise to the phenomenon of "tarnishment" whereby the reputed mark ceases to convey desirable messages to the public: hence the detriment to its distinctive character.

9–119C   It has been emphasised that detrimental effect or unfair advantage are requirements that need to be positively established.[69] The evidence of detriment may be argumentative and based upon the rule of probability. However the opponent must demonstrate why and how damage could be caused to the trade mark image in question, or undue advantage taken from that image.[70]

9–120   (1) An application for HOLLYWOOD for tobacco and smoking articles was successfully opposed in the light of the earlier registration of the same mark for chewing gum. The proprietor of the earlier mark established that in France its mark enjoyed a healthy, dynamic and youth oriented image which would be tarnished by the use of the same mark on tobacco products.[71]

(2) Opposition to registration of 'Duplo' for various goods in Classes 2,7,9 and 16 on the basis of the earlier trade mark 'duplo' for chocolate goods failed because the earlier mark was inherently weak and the distance between the goods rendered association improbable.[72]

(3) Application to register INTEL-PLAY in respect of "interlocking blocks being constructional toy puzzles" refused on the basis of the established reputation of the mark INTEL for computers and computer linked products. Use of the mark INTEL-PLAY on such unsophisticated goods would dilute the strength of the INTEL mark and reduce its distinctive character, which was founded on high-quality, technologically-based products with an international reputation.[73]

(4) Application to register the mark KINDER CARE in respect of educational services, nurseries and childminding was allowed despite the earlier registration and use of the mark KINDER in respect of sweets, snacks and pastry. None of the goods or services applied for generated any feeling of annoyance or disgust and it was not enough that consumers would think that KINDER CARE was an additional member of the KINDER family of marks.[74]

(5) Application to register the mark FLORIS in respect of a variety of household goods made of textiles was refused in the light of the earlier registration and use of the mark FLORIS in respect of, *inter alia*, luxury perfumes and toiletries. The use of the mark by the applicant would be likely to dilute the value and reputation of the earlier mark.[75]

9–121   Before the Registrar the following matters are considered relevant in considering whether the requirements of the prohibition are satisfied:[76]

(1) the inherent distinctiveness of the earlier trade mark;

---

[68] *Elleni Holding*, para.43.
[69] *Ferrero*, para.23.
[70] *Elleni Holding*, paras 45 and 46; see also *Spa Monopole v Spa-Finders Travel Arrangements (Spa Finders)*, Case R–131/2003-1, [2005] E.T.M.R. 9.
[71] *Hollywood v Souza Cruz* [2002] E.T.M.R. 64 (p.705) OHIM BoA.
[72] *Ferrero v Duplo*, Case R–802/1999-1, decision of June 5, 2000, OHIM BoA.
[73] *Intel Corp v Sihra* [2003] EWHC 17 (Ch); [2004] E.T.M.R. 44.
[74] *Ferrero v Kindercare Learning (KINDERCARE/kinder et al)*, Case R–1004/2000, [2005] E.T.M.R. 6, OHIM BoA
[75] *Floris v Istrad (FLORIS)*, Case R–470/2001-2, [2005] E.T.M.R. 8, OHIM BoA.
[76] See *Oasis Stores* [1998] R.P.C. 631; *"Audi-Med"* [1998] R.P.C. 863. OHIM takes a similar line: see, *e.g. Campomar's Application* [2000] E.T.M.R. 50.

(2) the extent of the reputation that the earlier mark enjoys;

(3) the range of goods or services for which the earlier trade mark enjoys a reputation;

(4) the uniqueness or otherwise of the mark in the market place;

(5) whether the respective goods/services, although dissimilar, are in some way related or likely to be sold through the same outlets;

(6) whether the earlier trade mark will be any less distinctive for the goods/services for which it has a reputation than it was before;

(7) whether the reputation of the earlier trade mark is likely to be damaged or tarnished in some significant or material way.

E. MEANING OF AN EARLIER TRADE MARK

All of the prohibitions of s.5(1), (2) and (3) of the 1994 Act are concerned with earlier trade marks. **9–122**

Section 6(1) of the Act identifies the various types of earlier trade mark in relation to which a conflict may arise. In summary they are earlier United Kingdom national registrations, registrations entitled to protection in the United Kingdom under the Madrid Protocol, Community trade marks and marks entitled to protection in the United Kingdom under the Paris Convention or the WTO Agreement (TRIPS)[77] as well-known trade marks. As will be seen, account is to be taken of appropriate priorities and specific provision is made in respect of applications and trade marks which have recently expired. **9–123**

Registered trade marks, the Madrid Protocol and Community trade marks

In the case of national registered trade marks, international registrations designating the United Kingdom and Community trade marks, earlier trade marks are those with a date of application for registration earlier than that of the trade mark in question, taking account (where appropriate) of any priority claimed.[78] **9–124**

In the case of all these types of trade marks, priority may be claimed under the Paris Convention for a period of six months from the date of filing of the first application for that trade mark in a Convention country.[79] So also priority may be claimed from a first filing in one of the countries with whom the United Kingdom has an agreement for the reciprocal protection of trade marks.[80] It is to be noted that the priority period runs from the first application. It is not possible to prolong the period by making applications in different countries and claiming priority from the later one. Priority rights are assignable.[81] **9–125**

The Registrar must therefore consider the mark the subject of the application, taking into account its priority claim and, in the light of that, whether there is an earlier relevant trade mark, taking into account its priority claim. It must also be borne in mind that it is possible for an application in respect of different goods or services to have different priority dates or for some of the goods or services to have a priority date earlier than the date of filing and for others to have the priority date of the date of filing. **9–126**

---

[77] The Patents and Trade Marks (World Trade Organisation) Regulations 1999, SI 1999/1899.

[78] 1994 Act, s.6(1)(a). And an International trade mark (UK) and Community trade mark may be converted into a national application, without loss of priority.

[79] See 1994 Act, ss.35 and 55, in the case of national registrations; Trade Marks (International Registration) Order 1996, Art.8, in the case of international registrations designating the UK; Community Trade Mark Regulation, Art.29, in the case of Community trade marks.

[80] Under the 1994 Act, s.36.

[81] s.35(6).

9–127   Where two applications are filed on the same day or claim the same priority date and are otherwise each acceptable, then the Registrar will allow both marks to proceed to registration.

9–128   A claim to priority will be accepted or rejected without considering whether the certified application is liable to succeed or fail in the convention country in which it is shown by the relevant certificate to have been accorded a filing date. The requirement is satisfied by evidence of a procedurally regular filing in the relevant convention country.[82]

9–129   In the case of Community trade marks, two other matters are notable. First, a Community trade mark application is, in Member States, to be treated as equivalent to a national filing under Article 32 of the CTM Regulation. Secondly, under the Community trade mark regime the proprietor of an earlier trade mark registered in the United Kingdom who applies for, or has secured registration of, an equivalent Community trade mark may surrender the later trade mark or allow it to lapse but retain seniority, that is to say he is deemed to continue to have the same rights as he would have had if the earlier trade mark had continued to be registered. The position of such a proprietor is preserved under the 1994 Act.[83] The seniority of a Community trade mark is to be considered.

Applications for registration

9–130   Earlier trade marks include applications for registration under the domestic regime, the Madrid Protocol and the Community trade mark system, which when registered would be "earlier trade marks".[84] The provision only operates subject to such an earlier application being registered. So the Registrar may suspend an application pending the resolution of any issues concerning the registrability of an earlier application.

Account to be taken of marks for a period of one year after expiry

9–131   The 1994 Act provides that a registration which has expired shall nevertheless continue to be taken into account in determining the registrability of a later mark for a period of one year after the expiry unless the Registrar is satisfied that there was no *bona fide* use of the mark during the two years immediately preceding the expiry.[85] The use of the term "expiry" suggests that it does not apply to marks which have been revoked or declared invalid, but is rather concerned with marks which have not been renewed by the due date. Where such a mark is cited then it may be possible to overcome the objection by suspending the application until the year has elapsed or seeking the consent of the original proprietor.

Marks entitled to protection as well-known marks

9–132   Earlier trade marks include marks which have not been registered or even used in this country where they are entitled to protection as well-known marks under the Paris Convention or the WTO Agreement (TRIPS).[86] The scope of protection afforded to such marks must also be considered and, in particular, the "protected" goods or services identified. This is discussed in paras 9–023 to 9–025.

---

[82] *FSS Trade Mark* [2001] R.P.C. 40.
[83] s.6(1)(b).
[84] s.6(2).
[85] s.6(3).
[86] s.56, as amended by SI 1999/1899 defines, for the purposes of the Act, trade marks which are

Position under the Community Trade Mark Regulation

Under the CTM system earlier trade marks comprise:[87]   **9–133**

(1) Community trade marks, national trade marks registered in any Member State, or, in the case of Belgium, the Netherlands or Luxembourg, at the Benelux Trade Mark Office and any trade marks registered under international arrangements which have effect in a Member State or in the Community[88] (*i.e.* under the Madrid system);

(2) applications for any such trade marks, subject to their registration;

(3) and any trade marks which, on the date of application for the Community trade mark, or on the date of priority where appropriate, are well-known in a Member State, in the sense in which the words "well known" are used in Article 6*bis* of the Paris Convention.

As under the TM Directive, account is to be taken, where appropriate, of claimed priorities.

F. ACTS OF AGENTS OR REPRESENTATIVES

The Act provides special protection against the unauthorised acts of agents or   **9–134**
representatives in seeking to register marks. If an application for registration of a trade mark is made by a person who is an agent or representative of a person who is the proprietor of the mark in a Paris Convention country then, if the proprietor opposes the application, registration shall be refused unless the agent or representative justifies his action.[89]

The Community trade mark system offers similar protection.[90]

3. Conflict with earlier rights

GENERAL

Section 5 of the 1994 Act also prohibits registration where or to the extent that   **9–135**
the use of the mark in the United Kingdom is liable to be prevented by what the Act describes as "earlier rights". These are defined by reference to two categories, namely, where the use of the trade mark is liable to be prevented:

(1) by virtue of any rule of law (in particular, the law of passing off) protecting an unregistered trade mark or other sign used in the course of trade; or

(2) by virtue of an earlier right other than those referred to in s.5(1)–(3) (earlier trade marks) or para.(a) above, in particular by virtue of the law of copyright, design right or registered designs.[91]

This provision implements the optional provisions of Article 4(4) of the TM   **9–136**
Directive. Depending upon the circumstances it may apply in respect of all or

---

entitled to protection under the Paris Convention or the WTO Agreement. For a discussion of the requirements for qualification, see Ch.14, paras 14–213 to 14–220.

[87] CTM Regulation, Art.8(2).

[88] Added by Council Regulation (EC) No. 992/2003. This amendment came into force on the date on which the Madrid Protocol entered into force with respect to the European Community, namely October 1, 2004.

[89] 1994 Act, s.60(1),(2) and (5), implementing Art.6 *septies* of the Paris Convention. s.60(4) also provides that the proprietor may apply for an injunction to restrain the use of the trade mark in the UK.

[90] CTM Regulation, Art.8(3). And see also Art.11 for a right equivalent to that provided by the 1994 Act, s.60(4).

[91] s.5(4).

only some of the goods or services the subject of the application.[92] Although not in terms so limited, for practical purposes the objections likely to be considered are those based upon the identified rights in passing off, copyright, design rights and registered designs.

9–137   The 1994 Act further specifies that the proprietor of the earlier right is the person so entitled to prevent the use of the trade mark, although it is to be noted that the Act does not require that the objection be taken by the proprietor of the earlier right. Nevertheless, identification of the proprietor may be important in two respects. First, if the objection is to be overcome by obtaining a consent under s.5(5), then the consent must be given by the proprietor of the earlier right. Secondly, if honest concurrent use is properly relied upon then the Registrar shall not refuse the application by reason of the earlier right unless objection on that ground is raised by the proprietor of the earlier right in opposition proceedings.[93]

THE PROTECTION OF AN UNREGISTERED TRADE MARK—PASSING OFF AND RELATED RIGHTS

9–138   This limb of the prohibition protects a goodwill established in a business conducted under an unregistered mark and imports into the relative grounds of objection a consideration of the requirements of the cause of action in passing off.[94] These are considered in detail in Ch.15.[95] The Registry accordingly looks for evidence of use sufficient to attract a relevant goodwill.[96]

9–139   The particular formulation of the provision suggests that the correct approach is to consider a normal and fair use of the mark the subject of the application in respect of the goods or services the subject of the application and whether or not this would result in passing off.[97] In this sense the test is different from that involved in a claim in passing off which would normally require a consideration of all of the circumstances of the defendant's trade.

9–140   It is suggested that the issue must be determined as at the date of the application for the mark in issue. The question is whether or not use of the mark applied for is liable to be prevented as at that date. If, however, the mark the subject of the application is already in use, then this may require consideration of the position at an earlier time too. The relevant date for proving reputation and goodwill

---

[92] So implementing the TM Directive, Art.13.

[93] 1994 Act, s.7(2).

[94] The prohibition has similarities to that provided by the 1938 Act, s.11, but important differences too. First, under the old law it was not necessary for the opponent to establish a reputation or goodwill. The question was determined having regard to the "user" of the earlier trade mark: *Berlei v Bali* ("Bali") [1969] R.P.C. 472. Secondly, it was not necessary to show deception in the sense required by passing off. It was enough if peoples' minds were put into a state of doubt or uncertainty: *Hack* (1940) 58 R.P.C. 91. Finally, it was not necessary to establish a likelihood of damage, let alone damage caused by the deception, which is a requirement of the cause of action in passing off.

[95] The basic principles were again explained by the House of Lords in terms of the "classical trinity" in *Reckitt v Coleman v Borden* ("Jif") [1990] R.P.C. 341. See, particularly, Lord Oliver at 406 and Lord Jauncey at 416. See also the Court of Appeal in *Consorzio del Prosciutto di Parma v Marks & Spencer* ("Parma Ham") [1991] R.P.C. 351 at 368, CA.

[96] *"Wackers"* [1999] R.P.C. 453.

[97] As under the 1938 Act: *Smith Hayden* ("Ovax") (1946) 63 R.P.C. 97 at 101; *Berlei v Bali* ("Bali") [1969] R.P.C. 472. This appears to be the approach adopted under the 1994 Act by the appointed person and the Registry: *"Wild Child"* [1998] R.P.C. 455; *"Corgi"* [1999] R.P.C. 549, both decisions of the appointed person; *Oasis Stores* [1998] R.P.C. 631, Regy.

in a claim for passing off is the date of commencement of the activities complained of.[98] If the applicant is the senior user then he should prevail.[99]

There are other relevant rules of law of a like nature. In particular under s.56 of the 1994 Act a proprietor of a trade mark which is entitled to protection under the Paris Convention or the WTO Agreement (TRIPS) as a well-known trade mark is entitled to restrain by injunction the use of that mark in the United Kingdom. Similarly, under s.60 of the Act the proprietor of a trade mark in a Paris Convention country may apply for an injunction to restrain the unauthorised use of that mark by an agent or representative. **9–141**

COPYRIGHT, DESIGN RIGHT AND REGISTERED DESIGNS

This limb of the prohibition deals with any mark, the use of which would result in the infringement of any other earlier right, in particular any copyright, design right or registered design.[1] This range of objections reflects the wide range of marks which may be registered under Act, including sounds, designs and the shapes of goods and their packaging:[2] but it had a parallel under the 1938 Act in the words of s.11.[3] **9–142**

POSITION UNDER THE COMMUNITY TRADE MARK REGULATION

Although there is a similar prohibition under the CTM system, it is cast in rather different terms. Article 8(4) of the CTM Directive provides: **9–143**

"Upon opposition by the proprietor of a non-registered trade mark or of another sign used in the course of trade of more than mere local significance, the trade mark applied for shall not be registered where and to the extent that, pursuant to the Community legislation[4] or the law of the Member State governing that sign,

(a) rights to that sign were acquired prior to the date of application for registration of the Community trade mark, or the date of the priority claimed for the application for registration of the Community trade mark;

(b) that sign confers on its proprietor the right to prohibit the use of a subsequent trade mark."

As in the case of the other relative objections, this ground may only be raised on opposition. The objection may be taken by the proprietor of the relevant earlier mark or sign or by any person authorised under national law to exercise those rights.[5] **9–144**

The rights generally contemplated are those based upon the use in the course of trade of non-registered trade marks and other signs (business and trade related **9–145**

---

[98] *"Pub Squash"* [1981] R.P.C. 429 at 494, (PC, NSW).

[99] *Croom's Trade Mark Application* [2005] R.P.C. 2.

[1] A consideration of the requirements of a cause of action to protect each of these rights is beyond the scope of this work and the reader is referred to a specialist text, such as *The Modern Law of Copyright* (3rd ed., Butterworths, London, 2000), *Copinger and Skone James on Copyright* (15th ed., Sweet & Maxwell, London, 2005), *Russell-Clarke and Howe* (7th ed., Sweet & Maxwell, London, 2005).

[2] See, *e.g. Team Lotus Ventures* [1999] E.T.M.R. 669.

[3] "It shall not be lawful to register as a trade mark or part of a trade mark any matter the use of which would ... be disentitled to protection in a court of justice, or would be contrary to law ..."; and see also: *"Karo Step"* [1977] R.P.C. 255; *"Oscar"* [1979] R.P.C. 173.

[4] The reference to Community legislation was added by Council Regulation (EC) No.422/2004. It appears to be concerned with certain indications of geographical orgin; see para.9–146.

[5] CTM Regulation, Art.43(1)(c).

identifiers[6]). National law will apply to determine the nature of the particular right invoked and the conditions which must be satisfied for its existence.[7]

9–146   There appears to be no objection based upon such rights outside those generated by use. So, for example, no mention is made of copyright or industrial property rights.[8] OHIM also applies Art.8(4) to designations of origin and geographical indications registered under Reg.2081/92 or the Lisbon Agreement.[9]

More than mere local significance

9–147   There is also an important requirement that the mark or sign is of more than mere local significance.

Quite what is meant by more than mere local significance is not explained but it appears to be a deliberate inclusion which is designed to cut out of consideration marks which have a reputation of only limited geographical and economic extent within any particular country.[10] This seems the correct interpretation of the provision as a whole which is concerned with the protection of unregistered marks *within* a Member State but which are not of *mere* local significance. It also appears to be the approach taken by OHIM.[11]

9–148   In accordance with this approach, OHIM considers an individual assessment must be made taking into account geographical criteria, the volume of sales, intensity of marketing and the population concerned. The fact that national law gives the holder of the sign a nation-wide right to prohibit the use of a subsequent trade mark does not ensure qualification, but may be a relevant consideration.[12]

9–149   In the UK, however, the provision has been given a very different interpretation.[13] It has been held that a mark should be considered as having mere local significance if its geographical spread is limited to substantially less than the whole of the European Union and that, from the perspective of the Community market in the goods or services in question, the mark is of little significance. If, however, the mark covers the whole or substantially the whole of the Community market or is significant there, then its Community impact will be too large to ignore and it will invalidate a subsequent application.[14]

---

[6] *EinStein Stadtcafe's Application* [2000] E.T.M.R. 952.

[7] The OHIM Opposition Guidelines, March 2004, Part 4, contain a table of national rights which constitute "earlier rights" in the sense of Art.8(4). For the UK, see the discussion in paras 9–135 to 9–142, of s.5(4) of the TM Act.

[8] Contrast the TM Directive, Art.4(4)(b). Instead the Regulation provides in Art.52(2) that these matters may be raised in proceedings for a declaration of invalidity or on the basis of a counterclaim in infringement proceedings.

[9] Some Member States are party to the Lisbon Agreement for the protection of Appellations of Origin and their International Registration (1958), as revised in Stockholm 1967, and amended on September 28, 1979.

[10] There is, however, a measure of protection for owners of such geographically limited rights in the CTM Regulation, Art.107. This provides that the proprietor of such a right may oppose the use of the Community trade mark in the territory where his right is protected in so far as the law of the Member State so permits, subject to acquiescence over a period of five years. So under the law of England a person with a goodwill of limited geographical extent could prevent the use of a Community trade mark in so far as it would result in passing off. It also provides that the proprietor of the Community trade mark cannot oppose the use of the earlier right, even if that right may no longer be invoked against the Community trade mark.

[11] *McCann-Erickson's Application* [2001] E.T.M.R. 52 (p.540); see also the OHIM Opposition Guidelines, March 2004, Part 4, para.5.3.

[12] *McCann-Erickson's Application* [2001] E.T.M.R. 52.

[13] *Compass Publishing v Compass Logistics* [2004] EWHC 520; [2004] R.P.C. 41. It is not apparent whether the Court was referred to *McCann- Erickson's Application* or the OHIM guidelines.

[14] As the Judge explained, any mark which is used in part of the Community but not all of it may be

4. Honest concurrent use

Section 7 of the 1994 Act preserves the notion of honest concurrent use in limited circumstances. It has no basis in the TM Directive. The section did not appear in the original Bill but in Committee an amendment was moved which would have had the effect that a mark was not to be refused registration where honest concurrent use had been made of it, notwithstanding that it conflicted with an earlier trade mark. It was considered that this amendment would have had the effect of preserving the effect of s.12(2) of the 1938 Act. The amendment was resisted by the Government on the basis that it was doubtful that it could be reconciled with the mandatory provisions of Article 4 of the Directive. This would seem to be correct. Articles 4(1) and (2) do not permit such an exception.[15] The current section was a compromise moved on the third reading of the Bill.[16]

9–150

There is no equivalent under the Community trade mark system.

Section 7 of the 1994 Act provides:

9–151

> (1) This section applies where on an application for the registration of a trade mark it appears to the registrar—
>> (a) that there is an earlier trade mark in relation to which the conditions set out in s.5(1), (2) or (3) obtain, or
>> (b) that there is an earlier right in relation to which the condition set out in s.5(4) is satisfied,
>
> but the applicant shows to the satisfaction of the registrar that there has been honest concurrent use of the trade mark for which registration is sought.
>
> (2) In that case the registrar shall not refuse the application by reason of the earlier trade mark or other earlier right unless objection on that ground is raised in opposition proceedings by the proprietor of that earlier trade mark or earlier right.

The Act therefore permits an applicant to rely upon honest concurrent use during the course of examination to defeat an objection raised on the basis of an earlier trade mark or earlier right. If the Registrar is satisfied that there has been honest concurrent use, as to which see below, then he must allow the application to proceed to advertisement and, if there is no opposition, to registration. If the proprietor of the earlier trade mark or earlier right opposes the application and the Registrar concludes that the opposition is properly founded and the ground of objection is a valid one, then he must refuse the application. He cannot at that stage rely upon honest concurrent use to dismiss the opposition.[17] Nevertheless it may be appropriate in evaluating the opposition to take into account any period of side by side use.[18]

9–152

Curiously s.7(2) refers only to an opposition by the proprietor of the earlier trade mark or other earlier right. On the words of the section it appears that if an opposition is entered by a party other than the proprietor of the earlier trade mark

9–153

---

called local. So, for example, a mark which is used in France, Spain, Germany Austria and Italy could be regarded as local.
[15] cf. Art.4(5) and (6).
[16] Hansard, H.L. Vol.553, col.71.
[17] *Road Tech Computer Systems v Unison Software* [1996] F.S.R. 805.
[18] As in *Codas Trade Mark* [2001] R.P.C. 14 (p.240).

or other earlier right and such a party relies upon that earlier trade mark or other earlier right, as he is entitled to, then the Registrar must take into account honest concurrent use and, in an appropriate case, allow the mark to proceed to registration. That party would then have to bring an application for a declaration under s.47 following registration. It is hard to reconcile this with the mandatory words of Article 4 of the TM Directive.

GENERAL PRINCIPLES

9–154   The 1994 Act defines honest concurrent use for the purposes of the section as such use in the United Kingdom, by the applicant or with his consent, as would formerly have amounted to honest concurrent use for the purposes of s.12(2) of the Trade Marks Act 1938. The effect of this section is therefore to introduce the old law of honest concurrent use into the new Act.

9–155   This is not a very satisfactory formula. Whilst it may be workable in the case of objections raised under s.5(1) or (2) of the 1994 Act it is hard to see how it can be applied in the case of an objection under s.5(3) which deals with the case of the use of the same or similar marks on goods or services which are not similar and where the objection does not call for a likelihood of confusion. There was no equivalent objection under the 1938 Act and circumstances which would have amounted to honest concurrent use for the purposes of s.12(2) are in large part concerned with the likelihood of confusion.[19] Much the same difficulties arise in the case of an application objectionable under s.5(4) of the 1994 Act.

MAIN MATTERS TO BE CONSIDERED

9–156   The main matters which the tribunal should take into account were laid down by Lord Tomlin in *Pirie*.[20] Briefly these matters are:

(1) The extent of use in time and quantity and the area of the trade;
(2) the degree of confusion likely to ensue from the resemblance of the marks which is to a large extent indicative of the measure of public inconvenience;
(3) the honesty of the concurrent use;
(4) whether any instances of confusion have in fact been proved; and
(5) the relative inconvenience which would be caused if the mark were registered.

The discretion of the tribunal is unfettered and concurrent registration may be allowed even where the possibility of confusion is considerable. Each case has to be determined on its own merits.[21]

HONESTY OF CONCURRENT USE

9–157   The concurrent use must be "honest".

"Knowledge of the registration of the opponent's mark may be an important

---

[19] See para.9–156.
[20] (1933) 50 R.P.C. 147 at 159, HL. Applied in *Electrix* [1954] R.P.C. 369 at 379. On appeal the questions which arose under the 1938 Act, s.12(2) had no application. See also *Fitton* (1949) 66 R.P.C. 110 at 112; *Peddie* (1944) 61 R.P.C. 31; *Spillers* (1952) 69 R.P.C. 327 at 330. For more recent illustrations see *"Star"* [1990] R.P.C. 522, Regy and *"Budweiser"* [1998] R.P.C. 669; [2000] R.P.C. 906, CA.
[21] A passage cited with approval by the CA in *"Budweiser"*, February 7, 2000 which emphasised that there are dangers in seeking to apply the five reasons found determinative in *Pirie* in every case.

factor where the honesty of the user of the mark sought to be registered is impugned, but where once that honesty of the user has been established, the fact of knowledge loses much of its significance, though it may be a matter not to be wholly overlooked in balancing the considerations for and against registration."[22]

Use in the genuine belief that the mark is not such as to cause confusion is "honest" use.[23] **9–158**

PUBLIC INTEREST

The tribunal should always consider the public interest. This has long been a matter taken into account in determining whether there is honest concurrent use.[24] Accordingly the Registrar should always consider whether the public are adequately protected. The tribunal will consider whether it is just to register, even if there is some confusion.[25] **9–159**

PERIOD OF USE

No fixed rule can be laid down as to the minimum period of honest concurrent use necessary to lead to registration. The Registrar looks for a reasonable period of use, usually about five years prior to the application date: but this is only a guideline. In *Peddie*,[26] the Registrar stated that he knew of "no reported case in which a period of concurrent use so short as two and a quarter years has been treated as sufficient to bring an application within the advantages of s.12(2) or the previous corresponding s.21 of the repealed Trade Marks Acts 1905 to 1919. But the circumstances here are exceptional" and registration was allowed. **9–160**

OR OTHER SPECIAL CIRCUMSTANCES

The 1994 Act does not permit other special circumstances to be taken into account.[27] **9–161**

5. General matters

WHEN THE OBJECTION MAY BE TAKEN

Any of the relative grounds of objection may be taken by the Registrar upon examination of the application under s.37 of the 1994 Act or by a third party upon an opposition under s.38(1) of the 1994 Act. Moreover, they may be the subject of third-party observations in writing to the Registrar under s.38(2). Following registration these grounds may be raised upon an application for a declaration of invalidity under s.47. **9–162**

---

[22] *per* Lord Tomlin in *Pirie* at 159, quoted in *Peddie* (1944) 61 R.P.C. 31 at 36, Regy.

[23] *"Bali" (No.2)* [1978] F.S.R. 193 at 220–221, but the applicant's knowledge of the opponent's mark was relevant on the question of discretion—no longer a material matter under the 1994 Act—and registration was refused.

[24] See *Ehrman* [1897] 2 Ch. 495; 14 R.P.C. 665; *Rosedale* [1968] F.S.R. 93.

[25] *"Buler"* [1975] R.P.C. 275; *"Star"* [1990] R.P.C. 522; *"Budweiser"* [2000] R.P.C. 906.

[26] (1944) 61 R.P.C. 31 at 36. See also *Smith Hayden* (1946) 33 R.P.C. 97 at 98 ("Ovax"), nine months not a long enough period; three and a half years use, on a larger scale than opponent, registration allowed, *"Buler"* [1975] R.P.C. 275; two years and 10 months use on a very large scale, registration allowed, *"Granada"* [1979] R.P.C. 303; four years use, starting small, not long and extensive enough to show likelihood of confusion, registration refused, *"Margaret Rose"* [1978] R.P.C. 55.

[27] In contrast to the position under the 1938 Act: see, *e.g. Peddie* (1944) 61 R.P.C. 31; *"Bud"* [1988] R.P.C. 535; *"Budweiser"* [2000] R.P.C. 906.

POSITION UNDER THE COMMUNITY TRADE MARK REGULATION

9–163   The position under the Community trade mark system is different. The relative grounds of objection may only be raised on opposition[28] or under Art.52.[29]

ONUS OF PROOF

9–164   There is no overall onus on the applicant either before the Registrar or in opposition proceedings. And so when an opponent raises objections under s.5 of the 1994 Act he must make them out.[30]

OVERCOMING THE OBJECTION-CONSENT OF THE PROPRIETOR OF THE EARLIER TRADE MARK OR RIGHT

9–165   No objection can be taken under s.5 of the 1994 Act where the proprietor of the earlier trade mark or other earlier right consents to the registration.[31] The Registrar has no discretion to refuse registration in a case where consent has been given but where he considers that confusion may result. The matter is left to the commercial judgment of the proprietor.

9–166   Other ways to overcome an objection include filing evidence of use, restricting the goods or services the subject of the application, offering a disclaimer or limitation and removal or limitation of the earlier trade mark and division of the application. These are discussed in Ch.5.

---

[28] See paras 9–022, 9–030, 9–095 and 9–144.
[29] Declaration of invalidity on application to OHIM or on the basis of a counterclaim in infringement proceedings.
[30] *"Audi-Med"* [1998] R.P.C. 859; *Oasis Stores* [1998] R.P.C. 631.
[31] s.5(5).

CHAPTER 10

VALIDITY AND REMOVAL OF TRADE MARKS FROM THE REGISTER

1. Preliminary matters

This chapter is concerned with certain aspects of the status of registered trade marks: principally with the ways in which a trade mark may be removed from the register but also the circumstances in which a registered trade mark loses some or all of its effect, through failure to meet the use conditions, as an obstacle to other marks or applications.

10–001

A mark may cease to be a registered trade mark in one of four ways. These are logically considered in the following order:

10–002

(1) Invalidity: a declaration of invalidity is made by the court or Registrar, upon application under s.47 of the Trade Marks Act 1994. The declaration may concern the whole or part of the registration.

(2) Revocation: the registration is revoked by the court or Registrar, upon application under s.46. Again, revocation may concern the whole or part of the registration.

(3) Surrender: the registration may be surrendered by the proprietor, pursuant to s.45. Again, the whole or part of the registration may be surrendered;

(4) Expiry: the registration is removed because it has expired and has not been renewed.

Invalidity and revocation are different. The essence of an invalidity attack is that the mark should never have been registered hence the cross-reference in s.47 to the absolute and relative grounds for refusal contained in ss.3 and 5. It is however possible to defeat an attack based on s.3(1)(b) to (d) grounds by showing that, since registration, the mark has in fact acquired distinctive character. By contrast, revocation is effectively dealing with the consequences of events over the period since registration: since registration, there has been a lack of genuine use in a five-year period, or the mark has become generic or misleading.

10–003

Each of the four ways outlined above produces a different temporal effect:

10–004

(a) A declaration of invalidity is the most serious. The consequence of such a declaration is that the registration is deemed never to have been made.[1]

(b) An order for revocation has effect from the date of the application for revocation, unless the court or Registrar decides that the grounds for revocation existed at some earlier date.

(c) A surrender would appear to take effect from the date when the Registrar publishes the amended entry in the Register, *i.e.* after the Registrar has approved the application to surrender.

(d) If a registration expires it enters a state of limbo for six months before the registration is removed from the Register. If, within that six-month period, an application to renew is filed with the appropriate fees, then the registration is renewed. Even after a registration has been removed, it may

---

[1] 1994 Act, s.47(6), subject to the proviso that "this shall not affect transactions past and closed". See para.10–034.

be restored upon application made within six months of removal, provided it is just to do so.

LOSS OF EFFECT AND THE "USE CONDITIONS"

10–005   Those familiar with CTM oppositions will know that it has always been a feature of the CTM system that if an earlier CTM[2] or national registration[3] is relied upon in an opposition, the applicant can request the proprietor to prove that the mark in question has been put to genuine use (or that there are proper reasons for non-use) in the five-year period preceding the date of publication of the CTM application. The requirement to prove use (in the preceding five years) also applies in applications for invalidity of a CTM registration[4] and also in counterclaims for invalidity in actions for infringement before a CTM Court.[5]

10–006   In so far as genuine use is proved (or proper reasons), the earlier registration can be relied upon but not otherwise. Logic would dictate that similar consequences would apply in proceedings for infringement: *i.e.* in so far as a CTM has not been put to genuine use in the preceding five years, there should be no infringement. However, no such provision appears to have been included in the CTM Regulation.

10–007   The TM Directive contained optional provisions covering all three situations: proceedings for invalidity, oppositions and infringement proceedings.[6] The first two have now been implemented in the UK through the insertion into the Act of subs.47(2A) and s.6A.[7] These provisions impose the "use conditions" which are effectively the same as the revocation provisions concerned with lack of genuine use. These "use conditions" apply to all applications published and any application for invalidity commenced after May 5, 2004.

STRUCTURE OF THIS CHAPTER

10–008   The structure of this chapter is as follows. In the remainder of this first section, we consider three preliminary topics: (1) the status of a registered trade mark and the onus of proof when an invalidity or revocation attack is made; (2) the important issue of estoppel/abuse of process and (3) we mention briefly the issue whether ss.46 and 47 contain a residual discretion (in the word "may") not to revoke or invalidate a registration, despite the fact that one or more grounds for revocation or invalidity, as the case may be, have been proved. The subsequent sections are:

2. Invalidity
3. Lack of Genuine Use
4. Common name in the trade
5. Marks which have become misleading
6. Procedure
7. Surrender
8. Expiry, renewal, removal and restoration

---

[2] Art.43(2) of the CTM Regulation.

[3] Art.43(3).

[4] Art.56(2) of the CTM Regulation. Note the phrase "provided the earlier Community trade mark has at that date been registered for non-use" appears to have been included in error.

[5] Art.96(5) of the CTM Regulation, as amended by Council Regulation (EC) No.422/2004.

[6] Arts 11(1) (re invalidity), (2) (opposition) and (3) (infringement).

[7] The Trade Marks (Proof of Use etc.) Regulations 2004 SI 2004/ 946.

STATUS OF A REGISTERED TRADE MARK AND ITS REGISTERED PROPRIETOR

Section 2(1) of the 1994 Act provides: **10–009**

"A registered trade mark is a property right obtained by the registration of the trade mark under this Act and the proprietor of a registered trade mark has the rights and remedies provided by this Act."

Section 72 provides: **10–010**

"In all legal proceedings relating to a registered trade mark (including proceedings for rectification of the register) the registration of a person as proprietor of a trade mark shall be prima facie evidence of the validity of the original registration and of any subsequent assignment or other transmission of it."

Section 72 is a slightly curious provision, but adopts the time-honoured word- **10–011** ing which can be traced back to the 1905 Act. It provides that the registration of a person now as the proprietor of a trade mark is *prima facie* validity of the registration when originally made. The effect of ss.72 and 2(1) appears to mean that as long as a trade mark remains registered it can be enforced, giving the rights and remedies provided by the Act which are now subject to the requirement of meeting the use conditions.[8] The fact of registration is *prima facie* evidence of the validity of the registration. Therefore, in the absence of any attack on a registered trade mark, it is assumed to be valid. Equally, unless attacked, any assignment or transmission of the mark (which has been entered on the Register) which has occurred since the mark was originally registered is assumed to be valid.

ONUS OF PROOF

With one notable exception, if an application is made for a declaration of invalid- **10–012** ity or for revocation, the onus lies on the person making the attack to prove the grounds of invalidity and/or revocation relied upon to the normal civil standard of the balance of probabilities. If one or more grounds are proved, this will automatically overcome the *prima facie* position provided for by s.72 of the 1994 Act. The rights and remedies, if any, which are then available in respect of the registered mark are subject to the temporal effects of the grounds relied upon.

The exception concerns applications to revoke for non-use. If any question **10–013** arises as to the use to which a registered trade mark has been put, it is for the proprietor to show what use has been made of the mark.[9] Therefore, an application to revoke for non-use places the onus of proof on the proprietor to prove the use which has been made of the mark. Equally, if the proprietor is not able to show genuine use, the onus rests on him to show that there were proper reasons for the non-use.

In addition, if an application for invalidity is based on any one of s.3(1)(b)–(d), **10–014** the onus of proving the ground relied upon rests on the applicant for invalidity. If the proprietor then wishes to overcome the ground for invalidity by proving that since registration the mark has acquired a distinctive character, then the onus of proving that obviously lies on the proprietor.

EVIDENTIAL BURDEN OF PROOF

The onus of proof, as explained above, does not change as proceedings progress. **10–015**

---

[8] See under "Loss of effect—the use conditions", above.
[9] 1994 Act, s.100.

By contrast, the evidential burden of proof may well move back and forth as the parties move through the stages of the proceedings. Section 72 of the 1994 Act indicates where the evidential burden lies at the outset of any legal proceedings. At that point, the registration itself is *prima facie* evidence of its validity and of the registration of the proprietor as proprietor. Any person wishing to attack the registration or the status of the proprietor must first present grounds which overcome the *prima facie* evidence of the registration. If such grounds are supported by evidence,[10] then the evidential burden shifts to the proprietor to produce evidence to the contrary. Ultimately, the validity of the registration is determined according to the normal civil standard of proof.

Estoppel and Abuse of Process

10–016   In *SPAMBUSTER*[11], Richard Arnold Q.C. (as a deputy Judge) considered the effects of cause of action estoppel and abuse of process in circumstances where successive attacks on a registered trade mark had been made. The owner of the trade mark SPAM had previously brought proceedings for invalidity of the mark SPAMBUSTER in the TM Registry under s.5(3) of the Act, relying on SPAM as a well-known mark. These proceedings failed and were not appealed. Subsequently, the same party brought High Court proceedings seeking (a) a declaration of invalidity under s.47(1) based on ss.3(1)(b), (c) & (d) & 3(6) (the allegation of bad faith was dropped in the course of the trial) and (b) revocation under s.46(1)(c). The deputy Judge held that (a) the remaining claims for a declaration of invalidity were barred by cause of action estoppel, notwithstanding that different grounds were relied upon and (b) all the remaining claims (for both invalidity and revocation) were an abuse of process on *Henderson v Henderson*[12] grounds.

10–017   The limits of the effects of cause of action estoppel and *Henderson v Henderson* abuse of process may require further consideration, for reasons explained below, but it is important to note what was not under consideration in SPAMBUSTER:

(1) As the deputy Judge made clear, he was not considering the position where a person who has unsuccessfully opposed an application then applies for a declaration of invalidity;[13]

(2) The reasoning does not automatically apply to successive applications for revocation. If different applications require consideration of the position at different dates or different periods of alleged lack of genuine use, no cause of action estoppel will arise and, generally, the later application will not constitute an abuse of process unless the position is more or less identical.

10–018   Even in the confines of the case, this was a strong decision. There are essentially two reasons why the position may require further consideration:

(1) first, the status of Registry proceedings and its role as a low-cost forum. It was accepted by the applicant that a decision of the Registrar was capable

---

[10] Again, allegations of non-use are the exception. In the normal way, an application for revocation for non-use must have some substance to it, otherwise it would be frivolous, vexatious and/or an abuse. Penalties are likely to be visited on frivolous applications or applications based on allegations which are untrue. Of course, the way in which the proprietor shows that an application is frivolous is by putting in evidence of (1) his use and (2) that the applicant knew of his use.

[11] *Hormel Foods Corporation v Antilles Landscape Investments N.V.* [2005] EWHC 13 (Ch), January 24, 2005.

[12] (1843) 3 Hare 100. See also *Johnson v Gore Wood & Co (No.1)* [2002] 2 A.C. 1, HL.

[13] See para.95.

of founding a plea of *res judicata* since such a decision is of a court of competent jurisdiction. Having analysed the law as it had developed in patent and registered design cases, the deputy Judge was of the view that there was no reason why the same should apply to trade marks. Despite the fact that Registry proceedings are more formal than they were, the Registry still constitutes a tribunal where costs recovery is usually limited and issues are dealt with in a more cost-effective manner than they would be in High Court proceedings, often markedly so. When considering abuse of process, the deputy Judge expressly recognised that the Registry is a low-cost and low-cost recovery forum. On cause of action estoppel, he seems to have treated the Registry as a forum equivalent to the High Court. However, it would be a pity if cause of action and abuse of process considerations caused the complexity of Registry proceedings to be increased to the level normally experienced in High Court proceedings.

(2) second, there are the competing public interests, which the deputy Judge naturally took into account. On the one hand, underlying both cause of action estoppel and abuse of process is the public interest in the finality of litigation. On the other hand, there are clear public interests underlying the removal of marks which are either invalidly registered or liable to be revoked. It is likely that the public interest is stronger when absolute grounds are invoked, in comparison to relative grounds. The issue is whether the right balance of public interests was achieved. In the absence of the findings on estoppel and abuse of process, the deputy Judge would have found the SPAMBUSTER registration invalid under ss.3(1)(c) and (b), he found the mark had not acquired distinctive character since registration and was also liable to revocation under s.46(1)(c) as of the date of application for revocation. The claimant was not able to benefit from these findings, although any other applicant would do so.

Whilst any tribunal must retain power to deal appropriately with vexatious **10–019** repetition of proceedings, and, in that regard, the tribunals of all Member States will be given a considerable margin of appreciation, the stringent application of these doctrines of English law is capable of having the effect that the conditions for obtaining and continuing to hold a registered trade mark may not, in general, be identical in all Member States.[14] The ECJ or the English Court of Appeal might take a different view.

A SUBSEQUENT APPLICATION FOR INVALIDITY AFTER AN UNSUCCESSFUL OPPOSITION

Notwithstanding the caveats mentioned above, it is unsafe to assume that an **10–020** unsuccessful opposition can be followed by a subsequent application for invalidity. If the grounds are more or less identical, the subsequent proceedings might well constitute an abuse of process, even if, as is usually the case, the evidence is improved second time around. In cases of commercial significance, it may be necessary to consider whether to withdraw an opposition which is based on less than the best evidence, retaining the opportunity to bring invalidity proceedings

DISCRETION?

Both subss.(1) and (2) of s.47 of the 1994 Act provide that: "The registration of a **10–021**

---

[14] cf. Recital 7 to the TM Directive.

trade mark may be declared invalid…". Equally, s.46(1) provides "The registration of a trade mark may be revoked on any of the following grounds…". Prior to the last edition, the use of the word "may" in s.46(1) gave rise to debate over whether that word provided a residual discretion not to revoke even though one of the grounds of invalidity or revocation has been made out. The debate arose particularly in cases of non-use, probably because the equivalent non-use provisions in the 1938 Act did contain a residual discretion.

10–022   There is no residual discretion in proceedings for invalidity or revocation.[15] With the benefit of hindsight, it is perhaps surprising that this was considered a serious issue. The fact that it was demonstrates how difficult it can be to break free of years of conditioning of the old law.

2. Invalidity

10–023   Section 47 of the 1994 Act sets out the grounds for invalidity of a registration. Subject to one exception, if the trade mark is found to have been registered in breach of any of the absolute or relative grounds for refusal contained in ss.3 and 5, then the registration is declared invalid. Attention is therefore directed primarily at the position at the date of application for the mark.

ABSOLUTE GROUNDS FOR INVALIDITY

10–024   If a trade mark was registered in breach of s.3 of the 1994 Act or any of the provisions referred to in that section,[16] it shall be declared invalid, subject only to one exception. The Act uses the expression "may be declared invalid", but the Directive says "shall be liable to be declared invalid". It is clear that "may" must be construed as "must" or "shall". There is no room nor any purpose for a residual discretion not to declare the mark invalid.[17]

10–025   The one exception is provided in s.47(1). If the ground for invalidity is one or more of subss.(1)(b), (c) or (d) of s.3 (no distinctive character, descriptive or generic), then the mark shall not be declared invalid if, in consequence of the use made of it, it has after registration acquired a distinctive character in relation to the goods or services for which it is registered. The wording is the same as that used in the proviso to s.3(1). Whereas the proviso operates to overcome these grounds if the mark has acquired a distinctive character before the date of application, this part of s.47(1) operates in the same way provided the mark has acquired a distinctive character "after registration". The wording appears to permit use prior to application and use prior to the date when the mark was actually put on the Register to contribute to the necessary distinctive character, which reflects reality in any case.

Section 47(1) raises the same issues as are raised under s.3(1). Reference is invited to the relevant part of Ch.8.

RELATIVE GROUNDS FOR INVALIDITY

10–026   Section 47(2) of the 1994 Act applies, by way of cross-reference, the relative

---

[15] For those who are interested in following the issue, reference is invited to the 13th Edition of this work, paras 9–12 to 9–16.

[16] This form of wording is appropriate since s.3 incorporates the provisions in s.4 which in turn incorporates parts of ss.57 and 58.

[17] See the discussion in para.10–021.

grounds contained in subss.(1), (2) and (3) of s.5 (conflict with earlier trade marks) and s.5(4) (conflict with earlier rights, including passing off). These grounds for invalidity are not available if the proprietor of the earlier trade mark or other earlier right has consented to the registration. This reflects the fact that these grounds may be raised by any person, whether they are entitled to an earlier trade mark or earlier right or not.

Section 47(2) raises the same issues as are raised under s.5. Reference is invited to the relevant parts of Ch.9.

WHEN MAY AN APPLICATION FOR INVALIDITY BE MADE

Generally, an application for a declaration of invalidity of a registered trade mark may be made at any time after the mark has been registered. The general position is subject to two areas of qualification. First, the transitional provisions of the 1994 Act and secondly, the effects of acquiescence under s.48(1). These are dealt with in turn. **10–027**

TRANSITIONAL PROVISIONS

The 1994 Act defined a trade mark registered under the 1938 Act as an "existing registered mark". At any time after the 1994 Act came into force, an application could be made to invalidate an existing registered mark under s.47. The transitional provisions provide that for the purposes of such an application, the provisions of the 1994 Act, with one exception, are deemed to have been in force at all material times. The exception is s.5(3) (identical or similar mark, goods or services not similar). In other words, the rules concerning distinctiveness and public policy contained in s.3 and the rules governing conflicts between registered marks and other rights in s.5, all of which had a rough equivalent in one form or another in the old Act are deemed to have applied at all times. Section 5(3) is excluded because there was nothing equivalent in the old Act. **10–028**

The effect of the transitional provisions creates the potential for a mark, whenever it was put on the United Kingdom Register, to face a challenge against the provisions of s.3. The potential for such a challenge under ss.5(1),(2) or (4) is much less significant, due to the acquiescence restriction contained in s.48(1)(a), to which we now turn. **10–029**

ACQUIESCENCE

For a person who is entitled to an earlier trade mark or earlier right, there is a restriction on his ability to raise grounds for invalidity based on his earlier trade mark or earlier right but not, it seems, any other grounds for invalidity. If such a person has acquiesced in the use of a registered trade mark in the United Kingdom for a continuous period of five years, during which time he was aware of such use, then he ceases to be entitled to apply for a declaration of invalidity of the registered mark based on any earlier trade mark or earlier right to which he is entitled.[18] It is suggested that this acquiescence restriction should apply even where there has been an assignment of the earlier trade mark or earlier right, provided that throughout the requisite five-year period both assignor and assignee were aware of and acquiesced in the use of the relevant registered trade mark. Thus, it certainly should not be possible to extend the period of acquiescence **10–030**

---

[18] 1994 Act, s.48(1)(a).

required by means of a sham assignment. Equally, any assignee of an earlier trade mark or earlier right must take the assignment subject to any accrued acquiescence right already established prior to the assignment.

PARTIAL INVALIDITY

10–031   If the grounds of invalidity exist in respect of only some of the goods or services for which the trade mark is registered, the trade mark is declared invalid as regards those goods or services only.[19] The remainder of the registration remains valid and enforceable. It is possible that issues might arise as to how the specification of goods or services should be divided in the event of partial invalidity. This type of issue is much more likely to arise in the case of partial revocation, and is discussed in detail below.

10–032   Neither the TM Directive nor the 1994 Act appear to contemplate partial geographical validity. This could arise in the following circumstances. The applicant for invalidity had and has a goodwill and reputation in a limited geographical area of the United Kingdom. Use of the registered mark in that limited area, but not outside it, would give rise to passing off and would have done so at the date of application for the mark. Although neither Art.13 nor s.47 contemplate this situation, it is suggested it should create no difficulty. In so far as the mark is invalid as covering the geographical area in question, it is declared invalid. Otherwise the validity of the registration is maintained, with a suitable geographical limitation being entered on the Register.

WHO MAY APPLY

10–033   Section 47(3) of the 1994 Act provides that any person can apply for a declaration of invalidity. This represents a change over the old law, where the applicant had to be a "person aggrieved". In practice this old requirement precluded intermeddlers but did little else except give rise to pointless argument over whether an applicant had *locus standi*. All that has been swept away.

EFFECT OF A DECLARATION OF INVALIDITY

10–034   If or to the extent that a trade mark is declared invalid, the registration is deemed never to have been made. The principal consequence of this provision is likely to be that potential liability for infringement disappears with the invalid registration. This deeming provision does not affect transactions past and closed. Thus a past assignment of the registration would not be affected, unless made on the strength of a representation that the mark was valid, which would give rise to a claim for damages/rescission. Equally, an agreement settling a claim for infringement could not be undone and would continue to be enforceable, unless the continued enforcement of an obligation depended upon the mark remaining on the Register. Any injunction previously granted to prevent further infringement of the registration in question would fall away as lacking foundation. If, however, the injunction was in absolute form, preventing any use of the mark XXXX, then the position is less clear. If there were dual claims for infringement of the registered trade mark and for passing off, then the injunction might continue to be supported by the claim for passing off and the continuing threat of damage to goodwill. If not, the injunction might be unenforceable as being in unreasonable restraint of trade.

---

[19] s.47(5).

In cases where the point mattered, it would be possible to apply to the court to determine whether the injunction should be varied or discharged.

INFLUENCE OF THE TM DIRECTIVE

Section 47 of the 1994 Act is the second part of the implementation of Arts 3 and 4 of the TM Directive and cross-refers back to ss.3 and 5, which constitute the first part. A question remains whether these two parts amount to full implementation of the Directive. The Directive uses the words "The following shall not be registered or if registered shall be liable to be declared invalid:" before setting out the absolute and relative grounds for both refusal and invalidity. That form of words suggests that if any of the grounds exist as at the date of application, then the application must be refused and that (subject to the acquiescence provisions) if any of the grounds exists at any later date, then the registration must be declared invalid. The United Kingdom has implemented the former but not the latter, since s.47 directs attention back to the date of application. It can be argued that the Directive should not be interpreted in this way since Art.12 (grounds for revocation) deals with the consequences of events which have occurred since the mark was put on the Register. There is some overlap between the grounds for revocation and the absolute grounds—(the mark has become the common name for the product or service—compare Art.12.2(a) and s.46(1)(c) with Art.3(1)(d) and s.3(1)(c), and the mark is liable to mislead the public—compare Art.12.2.(b) and s.46(1)(d) with Art.3.1(g) and s.3(3)(b))—which may indicate that it is not necessary to apply the absolute or relative grounds at any date other than the original date of application. However, there are other notable areas of overlap in the Directive which means that the existence of overlap in these provisions is not a reliable aid to construction, one way or the other. **10–035**

Section 47 also implements provisions of the Directive which support Arts 3 and 4, notably Art.13—if the grounds exist in respect of only some of the goods or services for which the mark is registered, then the invalidity extends only to those goods or services. **10–036**

THE APPROACH AT OHIM

We comment elsewhere on the respects in which the approach at OHIM differs on the application of the absolute and relative grounds for refusal.[20] Here there is one point to mention, largely of historical interest now, about how the OHIM Cancellation Divisions started to approach an invalidity attack, particularly when based on absolute grounds. Instead of deciding an invalidity attack on its merits and on the basis of the evidence put before it, the Cancellation Division initially[21] indicated that it treated the original decision of the Examination Division as involving an exercise of discretion which the Cancellation Division could not upset unless the Examination Division overlooked "substantial criteria" or was made on an insufficient basis. We pointed out in the previous edition that this approach was deeply flawed. It appears that the Cancellation Division now accept that they have to examine the grounds raised in the proceedings before them and make their own decision on them. **10–037**

---

[20] See generally, Chs 8 and 9.
[21] *Mortar & Pestle CTM* 172734, OHIM First Cancellation Division, January 31, 2000.

3. Revocation for lack of genuine use

10–038   The 1994 Act contains four grounds upon which the registration of a trade mark may be revoked. The first two concern lack of genuine use which, in brief outline, are:

(1) the mark has not been put into genuine use within five years of the date when the mark was put on the Register, and there are no proper reasons for the lack of use;

(2) there has been an uninterrupted period of five years in which no genuine use of the mark has occurred, and there are no proper reasons for the lack of use.

It has been customary to use the expression "non-use" when summarising the effect of these provisions, but perhaps it is better to say "lack of genuine use" to reflect more accurately the requirement of these provisions. The effect of revocation is that the life of the registration comes to an end. Unlike the effect of a declaration of invalidity under s.47, the registration continues to have effect whilst it was still "alive", *i.e.* prior to the date of revocation.

10–039   Clearly the two grounds raise a number of common issues. In fact the only difference between the two grounds is in how the requisite five-year period is fixed. In this section, we deal with the following issues: first, we outline the case law of the ECJ on "genuine use" and then deal with some subsidiary issues, followed by issues on timing; use of variants of the mark; proper reasons for non-use; and finally, partial revocation/partial enforcement.

GENUINE USE

10–040   One might have thought that the interpretation of "genuine use" had been authoritatively dealt with by the ECJ in *Ansul*. Certainly the ECJ thought so. When the later reference from the UK in *La Mer* came to be considered, the ECJ disposed of the reference using its abbreviated procedure[22], suitable for cases where the answers to the questions referred can be clearly deduced from existing case law or where the answer to the question admits of no reasonable doubt. Notwithstanding the ECJ's confidence, at the time of writing, there remains a degree of uncertainty in the UK at least about the true interpretation of "genuine use".

ANSUL[23]

10–041   The facts in *Ansul* were slightly unusual. Prior to the five-year period in issue, the owner of the mark MINIMAX in the Benelux had ceased to sell fire extinguishers under the mark, but had continued, in the five-year period, to maintain, check and repair equipment bearing the mark and to support the maintenance of previous installed MINIMAX extinguishers. These activities involved use of the mark in relation to the sale of component parts and extinguishing substances, on invoices for services and on strips and stickers sold to be put on extinguishers to show they had been serviced. The owner of the MINIMAX mark in Germany applied to revoke the Benelux registration for lack of genuine [in the Dutch language version: normaal] use.

---

[22] Notwithstanding resistance to that course from the referring Court: see [2003] EWHC 1382 (Ch).
[23] Case C–40/01 *Ansul BV v Ajax Brandbeveiliging BV* [2003] R.P.C. 40, p.717, E.C.J. March 11, 2003.

Notwithstanding the facts, the ECJ understood that it was being asked for an **10–042** interpretation of general application of the concept of "genuine use" in Art.12(1) of the TM Directive. As a preliminary matter, the Court considered whether the concept had to mean the same thing throughout the Community. Not surprisingly, the Court concluded it was necessary to provide a uniform interpretation of the concept and it did so in the following paragraphs:

35. "... the eighth recital in the preamble to the Directive states that trade marks 'must actually be used or, if not used, be subject to revocation'. 'Genuine use' therefore means actual use of the mark. That approach is confirmed, *inter alia*, by the Dutch version of the Directive, which uses in the eighth recital the words 'werkelijk wordt gebruikt', and by other language versions such as the Spanish ('uso efectivo'), Italian ('uso effettivo') and English ('genuine use').

36. 'Genuine use' must therefore be understood to denote use that is not merely token, serving solely to preserve the rights conferred by the mark. Such use must be consistent with the essential function of a trade mark, which is to guarantee the identity of the origin of goods or services to the consumer or end user by enabling him, without any possibility of confusion, to distinguish the product or service from others which have another origin.

37. It follows that 'genuine use' of the mark entails use of the mark on the market for the goods or services protected by that mark and not just internal use by the undertaking concerned. The protection the mark confers and the consequences of registering it in terms of enforceability vis-á-vis third parties cannot continue to operate if the mark loses its commercial *raison d'être*, which is to create or preserve an outlet for the goods or services that bear the sign of which it is composed, as distinct from the goods or services of other undertakings. Use of the mark must therefore relate to goods or services already marketed or about to be marketed and for which preparations by the undertaking to secure customers are under way, particularly in the form of advertising campaigns. Such use may be either by the trade mark proprietor or, as envisaged in Article 10(3) of the Directive, by a third party with authority to use the mark.

38. Finally, when assessing whether there has been genuine use of the trade mark, regard must be had to all the facts and circumstances relevant to establishing whether the commercial exploitation of the mark is real, in particular whether such use is viewed as warranted in the economic sector concerned to maintain or create a share in the market for the goods or services protected by the mark.

39. Assessing the circumstances of the case may thus include giving consideration, inter alia, to the nature of the goods or service at issue, the characteristics of the market concerned and the scale and frequency of use of the mark. Use of the mark need not, therefore, always be quantitatively significant for it to be deemed genuine, as that depends on the characteristics of the goods or service concerned on the corresponding market."

Later, the ECJ referred to "actual use of the mark under the conditions **10–043** described in paragraphs [35] to [39] of this judgment." The Court also declined to answer the second question referred, which invited the Court's view on the facts. It is for the national court to apply the interpretation of the Court to the resolution of the dispute before it.

LA MER

10–044   Under *Ansul*, the scale and frequency of use are to be taken into account, but the significance depends upon the market for the goods or services concerned. In *La Mer*, the scale of use over the five-year period was admitted to be minimal. The goods in question were "cosmetics containing marine products". The extent of the use shown was the importation into the UK of about £800 of such goods in five shipments over six months, the vast majority in one shipment. The items were in small containers bearing the mark, with recommended retail prices of between £5 and £30. The mark did not appear on any invoices or delivery notes. The goods were delivered to a company in Scotland. There was no evidence as to what happened to the goods thereafter, and no inference was (or could be) drawn about any other use (*e.g.* whether any of the goods were exposed for sale or sold to members of the public). About £600 of other goods bearing the mark were imported over the same period, and total sales to the company amounted to about £6,000. Before the end of the five-year period, the company in question was struck off. After the end of the five-year period, the proprietor of the mark appointed another distributor, but not for the goods in question.

10–045   The issue was whether the use proved constituted "genuine use". On appeal from the TM Registry, Jacob J. (as he then was) considered that the case raised the issue of whether "*de minimis*" use constituted "genuine use" and referred a series of questions to the ECJ on that issue. Jacob J. also ventured his own view on the issue, which was that provided the use was not token, there was no lower limit.[24] Following the judgment in *Ansul*, one question was withdrawn. The seventh question was concerned with whether it was legitimate to take into account events which occur after the five-year period in question.

10–046   In its reasoned Order, the ECJ recited paras 35–39 of its judgment in *Ansul* (set out above), and continued:

> "20. It follows from those considerations that the preservation by a trade mark proprietor of his rights is predicated on the mark being put to genuine use in the course of trade, on the market for the goods or services for which it was registered in the Member State concerned.
>
> 21. Moreover, it is clear from paragraph 39 of *Ansul* that use of the mark may in some cases be sufficient to establish genuine use within the meaning of the Directive, even if that use is not quantitatively significant. Even minimal use can therefore be sufficient to qualify as genuine, on condition that it is deemed to be justified, in the economic sector concerned, for the purpose of preserving or creating market share for the goods or services protected by the mark.
>
> 22. The question whether use is sufficient to preserve or create market share for those products or services depends on several factors and on a case-by-case assessment which is for the national court to carry out. The characteristics of those products and services, the frequency or regularity of the use of the mark, whether the mark is used for the purpose of marketing all the identical products or services of the proprietor or merely some of them, or evidence which the proprietor is able to provide, are among the factors which may be taken into account.

---

[24] *Laboratoire de la Mer Trade Mark* [2002] F.S.R. 51, p.790.

23. Similarly, as emerges from paragraphs 35 to 39 of *Ansul* set out above, the characteristics of the market concerned, which directly affect the marketing strategy of the proprietor of the mark, may also be taken into account in assessing genuine use of the mark.

24. In addition, use of the mark by a single client which imports the products for which the mark is registered can be sufficient to demonstrate that such use is genuine, if it appears that the import operation has a genuine commercial justification for the proprietor of the mark.

25. In those circumstances, it is not possible to determine a priori, and in the abstract, what quantitative threshold should be chosen in order to determine whether use is genuine or not. A de minimis rule, which would not allow the national court to appraise all the circumstances of the dispute before it, cannot therefore be laid down.

26. Finally, it can clearly be inferred from paragraph 36 of *Ansul* that, where use of the mark does not have as its essential aim the preservation or creation of market share for the goods or services which it protects, such use must be considered in fact to be intended to defeat any request for revocation. Such use cannot be characterised as genuine within the meaning of the Directive."

Evidently, the ECJ thought it was being asked to set a quantitative threshold **10–047** for "*de minimis*" use, and not surprisingly it declined to set any such rule. However, it is reasonably clear that the ECJ in *Ansul* did lay down a qualitative threshold, and confirmed this in *La Mer*. We suggest that is clear from the important reference to the "commercial *raison d'etre*" of a mark "which is to create or preserve an outlet for the goods …". This forms a particular part of the assessment whether there has been genuine use: "regard must be had to all the facts and circumstances relevant to establishing whether the commercial exploitation of the mark is real, in particular whether such use is viewed as warranted in the economic sector concerned to maintain or create a share in the market for the goods or services protected by the mark."

THE POSITION IN THE UK

The parties in *La Mer* put forward radically different interpretations of *Ansul* and **10–048** *La Mer*, which may be summarised as follows:

(1) the trade mark proprietor continued to argue that a dichotomy applied: provided use is shown which is not token and not merely internal, it must necessarily be external and for the purpose of preserving or creating a market share for the goods;

(2) the applicant for revocation argued that, leaving aside merely token use and internal use, genuine use requires use of the mark on the market, *i.e.* it must be directed to and come to the attention of the consumer or end user. Only in this way could the use be viewed as warranted in the economic sector concerned to maintain or create a share in the market for the goods.

Blackburne J. substantially agreed with the latter interpretation,[25] which we suggest accords with the tenor of the judgments of the ECJ. The proprietor's argument rests, essentially, on the use of the words "for the purpose of preserving or creating market share" in para.21 of *La Mer*. On the basis of those four words,

---

[25] *La Mer Technology Inc v Laboratoires Goemar SA* [2004] EWHC 2960 (Ch). See paras 28–34.

any use which is for the stated purpose would establish genuine use: *i.e.* any use which is not (a) token or (b) internal. As Blackburne J. noted, if the ECJ had intended this, it "could have easily said so and done so very shortly, on the reference to it by Jacob J., but did not." In fact, we suggest *Ansul* and the remainder of *La Mer* are inconsistent with the proprietor's argument.

10–049   Surprisingly, the Court of Appeal overturned the judgment of Blackburne J., holding, in effect that arms-length sales to the single UK importer constituted use of the mark on a relevant market for the goods.[26] On this reasoning, any use of a mark which is: (a) non-sham; and (b) external to the registered proprietor's undertaking will necessarily be on a market for the goods or services and will therefore constitute genuine use. Whilst such use is on a market, it does not seem likely that this was the market referred to by the ECJ in both *Ansul* and *La Mer*. Having referred to the essential function of a trade mark (to guarantee the identity of the origin of goods or services to the consumer or end user), the ECJ seem to require use of the mark on the market for the goods or services protected by the mark.[27] We consider the focus is the market for the end user of the goods or services in question.

10–050   It is possible that the Court of Appeal are right, and any non-sham use on any market constitutes genuine use. If the ECJ had meant to say this, the judgments in *Ansul* and *La Mer* would, we believe, have been rather different. We consider that the reasoning of the Court of Appeal is significantly out of step with *Ansul*, *La Mer* and numerous CFI decisions, as well as representing a retrograde step in this area of the law. The privilege of a trade mark registration requires that the mark must be put to genuine or real use. A generous period of five years is allowed for this, giving ample time for any real use to be made. If the mark is not put to genuine use, then you lose it. It remains to be seen whether the House of Lords will give leave to appeal and, if so, what view they take of the proper interpretation of *Ansul* and *La Mer*.

Other points arising from *Ansul*

10–051   First, pre-*Ansul*, the approach to "genuine use" in the UK tended to a two-stage test: (a) what use was shown? (b) was it genuine? *Ansul* requires a more holistic approach and a single question: has genuine use been established in all the circumstances?[28]

---

[26] *Laboratoires Goemar SA v La Mer Technology Inc* [2005] EWCA (Civ) 978, July 29, 2005. The Court of Appeal declined an invitation to make a reference to the ECJ on the question of "which market?". The judgments are unsatisfactory in a number of respects. For example, Mummery L.J. held that his analysis of the market produced a result which was compatible with various post-*Ansul* decisions of the CFI, including Case T–334/01 HIPOVITON, July 8, 2004; Case T–203/02 VITAFRUIT, July 8, 2004; Case T–356/02 VITAKRAFT, October 6, 2004. It is difficult to see how that could be so, unless the CFI use the expression "publicly and outwardly" simply to mean any use external to the undertaking. Similarly, Neuberger L.J. considered that any communication of the mark to a third party can be said to be "consistent with the essential function of a trade mark" as explained in *Ansul*. He could see no warrant for the requirement of Blackburne J. that the mark had to be communicated to ultimate consumers of the goods in question, despite: (a) the reference in *Ansul* to essential function; or (b) the CFI referring to "active functioning of the mark on the market".

[27] See *Ansul*, paras 36 & 37 and *La Mer*, para.20.

[28] One of the Registry's hearing officers has stated "When evidence is provided by a proprietor in defence of their registration, the Registrar would normally expect to see for example, figures detailing financial turnover or profit from sales of goods or services under the mark, details of exactly what goods or services have been offered under the mark, expenditure on advertising the mark with details of where and when the mark was advertised, exhibits demonstrating how the

Second, it is clear (as it always has been) that if the use was made for the   **10–052**
purpose of defeating a non-use attack, then it is not genuine use.[29]

Third, the broader approach taken in *Ansul* substantially reduces the scope for   **10–053**
argument on what were always, in truth, peripheral issues raised when a proprietor was struggling to demonstrate the normal type of use in the market
concerned. In the light of *Ansul* it is clear that genuine use must be demonstrated
(a) in relation to goods or services falling within the specification (b) in the relevant territory.

RELEVANT GOODS OR SERVICES

The use must be in relation to goods or services within the specification.[30] Use on   **10–054**
any other goods or services is irrelevant. If an issue arises as to whether particular
goods or services do or do not fall within the specification, it may be necessary to
construe what the words used in the specification actually mean. The general approach to construction has been described thus:

> "When it comes to construing a word used in a trade mark specification, one
> is concerned with how the product is, as a practical matter, regarded for the
> purposes of trade. After all, a trade mark specification is concerned with use
> in trade."[31]

The words in the specification must be construed as at the date of application
for the mark in question.

USE IN THE RELEVANT TERRITORY

It is axiomatic that the proprietor must prove genuine use in the relevant territory.   **10–055**
In cases where the proprietor has difficulty showing genuine use in the ordinary
course of trade, reliance is sometimes placed on (a) Internet use and (b) use in
publications which may be found in the territory. Whether these types of use
count as genuine use is a question of degree. The issue is double-edged in this
sense: what counts as genuine use in the course of trade in, say, the United
Kingdom should also count as use of the sign for the purposes of infringement.
The reverse is not necessarily true at all.

In *Crate & Barrel*,[32] the use relied on by the proprietor was basically held to be   **10–056**
use in the US and not in the UK. By contrast, the uses of the defendant which
were alleged to infringe the UK registration were (a) use on a website based in
Ireland and (b) use in an advertisement in a magazine published in the UK. Jacob
J. held that in deciding whether there was any use in the course of trade in relation to goods in the United Kingdom, the court should consider whether the defendant had any trade in the United Kingdom or had any customers buying goods
or services for consumption in the United Kingdom.

---

mark is promoted in advertising and how the mark was placed on goods in the marketplace."
Adrenalin SRIS O/336/99.

[29] The proposition hardly requires support from authority, but examples from the 1938 Act are:
Nerit [1982] F.S.R. 72, CA; *Concord* [1987] F.S.R. 209; *Huggars* [1979] F.S.R. 310; *Second
Sight* [1995] R.P.C. 423; *Trooper* [1994] R.P.C. 26; *Electrolux* (1954) 71 R.P.C. 23. Intermittent
or temporary use is usually an indicator of non-genuine use, even though wealthy traders may be
able to afford temporary use on a reasonably substantial scale. By contrast, steady use or use
backed by an intention to establish a market indicates genuine use.

[30] Under the 1938 Act, the proprietor could rely on use on goods of the same description, under
s.26(1). The only use which can be taken into account under the 1994 Act is use on goods or services for which the mark is registered.

[31] Jacob J. in *British Sugar plc v James Robertson & Sons Ltd* [1996] R.P.C. 281 at 288.

[32] *Euromarket Designs Inc v Peters and Crate & Barrel Ltd* [2001] F.S.R.20, p.288, Jacob J.

10–057　In essence, use of a mark on a website will only constitute use in a particular territory if the website is specifically aimed at and used by consumers in that territory. Likewise, use of a mark in foreign publications which happen to circulate in small quantities in the UK will not amount to or assist in showing genuine use.

TYPES OF USE

10–058　The 1994 Act does not specify any restrictions on the types of use which can be taken into account. However, bearing in mind s.46(1)(a) and (b) require "genuine use", it is suggested that the use must be as a trade mark, *i.e.* so as to indicate origin.[33] This point should not give rise to detailed debate over whether a trade mark reliably indicates origin. Alleged use should only be excluded if the "mark" is being used in a purely descriptive or decorative way. It should be fairly obvious whether or not such use has occurred.

10–059　The 1994 Act does provide some guidance as to what "use" encompasses. First, s.103(2) of the 1994 Act provides:

> "References in this Act to use (or any particular description of use) of a trade mark … include use (or that description of use) otherwise than by means of a graphic representation."

The principal effect of this provision is that oral use of a mark now counts as "use".

10–060　Secondly, the special case of goods made solely for export is dealt with in s.46(2) of the Act which provides:

> "…use in the United Kingdom includes affixing the trade mark to goods or to the packaging of goods in the United Kingdom solely for export purposes."

USE ON PROMOTIONAL ITEMS

10–061　Household consumer goods frequently feature "on-pack" promotions, where promotional items which have some link to the main product are offered either at a reduced price or given away in exchange for a stated number of vouchers. The promotional items feature the mark applied to the main product.[34] Their purpose is to advertise the main product. The issue is whether the mark on the promotional item is being used in relation to that item or whether, in reality, it is being used in relation to the main product. Under the 1938 Act, there was authority to the effect that use on promotional items was not use as a trade mark in relation to those goods, but constituted use in relation to the principal product.[35] This type of use is often intermittent and infrequent, but a well-informed proprietor will take steps to ensure that suitable promotional items appear at least every five years.

10–062　The proprietor would no doubt argue that he is using his mark in relation to the promotional product, because he has to select the quality of those products and put his reputation behind them. The fact that the mark is also advertising the main

---

[33] This argument failed on the facts in *Esquire* SRIS O/189/00, June 13, 2000, Regy.

[34] If the promotional item does not bear the mark, but is supplied in some way under the auspices of the mark, it is unlikely to constitute use of the mark in relation to the promotional items. See, *e.g. Elle T.M.* [1997] F.S.R. 529, Lloyd J., where the registered proprietor tried to rely on the endorsement in its ELLE magazine of cosmetic products marketed under other brands. This was held not use of the ELLE mark in relation to the cosmetics.

[35] *e.g.* Kodak on T-shirts was used in relation to the film, and not the T-shirts: *Kodak* [1990] F.S.R. 49.

product does not prevent it performing a dual function on the promotional item. Overall, it is difficult to see a court finding that this type of use was not genuine use in relation to the promotional items.[36] In addition it would be harsh to deprive the proprietor of the protection afforded to him by his registrations which covered promotional items, particularly if the same or closely similar mark was used in a different trade which might also be supported by use on similar promotional items.

TIMING

The prospective applicant for revocation wants to choose, within the constraints imposed by the 1994 Act and by the facts in question, the five-year period(s) which will maximise the chances of a successful challenge. Apart from the obvious constraint that a five-year period is required, the constraints imposed by the Act on the choice of a particular five-year period are as follows.   **10–063**

For a s.46(1)(a) type case (not put into genuine use within five years), the major constraint is the date when the registration formalities were completed for the mark in question. Essentially, s.46(1)(a) gives the proprietor a period of five years from the date when the mark is actually put on the Register to put his mark into genuine use. The relevant date can be found in the Register entry relating to the mark. The application for revocation can be brought as soon as five years has elapsed.[37] In fact, if an application under s.46(1)(a) is contemplated it is normally prudent to commence the application as soon as possible after the five-year period has elapsed, for reasons connected with other constraints imposed by the Act.   **10–064**

The second constraint is contained in s.46(3). If genuine use is commenced or resumed after the five-year period of non-use but before the application for revocation is made, then the application for revocation will fail. The general effect of this is that it is risky to delay commencing the application for revocation or to choose a five-year period which ended some time before the application was commenced, because the proprietor might be able to show genuine use in the interim period which will defeat the application.   **10–065**

This second constraint is subject to the qualification in the proviso to s.46(3). Essentially, it provides a three-month grace period after the end of the five-year period in question. Commencement or resumption of genuine use within that three-month period is disregarded unless preparations for the commencement or resumption began before the proprietor became aware that the application for revocation might be made. This creates something of a dilemma for the applicant for revocation. If he notifies the proprietor of his intention to bring an application at too early a stage, he might give the proprietor the chance to put his mark into use before the five-year period in contemplation had elapsed. The applicant then has to deal with the issue of whether the use was genuine or not, which it is better to avoid. If the notification comes too late, then the proprietor might have begun preparations for commencement or resumption of use before he was aware an application might be made, giving rise to the risk that the application would be   **10–066**

---

[36] In *Merc* [2001] R.P.C. 42, p.813, the promotional items sold by DaimlerChrysler were sweaters, anoraks, polo-shirts, scarves, T-shirts and baseball caps and they sustained a specification of goods limited to those items.
[37] Confirmed by the Court of Appeal in PHILOSOPHY DI ALBERTA FERRETTI [2002] EWCA Civ 921; [2003] R.P.C. 15, p.287.

defeated by commencement or resumption of use within the three-month grace period. Perhaps the best, but not necessarily perfect solution to the dilemma is to notify the proprietor as the five-year period expires. The applicant takes the risk that preparations for use have begun. If, however, it is clear that the preparations began precisely because the proprietor was aware that his five-year period was about to elapse, there would be a strong argument that he was not preparing for genuine use, but to use the mark for the purpose of defeating an application for revocation.

10–067   Of course, whether any of the constraints imposed by the Act actually operate depends on the facts of the particular situation. Generally, there are two types of situation. The first is where the applicant for revocation suspects that there has been no use of the mark in relation to any of the goods or services for which it is registered. In that type of situation, the applicant wants to choose a five-year period which will ensure success, and not trigger any use which might complicate the situation. The second type of situation is where the mark has been used in relation to particular goods or services, but the applicant for revocation is interested in cutting down the specification of goods or services to remove or reduce the risk of conflict. Again, the applicant wishes to choose a five-year period which will ensure success. In this second type of situation, there is less risk that the proprietor will be able to extend his use so as to cover the whole specification of goods or services. In this sense, the choice of five-year period is less constrained.

10–068   The facts are dictated by the actions or inaction of the proprietor of the mark. Although the applicant for revocation may well have some information about the lack of use of the mark, he may be able to obtain useful further information from the proprietor's response to an initial challenge of lack of use. However, the proprietor's response is likely to be cagey, so the applicant does not get to know the full facts until after his application has been commenced. Once the proprietor has filed his evidence of use and/or identified any alleged "proper reasons" for non-use, the applicant for revocation should consider whether a different five-year period of non-use can be identified which (1) avoids what appears to be genuine use by the proprietor and/or (2) avoids any periods of time which may be excused by the alleged "proper reasons" and/or (3) will not be defeated by genuine use commenced or resumed after the end of the five year period. Although these matters should be considered, it is frequently the case that there is no room for manoeuvre and the application must be fought on the original basis or settled/withdrawn.

10–069   It would seem obvious that any applicant must specify clearly in his application the five-year period or periods in which he alleges lack of genuine use, and particularly so if the or one of the periods he wishes to put in issue lies some time in the past.[38]

USE OF VARIANTS OF THE REGISTERED MARK

10–070   The first part of s.46(2) of the 1994 Act provides that "use of a trade mark includes use in a form differing in elements which do not alter the distinctive character of the mark in the form in which it was registered...". This requires a two-stage inquiry, as Lord Walker has confirmed:

---

[38] So held in *Saab AB v Saab Textiles Ltd* [2003] EWHC 1334, Jacob J. The pleading alleged non-use "for at least the last five years". This was rightly held to be too opaque to indicate a challenge going back to 1960!

"The first part of the necessary inquiry is, what are the points of difference between the mark as used and the mark as registered? Once those differences have been identified, the second part of the inquiry is, do they alter the distinctive character of the mark as registered?"[39]

He continued:

"The distinctive character of a trade mark (what makes it in some degree striking and memorable) is not likely to be analysed by the average consumer, but is nevertheless capable of analysis." "It is for the registrar, through the hearing officer's specialised experience and judgment, to analyse the "visual, aural and conceptual" qualities of a mark and make a "global appreciation" of its likely impact on the average consumer who: "normally perceives the mark as a whole and does not proceed to analyse its various details"."[40]

The advantage and importance of making the assessment using the viewpoint of the average consumer is that one avoids over-complicating the issue. It is a matter of impression.[41] If the variant passes the test, then the use of the variant must be taken into account.[42]   **10–071**

PROPER REASONS FOR NON-USE

References to "proper reasons for non-use" need to be interpreted in accordance with Art.19(1) of TRIPS which uses the expression "valid reasons based on the existence of obstacles" to the genuine use which is required. "Circumstances arising independently of the will of the owner of the trademark which constitute an obstacle to the use of the trademark, such as import restrictions on or other governmental requirements for goods or services protected by the trademark, shall be recognized as valid reasons for non-use."   **10–072**

Whether there are proper reasons for non-use is something to be decided in all the circumstances of the case. One factor which must always be taken into account is the legislative purpose of the non-use provisions (see above), which has been described as the requirement to use a trade mark or lose it. In *Invermont*,[43] the hearing officer gave some guidance, which has been applied subsequently: **10–073**

"... bearing in mind the need to judge these things in a business sense, and also bearing in mind the emphasis which is, and has always been placed on the requirement to use a trade mark or lose it, I think the word proper, in the context of section 46 means: apt, acceptable, reasonable, justifiable in all the circumstances.

I do not think that the term "proper" was intended to cover normal situations or routine difficulties. I think it much more likely that it is intended to cover abnormal situations in the industry or the market, or even perhaps some temporary but serious disruption affecting the registered proprietor's business. Normal delays caused by some unavoidable regulatory require-

---

[39] *per* Lord Walker in B quoting from BUD and BUDWEISER BUDBRAU [2003] R.P.C. 25, p.477 at p.490, para.4.3.

[40] Lord Walker in para.26 of the ECJ in Case C–342/97 *Lloyd Schuhfabrik Meyer GmbH v Klijsen Handel BV* [1999] E.C.R. I-3819.

[41] For examples, see *Elle T.M.* [1997] F.S.R. 529, Lloyd J. and the *Club Soda* decision, SRIS O/230/98, November 17, 1998, Regy.

[42] Under the 1938 Act, s.30(1) gave the Registrar a discretion to take account of use of marks not differing in their distinctive elements. There is no such discretion under the 1994 Act.

[43] [1997] R.P.C. 125.

ment, such as the approval of a medicine, might be acceptable but not, I think, the normal delays found in the marketing function. These are matters within the businessman's own control and I think he should plan accordingly."

10–074   As to the first paragraph, Park J. has commented that, whilst the adjectives set out there were well chosen, it must not be forgotten that the statutory word which must be applied is "proper" and not any of the near-synonyms suggested.[44] Some examples from decided cases are set out below. It is rare for "proper reasons for non-use" to be established. In the light of the approach to genuine use taken in *Ansul*, it seems likely that it should be even more difficult now to establish proper reasons for non-use.

(1) Apart from one period of a month, non-use attacks had been extant against the trade marks for over five years. Throughout that period, negotiations for licensing of the trade marks had been continuing, but the uncertainty created by the existence of the non-use attacks had meant that no licensing agreement could be concluded. It was held these were proper reasons for the non-use.[45]

(2) The proprietor intended to apply the mark to a new type of lollipop which required the development of a new manufacturing technique. The development process started in 1989, was brought in-house in 1991 and had not been completed in 1997, a year after the application to revoke was brought. The problems which had been encountered in the development process were described in evidence and apparently a team of three or four technical personnel had been working almost exclusively and almost continuously on the project. Commercial production was predicted for 2000. It was held there were proper reasons for the non-use. Arguments that (a) all the reasons for the non-use were within the proprietor's control; (b) that the proprietor should have put out some lollipops produced on unsatisfactory machinery; and (c) that the development process was a "normal situation or a routine difficulty" were rejected.[46]

(3) The sole proprietor of a business cited family considerations and recession in his industry as proper reasons for non-use. The family considerations failed on the facts. As for economic considerations, the hearing officer stated, correctly, that economic downturns, the cyclical nature of some industries, exchange rate movements, interest rate variations and the like have to be taken as part of the normal range of risks that must be accepted as part and parcel of running a business. No proper reasons.[47]

(4) The reason given for the non-use was characterised as a routine difficulty in business in generating funds for investment. No proper reasons.[48]

(5) It was claimed that the existence of a US trade embargo on goods from Cuba had prevented use of the mark and constituted proper reasons for non-use. The embargo had effect because the word HABANA formed part of the mark, and it would have been deceptive to use the mark on goods other than those emanating from Cuba. However, there was no evidence that the mark had ever been used, despite being registered for 26 years

---

[44] *Magic Ball* [2000] R.P.C. 439 at 442.
[45] *Worth* [1998] R.P.C. 875, Regy.
[46] *Magic Ball Trade Mark* [2000] R.P.C. 439, Park J.
[47] *Anglian Mode*, SRIS O/181/00, May 19, 2000, Regy.
[48] *Questo*, SRIS O/127/99, May 5, 1999, Regy.

before the embargo came into effect in 1962, some 33 years before the date of application for revocation. No proper reasons.[49]

(6) "A proprietor who does nothing for most of the five year period and then embarks on a procedure known to be lengthy but intended to lead to goods bearing the mark being produced for sale cannot ... say that the ordinary commercial delays in producing a new product bearing the mark amounted to proper reasons."[50]

WHAT PERIOD OF TIME MUST BE COVERED BY "PROPER REASONS"?

In the examples given above, where proper reasons were found, they happened to have extended over the entire five-year period of non-use. The issue which has, apparently, not yet arisen for decision is whether the "proper reasons" must excuse the entire five-year period of non-use[51] or whether it is sufficient for the proper reasons to cover a period of, say, a few months so that the period of non-use for which there are no proper reasons amounts to less than five years.   **10–075**

In CERNIVET,[52] Geoffrey Hobbs Q.C. as the Appointed Person held that, when considering whether there were proper reasons for non-use, it was necessary for the tribunal to be satisfied that in the absence of the suggested impediments to use there could and would have been genuine use of the mark during the relevant five-year period. This sensibly connects the "proper reasons" with the requirement to show genuine use within the generous period of five years.

Consideration of all the circumstances gives a certain room for manoeuvre even though there is no discretion involved and the tribunal must decide one way or another. For an individual, a short period of illness in the middle of the five-year period would not avoid revocation, whereas a longer and more serious condition might. Impecuniosity raises difficult questions.[53] In cases of real doubt, the tribunal may refuse the application for revocation, knowing that it is always open for a fresh application for revocation to be brought in a year or two and that use or lack of it in the interim will usually determine the matter. Against that, it should be borne in mind that five years is a generous period within which to require use, particularly in modern commerce.   **10–076**

PARTIAL REVOCATION AND PARTIAL ENFORCEMENT

Section 46(5) provides: "Where grounds for revocation exist in respect of only some of the goods or services for which the trade mark is registered, revocation shall relate to those goods or services only." Article 50(2) of the CTM Regulation is to the same effect.   **10–077**

Similarly, ss.6A(6) and 47(2E) provide: "Where an earlier trade mark satisfies the use conditions in respect of some only of the goods or services for which it is registered, it shall be treated for the purposes of this section as if it were registered   **10–078**

[49] *Cabanas Habana*, [2000] R.P.C. 26 Regy.

[50] *per* Peter Gibson L.J. in PHILOSOPHY DI ALBERTA FERRETTI [2002] EWCA Civ 921; [2003] R.P.C. 15, p.287 at p.298

[51] In PHILOSOPHY DI ALBERTA FERRETTI, the proprietor submitted that it would be inequitable if proper reasons for non-use had to extend throughout the five-year period. Peter Gibson L.J. appeared not to accept this submission, although there is no clear finding on this particular point. See paras 24 and 25 on p.297. In any event, the proprietor failed in its bid to establish proper reasons for the last 1 ½ years of the period.

[52] CERNIVET [2002] R.P.C. 30, p.585, see para.51.

[53] See para.52 in CERNIVET and the reference to *Woolly Bull Enterprises Pty Ltd v Reynolds* (2001) 51 I.P.R. 149, Fed. Court of Australia, Drummond J., paras 42 *et seq.*

only in respect of those goods or services." Articles 43(2) and 56(2) of the CTM Regulation are to similar effect.

10–079   In some cases, the application of these provisions will be straightforward. Some words from the specification of goods or services should obviously be discarded, it being equally obvious which words should remain. Alternatively, a more precise result may not be required, making no difference to the outcome. However, cases are likely to arise which involve significant issues over the extent to which the specification of goods or services should be cut down. Such issues are part of the wider issue of how specifications of goods and services should be worded under the new harmonised law of trade marks.

10–080   In the UK, there has been development of the law in this area but it has yet to be considered by the ECJ and is probably incomplete. To explain why, it is necessary to set out some of the detail.

THE PROBLEM AND THE REASONS FOR IT

10–081   The problem lies in over-wide specifications. As Jacob J. has observed:

> "The problem is that some of the language for specifications of goods is apt to be extremely wide." ... "Wide words can cover what are commercially quite different sorts of articles. So if one were to show use for just one of that sort, it would be commercial nonsense to maintain the registration for all goods covered by the wide words."[54]

And

> "There is an obvious strong public interest in unused trade marks not being retained on the registers of national trade mark offices. They simply clog up the register and constitute a pointless hazard or obstacle for later traders who are trying actually to trade with the same or similar marks. They are abandoned vessels in the shipping lanes of trade."[55]

10–082   Over-wide specifications result from three sources. First, under the Trade Marks Act 1938, if the defendant's goods did not fall within the specification, he did not infringe. The whole system (including the penumbra provided by "goods of the same description" as regards applications for other trade marks, plus the defence provided by another registration) involved the practice of drafting wide specifications of goods (and, latterly, services). Whatever the guidance given to ordinary people, any competent trade mark agent obtained the widest possible specification of goods for his client. This practice was ingrained and probably remains. Even now, at the application stage, unless the specification is very broad, the width of the specification rarely makes a difference, so nobody makes a fuss. This seems to be particularly true at OHIM, and this is the second source of the problem. The OHIM system seems to allow extremely wide and/or very long specifications and, at the application stage, there appears to be no way of cutting back on even very wide specifications of goods.[56] Third, having secured registration, the proprietor either does not use the mark at all, or often only on goods or services which are form only a limited part of the specification on the register.

---

[54] *Minerva Trade Mark* [2000] F.S.R. 734 at p738.
[55] *Laboratoire de la Mer Trade Marks* [2002] F.S.R. 51, p.790 at p.796, para.19(a). See also *Mercury* [1995] F.S.R. 850, Laddie J. at pp.863–5.
[56] A lack of intention to use does not constitute bad faith at OHIM, and bad faith can only be raised in invalidity proceedings. See, *e.g.* NAKED, Decision of the Cancellation Division of December 14, 2004.

We suggest that the new European law of trade marks requires a fundamentally **10–083** different approach to the drafting of specifications of goods and services.

THE UK APPROACH TO PARTIAL REVOCATION

Despite an initial difference of judicial opinion,[57] the UK courts have formulated **10–084** their approach which can be summarised in one sentence. The relevant test is: "A fair description which would be used by the average consumer for the products on which the mark has been used ..." A little more detail is required, from three passages. The approach was first formulated by Pumfrey J. in *Decon*[58] and *Merc*.[59] In the Court of Appeal, Aldous L.J. took the reasoning further, in FREESTYLE:[60]

> "29 ...Because of section 10(2) fairness to the proprietor does not require a wide specification of goods or services nor the incentive to apply for a general description of goods and services. As [counsel] pointed out to continue to allow a wide specification can impinge unfairly upon the rights of the public. Take for instance a registration for "motor vehicles" only used by the proprietor for motor cars. The registration would provide a right against a user of the trade mark for motor bikes under section 10(1). That might be understandable having regard to the similarity of the goods. However the vice of allowing such a wide specification becomes apparent when it is envisaged that the proprietor seeks to enforce his trade mark against use in relation to pedal cycles. His chances of success under section 10(2) would be considerably increased if the specification of goods included both motor cars and motor bicycles. That would be unfair when the only use was in relation to motor cars. In my view the court is required in the words of Jacob J to "dig deeper". But the crucial question is-how deep?
>
> 30. Pumfrey J was, I believe, correct that the starting point must be for the court to find as a fact what use has been made of the trade mark. The next task is to decide how the goods or services should be described. For example, if the trade mark has only been used in relation to a specific variety of apples, say Cox's Orange Pippins, should the registration be for fruit, apples, eating apples, or Cox's Orange Pippins?
>
> 31. Pumfrey J in *Decon* suggested that the court's task was to arrive at a fair specification of goods having regard to the use made. I agree, but the court still has the difficult task of deciding what is fair. In my view that task should be carried out so as to limit the specification so that it reflects the circumstances of the particular trade and the way that the public would perceive the use. The court, when deciding whether there is confusion under section 10(2), adopts the attitude of the reasonably informed consumer of the products. If the test of infringement is to be applied by the court having adopted the attitude of such a person, then I believe it appropriate that the court should do the same when deciding what is the fair way to describe the use that a proprietor has made of his mark. Thus the court should inform

---

[57] In *Premier Brands* [2000] F.S.R. 767, Neuberger J. applied a "blue pencil test" to the specification as it stood (although apparently he did not hear full argument on the point). In *Minerva*, Jacob J. disagreed, pointing out the reasons why a blue pencil test would normally be inappropriate.
[58] *Decon Laboratories Ltd v Fred Baker Scientific* [2001] R.P.C. 17.
[59] *DaimlerChrysler AG v Javid Alavi (t/a MERC)* [2001] R.P.C. 42, p.813.
[60] *Thomson Holidays Ltd v Norwegian Cruise Lines Ltd* [2002] EWCA Civ 1828 [2003] R.P.C. 32, p.586, CA.

itself of the nature of [the] trade and then decide how the notional consumer would describe such use."

10–085   In a further case in the Court of Appeal, ESB,[61] in which Pumfrey J. gave the main judgment, he explained the approach he had taken in *Decon*:

"51. In deciding the scope of the restriction in the Decon case, I took into account the intended use of the proprietor's goods, the channels of trade through which they were sold, and the likely purchasers of the goods. The limitation which was eventually arrived at encompassed the whole of the use which had taken place. Too wide a specification of goods will affect the rights of the public."

10–086   Finally, in ANIMAL,[62] Jacob J. took the approach of the average consumer a little further. Having referred to the "fair description" test, he said:

"20. The reason for bringing the public perception in in this way is because it is the public which uses and relies upon trade marks. I do not think there is anything technical about this: the consumer is not expected to think in a per-nickety way because the average consumer does not do so. In coming to a fair description the notional average consumer must, I think, be taken to know the purpose of the description. Otherwise they might choose something too narrow or too wide. Thus, for instance, if there has only been use for three-holed razor blades imported from Venezuela (Mr T.A. Blanco White's brilliant and memorable example of a narrow specification) "three-holed razor blades imported from Venezuala" is an accurate description of the goods. But it is not one which an average consumer would pick for trade mark purposes. He would surely say "razor blades" or just "razors". Thus the "fair description" is one which would be given in the context of trade mark protection. So one must assume that the average consumer is told that the mark will get absolute protection ("the umbra") for use of the identical mark for any goods coming within his description and protection depending on confusability for a similar mark or the same mark on similar goods ("the penumbra"). A lot depends on the nature of the goods—are they specialist or of a more general, everyday nature? Has there been use for just one specific item or for a range of goods? Are the goods on the High Street? And so on. The whole exercise consists in the end of forming a value judgment as to the appropriate specification having regard to the use which has been made."

COMMENTARY

10–087   The UK approach is fine so far as it goes and in many cases it will be sufficient, because a more precise result may not matter. However, it is a rather woolly approach. Although it includes consideration of the scope of protection provided by the specification of goods, what is absent is a more rigorous appreciation of the underlying policy considerations, and this may result in a slight misuse of the concept of the average consumer. The end result achieved in this sort of "value judgment" exercise can be affected significantly by the policy considerations that one starts with.

---

[61] *West v Fuller, Smith & Turner plc* [2003] EWCA Civ 48; [2003] F.S.R. 44, p.816. Pumfrey J. gave the main judgment, Arden and Schiemann L.JJ. agreeing.

[62] *H. Young (Operations) Ltd v Medici Ltd* [2003] EWHC 1589 reported as ANIMAL T.M. [2004] F.S.R. 19.

Consider the following examples, using the UK approach:

(1) In ESB, the mark was registered for "beer" but had only ever been used in relation to bitter. It was revoked down to "bitter beer" so that lager beer and stout were excluded, despite the fact that the consumer would encounter all three types of beer side by side in pub and off-licence.

(2) In ANIMAL, the mark was registered for "clothing" and had been used on a range of casual clothing of the "surfwear" type. The specification was not cut down, with the result that use of the mark ANIMALE in relation to elegant ladies clothing inevitably infringed.

(3) For the purposes of analysis, alter the facts of ANIMAL: Party A has a registration for "Clothing, including T-shirts" and has used the mark on T-shirts sold as part of a range of surfwear type clothing. Assume that "surfwear" is a recognised term in the clothing trade.[63] Party B sells a range of elegant ladieswear under the same mark, including silk T-shirts with screen-printed motifs. Assume that the respective goods have been on the market together for a time and there is no evidence of confusion in the market. If the specification is not cut back, a finding of infringement is inevitable, whereas if the specification were to be cut back (however difficult this might be), Party A would have to substantiate that there was a likelihood of confusion. If it can be said that the parties deal in commercially quite different sorts of goods, one would have thought that Party A should not have the benefit of the presumption of confusion, but should prove it.

10–088

UNDERLYING POLICY CONSIDERATIONS

The scope of protection afforded to a registered trade mark stems from the indissociable combination of mark plus specification.[64] In relation to one of those elements, in *Arthur et Félicie*[65] the ECJ stated that "The criterion of identity of the sign and trade mark must be interpreted strictly." The reason is because "the absolute protection... which is guaranteed by Article 5(1)(a) ... cannot be extended beyond the situations for which it was envisaged..." Absolute protection means that a likelihood of confusion is presumed without further investigation.[66] Parity of reasoning requires the same strict approach should be taken as regards the other element of the combination. Hence, when the eighth recital to the TM Directive says: "Whereas in order to reduce the total number of trade marks registered and protected in the Community and, consequently, the number of conflicts which arise between them, it is essential to require that registered trade marks must actually be used or, if not used, subject to revocation;", it is clear that the specification of goods or services must not extend beyond the actual use made of the mark. There is no warrant for absolute protection extending beyond the actual goods on which the trade mark is used. Furthermore,

10–089

---

[63] It would be prudent to have expert evidence on points of this nature, even though Judges sometimes believe such evidence is unnecessary. The vice is over-complication, but evidence of this nature does not need to be long or complicated.

[64] *Praktiker Bau- und Heimwerkermarkte AG*, Case C–418/02. Opinion of A.G. Léger dated January 13, 2005, Para.63 (of an unofficial translation) where he said: "the sign, on the one hand, and the products and services which that sign must be used to designate, on the other, constitute the two indissociable elements of registration which make it possible to determine the rights conferred by each trade mark registered."

[65] *Societe LTJ Diffusion S.A. v SA Sadas* Case C–291/00 [2003] F.S.R. 34, p.608. ECJ, para.50.

[66] (see, in particular, para.39 of the Opinion of A.G. Jacobs in *Societe LTJ Diffusion S.A. v SA Sadas* [2003] F.S.R. 1 at p.9–10. See also the decision of G. Hobbs Q.C. (the Appointed Person) in *Cycling Is...* [2002] R.P.C. 729 at 743, para.51.

if the over-wide specification needs to be cut back, it should be cut back to a reasonably precise description of the actual goods or services.

10–090   It is suggested that these considerations require a fairly rigorous approach to the drafting of specifications of goods and services—perhaps more rigorous than most practitioners contemplate because they are so accustomed to the practice which was prevalent under the 1938 Act, and now to what OHIM will allow.

10–091   In the light of these considerations, it is suggested that the correct approach under the 1994 Act should be as follows:

(1) If the court or Registry decides that there has been genuine use but only on a particular item or in relation to a particular service, the first question is whether the specification extends unduly beyond the item or service? If so, the inquiry is this: how would the notional reasonable man[67] describe that item? Naturally, the answer depends on all the circumstances, but the answer provides the wording appropriate for that item in the specification of goods.[68]

(2) If the mark has been used on many different items of a similar nature, there may come a stage where the notional reasonable man would say: "well, all those items are properly described by the collective term, X". It is then appropriate for that collective term to be used in the specification of goods.

(3) The words used in the Nice Classification act as a guide as to which items properly fall within which class, but it is not necessarily appropriate to populate one's specification of goods with terms used in the Nice Classification, unless those terms are prompted by the tests set out in paras one and two above.

10–092   It can be argued that such an approach could give rise to a proliferation of revocation applications seeking to cut down specifications of goods or services which were obtained under the old law. This would be unlikely to occur because that type of application for revocation is caused by a perceived conflict or restriction on the applicant's trading. Only the wealthiest of traders could afford to seek to restrict their competitor's specifications out of spite, and they would be well aware that the same action could probably be taken against their own registrations. Even if there were a number of applications of this nature, there is nothing wrong or to be feared by necessary adjustments to take account of the new law of trade marks. It would be far worse to allow one's approach to the new law to be influenced by wording in specifications of goods which happens to have lain undisturbed on the Register for years, unless that wording is examined and decided to be appropriate under the new law.

10–093   The only other objection which might be voiced against the approach advocated above, is that it could lead to a proliferation of evidence and argument about what the reasonable man would call a particular item. Any such fears would be groundless because:

---

[67] We suggest that the average consumer does not really have the right attributes for this task. The point is this: the average consumer is used on issues which require assessment of marks (distinctiveness, confusing similarity, identity) because it is at the level of the consumer that marks have their impact. Assessment of the appropriate terminology to be used in a specification of goods is a much more technical subject. The average consumer springs to mind, because an objective, impartial viewpoint is required. But the task has little in common with the other tasks ascribed to the average consumer. If, as we suggest, part of the inquiry looks at whether goods are commercially quite different, a view from the trade will be much more informative.

[68] This test should avoid the "red tea caddy" problem, posed by Neuberger J. in *Premier Brands* [2000] F.S.R. 767 at para.10–084. The description of the goods should be accurate but not overly detailed.

(a) the court and the Registry are quite capable of controlling unnecessary evidence and argument, and imposing appropriate sanctions;

(b) the proper description of the goods or services in question will often be found in the registrant's own commercial literature. For example, if he calls it a chopping board, that is the answer to the question above. It would be unreasonable of him to argue that the appropriate description was, say, a kitchen utensil in the absence of a range of items which would support the collective term;

(c) evidence need only be received from the trade regarding trade channels, sectors in the industry concerned or where there was a particular and specialised practice in the trade, for example the distinction between diesel engines of particular horsepower.

A REFERENCE TO THE ECJ

Sooner or later, this issue will have to be referred to the ECJ, as judges at various levels have indicated.[69] As Pumfrey J. observed in *Merc*:[70] "this raises a point of construction of and approach to Article 10 of the Directive, which is transposed into English law in s.46. It seems to me to be essential to know whether a registration is to be restricted to precisely the goods in respect of which use is shown or some other, wider class, and if so, what are the criteria by which that class is established." "…the degree of rigour to be applied when cutting down the scope of a specification for non-use is ultimately a matter upon which the guidance of the European Court of Justice is likely to be required: *DaimlerChrysler…* paragraphs 72 to 74."

10–094

4. Common name in the trade

Section 46(1)(c) provides:

10–095

"The registration of a trade mark may be revoked on any of the following grounds:

…

(c) that, in consequence of the acts or inactivity of the proprietor, it has become the common name in the trade for a product or service for which it is registered;".

DERIVATION[71]

The wording within subs.(c) of s.46 of the 1994 Act is virtually identical to Art.12(2)(a) of the TM Directive and Art.50(1)(b) of the CTM Regulation. The introductory words are different: the Directive provides "A trade mark shall also be liable to revocation if, after the date on which it was registered, …" which serves to make it clear that the ground is concerned with what has happened to the meaning conveyed by the mark since it was put on the Register. Section 46(1)(c) must be interpreted in that way.

10–096

Note that these introductory words from the Directive do not mean that

10–097

---

[69] In addition to the quoted passages, when giving judgment on an application to adjourn the appeal in ANIMAL, the Court of Appeal accepted that this was a referable issue. The appeal was not pursued.

[70] [2001] R.P.C. 42; [2001] E.T.M.R. 98, para.73.

[71] The 1938 Act, s.15, covered, *inter alia*, similar ground. It was invoked in very few cases. The 1994 Act, s.46(1)(c) was not derived in any way from s.15, but exclusively from the TM Directive.

consideration must be restricted to events (including, in particular, the acts or inactivity of the proprietor) after the date when the mark was put on the Register. The process by which the mark becomes the common name may have started long before that. This provision is concerned with whether the result specified has been achieved.

SCOPE OF THIS PROVISION AND RELATIONSHIP WITH SECTION 3(1)(D)

10–098   Although it is convenient to describe this ground using the shorthand "generic", the ground is more restricted than that and certainly more restricted than the "generic" absolute ground for refusal contained in s.3(1)(d) of the 1994 Act. Unlike s.3(1)(d), the word "exclusively" is not used, although the requirement that it, the registered mark, has become the common name, etc., means that the result is much the same.

TYPES OF MARKS AFFECTED

10–099   The requirement that the mark has become the common name in the trade seems to confine the operation of this provision to marks where the main or only distinctive element comprises a word or words, *i.e.* word marks and stylised word marks. It might possibly extend to other marks which can only be referred to, or which have come to be referred to, using words which are the common name in the trade for a product or service for which the mark is registered.

THE DECISION OF THE ECJ IN *BJÖRNEKULLA*

10–100   In *Björnekulla*[72] the mark BOSTONGURKA was alleged to have lost its distinctive character and become the common name in the trade for chopped pickled gherkins, the goods for which it was registered. The applicant for revocation relied on market surveys conducted amongst consumers. The owner of the mark relied on market surveys conducted amongst those in the trade. Hence, the ECJ was called upon to interpret Art.12(2)(a) of the TM Directive, focussing on the expression (in the English version) "in the trade".

10–101   The reasoning of the ECJ is worth consideration and proceeded as follows:

(1) Community provisions must be interpreted and applied in the light of all the language versions;

(2) Only two language versions (English and Finnish) referred to trade circles alone. The other nine language versions use expressions which encompass consumers and end users as well as those involved in distribution;

(3) Those considerations were supported by the general scheme and objectives of the Directive, starting from the essential function of a trade mark;

(4) Art.12(2)(a) addresses the situation where a trade mark is no longer capable of fulfilling its essential function;

(5) The focus is on the relevant product market for the goods in question and the role of the trade mark in that product market;

(6) Generally, the views of consumers or end users in the product market will play a decisive role, because the function of the trade mark as an indication of origin is of primary importance to them;

(7) "Accordingly, the relevant classes of persons comprise principally consumers and end users. However, depending on the features of the prod-

---

[72] Case C–371/02 *Björnekulla Fruktindustrier AB v Procordia Food AB* [2004] R.P.C. 45; [2004] E.T.M.R. 69, ECJ.

uct market concerned, the influence of intermediaries on decisions to purchase, and thus their perception of the trade mark, must also be taken into consideration."

The judgment is carefully worded to take account of the wide range of circumstances in which trade marks are encountered. For self-serve items where the consumer makes his or her own choice, the views of consumers or end users are likely to be decisive and the views of members of the trade almost irrelevant. For product markets where a member of the trade is normally involved in the purchasing process (*e.g.* purchases are made on the basis of advice or recommendation from someone in the trade) the views of the trade may be much more important. In specialist or industrial product markets the consumer or end user may be a member of the trade or have equivalent knowledge, and the views of the public may be completely irrelevant.

10–102

A QUESTION OF FACT

Whether a mark has become the common name in the trade for a product or service is a question of fact to be decided in the circumstances. It is a qualitative test rather than quantitative.[73] This ground depends on the evidence put forward in support of it. A tribunal would expect to see substantial independent evidence relating to the relevant product or service market. The evidence might come from surveys (as in *Björnekulla*), or from persons of standing within the trade or from trade organisations and the like, showing the mark in use as the common name in the trade for a relevant product or service.

10–103

What about the average consumer?

In the previous edition, we suggested that a tribunal should decide the question of fact looking through the eyes of the average person ["in the trade", now: in the product market concerned] who is reasonably well-informed and circumspect.[74] The adoption of a test of this type would help to avoid unnecessary argument about precisely how far it is necessary to prove the extent of use of the mark as the common name, and prevent overly repetitive evidence.[75]

10–104

The ECJ in *Björnekulla* did not mention the average consumer and it is difficult to discern the significance of this. On one view, it is not surprising because there was no issue in the reference which would have required mention of the average consumer. The other view is that the average consumer may not be appropriate since the reasoning of the ECJ indicates the hurdle is reasonably high. On balance, it would be surprising if the average consumer did not have a role to play. Depending on the product market concerned, it may be necessary to consider different "average consumers" representing the attributes of the relevant classes of person who have to be taken into account.

10–105

---

[73] *Hormel Foods Corporation v Antilles Landscape Investments N.V.* [2005] EWHC 13 (Ch); [2005] E.T.M.R. 54 (Ch), Richard Arnold Q.C. sitting as a Deputy Judge ("SPAMBUSTER"), para.166.
[74] An adaptation of the "average consumer" test. See elsewhere, in Chs 8, 9 & 14.
[75] In SPAMBUSTER [2005] EWHC 113; [2005] E.T.M.R. 54, Deputy Judge Richard Arnold Q.C. did not expressly invoke the average consumer in the service market concerned, but his findings of fact were plainly made from that viewpoint.

THE OR A COMMON NAME IN THE TRADE

10–106   The evidence in SPAMBUSTER[76] demonstrated that the mark was one of the common names in the trade for computer programming services to prevent or combat spam, but not the common name. Was this sufficient? The answer is clear from the reasoning in *Björnekulla* (see above). As the Deputy Judge held:[77] "…the purpose of these provisions… is to enable marks to be removed from the register if they cease to fulfil their essential function…If a trade mark has become a common name for goods or services for which it is registered, then it can no longer perform this essential function even if there are also other common names for those goods or services."

10–107   The requirement is that the mark has become the or a common name in the trade. There must, however, be a limit on this notion, and it is a question of degree. Some descriptive use of the mark does not make it the or a common name in the trade.[78] Likewise, where a mark has become a household name, some use by way of synecdoche does not mean the mark has become truly generic or that such use is due to the acts or inactivity of the proprietor.[79]

CAUSE AND CAUSATION

10–108   "in consequence of the acts or inactivity of the proprietor". These words reflect the fact that the proprietor bears the responsibility for ensuring that his mark continues to fulfil its essential function. Although a literal interpretation might indicate that the acts or inactivity of the proprietor must be the <u>cause</u>, there will always be other contributory causes. Hence it would be illogical to say that the acts or inactivity of the proprietor must be the sole cause. In SPAMBUSTER, the Deputy Judge held that it was sufficient if the [acts or] inactivity of the proprietor was <u>a</u> cause.[80] This may underestimate the significance of the role of the proprietor. These provisions clearly indicate focus on the acts or inactivity of the proprietor and not merely on the meaning conveyed by the mark. Whilst the acts or inactivity of the proprietor need not be the sole cause, they ought to be the main or a major cause of the end result.

ACTS OR INACTIVITY

10–109   Clearly all the circumstances must be taken into account and these will include:

(1) the nature of the mark itself. For example, if a proprietor manages to register (perhaps wrongly) a highly descriptive mark, he "bears a heavier burden to take steps to prevent it becoming a common name than one who registers an inherently distinctive mark."[81] If a term is already in wide use, a registration may well face a dual-pronged attack-invalidity under s. 47(1) and ss.3(1)(d) or (c) and revocation under s.46(1)(c).[82]

(2) the way it has been used by the proprietor. It is unlikely that a proprietor

---

[76] [2005] EWHC 113; [2005] E.T.M.R. 54.

[77] SPAMBUSTER, para.167.

[78] See the finding in SPAMBUSTER [2005] EWHC 113; [2005] E.T.M.R. 54 at para.173.

[79] See SPAMBUSTER, para.176.

[80] SPAMBUSTER [2005] EWHC 113; [2005] E.T.M.R. 54, para.171.

[81] SPAMBUSTER [2005] EWHC 113; [2005] E.T.M.R. 54, para.172.

[82] The mark VOICE PERSONALS faced the dual attack, which succeeded under s.47(1) and s.3(1)(d): SRIS O/388/99, November 3, 1999, Regy. The mark TCS (the standard abbreviation for Terne Coated Steel) was found invalid under s.47(1) and s.3(1)(b) and (c): SRIS O/351/99, October 8, 1999, Regy.

would deliberately set out to make his own mark generic, but it is entirely possible that a proprietor, having secured registration of a descriptive mark, might use his mark in the wrong way—so as to indicate the type of goods or services, rather than as an indication they emanate from him. Those would be circumstances in which his acts would cause the mark to become generic.

(3) what steps the proprietor has or has failed to take to seek to prevent generic use of his mark: e.g. by using the mark widely, publicising its registration, notifying appropriate bodies that it is registered, warning infringers, monitoring dictionaries[83] and use in the media.

The notion that a proprietor must police his mark does not impose an absolute **10–110** burden on the proprietor to eliminate all inappropriate use of his mark. A proprietor cannot be expected to undertake an uneconomic burden, but he will be expected to take all reasonable steps to ensure that his mark does continue to fulfil its essential function. In the past, it was generally the case that many years of neglect were required before a once-distinctive mark becomes the or a common name in the trade for the goods. Modern methods of communication, particularly involving the Internet, may speed up the process. Appropriate vigilance is required on the part of proprietors.

There are some recognised strategies for preventing a mark becoming generic. **10–111** A mark applied to a novel product can become the name of the product, particularly if it enjoys a period of monopoly protection. Shredded Wheat is an example.[84] The pharmaceutical industry is adept at avoiding this problem by coining a generic name for a newly invented drug as well as a trade mark. They can then place emphasis on their trade mark as identifying their drug, and the generic name is there to be used for all substitutes as and when they come on the market. This is one example of the need to police any reference by third parties to a trade mark to ensure that it is not used in a generic sense.

It is possible to conceive of circumstances where a mark might become the **10–112** common name for a product or service because of action by the state or some arm of government, which the proprietor attempted but failed to stop.[85] It would be harsh, in such circumstances, for the proprietor to lose his mark even though he did all that was economically possible to prevent the occurrence. Perhaps the overriding consideration has to be that marks which cease to be able to fulfil their essential function cannot remain registered as trade marks.[86] If the proprietor fails to prevent this occurring it should be attributable to his "inactivity", whatever the reason, and he is left to pursue whatever remedy he has against the entity responsible.

Examples:

First, take the facts of *Daiquiri Rum*: the mark was registered in 1922 for rum. **10–113** The cocktail (light rum, lime or lemon juice, sugar and ice) originated in Daiquiri

---

[83] The CTM Regulation Art.10, is a specific provision allowing the proprietor of a CTM to take steps to prevent or cure references in dictionaries and the like which use a CTM in a generic sense. There is no corresponding provision in the TM Directive or the 1994 Act.

[84] *The Shredded Wheat Co Ltd v Kellogg Co of Great Britain Ltd* (1940) 57 R.P.C. 137.

[85] An example of this was the adoption by the EU of the symbol for the Euro. It happened to be remarkably similar to a registered trade mark for goods and services in the financial field, owned by Thomas Cook. An action for damages by the owner of the mark against the Commission failed. See Case T–195/00, *Travelex Global and Financial Services Ltd (formerly Thomas Cook Group Ltd) v Commission*, CFI [2003] E.C.R. II-1677.

[86] Although s.46(1)(c) does not go that far.

in Cuba in about 1919, and became fashionable in the United Kingdom in the 1920s. Plainly "a Daiquiri" was a descriptive term for the cocktail. The mark was held to be an entry wrongly remaining on the Register under s.15 of the 1938 Act, because rum and a rum cocktail were goods of the same description. It is difficult to predict whether an application today under s.46(1)(c) of the 1994 Act would succeed. "Daiquiri" would not have become the or a common name for rum, however common its use as the name of a rum cocktail, but whether it would have retained any distinctive character is another matter.

10–114   Secondly, to alter the facts of *Jeryl Lynn*:[87] assume the mark Jeryl Lynn was registered when the vaccine was first developed in 1963. An invalidity attack in 1998 would fail, because the mark would not have been registered in breach of s.3 of the 1938 Act. However, a revocation action under s.46(1)(c) of the 1994 would succeed, because the mark had become the common name for the mumps vaccine.

10–115   Third, consider the mark "Piña Colada". It was registered (despite meaning "strained pineapple" in Spanish) in France for alcoholic beverages in 1974. Despite the fact that the owner of the mark had defended its mark against other applications, it had done nothing to counter general use of Piña Colada to designate a cocktail. By failing to take any steps to stop this use, the Court held the mark had become generic through the inactivity of the proprietor and the mark was revoked.[88]

5. Marks which have become misleading

10–116   Section 46(1)(d) of the 1994 Act provides:

> "The registration of a trade mark may be revoked on any of the following grounds:
>
> ...
>
> (d) that in consequence of the use made of it by the proprietor or with his consent in relation to the goods or services for which it is registered, it is liable to mislead the public, particularly as to the nature, quality or geographical origin of those goods or services."

DERIVATION

10–117   The wording within subs.(d) of s.46 of the 1994 Act is virtually identical to Article 12(2)(b) of the TM Directive and Article 50(1)(c) of the CTM Regulation. The introductory words in the Directive read "if, after the date on which it was registered, in consequence ...". Accordingly, s.46(1)(d) should be interpreted in that sense.

COMPARISON WITH SECTION 3(3)(B) OF THE 1994 ACT/ARTICLE 3(1)(G) OF THE TM DIRECTIVE

10–118   Section 3(3)(b) forbids the registration of a mark "if it is of such a nature as to deceive the public (for instance as to the nature, quality or geographical origin of the goods or service)." Thus, the same examples are used, yet slightly different

---

[87] [1999] F.S.R. 491, Laddie J.

[88] *Bardinet S.A. v Ego-Fruits SCP* [2002] E.T.M.R. 85, Cour d'Appel de Paris. Revocation did not save the defendant from infringing prior to the date of revocation, although the damages were fairly nominal— £100.

expressions define the heart of the provision: liable to mislead the public/of such a nature as to deceive the public. The difference appears to lie in the fact that the vice caught by s.3(3)(b) is inherent in the meaning of the mark itself, absent use, whereas the vice caught by s.46(1)(d) is a consequence of use. Apart from that, they are aimed at the same vice.

There are two differences of significance between ss.3(3)(b) and 46(1)(d). The **10–119** first relates to the date at which the position is assessed. As an absolute ground for refusal (and invalidity), s.3(3)(b) requires the position to be assessed at the date of application for the mark. Section 46(1)(d) requires the position to be assessed as at the date of application for revocation.[89] The second concerns the cause of the deceptiveness. Under s.3(3)(b), the cause does not matter: a deceptive mark shall not be registered. Section 46(1)(d) only operates if the deceptiveness has been caused by the use which has been made of the mark by the proprietor or with his consent. In other words it is deceptiveness for which the proprietor is responsible, although there is no requirement to prove "blameworthy conduct" as under the 1938 Act.[90] In these respects, s.46(1)(d) has a narrower ambit than s.3(3)(b) and a wider ambit than s.11 of the 1938 Act.

It is suggested that, like s.3(3)(b), s.46(1)(d) looks to the mark itself and **10–120** whether the mark itself is liable to mislead the public. However, unlike s.3(3)(b) (an absolute ground for refusal or invalidity), the liability to mislead must arise from the use made of the mark. Either way, "the court must have due regard... to the message which [the] trade mark conveys"[91]—it is that which must mislead. Section 46(1)(d) does not encompass passing off type deceptiveness. It is in the nature of an absolute objection and not a relative objection (in the sense of ss.3 and 5 respectively).

A QUESTION OF FACT

This ground of revocation raises a question of fact:[92] is the mark liable to mislead **10–121** the public in consequence of the use made of it? It is suggested that the tribunal must answer this question looking through the eyes of the average consumer of the products who is reasonably well informed and reasonably observant and circumspect.[93] In accordance with the judgment of the ECJ in *Björnekulla*, the court must have regard to the relevant product market concerned.[94] In *Scandecor*, the mark was known only in the trade and not to the general public. Hence, the relevant public were those in the trade. The question of fact must be answered having regard to matters as they now are [*i.e.* at the date of application for revocation], not as they were at some time in the past.[95]

APPLICATION

The application of this provision is likely to be relatively rare. In theory, one can **10–122**

---

[89] Confirmed by the Appointed Person (David Kitchin Q.C.) in *Elizabeth Emanuel*, O-017–04, January 16, 2004, at para.34. The Hearing Officer misunderstood para.49 of the opinion of Lord Nicholls in *Scandecor* to say that it was the date of the hearing.

[90] *GE* [1973] R.P.C. 297, HL. See at 334, *per* Lord Diplock.

[91] *per* Lord Nicholls, para.49 in *Scandecor Development AB v Scandecor Marketing AB* [2002] F.S.R. 7, p.122, HL.

[92] Lord Nicholls again, in para.49 of *Scandecor* [2002] F.S.R. 7.

[93] There is no direct authority to this effect, but it is clear that the average consumer test is of general application on all questions concerning confusion, distinctiveness and, here, whether a mark is liable to mislead the public. See Chs 8, 9 & 14.

[94] See the discussion above in relation to s.46(1)(c) at para.10–100.

[95] Lord Nicholls again, in para.49 of *Scandecor* [2002] F.S.R. 7.

postulate circumstances in which it becomes applicable and we set out some possibilities. As discussed later, in practice the facts can be complicated and/or give rise to difficult issues.

(1) As originally registered and used, the mark contained a correct allusion to the nature of the goods or services. There is a change in use, so that the mark is then used on goods or services which do not possess the quality to which the mark alludes. The mark is then liable to mislead the public and in consequence of the use made of it.

(2) The same would apply for a mark which alluded to the quality or geographical origin of the goods or services. Such a change of use can take place at any time, but is more likely to occur following assignment.

In *Smirnov*, a Russian company said to have been set up by direct descendants of the original Pierre Smirnov alleged that all the Smirnoff marks owned by Diageo should be revoked under s.46(1)(d) on the basis that any use of the Russian-sounding word Smirnoff misled the public into the belief that the vodka was made in Russia or that some part of its production occurred in Russia. The applicant for revocation argued that a "cause to wonder" test applied (cf. s.11 of the 1938 Act) but this argument was rejected, applying *Gorgonzola* (see para.10–125). The argument also failed on the facts.[96] An application to adduce survey evidence on appeal failed,[97] and the appeals were dismissed.[98] Although the identity and motives of the applicant are irrelevant, the allegation was probably not assisted by the fact that the Russian company was trying to hijack the UK market leading brand of vodka.

(3) If the mark is assigned without goodwill,[99] so that the mark and goodwill are separated, the mark is then likely to deceive the public as to origin.

(4) Equally, if the mark and goodwill become separated for some reason other than by an assignment without goodwill, the mark will then be liable to mislead the public.

(5) Separation of goodwill from the mark can occur through a sustained period of uncontrolled licensing in conjunction with the public coming to identify the licensee as the origin of the goods.

In practice, the first two examples are straightforward and the other three are frequently not. They require some further discussion.

MISLEADING AS TO TRADE ORIGIN?

10–123 An issue which remains unresolved is whether this provision applies where a mark becomes misleading as to trade origin.

There is one argument to support the notion that it does not. Section 3(3)(b) of the Act (Art.3(1)(g) of the Directive) uses the same examples—for instance/particularly as to the nature, quality or geographical origin of the goods—as in s.46(1)(d) (Art.12(2)(b) of the Directive) and none of these examples include deception as to trade origin. Indeed, deception as to trade origin invokes relative grounds for refusal and not absolute grounds because another trading reputation must be involved to give rise to the deception.

10–124 There are, however, more powerful factors to indicate that s.46(1)(d) should apply generally to any situation where a mark has become liable to mislead the

---

[96] SRIS O-523 to 526/01, Decisions of M. Knight Esq.
[97] Judgment of Pumfrey J. [2002] EWHC 2911, October 18, 2002.
[98] by Jacob J. April 7, 2003.
[99] See Ch.13.

public. The flaw in the argument set out above is that it transposes the context of the absolute grounds into the ground for revocation, and there is no warrant for doing that. Furthermore, it is difficult to think of any reason why, if a mark does mislead the public, it should escape revocation.[1]

Assuming that this provision is capable of applying in cases where a mark is misleading or is liable to be misleading as to trade origin, the next issue is to attempt to identify the principles which should apply.

APPLICABLE PRINCIPLES

The expression "liable to mislead the public" and variants of it are used in much Community legislation in the field of consumer protection. The ECJ has already given rulings on the interpretation of this type of expression and it is likely that the reasoning will be applied in the context of Art.12(2)(b) of the TM Directive. There are three applicable principles which can be deduced so far: **10–125**

(1) for a mark to be liable to mislead, it must be established, having regard to the opinions or habits of the consumers in question, that there is a real risk of their economic behaviour being affected.[2]

(2) the existence of actual deceit or a sufficiently serious risk that the consumer will be misled must be shown.[3]

(3) it is for the national court to assess the issue and in doing so it must take into account the presumed expectations of the average consumer who is deemed to be reasonably well-informed and reasonably observant and circumspect.[4]

Two cases illustrate the difficulties which can arise in practice. **10–126**

Consider example 3, above. The *Scandecor* case[5] provides a fruitful source of possible example facts. There the issue really turned on who owned the relevant goodwill. If you take the position as held by the Court of Appeal, the crucial factor leading to revocation was the assignment without goodwill.[6] By contrast, the House of Lords looked more closely at the assignment (in 1984), the licensing arrangement thereafter (1984–1994) and, in particular, the position of the UK companies when the licence was terminated. If the UK companies could establish a defence to infringement (use of own name), then that would clearly lead to revocation. If they could not establish that defence, the situation was more difficult.[7]

Consider example 4 above. The facts in *Elizabeth Emanuel* could not be simpler, but they raise a difficult issue. The well-known designer of bridal wear **10–127**

---

[1] Certainly the Appointed Person (David Kitchin Q.C.) in *Elizabeth Emanuel* considered the provision broad enough to cover the case before him. See para.47 of his decision: O-017–04. January 16, 2004.

[2] Case C–303/97 *Verbraucherschutzverein eV v Sektkellerei G. C. Kessler GmbH und Co* [1999] E.C.R. I-513.

[3] Case C–87/97 *Consorzio per la Tutela del Formaggio Gorgonzola v Kaserei Champignon Hofmeister and Eduard Bracharz* [1999] 1 C.M.L.R. 1203, para.41. Note that this is an application of the Community law concept of proportionality: measures implemented through Community provisions are appropriate for attaining the objective pursued and must not go beyond what is necessary to achieve it. See also Case C–315/92 *Verband Sozialer Wettbewerb* ("Clinique") [1994] E.C.R. I-317, Case C–470/93 *Mars* [1995] E.C.R. I-1923, and Case C–313/94 *Graffione* [1996] E.C.R. I-6039, para.24.

[4] See the cases referred to in the previous two footnotes.

[5] [1999] F.S.R. 26, CA and [2002] F.S.R. 7 (HL).

[6] For a summary of the position in the Court of Appeal See para.9–95 of the previous edition.

[7] The facts in *Scandecor* were complicated. Due to the fact that the case settled before the questions referred by the House of Lords to the ECJ were considered, it is somewhat difficult to predict what the outcome would have been. The case does not really shed much light on s.46(1)(d)

ceased any involvement with the company which carried her name in late 1997. The company already owned an "Elizabeth Emanuel" mark and applied for a further registration in March 1998. In due course, the designer applied to revoke the existing registration under s.46(1)(d) (in conjunction with opposing the application under s.3(3)(b)). The evidence established that, following her departure, a significant portion of the relevant public took the use of the mark to indicate that she was personally involved in the design and creation of the garments in question. The duration of the confusion was much more difficult to assess, but it continued into 2000. The rival arguments highlight the balance to be struck between freedom to assign (under s.24 of the Act) with protection of the public (under s.46(1)(d)). The designer's case applied orthodox ECJ principles: the issue must be considered from the point of view of the average consumer. If there was a real risk that the economic behaviour of such consumers would be affected by an inaccurate message being conveyed by the mark,[8] then it should be revoked. The owner of the mark argued that any confusion was an inevitable consequence of the sale of a business and could not be objectionable. As the Appointed Person indicated, that was a powerful argument applying to assignments in general, but the case involved a particular, personal goodwill. It will be interesting to see the extent to which the ECJ attempts to grapple with the balance between freedom to assign and not misleading the public.

10–128   Pending guidance from the ECJ, there are various reasons why situations of the type raised in *Elizabeth Emanuel* require a difficult balance to be struck:

    (1) if we leave aside purely altruistic applicants, the issue will normally arise in contested litigation in which success suits the commercial interests of the applicant, yet this is a provision which is designed to protect the public against misleading trade marks;

    (2) whilst there is a public interest underlying s.46(1)(d) (see below), there are countervailing public interests in allowing trade marks and businesses to be transferred and assigned;

    (3) if confusion does arise as the result of an assignment or new licensing of mark (and in many cases no relevant[9] confusion will arise), the confusion is at its height immediately after the assignment or new circumstance and usually dies off reasonably quickly. Any application for revocation usually comes some time afterwards. It would seem strange for an unscrupulous assignor to have the best chance of securing revocation of the marks he had just assigned. At the same time, part of the reason for purchasing a mark is the message the mark conveys to customers, perhaps the more so where a personal connection is involved. The assignee may not be particularly keen to disabuse customers of any misapprehension following the change in business circumstances.

10–129   In theory, some "confusion" may be caused by any assignment or new licensing of a mark. A period of temporary but not wide-scale confusion whilst the public adjust to the new state of affairs should not trigger this ground of revoca-

---

other than emphasising that it raises an issue of fact. The case is discussed in greater detail in Ch.13 in relation to assignments: see para.13–045.

[8] Applying the *Sekt* and *Gorgonzola/Cambozola* cases in the ECJ. See para.10–125.

[9] In theory, any trade mark owner is free to change the quality, place of production, or any attribute of the goods or services he provides under his mark. The House of Lords in *Scandecor* proceeded on the basis that the trade mark owner would look to his own interests to ensure that the public would not be misled by any such change. Whilst this is likely to be true in the normal run of business, different considerations apply when a mark or business is sold or transferred (one side wants the money, the other side wants the business) or when, as in Scandecor, there are two parties using the same mark.

tion, really on the basis that such a result would not be proportionate. Likewise, a period of uncontrolled licensing is unlikely to be sufficient unless, as indicated above, the period is sustained and is accompanied by the additional element of the public identifying the licensee as the source so that, as a matter of fact, the licensee can be said to be the owner of the goodwill in the mark.

Public interest

The public interest underlying s.46(1)(d) is slightly elusive. In one sense it is obvious that the public ought to be protected against trade marks which are misleading. However, this provision does no more than remove a registration of the trade mark from the register. It plays no role at all in preventing use of the misleading trade mark. Thus, the actual public interest has more to do with the dignity of the registration system itself and not allowing the imprimatur of registration to accompany a mark which has become misleading. Perhaps the public interest has to be viewed more broadly: the issue is whether the mark is liable to mislead the public: if the risk is sufficiently serious, the consequence under trade mark legislation is revocation of the mark. The same issue and finding of fact will give rise, under consumer protection legislation, to the prevention of use of the mark itself.

10–130

6. Procedure

Where to apply

If the trade mark in question is the subject of any proceedings in court, then any application for a declaration of invalidity or for revocation or for rectification of the register must be made to the court.[10] All proceedings under the 1994 Act must be brought in the Chancery Division.[11] Likewise, the Chancery Division of the High Court has been designated as the UK Community Trade Mark Court.[12] If the trade mark in question is not the subject of any proceedings in court,[13] then the applicant for invalidity or revocation or rectification has a free choice whether to make his application to the Registrar or to the court.[14] The Registrar does have power to refer any application for invalidity or revocation to the court.[15] This is likely to occur only in special circumstances.

10–131

Section 47(4) of the 1994 Act is a narrow provision which gives the registrar specific power to apply to the court for a declaration of invalidity "in the case of bad faith in the registration of a trade mark". This is presumably to cater for the situation where, after registration, it comes to the attention of the Registrar that the application was made in bad faith. The Registrar can then apply to the court, as a third party tribunal, rather than have to raise and decide the issue within the Registry.

10–132

---

[10] 1994 Act, ss.47(3)(a) and 46(4)(a).

[11] CPR Pt 63.13(2).

[12] See Practice Direction to CPR Pt 63, para.24. The actual designation was, by SI 1996/1908, the High Court.

[13] A search of the entry on the Register relating to the trade mark in question should reveal whether there are any proceedings on foot. Sometimes there is a slight delay between the commencement of proceedings and an entry appearing in the Register. A potential applicant can always ask the proprietor.

[14] s.47(3).

[15] ss.47(3)(b) and 46(4)(b).

APPLICATIONS TO THE COURT WHERE THERE ARE EXISTING PROCEEDINGS

10–133   If the applicant is a party to existing proceedings in court concerning the trade mark, then common sense and the overriding objective say that an application for a declaration of invalidity or revocation or rectification must be brought by way of counterclaim or other CPR Pt 20 claim.[16] Often such claims are made in response to a claim for infringement. If, however, the applicant is not a party to existing proceedings concerning the trade mark, he must still bring his application before the court.[17] It is then open to the court, or any of the parties to the proceedings, to consider whether all matters relating to the trade mark should be determined at the same time. Whatever the method of initiating the application in court, under the general CPR rules, the claimant is obliged to plead the objections to the validity of the registration or of any grounds of revocation or rectification on which he relies. A copy of any claim (whether Pt 20 claim or originating claim) together with "accompanying documents" must be served on the Registrar.[18] The Registrar is entitled to take such part in the proceedings as she may think fit, but need not serve a defence or other statement of case unless ordered to do so by the court.[19] Thereafter, the application for invalidity or revocation is dealt with as part and parcel of the action. If the case involves non-use, the registered proprietor is not generally required to put in his evidence of use until the normal exchange of witness statements, and this is one of the principal differences between proceeding in the Registry and court in such cases. Where any Order of the Court affects the validity of an entry in the register of trade marks, the court and the party in whose favour the Order was made must serve a copy on the Registrar within 14 days.[20]

APPLICATIONS TO THE COURT WHERE THERE ARE NO EXISTING
PROCEEDINGS

10–134   If there are no existing proceedings in court, an application for invalidity or revocation is initiated by issuing a claim form in the normal way.[21]

APPLICATIONS IN THE REGISTRY

10–135   The procedure is specified in the Trade Marks Rules 2000,[22] which reflect the latest improvements in practice and procedure in the Registry.[23] The procedure applicable for applications for revocation on grounds other than non-use is fairly standard, but the procedures for non-use and invalidity attacks are more complicated. In the case of non-use, the complication is the obligation on the pro-

---

[16] CPR Pt 63.15(1) seems to suggest this course is not obligatory, whereas it clearly should be. The previous version was mandatory.

[17] The old Practice Direction, Patents; etc. used to specify such a claim had to be brought under CPR Pt 8, a procedure which was not always appropriate. Now there is no such provision in the Practice Direction to CPR Pt 63, so the applicant can use an ordinary claim form or the Pt 8 route, as appropriate.

[18] CPR Pt 63.15(2) and Practice Direction, paras 23.1–16.1, 16.2.

[19] Practice Direction, CPR Pt 63, para.21.1. Frequently, the Registrar plays no part in the proceedings, simply requesting to be kept informed of the outcome.

[20] Practice Direction, CPR Pt 63, paras 22.1 & 15.1, 15.2.

[21] The old practice direction specified CPR Pt 8, which was often not appropriate. Now a normal claim form is used.

[22] SI 2000/136, as amended by SI 2001/3832 and SI 2004/947, set out in Appendix 2.

[23] The era of uninformative pleadings and repeated extensions of time for evidence has passed. Effectively, pleadings should emulate those in the High Court. See Tribunal Practice Note 1/2000. The Registry also has case management powers (see r.36).

prietor to file evidence of use or reasons for non-use with his counterstatement. In the case of invalidity applications, the complication is caused if a mark relied on has to meet the use conditions.

APPLICATIONS BASED ON LACK OF GENUINE USE

Applications for lack of genuine use are governed by (the new) rr.31, 31A and 31B of the Trade Marks Rules 2000. The following is a summary of the rules which govern up to four rounds of evidence. An application for revocation for non-use is initiated on Form TM 26(N)[24] together with a statement of grounds. Within three months the registered proprietor may file his counter-statement with Form TM8 and either two copies of his evidence of use or reasons for non-use. If those are not served, then the Registrar may treat him as not opposing the application. If they are served, then the Form TM8 and any evidence of use or reasons for non-use are sent to the applicant. The date on which this is done is the "initiation date".   **10–136**

Within three months of the initiation date, the applicant files his evidence, and the proprietor then has three months to file such evidence as he may consider necessary to support his case. If the applicant files no evidence, the proprietor may still file such evidence and has three months to do so starting from when he is notified by the registry that the applicant has filed no evidence. If the proprietor serves such a round of evidence, the applicant then has three months for evidence "strictly in reply" to the proprietor's evidence.   **10–137**

The Registrar has a discretion to give leave to either party to file evidence on such terms as she thinks fit. The Registrar shall send the statements of case (and evidence of use) received from one party to the other. Evidence served after the initiation date is not considered as filed unless it has been received by the Registrar accompanied by Form TM54 and sent to all other parties to the proceedings.   **10–138**

All the periods for filing evidence have expired, the Registrar asks the parties whether they wish to have a hearing. If any party requests to be heard, a notice of a date for the hearing is sent to the parties.   **10–139**

When a decision has been made on the application, written notice of the decision is sent to the parties, stating the reasons for it. For the purposes of any appeal, the decision dates from when notice of it is sent.

REVOCATION OTHER THAN NON-USE

The procedure on applications for revocation on grounds other than non-use is set out in (the new)[25] rr.32, 32A & 32B respectively of the 2000 Rules. The following is a summary. The application is made on Form TM26(O), accompanied by a statement of grounds, and the Registrar sends copies to the proprietor. Thereafter, the registered proprietor has six weeks to file a TM8 including his counterstatement, otherwise the Registrar may treat him as not opposing the application. The date on which the Registrar sends a copy of the TM8 to the applicant is the "initiation date".   **10–140**

Within six weeks of the initiation date, the applicant must file his evidence in support. If no evidence is served, he is deemed to have withdrawn the application   **10–141**

---

[24] The "N" evidently stands for "Non-use". Likewise, TM26(O) for applications on grounds "Other than Non-use", and TM26(I) for applications for invalidity.

[25] Subject to some complications which are no longer relevant, the new rules apply from May 2004.

unless the Registrar otherwise directs, and any such direction must be notified to the proprietor. Within six weeks of the evidence being filed (or the notification), the proprietor serves his evidence, with a further six weeks for evidence strictly in reply from the applicant.

The remainder of the procedure is as set out in the last numbered paragraph in the preceding section.

APPLICATIONS FOR INVALIDITY

10–142   The procedure on applications for invalidity is set out in (the new) rr.33, 33A & 33B respectively of the 2000 Rules. The following is a summary. The application is made on Form TM26(I), accompanied by a statement of grounds. Where the application is based on any registered trade mark, the statement of grounds must include:

(1) a representation of the mark;
(2) details of the authority with which the mark is registered;
(3) the registration number;
(4) the classes in respect of which it is registered;
(5) the goods and services in respect of which the mark is registered and the application is based; and
(6) a statement of use (where neither ss.47(2A)(a) or (b) applies to the mark).

Where the application for invalidity is based on an application for a mark, the grounds must include the matters set out under (1) to (5) above. Where a passing off ground is relied upon, the grounds must include a representation of the mark or sign in question and the goods or services in respect of which protection is claimed.

10–143   The Registrar sends the Form and the statement of grounds to the proprietor. Thereafter, the proprietor has six weeks to file a TM8 including his counter-statement, otherwise the Registrar may treat him as not opposing the application. The date on which the Registrar sends a copy of the TM8 to the applicant is the "initiation date".

10–144   Within six weeks of the initiation date, the applicant must file his evidence in support. If the proprietor has either denied or not admitted the truth of any matter set out in the statement of use, the applicant must file evidence supporting the statement of use. If no evidence is served by the applicant, he is deemed to have withdrawn the application unless the Registrar otherwise directs, and any such direction must be notified to the proprietor. Within six weeks of the evidence being filed (or the notification), the proprietor serves his evidence, with a further six weeks for evidence strictly in reply from the applicant.

The remainder of the procedure is as set out above.

APPEALS

10–145   The decision of the Registrar in invalidity or revocation proceedings may be appealed either to the appointed person or to the court.[26] The practice and procedure is dealt with in Ch.5.

INTERVENERS

10–146   A person, other than the registered proprietor, with an interest in any application

---

[26] 1994 Act, s.76.

to invalidate or revoke can apply under r.35 of the 2000 Rules for leave to intervene in the proceedings. The Registrar has a general discretion to grant leave upon such terms and conditions as are appropriate. Once leave has been given, the intervener is treated as a party to the proceedings for the purposes of the applicable rules, subject to any terms upon which leave was given.

7. Surrender

Section 45 of the 1994 Act allows the proprietor to surrender his registered trade **10–147** mark in respect of some or all of the goods or services for which it is registered. There was a similar provision in the 1938 Act. What is new in the 1994 Act is the provision, in s.45(2)(b) for rules for protecting the interests of other persons having a right in the registered trade mark. This provision is consistent with the greatly extended powers of licensing of trade marks which are available under the 1994 Act.[27] The relevant rule is r.26 of the Trade Mark Rules 2000.

THE PROCESS OF SURRENDER

The process of surrender is initiated by the proprietor sending a notice in the **10–148** prescribed form to the Registrar. Form TM22 is to be used for total surrender. For partial surrender the proprietor must specify on Form TM23 the goods or services in respect of which the registration is to be surrendered. The notice shall have no effect unless the proprietor gives the name and address of any person having a registered interest in the mark and certifies that any such person: (1) has been sent not less than three month's notice of the proprietor's intention to surrender the mark; or (2) is not affected; or (3) if affected, has consented.

Once a notice in proper form has been served, the Registrar makes the ap- **10–149** propriate entry in the Register and publishes it. Although r.26(2) of the 2000 Rules provides that the notice has no effect unless the prescribed conditions are satisfied, if it is later discovered that the notice was wrong it is difficult to see how the situation can be rectified once the surrender has taken effect.

"REGISTERED INTEREST"

Neither the 1994 Act nor the 2000 Rules contain any definition of "registered **10–150** interest", although s.25 of the Act shows the ambit of this expression. Section 25(1) refers to persons claiming to have an interest in or under a registered trade mark by virtue of a registrable transaction or claiming to be affected by such a transaction. Section 25(2) defines the different types of registrable transaction— assignments, grants of licences, grants of security interests, the making by personal representatives of an assent or orders for transfer of the court or other competent authority—all of which apply to the registered trade mark in question or any right in or under it. Rule 40 prescribes the information about a registrable transaction which must be entered on the Register. That information includes the identity of persons referred to in s.25(1) and other persons who have an interest in the transaction. Assuming that all registrable transactions have been properly registered, it should be possible to determine from the Register those persons who have a "registered interest" in the trade mark in question.

---

[27] See ss.29 to 31, dealt with in Ch.13.

8. Expiry, renewal, removal and restoration

EXPIRY AND RENEWAL

10–151   Under the 1994 Act, marks are registered and renewed for periods of 10 years.[28] The process of renewal begins with the Registry sending a notice to the proprietor informing him of the date of expiry and the manner in which the registration may be renewed. At any time within the six months prior to the date of expiry, the proprietor effects renewal of his registration by filing Form TM11 together with the appropriate fee. Renewal takes effect from the date of expiry of the previous registration.

10–152   If the renewal fee is not paid by the date of expiry, the mark is not immediately removed from the Register. First, the fact of non-payment of the renewal fee is published. The proprietor has a period of six months from the date of expiry within which to file a request for renewal together with the renewal fee and an additional renewal fee. Pending the filing of such a request, the registration is in limbo. It has expired but has not been removed from the Register.

EFFECT AFTER EXPIRY

10–153   A registration may continue to have effect after expiry, due to the definition in s.6 of "earlier trade mark". Section 6(3) provides that if registrations for United Kingdom or Community trade marks have expired, they shall continue to be taken into account as earlier trade marks for one year following expiry unless the Registrar is satisfied there has been no *bona fide* use of the mark during the two years immediately preceding the expiry.[29]

REMOVAL

10–154   If no request for renewal (with the necessary fees) is filed within the six months after expiry, then the mark is removed from the Register and the removal is published.

RESTORATION

10–155   The proprietor then has a further period of six months from the date of removal of the mark in which to file a request, on Form TM13 accompanied by the appropriate renewal fee and appropriate restoration fee, to restore the mark to the Register and renew the registration. The mark will only be restored and renewed if the Registrar is satisfied, having regard to the circumstances of the failure to renew, that it is just to do so. The fact of restoration is published, together with the date of restoration. Presumably the renewal takes effect from the date of expiry, as before. The status of the mark between the date of expiry and the date of restoration is unclear. It appears that if the mark is restored to the Register, the continuity of the registration is also restored. However, any claim for damages for infringement in the period between expiry and restoration would appear to have little merit.

---

[28] See, generally, the 1994 Act, ss.42, 43, and the Trade Mark Rules 2000, rr.27–30.
[29] 128 This is the UK's implementation of the optional provision in the TM Directive, Art.4.4(f). Even so, it is curious that reference was not made to "genuine" use.

CHAPTER 11

GEOGRAPHICAL INDICATIONS AND APPELLATIONS OF ORIGIN

1. Introduction

The use by traders of marks with geographical significance is both normal and problematic: it is normal to wish to indicate a connection with a particular geographic location, especially if that location gives to the product a cachet or characteristic it would not otherwise have; it is problematic if, in so doing, the trader seeks to fence off part of the commons which should be free to any other trader who does not mislead by using the geographical name.

11–001

The Trade Marks Act, 1938, excluded from registrability a mark which was, according to its ordinary signification, a geographical name[1] and the well-known "*York*" judgment of the House of Lords[2] indicated clearly the disquiet felt by the courts about the possibility that geographical names which others may legitimately wish to use could become the property of trade mark proprietors.[3] Of course, there are many geographical indications which are not (or are no longer) considered by the public to be indications of the geographical source of the goods in respect of which they are used (for example "Mont Blanc" for pens) and these may be registered with little difficulty.

11–002

In the field of passing off,[4] in appropriate cases the courts have shown themselves willing to protect groups of traders in a particular geographical location against misleading use of a geographical indication, for example "Champagne",[5] "Advocaat",[6] "Scotch whisky",[7] "Swiss".[8] Also, a remedy in passing off may be available to protect a geographical name for a beer, which name may indicate either: (1) that it is brewed in a particular place; or (2) that it is of a particular type associated with that place and so likely to appeal to a particular taste; or (3) that it is the product of one particular brewery at that place.[9] However, unlike elsewhere, there has been in English law no specific protection for "indica-

11–003

---

[1] See the 12th edition of this work, at paras 8–52 *et seq*. Such a mark could, however, be registered as a certification mark under s. 37 of the 1938 Act; for an example, see *Stilton* [1967] R.P.C. 173; also see Ch.12.

[2] [1984] R.P.C. 231, HL; *cf. Waterford T.M.* [1984] F.S.R. 390 (Irish Supreme Court).

[3] For one in the series of cases raising the issue of whether it is trade mark infringement to take whisky from a named distillery, to bottle and sell it as a product of that distillery, see *Allied Domecq v Murray McDavid* [1997] F.S.R. 864.

[4] See generally Ch.15.

[5] [1993] F.S.R. 141. See also Reg.823/87, as amended, which provides protection for the appellations of origin "Champagne" and "Cognac".

[6] [1980] R.P.C. 31, HL.

[7] [1970] R.P.C. 489.

[8] [1999] R.P.C. 826, C.A. It is interesting to compare this decision with that in Germany in which it was held not to be sufficient evidence of confusion for a finding of unfair competition where 10–15% of consumers assumed that chocolate bearing the words "Alpine Milk Chocolate" originated in Switzerland: *Suchard-Milka* [1987] G.R.U.R. 374 (Cologne Court of Appeals).

[9] *per* Robert Walker J. in *Barnsley Brewery v RBNB* [1997] F.S.R. 462, citing *Montgomery v Thompson* ("Stone Ale") [1891] A.C. 217.

tions of source" or "appellations of origin", both of which are included in "industrial property" in Article 1 of the Paris Convention 1883.[10]

11–004   The Trade Marks Act 1994 now provides in s.3(1)(c) that trade marks which consist exclusively of signs or designations which serve to indicate geographical origin should not be registered[11] and the *Windsurfing Chiemsee* judgment of the ECJ[12] has interpreted that provision to mean that "geographical names which are liable to be used by undertakings must remain available to such undertakings as indications of the geographical origin of the category of goods concerned".[13] Also, the 1994 Act provides in ss.49 and 50 for the registration of geographical names as certification and collective marks.[14] But, for agricultural products and foodstuffs, there is an EU system for the protection through registration of geographical indications and designations of origin.[15]

2. Regulation 2081/92 on the Protection of Geographical Indications and Designations of Origin for Agricultural Products and Foodstuffs

INTRODUCTION

11–005   Under Reg.2081/92[16] ("the Regulation"), as amended by Reg.535/97,[17] protection can be obtained for designations of origin and for geographical indications for agricultural products and foodstuffs. Wine products or spirit drinks are covered by other legislation.[18] Protection can be obtained by following the application procedure either in the Member State or in any other country belonging to the WTO[19] in which the geographical area is located. Once registered, the protection can be used to prevent commercial use of the particular designation or indication on products "comparable" to those for which it is registered. Also, the right may be used by any producer who comply with the conditions of production

---

[10] Art. 22(2) of the TRIPs Agreement provides that States must allow for remedies to prevent the public being misled as to the geographical origin of goods or use which constitutes unfair competition within Art.10 *bis* of the Paris Convention. In order to comply with its obligations under TRIPs, Malaysia has passed recently, *inter alia*, the Geographical Indications Act 2000.

[11] See Ch.8, paras 8–009 to 8–014.

[12] [1999] E.T.M.R. 585.

[13] [1999] E.T.M.R. 585, at para.30. See T.M.J. No. 6308 (22/12/99) for the consequential special notice changing Registry practice on the registration of geographical names; also, see Ch.7. In *Nordic Saunas Ltd's Trade Mark* [2002] E.T.M.R. 18 the Appointed Person (S. Thorley Q.C.) rejected a contention that it was only in rare cases that a mark indicating geographical origin could be registered without evidence of use: "Each geographical name must be considered in relation to the goods in question and where there is no current association of that geographical name with the goods in question, all relevant factors must be taken into account in assessing whether the name is capable of designating the geographical origin of that category of goods to the average consumer", at para.17.

[14] See Ch.12.

[15] In addition, Reg.2082/92 provides for Certificates of Specific Character (CSC), or Traditional Specialities Guaranteed (TSG), which relate to specific features which distinguish agricultural products or foodstuffs but not where, *inter alia*, they are due to geographical origin. The only one registered by the UK as at November 1, 2004 was Traditional Farmfresh turkey. These are beyond the scope of this work.

[16] [1992] O.J. L 208/1. The Regulation came into force on July 25, 1993.

[17] [1997] O.J. L 083/3.

[18] Geographical designations of origin for wines: Reg.2392/89; and geographical designations for spirits: Reg.1576/89. The latter reserves, *inter alia*, the designations "Ouzo" and "Grappa" to Greek and Italian producers, respectively.

[19] See below for the amendments made by Reg.692/2003 to deal with applications from nationals of WTO member countries.

laid down in the specification; it is not limited to those who made the application in the first place.

The legislation was passed to protect indications regarding the origin of agri-   **11–006**
cultural products and foodstuffs products and to harmonise equivalent national "registered designation of origin" systems which existed in most civil law Member States but were particularly important in Mediterranean economies such as Italy, France and Spain.[20]

The Regulation does not preclude national systems for the protection of   **11–007**
geographical indications where there is no link between the indication and quality,[21] as in paras 126 to 128 of the German *Markengesetz*,[22], provided that the protection is only given when there is a sufficiently serious risk of misleading consumers and that, in assessing the level of risk, the relevant criterion is the presumed expectations of an average consumer who is reasonably well-informed and reasonably observant and circumspect.[23] Similarly, the Regulation does not preclude the application in a particular Member State of a bilateral agreement with a non-Member State under which a simple and indirect indication of geographical origin in that non-Member State is given protection in the Member State, even if there is a risk of misleading consumers and the import of a product lawfully marketing in another Member State may be prevented.[24]

On the other hand, the European Court has declared that France was in breach of Article 28 of the Treaty by maintaining national legal protection for various regional labels such as "Savoie", "Corse" and "Limousin" after the transitional period provided by Article 17 of the Regulation.[25]

DESIGNATIONS FOR WHICH PROTECTION IS AVAILABLE

Two new forms of protection are provided by the Regulation, namely a protected   **11–008**
designation of origin ("PDO") and a protected geographical indication ("PGI").

---

[20] For the background to the Regulation, see Kolia, "Monopolising Names: EEC Proposals on the Protection of Trade Descriptions of Foodstuffs" [1992] E.I.P.R. 233.

[21] See the Opinion of A.G. Jacobs (at para.35) in *Warsteiner*, [2000] E.T.M.R. 734. This type of geographical indication has been described as "simple" or "quality-neutral": see Beier & Knaak, "Geographical Indications of Source in the E.C." (1994) 25 I.I.C. 1 at 2.

[22] For an explanation of these provisions, see Knaak, "Der Schutz geographischer Herkunftsangaben nach dem neuen Markenrecht" [1995] G.R.U.R. 98. Also, see the German Supreme Court decision in *Champagner bekommen Sekt bezahlen* [2002] E.T.M.R. 89 in which the association of Champagne houses succeeded in an action under para.127(3) of the *Markengesetz* against a computer reseller who advertised IBM products under the strapline "Get Champagne for the price of sparkling wine: IBM Aptiva now at a bargain price", the Supreme Court holding that Reg.2081/92 did not prevent such an action, at para.14.

[23] Reg.2081/92, at para.59, citing *Gut Springenheide* [1998] E.C.R. I-4657, paras 30–32. See also *Verbraucherschutzverein E.V. v Sektkellerei Kessler* [1999] E.T.M.R. 269, for a dispute concerning a German trade mark registered for almost 50 years and a description protected by EC Wine Regulation 2392/89: the ECJ found that it was "necessary to establish that the brand name is in fact likely to mislead the consumers concerned and thus affect their economic behaviour", at 281.

[24] *Budejovicky Budvar Narodni Podnik v Rudolf Ammersin* [2004] E.T.M.R. 243, ECJ, concerning a 1976 bilateral agreement between Austria and the Czechoslovak Republic.

[25] *Commission of the European Communities v Republic of France* [2003] E.T.M.R. 1043. It was stated by Commission official Bertold Schwab in "The Protection of Geographical Indications in the E.C." [1995] E.I.P.R. 242, that the stance of the Commission was clear: "Nationally protected names not communicated within the six month period [provided by Article 17] as also those which, although communicated, are subject to a decision of non-registration, will cease to be protected": at 245. As a result of the *Commission v France* judgment there must now be an argument that any certification marks for geographical designations or indications capable of being registered as PDOs or PGIs are wrongfully on the UK Register.

The European Court has held that both are intellectual property rights.[26] The PDO and PGI alike refer to the "name of a region, a specific place or, in exceptional cases, a country, used to describe an agricultural product or a foodstuff" originating in that area[27] with a further requirement depending on whether it is a PDO or PGI. The requirements for a PDO are the more onerous, namely that the quality or characteristics of the agricultural product or foodstuff are "essentially or exclusively due to a particular geographical environment"[28] and the production, processing and preparation must take place in that area (with some exceptions).[29] By contrast the PGI merely requires the agricultural product or foodstuff possess "a specific quality, reputation or other characteristics attributable" to the area and just one of the production, processing or preparation elements of the product needs to take place in that area.[30] Thus, all PDOs could fall within the definition of PGI but many PGIs would not be a PDO.[31]

11–009   Names that have become generic may not be registered[32] nor those which are likely to be confused with a plant variety or animal breed.[33] However, under Art.2.3 "certain traditional geographical or non-geographical names" (emphasis added) may be registered as PDOs if other conditions are satisfied: it is under this provision that "Feta" was registered for cheese, even though it is not a geographical name but rather derived from the Italian word for "slice". The registration was subsequently annulled after an ECJ ruling but re-instated after further consideration—see para.11–021.

THE APPLICATION PROCESS

11–010   Article 5 of the Regulation provides that only a group (or in limited circumstances a natural or legal person[34]) is entitled to apply for registration. "Group" is defined as any association of producers and/or processors working with the same agricultural product. Applications are to be sent to the relevant authority in the Member State in which the geographical area is located. In the United Kingdom applications are processed for England by the Department of Environment, Food and Rural Affairs, for Scotland by the Scottish Executive Environment and Rural Affairs Department (SEERAD), for Wales by the Welsh Assembly Government Food and Farming Development Division and for Northern Ireland the Department for Agriculture and Rural Development for Northern Ireland.[35]

---

[26] *Consorzio del Prosciutto di Parma* [2004] E.T.M.R. 314 and *Ravil and Bellon* [2004] E.T.M.R. 274.

[27] The words "exclusively or essentially" form part of the similar definition of "appellation of origin" in Art.2 of the 1958 Lisbon Agreement for the Protection of Appellations of Origin and their International Registration. The UK is not a party to this specialised Agreement under the Paris Convention.

[28] Art.2.

[29] Art.2(a).

[30] Art.2(b). In the case of applications based solely on reputation, this must be substantiated by relevant literature or consumer surveys.

[31] In *Carl Kühne v Jütro Konservenfabrik* [2002] E.T.M.R. 89, the application to register "Spreewälder Gurken" was made first as a PDO and then as a PGI, the latter with a considerably extended protected area.

[32] Art. 3.1. The provision defines a "name that has become generic" as one which has become "the common name of an agricultural product or a foodstuff" although it may relate to a place where it was originally produced or marketed. See discussion of "feta", at para.11–021.

[33] Art.3.2.

[34] See Reg.2037/93, [1993] O.J. L 185/05, Art.1, for the circumstances.

[35] On Form PFN 1 (issue 2003), which also relates to the Traditional Speciality Guaranteed sign, and is available on the DEFRA website *www.defra.gov.uk*).

Product types

The product types for which a PDO or PGI may be registered are beer; bread, **11–011** confectionery, pastry, cakes and other baker's wares; cheese; ciders; essential oils; fresh fish, molluscs and crustaceans and products derived from them; fresh meat and offal; fruit, vegetables and cereals; meat based products; natural gums and resins; oils and fats; olive oils; wine vinegar;[36] other agricultural products; other products of animal origin, for example eggs, honey, etc. Natural mineral waters and spring waters were included in Reg.2081/92 but removed by Reg.692/ 2003, subject to a transitional period until December 31, 2013 during which names already registered remain on the Register.[37]

Product specification

The application must include a product specification[38] to include, at least: **11–012**
(1) the name of the agricultural product or foodstuff, including the designation of origin or the geographical indication;
(2) a description of the agricultural product or foodstuff including the raw materials, if appropriate, and principal physical, chemical, microbiological and/or organoleptic characteristics of the product or the foodstuff;
(3) the definition of the geographical area;[39]
(4) evidence that the agricultural product or the foodstuff originates in the geographical area for the PDO or PGI, as appropriate;
(5) a description of the method of obtaining the agricultural product or foodstuff and, if appropriate, the authentic and unvarying local methods;
(6) the details bearing out the link with the geographical environment or the geographical origin for the PDO or PGI, as appropriate;
(7) details of the inspection structures to be put in place;
(8) the specific labelling details relating to the indication PDO or PGI, whichever is applicable, or the equivalent traditional national indications;
(9) any requirements laid down by Community and/or national provisions.

By Reg.692/2003 it has been provided explicitly that the product specification may include provisions relating to packaging "if the group making the request determines and justifies that the packaging must take place in the limited geographical area to safeguard quality, ensure traceability or ensure control".[40]

Examination

The Member State vets the application before forwarding it to the European   **11–013** Commission if it considers that it satisfies the requirements of the Regulation. The Commission must examine the application within six months to verify that it complies with Art.4 and if so publish the application in the Official Journal of the

---

[36] Added by Reg.692/2003 "to avoid a gap in the Community's protection provisions" (Recital 1).
[37] Art.15 of Reg.2081/92 as amended by Reg.692/2003. Mineral and spring waters remain regulated by Directive 80/777 of July 15, 1980, [1980] O.J. L 229 and its implementation in Member States.
[38] Art.4.
[39] In this context, it should be noted that the whole territory of a Member State cannot constitute a geographic area "capable of justifying an indication of origin": *Sekt* [1975] E.C.R. 181, at para.8.
[40] New Art.4(2)(e) of Reg.2081/92 introduced by Art.1(2) of Reg.692/2003.

European Communities for objections. The Commission is assisted by a committee composed of representatives of each Member State.[41]

Objections

11–014   Objections may be made both in Member States by interested parties before the application is submitted to the Commission by the national authority and by Member States within six months of publication in the Official Journal. Any "legitimately concerned natural or legal person"[42] with an objection must channel it through the appropriate authority in the Member State in which he resides or is established, although it is not clear what discretion the relevant Member State has in deciding whether and if so in what form to forward the objection to the Commission.[43] However, all objections made in the submitting Member State should be dealt with before submission to the Commission,[44] it is therefore critically important that any "legitimately concerned natural or legal person" in the UK should be made aware of any application the UK competent authority is proposing to submit to the Commission and be given a reasonable opportunity to object. At present, there is no specific mechanism for this.

11–015   To comply with Article 22 of the TRIPs Agreement, Reg.692/2003 amends Article 12 of 2081/92 to permit within the same timeframe objections to a proposed registration by "any natural or legal person that has a legitimate interest and is from a WTO member country or a third country recognised under the [reciprocity] procedure".[45] Such an objection, in duly substantiated form, must be submitted to the country in which the objector resides or is established, which will then transmit it to the Commission.[46]

It should be noted that trade mark owners themselves do not have any right to object directly to the European Commission but must submit their objections to the relevant national authority.

An objection from any natural or legal person with a legitimate interest, whether from a Member State or elsewhere, will only be admissible if:

(1) it shows that the application does not comply with the conditions for a PDO or PGI;

(2) it shows that the proposed name would jeopardise the existence of an identical or partly identical name or of a mark or the existence of products which have legally been on the market for at least five years prior to the publication of the application; or

(3) it indicates the name applied for is generic.[47]

If an objection is admissible, the Commission then asks the Member States to reach agreement amongst themselves within three months. If agreement is

---

[41] Art.15, known as the Regulatory Committee.

[42] Art.7.3.

[43] In the event that, for example, in the UK DEFRA were to decide not to forward the objection, the objecting party would need to apply for judicial review of that decision as there is no right for the objector to submit its objection directly to the Commission: *Molkerei Grobraunshain and Bene v Commission* [2002] E.T.M.R. 55, ECJ.

[44] *Carl Kühne v Jütro* [2003] E.T.M.R. 3, ECJ, at para.55. Also, Case T–215/00 *La Conqueste SCEA v Commission* [2002] E.C.R. I-1179 ECJ.

[45] New Art.12d of Reg.2081/92 introduced by Art.1(11) of Reg.692/2003.

[46] Art.12d of Reg.2081/92 introduced by Art.1(11) of Reg.692/2003

[47] Art.7.4, as amended by Reg.535/97 [1997] O.J. L 083/0003). The onus of proof is clearly on the national authority objecting.

reached to allow the application, it will be re-published if it has changed or be referred to the committee set up in accordance with Art.15.[48]

If no objections are received, there is no requirement imposed on the Commission to check for possible obstacles to registration, so it is important that trade mark owners and other interested parties keep themselves informed about applications and raise in good time any objections with the relevant authority of its Member State.[49] In this context, it is important to note that a PDO or PGI will not be registered where, in the light of a trade mark's reputation and renown and the length of time it has been used, registration is liable to mislead the consumer as to the true identity of the product.[50]   **11–016**

The Department for Environment, Food and Rural Affairs (DEFRA) maintains a complete list of PDOs and PGIs, which is also available at its web site: *www.defra.gov.uk.*

Names from third countries

Names from non-Member States of the Community may be registered under Art.12, which was amended by Reg.692/2003 to deal with reciprocity and equivalence. Provided the Commission decides, at the request of a non-Member State, that that country satisfies the equivalence conditions and offers identical or equivalent guarantees to those provided in Reg.2081/92, the procedure set out in Art.12(a) applies. Basically this mirrors that for applications from Member States but with a requirement that the application and accompanying documentation be in an official Community language or be accompanied by a translation in one of those languages.   **11–017**

Article 17

Article 17 provided for a six month period following entry into force of the Regulation for Member States to notify the Commission of names which either were already protected by national laws or were established by usage. These names were not subject to the opposition procedure set out in Art.7.[51]   **11–018**

The first group of PDOs and PGIs were approved under this "grandfather" provision in Reg.1107/96 on June 12, 1996[52] which gave Community-wide protec-

---

[48] Art.7.5.

[49] It has been reported in the Press that the application by the Melton Mowbray Pork Pie Association for registration as a PGI, which had been forwarded by DEFRA to the Commission, has been suspended after an objection from Northern Foods on a number of grounds including that the geographical area had been extended from the borough of Melton Mowbray, which has a ten mile radius, to an area of 1,800 square miles. As a last resort, an objector could apply for judicial review of a decision to forward an application to the Commission or indeed to disregard objections (see the comments of A.G. Jacobs in *Carl Kühne* [2002] E.T.M.R. 8 at para.77: "it is essential that interested third parties have the opportunity to make observations at national level with regard to designations which a Member State proposes to submit to the Commission ... and that national law provide a remedy where the competent authority has acted contrary to the Regulation." To this effect, see also *Molkerei Grossbraunshain and Bene v Commission* [2002] E.T.M.R. 605, ECJ).

[50] Art.14.3. The Commission Guidelines (2nd ed., August 2004) give the example of "Bayerisches Bier" which was applied for by a producer group in Germany. The Danish and Dutch Governments informed the Commission of the trade marks "Høker Bajer" and "Bavaria", respectively, but it was considered that registration of the PGI would not mislead consumers as to the identity of the product and the name was registered (at p.12).

[51] For an example of the problems this caused, see *Gorgonzola*, below at paras 11–036 to 11–038.

[52] [1996] O.J. L 148/1. Also, *Mölkerei Grossbraunshain & Bene v Commission* [2002] E.T.M.R. 605, in which the ECJ rejected a challenge to the validity of the implementing Regulation

tion to names (listed in the Annex to the Regulation)[53] which previously had only national protection.

Use

11–019   Only products that meet the requirements of the registered specification can bear the protected name and may be labelled with the indication PDO or PGI.[54] Producers who are not part of the original applicant group may, nevertheless, use the registered name if they can show that their product conforms fully with the registered specification.

Generic names

11–020   Although the requirements for product specifications under Art.4 may be satisfied, a name may not be registered if it has become generic under Art.3. To establish whether or not a name has become generic, account shall be taken of all factors, particularly the following:[55]

> (1) the existing situation in the Member States in which the name originates and in areas of consumption;
> (2) the existing situation in other Member States;
> (3) the relevant national or Community law.

11–021   The ECJ judgment in "Feta"[56] was concerned with whether the Commission had acted properly in registering "Feta" as a PDO under the simplified procedure in Art.17.[57] The Commission did not include the name "Feta" on the list of generic names[58] despite the majority of Member States asking it to do so. The applicant Governments[59] sought to challenge the registration, contending that the name "Feta" did not meet the conditions for registration as a PDO in Art.17.1[60] and also that it constitutes a generic name within the second and third indents of Art.3.1. The applicants noted that Feta had been lawfully produced in several Member States over a significant period.

11–022   The Commission contended that strict compliance with the conditions laid down in Art.3 was undertaken, but having regard to *Eportur v LOR SA and Confiserie du Tech SA*,[61] it was appropriate to pay particular attention to the situation in the Member State of origin. The European Court of Justice found that by following this judgment and relying on a survey result the Commission had mini-

---

whereby a particular PDO, Altenburger Ziegenkäse, was registered under the expedited procedure in Art.17 with a geographical area which the complainants alleged was too extensive.

[53] See para.11–029 for a list of the UK registrations. In *Chiciak and Fol* [1998] E.C.R. I-3315 a case involving the registered designation "Epoisses de Bourgogne", the ECJ found that after the entry into force of the Regulation, it is no longer open to Member States to legislate to give different protection to designations of origin for which it has requested registration at Community level.

[54] Art.8. Reg.2037/93 as modified by Regs 1428/97 and 1726/98 provides for the Community logo indicating a PGO or PDO and the terms for its use.

[55] Art.3.1.

[56] [1999] E.T.M.R. 478.

[57] Under Art.235 EC the applicant Member States sought annulment of the Commission's action.

[58] This was the first list published during 1996 pursuant to Reg.2081/92, Art.3, and consisted only of six cheeses; Cheddar, Gouda, Edam, Brie, Camembert and Emmenthal.

[59] French, German and Danish Governments.

[60] Art.17 established a registration procedure known as the "simplified procedure" applicable to names already existing. Art.17.2 requires compliance with Arts 2 and 4.

[61] [1992] E.C.R. I-5529,a case involving an action by a Spanish association of exporters of nougat called "Turron de Alicante" and "Turron de Jijona" against two French manufacturers of nougat with the same name.

mised the importance attached to the second and third requirements of Art.3.1.[62] The Commission had also made a distinction between generic names[63] and the names of products lawfully marketed. This distinction should not mean that a product legally marketed under a name in certain Member States cannot be taken into account when considering whether it has become generic within Art.3.1. Thus, the court found that the Commission had failed to take properly into account the fact that the name had been used for a considerable period in Member States other than Greece.[64] The Court of Justice upheld the applicants' plea alleging non-compliance with Art.17.2 and the contested Regulation was annulled to the extent that "Feta" was removed from the Register as a PDO. However, after further consideration, it has been reinstated on the Register by Reg.1829/2002, although there are pending a number of challenges to that decision.[65]

PROTECTION GRANTED

Registered names are protected against: **11–023**

(1) any direct or indirect use of a registered name for products not covered by the specification in so far as those products are comparable to the products registered or using the name exploits the reputation of the protected name;

(2) any misuse, imitation or evocation, even if the true origin of the product is indicated[66] or the name translated or accompanied by an expression such as "style", "type", "method", "as produced in", "imitation", or similar;

(3) any other false or misleading indication on packaging or advertising as to the provenance, origin or essential qualities of the product that may convey a false impression as to its origin;[67] and

(4) any other practice liable to mislead the public as to the true origin of the product.[68]

Protection by the Customs against misuse of PDOs and PGIs in international trade is introduced by Reg.1383/2003, which came into force on July 1, 2004. This provides for Customs to act either on a complaint or of their own volition.

The scope of protection accorded to names registered under the Regulation   **11–024** was analysed extensively by Lords Hoffmann and Scott in *Consorzio del Prosciutto di Parma v Asda Stores*[69] before the House of Lords referred to the European Court of Justice various questions on the interpretation of Reg.2081/

---

[62] These requirements are the existing situation in other Member States and relevant national and EC law.

[63] Art.3.

[64] Art.3.1, second indent. All factors in Art.3.1 must be taken into account.

[65] Including Case C–466/02 brought by Denmark against the Commission, seeking annulment on the ground *inter alia* that Danish production and marketing of feta does not give rise to a genuine risk of confusion because Danish legislation requires that such feta is described as "dansk feta". On May 10, 2005, A.G. Ruiz Jarebo gave his Opinion proposing the Court reject the challenges.

[66] In the *Gorgonzola/Cambozola* decision, [1999] E.T.M.R. 454, Jacobs A.G. noted the presence of these words in concluding that it was irrelevant that the Cambozola wrapping stated that it was a German soft cheese (at para.39). However, in earlier proceedings (June 1997) the Frankfurt Oberlandesgericht found that "Cambozola" did not damage "Gorgonzola" within the meaning of the Regulation, Art.13.1.b: [1999] E.T.M.R. 135.

[67] In the Control of Misleading Advertisements (Amendment) Regulations 2000 (SI 2000/ 914), which implement the Comparative Advertising Directive 97/55 [1997] O.J. L 290/17), products to which the Regulation applies are defined as "products with designations of origin", Art.3(1).

[68] Art.13.1. As an example, in *Bigi* [2003] E.T.M.R. 55, the ECJ questioned whether the word "parmesan" was generic and instead suggested (without deciding) that it was a French translation of the PDO "Parmigiano Reggiano".

[69] [1999] F.S.R. 563. The *Consorzio* had earlier been unsuccessful in an action for passing off against Marks & Spencer because both the first instance judge (Morritt J.) and the Court of Appeal (Balcombe, Nourse & Leggatt L.JJ.) considered the description "sliced Parma ham" to be

92. The claimant consortium of producers owned a PDO for Parma ham, whilst the defendant sliced, packaged and sold in sliced form, all in the United Kingdom, genuine Parma ham purchased in Italy from a member of the consortium: the consortium sought to stop this activity. After giving their own detailed analyses of the Regulation, the House of Lords referred three questions concerning its interpretation.

11–025   In declining to follow the guidance of A.G. Alber, the Court of Justice came down strongly in favour of the owners of PDOs, holding that the use of the PDO could be subject to a condition that the slicing and packaging of the product take place in the region of production provided such a condition is justified by the need to guarantee quality and authenticity.[70] However, in the particular case of "Prosciutto di Parma", which had been registered under the simplified procedure, the right could not be exercised because the condition had not been brought to the attention of third parties by adequate publicity (Reg.1107/96 merely provided that the name was registered under Art.17 of Reg.2081/92).[71]

ENFORCEMENT

11–026   Once names are registered, they are enforced in the United Kingdom by the Trading Standards (Environmental Health) Department of the various local authorities. However, to date no Statutory Instrument has been passed to implement the Regulation and so it is not clear how there can be enforcement without any detailed legislative provisions dealing, for example, with penalties or remedies. It is submitted that these would sensibly follow those provided for by trade descriptions legislation but at present there is a vacuum.

11–027   Despite this, in the *Parma Ham* case[72] the ECJ found that Reg.2081/92 has direct effect and "creates not only rights but also obligations for individuals, on which they may rely against other individuals before national courts.[73] In Germany the association of Gorgonzola cheese producers were permitted to bring proceedings (albeit unsuccessfully) under the Regulation against the producer of Cambozola cheese.[74]

11–028   All products registered are subject to inspection to ensure that the requirements of the specification are met.[75] Applicants nominate an inspection body and these bodies are required to comply with European Standard EN 45011. In some cases, government organisations perform this task whilst in others the trade associations themselves are responsible, for example, the Scottish Quality Beef and Lamb Association and the Stilton Cheese Makers' Association.

TRANSITION PERIOD

11–029   As noted above, within six months of the entry into force of the Regulation.

---

true and therefore no misrepresentation: [1991] R.P.C. 351. This preceded the introduction of the EC regime.

[70] [2004] E.T.M.R. 314, ECJ at paras 68–81.

[71] [2004] E.T.M.R. 314, at paras 91–96.

[72] [2004] E.T.M.R. 314[2004] E.T.M.R. 314; cf. *Matthew Gloag & Son Ltd v Welsh Distillers Ltd* [1998] E.T.M.R. 504, in which Laddie J. refused to strike out the plaintiff's statement of claim alleging breach of Reg.1576/89 on descriptions of spirits.

[73] At para.88. cf, judgment of Laddie J. in *Antonio Munoz y Cia SA v Frumar Ltd* [1999] F.S.R. 872, in which an attempt to enforce private rights allegedly arising under the EU Grape Regulations was rejected.

[74] *Consorzio per la Tutela del Formaggio Gorgonzola v Kaserei Champignon Hofmeister GmbH & Co KG* [1999] E.T.M.R. 135.

[75] Art.10. The costs of inspection must be borne by the producers using the protected name Art.10.7).

Article 17 of the Regulation allowed Member States to apply for registration, as a PDO or PGI, of marks legally protected in that Member State or, where there was no protection system, those names established by usage. Accepted applications were granted on June 12, 1996 under Reg.1107/96.[76]

It is interesting to note that both the description and the method of production in the specification of one of the UK PGIs granted under the Art.17 procedure, Scotch beef, have been amended by Reg.1215/2004 as the changes were considered to be significant.[77]

Under Article 13.1 of the Regulation, Member States were permitted to maintain national systems that permit the use of names given a PDO or PGI under Art.17 which may breach para.1(a) or (b) of Art.13 (see "Protection Granted", above at para.11-023) for a period of up to five years from registration.[78]   **11–030**

Further, Article 13.4 allows for the provision of a transitional period where an application has validly been objected to on the grounds that it jeopardises a pre-existing name or products on the market for at least five years. It appears that the Commission will allow the non-complying name to continue for up to five years before being phased out.[79]

CONFLICT WITH TRADE MARKS

In certain circumstances the existence of a trade mark may hinder or prevent the registration of a PDO or PGI: one of the grounds for objection is that "registration of the name proposed would jeopardize the existence of an entirely or partly identical name or of a mark, or the existence of products which have been legally on the market for at least five years preceding the date of the publication" of the application.[80]   **11–031**

Article 14.1 of the Regulation sets out the consequence of a PDO or PGI on a subsequent trade mark application relating to the "same type of product": it is submitted that this should be assessed in the same way as "similar goods" under s.5(2) of the 1994 Act. If the application for a trade mark was made after the date of publication of the application for the PDO or PGI, the trade mark application should be refused provided it impinges upon the protection granted to the PDO or   **11–032**

---

[76] [1996] O.J. L 148/01. For the UK, these were Orkney beef (PDO), Orkney lamb (PDO), Scottish beef (PGI), Scottish lamb (PGI), Shetland lamb (PDO); White Stilton and Blue Stilton cheese (PDO), West Country farmhouse Cheddar cheese (PDO), Beacon Fell traditional Lancashire cheese (PDO), Swaledale cheese and ewes' cheese (PDO), Bonchester cheese (PDO), Buxton blue (PDO), Dovedale cheese (PDO) and Single Gloucester (PDO); Herefordshire cider/perry (PGI), Worcestershire cider/perry (PGI), Gloucestershire cider/perry (PGI); Jersey Royal potatoes (PDO); Newcastle brown ale (PGI), Kentish ale and Kentish strong ale (PGI), Rutland bitter (PGI).

[77] Somewhat surprisingly, the specification originally described the product as derived from cattle finished in Scotland for a minimum period of three months and then slaughtered and dressed there. The amended description requires that the cattle be born, reared throughout their lives, slaughtered and dressed in Scotland.

[78] But not in the Member State which registered the PDO: thus, a dried, grated pasteurised cheese in powder form produced in Italy under the name "parmesan" for sale in France but not in Italy (because it did not comply with the PDO "Parmigiano Reggiano") could not benefit from the derogation, *Dante Bigi* [2003] E.T.M.R. 707, ECJ.

[79] Thus, Reg.2139/98 ([1998] O.J. L 270/07) adding "Jambon de Bayon" as a PGI permits various named Danish companies to continue marketing their products under the name for a period of three years from the publication of the Regulation, provided the label showed clearly the true origin of the Danish product.

[80] See Art.7.4, as amended by Reg.535/97. Prior to amendment the provision referred to "trade mark" rather than "mark": presumably, the latter is broader and would cover unregistered marks protectable in the UK under the law of passing off.

PGI under Art.13.[81] If registered despite the existence of an earlier PDO or PGI which it impinges upon, the trade mark shall be declared invalid, including trade marks applied for before publication (in the Official Journal) but registered after the publication.[82] Presumably, s.3(4) of the Act would be relied upon for such refusal or invalidity, although it is not clear by whom it should be declared invalid as there is no mechanism in the Act for *ex officio* removal.

11–033   However, Art.14.2 provides that a trade mark registered in good faith before publication of the application for a PDO or PGI may continue in force where there are no grounds for invalidity or revocation of the trade mark under Art.3(1)(c) and (g)[83] or Art.12(2)(b),[84] respectively, of the Trade Mark Directive[85] (ss.3(1)(c) and 3(3)(b) or s.46(1)(d) in the 1994 Act). This provision does not seem to cover the situation where the prior right is an unregistered mark capable of being protected under the law of passing off, so that use in good faith of such a mark may be stopped.[86] Also, it does not deal with the impact of the proviso to s.3(1) (Art.3(3)), which provides for the possibility of distinctive character acquired through use prior to the date of application for registration.

11–034   In addition, it is a ground for refusal of a PDO or PGI if, because of a trade mark's reputation and renown, registration would "be liable to mislead the consumer as to the true identity of the product."[87] It is not clear whether this provision relates only to registered trade marks but it is submitted that it is so limited as elsewhere in the Regulation references to trade marks are always in the context of the TM Directive (as seems to have been recognised in the 1997 amendment[88] to Art.7.4, which replaced "trade mark" with "mark").

11–035   Owners of an unregistered mark comprising or including a geographic name should consider registering it in order to avail themselves of this provision in case a future PDO or PGI conflicts with their mark. It is not clear how this may be affected by Article 13.4 of the Regulation (see "Transition Period", above at para.11–027).

THE *GORGONZOLA* CASE

11–036   The European Court of Justice case of *Consorzio per la Tutela del Formaggio Gorgonzola v Käserei Champignon Hofmeister GmbH & Co KG*[89] was an Art.234 (ex Art.177) reference from the Commercial Court of Vienna on the conflict between a PDO owned since 1996 by the claimant for a soft white cheese marbled

---

[81] It is understood that the UK Registry does not have a set practice of referring to the Register of PDOs and PGIs, although if an application is made in any of Classes 29, 30, 31, 32 or 33 the examiner would consult MAFF reference works and the MAFF website.

[82] Art.14.1.

[83] A trade mark should not be registered if it is of such a nature as to deceive the public, for instance as to the nature, quality or geographic origin of the goods.

[84] A trade mark may be revoked if "in consequence of the use made of it by the proprietor or with his consent in respect of the goods or services for which it is registered, it is liable to mislead the public, particularly as to the nature, quality or geographical origin" of the goods.

[85] 89/104. See *"Gorgonzola"*, at para.11–036.

[86] This would appear to be contrary to Art.24(5) of TRIPs. It is noteworthy in this context that, by Reg.123/97 (O.J. L 022, 24/1/1997), "Whitstable Oysters" is registered as a PGI: cf. *Free Fishers of Whitstable v Elliott* 4 T.L.R. 273 and *Whitstable Oyster Fisheries v Hayling* (1900) 17 R.P.C. 461; 18 R.P.C. 434, for passing off actions involving the name "Whitstable" in relation to oysters.

[87] Art.14.3.

[88] By Reg.535/97 ([1997] O.J. L 083/03).

[89] [1999] E.T.M.R. 454.

with blue mould, "Gorgonzola", and a registered trade mark owned since 1983 by the defendant in Austria used for a similar soft blue cheese, "Cambozola".[90]

The court found that use of the mark "Cambozola" "evoked" the term "Gorgonzola" since "Cambozola": "ends in the same two syllables and contains the same number of syllables, with the result that the phonetic and visual similarity between the two terms is obvious".[91] It further found that:

    "'evocation', as referred to in Article 13(1)(b) of Regulation No. 2081/92, covers a situation where the term used to designate a product incorporates part of a protected designation, so that when the consumer is confronted with the name of the product, the image triggered in his mind is that of the product whose designation is protected ....

    [It] is possible, ... for a protected designation to be evoked where there is no likelihood of confusion between the products concerned and even where no Community protection extends to the parts of that designation which are echoed in the term or terms at issue."[92]

However, by Article 14.2 of the Regulation, for the trade mark to be rendered invalid or revoked in such circumstances, then, provided it was applied for in good faith,[93] there must be shown to be grounds for invalidity or revocation under Article 3.1(c) and (g) and Article 12.2(b) of the Trade Mark Directive. The court found that it was for the national court to decide whether, on the facts, the conditions laid down in Article 14.2 of the Regulation would allow further use of the trade mark.

on Similar lines, the European Court of Justice held in *Gerolsteiner Brunnen*[94] that it was also for the national court to decide whether a likelihood of confusion between a registered trade mark ("Gerri") and an indication of geographical origin ("Kerry Spring", recognised as a mineral water by Ireland under Dir.80/777) entitled the trade mark proprietor to prevent such use. Such an assessment would require deciding whether the producer of the soft drink using water from a spring called "Kerry Spring" might be regarded as unfairly competing, particular having regard to the shape and labelling of the bottle, such that the use would not be in accordance with honest practices under Article 6(1)(b) of the TM Directive.[95] If the use were found to be in accordance with honest practices, the fact that the indication of geographical origin was being used as a trade mark would not prevent the user from availing itself of the defence.

Concurrent protection

It is not stated in the Regulation whether the same designation of origin or geographical indication could be registered under the Regulation and as a trade mark and this will depend on the particular national law in the Member State concerned.

11–037

11–038

11–039

11–040

---

[90] The conflict also concerned the 1951 Stresa Convention on the Use of Appellations of Origin and Designations of Cheese, to which both Italy and Austria were party.

[91] [1999] E.T.M.R. 454, at para.27.

[92] [1999] E.T.M.R. 454, at paras25 and 26.

[93] This will depend on whether the national court decides that the applicant "took all reasonable steps at the time of registration to satisfy himself that use of the mark was compatible with the national law (including any applicable international provisions) then in force": at para.51 of the A.G.'s Opinion.

[94] [2004] E.T.M.R. 40.

[95] [2004], at para.26.

Although in most cases in the United Kingdom ss.3(1)(c) and 3(3) of the 1994 Act are likely to prove insuperable obstacles to registration of PDOs or PGIs as trade marks, there appears no reason why, for example, the ducal crown used on Parma ham should not be registered and in appropriate circumstances benefit from the broad scope of protection given by s.10(3).

11–041   Another unclear area is the status of existing trade mark registrations for geographical names which have now been registered by the proprietors as PDOs or PGIs. It is submitted that such trade marks should not be permitted to remain on the Register as the two protection systems are contradictory and if the status of PDO or PGI has been granted, the trade mark should be subject to revocation under s.46(1)(c).[96]

11–042   On the other hand, it is stated expressly in para.3(1) of Sch.1 of the 1994 Act that "a collective mark may be registered which consists of signs or indications which may serve, in trade, to designate the geographical origin of the goods or services" provided that the proprietor may not prohibit the use of the mark by one entitled to use it "in accordance with honest practices" (para.3(2)). Thus, a PDO or PGI and a United Kingdom collective mark may co-exist. The same apparently applies to certification marks granted in accordance with s.50 and Sch.2, although after the *Commission v France* case there must be an argument that a PGI or PDO cannot also be a certification mark.[97]

---

[96] In this context it is interesting to note that "Newcastle Brown Ale" was registered as a trade mark in 1993 and also was one of the PGIs registered under the Art.17 fast-track procedure in 1996 (the applicant group was Scottish and Newcastle PLC, the proprietor of the trade mark). Also, "Rutland Bitter", another fast-track PGI, was registered as a trade mark in 1994 by the Grolsch-Ruddles Brewing Company Ltd.

[97] *Commission of the European Communities v Republic of France* [2003] E.T.M.R. 1043, ECJ.

CHAPTER 12

COLLECTIVE AND CERTIFICATION MARKS

1. Generally

The grant and treatment of collective and certification marks is governed by ss.49 **12–001**
and 50 of the Trade Marks Act 1994, together with Schs 1 and 2. Although "certification marks" have been a feature of the law of registered trade marks in the
United Kingdom since the Trade Marks Act 1905 (when they were called "stan-
dardisation marks"), it was not possible previously to obtain registration of a so-
called "collective mark".[1] Where a mark has been used by a number of traders[2],
the principal civil remedy against misleading use has been in passing off: the
"Swiss chocolate" type of case involves essentially the protection of a certification mark (which may also but need not be a collective mark).[3] However, the limitations of the action in passing off can be seen in the "Parma Ham" passing off
case,[4] in which it was found that the Italian association set up to protect the
"Prosciutto di Parma" designation of origin was not permitted under procedural
rules to bring a representative action on behalf of its members,[5] and in the "Food
Ireland"[6] case, in which a passing off claim brought by the plaintiff statutory body
established to promote the export of Irish foods failed because it was unable to
show that its logo was known in connection with any business in which it was
engaged.[7]

2. The Trade Marks Directive

Article 7*bis* of the Paris Convention requires countries of the Union "to accept **12–002**
for filing and to protect collective marks belonging to associations the existence
of which is not contrary to the law of the country of origin, even if such associations do not possess an industrial or commercial establishment". Thus, Article 15
of the Trade Marks Directive recognises the right of Member States to permit
registration of collective marks and of guarantee or certification marks. It
provides that Member States may introduce or maintain in effect provisions
governing the registration of such marks which may be additional to those set out
in Arts 3 and 12 (on absolute grounds for refusal or invalidity and revocation,
respectively).

In addition, Art.15(2) permits Member States to derogate from Article 3(1)(c) **12–003**

---

[1] See generally Belson, *Certification Marks* (Sweet & Maxwell, London, 2002).
[2] See Firth, *Collectivity, Control and Joint Adventure—Observations on Marks in Multiple Use* in
"Perspectives on Intellectual Property: Trade Marks Retrospective", vol.7 (Sweet & Maxwell,
London, 2000), pp.171–178.
[3] See Ch.15, paras 15–078 to 15–080.
[4] See Ch.15, at paras 15–058 and 15–079.
[5] [1991] R.P.C. 351 at 368, *per* Nourse L.J., following Morritt J. at first instance (at 357).
[6] *An Bord Trachtala v Waterford Foods* [1994] F.S.R. 316 (HC, Ireland).
[7] "[P]rovided the logo achieves, or helps to achieve, its object of identifying Irish food products
abroad with a pure and pollution-free environment, it is hardly a major consideration that the
name and reputation of the sponsoring body is not known to the prospective customers in Birmingham or Glasgow. It is "Food Ireland" that the logo seeks to promote, not [the plaintiff]": *per*
Keane J., at 323.

(s.3(1)(c) of the 1994 Act) on the non-registrability of signs or indications of geographical origin where the signs or indications in question may constitute collective, guarantee or certification marks. However, it is specifically provided that such a mark may "not entitle the proprietor to prohibit a third party from using in the course of trade such signs or indications, provided he uses them in accordance with honest practices in industrial or commercial matters; in particular, such a mark may not be invoked against a third party who is entitled to use a geographical name".

12–004   Where applications are made contemporaneously by the same party to register the identical mark for the same goods or services as both a collective or certification mark and as an ordinary trade mark, the Registry should object to the latter under s.3(1)(a) and s.3(3) (a) and/or (b). It is not possible to contend both that the mark satisfies the requirements of s.49 or s.50, as the case may be, and that the mark falls within the definition of "trade mark". Indeed, Sch.1, para.2 amends the definition in s.1(1) in relation to a collective mark so that it must function to distinguish the goods or services of members of the association from those of others.[8]

3. Collective marks

DEFINITION

12–005   Section 49 of the 1994 Act introduces into the United Kingdom registered trade mark law the "collective mark", which is defined as "a mark distinguishing the goods or services of members of the association which is the proprietor of the mark from those of other undertakings". The provisions applying to such marks are set out in Sch.1 to the Act.

WHO MAY OWN A COLLECTIVE MARK

12–006   There is no definition of "association" in the 1994 Act, although the CTM Regulation does contain one in Art.64(1): "Associations of manufacturers, producers, suppliers of services, or traders which, under the terms of the law governing them, have the capacity in their own name to have rights and obligations of all kinds, to make contracts or accomplish other legal acts and sue and be sued as well as legal persons governed by public law."

12–007   Examples of applicants for collective marks are professional bodies or trade associations, where certain professional levels or quality requirements are specified for membership. Frequently the applicant will be a company limited, for example, by guarantee, such as The Institute of Trade Mark Attorneys, and this poses no difficulties. However, where the applicant for registration of a collective mark is an unincorporated association, there must be serious concern that if granted in the name of the unincorporated association the mark will be invalid. It is understood from inquiries of the Registry that it will accept applications in the name of an unincorporated association, either with or without a list of members (although it suggests that a list not be filed as any change of membership would be viewed as an assignment and require appropriate notification and payment of

---

[8] See Practice Amendment Notice PAN 2/01, which also states that if the goods or services covered by the ordinary trade mark and the collective or certification mark are similar, confusion between the two categories of mark may give rise to revocation of the collective or certification version.

fee). This must be wrong: an unincorporated association cannot sue or be sued[9] as it has no legal capacity to enter into obligations or have rights in its own name. Thus, although s.49 provides that an "association" should be the proprietor of a collective mark, this presupposes that the association is a legal body[10] because otherwise the mark cannot be licensed or enforced by its proprietor. Also, by its wording s.49 would seem to rule out the possibility of the members of an unincorporated association applying for the mark because it would then not be the "association" which is the proprietor and the mark could not perform its function. The position is even clearer where the application is for a Community Trade Mark as Article 64(1) of the CTM Regulation makes it clear that legal personality is a pre-requisite for ownership.

THE FUNCTION OF COLLECTIVE MARKS

Signs which may be a collective mark are those which distinguish the goods or services of members of the association which is proprietor from those of other undertakings, and s.1(1) of the 1994 Act is to be construed accordingly.[11] The proprietor of a collective mark, which will be the association (if a legal entity), may also use the mark, unlike a certification mark which may not be used by its proprietor. **12–008**

INDICATIONS OF GEOGRAPHIC ORIGIN

As permitted by Article 15(2) of the TM Directive, para.3 of Sch.1 provides for the registration of indications of geographical origin, which may otherwise be unregistrable under s.3(1)(c) of the 1994 Act (although presumably could be registered as PDOs or PGIs).[12] Such a collective mark may not be used to prohibit the use of the sign in accordance with honest practices in industrial or commercial matters, particularly by a person entitled to use a geographical name.[13] **12–009**

MISLEADING MARKS

However, para.4 of Sch.1 of the 1994 Act excludes a mark from registrability as a collective mark "if the public is liable to be misled as regards the character or significance of the mark, in particular if it is likely to be taken to be something other than a collective mark". It is therefore open to the Registrar to require that a **12–010**

---

[9] See, *e.g. Artistic Upholstery Ltd v Art Forma (Furniture) Ltd* [2000] F.S.R. 311. As noted by *Shrivastava* [2000] I.P.Q. 112): "The implications of this case seem to be, that the goodwill accruing to an unincorporated association is held by its members on trust for each other": such an analysis would not assist the unincorporated association which purports to be the proprietor of a registered collective mark as the definition of collective mark in the 1994 Act, s.49 requires the proprietor to be the association.

[10] "An unincorporated association is not, of course, a legal person" *per* Lawrence Collins Q.C. in *Artistic Upholstery* [2000] F.S.R. 311, at 284. *Cf.* Manual of Patent Practice, UK Patent Office (4th ed. 1999), which sets out at para.7 those "persons" who may apply for a patent, which does not include "a firm, partnership or body which is unincorporate, although in such cases application may be made by individual partners jointly". Whilst the joint application route may be appropriate for partnerships, it is not clear that it is so for unincorporated associations.

[11] Sch.1, para.2.

[12] See Ch.12. It is not clear why an indication which could be registered as a PGI should also be proper subject-matter for a collective mark as the two systems, that for the protection of PDOs and PGIs and that for registered trade marks, have different and potentially conflicting scopes of protection.

[13] Sch.1, para.3(2). It is unclear why there is need for this provision in view of s.11(2)(b).

mark includes some indication that it is a collective mark.[14] In this context, it is worth mentioning the decision of Jacob J. in *Association of Certified Public Accountants v Trade Secretary*[15] where the learned judge confirmed a direction of the Secretary of State under s.32 of the Companies Act 1985 requiring the claimant to change its name within six weeks on the ground that using the word "certified" was misleading and likely to cause harm to the public. He found that the word "indicates, or is likely to indicate, to a substantial number of persons, that there is something objectively significant about the members' qualifications, training and experience".[16] It is interesting to speculate whether the Association would have succeeded in an application for a collective mark.

REGULATIONS

12–011   An applicant for a collective mark must file with the Registrar within nine months of the date of application[17] a copy of the regulations governing the use of the mark, on Form TM35.[18] The regulations must specify who is authorised to use the mark, the conditions for membership of the association and, if there are any (and there need not be), conditions of use, including any sanctions.[19] Once the regulations have been examined and approved by the Registrar (who must be satisfied that they are not "[c]ontrary to public policy or to accepted principles of morality"),[20] the application is published for opposition purposes as any "ordinary" mark would be but noting that the regulations are available for public inspection.

REGISTRATION

12–012   Once the application has been advertised and the opposition period expired, the mark proceeds to registration as any other mark would. Any amendments to the regulations must be approved by the Registrar.[21]

RIGHTS OF MEMBERS OF THE ASSOCIATION

12–013   Authorised users of registered collective marks are given the same rights as a licensee under ss.10(5), 19(2) and 89 of the 1994 Act,[22] and the same rights as are given by s.30 in relation to infringement are accorded to authorised users by para.12 of Sch.1.

ASSIGNMENT

12–014   It appears that a collective mark may be assigned without the consent of the Registrar (unlike certification marks: see below), although obviously the effect of the assignment ought not to be that any subsequent use is misleading.

---

[14] Such an amendment would not fall within s.39(2): see Sch.2, para.4, proviso 2.

[15] [1998] 1 W.L.R. 164.

[16] [1998] 1 W.L.R. 164, at 173.

[17] Trade Marks Rules 2000, SI 2000/136, r.22. This is made on Form TM3 with Part 9 filled in to indicate that the application is for a collective mark.

[18] 1994 Act, Sch.1, para.5(1).

[19] 1994 Act, Sch.1, para.5(2).

[20] 1994 Act, Sch.1, para.6(1).

[21] An application to amend should be made on Form TM36 and the Trade Mark Rules 2000 (SI 2000/136), r.23, sets out the procedure for dealing with such an application.

[22] Sch.1, para.11(a), (b) and (c).

REVOCATION

In addition to the grounds of revocation set out in s.46 of the 1994 Act for "ordinary" marks, the registration of a collective mark may be revoked on the ground (1) that the manner in which it has been used by the proprietor has caused it to become liable to mislead as regards its character or significance, (2) that the regulations have not been observed or enforced by the proprietor, or (3) that an inappropriate amendment has been made to the regulations.[23] Also, in addition to the usual grounds set out in s.47, a collective mark may be declared invalid on the ground that it was registered in breach of para.4(1)—it was misleading—or para.6(1)—the regulations should not have been approved.[24]

12–015

OTHER RESPECTS

In all other respects, the collective mark is treated as any other registered trade mark.

12–016

4. Certification marks

DEFINITION

The registration of certification marks is dealt with by s.50 of the 1994 Act.[25] The section defines such marks in relation to both goods and services, whereas under the 1938 Act they were available only for goods. The mark should indicate "that the goods or services in connection with which it is used are certified by [its] proprietor ... in respect of origin, material, mode of manufacture of goods or performance of services, quality, accuracy or other characteristics".

12–017

GRANTING AUTHORITY

Unlike under the Trade Marks Acts 1905, 1919 and 1938, where certain powers were reserved to the Board of Trade (for example, under s.62 of the 1905 Act the Board was required to decide whether it was "to the public advantage" to grant such a mark), the Registrar is the person responsible for considering applications for certification marks under the 1994 Act. Indeed, the whole emphasis of the certification mark as a special mark has changed and most provisions of the Act apply, along with the additions set out in Sch.2.

12–018

REGISTRABLE TRADE MARK

A trade mark applied for under s.50 of the 1994 Act must be a registrable trade mark, in the sense of ss.1 and 3. Thus, in the application by the Legal Aid Board for registration of "Legal Aid" the Registrar concluded that the applicant had failed to provide evidence that the public recognised the sign "Legal Aid" as a mark which certifies some aspect of the performance of legal services or conciliation services. Whilst the Registrar acknowledged that the public recognised "Legal Aid" as the State Assisted Financial Aid Scheme, this was an entirely different matter from recognition as the Legal Aid Board's certification mark. It was therefore found that the sign did not qualify for registration under the proviso to

12–019

---

[23] Sch.1, para.13.
[24] Sch.1, para.14.
[25] In the 1938 Act it was dealt with in s.37, replacing the 1905 Act, s.62.

s.3(1). On appeal, Sir Andrew Morrit V.C., held that as the mark had acquired a distinctive character through use, and there was no reason not to infer that the public understood the nature of the scheme operated by the Board, the mark was capable of registration as a certification mark.[26]

PROPRIETOR MAY NOT USE

12–020   The effect of s.50 of the 1994 Act is generally to allow associations and traders to register trade marks to be applied to goods and services certified by them, provided that they do not carry on a business involving the supply of goods or services of the kind certified.[27] About a dozen applications to register such marks were made each year under the 1938 Act and it is unlikely that there will be significantly higher numbers under the 1994 Act, especially in view of the introduction of collective marks.

THE REGIME

12–021   Section 50, Sch.2 and para.19 of Sch.3 of the 1994 Act (which deals with marks already registered under s.37 of the 1938 Act) set out the provisions specific to marks of this character; Sch.2 of the 1994 Act and r.22 of the 2000 Rules deal with the procedure on application to register, and r.23 with amendment of the deposited regulations; as noted above, all other sections of the 1994 Act apply to certification marks.[28]

ASSIGNMENT, ETC.

12–022   Under Sch.2, para.12 of the 1994 Act, assignment and other transmission require the consent of the Registrar before they are effective.

PROCEEDINGS CONCERNING CERTIFICATION MARKS

12–023   There has been little litigation concerning certification trade marks. The only two cases under the 1938 Act were concerned with the registrability of the mark "Stilton" for cheese[29] (which turned on the ordinary question of distinctiveness of

---

[26] SRIS 0/056/00, Regy and *Re Legal Aid Board's Trade Mark Application*, October 3, 2000, unreported.

[27] Counsel for Marks & Spencer in the *Parma Ham* case [1991] R.P.C. 351, suggested that the Consorzio could have applied for registration of Parma Ham as a certification mark under s.37 of the 1938 Act, but Nourse L.J. declined to comment on this possibility, whilst noting that the action brought was in passing off: "there may be some disappointment amongst the consortium and its members at what they regard as the shortcomings of English law. While the court can fully understand such feelings, they cannot be allowed to affect its decision on the questions before it": at 367. See now, of course, the *Parma Ham* judgment of the ECJ [2004] E.T.M.R. 314 and Ch.12.

[28] The 1938 Act adopted the different route of providing a separate code for certification marks (in ss.37, 68 and the First Schedule), with many remaining sections of the Act not applying, *e.g.* s.4 on infringement.

[29] " *Stilton*" [1967] R.P.C. 173. *Union Nationale* (1922) 39 R.P.C. 346, CA was the decision under the 1905 Act, s.62 embodying many of the principles which were then expressly set forth in the 1938 Act, s.37.

the mark rather than upon any point peculiar to certification trade marks),[30] and an application to expunge the mark "SeaIsland Cotton".[31]

REGULATIONS

As with collective marks, an applicant for registration of a certification mark must file draft regulations governing use of the mark[32] within nine months of the date of the application for registration.[33]   **12–024**

The following basic requirements must be covered in the regulations: (1) who is authorised to use the mark; (2) the characteristics to be certified by the mark; (3) how the certifying body is to test those characteristics and supervise the use of the mark; (4) the fees (if any) to be paid in connection with the operation of the mark; and (5) the procedures for resolving disputes.[34]

It is a ground of refusal by the Registrar that the regulations are unsatisfactory,[35] and a ground for revocation that the regulations are not observed.[36] Registration of a certification mark will be refused unless the applicant is competent to certify the goods or services for which the mark is to be registered.[37]   **12–025**

REGISTRATION PROCESS

Provided the requirements for the regulations set out in Sch.2, para.7(1) of the 1994 Act are met, the mark proceeds to publication, opposition and registration as any "ordinary" mark, although observations may be made on whether the regulations comply with the requirements.[38] The regulations are open to public inspection.   **12–026**

5. Differences between collective and certification marks

Certain marks may be registered either as a collective or a certification mark (or as both although it is difficult to envisage circumstances where this might be done). However, only the certification mark is available where the applicant is connected with those who wish to use the mark only through the certification pro-   **12–027**

---

[30] Although, in the nature of a certification mark, the kind of distinctiveness required was rather different from that needed for an ordinary mark, *i.e.* merely that the name should denote a cheese having particular properties and also one where a particular method of manufacture in a particular region had been used. A possible s.11 objection was overcome on the ground that all persons who were permitted to use the mark were bound under the regulations to observe the conditions as to process and district.

[31] [1989] R.P.C. 87. The application was made on three main grounds: (1) the proprietors were no longer competent to certify; (2) there had been failures to observe the provisions of the regulations; and (3) the registration of the marks was no longer to the public advantage. The Board of Trade found that, whilst the proprietor had not been competent to certify for certain periods and there had been breaches which were not to the public advantage, it had not been shown that any member of the public had suffered and the marks were not expunged.

[32] 1994 Act, Sch.2, para.6(1). For an example of part of such regulations, see "Stilton" at para.12–023 and the notes therein.

[33] On Form TM35: 2000 Rules, r.22.

[34] 1994 Act, Sch.2, para.6(2).

[35] In *Legal Aid Certification Mark Application*, SRIS 0/056/00, the hearing officer considered the deficiencies of greatest concern to be the actual characteristics to be certified, the tests necessary to ensure compliance, and the measures for supervision and control by the proprietors of the mark.

[36] 1994 Act, Sch.2, para.15(c).

[37] 1994 Act, Sch.2, para.7(1)(b). This was one of the issues raised in the *"Sea Island Cotton"* case, see para.12–023.

[38] Sch.2, para.9.

cess;[39] whereas, the members of an association may use, or not, the collective mark to indicate membership (and indirectly compliance with the conditions for that membership).[40] The certification mark is more akin to a consumer protection measure than is the collective mark: this is highlighted by the definition of the former as a sign capable of "distinguishing goods or services *which are certified from those which are not*"(italics added). By comparison, the function of a collective mark is to indicate a trade connection between the goods or services of members of the association and to distinguish them from those of other undertakings.

12–028   A certification mark may not be registered as an "ordinary" trade mark: its purpose is different. On the other hand, a registered collective mark can also be registered as a trade mark: an example is the logo of The Chartered Institute of Patent Agents.

---

[39] Examples include the "Woolmark", owned by I.W.S. Nominee Services Ltd (presumably a company connected with the International Wool Secretariat), and the "Kite" mark, owned by the British Standards Institution.

[40] For example, "Chartered Patent Agent" has been registered as a collective mark by The Chartered Institute of Patent Agents, as has the Chartered Institute's logo (which, as noted in the text, is also registered as a trade mark). Also, "Fellow of ITMA" and "Member of ITMA" have been registered as collective marks by The Institute of Trade Mark Attorneys.

CHAPTER 13

ASSIGNMENTS, TRADE MARKS AS PROPERTY CO-OWNERSHIP AND LICENCES

1. Outline

SCOPE OF CHAPTER

This chapter concerns the types of assignments permitted in respect of registered **13–001** and unregistered trade marks, and the manner in which they may be implemented. It also covers the nature of trade marks as items of personal property, and the statutory provisions governing co-ownership. Finally, it deals with licensing of registered trade marks, including addressing the rights of licensees to bring proceedings. In relation to the procedural aspects of registering licences and assignments, and of the bringing of infringement proceedings by licensees, fuller details are given in Chs 3 and 19, although this chapter deals with the consequences of non-registration of assignments and licences.

A common consideration underlying most of the above matters is the extent to **13–002** which a proprietor may deal with his mark without rendering it deceptive. This is not an issue which is new to the Trade Marks Act 1994, or even to the 1938 Act. Indeed, it is an issue which is inherent in the nature of trade marks: given that their function, or at least a major part of their function, is to indicate the origin of goods or services, it will always be open to debate as to how direct or how tenuous the connection between the proprietor and the goods or services may be without the mark becoming more misleading than informative. To understand these issues, and to follow the scheme of the 1994 Act and the problems likely to be involved in its application to dealings with trade marks, it is necessary to begin with a look at the position under the old Acts.

INTRODUCTION — THE OLD LAW AND POLICY

The assignment of registered marks is governed by rules contained in the 1994 **13–003** Act. These do not apply to unregistered marks.[1] They are radically different from the provisions of the Trade Marks Act 1938, being much more permissive.

Before 1938,[2] the rules governing assignment of registered and unregistered **13–004** trade marks were much the same. The theory underlying the rules during that period was that the public regarded a trade mark as indicating that the goods bearing the mark emanated from a particular business exclusively, and that, if the link between the mark and the business was broken, it would be contrary to public policy to recognise the continuance of any exclusive right to the mark. Thus,

---

[1] s.24(6).

[2] An outline of the historical position, including the common law, and a contrast with the 1994 Act may be found in *Scandecor Development v Scandecor Marketing* (HL) [2002] F.S.R. 7. See paras 13–047 to 13–056 as to the position following *Scandecor*.

under the Acts before 1938 and at common law, a trade mark and the goodwill of the business concerned had to be assigned together.

13–005   The 1938 Act relaxed that strict position. It was, however, still a major feature of the policy of the 1938 Act to control the manner in which trade marks could be assigned. In particular, although it was possible under the 1938 Act to assign a registered trade mark without goodwill,[3] such transactions were closely policed by the Registrar.[4]

13–006   There were further complications where common law trade marks were assigned at the same time as registered marks; the 1938 Act purported to allow an assignment of a common law trade mark without goodwill in those circumstances,[5] but it was never clear how in fact the assignee could acquire useful rights if he did not obtain the goodwill associated with the mark.[6]

13–007   The 1938 Act also contained detailed provisions controlling the manner in which related marks for similar goods might be assigned, to seek to avoid the danger of deception of the public.[7] Provided that the assignor of a mark complied with the various provisions of the 1938 Act, he would obtain a degree of comfort from the Registrar that the assignment made would be valid.[8]

13–008   The 1938 Act also contained detailed and complex provisions concerning registered user agreements, whose purpose was to regulate situations in which a registered mark was held by its proprietor but used by some other party pursuant to contractual relations between them.[9]

Change in policy

13–009   The 1994 Act contains no express restrictive provisions as to assignment of the kind referred to above. The proprietor's rights of assignment in relation to registered marks are broad and general and expressly extend to assignments without goodwill.[10] However, there is no provision guaranteeing that a trade mark assigned in that way will remain valid, or that the assignment will be valid, and there is also no mechanism to reassure an assignor of one of a number of related marks that they will all remain valid following assignment. There is no method for seeking the Registrar's views as to the effect of an assignment. The power to grant licences is broad and general. Nonetheless, as a general rule, the effect of the 1994 Act is to "[free] the law of registered trade marks from the straitjacket imposed by the statutory definitions of a trade mark in the 1905 Act and the 1938 Act."[11]

13–010   Since the 1994 Act contains general provisions providing for the revocation of

---

[3] And, in some situations, an unregistered trade mark: see below.

[4] Trade Marks Act 1938, s.22(7).

[5] Under the 1938 Act, s.22(3).

[6] There is a fuller discussion of these issues in Ch.13 of the previous edition of this work.

[7] Trade Marks Act 1938, s.22(4)–(6).

[8] See, *e.g.* Trade Marks Act 1938, s.22(5).

[9] 1938 Act, s.28, which operated in doctrinal terms by deeming use by a registered user to be used by the proprietor himself. The Act did not contain a general power to grant licences, and the 1905 Act had not permitted licences at all; if a registered mark were used on goods which did not emanate from the proprietor then the mark would be deceptive, while if the goods did emanate from him, no licence would be necessary in the first place.

[10] 1994 Act, s.24(1).

[11] *Scandecor* (HL) [2002] F.S.R. 7 at para.40. The decision is discussed in more detail at paras 13–047 to 13–056.

marks which become deceptive by reason of the manner of their use,[12] it seems clear that its overall scheme is to leave trade mark owners, within broad limits, to organise their own affairs, including by assignments and licences, so as to protect and increase their value, but with the sanction against dealings which lead to deception of the public being the potential revocation of the marks. This overall approach was reflected in the White Paper leading to the 1994 Act,[13] and in the permissive terms of Article 8 of the Directive. The interaction of the assignment and revocation provisions of the 1994 Act is considered in more detail below.

2. Assignments

THE NEW LAW OF ASSIGNMENT, AND TRADE MARKS AS PROPERTY

The provision of the 1994 Act dealing with assignment generally is s.24(1), which provides:
    13–011

> "A registered trade mark is transmissible by assignment, testamentary disposition or operation of law in the same way as other personal or moveable property.
>
> It is so transmissible either in connection with the goodwill of a business or independently."

It should be borne in mind that when a registered mark is transmitted by will, or corporate merger or operation of law in some other way, the register will not automatically be updated, and the registered proprietor will remain the same until the transmitting event and new proprietor are registered. Since certain important acts have to be done by the *registered* proprietor, the mere fact that legal title has passed is not enough fully to protect the new owner. For example, a counterstatement to a revocation claim has to be filed by the registered proprietor, and where the registered proprietor has merged into another corporation and so ceased to exist, the filing of a counterstatement by the new corporation does not satisfy the rules and revocation is liable to be granted.[14]
    13–012

Section 24 must be read in conjunction with s.22, which provides that:
    13–013

> "A registered trade mark is personal property (in Scotland, incorporeal moveable property)."

By s.27 of the 1994 Act, an application for a registered trade mark is subject to the same provisions, is therefore itself personal property[15], and may be assigned in the same way.
    13–014

---

[12] s.46(1)(d). see Ch.10 at paras 10–116 to 10–130.

[13] At para.4.36 the White Paper stated that: "Whatever may have been the position in 1938, the public is now accustomed to goods and services being supplied under licence from the trade mark owner. For example there has been the growth of franchising operations. The potential for deception is therefore less. Moreover the strongest guarantee that a proprietor will maintain control over the way in which his trade mark is used is that it is in his own interest to do so. A trade mark is a valuable piece of property, in terms both of its power to attract customers and of the royalties which can be demanded from licensees. Its value is however ultimately dependent upon its reputation with the public. If the proprietor tolerates uncontrolled use of his trade mark the value of his property will be diminished. In an extreme case the registration of the mark may become liable to be revoked if it has become deceptive or generic through such use. It is however the responsibility of the proprietor, not the Registrar, to prevent the devaluation of his own property." This section of the White Paper was quoted in *Scandecor* at para.37, and formed a significant part of the reasoning.

[14] *CERNIVET Trade Mark* [2002] R.P.C. 30.

[15] So that, for example, an application does not "evaporate" if a company owning it is dissolved, but is dealt with as other personal property of such a company, and may become *bona vacantia*: *Joe Cool (Manchester) Ltd's Trade Mark Application* [2000] R.P.C. 926, Regy.

These provisions do not arise out of the TM Directive, which does not deal expressly with assignment of registered trade marks.

TYPES OF ASSIGNMENT

Assignment of the whole mark, or partial assignment

13–015   The simplest kind of assignment is one of the whole of a trade mark and all interests in it, but it is not the only possibility. The 1994 Act allows for partial assignments as well, which may be limited so as to apply to only some of the goods or services for which the mark is registered, or so as to apply to use of the mark in a particular manner or in a particular locality.[16]

13–016   These latter two possibilities—assignments which are partial as to manner of use or as to locality—are not easy to understand. In particular, it is difficult to see how they could be implemented without rendering the mark concerned deceptive. For example, if a trade mark owner assigned to another trader the rights in his registration, but only south of Watford, how could members of the public, travelling around the country, realistically be expected to identify the source of goods bearing the mark? And when the goods concerned were transported between the territories of the two traders, the same problem would arise. It is suggested that unless a mark had only a strong local following to begin with, or unless the two traders concerned took care to use other, different, trade marks in addition to the partially assigned mark, deception would be highly likely, if not inevitable. This difficulty has been made more acute by the decision of the house of Lords in *Scandecor*.[17] One of the major reasons why it was held that the marks in question had not become deceptive, and why marks the subjective of an exclusive licence generally will not do so, was that they had only been used by one trader at a time,[18] so that the marks indicated a single trade source, complying with the definition of "trade mark" in s.1 of the 1994 Act. This reasoning is not really capable of application to marks divided as to locality or manner of use, which at first sight, on the reasoning of *Scandecor*, will generally tend to be deceptive.

13–017   Similar difficulties arise in connection with assignments which are partial as to the manner of use of a trade mark (bearing in mind that "manner" of use must mean something different from use in relation to a particular type of goods). For example, suppose an assignment is made of a trade mark but only in relation to the right to import goods bearing the mark, with the original owner retaining the rights of advertisement, sale and so forth: how could the mark continue to function as an indication of the origin of the goods, without deception?

Assignments by way of security; charges

13–018   A registered trade mark may be assigned by way of security in the same manner as for assignments generally.[19] It may also be charged in the same way as any other moveable property.[20] Where an assignment by way of security is made, there is frequently a licence back to the assignor, although in such cases it is not uncommon for the issue of control of the (new) licensee's use by the (new) proprietor to be overlooked.

---

[16] s.24(2).
[17] (HL) [2002] F.S.R. 7, discussed in more detail at 10–116 to 10–130.
[18] Paras 36–44 of the decision.
[19] s.24(4).
[20] s.24(5).

Assignment to be in writing and signed

By s.24(3) of the 1994 Act, an assignment of a registered trade mark is not effective unless it is in writing signed by or on behalf of the assignor or, if applicable, a personal representative.

13–019

3. Registration of assignments and other transactions

By s.5 of the 1994 Act, assignments and licences of registered trade marks are registrable transactions, and details of them may be entered in the Register on application by the proprietor, any other person claiming to have an interest in the mark, or anyone affected by the transaction concerned.[21]

13–020

Registration is not compulsory and the validity of a transaction between the parties to it is not *per se* affected by non-registration. However, there are two important reasons to register.[22] First, registration protects a person acquiring an interest in a trade mark from another person acquiring a conflicting interest. Secondly, registration is necessary for a licensee or assignee to be able to sue and obtain full relief for infringement.

13–021

The effects of a failure to register a registrable transaction are set out in s.25(3) and (4) of the 1994 Act.

13–022

Subsections (3) and (4) each provide for consequences which flow in the absence of an application for registration of a registrable transaction. Once the person seeking to register his interest has made an application, it therefore seems that his interest is protected. If there is a short gap thereafter before his interest or application to register appears on the Register, the risk appears to fall on any others who may be affected. A person who intends to acquire an interest in a trade mark may wish to search the Register more than once to try to avoid the danger this presents.

Section 25(3)(a) of the 1994 Act is a general provision relating to all registrable transactions and provides that until an application for registration has been made, "the transaction is ineffective as against a person acquiring a conflicting interest in or under the registered trade mark in ignorance of it". It is clear from the context, and as a matter of common sense, that the "it" of which the person acquiring the conflicting interest is required to be ignorant is the transaction, not the registered trade mark in question.

13–023

It is to be noted that the effect of s.25(3)(a) is to render the first transaction ineffective as against the later acquirer of an interest. It does not render the transaction ineffective generally. Further, it is only against a person later acquiring a

13–024

---

[21] See s.25(1) and (2). Full details of the procedure for registering such a transaction, and the matters to be registered are given Ch.3.

[22] A more minor reason is to give protection against the surrender by the proprietor of the mark.

conflicting interest that the earlier transaction is ineffective, and this may leave room for uncertainty.

13–025   Some later transactions will plainly confer a "conflicting" interest on the person concerned. If A assigns his mark to B, who fails to register, and then purports also to assign it to C, who is ignorant of the assignment to B, then the interest of C plainly conflicts with that of B.[23] Similarly, one would expect that if in the same situation C were granted an exclusive licence, that interest would conflict with B's, since B would not be able to use the trade mark himself were C's rights valid; presumably the consequence would be that as against C, B could not assert his title to the registered trade mark.[24]

13–026   However, what if merely a non-exclusive licence were granted to C? It is unclear whether that would be an interest conflicting with the interest of B, since it would not prevent B from exercising any of his rights under the registration. If it were not a conflicting interest, then B would seem to be able to assert his assignment from A, and thereby avoid the licence to C. Since this would be an unjust result for C, who may well have given valuable consideration to A, and since the situation would be the fault of B because of his failure to register, it is suggested that even a non-exclusive licence should be regarded as a potentially conflicting interest, on the basis that at the very least it deprives B of the ability to sue C under his registration.

13–027   Section 25(3) does not appear to be limited to the case where the person acquiring the potentially conflicting interest has given value for it. It is to be presumed that this omission was deliberate, and it would therefore seem that the section applies in cases where an interest has been granted by way of gift, or because a third party has provided value to procure its grant. It is also not an express requirement of s.25(3) that the person acquiring the potentially conflicting interest has acted in good faith, although it seems rather unlikely that such a person would act in bad faith *vis-à-vis* the person seeking to acquire an interest under an earlier unregistered transaction yet not (as the section does require) have knowledge of the earlier transaction.

NON-REGISTRATION OF TRANSACTIONS CONFERRING A LICENCE

13–028   Licences under registered trade marks are dealt with in more detail below, but it is convenient to deal here with the effect of a failure to register them.

Section 25(3)(b) of the 1994 Act is a provision dealing specifically with the effect of a failure to register a transaction conferring a licence. The person claiming to have become a licensee (whether exclusive or non-exclusive) does not obtain the rights relating to infringement provided by s.30 or 31 (as the case may be)[25] until an application is made to register the transaction in question. This may affect relations between that person and the proprietor, as well as the rights of that

---

[23] What would follow thereafter is unclear; one view is that since the assignment to B is ineffective as against C, C obtains title to the registered mark. However, this is not spelt out in the section as explicitly as one might expect were it to be the correct analysis, and it seems surprising that A can execute a good assignment to C at all, since he has lost anything to assign by virtue of his transaction with B. Nonetheless, it is suggested that the better view is that C becomes owner.

[24] How this would work in practice is very unclear, however, since as between A and B, B would be the owner of the mark, and could obtain registration (albeit subject to C's interest), although there would be no privity of contract between B and C so as to regulate the exclusive licence.

[25] The rights provided by ss.30 and 31 are set out in more detail below at paras 13–080 to 13–085.

person against infringers, since a licensee may frequently have the right to call upon the proprietor to bring infringement proceedings.[26]

EFFECT OF NON-REGISTRATION ON RIGHT TO FINANCIAL RELIEF

As is explained in Ch.18, both a licensee and a proprietor of a registered mark may obtain damages or an account of profits if successful in an infringement action. But as a result of s.25(4) of the 1994 Act the right to obtain financial relief generally depends on an application having been made to register the assignment or agreement whereby such a party obtained his interest. **13–029**

In general, s.25(4) has the effect that a failure to register that transaction will deprive the party concerned of the right to financial relief in respect of acts of infringement committed before the registration of the transaction (and if the transaction has not been registered at all, then no financial relief at all will be available). There are, however, two exceptions. **13–030**

First, there is a six month grace period. Provided an application for the registration of the transaction is made within that period from its date, full financial relief will be available under s.25(4)(a). Further, the grace period is extended by s.25(4)(b) if it was not practicable to apply for registration before the end of it, and provided that an application was made as soon as practicable. **13–031**

Section 25(4) is very similar in its structure and expression to s.68 of the Patents Act 1977, and it is suggested that authorities in relation to that provision will be relevant to the application of s.25(4). **13–032**

TRUSTS AND EQUITIES

By s.26(1) of the 1994 Act, no notice of any trust is to be entered on the Register, and the Registrar is not affected by trusts, even if notified of them. This does not prevent a trust being created and, as between the parties to it, enforced, but only their legal interests will be entered on the Register. **13–033**

APPLICATIONS AS OBJECTS OF PROPERTY

By s.27 of the 1994 Act, the provisions of ss.22–26 are applicable (with the necessary modifications set out in ss.27(2) and (3)) to applications for registration in the same way as to registered trade marks. As a result, applications for registration are also to be regarded as objects of property, and dealings in them should be registered in the same way as dealings in registered trade marks. **13–034**

4. Assignments without goodwill

MEANING OF GOODWILL

The meaning of goodwill is dealt with in detail in Ch.15. However, it is necessary to consider it to some extent here, since it is important to an understanding of the difficulties attendant on an assignment of a registered trade mark without goodwill. **13–035**

However, before embarking on a consideration of whether and how trade marks may be assigned without goodwill, it is worth appreciating that the vast majority of trade mark assignments include the transfer of goodwill. There is **13–036**

---

[26] Under s.30(2).

usually a specific reason if goodwill is omitted: frequently taxation, or price. Sometimes goodwill is separated from the connected trade mark by their being held by different companies within a group, causing no difficulty while they are in the same ultimate ownership, but giving rise to problems if they later become split.[27] The point to be appreciated in such situations is that even if there is a specific reason for not assigning the goodwill, it needs to be weighed against the possibly considerable risk that the mark in question will be rendered void or unenforceable as a result. Furthermore, if the goodwill is simply left to atrophy in the hands of the assignor of the trade mark, the assignee is likely, in practical terms, to gain the benefit of it. If that is so, it is likely to be preferable to assign it in a formal sense as well.

13–037   The nature of goodwill has been many times stated but has not been categorically defined. Its definition is complicated by the fact that to different people in different contexts it means different things. An accountant valuing a company's assets, for example, has a different view of goodwill than a trade mark lawyer. To the former, goodwill includes more or less anything intangible which brings in business, whether it arises from a distinctive trade mark, get-up, etc., or otherwise. To the latter, it is a much narrower notion. Goodwill also falls to be considered in the law of landlord and tenant, and of taxation.[28]

13–038   In the context of trade mark law, goodwill has been stated to represent, in connection with a business or business product, the value of the attraction to customers which the name and reputation possesses.[29] The matter was considered in *IRC v Muller's Margarine*,[30] where Lord Macnaghten said:

> "It [goodwill] is a thing very easy to describe, very difficult to define. It is the benefit and advantage of the good name, reputation and connection of a business. It is the attractive force which brings in custom. It is the one thing which distinguishes an old-established business from a new business at its first start. The goodwill of a business must emanate from a particular centre or source. However widely extended or diffused its influence may be, goodwill is worth nothing unless it has power of attraction sufficient to bring customers home to the source from which it emanates. Goodwill is composed of a variety of elements. It differs in its composition in different trades and in different businesses in the same trade. One element may preponderate here and another element there ... For my part, I think that if there is one element common to all cases of goodwill it is the attribute of locality. For goodwill has no independent existence. It cannot subsist by itself. It must be attached to a business. Destroy the business and the goodwill perishes with it, though elements remain which may perhaps be gathered up and revived again. No doubt, where the reputation of a business is very widely spread, or where it is the article produced rather than the producer of the article that has won popular favour, it may be difficult to lo-

---

[27] As, *e.g.* happened in *Scandecor Development v Scandecor Marketing* [2002] F.S.R. 7.

[28] See, *e.g. Whiteman Smith Motor Company v Chaplin* [1934] 2 K.B. 35, *IRC v Muller and Co's Margarine* [1901] A.C. 217. In the former case, the Court of Appeal considered a number of types of customers, including "cats", who continue to frequent a business after a change of ownership because of their attachment to the premises and relative indifference to the identity of the proprietor, and "dogs", who will continue to patronise the former proprietor elsewhere. The former are not the concern of the law of passing off, while the latter are. The law of landlord and tenant has regard to both.

[29] *Reuter v Mulhens (No.2)* (1953) 70 R.P.C. 235 at 254.

[30] [1901] A.C. 217 at 223.

calise the goodwill. But here, I think there is no difficulty ... Moreover, under the Stamp Act 1891, we are not required to define the local situation of the goodwill. We have only to determine whether it is or is not situate out of the United Kingdom."

Lord Lindley said:

13–039

"Goodwill regarded as property has no meaning except in connection with some trade, business or calling. In that connection I understand the word to include whatever adds value to a business by reason of situation, name and reputation, connection, introduction to old customers, and agreed absence from competition, or any of these things, and there may be others which do not occur to me. In this wide sense, goodwill is inseparable from the business to which it adds value, and, in my opinion, exists where the business is carried on. Such business may be carried on in one place or country or in several, and if in several there may be several businesses, each having a goodwill of its own."[31]

However difficult to identify, English goodwill appears to be a species of English personal property capable of being sold or charged or of being bequeathed by will.[32]

13–040

The proprietor of a mark may have a goodwill in England without having a place of business in England, but there must be a business in England.[33]

13–041

A vendor who sells the goodwill of his business may not afterwards destroy the goodwill which he has sold by soliciting his former customers.[34]

ASSIGNMENTS WITHOUT GOODWILL ARE PERMITTED

As is noted above,[35] assignments of registered trade marks, with or without goodwill, are permitted expressly by s.24 of the 1994 Act, and no special formalities are required to achieve them.[36] The important question, however, is whether and to what extent they can be achieved without rendering the mark in question liable to revocation under s.46.

13–042

RELATIONSHIP OF SECTION 24 TO SECTION 46: MARKS WHICH BECOME DECEPTIVE

Section 46(1)(d) of the 1994 Act provides that the registration of a trade mark may be revoked on the ground that:

13–043

"in consequence of the use made of it by the proprietor or with his consent in relation to the goods or services for which it is registered, it is liable to mislead the public, particularly as to the nature, quality or geographical origin of those goods or services."

---

[31] This passage was quoted by Byrne J. in *Rickersby v Reay* (1903) 20 R.P.C. 380 and by Romer L.J. in *Reuter v Mulhens* (1953) 70 R.P.C. 235 at 237, who found that goodwill had locality.

[32] *Reuter v Mulhens* (1953) 70 R.P.C. 235 at 254 *per* Evershed M.R.; *Adrema-Werke v Custodian of Enemy Property* [1957] R.P.C. 49 at 54.

[33] See *Star Industrial v Yap Kwee Kor* [1976] F.S.R. 256 (PC, Singapore); *"Advocaat"* [1980] R.P.C. 31 at 105, HL, *per* Lord Fraser. As to the question of foreign businesses with a reputation in the UK but no goodwill, see Ch.14.

[34] *Trego v Hunt* [1896] A.C. 7 and cases cited by Danckwerts J. in *Reuter v Mulhens (No.2)* (1953) 70 R.P.C. 102 at 121, and approved in CA.

[35] See para.13–011.

[36] Moreover, the 1994 Act does not contain the express provision against "trafficking"— *i.e.* dealing in the right to use a registered mark as a commodity in itself without its connoting a true connection in the course of trade—which was found in the 1938 Act, s.28(6), as to which see *"Holly Hobbie"* [1984] F.S.R. 199, HL.

13–044   The section focuses on the nature of use by or with the consent of the proprietor; on its face it would not seem that a danger of misleading the public which arises from some other factor would leave a mark liable to be revoked.

13–045   The important question which requires an answer is how far the permissive nature of s.24 can be pressed before the tension with s.46 becomes unbearable. Take an extreme example: Trader A has a business which he conducts under a registered trade mark. By reason of his use, he has acquired a goodwill in relation to the business conducted under the mark. A sells his registered mark to B. The agreement between A and B requires that A ceases to use the mark, which he does, but it leaves the goodwill with A and permits him to carry on business as before, selling the same goods to the same customers, which he also does. B begins to use the mark in the course of a new business, on goods covered by the registration, but which are different in quality to the goods of A, and which have no connection with A in any way.

13–046   What makes this an extreme example is A's continuing trade under a different mark while retaining the goodwill of the old, and the lack of connection of B's new business with A. However, one cannot avoid the conclusion that the public are liable to be misled; they are likely to get the mistaken impression that B's goods are the same as those formerly acquired from A, or are at least from the same trade source. Yet not only are the goods not the same, or from the same trade source, but they are actually still available from A. It is difficult to resist the conclusion that the registration of the mark is liable to be revoked. Yet the transaction between A and B which caused the problem does not on its face in any way offend the provisions of the 1994 Act concerning assignment. It was merely an assignment of a registered trade mark without goodwill, a thing expressly permitted. The issues raised by this kind of situation were analysed, to some extent at least, by the House of Lords in *Scandecor*.

THE DECISION OF THE HOUSE OF LORDS IN *SCANDECOR*

13–047   In *Scandecor Development v Scandecor Marketing*,[37] two Scandinavian partners began a successful business in posters, which operated throughout Europe and elsewhere through local subsidiaries, including one in the United Kingdom. The partners fell out and divided areas of the business among themselves. For a period of time the United Kingdom subsidiary controlled distribution in the United Kingdom, being an exclusive distributor of the parent company's products, and selling its own range of calendars, prints and frames. The mark in question, "Scandecor", was known to the trade, but not to the public.

In due course relations between the parties broke down altogether, and the parent company, which owned the relevant registrations, sued for infringement, and for passing off. The United Kingdom subsidiary, now no longer under the ownership of the parent, counterclaimed to revoke the marks and for passing off.

13–048   At first instance, the court held that although the parent company did not control the products of its former subsidiary, there was "a fairly general recognition" that the products emanated from Scandinavia. It also held that the parent owned the goodwill in relation to posters, and that the goodwill in relation to calendars and the like, generated by the trade of the United Kingdom subsidiary, was shared between it and the parent because of a misconception on the part of

---

[37] [1998] F.S.R. 500, [1999] F.S.R. 26 CA and [2002] F.S.R. 7 (HL).

customers that they came from the same source as the posters. Although there was confusion about the source of the goods, which could be relevant deception for the purposes of s.46, "indication of origin" in that section was not limited to an indication that the proprietor produced the goods. The relationship between the parent and the subsidiary constituted a sufficient connection.

The Court of Appeal overturned the decision, holding that the judge had erred **13–049** in finding that the parent could have a share in the goodwill as a result of an assumed and incorrect connection between the goods and the parent. It found that the subsidiary owned the relevant goodwill by reason of its having conducted the actual trade in the United Kingdom. The parent's counsel had conceded[38] that on that basis, the registered marks concerned had to be revoked under s.46, by reason of their being no longer distinctive. This concession appears to have been accepted without demur by the Court of Appeal which as a result did not hear full argument on the point and were not, it seems, directed to s.24.

The House of Lords reversed most of the reasoning of the Court of Appeal in **13–050** relation to issue of whether the registered marks had become deceptive under s.46, but adjourned a final decision pending a reference to the European Court of Justice. The nub of its reasoning was that the 1994 Act was intended to be highly permissive in relation to assignments, that the public have become used to marks being used under licences, even bare licences (so that they are no longer inherently deceptive, even if they were previously), and that provided a mark is used by only one trader at a time, it serves the proper function of a trade mark, and is not deceptive.

Somewhat similar hypothetical situations to those identified in para.13–045 **13–051** were also considered by the House of Lords in *Scandecor*,[39] where it was held that provided only one trader was carrying on use of a mark formerly owned by another, even in connection with another business, the mark would remain distinctive, and the "change in the source [of the goods] is not inherently deceptive. Such a change occurs whenever a trade mark changes hands." With respect, for reasons given below,[40] the change is deceptive, at least for a while, because the public will believe they are getting the same goods from the same source. This part of the decision in *Scandecor* may be better understood as being to the effect that such deception is not of a relevant kind, and will be excused by the courts so as to promote the objective of the assignment provisions of s.24 of the 1994 Act.

Other examples may be much less difficult in any event. If A has never used **13–052** the mark, or only barely used it, so that it has no, or only negligible, goodwill, then an assignment may be much less likely to cause the public to be misled. Similarly, the problems may be much less acute or enduring if A ceases his former trade upon assignment to B.[41] But dwelling on cases where the assignor has no goodwill does not really help to understand the relationship between ss.24 and 46. The basic problem arises not because the assignee does not acquire any

---

[38] Recorded at 45.

[39] [1998] F.S.R. 500, [1999] F.S.R. 26 CA and [2002] F.S.R. 7, at paras 42–44. The situations posited were of (a) a bare exclusive licence which terminated, with the trade reverting to the licensor and the former licensee ceasing trading, and (b) the same situation, but with the former licensee carrying on the same business under a different mark.

[40] para.13–052.

[41] Analogous to the first situation considered in *Scandecor* [1998] F.S.R. 500, [1999] F.S.R. 26 CA and [2002] F.S.R. 7.

goodwill in connection with the mark, but rather because the assignor keeps such goodwill.

13–053　　At one level, all transmissions of a trade mark, even with goodwill, are liable to mislead customers, at least for a while. If the founder of a family business retires, leaving it to his children, who already work in it, there may be some customers who will continue to patronise the business under the mistaken impression that the founder is still involved. However, this kind of false impression has never been an objection to an action in passing off[42] or to the registration of a trade mark. It is inevitable, and not regarded as damaging or contrary to the interests of the public or the policy of the law. Any difficulty which it presents is much outweighed by the desirability that a valuable asset such as goodwill be alienable in the right circumstances, and by the fact that the continuing use of a mark in such circumstances conveys far more accurate information (that the goods are from essentially the same source) than inaccurate information. This is the effect of the decision reached in *Scandecor*, as explained above.

13–054　　Moreover, it must be recognised that the conditions of modern commerce are far different from those prevailing when the earlier trade mark Acts (even the 1938 Act) were implemented.[43] Businesses are much larger, and the mobility of labour is much greater. Well-known trade marks rarely connote the involvement of a particular individual in the production of the goods concerned (no one imagines that there is a Mr Levi Strauss making jeans, for example), and there is a much greater public awareness that trade marks pass with the sale of businesses and are widely licensed.

13–055　　The result, it is suggested, is that the courts will have to continue to strike a balance in seeking to reconcile ss.24 and 46 of the 1994 Act. If any element of public deception leads to a mark becoming vulnerable to revocation, then s.24 will be deprived of meaning, while a reading of s.24 to the effect that any assignment of a mark is permitted without goodwill whatever the effect would be to promote unnecessary deception of the public, which it is the policy of the Act and the TM Directive to avoid. It is further suggested that transitory public confusion in the period immediately after the assignment of a mark ought to be accepted as inevitable, and merely part of the price for allowing assignment at all. This was the course taken by the House of Lords in *Scandecor*, as explained above, which gives greater weight to the policy of s.24 than of s.46. But *Scandecor* dealt with only a limited category of situations. Its reasoning[44] is confined to bare, exclusive licences. It did not deal at all with what one would expect to be permissible situations of multiple users of a trade mark (multiple non-exclusive licensees with quality control provisions in their licences), although one would expect that by extension of its reasoning, at least situations of multiple non-exclusive licences without quality control, would be at risk under s.46.

13–056　　A similar difficulty had to be grappled with under the 1938 Act, in connection with registered user agreements, licences, and the use of foreign proprietors' marks by domestic distributors in the absence of control generally. The cases were never entirely consistent, and it was hard to discern hard and fast rules as to

---

[42] On the contrary, it may well be passing off for a vendor of a business falsely to represent that he continues to have an involvement in it (see Ch.14), although to advertise his former connection is generally lawful (see, *e.g. Harrods v Schwartz-Sackin* [1986] F.S.R. 490).

[43] As the White Paper recognised, in the passage quoted in para.13–010, and in *Scandecor*.

[44] See para.36.

the connection in the course of trade which was required between the proprietor of a mark and the goods of his licensee in order to avoid the mark becoming deceptive.[45]

"UNDERTAKINGS"

An important issue left unresolved by *Scandecor*, and the subject of one of the questions referred to the European Court of Justice by the House of Lords, is what is meant by "an undertaking" in Art.2 of the Trade Marks Directive. The reason the question is important is that if "undertaking" has a broad meaning, so as to embrace, for example, a group of companies which present a single face to the world, then transactions between companies in that group will be far less likely to result in a mark being deceptive, because the mark will indeed always designate the goods of that "undertaking". On the other hand, if "undertaking" means a single legal entity, then intra-group transactions will continue to present greater problems.[46]

13–057

MARKS WHICH INHERENTLY DENOTE THE PROPRIETOR

A further series of questions which has been referred to the European Court of Justice relates to marks which inherently denote a connection with the (original) proprietor. The well-known dress designer Elizabeth Emanuel assigned a mark which consisted primarily of her name, along with the business concerned. The issue then arose of whether it became deceptive when she ceased to be involved with the business. The Appointed Person referred the issue to the European Court of Justice.[47] Although there is the risk of a somewhat elevated level of confusion in the wake of a sale of such a mark with its associated business, a decision that it is such as to render the mark invalid will mean that such marks will be effectively be incapable of assignment, which will be to the disadvantage of the proprietor as well as the purchaser. It is also hard to see how, if such a mark becomes invalid by assignment, it does not also become invalid on, *e.g.* the retirement of the individual denoted by the mark.

13–058

5. Unregistered trade marks

ASSIGNMENTS OF UNREGISTERED TRADE MARKS

Title to a trade mark could not at common law be assigned, and nor could it devolve in gross;[48] but unless the mark connoted a personal connection between its original owner and the goods in connection with which it was used, it could be assigned and transmitted, together with the goodwill of the business in such goods.

13–059

Until it was established that there could be property in a trade mark there could,

13–060

---

[45] Contrast *Bowden Brake v Bowden Wire* (1913) 30 R.P.C. 561 HL, on the one hand with *"Manus"* (1949) 66 R.P.C. 71, CA, and *"Bostitch"* [1963] R.P.C. 183 on the other. The House of Lords in *Scandecor* approved the corresponding paragraph of the last edition of this work, at para.31.

[46] *Scandecor*, paras 50–53.

[47] *Elizabeth Emmanuel's Application*, Appointed Person (David Kitchin Q.C.), decision O/017/04, January 17, 2004.

[48] See, *e.g. Pinto v Badman* (1891) 8 R.P.C. 181; *Thorneloe v Hill* [1894] 1 Ch. 569; *Ullman v Leuba* (1908) 25 R.P.C. 673.

of course, be no question of the assignment of trade mark rights,[49] although the successors of the original founders of a business no doubt took over and continued to use the old trade marks employed in it, and were protected when other traders sought to pass-off their goods as the goods of the lawful users of the marks.[50] But as soon as trade marks were recognised as the subjects of property, it followed that they were alienable, subject always to this, that the property was lost if the marks became deceptive.

TRANSFER BY IMPLICATION WITH GOODWILL

13–061 Conversely, it was held that the sale and transfer of the goodwill of a business assigned the trade marks used in the business to the purchaser and transferee by implication, and without any express grant being needed.[51] This is still the law.[52] It is a question of interpretation, to be gathered from the assignment as a whole, whether the trade marks do or do not pass, and an intention not to assign them may appear, notwithstanding the use of the word "goodwill" in the assignment.[53]

A difficult question of fact may arise, whether in particular circumstances a person has purchased the right to represent that he is the successor in business of another.[54]

ASSIGNMENT OF PART OF BUSINESS

13–062 There is no clear authority as to how far, at common law, a business might be split up and parts assigned separately with the relevant trade marks. The history of the "Sunbeam" trade mark[55] is an example of such a division having taken place, and the propriety of the transaction was not the subject of any criticism by the courts. Doubts have been expressed whether the rule in regard to assignments is as restrictive as a literal construction of the words of Fry L.J. in *Pinto v Badman*[56] might suggest. In *Sinclair*,[57] both Maugham J. (at 129) and Lawrence L.J. (at 139) were careful to avoid expressing an opinion that an assignment of part of a business with the relevant trade mark could not be valid at common law.

---

[49] See *per* Fry L.J. in *Pinto v Badman* (1891) 8 R.P.C. 181 at 194, quoting from *Leather Cloth v American Leather Cloth* (1863) 4 De. G.J.&S. 137.

[50] See, for instance, *Webster v Webster* (1791) 3 Swan 490, *per* Thurlow L.C., and *Motley v Downman* (1837) 3 My. & Cr. 1; 6 L.J. Ch. (NS) 308.

[51] *Shipwright v Clements* (1871) 19 W.R. 599; referred to in *Sinclair* (1932) 49 R.P.C. 123. See also *Currie v Currie* (1898) 15 R.P.C. 339, where goodwill was held to pass and therefore the trade marks.

[52] "He who sells the cow doubtless may reserve for himself the contractual right to sup the milk; but in the absence of any such agreement I should be slow indeed to hold that a foreign company was free to use a trade mark in competition in this country with the subsidiary company which it itself had created and then sold to the purchaser": *per* Megarry J. in *"Weston"* [1968] R.P.C. 167 at 183.

[53] *Roger* (1895) 12 R.P.C. 149.

[54] See *Rickersby v Reay* (1903) 20 R.P.C. 380. See also *Currie v Currie* (1898) 15 R.P.C. 339, where on dissolution of a partnership without any deed or formal agreement, one partner bought the share of the other partner in the assets, and these were held to include the goodwill and therefore the trade marks. In *Wood v Hall* (1916) 33 R.P.C. 16, it was contended that an assignment of particular brands and goodwill on the construction of the agreement comprised only the goodwill in the trade under the brands, but this contention failed.

[55] (1916) 33 R.P.C. 389.

[56] (1891) 8 R.P.C. 181 at 194–195: "The brand is an indication of origin...It can be assigned...when the origin is assigned with it. It cannot be assigned when it is divorced from its place of origin, or when, in the hands of the transferee, it would indicate something different to what it indicated in the hands of the transferor."

[57] (1932) 49 R.P.C. 123.

6. Co-ownership

Nature of co-ownership; co-proprietors' rights *inter se*

Co-ownership of registered trade marks is governed by s.23 of the 1994 Act, which is modelled on s.36 of the Patents Act 1977. Section 23(1) provides that where a mark is granted to two or more persons jointly, each is entitled to an equal undivided share in it, although they may modify that arrangement by agreement. There does not appear to be any limit to the number of co-proprietors permitted. **13–063**

Co-proprietors are entitled to use the trade mark for their own benefit, and they may do so without the permission of the other co-proprietor(s) and without accounting to them (s.23(3)). This extremely liberal provision may not be without its perils, however. Co-proprietors who each independently use the same mark on different goods without reference to one another must be at risk of rendering the mark deceptive and liable to revocation under s.46, for reasons similar to those discussed above in relation to assignments. **13–064**

Co-proprietors may not grant a licence under the trade mark, or assign or charge their share in it, without permission of the other co-proprietor(s).[58] This may in practical terms make it unlikely that ownership of a registered mark will pass into the hands of different parties who later use it without reference to one another, since an assignment or licence made in circumstances in which the formal consent of a number of parties is required is likely to be accompanied by contractual provisions as to the later use of the mark. **13–065**

Any co-proprietor may bring infringement proceedings, but all the co-proprietors must be joined as parties, by being added either as a claimant or defendant[59] (the purpose of their joinder being, of course, to ensure that they are bound by the decision and thus to prevent the defendant being sued more than once). A co-proprietor joined as defendant in those circumstances is not liable for costs. Interim relief can be sought by a single co-proprietor without joining the others at that stage.[60] **13–066**

Transitional arrangements as to co-ownership

The 1938 Act had a different scheme for shared ownership of registered trade marks, which was governed by the rather obscure s.63. That section did have the major advantage, however, that registration as joint proprietors was only permitted where the relations between the parties (presumably usually by contract or partnership) was such that each could only use the mark on behalf of all of them, in relation to goods with which they were all connected in the course of trade. Thus, the danger of deceptive use was greatly limited. **13–067**

Schedule 3 of para.7 of the 1994 Act governs the transition from s.63 of the 1938 Act to the new s.23. Paragraph 7 provides that so long as the arrangements between the parties remain of the kind described in s.63 of the 1938 Act (use by one on behalf of all, use only on goods with which all are connected), then the provisions of s.23(1) and (3), providing for ownership in undivided shares and permitting independent use, will not bite. Otherwise, s.23 takes effect as from the **13–068**

---

[58] 1994 Act, s.23(4).
[59] s.23(5).
[60] s.23(5).

commencement of the 1994 Act in relation to all existing registered trade marks in respect of which multiple proprietors were entered in the Register immediately before commencement.

13–069   What para.7 therefore means, in practical terms, is that the liberal provisions of s.23(1) and (3) will come into effect either when existing co-proprietors agree that they should and alter the arrangements between themselves to achieve that result, or when the arrangements between them are unilaterally changed by one or more of them without the agreement of the others, should that be possible.

7. Licensing of registered trade marks

OUTLINE OF THE LAW

13–070   Unlike the sections of the 1994 Act concerning assignments, its provisions concerning licences arise directly from Article 8 of the TM Directive.

Article 8(1) provides specifically that licences may be exclusive or non-exclusive, may relate to some or all of the goods or services for which the mark concerned is registered, and may be for all or part of the Member State to which the registration relates. These provisions are closely echoed in ss.28–30 of the 1994 Act, which also permit licences to be partial as to the manner of use of the mark.[61],[62]

13–071   Article 8(2) provides that the registered proprietor may sue for infringement a licensee who contravenes provisions of his licence as to duration, form in which the mark is used, the goods or services licensed, territory, or quality. No equivalent express provision is to be found in the 1994 Act, and it is most unclear how or whether its infringement provisions achieve the result intended by Art.8(2).

TYPES OF LICENCE, AND THEIR INCIDENTS

13–072   There are thus two main types of licence: exclusive and non-exclusive. In addition, either kind may be partial, covering only part of the scope of the registration.

These types of licence are provided for by s.28(1) of the 1994 Act. Section 28 also provides for the formalities of granting a licence (it is required to be in writing signed by or on behalf of the grantor: s.28(2)) and for sub-licences (which may be granted if the licence so provides: s.28(4)).

13–073   The additional significance of an exclusive licence is provided for in s.29.

The section defines an exclusive licence as being one which authorises the licensee to use the mark, as permitted by the exclusive licence, to the exclusion of all other persons, including the person granting the licence. Because of the reference to "the person granting the licence" and the provisions of s.28(4) as to sub-licences, it is clear that an exclusive licensee can grant an exclusive sub-licence (provided that his licence allows sub-licensing). Section 29(1) also makes it clear that an exclusive licence may be partial in just the same manner(s) as a non-exclusive licence.

13–074   In addition to the exclusive nature of his interest, and no doubt as a reflection of it, an exclusive licensee generally has greater rights in relation to infringers than does a non-exclusive licensee. This is discussed below.

---

[61] By s.28(1)(a).
[62] By s.28(1)(a).

The nature of a licence under the 1994 Act was held in *Northern & Shell v* **13–075**
Condé Nast [1995] R.P.C. 117 to be a bare permission to use the mark, not conferring on the licensee any proprietary right. By reason of that finding and by reason
of the manner in which ss.9 and 10 of the 1994 Act are phrased, it was further
held that a licensee cannot sue a person who has the consent of the proprietor for
their use of the trade mark. The remedy of a licensee in that situation lies, if at all,
in contract. It should be noted, however, that the decision in that case was based
on the construction of s.30 of the 1994 Act and the transitional provisions relating to it; the court did not refer expressly to s.31 (and its decision on the 1994 Act
was in any event obiter, since it had held that the defendant's acts were not an infringement under the 1938 Act, which continued to apply because of the
transitional provisions of the 1994 Act concerning continuing acts begun before
commencement). Section 31(1) of the 1994 Act provides that in relation to an
exclusive licence, the parties may provide that the licensee is to have "the same
rights and remedies ... as if the licence had been an assignment". Although the
second part of that subsection makes it clear that the proprietor still cannot be
sued for infringement by the exclusive licensee, and although subs.(2) stipulates
that the rights and remedies enjoyed are concurrent with those of the proprietor,
the subsection still seems to leave open the argument that the nature of the interest enjoyed by an exclusive licensee is more than a bare permission.[63]

BINDING ON SUCCESSORS (SUBJECT TO SECTION 25)

Under s.28(3) of the 1994 Act, licences are binding on a successor to the grantor's **13–076**
interest (and references to the consent of the proprietor elsewhere in the Act must
be construed accordingly, *i.e.* to refer to the consent of the proprietor or, in the
case of a licence, the predecessor who granted the licence).

At first sight, s.28(3) might be thought inconsistent with s.25, which, as is **13–077**
explained above, provides that licences, being registrable transactions, do not
bind unknowing parties to later inconsistent dealings unless an application for
registration has been made.[64] In fact, there is no inconsistency. Section 28 states
the general rule that successors are bound. It is necessary that there should be
such a provision, because there is of course usually no privity of contract between the grantee of the licence and the grantor's successor. However, s.25 has
the effect that s.28 will only bite when an application for registration of the licence
has been made (or when the successor has knowledge of the licence). Purchasers
of the grantor's interest without knowledge of the licence will not be bound in the
absence of an application for registration.[65]

By s.29(2), an exclusive licensee has "the same rights against a successor in **13–078**
title who is bound by the licence as he has against the person granting the
licence". It is most unclear what this adds to s.28(3), or indeed what the "rights"
referred to are, since the licensee's statutory rights appear to be transferred by
s.28(3) in any event, and the words used do not seem apt to describe contractual
rights. Nor, in general can the "rights" referred to be rights to bring infringement
proceedings against a successor, since even where an exclusive licensee has a

---

[63] It might be said that s.31(1) merely confers rights and remedies on the exclusive licensee in order
to found his ability to bring proceedings in his own name, but it is hard to see why s.31(1) need
have been in the form adopted for it merely in order to achieve that result.

[64] See para.13–027.

[65] Depending on the meaning of "conflicting interest" in s.25(3), which is considered in para.13–
026.

right to sue for infringement in his own name under s.31, he cannot sue the proprietor. It may be that the effect of s.29(2) is to allow an exclusive licensee to sue a successor to a grantor of an exclusive licence which grantor was not himself the proprietor but only an exclusive licensee himself, but why this should be so, and why s.29(2) should be drafted as it is to achieve such a result is equally unclear.

REGISTRATION OF LICENCES

13–079　Licences are registrable transactions. The matters which are required to be registered are considered in Ch.3. The consequences of failure to register are dealt with above.[66]

RIGHTS OF LICENSEES AS TO INFRINGEMENT PROCEEDINGS

13–080　The procedural details concerning the manner in which licensees may bring infringement proceedings, or cause them to be brought, are dealt with in Ch.19. This and the following section are concerned only with the question of what right a licensee has to bring proceedings, or to call on the proprietor to bring them.

13–081　The rights of licensees in case of infringement are dealt with in ss.30 and 31 of the 1994 Act. The general scheme is as follows.

By s.31, an exclusive licensee may, by contract with the proprietor of the mark, be given the same rights and remedies as if the licence had been an assignment, including the right to bring proceedings in his own name.[67] Such a right of action, if granted, is concurrent with that of the proprietor.[68] However, it is in no way compulsory for an exclusive licensee to be given such a right, as is clear from the permissive words of s.31(1), and indeed it is fairly clear from the wording of the section that if the agreement granting the licence is silent, then the exclusive licensee will not have his own right of action.

13–082　Section 30 deals with the rights of licensees generally, including, as the second part of s.30(1) makes clear, exclusive licensees not given their own right of action under s.31. Section 30 does not apply to exclusive licensees given their own right of action under s.31.

13–083　The general rule under s.30 is that a licensee is entitled to call on the proprietor (or, by s.30(7), an exclusive licensee having his own right of action from whom a non-exclusive sub-licence has been obtained) to bring infringement proceedings in relation to "any matter which affects his interests".[69] If the proprietor refuses to bring proceedings, or fails to do so within two months, then the licensee may sue himself as if he were the proprietor/exclusive licensee. In contrast with s.31(1), the rights given under s.30 arise automatically unless the licence agreement(s) through which the licensee derives his rights excludes them.[70]

13–084　Both s.30 and s.31 have unusual provisions entitling the court to award dam-

---

[66] See paras 13–028 to 13–032.

[67] s.31(1).

[68] s.31(2).

[69] Presumably this includes at least any infringement within the field of use, geographical area, and specification of goods and services covered by the licence, as well as any infringement causing loss and damage to the licensee. The general words used suggest a broad test, and one would also expect them to catch use on goods not identical to those for which the licensee is licensed, but only similar, provided that his commercial interests are affected. Whether a s.10(3) infringement would be caught may be more doubtful, since that kind of infringement is more directed at the integrity of the mark itself, more naturally the area of interest of the proprietor.

[70] s.30(2).

ages against an infringer to reflect loss to a licensee, even if the licensee is not a party to the proceedings. In such cases, the court may give directions requiring the claimant to hold such damages for the licensee.[71]

A licensee cannot successfully bring infringement proceedings against a person operating with the proprietor's consent, although he may have a claim for damages in contract against the proprietor.[72]   **13–085**

LICENCES RENDERING A REGISTERED MARK DECEPTIVE

Under the 1938 Act, a difficult problem, never satisfactorily resolved, was the degree of control which a trade mark proprietor had to exercise over the activities of those using his mark with his permission, in order to prevent it from becoming deceptive.[73] Although the more marginal cases dealt with under the 1938 Act are hard to reconcile one with another, it was fairly clear that a bare licence of a trade mark under which the licensor/proprietor has no control over the activities of the licensee would render the mark deceptive.[74] As with the tension between the provisions of the 1994 Act concerning assignments without goodwill and revocation in cases of deceptiveness, considered above, there is no express guidance in the Act as to what a proprietor can and cannot do by means of a licence. Even accounting for the broad and apparently liberal provisions of ss.20–30 of the 1994 Act, it must surely be the case, particularly where a proprietor ceases to use the mark himself and instead permits multiple licensees to do so without control, that registered marks can in principle be rendered invalid by inappropriate licensing.[75] As a practical matter, trade mark proprietors would be well advised to insert quality control provisions into their licences, requiring goods or services to meet objective, specified standards, at the very least. More so than before, the responsibility of ensuring that a trade mark is used properly rests with the proprietor.   **13–086**

TRANSITIONAL PROVISIONS

The transitional provisions of the 1994 Act relating to licences are to be found in Sch.3 of para.9. That paragraph provides that ss.28 and 29(2) (which concern licences generally and the rights of an exclusive licensee against a successor to the licensor) apply only to licences granted after commencement.[76] In relation to licences granted earlier, the 1938 Act continues to apply as to those matters. However, whether or not a licence falls to be assessed under the 1938 Act or the 1994 Act, if the issue is whether a mark has become deceptive under s.46, the question is to be determined as of the date mandated by s.46,[77] not the date of the licences concerned.   **13–087**

---

[71] ss.30(6) and 31(6). These provisions are covered in more detail in Ch.19.

[72] *Northern & Shell v Condé Nast* [1995] R.P.C. 117, but see the discussion in para.13–075, as to whether there may be some doubt over the position of an exclusive licensee under s.31.

[73] This has been touched on above: see in particular the discussion of *Scandecor* [1998] F.S.R. 500, [1999] F.S.R. 26 CA and [2002] F.S.R. 7.

[74] And there was also the provision of the 1938 Act, s.28(6), dealing with trafficking. See *Holly Hobbie* [1984] F.S.R. 199.

[75] If and to the extent that this situation gives rise to an objection to the validity of a mark, it is an objection under s. 46(1)(d) based on deceptiveness, and not an allegation of non-use under s.6(1)(a) or (b), since such use is with the consent of the proprietor for the purposes of the non-use provisions of the act, whether or not there has been sufficient control to avoid deceptiveness. See *SAFARI Trade Mark* [2002] R.P.C. 23.

[76] Sch.3, para.9(1).

[77] *Scandecor* [1998] F.S.R. 500, [1999] F.S.R. 26 CA and [2002] F.S.R. 7, at paras 45–49. Usually

13–088　Registered user agreements entered on the Register under the 1938 Act are to be transferred on commencement to the new Register and there take effect as if registered under s.25 of the 1994 Act.[78]

13–089　Applications for registration of registered user agreements not finally determined at commencement are either to be treated as being applications under s.25 of the 1994 Act, or under the old law, depending on whether they were still pending before the Registrar at commencement, or had been dealt with by him but not finally disposed of.[79]

8. Stamp duty

Abolition in relation to intellectual property

13–090　By s.129 of the Finance Act 2000, stamp duty was abolished on dispositions of, *inter alia*, "any trade marks". This appears to include both registered and unregistered marks (given that no indication to the contrary was given, and in the light of s.1 of the 1994 Act). It also extends to licences or any other right in respect of a trade mark.

13–091　Assuming that both registered and unregistered trade marks were meant by the expression, it ought to be the case that stamp duty is not payable on goodwill associated with trade marks, either. The reason is that, as is discussed above, an assignment of a common law trade mark without goodwill is contrary to public policy and void; the section cannot have been intended to promote or encourage such conduct. If goodwill in relation to unregistered marks is not stampable, then it would be illogical if goodwill in relation to registered marks were.

---

the date is that of the application to revoke, unless it is alleged that the grounds existed earlier. See Ch.10 for further detail.
[78] Sch.3, para.9(2).
[79] Sch.3, para.9(3), (4).

CHAPTER 14

THE DEFINITION OF INFRINGEMENT

1. Preliminary

In this chapter we consider the definition of infringement. It concerns national trade marks, international trade marks designating the United Kingdom under the Madrid Protocol and Community trade marks under the Community Trade Marks Regulation. There is a substantial consistency between the approaches adopted in relation to each. This is to be expected because the provisions of the 1994 Act are, in large measure, an implementation of the provisions of the Trade Marks Directive. But in important respects there are differences too. These are in part the inevitable result of the difference in nature between a national trade mark system applying only in one country and a Community system seeking to provide marks which have a unitary character and equal effect throughout the Community. They are also the result of the way the United Kingdom has chosen to implement particular provisions of the TM Directive and to add some home grown provisions of its own. In this chapter we also have regard to the marks of a somewhat different nature provided for under each system, namely collective and certification marks under the 1994 Act and collective marks under the CTM Regulation. These have slightly different provisions to those relating to other trade marks and to each other.

It is a notable feature of the 1994 Act that, in addition to the provisions relating **14–002** to infringement of registered trade marks, protection is conferred on the proprietors of well-known trade marks under the Paris Convention and under the WTO Agreement. This protection is dependent neither upon registration nor upon the proprietor establishing that he has any business in the United Kingdom.

The scheme of this chapter is to consider first, infringement in relation to **14–003** national trade marks and the limitations, exceptions and defences thereto, secondly the further rights conferred by the 1994 Act and finally the position under the Community trade mark system and, in particular, where and how it differs from that pertaining to national trade marks.

2. National registered trade marks

A. GENERAL

Introduction

The rights conferred by a national registered trade mark (and an international **14–004** registration designating the United Kingdom under the Madrid Protocol) are set out in ss.9 and 10 of the 1994 Act. They essentially implement Article 5 of the TM Directive. In construing these new provisions it is therefore generally not appropriate to look back at the Trade Marks Act, 1938, the White Paper or Hansard.[1] The provisions of the 1994 Act must be construed, so far as possible, in accordance with the provisions of the TM Directive.[2]

14–005   In the following sections of this chapter we consider the various elements necessary to establish infringement. It is important to have in mind that principles established in relation to the relative grounds of objection under s.5 are generally applicable to considerations of infringement under s.10, save that in the case of s.5 the comparison is between the earlier trade mark and the mark in respect of which registration is sought and under s.10 the comparison is between the registered mark and the alleged infringement. Accordingly, when we address the assessment of the likelihood of confusion under s.10(2), and the use of a sign in relation to goods or services which are not similar to those in respect of which the mark is registered under s.10(3), we refer back extensively to the consideration of these matters in Ch.9.

In the course of trade

14–006   All of the provisions in s.10 of the 1994 Act relating to infringement are qualified by the expression "uses in the course of trade a sign".[3] To constitute an infringement the sign[4] in issue must therefore be used in the course of trade. Broadly, use in the course of trade calls for use in the context of a commercial activity with a view to economic advantage, and not as a private matter.[5]

14–007   "Trade" is defined in s.103(1) of the 1994 Act as including any business or profession and, as under the 1938 Act, will include leasing, hire purchase and the like.[6] But it is to be noted that the trade does not necessarily have to be in the goods or services the subject of the registration.[7]

Activities in the course of trade include communications, for example by way of orders and invoices, with suppliers and trade customers.[8]

14–008   As under the 1938 Act, it should be no answer to an allegation of infringement that the purpose of the mark is to show a business connection with a foreign manufacturer entitled to use the mark in his own country, and not with the British owner of the mark.[9]

Whether rights limited to trade mark or service mark use

14–009   The question has arisen whether the expression "uses in the course of trade" carries with it the requirement that the offending sign must be used as a "trade mark" or "service mark", that is to say as an indication of origin, in order to infringe.[10] The answer to this question depends upon the correct interpretation of Article 5

---

[1] See, *e.g. British Sugar v James Robertson* [1996] R.P.C. 281 at 292; and *Philips v Remington* [1999] R.P.C. 809, CA. Although there are exceptions, notably 1994 Act, s.10(6).

[2] *Marleasing* [1990] E.C.R. I-4135

[3] Implementing the same words of TM Directive, Art.5(1) and (2).

[4] The term "sign" is used throughout the 1994 Act, s.10 to describe the mark used by the infringer.

[5] *Arsenal Football Club v Matthew Reed* [2003] R.P.C. 9, (ECJ) at para.40.

[6] *Aristoc v Rysta* (1945) 62 R.P.C. 65 at 83, HL.

[7] See paras 14–057 to 14–078.

[8] *Beautimatic v Mitchell* [2000] F.S.R. 267.

[9] See, *e.g.* "4711" (1953) 70 R.P.C. 235; *"Everglide"* [1964] R.P.C. 37 at 42.

[10] See, for example: *British Sugar v James Robertson* [1996] R.P.C. 281, a decision of Jacob J.; the court declined to follow the decision in "Wet Wet Wet", *Bravado Merchandising v Mainstream Publishing* [1996] F.S.R. 205, where the matter proceeded on a concession by counsel; *Philips v Remington* [1998] R.P.C. 283 at 311–312; [1999] R.P.C. 809, at 823, CA.

of the TM Directive. In some cases (particularly where the sign is identical to the registered mark and is used in relation to goods or services the subject of the registration) it may be of some importance.[11]

In *Arsenal Football Club v Matthew Reed*[12] the question was addressed by the **14–010** European Court of Justice in the context of a referral as to the scope of Art.5(1)(a). Mr Reed carried on business near the Arsenal football ground selling souvenirs and articles of clothing which bore the registered trade mark 'Arsenal'. In para.48 of the decision the Court affirmed the essential function of a trade mark:

"... is to guarantee the identity of origin of the marked goods or services to the consumer or end user by enabling him, without any possibility of confusion, to distinguish the goods or services from others which have another origin. For the trade mark to be able to fulfil its essential role in the system of undistorted competition which the Treaty seeks to establish and maintain, it must offer a guarantee that all the goods or services bearing it have been manufactured or supplied under the control of a single undertaking which is responsible for their quality."

The Court then considered the scope of the exclusive rights conferred. In paras **14–011** 51–54 it held:

"... the exclusive right under Art.5(1)(a) of the Directive was conferred to enable the trade mark proprietor to protect his specific interests as proprietor, that is, to ensure that the trade mark can fulfil its functions. The exercise of that right must therefore be reserved to cases in which a third party's use of the sign affects or is liable to affect the functions of the trade mark, in particular its essential function of guaranteeing to customers the origin of the goods.

The exclusive nature of the right conferred by a registered trade mark on its proprietor under Art.5(1)(a) of the Directive can be justified only within the limits of the application of that article ....

The proprietor may not prohibit the use of a sign identical to the trade mark for goods identical to those for which the trade mark is registered if that use cannot affect his own interests as proprietor of the mark, having regard to its functions. Thus certain uses for purely descriptive purposes are excluded from the scope of Art.5(1) of the Directive because they do not affect any of the interests which that provision aims to protect, and therefore do not fall within the concept of use within the meaning of that provision ..."

The Court concluded that the use of the mark 'Arsenal' was such as to create **14–012** the impression that there was a material link in the course of trade between the

---

[11] See, *e.g. Mars v Cadbury* [1987] R.P.C. 387: ("Treat Size" not used as a trade mark in relation to confectionery); *Mothercare v Penguin* [1988] R.P.C. 113: ("Mothercare" used as the title of a book not use as a trade mark); cf. *Games Workshop v Transworld Publishers* [1993] F.S.R. 705 (seriously arguable that the title on a series of books was used as a trade mark); *Unidoor v Marks & Spencer* [1988] R.P.C. 275 (at the interlocutory stage extreme doubt was expressed as to whether the defendants were using the slogan "Coast to Coast" as a trade mark on the front of shirts); *Musidor BV v Tansing (trading as Apple Music House)* (1994) 123 A.L.R. 593 (held by a majority of the Federal Court of Australia that use of the name 'Rolling Stones' on the cover of compact discs bearing bootleg recordings of live performances of the Rolling Stones group was not use as a trade mark); see also the further cases discussed in the text. See also *Animated Music Ltd's Trade Mark* [2004] E.T.M.R. 79 (in the context of an application for revocation for non use, use of "Nellie the Elephant" as the title of a book was not to be regarded as trade mark use in the absence of evidence it was perceived as an indication of origin).

[12] [2003] R.P.C. 9.

goods and the trade mark proprietor and there was a clear possibility that some consumers might interpret the use of sign as designating the proprietor as the undertaking of origin of the goods (paras 56 and 57). The use of the sign in issue was liable to jeopardize the guarantee of origin which constitutes the essential function of a trade mark and was consequently a use which the trade mark proprietor must be able to prevent (paras 60 and 61).

14–013   The case came back before the High Court and subsequently the Court of Appeal. In a judgment given on May 21, 2003,[13] the Court of Appeal interpreted the decision of the Court of Justice in a somewhat liberal way: the relevant consideration was not whether the use complained of was trade mark use but whether it was likely to affect or jeopardize the guarantee or origin which constitutes the essential function of the mark.[14]

14–014   On the following day, May 22, 2003, the House of Lords gave judgment in *R. v Johnstone*,[15] a case concerning criminal offences under s.92 of the 1994 Act. Lord Nicholls was in no doubt: the Court of Justice decided in *Arsenal* that non-trade mark use is not within s.10(1) to (3)[16]. Similarly, s.92 was to be interpreted as applying only when the offending sign is used as an indication of trade origin.[17]

14–015   Lord Walker observed that the Court of Justice had excluded use of a trade mark for purely descriptive purposes, but that there will be infringement if the sign is used, without authority, "to create the impression that there is a material link in the course of trade between the goods concerned and the trade mark proprietor".[18] He continued:[19]

> "The difficulty arises, I think, because between cases which are clearly at the opposite extremes of "distinctiveness" and "descriptiveness" there is something of a no man's land of debateable cases, and the problem of analysis varies with the character of the mark and the character of the goods to which it is affixed ….
>
> … Whatever uncertainties there are about the decision of the European Court of Justice in *Arsenal*, its likely effect is that the province of trade mark use has annexed a significant part of the no man's land in which elements of distinctiveness and descriptiveness overlap …"

14–016   Lord Walker was also of the view that trade mark use is a necessary ingredient of criminal liability under s.92.[20] Lord Hope, Lord Hutton and Lord Rodger agreed with the opinions of Lord Nicholls and Lord Walker.

14–017   Most recently the Court of Justice has clarified the correct approach in *Anheuser-Busch*:[21]

> "59. First, with respect to TM Directive, it follows from the Court's case-law on the definition of use by a third party, for which provision is made in Article 5(1) of that directive, that the exclusive right conferred by a trade mark was intended to enable the trade mark proprietor to protect his specific interests as proprietor, that is, to ensure that the trade mark can fulfil its

---

[13] [2003] EWCA Civ 696; [2003] R.P.C. 39.
[14] *Arsenal*, CA, at paras 32–47.
[15] [2003] U.K.H.L. 28; [2004] E.T.M.R. 2.
[16] *Johnstone* [2003] U.K.H.L. 28, at paras 13–17.
[17] *Johnstone* [2003] U.K.H.L. 28, at paras 25–31.
[18] *Johnstone* [2003] U.K.H.L. 28, at para.85.
[19] *Johnstone* [2003] U.K.H.L. 28, at paras 86 and 87.
[20] *Johnstone* [2003] U.K.H.L. 28, at para.88.
[21] *Anheuser-Busch v Budejovicky Budvar NP* Case C–245/02 [2005] E.T.M.R. 27.

functions and that, therefore, the exercise of that right must be reserved to cases in which a third party's use of the sign affects or is liable to affect the functions of the trade mark, in particular its essential function of guaranteeing to consumers the origin of the goods (see Case C–206/01 *Arsenal Football Club* [2002] E.C.R. I-10273, paras 51 and 54).

60. That is the case, in particular, where the use of that sign allegedly made by the third party is such as to create the impression that there is a material link in trade between the third party's goods and the undertaking from which those goods originate. It must be established whether the consumers targeted, including those who are confronted with the goods after they have left the third party's point of sale, are likely to interpret the sign, as it is used by the third party, as designating or tending to designate the undertaking from which the third party's goods originate (see, to that effect, *Arsenal Football Club* [2004] EWCA Civ 159, cited above, paras 56 and 57).

61. The national court must establish whether that is the case in the light of the specific circumstances of the use of the sign allegedly made by the third party in the main case, namely, in the present case, the labelling used by Budvar in Finland.

62. The national court must also confirm whether the use made in the present case is one 'in the course of trade' and 'in relation to goods' within the meaning of Article 5(1) of Directive 89/104 (see, *inter alia*, *Arsenal Football Club*, paras 40 and 41).

63. Where those conditions are satisfied, it follows from the case-law of the Court that, in the event of identity of the sign and the trade mark and of the goods or services, the protection conferred by Article 5(1)(a) of Directive 89/104 is absolute, whereas, in the situation provided for in Article 5(1)(b), the proprietor, in order to enjoy protection, must also prove that there is a likelihood of confusion on the part of the public because the signs and trade marks and the designated goods or services are identical or similar (see, to that effect, Case C–292/00 *Davidoff* [2003] E.C.R. I-389, paragraph 28, and Case C–291/00 *LTJ Diffusion* [2003] E.C.R. I-2799, paras 48 and 49).

64. However, where the examinations to be carried out by the national court, referred to in paragraph 60 of this judgment, show that the sign in question in the main case is used for purposes other than to distinguish the goods concerned—for example, as a trade or company name—reference must, pursuant to Article 5(5) of Directive 89/104, be made to the legal order of the Member State concerned to determine the extent and nature, if any, of the protection afforded to the trade-mark proprietor who claims to be suffering damage as a result of use of that sign as a trade name or company name (see Case C–23/01 *Robelco* [2002] E.C.R. I-10913, paras 31 and 34)."

The exposition of the law by the Court of Justice in *Anheuser-Busch* and by the House of Lords in *Johnstone* must be taken to be definitive. In order to establish infringement under s.10(1)–(3) a claimant must therefore prove that the defendant is using the sign in issue in a trade mark sense, that is to say as an indication of origin or so as to create the impression that there is a material link in the course of trade between the goods or services in issue and the trade mark   **14–018** proprietor.[22] Purely descriptive use cannot infringe.[23] If the sign is used in such a way that it both denotes origin and acts as a description—the no man's land identified by Lord Walker—then, it is submitted, such use will also infringe if the use is liable to jeopardise the guarantee of origin which constitutes the essential function of a trade mark.

14–019   Whether a sign is being used in a trade mark sense is a question of fact to be determined in the light of the specific circumstances of the use.[24] The test is how the sign would be perceived by the average consumer of the type of goods in question.[25]

14–020   Travelex registered and used in connection with their financial services a particular figurative sign comprising a "C" horizontally crossed in the middle by two parallel, curved strokes. They contended the Commission had infringed the trade mark by adopting and promoting the official symbol used for the euro currency. Held, the official euro symbol was not a sign affixed to products or services to distinguish them from other products and services thereby enabling the public to identify their origin, but instead denoted a currency unit. It therefore did not amount to use of a sign in the course of trade within the meaning of Article 5 of the Directive.[26]

Use in relation to goods or services

14–021   To constitute infringement under any head of s.10 of the 1994 Act, the mark must be used *in relation* to goods or services.[27]

(1) The defendant publishes a directory of trade marks which wrongly attributes the plaintiff's registered mark to another company. It is suggested this would not be use in relation to directories or, indeed, any goods.[28]

(2) The petitioner was the registered proprietor of the trade mark "Wet Wet Wet", the name of a pop group, registered in respect of, *inter alia*, books. The respondent published a book, about the group, bearing the title "A Sweet Little Mystery—Wet Wet Wet—The Inside Story". Lord McCluskey concluded the use of "Wet Wet Wet" was use in a trade mark sense of a sign identical to the registered trade mark on goods identical to those for which it was registered. But he found for the respondent under s.11(2): *Bravado Merchandising Services v Mainstream Publishing* [1996] F.S.R.

---

[22] Earlier decisions of the Court of Justice are consistent with this approach: *Robelco NV v Robeco Groep NV* [2002] E.C.R. I-10913, at paras 28–36; the European Court of Justice said, at para.31: "It follows that reinforced protection of a trade mark's distinctive character or reputation against certain uses of a sign other than for the purpose of distinguishing goods or services is not covered by Community harmonisation"; *BMW v Deenik* [1999] E.C.R. I-905; [1999] E.T.M.R. 339, where the European Court of Justice said, at para.38: "In that connection, it is true that the scope of application of Article 5(1) and (2) of the directive, on the one hand, and Article 5(5) on the other, depends on whether the trade mark is used for the purpose of distinguishing the goods or services in question as originating from a particular undertaking, that is to say, as a trade mark as such, or whether it is used for other purposes." This is the approach most recently adopted in the UK: *Electrocoin Automatics Ltd v Coinworld Ltd* [2004] EWHC 1498 (Ch); [2005] F.S.R. 7.

[23] See also *Michael Holterhoff v Ulrich Freisleben* [2002] E.C.R. I-4187, at para.17: "the proprietor of a trade mark cannot rely on his exclusive right where a third party, in the course of commercial negotiations, reveals the origin of goods which he has produced himself and uses the sign in question solely to denote the particular characteristics of the goods he is offering for sale so that there can be no question of the trade mark used being perceived as a sign indicative of the undertaking of origin".

[24] *Anheuser-Busch*, Case C–245/02 at para.61.

[25] *Sabel BV v Puma AG, Rudolf Dassler Sport* [1997] E.C.R. I-6191, 6224, para.23; *Johnstone* [2003] U.K.H.L. 28, at para.31 *per* Lord Nicholls, and at para.87, *per* Lord Walker.

[26] *Travelex Global v Commission* [2003] E.T.M.R. 90 (CFI).

[27] *Anheuser-Busch* Case C–245/02, at para.62.

[28] See, under the 1938 Act, *Ravok v National Trade Press* (1955) 72 R.P.C. 110.

205, Ct of Sess. The matter proceeded on a concession by counsel that trade mark use was essential and this, it has been suggested, led to a muddle. The learned judge ought to have found that the use in the title was not use in relation to the registered goods.[29]

(3) A manufacturer of confectionery sold candy sticks in packets containing a card bearing a photograph and description of a famous footballer. In some cases the player was wearing a playing strip bearing the well-known England team logo, showing three lions. The Football Association objected that this constituted an infringement of its registration of that logo as a trade mark in respect of cards. The learned judge held that the manufacturer was not even arguably using the logo, as such, in any real sense of the word "uses" and was certainly not using it as a sign in respect of its cards.[30]

(4) The use of "Kodak" on T-shirts was not use as a trade mark in relation to those goods; rather it was use in relation to films and plates.[31]

(5) An Internet service provider used the trade mark Avnet in relation to a service which involved giving to customers an email address and a Web page. In this way it provided a facility for each customer to advertise on the customer's own Web page. Held, this did not constitute use of the mark in relation to "advertising and promotional services".[32]

It seems likely that the important question will be how the average consumer understands the sign to be used.[33] No doubt if it is plain that the intention of the defendant is that the sign should be understood to denote the origin of the goods or services in the manner suggested by the claimant, then this will be likely to determine the issue. But often the defendant may reasonably contend that the use of the sign is not intended to be so understood and here, it is suggested, the defendant's intention cannot be determinative. The following examples, decided under the old law, illustrate the point; but now it must be remembered that use in relation to goods or services outside the scope of the registration can amount to infringement if the additional requirements of ss.10(2) or 10(3) of the 1994 Act are satisfied.

14–022

(1) The plaintiffs owned the trade mark "John Bull" for beer; the defendants owned it for "beer kits" to make beer at home. The defendants advertised their kits so as to call the beer to be made with them, as well as the kits themselves, "John Bull". Held, that this was an infringement under the 1938 Act even though there could never be any trade in beer made from the defendants' kits and even though the home made beer would never be "goods".[34]

(2) The plaintiffs were the registered proprietors of the device of a cow and the word "cow" in respect of matches. The defendants sold matches in

---

[29] *British Sugar v James Robertson* [1996] R.P.C. 281 at p.293. Jacob J. evidently felt strongly about this, stating: "I have no doubt that the learned Judge reached the right result. It would be fantastic if the new trade mark legislation had the effect of enabling quasi censorship of books about people or companies just because those people or companies had registered their names as trade marks for books".

[30] *Trebor Bassett Ltd v The Football Association* [1997] F.S.R. 211. Rattee J. felt it was quite unreal to say that the manufacturer was affixing the sign comprising the England logo to its cards, and therefore to goods within the meaning of the 1994 Act, s.10(4)(a), or that it was putting the cards on the market under the sign comprising the England logo within s.10(4)(b).

[31] *"Kodiak"* [1990] F.S.R. 49.

[32] *Avnet v Isoact* [1998] F.S.R. 16.

[33] See para.14–019.

[34] *Ind Coope v Paine* [1983] R.P.C. 326 at 327. A similar case is *Rolls Royce v Dodd* [1981] F.S.R. 517.

boxes having on them a device of a cow and the words "cow brand" to advertise their condensed milk. This was held to be an infringement under the 1905 Act and, it is suggested, the position would be the same under the 1994 Act.[35]

Activities which constitute use of a sign

14–023   It has never been the law that the spurious mark should be actually affixed to the goods, provided it was so used in relation to them as to be calculated to lead to the belief that the goods were designated by the mark. This position is maintained under the 1994 Act which, in s.10(4) and (5), follows the permissive provisions of Article 5(3) of the TM Directive in identifying the various activities which constitute use of a sign for the purposes of the infringement provisions. Section 10(4) specifies that a person uses a sign if, in particular, he:

(1) affixes it to goods or the packaging thereof;
(2) offers or exposes goods for sale, puts them on the market or stocks them for those purposes under the sign, or offers or supplies services under the sign;
(3) imports or exports goods under the sign; or
(4) uses the sign on business papers or in advertising.

It is notable that the definition is not exhaustive. Nevertheless it introduces a degree of clarity absent from the uncertain definition of use in s.68 of the 1938 Act. It should be read with the definition of use in s.103(2) of the 1994 Act which specifically includes use otherwise than by means of a graphic representation. In this section certain practical aspects of the definition are discussed.

Mere possession

14–024   It would appear that mere possession of goods bearing an offending sign is not an infringement, unless there is an intention to deal in them.[36] This mirrors the position under the 1938 Act.

Point of sale

14–025   A question arises as to whether the offending sign needs to be visible at the point of sale. It is submitted that this is not a requirement, provided that when the sign does become apparent it is understood to be a sign used in the course of trade in relation to the relevant goods.[37] This follows from the wide definition of "use" in s.103(2) of the 1994 Act[38] and the express provision that use of a sign includes use of the sign on business papers, presumably including such items as receipts.

---

[35] *Nitedals v Lehmann* (1908) 25 R.P.C. 793.

[36] See *Waterford Wedgwood v David Nagli* [1998] F.S.R. 92 at 105.

[37] This was generally accepted to be the position under the old law. See, *e.g. Esquire v Roopanand* [1991] R.P.C. 425 (Sup Ct of S.A.); *Cheetah Trade Mark* [1993] F.S.R. 263. It was also the intention of the Government, albeit that this is not a legitimate aid to interpretation; see, Hansard, HL, Vol. 552, col.740, Lord Strathclyde, Minister for State, Department of Trade and Industry: "The proposed new [s.103(2)] therefore covers not only audible use, but any use of a trade mark which is other than by graphic representation. This would, *e.g.* apply where a trade mark is encoded electronically in a video cassette. It is not visible at the time of sale, and only becomes so when the purchaser plays it. Another instance which has been mentioned is where goods, *e.g.* jewellery, are actually made in the shape of a protected trade mark. All those would be caught by the new provision." But cf. *Unilever (Striped Toothpaste)* [1980] F.S.R. 280.

[38] Contrast the position under the Trade Marks Act 1938, s.68(2), which provided (in relation to goods) that references to the use of a mark should be construed as references to the use of a printed or other visual representation of the mark, and that references to the use of a mark in rela-

Affixes the sign to goods or the packaging

A person who affixes an offending sign to the goods or to the packaging thereof is an infringer,[39] provided he does so in the course of trade. If the work is carried out by a sub-contractor then it appears that he also infringes. This will be so even if the goods are being manufactured here for export. **14–026**

As to packaging, this provision must be reconciled with s.10(5) which deals with the application of a registered trade mark to material intended to be used for labelling or packaging. This is simply done if this provision is limited to packaging actually enclosing the goods rather than intended to be used in that way in the future.[40] **14–027**

Offers or exposes goods for sale or offers or supplies services under the sign

A person uses a sign if he offers or exposes goods for sale, puts them on the market or stocks them for those purposes under the sign, or offers or supplies services under the sign.[41] This is much as under the 1938 Act but appears to extend a little further. In particular it is now expressly provided that the stocking of goods for sale under a sign is an infringement. This would seem to include the case of a trader using the trade mark as the name of a business dealing in the goods, for example as the name of a shop through which the goods are sold.[42] **14–028**

Imports or exports goods under the sign

A person uses a sign if he imports or exports goods under the sign.[43] Importation consists of bringing goods into the territorial jurisdiction; exportation consists of their removal from the territorial jurisdiction.[44] In the case of goods to be exported, there is no need to show that the goods in question have been placed before the consumer or end user in the United Kingdom.[45] **14–029**

It may be necessary to determine precisely who is responsible for the alleged importation or export. This may be the owner of the property or there may be other principals for whom the shippers are acting. In any case it is no answer that the goods were only inadvertently brought into the jurisdiction, nor that the goods are only temporarily here while in transit.[46] **14–030**

Use of the sign on business papers or in advertising

It is an infringement to use an offending sign on business papers or in advertising: **14–031**

---

tion to goods should be construed as references to the use thereof upon, or in physical or other relation to, goods.

[39] 1994 Act, s.10(4)(a).
[40] *Beautimatic v Mitchell* [2000] F.S.R. 267. See also paras 14–035 to 14–038.
[41] 1994 Act, s.10(4)(b).
[42] This would reflect the intention expressed in the White Paper, Reform of Trade Marks Law, September 1990, para.3.27: "The new law will make it clear that offering goods, or putting them on the market, or stocking them for these purposes, under a sign which resembles someone else's trade mark is an infringement. This will prevent a trader from using such a sign as the name of a business dealing in goods or services similar to those for which the trade mark is registered." This may be contrasted with the position under the 1938 Act illustrated by, *e.g. "Autodrome"* [1969] R.P.C. 564.
[43] 1994 Act, s.10(4)(c).
[44] *L.A Gear v Hi-Tec Sports* [1992] F.S.R. 121 at 129 to 130.
[45] *Beautimatic v Mitchell* [2000] F.S.R. 267
[46] *Waterford Wedgwood v David Nagli* [1988] F.S.R. 92.

this has always been the law.[47] But with the wider definition of use including oral use of a trade mark it will now be an infringement to advertise using an offending mark by, for example, radio or through oral use of the mark by salesmen.

14–032   Where the mark is used on business papers, such as invoices, it may, however, be important to determine in relation to which goods it is being used.

> Allegedly infringing invoices bearing the registered mark referred to labels. Held, in the particular circumstances of the case, the wording on the invoices was directed towards the labels to be manufactured, and to what was written on those labels, and not to the goods to which they might subsequently be affixed.[48]

14–033   Advertisement in the United Kingdom of goods situated abroad may also be an infringement, even if the person who places the advert has no intention to bring them into the jurisdiction. Many publications have circulations in a number of different territories. If a person places an advert containing an offending trade mark in such a publication, knowing it will reach the United Kingdom, then it appears he may well infringe.[49]

14–034   Special difficulties arise in the case of comparative advertising and this is addressed as a separate topic.[50]

Materials intended to be used for labelling, packaging, as business papers or for advertising

14–035   Section 10(5) of the 1994 Act provides that a person who applies a registered trade mark to material intended to be used for labelling or packaging goods, as business papers, or for advertising goods or services, shall be treated as a party to any use of the material which infringes the registered trade mark if, when he applied the mark, he knew or had reason to believe that the application of the mark was not duly authorised by the proprietor or a licensee.[51]

14–036   This subsection is new and extends the ambit of infringement beyond that provided by s.10(4)(a) and (d). Thus manufacturers of labels, bottles and other materials and others, such as printers, who apply a registered trade mark to material which is ultimately used to infringe will be party to, and liable for, that infringement if they knew or had reason to believe the application was not authorised. Accordingly, if the labelling or packaging is to be taken abroad and only to be applied to the goods outside the United Kingdom then there can be no infringement.[52]

14–037   As to the requirement of knowledge, the test to be applied is that laid down in *LA Gear v Hi-Tec Sports*.[53] In relation to "reason to believe", it must be considered whether the defendant knew of facts from which a reasonable man would have arrived at the belief that the application of the mark was not duly au-

---

[47] As to business papers, see, *e.g. "Cheetah"* [1993] F.S.R. 263: use of a mark on delivery notes and on invoices delivered long after sale constituted use of the mark in the course of trade and in relation to the goods.

[48] *Beautimatic v Mitchell* [2000] F.S.R. 267.

[49] For an example under the old law, see *Reuters v Mulhens* (1953) 70 R.P.C. 235 at 250, CA. The Internet raises special difficulties, see Ch.21.

[50] See paras 14–098 to 14–119.

[51] s.10(5).

[52] *Beautimatic v Mitchell* [2000] F.S.R. 267.

[53] [1992] F.S.R. 121 at 129 and at 138, CA. The same test was applied in *Beautimatic v Mitchell* [2000] F.S.R. 267.

thorised by the proprietor or a licensee. Moreover the phrase allows for a period of time to enable the reasonable man to evaluate the facts so as to convert the facts into a reasonable belief.[54]

In contrast to the words of s.10(4), this provision is framed in terms of "a person who applies a registered trade mark ...". Accordingly, it may be argued to be limited such that it only applies if the registered trade mark itself is applied, not a mark which is so similar as to be likely to cause confusion.[55] **14–038**

B. THE CATEGORIES OF INFRINGEMENT

Introduction: Identical marks, resembling marks and the likelihood of confusion, comparative advertising

Section 10 of the 1994 Act defines three different potential categories of infringement in implementing Article 5 of the TM Directive. The first involves the use of a sign which is identical to the registered trade mark in relation to goods or services which are identical with those for which the mark is registered. The second involves the use of a sign which is identical or similar to the registered trade mark and in relation to goods or services which are identical or similar to those for which the mark is registered. The third involves the use of a sign which is identical or similar to the registered trade mark and in relation to any goods or services whether or not they are similar to those for which the mark is registered. Each category has its own requirements which, in view of the complexity of the topic, are addressed in separate sections below. **14–039**

In addition to these three principal categories of infringement, the Act introduces a fourth category of infringement in s.10(6). This is a curious provision which has no clear foundation in the TM Directive and has no counterpart in the CTM Regulation. It contains, first of all, a saving in respect of the use by a person of a trade mark for the purpose of identifying goods or services as those of the proprietor or a licensee. But then it continues to create a further category of infringement by providing that any such use, other than in accordance with honest practices in industrial or commercial matters, shall be treated as infringing the registered trade mark if the use, without due cause, takes unfair advantage of, or is detrimental to, the distinctive character or repute of the trade mark. These two aspects of the subsection appear to render some, but only some, comparative advertisements an infringement and it has been so construed, as we explain below. **14–040**

The scope of the registration

Each of the three categories of infringement referred to above requires the identification of the goods or services the subject of the registered trade mark.[56] All goods and services are divided into a series of classes in accordance with the Nice Classification,[57] and the decision of the Registrar as to the class into which any particular goods or services fall is final.[58] Not only do all goods and services fall within one of the classes, sometimes, under the 1938 Act, the applicant sought **14–041**

---

[54] cf. *Monsoon v India Imports* [1993] F.S.R. 486.

[55] And possibly therefore primarily directed to counterfeiting.

[56] This was a matter of particular importance under the 1938 Act where infringement required use of the offending mark in relation to goods or services within the scope of the registration. It is of less importance under the 1994 Act because of the wider protection afforded by s.10(2) and (3).

[57] As discussed in Ch.4.

[58] 1994 Act, s.34(2).

or the Registrar required the goods or services of an application to be defined by reference to the class. Under the 1994 Act the application must identify the classes in respect of which registration is sought if it is to proceed to examination.[59]

14–042   In many cases the specification of goods or services of a registered trade mark is clear; but sometimes it is not, either because of the limitation to the goods or services of a class or because the description of goods or services is general or vague.

14–043   In any case where it must be determined into which class any particular goods or services fall, it is necessary to look at the Registrar's practice at the date of the registration.[60]

14–044   Where the description of goods or services is vague, a particular problem with services, it is necessary to interpret or construe the words used. Here one is concerned with how a product is, as a practical matter, regarded for the purposes of trade[61] or the meaning of the words of the specification as a matter of ordinary language.[62] In keeping with this approach, the test of whether particular goods fall within a specification of goods has been said to be a question for the consumer and not a matter to be determined by expert scientific evidence.[63] The meaning of the words must be determined as of the date of registration.[64]

14–045   In the case of services it has been said that:

> "specifications of services should be scrutinised carefully and they should not be given a wide construction covering a vast range of activities. They should be confined to the substance, as it were, the core of the possible meanings attributable to the rather general phrase."[65]

Section 10(1): Where the marks and the goods or services are identical

General

14–046   Section 10(1) of the 1994 Act reads:

> "A person infringes a registered trade mark if he uses in the course of trade a sign which is identical with the trade mark in relation to goods or services which are identical with those for which it is registered."

14–047   This subsection implements Article 5(1) of the TM Directive and represents the simple case. It requires identical marks and identical goods or services.

The sign must be used in the course of trade in relation to goods or services

14–048   This requirement is discussed in paras 14–006 to 14–038. Non-trade mark use does not infringe.

---

[59] If the applicant does not do this then the Registrar will suggest appropriate classes.

[60] *GE Trade Mark* [1969] R.P.C. 418 at 458; *Avnet v Isoact* [1998] F.S.R. 16; *British Sugar v James Robertson* [1996] R.P.C. 281.

[61] *British Sugar v James Robertson* [1996] R.P.C. 281.

[62] *Beautimatic v Mitchell* [2000] F.S.R. 267.

[63] *Unilever v Johnson Wax* [1989] F.S.R. 145, where a thick liquid lavatory cleaner was held not to fall within "common soap and detergents"; *Beautimatic v Mitchell* [2000] F.S.R. 267: held, as a matter of ordinary language, skin lightening cream and dry skin lotion were cosmetics; see also *Portakabin v Powerblast* [1990] R.P.C. 471.

[64] *Reed Executive plc v Reed Business Information Ltd* [2004] EWCA Civ 159; [2004] R.P.C. 40.

[65] *per* Jacob J. in *Avnet* [1998] F.S.R. 16; cited with approval by the CA in *Reed* [2004] EWCA Civ 159; [2004] R.P.C. 40 at para.43.

Comparison is mark for sign

The comparison is "mark for sign" and first requires the identification of the **14–049**
defendant's sign for the purposes of the comparison:

> "In most cases there will be no difficulty. It is either there or not. However it
> is possible for the sign to be hidden or swamped. No one but a crossword
> fanatic, for instance, would say that 'treat' is present in 'theatre atmosphere'.
> There is no question of that sort here, however. 'Treat' is there on the Rob-
> ertson products for all to see."[66]

But there will be cases where the matter is not clear, particularly where a **14–050**
distinctive element is used in conjunction with descriptive or semi-descriptive
words. If the additional words are wholly descriptive then they are unlikely to be
perceived as being part of the sign. If they are not wholly descriptive or are presented in a visually arresting way then they are more likely to be perceived as
part of the sign. Each case must depend upon its own facts and must be considered
from the perspective of the average consumer. In *Reed Executive plc v Reed
Business Information Ltd*[67] it was alleged that the trade mark "Reed" was
infringed by the use of, *inter alia*, "Reed Business Information". Jacob L.J. said,
at para.36:

> "It was over "Reed Business Information" that battle was joined. The com-
> posite is not the same as, for instance, use of the word "Reed" in the
> sentence: "Get business information from Reed." In the latter case the only
> "trade-marky" bit would be "Reed". In the former, the name as a whole is
> "Reed Business Information". The use of capital letters is of some visual
> significance—it conveys to the average user that "Business Information" is
> part of the name. If the added words had been wholly and specifically
> descriptive—really adding nothing at all (*e.g.* "Palmolive Soap" compared
> with "Palmolive") the position might have been different. But "Business In-
> formation" is not so descriptive—it is too general for that."

The sign and mark must be identical

Once the defendant's sign has been identified it must be compared with the **14–051**
registered mark to determine if it is identical. Again, this is a matter to be
considered from the perspective of the average consumer. A sign will be identical
with the registered mark where it reproduces, without any modification or addition, all the elements constituting the mark or were, viewed as a whole, it contains
differences so insignificant they may go unnoticed by the average consumer.[68]

Accordingly, in the case of any accused sign which has some visual signifi- **14–052**

---

[66] On the label marked "ROBERTSON'S Toffee TREAT": *British Sugar* [1996] R.P.C. 281, at 293
to 294.

[67] [2004] EWCA Civ 159; [2004] R.P.C. 40.

[68] *LTJ Diffusion v Sadas ("Arthur et Felicie")* [2003] F.S.R. 34. Applied by the CA in *Reed* (above);
see Jacob L.J. at paras 20–41: "Reed" not identical to "Reed Business Information". c.f. *BMW v
Deenik*, Case C–62/97, [1999] E.C.R. I-905: the expressions "BMW specialist", "Specialised in
BMWs", "Repairs and maintenance of BMWs" were in each case identical to "BMW". For other
cases on either side of the line see, by way of example: *Origins Natural Resources v Origin
Clothing* [1995] F.S.R. 280, one letter changing singular to plural was apparently sufficient to
take the matter out of s.10(1) and s.10(2). *IDG Communications Trade Mark* [2002] R.P.C. 10
(DIGIT and DIGITS not-identical); *Decon Laboratories v Fred Baker Scientific* [2001] R.P.C.
17 (both parties used the trade mark Decon with a descriptive suffix); *Asprey & Garrard v WRA
(Guns) Ltd* [2002] F.S.R. 30 summary judgment granted in respect of infringement of 'Asprey'
by the use of 'William R Asprey Esq.'; set aside on appeal on counsel's concession in the light of
the pending decision in *LTJ Diffusion*: [2002] F.S.R. 31.

cance, one must take that into account in considering the question of identity. The visual impact may be slight, but it will count even if the marks are identical to the ear. There can only be "identity" if there is both aural and visual identity.[69]

14–053 Similarly, it has been said that the mark and sign must be so close that one could be considered a counterfeit of the other. Any addition which has some trade mark significance cannot be ignored.[70]

14–054
(1) The claimant was proprietor of the trade mark "Vantage" for "operating incentive schemes". The defendant operated a loyalty card scheme under the words "Vantage Rewards". Held, on an application for summary judgment, the marks were identical because the word "Reward" was merely descriptive of the services offered.[71]

(2) The claimant was the proprietor of the registered mark "Decon" in respect of cleaning preparations and sold a range of such products under a series of names which included that mark. The defendant sold a cleaning preparation consisting of isopropyl alcohol under the name "Decon-Ahol". Held, the signs were identical. The suffix was descriptive and did not change the nature of the principal sign. The claimant actually used its mark in the same way and this use was well within the scope of the ordinary and fair use of the mark.[72]

(3) IBM was the proprietor of the trade mark WEBSPHERE in respect of, computer software and software for web site development. The defendant changed its name to Web-Spere Ltd and began to use the trade mark Web-Spere on its web site and in relation to computer software and Internet related computer services. Held, the marks were identical for the purposes of Art.9(1)(a) of the CTM Regulation. The marks sounded exactly the same and the presence of the hyphen would go unnoticed by the average consumer.[73]

The goods and services must be identical

14–055 The second fundamental requirement is that the sign is used in relation to identical goods or services to those the subject of the registration. This will depend upon what the specification means, a matter discussed in paras 14–041 to 14–045.

Distinguishing material is to be disregarded

14–056 If these requirements are satisfied then the statutory protection is absolute in the sense that the user cannot escape by showing that by something outside the actual mark itself he has distinguished his goods or services from those of the registered proprietor.[74] If he uses the mark as a sign and in the course of trade in relation to

---

[69] *Reed* [2004] EWCA Civ 159; [2004] R.P.C. 40, at para.32. See also *Philips v Remington* [2004] EWHC 2327 (Ch); [2005] F.S.R. 17 at paras 14–177 to 14–185.

[70] *Compass Publishing v Compass Logistics* [2004] EWHC 520 (Ch); [2004] R.P.C. 41: "Compass Logistics" not identical to "Compass".

[71] *AAH Pharmaceuticals v Vantagemax* [2002] EWHC 990 (Ch); [2003] E.T.M.R. 18.

[72] *Decon Laboratories v Fred Baker Scientific* [2001] R.P.C. 17 at p.293.

[73] *WebSphere Trade Mark* [2004] EWHC 529 (Ch); [2004] F.S.R. 39

[74] *Origins* [1995] F.S.R. 280; *British Sugar v James Robertson* [1996] R.P.C. 281; *Premier Brands v Typhoon* [2000] F.S.R. 767; *Volvo v Heritage* [2000] F.S.R. 253; *Decon Laboratories v Fred Baker* [2001] R.P.C. 17; *BP Amoco v John Kelly* [2002] F.S.R. 5 (Court of Appeal of Northern Ireland); *Saville Perfumery v June Perfect* (1941) 58 R.P.C. 147 at 161.

any of the goods or services the subject of the registration then there is, *prima facie*, infringement.[75]

Section 10(2): Where the marks and the goods or services are identical or similar

General

Section 10(2) of the 1994 Act reads: **14–057**

"A person infringes a registered trade mark if he uses in the course of trade a sign where because—

    (a) the sign is identical with the trade mark and is used in relation to goods or services similar to those for which the trade mark is registered, or

    (b) the sign is similar to the trade mark and is used in relation to goods or services identical with or similar to those for which the trade mark is registered,

there exists a likelihood of confusion on the part of the public which includes the likelihood of association with the trade mark."

This subsection implements Article 5(1)(b) of the TM Directive. It extends the **14–058** ambit of infringement in particular circumstances where neither the marks nor goods or services need be identical to those the subject of the registration. If the marks are identical or similar and the goods or services are identical or similar to those the subject of the registration and because of that similarity there exists a likelihood of confusion on the part of the public then there is infringement.

The words of the subsection and of the Directive are mirrored in the words of **14–059** s.5(2) of the 1994 Act and Article 4(1)(b) of the TM Directive which provide a corresponding relative ground of objection to the registration of a trade mark which conflicts with an earlier trade mark. Accordingly the approach to the construction and application of this infringement provision must be the same, save that now the comparison is between the registered trade mark and the allegedly offending sign. In this section of this chapter we identify the issues and indicate where they are discussed or where particular points relevant to infringement arise.

Comparison is mark for sign

As in the case of identity (above), the subsection requires identification of the **14–060** sign used by the defendant and a determination of the goods or services (if any) in relation to which he is using it.[76] This must be compared to a notional and fair use of the registered mark in relation to all of the goods and services covered by the registration.[77] If the mark has been used then the way it has been used can be said, at the very least *prima facie*, to be a paradigm case of the use of the mark in a normal and fair manner.[78]

---

[75] See paras 14–006 to 14–038 for a discussion of these requirements. In particular, non-trade mark use does not infringe.

[76] See paras 14–041 to 14–045 and paras 14–049 to 14–050 for a discussion of how these matters are determined.

[77] see, for example, *Compass Publishing v Compass Logistics* [2004] EWHC 520; [2004] R.P.C. 41.

[78] *Premier Brands v Typhoon Europe* [2000] F.S.R. 767.

Use in the course of trade in relation to goods or services

14–061   This requirement is discussed in paras 14–006 to 14–038. Non-trade mark use does not infringe.

The same or similar goods or services

14–062   The goods or services the subject of the registered mark and those the subject of any alleged infringing use must be the same or similar. It appears this is not only a relevant matter to take into account in assessing the likelihood of confusion but is also a threshold requirement before infringement can be found under this provision.[79] The matters to be taken into account in assessing identity of goods and services are discussed in paras 14–041 to 14–045. Assessment of the degree of similarity between goods or services is discussed in relation to s.5(2) of the 1994 Act.[80]

14–063   The claimant was the proprietor of the mark Viagra, registered in Class 5 in respect of veterinary preparations and pharmaceutical substances. The defendant proposed to market a beverage to be used as a mixer under the mark Viagrene. It became apparent that the defendant proposed to market its product as a drink capable of stimulating the libido of men and women by incorporating a natural herb which was thought to act directly on the reproductive organs. Held, once considered in the light of the defendant's intention, the similarity between the goods became more pronounced and that infringement under s.10(2) was established.[81]

The same or similar marks

14–064   The registered mark and the sign alleged to infringe must be identical or similar. Identity of marks is discussed in paras 14–051 to 14–054. Similarity of marks is a subject discussed in relation to s.5 of the 1994 Act.[82] In short, the condition of similarity requires the existence, in particular, of elements of visual, aural or conceptual similarity.[83]

There exists a likelihood of confusion

14–065   There can only be infringement where there exists a likelihood of confusion, which includes a likelihood of association. This requirement is fundamental to the provision.[84]

Confusion as to origin

14–066   The risk that the public might believe that the goods or services in question come from the same undertaking or, as the case may be, economically linked undertakings, constitutes a likelihood of confusion within the meaning of

---

[79] See Ch.9, paras 9–047 to 9–058.
[80] See Ch.9, paras 9–059 to 9–068.
[81] *Pfizer v Eurofood Link*, a decision of S. Thorley Q.C., [2001] F.S.R. 3.
[82] See Ch.9, paras 9–069 to 9–083.
[83] *Sabel v Puma* [1997] E.C.R. 1-6191; [1998] R.P.C. 199; *Lloyd Schufabrik Meyer v Kliysen Handel* [1999] E.T.M.R. 690; *Adidas-Salomon v Fitnessworld* [2004] E.T.M.R. 10 at p.129, para.28
[84] *Sabel* [1997] E.C.R. 1-6191; [1998] R.P.C. 199 and see the discussion in Ch.9, paras 9–045 to 9–046.

Art.5(1)(b) of the Directive.[85] In short, the sort of confusion required to satisfy this provision is confusion as to origin.

(1) The use by sales staff of the expressions "Premier Luggage" or "Premier Luggage Company" did not infringe the registered trade mark "Premier" for luggage in circumstances where there was no passing off and the claimants had failed to establish that members of the public would make a connection with the registered mark.[86] **14–067**

(2) The claimants ran employment agencies, provided temporary staff and were proprietors of the trade mark "Reed" in respect of employment agency services. The defendants used the word "Reed" in relation to their business of publishing various journals and magazines. They also ran a totaljobs.com recruitment website. A Yahoo search under the name "Reed" caused the totaljobs banner to appear. In addition the totaljobs site had the words "Reed Business Information" as a metatag. If a search was made under the phrase "Reed jobs" then the totaljobs site was listed, but in all cases under the claimants' site in the search results. Held, no infringement under s.10(2). As to the totaljobs banner, this contained no reference to the word Reed. It was fanciful to suggest that a search under the name "Reed" would make anyone think there was a trade connection between the totaljobs banner and the claimants, and it was arguable that such an invisible use was not use of a trade mark at all. As to the metatag use, it was obvious that anyone looking for the claimants' site would find it rather than totaljobs. Assuming that metatag use counted as use as a trade mark, there was no confusion; causing a site to appear in a search result, without more, did not suggest any connection with anyone else.[87]

Assessment of the likelihood of confusion

As in the case of s.5(2) of the 1994 Act, the words of s.10(2) and of Article 5(2)(b) of the TM Directive require that the likelihood of confusion is caused by the identity or similarity of the marks and the goods or services. That likelihood is to be assessed globally taking into account all relevant factors, including the degree of similarity between the relevant marks, the degree of similarity between the relevant goods or services, the likely perception of the marks in the minds of the average consumer of the goods or services in question and the degree of distinctiveness of the earlier mark. The discussion of these matters in relation to s.5 is relevant in relation to s.10 too.[88] **14–068**

(1) The claimant owned and operated a very successful inexpensive Japanese style noodle bar and restaurant under the trade mark "Wagamama". The defendant decided to set up an American theme restaurant with Indian décor and food and called it "Rajamama". The claimant thereupon commenced proceedings for passing off and trade mark infringement. Held, the marks were being used in relation to comparatively inexpensive restaurant services where imperfect recollection was likely to play an important role, and the fact that "Wagamama" was meaningless made imperfect recollection more likely. There was a substantial likelihood of confusion because some members of the public would think the marks **14–069**

---

[85] *Lloyd Schufabrik Meyer v Kliysen Handel* [1999] E.T.M.R. 690 at para.17; *Canon v MGM* [1998] E.C.R. I-5507, [1999] R.P.C. 117, para.29. See the discussion of this issue in Ch.9, para.9–046.

[86] *Premier Luggage & Bags Ltd v Premier (UK) Ltd* [2002] EWCA Civ 387; [2003] F.S.R. 5 at p.69.

[87] *Reed Executive plc v Reed Business Information Ltd* [2004] EWCA Civ 159; [2004] R.P.C. 40. See also the discussion in Ch.23.

[88] See Ch.8, where the approach to the assessment of the likelihood of confusion is considered in detail.

were the same and others that they associated in the sense that one was an extension of the other or otherwise derived from the same source.[89]

(2) The claimant imported and sold tea in the UK under the registered trade mark TY.PHOO. It also had the mark registered in respect of, *inter alia*, domestic utensils. The defendant imported and sold kitchen hardware under the trade mark TYPHOON. Held, there was a considerable degree of aural similarity between the marks, but visually it was not so significant and conceptually there was much less similarity. Overall the average consumer would not confuse the marks.[90]

(3) The claimant operated BP service stations under a livery consisting of the extensive application of a particular green colour to their prominent surfaces. It also registered as a trade mark the colour when applied to the exterior surfaces of such premises. The defendant operated a chain of ser-vice stations under the name TOP. These stations were subsequently given a new brand image in which green was adopted as the main colour (albeit of a slightly different shade to that of BP). Held, the claim for trade mark infringement succeeded. There was a likelihood of confusion when motor-ists travelling at speed saw a green station at a distance and made prepara-tions to turn off into the station; such motorists were liable to continue the manoeuvre even thought they might appreciate that the petrol was not that of BP as they neared the station.

Distinctive nature of the registered mark

14–070   If the registered mark has not been used then its inherent distinctiveness must be considered. If it has been used on a substantial scale then that may be taken into account in assessing its distinctiveness.[91]

14–071   (1) The claimant was the proprietor of the registered mark "Decon" in respect of cleaning preparations and sold a range of such products under a series of names which included that mark. The defendant sold a cleaning prepa-ration consisting of isopropyl alcohol under the name "Decon-Ahol". Held, in considering infringement under s.10(2), consideration of the rep-utation enjoyed by the mark was central. This was not a case in which it would be possible to substitute the defendant's products for those of the claimant. Nevertheless, the claimant enjoyed a substantial reputation under its mark, and that reputation extended to persons who might be purchasers of the defendant's products. In the circumstances there was a substantial likelihood of confusion.[92]

(2) The claimants were proprietors of a pictorial mark consisting of a colour reproduction of a "Malibu" bottle (having particular contours, a white co-lour and a dark brown cap) upon which there was no printing. It was registered in respect of coconut flavoured rum based drinks. The defen-dants sold a coconut liqueur under the SURFERS trade mark in a bottle of

---

[89] *Wagamama v City Centre Restaurants* [1995] F.S.R. 713.

[90] *Premier Brands v Typhoon Europe* [2000] F.S.R. 767.

[91] *Reed Executive plc v Reed Business Information Ltd* [2004] EWCA Civ 159; [2004] R.P.C. 40 at paras 79– 81, and 83–86. The consequences of an increase in distinctiveness will vary from case to case for it must ultimately be a question of fact as to whether two marks are confusingly simi-lar; see the discussion in Ch.9, paras 9–069 to 9–083.

[92] *Decon Laboratories v Fred Baker Scientific* [2001] R.P.C. 17. The court concluded the marks were identical: see illustration at para.14–054, but considered the issue under s.10(2) on the basis that it might be wrong.

shape. Held, there was a likelihood of confusion, and this conclusion was reinforced by the reputation attaching to the Malibu brand.[93]

(3) The claimant was the producer of Veuve Clicquot champagne and the owner of a registered trade mark consisting of the colour orange of a particular Pantone shade. The defendant began to sell a beer under the trade mark "Maleur" in champagne shaped bottles with a label on an orange background and presented in a box, the predominant colour of which was orange. Held, upholding a finding of infringement of the colour mark: the trade mark had only weak inherent distinctive power; however, it had acquired a highly distinctive character as a result of prolonged use in combination with the prestigious word mark "Veuve Clicquot Ponsardin". The difference between the opposed sign and the protected trade mark was barely perceptible and the use of the mark "Maleur" did not assist the defendant because it would be perceived as an independent sign.[94]

Evidence of actual confusion

Where the use of the offending sign results in actual confusion then this is likely to very persuasive. However, an absence of confusion may be attributable to the nature of the parties' respective presences in the market. For example, they may have traded in different geographical areas or carried on different core activities, but all within the scope of the registration.[95]   **14–072**

Distinguishing material is to be disregarded

The statutory protection is absolute in the sense that the user cannot escape by showing that by something outside the actual mark itself he has distinguished his goods or services from those of the registered proprietor.[96]   **14–073**

The average consumer

In brief summary, for the purposes of the global assessment and appreciation, the average consumer of the category of products concerned is deemed to be reasonably well-informed and reasonably observant and circumspect. However, account is to be taken of the fact that the average consumer only rarely has the chance to make a direct comparison between the different marks but must place his trust in the imperfect picture of them he has kept in his mind. It is also to be borne in mind that the average consumer's level of attention is likely to vary according to the category of goods or services in question.[97]   **14–074**

The average consumer test is conceptually different from the "substantial proportion of the public" test applied in passing off cases, but in the end they come to the same thing. If a "substantial proportion" of the relevant consumers are likely to be confused, so will the average consumer and vice versa. Both ap-   **14–075**

---

[93] *Guiness United Distillers & Vintners Amsterdam v Cooymans* [2004] E.T.M.R. 11, Court of Appeal of Den Bosch, Netherlands.

[94] *Emmanuel de Landtsheer v Veuve Cliquot Ponsardin, LVHM Fashion Group* [2005] E.T.M.R. 12, Court of Appeal of Brussels.

[95] see, for example, *Compass* [2004] EWHC 520; [2004] R.P.C. 41: the mark was registered in respect of business consultancy services. The defendant carried on business in a small way in the logistics sector of this market and this was not an area in which the claimant had traded.

[96] *Origins* [1995] F.S.R. 280; *British Sugar v James Robertson* [1996] R.P.C. 281; *Premier Brands v Typhoon* [2000] F.S.R. 767; *Volvo v Heritage* [2000] F.S.R. 253; *Decon Laboratories v Fred Baker* [2001] R.P.C. 17; *BP Amoco v John Kelly* [2002] F.S.R. 5 (Court of Appeal of Northern Ireland); *Saville Perfumery v June Perfect* (1941) 58 R.P.C. 147 at 161.

[97] *Lloyd Schufabrik Meyer v Kliysen Handel* [1999] E.T.M.R. 690 at para.26; *Gut Springenheide and Tusky* [1968] E.C.R. I-4657 at para.31.

proaches guard against too "nanny" a view of protection; to confuse only the careless or stupid is not enough.[98]

14–076   The correct test is whether there is *a risk* that the public might believe that the goods or services in question come from the same or economically linked undertakings.[99]

The date of assessment

14–077   As explained, it is now clear that the degree of distinctiveness of the registered mark, including that acquired through use, is likely to increase the risk of confusion. It is suggested the likelihood of confusion must exist, at the latest, at the date of commencement of the proceedings. But if relief is to be sought in respect of activities before that date then it would seem that the likelihood of confusion (and so also the distinctiveness of the registered mark) must have existed throughout the time that the activities complained of were conducted.

14–078   However this approach could create difficulties, particularly in the light of the "global assessment of the likelihood of confusion. So, for example, the reputation of the claimant and the activities of a defendant might not have been sufficient to create a likelihood of confusion at the date of the commencement of those activities. Subsequently, the reputation of the claimant might have increased such that there is a likelihood of confusion, but through no fault or act of the defendant. Accordingly, it might be argued, the relevant date for consideration of the issue should be the date of the commencement of the activities complained of or, in a *quia timet* action, the date of the threat.[1]

Section 10(3): Where the use of the sign without due cause takes unfair advantage of, or is detrimental to, the distinctive character or the repute of the trade mark

General

14–079   Section 10(3) of the 1994 Act (as amended by reg.7 of The Trade Marks (Proof of Use, etc.) Regulations 2004)[2] reads:

> "A person infringes a registered trade mark if he uses in the course of trade in relation to goods or services a sign which,

is identical with or similar to the trade mark,

where the trade mark has a reputation in the United Kingdom and the use of the sign, being without due cause, takes unfair advantage of, or is detrimental to, the distinctive character or repute of the trade mark."

14–080   This subsection implements the optional provision of Article 5(2) of the TM Directive. It provides an important ground of infringement in cases where a sign is used which is identical or similar to a registered trade mark which has a reputation in the United Kingdom. In such a case, use in the course of trade infringes if, being without due cause, it takes unfair advantage of, or is detrimental to, the distinctive character or repute of the registered trade mark. The words of the

---

[98] *Reed* [2004] EWCA Civ 159; [2004] R.P.C. 40 at para.82.

[99] *Thomson Holidays v Norwegian Cruise Lines* [2003] R.P.C. 32 at p.586, CA, applying the decision of the ECJ in *Canon* [1998] E.C.R. I-5507, [1999] R.P.C. 117at para.29. The court considered the trial judge had wrongly adopted the higher test of whether the public would believe the product was that of the proprietor or an associated product and had failed to make allowance for imperfect recollection (at para.56).

[1] cf. the position in relation to passing off, as to which see Ch.15.

[2] SI 2004/246. The Regulations came into force on May 5, 2004.

subsection mirror those of s.5(3) and accordingly the discussion of that provision in Ch.9 is equally applicable here, save as indicated below.[3]

Use in the course of trade in relation to goods or services

These requirements are discussed above.[4] The offending sign must be used in the course of trade as a trade mark.

14–081

The same or similar trade marks

The sign used by the defendant must be identified[5] and it must be identical or similar to the registered mark. Identity of marks is discussed in paras 14–051 to 14–054. Similarity of marks is a subject discussed in relation to s.5 of the 1994 Act.[6] In short, the condition of similarity requires the existence, in particular, of elements of visual, aural or conceptual similarity.[7]

14–082

All goods and services

The subsection clearly applies to all goods and services. In its original form the subsection closely followed Article 5(2) of the TM Directive. This permits Member States to provide that the proprietor shall have a right to prevent third parties from using an identical or similar trade mark in relation to goods or services which are *not similar* to those in respect of which it is registered where the earlier trade mark has a reputation and the use of the sign takes unfair advantage of or is detrimental to the distinctive character of the earlier trade mark. This raised the question whether such a right extended to identical or similar goods. However, in *Davidoff & Cie SA and Zino Davidoff SA v Goffkid* and *Adidas Salomon AG v Fitnessworld Trading Ltd* the European Court of Justice decided that Art.5(2) also applies to goods or services which are identical or similar to those in respect of which the earlier trade mark is registered.[8] These decisions are implemented in the amended subsection.

14–083

The registered mark must have a reputation

The registered trade mark must have a reputation in the United Kingdom.[9] Presumably the reputation must exist at the date of the alleged infringement. There is no requirement that the reputation must extend over the whole of the United Kingdom (or the Community, in the case of a Community trade mark). But it appears that it must exist in a substantial part of it.[10] There is no express requirement as to the extent of the reputation necessary, although the degree of required recognition must be considered to be reached when the mark is known by a significant part of the public concerned by the products or service covered by the

14–084

---

[3] See Ch.9, paras 9–088 to 9–121.
[4] See paras 14–006 to 14–038.
[5] As to identification of the sign used by the defendant, see paras 14–049 to 14–050.
[6] See Ch.9, paras 9–069 to 9–083.
[7] *Adidas-Salomon v Fitnessworld* [2004] E.T.M.R. 10, at para.28.
[8] See the discussion in Ch.9, paras 9–098 to 9–100.
[9] Or, in the case of a Community trade mark, a reputation in the Community: TM Directive, Art.4(3).
[10] *General Motors v Yplon* [1999] All E.R. (E.C.) 865; [1999] E.T.M.R. 950, at para.28.

trade mark.[11] Any genuine commercial use of a trade mark will generate at least some reputation, but it must now be doubted whether such a measurable but small reputation would be sufficient.[12]

Without due cause, taking unfair advantage, causing detriment

14–085 These are the most important words of the provision. The use must be without due cause and must take unfair advantage of or be detrimental to the distinctive character or the repute of the trade mark. These words are discussed in the context of objections to registration arising under s.5 of the 1994 Act.[13] But certain aspects of the requirement as it relates to infringement are discussed here.

Consumers must establish a link between the sign and the mark

14–086 The provision is not limited to use which is likely to cause confusion as to origin. But it is necessary that the degree of similarity between the mark with the reputation and the sign has the effect that the relevant section of the public establishes a link between the sign and the mark. The existence of such a link must be appreciated globally taking into account all factors relevant to the circumstances of the case.[14]

Without due cause

14–087 This requirement is discussed in Ch.9, paras 9–111 to 9–112. The burden lies on a defendant who wishes to establish that his activities fall within this exception.[15]

Unfair advantage or detriment

14–088 This requirement is discussed in Ch.9, paras 9–113 to 9–121. The link must be such as to cause actual detriment to or take unfair advantage of the distinctive character or repute of the earlier mark. Typically detriment may take the form of making the earlier mark either less attractive (tarnishing) or less distinctive (blurring); unfair advantage may take the form of free-riding on the coattails of a famous mark or trading on its reputation.

14–089 It is to be noted that s.10(2) refers to a "*likelihood* of confusion" whereas s.10(3) uses the words "*takes* unfair advantage of, or is detrimental to …".[16] This difference is wording is significant. It is not enough that the earlier mark is simply called to mind.[17] The existence of such unfair advantage or detriment cannot be assumed and must be established on the evidence.[18] Proof is required of real

---

[11] *General Motors* [1999] All E.R. (E.C.) 865; [1999] E.T.M.R. 950, at para.26. English law draws a distinction between reputation and goodwill. The former does not require any trade in this country; the latter requires at least some business here. See, *e.g. Star Industrial v Yap Kwee Kor* [1976] F.S.R. 256 (PC, Singapore) and Ch.15.

[12] In the light of *General Motors* [1999] All E.R. (E.C.) 865; [1999] E.T.M.R. 950. In contrast, in the field of passing off, a small trader with a limited clientele is as much entitled to protect his trade mark as a large concern.

[13] See Ch.9, paras 9–105 to 9–121 .

[14] See the discussion of this topic in Ch.9, paras 9–107 to 9–110; *Adidas-Salomon v Fitnessworld* [2004] E.T.M.R. 10, paras 28–31 and 38–41.

[15] *Premier Brands v Typhoon* [2000] F.S.R. 767.

[16] Corresponding to Arts 5.1(b) and 5.2 of the TM Directive; see also Art.9(1)(b) and (c) of the CTM Regulation.

[17] *Premier Brands v Typhoon* [2000] F.S.R. 767. For other illustrations, see *BASF v CEP*, Knox J., October 26, 1995, unreported; *Pebble Beach v Lombard Brands* [2003] E.T.M.R. 21 at p.252 (Outer House, Court of Session).

[18] *DaimlerChrysler v Javid Alavi* [2001] R.P.C. 42 at p.813; *Mastercard International v Hitachi Credit* [2004] EWHC 1623; (Ch) [2005] E.T.M.R. 10.

future unfair advantage or detriment; it must be shown to be a real as opposed to a theoretical possibility.[19]

The position is somewhat analogous to that in the US where protection is provided against the dilution of famous marks by the Federal Trademark Dilution Act which amended the Trademark Act of 1946 to provide a remedy against another person's commercial use of a mark or trade name if that use "causes dilution of the distinctive quality" of the famous mark.[20] It defines dilution as the "lessening of the capacity of a famous mark to identify and distinguish goods or services."[21] The Supreme Court has recently affirmed that the provision requires a showing of actual dilution, rather than a likelihood of dilution[22]   **14–090**

In circumstances where the use is such as to cause confusion as to the origin of the goods or services, then it would seem almost inevitable that the effect of that confusion will be to affect detrimentally the distinctive character and the reputation of the registered trade mark. It may also provide an unfair advantage to the alleged infringer. In such circumstances, and absent a specific defence, one can see a court readily finding infringement.[23] Such is also likely to be the case where it is apparent that the defendant is seeking to associate itself with the claimant.[24] But in other cases a court will require convincing evidence of detriment or unfair advantage. It seems the stronger the registered mark's distinctive character and reputation the easier it will be to accept that detriment has been caused to it.[25]   **14–091**

(1) The claimant imported and sold tea in the UK under the registered trade mark TY.PHOO. It also had the mark registered in respect of, *inter alia*, domestic utensils. The defendant imported and sold kitchen hardware under the trade mark TYPHOON. The claimant contended that the defendant's use of the mark TYPHOON would tarnish the TY.PHOON brand because of is association with the destructive power of cyclones and would reduce the uniqueness of the TY.PHOO brand by blurring. Held, there was a limited degree of association between the two marks but it would have no more than an inconsequential effect on the TY.PHOO brand.[26]   **14–092**

(2) The claimant made Mercedes motor cars and was the proprietor of vari-

---

[19] *Intel Corporation v Kirpla Singh Sihra* [2003] EWHC 17 (Ch); *Mastercard International v Hitachi Credit* [2004] EWHC 1623; (Ch) [2005] E.T.M.R. 10.

[20] 15 U.S.C. 1125(c)(1).

[21] 15 U.S.C. 1127.

[22] *Secret Catalogue Inc v Victor Moseley, dba Victor's Little Secret*, 123 S. Ct. 1115. The claimants owned the Victoria's Secret trade mark and operated hundreds of stores under the mark selling, *inter alia*, moderately priced, high quality, attractively designed lingerie. The defendant opened a store shortly before Valentine's day called Victor's Little Secret selling what was described as "unwholesome, tawdry merchandise" including lycra dresses, intimate lingerie and adult novelties. The Court of Appeals held: "While no consumer is likely to go to the Moseleys' store expecting to find Victoria's Secret's famed Miracle Bra, consumers who hear the name "Victor's Little Secret" are likely automatically to think of the more famous store and link it to the Moseleys' adult-toy, gag gift, and lingerie shop. This, then, is a classic instance of dilution by tarnishing (associating the Victoria's Secret name with sex toys and lewd coffee mugs) and by blurring (linking the chain with a single, unauthorised establishment). Given this conclusion, it follows that Victoria's Secret would prevail in a dilution analysis, ...". The Supreme Court reversed and remanded the summary judgment on the dilution count on the basis there was no evidence of any lessening of capacity of the Victoria's Secret mark to identify and distinguish the claimants' goods or services. At least where the marks at issue were not identical, the mere fact that consumers would mentally associate the junior user's mark with a famous mark was not sufficient to establish actionable dilution.

[23] See, *e.g. B.T. v One in a Million* [1998] F.S.R. 265; [1999] F.S.R. 1, CA.

[24] See, *e.g. Gleneagles Hotels v Quillco 100* [2004] E.T.M.R. 12.

[25] *General Motors* [1999] All E.R. (E.C.) 865; [1999] E.T.M.R. 950 at para.30. *Premier Brands v Typhoon* [2000] F.S.R. 767.

[26] *Premier Brands v Typhoon* [2000] F.S.R. 767.

ous trade mark registrations in respect of the words "Mercedes" and "Merc" in respect of vehicles. The defendant sold clothes under the trade mark "Merc" and was, so the claimant complained, concerned with "mods" and "skinheads" and its website contained links to "skinhead" sites which were distasteful. Held, there was no possibility of confusion as to origin and although the word "Merc" might be recognised by some people as an abbreviation of the "Mercedes" mark there was no evidence the defendant derived any advantage from this recognition. As to detriment, the claimant had not proved that the public made any connection between the disparaging use and the familiar "Mercedes" mark. It was not sufficient for the relevant public to see the word "Merc", note that it was a word used to refer to "Mercedes" motor cars, see the disagreeable website and register it as disagreeable, if nothing actually rubbed off on the claimant or on its marks.[27]

Merchandising

14–093   Famous trade marks are often used on t-shirts or other merchandise, being goods which are not similar to any goods sold by the registered proprietor. Traditionally such use might not even be considered trade mark use, let alone use which is calculated to cause confusion as to the origin of the goods.[28] But it seems such use is increasingly likely to be considered to fall into that area between the extremes of distinctiveness and descriptiveness identified by Lord Walker in *Arsenal*.[29] In such cases it may be anticipated the courts may now be more willing to find that such use is both trade mark use and use which is likely to establish a "link" between the sign and the registered mark. And it may well result in the traders in such goods benefiting from the reputation of the registered proprietor.[30]

Parody and satire

14–094   No defence of parody or satire is provided by the 1994 Act but it seems likely that if the use complained of is truly parodic or satirical then this is a matter which may be taken into account by the court in determining whether the use complained of is "without due cause". Nevertheless the scope for any such defence is likely to be limited where the other requirements necessary to establish infringement are satisfied. To fall within the scope of s.10 the use must be in the course of trade as a trade mark.[31] Accordingly any such use will be commercial and is likely to be for the purpose of furthering the sales of the defendant's goods or services. Assuming also that the use either causes detriment to the trade mark owner or provides an advantage to the alleged infringer it is suggested that

---

[27] *DaimlerChrysler v Javid Alavi* [2001] R.P.C. 42.

[28] See, *e.g. Unidoor v Marks & Spencer* [1988] R.P.C. 275; *"Kodiak"* [1990] F.S.R. 49; and for the titles of books, see *Mothercare UK v Penguin Books* [1988] R.P.C. 113; *Games Workshop v Transworld Publishers* [1993] F.S.R. 705.

[29] See the discussion in paras 14–015 to 14–018.

[30] Although not a legitimate aid to interpretation it is interesting that this was recognised at the Committee stage of the Bill (see, HL Official Report, Public Bill Committee, Trade Marks Bill, Second Sitting, January 18, 1994, cols. 35 and 36). Similarly in the White paper, Reform of Trade Marks Law, September 1990, it was noted at para.3.17: "A trade mark may acquire such a wide reputation in relation to particular goods that its use in relation to quite different goods is likely to lead the public into thinking that there is a trade connection. This is probably more so today, when consumers have grown accustomed to supermarkets selling a wide range of goods, or to manufacturers of unrelated goods who are part of the same economic group, than it was when the present law was passed in 1938. Moreover there has grown up the practice of using familiar trade marks to decorate such goods as T-shirts. If the owner of such a mark has no redress then other traders are able to benefit unjustly from his reputation. He may also be denied the opportunity to diversify the exploitation of his mark."

[31] See paras 14–006 to 14–038.

in most cases a defence of satire or parody is unlikely to be viewed by the court with much sympathy.

(1) The claimant's group produced and sold beer under a series of Carling **14–095** Black label trade marks. One of these consisted of a representation of Black Label stickers on the neck and body of a beer bottle. The stickers consisted of a combination of colours and wording including "Black Label" and "Carling Beer" and the phrases "America's lusty, lively beer" and "brewed in South Africa". The defendants sold t-shirts bearing the general colours and lay out of the registered mark but with different wording; the words "Black Label" were replaced with "Black Labour" and "Carling Beer" with "White Guilt". The phrases of the registered mark were replaced by "Africa's lusty, lively exploitation since 1652" and "No regard given worldwide". Held, the use complained of was materially detrimental to the trade mark concerned and the relief sought did not interfere with the defendant's freedom of expression because it could proclaim its message in a variety of other ways. Moreover, it was relevant to take into account the fact that the defendant was in the business of marketing clothing and using well-known marks for that purpose. Finally, the defendant's reliance on parody was misconceived because it was using the reputation of the claimant's mark in the course of trade in relation to goods to the detriment of the repute of the mark without justification.[32]

(2) Esso sought an interim injunction to prevent Greenpeace from reproducing on its website the ESSO trade mark in the form E££O. Held, in the light of the constitutional principle of freedom of speech, no injunction would be granted. Greenpeace's intention was to expose the activities of Esso for adversely affecting the environment without misleading the public as to the author of the communication. Further, Greenpeace was not aiming to commercialise its own products or services.[33]

The whole manner of the defendant's trade to be considered

In considering the application of this provision it seems that the whole manner **14–096** of the alleged infringer's trade may be open to scrutiny and to comparison with the manner of trade of the registered proprietor. A "mark for sign" test is likely to be inadequate to determine whether the use complained of has taken advantage of, or been detrimental to, the distinctive character or repute of the registered trade mark.[34]

Date of the assessment

It is suggested that the same considerations apply here as in relation to s.10(2).[35] **14–097**

Comparative advertising

The 1994 Act has a provision specifically drawn to address the issue of compara- **14–098** tive advertising. It is contained in s.10(6) of the Trade Marks Act and it provides some, but limited, protection against comparative advertising. It does so by creating what, on one view, is a further category of infringement in particular cases involving the use by a third party of a registered trade mark in a comparative

---

[32] *South African Breweries International (Sabmark International) v Laugh It Off Promotions*, SA Court of Appeal, Case 242/2003, September 16, 2004. The case was decided under s.34(1)(c) of the Trade Marks Act 1994 which is in substantially the same terms as s.10(3) of the 1994 Act.

[33] *Association Greenpeace France v SA Societe ESSO*; Cour d'Appel de Paris [2003] E.T.M.R. 66. At trial the action also failed: [2004] E.T.M.R. 90.

[34] As opposed to the position under the 1994 Act, s.10(1) and (2).

[35] See paras 14–077 and 14–078.

advertisement and where, in so doing, the third party uses the trade mark in relation to the goods or services of that proprietor. As will be seen, legislation in the United Kingdom curtailed the use of registered trade marks in comparative advertisements from 1938.[36] The present subsection reflects something of a sea change and the contemporary view, at least in this country, is that comparative advertisements which are fair and accurate do no harm and accordingly should not be prohibited by the use of registered trade marks.

Historical

14–099 Restrictions on the use of a trade mark in comparative advertising were first introduced into the Trade Marks Act 1938. Broadly, s.4(1)(b) of the Act prohibited the use of a mark likely to be taken as "importing a reference" to the registered proprietor or a registered user or to the goods of either of them.[37] The Mathys Report (British Trade Mark Law and Practice (Cmnd. 5601), May 1974, paras 80–88) recommended that such restrictions should remain but there is no specific provision to this effect in the TM Directive. The White Paper, Reform of Trade Marks Law, September 1990, noted at para.3.28, that comparative advertising was regarded as more acceptable than it used to be but it was still generally felt that an advertiser should not be free to ride on the back of a competitor's trade mark. Accordingly it was proposed that s.4(1)(b) of the 1938 Act would be replaced by a provision allowing a trade mark owner to restrain use in advertising which was contrary to honest practices in industrial or commercial matters and would take unfair advantage of or be detrimental to the distinctive character or repute of the trade mark. This is reflected too in the statement of Lord Strathclyde, Minister of State, Department of Trade and Industry, on behalf of the Government:

> "The government have been persuaded that there is no harm in comparative advertising … provided that it makes fair use of a registered trade mark for the purpose of informing the public. As foreshadowed in the White Paper, the Bill seeks to chart a middle course: allowing comparative advertising but providing safeguards for the owner of a registered trade mark."[38]

14–100 In substance this proposal is now embodied in s.10(6) of the 1994 Act. It is a hybrid derived originally from the Paris Convention (Art.10*bis*(2)): "honest practices in industrial and commercial matters" (and now in Article 6 of the TM Directive) and words found in Articles 4 and 5 of the Directive: "where use of the sign without due cause takes advantage of, or is detrimental to, the distinctive character or repute of the trade mark". As will be seen the courts have taken the view that the purpose of this provision is positively to permit comparative advertisements.

Section 10(6)

14–101 Section 10(6) of the 1994 Act is as follows:

---

[36] In the case of marks registered in Part A of the Register.

[37] s.4(1)(b), was introduced to overrule the case of *Irving's Yeast Vite v Horesenail* (1934) 51 R.P.C. 110, HL ("Yeast tablets. A substitute for Yeast-Vite" not an infringement of "Yeast-Vite"). It was applied most famously in *Bismag v Amblins* [1940] Ch. 667; 57 R.P.C. 209; see illustration in the text at para.14–115.

[38] Parliamentary Debates, HL Official Report, Public Bill Committee, Trade Marks Bill, Second Sitting, January 18, 1994, col.42.

"Nothing in the preceding provisions of this section shall be construed as preventing the use of a registered trade mark by any person for the purpose of identifying goods or services as those of the proprietor or a licensee.

But any such use other than in accordance with honest practices in industrial or commercial matters shall be treated as infringing the registered trade mark if the use without due cause takes advantage of, or is detrimental to, the distinctive character or repute of the trade mark."

It has no counterpart in the CTM Regulation and no direct foundation in the **14–102** TM Directive. It is divided into two parts. The first part is a saving where a registered trade mark is used in relation to the genuine goods. The second part qualifies the saving by providing that such use which is not in accordance with honest practices shall be treated as an infringement if it is use which, without due cause, takes advantage, of or is detrimental to, the distinctive character or repute of the trade mark.

Although, as noted above, the subsection was specifically introduced to ad- **14–103** dress the issue of comparative advertising, it is not in fact so limited, for it also covers any other use of a trade mark for the purpose of identifying the genuine goods or services of the proprietor. The two sorts of use are not quite the same. In the case of a comparative advertisement, the mark is primarily being used in relation to the genuine goods or services of the proprietor and those are not goods or services in which the advertiser is actually dealing.

It is of some importance to consider the nature of this subsection and the basis **14–104** for it because it may have implications in considering the proper interpretation of the CTM Regulation and indeed the extent of protection properly afforded under the TM Directive and the CTM Regulation to the use of a trade mark in relation to the genuine goods or services of the proprietor.

On one approach it may be argued that since the saving part of s.10(6) has no **14–105** clear foundation in the TM Directive it must be concluded that the legislature considered that use of a trade mark in a comparative advertisement does not fall within the rights conferred by a registered trade mark under Art.5(1) or (2) in the first place.[39] Were it otherwise the 1994 Act would have provided a defence or saving not sanctioned by the TM Directive. This is a matter developed in relation to the CTM Regulation in paras 14–229 to 14–237. As will be seen, if this is the correct interpretation of the Directive and the Act, then it would appear to have the consequence that comparative advertising using a Community trade mark is not an infringement under the CTM Regulation.

On the same approach the second half of the subsection may then be viewed as **14–106** permitted under the optional provisions of Article 5(5) of the TM Directive which states that paras 1–4 of Art.5 shall not affect provisions in any Member State relating to the protection against the use of a sign other than for the purpose of distinguishing goods or services, where use of that sign without due cause takes unfair advantage of, or is detrimental to, the distinctive character or the repute of the trade mark.

Another approach is to regard comparative advertising as something which, **14–107** *prima facie*, falls within Article 5(1) and 5(2) of the Directive and, accordingly,

---

[39] Although, of course, the Directive cannot be construed by reference to the Act. Some support for this argument may be derived from the decision of the ECJ in *Anheuser-Busch* [2005] E.T.M.R. 27. See para.14–017.

ss.10(1) and 10(2) of the Act.[40] After all, on a traditional analysis, such an advertisement does in one sense involve the use of the trade mark in relation to the goods or services of the proprietor[41] and for which, on this assumption, it is registered. In the High Court it has now been held that this is indeed the position.[42]

14–108   On this approach all such use is, *prima facie*, an infringement unless it is taken out of the scope of the prohibited field by s.10(6) which is then properly regarded as a qualified saving only. This is all very well in considering national registrations although, as already indicated, it is not a saving sanctioned by the TM Directive and it must be questioned whether it is therefore properly part of the law at all.[43] But it has important consequences in considering Community trade marks because, as also indicated, there is no equivalent provision in the TM Directive. Any saving of a comparative advertisement from infringement in the case of Community trade marks must therefore be found elsewhere and, in particular, in notions of consent, exhaustion or under Article 12 of the CTM Regulation.[44]

Interpretation and application

14–109   In a comparative advertisement the trade mark is being used to identify the goods or services of the proprietor or licensee. Accordingly such use will fall within the first paragraph of the subsection which sets out the freedom to use a trade mark to denote the goods or services of the proprietor or licensee in one's own advertisements. But the freedom is qualified by the proviso. Any use in a comparative advertisement which contravenes the proviso will amount to an infringement.

14–110   The meaning of the proviso has now been considered in a number of cases: *Barclays Bank v Advanta*;[45] *Vodafone Group v Orange*;[46] *BT v AT & T* (a decision of Mr Crystal Q.C., sitting as a deputy judge);[47] *Cable & Wireless v BT*.[48] In the latter case (at 389) Jacob J. quoted with approval the summary of the findings of Mr Crystal Q.C. with one qualification:

> "(1) The primary objective of section 10(6) of the 1994 Act is to permit comparative advertising (see Advanta at pages 312–313 and 315, and Vodafone at page [39]);[49]
>
> (2) As long as the use of a competitor's mark is honest, there is nothing wrong in telling the public of the relative merits of competing goods

---

[40] It now seems clear that the use by a person of a trade mark in relation to the genuine goods of the proprietor in which he is dealing does fall within Art.5(1): *BMW v Deenik* [1999] E.C.R. I-905; [1999] E.T.M.R. 339. But for the reasons indicated, this use is not quite the same as the use of a trade mark in a comparative advertisement.

[41] *Bismag v Amblins* [1940] Ch. 667; 57 R.P.C. 209; it will also be remembered that the CA considered that the use of the mark was used both in relation to the goods of the proprietor and of the advertiser. See also the discussion in relation to Community trade marks in paras 14–229 to 14–239.

[42] *British Airways v Ryanair* [2001] F.S.R. 32 at p.541

[43] Save in so far as it merely constitutes a repetition of savings or defences to be found elsewhere in the Directive and in particular, in Art.6(1): see para.14–171.

[44] Corresponding to the TM Directive, Art.6, implemented in the 1994 Act, s.11. See further in the discussion of the position in relation to Community trade marks in paras 14–229 to 14–237.

[45] [1996] R.P.C. 307.

[46] [1997] F.S.R. 34.

[47] December 18, 1996.

[48] [1998] F.S.R. 383. Now followed most recently in *Emaco Ltdv Dyson* [1999] E.T.M.R. 903. See also *MacMillan Magazines v RCN Publishing* [1998] F.S.R. 9.

[49] We have inserted the page references of the report of *Vodafone* in [1997] F.S.R. 34.

or services and in using registered marks to identify them (see Advanta page 315, Vodafone at page [39]);

(3) The onus is on the registered proprietor to show that the factors indicated in the proviso to section 10(6) exist (see Advanta at page 315, Vodafone at page [39]);

(4) There will be no trade mark infringement unless the use of the registered mark is not in accordance with honest practices (see Advanta at page 315);

(5) The test is objective: would a reasonable reader be likely to say, upon being given the full facts, that the advertisement is not honest?[50] (see Advanta at page 315, Vodafone at page [39]);

(6) Statutory or industry agreed codes of conduct are not a helpful guide as to whether an advertisement is honest for the purposes of section 10(6). Honesty has to be gauged against what is reasonably to be expected by the relevant public of advertisements for the goods or services in issue (see Advanta at page 316);

(7) It should be borne in mind that the general public are used to the ways of advertisers and expect hyperbole (see Advanta at page 315; cf. Vodafone at pages [38 to 39]);

(8) The 1994 Act does not impose on the courts an obligation to try and enforce through the back door of trade mark legislation a more puritanical standard than the public would expect from advertising copy (see Advanta at page 315; Vodafone at page [39]);

(9) An advertisement which is significantly misleading is not honest for the purposes of section 10(6) (see Advanta at page 316, Vodafone at pages [39 to 40];

I venture with diffidence to make a number of additional observations.

(10) The advertisement must be considered as a whole (cf. Advanta at pages 316–318);

(11) As a purpose of the 1994 Act is positively to permit comparative advertising, the court should not hold words in the advertisement to be seriously misleading for interlocutory purposes unless on a fair reading of them in their context and against the background of the advertisement as a whole they can really be said to justify that description;

(12) A minute textual examination is not something upon which the reasonable reader of a advertisement would embark;

(13) The court should therefore not encourage a microscopic approach to the construction of a comparative advertisement on a motion for interlocutory relief."

The qualification related to "honesty" and the nature of the objective test. Jacob J. considered that the test was objective in this sense: that one should ask whether a reasonable trader could honestly have made the statements he made based upon the information that he had (at 391).   **14–111**

All of these observations as to the meaning of "honest practices in industrial or commercial matters" must now be seen in the context of the decisions of the European Court of Justice concerning the same words in Article 6(1) of the TM   **14–112**

---

[50] In trade marks, there is no "one meaning" rule. If a comparison is significantly misleading on an objective basis to a substantial proportion of the reasonable audience, it is not an honest practice within the section: Vodafone at 39.

Directive.[51] The condition constitutes in substance the expression of a duty to act fairly in relation to the legitimate interests of the trade mark owner. In *Reed Executive v Reed Business Information*[52] Jacob L.J. indicated that notwithstanding his observation in *Cable & Wireless* he now inclined to the view that the test was objective and one of simple causation.[53]

14–113   Moreover, the matter should be considered from the perspective of the average consumer who is reasonably well-informed and reasonably observant and circumspect.[54] Such a person expects hyperbole and puff.[55]

14–114   Certainly the approach taken by the courts hitherto indicates that they are minded to take a liberal view of what is permissible; this is revealed by the suggestion that the purpose of the legislation is positively to permit comparative advertising[56] and the reference to a need for the advertising to be significantly misleading before it will be characterised as offensive. There has been no suggestion that the use of trade marks, even if not necessary, and denigrations of competitors goods are not permissible, provided that they are not significantly misleading. In these respects it may be contended that s.10(6), as interpreted by the courts, has been taken beyond any defence contemplated by the TM Directive or now reflected in the Comparative Advertising Directive.[57]

14–115   (1) The plaintiff, the bank Barclays, ran the Barclaycard credit business and was the proprietor of the registered trade mark BARCLAYCARD. The defendant, RBS Advanta, a joint venture owned by the Royal Bank of Scotland and Advanta Corporation, intended to offer a credit card under the name RBS Advanta VISA card. It issued advertising material identifying 15 ways the card was a better credit card than its competitors and a comparative table referring expressly to, *inter alia*, BARCLAYCARD. The plaintiff complained that the advertisement was misleading in that it made no mention of other ancillary benefits which the plaintiff offered and which the defendant did not have and that at least six of the 15 points identified were common to BARCLAYCARD as well. Held, refusing an interlocutory injunction, it was most unlikely any reasonable reader would take the view the advertisement was dishonest; the advertisement conveyed the message that the package, taken as a whole, offered the customer a better deal.[58]

(2) Vodafone and Orange operated rival cellular telephone networks. Orange adopted, for an advertising campaign, the slogan "On average, Orange users save £20 every month", a saving expressly stated to be in comparison with Vodafone's equivalent tariff. It was thereupon sued by Vodafone for malicious falsehood and trade mark infringement. Vodafone contended that the advertisement carried the message that on average Vodafone users would save £20 every month if they had instead been on Orange and in any event the notion of an average was inherently deceptive because the user profile was skewed with most users making relatively little usage of their phones. Held, the claim failed. The ordinary person would

---

[51] *BMW v Deenik* [1999] E.C.R. I-905, at paras 61–62; *Gerolsteiner Brunnen v Putsch*, Case C–100/02, [2004] R.P.C. 39 at para.24. See also paras 14–158 to 14–163.

[52] [2004] EWCA Civ 159; [2004] R.P.C. 40.

[53] [1998] F.S.R. 383, at paras 131 and 132.

[54] *British Airways v Ryanair* [2001] F.S.R. 32, at paras 30–31 (citing *Estée Lauder Cosmetics* [2000] I.P.&T. 380 and *Gut Springenheide* [1998] E.C.R. I-4657).

[55] *British Airways* [2001] F.S.R. 32 at para.32.

[56] cf. the legislative history, para.14–099.

[57] See paras 14–116 to 14–119.

[58] *Barclays Bank v Advanta* [1996] R.P.C. 307.

understand the advertisement to mean that, on average, if Orange users had been on Vodafone, they would have had to pay £20 more a month. Vodafone users would simply recognise that it might be cheaper to use Orange. It was not established that the advertisement was misleading.[59]

(3) British Telecom issued a brochure to small- and medium-sized customers containing the sentence: "Most customers who are using the best Cable & Wireless indirect price package will make savings by using the best package from BT". The brochure continued with an analysis of the costs of calling with BT and Cable & Wireless and a price comparison. The brochure was based upon an analysis carried out by Deloitte & Touche, a leading firm of chartered accountants. Cable & Wireless thereupon launched proceedings for trade mark infringement and sought an injunction pending trial. Held, refusing the injunction, much of the dispute turned on statistical models; it could not be said that honest traders, having the information which BT had, would not be prepared to make the statements which BT had made.[60]

(4) Ryanair placed a press advertisement under the headline "EXPENSIVE BA .... DS!' in which it compared a number of return air fare prices to European destinations with those of British Airways. Held, dismissing the claim, the comparisons were fair and offensive or vulgar abuse was not actionable as trade mark infringement.[61]

(5) The plaintiffs were the registered proprietors of the trade mark "Bisurated" for medicines. The defendants were selling in addition to their own medicines proprietary medicines of other manufacturers, including those of the plaintiffs. The defendants issued a pamphlet in which, after a preliminary statement as to the prices of patent medicines, there were set out two columns; in one, headed "List of advertised patent medicines sold by us", prescriptions including *inter alia* "Bisurated Magnesia Tablets" with an analysis and price; in the other, headed "Amblins Medicine (Brand) Prescriptions" (and opposite to the "Bisurated Magnesia Tablets"), the words "Bismuthated Magnesia Tablets", also with an analysis and price which was much lower than the other. The majority of the Court of Appeal held that the mark "Bisurated" was used in relation to both sorts of goods, the defendants' "Bismuthated" tablets as well as the plaintiffs'. Accordingly, under the Trade Marks Act 1938 there was infringement. There seems no doubt that under the 1994 Act the claim would have failed.[62]

The Comparative Advertising Directive

It is interesting to note that the approach of the courts to comparative advertising **14–116** and trade mark infringement is not fully consistent with Directive 97/55 of October 6, 1997 amending Directive 84/450 concerning comparative advertising.[63] The earlier Directive requires the prohibition of advertising which is misleading. The later Directive has a specific purpose of laying down the condi-

---

[59] *Vodafone v Orange* [1997] F.S.R. 34.
[60] *Cable & Wireless v British Telecommunications* [1998] F.S.R. 383.
[61] *British Airways* [2001] F.S.R. 32, at paras 34 and 35.
[62] *Bismag v Amblins* [1940] Ch. 667; 57 R.P.C. 209, CA. There were many cases under the 1938 Act, see the 12th edition of *Kerly*, paras 14–026 and 14–027 and supplement. For a more recent case, objectionable under the old law and which, it is suggested, would have been equally objectionable under the new, see *Compaq v Dell* [1992] F.S.R. 93.
[63] Directive 97/55, Art.3, allowed Member States up to 30 months to bring into force laws, regulations and administrative provisions necessary to comply with it.

tions under which comparative advertising is permitted.[64] The European Court of Justice has observed that the lawfulness of comparative advertising throughout the Community is to be assessed solely in the light of the criteria laid down by the Community legislature.[65]

14-117   For the purposes of these Directives comparative advertising means any advertising which explicitly or by implication identifies a competitor or goods or services offered by a competitor.[66] Article 3a of Directive 84/450 provides that comparative advertising shall, as far as the comparison is concerned, be permitted when the specified conditions are met. Those conditions are as follows:

(1) it is not misleading according to Arts 2(2), 3 and 7(1);[67]

(2) it compares goods or services meeting the same needs or intended for the same purpose;

(3) it objectively compares one or more material, relevant, verifiable and representative features of those goods and services, which may include price;

(4) it does not create confusion in the market place between the advertiser's trade marks, trade names, other distinguishing marks, goods or services and those of a competitor;

(5) it does not discredit or denigrate the trade marks, trade names, other distinguishing marks, goods, services, activities or circumstances of a competitor;

(6) for products with designation of origin, it relates in each case to products with the same designation;

(7) it does not take unfair advantage of the reputation of a trade mark, trade name or other distinguishing marks of a competitor or of the designation of origin of competing products;

(8) it does not present goods or services as imitations or replicas of goods or services bearing a protected trade mark or trade name.

The provision also includes specific restrictions relating to special offers.

14-118   Directive 84/450 allows an advertiser to state in comparative advertising the brand of a competitor's product where the comparison does not have the intention or effect of giving rise to such situations of unfair competition.[68]

14-119   The Directive has been implemented in the United Kingdom by the Control of Misleading Advertisements) (Comparative Advertisements) (Amendment) Regulations 2000 which came into force in April 2000.[69] These Regulations amend the Control of Misleading Advertisements Regulations 1988[70] by adding comparative advertisements to the regime governing misleading advertisements there set out. The responsibility for enforcement lies with the Director General of Fair Trading. It certainly appears that these Regulations are more restrictive than

---

[64] Directive 97/55, Art.1(2). The preamble to the Directive rather suggests (in Recitals 14–015) that comparative advertising that does not comply with Directive 97/55 would fall within the exclusive rights conferred by Directive 89/104 (the TM Directive).

[65] *Pippig Augenoptik v Hartlauer* [2004] E.T.M.R. 5, at paras 34–44.

[66] Directive 84/450, Art.2(2a). this is a broad definition covering all forms of comparative advertising. It is sufficient for there to be a statement referring even by implication to a competitor or to the goods or services which he offers: *Toshiba Europe v Katun Germany* [2001] E.C.R. I-7945, at paras 30 and 31; *Pippig Augenoptik v Hartlauer* [2004] E.T.M.R. 5, at paras 34–37.

[67] These provisions are set out in App.15. Misleading advertising is broadly defined as any advertising which in any way, including its presentation, deceives or is likely to deceive the persons to whom it is addressed or whom it reaches and which, by reason of its deceptive nature, is likely to affect their economic behaviour or which, for those reasons, injures or is likely to injure a competitor. See also *Toshiba Europe v Katun Germany* [2001] E.C.R. I-7945.

[68] *Pippig Augenoptik v Hartlauer* [2004] E.T.M.R. 5, at paras 45–51.

[69] SI 2000/914.

[70] SI 1988/915.

s.10(6) of the 1994 Act and that an advertisement may offend the Regulations even if it does not amount to an infringement of registered trade mark, at least on the approach to infringement adopted by the courts hitherto. Nevertheless, at least thus far, the High Court has held that Directive 97/55 does not affect the interpretation of the 1994 Act on the basis that it was not intended to amend the TM Directive.[71]

C. ANCILLARY MATTERS

Joint liability

Section 10(5) of the 1994 Act makes specific provision for the case where a person applies a registered trade mark to material intended to be used for labelling or packaging goods, as business papers or for advertising goods or services. The scope of this provision is discussed in para.14–035 *et seq.* In addition a person who becomes involved in counterfeiting or other infringement may be liable for directing, procuring or combining with others to infringe.[72]   **14–120**

Limitation as to validity

The rights given by a registered trade mark are not subject to an express limitation that the registration must be valid.[73] Nevertheless, under s.46 of the 1994 Act, a mark may be revoked with effect from the date of the application for revocation or, if the Registrar or court is satisfied that the grounds of revocation existed at an earlier date, that date. Furthermore, where the registration of a mark is declared invalid to any extent under s.47, then, to that extent, the registration is deemed never to have been made. Validity is considered elsewhere.[74] As before, an action for infringement is likely to be met by the defence that the mark is invalid and liable to be revoked and a counterclaim for a declaration of invalidity and for an order that the registration be removed from the Register.   **14–121**

Date from which rights are conferred

The rights of the proprietor have effect from the date of filing of the application for registration. But no infringement proceedings may be begun before the date on which the trade mark is in fact registered.[75] In this respect the position is the same as under the old law.[76]   **14–122**

Locality of infringement

Trade mark rights are territorial. An infringing act committed outside the United Kingdom cannot be sued upon as an infringement of a United Kingdom registered   **14–123**

---

[71] *British Airways v Ryanair* [2001] F.S.R. 32, at paras 24–28. cf. *Gillette v La-Laboratories*, Case C–228/03, decision of March 17, 2005, where the ECJ did apparently take account of Directive 84/450 in explaining the critieria to be applied in determining the scope of "honest practices" in Art.6 of the TM Directive; see particularly at paras 9 and 42–45.

[72] For an exposition of the relevant principles, see *CBS v Amstrad Consumer Electronics* [1988] 1 A.C. 1013. An example of their application is *White Horse Distillers v Gregson Associates* [1984] R.P.C. 61. This topic is discussed further in Ch.19.

[73] This position may be contrasted with that under the 1938 Act where, by s.4, it was specified that a registration gave exclusive rights, if valid.

[74] See Ch.10.

[75] 1994 Act, s.9(3) and s.40(3).

[76] As to offences and criminal proceedings, see Ch.20.

trade mark.[77] This may be a point of particular relevance in relation to magazines circulating in the UK and websites. The mere fact that websites can be accessed anywhere in the world does not mean that, for trade mark purposes, the law should regard them as being used everywhere in the world. It all depends upon the circumstances, particularly the intention of the website owner and what the reader will understand if he accesses the site.[78]

The claimant was the proprietor of the registered trade mark "Crate & Barrel" and ran a successful business in the US selling household goods and furniture under the mark. The Defendant ran a shop in Dublin called "Crate & Barrel" selling household goods and furniture. It had a website under the name and advertised in magazine which circulated in the UK and Ireland. Held, no infringement; a reasonable trader would not regard the activities of the defendant as use "in the course of trade in relation to goods" within the UK.[79]

Burden of proof

14–124 In cases of infringement the burden of proof lies upon the claimant, usually the proprietor of the mark, although in particular circumstances exclusive or even non-exclusive licensees can bring proceedings, joining the proprietor as co-claimant or defendant.[80] The burden of proof lies on the defendant to establish invalidity.

D. Savings and exceptions

Limitations entered onto the Register

14–125 Section 13 of the 1994 Act provides that where the registration of a trade mark is subject to a disclaimer or a limitation, then the rights conferred by s.9 are restricted accordingly. Similarities attributable to nothing more than that which is disclaimed can not support an action for infringement.[81]

Use on the genuine goods or services of the proprietor

14–126 It was recognised before the Trade Marks Act of 1938 that a proprietor should not have the right to stop the use of a trade mark in connection with what were usually described as "the genuine goods".[82] The reasoning for this limitation was that such use could not cause deception, which was the test of infringement. The Trade Marks Act 1938 incorporated a specific provision to deal with the issue,[83] a provision necessary because there were now cases deemed to be infringements

---

[77] But as for bringing proceedings here in respect of infringements of foreign trade marks and vice versa, see Ch.19.

[78] *1–800 Flowers v Phonenames* [2000] E.T.M.R. 369; *Euromarket Designs Inc v Peters* [2001] F.S.R. 20 at p.288; *Bonnier Media v Greg Lloyd Smith and Kestrel Trading Corp* [2002] E.T.M.R. 86. See further, Ch.23.

[79] *Euromarket Designs Inc v Peters* [2001] F.S.R. 20.

[80] See Ch.19.

[81] *The European v The Economist* [1998] F.S.R. 283, CA.

[82] *Champagne Heidsieck v Buxton* [1930] 1 Ch. 330; 47 R.P.C. 28; cf. *Farina v Silverlock* (1885) 1 K. & J. 509; 24 L.J.Ch. 632; 6 De G.M. & G. 214; 24 L.J. Ch. 11, a case prior to the earliest Registration Act.

[83] Trade Marks Act 1938, s.4(3)(a).

within s.4(1)(b) of that Act, where the use of the mark did not involve any likelihood of deception.[84]

The matter is dealt with expressly under the 1994 Act by s.10(6) which provides that, in these circumstances, and subject to the proviso, it is not an infringement to use the registered mark for the purpose of identifying goods or services as those of the proprietor or licensee.[85] **14–127**

In the straightforward case where the trader is doing no more than using the trade mark in relation to the genuine goods in which he is dealing, then there will plainly be no difficulty. A defence will be provided by s.11(2) or s.12 implementing Art.6(1) and Art.7 of the TM Directive, respectively.[86] But in other cases the matter will not be so clear. So for, example, the goods may have deteriorated or been altered or adulterated so as to affect their quality. In other cases bulk goods may simply have been broken down. In such cases, it is suggested, the principles of international exhaustion should be equally applicable.[87] **14–128**

(1) The claimant was the proprietor of the trade mark "Primark" for clothing. The defendant sold jeans under the name "Primark" which it claimed had been made by one of the claimant's suppliers as part of an order placed by the claimant. Held, finding infringement, for the jeans to become the claimant's goods it was not enough that they had been manufactured to its specification; it was necessary that they had been adopted by the claimant as its goods and this could happen no earlier than the time at which he accepted delivery and had an opportunity of satisfying himself that the goods were to the specification and to the requisite standard.[88] **14–129**

(2) The claimant was the proprietor of the trade mark PAG for batteries. It sold a battery called the PAG Lok which contained a number of rechargeable cells and an interface, also called the PAG Lok, which allowed it to be connected to the apparatus with which it was used. The defendant refurbished PAG Lok batteries by replacing the cells and sometimes the casings and then returned them to the original customer or sold them to third parties. Held, the goods were no longer the goods of the proprietor and accordingly s.10(6) was of no application.[89]

(3) The defendant, in business as a repairer of automatic transmissions of cars, built himself a car and got it up to look like one of the plaintiff's. The radiator was a Rolls Royce part bearing their trade mark. On an application for an interlocutory injunction, it was held there was an arguable case of infringement of trade mark notwithstanding that the only use of the mark was on the genuine part and the car.[90]

Parallel imports

The position in respect of goods put on the market in the EEA is governed by **14–130**

---

[84] *Bismag v Amblins* [1940] Ch. 667; 57 R.P.C. 209.

[85] See the discussion of this issue in paras 14–098 to 14–1108. Because of the dubious origin of this provision, it is suggested that the best approach is to follow the principles set out in the next paragraph.

[86] Provided they are goods which the trade mark owner has actually adopted as his own: *Primark Stores v Lollypop Clothing* [2001] F.S.R. 37 at p.637: see illustration (1) in the text.

[87] TM Directive, Art.7, discussed briefly in Ch.16. In short, there must be legitimate reasons for opposing the use of the mark: *BMW v Deenik* [1999] E.T.M.R. 339.

[88] *Primark Stores v Lollypop Clothing* [2001] F.S.R. 37.

[89] *PAG Limited v Hawk-Woods* [2002] F.S.R. 46.

[90] *Rolls-Royce v Dodd* [1988] F.S.R. 517, a decision under the 1938 Act but, it is suggested, the result under the 1994 Act would be the same.

s.12 of the 1994 Act.[91] It provides that a registered trade mark is not infringed by the use of the trade mark in relation to goods which have been put on the market in the EEA under that trade mark by the proprietor or with his consent, unless there are legitimate reasons for the proprietor to oppose further dealings in the goods. This is a complex topic and it is considered in detail in Ch.16.

14–131   If the goods were first put on the market outside the EEA then it now seems that there may be no exhaustion of trade mark rights unless consent has been given for the importation of those goods into the EEA.[92]

14–132   This is a dramatic change in the law, introduced by the implementation of the TM Directive. Hitherto it had seemed clear that the courts would not permit the use of United Kingdom registered trade marks to prevent the importation of goods, bearing a particular trade mark, where the goods were originally marketed by some branch of the enterprise of which the United Kingdom registered proprietor (or registered user under the 1938 Act) formed part. In effect the courts regarded the mark as applying to the genuine goods, the use having the consent of the registered proprietor.[93] Again this matter is addressed in detail in Ch.16.

E. DEFENCES TO AN ACTION FOR INFRINGEMENT OF A REGISTERED TRADE MARK

14–133   The defences discussed in this section must be considered together with the elements which a claimant is required to prove to make out a case of infringement. These are considered above. The most commonly cited defences are set out below:

(1) the activities complained of were performed with the consent of the proprietor;

(2) the use complained of is use in relation to the genuine goods or services;

(3) the registration is invalid or liable to be revoked;

(4) the defendant has an independent right to use the mark arising from his own registration;

(5) the defendant is using his own name and address;

(6) the defendant is using indications concerning the characteristics of his goods or services;

(7) the defendant is indicating the intended purpose of a product or service;

(8) the defendant has his own right to use the mark arising from an earlier right;

(9) miscellaneous and general defences.

(1) Consent

14–134   Section 9 of the 1994 Act makes it clear that the exclusive rights in a trade mark are infringed by the use of the trade mark in the United Kingdom without the consent of the proprietor. As such this is truly a requirement of the cause of action, rather than a defence. If the defendant relies upon a specific licence, then the evidential burden may shift onto him. Licences to use a registered trade mark may be general or limited and are discussed in detail in Ch.13.

---

[91] Implementing the TM Directive, Art.7.

[92] *Silhouette International v Hartlauer* [1999] F.S.R. 729; *Sebago v Unic* [2000] R.P.C. 63; cf. *Zino Davidoff v A & G Imports* [1999] R.P.C. 631.

[93] *Revlon* [1980] F.S.R. 50, CA; cf. if there was an express denial of a United Kingdom trade mark licence: *Castrol v Automotive* [1983] R.P.C. 315; or if the quality of the goods sold in each territory was different: *Colgate Palmolive v Markwell Finance* [1989] R.P.C. 497, CA.

(2) Use on the genuine goods or services

This is discussed at paras 14–126 to 14–132.   **14–135**

(3) Attack on the validity of the registration

A registration can be attacked in two ways. An application can be made for the   **14–136**
revocation of the registration and an application can be made for a declaration
that the registration of the trade mark is invalid.[94]

A registered trade mark can be revoked on any of the grounds set forth in s.46   **14–137**
of the 1994 Act. The grounds of revocation are discussed in detail in Ch.10. It
should be noted that if the grounds of revocation exist in respect of only some of
the goods or services for which the mark is registered, then the revocation will
relate to those goods or services only. Where a mark is revoked to any extent,
then the rights of the proprietor are deemed to have ceased to that extent as from
the date of revocation, or if the court or Registrar is satisfied that the grounds of
revocation existed at an earlier date, then as from that date.[95]

An application can be made for a declaration that the registration is invalid on   **14–138**
any of the grounds set forth in s.47 of the 1994 Act. These grounds are discussed
in detail in Ch.10. As in the case of revocation, if the grounds exist in relation to
only some of the goods or service for which the mark is registered, then the declaration will be made in respect those goods or services only. The grounds of invalidity relate to the original registration and accordingly, where a declaration of
invalidity is made to any extent, the registration is to that extent deemed never to
have existed; provided that this does not affect transactions past and closed.[96]

(4) Use of a registered trade mark

A registered trade mark is not infringed by the use of another registered trade   **14–139**
mark in relation to goods or services for which it is registered.[97] This defence was
introduced at the Report stage of the Bill and provides equivalent protection
under the new law to that previously afforded by s.4(4) of the Trade Marks Act
1938. The defence is not derived from the TM Directive and it has no parallel in
the CTM Regulation.[98]

For the defence to operate the defendant must be using the mark in the form in   **14–140**
which it is registered and in relation to the particular goods or services for which
it is registered. A court is likely to consider carefully whether or not these requirements are satisfied, as it did under the old law.[99]

    (1) The plaintiffs had the mark "Gor-Ray" registered for, *inter alia*, skirts; the   **14–141**
        defendants had the mark "Gilray" registered for dresses. The plaintiffs
        sued for infringement in respect of the use of "Gilray" on separate skirts.
        There was evidence that in the trade the term "dress" could cover a two-
        piece suit, including coat and skirt. Harman J. held that since the sale of a
        dress necessarily included the sale of the skirt of the dress, s.4(4) of the
        1938 Act applied. The Court of Appeal took the opposite view. Evershed

---

[94] The procedures involved are discussed in Chs 10 and 19.
[95] s.46(6).
[96] s.47(6).
[97] s.11(1).
[98] See para.14–245.
[99] See, in addition to the illustrations below, *Spillers* (1952) 69 R.P.C. 327; (1953) 70 R.P.C. 51,
    CA and (1954) 71 R.P.C. 234, HL; *Cluett, Peabody v McIntyre, Hogg* [1958] R.P.C. 335 at 355.

M.R. observed that "skirts are not, when treated separately, dresses"; and that "the right to use a trade mark for dresses ... does not involve the right to use that mark in respect of parts of dresses": *Gor-Ray v Gilray* (1952) 69 R.P.C. 99 at 106; 69 R.P.C. 199 at 205, 206, CA.

(2) The defendants had a registration of ECONCIL-VK, the plaintiff one of V-CIL-K. The defendant was restrained from using econoCIL-VK (the former letters being about four times smaller than the latter), the court holding that it is a question of fact whether a defendant is using his registered mark and that question is not to be answered by asking whether the mark used would be an infringement of the registered mark: *Lilly (Eli) v Chelsea Drug* [1966] R.P.C. 14.

Defendant not registered

14–142   The defence applies only to cases where the defendant is actually validly registered. If a defendant is threatened or sued and has not yet registered his mark, although it is capable of registration, then he ought immediately to apply for registration. In a proper case the court may stay proceedings in an action for infringement until an application for registration has been decided.

14–143   In various cases brought under the Trade Marks Act 1938 and earlier legislation, such applications were made and it is reasonable to suppose that under the 1994 Act the courts will adopt a similar approach; some illustrations are set out below.[1]

Examples of applications to stay infringement actions

14–144   (1) In *Electrolux v Electrix*[2] it was held that the mark was valid and infringed but that in view of the defendant's long concurrent use, relief should be suspended to give the defendants an opportunity to apply for registration. They did so, but failed.[3]

(2) In *Colibri v Markt*[4] the defendants, who were importers of products manufactured by a German firm, failed in their application for a stay of infringement proceedings pending the conclusion of opposition proceedings by the plaintiffs to the German firm's application for a trade mark containing the word "Colibri" as used in Germany and claimed in the action to have been used for 30 years; no particulars of such use had been supplied.

(3) In *Berlei v Bali*,[5] the defendants had been the registered proprietors of the mark "Bali" but this was expunged by the House of Lords on the grounds that it offended s.11 of the Trade Marks Act 1938. The defendants thereupon sought to register the mark under the provisions of s.12(2) of the 1938 Act and at the same time the plaintiffs pressed their action for infringement which had been commenced earlier. Megarry J. refused a stay, observing that a stay should only be granted where the interests of justice (taking into account the claims of both parties) required it. If an injunction were obtained in the action and the defendants subsequently were registered and thus obtained the protection of s.4(4) of the 1938 Act, the

---

[1] Other older cases are noted in the 12th edition of this book.
[2] (1953) 70 R.P.C. 127; (1954) 71 R.P.C. 23, CA.
[3] *"Electrix"* [1959] R.P.C. 283.
[4] [1959] R.P.C. 8.
[5] [1970] R.P.C. 469.

injunction could be qualified *ab initio* or varied when registration was effected.[6]

Effect of belated registration

If a defendant secures a registration of his mark, then the registration takes effect as of the date of filing of the application for registration. Activities before that date must therefore remain potential infringements, subject to any other defences available. **14–145**

If the defendant secures his registration before the commencement of proceedings against him, then the position is straightforward. If he secures his registration in the period between the commencement of proceedings and trial, then no injunction would be granted against him but damages could be awarded in respect of his activities prior to the application for registration. The most difficult cases will be those where the defendant hopes to secure a registration but is unlikely to do so before the trial. Here he would be well-advised to consider applying for a stay of the infringement action pending a final decision in respect of the application.[7] If such a stay is not ordered then, it is suggested, he should seek to have the grant of any relief stayed until the application has been decided or that he be given liberty to apply to have any injunction varied and that ancillary relief only be granted subject to a cross-undertaking and the giving of any necessary security. **14–146**

Validity of defendant's registration

A complete defence will only be available if the defendant's mark is validly registered. It should be noted that where the registration of a mark is declared invalid pursuant to an application made under s.47 of the 1994 Act, then it is deemed never to have been made. Where a registration is revoked to any extent under s.46, then the rights of the proprietor are deemed to have ceased to that extent as from the date of the application for revocation, or, if the Registrar or court is satisfied that the grounds for revocation existed at an earlier date, then that date. In both cases there will be no protection for the future. **14–147**

Any claimant who is met with a defence that the mark complained of is registered should therefore consider whether he has grounds to seek revocation of that registration or a declaration of invalidity in respect of it. It is to be noted however that the opportunity to apply for a declaration that the registration of a later trade mark is invalid is restricted by s.48. This important provision is discussed below. **14–148**

Effect of acquiescence

Section 48(1) of the 1994 Act provides that where the proprietor of an earlier trade mark or other earlier right has acquiesced for a continuous period of five years in the use of a registered trade mark in the United Kingdom, being aware of that use, there shall cease to be any entitlement on the basis of that earlier trade mark or other right— **14–149**

    (1) to apply for a declaration that the registration of the later trade mark is invalid; or

---

[6] For the form of order, see [1970] R.P.C. 469.
[7] See para.14–142.

(2) to oppose the use of the later trade mark in relation to the goods or services in relation to which it has been so used;

unless the registration of the later trade mark was applied for in bad faith.

14–150   This section implements Article 9 of the TM Directive but, at least in part, is swamped by the defence provided by s.11(1) which has no foundation in the Directive and is discussed in paras 14–139 to 14–148. Nevertheless this provision is important because it restricts the extent to which a declaration of invalidity may be sought in respect of a registered mark, and so also the opportunity for a claimant to attack the registered trade mark of the defendant and behind which it is sheltering.[8] Where the proprietor of the earlier registered mark has acquiesced as called for by the provision, then he may no longer apply for a declaration of invalidity or oppose the use of the later trade mark in relation to the goods or services in relation to which it has been so used, unless the registration of the later trade mark was applied for in bad faith.

14–151   It is suggested that the requirement of acquiescence appears to require no more or less than inaction with actual knowledge of the use. As in the case of the equivalent provision under the CTM Regulation, there seems to be little scope for importing into the provision English notions of acquiescence or estoppel[9] in the light of the express words relating to time and knowledge. Secondly, if bad faith is shown then it seems the limitation is not applicable in terms either of preventing the attack on the later registration or opposing its use.[10]

14–152   Where the provisions of s.48(1) apply, then the proprietor of the later mark is not entitled to oppose the use of the earlier trade mark or, as the case may be, the exploitation of the earlier right either. The use of the word oppose must be intended to include any attempt to prevent use by infringement proceedings.

(5) Use by a person of his own name or address, etc.

14–153   A registered trade mark is not infringed by the use by a person of his own name or address, provided the use is in accordance with honest practices in industrial or commercial matters.[11] This defence implements Article 6(1)(a) of the TM Directive.

Where the defence applies, then the defendant can use the name as a trade mark and a rival trader must sue, if at all, for passing off.[12]

"Name" of the defendant

14–154   It is plain that the defence applies to a natural person. There seems to be no sensible reason why it should not also apply to a company or firm, provided that the other requirements of the defence are met.The House of Lords has now said

---

[8] Although it seems that in an appropriate case the registration might be attacked on other grounds under s.46 and it will be noted that under s.46(2) the rights of the proprietor may be deemed to have ceased as of an earlier date if the Registrar or court is satisfied that the grounds for revocation existed at an earlier date.

[9] As in *Wilmott v Barber* (1880) 15 Ch. D. 96 at 105, *per* Fry J., (1881) 17 Ch.D. 772, CA; *Electrolux v Electrix* (1954) 71 R.P.C. 23 at 32 *et seq.*; *Bulmer v Bollinger* [1978] R.P.C. 78; *Habib Bank v Habib Bank* [1982] R.P.C. 1; [1981] 1 W.L.R. 1265, CA.

[10] As to the meaning of bad faith, reference is invited to the discussion in Ch.8.

[11] 1994 Act, s.11(2)(a).

[12] *Scandecor Development v Scandecor Marketing* [1998] F.S.R. 500; on appeal this issue was not addressed by the court, see [1999] F.S.R. 26. In this case it seems to have been assumed that the defence covered use of the name as a trade mark. The position was the same under the Trade Marks Act 1938, s.8: *Baume v Moore* [1957] R.P.C. 459 at 461 to 464; [1958] R.P.C. 226 at 235, CA.

that represents the "better view", albeit holding that the matter was not *acte clair*.[13] The Court of Justice has held that a party may, in principle, rely on the exception in relation to the use of a trade name.[14] Nothing in the TM Directive suggests that any distinction is to be drawn between natural persons, firms and companies.

If a corporate or firm name was adopted for the purpose of trading off any rep- **14–155** utation attaching to a registered trade mark or for passing off, then it would not satisfy the requirement of being in accordance with honest practices.[15] What goes for the formation of a new company must apply equally to a change of name by an existing company.[16]

The name of a person is the name by which he is known or called. So in the **14–156** case of a natural person it will include the name by which he is christened and the name by which he is usually known.[17] In the case of a company it will include its full corporate name and the name by which it is known to its customers; that is to say omitting such words at the end of the name as "Limited", "Corporation", "Incorporated" or other words or letters indicating corporate status.[18] By parity of reasoning, the defence will apply to business names of persons, firms and companies too, provided they are the names by which those persons, firms and companies are known.[19]

> The claimant was proprietor of the trade mark "Asprey" in relation to a wide **14–157** range of luxury goods, including guns, and had a long established reputation under the name in connection with its business conducted from premises in Bond Street. The second defendant, William Asprey, was a member of the Asprey family, and set up the first defendant, WRA (Guns) Ltd, which traded from premises in Mount Street. The full name of the second defendant, "William R. Asprey, Esquire" ran across the top of the shop. Held, finding passing off and trade mark infringement, the defence of use of own name could apply neither to the first defendant because it was not using its own name, nor to the second defendant because he was not himself trading. More-

---

[13] *Scandecor Development AB v Scandecor Marketing AB* [2001] 2 C.M.L.R. 30. The HL referred the question to the ECJ, but the case settled. In *Reed Executive plc v Reed Business Information Ltd* [2004] EWCA Civ 159, [2004] R.P.C. 40, the CA considered that this may be taken to be the settled opinion within the UK; cf. *NAD Electronics Inc v NAD Computer Systems Ltd* [1997] F.S.R. 380, where Ferris J. questioned whether the defence applied to the use of the corporate name of an artificial person such as a company. It should also be noted that a statement was entered into the minutes of the Council meeting at which the TM Directive was adopted, that the Council and Commission considered that the terms "his own name" applied only in respect of natural persons. Such minutes are not a legitimate aid to interpretation: *Antonissen* [1991] E.C.R. I-745; *Bautiaa and Société Française Maritime* [1996] E.C.R. I-505; but they do indicate that it is possible that the ECJ might take a different view. Under Trade Marks Act 1938, s.8, protection extended to the use by a company of its registered name: *Baume v A.H. Moore* [1957] R.P.C. 459; [1958] R.P.C. 226, CA; *Ballantine v Ballantyne, Stewart* [1959] R.P.C. 47 at 49; [1959] R.P.C. 273; *Parker-Knoll v Knoll International* [1961] R.P.C. 346, CA; [1962] R.P.C. 265, HL, and probably to a firm or business name.

[14] *Anheuser-Busch v Budejovicky Budvar, narodni podnik* Case C–245/02, decision of November 16, 2004, at para.81.

[15] *Asprey & Garrard v WRA (Guns)* [2002] F.S.R. 310 at p.487, CA. As Peter Gibson L.J. said: "... the defence has never been held to apply to names of new companies as otherwise a route to piracy would be obvious."

[16] *WebSphere Trade Mark* [2004] EWHC 529 (Ch); [2004] F.S.R. 39 at paras 37–38.

[17] *Mercury Communications v Mercury Interactive* [1995] F.S.R. 850.

[18] *Reed* [2004] EWCA Civ 159, [2004] R.P.C. 40 at para.115; *WebSphere Trade Mark* [2004] EWHC 529 (Ch); [2004] F.S.R. 39 at para.39; *Baume* [1957] R.P.C. at 461; *Parker-Knoll* [1962] R.P.C. at 275. It would appear that it is enough, for this element of the defence, if it is the name by which a foreign corporation is known in its own country. *Euromarket Designs v Peters* [2001] F.S.R. 20 at p.288 (para.39).

[19] *Mercury* [1995] F.S.R. 850 at 860–863.

over, any use which amounted to passing off could not be in accordance with honest practices.[20]

Use in accordance with honest practices

14–158   The defence will only apply if the defendant shows that his use is in accordance with honest practices in industrial and commercial matters. These words, derived from the TM Directive, also appear in s.10(6) of the 1994 Act. The Directive gives no assistance as to their interpretation.

14–159   It now seems clear that the test is an objective one.[21] The ECJ has said that the condition of honest practices constitutes in substance the expression of a duty to act fairly in relation to the legitimate interests of the trade mark owner.[22] The obligation is similar to that imposed on the reseller when he uses another's trade mark to advertise the resale of products covered by that mark.[23] The national court must carry out an overall assessment of all the circumstances, and, in particular, assess whether the defendant might be regarded as competing unfairly with the proprietor of the trade mark.[24]

14–160   The ECJ has provided some guidance as to how the test is to be applied. In *Anheuser-Busch* it explained that in assessing whether the condition of honest practices is satisfied, account must be taken first of the extent to which the use of the third party's trade name is understood by the relevant public, or at least a significant section of that public, as indicating a link between the third party's goods and the trade mark proprietor or a person authorised to use the trade mark, and secondly of the extent to which the third party ought to have been aware of that. Another factor to be taken into account when making the assessment is whether the trade mark enjoys a certain reputation in the member State in which it is registered and its protection is sought, from which the third party might profit in selling his goods.[25]

14–160A   In *Gillette* the ECJ explained that the use of a trade mark will not be in accordance with honest practices in industrial or commercial matters if, for example:

—it is done in such a manner as to give the impression that there is a commercial connection between the third party and the trade mark owner;
—it affects the value of the trade mark by taking unfair advantage of its distinctive character or repute;
—it entails the discrediting or denigrating of that mark;
—or where the third party presents its product as an imitation or replica of the product bearing the trade mark of which it is not the owner.[26]

14–160B   The national court must determine whether the use by the third party is in accordance with honest practices taking account of the above and the following further matters:

[20] *Asprey & Garrard v WRA (Guns) Ltd* [2002] F.S.R. 31 at 487, CA.
[21] *Reed* [2004] EWCA Civ 159, [2004] R.P.C. 40 at paras 131–132; see also in the context of s.10(6) the discussion at para.14–101 and, *Barclays Bank v Advanta* [1996] R.P.C. 307; *Vodafone Group v Orange* [1997] F.S.R. 34; *Cable & Wireless v BT* [1998] F.S.R. 383.
[22] *BMW v Deenik* [1999]E.C.R. I-905, at paras 61 to 62; *Gerolsteiner Brunnen v Putsch*, Case C–100/02, [2004] R.P.C. 39, at para.24. *Gillette v La-Laboratories*, Case C–228/03, decision of March 17, 2005, at para.41.
[23] *Gillette*, at para.41, citing *Parfums Christian Dior* [1997] E.C.R. I-6013, para.45; *BMW* [1999] E.C.R. I-905, para.61.
[24] *Gerolsteiner Brunnen*, Case C–100/02, [2004] R.P.C. 39, at paras 23–26.
[25] *Anheuser-Busch v Budejovicky Budvar, narodni podnik* Case C–245/02, decision of November 16, 2004; [2005] E.T.M.R. 286.
[26] *Gillette*, paras 40–49.

—the overall presentation of the product marketed by the third party, particularly the circumstances in which the mark of which the third party is not the owner is displayed in that presentation;

—the circumstances in which a distinction is made between that mark and the mark or sign of the third party;

—and the effort made by that third party to ensure that customers distinguish its products from those of which it is not the trade mark owner.[27]

In the UK the test has been formulated essentially as follows: would reasonable members of the trade concerned say, upon knowing all the relevant facts that the defendant knew, that the use complained of is honest?[28]

Use of the name as a trade mark does not prevent the application of the defence.[29]

14–161

> The claimant was the proprietor of the trade mark "Premier" in respect of luggage. The defendant used its name "The Premier Company (UK) Limited and the address "Premier House" on swing tags for the purpose of identifying the trade origin of the goods. There was no passing off and no desire by the defendant to take advantage of the reputation or goodwill of the claimant. Held: the swing tags were used for a legitimate commercial purpose and the defence applied.[30]

Moreover the defence may apply even if some confusion results.[31] The amount of confusion which can be tolerated is a question of degree. Only if objectively what the defendant does, in all the circumstances, amounts to unfair competition, will there be infringement. Relevant factors may include that fact that the defendant has set out to cause confusion or, conversely, taken reasonable steps to avoid confusion. All will turn on the overall circumstances of the case.[32]

14–162

If a defendant believes that what he is doing will not cause substantial confusion but has been shown to be wrong then he must stop at once. Moreover, he may well be liable for the damage that he has unwittingly caused in the past.[33]

14–163

(6) The use of indications concerning the characteristics of the goods, such as kind and quality

Section 11(2)(b) of the 1994 Act provides that a registered trade mark is not infringed by the use of indications concerning the kind, quality, quantity, intended purpose, value, geographical origin, the time of production of goods or rendering of services, or other characteristics of goods or services. Again, the use must be in accordance with honest practices in industrial or commercial matters. This provision implements Article 6(1)(b) of the TM Directive.

14–164

---

[27] *Gillette*, at para.46.

[28] *Volvo v Heritage* [2000] F.S.R. 253.

[29] *Gerolsteiner*, Case C–100/02, [2004] R.P.C. 39, at para.15; *Reed* [2004] EWCA Civ 159, [2004] R.P.C. 40, at paras 122–125.

[30] *Premier Luggage and Bags v Premier Company* [2002] EWCA Civ 387; [2003] F.S.R. 5, at p.69, CA. The same did not apply to the self introduction by sales staff as being from "Premier", of from "Premier Luggage" or "Premier Luggage Company" because in these cases the names used were abbreviations of the full company name.

[31] *Gerolsteiner*, Case C–100/02, [2004] R.P.C. 39, at para.25. A likelihood of aural confusion is not enough, of itself, to conclude that use is not in accordance with honest practices.

[32] *Reed* [2004] EWCA Civ 159, [2004] R.P.C. 40, at para.129. Such reasonable steps may include a search of the national and European registers of trade marks, and if alerted to a potentially conflicting mark, to have made reasonable investigation as to whether it has been used enough to have acquired a reputation or goodwill.

[33] *Reed* [2004] EWCA Civ 159, [2004] R.P.C. 40, at para.131.

General

14–165   The provision requires a consideration of two issues. First, it must be considered whether the use complained about is an indication concerning one of the specified or other characteristics of the goods or services, and secondly, whether the use is in accordance with honest practices in industrial or commercial matters. It is to be noted that the word "necessary" does not appear as a requirement in the provision.[34]

Use in a trade mark sense

14–166   An important question arises as to whether the use must be purely descriptive to fall within the exception or whether use by the defendant of the description in a trade mark sense, that is to say as an indication of origin, is also excepted.

14–167   It seems that various different sorts of trade mark use must be considered. First, there is the use of the indication in relation to the defendant's goods or services, but in such a way that the trade and public will think that the indication is being used by the defendant to denote the origin of the goods or services. An illustration of this under the old law is provided by the case of *Mars v Cadbury*[35] which involved the use by the defendants of the words "treat size" in relation to their confectionery, but with such size and prominence that the words had acquired a degree of distinctiveness.

14–168   Secondly, there is the use by the defendant of the claimant's mark in a comparative sense. One manufacturer may, for example, wish to claim that his goods are of the same quality, kind and have the same purpose as goods sold under a particular trade mark. In all these cases the registered trade mark is being used in a trade mark sense in relation to the goods of the proprietor: but it is also being used by way of description in relation to the goods of the defendant.[36]

14–169   Thirdly, there is the use by the defendant of the claimant's mark so as to indicate some characteristic of the defendant's goods or services. So, for example, the yarn of one producer might be used by another for the purpose of making clothes, goods may be impregnated with some chemical for the purpose of improving their qualities, instruments may be made of a particular alloy. In all these cases the original materials may have been sold under a particular trade mark which the producer of the finished goods wishes to refer to for the purpose of indicating the quality of his own goods.

14–170   As to the first category of uses, that is to say the use of the sign for the defendant's goods as a descriptor, the European Court of Justice has held that it is enough that a sign has some descriptive significance, even if it also has some trade mark significance. The only further question is whether it is used in accordance with honest practices in industrial or commercial matters.[37]

14–171   As to the second category of uses, Jacob J. considered this in *British Sugar*. He

---

[34] *Philips v Remington* [1999] R.P.C. 809 at 824, CA.

[35] [1987] R.P.C. 387.

[36] Or at least it would be so understood by someone familiar with English trade mark law: *Bismag v Amblins (Chemists)* [1940] Ch. 667; 57 R.P.C. 209.

[37] *Gerolsteiner*, Case C–100/02, [2004] R.P.C. 39, at para.15; as explained by Jacob L.J. in *Reed* [2004] EWCA Civ 159, [2004] R.P.C. 40, at paras 122–125. cf. the older cases: *British Sugar v James Robertson*. There it was held that one must first look at the whole context of the use to determine whether the use is descriptive or not. If the mark was being used as a trade mark for the defendant's goods, then it was not being used as a description: [1996] R.P.C. 281 at 297–300; see also *Philips Electronics v Remington* [1998] R.P.C. 283 at 313; [1999] R.P.C. 809, CA; *The*

considered that one must look at the whole context of the use, and then, provided the use was fair, he concluded that it does fall within the defence:

> "I see no reason why the provision does not permit a fair comparison between a trade mark owner's goods and those of the defendant. The comparison would have to be honest, but provided it was and was part of a genuine indication of, for instance, quality or price, I think it would be within the provision. Such honest comparative use might well upset the mark's proprietor (proprietors particularly do not like price comparisons, even if they are true) but would in no way affect his mark as an indication of trade origin. Indeed the defendant would be using the proprietor's mark precisely for its proper purpose, namely to refer to his goods. I can see nothing in the stated purpose of the Directive indicating that a trade mark monopoly should extend to the point of enabling a proprietor to suppress competition by use of his trade mark in this way."[38]

As to the third category of cases, it may be supposed that an English court will take much the same view as it has done in relation to comparative advertising in the *British Sugar* case. After all, this sort of use, provided it is fair and honest, is hardly more offensive than comparative advertising. **14–172**

> The claimant was the proprietor of the trade mark PAG for batteries. It sold a battery called the PAG Lok which contained a number of rechargeable cells and an interface, also called the PAG Lok, which allowed it to be connected to the apparatus with which it was used. The defendant refurbished PAG Lok batteries by replacing the cells and sometimes the casings and then returned them to the original customer or sold them to third parties. Held, there was no defence under s.11(2)(b) or (c) because the word PAG was not just being used to indicate that the reconditioned batteries were suitable for use for use in apparatus equipped with PAG Loks; it was also being used in relation to the batteries themselves.[39]

It is notable that there is a distinct difference in the wording of ss.11(2)(b) and (c) of the 1994 Act. The latter specifies that a trade mark is not infringed by the use of the trade mark where it is necessary to indicate the intended purpose of a product or service. It must be assumed that the words emphasised have a meaning, for otherwise intended purpose is already covered by the former provision. Hence it appears that the Directive contemplates that it is permissible to use the trade mark only where it is necessary to indicate the intended purpose of a product or service, but not otherwise. And yet on the approach of the English court it appears to be enough that the use is fair and honest. **14–173**

Use in accordance with honest practices

This requirement is discussed above in relation to the defence of use of own name. In this context certain additional points are worthy of note. Again the test must be objective, and it seems likely that one of the primary considerations will be whether or not the use is likely to cause significant confusion in practice.[40] All the circumstances must be considered. Where there is a valid intellectual prop- **14–174**

European v The Economist Newspaper [1998] F.S.R. 283 at 291, CA— obiter; D. Green & Co (Stoke Newington) and Plastico v Regalzone [2001] EWCA Civ 639, [2002] E.T.M.R. 22.

[38] above, at 298. See also *British Airways v Ryanair* [2001] F.S.R. 32 at paras 19–32.

[39] *PAG Limited v Hawk-Woods* [2002] F.S.R. 46 at p.723

[40] *Reed* [2004] EWCA Civ 159, [2004] R.P.C. 40, at paras 126–130 and see the discussion in paras

erty right, copying may be a commercial practice which is not honest. But copying *per se* is not a dishonest practice.[41]

(7) Intended purpose of a product or service

14–175   A registered trade mark is not infringed by the use of the trade mark where it is necessary to indicate the intended purpose of a product or service (in particular, as accessories or spare parts), provided the use is in accordance with honest practices in industrial or commercial matters.[42]

14–176   The subsection is concerned with all providers and services, not just accessories and spare parts, and provides protection similar to that afforded by s.4(3)(b) of the Trade Marks Act 1938. Here, and in contrast to the other provisions of s.11(2) of the 1994 Act, the provision expressly permits the use of the trade mark of the proprietor, provided the other specified conditions are satisfied.

Use is necessary

14–177   The TM Directive provides no guidance as to how use which is necessary may be distinguished from that which is not necessary. However, in *Gillette v La-Laboratories* the ECJ explained the criteria to be applied.[43]

"Use of the trade mark by a third party who is not its owner is necessary in order to indicate the intended purpose of a product marketed by that third party where such use in practice constitutes the only means of providing the public with comprehensible and complete information on that intended purpose in order to preserve the undistorted system of competition in the market for that product.

It is for the national court to determine whether ... such use is necessary, taking account of the nature of the public for which the product marketed by the third party in question is intended."

The Court also explained that the defence is not limited to accessories or spare parts and that Art.6(1)(c) makes no distinction between the possible intended purposes of products when assessing the lawfulness of the use of a trade mark. Accordingly, the criteria for assessing the lawfulness of the use of a trade mark with accessories or spare parts are no different from those applicable to other categories of possible intended purposes.

Other cases have also emphasised that the purpose of the provision is not to allow use of valid trade marks except where "necessary" to indicate the purpose.[44]

14–178   (1) BMW complained about a garage business which issued advertisements such as "Repairs and maintenance of BMW's" and used the descriptions "BMW specialist" and "Specialised in BMW's". Held, by the European Court of Justice, where an independent trader carried out the maintenance

---

14–158 to 14–163 cf. *The European v The Economist Newspapers* [1996] F.S.R. 431 at 446; [1998] F.S.R. 283, CA; *Philips v Remington* [1998] R.P.C. 283 at 313; [1999] R.P.C. 809. See also *Philips v Remington* [2004] EWHC 2327(Ch.); [2005] F.S.R. 17 at paras 189–197.

[41] *Philips v Remington* [1998] R.P.C. 283 at 313; [1999] R.P.C. 809.

[42] 1994 Act, s.11(2)(c). It implements Art.6(1)(c) of the TM Directive.

[43] Case C–228/03, decision of March 17, 2005, para.39.

[44] *Philips v Remington* [1998] R.P.C. 283 at 313; [1999] R.P.C. 809. The Court of Appeal stated (at [1999] R.P.C. 824): "The purpose of this subsection is to allow such use as 'This film is suitable for a Kodak camera'. The purpose is not to allow use of valid trade marks except where 'necessary' to indicate the purpose. The shape of a three headed rotary shaver does indicate the purpose of the product, but the particular shape is not necessary to make that indication"; see also *PAG Limited v Hawk-Woods* [2002] F.S.R. 46, at para.14–172 and the illustrations in the text. For a similarly restrictive view under the Benelux Trade Marks Act, see *Hermans Groep v Gillette Nederland* [2002] E.T.M.R. 12.

and repair of BMW cars or was a specialist in that field, that fact could not in practice be communicated to customers without the use of the BMW mark.[45]

(2) The defendant was an approved Volvo dealer but after the cessation of its authorised dealership began to use the word "Volvo" together with the words "Independent" and "Specialist", but in much smaller lettering. Held, the manner of use was calculated to cause confusion and accordingly did not satisfy the requirements of the defence under s.11(2)(c) of the 1994 Act.[46]

Use in accordance with honest practices

To satisfy the defence, the use must not only be necessary but also in accordance with honest practices. This requirement is discussed extensively in paras 14–158 to 14–163 and para.14–174, to which reference is invited.   **14–179**

In *Gillette v La-Laboratories*[47] the ECJ elaborated two further aspects of the requirement which have particular relevance to the defence under Art.(1)(c). First, whether the product marketed by the third party has been represented as having the same quality as, or equivalent properties to, those of the product bearing the mark is a factor which the court must take into consideration[48] Secondly, the defence does not cease to be applicable because the third party markets not only spare parts or accessories but also the product itself with which the spare parts or accessories are intended to be used.[49]

(8) Earlier right

Section 11(3) of the 1994 Act limits the right of a proprietor to take action against use of an earlier right. It says: **14–180**

"A registered trade mark is not infringed by the use in the course of trade in a particular locality of an earlier right which applies only in that locality.

For this purpose an "earlier right" means an unregistered trade mark or other sign continuously used in relation to goods or services by a person or a predecessor in title of his from a date anterior to whichever is the earlier of—

(a) the use of the first-mentioned trade mark in relation to those goods or services by the proprietor or a predecessor in title of his, or

(b) the registration of the first-mentioned trade mark in respect of those goods or services in the name of the proprietor or a predecessor in title of his; and an earlier right shall be regarded as applying in a particular locality if, or to the extent that, its use in that locality is protected by virtue of any rule of law (in particular, the law of passing off)."

This provision implements Article 6(2) of the Directive. It provides a defence in particular circumstances where the mark complained of has been used continuously from a date anterior to the earlier of the date of registration or the date of   **14–181**

---

[45] *BMW v Deenik* [1999] E.T.M.R. 339.
[46] *Volvo v Heritage* [2000] F.S.R. 253.
[47] Case C–228/03, decision of March 17, 2005.
[48] *Gillette* at para.47.
[49] *Gillette* at paras 50–53.

first use of the mark sued upon.[50] It has a number of elements which require consideration.

Earlier rights

14–182 Earlier rights are concerned with unregistered trade marks and signs. To qualify for protection the use of the defendant's trade mark or sign must first have been continuous in relation to the relevant goods or services. Secondly, it must have been by a person or a predecessor in title. Each of these requirements is discussed below. Thirdly, the defendant's trade mark or sign must have been used in relation to goods or services from a date prior to whichever is the earlier of the use of the claimant's trade mark in relation to those goods or services or the registration of that trade mark in respect of those goods or services, in each case by the proprietor or a predecessor in title of his. This aspect of the provision is all very well if the goods or services of the defendant are the same as those the subject of the registration or the use by the claimant or his predecessor. Under the old law this was necessarily the case. But the new law has extended the rights of proprietors over similar and even dissimilar goods and services to those the subject of the registration. In such cases it is very difficult to see how the provision can sensibly be applied, as shown by the following illustration:

> X is proprietor of the mark "Revue" registered in respect of sunglasses as of 1994 and has used the mark on a limited scale in respect of sunglasses since 1996. Y began to use the mark "Revue" for spectacle frames in 1996 and rapidly acquired a reputation and goodwill in the locality of his business. The similarity between the goods and the identity of the marks is such that there is a likelihood of confusion. X commences proceedings and Y claims to have a defence under s.11(3) of the 1994 Act. Y has used the mark in relation to spectacle frames from a date prior to the use by X of the mark in relation to spectacle frames or the registration by X of the mark in respect of spectacle frames. It is certainly arguable Y could sue a third party to prevent them from commencing business in his locality and trading off his reputation and goodwill.

Applying in a particular locality

14–183 The words of the provision appear to make it clear that it is concerned with the protection of persons who have made use of unregistered trade marks in localised areas only. The words "use in the course of trade in a particular locality of an earlier right which applies only in that locality" are drawn from Article 6(2) of the TM Directive which uses the words "an earlier right which only applies in a particular locality". Such persons may not have taken the steps necessary to oppose the registration asserted against them under the relative ground of objection provided by s.5(4) of the 1994 Act. Persons who have larger businesses must take steps either to oppose any registration which might interfere with that business or seek a declaration of invalidity under s.47 of the Act. The Act and the Directive give no guidance as to what constitutes a particular locality, but it is suggested that protection would be available where the defendant is able to point to any significant geographical limitation to its business in any country in the United Kingdom.

---

[50] As such it has a number of similarities to the Trade Marks Act 1938, s.7.

An earlier right applies in a locality if, or to the extent that, its use in that local- **14–184** ity is protected by virtue of any rule of law (in particular the law of passing off). So the use by the defendant must be protected. But use is not something which can be protected of itself. A goodwill is required. Accordingly it seems that the court will require that at least some goodwill has been generated in the locality in issue. The question then arises as to the date by which that goodwill must have been established. Although no date is specified, it seems from the provision as a whole that the goodwill must have been established at the earlier of the registration or the first use by the proprietor or a predecessor in title of his.

Continuously used

No exceptions are provided, as they are under s.46 of the 1994 Act, where there **14–185** are proper reasons for non-use. Nevertheless, it is suggested that the phrase "used continuously" must be given a reasonable business interpretation, as it was under the earlier legislation. So, even if the proprietor is not at any particular time actually supplying goods himself, there must be goods in the distribution chain, or on the market. It has been said: "A man who has a trade mark may properly have regard to the state of the market and the demand for the goods; it would be absurd to suppose that he lost his trade mark by not putting more goods on the market when it was glutted."[51] There must be more than occasional use of the mark, though not necessarily "every week or even every month."[52]

It is also suggested that the use must be genuine commercial use and not use effected purely for the purpose of securing a defence under this provision or its predecessor.[53]

Predecessor in title

These words appear to have been carried forward from s.7 of the 1938 Act. As **14–186** such it may be concluded they presuppose a valid transfer of the mark from the previous user. Assignments of unregistered trade marks are addressed in Ch.13.

(9) Miscellaneous and general defences

Personal estoppel

With the exception of the several matters which are considered below, there is **14–187** nothing peculiar to the law of trade marks to determine what agreements, or what circumstances constituting a personal estoppel, will prevent a claimant from suing a particular defendant for infringement (or in passing off).

Uncandid conduct

In *Maxwell v Hogg*[54] the defendants had received and published for reward from **14–188** the claimants, advertisements of an intended new magazine, bearing the title of a magazine which they were themselves preparing to publish, without warning the claimants of their own intention; and this uncandid conduct was held to be suf-

---

[51] *per* Chitty J. in *Mouson v Boehm* (1884) L.R. 26 Ch.D. 398.
[52] *Smith Bartlett v British Pure Oil* (1934) 51 R.P.C. 157 at 163.
[53] see, *ElectrIx* (1954) 71 R.P.C. 23, CA; *Nerit* [1982] F.S.R. 82, CA; cf. *Concord* [1987] F.S.R. 209.
[54] (1866–67) L.R. 2 Ch. App.307.

ficient ground for dismissing the cross-suit of the defendants for an injunction to prevent the claimants using the name; cf. *Electrolux v Electrix* (1954) 71 R.P.C. at pp.29–30, CA, where the claimants deliberately delayed replying to a letter asking them to agree to cancellation of their mark until they had used it for long enough to prevent its removal from the Register for non-use; the claimants nevertheless won.

Use outside registration

14–189   It is no ground of estoppel that the claimant extends the use of his mark to goods in respect of which it is not registered.[55]

Acquiescence and laches

14–190   The law on this subject used to be both rather technical and rather obscure, as is illustrated for example, by the "five probanda" referred to in *Willmott v Barber*.[56] It is now clear, however, that the relevant test is now the much broader one appearing in *Habib Bank v Habib Bank* [1982] R.P.C. 1, which is whether in all the circumstances it would be unconscionable to allow the claimant to maintain his claim. It is, however, clear that the matters which fall to be considered include the factors identified in the old cases: whether the proprietor induced or encouraged the defendant's behaviour, or represented to him that he was entitled so to act, the passage of time, reliance by and detriment to the defendant and so on.

14–191   Mere failure to sue, however, without some positive act of encouragement, is not in general enough to give a defence.[57] A defendant who infringes knowing of the claimants mark can hardly complain if he is later sued upon it,[58] nor is a defendant who starts to infringe without searching the Register of Trade Marks in any better position than if he had searched and so learned of the claimant's mark.[59] Acts of the proprietor done in ignorance of the infringement,[60] or even done without his own registration in mind,[61] will not amount to acquiescence. A defence of estoppel by acquiescence is to be distinguished from a defence that by delay the mark has become *publici juris*.[62]

Delay does not bar the right of action

14–192   In general mere delay after knowledge of infringement does not deprive the registered proprietor of a trade mark of his statutory rights or of the appropriate remedy for the enforcement of these rights.[63] But inordinate delay can exception-

---

[55] *Jay v Ladler* (1889) L.R. 40 Ch.D. 649; 6 R.P.C. 136 at 139.
[56] (1880) 15 Ch.D. 97.
[57] See paras 14–192 to 14–193, "delay."
[58] *Electrolux v Electrix* (1954) 71 R.P.C. 23 at 40, *per* Jenkins L.J.
[59] *Electrolux v Electrix* (1954) 71 R.P.C. 23.
[60] *Electrolux v Electrix* (1954) 71 R.P.C. 23, and see generally *De Bussche v Alt* (1878) L.R. 8 Ch.D. 286; *Willmott v Barber* (1881) 17 Ch.D. 772. *Habib* [1982] R.P.C. 1, can hardly be authority for the contrary proposition.
[61] *Electrolux v Electrix* (1954) 71 R.P.C. 23, *per* Jenkins L.J. at 41.
[62] *Bollinger v Goldwell* [1971] R.P.C. 412 (a defence that a mark has become *publici juris* is open to any defendant; a defence of acquiescence depends upon the facts relating to each defendant.).
[63] *per* Jenkins L.J. in *Electrolux v Electrix* (1954) 71 R.P.C. 23 at 41. As to delay of two years, see *Fullwood v Fullwood* (1878) L.R. 9 Ch.D. 176 at 178, approved by Harman J. in *Manus* (1948) 65 R.P.C. 329; and see *L.C. & D. Ry. v Bull* (1882) 47 L.T. 413; *Leibig's v Chemists' Co-operative* (1896) 13 R.P.C. 635, 736, a trade name and passing off case; *Poiret v Jules Poiret*

ally provide a defence,[64] and can also form a major ingredient in a case of acquiescence.[65]

1. The claimants used the expression "British Sherry" (and like expressions) **14–193** for over 100 years before the defendants (representing the producers of "real" sherry, *i.e.* a wine from the Jerez district of Spain) complained. The claimants were granted a declaration that they were entitled to continue such use, despite the finding that the name "sherry" was not apt to describe the claimants' products. Cross J. held that it would be "altogether unjust to allow the defendants to rely on the ignorance of their lawyers, excusable though it was, as to the law on the point in question before the decision in the *Spanish Champagne* case." *Vine Products v Mackenzie* [1969] R.P.C. 1 at p.26.

2. The defendants traded for some twelve years (about half of which were interrupted by the war) under their trade mark before the claimants sued. Held, that in the absence of some positive representation from the claimants there was no defence of delay or acquiescence: *Electrolux v Electrix* (1954) 71 R.P.C. 23.

Delay may modify the relief granted

Unexplained delay that offers no absolute defence may effect the nature of the **14–194** relief granted. It may cause the court to refuse an interim injunction, however.[66] There would appear to be no instance of refusal of a final injunction for mere delay, and in principle, such refusal would seem inappropriate. A short stay may be appropriate, though.

Where there had been over a year's delay in bringing the action, the injunction **14–195** was stayed for six weeks to allow the defendant time to make the arrangements necessary for the alterations of his trade name required by it: *Grant v Levitt* ("Globe Furnishing Co") (1901) 18 R.P.C. 361, CA. It may, of course, be possible for the claimant to show that the delay was reasonable.[67]

Deceptive trade mark and fraudulent trade

The court may refuse to interfere to protect the use of a deceptive trade mark or **14–196** to assist a trader who is using his mark for the purposes of a fraudulent trade. This principle was well-established in the Court of Chancery, and the maximum *ex turpi causa non oritur actio* is a rule of law. There is, however, a little modern authority on this matter, and the older cases are not very clearly related to the present law of registered marks. The following points, however, would seem sustainable.

It is of course a defence to an action for infringement, that the mark sued upon **14–197**

(1920) 37 R.P.C. 177 (a trade name case). See also *Vidal Dyes v Levinstein* (1912) 29 R.P.C. 245, where it is clearly stated that in the case of a patent, mere delay in enforcing rights did not affect the legal position.

[64] *Vine Products v Mackenzie (No.5)* [1969] R.P.C. 1.

[65] *Cluett, Peabody v McIntyre Hogg ("Arrow" shirts)* [1958] R.P.C. 335 at 354. There had been nearly 30 years delay; and it would seem that Upjohn J. was neither willing to allow the proprietors to use after all that time, nor happy to rest his judgment on delay alone.

[66] See Ch.19.

[67] As random instances of explanations of delay, that the courts would seem to have accepted, see *Daniel & Arter v Whitehouse* [1898] 1 Ch. 685; 15 R.P.C. 134 (claimants thought infringement had ceased); Rowlands. *Mitchell* (1896) 13 R.P.C. 457; (1897) 14 R.P.C. 37, but not reported on this point: infringer not worth suing; *Young v Holt* (1948) 65 R.P.C. 25 (some four months' delay whilst claimants made certain of the facts; account of profits granted, and not limited to the period after the claimants first complained to the defendants).

is invalid; and one ground of invalidity is that the mark is liable to mislead under s.46.[68] In practical terms, this may deal with nearly all situations likely to arise. The other branch of this proposition, concerned with claimants suing to protect a fraudulent trade, is discussed in para.14–203. In so far as the claimant seeks equitable relief, an injunction in particular, this is always in some degree discretionary.

Collateral misrepresentation

14–198   Where the false description was collateral and did not appear in the mark in question, and the claimant's trade was not shown to be fraudulent, the court decided that the claimant's legal right of action in respect of the defendant's infringement was not barred, and that he was consequently entitled to an injunction and costs: *Ford v Foster* (1871–72) L.R. 7 Ch. 611 ("Eureka Shirts").

14–199   The following are some miscellaneous examples of case where objections to the claimant's case on the ground of collateral misrepresentation failed: title of a magazine protected, although the magazine purported to be written by someone other than the author;[69] similar cases with regard to songs;[70] "Holloway's pills and ointment" protected, although the claimant called himself Professor Holloway without warrant, and published exaggerated commendations of his pills;[71] an objection on the ground that the claimants retained a brass plate on the door of their business premises, bearing their predecessor's name, overruled;[72] the claimants alleged that after registration of the mark "Kit" for coffee, fraudulent misrepresentions had been made, by the defendant's predecessors in title, that "Kit" coffee essence was the same as the claimants' "Camp" coffee essence;[73] held that, even if the misrepresentations should be proved, being extraneous to the mark, the use of the mark by the defendants was not necessarily deceptive.

False assertion of registration

14–200   Under s.95 it is a penal offence to describe a trade mark as registered when it is not. Such a misrepresentation has been sufficient to deprive the proprietor of a mark of an interlocutory injunction in a passing off action.[74] It has been submitted that relief should also be refused at trial, but there is no statutory provision to this effect.[75]

"Trade mark"

14–201   The description of an unregistered trade mark as a "trade mark" is no offence within s.95, and if the mark is, in fact, as it may be, a trade mark acquired by user, such description is not by itself a misrepresentation.

---

[68] See Ch.8.

[69] *Hogg v Kirby* (1803) 8 Ves. 215; 7 R.R. 30.

[70] *Chappell v Sheard* (1855) 2 K. & J. 117; *Chappell v Davidson* (1855) 2 K. & J. 123; 8 De G.M. & G. 1.

[71] *Holloway v Holloway* (1850) 13 Beav. 209.

[72] *Hudson v Osborne* (1869) 39 LJ.Ch. 79.

[73] *Paterson v Kit Coffee* (1910) 27 R.P.C. 594.

[74] *Johnson v Puffer* (1930) 47 R.P.C. 95.

[75] In *Sen Sen v Britten* [1899] 1 Ch. 692; 16 R.P.C. 137, Stirling J. said, "Of course, if the plaintiffs are brought within the terms of that section they must be denied relief." See also 6th ed. for earlier cases.

Misrepresentation abandoned before, or commencing after, action brought

A misrepresentation which has been corrected and abandoned before the action is no bar.[76] The same rule is said to apply to one adopted after the commencement of the action.[77] It is submitted that it can make no difference that the frauds commenced after the action was begun. The objection is that the claimant and his business are, when the court takes cognisance of the matter, unworthy of its protection or assistance. **14–202**

Fraudulent trade

Where the claimant uses the trade mark in aid of a fraudulent trade, the rule which bars his action is clear but even so, it may be proper to grant in injunction whose purpose is to put an end to the fraud.[78] **14–203**

A plea that the claimant made a practice of selling by short weight failed because it was not supported by the evidence.[79] A pianoforte tutor, described as "600th edition, specially revised by Hemy," although the musician referred to had not revised the work for ten years, was held not to be misleading, evidence being given that in the trade an issued of 250 was called an edition.[80] A trade in German cigars sold in boxes bearing a label with the words La Pureza (an old Havana brand), Habana, Ramon, Romedo and additional labels with other words and a sham address in Spanish was held to be fraudulent, the whole get-up being described by Bowen L.J. as "an elaborate concatenation of pictorial lies" intended to pass off the cigars as made in Havana, although evidence was given that the name "Havana" in the cigar trade indicates the shape of the cigar only.[81] The sale of English cigars under a label bearing the word Habana, in boxes marked "British Manufacture," was held not to be fraudulent in the absence of evidence that the claimants represented that their cigars were made in Havana.[82] The application of the name "California Syrup of Figs" to an aperient drug in which fig syrup was used as a flavouring only was held not to be a misrepresentation.[83] In another case[84] the claimants advertisement falsely stated that the basis of their Bile Beans was an Australian herb discovered by an eminent scientist, whose name was given. There was no such person, and the story of the discovery given in the advertisement was an invention. It was held that the misrepresentation was not a collateral one but affected the very essence of the article offered for sale. **14–204**

---

[76] *Benedictus v Sullivan* (1895) 12 R.P.C. 25.

[77] See *Siegert v Findlater* (1877–78) 7 Ch.D. 801 ("Angostura Bitters"); *Ford v Foster* (1872) L.R. 7 Ch. 611; *Faulder v Rushton* (1903) 20 R.P.C. 477 at 489.

[78] This would seem to be the implication of *Coles v Need* [1934] A.C. 82 at 89–90 (P.C., Australia). Note the further implication that the bar to the action in these cases is not absolute but discretionary. This, a passing off case, seems to be the most modern authority on the point.

[79] *Guinea Coal (Lee) v (Haley)* (1869) L.R. 5 Ch. 155.

[80] *Metzler v Wood* (1878) L.R. 8 Ch.D. 606.

[81] *Newman v Pinto* (1887) 4 R.P.C. 508; cf. *Fuente* [1891] 2 Ch. 166; 8 R.P.C. 214 and *Dexter* [1893] 2 Ch. 262; 10 R.P.C. 269.

[82] *Hargreaves v Freeman* [1891] 3 Ch. 39; (1891) 8 R.P.C. 237; cf. *Benedictus v Sullivan* (1895) 12 R.P.C. 25, where a Spanish look about the box, and the words "Fabrica de Tobaccos de la Vuetia Abago," was held not to be a representation of foreign manufacture in the face of the words "Regalia Britannica," "Londini"; and see *R. v Butcher* (1909) 99 L.T. 622; (1867-68) L.R. 3 Q.B. 335 and *Van der Leeuw* [1912] 1 Ch. 40; 28 R.P.C. 708.

[83] *California Fig Syrup v Taylor's* (1897) 14 R.P.C. 341, Kekewich J.; reversed on appeal on another point, 14 R.P.C. 564.

[84] *Bile Bean v Davidson* (1905) 22 R.P.C. 553; 23 R.P.C. 725.

F. Collective and certification marks

14–205 The provisions of the 1994 Act relating to infringement apply to collective and certification marks too, subject to the limitations and provisions of Schs 1 and 2 of the Act which apply to collective and certification marks respectively. These Schedules contain particular provisions which reflect the special nature of these marks. In this section we consider those provisions which relate to infringement.

Limitations on infringement provisions—indications of geographical origin

14–206 A proprietor of a collective or certification mark is not entitled to prevent a third party from using a sign or indication which may serve in trade to designate the geographical origin of the goods or services where the use is in accordance with honest practices in industrial or commercial matters.[85] This limitation reflects the opportunity to register such marks which might otherwise offend s.3(1)(c) of the 1994 Act.[86] The requirement that the use be in accordance with honest practices recurs throughout the infringement provisions, and it is to be expected that it will be interpreted consistently. Accordingly reference is invited to the discussion in paras 14–158 to 14–163, 14–174 and 14–179.

Infringement: rights of authorised users

14–207 There are particular provisions extending the rights given by collective and certification marks to authorised users.[87] Some are common to collective and certification marks. Others apply only to collective marks.

14–208 The common provisions apply to authorised users certain sections of the 1994 Act, just as they apply to a licensee of a trade mark. The sections so applied are s.10(5) (the authorised application of the mark to certain material), s.19(2) (order as to disposal of infringing goods, material or articles) and s.89 (request to Commissioners of Customs and Excise for the prohibition of importation of infringing goods, material or articles).[88] In addition it is provided that in infringement proceedings brought by the proprietor any loss suffered or likely to be suffered by authorised users is to be taken into account and the court may give appropriate directions as to the extent to which the claimant is to hold any proceeds on behalf of such users.[89]

14–209 In the case of collective marks, but not in the case of certification marks, and subject to any agreement to the contrary, an authorised user may call upon the proprietor to take action in respect of any matter which affects his interests and if he fails to do so, may take action himself, just as in the case of licensees.[90]

G. Transitional provisions

14–210 Existing registrations (whether registered in Part A or B of the register kept under the 1938 Act) were transferred on commencement of the 1994 Act to the Register

---

[85] Schs 1 and 2, para.3(2).
[86] Schs 1 and 2, para.3(1).
[87] These are the persons specified in the regulations governing the use of the marks.
[88] Sch.1, para.11; Sch.2, para.13.
[89] Sch.2, para.12(6); Sch.3, para.14.
[90] Sch.1, para.12(1)–(5).

kept under the Act and have effect for the purposes of infringement as if registered under the Act.[91]

In general, the scheme provided by the transitional provisions was that the old **14–211** law continued to apply to infringements committed prior to commencement and the new law applies in relation to acts committed after commencement.[92] Hence ss.9–12 of the Act (effects of registration) apply as from the date of commencement and s.14 (action for infringement) applies in relation to acts committed after commencement subject to certain savings. It is anticipated that the details of the transitional provisions are almost certainly now irrelevant. They are, however, considered in the 13th edition of Kerly, at paras 13–173 to 13–179.

3. Further rights conferred by the 1994 Act

THE PARIS CONVENTION AND TRIPS

The 1994 Act introduced into the law for the first time important provisions **14–212** based upon the provisions of the Paris Convention.[93] More recently the Act has been amended and modified in pursuance of the United Kingdom's obligations under the WTO Agreement and the Agreement on Trade Related Aspects of Intellectual Property Rights (TRIPS) which is an integral part of the WTO Agreement. Specifically for the purposes of this section it is to be noted that the provisions of ss.55–60 of the Act which are discussed below have been amended to extend their scope to include the WTO Agreement.[94] TRIPS provides, so far as material, that members shall comply with Art.6 of the Paris Convention and that nothing in the Agreement shall derogate from existing obligations that members may have to each other under the Paris Convention.

PROTECTION OF WELL-KNOWN MARKS UNDER ARTICLE 6BIS OF THE PARIS CONVENTION AND TRIPS

The 1994 Act confers a separate right to protection on the owners of well-known **14–213** trade marks under the Paris Convention and TRIPS. Section 56 of the Act gives effect to Article 6*bis* of the Paris Convention and to Article 16 of TRIPS so far as it refers to the protection of well-known trade marks.[95] A number of matters call for consideration; first, the necessary qualification for the right and secondly, the right and remedy provided and defences to it.

QUALIFICATION FOR THE RIGHT

The protection is provided to the proprietor of a trade mark which is entitled to **14–214** protection under the Paris Convention or TRIPS as a well-known trade mark.[96] Such a mark is defined as a mark which is well-known in the United Kingdom as

---

[91] Sch.3, para.2.
[92] Sch.3, para.4.
[93] The Paris Convention is set out in App.20.
[94] SI 1999/1899. The relevant provisions of TRIPS are set out in App.21.
[95] Art.6 *bis* is set out in full in App.20. It will be seen that there are other aspects of the provision, such as the prohibitions on registration, which are effectively implemented elsewhere in the Act. The relevant provisions of TRIPS are set out in App.21.
[96] 1994 Act, s.56(2).

being the mark of a person who is a national of a Convention country,[97] or who is domiciled in, or has a real and effective industrial or commercial establishment in, a Convention country, whether or not that person carries on any business, or has any goodwill in the United Kingdom.[98]

14–215   The latter words are of considerable significance and make this provision an important one. It is not a requirement that the proprietor has any goodwill or business in the United Kingdom. Accordingly, he need have no customers here. This is in contrast to the cause of action in passing off which calls for goodwill as a fundamental requirement.[99] All that is required is that the mark is "well-known" in the United Kingdom. No guidance is given in the Paris Convention as to what this means. TRIPS, on the other hand, provides that in determining whether a trade mark is well-known, members shall take account of the knowledge of the trade mark in the relevant sector of the public, including knowledge in the member concerned, which has been obtained as a result of the promotion of the trade mark. It is to be expected that, with this limited guidance, the provision will be construed as a matter of ordinary language so to require that the mark is well-established amongst, and familiar to, the interested public and so, in short, that the mark is famous. The original wording of the Paris Convention contemplates the use of the mark by the proprietor and by the other party in relation to "goods".[1] TRIPS provides that Art.6*bis* of the Paris Convention shall apply, *mutatis mutandis*, to services. In any event the 1994 Act is not so limited, providing as it does its own definition of a well-known trade mark and the extent of the right in respect of goods or services where the use is likely to cause confusion.[2]

14–216   There are a number or ways by which the proprietor may achieve qualifying status. In the case of an individual he may be a national of or domiciled in a Convention or member territory.[3] In the case of a body corporate or other legal entity, it may be established under the laws of that territory. Alternatively, in either case, it is sufficient if he has a real and effective industrial or commercial base in a Convention or member country.

Extent of the Right and Remedy

14–217   The proprietor of such a well-known trade mark is entitled to restrain by injunction the use in the United Kingdom of a trade mark which, or the essential part of which, is identical or similar to his mark, in relation to identical or similar goods or services, where the use is likely to cause confusion.[4] As in the case of the infringement provisions of s.10(2) of the 1994 Act, the provision calls for a consideration of the extent of the similarity of the goods or services in issue and

---

[97] s.56 defines the Paris Convention for the purposes of the Act as the 1883 Convention and any revisions or amendments to it. A Convention country is also defined as any party to the Convention other than the UK. All Members of TRIPS are now included.

[98] s.56(1).

[99] See the full discussion in Ch.15.

[1] It uses the words: "a mark ... used for identical or similar goods".

[2] s.56(2), and see below.

[3] "National" and "domicile" are not defined and it seems may depend upon the law of that territory. So, for example, British nationality is used to refer to the various forms of British national status and comprises, *inter alia*, the terms British citizen and British subject: see, for a full discussion, Halsbury's Laws, Vol. 4(2); a person is, in general, domiciled in the country in which he is considered by English law to have his permanent home (although a person may sometimes be domiciled in a country although he does not have his permanent home in it); see Dicey & Morris, *Conflict of Laws* (13th ed., Sweet & Maxwell, London, 2000), Ch.6.

[4] 1994 Act, s.56(2).

of the likelihood of confusion. The likelihood of confusion must be assessed globally taking into account all relevant factors, including the degree of similarity of the marks in issue, the degree of similarity between the relevant goods or services, the likely perception of the marks in the minds of the average consumer of the goods or services and the degree of distinctiveness of the well-known mark.[5] Nevertheless similarity between the goods or services does still seem to be a threshold requirement, as in the case of infringement.[6]

There appears to be no requirement that the use of the mark complained of has damaged or is likely to cause damage to the proprietor of the well-known mark. In this respect the right is again different from passing off, which not only requires the claimant to establish damage or, in the case of a *quia timet* action, the likelihood of damage, but also that the damage is the result of the misrepresentation and confusion. Correspondingly the right provided under s.57 is to an injunction only[7] and there appears to be no right to claim damages or an account of profits.   **14–218**

The right is expressly subject to the provisions of s.48. This makes provision in the case where the proprietor of an earlier trade mark or right has acquiesced for a continuous period of five years in the use of a registered trade mark in the United Kingdom, being aware of that use. Reference is invited to paras 14–149 to 14–152 for a consideration of that provision. In this context, it is to be noted that it is not clear if the defence applies only in circumstances where the mark complained of by the proprietor of the well-known mark has actually been registered. It is suggested, however, that this is not the intention behind s.56 and that such is made reasonably clear by the way s.48 is imported by reference and the use of the words "effect of acquiescence by proprietor of earlier trade mark". On this basis the defence would be made out where the proprietor of the well-known mark has taken no action for a continuous period of five years in the use of that mark in the United Kingdom when he was aware of that use.   **14–219**

Section 56(3) provides a saving in respect of the continuation of *bona fide*[8] use of a trade mark begun before the commencement of the section.[9]   **14–220**

NATIONAL EMBLEMS AND EMBLEMS OF INTERNATIONAL ORGANISATIONS

Sections 57 and 58 of the 1994 Act provide protection in respect of flags, armorial bearings, state emblems, official signs and hallmarks of Paris Convention or TRIPS member countries and emblems, names and abbreviations of international intergovernmental organisations. Such signs must be notified under the provisions of s.59 and then may not be registered without the authorisation of the competent authority of the Convention or member country or the international organisation in question. These matters are considered in detail in Ch.8. For the purposes of this chapter it is important to note that where the authorisation of the competent authority of the Convention or member country or international organisation would be required for registration of a trade mark, then that authority or organisation is entitled to restrain by injunction any use of that mark in the   **14–221**

---

[5] See paras 14–057 to 14–078.

[6] See para.14–062.

[7] And, presumably, and at the discretion of the court, an order for delivery up or destruction to support the injunction.

[8] For the meaning of this term, see *Baume v Moore* [1957] R.P.C. 459; [1958] R.P.C. 226, CA; and the 12th ed. of this book, para.15–33.

[9] October 31, 1994.

United Kingdom without its authorisation.[10] In the latter case, no rights are afforded against a person whose *bona fide* use of the trade mark began before January 4, 1962.[11]

ACTS OF AN AGENT OR REPRESENTATIVE

14–222   An agent or representative of any person who is a proprietor of a mark in any Convention or member country[12] may restrain any use of the mark in the United Kingdom which is not authorised by him[13] and unless the agent or representative justifies his action.[14] This is an important provision and it is designed to restrain an agent or representative from hijacking the mark of a foreign principal. It forms part of a set of provisions which also prohibit the registration of such a mark which is not authorised by the proprietor.[15] No injunction shall be granted in respect of a use in which the overseas proprietor has acquiesced for a continuous period of three or more years.[16]

UNAUTHORISED USE OF ROYAL ARMS

14–223   Section 99 of the 1994 Act prohibits the use, in connection with any business of the Royal arms or any arms closely resembling them, without the authority of Her Majesty and in such a way as to be likely to lead to the belief that the use is duly authorised. So also no one, without the authority of Her Majesty or a member of the Royal family, may use in connection with any business any device, emblem or title in such a manner as to be calculated to lead to the belief that he is employed by, or supplies goods or services to, Her Majesty or that member of the Royal family.[17] This is a provision which prevents unauthorised use of Royal warrants. An action may be taken to restrain the offending use by any person who is in fact authorised to use the arms, device, emblem or title in question or by the Lord Chamberlain or any person authorised by him.[18]

4. Community trade marks

A. INTRODUCTION

14–224   This section deals with the issues arising in respect of the infringement of Com-

---

[10] ss.57(6) and 58(4), respectively.

[11] s.58(5).

[12] Defined by the 1994 Act, s.55, as any country, other than the UK, which is a party to the Paris Convention and any revision or amendment to it and any member of TRIPS. It appears that it is not a requirement that the mark is registered in the Convention or member country of origin, although it seems that it must be in use and properly so by the person claiming to be the proprietor if he is to be so regarded. Although s.60 is not specifically referred to in SI 1999/1899, s.60 refers to " Convention country" as defined in s.55(1)(b) and that has been amended by SI 1999/1899 to refer to the WTO Agreement as well as the Paris Convention.

[13] s.60(4).

[14] s.60(5).

[15] s.60(2) and (3).

[16] s.60(6). No mention is made here of knowledge of the use, in contrast to the similar provisions in respect of acquiescence in s.48. It seems that the difference is probably attributable to the different origins of the provisions. S.48 implements the TM Directive, Art.9, which expressly refers to knowledge. S.60(6), on the other hand, implements Art.6 *septies* of the Paris Convention which provides that "Domestic legislation may provide an equitable time limit within which the proprietor of the trade mark must exercise the rights provided for in this Article". Accordingly it is suggested that a court would require knowledge of the offending use despite the absence of any express mention of it.

[17] s.99(1) and (2).

[18] s.99(4).

munity trade marks registered pursuant to Council Regulation 40/94 of December 20, 1993 (the CTM Regulation).[19] Such marks have a unitary character and equal effect throughout the Community. The use of a Community trade mark may not be prohibited, nor may it be revoked or declared invalid save in respect of the whole Community. Accordingly the effective working of the Community trade mark system will require a measure of harmonisation of the approaches of the courts of different countries on a scale not seen before.

The fundamental provisions concerning infringement are contained in s.2 of Title 2 of the CTM Regulation which makes provision in respect of the "Effects of Community Trade Marks". Article 14 provides that these effects are governed solely by the CTM Regulation but that in other respects, infringement of a Community trade mark is to be governed by the provisions of national law relating to infringement of national trade marks and in accordance with the provisions of Title X of the CTM Regulation. We discuss these further below and, in particular, the respects in which they differ from the infringement provisions relating to national registrations. **14–225**

Matters of jurisdiction and procedure in legal actions relating to Community trade marks are dealt with in Articles 90–104 of the CTM Regulation. Importantly these make provision in respect of the application of the Brussels Convention[20] and for the designation by Member States of national courts and tribunals of first and second instance as Community trade mark courts.[21] Such courts have exclusive jurisdiction for all infringement actions, for actions for declarations of non-infringement and for actions for revocation and for declarations of invalidity.[22] In England and Wales and Northern Ireland the High Court has been so designated and in Scotland the Court of Session.[23] The Court of Appeal has been designated the court of second instance. **14–226**

As explained further in Ch.19, in most circumstances where a Community trade mark court has jurisdiction it extends to acts of infringement committed or threatened within the territory of any of the Member States.[24] This makes a Community trade mark especially valuable. **14–227**

In the final part of this section we address the infringement aspects of Community Collective marks.

B. RIGHTS CONFERRED BY A COMMUNITY TRADE MARK

The general rights conferred by a Community trade mark in respect of the use of a sign which is the same as or similar to the trade mark are set out in Article 9(1) of the CTM Regulation. This mirrors the provisions of Article 5(1) and (2) of the TM Directive. So also Article 9(2) of the CTM Regulation identifies specific activities involving the use of the mark which may be prevented and which correspond to those identified in Article 5(2) of the TM Directive. Article 12 of the Regulation limits the effects of a Community trade mark in like manner to Article 6 of the TM Directive. Accordingly, it is to be expected that in the general case **14–228**

---

[19] See App.8.

[20] Arts 90, 93 and 94. There are also specific provisions in Art.105 dealing with cases involving Community and national trade marks. The application of these provisions and of the Brussels Convention is discussed further in Ch.19, relating to proceedings.

[21] Art.91.

[22] Art.92.

[23] Reg.6 of the CTM Regulations 1996, reproduced in App.13.

[24] Art.94.

the discussion in s.2, above of the various categories of infringement and their different requirements is equally applicable to Community trade marks. There are, however, potentially important differences too and these we discuss in the following sections.

Comparative advertising

14–229   The CTM Regulation contains no provision expressly dealing with the use of a Community trade mark in a comparative advertisement. In particular it has no provision corresponding to s.10(6) of the 1994 Act which regulates the position in the United Kingdom in relation to national trade marks and expressly permits the use of a national trade mark in a comparative advertisement unless the use is otherwise than in accordance with honest practices and would, without due cause, take unfair advantage of, or be detrimental to, the distinctive character or repute of the trade mark. Accordingly, it seems the position in relation to a Community trade mark must be considered as a matter of principle and of the proper construction of Article 9(1) of the Regulation.

14–230   When a trade mark of a competitor is used in an honest comparative advertisement which does not mislead, it is almost invariably used in a form which is identical to that the subject of the registration and, at least in one sense, in relation to the goods or services of the competitor which are identical to those in respect of which it is registered.[25] This is the consequence of comparing the goods or services being advertised to those the subject of the registered trade mark. The issue which must be determined is whether this activity offends against Article 9(1) of the Directive.

14–231   Article 9(1)(a) confers on the proprietor exclusive rights therein and, in particular, the right to prevent third parties, not having his consent, from using in the course of trade any sign identical with the Community trade mark in relation to goods or services in respect of which it is registered. On the face of it that is exactly what the comparative advertiser is doing and so rendering it at least arguable that there is infringement.[26]

14–232   Nevertheless this may be considered a most unattractive result. After all the advertiser has done no more than use the mark of the competitor in relation to the competitor's own goods or services and for the purpose of indicating the origin of those goods or services in the competitor, that is to say in a manner which is entirely consistent with the essential function of the trade mark. A number of arguments may be deployed to avoid a finding of infringement in such a case. These are discussed below.

14–233   First, it may be contended that the use of a competitor's trade mark in a comparative advertisement simply does not fall within the scope of Art.9 at all, upon its proper construction. Art.9(1) is concerned with the use by a person of a trade mark in relation to goods or services which he himself is dealing with in the course of trade. As such he is using the mark for the purposes of distinguishing his own goods or services. This interpretation is consistent with the provisions of Art.9(2) which, so far as subparagraphs (a)–(c) are concerned, is clearly only concerned with goods or services in which that person is himself dealing.

---

[25] See the discussion of comparative advertising in relation to national registrations in paras 14–098 to 14–119.

[26] This is how the English High Court has construed s.10(1) of the 1994 Act, corresponding to Art.5.1(a) of the TM Directive: *British Airways v Ryanair* [2001] F.S.R. 32.

Subparagraph (d), namely the use of the sign on business papers and in advertising, should, it may be argued, be construed in a like manner. A person who uses a trade mark of a rival in a comparative advertisement is not using the mark for the purposes of distinguishing any goods or services in which he himself is dealing.[27]

Secondly, and on the assumption that the use of the trade mark does fall within the scope of Art.9 then, it may be contended, use in accordance with honest practices is protected by the provisions of Art.12(b).[28]   **14–234**

Thirdly, it may be argued that the competitor must be taken to have consented   **14–235**
to the use of his mark in relation to his own goods and services and which he has marketed under the mark. As a matter of English law it is well-established that, absent an agreement to the contrary, a person who purchases an article is free to do with it what he will and that includes the freedom to market it and sell it on to others under the mark.[29] Accordingly, it may be argued, he has consented to the use of his mark in relation to his own goods or services and in any way which is not misleading.[30]

Fourthly, in cases involving goods marketed under a trade mark in the Community, the rights of the proprietor in the United Kingdom are curtailed by Article   **14–236**
13 of the Regulation, which provides that a Community trade mark shall not entitle the proprietor to prohibit its use in relation to goods which have been put on the market in the Community under that trade mark by him or with his consent.[31] Accordingly, it may be argued, it cannot be an infringement to use such a registered mark in relation to such goods in a comparative advertisement.

Neither the third nor the fourth argument is wholly satisfactory. The former   **14–237**
relies upon a general inference of consent and might be avoided by express words in the agreement of sale to the contrary. The latter relies upon a provision which only deals expressly with the position in relation to goods and, moreover, the provision is obviously primarily directed against attempts to prevent subsequent dealings in and commercialisation of such goods.

Joint liability

There is no express provision in the CTM Regulation addressing the issue of   **14–238**
joint liability for infringement. This position is to be contrasted with s.10(5) of the 1994 Act which makes provision in respect of materials intended to be used for labelling, packaging as business papers or for advertising.[32] As in the case of national trade marks, a person who becomes involved in counterfeiting or other

---

[27] This argument has the added benefit of introducing a measure of consistency with Art.5 of the TM Directive and s.10(6) of the UK Act. The provisions of the Directive, Art.5(1) and (2), are in like terms to the CTM Regulation, Art.9(1). Art.5(5) of the Directive provides that the earlier paragraphs shall not affect provisions in Member States relating to the protection against the use of a sign other than for the purposes of distinguishing goods or services, where use of that sign without due cause takes unfair advantage of, or is detrimental to, the distinctive character or repute of the trade mark. This provision appears to be the foundation of the 1994 Act, s.10(6) and it has no counterpart in the CTM Regulation.

[28] Corresponding to the TM Directive, Art.6(1)(d) and implemented by the 1994 Act, s.11(2)(b). In *British Sugar* and in *British Airways*, Jacob J. considered that the provision was apt for this purpose, see the discussion in paras 14–168 to 14–171.

[29] *Betts v Wilmott* (1871) 6 Ch. App. 239; *National Phonographic Co of Australia v Walter T Menck* [1911] A.C. 337; *Zino Davidoff v A&G Imports* [1999] R.P.C. 631, an interim decision on the issue of international exhaustion and now the subject of a reference to the ECJ.

[30] As in *Revlon* [1985] F.S.R. 80, CA; cf. *Colgate Palmolive v Markwell Finance* [1989] R.P.C. 497, CA.

[31] Subject to the provisions of Art.13(2) which do not bear on this issue.

[32] See the discussion at paras 14–035 to 14–038.

infringement may nevertheless be liable for directing, procuring or combining with others to infringe.[33]

Reproduction of Community trade marks in dictionaries

14–239   One of the important limitations in the prohibition of the use of national trade marks arises from the requirements that the offending sign be used in the course of trade and in relation to particular goods or services.[34] While not expressly importing a requirement that the offending sign be used in a trade mark sense, these requirements may nevertheless amount to much the same thing in many cases. The TM Directive addresses this issue at least in part by including a remedy against the generic use of a Community trade mark in a dictionary or the like. Such use can be very damaging in reducing the distinctiveness of a trade mark. Accordingly, Article 10 of the CTM Regulation provides that if the reproduction of a Community trade mark in a dictionary, encyclopaedia or similar reference work gives the impression that it constitutes the generic name of the goods or services for which the trade mark is registered, the publisher of the work shall, at the request of the proprietor of the Community trade mark, ensure that the reproduction of the trade mark at the latest in the next edition of the publication is accompanied by an indication that it is a registered trade mark.[35] It would seem that this right is enforceable by injunction.

Prohibition on the use of a Community trade mark registered in the name of an agent or representative

14–240   Articles 11 and 18 of the CTM Regulation make provision for the protection of a proprietor where an agent or representative registers and uses the mark without his authorisation. In such a case the proprietor is entitled to oppose the use of the mark and to demand an assignment in his favour of the registration unless the agent or representative justifies his action. It would therefore seem that a number of requirements must be satisfied for the remedies (presumably by injunction) to be available. First, the mark must have been registered by the agent or representative. Secondly, the claimant must be the true proprietor of that registration.[36] Thirdly, the proprietor must show that the registration was secured and that the agent or representative is using the mark or threatening to use it without his authorisation.

C. SAVINGS, EXCEPTIONS AND DEFENCES

Introduction

14–241   Just as for the rights conferred by Community trade marks, the CTM Regulation contains much the same savings, exceptions and defences as does the TM Directive for national registered trade marks. So, Article 12 of the Regulation provides for limitations of the effects of Community trade marks in like form to Article 6(1) of the TM Directive where a third party is using his own name and address, or indications concerning the characteristics of the goods or services or a trade

---

[33] For an exposition of the relevant principles, see *CBS v Amstrad Consumer Electronics* [1988] 1 A.C. 1013.

[34] See the TM Directive, Art.5(1) and (2) and the discussion in paras 14–006 to 14–022. The same words appear in the CTM Regulation, Art.9(1).

[35] There is no equivalent provision in the TM Directive.

[36] And here satisfy the conditions of Art.5.

mark where it is necessary to indicate the intended purpose of a product or service, in particular as accessories or spare parts.[37] Similarly, Article 13 of the
Regulation provides for the exhaustion of the rights conferred by a Community
trade mark where goods have been put on the market in the Community under
that trade mark by the proprietor or with his consent. This corresponds to Article
7 of the TM Directive.[38]

Infringement proceedings may also be defended by an attack on the registra-   **14–242**
tion which may be brought by counterclaim. So, Article 50 of the Regulation
provides for revocation in the event of non-use; if the mark has become the common name in the trade for a product or service in respect of which it is registered;
if it has become deceptive; or if the proprietor is no longer properly qualified
under Art.5.[39] It may also be declared invalid if it was registered contrary to any
of the absolute or relative grounds of objection,[40] and subject to the limitations, in
the event of acquiescence, provided by Art.53. Where the grounds for revocation
or for a declaration of invalidity exist in respect of only some of the goods or services in respect of which the mark is registered, then it may be revoked or
declared invalid in respect of those goods or services only. All these matters may
also be raised by way of defence to an action for infringement.[41]

In the following parts of this section we therefore discuss particular aspects in   **14–243**
which it appears that the savings and defences in respect of Community trade
marks may differ from those pertaining to national registrations under the 1994
Act and the TM Directive.

Use in relation to genuine goods or services

There is no specific provision in the CTM Regulation affording a defence in re-   **14–244**
spect of the use of the mark in relation to the goods or services of the proprietor.
This position is to be contrasted with the position under the 1994 Act in relation
to national registrations. Here a specific defence is provided under s.10(6), subject
to the proviso that it must be in accordance with honest practices. Nevertheless, it
would seem inconceivable that a different result should be arrived at depending
on whether the mark in issue is a Community or a national registration. Indeed it
seems such a result would be prohibited because s.10(6) is not expressly
sanctioned as a defence in the TM Directive, so effectively barring any attempt to
construe it as affording a broader measure of protection.

Use of a registered Community trade mark

There is no provision under the CTM Regulation providing an absolute defence   **14–245**
to infringement of a registered Community trade mark where the alleged infringer
is using a registered Community trade mark in relation to goods or services in respect of which it is registered.[42] This is so whether the mark complained of is
registered as a national trade mark under the 1994 Act or is a Community trade
mark registered under the CTM Regulation. Instead, the CTM Regulation

---

[37] For a discussion of these limitations reference is invited to paras 14–153 to 14–179.
[38] For a discussion of this provision and the other aspects of exhaustion, reference is invited to
Ch.16.
[39] Art.50, discussed in Ch.16.
[40] Arts 51 and 52, discussed in Ch.16. The absolute and relative grounds of objection are discussed
in Chs 8 and 9, respectively.
[41] Art.95(3).
[42] In contrast to the position under the 1994 Act, s.11(1) in respect of national registrations and the

provides for a measure of protection where the proprietor of an earlier trade mark has acquiesced in the use of the later Community trade mark.

14–246   The owner of an earlier Community trade mark may take action against the user of a later Community trade mark in relation to goods or services in respect of which it is registered save as prohibited by Art.53(1). This provides that where the proprietor of the earlier mark has acquiesced for a period of five years in the use of the later mark in the Community, while being aware of such use, then he shall no longer be entitled on the basis of the earlier mark either to apply for a declaration that the later trade mark is invalid or to oppose the use of the later mark in respect of the goods or services for which the later mark has been used, unless registration of the later trade mark was applied for in bad faith.[43] Correspondingly, in these circumstances, the proprietor of the later Community trade mark is not then entitled to oppose the use of the earlier right either.[44]

14–247   A number of points in this limitation require consideration. First, in the context of this provision acquiescence appears to require no more or less than inaction with actual knowledge of the use. Secondly, if bad faith is shown then it seems the limitation is not applicable in terms either of preventing an attack on the later registration or opposing its use.[45]

Use of an earlier right

14–248   As will be seen from the next section, where the proprietor of an earlier right has acquiesced in the use of a later Community trade mark in a Member State, then his opportunity to oppose the use of the later trade mark is restricted. In these circumstances the proprietor of the later Community trade mark is not entitled to oppose the use of the earlier right.[46] There is also a provision restricting the opportunity of the proprietor of a Community trade mark to take action against the user of an earlier right which applies only in a particular locality.[47]

D. NATIONAL LAWS PROHIBITING THE USE OF COMMUNITY TRADE MARKS

14–249   The Community trade mark system provides a measure of protection against the use of a Community trade mark in any particular Member State, including the United Kingdom. These measures fall into two categories, earlier rights of a general nature and earlier rights which apply only in a particular locality. Each is dealt with below.

Earlier rights

14–250   Article 106 of the CTM Regulation makes it clear that, save unless otherwise provided for, the Regulation does not affect any earlier rights which may exist under the laws of any Member State, to take action against the use of a later

---

defence there provided in the case of the use of another national registration in relation to goods or services in respect of which it is registered.

[43] Art.53(1).

[44] Art.53(3).

[45] As to the meaning of bad faith, reference is invited to the discussion in Ch.8.

[46] Art.53. See paras 14–249 to 14–254.

[47] Art.107. This reflects the inability of the user of such a mark to oppose the registration of the Community mark under Art.8(4). This provision and the meaning of "in a particular locality" are discussed in Ch.9. See also paras 14–255 to 14–257.

Community trade mark in that Member State.[48] Particular provision is made in respect of earlier national trade marks, international marks under the Madrid Protocol designating the United Kingdom, well-known marks under Article 6*bis* of the Paris Convention or the WTO Agreement (TRIPS) and other non-registered trade marks or other signs used in the course of trade of more than mere local significance which may be protected by an action for passing off in the United Kingdom.[49]

The owner of any of the above rights may take action in the United Kingdom in respect of the use in the United Kingdom of a Community trade mark unless he has acquiesced, for a period of five successive years, in the use of the Community trade mark in the United Kingdom while being aware of such use. In those circumstances he is no longer entitled to apply for a declaration that the later Community trade mark is invalid or to oppose its use, unless registration of the Community trade mark was applied for in bad faith.[50] This provision raises the same issues of interpretation discussed above in relation to earlier Community marks. The points there considered are equally applicable in this context. **14–251**

Where there has been acquiescence then the proprietor of the later Community trade mark is nevertheless not entitled to oppose the use of the earlier right.[51] **14–252**

Another category provided for is the case where the use of a Community trade mark in the United Kingdom would offend against a right to a name, a right of personal portrayal, a copyright or other industrial property right.[52] Here it is clear that in so far as any such rights may exist in the United Kingdom they may be enforced against the use of the Community trade mark in the United Kingdom.[53] **14–253**

In a final catch all, the Regulation provides that it shall, unless otherwise provided for, not affect the right to bring proceedings under the civil, administrative or criminal law of a Member State or under the provisions of Community law for the purpose of prohibiting the use of a Community trade mark, to the extent that the use of a national trade mark may be prohibited under the law of that Member State or under Community law.[54] **14–254**

Use and protection of an earlier right in a particular locality

The Community trade mark system affords protection to the proprietor of an earlier right which exists only in a particular locality through the provisions of Article 107 of the CTM Regulation.[55] This provides that the proprietor of such an earlier right may oppose the use of the Community mark in the territory where **14–255**

---

[48] As from May 1, 2004, Art.159a came into force. This relates to the enlargement of the Community and provides that as from the date of accession of the new Member States, a Community trade mark registered or applied for pursuant to the TM Regulation before the date of accession shall be extended to the territory of those Member States. The use of a Community trade mark which has been so extended may be prohibited pursuant to Arts 106 or 107, if the earlier trade or other earlier right was registered, applied for or acquired in good faith in the new Member State prior to the date of accession of that State; or, where applicable, has a priority date prior to the date of accession of that State.

[49] And set out in Art.8(2) and (4). The meaning of "more than mere local significance" is discussed in Ch.9 and see also paras 14–255 to 14–257.

[50] Arts 106 and 53(2).

[51] Art.53(3). And see paras 14–255 to 14–257 in relation to the position of earlier rights in a particular locality.

[52] As provided for in Art.52(2).

[53] Art.106(1).

[54] Art.106(2). *e.g.* under EC Regulation 2081/92 on the Protection of Geographical Indications and Designations of Origin, Art.13.

[55] See also para.14–248 and Ch.9.

his right is recognised and protected in so far as the local law so permits.[56] So, in the United Kingdom, where local goodwill is indeed protectable by an action for passing off, it seems the proprietor of the earlier right may apply for an injunction to restrain the use of the Community trade mark and other relief in so far as the use of the Community trade mark will result or has resulted in passing off.[57] This right ceases to apply if the proprietor of the earlier right has acquiesced in the use of the Community trade mark in the United Kingdom for a period of five successive years, he being aware of such use, unless the Community trade mark was applied for in bad faith.[58]

14–256   Importantly, the proprietor of the Community trade mark may not oppose the use of the earlier right, even though that right may no longer be invoked against the Community trade mark, through acquiescence.[59]

14–257   The scope of the defence mirrors the protection afforded to proprietors of earlier rights of more than mere local significance by Arts 52, 53 and 106. The proprietor of such an earlier right may seek a declaration of invalidity under Art.52 unless he has acquiesced in the use of the Community trade mark and, even then, under Art.53, the proprietor of the Community mark may not oppose the use of the earlier right. The boundary beyond which an earlier right ceases to be of mere local significance is a matter discussed in Ch.9 and must be regarded as somewhat uncertain. Accordingly, a defendant with an earlier right would be well-advised to plead a defence under Art.107(3) and not rely solely on Arts 52 and 53.[60]

E. COMMUNITY COLLECTIVE MARKS

14–258   Community collective marks are generally treated in the same way as ordinary Community trade marks by the CTM Regulation for the purposes of infringement but with two particular modifications which are necessary to take account of their special nature.

Limitations on infringement provisions-indications of geographical origin

14–259   A Community collective mark does not entitle the proprietor to prohibit a third party from using in the course of trade a sign or indication which may serve in trade to designate the geographical origin, provided such use is in accordance with honest practices in industrial or commercial matters.[61] This limitation is also found in the provisions relating to national collective and certification marks and similarly reflects the ability to register Community collective marks which designate the geographical origin of the goods or services.[62]

---

[56] See para.14–250 as to the position in new Member States.

[57] Art.107(1).

[58] Art.107(2). By acquiescence it would seem the Regulation requires no more than inactivity knowing of the use of the Community trade mark. See para.14–247; as to the meaning of bad faith, reference is invited to the discussion in Ch.8.

[59] Art.107(3).

[60] See also paras 14–250 to 14–254. As discussed in Ch.9, in *Compass Publishing v Compass Logistics* [2004] EWHC 520; [2004] R.P.C. 41 the court took what might be described as a generous view of the scope of the boundary and found the earlier right was not of more than mere local significance; but it seems the defendant had not attempted to run the Art.107 defence.

[61] Art.64(2).

[62] The provisions relating to national collective and certification marks also require the use to be in accordance with honest practices; see para.14–206.

Persons who are entitled to bring an action for infringement

Proceedings for infringement of the collective mark may be brought by the proprietor and anyone who has the authority to use it.[63] The proprietor is entitled to claim compensation on behalf of persons who have authority to use the collective mark where they have sustained damage through its unauthorised use.[64] **14–260**

---

[63] Art.70(1), applying the provisions of Art.22(3) and (4).
[64] Art.70(2).

CHAPTER 15

THE ACTION FOR PASSING OFF

STRUCTURE OF THIS CHAPTER

15–001 This chapter attempts to set out the substantive law of passing off, as well as points of practice peculiar to passing off actions. Other points of practice and the relief available in an action for passing off are dealt with in Ch.19. As in previous editions, this very long chapter is broken up into sections, principally according to the type of misrepresentation involved:

1. Foundation and Nature of the Action;
2. The Limits of Passing Off;
3. Goodwill;
4. Direct Misrepresentation as to Business or Goods;
5. Imitations of Trade or Service Marks;
6. Trading Names;
7. Imitation of Get-up;
8. Proof of Likelihood of Deception;
9. Defences.

15–002 Inevitably, the same questions tend to arise whatever the type of misrepresentation, leading to some repetition on the one hand and cross-referencing to avoid repetition on the other. Some of the more important common points are dealt with at the beginning of this chapter, where we have also attempted to point out some of the limits of the law of passing off and certain situations which fall outside its scope.

15–003 In reading this chapter, the age of a cited case should be borne in mind. Whilst the principles of law have not changed in recent times, there has been a distinct tendency for judicial opinion to become less robust in character and more careful of those who complain of deception. Thus cases which are still good law might well be decided differently today.[1] Even absent changes in judicial approach, the requirement that a claimant prove that a misrepresentation by the defendant is likely to give rise to deception on the part of the public expressly links the tort to the preconceptions and reactions of the public. As the attributes of the public have changed over time, so too might the outcome of particular cases.

---

[1] The case of *Ainsworth v Walmsley* (1865–66) L.R. 1 Eq. 518, may serve as an instance. Undoubtedly there was passing off; the defendant expressly asserted that his goods were the claimant's, which was untrue (although the defendant may not have known it). But the court declared that anyone believing the assertion "would have had only their own folly to complain of", for they ought to have known that the goods were probably "doctored", and refused relief. It is hard to imagine such a judgment today. Nevertheless, deception remains and essential requirement of the tort, and merely demonstrating that as a result of the similarities between two marks "people make assumptions, jump to unjustified conclusions, and put two and two together to make five" does not suffice to establish passing off *HFC Bank plc v Midland Bank plc* [2000] F.S.R. 176, a passage cited with approval by Chadwick L.J. in *Premier Luggage & Bags Ltd v Premier Co (UK) Ltd* [2003] F.S.R. 5

1. Foundation and nature of the action

INTRODUCTION

Passing off is a single common law cause of action which can apply in a very   **15–004**
wide range of factual situations. The breadth of the tort is such that, despite some
views to the contrary, it now appears to be generally accepted that it is permissible to define two forms of the cause of action: the classic form, defined by the
"classical trinity", and the "extended form", typified by the Champagne[2], Sherry[3]
and Advocaat[4] cases. These two forms are not different torts, it is simply more
convenient for the purposes of analysis of a particular case to define passing off
by reference to one or other of these forms. This highlights a common problem in
passing off cases: however authoritative the source used for a definition of the
elements of the tort, it is frequently the case that further authority is required to
emphasise particular features of the tort as they apply to the facts of the case.[5]
Even the "classical trinity" of reputation, misrepresentation and damage to
goodwill can be misunderstood without further explanation. Accordingly, in attempting to "define" the cause of action in passing off, it is necessary to look at
several different dicta, although the starting point must be *Jif*.[6]

THE CLASSICAL TRINITY, RESTATED IN *JIF*

The "Jif Lemon" case is important in at least two respects. First, the House of   **15–005**
Lords confirmed that each passing off case depended on its own facts.[7] Secondly,
their Lordships reverted to the "classical trinity" for their definition of the elements of the cause of action. Lord Oliver put the matters a successful claimant
must prove as follows:

"First, he must establish a goodwill or reputation attached to the goods or services which he supplies in the mind of the purchasing public by association with
the identifying 'get-up' (whether it consists simply of a brand name or a trade description, or the individual features of labelling or packaging) under which his
particular goods or services are offered to the public, such that the get-up is recognised by the public as distinctive specifically[8] of the plaintiff's goods or services.

Secondly, he must demonstrate a misrepresentation by the defendant to the
public (whether or not intentional) leading or likely to lead the public to belief
that the goods or services offered by him are the goods or services of the plaintiff.

Thirdly, he must demonstrate that he suffers or, in a *quia timet* action, that he is
likely to suffer damage by reason of the erroneous belief engendered by the

---

[2] *Bollinger v Costa Brava Wine* [1960] R.P.C. 16.
[3] *Vine Products v Mackenzie* [1969] R.P.C. 1.
[4] *Warnink v Townend* [1980] R.P.C. 31, HL.
[5] Gummow J. has remarked "… it is to be observed that the law of passing off contains sufficient
nooks and crannies to make it difficult to formulate any satisfactory definition in short form.":
Conagra Inc v McCain Foods (Australia) Pty Ltd (1992) 106 A.L.R. 465 at 518.
[6] *Reckitt & Colman Products Ltd v Borden* [1990] R.P.C. 341, HL.
[7] See further, paras 15–015 to 15–017.
[8] Note that the requirement that get up is distinctive specifically of the claimant's goods or services
does not mean that the get up must be distinctive of claimant's goods or services to the exclusion
of all others. By way of example see *Associated Newspapers Limited v Express Newspapers*
[2003] F.S.R. 51.

defendant's misrepresentation that the source of the defendant's goods or services is the same as the source of those offered by the plaintiff."[9]

15–006   Lord Jauncey stated the principles thus:[10]

> "[quoting Lord Langdale] 'a man is not to sell his own goods under the pretence that they are the goods of another man ...' Accordingly a misrepresentation achieving such a result is actionable because it constitutes an invasion of proprietary rights vested in the plaintiff. However, it is a prerequisite of any successful passing off action that the plaintiff's goods have acquired a reputation in the market and are known by some distinguishing feature. It is also a prerequisite that the misrepresentation has deceived or is likely to deceive and that the plaintiff is likely to suffer damage by such deception. Mere confusion which does not lead to a sale is not sufficient."

> "It is not essential ... that the defendant should misrepresent his goods as those of the plaintiff. It is sufficient that he misrepresents his goods in such a way that it is a reasonably foreseeable consequence of the misrepresentation that the plaintiff's business or goodwill will be damaged."

15–007   These and other statements cited below reflect the fact that, within the action for passing off, "there are accommodated and adjusted inter se three sets of interests. There is the plaintiff's interest in protecting his skill, effort and investment, the interest of the defendant in freedom to attract purchasers for his goods and services, and the interest of consumers in having available a range of competitive goods and services for selection by consumers without the practice upon them of misrepresentations."[11]

THE EXTENDED FORM

15–008   The reversion to the classical trinity in *Jif* followed the attempt by Lords Diplock and Fraser in *Advocaat* to formulate general propositions of the law of passing off to take account of its "extended form". Lord Diplock's formulation was as follows:[12]

> "My Lords, *Spalding v Gamage* and the later cases make it possible to identify five characteristics which must be present in order to create a valid cause of action for passing off: (1) a misrepresentation (2) made by a trader in the course of trade, (3) to prospective customers of his or ultimate consumers of goods or services supplied by him, (4) which is calculated to injure the business or goodwill of another (in the sense that this is a reasonably foreseeable consequence) and (5) which causes actual damage to a

---

[9] At p.406.

[10] At pp.416–7.

[11] *per* Gummow J. (as he then was, in the Federal Court of Australia) in *Hogan v Pacific Dunlop Ltd* (1988) 83 A.L.R. 403. His observations were expressed in relation to the action for passing off "as presently understood in Australia". The law in Australia has diverged somewhat from the law in the UK, notably in territorial considerations, but this general comment holds good. He repeated these notions in *ConAgra Inc v McCain Foods (Aus) Pty Ltd* (1992) 106 A.L.R. 465 at 517.

[12] Accompanied by this warning: "In seeking to formulate general propositions of English law, however, one must be particularly careful to beware of the logical fallacy of the undistributed middle. It does not follow that because all passing off actions can be shown to present these characteristics, all factual situations which present these characteristics give rise to a cause of action for passing off."

business or goodwill of a trader by whom the action is brought (or in a quia timet action) will probably do so."[13]

Lord Fraser in the same case also advanced a five characteristic formulation:　　**15–009**

"It is essential for the plaintiff in a passing-off action to show at least the following facts:

(1) That his business consists of, or includes, selling in England a class of goods to which the particular trade name applies;

(2) That the class of goods is clearly defined, and that in the minds of the public, or a section of the public, in England, the trade name distinguishes that class from other similar goods;

(3) That because of the reputation of the goods, there is goodwill attached to the name;

(4) That he, the plaintiff, as a member of the class of those who sell the goods, is the owner of goodwill in England which is of substantial value;

(5) That he has suffered or is *really likely*[14] to suffer, substantial damage to his property in the goodwill by reason of the defendants selling goods which are falsely described by the trade name to which the goodwill is attached."[15]

It is evident that the two formulations are different, yet they should be regarded　　**15–010** as complementary.[16] Note particularly Lord Fraser's emphasis on the need to prove that the plaintiff "has suffered, or is really likely to suffer substantial damage to his property in the goodwill." The goodwill must be in the country concerned.[17]

CLASSICAL TRINITY VERSUS EXTENDED FORM

In *Advocaat* (at pp.94–5), Lord Diplock identified the features which distin-　　**15–011** guished the "extended form" of the tort from the classic form:

"The features which distinguish it from all previous cases were (a) that the element in the goodwill of each of the individual plaintiffs that was represented by his ability to use without deception (in addition to his individual house mark) the word 'Champagne' to distinguish his wines from sparkling wines not made by the champenois process from grapes produced in the Champagne district of France, was not exclusive to himself but was shared with every other shipper of sparkling wine to England whose wines could satisfy the same condition and (b) that the class of traders entitled to a proprietary right in 'the attractive force which brings in custom' represented by the ability without deception to call one's wines 'Champagne' was capable of continuing expansion, since it might be joined by any future shipper of wine who was able to satisfy that condition."

---

[13] [1980] R.P.C. 31 at 93.

[14] These italics in the original judgment appear in the report at [1980] R.P.C. 31 at 106, but not in the report at [1979] A.C. 731 at 756. The advantage of these words is that they emphasise the element of proportionality: is the damage sufficiently serious? cf. Lloyd J. in *HFC Bank plc v Midland Bank plc* [2000] F.S.R. 176 (settled on appeal).

[15] At 105–106 of the R.P.C. report.

[16] See *Anheuser Busch* [1984] F.S.R. 413 at 463, CA.

[17] See *per* Lord Fraser where he speaks of "goodwill in England" and *Star Industrial v Yap Kwee Kor* [1976] F.S.R 256 (PC, Singapore).

15–012   These distinguishing features were cited with approval by Chadwick L.J. in *Chocosuisse*.[18]

SUMMARY OF THE CURRENT APPROACH

15–013   The present position may be summarised as follows:

(1) for passing off in its classic form, the classical trinity, as expounded in *Jif* and other cases, should normally be applicable and be applied;

(2) for passing off in its extended form, one can apply either the classical trinity or the Advocaat tests. Judicial preference seems to vary. In *Parma Ham*,[19] the Court of Appeal welcomed the reversion in *Jif* to the classical trinity. Subsequently, the Court of Appeal has been content to utilise the Advocaat tests in *Elderflower Champagne*[20] and *Chocosuisse*;

(3) there is nothing inherently wrong in applying the Advocaat tests to cases of passing off in its classic form,[21] but doing so might raise the suspicion that the case falls into Lord Diplock's "undistributed middle". The modern trend is to use the classical trinity. See, for example, the view of Nourse L.J. in *Parma Ham*:

> "Although those speeches [of Lord Diplock and Lord Fraser] are of the highest authority, it has been my experience, and it is now my respectful opinion, that they do not give the same degree of assistance in analysis and decision as the classical trinity of (1) a reputation (or goodwill) acquired by the plaintiff in his goods, name, mark etc., (2) a misrepresentation by the defendant leading to confusion (or deception), causing (3) damage to the plaintiff."[22]

See also similar views expressed by Millett L.J. in *Harrods Ltd v Harrodian School Ltd.*[23]

15–014   The advantage of the classical trinity, as restated in *Jif*, is that attention is properly drawn to the essential relationships between the three elements. In a true case of passing off, all three elements are intertwined. It is the existence of a mark or get-up with reputation distinctive specifically of the claimant's goods or services which provides the necessary foundation for misrepresentation; the misrepresentation must be one which causes or is likely to cause damage to goodwill (in other words, the misrepresentation must be "operative" in the transaction and causative of the damage claimed); and damage to goodwill is at the heart of the cause of action. Goodwill itself is generated by trading activity, which is usually the source of reputation. But the existence of a reputation does not automatically establish goodwill. A claimant may be able to demonstrate a reputation in the United Kingdom giving rise to people being misled by the defendant's activities, but if he has no goodwill here, his claim will fail.[24] All these concepts are explained in further detail below.

A QUESTION OF FACT

15–015   It has always been the law that every case in which passing off is alleged turns on

---

[18] [1999] R.P.C. 826, CA.

[19] [1991] R.P.C. 351 at 369.

[20] [1993] F.S.R. 641.

[21] In *Bristol Conservatories Ltd v Conservatories Custom Built Ltd* [1989] R.P.C. 455 at 466, Ralph Gibson L.J. observed that the probanda formulated by Lords Diplock and Fraser would not, *e.g.* allow for cases of so-called "reverse" passing off (see below at para.15–129).

[22] At 568.

[23] [1996] R.P.C. 697 at 711.

[24] See, *e.g. Budweiser*, which should properly be regarded as an instance of the collision of independent rights in the name Budweiser, giving rise to no liability on either side: [1984] F.S.R. 413.

its own facts. The question whether the use of particular indicia results in passing off the goods or services of the defendant as those of the claimant is often one of difficulty, but it is in substance a question of fact:

"The principle of law may be very plainly stated, that nobody has any right to represent his goods as the goods of somebody else. How far the use of particular words, signs, or pictures, does or does not come up to the proposition enunciated in each particular case must always be a question of evidence, and the more simple the phraseology, the more like it is to a mere description of the article sold, the greater becomes the difficulty of proof, but if the proof establishes the fact, the legal consequence appears to follow."[25]

So, each of the elements of the claim requires the necessary facts to be established. Often the presence of a misrepresentation has to be inferred from the circumstances: **15–016**

"The basis of a passing-off action being a false representation by the defendant, it must be proved in each case as a fact that the false representation was made. It may, of course, have been made in express words, but cases of express misrepresentation of this sort are rare. The more common case is where the representation is implied in the use or imitation of a mark, trade name or get-up with which the goods of another are associated in the minds of the public, or of a particular class of the public. In such cases the point to be decided is whether, having regard to all the circumstances of the case, the use by the defendant in connection with the goods of the mark, name or get-up in question impliedly represents such goods to be the goods of the plaintiff, or the goods of the plaintiff of a particular class or quality, or, as it is sometimes put, whether the defendant's use of such mark, name or get-up is calculated to deceive. It would, however, be impossible to enumerate or classify all the possible ways in which a man may make the false representation relied on."[26]

For those analysing or applying the law, two important consequences follow: **15–017**

First, each case depends on the evidence, but it is not always easy to predict what the evidence will prove. In straightforward cases, personal expectations or predictions as to the effect of the insignia complained of coincide with what happens in reality. The cases which present the greatest difficulty are those in which the evidence establishes an unusual result. Difficult cases are won and lost on the evidence.[27] Jacob L.J. has observed:

"And even if one's own opinion is that deception is unlikely though possible, convincing evidence of deception will carry the day. The Jif lemon case ... is a recent example where overwhelming evidence of deception had that effect. It was certainly my experience in practice that my own view as to the likelihood of deception was not

---

[25] per Halsbury L.C. in "Camel Hair Belting" Reddaway v Banham) [1896] A.C. 199 at 204; 13 R.P.C. 218 at 224. For the case of "business" rather than "goods", see per Lord Simonds in Office Cleaning v Westminster (1946) 63 R.P.C. 39 at 42. See per Lord Parker in Spalding v Gamage (1915) 32 R.P.C. 000 at 283, 284, 285, quoted below. See generally Kay and Lindley L.JJ. in "Yorkshire Relish" (1896) 2 Ch. 54; 13 R.P.C. 235, and Lord Davey in Cellular Clothing v Maxton [1899] A.C. 326 at 343; 16 R.P.C. 397 at 408. See also Buckley L.J. in Brinsmead v Brinsmead (1913) 30 R.P.C. 493 at 506, 507; Baume v Moore [1958] R.P.C. 226 at 229, per Romer L.J.; Danckwerts J. in Adrema v Adrema GmbH [1958] R.P.C. 323.

[26] per Lord Parker in Spalding v Gamage (1915) 32 R.P.C. 273 at 284.

[27] cf. Jif where all the arguments raised by the defendants on appeal were defeated by the findings of fact.

always reliable. As I grew more experienced, I said more and more 'it depends on the evidence'."[28]

Secondly, the use of previous decisions as authorities requires care. There is a fine line between the citation of previous passing off cases to demonstrate principles of law and reliance on cases by way of factual analogy. Often it is necessary to understand the underlying facts to put particular *dicta* into their proper context, but sometimes the unspoken suggestion is that a factual analogy may also be drawn. Unless the facts are virtually identical, this simply creates unnecessary work. In the words of Lord Oliver in the Jif Lemon case "... this is not a branch of the law in which reference to other cases is of any real assistance except analogically".[29]

REPUTATION

15–018   It is essential to the success of any claim in respect of passing off, based on the use of a given mark, get-up or other indication of origin, for the claimant to show that this had (at the relevant date) become by user in this country distinctive, to some section of the public, if not of the claimant's goods or business alone, at least of a defined class of goods or business to which those of the claimant belong.

"It is, of course, essential to the success of any claim in respect of passing-off based on the use of a given mark or get-up that the plaintiff should be able to show that the disputed mark or get-up has become by user in this country distinctive of the plaintiff's goods so that the use in relation to any goods of the kind dealt in by the plaintiff or that mark or get-up will be understood by the trade and the public in this country as meaning that the goods are the plaintiff's goods. The gist of the action is that the plaintiff, by using and making known the mark or get-up in relation to his goods, and thus causing it to be associated or identified with those goods, has acquired a quasi-proprietary right to the exclusive use of the mark or get-up in relation to goods of that kind, which right is invaded by any person who, by using the same or some deceptively similar mark or get-up in relation to goods not of the plaintiff's manufacture, induces customers to buy from him goods not of the plaintiff's manufacture as goods of the plaintiff's manufacture, thereby diverting to himself orders intended for and rightfully belonging to the plaintiff."[30]

15–019   The mark or other indication concerned need not be universally known. A small trader with limited clientele is as much entitled to protect his brands and business name as any large concern.[31] The overriding consideration, in judging extent of reputation, is whether the claimant has built up a goodwill to the point where substantial damage will be caused to it by the acts he complains of.[32]

---

[28] Prior to his elevation to the Court of Appeal, in *Neutrogena Corporation v Golden Ltd* [1996] R.P.C. 473 at 482 (upheld on appeal).

[29] *Reckitt & Colman Products Ltd v Borden* [1990] R.P.C. 341, HL p.406.

[30] *per* Jenkins L.J. in "Turmix" *Oertli v Bowman*) [1957] R.P.C. 388 at 397. cf. with *"Manus"* (1948) 65 R.P.C. 329 at 339. See also below, paras 15–138 to 15–140. As to the need to show user in this country, see below, para.15–070.

[31] *Chelsea Man* [1985] F.S.R. 567 at 574, upheld on appeal [1987] R.P.C. 189.

[32] This is a question of degree. For two similar cases falling on either side of the line see *Hart v Relentless Records Ltd* [2003] F.S.R. 36 (goodwill too small for any likelihood of damage) and *Sutherland v V2* [2002] E.M.L.R. 28 (goodwill small but commercial, and liable to be "swamped" if defendant not restrained).

The relevant date, when it comes to proving reputation is the date when the defendant commenced the acts complained of.[33]

It is rare for a passing off action to be begun unless the goods concerned have   **15–020**
some sort of reputation, so that reported cases in which the claimant failed because the name, mark or get-up relied upon simply was not well enough known are rare; though cases in which the badge concerned is associated with the defendant rather than the claimant are sometimes found.[34] In general, however, where a claimant loses through failure to prove his reputation (as distinct from failure to show a deceptive resemblance of the defendant's badge to his) his difficulty is the subtler one that the badge relied on, however well-known, does not indicate a common trade origin for his and the defendant's goods.

(1) In an action concerning "Old Innishowen" whiskey, it was established   **15–021**
    that the name "Old Innishowen" had once been generally known as meaning illicit pot-still whiskey or "poteen", with the result that its use on the claimants' and defendant's whiskeys was less a representation as to trade origin than a representation that the whiskey resembled poteen: "Old Innishowen" (*Watt v O'Banlon*) (1886) 4 R.P.C. 1.

(2) An action by the manufacturers of the "Rolls" razor against the manufacturers of a "Rolls" cigarette lighter failed. The court was clearly inclined to the view that where two dissimilar products were both called "Rolls" the public would consider that they both claimed to be in the "Rolls Royce" class rather than that they had a common trade origin: *Rolls Razor v Rolls Lighters* (1949) 66 R.P.C. 137 at 142.

(3) In an action in which the passing off alleged was the mere sale of copies of the claimants' trinkets, a motion for interlocutory injunction failed in the absence of evidence that any degree of resemblance between the goods would be taken as indicating a common trade origin: *British American Glass v Winton* [1962] R.P.C. 230.

(4) Where the claimants' carpet-shampooing device was sold as the "Countess Shampoomatic," and the defendants marketed an "Addis Shampoomatic", an interlocutory injunction was refused in the absence of evidence of actual confusion: "Shampoomatic" (*Countess Housewares v Addis*) [1964] R.P.C. 251.

(5) The claimants had a reputation in the United Kingdom as importers of foreign racing bicycling accessories, under the trade mark "Evian". One item imported by them was a cyclist's plastic water-bottle, marked "Evian", devised by the proprietors of the well-known "Evian" natural mineral water to advertise their water. An action for passing off against the sale of similar bottles not imported by the claimants failed because (*inter alia*) they did not prove that the "Evian" bottles were in this country distinctive of them and not of the proprietors of the water: *Evian v Bowles* [1965] R.P.C. 327.

(6) Similarly where a defendant (truthfully) described his goods as "Guy Laroche designed for Marcel Fenez" the claimants, as exclusive English agents for the Paris couturier Guy Laroche, failed because they had no reputation in that name: *Poister v Fenez* [1965] R.P.C. 187.

---

[33] *"Pub Squash"* [1981] R.P.C. 429 at 494 (PC, N.S.W.); *J. C. Penney v Penneys* [1975] F.S.R. 367 at 374 and 381, CA. In *Teleworks Ltd v Telework Group plc* [2002] R.P.C. 27 the claimant unsuccessfully sought to rely upon the goodwill that the defendant could be expected to acquire through future expansion of trade. The court correctly rejected the consideration of such "future goodwill" as wrong in principle.

[34] "Turmix," *Oertli v Bowman*) [1957] R.P.C. 388 at 397, CA; approved [1959] R.P.C. 1, HL, is one such.

(7) Where the claimant had done nothing to indicate its connection with the mark "Coast to Coast", instead using it mainly as a slogan on T-shirts, Whitford J. expressed the view at the interlocutory stage that the claimant would have difficulty in establishing reputation: *Unidoor v Marks & Spencer* [1988] R.P.C. 275.

TIME NEEDED TO ACQUIRE REPUTATION

15–022   It is easier to establish a reputation where a mark has been used for a substantial period of time, but no length of time during which the claimant or his predecessors must have used the marks in question can be laid down.[35] In each case the question must be, has the claimant acquired a sufficient reputation?

(1) The "Fletcher" and "Challenge" companies, both well-known New Zealand companies, announced a merger under the name "Fletcher Challenge". Within a few hours of this being announced in Australia, the defendants reserved the name "Fletcher Challenge Pty." at an Australian companies registry. A passing off injunction was granted by the New South Wales court: *Fletcher Challenge v Fletcher Challenge Pty* [1982] F.S.R. 1.[36]

(2) A period of six months was insufficient to establish a reputation in the name "The Gold AM" for a radio programme comprising "Golden Oldies": *County Sound v Ocean Sound* [1991] F.S.R. 367. This is an indication of the difficulty in establishing a descriptive name as distinctive.

(3) Where the defendant advertises his goods and workmanship by showing photographs of the claimant's goods and workmanship, the defendant may, simultaneously, be contributing to the goodwill and reputation of the claimant and making a misrepresentation sufficient to found a passing off action: see *Bristol Conservatories v Conservatories Custom Built Ltd* [1989] R.P.C. 455.

MISREPRESENTATION

15–023   The passages cited above demonstrate that misrepresentation lies at the heart of an action for passing off. They also demonstrate that a successful claimant must prove not only the fact of misrepresentation but also that the misrepresentation was operative or material,[37] in the sense that the allegedly misleading indicia was at least a cause[38] of deception or its likelihood amongst the relevant class of consumers and hence damaging to the claimant's goodwill. The existence and effect of misrepresentation in any case is a matter for the court to decide.[39]

15–024   As Lord Parker observed in *Spalding v Gamage*,[40] it would be impossible to enumerate or classify all the possible ways in which a man might make the false representation relied on. Later sections in this chapter set out the variety of pos-

[35] Cases where comparatively short times have been sufficient: *Stannard v Reay* [1967] R.P.C. 589 (three weeks sufficient for "Mr. Chippy"); *McAndrew v Bassett* ("Anatolia Liquorice") (1864) 4 De. G.J. & S. 380 (one and one-half months sufficient); *Allen v Brown Watson* [1965] R.P.C. 191 (heavy pre-publication advertising sufficient); cf. *Compatibility Research v Computer Psyche* [1967] R.P.C. 201, illustration 5, para.15–140 (one month insufficient for descriptive device). See also *BBC v Talbot* [1981] F.S.R. 228; *Elida Gibbs v Colgate Palmolive* [1983] F.S.R. 95; *My Kinda Bones v Dr Pepper's Stove* [1984] F.S.R. 289; *Marcus Publishing v Hutton-Wild* [1990] R.P.C. 576.
[36] Similarly, but without the foreign element: *Glaxo plc v Glaxowellcome Ltd* [1996] F.S.R. 388, Lightman J.
[37] See especially Lord Oliver's third requirement, and Lord Jauncey, above, at paras 15–005 and 15–006, respectively.
[38] *My Kinda Town v Soll* [1983] R.P.C. 407, CA.
[39] See below, paras 15–192 to 15–194.
[40] (1915) 32 R.P.C. 273 at 284, cited above at para.15–016.

sible misrepresentations which have given rise to liability. Not all representations made in commerce as to a connection between the claimant and the goods or services of the defendant will suffice. As Goff L.J. observed in *Bulmer v Bollinger*:[41]

> "Not every kind of connection claimed will amount to passing off; for example, if one says that one's goods are very suitable to be used in connection with the plaintiff's. On the other hand in my view there can be a passing off of goods without representing that they are actually the well known goods which the plaintiff produces or a new line which he is supposed to have started. It is sufficient in my view if what is done represents the defendant's goods to be connected with the plaintiff's in such a way as would lead people to accept them on the faith of the plaintiff's reputation. Thus for example it would be sufficient if they were taken to be made under licence, or under some trading arrangement which would give the plaintiff some control over them...."

Millett L.J. was prepared to go slightly further in *Harrods v Harrodian School*. **15–025** Having quoted the passage above, he stated:[42]

> "It is not in my opinion sufficient to demonstrate that there must be a connection of some kind between the defendant and the plaintiff, if it is not a connection which would lead the public to suppose that the plaintiff has made himself responsible for the quality of the defendant's goods or services."

PROOF OF FRAUDULENT INTENTION IS NOT ESSENTIAL

Passing off cases are often cases of deliberate and intentional misrepresentation, **15–026** but it is well settled that fraud is not a necessary element of the right of action,[43] and the absence of an intention to deceive is not a defence.[44] Moreover, literal truth is not necessarily innocent of misrepresentation.

> "If a man makes a statement which is true, but which carried with it a false representation and induces the belief that his goods are the plaintiff's goods, he will be restrained by injunction. He cannot rely on the fact that his statement is literally and accurately true if, notwithstanding the truth, it carries with it a false representation."[45]

Proof of fraudulent intention may, however, materially assist a claimant in **15–027** establishing probability of deception.[46]

It should be remembered that deliberate imitation of another's goods, get-up, **15–028** method of trading or trading style does not necessarily involve fraud; a trader is

---

[41] [1978] R.P.C. 79 at 117.

[42] [1996] R.P.C. 697 at 713, relying also on Farwell J. in *British Legion v British Legion Club (Street) Ltd* (1931) 48 R.P.C. 555, where the judge considered that the public would take the defendant club to be "connected in some way" with the plaintiff. But he explained this by saying that some persons would think that it was "either a branch of the plaintiff or a club in some way amalgamated with or under the supervision of the plaintiff and for which the plaintiff had in some way made itself responsible."

[43] *Reddaway v Bentham* [1892] 2 Q.B. 639; 9 R.P.C. 503 at 507, CA; Halsbury L.C. in *Cellular Clothing v Maxton* [1899] A.C. 326 at 334; 16 R.P.C. 397 at 404. But cf. the cases on enabling others to pass-off, para.15–201.

[44] *Baume v Moore* [1958] R.P.C. 226 at 228.

[45] *per* Buckley L.J. in *Brinsmead v Brinsmead* (1913) 30 R.P.C. 493 at 506.

[46] See below, para.15–199, and *O.T. v Cumming* (1915) 32 R.P.C. 69. For if the defendant set out to deceive, the court will readily infer that he succeeded. Fraudulent intent may be implied where the defendant continues to use deceptive marks after complaints have been made to him: *Johnston v Orr Ewing* (1882) 7 App.Cas. 219 at 229; *Weingarten v Bayer* (1906) 22 R.P.C. 341 at 357, HL.

entitled to sail close to the wind, so long as he steers clear of actual misrepresentation.[47] It is, in particular, lawful for a trader to suggest to purchasers that his goods are equivalent to, or a substitute for, those of another,[48] and to choose marks and styles appropriate to that. Furthermore, the cases would seem to imply that it is lawful to adopt a mark so close to another's that customers (whilst aware that there are two marks) will not bother to distinguish between them;[49] something that can cause very great damage as well as great resentment. On the other hand, a conscious decision on the part of a defendant "is not something which the court is bound to disregard".[50]

DAMAGE

15–029   Proof of damage is not in every case essential to enable the claimant to maintain his action,[51] it depends on the circumstances. If the claimant shows that the defendant is acting so as to pass-off goods as those of the claimant which are not the claimant's it will generally be assumed that the claimant is thereby prevented from selling as many of the goods as he otherwise would; while even if there is no direct loss of sales (as where claimant and defendant are not in direct competition) the confusion between the two suppliers puts the claimant's goodwill at risk. There is indeed some authority for the proposition, that any unauthorised appropriation of or profit from another's business goodwill or professional reputation[52] or business goodwill,[53] inasmuch as it deprives the claimant of the opportunity to exploit his goodwill himself if nothing else. But this doctrine is by no means firmly established, and where the claimant is not a trading business especially, he may well be required to establish a likelihood of actual financial loss from the defendant's actions.[54] Thus it has been held that the assumption of a name,[55] or an address,[56] similar to the name or address of the claimant, without malicious intent, although it may cause annoyance and inconvenience to him—for instance, by delaying his letters—is not actionable unless it is shown to be

---

[47] So Roxburgh J. frequently observed, *arguendo*. He appears never to have put the observation into a judgment, but *Day v Kennedy* (1952) 70 R.P.C. 19 at 21, 22 comes close to it; cf. *per* Greene M.R. in *Wright Layman & Umney v Wright* (1949) 66 R.P.C. 149 at 152: "Honest men do not sail near to the wind." But that referred to a man who had passed off. See also, para.15–040.

[48] cf. para.15–113 and *King v Gillard* (1905) 22 R.P.C. 327, CA (a "get-up" case).

[49] cf. *Goya v Gala* (1952) 69 R.P.C. 188; there are similar cases, but the point seems never to have been expressly decided.

[50] *United Biscuits v Asda Stores* [1997] R.P.C. 513 at 531. The defendant had aimed to avoid passing off but deliberately sailed close to the wind in selecting the packaging and name for its "Puffin" biscuits, an intended own-brand equivalent to the claimant's "Penguin".

[51] *Procea v Evans* (1951) 68 R.P.C. 210, and see *Associated Newspapers v Insert Media* [1991] F.S.R. 380, CA, where the misrepresentation was that the claimants must have authorised and taken responsibility for the defendant's activities, the parties were appealing to the same customers and it was held the defendant intended to exploit the claimant's goodwill (distinguishing *Stringfellow* [1984] R.P.C. 501, CA, a case where little, if any, overlap existed and there was no attempt to trade on the claimant's goodwill).

[52] *Henderson v Radio Corp* [1969] R.P.C. 218 (High Ct, Aust.).

[53] *Lego v Lego M. Lemelstrich* [1983] F.S.R. 155; but cf. "Judge Dredd," para.22–027. See also *Blazer v Yardley* [1992] F.S.R. 501, where there was no overlap in trade, but it was accepted there was a serious issue to be tried that the defendant's products might be associated with the claimant. Although an interlocutory injunction was refused on the balance of the risk of injustice, Aldous J. stated that use of the claimant's goodwill by definition causes injury to the claimant and lays open that goodwill to damage by the actions of the defendant.

[54] *Morecombe v Mecca* [1966] R.P.C. 423 (beauty contests).

[55] *Borthwick v Evening Post* (1888) L.R. 37 Ch.D. 449; *Du Boulay v Du Boulay* (1867–69) L.R. 2 P.C. 430.

[56] *Day v Brownrigg* (1878–79) 10 Ch.D. 294; *Street v Union Bank of Spain and England* (1885) L.R. 30 Ch.D. 156 (adoption by the defendants (bankers) of the same cypher telegraphic address as that of the claimant).

calculated to injure him in his business. No action lies at the suit of any private person for deception practised upon the public, unless it incidentally causes, or is calculated to cause, damage to him as an individual; if this is not the case, the wrongdoer can only be punished through the criminal law, or in a civil action on information brought in the name of the Attorney-General.[57] In a passing off action the court is not concerned with the truth or falsity of statements in the defendant's advertisements except so far as they tend to induce the belief that the defendant's goods or business are the claimant's.[58]

INFERIORITY OF THE SPURIOUS GOODS NEED NOT BE SHOWN

It is immaterial to the existence of the claimant's right of action that the goods passed off as his are as good as or better than his own;[59] or that the defendant does not undersell him.[60] When it comes to assessment of damages, all such matters are material.[61]   **15–030**

COMPARISON WITH THE ACTION FOR THE INFRINGEMENT OF A TRADE MARK

As a matter of legal history, it may be said that the actions for infringement of trade mark and for passing off have a common origin—the latter is a generalisation of the old action for infringement—but they are now distinct. With the new law of trade marks, the two causes of action have converged somewhat, in the sense that a wider variety of indicia may now be eligible for registration, and reputation can (under s.10(2) of the 1994 Act) and must (under s.10(3)) be relevant. Nonetheless it remains the case that the cause of action in passing off is wider and more flexible, giving protection to all the means by which the claimant's trade or goods may be identified with him, and not just those which he has managed to get registered. It is also more onerous, in the sense that the claimant must prove his reputation and that the defendant's activities involve a false representation damaging to the claimant's goodwill.   **15–031**

The main consequence of this need to prove in each case that a false representation has been made is less that an action for passing off differs from an action for infringement of trade mark (they do not in general differ greatly) than that a registered trade or service mark is a species of property, and may be regarded as such, to an extent that the right to sue for passing off cannot. Whilst there is no doubt that goodwill may be a saleable asset, and it is goodwill, or reputation, that founds most passing off actions, it must be remembered that transactions in goodwill do not necessarily give rights against third persons: the "purchaser" of the "right" to use a certain name or badge acquires no right of action, unless he can show that the use of it by others will amount to false representation.   **15–032**

WHERE TRADE MARK ACTION FAILS, PASSING OFF ACTION MAY SUCCEED ON THE SAME EVIDENCE

A claimant may fail to make out a case of infringement of a trade mark for vari-   **15–033**

---

[57] *per* Cotton L.J. in *Native Guano v Sewage Manure* (1889) 6 R.P.C. 125, at 128; the proposition seems correct, notwithstanding the criticism of this case in "Advocaat", *Warnink v Townend* [1980] R.P.C. 31; see also *Clark v Freeman and Williams v Hodge,* cited below.
[58] *Bowden Brake v Bowden Wire* (1913) 30 R.P.C. 580 at 618.
[59] *Blofeld v Payne* (1833) 4 B. & Ad. 410; *Edelsten v Edelsten* (1863) 1 De G.J. & S. 185, Westbury L.C.; *per* Lord Blackburn in *Singer v Loog* (1882–83) L.R. 8 App.Cas. 15 at 29.
[60] *per* Joyce J. in *Spicer v Spalding & Hodge* (1915) 32 R.P.C. 52 at 59.
[61] See paras 19–127 to 19–142.

ous reasons and may yet show that by imitating the mark claimed as a trade mark, or otherwise, the defendant has done what is calculated to pass off his goods as those of the claimant. A claim in "passing off" has generally been added as a second string to actions for infringement, and has on occasion succeeded where the claim for infringement has failed.[62]

THE TRADE MARKS ACT AFFORDS NO BAR TO A PASSING OFF ACTION

15–034   Subject to possibly one qualification,[63] nothing in the Trade Marks Act 1994 affects a trader's right against another in an action for passing off.[64] It is, therefore, no bar to an action for passing off that the trade name, get-up or any other of the badges identified with the claimant's business, which are alleged to have been copies or imitated by the defendant, might have been, but are not registered as, trade marks, even though the evidence is wholly addressed to what may be a mark capable of registration. Again, it is no defence to passing off that the defendant's mark is registered.[65] The Act offers advantages to those who register their trade marks, but imposes no penalty upon those who do not. It is equally no bar to an action for passing off that the false representation relied upon is an imitation of a trade mark that is incapable of registration.[66] A passing off action can even lie against a registered proprietor of the mark sued upon.[67] The fact that a claimant is using a mark registered by another party (or even the defendant) does not of itself prevent goodwill being generated by the use of the mark, or prevent such a claimant from relying on such goodwill in an action against the registered proprietor.[68] Such unregistered marks are frequently referred to as "common law trade marks".

NEW CASE OF FRAUD OR OF PASSING OFF RAISED AT THE TRIAL

15–035   If a charge of fraud is to be made at the trial, it is essential that it should be put forward clearly and prominently on the pleadings.[69] But the fact that the claimants have not pleaded fraud does not exclude the court from considering whether fraud in fact existed.[70] A claimant who has raised no issue upon his pleadings except in regard to the infringement of his trade mark has been refused leave to

---

[62] *Hart v Colley* (1890) L.R. 44 Ch.D. 193; 7 R.P.C. 93. *Jay v Ladler* (1888) 40 Ch.D. 649; 6 R.P.C. 136; *Montgomery v Thompson*, 41 Ch.D. 35; 6 R.P.C. 404; [1891] A.C. 217; 8 R.P.C. 361 (CA and HL); *"Yorkshire Relish"* [1897] A.C. 710; 14 R.P.C. 720; *Barber v Manico* (1893) 10 R.P.C. 93. More recently, see *United Biscuits v Asda Stores* [1997] R.P.C. 513.

[63] See s.48 (effect of acquiescence) (especially s.48(1)(b)) which relates to unregistered as well as registered trade marks, and consequently, though its provision so far as common law rights are concerned are probably only declaratory, must be regarded as qualifying the general provisions of s.2. S.22(3), dealing with assignments, also affects common law rights.

[64] This is expressly declared by s.2(2), but the law was the same under the earlier Acts which, prior to the 1905 Act, contained no such express provision.

[65] See para.15–209.

[66] "Camel Hair Belting" *Reddaway v Banham*), quoted above, para.15–015, was such a mark; it was hopelessly descriptive.

[67] e.g. *Thorne v Pimms* (1907) 26 R.P.C. 221; see also para.15–068 No.3.

[68] See *Inter Lotto (UK) v Camelot Group plc* [2004] R.P.C. 9; see also para.15–209.

[69] *Leahy, Kelly v Glover* (1893) 10 R.P.C. 141, HL; *Claudius Ash v Invicta* (1911) 28 R.P.C. 252 and 597; 29 R.P.C. 465; cf. *United Kingdom Tobacco v Malayan Tobacco* (1933) 51 R.P.C. 11, PC (fraud neither pleaded nor suggested in cross-examination; finding of fraud unjustified); *Bulmer v Bollinger* [1978] R.P.C. 79; and see now, CPR 16PD–009. 2(1).

[70] *John Walker v Ost* [1970] R.P.C. 489 (fraud was found but not pleaded); *Midland Counties Dairy v Midland Dairies* (1948) 65 R.P.C. 429; *Bulmer v Bollinger* [1978] R.P.C. 79.

amend his claim at the trial so as to start a fresh case of "passing off" in order to save his action.[71]

2. The limits of passing off

WHAT IS AND WHAT IS NOT PASSING OFF

It may aid understanding to examine briefly some examples of situations which **15–036** lie outside or around the limits of the law of passing off. Some activities which would constitute unfair competition in continental countries clearly lie outside the scope of the tort. This type of case often lacks one of the essential elements of passing off. We discuss these types of cases first. The cases which are most difficult are those where, at first sight, each of the three elements appears to be present yet closer analysis reveals that, for example, apparent deception is being caused by something other than the alleged misrepresentation, or the damage complained of is dilution of distinctiveness which may not be caused by any deception at all. These cases require a clear understanding of the concepts involved and we discuss some of the common points below. These are also illustrated, of course, throughout this entire chapter.

PASSING OFF IS NOT A GENERAL TORT OF UNFAIR COMPETITION

Article 10*bis* of the Paris Convention stipulates that the Convention countries are **15–037** bound to assure to persons entitled to the benefits of the Convention an effective protection against unfair competition. Any act of competition contrary to honest practices in industrial or commercial matters constitutes an act of unfair competition. The term "unfair competition" is used in the broad sense adopted by countries such as France, Germany and Switzerland.

Under Article 10*ter*, Convention countries are bound to provide nationals of **15–038** other Convention countries with appropriate legal remedies to repress effectively the acts referred to in Arts 9 (seizure on importation of goods unlawfully bearing a mark or trade name), 10 (seizure on importation of goods unlawfully bearing false indications as to their source or identity of the producer) and 10*bis*.

English law purports to (but does not fully) comply with the United Kingdom's **15–039** obligations as a member of the Paris Convention through the mixture of passing off, malicious falsehood and a variety of criminal statutory provisions to which must be added an ever increasing amount of legislation emanating from the EU. Most continental European countries provide a generalised cause of action in "unfair competition". It is clear that English law does not. However, it will be found that acts of "unfair competition" likely to cause any real damage to other

---

[71] *Native Guano v Sewage Manure* (1887) 4 R.P.C. 478; 8 R.P.C. 125 (CA and HL); but the whole case was a mess, see *per* Lord Diplock in "Advocaat" at [1980] R.P.C. 96. Leave was granted, the defendants not objecting, in *Jay v Ladler* (1888) 40 Ch.D. 649; 6 R.P.C. 136, and also in *Barberb v Manico* (1893) 10 R.P.C. 93, where the defendants raised the objection. But see *Andrew v Kuehnrich* (1913) 30 R.P.C. 93, where at the trial the claimants were given leave to amend so as to claim clearly for infringement as well as passing off. cf. *Cellular Clothing v White* (1953) 70 R.P.C. 9, where the claimants, having included in their writ claims both in infringement and in passing off, limited their statement of claim to passing off, then sought at the trial to add a claim for relief for infringement; Harman J. refused leave, saying that claim had been abandoned. But where claimants had claimed for passing off in their writ, but not in their statement of claim, and had, on an application in chambers stated that they claimed only for infringement of trade mark, they were, nevertheless, allowed to amend by adding a claim for passing off, shortly before the trial: *Rossell v Hodges* (1918) 35 R.P.C. 285.

traders are with few, if any, exceptions within the concept of passing off, as now understood, or more rarely within malicious falsehood, whilst acts of unfair competition likely to cause real damage to the consuming public are within the criminal law, especially that relating to false trade descriptions. There is no doubt that a broad concept of "unfair competition" would benefit some claimants who lie outside the limits of passing off, particularly those who have trouble establishing the necessary goodwill to found the action.

IT IS NOT A TORT OF MISREPRESENTATION WHICH INJURES ANOTHER TRADER

15–040   The limits of the law of passing off are essentially defined by the classic and extended forms of the tort explained above, even though it has been acknowledged that there may be cases which meet the criteria of the extended form yet still do not amount to passing off—the so-called undistributed middle. However, even what is now characterised as the classic form of passing off has often been treated as only a special instance of a more general rule that any misrepresentation calculated to give one trader the benefit of another's goodwill is actionable; or even more generally that any "misrepresentation ... calculated to injure another in his trade or business" is to be regarded as passing off.[72] The principle has been even more broadly stated:[73]

> "In the interests of fair trading and in the interest of all who may wish to buy or sell goods the law recognises that certain limitations upon freedom of action are necessary and desirable. In some situations the law has had to resolve what might at first appear to be conflicts between competing rights. In solving the problems which have arisen there has been no need to resort to any abstruse principles but rather ... to the straightforward principle that trading must not only be honest but must not even unintentionally be unfair."

15–041   More recent attempts to invoke a tort of unfair competition or to expand passing off to cover such acts have been rebuffed:[74]

(1) In Insert Media, at the interim stage, the claimant argued (in addition to passing off) a separate and distinct cause of action to the effect that the law would prevent deliberate acts calculated to cause damage to the claimant's goodwill, based on *Emperor of Austria v Day*[75] and *Kingdom of Spain v Christie*.[76] This claim was rejected, even without the benefit of full argument.[77]

(2) Similarly in *Hodgkinson & Corby v Wards*: "I turn to consider the law and begin by identifying what is not the law. There is no tort of copying. There is no tort of taking a man's market or customers. Neither the market nor the customers are the plaintiff's to own. There is no tort of making use of another's goodwill as such. There is no tort of competition. I say this

---

[72] *per* Parker J. in *Burberry v Cording* (1909) 26 R.P.C. 693 at 701.

[73] *per* Lord Morris in *Parker-Knoll v Knoll International* [1962] R.P.C. 265 at 278.

[74] Though note the *obiter* comments of Aldous L.J. at paras 70 and 71 of *Arsenal Football Club plc v Reed* [2003] R.P.C. 39 alluding to the possible expansion of the tort. However, note *L'Oreal v Bellure* [2005] EWCH 269 (Ch) where a claim founded in unfair competition or "passing off absent deception, was referred to as hopeless on the present state of the law".

[75] (1861) 3 De. G.F.& J. 217.

[76] [1986] 1 W.L.R. 1120.

[77] *Mail Newspapers v Insert Media* [1987] R.P.C. 521. The claimant succeeded at full trial in its claim in passing off. See *Associated Newspapers v Insert Media* [1991] F.S.R. 380, CA.

because at times the plaintiffs seemed close to relying on such torts", *per* Jacob J.[78]

(3) In *BBC v Talksport*[79] the claimant argued that the coverage provided by the defendant of Euro 2000 football matches gave rise to the false impression that the matches were being broadcast live. The judge accepted that that this misrepresentation was being made, but held that the claimant "live broadcasting" was no more than a description of the claimant's activities and did not give rise to protectable goodwill owned by the claimant.

AT COMMON LAW THERE IS NO PROPRIETARY RIGHT IN A NAME OR GET-UP

It is well settled that (unless registered as a trade mark) no one has a monopoly in his brand name or get up, however familiar these may be. Passing off is a wrongful invasion of a right of property vested in the claimant; but the property which is protected by an action for passing off is not the claimant's proprietary right in the name or get-up which the defendant has misappropriated, but the goodwill and reputation of his business which is likely to be harmed by the defendant's misrepresentation.[80]   **15–042**

THE DISTINCTION BETWEEN CONFUSION AND DECEPTION

In many authorities the terms "confusion" and "deception" are used to mean the same thing.[81] However, it is necessary to distinguish between "mere confusion" on the one hand and deception or its likelihood on the other. Mere confusion does not indicate or establish passing off. See the following: **15–043**

(1) "Then it is said—and again there is no disagreement as to this—that the mere fact that the produce of the appellants and that of the respondents may be confused by members of the public is not of itself sufficient."[82]   **15–044**

(2) "It is also a prerequisite that the misrepresentation has deceived or is likely to deceive and that the plaintiff is likely to suffer damage by such deception. Mere confusion which does not lead to a sale is not sufficient. Thus, if a customer asks for a tin of black shoe polish without specifying any brand and is offered the product of A which he mistakenly believes to be that of B, he may be confused as to what he has got but he has not been deceived into getting it. Misrepresentation has played no part in his purchase."[83]

(3) "No one is entitled to be protected against confusion as such. Confusion may result from the collision of two independent rights or liberties and where that is the case neither party can complain; they must put up with the results of the confusion as one of the misfortunes which occur in life.

---

[78] [1995] F.S.R.169.

[79] [2001] F.S.R. 6.

[80] See Millett L.J. in *Harrods Ltd v Harrodian School Ltd* [1996] R.P.C. 697 at 711.

[81] The prevalence of the use of "confusion" rather than "deception" may be caused by a certain squeamishness on the part of claimants and judges to brand defendants as responsible for deception when there is no deliberate intent to deceive. "Deception" should not be seen as a term of opprobrium, except in cases of fraud.

[82] *per* Lord Oliver in *Jif* [1990] R.P.C. 341 at 412.

[83] *per* Lord Jauncey in *Jif* [1990] R.P.C. 341 at 417.

The protection to which a man is entitled is protection against passing off, which is a quite different thing from mere confusion."[84]

(4) "At the heart of passing off lies deception or its likelihood ... Never has the tort shown even a slight tendency to stray beyond cases of deception."[85]

(5) "Secondly, 'to deceive' is one thing. To 'cause confusion' is another. The difference is this: when you deceive a man, you tell him a lie. You make a false representation to him and thereby cause him to believe a thing to be true which is false. You may not do it knowingly, or intentionally, but you still do it, and so you deceive him. But you may cause confusion without telling him a lie at all, and without making any false representation to him. You may indeed tell him the truth, the whole truth and nothing but the truth, but still you may cause confusion in his mind, not by any fault of yours, but because he has not the knowledge or ability to distinguishing it from other pieces of truth known to him or because he may not even take the trouble to do so."[86]

15–045   The position is complicated somewhat by the fact that the dividing line between confusion (no passing off) and deception (resulting in passing off) may seem to vary according to the facts of particular cases. This can lead to circular reasoning: an event was an instance of deception because the court found passing off and vice versa. However, the real distinction between mere confusion and deception lies in their causative effects. Mere confusion has no causative effect (other than to confuse lawyers and their clients), whereas if, in answer to the question: "what moves the public to buy?", the insignia complained of is identified, then it is a case of deception. The distinction is blurred somewhat by cases where instances of what would appear to be deception were proved, yet those instances were treated as being "mere confusion" for which the defendant was not held responsible:

(1) Confusion caused by descriptive names: The parties trade under names which are purely descriptive (for example Office Cleaning) and some members of the public mistakenly suppose the defendant's product or service is that of the claimant: for example *Office Cleaning Services v Westminster Office Cleaning Association* 63 R.P.C. 39 at 43, *per* Lord Simonds; *Jif* [1990] R.P.C. 341 at 412, *per* Lord Oliver.

(2) Confusion caused by cessation of a *de facto* monopoly: the claimant has enjoyed a *de facto* monopoly in a particular product; the defendant breaks the monopoly and some members of the public continue to assume, for a time, that the defendant's product is the claimant's: for example My *Kinda Town v Soll* [1983] R.P.C. 407, CA; and see *Jif* [1990] R.P.C. 341 at 412, *per* Lord Oliver.

(3) Confusion caused by lack of source motivation: some members of the public purchase the defendant's product whilst under the impression that it is the claimant's product, but they do not care either way: for example *Hodgkinson & Corby v Wards* [1994] 1 W.L.R. 1564 at 1574G–1575A, 1576G–1577B.

(4) Confusion caused by features common to the trade: some members of the public are under the impression that the defendant's product emanates from the claimant because of his use of features common to both which are also common to the trade as a whole: for example *Payton v Snelling*

---

[84] See *Marengo v Daily Sketch* [1992] F.S.R. 1 at 2, CA *per* Lord Greene M.R.

[85] *Hodgkinson & Corby v Wards* [1994] 1 W.L.R. 1564, Jacob J. at 1570.

[86] *Parker-Knoll Limited v Knoll International Limited* [1962] R.P.C. 265 HL, Lord Denning at 274, lines 1–10.

17 R.P.C. 48 at 57, CA; *Williams v Bronnley* (1909) 26 R.P.C. 765; *Jif* [1990] R.P.C. 341 at 412, *per* Lord Oliver.

(5) Administrative confusion caused by similarities between marks, without there being any mistaken belief as to the trade origin of the goods or services in issue. HFC complained of the adoption by Midland Bank plc of the mark HSBC and adduced evidence from a substantial number of members of the public who had been confused by the similarity between the names. However, only those who were not aware of HFC were confused and the action therefore failed *HFC Bank plc v Midland Bank plc* [2000] F.S.R. 176.

COMMON FIELD OF ACTIVITY

There is no rule that the defendant must operate in the same field of activity as the claimant.[87] However, this does not mean an examination of their respective fields of activity is irrelevant. The more remote the activities of the parties, the stronger the evidence needed to establish misrepresentation and the real likelihood of damage that are prerequisites of a right of action in passing off. Although this is a question of fact to be determined in the circumstances of the particular case, instances of decisions may be helpful and are given below.   **15–046**

It may be said generally that establishing passing off by goods in which the claimant does not trade calls for special evidence to establish that the defendant's actions will induce the belief, if not that his goods are those of the claimant[88] at least that his business is an extension of[89] or somehow connected with[90] that of the claimant, or his goods somehow approved or authorised by the claimant.[91] Where the fields of activity of the parties are different, the burden of proving that the defendant causes real likelihood of damage to the claimant is a very heavy one.[92] There is some authority for saying that goodwill may extend to natural future extensions of a business, so that a claimant may be entitled to prevent use of his name or marks on goods he expects to sell in the future.[93] However, the better view is that although a claimant's goodwill may suffice to render the activities of a defendant in relation to such goods a misrepresentation, the only goodwill relevant when considering whether such a misrepresentation has in fact occurred or amounts to passing off is the goodwill which has been generated by actual use of the mark in issue at the date upon which the defendant commenced the activi-   **15–047**

---

[87] *Harrods v Harrodian* [1996] R.P.C. 697.

[88] As in *"Treasure Cot"*, where the judge (Harman J.) granted a declaration against use on dolls' cots of a mark established for babies' cots: (1950) 67 R.P.C. 89 (almost the only case in which he found for a plaintiff in passing off in the absence of fraud) having previously doubted whether a manufacturer could ever monopolise a mark outside his own line of business, in *Rolls Razor v Rolls (Lighters)* (1949) 66 R.P.C. 137 at 142 (an appeal failed, see at 299); and see the old case of *Warwick v New Motor* (1910) 27 R.P.C. 161 (cycle tyres and motor tyres); cf. from the same period, *Lucas v Fabry* (1906) 23 R.P.C. 33 (cycle accessories and cycle tyres), relief refused. The real point in such cases will ordinarily be the need to show damage to the claimant's goodwill.

[89] *Eastman v Griffiths* (1898) 15 R.P.C. 105 ("Kodak" for bicycles: the judge found that there was an "intimate connection" between the photographic and cycle trades, so much so that Kodak would probably take to making bicycles).

[90] *Manchester Brewery v North Cheshire* [1899] A.C. 83, HL, and see *Bulmer v Bollinger* and *Harrods v Harrodian* [1996] R.P.C. 697.

[91] As in *Morny v Ball & Rogers*, listed below at para.14–044.

[92] *"Stringfellows"* [1984] R.P.C. 501 at 546, 547, CA.

[93] *Eno v Dunn* (1890) L.R. 15 App. Cas. 252 at 258, HL; *"Morning Mail"* (1885) 54 L.J.Ch. 1059 *per* Cotton, L.J.); *Dunlop v Dunlop Lubricant* (1899) 16 R.P.C. 12; and cf. the cases on foreign companies hoping to trade here, above, para.14–056.

ties complained of.[94] The Court of Appeal in "Stringfellows" doubted that loss of a possible field for "merchandising" of the mark concerned was a permissible head of damage in passing off.[95]

15–048   "Character merchandising" presents problems here. Unless the public can be shown to be well aware of merchandising in the particular field,[96] there will, in general, be no obvious link between the production of television programmes or films (let alone, a pure "merchandising" operation) and the manufacture of toys, clothes, sweets or anything else with which characters' names may be profitably used. Once merchandising is well under way, someone will have a goodwill, but before then, any goodwill is likely to belong to the defendant who is using the name without a licence rather than to the producer of the programme or film or his licensee.[97] Commercially speaking, however, the defendant may be appropriating an asset of considerable value.

Relief granted

15–049   Sunglasses and smoking goods: *Dunhill v Sunoptic* [1979] F.S.R. 337, CA (special evidence that reputation extended that far: at 362); scent packaged with genuine "foambath": *Morny v Ball & Rogers* [1978] F.S.R. 91 ("strongly arguable case"); cigarettes and whisky: *John Walker v Rothmans* [1978] F.S.R. 357 (both "Red Label" and some similarity of get up: "serious question," although not sufficient likelihood of damage for injunction pending trial); T-shirts and motor cars: *"Golden Jet"* [1979] R.P.C. 19 (some evidence car manufacturer's emblem had been used on T-shirts); spare car parts service and traffic information system using special car radios: *BBC v Talbot* [1980] F.S.R. 228; "escort agency" and club: *Annabel's v Schock* [1972] R.P.C. 838, CA; toilet paper and plastic gloves or babies' pants: *L.R.C. v Lilla Edets* [1973] R.P.C. 560 (both "Mangold"); electronic check-out system and electronic equipment such as computer-aided design system: "Computervision" [1975] R.P.C. 171; protective clothing and pollution control: *Ames Crosta v Pionex* [1977] F.S.R. 46; children's plastic toys and plastic irrigation equipment: " *Lego*" [1983] F.S.R. 155—a decision which shows how far the courts can go when the name is both highly distinctive and very famous;[98] advertising material inserted into newspapers: *Associated Newspapers v Insert Media* [1991] F.S.R. 380, CA; building society and estate

---

[94] The concept of "future goodwill" has been rejected as inconsistent with the decision of the Privy Council in the *Pub Squash* case. *Teleworks Ltd v Telework Group plc* [2002] R.P.C. 7.

[95] *"Stringfellows"* [1984] R.P.C. 501 at 547. Of course, any adoption of a name by others reduces the potentialities for merchandising: whether that reduction is connected with the suggestion that the name as so used denotes a connection with the claimant is another matter. Merchandising in remote fields could be the more affected, if it became known that the name concerned did not necessarily relate to the claimant. Nevertheless, this was accepted as a head of damage in the earlier case of " *Lego*" [1983] F.S.R. 155 at 194–195.

[96] As in *Mirage Studios v Counter-Feat Clothing Co Ltd* [1991] F.S.R. 145 (Browne-Wilkinson V.C.)—Ninja Turtles. The defendant's name did not help. cf. *BBC Worldwide v Pally Screen Printing* [1998] F.S.R. 665, Laddie J. "Teletubbies", where the claimant failed to secure summary judgment against a producer of T-shirts bearing pictures of the Teletubbies. See generally, Ch.22, paras 22–024 to 22–032.

[97] "Kojak" *Tavener Rutledge v Trexapalm*) [1977] R.P.C. 275: the defendants, not the plaintiffs, had a licence from the owners of the TV series, but the plaintiffs had the reputation and goodwill and were granted an interlocutory injunction. *Likewise in Nice and Safe Attitude Ltd v Piers Flook* [1997] F.S.R. 14 (on evidence that the defendant had a licence from NASA and claimant did not, defendant's attempt to modify undertakings failed because claimant had built up (somewhat parasitically) sufficient goodwill for clothing); "Dallas" *Lorimar v Sterling*) [1982] R.P.C. 395 (South Africa; reviewing the English cases); " *Wombles*" [1977] R.P.C. 99 (hiring out of rubbish skips: no common field of activity).

[98] Note that on similar facts the plaintiff lost in Australia even though the action was based on the

agency: *Nationwide Building Society v Nationwide Estate Agents Ltd* [1987] F.S.R. 579 (although interlocutory relief refused on other grounds); hi-fi equipment and computer systems (fields which were converging): *NAD Electronics Inc v NAD Computer Systems Ltd* [1997] F.S.R. 380.

Relief refused

"Ugly contest" film and beauty contest: *"Miss Alternative World"* [1981] F.S.R. 309, CA; cars and cinemas: *Granada v Ford* [1973] R.P.C. 49; builders' subcontracting, in particular plastering and building materials: *Unitex v Union Texturing* [1973] R.P.C. 119, CA; pop star and pictures of him: *Merchandising Corp of America v Harpbond* [1983] F.S.R. 32, CA; cable television and television programmes (in USA) and video hire business: *Home Box Office v Channel 5 Home Box Office* [1982] F.S.R. 449; night club and frozen chips: *Stringfellows* [1984] R.P.C. 501, CA; clothing and shipping and container leasing: *Ocean Pacific Sunwear v Ocean Pacific Enterprises* (1990) 17 I.P.R. 405; clothing and toiletries: *Blazer v Yardley* [1992] F.S.R. 501; high quality food retailing in the United Kingdom and lower quality food wholesaling, mainly abroad: *Fortnum & Mason v Fortnam Ltd* [1994] F.S.R. 438; amusement parks and hotels: *Walt Disney Productions v Fantasy Hotel Inc* (1995) 31 I.P.R. 233; fungicide and directory: *BASF v CEP(UK)* (1996) 35 I.P.R. 241 (Knox J.); department store and preparatory school: *Harrods Ltd v Harrodian School* [1996] R.P.C. 697, CA; Golf course and whisky: *Pebble Beach Company v Lombard Brands Limited* [2003] E.T.M.R. 21 (Court of Session).

15–050

DISTINGUISHING BETWEEN REPUTATION AND GOODWILL

The concepts of reputation and goodwill are very closely related, not least because they are generated in the vast majority of cases by the same trading activity. However, it will aid understanding of difficult cases to have clearly in mind the difference between reputation and goodwill, since they are not synonymous. As "the attractive force which brings in custom", goodwill is a form of legal property, representing the connection between business and customer. Reputation is a matter of fact: to what extent is the indicium in question known in the public mind? The existence of reputation does not require there to be a business in this country, whereas there must be some business or market in this country for goodwill to exist.

15–051

The cases concerning the territoriality of goodwill (discussed above) demonstrate the distinction between goodwill and reputation. If goods bearing the relevant indicia are in or about to be[99] in circulation in this country, then both reputation and goodwill exist here. If the goods are not in circulation and not about to be in circulation, there is no business and no goodwill here, even if the goods are known here (reputation) and the public would buy the goods if they were available here.[1] The provision of services creates different problems. If the services are in fact provided abroad, the presence of customers here would appear to es-

15–052

Trade Practices Acts 1974 which provides a remedy at least as wide as passing off: *Lego Australia v Paul's* (1982) 42 A.L.R. 344.
[99] Pre-launch publicity establishes a connection between business and customer, the desire to purchase being fulfilled when the goods become available.
[1] As in *Budweiser*, see para.15–073.

tablish reputation but not goodwill unless some business was actually transacted here.[2]

DILUTION OF DISTINCTIVENESS AS A HEAD OF DAMAGE

15–053   Dilution or erosion of distinctiveness is usually (but not always) raised as a head of damage by a claimant who has difficulty in demonstrating any other way in which his goodwill is being damaged by the alleged misrepresentation.[3] In other words, a claim which depends upon dilution as the sole head of damage normally needs to be treated with some caution. Millett L.J. has explained why:

> "Erosion of the distinctiveness of a brand name has been recognised as a form of damage to the goodwill of the business with which the name is connected in a number of cases, particularly in Australia and New Zealand; but unless care is taken this could mark an unacceptable extension to the tort of passing off. To date the law has not sought to protect the value of a brand name as such, but the value of the goodwill which it generates; and it insists on proof of confusion[4] to justify its intervention. But the erosion of the distinctiveness of a brand name which occurs by reason of its degeneration into common use as a generic term is not necessarily dependent upon confusion at all…. I have an intellectual difficulty in accepting the concept that the law insists on the presence of both confusion and damage and yet recognises as sufficient a head of damage which does not depend on confusion."[5]

15–054   Dilution or erosion of distinctiveness has been accepted as a legitimate head of damage by the Court of Appeal in two cases: *BT v One in a Million*[6] ("Internet domain names") and *Taittinger v Allbev*[7] ("Elderflower Champagne"). These cases appear to show that the claimant either has to prove fraud or requires something akin to a monopoly interest in the name or indicia so that there is real damage to the exclusivity in the name. In the former case, the trade name "Marks and Spencer" was unusual and famous, so that its inclusion in an Internet domain name rendered the domain name itself an instrument of deception. Erosion of distinctiveness was a but not the only head of (threatened) damage. In the latter case it was. The Champagne houses effectively claimed a monopoly in the term, at least in the drinks field. However, whether the claimant is entitled to exclusivity or a monopoly in a particular name or trading indicia begs the question as to whether passing off is established or not. As Millett L.J. indicated, one should concentrate on whether the essential requirements for passing off have been proved. If relevant deception has been proved, it will rarely be necessary for a

---

[2] In *Sheraton*, there was some business transacted here: in *Crazy Horse*, there was not. In *The Hit Factory*, no business was conducted here, but the judge held that the mere presence of customers here for services provided in the US was sufficient use in this country to establish a goodwill here.

[3] In the UK, claims of damage by dilution became familiar since they were often raised by claimants seeking to bolster their irreparable damage in order to secure an interlocutory injunction. In that context, the claims were questioned rarely, if at all, not least because other heads of damage were invariably relied upon. Note that "dilution" is accepted in the US as relevant damage, but only in the context of various statutory provisions. US common law has never recognised "dilution" as a head of damage.

[4] In this passage it is evident that Millett L.J. is using "confusion" as meaning "deception".

[5] *per* Millett L.J. in *Harrods Ltd v Harrodian School Ltd* [1996] R.P.C. 697 at 715–716.

[6] [1999] F.S.R. 1, CA.

[7] [1993] F.S.R. 641, CA.

claimant to rely upon dilution alone.[8] Two areas in which dilution of goodwill is of more central importance are cases involving celebrity endorsement[9] and those in which co-owners of goodwill are in dispute, the actions of one blurring or diminishing the goodwill of another.[10]

3. Goodwill

Since the purpose of a claim in passing off is to protect goodwill, and essential ingredients in the tort are the existence of goodwill and actual or threatened damage to it, it is as well to identify, as best we can, what goodwill is and the goodwill which is relevant to a claim in passing off. In many situations, the existence and ownership of goodwill are readily apparent or not worth disputing. However, the resolution of disputes over the ownership of goodwill and issues concerning the territoriality of goodwill sometimes require a more precise identification of what is required to found a passing off action.

15–055

WHAT CONSTITUTES GOODWILL

The nature of goodwill has been stated many times, but has not been defined. It is probably not capable of precise definition. In the context of passing off, it has been stated to represent, in connection with any business or business product, the value of the attraction to customers which the name and reputation possesses.[11] It is often described as "the attractive force which brings in custom", an extract from the classic statements[12] concerning goodwill in *IRC v Muller's Margarine*[13] by Lords Macnaghten and Lindley. The particular issue in that case was whether the goodwill of a business was located in Germany or in England, for the purposes of the Stamp Acts. That context has undoubtedly contributed to the current view, in English law, that goodwill is "local in character and divisible",[14] a view not shared in Australia, in particular.[15]

15–056

Note that the goodwill required to sustain a passing off action is not necessarily the same as goodwill referred to in other contexts.[16] In *Patience & Nicholson*

15–057

---

[8] For those interested in further detail on dilution, see the article by *Hazel Carty* (1996) 112 L.Q.R. 632.

[9] *Irvine v Talksport* [2002] F.S.R. 60.

[10] *Sir Robert McAlpine Ltd v Alfred McAlpine* [2004] R.P.C. 36.

[11] *Reuter v Mulhens* (1953) 70 R.P.C. 235 at 254.

[12] The relevant passages are cited in Ch.13, at paras 13–037 and 13–038.

[13] [1901] A.C. 217 at 223.

[14] Lord Diplock, giving the opinion of the Privy Council in *Star Industrial v Yap Kwee Kor* [1976] F.S.R 256 (PC, Singapore).

[15] See further, at paras 15–070 and 15–071.

[16] For example, an accountant's notion and valuation of the goodwill of a company, would include "passing off" goodwill, but probably much else besides. The various elements of goodwill (for the purposes of landlord and tenant law) were colourfully described by Scrutton L.J. in *Whiteman Smith Motor Company v Chaplin* [1934] 2 K.B. 35 at 42, as follows: "A division of the elements of goodwill was referred to during argument and appears in Mr Merlin's book [on the Landlord and Tenant Act] as 'cat, rat and dog' basis. The cat prefers the old home though the person who has kept the house leaves. The cat represents that part of the customers who continue to go to the old shop, though the old shopkeeper has gone; the probability of their custom may be regarded as an additional value given to the premises by the tenant's trading. The dog represents that part of the customers who follow the person rather than the place; these the tenant may take away with him if he does not go too far. There remains a class of customer who may neither follow the place nor the person, but drift away elsewhere. They are neither a benefit to the landlord nor to the tenant, and have been called 'the rat' for no particular reason expect to keep the epigram to the animal kingdom. I believe my brother Maugham has introduced the rabbit, but I will leave him to explain the position of the rabbit. It is obvious that the division of customers into 'cat, rat and

(NZ) Ltd v Cyclone Hardware[17] the Court of Appeal of New Zealand distinguished between the goodwill arising from the use of a trade mark in connection with specific goods and services and that associated with the use of the same sign as the trading name of a company. Care must be taken to identify the relevant goodwill for the purposes of a claim in passing off, and to ensure that such goodwill is in fact owned by the intended claimant.

WHO MAY BRING AN ACTION

15–058 There are really only two requirements: first, the claimant must own or have a sufficient property interest[18] in the requisite goodwill; secondly, the goodwill so owned must be the goodwill which is really likely to be damaged by the alleged misrepresentation.

The first requirement is satisfied by virtually all types of legal person which carry on commercial activity: individuals, partnerships, corporations: but probably not by unincorporated associations,[19] who must bring their action in a different guise. Any dispute over precisely which of a group of companies owns the requisite goodwill is normally avoided by having sufficient of the companies as claimants and/or brushed aside.[20] Some illustrations of the limits of "commercial activity" are discussed below. The second requirement poses no problem in the typical passing off case, but trade associations in particular fall foul of it:

(1) Chocosuisse was a trade association representing the interests of Swiss chocolate manufacturers. Chadwick L.J. was "unable to identify any business interest or goodwill which the trade association Chocosuisse is entitled to protect in an action in England for passing off against a trader. Chocosuisse does not manufacture or sell Swiss chocolate.": *"Chocosuisse"*.[21] It would be otherwise if a trader was misrepresenting himself to be a member of the association, (see below).

(2) The claimant's logo promoted Irish food and not the claimant nor any business in which it was engaged: An *Bord Trachtala v Waterford Foods*.[22]

THE NEED FOR SOME FORM OF COMMERCIAL ACTIVITY

15–059 It seems clear that the claimant in an action for passing off must show, if not that

---

dog' must vary enormously in different cases and different circumstances.' Not all these animals would be relevant in passing off. The dog is really the one who counts—for it is he who wants to deal with a particular enterprise. The cat is really only relevant to the situation where a business is continued in the same location under a new proprietor.

[17] [2002] F.S.R 40.

[18] cf. the Champagne type case.

[19] cf. *Workman v Johns* [1960] R.P.C. 265 at 269 ("Dog Defence") with *British Legion v British Legion Club* (1931) 48 R.P.C. 555 at 562, and consider also precisely how the unincorporated association is supposed to own goodwill. This may well depend on the constitution of the particular association; in *Artistic Upholstery Ltd v Art Forma* [2000] F.S.R. 311 the constitution and rules of the Long Eaton Guild of Furniture Manufacturers were such that the members could hold property on behalf of the guild, subject to their rights and liabilities towards one another as guild members. Consider also the illustrations below.

[20] As in *Dawnay, Day & Co Ltd v Cantor Fitzgerald International* [2000] R.P.C. 669 and *William Grant & Sons Ltd v Glen Catrine Bonded Warehouse Ltd* [1999] E.T.M.R. 675, Court of Session.

[21] *"Chocosuisse"* [1999] R.P.C. 826, CA. The same point could have been made in *Parma Ham* but it was not disputed there. In *Scotch Whisky Association v J.D. Vintners Ltd* (March 6, 1996) [1997] Eur. L.R. 446, Sir Richard Scott V.C. said it was rightly accepted that the association had no cause of action in passing off.

[22] [1994] F.S.R. 316 (Keane J., HC, Eire).

he has some sort of business which is threatened by the defendant's activities, at least that his interest is something akin to that of the owner of a business.[23]

"It should never be forgotten that in these cases the sole right to restrain anybody from using any name he likes in the course of any business he chooses to carry on is a right in the nature of a trade mark, that is to say, a man has a right to say, 'You must not use a name, whether fictitious or real— you must not use a description, whether true or not, which is to represent, or calculated to represent, to the world that your business is my business, and so, by a fraudulent misstatement, deprive me of the profits of the business which would otherwise come to me.' An individual plaintiff can only proceed on the ground that having established a business reputation under a particular name, he has a right to restrain anyone else from injuring his business by using that name."[24]

The business concerned certainly need not be a trading business in any ordinary sense.

Many instances will be found later in this chapter. Actions about business names as distinct from trade marks are often concerned with service industries rather than trading: seein particular the illustrations to paras 15–161 to 15–164. There are a number of instances of actions for the passing off of books, plays, films: see the illustrations in paras 15–170 to 15–172. Other instances include disputes between rival beauty contests: *Morecambe v Mecca* [1962] R.P.C. 145 (no real risk of damage and names not close enough); *Miss World v James St.* [1981] F.S.R. 309, CA (beauty contest and "ugly contest" film: activities too different); business of looking after children: *Deane v Schofield* [1962] R.P.C. 179; clubs of one sort or another: *Annabel's v Schock* [19] R.P.C. 847, CA (club and escort agency sufficiently "related" for injunction to be granted); *Ad-Lib Club v Granville*, below; almost anything fairly called a business will do, but the further one gets from trade the harder, it would seem, to persuade a court to take the complaint seriously. **15–060**

PROFESSIONAL ASSOCIATIONS AND OTHER INSTITUTIONS AND ORGANISATIONS

It is clear that a professional association of sufficient standing may sue to prevent others imitating either its name or the initials by which qualified persons indicate their membership of it. Similarly, with charitable institutions and perhaps even religious organisations:[25] **15–061**

(1) In *Society of Accountants and Auditors v Goodway*,[26] the claimant society sued to restrain non-members from using a name which was calculated to

[23] *Kean v McGivan* [1982] F.S.R. 119, CA; (name of political party, injunction refused). cf. *Burge v Haycock* [2002] R.P.C. 28, CA (Non-profit lobbying organisation, "The Countryside Alliance", successfully restrained the defendant from standing for political office as Countryside Alliance candidate).

[24] *Levy v Walker* (1878–79) L.R. 10 Ch.D. 436 at 447, *per* James L.J.

[25] See the Australian case of *A.G. v Holy Apostolic & Catholic Church of the East* (1991) 98 A.L.R. 327, Supreme Court of N.S.W.—Young J., but note that English law is stricter on the requirement for goodwill.

[26] [1907] 1 Ch. 489; 24 R.P.C. 159. A similar decision was given in *Scotland in Society of Accountants in Edinburgh v Corporation of Accountants* (1903) 20 R. 750. See also *Tones and Moore v Merchant Service Guild* (1908) 25 R.P.C. 474; *British Legion v British Legion Club* (1931) 48 R.P.C. 555; *Clock v Clock House* (1936) 53 R.P.C. 269; *Walter v Ashton* [1902] 2 Ch. 282. There have been in addition a number of unreported cases in which professional associations have secured interlocutory injunctions to protect their names or initials, whilst proposed

represent them as being members of it, and it was held that it suffered a legal injury thereby, inasmuch that it was of pecuniary value to the society to have as many members as possible, and that the acts complained of, by reducing its status, might affect the number of its members.

(2) In *Society of Incorporated Accountants v Vincent*[27] the plaintiff society was granted an injunction to restrain the use of the letters "F.S.A.A." or of any other letters or designation likely to induce the belief that the defendant was a fellow of the society.

(3) In *Australian Society of Accountants v Federation of Australian Accountants Inc*[28] the defendant was restrained from offering professional accounting qualifications which were solely offered by the claimant, for a price—this was sufficient to constitute trade.

(4) The British Legion (an ex-servicemen's organisation formed after the 1915–1918 war) sued to prevent the use of the words "British Legion" in the name of a local club. It was contended that, even allowing a possibility of confusion, there could be no damage to the claimants. It was held that if the defendant club got into trouble, this must inevitably reflect discredit on the claimants, and an injunction was granted: *British Legion v British Legion Club*.[29]

(5) The defendants were restrained from using an accident helpline number which was very similar to the claimant's: *The Law Society of England & Wales v Griffith*.[30]

(6) The scope of the action in passing off was held wide enough to include deception of the public by one charity such that the goodwill of another was appropriated: *The British Diabetic Association v The Diabetic Society*.[31]

(7) No interlocutory injunction was granted on the balance of the risk of injustice, and the evidence of reputation was scanty, but the claimant charitable institution was entitled to bring an action: *British Association of Aesthetic Plastic Surgeons v Cambright Ltd*.[32]

(8) A member of an unincorporated association, the Long Eaton Guild of Furniture Manufacturers, acting on its own behalf and on behalf of other members of the guild, was entitled to restrain a former member from using the name of the exhibition at which the members exhibited their furniture in connection with an unrelated exhibition.[33]

INDIVIDUAL TRADERS AND PERSONALITIES

15–062   The position of an individual trader carrying on business presents no difficulty.

---

company names which would obviously be objectionable in this sort of way are known to have been rejected or refused by the Registrar of Companies; for instance (it is believed), certain names of the form "Institution of … Engineers.

[27] (1954) 71 R.P.C. 325; cf. *A.G. and General Council of Medical Education v Barrett Proprietaries* (1933) 50 R.P.C. 45; an action to restrain the use by the defendants of the letters B.P., being the initial letters of British Pharmacopeia, failed; no evidence of fraud.

[28] (1988) 9 I.P.R. 282.

[29] (1931) 48 R.P.C. 555. The point had arisen before, and it was proved that in all other instances, clubs adopting a title including the words "British Legion" had agreed to accept supervision by the plaintiffs.

[30] [1995] R.P.C. 16, Aldous J.

[31] [1996] F.S.R. 1, Robert Walker J.

[32] [1987] R.P.C. 549, Scott J. and see *Guide Dog Owners & Friends Association Inc v Guide Dog Association of NSW & ACT* (1999) 43 I.P.R. 531, FCA.

[33] *Artistic Upholstery Ltd v Art Forma* [2000] F.S.R. 311.

The old case of *Clark v Freeman* would be decided differently today.[34] Sir J. Clarke, an eminent physician, failed to restrain the defendant from selling a quack medicine as "Sir J. Clarke's Consumption Pills", on the basis that he carried on no business of pill-making.

Although in English law passing off does not extend so as to provide a "right of personality", covering character merchandising, it is now clear that celebrity endorsement of goods or services does fall within the scope of passing off. The claimant in such an endorsement case must show not only that at the time of the act complained of he had a significant reputation and goodwill (in his area of celebrity) but also that the actions of the defendant gave rise to a false message to the defendant's market that the celebrity had endorsed the defendant's products. In the light of the decision of Laddie J. in *Irvine v Talksport*,[35] upheld on appeal, the "Uncle Mac"[36] decision is no longer good law.[37]

15–063

(1) In *Irvine v Talksport* the image of a well-known racing driver carrying a radio bearing the defendant's station name was used by the defendant on the front cover of a promotional brochure. Held that the photograph constituted a misrepresentation that the racing driver was endorsing the radio station.

(2) In *Kaye v Robertson* [1991] F.S.R. 62 CA, the claimant was held not to be in the position of a trader in relation to the interest in the story regarding the celebrity's accident and recovery.

(3) In *Hogan v Pacific Dunlop*[38] the actor who played Crocodile Dundee in the film of that name succeeded in an action for passing off against the defendant who had produced a television commercial which was easily recognisable as a parody of a scene from the film known as the "knife scene". The Crocodile Dundee character was an extension or exaggeration of the claimant's own personality, as projected in various television advertisements in which he had appeared.

OWNERSHIP OF GOODWILL

Identification of the person who benefits from and therefore owns the attractive force which brings in custom is straightforward in the old-fashioned case of a shop selling its own produce. As commerce has grown in complexity and particularly with the advent of the Internet, there are myriad ways in which goods reach the ultimate consumer and a number of traders are likely to be involved in that process. In these circumstances, issues can arise as to who is the owner of the relevant goodwill. So far as the provision of services is concerned, there tends,

15–064

---

[34] Lord Selborne said the case had seldom been cited except to be disapproved: *Riviere* (1884) 26 Ch. D. 48. See also *Maxwell v Hogg* (1867) L.R. 2 Ch. 307; *Springhead v Riley* (1868) L.R. 6 Eq. 551; *British Medical Association v Marsh* (1931) 48 R.P.C. 565 at 574, where Maugham J. reviewed the authorities since *Clark v Freeman*. See also " *Albert Hall*" (1934) 51 R.P.C. 398. cf. the case of the name of a private house, para.15–029; and cf. *Tolley v Fry* [1931] A.C. 333.

[35] [2002] F.S.R. 60 and [2003] F.S.R. 35, CA.

[36] *McCulloch v May* (1947) 65 R.P.C. 58. The claimant was a well-known broadcaster on the Children's Hour programme of the BBC under the name "Uncle Mac". The defendants began selling a cereal under the name "Uncle Mac". It was held that as the claimant was not engaged in any degree in producing or marketing cereals, there could not be passing off by the defendants of any goods or business of the claimant. This decision was founded on a requirement for a common field of activity if passing off were to be proved. No such requirement now exists in England.

[37] See also the character merchandising cases, discussed below and Ch.22 at paras 22–024 to 22–032.

[38] (1988) 83 A.L.R. 403, Gummow J. and (1989) 87 A.L.R. 14 (Sheppard, Beaumont and Burchett JJ.) See also 10th *Cantanae Pty Ltd v Shoshana Pty Ltd* (1987) 79 A.L.R. 299 (Wilcox, Pincus and Gummow JJ.) (failed to establish misrepresentation).

necessarily, to be a somewhat more direct relationship between the provider of the service and the consumer. Even here, modern commercial methods, franchising for example, tend to increase the divide between the owner of the goodwill and the consumer. Likewise with the provision of information over the Internet.

15–065   Similar issues arise when two parties originally connected with goods or services become estranged: who is entitled to the goodwill? The resolution of these issues is not always easy.[39] Ultimately, the issue as to who owns the goodwill is a question of fact, to be determined in all the circumstances. Normally, the issue is decided by the answer to this question:[40] of whom is the indicia (whether it be a name, mark or get-up) distinctive? It is important to determine the nature of the former relationship between the estranged parties. Former members of a partnership are generally not entitled to a share in the goodwill thereof on dissolution of the partnership or on their departure. Goodwill generated by a partnership is a partnership asset. On dissolution the partners may require it to be sold and divide the proceeds, as with any other asset, but are not each entitled to a "share" of the goodwill unless the partnership deed provides otherwise.[41]

15–066   There have been a number of cases which have taken the form of passing off actions but can also be regarded as disputes over the ownership of goodwill. There are other cases where goodwill has been divided lawfully or shared. In such cases it is now clear that those entitled to the goodwill cannot interfere with each other, but all have a right against third parties. A joint owner of such goodwill may be restrained from acting to diminish the goodwill of a co-proprietor: "Just as a sole owner's rights in his goodwill should not be reduced, blurred or diminished, nor should a joint owner's whether at the hands of the other joint owner or a third party".[42] The issue of co-ownership arises most often across territorial boundaries, discussed next. There are a number of further examples in various parts of this chapter.[43]

FOREIGN MANUFACTURERS

15–067   A foreign manufacturer, who does not trade in this country but whose goods are sold in this country, may well acquire a protectable goodwill in his trade name or trade marks.[44] There will then be what in principle is a pure question of fact, whether the goodwill is that of the foreign manufacturer or the importer.[45] This is the sort of question of fact on which a court's finding is easily influenced by its feelings as to the merits of the case; the objection that an importer has no independent goodwill, so often successful when raised on behalf of the manufacturer of a trader dealing in the manufacturer's own goods[46], is likely to be brushed aside as a mere technicality when made by a defendant having no connection with the "genuine" goods.

---

[39] See, *e.g. Scandecor Development v Scandecor Marketing* [1999] F.S.R. 26, CA.
[40] Note that the views of persons in the trade (who generally know with whom they are dealing) may not indicate the "right" answer to this question.
[41] See *SAXON Trade Mark* [2003] F.S.R. 39 *Byford v Oliver*); cf. *Burchell v Wilde* [1900] 1 Ch. 551.
[42] *Sir Robert McAlpine Ltd v Alfred McAlpine Limited* [2004] R.P.C. 36 at para.49.
[43] See paras 15–084 and 15–085, 15–118 to 15–123, and 15–224 and 15–225.
[44] See, *e.g.* "Panhard," illustration (1), below at para.15–076.
[45] cf. *Reuter v Mulhens* (1953) 70 R.P.C. 102; [1954] Ch. 50; 70 R.P.C. 235, CA ("4711") and *Adrema v Adrema-Werke* [1958] R.P.C. 323 (both enemy-property cases) with *"Manus"* (1948) 65 R.P.C. 329; (1949) 66 R.P.C. 71.
[46] See *Imperial Tobacco v Bonnan*; illustration (2) para.15–085; *Dental Mfg v de Trey* [1912] 3 K.B. 76; 29 R.P.C. 617; *"Manus"* above; *Roberts Numbering Machine v Davis* (1936) 53 R.P.C.

(1) The claimant, an American manufacturer was the developer of a natural **15–068** health care product to prevent snoring called "Snorenz". The defendant was the claimant's UK distributor. The defendant's packaging and promotion did not identify the claimant as the source of the product. Held, there is no general presumption that goodwill is owned by a foreign manufacturer rather than a UK distributor (or, presumably, vice versa). The question of ownership is one of fact in each case, and in the light of the packaging and marketing, the claimant's lack of trade in the UK, the fact that it was the defendant to whom trade customers turned in case of any defect and the absence of any evidence that the ultimate customer knew of the claimant's role or cared who had developed the product, the claim failed. *MedGen Inc v Passion for Life Products Ltd* [2001] F.S.R. 30.

(2) The claimants were American manufacturers of arc-lamps. An English syndicate had lamps made to their order by the claimants and sold them in England under the mark "Stewart". Later, the syndicate's business passed to the defendants, who took to getting lamps from an English manufacturer, and the American claimants set up a sales agency over here. Both parties claimed the exclusive right to call their lamps "Stewart". It was held that the goodwill in the mark had belonged to the syndicate and so had passed to the defendants; so the defendants got the injunction: *Defries v Electric Accessories* (1906) 23 R.P.C. 341.

(3) The firm of Köpke, wine merchants, had previously imported wine from the Quinta de Roriz vineyard in Portugal. At a later stage, they registered a trade mark for wine, "Köpke Roriz", and took to selling under it wine, much of which did not come from the Quinta de Roriz. There was evidence of representations to the public that there was a connection with the Quinta de Roriz. The owners of the vineyard were granted an injunction against Köpke restraining them from selling any other wine under the name "Roriz", the fact that the mark was registered being irrelevant: *Van Zeller v Mason, Cattley* (1907) 25 R.P.C. 37.

Even though the claimant is a foreign manufacturer, and the defendant's goods **15–069** come from the same foreign country, it may be proper to try in this country an action about passing off here, and to allow service of the writ upon the foreign supplier of the defendant's goods for that purpose.[47]

It is not necessary that the association of the claimant's mark with his goods should be known all over the country, or to every person in the area where it is known best.[48]

THE TERRITORIAL NATURE OF GOODWILL

The claimant in an action founded on passing off in the United Kingdom must of **15–070** course prove that the acts complained of amount to a misrepresentation: which will normally involve proof that he has a reputation in this country—that the disputed badge, trade mark or trade name, is in this country distinctive of his

79. cf. *Sturtevant Engineering v Sturtevant Mill* (1936) 53 R.P.C. 430 and *Suhner v Suhner* [1967] R.P.C. 336.

[47] "Harris Tweed" *Macaulay v Hepworths*) [1961] R.P.C. 184. In the end, however, the dispute was tried in Scotland: *Argyllshire Weavers v A Macaulay (Tweeds) Ltd (No.3)* [1964] R.P.C. 477. As to jurisdiction over defendants from EEC countries, see Civil Jurisdiction and Judgments Act 1982, Sch.1, art.5(3).

[48] *Faulder v Rushton* (1903) 20 R.P.C. 477, CA ("Silverpan Jam"); and para.15–096 (area), and paras 15–090 to 15–092 (secondary distinctive meaning).

goods or business.[49] But he must do more: since an essential ingredient of passing off is damage (or prospective damage) to goodwill, he must show that he had, at the date when the defendants started up,[50] in this country not merely a reputation but also a goodwill capable of being damaged. Goodwill, however, is local:[51] it is situated where the business is. Thus a foreign claimant may have a reputation in this country—from travellers or periodicals of international circulation or, increasingly, from exposure on the Internet—yet still fail in an action for passing off because he has here no business and so no goodwill. Such cases have been not uncommon in recent years, and have caused considerable difficulty. Where there is a substantial reputation here, our courts will often accept minimal evidence that a business exists here;[52] but there has to be some.

15–071   The decisions on this point are not easy to reconcile and in some the reasoning is artificial. The more difficult cases raise fundamental questions about whether goodwill must be treated as local or whether it is time to recognise the existence of international goodwill.[53] If goodwill has to be treated as local, then the debate turns to what is required to establish a goodwill in this country: is it sufficient merely to have customers here, in circumstances where no business is being carried on in the United Kingdom?[54] If goodwill does not have to be treated as local,[55] then the focus of the action shifts effectively (as it has done in the Republic of Ireland,[56] Canada,[57] Australia,[58] New Zealand,[59] and elsewhere)[60] to the

---

[49] *Oertli v Bowman* [1957] R.P.C. 388 at 397, CA; [1959] R.P.C. 1, HL ("Turmix"). See also *Goodfellow v Prince* (1887) L.R. 35 Ch.D. 9, CA.

[50] *Anheuser-Busch v Budejovicky Budvar* [1984] F.S.R. 413 at 462, CA.

[51] *Star Industrial v Yap Kwee Kor* [1976] F.S.R 256 (PC, Singapore).

[52] See *Poiret*, illustration 2, at para.15–076; *Penney v Punjabi Nick* [1979] F.S.R. 26 (Hong Kong: presence of retail trader's purchasing subsidiary in the then Colony enough to support passing off action against another retailer); *Globelegance v Sarkissian* [1974] R.P.C. 603; *Esanda v Esanda Finance* [1984] F.S.R. 96 (N.Z.; Australian company suing in New Zealand.); *Nishika v Goodchild* [1990] F.S.R. 371, Knox J., where the way in which the defendant misrepresented his connection with the claimant's foreign business actually established a sufficiently protectible goodwill here. cf. *Bristol Conservatories* [1989] R.P.C. 455, CA.

[53] See "The Hit Factory", *Pete Waterman Ltd v CBS United Kingdom Ltd* (1990) 20 I.P.R. 185, Browne-Wilkinson V.C.

[54] The positive answer to this question given in "The Hit Factory", requires distinct modification of the traditional notions of goodwill.

[55] The cases which underpin this approach in English law could have been decided on other grounds: notably: *Crazy Horse* (lack of sufficient reputation, a case dismissing an application for an interlocutory injunction); *Star Industrial* (lack of sufficient reputation in Singapore, the slight trading relied on having ceased three years previously); *Budweiser* (collision of independent rights. Whitford J. at first instance drew the analogy with honest concurrent user from the 1938 Act). The notion that goodwill must be local stems from *IRC v Muller* (a case about the Stamp Act). The fact that the notion of local goodwill was consistent with most trading arrangements then does not mean that it is necessary to adhere to it now. Obviously, this is a House of Lords point.

[56] In the Republic of Ireland it is the presence of customers, rather than any actual trade, which gives rise to the right to bring a passing off claim: *DSG Retail Ltd v PC World Ltd* [1998] E.T.M.R. 321.

[57] *Orkin Exterminating Co Inc v Pest Co of Canada Ltd* (1985) 19 D.L.R. (4th) 90. (Ontario CA; claimant providing services to real property in the United States with customers in Canada who owned United States property but with no Canadian business, held to have a protectable goodwill in Canada).

[58] See *ConAgra*, (1992) 106 A.L.R. 465. at No.10, para.15–007, at and the discussion of the Australian and other cases there. Note in particular, the role of fraud in the pre-Crazy Horse cases: see Gummow J. at 519–523, citing in particular, Farwell J. in *Panhard Levassor, arguendo*: the defendants either meant "to steal the plaintiffs' business or to prevent them having any in England": "they are wrong on either alternative".

[59] *Dominion Rent A Car v Budget Rent A Car System* (1987) 9 I.P.R. 367, although there has been disagreement from Casey J. in particular, who dissented in *Dominion* and followed the English approach in *Esanda Ltd v Esanda Finance Ltd* [1984] F.S.R. 96 at 100.

[60] e.g. in Hong Kong see *Ten-Ichi v Jancar* [1990] F.S.R. 151 (H.K., H Ct); in *India Apple Com-*

existence of an international reputation and damage to it.[61]

Some versions of this type of case present no real difficulty. The first is, where **15–072** the claimant has no significant reputation here: the name or mark was in origin his, and he may hope to exploit it here someday, but it is not yet here associated in the public mind with any business or any goods. Clearly, his action must fail.[62] This category overlaps the "merchandising" cases discussed below, where the defendant adopts the name of (say) a film or television character before the promoter's "merchandising" operations are under way.[63] The second is, where the claimant simply cannot show damage: it is annoying to him to have his name or mark copied in a foreign country, but he has no business there and his profits are in no way diminished thereby.[64] More difficult is the case where he has a substantial reputation, which he hopes or even positively intends to exploit by business activities here.[65] The court will then no doubt accept very small indications that exploitation has actually started as justifying intervention.[66] There remain, however, cases where there is a reputation, where there is damage—there may be customers here, even though no business is carried on here and no goods are sold nor services provided here[67]—but the goodwill is situate elsewhere. As will be seen, this type of case is not new, but the problem has become more acute with the increase in international travel, the growth of multinational businesses and the increasing influence of the Internet. Clarification of the law on this point

---

puter Inc v Apple Leasing Industries Ltd (1992) 22 I.P.R. 257 (HC, Delhi); *Calvin Klein Inc v International Apparel Syndicate* [1995] F.S.R. 515 (HC, Calcutta); *Yahoo! Inc v Akash Arora* [1999] F.S.R. 931 (HC, Delhi).

[61] cf. Learned Hand J. in *Yale Electric Corp v Robertson* 26 F. 2d 972 (1928) at 974: "If another uses [the claimant's mark], he borrows the owner's reputation, whose quality no longer lies within his own control. This is an injury, even though the borrower does not tarnish it, or divert any sales by its use; for a reputation, like a face, is the symbol of its possessor and creator, and another can use it only as a mask. And so it has come to be recognised that, unless the borrower's use is so foreign to the owner's as to insure against any identification of the two, it is unlawful."

[62] *Elida Gibbs v Colgate-Palmolive* [1983] F.S.R. 95, where the defendants, knowing of the claimants' intended launch, got their advertisements in the day before, and the claimants got an interlocutory injunction, may be considered the exception that proves the rule.

[63] See para.15–048 and the footnotes thereto; cf. *Tavener Rutledge v Trexapalm* [1977] R.P.C. 275 ("Kojak"): the defendants, not the claimants, had a "licence" from the owners of the television series, but the claimants had the reputation and goodwill and an interim injunction was granted.

[64] *Lyngstad v Anabas* [1977] F.S.R. 62 (foreign pop-group with no merchandising here); *Wienerwald v Kwan* [1979] F.S.R.381 (Hong Kong: "international" reputation only).

[65] *Athlete's Foot v Cobra* [1980] R.P.C. 343 (intention to merchandise here, but nobody here yet in trading relation with claimant: no passing off rights); *Amway v Eurway* [1972] F.S.R. 213 (US company about to trade here which has publicised that: no claim in passing off); *Home Box Office v Channel 5 Home Box Office* [1982] F.S.R. 449 (US cable TV company with only slight business links here—held to have sufficient activity to create arguably a goodwill here); *BBC v Talbot* [1980] F.S.R. 228 (said that preparations for an operation may create protectible goodwill; but no foreign element); *Baskin-Robbins v Gutman* [1976] F.S.R. 545 (the claimant hoped or intended to merchandise here; the defendant offered an undertaking: the judge refusing to follow Star Industrial). In another case the same judge, Graham J., refused to follow "Crazy Horse" as inconsistent with the Rome Treaty: *Maxim's v Dye* [1977] F.S.R. 364. See also "Rib Shack," *My Kinda Bones v Dr. Pepper's Stove* [1984] R.P.C. 289, where the cases are reviewed: substantial preparations for trade here and substantial reputation but no actual trade: statement of claim not struck out. An extreme case was *Fletcher Challenge v Fletcher Challenge Pty.* [1982] F.S.R. (NSW; a few hours' reputation only; the court refused to follow "Crazy Horse.") This is, of course, just the sort of situation where anticipatory registration of a service mark is called for.

[66] As in *BBC v Talbot* [1980] F.S.R. 228.

[67] As in *Pete Waterman Ltd v CBS United Kingdom Ltd* (1990) 20 I.P.R. 185, "The Hit Factory" where Sir Nicholas Browne-Wilkinson V.C., clearly favouring the Australian approach, observed: "In my view, the law will fail if it does not try to meet the challenge thrown up by trading patterns which cross national and jurisdictional boundaries due to a change in technical achievement. The problem is particularly acute with service industries…As a matter of legal principle, I can see no reason why the courts of this country should not protect the trading relationship between a foreign trader and his United Kingdom customers by restraining anyone in this country from passing himself off as the foreign trader."

may be some time coming for three reasons: first, a claimant may be able to avoid tackling this issue by proving that the conduct complained of is actionable under the law of a foreign country and the defendant should be restrained here (see below); secondly, if the claimant can show that he is "well-known" in the United Kingdom, he can rely on s.56 of the Trade Marks Act 1994 and any accompanying passing off claim may not need to be decided; thirdly, special facts are required, the more so because of the previous two points.

15–073   (1) The claimants were proprietors of an establishment in Paris called "Crazy Horse Saloon". The defendants set up an establishment in London (in some respects similar), advertising it as "Crazy Horse Saloon comes to London". There was evidence of deception and confusion amongst the public in this country. The claimants had circulated publicity material in English through travel agencies in this country but they had no office in this country and took no bookings here. Held, distinguishing the "Sheraton" case (at para.15–076), that the claimants had failed to show a reputation acquired by user[68] in this country on which an action in passing off could be based: *Bernardin v Pavilion Properties* [1967] R.P.C. 581.

(2) The claimants, American brewers of "Budweiser" beer, sued for passing off by sales of Czech "Budweiser". At the date when the Czech brewery entered the United Kingdom market, the claimants had some reputation in this country but no customers here, so no local goodwill: their beer had been on sale in American bases here, but that belonged to their US goodwill: *Anheuser-Busch v Budejovicky Budvar* [1984] F.S.R. 413, CA, approving *"Athlete's Foot"* [1980] R.P.C. 343, with the warning that "customers" for this purpose include ultimate retail customers, not merely people buying direct from the claimant (at 465).

(3) The claimants had a shop in Belfast. They advertised throughout Ireland and had customers in Eire. It was held that they had a protectable goodwill in Eire. "Crazy Horse" was not followed, the Irish court approving a comment in the tenth edition of this work to the effect that the decision in "Crazy Horse" was unreasonable: *"C. & A."* [1978] F.S.R. 126.

15–074   Suppose that the claimant in "Crazy Horse" had been established not in Paris, but in Berwick-on-Tweed, with customers both sides of the border between England and Scotland, and suppose an imitation over the border. Obviously, an action for passing off would have succeeded: yet strictly speaking, the goodwill would be in Berwick alone.[69]

15–075   It is, of course, open to the Australian,[70] Irish and other[71] courts simply to say that English law is wrong. Most business men certainly, and probably most lawyers, would agree that the very technical rules as to localisation of goodwill have no relevance here, and that in any real sense a business has goodwill, that the court should protect, throughout its catchment area and not merely where the

---

[68] There is, of course, good authority for the phrase "reputation acquired by user", but it is submitted that the real point is that the reputation in such cases is unaccompanied by goodwill.

[69] Note the emphasis on "England" in Lord Fraser's propositions, cited above, para.15–009. This "Berwick" example (and the Irish one, below) do not quite comply even with the later customers in this country test of Athlete's Foot and "Budweiser" (illustration (2), above), since there are no sales actually in the country; even "Sheraton," illustration (3) below, admittedly a borderline case, comes a little closer.

[70] See *ConAgra Inc v McCain Foods (Aust) Pty Ltd* (1992) 106 A.L.R. 465 and particularly the exhaustive analyses of the cases by Lockhart J. at 473–490 (English cases), 490–501 (cases from other jurisdictions) and by Gummow J. at 529–536.

[71] See paras 15–007 to 15–009 and the footnotes therein.

business is carried on.[72] But if we accept that, in English law, C. & A.'s Irish goodwill was localised in Northern Ireland, does it follow that their action should have failed? If the name "C. & A." had been used by an Eire business, not in Eire but in Northern Ireland, the Irish court would, under the usual rules about foreign torts, have had jurisdiction to intervene.[73] It can hardly prevent the court's having jurisdiction over a tort, that it was partly committed at home and not abroad. Perhaps what was wrong in "Crazy Horse" was that the action was framed as an English passing off and not as "concurrence deloyale"?

(1) The claimants, French car manufacturers, had no place of business in England, but a number of English people had purchased their cars and brought them back to this country. They were held to have a reputation and a market in England which the court would protect: *Panhard et Levassor v Panhard Levassor Motor Co* (1901) 18 R.P.C. 405.

15–076

(2) The claimant, a Paris couturier, had customers but no place of business here. It is not clear that any sales took place here, but he occasionally visited England; in particular, a show of his dresses had been held at 10 Downing Street, London. His action for passing off by the use of "Poiret" here succeeded: *Poiret v Poiret* (1920) 37 R.P.C. 177.

(3) The claimants owned a chain of hotels in the United States and other foreign countries, the principal hotels being called "Sheraton Hotels". There was some evidence of advertising reaching this country and bookings being taken at an office kept by the claimants here. The defendant company, "Sheraton Motels Ltd.", proposed to set up an hotel in this country. An interlocutory injunction was granted, the court observing that there could be only one reason for the defendants' choice of "Sheraton" as part of their name: *"Sheraton"* [1964] R.P.C. 202; following *Poiret v Poiret*, above.

(4) The defendant asserted a concurrent right to use "The Hit Factory" for a recording studio in London, based on its long established and *bona fide* use of that term in America as part of its business operating recording studios which had an international clientele and reputation. In answer, the claimant asserted the defendant had no protectable goodwill in England, as it had no place of business nor rendered any services here. Browne-Wilkinson V.C. held (a) the existence of a severable English goodwill attached to a place of business in this country is not the basis of a right in passing off. All that was necessary was a trade connection here, which will normally consist of customers forming part of the goodwill, wherever it is situate, which goodwill is being invaded by the acts of the defendant in this country, but that (b) that approach was not open, as being contrary to the decision of the Court of Appeal in Budweiser and therefore (c) the presence of customers in this country is sufficient to constitute the carrying on of a business here, whether or not there is a place of business or whether services are provided here. Once it is found there are customers, it is open to find that there is a business here to which the local goodwill is attached; and (d) to the extent that the Crazy Horse decision was authority

---

[72] A Canadian appellate court has explicitly taken this view, preferring the Irish approach to the English and saying that the definition of "goodwill" used in the English cases was not necessarily appropriate to passing off: *Orkin v Pestco* (1985) 19 D.L.R. 90.

[73] See para.19–040.

to the contrary, he preferred not to follow it: "The Hit Factory", *Pete Waterman Ltd v CBS United Kingdom Ltd.*[74]

EXTINCTION OR ABANDONMENT OF GOODWILL

15–077   If a business ceases or suspends trading temporarily, there remains a residual goodwill which the claimant might wish to sell or use in a reopened business.[75] If once the business is definitely abandoned, however, so that the claimant no longer owns goodwill, there can be no passing off.[76] Where no positive decision is made to abandon goodwill, but trade under the mark has nonetheless ceased with no concrete plan for restarting operations, the question of whether any residual goodwill survives, and for how long, is a question of fact in each case.[77]

SHARED REPUTATION

15–078   The claimant in a passing off action need not show that the badge the defendant has taken denotes his goods or business exclusively if the defendant has no right to use it at all:[78] it is enough for him to show that he is one of a definite and ascertainable class[79] of those who are entitled to use it and who consequently suffers damage from its misuse. But if the badge is independently properly used by others than himself, the difficulty of showing that its use by the defendant is calculated to injure his goodwill may be greatly increased.[80] It is accordingly desirable, where the right to use a badge is shared, that as many as practicable of those entitled to use it should join in an action to protect it.[81]

15–079   (1) Two firms were separately carrying on business as watchmakers under the name Dent. Held, that either might sue a third who had set up a similar business under the same name: *Dent v Turpin* (1861) 2 J. & H. 139.[82]

            (2) The defendants sold Spanish sparkling wine as "Spanish Champagne." The larger producers of Champagne joined together to sue for passing off. Held, that any one producer could have sued: *Bollinger v Costa Brava* [1960] R.P.C. 16; [1961] R.P.C. 116 at 120; approved HL in "Advocaat," above. See also *Comité Interprofessionnel du Vin de Champagne v Wineworths Group* [1991] 2 N.Z.L.R. 432.

---

[74] (1990) 20 I.P.R. 185 at 208/209. His desire to find a way round the obstacles highlights the artificiality of the requirement of goodwill in difficult cases such as the one before him.

[75] *Ad-Lib Club v Granville* [1970] 2 All E.R. 300; [1972] R.P.C. 673 (reputation proved four years after business closed. No intention to abandon goodwill); cf. *Kark v Odhams* [1962] R.P.C. 163 (illustration 5, para.H-14–226); *Levey v Henderson-Kenton* [1974] R.P.C. 617; *Thermawear v Vedonis Thermawarm* [1982] R.P.C. 44 (mark little used for five years before writ).

[76] *Star Industrial v Yap Kwee Kor* [1976] F.S.R. 256 (PC, Singapore: business in Singapore closed down and goodwill disposed of).

[77] By way of example, see *Sutherland v V2 Music* [2002] E.M.L.R. 28 (the *Liberty* Case).

[78] *Bollinger v Costa Brava* [1960] R.P.C. 16 at 25; *Vine Products v Mackenzie* [1969] R.P.C. 1 ("British Sherry"); *John Walker v Ost* [1970] R.P.C. 489 ("Scotch Whisky"). It may be noted that *Dent v Turpin*, illustration (1), below, was a case of "concurrent" rights of the Dents in the mark; the "Aladdin" case, illustration 3, one of "joint" ownership; whereas Bollinger v. Costa Brava, above, illustration (2), below, is something between the two, with no true trade mark analogy. As in trade mark cases, there is no express authority that the proposition in the text applies to cases of joint ownership, but on general principles it should.

[79] " *Advocaat*" [1980] R.P.C. 31 at 104–105, HL.

[80] See *Jamieson v Jamieson* (1898) 15 R.P.C. 169 at 193; note that the action failed because the defendants had not used anything identified with the claimant, at 182, not because there were other Jamiesons in the trade in Aberdeen. See also *Whitstable Oyster v Hayling Fisheries* (1901) 17 R.P.C. 461; 18 R.P.C. 434 and *Mappin and Webb v Leapman* (1905) 22 R.P.C. 398.

[81] Alternatively, since there is a common interest, common grievance and remedy beneficial to all, it may be appropriate for some to sue in a representative action on behalf of all: *Bollinger v Goldwell* [1971] R.P.C. 412.

[82] Expressly approved by Lord Diplock in " *Advocaat*" [1980] R.P.C.31, at 742.

(3) A heavy metal band had traded under the name SAXON from the 1970s to 1985. Legally the band could be viewed as a partnership at will. The band split in 1985, but a new band (containing some members of the original SAXON) began to trade under the mark SAXON and continued to do so until 1995. Independent goodwill in the mark SAXON had been generated by each of the two bands and irrespective of the rights as between those two, each could restrain third parties from trading under the mark: *Byford v Oliver* [2003] E.M.L.R. 20.

(4) An oil company and a lamp maker jointly set up a trade in lamp oil, which was supplied by the oil company under the trade mark used by the lamp maker for its lamps. When inferior oil was passed off for theirs, they sued successfully as joint claimants: *Shell-Mex and Aladdin v Holmes* (1937) 54 R.P.C. 287.

(5) One of a set of estate agents, operating in different towns, all known as "Parkers", sued one J.T. Parker to restrain him from doing the same. On a motion for interlocutory injunction (which was granted) the court declined to consider the relevance of the other companies, "for the purpose of this motion, where the claimants are not claiming any exclusive right to the use of the word 'Parkers' but are claiming merely to restrain the defendant from representing his business as being the business of the plaintiffs": *Parker v Parker* [1965] R.P.C. 323 at 325.

(6) The Consorzio del Prosciutto di Parma was a body corporate established under the law of Italy, whose members were producers of Parma ham and whose objects were to protect and promote the reputation of Parma ham. Although entitled to sue in passing off on its own behalf, the Consorzio could not sue on behalf of its member producers as their interests were not the same. The judge gave leave to amend to join representative producers of Parma ham as additional claimants: [1991] R.P.C. 351 at 357, *per* Morritt J, upheld by the Court of Appeal.[83]

The product names concerned in such cases as "Spanish Champagne" and **15–080** "Advocaat" (examples (1) and (2) above) are, of course, not trade marks in the ordinary sense at all; rather, they are analogous to the "certification marks" discussed at ch.11. But where passing off is concerned, there is no real dividing line between such cases and cases such as "Dent" (illustration (1) above) where an ordinary trade mark is shared. Note that where two or more parties share reputation in a mark, one may be restrained from damaging the goodwill owned by the others.[84]

Where a number of companies within a group all trade under a common name, **15–081** the courts will usually accept that the goodwill is shared: in "Dawnay, Day",[85] the Court of Appeal found it unnecessary to analyse the ownership of the trading name to decide whether it belonged to the holding company or was shared, holding that each company in the group had a legitimate interest for passing off purposes, *per* Sir Richard Scott V.C.

---

[83] In *Scotch Whisky Association v J.D. Vintners*, [1997] Eur. L.R. 446, Sir Richard Scott V.C. stated that he could see no basis "on which a trade association could maintain a passing off action based on conduct which constitutes a passing off by the defendant of its products for those of the members of the trade association". In *"Chocosuisse"* Chadwick L.J. adopted this reasoning (rather than that of Parma Ham) in stating that there was no business interest or goodwill which Chocosuisse, the trade association, was entitled to protect in a passing off action. Whilst he noted that it would be "convenient" to permit such a representative action, Chadwick L.J. considered that the correct route lay in an alteration of the Rules of Court, at 843–844. The position under CPR 19.6 remains essentially the same as it was under RSC Order 15 r.12.

[84] *Sir Robert McAlpine Ltd v Alfred McAlpine plc* [2004] R.P.C. 36.

[85] See para.15–155.

THE CLAIMANT HIMSELF MAY BE UNKNOWN TO CUSTOMERS

15–082   It is not necessary to show that the customers who knew the goods of the claimant's firm by a particular name or get-up knew anything whatever about the claimant.[86] It is immaterial that they did not even know his name,[87] for it is sufficient to prove that purchasers of his goods recognised, by the use of the marks in question in connection with them, that they were goods of a particular class, and to show that such class is, in fact, constituted by his goods.[88]

15–083   (1) Thus in "Yorkshire Relish", the claimant's sauce was made according to a secret recipe, and was always bought and sold by the name alone. The defendants made a sauce described as a "wonderful match" of the claimant's, and their contention was that the public knew and cared nothing about the actual manufacturer, but wanted only the sauce known as "Yorkshire Relish". The contention failed. Lord Herschell said:

> "I think that the fallacy of the appellants' arguments rests on this: that it is assumed that one trader cannot be passing-off his goods as the manufacture of another unless it be shown that the persons purchasing the goods know of the manufacturer by name, and have in their mind when they purchase the goods that they are made by a particular individual. It seems to me that one man may quite well pass off his goods as the goods of another, if he passes them off to people who will accept them as the manufacture of another, though they do not know that other by name at all. In the present case it seems to me that 'Yorkshire Relish' meant the manufacture of a particular person": *Powell v Birmingham Brewery* [1897] A.C. 710 at 715.

(2) The claimants were manufacturers of washing-blue. Their blue did not bear their name, but was sold in bags distinguished by a protruding stick, or "dolly". It was shown that the purchasers of the claimants' blue included many persons of the poorer classes, to whom their name was unknown, and who distinguished their goods by the presence of the dolly, not infrequently asking for it as "dolly blue". The defendants marketed a blue in bags with a dolly and bearing their name. Held, that there was passing off, the defendants' name in the circumstances being inadequate to distinguish their goods: *Edge v Niccolls* [1911] A.C. 693; 28 R.P.C. 582.

(3) The claimants sold their drug in green and black capsules. The defendants proposed to sell the same drug in similar capsules, arguing that the medical profession would not be deceived and that patients were only concerned with getting the same drug as they had had before. Held that the "same again" included not only the drug, but the drug manufactured by the same manufacturer. "Now I myself never received from the defendants a satisfactory answer to the plain question: why do they wish to market their goods in green and black? I can only answer that they wish so to do in order to attract to themselves some part of the claimants' goodwill and trade on their reputation and in fact to represent to the public that their goods are the goods of the claimants. That ... is exactly the clas-

---

[86] *United Biscuits v Asda* [1997] R.P.C. 513.

[87] *Lever v Goodwin* (1887) 36 Ch.D. 1; 4 R.P.C. 492, CA ("Sunlight Self-Washer Soap"); see "Yorkshire Relish" illustration below; *"Jif"* [1990] R.P.C. 341, at 406, *per* Lord Oliver.

[88] Paragraph (which has been in this work since at least 1910) quoted by Jenkins L.J. in *Oertli v Bowman* [1957] R.P.C. 388 at 397. It was also approved by Harman and Russell L.JJ. in *Hoffmann-La Roche v D.D.S.A.* [1969] F.S.R. 410 at 416, 421.

sic case of passing-off,": *per* Harman L.J. in *Hoffmann-La Roche v D.D.S.A.* [1969] F.S.R. 410 at 419.

ASSIGNMENT AND DEVOLUTION OF TRADING NAME, ETC.

The right to protect the goodwill of a business against the use of deceptive imita-   **15–084**
tions will pass to an assignee of the goodwill. Under s.22(3) of the Trade Marks
Act, 1938, unregistered trade marks could in some cases be assigned without the
goodwill of the business in which they were used, and it must be presumed that in
such cases[89] Parliament intended to give the assignee of the mark without
goodwill the right to sue for passing off. However, there is no corresponding provision in the 1994 Act and the general rule as to right to sue in passing off must
be taken to now apply generally: only the owner of goodwill can sue to protect
it.[90] Thus, in general, if the things which the defendant has copied denote a connection, not with the claimant, but with someone else, the claimant can have no
claim to sue in respect of any deception which their use may cause.[91]

(1) A jury found that the defendant had both infringed the claimant's trade   **15–085**
    mark and had passed off his goods as those of the claimant. On appeal it
    appeared that the label and brand copied by the defendant had, not long
    before the commencement of the action, been assigned, without the busi-
    ness with which they were connected, by certain third parties to the
    claimant. Upon this ground the Court of Appeal set aside the verdict and
    entered judgment for the defendants, notwithstanding the finding as to
    passing off. The case, so far as regards passing off, was not expressly
    referred to in the judgments, but the principles stated were as applicable to
    that as to the case for infringement: *Pinto v Badman* (1891) 8 R.P.C. 181.

(2) A manufacturing company in England, with a world-wide business in
    "Gold Flake" cigarettes, had sold to the claimant company, who were
    importers in India, the goodwill in India together with trade marks and
    other rights and assets in India. After the transfer the manufacture was
    carried on in England by the transferor company for the claimants. The
    defendants purchased a large quantity of the same brand of cigarettes
    from the British Army Canteen authorities, which had been originally
    purchased from the manufacturing company. It was held that the claimant
    company had acquired no independent reputation as importers, the reputa-
    tion in India of the brand of "Gold Flake" cigarettes being that of the
    maker and not of the claimant's company as importers; and that the
    defendants were in no way passing off the cigarettes sold by them as the
    claimant company's goods: *Imperial Tobacco of India v Bonnan* (1924) 4
    R.P.C. 441. It would seem to follow from the decision in *"Bostitch"*
    [1963] R.P.C. 183 that even if the claimant company had itself undertaken
    manufacture of its cigarettes the reputation in the mark might well have
    remained that of the transferor: cf. *Diehl* [1970] R.P.C. 435 (where the
    mark was the importer's and not the manufacturer's).

(3) The claimant claimed only as the mortgagee of a business and its name,
    and had never used, and did not intend to use, the name. The defendant

---

[89] And it would seem, only in such cases: see *per* Lord Diplock in *Star Industrial v Yap Kwee Kor* [1976] F.S.R. 256 at 272 (PC, Singapore).
[90] *Thorneloe v Hill* [1894] 1 Ch. 569; 11 R.P.C. 61 ("John Forrest"). Nor can goodwill be licensed to another: *Star Industrial v Yap Kwee Kor* [1976] F.S.R. 256.
[91] Where goodwill is shared between a number of traders, all of whom are entitled to use the partic-
ular badge, any one of them may sue a trader using it with no right to do so at all: see discussion
of *Bollinger v Costa Brava* [1960] R.P.C. 16, paras 15–078 to 15–081.

had bought the business, subject to the mortgage, and the claimant sued to prevent him trading under the old name without paying off the mortgage. The action was dismissed: *Beazley v Soares* (1882) L.R. 22 Ch.D. 660.

USE OF THE NAME OR DESCRIPTION OF THE GOODS

15–086   In an action for passing off[92] by the use of a supposed trade mark, it is ordinarily enough for the defendant to show that the mark is a mere name for the goods, regardless of trade origin, and that he has used it accurately—whether the supposed mark be an expression that once was or might have been a trade mark like "Liebig's Extract",[93] "Chlorodyne",[94] "Linoleum",[95] "Wellington Boots", "Gladstone Bag" and "Hansom Cab"; or is a mere description of the goods, denoting only their pattern,[96] mode of manufacture,[97] or sale,[98], type[99], ingredients[1] quality,[2] or place of origin.[3] But as the cases just cited show, such a defence has often failed, the claimant showing that the expression concerned is distinctive of his

---

[92] *Gamage v Randall* (1899) 16 R.P.C. 185 ("Shortland" shoes); illustration (1), para.15–098; the "Hommel's Haematogen" cases: *Hommel v Bauer* (1905) 22 R.P.C. 43 and *Hommel's v Hommel* (1912) 29 R.P.C. 378—all instructive without perhaps being sound. cf. also the cases on descriptive trading names, paras 15–090 to 15–094.

[93] *Liebig's v Hanbury* (1867) 17 L.T.(N.S.) 298; *Liebig v Anderson* (1886) 55 L.T. 206; and cf. *Same v Chemists' Co-operative* (1896) 13 R.P.C. 736.

[94] *Browne v Freeman (No. 1)* (1864) 12 W.R. 305; (No. 2) [1873] W.N. 178.

[95] *Linoleum v Nairn* (1877–78) 7 Ch.D. 834. cf. *Chesebrough* (1901) 18 R.P.C. 191; 19 R.P.C. 342 ("Vaseline" not descriptive).

[96] *Burberry v Cording* (1909) 26 R.P.C. 693; *Winser v Armstrong* (1899) 16 R.P.C. 167 ("Winser Interceptors"). In *Cordes v Addis* (1923) 40 R.P.C. 133, held that in this country the word "Prophylactic" was descriptive of a particular shape and make of toothbrush. But a word may be shown by evidence to indicate a particular pattern of goods when made by a particular manufacturer, and thus to be distinctive: *Whitfield* [1909] 2 Ch. 373; 26 R.P.C. 657 ("Lawson Tait Bedsteads"; a registration case).

[97] *Singer v Wilson* (1875) 2 Ch.D. 434; 3 App.Cas. 376; *Same v Loog* (1877) 18 Ch.D. 395; 8 App.Cas. 15; *Same v Spence* (1893) 10 R.P.C. 297; *Same v British Empire* (1903) 20 R.P.C. 313 ("Singer System," "Singer Sewing Machine"). In the last two cases and in *Daimler v London Daimler* (1907) 24 R.P.C. 379 ("Daimler"), the claimants, after failing in previous actions, established that the name had become distinctive. See also *Bowden Brake v Bowden Wire (No.2)* (1913) 30 R.P.C. 56 ("Bowden Control" held to be descriptive). In *Bechstein v Barker* (1910) 27 R.P.C. 484, the claimants obtained an injunction against passing off by the use of the word "Bechstein", the defendants having sold pianos not of the claimants' manufacture as "Bechstein Model Pianos".

[98] *Symington v Footman* (1885) 56 L.T. 696 ("Guaranteed Corset").

[99] In *Armstrong Oiler v Patent Axlebox* (1910) 27 R.P.C. 362, the claimants, who were makers of oilers for the axles of railway carriages claimed that "Armstrong Oilers" meant their oilers, and failed to restrain the defendants from supplying their own goods as "Armstrong Type Oilers". In *Universal Winding v Hattersley* (1915) 32 R.P.C. 479, held that the defendants were entitled to make and advertise for sale universal machinery by the names "Universal Wind" or "Universal Machine" or "Universal Winding Machinery"; cf. the interlocutory injunction granted in *A. v Roe v Aircraft Disposal* (1920) 37 R.P.C. 249 restraining the defendants from selling or offering for sale aeroplanes not being of the claimant's manufacture as "Avro" goods, with the addition assented to by the claimants that that was not to prevent the defendants from selling aeroplanes made according to the design "Avro 504 K" as aeroplanes "Avro type" or "type Avro". "Edison" was held to be distinctive: *Edison Storage Batteries v Britannia* (1931) 48 R.P.C. 350. cf. "Blue Orchid", distinctive but not descriptive, in *Delavelle v Stanley*; "Crystal" (for a ball-point pen, transparent and made from moulding powder such as the trade called "crystal" powders) protected by interlocutory injunction: *Biro Swan v Tallon* [1961] R.P.C. 326.

[1] In *Boake, Roberts v Wayland* (1909) 249 R.P.C. 251, the claimants established that K.M.S. (the initial letters of Kalium Meta Sulphite) meant their goods; cf. *White, Tomkins v United Confectionery* (1914) 31 R.P.C. 430 (picture indicating flavour of jelly preparation) and *Woodward v Boulton Macro* (1915) 32 R.P.C. 173 (Gripe Water). See also *Horlick's v Summerskill* (1916) 34 R.P.C. 63, HL; *Newton Chambers v Neptune* (1935) 52 R.P.C. 399 ("Medicated with "Izal"; but "medicated" and "with" too small, so that the effect was use of "Izal" as a trade mark).

[2] Where "Vacuum Oil" meant the claimants' oil, the defendants, who described their oil as "Vacuum Motor Oil A Quality", were restrained: *Vacuum Oil v Gooch* (1909) 27 R.P.C. 76; *Sharpe v Solomon* (1915) 32 R.P.C. 15 ("Classic" as applied to artistic goods).

[3] " *Rugby Portland Cement*" (1892) 9 R.P.C. 46, CA; " *Whitstable Oysters*" (1901) 18 R.P.C. 434, CA. But the defence failed in *Seixo v Provezende* (1885) L.R. 1 Ch. 192 ("Seixo Wine"); *Wother-*

goods or business; and a claimant alleging this will in most instances be able to show enough of an arguable case to support a claim for an interlocutory injunction.

The claimant was the owner of the trade mark "Aertex", for underwear, etc. The action was based on trap orders, the claimant alleging that goods not of its manufacture had been supplied to persons asking for "Aertex". In the course of the argument, counsel for the claimant conceded that some members of the public used the word "Aertex" as the description of a type of cellular fabric. The judge observed that this admission was fatal to the case, unless it was made clear to the shop assistant that this "customer" was not using the word "Aertex" descriptively: "If customers do use the word descriptively, 50 trap orders will not help you": *Cellular Clothing v White & Co* (1953) 70 R.P.C. 9 at 11, *per* Harman J., *arguendo*. But cf. the "Corona" case, illustration (1), para.15–090. **15–087**

If, however, the description is used inaccurately, its use may amount to passing off, actionable by those whose are able properly to use it.[4] **15–088**

Thus in particular cases the facts may justify the contention that in relation to accessories for use with a proprietary article, use of the brand name of the article means only that it is such an accessory.[5]

(1) In an action for passing off of photographic film, the defendants alleged that, when applied to films, names such as "Kodak" and "Brownie" merely meant to the general public films for "Kodak" or "Brownie" cameras. The defence failed on the facts, the judge finding that these names meant only Kodak Ltd's films for those cameras: *Kodak v London Stereoscopic* (1903) 20 R.P.C. 337. **15–089**

(2) The claimants, manufacturers of "Gledhill" cash tills, sued a defendant who produced paper rolls for those tills and sold them as "Gledhill rolls" (or "Gledhill coils") and in boxes stamped "Gledhill". The evidence was that this had been going on for some years, with various makes of till; that the defendants' customers (who were traders) habitually ordered what they knew were the defendants' goods as "Gledhill rolls" (or "coils"), and (from the defendants' customers) that this was normal practice in the trade and never gave rise to complaints. The claimants weakened their case by objecting to the defendants' price list, which (arranged in columns headed "make of till", "dimensions", "price") struck the Court of Appeal as eminently fair. Held that such terms as "Gledhill rolls" had acquired the secondary meaning of "rolls to fit Gledhill tills", and the action failed: *Gledhill v British Perforated* (1911) 28 R.P.C. 429 (Eve J.), 714, CA.

DESCRIPTIVE NAMES MAY BE DISTINCTIVE TO SOME

A word may be distinctive of the claimants' goods to the majority of people, but to some people the same word may indicate a characteristic of the goods, for instance, size and shape. **15–090**

---

spoon v Currie (1872) L.R. 5 H.L. 508 ("Glenfield Starch"); see also "Reading Biscuit" *Huntley and Palmer v Reading Biscuit)* (1893) 10 R.P.C. 277; *Bewlay v Hughes* (1898) 15 R.P.C. 290 ("Dindigul Cigars"); and "London Candles", at para.15–091.

[4] See para.15–078, on "Shared reputation" and cf. para.15–141.

[5] This is not a contention likely to meet much favour from the court, since the defendant in such cases could easily avoid any possible ambiguity; but see the examples below; cf. *Neostyle v Ellams* (1904) 21 R.P.C. 185, 569, where it was held on the facts that, although "Neostyle" in England denoted the name of the claimants' duplicating machine, the claimants had no exclusive right to it for accessories. See also *Yost v Typewriter Exchange* (1902) 19 R.P.C. 422 (Yost pads for a Yost typewriter).

(1) The word "Corona", a name distinctive of the claimants' brand of cigars, had also acquired a meaning descriptive of size and shape, irrespective of brand, so that a request for "a Corona cigar" was ambiguous. The defendant was held to have set up a claim to do that which would, in the majority of cases, be passing off goods, and Russell J. granted an injunction restraining the sale or supply in response to any order for "some cigars, Coronas", or "Corona cigars", or a "Corona cigar", or "Coronas", or a "Corona", cigars or a cigar not of the Corona brand, unless it be first clearly ascertained that the customer who gives the order does not require cigars or a cigar of the Corona brand and no other brand. On appeal the Court of Appeal affirmed the order of Russell J. with the addition of the words "or unless it was made clear to him by word of mouth or otherwise that the cigar supplied was of a brand other than the claimants' brand": *Havana v Oddenino* [1923] 2 Ch. 243; 40 R.P.C. 229; [1924] 1 Ch. 179; 41 R.P.C. 47.

(2) The claimants claimed that "Staunton" as applied to chessmen indicated their manufacture exclusively, whilst the defendant's case was that the name was merely descriptive of chessmen made according to designs produced by the famous chess player. There was evidence that the claimants' claim was generally recognised in the trade, other makers' goods being advertised as "Staunton pattern" and the like. It was held that the public generally regarded the name as descriptive; an injunction was granted in the court of first instance restraining the use of the words "genuine Staunton". This was discharged by the Court of Appeal on the ground that if the name was descriptive, the addition of the word "genuine" could make no difference: *Jacques v Chess* (1940) 57 R.P.C. 77. It is interesting here to compare the observation of Lord Hunter, a quarter of a century later, that "the word 'genuine' has almost begun to acquire a connotation as sinister as the word 'type'": "*Harris Tweed*" [1964] R.P.C. 477 at 550; cf. at 510.[6]

(3) The claimants, Purefoy Engineering, were suppliers of standard engineering components, which were identified in their trade by code numbers given in their catalogue. The defendants took to supplying a similar range of components. The claimants sent a series of "trap orders" to the defendants, for components described as "Purefoy", followed by the claimants' code number. There was evidence that to many people in engineering concerns, such a designation was merely descriptive of the component and did not mean a component made by "Purefoy". The Court of Appeal held that the defendants ought not to supply their own products upon such orders without inquiry whether the claimants' goods were intended or merely an equivalent, and granted an injunction in "Corona" form: *Purefoy v Sykes Boxall* (1954) 71 R.P.C. 227; (1955) 72 R.P.C. 89 at 93, CA. There was extraneous evidence that the defendants were not unwilling to pass off if they could. This case was followed in *Bostitch v McGarry & Cole* [1964] R.P.C. 173 (where the defendants, formerly sole suppliers of "Bostitch" goods, continued after severance of relations with the claimants to supply their own equivalent goods "without first making it perfectly clear to the inquirer that they cannot supply him with the article he wants, and leaving him an interval to decide what he is going to do,") but it must not be taken as deciding that "if a plaintiff establishes in any given case that A has ordered particular goods under a mark which is

---

[6] cf. *Cocks v Chandler* (1870–71) L.R. 11 Eq. 446 and *Allen v Original Samuel Allen* (1915) 32 R.P.C. 33 (illustration (6), above, para.15–122) where the added word was "original".

established as B's mark and is then supplied with some other goods passing-off must necessarily be established": *per* Whitford J. in *Broad v Cast Iron Drainage* [1970] F.S.R. 363 at 371.

(4) The defendant adopted the word "Gloss" for its range of cosmetics. The claimants were the makers of a successful television soap opera "Gloss" and a company licensed to use the name "Gloss" on a range of toiletries and cosmetics (although it had not yet started doing so). In granting an interlocutory injunction, the judge concluded that the word was almost meaningless in descriptive terms when used on its own. (Counsel for the defendant had conceded the existence of a "merchandising" right): *TVNZ v Gloss Cosmetic Suppliers* (1991) 19 I.P.R. 663 (HC, N.Z.).

It is not uncommonly found that marks which many members of the public use **15–091** descriptively are, nevertheless, fully distinctive to those in the trade.[7] Such marks are of exceptional value. Whilst they are not easy to protect merely by proceedings for passing off, if they are registered they can without undue difficulty be protected by proceedings for infringement.[8]

Words and terms which *prima facie* are merely descriptive in the sense just explained may, by use and reputation, acquire a secondary distinctive meaning,[9] so that they may be practically monopolised for use in connection with certain classes of goods by a particular trader, since their employment by anyone else would be calculated to deceive.[10]

The claimant had a trade mark "Apollo" (for chicken essence) which (as is **15–092** usual in Chinese speaking countries like Singapore) was habitually used in the form of Chinese characters with rough phonetic resemblance to "Apollo" and with an alternative meaning thought to be attractive (here, "beneficial for restoring strength"). The defendant used as a trade mark similar Chinese characters with a similar punning meaning. In an action for passing off, held, that the claimant must show that his Chinese mark had acquired a secondary meaning denoting his goods, and this he failed to do: *McAlister v Pasuma* [1975] R.P.C. 601 (HC, Singapore). This would seem to be the wrong test: the question should surely have been, whether the parties' marks were recognised by the public as being trade marks (which they probably were) and if so, whether they were confusingly similar.

JUDGMENT OF PARKER J. IN *BURBERRYS V CORDING*

In a case in which the claimants were claiming that the words "Slip-On" were **15–093** distinctive of their goods,[11] Parker J. summarised the principles of law applicable to the case in the following passage:

"The principles of law applicable to a case of this sort are well known. On

---

[7] *e.g.* "*Gramophone*" [1910] 2 Ch. 423; followed in *Antec International v South Western Chicks* [1998] F.S.R. 738, at 744 (finding "Farm Fluid" sufficiently distinctive to justify grant of an interlocutory injunction).

[8] Although such marks are unregistrable, a registration already in existence may well be valid.

[9] Above, para.102.

[10] See the cases cited in para.15–086, and *Montgomery v Thompson* [1891] A.C. 217; 8 R.P.C. 361 ("Stone Ales" HL). In *Price's Patent Candle v Ogston and Tennant* (1909) 26 R.P.C. 797 (Scotland) it was found that in Morocco "London Candles" meant the claimants' candles. See further *Reddaway v Banham* [1896] A.C. 199 at 210; 13 R.P.C. 218, HL; the judgment of Kennedy L.J. in *Daimler v London Daimler* (1907) 24 R.P.C. 379; and the judgment of Parker J. in *British Vacuum Cleaner v New Vacuum Cleaner* (1907) 24 R.P.C. 641; cf. *Treasure Cot v Hamleys* (1950) 67 R.P.C. 89 ("Treasure" when applied to a cot held to be a fancy word).

[11] *Burberrys v Cording* (1909) 26 R.P.C. 693 at 701.

the one hand, apart from the law as to trade marks, no one can claim monopoly rights in the use of a word or name. On the other hand, no one is entitled by the use of any word or name, or indeed in any other way, to represent his goods as being the goods of another to that other's injury. If an injunction be granted restraining the use of a word or name it is no doubt granted to protect property, but the property, to protect which it is granted, is not property in the word or name, but property in the trade or goodwill which will be injured by its use. If the use of a word or name be restrained, it can only be on the ground that such use involves a misrepresentation, and that such misrepresentation has injured, or is calculated to injure, another in his trade or business. If no case of deception by means of such misrepresentation can be proved it is sufficient to prove the probability of such deception, and the court will readily infer such probability if it be shown that the word or name has been adopted with any intention to deceive. In the absence of such intention, the degree of readiness with which the court will infer the probability of deception must depend on the circumstances of each particular case, including the nature of the word or name, the use of which is sought to be restrained. It is important for this purpose to consider whether the word or name is prima facie in the nature of a fancy word or name, or whether it is prima facie descriptive of the article in respect of which it is used. It is also important for the same purpose to consider its history, the nature of its use by the person who seeks the injunction, and the extent to which it is or has been used by others. If the word or name is prima facie descriptive or be in general use, the difficulty of establishing the probability of deception is greatly increased. Again, if the person who seeks the injunction has not used the word or name simply for the purpose of distinguishing his own goods from the goods of others, but primarily for the purpose of denoting or describing the particular kind of article to which he has applied it, and only secondarily, if at all, for the purposes of distinguishing his own goods, it will be more difficult for him to establish the probability of deception. But whatever be the nature or history of the word or name, in whatever way it has been used, either by the person seeking the injunction or by others, it is necessary where there has been no actual deception, to establish at least a reasonable[12] probability of deception."

MARKS MORE-OR-LESS DESCRIPTIVE

15–094   There is, of course, no sharp division between marks that are descriptive and marks that are not: descriptiveness is a matter of degree.[13] As with trade names,[14] to the extent that a trader chooses a descriptive mark, he must expect others to use similarly descriptive marks so that confusion may be inevitable. The courts have sometimes (but not always) had regard to this, and accepted relatively small differences between descriptive marks as sufficient to avoid passing off.[15]

---

[12] See as to "reasonable", here, *Delavelle v Stanley* (1946) 63 R.P.C. 103 at 105.

[13] See the discussion of descriptive marks in Ch.7.

[14] "Office Cleaning" para.15–147.

[15] See here the lists in App.31, noting that there is here a distinction to be drawn between passing off and trade mark infringement (see paras 17–003 to 17–005); and see *McCain v Country Fair* [1981] R.P.C. 69, CA (only the descriptive part of the claimants' mark taken, no passing off); *Fisons v Godwin* [1976] R.P.C. 653 is similar; but cf. *Carlsberg v Tennent* [1972] R.P.C. 847

WORD FORMERLY COMMON TO TRADE

A word which has, at one time, been in common use in a trade with a mere **15–095** descriptive meaning may subsequently come to have special reference to the goods of a particular trader, who will then be entitled to prevent others using it without sufficiently distinguishing their goods.[16]

A word which has denoted the goods of two or three separate firms may come to denote the goods of one only: *Worcester Royal Porcelain v Locke* (1902) 19 R.P.C. 479, where the claimants were the successors of all the three firms who had previously used the term "Worcester" to denote their goods.

AREA

Where a word which is *prima facie* descriptive is claimed as his trade mark by **15–096** the claimant, he must show that it has acquired a distinctive meaning "amongst those who are purchasers of the goods" in question[17] within a definite area. Such area must extend to a large part of England and Wales, and include the district in which the defendant trades or proposes to trade.[18] If the word still continues to be used and understood with its original descriptive meaning by any considerable section of such persons, it cannot be monopolised.[19] The more appropriate the words claimed are as a description of the goods or of some characteristic of the goods, the greater is the burden of proof required from the claimant.[20]

THE QUESTION OF FACT

The question of fact which has to be answered in the cases under consideration **15–097** has, accordingly, a negative as well as an affirmative part: Does the word in dispute mean the claimant's goods and not goods (by whomsoever made) of a particular pattern or description?[21] The first part of the question alone is not enough:

"Where a word is prima facie the name or description of an article, evidence

---

(OH, Sc.), where an interim interdict was granted to protect the mark "Special brew" for beer; there was some similarity of get-up and the goods were intended to be directly competitive.

[16] *Daimler Motor v London Daimler* (1906) 23 R.P.C. 718; 24 R.P.C. 379.

[17] This was Lord Herschell's phrase in *Reddaway v Banham* [1896] A.C. 199 at 208; 13 R.P.C. 218 at 227.

[18] *Chivers v Chivers* (1900) 17 R.P.C. 420 at 429; *Faulder v Rushton* (1903) 20 R.P.C. 477, CA and the judgment of Moulton L.J. in *Star Cycle v Frankenburgs* (1907) 24 R.P.C. 405 at 414—small local *bona fide* users, which had been proved, did not affect his mind much with regard to the issue, the general reputation of the claimants under the name "Star Cycle". See also the judgment of Lord Shand in *Cellular Clothing v Maxton* [1899] A.C. 326; 16 R.P.C. 397(nn.78 and 85) at 408. In *Thorne v Sandow* (1912) 29 R.P.C. 440 at 453 evidence did not suffice to prove that throughout the country "Health Cocoa" had acquired a secondary meaning. See also cases as to registration, in which distinctiveness can only be established in particular districts.

[19] *Parsons v Gillespie* [1898] A.C. 239; 15 R.P.C. 57, PC ("Flaked Oatmeal"); *Cellular Clothing v Maxton* [1899] A.C. 326; 16 R.P.C. 397 at 403, HL. Where the only evidence that the word "Chequerboard" for fencing was distinctive of the claimants' fencing was that of persons in a special position to know of the origin of the goods, the action failed: *T. & C. v Victoria* (1931) 48 R.P.C. 148.

[20] *Randall v Bradley* (1907) 24 R.P.C. 657; affirmed at 773. The action of the claimants (The American Shoe Co) to restrain the defendants trading as The Anglo-American Shoe Co was dismissed. *Hommel v Bauer* (1905) 22 R.P.C. 43: "Haematogen" for a medicine held not to be distinctive. "The 'Camel Hair Belting' case may be an example of what, under ordinary circumstances, it would be very difficult to establish": *per* Halsbury L.C. in *Cellular Clothing* [1899] A.C. 326 at 336; 16 R.P.C. 397 at 405. See also the judgment of Parker J. in *Burberrys v Cording* (1909) 26 R.P.C. 693 at 701, 704 and 709 ("Slip-On" coats), cited above at para.15–093.

[21] *Gamage v Randall* (1899) 16 R.P.C. 185 at 196; *Reddaway v Banham* [1896] A.C. 199; 13 R.P.C. 218 ("Camel Hair Belting").

that it is also generally associated with the name of a particular maker is by no means conclusive that it has become a distinctive work which cannot be used of the same article when made by others without risk of deception".[22]

15–098   (1) In a dispute about the appellation "Shorland" for cycling shoes—a Mr Shorland, a well-known cyclist, having lent his name to the shoe—the defence was that the term was descriptive of the particular pattern of shoe. There was evidence that a number of makers used the name, apart from its use by Gamage's, the claimants; and some evidence that without Gamage's name a "Shorland" shoe would not be taken as made by Gamages. The jury found for the defendants and the Court of Appeal upheld the judgment: *Gamage v Randall* (1899) 16 R.P.C. 185. No doubt it would inevitably have told against the claimants that they had persistently associated their own name with "Shorland" when advertising the shoe. But the question actually put to the jury made a verdict for the defendants a foregone conclusion:

"If a man goes into a shop which is not Gamages ... and says 'Give me a pair of Shorland shoes' and shoes of this type were produced with no stamp of Gamages' name upon it, do you think that that man understands or believes that he is getting a shoe that comes from Gamages' shop?": see at 196.

If that be a fair question, no retailer can have a valid trade mark. In these days also, the idea that Gamages could, by securing Mr Shorland's permission for use of his name, get some sort of *prima facie* right to it would have been more familiar to the jury and even the judge: cf. paras 15–086, 15–097,15–098.

(2) In "Camel Hair Belting" the following questions were put to the jury—with the approval, it is clear, of the House of Lords: (a) Does "Camel Hair Belting" mean belting made by the plaintiffs as distinct from belting made by other manufacturers? (b) Does it mean belting of a particular kind, without reference to any particular maker? (c) Do the defendants so describe their belting as to be likely to mislead purchasers, and to lead them to buy the defendants' belting as and for the plaintiffs' belting? (d) Did the defendants endeavour to pass off their goods as and for the plaintiffs' goods, so as to be likely to deceive purchasers? The jury said "Yes" to (a), (c) and (d), and "No" to (b); judgment for the plaintiffs.

(3) Where the claimant had been selling, for less than a year, beers under the name "Newquay Real Steam Beer", the court found there to be a serious issue to be tried as to whether the word "Steam" was entitled to protection. The judge did not consider that the adoption of the name by the claimant with the intention of conveying an aura of purity, strength and old-fashioned character put it into the category of descriptive marks described in *Burberry v Cording* by Parker J.: *Island Trading v Anchor Brewing* [1989] R.P.C. 287a.[23]

SECONDARY MEANING NOT ACQUIRED WHILE NO COMPETITION

15–099   If the claimant has had a monopoly in fact of the goods, his difficulty in showing that the name he called them by is distinctive of his goods is increased.[24] In particular, reputation in get-up sufficient to found an action for passing off is not

---

[22] *per* Parker J., *Burberrys v Cording* (1909) 26 R.P.C. 693 at 704 (cited above, para.15–093).

[23] The judge granted an interlocutory injunction in relation to keg beer but not bottled beer, because there was a greater chance of confusion with the former: at 306.

[24] *British Vacuum Cleaner v New Vaccuum Cleaner* (1907) 24 R.P.C. 641 at 652, citing Lord

established merely by proof of large sales of a unique product:[25] "if any confusion has taken place it can only be the type of confusion which inevitably occurs when the first competitors appear on the scene to break—and to break quite legitimately—the monopoly previously enjoyed in the use of a new product", *per* Sir Allan Huggins V.P. in *Interlego v Tyco*.[26] However, in order to succeed in a defence based on what was described in *"Jif"* as "the monopoly assumption" it must be shown that the claimant's mark (or get-up) is "either so ordinary or in such common use that it would be unreasonable that he should claim it as applicable solely to his goods": *per* Lord Oliver, at 413.

(1) A number of grocers proved that when asked by their customers for **15–100** "Flaked Oatmeal" they supplied the claimant's goods; but there was no evidence of actual deception or confusion, and the value of the evidence first mentioned was discounted by the fact that it wholly or chiefly referred to a period when there were no other goods of the kind in question in the market besides the claimant's goods. The claimant failed: *Parsons v Gillespie* [1898] A.C. 239 at 254; 15 R.P.C. 57 at 62.

(2) The claimants' evidence consisted of: (a) their own advertisements, in which they used the word "cellular" to describe their cloth, but did not suggest that its use distinguished their cloth from cloth of a similar description made by others;[27] (b) statements of witnesses who said they understood "cellular goods" to mean the goods of the claimants, but who did not say that they knew of any other manufacturers making similar classes of goods; and (c) consent orders for injunctions obtained against other persons who had used the name. The claimants failed: *Cellular Clothing v Maxton* [1899] A.C. 326 at 345; 16 R.P.C. at 410.

(3) The name "Shredded Wheat" had been used for many years as the name of a breakfast food, originally a patented article. The name was appropriate as a description of the article, as was emphasised by the use of such advertising slogans as "It's all in the shreds"; and even after expiry of the patent, the users of the name were the only makers of that type of breakfast food. The mark "Shredded Wheat" was held invalidly registered, both in England and in Canada: *Canadian Shredded Wheat v Kellogg* (1938) 55 R.P.C. 125; *"Shredded Wheat"* (1938) 55 R.P.C. 55, 271; (1940) 57 R.P.C. 137, HL.

(4) The claimants had a restaurant called "Chicago Pizza Pie Factory", whose main business was selling what they called a "Chicago Pizza". The defendants opened a very similar restaurant called "L.S. Grunts Chicago Pizza Company". There was evidence of substantial confusion between the two; but it was held that since the claimants had given the name "Chicago Pizza" to this dish, they were not entitled to rely as passing off on confusion resulting from the defendants calling it that too: *My Kinda Town v Soll* [1983] R.P.C. 407, CA.

(5) For many years the claimant had sold cigarette papers in three weights,

---

Davey in " *Cellular Clothing*" at 16 R.P.C. 309. "To succeed in such a case [the claimant] must demonstrate more than simply the sole use of the description term. He must demonstrate that it has become so closely associated with his goods as to acquire the secondary meaning not simply of goods of that description but specifically of goods of which he and he alone is the source"; *per* Lord Oliver in *"Jif"* [1990] R.P.C. 341c, at 413.

[25] *Jarman & Platt v Barget* [1977] F.S.R. 260, CA; cf. " *Jif*".

[26] [1985–1987] 7 I.P.R. 417 (CA, –HK).

[27] It is not sufficient to show extensive advertising apart from the effect of the advertisement. "To make an advertisement relevant you must show that it had an effect": *per* Vaughan Williams L.J. in *Christy v Tipper* (1904) 21 R.P.C. 97 at 101. See also *Chivers v Chivers* (1900) 17 R.P.C. 420 at 431.

each indicated by a colour on the packaging: red, blue and yellow. The defendant launched its own three weights of cigarette papers, whose packaging was readily distinguishable from the claimant's although they also used red, blue and yellow to indicate the three weights. Passing off was alleged on the basis that: (a) the claimant's papers were never on display, being kept under the counter; and (b) that people would ask for a packet of "reds" and be supplied with the defendant's papers. The judge thought that it was by no means clear that a request for "reds" meant the claimant's goods as opposed to papers of that weight. He also thought that any confusion could be avoided by the claimant's ensuring that their goods were put on display; interlocutory relief was refused: *Rizla v Bryant & May* [1986] R.P.C. 389.

15–101   It was stated by Slade L.J. in the Court of Appeal in *"Jif"* [1990] R.P.C. 341, that the so-called monopoly assumption point, *i.e.* if a claimant has had a monopoly his difficulty in showing that the name (or get-up) is distinctive is increased, makes more difficult the defendant's case once the claimant has established a proprietary right in the name or get-up.

"If a trader enters the market with a class of goods, which have already for many years been sold under a particular get-up by another trader and have by reason of such get-up become identified in the minds of the public as the products of that trader, it is in my judgment ordinarily necessary, if he is to avoid the risk of misrepresentation, for him to take all the greater pains to ensure that there are sufficient distinguishing features between the get-up of his goods and those of the other trader. Potential competitors in this class of case may thus be well advised to enter the field quickly, if at all, before a reputation has been established." (at 392).[28]

In the House of Lords, Lord Oliver emphasised the need for the new entrant "to see that the goods can be really distinguished" (citing Romer L.J. in *Payton v Snelling*), at 414.

WHERE CLAIMANTS HAVE OTHER, SPECIAL NAMES FOR GOODS

15–102   The fact that the claimant has for some of his goods a special name does not necessarily negative his right to a more general name.[29]

In "Worcester China" the claimants had used the terms "Royal Worcester" and "Grainger's Worcester China" for some of their goods, and it was contended that by their conduct they had abandoned or lost their rights in "Worcester China" simpliciter, but this defence failed: (1902) 19 R.P.C. 479.

But the use of such special names is a matter to be considered.[30]

Name of introducer or patentee

15–103   The name of the inventor or first introducer of goods which are new to the market, or the name which he gives to those he manufactures or sells, is very readily adopted as the name of goods by whomsoever they are made; and in the case of

---

[28] See also *United Biscuits v Asda* [1997] R.P.C. 513 at 524 (Robert Walker J.) The judge considered that the court was not bound to disregard the fact that the defendant had taken a conscious decision to live dangerously: at 531.

[29] *Ford v Foster* (1872) L.R. 7 Ch. 611 at 628.

[30] *Fels v Thomas* ("Naphtha Soap") (1903) 21 R.P.C. 85 at 88, CA. The idea that goods habitually carry two trade marks—one the maker's "house mark", the other denoting the particular product, for the thing to be called by—was not always recognised in the earlier cases; but it seems to be well understood now.

goods made under a patent, the court is careful not to extend the patentee's monopoly by forbidding other manufacturers, after the patent has expired, to sell goods lawfully made by them according to its specification under the only name by which they are known.[31]

The name of the first maker or inventor is often understood to imply the good quality of work or materials which has brought the new goods into favour rather than the mode of manufacture or the nature of the ingredients employed.[32] Where this is the case, the use of the name by traders who have no connection with him must almost always be calculated to deceive.

NAMES MAY BECOME PUBLICI JURIS

Names which once carried a distinctive reference to a particular trader may, in consequence of successful piracies, or of their use by the trader himself for goods which are the goods of others, or are put forward as such,[33] or for other reasons,[34] lose it and fall into common use and become *publici juris*, in the same way as trade marks may be lost or abandoned.[35] The proper test whether an exclusive right has become *publici juris* is whether the use of the trade mark by other persons has ceased to deceive the public as to the maker of the article.[36] Accordingly, evidence is admissible to show that a word which was once distinctive of a particular trader's goods has become common in the trade. But, where the distinctive meaning alleged is proved to hold generally for the trade and public, cases of small local use for the goods of other traders will not have much effect to displace the evidence.[37] So also, piracy which exceeds in volume the genuine goods may fail to destroy the reputation of a mark, if it remains surreptitious, so that the ultimate consumer never appreciates the true position. **15–104**

(1) The mark "Harris Tweed" acquired a widespread reputation as denoting tweed, made in the island of Harris or a neighbouring island, which was essentially the product of a cottage industry. At times after the 1915–1918 War, much if not most of what was sold as "Harris Tweed" consisted of machine-made imitations. But these remained surreptitious, with the result that the reputation of the mark was never destroyed, though it became modified in the course of time: *"Harris Tweed"* [1964] R.P.C. 477 at 506, 509, 513–570; cf. *"Maizena"* [1894] A.C. 275; 11 R.P.C. 281 at 293, where substantially the same test was applied but the case went the other way (PC, Australia). **15–105**

(2) Where it was proved that the supposed proprietor of an unregistered trade mark had licensed its use by another manufacturer (with whom he was not connected, and over whom he had no control), an action to prevent its use by a third manufacturer was dismissed: for the use under licence must either have been a fraud on the public or else have destroyed any goodwill

[31] *"British Vacuum Cleaner"* (1907) 24 R.P.C. 641 at 652, and cases there cited.
[32] See *Massam v Thorley's*, above. And cf. the cases on designers' names, etc., at paras 15–157, 15–158.
[33] *Wolff v Nopitsch* (1900) 17 R.P.C. 321 at 330; on appeal (1901) 18 R.P.C. 27, CA.
[34] See "Gledhill Coils", para.15–089, illustration (2), above.
[35] Ch.9.
[36] *Ford v Foster* (1872) L.R. 7 Ch. 611 at 628 ("Eureka" shirts); followed in *Treasure Cot v Hamleys* (1950) 67 R.P.C. 89 at 90 ("Treasure" for dolls' cots not *publici juris*). Test approved as a basis of a defence: *Bollinger v Coldwell* [1971] F.S.R. 405.
[37] *Star Cycle v Frankenburgs* (1907) 24 R.P.C. 405, Moulton L.J.; and cf. "Area", above, para.15–096; cf. the "Iron-Ox" case, above, para.15–141, illustration; and *Goddard v Watford Co-operative Society* (1924) 41 R.P.C. 218 at 231–232.

the licensor may have had: "John Forrest" *Thorneloe v Hill*) (1894) 11 R.P.C. 61 at 71. Compare *"Bostitch"* [1963] R.P.C. 183, in which the question of validity of a registered mark, whose proprietor had allowed manufacture to be carried on by another company was tested in a very similar way.

NAME MAY BECOME ASSOCIATED WITH ANOTHER TRADER

15–106   The question is, what is the meaning of the name for the time being? It is possible, therefore, for a word which has at one time been the trade mark of one trader to become so identified with the goods of a rival trader as afterwards to become the trade mark of the latter, who may thereby acquire an exclusive right to its use,[38] or, if its association with the original owner has continued, a right concurrent with his right.[39] But in some circumstances—it is none too clear which—a party may be held debarred from setting up such a case, on the ground that his use was wrongful, and he may not rely on his own wrong.

15–107   The claimants were Swedish, the defendants their British agents. When supplies from Sweden were cut off during the Second World War, the defendants replaced them by British goods, using the same trade mark. It was agreed that they should use the claimant's designs and should use the mark so as to maintain the claimant's goodwill. After the war, the defendants sought to show that the goodwill was now theirs, but were held disentitled by their breach of the agreement from doing so: *"Manus"* (1949) 66 R.P.C. 71 at 76, CA.

DISCLAIMED WORD

15–108   That a claimant has applied, in order to secure registration of a mark, to disclaim some word, device or other thing found in it, should not prevent his establishing if he can that its use by others is deceptive, so as to found an action for passing off,[40] although he may be obliged to prove why he decided to disclaim and how the situation has changed since he did so. In the case of a word or mark which has been expunged from the Register, even though it was expunged without the claimant's assent, the removal of the mark does not and never did prevent the claimant from showing that the mark is, nevertheless, distinctive of his goods.[41] The court may, however, infer that other traders have refrained from using the word, not because they knew it to mean the claimant's goods, but merely because of the registration.[42] A trade mark which has never been registered, or which has been removed from the Register, may be the basis of a passing off case,[43] for

---

[38] *Daniel and Arter v Whitehouse* [1898] 1 Ch. 685; 15 R.P.C. 134 at 140 ("Brazilian Silver"); *Jaeger v Jaeger Co* (1927) 44 R.P.C. 437 at 448, CA. This was also the contention of the former marketing company for the overseas supplier in *Essex Electric v IPC Computer (U.K.)* [1991] F.S.R. 690, where the claimant succeeded in its application for an interlocutory injunction to restrain threats of passing off.

[39] *Edge v Gallon* (1899) 16 R.P.C. 509 ("Dolly Blue").

[40] 1994 Act, s.13.

[41] See "Yorkshire Relish" (para.15–083, illustration (1)), and "Stone Ales" (para.15–111).

[42] *Hommel v Bauer* (1904) 21 R.P.C. 576 at 587; (1905) 22 R.P.C. 43, CA, approving the judgment below. *Sed quaere*: if in trade the mark concerned does denote the claimant's goods exclusively, why should it matter how that happened?

[43] *Parker-Knoll v Knoll International* [1962] R.P.C. 265, HL; (mark "Knoll" not validly registrable, but use by defendants passing off); cf. para.15–033.

instance, a descriptive word, to which the claimant has a right that is not exclusive.[44]

GEOGRAPHICAL NAMES

Most geographical names are *prima facie* descriptive, of goods originating or a business carried on in the place concerned; they may by use come to distinguish a particular manufacturer or a particular undertaking, but can never entirely lose their primary significance.[45] Accordingly: "In the case of trade names which are prima facie geographically descriptive, a special order has sometimes been made in order to avoid any interference with the honest and proper use of them by persons other than the owner of the trade name."[46] However, reputation may attach to a geographical name that remains purely descriptive of a place or area, so that the right to attach it to goods or business may form part of the goodwill of those who are duly associated with that place or area: in which case, wrongful or dishonest use of that name will be actionable.[47]

15–109

(1) The claimant, being owner of all the collieries in Radstock, except a very small one, traded as the "Radstock Coal Co", and the defendants began to sell coal under the same name, and also as "The Radstock Colliery Proprietors". An injunction was granted "to restrain the defendants, unless and until they shall acquire a colliery or coal mine within the parish of Radstock, from trading under, or using the name or style of 'The Radstock Colliery Proprietors', or any other name or style signifying that the defendants or either of them are proprietors of any colliery or collieries at Radstock": *Braham v Beachim* (1878) 7 Ch.D. 848. Subsequently the defendants acquired a colliery, but not in Radstock, and began to trade as "The Radstock Coal and Waggon Co, Colliery Proprietors, Radstock, Somerset", and a motion to commit for breach of the injunction was refused on the ground that the terms used by them did no more than imply that they were proprietors of collieries, and that their place of business was at Radstock, and this was true: (1878) Seb.Dig. at 633, Fry J.

15–110

(2) On a finding that the name "Whitstable Native Oysters" meant the claimants' oysters, and could not be fairly used of French oysters relaid and brought to maturity at Whitstable, the court granted an interlocutory injunction to restrain the use of "Native"; no order as to "Whitstable": *Free Fishers of Whitstable v Elliott*, 4 T.L.R. 273; [1888] W.N. 27. In the later case of *Whitstable Oyster Fisheries v Hayling* (1900) 17 R.P.C. 461; 18 R.P.C. 434, it was decided that "Whitstable", as applied to oysters, was descriptive of the place where the oysters reach maturity.

(3) The claimant owned the only quarry in Brereton (in Chester) producing foundry sand. The defendant sold foundry sand as "Brereton sand". There was another Brereton in Staffordshire. An interlocutory injunction was

[44] See para.15–078.
[45] cf. the discussion of distinctiveness of geographical trade marks, above, Ch.9. Also, see Ch.11, on geographical indications.
[46] These words appeared in the 9th edition of this work and were quoted by Plowman J. in *Bach & Jackson v Cowan* [1969] R.P.C. 156. In that case the defendant who had recently commenced his hotel business near the claimants' hotel under the name "Pembridge Hotel" was restrained from so doing upon evidence that the claimants' hotel was known as "the Pembridge" even though its full name was the "Pembridge Gardens Hotel". Both hotels were in an area of London where the names of many roads were prefaced by the word "Pembridge".
[47] para.15–078; "Spanish Champagne" and "Sherry" cases; *John Walker v Henry Ost* [1970] R.P.C. 489 (a "Scotch whisky" case); but cf. *Lang v Goldwell* [1977] F.S.R. 353 (OH, Sc) (marketing a drink containing whisky so as to suggest a greater connection with Scotland than it does have, held not passing off).

granted restraining the defendant from selling foundry sand as "Brere-ton", "except sand quarried in the parish of Brereton in the county of Chester or any other parish bearing the name of Brereton"—with a gen-eral prohibition of passing off also: *Smith v Fieldhouse* [1961] R.P.C. 110.

(4) In the "Spanish Champagne" case, where a number of champagne pro-ducers sued in respect of the sale of Spanish sparkling wine as "Spanish Champagne", an injunction was granted restraining the defendants from passing off "as and for wine produced in the district of France known as the Champagne District wine not so produced by advertising, offering for sale or selling the same as Spanish Champagne or under any other name or description that includes the name Champagne": [1961] R.P.C. 116 at 127; [1960] R.P.C. 16 at 17. Any one of them, with substantial English goodwill in the name "Champagne", could have sued: see *"Advocaat"* [1980] R.P.C. 31, HL; *Bulmer v Bollinger* [1978] R.P.C. 79, CA; (where, however, the description "Champagne perry" for perry made sparkling otherwise than by the champagne process and sold in bottles very differ-ent from champagne bottles, was held not deceptive).

(5) The injunction granted in the "Sherry" case restrained the claimants (who had been sued on a counterclaim) "from using in the course of trade the word 'sherry' in connection with any wine not being wine coming from the Jerez district of Spain otherwise than as part of one or more of the phrases 'British Sherry', 'English Sherry', 'South African Sherry', 'Cyprus Sherry', 'Australian Sherry' and 'Empire Sherry'". The excepted phrases would not have been permitted if there had not been acquies-cence: [1969] R.P.C. 1 at 32. Both the "Champagne" and "Sherry" cases were followed in the "Whisky" case, *John Walker v Ost* [1970] R.P.C. 489.

(6) The defendants were marketing a non-alcoholic drink under the name "Elderflower Champagne" in a bottle made up to look like a champagne bottle. In a representative capacity, the champagne house Taittinger sued for passing off. The Court of Appeal found there to have been a misrepre-sentation that the product was champagne or in some way associated with it and many members of the public would be deceived: *Taittinger v Allbev* [1993] F.S.R. 641, CA. The court also granted an injunction restraining the use under EC Regulation 823/87 protecting the term "Champagne", at 673.

(7) Where the name "Banbury" was distinctive of the claimants, the follow-ing qualification was added to the defendant's undertaking not to trade under that name, "Provided that nothing in the aforementioned undertak-ing shall prevent the defendant from making bona fide use of the word 'Banbury' as part of the address on any business for the time being bona fide carried on by it in the Borough of Banbury": *Banbury Buildings v Sectional Concrete* [1970] R.P.C. 463. An injunction restraining the use of "Banbury" simpliciter would have prevented the defendant from carry-ing on its trade in Banbury altogether, since it could not have used its address.

15–111   "Thus cases of this sort fall into two categories: those where the question is whether the defendant has made a misleading use of a geographical appellation; and those where the allegation is that, although as a geographical appellation the expression complained of may have been accurately used, its use is calculated to represent that the goods are the claimant's".[48] To succeed under the former head, it is enough for the claimant to prove "(1) that he produces the substance in a given place; (2) that no one else produces the substance in that place; (3) that the defendant is selling the substance with the name of that place as a description; and (4) that there is likely to be deception of the public"[49]; although, as "Spanish Champagne" cited above shows, there are other ways of making out a case. It has been said that to succeed under the second head, the claimant must prove that the appellation in dispute hasceased to have a purely descriptive meaning as in "Stone Ales,"[50] where, although the right of the appellant to state that his beer was brewed at Stone was recognised, it was held to be subject to an obligation not to do so in any manner calculated to cause the appellant's beer to be passed off as that of the respondents, which was commonly known as "Stone Ale."[51] If, as required by the rule laid down in the authorities, cited above, the claimant proves that an apparently descriptive word which he claims to appropriate has ceased to have a purely descriptive meaning, it may be difficult to imagine how the defendant can be truthfully using the word with that meaning unless the context makes this clear. However, that rule is not easily reconciled with the decision in "Office Cleaning":[52] a business (or trading) name rather than a trade mark case, but there is no line to be drawn between passing off of goods and of a business.[53] Thus, in *Provident Financial v Halifax Building Society*,[54] where the claimant was one of the leading motor insurance underwriters and had traded under the name "Halifax Insurance" for more than 25 years, an interlocutory injunction was granted to restrain the defendant from selling motor insurance under the name "Halifax".

4. Direct misrepresentation as to business or goods

REPRESENTATION AS TO GOODS OR SERVICES

Where there is a direct misrepresentation by the defendant that the goods he sells   **15–112**
or services he offers are the goods or services of the claimant, the case presents
no difficulty, though in earlier days the principle was not clearly understood, and

---

[48] These words (from the 9th edition) were also approved by Plowman J. in *Bach & Jackson v Cowan* [1969] R.P.C. 156.

[49] "Brereton sand" case [1961] R.P.C. 110 at 114, illustration (3), at para.5–110.

[50] *Worcester Royal v Locke* (1902) 19 R.P.C. 479. See also "Yorkshire Relish" (para.15–083); and cf. also in *Hopton Wood v Gething* (1910) 27 R.P.C. 605 at 623–624; held that "Hopton" or "Hopton Wood" in connection with stone did not connote stone from the claimants' quarries only or from a particular seam. In *Grand Hotel v Wilson* [1904] A.C. 103; 21 R.P.C. 117, held that the defendants were entitled to indicate that their mineral waters came from springs at Caledonia; cf. *Rey v Lecouturier* [1908] 2 Ch. 715; [1910] A.C. 262; 25 R.P.C. 275; 27 R.P.C. 268 at 278, HL ("Chartreuse"). In *Price's Patent Candle v Ogston and Tennant* (1909) 26 R.P.C. 797 at 813, (para.15–091), the defendants were restrained from selling their candles as "London candles" without distinguishing. In *Brock v Pain* (1911) 28 R.P.C. 697, the claimants established that "Crystal Palace" fireworks meant their fireworks, notwithstanding their contract to give displays at the Crystal Palace had ended.

[51] In *Barnsley Brewery v RBNB* [1997] F.S.R. 462, Robert Walker J. referred to the *"Stone Ales"* case [1891] A.C. 217 in finding that the claimant did not have a strong case for asserting exclusive entitlement to the mark "Barnsley Bitter". He noted that the claimants in " *Stone Ales*" had been brewing in Stone for over 100 years and were the only significant brewery in the town: at 468.

[52] See para.15–147.

[53] *Bulmer v Bollinger* [1978] R.P.C. 79, CA.

[54] [1994] F.S.R. 81.

innocence was sometimes accepted as a defence.[55] The fact that a company may have used its own name in making a misrepresentation is irrelevant.[56]

REPRESENTATION AS TO NATURE OF GOODS OR SERVICES

15–113   In general, no action lies for passing off goods as "similar to"[57] or better than[58] or a substitute for[59] those of another, even though that other offers to show that the statements are untrue and are injurious to him.[60] However, as noted by Aldous J. in *Ciba-Geigy v Parke Davis*,[61] "care must be taken in applying in 1993 general statements of the law made in 1898". Goodwill may lie in a reputation for selling particular goods, and if so a false representation by another that his goods are those goods will be actionable.[62] On the other hand, it is not sufficient that the defendant makes a false representation, it must be a false representation related to the claimant's product or goodwill.[63]

15–114   The defendant carried on a business of designing and building exhibition stands under the name "Tabasco Design", on the basis that one of the designers used by the defendant was "hot". The makers of the well-known "Tabasco" sauce failed in its application for interim relief: *McIlhenny v Blue Yonder* (1998) 39 I.P.R. 187.

> "I accept—it is not in controversy—that [the defendant], in adopting the name Tabasco, sought to take advantage of a well-known characteristic of the [claimant's] product. But there is an appropriation only if some property or right is taken and the appropriation, if there is one, is wrongful only if a rule or principle of law forbids it... . Authority binding on this court requires me to hold that there is no passing off in the absence of a representation of connection between the [defendant] or its services on the one hand and the [claimant] or its product on the other", *per* Lehane J. at 201.

15–115   In particular, a descriptive term (geographical or otherwise) may denote the goods of a particular trader or a definable class of traders, so that the reputation of

---

[55] See *Ainsworth v Walmsley* (1866) L.R. 1 Eq. 518. Upon the facts proved, nowadays the claimant would probably succeed. The court treated the representation as equivalent to a warranty to the purchaser and no more. cf. the defence of "acting innocently" under the Merchandise Marks Act 1887, s.2(2)(c): *Christie v Cooper* [1900] 2 Q.B. 522.

[56] *NAD Electronics v NAD Computer Systems* [1997] F.S.R. 380 at 392, *per* Ferris J. and see paras 15–213 to 15–218.

[57] *Magnolia Metal v Tandem Smelting Syndicate* (1900) 15 R.P.C. 701; 17 R.P.C. 477, HL; *Broad v Graham Building Supplies (No.1)* [1969] R.P.C. 285 ("as"); *Broad v Cast Iron Drainage* [1970] F.S.R. 363 ("similar to").

[58] *White v Mellin* [1895] A.C. 154.

[59] " *Yeast-Vite*" (1934) 51 R.P.C. 110, HL.

[60] *Hubbuck v Wilkinson* [1899] 1 Q.B. 86; and see cases last cited. This is a matter of public policy, which has developed over the years, so that the courts may well now intervene where a century ago they would not have: see *per* Lord Diplock in " *Advocaat*" [1980] R.P.C. 31, especially at 94. For example, in *Ciba-Geigy v Parke Davis* [1994] F.S. R. 8, the judge noted that "the common law could apply different standards to statements about pharmaceuticals to those made about flour", at 21.

[61] [1994] F.S.R. 8 at 20.

[62] " *Angostura Bitters*" (1878) 7 Ch.D. 801; "*Yorkshire Relish*" [1897] A.C. 710, 14 R.P.C. 720, HL; *Masson, Seeley v Embossotype* (1924) 41 R.P.C. 160, illustration para.15–133; *Combe v Scholl* [1980] R.P.C. 1; and the "Champagne" line of cases cited below.

[63] *Schulke & Mayr U.K. v Alkapharm U.K.* [1999] F.S.R. 161. In *Dr Martens v Figgins* (1999) 44 I.P.R. 281, it was held that use of the words "The Original" on the defendant's look-alike footwear was sufficient to find passing off, even though the product bore the words "Made in Australia" on the instep: "a potential purchaser or consumer cannot be expected to undertake a reasoned analytical exercise when confronted with [the defendant's product]", *per* Goldberg J. at 389 (although passing off was not found in relation to another defendant who used a distinctive mark on "look-alike" products, at 329).

goods so described is part of those traders' goodwill: in *"Chocosuisse"* [1999] R.P.C. 826, CA, it was held that the words "Swiss chocolate" were taken by a significant section of the public in England to mean (and to mean only) chocolate made in Switzerland, *per* Chadwick L.J. at 836. Where this is so, a false use of that description for goods not entitled to it will be actionable.[64] But the term must be precise enough to define with reasonable precision the type of product that has acquired the reputation.[65]

REPRESENTATION AS TO BUSINESS

Cases in which the defendant directly represents that his business is the claimant's business, or a branch of it, or connected with it,[66] are equally clear as soon as the false representation is made out.   **15–116**

In *Law Society of England and Wales v Griffiths* [1995] R.P.C. 16, the defendants had adopted a telephone number 0800 192939 extremely close to that used for the claimant's "Accident Line" under which the public could telephone 0500 192 939 for advice on personal injuries and referral to a panel solicitor. It was held, in granting an interlocutory injunction, that "[a] person who takes steps which will lead a person who acts in a particular way to conclude that his business is that of another is guilty of passing off just as much as a person who states that his business is that of another".[67]

Where in Malaysia the defendant had chosen as its name a French name used by the claimant, it was held that, French hardly ever being used in Malaysia, this constituted passing off even without any evidence being adduced by the defendant as to what business activity it was engaged in: *Compagnie Générale des Eaux v Compagnie Général des Eaux Sdn Bhd* [1997] F.S.R. 610 (HC Malaysia).   **15–117**

However, in relation to services, very substantial differences between the get-up of the claimant's restaurants and of the defendant's hotel were sufficient to defeat a claim of passing off, even though the court accepted that the defendant had been opportunistic in its adoption of the name and saw the possibility of extracting "greenmail": *TGI Friday's Aust v TGI Friday's* (1999) 45 I.P.R. 43 (Fed. Ct. of Australia), *per* the Full Court.[68]

PAST MEMBERS OF BUSINESS

A partner or employee who has left a well-known firm and set up a similar busi-   **15–118**

---

[64] *"Advocaat"* [1980] R.P.C. 31, HL, approving (at 95, 105); *"Spanish Champagne"* [1960] R.P.C. 16 at 31. Any member of the class suffering substantial damage may sue; or some may sue on behalf of the class in a representative action: see para.15–078.

[65] *"Advocaat"* [1980] R.P.C. 31, at [1980] R.P.C. 98 at 104–105, HL. In *"Chocosuisse"* [1999] R.P.C. 826, the definition of the type of product in which the reputation subsisted was amended in the Court of Appeal to include the absence of added vegetable fat, upon application by the Swiss chocolate manufacturers: at 840.

[66] *Walter v Ashton* [1902] 2 Ch. 282. The CA said that this case was decided on too narrow a ground: *Harrods v R. Harrod* (1924) 41 R.P.C. 74. *Pompadour v Frazer* [1966] R.P.C. 7, where interlocutory relief was refused upon a false representation that the defendant (a former manufacturer of the claimant's goods) was still manufacturing for them, on the ground that this was not passing off, should not be taken as deciding that; it appears rather that the wrong form of injunction was asked for. The court seems in fact to have regarded the case as analogous to that of a representation of the sort of "business connection" discussed in the following paragraph: see at p.10.

[67] *per* Aldous J, at 21.

[68] Citing with approval the statement of Lockhart J. in *ConAgra Inc v McCain Foods (Aust)* (1992) 33 F.C.R. 302, that "… deliberate copying of the plaintiff's goods does not always evidence an intention to deceive; it may indicate nothing more than realisation that the plaintiff has a useful idea which the defendant can turn to his own advantage, though not intending to pass off his goods as those of the plaintiff": at 345.

ness of his own is entitled to advertise his former connections,[69] unless restrained from doing so by contract with his late partners or employers,[70] but he must take care to do it so as not to suggest that the connection is still existing between them and him[71], or that they have ceased to carry on business and he is their successor.[72] It would seem that this principle extends to other types of business connection, such as that of a supplier of the goods sold by a business.[73]

15–119   The same rule holds good of a trader who,[74] or whose trustee in bankruptcy,[75] has sold the goodwill of his business. It is important to specify clearly in the sale agreement the future use of names used in the business.[76]

15–120   Particularly difficult problems may arise upon the severance of business relations between, say, a manufacturer and the distributor of his goods. Where the distributor (claimant) had been selling for a number of years under the mark "Gro-Shield" products manufactured by the supplier (defendant) and had been co-operating with the supplier, upon termination of the commercial relationship (and therefore the trade mark licence) it was held that the goodwill in the mark was owned jointly.[77]

15–121   Where the goodwill of the common business has been attached to the manufacturer's name or mark, it is tempting for the distributor to act improperly in trying to sell his new, competing lines to customers for the old.[78] Where the goodwill has belonged to the distributor, it is tempting for the manufacturer to approach customers and explain that the goods were really his. Whilst the cruder forms of passing off, which may well be unintentional—sales of the "new" lines in response to orders for the old, and the like—can easily enough be stopped in most cases, experience suggests that there are subtler ways of filching goodwill that the courts are at best moderately competent to stop.[79]

15–122   (1) The son of the claimant left his father's employment, and described

---

[69] *Clark v Leach* (1862) 32 Beav 14, Romilly M.R. and Westbury L.C.

[70] As in *Wolmershausen v O'Connor* (1877) 36 L.T.(N.S.) 921 and *Selby v Anchor Tube* [1877] W.N. 191, where the style and goodwill passed, under the articles, to one partner on a dissolution. An employee must not use information acquired in his employment to enable him to solicit his employer's customers to deal with him after he has left the employment: *Robb v Green* [1895] 2 Q.B. 1 at 315. See also *Pullman v Pullman* (1919) 36 R.P.C. 240 and *Harrods v Schwartz-Sackin* [1991] F.S.R. 209, CA, in which the contractual restriction was held to come to an end with the termination of the concession agreement. As to sales of goodwill, see Ch.12.

[71] *Burgess v Burgess* (1853) 3 De G.M. & G. 896; illustration (1), below; *Van Oppen v Van Oppen* (1903) 20 R.P.C. 617. Also, see *Hookham v Pottage* (1872–73) L.R. 8 Ch. App 91, followed in *Harrods v Schwartz-Sackin* [1986] F.S.R. 490 at 494.

[72] See the cases next cited and *Laboucheère v Dawson* (1871–72) L.R. 13 Eq. 322.

[73] *Pompadour v Frazer* [1996] R.P.C. 7 at 10.

[74] *Churton v Douglas* (1859) John. 174; *Fullwood v Fullwood* [1873] W.N. 93 and 185.

[75] *Hudson v Osborne* (1869) 39 L.J.Ch. 79.

[76] See *Greg Cotton Motors v Neil & Ross Neilson* (1983–84) 2 I.P.R. 214, for an example of the consequences of not including such a provision.

[77] *Gromax Plasticuleure v Don & Law Nonwovens* [1999] R.P.C. 367: "Gromax, having had the benefit of the distributorship agreement, must now bear that as its burden", *per* Lindsay J. at 389. cf. *Watson v Dolmark Industries* (1991–92) 23 I.P.R. 363, in which Gault J. refused to extend the right to licence unregistered marks beyond where there has been a clear connection in the course of trade between the licensed marks and the goods involved and clear marking of the goods informing purchasers of the true position: at 372.

[78] In *C-Shirt v Barnett* (1997) 37 I.P.R. 315, Lehane J. rejected an argument by the claimant that its former distributor owed it a fiduciary duty not to compete with similar products.

[79] Disputes in circumstances akin to those discussed in the text are reported in *Hilti v Ucan* [1963] R.P.C. 160; [1964] R.P.C. 206 and in *Bostitch v McGarry & Cole* [1964] R.P.C. 173. The subtler cases tend never to come to trial. That where the goodwill belongs to the factor, the manufacturer may neither use the factor's marks nor prevent the factor finding another manufacturer is clear from *Defries v Electric & Ordnance* (1906) 23 R.P.C. 341; cf. *Van Zeller v Mason, Cattley* (1908) 25 R.P.C. 37 (where the mark was the name of a vineyard, and the merchant was held not entitled to use it for other wines). cf. also *"Diehl"* [1970] R.P.C. 435 at 446, where the importer

himself as "late of 107, Strand": *Burgess v Burgess* (1853) 3 De G.M. & G. 896. An injunction was granted to restrain him from continuing to do so.

(2) A doorplate, bearing the words "Scott and Nixon, late Robert and Walter Scott", was held to be a representation that Walter Scott had retired and that Scott and Nixon were carrying on the business of his old firm: *Scott v Scott* (1866) 16 L.T.(N.S.) 143.

(3) In a case where no connection had existed between the defendants and the claimants, but the defendants, having obtained a lease of clay mines formerly leased to the claimants, described themselves in advertisements (referring not only to the mines, but also to certain works where they had carried on a trade similar to that of the claimants) as "E. and J. Pearson (late Harpers and Moore)", the description was held to be a representation calculated to lead the public to believe that the claimants had retired from business: *Harper v Pearson* (1860) 3 L.T.(N.S.) 547.

(4) The defendant had formerly been the managing director of the claimant company but had severed his connection with them, and set up his own competing business. He had in his possession a book of vouchers issued by the claimants and bearing the defendant's name as their managing director, and had used one of these vouchers in the course of his own business. It was held that this was a representation that the business carried on by the defendant was connected with, or was that carried on by, the claimant company. An injunction was granted restraining the defendant from continuing such representation: *Fairest v Fairest* (1949) 66 R.P.C. 275. In a more recent decision in Singapore, the defendant left on shelves readily accessible to students study notes belonging to her former franchisor and an injunction was granted restraining her from passing them off as her own: *John Robert Powers School Inc v Tessensohn* [1995] F.S.R. 947 (CA, Sing.).[80]

(5) Where the claimant and defendant were carrying on business as rival dentists in the same street, and, on the expiration of his tenancy, the claimant was compelled to remove, and the defendant put up a board describing himself as the "old-established dentist", this was held to be a representation that the claimant had removed to the defendant's place of business: *Mallan v Davies* (1887) 3 T.L.R. 221.

(6) Samuel Allen sold his business; it passed to a company, Samuel Allen & Sons Ltd, and thence to D. Samuel Allen later formed a new company (in the same trade) which advertised its goods as those of "Original Samuel Allen". This inconvenienced D., who in retaliation formed a new company under the name "Original Samuel Allen & Sons Ltd" (it was refused registration as "Samuel Allen & Sons Ltd," the old name, by reason of another of Samuel Allen's companies). Samuel Allen sued D.'s new company to restrain the use of that name. It was held that "Original Samuel Allen & Sons Ltd." could mean the business that originally was Samuel Allen & Sons Ltd; and that to succeed, Samuel Allen would have to show that "Original Samuel Allen" had acquired the secondary meaning of his own new business: *Allen v Original Samuel Allen* (1915) 32 R.P.C.

---

of goods was held entitled as against their manufacturer to retain ownership of the registration of the mark the goods were sold under, but nevertheless it was suggested as possible that use of this mark upon goods of another manufacturer might be deceptive. An instance where the mark was the (foreign) manufacturer's and the (British) merchant was restrained from using it is *"Manus"* (1949) 66 R.P.C. 71. See also paras 15–070 to 15–076.

[80] The court referred to the Bristol Conservatories case, above, as one concerning "inverse" passing off: at 954.

33. All in all, it is perhaps surprising that Samuel Allen was claimant and not defendant.

(7) The claimant acquired the business of a former competitor Yencken Sandy Glass but the purchase agreement stated specifically "the goodwill of the business shall not pass to the purchaser" (apparently for accounting reasons). The claimant then ceased to use the name Yencken Sandy Glass and the defendant started to do so. The claimant succeeded in its application for injunctive relief on the grounds *inter alia* of passing off, as it was still well-known in the trade and amongst certain member of the public that the claimant had acquired the business known as "Yencken Sandy Glass": *ACI v Glamour Glaze* (1987—88) 11 I.P.R. 269.[81]

15–123 Where companies had a common origin, both being subsidiaries of a common parent, it did not constitute passing off for a United Kingdom branch of a foreign corporation to state its ownership on its headed paper and employees' business cards: *Anderson & Lemke Ltd v Anderson & Lemke Inc* [1989] R.P.C. 124. Although the judge (Hoffmann J.) considered that the casual reader might wonder what, if any, connection there was between the United Kingdom and US companies: "this puzzle is caused by the lawful existence of the two companies with similar names and not by any representation by the defendants." It is important to note that the defendant had adopted the trading style "Business Advertising Europe" and the judge also took comfort from the relative sophistication of the market in which the parties operated.

FALSE CLAIM TO BE AUTHORISED RE-SELLER / LICENSEE

15–124 Another category of false representation of a business connection which has sometimes come before the courts is where the defendant has pretended to be agent for the sale of the claimant's goods.[82]

A retailer of electronic equipment, selling "grey" imports, modified by it for United Kingdom use, held itself out as an authorised dealer of the manufacturer and purported to sell with the manufacturer's guarantee, which such goods did not have. It was ordered, on motion, not to deal in the claimant's goods without labelling them to say it was not an authorised dealer and there was no manufacturer's guarantee and to say if the goods had been modified: *Sony v Saray* [1983] F.S.R. 302, CA. This was an extreme case: the defendant already had a bad trading reputation.[83] More recently, the import and sale in the UK of software intended for bundled sale in the USA was held not only to constitute an infringement of the copyright in the software, but also to constitute passing off in that the sale of the software under the manufacturer's marks in the UK constituted a misrepresentation that the software licensed for use in the UK.[84] The sale of goods that are identical to genuine authorised products but that were manufactured without the authorisation of the trade mark owner constituted passing off unless

---

[81] Citing *Ad Lib Club v Granville* [1972] R.P.C. 673, see para.15–060.

[82] *e.g. "The Linden Singers." Galer v Walls, The Times*, August 6, 1964 (injunction sought to restrain the defendant from, *inter alia*, "using notepaper that purported to be the notepaper of [the group of singers, 19 of whose members were claimants], or otherwise representing that he had any authority to act for or on behalf of the group"; an undertaking was given).

[83] The Canadian Supreme Court has recognised that an action for passing off may be a disguised way of preventing parallel imports and refused any relief on somewhat similar facts, *Consumers Distributing v Seiko* (1985) 1 C.P.R. (3d) 12. For EC problems relating to the use of passing off to prevent parallel imports, see Ch.16, and particularly paras 16–047 to 16–051.

[84] *Microsoft Corp v Computer Future* [1998] E.T.M.R. 597.

and until the trade mark owner adopted the goods, taking responsibility for their quality and origin.[85]

Use in metatags

With the increase in importance of Internet trading and promotion, the use of third party trade marks in metatags (the unseen text on Internet web pages scanned by search engines) and other mechanisms to achieve the aim of having a party's web page offered by search engines in response to a search for the third party site is viewed by trade mark proprietors with increasing concern. The present attitude of the Court of Appeal as to whether such "invisible" use of a trade mark can amount to passing off is sceptical.[86] It is submitted that such invisible use might very well amount to a misrepresentation in some circumstances, but that absent other factors, it is perhaps unlikely that any such misrepresentation would lead to deception on the part of the public. If nobody is misled or likely to be misled, there can be passing off. As ever, the outcome of each case will be dependant on the particular facts.

15–125

Direct false statement

There may of course be a direct statement by the defendant that he is selling the claimant's goods when he is not, as in those cases where the defendant sells counterfeit goods.[87] But the cases of direct false statements found in the reports are mostly more complex than that: sales of inferior goods of the claimant's own merchandise, for instance:[88] others include placing a deceptive name or title on the facia of a shop,[89] or opening and replying to letters addressed to or intended for the claimant and executing the orders contained therein,[90] or supplying the defendant's goods in pursuance of an order for the claimant's goods, without informing the customer of substitution,[91] or inserting advertising material between the pages of national newspapers without the publishers' consent.[92] It may be assumed that more common in practice are false statements made orally, in meetings with customers or over the telephone. The difficulty of proof where such representations are made orally probably accounts for the small number of reported cases of this type.[93] The right to sue is not dependent on the false representation being made in any special way.[94]

15–126

---

[85] *Primark Stores Ltd v Lollypop Clothing Ltd* [2002] F.S.R. 60.

[86] *Reed Executive plc v Reed Business information Ltd* [2004] R.P.C. 40.

[87] For a recent example, see *Gillette UK v Edenwest* [1994] R.P.C. 279, in which Blackburne J. found that dishonesty on the defendant's part is not necessary before an award of meaningful damages for passing off: at 291.

[88] As in *Spalding v Gamage* (1915) 32 R.P.C. 273, HL (advertising obsolete model as the new one); *Gillette v Franks* (1924) 41 R.P.C. 499 (second-hand razor-blades sold as new); and cf. *Masson, Seeley v Embossotype* (1924) 41 R.P.C. 160 (illustration at para.15–133).

[89] *e.g., Hookham v Pottage* (1872) L.R. 8 Ch. 91. As to the purchase of a building with the vendor's name built into it, see *Boussod, Valadon v Marchant* (1908) 25 R.P.C. 42, CA. As to names of places of business, see para.15–159.

[90] *Edgington v Edgington* (1864) 11 L.T.(N.S.) 299 (a single instance proved, injunction refused).

[91] *British Leather Cloth v Dickens & Cooper* (1914) 31 R.P.C. 337.

[92] *Associated Newspapers v Insert Media* [1991] F.S.R. 380.

[93] *e.g. Law Society v Griffiths* [1995] R.P.C. 16.

[94] See, *e.g. Illustrated Newspapers v Publicity Services* (1938) 55 R.P.C. 172 (binding in of a "supplement" to copies of claimants' publications); *Morny v Ball & Rogers* [1978] F.S.R. 91 (selling scent packaged together with genuine "Morny" "Foambath"); *Insert Media* [1991] F.S.R. 380.

False claims to the prizes, medals, patents, copyright or praise
due to another

15–127   False claims to the prizes, medals, recommendations or other forms of praise which, in fact, have been gained by the claimant,[95] or to patents under which the claimant and not the defendant is working,[96] require special consideration. If such claims enable the maker to pass his goods or business off as those of the person really entitled to the medals, prizes or patents, the matter is clear. If they do not, then there is old authority for saying that no case can be made.[97] The tendency of the courts in recent years, however, has been to treat all such misrepresentations as actionable if a real probability of damage to the claimant is shown. Merely to reproduce on a label representations of gold medals won by other traders could hardly so influence customers—in these days, at least—as to be a substantial ingredient in passing off; at most it could be evidence of bad faith.

15–128   (1) The claimant's goods were the subject of a television demonstration in which the claimant's identity was not disclosed. The defendants then falsely advertised their similar goods as being "as shown on television". It was held that this was a proper case for an interim injunction but that an undertaking should be accepted in lieu: *Copydex v Noso* (1952) 69 R.P.C. 38.

        (2) The proprietors of a pipe band well-known as "The Dagenham Girl Pipers", failed to obtain interim relief against the proprietor of a newly established band billed as the "The Famous London Girl Pipers", although the costumes used and the performances of the two bands were similar and the use of the term "famous" was ground for suspicion as to the defendants' intentions: *Dagenham Girl Pipers v Vishnu Pather* (1952) 69 R.P.C. 1.

        (3) The English goodwill of a German manufacturer of eau-de-Cologne was expropriated during the war, and was in due course transferred to an English company. The English company sold its eau-de-Cologne (which was not made to the original German formula) under labels copied from those of the German company, the labels including representations of medals won by the German company. This was held legitimate, the goodwill being vested in the English company; the medals were treated as simply part of the get-up: *Reuter v Mulhens* (1953) 70 R.P.C. 102 at 121.

        (4) An action for passing off, alleging that a book was one prescribed for an examination whereas it was the claimant's book that was prescribed, failed on the ground that any such representation was only as to quality and that there had been no passing off: *Cambridge University Press v University*

---

[95] *National Starch v Munn's* [1894] A.C. 275 at 281; 11 R.P.C. 294, PC (reference to claimant's medals held a mere disreputable advertising trick). In *King v Gillard* (1905) 22 R.P.C. 327, CA, the defendants' representations as to medals, etc., were held at the trial to be untrue, and they were for that reason deprived of costs; reversed in the CA, as any false claims to awards were irrelevant to the particular issue of passing off, and so not proper to be considered in awarding costs. See also *Reuter v Mulhens* (1953) 70 R.P.C. 102 at 108, 121, illustration (3) below.

[96] *Lawrie v Baker* (1885) 2 R.P.C. 213; cf. *Pneumatic Rubber Stamp v Linder* (1898) 15 R.P.C. 525. It was argued in *Hospital for Sick Children v Walt Disney* [1966] R.P.C. 246 that there could be passing off by misrepresenting that a film was made under licence from the copyright owner-the action failed on the facts, no comment being made as to whether the cause of action lay.

[97] *Tallerman v Dowsing* [1900] 1 Ch. 1 (interlocutory injunction refused); though these days a court might well find passing off on such facts—the case is rather similar to *Masson, Seeley v Embossotype* (1924) 41 R.P.C. 160 (illustration para.15–133) where the claimant won. In *Testro Bros v Tennant* (1983–84) 2 I.P.R. 469, the Supreme Court of N.S.W. declined to follow *Tallerman v Dowsing*, stating that the case was not "of much, if any, authority": *per* Holland J. at 474.

Tutorial Press (1928) 45 R.P.C. 335. It is submitted that such facts would be decided differently today and passing off found.[98]

(5) The defendant was selling goods, not manufactured by or under licence from the claimants, bearing the words "manufactured under Ormond Patent No. 273,392". It was held that, assuming these words meant that the defendant had been licensed by the claimants and were untrue, there was no evidence that the claimants were making or selling goods of the kind in question; and accordingly no cause of action had been established: *Ormond v Knopf* (1932) 49 R.P.C. 634.

(6) It has been said that imitations of the descriptive and commendatory inscriptions and of the directions for use printed on the covers of patent medicines and proprietary articles were once common: *Franks v Weaver* (1847) 10 Beav 297, Langdale M.R., and *Massam v Thorley's* (1880) 14 Ch.D. 748, CA are instances. However, it is unlikely that a court would now tolerate them.

"REVERSE" PASSING OFF

As discussed above,[99] the classic case of passing off is where the defendant misrepresents his goods as those of the claimant, although as Lord Jauncey stated in *Jif Lemon*:[1] "It is not essential ... that the defendant should misrepresent his goods as those of the plaintiff. It is sufficient that he misrepresents his goods in such a way that it is a reasonably foreseeable consequence of the misrepresentation that the plaintiff's business or goodwill will be damaged."[2]   **15–129**

In *Bristol Conservatories v Conservatories Custom Build* [1989] R.P.C. 455, the defendant's salesman showed prospective customers an album of photographs of conservatories, some of which were of conservatories designed and built by the claimant. Although there was no allegation that anyone looking at the photographs would associate any with the claimant, the Court of Appeal found that there was a reasonable claim for passing off,[3] because if a customer ordered a conservatory from the defendant in response to the photographs he would be supplied with a conservatory not of the stated commercial source but of the defendant's manufacture. The court specifically declined to decide whether there is a form of tort known as "reverse passing off", preferring to find the facts alleged as within the tort of passing off.[4]   **15–130**

Counsel for the claimant had contended that as a result of the defendant's use of the photographs customers were misled into believing (1) that the defendant was the company which produced the conservatory, (2) that its designs were the same as in the album, and (3) that the defendant had a well-established business. It is submitted that the only misrepresentation on its own actionable in passing off was (1) and that falls squarely within the wrong envisaged by Lord Jauncey and   **15–131**

---

[98] See discussion below of "reverse" passing off.

[99] At para.15–013 *inter alia*.

[1] [1990] R.P.C. 341, at 417.

[2] His Lordship also referred to the classic statement of Lord Langdale in *Perry v Truefitt* (1842) 6 Beav 66 at 73: "A man is not to sell his own goods under the pretence that they are the goods of another man."

[3] Applying *Samuelson v Producers Distributing* (1931) 48 R.P.C. 580, CA and *Plomien Fuel Economiser v National School of Salesmanship* (1943) 60 R.P.C. 209, CA: the judgment in the former case appears to have been based on the principle, as expressed by Romer L.J. (at 593) "that the court will always interfere by injunction to restrain irreparable injury being done to the plaintiff's property" (in that case, the plaintiff's copyright). The Scottish case of *John Henderson v A. Munro* (1905) 7 F. 636 (Ct of Sess) was also referred to with approval.

[4] *per* Ralph Gibson L.J., at 464.

it is unnecessary to rely on any extension of classic principles. Although it was open to the defendant to use photographs of the claimant's product to indicate that it could make products like it,[5] it went further and made an actionable misrepresentation which could have caused damage to the claimant in the form of lost sales (in the sense that all the defendant's potential customers could have been customers of the claimant had not the misrepresentation been made).

15–132   Notwithstanding Bristol Conservatories, passing off is not a tort providing a remedy in all cases of deception: it is submitted that Laddie J. went too far in *Matthew Gloag v Welsh Distillers*[6] when he refused the defendant's application to strike out the claimant's claim for passing off. The defendant sold as "Welsh whisky" a product which was, in reality, Scotch whisky purchased by them in bulk, bottled and then sold. The claimant claimed that this constituted "reverse passing-off" and relied on Bristol Conservatories. The judge found that this was arguable. This cannot be right: passing off does not extend to misstatements in the abstract, it is not a tort covering all misdescriptions of products: there must be an actionable misrepresentation which harms the claimant's goodwill in a name or get-up,[7] mere appropriation is not sufficient. Although the defendant's actions may have contravened trade descriptions legislation or EU regulations, there was no representation connecting the "Welsh whisky" product with anyone other than the defendant.[8] This can be contrasted with Bristol Conservatories where the photographs were equivalent to such a representation.[9]

SYSTEM OF ADVERTISING

15–133   The mere adoption by one person of a system of advertising similar to that used by a rival trader will not support a passing off action[10] nor will the mere adoption of a similar system of window-dressing or decoration of a shop.[11]

The claimants were suppliers of type for use in a particular sort of printing machine. The defendants supplied type of an inferior sort for the same machine. The defendants circulated price lists which were practically copies of the claimants', and used samples of work done with the claimants' type for showing to prospective customers. It was found that the defendants were deliberately attempting to find a market for their goods by suggesting (contrary to the fact) that they were the same as the claimants. The claimants were granted an injunction: *Masson, Seeley v Embossotype* (1924) 41 R.P.C. 160.[12]

15–134   Such untrue statements, in a defendant's advertisements, as "the only genuine

---

[5] *e.g. Broad v Cast Iron Drainage* [1970] F.S.R. 363.

[6] [1998] F.S.R. 718.

[7] See *"Pub Squash"* [1981] R.P.C. 429 (PC, N.S.W.). See *Snyman v Cooper* (1991) 19 I.P.R. 471 for an example of a case in which the judge had no difficulty in finding that the defendant's misleading reference in advertising to a location in which only the claimant had a shop constituted passing off.

[8] See the analysis of the case law by Fisher J. in " *Tot Toys*" (1993) 25 I.P.R. 337, in which the judge concludes: "Source motivation is and always has been an essential ingredient of diversion passing off" (at 365).

[9] For an earlier case on the same lines, see *Masson, Seeley*, at para.15–133.

[10] *Wertheimer v Stewart, Cooper* (1906) 23 R.P.C. 481. *Elida Gibbs v Colgate-Palmolive* [1983] F.S.R. 95 *contra*—but there the parties were agreed that if they both used the same "motif" (analogy between teeth and trees), confusion would result: see at 97. Also, *"Pub Squash"* [1981] R.P.C. 429 (PC, N.S.W.)

[11] *Plotzker v Lucas* (1907) 24 R.P.C. 551; *Bravingtons v Barrington Tennant* [1957] R.P.C. 183.

[12] cf. *Ciba-Geigy v Parke Davis* [1994] F.S. R. 8.

Bowden Control wires"[13] are only material in so far as they tend to induce the belief that the defendant's goods are the claimant's.[14]

Where the defendant used in a comparative advertisement for its generic equivalent pharmaceutical an image (an apple) which the claimant had used for some years in its advertising and promotion of its formerly patented drug, it was held to be unarguable that this constituted passing off.[15]

PASSING OFF ONE QUALITY OF GOODS FOR ANOTHER

It is in general a defence to an action for passing off goods as those of the claimant that the goods were the claimant's. This defence will not succeed, however, where the goods have been altered or mutilated,[16] or allowed to deteriorate so as not to be the same goods.[17] Furthermore, the court will intervene where one quality of manufacturer's goods is passed off as another quality,[18] as, for example, the sale by the defendants of Continental quality of the claimants' champagne as claimants' English quality.[19] But in order to establish such a case, there must be a definite superior class of article for which the goods of the other class are passed off.[20] The existence of two classes must be established:[21] in *Parma Ham v Marks & Spencer*;[22] Morritt L.J. commented: "[t]he reason for this requirement… is that the court is one of law and not gastronomy and does not adjudicate on the relative merits of particular products".[23] Furthermore, there cannot in general be passing off where the claimant's goods are sold unaltered and with unaltered labels, even though they are goods he does not himself sell in the country.[24]

15–135

The sale of second-hand goods as new is actionable, by the trader whose name or mark they bear, provided always he can show that he is likely to suffer damage

15–136

---

[13] *Bowden Brake v Bowden Wire* (1913) 30 R.P.C. 609, Warrington J.

[14] As to the continuing effect of a misleading advertisement, see *per* Lord Parker in *Spalding v Gamage* (1915) 32 R.P.C. 273 at 288.

[15] *Ciba-Geigy v Parke Davis* [1994] F.S.R. 8. On the claimant's submission that the advertisements were "knocking advertisements" which wrongfully appropriated the claimant's goodwill, Aldous J. stated: "I believe the advertisements are examples of comparative advertising. Such advertisements are perfectly proper unless registered trade marks are used [the case was prior to the 1994 Act]. They are not knocking advertisements in that they do not suggest that the plaintiff's product is a bad product; they only seek to suggest that the defendant's product is as good a product. Such statements are not actionable according to common law" (at 22–23).

[16] *Westinghouse v Varsity Eliminator* (1935) 52 R.P.C. 295. Also, see *IBM v Phoenix* [1994] R.P.C. 251, in which the claimants claimed that the use of "IBM manufactured" on memory cards reworked by the defendant constituted passing off and the court refused to strike out the defence that there was no misrepresentation.

[17] See *Wilts United Dairies v Robinson* (illustration below) [1958] R.P.C. 94 at 102, CA.

[18] *Spalding v Gamage* (1915) 32 R.P.C. 273 at 284, *per* Lord Parker. See also *Teacher v Levy* (1906) 23 R.P.C. 117. As to damages in *Spalding v Gamage*, see (1918) 35 R.P.C. 101, CA.

[19] *Champagne Heidsieck v Scotto and Bishop* (1926) 43 R.P.C. 101. Contrast *Champagne Heidsieck v Buxton* (1929) 47 R.P.C. 28. In *Re "Grand Marnier" Liqueur* [1994] F.S.R. 61 the Oberlandesgericht in Frankfurt found that it would be contrary to Art.30 (now 28) of the EC Treaty for national unfair competition law to be used to prohibit use of confusing get-up on an inferior quality product produced alongside a better quality product in a similar get-up by the same producer in another EC Member State.

[20] *Hunt, Roope, Teage v Ehrmann* [1910] 2 Ch. 198; 27 R.P.C. 512.

[21] *Harris v Warren* (1918) 35 R.P.C. 217. And see illustration para.15–137(1).

[22] [1991] R.P.C. 351, CA.

[23] [1991] R.P.C. 351 at 363.

[24] *Revlon v Cripps & Lee* [1980] F.S.R. 85, CA: this is quite apart from the EU law objections to restraints on parallel imports from other EU countries: cf. Ch.15. But there is no absolute rule excluding passing off in such cases: cf. *Wilkinson Sword v Cripps & Lee* [1982] F.S.R. 16, where passing off was alleged by sale in the UK of blades of export *i.e.* inferior quality; the court refused to strike the claim out; *Colgate Palmolive v Markwell Finance* [1989] R.P.C. 497, CA, in which passing off was found by reason of the inferior quality of the genuine "Colgate" toothpaste imported from Brazil.

thereby.[25] The sale of second-hand goods bearing the claimant's mark without any indication whether or not they are new goods may or may not be deceptive according to the circumstances of the sale. The character of the shop, the price and the appearance of the goods may affect the mind of the customer.[26]

15–137

(1) The defendants were wholesale grocers. They sold old stock (at least 20 months old) of the claimants' condensed milk to grocers at reduced prices, with a recommendation that it be resold at the price ruling before an increase made less than two months before, but without any warning as to its age. Condensed milk begins to deteriorate after six months. The tins were not distinguishable from new stock except by opening them. Held, that the defendants were representing that this was fresh stock: *Wilts United Dairies v Thomas Robinson* [1958] R.P.C. 94, CA. In *Parma Ham v Marks & Spencer*, Leggatt L.J. contrasted this case from that before him: "a purchaser of pre-sliced Parma ham cannot be said to have been supplied with something other than what it is described as being, and what he can see it is, assuming that it was from a Parma ham that the slices came", (at 382).

(2) Injunctions will be granted to restrain the selling of second-hand motor-cars as "new": and for this purpose a car ceases to be "new" as soon as it has been sold retail, registered and driven away by the purchaser: after that the manufacturer's obligations (in respect of defects and of servicing) are no longer those belonging to a new car: *Morris Motors v Lilley* [1959] 1 W.L.R. 1184. But if that is so, an injunction against selling cars as "new" is not in proper form, since (with "new" bearing a special meaning) it may act as a trap: *Morris Motors v Phelan* [1960] R.P.C. 209; cf. *Vanden Plas v Cars & Caravans* [1965] F.S.R. 93. Furthermore, to describe a car as "brand new" may well not imply that it is "new" in that special sense: *Standard Motor v Grantchester Garage* [1960] R.P.C. 211.

(3) Where the defendant sold unfinished rejects from the claimant's manufacture under the claimant's mark, without explanation, an injunction was granted to restrain the defendant from passing off goods "not of the plaintiff's finished manufacture or merchandise as and for", the plaintiff's goods: *Britains v Morris* [1961] R.P.C. 217 ("Swoppets").

(4) The claimant published an unexpurgated edition of a salacious book previously only published in expurgated form. The claimant used for his edition an altered title. The defendant republished the expurgated edition, giving it the claimant's altered title and was restrained by interlocutory injunction from so doing: *Allen v Brown Watson* [1965] R.P.C. 191.

(5) The defendants sold second-hand denim garments including jeans labelled "Levi's" which had been imported from the USA. The defendants altered such jeans in a number of ways, for example by patching, colouring or cutting off part of the legs, and supplied them to retailers with an additional label bearing the mark "Revise". It was held that this constituted passing off because *inter alia* both the claimant's new products (including new second-hand look jeans) and the defendant's altered products were sold alongside each other in shops which sold new goods to the same range of consumers, as well as the fact that the "Revise" label was usually in close proximity to a number of the trade marks of Levi Strauss and the mark

---

[25] See, *e.g.* cases on selling second-hand cars as new: *Morris Motors v Lilley* [1959] 1 W.L.R. 1184; *Morris Motors v Phelan* [1960] 1 W.L.R. 352, 566, illustration (2), below; and razor blades: *Gillete v Franks* (1924) 41 R.P.C. 499; *Gillette v Diamond Edge* (1926) 43 R.P.C. 310 (interim injunction granted).

[26] *General Electric v Pryce's* (1933) 50 R.P.C. 232.

"Revise" had been chosen so as to suggest Levi's: *per* Sheppard J., at 209 in *Wingate Marketing v Levi-Strauss* (1993–94) 28 I.P.R. 193 (Fed. Ct. of Australia, Full Court).

(6) Where the defendant sold lenses "to suit" the claimant's helmets, it was held arguable that this constituted passing off where the claimant's helmets fitted with the defendant's lenses would not comply with health and safety regulations: *Hodge Clemco v Airblast* [1995] F.S.R. 806. The case was described by the judge, Jacob J., as at "the outer limits of the tort of passing off", at 809.[27]

5. Imitations of trade or service mark

The mark or name (or get-up, see below) must be associated with the goods or business of the claimant   **15–138**

Actions based upon direct misrepresentation are comparatively rare. The claimant's case more commonly is that the defendant has copied or imitated the trading name, the trade mark, the get-up or some other badge or description by which the claimant's business or goods are known to be his. The cases concerned with trading names, and the cases concerned with get-up, are specially considered in later sections of this chapter.[28] The present section is accordingly concerned generally with matters common to all cases of misrepresentation by the use of badges of trade, and with misrepresentation by the use of trade and service marks in particular.

Where the charge is one of indirect misrepresentation of this sort, the case is usually based on the allegations that (a) a mark, get-up, etc., is distinctive of the claimant's goods exclusively and that (b) the defendant has used the mark or get-up or an imitation so close as to be likely to deceive. It may be fallacious to treat the two allegations as propositions which must be established separately. What has to be proved is one proposition, namely that the defendant's conduct is likely to lead to passing off.[29] Nevertheless, the claimant must establish on the one hand that the badge of trade concerned has been used for goods or a business that are not his—or at least that have no right to the badge[30] —so as to be recommended by it.[31] On the other hand, if the claimant cannot prove the association, in this country, of the mark or get-up concerned with goods that in fact are his (or, in the case of a trading name, associated with his business) the action fails in limine.[32] The foundation of an ordinary[33] passing off case: **15–139**

"is that the party alleging it should prove, in the first instance, that any name

---

[27] See also *SDS Biotech v Power Agrichemicals* [1995] F.S.R. 797 (whether unauthorised use on fungicide of MAFF number gave rise to a cause of action in passing off for authorised traders on the basis of "Advocaat" [1980] R.P.C. 31, HL; summary judgment was refused by Aldous J.).

[28] See Sections 6 and 7 below.

[29] *Magnolia Metal v Tandem Smelting* (1900) 17 R.P.C. 477 at 486, *per* Lord Halsbury; *Office Cleaning v Westminster* (1946) 63 R.P.C. 39 at 42, *per* Lord Simonds (a trading name case), is to the same effect.

[30] *e.g.* when one quality of goods is passed off for another, all of the same manufacture: para.15–135.

[31] Note that the badge, even if a trade mark, need not be placed upon the goods, nor even necessarily used in a way that would infringe a registered mark: it is a pure question of fact whether the use made of the badge is deceptive or not. An injunction will be granted against the particular mischief that has occurred: see the injunctions in *Hendriks v Montagu* (1881) 17 Ch.D. 638; *Massam v Thorley* (1880) 14 Ch.D. 748.

[32] "Turmix" *Oertli v Bowman*) [1957] R.P.C. 388 at 397, CA; approved [1959] R.P.C. 1, HL.

[33] There are of course other sorts of case: where the claimant is not a trader or goods are not involved; or of "Advocaat" type, see para.15–078.

which he claims as his trade name has been so extensively used in connection with his manufacture or with the goods which he sells that his goods have come to be known in the market by that name; that anyone using that name would intend to refer to his goods, and that anyone to whom the name was used would understand that his goods were referred to."[34]

15–140 Furthermore, in order to establish passing off in this way, it must be shown that what the defendant has taken is in itself sufficiently distinctive of the claimant,[35] and further that the confusion or deception relied upon as causing damage to the claimant is caused by the taking of that distinctive matter.[36]

(1) The publishers and owners of the British Pharmacopoeia failed in an action against Barrett Proprietaries, makers and vendors of medical preparations, to restrain them from using the letters B.P. in connection with such goods, there being no evidence what the public would understand by those letters: Att.Gen. and the *General Medical Council v Barrett* (1933) 50 R.P.C. 45.

(2) Three days' use of the name of a new weekly newspaper (of which 15 copies had been sold before the defendants' publication began) was held insufficient to give the owners any right to stop use of the name for a rival paper. The larger sale of the claimants' paper after the defendants started publication was immaterial: *Licensed Victuallers v Bingham* (1888) L.R. 38 Ch.D. 139; cf. *Maxwell v Hogg* (1867) L.R. 2 Ch. 307.

(3) The claimants were manufacturers of tobacco-pipes. They had for many years marked their pipes with an inlaid white spot on the stem. The defendants started selling pipes with a spot on the stem, but larger and coloured. It was held that if spots on pipe stems were distinctive of the claimants at all, this was so of small white spots only, and the action failed: *Dunhill v Bartlett* (1922) 39 R.P.C. 426.

(4) The claimants had a mark for sarongs showing a native cap with the words "Chop Topi Achai". The defendants sold sarongs bearing a label incorporating a markedly different native cap. The claimants alleged that their goods were known as "Chop Topi" ("Cap Brand") sarongs, so that use by others of a sarong mark including any sort of topi (or cap) would be deceptive: but it was held that no such distinctiveness of "Chop Topi" was established: *Mohamed Noordin v Abdul Kareem* (1931) 48 R.P.C. 491. If the fact of distinctiveness had been proved, it would seem that the action would have succeeded; cf. the cases on "essential features" of a trade mark, paras 17–028 to 17–033.

(5) The claimants in October commenced a new kind of business in the United Kingdom—that of arranging introductions between members of the opposite sex by means of a computer. They used in connection with their business a symbol consisting of a heart combined with the standard biological symbols for male and female. The defendants commenced a similar business in November, using a similar symbol. Stamp J. held that the evidence did not show that the symbol had, in the short time of use, become exclusively associated with the claimants, particularly because of its descriptive nature. "A trader who sets up a new trade has no monopoly of that trade or of the manner of carrying it on, and he cannot prevent a rival trader copying his ideas, notwithstanding that confusion may be

---

[34] *Leahy, Kelly v Glover* (1893) 10 R.P.C. 141 at 155.
[35] *Imperial v Phillip Morris* [1984] R.P.C. 293, citing *Payton v Snelling* (1900) 17 R.P.C. 48, CA (get-up, of which part common).
[36] *My Kinda Town v Soll* [1983] R.P.C. 407, CA, illustration (4), para.15–100.

caused": *Compatibility Research v Computer Psyche* [1967] R.P.C. 201; cf. *Stannard v Reay* [1967] R.P.C. 589, where the claimants commenced their business in the Isle of Wight using a mobile fish and chip van under the name "Mr. Chippy" only three weeks before the defendants did the same thing, but were able to show a considerable drop in earnings and other facts showing a likelihood that the name had achieved at least a degree of distinctiveness in the short period of time involved so that an interlocutory injunction was granted.

(6) An interlocutory injunction was granted restraining use for the defendant's mechanical excavators of "580", the claimant's type number: *Hymac v Priestman* [1978] R.P.C. 495.

(7) A service mark case: the claimants were the suppliers of the materials used in a particular permanent-waving process, known as a "Jamal wave". The defendant, asked by customers for a "Jamal wave," used other materials. On evidence suggesting that people asking a hairdresser for a "Jamal wave" wanted to be waved by the claimant's process, held that this was a sort of passing off: *Sales Affiliates v Le Jean* (1947) 64 R.P.C. 103. The court seemed remarkably doubtful whether this was passing off at all; but no new principle seems to have been involved.

LITERALLY TRUE DESCRIPTION MAY MISLEAD

"Even a description of goods which is literally true may be so framed as to deceive";[37] "a statement that is literally true, but which is intended to convey a false impression ... is not sterling coin."[38]   **15–141**

Where an ingredient, oxide of iron, was used in making medicinal tablets merely to justify the use of the name "Compound Iron Oxide Tablets", and the name was chosen because it would lead to confusion with the claimants' "Iron-Ox Tablets", and not because it could be said correctly to describe the article, an injunction was granted against the use of the term "iron oxide" without "better distinguishing" the defendants' goods from those of the claimants. The claimants' goods did not contain oxide of iron, which was practically useless as a drug, and the name "Iron-Ox Tablets" was held to indicate their tablets and was not associated by the public with any particular drug: *Iron-Ox v Co-operative Wholesale Society* (1907) 24 R.P.C. 425. That other traders had adopted (sporadically and locally) the same stratagem was not treated as affecting the issue: cf. below, para.15–104.

BADGES OF ALLEGIANCE

The issue of whether or not the use of a device or mark to denote support for a sporting club or as a badge of allegiance constitutes a misrepresentation that the goods to which the device or mark is applied originate from that club is a question of fact in each case. The courts have considered the question in connection with the red rose emblem used as a badge of allegiance by supporters of the England Rugby Union team and also in connection with "unofficial" Arsenal   **15–142**

---

[37] *per* Lord Davey in *Grand Hotel v Wilson* (1904) 21 R.P.C. 117 at 134, PC; *Reddaway v Banham* [1896] A.C. 199 at 212; 13 R.P.C. 218 at 233.
[38] *per* Lord Macnaghten.

Football Club merchandise.[39] In each case it was held at first instance that the use of the marks or devices in issue did not denote trade origin, and therefore did not constitute a misrepresentation for the purposes of passing off. The passing off decision in *Arsenal v Reed* at first instance was not appealed, but Aldous L.J. nevertheless expressed doubt as to whether it was correct.[40]

6. Trading names[41]

INTRODUCTORY

15–143   The name under which a business trades will almost always be a trade mark[42] (or if the business provides services, a service mark, or both). Independently of questions of trade or service mark, however, the name of a business (a trading business or any other[43]) will normally have attached to it a goodwill that the courts will protect. An action for passing off will then lie wherever the defendant company's name, or its intended name, is calculated to deceive, and so to divert business from the claimant, or to occasion a confusion between the two businesses. If this is not made out there is no case.[44] The ground is not to be limited to the date of the proceedings; the court will have regard to the way in which the business may be carried on in the future, and to its not being carried on precisely as carried on at the date of the proceedings.[45] Where there is a probability of confusion in business, an injunction will be granted even though the defendants adopted the name innocently[46] and even though the claimant has decided no longer to use the name.[47]

DESCRIPTIVE NAMES

15–144   Where the claimant's name is descriptive of its business (or is geographically

---

[39] *RFU v Cotton Traders Limited* [2002] E.T.M.R. 76 (the England rose case) and *Arsenal Football Club plc v Reed* [2001] R.P.C.46.

[40] [2003] R.P.C. at paras 70 and 71.

[41] In previous editions of this work, this section was entitled "Business Names", which because of the expansion of the subject-matter has become slightly misleading.

[42] It is very difficult to avoid using the name of a trading business as a trade mark: see *Reuter v Mulhens* (1953) 70 R.P.C. 235 ("4711"; note the summary way in which the issue of infringement was disposed of); *Wright, Layman & Umney v Wright* (1949) 66 R.P.C. 149.

[43] See paras 15–172 to 15–174, as to actions for passing off by claimants who have no business in the ordinary sense; as to service trades, cf. *Harrods*.

[44] See *Electromobile v British Electromobile* (1908) 25 R.P.C. 149; *British Vacuum Cleaner v New Vacuum Cleaner* [1907] 2 Ch. 312; 24 R.P.C. 641. It is essential that there should be tangible probability of injury to the property of the claimants; but under the word "property" may well be included the trade reputation of the claimants: *per* Sargant L.J. in *Harrods v Harrod* (1924) 41 R.P.C. 74 at 86, commenting on *Walter v Ashton* [1902] 2 Ch. 282. In Harrod, the claimants' business comprised a banking department, and the defendant company was registered with the object of carrying on a moneylender's business and it was held that its name was chosen fraudulently.

[45] *Ouvah Ceylon Estate v Uva Ceylon Rubber Estates* (1910) 27 R.P.C 753 at 756, CA; cf. *Scottish Union and National Insurance v Scottish National Insurance* (1909); 26 R.P.C. 105 (defendant company did not intend to carry on any other business than marine insurance, whereas the claimants were a fire and life insurance company).

[46] See, *e.g. Ouvah Ceylon Estates v Uva Ceylon Rubber Estates* (1910) 27 R.P.C. 753, CA (innocence of defendants assumed, but injunction granted); the point is too well established for other instances to call for notice.

[47] In *WMC v Westgold* (1998) 39 I.P.R. 319 (Fed. Ct. of Aust.) the evidence showed that the claimants were still well-known by the name "Western Mining" even though they had decided a year previously to cease use of it. The judge granted a permanent injunction. This can be contrasted with *Elders IXL v Australian Estates* (1986–1988) 10 I.P.R. 575 (Fed. Ct. of Aust.) in which an action for passing off failed because neither of the claimants had used the name "Australian Estates" since acquiring three years earlier the business previously well-known under that name.

descriptive)[48] the mere fact that the defendant adopts a name containing the same descriptive words will not establish any sort of case of passing off; a trader cannot monopolise a mere description.[49] The claimant must (as in any other passing off case) establish that the use by the defendants of their trading style is calculated to lead to the belief that their business is the business of the claimant.[50] To do so, it must, in the ordinary way, establish its reputation: that is, that a substantial number of persons associate the words concerned with its business and its alone; as in any ordinary passing off action. But the claimant need not establish that the words concerned have ceased to be descriptive or have acquired a secondary meaning[51] if it can prove its case without.[52] The special character of such cases lies in this: that where a business adopts a name containing words in common use, some risk of confusion may be inevitable, and that risk must be run unless the first such business is allowed an unfair monopoly in those words.[53] In such cases the court will accordingly accept comparatively small differences as sufficient to distinguish,[54] unless the facts nevertheless show serious passing off.[55]

As stated by Templeman L.J. in *McCain International v Country Fair* [1981] R.P.C. 69: "if the plaintiffs introduce a novel product with novel words, but they take the risk of choosing descriptive words, then they run the risk that the defendants cannot be prevented from using those same descriptive words so long as they make it clear that their brands of the product are not the same as the brand of the plaintiffs" (at 81).[56]   **15–145**

There may, of course, be strong commercial reasons for choosing a descriptive business name (just as, for short-lived products for example, there may be strong commercial reasons for choosing a descriptive trade mark); and those reasons are likely to be particularly cogent just in the sort of case where a very strong reputation is difficult to establish: so that an action for passing off will be unlikely to succeed in view of the descriptiveness of the name, whilst on the other hand com-   **15–146**

---

[48] *Bristol-Myers v Bristol Pharmaceutical* [1968] R.P.C. 259, see para.15–109, and compare the "geographical" cases, Ch.11.

[49] See *Equity Access v Westpac* (1989) 16 I.P.R. 431, in which Hill J. noted: "Just as the distinction between descriptive and fancy names is not a distinction in law so too is it wrong to see the distinction in black and white terms. The reality is that there is a continuum with at the extremes purely descriptive names at the one end, completely invented names at the other and in between names that contain ordinary English words that are in some way or other at least partly descriptive. The further along the continuum towards the fancy name one goes, the easier it will be for a plaintiff to establish that the words used are descriptive of the plaintiff's business. The closer along the continuum one moves towards a merely descriptive name the more a plaintiff will need to show that the name has obtained a secondary meaning, equating it with the products of the plaintiff (if the name admits of this, a purely descriptive name probably will not) and the easier it will be to see a small difference in names as adequate to avoid confusion": at 448.

[50] *Office Cleaning v Westminster* (1946) 63 R.P.C. 39 at 42, HL.

[51] *Office Cleaning v Westminster* (1946) 63 R.P.C. 39 at 41.

[52] See comment by Roxburgh J. on the " *Office Cleaning* " case in *General Radio v General Radio (Westminster)* [1957] R.P.C. 471 at 479–480.

[53] Such a monopoly "might even deter others from pursuing the occupation which the words described" *per* Stephen J. in *Hornsby Building Information Centre v Sydney Building Information Centre* (1978) 140 C.L.R. 216.

[54] *Office Cleaning v Westminster* (1946) 63 R.P.C. 39, HL. More recently, see *Morgan Banks v Select Personnel* (1991) 20 I.P.R. 289 (CA (N.S.W.)): "Select Personnel"/"Select Appointments".

[55] *e.g. Legal and General v Daniel* [1968] R.P.C. 253 (claimants known as "Legal and General", defendants using the business name "Legal & General Enquiry Bureau", but putting the emphasis on "Legal & General", interlocutory injunction granted, CA); *Effluent Disposal v Midlands Effluent Disposal* [1970] R.P.C. 238 (addition of "Midlands" "no distinction at all" because both businesses carried on in the Midlands, interlocutory injunction granted); *Berkeley Hotel v Berkeley International* [1971] F.S.R. 300 (addition of "International" to "Berkeley Hotel" no distinction. cf. the "Hotel International" case).

[56] Referred to by Burchett J. in *Film Investment Corp v Golden Editions* (1994) 28 I.P.R. 1 at 19 (Fed. Ct. of Aust), rejecting a claim of passing off by the use of the words "animated classics".

petition from a concern of somewhat similar name can be particularly damaging. Thus the action may be least likely to succeed just where its success could be commercially most valuable. But such actions seldom go beyond the stage of an application for an interim injunction;[57] and here the current practice, under which a claimant need show only an arguable case,[58] means that relief will now be granted in many more instances than the old precedents might suggest.

15–147

(1) In the case of two companies doing business as office cleaners in the same area, it was held that the difference between "Office Cleaning Services" and "Office Cleaning Association" was sufficient: notwithstanding that "Office Cleaning Association" was not the defendant's corporate title: *Office Cleaning v Westminster*, above.

(2) See "General Radio," illustration (3), below, para.15–287.

(3) Where the claimant had had fruitless discussions with the defendant for the "anglicisation" of its US software product "BizPlan Builder" and the defendant later launched its own similar product under the name "BusinessPlan Builder", an interlocutory injunction was granted. The judge (Knox J.) referred, on the issue as to whether "BizPlan Builder" was purely descriptive, to the fact that the defendant had registered its version "BusinessPlan Builder" as a service mark: "they may have been wrong in their implicit assertion that the mark is capable of being distinctive, but it is difficult for them at this stage to contend that they were not arguably right", at 939. *Jian Tools* for *Sales v Roderick Manhattan Group* [1995] F.S.R. 924.

(4) The name "Fantasyland" had been used for more than 35 years by the claimants, Walt Disney Productions, for theme parks, which had been advertised extensively. The court rejected a contention that the name was descriptive (although recognising that it is formed by combining two ordinary words) and granted an injunction restraining use by the defendant of the name on an amusement area described in advertising literature as "an indoor Disneyland": *Triple Five Corp v Walt Disney Productions* (1995) 29 I.P.R. 639 (CA of Alberta).

(5) The claimant had sold for many years a product called "Bar's Bugs", used for cleaning car windscreens. The defendant launched a similar product called "Bug Off". In granting an interlocutory injunction, the judge said, of the name: "When one takes an unusual word like "bug", even though it is a word commonly in use now in this country, and uses it to describe a product, if that word has been used by another party where the word would not normally be used, there is an obligation on the person coming into the market to ensure his product is not confused"; *Bars Products v Holt Lloyd* (1991) 20 I.P.R. 87 at 92 (HC (N.Z.)).

(6) Further instances: "Music Corporation" was held not descriptive in the above sense: *Music Corp of America v Music Corp (Great Britain)* (1947) 64 R.P.C. 41; so was "Computervision" for electronic equipment: *Computervision v Computer Vision* [1975] R.P.C. 171. So was "Midland Dairies" for an ice-cream business: *Midland Counties v Midland* (1948) 65 R.P.C. 429. "Cool Foods" was held too close to "Chill Foods," although one was wholesale and the other retail: [1977] R.P.C. 522, (O.H., Sc.). But injunctions have been refused on "Self Drive" (*Drive Yourself v Par-*

---

[57] In refusing to grant an interlocutory injunction (but ordering a speedy trial) in *Stacey v 20/20 Communications* [1991] F.S.R. 49, Millett J. noted that the scale of the claimant's business was small and the name at issue (20/20 Telecom) had been adopted by a number of companies in the communications industry: at 53.

[58] See paras 19–078 to 19–097.

ish [1957] R.P.C. 307); "Credit Management" ([1961] R.P.C. 157) and "Tape Recorder Centre" (*Sylpha v Tape Recorders* [1961]) R.P.C. 27, one wholesale and the other retail); and injunctions were refused in *Salaried Persons Post Loans v Postal and Salaried Loans of Glasgow* [1966] R.P.C. 24, Sc.) and in *Premier Motor Co v Premier Driving School* [1962] R.P.C. 222). In *Technical Productions v Contemporary Exhibitions* [1961] R.P.C. 242, the court refused an interlocutory injunction to restrain the defendants holding an exhibition with a title including "refrigeration" at about the same time as and at a near-by hall to the plaintiffs'. An interlocutory injunction was refused in *Coral Index v Regent Index* [1970] R.P.C. 147 because the only similarity between the parties' names was the word "Index" which was descriptive of their businesses of accepting wagers on the Financial Times Share Index; a final injunction was refused in *Industrial Furnaces v Reaves* [1970] R.P.C. 605 at 625 (addition of "Reaves" to the descriptive words "Industrial Furnaces" a "sufficient difference to avert confusion"); an interlocutory injunction was refused in *Pet Library v Ellson* [1968] F.S.R. 359 ("Ellson's Pet Library", a "plain case"); an interlocutory injunction was refused in *Park Court Hotel v Trans-World* [1970] F.S.R. 89 ("Hotel International" and "London International Hotel"); an interlocutory injunction was refused in *County Sound v Ocean Sound* [1991] F.S.R. 367 ("The Gold A.M." too descriptive, not long enough use), referring to *McCain International v Country Fair* [1981] R.P.C. 69 ("Oven Chips"). It is of course helpful to a defendant if there are differences in field of activity and if the customers are businesses likely to be clear who they are dealing with, as in "Credit Management", above.

Taking an existing name as a whole

If a new company takes the whole name of a subsisting company, even though that name is of a descriptive character, there is a high probability of deception. **15–148**

(1) The Manchester Brewery Co Ltd had a brewery and a large business at Manchester. A new company which had acquired a brewery at Macclesfield with a business extending to Manchester, as well as other towns attached to it, was restrained from trading as the "North Cheshire and Manchester Brewery Co Ltd" on the ground that the use of the name would amount to a representation that the new company was an amalgamation comprising the business of the complainants: *Manchester Brewery v North Cheshire.*[59]

(2) An injunction was refused against a defendant trading under a name whose initials were the claimant's name: but it appears that the court would have intervened if the defendant had traded under its initials: *I.D.W. v Duncan Harris* [1975] R.P.C. 178. cf. an older case, *A.G.S. v Aeroplane General Sundries*, where the defendants in effect tried to persuade customers that the initials "A.G.S." meant them; held passing off, notwithstanding that the initials "A.G.S." were in general use to describe the "sundries" in which both companies dealt: (1918) 35 R.P.C. 127, CA.

But there is no rule of law that the use of a descriptive word in the name of a new company is deceptive and, therefore, unlawful if it forms part or even the whole of the name of a previously existing company engaged in a similar trade.[60]

---

[59] [1899] A.C. 83.
[60] In *Aerators v Tollit* (1902) 19 R.P.C. 418, a claim to stop "Automatic Aerator Patents Ltd" failed; *British Vacuum Cleaner v New Vacuum* [1907] 2 Ch. 312; 24 R.P.C. 641; *Randall v Bradley*

NAME SUGGESTING A BRANCH OR AGENCY

15–149   If the name of the defendant company is one which is calculated to lead to the belief that it is an agency, branch or department of the claimant company, an injunction will be granted,[61] unless, of course, what is suggested is true.[62] In *Harrods v Harrodian School* [1996] R.P.C. 697, Millett L.J. considered that it was "the gist of the matter" whether people would think that the defendant was "either a branch of the plaintiff or a client in some way amalgamated with or under the supervision of the plaintiff and for which the plaintiff had in some way made itself responsible" (emphasis added by the judge).[63]

NAME COMPRISING CLAIMANT'S TRADE MARK

15–150   Injunctions have been granted, in a number of cases, to restrain a defendant from trading under a name resembling or including the claimant's trade mark, as distinct from the claimant's trading name. An injunction against use of the claimant's trade mark as a trade mark, and an injunction against use of it in a trading style, do not necessarily go together, for the types of confusion they are intended to prevent are different. If, however (as must often be the case), use of the claimant's mark in the defendant's trading style leads to its application by others to the defendant's goods, the claimant is entitled to an injunction against such use.[64] It would furthermore seem obvious that if the trade mark is a really inherently distinctive one (as in the "Kodak" case, below) most customers will assume that any company with that mark in its name is either an offshoot of the owner of the mark or that owner having changed its name.

(1)   The claimants, proprietors of "Wright's Coal Tar Soap", sold, *inter alia*, baby powder under their mark "Wright's". The defendant, W.F.T. Wright, trading as "Wright's Chemical Company", also sold baby powder. At the trial, it was found that the defendant had passed his baby powder off as "Wright's" (and he was enjoined from marking his goods "Wright's"), but in spite of a finding that his use of the name "Wright's Chemical Company" had caused dealers in baby powder to call his goods "Wright's" the trial judge refused an injunction against trading under the name "Wright", since it was his own name. The Court of Appeal considered this illogical, and enjoined him from trading under a name of which "Wright" or "Wright's" formed part without clearly distinguishing his business from that of the claimants: *Wright, Layman & Umney v Wright* (1949) 66 R.P.C. 149.

(1907) 24 R.P.C. 657 at 773 ("Anglo-American Shoe Co"); *Electromobile v British Electromobile* (1907) 24 R.P.C. 688; 25 R.P.C. 149.

[61] *Lloyd's v Lloyd's (Southampton)* (1912) 29 R.P.C. 433. However it may not be possible to obtain an interlocutory injunction since there may not be an immediate danger of irreparable damage to the claimant, see *Marathon Oil v Marathon Shipping* [1968] R.P.C. 443. See also paras 15–046 to 15–050, as to the relevance of a common field of activity. Also, on domain names suggesting a similar connection, see the "Yahoo®" case, at para.15–150, illustration (4).

[62] As in *Habib Bank v Habib Bank Zurich* [1982] R.P.C. 1: use by defendants of "Habib" was a representation only of some sort of connection with the claimants, and the defendants had in fact originally been set up by the claimants. But note that the claimants had not only set the defendants up in Zurich, but helped to establish them over here: a former associate, coming newly over here where only the claimant was known, could expect little encouragement from the courts. See also *Scandecor Development v Scandecor Marketing* [1999] F.S.R. 26, CA.

[63] At 712–713, citing Farwell J. in *British Legion v British Legion Club* (1931) 48 R.P.C. 555. For a similar analysis, see *Triple Five v Walt Disney* (1995) 29 I.P.R. 639 (CA, Alberta).

[64] See examples below, but cf. "Amami", *Prichard and Constance v Amata* (1925) 42 R.P.C. 63; where a business name injunction was refused. Note the part played in these cases by disputes as to the form of injunction.

(2) The claimant owned a trade mark, "Kodak", well-known for cameras and films. The court enjoined the "Kodak Cycle Co Ltd.", and another company which had promoted it, from carrying on business under any name comprising the word "Kodak". There was some suggestion that the trades in cameras and in bicycles went together: *Eastman v Griffiths* (1898) 15 R.P.C. 105.

(3) The claimants had a trade mark of which the essential feature was the word "June". The defendants, June Perfect Limited, trading in the same sorts of goods, marked their goods "June". The defendants sold only to Woolworths (who did not confuse them with the claimants) and retail purchasers were not necessarily aware of the defendants' trading style. The House of Lords, whilst dismissing appeals against injunctions granted by the Court of Appeal to restrain infringement and passing off by the use of the word "June", varied the order by omitting a third injunction which had been granted restraining the defendants from carrying on business (in the goods concerned) under any name comprising the word "June" and calculated to deceive the public into the belief that they were the same company as, or connected with, the claimants. The reason for refusing this injunction was that, in the view of the House of Lords, the first defendants could by taking proper precautions sell and deal with the three articles concerned in connection with their name June Perfect Ltd, while clearly distinguishing those goods from the goods of the claimants: *Saville Perfumery v June Perfect* (1941) 58 R.P.C. 147, HL, speech of Lord Maugham at 176.

(4) The claimant owned many trade mark registrations around the world for the mark "Yahoo!' and had made an application for registration of it in India. The defendant used the trading name "Netline Internet Solutions" but registered the domain name yahooindia. com. In finding that Internet users would likely be deceived into believing a common source or a connection and that domain names performed the same function as trade marks, the court granted an interlocutory injunction: *Yahoo! Inc v Akash Arora* [1999] F.S.R. 931 (HC, Delhi).

NAME NEED NOT BE THE CLAIMANT'S "REAL" NAME

The name sued upon need not be the personal or corporate name of the claimant.[65]   **15–151**
It need not even be that of a predecessor in business, for a business may lawfully adopt and operate under any name which is unappropriated for businesses of the same kind, and when the name has become its by repute, it is as well entitled to protection for that name as for its own.[66]

(1) Where the claimants made and sold a sauce which they called by the name of one of their servants, "Holbrook's Worcester Sauce", and the servant left them and joined the defendants, who advertised that they had acquired the right to make "Holbrook's Worcester Sauce", it was shown that the sauce sold by the claimants was well-known as theirs by the name. It was

---

[65] An assumed name may be part of the goodwill of a business, and the right to use it sold as part of the goodwill, as in *Pomeroy v Scale* (1907) 24 R.P.C. 177 and cases cited below.

[66] *Isaacson v Thompson* (1871) 41 L.J.Ch. 101 ("Mme Elise"). The names may be the colloquial name of the claimants: *Heels v Stafford Heels* (1927) 44 R.P.C. 299, the claimants being known as Heels of Stafford; *Dickinson v Apsley Press* (1937) 54 R.P.C. 219, the claimants carrying on business at Apsley Mills and being known as "Apsley". In *British Diabetic Association v Diabetic Society* [1996] F.S.R. 1, Robert Walker J., in referring to the "Heels" case, noted "the fact that members of the public make mistakes about a person's name—even that such mistakes are, in absolute terms, numerous—cannot by itself lead to the conclusion that every mistaken variant of a business name is entitled to the same protection as the correct name".

held that they had a right to the name in question, and that Holbrook could not sell it to the defendants, and an interlocutory injunction was granted: *Birmingham Vinegar Brewery v Liverpool Vinegar* [1888] W.N. 139. In that case the sauce was identified by the name with the claimants, and not with Holbrook; an opposite result would have been reached if the name had been understood to indicate that the latter person was the actual maker of the goods, and that they were his goods of which the claimants happened to be vendors: see next illustration.

(2) The claimant had organised a series of concerts, conducted by one Herr Richter and known as "Richter Concerts", for many years, when Herr Richter made arrangements to conduct the rival concerts of the defendants. It was held that the defendants might rightly advertise their series under the name, since it was understood to mean, not concerts got up by the claimant, but anybody's concerts conducted by Richter: *Franke v Chappell* (1887) 57 L.T. (N.S.) 141.

ASSIGNMENT OF TRADING NAME TO OR BY A LIMITED COMPANY

15–152   A limited company, by the purchase of a business, often becomes entitled to a name which is different from its registered name, and so becomes entitled, if it does not abandon the name, to prevent others so using it as to represent that they are carrying on the business formerly carried on under it: moreover, the company could sell the name with the goodwill.[67] If a limited company sells its goodwill, a third person will not be permitted after the dissolution of that company to adopt its name, so as to lead to the belief that his business is that formerly carried on by the company and so to injure the purchaser.[68]

Licensing of trade name: "franchising"

15–153   An Australian company, J.H. Coles Pty. Ltd, authorised a shopkeeper to call his shop "J.H. Coles 3d., 6d. and 1s. Stores", the arrangement being that the goods sold in the shop would come from the J.H. Coles company. (There seems to have been a chain of such shops.) The Privy Council (deciding in favour of the company a dispute as to the shopkeeper's right to go on using the name after the authority was determined) appears to have considered this a proper way of working, so long as a connection in the course of trade was maintained between the J.H. Coles company and the goods sold in the shop: *Coles v Need* (1933) 50 R.P.C. 379. This sort of "franchising" operation has of course since become common; it would probably now be held that not only the franchisor but also any franchisee substantially affected could sue to protect the right to the name. In a different context (a restrictive covenant case), Neuberger J. noted of a franchise relationship: "the franchisor ... and the franchisee ... each have a business. They are symbiotic businesses, and the goodwill provision ... indicates that the franchisee ... has the benefit of the goodwill as long as he is franchisee": *Dyno-Rod v Reeve* [1999] F.S.R. 148 at 153.

A NEW COMPANY MAY CONTINUE AN ESTABLISHED NAME

15–154   A limited company formed to take over a business may adopt and use a name

---

[67] *Macmillan v Ehrmann* (1904) 21 R.P.C. 357, 647; *Pearks, Gunston v Thompson, Talmey* (1901) 18 R.P.C. 185.

[68] *Montreal Lithographing v Sabiston* [1899] A.C. 610 (PC); *Townsend v Jarman* (1900) 17 R.P.C. 649.

embodying a name under which the business has already been lawfully and properly carried on.[69]

However, the purchase of the goodwill of a business (together with the right for the acquirer to represent itself as continuing the former business) does not imply a right to use the trading name formerly used in that business.

In *Dawnay, Day v Cantor Fitzgerald* [2000] R.P.C. 669, CA, the court-appointed administrator of a deadlocked company (50 per cent owned by the claimant) had sold to the defendant the assets of the business carried on under the name "Dawnay, Day Securities" ("DDS"). The sale agreement also gave the defendant the right to use the name DDS "so far as it is lawfully able to do so". The Court of Appeal upheld the judgment of Lloyd J. finding passing off. Although the joint venture agreement setting up DDS was silent as to the name under which the new company would trade, one of its provisions permitted the parties "to make it known that the Company is part of the Dawnay, Day Group". The Vice-Chancellor, Sir Richard Scott, found that it was implicit that such use would stop when it was no longer true and, referring to *Coles v Need*,[70] that the defendant could not show that the use of the name by the joint venture had had "the effect that the style has ceased to be distinctive of the licensor", *i.e.* the claimant. The case highlights the importance of regulating expressly by contract the use of trading names by third parties, including joint venture companies.

15–155

RIGHT TO USE A NAME NOT ATTACHED TO ANY GOODWILL CANNOT BE SOLD

A vendor who has no business goodwill to sell cannot convey any right to the use of a business or trading name: and in particular, a man cannot give to another the right that he himself may have[71] to trade under his own name.

15–156

The claimants, Kingston, Miller & Co Ltd, were caterers. Thomas Kingston, one of their managers and well-known to customers, left them to become managing director of a new catering company, Thomas Kingston & Co Ltd. It was contended that he had something in the nature of goodwill attached to his name of which he could give the benefit to the defendant company, namely, qualifications such as personal skill and experience in the business. But it was held that he had nothing in the nature of goodwill to transfer, and that, although he could make use of his personal qualifications, the name was not incident to that qualification in the sense that it could be transferred to a third person and give to that third person the right to use it regardless of the fact that it might mislead the public: *Kingston, Miller v Kingston* [1912] 1 Ch. 575; 29 R.P.C. 289.[72]

Where a person bearing the surname in dispute is associated with the business in the capacity of designer, or something of that sort, it may be proper to say so; but only the purchase of an existing goodwill, associated with a particular trading style, can give any special right to the use of that style.[73] An existing goodwill in a rather different trade may suffice to prevent passing off; but an attempt to justify

15–157

---

[69] So that cases where the defendant has done this are treated by the court as "ordinary use of own name" cases, as in *Chivers v Chivers* (1900) 17 R.P.C. 420, Farwell J. at 426. This was fully recognised in *Tussaud v Tussaud* (1890) L.R. 44 Ch.D. 678, where, however, the condition did not obtain.

[70] (1933) 50 R.P.C. 379.

[71] See paras 15–213 to 15–218.

[72] *Fine Cotton Spinners v Harwood Case* [1907] 2 Ch. 184 at 190; 24 R.P.C. 533 at 538.

[73] cf. the previous paragraph and *Tussaud v Tussaud* (1890) 44 Ch.D. 678.

adoption of a questionable name by purchase of a goodwill associated with different goods may well be viewed with suspicion by the court.[74]

15–158   Henry Meadows Ltd, manufacturers of internal combustion engines, called an engine designed by one Dorman a "Meadows-Dorman" engine. In an action for passing off brought by W.H. Dorman & Co, Meadows contended that they were entitled to use the name "Dorman" to indicate the designer. A qualified injunction only was granted as to use of the name "Dorman", but an absolute injunction restraining use of the term."Meadows-Dorman" for the engines: *Dorman v Meadows* [1922] 2 Ch. 332; cf, as to the goodwill in the name of a designer, *Bentley v Lagonda* (1947) 64 R.P.C. 33 at 38–40; and *Birmingham Vinegar Brewery v Liverpool Vinegar Co* [1888] W.N. 139; illustration (1), above, para.15–151.

NAME OF BUSINESS HOUSE OR FACTORY

15–159   The name of a shop[75] or factory[76] may in effect be a trading name or trade mark, to which goodwill attaches, and entitled accordingly to protection against use of similar names so as to pass off. Furthermore, the use of a similar address may be an ingredient in passing off, particularly where businesses have similar names.[77] There is no right to the exclusive use of the name of a mere private house,[78] and no cause of action arises where, although the defendant has adopted, for business purposes, an address likely to be confused with that of the claimant,[79] yet the businesses of the parties are so different that only inconvenience can result and no damage to the claimant's goodwill.[80] Thus, in *Harrods v Harrodian School*[81] Millett L.J. considered that "[c]ustomers of the plaintiff ... would ... be incredulous if they were told that Harrods had opened a preparatory school".

---

[74] *Holloway v Clent* (1903) 20 R.P.C. 525; *Rodgers v Hearnshaw* (1906) 23 R.P.C. 349.

[75] *Boussod, Valadon v Marchant* (1907) 24 R.P.C. 665; 25 R.P.C. 42 ("Goupil Gallery"); *Bodega v Owens* (1890) 7 R.P.C. 31; 23 L.R.Ir. 371 ("Bodega Wine Shop"). In *Clock v Clock House* (1936) 53 R.P.C. 269, an injunction was granted restraining the defendants from carrying on business under certain names of which Clock formed part, but limited to particular premises about five miles distant from the claimants' premises, as well as an injunction in more general terms. See also *Madeira House v Madeira House (London)* (1930) 47 R.P.C. 481 (interlocutory injunction granted). In *J. Lyons v G. & K. Restaurants* (1955) 72 R.P.C. 259 (rival restaurants both styled "Egg and Bacon") the court indicated that even had the defendants not offered undertakings they would not have been ordered to change the words on facia of shop. The defendants in fact undertook to change to "Eggs and Bacon". In *Cooper and M'Leod v Maclachlan* (1902) 18 R.P.C. 380, 19 R.P.C. 27, the defendant was held entitled to use "Castle Brewery", which the claimants also used, there being no probability of deception. As to assignment of marks having a local connotation, see Ch.13.

[76] *Braham v Beachim* (1878) 7 Ch.D. 848, Fry J. ("Radstock Colliery"); *Montgomery v Thompson* [1891] A.C. 217; 8 R.P.C. 361 ("Stone Brewery"). In *Dickinson v Apsley Press* (1937) 54 R.P.C. 219, the successful defendants carried on business as papermakers and printers at Apsley Mills and were known to their customers as "Apsley".

[77] *Pullman v Pullman* (1919) 36 R.P.C. 240. cf. *Nicholson v Buchanan* (1900) 19 R.P.C. 321 ("Black Swan Distillery"), where the business names and businesses were distinct and relief was refused. In *General Equity v General Corp* (1995) 32 I.P.R. 481 (Fed. Ct of Aust.) the fact that the defendant was trading from next door to premises widely known as the claimant's was viewed unfavourably when coupled with the defendant's adoption of the name "Central" and a similar logo to that of the claimant; notwithstanding these misrepresentations the claim of passing off was dismissed as in two and one-half years there was no evidence of confusion.

[78] *Day v Brownrigg* (1878–79) L.R. 10 Ch.D. 294.

[79] cf. *Law Society of England & Wales v Griffiths* [1996] F.S.R. 739, in which a very similar telephone number was the reason for the successful application for an interlocutory injunction.

[80] *Street v Union Bank* (1885) 30 Ch.D. 156; the claimants were advertising agents; the defendant bank adopted (and registered with the GPO) a cable address that the claimants had used for many years. Confusion occurred but an injunction was refused. A claim by the owners of the Royal Albert Hall to restrain Albert Edward Hall from calling his orchestra "Albert Hall Orchestra" was refused as not being liable to cause confusion; the claimants let the hall for entertainments but did not employ any orchestra: *Corporation of Hall of Arts and Sciences v Hall*, 51 R.P.C. 398.

[81] [1996] R.P.C. 697, at 717.

Cases in which a business has been moved from the shop or factory whose **15–160** name is associated with it, and the new owner of the building wants to continue to use the old name, may present a little difficulty. On the one hand, it would seem clear that the new owner is not entitled to use the old name as a means of passing off his business as that of the original owner.[82] On the other hand, the disputed name may be known as that of the building rather than of the business carried on there;[83] and furthermore there would seem to be a presumption that the sale of premises, known by a name, carries with it (in the absence of covenants to the contrary) the right to keep that name for them.[84] The issue of covenants should always be borne in mind by the vendors of property bearing a particular name: it would presumably have been open to the vendor of "the Harrodian Club site" to have secured a covenant not to use the name "Harrodian" or anything confusingly similar in connection with a business carried on from the site.

COMPANY NAMES

Most recent authorities on trading names concern the names of limited companies **15–161** rather than of individuals or of partnerships. The relief claimed in such cases may well include an injunction that will require the defendant to take steps to change its name.[85]

Where an injunction is granted against a limited company carrying on business **15–162** under its registered name, the injunction is usually suspended for a short time to allow the company to change its name.[86]

Where individuals or companies have tried to make a business out of setting **15–163** up numbers of limited companies with well-known names, which they then try to sell to the owners of those well-known names, the courts have in recent years been robust in their treatment of such behaviour. In *Direct Line Group v Direct Line Estate Agency Ltd* [1997] F.S.R. 374, Laddie J., granted an interlocutory injunction in a passing off case brought against three companies with "Direct Line" in their name, noting that the two individual defendants had been behind the registration of a large number of other famous company name registrations. Indicative of the displeasure with which the court viewed such activities, a lump sum order for costs was made with payment to be made within 14 days. Similarly, in *Glaxo v Glaxowellcome* [1996] F.S.R. 388, Lightman J. granted a mandatory injunction requiring the defendant company and the defendant subscribers to take

---

[82] *Rickersby v Reay* (1903) 20 R.P.C. 380 (owner entitled to keep name, but advised by court not to use it, as making distinction from former occupier's business harder); *Berkeley v Berkeley International* [1971] F.S.R. 300 (hotel on old site of claimant's: interlocutory injunction granted). The latter case was referred to in *Pontiac v CDL Hotels* [1998] F.S.R. 839 at 869–870 in which the court granted an injunction restraining the defendant from using the name "Millennium" for hotel services because of the strong likelihood of a deception that they were associated with the claimant's Millenia property complex, which included the "Ritz Carlton, Millenia Singapore" hotel.

[83] As in *Rickerby v Reay*, above; *Nicholson v Buchanan*, above. *Mason v Queen* (1886) 23 S.L.R. 641 would seem, if not decided on wrong principles, to be to the same effect—not all the old cases show a full recognition of the law of passing off.

[84] "Goupil Gallery," above, at (1908) 25 R.P.C. 53, CA, *per* Fletcher Moulton, L.J.

[85] See under "Relief," para.19–049, and, *e.g. Manchester Brewery v North Cheshire* [1899] A.C. 83. See *Hendriks v Montagu* (1881) 17 Ch.D. 638 for one form of injunction. Non-profit making companies stand in the same position as trading companies in this respect: *Lagos Chamber of Commerce v Registrar of Companies* (1955) 72 R.P.C. 263, PC.

[86] See, for instance, *Lloyd's v Lloyd's (Southampton)* (1912) 29 R.P.C. 433; *Midland Counties Dairy v Midland Dairies* (1948) 65 R.P.C. 429; *Letters v Letters (Craigton)* [1967] R.P.C. 209 (Scots).

all steps as lay within their power to change the name of the company.[87] The judge found the defendants to be engaged in a dishonest scheme to appropriate the goodwill of the claimants.

15–164   In *Ben & Jerry's Homemade v Ben & Jerry's Ice Cream Limited*, unreported judgment of Ferris J., January 19, 1995, an interlocutory injunction was refused as there was no evidence that the defendant had traded and assertions that it had no intention of doing so. This must be wrong as otherwise why incorporate a company under such a distinctive name. Thus, in *Fletcher Challenge v Fletcher Challenge Pty Ltd* [1982] F.S.R. 1 (S.C., N.S.W.), an injunction was granted in almost identical circumstances to those in Ben & Jerry's. The *Fletcher Challenge* case was referred to with approval by Aldous L.J. in the domain name case, *BT v One in a Million* [1999] F.S.R. 1.[88] In that judgment, Aldous L.J. reviewed the history of passing off cases in which the defendant had equipped himself with means of identification similar to the claimant. He concluded that "there can be discerned from the cases a jurisdiction to grant injunctive relief where a defendant is equipped with or is intending to equip another with an instrument of fraud... A name which will, by reason of its similarity to the name of another, inherently lead to passing off is such an instrument": at 18.

AUTHOR'S OR ARTIST'S NAME OR *NOM-DE-PLUME*

15–165   An author can restrain the publication under his name of books which are not written by him, on the same principles as a trader can obtain an injunction to protect his trade name or that of his goods.[89]

In *Clark v Associated Newspapers* [1998] R.P.C. 261 the defendant newspaper The Evening Standard published a spoof diary under the title "Alan Clark's Secret Political Diary". The claimant, a well-known politician and diarist, successfully sued for passing off and false attribution (see below). The judge (Lightman J.) found that the layout of the diary in the newspaper "succeeded too well in making the articles look real" and the "contrary representations" (for example the use of the word "Secret" in the title and the content-in part "obvious fantasy, incredible and wild exaggeration") did not sufficiently correct the deception of a substantial number of readers. The judge emphasised that despite his findings the judgment should be no bar to parodies.

15–166   On the other hand, an attempt by the estate of James Joyce to restrain the publication of an unauthorised edition of *Ulysses* by way of the law of passing off failed because the claimant was unable to identify a class of goods identified by the public as "authorised" editions of the author's work.[90]

15–167   A cartoonist may sue upon the use by a rival cartoonist of a confusingly similar signature,[91] or an actor to protect his stage name.[92] A nom-de-plume *prima*

---

[87] Note that the Court has no jurisdiction to order the Registrar of Companies to change the name of a company, circumventing the requirement under s.28(1) of the Companies Act 1985 for a special resolution to change a company name: *Halifax plc v Halifax Repossessions Ltd* [2004] EWCA Civ 331 CA.

[88] On domain names generally, see Ch.23.

[89] *Lord Byron v Johnson* (1816) 2 Mer. 29; cf. *Barnard v Pillow* [1868] W.N. 94 (music) and *Martin v Wright* (1833) 6 Sim. 297 (copy of work of diorama painter).

[90] *Sweeney v Macmillan Publishers Ltd* [2002] R.P.C. 35.

[91] *Marengo v Daily Sketch* (1948) 65 R.P.C. 242 ("Kem" and "Kim"), HL.

[92] *Hines v Winnick* [1947] Ch. 708; 64 R.P.C. 113 ("Dr. Crock and his Crackpots"). Although

facie belongs to the author and is considered to be his stock-in-trade.[93] Disputes as to the ownership of a nom-de-plume, however, normally arise as between author and publisher; and such disputes have in practice been treated as pure questions of contractual right as between the parties, without regard to the considerations peculiar to disputes over a trade mark.[94] Further, it has been held that the writer of a work can maintain an action against the owner of the copyright for the damage occasioned to his reputation by the publication of a new edition of the book, purporting to be prepared by him, but in fact not so prepared.[95]

The author's right to prevent the work of another being passed off as his is quite distinct from the moral right which he may have in his own work; a right contained in s.84 of the Copyright, Designs and Patents Act 1988, under which an author has the right not to have any "literary, dramatic, musical or artistic work" falsely attributed to him.[96] But in the case of a serial publication, the right to use the name of the original author or editor may be part of the goodwill of the business of conducting it, so as to pass on a sale of the goodwill:[97] the original author's name, indeed, becomes a trade mark[98] in the same way as the name of the author of a text-book running into several editions becomes a trade mark.[99]   **15–168**

Upon the principle already stated,[1] the right here under consideration will not enable an author to stop the republication under his name of his own, non-copyright work.[2]

Where the defendants had acquired the English copyright in an old song which the composer, who had a great reputation and a large sale, considered to be without merit, it was held that the composer's rights against the defendants were qualified and restricted by the defendants' right to state that the song was by the composer. The claimant asked for an injunction to restrain the defendants from representing that the song was a new song of the composer, but it was held that the claimant had not alleged and proved what must be proved in an action for passing off goods of one class or quality for the claimants' goods of another class or quality, namely, the existence of the two classes of goods: *Harris v Warren & Phillips* (1918) 35 R.P.C. 217.   **15–169**

---

pleaded as a case of passing off one musical sketch for another, the case was decided as one in which to the public the claimant himself was "Dr. Crock".

[93] *Landa v Greenberg* (1908) 24 T.L.R. 441 ("Aunt Naomi"); referred to in *Modern Fiction v Fawsett* (1949) 66 R.P.C. 230 at 248 ("Ben Sarto"); *Forbes v Kemsley Newspapers* (1951) 68 R.P.C. 183 ("Mary Delane").

[94] There is always a tendency for disputes as to the ownership of a mark or of goodwill to be decided purely in terms of rights *inter partes*: see, *e.g. Manus v Fullwood & Bland* (1949) 66 R.P.C. 71, CA (dispute between manufacturer and agent); *"Oranje" v Kuys* [1973] 1 W.L.R. 1126 (PC, N.Z.: Ownership of newspaper title). But the decisions on noms-de-plume seem to show no recognition that the subject of the dispute is of the nature of a trade mark at all.

[95] *Archbold v Sweet* (1832) 1 M. & R. 162; 5 C. & P. 219. In *Lee v Gibbings* (1892) 66 L.T. 263, the question was one of libel; interim injunction refused.

[96] See *Clark v Associated Newspapers* [1998] R.P.C. 261 and, on the predecessor s.43 of the Copyright Act 1956, *Moore v News of the World* [1972] 1 Q.B. 441.

[97] *Ward v Beeton* (1874–75) L.R. 19 Eq. 207 ("Beeton's Christmas Annual"). Presumably, on such a sale, the court would imply the necessary licence for the use of an author's name, to exclude s.84 of the Copyright, Designs and Patents Act 1988. It appears from the cases on this point to have been customary to refer to the goodwill in the business of conducting a serial publication as the "copyright" in the publication.

[98] cf. *Condy v Mitchell* (1877) 37 L.T.(N.S.) 766 ("Condy's Fluid").

[99] "Kerly" is clearly a trade mark.

[1] See para.15–165.

[2] *Clemens v Belford* (1883) 14 Fed.Rep. 728, US ("Mark Twain").

TITLE OF NEWSPAPER, OTHER PERIODICAL, BOOK, FILM

15–170   Titles of books, newspapers or other publications also are in principle protected in the same way as business names: no cause of action arises, therefore, unless it is shown that the title is known to indicate the claimant's book or paper, so that its use by the defendant would be calculated to lead to deception; and that the circumstances are such as to permit of such deception.[3] There is usually no copyright in such titles.[4]

15–171   The cases show that it has become difficult, though not impossible to persuade a court that the use of similar or even closely similar names for rival newspapers or periodical publications will result in passing off; of course, most periodical titles in particular are largely descriptive; even in comparison with the cases on descriptive trading names generally,[5] it is comparatively rare for actions on titles of publications to achieve any success. However, two recent cases have bucked this trend, and may indicate a greater willingness by the courts to restrain such use.

(1) The publishers of the *Daily Mail* and *Mail on Sunday* were granted an injunction to restrain the proposed launch of a new evening newspaper under the tile *London Evening Mail*: *Associated Newspapers Limited v Express Newspapers* [2003] F.S.R 51.

(2) An interim injunction was granted to the publisher of a range of free newspapers entitled *Bedfordshire on Sunday, Dunstable on Sunday Leighton Buzzard on Sunday, Milton Keynes on Sunday, Hertfordshire on Sunday* and *Royston on Sunday* restrain the sale of a free Sunday paper entitled *Northants on Sunday*: *Local Sunday Newspapers Ltd v Johnston Press plc* (2001) 24(9) I.P.D. 24062.

(3) An interlocutory injunction was granted to the proprietors of a periodical publication for children called *Eagle* against the use of the word "Eagle" in the name of a children's holiday camp: *Hulton v White Eagle* (1951) 68 R.P.C. 126.

(4) The proprietors of two weekly newspapers, the *London Weekly Advertiser* and the *National Advertiser*, sued to restrain the use by a similar periodical of the title *National Weekly*. No order was made on the motion on the defendants giving an undertaking in the "Teofani" or "Corona"[6] form: *Brittain v Trade & Commercial Press* [1957] R.P.C. 134.

(5) The proprietors of a London daily newspaper, *The Morning Post*, sought to restrain the publishers of a new evening newspaper from calling their paper *The Evening Post*. The Court of Appeal, holding, as an inference of fact, that there was no probability of the defendants' paper being taken for the claimants', or being taken to have any connection with it so as to cause damage to the claimants, dismissed the action: *Borthwick v Evening Post* (1888) 37 Ch.D. 449, CA.

(6) The owners of the *Evening Times* published in Glasgow were held not entitled to restrain the publication of a paper of the same name published in London, there being no competition and no resemblance between the papers: *Outram v London Evening Newspapers* (1911) 28 R.P.C. 308. Similarly the American proprietors of a shilling monthly magazine called

---

[3] *Mathieson v Pitman* (1930) 47 R.P.C. 541 (How to Appeal against Your Rates was held not to have acquired a secondary or special meaning).
[4] *Mathieson v Pitman* (1930) 47 R.P.C. 541, at 549.
[5] See para.15–100.
[6] See *Teofani v Teofani* (1913) 30 R.P.C. 446; *Havana Cigar v Oddenino* (1924) 41 R.P.C. 47.

Everybody's Magazine failed to obtain an injunction against the proprietors of a penny weekly paper known as *Everybody's Weekly*, there being no competition and no resemblance except in the word "Everybody's": *Ridgeway v Amalgamated Press* (1912) 29 R.P.C. 130.

(7) In an action to restrain use of the periodical name "Today", by claimants who had published a periodical under that name in the past, but nine years ago had "incorporated" it in another periodical, retaining a mere mention of "Today" on the inside frontispiece, it was held that the claimants no longer had a sufficient reputation to maintain the action: the right to the name of a periodical is not like a trade mark, which, once registered, remains effective until abandoned: *Kark v Odhams* [1962] R.P.C. 163.

(8) Other older cases where injunctions were refused: "Magazine of Fiction" (*Stevens v Cassell* (1913) 30 R.P.C. 199), "How to Appeal Against Your Rates" (*Mathieson v Pitman*) (1930) 47 R.P.C. 541); and to "Adventure" against "Hutchinson's Adventure Story Magazine" (*Ridgeway v Hutchinson* (1923) 40 R.P.C. 335). "Rubber & Plastic Age" against "Rubber & Plastics Weekly" (*Technial Rubber & Press v Maclaren* [1961] R.P.C. 264); to "Maidenhead Advertiser" (known locally as "The Advertiser") against "New Advertiser" (distributed free; *Bayliss v Darlenko* [1974] F.S.R. 284); to "Morning Star" against "The Star" (no arguable case: *Morning Star v Express* [1979] F.S.R. 113); to "Athletics Weekly" against "Athletics Monthly" (with a different get-up: *World Athletics v Webb* [1981] F.S.R. 27, CA); to "Sunday below" (with small Kent circulation) against "South East Sunday below" (*Thomson v Kent Messenger* [1975] R.P.C. 191); to a periodical "Newsweek" against a BBC feature of the same name (in spite of possibility of ambiguous quotations, etc.: *Newsweek v BBC* [1979] R.P.C. 441, CA). See further *Allen v Brown Watson* [1965] R.P.C. 191, illustration 4, para.15–137.

(9) Amongst newer cases, injunctions were refused to: *Advancing Magazine Publishing v Redwood Publishing* [1993] F.S.R. 449. There was no arguable case that a magazine entitled *BBC Gourmet Good Food* would be confused with the title *Gourmet*. *County Sound v Ocean Sound* [1991] F.S.R. 367 above, para.15–147 illustration 6, a case involving the name of a radio programme ("The Gold A.M."). *Management Publications v Blenheim Exhibitions Group* [1991] F.S.R. 348 and 550, CA: the claimants argued that the public would think that the two publications Management Today and Security Management Today were connected. Held, arguable case in passing off; injunction refused on the balance of convenience. *Marcus Publishing v Hutton-Wild* [1990] R.P.C. 576, CA, above, para.15–022. *Tamworth Herald v Thomson Free Newspapers* [1991] F.S.R. 337: the claimant published the *Tamworth Herald* and a free sheet, the *Tamworth Herald Extra*. The defendants proposed to rename *Tamworth Trader* the *Tamworth Herald* and below. The mastheads looked different and would make it clear that the paper had been renamed. Held, no arguable case.

(10) For other cases where an injunction was granted: Amongst older cases, "Morning Mail" (*Walter v Emmott*, above); "The Grocer" (*Reed v O'Meara* (1904) 21 L.R.Ir. 216); and on the ground of gross fraud in "Bradshaw" (*Blacklock v Bradshaw's* (1926) 43 R.P.C. 27); Amongst more recent cases see *Morgan Grampian v Training Personnel* [1992] F.S.R. 267. The claimants published a series of titles including the expression "What's New In ...". The defendants had used the title "Training Personnel", but changed it to "What's New In Training". An injunction was granted on the balance of convenience.

PLAYS, FILMS, ETC.

15–172   An author of a play or musical sketch has similarly the right to prevent another person from passing off as a film version of the play or sketch something which is not such a version.[7]

(1) The authors and owners of the copyright in a play called "Sealed Orders" sought to restrain the defendants from using and advertising a film under that name. The action was settled by the defendants agreeing to change the name of their film play to "Orders under Seal", and paying the costs: *Raleigh v Kinematograph Trading* (1914) 31 R.P.C. 143.

(2) An Australian court granted relief to the owners of a television series against a series with similar title, characters and leading actor: *Hexagon v A.B.C.* [1976] R.P.C. 628.

VOICE OF ACTOR

15–173   An application for an interlocutory injunction to restrain the broadcast of an alleged imitation of the claimant's voice in advertisements on commercial television on the grounds of libel, malicious falsehood and passing off was refused in view of the established practice not to grant interlocutory relief on the ground of libel and that if a claim for passing off was maintainable it would involve the same issues as in libel: *Alastair Sim v Heinz* [1959] R.P.C. 75. I the light of the decision in *Irvine v Talksport*[8] the outcome of this case result might well have been different if decided today.

INJUNCTION AGAINST SIGNATORIES OF MEMORANDUM OF ASSOCIATION

15–174   In *Panhard et Lavassor v Panhard-Levassor*[9] the injunction was granted against the defendant company and also against the seven signatories of the memorandum of association forbidding them to use the names Panhard and Levassor, and also forbidding the signatories to allow the company to remain registered under its then present name. But when in *Allen v Original Samuel Allen* (1915) 32 R.P.C. 33 the claimant sued two solicitors' clerks who had signed the defendant company's memorandum of association, the claim against them was simply rejected as "founded on some misapprehension of the effects of the 'Panhard' case."

7. Imitation of get-up

15–175   It is usually true in some degree that a trader's goods are recognised as his by their general appearance, or "get-up". Accordingly, resemblance of get-up is not uncommonly an ingredient in passing off, and it is possible for imitation of get-up

---

[7] *Samuelson v Producers* (1931) 48 R.P.C. 447 and 580 (theatrical sketch The New Car and cinematograph film His First Car). *Hines v Winnick* (1947) 64 R.P.C. 113 ("Dr. Crock and his Crackpots"), sometimes considered as a "stage name" case, was pleaded as passing off one "musical sketch" for another. In an earlier case, *Houghton v Film Booking* (1931) 48 R.P.C. 329, the evidence did not establish that the title "The Younger Generation" used in connection with a film meant in the mind of the film-going public a film based on the play of that name by the claimant. In *Loews v Littler* (1955) 72 R.P.C. 166, held that claimants had not established that the title "Merry Widow" denoted the musical version they owned. See also the form of undertaking agreed in *20th Century-Fox v Gala Film* [1957] R.P.C. 105, in respect of use as title for films of "Anastasia".

[8] [2002] F.S.R. 60.

[9] [1901] 2 Ch. 513; 18 R.P.C. 405, followed in *Suhner A.G. v Suhner Ltd* [1967] R.P.C. 336, in which the *Allen* case was not cited.

alone to amount to passing off. Such cases are rare, since few traders rely on get-up alone to distinguish their goods, so that trade names and word trade marks are ordinarily present too, and in these days, in this country,[10] a difference in names is enough to warn the public that they are getting one trader's goods and not the other's.[11] Accordingly, there can hardly be passing off by get-up alone (in the usual sense of substitution of one make of a product for another) unless the resemblance between the goods is extremely close, so close that it can hardly occur except by deliberate imitation; and even that may not be enough.[12] But there are forms of passing off in which a difference of name is not important: for example, where the goods themselves are distinct enough from the claimant's for a different product name to be expected.[13]

The relative importance to be attributed to names and word marks on the one hand, and to get-up on the other, is a matter upon which different people have different views; with the result that the outcome of disputes about get-up is exceptionally hard to predict.[14]

What is compendiously called the "get-up" of goods—the dress in which they **15–176** are presented to the buyer[15] comprises, in particular, the size and shape of the packages,[16] where the goods have no definite outline, or none which is shown to the buyer, the material, colour[17] and decoration of their wrappers, and the lettering and arrangement of their labels.[18] Where what the buyer sees are the goods themselves, not the packaging, get-up may consist in some capricious or fanciful addition to the goods themselves: paintwork, for instance[19] or colouring,[20] or

---

[10] cf. *White, Hudson v Asian* [1965] R.P.C. 45 (PC, Singapore): Asian customers may be unable to read rival names in roman letters. However, nowadays illiteracy is "an evaporating consideration" in get-up cases: *per* CA Sing. in *Tong Guan Food Products v Hoe Huat Hng Foodstuffs* [1991] 2 M.L.J. 361 at 367.

[11] *Saper v Specter's* (1953) 70 R.P.C. 173 at 178; and see below.

[12] Compare *Saper v Specter's*, above, with *Tavener Rutledge v Specter's* [1959] R.P.C. 83 at 84; 355, CA; note the indication in both cases of deliberate copying of the claimant's get-up, and note that even in the later case an interlocutory injunction was refused: [1957] R.P.C. 498 at 501–502.

[13] And cf. the "Carvino" case, where the defendant altered the name (only) and printed "new name" on the label: (1912) 29 R.P.C. 81: or so the judge below found; but the Court of Appeal, in the absence of serious evidence of confusion, found this get-up not deceptive.

[14] cf. *New Way v Lucking* [1960] R.P.C. 147 with the two Specters cases cited above. Differences in the weight allowed to evidence of conscious imitation, and in willingness to infer a fraudulent intention, play their part here too; cf. also the majority and minority views in the Irish case of *Adidas v O'Neill* [1983] F.S.R. 76 (SC, Ir.).

[15] "The get-up of an article means a capricious addition to the article itself, the colour, or shape, it may be, of the wrapper, or anything of that kind; but I strongly object to look at anything that has a value in use as part of the get-up of the article": *per* Fletcher Moulton L.J. in *Williams v Bronnley* (1909) 26 R.P.C. 765 at 773; a case described by Walton J. in *"Jif"* [1990] R.P.C. 341, as "Quite ridiculous": at 355. In *"Roho"*, Jacob J. considered that this passage is not consistent with *Edge v Niccolls* [1911] A.C. 693; 28 R.P.C. 582, and stated: "Even if one adopts the notion 'capricious feature' rather than 'capricious addition' (so as to get rid of the way the concept of the article on the one hand and a mark or the like being added to it), one ends up with arguments about the necessity of a particular shape: the plaintiff says 'well you could have made it work the same way but made it look different' and the defendant says 'no I couldn't because of such and such technical reason—the shape of my goods is dictated by utility'. The law of registered designs shows what a horrendous road that is, and I cannot think it has any place in a passing off action where the public are being deceived": at 177.

[16] In *Jones v Hallworth* (1897) 14 R.P.C. 225, the colours, patterns, shape and sizes of the claimant's "Selvyt" dusters were imitated; cf. *Jones v Anglo-American Optical* (1912) 29 R.P.C. 1 and 361, the action failed. In *Elliott v Hodgson* (1902) 19 R.P.C. 518, Buckley J., flat-ended cigars were imitated.

[17] As in *White, Hudson v Asian* [1965] R.P.C. 45.

[18] In *Parker and Smith v Satchwell* (1900) 17 R.P.C. 713 the show-cards on which the defendant's goods were sold closely resembled those used by the claimants.

[19] See *Terrapin v Ariston* [1964] F.S.R. 218 at 224, *per* Denning M.R.

fanciful shaping[21] of the goods. Possibly, even purely functional features may give a distinctive get-up that will support an action for passing off[22]: in *Kemtron*, it was found that an utilitarian feature may constitute get-up provided it is distinctive and open to argument that a combination of utilitarian features may be protected, again as long as distinctive[23]; whereas in *Interlego v Tyco*[24], Sir Allan Huggins V.P. rejected this. The better position is that adopted by Fisher J. in *Tot Toys v Mitchell*,[25] that the copying of a functional feature may support a passing off action but only where the get-up in question comprises the capricious way in which an essentially utilitarian objective has been expressed.[26] Thus features of an article which are dictated solely by function are not protected in passing off.[27] In addition, such a passing off action would be likely to succeed only in those unusual cases, such as *Edge v Niccolls* and *"Jif"*, where the shape has become distinctive on its own, rather than in conjunction with a word mark, and the defendant has not clearly distinguished his goods.[28]

15–177   But cases involving the shape of goods—and today most get-up disputes involve the shape of the goods—do present special difficulties. In the absence of deception or confusion, and in the absence of some patent or design monopoly, enforceable copyright, or now registered trade mark,[29] it is not unlawful to copy another's goods,[30] and the courts have shown themselves astute to reject attempts to prevent copying of goods under the guise of passing off actions.[31] Indeed, there is authority for saying that, regardless of any other considerations, the mere copying of goods as distinct from the copying of something capriciously added to the goods can never amount to passing off.[32] This is hardly a satisfactory approach: it is not easy to see why misleading of the public by close imitation of

---

[20] As in *Hoffmann-La Roche v D.D.S.A.*, above, para.15–084, illustration (3) (colouring of pharmaceutical capsule): cf. *Roche v Berk* [1973] R.P.C. 473, where the goods were "typical pills" and relief was refused.

[21] *e.g.* the "Toofies" case, illustration (1), para.15–185. See also *Adcock-Ingram v Beecham* [1978] R.P.C. 232 (South Africa: Domed top on an aerosol can held distinctive, but as usual there were differences preventing imitation of that causing passing off).

[22] *Kemtron v Jimmy's* [1979] F.S.R. 86 (Hong Kong). In noting that despite both parties' products bearing their respective trade marks there did not appear to be any "source motivation" evidence referred to in the judgment, Jacob J. did not consider *Kemtron* "a helpful case", in *" Roho"* [1995] F.S.R. 169 at 179.

[23] Ibid., at 93–94.

[24] (1985–87) 7 I.P.R. 417 (CA,-H.K.).

[25] (1993) 25 I.P.R. 337 at 350 (HC (N.Z.)).

[26] "[I]f there are no obvious alternatives to the way in which an original or unusual idea has been expressed, the very originality or unusualness may help rather than hinder the defendants" (at 355); cf, the judgments of Jacob J. and Aldous L.J. in *Philips v Remington*, op. cit., on the meaning of s.3(2)(b) of the 1994 Act: according to Aldous L.J. its purpose was to exclude from registration shapes dictated by technical considerations: at 821.

[27] This is considered a matter of public policy by the High Court of South Africa. *Triomed (Pty) Limited v Beecham Group plc* [2001] F.S.R. 583.

[28] See para.15–180.

[29] As to which, see Ch.8.

[30] It was decided by Lehane J. in *Philips v Remington* (1998) 39 I.P.R. 283 that "unless Philips is entitled to a monopoly in that configuration [of its razor head] by virtue of particular intellectual property rights *e.g.* registered trade marks or registered designs) then another trader may copy it provided that it is clearly indicated that the copied product is not a Philips but a product of the other trader": at 294. The learned judge considered it unnecessary to add "this machine is not a Philips".

[31] See, *e.g. Interlego v Croner* (1991) 21 I.P.R. 373 (Fed. Ct. of Aust.) at 47, where mere copying of the claimant's plastic bricks was found not to constitute passing off (although passing off was found for other reasons): "The matters I have to be careful about are that confusion itself is not enough and that one must guard against cases in which customers or potential customers have been misled not by anything done by a defendant but rather by their own misconceptions or misunderstandings": *per* Sheppard J.

[32] *Terrapin v Ariston*, above, comes very close to deciding just that, quoting Fletcher Moulton L.J.

goods should be treated any differently from misleading of the public in any other way, whilst the distinction between the goods in themselves and features added capriciously to them belongs, perhaps, more to the realms of metaphysics than of commercial design.[33] Certainly there has been a tendency to adopt this approach to deal with such cases according to the ordinary principles governing passing off—whilst scrutinising the claimant's evidence of reputation with care, to make sure that any preference shown by the public for his goods results from their associating the particular design or style concerned with the claimant, not merely from a preference for that particular style or design.[34]

At the same time as the courts have shown a certain tendency to reject out of hand allegations of passing off based merely on copying of the design of the goods,[35] they have shown a complementary tendency to treat as inherently unlawful the copying of fanciful characteristics of goods or packaging.[36] This, too, however, involves a departure from the principles laid down in the earlier authorities. "Apart from monopolies conferred by patents, and apart from protection afforded by registration, it is open to anyone to adopt the ideas or devices of his neighbours and apply them to his own goods provided he clearly distinguishes his goods from those of his neighbour": a proposition which, stated with reference to a fanciful feature of the goods (a white inlaid spot in the wood of a tobacco-pipe near the join to the mouthpiece),[37] would seem to be equally applicable to novelties of packaging. To the same effect more recently: "Some think that copying is unethical; others do not. Often the copyist of today becomes the innovator of tomorrow. Copying is said by some to be the lifeblood of competition, the means of breaking *de facto* market monopolies and keeping down the price of articles not protected by special monopolies such as patents or registered designs. Others say that copyists are parasites on innovators. None of this matters.

15–178

---

in *Williams v Bronnley* as authority. See also *Benchairs v Chair Centre* [1974] R.P.C. 429 (mere copying of goods not a representation as to trade origin); *Hawkins v Flude's* [1957] R.P.C. 8; and see also the warning in Jarman & Platt v Barget [1977] F.S.R. 260, CA, that large sales of a unique product do not prove that its get-up has a reputation that will support a passing off action—other evidence of reputation may be hard to get. A case that went the other way is *Plix v Winstone* [1986] F.S.R. 63 (HC, N.Z.: "Pocket packs" for Kiwi fruit).

[33] It has been accepted for many years, by some designers, that fanciful features are only permissible if they do appear to be integral parts of the design. It is, indeed, interesting to compare this question with the corresponding question arising in the law of registered industrial design itself. It was contended many years ago that to qualify for protection by registration an industrial design must involve some purely ornamental feature added to the article. The House of Lords in due course rejected the contention *Hecla Foundry v Walker, Hunter* (1889) 6 R.P.C. 554 at 558–559). It was later held that a design might come too close to being merely the bare bones of an article to be registrable *Tecalemit v Ewarts (No.2)* (1927) 44 R.P.C. 503 at 507–508); but even that proposition may well go too far—cf. *Cow v Cannon* [1959] R.P.C. 347 at 353, CA. It is by no means clear that the proposition discussed in the text has any greater merit than the propositions rejected in the design cases, or that the proposition that there can be no action for passing off merely for copying what could have been registered as a design has any greater merit than the proposition (equally rejected by the courts) that nothing protectable by a patent could be a registrable design.

[34] *British American Glass v Winton* [1962] R.P.C. 230 (copying of ornamental dogs sold without packaging); *Hawkins & Tipson v Fludes* [1957] R.P.C. 8 at 11; and *Gordon Fraser v Tatt* [1966] R.P.C. 505 (copying of style of claimants' greeting cards) would seem to illustrate this approach to such matters. It has been argued that the law has gone too far in protecting products by passing off actions: see Evans "Passing-Off: The Problem of Product Simulation" [1968] M.L.R. 642.

[35] On the obstacles facing the registrability of shapes as trade marks, see Ch.9.

[36] It is difficult to account otherwise for the decision in *New Way v Lucking* [1960] R.P.C. 147.

[37] "White Spot Pipe" case *Dunhill v Bartlett & Bickley)* (1922) 39 R.P.C. 426 at 438. Note the completely literal way in which (it would seem) the judge concerned used the word "distinguish": a large red spot and a small white spot do not look alike, and that is the whole of the case.

Certainly it is not the law that copying as such is unlawful: the common law ... leans against monopolies", *per* Jacob J. in *"Roho"*.[38]

15–179   (1) The claimants sold bags of laundry blue, each bag holding a stick or "dolly" of a particular form. The evidence showed that customers bought entirely by the appearance of the goods, relying in particular on the "dolly". The defendants adopted a similar dolly, and the presence on their goods of their name was in these circumstances held an insufficient distinction: *Edge v Niccolls* [1911] A.C. 693; 28 R.P.C. 582. cf. *Coca-Cola v Barr* [1961] R.P.C. 387, where the use of bottles shaped like the claimants, and unlabelled, was considered deceptive: but an interim interdict was refused in respect of drinks of a different colour from the claimants.

         (2) The claimants sold their soap in packets wrapped up in a peculiar parchment paper, with "Sunlight Self-Washer" printed in spaced type upon the wrapper; the defendants began to use similar packets and paper, with the words "Goodwin's Self-washing Soap" printed upon it in similar type. It was treated as an obvious case of fraud: *Lever v Goodwin* (1887) 36 Ch.D. 1; 4 R.P.C. 492. cf. *Lever v Bedingfield* (1899) 16 R.P.C. 3.

THE "JIF" CASE

15–180   In the *"Jif"* case,[39] Reckett & Colman established that the "Jif" lemon-shaped plastic container had acquired a secondary significance. The question then came down to whether Borden, in adopting containers having the most striking feature of the "Jif" get-up, had taken sufficient steps to distinguish their products. It was found that they had not; this despite the fact that the Borden lemons did have labels which were marked "Realemon". The case can be understood in the light of the particular findings of fact; namely that for customers a crucial point of reference was the lemon shape and that virtually no attention was paid to the label. Shoppers had no reason to read the label or pay any attention to it in order to obtain the goods they required.

15–181   Borden deployed a number of arguments. First, they contended that a distinction must be drawn between a manufactured article itself, and the special trade insignia (such as get-up) used to designate its trade origin. The article itself could not constitute the special insignia of its own origin. Lord Oliver dealt with the argument by rejecting the suggestion that the container was an object in itself rather than part of the get-up. Lord Jauncey, who gave the other principal speech, adopted the more robust position that the shape and configuration of the article could be protected against deception and confusion. He concluded (at 426):

> "this principle [that no man may sell his goods under the pretence that they are the goods of another] applies as well to the goods themselves as to their get-up. A. markets a ratchet screwdriver with a distinctively shaped handle. The screwdriver has acquired a reputation for reliability and utility and is generally recognised by the public as being the produce of A. because of the handle. A. would be entitled to protection against B. if the latter sought to market a ratchet screwdriver with a similarly shaped handle without taking sufficient steps to see that the public was not misled into thinking that his product was that of A."

---

[38] [1995] F.S.R. 169 at 173.
[39] [1990] R.P.C. 341.

The critical point here is that the defendant had not taken sufficient steps to avoid deception.[40]

15–182

Borden also contended that mere confusion was not sufficient to found the cause of action; they argued that all that they had done was to adopt a descriptive device and that Reckitt & Colman were not entitled to relief simply because they had used the same device as descriptive of their own goods and had been the only people previously to adopt that description. This, of course, was not a novel proposition. It is well established that where a descriptive term is used, a claimant must show more than simply the sole use of it. He must show that it has acquired secondary meaning not simply of the goods of that description, but also of goods of which he, and he alone, is the source. The difficulty facing Borden was that the trial judge had found as a fact that the "Jif" lemon container was so distinctive.[41]

15–183

Reckitt & Colman, for their part, accepted that they had to establish deception and confusion and argued that the crucial question is "What moves the public to buy?", a question taken from the judgment of Judge Learned Hand in *Crescent Tool Co v Kilborn & Bishop* (1917) 147 F. 299 (a case about a copy of an adjustable wrench sold under the trade mark "Crescent").[42] Although not expressly referred to in the speeches, it appears (particularly from the passage cited above from the speech of Lord Jauncey) that this was accepted. What a claimant has to do is to prove that it is deception which moves the public to buy the defendant's goods. If successful, the claimant has proved both the fact of misrepresentation and that the misrepresentation was operative. Lord Oliver rejected Borden's contention that there was sufficient differentiation to avoid confusion: "it can be no answer, in a case where it is demonstrable that the public has been or will be deceived, that they would not have been if they had been more careful, more literate or more perspicacious. Customers have to be taken as they are found": at 415.[43]

CLAIMANT MUST PROVE REPUTATION

15–184

As in any other passing off case, a claimant relying upon get-up must prove his reputation: he must prove, that is, that the get-up concerned indicates his goods and no one else's.[44] In particular, he must show that distinctiveness lies in the get-up and not (for instance) in his name or trade marks, if those appear on the

---

[40] See also the statement of Glidewell L.J. in the CA: "I wish only to emphasise ... that if a trader has in fact obtained a monopoly in selling goods in a particular get-up, the longer the monopoly subsists the greater becomes the obligation on another trader who wishes to sell similar goods in competition to ensure that the get-up of his goods is sufficiently distinguished from those already on the market": at 396.

[41] Lord Oliver expressed surprise at the findings at trial of confusion but stated: "it has to be borne in mind that ... the primary retail outlets for these products are supermarkets ... and the purchasing member of the public is reliant on his own perception or recollection, unassisted by the opportunity of side-by-side comparison": at 407.

[42] Also referred to by Jacob J. in " *Roho* " [1995] F.S.R. 169 at 178, as a question which "exactly encapsulates what must be shown" by a claimant. In *Kimberley-Clark v Fort Sterling* [1997] F.S.R. 877, Laddie J., considered that Jacob J. did not intend to suggest that the claimant must show that sales will be diverted but rather was addressing the question of whether the goodwill and misrepresentation requirements were satisfied: at 889–890.

[43] See also *Clark v Associated Newspapers* [1998] R.P.C. 261.

[44] See para.15–018; and *Jones v Anglo-American* (1912) 29 R.P.C. 361; *Saper v Specter's* (1953) 70 R.P.C. 173 at 174. "If reputation is not established, the question of confusion does not arise", *per* Megaw L.J. in *Jarman & Platt v Barget* [1977] F.S.R. 260 at 270. Also, *"Jif"* [1990] R.P.C. 341, *per* Lord Oliver, at 406.

goods.[45] Thus, if a claimant by his cautions and advertisements shows that he relies wholly or mainly on his trade mark or business name, he makes his case on general get-up, apart from trade mark or business name, more difficult to establish.[46] A trader who introduces a new feature into the get-up of his goods does not thereby acquire any proprietary interest in it, so as to be able to prevent its use by competitors, until it has become so identified with his goods that its use by others is calculated to deceive.[47] No case can be made merely[48] by showing an imitation of the parts of the get-up of goods which are common to the trade.[49] But very little evidence of user may be sufficient to establish distinctiveness where the get-up is not only novel but striking,[50] even though it consists of a combination of commonly used parts. The case is then analogous to that of a "fancy word": in *United Biscuits v Asda* [1997] R.P.C. 513, Robert Walker J. considered that the words "Penguin" and "Puffin" were "fancy" in the sense that "an unpalatable bird has no obvious connection with a chocolate-coated sandwich biscuit", at 532. Where the goods themselves are unique, however, merely showing large sales does not prove that their get-up enjoys a reputation.[51]

15–185 (1) The claimants had for some months sold bubble gum in the shape of a set of false teeth, and labelled "Toofy's Bubble Gum". The defendants marketed a similar article, labelled "Margo's Toofies Bubble Gum". On a motion for an interlocutory injunction, the defendants offered an undertaking not to use the word "Toofy's" or "Toofies", and an injunction was refused: Harman J. observing that the claimants "have not shown that any

---

[45] See *Schweppes v Gibbens* (1905) 22 R.P.C. 113, 601 (HL); *King v Gillard* (1905) 22 R.P.C. 327, CA; and the cases cited in para.15–184 therein, especially *Payton v Snelling*. See *Tot Toys v Mitchell*, (1993) 25 I.P.R. 337: "The capricious get-up must be a sine qua non for customer recognition even though it may not be its sole cause" *per* Fisher J. at 355).

[46] *Imperial Tobacco v Purnell* (1904) 21 R.P.C. 368, 598; and see *Coleman v Smith* (1912) 29 R.P.C. 81; *Hennessy v Keating* (1908) 25 R.P.C. 125 and 361 (HL).

[47] Thus, in *Klissers Farmhouse Bakeries v Harvest Bakeries* [1989] R.P.C. 27, Casey J. rejected the claimant's claim of distinctiveness in the use on bread packaging of check or gingham patterns, whilst noting the importance of the fact that the defendant's packaging had a label showing clearly the maker's name and mark: at 37. Bisson J. found that checks were a common feature of the trade: at 44.

[48] But where the colouring of the claimants' label was common to the trade, and the goods were sold under different names, yet the defendants' label contained features liable to be confused with those of the claimants' label and seemed to have been designed with that object, the claimants were held to be entitled to succeed both on infringement and passing off: *Bryant & May v United Match* (1933) 50 R.P.C. 12.

[49] In *Payton v Snelling* [1901] A.C. 308; 17 R.P.C. 628, the claimants had been the first to put coffee in tins enamelled in bright colours; held that the claimants had no monopoly in such tins; and in *Williams v Bronnley* (1909) 26 R.P.C. 481, 765, the claimants had been the first and, for years, the only persons to put on the market shaving-sticks in tin-lined boxes with maroon covers, but at the date of the action these features were held to be common. See also *Hubbuck v Brown* (1900) 17 R.P.C. 148 at 154 (upheld CA, at 638) as to the fashion of the market. In *White, Tomkins v United Confectionery* (1914) 31 R.P.C. 430, it was held that, although the claimants were the only persons who had used a picture of a particular fruit to denote the flavour of their jelly crystals, they had not shown that the particular device was identified with their goods. In *Hawkins & Tipson v Flude's* [1957] R.P.C. 8, action dismissed as claimants had not discharged onus upon them of showing patterns woven into their matting to be distinctive of themselves. In *Politechnika I. Pari v Dallas Print* [1982] F.S.R. 529, the makers of "Rubik" cubes failed to establish that the appearance of the cube denoted their goods. On the other hand, in *EMAP v Security Publications* [1997] F.S.R. 891, the particular combination of features used on the cover of the claimant's classic car magazine was found sufficiently distinctive to justify granting an interlocutory injunction; and in *"Jif"* [1990] R.P.C. 341, Lord Oliver commented of the *Williams v Bronnley* line of cases: "[they] established no fresh principle of law, and are really of very little assistance": at 412.

[50] *Weingarten v Bayer* (1905) 22 R.P.C. 341, HL ("Erect Form" with "corsets" written in a flourish of the "E").

[51] *Jarman & Platt v Bargett* [1977] F.S.R. 260, CA; but large sales of goods under a unique get-up "must go some way" to such proof: *Sodastream v Thorn Cascade* [1982] R.P.C. 459 at 469, CA (CO_2 in grey cylinders).

member of the public, seeing bubble-gum in the shape of false teeth, will associate it with any particular manufacturer at all"; and that the claimants had to prove "that bubble gum cannot be made in that shape without representing to the trade and to the public that those goods are the goods of the plaintiffs": *Blundell v Margolis* (1951) 68 R.P.C. 71.

(2) The petitioners had for a long period sold whisky in bottles of a special shape which had become known as "Dimple" bottles, the whisky being known as "Dimple" Whisky. Interim relief was first granted, and later a perpetual interdict, against use by the defendants of similar bottles: *Haig v Forth Blending* (1952) 69 R.P.C. 323 and (1953) 70 R.P.C. 259.[52]

(3) The claimant had for many years sold a chocolate-coated confectionery product called "Pineapple Lumps", for the previous four years in three sizes of bag with a particular design. The defendant acquired from the receiver a confectionery business which had been marketing *inter alia* a product called "Pineapple Chunks" for many years. The defendant re-designed the packaging and relaunched the product in bags of three sizes the same as those of the claimant (which were an industry norm). An interlocutory injunction was granted, the judge noting the prevalence of impulse purchasing of the particular products: *Griffin v Regina* (1991) 19 I.P.R. 425 (HC (N.Z.)).

"LOOK-ALIKES"

In a "look-alike" case, the defendant supermarket chain sold a chocolate-coated **15–186** sandwich biscuit under the name "Puffin" and the predominantly red packaging included a cartoon depiction of a puffin. The claimant, who had sold successfully for a number of years a similar biscuit called "Penguin" in predominantly red packaging, sued for passing off (and trade mark infringement). In finding passing off, Robert Walker J. found that a substantial number of consumers would think the two products came from the same manufacturer: *United Biscuits v Asda* [1997] R.P.C. 513 at 538. The case highlights the practice in recent years of supermarkets marketing their own-brand "look-alike" products to compete with well-known brand leaders and makes clear that where the "look-alike" comes too close to the product it is designed to compete with, there will be passing off. On the other hand where there is clear differentiation, although the "look-alike" has been inspired by the original product, there will be neither misrepresentation nor deception.

In *"Roho"* Jacob J. found the claimant had failed to establish that the shape of **15–187** their cushion, which the defendant had copied was the "crucial point of reference" for those who wanted specifically a Roho cushion made by the claimant. Despite the evidence that almost all those who saw the defendant's product (or a photograph of it) reacted by saying "that is a Roho", this did not prove the customers wanting a Roho cushion would be deceived into buying the defendant's.[53]

IMITATION OF PART OF GET-UP

It is not necessary for passing off that every part of the get-up should be imitated, **15–188**

---

[52] But in *Haig v Brooks* (1955) 72 R.P.C. 247, interim injunction refused as claimants had not shown that there was any likelihood of the public being deceived by the shape of the defendants' bottles.

[53] [1995] F.S.R. 169, at 179–181.

for, though no exclusive right to the use of any single feature of it which is not a registered trade mark is recognised, yet a part of the get-up—a picture, for instance, which is used on the label or wrapper—may be shown to be so identified with the claimant's goods that its use for similar goods is calculated to pass them off as his. The picture, in effect, may become a "common law trade mark".[54]

15–189 The claimant used the device of a lady and a bear, in his trade as a furrier, by attaching it to the wrappers and boxes in which he sent out his goods, but he had registered it only as a trade mark for sealskin mantles and coats. The defendant began to issue a circular, bearing a similar mark, in connection with his trade which was also that of a furrier. Two injunctions were granted, one restricted to the mantles and coats, to restrain infringement of the trade mark, the other, not so restricted, to restrain the defendant from using the device so as to deceive the public: *Jay v Ladler* (1888) 40 Ch.D. 649; 6 R.P.C. 136.

15–190 On the other hand, the imitation of a number of things, each of which is in itself not distinctive of the claimant's goods, may make a strong case on account of the cumulative effect of the detailed resemblances.[55] The taking by the defendant of a word or words, which though not distinctive, form a prominent part of the claimant's label, may strongly contribute to the passing off.[56]

Only things which are put prominently forward so as to be likely to catch the eye of a purchaser and remain in his memory need generally be considered. Thus, the printing on the back or sides of a box may usually be disregarded in considering whether the get-up of goods is likely to deceive.[57]

GET-UP OF A BUSINESS

15–191 Passing off by get-up is not confined to goods; thus there have been actions relating to passing off by the get-up of a shop[58] and of an omnibus.[59] A recent action in which the get up of retail premises, which failed on the facts, was *BP Amoco v John Kelly plc*.[60] In *Taylor Bros v Taylor Group* (1991) 19 I.P.R. 615 (CA (N.Z.)), the court found it a breach of an earlier injunction, which prohibited the defendant from trading under or by reference to the name "Taylors", for the get-up of the shop to be used in such a way as to suggest continuity, even though the trad-

---

[54] See at para.15–179, and *Weingarten v Bayer*, (1905) 22 R.P.C. 341.

[55] *Lever v Goodwin* (1887) 36 Ch.D. 1, at 4 R.P.C. 505–506, CA, and compare with *Lever v Bedingfield* (1899) 16 R.P.C. 3. See also *Williams v Bromley* (1909) 26 R.P.C. 481 at 486: "I am not prepared to say that there may not be cases in which a trader may acquire by user an exclusive right of monopoly in respect of a combination of two or more matters, which by themselves are absolutely common to the trade," *per* Neville J. See also *Christiansen's T.M.* (1886) 3 R.P.C. 54, CA.

[56] As the words "Self Washer" in *Lever v Goodwin* (1887) 36 Ch.D. 1; 4 R.P.C. 492. See also *Knott v Morgan* (1836) 2 Keen 213, at para.15–191.

[57] *per* Kekewich J. in *Lever v Bedingfield* (1898) 15 R.P.C. 453 at 462 (a box of tablets of soap). Also, *Smith's Potato Crisps v Paige's Potato Crips* (1928) 45 R.P.C. 132: "there is a distinguishing feature in the Defendants' [product] which ought not to be overlooked by any observer with his wits reasonably about him", *per* Lord Hanworth M.R. at 146.

[58] *Laraine Day v Kennedy* (1953) 70 R.P.C. 19; the action failed, but on the facts. In *My Kinda Town v Soll* [1983] R.P.C. 407, it was sought to argue that the get-up of the defendant's restaurant caused deception but the Court of Appeal found that the pleadings did not disclose such an assertion: *per* Oliver L.J. at 419.

[59] *Knott v Morgan* (1836) 2 Keen 213; the fraud consisted in the imitation of the painting of the claimants' omnibuses, the uniforms of their servants and the use of their descriptive title—The London Conveyance Co: *London General Omnibus v Felton*, 12 T.L.R. 213; and *London Road Car v Era Omnibus*, *The Times*, June 23, 1898; *The Times*, April 28, 1899, similar.

[60] [2002] F.S.R 5 The claimant sought to rely on the use of a particular shade of green on the canopy of the defendant's petrol station as constituting a misrepresentation. Held other features (such as the defendant's logo) would dispel any deception engendered by the use of the colour.

ing name had been changed to "Laytons": "[t]he signs at the premises and on the vans and the stationery used ... corresponds exactly with the get-up previously used by the [defendant]", at 619–620, *per* Cooke P.

8. Proof of likelihood of deception

GENERALLY[61]

In the common case the court must be satisfied that the defendant's conduct is calculated[62] to pass off other goods as those of the claimant, or, at least, to produce such confusion in the minds of probable customers or purchasers or other persons with whom the claimant has business relations[63] as would be likely to lead to the other goods being bought and sold for his.[64] This is the foundation of the action. Similarly with any other sort of passing off. The claimant has to prove that it is deception which moves the public to buy the defendant's goods.

15–192

> "... is it, on a balance of probabilities, likely that ... a substantial number of [the relevant class[65]] will be misled into purchasing the defendant's [product] in the belief that it is the respondent's [product].": *per* Lord Oliver in Jif.[66]

Mere confusion is not enough.[67] No one is entitled to be protected against confusion as such.[68] At the heart of passing off lies deception or its likelihood. Never has the tort shown even a slight tendency to stray beyond cases of deception. Were it to do so it would enter the field of honest competition, declared unlawful for some reason other than deceptiveness.[69]

15–193

The onus of proving deception or its likelihood is upon the claimant.

The question of likelihood of deception is for the court (not the witnesses) to decide "looking at the documents and evidence before him."[70] Evidence may be called on the point, but is not essential except in cases of doubt,[71] and the assistance it gives to the court will be of a limited nature unless it includes evidence of actual deception[72] apart from cases turning on the circumstances and practices of

15–194

---

[61] As to the tests to be applied in comparing marks, see Ch.17 on "Deceptive Resemblance." In particular, as to evidence on deceptiveness of resemblance see, para.17–061 to 17–074.

[62] "calculated" in the sense of being the reasonably foreseeable consequence. Fraud is not required.

[63] As in *Pullman v Pullman* (1919) 36 R.P.C. 240.

[64] *Schweppes v Gibbens*, above, para.15–184.

[65] In that case, the relevant class of persons were members of the public. In general the relevant class are "purchasers or probable purchasers of goods of the kind in question": Viscount Maugham, *Saville Perfumery v June Perfect* (1941) 58 R.P.C. 147 at 176.

[66] [1990] R.P.C. 341 at 407. This passage indicates that below-sale confusion can really only be relevant in passing off if the confusion persists through and results in a second/subsequent purchase. The contrary reasoning in *Levi's v Kimbeyr Investments* [1994] F.S.R. 335, High Ct. N.Z., is not convincing.

[67] *Marcus Publishing plc v Hutton-Wild Communications Ltd* [1990] R.P.C. 576 C.A. *per* Dillon L.J. at 580; *County Sound plc v Ocean Sound Ltd* [1991] F.S.R. 367 CA, *per* Nourse L.J. at 376; quoting Lord Greene M.R. in *Marengo v Daily Sketch and Sunday Graphic Ltd* (May 17, 1946) now reported at [1992] F.S.R. 1.

[68] Lord Greene M.R. in *Marengo* (May 17, 1946) now reported at [1992] F.S.R. 1. The passage in question was not questioned when the decision of the CA was reversed on the facts by the House of Lords: (1948) 65 R.P.C. 242.

[69] Jacob J. in *Hodgkinson & Corby Ltd v Wards Mobility Ltd* ("Roho") [1994] 1 W.L.R. 1564.

[70] *Spalding v Gamage* (1915) 32 R.P.C. 273 at 286, HL, *per* Lord Parker of Waddington; it is clear in the context (see the next proposition) that he was contemplating deciding upon the documents alone—as in trade mark cases.

[71] *Spalding v Gamage* (1915) 32 R.P.C. 273.

[72] *Parker-Knoll v Knoll International* [1962] R.P.C. 265 at 285, *per* Lord Hodson, citing *Spalding v*

the particular trade.[73] As in trade mark infringement, expert evidence is of limited use and admissibility.[74] The judge is entitled to give effect to his own opinion as to the likelihood of deception and, in doing so, is not confined to the evidence of the witnesses called at trial.[75] The issue is whether a substantial[76] or large[77] number of relevant trade or public have been misled or are likely to be misled. The deception must be more than momentary and inconsequential.[78]

(1) An advertisement intended as "comparative advertising" was held to involve passing off on evidence showing that many people took it as an advertisement for the claimants' goods, asserting that they were obtainable from the defendants' outlets: *McDonald's v Burgerking* [1986] F.S.R. 45.

(2) The claimant had sold lemon juice in yellow, lemon-sized squeezy packs for many years. The defendant introduced their similarly packaged lemon juice, with a prominent neck label.[79] As the trial judge found, "[t]here would be no difficulty in a careful shopper coming to the conclusion that [none of the defendant's products] was a Jif lemon—it would merely be a question of her ... reading the label." However, on evidence from members of the public who had taken part in a realistic survey, the trial judge found as facts that "The crucial point of reference for a shopper who wishes to purchase a Jif squeezy lemon is the lemon shape itself. Virtually no, if any, attention is paid to the label." The lemon shape had acquired a secondary meaning: *Jif* [1990] R.P.C. 341.

(3) A weekly column in the *Evening Standard* newspaper was entitled "Alan Clark's Secret Political Diary". The articles were parodies of the well-known diaries of Alan Clark. On evidence showing that a number of "rational men" and women believed the articles to have been written by the claimant, passing off was held established. Since the issue was one of authorship, it did not matter that some had not read the articles and merely skim read the newspaper: *Alan Clark v Associated Newspapers Ltd* [1998] R.P.C. 261.

Gamage, above. Jacob J. in *Neutrogena Corporation v Golden Ltd* [1996] R.P.C. 473 (upheld on appeal) made various observations concerning the provision of evidence of deception: (at 483): "The principal advantage [of members of the public giving their evidence in chief by direct oral examination rather than by confirmation of their witness statements] was that they were able to give their account of events directly to me in their own words without any leading." Generally, market surveys, with statistical analysis of the results, are (at 485–486) "unnecessarily elaborate in a passing off action. The court in a passing off case is not concerned with statistical precision. What it wants to know is whether or not there is a substantial degree of deception or confusion. Moreover pure questionnaire evidence is seldom helpful ... But unless one can have some real evidence, tested in cross-examination, one cannot really be sure of what was passing through people's minds. Those cases where surveys have proved to be useful have all involved some of the 'pollees' coming to court". In practice, surveys are used now to find witnesses who were allegedly deceived.

[73] *The European Ltd v The Economist Newspaper Ltd* [1998] F.S.R. 283 at 291, CA; and *Alan Clark v Associated Newspapers Ltd* [1998] R.P.C. 261, Lightman J. at 271, para.3.

[74] See para.17–063.

[75] Lord Diplock in *GE Trade Mark* [1973] R.P.C. 297 at 321, cited by Morritt L.J. in *Neutrogena* [1996] R.P.C. 473 at 495.

[76] It is not necessary to or to be able to extrapolate from the evidence so as to arrive at any quantitative or qualitative measure of the deception caused by the defendant. See Morritt L.J. in *Neutrogena* [1996] R.P.C. 473, at 505. In cases which are near the borderline (and *Neutrogena* was such a case), the Court has to take account of the fact that "... there are always some people who are confused and even when products and names are well-differentiated, mistakes do occur". See Jacob J. in *Neutrogena* , at 482. See also *Irvine v Talksport* in which Laddie J. held that the evidence of a single individual was sufficient to support a claim in passing off, on the basis that a "not insignificant" section of the relevant market would be deceived [2002] F.S.R. 60.

[77] *Saville Perfumery Ltd v June Perfect Ltd* (1941) 58 R.P.C. 147 at 175–176, HL.

[78] *Cadbury-Schweppes Pty Ltd v The Pub Squash Co* [1981] 1 W.L.R. 193 at 205B, PC.

[79] Photographs of the products are at [1990] R.P.C. 341 at 343.

It is not a defence to prove that there are persons who purchase the goods of a defendant who are not misled, if it is established that there are a large number of persons who are.[80]

THE STANDARD REQUIRED

"The essence of the action for passing off is a deceit practised on the public and it can be no answer, in a case where it is demonstrable that the public has been or will be deceived, that they would not have been if they had been more careful, more literate or more perspicacious. Customers have to be taken as they are found."*per* Lord Oliver and *per* Lord Jauncey: "There is ample authority for the view that you must take customers as you find them including the imprudent and the unwary: *R. Johnston & Co v Archibald Orr-Ewing & Co* (1882) 7 App. Cas. 219, Lord Selborne L.C. at page 225, Lord Blackburn at page 229; *Powell v Birmingham Vinegar Brewery Co* [1896] 2 Ch. 54, Lindley L.J., at page 68.": *Jif*.[81]   **15–195**

Despite the consistency in this approach for well over a century, the issue arises as to whether the influence of judgments of the European Court of Justice will lead to or require the adoption of the "average consumer" test. This test was developed[82] by the Court in a series of cases in which it had to weigh the risk of consumers being misled against the requirement of the free movement of goods. Essentially, whenever a national court has to determine whether something would mislead the public: "it is necessary to take into account the presumed expectations of an average consumer who is reasonably well informed and reasonably observant and circumspect." The test, based on the principle of proportionality, has a number of advantages. First, it is a uniform test applicable throughout the EEA.[83] Secondly, the test is obviously one for the court to decide. Thirdly, it encourages economy of evidence.[84]   **15–196**

Although the average consumer test was first advocated by the ECJ in a case involving inter-state trade, it has rapidly pervaded the purely national context[85] to ensure a uniform approach to the issue of likelihood of confusion in the law of   **15–197**

---

[80] *per Viscount Maugham, Saville Perfumery v June Perfect* (1941) 58 R.P.C. 147 at 175. cf. *Marengo v Daily Sketch* (1948) 65 R.P.C. 242 at 252, HL (defendant's mark ambiguous). "… where it appears to the eye of the court that there is likely to be deception, and there is evidence of rational men that they have been deceived there is little value in the evidence of witnesses who say they have not been deceived.": *per* Lord Simonds at 250. And see *Neutrogena Corporation v Golden Ltd* [1996] R.P.C. 473 at 491: "There is passing off even if most of the people are not fooled most of the time but enough are for enough of the time. By 'enough' I mean a substantial number of the plaintiff's customers or potential customers deceived for there to be a real effect on the plaintiff's trade or goodwill.": Morritt L.J. quoting Jacob J. at first instance.

[81] [1990] R.P.C. 341 at 415 and 423, respectively. This does not mean, as Lord Jauncey pointed out, that customers who through a lack of interest or idleness have deliberately disregarded distinct labelling of different brands of goods. See also Lightman J. in *Alan Clark* [1998] R.P.C. 261 at 271: "no claim lies if they are indifferent or careless as to [the indicia in dispute]—in that case "who is the author".

[82] The development is described by A.G. Fennelly in Case C–220/98 *Estée Lauder Cosmetics GmbH v Lancaster Group GmbH* September 16, 1999. It was first properly formulated in *Gut Springenheide and Tusky v Oberkreisdirektor Steinfurt* [1998] E.C.R. I-4657.

[83] This does not mean that the test will give the same result in every country. The European Court has recognised that social, cultural or linguistic factors may justify a different conclusion in one Member State to others.

[84] The Court of Appeal in *Bach and Bach Flower Remedies Trade Marks* [2000] R.P.C. 513, not only extended the average consumer test to distinctiveness, but also took the opportunity to use it to discourage repetitive evidence. See *per* Morritt L.J. at 526 and Chadwick L.J. at 534.

[85] One of the recent cases before the Court was a claim brought under German legislation by a German trade association against a German company in the context of a beer brewed in Germany. At least A.G. Jacobs considered that Art. 30 (now 28) of the Treaty was applicable on the basis of the potential effects of the national legislation on intra-Community trade. A.G. Jacobs was of the opinion that the average consumer test applied: Case C–312/98 *Schutzverband gegen Unwesen in*

registered trade marks under ss.5(2) and 10(2)/Arts 4(1)(b) and 5(1)(b), and possibly to the issue of distinctiveness also, if, as seems likely, the ECJ follow the lead of the Court of Appeal in *Bach Flower Remedies* [2000] R.P.C. 513. Strictly, the ECJ can only influence the law of passing off to the extent that it has effects on the free movement of goods which cannot be objectively justified,[86] and this is unlikely to occur. Even so, the pressure for the uniform adoption of the average consumer test is likely to increase, both at European and national level.[87]

15–198   At first sight, there seems to be no appreciable difference between the traditional approach in passing off cases and the "average consumer" test. If there is any difference, the "average consumer" appears to be more careful and therefore less likely to be misled than the imprudent or the unwary, which an English court would be entitled to take into account. Bearing in mind the scrutiny which is applied in English courts to evidence of alleged deception, once an English court has decided a likelihood of deception exists, it is very difficult to see that the judge would conclude that he had not also just applied the average consumer test. Otherwise, and if the tests were different, the application of the average consumer test might entail a risk of the public being deceived.[88]

FRAUDULENT INTENTION

15–199   If it is shown to have been intended by the defendant to deceive the burden of proof is much lighter[89] and the court will not generally push the inquiry further.[90]

But the intention is only evidence of the actual deception or probability of deception which may be inferred from it.[91] If the court does not believe that there is any probability of deception, the action must fail.[92] The law does not take notice of a fraudulent intention in a man's mind if he does nothing to carry out the fraud.[93]

> "When once you establish the intent to deceive, it is only a short step to proving that the intent has been successful, but still it is a step, even though it be a short step."[94]

---

der Wirtschaft e.v. v Warsteiner Brauerei Haus Cramer GmbH & Co KG. Opinion of A.G. Jacobs, May 25, 2000.

[86] See further, Ch.15.

[87] Even if this test is uniformly adopted, and leaving aside social, cultural and linguistic differences between countries, it does not mean that the same standard is being applied everywhere. The average consumer test is one part of the story, the other part being the rigour with which the court scrutinises purported evidence of deception. The English approach is one of the most rigorous (witness the general lack of faith placed in market surveys), whereas courts in other jurisdictions appear to place great faith in precise statistics drawn from market surveys which would be treated very differently by an English judge.

[88] In *Reed Executive plc v Reed Business Information* [2004] R.P.C. 40 at para.82 Jacob L.J. expressed the view that the average consumer test and the "substantial proportion" test differ conceptually but come to the same result.

[89] *Taylor v Taylor* (1854) 2 Eq.Rep. 290; 23 L.J.Ch. 255.

[90] *Rolls Razor v Roll (Lighters)* (1949) 66 R.P.C. 299 at 303, CA.

[91] "Why should we be astute to say that (the defendant) cannot succeed in doing what he is straining every nerve to do?" Lindley L.J. asked in *Slazenger v Feltham* (1889) 6 R.P.C. 531 at 538. cf. *per* Lord Macclesfield in *Mitchell v Reynolds*, 1 Sm.L.C. (10th ed.) at 391. "He only can suffer by his knavery, and surely Courts of Justice are not concerned lest a man should pay too dear for being a knave." "If you find a defendant who is a knave, you may presume he is not a fool": *per* Cozens-Hardy M.R. in *Claudius Ash v Invicta* (1912) 28 R.P.C. 597 at 603: but note (below) that the HL took a different view of the case.

[92] cf. above, para.15–194.

[93] *Lever v Bedingfield* (1899) 16 R.P.C. 3, CA, overruling 15 R.P.C. 453, Kekewich J. See *Claudius Ash v Invicta* (1912) 29 R.P.C. 465, HL; *"Pub Squash"* [1981] R.P.C. 429 at 493–4 (PC, N.S.W.).

[94] *per* Lord Esher M.R. in *Reddaway v Banham* (1895) 12 R.P.C. 83 at 89.

The existence of unexpected and unexplained similarities[95] between the goods **15–200** of the defendant and those of the claimant or of similarities which have been modified by colourable differences[96] or by differences and distinctions so arranged as to escape notice;[97] the use by the defendant of descriptions, which, as applied to himself or his own trade, are inaccurate, and by reason of their inaccuracy approach more nearly to the proper description of the claimant,[98] and the gradual approximation of the defendant's names, get-up or description to those of the claimant,[99] are all obvious badges of fraudulent intention frequently recurring in the cases which come before the court.[1]

ENABLING PASSING OFF BY OTHERS

Deception by the deliberate fraud of a third party, for example a retailer,[2] where **15–201** the defendant's mark when fairly used is not calculated to deceive, is not imputable to the defendants.[3] On the other hand, it is a common cause of complaint against defendants who are manufacturers that they are putting an instrument of fraud in the hands of retailers; and the complaint is sound in law. Indeed, the rule goes further. "No man is permitted to use any mark, sign or symbol, device or other name, whereby, without making a direct false representation himself to a purchaser who purchases from him, he enables such purchaser to tell a lie or to make a false representation to somebody else who is the ultimate customer."[4] Nor is it permissible so to mark or describe goods that (even though the defendant may be careful to avoid himself marking the goods with, or advertising them under, a mark that would deceive) subsequent purchasers are induced so to mark them.[5]

It used to be thought[6] that the tort of passing off is complete only when deceptive goods are sold to a middleman. However, it was held in *BT v One in a Million* that the tort is committed where a defendant has equipped himself or intends **15–202**

---

[95] *per* Earl Loreburn in *Claudius Ash v Invicta* (1912) 29 R.P.C. 465 at 475; neither fraud nor probability of deception was proved.

[96] *Slazenger v Feltham* (1889) 6 R.P.C. 531, CA ("Demon", "Demotic").

[97] *e.g.* "late of", etc. in small letters, para.15–122.

[98] *Holloway v Holloway* (1850) 13 Beav 209. And see *Middlemas v Molivar* (1921) 38 R.P.C. 97 (mark used by defendant not quite his original name, let alone the name he usually used); also see paras 15–113 to 15–115, and cases there cited.

[99] *Boulnois v Peake* (1868) 13 Ch.D. 521 n., "Carriage Repository" changed to "New Carriage Bazaar"; *Apollinaris v Herrfeldt* (1887) 4 R.P.C. 478, CA ("Apollinis"); *Sanitas v Condy* (1886) 4 R.P.C. 195, 530: 56 L.T. 621 ("Condi-Sanitas"). Lord Macnaghten in the " *Camel Hair Belting*" case (1896) 13 R.P.C. 218 at 233. See also *Colman v Farrow* (1898) 15 R.P.C. 198.

[1] See further paras 15–221 and 15–222.

[2] As in *Bovril v Bodega* (1916) 33 R.P.C. 153, where the defendants supplied Oxo-and-Soda when Bovril-and-Soda was asked for.

[3] *Payton v Snelling* [1901] A.C. 308, 17 R.P.C. 628 at 635, HL; *Schweppes v Gibbens* (1905) 22 R.P.C. 113 at 120, 121, CA 601; *Hennessy v Keating* (1908) 25 R.P.C. 361 at 367, HL. See *Paterson v Kit Coffee* (1910) 27 R.P.C. 594 (fraud of predecessors).

[4] *Singer v Loog* (1880) 18 Ch.D. 395 at 412, cited with approval by Lord Macnaghten in " *Camel Hair Belting*" [1896] A.C. 199 at 215–216. Hence the established practice of granting injunctions in the form "so as to pass-off or enable others to pass-off"; note that the word is "enable", not "cause", assuming fraud on the part of the "others". See further, *Draper v Trist* (1939) 56 R.P.C. 429 at 435, 439, CA (citing *Lever v Goodwin* (1887) 36 Ch.D. 1 at 7). *Trist* was a case on damages: which means that the precise extent of the defendants' wrongful acts was of real importance.

[5] See " *Harris Tweed*" [1964] R.P.C. 477 at 542 *et seq.*, and at 509, where this is called a "typical passing-off situation".

[6] Based on *My Kinda Town v Soll* [1983] R.P.C. 15 at 49, where the judge cited, a number of cases in particular *Edelsten v Edelsten* (1863) 1 De G, J. & S. 185. (My Kinda Town, the "Chicago Pizza" case, was overruled by the CA, but on another point: [1983] R.P.C. 407).

to equip another with an instrument of fraud, even though such cases are probably mere *quia timet* actions.[7]

The defendants were so-called cybersquatters who registered Internet domain names such as marksandspencer.com, comprising the names of well-known companies. The Internet domain names themselves were held by the Court of Appeal to be instruments of fraud: *BT v One in a Million*.[8]

15–203   The supply of (or even the mere authorisation to use) instruments of deception which the defendant knows are going to be used for passing off (even abroad) is itself a form of passing off which is actionable and takes place when the supply or authorisation occurs.[9]

(1) The defendant supplied from England to purchasers in Ecuador single malt whisky together with labels ("Scottish Archer") and empty bottles. The defendant further authorised his Ecuadorian purchaser to use other labels ("White Abbey") which bore his address and which he had registered as a trade mark in Ecuador. The purchaser, to the defendant's knowledge, mixed the whisky with local cane spirit and used the labels on the bottles. The labels were calculated to lead to the belief that the contents were genuine blended Scotch whisky. The defendant was restrained, by Foster J. "from supplying ... any Scotch Whisky or bottles or labels or other things or documents and from permitting and/or licensing the use of any trade marks or label for the purpose of enabling and/or which are calculated to enable spirits that consist of or include spirits that [are] not [Scotch Whisky] to be passed off in any country as and for Scotch Whisky": *John Walker v Ost* [1970] R.P.C. 489 at 513. Note that a proviso to the injunction, permitting honest supply of goods which could be used as instruments of deception, was added. *John Walker v McGibbon* [1975] R.P.C. 506 (OH, Sc.) was a similar case, where the actual sales complained of took place in Scotland.

(2) In a somewhat similar case, an exporter of whisky for foreign admixture who had given the foreign purchaser inadequate advice for avoiding passing off was held liable; the court observing that such an exporter is himself liable only if he "takes part in the passing off": *White Horse v Gregson* [1984] R.P.C. 84 at 88–9.

PROOF OF ACTUAL DECEPTION

15–204   Instances of actual deception need not be proved if the court is otherwise satisfied of the probability of deception;[10] although in the absence of cases of actual decep-

---

[7] *BT v One in a Million* [1999] 1 W.L.R. 903 at 920, CA *per* Aldous L.J. See also at 915–920 for his analysis of the cases.

[8] [1999] 1 W.L.R. 903. "Whether any name is an instrument of fraud will depend upon all the circumstances. A name which will, by reason of its similarity to the name of another, inherently lead to passing off, is such an instrument. If a name would not inherently lead to passing off, it does not follow that it is not an instrument of fraud. The court should consider the similarity of the names, the intention of the defendant, the type of trade and all the surrounding circumstances. If it be the intention of the defendant to appropriate the goodwill of another or enable others to do so, I can see no reason why the court should not infer that it will happen, even if there is a possibility that such an appropriation would not take place.": Aldous L.J. at 920.

[9] *John Walker v Ost* [1970] R.P.C. 489 (illustration below). See also *Saper v Specter's* (1953) 70 R.P.C. 173 at 178–179. Note (at 175) that the box-maker showed the claimants' box to the defendants and solicited orders for an imitation.

[10] See para.15–194, and Parker J. in *Iron-Ox v Co-operative Wholesale Society* (1907) 24 R.P.C. 425 at 430; *Delavelle v Stanley* (1943) 60 R.P.C. 103 *quia timet* action) ("Blue Orchid").

tion the evidence adduced must be "of the most cogent sort".[11] On the other hand, cases of actual deception are not necessarily conclusive: for example, where their number is comparatively insignificant;[12] or where the defendant has done nothing but what he was entitled to do, as where he has only used marks common to the trade. Furthermore, people who allow themselves to be deceived seldom make good witnesses, with the result that their evidence can usually be brushed aside by a judge who is not otherwise convinced. Indeed evidence relied upon as demonstrating deception may in fact be taken to prove the contrary.[13]

ALL THE CIRCUMSTANCES TO BE CONSIDERED

All the circumstances of the case must be considered. Thus where the mark in question is not attached to the goods themselves so as to reach the ultimate purchasers, it may be clear that the trade purchasers to whom the defendant's business is confined are not in danger of being deceived.[14] **15–205**

Where the alleged passing off is in response to oral orders, the evidence should be clear, and "trap orders" in particular (orders given by agents of the claimant, with the possibility of passing off in mind) must be both clear and fair.[15] This is of particular importance where the claimant's mark resembles a word which is descriptive.[16]

Where assistants on being asked for "Glacier Mints" supplied other mints of a similar kind which were known locally as "glassy mints," the claimants were held not to have made out their case, there being ample possibility of there having been the misunderstanding which was said to have occurred: *Fox's v Jobbings* (1932) 49 R.P.C. 352.

Where the defendant in response to an order for the claimants' goods by their trade name supplies his own goods, it is no defence to say that the persons giving the orders could have discovered, by examination, that the goods supplied did not in fact bear the name.[17] **15–206**

Obvious differences between the goods themselves are very material to the question of probability of deception.[18]

---

[11] *per* Harman J. in *Gor-Ray v Gilray* (1952) 69 R.P.C. 99 at 105–106; on appeal, 69 R.P.C. 199. cf. *per* Roxburgh J. in *Tavener Rutledge v Specters* [1957] R.P.C. 498 at 502.

[12] *Rutter v Smith* (1901) 18 R.P.C. 49; and above, para.15–194; and *Neutrogena* [1996] R.P.C. 473.

[13] See below, Defences. In *King v Gillard* (1905) 22 R.P.C. 327 at 337 the defendant copied some common elements from the claimant's box.

[14] *Star Cycle v Frankenburgs* (1907) 24 R.P.C. 46, 405 (use only in trade price lists, etc.); *Fairbank v Cocos Butter* (1904) 21 R.P.C. 23.

[15] See as to the requirements for a trap order, *Procea v Evans* (1951) 68 R.P.C. 210; *Stillitz v Jones & Higgins* (1943) 60 R.P.C. 15; *Cellular Clothing v White* (1953) 70 R.P.C. 9 at 14. See also Chadwick J. in *Marie Claire v Hartstone Hosiery Ltd* [1993] F.S.R. 692.

[16] See *Procea v Evans*, above("process" bread); *Cellular Clothing v White*, above, 70 R.P.C. 9 at 11.

[17] *Pearson v Valentine* (1917) 34 R.P.C. 267 ("Matamac") followed in *French v Rind* [1958] R.P.C. 82. See also *Purefoy Engineering v Sykes, Boxall* (1955) 72 R.P.C. 89 at 93–94, CA; *Procea v Evans* (1951) 68 R.P.C. 210 at 212. *Broad v Cast Iron Drainage* [1970] F.S.R. 363, which might appear authority for a different view, depends on the defendant's making it clear what was being supplied before delivery of the goods: see at 368.

[18] *Coleman v Brown* (1899) 16 R.P.C. 619 ("Wincarnis, Vincalis"); *Reddaway v Irwell* (1907) 23 R.P.C. 621; 24 R.P.C. 203 ("Lancashire" for hair belting, "Lanco" for balata belting); *Nugget v Harboro'* (1912) 29 R.P.C. 133 (boot polish and rubber heels). See also *Wilson's v Meynell* (1929) 46 R.P.C. 80. See further, para.15–046, "Common field of activity".

9. Defences

15–207   The defences, other than a simple denial of the acts alleged, which are commonly set up, may be tabulated as follows: that

(1) The name or other badge, which the claimant charges the defendant with having imitated, carried no distinctive reference to the claimant's goods or business.

(2) The defendant has an independent or a concurrent right to use it.[19]

(3) The name or other badge which the defendant is using is not such, or is not so used, as to be calculated to pass off any goods for those of the claimant.[20]

(4) The claimant is debarred from suing the defendant for all or part of the relief he seeks by (a) an agreement, or some personal estoppel[21] (other than those next alluded to); (b) acquiescence;[22] (c) delay;[23] (d) deceptive use of the name or badges he relies on, or because his trade is fraudulent;[24] or (e) EU law.[25]

(5) There is no likelihood of appreciable damage.

(6) The claimant has no goodwill in this country.[26]

(1) Denial of reputation

15–208   This is a traverse of part of the claimant's case. It may take the form of an allegation that the name or other badge is merely descriptive or has become common.[27] If so, the defence falls under the second head (no misrepresentation) also; and such a positive case must be pleaded. Where the defendant's case is that the claimant has used the badge for too short a time, or in the wrong way, for it to have become distinctive, those points should be pleaded.

(2) Concurrent right

15–209   The most important question here is the right of a man, apart from restriction by contract, to trade honestly under his own name. Also of importance are issues arising from the transfer of goodwill on dissolution of a business. These matters are discussed in detail below. The statutory right of use given by registration of a mark does not provide a defence to proceedings for passing off by the use of the mark;[28] although it is normally expedient for the claimant in such cases to apply to revoke the registration. Where a party applies to register a mark but does not

---

[19] See, as to the right to trade under one's own name, below and para.15–227 and as to the right to describe honestly the place or origin, etc., of his goods, at para.15–086, and further, Ch.14, "Infringement".

[20] Above para.15–192; and Ch.19. As to cases where the claimant is not a trader, so that there are no goods, see paras 15–059 and 15–060.

[21] At para.14–187.

[22] At paras 14–190 to 14–193.

[23] At para.14–194.

[24] At para.14–196.

[25] See Ch.15.

[26] See paras 15–070 to 15–076.

[27] Above para.15–104.

[28] 1994 Act, s.2(2): "… nothing in this Act affects the law relating to passing off". *Van Zeller v Mason, Cattley* (1907) 25 R.P.C. 37; *Lyle & Kinahan* (1907) 24 R.P.C. 249 at 262; *Eli Lilly v Chelsea Drug* [1966] R.P.C. 14 at 18. cf. in this connection the limited scope of s.11(1) with the width of the final provision of s.2. Registration gives the sort of *prima facie* case of right to the

immediately use it, and another party uses the mark and generates sufficient goodwill to support a passing claim prior to the first use by registered proprietor, an impasse ensues. The proprietor of the mark, if valid, may restrain use by the owner of the goodwill. However the proprietorship of the trade mark provides no defence to a passing off claim by the owner of the goodwill, notwithstanding the fact that such goodwill was generated after the application to register the mark.[29]

(3) Denial of deception

This defence also is a mere traverse. It has been considered already.[30]   **15–210**

(4) Estoppel

The defences collected under the fourth head are precisely analogous to those   **15–211**
discussed in Ch.14;[31] they depend on the same considerations and are governed by the same rules.

(5) Likelihood of damage

This defence is mainly applicable where the claimant is not a trader;[32] in business   **15–212**
name cases where the businesses are not in effective competition;[33] or in cases where the parties deal in different goods.[34] But it may serve in other cases where the matters complained of are too trivial to call for intervention of the court, and may in particular serve to answer a claim for interlocutory relief. This may also apply where the goodwill relied upon by a claimant is small.[35]

CONCURRENT RIGHT: USE OF ONE'S OWN NAME[36]

Once the claimant has proved the elements necessary for passing off, and in par-   **15–213**
ticular deception of the public or its likelihood, the concept that the defendant escapes liability because he is making "bona fide" use of his own name, is a difficult one.[37]

The precise nature and extent of this "defence" are none too clear, the rather

---

mark that may affect interlocutory decisions, for instance, provided the mark is not vulnerable for non-use.

[29] See *Inter Lotto (UK) v Camelot Group plc* [2004] R.P.C. 9.
[30] See paras 15–192 to 15–198.
[31] See para.14–187.
[32] See paras 15–165 to 15–169.
[33] *e.g.* the newspaper-title cases, para.15–170.
[34] Since (above, para.15–029) actual damage is not necessary to this cause of action, the claimant who does succeed at the trial in establishing passing off in spite of differences in goods or business will normally have his injunction, although he may be well advised not to take an inquiry as to damages. In interlocutory proceedings, where the case cannot be fully gone into, and where the test is rather whether irreparable damage will result if matters continue as they are until the trial, such matters as differences between the goods are of greater weight. See, *e.g. Lyons Maid v Trebor* [1967] R.P.C. 222 at 226.
[35] For a case in which the goodwill relied upon by the claimant was too small for there to be any likelihood of real damage being suffered by the claimant see *Hart v Relentless Records Ltd* [2003] F.S.R. 36.
[36] This "defence" is different to that provided in the Trade Marks Act 1994, s.11(2)(a).
[37] Most, if not all of the cases can be explained on normal principles of passing off (as now understood), without the need for any specific defence but probably only the House of Lords is in a position to explain away all the authorities on this basis. Part of the problem lies in the failure to distinguish clearly between deception and mere confusion. If what we would call "mere confusion" was thought to give rise to liability for passing off, then one can see room for this defence. On the contrary, if passing off is properly limited to cases involving deception or its likelihood. McGechan J. in *Taylors' Bros Ltd v Taylors' Group Ltd* [1988] 2 N.Z.L.R. 1 at 23, having stated correctly that (a) the "defence" does not apply if there is actual deception, (b) the "defence" is not

numerous authorities on the point being difficult to reconcile.[38] The defence is certainly of very limited scope, if indeed it exists at all. Although no superior court has as yet gone so far as to say the defence does not exist, Jacob LJ has made his scepticism as to the practical effect of the defence clear:[39]

> "The Judge rightly observed that the passing-off defence is narrow. Actually no case comes to mind in which it has succeeded. Because the test is honesty, I do not see how any man who is in fact causing deception and knows that to be so can possibly have a defence to passing off."

15–214   If the honest use of one's own name is truly a defence to a passing off claim, then it must apply even if all other elements of the tort are made out by the claimant. This is understandably unattractive to the courts: if the use of by a defendant of a mark constitutes a misrepresentation leading to deception and damage (as it must be if passing off is to be established) the mere fact that through an accident of birth the mark used is the defendant's own name would save the defendant from passing off. In modern trading conditions, any individual (or company) can adjust their trading style, if they so wish, so as to eliminate deception on the part of the public. In such circumstances, it is difficult to see the justification for upholding any absolute right to trade under one's own name when balanced against the deception of the public or the likelihood of such deception.

15–215   The origins of the "defence" lie in certain *dicta* of Romer J. Certainly, the defence does not extend to allowing use of the trader's own name in relation to goods so as to pass off:

> "To the proposition of law that no man is entitled so to describe his goods as to represent that the goods are the goods of another, there is no exception."[40]

15–216   The difficulty arises on the other half of Romer J.'s proposition:

> "To the proposition of law that no man is entitled to carry on his business in such a way as to represent that it is the business of another, or is in any way connected with the business of another, there is an exception, that a man is entitled to carry on his business in his own name so long as he does not do anything more than that to cause confusion with the business of another, and so long as he does it honestly."[41]

---

required if there is "mere confusion", because there is no passing off, appears to suggest, therefore (c) the "defence" only runs where the court has found only a likelihood of deception. This is a valiant attempt to reconcile the authorities, but it is very difficult to justify such distinctions as a matter of principle—the defence would depend on whether instances of deception came to the claimant's attention. Whether they do or not depends on the circumstances, but it is easy for a court to accept that most do not.

[38] See the analysis of the cases in Boswell Circus *Boswell–Wilkie Circus v Brian Boswell Circus* [1985] F.S.R. 434 (SC, S.A., Natal)), on appeal [1986] F.S.R. 479. See also the analysis of Somers J. in *New Zealand Farmers' Co-operative Association of Canterbury Ltd v Farmers' Trading Co Ltd* (1979) 1 N.Z.I.P.R. 212, summarised by McGechan J. (upheld on appeal) in *Taylor Bros Ltd v Taylor Group Ltd* [1988] 2 N.Z.L.R. 1.

[39] *Reed Executive plc v Reed Business Information Ltd* [2004] R.P.C. 40. See also the comments of Jacob L.J. in *I.N. Newman Limited v Richard T Adlem* [2005] EWCA (Civ) 741 at paras 46 and 47.

[40] *Rodgers v Rodgers* (1924) 41 R.P.C. 277 at 291, *per* Romer J., approved in *Parker-Knoll v Knoll International* [1962] R.P.C. 265, at 279 (Lord Morris) and 284 (Lord Hodson), Lord Guest (at 287) concurring, HL.

[41] *Rodgers v Rodgers* (1924) 41 R.P.C. 277.

This proposition, which seems to have originated with Romer J.[42] was doubted **15–217** by most of the House in *Knoll*.[43] The question is how far it extends. Given that there is no defence, if passing off results from use of the name on goods,[44] or if goods are sold under it,[45] and given that the same must surely be true in relation to services, what is there left that the owner of the name can do? Arguably, the matter turns on the word "confusion." Whenever two people or two companies have the same or similar names, some other people will be uncertain whether they are really the same, or somehow related; that sort of confusion does not in itself involve any misrepresentation by either, so that there will be no passing off.[46] But if that is all this "exception" amounts to, the rule is no different from that governing other sorts of descriptive marks; nor any different from that for marks used on goods:[47]

> "It is a question of fact, to be decided on the evidence, whether it is proved that a name or mark has acquired a secondary meaning so that it denotes or has come to mean goods made by a particular person and not goods made by any other person, even though such other person may have the same name. If it is proved on behalf of a claimant that a name or mark has acquired such a secondary meaning, then it is a question for the court whether a defendant, whatever may be his intention, is so describing his goods that there is a likelihood that a substantial section of the purchasing public will be misled into believing that his goods are the goods of the claimant."[48]

It is clear that any exception does not extend to use of abbreviations of the **15–218** name, where the abbreviation increases the risk of confusion.[49] If necessity is indeed the basis of the exception, no abbreviation falls within its scope.

The claimants, whose principal product was "Wrights' Coal Tar Soap", also used the style "Wrights" on other goods including talcum powder. The defendant, William Frederick Thomas Wright, had commenced to sell toilet preparations about 1934 under the name W. F. T. Wright and about 1943 he changed his trading style to "Wrights' Chemical Company". The claimants at first instance were granted an injunction to restrain the defendant from "passing-off as and for the goods of the claimants pharmaceutical and toilet goods not of the claimants' manufacture or merchandise by the use upon or in connection therewith of the name 'Wright' or 'Wright's' without clearly distinguishing such goods from

---

[42] Boswell Circus, above, at 462 but see *Saunders v Sun Life* [1894] 1 Ch. 537.

[43] Lord Guest at 287; and two dissentients: Lord Denning at 277 and Lord Devlin at 291.

[44] *Wright, Layman & Umney v Wright* (1949) 66 R.P.C. 149 at 150–151, CA, illustration below, unaffected, on this point, by the doubts expressed in *Knoll*. The distinction is between using his name as a name and using it as a trade mark; cf. using a defendant's address, *Banbury Bldgs. v Sectional* [1970] R.P.C. 463.

[45] *Parker-Knoll v Knoll International* [1962] R.P.C. 265, note that the word "Knoll" in question, was held not to be distinctive of the claimants. *Baume v Moore* [1958] R.P.C. 226 at 236, CA.

[46] Or there may be some historical connection, as in *Habib Bank* [1982] R.P.C. 1 at 31–32, CA.

[47] This is effectively the conclusion reached in New Zealand. When summarising the analysis of Somers J. in the Farmers case (at para.15–213), McGechan J., in *Taylor Bros Ltd v Taylors Group Ltd* [1988] 2 N.Z.L.R. 1, acknowledged three limitations on the ostensible scope of this "defence": "The name used, to come within the exception, must be the actual name of the defendant." "The exception does not extend to the use of the name "if it will deceive as distinct from merely causing confusion'" "The exception extends to companies 'with an established business' but 'not to new companies'." It would seem to follow from this last point that any exception would not extend to companies extending into new areas, either geographical or fields of business.

[48] *per* Lord Morris, *Parker-Knoll v Knoll International* [1962] R.P.C. 265 at 279.

[49] *Wright, Layman & Umney v Wright* (1949) 66 R.P.C. 149 at 150 *arguendo*), 156; *General Radio v General Radio (Westminster)* [1957] R.P.C. 471; cf. *Aubanel & Alabaster v Aubanel* (1949) 66 R.P.C. 343.

those of the claimants"; as Greene M.R. said, a common form injunction, according to his recollection and experience. But the claimants were held by the judge not to be entitled to restrain the defendant from carrying on business under a name of which "Wright" or "Wrights" formed part: the real risk of confusion, he said, was in regard to goods sold to the public and not between the respective trading styles by which they were known to the trade. Upon appeal it was held that the second injunction should be granted. The first would give no protection against, for instance, supply of the wrong goods by wholesalers as a result of treating both sorts of goods as "Wrights". The Master of the Rolls stated: "If a man uses his own name and uses it honestly and fairly, and is doing nothing more, he cannot be restrained if confusion results. Once he oversteps the line and confusion results or is calculated to result, the fact that he is using something approaching his own name is no justification":[50] *Wright, Layman & Umney v Wright* (1949) 66 R.P.C. 149 at 153, 154. See also where John Thomas Parker formerly connected with a company carrying on business as estate agents under the name "Parkers", set up in business on his own in the same area also as "Parkers", an interlocutory injunction was granted to restrain him from doing so; the judge remarking: "The question is not simply whether the defendant can be prevented from using his own name but whether the defendant can be prevented from garnishing that name ... in such a way that it looks as if the name were being used not by him but by the claimants": *Parker v Parker* [1965] R.P.C. 323.

COMPANY NAMES

15–219   If the defence exists (see above), it appears to extend to a company with an established business[51] or to a company formed to carry on an established business[52] but the exception does not extend to a company with an established business adopting a new name[53] or to the name of a new company conducting a new business, notwithstanding that the name in dispute may be the personal name of a promoter or other person connected with the company.[54]

15–220   "A new company with a title of which the name 'A', for instance, forms part has none of the natural rights that an individual born with the name 'A' would have."[55]

(1) A German company, which manufactured "Adrema" addressing machines, had, before the war, formed an English company "Adrema Ltd" for the purpose of its trade in the United Kingdom, and allowed the English subsidiary to acquire the entire United Kingdom goodwill in the

---

[50] This observation would not seem to be affected by the criticism of other remarks of Greene M.R. in this case made in *Parker-Knoll v Knoll International*, at [1962] R.P.C. 279 and 284, provided— see para.15–217—it is understood as limited to use of the name as a trading style, and not as extending to use of the name as a trade mark for the goods.

[51] This follows from *Parker-Knoll v Knoll International* [1962] R.P.C. 265, notwithstanding Harman L.J. *arguendo* in later proceedings in the same case at [1962] R.P.C. 255; cf. at 258. It should be noted, however, that the cases on foreign companies are not altogether easy to reconcile: see the "Adrema" and "Sturtevant" cases, illustration (1), below.

[52] Since the right to use the name is assignable to the company as part of the goodwill of the business: above, para.15–152.

[53] For a recent example, see *Asprey & Garrard v WRA (Guns)* [2002] F.S.R. 41. See also *HFC Bank plc v Midland Bank plc* [2000] F.S.R. 176 at 201–202, Lloyd J. (The case settled on appeal, but any appeal was not going to turn on this point).

[54] *Kingston, Miller v Kingston* [1912] 1 Ch. 575, 29 R.P.C. 289, illustration above, para.15–156; *Fine Cotton Spinners v Cash* [1907] 2 Ch. 184; 24 R.P.C. 533. cf. *Boswell Circus* [1985] F.S.R. 434 at 445, where the South African judge treated the defendant company and "the man behind it" as "for all practical purposes, indistinguishable".

[55] *per* Joyce J., *Fine Corton Spinners v Cash*, above, at 24 R.P.C. 538.

mark "Adrema". As a result of the war, the two companies ceased to be connected. After the war, the German company (now called "Adrema-Werke GmbH") sought to use its name in trading in its machines in the United Kingdom. When sued by the English company for passing off it offered to submit to a qualified injunction; but Danckwerts J. followed the rather similar "Sturtevant" case and granted an absolute injunction (see para.19–066). The bona fides of the German company were in doubt, but the decision did not rest upon that; whilst in the "Sturtevant" case the defendant was an English company newly formed by a foreign parent, but that made no difference—the result (see *per* Danckwerts J. at [1958] R.P.C. 332) would have been the same if the parent itself had begun to trade here: *Adrema v Adrema-Werke* [1958] R.P.C. 323; *Sturtevant Engineering v Sturtevant Mill* (1936) 53 R.P.C. 430. The distinction from "Knoll",above where the right of the American Knoll company to trade under its own name in this country (by itself or by a British subsidiary) was recognised in spite of passing off, is to be found (it would seem) in the circumstance that in the "Adrema" and "Sturtevant" cases the British goodwill of the foreign company's business had passed to the claimant, leaving the foreign company somewhat in the position of a vendor of goodwill seeking to go on using the marks in which that goodwill is embodied. In the "Knoll" cases, the parties had never been connected.

(2) The claimant, E. V. Hawtin Ltd, was an importer of gloves, of considerable reputation, and alleged that it was known as "Hawtin" or "Hawtins". Its gloves came from Hong Kong. Two merchants, one of them John F. Hawtin, formed a company John F. Hawtin & Co Ltd, which soon began to import gloves from Hong Kong. Both companies dealt only with the trade, and there was no indication of fraud. Roxburgh J. observed that whilst the defendant could not rely on any exception to any rule (its name could not be treated as that of John F. Hawtin, carrying on business alone or with partners), it had on the facts "a fairly strong moral case". He found the evidence of actual confusion inadequate, and refused an interlocutory injunction: *Hawtin v Hawtin* [1960] R.P.C. 95. It is always open to the court, where a defendant has a moral case but is in difficulties over the law, to prove hard to satisfy on questions of fact.

(3) The claimant, General Radio Co, was an American company but also well-known in this country. The defendant, General Radio Co (Westminster) Ltd was a newly formed British company. The defendant, under the name "General Radio Co", advertised American radio equipment for sale. In spite of an undertaking by the defendant not to put further advertisements in the press, Roxburgh J. granted an *ex parte* interim injunction to the claimant, restraining the defendant from carrying on business under any name containing the words "General Radio Co" except their own name "General Radio Co (Westminster) Ltd". But he refused to grant, *ex parte*, an injunction against trading under their full name: *General Radio v General Radio (Westminster)* [1957] R.P.C. 471. On the full hearing of the motion, an injunction until trial was granted restraining the defendant "from trading in electrical or electronic apparatus under any name containing the words 'General Radio Co' without clearly distinguishing their goods from those of the claimant: but this order is not to prevent the defendant from trading in their corporate name, provided that equal prominence is given to the words 'Westminster' and 'Limited' as the words of 'General Radio Co'." (at [1957] R.P.C. 496).

(4) "It is a very strong thing, in the absence of fraud …, to grant an injunction which would force the defendant company to change its name before the

trial, and really, for practical purposes, decide the issues between the parties before the trial,": *per* Cross J. in *Mansfield v Gaygirl* [1968] F.S.R. 144. An injunction against issuing advertisements to the public under the company name was granted.

RELEVANCE OF FRAUD

15–221   In the light of the authorities cited above, it would seem clear that in cases of passing off of goods[56] and in cases involving new companies[57] the relevance of the presence or absence of fraudulent intent in "own name" cases is precisely the same as in any other passing off case.[58] But in cases of confusion of businesses (as distinct from goods), where the defendant is trading under his own name, the claimant must at least prove not merely that some confusion has occurred or is probable but also that the defendant's trading is, if not dishonest, at least unintentionally deceptive. In satisfying a court of this, a strong suspicion of fraudulent intention is naturally of great assistance.

PROXIMITY MAY BE A BADGE OF FRAUD

15–222   The proximity of the place where the defendant sets up his business to that where a well-known firm is already trading may be evidence to show that, although trading under his own name, the defendant is seeking to take fraudulent advantage of its similarity to the claimant's name. The case of somebody finding a man named Bass and setting up a brewery at Burton as Bass & Co,[59] and the case of a man starting business as a banker in the Strand under the name of Coutts,[60] have been cited as instances in which it is scarcely conceivable that the use of the name could be honest.

ASSUMED NAME OR PEN NAME

15–223   Whether or not the same considerations of law as regards a man carrying on a business under his own name apply in the case of a man carrying on a business under an assumed name has not been decided.[61] It has been held that there is no special right to trade under one's nickname.[62]

> (1) Jay's Ltd, a London concern, sued to restrain a small Brighton shop from trading as "Jays". There was some evidence of confusion. The defendants, two partners, said that one of them was called Jay; and to evidence from the claimants that her real name was Jacobi replied that she had, when employed by a larger Brighton shop, become known to people in Brighton as "Miss Jay". Eve J. found for the defendants, saying: "The defendant, therefore, as the owner by reputation of the surname 'Jay', has the right to trade under that name": *Jay's v Jacobi* (1933) 50 R.P.C. 132. But when this case was cited in the "Wrights" case, Greene M.R. said of it: "It is perfectly true that the name in which the defendant was carrying on her

---

[56] *Parker-Knoll v Knoll International* [1962] R.P.C. 265 at 284, *per* Lord Hodson.

[57] *Fine Cotton Spinners v Cash* [1907] 2 Ch. 184 at 190; 24 R.P.C. 533 at 538.

[58] *Parker-Knoll v Knoll International* [1962] R.P.C. 265 at 285; see also para.15–192.

[59] James L.J. in *Massam v Thorley* (1880) 14 Ch.D. 748 at 757.

[60] Chitty J. in *Melachrino v Melachrino Co* (1887) 4 R.P.C. 215 at 221.

[61] The HL in *Marengo v Daily Sketch* (1948) 65 R.P.C. 242 ("Kem" and "Kim"), left the point open.

[62] *Biba Group v Biba Boutique* [1980] R.P.C. 413. The defendant prejudiced his case by displaying one of the claimants' advertisements whilst saying he had never heard of them. See also *NAD Electronics Inc v NAD Computer Systems Ltd* [1997] F.S.R. 380. The man behind the defendant had the nickname Nad, but the judge was not entirely satisfied as to his *bona fides*.

business at Hove was not her own name in the strict sense; but the judge found that in carrying on that business in that name, which was not her own name, there was no probability of confusion with the well-known business of Jay's in London. Once he had found that, she could carry on her business in the name she was using, since there was no probability of confusion. The reasoning in that case was that there was no probability of confusion. Had Eve J. found on the facts that there was a probability of confusion, I cannot doubt that in the circumstances he would have granted an injunction." The rest of the Court of Appeal concurred: *Wright, Layman & Umney v Wright* (1949) 66 R.P.C. 149 at 153.

(2) In *Richfield v Speedy Cables* the claimants' complaint was that the defendants had sent out a number of business letters signed "Thomas Richfield". There was a Thomas Richfield prominently associated with the claimants. There were Richfields who were directors of the defendant company but none of them were called Thomas. The signatory of the letter was the stepson of one of them, whose name was not originally Richfield at all but who had called himself "Thomas Richfield" for some years; he was not a director or officer of the defendant company, although he performed "most of the functions of either a director or a secretary". Harman J. granted an interlocutory injunction restraining the defendants from using in connection with their business the name "Thomas Richfield" at all, or using "Richfield" without clearly distinguishing their business from the claimants'—this last, so that the actual Richfield directors could sign letters in their own names: [1957] R.P.C. 47. The action never came to trial.

(3) A company formed to take over a business run by traders named Israel and Seabrook was named "Rael-Brook Limited", and two directors, a Mr Seabrook and a Mr Israel, changed their names respectively to Harry Rael-Brook and Graham Rael-Brook. Graham Rael-Brook left the company to become managing director of a company with an entirely different name, trading in similar goods. An *ex parte* application to stop him using his name in advertisements of his company failed.[63] It seems clear that the court regarded this as an "own name" case. It was conceded that Graham Rael-Brook should not use "Rael-Brook" without the Graham.

OTHER CASES OF CONCURRENT RIGHT

There are other cases best considered as cases where the defendant has as good a title to use the mark or name complained of as the claimant has to use the mark or name with which (as he alleges) it is likely to be confused: as, for instance, where the defendant has been using his mark or name for nearly as long as the claimant has his;[64] or where both parties are equally unmeritorious.[65] Since, however, there is really no such thing as a right to use a mark or name,[66] such cases require more careful analysis for the purpose of pleading a defence. They may be classified as cases where the mark or name whose use is complained of is distinctive of the defendant, not of the claimant; cases where each party has established an independent reputation and goodwill in particular geographical areas, the dispute

15–224

---

[63] *Rael-Brook v Head Shirts* [1963] R.P.C. 6.

[64] cf. the limited defence under s.11(3) to actions for infringement, para.14–180.

[65] cf. *Rolls Razor v Rolls (Lighters)* (1949) 66 R.P.C. 137 at 143; 299 at 301, CA: name "Rolls" adopted by both parties to suggest the quality of a "Rolls-Royce" car.

[66] As distinct from a right to prevent others using it. Note that even the limited right of use given by s.11(1) of the Trade Marks Act gives no defence against proceedings for passing off.

arising because one or both have expanded into the area of the other; cases where it is common to the trade, or otherwise not distinctive of either party;[67] cases where in the circumstances the defendant has sufficiently distinguished his goods from those of the claimant;[68] cases where there is no real likelihood of damage;[69] cases where as between claimant and defendant the right to the goodwill the claimant seeks to protect is vested in the defendant, or in neither, or is shared between them;[70] cases where the claimant has no goodwill.[71]

Certain cases of transfer of dissolution of a business here call for more detailed discussion.

PURCHASER OF GOODWILL

15–225   The purchaser of the goodwill of a business (or a partner succeeding to it under agreement upon dissolution of partnership) will normally[72] have the right to use the trade name and trade marks under which the business was conducted,[73] even though they comprise the personal name of a late partner,[74] or of any other late owner of the goodwill, but not so as to cast any risk of liability upon the late partner or owner[75] by using his personal name in such manner as to represent that he is still a member of the firm, or carrying on the business.[76]

Partners after dissolution

15–226   On the dissolution of a partnership, the goodwill is normally sold; in which case,

---

[67] As to marks common to the trade, see para.14–171; as to "otherwise", cf. the Rolls case, above: or the case of a get-up newly adopted by both parties, or of a descriptive mark.

[68] e.g. the "small differences" that suffice to distinguish two names that are equally descriptive: *Office Cleaning v Westminster* (1946) 63 R.P.C. 39 at 43—or two names or marks that have long been used side-by-side.

[69] e.g. cases where no trade is involved (paras 15–059 and 15–060.); cases where marks have long been used side-by-side without appreciable confusion.

[70] cf. the discussion above, para.15–165 of disputes over noms-de-plume; and *Technical Waxes v Whitehead* (1953) 70 R.P.C. 230 at 232–233 (defendants alleged right by agreement to use marks concurrently with claimants; but interlocutory injunction granted for protection of public).

[71] e.g. *Anheuser-Busch Inc v Budejovicky Budvar Narodni Podnik* [1984] F.S.R. 413, CA.

[72] Obviously it depends upon the circumstances and terms of the agreement of sale and purchase. See, e.g. *Dawnay, Day & Co Ltd v Cantor Fitzgerald International* [2000] R.P.C. 669.

[73] *Levy v Walker* (1879) 10 Ch.D. 436, CA; *Currie v Currie* (1898) 15 R.P.C. 339, Ct of Sess ("Prince Charlie"); *Rickersby v Reay* (1903) 20 R.P.C. 380 at 388. For cases of colourable purchase of a goodwill, see paras 15–084 and 15–085.

[74] *Condy v Mitchell* (1877) 37 L.T. (N.S.) 268, 766. ("Condy's Fluid Co"); *Chappell v Griffith* (1885) 53 L.T. (N.S.) 459.

[75] *Chatteris v Isaacson* (1887) 57 L.T. (N.S.) 177. The vendor of the business of "Mme. Elise" agreed that the purchaser should have the exclusive right to use the name "Mme. Elise & Co". Mme. Elise was his wife's name. Held, the purchaser might use the name only with the addition "& Co" In *Burchell v Wilde* [1900] 1 Ch. 551, it was held that, upon the division of a solicitor's business between the partners on dissolution, the partner whose name was Burchell would run no risk by reason of the use by the other of the old name, "Burchell & Co". Notice of the change had been given to all the clients. The defendants, in fact, undertook to carry on in business under a different name, namely, Burchell, Wilde & Co In *Townsend v Jarman* [1900] 2 Ch. 698; 17 R.P.C. 649, the claimant bought the business of Jarman & Co Ltd, seedsmen, from a company to whom he and the defendant had, on the dissolution of their partnership, transferred it. He carried on business as "Jarman & Co", and it was held that the defendant could not complain of this. The defendant had sold the business premises, on which his name "E. J. Jarman" was cut, to the company, who had transferred them to the claimant. It was held that the defendant could not compel the claimant to remove the name.

[76] *Thynne v Shove* (1890) L.R. 45 Ch.D. 577, Ch. D. These partnership cases are not easy to understand. It is difficult to see how continuation of a business under its own name could render former partners liable for its activities; and the cases seem to distinguish here—or some of them do—between cases where the goodwill is actually assigned to the new owners and cases where they merely acquire the business with no explicit assignment of goodwill. It would seem, accordingly, that such cases cannot be considered merely as cases involving passing off, and reference to specialist works on partnership may here be desirable.

in the absence of special agreement, the right to use the partnership name belongs to the purchaser.[77] But the partners may agree to divide up the goodwill, and if they do, they will each be entitled to make use of the name, in a business similar to that of the partnership, so long as they do not do so deceptively and in particular, do not represent that the others are still their partners.[78]

Trader may use his name after the sale of his business, where no contrary agreement

Where the goodwill of an unincorporated business is sold, or is taken over on the dissolution of a partnership by agreement, without any restrictive condition being imposed upon the late owner or the retiring partner which restrains him from exercising his ordinary right, he is at liberty to start in the same trade again at once under his own name, even though it be the same as, or be similar to, the name under which the old business was, and continues to be, carried on:[79] provided that he does so honestly and without representing to customers that his new business continues or is connected with the business that he has sold.[80] An agreement for the sale of a business carried on under the proprietor's personal name should, accordingly, normally contain appropriate restrictions on his using the name again. The sale of a business conducted by a limited company involving transfer of ownership of the company, raises different considerations, since there can hardly be any justification for giving a similar name to any other company.[81] Even so restrictions on individuals concerned with the old management may be desirable.   **15–227**

Even in the absence of express restrictions the vendor or retiring partner could not trade under the old name if it differed from his own personal name.[82]

FORCED SALE OF GOODWILL

A trustee in bankruptcy has no power to contract on behalf of the bankrupt, and the bankrupt is not a grantor so as to be bound by the rule applied in *Trego v Hunt*.[83] The sale of the goodwill of his business in the bankruptcy, accordingly, throws no obligation upon the bankrupt trader, other than the obligation of the   **15–228**

---

[77] It is part of the partnership assets: *Re David and Matthews* [1899] 1 Ch. 378. For a recent consideration of this point, see *SAXON Trade Mark* [2003] F.S.R. 704 *Byford v Oliver*).

[78] *Burchell v Wilde* [1900] 1 Ch. 551 (Burchell & Co).

[79] *Labouchère v Dawson* (1872) L.R. 13 Eq. 322.

[80] See below. The cases on this point are old ones, and share the characteristic vagueness of the older "own name" cases. It would seem from the judgment of Parker J., in *Pomeroy v Scale* (1907) 24 R.P.C. 177 at 187, that if mere use of his name without proper explanation must necessarily make such a representation, he may not use the name without making the explanation, to each customer if necessary. Buckley J. at 181, put the law slightly differently, but it is submitted that Parker J. would probably be followed today. Probably the vendor may use his own name again, notwithstanding that he thereby reminds customers that he used to be connected with the business sold (provided he does no more), but only on condition that it is absolutely clear that the two businesses are distinct. In *Aubanel & Alabaster v Aubanel* (1949) 66 R.P.C. 343, the case was treated as on all fours with any ordinary "own name" case: but then, the sale had been some 15 years before, and an injunction was nevertheless granted. This footnote (in the 13th edition) was cited with approval by Jacob L.J. in *I.N. Newman Limited v Richard T Adlem* [2005] EWCA (Civ) 741 at paras 29 to 32. The vendor of such a business is under a positive duty to make it clear that any new business under his own name is distinct from the business sold.

[81] See the discussion, para.15–219, illustration (1), of the "Adrema" and "Sturtevant" cases. There is indeed some difficulty in reconciling the various lines of authority, and the "Labouchère" case cited in para.15–227 might well not be followed today.

[82] The grant would then pass the exclusive right to the name: *Pomeroy v Scale* (1901) 24 R.P.C. 177, but see as to this case, above. See also cases cited in the last three footnotes.

[83] [1896] A.C. 7; see next note.

general law, not to represent that the business is still carried on by him.[84] The purchaser can accordingly restrain the bankrupt from using a firm name, but not from using his own name.[85]

(1) The claimant had had a cigar factory at Manila, which, owing to events consequent on the 1915–1918 War, passed into other hands. The claimant retained a factory in Hong Kong and had sold cigars in Shanghai from that factory under similar names and marks to those on the Manila cigars. It was held that the defendant company, assignees of the Manila business, who sold cigars in Shanghai made in the Manila factory, were entitled to do so under similar marks so long as they did not represent their goods to be those of the claimant: *Ingenohl v Wing On* (1927) 44 R.P.C. 343, PC.

(2) A group of companies traded in the financial sector under the name "Dawney, Day". One company in the group was a joint venture, the management of which became deadlocked. An administration order was made with directions for the sale of the business. The administrator sold the business and its goodwill to the defendants, with the right to use the business name "Dawnay, Day Securities" "so far as it is lawfully able to do so…". Companies representing the Dawnay, Day group succeeded in preventing the defendants from continuing to use the "Dawnay, Day" name: *Dawnay, Day & Co Ltd v Cantor Fitzgerald International*.[86]

The vendor must not represent that his business is the old business, or its successor

15–229   The vendor of a business must do nothing, after the sale, which is calculated to suggest that he is still carrying on the old business.[87]

A partner, who, after he had sold his share in the business of "John Douglas & Co." to his co-partners, continued to trade as "Churton, Bankart and Hirst, late John Douglas and Co.", was restrained from trading as "John Douglas & Co.," or representing that his new business was a continuation of the old business: *Churton v Douglas* (1859) L.J.Ch. 841.

15–230   The question whether the late owner of a business which has passed into other hands is representing that he is still carrying it on or that a new business of his is its successor, or is only fairly working and advertising the latter business as his own, may be one of difficulty.

The partnership between the parties having expired by effluxion of time, and the goodwill passing under the partnership articles to the claimant, but without any restrictive covenant binding the defendant not to use the firm name or any similar name, the defendant was restrained from issuing a circular to the old customers stating the fact of dissolution and that he had joined a new firm, and

---

[84] *Walker v Mottram* (1881–82) L.R. 19 Ch.D. 355, CA. In *Trego v Hunt* [1896] A.C. 7. Lord Macnaghten said: "There is all the difference in the world between the case of a man who sells what belongs to himself and receives the consideration, and the man whose property is sold without his consent by his trustee in bankruptcy, and who comes under no obligation, express or implied, to the purchaser from the trustee." See also *Greener v Morris* [1914] 1 Ch.D. 562 at 566; and as to the effect of a vesting order under Enemy Property legislation, *Reuter v Mulhens* (1953) 70 R.P.C. 235.

[85] *Wood v Hall* (1916) 33 R.P.C. 16, Younger J. (sale of goodwill by trustee of deed of arrangement for creditors).

[86] [2000] R.P.C. 669. The Court of Appeal held that the licence to the joint venture company to use the Dawnay, Day name must have been subject to the implied condition that the company would continue to be part of the group.

[87] See *May v May* (1914) 31 R.P.C. 324. As to subsequent use by the vendor of his own name, see above.

asking the customers for a "continuance" of their custom. This was held to be a suggestion, that he was about to carry on, not merely a similar business, as he lawfully might, but the identical business which had passed to the claimant: *Mogford v Courtenay* (1881) 45 L.T. (N.S.) 303. There is some later authority[88] that he ought to have been restrained from privately soliciting the old customers to deal with him in any terms whatsoever.

---

[88] *Re David and Matthews* [1899] 1 Ch. 378; but the matter is more complex than that: see works on confidential information.

CHAPTER 16

LIMITATIONS ON ENFORCEMENT AND EXPLOITATION

1. Introduction

16–001　This chapter is concerned with certain limitations on enforcement of registered trade marks, over and above the standard defences to an action for infringement. The limitations discussed in this chapter are essentially derived from law developed at Community and now European Union level. They divide into two principal topics:[1] the first is principally concerned with what has become known as "exhaustion of rights" and the second is concerned with the application of the competition laws of the European Union and the United Kingdom to the exploitation and enforcement of registered trade marks.

16–002　The function of this chapter is to examine in detail these limitations on the exploitation and enforcement of trade marks. It is beyond the scope of this work to examine wider questions of EU law, of Commission practice or general United Kingdom competition law and practice. For these the reader is referred to more general works.[2]

STRUCTURE OF THIS CHAPTER

16–003　The two principal topics identified above-relating to "exhaustion" and "competition" respectively-are dealt with in turn. However, the first topic is conveniently divided under a number of headings. First, it is necessary to explain how the rule of "exhaustion of rights" applies at the level of individual Member States. Section 12 of the Trade Marks Act 1994, derived from Article 7 of the Trade Marks Directive, is one manifestation of the rule. Neither s.12 nor Art.7 contain the whole story. Both carry with them the accumulated case law of the ECJ concerning the application of Arts 28 and 30 (formerly Arts 30 and 36) in the field of trade marks and will fall to be interpreted in accordance with any new case law in this area. Accordingly, interpretation of s.12/Art.7 requires a thorough understanding of the existing case law relating to exhaustion of trade mark rights and how it has developed. The development has been somewhat haphazard. In particular, it will be seen that misconceptions about the proper level of trade mark

---

[1] Of course, these are not the only aspects of EU law which are now relevant to the UK law of registered trade marks. The harmonisation of the laws of Member States relating to trade marks is dealt with subject by subject in other chapters.

[2] See, *e.g.* Bellamy and Child, *European Community Law of Competition* (5th ed., ed.Roth, Sweet & Maxwell, London, 2001). A full examination of Community law is contained in the *Encyclopaedia of European Community Law* (ed. Merkin, Sweet & Maxwell, London). A particularly helpful work on Commission practice and procedure is Kerse and Khan, *EC Antitrust Procedure* (5th ed., Sweet & Maxwell, London, 2005).

protection[3] underlie some of the more problematic decisions of the European Court in this field.[4]

The application of the rule of exhaustion in straightforward situations involving intra-EU trade calls for little comment. However, the precise limits of the rule, as developed by the European Court, are still being explored, particularly in the repackaging cases. Further current issues are whether the rule applies at all to parallel imports into the EEA, and the position as regards goods which do not originate in the EEA but which are first put on the market in one of the EEA countries which is not also an EU State. An issue which has yet to arise, but was foreshadowed in *Dior* concerns whether s.12(2)/Art.7(2) creates a new right. The resolution of these and other undecided issues is greatly assisted by a clear understanding of the principles of EU law involved and how they interact. The foregoing gives some explanation as to the structure of this Chapter, which is as follows:

   2. Section 12/Article 7 in the Hierarchy of EU Law
   3. The Development and Application of "Exhaustion of Rights"
   4. Repackaging, Relabelling and Rebranding
   5. Parallel Imports into the EEA
   6. The Dior Problem
   7. Competition Laws of the EU and the United Kingdom
   8. Arts 81 and 82
   9. Competition Act 1998
  10. Trade Marks and Restraint of Trade

16–004

2. Section 12/Article 7 in the hierarchy of EU law

INTERPRETATION OF SECTION 12/ARTICLE 7

Section 12 of the 1994 Act provides as follows:

16–005

"Exhaustion of rights conferred by registered trade mark

12—(1) A registered trade mark is not infringed by the use of the trade mark in relation to goods which have been put on the market in the European Economic Area under that trade mark by the proprietor or with his consent.

   (2) Subsection (1) does not apply where there exist legitimate reasons for the proprietor to oppose further dealings in the goods (in particular, where the condition of the goods has been changed or impaired after they have been put on the market)."

Section 12 is derived from Article 7 of the TM Directive. The reference in s.12 to the EEA, as opposed to the reference in the original version of Art.7 to "the Community", is the result of the EEA Agreement.[5] The other slight differences in

---

[3] The context requires a precise evaluation of the function of trade marks, something which is not required in the context of inherent registrability of a mark. There, a mark need only satisfy the minimum requirement of having a distinctive character, and no further investigation of function is required.

[4] Although it should be said that the European Court has had admirable guidance from A.G. Jacobs in most of the important trade mark cases of the 1990s, from Hag II onwards.

[5] Effective from January 1, 1994. The original Art.7(1) in the Directive was replaced by a version set out in Annex XVII to the EEA Agreement. Essentially, "in the Community" was replaced with "in a Contracting Party".

wording appear immaterial.[6] Since s.12 must be interpreted consistently with Art.7, unless that is impossible,[7] and since consistent interpretation appears possible, in the remainder of this discussion s.12 and Art.7 are treated as being identical.

16–007   At the basic level, s.12 poses few problems. Once goods have been put on the market by the proprietor or with his consent, his registered trade mark rights cannot be used to prevent further dealings in the goods. The registered trade mark right is said to have been "exhausted" by the first marketing of the goods bearing the trade mark. The limitation contained in s.12(1) has particular relevance in the context of free movement of goods throughout the EEA. Once goods have been placed on the market anywhere in the EEA, national trade mark rights cannot be used to prevent their movement anywhere in the EEA.

One (perhaps unintentional) effect of s.12(1) is that it applies whether or not any inter-state trade is involved. It lays down the rule for domestic exhaustion of rights of trade marks as well as the rule for inter-EEA trade.

16–008   The limitation contained in s.12(1) is not absolute. The trade mark proprietor may use his registered trade mark rights to oppose further dealings in the goods where there exist legitimate reasons to do so. Section 12(2) gives some non-exhaustive examples of what may constitute legitimate reasons-where the condition of the goods is changed or impaired after they have been put on the market. Other examples of "legitimate reasons" are contained in the case law of the ECJ, particularly under Art.30 (ex.36).[8]

16–009   An independent garage in the Netherlands specialised in the sale of second-hand BMW cars and in repairing and maintaining BMWs. Complaint was made of the use of the BMW mark in advertisements for these goods and services: "BMW Specialist"; "Specialised in BMWs"; "Repairs and maintenance of BMWs". The ECJ held:

(1) In relation to the advertisements for second-hand BMWs, if the trade mark was used in a reseller's advertising in such a way as to give rise to the impression that there is a commercial connection between the reseller and the proprietor, that might give a legitimate reason within Art.7(2). Whether the advertising created that impression is a matter for the national court. On the other hand, if there is no risk that the public will be led to believe there is a commercial connection, the mere fact that the reseller derives an advantage from using the mark in advertisements, provided they are honest and fair, in that they lend an aura of quality to his business does not constitute a "legitimate reason".

(2) In relation to the advertisements for services, Article 7 had no application, but Art.6 had to be interpreted in the same way, as seeking "to reconcile the fundamental interests of trade mark protection with those of the free movement of goods and freedom to provide services in the common market". The same reasoning applied. *BMW v Deenik*.[9]

16–010   As soon as one moves beyond the basic level, problems begin to appear which

---

[6] Art.7(2) uses the expression "further commercialization of the goods", whereas s.12(2) refers to "further dealings in the goods". In *Paranova* [1996] E.C.R. I-3457 and *Dior* [1998] 1 C.M.L.R. 737, A.G. Jacobs commented that "commercialization" in the English version of the Directive appears to be a literal translation of the French word "commercialisation", whereas it would be more normal in English to speak of "further marketing of the goods".

[7] *Marleasing* [1990] E.C.R. I-4135; and *Webb v EMO Air Cargo* [1993] 1 W.L.R. 49.

[8] See ss.3, 4 and 6 of this chapter at paras 16–021, 16–054 and 16–100 respectively.

[9] [1999] E.C.R.-I 905; [1999] E.T.M.R. 339.

cannot be satisfactorily resolved simply from the wording used in s.12/Art.7. For example:

> what is the precise scope of the expression "under that trade mark by the proprietor or with his consent"?
>
> how should "consent" be interpreted?
>
> what can constitute a "legitimate reason"?
>
> is "exhaustion" the correct concept?
>
> and, at a deeper level, does the wording of s.12(1) faithfully reflect the state of affairs presented by the EEA Agreement?

The first point is answered below. The second point lies at the heart of the issue concerned with parallel imports into the EEA.[10] The third point lies at the heart of the repackaging cases.[11] The fourth point lies at the heart of a problem which the European Court has created for itself in Dior and which it will have to tackle at some point in the future.[12] This problem relates to the scope of protection afforded to, and the true function of, a registered trade mark. The final point gives a further twist to the issue of parallel imports into the EEA.

"Under that trade mark"

Article 7 of the TM Directive is virtually identical to Article 13 of the Community Trade Marks Regulation. Despite the fact that the CTM Regulation was passed some six years after the Directive, the *travaux preparatoires* make it clear that the two provisions were drafted at the same time.[13] Both provisions apply to goods put on the market in the EEA under that trade mark. That expression is apt for a CTM, but is rather clumsy when transposed into the TM Directive. In the context of the Directive, it must be interpreted as referring not only to the particular national registered trade mark but also all trade marks which: (1) are owned by the same proprietor or by another entity which is economically linked;[14] (2) are identical or virtually identical;[15] and (3) either registered or unregistered[16] which are used by the proprietor or with his consent for putting goods on the market in any state of the EEA. The alternative interpretation is untenable, that it refers only to the particular national trade mark. This is but one example which demonstrates that the proper interpretation of s.12/Art.7 requires knowledge of the accumulated case law of the ECJ on Arts 28 and 30 (formerly Arts 30 and 36) in the field of trade marks.

16–011

---

[10] See s.5, at para.16–081.

[11] See s.4, at para.16–054.

[12] See s.6, at para.16–100.

[13] The *travaux preparatoires* also show that the original proposals for the CTM Regulation and TM Directive incorporated a rule of international exhaustion (COM (80) 635 final: [1980] O.J. C 351/1). In 1983, the European Parliament proposed the deletion of the rule of international exhaustion and substitution of a rule of Community-wide exhaustion ([1983] O.J. C 307/46), a proposal which was adopted by the Commission (COM (84) 470 final—for the Regulation; COM (85) 793 final for the Directive). As for the exceptions to exhaustion early attempts to codify the existing case law of the European Court were abandoned, giving rise to the expression "legitimate reasons", which is wide enough to catch all relevant existing and future case law of the ECJ.

[14] See, *e.g. IHT Internationale Heiztechnik v Ideal Standard* [1994] E.C.R. I-2789 at 2847, para.34; [1994] 3 C.M.L.R. 857; [1995] F.S.R. 59.

[15] The case law of the ECJ brushes aside slight differences in marks used in different Member States, *e.g.* Cotonelle/Cottonelle and goes further in the repackaging cases, allowing rebranding, provided it is objectively necessary *e.g.* Dalacine/Dalacin C/Dalacin) where different marks are used in different Member States. See further at para.16–063.

[16] cf. *Merck v Stephar* [1981] E.C.R. 2063; [1981] 3 C.M.L.R. 463. See further at para.16–024.

16–012   In two repackaging cases, the European Court has explained the proper approach to the interpretation of Art.7. In *Paranova*,[17] the Court held that:

(a)   Art.7 comprehensively regulates the question of exhaustion of trade mark rights for products traded in the Community [now EEA];

(b)   the Directive must be interpreted in the light of the Treaty rules on free movement of goods;

(c)   Art.7(1) reiterates the case law of the Court based on Arts [28 and 30] (ex.30 and 36); and

(d)   Art.7(2) must be interpreted in the same way as Art.[30] (ex.36).

These principles were confirmed in *Loendersloot*.[18] The reason why Art.7 must be interpreted in the same way as Art.30 of the Treaty[19] is because, in the context of trade marks, both provisions are intended to reconcile the fundamental interest in protecting trade mark rights with the fundamental interest in the free movement of goods within the Common Market. In order to resolve the finer points of the repackaging cases and the issue over parallel imports into the EEA, it helps to have a precise understanding of how this process of reconciliation works. A comprehensive interpretation of Art.7 requires us to start from first principles.

THE CONFLICT BETWEEN NATIONAL TRADE MARK RIGHTS AND THE FREE MOVEMENT OF GOODS

16–013   One of the principal objectives of the Treaty of Rome was and remains to establish a single or internal market comprising the territories of all the Member States "characterised by the abolition, as between Member States, of obstacles to the free movement of goods, persons, services and capital".[20] It has long been recognised that a conflict exists between the aim of a single market and the presence of national intellectual property rights, which are particularly suited to dividing up the market along national boundaries.

16–014   In order to resolve the conflict in the field of trade marks, the European Court has had to balance the competing interests: the fundamental aim of the single market and the free movement of goods in the Community against the fundamental interest in the protection of trade mark rights. The way in which the balance is achieved depends upon the relative status of the interests or principles involved.

THE PRINCIPLES ENSHRINED IN THE TREATY

16–015   At the highest level are the principles set out in the EC Treaty (originally the Treaty of Rome).[21]

Article 2: "The Community shall have as its task, by establishing a common market and an economic and monetary union and by implementing common policies or activities referred to in Articles 3 and 4, to promote throughout the

---

[17] *Bristol Myers Squibb v Paranova* [1996] E.C.R. I-3457 (ECJ); [1996] F.S.R. 225 (AG); and [1997] F.S.R. 102 (ECJ). See furthe at para.16–060.

[18] [1997] E.C.R. I-6227, para.18.

[19] Note that it is not permissible to interpret s.12 directly in relation to Art.30 (ex.36). As a national measure implementing a provision of the Directive, s12 must be interpreted consistently with Art.7. Art.7 may then be interpreted in the light of Art.30 and applicable case law, even though the result may be exactly the same: see *Paranova* [1996] E.C.R. I-3457, paras 25, 26; [1997] F.S.R. 102.

[20] EC Treaty, Art.3(a).

[21] The EC Treaty has been amended by the Single European Act 1986, the Treaty on European Union (the EU Treaty) in 1992 and the Treaty of Amsterdam 1997. Art.12(1) caused renumbering of some of the most familiar Articles. Hence the familiar old Arts 30 and 36 are 28 and 30, and the old Arts 85 and 86 are now 81 and 82.

Community a harmonious, balanced and sustainable development of economic activities, …".

Article 3: "For the purposes set out in Article 2, the activities of the Community shall include, as provided in this Treaty and in accordance with the timetable set out therein:

(a) the prohibition as between Member States, of customs duties and quantitative restrictions on the import and export of goods, and of all other measures having equivalent effect, …

(b) an internal market characterised by the abolition, as between Member States, of obstacles to the free movement of goods, persons, services and capital;

…

(g) a system ensuring that competition in the internal market is not distorted;
…"

Article 28 (ex.30): "Quantitative restrictions on imports and all measures having equivalent effect shall be prohibited between Member States." **16–016**

Article 30 (ex.36): "The provisions of [Article 28] shall not preclude prohibitions or restrictions on imports, exports or goods in transit justified on the grounds of … the protection of industrial and commercial property. Such prohibitions or restrictions shall not, however, constitute a means of arbitrary discrimination or a disguised restriction on trade between Member States."

Article 295 (ex.222): "This Treaty shall in no way prejudice the rules in Member States governing the system of property ownership." **16–017**

COMMUNITY LEGISLATION

At the second level, for our purposes, are provisions of Community legislation made pursuant to the powers conferred in the EC Treaty. The relevant legislation comprises the CTM Regulation and the Trade Marks Directive. **16–018**

UNITED KINGDOM LEGISLATION

First, it is necessary to have regard to s.2(1) of the European Communities Act 1972, which expressly provides for the supremacy of the Community Treaties, although the key Treaty referred to in the Act is the Treaty establishing the European Community—the " E.C. Treaty":[22] **16–019**

"all such rights, powers, liabilities, obligations and restrictions from time to time created or arising by or under the Treaties, and all such remedies and procedures from time to time provided for by or under the Treaties, as in accordance with the Treaties are without further enactment to be given legal effect or used in the United Kingdom shall be recognised and available in law, and be enforced, allowed and followed accordingly."

In the context of the Trade Marks Act 1994, that provision serves to reinforce what is already obvious: that the relevant provisions of the 1994 Act implement and are derived from the Trade Marks Directive. However, s.12/Art.7 represent just one manifestation of the more general rule known as "exhaustion of rights", and in order to explain how the hierarchy of interests is reconciled, it is necessary to track something of the development of the "exhaustion of rights" rule. **16–020**

---

[22] Other treaties are also within the scope of the Act, but they have no relevance to trade mark law. The EC Treaty was previously known as the Rome Treaty. The EC Treaty has been amended by the Single European Act 1986, the Treaty on European Union (the EU Treaty) signed at Maastricht in 1992 and the Treaty of Amsterdam 1997.

3. The development and application of "exhaustion of rights"

INTRODUCTION

16–021 The "exhaustion of rights" principle was developed by the European Court in a series of cases in the 1970s. Seeking to prevent the use of industrial property rights to divide the Common Market, the Court initially sought to achieve its purpose via the use of Art.81 (ex.85). This had a number of difficulties so, once the route via Arts 28 and 30 (ex.30–36) was seen, Art.85 ceased to play a significant role in the development. This switch is an indication of the rather haphazard development of the principle.

PRINCIPLE OF EXHAUSTION OF RIGHTS

16–022 "The proprietor of an industrial or commercial property right protected by the law of a Member State cannot rely on that law to prevent the importation of a product which has lawfully been marketed in another Member State by the proprietor himself or with his consent."[23]

16–023 This principle does not depend upon whether the first marketing is in a Member State where there is an industrial property right. It is enough that the goods are put into free circulation by or with the consent of the holder of the right.

16–024 Merck could not obtain a patent in Italy although they patented the drug concerned in every other Member State. The defendants imported Merck's product marketed by Merck in Italy. Held: The free movement rules of the Treaty prevented Merck from asserting their Dutch patent to prevent sales in Holland: *Merck v Stephar*.[24]

16–025 It follows that the expression "exhaustion of rights" is not wholly apt; there need be no right exhausted in the Member State of first marketing, nor does the rule apply where the holder of the right has received a royalty under his right from a compulsory licensee.[25] Nonetheless, the expression is now firmly established.[26]

EVOLUTION OF "EXHAUSTION OF RIGHTS"

16–026 The first step was the creation of the distinction between the existence of the property right and its exercise. This step was necessary to overcome Art.222 (now 295): "This Treaty shall in no way prejudice the rules in Member States governing the system of property ownership."

  1. Grundig, of Germany, appointed Consten their "sole representative" in France. Consten registered GINT (Grundig INTernational) in France subject to a declaration that it was intended to be placed solely on Grundig's goods. Additionally, Consten undertook to transfer the mark to Grundig (or abandon it altogether) if they ceased to be sole distributors.

---

[23] *Terrapin v Terranova* [1976] E.C.R. 1039 at 1061, para.6; [1976] 2 C.M.L.R. 482 at 505–506; *Merck v Stephar* [1981] E.C.R. 2063; [1981] 3 C.M.L.R. 463.

[24] [1981] E.C.R. 2063; [1981] 3 C.M.L.R. 463.

[25] Case 19/84 *Pharmon v Hoechst* [1985] 3 C.M.L.R. 775, ECJ (no right of free circulation for drugs sold by compulsory licensee). The compulsory licence is regarded as a state measure, not a permission from the holder of the right.

[26] In the 12th edition of this work, the rule was called the free circulation rule. We continue to consider the notion of "free circulation" as more accurate, but "exhaustion of rights" is very firmly established *e.g.* in s.12/Art.7) despite being something of a misnomer, as explained in the text.

Grundig used the GINT mark on all their goods, including their German goods. Consten sought to use the GINT trade mark to prevent parallel imports from Germany of Grundig goods. A complaint to the Commission that Grundig and Consten had infringed Art.85 (now 81) was upheld by the Court. The Court recognised the French registration but went on to say "the fact nevertheless remains that it was by virtue of an agreement with Grundig that it was able to effect registration." "Articles 36, 222 and 234 of the Treaty ... do not exclude any influence whatever of Community law on the exercise of national industrial property rights."[27] Consten was restrained from using its national trade mark rights to prevent parallel imports.

Following Grundig, this dichotomy between *existence* and *exercise* of industrial property rights became well established.[28]

The second step involved the shift from emphasis on Art.85 (now 81) to Art.30 (now 28). The crucial piece of evolution was the decision to treat the reference in Art.30 to "measures having equivalent effect" as including all industrial property rights. This led, eventually, to the implementation of the three stage test which was inherent in what was Arts 30–36. First, Art.30 contained the overriding rule "without prejudice to the following provisions" that quantitative restrictions on imports and all measures having equivalent effect between Member States were prohibited. Secondly, of the following provisions, only Art.36 provided a possible justification for the enforcement of an industrial property right so as to prohibit such imports. But the enforcement must be "justified on grounds of ... the protection of industrial and commercial property." And, thirdly, there is no justification if such enforcement constitutes "a means of arbitrary discrimination or disguised restriction upon trade between Member States." **16–027**

The shift to Art.30 took place in the early 1970s. In *Grundig* there had been some almost passing reference to Art.36, but the reference was a little muddled and seems to have been on the basis that Art.36 operated, by way of analogy, as an exception to Art.85. The cases following first indicated the difficulty of the Art.85 approach and then its virtual abandonment. **16–028**

2. Sirena in Italy had acquired the trade marks "Prep" and "Good Morning" by a series of transactions in the 1930s and 1940s. In part there was an assignment from a United States corporation, Mark Allen, and in part (as part of the arrangements with Mark Allen, however) an original registration in the name of Sirena. Novimpex imported goods bearing the marks into Italy from a German licensee of Mark Allen. The European Court reasoned that the original arrangements between Mark Allen and Sirena fell within Art.85 because, although they were apparently over, as active trading arrangements, "it is both necessary and sufficient that they continue to produce their effects after [the Treaty entered into force]": *Sirena v Eda*.[29]

This reasoning was clearly particularly artificial. The transactions had occurred years before the Treaty. Moreover there were considerable difficulties about the

---

[27] *Consten and Grundig v Commission* [1966] E.C.R. 429 at 345; [1966] C.M.L.R. 418 at 476.
[28] See, *e.g. Merck* [1981] E.C.R. 2063 at 2082, para.11, by the date of which the dichotomy is taken for granted.
[29] [1971] E.C.R. 69 at 83, para.12; [1971] C.M.L.R. 260 at 274. Note that the translation in C.M.L.R. is not exactly the same as that in E.C.R. The latter is the authoritative text. The Italian court's final ruling against Sirena, following the Art.177 reference, is reported at [1975] 1 C.M.L.R. 409.

status of the assignment. It seemed to follow that the original assignment to Sirena was invalid—which was a patently absurd result.[30]

16–029   Neither in *Sirena* nor in the next case *Deutsche Grammophon v Metro*, was there an express reference to Art.30 itself. But *Deutsche Grammophon* saw a much greater emphasis on the rules for the free movement of goods. The Art.85 reasoning of the earlier cases could hardly be applied because there was no agreement or the like involved. The case represents the first stage in the shift from Art.85 to Art.30.

> 3. DG sued Metro in Germany for copyright (strictly "distribution right") infringement in respect of the latter's importation and sale of DG made records from France. The action failed.

16–030   The Court noted that even if the exercise of the right did not fall within Art.85, the free movement rules should be considered. It stated that the effect of Art.36 "only admits derogations from [the free movement principle] to the extent to which they are justified for the purpose of safeguarding rights which constitute the specific subject-matter of such property". And it went on to state that the use of industrial property rights on the sole ground that initial distribution did not take place on the national territory concerned would be repugnant to the Treaty if it thereby isolated national markets. It concluded by its first formulation of the free movement rule in the following terms:

> "It would be in conflict with the provisions prescribing the free movement of products within the common market for a manufacturer of sound recordings to exercise the exclusive right to distribute the protected articles, conferred upon him by the legislation of a Member State, in such a way as to prohibit the sale in that State of products placed on the market by him or with his consent in another Member State solely because such distribution did not occur within the territory of the first Member State": *Deutsche Grammophon v Metro*.[31]

16–031   A number of cases following *Deutsche Grammophon v Metro* saw a natural expansion of the rule first stated in its narrow form as above. Thus it was applied to trade marks and patents. It reached its most general form, as applying to all forms of industrial property and whether or not a particular national right was exhausted, in *Merck*. And, through successive cases, the Court clarified the legal basis of the rule by particular reference to Art.30.

"ESSENTIAL FUNCTION" AND "SPECIFIC SUBJECT-MATTER" OF TRADE MARKS

16–032   Concepts of particular importance which were developed along with the rule as to goods in free circulation were the notions of the "essential function" and "specific subject-matter" of an industrial property right. When inter-state trade may be affected by the enforcement of such a right, such enforcement must be justified on the grounds of protection of the right. In deciding what is or is not justified, regard must be had to what is the essential purpose or function of the right. Initially, the Court was prepared to be bold in declaring the essential purpose—the specific subject-matter—narrowly so that interferences to inter-state trade were kept to a minimum. This was probably the result of the early

---

[30] And one which the Italian court refused to find in the subsequent proceedings by resorting to a fairly artificial process of reasoning—see [1975] 1 C.M.L.R. 409.

[31] [1971] E.C.R. 487 at 499–500; [1971] C.M.L.R. 631 at 656–658, para.13.

perception that trade marks were somehow less worthy of protection than other industrial property rights.[32] The balance did not begin to be restored until *HAG II*.

The first reference to "specific subject-matter" arose in *Deutsche Grammophon*.[33] Since then the concept has widened. In relation to patents the Court has said "the substance of a patent right lies essentially in according the inventor an exclusive right of first placing the product on the market."[34] The Court's definition of the specific subject-matter of trade mark rights was first given in *Centrafarm v Winthrop*,[35] and was as follows:

    16–033

> "In relation to trade marks, the specific subject-matter of the industrial property is the guarantee that the owner of the trade mark has the exclusive right to use that trade mark, for the purpose of putting products protected by the trade mark into circulation for the first time, and is therefore intended to protect him against competitors wishing to take advantage of the status and reputation of the trade mark by selling products illegally bearing that trade mark."

In *HAG I*,[36] the Court referred to the "basic function" of a trade mark as being "to guarantee to consumers that the product has the same origin" and in *Pfizer* it was stated:

    16–034

> "The main function of a trade mark is to give the consumer or final buyer a guarantee of the identity of origin of the marked product, by enabling him to distinguish this product, with no risk of confusion, from products of a different origin."

The decision in *HAG I* was eventually reversed by the European Court in *HAG II*[37] (see below). In *HAG II*, the Court clearly recognised the essential value of trade marks. They enable enterprises to gain customers by the quality of their goods and services, and for that purpose a trade mark must constitute a guarantee that all products bearing it have been manufactured under the supervision of a single enterprise. The Court restated that the specific subject-matter of a trade mark is:

    16–035

> "to grant the owner the right to use the mark for the first marketing of a product and, in this way to protect him against competitors who would like to abuse the position and reputation of the mark by selling products to which the mark has been improperly affixed."

---

[32] The marks at issue in *Sirena v Eda*, "Prep" and "Good Morning" no doubt contributed to this perception: "The exercise of a trade-mark right is particularly apt to lead to a partitioning of markets, and thus to impair the free movement of goods between States which is essential to the Common Market. Moreover, a trade-mark right is distinguishable in this context from other rights of industrial and commercial property, inasmuch as the interests protected by the latter are usually more important, and merit a higher degree of protection, than the interests protected by an ordinary trade mark.": [1971] E.C.R. 69 at 82, para.7; [1971] C.M.L.R. 260 at 273.

[33] [1971] E.C.R. 487 at 500, para.11; [1971] C.M.L.R. 631 at 657: " Art.36 only admits derogations from that freedom [*i.e.* of inter-State trade] to the extent to which they are justified for the purpose of safeguarding rights which constitute the specific subject-matter of such property."

[34] *Merck* [1981] E.C.R. 2063 at 2081, para.9; [1981] C.M.L.R. 463 at 481, para.9. And see also *Centrafarm v Sterling Drug*, [1974] E.C.R. 1147; [1974] 2 C.M.L.R. 480, at para.9: "In relation to patents, the specific subject-matter of the industrial property is the guarantee that to the patentee, to reward the creative effort of the inventor, has the exclusive right to use an invention with a view to manufacturing industrial products and putting them into circulation for the first time, either directly or by the grant of licences to third parties, as well as the right to oppose infringements."

[35] [1974] E.C.R. 1183 at 1194, para.8; [1974] 2 C.M.L.R. 480 at 508. Note: the unofficial C.M.L.R. translation of this paragraph is significantly different.

[36] [1976] E.C.R. 1039 at 1061, para.6; [1976] 2 C.M.L.R. 482 at 506.

[37] [1990] I E.C.R. 3711; [1990] 3 C.M.L.R. 571; [1991] F.S.R. 99.

16–036   And the essential function of a trade mark was stated to be:

> "to give the consumer or final user a guarantee of the identity of the origin of the marked product by enabling him to distinguish, without any possible confusion, that product from others of a different provenance."

16–037   It will be seen below that, although these concepts of essential function and specific subject-matter have retained a core consistency, they are used flexibly to adapt to particular situations which come before the European Court. This is readily apparent in the repackaging cases, which are discussed in detail in the next section of this chapter.

GOODS OF DIFFERENT QUALITY IN DIFFERENT STATES

16–038   Situations of this type fall to be decided under s.12 of the 1994 Act and Article 7 of the TM Directive. Bearing in mind that Art.7 must be interpreted in the same way as Art.30 (ex.36) of the EC Treaty, one can predict the outcome of the two typical situations which might arise.

16–039   The first is where the trade mark owner markets goods of different quality under the same mark in different Member States. He cannot use his trade mark rights to prevent the free movement of both types of goods throughout the EEA. The most that local law can require is that the public are warned of the different quality of the imported goods.

16–040   Imerco, in Denmark, ordered from Broadhurst in the United Kingdom, china services having a particular decoration. Strict quality standards were set, with the result that some 1,000 sub-standard services were rejected. Imerco agreed with Broadhurst that the latter could sell the rejects but not in Scandinavia. Broadhurst sold some of the rejects to United Kingdom wholesalers with a prohibition on resale to Denmark. Dansk Supermarket purchased some of the rejects and put them on sale in Denmark. Imerco sued in Denmark for trade mark and copyright infringement. The European Court held that the enforcement of those rights was prevented by Art.30 (now 28), although that did not preclude the possibility of action under consumer protection laws if the conditions of actual sale to the public infringed those laws. *Dansk Supermarked v Imerco*.[38]

16–041   The second situation is where the proprietor markets goods of one quality under one mark in some Member States and goods of another quality under a different mark in different Member States. Free circulation of both types of goods could not be prevented. On the other hand, a parallel trader could not substitute one mark for the other just because the first mark was better known in a particular Member State.

MARKS OF COMMON ORIGIN

16–042   "Marks of common origin" is a shorthand for the situation which sometimes arises where marks, originally in common ownership, become divided between separate undertakings. This situation raises particular problems in deciding how to balance the free movement of goods in the EEA against the enforcement of trade mark rights. Initially, the European Court did not get the balance quite right, probably because at the time it perceived trade mark rights to be less worthy of protection than other industrial property rights.

1. Originally the HAG trade mark was owned in Germany and Benelux by

---

[38] [1981] E.C.R. 181; [1981] 3 C.M.L.R. 590.

HAG Germany. In 1935 the Belgian and Luxembourg trade mark registrations were transferred to a subsidiary, HAG Belgium. HAG Belgium was confiscated during the war as being enemy property. As a result, the HAG trade marks in Germany on the one hand and Belgium and Luxembourg on the other were vested in entirely separate enterprises. By the date of the action, the Benelux rights had become vested in Van Zuylen Freres. HAG Germany, through an agent, sought to sell its HAG coffee in Luxembourg whereupon VZF sued for infringement. Held (on a reference to the European Court) that "one cannot allow the holder of a trade mark to rely on the exclusiveness of a trade mark right-which may be the consequence of the territorial limitation of national legislation-with a view to prohibiting the marketing in a Member State of goods legally produced in another Member State under an identical trade mark having the same origin": HAG I.[39]

This so-called "common origin" rule went further than the doctrine of exhaustion of rights. In particular it did not depend on any exercise of the right of first marketing. Each of the owners of a divided mark was entitled to sell throughout the Community under the mark, whether by himself or through others. The opportunity to reconsider this rule arose in *HAG II*.   **16–043**

2. After the decision in HAG I, the VZF firm was purchased by a Swiss company which disposed of most of VZF's coffee business apart from the HAG trade marks. The firm was transformed into a subsidiary of its new owner, trading under the name SA CNL-SUCAL NV ("HAG Belgium"). HAG Belgium then began to supply HAG coffee to the German market, whereupon HAG Germany sued in Germany for infringement. Held (on a reference to the European Court) Arts 30 and 36 do not preclude the exercise by a party of trade mark rights to oppose the importation of similar goods marked with the same or confusingly similar trade mark "even though the mark under which the disputed products are imported originally belonged to a subsidiary of the enterprise which opposes the importation and was acquired by a third enterprise as a result of the expropriation of that subsidiary." "Free movement of the goods would undermine the essential function of the trade mark": HAG II.[40]

HAG II involved a recognition by the European Court of the essential value of trade marks in enabling enterprises to gain customers by the quality of their goods or services. For that purpose a trade mark must constitute a guarantee that all products bearing it have been manufactured under the supervision of a single enterprise.[41] The severity of the "common origin" rule was relaxed, although the judgment in HAG II left a number of issues unresolved.   **16–044**

3. The mark "Tayto" was devised by a trader in the Republic of Ireland. An agreement in 1956 gave the use of the "Tayto" name together with selling and production rights in Northern Ireland to the claimant and in due course the claimant obtained a registration for the mark in the United Kingdom. Both traders flourished and competed in each other's territories but kept to their respective territories in their use of the Tayto mark. By the time the United Kingdom and Ireland joined the EC, the restrictive aspects of the 1956 agreement had ceased to be operative. The defendant imported

[39] *HAG I* [1974] E.C.R. 731 at 734, para.12; [1974] 2 C.M.L.R. 127 at 143. The language of the C.M.L.R. report is different but not, in this instance, materially so.
[40] *HAG II* [1990] I E.C.R. 3711; [1990] 3 C.M.L.R. 571; [1991] F.S.R. 99.
[41] Perhaps the surprising aspect of HAG II is the emphasis on the fact that national trade marks are territorial and the function of a trade mark must also be seen as territorial.

crisps into Northern Ireland from the Republic and was sued for passing off and trade mark infringement. Held (before HAG II was decided) that on the facts, the common origin doctrine from HAG I did not apply because the marks had never been in common ownership; nor were they the result of a subdivision of trade mark rights by agreement. *Tayto (Northern Ireland) Ltd v McKee*.[42]

16–045   One of the issues left unresolved in HAG II was whether the common origin doctrine applies if a mark is divided voluntarily but not as part of a deliberate market sharing arrangement? This issue arose in *Ideal Standard*.

> 4. Registrations of the mark "Ideal Standard" for heating installations and sanitary ware in France and Germany were originally held by national subsidiaries (SA and GmbH, respectively) in the same group. Economic difficulties in about 1976 led to the group ceasing its activities in heating installations, GmbH trading in sanitary ware only, and eventually to the assignment by SA of its business interests in heating installations together with the French trade mark for heating installations to CICH. SA retained the trade mark for sanitary ware. IHT, the German subsidiary of CICH, began to sell heating installations in Germany under the Ideal Standard mark. GmbH sued for infringement of its registration relating to sanitary ware. The European Court held that the considerations in HAG II applied whether the splitting of the trade mark was compulsory or by voluntary assignment: *Ideal Standard*.[43]

Essentially, cases involving marks of common origin will be decided on mainstream principles developed under Arts 28 and 30 (ex.30 and 36), there being no special or separate doctrine relating to marks of common origin.[44]

16–046   There is one further aspect of *Ideal Standard* which is worthy of note. It was argued that the assignment of the mark carried with it an implied consent to the assignee putting goods bearing the mark into circulation. This was rejected, on the basis that the consent implicit in an assignment is not the consent required for application of the doctrine of exhaustion of rights.

FREE MOVEMENT OF GOODS, CONSUMER PROTECTION AND UNFAIR COMPETITION/PASSING OFF

16–047   Most, if not all, Member States have national provisions which can be described generally as preventing unfair competition. Increasingly, areas previously covered by general unfair competition provisions are being supplanted by EU legislation—there are, for example, a number of Directives which are concerned with consumer protection.[45] Since all these measures can interfere with the free movement of goods, the question arises as to how the conflict is resolved.

16–048   Initially, the Court appeared to accept that the need to protect producers against unfair competition and consumers against deception regarding the origin of

---

[42] [1991] 3 C.M.L.R. 269 (High Court, Northern Ireland). For another pre-HAG II decision, see *Re "Klint"* [1988] 1 C.M.L.R. 340, a decision of the German Federal Supreme Court.

[43] *IHT Internationale Heiztechnik v Ideal Standard GmbH* [1994] E.C.R. I-2789.

[44] Even before HAG II, it had been decided that the common origin doctrine did not apply where the trade mark rights were divided between the Community and elsewhere: *EMI v CBS* [1976] E.C.R. 811; [1975] 2 C.M.L.R. 235 (the trade mark "Columbia" in the hands of EMI throughout the EEC and in the hands of CBS in the USA as a result of past and now-spent agreements, mergers and de-mergers. EMI held entitled to prevent sale of CBS "Columbia" records unless the word "Columbia" was obliterated).

[45] *e.g.* Directive 79/112 on the labelling, presentation and advertising of foodstuffs; Directive 84/450 on misleading advertising.

products could constitute justification on grounds of public policy under Art.36 (now 30). Subsequent case law has made it clear that, since Art.36 (now 30) derogates from a fundamental rule of the Treaty enshrined in Art.30 (now 28), it must be interpreted strictly and cannot be extended to objectives—such as protection against unfair competition and consumer protection—which are not expressly referred to in Art.36.[46] The justification for the restriction on the free movement of goods must be found elsewhere.[47]

In *Cassis de Dijon*[48] the Court first articulated a formula whereby the restriction on free movement of goods caused by national unfair competition legislation could be justified in order to satisfy overriding or mandatory requirements, which include protection against unfair competition and the defence of the consumer, provided that the legislation is proportionate to its objective. The objective must not be capable of being achieved by measures which are less restrictive of intra-Community trade.[49] In the application of this formula, the risk of misleading consumers cannot override the requirements of the free movement of goods unless the risk is sufficiently serious.[50] In assessing the level of risk, the relevant criterion is the presumed expectations of an average consumer who is reasonably well-informed and reasonably observant and circumspect.[51]   **16–049**

In Italy, the registration of "Cotonelle" for toilet paper was declared invalid as being liable to mislead the public into thinking the goods contained cotton, when they did not. In addition, the proprietor was ordered to cease use of the mark, under unfair competition laws. Use of the mark "Cottonelle" continued in France and Spain, where the registrations survived. Fransa parallel imported French goods into Italy. Graffione, a former wholesaler of the products in Italy, objected on the grounds of unfair competition. It was not clear whether the prohibition on use of the mark in Italy applied only to the (former) proprietor or to all. If the former, then unfair competition law could not be used to prevent Fransa parallel importing because Graffione had the ability to do the same. If the prohibition applied to all use of the mark in Italy, then the prohibition had to be necessary to ensure consumer protection, proportionate to that objective and incapable of being achieved by measures which are less restrictive of intra-Community trade. "The national court must, in particular, examine whether the risk of misleading consumers is sufficiently serious to be able to override the requirements for the free movement of goods": *Fratelli Graffione SNC v Ditta Fransa*.[52]   **16–050**

In the United Kingdom context, cases of this type are rare, probably because the argument that the free movement of goods requires deception of the public in   **16–051**

---

[46] See, *e.g. Commission v Ireland* [1981] E.C.R. 1625, paras 7–8; *Kohl v Ringelhan & Rennett* [1984] E.C.R. 3651, para.14.

[47] See the Opinion of A.G. Jacobs in Case C–312/98, *Schutzverband gegen Unwesen in der Wirtschaft e.V. v Warsteiner Brauerei Haus Cramer GmbH & Co KG*, of May 25, 2000, paras 55–56.

[48] [1979] E.C.R. 649; [1979] 3 C.M.L.R. 494.

[49] " *Cassis de Dijon*" [1979] E.C.R. 649, para.8; *Pall v Dahlhausen* [1990] E.C.R. I-4827, para.12, para.12; *Yves Rocher* [1993] E.C.R. I-2361, para.12; and *Mars* [1995] E.C.R. I-1923, para.15.

[50] *Graffione* [1996] E.C.R. I-6039, para.24, and see para.16–050.

[51] *Gut Springenheide and Tusky v Oberkreisdirektor Steinfurt* [1998] E.C.R. I-4657, paras 30–32. Those interested in the development of the "average consumer" test should consult paras 23–29 of the Opinion of A.G. Fennelly in Case C–220/98, *Estée Lauder Cosmetics v Lancaster Group*, September 16, 1999. Of course, the test has now been deployed in the field of registered trade marks, in *Lloyd Schuhfabrik Meyer v Klijsen Handel* [1999] E.C.R. I-3819, para.26, to the global assessment required for infringement under the 1994 Act, s10(2), and by the Court of Appeal in *Bach and Bach Flower Remedies Trade Marks* [2000] R.P.C. 513, to the test for distinctiveness.

[52] [1996] E.C.R. I-6039; [1997] F.S.R. 538.

the United Kingdom is a difficult one. There is greater scope for conflict with more general laws of unfair competition, which do not necessarily depend on proof of deception or its likelihood. It is possible to conceive of a claim in passing off where the Court would have to balance the risk of deception against the requirement for the free movement of goods, particularly if the case was near the borderline, where the risk was slight and only applied to a limited class of people.[53] The wider issue of whether the "average consumer" test should be adopted generally in the law of passing off is dealt with in Ch.14.

"ARBITRARY DISCRIMINATION OR A DISGUISED RESTRICTION"

16–052   The last sentence of Art.30 (ex.36) must be seen as a potent reserve weapon available against any attempt to use industrial property rights artificially to divide the EEA, supposing that any such attempt has otherwise overcome the free circulation rules.

APPLICATION TO SERVICE MARKS

16–053   The considerations discussed above are not directly applicable to trade marks used in relation to services. However, the European Court would no doubt regard as equally objectionable any use of a mark registered in respect of services to interfere with the free circulation of goods or services within the EEA, should suitable facts arise.

4. Repackaging, relabelling and rebranding[54]

16–054   In a previous edition of this work,[55] it was stated, somewhat optimistically, that the limitation of trade mark rights in repackaging cases was now settled-trade mark rights (if enforceable by national law)[56] cannot be enforced to prevent parallel imports from elsewhere in the EEA where the importer has re-packaged the goods fairly. If anything, the position is now less clear than it appeared at the time of that edition. This area of the law has now become a maze of arcane rules which seem to be developed for their own sake rather than because they are justified by any fundamental trade mark reason. The ECJ seems to have missed several opportunities to take a robust view and to say that the rights of the trade mark proprietor were exhausted when the goods were first put on the market in the EEA. As Jacob L.J. has observed,[57] there are other areas of law which are well equipped to deal with any later dealings which are unfair. Unless or until the ECJ undertakes a major review of the law in this area, we are stuck with an increasingly complex and unreal set of rules. Again, it seems sensible to summarise the evolution of the law in this area to explain its current state.

16–055   The clearer case is where the condition of the goods (as opposed to their packaging) has been altered after they have been put on the market, particularly where the alteration comprises the addition of a component not approved by the

---

[53] Equally, on suitable facts, an order of the "without sufficiently distinguishing" type could be too restrictive of inter-state trade.

[54] "Re-affixing" is the term used by the European Court to describe the situation where the mark on the goods is replaced by the mark used in the country of import—"rebranding" would seem to be a more accurate term.

[55] 12th ed., 1986.

[56] See the 1994 Act, s.10(6).

[57] *Boehringer Ingelheim v Swingward & Dowelhurst* [2004] E.W.C.A. Civ 129, paras 18–21.

trade mark proprietor.[58] The remainder of this discussion addresses the situation where the condition of the actual goods has not been altered, only their packaging.

Originally, different principles were thought to apply to cases of repackaging **16–056** (where the same mark was used in the relevant Member States) as opposed to the rebranding or re-affixing cases (where the trade mark owner used different marks in different Member States and the parallel importer affixed the mark used in the country of importation). However, by the time of *Pharmacia*,[59] it was realised that repackaging, relabelling and rebranding shade into one another, raising very similar issues. It was in *Pharmacia* that the European Court held that the same principles apply.

The commercial significance of repackaging by parallel importers, particularly **16–057** but not exclusively in the field of pharmaceuticals, has required further definition of how the balance is to be struck between the basic interests in free movement of goods and in trade mark rights. In seeking to strike this balance, the decisions of the European Court have again displayed a tendency to be influenced by the particular facts of the case, which have produced some unfortunate consequences-particularly the requirement that the repackager must give notice to the proprietor. Again, the notions of "specific subject-matter" and "essential function" are used to explain how the balance is to be achieved.

SPECIFIC SUBJECT-MATTER

Part of the specific subject-matter is the right to prevent use of the trade mark **16–058** which is liable to impair the guarantee of origin, as stated in *Hoffmann-La Roche*:

"In relation to trade marks, the specific subject-matter of the industrial property is the guarantee that the owner of the trade mark has the exclusive right to use that trade mark, for the purpose of putting products protected by the trade mark into circulation for the first time, and is therefore intended to protect him against competitors wishing to take advantage of the status and reputation of the trade mark by selling products illegally bearing that trade mark. In order to answer the question whether that exclusive right involves the right to prevent the trade-mark being affixed by a third person after the product has been repackaged, regard must be had to the essential function of the trade-mark, which is to guarantee the identity of the origin of the trade-marked product to the consumer or ultimate user, by enabling him without any possibility of confusion to distinguish that product from products which have another origin. This guarantee of origin means that the consumer or ultimate user can be certain that a trade-marked product which is sold to him has not been subject at a previous stage of marketing to interference by a third person, without the authorisation of the proprietor of the trade-mark, such as to affect the original condition of the product. The right attributed to the proprietor of preventing any use of the trade-mark which is likely to

---

[58] See *Sony Computer Entertainments v Tesco* [2000] E.T.M.R. 102. To make French Sony Playstations work in the UK, adaptors were added to the box. The origin of the adaptors was not made clear.

[59] *Pharmacia & Upjohn v Paranova* October 12, 1999. See further at para.16–060.

impair the guarantee of origin so understood is therefore part of the specific subject-matter of the trade-mark right."[60]

16–059   Eurim-Pharm imported an antibiotic sold under the trade mark Vibramycin. They re-packaged the goods to comply with German rules but in such a way that the trade mark was clearly visible. The re-packaging made it clear that the goods were imported and that Eurim-Pharm was responsible for the re-packaging. The European Court held that the German trade mark was unenforceable because the "consumer or final buyer cannot be misled as to their origin": *Pfizer v Eurim-Pharm*.[61]

THE *PARANOVA* CONDITIONS

16–060   In *Paranova*,[62] the Court summarised and elaborated on the previous re-packaging cases as follows:

"Save in the circumstances defined in Article 7(1), Article 7(2) of [the Directive] precludes the owner of a trade mark from relying on his rights as owner to prevent an importer from marketing a product which was put on the market in another Member State by the owner or with his consent, even if that importer repackaged the product and reaffixed the trade mark to it without the owner's authorisation.

Article 7(2) of [the Directive] must be interpreted as meaning that the trade mark owner may legitimately oppose the further marketing of a pharmaceutical product where the importer has repackaged the product and re-affixed the trade mark unless:

(1) it is established that reliance on trade-mark rights by the owner in order to oppose the marketing of repackaged products under that trade mark would contribute to the artificial partitioning of the markets between Member States; such is the case, in particular, where the owner has put an identical pharmaceutical product on the market in several Member States in various forms of packaging, and the repackaging carried out by the importer is necessary in order to market the product in the Member State of importation, and also carried out in such conditions that the original condition of the product cannot be affected by it; that condition does not, however, imply that it must be established that the trade-mark owner deliberately sought to partition the markets between Member States; [the "market partitioning condition"]

(2) it is shown that the repackaging cannot affect the original condition of the product inside the packaging; such is the case, in particular, where the importer has merely carried out operations involving no risk of the product being affected, such as, for example, the removal of blister packs, flasks, ampoules or inhalers from their original external packaging and their replacement in new external packaging, the fixing of self-stick labels on the inner packaging of the product, the addition to the packaging of new user instructions or information, or the insertion of an extra article; it is for the national court

---

[60] *Hoffmann-La Roche v Centrafarm* [1978] E.C.R. 1139 at 1164, para.7; [1978] 3 C.M.L.R. 217, para.14.

[61] [1981] E.C.R. 2913; [1982] 1 C.M.L.R. 406, applying the criteria in *Hoffmann-La Roche* , at para.14. Photographs of the goods both before and after re-packaging appear at [1982] E.I.P.R. 84.

[62] *Bristol-Myers Squibb v Paranova A/S* [1996] E.C.R. I-3457; [1996] E.T.M.R. 1.

to verify that the original condition of the product inside the packaging is not indirectly affected, for example, by the fact that the new external or inner packaging of the repackaged product or new user instructions or information omits certain important information or gives inaccurate information, or the fact that an extra article inserted in the packaging by the importer and designed for the ingestion and dosage of the product does not comply with the method of use and the doses envisaged by the manufacturer;

(3) the new packaging clearly states who repackaged the product and the name of the manufacturer in print such that a person with normal eye-sight, exercising a normal degree of attentiveness, would be in a position to understand; similarly, the origin of an extra article from a source other than the trade mark owner must be indicated in such a way as to dispel any impression that the trade mark owner is responsible for it; however, it is not necessary to indicate that the repackaging was carried out without the authorisation of the trade mark owner;

(4) the presentation of the repackaged product is not such as to be liable to damage the reputation of the trade mark and of its owner; thus, the packaging must not be defective, of poor quality, or untidy; and

(5) the importer gives notice to the trade mark owner before the repackaged product is put on sale, and, on demand, supplies him with a specimen of the repackaged product."[63]

The propositions concerning Article 7(1) of the TM Directive were stated in terms which apply to all goods, whereas the specific guidelines on Art.7(2) (the so-called Paranova conditions) were stated in terms which applied only to pharmaceutical products. In *Loendersloot*,[64] the Court treated the Paranova conditions as applicable to all goods, with only minor variations. One particular variation from Loendersloot (a relabelling case) should be noted: **16–061**

"The person carrying out the re-labelling must, however, use the means which make parallel trade feasible while causing as little prejudice as possible to the specific subject matter of the trade mark right. Thus, if the statements on the original labels comply with the rules on labelling in force in the Member State of destination, but those rules require additional information to be given, it is not necessary to remove and reaffix or replace the original labels, since the mere application to the bottles in question of a sticker with the additional information may suffice."[65]

The principles stated in *Hoffmann-La Roche* were extended in *Dior*: **16–062**

"According to the case law of the Court concerning the repackaging of trademarked goods, the owner of a trade mark has a legitimate interest, related to the specific subject-matter of the trade mark right, in being able to oppose the commercialisation of those goods if the presentation of the repackaged goods is liable to damage the reputation of the trade mark."[66]

---

[63] [1996] E.C.R. I-3457 at 3543–3545; cf. [1996] E.T.M.R. 1 at 21. Note that the E.T.M.R. report does not include the Court's answers to the questions referred. The passages quoted are answers 2 and 3.

[64] *Frits Loendersloot v George Ballantine & Son Ltd* [1997] E.C.R.-I 6227, where the parallel traders removed the original labels to strip off identification codes and replaced them with original labels or copies.

[65] [1997] E.C.R.-I 6227 at 6260, para.46.

[66] *Parfums Christian Dior v Evora* [1998] 1 C.M.L.R. 737 at 766, para.43.

PHARMACIA

16–063 Pharmacia marketed an antibiotic, clindamycin, under a variety of marks. It used the trade mark "Dalacin" in Denmark, Germany and Spain, the trade mark "Dalacine" in France and the trade mark "Dalacin C" in the other Member States. The existence of the different marks was explained by an agreement with American Home Products in 1968 pursuant to which AHP assisted Pharmacia in obtaining suitable trade mark protection. The parallel importer, Paranova, had two sources of the drug: it purchased capsules in France (Dalacine) and injection phials in Greece (Dalacin C). After repackaging, the drugs were marketed in Denmark under the mark Dalacin. The Court affirmed and elaborated on the test of necessity: *Pharmacia*.[67]

16–064 The Court clarified, in *Pharmacia*, what was meant by the first *Paranova* condition relating to market partitioning. It held that this meant the replacement of the trade mark must be objectively necessary if the proprietor is to be precluded from opposing it and added (at paras 43–49):

"It follows that it is for the national courts to examine whether the circumstances prevailing at the time of marketing made it objectively necessary to replace the original trade mark by that of the importing Member State in order that the product in question could be placed on the market in that State by the parallel importer. This condition of necessity is satisfied if, in a specific case, the prohibition imposed on the importer against replacing the trade mark hinders effective access to the markets of the importing Member State. That would be the case if the rules or practices in the importing Member State prevent the product in question from being marketed in that State under its trade mark in the exporting Member State. This is so where a rule for the protection of consumers prohibits the use, in the importing Member State, of the trade mark used in the exporting Member State on the ground that it is liable to mislead consumers.

In contrast, the condition of necessity will not be satisfied if replacement of the trade mark is explicable solely by the parallel importer's attempt to secure a *commercial advantage*." (emphasis added).

16–065 Quite how the national courts are supposed to decide the postulated antithesis between "effective access to the market" and "commercial advantage" was not explained. Naturally that issue arose shortly afterwards, in *Dowelhurst*.

THE *DOWELHURST* SAGA[68]

16–066 Four drug companies brought proceedings against parallel importers who engaged in various forms of repackaging. The drugs in question were genuine, identical to those on the UK market, but obtained in other Member States of the EEA. Due to regulatory requirements, the boxing, labelling and information leaflets are not suitable for use in the UK. Hence the parallel importers make

---

[67] Case C–379/97, *Pharmacia & Upjohn v Paranova*, October 12, 1999, [1999] All E.R. (E.C.) 880; [2000] F.S.R. 621, cited passages at 631.
[68] The various judgments issued so far are as follows: (1) *Glaxo v Dowelhurst & Swingward* [2000] E.T.M.R. 415; [2000] F.S.R. 529, Laddie J.—his "first judgment" in which he made a reference to the ECJ: (2) Case C–143/00 *Boehringer Ingelheim v Swingward & Dowelhurst*, ECJ, April 23, 2002; (3) Laddie J.'s second judgment, February 6, 2003; (4) Main judgment of the Court of Appeal [2004] EWCA Civ 129, March 5, 2004; (5) Further judgment of the Court of Appeal, deciding the form of questions to refer to the ECJ [2004] EWCA Civ 757, June 17, 2004, giving rise to Case C–348/04.

changes. Since different issues may arise depending on the type of change undertaken, it is necessary to summarise them:

(1) "reboxing" is self-evident. Usually, the trade mark is re-affixed to the new
    box and the fresh information leaflet, but sometimes only the generic
    name of the drug is put on the box and leaflet. This results in "de-
    branding" or "partial de-branding" because the trade mark often remains
    on the blister packs and on the pills themselves;

(2) "co-branding" occurs where the new boxes carry the trade mark together
    with branding or get-up distinctive of the parallel importer;

(3) "stickering" involves sticking a new label to an original foreign language
    box plus replacement of the information leaflet;

(4) a further relevant fact[69] was that each importer indicated clearly on the
    new box or sticker that the goods were procured in the EU and repack-
    aged by the importer.

The saga commenced in 1999, and may conclude in 2007. Throughout, the   **16–067**
drug companies have focused in particular on (a) whether the repackaging was
"necessary" and (b) the lack of notice given by the parallel importers. As Laddie
J. commented in his first judgment, these issues were only manifestations of a
fundamental difference of view between the parties as to how domestic trade
mark law and the principle of the free movement of goods and exhaustion of
rights under the Treaty were to be reconciled.

The drug companies appeared to treat the *Paranova/Pharmacia* guidelines as   **16–068**
establishing virtually a stand-alone test with which the parallel traders had to
prove compliance in order to avoid infringement. They also took the view that
virtually any type of repackaging, overlabelling and advertising carried out by
the parallel importers was not "necessary",[70] contending that "necessary" meant
essential and not commercially desirable. Even if the re-packaging was necessary, the drug companies initially contended that no notice had been given, but
later accepted that they had received notice once the repackaged product appeared on the market.

The first reference to the ECJ

The questions referred by Laddie J. were treated by the ECJ as raising three is-   **16–069**
sues:

(1) clarification of the concept of the specific subject-matter of the trade mark
    in order to determine the circumstances in which a trade mark proprietor
    may rely on its trade mark rights to prevent repackaging;[71]

(2) clarification of the circumstances in which repackaging can be considered
    necessary;

(3) questioning whether the giving of notice was necessary and if so, the
    length of notice and the consequences of failure to give notice.

Specific subject-matter of a trade mark

Based on the evidence, Laddie J. made findings of fact which led him to the   **16–070**
conclusion that the repackaging in issue did not harm or even put at risk what he

---

[69] At least, this was the assumption on which the case was conducted.

[70] See, *e.g.* para.94–95 of Laddie J.'s first judgment [2000] E.T.M.R. 415 at 453; [2000] F.S.R. 529
at 564.

[71] The ECJ saw no need to distinguish between the various changes in issue and used the global
term "repackaging".

understood to constitute the specific subject matter of the trade marks. The ECJ reacted to this by affirming (perhaps even extending slightly) the concept of the specific subject matter. Based on *Hoffmann-La Roche* and *Paranova*, the Court stated:[72]

> "...it is the repackaging of the trade-marked pharmaceutical product in itself which is prejudicial to the specific subject-matter of the mark, and it is not necessary in that context to assess the actual effects of the repackaging by the parallel importer."

> "Thus, it is clear from settled case-law that the change brought about by any repackaging of a trade-marked pharmaceutical product—creating by its very nature the risk of interference with the original condition of the product—may be prohibited by the trade mark proprietor unless the repackaging is necessary in order to enable the marketing of the products imported in parallel and the legitimate interests of the proprietor are also safeguarded (see to that effect, [*Paranova*], paragraph 57)."

NECESSITY

16–071   On the meaning of "necessary", the Court stated:

> "replacement packaging of pharmaceutical products is objectively necessary ...if, without such repackaging, effective access to the market concerned, or to a substantial part of that market, must be considered to be hindered as the result of strong resistance from a significant proportion of consumers to relabelled pharmaceutical products."

16–072   This interpretation of "necessary" was a long way short of the drug companies' contention. As Jacob L.J. put it on appeal:[73] "This is important—"a strong resistance from a significant proportion of consumers" is enough to count as a "hindrance". The parallel importers are entitled to do more than just render the packaging lawful for UK marketing—they are entitled to replace the packaging if that is what is necessary to overcome a strong resistance in the market to relabelled boxes."

NOTICE

16–073   In his first judgment, Laddie J. traced the development of the requirement for notice from *Hoffmann-La Roche* through the later cases, citing an observation of A.G. Jacobs from *Paranova*:[74]

> "The precise justification for a requirement that the trade mark owner must receive prior notice of the repackaging is not clear from the judgment in *Hoffmann La-Roche v Centrafarm*, and there may be circumstances in which such notice would be superfluous."

16–074   Both A.G. Jacobs and the Court declined the invitation to reconsider the

---

[72] Case C–143/00 *Boehringer Ingelheim v Swingward & Dowelhurst*, ECJ, April 23, 2002, paras 30 and 34. The ECJ very much followed A.G. Jacobs' Opinion. He stated "It must be borne in mind that repackaging a product which bears a trade mark, whether or not the trade mark is reaffixed to the new external packaging or simply removed and not replaced, is a particularly intrusive form of trade mark infringement." This perhaps explains why "since repackaging was liable to impair the guarantee of origin"..."there may be cases where the trade mark owner can so rely on his rights even if it might appear in a particular case that there is no actual harm to the specific subject-matter or essential function of his mark".
[73] [2004] EWCA Civ 129, para.38.
[74] [1996] E.C.R. I-3457 at 3496, para.86. In *Dowelhurst*, see paras 135, 193(I).

requirement for notice. It "enables the proprietor to check that the repackaging is not carried out in such a way as directly or indirectly to affect the original condition of the product and that the presentation after repackaging is not such as to damage the reputation of the trade mark. It also affords the trade mark proprietor a better possibility of protecting himself against counterfeiting." It appears that the Court considered the giving of notice and provision of a sample as not posing any practical problem for the parallel importers, apparently blind to the realities as described in Laddie J.'s first judgment.

The Court also indicated that a reasonable period of notice would be 15 working days, the exact period being a matter for the national court to decide. The Court expressly affirmed that notice had to be given by the parallel importer and that, if no such notice was given, there would be infringement. It is impossible to understand the basis for these requirements, but at least they are clear and precise and can be applied mechanically.[75] Nonetheless, some important issues about notice remain. **16–075**

BACK TO THE UK—THE DIFFERENCE BETWEEN THE LEGAL RIGHT AND THE PURPOSE OF IT

Laddie J. interpreted the Court's answer on specific subject matter as creating "an irrebuttable legal fiction unconnected with the facts." This pervaded the whole of his second judgment and led him to find that even where he found the reboxing necessary, the de-branding, partial debranding and co-branding resulted in infringement[76] (essentially the opposite of the views he expressed in his first judgment). The Court of Appeal disagreed with his interpretation. Had the matter been free from doubt, the Court of Appeal would have found no infringement. They held that Laddie J. had misinterpreted the Court's answers on specific subject matter which had led him into error on the requirement of necessity. Jacob L.J. explained that the specific subject matter is *the legal right*, as opposed to *the purpose of the legal right*, which is to protect the reputation in the trade mark. He observed that the five *Paranova* conditions are all about protecting the reputation of the mark. Hence: "A fair summary of the position may be that (1) reaffixing creates a risk of jeopardising the reputation (2) but if the conditions are satisfied that risk is removed." **16–076**

THE SECOND REFERENCE TO THE ECJ

The Court of Appeal concluded that these issues were not *acte clair* and required a further reference. They noted that a number of national courts in other Member States at the highest level had adopted the "necessity" test espoused by the drug companies and accepted by Laddie J. in his second judgment, whereas the EFTA Court of Appeal had come to the opposite conclusion in a co-branding case: *Paranova v Merck*.[77] The difference really lies in whether the necessity test applies to the act of repackaging, or to the presentation of the repackaged product. **16–077**

The Court of Appeal has referred a range of questions[78] in the hope that the ECJ will provide a single comprehensive code setting out all the rules. Tradition- **16–078**

---

[75] See the observations of Jacob L.J., [2004] EWCA Civ 129, paras 100–102.

[76] He found the stickered products did not infringe and the appeal against this was dismissed.

[77] [2003] C.M.L.R. 7.

[78] To be found either in [2004] EWCA Civ 757, or on the ECJ website *www.curia.eu.int* under the case reference C–348/04. There are five questions relating to reboxed products, including co-

ally, the Court tends only to provide the answers it considers are necessary. In this instance, it might see that a single comprehensive code is required.

"DISGUISED RESTRICTION"

16–079   Oxazepam was sold in the United Kingdom under the mark Serenid D and in the Netherlands under the mark Seresta by two different companies within the same group. The parallel importer claimed that it was entitled to import Serenid D from the United Kingdom into Holland to sell it there under the Seresta mark. The European Court ruled that the mark owner was justified (within the meaning of Art.36) in preventing the application of his mark to the goods even though he had marketed those goods under a different mark elsewhere in the Community. However, it went on to hold that the exercise of the right may constitute a disguised restriction on trade within the meaning of Art.36. It indicated that such would be the case if the mark proprietor had pursued a policy of using different marks in different Member States in order to partition the Common Market: *Centrafarm v American Home Products*.[79]

16–080   It has yet to be decided what constitutes a practice which gives rise to a "disguised restriction". It should be enough to show that partitioning of the market was an obvious consequence of the policy (the "objective" test), the alternative being a subjective test that partitioning must have been the purpose behind the policy. The European Court is likely to prefer the former view, on the basis that a man must be taken to intend the foreseeable consequences of his own acts.[80] The Court is also likely to take the view that the bigger pharmaceutical companies are well aware of the consequences of adopting different marks in different territories.

5. Parallel imports into the EEA

SUMMARY

16–081   In theory, parallel imports into the EEA could be dealt with according to one of three possible regimes:

1. International exhaustion—with the result that trade mark rights cannot be used to prevent imports into the EEA of goods placed on the market anywhere in the world under the trade mark (subject to Art.7(2) of the TM Directive considerations);
2. Community or EEA-wide exhaustion—with the result that EEA trade mark rights can be used to prevent, without consent (which, in practice, will have to be virtually express consent), imports into the EEA of goods placed on the market elsewhere in the world bearing the trade mark;
3. Some intermediate possibility, decided on a case-by-case basis.

16–082   The European Court ruled out option 1, in *Silhouette* and *Sebago*. Option 3 would probably create chaos. Not surprisingly, in *Davidoff* the European Court decided that option 2 applied. A related issue concerns the status of parallel

---

branding and de-branding issues, five questions relating to overstickered products and four relating to notice *e.g.* does the infringement continue indefinitely or until the trade mark proprietor becomes aware, what should the financial remedies be).

[79] [1978] E.C.R. 1823; [1979] 1 C.M.L.R. 326.

[80] The German Supreme Court has, however, preferred the subjective view: *Hoffmann-La Roche v Centrafarm* [1984] 2 C.M.L.R. 561 (replacement not allowed because difference in packs between different states not intended to partition market artificially).

imports into EEA countries which are not also EU Member States. This is dealt with at the end of this section.

THE APPLICABLE PRINCIPLES

As explained above, the decisions of the European Court in this area of the law **16–083** can be analysed according to the hierarchy of principles. For present purposes, the overriding principles concern the single market and the free movement of goods within that market of the EEA—Arts 2, 3 and 28. Industrial property rights are accommodated according to the terms of Art.30. The corollary is that if the enforcement of an industrial property right does not interfere with those principles (nor the competition principles) then it is left unaffected.

SILHOUETTE AND *SEBAGO*

The case law of the European Court has demonstrated that the principles referred **16–084** to in the preceding paragraph do have a role to play in cases where products are parallel imported into the EEA. If one Member State were to implement a rule of international exhaustion of trade mark rights, then genuine products placed on the market anywhere in the world under a particular trade mark could be imported into that Member State, and a national trade mark could not be enforced to prevent such imports.[81] Those products would then be on the market within the EEA. Either they would be permitted to circulate freely within the EEA or, possibly, Member States which did not agree with international exhaustion might seek to restrict their circulation as goods which were not legitimately put on the market in the EEA. The consequence would be either that a rule of international exhaustion would have been imposed on the EEA by one country or there would be considerable interference in the operation of the single market. It was therefore inevitable that the European Court would rule, as in *Silhouette* and *Sebago*, that no Member State may impose a rule of international exhaustion.[82]

(1) Some 21,000 pairs of out-of-fashion sunglasses bearing the mark Silhouette were sold by a representative of the Austrian trade mark proprietor to Bulgaria, apparently on condition that they should be sold in Bulgaria or in the former states of the USSR and not exported to other countries. This condition was not proved so the reference to the European Court proceeded on the assumption that no consent had been given that the sunglasses could be put on the market in Austria. In those circumstances, the parallel importer argued that Article 7 of the Directive left it open to Member States to provide for international exhaustion. This was rejected, the European Court holding that Art.7 could not be interpreted as leaving it open to the Member States to provide in their domestic law for exhaustion of the rights conferred by a trade mark in respect of products put on the market in non-member countries. Essentially, if one Member State

---

[81] Presumably the national court would refuse to enforce a CTM, for the same reasons.
[82] Before *Silhouette* was decided, the EFTA Court issued an Advisory Opinion to a court in Norway (an EEA country, but not a member of the EU) on Art.7(1) of the TM Directive. The EFTA Court concluded that Art.7(1) left it open to EFTA states to decide whether they wish to introduce or maintain the principle of international exhaustion with regard to goods originating from outside the EEA. This conclusion was reached on the basis that the purpose of the EEA is different to the EC/EU, and that the principle of free movement of goods in the EEA applies only to goods originating in the EEA, whereas for the EC the principle applies to any goods which are put on the market in the Community. Therefore the EEA principle of free movement of goods did not apply to the Maglite torches which originated and were parallel imported from the USA: *Mag Instrument Inc v California Trading Co* [1998] E.T.M.R. 85. See paras 16–096 to 16–099.

imposed a rule of international exhaustion, this would either mean international exhaustion applied throughout the EEA or it would give rise to barriers within the EEA to the free movement of goods. On the facts before the Court, there was no issue concerning consent within Art.7(1): Silhouette.[83]

(2) Sebago sold shoes under the trade marks "Docksides" and "Sebago". Genuine shoes were obtained from El Salvador and sold in Belgium by GB-Unic. Before the Belgian courts, GB-Unic ran two arguments: the first was that Sebago had not prohibited export from El Salvador and accordingly should be deemed to have given implied consent to the marketing of the goods in the Community. This argument was dismissed on the facts. The second argument, which was the only one referred to the European Court, was to the effect that, to prove consent, it was sufficient to show that the same type of goods bearing the marks had been lawfully marketed in the EEA with the consent of the proprietor. This argument was dismissed, because it would, for practical purposes, impose a rule of international exhaustion for all parallel imports: Sebago.[84]

16–085   The outcome of these cases was not at all surprising bearing in mind that during the drafting of the CTM Regulation and the TM Directive, the decision was taken not to introduce a rule of international exhaustion. The only other alternative was Community or EEA-wide exhaustion, which is what Article 13 of the CTM Regulation and Article 7 of the Directive provide.

The next stage

16–086   The next stage is, effectively, a refinement of the reasoning underlying *Silhouette* and *Sebago*. If no Member State is permitted to impose a rule of international exhaustion, it must follow that no Member State may implement a rule having equivalent effect. This would occur if one Member State adopted an approach to Article 7 of the TM Directive, and particularly to the issue of consent within Article 7(1) which was radically different to the approach adopted in other Member States. The corollary of this is that, given the same facts, the courts in all Member States ought to reach the same decision on whether or not consent had been given to the products being put on the market in the EEA. This was one of the issues which the ECJ decided in the conjoined *Davidoff* and *Levi* cases.

The *Davidoff* and *Levi* cases

16–087   (3) Aftershave bearing the mark "COOL WATER" was manufactured in France for distribution worldwide. The parallel imports were obtained from Singapore, where the distributor had undertaken not to sell outside his Territory and to oblige his customers to refrain from such sales. No other contractual restrictions were imposed. The product codes on the goods had been partly obliterated, to impede tracing of the source of the

---

[83] [1998] F.S.R. 729. ECJ. cf. *Javico* at para.16–141.

[84] [2000] R.P.C. 63, A.G. and ECJ. Although the *Sebago* (the so-called "all or none") argument was dismissed as not relevant in *Davidoff* by Laddie J., there was a sound basis for it. The argument was based on the essential function of a trade mark, *i.e.* to guarantee to the consumer the identity of the product's origin, the object being to enable him to distinguish that product without any risk of confusion from those of different origin. GB-Unic were arguing that the mark on the genuine goods sold by them continued to perform this essential function (see, in particular, para.16 of the judgment). To put this argument in another way, the sale of the genuine goods by GB-Unic caused no damage to the specific subject matter of the trade mark. The fact that this reasoning was rejected is a further indication that the issue of parallel imports from outside the EEA has nothing to do with the function of trade marks and depends upon economic policy. See further at para.16–089.

parallel goods. The parallel importers argued that the trade mark proprietor had impliedly consented to the goods being imported into the EEA: *Davidoff*.

(4) Levi 501 jeans were manufactured in the US, Canada and Mexico. Quantities of those jeans were obtained by Tesco and Costco from authorised retailers in those countries and from "accumulators" who buy up spare stocks from authorised retailers. Tesco admitted it knew that Levi did not wish their jeans to be sold in the EEA otherwise than through their authorised retailers. Costco maintained it was unaware of this. Again, the principal issue was implied consent: *Levis v Tesco*, *Levis v Costco*.

THE DECISION OF THE ECJ

The ECJ dealt with the *Davidoff* and *Levis* references together.[85] The judgment was predictable. The reasoning may be summarised in the following steps:

16–088

(1) Arts 5–7 of the Directive embody a complete harmonisation of the rules relating to the rights conferred by a registered trade mark.

(2) The "consent" referred to in Arts 5 and 7 is tantamount to the proprietor's renunciation of his exclusive right under Art.5 and therefore constitutes the decisive factor in the extinction of that right.

(3) If the concept of consent were a matter for the national laws of Member States, protection would vary. Therefore, it was necessary for the ECJ to supply a uniform interpretation of the concept of consent to the placing of goods on the market within the EEA.

(4) In view of its serious effect in extinguishing the exclusive rights of the trade mark proprietor, consent must be so expressed that an intention to renounce those rights is unequivocally demonstrated.

(5) Consent will normally have to be express, although it is conceivable that implied consent may be inferred from facts and circumstances prior to, simultaneous with or subsequent to the placing of the goods on the market outside the EEA which, in the view of the national court, unequivocally demonstrate that the proprietor has renounced its rights.

(6) Consent cannot be inferred from mere silence on the part of the trade mark proprietor. More specifically, implied consent cannot be inferred from:

    (a) the fact that the proprietor has not communicated his opposition to goods placed on the market outside the EEA being placed on the market within the EEA;

    (b) the fact that the goods carry no warning of a prohibition on their being placed on the market within the EEA;

    (c) the fact that the proprietor imposed no contractual restrictions when selling the goods;

    (d) the fact that, under the law governing the contract of sale by the proprietor, the property right transferred includes, in the absence of contractual reservations, an unlimited right of resale or, at least, a right to market the goods within the EEA.

(7) Ignorance on the part of the trader importing the goods into the EEA is irrelevant.

As predicted in the previous edition, the issue raised by parallel imports into

16–089

---

[85] Joined Cases C–414/99 to C–416/99, *Zino Davidoff v A&G Imports Ltd, Levi Strauss v Tesco, Levis Strauss v Costco*. ECJ November 20, 2001 [2001] E.C.R. I-8691; [2002] Ch. 109; [2002] R.P.C. 20; [2002] E.T.M.R. 9.

the EEA has nothing to do with the essential function of a trade mark or whether a trade mark should confer the ability to interfere with this type of activity. It is purely a matter of economic policy of the EU and EEA.[86] The Community legislature has allowed the proprietor of the trade mark to control the initial marketing in the EEA of goods bearing his mark.[87] The practical result is that parallel imports into the EEA will result in infringement unless the trade mark proprietor has given consent. Cases of implied consent are likely to be very rare. In practice, unless express consent has been given, parallel imports into the EEA are most likely to result in infringement.[88]

FUTURE POLICY

16–090   Any fundamental change in this area is dependent upon economic policy. The whole question of international exhaustion proved so contentious that it was not possible to agree on a position at the Uruguay Round of GATT which resulted in TRIPS.[89] The perception is that unilateral adoption of international exhaustion by the EEA would almost certainly cause significant damage to the economies of countries within the EEA. The only feasible options appear to be bilateral treaties between the EEA and major trading partners such as the US and Japan.[90] It is very difficult to predict when such developments might occur. In the absence of a change in policy, the remaining issues are relatively minor, concerning (a) the burden of proof and (b) the issue of what "putting on the market" entails.

BURDEN OF PROOF

16–091   The net effect of *Silhouette*, *Sebago* and *Davidoff* appeared to place the burden of proving consent firmly on the parallel importer, with all the difficulties that entails. However, shortly after *Davidoff*, the ECJ was called upon to analyse the effect of the burden of proof in slightly different circumstances.

(5) The proprietor of the mark *Stüssy* invited the inference that the goods bearing the mark were placed on the market for the first time outside the EEA, relying on his exclusive distribution system inside the EEA, and contended it was for the defendant to prove consent to marketing within the EEA. The defendant invited the inference that the goods were first

---

[86] Despite the fact that the ECJ had decided the issues firmly against the parallel importers, Tesco and Costco attempted a last stand, arguing that (1) they had a defence under section 10(6) (especially bearing in mind their rights under the ECHR, art.1 of the First Protocol, to own and dispose of property and Art.10, the right to freedom of expression), (2) under Community law, Art.7 of the Directive had to be interpreted so as to respect those fundamental rights of the defendants; (3) if it wasn't, Art.7 is inconsistent with Arts 28–30 of the Treaty. In rejecting all these points, Pumfrey J. observed that aspects of these points had been argued before the ECJ and rejected, expressly or impliedly and others had been rejected in previous judgments of the ECJ *e.g. EMI v CBS*, Case 51/75, [1976] E.C.R. 811); *Levis v Tesco & Costco* [2002] EWHC 1556 (Ch).

[87] *Davidoff*, para.33

[88] See, *e.g.* Quiksilver [2005] F.S.R. 8 and *Hewlett-Packard v Expansys* [2005] EWHC 1495, Laddie J., and *Sony v Nuplayer* [2005] EWHC 1522, Lawrence Collins J.

[89] See TRIPS, Art.6.

[90] In its Explanatory Memorandum proposing Community-wide exhaustion for the CTM Regulation (and hence the TM Directive), the Commission stated "On the question of international exhaustion of the rights conferred by the Community trade mark, the Commission has formed the view that the Community legislator should refrain from introducing this principle and make do with the rule of Community-wide exhaustion. The Community must, however, be empowered to conclude, at some future time with important trading partners, bilateral or multilateral agreements whereby international exhaustion is introduced by the contracting parties. The restriction to Community-wide exhaustion, however, does not prevent national courts from extending this principle, in cases of a special nature, in particular where, even in the absence of a formal agreement, reciprocity is guaranteed." COM (84) 470 final, July 31, 1984.

placed on the market within the EEA, contending that the proprietor had failed to prove that his distribution system was impervious. Accordingly, the defendant argued that the rights of the proprietor had been exhausted: *Van Doren + Q*

Observing that the burden of proof was a rule of evidence of the national court, the ECJ ruled:[91]

(1) a rule of evidence placing the burden of proving consent, for the purposes of Articles 5 and 7 of the Directive, on the defendant was consistent with Community law and, in particular, those Articles;

(2) that rule of evidence may need to be qualified where the defendant succeeds in establishing that there is a real risk of partitioning of national markets if he bears the burden of proving that the goods were placed on the market in the EEA. The Court accepted there was a real risk where the trade mark proprietor uses an exclusive distribution system in the EEA. In those circumstances, it is for the trade mark proprietor to prove that the goods were initially placed on the market outside the EEA by him or with his consent. If such evidence is adduced, it is for the defendant to prove consent to the subsequent marketing of the goods in the EEA.

It is not immediately clear why the mere use of an exclusive distribution system in the EEA should be a prime example of circumstances giving rise to a real risk of partitioning of national markets. The ECJ appears to have been concerned with two possibilities: first, that the parallel trader would never have been able to prove that the goods were put on the market in the EEA and/or second, if the parallel trader did identify his source of supply within the EEA, the trade mark proprietor would have then taken steps to close the breach in his exclusive distribution system. The vice appears to lie with exclusive distribution systems, which can really only be tackled under competition law.

16–092

PEAK PERFORMANCE

At what point can goods be said to have been "put on the market" within the EEA? The answer is not what that expression indicates at first sight.

16–093

(6) A Swedish parallel trader obtained a consignment of clothes bearing the mark Peak Performance. The consignment comprised out of date styles. All the clothes had been manufactured outside the EEA and imported into the EEA by the trade mark proprietor for sale in the EEA. The clothes had been offered for sale in a store in Copenhagen, but remained unsold and the property of a sister company of the Danish proprietor. The unsold clothes were sold to a French company on condition they were not to be sold in European countries other than Russia or Slovenia, apart from 5 per cent of the consignment which could be sold in France. The parallel trader had no knowledge of this restriction.

The parallel trader contended that the rights of the trade mark proprietor had been exhausted either (a) when the goods were imported into the EEA for sale; (b) when the goods were put on the market in the store in Copenhagen and offered to consumers or (c) when the consignment was sold in the EEA to the French undertaking, regardless of whether any restriction had been placed on resale: *Peak Performance*.[92]

The ECJ interpreted "put on the market" as meaning, in effect, "released into

16–094

---

[91] Case C–244/00, *Van Doren + Q GmbH v Lifestyle sports* [2003] E.C.R. I-3051; [2003] E.T.M.R. 75 ECJ. See paras 35–41 in particular.
[92] Case C–16/03, *Peak Holding AB v Axolin-Elinor AB* [2005] E.T.M.R. 28.

the market by an act of sale". A little more detail is required to explain the subtleties, not least because at a crucial point, the ECJ introduces the unexplained concept of the proprietor being able to "realise the economic value of his trade mark".

16–095   Clearly the ECJ did not favour the literal meaning of the expression "put on the market", since it would depend which "market" was under consideration—wholesale, retail etc.—and would have occurred, at the latest, when the goods were put on retail sale to consumers. So, the ECJ went back to first principles, as expressed in previous judgments, and found the answer in the distinction between initial marketing and further marketing in the EEA:

(1) By Articles 5 and 7 of the Directive, the Community legislature allowed the proprietor of the trade mark the right to control the initial marketing in the EEA of goods bearing the trade mark: *Sebago*, para.21 (confirmed in *Davidoff*, para.33)

(2) Art.7(1) makes possible the further marketing of an individual item of a product bearing the trade mark without the trade mark proprietor being able to oppose that: *BMW*, para.57, *Sebago*, para.20;

(3) In order to fulfil its essential role in the system of undistorted competition which the EC Treaty seeks to establish, a trade mark must offer a guarantee that all the goods or services bearing it have been manufactured or supplied under the control of a single undertaking which is responsible for their quality: *Philips*, para.30;

(4) Therefore, the ECJ reasoned, "A sale which allows the trade mark proprietor to realise the economic value of his trade mark exhausts the exclusive rights conferred by the Directive, more particularly the right to prohibit the acquiring third party from reselling the goods."[93]

This last step is difficult to follow. The exclusive rights conferred by Art.5 do not normally extend to "the right to prohibit the acquiring party from reselling the goods" because selling the goods to a third party exhausts those exclusive rights. However the use of this tortuous language is explained by analysis of the Opinion of A.G. Stix-Hackl.[94] Evidently the case involved discussion of whether goods were put on the market by a sale by the trade mark proprietor to a related company or by delivery to a forwarding agent. In addition, the Court appears to have taken account of possible complications caused by reservation of title clauses and goods delivered on a sale or return basis. On the "economic" approach taken by the Advocate-General, a change of ownership of the goods is not relevant, the decisive event being "the transfer of the actual right of disposal of the goods". Until the right of disposal is transferred, the trade mark proprietor retains his interest in controlling the quality of the goods. It seems that realising the economic value of the trade mark means a sale to an objectively independent third party who acquires the actual right of disposal of the goods. We think this concept is best summarised as a "release into the market by an act of sale".

Parallel imports into EEA Member States which are not EU Member States

16–096   There is a possible breach in the "fortress Europe" established by the adoption of

---

[93] *Peak*, para.40.
[94] See paras 17, 40–43 including the footnotes.

EEA-wide exhaustion. The *Mag Instrument*[95] case highlights an imbalance resulting from the EEA Agreement. Essentially, the EU states[96] operate the principle of
free movement for any goods put on the market in the EEA whereas EEA states
which are not EU States (namely Norway, Iceland and Liechtenstein) only operate the principle of free movement for goods originating in the EEA.[97] Part of the
EEA Agreement effectively extended Article 7(1) of the TM Directive so that it
applied to goods put on the market in the EEA.[98] In return, it appears that the
EFTA states were or are supposed to adjust their intellectual property laws to
give at least the level of protection for intellectual property prevailing in the
Community when the EEA Agreement was signed[99] —and part of this protection
is the EEA-wide exhaustion provided for in Article 7(1) of the TM Directive.
This does not seem to have occurred and will not occur unless Norway, Iceland
and Liechtenstein either join the EU or provide for the same degree of exhaustion
as EU states, namely EEA-wide and no broader.

    Due to the different principles in the EEA Agreement, the EFTA Court in *Mag*   **16–097**
Instrument was able to advise the Norwegian court that it is for EFTA states to
decide whether they wish to introduce or maintain the principle of international
exhaustion of rights conferred by a trade mark with regard to goods originating
outside the EEA. The EFTA Court noted that it was established Norwegian law
that international exhaustion applies for trade marks. If Iceland and Liechtenstein
also apply international exhaustion, any one of those three countries appear to
provide an entry point into the EEA for parallel imports of goods which originate
outside the EEA. Once those goods are placed on the market[1] in Norway, Iceland
or Liechtenstein, the only issue remaining under Art.7(1) (as amended) of the
TM Directive is whether the goods were put on the market (in the EEA) with the
consent of the proprietor of the mark. It would seem that this consent issue must

---

[95] *Mag Instrument Inc v California Trading Co* [1998] E.T.M.R. 85. The EFTA Court concluded
that Art.7(1) left it open to EFTA states to decide whether they wish to introduce or maintain the
principle of international exhaustion with regard to goods originating from outside the EEA.

[96] At the time of the EEA Agreement, the Member States of the EC were Belgium, Denmark, Germany, Greece, Spain, France, Ireland, Italy, Luxembourg, Netherlands, Portugal and the UK. Of
the EFTA states who signed the EEA Agreement, Austria, Finland and Sweden joined the EU as
from January 1, 1995.

[97] EEA Agreement, Art.8(2), applying in the field of IP rights via Arts 11 and 13 EEA (corresponding to Arts 28 and 30 EC).

[98] EEA Agreement, Annex XVII, para.4(c), replaced the original Art.7(1) with the following: "The
trade mark shall not entitle the proprietor to prohibit its use in relation to goods which have been
put on the market in a Contracting Party under that trade mark by the proprietor or with his
consent." [1994] O.J. L 1/483. Effectively, "Contracting Party" means any state of the EEA.

[99] Protocol 28 on Intellectual Property ([1994] O.J. L 1/194) contains the following provisions:
Article 1(2): "Without prejudice to the provisions of this Protocol and of Annex XVII, the
Contracting Parties shall upon the entry into force of the Agreement adjust their legislation on
intellectual property so as to make it compatible with the principles of the free circulation of
goods and services and with the level of protection of intellectual property attained in Community law, including the level of enforcement of those rights. Art.1(3): "Subject to the
procedural provisions of the Agreement and without prejudice to the provisions of this Protocol
and of Annex XVII, the EFTA States will adjust, upon request and after consultation between the
Contracting Parties, their legislation on intellectual property in order to reach at least the level of
protection of intellectual property prevailing in the Community upon signature of this
Agreement." Art.2 Exhaustion of Rights "(1) To the extent that exhaustion is dealt with in Community measures or jurisprudence, the Contracting States shall provide for such exhaustion of
intellectual property rights as laid down in Community law. Without prejudice to the future
developments of case-law, this provision shall be interpreted in accordance with the meaning
established in the relevant rulings of the Court of Justice of the European Communities given
prior to the signature of this Agreement."

[1] This would require payment of customs tariffs—see A.G. Warner in *EMI v CBS* [1976] E.C.R.
811 at 860. Mere trans-shipment through Norway would mean the goods were not put on the
market there.

be decided according to the law of the state concerned, not least because applying the law of any other Member State would be entirely arbitrary. Presumably, under Norwegian law, the application of international exhaustion also means that the proprietor is deemed to have consented to the goods being placed on the market in Norway. Even though the proprietor of the mark would say he had given no consent at all, giving him the ability to withhold consent would negate the rule of international exhaustion. Equally, allowing the law of any other Member State to determine the issue of consent (in accordance with guidance from the ECJ) would negate the ability of Norway to maintain a rule of international exhaustion.

16–098   If this analysis of the consent issue is correct, then Art.7(1) as amended has the consequence that no national trade mark right in the EEA can be used to prevent the free movement of those goods throughout the EEA. It would require tortuous reasoning to hold that the imbalance between EU and EFTA states constituted "legitimate reasons" for opposing importation into the EU.

16–099   The final point to note is the position of a CTM. Unlike Article 7(1) of the TM Directive, the EEA Agreement effected no extension of the exhaustion provision for CTMs in Art.13(1) from "the Community" to "the EEA". For a CTM the territorial effect of the exhaustion provision coincides with the territorial effect of the CTM.[2] Therefore, unless or until Norway, Iceland and Liechtenstein join the CTM system, a CTM is not exhausted by goods under that mark[3] being placed on the market in any of those countries. It follows that Article 13(1) of the CTM Regulation would not prohibit the use of the CTM to prevent importation of those goods into the EU. By analogy with Article 7 of the TM Directive and the *Paranova* judgment,[4] one would expect the ECJ to hold that Article 13 of the CTM Regulation comprehensively regulates the question of exhaustion of CTM rights. Indeed, there would be no reason to override Article 13 of the CTM Regulation because the EEA principle of the free movement of goods applies only to goods originating in the EEA. Arts 11 and 13 EEA would not apply. By analogy with *Silhouette*, the principle of free movement of goods in the EU would require that Article 13 of the CTM Regulation was not overridden.

6. The *Dior* problem

What is the problem?

16–100   The problem is whether s.12(2)/Art.7(2) creates a new right enforceable by the proprietor of a registered trade mark, over and above the infringement rights conferred by ss.9 and 10/Art.5, as limited by ss.11 and 12(1)/Arts 6 and 7. This problem manifested itself in *Dowelhurst* in a slightly different guise. There the claimants asserted a new or "stand-alone" right conferred by the case law of the ECJ on repackaging.[5] It has been suggested above that the claim in *Dowelhurst* can and should be defeated simply by putting the principles drawn from the case law into their proper context. The claim in *Dior* was linked more directly to

---

[2] A CTM covers all countries of the EU.
[3] Note that the interpretation of these words in the CTM context is very different to the interpretation appropriate in the national context. The different interpretation is permissible and is indeed required by the purpose of the respective provisions. See para.16–011.
[4] See para.16–012.
[5] The *Dowelhurst* claim could equally well have been formulated directly under s.12(2)/ Art.7(2), since the ECJ has already held (in *Paranova*), that Art.7 must be interpreted in the same way as Art.30 (ex.36).

Art.7(2). Although the claim in *Dior* was rejected, the reasoning has merely postponed the problem. As in *Dowelhurst*, the answer to this problem lies in placing it in its proper context.

DIOR

In *Dior*, the goods were genuine, obtained by means of parallel imports. Dior   **16–101** complained that the advertising for sale of the parallel imports did not correspond to the luxurious and prestigious image of the Dior marks. The European Court held that a trade mark proprietor cannot rely on Article 7(2) of the TM Directive to oppose the use of the trade mark by a reseller who habitually markets articles of the same kind, but not necessarily of the same quality, as the trade-marked goods, in ways customary in the reseller's sector of trade, for the purpose of bringing to the public's attention the further commercialisation of the goods, unless it is established that, given the specific circumstances of the case, the use of the trade mark for this purpose seriously damages the reputation of the trade mark.

This conclusion was the result of two factors. The first was the readiness of the   **16–102** Court to treat the fourth *Paranova* guideline[6] as capable of establishing a "legitimate reason" by itself. The second was the readiness to extend that guideline so that it applied not only to changes to the physical condition of the goods, but also to the mental condition of the goods. The Court had re-phrased the key question for its consideration in effect in the following way:

Do the following constitute legitimate reasons within Art.7(2):

— "where the advertising function of the trade mark is endangered by the fact that, as a result of the manner in which the reseller uses the trade mark in order to attract public attention, he damages the luxurious and prestigious image of the trade mark, and

— where, as a result of the way in which the reseller advertises the goods, their 'mental' condition, that is to say the allure, prestigious image and aura of luxury which they have as a result of the manner in which the trademark owner has chosen to present and advertise the goods using his trade mark rights, is changed or impaired."[7]

Phrasing the question in this way entails the unquestioning acceptance that a   **16–103** registered trade mark with a luxurious and prestigious image has an advertising function which should be protected. A.G. Jacobs correctly concluded that any advertising function of a trade mark is merely a derivative of the origin function. Despite giving a warning that "the circumstances in which a trade mark owner can invoke his trade mark rights in order to protect his reputation should not be construed too widely", even he seems to have accepted the principle that the trade mark should be protected from damage which is solely caused to the advertising function.[8] All of this discussion about the extent to which a trade mark must be protected took place in the context of striking the balance between free movement of goods and trade mark rights, and quite independently of and without apparent reference to the infringement provisions.

---

[6] See para.16–060.
[7] See para.39 of the judgment. *Parfums Christian Dior S.A. v Evora B.V.* [1997] E.C.R. I-6013 at 6047; [1998] R.P.C. 166 at 194.
[8] See his Opinion, para.42. [1997] E.C.R. I-6013 at 6027; [1998] R.P.C. 166 at 180/1.

The natural conclusion from *Dior*

16–104   Both *Dowelhurst* and *Dior* contained the element of inter-state trade. Section 12/ Art.7 are not limited to situations which involve inter-state trade. They apply equally in a purely national context. Therefore, it can be argued that *Dior* establishes that s.12(2)/Art.7(2) gives the proprietor a right to interfere in reselling of genuine goods, even in a purely national context, provided the activity of the reseller "seriously damages the reputation of the trade mark".

Support from the notion of "exhaustion"

16–105   The argument that s.12(2)/Art.7(2) creates a new right is supported by the concept of "exhaustion of rights" which those provisions are meant to embody. By nature, any "legitimate reason" within s.12(2)/Art.7(2) must arise or manifest itself after the first marketing of the goods. If the trade mark right is truly "exhausted" by first marketing, the existence of legitimate reasons under s.12(2) of the 1994 Act must either revive the exhausted right or create a new right. Since the former is a contradiction in terms, the notion of "exhaustion" tends to suggest that s.12(2) creates a new right, whereas the alternative notion (that the rule is one of free circulation) does not.

The answer to the problem

16–106   It is suggested that the correct answer to the problem is that s.12(2)/Art.7(2) does not create any new right for the proprietor of a trade mark. There is one principal reason why this should be the correct answer. It should be obvious from the TM Directive that, in so far as the advertising function of a trade mark is protected, the protection is conferred directly by s.10/Art.5 (and not via the back door of s.12(2)/Art.7(2)). The corollary is that if this is not the correct answer, then via the back door route of s.12(2)/Art.7(2), the case law of the ECJ has created a new right for the proprietor of a trade mark. There was no such right available in the United Kingdom under the Trade Marks Act 1938. Since many EU countries applied a rule of international exhaustion before the TM Directive was implemented, it seems most unlikely that any other EU country previously conferred such a right. It cannot have been intended that the developing case law of the ECJ could create such a right.

16–107   One consequence of this reasoning is that, when the European Court is seeking to strike the appropriate balance between the fundamental interest in the free movement of goods and the fundamental interest in trade mark (or other industrial property) rights (whether under Art.7(2) or Article 30 of the Treaty), it should have regard to the degree of protection afforded to the trade mark by the infringement provisions and not examine in the abstract the protection which the trade mark appears to deserve on the facts of the particular case.[9] In other words, it is necessary to achieve consistency between the protection available in the national context and the protection available in a context which involves inter-state trade. The latter protection may be less than the former, due to the overriding principle of free movement of goods, but it should never be greater.

---

[9] Without the anchor of the infringement provisions, it is difficult to resist providing some protection against damage which can be seen to be real. Hence unsuccessful claimants in cases like *Paranova* and *Dior* manage to extract a concession from the European Court in, *e.g.* the requirement for notice and the exception for serious damage to reputation, when the right answer is that trade mark proprietors should do without, and lump it.

If it is thought that the advertising function of a trade mark deserves protection **16–108** over and above that conferred in s.10/Art.5, then that is a matter for Community legislation and not otherwise.

7. Competition laws of the EU and the United Kingdom

The competition laws of the European Community[10] and the United Kingdom **16–109** both impose important limitations on the exploitation and enforcement of trade marks. EC competition law applies by virtue of s.2(1) of the European Communities Act 1972.

The Competition Act 1998[11] introduced into United Kingdom law a domestic **16–110** competition regime which is modelled on the relevant provisions of the EC Treaty, and as a result it is likely that the exploitation and enforcement of trade marks within the United Kingdom will be subject to more limitations than was previously the case (or at any rate that competition law issues will now be raised more frequently both in negotiation and in legal proceedings).

8. Articles 81 and 82[12]

THE NATURE OF ARTICLES 81 AND 82

The basic purpose of Arts 81 and 82 of the EC Treaty[13] is to control certain types **16–111** of agreements-using that term in a broad sense (Article 81—ex Art.85) and certain types of monopolistic behaviour (Art.82—ex Art.86). Neither provision is directed particularly at trade marks or even intellectual property rights at all (and indeed the EC Treaty states in Art.295 (ex.Art.222) "this Treaty shall in no way prejudice the rules in Member States governing the system of property ownership"). However, the manner in which such rights are exercised (whether by direct enforcement in the courts or by way of agreements) can fall within the general ambit of the provisions. Jurisdiction concerning breaches of either Article is given both to national competition authorities and courts and to the European Commission by virtue of Reg.1/2003, which replaced Reg.17/62 with effect from May 1, 2004 as the basic implementing Regulation for the Treaty provisions on competition. Appeal against a Commission decision lies to the European Court of First Instance ("C.F.I."), which has jurisdiction to determine at first instance actions against the Commission relating to the enforcement of EC competition rules.[14] The Commission has power to order undertakings to cease their violations[15] and to fine parties for such violations.[16]

In addition, in some cases breaches of either Article may directly affect the **16–112** enforceability of intellectual property rights—so that the breach may be pleaded

---

[10] From January 1, 1994 these were extended by the European Economic Area Agreement (the EEA Agreement) to Iceland, Norway and Liechtenstein, member states of the European Free Trade Area (EFTA). Switzerland, although a member of EFTA, did not accede to the EEA Agreement. The EEA Agreement, Arts 53 and 54, reproduce the EC Treaty, Arts 81 and 82.

[11] The Act came into force on March 1, 2000.

[12] Ex Arts 85 and 86: the renumbering results from the Treaty of Amsterdam 1997, Art.12(1).

[13] App.7.

[14] By virtue of Arts 229, 230 and 232 (ex. Arts 172, 173 and 175) of the EC Treaty and Art.31 of Reg.1/2003 (which confers unlimited jurisdiction on the Court of Justice to review decisions which impose fines or periodic payments.) Appeal from a judgment of the C.F.I. lies to the Court of Justice ("E.C.J.").

[15] Reg.1/2003, Art.7(1).

[16] Reg.1/2003, Art.23, although such fines are expressed not to be of a criminal nature Art.15(5).)

by way of defence to an infringement action[17] —and also of an agreement exploiting intellectual property rights, which by Art.81(2) is void if contrary to Art.81(1)
and not exempt pursuant to Art.81(3). A breach may also give rise to a claim by a
party injured.[18]

BREACH AS A DEFENCE

16–113   Before turning to the manner in which Arts 81 and 82 may affect exploitation of
trade mark rights, otherwise than by affecting enforcement, it is convenient to
consider the extent to which breach of the Articles can constitute a defence to
infringement. It has already been noted that the development of the free movement rules under Arts 28 and 30[19] has affected considerably the enforcement of
trade marks within the Community.[20]

16–114   This use of Arts 28 and 30 has been so significant that all cases where a so-
called "Eurodefence" has been successful before the English courts can now be
explained as applications of those rules. Thus cases of attempts to divide the
geographic territory of the European Community by way of partial assignments
or licences for limited parts only of the Community are usually dealt with by application of the doctrine of "first marketing".[21] It is difficult therefore to see any
significant need for an independent defence of breach of Arts 81 or 82 where the
free circulation rules are invoked. However, the jurisdiction to recognise the
defence clearly exists (and in the United Kingdom has become more important as
a result of the Competition Act 1998). Thus in *Sirena*[22] the ECJ said:

> "A trade-mark right, as a legal entity, does not in itself possess those ele-
> ments of contract or concerted practice referred to in Article 85(1) [now
> 81(1)]. Nevertheless, the exercise of that right might fall within the ambit of
> the prohibitions contained in the Treaty each time it manifests itself as the
> subject, the means or the result of a restrictive practice."[23]

16–115   In *Sirena* itself the ECJ went on to hold that the past assignments amounted to
a "restrictive practice" and that accordingly the assigned mark could not be
enforced to prevent what were effectively parallel imports. The Court also
indicated that the exercise of a trade mark right might be prohibited under Art.86
[now 82] of the Treaty.[24]

16–116   The ECJ has also said:

> "The proprietor of an exclusive right may not rely on his right if the prohibi-
> tion on importation or marketing of which he wishes to avail himself could
> be connected with an agreement or practice in restraint of competition within
> the Community contrary to the provisions of the Treaty, in particular those
> of Art.85(1) [now 81(1)]": *Keurkoop v Nancy Kean*.[25]

WHAT TYPE OF BREACH GIVES RISE TO A DEFENCE?

16–117   However, although the defence of breach of Art.81 or Art.82 is established in

---

[17] See paras 16–113 to 16–116.
[18] See para.16–112.
[19] Formerly Arts 30 and 36, respectively.
[20] See paras 16–021 to 16–037.
[21] See *IHT v Ideal Standard* [1994] F.S.R. 59; and *Cnl-Sucal v Hag* ("Hag II") [1990] 3 C.M.L.R.
    571 (which effectively overruled *Hag I* [1976] E.C.R. 1039.).
[22] [1971] E.C.R. 69 at 84, para.9.
[23] See paras 16–127 to 16–143.
[24] [1971] E.C.R. 69 at 85, paras 14–16.
[25] [1982] E.C.R. 2853; [1983] 2 C.M.L.R. 47, para.26.

general terms, it is rare for it to be used successfully beyond the area covered by the free circulation rules. It cannot be the case that any party in breach of either Article simply is unable to enforce his trade mark or other rights as some sort of outlaw.[26] There has to be some close nexus[27] between the proposed exercise of trade mark rights and the breach.[28]

There was in the early years after the accession of the UK to the then European Economic Community a tendency for defendants to put forward "Euro-defences" based on Arts 81 and 82 liberally,[29] but the courts generally adopted a robust attitude and, save in genuine free circulation cases, they have not succeeded.[30] The general attitude now to such defences was summarised by Neuberger J. in *Sandvik AB v KR Pfiffner (United Kingdom) Ltd*:   **16–118**

> "On the one hand, the court should not make it too easy for a defendant to raise what turns out to be a baseless allegation of Article 86 [ex 82] infringement against a plaintiff, with a view to frightening off the plaintiff or at least increasing the cost and delay to the plaintiff, in establishing his right. On the other hand, it would be wrong to make it too difficult for a defendant with a valid case of Article 86 [now 82] infringement to put his case before the court".[31]

The courts have tended to ignore the fact that in any actual case of breach of Arts 81 or 82 the defendant has the additional remedy of a complaint to the European Commission, formerly under Reg.17/62 and now under Reg.1/2003, Art.7(2).[32] Such a complaint can be effective, and the Commission has power to take immediate action by way of interim measures[33] (it should be noted, however, that the Commission has no power to award damages to an aggrieved party).   **16–119**

However, it has been held that where the Commission has not yet made a final decision on a complaint, it is open to (and indeed incumbent upon) an English court to find a just way of regulating the position between the parties in English   **16–120**

---

[26] See *ICI v Berk* [1981] 2 C.M.L.R. 91; [1981] F.S.R. 1 at 6, *per* Megarry V.C.

[27] *per* Peter Gibson J. in *Holleran v Daniel Thwaites plc* [1989] 2 C.M.L.R. 917.

[28] Some of the difficulties of any more general rule were pointed out by Megarry V.C. in *ICI v Berk* [1981] 2 C.M.L.R. 91, where a plea of abuse of dominant position (by imposing unfair prices) was struck out because there was no nexus between the abuse and the plaintiffs' cause of action. A case of a close nexus appears to be *L'Oréal* [1980] E.C.R. 3775. In *Nancy Kean*, at para.16–116 the ECJ said "it is for the national court to ascertain in each case whether the exercise of the exclusive right in question leads to one of the situations which fall under the prohibitions contained in Art. 85 [now 81] and which may, in the context of the exercise of exclusive rights to designs take very different forms, such as, for example, the situation where persons simultaneously or successively file the same design in various member-States in order to divide up the markets within the Community among themselves" (para.28). The same would obviously apply to trade marks used in this way.

[29] See, *e.g. British Leyland v T.I. Silencers* [1981] F.S.R. 213; [1981] 2 C.M.L.R. 75, C.A.; *ICI v Berk*, at para.16–117; *Hoover v Hulme* [1982] F.S.R. 565; *Who Group Ltd v Stage One* [1980] F.S.R. 268; *Application des Gaz v Falks Veritas* [1975] R.P.C. 421.

[30] Although in one case the English Court of Appeal, CA, was persuaded that a Euro-defence to the effect that by reason of the EEC-Portugal trading agreement the free circulation rules applied to EEC-Portuguese trade was so strong as to make the plaintiffs' case unarguable: *Polydor v Harlequin* [1980] 2 C.M.L.R. 413; [1980] F.S.R. 362. This decision was reversed by the ECJ on the reference made by that Court of Appeal: [1982] 1 C.M.L.R. 677.

[31] [2000] F.S.R. 17 at 68.

[32] Although in a decision shortly after UK accession, Graham J. in *Aero Zipp Fasteners Limited v YKK Fasteners (UK) Limited* [1973] C.M.L.R. 819, refused to strike out an unparticularised defence founded on Arts 85 and 86 (now 81 and 82) on the ground that the European Commission had already initiated proceedings, which the judge considered would only have occurred if the Commission was "satisfied that there is at least a prima facie case".

[33] Art.8, Reg.1/2003, [2003] O.J. L 1/1, in cases of urgency due to the risk of serious and irreparable damage to competition.

proceedings.[34] Notwithstanding this, Art.16(1) of Reg.1/2003 now states that national courts "cannot take decisions running counter to the decision adopted by the Commission. They must also avoid giving decisions that would conflict with a decision contemplated by the Commission in proceedings it has initiated. To that effect, the national court may assess whether it is necessary to stay its proceedings". In addition, Art.15(1) provides for national courts in proceedings involving the application of Art.81 or Art.82 to ask the Commission for its opinion concerning the application of the Community competition rules (or indeed to ask the Commission to transmit information in its possession).

16–121   Where the Commission had issued a Statement of Objections, it was held by the Court of Appeal that the national court was not obliged to stay proceedings pending a decision, provided that the case was not clearly in favour of either the claimant or the defendant.[35] As emphasised by Reg.1/2003, what should be avoided by national courts is taking decisions which may conflict with those of the Commission or those contemplated by the Commission in proceedings it has initiated.[36] Once a decision has been issued by the Commission, it is legally binding on national courts and such courts may not allow a party whose position was rejected by the Commission to re-litigate the question. Similarly, if proceedings are already afoot but suspended, the national court should decide the case in the same way as the Commission.[37]

BREACH GIVING RISE TO A CLAIM

16–122   It is clear that any party directly affected by a breach of either Art.81 or Art.82 can not only complain to the European Commission,[38] but can also sue in the national courts for an injunction to restrain continued breach[39] and for damages.[40] So far as trade marks are concerned however, it is difficult to envisage circumstances where this rule may apply.[41] Perhaps a parallel importer whose supplies of the trade-marked goods were withheld as a result of collusion between the

---

[34] *Fyffes v Chiquita Brands International* [1993] F.S.R. 83 at 100.

[35] "The Court's concern is to avoid inconsistent decisions. There is no ground for seeking to prohibit the preparation of an action for trial so long as it does not lead to a decision in advance of a decision by the Commission": *per* Sir Thomas Bingham M.R. in *MTV Europe v BMG Records (UK) Ltd* [1997] Eu.L.R. 100 at 108, upholding the decision of the trial judge (Evans-Lombe J.) to allow the action to proceed to setting down.

[36] Art.16(1), Reg.1/2003, [2003] O.J. L 1/1.

[37] Art.16(1), Reg.1/2003, [2003] O.J. L 1/1. See also *Iberian v BPB and British Gypsum* [1997] I.C.R. 164, and the commentary on it by the judge, Mr Justice Laddie, in "Community Competition Law in English Courts" in Andenas and Jacobs (eds), *European Community Law in the English Courts* (Clarendon Press, Oxford, 1998), pp.177–178.

[38] Under Reg.1/2003, [2003] O.J. 1/1, which makes the procedure for complaints more effective than it was under Reg.17/62.

[39] *Cutsforth v Mansfield Inns* [1986] 1 All E.R. 577.

[40] In *Courage Ltd v Crehan* [2001] E.C.R. I-6297, the ECJ made it clear that there must be available in national courts the right to obtain damages from the breaching party; see also the *Commission Notice on Cooperation*, [2004] O.J. C 101/54. See also *Bourgoin v Ministry of Agriculture* [1986] 2 C.M.L.R. 267, CA (action against Government for breach of Art.30 [now 28] actionable as breach of statutory duty where there is an abuse of power). For earlier cases, see *Application des Gaz v Falks Veritas* [1975] R.P.C. 421, CA; *BRT SABAM* [1974] E.C.R. 51, 333 (ECJ).

[41] See *Glaxo Group Ltd v Dowelhurst Ltd* [2000] F.S.R. 371, in which the defendants sought to amend their defences and have permission to make counterclaims based on Art.81(1): in allowing the amendments, even though he considered the evidence of a concerted practice to be "thin", the judge noted "Issues arising under Article 81(1) are likely to add significantly to the costs and duration of a trial and care must be taken to distinguish between an honestly held persecution complex and evidence of collaboration": at 384.

manufacturer and his distributors could sue.[42] But he would have to prove that his inability to obtain the goods was indeed the result of a deliberate attempt to partition the Community.

"MAY AFFECT TRADE BETWEEN MEMBER STATES"

No question under Art.81 or Art.82 can arise unless the conduct concerned "may affect trade between Member States",[43] although obviously in the United Kingdom a question may then arise under the Competition Act 1998.[44] This is thus a jurisdictional requirement dividing the competences of the Community and national competition authorities.[45] The Commission has set out the conditions to be met in order for an agreement to come within the concept of no appreciable effect on trade and therefore fall outside Art.81:[46] in the case of licence agreements (a) the aggregate annual Community-wide turnover of the licensees in the product and the licensor's own turnover should not exceed €40 million *and* (b) the aggregate market share of the parties on any relevant market within the Community affected by the agreement should not exceed 5 per cent.[47] Thus, it needs to be determined what the relevant market is in the context of reviewing a trade mark licence to decide whether it is "de minimis".[48] A possibility of such an effect on inter-State trade will suffice.[49] The Commission has in the past taken a rather liberal view of the requirement,[50] but recently there has been a marked change in this attitude and a willingness on the part of the Commission to cede responsibility to national authorities.[51] The United Kingdom courts have been reluctant to find an effect on inter-State trade on too speculative a basis and evi-

16–123

---

[42] However, it should be borne in mind that unilateral conduct does not fall within Art.81: in *Adalat* [1996] O.J. L 201/1 the Commission found Bayer to be acting contrary to Art.81(1) by refusing to supply pharmaceutical wholesalers who were involved in parallel trading. The CFI annulled the Commission's decision requiring Bayer to resume supply, on the ground that it raised "the particularly delicate question as to the circumstances in which a refusal to sell is capable, when it occurs in the context of continuing commercial relations, of constituting one of the aspects of an agreement containing an export prohibition" and that it did not appear on the evidence that there was sufficient consent by the other wholesalers to Bayer's refusal to supply to create an agreement falling within Art.85(1): [1996] E.C.R. II-383, at paras 41–52. The Court of Justice *Bunderverband der Arzneimittel-Importeure v Commission* [2004] 4 C.M.L.R. 653) dismissed the Commission's appeal against this finding, holding that the mere fact that a measure adopted by a manufacturer, which has the object or effect of restricting competition, falls within the context of continuous business relations between the manufacturer and its wholesalers is not sufficient for a finding that such an agreement exists, at para.141.

[43] These words appear in each Article.

[44] See paras 16–147 to 16–152.

[45] On the relationship between Community and national competition laws, see Reg.1/2003, [2003] O.J. 1/1 and the Guidelines thereto.

[46] Commission Guidelines on the effect on trade concept contained in Arts 81 and 82 of the Treaty, [2004] O.J. C 101/81.

[47] Commission Guidelines on the effect on trade concept contained in Arts 81 and 82 of the Treaty, [2004] O.J. C 101/81, at para.52.

[48] For further guidance, see *Volk* [1969] E.C.R. 295; [1969] C.M.L.R. 273; *Baeguelin I* [1971] E.C.R. 949; [1972] C.M.L.R. 81; *La Technique Miniere (LTM)* [1966] E.C.R. 337; [1966] C.M.L.R. 357; *Hugin* [1979] E.C.R. 1869; [1979] 3 C.M.L.R. 345; *European Night Services* [1998] 5 C.M.L.R. 718.

[49] *Michelin* [1983] E.C.R. 3461, para.104.

[50] See, *e.g. Michelin* [1982] 1 C.M.L.R. 643 at 663; *Advocaat Zwarte Kip* [1974] 2 C.M.L.R. D79 at D85; *AOIP/Beyrard* [1976] 1 C.M.L.R. D14; *SABA* [1976] 1 C.M.L.R. D61, cf. *SAFCO* [1972] C.M.L.R. D83.

[51] See Reg.1/2003 ,[2004] O.J. L 1/11, Ch. IV on Co-operation between the Commission and the competition authorities of the Member States; and Commission Notice on the Cooperation Between the Commission and the Courts of the EU Member States in the Application of Arts 81 and 82 EC, [2004] O.J. C 101/54.

dence must be shown of a definite effect on past trade or a real likelihood of future trade being affected.[52]

SCOPE OF ARTICLE 82

16–124   In order to establish a breach it is of course first necessary to establish that a party is in a dominant position within the Community. There is now a substantial body of authority on what amounts to a "dominant position."[53] As a preliminary step, it is necessary to establish the "relevant market" (for example the class of goods or services concerned) and then determine whether the party concerned is dominant in that market, for example, is in a position to prevent effective competition or otherwise to act without regard to its competitors. So far as industrial property rights are concerned, the ECJ has clearly established that their mere existence does not constitute a "dominant position". Thus in *Sirena* the Court said:[54] "the proprietor of a trademark does not enjoy a 'dominant position' within the meaning of Article 86[now 82] merely because he is in a position to prevent third parties from putting into circulation, on the territory of a Member State, products bearing the same trademark."[55]

16–125   What more is needed to establish a "dominant position"? In *Sirena* the Court suggested that "the proprietor should have the power to impede the maintenance of effective competition over a considerable part of the relevant market, having regard in particular to the existence and position of any producers or distributors who may be marketing similar goods or goods which may be substituted for them".[56] It is possible therefore that a particularly well-known trade mark might have such a powerful goodwill that others could not effectively compete. In such a case the marked product might constitute a relevant market in its own right and the proprietor of the mark may be in a dominant position.[57] It would by no means follow, however, that the enforcement of rights in such a mark would be forbidden absolutely. That would depend upon whether or not the type of enforcement concerned could be held an "abuse" of the dominant position.[58]

16–126   So far as "abuse" of a dominant position arising from monopoly rights is

---

[52] In *Chiron v Murex (No.2)* [1994] 1 C.M.L.R. 410, CA, the court struck out a pleading of abuse contrary to Art.86 [82] as there was no effect on trade between Member States; see also *Duracell v Ever Ready* [1989] R.P.C. 731 and *Sport International B.V. v Hi-Tec Sports Ltd* [1990] F.S.R. 312 at 318, *per* Hirst J.

[53] See, *e.g. United Brands* [1978] E.C.R. 207; [1978] 3 C.M.L.R. 83; *Hugin* [1979] E.C.R. 1969; [1879] 3 C.M.L.R. 345; *Commercial Solvents* [1974] E.C.R. 223; [1974] C.M.L.R. 309; *Hoffmann-La Roche* [1979] E.C.R. 461; [1979] 3 C.M.L.R. 211; *Volvo v Veng* [1988] E.C.R. 6211; *AKZO Chemie* [1991] E.C.R. I-3359; and, generally, Bellamy & Child, *Common Market Law of Competition* (4th ed., Sweet and Maxwell, London) Ch.7.

[54] [1971] E.C.R. 69 at 83, para.16; [1971] C.M.L.R. 260 at 275 (there is a slight difference in language in this unofficial report).

[55] See also *EMI v CBS* [1976] E.C.R. 811 at 849, para.36; [1976] 2 C.M.L.R. 235; *Parke Davis* [1968] E.C.R. 81; [1968] C.M.L.R. 47 (patents); *DG v Metro* [1971] E.C.R. 487; [1971] C.M.L.R. 631 (copyright).

[56] *Sirena* [1971] E.C.R. 69, para.16. See also *Parke Davis* [1968] E.C.R. 55; *Volvo v Veng* [1988] E.C.R. 6211; *CICRA v Renault* [1988] E.C.R. 6039.

[57] In *United Brands* [1978] E.C.R. 207; [1978] 1 C.M.L.R. 429, the ECJ included in the factors which were important in finding dominance, the quality control imposed in relation to its well-known trade mark Chiquita. In a UK context, it was unsuccessfully alleged that The Post Office had breached the Competition Act equivalent of Art.82 by licensing its Royal Mail logo to a related party; it was contended that this would give its licensee an overwhelming advantage: *Claritas (UK) Ltd v The Post Office* [2001] E.T.M.R. 679.

[58] In *Tierce Ladbroke v Commission* [1997] 5 C.M.L.R. 309, the Court of First Instance held (at para.131) that for a refusal to licence copyright to amount to an abuse, it had to be related to either a product or a service which was essential for the exercise of the activity in question, in that there was no real or potential substitute. It is difficult to envisage this test being satisfied in rela-

concerned, the Court has clearly contemplated that overpricing may constitute an abuse.[59] But it is difficult to see why, given such overpricing, the trade mark right should be wholly unenforceable.[60]

The Commission has held it to be an abuse of a dominant position for a party in such a position to register in one part of the Community a mark it knows or ought to know is used by a competitor elsewhere in the Community.[61]

SCOPE OF ARTICLE 81

There is now a considerable amount of authority both of the ECJ and of the European Commission concerning the ambit of Art.81(1) and the circumstances in which, even though an agreement might fall within Art.81(1), the parties to it can claim the benefit of Art.81(3),[62] or fall within the various "block exemptions".[63] They cannot be discussed fully here: we confine ourselves to agreements relating to trade marks and allied matters.[64] Speaking generally, however, any arrangement intended for (or which has the effect of) partitioning the EC or restricting competition is almost certainly offensive, provided that trade between Member States is or may be affected.[65]

16–127

---

tion to a refusal to licence a trade mark. Also, see *Biotrading & Financing v Biohit Ltd* [1998] F.S.R. 109, in which Aldous L.J. reiterated that enforcement of copyright cannot by itself be an abuse: at 133.

[59] *Sirena* [1971] E.C.R. 69, para.17.

[60] See *I.C.I. v Berk* at para.16–117. Similarly, it is difficult to envisage circumstances in which the "essential facilities" notion developed by the ECJ in *Volvo v Veng* [1988] E.C.R. 6211; [1989] 4 C.M.L.R. 122; and *RTE and ITP* [1995] E.C.R. I-743; [1995] 4 C.M.L.R. 718 would be applied to trade marks as the specific subject-matter does not lend itself to the market-foreclosing behaviour resulting from a refusal to license patents or copyright. In Case C– 53/03 *Synetairismos Farmakopoion v GlaxoSmithkline*, October 28, 2004, unreported, A.G. Jacobs advised that "a dominant pharmaceutical undertaking will not necessarily abuse its dominant position by reason of its refusal to supply in full the orders placed with it by pharmaceutical wholesalers even when its intention is thereby to limit parallel trade", at para.53.

[61] *Osram/Airam Settlement* [1982] 3 C.M.L.R. 614; [1983] F.S.R. 108.

[62] Until May 1, 2004, Art.9(1) of Reg.17, gave the Commission the exclusive power to grant exemptions, whereas now Art.2 of Reg.1/2003, [2003] O.J. L 1/1, imposes on the person claiming the benefit the burden of proof that the conditions of Art.81(3) are satisfied, either in proceedings before a national court or the Commission on a complaint. Although by Art.4(2)(iii) of Reg.17, trade mark (and other industrial property) assignments or licences to which not more than two undertakings were party did not need to be notified as long as they only imposed restrictions on the exercise of the rights by the assignee or licensee, there is no corresponding exemption in Reg.1/2003 and therefore companies and their advisers themselves must now come to their own assessment as to whether Art.81(3) applies: see Guidelines on the application of Art.81(3), [2004] O.J. C 101/97. Clearly, this would not be the case where the restrictions go beyond the specific subject-matter of the trade mark: in *Windsurfing International Inc v Commission* [1986] E.C.R. 611; [1986] 3 C.M.L.R. 489, the ECJ held that the exception in Reg.17 did not apply where the restrictions covered goods not covered by the patent and there was a no-challenge clause affecting both patents and trade marks; also the trade mark delimitation agreement in *BAT "Toltecs"* [1985] F.S.R. 533, fell outside the exception.

[63] Commission had developed the practice of issuing so-called comfort letters by which it closed its file on a particular agreement without granting either a negative clearance or individual exemption; this will now only be done in exceptional circumstances under the new regime introduced by Reg.1/2003 ,[2003] O.J. L 1/1.

[64] See generally the article by the late Judge Joliet (of the ECJ) Trademark Licensing Agreements under the EEC Law of Competition (1983–84) 5 Northwestern Journal of International Law & Business 755.

[65] Note the comment of Judge Bellamy of the ECJ: "an effects-based system in its pure form is frankly unmanageable. It is totally impractical. If you adopt a wide-ranging test like that adopted by the Court of Justice in Consten and Grundig, in the mid 1960s, you immediately find that to make it workable you have to adopt a whole series of exemptions and exceptions, in order to give back to business the legal certainty that it needs and to reduce the administration burden on the authority to within manageable limits" in *The Europeanisation of United Kingdom Competition Law* (eds. Green & Robertson), 1999. Howver, there is a strong argument that the recent reforms have once again removed legal certainty from business.

(1) Assignments of trade marks

16–128   The ECJ has made it clear that any assignment of a trade mark for part of the Community only should not in itself be viewed as having the effect of partitioning the market.[66] Nevertheless, an assignment of a mark (or an agreement to assign) for part of the market alone may fall within Art.81(1) in certain circumstances. As a practical matter, however, it cannot vest in the assignee absolute protection for the countries for which he has taken an assignment: he may be exposed to parallel imports from the remainder of the Community. If, however, the parties go further than a mere assignment, and actively (either by terms of the agreement or by their conduct) seek to partition the Community then there will be a breach of Art.81(1).[67] Indeed an attempt to enforce a trade mark to prevent parallel imports with knowledge of the competition rules may increase the gravity of the breach.

(2) Exclusive licences

16–129   United Kingdom law recognises in s.31(1) of the Trade Marks Act 1994 that trade marks may be licensed exclusively, provided the requirements of s.28(2)[68] are complied with.[69] At one time the Commission took the view that all exclusive licences of industrial property rights fell within Ar.85(1) (now 81(1)) and, if they were to be justified at all, needed exemption under Art.5(3) (now 81(3)).[70] As a result of the *Maize Seed* case[71] that view was modified: the European Court drew a distinction between "open" and "closed" exclusive licences. An "open" exclusive licence is one whereby the owner of the right merely undertakes not to grant other licences in the territory concerned and not himself to compete with his licensee in that territory. Such a licence will not normally fall within Art.81(1), although the particular facts will have to be examined to discover whether the licence has the effect of preventing or distorting competition within the EC.[72] But if the parties go further, and by their agreement seek to confer absolute territorial protection on the licensee, so that parallel importers or licensees from other ter-

---

[66] *IHT Internationale Heiztechnik v Ideal-Standard* [1994] E.C.R. I-2789.

[67] *IHT Internationale Heiztechnik v Ideal-Standard* [1994] E.C.R. I-2789, "Before a trade mark assignment can be treated as giving effect to an agreement prohibited under Article 85 [now 81], it is necessary to analyse the context, the commitments underlying the assignment, the intention of the parties and the consideration for the assignment": at para.59. Also, see *Tepea* [1978] E.C.R. 1391; [1978] 3 C.M.L.R. 392.

[68] "A licence is not effective unless it is in writing signed by or on behalf of the grantor."

[69] See Ch.12.

[70] The argument was that the grant of such a licence was restrictive of trade because it prevented the licensor from granting licences to others, see, *e.g. Burroughs* [1972] C.M.L.R. D67; *Kabelmetal* [1975] 2 C.M.L.R. D40; *AOIP/Beyrard* [1976] 1 C.M.L.R. D14. It followed from this that if there were to be exclusive licences within the Community at all, they would need exemption under Art. 85(3) (now 81(3)). In *Campari* the exclusivity was exempted: (1978) 22 C.M.L.R. 397.

[71] *Nungesser* [1982] E.C.R. 2015; [1983] 1 C.M.L.R. 278.

[72] Thus the Commission held a 10-year exclusive trade mark licence for the whole EC granted on the occasion of the grantor's transfer of its European business to the grantee as constituting protection against competition for an unreasonable length of time: *Tyler* [1982] 3 C.M.L.R. 613; [1973] F.S.R. 109. On the other hand, a three-year non-compete clause included in a sale of a business with goodwill was held not to fall within Art.85(1) (now 81(1)); *Mecaniver/PPG* [1985] O.J. L 35/54; [1985] C.M.L.R. 359. In *Nutricia* [1984] 2 C.M.L.R. 165, the Commission indicated the principles under which an allowable period for a non-compete clause on the sale of a business may be set (four years for a low technology business of sauces and pickles). The benefits of the vertical restraints block exemption, above, are not available where the agreement includes a non-compete obligation the duration of which is either indefinite or exceeds five years: Art.5(1).

ritories are excluded, then the licence will be "closed" and fall foul of Art.81(1).[73] The difference can perhaps be put in this way: that exclusive licences may be granted, provided they do not go so far as to attempt to circumvent the free movement rules.

In *Moosehead/Whitbread*[74] the Commission found that an exclusive trade mark **16–130** licence to brew and market beer in the United Kingdom under the "Moosehead" mark fell within Art.81(1). The Commission considered that the exclusivity, coupled with a prohibition on active sales outside the United Kingdom and a ban on marketing competing brands, could affect trade between Member States. However, an individual exemption was granted in view of the competitive state of the United Kingdom beer market.

(3) Block exemptions

So far as patents and know-how, as well as software and designs, are concerned, **16–131** the Commission has issued a new block exemption covering technology transfer agreements (including exclusive licences) (TTBER).[75] "[I]n order to simplify the regulatory framework and its application", this no longer lists the exempted clauses but rather only 'hardcore restrictions' which may not be included in technology transfer agreements.[76] The TTBER emphasises[77] that there is no presumption of illegality of a technology transfer agreement falling outside its scope provided it does not contain one of the hardcore restrictions of competition set out in Art.4 contains certain provisions as to what can and cannot be done by way of ancillary clauses concerned with trade marks.[78] There is also another recent block exemption covering vertical agreements and concerted practices[79] which contains an important provision on intellectual property rights: "The exemption provided for in paragraph 1 shall apply to vertical agreements containing provisions which relate to the assignment to the buyer or use by the buyer of intellectual property rights, provided that those provisions do not constitute the primary object of such agreements and are directly related to the use, sale or resale of goods or services by the buyer or its customers."[80] Thus the exemption depends on whether the trade mark licence is or is not the "primary object" of the agreement, where distribution of goods or services and a licence of trade marks

---

[73] above.

[74] [1990] O.J. L 100/32.

[75] Reg.772/2004: [2004] O.J. L 123/11, which should be read in conjunction with the associated Guidelines, [2004] O.J. C 101/2. Agreements entered into prior to April 30, 2004 and which comply with the previous Regulation, Reg.240/96, but not the new conditions for exemption are granted a transitional period of approval until March 31, 2006, Art.10.

[76] [2004] O.J. L 123/11 at Recital 4.

[77] Guidelines, [2004] O.J. C 101/2 paras 9 and 130.

[78] Namely Art.1.1(7) accepts "an obligation on the licensee to use only the licensor's trade mark or get-up to distinguish the licensed product during the term of the agreement, provided that the licensee is not prevented from identifying himself as the manufacturer of the licensed products"; and Art.2.1(11) "obligation on the licensee to mark the licensed product with an indication of the licensor's name or of licensed patent."

[79] Reg.2790/99: [1999] O.J. 336/21, applied from June 1, 2000: until that date, there applied the previous block exemptions on exclusive distribution and exclusive purchasing (Regs 1983/83 and 1984/83 respectively: [1983] O.J. L 173) and on franchising (Reg.4087/88: [1988] O.J. L 359/46).

[80] Art.2(3).

are included in the same agreement. These clauses are a good guide as to some types of clause which may be acceptable in other forms of licence.[81]

(4) Licences generally

16–132   It is of course essential in relation to a trade mark licence that there be a right of quality control by the licensor.[82] So to that extent the licensee is put under a requirement that might be suggested is restrictive of competition within the Community and so theoretically caught by Art.81(1). Such a suggestion is clearly wrong. Unless the licence contains other terms (for example a requirement forcing the licensee to use the mark) the licensee is merely given a permission to use the mark where he complies with the quality control provisions.[83] It is noteworthy that the Commission has never considered quality control provisions in a patent licence as restrictive where they were "indispensable for the technically perfect exploitation" of the patent.[84] Since quality control is of the essence of a valid trade mark licence the same reasoning must apply to such licences.[85]

(5) "No challenge" clauses

16–133   It seems clear that clauses in agreements forbidding the licensee to challenge the validity of the licensed right usually fall within Art.81(1).[86] However, where it is necessary in order to establish a trade mark in an already crowded market, such a clause may be acceptable.[87] A clause permitting the licensor to terminate the licence if such a challenge is made is likely to be acceptable.[88]

16–134   This rule can pose special difficulties in the way of the settlement of litigation: in particular where the validity of the claimant's right is contested, the claimant will normally desire to see that right recognised in any settlement. Even so, and

---

[81] Note that the Guidelines on the TTBER state that it will be applied by analogy to certain agreements not falling within its scope but expressly not to trade mark licences, para.53. The practical effect of this is that great care needs to be given to the terms of a trade mark licence as there is no longer the possibility of notifying or requesting individual exemption but rather a self-assessment must be conducted and the ultimate test of that assessment will be either in litigation to enforce the agreement's provisions or if the Commission launches an investigation.

[82] See Ch.12.

[83] e.g. *Campari* (1978) 22 C.M.L.R. 397, in which the Commission found that Art.85(1) [now 81(1)] does not catch production standards or the licensor's right to inspect and sample: at 408.

[84] See Notice of December 24, 1962 ("the Christmas Message"); *Burroughs* [1972] C.M.L.R. D67; *Raymond/Nagoya* [1972] C.M.L.R. D45. Under Reg.240/96 an obligation on the licensee to accept quality specifications not necessary for a technically satisfactory exploitation of the licensed technology, and to allow the licensor to carry out related checks, was a grey clause acceptable (Art.4(2)(a)) as long as the agreement was notified and the Commission did not oppose an exemption within four months (Art.4(1)). With the new regime of non-notification, see Reg.772/2004, [2004] O.J. L 123/11, only hardcore restrictions (or black) clauses are specifically proscribed.

[85] Thus in *Carlsberg* [1984] O.J. C 27/4; [1984] 1 C.M.L.R. 305, the Commission clearly accepted quality control clauses in a much wider commercial agreement, also *Moosehead/Whitbread* [1990] O.J. L 100/32at para.16-130. Of course where quality control conditions are imposed on more than one licensee there may be a breach of Art.81(1) if different standards are applied to equivalent licensees, see: *Carlsberg* [1985] C.M.L.R. 735 at 734.

[86] *BAT "Toltecs"* [1985] 2 C.M.L.R. 470; [1985] F.S.R. 533, at paras 34–5 (ECJ); *Davidson* [1972] C.M.L.R. D52; *Raymond/Nagoya* [1972] C.M.L.R. D45; *Kabelmetal* [1975] 2 C.M.L.R. D40; *AOIP* [1976] 1 C.M.L.R. D15; *Goodyear* [1975] 1 C.M.L.R. D31. The common law rule (based upon the analogy with the law of landlord and tenant) that even in the absence of an express no challenge clause the licensee cannot challenge the title of the right licensed is clearly abrogated so far as agreements affecting trade between Member States are concerned and in domestic situations presumably, may now contravene the Competition Act 1998 (see paras 16–147 to 16–152).

[87] See *Moosehead/Whitbread* [1990] O.J. L 100/32at para.16-130, in which the Commission found that such an obligation did not restrict competition within the meaning of Art.81(1).

[88] See Art.5(1)(c) of the Technology Transfer Block Exemption 772/2004, which accepts "the possibility to provide for termination of the technology transfer agreement in the event that the licensee challenges the validity of one or more of the licensed intellectual property rights".

despite the general desirability of encouraging settlement of litigation, the Commission has taken the view that parties may not "reinforce" by contract industrial property rights,[89] although to decide whether such reinforcement has taken place may involve difficult issues of likelihood of confusion on which reasonable people may disagree. In some cases it may be possible to argue that a particular "no challenge" clause is outside Art.81(1)[90] or should benefit from Art.81(3). In general terms this should be so in any case where there is a *bona fide* dispute being settled (although the respective size of the parties should always be considered when evaluating the legitimacy of the settlement). Of course it is equally clear that a "no challenge" clause in respect of a virtually bogus trade mark right could in practice amount to no more than a market-sharing agreement and no doubt such a clause could itself be challenged.[91]

It should be borne in mind by those drafting trade mark delimitation agreements that, where the agreement is for an indefinite period, the validity of a "no challenge" clause may depend on whether the trade mark in question remains in use, or at least is used sufficiently to maintain a trade mark registration.[92]   **16–135**

(6) Agreement to minimise confusion

It seems clear that an agreement (for example between holders of a mark of "common origin") merely designed to avoid confusion but not to partition the Community is outside Art.81(1).[93] However, a trade mark delimitation agreement would fall within Art.81(1) where it is not evident that the holder of an earlier trade mark could have recourse to national law to prevent the holder of a later mark from using it in one or more Member States.[94]   **16–136**

---

[89] There is no distinction to be made between agreements putting an end to litigation and other agreements: *Bayer v Sullhofer* [1990] 4 C.M.L.R. 182; cf. the suggestion by Neill L.J. in *Apple Corps Ltd v Apple Computer Inc* [1991] C.M.L.R. 397, that such a distinction may be relevant in restraint of trade.

[90] *Penneys* [1978] 2 C.M.L.R. 100 (settlement of major trade mark and passing off litigation. "No-challenge" for five years accepted as not restrictive, this being the normal period after which a mark is vulnerable for non-use, settlement related solely to trade marks).

[91] *Sirdar/Phildar* [1975] 1 C.M.L.R. D83, appears to be such a case. The marks were fairly obviously not confusable (and were held so on motion: [1975] 1 C.M.L.R. 378; [1975] F.S.R. 309). BAT "Toltecs" is another such case: see Commission decision [1982] O.J. L 379/19; [1983] 1 C.M.L.R. 412, at paras 43–44. The decision itself was upheld by the ECJ ([1985] 2 C.M.L.R. 470; [1985] F.S.R. 533), although the Court refrained from commenting on this point (para.35). But the suggestion in the decision of the Commission that the agreement would be caught even if the marks were confusingly similar appears to go too far. Taken logically it would mean that parties could not settle infringement and passing off cases at all. The only way the holder of the right could prevent imports would be by success in a fought action.

[92] In *Apple Corps Ltd v Apple Computer Inc* [1991] 3 C.M.L.R. 49, Neill L.J. stated: "It is plain that to enforce ... the 'no-challenge' restrictions in the 1981 Agreement it will be necessary for Apple to prove that they have used the marks at the relevant times in the course of their businesses. The actual use of the marks by Apple will be one of the central issues for the court to determine": at para.80. See also, *Sport International Bussum v Hi-Tec Sports* [1990] F.S.R. 312, in which a mandatory injunction was granted to restrain an opposition contrary to the terms of a settlement agreement; rejecting an argument that this was equivalent to a no-challenge clause and therefore contrary to Art.85 [now 81].

[93] *Persil* [1978] 1 C.M.L.R. 395; *Velcro/Aplix* [1989] 4 C.M.L.R. 157. Clearly there is a difference between such an agreement between persons who have concurrent rights to use a mark throughout the EC and an agreement where there are no such rights *e.g.* in a Terrapin-like case). In the latter, more restrictive conditions ought to be acceptable, but the Commission might well not agree: see *Sirdar/Phildar* [1975] 1 C.M.L.R. D83.

[94] The *Community v Syntex Corp* [1990] 4 C.M.L.R. 343; [1990] F.S.R. 529: the Commission closed its file when the parties amended the agreement to provide for co-existence in all Member States.

(7) Obligation on patent licensee to use licensor's mark

16–137   This clause has been held unobjectionable where the licensee is permitted also to use his own mark.[95] It is not clear what attitude the Commission would take where the licensee under a patent was compelled to use the licensor's mark only, with the result that on expiry of the licence and patent the licensee would find it difficult to continue the business formerly conducted by it. On one view the licensee would be in no worse position than any third party entering the market after expiry of the patent and so the clause is not restrictive. But in practice the clause could have a devastating effect on the licensee's continued ability to conduct his business and the Commission might hold the clause in substance restrictive.

(8) Settlements of actions

16–138   Even some settlements of actions can be invalidated under Art.81(1).

BAT owned the dormant mark "Dorcet" in Germany and sued a relatively small defendant using the mark "Toltecs Special". Although the "Dorcet" registration was open to cancellation, BAT secured a settlement which was heavily disadvantageous to the defendant. The ECJ held that the agreement was invalid: in substance it served no purpose other than for BAT to control and in the end prevent distribution of the defendant's tobacco in Germany.[96]

16–139   This decision is of particular significance: large companies frequently own considerable portfolios of registered marks which are either wholly unused or have only token use. If they use such marks to oppress other, genuine, traders they may well be acting in breach of Art.82 and any settlement achieved may fall foul of Art.81(1).

16–140   It is important to bear in mind that a settlement agreement which did not fall within Art.81(1) at the time it was entered into, may do so subsequently if circumstances change and the agreement is no longer not restrictive of competition, for example because marks have become susceptible to attack on the grounds of non-use or have been abandoned.[97] Also, where a global or EC-wide trade mark delimitation (or settlement) agreement is entered into for an indefinite period, it is essential that the parties try to anticipate business developments which may later make the field of use unacceptable to one of the parties.[98]

(9) Selective distribution

16–141   It is of course common for manufacturers to distribute their wares through a network of dealers. The agreements with such dealers may, if restrictive of inter-

---

[95] *Burroughs* [1972] C.M.L.R. D67. The Technology Transfer Block Exemption (Reg.240/96) included in the clauses generally not restrictive of competition (grey clauses), an obligation on the licensee to use only the licensor's trade mark or get up provided the licensee is permitted to identify itself as the manufacturer (Art.1(7) and an obligation on the licensee to mark the licensed product with an indication of the licensor's name (Art.2.1(11)).

[96] *BAT "Toltecs"* [1985] 2 C.M.L.R. 470; [1985] F.S.R. 533.

[97] For an example, see *Apple Corps Ltd v Apple Computer Inc* [1991] 3 C.M.L.R. 49, particularly Nicholls L.J. at para.113.

[98] In *Apple* [1991] 3 C.M.L.R. 49, the computer industry developed in ways unforeseen at the date of the agreement and by the time of the dispute six years later the "music" and "computer" markets "were no longer different, separate or distinct": *per* Neill L.J., para.23.

state trade, fall within Art.81(1).[99] Any attempt to use passing off rights to prevent parallel imports where the alleged misrepresentation relates to the nature of a dealer (or the giving of a guarantee), may fail if there was a related breach of Art.81(1).[1] In *Javico v Yves St Laurent*[2] the ECJ held that a selective distribution system outside the Community may fall foul of Art.81(1) if the agreement contains a provision restricting sales into the Community:[3] this is an area in which one can envisage further attempts by parallel importers to resist attacks by national or EC trade mark proprietors on grey imports into the EC from outside and highlights the importance of reading trade mark legislation bearing in mind the overarching reach of EC and UK competition laws.

(10) "Franchise agreements"

These present enormous diversity. The ECJ has noted three types particularly: **16–142**

"service franchise agreements, by which the franchisee offers services under the sign and trade name, or indeed the trade mark, of the franchisor and complies with the franchisor's directives; production franchise agreements by which the franchisee himself manufactures, according to the instructions of the franchisor, products which he sells under the franchisor's trade mark; and finally, distribution franchise agreements by which the franchisee restricts himself to the sale of certain products in a shop carrying the mark of the franchisor."[4]

In relation to the third type of agreement there will not normally be a breach of **16–143**
Art.81(1) by a clause protecting the franchisor's know-how. Nor will there be a breach by a clause which enables the franchisor to take appropriate measures to preserve the identity and reputation of the network which is symbolised by the mark, at least where such clauses are indispensable for this purpose.[5]

PROCEDURAL QUESTIONS

Questions of Community law may arise in essentially two different contexts, **16–144**
namely in proceedings before a national court, or as a result of some direct action involving the European Commission. Where a point arises in proceedings before a national court (or tribunal)[6] it may, under Art.234 (formerly 177), be referred to the ECJ.[7]

Whenever an agreement was thought potentially to fall within Art.81 it was **16–145**
possible previously for an application to be made to the Commission for "nega-

---

[99] See, *e.g. Hasselblad v Commission* [1984] E.C.R. 883; [1984] 1 C.M.L.R. 559; [1984] F.S.R. 321, ECJ; *AEG-Telefunken* [1983] E.C.R. 3151, ECJ.

[1] Thus the decision in *Sony v Saray* [1983] F.S.R. 302, CA might well have gone the other way if the defendants had not actually had to modify the parallel-imported television sets and they had been imported from an EC Member State.

[2] [1998] 5 C.M.L.R. 172.

[3] As long as the effects within the Community are appreciable: [1998] 5 C.M.L.R. 172, para.26.

[4] *Pronuptia* [1986] 1 C.M.L.R. 414, para.13.

[5] *Pronuptia* [1986] 1 C.M.L.R. 414, para.17. This ruling provides a fairly strong indication that a normal trade mark licence agreement with quality control provisions would equally not fall within Art.81(1).

[6] On which see the Opinion of A.G. Jacobs, at paras 17 *et seq.*, in *Synetairismos Farmakopoion v GlaxoSmithkline* (C–53/03), October 28, 2004, unreported: if the ECJ follows the Opinion the Appointed Person would clearly fall within the scope of bodies which may make references.

[7] See the Civil Procedure Rules, RSC, Ord.114 (contained in Sch.1 and re-enacted by Pt 50, CPR) as to the principles under which references are made. The main purpose of such a reference is to ensure that Community law is applied uniformly by national courts: *Foto-Frost* [1987] E.C.R. 4199.

tive clearance" or exemption, but this possibility has been removed now by Reg.1/2003 and parties to an agreement must make their own assessment at their own risk.[8] Such an assessment may have to include the pro-and anti-competitive balance of an agreement in order to decide whether it benefits from the "rule of reason" contained in Art.81(3).[9] By Art.6 of Reg.1/2003 national courts are given the power to apply Arts 81 and 82 and therefore by implication to decide on whether an agreement should benefit from Art.85(3). Where proposed arrangements give rise to "genuine uncertainty because they present novel or unresolved questions" informal guidance may be sought from the Commission[10] but it is clear that this will only be given in very unusual situations.

EFFECT OF COMMUNITY LAW ON REGISTRABILITY OR VALIDITY AS SUCH

16–146   It seems clear on general principles that no registration can be made of a mark whose use is, under the EC Treaty or regulations, directly contrary to law.[11] But are there cases where registration can be refused because it would in some way infringe Arts 81 or 82? In principle there seems no reason why not. It would be necessary to prove that the registration formed part of some abusive conduct (for example part of a deliberate market dividing campaign). But given such proof and a sufficiently close nexus between the proposed registration and the abuse, it seems to follow that registration of the mark concerned would, in any event, be contrary to public policy and therefore excluded under s.3(3)(a) of the Trade Marks Act 1994.

9. Competition Act 1998

16–147   The Competition Act 1998, which came into force on March 1, 2000,[12] introduced a new regime to deal with restrictive agreements (Chapter I) and abuses of market power (Chapter II), respectively modelled on Art.81 and Art.82 of the EC Treaty. It is stated expressly that the provisions must be interpreted and applied consistently with judgments of the ECJ and have regard to statements and decisions of the European Commission.[13] The Act repeals the Restrictive Trade Practices Act 1976, the Resale Prices Act 1976 and the provisions of the Competition Act 1980 dealing with anti-competitive practices.

16–148   Agreements which do not have an "appreciable effect on competition" will not be caught by the Chapter I prohibition. In general, an agreement is unlikely to have an appreciable effect where the combined market shares of the parties

---

[8] It is important to bear in mind that the Commission's interpretation of Art.81 has diverged not infrequently from that of the Court of Justice: see, *e.g. Schöller* [1995] E.C.R. II-1611 and *Langnese-lglo v Commission* [1995] E.C.R. II-1533.

[9] As Art.81(3) was characterised by the C.F.I. in *Van den Berg Foods v Commission* [2004] 4 C.M.L.R. 1.

[10] Commission Notice on Informal Guidance Relating to Novel Questions Concerning Arts 81 and 82 that Arise in Individual Cases (Guidance Letters), [2004] O.J. C 101/78.

[11] *e.g.* contrary to EC wine regulations, as was suggested (without success on the facts) in *Domgarden* [1982] R.P.C. 155.

[12] A transitional period of one year generally applies to any agreement made before the Act came into force: Sch.13, para.19(1).

[13] s.60. "Different treatment for intellectual property rights under the Competition Act regime and the European regime seems neither necessary nor desirable and is likely to increase the burden on business of compliance", in "Exclusion of Vertical Agreements: Consultation on a draft Order" (Doc URN 88/1030), para.22. This ignores the question as to whether judgments of the ECJ which are based expressly or implicitly on the overriding aim of creating a Common Market should be followed with reference to the UK Act in respect of which such an aim is irrelevant.

involved does not exceed 25 per cent.[14] So-called "small agreements" which are not price-fixing agreements are given limited immunity[15]: the Chapter I prohibition does not apply to agreements between undertakings the combined turnover of which does not exceed €20 million in the year before the infringement occurred,[16] and the Chapter II prohibition does not apply to conduct of any undertaking whose turnover does not exceed €50 million.[17]

Most vertical agreements are excluded from the Chapter I prohibition:[18] a   **16–149**
"vertical agreement" is defined as:

> "an agreement between undertakings, each of which operates, for the purposes of the agreement, at a different level of the production or distribution chain, and relating to the conditions under which the parties may purchase, sell or resell certain goods or services and includes provisions contained in such agreements which relate to the assignment to the buyer or use by the buyer of intellectual property rights, provided that those provisions do not constitute the primary object of the agreement and are directly related to the use, sale or resale of goods or services by the buyer or its customers." (emphasis added)[19]

Thus, where a vertical agreement contains trade mark provisions ancillary to the main purpose, for example a distribution agreement, it will be excluded.

An agreement which falls within the Chapter I prohibition may be exempted in   **16–150**
three ways: (1) by being granted, on application, an individual exemption;[20] (2) by falling within a block exemption;[21] or (3) by benefiting from a parallel exemption where it is covered by an EC individual or block exemption,[22] or would be so covered if it had an effect on trade between Member States of the EC. The exemption criteria[23] to be applied by the Office of Fair Trading (OFT) are very similar to Art.81(3).

The Chapter II prohibition covers the abuse of a dominant position in the   **16–151**
market.[24] Unlike Art.82, which requires a dominant position in the whole or a substantial part of the Community, the provision does not limit its impact in this way: therefore, local dominance would still fall foul of the prohibition.[25]

In *Claritas (UK) Ltd v The Post Office*[26] it was alleged unsuccessfully that a   **16–152**
trade mark licence to use the Royal Mail logo granted by The Post Office to a 30 per cent-owned subsidiary which collected direct mail data constituted an abuse

---

[14] Director-General of Fair Trading's guidelines on The Chapter I Prohibition, March 1999 (OFT 401), paras 2–18 to 2–22.

[15] s.39. The immunity does not go to substance, may be withdrawn and does not affect third parties.

[16] Competition Act 1998 (Small Agreements and Conduct of Minor Significance) Regulations 2000, SI 2000/262, Art.3.

[17] ibid., Competition Act 1998 (Small Agreements and Conduct of Minor Significance) Regulations 2000, SI 2000/262, Art.4.

[18] s.50 and the Competition Act 1998 (Land and Vertical Agreement Exclusion) Order 2000, SI 2000/310.

[19] See paras 16–113 to 16–116, Art.2. cf. the Vertical Restraints Block Exemption 2790/99, Art.2(3) which is in identical terms.

[20] ss.4 and 5.

[21] ss.6–8.

[22] s.10(1).

[23] s.9. They include, in s.9(a)(ii), "promoting technical or economic progress", which may be relevant for intellectual property licences: cf. *Campari* (1978) 22 C.M.L.R. 397.

[24] s.18.

[25] DGFT Guidelines "Market definitions", Part 4.

[26] [2001] E.T.M.R. 679.

of a dominant position contrary to the Chapter II prohibition contained in s.18(1) of the Act.[27]

10. Trade marks and restraint of trade

16–153   In a settlement agreement governing the use by the parties of their respective trade marks in many countries around the world, the English court did not consider relevant whether particular provisions (in particular the field of use and no challenge clauses) contravened foreign laws, where the parties had chosen English law in the choice of law clause: *Apple Corp Ltd v Apple Computer Inc.*[28]

16–154   Where a trade mark dispute has been resolved by a settlement agreement, the terms of which were arrived at through "proper negotiation between commercial parties",[29] there is a "threshold requirement" to be satisfied by the restrained party before the common law restraint of trade doctrine applies.[30] The presumption is that the restraints included in the settlement agreement are reasonable[31] and in any action to enforce the terms the onus is on the defendant to show that there is something which justifies avoiding the agreement.

16–155   If the party restrained were to succeed in rebutting that presumption, by for example raising serious questions as to whether there was genuine use of the marks in issue at the time of the agreement, then in order to establish that the agreement was enforceable under the law of restraint of trade, it would be necessary for the party relying on it to prove (1) that the restraints contained in it were imposed for the purpose of protecting legitimate interests; and (2) that the restraints were no more than were necessary to protect those interests.[32]

16–156   It should be noted that the broadened scope of infringement in the Trade Marks Act 1994, especially ss.10(3) and 56, makes the question as to whether a particular registered mark has been used in relation to particular goods less clearly rele-

---

[27] There was no evidence before the court as to the terms of the licence or whether it was exclusive. In addition, Lawrence Collins J. rejected the argument that the Post Office was abusing its dominant position in the market for mail delivery by acts which had an effect in a market in which it was not dominant, the collection and exploitation of direct mail data: following *Tetra Pak II* [1996] E.C.R. I-5951 at 6008, he found that in principle the dominated market and the market affected by the abuse must be the same (at para.44).

[28] [1992] F.S.R. 431. "There must be cases in modern commercial life where world-wide restrictions will be necessary and proper. What the parties to commercial agreements require is certainty and it is natural, and generally desirable, that they should seek to identify a single system of law to govern their relationship": *per* Ferris J. at 456.

[29] *Per* Jacob J. and adopted by the Court of Appeal in *World Wide Fund v World Wrestling Federation* [2002] E.T.M.R. 564 at para.63.

[30] [2002] E.T.M.R. 564, at para.49. At first instance, the judge formulated a three stage test: "a restraint imposed by an intellectual property dispute settlement should only be regarded as falling within the restraint of trade doctrine (and thus require justification) if the restrained party can show that: (a) the restraint actually imposes a real fetter on his trade; and (b) the restraint goes beyond any reasonably arguable scope of protection of the intellectual property right in issue. If the restrainee can show that, the restrainor may nonetheless justify by showing (c) that the restraint nonetheless provides a protection that he reasonably needs." (At para.28) However, whilst agreeing that there was a threshold requirement, the Court of Appeal did not consider it necessary or appropriate to lay down a test (at para.49).

[31] [2002] E.T.M.R. 564, Carnwath L.J. (on behalf of the Court) in *World Wide Fund*, at para.48.

[32] See *Apple Corp v Apple Computer*, [1991] 3 C.M.L.R. 49, CA, at paras 22 and 102: it was common ground in this case that enforceability depended on whether the restrictions were reasonably necessary to protect the claimant's interests. In this context, Nicholls L.J. considered that "the essence of Article 85 is not substantially different from the common law principles concerning unreasonable restraints of trade": para.109. In *World Wide Fund* [2002] E.T.M.R. 564, it was noted by the Court of Appeal that an Art. 81 issue may arise if a restraint was reasonable at the time the agreement was made but has subsequently become unreasonable through no fault of the parties (although on the facts of the case that was not pertinent as the contract had become more onerous only because the defendant had breached it), at para.64 adopting with approval the view of the trial judge.

vant than hitherto to the analysis of what are the legitimate interests being protected and the reasonableness of the restraints. Clearly the increased scope of protection must have widened in turn the scope of restrictions which would be reasonable to include in an agreement settling a trade mark dispute.

Also, it is difficult to envisage circumstances in which the common law of restraint of trade would now be applicable rather than the Competition Act 1998[33] and the question as to whether domestic or EU competition rules are applicable will depend upon whether there is an effect on inter-State trade.[34]   **16–157**

In *Jobserve Ltd v Skillsite Ltd*,[35] where the claimant brought committal   **16–158** proceedings for alleged breach of a consent order in a database right case, the judge dismissed peremptorily an argument that undertakings which went beyond those which a court could give by way of relief were in restraint of trade and/or in breach of the Chapter 1 prohibition in s.2 of the Competition Act. He stated that this would need to be established by evidence: "[a]n effect on trade is only relevant for the purposes of the Act if it is material, and that involves an examination of the product market, the geographical market and then economic effect of the agreement."[36] It is submitted this cannot be correct: either the restraint of trade doctrine or the Competition Act must catch any provision in a settlement of an intellectual property dispute which clearly goes beyond the legitimate subject-matter of the rights in dispute. In those circumstances the giver of the undertaking cannot be prevented from doing what everybody else in the market, however defined, is free to do.[37]

---

[33] If the Competition Act 1998 were to be applied today to facts as in the *Apple* case, the analysis would be likely to be more favourable to the defendant's contention that market conditions had altered sufficiently since the parties entered into the delimitation agreement that it had become anti-competitive.

[34] In *Apple* [1991] 3 C.M.L.R. 49, Nicholls L.J. considered that "the essence of Article 85 [81] is not substantially different from the common law principles concerning unreasonable restraints of trade": para.109. In *World Wide Fund* [2002] E.T.M.R. 564, at para.64, it was noted by the Court of Appeal that an Art.81 issue may arise if a restraint was reasonable at the time the agreement was made but has subsequently become unreasonable through no fault of the parties (although on the facts of the case that was not pertinent as the contract had become more onerous only because the defendant had breached it), adopting with approval the view of the trial judge.

[35] [2004] F.S.R. 762.

[36] *per* Lewison J. at para.27.

[37] It is submitted that the judge in *Jobserve* [2004] F.S.R. 762, erred in applying *Haddonstone Ltd v Sharp* [1996] F.S.R. 767, CA, to the facts before him. In that case the settlement provision which relieved the claimant from the need to prove copying if the defendant continued to make urns to the claimant's design flowed from the legitimate subject-matter of the right in dispute and was a fair restriction on the defendant's freedom to trade in future, whereas in *Jobserve* the restraint had the consequence that the defendant could not in practice compete with the claimant (especially bearing in mind that the restraint was without limit in time).

CHAPTER 17

ASSESSING THE DEGREE OF RESEMBLANCE OR SIMILARITY BETWEEN MARKS OR GET-UP

1. Outline, the tests, and onus

INTRODUCTORY

17–001 Ever since the seventh edition of this work, published in 1951, there has been a chapter entitled "deceptive resemblance", whose function has been to consider the degree and nature of resemblance between the parties' respective marks (or get-ups) required for an action in passing off or trade mark infringement, or for an opposition to registration, to succeed, as well as the procedure and evidence appropriate to prove such.

17–002 Until the 12th edition of this work "deceptive resemblance" was a pithy and fairly accurate title; it reflected the test for actionability in passing off,[1] as well as the test for near resemblance of marks under the Trade Marks Act 1938.[2] For the 13th edition, however, we felt that it was time to change the title of the chapter, mainly to reflect the changes brought by the Trade Marks Act 1994.

17–003 Since the 13th edition, there has been yet further very substantial analysis by the ECJ and by national courts of the nature of the relationship between a registered mark and another mark which is necessary in order for there to be infringement (or for the former to block the registration of the latter). It is now very difficult to assimilate the test for infringement of a registered trade mark (where the marks are similar but not identical) with the test for passing off, at a theoretical level at least, although the "global" nature of the test for infringement of a registered mark under the jurisprudence of the ECJ suggests that there will be little practical difference. But the evidence and procedure under English law remains largely the same for both, and has been little affected by changes in the law since the previous edition.

17–004 As result, this chapter will deal less than before with the nature of the test for infringement of a registered trade mark. That issue is considered in detail in Chs 9 and 14. This chapter will deal with it only fairly briefly; it will, as ever, deal with "rules of comparison" relevant to determining whether two marks are so similar as to be likely to lead to confusion. They are no more "rules" in the strict sense than they ever were; they are included mainly because their application to passing off is undiminished, but also because under the "global" test for trade mark infringement they appear relevant, and correspond quite well with the principles set out in Ch.9. Nonetheless, there is little or no authority considering

---

[1] Where it is often said that mere confusion is not enough, but a misrepresentation must be shown. See Ch.15.

[2] Which was defined in s.68 of the 1938 Act as "a resemblance so near as to be likely to deceive or cause confusion".

the extent to which those rules *per se* apply to infringement of registered trade marks.

In the introduction to the chapter on "deceptive resemblance" in previous editions of this work, there was always a warning to the effect that care should be taken in applying the rules set out, because of their different manner of application to passing off and to registered trade marks. Now, the warning must be reinforced: that in reading the rules and authorities set out below, one must have regard to whether the 1938 Act, the 1994 Act or passing off (or more than one of them) is under consideration.   **17–005**

SCOPE OF CHAPTER

This chapter first identifies the contexts in which the resemblance of marks falls to be considered for the purposes of this work. Thereafter it covers the level of confusion or deception required and the persons who must be confused or deceived. Then the numerous rules of comparison are discussed, subject to the caveat set out above.   **17–006**

Finally, this chapter deals with evidence of confusion or deception and the manner in which it may be gathered and presented to the court. This section covers "survey" evidence and evidence from the public generally. In considering survey evidence, consideration is also given to the increasing role of such evidence in showing what significance marks have to the public, in addition to its use to show confusion or deception.   **17–007**

This chapter should be read in conjunction with App.31 which contains a list of cases in which contentions of likely confusion or deception have succeeded or failed. As ever, the reader is warned that the cases mentioned there all turned on their own facts, and many were decided under the Acts of 1938 and before.   **17–008**

PROCEEDINGS TO WHICH THIS CHAPTER RELATES, AND ONUS

The main different types of proceedings in which the question of deception or confusion arises are summarised in the paragraphs which follow, and some observations relevant to the proceedings in question are added.   **17–009**

(1) On an application to register, the Registrar or an opponent may object that the trade mark is not registrable by reason of s.5[3] of the 1994 Act. There is no overall onus one way or the other when the Registrar considers the application,[4] but on an opposition, the onus is on the opponent to make out any grounds on which he relies.[5] These matters are considered in more detail in Ch.5.

(2) On an application to invalidate a registration under s.47 (by reference back to s.5),[6] the onus is on the applicant for invalidity, by reason of the presumption of validity contained in s.72.

---

[3] And note that s.5(4) includes passing off against an earlier mark as a ground for refusing registration.

[4] *"Eurolamb"* [1997] R.P.C. 279; *Procter & Gamble (soap tablet shape)* [1998] R.P.C. 710; *Procter & Gamble (bottle shape)* [1999] R.P.C. 673, CA.

[5] *"Audi-Med"* [1998] R.P.C. 863; *Oasis Stores* [1998] R.P.C. 631. If, however, the evidence led in order to have the application accepted is rejected on opposition, then there is no overall onus: *Dualit* [1999] R.P.C. 304.

[6] The onus is the same whether the application is made as a counterclaim in infringement proceedings, or on its own by originating process.

(3) In an action for infringement (see Ch.14),[7] the onus is on the claimant.

(4) In an action for "passing-off"[8] (see Ch.15), the onus is on the claimant.

(5) In both infringement and passing off, in applications for interim injunctions. Here, although the onus is on the claimant, he need show only an arguable case (see Ch.19).

LIKELIHOOD OF CONFUSION AND OTHER SIMILAR TESTS IN THE 1994 ACT

17–010   In addition to the above situations, which are certainly the main ones, the following sections of the 1994 Act require consideration of the degree of resemblance between marks:[9]

(1) Under ss.16 to 19 (delivery up), remedies are available in relation to signs "identical or similar to" a registered trade mark.[10]

(2) Under s.46(2), use by the proprietor of a mark "differing in elements which do not alter the distinctive character of the mark" as registered counts as use for the purposes of meeting an allegation of invalidity through non-use.[11]

(3) Under s.56(2), the proprietor of a well-known mark within the meaning of the Paris Convention may obtain an injunction to restrain the use of "a trade mark which, or the essential part of which, is identical or similar to the [well-known] mark, in relation to identical or similar goods or services, where the use is likely to cause confusion."

(4) Under ss.57 and 58, national emblems and emblems of certain international organisations are protected against unauthorised registration of marks consisting of or comprising those emblems or "anything which from a heraldic point of view imitates any such flag or other emblem ...". Section 57 also invokes the test of whether the emblem sought to be registered suggests a connection with the international organisation concerned or is likely to mislead as to the existence of such a connection.

(5) Under s.92 (criminal sanctions) and s.97 (forfeiture in connection with criminal proceedings), the test of whether a sign is identical to "or likely to be mistaken for" the registered mark is employed.[12] It has now been held that this test cannot be satisfied unless the test for infringement under s.10 is satisfied.[13]

(6) Under the provisions relating to the powers of the Commissioners of Customs and Excise under Community legislation (which do not arise directly from the 1994 Act, but are closely related to it).[14] The powers of the Commissioners under domestic legislation operate by reference to the definition of "infringing goods" in s.17, which is mentioned above.[15]

(7) Under s.99, use of the Royal or arms "so closely resembling the Royal arms as to be calculated to deceive" in "such manner as to be calculated to lead to the belief that" the defendant is "duly authorised to use" them, is prohibited. This appears to be a passing off kind of test.

---

[7] If brought under s.10(2) or 10(3); there is no requirement of confusion under s.10(1), that is to say if the alleged infringing sign is identical to the registered mark and is used on goods identical to those the subject of the registration. The same applies, *mutatis mutandis*, to infringement of CTMs.

[8] Including where passing off is invoked as an "earlier right" under s.5(4).

[9] Or between marks and signs.

[10] And in addition it is required that the application of the sign should infringe the registration: see Ch.19.

[11] See Ch.10.

[12] See Ch.20.

[13] *R. v Johnstone* [2003] F.S.R. 42.

[14] See Ch.21.

[15] See s.89.

BASIC TEST UNDER THE 1994 ACT

Before proceeding any further, it is worth setting out the main elements of the basic test which will be applied under the 1994 Act, as explained by the ECJ in *Sabel v Puma* and *Lloyd Schuhfabrik v Meyer*.[16] The test is considered in much more detail in Ch.9. **17–011**

(1) It is a global test taking account of all factors relevant to the parties' marks and the goods or services in issue.

(2) The relevant factors include the degree and nature of use of the claimant's registered mark, its inherent and acquired distinctiveness.

(3) The similarity of the goods/services as well as of the marks themselves is a part of the consideration.

(4) The visual, oral and conceptual[17] similarity of the marks must be considered.

(5) Particular regard is to be had to the dominant and distinctive elements of the marks.[18]

(6) The sort of confusion required to satisfy the test is confusion as to origin.

2. Persons to be considered

WHOM THE MARK MUST BE CALCULATED TO DECEIVE

This is an area where some care is needed, for under previous Trade Mark Acts, the test did not materially differ from the test in passing off. It is no longer clear that this is the case. **17–012**

In relation to registered trade marks, the relevant standard is to be found in *Lloyd Schuhfabrik v Meyer*,[19] which was considered and adopted by the Court of Appeal in *Bach Flower Remedies v Healing Herbs*[20] (in the context of distinctiveness). The relevant person, according to the decision in *Lloyd*,[21] is the average consumer, who is considered to be "reasonably well informed and reasonably observant and circumspect", although taking account of the fact that such a person will rarely have the opportunity to make a direct comparison, but rather has to rely on "the imperfect picture of them that he has kept in his mind". **17–013**

In passing off, the persons to be considered in estimating whether the resemblance between the marks in question is likely to deceive are all of those who are likely to become purchasers[22] of the goods upon which the marks are used, provided that such persons use ordinary care[23] and intelligence. **17–014**

It may be, and time will tell, that these tests are not the same, and that the ref- **17–015**

---

[16] [1998] R.P.C. 199 and [1999] F.S.R. 627. And see Ch.9.

[17] *Sabel v Puma* also refers to "analogous semantic content".

[18] See, *e.g. The European v The Economist* [1998] F.S.R. 283; [1996] F.S.R. 431 where the common element between the parties' marks was not distinctive, and the action failed. The case is also interesting because the Court of Appeal endorsed the judge's decision to treat the case as one of passing off, even though trade mark infringement was alleged.

[19] [1999] F.S.R. 627.

[20] [2000] R.P.C. 513.

[21] In particular, para.27 of the judgment.

[22] See, *e.g.* in *"G.E."* [1973] R.P.C. 297 at 321–322 HL, the distinction drawn between goods sold in a specialised market and goods sold to the general public for consumption or domestic use.

[23] *Christiansen* (1886) 3 R.P.C. 54 at 62, CA; *Coombe v Mendit* (1913) 30 R.P.C 709 at 717. The older cases regarding the standard of attention or carefulness to be expected of the ordinary member of the purchasing public are reviewed by the Assistant Registrar in *Angus* (1943) 60 R.P.C. 29 at 31. See also Ch.15, and the cases below concerning differing levels of care in relation to different kinds of goods and services.

erence in *Lloyd* to a "reasonably well informed and reasonably observant and circumspect" average consumer will have the effect that a likelihood of confusion for the purposes of the 1994 Act will be harder to show than a likelihood of deception for the purposes of passing off, owing to the different notional persons to be considered. This would be unfortunate, and may seem unlikely given that the two areas in many other ways recognise similar considerations, for example, the doctrine of imperfect recollection, and the notion of the "idea" of the mark.[24] In *Reed Executive Plc v Reed Business Information Ltd.*[25] the Court of Appeal held that the tests are conceptually different but equivalent in practice.

THE ULTIMATE PURCHASERS

17–016   It is clearly not enough to show that retailers buying goods for resale would not be deceived, since they might themselves fraudulently or carelessly make use of the ambiguous character of the trade mark to deceive their customers, the ultimate purchasers[26] —or more likely, in these days of self-service, allow customers to deceive themselves. Dealers who buy from the manufacturers in order to sell by retail may be aware of attempted infringements and be parties to the fraud.[27]

17–017   Some marks are only used in the trade,[28] and in such cases it is submitted that it is traders, rather than members of the public, who are to be considered.[29] It may, consequently, be hard to prove a likelihood of confusion or deception in such cases because they are likely to have a clear idea from whom they buy.

STANDARD OF CARE TO BE EXPECTED

17–018   As is noted above in relation to *Lloyd*, and as common experience shows, consumers' attention will vary depending on the kind of goods which they are buying, and not all classes of consumers will exercise the same level of care in choosing products.

Many older cases have considered this general issue, including cases going back to times when many consumers were illiterate (likely to be relevant now only in relation to goods for export, or aimed at children).[30]

17–019   In considering all of the authorities below, it must be borne in mind that they were decided in relation to passing off or under older Trade Mark Acts. With that said, the general principles are as follows:

---

[24] See paras 17–028 and 17–050.

[25] [2004] R.P.C. 40 at para.82.

[26] *Wilkinson v Griffith* (1891) 8 R.P.C. 370 at 374. See Mellish L.J. in *Ford v Foster* (1872) L.R. 7 Ch. App. 611 at 616; and Lord Selborne in *Singer v Loog* (1882) L.R. 8 App.Cas.15; and *Powell v Birmingham Vinegar*(1886) in the CA; 13 R.P.C. 235 at 250; and *Edge v Niccolls* [1911] A.C. 693; 28 R.P.C. 582 at 593.

[27] *Lever v Goodwin* (1887) L.R. 36 Ch.D. 1; 4 R.P.C. 492 at 498.

[28] *e.g.* as in *Scandecor v Scandecor* [1999] F.S.R. 26; [1998] F.S.R. 500, [2002] F.S.R. 7.

[29] And this appears to be consistent with the exhortation in *Sabel* and *Lloyd* that all the relevant circumstances are to be considered.

[30] Note that this point certainly is in keeping with *Lloyd* and the position under the 1994 Act, as considered above. See, for older cases, *Lever v Goodwin* (1887) L.R. 36 Ch.D. 1; 4 R.P.C. 492. *per* Lord Gorell in *Edge v Niccolls* (1911) 28 R.P.C. 582 at 593. In one case in which the goods (lemonade powders) were largely bought by children, and it was suggested that they would be more easily deceived than adults, Byrne J. stated that, having regard to the nature of the goods which they would be likely to purchase for themselves, they would be less likely to be deceived than grown-up people: *Clark v Sharp* (1898) 15 R.P.C. 141 at 149, settled on appeal (1898) 15 R.P.C. 268.

(1) It must not be assumed that a very careful or intelligent examination of the mark will be made;[31]

(2) But, on the other hand, it can hardly be significant that unusually stupid people,[32] "fools or idiots",[33] or a "moron in a hurry"[34] may be deceived.

(3) If the goods are expensive or important to the purchasers and not of a kind usually selected without deliberation,[35] and the customers generally educated persons, these are all matters to be considered.[36]

(4) If some parts of the mark are common, one must consider whether people who know the distinguishing characteristics of the opponents' mark would be deceived.[37]

NEW TYPES OF MARK

A novel feature of the 1994 Act is the possibility of registering new types of marks such as smells, sounds, and three-dimensional shapes. Their inherent registrability is considered in Ch.8. Although their practical significance has yet to be assessed, it is now possible that one will have to inquire whether a smell mark is infringed by a graphical representation, or a sound mark by a smell, or a three-dimensional mark by a two-dimensional representation of it.   **17–020**

It is tentatively suggested that in determining cases of this kind, the rules of comparison used for traditional marks will still fall to be applied in general, with the caveat that some of them will be of no, or only very limited, relevance to certain kinds of comparisons. For example, the importance of the first syllable would be of no relevance in relation to marks consisting of a smell (although by close analogy it might be relevant to marks consisting of a musical phrase). It is also suggested that the rule of comparison which will be of the greatest importance in relation to such marks is that which requires attention to the "idea of the mark". Thus, for example, by the application of that rule one would expect a mark consisting of the smell of roses probably to be infringed by a picture of a rose.[38]   **17–021**

---

[31] *Wotherspoon v Currie* (1871–72) L.R. 5 H.L. 508 at 519; "Ordinary purchasers purchasing with ordinary caution": *Seixo v Provezende* (1865–66) L.R. 1 Ch. 192; "Ordinary" or "incautious" purchasers: *Powell v Birmingham Vinegar* (1896) 13 R.P.C. at 258; not "persons of an ideal character who either are particularly innocent or too easily deceived": *Payton v Snelling Lampard & Co Ltd* (1900) 17 R.P.C. 48 at 57; 17 R.P.C. 628; and see Kekewich J. in *Marshall v Sidebotham* (1901) 18 R.P.C. 43 at 49 and *Alaska Packers v Crooks* (1901) 18 R.P.C. 129 at 137: "The unwary customer is extremely difficult to find"; but cf. *Currie* (1896) 13 R.P.C. 681, where the same judge had twice referred in the case to the "ordinary or unwary purchaser". in contrast to "intelligent persons".

[32] *Payton v Titus Ward* (1900) 17 R.P.C. 58 at 67; *Scottish Union and National Insurance v Scottish National Insurance* (1909) 26 R.P.C. 105 at 112; *Crook* (1914) 31 R.P.C. 79 at 85.

[33] Jessel M.R. in *Singer Machine Manufacturers v Wilson* (1875–76) L.R. 2 Ch.D. 434 at 447; *Smith* (1913) 30 R.P.C. 363 at 366.

[34] *Morning Star v Express Newspapers* [1979] F.S.R. 113.

[35] Thus far, this principle is in keeping with *Lloyd*.

[36] See *HFC v Midland* [2000] F.S.R. 176 at 184, and the contrast with "Jif", *Reckitt & Colman Products Ltd v Borden Inc (No.3)* [1990] R.P.C. 341. *Pianotist* (1906) 23 R.P.C. 774 ("Neola," "Pianola"); and see *Claudius Ash v Invicta* (1911) 28 R.P.C. 597; 29 R.P.C. 465, CA and HL where the customers were dentists and their assistants. *Rysta* (1943) 60 R.P.C. 87 at 106, *per* Greene M.R.

[37] See Romer L.J. in *Payton v Snelling* (1900) 17 R.P.C. 48 at 57 (on appeal, 17 R.P.C. 628, HL; and *Same v Titus Ward* (1900) 17 R.P.C. 58 at 67 (passing off cases); also *Alaska Packers v Crooks*, and *Marshall v Sidebotham* in point 1.

[38] For some new marks, this test may, however, have to modified in order to limit the proprietor to a fair degree of protection. For example, where a colour is registered, the "idea" of the mark may simply be, say, orange. To confer a monopoly in the use of orange for a whole category of goods on that basis would, it is suggested, be excessive.

3. Rules of comparison

WHAT AMOUNT OF RESEMBLANCE IS LIKELY TO CONFUSE OR DECEIVE;
PROPORTION OF PUBLIC REQUIRED TO BE DECEIVED

17–022   Two important, and related, questions which arise are: what degree of resemblance must be shown to demonstrate a likelihood of confusion or deception? And, what proportion of the public must be confused or deceived for the test to be satisfied?

The first question must be answered with regard to the principle that similarity *per se* is acceptable, so long as it does not lead to confusion.[39] Strictly, the second question is quite probably only relevant to passing off now; since under the 1994 Act the issue is whether there is a likelihood of confusion. They are clearly closely related ideas, though: the greater the likelihood, the more people will be confused.

17–023   It is not, however, possible to discover from the decided cases any absolute standard as to the amount of resemblance which may suffice to deceive or cause confusion. As Lord Cranworth said in *Seixo v Provezende*:[40] "What degree of resemblance is necessary ... is from the nature of things incapable of definition a priori." Nor is the standard always the same: thus in the case of pharmaceutical products, in the absence of restrictions upon their distribution, it is more important that the public should be protected from the consequences of deception and confusion.[41] It follows that, except in so far as they lay down any general principle, the decided cases are of little assistance in the determination of new questions of fact raised upon other materials.

17–024   In all cases, as stated above, it should be borne in mind that a decision on the question whether a mark so nearly resembles another as to be likely to deceive or cause confusion is not an exercise of discretion by a tribunal but a finding of fact.[42]

17–025   As to the number of persons required to be confused or deceived before an action will succeed, the test is whether, on the balance of probabilities, a substantial number of persons would be.[43] The test has sometimes been phrased as "more than de minimis" or "above a trivial level", but these expressions were disapproved in *Neutrogena v Golden*,[44] in particular on the basis that they do not necessarily connote the opposite of substantial. In that case, the claimant succeeded although the percentage of persons shown to be confused was really quite small, on the basis that although it was not possible to arrive at any quantitative or qualitative measure of the confusion, it was substantial.

---

[39] *e.g. The European v Economist Newspapers* [1996] F.S.R. 431 and [1998] F.S.R. 283.

[40] (1865) L.R. 1 Ch. 192, cited by Luxmoore L.J. in *Rysta* (1943) 60 R.P.C. 87 at 108.

[41] *Harker Stagg* (1953) 70 R.P.C. 205. See also *Vitamins (No.2)* [1956] R.P.C. 1 at 13. The position is otherwise where restrictions upon distribution do exist (see, *e.g. Geigy v Chelsea Drug* [1966] R.P.C. 64) unless it can be shown that the public will be deceived despite such restrictions *Hoffman–La Roche v D.D.S.A.* [1969] F.S.R. 410). Furthermore, where there is a possible doubt, a pharmacist will normally check: *Glaxo v Pharmax* [1976] F.S.R. 278. Even so, the special risk to patients may make even minimal confusion unacceptable: *Sterwin v Brocades* ("Danol", "De-Nol") [1979] R.P.C. 481.

[42] *Rysta* (1943) 60 R.P.C. 87 at 105, *per* Greene M.R.

[43] See *Neutrogena v Golden* [1996] R.P.C. 473, *Reckitt & Colman v Borden* [1990] R.P.C. 341, *Saville Perfumery v June Perfect* (1941) 58 R.P.C. 147, and *Re Smith Hayden's & Co Application* (1946) 63 R.P.C. 97.

[44] [1996] R.P.C. 473.

It should be noted that with the exception of *The European*,[45] the authorities **17–026** referred to above were decided in the context of passing off and/or the 1938 Act.

THE TRIBUNAL CAN FORM ITS OWN OPINION

It has long been established that evidence of the likelihood of confusion or decep- **17–027** tion led at trial is not necessary, or, when it is led, decisive. The judge is not confined to such evidence, and is entitled to form his own view: "GE" Trade Mark,[46] *Re Christiansen's Trade Mark*,[47] *Spalding v Gamage*,[48] *Neutrogena v Golden*.[49] In appropriate circumstances the court is entitled to reach such a view on a summary basis.[50]

IDEA OF THE MARK

Two marks, when placed side by side, may exhibit many and various differences, **17–028** yet the main idea left on the mind by both may be the same. A person acquainted with one mark, and not having the two side by side for comparison, might well be deceived, seeing the second mark on other goods, into a belief that he was deal- ing with goods which bore the same mark as that with which he was acquainted. Thus, for example, a mark may represent a game of football; another mark may show players in a different dress, and in very different positions, and yet the idea conveyed by each might be simply a game of football.[51] It would be too much to expect that persons dealing with trade-marked goods, and relying, as they frequently do, upon marks, should be able to remember the exact details of the marks upon the goods with which they are in the habit of dealing. Marks are remembered rather by general impressions or by some significant detail than by any photographic recollection of the whole.[52] Moreover, variations in details might well be supposed by customers to have been made by the owners of the trade mark they are already acquainted with for reasons of their own.[53]

When the question arises whether a mark so resembles another mark as to be **17–029** likely to deceive or cause confusion, it should be determined by considering what is the leading characteristic of each. The one might contain many, even most, of the same elements as the other, and yet the leading, or it may be the only, impres- sion left on the mind might be very different. On the other hand, a critical comparison of two marks might disclose numerous points of difference, and yet the idea which would remain with any person seeing them apart at different times might be the same. Thus it is clear that a mark is infringed if the essential features, or essential particulars of it, are taken.[54] In cases of device marks, especially, it is helpful before comparing the marks to consider what are the essentials of the

---

[45] *The European v Economist Newspapers* [1996] F.S.R. 431; [1998] F.S.R. 283.
[46] [1973] R.P.C. 297.
[47] (1886) 3 R.P.C. 54.
[48] (1915) 32 R.P.C. 273.
[49] [1996] R.P.C. 473.
[50] *Musical Fidelity v Vickers* [2003] F.S.R. 50.
[51] cf. *Barker* (1885) 53 L.T. 23 ("Huntsman" or "Sportman's" cherry brandy); *Reynolds v Laffeaty's* [1957] R.P.C. 311, CA; [1958] R.P.C. 387 ("Watermatic" an infringement of "Aquamatic" for water-pistols).
[52] *De Cordova v Vick* (1951) 68 R.P.C. 103 at 106, PC.
[53] *R. Johnston & Co v Orr-Ewing* (1882) L.R. 7 App.Cas. 219 (illustration (1), below); *Ravenhead Brick v Ruabon* (1937) 54 R.P.C. 341 at 349 ("Rus" and "Sanrus"). *Yahoo! v Akash Arora* [1999] F.S.R. 931 (HC Delhi).
[54] *De Cordova v Vick* (1951) 68 R.P.C. 103 at 106; *Taw v Notek* (1951) 68 R.P.C. 271; *Murphy* (1890) 7 R.P.C. 163. See also *Bale & Church v Sutton Parsons* (1934) 51 R.P.C. 129, *per* Romer

claimant's device;[55] with word marks, the court is apt to be more impressed by the dangers of giving the claimant what amounts to a monopoly in a large class of words.[56]

17–030   A similar question may arise where the defendant has added a prefix or suffix to a word mark of the claimant. Such cases have sometimes been disposed of merely by saying that the defendant is necessarily using the claimant's mark; but the sounder approach is to treat the defendant's mark as a combination having "one individual thing which is a monopoly of the plaintiff".[57] It is then necessary to consider how important that thing is to the whole. So also, where the defendant's mark is part of the claimant's. Where a suffix is merely descriptive or simply makes the mark more specific, it will not avoid infringement,[58] and so too where it is apt to suggest an addition to a range of goods.[59]

17–031   To refer in this context to "essential particulars" (which was the expression used in s.9 of the 1938 Act and hence should be regarded with a little caution if authorities based on it are sought to be used in the context of the 1994 Act) suggests that it may be convenient to put the question in the form, whether the defendant has taken those features which give the claimant's mark that distinctiveness needed to support the registration?[60] Such an approach is sometimes convenient; but it does not follow that there can be no infringement unless what the defendant has taken is a registrable mark.[61] A more contemporary way of expressing this idea, put the other way around, is that the central idea of the claimant's mark is of great importance in the comparison, but only if it is distinctive in nature; this was the way it was put by the Court of Appeal in *The European v The Economist*.[62]

17–032   The importance of having regard to the idea of the mark is such that it may well result in a finding that there is no likelihood of confusion even though in other ways the marks are very similar. For example, registration of LANCER was allowed despite the presence on the Register of LANCIA because, despite the considerable similarity to the ear, the ideas conveyed were very different.[63]

17–033   (1) Both the plaintiff's and the defendant's marks consisted of tickets bearing

---

L.J. It is less usual for decisions upon applications to register to refer to "essential features": partly, perhaps, because device marks are rarely concerned (cf. below), partly because the sort of evidence used in such cases seldom lends itself to such an approach.

[55] *De Cordova v Vick* (1951) 68 R.P.C. 103; *Taw v Notek* (1951) 68 R.P.C. 271; *Saville Perfumery v June Perfect* (1941) 58 R.P.C. 147 were all cases where the plaintiff's mark was a device mark.

[56] See *London Lubricants* (1925) 42 R.P.C. 264 at 278 ("Tripcastroid"). See also *De Cordova v Vick* (1951) 68 R.P.C. 103 *Hassan El - Madi* (1954) 71 R.P.C. 281 at 289. There are exceptions, however, like the "*Parker-Knoll*" case [1962] R.P.C. 265, where "Knoll" was treated as an essential feature of the mark "Parker-Knoll"; and see the G.E.C. cases (illus.(12) and (13) at para.17–033 as to initial marks.

[57] *Sanitas v Condy* (1886) 4 R.P.C. 580. cf. *Ravenhead Brick v Ruabon* (1937) 54 R.P.C. 341, where "Rus" was held to be infringed by "Sanrus".

[58] See *Yahoo! v Akash Arora* [1999] F.S.R. 931, (HC Delhi).

[59] As in *Portakabin v Powerblast* [1990] R.P.C. 471: "Porta" infringed by "Portablast".

[60] And this kind of reasoning was adopted and even decisive in *The European v The Economist* [1996] F.S.R. 431, [1998] F.S.R. 283, where the claimant's mark's main feature was the word "European", but that word had been disclaimed from the registration.

[61] Such a contention was expressly rejected in "*Electrix*" [1959] R.P.C. 283 ("Electrix" held unregistrable, as phonetic equivalent of "electrics", for electrical equipment, notwithstanding that it had been held to infringe "Electrux"). But cf., for instance, *Jeyes v Aliamaid (No.1)* (1955) 72 R.P.C. 277, where the contention that "J" infringed "Jeyes" might well have been better received if "J" had not so obviously been a mark no trader might monopolise.

[62] [1996] F.S.R. 431; [1998] F.S.R. 283. And see also *United Biscuits v Asda* [1997] R.P.C. 513, "*Penguin*" *v* "*Puffin*"), where the passing off claim succeeded, but a trade mark infringement claim based on a "Penguin" mark failed, because there was no pictorial element to the registered mark.

[63] *LANCER Trade Mark* [1987] R.P.C. 303. For another example, see *Rygrange Ltd's Applications*

pictures of two elephants with a banner between them, the figures being differently arranged. Lord Selborne said:[64] "Although the mere appearance of these two tickets could not lead anyone to mistake one of them for the other, it might easily happen that they might both be taken by natives of Aden or of India, unable to read and understand the English language, as equally symbolical of the plaintiff's goods.": *Johnston v Orr-Ewing* (1882) 1 App.Cas. 219.[65]

(2) The registered mark included the words "The Cock o' the North" with a picture of a cock. The applicant's mark consisting of a similar cock was refused, both marks being for Scotch whisky: *Curries* (1896) 13 R.P.C. 681. See however *Fromex SA's Application* [1999] E.T.M.R. 989, OHIM.

(3) In *Danish Bacon*[66] Luxmoore J. upheld the decision of the Registrar refusing to register the applicants' device marks consisting of representations of pigs on the grounds that the marks would conflict with the opponents' trade marks one being a picture of three pigs, but quite different from the applicants' picture of three pigs, and the other consisting of the words "Three Pigs Brand".

(4) In the Cat and Barrel cases[67] it was found that the plaintiffs' trade mark had come to be known as the "Cat and Barrel Brand", and the marks held to be infringements included combinations of a cat and barrel differing to a considerable extent from that which appeared in the plaintiffs' mark.

(5) On the other hand, an application for a mark consisting of the head of a Red Indian was allowed to proceed to advertisement notwithstanding the presence on the Register of a mark consisting of a Red Indian on horseback and the words "Red Indian", which were disclaimed, but this was on the ground that there had been substantial use of the applicant's mark: *Carborundum* (1909) 26 R.P.C. 504.

(6) In a case where the plaintiffs were suing to restrain the infringement of their registered trade mark "999" by the use of "99" and the words "double nine", and they had several other triple numbers also registered, it was suggested that the idea of their mark was the repetition of a digit. It was held that the idea of the mark was at the most triplication, and that there was no infringement, and a claim for passing off also failed: *Ardath Tobacco v Sandorides* (1925) 42 R.P.C. 50.

(7) Both the plaintiffs and the defendants used as their trade mark for motor lamps devices in which a pair of motor-car headlamps were represented as the eyes of a cat, seen full-face. The devices were otherwise very different: the one, essentially a distorted line drawing of an old-fashioned motor-car (with the word "Taw", although that was disclaimed); the other a detailed representation of the head of a cat, with the word "Notek". But it was held that the idea of the marks was the same, and that there was infringement: *Taw v Notek* (1951) 68 R.P.C. 271.

(8) Where the opponents were owners of a very well-known mark, consisting of a dog looking into a gramophone with the words "His Master's Voice",

---

[2001] E.T.M.R. 78, where the Registry held that UNITED and MANCHESTER UNITED were not too close, because of the great difference in idea conveyed.

[64] At 225. See also *Baschiera* (1889) 33 S.J. 469; 5 T.L.R. 480; the ground of rejection was that "the dominating portion of each mark was a lion, and the goods were designated by the prevailing feature according to the custom of the trade"; and *Christiansen* (1886) 3 R.P.C. 54, the "Taendstikker" case (matchbox labels).

[65] See also *Hollins v Cotella* (1937) 54 R.P.C. 81.

[66] (1934) 51 R.P.C. 148.

[67] *Boord & Son v Huddart* (1904) 21 R.P.C. 149; *Same v Thom & Cameron Ltd* (1907) 24 R.P.C. 697, IH, Scotland. The "Eastern Dye Works" case, *Greisheim Electron* (1910) 27 R.P.C. 201 is another illustration of the principle.

an application to register "Pup" for similar goods was allowed, since it did not appear that the opponents' mark was regarded by the public as a "puppy" mark: *Kolster Brandes* (1933) 50 R.P.C. 198.

(9) Where the opponents had for many years used "Ace" as a mark (without registering it), an application to register a device of aces with the word "Ace" was refused notwithstanding an offer to disclaim the word "Ace"; since regardless of any disclaimer, goods so marked would be referred to as "Ace" goods: *Mellor* (1948) 65 R.P.C. 238; but "ACEC" was allowed in the face of "Ace", one being a word, the other merely a set of initials: *ACEC* [1965] R.P.C. 369.

(10) A mark containing prominently the representation of half an apple was refused registration on account of the words "Apple Brand" in two registered marks: *Pomril* (1901) 18 R.P.C. 181.[68]

(11) Where on an application to register a mark consisting of four pictures in separate panels, one of which represented a ship, and the application was opposed by the owners of a mark consisting of a ship whose goods had become known as "Ship Brand", it was held that the picture of a ship in the mark applied for, if it stood alone, would lead to confusion and that the four pictures were not combined in such a way as to take from the picture of a ship its individual significance and that therefore there was a probability of deception: *Huxley* (1924) 41 R.P.C. 423.[69]

(12) On an interlocutory motion to restrain infringement of a mark "GEC" by the use of the mark "CEC", the court said that "The resemblance could hardly be closer, short of actual identity, and might well confuse anyone not having special knowledge." A contention that the defendants' goods were of a highly specialised character, such that customers for them would not be confused, failed on the ground that the plaintiffs' goods covered a very wide range and the matter must be considered "over the whole range of potential customers for goods protected by the plaintiff company's marks": *General Electric v Consolidated Electrodynamics* [1963] R.P.C. 1 at 3, 4. However "MEM" was allowed against opposition by "GEM" (for razor blades), M and G being visually distinct and the ideas of the two words being different: *MEM* [1965] R.P.C. 347.

(13) The (British) General Electric Company had a mark consisting of the initials "G.E.C." in script lettering. The (American) General Electric company used the initials "G.E." in script lettering in a "rondel". The two were held confusingly similar, even though they could confuse only by suggesting the confusingly similar company names: " *G.E*" [1973] R.P.C. 297 (HL at 317, 322).

(14) Where an opponent had used "Liebling" for Rhine wines, registration of "Rheinliebling" for such wines was refused: " *Rheinliebling*" [1966] R.P.C. 68.

(15) The plaintiff's mark comprised an oval border, which enclosed "Laura Ashley", and a botanical sprig. The defendant's mark comprised a similar oval border, enclosing "Coloroll", and a different sprig. The plaintiff contended that the essential feature of the mark was the oval border. Whitford J. disagreed. His initial view was that the essential feature was "Laura Ashley" and the evidence did not persuade him from that view: *Laura Ashley v Coloroll* [1987] R.P.C. 1.

(16) The claimant had a registration for "European" with other elements, which

---

[68] See also *Forth & Clyde v Sugg* (1928) 45 R.P.C. 382, where "Red Knight" was held to be infringement of "Silent Knight" (gas fires; there was evidence of actual confusion).

[69] See also *Connor* (1924) 41 R.P.C. 458: two very different devices, both with word "Sterling".

it used as a banner for a newspaper. The defendant also used a banner with "European" in it, also with other elements which differed from the claimant's. The claim failed because "European" was disclaimed from the registration, so although the central idea of the marks was very close, that was not relevant: *The European v The Economist* [1996] F.S.R. 431, [1998] F.S.R. 283.

(17) "Zinc" was infringed by "Zn", the chemical symbol for zinc: *Conran v Mean Fiddler* [1997] F.S.R. 856.

WHERE THE GOODS ARE KNOWN BY A NAME SUGGESTED BY THE MARK

Cases in which the goods of a particular trader have become known by a name **17–034** derived from his trade mark may be considered as carrying a stage further the concept of the "idea of a mark". In these special cases,[70] any other mark which would be likely to suggest the use of the same name for the goods on which it is used, so resembles the former as to be likely to deceive. With the present-day predominance of "word" as distinct from "label" marks, this sort of case is now very rare; though similar considerations could arise in disputes over rival logos. The matter is discussed at length in all earlier editions of this work.

(1) Where the trade mark of the plaintiff was a crown and the word "Seixo", and his goods had in consequence come to be known in the market as "Crown-Seixo" wine, the defendants were restrained from using marks which led their wine to be described by the same name, although evidence was given that "Seixo" was a common word in Portuguese: *Seixo v Provezende* (1865) L.R. 1 Ch. 192.[71]

(2) "L'AMY" was refused under s.12 of the 1938 Act for a mark consisting of a device with a small "LAMY"; notwithstanding that "LAMY" (a foreign surname) was disclaimed: there was no other way of "naming" the goods carrying the LAMY mark: *L'AMY* [1983] R.P.C. 137 at 143, Regy.

---

[70] Note that what is said here assumes that it is proved that the goods have become so known: mere surmise that they may have become so known amounts to little more than argument as to what the idea of the mark is. cf. *Holbrooks* (1909) 26 R.P.C. 791, where the opponents' goods were sold under a name other than that suggested by the applicant's mark. And see *Angus Watson* (1911) 28 R.P.C. 313, Parker J., where the applicants were the registered owners of the trade mark "Skipper" for sardines, and the opponents owned the same word for all other goods in the same class, including tinned salmon. The applicants sought to register for such goods a label with the word "Sailor" prominently appearing under a picture of a sailor, and the opponents alleged that goods sold under that label would by reason of the applicants' own use of the word "Skipper" for sardines become known as "Skipper" salmon, etc.; on appeal to the court the opposition was disallowed, the applicants consenting to amend by altering the word "Sailor" to "Sailor Brand".

[71] Other cases are: *Orr-Ewing v Johnston* (1880) 13 Ch.D. 434; 7 App.Cas. 219 ("Two Elephant Yarns"); *Speer* (1887) 4 R.P.C. 521 ("Dog, Tower, and Harp Linen"); *Des Verreries de l'Etoile* [1894] 1 Ch. 61; 10 R.P.C. 436; [1894] 2 Ch. 26; 11 R.P.C. 142 ("Red Star Glass"); *Wilkinson v Griffith* (1891) 8 R.P.C. 370 ("Red Medal Polish"); *John Dewhurst & Sons Ltd's Trade Mark* [1896] 2 Ch. 137; 13 R.P.C. 288 ("Golden Fan Cotton"); *Currie* (1896) 13 R.P.C. 681 ("Cock o' the North Whisky"); the Cat and Barrel cases, and Eastern Dye Works cited above. In *Cowie v Herbert* (1897) 14 R.P.C. 436, Ct of Sess, such a case was set up by the plaintiffs, but failed ("El-Musjid"), as also did the plaintiffs in *Lever v Bedingfield* (1899) 16 R.P.C. 3, where the plaintiffs had a small picture of a laundry-maid on the label, and the defendant had the words "Red Maid", and the plaintiffs relied *inter alia* on that. See also *Dubonnet* (1915) 31 R.P.C. 453; 32 R.P.C. 241. In *Tatem v Gaumont* (1917) 34 R.P.C. 181 CA, the plaintiffs, who alleged that their mark had caused the goods to be known as "Black Cat Films", failed in an infringement action to restrain the use of a quite different mark in which a black cat appeared. See also "Ship Brand", *Prices' v Jeyes'* (1902) 19 R.P.C. 17 compromised on the plaintiff's appeal; cf. also *Pomril* (1901) 18 R.P.C. 181 ("Apple Brand" cider). A somewhat similar point arose in a case in which the applicants and opponents were both companies whose names included the surname "Cording"; it was held that, in the circumstances, the mark "Gnidroc", being the name "Cording" reversed, was calculated to deceive, and registration was refused; but, the opponents not objecting, the application was allowed to proceed in the form "Nidroc": *Cording* (1916) 33 R.P.C. 83 and 325 HL.

THE MARK AS A WHOLE: COMMON ELEMENTS

17–035   The trade mark is the whole thing—the whole picture in relation to each of the marks being compared has to be considered. There may be differences in the parts of each mark, but it is important to consider the mode in which the parts are put together and to judge whether the dissimilarity of the part or parts is enough to make the whole dissimilar.

17–036   In the case of the application to register "Erectiko",[72] Farwell J. said: "I do not think it is right to take a part of the word and compare it with a part of the other word; one word must be considered as a whole and compared with the other word as a whole ... I think it is a dangerous method to adopt to divide the word up and seek to distinguish a portion of it from a portion of the other word."

17–037   Both the applicant and the opponent were mustard merchants, and both used square boxes covered with yellow labels printed in black and red; these boxes were common to the trade. The applicant placed upon his labels a picture of a charging buffalo, and the opponent a picture of a bull's head; both pictures were contained within silver rings, and these rings were also common to the trade. Stirling J. said that the buffalo and the bull's head, as printed in the Trade Marks Journal, were very different, but when they were placed upon the coloured labels, the applicant's label too closely resembled that of the opponent to be admitted to the Register: Farrow's Trade Mark.[73]

17–038   It has been said that if the only resemblances between the two marks are in parts which are common, so that the owner of the one has taken nothing which is peculiar to the other, then there is at all events no infringement,[74] at any rate unless the claimant has a distinctive arrangement of the common elements. But this approach is hardly suited to a comparison of word marks; and even in relation to label marks or other features of get-up, it would seem more appropriate to consider the case as a whole, with due regard to the background provided by any other marks shown to be in use.

ELEMENTS IN COMMON USE: SOME DICTA

17–039   In *Broadhead*,[75] Evershed M.R., following the observations of Lord Russell in *Coca Cola of Canada v Pepsi Cola of Canada*,[76] stated: "Where you get a common denominator, you must in looking at the competing formulae pay much more regard to the parts of the formulae which are not common—although it does not flow from that that you must treat the words as though the common part was not there at all." Where common parts are included in the trade marks to be

---

[72] *Bailey* (1935) 52 R.P.C. 136 at 151, opposed by the proprietors of the trade mark "Erector". Registration refused. See *Broadhead* (1950) 67 R.P.C. 113 at 119. See *per* Evershed M.R. in *Electrolux v Electrix (No.2)* (1954) 71 R.P.C. 23 at 31.

[73] (1890) 7 R.P.C. 260; 63 L.T. 233.

[74] *The European v The Economist* [1996] F.S.R. 431, [1998] F.S.R. 83; *Jamieson v Jamieson* (1898) 15 R.P.C. 169; *Payton v Snelling* (1900) 17 R.P.C. 48, especially at 56 (affirmed by HL, 17 R.P.C. 628); *Payton v Titus Ward* (1900) 17 R.P.C. 58 at 63, all passing off cases; *Marshall v Sidebotham* and *Alaska Packers v Crooks*, above (trade mark and passing off).

[75] (1950) 67 R.P.C. 209 at 215, where a dispute arose as to an admission as to what was fair use of marks "Alka-vescent" and "Alka-Seltzer".

[76] (1942) 59 R.P.C. 127; "Pepsi-Cola" held not an infringement of "Coca-Cola," "Cola" being common to the trade; applied also in *Demuth* (1948) 65 R.P.C. 342 ("Seda Seltzer" not too close to "Alka Seltzer", "Seltzer" being common to the trade).

compared, or in one of them, the proper course is to look at the marks as wholes, and not to disregard the parts which are common.[77]

In the "Kleenoff" case,[78] Maugham L.J. said: "In the present case my view is that the test of infringement where the trade mark has a descriptive element is the same as the test where it has no descriptive element, except so far as the descriptive element is itself common to the trade." **17–040**

In *Harrods*,[79] the Registrar stated: "It is a well-recognised principle that has to be taken into account in considering the possibility of confusion arising between any two trade marks, that, where those two marks contain a common element which is also contained in a number of other marks in use in the same market, such a common occurrence in the market tends to cause purchasers to pay more attention to the other features of the respective marks and to distinguish between them by those features. This principle clearly requires that the marks comprising the common element shall be in fairly extensive use and, as I have mentioned, in use in the markets in which the marks under consideration are being or will be used." **17–041**

"It is not right to pull the words to pieces, ACCU- for one part and -IST and -LARM for the other part, next to argue that ACCU reminds you of 'accurate', no matter what the suffix, and to conclude that the upshot will be a monopoly in the natural word": *per* Harman L.J. in *Accutron*.[80] **17–042**

In *The European v The Economist*,[81] Millett L.J. said: "... 'European' is the most prominent feature of the plaintiff's mark, but ... it is not a made-up or invented word but an ordinary word in common use, capable of being used most naturally in a descriptive manner, and in the case of the defendant's newspaper used to describe its character and contents. ... Where descriptive words are included in a registered trade mark, the courts have always and rightly been exceedingly wary of granting a monopoly in their use." **17–043**

In *The European*, it so happened that the common element was disclaimed from the registration. Disclaimers may no longer be imposed under the 1994 Act, and if registrations are granted containing common elements without a disclaimer, it is suggested that the approach of identifying and allowing for common matter will increase in practical importance very considerably. **17–044**

IMPORTANCE OF FIRST SYLLABLE

It has been accepted in several reported cases that the first syllable of a word mark is generally the most important. It has been observed in many cases that **17–045**

---

[77] See above and also *Christiansen* (1886) 3 R.P.C. 54 at 61, CA. The fact that a part of the mark is common must be taken into consideration, and if the common feature appears in an unusual way that is an element to be considered: *Orr-Ewing v Registrar* (1878–79) 4 App.Cas. 479.

[78] *Bale & Church v Sutton* (1934) 51 R.P.C. 129 at 144, CA ("Kleenup" held to infringe "Kleenoff," on domestic cleaning material). Typical cases of this sort are "Accutron", [1966] R.P.C. 152, and *"Rheinliebling"* [1966] R.P.C. 68; for cases where the descriptive element was common to the trade, see above.

[79] (1935) 52 R.P.C. 65 at 70. "Hyde Park" for cigarettes opposed by proprietors of marks containing the words "Park" or "Park Drive". Application allowed subject to limitation.

[80] [1966] R.P.C. 152 at 158. Subsequently "Bulova Accutron" was also refused, the grounds being that the mark would be taken to be two trade marks, namely, a "house name" together with the trade mark "Accutron": *"Bulova Accutron"* [1969] R.P.C. 102.

[81] [1998] F.S.R. 283 at 289–290.

there is a "tendency of persons using the English language to slur the terminations of words".[82]

GROUPS OF RELATED MARKS

17–046   Where there are a "series" of marks, registered or unregistered, but in use, having a common feature or a common syllable and where all the marks in such a series belong to an opponent, these are generally circumstances adverse to an applicant for a mark containing the common feature, since the public might think that such a mark indicated goods coming from the same source;[83] the strength of this "series" objection depending on how distinctive the common feature is.[84] If the marks in the series are owned by different persons, this tends to negative any proprietorial signification of the common feature and so may assist the applicant,[85] unless the common feature is descriptive of a class of goods narrower or different from the goods in respect of which registration is sought. If the marks in a series are merely on the Register, but are not shown to be in use and so known to the public, the above considerations do not apply, and such marks must be considered individually only.[86]

EAR AS WELL AS EYE MUST BE CONSIDERED

17–047   The importance of aural similarity is expressly recognised in the jurisprudence of the ECJ: see para.17–011. This is especially important now that infringement can be committed by oral use of a mark.[87]

The resemblance between two marks must be considered with reference to the

---

[82] *London Lubricants* (1925) 42 R.P.C. 264 at 279, CA; "Tripcastroid"), *per* Sargant L.J.; *Enoch* (1947) 64 R.P.C. 119, "Vivicyllin" allowed notwithstanding "Cyllin", at 122; *Bayer* (1947) 64 R.P.C. 125 at 128, "Diasil" allowed notwithstanding "Alasil"; *Demuth* (1948) 65 R.P.C. 342 at 346; "Seda Seltzer" allowed notwithstanding "Alka Seltzer"; *Fitchetts v Loubet* (1919) 36 R.P.C. 296, "Rito" allowed notwithstanding "Lito" and "Yto"; *Fox* (1920) 37 R.P.C. 37, "Motrate" allowed notwithstanding "Filtrate"; "Cal-U-Test" allowed notwithstanding 12 other "Test" marks with different prefixes, *Cal-U-Test* [1967] F.S.R. 39; *Capsuloid* (1906) 23 R.P.C. 782, "Tablones" too near "Tabloids"; *Accutron* [1966] R.P.C. 152, "Accutron" too near "Accurist" for watches; and *Buler* [1966] R.P.C. 141, "Buler" too near "Bulova" for watches, are instances of paired marks with common first parts; note that in the first case, where the common part is descriptive, the Registrar refused registration; in the second, where the common part has no separate meaning, he would have allowed registration but the court did not; cf. the quotation, at para.17–040, from the "Kleenoff" case. But cf. *Aristoc v Rysta* 62 R.P.C. 65; *Reynolds v Laffeaty* [1957] R.P.C. 311, CA (interim proceedings), [1958] R.P.C. 387 (final proceedings); "Watermatic" too near "Aquamatic" for water-pistols; *Geigy v Chelsea Drug* [1966] R.P.C. 64 ("butazolidin" not infringed by "butazone"). "Bensyl" too close to "Bentasil" and "Benvil": *BENSYL Trade Mark* [1992] R.P.C. 529. "Neutralia" confusingly similar to "Neutrogena": *Neutrogena v Golden* [1996] R.P.C. 473.

[83] e.g. *Accutron* [1966] R.P.C. 152 (opposition by proprietor of "Accurist" and "Accularm"); *Flowstacka* [1968] R.P.C. 66.

[84] "*Frigiking*" [1973] R.P.C. 739 ("King" not distinctive enough for a "series" objection to have much weight).

[85] *Beck, Koller* (1947) 64 R.P.C. 76: "Plyophen" refused in view of many other marks commencing with "Plio"; *British Lead Mills* [1958] R.P.C. 425. ("Welloy" refused: opponents owned many marks beginning with "Wel").

[86] "*Semigres*" [1979] R.P.C. 330 (Registry; refused for a series of "Sem-" marks); citing *Beck, Koller* (1947) 64 R.P.C. 76.

[87] See Ch.14.

ear as well as to the eye.[88] Whether confusion will arise in the course of telephone conversations must also be considered.[89]

For a recent case where two marks different in appearance were nonetheless held sufficiently similar to the ear for one to block the registration of the other, see Northern Foods Application,[90] where the decision was based on the fact that German speakers would pronounce the two marks (FOX'S, FUCHS) very similarly.

Examination of reported cases shows that where the marks are meaningless   **17–048** words, or words of essentially similar character, the courts give as much weight to phonetic as to visual resemblance.[91] But for a mere accidental phonetic resemblance (in the sense that the idea of the marks, once properly grasped, is quite different) to convince the court of deceptive resemblance calls for something special: for a convincing demonstration that some context likely to occur in actual commerce would convert the accidental resemblance into something approaching identity of sound.[92] However, careless pronunciation and the fact that the actual purchaser may be buying for someone else are both relevant.[93]

Since all the circumstances of the trade are to be considered, it is relevant to   **17–049** inquire whether and to what extent the customer has to call for goods by name in order to buy them. In public houses, drinks will be offered and ordered orally by name and the likelihood of confusion owing to similarity in the sound of the marks may be high. On the other hand, in supermarkets these days the customer normally takes goods off the shelf without asking for assistance, and the goods bear trade marks prominently where they are easy to see. In such circumstances, Whitford J. observed in *Mars v Cadbury*[94] (the "Treat Size" case), the importance of the sound of a mark may be diminishing.

---

[88] *County Chemical Application* (1937) 54 R.P.C. 182 at 185 ("Arlette"). *"June Perfect"* (1941) 58 R.P.C. 147 at 161. A good example of the possibility of oral confusion being decisive is *Philips* [1969] R.P.C. 78. The two marks were visually entirely different, but because the applicants' mark contained the word "Philips" there was a distinct possibility of oral confusion with the defendants' signature mark which ended with the surname "Phillips".

[89] *Magdalena Securities* (1931) 48 R.P.C. 477 at 487 ("Ucolite" held by court to be too near "Co-alite" for registration); *Bayer* (1947) 64 R.P.C. 125 at 133; *Rheinliebling* [1966] R.P.C. 68 at 74 (not apparent over telephone whether mark was one word or two); *Morcream v Heatherfresh* [1972] R.P.C. 799 (trade name case; too close to "Everfresh", on telephone only; injunction granted specifically against business on telephone).

[90] [2002] E.T.M.R. 48.

[91] Thus in *Ouvah Ceylon v Uva Ceylon* (1910) 27 R.P.C. 645 at 753, the plaintiffs obtained an injunction against the defendants' use of their name, the first word in each being a different spelling of the name of the same district. See also the cases establishing that a mark is unregistrable if it is a phonetic equivalent of an unregistrable mark; *e.g.* "Dex" for bolts ("Deck bolts"), *National Machinery* (1941) 58 R.P.C. 128; "Pirle" (because of "pearl"), *Ripley* (1895) 15 R.P.C. 151; "Electrix" ("electrics" admitted unregistrable), *"Electrix"* [1959] R.P.C. 283; and "Orlwoola", ("all wool"), *Orlwoola* [1910] 1 Ch. 130; 26 R.P.C. 683, 850.

[92] cf. *"Kidax"* [1960] R.P.C. 117 ("Kidax" registered notwithstanding "Daks", for clothing: court not convinced anyone would ask for "Kiddies' Daks"); *Jeyes v Aliamaid* (1955) 72 R.P.C. 277 (court not convinced anyone would ask just for "3 Jeyes'" (or "J's'"), and possible confusion between "3 bottles of 'J'" and "3 bottles of 'Jeyes'" not sufficient to justify a monopoly of the letter "J"); *Broadhead* (1950) 67 R.P.C. 209 (real possibility of confusion between "Alka-Seltzer' Effervescent Tablets" and " 'Alka-Vescent' Seltzer Tablets"; registration of "Alka-Vescent" refused). *"Nerit"* [1982] F.S.R. 72, CA, probably goes too far, holding (at 79) that since "Nerit" was too close to "Merit" only phonetically and the idea was different, "Nerit" was registrable as a new mark; but the point is the same. cf. *"Kwik Kopy"* [1982] R.P.C. 102: mark visually distinctive but phonetically just "Quick Copy" so unregistrable.

[93] *"Inadine"* [1992] R.P.C. 421.

[94] [1987] R.P.C. 387.

IMPERFECT RECOLLECTION

17–050   This aspect of the comparison between marks has also been adopted by the ECJ in relation to the ordinary consumer test: see paras 17–012 to 17–015.

17–051   It is clear as a matter of commonsense that the tribunal ought not merely to look at the marks as they stand side by side; it is most unlikely in most cases that the customer will have an opportunity for such a comparison. He can only rely on his recollection of the mark he is used to seeing on the goods he is seeking to buy, and allowance must be made for this in estimating the probability of deception. Any other rule would be of no practical use.[95] It has to be borne in mind that the ordinary purchaser has only "an ordinary memory".[96]

> "The question is not whether if a person is looking at two trade marks side by side there would be a possibility of confusion; the question is whether the person who sees the proposed trade mark in the absence of the other trade mark, and in view only of his general recollection of what the nature of the other trade mark was, would be liable to be deceived and to think that the trade mark before him is the same as the other, of which he has a general recollection."[97]

17–052   "Whether there has been trade mark infringement is more a matter of feel than science. I have borne in mind all of the arguments advanced by the defendant. However in this case it is significant that the marks are being used in relation to comparatively inexpensive restaurant services. This is an area where imperfect recollection is likely to play an important role. Furthermore the fact that the plaintiff's mark is quite meaningless means that imperfect recollection is more likely.": Laddie J. in *Wagamama v City Centre Restaurants*;[98] Wagamama infringed by Rajamama (and also passing off). See also *De Cordova v Vick*,[99] from which Laddie J. quoted thereafter.

17–053   That one of two words was in English and the other in a foreign language would, in general, diminish the probability of confusion through "imperfect recollection".[1]

MARKS TO BE COMPARED AS SEEN IN ACTUAL USE

17–054   This consideration is inherent to the test in passing off; the question as to what extent registered marks are to be considered strictly as they appear on the Register is dealt with in Ch.8.

17–055   Thus, under the 1938 Act the position was that in comparing marks regard must be had not only to their form as they appear on the Register,[2] but also to the

---

[95] *Seixo v Provezende* (1865–66) L.R. 1 Ch. App. 192; *Wilkinson v Griffith* (1891) 8 R.P.C. 370; *Hubbuck v Brown* (1900) 17 R.P.C. 638 at 645. *Ravenhead Brick v Ruabon* (1937) 54 R.P.C. 341 at 349, *per* Simonds J.: "Sanrus" held to be an infringement of "Rus". "*Coca Cola*" (1942) 59 R.P.C. 127 at 133; "*Ovax*" (1946) 63 R.P.C. 97.
[96] *per* Romer L.J., "*Kleenoff*" (1934) 51 R.P.C. 129 at 141.
[97] *Sandow* (1914) 31 R.P.C. 196 at 205, *per* Sargant J.
[98] [1995] F.S.R. 713 at 733.
[99] (1951) 68 R.P.C. 103 at 106.
[1] "*Solibrisa*" (1948) 65 R.P.C. 17 at 22.
[2] Jessel M.R. held, in several cases, that the Register only should be looked at: *Re Jelley* (1878) 51 L.J. Ch. 639n; *Robinson* (1880) 29 W.R. 31; *Mitchell v Henry* (1880) L.R. 15 Ch.D. 181; but in the latter case the CA dissented from his opinion and overruled his decision; *Christiansen* (1886) 3 R.P.C. 54; *Lyle and Kinahan* (1907) 24 R.P.C. 37 and 249.

appearance they would present in actual use when fairly and honestly used;[3] to the nature of the goods upon which they are to be employed; to the character and size of the marks themselves; and to the probabilities of their becoming partially or wholly blurred or modified as ordinarily stamped or printed, or by ordinary wear and tear.[4] A mark which is used for hardware goods, and is stamped upon them with a die, is not likely to appear so definitely or to be so readily distinguishable from a similar mark as one which is engraved or printed upon a paper label and so attached to the goods.[5]

Some marks continue to indicate origin well after the point of sale, and it is suggested that that also is a circumstance which ought to be taken into account. In *Levi Strauss v Kimbyr Investments*,[6] the plaintiff's "tab" mark was held infringed because after sale, when the customer was wearing the jeans and all point of sale material had been removed, the "tab" still functioned as an indication of origin.   **17–056**

COLOUR

Where marks are used in colour, it may undoubtedly affect the likelihood of confusion that the colours are or are not the same. Whilst, however, this is often a circumstance of great importance in relation to passing off, it is (except in the rare cases where a mark is registered in particular colours only) ordinarily of less importance in considering infringement: for the owner of a registered mark may use it in any colour. Even so, however, colour should seldom be entirely ignored.   **17–057**

(1) Since the registered proprietor of the device of a star could use it in any colour, the words "Red Star" would be as objectionable as the word star by itself: *Des Verreries de l'Etoile* [1894] 1 Ch. 61; 10 R.P.C. 436; [1894] 2 Ch. 26; 11 R.P.C. 142 ("Red Star Brand").

(2) The words "The Golden Fan Brand" were refused registration as an essential particular of a mark, on account of the presence on the Register of a fan which was in fact coloured gold in use: *Dewhurst* [1896] 2 Ch. 137; 13 R.P.C. 288.

(3) A triangular frame with the picture of a church inside was rejected on the ground that it would, if the whole were coloured red, too nearly resemble Bass's well-known solid red triangle: *Worthington's Case* (1880) L.R. 14 Ch.D. 8 (these days it might well be held that a monopoly over triangles generally on this possibly rather speculative basis would be too broad); and see *Hanson* (1887) 37 Ch.D. 112 (red, white & blue coffee label not distinctive without colours).

(4) In an action for infringement of several marks, of which the essential feature was the initials "B.P.", the defendants had used the initials "E.P.", always displayed in black on a yellow ground, whereas the plaintiffs' mark was displayed in yellow on green. The possibilities of confusion alleged by the plaintiffs essentially concerned use of the marks by such displays at filling stations. Held that the difference in colour was irrelevant to the question of infringement: *British Petroleum v European Petroleum* [1968] R.P.C. 54 at 64. Doubtless the position would have been otherwise if the mark had been registered in respect of a particular colour.

---

[3] *"June"* (1941) 58 R.P.C. 147 at 161; *"Ovax"* (1946) 63 R.P.C. 97.
[4] *Lyndon* (1886) 32 Ch.D. 109; 3 R.P.C. 102, CA; *Haines, Batchelor* (1888) 5 R.P.C. 669.
[5] *Haines, Batchelor* (1888) 5 R.P.C. 669 (dog and pig stamps: the objection failed).
[6] [1994] F.S.R. 335 (N.Z.). But see Ch.14, in relation to the value of this authority.

SIZE

17–058   Size is not in itself a material factor in the comparison: a trade mark owner may use his mark in any size.[7] Where, however, the small size of the mark is such as to render it indistinct, this is material on the basis of the principle already stated. Whether there can be infringement by a mark so small as to be entirely invisible to the naked eye, *quaere*.[8]

ALL THE CIRCUMSTANCES OF THE TRADE TO BE CONSIDERED

17–059   Further, the court must have regard to all the circumstances of the trade[9] in which the marks in question are employed, or are to be employed, and in particular (1) to the nature of the market, whether a home or a foreign one; (2) to the number of other trade marks similar to the contrasted marks already circulating in connection with the same description of goods; (3) to the common marks which are or may be combined with the contrasted marks or either of them; and, generally(4) to the customs and usages of the trade. As with the considerations identified in the foregoing sections, the relevance of all the circumstances of the trade has been endorsed by the ECJ.[10]

17–060   In passing off actions, also, the circumstances of the trade may be highly material to the question of confusion.[11] In *Portakabin v Powerblast*,[12] relevant circumstances included the fact that the range of the plaintiff's potential customers for its portable buildings was wide enough to include customers for the defendant's shot-blasting units.

It may also be relevant that goods are sometimes bought for others, and that the customer may not know the purpose for which the goods are acquired: "Inadine".[13]

4. Evidence—general considerations

THE ROLE OF EVIDENCE ON THE QUESTION OF RESEMBLANCE

17–061   The question of whether two marks are deceptively or confusingly similar to one another is for the judge to decide, and as is noted above, he is entitled to make a decision based on his own experience even in the absence of evidence.[14] Thus it has been said that the question of whether the resemblance is too close is one for the tribunal and not the witness.[15]

17–062   It has also been said that:

---

[7] *Speer* (1887) 4 R.P.C. 521; 55 L.T. 880. But he may not use part of the mark one size and part another size if the mark is thereby rendered deceptive: *Lilly (Eli) v Chelsea Drug* [1966] R.P.C. 14.

[8] *"Everglide"* [1964] R.P.C. 37 (mark just visible).

[9] *Cochrane v MacNish* [1896] A.C. 225; 13 R.P.C. 100 ("Club Soda"); *Coats* (1936) 53 R.P.C. 355 ("Sheen").

[10] See para.17–011, and Ch.9.

[11] See, *e.g. Hayter v R.B.H.S.* [1977] F.S.R. 285, CA ("B.J.S. Motor Syndicate" not too close as a business name to "J.S.B. Policies", in view of practices at Lloyd's); *Berkeley Hotel v Berkeley International* [1972] R.P.C. 237 at 244 (relevant to the risk of confusion, that defendants' hotel was to be on plaintiffs' old site).

[12] [1990] R.P.C. 471.

[13] [1992] R.P.C. 421.

[14] See *Spalding v Gamage* and *Neutrogena*, (1915) 32 R.P.C. 273; [1996] R.P.C. 473.

[15] This statement in the 12th edition of this work was expressly approved by Dillon L.J. in *Mothercare v Penguin Books* [1988] R.P.C. 113, and referred to by Knox J. in *Island Trading v Anchor Brewing* [1989] R.P.C. 287a. See also *Harker Stagg* (1954) 71 R.P.C. 136 at 140; *Payton v Snel-*

"The question of infringement, the question whether one mark is likely to cause confusion with another, is a matter upon which the judge must make up his mind and which, he and he alone, must decide. He cannot abdicate the decision in that matter to witnesses before him. On the other hand, it is equally true that he must be guided in all these matters by the evidence before him and where the evidence is that there has been no confusion that is a material matter which the judge must take into account."[16]

EXPERT AND TRADE EVIDENCE — ADMISSIBILITY

Leaving aside for the moment "survey" evidence, which is a separate matter considered below,[17] the admissibility of expert evidence depends on the purpose of adducing the evidence, and the nature of the trade in question.   **17–063**

Thus evidence of the circumstances of the trade, the manner in which goods are sold and so on is always admissible[18] (although if the trade is one with which the judge may be expected to have experience of his own, it may be of limited value). Thus, evidence may be given, by retailers,[19] as to the phrases used by customers in asking for goods,[20] and as to the proper inference to be drawn from the wording of the requests.[21] Similarly, a wholesaler may give evidence as to the likely effect on his system of handling orders of concurrent use of the two marks.[22]   **17–064**

However, the admissibility of direct evidence of an "expert" to the effect that there is likely to be confusion depends on the trade. Evidence concerning a specialist field is much more likely to be admitted than evidence concerning mundane, everyday purchases such as groceries.[23] There does not, however, seem to be a clear dividing line between what is permitted and what is not.   **17–065**

---

ling (1900) 17 R.P.C. 628 (alleged passing off by get-up) at 635, *London General Omnibus Co v Lavell* [1901] 1 Ch. 135; 18 R.P.C. 74; *North Cheshire Brewery v Manchester Brewery* [1899] A.C. 83.

[16] *Electrolux v Electrix (No.2)* (1954) 71 R.P.C. 23 at 31, *per* Evershed M.R. ("Electrux" and "Electrix"). See also *Cowie v Herbert* (1897) 14 R.P.C. 436 ("Town Hall") no proof of confusion; *"Kidax"* [1960] R.P.C. 117 at 122, CA. See further as to evidence that there has been no confusion in practice, and/or a lack of positive evidence of confusion, paras. 17–072 to 17–074.

[17] See paras 17–082 to 17–089.

[18] This kind of evidence has long been regarded as being of informative value for the court, as was confirmed in *Dalgety Spillers v Food Brokers* [1994] F.S.R. 504. Other cases include *George Ballantine v Ballantyne Stewart* [1959] R.P.C. 47, 186; *Sodastream v Thorne Cascade* [1982] R.P.C. 459; *Guccio Gucci v Paolo Gucci* [1991] F.S.R. 89; and *Taittinger v Allbev* [1993] F.S.R., 641; *NAD Electronics v NAD Computer Systems* [1997] F.S.R. 380. For older cases, see, *e.g. Electrolux v Electrix (No.2)* (1953) 70 R.P.C. 127 at 131; following Warrington J. in *Schweppes v Gibbens* (1905) 22 R.P.C. 113 at 119; Lord Parker in *Spalding v Gamage* (1915) 32 R.P.C. 273 at 286. See also " *Diasil*"(Bayer) (1947) 64 R.P.C. 125, where conditions of sale and purchase of the goods were considered at length, and weight given to the fact that they could be supplied on prescription only; *Players* (1965) R.P.C. 363 (relevant that chocolate cigarettes and real cigarettes are sold in the same shops) and *Picot v Goya* (1967) R.P.C. 573 (oral confusion not so important because the goods, perfumes, always purchased over the counter and not by telephone).

[19] Evidence from others closely connected with the retail trade may be easier to secure and equally admissible: *e.g.* from the claimant's own sales representatives, from their own observations whilst in customers' shops.

[20] *Elliott Optical* (1952) 69 R.P.C. 169 at 173.

[21] *Sales Affiliates v Le Jean* (1947) 64 R.P.C. 103 at 110; *"Glastonburys"* (1938) 55 R.P.C. 253 at 262; *Ballantine v Ballantyne, Stewart* [1959] R.P.C. 273 at 280.

[22] See the defendants' evidence in "Sunniwite" para.17–069 and footnotes therein, at 95–96.

[23] Contrast *"GE"* [1973] R.P.C. 297 at 321–322 with *Dalgety Spillers v Food Brokers* [1994] F.S.R. 504.

17–066   Thus evidence of this kind was admitted in *Guccio Gucci v Paolo Gucci*[24] (designer clothes), but rejected in *The European v The Economist*[25] (newspapers), admitted in *Antec v South-Western Chicks* (agricultural disinfectant), and in *NAD Electronics v NAD Computer Systems*[26] (hi-fi and computers). In *United Biscuits v Asda*,[27] (chocolate biscuits), the evidence was not rejected entirely, but firmly given second place after the judge's own impression.

17–067   The contrast between what is admissible and what is not is well illustrated by *Island Trading v Anchor Brewing*,[28] where the judge admitted evidence that the public identified the plaintiff's product as "Steam beer",[29] and ordered it as such, but rejected evidence from the trade that the public might be confused.

17–068   The overall position in relation to the 1994 Act was stated in *Bach Flower Remedies v Healing Herbs*[30] (a case concerned with distinctiveness under s.3 of the 1994 Act rather than infringement under s.10 or relative grounds for refusal under s.5, but relevant nonetheless), as follows:

> "The task for the court is to inform itself, by evidence, of the matters of which a reasonably well informed and reasonably observant and circumspect consumer of the products would know; and then, treating itself as competent to evaluate the effect which those matters would have on the minds of such a person with that knowledge, ask the question."[31]

17–069   In some cases it may not be entirely easy to distinguish between direct evidence that there is a likelihood of confusion, and evidence about the circumstances of the trade or whether there has been confusion. In *Neutrogena v Golden*,[32] shopkeepers gave evidence that they were content to stock both parties' products, and had not themselves experienced any signs of confusion. This was held relevant and admissible, although the judge declined to rely on it for other reasons.[33]

17–070   Evidence as to other related marks or names in use in the trade is of value; but mere evidence of entries on the Register of Trade Marks, without evidence of whether and to what extent the marks or names concerned are used, is of little or no value. Further, regard must be had to the number of different owners of the marks. Evidence that marks were accepted onto the Register without objection is at most evidence of the opinion of the Registrar, and is completely irrelevant in the absence of evidence as to his reasons.[34]

17–071   The court may properly refer to dictionaries in order to ascertain not only the

---

[24] [1991] F.S.R. 89.

[25] [1996] F.S.R. 431; [1998] F.S.R. 283. The statement by Millett L.J. at 291 that the trade evidence was inadmissible must, it is suggested, be understood in context and not as a general rule that such evidence of likelihood of confusion is always inadmissible.

[26] [1997] F.S.R. 380.

[27] [1997] R.P.C. 513 at 538.

[28] [1989] R.P.C. 287a.

[29] And also evidence about publicans' policy in the light of likely customer reaction.

[30] [2000] R.P.C. 513.

[31] *per* Chadwick L.J. at 535.

[32] [1996] R.P.C. 473 at 501–502.

[33] Similar evidence was led in *Lever Bros v Sunniwite* (1949) 66 R.P.C. 84 at 92 et seq., 97–98 (Romer J.; "Sunlight" and "Sunniwite"). Those of the defendants' witnesses who said in cross-examination that they would, or did, stock "Sunniwite" as well as "Sunlight" were then asked whether they would say the same if it were not "Sunniwite" but "Sunwhite"; a question admitting of no satisfactory answer.

[34] *Neutrogena v Golden* [1996] R.P.C. 473 at 502–503, referring to *Goya v Gala of London* (1952) 69 R.P.C. 188. Entry is not evidence of use: *Willesden Varnish v Young* (1922) 39 R.P.C. 285 at 288, 292; "*Daisil*" (1947) 64 R.P.C. 125 at 128; the point was not raised on appeal. As to the old

meaning of a word but also the use to which the thing (if it be a thing) denoted by the word is commonly put.[35] But statements in year books, etc., as to words being trade marks have been held inadmissible.[36]

PRESENCE OR ABSENCE OF EVIDENCE OF ACTUAL CONFUSION OR DECEPTION

Proof of actual deception, if the mark is in the opinion of the tribunal likely to deceive, is unnecessary.[37] Nevertheless, if one or more cases of actual deception are made out to the satisfaction of the court, this will, of course, afford very strong evidence that the resemblance between the marks in question is so close as to be likely to deceive.[38] However, the deception proved must be of the kind relevant to infringement or passing off; mere "administrative" confusion such as misdirected post and the like will not assist.[39]   **17–072**

The absence of evidence of actual deception is a circumstance which varies greatly in weight according to the nature of the case. Even where the proper inference to be drawn is that there has been no confusion,[40] this cannot be conclusive by itself:[41] the decision is for the court, which cannot abdicate it in favour of the witnesses.[42] Nevertheless, where the marks have been circulating side by side in the market[43] where deception is alleged to be probable, the fact that no one appears to have been misled is very material,[44] unless satisfactorily explained. On the other hand, if one or both of the marks is new or nearly new, there can have been no opportunity or little opportunity, for deception to occur.[45] Where   **17–073**

Business Names Register, see *General Radio v General Radio (Westminster)* [1957] R.P.C. 471 at 491; note the greater weight given to the telephone directory.

[35] *Coca-Cola of Canada v Pepsi Cola of Canada* (1942) 59 R.P.C. 127 at 153.

[36] *Havana Cigar v Oddenino* (1923) 40 R.P.C. 229 at 241; *Jacques v Chess* (1939) 56 R.P.C. 415; *Delavelle Stanley* (1946) 63 R.P.C. 103 at 109; *Sales Affiliates v Le Jean* (1947) 64 R.P.C. 103 at 110.

[37] See para.17–061, (judge can make his own decision).

[38] See, *e.g Saville Perfumery v June Perfect* (1941) 58 R.P.C. 147 at 174, *per* Viscount Maugham, HL.

[39] See, *e.g. The European v The Economist* [1998] F.S.R. 283, [1996] F.S.R. 431; *HFC v Midland* [2000] F.S.R. 176, CA.

[40] This does not always follow: evidence of actual deception is notoriously difficult to secure. Besides, "the more complete the deception, the less likely its detection" (*"Electrix"* (1953) 70 R.P.C. 127 at 132, *per* Lloyd-Jacob J.). It seems clear, in fact, that commercially the real harm arising from the use of confusingly similar marks may often be that the public, whilst aware that there are two brands of goods, cease to care which is which-in which case convincing evidence of confusion could hardly be obtainable. In *Neutrogena v Golden* [1996] R.P.C. 473, the trial judge rejected the evidence of retailers that they had not noticed any confusion on the basis that, inherently, it would not become apparent in the shop, but only afterwards.

[41] *Edelsten v Edelsten* (1863) 1 De G.J. & S. 185; *Campania Générale de Tobacos v Rehder* (1887) 5 R.P.C. 61; *Paine v Daniells* [1893] 2 Ch. 567, 10 R.P.C. 217.

[42] See para.17–061.

[43] If the marks have been used at different ends of the market in the goods concerned, this will explain absence of confusion: *"Bali"* [1969] R.P.C. 472, HL; *"Da Vinci"* [1980] R.P.C. 237 (Registry; too close to "Vincci"). Geographical separation of businesses may equally explain absence of confusion.

[44] For recent examples of this kind of reasoning, see *Laura Ashley v Coloroll* [1987] R.P.C. 1; *Elvis Presley Trade Mark* [1999] R.P.C. 567; [1997] R.P.C. 543, CA. Older cases include *Lambert* (1888) 6 R.P.C. 344; 61 L.T. 138, CA; and *Baker v Rawson* (1890) 45 Ch.D. 519; 8 R.P.C. 89 at 107. *"Kidax"* [1959] R.P.C. 295 at 308; *Cowie v Herbert* (1897) 14 R.P.C. 436 at 448 (IH). See also *"Solavoid"* [1977] R.P.C. 1 at 29, PC (N.Z., citing the corresponding passage to this from the 10th edition of this work).

[45] See, *e.g. Kimberley Clark v Fort Sterling* [1997] R.P.C. 877. A fortiori in a *quia timet* action such as *"Jif"* [1990] R.P.C. 341.

the defendants in a passing off action had issued deceptive literature, it was quite open to the court to draw an inference that some people were deceived.[46]

17–074   The owner of a trade mark is not bound to wait before taking action to see whether his customers will in fact be deceived, for "the very life of a trade mark depends upon the promptitude with which it is vindicated."[47] If he does wait, and fails nevertheless to secure evidence of actual confusion, this will suggest that the risk to his business is small, and incline a court to refuse interim relief at least.[48]

5. "Survey" evidence and other evidence from consumers

INTRODUCTION

17–075   It is common in actions for passing off and trade mark infringement for evidence to be adduced which concerns the reactions of members of the public to the marks or get-ups the subject of the proceedings, in circumstances where the party to the litigation has gone out to find or create such evidence (as opposed to passively receiving spontaneous evidence of confusion). Probably such evidence is most commonly led by the claimant in order to seek to demonstrate that the defendant's mark or get up is confusingly similar to, or deceptively resembles, his own. Although that is the main purpose of this kind of evidence, it is also sometimes adduced to show what the public understands by the parties' marks, or whether they are distinctive, or understood to indicate origin.[49]

17–076   This kind of evidence is often generically referred to as "survey evidence", but this term is misleading if used indiscriminately, and in fact evidence of this general kind takes a number of forms, apart from surveys in the strict sense.

17–077   When one refers to a "survey" in the strict sense, what is meant is an exercise in which a substantial number of persons are asked a series of questions according to explicit detailed instructions. Thereafter, the totality of their responses are collated and presented in the form of statistics, such as: "53% of those asked thought that the defendant's product was a new line from the claimant." This kind of exercise is similar in many ways to market research surveys, and is often designed and/or supervised and/or carried out by persons who have gained their experience in market research organisations such as MORI or Gallup.

17–078   However, the term "survey evidence" is also used more loosely to refer to any organised exercise whose objective is to seek and obtain evidence from a number of members of the public. A better and more accurate general term for this sort of activity, often used by practitioners these days, is "witness collection programme" or "witness gathering exercise".[50] One reason why the terms have tended to be blurred together is that, as practitioners are well aware, it can often happen that

---

[46] *Plomien Fuel Economiser v National School of Salesmanship* (1943) 60 R.P.C. 219.

[47] *Johnston v Orr-Ewing* (1879–80) L.R. 13 Ch.D. 434 at 464.

[48] Whilst the absence of actual confusion can often be explained (see above), most likely explanations (except in particular that confusion is taking place undetected) equally imply that little confusion is likely in the immediate future, so tilting the balance of convenience against the claimant, *e.g.* geographical separation: *Evans v Eradicure* [1972] R.P.C. 808.

[49] *e.g. Bach Flower Remedies v Healing Herbs* [2000] R.P.C. 513. For reasons explained at the end of this section, "survey" evidence to demonstrate that a mark is or is not understood as denoting a source of origin may well become more common in future under the 1994 Act.

[50] *e.g.* in *Bach Flower Remedies v Healing Herbs* [2000] R.P.C. 513 at para.49.

although the court is not taken with a survey qua survey, it is nonetheless swayed by the oral evidence of some of the subjects.[51]

Since their introduction in English litigation in the late 1960s and early 1970s[52]   **17–079**
surveys have not, it has to be said, achieved great impact, although there have been instances where they have been given considerable weight. The complexities involved in their preparation, the frequency with which leading or other inappropriate questions are asked, and the general approach that in relation to ordinary consumer goods the court can make its own decision, have all led to a rather hostile attitude. In *Neutrogena v Golden*,[53] Jacob J. said:

> "[P]ure questionnaire evidence is seldom helpful—there are almost inevita-   **17–080**
> ble faults with the questions or the recordal of the answers as well as in later stages of the processing. Of course the court needs to know what evidence was collected, and needs to have the full picture, including particularly what failed surveys, if any there were. But unless one can have some real evidence, tested in cross-examination, one cannot really be sure of what was passing through people's minds. Those cases where surveys have proved to be useful have all involved some of the "pollees' coming to court.""

The ECJ has now given surveys a similarly lukewarm reception in *Gut Spring-*   **17–081**
enheide,[54] where it held that in general it and the national courts could be expected to make decisions as to the likely state of mind of the "average consumer" without assistance, but that surveys were not ruled out by Community law in difficult cases.

SURVEYS—RULES

The basic rules for the conduct of a survey, in order for it to be probative, were   **17–082**
set out by Whitford J. in *Imperial v Philip Morris* [1984] R.P.C. 293 at 302–303. The requirements are:

(1) All surveys conducted, their methodology and results must be disclosed.
(2) The totality of all answers must be disclosed.
(3) The questions asked must not be leading.
(4) The questions asked must not lead the interviewee into a field of speculation upon which he would not otherwise have embarked.
(5) Exact answers and not abbreviations must be provided.
(6) Coding must be accurately carried out,[55] and the coding methods disclosed.
(7) The instructions given to the interviewers must be disclosed.

An example of leading questions and of questions based on a false premise   **17–083**
may be found in *Scott v Nice-Pak*,[56] where, despite the fact that it was not on the market, the consumers were asked if they had bought the defendant's product. The survey was also criticised for providing only "yes" and "no" options in answer to certain questions where the respondents might not know the answer or might be doubtful.

---

[51] In *Bach* the evidence was rejected under either rubric, but the court plainly accepted that a survey could be deployed as a witness gathering exercise.
[52] Early cases included *Coca Cola v Struthers* [1968] R.P.C. 231, and *"GE"* [1969] R.P.C. 418 (at first instance; the Court of Appeal accepted it, but the House of Lords gave it little weight: [1970] R.P.C. 339 and [1973] R.P.C. 297).
[53] [1996] R.P.C. 473 at 486.
[54] [1998] E.C.R. I-4657.
[55] But preferably not on the spot by the interviewer: *Scott v Nice Pak* [1989] F.S.R. 100; [1988] F.S.R. 125.
[56] [1989] F.S.R. 100; [1988] F.S.R. 125, CA.

17–084   The net effect of these rules, necessary as they are, is that it is very difficult to design a survey which will pass muster in court, and their design has become a very specialised art. One technique which improves the chances of useful evidence being obtained is to begin with a very open question, such as "what can you tell me about this product?", and to move on to ones which are gradually more specific, such as "can you tell me who makes this product?". The evidence of respondents who give useful answers to the very broad question is then untainted, while leaving an opportunity still to get evidence from persons who misunderstand what the interest of the interviewer is:[57] very broad questions are apt to receive an answer quite unrelated to the get up or mark of interest. For example, it is not uncommon for respondents to say "it looks expensive" or something of that kind, which may be of tangential relevance, and does not mean that the respondent has nothing to say about the principal question. When they are directed a little more, for example by asking about the origin of the goods, they may then give relevant evidence, although there is of course the risk of an accusation of leading.

SUCCESSFUL AND UNSUCCESSFUL SURVEYS

17–085   *Lego v Lego Lemelstrich* [1983] F.S.R. 155—evidence accepted.

Imperial Group v Philip Morris [1984] R.P.C.293, para.17–082—rejected.

Unilever v Johnson Wax [1989] F.S.R. 145, survey as part of an omnibus survey[58]—rejected.

"Jif" [1990] R.P.C. 341—accepted to varying degrees by the judge, the Court of Appeal and the House of Lords, but strongly supported by "live" evidence.

United Biscuits v Burtons [1992] F.S.R. 14—rejected.[59]

The European v The Economist [1996] F.S.R. 431 and [1998] F.S.R. 283—rejected by the judge and the Court of Appeal (question on a false basis—persons who had never seen the defendant's product presented with the top half of the front page only).

Neutrogena v Golden [1996] R.P.C. 473—the plaintiff produced the questionnaires used, but did not rely on them, only on oral evidence from some of the persons interviewed, which was accepted. The defendant's internal market research (not for the purposes of litigation) was relied on as showing confusion.

Pontiac Marina v CDL Hotels [1997] F.S.R. 725 (High Court of Singapore)—short and uncomplicated survey accepted.

Kimberley Clark v Fort Sterling [1997] F.S.R. 877—surveys held of limited quantitative value but of some qualitative value as an indication of the attractiveness of the claimant's mark and of whether it overwhelmed the disclaiming material.

Weight Watchers (UK) v Tescos Stores [2003] EWHC 1109 Ch.—rejected because questions leading.

Neil King's Application [2000] E.T.M.R. 22— survey rejected because a single small sample taken on one street not representative of the public. In

---

[57] This approach was endorsed by Lindsay J. in *Weight Watchers (UK) v Tescos Stores* [2003] EWHC 1109 Ch., para.24.

[58] An omnibus survey is a long set of questions on a wide range of topics sent to consumers on a regular basis. Interested parties pay for questions to be included.

[59] Evidence obtained with a "tachistoscope" was also rejected in this case, as well as in *Laura Ashley v Coloroll* [1987] R.P.C. 1.

addition, the population considered was persons aged 17–55, but no explanation was given for the choice, and the questionnaires did not reveal that the respondents had been asked if they fell in the population.

ADMISSIBILITY

Under the Rules of the Supreme Court and the Civil Evidence Act 1968, there were considerable complications as to the admissibility of survey evidence. A particular problem was that factual proof of what took place during the interviews was necessary, but that if a Civil Evidence Act Notice were served in relation to the interviewee's responses, the opposing party could generally require their attendance.[60] There was also a particular difficulty in the treatment of the evidence of the market researcher who reported on the surveys, since in strict terms his evidence could be said to contain or refer to second or third hand hearsay.[61] Moreover, it was suggested that such an expert could not give evidence on the ultimate matter to be decided by the court (whether or not there was a likelihood of deception).   **17–086**

These difficulties led to a number of rather unsatisfactory decisions. For example, in the course of "*Jif*", a decision was given[62] that the person giving evidence as to the surveys was not an expert at all, on the basis that he was merely reporting the results. This analysis, it is suggested, cannot be supported, at least where, as in most cases, evidence is given about general and desirable practice in market research.   **17–087**

In practice, the Civil Evidence Act requirements were honoured more in the breach than in the observance. In some cases the parties agreed to waive them. Happily these formal difficulties, such as they were, have been removed by the combined effects of the Civil Evidence Act 1995, and Pt 8 of the Civil Procedure Rules, which now permit the admission of most hearsay evidence subject to the court's ability to give it such weight as it thinks fit, without the necessity of the witness being brought to court, even if not beyond the seas, etc.   **17–088**

CASE MANAGEMENT OF SURVEY EVIDENCE

Surveys, even as witness collection exercises, are apt to throw up a large number of respondents. This does not mean that the party relying on the survey is entitled as of right to lead oral evidence from every single one which supports his case. The court has general power under the CPR to restrict the number of "live" witnesses to be called, having regard to the overriding objective in Pt 1 of the CPR. Thus in *HFC v Midland*,[63] in advance of trial, the judge limited the claimant to its 20 (later increased to 27) best witnesses. Subsequently, the claimant was permitted to serve Civil Evidence Act Notices in relation to all respondents, not in order   **17–089**

---

[60] Unless they were beyond the seas, ill or untraceable. Most of them tended to be ordinary members of the public in the UK and therefore available to give evidence if required.

[61] See *"GE"* [1970] R.P.C. 339, CA; *Customglass v Salthouse* [1976] R.P.C. 589; *Lego v Lego Lemelstrich* [1983] F.S.R. 155. In the last case, the conclusion was reached that the evidence went to prove public opinion, an external fact, and was therefore not subject to the hearsay rules. The admission of survey-type evidence on interim applications was easier because hearsay was expressly permitted on such occasions under the rules.

[62] [1987] F.S.R. 407.

[63] Unreported, Laddie J., May 18, 1999.

to use their evidence to show confusion, but in order to show that the 27 who were to give oral evidence were representative.[64]

This practice was mentioned and expressly approved in *Bach Flower Remedies v Healing Herbs*.[65]

SURVEYS TO PROVE MEANING TO THE PUBLIC

17–090   In addition to demonstrating the likelihood of confusion or deception, surveys may be used to show that a party's mark is known to the public, and what it means to them. This is of relevance not only in the context of civil proceedings for passing off or trade mark infringement, but also in relation to applications to register, and oppositions under s.3 of the 1994 Act. It is clear from cases such as *Windsurfing Chiemsee Produktions v Huber*[66] (ECJ) that in such cases, evidence will be required more than ever. Windsurfing was adopted and applied in *Bach Flower Remedies v Healing Herbs*.[67]

17–091   Surveys for such purposes will require different planning from those intended to produce evidence of deception or confusion. They may, in particular, require a different approach to sample selection. In *Dualit's Application*,[68] the survey was rejected because the sample was limited to the class of persons likely to buy the applicant's products, and by eliminating those who said that design was not important to them as a function. Whether such criticisms would lie against a survey intended to show confusion in a relevant section of the public is doubtful.

17–092   Surveys for this purpose will always be difficult to conduct, because it is not sufficient merely to establish recognition of the "trade mark" in question: distinctiveness has to be shown. See, *e.g. Nestlé's Application*.[69] Furthermore, avoiding leading questions will be more of a challenge than usual, because it will be necessary to avoid suggesting to the respondents that the mark in question is even capable of being a trade mark/denoting origin. For an attempt which was unsuccessful for this reason, see *Yakult Honsha KK's Application*.[70]

---

[64] Also unreported, Laddie J.
[65] [2000] R.P.C. 513 at para.35, *per* Morritt L.J.
[66] [1999] E.T.M.R. 585.
[67] [2000] R.P.C. 513.
[68] [1999] R.P.C. 890.
[69] [2003] F.S.R. 37.
[70] [2001] R.P.C. 39.

CHAPTER 18

TRADE LIBEL AND THREATS

1. Outline of chapter

INTRODUCTION

This chapter is concerned with the tort known as trade libel, and with the statu-   **18–001**
tory action for threats of proceedings for trade mark infringement, which is new
to the 1994 Act, although similar provisions have been in force in relation to
patents and designs for some time.[1]

In addition, there are a number of references in this chapter to infringement of   **18–002**
registered trade marks under s.10(6) of the Trade Marks Act 1994, the provision
mainly concerned with comparative advertising. Section 10(6) is dealt with in
full in Ch.14, but it is necessary and desirable to refer to it in the context of trade
libel, partly because many of the most relevant cases have involved both causes
of action, partly because the kinds of behaviour they are meant to address are
very similar, and partly because many of the same policy considerations underlie
them.

TERMS USED

This chapter is entitled "trade libel", but there are a number of names for the   **18–003**
same tort, including slander of goods, malicious falsehood and injurious
falsehood. These terms are used interchangeably in the authorities and in this
chapter, although the more modern judgments seem to use the name "malicious
falsehood" more than any other. That expression may well be the most apt in any
event because it emphasises the crucial importance of malice, while the terms
"slander of goods" and "trade libel" give too narrow an impression of the scope
of the tort, since it protects financial interests generally and not just commercial
ones.[2] Those terms also give perhaps too much of an impression of proximity to
the torts of slander and libel, which are related to malicious falsehood in many
respects, but are also very different in others.[3]

---

[1] Patents Act 1977, s.70, and the Copyright, Designs and Patents Act 1988, s.253.

[2] See, *e.g. Shepherd v Wakeman* (1662) 1 Sid 79, where the plaintiff lost her prospects of marriage
owing to a false and malicious claim that she was already married to the defendant; and *Joyce v
Sengupta* [1993] 1 W.L.R. 337, where the plaintiff's claim was that she would be hindered in
finding further employment involving positions of trust owing to a false assertion that she had
stolen her employer's confidential papers. Her interest was not as a trader, but the falsehood affected her financial position.

[3] The principle differences are that in libel and slander the claimant's reputation is protected, and
hence the statement complained of must be defamatory before a claim can succeed, whereas in
malicious falsehood any false statement is actionable provided that it is calculated to cause
financial damage, and is made maliciously. In malicious falsehood the claimant must prove
malice and bears the burden of proving falsity, whereas in defamation falsity is presumed and the
defendant must prove the statement to be true.

18–004   It is worth noting that the Defamation Act 1952[4] recognises that these various terms denote forms of the same general tort, by the use in s.3(1) of the expression "slander of title, slander of goods, and other malicious falsehood".

POLICY

18–005   The following are the main policy considerations underlying the law of malicious falsehood. They are worth setting out at this stage because they form an obvious and major part of the courts' reasoning in dealing with this cause of action. The policy considerations come particularly to the fore in the kind of cases with which this work and this chapter are concerned, namely disputes between rival traders as to statements made by one about the goods or business of another.

     The first main policy objective is the protection of economic interests. This is the *raison d'etre* of the tort as a whole.

18–006   The second main policy consideration is the promotion of competition. The courts recognise that an important vehicle for competition is the ability of one trader to seek to inform the public that his goods are available to be bought and that they have, or may have, advantages over the goods of another trader. This objective is so important that the courts may even permit a trader knowingly to make false statements about his goods in comparison with another trader's. See for example, the speech of Lord Diplock in the *Advocaat* case[5] (in the context of passing off, but with general application on this issue):

> "... in an economic system which has relied on competition to keep down prices and to improve products there may be practical reasons why it should have been the policy of the common law not to run the risk of hampering competition by providing civil remedies to everyone competing in the market who has suffered damage to his business or goodwill in consequence of inaccurate statements of whatever kind that may be made by rival traders about their own wares. The market in which the action for passing off originated was no place for the mealy mouthed; advertisements are not on affidavit; exaggerated claims by a trader about the quality of his wares, assertions that they are better than those of his rivals even though he knows this to be untrue, have been permitted by the common law as venial 'puffing' which gives no cause of action to a competitor even though he can show that he has suffered actual damage in his business as a result."

18–007   This policy consideration is also reflected in the requirement of this tort that malice must be proved. This can be a major difficulty in the path of a claimant suing for malicious falsehood, and the practical result is that a trader who honestly believes what he is saying cannot successfully be sued,[6] at least until the aggrieved rival puts him on notice by demonstrating the falsity of the statement to a sufficient degree of certainty. Moreover, although in the tort of malicious falsehood generally malice can arise in making a false statement for improper motives, the law recognises that the desire of a trader to earn custom at the expense

---

[4] See para.18–033.

[5] [1979] A.C. 731 at 742, quoted by Aldous J. in *Ciba-Geigy v Parke Davis* [1994] F.S.R. 8 at 20–21, a case about malicious falsehood. The circumstances in which this kind of statement is allowed are considered in more detail below.

[6] Even if his belief is not based on reasonable grounds, so long as he is not reckless as to the truth of what he says. Malice is considered in more detail in paras 18–062 to 18–075.

of his rivals is perfectly proper.[7] Recent cases have emphasised that an allegation of malice is generally treated as tantamount to one of dishonesty, so that it should be treated with the same circumspection as one of fraud.[8]

The third main policy consideration is the protection of free speech. This **18–008** overlaps with the previous consideration, but is of broader application. Its most important practical consequence is the rule, applicable in and arising from the law of defamation, that interim[9] relief is not available to restrain an alleged falsehood if the defendant has an arguable case that the statement in question is true. The law is in a somewhat unclear and unsatisfactory state as to whether and to what extent this rule applies where another cause of action based on the same facts is pleaded as well as or in place of malicious falsehood. At the very least it is clear that in such cases preservation of freedom of speech is an important factor in assessing the balance of convenience.

In addition to the general rule against interim relief, the law of malicious false- **18–009** hood has recently been affected in a number of more minor ways by Article 10 of the European Convention on Human Rights. See the references below to *IBM v Web-Sphere*, *Ferguson v Associated Newspapers* (both relating to the likelihood of damage required under s.3 of the Defamation Act 1952) and *O'Shea v MGN* (concerning whether "lookalike" pictures in a derogatory context may be actionable).

The fourth policy consideration is that the courts are not the appropriate forum **18–010** for resolving differences of opinion between traders as to which party's goods or services are better. The reluctance to deal with this kind of case was made clear over a hundred years ago, and seems to be based both on the courts' unsuitability to determine such issues, and the concern that a large number of time-consuming actions would fall to be tried, and so take up the courts' resources, which could be better used. For example, in *White v Mellin* [1895] A.C. 154, Lord Herschell L.C. said (at 165):

> "If an action will not lie because a man says that his goods are better than his neighbour's, it seems to me impossible to say that it will lie because he says that they are better in this or that or the other respect. Just consider what a door would be opened if this were permitted. That this sort of puffing advertisement is in use is notorious; and we see rival cures advertised for particular ailments. The Court would then be bound to inquire, in an action brought, whether this ointment or this pill better cured the disease which it was alleged to cure, whether a particular article of food was in this respect or that better than another. Indeed, the Courts of law would be turned into a machinery for advertising rival productions by obtaining a judicial determination which of the two was better."

And as a result the courts have preferred to leave determination of which **18–011** trader's goods are better, and statements about which are better, to be determined by the market and the advertising authorities. The courts' scepticism has remained, and has been reinforced to some extent by cases involving malicious falsehood and s.10(6) trade mark infringement brought in the years since the

---

[7] See the section on malice, below.

[8] *Webster v British Gas* [2003] EWHC 1188 (QB), May 23, 2003 (Tugendhat J.), para.28, referring to *Komarek v Ramco* (unreported), December 17, 2002 (Eady J.).

[9] The expression "interim" relief (or injunction) is used herein in preference to the term "interlocutory" as used before the introduction of the Civil Procedure Rules in 1999.

introduction of the 1994 Act. A number of them seem to have been brought against a background of ferocious competition between the parties in the marketplace and personal feelings on the part of their managements, as much to prove a point as to obtain compensation for an injury suffered. In at least one case the trial judge has made strong and explicit statements to such effect in giving judgment: see *Emaco Ltd v Dyson Appliances Ltd.*[10] refusing to award either side any costs:

> "[E]ach side is (as I said earlier when delivering judgment on the question of relief) intent on using these proceedings...as weapons in a continuing and, it appears, increasingly bitter advertising war...A party who approaches litigation in that way must expect (at the very least) to do so at his own expense.
>
> In all the circumstances, the right course to take in relation to costs, in my judgment, is to leave the costs where they lie: In other words, each party should pay its own costs. If (as I would hope) that serves to discourage other parties from using the courts as a forum for a continuing advertising war, that can only be in the interest of the public, and in particular of other litigants waiting to have their cases heard."

STATEMENT MAY BE A PERSONAL LIBEL; RELATIONSHIP WITH LIBEL

18–012 A disparaging statement with regard to a trader's goods may be an ordinary libel upon the trader personally and, accordingly, be actionable. Such, for instance, would be the case if the goods were described as worthless[11] or spurious.[12] To write of a trader that he sells such goods may well be defamatory, and all the more so if it is suggested that he does so knowingly. Ordinary libel is a matter beyond the scope of this book, and specialist works on defamation should be consulted.

18–013 It is, however, worth noting at this stage an important practical advantage of the action for malicious falsehood, which is that legal aid is not available to bring a claim in respect of defamation, but may be in respect of malicious falsehood. Where a claim could potentially be pleaded either way, there is nothing wrong in pleading it in malicious falsehood, even if that is done in order to obtain legal aid. It is not an abuse of process to do so, even if the amount of damages which may be obtained in malicious falsehood is small in comparison with what might be obtained if the same action were based in defamation: *Joyce v Sengupta*.[13] A side effect is that the right to a jury trial will not apply if the claim is brought in malicious falsehood.

RELATIONSHIP OF TRADE LIBEL WITH THE ACTION FOR THREATS

18–014 The action for threats is considered in detail below, but a few useful comparisons can be drawn at this stage.

As will be explained below, the action for threats provided for by the 1994 Act is new and little litigated so far, but is very similar to long-standing provisions concerning threats of actions for patent infringement.

18–015 Malicious falsehood and statutory actions for threats have a number of things

---

[10] The case is reported at [1999] E.T.M.R. 903; the judge made the above observations at a later unreported hearing.
[11] *British Empire v Linotype* (1898) 79 L.T. 8.
[12] *Liebig's Extract of Meat Co v Anderson* (1886) 55 L.T. 206.
[13] [1993] 1 W.L.R. 337, CA.

in common. The purpose of each is to restrain the making of false and damaging statements about a trader's goods or business. In each case, it is open to the person making the damaging statement to do so if the statement is true.

However, the statutory actions for threats exist in recognition of the fact that **18–016** allegations that a trader's goods infringe the intellectual property rights of one of his rivals call for particularly firm treatment. There are a number of reasons for this.

First of all, threats are inherently likely to be taken seriously. Rarely if ever **18–017** can they be "puffs". Moreover, threats are particularly pernicious in their effect on the potential customers of the trader whose goods are said to infringe. A potential customer who reads "knocking copy" directed at one of his suppliers only has to be concerned about the quality of the goods he is buying, and is likely to feel able to assess that for himself. But a threat of an infringement action is different; even if the threat is directed to the supplier and not the customer, the customer will fear that he will be unable to obtain supplies at all from that source, or that if he does, he will be in difficulty selling them on, and may even himself be sued.

There is also the consideration that intellectual property rights are potent tools **18–018** in business, and that if a trader is granted such a monopoly he should be required to vindicate it directly and properly by showing infringement of a valid right, rather than driving off other traders by the use of threats.

These issues are reflected in the different law and procedure applicable to the **18–019** common law action for malicious falsehood and the statutory one for threats. In malicious falsehood, the claimant must prove that the statement is false and made maliciously; in threats the onus lies on the owner of the right to prove that there has been infringement if he wishes to justify the threat, and there is no requirement of any mental element.

Procedurally, the difference between the actions of most importance is the **18–020** potential availability of interim relief to restrain threats even if the defendant right holder has an arguable case that the threat was justifiable. Interim relief is made available in recognition of the damage which threats can do and of the speed with which they can do it.

RELATIONSHIP WITH SECTION 10(6) INFRINGEMENT

Within the scope of this work, the main significance of the action for malicious **18–021** falsehood and the provisions of s.10(6) are in the field of comparative advertising. Since the 1994 Act came into force, there have been a number of cases where both causes of action were pleaded in respect of the same advertisement or series of advertisements.[14]

In this field, the two causes of action are directed at similar kinds of behaviour, **18–022** although they are aimed at protecting rather different interests. The action for trade mark infringement protects the claimant's interest in the registered mark (and hence the requirement that the use complained of must take unfair advantage, or be detrimental to, the distinctive character of the mark),[15] while the action for malicious falsehood protects the claimant's economic interests generally, whether or not his trade mark is used.

---

[14] See, e.g. *Vodafone v Orange* [1997] F.S.R. 34; *MacMillan v RCN Publishing* [1998] F.S.R. 9; *Cable & Wireless v BT* [1998] F.S.R. 383; *Emaco v Dyson Appliances* [1999] E.T.M.R. 903, *British Airways v Ryanair* [2001] F.S.R. 32.
[15] The proviso to s.10(6); and see Ch.14.

18–023   That said, in cases where the defendant has used the claimant's registered trade mark in the advertisement complained of, an action for infringement is more favourable to the claimant than an action for malicious falsehood in two very significant respects.

18–024   The first main advantage is that malice need not be proven, there being no subjective mental element under s.10(6).[16] The second is that that the advertisement will offend under the Act if it is misleading to a substantial proportion of the public, so that the claimant can succeed if the advertisement has two plausible meanings, one of which is false. In malicious falsehood, by contrast, the statement complained of must be given a single meaning, which is either true or false.[17]

18–025   Given these advantages, why would one allege malicious falsehood if a claim for infringement of a registered mark were available? One possible reason would be if there were a threat to the validity of the registration in question, although in most of the reported cases to date there has not been a counterclaim for revocation, probably because the actions have tended to be brought by established claimants with established marks.

18–026   Another reason which has been suggested by practitioners is the availability of potentially more extensive disclosure in connection with the issue of malice, such as documents revealing the thinking and planning behind the advertisement complained of. This reasoning is probably mistaken; although the test for "honest practices" under s.10(6) is basically an objective one,[18] documents showing what inquiries and checks the defendant made, planning undertaken, research into how it was expected that consumers would see the advertisement and so on are surely relevant to it.[19] So disclosure ought to be essentially the same in respect of the two causes of action, although its precise scope will of course depend on the pleadings.

18–027   One instance where it might genuinely be worth continuing with both causes of action is if there is good reason to believe that the defendant, even if found to infringe the claimant's trade mark, might continue with a modified advertisement making essentially the same statement but without use of the claimant's trade mark.

18–028   The courts have shown an awareness that a claim for malicious falsehood may be an unnecessary and burdensome addition to an action for trade mark infringement. In *Cable & Wireless v BT* [1998] F.S.R. 383 at 386, Jacob J. persuaded the claimant to limit its claim to trade mark infringement for that very reason. Although in that case (decided before the Civil Procedure Rules came into force) the claimant voluntarily dropped its claim for malicious falsehood, it would certainly be very much within the spirit of the Rules for the court to use its case management powers to remove an unnecessary claim for malicious falsehood from an action even if the claimant did not agree, on the basis that the cost and effort involved was not proportionate. Of course, it would not be appropriate to do so if there were a serious counterclaim to revoke the registration concerned.

---

[16] The test for "honest practices" under s.10(6) is probably whether, objectively assessed, an honest trader possessed of the information which could be obtained by reasonable inquiries, could reasonably make the statement concerned. See Ch.14, for more details.

[17] See paras 18–058 to 18–060.

[18] See above and Ch.14.

[19] Just as in passing off, where intention to deceive is not a necessary element of the tort, but may be most relevant if shown. See Ch.15

In *British Airways v Ryanair*[20] Jacob J. considered the issue again. He rejected the possibility of the defendant changing the alleged offending material as being too speculative. He also rejected the claimant's further arguments that damages can be recovered for malicious falsehood without proof of damage to reputation (because there no such proof is needed in relation to trade mark infringement either), and that s.10(6) of the 1994 Act is of doubtful status and effect (because there is no serious school of thought that it imposes a higher standard of liability than malicious falsehood). Jacob J. identified a further possible reason, not advanced by the claimant: that victory in a trade mark infringement claim does not sound as good as victory in a malicious falsehood claim.

18–029

There seems very little reason in most cases to plead malicious falsehood in addition to trade mark infringement, and given judicial pronouncements against the practice of doing so, it seems likely that claimants who advance both causes of action will suffer adverse consequences in costs.

2. Trade libel generally

ELEMENTS OF THE TORT

The essential elements of the tort are: (1) that the defendant has published about the claimant words which are false; (2) that they were published maliciously; and (3) that special damage has followed as the direct and natural result of their publication. A statement of the essential elements in a modern authority may be found in *Kaye v Robertson* [1991] F.S.R. 62 at 67, *per* Glidewell L.J.

18–030

The third requirement, special damage, was relaxed by the Defamation Act 1952: see below.

(a) Traders were restrained from advertising, or representing, or suggesting in their advertisements or circulars, that they or the proprietors of their testator's business, were alone possessed of the secret recipe for cattle food and from representing or suggesting, or doing anything calculated to represent or suggest, that the cattle food manufactured by the plaintiffs[21] was spurious or not genuine: *Thorley's v Massam (No.2)* (1880) L.R. 14 Ch.D. 763. Subsequently, the executors succeeded in a trade name and passing off action against the company.

18–031

(b) Circulars suggested that the goods of the plaintiff were not genuine, but were imitations of goods sold by the defendants; their publication was restrained: *Thomas v Williams (No.1)* (1880) L.R. 14 Ch. D. 864.

(c) The defendant had written that the plaintiffs were proposing to make use of a patented invention of the defendant which he had himself abandoned, leading to a construction that was "inadequate". It was held that this was actionable as a false and malicious statement: *London Ferro-Concrete v Justicz* (1951) 68 R.P.C. 65 at 261.

(d) The plaintiff's landlord, by maliciously asserting that he was no longer a tenant or available, got him struck off his suppliers' register: injunction granted: *Joyce v Motor Surveys* [1948] Ch. 252.

(e) The sale of old tinned milk manufactured by the plaintiffs as and for the plaintiffs' current stock was held to be passing off and a malicious false-

---

[20] [2001] F.S.R. 32 paras 9–14.

[21] Parties are referred to as the "plaintiff" herein in relation to cases which were decided before the introduction of the Civil Procedure Rules in 1999. In relation to cases taking place since then, and in relation to hypothetical examples, the expression "claimant" is used.

hood calculated to injure the plaintiffs' reputation: *Wilts United Dairies v Robinson* [1957] R.P.C. 220 and [1958] R.P.C. 94.

(f) An allegation in a medical publication that a dentist used an unsatisfactory technique was held capable of bearing a defamatory meaning and it was unnecessary to plead malice as the action was for libel: *Drummond-Jackson v British Medical Association* [1970] 1 W.L.R. 688.

PROOF OF DAMAGE

18–032 In an action for trade libel it used to be held that special damage was the gist of the action, though it was sufficient for grant of an injunction to prove likelihood of actual damage.[22]

If the injury is proved trifling and no threat to repeat the publication is proved, the action may be dismissed.[23]

The interruption of an illegal trade cannot be legal damage.[24]

DEFAMATION ACT 1952

18–033 The general rule as to proof of damage was modified by s.3(1) of the Defamation Act 1952 which provides:

"In an action for slander of title, slander of goods or other malicious falsehood, it shall not be necessary to allege or prove special damage—

(a) if the words upon which the action is founded are calculated to cause pecuniary damage to the plaintiff and are published in writing or other permanent form;[25] or

(b) if the said words are calculated to cause pecuniary damage to the plaintiff in respect of any office, profession, calling, trade or business held or carried on by him at the time of publication."

18–034 Although at first sight this provision is quite liberal and would seem to set only a low hurdle for claimants, in *Ferguson v Associated Newspapers*,[26] Gray J. held that, in the light of Article 10 of the European Convention on Human Rights, which requires any restriction on the freedom of expression to eb strictly justified as necessary in a democratic society, "calculated" should be interpreted as meaning "likely" or "probable" in an objective sense, rather than something which might well happen or was a possibility.

3. "Puffery" not actionable; rival traders

GENERAL

18–035 It is often said that "mere puffs" of the defendant's own goods, or statements that the defendant's goods are better than the claimant's, are not actionable, even if untrue and the cause of damage. In some authorities it is also remarked that such

---

[22] *Thomas v Williams (No.1)* (1880) L.R. 14 Ch.D. 864; *Reuter v Mulhens (No.2)* (1953) R.P.C. 102 at 116 (in the CA at 70 R.P.C. 235, the point was not argued).

[23] *Dicks v Brooks (No.2)* (1880) L.R. 15 Ch.D. 22.

[24] *Royal Baking Powder* (1900) 18 R.P.C. 95, *per* Lord Davey, Lord Robertson.

[25] Under the 1952 Act, s.5(2), the broadcasting of words is to be treated as being in permanent form.

[26] Unreported, December 3, 2001, followed in *IBM v Web-Sphere*, March 17, 2004 (Lewison J.), [2004] EWHC 529.

statements are not actionable even if the defendant knows them to be false.[27] It is not easy to reconcile all of these statements unless they are read carefully, and many of the broader ones were made obiter.

The two leading cases are *White v Mellin*,[28] and *Hubbuck v Wilkinson*.[29] A **18–036** clear and useful modern analysis of these and other cases is to be found in *De Beers Abrasive Products v International General Electric Co*[30] *White v Mellin* and *Hubbuck v Wilkinson* were both decided before the Defamation Act 1952, at a time when it was always a requirement to plead and prove special damage in order to succeed in a claim for malicious falsehood. This requirement is important to the reasoning in both decisions, and this must be borne in mind in reading them.

In *White v Mellin*, the defendant bought baby food from the plaintiff and sold it **18–037** on to the public. He attached to the packaging of the plaintiff's food a label which stated that the defendant's own brand of baby food, called "Dr Vance's", was "more nutritious and healthful than any other yet offered". The action failed on appeal to the House of Lords. Lord Herschell L.C. found that the label was sufficiently directed at the plaintiff by reason of being attached to his goods (at 158), and while he doubted whether the label had been shown falsely to disparage the plaintiff's goods, he went on to consider the position on the assumption that it had (at 159). On that basis, he considered that the action should fail because the label was a common kind of puff which the public would not seriously take to mean that the plaintiff's goods were not good, or were less good than anyone else's (at 160). While he also held that there was no malice, there being no evidence of intention to injure the defendant or of a lack of belief by the defendant that what he had said was true (at 161), the primary reason for his decision was the general nature of the statement. That appears from the following passages (at 164):

"I entertain very grave doubts whether any action could be maintained for an alleged disparagement of another's goods, merely on the allegation that the goods sold by the party who is alleged to have disparaged his competitor's goods are better either generally or in this or that particular respect than his competitors' are... . I am dealing with the class of cases which is now before us, where the only disparagement consists in vaunting the superiority of the defendant's own goods."

He rejected a suggestion that a claim that the defendant's goods were more **18–038** nutritious and healthful was not merely a matter of opinion but one of fact (at 165), and he held that there would be no cause of action whether the defendant claimed that his goods were better generally, or in one or more particular respects (also at 165).

Lords Watson and Shand both held that a statement that the defendant's goods are better than the plaintiff's is "a disparagement of which the law takes no cognizance" (at 167 and 171).

However, none of the speeches appears to have been on the basis that the truth **18–039** or falsity of the statement made was not capable of being determined. Lord Morris, for example, stated that "A party does not lay himself open to action who *bona fide* praises his goods as better than another's, and it cannot give a cause of

---

[27] See the reference to the speech of Lord Diplock in *Advocaat*, para.18–006, [1979] A.C. 731.
[28] [1894] 3 Ch. 276.
[29] [1899] 1 Q.B. 86.
[30] [1975] F.S.R. 323.

action because on the trial of those competing articles the defendant's article may be ascertained not to be better than the plaintiff's" (at 170). The decision seems primarily to be based on the assumption that the public do not see mere praise of one trader's goods as seriously denigrating those of the trader with whom the comparison is made, and on the policy ground that the courts should not try such disputes between rival traders.[31]

18–040   In *Hubbuck v Wilkinson*, the defendant published a circular which purported to give details of trials comparing the parties' respective zinc paints, the conclusion being that the defendant's had a slight advantage, but that for all practical purposes the paints were equal. The defendant's paint was much cheaper. The plaintiff alleged that the results reported in the circular were not true.

18–041   Following *White v Mellin* the Court of Appeal struck out the plaintiff's claim, on the basis that a statement that the defendant's product was as good as or better than the plaintiff's was not actionable, even if false, the cause of loss, and made maliciously (at 91).

18–042   In *De Beers*, the defendant had again published the purported results of a series of comparative tests on the parties' products, which in this case were diamond abrasives (the plaintiff's being natural and the defendant's synthetic). The results given were specific and quantitative, and gave the impression that the plaintiff's abrasives wore unacceptably quickly when used on granite (and the judge considered that that would imply a more general problem with cutting power—at 329).

18–043   The defendant applied unsuccessfully to strike out the claim. In the course of a detailed review of the cases, Walton J. identified two different kinds of extreme case: in the first, a defendant asserts that his goods are the best in the world. That is only a more dramatic way of saying that his goods are better than the claimant's, and is not actionable. In the second kind of case, the defendant asserts that his goods are better than the claimant's by reason of the claimant's goods being "rubbish" (at 329). That, he considered, would be actionable on the basis of the speech of Lord Shand in *White v Mellin*.

18–044   Walton J. went on to assess how to decide cases falling between those extremes. He considered two tests. The first was whether a reasonable man would consider the defendant's claim to be a serious one. The second was whether the defendant had pointed to a specific deficit in the claimant's goods (at 329). He preferred the first test because it would inherently cope with situations where the defendant's claim would not be taken seriously because, for example, it had been expressed in a light-hearted way. However, both tests were consistent with the authorities and would give the same result in the instant case.

18–045   *Hubbuck v Wilkinson*, despite its superficial similarities, was distinguished on the basis that a statement that the parties' products were equal was not likely to be taken seriously, and because there was no real disparagement of the plaintiff's paint. The statement by the defendant about the parties' abrasives was to be taken seriously because it was presented as a proper scientific test, and could be actionable if it contained disparaging statements (at 332).

18–046   It is suggested that three related points of principle can be discerned from these cases. They are (1) the statement complained of must specifically denigrate the claimant in order for it to be actionable; (2) the statement will not be actionable

---

[31] See para.18–010.

unless it is likely to be taken seriously; and (3) general praise of the defendant's goods is not actionable.

STATEMENT MUST SPECIFICALLY DENIGRATE THE CLAIMANT

This proposition follows from *White v Mellin* and *Hubbuck v Wilkinson*. It was recently confirmed in *Schulke & Mayr v Alkapharm*,[32] where the advertisement complained of contained statements about the defendant's goods which were alleged to be untrue, but did not refer to the plaintiff's or its goods at all. The claim was struck out.

18–047

It is also clear from those cases that the denigration must be specific; although a statement that the defendant's goods "are the best" implies that the claimant's are not as good, it does not denigrate them. It also offends the third principle, below.

18–048

STATEMENT MUST BE INTENDED TO BE TAKEN SERIOUSLY

This also follows from the nineteenth century cases, and was made more explicit in *De Beers*. Note that in none of those cases was any evidence led as to whether the statements were likely to be taken seriously; the court reached its own conclusions.

18–049

The matters which will determine whether a statement is likely to be taken seriously will include its level of generality (detailed data with specific conclusions as presented in *De Beers* is more likely to be taken seriously than wide statements about comparative quality of the kind found in *Hubbuck v Wilkinson*), and its tone. A humorous advertisement may well not be taken seriously: an example was given in *De Beers* of a maker of amphibious cars alleging that his goods were better than a Rolls Royce, because the latter would sink. It was also suggested in that case that a statement may be so vituperative that it would not be taken seriously (at 329).

18–050

This principle would appear to be obvious in any event from the basic elements of the tort, since a statement which is not likely to be taken seriously can rarely, if ever, be damaging or calculated to cause damage.

18–051

MERE GENERAL PRAISE OF THE DEFENDANT'S GOODS IS NOT ACTIONABLE

General praise of the defendant's goods will usually not be actionable for one of the two foregoing reasons in any event: it will not denigrate the claimant's goods, and is unlikely to be taken seriously. However, it is clear from the nineteenth century cases, in particular from *Hubbuck v Wilkinson* (at 91), that this is an independent principle. General praise is not actionable even if false, damaging and made maliciously.

18–052

SPECIFIC FALSE COMPARISONS WHICH DO NOT DENIGRATE THE CLAIMANT

The recent malicious falsehood cases concerned with comparative advertising[33] have mostly concerned price comparisons, in which the defendant has claimed to be cheaper by some specific percentage or amount of money per month. The claimant's allegations have been that the defendant's statement is false, or calculated on a wrong basis, or an inappropriate comparison.

18–053

---

[32] [1999] F.S.R. 161.
[33] See para.18–021 and the footnote therein.

18–054   It is open to question how these cases fit in with the general principles above, which require that the claimant's goods be specifically denigrated. It may be that a price comparison for specific goods asserts that the claimant is more expensive than the defendant, but unless there is an implicit statement that the claimant's goods are unjustifiably expensive, does that really denigrate him or his goods? If, as seems to be the case, it does not, can it be actionable?

18–055   This point was not argued in any of the recent cases referred to above or, it seems, in any of the authorities considered by Walton J. in *De Beers*. But it did fall to be considered in *DSG Retail v Comet Group plc*,[34] where the following statement from the previous edition of this work was approved:[35]

> "In principle, it seems that such statements ought to be actionable. They are by their nature intended and likely to be taken seriously, their prevention would not interfere with the defendant's ability to praise his own goods generally and in broad terms, they are directed specifically at the claimant, and they are intended and likely to draw business directly from the claimant to the defendant, to the claimant's detriment. It can perhaps be said that statements of this kind are so specifically aimed at the claimant, and are so directly in comparison with the defendant, that a slightly wider meaning of "denigrate" or "disparage" is appropriate."

4. Construing the statement, and falsity

GENERAL STANDARD, EVIDENCE

18–056   The meaning of the statements complained of is determined by the court itself, and (unless circumstances are proved tending to show that their actual meaning, in the particular case, is different from the natural meaning), evidence cannot be adduced to prove that they were not understood according to it.[36] Because the meaning is determined by the Court, in the right circumstances it can be decided on a summary basis or interim application. See for example *Douglas v Hello! (No.1)*,[37] where the Court of Appeal, on appeal from the grant of an interim injunction, held that "exclusive photographs" meant only that the defendant had exclusive rights over the specific photographs printed by it (which was true), and not that it had exclusive rights over the event photographed (which was not).

18–057   The court will take a practical approach in its reading of the statements complained of, with regard to the fact that the public expect a degree of hyperbole in advertising. In *De Beers Abrasive Products v International General Electric Co*,[38] Walton J. said (at 328): "in the kind of situation where one expects, as a matter of ordinary common experience, a person to use a certain amount of hyperbole in the description of goods, property or services, the courts will do what any reasonable man would do, namely, take it with a large pinch of salt."

---

[34] [2002] F.S.R. 58.
[35] At paras 17–20. See also the reference in para.17 to *Jupiter Unit Trust Managers v Johnson Fry Asset Managers plc*, unreported, Morland J., April 19, 2000.
[36] *Royal Baking Powder* (1900) 18 R.P.C. 95 at 101, HL. In *McDonald's v Burgerking* [1986] F.S.R. 45, the judge appears to have had regard to evidence from members of the public as to how they had in fact understood the advertisement concerned, but there was also a claim for passing off, to which that evidence was primarily directed. It is suggested that normally in a trade libel case, the general rule is that evidence about the meaning of the statements in issue is not admissible. This is related to the "one meaning" rule, as to which see below.
[37] [2001] F.S.R. 40.
[38] [1975] F.S.R. 323.

See also *McDonald's Hamburgers v Burgerking*:[39] "Advertisements of this kind are not to be read as if they were some testamentary provision in a will or a clause in some agreement with every word being carefully considered and the words as a whole being compared."

The onus is on the claimant to prove falsity, since it is an essential element of the tort.

"ONE MEANING" RULE

In defamation, there is a rule that a statement which is alleged to be defamatory has only one true meaning,[40] and that is so even if in fact some members of the public would understand it to mean one thing and others another. A claimant cannot succeed by showing that a reasonable proportion of the public would understand the statement in a defamatory sense. This is a principle of long standing, with its origins and rationale probably lying in the fact that defamation actions are usually tried with juries. It was recently confirmed in *Charleston v News Group Newspapers*.[41]
          18–058

It appears that the same rule applies to malicious falsehood, although some doubts have been expressed about whether that is so. In *Vodafone v Orange* [1997] F.S.R. 34, Jacob J. accepted on the authority of *Charleston* that the "one meaning" rule applied to malicious falsehood, the contrary not having been argued. He pointed out, though, that the jury-trial basis for the rule in defamation might not apply to the same extent in malicious falsehood. First, because there is no general right of jury trial in the latter case, and second, because a single meaning needs to be determined in defamation actions so as to assess quantum for damage to the claimant's reputation. In malicious falsehood, by contrast, damages are awarded to compensate for pecuniary loss. So long as the words complained of caused the loss in question, it may be that their precise meaning does not matter.
          18–059

In addition, the "one meaning" rule for malicious falsehood appears strange when, as frequently happens, it falls to be applied in the same action as passing off or infringement under s.10(6) of the 1994 Act. In the latter two torts, it is sufficient if a proportion of the public would be misled by the statement concerned.[42] It seems odd that a claimant may succeed in those causes of action but fail, on the same facts, in a claim for malicious falsehood (assuming malice and likelihood of damage can be shown). That would happen if the statement concerned would be likely to be, and has been, understood by a significant number of persons in a false and damaging sense, but not in its "one meaning". It is hard to see why, in justice, a claimant should fail in a claim for malicious falsehood in such a situation.
          18–060

"LOOKALIKES"

It has been held that publication of a photograph, which is not of the claimant but which bears such a strong resemblance that it would be taken by readers to be the
          18–061

---

[39] [1986] F.S.R. 45 at 58.

[40] Leaving aside cases where by reason of circumstances extrinsic to the statement, a legal innuendo is alleged.

[41] [1995] 2 All E.R. 313.

[42] See Chs 14 and 15. The proportion of the public which need be misled for an action in passing off to succeed may simply be more than *de minimis*.

claimant, and which is in such a setting as to convey a derogatory message about the claimant, would have been actionable in defamation prior to the European Convention on Human Rights, but is no longer.[43] The defendant published pictures of a model looking very much like the claimant in advertisements for pornographic Internet services. Morland J held that under the strict rules applicable to defamation, the publication would be actionable if it gave the impression that the claimant was willingly engaged in such activities, but that such liability would be inconsistent with Article 10 of the Convention because it would impose an impossible burden on any publisher of photographs, which are themselves essential to reporting.

It is, however, unlikely that this exemption from liability would be extended to malicious falsehood, since it would not impose an undue or impossible burden on a publisher to refrain from publications known to be false.

5. Malice

MEANING

18–062   The definitions of malice given in the authorities are complex and somewhat unsatisfactory. For example, in *Balden v Shorter*,[44] Maugham J. approved the following statement:

> "… it is now apparently settled that malice in the law of slander of title and other forms of injurious falsehood means some dishonest or otherwise improper motive. A bona fide assertion of title, however mistaken, if made for the protection of one's own interest or for some other proper purpose, is not malicious."

18–063   Thus an allegation of malice is one of dishonesty or at least improper motive, and is akin to an allegation of fraud.[45]

18–064   In the same case, Maugham J. also said that malice "in the sense of a wrongful intention to injure the plaintiffs" was required. This is, or may be, a somewhat different requirement. Sometimes, an intention to injure "without just cause" is stated to be a requirement of the tort, and again, this is not, on the face of it, quite the same as "improper motive".

18–065   Despite these apparent inconsistencies, certain key principles are clear enough. First of all, malice involves a subjective state of mind on the part of the defendant. Even if the defendant had no positive justification for making the statement complained of, it is still necessary to show that he had the necessary mental element of ill-will, intention to injure or the like. Secondly, the reason for the defendant's statement is relevant. If he was seeking to defend his own lawful interest, then the fact that he knew that the claimant would be damaged does not constitute malice. In this connection, it is recognised that a trader's desire to promote his business at the expense of his rivals is a proper one: see *White v Mel-*

---

[43] *O'Shea v MGN Ltd*, [2001] E.M.L.R. 40.

[44] [1933] Ch. 427 at 430, referring to the 7th ed. of *Salmond on Torts*. Followed in *Loudon v Ryder (No.2)* [1953] Ch. 423, in *London Ferro-Concrete v Justicz* (1951) 68 R.P.C. 65 at 261 and in *Eothen Films v Industrial and Commercial Education* [1966] F.S.R. 356, CA. That good faith excludes malice was confirmed by the House of Lords in *Spring v Guardian Assurance* [1994] 3 W.L.R. 354, *e.g.* at 379, *per* Lord Slynn.

[45] See para.18–007.

lin and *Hubbuck v Wilkinson*.[46] Thirdly, knowledge of the falsity of the statement made amounts to malice.

It was held by the Court of Appeal in *Spring v Guardian Assurance*[47] that the meaning of malice is the same in this tort as in defamation, so authorities from that field may be considered for assistance.

18–066

KNOWLEDGE OF FALSITY OR RECKLESSNESS

Since the promotion of one trader at the expense of his rivals is regarded as a proper objective for the purposes of this tort, the most important kind of malice in the context of this work is knowledge on the part of the defendant that the statement he has made is false (or recklessness as to its truth).[48]

18–067

Knowledge of falsity amounts to malice without any more having to be proven. Such a state of mind obviously excludes any suggestion of *bona fides* on the part of the defendant.

"Recklessness" in this context is a subjective concept. It means that the defendant made the false statement without considering or caring whether or not it was true.[49] It is not the same as carelessness.[50] Recklessness is excluded by a belief on the part of the defendant that the statement was true, even if that belief was irrational.[51]

18–068

What if the defendant did not believe himself to be making the statement alleged by the claimant (or did not turn his mind to it), but a different statement, which he believed to be true? In principle, it would seem that such a state of mind does not amount to malice. There is some support for this view in *McDonald's v Burgerking* [1986] F.S.R. 45 at 60. It was alleged that the advertisement complained of had falsely stated (by implication, rather than expressly) that McDonald's Big Macs were not 100 per cent pure beef. The judge rejected McDonald's case on malice on the basis that the relevant employees of Burgerking never intended to suggest that McDonald's products were not 100 per cent beef.

18–069

GENUINE BUT IRRATIONAL BELIEF IN TRUTH

A genuine belief in the truth of the statement made negates malice, in the absence of some other improper motive.[52]

18–070

EFFECT OF NOTICE OF FALSITY

It not infrequently happens that although the claimant has difficulty in proving that the defendant acted with malice in making the initial publication, events during the proceedings themselves make it clear that the statement was false. In

18–071

---

[46] [1895] A.C. 154 at 160–161; [1899] 1 Q.B. 86 at 94.

[47] [1993] 2 All E.R. 273. Note that the Court of Appeal's decision was overturned by the House of Lords (see note above), although not on this point.

[48] It was confirmed that this state of mind amounts to malice in *Kaye v Robertson* [1991] F.S.R. 62 at 67. Glidewell L.J. also stated that for malice to be shown it was necessary that the words concerned were calculated to cause damage. It is suggested that this simply meant that the words must be likely to damage the plaintiff, thereby preventing the making of false but apparently innocuous statements from being malicious. It does not add the requirement of intention to injure. In practical terms it will rarely make any difference, since either special damage or words calculated to cause pecuniary damage are requirements of the tort in any event.

[49] See *Horrocks v Lowe* [1975] A.C. 135, *per* Lord Diplock.

[50] *Balden v Shorter* [1933] Ch. 427 and *Loudon v Ryder (No.2)*.

[51] See *Horrocks v Lowe* [1975] A.C. 135.

[52] See *Horrocks v Lowe* [1975] A.C. 135.

those circumstances, the claimant may be able to obtain relief despite his difficulties in showing that the initial publication was tortious, particularly if the defendant evinces an intention to repeat the statement.

18–072   For example, in *Kaye v Robertson*,[53] the statement complained of was to the effect that the plaintiff had consented to an interview following a car accident in which he suffered head injuries. In fact, he had not consented, and the question arose of whether the defendant had known of his lack of consent. The Court of Appeal held on the evidence that the defendant's staff realised that the plaintiff was unable to consent from his condition during the interview. It also said that even if that had not been so, the affidavit sworn on the claimant's behalf would have put the defendant on notice of the statement's falsity so that "any subsequent publication of the falsehood would inevitably be malicious". An interim injunction was granted.

IMPROPER PURPOSE

18–073   As is pointed out above, in the world of commerce it will be rare that malice consists purely in making a statement with an improper purpose. The maker of the statement will usually be seeking to promote his own sales, which is not improper. However, it is not at all impossible.

IMPROPER PURPOSES INCLUDE SHEER SPITE, REVENGE AND THE LIKE.

Delay in suing not evidence of malice

18–074   Upon an application for an interim injunction to restrain the publication of threats[54] by the defendant, it is not sufficient proof, if it is any evidence at all, of want of good faith, to show that he has commenced an action for infringement of trade mark, or for passing off goods against the claimant, but has neglected to apply in it for an interim injunction;[55] nor to show even a long delay in bringing an action for infringement, if the delay is properly explained.[56]

LIBEL ON INVENTOR

18–075   In an action brought for falsely and maliciously publishing passages in a book depriving the plaintiff of the credit for being the first inventor of a machine, the statement of claim was struck out on the ground that the passages complained of were not libellous. But Vaughan Williams L.J. said that he must not be supposed in any way to be affirming such a proposition as that you cannot libel anyone by denying his title to a reputation which he may have obtained as an inventor or as a man of science: *Wilde v Thompson*.[57]

---

[53] [1991] F.S.R. 62 at 68. See also *Loudon v Ryder (No.2)* [1953] Ch. 423, where malice was not proven but declaratory relief was granted; and by way of contrast, *Reuter v Mulhens (No.2)* (1953) 70 R.P.C. 102 at 235, CA, where a declaration was refused.

[54] In respect of threats of trade mark infringement proceedings, there is now a statutory right of action which does not depend on absence of good faith (as to which, see below) but for some other kinds of threats the action for malicious falsehood is still appropriate.

[55] *Anderson v Liebig's* (1881) 45 L.T. (N.S.) 757.

[56] *Incandescent Gas Light v Sunlight* (1897) 14 R.P.C. 180.

[57] (1903) 20 R.P.C. 361 at 775.

6. Proceedings

SOLICITOR OR OTHER AGENT

There is old authority to the effect that a solicitor who has made a publication **18–076**
merely as agent for the real defendants should not normally be joined as a
defendant.[58] Frequently in such instances it will be hard to prove or even plead
that the solicitor acted with malice in the initial publication, since in most cases
he will have acted *bona fide* in accordance with his instructions. There is plainly
no rule of law that a solicitor in such situations may not be sued though, and there
are a number of instances where they have been.[59] In particular, it may be necessary or desirable to sue the solicitors to the "real" defendants if the latter would
not be able to pay any damages which might be awarded.

PUBLICATION OF AN APOLOGY

The publication of an apology actually made by the plaintiffs to the defendants is **18–077**
justifiable, though it may have been extracted from the plaintiffs under duress of
civil or criminal proceedings in respect of the false marking of their goods.[60]

NO INTERIM INJUNCTION WHERE JUSTIFICATION ARGUABLE

It has long been the position in the law of defamation that an interim injunction **18–078**
will not be granted to restrain the publication of an alleged defamatory statement
if the defendant states an intention to justify the statement, and the statement is
such that a reasonable jury could find it to be true.[61]

This rule also applies to claims for malicious falsehood by virtue of the deci- **18–079**
sion of the Court of Appeal in *Bestobell Paints v Bigg*,[62] and is an exception to
the principles of *American Cyanamid*.[63]

The modern rationale for the rule is the protection of freedom of speech[64], al- **18–080**
though historically its origins were connected with the respective functions of the
judge and jury in defamation actions.

INTERIM INJUNCTION IN OTHER CASES

Although the general rule in *Bestobell Paints v Bigg* will usually prevent a suc- **18–081**
cessful application for an interim injunction to restrain an alleged malicious
falsehood, there are exceptions.

First, an interim injunction may be granted (and provided that there is a likeli-

---

[58] *Incandescent v Sunlight* (1897) 14 R.P.C. 180 at 186, 190.
[59] See *Mentmore v Fomento* (1955) 72 R.P.C. 157, where the solicitor was made a party and an
undertaking given on his behalf; *CHC v Hopkins & Wood* [1993] F.S.R. 241 (the action
subsequently failed); and *Brain v Ingledew Brown Bennison & Garrett (No.1)* [1996] F.S.R. 341
(this was a threats case under the Patents Act 1977. Threats of trade mark proceedings are dealt
with in more detail below, but note that that tort does not have a mental element, and therefore
does not present the difficulty of proving malice on the part of a professional adviser).
[60] *Fisher v Apollinaris* (1874–755) L.R. 10 Ch. App. 297.
[61] *Bonnard v Perryman* [1891] 2 Ch. 269.
[62] [1975] F.S.R. 421.
[63] *Herbage v Times Newspapers, The Times*, May 1, 1981.
[64] See, *e.g. Microdata v Rivendale* [1991] F.S.R. 681.

hood of damage, presumably usually will be) where the statement is so unarguably false that only an unreasonable jury could accept it as true.[65]

18–082   Secondly, an interim injunction may be granted where the dispute between the parties is over the meaning of the statement in question, it being clear that the statement is false if it bears the meaning for which the claimant contends. For example, in *Compaq v Dell*,[66] the defendant had published a number of advertisements comparing the parties' prices for various personal computers. The plaintiff's computers shown in the advertisements differed materially from the defendant's (the judge holding that no reasonable jury could find otherwise), but the plaintiff alleged that the advertisement suggested that they were essentially the same. The defendant denied that such a suggestion was made. In those circumstances, Aldous J held that the principles from *American Cyanamid* should be applied, but that potential interference with the defendant's freedom of speech was a relevant factor to take into account in assessing the balance of convenience. On that basis, he granted an interim injunction.

18–083   Thirdly, there are circumstances where an interim injunction may be granted when a cause of action other than malicious falsehood is relied on, even though malicious falsehood is or could be pleaded as well. This principle has been considered in a number of cases, and the resulting position is not clear or satisfactory.

18–084   In *Microdata v Rivendale*,[67] the defendant had alleged that the plaintiff had no right to deal in certain computer software which it was seeking to sell to its customers. The plaintiff framed its case in interference with contractual relations rather than malicious falsehood, and the Court of Appeal held that in those circumstances the Bestobell rule did not apply, and "ought not to be applied any further than is necessary to preserve the fundamental right of free speech".[68] It is notable that the facts of the case reeked of bad faith on the part of the defendant, and this may well have had an effect on the result.

18–085   A similar situation arose in *Western Front v Vestron*[69] (although the defendant's conduct was not so obviously blameworthy). Counsel for the defendant sought to criticise the reasoning of the court in *Microdata v Rivendale*, but the judge held himself to be bound by it, despite considerable reservations and with the hope that it would be reconsidered. The same happened in *Consorzio del Prosciutto di Parma v Marks & Spencer*,[70] a passing off case, where Morritt J. held that *American Cyanamid* should be applied, but with the importance of freedom of speech being considered as part of the balance of convenience.

18–086   The whole line of authority was considered by Ferris J. in *Essex Electric v IPC Computers*.[71] There, the plaintiff sued for malicious falsehood and interference with contractual relations. While it accepted that the *Bestobell* rule applied to the former claim, it relied on *Microdata v Rivendale* to seek an interim injunction in respect of the latter, and it succeeded. Ferris J. took the same course as Morritt J. had.

---

[65] *Kaye v Robertson* [1991] F.S.R. 62.
[66] [1992] F.S.R. 93.
[67] [1991] F.S.R. 681.
[68] *per* May L.J. at 686.
[69] [1987] F.S.R. 66.
[70] [1990] F.S.R. 530.
[71] [1991] F.S.R. 690.

An interim injunction was also granted in *Gulf Oil v Page*[72] where, in an action for libel, conspiracy was also pleaded.

The state of affairs arrived at in this line of cases is, it is suggested, unsatisfactory and rather arbitrary. If the reason for the *Bestobell Paints v Bigg* rule is a policy decision that restraining arguably truthful statements prior to trial is unacceptable because of its impact on freedom of speech, then one would not expect its scope to be limited to a particular cause of action. There is no persuasive reason in the cases why interference with contractual relations, say, should be treated any differently from malicious falsehood. The reason given in *Microdata v Rivendale*, that a different interest may be protected by the former tort,[73] is not convincing, it is suggested. In each case the commercial interest protected is the ability of the claimant to do business with his customers, without interference by damaging statements from the defendant, and that is so regardless of the cause of action pleaded. It having been decided that that interest should yield to the defendant's interest in being able to exercise free speech (at least until trial and provided that the statement is at least arguably true), that decision ought in principle to apply whatever the cause of action. Moreover, the addition of a cause of action other than malicious falsehood may be either specifically designed to obtain an interim injunction by avoiding the *Bestobell Paints v Bigg* rule (as may have been the case in *Essex Electric v IPC*, where the real gist of the complaint was the defendant's statements and not the plaintiff's specific contracts with its customers), or available only fortuitously (in *Gulf Oil v Page* an interim injunction based on a claim in conspiracy was granted since the defendant had assistance in publishing the statement. Presumably if he had acted alone then the only claim would have been for defamation or malicious falsehood and no interim injunction would have been available. This is not a rational distinction.) **18–087**

In addition, there are other authorities which go the other way, and so suggest that the rule against interim injunctions where the statement is capable of justification applies more broadly than where the only claim is for malicious falsehood. See, for example, *Sim v H.J. Heinz* [1959] R.P.C. 75, CA and *Lord Brabourne v Hough* [1981] F.S.R. 79. In the latter case, the defendant intended to publish a biography of Lord Louis Mountbatten and to claim that it was authorised. The plaintiff alleged that it was not, and sued in passing off (and for interference with contractual relations, but not for defamation or malicious falsehood). An interim injunction was refused by analogy to the rule in defamation and malicious falsehood. In the former case, the well-known actor Alastair Sim complained that his voice had been imitated by an actor. He sued for libel, malicious falsehood and passing off, but an interim injunction was refused by reference to the rule applicable in libel cases. **18–088**

It is suggested that a proper analysis of all these cases is assisted by bearing in mind once again the analysis behind the decision in *Compaq v Dell*. Where there is no doubt that the statement complained of has been made, but the issue is whether it is true or false, then in principle the rule in *Bestobell Paints v Bigg* ought to apply regardless of the precise cause of action. Where the statement complained of is not express and is said to have been made by implication or innuendo or get-up (as in *Compaq v Dell* itself, and in most passing off cases, **18–089**

---

[72] [1987] Ch. 327.
[73] As is suggested in the section of the judgement of Griffiths L.J. quoted in *Essex Electric* at 702, and also in the judgment of May L.J. quoted there.

certainly including the *Parma Ham* case), but it is plainly false if it has been made, then *American Cyanamid* ought to be applied, with the issue of free speech falling to be considered as an element of the balance of convenience, unless it is possible also to decide on a summary basis whether the statement has been made.[74] On this basis, *Lord Brabourne v Hough* was rightly decided (since, unusually for a passing off case, it was clear that the statement was made but not whether it was true), but *Sim v H.J. Heinz* may be regarded as a doubtful application of the *Bestobell Paints v Bigg* rule, since if the advertisement did in fact suggest that Alastair Sim had done the voiceover, it was unarguably false (the result might still have been the same, of course).

ACTION SURVIVES TO EXECUTORS

18–090 Because the cause of action in malicious falsehood protects financial interests, rather than the claimant's reputation, a claim survives the death of the claimant.[75]

LIMITATION

18–091 The limitation period in relation to trade libel is one year, by virtue of s.4A of the Limitation Act 1980, as amended by s.5(2) of the Defamation Act 1996.

RELIEF AND REFUSAL OF RELIEF

18–092 The relief available to a successful claimant in malicious falsehood is damages (or an inquiry as to damages) and an injunction to restrain repetition of the statement concerned. The injunction ought only to restrain the repetition of the statement complained of or an equivalent statement, *i.e.* statements which have been found to be false.

18–093 Relief (and particularly costs) may be refused where one or both parties are conducting the proceedings for the purposes of publicity rather than in pursuit of genuine grievances: *Emaco v Dyson Appliances*.[76]

DISCLOSURE OF ADDRESSEES OF FALSEHOODS

18–094 The court has power in an appropriate case to order, before trial, disclosure of the names and addresses of those persons to whom allegedly malicious false statements have been made, so that the claimant can seek to mitigate its loss by disabusing them of any false impression: *CHC Software v Hopkins & Wood* [1993] F.S.R. 241.

7. Misleading reports of proceedings

MAY BE MALICIOUS FALSEHOOD

18–095 A false statement about proceedings may be a malicious falsehood provided that it satisfies the usual elements of the tort. So, for example, falsely to state that a person is a party to an action when he in fact is not, or to state that proceedings have been brought to a successful conclusion when they have not, would plainly be actionable (given malice and likelihood of damage). However, to state cor-

---

[74] As was done in *Douglas v Hello!* [2001] F.S.R. 40.
[75] *Hatchard v Mege* (1887) 18 Q.B.D. 771, Law Reform Act (Miscellaneous Provisions)1934, s.1(1).
[76] [1999] E.T.M.R. 903.

rectly that proceedings are underway, if true, is not actionable, and nor, probably, is it capable of being a malicious falsehood to state that a party is confident, or even very confident, about the outcome of proceedings.[77] Such statements are unlikely to be taken seriously in any event.

MAY BE CONTEMPT ALSO

Statements about pending proceedings may also amount to a contempt of court, if **18–096** they are likely to prejudice the conduct or fair trial of the proceedings, and this may be so even if the statements are true. Again, however, confident statements about the likely outcome will usually not be wrongful; they are unlikely to affect the outcome, especially since most civil cases are not now heard by juries, and this kind of statement is not likely to affect potential witnesses.[78]

Contempt of court generally is outside the scope of this work; the reader should refer to specialist works.

8. Threats

BACKGROUND TO THE PROVISIONS

It has been recognised for many years, in the context of patents that threats of **18–097** proceedings may be extremely pernicious. Some of the reasons for this are considered above.[79] As a result, a statutory action for threats of patent infringement was introduced. It is now enacted by s.70 of the Patents Act 1977. There are parallel provisions in respect of registered and unregistered designs: s.26 of the Registered Designs Act 1949 and s.253 of the Copyright, Designs and Patents Act 1988.

The 1994 Act has for the first time introduced a provision making threats of trade mark infringement proceedings actionable. The relevant provision is s.21.

ANALOGY TO PROVISIONS ABOUT THREATS UNDER THE PATENTS ACT

Section 21 of the 1994 Act was not introduced to give effect to any provision of **18–098** the Trade Marks Directive. It is a domestic provision passed in order to extend the threats action available in relation to patent infringement to the field of trade marks, as its close similarity to s.70 of the Patents Act 1977 makes clear. It therefore is to be construed in that context rather than in the context of the Directive. The approach of construing s.21 by reference to s.70 of the Patents Act 1977 was followed in *Prince plc v Prince Sports Group Inc*[80] Although there are differences in wording between the sections, in most cases it may be expected that the authorities in relation to s.70 will be applied to s.21.

MAY BE MALICIOUS FALSEHOOD

In principle, an allegation that the goods of one trader infringe the registered **18–099** trade mark of another may be a malicious falsehood. However, proving malice and falsity, particularly at an interim stage, will be difficult. If the person making

---

[77] See *Goulard v Lindsay* (1887) 4 R.P.C. 189.

[78] See, *e.g. Carl Zeiss Stiftung v Rayner & Keeler* [1961] R.P.C. 1; *Easipower v Gordon Moore* [1963] R.P.C. 8.

[79] See paras 18–017 to 18–019.

[80] [1998] F.S.R. 21.

the threat has a *bona fide* belief in its truth, then a claim for malicious falsehood should fail. It is therefore hard to think of any reason to bring an action for malicious falsehood if a claim under the 1994 Act is available.

THE ACTION FOR THREATS

18–100   Section 21 provides:

(1) Where a person threatens another with proceedings for infringement other than—

(a) the application of the mark to goods or their packaging,

(b) the importation of goods to which, or to the packaging of which, the mark has been applied, or

(c) the supply of services under the mark,

any person aggrieved may bring proceedings for relief under this section.

(2) The relief which may be applied for is any of the following—

(a) a declaration that the threats are unjustifiable,

(b) an injunction against the continuance of the threats,

(c) damages in respect of any loss he has sustained by reason of the threats;

and the plaintiff is entitled to such relief unless the defendant shows that the acts in respect of which proceedings were threatened constitute (or if done would constitute) an infringement of the registered trade mark concerned.

(3) If that is shown by the defendant, the plaintiff is nevertheless entitled to relief if he shows that the registration of the trade mark is invalid or liable to be revoked in a relevant respect.

(4) The mere notification that a trade mark is registered, or that an application for a trade mark has been made, does not constitute a threat of proceedings for the purposes of this section.

18–101   Hence, the pattern of the section is as follows (the individual issues are considered in more detail below).

18–102   First, the claimant must show that a threat has been made, which threat is not in relation to one of the matters listed in subs.(1)(a)–(c). The matters excepted by subs.(1)(a)–(c) may be referred to as "primary" infringements. So, broadly speaking, the claimant has to prove that the threat was made in respect of secondary infringement, which generally means dealing in infringing goods other than by importation or manufacture.

18–103   Secondly, the claimant must show that he is a "person aggrieved".

If the claimant proves those matters, then he is entitled to succeed unless the defendant, the person who has made the threat, proves that there has in fact been an infringement (or, that there would be an infringement if the claimant carries out the acts in question in future).

18–104   If the person making the threat proves that there has been or would be an infringement, then the claimant may yet succeed if he proves that the registration concerned is invalid or liable to be revoked "in a relevant respect".[81]

18–105   The section thus makes it clear that the claimant bears the onus of proving that

---

[81] Presumably, this means that the claimant will succeed if the threat is at least in part in relation to goods or services for which the registration is invalid, rather than only if the threat is wholly in relation to goods or services for which it is invalid. In other words, the claimant is entitled to succeed if, by reason of the partial validity of the registration, the threat is partly, but not entirely, justifiable. This is consistent with the words used ("a relevant respect", rather than "all relevant respects"), and with the policy of the section.

there has been a threat, that he is aggrieved, and, if infringement is proven, that the registration concerned is invalid. The person making the threat bears the onus of proving infringement.

Note that there is no requirement in the section that the person aggrieved must be the same as the person against whom it is threatened that proceedings will be brought. They may be different persons, and in fact the most important cases where threats proceedings are brought are instances where they are different persons, as where a trader sues in relation to threats made to his customers or his suppliers. **18–106**

WHAT THREATS ARE ACTIONABLE-PRIMARY INFRINGERS, SERVICES

Under s.70(4) of the Patents Act 1977, threats in relation to importation and manufacture are exempted from being actionable. Section 21 of the 1994 Act is in similar terms, although primary acts of infringement are excluded from the definition of the tort itself rather than being the subject of a separate exception as in s.70(4). **18–107**

The rationale for the distinction is to strike a balance between the legitimate interest of the patentee or trade mark owner in warning infringers, and the right of others not to be vexed by threats without actually being sued. A direct warning to the source (in the United Kingdom) of infringing goods is therefore allowed, but threats to his customers may be actionable, because of the danger that they will stop patronising him whether or not the allegation of infringement is a good one. **18–108**

However, s.70 of the Patents Act 1977 has caused some difficulties, because the exception from actionability is expressed by reference to the alleged infringing act, and not by reference to the person threatened. Hence, if a manufacturer is threatened in relation to his subsequent dealings in the products which he has made (secondary infringements) as well as in relation to the manufacture itself (primary infringement), then s.70(4) will not apply, and the threat is actionable.[82] It seems likely that the same result would be achieved in relation to s.21 of the 1994 Act.[83] Although this position is in keeping with the words of both Acts, it gives rise to a curious result, because a threat to a manufacturer which relates exclusively to manufacture is not actionable (even though the manufacturer will almost certainly infer that he would also be sued in respect of sale of the same product), while a threat which mentions sale of the same goods, which would be understood to have exactly the same impact, is. **18–109**

The upshot is that a primary infringer may be threatened with impunity, provided that the threat is carefully expressed to relate to primary infringement alone. Accordingly, letters of threat need to be drafted with great care. Logically, it could follow that a threat expressed to be purely in relation to primary infringement but which is sent to a person who only carries on activities capable of being secondary infringements would not be actionable. However, such a threat might well be construed to be an implicit threat in relation to secondary infringement as well, especially if its sender was aware that the recipient did not carry on acts **18–110**

---

[82] See *Cavity Trays v RMC Panel Products* [1996] R.P.C. 361; *Therm-A-Stor v Weatherseal Windows* [1981] F.S.R. 579; *Johnson Electric v Mabuchi Motor* [1986] F.S.R. 280 at 288; and *Bowden v Acco* [1990] R.P.C. 427.

[83] Such was accepted by the judge in *Prince plc v Prince Sports Group Inc* [1998] F.S.R. 21 at 33, although the contrary was not argued.

capable of being a primary infringement, and/or if the expression of the letter appeared to be a device to avoid the statutory threats provisions.[84]

18–111   Section 21 recognises a category of primary infringer which is not relevant under the Patents Act 1977, namely suppliers of services. By their nature, of course, services cannot be passed down a chain of supply, and customers in receipt of services will not usually infringe a trade mark under which those services are supplied. The result is that threats in relation to services do not present the same danger of damage as threats in relation to goods, and accordingly they are excluded from the ambit of s.21.

18–112   In *Prince plc v Prince Sports Groups Inc*,[85] the plaintiff only provided services, having, on the evidence before the court, no trade in goods. The threat complained of merely asserted the defendant's various trade marks, without stating whether it was intended to sue the plaintiff in relation to goods or services. Because the plaintiff only supplied services, the defendant argued that the threat should be construed as extending only to services, and hence outside s.21. Neuberger J. held[86] that because s.21 is concerned to prevent threats being made casually or recklessly, it is incumbent on a person who wishes to take advantage of one of the excepting paragraphs of subs.(1) to indicate so in terms. It is suggested, however, that there is nothing in the words of s.21 to require such a person to express his reliance on any of the exceptions in terms, and in *Brain v Ingledew Brown Bennison & Garrett*,[87] the Court of Appeal rejected the argument that a general threat should usually be regarded as a threat in respect of all potentially infringing acts. Rather, it is a question of construction in the particular circumstances which prevail. Aldous L.J. said (at 352):

> "Even if it be assumed that the letter contained a threat in general terms it does not follow that the recipient would read it as making a threat of proceedings in respect of all potentially infringing acts. A letter such as [the one in question], when written to a person who only operated a process, could be understood as being a threat of infringement by carrying out the process; whereas a letter written in general terms to a person who not only carried out the process but sold the products of that process, could be understood in a different way."

THREATS IN RELATION TO APPLICATIONS FOR A TRADE MARK

18–113   Under s.70 of the Patents Act 1977, it is actionable to make a threat of infringement in relation to an application for a patent which has not been granted: *Brain v Ingledew Brown Bennison & Garrett (No.1)*.[88] The decision in that case depended on the construction of s.69 of the Patents Act 1977 (giving various rights in relation to applications for patents which can be asserted retrospectively once the patent is granted). That section has no exact parallel in the 1994 Act, but it seems likely that the same result would be achieved, and a threat made in relation to an

---

[84] See, *e.g. L'Oréal v Johnson & Johnson* [2000] F.S.R. 686, where the judge held that a letter which expressly asserted that the trade mark owner had not decided whether to sue was an implicit threat. Important factors included the deliberate obscurity of the letter and the fact that proceedings in Ireland were already on foot and were referred to in the letter.
[85] [1998] F.S.R. 21.
[86] At 33.
[87] [1996] F.S.R. 341.
[88] [1996] F.S.R. 341.

application for a trade mark is actionable.[89] In any event, such a threat will normally be understood to be a threat to bring proceedings once registration is achieved, and will therefore be actionable on that basis.[90]

In addition, s.21(4) of the 1994 Act, which exempts from actionability a mere **18–114** notification of a registration, also exempts notification that an application has been made, and such a provision would not have been necessary unless it were contemplated that a threat in relation to an application could be actionable.

The fact that a threat may be made in relation to an ungranted application may **18–115** cause difficulties if the application remains ungranted by the time of trial. In *Brain v Ingledew Brown Bennison & Garrett (No.2)*,[91] Laddie J. held that the court would not allow a trial on hypothetical patent claims which might not be granted, but rather that a person making threats in respect of an application for a patent took the risk that it would not be granted by trial, and he struck out the defence of justification. The same reasoning would presumably apply in relation to the 1994 Act. Although it is probably less common for the specification of goods for a trade mark to change during prosecution than for the claims of a patent to be amended, there obviously remains the possibility that a trade mark application will not be granted at all.

Person Aggrieved

The requirement that the claimant be a person aggrieved by the threat in question **18–116** is not a difficult one to satisfy. Save perhaps in very exceptional circumstances, the person threatened is always aggrieved, and so is anyone else who can show that his commercial interests are or are likely to be adversely affected in a real as opposed to a fanciful or minimal way.[92] Clearly, a person whose customers or suppliers are threatened will be a person aggrieved, and that is so even if he manages to assuage their fears so that no recoverable loss is suffered.[93]

A person involved in the management of a company may be a person aggrieved **18–117** if he has sufficient personal interest in the effect of the threats, for example if the company threatened is simply a vehicle for the commercial interests of the principal shareholder and executive.[94]

Construing the alleged threat

Construing an alleged threat is a practical matter, to be decided on the basis of the **18–118** effect it would have on an ordinary reader, and should not be an exercise in unrealistic forensic analysis.[95] It is a jury-type question to be decided against the appropriate matrix of fact. A letter which is innocuous on its face may be a threat when placed in context (and the reverse is possible, though less likely).[96] For

---

[89] Since it is recognised that an actionable threat can be made by someone who has no patent at all, this result is obviously right: see *Brain* at 347, approving a statement by the judge at first instance to that effect.

[90] See *per* Aldous L.J. in *Brain* at 347–348.

[91] [1997] F.S.R. 271.

[92] See *Prince plc v Prince Sports Group Inc* [1998] F.S.R. 21 at 33 to 34, referring to *Brain v Ingledew Brown Bennison & Garrett (No.1)* [1996] F.S.R. 341.

[93] *Brain v Ingledew Brown Bennison & Garrett (No.3)* [1997] F.S.R. 511.

[94] *Brain v Ingledew Brown Bennison & Garrett (No.3)* [1997] F.S.R. 511.

[95] *Brain v Ingledew Brown Bennison & Garrett (No.3)* [1997] F.S.R. 511; *L'Oréal v Johnson & Johnson* [2000] F.S.R. 686.

[96] *Brain v Ingledew Brown Bennison & Garrett (No.1)* [1996] F.S.R. 341 at 349.

these reasons, the question of whether a threat has been made will usually require a trial, although not always.[97]

18–119   A series of letters should be looked at as a whole to determine whether they contain a threat.[98] However, if an earlier letter in a series makes a threat, the threat is not negated by a later explanation, although the relief to be granted could be affected.[99]

AVAILABILITY OF INTERIM RELIEF

18–120   An interim injunction is available to restrain the making of threats, notwithstanding the rule in *Bestobell Paints v Bigg*[1] in relation to malicious falsehood. The reason is that threats cause severe damage quickly, and the statutory provisions against them would be of little use if the remedy of an interim injunction were not available. See *Johnson Electric v Mabuchi Motor*.[2]

DEFENCES

18–121   Justification, *i.e.* proof that the acts the subject of the threat are or would be an infringement, is a defence by virtue of s.21(2) of the 1994 Act. Where the person threatened has not yet done the acts concerned, it may be more difficult to show that they would infringe (certainly if the infringement in question would be under s.10(2), where surrounding circumstances would be relevant), but given the policy of s.21 and the courts' attitude to threats, it is highly likely that that would be held to be a risk taken by the person making the threat.

18–122   Mere notification that a trade mark is registered, or that an application has been made, is not actionable by virtue of s.21(4). However, persons seeking to take advantage of that provision should be very careful not to go even a fraction further than what is permitted, lest a threat be inferred.[3] Probably the most cautious and only truly safe approach is to say "In accordance with s.21(4) of the Trade Marks Act 1994 I hereby notify you that the mark XYZ is a registered trade mark appearing on the Register of Trade Marks as number 123,456.", and absolutely nothing more.

EFFECT OF ISSUING PROCEEDINGS BEFORE MAKING THREAT

18–123   It is not actionable as a threat to report the mere existence of proceedings, subject to the comments above about the risk of malicious falsehood and contempt of court.[4]

RELIEF

18–124   The relief available under s.21 is set out in subs.(2): a declaration that the threats are unjustifiable, an injunction, and damages. Although the subsection is phrased in terms which suggest that the grant of that relief is mandatory once the claimant proves his case, it is clear that the court retains its general discretionary

---

[97] *Brain v Ingledew Brown Bennison & Garrett* [1996] F.S.R. 341, although summary judgment was given in *Prince plc v Prince Sports Group Inc* [1998] F.S.R. 21.
[98] *Brain v Ingledew Brown Bennison & Garrett (No.3)* [1997] F.S.R. 511 at 521.
[99] *Prince plc v Prince Sports Group Inc* [1998] F.S.R. 21 at 27–28.
[1] [1975] F.S.R. 421.
[2] [1986] F.S.R. 280.
[3] For an example of how not to proceed, see *L'Oréal v Johnson & Johnson* [2000] F.S.R. 686.
[4] See, *e.g. Carl Zeiss Stiftung v Rayner & Keeler* [1961] R.P.C. 1; *Easipower v Gordon Moore* [1963] R.P.C. 8.

jurisdiction.[5] Hence, although an injunction and an inquiry will usually be granted, it is not automatic. In particular, an inquiry may not be granted if there is no evidence of loss.[6]

Except in unusual circumstances, relief going beyond that specified in s.21 will not be granted. The legislature has decided what relief is appropriate.[7]

COMMUNITY TRADE MARKS

The provisions of s.21 apply to Community Trade Marks pursuant to para.4 of the Community Trade Mark Regulations 1996.[8]   **18–125**

THREATS MADE "WITHOUT PREJUDICE"

It is an abuse of process to plead that a threat was made at a "without prejudice" meeting, and an action based on such a plea will be struck out.[9]   **18–126**

---

[5] *Prince plc v Prince Sports Group Inc* [1998] F.S.R. 21; *Brain v Ingledew Brown Bennison & Garrett (No.3)* [1997] F.S.R. 511 at 526, relying on *Allied Maples v Simmons & Simmons* [1995] 1 W.L.R. 1602.

[6] *Prince plc v Prince Sports Group Inc* [1998] F.S.R. 21 at 36–37, where an inquiry was refused initially with leave to the plaintiff to lead evidence of damage, which it later did. See also *Brain v Ingledew Brown Bennison & Garrett (No.3)* [1997] F.S.R. 511 at 525–528, where Laddie J held that usually an inquiry will follow from a finding of an actionable threat, and ordered an inquiry with considerable misgivings, on the basis that the evidence of damage was slight but not such as to be rejected altogether. That was a legal aid case; the inquiry is normally of course at the claimant's risk as to costs: *McDonald's v Burgerking* [1987] F.S.R. 112.

[7] *Prince plc v Prince Sports Group Inc* [1998] F.S.R. 21 at 41–42.

[8] See App.14.

[9] *Unilever v Procter & Gamble* [2000] F.S.R. 344.

CHAPTER 19

CIVIL PROCEEDINGS FOR TRADE MARK INFRINGEMENT AND PASSING OFF

1. Scope of chapter

19–001 The substantive law of registered trade marks and passing off has largely already been considered. The present chapter is concerned essentially with matters of practice and procedure. The matters covered include the requirements to be satisfied before an action may be brought, jurisdictional matters as to the proper forum for such disputes, both domestic and international remedies, both interim and final, costs, and appeals. Many of the issues covered are common to passing off as much as to trade mark infringement, although a number of formal matters are applicable only to the latter.

Certain aspects of civil litigation concerned specifically with Community Trade Marks are not dealt with here, but rather in Ch.6.

2. Statutory action for infringement

INFRINGEMENT OF MARK CONTRASTED WITH PASSING OFF

19–002 Although many of the principles applicable are common to both forms of action (and the two are frequently combined in a single action), it is important to bear in mind the differences between actions which are brought to prevent or to recover damages for the infringement of trade mark, and those which are compendiously described as "passing-off actions." In an action of the first kind the claimant complains that the defendant has infringed his mark by using an identical or similar mark, and he relies on his statutory title to the exclusive use of the mark in question for the goods or services specified in his registration, or goods or services similar thereto;[1] in an action of the second kind the claimant's case is less specialised, for he complains that the defendant is using means which are calculated to pass-off, or to cause to be passed-off, the goods or business of the defendant as and for those of the claimant, and the means may or may not comprise or consist of the taking of a mark, either registered or not.

19–003 An action for infringement is necessarily an action upon a registered mark, by reason of s.2(2) of the 1994 Act which provides as follows:

> "No proceedings lie to prevent or recover damages for the infringement of an unregistered trade mark as such; but nothing in this Act affects the law relating to passing off."

EFFECTS OF SECTION 2(2)

19–004 It is questionable whether s.2(2) or its predecessors were necessary, since there

---

[1] Or even, under the 1994 Act, s.10(3), dissimilar goods.

probably never was any right of action for infringement of an unregistered trade mark, other than an action for passing off by the use of the mark.[2]

The express words in the second part of s.2(2), preserving the law of passing off from being altered by the 1994 Act, mean that it is no defence to an action for passing off that the defendant is registered as proprietor of the mark which he is using;[3] but, where this is the case it is usual for the claimant at the same time to apply to have the registration revoked.[4]   **19–005**

Under the 1938 Act, the provision equivalent to s.2(2)[5] was held not to affect the right of the owner of an unregistered trade mark to oppose a potentially conflicting registration,[6] and no doubt the same would apply in relation to the 1994 Act.   **19–006**

RIGHT TO SUE FOR INFRINGEMENT OF A REGISTERED TRADE MARK

The claimant in an action for infringement of a registered mark must generally establish his title to sue either as proprietor or as an exclusive licensee, although in certain instances a licensee with no general right of action may be entitled to sue if the proprietor fails to do so when called upon.[7] He must then prove that the defendant has acted or threatens to act in such a way as to infringe the right conferred by registration as defined by the 1994 Act.   **19–007**

These subjects, the relief which may be obtained, and the procedure to be followed will now be examined.

3. The claimant's title—infringement of registered marks

TITLE CONFERRED BY REGISTRATION

The claimant's title as proprietor under the 1994 Act depends on the existence of a valid registration.[8] The fact that a person is registered as proprietor of a mark is *prima facie* evidence of the validity of the original registration and of any subsequent assignment or transmission thereof.[9]   **19–008**

The action may not be commenced until the mark is on the Register, notwithstanding that a registration once applied for will (if in due course achieved) date back to the application.[10] Under previous Acts, an assignee could commence an action for infringement of a mark on the Register without registration of the assignment,[11] and it would seem that that should still be the position, in particular because ss.9, 10 and 14 of the 1994 Act refer to "the proprietor" rather than "the registered proprietor", and because s.25, dealing with the consequences of non-registration, provides for an inability to obtain damages in certain circumstances, but not an inability to bring or maintain an action altogether. It should be noted   **19–009**

---

[2] The reason for insertion of this or similar provisions in successive Trade Marks Acts is discussed further in the earlier editions of this work.

[3] *Inter Lotto v Camelot Group* [2004] R.P.C. 9, CA.

[4] *e.g. Rey v Lecouturier* [1910] A.C. 262; 27 R.P.C. 268.

[5] s.2.

[6] *Mellor* (1948) 65 R.P.C. 238, Regy.

[7] See Ch.13.

[8] 1994 Act, s.9.

[9] s.72.

[10] ss.9(3) and 40(3).

[11] *Ihlee v Henshaw* (1886) 31 Ch.D. 323; 3 R.P.C. 15. This case was decided on the 1883 Act, but the position would seem to be unchanged.

that in relation to copyright infringement proceedings, an equitable owner may bring an action before obtaining legal title, provided that he either perfects his title before judgement or joins the legal owner,[12] so as to remove the risk that the defendant may be sued again. Assuming that an action may be brought by a trade mark proprietor whose interest is not on the Register, one would expect similar procedural safeguards to be required.

EXCLUSIVE LICENSEE AS CLAIMANT IN HIS OWN RIGHT

19–010   Unless their licence provides otherwise, licensees under a registered trade mark may bring proceedings to restrain infringements which affect them, should the proprietor fail to do so: this is dealt with in the next section. The present section is concerned with the interest of an exclusive licensee who is positively given, by his licence agreement, the right to sue in his own name. The nature of the interest which the exclusive licensee obtains in such a situation is dealt with in Ch.12. Here, we deal with procedural matters concerning an exclusive licensee in such a situation.

19–011   As will appear below, the fact that an exclusive licensee has a right to sue in his own name affects not only the manner in which he may bring proceedings, but also, in certain circumstances, the manner in which the proprietor may do so.

19–012   The rights of action which an exclusive licensee obtains under s.31 of the 1994 Act are concurrent with those of the proprietor,[13] and the defendant may avail himself of any defence which would have been available to him had the proprietor brought the action[14] (and it appears that this includes personal defences such as licence or acquiescence).

19–013   By s.31(4):

> "Where proceedings for infringement of a registered trade mark brought by the proprietor or an exclusive licensee relate wholly or partly to an infringement in respect of which they have concurrent rights of action, the proprietor, or, as the case may be, the exclusive licensee may not, without the leave of the court, proceed with the action unless the other is joined as a plaintiff or added as a defendant."

Thus, for example, if an exclusive licence relates to some but not all of the types of goods the subject of a registration, and gives the licensee a right to sue in his own name, and an infringer uses the mark on those types of goods, or on those types of goods and other goods covered by the registration but not by the licence, then the proprietor and the licensee can both sue, but both must be made parties.

19–014   Joinder of the additional party is not required in order to obtain interim relief.[15]

---

[12] See *e.g. Orwin v Attorney-General* [1998] F.S.R. 415, and generally *Copinger and Skone James on Copyright* (15th ed., Sweet and Maxwell, London, 2005) at para.5–186.

[13] s.31(2). Of course, the exclusive licensee's rights to use the registered mark and to sue for infringements of it need not extend across the whole scope of the registration; the licence may be partial, limited to certain goods, or areas, or manners of use, as is explained in Ch.13. Where the licence is partial, the rights of the exclusive licensee and the proprietor will only be concurrent in relation to those parts of the registration over which the licensee has rights; in relation to the remainder, the proprietor alone will have rights: such is clear from the wording of ss.28 and 31, particularly s.31(4).

[14] s.31(3).

[15] s.31(4), last sentence.

Where a proprietor or licensee is joined to proceedings under s.31(4) but takes no part, then he shall not be made liable for any costs.[16]

Somewhat peculiarly, s.31(8) appears to allow the proprietor and exclusive licensee to contract out of the provisions of s.31(4) and (5). While one can understand the possibility that they might wish to make a contractual agreement as to the costs of proceedings brought by the one without the involvement of the other (since the other may yet derive a benefit from them), it seems surprising that the parties should be able to vary the requirement of s.31(4) that both should be joined if their rights are concurrent, since such provisions are usually made in order to protect a defendant from being sued twice for the same infringement. By contrast, s.30, considered below, does not allow the parties to modify the provisions equivalent to s.31(4) and (5) by agreement between themselves.   **19–015**

The relationship between proprietor and licensee may also affect the relief which each can obtain (particularly as to damages and delivery up) in an action for infringement where their rights are concurrent. The 1994 Act deals with these issues in the broad and flexible provisions of s.31(6) and (7).   **19–016**

Section 31(6) provides that, where there are concurrent rights of action, the court is to take the terms of the licence into account in assessing damages, as well as any award of damages already made.[17] It is clear that the purpose of requiring reference to the terms of the licence is not simply to avoid the proprietor or licensee being awarded a sum which exceeds the actual damage to him, allowing for the licence, since the section provides that the court may, if they are not both parties,[18] direct that the one is to hold relevant proceeds on behalf of the other. In other words, the section expressly envisages that one of them may recover damages to reflect loss to the other, even though that other is not a party. This is an unusual approach; it is even possible to imagine a party being awarded damages from infringement proceedings of which he is not aware, and it certainly could happen that a proprietor or licensee recovers damages which have been assessed in a manner over which he had no control. It appears that in general it would be much more desirable that both holders of concurrent rights should generally be made parties, which makes it all the more strange that the parties are apparently able to contract out of s.31(4), and, indeed, s.31(6).[19]   **19–017**

The court may not award an account of profits if an award of damages has been made or an account already directed in favour of the other party with a concurrent right.[20] If an account is ordered, the court is to apportion the proceeds in a manner which it considers just, having regard to the licence agreement.[21] These provisions apply whether or not both of the concurrent right holders are parties to the action.   **19–018**

As to delivery up, s.31(7) provides that the proprietor must notify an exclusive licensee with a concurrent right of action of any application for an order under s.16,[22] and empowers the court to make an order under s.16 upon the ap-   **19–019**

---

[16] s.31(5).
[17] s.31(6)(a).
[18] As may happen if the court gives permission for one to be omitted under s.31(4), or, apparently, if the licence agreement permits one to proceed without the other.
[19] By s.31(8), referred to above.
[20] s.31(6)(b).
[21] s.31(6)(c).
[22] The provisions of s.16 are considered below in paras 19–110 to 19–114.

plication of an exclusive licensee, having regard to the terms of the licence.[23] Of course, if both are parties to the action then the licensee will presumably know of the application anyway, but there could be a problem if, as is possible, the licensee is a party while the proprietor is not. For some reason the section does not expressly require the licensee to give the proprietor notice of an application by him.

19–020   In no circumstances can the exclusive licensee sue the proprietor: his remedy against the proprietor lies, if anywhere, in contract. See *Northern & Shell v Condé Nast*.[24]

LICENSEES WITHOUT THEIR OWN RIGHT OF ACTION

19–021   Section 30 of the 1994 Act confers a more limited right of action than does s.31. It confers such a right on non-exclusive licensees and on exclusive licensees whose agreement with the proprietor takes them outside s.31. The provisions of ss.30 and 31 are mutually exclusive, since s.30(1) excludes from the provisions of that section exclusive licensees having a right of action under s.31.

19–022   Unless the right is excluded by the agreement(s) from which he derives his licence, a licensee may, under s.31(2) call upon the proprietor to take infringement proceedings in respect of any matter "which affects his interests".[25] If the proprietor refuses to bring proceedings, or fails to do so within two months after being called upon, then the licensee may bring proceedings in his own name as if he were the proprietor.[26] As with s.31(4) and (5), s.30(4) and (5) provide that the proprietor must be joined as a party unless the court permits otherwise, but that that requirement is not to affect the granting of interim relief, and that the proprietor is not liable for costs if he does not take part in the proceedings.

19–023   Section 30 is unclear as to the remedies which a licensee may obtain if successful in an action brought under s.30, and a particular question appears to arise over his right to recover damages. On the one hand, the section provides for the licensee to sue "as if he were the proprietor",[27] and this coupled with s.14(2), which provides that all relief is available to the proprietor in an infringement action as would be available in respect of the infringement of any other property right, would suggest that damages ought to be available. However, s.30 lacks the provision of s.31 giving an exclusive licensee "the same rights and remedies" as if the mark had been assigned to him, and s.30(6) provides that in infringement proceedings brought by the proprietor loss suffered by a licensee is to be taken into account, without stipulating what is to be done if the licensee is the claimant. This is to be contrasted with s.31(6), where it is plainly envisaged that both the proprietor and the exclusive licensee may recover damages.

---

[23] It is not altogether clear on the wording of s.31(7) whether the licensee's right to apply under s.16 is contingent on, and to be exercised only in the context of, an application by the proprietor, or whether it is wholly independent. Since s.31(1) provides that the parties may by agreement confer on the licensee all the same rights and remedies as if the licence had been an assignment (albeit subject to the following provisions of s.31), and since if the right to apply under s.16 were contingent then there could be cases where no claimant could apply for delivery up (if the licensee were the only claimant), it appears that the right must be independent. However, the existence of the curious requirement that the proprietor must notify the licensee of an application under s.16 without a corresponding requirement that the licensee notify the proprietor may tend to suggest the contrary.

[24] [1995] R.P.C. 117, considered further in Ch.13.

[25] The scope of this term is considered in Ch.13.

[26] s.31(3).

[27] s.30(3).

Since it is plainly envisaged that damages may be recovered by the proprietor **19–024** to reflect loss to a non-exclusive licensee (as a result of s.30(6)), and since it is envisaged that sums recovered as a result should be held for and pass to the licensee, it is clear that there is no intention in s.30 to exclude such persons from recovering financial relief altogether. Hence the better view probably is that a non-exclusive licensee can recover damages under s.30. It is unsatisfactory, however, that this does not explain the differences between ss.30 and 31 referred to above. A further possibility is that a non-exclusive licensee may recover damages as a result of s.30, but only through the medium of the proprietor (who will usually also be a party under s.30(4)).

There is no provision under s.30 entitling a non-exclusive licensee to take **19–025** advantage of the statutory provisions relating to delivery up. This is an unfortunate omission, but it may be that the non-exclusive licensee could obtain delivery up by relying on the common law rights of a property owner as preserved by s.14 of the 1994 Act.

Although it is not expressly stated, it seems that, whatever the position in rela- **19–026** tion to damages, a non-exclusive licensee must at the very minimum have the right to obtain an injunction to restrain further infringements through proceedings under s.30; without it, the ability to bring an action at all would be worthless. Obtaining an interim injunction is plainly contemplated by s.30(4). Assuming that an injunction to restrain infringement is available in proceedings brought under s.30, this would provide another basis for the remedy of delivery up, which the common law has traditionally treated as a head of mandatory relief which may be awarded to ensure compliance with a prohibitory injunction.

CO-PROPRIETORS

Each co-proprietor may sue for infringement in his own right, and the permission **19–027** of the other co-proprietors is not required to do so.[28] However, all the other co-proprietors must be joined as a claimant or a defendant before the action can proceed, unless the court gives permission for their omission.[29] There are the usual provisos that interim relief can be obtained without the joinder of all the co-proprietors, and that those joined as parties but who do not take part are not liable for costs.[30]

CONCURRENT REGISTRATIONS

Where, as distinguished from a registration owned by co-proprietors, there are **19–028** concurrent registrations of resembling marks, the use of a mark by a stranger may be an infringement of the right of more than one proprietor. In such cases any of the registered proprietors can sue by himself and obtain an injunction.[31] The assessment of damages may present some difficulty; and unless the proprietors of all the marks were parties, an account of profits could presumably not be ordered.

[28] This is clear from the structure of s.23(4) and (5).
[29] s.32(5).
[30] s.32(5).
[31] This follows from ss.9 and 10 of the Act.

19–029   Infringement of a registered mark being an interference with a right of property[32] injuring the estate of the proprietor, proceedings may be begun or continued by the executors of a deceased proprietor.[33] Beneficiaries under a will or intestacy who become entitled to the mark can secure registration and sue as proprietors.[34] The authorities for these propositions were decided under previous Acts, but the position ought to be the same, since the fundamental nature of the proprietor's right, as one of property, has not changed.

4. Commencement of passing off or infringement action

In what court an infringement or passing off action should be commenced

19–030   Passing off claims may be brought in the Chancery Division, the Patents County Court or a County Court where there is a Chancery District Registry (currently Birmingham, Bristol, Cardiff, Leeds, Liverpool, Manchester and Newcastle upon Tyne).[35]

19–031   Claims relating to registered trade marks may now be brought in the same courts as those listed in para.19–030; the jurisdiction of the Patents County Court was recently extended to such claims.[36]

5. Service out of the jurisdiction

Service out of the jurisdiction without permission

19–032   Service out of the jurisdiction is now dealt with in Pt 6 of the CPR. There are two different schemes relevant to this work: service without leave in cases provided for by Council Regulation (EC) No. 44/2001 (formerly the Brussels Convention), which is dealt with by r.6.19(1),[37] and service where leave is required, in all other cases, which is dealt with in r.6.20 of the CPR.

19–033   The scheme in relation to service without permission of the court under r.6.19(1) is that it is permitted so long as (1) the defendant is domiciled in a relevant territory covered by Regulation (EC) No. 44/2001 (including the United Kingdom), (2) the same cause of action is not being litigated between the same parties in any of those countries, and (3) the claim is one which the United Kingdom court has power to determine under the 1982 Act.

19–034   The basic rule of Regulation (EC) No. 44/2001 is that defendants should be sued in the courts where they are domiciled.[38] However, in cases concerning tort, a defendant may also be sued, if desired, in the courts of the state where the

---

[32] s.14.

[33] *Oakey v Dalton* (1887 L.R. 35 Ch.D. 700: 4 R.P.C. 313.

[34] *Massam v Thorley's* (1880) 14 Ch.D. 748 at 754 (C.A.).

[35] CPR, Part 63.13 and 63PD 18.1–18.3.

[36] High Court and County Court Jurisdiction (Amendment) Order SI 2005/587. Strictly speaking there seems to be an inconsistency between the nomination of the Patents County Court by Art.3 of the 2005 Order on the one hand, and CPR 63PD 18.3 which excludes the Patents County Court, but the clear intention is that the former should prevail, and presumably the Practice Direction will be brought into conformity soon.

[37] r.6.19(2) contains provisions in relation to other enactments.

[38] Brussels Convention, Art.2, which forms Sch.1 to the 1982 Act.

harmful act occurred.[39] Hence in the case of infringements committed in this jurisdiction, proceedings may be served without leave on a defendant domiciled in a state to which r.6.19(1) applies.

SERVICE OUT WITH THE PERMISSION OF THE COURT

Service out with the permission of the court under r.6.20 of the CPR follows a **19–035** somewhat similar pattern; a defendant domiciled in this jurisdiction may be served abroad under r.6.20(1), and in the case of claims in tort, a defendant domiciled abroad may be served with proceedings under r.6.20(8) if damage was sustained, or if the act leading to damage was committed, here. In addition, service out may be allowed if a claim is made for an injunction to restrain a defendant from doing, or order him to do, an act in the jurisdiction, under r.6.20(2). The procedure to be followed in making an application for service out under r.6.20 is set out in r.6.21. Such an application is by no means a formality; the claimant must satisfy the court that its claim raises a serious issue to be tried,[40] and that the High Court is the appropriate forum.[41]

6. Jurisdiction over foreign trade marks

COURTS TRYING INFRINGEMENT OF FOREIGN TRADE MARKS

Difficult problems may arise where the courts of one state attempt to try the in- **19–036** fringement of a trade mark registered in another state, even if that other state is a member state of the EU and hence subject to Regulation (EC) No.44/2001. The problems are particularly acute if the validity of the registration is attacked or likely to be attacked.

It will be observed that in principle under Regulation (EC) No.44/2001 a court **19–037** in, say, England may try a claim against a person domiciled here in which the allegation is that that person infringed, say, a French trade mark. Indeed, the general rule is that such a person should be sued in the place of domicile. There would also be the option, in that example, of suing such a person in France, the place of the tort[42], under article 5(3). That an action for infringement of a foreign intellectual property right may be tried in the United Kingdom was confirmed in *Pearce v Ove Arup* [1999] F.S.R. 525, CA, where it was held that the High Court had jurisdiction to try an action in which infringement of Dutch copyright by the construction of a building in the Netherlands was alleged (the reason for the action being brought in the United Kingdom was the availability of legal aid here). That case also established that the old double actionability rule did not apply to

---

[39] Sch.1, art. 5(3). This has been interpreted by the ECJ to allow a defendant to be sued either where the tortious act was committed or where the damage which it caused was suffered: *Handelskwerkerij v Mines de Potasses d'Alsace* [1976] E.C.R. 1735.

[40] *Seaconsar v Bank Markazi* [1994] 1 A.C. 438.

[41] This is a matter of weighing a number of factors, the basic principles being set out in *Spiliada Maritime v Cansulex* [1987] A.C. 460. In relation to trade mark infringement and passing off, if the acts complained of took place in the UK then it is highly likely that the High Court will be the *forum conveniens* because of the need for evidence from the trade and public, and because of the desirability of having a tribunal familiar with commerce in the UK.

[42] Registered trade marks are territorial, and so can only be infringed in their country of registration: see the 1994 Act, s.9, which makes it clear that the proprietor has the exclusive rights to the mark in the UK, and *LA Gear v Whelan* [1991] F.S.R. 670, followed in *Waterford v David Nagli* [1998] F.S.R. 92.

cases concerning territorial intellectual property rights.[43] The case is unclear as to what the position is in relation to trying in the United Kingdom alleged infringements of trade marks registered in states which are not covered by Regulation (EC) No.44/2001.[44]

19–038   However, the ability in principle to sue in the United Kingdom for infringement of foreign intellectual property rights is considerably complicated in the context of trade marks by the fact that they are registered rights, and Article 22(4) of Regulation (EC) No.44/2001 (formerly Article 16 of the Brussels Convention) provides that in the case of "proceedings concerned with the registration or validity of patents, trade marks, designs, or other similar rights required to be deposited or registered", the courts of the state in which registration has taken place are to have exclusive jurisdiction, regardless of domicile and overriding the provisions of Art.5. In the context of patents, there have been numerous attempts, most frequently and most successfully in the courts of the Netherlands, to sue for infringement of rights registered abroad. The attraction of doing so is not so much the ability to sue in the Netherlands rather than elsewhere in respect of infringements taking place in a single European jurisdiction, but rather to seek to obtain a "pan-European" injunction, covering numerous jurisdictions, from a single set of proceedings.[45] There has been considerable debate about whether such an approach is permitted under the Conventions, because although proceedings for patent infringement do not *per se* necessarily involve questions of validity, it is of course extremely common for a defendant in a patent action to defend himself by alleging the invalidity of the patent in suit; and it is quite clear that that question can only be tried in the state where the patent is registered. At least in the United Kingdom view of patent litigation, an infringement action concerns validity to the extent that the scope of the claims bears on both, particularly where there is a "squeeze", although in continental jurisdictions the connection is not seen as being so close. The question of whether such pan-European proceedings in respect of patent infringement may be brought in a single European jurisdiction has been considered on a number of occasions by the United Kingdom courts, and indeed reference to the ECJ has been made, although until recently the proceedings concerned all ended before the ECJ could rule.[46]

19–039   This does not mean, however, that the position will be the same in relation to

---

[43] It had previously been suggested, *e.g.* in *Def Lepp Music v Stuart-Brown* [1986] R.P.C. 273, that because the law of the UK as to copyright is territorial, so that an act would only be an infringement if committed in the UK, the requirement of the double actionability rule that the act complained of be tortious under the *lex fori* could not be met. The Court of Appeal rejected the argument in *Pearce v Ove Arup* (at 559–561), but it had in any event been overtaken by the passage of the Private International Law (Miscellaneous Provisions Act) 1995, ss.10–12.

[44] In *Tyburn Productions v Doyle* [1991] Ch. 75, Vinelott J., held on the basis of *British South Africa Company v Companhia de Mocambique* [1893] A.C. 602 that a claim in respect of US copyright was not justiciable in the UK. The Mocambique case was considered in detail by the Court of Appeal in *Pearce*, and while it was clearly decided that its effect had been abrogated by the 1982 Act for those states covered by it, there is no clear decision as to the rest of the world, and the *Tyburn* case was neither expressly approved nor disapproved. It is, however, not easy to see how the 1982 Act would affect the position as to the rest of the world. The correctness of the decision in *Tyburn* was doubted in *R Griggs Group v Evans* [2004] F.S.R. 48, where Peter Prescott Q.C., sitting as a deputy High Court Judge, held that the ownership of Australian copyrights was justiciable in the UK.

[45] This approach is assisted by Art.6(1), which permits the joinder of additional defendants in proceedings instituted in a given jurisdiction against one defendant.

[46] See, *e.g. Fort Dodge Animal Health* [1998] F.S.R. 222, CA. For a view from another European jurisdiction, see *Expandable Grafts v Boston Scientific* [1999] F.S.R. 352, Court of Appeal of the Hague, which seems to be converging with the UK position, and moving towards an acceptance that Art.22 prevents multi-jurisdictional decisions on the substantive merits, although not interim

registered trade marks, for two reasons. First, in many more trade mark cases than patent cases, there is no serious attack on the validity of the claimant's registration. In such cases, Art.22 probably ought to have no effect; the only issue is infringement, and that is triable outside the state where the right is registered, under Art.5(3) as interpreted in *Pearce*. Secondly, where the validity of a trade mark registration is attacked in infringement proceedings, it is usually much less connected with the infringement issues than is the case in patent infringement proceedings, so that it may be harder to say that the infringement proceedings "concern" validity.

PASSING OFF ABROAD

Passing off is a tort, and passing off which has taken place abroad may be sued **19–040** for in England, subject to the defendant being a person over whom the English court can and will exercise jurisdiction. Formerly, it was necessary to satisfy the double actionability rule,[47] but that has been changed by ss.10–12 of the Private International Law (Miscellaneous Provisions) Act 1995. In general now, only the law of the country where the passing off has been committed will be relevant. It will be necessary to lead evidence of that law rather than merely relying on the presumption that it is the same as the law of England: *Alfred Dunhill v Sunoptic*,[48] *Waterford v David Nagli*.[49]

The difficulties of jurisdiction posed by Article 22 of the Brussels Convention **19–041** in relation to registered trade marks[50] do not apply to passing off, which does not depend on the existence of a registered right, or other statutory monopoly, and is justiciable here under the general principles of conflict of laws and/or under Arts 2 and 5.

LIS ALIBI PENDENS: ARTICLES 27 AND 28 AND FORUM CONVENIENS

Because more than one court may have jurisdiction over the same claim under **19–042** Regulation (EC) No.44/2001 (most commonly, for example, the court of the defendant's domicile under Art.2 and the court of the place of the tort under Art.5), it is necessary that there should be rules to determine which court should proceed if the same or related claims are sought to be brought in more than one court. Art.27 provides that where the same claim between the same parties is brought in more than one court, the court second seised must decline jurisdiction.[51] Article 28 provides that if related claims are brought in different courts ("related" meaning that they need not be identical as to parties or claims, but must present the risk of giving rise to irreconcilable decisions), the court second seised may decline jurisdiction; it has a discretion whether or not to do so. For an application of these principles, see for example *Mecklermedia v DC Congress* [1997] F.S.R. 627.

Similar problems may arise outside the ambit of Regulation (EC) No.44/2001, **19–043**

---

or accelerated hearings. However, see also the opinion of the A.G. in C–4/03, *GAT v LuK*, which is to the opposite effect.

[47] *i.e.* that the acts complained of would be passing off if committed in the UK and would be actionable in the country where they were committed. See, *e.g. Walker v Ost* [1970] R.P.C. 489 at 509. See also para.19–037 and notes therein.

[48] [1979] F.S.R. 337.

[49] [1998] F.S.R. 92.

[50] Nor does the Tyburn Productions/Mocambique point concerning copyright, referred to above, arise.

[51] This does not preclude an application for interim relief, however, under Art.31.

either in the context of an application to serve out of the jurisdiction with permission (or an application to set aside leave), or in the context of an application to restrain proceedings abroad. In any such case the question for the court is which jurisdiction is the forum conveniens for the dispute. Although the evidential onus may vary depending on the nature of the application, the main relevant matters are set out in *Spiliada Maritime v Cansulex* [1987] A.C. 460.

7. Vicarious and joint liability

19–044   For the general principles applicable in relation to joint liability based on procurement or common design, see *CBS v Amstrad*, and *Crédit Lyonnais v ECGD*.[52]

EMPLOYER RESPONSIBLE FOR SERVANT'S ACTS

19–045   An employer will be held responsible for the wrongful acts of infringement or passing off on the part of his servant done in the course of the employer's business and within the scope of the employment, notwithstanding that the acts were done without the employer's knowledge,[53] or even contrary to his express orders.[54] But it does not follow that an injunction will be granted in every case where this is established.[55]

AGENTS AND PARTNERS OF INFRINGER

19–046   The action is one of tort, and, consequently, every infringer is liable to be sued, whether he acted on his own behalf or as agent for a principal. But a mere servant (as distinct from an employee who has direction of the infringer's affairs)[56] should not, without some special reason, be added as a defendant.[57]

DIRECTORS AND PROMOTERS

19–047   Directors of a limited company which infringes are not liable merely because they are directors, but only for infringing acts that they personally have committed or directed.[58] Accordingly, in cases where it is desirable to join directors as defendants—as it well may be,[59] especially in view of the modern practice of forming companies without available assets to carry on any doubtful activity—specific infringements should be alleged against them. Persons directly respon-

---

[52] [1998] R.P.C. 567; [1998] 1 Lloyd's Rep. 19.
[53] *Cusenier v Gaiety Bars* (1902) 19 R.P.C. 357; and *Havana Cigar Factories v Tiffin* (1909) 26 R.P.C. 473, where the Court of Appeal held the defendant company liable for the acts of the persons entrusted by it with the selling of the particular goods.
[54] *Grierson, Oldham v Birmingham Hotel* (1901) 18 R.P.C. 158 ("Big Tree Brand") where an hotel company was held responsible for passing off by waiters contrary to orders; *Monro v Hunter* (1904) 21 R.P.C. 296. cf. a Scottish case, *Montgomerie v Young* (1904) 20 R.P.C. 781; 21 R.P.C. 285, I.H. reversing the Lord Ordinary.
[55] *Lever Bros v Masbro* (1912) 29 R.P.C. 34, and 225 CA.
[56] *Adrema v Adrema-Werke* (1954) 71 R.P.C. 345.
[57] cf. *Daniel and Arter v Whitehouse* (1898) 16 R.P.C. 71 (a motion to commit).
[58] See the discussion of earlier cases in *Evans v Spritebrand* [1985] F.S.R. 267, CA. Note in particular that *White Horse v Gregson* [1984] R.P.C. 61 at 91 (an unusual case, of failure to prevent passing off abroad rather than positively committing it) goes too far in holding that "before a director can be held personally liable for a tort committed by his company he must not only commit or direct the tortious act or conduct but he must do so deliberately or recklessly and so as to make it his own, as distinct from the act or conduct of the company."
[59] cf. *Adrema v Adrema-Werke* (1954) 71 R.P.C. 345 at 347: "Right and proper" to join directors as defendants. But see *Premier Luggage v The Premier Company* [[2001] F.S.R. 29, where the managing director of the defendant company was held not liable on the basis that he was only one of three directors, and there was no evidence that he himself had done the acts concerned (decision not reviewed on appeal at [2003] F.S.R. 5.

sible for the promotion of a company for the purpose of doing a wrongful act may be liable:[60] this would seem to extend to a holding company forming a subsidiary for purposes of infringement. Where personal defendants are joined in such cases, particulars of the acts relied on will be ordered where necessary.[61] The numerous authorities in this area were recently helpfully summarised in *MCA Records v Charly Records*.[62]

PARENT AND GROUP COMPANIES

Similarly, it is frequently sought to join as a defendant the parent of the company actually carrying on the allegedly infringing acts, either in order to be able effectively to enforce any award for damages, or for disclosure. In such cases, it is not enough to show that the parent company knew and approved of the acts concerned,[63] or even that it knowingly assisted the conduct in question.[64] It must be shown either that it procured or induced or conspired in the commission of the conduct, or was involved in its commission.[65]   **19–048**

8. The relief granted

OUTLINE OF THE TYPES OF RELIEF AVAILABLE

In general, the relief available to a successful claimant is much the same whether he succeeds for registered trade mark infringement, for passing off, or both. However, as will appear below, the 1994 Act has introduced a new statutory regime relating to erasure and delivery up[66] which applies to actions for infringement and not to passing off. In certain areas, this may give a registered owner broader protection than the common law remedies previously available.   **19–049**

By s.14 of the 1994 Act, all relief is available in an action for infringement of a registered trade mark as is available in respect of any other property right. The section does not appear to suggest that the statutory remedies provided by s.15–19 replace the remedies available at common law and in equity for invasions of property rights, so it appears that they are concurrent. This is unlikely to be of great practical significance unless there is some formal or procedural difficulty with proceeding by the statutory route, in which case a claimant may wish to rely on his common law and equitable rights.[67]   **19–050**

In general, a successful claimant may obtain an order for (1) an injunction restraining further infringements of his rights; (2) the delivery up for the destruction of, or for the erasure of the marks from, any goods already marked with the   **19–051**

---

[60] *Panhard et Levassor v Panhard Levassor Motor Co* [1901] 2 Ch. 513; 18 R.P.C. 405. Contrast *Pritchard & Constance v Amata* (1925) 42 R.P.C. 63 at 73.

[61] *British Thomson-Houston v Irradiant* (1924) 41 R.P.C. 338.

[62] [2002] F.S.R. 26, and see also the useful summary in the judgment at first instance: [2000] E.M.L.R. 743.

[63] As in, *e.g. Mead v Riverwood* [1997] F.S.R. 484.

[64] *Crédit Lyonnais v ECGD* [1998] 1 Lloyd's Rep. 19.

[65] *Crédit Lyonnais* [1998] 1 Lloyd's Rep. 19; *Unilever v Chefaro* [1994] F.S.R. 135. A list of most of the numerous authorities on this topic may be found in *Sepracor v Hoechst Marion Roussel* [1999] F.S.R. 746.

[66] ss.15–19.

[67] 1994 Act, s.2(1), states that "the proprietor of a registered trade mark has the rights and remedies provided by this Act", and it has been suggested that this means that the only remedies available to a proprietor are, as a result, those given by the Act. However, it seems that this cannot be right, if for no other reason than that there is no statutory provision for the grant of an injunction. Moreover, the words of s. 2(1) do not suggest that the proprietor has no other rights or remedies.

spurious mark and in the possession or under the control of the defendant, as well as of deceptive labels, advertising material, etc.; (3) and an inquiry as to damages in respect of the past infringement, or in lieu, an account of the profits made by the defendant by the sale of the spuriously marked goods.

In addition to the relief obtainable by an action for infringement, the Act provides machinery for causing infringing goods to be treated as prohibited imports.[68]

SUBMISSION OF ORDER TO REGISTRAR

19–052   Under CPR 63PD 22.1 the successful party in any matter which affects the validity of an entry in the Register is required to serve a copy of the order made on the Registrar.

9. Final injunctions

GENERAL CONSIDERATIONS

19–053   In general, a claimant whose rights have been invaded will obtain an injunction to restrain further wrongs from being committed against him, but his entitlement is not absolute. The exceptions to the general rule are much the same for passing off as for trade mark infringement, and they are considered together below.

19–054   The form of injunction granted may, by contrast, differ substantially depending on the cause of action, for passing off does not give an absolute exclusive right to use a mark, so that the injunction granted may be framed to allow the defendant to continue to use the offending mark provided that he does not cause deception. This is often phrased as a positive obligation on him sufficiently to distinguish his goods from the claimant's. These matters are considered below, separately for passing off and for infringement of registered marks.

FURTHER INFRINGEMENT MUST BE THREATENED OR BE LIKELY TO OCCUR

19–055   The grant of an injunction in trade mark and passing off cases is governed by the general rules applicable where other rights are concerned. There must be some threat or probability that the infringement will be commenced, continued, or repeated, or the court will not interfere.[69] If an actual infringement is shown to have occurred, that is usually sufficient and the claimant is not bound to wait until it has been frequently repeated, or until warning has been given and been disregarded,[70] for "the life of a trade mark depends upon the promptitude with which it is vindicated."[71]

19–056   (1) In *Steiner v Stevens* it was held that the plaintiffs were entitled to an injunction and costs though the evidence showed that the sale was due to a

---

[68] See Ch.20.

[69] An act having a continuing effect, *e.g.* the issue of a large number of circulars, is not sufficiently met by the offer of an undertaking not to repeat it, without anything to neutralise the effect of what has been done: *Yeatman v Homberger* (1912) 29 R.P.C. 561 and 645; *Hindhaugh v Inch* (1923) 40 R.P.C. 368; *Spalding v Gamage* (1915) 32 R.P.C. 273 at 289, 290, HL. The court will presume that a trader will use his mark so as not to be deceptive, if it is capable of being used without the probability of being deceptive, unless some reason to the contrary is shown: *Kutnow* (1893) 10 R.P.C. 401.

[70] See *Upmann v Forester* (1883) L.R. 24 Ch.D. 231.

[71] *Johnston v Orr-Ewing* (1882) 7 App.Cas. 219 at 229, 230.

mistake, but the defendant had refused to make any apology or offer any undertaking.[72]

(2) In *Myers v Fields*[73] infringement was by mistake and there was no apparent probability of the defendants repeating it. No injunction was granted but (the defendants having denied the infringement) the plaintiffs were granted a declaration: the order reciting that in the opinion of the court the acts complained of were inadvertent.

If the action is commenced before any undertaking has been given, a subsequent offer or even an undertaking out of court will not usually be sufficient unless an undertaking is offered in the defence,[74] although in some instances, the undertaking of an innocent infringer has been accepted by the court.[75] If an offer is made on an application for an interim injunction, the fact that the offer was made should be recited in the order on the motion,[76] and if the defendant wishes to adhere to the offer, it should be repeated in the defence. Where the defendant makes an offer in the defence to give an undertaking or submit to an injunction, the claimant is entitled to apply for an order embodying the offer, and to the costs even if the costs are not offered, and even if the relief offered is much less than claimed.[77] It is not necessary that any actual infringement should have occurred if it is proved that the defendant contemplates committing or has threatened to commit one,[78] and it is sufficient evidence of this that he is in possession of a considerable quantity of spuriously marked goods, even though it is only as a forwarding agent.[79]

19–057

ENFORCING AGREED TERMS

Where, as is not uncommon, an action is settled and a "Tomlin" order made staying proceedings, on terms scheduled to the order, except for the purpose of enforcing the terms, the court (in case the terms are not observed) can grant an injunction and order an inquiry as to damages on application in the original action[80] by the aggrieved party.[81] The court will not enforce such terms if they are too vague.[82]

19–058

FORM OF INJUNCTION—INFRINGEMENT OF A REGISTERED TRADE MARK

The usual form of injunction simply restrains infringement of the mark concerned, referring to it by number. This kind of order, expressed by reference simply to the right infringed, is the usual one in intellectual property cases.[83] Frequently, the particular infringement of which the defendant has been proved to have been guilty is expressly referred to in the order, a general restraint being added.

19–059

---

[72] [1957] R.P.C. 439.
[73] (1954) 71 R.P.C. 435.
[74] *Fram v Morton* (1922) 40 R.P.C. 33, CA.
[75] *Rose v Loftus* (1878) 47 L.J. Ch. 576.
[76] *Stillitz v Jones & Higgins* (1943) 60 R.P.C. 15.
[77] *Clark v Clark's Shoe Service* (1935) 52 R.P.C. 254, following *Winkle v Gent* (1914) 31 R.P.C. 473.
[78] *Emperor of Austria v Day and Kossuth* (1861) 3 De G.F. & J. 217 at 240, 247–249.
[79] *Upmann v Elkan* (1871–72) L.R. 12 Eq. 140; (1871–72) L.R. 7 Ch. App. 130; or a commission agent: *Catterson v Anglo-Foreign* (1911) 28 R.P.C. 74.
[80] See *Phillips v Clarke* [1970] Ch. 322.
[81] *Hyatt v Pollard* (1935) 52 R.P.C. 115. See also *Green v Rozen* [1955] 2 All E.R. 797.
[82] *Wilson & Whitworth v Express & Independent Newspapers* [1969] R.P.C. 165.
[83] See, *e.g. Spectravest v Aperknit* [1988] F.S.R. 161 at 170, *Coflexip v Stolt Comex* [2001] R.P.C. 9.

19–060   However, although the usual order is in terms of the right infringed, the court retains a discretion to craft the injunction to the circumstances of the case (or, as mentioned above, to grant no injunction). In particular, where an infringement is such that an injunction of some kind is appropriate, but a general restraint against infringement would be an unfair imposition on the defendant because it would force him to steer a wide course so as to avoid it, or because the right alleged to be infringed is a narrow or geographically limited one, and the infringement was inadvertent or innocent, a narrowly drawn injunction directed only at the specific acts found to infringe may be granted.[84]

19–061   The court will not usually in anticipation lay down a course of conduct for the defendant.[85] It is not the practice of the court to say in advance what is or is not sufficient to distinguish between marks.[86]

19–062   As it is not usually an infringement to use the claimant's mark upon his own goods, that is, goods which possess the attribute connoted by the mark,[87] the injunction can be expressed so as to prevent this being a breach of its terms.[88]

19–063   Where mere use of the defendant's own name would be *prima facie* a breach of the injunction, it is possible to include in the order an express reference to s.11 of the 1994 Act.[89]

A special order may be appropriate where the defendant is applying to register his infringing mark.[90]

FORM OF INJUNCTION — PASSING OFF ACTION

19–064   The form of the injunction granted varies considerably, according to the nature of the deceptive representation which the defendant is shown to have made use of, or threatened to make use of.

A declaration may be granted and not an injunction, in the absence of a threat by the defendants to continue the acts complained of.[91]

19–065   Where a defendant has imitated or adopted the claimant's distinctive trade mark or business name, the order may be an absolute injunction that he shall not use or carry on business under that name.[92] In a case before 1938[93] the court refused to grant an absolute injunction against selling goods under an unregistered mark, saying that the defendant would be entitled if he wished to sell under the mark with an explanation that the goods were not those of the plaintiff. This has

---

[84] *Microsoft v Plato* [1999] Masons C.L.R. 370, *Associated Newspapers v Express Newspapers* [2003] F.S.R. 51 at para.49.

[85] *Kerfoot v Cooper* (1908) 25 R.P.C. 508 ("Sweet Lips Cachous").

[86] *Brittain v Trade & Commercial Press* [1957] R.P.C. 134.

[87] See, *e.g. Condy v Taylor* (1887) 56 L.T. 891. Use of the mark on the claimant's "own" goods may be an infringement in some cases concerned with parallel imports, or with repackaging under the 1994 Act, s.12. The matter is discussed in more detail in Chs 13 and 15.

[88] cf. the "passing-off" case *Braham v Beachim* (1878) 7 Ch.D. 848.

[89] The CA did so in *Parker-Knoll v Knoll International* [1961] R.P.C. 346—a case decided under the 1938 Act, where s.8 was the relevant provision; see the order, printed at 373. The House of Lords showed no disapproval ([1962] R.P.C. 265 at 278, 283, 287, 288, 292); but Harman L.J. disapproved strongly, describing the order as made as a contradiction in terms: [1962] R.P.C. 243 at 256.

[90] See *Berlei v Bali* [1972] R.P.C. 568.

[91] *Treasure Cot v Hamleys* (1950) 67 R.P.C. 89. Liberty to apply for an injunction was granted.

[92] As in *Hendriks v Montagu* 17 Ch.D. 638. See *Manus v Fullwood & Bland* (1949) 66 R.P.C. 71 at 77; the order is quoted at (1949) 66 R.P.C. 285 at 286, *per* Roxburgh J. cf. *Aubanel & Alabaster v Aubanel* (1949) 66 R.P.C. 343 at 347, where the injunction was qualified.

[93] *Lissen v Harley* (1929) 46 R.P.C. 11; cf. *La Radiotechnique v Weinbaum* [1928] Ch. 1; 44 R.P.C. 361, where it was suggested that a claim for an absolute injunction might make the action not an action for passing off but one for infringement of an unregistered trade mark and so unsustainable.

not been the practice, and it is not thought that the argument would appeal to a modern court as applicable in every case.

(1) There are circumstances—for instance, in the bars of busy public **19–066** houses—where it is virtually impossible for managers to prevent supply of any available brand of a commodity, regardless of what is asked for. The court may then, passing off having been proved, be asked to limit the injunction granted to what is practicable whilst continuing to sell goods other than the claimant's. In some cases it will;[94] in others it will not.[95]

(2) In a dispute between a British company and its former German parent, as to the right to use the mark "Adrema" which formed the main part of each party's name, it was held that the goodwill connected with that mark in the United Kingdom belonged to the British company, the plaintiff, exclusively. An injunction was granted restraining the defendant from selling, advertising or offering for sale in the United Kingdom any addressing or costing machines or equipment therefore under any name or mark comprising the name or mark "Adrema" or any other name or mark so closely resembling the name or mark "Adrema" as to be calculated to pass-off or enable others to pass-off such machines or equipment as and for the plaintiffs' machines or equipment: *Adrema v Adrema- Werke* [1958] R.P.C. 323 at 332, following *Sturtevant Eng. v Sturtevant Mill* (1936) 53 R.P.C. 430. But Upjohn L.J. has said: "Perhaps that can be justified on the facts of that case but the general practice is to grant an injunction in the qualified form where the defendant is only using his own name": *Parker-Knoll v Knoll International* [1961] R.P.C. 346 at 362.

QUALIFIED INJUNCTIONS

In a case where it may be possible for the defendant to use the mark or name in **19–067** question without passing off, the injunction is granted in qualified form.[96]

Where the mark or name is one in which the claimant cannot claim an exclusive right, but which to many people indicates his goods or business, it is proper to qualify the injunction against using it by such words as "without clearly" (or "sufficiently") distinguishing his goods from the claimant's.[97] In cases where use of the mark or name without qualification need not be deceptive, an even weaker form may be employed: the prohibition being qualified by the addition "so as to represent" or "so as to lead to the belief" that the defendant's goods or business

---

[94] If rival brands are established on the market, a defendant in such cases cannot comply with an absolute injunction by switching to one claimant's goods without laying himself open to attack by the rival suppliers.

[95] *Showerings v Entam* [1975] F.S.R. 45.

[96] See, *e.g. Massam v Thorley's* (1880) 14 Ch.D. 748 at 762, CA. For a form of injunction in a business name case in which the plaintiffs had not an exclusive but only a qualified right in a particular word, see *Daimler (1904) v London Daimler* (1907) 24 R.P.C. 379. As to "own name" cases generally, see *Parker-Knoll v Knoll International* [1961] R.P.C. 346, at para.19–066.

[97] See the "Stone Ales" case, *per* Lord Watson and Lord Macnaghten: *Montgomery v Thompson* [1891] A.C. 217; 8 R.P.C. 361; see also *Thompson v Bent's Brewery* (1891) 8 R.P.C. 479. In *Magnolia Metal v Atlas Metal* (1897) 14 R.P.C. 389, Collins J. granted an injunction in this form, and the plaintiffs unsuccessfully appealed asking for an absolute prohibition, cf. the form in *Short's v Short* (1914) 31 R.P.C. 294 at 300. Injunctions were granted in this form, for instance, in the following cases: *Seixo v Provezende* (1865) L.R. 1 Ch.192; *Johnston v Orr-Ewing* (1882) 13 Ch.D. 434; 7 App.Cas. 219 at 234n; *Powell v Birmingham Brewery* ("Yorkshire Relish") [1897] A.C. 710; *Bewlay v Hughes* (1898) 15 R.P.C. 290 ("Dindigul Cigars"); *Grezier v Autran* (1896) 13 R.P.C. 1, and *Rey v Lecouturier* (1908) 25 R.P.C. 265; [1910] A.C. 262; 27 R.P.C. 268, HL (both "Chartreuse"). See also Lord Macnaghten in *Reddaway v Banham* [1896] A.C. 199 at 221; 13 R.P.C. 218 at 234.

are the claimant's.[98] In the special case of a word that is used by some as a description of the goods, although to some it is a trade mark of the claimant, what is known as the "Havana" or "Corona" form may be adopted,[99] the prohibition being qualified by such words as "without making it clear to the customer that it is not of the goods of the claimant".

19–068

(1) The Pinet cases illustrate the different cases to which the absolute and the limited forms of injunctions are respectively applicable. In the first case it was supposed that the assignor to the defendant company had traded under his own name, "Pinet", and a limited injunction was granted. Subsequently it was discovered that this was not his own name, but a name adopted for the purpose of fraud, and thereupon an absolute injunction was decreed: *Pinet v Maison Pinet* (1897) 14 R.P.C. 933; *Pinet v Maison Louis Pinet* (1898) 15 R.P.C. 65.

(2) In "Stone Ales" above, "Stone" being the name of the town where the plaintiff's ales were made, the qualified form of injunction—"without clearly distinguishing"—would normally have been appropriate. Nevertheless, an injunction to restrain the defendant (*inter alia*) from selling beer not of the plaintiff's manufacture, under the term "Stone Ales" or "Stone Ale", or in any way so as to induce the belief that such ale was of the plaintiff's manufacture, was maintained, the court holding that the ordinary qualified form of injunction would be more stringent, as it would in effect prevent the defendant using the term "Stone Ale" at all.

(3) The plaintiff had trade marks, registered for perfumery and toilet articles, of which the word "June" was the essential feature. The defendants, June Perfect Ltd, sold hair lotions, shampoos and lipsticks, bearing their name, to Messrs. Woolworths, who put them on retail sale, thereby passing them off as the plaintiff's. The Court of Appeal granted injunctions against infringement of trade mark; against passing off by use of the word "June"; and against continuing to trade in those articles under the name " *June Perfect Ltd.*" (see 68 R.P.C. at 166, 167, 168); but limited the passing off injunction to the three specific articles mentioned, and qualified it by the words "without clearly distinguishing, etc." (see 68 R.P.C. at 167). The House of Lords discharged the injunction against trading under the defendants' existing name, since they traded only with retailers, who need not be misled. The House observed that the other two injunctions should give adequate protection; whilst the form adopted for the passing off injunction supported the view that the defendants might "be able by proper precautions to sell the three articles in connection with their name of June Perfect Ltd. while clearly distinguishing those goods from the [plaintiffs'] goods": *Saville Perfumery v June Perfect* (1941) 58 R.P.C. 147 at 176.

(4) The term "Goddard's Plate Powder," originally meaning the powder of a Mr Goddard, had come to mean the goods of the plaintiff only, except to a small number of people who accepted powder made by Goddard's daughter. The defendants, when asked for "Goddard's Plate Powder,"

---

[98] e.g. *Slazenger v Feltham* (1889) 6 R.P.C. 531 (injunction against stamping "Demotic" on lawn-tennis racquets qualified by CA by adding "so as to represent that [they] are manufactured by the plaintiffs, or in any other way from passing off, etc."). In *Redwing v Redwing Forest* (1947) 64 R.P.C. 67, it was disputed how much of the order the qualifying words governed.

[99] From the "Corona" case, *Havana Cigar v Oddenino* [1923] 2 Ch. 243; 40 R.P.C. 229. A declaration in this form was granted (in similar circumstances) in *Treasure Cot v Hamleys* (1950) 67 R.P.C. 89 at 94: "A declaration that the defendants are not entitled to sell as 'Treasure Cots' any toy cots not supplied by or through the plaintiffs without making it clear to the customer that they are not connected with the plaintiffs." Another example is *Purefoy v Sykes Boxall* (1955) 72 R.P.C. 89 CA. As to what does "make it clear", cf. *Bostitch v McGarry & Cole* [1963] R.P.C. 183.

supplied Miss Goddard's plate powder without explanation or inquiry. An injunction was granted in the "Havana" form: *Goddard v Watford Co-op* (1924) 41 R.P.C. 218.

(5) The plaintiffs were credit-check traders (that is, provided the money for credit sales by retail traders), working by the issue of documents known in the area concerned as "Ideal Checks". The defendants were retail traders. The plaintiffs having refused to supply their "Ideal Checks" to the defendants, the defendants obtained credit checks from another company and (with fraudulent intent) advertised them as "Ideal Checks". The use of the defendants' name "The Ideal Clothing Co" was not calculated to deceive. An injunction was granted "restraining the defendants ... from using any form of words in newspaper advertisements or otherwise calculated to deceive persons into the belief that the defendants' said business is carried on by the plaintiffs or is in any way connected with the plaintiffs' business as credit check traders or that the defendants are authorised to issue or accept Ideal Checks": *Ideal General v Ideal Clothing* [1957] R.P.C. 252 at 259.

The qualification "without clearly distinguishing" is precise enough, and the order should not go into further detail. "It has been said many times that it is no part of the function of this court to examine imaginary cases of what the defendant could or could not do under this form of injunction. The best guide, if he is an honest man, is his own conscience; and it is certainly not the business of this court to give him instructions or hints as to how near the wind he can sail."[1] **19–069**

TEMPORARY OR CONTINGENT PROHIBITION

The defendant has, in some instances been restrained from using a word or words which could not be used by him at all, except deceptively, so long as this should continue to be the case; for instance, from calling his bitters "Angostura Bitters" until he should find out how to make the real "Angostura Bitters";[2] or from using the name "Radstock Colliery Proprietors" until he should be able to sell coal from Radstock.[3] **19–070**

NO RULE AS TO WHAT DISTINCTION IS SUFFICIENT

No general rule can be laid down as to what additions to the objectionable matter will be sufficient to effect the requisite distinction.[4] **19–071**

It must depend upon the circumstances of each case.[5] It is no answer to say that the custom of the trade is not to distinguish.[6]

(1) Since the decision in *Reddaway v Banham*, there have been three reported cases as to "camel-hair" belting in which the question has arisen whether the defendant sufficiently distinguished, namely, *Reddaway v Ahlers* (1902) 19 R.P.C. 12; *Reddaway v Frictionless Engine Packing* (1902) 19 **19–072**

---

[1] *per* Greene M.R., *Wright, Layman & Umney v Wright* (1949) 66 R.P.C. 149 at 152. See also *Letters v Letters (Craigton)* [1967] R.P.C. 209, SC; *Sterling Winthrop v Bayer* [1967] R.P.C. 326 and *Bach & Jackson v Cowan* [1969] R.P.C. 156 at 164 for examples of courts' refusals to tell a defendant how far he can go.

[2] *Siegert v Findlater* (1878) 7 Ch.D. 801.

[3] *Braham v Beachim* (1878) 7 Ch. D 848.

[4] "No court has ever said how the distinction is to be made": *per* Sterling J. in *Powell v Birmingham Vinegar* [1896] 2 Ch. 54 at 64. Also *Kerfoot v Cooper* (1908) 25 R.P.C. 508. See also *Clark v Associated Newspapers* [1998] R.P.C. 281.

[5] See *Warsop v Warsop* (1904) 21 R.P.C. 481, where "A. Warsop" was held to be sufficiently distinguished from "B. Warsop & Sons Ltd".

[6] *Reddaway v Ahlers*, illustration 1, below.

R.P.C. 505; and *Reddaway v Stevenson* (1903) 20 R.P.C. 276. In the second of these cases it was held that the prefixing of the defendant's name was sufficient, although they were not manufacturers, but the result was different in the last case, where it was pointed out that each case must rest on its own facts.

(2) The plaintiffs being the owners of natural springs at Caledonia, Ontario, sold the water as "Caledonia Water" or "Caledonia Springs Water". They had, however, no exclusive right to the word "Caledonia", and the defendants, who owned springs in the same neighbourhood and sold "Natural Saline water from the New Springs at Caledonia", were held to have sufficiently distinguished: *Grand Hotel v Wilson* [1904] A.C. 103; 21 R.P.C. 117, PC.

(3) In an action of Parker-Knoll Ltd. against an American company. Knoll International Ltd, the use by the defendants of the mark "Knoll" or "Knoll International" was held to be deceptive, and an injunction granted against doing so without clearly distinguishing their goods. It was later held that both use of the mark "Knoll International of U.S.A." and use as a mark of stylised initials "K.I." (with an indication whose initials they were) were breaches of the injunction: *Parker-Knoll v Knoll International* [1962] R.P.C. 243 (Wilberforce J. and CA). But a later motion for contempt based on the use of "Knoll International", failed so far as passing off went, the plaintiffs having failed—as in National Advertiser, below—to prove that the distinction was inadequate: *Parker Knoll v Knoll Overseas* [1985] F.S.R. 349 at 363–364.

(4) Where the plaintiffs had two weekly papers, the London Weekly Advertiser and (much less well-known) the National Advertiser almost identical in content, and the defendants adopted the title "National Weekly", it was held that in this exceptional case printing "No connection with any other paper whatsoever" might be a sufficient distinction: for those likely to be confused could be people who knew the National Advertiser only as a subsidiary of the London Weekly Advertiser: *Brittain v Trade & Commercial Press (No. 2)* [1957] R.P.C. 271.

19–073   Where the order is in respect of a word which has, in fact become the claimant's trade mark, used as the name of the claimant's goods, the most careful differentiation of the get-up of the goods,[7] and the greatest possible prominence of the defendant's own name[8] upon his labels may not be enough. In such cases the limitation of the order is more likely to mislead the defendant than to protect him in his assumed right to use the word.

INJUNCTION DIRECTED TO FUTURE CONSIGNMENTS OF GOODS ONLY

19–074   In a case where the plaintiffs refrained from taking proceedings on learning that the defendants had received a small quantity of the infringing goods, but waited until they had got a larger consignment, Malins V.C. ordered the injunction to be directed to stop the sale of future consignments only.[9] It is submitted, however, that the calculated conduct of the plaintiffs was not a sufficient reason for allowing the goods already received to be sold under the deceptive labels. It has

---

[7] In *Powell v Birmingham Vinegar* the bottles and labels on the defendants' "Yorkshire Relish" were totally different from those of the plaintiffs. They are shown in (1896) 13 R.P.C. at 237, 238 and 240.

[8] In *Daniel and Arter v Whitehouse* (1898) 16 R.P.C. 71, "F. Whitehouse's Brazilian Silver" was held to be an infringement of an order not to use "Brazilian Silver" without distinguishing, etc.

[9] *Anglo-Swiss v Swiss* [1871] W.N. 163.

certainly been held that acquiescence, not sufficient to bar the claimant's right, may, in some classes of action, cause the court to refuse relief by injunction, and to grant the claimant damages only,[10] but the case last referred to did not involve any continuing fraud or deception.[11]

MANDATORY INJUNCTIONS; ORDERS TO CHANGE NAME

The court has power to make mandatory as well as prohibitory injunctions. Procedurally, mandatory injunctions may be more difficult, because they require to be policed, but this is simply a factor to be considered (and in relation to interim injunctions it is a matter going to the balance of convenience, since it may be more prone to cause injustice than an order preserving the status quo).[12]   **19–075**

Mandatory relief in a passing off action may include an order to compel the defendants to state that they are not connected with the claimant, where they are selling the claimant's goods but also falsely giving the impression that they are authorised agents.[13]   **19–076**

A defendant whose company name is inherently deceptive may be ordered to change its name. Such an order may even be made at an interim stage: *Glaxo v Glaxowellcome*.[14] Likewise, a company registering a websitewith a name which is so inherently deceptive as to amount to an instrument of fraud may be ordered to change the name of the site or to transfer it to the claimant: *Marks and Spencer v One-in-a-million*[15] (the order there being made following a successful application for summary judgment). Formally speaking, an order should be obtained against the members of such a company requiring them to change the name, since the court has no power to give authority to do so to any other person: *Halifax plc v Halifax Reposessions Ltd* [2004] F.S.R. 45.   **19–077**

10. Interim injunctions

OUTLINE

The claimant in an infringement or passing off action may apply for an interim injunction to restrain the defendant, until the hearing of the action or further order, from continuing or committing the infringement or deceptive conduct of which he complains. Quite apart from the advantages of stopping the infringement without delay, experience shows that a successful application for an interim injunction frequently puts an end to the litigation and the infringement, with a great saving in expense compared with a full trial.   **19–078**

However, in recent years there has been a growing trend for applications for interim injunctions, when made, to be refused or adjourned to trial, with an order   **19–079**

---

[10] *Sayers v Collyer* (1884) 28 Ch.D. 103, *per* Fry L.J. A case relating to a restrictive covenant in regard to buildings. In a passing off action a delay of three and a half years was under the circumstances of the case held not to disentitle the plaintiffs to an injunction: *Reddaway v Stevenson* (1903) 20 R.P.C. 276 (injunction but no damages).

[11] The action for infringement may wholly fail, because the defendant has used the plaintiff's mark so long that there is no longer any deception, as in *Londonderry v Russell* (1886) 2 T.L.R. 843; 3 T.L.R. 360.

[12] *Nottingham Building Society v Eurodynamics* [1993] F.S.R. 468. [1995] F.S.R. 605, CA.

[13] *Sony v Saray* [1983] F.S.R. 302, where it was held that undertakings from the defendants were worthless, and they were ordered to put disclaiming stickers on goods of the claimants sold by them.

[14] [1996] F.S.R. 388.

[15] [1998] F.S.R. 265, [1999] F.S.R. 1.

for a speedy trial. In some cases, trials have taken place within two or three months from the issuing of proceedings, which used to be the kind of period taken for a full scale application for an interim injunction to come on for hearing in the 1980s and early 1990s. This kind of order has much more frequently been made in cases where there is a legitimate dispute between the parties as to the defendant's right to use the name or mark concerned; it is not really of application in counterfeiting cases.

APPLICATIONS WITHOUT NOTICE

19–080   Where an application for relief is made without notice, especially, there is an obligation upon the applicant to make full disclosure to the court of all facts material to the application. An order made upon evidence not making full disclosure will usually be discharged, or not continued; but this does not prevent a further application once full disclosure has been made,[16] and there remains a discretion not to discharge the order if justice requires that some relief be continued.[17] The Court has power, in appropriate circumstances, to grant relief even against defendants whose name the claimant does not know, or whom the claimant knows only by description.[18]

APPEAL FROM THE GRANT OR REFUSAL OF INTERIM RELIEF

19–081   In present practice, the decision upon an application for an interim injunction is essentially an exercise of judicial discretion, with which the Court of Appeal will interfere only where the decision below is wrong in principle.[19]

THE GENERAL TEST FOR THE GRANT OF AN INTERIM INJUNCTION

19–082   In general, applications for interim relief are decided on the *American Cyanamid* principles: in outline, this means that a claimant must show an arguable case against the defendant, and that (if he is right) continuance of the defendant's activities until the trial is likely to cause substantial damage to him that is irreparable in the sense that it will not be compensated by an order for damages at the trial.[20] Damages may be an inadequate remedy either because the defendant is or will be unable to pay, or because the nature of the damage being sustained by the claimant is such that it cannot be assessed in money terms or repaired by the expenditure of money after success at trial. The potential damage to the claimant which must be considered is limited to damages which he could recover at trial if successful: damages which would be suffered but which would be too remote to recover are irrelevant: *Peaudouce v Kimberley Clark*.[21]

19–083   In trade mark infringement cases irreparable damage, in this sense, is relatively easily shown, since infringement may easily destroy the value of a mark or at least nullify expensive advertising in a way that is hard to quantify for the

---

[16] *Yardley v Higson* [1984] R.P.C. 304, CA.
[17] *Brink's-Mat v Elcombe* [1988] 1 W.L.R. 1350.
[18] *Bloomsbury Publishing Group v News Group Newspapers* [2003] F.S.R. 45.
[19] *Elan Digital v Elan Computer* [1984] F.S.R. 373 at 384, 386, CA.
[20] *American Cyanamid v Ethicon* [1975] A.C. 396; [1975] R.P.C. 513, HL (a patent infringement case). This marked a major change in the practice on such applications, so that previous authorities are now of little or no value. Furthermore, the balance of convenience is so much a matter of personal judgment of the special facts of the particular case, that later decisions are rarely of much help either.
[21] [1996] F.S.R. 680.

purposes of an inquiry into damages.[22] This has more recently come to be referred to, in cases where the defendant's conduct is not directly damaging but merely reduces the distinctive character of the claimant's mark, as "dilution". It is, however, an important and recognised head of recoverable damage which has been successfully invoked by claimants on a number of occasions.[23] However, where the proprietor has licensed the mark it is likely that damages will be an adequate remedy.[24]

Where all that can be shown, however, is that some damage is likely and ought not to be allowed to go on for too long, an order for a speedy trial may be more appropriate than an injunction, as has been mentioned above.   **19–084**

The defendant may meet the application by showing that he genuinely intends to defend[25] and that he also would (if an injunction were granted and were shown at the trial to have been unjustified) suffer damage not reparable by an order for damages under the cross-undertaking that accompanies any interim injunction. If the defendant is able so to do,[26] the matter then depends on the "balance of convenience":[27] that is, on the relative extent of the damage to one or other party if the injunction is or is not granted. The ability of the parties to meet an order for damages on the scale contemplated will be relevant.[28] In general, the likelihood that one or other party will succeed at the trial is not a relevant consideration: but the likely extent of confusion or deception clearly may be;[29] whilst in cases where the interim proceedings are likely to determine the dispute finally, one way or the other, the probabilities of success are clearly relevant.[30]   **19–085**

APPLICATION OF *AMERICAN CYANAMID* PRINCIPLES TO TRADE MARK CASES

While it has been confirmed that *American Cyanamid* principles apply in general to applications for interim relief in trade mark and passing off cases,[31] there are certain important considerations, specific to such actions, which need to be borne in mind. In particular, although it is usually neither necessary nor appropriate to assess the degree of probability of success which the claimant's action has (provided that it is arguable, and subject to the principle of *American Cyanamid* that the merits may be resorted to as a "tie-breaker" if the balance of convenience is very even),[32] in trade mark and passing off cases, it is very hard to avoid doing so, since the better the claimant's case on the likelihood of deception (frequently the major issue) the greater the harm which he is likely to suffer. Accordingly, in   **19–086**

---

[22] *Elan Digital v Elan Computers* [1984] F.S.R. 373 at 385, CA; defendants' proposed operations, though in a different field from the plaintiffs, would "swamp" the plaintiffs' goodwill; grant of injunction upheld. See below for further authorities in relation to the "swamping" argument.

[23] See the discussion on dilution in Ch.14. For a recent example see *Scotch Whisky Association v Glen Kella Distillers* [1997] E.T.M.R. 470.

[24] *Weight Watchers v Tesco* [2003] EWHC 1109 (Ch).

[25] *Smith & Nephew v 3M* [1982] R.P.C. 92, CA: (patent case).

[26] But to do so he must be specific, and give details. If he leaves the court in doubt as to the size of the problems which an interim injunction would occasion, he risks the court finding against him: *Antec v South Western Chicks* [1997] F.S.R. 278.

[27] *American Cyanamid v Ethicon* [1975] A.C. 396; [1975] R.P.C. 513, at para.19–082.

[28] For an example of a case where the defendant's inability to pay was a significant factor in the grant of an interim injunction, see *The Law Society v Society of Lawyers* [1996] F.S.R. 739. See also *Antec v South Western Chicks* [1997] F.S.R. 278, where ability to pay was a factor.

[29] See para.19–086.

[30] See para.19–087.

[31] See, *e.g. County Sound v Ocean Sound* [1991] F.S.R. 367, CA.

[32] This principle was applied in, *e.g. Mirage Studios v Counter-Feat Clothing* [1991] F.S.R. 145.

appropriate cases, where the state of the evidence permits it, the court may seek to weigh up the merits in deciding whether to grant interim relief. This was confirmed in, for example, *Financial Times v Evening Standard*[33], and more recently in *Antec v South Western Chicks*[34] and *SmithKline Beecham v Antigen Pharmaceuticals*.[35] However, such an approach is not always necessary, since factors other than the relative merits may be determinative of the application, and where the facts are sufficiently complex, carrying out a "not-so-mini" trial to assess the merits will not be appropriate: *Blazer v Yardley*.[36]

19–087   Additionally, there are cases where it is clear that the outcome of an application for interim relief will decide the whole action, in particular where the application is made before or soon after the defendant has started to use the mark alleged to infringe, and in circumstances where it is clear that he will have to abandon it permanently for another if an injunction is granted. In such cases, the court may have to do the best it can to assess the merits and grant or refuse an injunction based on its conclusion.[37]

19–088   There has also been a tendency on the part of the courts to be willing to assess the merits at the interim stage, and to decide the application on that basis, where it is clear that the arguments of one side or the other on the issue of likelihood of confusion are hopeless or close to hopeless. Examples of such cases include *Furnitureland v Harris*,[38] *Financial Times v Evening Standard*,[39] *Tamworth Herald v Thomson*,[40] *United Biscuits v Burton Biscuits*,[41] (part of case held unarguably bad, part held arguable) *Advance Magazines v Redwood*,[42] *Rizla v Bryant and May*.[43] This is in no way a departure from the *American Cyanamid* principles, which require the court first of all to decide whether there is a triable issue; it is rather a result of the fact that in passing off and trade marks cases, the court is able to assess the factual issue of likelihood of confusion on the basis of its own impression and experience.

STATUS QUO

19–089   Where convenience is evenly balanced, the court should incline towards preserv-

---

[33] [1991] F.S.R. 7 at 10–11
[34] [1997] F.S.R. 278, citing *Series 5 Software v Clarke* [1996] F.S.R. 273.
[35] [1999] E.T.M.R. 512 (HC, Ireland)—little confusion apparent despite aggressive marketing by the defendants.
[36] [1992] F.S.R. 501 at 506–507.
[37] See *NWL Ltd v Woods* [1979] 1 W.L.R. 1294 and *Cayne v Global Natural Resources* [1984] 1 All E.R. 225 generally in relation to the principle of assessing the merits where an interim decision is likely to decide the dispute finally. For authorities in the field of passing off and trade mark infringement specifically, see *Boots v Approved Prescription Services* [1988] F.S.R. 45; *Post Office v Interlink* [1989] F.S.R. 369; *Stacey v 2020 Communications* [1991] F.S.R. 49; *Gala of London v Chandler* [1991] F.S.R. 294; *Management Publications v Blenheim Exhibitions* [1991] F.S.R. 348 and 550, CA; *Blazer v Yardley* [1992] F.S.R. 501; *BBC v Talbot* [1980] F.S.R. 228; *Parnass/Pelly v Hodges* [1982] F.S.R. 329; *Elan Digital v Elan Computers* [1984] F.S.R. 373 at 386, CA; *BBC v Talksport Ltd* [2001] F.S.R. 6. In *Entec v Abacus* [1992] F.S.R. 332, CA, a copyright case, the defendant successfully defeated an application for an interim injunction by arguing that the grant of one would cause its bankruptcy and hence there would never be a trial. The argument succeeded on the basis of the Cayne principle.
[38] [1989] F.S.R. 536.
[39] [1991] F.S.R. 7.
[40] [1991] F.S.R. 337.
[41] [1992] F.S.R. 14.
[42] [1993] F.S.R. 449.
[43] [1986] R.P.C. 389.

ing the "status quo"[44]: that is to say, the *status quo ante bellum*, so that the Court should here look for the *casus belli* with a view to intervening against it.[45] In general, the status quo is the state of affairs existing immediately before the issue of the proceedings, or, if there has been unreasonable delay between the issue of the proceedings and the application for an injunction, immediately before the application: *Garden Cottage Foods v Milk Marketing Board*.[46]

However, care is needed in this analysis, and it may not be so simple as to say   **19–090**
that the status quo, in the case of a newly launched product which is alleged to infringe, is that the product is not on the market. In *Blazer v Yardley*,[47] where the defendant had recently launched a product which the plaintiff alleged amounted to passing off, it was held that granting an injunction would not preserve the status quo. The status quo was not limited to the presence or absence of the defendant from the market, but also included the state of the market, which would be changed by the grant of an injunction. Moreover, since an injunction would effectively prevent the defendant from returning to the disputed name for all time, that would also be a change to the status quo, in which the use of the name by the defendant was a possibility. By contrast, in *Morgan-Grampian v Training Personnel*,[48] the defendant changed the name of an existing publication to one alleged to constitute passing off, and the court held that the status quo would be preserved by the grant of an injunction. In *Reckitt & Colman v Borden*[49] (the "Jif" case), it was held that the grant of an interim injunction would preserve the status quo, the defendant's product not having been launched.

A related issue is the question of defendants who act with "eyes open", in the   **19–091**
sense of knowing that the claimant may object to their conduct, it sometimes being argued that such persons are undeserving of sympathy. There is something a little illogical about the argument, since it would seem wrong to count against such a defendant the fact that he has considered his proposed conduct and concluded that it would be lawful, particularly when there is a good chance that his conclusion is correct. However, it has been taken into account in favour of claimants in a number of cases, and in particular it has been held that where a defendant presses on boldly with a high risk strategy knowing of a likely objection from the claimant, doing so should not improve his position in relation to the assessment of the status quo or the balance of convenience: *Peaudouce v Kimberley Clark*.[50]

OTHER FACTORS RELEVANT TO THE BALANCE OF CONVENIENCE

It is probably impossible to list all of the matters which may be relevant in rela-   **19–092**
tion to the balance of convenience, but in addition to the matters referred to above, the following have been recognised as being of weight.

The defendant's freedom of speech is a relevant factor. This issue is considered

---

[44] *American Cyanamid v Ethicon* [1975] A.C. 396; [1975] R.P.C. 513, at para.19–082.
[45] *Metric Resources v Leasemetrix* [1979] F.S.R. 571 (passing off case). See also, as to "status quo", *Dunhill v Sunoptic* [1979] F.S.R. 337 at 376, CA (passing off case).
[46] [1984] A.C. 130.
[47] [1992] F.S.R. 501.
[48] [1992] F.S.R. 267.
[49] [1987] F.S.R. 228.
[50] [1996] F.S.R. 681, and see also *Jian Tools v Roderick* [1995] F.S.R. 924, *Morgan-Grampian v Training Personnel* [1992] F.S.R. 267, where a lack of prudence by the defendant in not checking whether the name objected to was already in use was held against it on the balance of convenience.

in detail in Ch.17 in connection with malicious falsehood, where it is more relevant, but even in a "pure" passing off case, it has been held that freedom of speech is a relevant factor: *Consorzio del Prosciutto di Parma v Marks & Spencer*.[51]

19–093   Another factor of importance in certain cases is "swamping", which is to say that where the defendant is a much bigger concern than the claimant, it may be that his use will be so extensive that by trial the claimant's reputation will have been overwhelmed. This is of course a rather unusual situation, but it can be a very significant point, as for example in *Provident Financial v Halifax Building Society*.[52]

COMPROMISE OF INTERIM APPLICATION; VARIATION OF INTERIM ORDER

19–094   It often happens that the interim application is settled by the defendant offering, and the claimant accepting, a compromise in the form of an undertaking or injunction giving part of what was sought. Where this is done, however, the parties will be bound by it: a claimant who finds confusion worse than he supposed cannot come back to ask for more,[53] nor can a defendant whose offer was based on a wrong view of the law ask to be released.[54] Where the court has already made an order giving directions, upon undertakings by the defendant, it will not normally entertain an application for summary judgment, because to do so is to some extent inconsistent with the giving of directions for disclosure and pleadings, although it has jurisdiction to do so, and may do so if there has been a change of circumstances since the order for directions.[55]

19–095   It is also possible to apply to vary an interim order. The court will not, however, do so unless there has been a significant change in circumstances: *Gordino Ltd v Burgess*.[56]

INTERIM INJUNCTION REFUSED ON ACCOUNT OF DELAY

19–096   Any significant, unnecessary delay in applying for interim relief is likely to tilt the balance of convenience against the claimant.[57] That does not mean that proceedings should be started without warning; delay due to failure of the defendants to answer letters may be excused.[58] Also, a degree of hesitation owing to a desire to avoid litigation is understandable and not normally a bar to relief.[59] A confidential notification by a defendant to a claimant of an intended course of action is nonetheless a notification, and delay thereafter is relevant: *Silicon Graphics v Indigo Graphic*.[60]

INTERIM INJUNCTION LIMITED AS CLOSELY AS POSSIBLE

19–097   The interim injunction, being intended only to preserve the claimant's right from

---

[51] [1990] F.S.R. 530.
[52] [1994] F.S.R. 81.
[53] *GCT v Laurie Marsh* [1973] R.P.C. 432 (passing off case).
[54] *Chanel v Woolworth* [1981] F.S.R. 196, CA.
[55] *Fabre v Ronco* [1984] F.S.R. 148.
[56] [1988] 1 W.L.R. 890, CA.
[57] The older cases, indicating that avoidable delay is an absolute bar to interim relief, are in general not now followed; but it remains true that all reasonable speed in making the application is desirable.
[58] "Under Six Club" (*Deane v Schofield*) [1962] R.P.C. 179: penalty in costs, where a letter would have sufficed to stop the acts complained of.
[59] "Oxford Marmalade", *CPC v Keenan* [1986] F.S.R. 527.
[60] [1994] F.S.R. 403.

serious detriment until the hearing, is, at any rate in cases which appear to be doubtful or honestly disputed, limited as closely as possible to what is sufficient to attain that end.[61] The claimant must give a cross-undertaking to abide by any order of the court as to damages for the loss (if any) occasioned by it to the defendant, should it turn out at the trial that it ought not to have been granted. If an undertaking to the court is given in lieu of an interim injunction there is similarly inserted in the order a cross-undertaking in damages. Where the claimant is a foreign corporation it and its British subsidiary may give the cross-undertaking.[62]

11. Enforcement and breaches of injunctions

ENFORCEMENT OF THE INJUNCTION

Breaches of an injunction or undertaking are contempts of court, which may be punished by the committal of the guilty person, or by ordering him to pay a fine or costs. Before the court will punish a breach of an injunction or undertaking, it must be clear that a breach has been committed.[63] Accordingly, where an injunction is granted in general terms, and the defendant is not doing the specific thing on which the judgment was founded; or the injunction having been obtained by default, no specific thing has been admitted or found to be an infringement; the claimant may, when moving for contempt, be in some difficulty:[64] for it is inconvenient to try an action upon such a motion. **19–098**

Where the defendant under an injunction or an undertaking wishes to be relieved therefrom in respect of particular acts he may apply to the court, but must make out a case in favour of that relief.[65] **19–099**

UNINTENTIONAL BREACH OF THE INJUNCTION

It may be assumed that, if the court is satisfied that the defendant has honestly tried to comply with its order, it will be unwilling to send him to prison because he has failed in his endeavour. But the court has jurisdiction to commit for disobedience to an order which is not shown to have been wilful.[66] If the defendant is in the wrong, even though by mistake or misfortune, he may be ordered to pay the costs of the application.[67] In recent years, a more forgiving attitude has been taken by the courts, and in one case, where the defendant was striving honestly to obey an order made without notice in the absence of the supervising solicitor, **19–100**

---

[61] *Biro-Swan v Tallon* [1961] R.P.C. 326; *Bowater-Scott v Modo* [1969] F.S.R. 330 (passing off injunction refused where registered trade mark injunction sufficient).

[62] *Hobart v Cannon* [1959] R.P.C. 269; *Ferragamo v Lotus* (1950) 67 R.P.C. 175.

[63] See, *e.g. Redwing v Redwing Forest* (1947) 64 R.P.C. 67 (passing off case; undertaking broken only on one of two possible constructions; no order on motion for sequestration).

[64] *Ripley v Arthur* (1902) 19 R.P.C. 443, a passing off case; *Multiform v Whitmarley* [1957] R.P.C. 260 at 262, HL. Accordingly, the claimant in such a case will normally do better to start a fresh action, although where the defendant is doing the specific thing forbidden by the earlier injunction, contempt proceedings are the only proper remedy; *Sterling-Winthrop v Bayer* [1966] R.P.C. 477. Often an injunction is not of much value against a wrongdoer who is both astute and determined. Fortunately, few wrongdoers are either, let alone both.

[65] *Sterling-Winthrop v Bayer* [1967] R.P.C. 326. The court will seldom relieve from an undertaking or an injunction made by consent, by way of compromise with the claimant's demands: see *Chanel v Woolworth* [1981] F.S.R. 196 at para.19–094.

[66] *Hewitt v Mansell*, 29 S.J. 66. In *Parker v Cooper* (1901) 18 R.P.C. 319, Cozens-Hardy J. refused to commit the defendant for an isolated instance of passing off by the defendant's son without the defendant's knowledge.

[67] *Daniel and Arter v Whitehouse* (1898) 16 R.P.C. 71; *Vine Products v Mackenzie* [1968] F.S.R. 625. cf. *Frenkel v Orru* [1968] R.P.C. 49 (special circumstances, no order for costs).

who had gone away to serve another defendant, the claimant was ordered to pay the costs of the application to commit, even though technically a breach had been committed: *Adam Phones v Goldschmidt*.[68] The same attitude may be taken by the court where an employee has committed a breach and so put his employer in technical contempt despite that employer's best efforts to avoid such a situation arising.[69] In any event an order restraining a defendant from doing acts through its agents and so forth does not impose an obligation on it to prevent all restrained actions by such persons, but only those over which it has some control.[70]

CHOICE OF A NEW MARK BY THE DEFENDANT

19–101   The court will not compel an honest trader to alter his mark more than is necessary to protect the claimant's rights. But the court will not usually assist a defendant by indicating how far he may safely go.[71]

DELAY IN APPLICATION TO COMMIT

19–102   If the claimant delays taking steps to enforce the injunction for a considerable time after he knows of the fresh infringement, the delay may cause the court to refuse to commit.[72]

12. Erasure, destruction, delivery up

STATUTORY REMEDIES FOR INFRINGEMENT OF REGISTERED MARKS

19–103   In addition to the common law and equitable remedies available in respect of passing off and trade mark infringement by virtue of their being actions in tort, there is now a statutory regime providing for erasure of infringing marks, and destruction or delivery up of offending goods. These remedies are to be found in ss.15–19 of the 1994 Act. These remedies apply only to actions for infringement of a registered mark, not to passing off claims, in respect of which only the former common law remedies are available.

TO WHAT ARTICLES THE STATUTORY REMEDIES APPLY

19–104   The statutory remedies apply to "infringing goods", "infringing material", and "infringing articles". These terms are defined in s.17(2), (4) and (5) respectively of the 1994 Act.

In broad terms, goods are "infringing goods" if, first, they bear (or their packaging bears) the registered mark in question, or a mark similar to it, and, secondly, the application of the mark to them was, or, had it been done in the United Kingdom, would have been, an infringement of the registration. Section 17(2)(c) broadens the definition to a rather unclear extent by including goods in relation to which "the sign has otherwise been used ... in such a way as to infringe the registered trade mark."

---

[68] [2000] F.S.R. 163. See also *Bhimji v Chatwani* [1991] 1 W.L.R. 989, *BT v Nextcall* [2000] E.T.M.R. 943 Jacob J., January 25, 2000.

[69] See *BT v Nextcall*; *Showerings v Entam* [1975] F.S.R. 45.

[70] *World Wildlife Fund v THQ/Jakks Pacific* [2004] F.S.R. 10.

[71] cf. *Kerfoot v Cooper* (1908) 25 R.P.C. 508; and see the passing off cases, at paras 19–067 to 19–069.

[72] See Turner L.J. in *Rodgers v Nowill* (1847) 3 De G.M. & G. 614; 22 L.J.Ch. 404. But delay is not a defence, *Chanel v F.G.M. Cosmetics* [1981] F.S.R. 471.

Section 17(2) of the 1994 Act is silent as to the notional circumstances in **19–105** which it is to be assumed that the offending mark was applied to the goods outside the United Kingdom for the purposes of the test under s.17(2)(b). Decisions under related provisions of copyright law suggest that what should be considered is application by the persons who did in fact mark the goods (see, for example, *CBS v Charmdale*).[73] In most situations, particularly where the goods are counterfeit, this nuance will not matter. But where the goods have been marked by a person in some way connected with the claimant, perhaps by virtue of being a company in common ownership, or holding some kind of licence, it could be of great importance. This is particularly so having regard to the English courts' reluctance to permit trade marks to be used to prevent the importation of goods put on the market by a company related to the United Kingdom trade mark owner, as in *Revlon v Cripps & Lee*.[74]

Goods are not capable of being "infringing goods" if by virtue of an enforceable Community right, they may lawfully be imported into the United Kingdom.[75]

"Infringing materials" are defined by s.17(4), and are materials such as labels, **19–106** wrappers, business papers or advertising materials which, first, bear the registered mark or a mark similar to it, and, secondly, are used, or intended to be used, in a manner which would infringe. It is plain from the words of s.17(4) that the intention required is merely intention to use. There is no requirement that the person concerned should know or intend that such use would amount to an infringement.

"Infringing articles" are defined by s.17(5). They must satisfy a two-stage test. **19–107** First, they must be specifically designed or adapted for making copies of a sign identical or similar to the registered mark in question. Secondly, the person possessing them must know or have reason to believe that they have been used or are to be used to make infringing goods or materials. The section is, regrettably, unclear as to what this involves, since the reference back to infringing materials itself involves incorporation of the mental element of s.17(4). As a minimum, it is suggested that the person in possession of the allegedly infringing article must know that it will be used to make materials and what the manner of use of those materials will be (even if he may be ignorant as to whether that use would infringe).

STATUTORY ORDER FOR ERASURE, REMOVAL OR OBLITERATION

By s.15 of the 1994 Act, the court may order a person who has been found to **19–108** infringe a registered trade mark to cause the offending sign to be erased, removed or obliterated from any infringing goods, materials or articles in his possession, custody or control. If it is not reasonably practicable for the sign to be erased, the person may be ordered to destroy the goods, materials or articles in question.

Of course, many unsuccessful defendants in trade mark actions, particularly of **19–109** the kind involving counterfeiting, may not be trustworthy, and to put the erasure of the offending mark or destruction of the offending goods in their hands would just be a recipe for them to be spirited away only to appear somewhere else. For this reason, s.15(2) permits the court, where an order under s.15(1) has not been complied with, or seems unlikely to be complied with, to direct that the goods,

---

[73] [1981] Ch. 91.
[74] [1980] F.S.R. 85. And see Ch.15, generally.
[75] 1994 Act, s.17(3).

materials or articles be delivered up to some other person for erasure or destruction. It is to be assumed that frequently the person to whom they are so delivered up will be the claimant.

It is important to note, by contrast with s.16 (which is considered below), that for the court to exercise its powers under this provision, a finding of infringement must have been made against the person in possession of the goods, materials or articles concerned.

STATUTORY ORDER FOR DELIVERY UP

19–110   Section 16 of the 1994 Act permits a trade mark proprietor to apply to the court for an order for the delivery up (to himself or to someone else directed by the court) of infringing goods, materials or articles in the possession, custody or control of another person in the course of a business. Relief under s.16 may be sought in the same application as relief under s.19 (as to which, see below).[76]

19–111   An order under s.16 may not be made after the period provided for by s.18 (which is considered in more detail below, but is basically six years from the date of application of the mark), and may not be made unless the court also makes, or it appears that there are grounds for making, an order under s.19 (which is considered below and relates to disposal of infringing goods, materials or articles).

19–112   It is important to note that while s.16 requires that the goods, materials or articles in question must be "infringing", it does not require that the person against whom the order is sought must have infringed within the meaning of s.10, or intend to do so. An order under the section may therefore be made against a person who is merely the keeper of infringing goods, etc.

19–113   This raises the question of the level of proof required under the section. Of course, if the person against whom delivery up is sought has lost an infringement action against the proprietor of the mark there should be no difficulty. Likewise, if the proprietor has succeeded in relation to certain kinds of goods at a trial there should be little difficulty in satisfying the court under s.16 even if the application is made against someone other than the unsuccessful defendant. But what if an application is made under s.16 against an innocent person who does not know whether the goods in question are infringing, in circumstances where the proprietor has not previously vindicated his rights? It is suggested that the right answer is that in such cases the applicant must show on the balance of probabilities that the goods are in fact infringing, not merely that they might be or are arguably so. In the context of the very similar provisions of the Copyright, Designs and Patents Act 1998, ss.99 and 114, it has been suggested that the lower standard of proof is correct,[77] but that seems wrong in principle.[78]

19–114   The person to whom delivery up is made must keep the infringing goods, materials or articles pending the making of an order under s.19 of the 1994 Act.[79]

---

[76] *Miller Brewing Co v The Mersey Docks and Harbour Company* [2003] F.S.R. 5.

[77] *Lagenes v It's At* [1991] F.S.R. 492.

[78] For a cogent criticism of the decision and an explanation as to why the proper view is that the goods must be shown actually to be infringing, see Laddie Prescott & Vitoria, *Modern Law of Copyright*, (3rd ed., Butterworths, London, 2000) paras 39.54 and 71.

[79] s.16(3).

APPLICATION FOR ORDER FOR DISPOSAL

At the same time as,[80] or after, an application for delivery up under s.16 of the **19–115**
1994 Act has been made, a further application may be made for an order dealing
with the disposal of the goods, materials or articles concerned. The possible
outcomes are an order for destruction, an order for forfeiture, or no order.
Unfortunately, there is no apparent jurisdiction under s.19 to order removal or
erasure of the mark, as there is under s.15. Proceedings under s.19 are civil
proceedings and therefore within the Brussels Convention.[81]

In deciding what order, if any, to make, the court must consider the other rem- **19–116**
edies available to the trade mark owner in an infringement action, and whether
they would be adequate to compensate the proprietor and any licensee, and
protect their interests. This rather complicates matters, since one remedy available in infringement proceedings (but not under s.19) is removal or erasure of the
mark. It therefore seems open to the court to decide that removal would be sufficient protection, but not open to it to order it, unless and until infringement
proceedings are successfully brought. This is illogical, and it is suggested that the
court would only decline to order forfeiture or destruction on that basis if infringement proceedings could be brought relatively easily and swiftly. If the
bringing of infringement proceedings would be difficult or lengthy (perhaps
because identifying the infringer would be a problem—recalling that the infringer
may not himself be a party to proceedings under s.19), it is suggested that the
court will be inclined to order destruction or forfeiture.

Section 19(1) contemplates that an order for forfeiture in favour of the propri- **19–117**
etor may be made, and presumably would be seriously considered in a case where
his financial remedies appeared inadequate because of the impecuniosity of the
defendant.

If the court decides that no order is appropriate, then the goods are to be
returned to the person from whom they were delivered up.[82]

Any person having an interest in the goods is entitled to appear in proceedings **19–118**
under s.19. A "person having an interest" is not defined in the section, save that
s.19(6) states that it includes any person in whose favour an order under the
equivalent provisions of the Copyright, Designs and Patents Act 1988 could be
made. It is suggested that the term should be understood broadly so as to include
anyone whose financial interests could be affected by the forfeiture or destruction
of the goods, and any person responsible for their safekeeping. Thus their owner,
their bailee, any person having a security interest in them, any person who has
sought to buy or sell them, and any person having the benefit of a court order relating to them should all be included. It is certainly clear that more than one
person may have an interest in the same goods, and where that is so, the court
must make such order as it thinks just.[83] This will involve identifying those parties whose interests would be served by the permanent removal of the goods from
circulation (such as the proprietor of the registered mark in question), and those
parties who would lose financially as a result (such as an owner of the goods who
is innocent of any infringement), and balancing their needs. This may be

---

[80] *Miller Brewing Co v The Mersey Docks and Harbour Company* [2003] F.S.R. 5.
[81] *Unic Centre v Harrow Magistrates Court* [2000] F.S.R. 667.
[82] s.19(5).
[83] s.19(4).

particularly difficult if, as is suggested above, an order for erasure or obliteration is not available under s.19 of the 1994 Act.

19–119   A person having an interest in infringing goods may also appeal against any order made under s.19, even if he did not appear at the hearing.[84] The order is not to be carried into effect until the time for appeal has expired and any appeal made has been finally determined.[85]

19–120   Although s.19 provides that rules of court may be made as to the service of notice on persons having an interest in infringing goods, materials or articles, none have been made. It is therefore suggested that the ordinary forms of application for interim or final relief be used. A person having an interest in such goods is entitled to appear whether served with a notice or not.[86]

PERIOD AFTER WHICH STATUTORY DELIVERY UP IS NOT AVAILABLE

19–121   By s.18 of the 1994 Act, delivery up is not available after the expiry of six years from the application of the infringing mark to infringing goods or their packaging, or to infringing materials, or from the making of infringing articles. If the proprietor of the trade mark was under a disability during that period or was prevented by fraud or concealment from finding out the facts entitling him to apply for delivery up, the period of six years runs from the time when his disability ends or when he could with reasonable diligence have found out the facts entitling him to apply.

REMEDIES AVAILABLE UNDER THE COURT'S GENERAL POWERS

19–122   We now consider the relief available other than under the 1994 Act.

ERASURE OF THE SPURIOUS MARKS

19–123   The court not only forbids further infringement by its injunction, but, where the defendant is proved to have spuriously marked articles in his possession or under his control, it usually orders the erasure of the marks,[87] or the delivery up of the marked articles for that purpose, or, if erasure is impracticable, for destruction.

19–124   Thus, in *Slazenger v Feltham*,[88] where the word "Demotic", an infringement of the plaintiffs' mark "Demon", was stamped upon the defendants' tennis racquets, it was ordered that the defendants should make an affidavit verifying the number of the racquets and that they should either deliver up the racquets to the plaintiffs to be destroyed, or satisfactorily erase from them the name "Demotic" in the presence of the plaintiffs or their agent.

19–125   In the same way, the court usually orders obliteration of the mark from labels, wrappings, advertising "literature", etc., in the defendant's possession, with delivery up as an alternative.

The order for delivery up or obliteration may be stayed pending an appeal.

---

[84] s.19(3)(b).
[85] s.19(3).
[86] s.19(3)(a).
[87] *Dent v Turpin* (1861) 2 J. & H. 139; 30 L.J.Ch. 495; *Upmann v Elkan* (1871) L.R. 7 Ch. 130.
[88] (1889) 6 R.P.C. 531; 5 T.L.R. 365.

DELAY

A claimant may fail to get an order for delivery up if he unduly delays the com-   **19–126**
mencement of his action.[89]

13. Financial remedies—damages and accounts of profits

NO DISTINCTION BETWEEN INFRINGEMENT AND PASSING OFF

So far as concerns the relief by way of damages or an account of profits there ap-   **19–127**
pears to be no reason to distinguish between actions for infringement and actions
for passing off. However in passing off actions where the claimant is not a trader
in the ordinary sense, a claim for damages may present difficulties: see Ch.14.

NOMINAL DAMAGES

It was long ago decided at common law that the mere proof of an infringement   **19–128**
entitles the claimant to damages.[90] Consequently, no allegation of special damage
is a necessary part of his case.[91] The natural consequence of an infringement,
even though it be made in complete ignorance of the claimant's rights, is that the
infringer must pay at least nominal damages, and the costs of action: so that, if he
acted under the direction of a third person, he may reasonably compound with the
proprietor of the mark on these terms, and claim an indemnity from his principal.[92]

ONUS OF SHOWING SUBSTANTIAL DAMAGE LIES ON THE CLAIMANT

In order to obtain an order for an account of profits or an inquiry as to damages,   **19–129**
the claimant need in general only show that he may be able to recover substantial
damages. This is not a high hurdle at all, and in general the attitude of the court is
that the defendant can be protected against the costs of an inquiry or account
which results in no, or only a very small award, by making a payment into court
and thus letting the claimant bear the risk of the costs of the proceeding. Hence
an inquiry should be ordered even if the court feels serious doubt about the
claimant's ability to recover any substantial amount.[93] However, this attitude is
taken even where the claimant is legally aided so that the defendant cannot obtain
substantial protection by way of a payment in.[94]

However, where the claimant fails to clear this low threshold, the court may   **19–130**
award nominal damages or fix a sum without ordering an account or an inquiry as

---

[89] *County Chemical v Frankenburg* (1904) 21 R.P.C. 722: five months' delay before complaint; the
boxes complained of being capable of being used in ways not a breach of the injunction.

[90] *Blofeld v Payne* (1833) 4 B. & Ad. 410. The jury gave him a farthing.

[91] *Rodgers v Nowill* (1847) 5 C.B. 109. See also *Reddaway v Bentham* [1892] 2 Q.B. 639; 9 R.P.C.
503.

[92] *Dixon v Fawcus* (1861) 3 E. & E. 537. As to third party procedure for claiming an indemnity, see
Hennessy v Dompåe (1902) 19 R.P.C. 333.

[93] If the claimant is successful on an application for summary judgment but has not led evidence of
loss and damage, the court may allow him a further opportunity to submit evidence in support of
an order for an inquiry or account. See *Prince plc v Prince Sports Group Inc* [1998] F.S.R. 21;
Beautimatic v Mitchell [2000] F.S.R. 267.

[94] See, *e.g. Brain v Ingledew Brown Bennison & Garrett (No.3)* [1997] F.S.R. 511 at 525–8, *Mc-
Donald's v Burgerking* [1987] F.S.R. 112.

to damages. In exceptional circumstances, that course may be followed if the evidence of damage is not sufficient to justify the costs of an inquiry.[95]

19–131   If the claimant pursues an inquiry or account, the onus of showing what loss he has actually sustained by reason of the defendant's conduct lies upon him. It cannot be presumed, in the absence of evidence, that the amount of goods sold by the defendant under an infringing trade mark would, but for the defendant's unlawful use of the claimant's mark, have been sold by the claimant.[96] The proper form of an order for an inquiry as to damages occasioned by the infringement of a mark is, therefore, what damage (if any) has the claimant sustained by reason of the acts, repetition of which is restrained by the judgment.[97]

BASIC PRINCIPLES FOR ASSESSING DAMAGES

19–132   The basic principles for the assessment of damages in a patent case were considered by Jacob J. in *Gerber v Lectra*.[98] The following principles are applicable to trade mark infringement:

(1) Damages are compensatory only, to put the claimant in the same position he would have been in had the wrong not been sustained.[99]

(2) The burden of proof lies on the claimant, but damages are to be assessed liberally.[1]

(3) Where the claimant has licensed his right, the damages are the lost royalty.[2]

(4) It is irrelevant that the defendant could have competed lawfully.[3]

(5) Where the claimant has exploited his right by his own sales, he can claim lost profit on sales by the defendant he would have made otherwise, and lost profit on his own sales to the extent that he was forced by the infringement to reduce his own price.

19–133   Jacob J. also held as part of principle (5) that a claimant who obtains damages for sales by the defendant which he has proved would have been made by him in the absence of the infringement, will be entitled to damages on the basis of a reasonable royalty for all the other infringements, but it has been doubted whether this particular principle applies to trade mark cases.[4]

19–134   It is important to note that in assessing damages for lost sales on a compensatory basis, it will be necessary for the court to determine what proportion of the defendant's customers have been confused. The claimant is not entitled to dam-

---

[95] cf. the passing off cases, such as *Rose v Loftus* (1878) 47 L.J.Ch. 576; *Samuelson v Producers* (1931) 48 R.P.C. 580 at 590.

[96] *Leather Cloth v Hirschfeld* (1865) L.R. 1 Eq. 299; *Magnolia Metal v Atlas Metal* (1879) 14 R.P.C. 389, CA; *Alexander v Henry* (1895) 12 R.P.C. 360, illustration 2, below. In the first two of these cases, the plaintiffs were given nominal damages only; but this would in general seem to be inappropriate (except in a *quia timet* action): a finding of passing off almost necessarily implies that some damage will have been caused, and in recent times courts have customarily so assumed—as in the later cases cited below.

[97] *Spalding v Gamage* (1915) 32 R.P.C. 273, HL; (1918) 35 R.P.C. 101, CA.

[98] [1995] R.P.C. 383.

[99] *General Tire v Firestone* [1976] R.P.C. 197.

[1] *General Tire v Firestone* [1976] R.P.C. 197.

[2] *General Tire v Firestone* [1976] R.P.C. 197. Jacob J. held in *Gerber* that this follows from the first proposition. It is less likely to be of application in trade mark cases than in patent cases because the prevalence of exploitation by licensing is less.

[3] *United Horse-Shoe v Stewart* (1888) 5 R.P.C. 260.

[4] *Dormeuil v Feraglow* [1990] R.P.C. 449. The case did not decide that damages assessed as a royalty were not available; it merely held that their availability or otherwise should not be decided on an application for an interim payment, and that there was no binding authority that they were available. In support of the argument that damages assessed on the "user" principle are available, see *Stoke on Trent City Council v W&J Wass* [1988] 1 W.L.R. 1406; *Meters v Metropolitan Gas Meters* (1911) 29 R.P.C. 157.

ages for sales to persons who have not been misled, since he has suffered no loss in respect of them, and, arguably, no actionable wrong has been committed in respect of sales to them.[5] If he were to recover damages in relation to such persons, he would be over-compensated. This principle distinguishes passing off and trade mark infringement from other intellectual property proceedings such as those for patent infringement, where all the defendant's activities of a given kind infringe.

OTHER HEADS OF DAMAGE

In general, the only injury which is done by an infringement is that the defendant's goods or services are sold instead of those of the claimant, and the sale of the latter is, in some degree, diminished in consequence. But it may appear that further damage has been done, for instance, where spurious goods are so inferior to the genuine as to injure the trade reputation of the claimant,[6] or where the stress of the competition compels the claimant to lower his prices and thus suffer loss. **19–135**

The cost of advertisements to counteract the effect of the defendant's conduct may be taken into account.[7] Further, the legal costs of putting on notice foreign manufacturers of infringing materials have been held recoverable.[8] **19–136**

In the area of damages for patent infringement it has been held that, provided causation is shown, and subject to the normal rules as to remoteness of damage, it is possible to recover damages for items sold as a result of an infringing sale, even if such ancillary items do not themselves infringe.[9] There appears no reason why this principle should not apply to trade mark infringement in appropriate circumstances. **19–137**

DAMAGE CAUSED TO SUBSIDIARY

In principle, a claimant may recover damages suffered by a subsidiary company, provided that he himself has a cause of action, and the damage to the subsidiary causes damage to him. But in such cases, the claimant must prove the quantum of his loss properly; it is not to be assumed that the loss of a pound by the subsidiary will necessarily result in the same loss to the parent.[10] **19–138**

DATE TO WHICH DAMAGES ARE RECKONED

If the infringement is a continuing one, the damages ought to be assessed down to the time of the assessment. **19–139**

Examples:

(1) In a case where the plaintiffs were foreign manufacturers, and the defendants, former British agents for the plaintiffs, claimed that the mark in suit now belonged to them, it was held (a) that the acts of the defendants had delayed the plaintiffs' resumption of trade in this country by many years; (b) that damages were recoverable for this although the plaintiffs might have disregarded the defendants' claim and resumed trade at an

---

[5] See *Spalding v Gamage* (1915) 32 R.P.C. 273, HL; (1918) 35 R.P.C. 101 at para.19–031, and *Draper v Trist* (1939) 56 R.P.C. 429.

[6] As in *Alexander v Henry*, illustration 2, below.

[7] *Spalding v Gamage* (1918) 35 R.P.C. 101, CA.

[8] *Dormeuil v Feraglow* [1990] R.P.C. 449.

[9] *Gerber v Lectra* [1995] R.P.C. 383; [1997] R.P.C. 443, CA.

[10] See *Gerber v Lectra* [1995] R.P.C. 383 [1997] R.P.C. 443, at para.19–132.

earlier date; (c) judgment for infringement of trade mark and passing off had not restored the plaintiffs' goodwill in its entirety; and (d) that the profits made by the defendants were not the measure of the damage suffered by the plaintiffs: *Manus v Fullwood* (1954) 71 R.P.C. 243 (£10,000 damages awarded).

(2) Where by a persistent course of fraudulent imitation of the plaintiffs' mark the defendants succeeded in so damaging the plaintiff's goodwill in Mexico as to destroy their control of the Mexican market for their goods, with the result that thereafter the defendants could compete effectively with the plaintiffs in Mexico without further infringement, the damage done to the plaintiffs by the subsequent lawful competition—loss of business, and loss of profit through forced reduction of prices—was held attributable to the infringement: *Alexander v Henry* (1895) 12 R.P.C. 360.

Innocence no defence to damages

19–140   A defendant cannot avoid an order for an inquiry by showing that he infringed innocently. The claimant has a right to damages regardless of the defendant's state of mind, and that is so regardless of whether the cause of action is infringement of a registered mark, or passing off.[11]

Order for account

19–141   The ordinary form of the order for an account directs an account of the profits made by the defendant in selling or otherwise disposing of the goods bearing the spurious mark or marks, to be taken by the master, with liberty to apply.

19–142   The account should not be limited to sales made to persons who bought the goods as and for the goods of the claimant, by reason of the use of the infringing mark upon them.[12] The mischief done by the spurious marking of the goods is not merely that it is calculated to deceive immediate purchasers from the infringers, but that it puts "a weapon calculated to be fraudulently used by the middlemen"[13] into their hands, by which they may intentionally, or not, deceive the ultimate purchasers. The account should be of such profits as ought to be treated as having been improperly made by the defendant.[14]

Basic principles applicable to an account

19–143   Accounts of profits in trade mark cases have been rare in the United Kingdom, but the following are probably sound basic principles:

(1) An account is confined to profits actually made, its purpose being to deprive the defendant of unjust enrichment rather than to punish him.[15]

(2) An account is addressed to identifying profits caused, in the legal sense, by the infringement.[16]

---

[11] *Gillette v Edenwest* [1994] R.P.C. 279; *Spalding v Gamage* (1915) 32 R.P.C. 273 at 283, HL; *Henry Heath v Gorringe* (1924) 41 R.P.C. 457.

[12] *Lever v Goodwin* (1887) 36 Ch.D. 1; 4 R.P.C. 492.

[13] *Price's Patent Candle v Ogston and Tennant* (1909) 26 R.P.C. 797 at 814. See also *Saxlehner v Apollinaris* [1897] 1 Ch. 893; 14 R.P.C. 645.

[14] *My Kinda Town v Soll* [1982] F.S.R. 147.

[15] *My Kinda Town v Soll* [1982] F.S.R. 147; *Celanese v BP* [1999] R.P.C. 203.

[16] *Celanese v BP* [1999] R.P.C. 203.

(3) The fact that the defendant's profits could have been made in a non-infringing fashion is irrelevant.[17]

(4) The claimant must take the defendant as he finds him, and may not argue that the defendant could have made greater profits by trading in a different fashion.[18]

(5) Where only parts of the defendant's activities infringed, profits attributable to the non-infringing parts are not caused by the infringement, and the overall profits must be apportioned.[19]

(6) Overheads should be dealt with so as to arrive as closely as possible at the true profit.[20]

(7) The defendant cannot generally deduct opportunity cost.[21]

(8) General overheads may be apportioned to the infringing activity, subject to the above principles.[22]

ELECTION BETWEEN DAMAGES AND PROFITS

Damages are a matter of right; the account of profits is an equitable remedy and the court has a discretion whether or not to grant it. Accordingly, a successful claimant in an infringement action is entitled to an inquiry as to damages (at his own risk as to costs) in any case where there is a prospect that the inquiry would reach a positive result;[23] whilst only in certain cases will the court grant an account of profits. In these cases, the claimant has an option (exercisable at the conclusion of the hearing of the case) to claim either damages or profits: he cannot have both.[24] Accordingly, it is usual in particulars of claim to ask for the two in the alternative. The principle upon which the court grants an account of profits is that where one party owes a duty to another, the person to whom the duty is owed is entitled to recover from the other party every benefit which that other party has received by virtue of his fiduciary position if in fact he has obtained it without the knowledge or consent of the party to whom he owed the duty.[25] An account is generally refused if the defendant had no knowledge of the claimant's mark and, when ordered, is limited to the period during which such knowledge had existed; whilst knowledge or absence of knowledge does not affect the right to damages.[26]   **19–144**

A claimant who has been successful in an action for trade mark infringement or passing off may not have sufficient knowledge of the defendant's activities to make an informed decision as to whether he should seek an inquiry as to damages or an account of profits. In such a case he may seek disclosure before making his election: *Island Records v Tring*.[27] Disclosure given in such circumstances should be limited to that which is necessary for the claimant to make an informed decision within a reasonable time; he is not entitled to all the disclosure which   **19–145**

---

[17] *Celanese v BP* [1999] R.P.C. 203.

[18] *Celanese v BP* [1999] R.P.C. 203; *Dart v Decor* [1994] F.S.R. 567.

[19] *Celanese v BP* [1999] R.P.C. 203.

[20] *Dart v Decor* [1994] F.S.R. 567.

[21] *Dart v Decor* [1994] F.S.R. 567.

[22] *Dart v Decor* [1994] F.S.R. 567.

[23] See *e.g. McDonalds v Burgerking* [1987] F.S.R. 112.

[24] *Neilson v Belts* (1871) L.R. 5 H.L. 1; followed in *De Vitre v Betts* (1868) L.R. 6 H.L. 319. See *per* Cotton L.J. in *Lever v Goodwin* (1887) 36 Ch.D. 1; 4 R.P.C. 492.

[25] *Electrix* (1953) 70 R.P.C. 158.

[26] See paras 19–140 to 19–142.

[27] [1995] F.S.R. 560.

would be given in the inquiry, and in appropriate circumstances an audited schedule of infringing dealings may be a substitute for documentary disclosure.[28]

REFUSAL BECAUSE OF DELAY OR ACQUIESCENCE

19–146   The court may refuse to order an account of profits,[29] or order it to be taken only from the date of the letter before action,[30] where the claimant has neglected to take proceedings after becoming aware of the infringement. There have been passing off cases in which damages were refused to the claimant on the ground of delay verging on acquiescence;[31] but it is not easy to see on what principle, nor how this could be right in actions for infringement.

19–147   In a case where there had been some delay, and some amount of misrepresentation in his business on the plaintiff's part, and the defendant's proper trade was larger than that of the plaintiffs, the account was limited to profits earned since the commencement of the suit: *Ford v Foster* (1872) L.R. 7 Ch. 611 at 633.

PROFITS OR DAMAGES ONLY GO BACK FOR SIX YEARS

19–148   Damages can only be recovered, and the profits to be included in the account can only be reckoned, in respect of infringements occurring less than six years before the issue of the proceedings,[32] subject to the exception in the case of concealed fraud which is part of the general law.

COSTS OF INQUIRY OR ACCOUNT

19–149   The costs of the inquiry as to damages or the account of profits should generally be reserved until the result of the inquiry or account is known,[33] at any rate. If no damages or profits are found to have been incurred or made[34], or if the proceedings subsequent to the judgment are oppressively conducted by the claimant, or if the defendant has made a sufficient offer,[35] the claimant ought to pay the costs. But where the defendant had filed a false affidavit greatly understating the number of goods sold, although the account showed that he had made no profit, Chitty J. said it was a case for investigation, and allowed the plaintiff costs.[36]

14. Costs

COSTS IN THE DISCRETION OF THE JUDGE

19–150   Subject to the provision in s.73 of the 1994 Act as to the effect of a "certificate of

---

[28] *Island Records v Tring* [1995] F.S.R. 560.

[29] *Harrison v Taylor* (1865) 11 Jur.(N.S.) 408; 12 L.T. (N.S.) 339; *Beard v Turner* (1866) 13 L.T. (N.S.) 746. Or, perhaps, only down to the date when the claimants learnt of the infringement: *Electrolux v Electrix* (1953) 70 R.P.C. 158. See also *Crossley v Derby* (1834) 1 Webster's P.C. 119, a patent case.

[30] *Lever v Sunniwite* (1949) 66 R.P.C. 84; cf. *Young v Holt* (1948) 65 R.P.C. 25 ("Mendoza").

[31] *Reddaway v Stevenson* (1903) 20 R.P.C. 276, three years' delay before action; *Gledhill v British Perforated* (1911) 28 R.P.C. 429, delay of over two years.

[32] *per* Mellish L.J. in *Ford v Foster* (1872) L.R. 7 Ch. 611 at 633; Limitation Act 1980, s.2. See also *Electrolux v Electrix* (1953) 70 R.P.C. 158.

[33] *per* Fry J. in *Slack v Midland Ry* (1880–81) 16 Ch.D. 81, a case of nuisance.

[34] *Tonge v Ward* (1869) 21 L.T. (N.S.) 480.

[35] *Fettes v Williams* (1908) 25 R.P.C. 511, a design case, in which the damages were assessed at less than the amount of the offer, and the plaintiffs were ordered to pay the costs of the inquiry and of the further consideration. See also *Draper v Trist* (1939) 56 R.P.C. 225.

[36] *Dicks v Jackson*, March 31, 1884, cited *Sebastian's Law of Trade Marks* (5th ed., London, 1911), p.251.

contested validity", as to which see below, the costs of and incident to an action for the infringement of a trade mark, as the costs in any other action, are in the discretion of the court, and the court has full power to determine by whom and to what extent such costs shall be paid. There is now a substantial body of authority relating to decisions on costs under the CPR; dealing with all of it would be outside the scope of this work, and what follows is intended to deal with those parts particularly significant to trade marks and passing off, or where there are special principles applying to those matters.

UNSUCCESSFUL PARTY USUALLY ORDERED TO PAY COSTS

The court or judge in general follows the ordinary rule that the unsuccessful party shall pay the costs of the litigation. This principle is now expressly incorporated in the rules under r.44.3(2) of the CPR. Most of the authorities referred to below are from before the introduction of the CPR, and should therefore be approached with a little care, but in general the principles have not changed so much as to render them inapplicable. They remain useful guides. **19–151**

Where each party is successful on part of the case, it is usual to give whichever party succeeds on the dispute as a whole the costs, save so far as these are increased by the issues upon which he has failed;[37] unless there was only one main issue.[38] More rarely, the costs of the different issues are ordered to be separately assessed, and given to the party succeeding on them, but the CPR now deprecates this practice, and in so far as it is practicable, the court ought instead to award the winning party either a proportion of his costs, or his costs from a certain date.[39] Costs may also be refused where a party wrongly refuses mediation. For a discussion of such circumstances see *Reed Executive plc v Reed Business Information Ltd (No.2)* [2005] F.S.R. 3, paras 31–47. **19–152**

In carrying out this assessment, the court is to consider all the circumstances, including the parties' conduct before and after proceedings began, and whether and to what extent a party has been successful.[40] **19–153**

In some cases of isolated instances of infringement or passing off, the claimant has been refused relief at the trial, and been ordered to pay the costs of the action.[41]

OFFER BY DEFENDANT, OR BY CLAIMANT

The procedure relating to offers and payments into court is now codified by Pt 36 of the CPR. **19–154**

An unsuccessful defendant must usually pay costs, although he has only defended a mark which he honestly adopted without being aware of its too great

[37] *Saxlehner v Apollinaris* [1897] 1 Ch. 893; [1897] 1 Ch. 893; *Lever v Bedingfield* (1898) 15 R.P.C. 453; *Hipkins v Plant* (1898) 15 R.P.C. 294.
[38] The court has often made some rough apportionment of costs, without giving detailed reasons for it: as in *Bourne v Swan & Edgar* (1903) 20 R.P.C. 105.
[39] CPR, r.44.3(7).
[40] CPR, r.44.4(4) and (5).
[41] *Leahy v Glover* (1893) 10 R.P.C. 141 HL, and *Rutter v Smith* (1901) 18 R.P.C. 49, where only a single act of passing off by a servant, since discharged, was proved, and costs were given against the plaintiffs; and see the other similar cases cited below in relation to trap orders, see paras 19–212. In *Burberry v Watkinson* (1906) 23 R.P.C. 141, Warrington J., in a case where the defendant had been misled by his supplier, refused to order any injunction and made no order for costs. But cases differ: cf. *Bass, Ratcliff and Gretton v Laidlaw* (1909) 26 R.P.C. 211; *Kodak v Grenville* (1908) 25 R.P.C. 416; and *Myers v Fields* (1954) 71 R.P.C. 435.

resemblance to the claimant's mark,[42] and though he has acted without fraud and in ignorance of the claimant's rights.[43] But by offering the claimant all that he is entitled to,[44] that is, in the case of the innocent holder[45] of spuriously marked goods, an undertaking[46] not to part with them until the spurious marks have been removed,[47] and all requisite information to enable the claimant to stop the infringement,[48] and the payment of the assessed costs (if any) already incurred by him in the action, if an action has been commenced—the defendant may escape liability for subsequent costs.[49] If the claimant, after such an offer has been made, commences or continues proceedings against the defendant making it, he will usually be ordered to pay him his costs subsequently incurred.[50] A letter offering too little too late will not assist a defendant.[51]

19–155   Under Pt 36 of the CPR, a claimant may now make an offer to settle proceedings. He may offer to accept less than is sought by his statement of case, with the sanction against the defendant that if he in fact obtains more than that offered, his recovery in costs, and in interest on costs, may be increased.[52]

NOTICE OF ACTION IS UNNECESSARY

19–156   Formally, no notice need be given to the alleged infringer before the action is brought.[53] But even before the CPR it was considered bad practice to sue without warning, in the absence of some special reason for doing so.[54] Moreover, there may be a risk when an action is commenced without warning, especially against a mere retailer, that the defendant may satisfy the court that the infringement was

---

[42] *Blair v Stock* (1884) 52 L.T. 123; cf. the registration case, *Hyde* (1878) 7 Ch.D. 724.

[43] *Edelsten v Edelsten* (1863) 1 De G.J. & S. 185.

[44] But where the defendants altered their mark after action, but declined to give an undertaking and pay the costs of the action, an injunction was granted and they were ordered to pay costs: *Spicer v Spalding & Hodge* (1915) 32 R.P.C. 52; and see *Steiner v Stevens* [1957] R.P.C. 439.

[45] In a case of fraud, the claimant may, notwithstanding that the defendant has made a full offer to submit, be allowed the whole costs although he proceeds to trial: *Jameson v Clarke* (1902) 19 R.P.C. 255.

[46] The claimant is not bound to accept an undertaking in the case of an infringer with notice, or where there is reasonable risk that it will be necessary to take steps to enforce it. In such a case the claimant will usually be allowed the costs of a motion for judgment: *Gandy Belt v Fleming, Birkby* (1901) 18 R.P.C. 276; but at all events the defendant must pay the costs of the claimant obtaining an injunction by consent: *Slazenger v Pigott* (1895) 12 R.P.C. 439. cf. *Jenkins v Hope* [1896] 1 Ch. 278; 13 R.P.C. 57 (a patent case, where the plaintiff ought to have accepted an undertaking, the infringement being very small).

[47] Except, perhaps, by returning them to the consignor: see *Upmann v Elkan* (1871) L.R. 7 Ch. 130.

[48] The claimant is not entitled to the publication of an apology: *British Blue Spot v Keene* (1931) 48 R.P.C. 375, though it may be reasonable to ask for an apology and undertaking in lieu of an injunction in open court, and to apply for an injunction if this is refused: *Kodak v Illingworth* (1925) 43 R.P.C. 33; or to receive a list of the defendant's customers, if not entitled to an inquiry or account: *Hipkins v Plant* (1898) 15 R.P.C. 294.

[49] But the defendant must not ask for a term to which he is not legally entitled, as, for instance, that the claimant should not advertise the undertaking: *Hipkins v Plant* (1898) 15 R.P.C. 294; *Clay v Godfrey Phillips* (1910) 27 R.P.C. 508.

[50] CPR, r.36.20. *Slazenger v Spalding* (1910) 27 R.P.C. 20; *Rippingille's v Clarke's* (1917) 34 R.P.C. 365. In *Catterson v Anglo Foreign* (1911) 28 R.P.C. 74, the defendants, who were commission agents and alleged that they were innocent importers from abroad, were held not to have met the plaintiff's complaint in a proper manner, and an injunction was granted with costs.

[51] *Colgate Palmolive v Markwell Finance* [1990] R.P.C. 197.

[52] CPR, r.36.21.

[53] The very life of a trade mark depends upon the promptitude with which it is vindicated: *Johnston v Orr-Ewing* (1882) 7 App.Cas. 219. And see *Customagic v Headquarter & General* [1968] F.S.R. 150 (two successful trap orders justified immediate proceedings without warning).

[54] *e.g.* because an application for an Anton Piller order is to be made, or in counterfeiting cases generally.

inadvertent and that there was no reason for apprehending any repetition.[55] Further, the court may not award the claimant his costs if the defendant would have been willing to concede the claimant's demand if notice had been given.[56]

With the introduction of the CPR, these considerations have even more force. It is a principal focus of the CPR to encourage parties to enter into a dialogue, and to exchange information, before proceedings are begun. The object is to promote settlements by avoiding the entrenchment which can result from proceedings being begun. In many fields of litigation there are formal pre-action protocols as a result.[57] There is none in intellectual property matters,[58] but it still is likely that the precipitate bringing of proceedings will result in the claimants being punished in costs. Furthermore, the Practice Direction relating to pre-action protocols contains, in para.5, general provisions to be met in cases not specifically covered by their own protocol.

19–157

INSTANCES OF CLAIMANTS DEPRIVED OF COSTS

Again, it should be borne in mind that the following cases were decided before the introduction of the CPR.

19–158

(1) Where the plaintiff was entitled to an injunction only, and his right to this was admitted on the second day of the trial, he was given costs up to that time, and was ordered to pay the subsequent costs: *Magnolia Metal v Atlas Metal* (1897) 14 R.P.C. 389 at 400 (passing off).

(2) In a passing off case, in which the defendants offered any undertaking at an early stage of the trial, and the plaintiffs refused the offer, and pressed for an injunction and it was held that there had been no fraud, and that, if any wrongful acts had been done, they had been done accidentally or by inadvertence, and an injunction was refused, no order was made as to costs; and an appeal by the plaintiffs was dismissed with costs: *Lever v Masbro' Equitable* (1912) 29 R.P.C. 33 and 225.

(3) Where an action was brought for infringement and passing off by the use of a label, and the defendants offered to submit to an injunction as regards the trade mark, but not as regards passing off by use of the mark, the plaintiffs were held entitled to go on and seek an injunction against passing off: *Hat Manufacturers v Tomlin* (1906) 23 R.P.C. 413; but plaintiffs who in such a case accepted the offer, but afterwards continued the action as regards passing off, were ordered to pay the costs from the date of the offer: *Vernon v Buchanan's* (1906) 23 R.P.C. 17.

(4) Where wharfingers with whom the spuriously marked goods had been warehoused in the ordinary course of trade, and who were entitled to a lien for their charges, were added as defendants, and the plaintiffs proceeded to trial against them, the Court of Appeal, reversing Fry J., ordered that their costs of action should be paid by the plaintiffs: *Moet v Pickering* (1878) 8 Ch.D. 372.

(5) In a trivial case, where an action had been commenced without notice against the innocent purchaser of an inconsiderable quantity of spuriously

---

[55] *e.g. Leahy v Glover* (1893) 10 R.P.C. 141; *Bass v Laidlaw* (1909) 26. R.P.C. 211. Contrast *Bovril v Bodega* (1916) 33 R.P.C. 153 at 155 and *Steigumingner v Stevens* [1957] R.P.C. 439.

[56] See, *e.g. Ucan v Hilti* [1968] F.S.R. 248 (motion launched without notice and defendants gave undertaking before hearing, defendants' costs in cause).

[57] And CPR, r.26.4 allows the stay of proceedings at an early stage in order to allow negotiations to take place.

[58] Partly because the statutory threats provisions make it difficult to enter into a dialogue with a secondary infringer without the potential claimant being at risk of committing an actionable threat.

marked goods, and he at once submitted to do as the court directed, costs were refused: *American Tobacco v Guest* [1892] 1 Ch. 630; 9 R.P.C. 218.[59]

OTHER INSTANCES

19–159   Costs have been refused to a successful claimant because he claimed an injunction too wide in its terms.[60] Where the plaintiffs set up claims to a copyright in a music tutor, as well as an exclusive right to its title, and failed as to the copyright, they were allowed only half their taxed costs of action.[61] On similar grounds, claimants have been ordered to pay,[62] or have been deprived of,[63] the costs occasioned by allegations which they have failed to prove, although they have succeeded and obtained the general costs of their actions. But where the plaintiff, in an action for infringing his trade mark and also for passing off, failed as regards the infringement in respect of some of the goods for which he used, but had not registered, the trade mark, and succeeded as to the rest of the action, and the defendant was held to have been guilty of deliberate infringement in breach of an undertaking previously given by him, the plaintiff was not deprived of his costs.[64] If the claimant's case had been overlaid with unnecessary evidence, he may be deprived of the costs of such evidence.[65] Where a claimant, acting reasonably, launches a motion for an interim injunction, but the position changes before the hearing, so that he no longer seeks relief, the appropriate course may be to adjourn the application to the trial of the action with the costs of both parties being costs in the case.[66]

19–160   In relation to applications for interim injunctions, the general position now is that where the decision is reached on the balance of convenience, costs are likely to be reserved, and a defendant who concedes in the light of the position on the balance of convenience should not be worse that one who fights and loses on that issue.[67] The position is otherwise where the applicant fails and the failure arises out of his own evidence.[68]

DEFENDANT DEPRIVED OF COSTS

19–161   (1) Successful defendants have been deprived of their costs where the evidence made it clear that they had acted, or intended to act, dishonestly.[69] Thus, where features of the defendants' wrapper had been taken from the plaintiffs', but not so as to infringe the plaintiffs' rights, the Court of Appeal, whilst dismissing the action and giving the defendants the costs of their successful appeal, refused to give them costs of the action: *Lever v*

---

[59] cf. *Rose v Loftus* (1878) 47 L.J.Ch. 576.

[60] In *Rodgers v Rodgers* (1924) 41 R.P.C. 277, where the court was of the opinion that the case might never have been contested if the plaintiffs' claim had not been too wide, no costs were awarded.

[61] *Metzler v Wood* (1878) 8 Ch.D. 606.

[62] *Saxlehner v Apollinaris* [1897] 1 Ch. 893; 14 R.P.C. 645.

[63] *Montgomerie v Young* (1903) 20 R.P.C. 781. On appeal the defendants wholly succeeded: (1904) 21 R.P.C. 285. In *O.T. v Cumming* (1915) 32 R.P.C. 69 (Scot.) the plaintiffs, having failed in personal charges of fraud against the defendants, were given, although successful in the action, three-fourths only of their costs.

[64] *Jay v Ladler* (1888) 40 Ch.D. 649; 6 R.P.C. 136, *Hodgson v Kynoch* (1898) 15 R.P.C. 465.

[65] *Daimler v London Daimler* (1907) 24 R.P.C. 379, plaintiffs given one-half costs of evidence.

[66] *Leng v Gold Star* [1967] F.S.R. 75.

[67] *Picnic At Ascot v Kalus Derigs* [2001] F.S.R. 2.

[68] *Local Sunday Newspapers v Johnston Press*, unreported, June 19, 2001 (Neuberger J.).

[69] As in *Claudius Ash v Invicta* (1912) 29 R.P.C. 465, HL; (see at 470, 476) and *Lambert & Butler v Goodbody* (1902) 19 R.P.C. 377 at 383. But there are limits to the discretion to deprive a successful defendant of its costs: *King v Gillard* (1905) 22 R.P.C. 327 at 332, CA.

Bedingfield (1899) 16 R.P.C. 3. In *Coca Cola v Mabe*[70] the costs of a successful Norwich Pharmacal application incurred by the claimant and paid to the third party in question were set off against the defendant's costs, even when the claimant discontinued, because of the defendant's improper conduct in opposing an entry and search order, which had led to his committal for contempt.

(2) In cases in which the claimant fails because he is carrying on a fraudulent trade, and the defendant stands in *pari delictu*, the practice has been to dismiss the action without costs.[71]

(3) A successful defendant has been deprived of costs because he has made an unfounded charge of fraud.[72]

(4) Where defendants in a passing off action, represented by the same solicitors, severed in defence, and the taxing master disallowed some of the costs of separate defences and the briefs at the trial on the ground that the companies and their defences were practically identical, it was held that this was a matter which the court had power to review, that the defences were not practically identical, and that the items should not have been altogether struck out: *Spalding v Gamage* [1914] 2 Ch. 405; 31 R.P.C. 431.

IMMEDIATE PAYMENT OF COSTS

There are two methods under the CPR by which immediate payment of costs by a successful party may be achieved. In relation to hearings of less than a day, the judge or master hearing the application ought usually to assess the costs himself and order payment.[73] Where an order for costs is made in a party's favour but detailed assessment is ordered, the court may make an order for an amount to be paid on account.[74]   **19–162**

CERTIFICATE OF CONTESTED VALIDITY

Section 73 of the 1994 Act (s.60 of the 1938 Act was to the same effect) provides that in any proceedings before the court in which the validity of the registration of a registered trade mark is contested and is decided in favour of the proprietor of the trade mark, the court may certify to that effect. In any subsequent proceeding in which the validity of the registration comes into question the proprietor of the trade mark on obtaining a final order or judgment in his favour is entitled to have his full costs "as between solicitor and client", unless the court directs that he ought not to have them.[75]   **19–163**

As the CPR now stands, however, whilst it is hardly open to the rules to override the Act, there would seem to be no machinery for giving effect to the specific provision as to costs "as between solicitor and client": the court may order costs to be assessed either on the standard or on the indemnity basis: CPR, r.44.4. It therefore seems that in practice the only order which can be made is for assessment on the indemnity basis which does, in practice, give the successful party an appreciably higher level of return.   **19–164**

---

[70] [2002] F.S.R. 47.

[71] *Newman v Pinto* (1887) 4 R.P.C. 508; 57 L.T. 31, CA; *Thorneloe v Hill* (1894) 11 R.P.C. 61.

[72] *Hargreaves v Freeman* [1891] 3 Ch. 39; 8 R.P.C. 237, but cf. *King v Gillard* [1905] 2 Ch. 7; 21 R.P.C. 589; 22 R.P.C. 327.

[73] CPR, Pt 44 PD, paras 4.3 and 4.4.

[74] CPR, r.44.3(8), and see *Mars v Teknowledge* [2000] F.S.R. 138.

[75] Instances of grant of a certificate were *Imperial Tobacco v De Pasquali* (1918) 35 R.P.C. 185, CA; *Bentley v Lagonda* (1947) 64 R.P.C. 33; *Pan Press* (1948) 65 R.P.C. 193; *Manus v Fullwood & Bland* (1948) 65 R.P.C. 329.

19–165   The validity of a trade mark may be affected by events occurring at any time, so that although validity may have been established in one case, there may subsequently arise further grounds for questioning validity, and this may be a reason for certifying in later proceedings that solicitor and client costs should not be ordered.

19–166   Under the 1938 Act, a certificate was granted where the question of validity was argued, although there was no application to revoke or rectify.[76] The grant is a matter of discretion and has been refused where an application to rectify was abandoned without argument.[77] An application to rectify the Register under s.26 of the 1938 Act on the grounds of non-use was held not to attack validity, so that on its failure a certificate was not given.[78]

The order granting a certificate was held not to be appealable under earlier Acts.[79]

15. Appeal

STAY PENDING APPEAL

19–167   Where a claimant is successful at trial he is usually entitled to an injunction pending appeal, and the onus is on the defendant to apply for a stay. The application for a stay is dealt with on much the same principles as an application for an interim injunction, in the sense that the court must do the best it can to secure justice in the long term, having regard to the fact that its decision may be overturned in the Court of Appeal.[80] However, the fact that the claimant has been successful is the most material factor to bear in mind, and it should be appreciated that a stay deprives the successful claimant, at least for a while, of the fruits of success. A claimant who successfully resists a stay must normally give a cross undertaking in damages.[81] In some cases, the defendant will be required to secure moneys for the payment of damages as a term of the stay.[82]

19–168   A stay of an order for delivery up is more readily granted, for obvious practical reasons, providing that satisfactory steps can be taken to prevent the goods in question from entering circulation in the meantime.[83]

19–169   An inquiry as to damages or an account of profits is not usually stayed pending appeal, and a claimant who wishes to press ahead with one is normally entitled to

---

[76] *Major v Franklin* (1908) 25 R.P.C. 406.

[77] Certificate refused in *Bourne v Swan and Edgar* (1903) 20 R.P.C. 105.

[78] *Lever v Sunniwite* (1949) 66 R.P.C. 84. See also *Parkington* (1946) 63 R.P.C. 171, where an application was made to limit the area of use of the registered mark under the 1938 Act, s.26(2), and it was held that the applicant's use had not been honest concurrent use within the meaning of s.12(2) of that Act. A certificate of validity was refused.

[79] *Haslam v Hall* (1888) 5 R.P.C. 144 (a patent case where the court had found the patent partially invalid). The point there taken by the CA, that their jurisdiction is limited to appeals from judgments and orders (which a certificate is not) would seem equally relevant to the current Supreme Court Act 1981.

[80] See *Minnesota Mining and Manufacturing v Johnson & Johnson* [1976] R.P.C. 671, CA; *Minnesota Mining and Manufacturing v Rennicks* [1992] R.P.C. 331.

[81] *Minnesota Mining and Manufacturing v Rennicks* [1992] R.P.C. 331.

[82] As in "Oxford Marmalade", *CPC v Keenan* [1986] F.S.R. 527, where the defendant undertook to pay 10% of receipts into a joint account.

[83] *e.g.* granted in *Parker and Smith v Satchwell* (1901) 18 R.P.C. 299, where the delivery up was stayed, although a stay of the injunction was refused. Also *Presto v Orme, Evans* (1900) 17 R.P.C. 218 at 227; and *Gillette v Anglo-American* (1912) 29 R.P.C. 341.

do so at his own risk as to costs should the decision in his favour be overturned on appeal. The same applies to an assessment of costs.[84]

A stay of the injunction pending an appeal from the Court of Appeal to the **19–170** House of Lords, the defendants undertaking to keep an account, was granted in a patent case on the ground of difference of opinion in the court, coupled with the fact that there was no possible doubt as to the plaintiffs getting their damages if an appeal failed: *Consolidated Pneumatic v Dark*.[85]

INTERIM INJUNCTION CONTINUED OVER APPEAL

In a case where the plaintiffs were disputing the right of the defendant to certain **19–171** marks registered in his name, but failed both at the trial and in the Court of Appeal, the judge of first instance suspended over the appeal the discharge of an interim injunction against dealing with the marks; the Court of Appeal, whilst granting leave to appeal to the House of Lords, refused to continue the injunction, the defendants having offered undertakings: *Adrema-Werke v Custodian of Enemy Property*.[86]

APPEAL EXPEDITED

In a case where the defendant desired to appeal against an injunction which the **19–172** plaintiff had obtained, the court on his application, and on the ground that the continuance of the injunction would do irreparable damage to his business, advanced the case to the head of the list.[87]

STAY OF ORDER FOR NEW TRIAL

An application to stay a new trial ordered to take place by the Court of Appeal, **19–173** pending an appeal against the order to the House of Lords, was refused in *Edge v Johnson*.[88]

APPEAL IN CASE OF FRAUD

Where the judge of first instance has found, or has refused to find, fraud, the **19–174** Court of Appeal is usually very unwilling to reverse his finding; but there are some cases in which this has been done.

(1) In a trade name case a finding of fraud was reversed, the court being able to act without relying on the evidence of the defendant, which the judge below had not believed: *Jamieson v Jamieson* (1898) 15 R.P.C. 169.

(2) In a case in which the judge below found that the get-up of the defendants' goods was calculated to deceive, and expressed his dissatisfaction with the defendants' principal witness, and said that he could not exonerate the defendants from intention to deceive, the Court of Appeal held that these reflections were unjustified, and that the get-up was in fact not calculated

---

[84] *Minnesota Mining & Manufacturing v Rennicks* [1992] R.P.C. 331; *Lucas v Gaedor* [1978] R.P.C. 389.

[85] (1907) 24 R.P.C. 593 at 640.

[86] [1956] R.P.C. 301 at 306; [1957] R.P.C. 49 at 60, CA.

[87] *Lazenby v White* (1870–71) L.R. 6 Ch. 89, CA. But the main argument in the case, that if the defendant succeeded on the appeal he would not be compensated for the stopping of his business, is not in these days necessarily so cogent: the CA will, in a proper case, require the claimant to give a cross-undertaking in damages pending appeal.

[88] (1892) 9 R.P.C. 134.

to deceive: *Coleman v Smith* [1911] 2 Ch. 572; 28 R.P.C. 645; 29 R.P.C. 81.[89]

(3) In *Jif*,[90] the Court of Appeal held that the evidence before the trial judge was not sufficient to support his findings of fraudulent intention by the defendants.

COSTS OF APPEAL

19–175   The costs of an appeal are normally given to the party succeeding in the appeal, notwithstanding that there may have been good reason for depriving him of his costs below.[91]

16. Practice and evidence

PLEADING

19–176   There is no reason to think that the CPR changes the principles set out below, which are as much a matter of common sense and fairness as anything else, although it may be that pleadings will be fuller under the CPR than previously.

19–177   The ordinary rules as to pleadings apply to actions for the infringement of trade marks. If fraud is alleged it must be clearly pleaded.[92] Material facts only should be pleaded. Thus, for example, where a party alleges a continuing course of the exercise of quality control (so as to show a "connection in the course of trade") he need not give particulars of the vast number of details involved.[93]

19–178   If the claimant alleges that actual deception has occurred, he will be ordered to give particulars of the person deceived.[94] So also if he relies upon trap orders. If the defendant pleads that the claimant's registration is invalid, he must give particulars of the invalidity alleged.[95]

19–179   Where a defendant alleges common use of the mark in question, he is likely to be ordered to give particulars of such use.[96] If reliance is placed by the defendant on use by other traders of marks with features similar to those of the claimant's mark, so as to support a contention that the claimant's right is limited to certain

---

[89] See also *Claudius Ash v Invicta* (1911) 28 R.P.C. 252 and 597; (1912) 29 R.P.C. 465; *Williams v Bronnley* (1909) 26 R.P.C. 481 and 765.

[90] [1990] R.P.C. 341.

[91] *Newman v Pinto* (1887) 57 L.T. 31; 3 T.L.R. 685; 4 R.P.C. 508.

[92] See, *e.g. Claudius Ash v Invicta* (1912) 29 R.P.C. 465, HL.

[93] *General Electric v Simplex-G.E.* [1971] R.P.C. 351; [1971] F.S.R. 106.

[94] *Humphries v Taylor* (1888) L.R. 39 Ch.D. 693; 5 R.P.C. 687; *Whitstable Oyster Fishery v Hayling* (1900) 17 R.P.C. 461; (1901) 18 R.P.C. 434; and where a claimant at the trial desires to give evidence of such a case which has not been pleaded, the defendant will generally be entitled to ask for an adjournment, as in *Lines Brothers v Farris* (1925) 43 R.P.C. 64 at 68.

[95] Intellectual Property Proceedings Practice Direction, CPR Specialist Proceedings Practice Direction 2D, para.24.2.

[96] *Aquascutum v Moore* (1903) 20 R.P.C. 640; *Schweppes v Gibbens* (1905) 22 R.P.C. 113 at 116. But if a defendant pleads that the article in question is generally known by the name which the claimant alleges is distinctive, and does not rely on particular users, he will not be ordered to give particulars of the general knowledge: *Boake Roberts v Wayland* (1909) 26 R.P.C. 249. Formerly, in a passing off case, a bare denial by the defendant of the claimant's allegation that a mark is distinctive of his goods will not entitle the claimant to ask for particulars of use by other traders (*La Radiotechnique v Weinbaum* (1927) 44 R.P.C. 361), but this is likely to be changed under the CPR, certainly if the plea is not simply to found a case that the claimant's use has not been sufficiently extensive to make the mark distinctive, but is on the footing of a positive allegation that use by others is such that distinctiveness is lacking.

features, particulars of such use should be given.[97] Where a defendant alleges use by himself he may be ordered to give particulars of the user alleged.[98]

Where a defendant pleaded that the acts complained of were done by an employee outside his authority and contrary to express instructions given by the defendant, he was ordered to give particulars of the instructions.[99] **19–180**

Where a defendant pleads that the words complained of are a *bona fide* description of the character or quality of his goods, he may be ordered to give particulars of the character or quality which the words describe.[1] **19–181**

In a passing off case in which the plaintiffs alleged that their cigars had come to be known by a name consequent on the use of red bands, they were ordered to give particulars of the date when the cigars first became so known.[2] **19–182**

DISCLOSURE OF DOCUMENTS

The ordinary rules governing disclosure, set out in Pt 31 of the CPR, also apply to trade mark actions. But a process which enables a rival trader to extract from his opponent information concerning his customers, his trade, and his mode of doing business is extremely likely to be abused; whilst in cases where a large business is affected, even the ordinary order for disclosure of documents may be very oppressive.[3] The court, therefore, will, upon a proper case being shown, modify the common orders so that they shall occasion no more inconvenience to the party to whom they are directed than is necessary to ascertain the rights of his opponent.[4] These principles are now expressly reflected in the CPR, which limits the extent of standard disclosure,[5] and requires a search for documents which is no more than is reasonable in the circumstances, having regard to the number of documents involved, the nature and complexity of the proceedings, the ease and expense of retrieving the documents concerned, and the significance of documents likely to be found.[6] A party must make it clear what documents he has not felt it reasonable to search for.[7] **19–183**

Documents given on disclosure may not be used for any purposes other than the proceedings in which they are disclosed,[8] unless read or referred to in open court, or the court or the disclosing party (and the person to whom the document belongs, if different) gives permission. Under the old Rules of Court, permission to use disclosed documents for other purposes would only be given in exceptional circumstances,[9] and it seems that this standard is likely to be maintained, since the purpose of the rule is to encourage frank disclosure by giving proper protection to the disclosing party. An exception exists in relation to "Anton Piller" search orders, which may more readily, with permission, be used to commence **19–184**

---

[97] *Willesden Varnish v Young & Marten* (1922) 39 R.P.C. 285 at 289.
[98] *Beindorff v Chambers* (1928) 45 R.P.C. 122.
[99] *Boston Marine v Wheeler & Thomson* (1954) 71 R.P.C. 432 (passing off case).
[1] *Coca Cola v Duckworth* (1928) 45 R.P.C. 225.
[2] *Imperial Tobacco v Purnell* (1903) 20 R.P.C. 719.
[3] *Wills* [1892] 3 Ch. 201; 9 R.P.C. 346, CA.
[4] *Andrew v Kuehnrich* (1912) 29 R.P.C. 698, CA.
[5] r.31.6.
[6] r.31.7.
[7] r.31.7(3).
[8] CPR, r.31.22.
[9] *Crest Homes v Marks* [1987] A.C. 289.

proceedings against third parties shown by the seized material to be involved in infringing the claimant's rights.[10]

Disclosure of sales

19–185   Disclosure in regard to the sales effected by the defendant under the disputed mark is not, in general, where the infringement is denied, material, until the fact that the mark is an infringement of the claimant's rights has been decided.[11] After an account of profits or an inquiry as to damages has been directed, full disclosure will generally be ordered, although in some cases, audited schedules of sales may be ordered instead, or by agreement.[12]

19–186   Disclosure of the identity of suppliers or customers is not infrequently sought at an interim stage by a claimant seeking to trace the source and destination of goods which have passed through a defendant's hands. There is certainly jurisdiction to grant such an order,[13] but it will be exercised with care, and in particular it is usually easier to get disclosure of suppliers' names than customers, because that relief is more helpful to the claimant and less potentially damaging to the defendant.[14] Fear of violence by the person whose identity is ordered to be disclosed is not an answer to such an application except in extraordinary circumstances: *Coca Cola v Gilbey*.[15]

"Anton Piller," "Mareva" and similar orders

19–187   During the 1970s the courts evolved a number of remedies of particular value in cases of serious or deliberate violations of industrial property rights. In particular it is now possible in strong cases to obtain orders, without notice being given to the defendant, requiring the defendant to permit the claimant's solicitors to search premises for infringing goods or documents relating thereto[16] and to require the defendant forthwith to disclose his source of supply of such goods.[17] Similarly there is power to "freeze" a defendant's assets where there is evidence of a risk that such assets will be dissipated before a money judgment can be enforced.[18] These and other similar orders may now even be made against defendants known only the claimant by description and not by name.[19]

19–188   These orders are now, under the CPR, referred to as "freezing orders" and "search orders", respectively, and are provided for by r.25(1)(f) and (h) of the

---

[10] See *Sony v Anand*; *Seiko Time v Domicrest* [1981] F.S.R. 398. By contrast see *Cobra v Rata* [1997] F.S.R. 317, where leave to use documents obtained on an Anton Piller raid in support of contempt proceedings was refused.

[11] See, *e.g. Benbow v Low* (1880) 16 Ch.D. 93.

[12] *Leather Cloth v Hirschfeld* (1865–66) 1 H. & M. 295; *Powell v Birmingham Brewery* (1897) 14 R.P.C. 1; *Saccharin v Chemicals and Drugs* [1900] 2 Ch. 556; 17 R.P.C. 612; *"Manus"* (1949) 66 R.P.C. 285.

[13] *Lagenes v It's At* [1991] F.S.R. 492.

[14] *Jade v Antiference* [1996] F.S.R. 461; *Sega v Alca* [1982] F.S.R. 516; *Charles of the Ritz v Jory* [1986] F.S.R. 14 Ch. D.

[15] [1996] F.S.R. 23.

[16] *Anton Piller v Manufacturing Processes* [1976] Ch. 55; [1976] R.P.C. 719.

[17] *EMI v Sarwar* [1976] F.S.R. 146.

[18] The "Mareva" injunction, the power to grant which was specifically confirmed by the Supreme Court Act 1981, s.37(3).

[19] *Bloomsbury Publishing Group v News Group Newspapers* [2003] F.S.R. 45.

CPR. A considerable body of authority in relation to them has grown up since their invention, and the reader is referred to specialised works on the topic.[20]

DISCLOSURE AGAINST A THIRD PARTY

There is power to order disclosure of the identity of the true tortfeasor against an innocent third party who gets "mixed up" in transactions relating to infringing goods.[21] This includes the jurisdiction to order disclosure so as to enable the claimant to effect service when he already knows the identity of the intended defendant.[22] The jurisdiction has been extended by analogy to situations where the defendant's identity is known, but the claimant is not in possession of information necessary to make a claim against that defendant, which information is held by a third party innocently involved in the alleged wrongdoing.[23]   **19–189**

INTERIM INJUNCTION AGAINST INNOCENT THIRD PARTY

There is also power to obtain an interim injunction against a third party, for example a carrier, who happens to have custody or control of goods which infringe a claimant's rights.[24] Reference should also be made to the section above dealing with applications for delivery up under s.19 of the 1994 Act.[25]   **19–190**

DOCUMENTS REFERRED TO IN THE PLEADINGS, ETC.

Production and inspection of copies of documents which are referred to in any statement of case, witness statement, witness summary or affidavit may be ordered.[26]   **19–191**

EVIDENCE OF TITLE

Registration is *prima facie* evidence of the validity of the original registration and of all assignments and transmissions of the mark (s.72 of the 1994 Act).   **19–192**

TRAP ORDERS

In general, proof of a single act of infringement by the defendant is sufficient to justify the claimant in bringing his action, and the evidence relied on is frequently the sale by the defendant of the spurious goods to the claimant or his agent, who has bought them merely for the purpose of procuring evidence. Though orders of this sort, generally referred to as "trap orders", have not infrequently been the subject of unfavourable comment, they are often the only means by which evidence can be obtained, and, if they are fairly given, there is no impropriety in adopting this procedure.[27] The object is to show what the defendant is doing or what is likely to be the result of some ambiguous advertisement or marking, and   **19–193**

---

[20] See, *e.g.* S. Gee, Mareva Injunctions and Anton Piller Relief *Mareva and Anton Piller Orders*, (4th ed., Sweet and Maxwell, London, 1998).

[21] *Norwich Pharmacal v Customs & Excise* [1974] A.C. 133; [1974] R.P.C. 101, HL. And see now CPR, rr.31.17 and 18.

[22] *Coca Cola v BT* [1999] F.S.R. 518: disclosure in relation to mobile telephone customer ordered so as to effect service.

[23] *Carlton Film Distributors v VCI* [2003] F.S.R. 47.

[24] *Norwich Pharmacal v Customs & Excise in the CA* at [1974] A.C. 133 at 146; [1972] R.P.C. 743. The decision in the HL does not affect this point. See also *Washburn v Cunard* (1889) 6 R.P.C. 398 and *Smith, Kline & French v Harbottle* [1980] R.P.C. 363.

[25] See paras 19–110 to 19–125.

[26] CPR, r.31.14.

[27] *Wakefield v Purser* (1934) 51 R.P.C. 167 at 171; *Walt Disney Productions v Gurvitz* [1982]

the orders must, therefore, be fairly given, and of a character which is not unlikely to occur in ordinary practice.[28] Orders in writing, where they are practicable, are to be preferred; but in a class of business where orders are nearly always oral, a written order may inevitably arouse suspicion and, therefore, be of no practical use. In all cases the defendant should be promptly informed as to what is alleged to have occurred so that he may have the opportunity of investigating the incidents while the recollection of those concerned is fresh.[29] All the circumstances surrounding trap orders have to be scrutinised with great care.[30] The courts will not necessarily grant relief in respect of isolated instances which may not be sufficient to prove any apprehension that passing off is likely to occur, and the needs of the case may sometimes be met by a special order as to costs.[31]

STAY OF OTHER PROCEEDINGS

19–194 Where High Court proceedings involve the same or very similar issues to those raised in proceedings in an inferior tribunal such as the Registry, an injunction may be granted restraining a party from pursuing those other proceedings, as happened in *Sears v Sears Roebuck*.[32]

F.S.R. 446 (a contempt case). In *Marie Claire v Hartstone* [1993] F.S.R. 692, the defendant argued that the plaintiff's solicitors had practised a deception during their involvement in a trap purchase. Chadwick J. held that there was nothing, from the perspective of the court, wrong in the solicitors' involvement, since the plaintiff itself would have been entitled to make the trap order, and if nothing else the solicitor's presence ensured an accurate record. He pointed out, however, that the deceptive nature of the trap order might be a matter for the Law Society. See Ch.24, in relation to the potential impact of human rights issues on the use of trap orders.

[28] *California Fig Syrup v Taylor's* (1897) 14 R.P.C. 564, CA; *Carr v Crisp* (1902) 19 R.P.C. 497, Byrne J.

[29] e.g. *Fox's Glacier Mints v Jobbings* (1932) 49 R.P.C. 352; *Hampshire v General Kaputine* (1930) 47 R.P.C. 437 at 444; *Broad v Cast Iron Drainage* [1970] F.S.R. 363.

[30] *Stillitz v Jones and Higgins* (1943) 60 R.P.C. 15 at 17.

[31] *Hennessy v Kennett* (1877) Seb.Dig. at 331, Malins V.C.; cf. *Leahy, Kelly v Glover* (1893) 10 R.P.C. 141, HL, where a single instance of the sale of goods by the defendant's shopwoman, not shown to have been with his authority, was considered insufficient to support a case of passing off; *Rutter v Smith* (1901) 18 R.P.C. 49; and *Knight v Crisp* (1904) 21 R.P.C. 671 similar cases; *Burberry v Watkinson* (1906) 23 R.P.C. 141, an isolated instance of mistake; and *Armstrong Oiler v Patent Axlebox* (1910) 27 R.P.C. 362, an isolated instance of a mistake by a workman, and the plaintiffs, who failed on the rest of the case, were ordered to pay the costs, except so far as they had, down to the giving of an undertaking, been increased by this complaint. See also *Carr v Crisp* (1902) 19 R.P.C. 497, where Byrne J. said that if one instance only had been proved he would have followed *Leahy v Glover*; and *Kodak v Grenville* (1908) 25 R.P.C. 416, where the only question was as to costs; cf. *Hennessy v Neary* (1902) 19 R.P.C. 36 (Ireland). In *French v Rhind* [1958] R.P.C. 82 (a passing off case) it was contended that the manner of conducting the oral trap order was unsatisfactory; but unsuccessfully, following *Pearson v Valentine* (1917) 34 R.P.C. 267, where it was held that it was not sufficient for a person who receives an order for a particular brand to send another brand and leave it to the customer to find out himself that it is a different brand. See further *L'Oreal v Coiffeur Supplies* [1961] R.P.C. 219 (interim injunctions granted on a single written trap order); *Cellular Clothing v White* (1953) 70 R.P.C. 9 (*arguendo*, observations on possible ambiguities in trap orders; need to give notice at once); and contrast *Bostitch v McGarry & Cole* [1964] R.P.C. 173 at 177 with *Hilti v Ucan* [1963] R.P.C. 160; [1964] R.P.C. 206 (both cases of defendants who had ceased to sell goods bearing the plaintiffs' mark; in "Bostitch", there was delivery of the defendants' goods on written trap orders for the plaintiffs', interim injunction granted; in "Hilti", such an injunction was refused on a single trap order—in writing, but handed over, not sent by post—and again on a verbal trap order, there being a conflict of evidence). See also *Showerings v Blackpool Tower* [1975] F.S.R. 40.

[32] [1993] R.P.C. 385, since upheld in the Court of Appeal (where the Registry had refused a stay) and see generally Ch.5, for the circumstances in which the Registry will itself order a stay.

CHAPTER 20

CRIMINAL PROCEEDINGS

1. Outline

The Trade Marks Act 1994 creates two main categories of offences. The first, which is likely to be of far greater practical importance of the two, concerns "unauthorised" use of a trade mark (ss.92 and 93). It is primarily aimed at counterfeiting, but as will be suggested below, it seems that the definitions of the offences created are so broad that many other kinds of behaviour will or may also amount to a criminal offence. Similar offences, but of more restricted scope, were previously provided for by the Copyright, Designs and Patents Act 1988,[1] which was added by amendment as ss.58A–58D into the Trade Marks Act 1938.   **20–001**

The second category of offence concerns making false statements about the registered status of a mark, either by falsifying the Register or entries in it (s.94 of the 1994 Act), or by representing that a mark is registered when in fact it is not (s.95). Similar provisions were contained in the 1938 Act.[2]   **20–002**

In addition, it is an offence to make unauthorised use of the Royal arms (s.99 of the 1994 Act).   **20–003**

This chapter also covers forfeiture of counterfeit goods (ss.97 and 98).

2. Offences involving unauthorised use

UNAUTHORISED USE-GENERAL SCHEME OF SECTION 92

Subsections (1) to (3) of s.92 of the 1994 Act, each create separate offences. In outline,[3] subs.(1) concerns applying an offending mark to goods or dealing in or keeping goods carrying such a mark; subs.(2) concerns the making use or keeping of packaging or documents bearing an offending mark, and subs.(3) concerns making or keeping articles designed for reproducing an offending mark.   **20–004**

The offences created by the section all require that the defendant's use be in relation to goods. It is not an offence to misuse a mark in relation to services, or in the creation of advertising or other materials for services.[4]   **20–005**

Since the last edition of this work, the House of Lords in *R. v Johnstone*[5] has ruled (contrary to the impression many practitioners and commentators gained from the wording of s.92) that in order for an offence to be committed, there must be infringement of the mark in question (and thus civil defences such as those   **20–006**

---

[1] s.300.
[2] ss.59 and 60.
[3] The acts to which each of the subsections relate are considered in more detail in paras 20–019 to 20–026.
[4] In principle, it seems it would be possible to commit an offence by using on goods a mark identical to one registered in respect only of services, provided that the mark was a famous one, since s.92(4)(b), discussed below, contains no limitation to marks registered in respect of goods.
[5] [2003] F.S.R. 42.

under s.11 are defences under s.92), and further, that infringement requires use as a trade mark.[6]

20–007   Subsection (5), which is discussed below, provides a further defence if the defendant believed on reasonable grounds that his acts were not infringements.

It does not seem to be an element of any of the offences under s.92 of the 1994 Act, that the defendant mislead or intend to mislead his customers into thinking that the goods in which he is dealing or intending or preparing to deal, are genuine. The offences will be committed even if the defendant's customers are well aware that the goods are counterfeit (provided that such awareness does not provide a defence to infringement, which it usually will not, and certainly not in relation to use of an identical mark on identical goods).[7] This will avoid the problems which have arisen in some cases under the Trade Descriptions Act where defendants have avoided liability by selling counterfeit goods at stalls bearing a warning that the goods are fake.[8]

20–008   For the purposes of s.92, "registered trade mark" includes both Community trade marks and protected international trade marks (UK).[9]

MENS REA

20–009   There is no requirement of dishonest conduct in the definitions of these offences. Save in respect of ss.92(2) and (3) of the 1994 Act, the only *mens rea* required is that the defendant act with a view to gain for himself or with intent to cause loss to another.[10] "With a view to" has been held to have a broad meaning, simply to the effect that the defendant had something in his contemplation, not necessarily something he wanted or intended to happen but something which might realistically occur, and is to be contrasted with "with intento to".[11] It appears that "with a view to gain" will virtually always be established if the defendant's acts are done for any kind of commercial purpose, including selling or advertising goods bearing an offending mark, or keeping them with a view to selling them, or even keeping them for security for a debt.[12]

20–010   Section 92(2) requires, in addition, that the materials to which the mark is applied be intended to be used for labelling or packaging goods, or as a "business

---

[6] As to which, see further Ch.14. Lord Nicholls (para.34) identified one possible aspect in which infringement under the civil provisions of the 1994 Act might not have to be proved: infringement under the civil provisions requires the accused use to be "in the course of trade", but the same requirement does not appear in all the relevant provisions of s.92. As Lord Nicholls pointed out, the difference is not likely to be material, because s.92 does require the acts to be done "with a view to gain for himself or another, or with intent to cause loss to another."

[7] See further Ch.14.

[8] See *Kent County Council v Price* [1993] 9 E.I.P.R. D-224, a Trade Descriptions Act case, and contrast *Akhtar v Grout* (1998) 10 I.P.R. 714, a prosecution under s.92, where the defendant, who was convicted, described his counterfeit goods to persons making a trap purchase by saying that "They are not real, but they are good." See, below, however, as to the situation where the marks are not identical. See also *Torbay Council v Satnam Singh* [2000] F.S.R. 158 at 161, for a statement concerning the policy of these provisions which is in keeping with the above approach, but note that that decision was overruled in *R. v Johnstone* on the specific question of whether a belief that a mark was not registered constitutes a defence under s.92(5).

[9] Community Trade Mark Regulations 1996, reg.7 (SI 1996/1908), Trade Marks (International Registration) Order 1996, art.17 (SI 1996/714).

[10] s.92(1) also requires that keeping material marked with an offending sign in the course of a business be "with a view" to dealing in the goods. This is probably an objective test and is unlikely to be of much practical significance.

[11] *R. v Zaman* [2003] F.S.R. 13.

[12] As in *R. v Zaman*.

paper",[13] or for advertising goods. This is very likely to be evident from the materials themselves.

Section 92(3) requires, in addition to having a view to gain or intention to cause loss, that the defendant knows or had reason to believe that the article specifically designed or adapted to copy the offending mark has been used or is intended to be used to produce goods or material for labelling or packaging goods, or as a business paper in relation to goods, or for advertising goods.[14] There is no requirement that the defendant knows that the use of materials made with the article in question would be wrongful.   **20–011**

The overall result is that in many, and perhaps most, practical cases, the *mens rea* of these offences will follow almost automatically from the commission of the offending act, and a defendant who believed that his acts did not infringe will bear the onus of proving that that was the case, under s.92(5). In addition, he will have to prove that he had reasonable grounds for such a belief. What those grounds might be, and the nature of the onus on the defendant, is considered below.[15] A defendant who gives no thought to whether his acts would infringe, but had no reason to believe that they did, will be in danger of committing an offence without any ill motive at all. For this reason alone, it appears that s.92 goes well beyond counterfeiting, even after the decision of the House of Lords in *Johnstone*; although the decision requires the prosecution to show infringement under the civil provisions of the 1994 Act, those civil provisions have no significant mental element.   **20–012**

Marks need not be identical

In addition to the readily satisfied requirements of the mens rea of these offences, it should be noted that the offending mark does not have to be identical to the registered mark in question: it may be merely "likely to be mistaken" for it. This expression is not the same as that used in the section of the 1994 Act dealing with infringement by use of a similar mark,[16] but following the decision in *Johnstone*, the difference is probably not very material, since the prosecution will have to satisfy both the test of s.10(2) and of s.92, even if they are different. If anything the language used in s.92 suggests a somewhat narrower test, focusing solely on whether the marks are similar enough to be mistaken one for another. This was the intention of the legislature.[17]   **20–013**

The fact that the marks need not be identical and may be merely similar is an-   **20–014**

---

[13] This rather clumsy term presumably covers documents such as invoices, delivery notes, catalogues and the like.

[14] The subsection is unclear as to whether the defendant must know or have reason to believe that the mark will be used on goods for which the relevant registered trade mark is in fact registered (use on goods for which it is not registered will not normally be an offence, because of the operation of subs.(4)), or merely for goods generally. It is suggested that the former is the better view, since it would be strange if a person committed an offence by creating material for copying a mark whose use in due course could not itself be an offence. Of course, in many instances it will be perfectly clear from the surrounding circumstances that the mark was intended to be used on goods for which the relevant registered mark was registered.

[15] paras 20–031 to 20–039.

[16] s.10(2). See Ch.14.

[17] H.L. Public Bill Committee, Fourth Sitting, January 20, 1994, col.96. It is to be hoped that the question of whether the offending sign is likely to be mistaken for the registered mark in question is to be determined by reference to the sign and mark alone, though. If the surrounding circumstances are to be taken into account, then it might be that the problems associated with the Trade Descriptions Act 1968, where the defendant describes the offending goods as "brand copies", or otherwise makes it clear that they are not genuine, will recur: see the reference to *Kent County Council v Price* [1993] 9 E.I.P.R. D-224. It is also hard to see how the likely circumstances sur-

other reason why s.92 extends well beyond counterfeiting. A requirement that the marks be absolutely identical would allow the section to be avoided too easily by counterfeiters, merely by a trivial change to the mark. However, the test used by the section means that a criminal offence may be committed by a person using a mark which the court finds is too similar to a registered mark, even if there were real differences between the marks, and there had been no conscious or dishonest copying of the registered mark in question.

20–015   Whether two non-identical marks are sufficiently close to one another for there to be a likelihood of confusion between them is frequently difficult to judge, and reasonable minds can honestly differ. Many infringement actions have taken place where a defendant has created his own mark with every honest intention, in ignorance of the registered mark in question, and the court has later found that the similarity is sufficient for there to be infringement.

20–016   It is unsatisfactory that the section is so likely to impose criminal liability on the defendant in such a situation, who very probably will not be able to prove that he believed on reasonable grounds that he would not be infringing, since he will not have considered the matter at all and will have had no grounds to think that he did not infringe. A defendant may be able to argue that it is not clear beyond a reasonable doubt that the offending sign is likely to be mistaken for the registered mark, but that is plainly an uncertain course, and it may perfectly well be that the sign in question is likely to be so mistaken, even though independently designed. This problem has not been ameliorated by the decision of the House of Lords in *Johnstone*; it did not arise for consideration there. The House of Lords did decide that s.92(5) would provide a defence if the defendant had reasonable grounds to believe the mark was not registered, or that the goods were "genuine".[18] But where a trader deals with goods which are not counterfeits, yet have a mark potentially confusingly similar to a registered mark, of which he is unaware, he may well, in all honesty, have no reason at all to consider whether there might be infringement.

REQUIREMENT THAT THE PROPRIETOR DID NOT CONSENT

20–017   Subsections (1)–(3), of s.92 of the 1994 Act, each stipulate that the defendant must have acted without the consent of the proprietor of the registered trade mark in question (and the requirement would probably follow in any event from the decision in *Johnstone* that there must be civil infringement for the offence to be committed). The drafting of the subsections make it clear that this is a positive element of the offence for the prosecution to prove, rather than a defence on which the defendant bears the onus.

20–018   This may be of some significance in cases where a defendant is dealing in goods which are very similar to the proprietor's genuine goods, or where he is dealing in "grey" goods. In such situations it can be quite difficult, even in civil proceedings, to prove whether the goods are genuine or fake, or whether their sale in the United Kingdom was consented to by the proprietor, explicitly or impliedly. Proving these matters to the criminal standard will of course be much more difficult still.

---

rounding the ultimate sale to the public can be assessed in relation to a defendant who is prosecuted for applying the mark to the goods, or for keeping goods bearing an offending sign.

[18] Paras 42–55, and see paras 20–031 to 20–039.

ACTS CONSTITUTING OFFENCES UNDER SECTION 92

Subsection 92(1) of the 1994 Act makes it an offence to: **20–019**

  (a) apply to goods or their packaging a sign identical to, or likely to be mistaken for, a registered trade mark; or

  (b) sell or let for hire, offer or expose for sale or hire or distribute, goods which bear, or the packaging of which bears, such a sign; or

  (c) have in the defendant's possession, custody or control in the course of a business any such goods with a view to the doing of anything, by himself or another, which would be an offence under (b).

As one would expect, the offence is committed whether the offending sign is **20–020** on the goods themselves or on their packaging. But it does not appear that the offence is committed by selling unlabelled goods in connection with documents such as invoices which describe the goods by reference to the offending sign. That situation would be covered by subs.(2).

Keeping unauthorised goods under subs.(1)(c) is only an offence if done in the **20–021** course of a business. This limitation is necessary to prevent consumers who buy counterfeit goods from committing an offence in keeping the goods at their homes. By necessary implication, though, it means that consumers who privately sell on counterfeit goods which they have bought (even a single item), even if they did not know that the goods were counterfeit, may be committing an offence.

Subsection (1)(c) also only makes it an offence to keep goods or their packag- **20–022** ing bearing an offending sign if it is with a view to dealing in them by way of sale, hire or the like under subs.(1)(b). This means that some limited categories of business may be entitled lawfully to keep infringing materials, for example for the purposes of scrapping or recycling them.

Subsection (2) makes it an offence to: **20–023**

  (a) apply a sign identical to, or likely to be mistaken for, a registered trade mark to material intended to be used—

    (i) for labelling or packaging goods,

    (ii) as a business paper in relation to goods, or

    (iii) for advertising goods, or

  (b) use in the course of business material bearing such a sign in relation to goods, or for advertising goods, or

  (c) have in the defendant's possession, custody or control in the course of a business any such material with a view to the doing of anything, by himself or another, which would be an offence under (b).

As has been mentioned above, "business paper" is a curious term. It is not fur- **20–024** ther defined in the 1994 Act. It appears that the term was probably used with the intention of covering all kinds of documents which might bear a trade mark and be used in connection with goods, so as to cover invoices, price lists and so on. There is nothing, however, in the subsection to require that the "business paper" be of a kind likely to be seen by a customer, although such papers are plainly covered. So, for example, the internal papers of a business such as inventory lists, which no customer would ever be likely to see, would seem to fall within the definition.

Subsection (3) makes it an offence to: **20–025**

  (a) make an article specifically designed or adapted for making copies of a sign identical to, or likely to be mistaken for, a registered trade mark; or

(b) have such an article in the defendant's possession, custody or control in the course of a business.

20–026   The defendant must also know that the article has been, or is to be used to produce goods, or material for labelling or packaging goods, as a business paper in relation to goods, or for advertising goods.

The Goods in Question; Well-known Marks

20–027   By s.92(4), no offence is committed under s.92 unless the goods in question are those for which the trade mark concerned is registered, or the trade mark "has a reputation in the United Kingdom and the use of the sign takes or would take unfair advantage of, or is or would be detrimental to, the distinctive character or the repute of the trade mark". The degree of repute required to satisfy this test is considered in Chs 9 and 14.

20–028   The second limb of s.92(4) echoes the words of s.10(3).[19] Its effect will be that an offence may be committed by the use of well-known marks on goods for which they are not registered, and this is likely to be of particular importance in connection with the sale of counterfeit souvenir items of small value which are not the kind of goods produced by the registered proprietor.

20–029   Proof that the use of a mark in such circumstances takes unfair advantage of it will often follow from the fact that the defendant is using the presence of the mark to sell his goods and turn a profit. Alternatively, use of a prestigious mark on cheap counterfeits may well be detrimental to its repute. These are not matters which are likely to cause any great practical problems of proof.

20–030   However, proving the existence of a reputation in the context of a criminal prosecution and to the criminal standard of proof may be difficult in practice.[20] Much of the evidence relied upon in civil proceedings to prove reputation would not be admissible in criminal proceedings, in particular because of the hearsay rules.

Defence of Reasonable Belief of Non-infringement

20–031   Section 92(5) provides that:

> "It is a defence for a person charged with an offence under this section to show that he believed on reasonable grounds that the use of the sign in the manner in which it was used, or was to be used, was not an infringement of the registered trade mark."

20–032   The House of Lords in *Johnstone*[21] confirmed that the onus of proof is on the person charged, and carries with it a persuasive burden. It appears at first reading that the test is two-fold. First, the defendant must have in fact believed that his acts did not or would not infringe. That appears to be a subjective test. Secondly, the defendant must have had reasonable grounds for that belief.

20–033   The subsection does not say that the defence is made out if the defendant merely proves that there was in fact no infringement, but this now follows from the main part of the decision in *Johnstone*.

---

[19] See Ch.14.

[20] Unless the court can be persuaded to take judicial notice of the reputation of extremely well-known marks such as Coca-Cola and the like.

[21] [2003] F.S.R. 42, paras 44–55. There had been contradictory authority of the Court of Appeal on the point, in *R. v S (Trademark Defence)* [2002] EWCA Crim 2558, and in the Court of Appeal in *Johnstone* itself. The House of Lords held that the social and economic conditions relating to counterfeit goods justified placing the onus on the defendant, having due regard to the presumption of innocence under art.6(2) of the European Convention on Human Rights.

A potentially difficult question arises in relation to a person dealing in goods   **20–034**
who never turns his mind to the issue of whether they infringe or not. There is
nothing in the subsection to indicate that the defence extends to such a person,
even if there were reasonable grounds available to him for believing that the
goods did not infringe had he inquired.

However, it should be appreciated that the subsection surely does not require a   **20–035**
trader to give his mind to the law of registered trade marks in conducting his
business. He must be entitled to some extent to form a lay view of the situation,
particularly if the issue is whether the goods are genuine or not, and the purchaser
has no reason to think that they are not. So a trader who buys full price goods
bearing a registered mark from a reputable source, perhaps one of the trade mark
proprietor's own distributors, should be entitled to say "I did not think about the
law specifically, but I thought that these were 'genuine' goods because of where
they came from".[22] Of course, the situation would be different if the goods were
bought at an unusually low price or from a "grey" importer.

On the other hand, what of a defendant who obtains legal advice that his deal-   **20–036**
ings in goods bearing a trade mark do not infringe, or reaches that conclusion
himself on considering the law? This will have little significance in relation to
outright counterfeiting cases, but as is observed above, the offences under s.92
cover many other kinds of behaviour.

Assuming that the defendant properly instructed his lawyers about the facts[23]   **20–037**
(or that his own deliberations were reasonably competent), it may well be that the
defence under s.92(5) would be available.

Although ignorance of the criminal law is not a defence, a mistake about the   **20–038**
civil law can negative *mens rea*.[24]

An honest and reasonable belief that the mark concerned is not registered may   **20–039**
provide a defence under s.92. The decision to the contrary of the Court of Appeal
in *Torbay Council v Satnam Singh* [2000] F.S.R. 158[25] was reversed by the House
of Lords in *Johnstone*, which held that there was no rational basis for distinguishing between persons who honestly believe there was no infringement of a mark
of which they were aware, and persons who honestly believe there was no
registration at all. However, the circumstances in which a person can have an
honest but erroneous belief on reasonable grounds that a mark is not registered,
are likely to be rare. It is very easy to find out, reliably, whether a mark is
registered, and it is to be doubted whether merely ebing told by a supplier of
potentially counterfeit goods that there is no registration will constitute reasonable grounds.

---

[22] And this appears consistent with the decision in *Johnstone*, para.53.

[23] Legal advice based on erroneous instructions would surely not provide "reasonable" grounds for
a belief that the acts would not infringe, especially if the instructions given were deliberately
wrong or incomplete.

[24] See, *e.g. R. v Smith (David Raymond)* [1974] Q.B. 354, where a mistaken belief as to the ownership of property was a defence to a charge of criminal damage. And see generally Archbold, 1999
edition, s.17–22 at p.1503. It is suggested that the position under s.92 is different from that under
the civil provisions of the Copyright, Designs and Patents Act 1988 (and previously the Copyright Act 1956). There, what is required is knowledge of the facts, not an appreciation of the legal
conclusion which would follow from them: see, *e.g. Sillitoe v McGraw Hill Book Co (UK) Ltd*
[1983] F.S.R. 545. However, s.92 draws a distinction between the reasonable grounds and the
objective belief of the defendant; they are separate matters. In addition, being a criminal provision it should be construed more narrowly.

[25] Which had been followed in *R. v Keane* [2001] F.S.R. 63 but doubted by a differently constituted
Court of Appeal in *R. v Rhodes* [2003] F.S.R. 9 (which had overturned a conviction where the
defence was that the counterfeiting was so convincing that the defendants had not realised the
goods were not genuine).

EVIDENCE

20–040   Expert evidence is admissible both in relation to whether the goods concerned are genuine and, apparently, as to whether they would infringe the trade mark concerned: *Akhtar v Grout* (1998) 10 I.P.R. 714 at 717–718.[26] The second proposition is rather puzzling, and the case is probably best understood as being to the effect that expert evidence is admissible on the question of whether the public is likely to mistake the offending signs for the registered marks. For some reason the justices did not make a finding as to whether the offending signs and the registered marks were identical (at 716D–E), and therefore received evidence on the issue of whether the signs were likely to be mistaken for the marks. To decide that issue, the court held that they were entitled to hear evidence as to whether the signs infringed the marks.

3. Offences of unauthorised use—procedure

WHO CAN PROSECUTE; RELATIONSHIP WITH CIVIL PROCEEDINGS

20–041   Under s.6(1) of the Prosecution of Offences Act 1985, any person[27] can bring a prosecution under s.92 of the 1994 Act.[28]

As a result, the trade mark proprietor may himself bring a private prosecution. In counterfeiting cases, there is nothing wrong with this, but because of the wide scope of s.92 there is a risk that trade mark owners will bring private prosecutions against other traders where there has been no dishonesty, and the question of whether there is infringement is genuinely debatable, perhaps because of differences between the two marks in question. A trade mark owner might opt for a prosecution instead of or as well as a civil proceedings in such circumstances for a number of reasons. One might be cost, but another less palatable reason would be to put pressure on the defendant.

20–042   There has been a recent trend for copyright owners to bring private prosecutions in cases which would more normally be the subject of civil proceedings.

20–043   In *Thames & Hudson v DACS* [1995] F.S.R. 153, the defendant to criminal proceedings, a well-known art publisher, reacted by seeking a declaration of non-infringement in the High Court, and an injunction restraining DACS from continuing with the prosecution. DACS had prosecuted all the directors of the company in the criminal proceedings, and it was said that that was done without inquiry as to who was actually responsible, and was an indication of a desire to pressurise the company. The court refused to stay the proceedings, on the basis that Parliament had elected to make certain kinds of copyright infringement a crime, and had not limited the statutory provisions to "pirates". However, the judgment also indicated that the High Court was a more suitable forum for determining such disputes, and that the magistrates might wish to adjourn the criminal proceedings pending the resolution of the High Court action.

---

[26] And see also *R. v Wakefield* [2004] EWCA Crim 2278, para.17, where a witness gave expert evidence as to why he thought recordings were bootlegged, and that record companies do not consent to bootlegged recordings. The evidence was admitted.

[27] There is conflicting authority as to whether a corporation is a "person" for the purposes of being able to bring a prosecution. An unincorporated association clearly is not, though. See *R. v Ealing Justices, ex p. Dixon* [1990] 2 Q.B. 91. This issue is mainly a formal one, though, since if a corporate trade mark owner wishes to bring a prosecution it can always do so by an employee.

[28] Although under the 1985 Act, s.6(2), the DPP can take over the conduct of any prosecution, and under s.23 he may thereafter decide not to proceed with it.

A similar approach may be expected under s.92, but there is an additional complication to be considered where there is an issue over the validity of the trade mark in question. Under s.92, the offence is only committed by the use of a "registered" mark. At least in relation to a declaration of invalidity under s.47 of the 1994 Act, and in many practical situations in relation to revocation under s.46, once a mark is revoked or declared invalid, its registration is treated as never having taken place.[29]   **20–044**

It would therefore appear that, in principle, revocation of the trade mark in question or a declaration of invalidity under ss.46 or 47 would date back, and prevent the commission of an offence under s.92. However, it seems that the mark would actually have to be revoked or declared invalid, and only the Registrar or the court can do that.[30] "The court" is defined by s.75 as being, in England and Wales, the High Court.[31] A criminal court cannot therefore deal with revocation or a declaration of invalidity (and in any event its procedures are not suitable for doing so).   **20–045**

It would therefore seem that if a defendant wishes to challenge the validity of a trade mark as a defence under s.92,[32] there would have to be a stay of the criminal proceedings to allow an opportunity for that to be done in the High Court or the Registry.   **20–046**

OBLIGATION ON LOCAL WEIGHTS AND MEASURES AUTHORITY TO ENFORCE

Under s.93(1) of the 1994 Act, the local weights and measures authority in England and Wales is charged with enforcing within their areas the provisions of s.92. In Northern Ireland, the duty is on the Department of Economic Development.[33]   **20–047**

For the purposes of enforcing the provisions of s.92, they are given the same powers which they have under the Trade Descriptions Act 1968, ss.27, 28, 29 and 33. In addition, any enactment which authorises the disclosure of information for the purposes of enforcement of the Trade Descriptions Act 1968 also applies in relation to s.92 of the 1994 Act.[34]   **20–048**

PENALTIES AND PROCEDURE UNDER SECTION 92

Offences under s.92 of the 1994 Act are triable either way.   **20–049**

---

[29] s.46 actually provides that the "rights of the proprietor shall be deemed to have ceased" as from the date of the application to revoke, or any earlier date on which the Registrar or court is satisfied the grounds for revocation existed. This may leave open the possibility that a prosecution could be brought on a mark which is liable to be revoked, on the basis that the registration is not deemed never to have existed but only the proprietor's rights under it, although the distinction is at best a very fine one. Unless an application to revoke has been brought before a prosecution begins, a defendant relying on s.46 would have to show that the grounds for revocation existed at the time of the alleged offence. This situation seems to be potentially inconsistent with the Trade Marks Directive, Art.11, which provides that a non-used mark liable to revocation for non-use should not have effect in infringement proceedings or in relation to relative grounds for refusal of registration.

[30] ss.46(4) and 47(3).

[31] Unless the context otherwise requires, and there is nothing in the context of ss.46 or 47 to change the meaning of "court". On the contrary, they obviously mean the High Court.

[32] Once registration was proved, validity would be presumed under s.72 of the Act, and the onus would be on the defendant to prove that the mark was liable to be revoked or was invalid.

[33] s.93(3).

[34] s.93(4).

On summary conviction, a defendant is liable to up to six months in prison, or a fine not exceeding the statutory maximum.[35]

20–050   On conviction on indictment, a defendant is liable to up to 10 years in prison or an unlimited fine.[36] While 10 years in prison may seem like a severe sentence, there is authority in relation to copyright offences that they are serious offences of dishonesty akin to theft,[37] and counterfeiting may involve very large sums.

4. Falsifying the register

FALSIFICATION OF REGISTER

20–051   By s.94(1) of the 1994 Act it is an offence to make, or cause to be made, a false entry in the Register, knowing or having reason to believe it to be false. This refers to actually meddling with the Register itself, and it is not likely that this provision will be of much practical importance.

20–052   By s.94(2) it is an offence to make, or cause to be made, anything which falsely purports to be a copy of an entry in the Register, or to tender, or cause to be tendered, in evidence such a thing, knowing or believing that the thing is false. This subsection would cover, for example, making a forged certificate of registration.

PENALTIES AND PROCEDURE UNDER SECTION 94

20–053   Offences under s.94 of the 1994 Act are triable either way, and the penalties are the same as under s.92, except that the maximum period of imprisonment following conviction on indictment is only two years.[38]

5. Falsely representing a mark as registered

FALSELY REPRESENTING MARK AS REGISTERED

20–054   Under s.95(1) of the 1994 Act, it is an offence falsely to represent a mark as being registered when it is not, or to make a false representation as to the goods or services for which a mark is registered, knowing or having reason to believe that the representation is false.

20–055   There is a presumption that the word "registered" or any other word or symbol importing a reference to registration (an example would be the R in a circle) is a representation as to registration. Since goods may find their way into the United Kingdom bearing marks which are registered abroad but not here, the presump-

---

[35] s.92(6)(a). The statutory maximum is presently £5,000: Criminal Justice Act 1982, s.37(2) as amended by the Criminal Justice Act 1991, s.17(2).

[36] 1994 Act, s.92(6)(b).

[37] *R. v Carter* [1993] F.S.R. 303. For other examples see *R. v Ansari* [2001] 1 Cr. App. R. (S.) 94, and, by contrast, *R. v Passley* [2004] 1 Cr. App. R. (S).) 70, where a sentence of 21 months in respect of counterfeit videos was reduced on appeal to one of 12 months because the defendant's venture, though profitable, had lacked investment and sophisticated technology. The decision in *Carter* that the offence is akin to theft is supported by the decision of the Court of Appeal in *R. v Davies* [2004] F.S.R. 24 that a conviction under s. 92 can found a confiscation order under s.71of the Criminal Justice Act 1988 even where the indictment did not allege selling or offering for sale the infringing goods, on the basis that by applying labels to counterfeits, or preparing to make such labels, the defendant was stealing the marks.

[38] s.94(3).

tion can be rebutted by showing that the reference is to registration abroad, and that there, in fact, is a foreign registration for the goods or services in question.[39]

It should also be noted that falsely representing that a mark is registered might affect a claim for passing off based on the mark in question.[40]   **20–056**

PENALTIES AND PROCEDURE UNDER SECTION 95

Offences under s.95 of the 1994 Act are only triable summarily, and on conviction the maximum penalty is a fine at level 3 on the standard scale.[41]   **20–057**

CTMs AND PROTECTED INTERNATIONAL TRADE MARKS (UK)

Virtually identical provisions apply to making misrepresentations about Community trade marks and protected international trade marks (UK).[42] The penalties are the same as under s.95 of the 1994 Act.   **20–058**

6. Forfeiture of counterfeit goods and the like

FORFEITURE OF COUNTERFEIT GOODS, ETC.: OVERVIEW

Sections 97 and 98 of the 1994 Act[43] give the criminal courts powers to order the forfeiture of goods, packaging materials, labelling materials or business papers bearing a mark the same as a registered trade mark[44] or likely to be mistaken for it. Articles designed for making copies of such a mark may also be forfeit. Although the provisions are enforced by criminal courts, they are civil proceedings; local authorities have duties to prosecute, but no duty or exclusive status to bring forfeiture proceedings.[45] The relief obtained under the forfeiture provisions is granted according to a determination of private interests. Because the proceedings are civil proceedings, findings in other proceedings that goods are not counterfeit may operate by way of estoppel in them.[46]   **20–059**

The general scheme of the forfeiture powers is that goods, which come into the hands of a person in connection with the investigation or prosecution of counterfeiting-type offences, can be forfeited by an order of the relevant court. The order can be made in the course of a prosecution, but it is not necessary that there should be a prosecution so long as it appears that an offence of the relevant kind has been committed in relation to the goods.[47]   **20–060**

---

[39] s.95(2).

[40] Interlocutory relief was refused on this basis in *Johnson v Puffer* (1930) 47 R.P.C. 95. There is however no case where relief has been refused at trial on this basis, and it is doubtful whether this approach is in keeping with modern practice. See also *Jamieson v Jamieson* (1898) 15 R.P.C. 169 at 191, *per* Vaughan Williams L.J.

[41] Presently £1,000: Criminal Justice Act 1982, s.37(2) as amended by the Criminal Justice Act 1991, s.17(2).

[42] Community Trade Mark Regulations 1996, reg.8 (SI 1996/1908), Trade Marks (International Registration) Order 1996 art.18 (SI 1996/714), Apps 14 and 20.

[43] s.97 sets out the powers of forfeiture for England, Wales and Northern Ireland, which are considered in more detail below. s.98 creates similar powers applicable in Scotland.

[44] "Registered trade mark" includes for these purposes a Community trade mark or a protected international trade mark (UK): Community Trade Mark Regulations 1996 reg.7 (SI 1996/1908), Trade Marks (International Registration) Order 1996 (as amended) art.17 (SI 1996/714).

[45] *UNIC Centre Sarl v Brent and Harrow Trading Standards Office* [2000] F.S.R. 667.

[46] *UNIC Centre Sarl v Brent and Harrow Trading Standards Office* [2000] F.S.R. 667.

[47] s.97(2)(b).

20–061   Persons aggrieved by a forfeiture order are entitled to appeal against it.[48]

Goods which are ordered to be forfeited are normally to be destroyed, but it is possible that instead the offending mark may merely be obliterated from them.

Circumstances in which a section 97 application can be made

20–062   An application under s.97 of the 1994 Act may be made whenever any person comes into possession of goods of the kind described above in connection with the investigation or prosecution of a "relevant offence". "Relevant offence" includes any offence under s.92, or under the Trade Descriptions Act 1968, or any offence involving dishonesty or deception.[49]

20–063   It is not a requirement of s.97 of the 1994 Act that the goods in question actually be counterfeit, so long as a relevant offence has been committed in relation to them.[50] Since theft is a relevant offence, for example, the section could extend to stolen goods even if it were unknown, or could not be proved, whether or not they were counterfeit.

20–064   It is also not a requirement that the goods in question should be in the possession of the police or the prosecution. They could be in the possession of the trade mark owner, or of trading standards officers, or anyone else, so long as they came into the possession of that person in connection with the investigation or prosecution of a relevant offence.[51]

20–065   Presumably, though, no forfeiture order can be made until the goods in question are taken away from the counterfeiter or thief by some means, first because he will not have obtained possession in connection with the investigation or prosecution, and secondly because the right to apply for forfeiture resides with the person in possession.

Where the application should be made

20–066   If proceedings for a relevant offence relating to the goods concerned have been brought, then the application under s.97 of the 1994 Act may be made to the court dealing with those proceedings.[52] That will be a magistrates'c court or the Crown Court, depending on whether the offences are being tried summarily or not. If no application has been made to a court trying the relevant offence, then the application may be made to a magistrates' court.[53] It appears from the permissive words of the section that an application to a magistrates' court can be made either if there is no prosecution at all, or if there is a prosecution but no application for forfeiture is made in the course of it.

A relevant offence must have been committed

20–067   Forfeiture can only be ordered if the court is satisfied that a relevant offence has been committed in relation to the goods concerned. This may well be obvious as a result of a conviction being achieved. In addition, the court can infer the commission of a relevant offence in relation to one set of goods if it is satisfied that a

---

[48] s.97(3).
[49] s.97(8).
[50] s.97(3).
[51] s.97(1).
[52] s.97(2)(a).
[53] s.97(2)(b).

relevant offence has been committed in relation to other goods which are representative of them.[54]

APPEAL FROM ORDER FOR FORFEITURE OR REFUSAL

A person aggrieved[55] by the making or refusal of a forfeiture order may appeal to the crown court (in England and Wales) or the county court (in Northern Ireland).[56]   **20–068**

Regrettably, this leaves it most unclear how, if at all, an appeal can be made against the decision of a Crown Court, trying a relevant offence on indictment, in relation to the making or refusal of a forfeiture order.   **20–069**

DISPOSAL OF FORFEITED GOODS

Generally, as mentioned above, goods the subject of a forfeiture order are to be destroyed in accordance with the court's directions.[57] Alternatively, there is power to release the goods to a person specified by the court on condition that that person removes the offending mark, and complies with any order to pay costs made against him in the forfeiture proceedings.[58] The language of this provision suggests that it is principally directed to letting a defendant keep counterfeit goods if it is expected that the mark can and will satisfactorily be removed, but it is not so limited. It could extend, for example, to allowing the return to their owner of stolen counterfeit goods.   **20–070**

7. Misuse of Royal arms, devices, emblems and titles

UNLAWFUL USE OF ROYAL ARMS

Use of the Royal arms (or arms so closely resembling the Royal arms as to be calculated to deceive), without the permission of the Queen, in a manner calculated to lead to the belief that the user is duly authorised to use them, is an offence. It is triable summarily only and may be punished by a fine not exceeding level 2 on the standard scale.[59]   **20–071**

In addition, it is forbidden, without the authority of the Queen or other member of the Royal family, to use any device, emblem or title in a manner calculated to lead to the belief that the person so using it is employed by, or supplies goods or services to the Queen or that member of the Royal family.[60] It is not an offence to do so, but such acts (and acts amounting to an offence under s.99(1) of the 1994 Act) may be restrained by an injunction in proceedings brought by a person who is authorised to use the device, emblem or title in question, or by any person authorised by the Lord Chamberlain to take such proceedings.[61]   **20–072**

---

[54] 1994 Act, s.97(4).
[55] This will include, presumably, at least, the investigating and prosecuting agencies, the defendant, the owner of the goods, and the owner of the trade mark in question.
[56] s.97(5).
[57] s.97(6).
[58] s.97(7).
[59] ss.99(1) and (3). Level 2 on the standard scale is presently set at £500: Criminal Justice Act 1982, s.37(2), as amended by the Criminal Justice Act 1991, s.17(2).
[60] 1994 Act, s.99(2).
[61] s.99(4).

20–073   These provisions do not affect the right of the owner of a trade mark which includes such arms, devices, emblems or titles to use that trade mark.[62]

8. Offences by partnerships and bodies corporate

GENERAL PROVISIONS ABOUT OFFENCES BY PARTNERSHIPS

20–074   By s.101(1) of the 1994 Act, proceedings for offences alleged to have been committed by a partnership must be brought against the partnership in the name of the firm and not of the partners.

20–075   However, s.101(1) does not affect the liability of individual partners. By s.101(4), where a partnership commits an offence under the 1994 Act, all the partners are guilty and liable to be punished unless they are proved to have been ignorant of the offence or to have attempted to prevent it. The offence under s.101(4) renders each partner liable at the time of commission of the offence by the partnership, and the dissolution of the partnership before the trial does not prevent the partners being convicted.[63]

20–076   Section 101(2) provides that a partnership is to be treated as a body corporate for the purposes of proceedings for an offence under the 1994 Act in relation to (a) any rules of court relating to the service of documents, and (b) certain procedural provisions of the Magistrates' Courts Act 1980.[64]

20–077   If a partnership is fined for an offence under the 1994 Act, the fine must be paid out of partnership assets.[65]

PROVISIONS CONCERNING OFFENCES BY BODIES CORPORATE

20–078   Where a body corporate has committed an offence under the 1994 Act, and it is proved that it did so with the consent or connivance of a director, manager, secretary or other similar officer, or a person purporting to act in such a capacity, that person is also guilty of the offence and liable to be punished.[66]

20–079   This provision concerns the circumstances in which an officer of the company is himself liable for the company's crime. It does not address the separate question of when the company is liable for acts of its officers, which will fall to be determined under the general criminal law, and is outside the scope of this book.

---

[62] s.99(5).
[63] *R. v Wakefield* [2004] EWCA Crim 2278, para.15.
[64] Specified in s.101(2)(b).
[65] s.101(3).
[66] s.101(5).

CHAPTER 21

CUSTOMS POWERS AND PROCEDURES

1. Scope of chapter

In addition to civil and criminal remedies for trade mark infringement, the Trade Marks Act 1994 provides for trade mark owners to invoke the powers of the Commissioners of Customs and Excise to seize infringing goods on their entry into the United Kingdom. Moreover, European legislation has been introduced which seeks to restrict the circulation of "counterfeit" goods within the EU. This legislation extends to, among other things, certain categories of goods and articles which infringe registered trade mark rights, whether those rights arise under national legislation or under the Community Trade Marks Regulations. These two regimes are referred to in this chapter as "the domestic regime" and "the European regime".   **21–001**

It is not the goal of this chapter to explore the full scope of Customs' powers in relation to goods bearing trade marks, or of all the procedural complications involved. To do so would involve a consideration of many aspects of the Customs and Excise Management Act 1979 ("CEMA 1979") and the Community Customs Code. The result would be excessively lengthy, and although Customs' powers are important, they are on the fringes of the main concerns of this work.   **21–002**

Rather, this chapter is intended to indicate the broad scheme of Customs' powers in relation to goods bearing registered trade marks, to point to the United Kingdom and European legislation which enacts those powers, to indicate how the domestic regime and the European regime interrelate, and to explain in outline the procedure involved in forfeiture proceedings.   **21–003**

2. Legislation making up the domestic regime

The domestic regime begins with s.89(1) of the 1994 Act, which provides that the proprietor of a registered trade mark[1] may give a notice to the Commissioners of Customs and Excise ("the Commissioners") asking that infringing goods, materials or articles[2] expected to arrive in the United Kingdom be treated as prohibited goods.   **21–004**

By s.89(2), where such a notice is in force, the importation of those goods is prohibited.[3]

Section 90 gives the Commissioners power to make rules specifying the form in which a notice under s.89 is to be given, and requiring the person giving notice to furnish evidence and to comply with other conditions specified in the regulations.   **21–005**

---

[1] For the purposes of ss.89, 90 and 91, "registered trade mark" has been extended to include CTMs and international registrations with effect in the UK: Community Trade Mark Regulations 1996, Reg.6 and Trade Marks (International Registration) Order 1996, Art.16.

[2] These terms import the definitions from s.17, which is explored in more detail in Ch.19.

[3] There is an exception for goods imported for private and domestic use.

The result of the importation of such goods being prohibited is that they fall under the provisions of the Customs and Excise Management Act 1979.[4]

21–006   Rules under s.90 have been made: the Trade Marks (Customs) Regulations 1994.[5] Their general effect is to specify the form of notice to be used,[6] to stipulate a fee,[7] to require the giving of such security as the Commissioners require (failing which the notice is ineffective),[8] to indemnify the Commissioners against liability for detaining the goods or for anything happening during their detention,[9] and to require the applicant to provide the Commissioners with the certificate of registration of the mark concerned, together with evidence of renewal.[10]

3. Legislation making up the community regime

21–007   The relevant European legislation consists of Council Regulation 1383/2003, referred to below as the "Counterfeit and Pirated Goods Regulation",[11] whose provisions are implemented in the United Kingdom by the Goods Infringing Intellectual Property Rights (Customs) Regulations 2004.[12]

21–008   The UK Regulations track the provisions of the Counterfeit and Pirated Goods Regulation fairly closely, principally by means of expressly adopting identical definitions by reference.[13] For example, "application" under the UK Regulations is defined as having the same meaning as under Article 5 of the Counterfeit and Pirated Goods Regulation, and thereby the detailed requirements of that Article are imported into the UK Regulations, together with such requirements as the giving of an indemnity by the right-owner to Customs and Excise, and an undertaking to pay storage costs.[14] Likewise, provision for the stipulation of the form of application to be used is automatically brought into the UK Regulations.[15]

21–009   The principal effect of the UK Regulations[16] is to apply the provisions of the CEMA 1979 referred to above[17] to counterfeit goods as defined by the Counterfeit and Pirated Goods Regulation[18] (which include goods offending against national registrations and CTMs). It should be noted that this regime does not apply to goods which also infringe one or more of a number of other intellectual property rights as set out in reg.8(1); proceedings in respect of such goods fall under reg.9 and must be brought (in England and Wales) in the High Court or a designated patents county court.[19]

---

[4] CEMA 1979, s.49, renders goods whose importation is prohibited under any enactment liable to forfeiture; s.139 gives the power to seize goods liable to forfeiture; and Sch.3 contains the procedure relating to proceedings to condemn goods so seized.
[5] SI 1994/2625.
[6] reg.2 and the Schedule.
[7] reg.3.
[8] reg.4.
[9] reg.5.
[10] reg.6.
[11] App.25.
[12] SI 2004/1473, App.26.
[13] reg.2.
[14] Article 6, as invoked by Art.5(5).
[15] Arts 5(5) and 21(2).
[16] reg.7.
[17] s.139 and Sch.3.
[18] In Art.2(1)(a).
[19] reg.9(6)(a), which also provides for the appropriate court and originating process in Northern Ireland and Scotland.

4. Interaction of the two regimes

It should first be appreciated that by virtue of s.89(3) of the 1994 Act, the domestic regime is excluded wherever the European regime applies. With that said, the general pattern is as follows:

21–010

(1) The domestic regime applies to goods, materials or articles which are expected to arrive in the United Kingdom from outside the EEA, or from within the EEA but which have not been in free circulation there;[20]

(2) The domestic regime applies to United Kingdom registered trade marks and CTMs and international registrations with effect in the UK;[21]

(3) The European regime, so far as it relates to registered trade marks, applies to "counterfeit goods".[22] This term is explained in more detail below, but it should be noted at this stage that it is not as extensive as "infringing goods" under the 1994 Act;

(4) The European regime applies to materials offending against United Kingdom registered trade marks and CTMs;[23]

(5) The European regime comes into operation where goods suspected of being counterfeit are entered for free circulation, export or re-export, or are found in the course of checks on goods under customs supervision.[24]

5. "Counterfeit goods"

"Counterfeit goods" are defined in Article 1(2)of the Counterfeit and Pirated Goods Regulation, as:

21–011

"(i) goods, including the packaging thereof, bearing without authorisation a trademark identical to the trademark validly registered in respect of the same type of goods, or which cannot be distinguished in its essential aspects from such trade mark, and which thereby infringes the trademark-holder's rights under Community law as provided for by Council Regulation (EC) No. 40/94 of December 20, 1993 on the Community trademark or the law of the Member Statein which the application for action by the customs authorities is made;

(ii) any trademark symbol (including a logo, label, sticker, brochure, instructions for use or a guarantee document bearing such a symbol), even if presented separately, on the same conditions as the goods referred to in point (i);

(iii) packaging materials bearing the trademarks of counterfeit goods, presented separately, on the same conditions as the goods referred to in point (i)."

And thus explicitly include packaging and business papers relating to the counterfeit goods (by contrast with the predecessor provision in the 1994 Regulation dealing with counterfeit goods.

This makes it clear that infringement under the 1994 Act or the CTM Regulation is necessary but not sufficient for goods sought to be seized under the European regime to be "counterfeit". In addition, the goods must bear the alleged infringing mark without authorisation, that mark must be identical to the

21–012

[20] 1994 Act, s.89(1)(b).
[21] See para.21–004 and the notes therein.
[22] Counterfeit and Pirated Goods Regulation, Art.2(1)(a).
[23] Counterfeit and Pirated Goods Regulation, Art.2(1)(a).
[24] Counterfeit and Pirated Goods Regulation, Art.1(1).

registered mark or such that it "cannot be distinguished in its essential aspects" therefrom (plainly a stricter test than that of s.10(2) of the 1994 Act or the equivalent provisions of the CTM Regulation), and it must be used on goods "of the same type" as those for which the complainant's mark is registered (again, plainly a stricter test).

21–013   Moreover, Art.3 provides that the Counterfeit and Pirated Goods Regulation does not apply to goods which bear a trade mark with the consent of its holder but which have been "placed in one of the situations referred to in Art.1(1) without the latter's consent" or "which have been manufactured or are protected by another intellectual property right referred to in Art.2(1) under conditions other than those agreed with the right-holder. The effect of these obscurely-worded provisions is thought to be that the Regulation does not apply to "grey" goods or to goods made by the holder of a licence, but outside or in breach of the licence terms.

21–014   As a result, "counterfeit goods" as defined in the Counterfeit and Pirated Goods Regulation is likely to exclude most parallel imports, and many goods in respect of which infringement is merely strongly arguable. It will only clearly catch goods which are counterfeit in the sense that the man in the street would use that expression: outright forgeries. It does however include goods temporarily in a Member State while in transit between two non-Member States: *Polo/Lauren Co v PT Dwidua Langgeng Pratama International* [2000] E.T.M.R. 535.

6. Procedure in relation to goods seized by Customs

21–015   Once goods have been seized as liable to forfeiture, either under the domestic or the European regime, the governing provision is Sch.3 of the CEMA 1979.

21–016   The Commissioners are first required to serve notice of seizure on the owner(s) of the item(s) seized.[25] A period of one month is then allowed for any person who alleges that the goods were not in fact liable to forfeiture to give notice to the Commissioners to that effect.[26] The notice must give the name and address of a solicitor in the United Kingdom authorised to accept service, and various other details such as the applicant's name and address.[27] If no notice under para.3 is given, or if the requirements to provide information under para.4 are not met, then the disputed items are deemed to have been forfeited.[28]

Assuming, however, that a proper notice is served in time, the onus falls on the Commissioners to begin proceedings for condemnation by the court.[29] These are called condemnation proceedings.

7. Condemnation proceedings

21–017   Condemnation proceedings are civil proceedings, and may be begun in either a magistrates' court[30] or in the High Court. Although the proceedings are begun by the Commissioners, as is explained above, and somewhat confusingly in the light

---

[25] Sch.3, para.1(1). There are a few exceptions, which are listed in para.1(2).
[26] Sch.3, para.3.
[27] Sch.3, para.4.
[28] Sch.3, para.5.
[29] Sch.3, para.6.
[30] By Sch. 3, para.9, a magistrates' court has jurisdiction if the place of the offence (if any) leading to seizure, or the place of seizure, or the claimant's residence falls within its geographical jurisdiction.

of the Woolf reforms and the CPR, the person alleging that the goods concerned are not liable to forfeiture is called the "claimant".[31]

In any condemnation proceedings, whether begun in the High Court or the magistrates' court, the claimant or his solicitor must swear that the claimant owned the disputed goods at the time of the seizure.[32] In High Court proceedings, the claimant must give security for the Commissioners' costs as ordered by the court.[33] Default of either of those procedural steps results in the court giving judgment for the Commissioners.[34] **21–018**

An appeal lies from the magistrates' court to the Crown Court.[35] An appeal in the High Court falls under the normal rules for appeals under the CPR.

Where a thing is in due course condemned as forfeited, then forfeiture, has effect from the date when the liability to forfeiture arose.[36]

8. Prospective powers under the European regime

A feature of the European regime not found in the domestic regime is that if goods are found in the course of searches or investigations by Customs which are believed to be counterfeit goods within the meaning of the European regime, Customs may inform the owner of the trade mark concerned, and may suspend release of the goods concerned or detain them for three working days to enable the owner to make an application for the seizure of the goods.[37] **21–019**

Article 9(3) of the Counterfeit and Pirated Goods Regulation requires the customs authorities to inform the trade mark owner, on request, of the name and address (if known) of the consignee and consignor of the goods, the declarant or holder of the goods, and the origin and provenance of the goods. There in no specific authorisation for Customs to do so in the UK Regulations, notwithstanding that in the absence of such information the trade mark owner may be unable to bring proceedings, as was recognised by the European Court of Justice in *Re Adidas*.[38] There, it was held that national law would be in contravention of the Regulation if it prohibited provision of such information to the trade mark owner. However, reg.11 of the UK Regulations provides sanctions for the misuse of information provided under Article 9(3) of Counterfeit and Pirated Goods Regulation, and it is therefore clear that the Commissioners do have such power. **21–020**

9. Power of the Commissioners to disclose information

By the very nature of their functions, the Commissioners frequently learn, in policing the entry into the United Kingdom of potentially infringing goods, of activities which amount to breaches of the criminal law. By s.91 of the 1994 Act, the Commissioners are specifically empowered to authorise the disclosure to any person who has a function in connection with the investigation or prosecution of offences under s.92 of the 1994 Act, or under the Trade Descriptions Act 1968, of information relating to infringing goods, materials or articles. It is suggested that **21–021**

---

[31] s.1.
[32] Sch.3, para.10(1).
[33] Sch.3, para.10(2).
[34] Sch.3, para.10(3).
[35] Sch.3, para.11(1).
[36] Sch. 3, para.7.
[37] Counterfeit and Pirated Goods Regulation, Art.4(1), and reg.4 of the UK Regulations.
[38] [2000] F.S.R. 227.

this section must be construed to mean potentially infringing goods, materials or articles, since otherwise the provision would be deprived of much or all of its utility.

CHAPTER 22

MERCHANDISING AND TRADE MARKS

GENERALLY

Over recent years, the business of merchandising using the names and images of celebrities and fictional characters has grown exponentially and even a decade ago was described as "probably a multi-billion dollar industry in the Western world".[1] The business can be divided into three categories: (1) the exploitation of fictional or long-dead historical characters; (2) the exploitation of the fame of a celebrity during his or her lifetime; and (3) the exploitation of the enduring fame of a celebrity after her or his death. Whilst there are many aspects in common in the way the law treats the three categories, there are important differences.   **22–001**

The exploitation in question will usually involve the licensing or, more appropriately, granting consent to use of the name at issue together with either one or a number of images: in the first category, an example would be Disney characters such as Donald Duck and Mickey Mouse; current examples of the second category would be Tiger Woods and Anna Kournikova;[2] and the third category would include Elvis Presley and Diana, Princess of Wales. Of course, it could be that an historical figure in the third category, such as Robin Hood or Pocahontas, may transfer to the first category as a result of a film, for example.   **22–002**

Under English law, there is no right of personality as such,[3] nor indeed a right of privacy.[4] But, as pointed out by Laddie J.: "To stop the use of the whole or part of [a person's] name by another [that person] must show that as a result of such use, the other person is invading some legally recognised right".[5] Recent cases have illustrated the difficulties with protecting such names or likenesses under passing off and trade mark law. In important respects in this area, the law in England has diverged from that elsewhere in the Commonwealth, such as Australia[6] and Canada,[7] where more expansive protection has been accorded.[8]   **22–003**

---

[1] per Anderson J. in *Tony Blain v Splain* [1994] F.S.R. 497 at 498 (HC (NZ)): a case involving the merchandising of the musical group Metallica and Paul McCartney.

[2] For an example of an "image rights" licensing structure set up by professional sportsmen, see *Sports Club plc v Inspector of Taxes* [2000] Special Commissioners' Decisions 253 (and the article discussing the case, Newth, "Performance and Image", in *Taxation*, 150 (2001) February 22, 2001, which reveals that the case involved players David Platt and Dennis Bergkamp and their employer Arsenal).

[3] See, generally, Frazer, *Appropriation of Personality—A New Tort?* (1983) 99 L.Q.R. 281, which proposes a statutory tort of appropriation of personality.

[4] See Lindsay J. in *Douglas v Hello! Ltd (Trial Action: Breach of Confidence) (No.6)* [2003] 2 All E.R. 996 at para.229 for a review of the recent authorities, concluding "[s]o broad is the subject of privacy and such are the ramifications of any free-standing law in the area that the subject is better left to Parliament" citing Lord Woolf in *A v B plc* [2002] 2 All E.R. 545 at para.11 (vi), to the same effect. In *Douglas v Hello! Ltd* [2005] EWCA Civ 595 the Court of Appeal seem to categorise the claim as one unjust enrichment, at paras 96 and 97.

[5] *"Elvis Presley"* [1997] R.P.C. 543 at 547; followed in *Diana, Princess of Wales' Trade Mark Application* [2001] E.T.M.R. 25 (T.M. Registry) at para.7.

[6] See, *e.g.* the judgments in *Hogan v Pacific Dunlop*, 12 I.P.R. 225 (Gummow J.) and, on appeal,

22–004   As mentioned above, merchandising commonly will involve the licensing[9] of the name or names in question, frequently together with copyright works (such as photographs or drawings), for use on or in relation to particular goods or services. The licences will usually specify quality standards to be complied with by the licensee. The detail and exercise of quality control varies enormously: in the licences of the character *"Holly Hobbie"*[10] for use on a wide range of products the quality control exercisable was described by Lord Brightman as "slight", whereas in other agreements very detailed standards are specified and policed.[11]

22–005   As well as registered designs[12] and copyright,[13] both registered trade marks and the law of passing off have been relied upon by licensors and licensees to prevent the sale of unauthorised products, in many cases unsuccessfully on the facts. However, in appropriate circumstances the use of either or both should be considered.

1. Registered trade marks

REGISTRATION

22–006   Historically, in the United Kingdom it has been difficult to register as trade marks the names or images on which a merchandising programme is based: under the Trade Marks Act 1938, for example, the mark "Tarzan" was refused registration for films and tapes, and "games, toys and playthings" on the ground that it had a direct reference to the character and quality of the goods.[14] In the words of Salmon L.J.:

> "there is nothing at all in the word TARZAN which would suggest to the public or to the trade that a film or magnetic tape recording had anything to

---

Pacific Dunlop Ltd v Hogan, 14 I.P.R. 398 (Sheppard, Beaumont and Burchett JJ., Fed. Ct of Australia): a case about a television advertisement for shoes which was an obvious parody of a scene featuring the Crocodile Dundee character played by Paul Hogan in the film "Crocodile Dundee". The parody had not been authorised by or on behalf of Paul Hogan. Gummow J. at first instance and the Full Court on appeal (Sheppard J. dissenting) found passing off.

[7] See, *e.g. Krouse v Chrysler* (1973) 40 D.L.R. (3d) 15 and *Paramount Pictures v Howley*, 39 C.P.R. 3d. 419, *per* Van Camp J. (another case involving "Crocodile Dundee").

[8] *cf.* the South African case of *Lorimar v Sterling* [1982] R.P.C. 395, involving names from the television series "Dallas". The court found passing off not established on the basis that character merchandising was not so well-known in the country that without proper evidence it could be assumed that the man in the street had any knowledge of it, *per* Van Dijkhorst J. at 418: "the fact that the names are used in fields totally unrelated to that in which Lorimar does business in South Africa, is of extreme importance. Without any inclination of Lorimar to enter these fields, the public would not expect this American television producer to start manufacturing clothes in South Africa or cater for our culinary tastes, or become interested in those businesses".

[9] All relevant "rights" will often be vested in a merchandising agent, either by way of assignment or licence, and thence licensed or sub-licensed, as the case may be, for particular territories and products.

[10] *American Greetings Corp* [1984] 1 W.L.R. 189 at 197.

[11] *e.g.* the case of *Children's Television Workshop v Woolworths* [1981] R.P.C. 187, involved the licensing of the Muppets characters under agreements containing rigorous quality standards which were enforced strictly.

[12] The use of registered designs to protect characters has increased since the tightening of the rules regarding series applications under s. 41(2) Trade Marks Act 1994, see Registry Work Manual (as at October 1, 2004), Ch.6, para.34 (following the decision of the Appointed Person in *Digeo Broadband Inc's Trade Mark Application* [2004] R.P.C. 32) which contains an example of an acceptable and unacceptable character mark series, at para.34.2.12.

[13] See, for example, *Mirage Studios v Counter-Feat Clothing Co Ltd* [1991] F.S.R. 145, in which the defendants tried unsuccessfully to avoid infringing the claimant's copyright by engaging an artist to create figures similar to the humanoid turtle characters, the Teenage Mutant Ninja Turtles.

[14] *"Tarzan Trade Mark"* [1970] R.P.C. 450, CA. As noted by Edmund-Davies L.J., the decision on games, toys and the like was not so straightforward as that on films and tapes and turned on the applicant's evidence that such products were "centred on" the Tarzan character (at 457 and 459).

do with the applicant or with anyone else. The word TARZAN when used in connection with a film suggests—and suggests only—that the film has something to do with the well-known fictional person, Tarzan, a man of great strength and agility."[15]

More recently (but also under the Trade Marks Act 1938), the Court of Appeal **22–007** upheld a judgment of Laddie J.[16] allowing an opponent's appeal against the Registrar's decision to allow registration of "Elvis", "Elvis Presley" and "signature 'Elvis A. Presley'" for goods in Class 3.[17] The applications were made by Elvis Presley Enterprises Inc, which carried on the merchandising activities previously engaged in by or on behalf of the singer when he was alive. Robert Walker L.J. agreed with the conclusion of Laddie J. that the "Elvis" mark had very little distinctiveness, noting:

> "That conclusion was reached by a number of intermediate steps, one of which was the judge's finding that members of the public purchase Elvis Presley merchandise not because it comes from a particular source, but because it carries the name or image of Elvis Presley".[18]

The court (Simon Brown, Morritt and Robert Walker L.JJ.) therefore agreed **22–008** with the judge that the "Elvis" mark lacked the distinctiveness required by s.9 of the 1938 Trade Marks Act, and that it was not a word having no direct reference to the character or quality of the goods as required by s.9(1)(b). Morritt L.J. noted in this context that "it is necessary in applying [s.9(1)] (b) to keep in mind that part of the definition of trade mark which requires that the mark is capable of indicating a connection in the course of trade between the goods and [the applicant]".[19] It was critical to the judgments in this case that the goods for which registration was being sought were what Laddie J. characterised as "memorabilia or momentoes" of Elvis Presley, thus making almost inevitable the conclusion that the marks being applied for were neither distinctive nor to be used as trade marks.[20] It is suggested below that an application under the 1994 Act for a similar type of mark which it is intended to merchandise would not necessarily be decided the same way: the "*Elvis*" case was unusual and highlighted well some of the problems in this area, but should not be taken as authority for the proposition that the names of celebrities (whether living or dead) may not be registered as trade marks.

In addition to problems with distinctiveness, the 'owner' of a name or mark **22–009** which it is intended to merchandise has had in the past to overcome the fact that in the UK the whole area of licensing of trade marks was one with which the legislature[21] and to a certain extent the courts[22] were uncomfortable. Thus, in

---

[15] *"Tarzan Trade Mark"* [1970] R.P.C. 450, at 456.
[16] [1997] R.P.C. 543.
[17] [1999] R.P.C. 567.
[18] At 585.
[19] At 592.
[20] As defined in the 1938 Act, s.68(1).
[21] As can be seen from the fiction in the 1938 Act whereby use by a licensee (or registered user) was deemed to be use by the proprietor.
[22] See, *e.g. "Pussy Galore" Trade Mark* [1967] R.P.C. 265, in which a company associated with Ian Fleming failed in its application to register "Pussy Galore", the name of a character in the book "Diamonds are Forever". The Board of Trade held that there was no sufficient intention to use (a decision which in earlier editions of this work is characterised as "irreconcilable with the line of cases beginning with *"Bostitch"* : see 11th ed. at para.2–04).

"Holly Hobbie"[23] the House of Lords upheld the Registrar's refusal to register the name of the character in respect of 12 different classes of goods to be made exclusively by the applicant's licensees. The court held that this would constitute "trafficking in the mark"[24] contrary to s.28(6) of the 1938 Act. Lord Bridge (who concurred in the judgment with reluctance) expressed the opinion that s.28(6) "has become a complete anachronism and that the sooner it is repealed the better".[25] The 1994 Act does not contain an equivalent provision and indeed the underlying tenor of that Act is that trade marks may be dealt with as commodities in their own right.

22–010   As explained elsewhere,[26], under s.1(1) of the 1994 Act in order to be registered as a trade mark a sign must be capable of distinguishing the goods or services of the proprietor from those of other undertakings and also must not be excluded from registrability by the absolute grounds for refusal set out in s.3. Thus, the sign "Johnny Wilkinson" may be refused for certain goods on the ground that, as a relatively common name, it is devoid of any distinctive character contrary to s.3(1)(b)[27] (unless it falls within the proviso because, as a result of the use made of it, it has in fact acquired a distinctive character in relation to the relevant goods or services, for example rugby boots). Where the application is for goods which the average consumer would obviously associate with the celebrity and expect that his or her name on products would be by way of endorsement, for example golfing equipment by Tiger Woods, there should be no difficulty with the application, but when the application relates to goods or services far from the field of activity of the celebrity it should be subject to further inquiry.[28] As was noted in *Diana, Princess of Wales Trade Mark Application*,[29] "the use of a famous name for product endorsement purposes is not trade mark use unless the proprietor of the 'mark' takes responsibility for the quality of the goods/services to which it is applied."

22–011   The Registry Work Manual notes that where an application is for the name of a famous person "it is possible that, when used in relation to certain goods/services, the name may appear to the average consumer as an indication that the goods/services are *about* the person whose name it is rather than as an indication that the goods/services are supplied by, or under the control of, one undertaking."[30] The Work Manual considers that such a perception, of the names as 'mere image carriers', is likely where the goods are posters, photographs, transfers and figu-

---

[23] *American Greetings Corp's Application* [1984] 1 W.L.R. 189.

[24] "Trafficking" means, in the words of Lord Brightman (expressly agreed to by Lord Bridge, at 191), "dealing in a trade mark primarily as a commodity in its own right and not primarily for the purpose of identifying or promoting merchandise in which the proprietor of the mark is interested": at 198.

[25] At 192.

[26] See Ch.2, generally.

[27] As to the meaning of s.3(1)(b), see Ch.7 generally. In order to satisfy the Registry that the mark has distinctive character, it would be necessary to adduce evidence as to how it would be viewed by the average consumer described by the ECJ in *Gut Springenheide* [1998] E.C.R. I-4567 (at para.31) and *Lloyd Schuhfabrik* [1999] E.T.M.R. 690 (at para.26).

[28] The Registry may require additional information from the applicant under the Trade Mark Rules 2000, r.57 (formerly r.51).

[29] [2001] E.T.M.R. 25 at para.13.

[30] See Ch.6, section 21 Work Manual as at October 1, 2004. Also, *Linkin Park LLC'S Application* [2005] E.T.M.R. 172, TM Registry, upheld by the Appointed Person, February 7, 2005, unreported, at para.18–068 (on which see Simon, *CDs, Celebrities, and Merchandise* [2005] E.I.P.R. 265)

rines,[31] as would be the case also with pictures of famous people, although each case will be considered on its own merits.[32] It is clear that where there is a doubt whether the name in question is capable of distinguishing in a trade mark sense, the applicant should be given the benefit of that doubt.[33]

Whilst it may be that the name of a celebrity such as Andre Agassi has been used on a variety of products over the years, usually to indicate an endorsement, there seems no reason under the 1994 Act why a company set up by Mr Agassi to exploit his renown through merchandising should not make a successful application for registration in relation to, for example, clothing or chinaware. Under the Act it should not be the function of the Registrar to refuse applications for marks which are capable of distinguishing merely because they may be used other than as a trade mark, for example as decoration on a plate or mug. If after registration they are in fact not used as a trade mark, they may be removed by reason of such non-use or use on an application under s.46(1)(a) or (c), respectively. Of course, if it is clear from the circumstances (or as a result of evidence provided under r.57 TM Rules 2000) that the mark will be used only for the purpose of decoration, the application should be refused.

22–012

As far as fictional characters are concerned, in *Animated Music Ltd's Trade Mark: Application for Revocation*[34] it was held in the Registry that the use of the name of a character (Nellie the Elephant) in the title of a book was not to be regarded as trade mark use in the absence of evidence that the name was perceived by the relevant consumers as being an indication as to the origin of the goods.[35] The Registrar referred[36] to a decision of the OHIM Opposition Division in *Francis Fitzpatrick v Disney Enterprises*,[37] in which the Opposition Division found that use of the names of various characters including Winnie the Pooh in videos and books, often in the title, did not prove that the characters were well-known as trade marks: "Characters of fiction may be trade marks, there is nothing to exclude them from acting as such. However, what makes them trade marks is either the fact of registration as trade marks or use in such a way that they will be seen as trade marks. Even when they enjoy registration the question of reputation and renown will depend on the ability of the public to identify them as indicators of origin; and not to simply see them as characters or titles or items of decoration."

22–013

In addition, there are certain names, especially of deceased celebrities such as Diana, Princess of Wales or Elvis Presley, which as a result of the way in which they have been used may be of such a nature that registration should be refused on the basis that if used on goods the public would be deceived as to their significance, contrary to s.3(3)(b). Also, because they are no longer "capable of distinguishing" origin as required by s.1(1). The same objections were raised successfully to the registration by the English Rugby Football Union as a CTM of a red rose emblem: the judge holding that the emblem was primarily a descrip-

22–014

---

[31] See Ch.6, section 21.2 Work Manual as at October 1, 2004.
[32] Ch.6, section 21.5 of the Work Manual (as at October 1, 2004).
[33] See *Linkin Park LLC'S Application*, Appointed Person (Richard Arnold Q.C.), February 7, 2005, unreported, at paras 65 and 68, agreeing.
[34] [2004] E.T.M.R. 1076, T.M. Registry.
[35] [2004] E.T.M.R. 1076, at para.21.
[36] [2004] E.T.M.R. 1076, at para.28.
[37] No.951/2001 (unreported).

tive or generic sign and not an indication of a trade connection between the goods bearing it and the RFU.[38]

22–015   An issue which arises not infrequently in cases involving celebrities is the use by different parties of a relatively common surname. For example, a recent decision concerned the distinctiveness for trade mark purposes of the relatively uncommon surname of celebrity designer Alexander McQueen who, on the basis *inter alia* of his registered mark "Alexander McQueen", opposed an application to register McQueen Clothing Co[39] In finding that the hearing officer had erred in holding that the presence of the name McQueen in both marks was sufficient to bring the marks into conflict under s.5(2)(b), the Appointed Person (G. Hobbs Q.C.) found that there was no evidence that the word McQueen on its own would be interpreted by the average consumer as a reference to Alexander McQueen: "the distinctive character of the mark 'Alexander McQueen' resides in the forename/surname combination"[40] and the marks could "coexist in the market-place without giving rise to a likelihood of confusion."

22–016   Where an application for registration of the name of a celebrity is made by, or has been registered by, an unconnected party, it should be refused or declared invalid, as the case may be, on the basis of its being likely to mislead the public (s.3(3)(b)) or as being made in bad faith (s.3(6)).[41]

INFRINGEMENT

22–017   In *"British Sugar"*[42] Jacob J. rejected the argument that for there to be infringement the defendant's use must be as a trade mark.[43] On the other hand, when considering the judgment of Lord McCluskey in *Bravado Merchandising*[44] the learned judge expressed the view that where "Wet Wet Wet", the name of a pop group, was used in the title of an unauthorised biographical book it did not infringe the group's registration in respect of books:[45] it merely referred to the pop group. He did not consider it necessary for the defendant to have to rely on the defence in s.11(2)(b), as there was not even use falling within s.10.[46]

22–018   It had been hoped that the case of *Arsenal v Reed* would clarify once and for all whether the unauthorised use on scarves and the like of a football club name registered by that club as a trade mark would constitute infringement, and indeed whether ss.10(1), (2) and (3) required trade mark use. This it did not do: the European Court of Justice decided that the exclusive right given to the registered proprietor of a mark was conferred in order to enable him to prevent "cases in which a third party's use of the sign affects or is liable to affect the functions of the trade mark, in particular its essential function of guaranteeing to consumers

---

[38] *Rugby Football Union and Nike European Operations Netherlands B.V. v Cotton Traders Ltd*, [2002] E.T.M.R. 861 at paras 52 and 53.

[39] *Croom's Trade Mark Application* [2005] R.P.C. 2.

[40] *Croom's Trade Mark Application* [2005] R.P.C. 2, at para.33, citing the example "Harry qualifies Potter and vice versa" put forward by Jacob L.J. in *Reed Executive plc v Reed Business Information Ltd* [2004] R.P.C. 767 at para.26. He could perhaps also have cited the observation at para.86 that "[t]he average consumer will be alert for differences—just in the same way as one distinguishes WH Smith from other Smiths by the initials."

[41] On bad faith generally, see Ch.8 paras 8–239 to 8–246.

[42] [1996] R.P.C. 281.

[43] See also, Aldous L.J. in *One in a Million* [1999] F.S.R. 1.

[44] [1996] F.S.R. 205, Ct. of Sess.

[45] This was surely an example of a mark which should not have been allowed on the Register without evidence that it could function as a badge of origin.

[46] See also *Trebor Bassett v The Football Association* [1997] F.S.R. 211.

the origin of the goods",[47] but did not answer the question posed as to whether trade mark use was required before there could be infringement. In turn, back in England the Court of Appeal found that "the trade marks, when applied to the goods, were purchased and worn as badges of support, loyalty and affiliation to Arsenal, but that did not mean that the use by a third party would not be liable to jeopardise the functions of the trade marks, namely the ability to guarantee origin. To the contrary, the wider and more extensive the use, the less likely the trade marks would be able to perform their function."[48] Although expressly not necessary to dispose of the appeal, Aldous L.J. considered that the evidence[49] showed that the use of the sign Arsenal on scarves and hats indicated trade origin.[50]

However, the difficulty of applying the E.C.J. judgment to real-life situations **22–019** was highlighted by Lord Walker in *R. v Johnstone*[51] when he commented that "the problem of analysis varies with the character of the mark and the character of the goods to which it is affixed. Disputes about books, and scarves, and compact discs, cannot easily be resolved by a single test. Most people would have an intuitive feeling that to label a compact disc with the words "Rolling Stones" is less purely descriptive than entitling a biography "Wet Wet Wet". That is no doubt because a group of musicians are in some sense the authors (or at least the performers) of what is on the disc, but are not the authors of an unauthorised book about themselves. But in that case is not their real grievance infringement of their copyright or their performing rights, rather than of their trade mark?"[52] (It is also worthwhile noting that Lord Nicholls found that the trade mark use issue has been "laid to rest" by the E.C.J. judgment in *Arsenal* and therefore "[n]on-trade mark use is not within s.10(1) to (3).")[53]

It seems, therefore, that whether a registered trade mark comprising the name **22–020** of a celebrity or of a fictional character is infringed by use on china, posters, T-shirts and the like will depend on the circumstances, both of the use by the proprietor and the type of use by the alleged infringer.[54] If the public has been educated that the mark is a badge of origin (in the wider sense including approval, selection and endorsement), perhaps by the use of words such as "licensed by" or "official", there will be infringement. However, if the purchaser of a mug with the name (and/or photograph) of their hero or heroine decorating it is indif-

---

[47] [2003] E.T.M.R. 227, E.C.J., at para.51.

[48] [2003] E.T.M.R. 895, CA, *per* Aldous L.J. at para.48.

[49] Cornish notes that the judge's "readiness to generalize from rather thin evidence is apparent", *Intellectual Property: Omnipresent, Distracting, Irrelevant?* (Clarendon Law Lectures 2004, OUP), at p.96.

[50] [2003] E.T.M.R. 895, CA, at para.69. One wonders what the learned judge's analysis would have been of replica Arsenal shirts bearing the following signs: O2 (the sponsor of the team), the Nike swoosh device (the well-known device mark of the manufacturers of the kit), the Arsenal shield device featuring both the registered trade marks "Arsenal" and the cannon logo, together with the name and number of the player in question (which may be registered, as with the name and number of Eric Cantona while he was with Manchester United). The average consumer would certainly need to be very sophisticated in his consideration of the functions fulfilled by each sign and presumably only one is the indication of origin.

[51] [2003] F.S.R. 748, HL.

[52] [2003] F.S.R. 748, HL, at para.86.

[53] [2003] F.S.R. 748, HL, at paras 16 and 17. An Italian District Court ruling after the E.C.J.'s *Arsenal* judgment found that the unauthorised use of the Inter Milan trade marks on hats, scarves, key rings and the like offered for sale to team supporters did not infringe as such use had a merely evocative function as a badge of allegiance; whereas it would constitute trade mark infringement if used on sportswear where the court considered it would be perceived as an indication of origin, Decision of the Tribunale di Milano (*Inter/Gua Giu*), December 5, 2002, unreported.

[54] Similar issues arise with retail marks; see the judgment of Jacob J. in *Euromarket Designs Inc v Peters* ("Crate & Barrel"), [2001] F.S.R. 20.

ferent as to who makes it or is responsible for the name being on it, this should not constitute infringement of the registered mark. Similarly, if the court finds that the relevant consumer would view the use of the mark as being mere decoration, this would not constitute trade mark infringement.[55]

22–021   What is clear is that the earlier the name is registered as a trade mark and the more diligent the owner is in educating the public as to the selection and endorsement functions it performs, the greater the scope of protection the mark will be accorded. The corollary of this is that the more famous a person is when considering registering his or her name as a mark, the more difficult it will be to protect it, both by registration and if registered in infringement proceedings.

22–022   Where the name of the celebrity is distinctive in itself, either because it has been chosen as such or it is an unusual surname, it is arguable that registration may give a more limited scope of protection than usual. Thus, in *Succession Picasso v DaimlerChrysler A.G.*[56] the Third Board of Appeal at OHIM found that "the inherent distinctive character of the sign 'Picasso' is so high that any perceptible difference may be apt to exclude any likelihood of confusion on the side of the consumers concerned."[57] On appeal, the CFI rejected the argument, based on *Puma v SABEL*[58] and *Canon*,[59] that the renown of the Picasso name meant that the registered trade mark should have broader protection: "[t]hat the word sign Picasso is well-known as corresponding to the name of the famous painter Pablo Picasso is not capable of heightening the likelihood of confusion".[60]

CRIMINAL PROCEEDINGS

22–023   Where a "merchandising mark" has been registered the proprietor may be able to rely on the criminal provisions in s.92 and following of the Trade Marks Act 1994.[61] Importantly, however, there is available the reasonable belief defence in s.92(5) which is available both (i) where the defendant believes on reasonable grounds that his use of the sign does not infringe a registered trade mark of whose existence he is aware and (ii) where he believes he does not infringe because he reasonably believes that no relevant trade mark is registered.[62] The burden of proving the relevant facts on the balance of probability lies on the defendant.[63] In such circumstances, a registered trade mark, perhaps of dubious validity, is of great value to its proprietor.

PASSING OFF

22–024   Where the name or character which is the subject-matter of a merchandising programme has not been registered as a trade mark, either because this step has not been taken or it has been refused, the "owner" of the name or character may seek

---

[55] A question of fact for the national court according to the E.C.J. in *Adidas-Salomon v Fitnessworld*, [2004] E.T.M.R. 10.

[56] Case Note, [2002] E.T.M.R. 953.

[57] [2002] E.T.M.R. 953, at para.20 of the decision, Case R–0247/2001, rejecting the opposition to the application for 'Picaro' (apparently a character taken from Spanish literature) based on the registered mark 'Picasso'.

[58] [1997] E.C.R. I-6191, ECJ.

[59] [1998] E.C.R. I-5507, ECJ.

[60] Case T–185/02, June 22, 2004, unreported, at para.61.

[61] As to which generally, see Ch.19.

[62] *per* Lord Nicholls in *R. v Johnstone* [2003] F.S.R. 748 at para.43, overruling *Torbay Council v Satnam Singh* [2000] F.S.R. 158.

[63] [2003] F.S.R. 748, HL, at paras 46 and 53, noting that counterfeiting "is a serious contemporary problem", at para.52.

to prevent unauthorised use through the medium of a passing off action. Again, there are difficulties due to the nature of the right protected by such cause of action.[64]

The classic trinity of reputation/goodwill, misrepresentation and damage has **22–025** proved troublesome for claimants seeking to prevent the unauthorised use of a name or character on a wide range of goods. Where the name or character has not been used in the United Kingdom in connection with the particular products in respect of which relief is being sought, the territorial nature of goodwill has posed a problem.

A local English company, seeing the success of the television series "Kojak" **22–026** in which the main character sucked lollipops, adopted the name "Kojakpops" for its lollipops. On the basis of its use it brought an action for passing off against the company which had been granted a licence to sell lollipops under the "Kojak" name by the US makers of the television series. In granting an interim injunction to the local 'interloper', Walton J. described the licence as "writ on water": *Tavener Rutledge v Trexapalm* [1977] R.P.C. 275.[65]

Similarly, the "common field of activity" question[66] has proved problematic in **22–027** passing off cases involving merchandising activity and even though it is now clear that this is not a requirement, it still imposes a significant evidential burden on the claimant in such cases, who must prove both misrepresentation and a real likelihood of damage.[67] In this context it is important for the claimant to adduce evidence of licensing activities or at least an intention to engage in them.[68]

An express misrepresentation as to approval or endorsement, for example by **22–028** stating that products are "official" when they are not, clearly constitutes passing off. In *Irvine v Talksport Ltd*,[69] the Formula 1 racing driver Eddie Irvine succeeded in his claim for passing off against the operator of a radio station which used without consent in its promotional materials a doctored photograph of Mr Irvine holding a portable radio bearing the words "Talk Radio". At first instance,[70] Laddie J. reviewed in detail the authorities on false endorsement and concluded

---

[64] As to which generally, see Ch.15. Hobbs commented in 1980 that "In England …the law has tended to part company with commerce in the case of a licence to use unregistered marks and insignia, or material which is not the subject of copyright in the hands of the licensor" in Passing Off and the *Licensing of Merchandising Rights* [1980] E.I.P.R. 47, and little has changed since.

[65] And see generally para.15–048.

[66] See generally paras 15–046 to 15–050, and the cases there cited.

[67] See, *e.g. Lyngstad v Anabas* [1977] F.S.R. 62 (a case involving the unauthorised use of photographs of the pop group Abba on badges, T-shirts and pillowslips), in which Oliver J. stated: "I am entirely unsatisfied that there is any real possibility of confusion. I do not think that anyone … receiving the goods…could reasonably imagine that all the pop stars … were giving their approval to the goods offered or that the defendants were doing anything more than catering for a popular demand among teenagers for effigies of their idols": at 68. Also see, in relation to the fictional characters, the Wombles, *Wombles v Womble Skip Hire* [1975] F.S.R. 488, cf. *IPC Magazines v Black & White Music* ("Judge Dredd") [1983] F.S.R. 348, where Goulding J. found that a substantial number of people would assume that the plaintiff, owners of the copyright in the comic strip "Judge Dredd", had endorsed the defendant's record containing a song called "Judge Dredd". Despite this, he refused an interim injunction as he could see no likelihood of damage.

[68] See *Stringfellow v McCain Foods* [1984] R.P.C. 501, CA, in which Slade L.J. noted that the claimant had never contemplated exploitation of his name through merchandising, at 545; he also doubted whether the loss of a possible field for merchandising constituted a permissible head of damage in passing off, at 547. In his article cited at para.22–024, Hobbs comments: "In an era of systematic commercialisation, it ought to be possible to establish that injury to a licensing pro-gramme is the natural and foreseeable consequence of the pre-emptive marketing of unlicensed merchandise. From there it is a very short step to the full protection of merchandising rights in England" (at 51).

[69] [2003] F.S.R. 619, CA.

[70] [2002] F.S.R. 60.

that "Mr Irvine has a property right in his goodwill which he can protect from unlicensed appropriation consisting of a false claim or suggestion of endorsement of a third party's goods or business";[71] a conclusion upheld by the Court of Appeal. However, the judge's award of £2,000 as a reasonable endorsement fee, assessed on the basis of the principles set out by Lord Wilberforce in *General Tire*,[72] *i.e.* the fee which on a balance of probabilities the defendant would have had to pay in order to obtain lawfully that which it had obtained unlawfully[73] was increased to £25,000 as the minimum the defendant would have had to pay.[74]

22–029   On the other hand, in *Harrison and Starkey v Polydor*[75] George Harrison and Ringo Starr failed in a passing off action to prevent the issue of a record album of taped interviews with a journalist. The album sleeve was to have printed prominently on the front cover the words "The Beatles" and "from the David Wigg Interviews", together with a number of photographs of The Beatles. An interim injunction was refused by Walton J. as there was no real prospect of the plaintiffs succeeding at trial. There had been no misrepresentation either express or implied.

22–030   Evidence must be adduced by the claimant to establish the presence of a misrepresentation and in *Mirage Studios v Counter-Feat*[76] the claimant succeeded in showing that "a substantial number of the buying public now expect and know that where a famous cartoon or television character is reproduced on goods, that reproduction is the result of a licence granted by the owner of the copyright or owner of other rights in the character".[77] The Vice-Chancellor distinguished the *Wombles*, *Kojak* and *Abba* cases[78] on the ground that these had been concerned only with the licensing of names as opposed to the licensing of copyright material.[79] In *Elvis Presley*[80] Robert Walker L.J. commented that he found the Vice-Chancellor's judgment "very clear and convincing".[81]

22–031   Notwithstanding these developments, for a passing off action to succeed it remains critical to prove that there has been a relevant misrepresentation, *i.e.* one which damages (or is likely to damage) goodwill. Thus, in *BBC Worldwide v Pally Screen Printing*,[82] a case involving unauthorised use of pictures of the "Teletubbies" characters on T-shirts, Laddie J. refused an application for summary judgment on the issues of copyright infringement and passing off. Of the latter, he considered that

> "it inevitably must be a question of fact whether or not members of the public seeing the T-shirts at issue will be deceived … the plaintiffs will need to show that members of the public would look at this type of artwork and

---

[71] [2002] F.S.R. 60, at para.75.

[72] *General Tire and Rubber Co v Firestone Tyre and Rubber Co Ltd (No.2)* [1976] R.P.C. 197, HL.

[73] *per* Jonathan Parker L.J. [2003] F.S.R. 619 at para.106.

[74] *per* Jonathan Parker L.J. [2003] F.S.R. 619, at para.114.

[75] [1977] F.S.R. 1.

[76] [1991] F.S.R. 145.

[77] *per* Sir Nicolas Browne-Wilkinson, V.C. See also another case involving the "Teenage Mutant Ninja Turtles" characters, *Surge Licensing v Pearson* 21 I.P.R. 228 (Fed. Ct of Australia), in which Einfield J. found that no evidence was required of consumers being actually misled or deceived: the position is different in England and any claimant would be well advised to adduce such evidence.

[78] At para.22–027.

[79] At 158, suggesting also that they may require reconsideration at some point if the evidence before the court as to the public awareness of character merchandising is more favourable.

[80] [1999] R.P.C. 567.

[81] At 582.

[82] [1998] F.S.R. 665.

consider it to represent the plaintiffs or products made with the plaintiffs' approval. It seems to me that it is quite possible that members of the public will look at T-shirts bearing this artwork and think no more than it is artwork bearing illustrations of well-known television characters without having any regard whatsoever to the source of supply and without having any regard as to whether or not these T-shirts were put out with the sanction of or under the aegis of the plaintiffs."[83]

In other words, the claimant should not rely on the court assuming the misrep-   **22–032**
resentation required to found the cause of action. Thus, the makers of the television soap "Neighbours" failed to prevent the sale of an unauthorised magazine "Neighbours Who's Who" and in its application to have ordered a disclaimer to the effect that the magazine was unofficial.[84] The judge, Millett J., expressed grave doubts whether there was even a serious question to be tried, commenting "I take the view that the word "Neighbours" on the frontispiece, plainly the identical logo of the show, is not intended to intimate to members of the public that it is a publication made or authorised by those responsible for the show. It refers not to the source or parentage of the publication, but to its contents."[85]

DOMAIN NAMES

Problems arising from the unauthorised registration of celebrity or character   **22–033**
names as domain names are dealt with in Ch.23.

---

[83] At 674.
[84] *Grundy Television Pty Ltd v Starttrain Ltd* [1988] F.S.R. 581. To the obvious surprise of the judge, the defendant offered undertakings not to use the word "Neighbours" in the same script as the claimant's logo or any script colourably similar thereto.
[85] [1988] F.S.R. 581, at 583.

CHAPTER 23

THE INTERNET

INTRODUCTION

23–001   Some characterise the Internet as spawning a series of wholly new problems for the law, particularly in the field of registered trade marks and passing off. In fact, the Internet has done no more than to throw up existing, sometimes familiar, issues in a different guise. There are three areas for discussion: registration of domain names, jurisdiction/infringement and metatags or other "invisible use". All three areas require some knowledge of how the Internet works and the terminology used. These subjects are dealt with in the next section.

1. Mechanics

23–002   The Internet is a large network of linked computers. It is, in effect, a high-speed electronic postal system. The principal reason why it "works" at a practical level is due to the speed of communication and the method by which individual computers are identified. For the most part, we need only concern ourselves with the end points of communication. At one end is the user accessing the Internet from, usually, a PC. At the other end is a server, on which is stored in electronic form, the website which the user wishes to access. The user gains access to the Internet at a gateway, either via an Internet service provider (ISP) or via a smaller, usually internal, network called an Intranet.[1] In the middle is a highly sophisticated network comprising router and other computers linked together.

23–003   Computers connected to the Internet have unique numerical addresses (for example, 1.256.123.123) so that electronic information is delivered to the right place. To make these identification numbers more user friendly, they can be associated with identifiers consisting of alphanumeric characters. These identifiers are Internet domain names. Because they are made up from alphanumeric characters, it is possible for the sequence of characters to spell out words and hence trade marks or other signs used by businesses.

ANATOMY OF A DOMAIN NAME

23–004   A typical domain name might appear as follows: *www.squiffo.com*. The www. element of the name is an abbreviation of "world wide web" and merely indicates that the expression is a domain name accessible via the Internet.[2] Most people are now familiar with the suffix .com, which identifies one of the Top Level Domains, or TLDs. In our example, squiffo is the second part of the domain name and is called a Second Level Domain (or SLD). This is a sequence of characters which

---

[1] Intranets frequently have a permanent telephone connection to the Internet.
[2] When accessing the website at *www.squiffo.com*, one often sees "http://www.squiffo.com/index.htm" or "…index.html". The letters "http" and "htm" or "html" indicate the language of the communication: HyperText Transfer Protocol and HyperText Markup Language.

is unique within the set of .com domain names and therefore operates as a unique identifier. TLDs can be categorised as sponsored (or sTLDs) or un-sponsored (also known as generic or gTLDs). gTLDs are open for registration by all, irrespective of the nature of the use to which they are intended to be put, but are generally understood to denote a particular type of registrant. Thus .biz generally denotes a business, .name an individual and so on.[3]

sTLDs are regulated by a particular organisation and only registrants that meet certain qualification criteria are permitted to register such domains. At present the sTLDs include .gov (restricted to US governmental use), .mil (restricted to US military use), .aero (for the aviation community), .coop (for cooperatives), .edu (for universities) and .museum (restricted to use by museums). There are presently plans to increase the number of sTLDs significantly, to include such domains as .asia, .travel and .post among others. The next category of TLDs is the two letter country code or ccTLDs such as .uk, .fr, .de and .tm.[4] Within the .uk and other ccTLDs, by convention a series of generic or sponsored Second Level Domains are used such as .co, .org, .net and .gov, etc. Thus, in the domain name *www.squiffo.co.uk*, the Third Level Domain is squiffo and is a unique alphanumeric sequence within the .co.uk subset and therefore provides this domain name with a means of unique identification. **23–005**

There is no central authority regulating the Internet, which is almost entirely governed by convention. The convention, for an American user of the Internet, is that a .com domain name generally indicates an American commercial entity, likewise with .org, an American organisation. For a user of the Internet outside the US, a .com domain name may indicate an American commercial entity or an international commercial entity (with or without a business in the US). A .co.uk suffix generally indicates a United Kingdom commercial entity and a .net.de generally indicates a German network, for example. Normally one would expect a website with an address ending in the suffix .co.uk to be situate in the United Kingdom. However, all these indications may or may not be true. A .com website may well not be operated by an international commercial entity and the server upon which the website is stored may well not be situated in the USA, though frequently they are. Likewise with a .co.uk website. The domain name *www.squiffo.co.uk* may do nothing more than link directly to the website identified by *www.squiffo.com* or it may identify a website which is wholly unrelated to that found at the .com address. **23–006**

REGISTRATION OF INTERNET DOMAIN NAMES

Registration of domain names is handled by a number of organisations. The Internet Corporation for Assigned Names and Numbers (ICANN) is responsible for managing and co-ordinating the domain name system but not all domain name registrar services are accredited by ICANN. Generally there is one organisation which oversees registration in each country, but there may be several organisations acting as registrars, particularly in those countries where Internet use is well established. The identities of the registrar services which administer the gTLDs and sTLDs can be found at the ICANN website at *www.icann.org* are currently **23–007**

---

[3] There are presently seven gTLDs: .biz, .com, .info, .name, .net, .net, .org and .pro.
[4] Identifying the UK, France, Germany and Turkmenistan, respectively. The .tm domain has been suspended, a victim of its own success.

administered by Network Solutions Inc. Many domain names with the .uk suffix are administered by Nominet UK Limited.[5]

23–008   To date, registration of domain names has been conducted by the various registrar organisations on a first-come, first-served basis. Some national registries do impose nationality restrictions on the applicant, for example the French authority requires the owner of a .fr registration to be a French national or domiciled in France. Such restrictions are not imposed for other domains.

23–009   To select a domain name, it must be, therefore, decided which Top Level Domain is required. Usually, the applicant will choose the most logical country so that a United Kingdom-based entity might choose the .uk Top Level Domain. However, the US domains, .com, .org, and .net, are perceived as having a certain cachet connoting an international business profile.

23–010   Having selected the Top Level Domain, the applicant should then select an appropriate Second Level Domain according to the nature of the applicant entity (with the US domains, the Top Level Domain will signify this and the choice of the Top Level Domain name will be influenced by the applicant's nature). Having selected the appropriate Top (and if applicable, Second) Level domain, the applicant should then select a unique alphanumeric Third Level (Second Level in the case of US domains). This should comprise no fewer than two and, for some registration authorities, no more than 26 standard ASCII characters, none of which must be a space break[6] or a forward slash. Some registration authorities have differing rules on the number of characters.

23–011   Once the name has been chosen, it is advisable to check that the name is available. The whole combination of Levels in the name must be unique in order correctly to identify the user. As far as the registration authorities are initially concerned, the domain name required merely has to be unique. A simple check can be conducted on the Internet. Many registration authorities provide a search engine on their websites to allow one to check on the availability of a chosen domain name or to check details of the owner of a domain name already registered. These searches are known as "whois" searches. To locate the website for the appropriate country registration authority, simply use the domain name formula, *www.nic.*+country Top Level Domain. For example the TLD for the United Kingdom authority is .uk and the website can be located at *www.nic.uk*. Other examples are *www.nic.fr* for France or *www.nic.de* for Germany (Deutschland and hence ".de").

23–012   Clearly, the most desirable part of a domain name is the unique Second/Third Level domain within the Top/Second Level Domain. If this is not available within the chosen Top/Second Level, then it should be remembered that it may be available in an alternative Top Level: the Third Level Domain is only unique to its Top/Second Level. For example, if squiffo.com were taken, the applicant might try for squiffo.org or squiffo.co.uk or even squiffo1.com. It is feasible and permissible that all these domains with the same squiffo Third/Second Level element could be owned by different entities because they are in different Top/Second Level Domains.

---

[5] In fact Nominet administers the following SLDs: .co.uk, .org.uk, .plc.uk, ltd.uk, .net.uk, .sch.uk, but not .ac.uk, .gov.uk, .nhs.uk, .police.uk, or .mod.uk. At the time of writing, proposals for new SLDs are being considered by Nominet, in line with new TLDs by ICANN.

[6] The convention is that spaces in a trade mark or trade name are either left out or indicated by hyphens, *e.g.* marksandspencer.com or marks-and-spencer.com.

The application is made via electronic mail to the appropriate registration **23–013** authority for the chosen Top Level Domain using an application template which can be downloaded from that authority's website. The ability to file domain names is given to members of the domain name authority. Membership can be obtained by anyone; however, most applications are made via a domain name registration company or Internet service provider (ISP) who will make an application on behalf of its client.

The information required to file a domain name application is straightforward: **23–014** the name and address of the applicant (including email address), the name and address of the owner's systems administrator, the name and address of the owner's technical contact, the name and address of a billing contact, and finally the identity code of the computer server owned by the applicant to which the domain name will direct web communications. Very often the Internet service provider will provide details of its technical and administrative contacts and server identity on behalf its client because the website to which the domain name will eventually point is inactive or "parked".

A fee is payable on application. The domain names are allocated on a "first **23–015** come, first served" basis. A registration lasts for two years and can be renewed upon payment of a fee. If the name is not renewed it will become available again for another owner to acquire.

TRANSACTIONS INVOLVING DOMAIN NAMES

It is possible to transfer the ownership of an Internet domain name. Upon the **23–016** grant of registration for a domain name, following a successful application and payment of the registration fee, a certificate is issued. The certificate contains a transfer document which can be detached and returned to the registration author- ity stating the new owner's details. The transfer document is also available on the Internet.

THE LINK BETWEEN TRADE MARKS AND DOMAIN NAMES

A domain name registration as such is not an intellectual property right: it is a **23–017** contract with the registration authority controlling the Top Level Domain concerned allowing communications to reach the domain name owner's com- puter via Internet links channelled through the registration authority's server. It does not create a monopoly or any other form of exclusive right. It is in many ways akin to a company name registration which is a unique identifier of a certain company but of itself confers no intellectual property right.

However, there are important intellectual property implications arising out of **23–018** the use of a verbal expression (which a domain name ostensibly is) in the course of trade. The Top and Second Level Domain elements for national registrations and the Top Level Domain for US domain names are generic and do not generate any form of allied IP rights. The rest of a domain name is user defined and may well spell out a trade mark or other sign used in trade leading to trade mark in- fringement issues and possible passing off.

USE OF DOMAIN NAMES

Once registered, a domain name may be used in various ways. Generally, a **23–019** domain name forms part of a website address (technically known as an URL: Unique Resource Locator). It may also be used as part of an email address, for example info@squiffo.com. Domain names are often used in advertising to point people to information about an organisation: increasingly, they identify a company or organisation. It is also, of course, possible to register a domain name and do nothing with it except keep the registration.

ACCESSING A WEBSITE

23–020   From a technical point of view, the following is a rather crude simplification of what happens when a user accesses a website. However, we believe it to be accurate enough for the purpose of analysis.

23–021   The user at his or her PC connects to the Internet, either via an ISP or via an Intranet. The user identifies the website which he or she desires to visit. This is done either by typing in the domain name or by selecting the website from a search listing or a hyperlink. The last command from the user, either pressing the return key or clicking on the domain name shown on screen, sends an electronic message equivalent to: "please send the web page identified by the domain name". The message is routed through to the web server on which the website is stored. The web server receives the message and responds by sending an electronic message containing the web page back to the PC of the user. The web page is received by the PC and displayed on the user's screen. Frequently, the first web page received will direct the user to other web pages which form part of the whole website. The user selects a second web page by clicking on the hyperlink. Thus, the user sends a second message "please send me the web page" identified and so the process continues. In between sending and receiving messages, the user's computer is sitting there waiting. Likewise, once the web server has received, processed and responded to the user's request, it is either waiting for another request or dealing with a request from a different user. The closest analogy is a mail order catalogue which is sent out page by page, upon specific request, the whole process taking seconds rather than the days which would be required to conduct the process by post.

23–022   So far we have only been considering web pages which provide information. If it is possible to make purchases at the website, then the same process applies. The product in question is identified on a particular web page which is being viewed by the user. The web page will have some means by which the user can indicate that he or she wishes to purchase the product. Thus an electronic message is sent "I wish to purchase" in conjunction with the message "please send the next page", which may indicate stock levels and/or contain a request as to how the user is going to pay. So the exchange of messages continues until the transaction is completed. In the absence of any indication to the contrary, the normal rules of offer and acceptance will indicate when and where the contract of purchase was made. Frequently, the terms and conditions on a website will specify when and where a contract is made and the law which governs the contract or, if it does not, those matters will have to be deduced from the circumstances. Again, the closest analogy to a purchase made over the Internet is a purchase made by post from a mail order catalogue.

OTHER ANALOGIES

23–023   Other analogies have been suggested, largely to suit the argument being presented. Thus a defendant, seeking to argue that his use of a mark on his website only occurs abroad, has argued that someone accessing his website from the

United Kingdom should be likened to the use of a "super-telescope", the eye-piece of which is at the user's PC, focused on the website situate at the web server. Even though this "super-telescope" analogy has been accepted as apt on the facts of one case,[7] the explanation above shows that it is inaccurate.

METATAGS/"INVISIBLE USE"

The pages which make up a website are stored and transmitted electronically. A **23–024** web page typically comprises a mixture of text and pictures. The creator of a web page uses one of a number of specialist software languages to give each piece of text and each picture its location on the page. In this way, a web page is built up electronically to produce the effect seen on screen. Underlying what is seen on the user's screen is a mass of hidden software commands.

Most people are aware of the use of search engines to locate particular items of **23–025** interest on the Internet. The ability of a particular search engine to locate what you are looking for depends on whether that search engine has digested the contents of the web page you are looking for. Search engines can digest different levels of information provided by a web page, but generally, search engines work on more than the user sees on his screen. As the Internet has grown, so the number of "hits" produced by any particular search have increased. Techniques have been developed to ensure that your website comes at or near the top of the list of "hits". One of these techniques uses metatags. As the name suggests, these are hidden tags, included in the software which makes up a web page, read by the search engines but not generally visible on the user's screen.[8] Thus, for example, a retailer of sports clothing might put the name of a famous footballer in a metatag to attract search engines to his website. The system is obviously open to abuse. Typical modes of abuse are (1) the use of a competitor's name or trade mark as metatags which can either attract users direct to the website or place the website address in close juxtaposition to that of the competitor in a search listing and (2) the use of the names of famous people or of famous trade marks as metatags although there is no connection between the website in question and the name or mark used.

Another way in which a trade mark or sign may be used to improve the way in **23–026** which a website is displayed by a particular search engine is the use of sponsored links triggered by particular keywords. Thus the company providing a search engine may allow a party to register particular words in a database so that whenever the words registered are typed into the search engine an advertisement for the party which registered the words, and a link to that party's website, appear in a prominent position near the search results otherwise produced by the search engine. If a competitor were to register a party's trade mark in such a manner, the results displayed by the search engine might well be the proprietor of the trade mark at the head of the search results and the competitor's details alongside.

The attitude of the Court of Appeal in *Reed Executive plc v Reed Business in-* **23–027** *formation Ltd* as to whether "invisible" use of a trade mark (as a metatag or otherwise) can amount to passing off or trade mark infringement is somewhat

---

[7] *Euromarket Designs Inc v Peters* [2001] F.S.R. 20.
[8] Unless the viewer takes steps to view the source code for the page displayed in the browser.

sceptical.[9] Jacob L.J. expressed doubts as to whether such use alone would ever give rise to a likelihood of confusion or to deception in for the purposes of passing off and (*obiter dictum*) whether use as a metatag was use for the purposes of trade mark infringement at all. On the other hand, the French court has taken a different approach and held that the registration as keywords by Google France (the French version of a prominent search engine) of words which constitute a third party trade mark amounted to the use by Google France of the mark for the purposes of trade mark infringement.[10] The Italian, Benelux and German courts have adopted similar attitudes in respect of keyword use. These matters are addressed in detail at paras 23–063 to 23-070.

2. Disputes over domain name registrations

23–028   Disputes over domain name registrations fall into one of two categories:

(1) there are some domain names which so obviously refer to and identify a particular business or entity, that their registration by a third party amounts to illegitimate hijacking of the name;

(2) there are far more domain names which could be legitimately registered and used by more than one person or business. A particular domain name is secured by the first to register and, in the vast majority of cases, all the others who might like that particular domain name cannot challenge the registration. An example of this type of case is *Pitman Training Ltd v Nominet UK*[11] where there were two independent businesses entitled to trade under the name Pitman. The registration of pitman.co.uk by one could not be disturbed by the other.

23–029   Both situations arise because, hitherto, the Internet has been governed by convention. It has taken some time to find ways to deal with the illegitimate hijacking of domain names, but in general terms, there are three routes by which a dispute may be resolved:

(a) A claimant can bring proceedings for passing off and/or infringement of registered trade mark. The basis for such claims over Internet domain names was clearly established by the Court of Appeal in *One in a Million*.

(b) In late 1999 a dispute resolution policy was launched by ICANN[12] relating to .com, .net and .org TLDs. It has also been adopted by the registries responsible for administering certain ccTLDs. The policy is operated at the WIPO[13] Arbitration and Mediation Centre and by various other bodies. It provides a mechanism for actually deciding disputes over domain name registrations outside formal litigation. However, if the unsuccessful party in ICANN proceedings is entitled to issue proceedings in a national court and does so within ten days of notification of the decision, the effect of the ICANN decision will be suspended pending the outcome of such proceedings.

(c) Most domain name Registrars operate a "Dispute Resolution Service".

---

[9] [2004] R.P.C. 40.

[10] *Viaticum v Google France* [2004] E.T.M.R 63.

[11] [1997] F.S.R. 797, Sir Richard Scott V.C. A case which establishes that in the United Kingdom, no liability attaches to the Registrar of the domain name for having registered it. The same position applies in the US.

[12] The Uniform Domain Name Dispute Resolution Policy adopted by ICANN, August 26, 1999. The policy has also been adopted by certain managers of ccTLDs such as .nu, .tv and .ws, from Niue, Tuvalu and Samoa.

[13] The World Intellectual Property Organisation, based in Geneva. For further details see the website at *www.wipo.org*.

These schemes range from those designed to assist the resolution of disputes by agreement between the parties, which are of little practical use, to those of a similar nature to the ICANN procedure, such as the procedure implemented in the United Kingdom by Nominet.

Each of these three methods of challenge are now examined.

ONE IN A MILLION[14]

The defendants were dealers in domain names who had registered a number of names which incorporated the names of well-known English companies, such as marksandspencer.com, marksandspencer.co.uk, sainsbury.com, virgin.org, bt.org, britishtelecom.com, ladbrokes.com. Although the judge at first instance granted summary judgment for passing off and s.10(3) of the Trade Marks Act 1994 infringement, he did not accept that the mere registration of the domain names constituted passing off. Giving the judgment of the Court of Appeal, Aldous L.J. held that a mere registration could give rise to liability for passing off on two bases. The first was a traditional analysis of reputation, misrepresentation and damage:

> "The placing on a register of a distinctive name such as "marksandspencer" makes a representation to persons who consult the register that the registrant is connected or associated with the name registered and thus the owner of the goodwill in the name. Such persons would not know of One in a Million and would believe they were connected or associated with the owner of the goodwill in the domain name they had registered. Further, registration of the domain name including the words "Marks & Spencer" is an erosion of the exclusive goodwill in the name which damages or is likely to damage Marks & Spencer plc."[15]

For the second basis, Aldous L.J. analysed the passing off case law concerned with "instruments of deception" and concluded that, in appropriate circumstances, the registration of a domain name can itself constitute an instrument of deception or fraud, leading to liability for passing off.

> "It follows that a court will intervene by way of injunction in passing off cases in three types of case. First, where there is passing off established or it is threatened. Second, where the defendant is a joint tortfeasor with another in passing off, actual or threatened. Third, where the defendant has equipped himself with or intends to equip another with an instrument of fraud. This third type of case is probably a mere quia timet action".[16]

Whether a registration constitutes an instrument of fraud depends on all the circumstances. There are essentially two types of case. Some names are so distinctive, denoting one trader and nobody else, that the conclusion may be drawn from the domain name itself. Thus:

> "I also believe that domain names comprising the name "Marks & Spencer" are instruments of fraud. Any realistic use of them as domain names would result in passing off ...".[17]

The second type of case was illustrated by the other domain names in issue,

23–030

23–031

23–032

23–033

---

[14] *British Telecommunications plc v One in a Million Ltd* [1999] 1 W.L.R. 903; [1999] F.S.R. 1, CA.

[15] [1999] 1 W.L.R. 903 at 924 F–H; [1999] F.S.R. 1 at 23.

[16] [1999] 1 W.L.R. 903 at 920 F–G; [1999] F.S.R. 1 at 18.

[17] [1999] 1 W.L.R. 903 at 925A; [1999] F.S.R. 1 at 23. cf. *Phones 4U Ltd v Phone 4U.co.uk Inter-*

since Aldous L.J. accepted that there are people called Sainsbury and Ladbroke and companies, other than Virgin and BT, who could legitimately use the other domain names in issue. Despite that, the circumstances of the defendant's conduct in that case required the same conclusion as for the domain names incorporating marksandspencer.[18]

Finally, the finding of a s.10(3) of the 1994 Act infringement was upheld, on the basis of sufficient threat to infringe.

APPLICATION OF THE DECISION IN *ONE IN A MILLION*

23–034   Naturally, the reasoning of the Court of Appeal in *One in a Million* is not restricted to domain names. The reasoning was based, in part, on cases concerning the registration of company names.[19] It is obviously applicable to cases concerning the registration of company names and, indeed to any system of registration[20] which is publicly accessible, where the thing registered may spell out a trade mark and is liable to be used in trade.

JURISDICTION

23–035   For this type of claim, jurisdiction depends on the domicile of the registrant of the domain name and not upon the country where the domain name Registrar is based. Thus, it is appropriate to deal with an English hijacker in England, whether he has registered a .com name or a domain name indicating some other country. If the claimant does not have registered or common law rights in the domicile of the hijacker, he may be able to bring a claim under s.56 (well-known marks) of the 1994 Act. Failing that, he will have to persuade a court in his own country to exercise extra-territorial jurisdiction over the defendant and generally this requires some substantial link between that country and the defendant.

ICANN

23–036   In October 1999, the Internet Corporation for Assigned Names and Numbers (ICANN) launched a Domain Name Dispute Resolution Policy that is now exercised by the World Intellectual Property Organisation and certain other organisations. The Policy currently applies only to names in the .com, .net, and .org Top Level Domains and certain country code domain names. If the system proves successful, it may well be adopted by other registries in the future.

23–037   When applying for registration of a domain name in a Top Level Domain operated by a registration authority subscribing to the ICANN Policy, the applicant agrees that:

(1) all statements made in the application are true and accurate; and

---

net Limited [2005] EWCH 334 (Ch) in which insufficent goodwill in the mark "Phones4U" had been generated for the defendants use to constitute a misrepresentation.

[18] The claimant's case is always assisted if the defendant registers the name and then offers to sell it to the claimant. Alternatively, the defendant may advertise the domain name for sale at a price which reflects how well-known the claimant is. More difficult are the cases where the defendant registers the name and is then careful not to make overt offers to sell. Those defendants then wait for the claimant to make them an offer. However, such a blocking registration may deprive the claimant of the ability to exploit his goodwill as he would like, and Aldous L.J.'s analysis means that, in appropriate circumstances, a blocking registration gives rise to liability.

[19] *Glaxo v Glaxowellcome* [1996] F.S.R. 388; *Direct Line Group v Direct Line Estate Agency Ltd* [1997] F.S.R. 374.

[20] e.g. alphanumeric telephone numbers: cf. *1–800 FLOWERS Inc v Phonenames Ltd* [2002] F.S.R. 12 CA.

(2) to the applicant's knowledge, the registration of the domain name will not infringe the rights of a third party; and

(3) it will not knowingly use the domain name in violation of any applicable laws or regulations.

The registration authority will cancel, transfer or otherwise change a domain name if the registrant so instructs it, if a competent court orders it, or upon a decision of an administrative panel (such as WIPO, Disputes.org/eResolution.ca Consortium, or the National Arbitration Forum) employing the ICANN Policy. The matter is decided by either an individual expert or, at the election of the complainant, a panel of three experts.

23–038

SUBSTANTIVE RULES[21]

In disputes to which the ICANN Policy pertains and pursuant to para.4(a) of the Policy the claimant must assert and prove that:

23–039

(1) the disputed domain name is identical or confusingly similar to a trade mark or domain name in which the complaining party has rights; and

(2) the registered party has no rights or legitimate interests in respect of the domain name; and

(3) the registered party is has registered or is using the domain name in bad faith.

Paragraph 4(b) of the Policy sets out the following non-exhaustive list of circumstances which will be taken as constituting evidence of "bad faith":

23–040

(a) where the circumstances surrounding the registration of the domain name indicate that it was primarily acquired for the purpose of selling, renting or otherwise transferring the domain name registration to the complainant owning the trade mark rights to the name, or to a competitor of the claimant, for valuable consideration in excess of documented out-of-pocket expenses relating directly to the domain name acquisition; or

(b) where the domain name has been registered to prevent the owner of trade mark rights in the name from reflecting the mark in a corresponding domain name where the registrant has engaged in a pattern of such conduct; or

(c) where the domain name has been registered primarily for the purpose of disrupting the business of a competitor; or

(d) where by using the domain name the registrant has attempted to attract commercial gain by luring Internet users to its website by creating a likelihood of confusion with the complainant's mark as to the source, sponsorship, affiliation or endorsement of its website or of a product on the website.

A claim under the Policy can be defeated if the registrant provides evidence that it has a right or legitimate interest in the domain name. Paragraph 4 (c) of the Policy identifies the following circumstances a constituting such a legitimate interest or right:

23–041

(i) that before notification of the dispute, its use (or demonstrable preparations for use) of the domain name or a name corresponding to it, was in connection with the *bona fide* offering of goods or services; or

(ii) that it has been commonly known by the domain name even if no trade mark rights have been acquired; or

---

[21] The ICANN Policy, Rules and Supplemental Rules, together with guidelines for complainant and respondent can all be found on the WIPO website at *www.wipo.org*.

(iii) that it is making legitimate non-commercial or fair use of the domain name without an intent to reap financial gain, to mislead consumers, or to tarnish the trade mark in issue.

OUTLINE PROCEDURE

23–042   The complaint should be filed with the organisation operating the Policy (such as WIPO) in both hard copy and by email. The complaint must contain full contact details of the complainant and his agent; an indication of the preferred means of communication; an indication of whether the matter is to be heard by one expert or a panel of three; the name and address of the respondent; details of the trade mark on the basis which the complaint is made (including details of the goods and services concerned); and a description of the grounds for complaint.

23–043   If the complaint is in order, it is sent to the registrant/respondent within three days of receipt. The respondent has 20 days to submit a response to the complaint. A written decision is produced within 14 days of receipt of the papers by the expert(s). Within three days of the decision, it is communicated to the registration authority, the parties, ICANN and the organisation through which the complaint was channelled. A majority decision by a panel of three experts is final. However, the ICANN procedure does not preclude a party from submitting the dispute to a relevant court and para.4(k) of the Policy provides that if WIPO is provided with official court documentation relating to such a proceedings within 10 working days of the decision, no further action will be taken until the legal action has been resolved.

THE ICANN POLICY IN PRACTICE

23–044   The ICANN Policy, as operated by WIPO, is very popular.[22] The procedure is quicker and cheaper than normal litigation. The jurisdiction is international in nature. There is a relatively high success rate for complainants.[23] In certain circumstances, the ICANN Policy produces an outcome for a claimant which he or she would not achieve under the law of passing off or infringement of registered trade mark.

(1) The domain names jeanettewinterson.com, jeanettewinterson.org and jeanettewinterson.net were required to be transferred to the well-known author. Having referred to *One in a Million*, the panel observed that "In this case, the issue is not whether the Respondent has committed passing-off by registering the three domain names in issue, it is merely whether under English common law unauthorised use of a mark can be restrained other than by an action for infringement of a trade mark." and "The case for decision here does not concern whether or not passing-off has occurred but whether the Complainant has rights in her name sufficient to constitute a trade mark for the purposes of para 4a of the Policy."[24]

(2) juliaroberts.com was required to be transferred to the well-known actress. In her case, an American panel referred to the Jeanette Winterson decision and observed: "The Policy does not require that the Complainant should have rights in a registered trade mark or service mark. It is sufficient that

---

[22] Over 1000 cases have been referred each year since the scheme's inception.

[23] To the end of December 2004, 70% of cases had been decided in favour of the complainant, 13% in favour of the respondent and 23% of cases had been withdrawn.

[24] Case No.D2000-0235: *Jeanette Winterson v Mark Hogarth* [2000] E.T.M.R. 783.

the Complainant should satisfy the Administrative Panel that she has rights in a common law trademark or sufficient rights to ground an action for passing off."[25] This decision confirms a literal interpretation of para.4(a) of the Policy. The complainant need not have sufficient rights to succeed in law against this respondent, but he or she must have some "rights" in the name. It may be sufficient to show that "rights" exist in one country which the Panel thinks is significant.

(3) Gordon Sumner, professionally known as "Sting", failed in his attempt to have the domain name sting.com transferred or cancelled. The Panel thought that the ICANN Policy had not intended to create or enforce personality rights, and distinguished the Jeanette Winterson and Julia Roberts decisions on the facts, accepting that there were a number of legitimate uses for sting.com. In spite of the fact that the respondent had offered to sell the domain name to the complainant for reportedly $25,000, this did not mean that the domain name had been registered in bad faith some five years previously. This approach is similar to that required in *One in a Million*: examine all the circumstances. This, and other decisions where the complainant has failed, shows that the Policy only works in favour of the complainant in cases which are reasonably clear cut.[26]

If the Panel finds that a complaint was brought in bad faith, whether to harass the registrant or as an attempt at "reverse domain name hijacking" it may dismiss the complaint as an abuse of process. The Panel adopted this approach in refusing a complaint by Nestlé, owners of the trade mark MAGGI, over the registration of the domain name maggi.com by one Romeo Maggi for the purposes of a family website.[27] **23–045**

Most disputes are decided by one expert, drawn from the country in question.[28] This has the distinct advantage that the expert has the necessary knowledge of the local law and can also take into account generally accepted local practices and customs. **23–046**

However, it is not all plain sailing. There are still some quite wide differences in the approach taken by experts from different countries. Thus one panel decided that mere registration of a domain name could not constitute bad faith, whereas other panels have decided the exact opposite. The desire to maintain a simple and cheap procedure can result in procedural unfairness: the complainant has no automatic right to respond to the contentions made by the respondent, and it is impossible for the complainant to anticipate every manoeuvre which a respondent may make. There is little opportunity to dispute assertions which are put forward as facts, or statements of intention put forward by registrants. Relatively speaking, it provides a cheaper and quicker solution than litigation, but it has its limitations. **23–047**

The Nominet UK Dispute Resolution Service

Some domain name registrars operate their own dispute resolution services with regard to the Top Level Domains they control. Nominet UK Limited in the United **23–048**

---

[25] Case No.D2000-0210: *Julia Fiona Roberts v Russell Boyd* .

[26] See, *e.g.* fuji.com (respondent had been trading under the Fuji name since 1992); sampdoria.com (complainant failed to prove bad faith, the respondent claimed that he would use the domain name to develop a sport and football fan related website).

[27] See, *e.g.* Case No. D2001-0916: *Nestlé v Pro Fiducia Treuhand AG* [2002] E.T.M.R. 351.

[28] There appears to be a reasonably high correlation between domicile of complainant and domicile of respondent.

Kingdom is a good example. A structured procedure has been set out by Nominet encompassing informal mediation of complaints followed by a formal decision by an appointed expert. Either party has a right to appeal the decision of the appointed expert, and appeals are heard by a panel of three appointed experts. If legal proceedings in the UK are issued before or during the course of dispute resolution proceedings and drawn to the attention of Nominet, the Nominet proceedings are suspended.

SUBSTANTIVE RULES[29]

23–049   In order to succeed in a complaint the complainant must prove on the balance of probabilities that it has rights enforceable under English law in respect of a name or mark identical with or similar to the domain complained of, and that the domain constitutes an "Abusive Registration". An Abusive Registration is defined as a domain which either was registered or has been used in a manner which took unfair advantage of or was detrimental to the complainant's rights. This broad definition is clarified by a non-exhaustive list of factors which may provide evidence of that a domain is an Abusive Registration, including:

    (a) evidence that the domain was registered primarily to be sold, as a blocking registration or to unfairly disrupt the complainant's business;

    (b) evidence that the domain name is being used in a way that has confused people into believing that it is connected with the complainant;

    (c) evidence that the registrant has given false contact details; or

    (d) evidence that the complainant has been using the domain name exclusively and paid for the registration, notwithstanding the fact that it is held in the registrant's name.

If a registrant has been found to have made an Abusive Registration in three or more cases in the two years before that complaint was filed, there a rebuttable presumption arises that the domain name in issue is also an Abusive Registration.

23–050   The following factors are regarded by Nominet as providing evidence that a domain name is not an Abusive Registration:

    (a) That before being made aware of the complaint the registrant has used or prepared to use the domain name in connection with a genuine offering of goods or services, has become commonly known by the name or legitimately connected with a mark similar or identical to the name or has made legitimate non-commercial use of the domain name.

    (b) That the domain name is generic or descriptive and the registrant is making fair use of it. Such fair use may be in respect of sites operated solely in tribute to or criticism of the complainant.

OUTLINE PROCEDURE

23–051   The complaint must be submitted in hard copy and electronic form to Nominet UK. It must be limited to 2000 words, and should identify the domain name, the rights relied upon by the complainant in the name or mark and why the domain name should be considered an Abusive Registration. The complainant must also state that it submits to the exclusive jurisdiction of the English courts with respect to any legal proceedings seeking to reverse the effect of a decision under the procedure. Nominet will send a copy of the complaint to the respondent. Within 15 days of receipt from Nominet of the complaint, the respondent must

---

[29] The Nominet dispute resolution rules and policy can be found at *www.nic.uk*.

submit its response, again limited to 2000 words. The response is sent to the complainant, who has a further five days to file a reply.

Within three days of receipt of the complainant's reply, if any, Nominet UK will commence informal mediation between the parties. If that mediation does not lead to an acceptable resolution of the matter within a further 10 days, an expert will be appointed and unless the expert calls for an in person hearing, the decision will be made on the papers and provided to the parties within 10 days of the appointment of the expert. Either party may appeal the decision of the expert as of right. Appeals are determined by a panel of three experts.   **23–052**

As with the ICANN procedure, the Nominet UK dispute resolution service has proved popular with users. The service was launched in September 2001, and since that date an average of 50 cases per month have been received. As of November 2004, 56 per cent of cases which reached the informal mediation stage were compromised. The complainant was successful in 78 per cent of the cases which were referred to an expert for determination. Only six appeals have been lodged, of which two were successful and four upheld the first instance decision.   **23–053**

3. Jurisdiction and infringement

The type of problem raised by use of marks on the Internet is best illustrated with an example. Take the situation where the same trade mark is owned and used by independent companies in the US and the United Kingdom. Each company has a website (squiffo.com and squiffo.co.uk respectively) which provides information about the company and its products and which features prominent use of the mark. Obviously, both websites can be accessed by an Internet user from anywhere in the world, raising the possibility that someone in the United Kingdom who is familiar with the UK company will encounter the website of the US company, and vice-versa.[30] The further stage in the example is where one or both companies offers goods or services for sale on their respective websites.   **23–054**

Does the use of the trade mark by the US company on its US website constitute infringement of the United Kingdom registered trade mark, and vice-versa? Claimants in this type of situation have argued that use of the trade mark on a website constitutes use of the trade mark throughout the world because the website can be accessed throughout the world.[31] This argument must be wrong and was rejected at first instance and on appeal in *1–800-FLOWERS*.[32] The analogy that the website owner automatically "puts a tentacle onto the user's screen" was also rejected in the same case. At the other extreme, defendants argue that the trade mark is only being used in the country where the web server is situate. This argument may or may not be right, it depends on the circumstances. Defendants also argue that a person in the United Kingdom who accesses a US website is   **23–055**

---

[30] This problem is no different from that raised by the two companies advertising in national magazines which happen to spill over in small quantities to the other territory.

[31] An example of the unfairness which can occur if this argument is accepted is provided by the decision of the Nanterre Court of Appeals in France in *SG2 v Brokat Informationssysteme GmbH*, October 13, 1996. The French claimant had registered "payline" in France for an Internet payment system. The German defendant had registered the same mark in Germany and sold its Internet payment system "Brokat-payline" on the Internet at its site at *www.brokat.de*. The defendant had not sold its system in France and did not intend to do so, because it would infringe French national cryptography regulations. Despite that, the French court granted an injunction preventing the defendant using "payline" in France in any form which extended to the use on the Internet. The court reasoned that the defendant's website could be accessed worldwide and this meant that an infringement had taken place in France.

[32] *1–800 FLOWERS Inc v Phonenames Ltd* [2002] F.S.R. 12 CA, [2000] F.S.R. 697 at first instance.

"visiting" the US or using a "super-telescope"[33] to view something in the US from the United Kingdom. This analogy is factually incorrect, as explained above at paras 23–020 to 23–023.

23–056   What is obvious from this example is that a measure of reciprocity is required from the courts of the respective countries, but where is the dividing line? Although this type of conflict is perhaps most likely to arise between the US[34] and the United Kingdom, one can certainly envisage the same conflict arising between two EU countries where the law should be exactly the same.

23–057   The dividing line is indicated by normal principles. Infringement in the United Kingdom requires use of the sign in the course of trade in relation to goods or services in the United Kingdom. So the use on the US or any foreign website must constitute use in the course of trade in the United Kingdom before it can amount to infringement of a United Kingdom registered trade mark or, for that matter, passing off in the United Kingdom. This is a question of fact to be decided in all the circumstances:

> "There is something inherently unrealistic in saying that A "uses" his mark in the United Kingdom when all he does is to place the mark on the Internet, from a location outside the United Kingdom, and simply wait in the hope that someone from the United Kingdom will download it and thereby create use on the part of A ...
>
> ... the very idea of "use" within a certain area would seem to require some active step in that area on the part of the user that goes beyond providing facilities that enable others to bring the mark into the area. Of course, if persons in the United Kingdom seek the mark on the Internet in response to direct encouragement or advertisement by the owner, the position may be different; but in such a case the advertisement or encouragement in itself is likely to suffice to establish the necessary use."[35]

23–058   If a website based in the US is directed at customers in the United Kingdom and seeks orders for delivery to the United Kingdom, the proprietor goes beyond merely waiting in the hope of custom in the United Kingdom. Such custom is in effect solicited. The issue does not depend on what the website owner says in evidence about his intentions or encouragement. The inquiry must be objective: what would the reasonable user understand looking at this website? Thus, Jacob J. (as he then was) in Euromarket Designs said: "... there must be an inquiry as to what the purpose and effect of the advertisement in question is."[36] and "One needs to ask whether the defendant has any trade here, customers buying goods or services for consumption here." Of course, infringement does not require the

---

[33] An analogy accepted on the facts in *Euromarket Designs Inc v Peters* [2001] F.S.R. 20.

[34] The US courts have also rejected the concept that use on a website is use worldwide. For example, in *Playboy Enterprises v Chuckleberry Publishing Inc* (1996) 39 U.S.P.Q. 2d 1746 (District Court of the Southern District of New York), the claimant tried to enforce a 1981 injunction preventing the defendant distributing and selling its Italian "Playmen" men's magazine in the US, against the defendant's Italian website which offered access to various photos at two levels: "Playmen-Lite", which was free, and "Playmen-Pro", which required payment. The claimant argued that the defendant should improve its password system so as to eliminate users from the US. The court held that the use of "Playmen" was simply on the home page in respect of Italian services. The fact that the website was accessible from the US did not result in breach of the US injunction.

[35] *1–800-FLOWERS*, Buxton L.J. at paras 137–138. Note that *1–800-FLOWERS* was a case concerning revocation for non-use.

[36] There being no difference in this context between an advertisement on a website and one in a magazine with international circulation. See Jacob J. in *Euromarket Designs Inc v Peters* [2001] F.S.R. 20, para.15.

defendant to have an established trade in the United Kingdom, the only requirement is for use in the course of trade. However, the extent of the defendant's
trade with customers in the United Kingdom will be an important factor in the inquiry whether there is use in the course of trade in the United Kingdom.

When making this type of inquiry, Jacob L.J. has very sensibly suggested that **23–059**
Internet users are reasonably robust when selecting what to look at or investigate
further, and use a lot more common sense than most claimants would like. His
views may be explained in the following propositions:

(1) The reasonable person,[37] using the Internet expects a search to produce a
lot of irrelevant sites, and expects many to be foreign.[38] It follows that the
mere fact that a search reveals a reference to a trade mark on a foreign
website does not begin to establish use of the sign in the course of trade in
the United Kingdom for the purposes of infringement.

(2) Even if it is not immediately obvious from the search results that a site is
irrelevant and the user decides to visit an identified site, that does not establish use in the United Kingdom. The user will be able to see fairly
quickly that the site is irrelevant, "he will simply say 'this is not for me'
and move on".[39]

On the basis of those propositions, one can suggest the following further **23–060**
propositions:

(a) The expectation that many sites will be foreign means that the user takes
at least some notice of the information provided to him about the nationality of the website. That information may be part of the domain name[40] or
part of the content of the site.

(b) The appearance of a mark on a foreign website will constitute use of the
mark in the course of trade in the United Kingdom if, objectively speaking, the website is aimed at or intended for consumers in the United
Kingdom, even if the United Kingdom is only one of the intended markets.

(c) If a significant number of customers in the United Kingdom have
purchased goods bearing a mark through a foreign website, then use in the
course of trade in the United Kingdom will have been established.

(d) If the only evidence of purchases being made from the United Kingdom is
trap purchases conducted on behalf of the claimant, then there is probably
no use in the United Kingdom, unless the operation has only just
commenced.

It is relatively easy for website owners to make it clear on their website whether **23–061**
they wish to and therefore do conduct trade with consumers in foreign countries.
A prominent disclaimer may be shown on the home page; alternatively, the terms
and conditions of sale may stipulate that products are not for sale to foreign
countries; alternatively, the payment methods may themselves prevent sales to
foreign countries;[41] alternatively, the screen on which the user enters the shipping
address may not accept a foreign address.[42] In most cases, these types of indications should be determinative, although there will always be the rare case where
they are used to conceal the true position.

---

[37] Perhaps even "the average consumer".
[38] *Euromarket Designs* [2001] F.S.R. 20, para.23. Also *Avnet Inc v Isoact Ltd* [1998] F.S.R. 16, Jacob J.
[39] *1–800-FLOWERS* [2000] F.S.R. 697 at 705, first instance.
[40] *e.g.* crateand barrel-ie.com or crateandbarrel.ie, as in *Euromarket Designs* [2001] F.S.R.20.
[41] Leaving aside the possibility that, *e.g.* an American in London may be able to buy from a US
website because he uses his US credit card.
[42] *e.g.* a US website may require the prospective purchaser to select a US state for his shipping
address.

Liability of Internet Service Providers

23–062 In the United Kingdom, no liability attaches to the Registrar of the domain name merely for having registered it.[43] The Electronic Commerce Directive[44] has harmonised the position on liability of Internet service providers throughout Europe. Where a party acts as mere conduit for the transmission of data, caches such data for the sole purpose of making its transmission more efficient or acts as a host for a website, that party is excluded from criminal or civil liability in respect of such acts in the following circumstances:

(1) In the case of transmission of information, if the party did not initiate the transmission, select the recipient of the transmission or select or modify the data so transmitted, it escapes liability. Thus a service provider involved in the transmission of communications to or from offending websites or of advertisements for such websites escapes liability as a joint tortfeasor.[45]

(2) In the case of caching information, if the party did not modify the information and acts expeditiously to remove or disable access to that information on obtaining knowledge that a court has ordered such removal or disablement. Thus a service provider involved in the caching of information from a website for the purposes of making its transmission more efficient is not liable in respect of infringements on the website if it acts expeditiously to remove or disable access to that information.[46]

(3) In the case of hosting information, where a party hosts information provided by its customers (such as a website) then if that party does not have actual knowledge of any unlawful activity and in the case of a civil claim, is not aware of matters from which it would have been apparent that the activity or information it is hosting is unlawful, and if upon becoming aware or gaining such knowledge, it acts expeditiously to remove or disable access to the information. Thus a service provider which is hosting an infringing website has no liability for the infringement if it does not know or have reason to believe that it infringes, and if it takes down the website promptly when if becomes aware or is given reason to believe that it is unlawful.[47]

4. Metatags and "invisible use"[48]

23–063 As mentioned above, trade marks or names belonging to others can be used in metatags or to otherwise optimise the position of a website within the result of an Internet search. Generally, three situations arise. The first is where a trade mark or name of a competitor is so used; the second is where a famous trade mark is used, but generally the goods or services are different; the third is where the name of a famous person is used.

23–064 Common to all situations where the allegedly infringing mark is contained in a metatag or used as an advertising keyword is the issue of whether such use constitutes use of the mark for the purposes of infringement of registered trade mark

---

[43] *Pitman Training Ltd v Nominet UK* [1997] F.S.R. 797, Sir Richard Scott V.C. The same position applies in the US.

[44] 2000/31/EC, implemented in the UK by the Electronic Commerce (EC Directive) Regulations 2002 (SI 2002/2013).

[45] Art.12.

[46] Art.13.

[47] Art.14.

[48] Reference is invited to the short explanation at paras 23–024 to 23–027.

and/or passing off. Prior to the decision of the Court of Appeal in *Reed Executive*[49] it seemed clear that under the 1994 Act use of a mark in a metatag does constitute use of the sign for the purposes of infringement.[50] The fact that the metatag is normally not seen should not make any difference, due to s.103(2) which specifically includes use "otherwise than by means of a graphic representation". Likewise, for passing off: the fact that the user may not see the metatag might be thought not to remove the misrepresentation. However, the views expressed by Jacob L.J. in Reed cast doubt on whether metatag (or other invisible use) is likely to give rise to a misrepresentation or deception for the purposes of passing off, or to a likelihood of confusion for the purposes of trade mark infringement. Further and more fundamentally, although not expressing a firm view on the point, Jacob L.J. made clear that he doubted whether such use constituted use for the purposes of trade mark infringement under the 1994 Act.

REED EXECUTIVE PLC

The relevant dispute in *Reed* concerned the use of the word REED within the sign REED BUSINESS INFORMATION as a metatag on the defendant's website and as a keyword for the generation of Internet advertising. Passing off and trade mark infringement under ss.10(1) and 10(2) of the 1994 Act were alleged. Jacob L.J. held that there was no identity between the sign used by the defendant and the mark registered. As a result, the infringement claim under s.10(1) failed. The passing off claim and the allegation of infringement under s.10(2) were rejected on the grounds that in all the circumstances the Defendant's use it did not constitute a misrepresentation leading to deception and would not be likely to give rise to confusion, respectively. **23–065**

Although expressed in strong terms, the findings on deception and likelihood of confusion were dependant on the particular evidence before the court. However, at pars 140 and 149(a) of *Reed*, Jacob L.J. raises the more fundamental question of whether metatag use or other invisible use of a trade mark constitutes use of a trade mark at all for the purposes of infringement. In the light of his decisions on absence of identity between the mark and sign, and on the absence of deception and confusion, he did not express a final opinion, but the question is of considerable importance and until a definitive answer has been provided, a degree of uncertainty is cast over the issue of infringement by such "use". **23–066**

The difficulty identified by Jacob L.J. is whether the use of a mark as a metatag or an advertising keyword constitutes use which is capable of affecting the functions of a trade mark, given that in normal operation the consumer will not be aware of the use by the defendant itself, merely of the results of the use (the display of a competitor's advertisement or a higher position on a search engine result table). In many circumstances it is the consumer who has typed in the mark in issue, and the only visible use in the search results may be the words remaining in the search window on the consumer's screen, alongside the advertisements and **23–067**

---

[49] *Reed Executive plc v Reed Business Information Limited* [2004] R.P.C. 40.
[50] Accepted in *Road Tech Computer Systems Limited v Mandata (Management and Data Services) Limited*, [2000] E.T.M.R. 970, a decision of Master Bowman essentially concerning *quantum* of damages. The defendant had admitted trade mark infringement but not passing off. Summary judgment was granted for both. There are a number of US decisions in which infringement has been found: *Niton Corp v Radiation Monitoring Devices Inc; Playboy Enterprises Inc v Calvin Designer Label;* and *Brookfield v West Coast Entertainment.*

search results complained of.[51] A further difficulty identified in *Reed* is the issue of whether, assuming such use was capable of constituting use for the purposes of trade mark infringement, it would also constitute use for the purposes of defeating an application to revoke for non-use? In response to the latter point, it is difficult to see how "invisible" or metatag use could be use in order to create or preserve an outlet for goods and services as required by *Ansul*.[52]

23–068   The approach adopted in France,[53] Benelux,[54] Germany[55] and Italy[56] has been that use of a third party mark as an Internet advertising keyword or a metatag can be restrained as trade mark infringement.[57] However, the analysis in the reported decisions of which goods or services the mark has been "used" in relation to, and by whom they have been used, does not seem to have been undertaken with any great rigour.

23–069   Apart from the common issue identified above, the three situations fall to be determined on normal principles. In the first situation, use of a competitor's mark is likely to be used in relation to identical goods (hence a s.10(1) infringement) or at least similar goods (s.10(2) infringement). Use of a famous mark may constitute a s.10(3) infringement[58] or may be restrained under s.56 of the 1994 Act. Both the first and second situations may result in passing off if there is a likelihood of deception on the part of the public.

23–070   The third situation presents the usual problems for celebrities where their names are used by unconnected traders. It will only be in rare cases that the celebrity has a valid trade mark registration which is infringed or is actionable under the law of passing off. The ICANN Dispute Resolution Policy is confined to domain name registrations and there is little or no prospect of those services being extended so as to provide a general jurisdiction over the Internet.

---

[51] The use of analogies in connection with the Internet can be counterproductive, but the position is perhaps analogous to a consumer asking to be provided with information by reference to a particular trade mark, and being offered instead information or advertising relating to a competitor's goods.

[52] *Ansul v Ajax* [2003] E.C.R I-2439 (C40/01).

[53] *Viaticum v Google France* [2004] E.T.M.R 63. Use of a mark as an advertising keyword.

[54] *VNU Business Publications BV v Monster Board BV* [2002] E.T.M.R. 111 Hague District Court. Use of a mark as an advertising keyword.

[55] *Estée Lauder v Fragrance Counter Inc* [2000] E.T.M.R.] 843, Hamburg District Court. Use of a mark as an advertising keyword.

[56] *Trieste e Venezia Assicurazioni Genertel SPAv Crowe Italia* [2001] E.T.M.R 66 Tribunal of Rome (Ninth section). Metatag use.

[57] Both on the part of the company offering the keyword advertising service and the client procuring those services. If the party providing such services is liable, it is difficult to see how the client procuring that use of the mark is not liable as a joint tortfeasor.

[58] cf. *BT v One in a Million* [1999] 1 W.L.R. 903, CA.

CHAPTER 24

MISCELLANEOUS

1. Company and business names

COMPANY NAMES

A spurious argument used frequently by potential defendants in passing off or trade mark infringement actions is that they have registered the name in question as a company name and therefore must be entitled to use it. This is not so.[1] **24–001**

The choice of company names is regulated by ss.26–34 of the Companies Act 1985.[2] Certain names (for example, those suggesting a connection with the Government or a local authority, or implying national or international renown) require the consent of the Secretary of State (in practice through the Registrar of Companies) before they may be included in a company name placed on the Companies Register.[3] Also, it is not permitted to register as a company name a name which is "the same as" one already on the Companies Register.[4] **24–002**

Once a company has registered its name, the Secretary of State may require it to change its name if it is the same as or too like another name on the Companies Register.[5] The procedure is cumbersome and in recent times the trade mark infringement and/or passing off action has been used far more to secure the change of name of the later registrant.[6] If the claimant's trade mark infringement and/or passing off action is successful, the directors of the offending company will be ordered to procure a change of name to a name which is not "the same as" or "too like" that of the claimant. Under s.28(1) of the Companies Act 1985, the members of a company must pass a special resolution in order to change its name and no other manner of change is possible. This means that even if (and in contempt of court) the defendant company fails to have passed a special resolution and change its name, the courts do not have power either to order the Registrar of Companies to change the name or to appoint a person to execute a document under an order requiring the directors of the company to procure a change of name (the latter under R.S.C. Order 45, r.8).[7] **24–003**

Additionally, under s.32 of the Companies Act 1985, the Secretary of State has **24–004**

---

[1] See generally Ch.14.

[2] Together with the Company and Business Names (Chamber of Commerce, Etc) Act 1999.

[3] Companies Act 1985, s.26(2) and Company and Business Names Regulations 1981, SI 1981/1685 (as amended).

[4] s.26(1)(c). In deciding whether a proposed name is "the same as" an existing company name, the Registrar of Companies ignores punctuation, the company's status (*i.e.*, the contractions and abbreviations "Ltd", "PLC", etc.), "The" at the beginning of the name, and words such as "Company" (or "Co.") and "and Company" (or "& Co.").

[5] s.28(2).

[6] See Ch.14, paras 14–179 to 14–080, and especially the decision in *Glaxo plc v Glaxowellcome Ltd* [1996] F.S.R. 388.

[7] *Halifax PLC v Halifax Repossessions Ltd* [2004] F.S.R. 903 at para.21.

power to require a company to change its name at any time if harm to the public is likely to be caused by its name being misleading.[8]

24–005 Further restrictions on the use of particular words in company names are prescribed in various Acts of Parliament, such as the use of the word "Olympic"[9] and words which relate to regulated professions, such as "pharmacist".[10]

BUSINESS NAMES

24–006 Save in relation to companies incorporated outside Great Britain (see below at paras 24–008 and 24–009), there is no longer any obligation to register a business name where a person or company is carrying on business under a name different from his or its true name. However, under the provisions of the Business Names Act 1985, if another name is used, all normal business documents are required to state the true name of the persons or company using the business name and an address for service.[11] Also, at any premises where the business is carried on and to which customers or suppliers have access, a notice specifying this information must be displayed in a prominent position.[12] There are minor penalties for non-compliance. Also, a firm or company in breach of the disclosure provisions may lose contractual rights in an action against a party who can show that the breach has caused him financial loss or an inability to bring a claim against the claimant.[13]

24–007 Section 3 of the Business Names Act 1985 provides the power for the Secretary of State to issue regulations specifying words and expressions which may not be used as part of a business name without his approval and identical restrictions apply as in relation to company names (see above at para.24–005).[14]

OVERSEA COMPANIES

24–008 Under Sch.21A[15] of the Companies Act 1985 an oversea company[16] which has a branch in Great Britain must inform the Registrar of Companies, amongst other matters, if the name of the company is different from the name under which the business in Great Britain is carried on by the branch.[17] The Registrar of Companies keeps an index of the names of the branches registered under Sch.21A.[18]

---

[8] See *Association of Certified Public Accountants v Secretary of State for Trade & Industry* [1998] 1 W.L.R. 164.

[9] Olympic Symbol etc. (Protection) Act 1995.

[10] Medicines Act 1968, s.78.

[11] s.4 (1)(a). There is an exception for partnerships and limited liability partnerships (LLPs) of more than 20 persons, which must maintain at their principal place of business a list of the names of all the partners or members (in the case of LLPs) provided that: (1) none of the names of the partners or members appear in the document in question otherwise than in the text or as a signatory; and (2) the document states in legible characters the address of the partnership's or LLP's principal place of business and a list of the partners' or members' names is open to inspection at that place (ss.4(3) and 4(3)(A).

[12] See s.4(1)(b). It should be noted that the so-called "Certificate of Registration" issued by a company in Birmingham, National Business Register plc, is of no greater legal significance than a plain piece of paper with the required information on it.

[13] s.5.

[14] The Company and Business Names Regulations 1981, SI 1981/1685 (as amended), have effect now as if made under s.3.

[15] Given effect by s.690A(2), implementing the Eleventh Company Law Directive 89/666.

[16] As defined in s.744.

[17] Sch.21A, para.3(d). The information specified in para.3 must be notified within one month of the company having opened a branch in Great Britain: para.1(1).

[18] Companies Act 1985, s.714(1)(aa).

There is no corresponding obligation in s.691 where an oversea company establishes a place of business in Great Britain (but not a branch).[19]

Within 12 months of the provision of the information required by either s.691 **24–009** or Sch.21A as appropriate, s.694 provides that the Secretary of State may object if the name would not be permitted as the name of a domestic company or if it is too like a name already on the Register,[20] and two months thereafter the oversea company must cease to carry on business under that name.[21]

2. Human rights and trade marks

The Human Rights Act 1998 ("HRA") gives further effect to the rights and **24–010** freedoms protected by the European Convention on Human Rights[22] ("the Convention"). The commencement date of the HRA was October 2, 2000. From that date, primary and subordinate legislation must be read and given effect to by the courts in a way compatible with the Convention[23] and taking into account the decisions and opinions of the European Court of Human Rights.[24]

The HRA is not directly justiciable by individuals *per se*, but rather aims at the **24–011** protection of the human rights of individuals against the abuse of power by the State.[25] Under the provisions of the HRA, it would be unlawful for a public authority to act in a manner which is incompatible with the Convention.[26] For these purposes, the Act makes it clear that "public authority" includes a court or tribunal.[27] Thus, in *Dyson Ltd's Trade Mark Application*[28] it was unsuccessfully contended by the appellant from an *ex parte* hearing officer decision to refuse registration under s.3 TMA that the appeal should be by way of a re-hearing if it was to be compliant with Art.6 of the Convention (under which everyone is entitled to a fair and public hearing by an independent and impartial tribunal). Although Patten J. accepted that the resolution of the appeal was "a prerequisite to the enjoyment of the property right obtained by the registration of a trade mark under the 1994 Act",[29] he did not consider it necessary to conduct a re-hearing of any appeal from an *ex parte* decision but rather appeal by way of review should be the norm.[30] On the other hand, an Art.6 objection succeeded before the Appointed Person (S. Thorley Q.C.) in *Silver Spring Mineral Water Co Ltd's Trade Mark Application (No.1)*[31] where a mark had been refused on the basis of an Appointed Person decision given after the hearing of the opposition in issue and without giving either party the opportunity of addressing him on that decision. As a result the matter was remitted to the Registry for hearing before a different hearing officer.

---

[19] The documents to be delivered to the Registrar are set out in s.691 but do not include an equivalent to Sch.21A, para.3(d).

[20] s.694(1) and (2).

[21] s.694(6).

[22] Convention for the Protection of Human Rights and Fundamental Freedoms (Rome, November 4, 1950; TS 71 (1953); Cmnd 8969).

[23] s.3 of the Act.

[24] s.2.

[25] *per* Lord Irvine, HL Report, 29.1.98, col.422.

[26] s.6(1).

[27] s.6(3) states "In this section 'public authority' includes (a) a court or tribunal, and (b) any person certain of whose functions are functions of a public nature."

[28] [2003] R.P.C. 821.

[29] *Dyson Ltd's Trade Mark Application* [2003] R.P.C. 821, at para.12.

[30] At para.14.

[31] [2003] R.P.C. 21.

24–012   A "person", which includes a corporate entity,[32] may only contend that a public authority has acted (or proposes to act) in a way which is unlawful under the Act if that person is (or would be) the victim of the unlawful act. It must however be borne in mind that the European Court of Human Rights has held that the State has a positive obligation to prevent one person's rights being breached by another private person.[33] In view of this, a court should at all appropriate times consider and apply the Convention in any proceedings, and not merely in actions against a public body allegedly acting contrary to it: for example, in *Levi Strauss & Co v Tesco Stores Ltd*[34] it was noted that "unless s.10(6) of the Trade Marks Act 1994 is read so as to fully protect [the Convention] rights, there is a failure to comply with s.3 of the HRA."[35]

24–013   Under the HRA it is accepted that the court has wide discretionary powers and may grant such relief as it considers just and appropriate,[36] and therefore will have the power to grant injunctions and award damages where in all the circumstances such an award is necessary.[37]

24–014   With these wide powers and obligations given to and imposed upon the courts, human rights arguments have been and will be raised in many types of legal proceedings, including those concerning the enforcement of intellectual property rights. However, in *D (A Child) v Walker*[38] Lord Woolf made it quite clear that at least the higher courts would not be sympathetic to such arguments being raised speculatively: "When the Act of 1998 becomes law, counsel will need to show self-restraint if it is not to be discredited".[39] In intellectual property cases at least, it is fair to say that to date a certain degree of self-restraint has been shown.

24–015   The principle perhaps of most relevance to trade mark infringement and passing off or trade libel actions is the right to Freedom of Expression set out in Art.10 of the Convention. This states that:

"1. Everyone has the right to freedom of expression. This right shall include freedom to hold opinions and to receive and impart information and ideas without interference by public authority and regardless of frontiers ...

2. The exercise of these freedoms, since it carries with it duties and responsibilities, may be subject to such formalities, conditions, restrictions or penalties as are prescribed by law and are necessary ... for the protection of the reputation or rights of others, for preventing the disclosure of information received in confidence ..."

24–016   This Article covers commercial free speech.[40] However, in the context of private rights such as trade marks, it must be borne in mind, as was noted in *R. v*

---

[32] *Autronic AG v Switzerland* (1990) 12 E.H.R.R. 485, Eu Ct HR.
[33] *X and Y v Netherlands* [1986] 8 E.H.R.R. 235.
[34] [2003] R.P.C. 319.
[35] *Levi Strauss & Co v Tesco Stores Ltd* [2003] R.P.C. 319, at para.22.
[36] s.8(1).
[37] s.8(3).
[38] [2000] 1 W.L.R. 1382. As the Civil Procedure Rules have as their overriding objective "enabling the court to deal with cases justly" (r.1.1), the Master of the Rolls considered that the Human Rights Act point did not add anything: at 1386–1387.
[39] At 1387.
[40] *Markt Intern Verlag v Federal Republic of Germany* (1990) 12 E.H.R.R. 161, E Ct HR; *Casado Coca v Spain* (1994) 18 E.H.R.R. 1, E Ct HR; *Jacubowski v Germany* (1995) 19 E.H.R.R. 64, E Ct HR and *Hertel v Switzerland* (1999) 28 E.H.R.R. 534 E Ct HR, where the Court held that an injunction restraining a scientist from disseminating views that microwave ovens were dangerous was disproportionate to the legitimate aim of protecting the rights of others, in particular the rights of manufacturers and suppliers of microwave ovens to be protected from acts of unfair competition.

Secretary of State for Health Ex.p. British American Tobacco,[41] that "[i]t is accepted that freedom of commercial expression has been treated traditionally as of less significance than freedom of political or artistic expression".[42] The *BAT* case involved a challenge (with significant implications for the use of trade marks in the tobacco sector) to the lawfulness of the Tobacco Advertising and Promotion (Point of Sale) Regulations 2004 on the ground that they are disproportionately restrictive of advertising at the point of sale and therefore impair the "very essence" of commercial free speech, contrary to Art.10.[43] The court rejected the challenge, finding that the Regulations were "proportionate"[44] to the legitimate aim of protecting public health (and therefore fell within the restrictions to the right permitted by Art.10(2)).[45]

In *Ghazilian's Trade Mark Application*[46] the Appointed Person (S. Thorley   **24–017**
Q.C.) declined to comment on the contention by counsel for the Registrar that a refusal of registration of a trade mark on the s.3(3) TMA ground that it is contrary to accepted principles of morality did not place any restriction on the applicant's right of expression (as it could still be used notwithstanding refusal of registration.)[47] Upholding the refusal to register "Tiny Penis", he suggested that the difference between the analysis under s.3(3) TMA and the Convention position that the freedom should be interfered with only where there is a pressing social need to do so, was "merely a matter of words."[48]

Section 12 of the HRA places an obligation on the court, where it is consider-   **24–018**
ing whether to grant any relief in a case, to consider whether such relief may adversely affect the Convention right to freedom of expression.[49] Accordingly, it is possible for an individual or company (with its own rights to commercial free speech)[50] to request in the context of a trade mark infringement action that the court protects its right to freedom of expression. In strict terms, the award by the court of any injunctive relief preventing a defendant from using (and infringing) a registered trade mark would constitute a fetter on that defendant's freedom of expression. However, the provisions of Art.10(2) of the Convention clearly contemplate this and recognise that the court may grant such injunctions (and other relief) as the right to freedom of expression is subject to such restrictions as are prescribed by law and are necessary for the protection of the rights of others (which term includes trade marks). Thus, in the context of trade mark exhaustion, "[t]he legislator must hold the balance ... between the right of the owner of the trade mark on the one hand, and the right to convey information about the origin of the goods on the other."[51]

Notwithstanding this, there are clearly limits to the extent to which such a re-   **24–019**

---

[41] [2004] E.W.H.C. 2493 (Admin).

[42] *per* McCombe J.at para.28. In *Levi Strauss & Co* [2003] R.P.C. 319, the right was described by Pumfrey J. as "weak", at para.41.

[43] [2004] EWHC 2493 (Admin), at para.13 summarising the claimants' case.

[44] As to which, see Lord Steyn in *R. v Secretary of State Ex.p. Daly* [2001] 2 A.C. 532, HL at 547–8.

[45] At paras 51–55.

[46] [2002] R.P.C. 33.

[47] A similar argument in relation to copyright was put forward and accepted in *Ashdown v Telegraph Group Ltd* [2002] R.P.C. 5, CA, particularly *per* Lord Phillips M.R at para.39.

[48] [2002] R.P.C. 628, at para.21.

[49] s.12(1).

[50] Subject to the caveat expressed by McCombe J. in *BAT* [2004] EWHC 2493 (Admin.) as to the treatment of commercial as opposed to political or artistic free speech.

[51] *per* Pumfrey J. in *Levi Strauss & Co* [2003] R.P.C. 319, at para.41.

striction is permissible and, where such a defence is raised, under s.12(3) the
court must be satisfied that the applicant for relief is "likely to establish" its case.
In the first *Douglas v Hello! Ltd*[52] case (involving a conflict between the right to
respect for private and family life in Art.8(1) and the right to freedom of expression in Art.10), Keene L.J. found that the section "requires the court to look at the
merits of the case and not merely to apply the *American Cyanamid* test.[53] Thus
the court has to look ahead to the ultimate stage and to be satisfied that the scales
are likely to come down in the applicant's favour."[54] In *Cream Holdings Ltd v
Banerjee*[55] it was made clear by Lord Nicholls that the degree of likelihood of
success at the trial needed to satisfy s.12(3) depends on the circumstances: "the
general approach should be that courts will be exceedingly slow to make interim
restraint orders where the applicant has not satisfied the court he will probably
('more likely than not') succeed at the trial …. But there will be cases where it is
necessary for a court to depart from this general approach and a lesser degree of
likelihood will suffice as a prerequisite."[56] It remains to be seen whether such an
analysis can and will be applied to publication in a broad sense (so as to include
the sale of trade marked products, for example) rather than be limited to cases
where the freedom of the Press is at issue.

24–020   In *Douglas v Hello!*,[57] in the appeal against the grant of an interim injunction,
Sedley L.J. noted that Art.10 requires the court "if the common law did not already do so" to have full regard for the defendant's right to freedom of expression when deciding if an injunction was appropriate.[58] Even before the HRA, in
defamation actions (including trade libel)[59] the courts were reluctant to restrict
the right to free speech unless absolutely necessary. As acknowledged by Sedley
L.J., at the interim stage the courts generally would not grant an injunction to
prevent alleged libels if a defendant has pleaded justification and had reasonable
grounds for so doing. Unsurprisingly, the HRA has not altered that practice which
was extended to cases such as *Sim v Heinz*[60] and *Lord Brabourne v Hough*[61]
where the alleged misrepresentation was pleaded in passing off; in the first case,
concerning an actor imitated in an advertisement, and the second, an alleged unauthorised biography of Lord Mountbatten. In both cases the injunction was
refused as the defendant stated that he intended to justify his claim.

24–021   Again before the passage of the HRA, in *Consorzio del Prosciutto di Parma v
Marks & Spencer*[62] the court considered the question of commercial free speech
in deciding to refuse the claimant's application for an interim injunction. Here,
Marks & Spencer submitted that they should not be prevented from truthfully
informing the public what type of ham they were selling. In assessing the balance

---

[52] [2001] F.S.R. 732.
[53] [1975] A.C. 396.
[54] [2001] F.S.R. 732, at para.150. Brookes L.J. expressed considerable hesitation on the question as
to whether, even though he considered the balance of convenience lay in the defendant's favour,
an injunction should nevertheless be granted; in the end he accepted the argument put forward by
Sedley L.J. (at para.144) that the case was just on the wrong side of the line for the grant of the
discretionary remedy of an injunction.
[55] [2004] 3 W.L.R. 918, HL.
[56] [2004] 3 W.L.R. 918, HL, at para.22.
[57] [2001] F.S.R. 732.
[58] At para.139.
[59] See Ch.18.
[60] [1959] R.P.C. 75.
[61] [1981] F.S.R. 79.
[62] [1991] R.P.C. 351, CA.

of convenience, the court at first instance stated that it did not consider the claimant's case "warrants the interference with free speech which the grant of injunctions would involve". In this area it seems unlikely that Art.10 adds anything to the role which considerations of free speech played previously in judicial reasoning and decision-making.

The court's comments in *Ciba-Geigy v Parke Davis*,[63] a comparative advertising case, also are worth remembering. In this passing off action, Aldous J. said the fact that the alleged misrepresentation could be pleaded in both passing off and in trade libel did not mean that an injunction to restrain the alleged misrepresentation must be refused. In addition, and perhaps more importantly, he added that if he had come to a conclusion that there was a serious issue to be tried, it would have been both appropriate and possible to formulate an injunction to restrain the alleged misrepresentation without substantially infringing upon the defendant's right to free speech. The issue for the court taking into account the Human Rights Act would be whether the injunction, and its form, is necessary for the protection of the "rights and freedoms of others" under Art.8,[64] which are "as material as the … right of free expression."[65] In this context, arguments may be raised as to whether the specific subject-matter of a trade mark right is being protected.[66] **24–022**

The two other Convention rights which may be of relevance in litigation concerning trade marks are the right to respect for private and family life in Art.8 of the Convention ("Everyone has the right to respect for his private and family life, his home and his correspondence") and the right to property contained in Art.1 of Protocol No.1 to the Convention ("Everyone has the right to peaceful enjoyment of his possessions. No one shall be deprived of his possessions except in the public interest …", Art.1 of Protocol No.1). Both are subject to "public interest" type exceptions and, as was noted by Pumfrey J. in relation to the latter,[67] the scope of the discretion accorded to the legislature by this exception is wide.[68] **24–023**

In *Irvine v Talksport Ltd*[69] the possibility that these two Articles were relevant to a claim of passing off by false endorsement was raised and rejected by the judge at first instance, Laddie J., although he suggested that had the law not developed sufficiently to cover such a claim it may have been necessary to rely on human rights points to "give the final impetus" to reach the desired result of preventing such a falsehood.[70] **24–024**

The former is likely to be raised in relation to evidence of wrongdoing obtained by questionable means, for example by trap orders or surveillance, although in *R.* **24–025**

---

[63] [1994] F.S.R. 8.

[64] "[W]hether introduced indirectly through s.12 or directly by virtue of s.6", *per* Sedley L.J., *Douglas v Hello! Ltd* [2001] F.S.R. 732, at para.139. In the appeal against the judgment at trial, [2005] EWCA Civ 595, the Court of Appeal (Lord Phillips M.R., Clarke and Neuberger L.JJ.) considered that the claimants had a "virtually unanswerable" (at para.253) privacy claim which may well have been enough to justify summary judgment (at para.259).

[65] [2001] F.S.R. 732, at para.136.

[66] cf. Ch.16.

[67] In *Levi Strauss & Co* [2003] R.P.C. 319, at para.40.

[68] *Citing Mellacher v Austria* (1990) 12 E.H.R.R. 391.

[69] [2002] F.S.R. 943.

[70] [2002] F.S.R. 943, at para.77, quoting Sedley L.J. in *Douglas v Hello!* [2001] F.S.R. 732.

v Broadcasting Standards Commission Ex p. British Broadcasting Corporation[71] it was left open by the Court of Appeal whether a company has a right to respect for its private life under Art.8.

24–026   Both the right to freedom of expression in Art.10 and the right to property in Protocol No. 1 were referred to by Pumfrey J. in *Levi Strauss & Co v Tesco Stores Ltd*[72] as requiring the court to interpret the infringement provisions (and in particular s.19(6)) of the 1994 Act in such a way as to protect those rights.[73] Notwithstanding this, he found devoid of any substance[74] the defendants' arguments that Art.7 of the TM Directive (on exhaustion) must be interpreted in such a way as to protect the purchaser's right of resale which it was contended is an aspect of the right to respect for property.

24–027   Similarly, a rejection of a trade mark application by the Registry would not seem to be susceptible to challenge under Art.1: in *British American Tobacco v The Netherlands*,[75] a case involving a challenge to a refusal to grant a patent, the European Commission on Human Rights concluded that Art.1 of Protocol No.1 applied only to existing possessions and did not guarantee any right to acquire property.[76]

---

[71] [2000] E.M.L.R. 587.

[72] [2003] R.P.C. 319.

[73] [2003] R.P.C. 319, at para.22.

[74] At paras 38–44, noting that the same issues had been addressed to the ECJ and the A.G. had expressed the view that they "do not really appear to be cogent", quoted by Pumfrey J. at para.42.

[75] (1996) 21 E.H.R.R. 409.

[76] Citing *Van der Mussele* (1984) 6 E.H.R.R. 163, para.48.

APPENDICES

PART I

KEY STATUTES

APPENDIX 1

Trade Marks Act 1994

1994 CHAPTER 26

An Act to make new provision for registered trade marks, implementing Council **A1–001**
*Directive No. 89/104/EEC of 21st December 1988 to approximate the laws of
the Member States relating to trade marks; to make provision in connection with
Council Regulation (EC) No. 40/94 of 20th December 1993 on the Community
trade mark; to give effect to the Madrid Protocol Relating to the International
Registration of Marks of 27th June 1989, and to certain provisions of the Paris
Convention for the Protection of Industrial Property of 20th March 1883, as
revised and amended; and for connected purposes.*

[21st July 1994]

ARRANGEMENT OF SECTIONS
Part I
REGISTERED TRADE MARKS
Introductory

PART I

REGISTERED TRADE MARKS

Introductory

Trade marks

A1–002   **1.**—(1) In this Act a "trade mark" means any sign capable of being represented graphically which is capable of distinguishing goods or services of one undertaking from those of other undertakings.

A trade mark may, in particular, consist of words (including personal names), designs, letters, numerals or the shape of goods or their packaging.

(2) References in this Act to a trade mark include, unless the context otherwise requires, references to a collective mark (see section 49) or certification mark (see section 50).

Registered trade marks

2.—(1) A registered trade mark is a property right obtained by the registration   **A1–003**
of the trade mark under this Act and the proprietor of a registered trade mark has
the rights and remedies provided by this Act.

(2) No proceedings lie to prevent or recover damages for the infringement of
an unregistered trade mark as such; but nothing in this Act affects the law relating
to passing off.

Grounds for refusal of registration

Absolute grounds for refusal of registration

3.—(1) The following shall not be registered—   **A1–004**
  (a) signs which do not satisfy the requirements of section 1(1),
  (b) trade marks which are devoid of any distinctive character,
  (c) trade marks which consist exclusively of signs or indications which may
      serve, in trade, to designate the kind, quality, quantity, intended purpose,
      value, geographical origin, the time of production of goods or of render-
      ing of services, or other characteristics of goods or services,
  (d) trade marks which consist exclusively of signs or indications which
      have become customary in the current language or in the *bona fide* and
      established practices of the trade:
Provided that, a trade mark shall not be refused registration by virtue of
paragraph (b), (c) or (d) above if, before the date of application for registration, it
has in fact acquired a distinctive character as a result of the use made of it.

(2) A sign shall not be registered as a trade mark if it consists exclusively of—
  (a) the shape which results from the nature of the goods themselves,
  (b) the shape of goods which is necessary to obtain a technical result, or
  (c) the shape which gives substantial value to the goods.

(3) A trade mark shall not be registered if it is—
  (a) contrary to public policy or to accepted principles of morality, or
  (b) of such a nature as to deceive the public (for instance as to the nature,
      quality or geographical origin of the goods or service).

(4) A trade mark shall not be registered if or to the extent that its use is
prohibited in the United Kingdom by any enactment or rule of law or by any provision of Community law.

(5) A trade mark shall not be registered in the cases specified, or referred to, in
section 4 (specially protected emblems).

(6) A trade mark shall not be registered if or to the extent that the application
is made in bad faith.

Specially protected emblems

4.—(1) A trade mark which consists of or contains—   **A1–005**
  (a) the Royal arms, or any of the principal armorial bearings of the Royal
      arms, or any insignia or device so nearly resembling the Royal arms or
      any such armorial bearing as to be likely to be mistaken for them or it,
  (b) a representation of the Royal crown or any of the Royal flags,
  (c) a representation of Her Majesty or any member of the Royal family, or
      any colourable imitation thereof, or
  (d) words, letters or devices likely to lead persons to think that the applicant
      either has or recently has had Royal patronage or authorisation,

shall not be registered unless it appears to the registrar that consent has been given by or on behalf of Her Majesty or, as the case may be, the relevant member of the Royal family.

(2) A trade mark which consists of or contains a representation of—

  (a) the national flag of the United Kingdom (commonly known as the Union Jack), or

  (b) the flag of England, Wales, Scotland, Northern Ireland or the Isle of Man,

shall not be registered if it appears to the registrar that the use of the trade mark would be misleading or grossly offensive.

Provision may be made by rules identifying the flags to which paragraph (b) applies.

(3) A trade mark shall not be registered in the cases specified in—

  section 57 (national emblems, &c. of Convention countries), or
  section 58 (emblems, &c. of certain international organisations).

(4) Provision may be made by rules prohibiting in such cases as may be prescribed the registration of a trade mark which consists of or contains—

  (a) arms to which a person is entitled by virtue of a grant of arms by the Crown, or

  (b) insignia so nearly resembling such arms as to be likely to be mistaken for them,

unless it appears to the registrar that consent has been given by or behalf of that person.

Where such a mark is registered, nothing in this Act shall be construed as authorising its use in any way contrary to the laws of arms.

(5) A trade mark which consists of or contains a controlled representation within the meaning of the Olympic Symbol etc. (Protection) Act 1995 shall not be registered unless it appears to the registrar—

  (a) that the application is made by the person for the time being appointed under section 1(2) of the Olympic Symbol etc. (Protection) Act 1995 (power of Secretary of State to appoint a person as the proprietor of the Olympics association right), or

  (b) that consent has been given by or on behalf of the person mentioned in paragraph (a) above.

Amendment

Subs.(5) was added by the Olympic Symbol etc. (Protection) Act 1995, s.13.

Relative grounds for refusal of registration

A1–006   **5.**—(1) A trade mark shall not be registered if it is identical with an earlier trade mark and the goods or services for which the trade mark is applied for are identical with the goods or services for which the earlier trade mark is protected.

(2) A trade mark shall not be registered if because—

  (a) it is identical with an earlier trade mark and is to be registered for goods or services similar to those for which the earlier trade mark is protected, or

  (b) it is similar to an earlier trade mark and is to be registered for goods or services identical with or similar to those for which the earlier trade mark is protected,

there exists a likelihood of confusion on the part of the public, which includes the likelihood of association with the earlier trade mark.

(3) A trade mark which—

    (a) is identical with or similar to an earlier trade mark,

    (b) [...]

shall not be registered if, or to the extent that, the earlier trade mark has a reputa-tion in the United Kingdom (or, in the case of a Community trade mark **or international trade mark (EC)**, in the European Community) and the use of the later mark without due cause would take unfair advantage of, or be detrimental to, the distinctive character or the repute of the earlier trade mark.

(4) A trade mark shall not be registered if, or to the extent that, its use in the United Kingdom is liable to be prevented—

    (a) by virtue of any rule of law (in particular, the law of passing off) protect-ing an unregistered trade mark or other sign used in the course of trade, or

    (b) by virtue of an earlier right other than those referred to in subsections (1) to (3) or paragraph (a) above, in particular by virtue of the law of copy-right, design right or registered designs.

A person thus entitled to prevent the use of a trade mark is referred to in this Act as the proprietor of an "earlier right" in relation to the trade mark.

(5) Nothing in this section prevents the registration of a trade mark where the proprietor of the earlier trade mark or other earlier right consents to the registration.

Amendment

Words omitted in subs.(3) were repealed by the Trade Marks (Proof of Use, etc.) Regulations (SI 2004/946), reg.7(2)(b) and words inserted by the Trade Marks (International Registrations Designating the European Community, etc.) Regulations (SI 2004/2332), reg.3.

Meaning of "earlier trade mark"

6.—(1) In this Act an "earlier trade mark" means—   A1–007

    (a) a registered trade mark, international trade mark (UK), Community trade mark **or international trade mark (EC)** which has a date of application for registration earlier than that of the trade mark in question, taking ac-count (where appropriate) of the priorities claimed in respect of the trade marks,

    (b) a Community trade mark or international trade mark (EC) which has a valid claim to seniority from an earlier registered trade mark or international trade mark (UK),

    (ba) a registered trade mark or international trade mark (UK) which—

        (i) has been converted from a Community trade mark or interna-tional trade mark (EC) which itself had a valid claim to seniority within paragraph (b) from an earlier trade mark, and

        (ii) accordingly has the same claim to seniority, or

    (c) a trade mark which, at the date of application for registration of the trade mark in question or (where appropriate) of the priority, claimed in re-spect of the application, was entitled to protection under the Paris Convention **or the WTO agreement** as awell known trade mark.

(2) References in this Act to an earlier trade mark include a trade mark in re-spect of which an application for registration has been made and which, if registered, would be an earlier trade mark by virtue of subsection (1)(a) or (b), subject to its being so registered.

(3) A trade mark within subsection (1)(a) or (b) whose registration expires shall continue to be taken into account in determining the registrability of a later mark for a period of one year after the expiry unless the registrar is satisfied that there was no *bona fide* use of the mark during the two years immediately preceding the expiry.

Amendments

The reference to the WTO Agreement was added by the Patents and Trade Marks (World Trade Organisation) Regulations SI 1999/1899, reg.13.

Words inserted in subs.(1)(a)and subs.(1)(b)–(ba) substituted for subs.(1)(b) by the Trade Marks (International Registrations Designating the European Community, etc.) Regulations (SI 2004/2332), reg.4(b).

Raising of relative grounds in opposition proceedings in case of non-use

A1–008   **6A.—(1) This section applies where—**
  (a) an application for registration of a trade mark has been published,
  (b) there is an earlier trade mark in relation to which the conditions set out in section 5(1), (2) or (3) obtain, and
  (c) the registration procedure for the earlier trade mark was completed before the start of the period of five years ending with the date of publication.
(2) In opposition proceedings, the registrar shall not refuse to register the trade mark by reason of the earlier trade mark unless the use conditions are met.
  (3) The use conditions are met if—
  (a) within the period of five years ending with the date of publication of the application the earlier trade mark has been put to genuine use in the United Kingdom by the proprietor or with his consent in relation to the goods or services for which it is registered, or
  (b) the earlier trade mark has not been so used, but there are proper reasons for non-use.
  (4) For these purposes—
  (a) use of a trade mark includes use in a form differing in elements which do not alter the distinctive character of the mark in the form in which it was registered, and
  (b) use in the United Kingdom includes affixing the trade mark to goods or to the packaging of goods in the United Kingdom solely for export purposes.
(5) In relation to a Community trade mark, any reference in subsection (3) or (4) to the United Kingdom shall be construed as a reference to the European Community.
(6) Where an earlier trade mark satisfies the use conditions in respect of some only of the goods or services for which it is registered, it shall be treated for the purposes of this section as if it were registered only in respect of those goods or services.
  (7) Nothing in this section affects—
  (a) the refusal of registration on the grounds mentioned in section 3 (absolute grounds for refusal) or section 5(4) (relative grounds of refusal on the basis of an earlier right), or
  (b) the making of an application for a declaration of invalidity under section 47(2) (application on relative grounds where no consent to registration).

Amendment

Section 6A added by the Trade Marks (Proof of Use, etc.) Regulations (SI 2004/946), reg.4.

Raising of relative grounds in case of honest concurrent use.

7.—(1) This section applies where on an application for the registration of a   **A1–009**
trade mark it appears to the registrar—

(a) that there is an earlier trade mark in relation to which the conditions set out in section 5(1), (2) or (3) obtain, or

(b) that there is an earlier right in relation to which the condition set out in section 5(4) is satisfied,

but the applicant shows to the satisfaction of the registrar that there has been honest concurrent use of the trade mark for which registration is sought.

(2) In that case the registrar shall not refuse the application by reason of the earlier trade mark or other earlier right unless objection on that ground is raised in opposition proceedings by the proprietor of that earlier trade mark or other earlier right.

(3) For the purposes of this section "honest concurrent use" means such use in the United Kingdom, by the applicant or with his consent, as would formerly have amounted to honest concurrent use for the purposes of section 12(2) of the Trade Marks Act 1938.

(4) Nothing in this section affects—

(a) the refusal of registration on the grounds mentioned in section 3 (absolute grounds for refusal), or

(b) the making of an application for a declaration of invalidity under section 47(2) (application on relative grounds where no consent to registration).

(5) This section does not apply when there is an order in force under section 8 below.

Power to require that relative grounds be raised in opposition proceedings

8.—(1) The Secretary of State may by order provide that in any case a trade   **A1–010**
mark shall not be refused registration on a ground mentioned in section 5 (relative grounds for refusal) unless objection on that ground is raised in opposition proceedings by the proprietor of the earlier trade mark or other earlier right.

(2) The order may make such consequential provision as appears to the Secretary of State appropriate—

(a) with respect to the carrying out by the registrar of searches of earlier trade marks, and

(b) as to the persons by whom an application for a declaration of invalidity may be made on the grounds specified in section 47(2) (relative grounds).

(3) An order making such provision as is mentioned in subsection (2)(a) may direct that so much of section 37 (examination of application) as requires a search to be carried out shall cease to have effect.

(4) An order making such provision as is mentioned in subsection (2)(b) may provide that so much of section 47(3) as provides that any person may make an application for a declaration of invalidity shall have effect subject to the provisions of the order.

(5) An order under this section shall be made by statutory instrument, and no

order shall be made unless a draft of it has been laid before and approved by a resolution of each House of Parliament.

No such draft of an order making such provision as is mentioned in subsection (1) shall be laid before Parliament until after the end of the period of ten years beginning with the day on which applications for Community trade marks may first be filed in pursuance of the Community Trade Mark Regulation.

(6) An order under this section may contain such transitional provisions as appear to the Secretary of State to be appropriate.

Effects of registered trade mark

Rights conferred by registered trade mark

A1–011 9.—(1) The proprietor of a registered trade mark has exclusive rights in the trade mark which are infringed by use of the trade mark in the United Kingdom without his consent.

The acts amounting to infringement, if done without the consent of the proprietor, are specified in section 10.

(2) References in this Act to the infringement of a registered trade mark are to any such infringement of the rights of the proprietor.

(3) The rights of the proprietor have effect from the date of registration (which in accordance with section 40(3) is the date of filing of the application for registration):

Provided that—

(a) no infringement proceedings may be begun before the date on which the trade mark is in fact registered; and

(b) no offence under section 92 (unauthorised use of trade mark, &c. in relation to goods) is committed by anything done before the date of publication of the registration.

Infringement of registered trade mark

A1–012 10.—(1) A person infringes a registered trade mark if he uses in the course of trade a sign which is identical with the trade mark in relation to goods or services which are identical with those for which it is registered.

(2) A person infringes a registered trade mark if he uses in the course of trade a sign where because—

(a) the sign is identical with the trade mark and is used in relation to goods or services similar to those for which the trade mark is registered, or

(b) the sign is similar to the trade mark and is used in relation to goods or services identical with or similar to those for which the trade mark is registered,

there exists a likelihood of confusion on the part of the public, which includes the likelihood of association with the trade mark.

(3) A person infringes a registered trade mark if he uses in the course of trade, **in relation to goods or services**, a sign which—

(a) is identical with or similar to the trade mark,

(b) [...]

where the trade mark has a reputation in the United Kingdom and the use of the sign, being without due cause, takes unfair advantage of, or is detrimental to, the distinctive character or the repute of the trade mark.

(4) For the purposes of this section a person uses a sign if, in particular, he—

(a) affixes it to goods or the packaging thereof;

(b) offers or exposes goods for sale, puts them on the market or stocks them for those purposes under the sign, or offers or supplies services under the sign;

(c) imports or exports goods under the sign; or

(d) uses the sign on business papers or in advertising.

(5) A person who applies a registered trade mark to material intended to be used for labelling or packaging goods, as a business paper, or for advertising goods or services, shall be treated as a party to any use of the material which infringes the registered trade mark if when he applied the mark he knew or had reason to believe that the application of the mark was not duly authorised by the proprietor or a licensee.

(6) Nothing in the preceding provisions of this section shall be construed as preventing the use of a registered trade mark by any person for the purpose of identifying goods or services as those of the proprietor or a licensee.

But any such use otherwise than in accordance with honest practices in industrial or commercial matters shall be treated as infringing the registered trade mark if the use without due cause takes unfair advantage of, or is detrimental to, the distinctive character or repute of the trade mark.

Amendment

Words inserted in subs.(3) and words omitted were repealed by the Trade Marks (Proof of Use, etc.) Regulations SI (2004/946), reg.7.

Limits on effect of registered trade mark

11.—(1) A registered trade mark is not infringed by the use of another **A1–013** registered trade mark in relation to goods or services for which the latter is registered (but see section 47(6) (effect of declaration of invalidity of registration)).

(2) A registered trade mark is not infringed by—

(a) the use by a person of his own name or address,

(b) the use of indications concerning the kind, quality, quantity, intended purpose, value, geographical origin, the time of production of goods or of rendering of services, or other characteristics of goods or services, or

(c) the use of the trade mark where it is necessary to indicate the intended purpose of a product or service (in particular, as accessories or spare parts),

provided the use is in accordance with honest practices in industrial or commercial matters.

(3) A registered trade mark is not infringed by the use in the course of trade in a particular locality of an earlier right which applies only in that locality.

For this purpose an "earlier right" means an unregistered trade mark or other sign continuously used in relation to goods or services by a person or a predecessor in title of his from a date prior to whichever is the earlier of—

(a) the use of the first-mentioned trade mark in relation to those goods or services by the proprietor or a predecessor in title of his, or

(b) the registration of the first-mentioned trade mark in respect of those goods or services in the name of the proprietor or a predecessor in title of his;

and an earlier right shall be regarded as applying in a locality if, or to the extent that, its use in that locality is protected by virtue of any rule of law (in particular, the law of passing off).

Exhaustion of rights conferred by registered trade mark

A1–014   12.—(1) A registered trade mark is not infringed by the use of the trade mark in relation to goods which have been put on the market in the European Economic Area under that trade mark by the proprietor or with his consent.

(2) Subsection (1) does not apply where there exist legitimate reasons for the proprietor to oppose further dealings in the goods (in particular, where the condition of the goods has been changed or impaired after they have been put on the market).

Registration subject to disclaimer or limitation

A1–015   13.—(1) An applicant for registration of a trade mark, or the proprietor of a registered trade mark, may—

　　(a) disclaim any right to the exclusive use of any specified element of the trade mark, or
　　(b) agree that the rights conferred by the registration shall be subject to a specified territorial or other limitation;

and where the registration of a trade mark is subject to a disclaimer or limitation, the rights conferred by section 9 (rights conferred by registered trade mark) are restricted accordingly.

(2) Provision shall be made by rules as to the publication and entry in the register of a disclaimer or limitation.

Infringement proceedings

Action for infringement

A1–016   14.—(1) An infringement of a registered trade mark is actionable by the proprietor of the trade mark.

(2) In an action for infringement all such relief by way of damages, injunctions, accounts or otherwise is available to him as is available in respect of the infringement of any other property right.

Order for erasure &c. of offending sign

A1–017   15.—(1) Where a person is found to have infringed a registered trade mark, the court may make an order requiring him—

　　(a) to cause the offending sign to be erased, removed or obliterated from any infringing goods, material or articles in his possession, custody or control, or
　　(b) if it is not reasonably practicable for the offending sign to be erased, removed or obliterated, to secure the destruction of the infringing goods, material or articles in question.

(2) If an order under subsection (1) is not complied with, or it appears to the court likely that such an order would not be complied with, the court may order that the infringing goods, material or articles be delivered to such person as the court may direct for erasure, removal or obliteration of the sign, or for destruction, as the case may be.

Order for delivery up of infringing goods, material or articles

A1–018   16.—(1) The proprietor of a registered trade mark may apply to the court for an order for the delivery up to him, or such other person as the court may direct, of any infringing goods, material or articles which a person has in his possession, custody or control in the course of a business.

(2) An application shall not be made after the end of the period specified in section 18 (period after which remedy of delivery up not available); and no order shall be made unless the court also makes, or it appears to the court that there are grounds for making, an order under section 19 (order as to disposal of infringing goods, &c.).

(3) A person to whom any infringing goods, material or articles are delivered up in pursuance of an order under this section shall, if an order under section 19 is not made, retain them pending the making of an order, or the decision not to make an order, under that section.

(4) Nothing in this section affects any other power of the court.

Meaning of "infringing goods, material or articles"

17.—(1) In this Act the expressions "infringing goods", "infringing material"   **A1–019**
and "infringing articles" shall be construed as follows.

(2) Goods are "infringing goods", in relation to a registered trade mark, if they or their packaging bear a sign identical or similar to that mark and—

- (a) the application of the sign to the goods or their packaging was an infringement of the registered trade mark, or
- (b) the goods are proposed to be imported into the United Kingdom and the application of the sign in the United Kingdom to them or their packaging would be an infringement of the registered trade mark, or
- (c) the sign has otherwise been used in relation to the goods in such a way as to infringe the registered trade mark.

(3) Nothing in subsection (2) shall be construed as affecting the importation of goods which may lawfully be imported into the United Kingdom by virtue of an enforceable Community right.

(4) Material is "infringing material", in relation to a registered trade mark if it bears a sign identical or similar to that mark and either—

- (a) it is used for labelling or packaging goods, as a business paper, or for advertising goods or services, in such a way as to infringe the registered trade mark, or
- (b) it is intended to be so used and such use would infringe the registered trade mark.

(5) "Infringing articles", in relation to a registered trade mark, means articles—

- (a) which are specifically designed or adapted for making copies of a sign identical or similar to that mark, and
- (b) which a person has in his possession, custody or control, knowing or having reason to believe that they have been or are to be used to produce infringing goods or material.

Period after which remedy of delivery up not available

18.—(1) An application for an order under section 16 (order for delivery up of   **A1–020**
infringing goods, material or articles) may not be made after the end of the period of six years from—

- (a) in the case of infringing goods, the date on which the trade mark was applied to the goods or their packaging,

(b) in the case of infringing material, the date on which the trade mark was applied to the material, or

(c) in the case of infringing articles, the date on which they were made, except as mentioned in the following provisions.

(2) If during the whole or part of that period the proprietor of the registered trade mark—

(a) is under a disability, or

(b) is prevented by fraud or concealment from discovering the facts entitling him to apply for an order,

an application may be made at any time before the end of the period of six years from the date on which he ceased to be under a disability or, as the case may be, could with reasonable diligence have discovered those facts.

(3) In subsection (2) "disability"—

(a) in England and Wales, has the same meaning as in the Limitation Act 1980;

(b) in Scotland, means legal disability within the meaning of the Prescription and Limitation (Scotland) Act 1973;

(c) in Northern Ireland, has the same meaning as in the Limitation (Northern Ireland) Order 1989.

Order as to disposal of infringing goods, material or articles

A1–021   **19.**—(1) Where infringing goods, material or articles have been delivered up in pursuance of an order under section 16, an application may be made to the court—

(a) for an order that they be destroyed or forfeited to such person as the court may think fit, or

(b) for a decision that no such order should be made.

(2) In considering what order (if any) should be made, the court shall consider whether other remedies available in an action for infringement of the registered trade mark would be adequate to compensate the proprietor and any licensee and protect their interests.

(3) Provision shall be made by rules of court as to the service of notice on persons having an interest in the goods, material or articles, and any such person is entitled—

(a) to appear in proceedings for an order under this section, whether or not he was served with notice, and

(b) to appeal against any order made, whether or not he appeared;

and an order shall not take effect until the end of the period within which notice of an appeal may be given or, if before the end of that period notice of appeal is duly given, until the final determination or abandonment of the proceedings on the appeal.

(4) Where there is more than one person interested in the goods, material or articles, the court shall make such order as it thinks just.

(5) If the court decides that no order should be made under this section, the person in whose possession, custody or control the goods, material or articles were before being delivered up is entitled to their return.

(6) References in this section to a person having an interest in goods, material or articles include any person in whose favour an order could be made under this section or under section 114, 204 or 231 of the Copyright, Designs and Patents Act 1988 (which make similar provision in relation to infringement of copyright, rights in performances and design right).

Jurisdiction of sheriff court or county court in Northern Ireland

20. Proceedings for an order under section 16 (order for delivery up of infring-   **A1–022**
ing goods, material or articles) or section 19 (order as to disposal of infringing
goods, &c.) may be brought—

   (a) in the sheriff court in Scotland, or
   (b) in a county court in Northern Ireland.

This does not affect the jurisdiction of the Court of Session or the High Court
in Northern Ireland.

Remedy for groundless threats of infringement proceedings

21.—(1) Where a person threatens another with proceedings for infringement   **A1–023**
of a registered trade mark other than—

   (a) the application of the mark to goods or their packaging,
   (b) the importation of goods to which, or to the packaging of which, the
       mark has been applied, or
   (c) the supply of services under the mark,

any person aggrieved may bring proceedings for relief under this section.

   (2) The relief which may be applied for is any of the following—

   (a) a declaration that the threats are unjustifiable,
   (b) an injunction against the continuance of the threats,
   (c) damages in respect of any loss he has sustained by the threats;

and the plaintiff is entitled to such relief unless the defendant shows that the acts
in respect of which proceedings were threatened constitute (or if done would
constitute) an infringement of the registered trade mark concerned.

   (3) If that is shown by the defendant, the plaintiff is nevertheless entitled to
relief if he shows that the registration of the trade mark is invalid or liable to be
revoked in a relevant respect.

   (4) The mere notification that a trade mark is registered, or that an application
for registration has been made, does not constitute a threat of proceedings for the
purposes of this section.

Registered trade mark as object of property

Nature of registered trade mark

22. A registered trade mark is personal property (in Scotland, incorporeal   **A1–024**
moveable property).

Co-ownership of registered trade mark

23.—(1) Where a registered trade mark is granted to two or more persons   **A1–025**
jointly, each of them is entitled, subject to any agreement to the contrary, to an
equal undivided share in the registered trade mark.

   (2) The following provisions apply where two or more persons are co-
proprietors of a registered trade mark, by virtue of subsection (1) or otherwise.

   (3) Subject to any agreement to the contrary, each co-proprietor is entitled, by
himself or his agents, to do for his own benefit and without the consent of or the
need to account to the other or others, any act which would otherwise amount to
an infringement of the registered trade mark.

   (4) One co-proprietor may not without the consent of the other or others—

> (a) grant a licence to use the registered trade mark, or
> (b) assign or charge his share in the registered trade mark (or, in Scotland, cause or permit security to be granted over it).

(5) Infringement proceedings may be brought by any co-proprietor, but he may not, without the leave of the court, proceed with the action unless the other, or each of the others, is either joined as a plaintiff or added as a defendant.

A co-proprietor who is thus added as a defendant shall not be made liable for any costs in the action unless he takes part in the proceedings.

Nothing in this subsection affects the granting of interlocutory relief on the application of a single co-proprietor.

(6) Nothing in this section affects the mutual rights and obligations of trustees or personal representatives, or their rights and obligations as such.

Assignment, &c. of registered trade mark

A1–026   **24.**—(1) A registered trade mark is transmissible by assignment, testamentary disposition or operation of law in the same way as other personal or moveable property.

It is so transmissible either in connection with the goodwill of a business or independently.

(2) An assignment or other transmission of a registered trade mark may be partial, that is, limited so as to apply—

> (a) in relation to some but not all of the goods or services for which the trade mark is registered, or
> (b) in relation to use of the trade mark in a particular manner or a particular locality.

(3) An assignment of a registered trade mark, or an assent relating to a registered trade mark, is not effective unless it is in writing signed by or on behalf of the assignor or, as the case may be, a personal representative.

Except in Scotland, this requirement may be satisfied in a case where the assignor or personal representative is a body corporate by the affixing of its seal.

(4) The above provisions apply to assignment by way of security as in relation to any other assignment.

(5) A registered trade mark may be the subject of a charge (in Scotland, security) in the same way as other personal or moveable property.

(6) Nothing in this Act shall be construed as affecting the assignment or other transmission of an unregistered trade mark as part of the goodwill of a business.

Registration of transactions affecting registered trade mark

A1–027   **25.**—(1) On application being made to the registrar by—

> (a) a person claiming to be entitled to an interest in or under a registered trade mark by virtue of a registrable transaction, or
> (b) any other person claiming to be affected by such a transaction,

the prescribed particulars of the transaction shall be entered in the register.

(2) The following are registrable transactions—

> (a) an assignment of a registered trade mark or any right in it;
> (b) the grant of a licence under a registered trade mark;
> (c) the granting of any security interest (whether fixed or floating) over a registered trade mark or any right in or under it;
> (d) the making by personal representatives of an assent in relation to a registered trade mark or any right in or under it;

(e) an order of a court or other competent authority transferring a registered trade mark or any right in or under it.

(3) Until an application has been made for registration of the prescribed particulars of a registrable transaction—

(a) the transaction is ineffective as against a person acquiring a conflicting interest in or under the registered trade mark in ignorance of it, and

(b) a person claiming to be a licensee by virtue of the transaction does not have the protection of section 30 or 31 (rights and remedies of licensee in relation to infringement).

(4) Where a person becomes the proprietor or a licensee of a registered trade mark by virtue of a registrable transaction, then unless—

(a) an application for registration of the prescribed particulars of the transaction is made before the end of the period of six months beginning with its date, or

(b) the court is satisfied that it was not practicable for such an application to be made before the end of that period and that an application was made as soon as practicable thereafter,

he is not entitled to damages or an account of profits in respect of any infringement of the registered trade mark occurring after the date of the transaction and before the prescribed particulars of the transaction are registered.

(5) Provision may be made by rules as to—

(a) the amendment of registered particulars relating to a licence so as to reflect any alteration of the terms of the licence, and

(b) the removal of such particulars from the register—

(i) where it appears from the registered particulars that the licence was granted for a fixed period and that period has expired, or

(ii) where no such period is indicated and, after such period as may be prescribed, the registrar has notified the parties of his intention to remove the particulars from the register.

(6) Provision may also be made by rules as to the amendment or removal from the register of particulars relating to a security interest on the application of, or with the consent of, the person entitled to the benefit of that interest.

Trusts and equities

26.—(1) No notice of any trust (express, implied or constructive) shall be entered in the register; and the registrar shall not be affected by any such notice.   **A1–028**

(2) Subject to the provisions of this Act, equities (in Scotland, rights) in respect of a registered trade mark may be enforced in like manner as in respect of other personal or moveable property.

Application for registration of trade mark as an object of property

27.—(1) The provisions of sections 22 to 26 (which relate to a registered trade mark as an object of property) apply, with the necessary modifications, in relation to an application for the registration of a trade mark as in relation to a registered trade mark.   **A1–029**

(2) In section 23 (co-ownership of registered trade mark) as it applies in relation to an application for registration the reference in subsection (1) to the granting of the registration shall be construed as a reference to the making of the application.

(3) In section 25 (registration of transactions affecting registered trade marks)

as it applies in relation to a transaction affecting an application for the registration of a trade mark, the references to the entry of particulars in the register, and to the making of an application to register particulars, shall be construed as references to the giving of notice to the registrar of those particulars.

Licensing

Licensing of registered trade mark

A1–030   **28.**—(1) A licence to use a registered trade mark may be general or limited.
A limited licence may, in particular, apply—
   (a) in relation to some but not all of the goods or services for which the trade mark is registered, or
   (b) in relation to use of the trade mark in a particular manner or a particular locality.
(2) A licence is not effective unless it is in writing signed by or on behalf of the grantor.
Except in Scotland, this requirement may be satisfied in a case where the grantor is a body corporate by the affixing of its seal.
(3) Unless the licence provides otherwise, it is binding on a successor in title to the grantor's interest.
References in this Act to doing anything with, or without, the consent of the proprietor of a registered trade mark shall be construed accordingly.
(4) Where the licence so provides, a sub-licence may be granted by the licensee; and references in this Act to a licence or licensee include a sub-licence or sub-licensee.

Exclusive licences

A1–031   **29.**—(1) In this Act an "exclusive licence" means a licence (whether general or limited) authorising the licensee to the exclusion of all other persons, including the person granting the licence, to use a registered trade mark in the manner authorised by the licence.
The expression "exclusive licensee" shall be construed accordingly.
(2) An exclusive licensee has the same rights against a successor in title who is bound by the licence as he has against the person granting the licence.

General provisions as to rights of licensees in case of infringement

A1–032   **30.**—(1) This section has effect with respect to the rights of a licensee in relation to infringement of a registered trade mark.
The provisions of this section do not apply where or to the extent that, by virtue of section 31(1) below (exclusive licensee having rights and remedies of assignee), the licensee has a right to bring proceedings in his own name.
(2) A licensee is entitled, unless his licence, or any licence through which his interest is derived, provides otherwise, to call on the proprietor of the registered trade mark to take infringement proceedings in respect of any matter which affects his interests.
(3) If the proprietor—
   (a) refuses to do so, or
   (b) fails to do so within two months after being called upon,

the licensee may bring the proceedings in his own name as if he were the proprietor.

(4) Where infringement proceedings are brought by a licensee by virtue of this section, the licensee may not, without the leave of the court, proceed with the action unless the proprietor is either joined as a plaintiff or added as a defendant.

This does not affect the granting of interlocutory relief on an application by a licensee alone.

(5) A proprietor who is added as a defendant as mentioned in subsection (4) shall not be made liable for any costs in the action unless he takes part in the proceedings.

(6) In infringement proceedings brought by the proprietor of a registered trade mark any loss suffered or likely to be suffered by licensees shall be taken into account; and the court may give such directions as it thinks fit as to the extent to which the plaintiff is to hold the proceeds of any pecuniary remedy on behalf of licensees.

(7) The provisions of this section apply in relation to an exclusive licensee if or to the extent that he has, by virtue of section 31(1), the rights and remedies of an assignee as if he were the proprietor of the registered trade mark.

Exclusive licensee having rights and remedies of assignee

31.—(1) An exclusive licence may provide that the licensee shall have, to such **A1–033** extent as may be provided by the licence, the same rights and remedies in respect of matters occurring after the grant of the licence as if the licence had been an assignment.

Where or to the extent that such provision is made, the licensee is entitled, subject to the provisions of the licence and to the following provisions of this section, to bring infringement proceedings, against any person other than the proprietor, in his own name.

(2) Any such rights and remedies of an exclusive licensee are concurrent with those of the proprietor of the registered trade mark; and references to the proprietor of a registered trade mark in the provisions of this Act relating to infringement shall be construed accordingly.

(3) In an action brought by an exclusive licensee by virtue of this section a defendant may avail himself of any defence which would have been available to him if the action had been brought by the proprietor of the registered trade mark.

(4) Where proceedings for infringement of a registered trade mark brought by the proprietor or an exclusive licensee relate wholly or partly to an infringement in respect of which they have concurrent rights of action, the proprietor or, as the case may be, the exclusive licensee may not, without the leave of the court, proceed with the action unless the other is either joined as a plaintiff or added as a defendant.

This does not affect the granting of interlocutory relief on an application by a proprietor or exclusive licensee alone.

(5) A person who is added as a defendant as mentioned in subsection (4) shall not be made liable for any costs in the action unless he takes part in the proceedings.

(6) Where an action for infringement of a registered trade mark is brought which relates wholly or partly to an infringement in respect of which the proprietor and an exclusive licensee have or had concurrent rights of action—

(a) the court shall in assessing damages take into account—
    (i) the terms of the licence, and
    (ii) any pecuniary remedy already awarded or available to either of them in respect of the infringement;

(b) no account of profits shall be directed if an award of damages has been made, or an account of profits has been directed, in favour of the other of them in respect of the infringement; and

(c) the court shall if an account of profits is directed apportion the profits between them as the court considers just, subject to any agreement between them.

The provisions of this subsection apply whether or not the proprietor and the exclusive licensee are both parties to the action; and if they are not both parties the court may give such directions as it thinks fit as to the extent to which the party to the proceedings is to hold the proceeds of any pecuniary remedy on behalf of the other.

(7) The proprietor of a registered trade mark shall notify any exclusive licensee who has a concurrent right of action before applying for an order under section 16 (order for delivery up); and the court may on the application of the licensee make such order under that section as it thinks fit having regard to the terms of the licence.

(8) The provisions of subsections (4) to (7) above have effect subject to any agreement to the contrary between the exclusive licensee and the proprietor.

Application for registered trade mark

Application for registration

A1–034   **32.**—(1) An application for registration of a trade mark shall be made to the registrar.

(2) The application shall contain—
    (a) a request for registration of a trade mark,
    (b) the name and address of the applicant,
    (c) a statement of the goods or services in relation to which it is sought to register the trade mark, and
    (d) a representation of the trade mark.

(3) The application shall state that the trade mark is being used, by the applicant or with his consent, in relation to those goods or services, or that he has a *bona fide* intention that it should be so used.

(4) The application shall be subject to the payment of the application fee and such class fees as may be appropriate.

Date of filing

A1–035   **33.**—(1) The date of filing of an application for registration of a trade mark is the date on which documents containing everything required by section 32(2) are furnished to the registrar by the applicant.

If the documents are furnished on different days, the date of filing is the last of those days.

(2) References in this Act to the date of application for registration are to the date of filing of the application.

Classification of trade marks

34.—(1) Goods and services shall be classified for the purposes of the registra- **A1–036**
tion of trade marks according to a prescribed system of classification.

(2) Any question arising as to the class within which any goods or services
fall shall be determined by the registrar, whose decision shall be final.

Priority

Claim to priority of Convention application

35.—(1) A person who has duly filed an application for protection of a trade **A1–037**
mark in a Convention country (a "Convention application"), or his successor in
title, has a right to priority, for the purposes of registering the same trade mark
under this Act for some or all of the same goods or services, for a period of six
months from the date of filing of the first such application.

(2) If the application for registration under this Act is made within that six-
month period—

(a) the relevant date for the purposes of establishing which rights take precedence shall be the date of filing of the first Convention application,
and

(b) the registrability of the trade mark shall not be affected by any use of the
mark in the United Kingdom in the period between that date and the date
of the application under this Act.

(3) Any filing which in a Convention country is equivalent to a regular national
filing, under its domestic legislation or an international agreement, shall be treated
as giving rise to the right of priority.

A "regular national filing" means a filing which is adequate to establish the
date on which the application was filed in that country, whatever may be the
subsequent fate of the application.

(4) A subsequent application concerning the same subject as the first Convention application, filed in the same Convention country, shall be considered the
first Convention application (of which the filing date is the starting date of the period of priority), if at the time of the subsequent application—

(a) the previous application has been withdrawn, abandoned or refused,
without having been laid open to public inspection and without leaving
any rights outstanding, and

(b) it has not yet served as a basis for claiming a right of priority.

The previous application may not thereafter serve as a basis for claiming a
right of priority.

(5) Provision may be made by rules as to the manner of claiming a right to
priority on the basis of a Convention application.

(6) A right to priority arising as a result of a Convention application may be
assigned or otherwise transmitted, either with the application or independently.

The reference in subsection (1) to the applicant's "successor in title"shall be
construed accordingly.

Claim to priority from other relevant overseas application

36.—(1) Her Majesty may by Order in Council make provision for conferring **A1–038**
on a person who has duly filed an application for protection of a trade mark in—

(a) any of the Channel Islands or a colony, or

(b) a country or territory in relation to which Her Majesty's Government in the United Kingdom have entered into a treaty, convention, arrangement or engagement for the reciprocal protection of trade marks,

a right to priority, for the purpose of registering the same trade mark under this Act for some or all of the same goods or services, for a specified period from the date of filing of that application.

(2) An Order in Council under this section may make provision corresponding to that made by section 35 in relation to Convention countries or such other provision as appears to Her Majesty to be appropriate.

(3) A statutory instrument containing an Order in Council under this section shall be subject to annulment in pursuance of a resolution of either House of Parliament.

Registration procedure

Examination of application

A1–039   **37.**—(1) The registrar shall examine whether an application for registration of a trade mark satisfies the requirements of this Act (including any requirements imposed by rules).

(2) For that purpose he shall carry out a search, to such extent as he considers necessary, of earlier trade marks.

(3) If it appears to the registrar that the requirements for registration are not met, he shall inform the applicant and give him an opportunity, within such period as the registrar may specify, to make representations or to amend the application.

(4) If the applicant fails to satisfy the registrar that those requirements are met, or to amend the application so as to meet them, or fails to respond before the end of the specified period, the registrar shall refuse to accept the application.

(5) If it appears to the registrar that the requirements for registration are met, he shall accept the application.

Publication, opposition proceedings and observations

A1–040   **38.**—(1) When an application for registration has been accepted, the registrar shall cause the application to be published in the prescribed manner.

(2) Any person may, within the prescribed time from the date of the publication of the application, give notice to the registrar of opposition to the registration.

The notice shall be given in writing in the prescribed manner, and shall include a statement of the grounds of opposition.

(3) Where an application has been published, any person may, at any time before the registration of the trade mark, make observations in writing to the registrar as to whether the trade mark should be registered; and the registrar shall inform the applicant of any such observations.

A person who makes observations does not thereby become a party to the proceedings on the application.

Withdrawal, restriction or amendment of application

A1–041   **39.**—(1) The applicant may at any time withdraw his application or restrict the goods or services covered by the application.

If the application has been published, the withdrawal or restriction shall also be published.

(2) In other respects, an application may be amended, at the request of the applicant, only by correcting—

(a) the name or address of the applicant,

(b) errors of wording or of copying, or

(c) obvious mistakes,

and then only where the correction does not substantially affect the identity of the trade mark or extend the goods or services covered by the application.

(3) Provision shall be made by rules for the publication of any amendment which affects the representation of the trade mark, or the goods or services covered by the application, and for the making of objections by any person claiming to be affected by it.

Registration

40.—(1) Where an application has been accepted and—   **A1–042**

(a) no notice of opposition is given within the period referred to in section 38(2), or

(b) all opposition proceedings are withdrawn or decided in favour of the applicant,

the registrar shall register the trade mark, unless it appears to him having regard to matters coming to his notice **since the application was accepted that the registration requirements (other than those mentioned in section 5(1), (2) or (3)) were not met at that time.**

(2) A trade mark shall not be registered unless any fee prescribed for the registration is paid within the prescribed period.

If the fee is not paid within that period, the application shall be deemed to be withdrawn.

(3) A trade mark when registered shall be registered as of the date of filing of the application for registration; and that date shall be deemed for the purposes of this Act to be the date of registration.

(4) On the registration of a trade mark the registrar shall publish the registration in the prescribed manner and issue to the applicant a certificate of registration.

Amendment

Words substituted by the Trade Marks (Proof of Use, etc.) Regulations (SI 2004/946), reg.5.

Registration: supplementary provisions

41.—(1) Provision may be made by rules as to—   **A1–043**

(a) the division of an application for the registration of a trade mark into several applications;

(b) the merging of separate applications or registrations;

(c) the registration of a series of trade marks.

(2) A series of trade marks means a number of trade marks which resemble each other as to their material particulars and differ only as to matters of a non-distinctive character not substantially affecting the identity of the trade mark.

(3) Rules under this section may include provision as to—

(a) the circumstances in which, and conditions subject to which, division, merger or registration of a series is permitted, and

(b) the purposes for which an application to which the rules apply is to be treated as a single application and those for which it is to be treated as a number of separate applications.

Duration, renewal and alteration of registered trade mark

Duration of registration

A1–044   **42.**—(1) A trade mark shall be registered for a period of ten years from the date of registration.

(2) Registration may be renewed in accordance with section 43 for further periods of ten years.

Renewal of registration

A1–045   **43.**—(1) The registration of a trade mark may be renewed at the request of the proprietor, subject to payment of a renewal fee.

(2) Provision shall be made by rules for the registrar to inform the proprietor of a registered trade mark, before the expiry of the registration, of the date of expiry and the manner in which the registration may be renewed.

(3) A request for renewal must be made, and the renewal fee paid, before the expiry of the registration.

Failing this, the request may be made and the fee paid within such further period (of not less than six months) as may be prescribed, in which case an additional renewal fee must also be paid within that period.

(4) Renewal shall take effect from the expiry of the previous registration.

(5) If the registration is not renewed in accordance with the above provisions, the registrar shall remove the trade mark from the register.

Provision may be made by rules for the restoration of the registration of a trade mark which has been removed from the register, subject to such conditions (if any) as may be prescribed.

(6) The renewal or restoration of the registration of a trade mark shall be published in the prescribed manner.

Alteration of registered trade mark

A1–046   **44.**—(1) A registered trade mark shall not be altered in the register, during the period of registration or on renewal.

(2) Nevertheless, the registrar may, at the request of the proprietor, allow the alteration of a registered trade mark where the mark includes the proprietor's name or address and the alteration is limited to alteration of that name or address and does not substantially affect the identity of the mark.

(3) Provision shall be made by rules for the publication of any such alteration and the making of objections by any person claiming to be affected by it.

Surrender, revocation and invalidity

Surrender of registered trade mark

A1–047   **45.**—(1) A registered trade mark may be surrendered by the proprietor in respect of some or all of the goods or services for which it is registered.

(2) Provision may be made by rules—

(a) as to the manner and effect of a surrender, and

(b) for protecting the interests of other persons having a right in the registered trade mark.

Revocation of registration

46.—(1) The registration of a trade mark may be revoked on any of the follow-   **A1–048**
ing grounds—

(a) that within the period of five years following the date of completion of the registration procedure it has not been put to genuine use in the United Kingdom, by the proprietor or with his consent, in relation to the goods or services for which it is registered, and there are no proper reasons for non-use;

(b) that such use has been suspended for an uninterrupted period of five years, and there are no proper reasons for non-use;

(c) that, in consequence of acts or inactivity of the proprietor, it has become the common name in the trade for a product or service for which it is registered;

(d) that in consequence of the use made of it by the proprietor or with his consent in relation to the goods or services for which it is registered, it is liable to mislead the public, particularly as to the nature, quality or geographical origin of those goods or services.

(2) For the purposes of subsection (1) use of a trade mark includes use in a form differing in elements which do not alter the distinctive character of the mark in the form in which it was registered, and use in the United Kingdom includes affixing the trade mark to goods or to the packaging of goods in the United Kingdom solely for export purposes.

(3) The registration of a trade mark shall not be revoked on the ground mentioned in subsection (1)(a) or (b) if such use as is referred to in that paragraph is commenced or resumed after the expiry of the five year period and before the application for revocation is made:

Provided that, any such commencement or resumption of use after the expiry of the five year period but within the period of three months before the making of the application shall be disregarded unless preparations for the commencement or resumption began before the proprietor became aware that the application might be made.

(4) An application for revocation may be made by any person, and may be made either to the registrar or to the court, except that—

(a) if proceedings concerning the trade mark in question are pending in the court, the application must be made to the court; and

(b) if in any other case the application is made to the registrar, he may at any stage of the proceedings refer the application to the court.

(5) Where grounds for revocation exist in respect of only some of the goods or services for which the trade mark is registered, revocation shall relate to those goods or services only.

(6) Where the registration of a trade mark is revoked to any extent, the rights of the proprietor shall be deemed to have ceased to that extent as from—

(a) the date of the application for revocation, or

(b) if the registrar or court is satisfied that the grounds for revocation existed at an earlier date, that date.

Grounds for invalidity of registration

47.—(1) The registration of a trade mark may be declared invalid on the ground   **A1–049**

that the trade mark was registered in breach of section 3 or any of the provisions referred to in that section (absolute grounds for refusal of registration).

Where the trade mark was registered in breach of subsection (1)(b), (c) or (d) of that section, it shall not be declared invalid if, in consequence of the use which has been made of it, it has after registration acquired a distinctive character in relation to the goods or services for which it is registered.

(2) The registration of a trade mark may be declared invalid on the ground—

  (a) that there is an earlier trade mark in relation to which the conditions set out in section 5(1), (2) or (3) obtain, or

  (b) that there is an earlier right in relation to which the condition set out in section 5(4) is satisfied,

unless the proprietor of that earlier trade mark or other earlier right has consented to the registration.

(2A) But the registration of a trade mark may not be declared invalid on the ground that there is an earlier trade mark unless—

  (a) the registration procedure for the earlier trade mark was completed within the period of five years ending with the date of the application for the declaration,

  (b) the registration procedure for the earlier trade mark was not completed before that date, or

  (c) the use conditions are met.

(2B) The use conditions are met if—

  (a) within the period of five years ending with the date of the application for the declaration the earlier trade mark has been put to genuine use in the United Kingdom by the proprietor or with his consent in relation to the goods or services for which it is registered, or

  (b) it has not been so used, but there are proper reasons for non-use.

(2C) For these purposes—

  (a) use of a trade mark includes use in a form differing in elements which do not alter the distinctive character of the mark in the form in which it was registered, and

  (b) use in the United Kingdom includes affixing the trade mark to goods or to the packaging of goods in the United Kingdom solely for export purposes.

(2D) In relation to a Community trade mark, any reference in subsection (2B) or (2C) to the United Kingdom shall be construed as a reference to the European Community.

(2E) Where an earlier trade mark satisfies the use conditions in respect of some only of the goods or services for which it is registered, it shall be treated for the purposes of this section as if it were registered only in respect of those goods or services.

(3) An application for a declaration of invalidity may be made by any person, and may be made either to the registrar or to the court, except that—

  (a) if proceedings concerning the trade mark in question are pending in the court, the application must be made to the court; and

  (b) if in any other case the application is made to the registrar, he may at any stage of the proceedings refer the application to the court.

(4) In the case of bad faith in the registration of a trade mark, the registrar himself may apply to the court for a declaration of the invalidity of the registration.

(5) Where the grounds of invalidity exist in respect of only some of the goods

or services for which the trade mark is registered, the trade mark shall be declared invalid as regards those goods or services only.

(6) Where the registration of a trade mark is declared invalid to any extent, the registration shall to that extent be deemed never to have been made:

Provided that this shall not affect transactions past and closed.

Amendment

Subs.(2A) to (2E) added by the Trade Marks (Proof of Use, etc.) Regulations (SI 2004/946), reg.6.

Effect of acquiescence

48.—(1) Where the proprietor of an earlier trade mark or other earlier right has acquiesced for a continuous period of five years in the use of a registered trade mark in the United Kingdom, being aware of that use, there shall cease to be any entitlement on the basis of that earlier trade mark or other right— **A1–050**

(a) to apply for a declaration that the registration of the later trade mark is invalid, or

(b) to oppose the use of the later trade mark in relation to the goods or services in relation to which it has been so used,

unless the registration of the later trade mark was applied for in bad faith.

(2) Where subsection (1) applies, the proprietor of the later trade mark is not entitled to oppose the use of the earlier trade mark or, as the case may be, the exploitation of the earlier right, notwithstanding that the earlier trade mark or right may no longer be invoked against his later trade mark.

Collective marks

Collective marks

49.—(1) A collective mark is a mark distinguishing the goods or services of members of the association which is the proprietor of the mark from those of other undertakings. **A1–051**

(2) The provisions of this Act apply to collective marks subject to the provisions of Schedule 1.

Certification marks

Certification marks

50.—(1) A certification mark is a mark indicating that the goods or services in connection with which it is used are certified by the proprietor of the mark in respect of origin, material, mode of manufacture of goods or performance of services, quality, accuracy or other characteristics. **A1–052**

(2) The provisions of this Act apply to certification marks subject to the provisions of Schedule 2.

PART II

COMMUNITY TRADE MARKS AND INTERNATIONAL MATTERS

Community trade marks

Meaning of "Community trade mark"

51. In this Act— **A1–053**

"Community trade mark" has the meaning given by Article 1(1) of the Community Trade Mark Regulation; and

"the Community Trade Mark Regulation" means Council Regulation (EC) No. 40/94 of 20th December 1993 on the Community trade mark.

Power to make provision in connection with Community Trade Mark Regulation

A1–054   **52.**—(1) The Secretary of State may by regulations make such provision as he considers appropriate in connection with the operation of the Community Trade Mark Regulation.

(2) Provision may, in particular, be made with respect to—

(a) the making of applications for Community trade marks by way of the Patent Office;

(b) the procedures for determining *a posteriori* the invalidity, or liability to revocation, of the registration of a trade mark from which a Community trade mark claims seniority;

(c) the conversion of a Community trade mark, or an application for a Community trade mark, into an application for registration under this Act;

(d) the designation of courts in the United Kingdom having jurisdiction over proceedings arising out of the Community Trade Mark Regulation.

(3) Without prejudice to the generality of subsection (1), provision may be made by regulations under this section—

(a) applying in relation to a Community trade mark the provisions of—

(i) section 21 (remedy for groundless threats of infringement proceedings);

(ii) sections 89 to 91 (importation of infringing goods, material or articles); and

(iii) sections 92, 93, 95 and 96 (offences); and

(b) making in relation to the list of professional representatives maintained in pursuance of Article 89 of the Community Trade Mark Regulation, and persons on that list, provision corresponding to that made by, or capable of being made under, sections 84 to 88 in relation to the register of trade mark agents and registered trade mark agents.

(4) Regulations under this section shall be made by statutory instrument which shall be subject to annulment in pursuance of a resolution of either House of Parliament.

The Madrid Protocol: international registration

The Madrid Protocol

A1–055   **53.** In this Act—

"the Madrid Protocol" means the Protocol relating to the Madrid Agreement concerning the International Registration of Marks, adopted at Madrid on 27th June 1989;

"the International Bureau" has the meaning given by Article 2(1) of that Protocol; and

"international trade mark (EC)" **means a trade mark which is entitled to protection in the European Community under that Protocol**;

"international trade mark (UK)" means a trade mark which is entitled to protection in the United Kingdom under that Protocol.

Amendment

Definition inserted by the Trade Marks (International Registrations Designating the European Community, etc.) Regulations (SI 2004/2332), reg.5.

Power to make provision giving effect to Madrid Protocol

54.—(1) The Secretary of State may by order make such provision as he thinks fit for giving effect in the United Kingdom to the provisions of the Madrid Protocol.

    A1–056

(2) Provision may, in particular, be made with respect to—

    (a) the making of applications for international registrations by way of the Patent Office as office of origin;

    (b) the procedures to be followed where the basic United Kingdom application or registration fails or ceases to be in force;

    (c) the procedures to be followed where the Patent Office receives from the International Bureau a request for extension of protection to the United Kingdom;

    (d) the effects of a successful request for extension of protection to the United Kingdom;

    (e) the transformation of an application for an international registration, or an international registration, into a national application for registration;

    (f) the communication of information to the International Bureau;

    (g) the payment of fees and amounts prescribed in respect of applications for international registrations, extensions of protection and renewals.

(3) Without prejudice to the generality of subsection (1), provision may be made by regulations under this section applying in relation to an international trade mark (UK) the provisions of—

    (a) section 21 (remedy for groundless threats of infringement proceedings);

    (b) sections 89 to 91 (importation of infringing goods, material or articles); and

    (c) sections 92, 93, 95 and 96 (offences).

(4) An order under this section shall be made by statutory instrument which shall be subject to annulment in pursuance of a resolution of either House of Parliament.

The Paris Convention: supplementary provisions

The Paris Convention

55.—(1) In this Act—

    A1–057

    (a) "the Paris Convention" means the Paris Convention for the Protection of Industrial Property of March 20th 1883, as revised or amended from time to time,

    (aa) "the WTO agreement" means the Agreement establishing the World Trade Organisation signed at Marrakesh on 15th April 1994, and

    (b) a "Convention country" means a country, other than the United Kingdom, which is a party to that Convention.

(2) The Secretary of State may by order make such amendments of this Act, and rules made under this Act, as appear to him appropriate in consequence of any revision or amendment of the Paris Convention **or the WTO agreement** after the passing of this Act.

(3) Any such order shall be made by statutory instrument which shall be subject to annulment in pursuance of a resolution of either House of Parliament.

Amendment

The references to the WTO Agreement was added by the Patents and Trade Marks (World Trade Organisation) Regulations 1999, SI 1999/1899.

Protection of well-known trade marks: Article 6bis

A1–058

56.—(1) References in this Act to a trade mark which is entitled to protection under the Paris Convention **or the WTO agreement** as a well known trade mark are to a mark which is well-known in the United Kingdom as being the mark of a person who—

(a) is a national of a Convention country, or

(b) is domiciled in, or has a real and effective industrial or commercial establishment in, a Convention country,

whether or not that person carries on business, or has any goodwill, in the United Kingdom.

References to the proprietor of such a mark shall be construed accordingly.

(2) The proprietor of a trade mark which is entitled to protection under the Paris Convention **or the WTO agreement** as a well known trade mark is entitled to restrain by injunction the use in the United Kingdom of a trade mark which, or the essential part of which, is identical or similar to his mark, in relation to identical or similar goods or services, where the use is likely to cause confusion.

This right is subject to section 48 (effect of acquiescence by proprietor of earlier trade mark).

(3) Nothing in subsection (2) affects the continuation of any *bona fide* use of a trade mark begun before the commencement of this section.

Amendment

The references to the WTO Agreement was added by the Patents and Trade Marks (World Trade Organisation) Regulations 1999, SI 1999/1899.

National emblems, &c. of Convention countries: Article 6ter

A1–059

57.—(1) A trade mark which consists of or contains the flag of a Convention country shall not be registered without the authorisation of the competent authorities of that country, unless it appears to the registrar that use of the flag in the manner proposed is permitted without such authorisation.

(2) A trade mark which consists of or contains the armorial bearings or any other state emblem of a Convention country which is protected under the Paris Convention **or the WTO agreement** shall not be registered without the authorisation of the competent authorities of that country.

(3) A trade mark which consists of or contains an official sign or hallmark adopted by a Convention country and indicating control and warranty shall not, where the sign or hallmark is protected under the Paris Convention **or the WTO agreement,** be registered in relation to goods or services of the same, or a similar kind, as those in relation to which it indicates control and warranty, without the authorisation of the competent authorities of the country concerned.

(4) The provisions of this section as to national flags and other state emblems, and official signs or hallmarks, apply equally to anything which from a heraldic point of view imitates any such flag or other emblem, or sign or hallmark.

(5) Nothing in this section prevents the registration of a trade mark on the application of a national of a country who is authorised to make use of a state

emblem, or official sign or hallmark, of that country, notwithstanding that it is similar to that of another country.

(6) Where by virtue of this section the authorisation of the competent authorities of a Convention country is or would be required for the registration of a trade mark, those authorities are entitled to restrain by injunction any use of the mark in the United Kingdom without their authorisation.

Amendment

The references to the WTO Agreement was added by the Patents and Trade Marks (World Trade Organisation) Regulations 1999, SI 1999/1899.

Emblems, &c. of certain international organisations: Article 6ter

58.—(1) This section applies to—   A1–060
    (a) the armorial bearings, flags or other emblems, and
    (b) the abbreviations and names,
of international intergovernmental organisations of which one or more Convention countries are members.

(2) A trade mark which consists of or contains any such emblem, abbreviation or name which is protected under the Paris Convention **or the WTO agreement** shall not be registered without the authorisation of the international organisation concerned, unless it appears to the registrar that the use of the emblem, abbreviation or name in the manner proposed—
    (a) is not such as to suggest to the public that a connection exists between the organisation and the trade mark, or
    (b) is not likely to mislead the public as to the existence of a connection between the user and the organisation.

(3) The provisions of this section as to emblems of an international organisation apply equally to anything which from a heraldic point of view imitates any such emblem.

(4) Where by virtue of this section the authorisation of an international organisation is or would be required for the registration of a trade mark, that organisation is entitled to restrain by injunction any use of the mark in the United Kingdom without its authorisation.

(5) Nothing in this section affects the rights of a person whose *bona fide* use of the trade mark in question began before 4th January 1962 (when the relevant provisions of the Paris Convention entered into force in relation to the United Kingdom).

Amendment

The references to the WTO Agreement was added by the Patents and Trade Marks (World Trade Organisation) Regulations 1999, SI 1999/1899.

Notification under Article 6ter of the Convention

59.—(1) For the purposes of section 57 state emblems of a Convention country   A1–061
(other than the national flag), and official signs or hallmarks, shall be regarded as protected under the Paris Convention only if, or to the extent that—
    (a) the country in question has notified the United Kingdom in accordance with Article 6ter(3) of the Convention that it desires to protect that emblem, sign or hallmark,
    (b) the notification remains in force, and

(c) the United Kingdom has not objected to it in accordance with Article 6ter(4) or any such objection has been withdrawn.

(2) For the purposes of section 58 the emblems, abbreviations and names of an international organisation shall be regarded as protected under the Paris Convention only if, or to the extent that—

(a) the organisation in question has notified the United Kingdom in accordance with Article 6ter(3) of the Convention that it desires to protect that emblem, abbreviation or name,

(b) the notification remains in force, and

(c) the United Kingdom has not objected to it in accordance with Article 6ter(4) or any such objection has been withdrawn.

(3) Notification under Article 6ter(3) of the Paris Convention shall have effect only in relation to applications for registration made more than two months after the receipt of the notification.

(4) The registrar shall keep and make available for public inspection by any person, at all reasonable hours and free of charge, a list of—

(a) the state emblems and official signs or hallmarks, and

(b) the emblems, abbreviations and names of international organisations,

which are for the time being protected under the Paris Convention by virtue of notification under Article 6ter(3).

(5) Any reference in this section to Article 6ter of the Paris Convention shall be construed as including a reference to that Article as applied by the WTO agreement.

Amendment

The reference to the WTO Agreement was added by the Patents and Trade Marks (World Trade Organisation) Regulations 1999, SI 1999/1899.

Acts of agent or representative: Article 6septies

A1–062   **60.**—(1) The following provisions apply where an application for registration of a trade mark is made by a person who is an agent or representative of a person who is the proprietor of the mark in a Convention country.

(2) If the proprietor opposes the application, registration shall be refused.

(3) If the application (not being so opposed) is granted, the proprietor may—

(a) apply for a declaration of the invalidity of the registration, or

(b) apply for the rectification of the register so as to substitute his name as the proprietor of the registered trade mark.

(4) The proprietor may (notwithstanding the rights conferred by this Act in relation to a registered trade mark) by injunction restrain any use of the trade mark in the United Kingdom which is not authorised by him.

(5) Subsections (2), (3) and (4) do not apply if, or to the extent that, the agent or representative justifies his action.

(6) An application under subsection (3)(a) or (b) must be made within three years of the proprietor becoming aware of the registration; and no injunction shall be granted under subsection (4) in respect of a use in which the proprietor has acquiesced for a continuous period of three years or more.

Miscellaneous

Stamp duty

A1–063   **61.** […]

Amendment

Section 61 repealed by the Finance Act 2000, Sch.40, Pt III, para.1.

PART III

ADMINISTRATIVE AND OTHER SUPPLEMENTARY PROVISIONS

The registrar

The registrar

62. In this Act "the registrar" means the Comptroller-General of Patents, Designs and Trade Marks.

A1–064

The register

The register

63.—(1) The registrar shall maintain a register of trade marks.

A1–065

References in this Act to "the register" are to that register; and references to registration (in particular, in the expression "registered trade mark") are, unless the context otherwise requires, to registration in that register.

(2) There shall be entered in the register in accordance with this Act—

(a) registered trade marks,

(b) such particulars as may be prescribed of registrable transactions affecting a registered trade mark, and

(c) such other matters relating to registered trade marks as may be prescribed.

(3) The register shall be kept in such manner as may be prescribed, and provision shall in particular be made for—

(a) public inspection of the register, and

(b) the supply of certified or uncertified copies, or extracts, of entries in the register.

Rectification or correction of the register

64.—(1) Any person having a sufficient interest may apply for the rectification of an error or omission in the register:

A1–066

Provided that an application for rectification may not be made in respect of a matter affecting the validity of the registration of a trade mark.

(2) An application for rectification may be made either to the registrar or to the court, except that—

(a) if proceedings concerning the trade mark in question are pending in the court, the application must be made to the court; and

(b) if in any other case the application is made to the registrar, he may at any stage of the proceedings refer the application to the court.

(3) Except where the registrar or the court directs otherwise, the effect of rectification of the register is that the error or omission in question shall be deemed never to have been made.

(4) The registrar may, on request made in the prescribed manner by the proprietor of a registered trade mark, or a licensee, enter any change in his name or address as recorded in the register.

(5) The registrar may remove from the register matter appearing to him to have ceased to have effect.

Adaptation of entries to new classification

A1–067   **65.**—(1) Provision may be made by rules empowering the registrar to do such things as he considers necessary to implement any amended or substituted classification of goods or services for the purposes of the registration of trade marks.

(2) Provision may in particular be made for the amendment of existing entries on the register so as to accord with the new classification.

(3) Any such power of amendment shall not be exercised so as to extend the rights conferred by the registration, except where it appears to the registrar that compliance with this requirement would involve undue complexity and that any extension would not be substantial and would not adversely affect the rights of any person.

(4) The rules may empower the registrar—
    (a) to require the proprietor of a registered trade mark, within such time as may be prescribed, to file a proposal for amendment of the register, and
    (b) to cancel or refuse to renew the registration of the trade mark in the event of his failing to do so.

(5) Any such proposal shall be advertised, and may be opposed, in such manner as may be prescribed.

Powers and duties of the registrar

Power to require use of forms

A1–068   **66.**—(1) The registrar may require the use of such forms as he may direct for any purpose relating to the registration of a trade mark or any other proceeding before him under this Act.

(2) The forms, and any directions of the registrar with respect to their use, shall be published in the prescribed manner.

Information about applications and registered trade marks

A1–069   **67.**—(1) After publication of an application for registration of a trade mark, the registrar shall on request provide a person with such information and permit him to inspect such documents relating to the application, or to any registered trade mark resulting from it, as may be specified in the request, subject, however, to any prescribed restrictions.

Any request must be made in the prescribed manner and be accompanied by the appropriate fee (if any).

(2) Before publication of an application for registration of a trade mark, documents or information constituting or relating to the application shall not be published by the registrar or communicated by him to any person except—
    (a) in such cases and to such extent as may be prescribed, or
    (b) with the consent of the applicant;
but subject as follows.

(3) Where a person has been notified that an application for registration of a trade mark has been made, and that the applicant will if the application is granted bring proceedings against him in respect of acts done after publication of the ap-

plication, he may make a request under subsection (1) notwithstanding that the application has not been published and that subsection shall apply accordingly.

Costs and security for costs

68.—(1) Provision may be made by rules empowering the registrar, in any **A1–070** proceedings before him under this Act—
- (a) to award any party such costs as he may consider reasonable, and
- (b) to direct how and by what parties they are to be paid.

(2) Any such order of the registrar may be enforced—
- (a) in England and Wales or Northern Ireland, in the same way as an order of the High Court;
- (b) in Scotland, in the same way as a decree for expenses granted by the Court of Session.

(3) Provision may be made by rules empowering the registrar, in such cases as may be prescribed, to require a party to proceedings before him to give security for costs, in relation to those proceedings or to proceedings on appeal, and as to the consequences if security is not given.

Evidence before registrar

69. Provision may be made by rules— **A1–071**
- (a) as to the giving of evidence in proceedings before the registrar under this Act by affidavit or statutory declaration;
- (b) conferring on the registrar the powers of an official referee of the Supreme Court as regards the examination of witnesses on oath and the discovery and production of documents; and
- (c) applying in relation to the attendance of witnesses in proceedings before the registrar the rules applicable to the attendance of witnesses before such a referee.

Exclusion of liability in respect of official acts

70.—(1) The registrar shall not be taken to warrant the validity of the registra- **A1–072** tion of a trade mark under this Act or under any treaty, convention, arrangement or engagement to which the United Kingdom is a party.

(2) The registrar is not subject to any liability by reason of, or in connection with, any examination required or authorised by this Act, or any such treaty, convention, arrangement or engagement, or any report or other proceedings consequent on such examination.

(3) No proceedings lie against an officer of the registrar in respect of any matter for which, by virtue of this section, the registrar is not liable.

Registrar's annual report

71.—(1) The Comptroller-General of Patents, Designs and Trade Marks shall **A1–073** in his annual report under section 121 of the Patents Act 1977, include a report on the execution of this Act, including the discharge of his functions under the Madrid Protocol.

(2) The report shall include an account of all money received and paid by him under or by virtue of this Act.

Legal proceedings and appeals

Registration to be prima facie evidence of validity

A1–074   **72.** In all legal proceedings relating to a registered trade mark (including proceedings for rectification of the register) the registration of a person as proprietor of a trade mark shall be prima facie evidence of the validity of the original registration and of any subsequent assignment or other transmission of it.

Certificate of validity of contested registration

A1–075   **73.**—(1) If in proceedings before the court the validity of the registration of a trade mark is contested and it is found by the court that the trade mark is validly registered, the court may give a certificate to that effect.

(2) If the court gives such a certificate and in subsequent proceedings—

    (a) the validity of the registration is again questioned, and

    (b) the proprietor obtains a final order or judgment in his favour,

he is entitled to his costs as between solicitor and client unless the court directs otherwise.

This subsection does not extend to the costs of an appeal in any such proceedings.

Registrar's appearance in proceedings involving the register

A1–076   **74.**—(1) In proceedings before the court involving an application for—

    (a) the revocation of the registration of a trade mark,

    (b) a declaration of the invalidity of the registration of a trade mark, or

    (c) the rectification of the register,

the registrar is entitled to appear and be heard, and shall appear if so directed by the court.

(2) Unless otherwise directed by the court, the registrar may instead of appearing submit to the court a statement in writing signed by him, giving particulars of—

    (a) any proceedings before him in relation to the matter in issue,

    (b) the grounds of any decision given by him affecting it,

    (c) the practice of the Patent Office in like cases, or

    (d) such matters relevant to the issues and within his knowledge as registrar as he thinks fit;

and the statement shall be deemed to form part of the evidence in the proceedings.

(3) Anything which the registrar is or may be authorised or required to do under this section may be done on his behalf by a duly authorised officer.

The court

A1–077   **75.** In this Act, unless the context otherwise requires, "the court" means—

(a) in England and Wales, **the High Court or a county court having jurisdiction by virtue of an order made under section 1 of the Courts and Legal Services Act 1990,**

(aa) in Northern Ireland, the High Court, and

(b) in Scotland, the Court of Session.

Amendment

Words inserted in subs.(a) and (aa) by the High Court and County Courts Jurisdiction (Amendement) Order 2005 (SI 2005/587), art.4.

Appeals from the registrar

76.—(1) An appeal lies from any decision of the registrar under this Act, except **A1–078** as otherwise expressly provided by rules.

For this purpose "decision" includes any act of the registrar in exercise of a discretion vested in him by or under this Act.

(2) Any such appeal may be brought either to an appointed person or to the court.

(3) Where an appeal is made to an appointed person, he may refer the appeal to the court if—

    (a) it appears to him that a point of general legal importance is involved,

    (b) the registrar requests that it be so referred, or

    (c) such a request is made by any party to the proceedings before the registrar in which the decision appealed against was made.

Before doing so the appointed person shall give the appellant and any other party to the appeal an opportunity to make representations as to whether the appeal should be referred to the court.

(4) Where an appeal is made to an appointed person and he does not refer it to the court, he shall hear and determine the appeal and his decision shall be final.

(5) The provisions of sections 68 and 69 (costs and security for costs; evidence) apply in relation to proceedings before an appointed person as in relation to proceedings before the registrar.

(6) In the application of this section to England and Wales, "the court" means the High Court.

Amendment

Subs.(6) inserted by the High Court and County Courts Jurisdiction (Amendement) Order 2005 (SI 2005/587), art.4.

Persons appointed to hear and determine appeals

77.—(1) For the purposes of section 76 an "appointed person" means a person **A1–079** appointed by the Lord Chancellor to hear and decide appeals under this Act.

(2) A person is not eligible for such appointment unless—

    (a) he has a 7 year general qualification, within the meaning of section 71 of the Courts and Legal Services Act 1990;

    (b) he is an advocate or solicitor in Scotland of at least 7 years' standing;

    (c) he is a member of the Bar of Northern Ireland or solicitor of the Supreme Court of Northern Ireland of at least 7 years' standing; or

    (d) he has held judicial office.

(3) An appointed person shall hold and vacate office in accordance with his terms of appointment, subject to the following provisions—

    (a) there shall be paid to him such remuneration (whether by way of salary or fees), and such allowances, as the Secretary of State with the approval of the Treasury may determine;

    (b) he may resign his office by notice in writing to the Lord Chancellor;

    (c) the Lord Chancellor may be notice in writing remove him from office if—

        (i) he has become bankrupt or made an arrangement with his creditors or, in Scotland, his estate has been sequestrated or he has executed a trust deed for his creditors or entered into a composition contract, or

    (ii) he is incapacitated by physical or mental illness,

or if he is in the opinion of the Lord Chancellor otherwise unable or unfit to perform his duties as an appointed person.

    (4) The Lord Chancellor shall consult the Lord Advocate before exercising his powers under this section.

Amendment

    By SI 1999/17, art.3, Sch.1, para.17, the Secretary of State's functions under s.77(4) are to be treated for the purposes of the Scotland Act 1998, s.63, as being exercisable in or as regards Scotland. By SI 1999/678, art.2(1), the functions of the Lord Advocate under this section are transferred to the Secretary of State.

Rules, fees, hours of business, &c.

Power of Secretary of State to make rules

A1–080   **78.**—(1) The Secretary of State may make rules—

    (a) for the purposes of any provision of this Act authorising the making of rules with respect to any matter, and

    (b) for prescribing anything authorised or required by any provision of this Act to be prescribed,

and generally for regulating practice and procedure under this Act.

    (2) Provision may, in particular, be made—

    (a) as to the manner of filing of applications and other documents;

    (b) requiring and regulating the translation of documents and the filing and authentication of any translation;

    (c) as to the service of documents;

    (d) authorising the rectification of irregularities of procedure;

    (e) prescribing time limits for anything required to be done in connection with any proceeding under this Act;

    (f) providing for the extension of any time limit so prescribed, or specified by the registrar, whether or not it has already expired.

    (3) Rules under this Act shall be made by statutory instrument which shall be subject to annulment in pursuance of a resolution of either House of Parliament.

Fees

A1–081   **79.**—(1) There shall be paid in respect of applications and registration and other matters under this Act such fees as may be prescribed.

    (2) Provision may be made by rules as to—

    (a) the payment of a single fee in respect of two or more matters, and

    (b) the circumstances (if any) in which a fee may be repaid or remitted.

Hours of business and business days

A1–082   **80.**—(1) The registrar may give directions specifying the hours of business of the Patent Office for the purpose of the transaction by the public of business under this Act, and the days which are business days for that purpose.

    (2) Business done on any day after the specified hours of business, or on a day which is not a business day, shall be deemed to have been done on the next business day; and where the time for doing anything under this Act expires on a day which is not a business day, that time shall be extended to the next business day.

(3) Directions under this section may make different provision for different classes of business and shall be published in the prescribed manner.

The trade marks journal

81. Provision shall be made by rules for the publication by the registrar of a journal containing particulars of any application for the registration of a trade mark (including a representation of the mark) and such other information relating to trade marks as the registrar thinks fit. **A1–083**

Trade mark agents

Recognition of agents

82. Except as otherwise provided by rules, any act required or authorised by this Act to be done by or to a person in connection with the registration of a trade mark, or any procedure relating to a registered trade mark, may be done by or to an agent authorised by that person orally or in writing. **A1–084**

The register of trade mark agents

83.—(1) The Secretary of State may make rules requiring the keeping of a register of persons who act as agent for others for the purpose of applying for or obtaining the registration of trade marks; and in this Act a "registered trade mark agent" means a person whose name is entered in the register kept under this section. **A1–085**

(2) The rules may contain such provision as the Secretary of State thinks fit regulating the registration of persons, and may in particular—

(a) require the payment of such fees as may be prescribed, and

(b) authorise in prescribed cases the erasure from the register of the name of any person registered in it, or the suspension of a person's registration.

(3) The rules may delegate the keeping of the register to another person, and may confer on that person—

(a) power to make regulations—

(i) with respect to the payment of fees, in the cases and subject to the limits prescribed by the rules, and

(ii) with respect to any other matter which could be regulated by the rules, and

(b) such other functions, including disciplinary functions, as may be prescribed by the rules.

Unregistered persons not to be described as registered trade mark agents

84.—(1) An individual who is not a registered trade mark agent shall not— **A1–086**

(a) carry on a business (otherwise than in partnership) under any name or other description which contains the words "registered trade mark agent"; or

(b) in the course of a business otherwise describe or hold himself out, or permit himself to be described or held out, as a registered trade mark agent.

(2) A partnership shall not—

(a) carry on a business under any name or other description which contains the words "registered trade mark agent"; or

(b) in the course of a business otherwise describe or hold itself out, or permit itself to be described or held out, as a firm of registered trade mark agents,

unless all the partners are registered trade mark agents or the partnership satisfies such conditions as may be prescribed for the purposes of this section.

(3) A body corporate shall not—

(a) carry on a business (otherwise than in partnership) under any name or other description which contains the words "registered trade mark agent"; or

(b) in the course of a business otherwise describe or hold itself out, or permit itself to be described or held out, as a registered trade mark agent,

unless all the directors of the body corporate are registered trade mark agents or the body satisfies such conditions as may be prescribed for the purposes of this section.

(4) A person who contravenes this section commits an offence and is liable on summary conviction to a fine not exceeding level 5 on the standard scale; and proceedings for such an offence may be begun at any time within a year from the date of the offence.

Power to prescribe conditions, &c. for mixed partnerships and bodies corporate

A1–087   85.—(1) The Secretary of State may make rules prescribing the conditions to be satisfied for the purposes of section 84 (persons entitled to be described as registered trade mark agents)—

(a) in relation to a partnership where not all the partners are qualified persons, or

(b) in relation to a body corporate where not all the directors are qualified persons,

and imposing requirements to be complied with by such partnerships or bodies corporate.

(2) The rules may, in particular—

(a) prescribe conditions as to the number or proportion of partners or directors who must be qualified persons;

(b) impose requirements as to—

(i) the identification of qualified and unqualified persons in professional advertisements, circulars or letters issued by or with the consent of the partnership or body corporate and which relate to its business, and

(ii) the manner in which a partnership or body corporate is to organise its affairs so as to secure that qualified persons exercise a sufficient degree of control over the activities of unqualified persons.

(3) Contravention of a requirement imposed by the rules is an offence for which a person is liable on summary conviction to a fine not exceeding level 5 on the standard scale.

(4) In this section "qualified person" means a registered trade mark agent.

Use of the term "trade mark attorney"

A1–088   86.—(1) No offence is committed under the enactments restricting the use of certain expressions in reference to persons not qualified to act as solicitors by the use of the term "trade mark attorney" in reference to a registered trade mark agent.

(2) The enactments referred to in subsection (1) are section 21 of the Solicitors Act 1974, section 31 of the Solicitors (Scotland) Act 1980 and Article 22 of the Solicitors (Northern Ireland) Order 1976.

Privilege for communications with registered trade mark agents

87.—(1) This section applies to communications as to any matter relating to the protection of any design or trade mark, or as to any matter involving passing off. **A1–089**

(2) Any such communication—
- (a) between a person and his trade mark agent, or
- (b) for the purpose of obtaining, or in response to a request for, information which a person is seeking for the purpose of instructing his trade mark agent,

is privileged from, or in Scotland protected against, disclosure in legal proceedings in the same way as a communication between a person and his solicitor or, as the case may be, a communication for the purpose of obtaining, or in response to a request for, information which a person is seeking for the purpose of instructing his solicitor.

(3) In subsection (2) "trade mark agent" means—
- (a) a registered trade mark agent, or
- (b) a partnership entitled to describe itself as a firm of registered trade mark agents, or
- (c) a body corporate entitled to describe itself as a registered trade mark agent.

Power of registrar to refuse to deal with certain agents

88.—(1) The Secretary of State may make rules authorising the registrar to refuse to recognise as agent in respect of any business under this Act— **A1–090**
- (a) a person who has been convicted of an offence under section 84 (unregistered persons describing themselves as registered trade mark agents);
- (b) an individual whose name has been erased from and not restored to, or who is suspended from, the register of trade mark agents on the ground of misconduct;
- (c) a person who is found by the Secretary of State to have been guilty of such conduct as would, in the case of an individual registered in the register of trade mark agents, render him liable to have his name erased from the register on the ground of misconduct;
- (d) a partnership or body corporate of which one of the partners or directors is a person whom the registrar could refuse to recognise under paragraph (a), (b) or (c) above.

(2) The rules may contain such incidental and supplementary provisions as appear to the Secretary of State to be appropriate and may, in particular, prescribe circumstances in which a person is or is not to be taken to have been guilty of misconduct.

Importation of infringing goods, material or articles

Infringing goods, material or articles may be treated as prohibited goods

89.—(1) The proprietor of a registered trade mark, or a licensee, may give notice in writing to the Commissioners of Customs and Excise— **A1–091**

(a) that he is the proprietor or, as the case may be, a licensee of the registered trade mark,

(b) that, at a time and place specified in the notice, goods which are, in relation to that registered trade mark, infringing goods, material or articles are expected to arrive in the United Kingdom—

   (i) from outside the European Economic Area, or

   (ii) from within that Area but not having been entered for free circulation, and

(c) that he requests the Commissioners to treat them as prohibited goods.

(2) When a notice is in force under this section the importation of the goods to which the notice relates, otherwise than by a person for his private and domestic use, is prohibited; but a person is not by reason of the prohibition liable to any penalty other than forfeiture of the goods.

(3) This section does not apply to goods placed in, or expected to be placed in, one of the situations referred to in Article 1(1), in respect of which an application may be made under Article 5(1), of Council Regulation (EC) No. 1383/2003 concerning customs action against goods suspected of infringing certain intellectual property rights and the measures to be taken against goods found to have infringed such rights.

Amendment

Subs.(3) substituted by the Goods Infringing Intellectual Property Rights (Customs) Regulations 2004 (SI 2004/1473).

Power of Commissioners of Customs and Excise to make regulations

A1–092   **90.**—(1) The Commissioners of Customs and Excise may make regulations prescribing the form in which notice is to be given under section 89 and requiring a person giving notice—

(a) to furnish the Commissioners with such evidence as may be specified in the regulations, either on giving notice or when the goods are imported, or at both those times, and

(b) to comply with such other conditions as may be specified in the regulations.

(2) The regulations may, in particular, require a person giving such a notice—

(a) to pay such fees in respect of the notice as may be specified by the regulations;

(b) to give such security as may be so specified in respect of any liability or expense which the Commissioners may incur in consequence of the notice by reason of the detention of any goods or anything done to goods detained;

(c) to indemnify the Commissioners against any such liability or expense, whether security has been given or not.

(3) The regulations may make different provision as respects different classes of case to which they apply and may include such incidental and supplementary provisions as the Commissioners consider expedient.

(4) Regulations under this section shall be made by statutory instrument which shall be subject to annulment in pursuance of a resolution of either House of Parliament.

(5) Section 17 of the Customs and Excise Management Act 1979 (general provisions as to Commissioners' receipts) applies to fees paid in pursuance of regulations under this section as to receipts under the enactments relating to customs and excise.

Power of Commissioners of Customs and Excise to disclose information

91. Where information relating to infringing goods, material or articles has been obtained by the Commissioners of Customs and Excise for the purposes of, or in connection with, the exercise of their functions in relation to imported goods, the Commissioners may authorise the disclosure of that information for the purpose of facilitating the exercise by any person of any function in connection with the investigation or prosecution of an offence under section 92 below (unauthorised use of trade mark, &c. in relation to goods) or under the Trade Descriptions Act 1968.

A1–093

Offences

Unauthorised use of trade mark, &c. in relation to goods

92.—(1) A person commits an offence who with a view to gain for himself or another, or with intent to cause loss to another, and without the consent of the proprietor—

A1–094

    (a) applies to goods or their packaging a sign identical to, or likely to be mistaken for, a registered trade mark, or

    (b) sells or lets for hire, offers or exposes for sale or hire or distributes goods which bear, or the packaging of which bears, such a sign, or

    (c) has in his possession, custody or control in the course of a business any such goods with a view to the doing of anything, by himself or another, which would be an offence under paragraph (b).

(2) A person commits an offence who with a view to gain for himself or another, or with intent to cause loss to another, and without the consent of the proprietor—

    (a) applies a sign identical to, or likely to be mistaken for, a registered trade mark to material intended to be used—

      (i) for labelling or packaging goods,

      (ii) as a business paper in relation to goods, or

      (iii) for advertising goods, or

    (b) uses in the course of a business material bearing such a sign for labelling or packaging goods, as a business paper in relation to goods, or for advertising goods, or

    (c) has in his possession, custody or control in the course of a business any such material with a view to the doing of anything, by himself or another, which would be an offence under paragraph (b).

(3) A person commits an offence who with a view to gain for himself or another, or with intent to cause loss to another, and without the consent of the proprietor—

    (a) makes an article specifically designed or adapted for making copies of a sign identical to, or likely to be mistaken for, a registered trade mark, or

    (b) has such an article in his possession, custody or control in the course of a business,

knowing or having reason to believe that it has been, or is to be, used to produce goods, or material for labelling or packaging goods, as a business paper in relation to goods, or for advertising goods.

(4) A person does not commit an offence under this section unless—

    (a) the goods are goods in respect of which the trade mark is registered, or

    (b) the trade mark has a reputation in the United Kingdom and the use of the sign takes or would take unfair advantage of, or is or would be detrimental to, the distinctive character or the repute of the trade mark.

(5) It is a defence for a person charged with an offence under this section to show that he believed on reasonable grounds that the use of the sign in the manner in which it was used, or was to be used, was not an infringement of the registered trade mark.

(6) A person guilty of an offence under this section is liable—

    (a) on summary conviction to imprisonment for a term not exceeding six months or a fine not exceeding the statutory maximum, or both;

    (b) on conviction on indictment to a fine or imprisonment for a term not exceeding ten years, or both.

Search warrants

A1–095   **92A.—(1) Where a justice of the peace (in Scotland, a sheriff or justice of the peace) is satisfied by information on oath given by a constable (in Scotland, by evidence on oath) that there are reasonable grounds for believing—**

    (a) that an offence under section 92 (unauthorised use of trade mark, etc. in relation to goods) has been or is about to be committed in any premises, and

    (b) that evidence that such an offence has been or is about to be committed is in those premises, he may issue a warrant authorising a constable to enter and search the premises, using such reasonable force as is necessary.

(2) The power conferred by subsection (1) does not, in England and Wales, extend to authorising a search for material of the kinds mentioned in section 9(2) of the Police and Criminal Evidence Act 1984 (c. 60) (certain classes of personal or confidential material).

(3) A warrant under subsection (1)—

    (a) may authorise persons to accompany any constable executing the warrant, and

    (b) remains in force for 28 days from the date of its issue.

(4) In executing a warrant issued under subsection (1) a constable may seize an article if he reasonably believes that it is evidence that any offence under section 92 has been or is about to be committed.

(5) In this section "premises" includes land, buildings, fixed or moveable structures, vehicles, vessels, aircraft and hovercraft.

Amendment

Section 92A added by the Copyright, etc. and Trade Marks (Offences and Enforcement) Act 2002, s.6.

Enforcement function of local weights and measures authority

A1–096   **93.**—(1) It is the duty of every local weights and measures authority to enforce within their area the provisions of section 92 (unauthorised use of trade mark, &c. in relation to goods).

(2) The following provisions of the Trade Descriptions Act 1968 apply in relation to the enforcement of that section as in relation to the enforcement of that Act—

    section 27 (power to make test purchases),

section 28 (power to enter premises and inspect and seize goods and documents),

section 29 (obstruction of authorised officers), and

section 33 (compensation for loss, &c. of goods seized).

(3) Subsection (1) above does not apply in relation to the enforcement of section 92 in Northern Ireland, but it is the duty of the Department of Economic Development to enforce that section in Northern Ireland.

For that purpose the provisions of the Trade Descriptions Act 1968 specified in subsection (2) apply as if for the references to a local weights and measures authority and any officer of such an authority there were substituted references to that Department and any of its officers.

(4) Any enactment which authorises the disclosure of information for the purpose of facilitating the enforcement of the Trade Descriptions Act 1968 shall apply as if section 92 above were contained in that Act and as if the functions of any person in relation to the enforcement of that section were functions under that Act.

(5) Nothing in this section shall be construed as authorising a local weights and measures authority to bring proceedings in Scotland for an offence.

Falsification of register, &c.

94.—(1) It is an offence for a person to make, or cause to be made, a false   **A1–097**
entry in the register of trade marks, knowing or having reason to believe that it is false.

(2) It is an offence for a person—
 (a) to make or cause to be made anything falsely purporting to be a copy of an entry in the register, or
 (b) to produce or tender or cause to be produced or tendered in evidence any such thing,

knowing or having reason to believe that it is false.

(3) A person guilty of an offence under this section is liable—
 (a) on conviction on indictment, to imprisonment for a term not exceeding two years or a fine, or both;
 (b) on summary conviction, to imprisonment for a term not exceeding six months or a fine not exceeding the statutory maximum, or both.

Falsely representing trade mark as registered

95.—(1) It is an offence for a person—   **A1–098**
 (a) falsely to represent that a mark is a registered trade mark, or
 (b) to make a false representation as to the goods or services for which a trade mark is registered

knowing or having reason to believe that the representation is false.

(2) For the purposes of this section, the use in the United Kingdom in relation to a trade mark—
 (a) of the word "registered", or
 (b) of any other word or symbol importing a reference (express or implied) to registration,

shall be deemed to be a representation as to registration under this Act unless it is shown that the reference is to registration elsewhere than in the United Kingdom and that the trade mark is in fact so registered for the goods or services in question.

(3) A person guilty of an offence under this section is liable on summary conviction to a fine not exceeding level 3 on the standard scale.

Supplementary provisions as to summary proceedings in Scotland

A1–099   **96.**—(1) Notwithstanding anything in **section 136 of the Criminal Procedure (Scotland) Act 1995**, summary proceedings in Scotland for an offence under this Act may be begun at any time within six months after the date on which evidence sufficient in the Lord Advocate's opinion to justify the proceedings came to his knowledge.

For this purpose a certificate of the Lord Advocate as to the date on which such evidence came to his knowledge is conclusive evidence.

(2) For the purposes of subsection (1) and of any other provision of this Act as to the time within which summary proceedings for an offence may be brought, proceedings in Scotland shall be deemed to be begun on the date on which a warrant to apprehend or to cite the accused is granted, if such warrant is executed without undue delay.

Amendment

Words substituted by the Criminal Procedure (Consequential Provisions) (Scotland) Act 1995, Sch.4, para.92(2).

Forfeiture of counterfeit goods, &c.

Forfeiture: England and Wales or Northern Ireland

A1–100   **97.**—(1) In England and Wales or Northern Ireland where there has come into the possession of any person in connection with the investigation or prosecution of a relevant offence—

(a) goods which, or the packaging of which, bears a sign identical to or likely to be mistaken for a registered trade mark,

(b) material bearing such a sign and intended to be used for labelling or packaging goods, as a business paper in relation to goods, or for advertising goods, or

(c) articles specifically designed or adapted for making copies of such a sign,

that person may apply under this section for an order for the forfeiture of the goods, material or articles.

(2) An application under this section may be made—

(a) where proceedings have been brought in any court for a relevant offence relating to some or all of the goods, material or articles, to that court;

(b) where no application for the forfeiture of the goods, material or articles has been made under paragraph (a), by way of complaint to a magistrates' court.

(3) On an application under this section the court shall make an order for the forfeiture of any goods, material or articles only if it is satisfied that a relevant offence has been committed in relation to the goods, material or articles.

(4) A court may infer for the purposes of this section that such an offence has been committed in relation to any goods, material or articles if it is satisfied that such an offence has been committed in relation to goods, material or articles which are representative of them (whether by reason of being of the same design or part of the same consignment or batch or otherwise).

(5) Any person aggrieved by an order made under this section by a magistrates' court, or by a decision of such a court not to make such an order, may appeal against that order or decision—

(a) in England and Wales, to the Crown Court;

(b) in Northern Ireland, to the county court;

and an order so made may contain such provision as appears to the court to be appropriate for delaying the coming into force of the order pending the making and determination of any appeal (including any application under section 111 of the Magistrates' Courts Act 1980 or Article 146 of the Magistrates' Courts (Northern Ireland) Order 1981 (statement of case)).

(6) Subject to subsection (7), where any goods, material or articles are forfeited under this section they shall be destroyed in accordance with such directions as the court may give.

(7) On making an order under this section the court may, if it considers it appropriate to do so, direct that the goods, material or articles to which the order relates shall (instead of being destroyed) be released, to such person as the court may specify, on condition that that person—

(a) causes the offending sign to be erased, removed or obliterated; and

(b) complies with any order to pay costs which has been made against him in the proceedings for the order for forfeiture.

(8) For the purposes of this section a "relevant offence" means an offence under section 92 above (unauthorised use of trade mark, &c. in relation to goods) or under the Trade Descriptions Act 1968 or any offence involving dishonesty or deception.

Amendment

A modified form of this section applies under the Olympic Symbol etc. (Protection) Act 1995, s.11.

Forfeiture: Scotland

98.—(1) In Scotland the court may make an order for the forfeiture of any—   **A1–101**

(a) goods which bear, or the packaging of which bears, a sign identical to or likely to be mistaken for a registered trade mark,

(b) material bearing such a sign and intended to be used for labelling or packaging goods, as a business paper in relation to goods, or for advertising goods, or

(c) articles specifically designed or adapted for making copies of such a sign.

(2) An order under this section may be made—

(a) on an application by the procurator-fiscal made in the manner specified in **Section 134 of the Criminal Procedure (Scotland) Act 1995**, or

(b) where a person is convicted of a relevant offence, in addition to any other penalty which the court may impose.

(3) On an application under subsection (2)(a), the court shall make an order for the forfeiture of any goods, material or articles only if it is satisfied that a relevant offence has been committed in relation to the goods, material or articles.

(4) The court may infer for the purposes of this section that such an offence has been committed in relation to any goods, material or articles if it is satisfied that such an offence has been committed in relation to goods, material or articles which are representative of them (whether by reason of being of the same design or part of the same consignment or batch or otherwise).

(5) The procurator-fiscal making the application under subsection (2)(a) shall serve on any person appearing to him to be the owner of, or otherwise to have an interest in, the goods, material or articles to which the application relates a copy of the application, together with a notice giving him the opportunity to appear at the hearing of the application to show cause why the goods, material or articles should not be forfeited.

(6) Service under subsection (5) shall be carried out, and such service may be proved, in the manner specified for citation of an accused in summary proceedings under the **Criminal Procedure (Scotland) Act 1995**.

(7) Any person upon whom notice is served under subsection (5) and any other person claiming to be the owner of, or otherwise to have an interest in, goods, material or articles to which an application under this section relates shall be entitled to appear at the hearing of the application to show cause why the goods, material or articles should not be forfeited.

(8) The court shall not make an order following an application under subsection (2)(a)—

- (a) if any person on whom notice is served under subsection (5) does not appear, unless service of the notice on that person is proved; or
- (b) if no notice under subsection (5) has been served, unless the court is satisfied that in the circumstances it was reasonable not to serve such notice.

(9) Where an order for the forfeiture of any goods, material or articles is made following an application under subsection (2)(a), any person who appeared, or was entitled to appear, to show cause why goods, material or articles should not be forfeited may, within 21 days of the making of the order, appeal to the High Court by Bill of Suspension; and **Section 182(5)(a) to (e) of the Criminal Procedure (Scotland) Act 1995** shall apply to an appeal under this subsection as it applies to a stated case under Part II of that Act.

(10) An order following an application under subsection (2)(a) shall not take effect—

- (a) until the end of the period of 21 days beginning with the day after the day on which the order is made; or
- (b) if an appeal is made under subsection (9) above within that period, until the appeal is determined or abandoned.

(11) An order under subsection (2)(b) shall not take effect—

- (a) until the end of the period within which an appeal against the order could be brought under the **Criminal Procedure (Scotland) Act 1995**; or
- (b) if an appeal is made within that period, until the appeal is determined or abandoned.

(12) Subject to subsection (13), goods, material or articles forfeited under this section shall be destroyed in accordance with such directions as the court may give.

(13) On making an order under this section the court may if it considers it appropriate to do so, direct that the goods, material or articles to which the order relates shall (instead of being destroyed) be released, to such person as the court may specify, on condition that that person causes the offending sign to be erased, removed or obliterated.

(14) For the purposes of this section—

"relevant offence" means an offence under section 92 (unauthorised use of trade mark, &c. in relation to goods) or under the Trade Descriptions Act 1968 or any offence involving dishonesty or deception,

"the court" means—
> (a) in relation to an order made on an application under subsection (2)(a), the sheriff, and
>
> (b) in relation to an order made under subsection (2)(b), the court which imposed the penalty.

Amendment

A modified form of this section applies under the Olympic Symbol etc. (Protection) Act 1995, s. 12. The amendments shown above were effected by the Criminal Procedure (Consequential Provisions) (Scotland) Act 1995.

PART IV

MISCELLANEOUS AND GENERAL PROVISIONS

Miscellaneous

Unauthorised use of Royal arms, &c.

99.—(1) A person shall not without the authority of Her Majesty use in connection with any business the Royal arms (or arms so closely resembling the Royal arms as to be calculated to deceive) in such manner as to be calculated to lead to the belief that he is duly authorised to use the Royal arms.   **A1–102**

(2) A person shall not without the authority of Her Majesty or of a member of the Royal family use in connection with any business any device, emblem or title in such a manner as to be calculated to lead to the belief that he is employed by, or supplies goods or services to, Her Majesty or that member of the Royal family.

(3) A person who contravenes subsection (1) commits an offence and is liable on summary conviction to a fine not exceeding level 2 on the standard scale.

(4) Contravention of subsection (1) or (2) may be restrained by injunction in proceedings brought by—
> (a) any person who is authorised to use the arms, device, emblem or title in question, or
>
> (b) any person authorised by the Lord Chamberlain to take such proceedings.

(5) Nothing in this section affects any right of the proprietor of a trade mark containing any such arms, device, emblem or title to use that trade mark.

Burden of proving use of trade mark

100. If in any civil proceedings under this Act a question arises as to the use to which a registered trade mark has been put, it is for the proprietor to show what use has been made of it.   **A1–103**

Offences committed by partnerships and bodies corporate

101.—(1) Proceedings for an offence under this Act alleged to have been committed by a partnership shall be brought against the partnership in the name of the firm and not in that of the partners; but without prejudice to any liability of the partners under subsection (4) below.   **A1–104**

(2) The following provisions apply for the purposes of such proceedings as in relation to a body corporate—
> (a) any rules of court relating to the service of documents;

(b) in England and Wales or Northern Ireland, Schedule 3 to the Magistrates' Courts Act 1980 or Schedule 4 to the Magistrates' Courts (Northern Ireland) Order 1981 (procedure on charge of offence).

(3) A fine imposed on a partnership on its conviction in such proceedings shall be paid out of the partnership assets.

(4) Where a partnership is guilty of an offence under this Act, every partner, other than a partner who is proved to have been ignorant of or to have attempted to prevent the commission of the offence, is also guilty of the offence and liable to be proceeded against and punished accordingly.

(5) Where an offence under this Act committed by a body corporate is proved to have been committed with the consent or connivance of a director, manager, secretary or other similar officer of the body, or a person purporting to act in any such capacity, he as well as the body corporate is guilty of the offence and liable to be proceeded against and punished accordingly.

Interpretation

Adaptation of expressions for Scotland

A1–105   **102.** In the application of this Act to Scotland—
"account of profits" means accounting and payment of profits;
"accounts" means count, reckoning and payment;
"assignment" means assignation;
"costs" means expenses;
"declaration" means declarator;
"defendant" means defender;
"delivery up" means delivery;
"injunction" means interdict;
"interlocutory relief" means interim remedy; and
"plaintiff" means pursuer.

Minor definitions

A1–106   **103.**—(1) In this Act—
"business" includes a trade or profession;
"director", in relation to a body corporate whose affairs are managed by its members, means any member of the body;
"infringement proceedings", in relation to a registered trade mark, includes proceedings under section 16 (order for delivery up of infringing goods, &c.);
"publish" means make available to the public, and references to publication—

(a) in relation to an application for registration, are to publication under section 38(1), and

(b) in relation to registration, are to publication under section 40(4);

"statutory provisions" includes provisions of subordinate legislation within the meaning of the Interpretation Act 1978;
"trade" includes any business or profession.

(2) References in this Act to use (or any particular description of use) of a trade mark, or of a sign identical with, similar to, or likely to be mistaken for a trade mark, include use (or that description of use) otherwise than by means of a graphic representation.

(3) References in this Act to a Community instrument include references to any instrument amending or replacing that instrument.

Index of defined expressions

104. In this Act the expressions listed below are defined by or otherwise fall to be construed in accordance with the provisions indicated—   **A1–107**

account of profits and accounts (in Scotland)	section 102
appointed person (for purposes of section 76)	section 77
assignment (in Scotland)	section 102
business	section 103(1)
certification mark	section 50(1)
collective mark	section 49(1)
commencement (of this Act)	section 109(2)
Community trade mark	section 51
Community Trade Mark Regulation	section 51
Convention country	section 55(1)(b)
costs (in Scotland)	section 102
the court	section 75
date of application	section 33(2)
date of filing	section 33(1)
date of registration	section 40(3)
defendant (in Scotland)	section 102
delivery up (in Scotland)	section 102
director	section 103(1)
earlier right	section 5(4)
earlier trade mark	section 6
exclusive licence and licensee	section 29(1)
infringement (of registered trade mark)	section 9(1) and (2) and 10
infringement proceedings	section 103(1)
infringing articles	section 17
infringing goods	section 17
infringing material	section 17
injunction (in Scotland)	section 102
interlocutory relief (in Scotland)	section 102
the International Bureau	section 53
international trade mark (EC)	section 53
international trade mark (UK)	section 53
Madrid Protocol	section 53
Paris Convention	section 55(1)(a)
plaintiff (in Scotland)	section 102
prescribed	section 78(1)(b)
protected under the Paris Convention —well-known trade marks	section 56(1)

—state emblems and official signs or hallmarks	section 57(1)
—emblems, &c. of international organisations	section 58(2)
publish and references to publication	section 103(1)
register, registered (and related expressions)	section 63(1)
registered trade mark agent	section 83(1)
registerable transaction	section 25(2)
the registrar	section 62
rules	section 78
statutory provisions	section 103(1)
trade	section 103(1)
trade mark	
—generally	section 1(1)
—includes collective mark or certification mark	section 1(2)
United Kingdom (references include Isle of Man)	section 108(2)
use (of trade mark or sign)	section 103(2)
well-known trade mark (under Paris Convention)	section 56(1)

Amendment

The entry "international trade mark (EC) section 53" inserted by the Trade Marks (International Registrations Designating the European Community, etc.) Regulations (SI 2004/2332), reg.6.

Other general provisions

Transitional provisions

A1–108 **105.** The provisions of Schedule 3 have effect with respect to transitional matters, including the treatment of marks registered under the Trade Marks Act 1938, and applications for registration and other proceedings pending under that Act, on the commencement of this Act.

Consequential amendments and repeals

A1–109 **106.**—(1) The enactments specified in Schedule 4 are amended in accordance with that Schedule, the amendments being consequential on the provisions of this Act.

(2) The enactments specified in Schedule 5 are repealed to the extent specified.

Territorial waters and the continental shelf

A1–110 **107.**—(1) For the purposes of this Act the territorial waters of the United Kingdom shall be treated as part of the United Kingdom.

(2) This Act applies to things done in the United Kingdom sector of the continental shelf on a structure or vessel which is present there for purposes directly connected with the exploration of the sea bed or subsoil or the exploitation of their natural resources as it applies to things done in the United Kingdom.

(3) The United Kingdom sector of the continental shelf means the areas designated by order under section 1(7) of the Continental Shelf Act 1964.

Extent

108.—(1) This Act extends to England and Wales, Scotland and Northern Ireland.   **A1–111**

(2) This Act also extends to the Isle of Man, subject to such exceptions and modifications as Her Majesty may specify by Order in Council; and subject to any such Order references in this Act to the United Kingdom shall be construed as including the Isle of Man.

Commencement

109.—(1) The provisions of this Act come into force on such day as the Secre-   **A1–112** tary of State may appoint by order made by statutory instrument.

Different days may be appointed for different provisions and different purposes.

(2) The references to the commencement of this Act in Schedules 3 and 4 (transitional provisions and consequential amendments) are to the commencement of the main substantive provisions of Parts I and III of this Act and the consequential repeal of the Trade Marks Act 1938.

Provision may be made by order under this section identifying the date of that commencement.

Short title

110. This Act may be cited as the Trade Marks Act 1994.   **A1–113**

SCHEDULES

Section 49   SCHEDULE 1

COLLECTIVE MARKS

General

1. The provisions of this Act apply to collective marks subject to the following   **A1–114** provisions.

Signs of which a collective mark may consist

2. In relation to a collective mark the reference in section 1(1) (signs of which a trade   **A1–115** mark may consist) to distinguishing goods or services of one undertaking from those of other undertakings shall be construed as a reference to distinguishing goods or services of members of the association which is the proprietor of the mark from those of other undertakings.

Indication of geographical origin

3.—(1) Notwithstanding section 3(1)(c), a collective mark may be registered which   **A1–116** consists of signs or indications which may serve, in trade, to designate the geographical origin of the goods or services.

(2) However, the proprietor of such a mark is not entitled to prohibit the use of the signs or indications in accordance with honest practices in industrial or commercial matters (in particular, by a person who is entitled to use a geographical name).

Mark not to be misleading as to character or significance

4.—(1) A collective mark shall not be registered if the public is liable to be misled as   **A1–117**

regards the character or significance of the mark, in particular if it is likely to be taken to be something other than a collective mark.

(2) The registrar may accordingly require that a mark in respect of which application is made for registration include some indication that it is a collective mark.

Notwithstanding section 39(2), an application may be amended so as to comply with any such requirement.

Regulations governing use of collective mark

A1–118   **5.**—(1) An applicant for registration of a collective mark must file with the registrar regulations governing the use of the mark.

(2) The regulations must specify the persons authorised to use the mark, the conditions of membership of the association and, where they exist, the conditions of use of the mark, including any sanctions against misuse.

Further requirements with which the regulations have to comply may be imposed by rules.

Approval of regulations by registrar

A1–119   **6.**—(1) A collective mark shall not be registered unless the regulations governing the use of the mark—

(a) comply with paragraph 5(2) and any further requirements imposed by rules, and

(b) are not contrary to public policy or to accepted principles of morality.

(2) Before the end of the prescribed period after the date of the application for registration of a collective mark, the applicant must file the regulations with the registrar and pay the prescribed fee.

If he does not do so, the application shall be deemed to be withdrawn.

A1–120   **7.**—(1) The registrar shall consider whether the requirements mentioned in paragraph 6(1) are met.

(2) If it appears to the registrar that those requirements are not met, he shall inform the applicant and give him an opportunity, within such period as the registrar may specify, to make representations or to file amended regulations.

(3) If the applicant fails to satisfy the registrar that those requirements are met, or to file regulations amended so as to meet them, or fails to respond before the end of the specified period, the registrar shall refuse the application.

(4) If it appears to the registrar that those requirements, and the other requirements for registration, are met, he shall accept the application and shall proceed in accordance with section 38 (publication, opposition proceedings and observations).

A1–121   **8.** The regulations shall be published and notice of opposition may be given, and observations may be made, relating to the matters mentioned in paragraph 6(1).

This is in addition to any other grounds on which the application may be opposed or observations made.

Regulations to be open to inspection

A1–122   **9.** The regulations governing the use of a registered collective mark shall be open to public inspection in the same way as the register.

Amendment of regulations

A1–123   **10.**—(1) An amendment of the regulations governing the use of a registered collective mark is not effective unless and until the amended regulations are filed with the registrar and accepted by him.

(2) Before accepting any amended regulations the registrar may in any case where it appears to him expedient to do so cause them to be published.

(3) If he does so, notice of opposition may be given, and observations may be made, relating to the matters mentioned in paragraph 6(1).

Infringement: rights of authorised users

A1–124   **11.** The following provisions apply in relation to an authorised user of a registered collective mark as in relation to a licensee of a trade mark—

(a) section 10(5) (definition of infringement: unauthorised application of mark to certain material);

(b) section 19(2) (order as to disposal of infringing goods, material or articles: adequacy of other remedies);

(c) section 89 (prohibition of importation of infringing goods, material or articles: request to Commissioners of Customs and Excise).

12.—(1) The following provisions (which correspond to the provisions of section 30 (general provisions as to rights of licensees in case of infringement)) have effect as regards the rights of an authorised user in relation to infringement of a registered collective mark.   **A1–125**

(2) An authorised user is entitled, subject to any agreement to the contrary between him and the proprietor, to call on the proprietor to take infringement proceedings in respect of any matter which affects his interests.

(3) If the proprietor—

(a) refuses to do so, or

(b) fails to do so within two months after being called upon,

the authorised user may bring the proceedings in his own name as if he were the proprietor.

(4) Where infringement proceedings are brought by virtue of this paragraph, the authorised user may not, without the leave of the court, proceed with the action unless the proprietor is either joined as a plaintiff or added as a defendant.

This does not affect the granting of interlocutory relief on an application by an authorised user alone.

(5) A proprietor who is added as a defendant as mentioned in sub-paragraph (4) shall not be made liable for any costs in the action unless he takes part in the proceedings.

(6) In infringement proceedings brought by the proprietor of a registered collective mark any loss suffered or likely to be suffered by authorised users shall be taken into account; and the court may give such directions as it thinks fit as to the extent to which the plaintiff is to hold the proceeds of any pecuniary remedy on behalf of such users.

Grounds for revocation of registration

13. Apart from the grounds of revocation provided for in section 46, the registration of a collective mark may be revoked on the ground—   **A1–126**

(a) that the manner in which the mark has been used by the proprietor has caused it to become liable to mislead the public in the manner referred to in paragraph 4(1), or

(b) that the proprietor has failed to observe, or to secure the observance of, the regulations governing the use of the mark, or

(c) that an amendment of the regulations has been made so that the regulations—

(i) no longer comply with paragraph 5(2) and any further conditions imposed by rules, or

(ii) are contrary to public policy or to accepted principles of morality.

Grounds for invalidity of registration

14. Apart from the grounds of invalidity provided for in section 47, the registration of a collective mark may be declared invalid on the ground that the mark was registered in breach of the provisions of paragraph 4(1) or 6(1).   **A1–127**

Section 50   SCHEDULE 2

CERTIFICATION MARKS

General

1. The provisions of this Act apply to certification marks subject to the following provisions.   **A1–128**

Signs of which a certification mark may consist

2. In relation to a certification mark the reference in section 1(1) (signs which a trade mark may consist) to distinguishing goods or services of one undertaking from those of other undertakings shall be construed as a reference to distinguishing goods or services which are certified from those which are not.   **A1–129**

Indication of geographical origin

A1–130   **3.**—(1) Notwithstanding section 3(1)(c), a certification mark may be registered which consists of signs or indications which may serve, in trade, to designate the geographical origin of the goods or services.

(2) However, the proprietor of such a mark is not entitled to prohibit the use of the signs or indications in accordance with honest practices in industrial or commercial matters (in particular, by a person who is entitled to use a geographical name).

Nature of proprietor's business

A1–131   **4.** A certification mark shall not be registered if the proprietor carries on a business involving the supply of goods or services of the kind certified.

Mark not to be misleading as to character or significance

A1–132   **5.**—(1) A certification mark shall not be registered if the public is liable to be misled as regards the character or significance of the mark, in particular if it is likely to be taken to be something other than a certification mark.

(2) The registrar may accordingly require that a mark in respect of which application is made for registration include some indication that it is a certification mark.
Notwithstanding section 39(2), an application may be amended so as to comply with any such requirement.

Regulations governing use of certification mark

A1–133   **6.**—(1) An applicant for registration of a certification mark must file with the registrar regulations governing the use of the mark.

(2) The regulations must indicate who is authorised to use the mark, the characteristics to be certified by the mark, how the certifying body is to test those characteristics and to supervise the use of the mark, the fees (if any) to be paid in connection with the operation of the mark and the procedures for resolving disputes.
Further requirements with which the regulations have to comply may be imposed by rules.

Approval of regulations, &c.

A1–134   **7.**—(1) A certification mark shall not be registered unless—
     (a) the regulations governing the use of the mark—
         (i) comply with paragraph 6(2) and any further requirements imposed by rules, and
         (ii) are not contrary to public policy or to accepted principles of morality, and
     (b) the applicant is competent to certify the goods or services for which the mark is to be registered.

(2) Before the end of the prescribed period after the date of the application for registration of a certification mark, the applicant must file the regulations with the registrar and pay the prescribed fee.
If he does not do so, the application shall be deemed to be withdrawn.

A1–135   **8.**—(1) The registrar shall consider whether the requirements mentioned in paragraph 7(1) are met.

(2) If it appears to the registrar that those requirements are not met, he shall inform the applicant and give him an opportunity, within such period as the registrar may specify, to make representations or to file amended regulations.

(3) If the applicant fails to satisfy the registrar that those requirements are met, or to file regulations amended so as to meet them, or fails to respond before the end of the specified period, the registrar shall refuse the application.

(4) If it appears to the registrar that those requirements, and the other requirements for registration, are met, he shall accept the application and shall proceed in accordance with section 38 (publication, opposition proceedings and observations).

A1–136   **9.** The regulations shall be published and notice of opposition may be given, and observations may be made, relating to the matters mentioned in paragraph 7(1).

This is in addition to any other grounds on which the application may be opposed or observations made.

Regulations to be open to inspection

10. The regulations governing the use of a registered certification mark shall be open to public inspection in the same way as the register.　　　　　　　　　　　　　　　　　　**A1–137**

Amendment of regulations

11.—(1) An amendment of the regulations governing the use of a registered certification mark is not effective unless and until the amended regulations are filed with the registrar and accepted by him.　　　　　　　　　　　　　　　　　　**A1–138**

(2) Before accepting any amended regulations the registrar may in any case where it appears to him expedient to do so cause them to be published.

(3) If he does so, notice of opposition may be given, and observations may be made, relating to the matters mentioned in paragraph 7(1).

Consent to assignment of registered certification mark

12. The assignment or other transmission of a registered certification mark is not effective without the consent of the registrar.　　　　　　　　　　　　　　　　　　**A1–139**

Infringement: rights of authorised users

13. The following provisions apply in relation to an authorised user of a registered certification mark as in relation to a licensee of a trade mark—　　　　　　　　　　**A1–140**

  (a) section 10(5) (definition of infringement: unauthorised application of mark to certain material);

  (b) section 19(2) (order as to disposal of infringing goods, material or articles: adequacy of other remedies);

  (c) section 89 (prohibition of importation of infringing goods, material or articles: request to Commissioners of Customs and Excise).

14. In infringement proceedings brought by the proprietor of a registered certification mark any loss suffered or likely to be suffered by authorised users shall be taken into account; and the court may give such directions as it thinks fit as to the extent to which the plaintiff is to hold the proceeds of any pecuniary remedy on behalf of such users.　　**A1–141**

Grounds for revocation of registration

15. Apart from the grounds of revocation provided for in section 46, the registration of a certification mark may be revoked on the ground—　　　　　　　　　　　　　**A1–142**

  (a) that the proprietor has begun to carry on such a business as is mentioned in paragraph 4,

  (b) that the manner in which the mark has been used by the proprietor has caused it to become liable to mislead the public in the manner referred to in paragraph 5(1),

  (c) that the proprietor has failed to observe, or to secure the observance of, the regulations governing the use of the mark,

  (d) that an amendment of the regulations has been made so that the regulations—

    (i) no longer comply with paragraph 6(2) and any further conditions imposed by rules, or

    (ii) are contrary to public policy or to accepted principles of morality, or

  (e) that the proprietor is no longer competent to certify the goods or services for which the mark is registered.

Grounds for invalidity of registration

16. Apart from the grounds of invalidity provided for in section 47, the registration of a certification mark may be declared invalid on the ground that the mark was registered in breach of the provisions of paragraph 4, 5(1) or 7(1).　　　　　　　　　　**A1–143**

Section 105　　　　　　　　　　SCHEDULE 3

TRANSITIONAL PROVISIONS

Introductory

1.—(1) In this Schedule—　　　　　　　　　　　　　　　　　　　　　　**A1–144**

"existing registered mark" means a trade mark, certification trade mark or service mark registered under the 1938 Act immediately before the commencement of this Act;

"the 1938 Act" means the Trade Marks Act 1938; and

"the old law" means that Act and any other enactment or rule of law applying to existing registered marks immediately before the commencement of this Act.

(2) For the purposes of this Schedule—

(a) an application shall be treated as pending on the commencement of this Act if it was made but not finally determined before commencement, and

(b) the date on which it was made shall be taken to be the date of filing under the 1938 Act.

Existing registered marks

A1–145   **2.**—(1) Existing registered marks (whether registered in Part A or B of the register kept under the 1938 Act) shall be transferred on the commencement of this Act to the register kept under this Act and have effect, subject to the provisions of this Schedule, as if registered under this Act.

(2) Existing registered marks registered as a series under section 21(2) of the 1938 Act shall be similarly registered in the new register.

Provision may be made by rules for putting such entries in the same form as is required for entries under this Act.

(3) In any other case notes indicating that existing registered marks are associated with other marks shall cease to have effect on the commencement of this Act.

A1–146   **3.**—(1) A condition entered on the former register in relation to an existing registered mark immediately before the commencement of this Act shall cease to have effect on commencement.

Proceedings under section 33 of the 1938 Act (application to expunge or vary registration for breach of condition) which are pending on the commencement of this Act shall be dealt with under the old law and any necessary alteration made to the new register.

(2) A disclaimer or limitation entered on the former register in relation to an existing registered mark immediately before the commencement of this Act shall be transferred to the new register and have effect as if entered on the register in pursuance of section 13 of this Act.

Effects of registration: infringement

A1–147   **4.**—(1) Sections 9 to 12 of this Act (effects of registration) apply in relation to an existing registered mark as from the commencement of this Act and section 14 of this Act (action for infringement) applies in relation to infringement of an existing registered mark committed after the commencement of this Act, subject to sub-paragraph (2) below.

The old law continues to apply in relation to infringements committed before commencement.

(2) It is not an infringement of—

(a) an existing registered mark, or

(b) a registered trade mark of which the distinctive elements are the same or substantially the same as those of an existing registered mark and which is registered for the same goods or services,

to continue after commencement any use which did not amount to infringement of the existing registered mark under the old law.

Infringing goods, material or articles

A1–148   **5.** Section 16 of this Act (order for delivery up of infringing goods, material or articles) applies to infringing goods, material or articles whether made before or after the commencement of this Act.

Rights and remedies of licensee or authorised user

A1–149   **6.**—(1) Section 30 (general provisions as to rights of licensees in case of infringement) of this Act applies to licences granted before the commencement of this Act, but only in relation to infringements committed after commencement.

(2) Paragraph 14 of Schedule 2 of this Act (court to take into account loss suffered by authorised users, &c.) applies only in relation to infringements committed after commencement.

Co-ownership of registered mark

7. The provisions of section 23 of this Act (co-ownership of registered mark) apply as **A1–150** from the commencement of this Act to an existing registered mark of which two or more persons were immediately before commencement registered as joint proprietors.

But so long as the relations between the joint proprietors remain such as are described in section 63 of the 1938 Act (joint ownership) there shall be taken to be an agreement to exclude the operation of subsections (1) and (3) of section 23 of this Act (ownership in undivided shares and right of co-proprietor to make separate use of the mark).

Assignment, &c. of registered mark

8.—(1) Section 24 of this Act (assignment or other transmission of registered mark) ap- **A1–151** plies to transactions and events occurring after the commencement of this Act in relation to an existing registered mark; and the old law continues to apply in relation to transactions and events occurring before commencement.

(2) Existing entries under section 25 of the 1938 Act (registration of assignments and transmissions) shall be transferred on the commencement of this Act to the register kept under this Act and have effect as if made under section 25 of this Act.

Provision may be made by rules for putting such entries in the same form as is required for entries made under this Act.

(3) An application for registration under section 25 of the 1938 Act which is pending before the registrar on the commencement of this Act shall be treated as an application for registration under section 25 of this Act and shall proceed accordingly.

The registrar may require the applicant to amend his application so as to conform with the requirements of this Act.

(4) An application for registration under section 25 of the 1938 Act which has been determined by the registrar but not finally determined before the commencement of this Act shall be dealt with under the old law; and sub-paragraph (2) above shall apply in relation to any resulting entry in the register.

(5) Where before the commencement of this Act a person has become entitled by assignment or transmission to an existing registered mark but has not registered his title, any application for registration after commencement shall be made under section 25 of this Act.

(6) In cases to which sub-paragraph (3) or (5) applies section 25(3) of the 1938 Act continues to apply (and section 25(3) and (4) of this Act do not apply) as regards the consequences of failing to register.

Licensing of registered mark

9.—(1) Sections 28 and 29(2) of this Act (licensing of registered trade mark; rights of **A1–152** exclusive licensee against grantor's successor in title) apply only in relation to licences granted after the commencement of this Act; and the old law continues to apply in relation to licences granted before commencement.

(2) Existing entries under section 28 of the 1938 Act (registered users) shall be transferred on the commencement of this Act to the register kept under this Act and have effect as if made under section 25 of this Act.

Provision may be made by rules for putting such entries in the same form as is required for entries made under this Act.

(3) An application for registration as a registered user which is pending before the registrar on the commencement of this Act shall be treated as an application for registration of a licence under section 25(1) of this Act and shall proceed accordingly.

The registrar may require the applicant to amend his application so as to conform with the requirements of this Act.

(4) An application for registration as a registered user which has been determined by the registrar but not finally determined before the commencement of this Act shall be dealt with under the old law; and sub-paragraph (2) above shall apply in relation to any resulting entry in the register.

(5) Any proceedings pending on the commencement of this Act under section 28(8) or (10) of the 1938 Act (variation or cancellation of registration of registered user) shall be dealt with under the old law and any necessary alteration made to the new register.

Pending applications for registration

A1–153 **10.**—(1) An application for registration of a mark under the 1938 Act which is pending on the commencement of this Act shall be dealt with under the old law, subject as mentioned below, and if registered the mark shall be treated for the purposes of this Schedule as an existing registered mark.

(2) The power of the Secretary of State under section 78 of this Act to make rules regulating practice and procedure, and as to the matters mentioned in subsection (2) of that section, is exercisable in relation to such an application; and different provision may be made for such applications from that made for other applications.

(3) Section 23 of the 1938 Act (provisions as to associated trade marks) shall be disregarded in dealing after the commencement of this Act with an application for registration.

Conversion of pending application

A1–154 **11.**—(1) In the case of a pending application for registration which has not been advertised under section 18 of the 1938 Act before the commencement of thisAct, the applicant may give notice to the registrar claiming to have the registrability of the mark determined in accordance with the provisions of this Act.

(2) The notice must be in the prescribed form, be accompanied by the appropriate fee and be given no later than six months after the commencement of this Act.

(3) Notice duly given is irrevocable and has the effect that the application shall be treated as if made immediately after the commencement of this Act.

Trade marks registered according to old classification

A1–155 **12.** The registrar may exercise the powers conferred by rules under section 65 of this Act (adaptation of entries to new classification) to secure that any existing registered marks which do not conform to the system of classification prescribed under section 34 of this Act are brought into conformity with that system.

This applies, in particular, to existing registered marks classified according to the pre-1938 classification set out in Schedule 3 to the Trade Marks Rules 1986.

Claim to priority from overseas application

A1–156 **13.** Section 35 of this Act (claim to priority of Convention application) applies to an application for registration under this Act made after the commencement of this Act notwithstanding that the Convention application was made before commencement.

A1–157 **14.**—(1) Where before the commencement of this Act a person has duly filed an application for protection of a trade mark in a relevant country within the meaning of section 39A of the 1938 Act which is not a Convention country ("a relevant overseas application"), he, or his successor in title, has a right to priority, for the purposes of registering the same trade mark under this Act for some or all of the same goods or services, for a period of six months from the date of filing of the relevant overseas application.

(2) If the application for registration under this Act is made within that six-month period—

    (a) the relevant date for the purposes of establishing which rights take precedence shall be the date of filing of the relevant overseas application, and

    (b) the registrability of the trade mark shall not be affected by any use of the mark in the United Kingdom in the period between that date and the date of the application under this Act.

(3) Any filing which in a relevant country is equivalent to a regular national filing, under its domestic legislation or an international agreement, shall be treated as giving rise to the right of priority.

A "regular national filing" means a filing which is adequate to establish the date on which the application was filed in that country, whatever may be the subsequent fate of the application.

(4) A subsequent application concerning the same subject as the relevant overseas application, filed in the same country, shall be considered the relevant overseas application (of which the filing date is the starting date of the period of priority), if at the time of the subsequent application—

    (a) the previous application has been withdrawn, abandoned or refused, without having been laid open to public inspection and without leaving any rights outstanding, and

    (b) it has not yet served as a basis for claiming a right of priority.

The previous application may not thereafter serve as a basis for claiming a right of priority.

(5) Provision may be made by rules as to the manner of claiming a right to priority on the basis of a relevant overseas application.

(6) A right to priority arising as a result of a relevant overseas application may be assigned or otherwise transmitted, either with the application or independently.

The reference in sub-paragraph (1) to the applicant's "successor in title" shall be construed accordingly.

(7) Nothing in this paragraph affects proceedings on an application for registration under the 1938 Act made before the commencement of this Act (see paragraph 10 above).

Duration and renewal of registration

15.—(1) Section 42(1) of this Act (duration of original period of registration) applies in relation to the registration of a mark in pursuance of an application made after the commencement of this Act; and the old law applies in any other case.   **A1–158**

(2) Sections 42(2) and 43 of this Act (renewal) apply where the renewal falls due on or after the commencement of this Act; and the old law continues to apply in any other case.

(3) In either case it is immaterial when the fee is paid.

Pending application for alteration of registered mark

16. An application under section 35 of the 1938 Act (alteration of registered trade mark) which is pending on the commencement of this Act shall be dealt with under the old law and any necessary alteration made to the new register.   **A1–159**

Revocation for non-use

17.—(1) An application under section 26 of the 1938 Act (removal from register or imposition of limitation on ground of non-use) which is pending on the commencement of this Act shall be dealt with under the old law and any necessary alteration made to the new register.   **A1–160**

(2) An application under section 46(1)(a) or (b) of this Act (revocation for non-use) may be made in relation to an existing registered mark at any time after the commencement of this Act.

Provided that no such application for the revocation of the registration of an existing registered mark registered by virtue of section 27 of the 1938 Act (defensive registration of well-known trade marks) may be made until more than five years after the commencement of this Act.

Application for rectification, &c.

18.—(1) An application under section 32 or 34 of the 1938 Act (rectification or correction of the register) which is pending on the commencement of this Act shall be dealt with under the old law and any necessary alteration made to the new register.   **A1–161**

(2) For the purposes of proceedings under section 47 of this Act (grounds for invalidity of registration) as it applies in relation to an existing registered mark, the provisions of this Act shall be deemed to have been in force at all material times.

Provided that no objection to the validity of the registration of an existing registered mark may be taken on the ground specified in subsection (3) of section 5 of this Act (relative grounds for refusal of registration: conflict with earlier mark registered for different goods or services).

Regulations as to use of certification mark

19.—(1) Regulations governing the use of an existing registered certification mark   **A1–162**

deposited at the Patent Office in pursuance of section 37 of the 1938 Act shall be treated after the commencement of this Act as if filed under paragraph 6 of Schedule 2 to this Act.

(2) Any request for amendment of the regulations which was pending on the commencement of this Act shall be dealt with under the old law.

Sheffield marks

A1–163   **20.**—(1) For the purposes of this Schedule the Sheffield register kept under Schedule 2 to the 1938 Act shall be treated as part of the register of trade marks kept under that Act.

(2) Applications made to the Cutlers' Company in accordance with that Schedule which are pending on the commencement of this Act shall proceed after commencement as if they had been made to the registrar.

Certificate of validity of contested registration

A1–164   **21.** A certificate given before the commencement of this Act under section 47 of the 1938 Act (certificate of validity of contested registration) shall have effect as if given under section 73(1) of this Act.

Trade mark agents

A1–165   **22.**—(1) Rules in force immediately before the commencement of this Act under section 282 or 283 of the Copyright, Designs and Patents Act 1988 (register of trade mark agents; persons entitled to described themselves as registered) shall continue in force and have effect as if made under section 83 or 85 of this Act.

(2) Rules in force immediately before the commencement of this Act under section 40 of the 1938 Act as to the persons whom the registrar may refuse to recognise as agents for the purposes of business under that Act shall continue in force and have effect as if made under section 88 of this Act.

(3) Rules continued in force under this paragraph may be varied or revoked by further rules made under the relevant provisions of this Act.

Section 106(1)   SCHEDULE 4

CONSEQUENTIAL AMENDMENTS

General adaptation of existing references

A1–166   **1.**—(1) References in statutory provisions passed or made before the commencement of this Act to trade marks or registered trade marks within the meaning of the Trade Marks Act 1938 shall, unless the context otherwise requires, be construed after the commencement of this Act as references to trade marks or registered trade marks within the meaning of this Act.

(2) Sub-paragraph (1) applies, in particular, to the references in the following provisions—

Industrial Organisation and Development Act 1947	Schedule 1, paragraph 7
Crown Proceedings Act 1947	section 3(1)(b)
[...]	
Printer's Imprint Act 1961	section 1(1)(b)
Patents Act 1977	section 19(2) section 27(4) section 123(7)
Unfair Contract Terms Act 1977	Schedule 1, paragraph 1(c)
Judicature (Northern Ireland) Act 1978	section 94A(5)
State Immunity Act 1978	section 7(a) and (b)
Supreme Court Act 1981	section 72(5) Schedule 1, paragraph 1(i)

Civil Jurisdiction and Judgments Act 1982	Schedule 5, paragraph 2 Schedule 8, paragraph 2(14) and 4(2)
Value Added Tax Act 1983	Schedule 3, paragraph 1
Companies Act 1985	section 396(3A)(a) or (as substituted by the Companies Act 1989) section 396(2)(d)(i) section 410(4)(c)(v) Schedule 4, Part I, Balance Sheet Formats 1 and 2 and Note (2) Schedule 9, Part I, paragraphs 5(2)(d) and 10(2)
Law Reform (Miscellaneous Provisions) (Scotland) Act 1985	section 15(5)
Atomic Energy Authority Act 1986	section 8(2)
Companies (Northern Ireland) Order 1986	article 403(3A)(a) or (as substituted by the Companies (No.2) (Northern Ireland) Order 1990)article 403(2)(d)(i) Schedule 4, Part I, Balance Sheet Formats 1 and 2 and Note (2) Schedule 9, Part I, paragraphs 5(2)(d) and 10(2)
Consumer Protection Act 1987	section 2(2)(b)
Consumer Protection (Northern Ireland) Order 1987	article 5(2)(b)
Income and Corporation Taxes Act 1988	section 83(a)
Taxation of Chargeable Gains Act 1992	section 275(h)
Tribunals and Inquiries Act 1992	Schedule 1, paragraph 34.

Amendment

References to the Plant Varieties and Seeds Act 1964, s.5A(4), and the Northern Ireland Constitution Act 1973, Sch.3, para.17, were repealed by the Plant Varieties Act 1997 and the Northern Ireland Act 1998 respectively.

Reference to Horticulture Act 1960 s.15(1)(b) was repealed by the Statute Law (Repeals) Act 2004, Sch.1, Pt 2, para.1.

2.—(1) The Patents and Designs Act 1907 is amended as follows.　**A1–167**

(2) In section 62 (the Patent Office)—
  (a) in subsection (1) for "this Act and the Trade Marks Act 1905" substitute "the Patents Act 1977, the Registered Designs Act 1949 and the Trade Marks Act 1994"; and
  (b) in subsections (2) and (3) for "the Board of Trade" substitute "the Secretary of State".

(3) In section 63 (officers and clerks of the Patent Office)—
  (a) for "the Board of Trade" in each place where it occurs substitute "the Secretary of State"; and
  (b) in subsection (2) omit the words from "and those salaries" to the end.

(4) The repeal by the Patents Act 1949 and the Registered Designs Act 1949 of the whole of the 1907 Act, except certain provisions, shall be deemed not to have extended to the long title, date of enactment or enacting words or to so much of section 99 as provides the Act with its short title.

Patents, Designs, Copyright and Trade Marks (Emergency) Act 1939 (c.107)

3.—(1) The Patents, Designs, Copyright and Trade Marks (Emergency) Act 1939 is amended as follows.　**A1–168**

(2) For section 3 (power of comptroller to suspend rights of enemy or enemy subject) substitute—

Power of comptroller to suspend trade mark rights of enemy or enemy subject

3.—(1) Where on application made by a person proposing to supply goods or services of any description it is made to appear to the comptroller—

     (a) that it is difficult or impracticable to describe or refer to the goods or services without the use of a registered trade mark, and

     (b) that the proprietor of the registered trade mark (whether alone or jointly with another) is an enemy or an enemy subject,

the comptroller may make an order suspending the rights given by the registered trade mark.

(2) An order under this section shall suspend those rights as regards the use of the trade mark—

     (a) by the applicant, and

     (b) by any person authorised by the applicant to do, for the purposes of or in connection with the supply by the applicant of the goods or services, things which would otherwise infringe the registered trade mark,

to such extent and for such period as the comptroller considers necessary to enable the applicant to render well-known and established some other means of describing or referring to the goods or services in question which does not involve the use of the trade mark.

(3) Where an order has been made under this section, no action for passing off lies on the part of any person interested in the registered trade mark in respect of any use of it which by virtue of the order is not an infringement of the right conferred by it.

(4) An order under this section may be varied or revoked by a subsequent order made by the comptroller."

(3) In each of the following provisions—

     (a) section 4(1)(c) (effect of war on registration of trade marks),

     (b) section 6(1) (power of comptroller to extend time limits),

     (c) section 7(1)(a) (evidence as to nationality, &c.), and

     (d) the definition of "the comptroller" in section 10(1) (interpretation),

for "the Trade Marks Act 1938" substitute "the Trade Marks Act 1994".

Trade Descriptions Act 1968 (c.29)

A1–169   **4.**—(1) In the Trade Descriptions Act 1968, in section 34 (exemption of trade description contained in pre-1968 trade mark)—

     (a) in the opening words, omit "within the meaning of the Trade Marks Act 1938"; and

     (b) in paragraph (c), for "a person registered under section 28 of the Trade Marks Act 1938 as a registered user of the trade mark" substitute," in the case of a registered trade mark, a person licensed to use it".

Solicitors Act 1974 (c.47)

A1–170   **5.**—(1) Section 22 of the Solicitors Act 1974 (preparation of instruments by unqualified persons) is amended as follows.

(2) In subsection (2)(aa) and (ab) (instruments which may be prepared by registered trade mark agent or registered patent agent) for, "trade mark or service mark" substitute "or trade mark".

(3) In subsection (3A) (interpretation)—

(a) in the definition of "registered trade mark agent" for "section 282(1) of the Copyright, Designs and Patents Act 1988" substitute "the Trade Marks Act 1994"; and

(b) in the definition of "registered patent agent" for "of that Act" substitute "of the Copyright, Designs and Patents Act 1988".

House of Commons Disqualification Act 1975 (c.24)

6.—(1) In Part III of Schedule 1 to the House of Commons Disqualification Act 1975 (other disqualifying offices), for the entry relating to persons appointed to hear and determine appeals under the Trade Marks Act 1938 substitute— **A1–171**

> "Person appointed to hear and determine appeals under the Trade Marks Act 1994."

Restrictive Trade Practices Act 1976 (c.34)

7.—(1) In Schedule 3 to the Restrictive Trade Practices Act 1976 (excepted agreements), for paragraph 4 (agreements relating to trade marks) substitute— **A1–172**

"**4.**—(1) This Act does not apply to an agreement authorising the use of a registered trade mark (other than a collective mark or certification mark) if no such restrictions as are described in section 6(1) or 11(2) above are accepted, and no such information provisions as are described in section 7(1) or 12(2) above are made, except in respect of—

(a) the descriptions of goods bearing the mark which are to be produced or supplied, or the processes of manufacture to be applied to such goods or to goods to which the mark is to be applied, or

(b) the kinds of services in relation to which the mark is to be used which are to be made available or supplied, or the form or manner in which such services are to be made available or supplied, or

(c) the descriptions of goods which are to be produced or supplied in connection with the supply of services in relation to which the mark is to be used, or the process of manufacture to be applied to such goods.

(2) This Act does not apply to an agreement authorising the use of a registered collective mark or certification mark if—

(a) the agreement is made in accordance with regulations approved by the registrar under Schedule 1 or 2 to the Trade Marks Act 1994, and

(b) no such restrictions as are described in section 6(1) or 11(2) above are accepted, and no such information provisions as are described in section 7(1) or 12(2) above are made, except as permitted by those regulations.".

Copyright, Designs and Patents Act 1988 (c.48)

8.—(1) The Copyright, Designs and Patents Act 1988 is amended as follows. **A1–173**

(2) In sections 114(6), 204(6) and 231(6) (persons regarded as having an interest in infringing copies, &c.), for "section 58C of the Trade Marks Act 1938" substitute "section 19 of the Trade Marks Act 1994".

(3) In section 280(1) (privilege for communications with patent agents), for "trade mark or service mark" substitute "or trade mark".

Tribunals and Inquiries Act 1992 (c.53)

9. In Part I of Schedule 1 to the Tribunals and Inquiries Act 1992 (tribunals under direct supervision of Council on Tribunals), for "Patents, designs, trade marks and service marks" substitute "Patents, designs and trade marks". **A1–174**

Section 106(2)   SCHEDULE 5

REPEALS AND REVOCATIONS

A1–175

Chapter or number	Short title	Extent of repeal or revocation
1891 c. 50	Commissioners for Oaths Act 1891	In section 1, the words "or the Patents, Designs and Trade Marks Acts, 1883 to 1888,".
1907 c. 29.	Patents and Designs Act 1907	In section 63(2), the words from "and those salaries" to the end.
1938 c. 22.	Trade Marks Act 1938.	The whole Act
1947 c. 44.	Crown Proceedings Act 1947.	In section 3(1)(b), the words "or registered service mark".
1949 c. 87.	Patents Act 1949.	Section 92(2).
1964 c.14.	Plant Varieties and Seeds Act 1964.	In section 5A(4), the words "under the Trade Marks Act 1938".
1967 c. 80.	Criminal Justice Act 1967.	In Schedule 3, in Part I and IV, the entries relating to the Trade Marks Act 1938.
1978 c. 23.	Judicature (Northern Ireland) Act 1978.	In Schedule 5, in Part II, the paragraphs amending the Trade Marks Act 1938.
1984 c. 19.	Trade Marks (Amendment) Act 1984.	The whole Act.
1985 c. 6.	Companies Act 1985.	In section 396— (a) in subsection (3A)(a), and (b) in subsection (2)(d)(i) as inserted by the Companies Act 1989, the words "service mark,".
1986 c. 12.	Statute Law (Repeals) Act 1986.	In Schedule 2, paragraph 2.
1986 c. 39.	Patents, Designs and Marks Act 1986.	Section 2. Section 4(4). In Schedule 1, paragraphs 1 and 2. Schedule 2.
S.I. 1986/1032 (N.I. 6).	Companies (Nothern Ireland) Order 1986.	In article 403— (a) in paragraph (3A)(a), and (b) in paragraph (2)(d)(i) as inserted by the Companies (No.2) (Northern Ireland) Order 1990, the words "service mark,".
1987 c. 43.	Consumer Protection Act 1987.	In section 45— (a) in subsection (1), the definition of "mark" and "trade mark"; (b) subsection (4).
S.I. 1987/2049.	Consumer Protection (Northern Ireland) Order 1987.	In article 2— (a) in paragraph (2), the definition of "mark" and "trade mark"; (b) paragraph (3).
1988 c. 1.	Income and Corporation Taxes Act 1988.	In section 83, the words from "References in this section" to the end.

Chapter or number	Short title	Extent of repeal or revocation
1988 c. 48.	Copyright, Designs and Patents Act 1988.	Section 282 to 284.
		In section 286, the definition of "registered trade mark agent". Section 300.
1992 c. 12.	Taxation of Chargeable Gains Act 1992.	In section 275(h), the words "service marks" and "service mark".

PART II

REGISTRY MATERIALS

This appendix contains the Trade Mark Rules 2000 in their complete form as **A2–001** they stand following the amendments made by the Trade Marks (Amendment) Rules 2001 (SI 2001/3832) and the Trade Marks (Amendment) Rules 2004 (SI 2004/947).

The appendix does not show the text deleted by the amending rules, and nor does it show the text inserted by them differently from the original text. Doing either or both tends to obscure the present form of the rules. Instead, the list of rules in the Arrangement of Rules section below has been marked to show which rule was changed by the 2001 amendments and which by the 2004 amendments (the latter by a single asterisk and the latter by a double asterisk).

The transitional provisions of the 2004 amending rules appear at the end of this appendix since they still have some relevance for applications made and proceedings instituted before those amendments came into force on May 5, 2004.

The Trade Marks Rules 2000 as amended (with 2004 transitional provisions)

SI 2000/136

ARRANGEMENT OF RULES

PRELIMINARY

A2–002 *The Secretary of State, in exercise of the powers conferred upon him by sections 4(4), 13(2), 25(1), (5) and (6), 34(1), 35(5), 38(1) and (2), 39(3), 40(4), 41(1) and (3), 43(2), (3), (5) and (6), 44(3), 45(2), 63(2) and (3), 64(4), 65, 66(2), 67(1) and (2), 68(1) and (3), 69, 76(1), 78, 80(3), 81, 82 and 88 of, paragraph 6(2) of Schedule 1 to, paragraph 7(2) of Schedule 2 to, and paragraphs 10(2), 12 and 14(5) of Schedule 3 to, the Trade Marks Act 1994, after consultation with the Council on Tribunals pursuant to section 8(1) of the Tribunals and Inquiries Act 1992, hereby makes the following Rules:-*

Preliminary

Citation and commencement

A2–003 **1.** These Rules may be cited as the Trade Marks Rules 2000 and shall come into force on 17th February 2000.

Interpretation

A2–004 **2.**—(1) In these Rules, unless the context otherwise requires—

"the Act" means the Trade Marks Act 1994;

"the Journal" means the Trade Marks Journal published in accordance with rule 71 below;

"the Office" means the Patent Office;

"old law" means the Trade Marks Act 1938 (as amended) and any rules made thereunder existing immediately before the commencement of the Act;

"proprietor" means the person registered as the proprietor of the trade mark;

"publish" means publish in the Journal;

"send" includes give;

"specification" means the statement of goods or services in respect of which a trade mark is registered or proposed to be registered;

"United Kingdom" includes the Isle of Man.

(2) In these Rules, except where otherwise indicated, a reference to a section is a reference to that section in the Act, a reference to a rule is a reference to that rule in these Rules, a reference to a Schedule is a reference to that Schedule to these Rules and a reference to a form is a reference to that form as published by the registrar under rule 3 below.

(3) In these Rules references to the filing of any application, notice or other document, unless the contrary intention appears, are to be construed as references to its being delivered to the registrar at the Office.

Forms and directions of the registrar under s.66

A2–005 **3.**—(1) Any forms required by the registrar to be used for the purpose of registration of a trade mark or any other proceedings before her under the Act pursuant to section 66 and any directions with respect to their use shall be published and any amendment or modification of a form or of the directions with respect to its use shall be published.

(2) A requirement under this rule to use a form as published is satisfied by the use either of a replica of that form or of a form which is acceptable to the registrar and contains the information required by the form as published and complies with any directions as to the use of such a form.

Requirement as to fees

4.—(1) The fees to be paid in respect of any application, registration or any other matter under the Act and these Rules shall be those (if any) prescribed in relation to such matter by rules under section 79 (fees).   **A2–006**

(2) Any form required to be filed with the registrar in respect of any specified matter shall be subject to the payment of the fee (if any) prescribed in respect of that matter by those rules.

Application for registration

Applications for registration; s.32 (Form TM3)

5.—(1) An application for the registration of a trade mark shall be filed on Form TM3 and shall be subject to the payment of the application fee and such class fees as may be appropriate.   **A2–007**

Claim to priority; ss.35 & 36

6.—(1) Where a right to priority is claimed by reason of an application for protection of a trade mark duly filed in a Convention country under section 35 or in another country or territory in respect of which provision corresponding to that made by section 35 is made under section 36, particulars of that claim shall be included in the application for registration under rule 5 above and, where no certificate as is referred to in paragraph (2) below is filed with the application, such particulars shall include the country or countries and the date or dates of filing.   **A2–008**

(2) Unless it has been filed at the time of the filing of the application for registration, there shall be filed, within three months of the filing of the application under rule 5, a certificate by the registering or other competent authority of that country certifying, or verifying to the satisfaction of the registrar, the date of the filing of the application, the country or registering or competent authority, the representation of the mark, and the goods or services covered by the application.

Classification of goods and services; s.34

7.—(1) For the purposes of trade mark registrations dated before 1st January 2002, goods and services shall be classified in accordance with Schedule 3, except where a specification is reclassified under rule 46 below to Schedule 4.   **A2–009**

(2) For the purposes of trade mark registrations dated on or after 1st January 2002, goods and services shall be classified in accordance with Schedule 4, which sets out the latest version of the classes of the International Classification of Goods and Services.

Application may relate to more than one class and shall specify the class (Form TM3A)

8.—(1) An application may be made in more than one class of Schedule 4.   **A2–010**

(2) Every application shall specify—
    (a) the class in Schedule 4 to which it relates; and
    (b) the goods or services which are appropriate to the class and they shall be described in such a way as to indicate clearly the nature of those goods

or services and to allow them to be classified in the classes in Schedule 4.

(3) If the application relates to more than one class in Schedule 4 the specification contained in it shall set out the classes in consecutive numerical order and the specification of the goods or services shall be grouped accordingly.

(4) If the specification contained in the application lists items by reference to a class in Schedule 4 in which they do not fall, the applicant may request, by filing Form TM3A, that his application be amended to include the appropriate class for those items, and upon the payment of such class fee as may be appropriate the registrar shall amend his application accordingly.

Determination of classification

A2–011   **8A.**—(1) Where an application does not satisfy the requirements of rule 8(2)(b) or 8(3), the registrar shall send notice thereof to the applicant.

(2) A notice sent under paragraph (1) shall specify a period, of not less than two months, within which the applicant must satisfy those requirements.

(3) Where the applicant fails to satisfy those requirements before the expiry of the period specified under paragraph (2) his application shall be treated as abandoned.

Prohibition on registration of mark consisting of arms; s.4

A2–012   **9.** Where a representation of any arms or insignia as is referred to in section 4(4) appears in a mark, the registrar shall refuse to accept an application for the registration of the mark unless satisfied that the consent of the person entitled to the arms has been obtained.

Address for service (Form TM33)

A2–013   **10.**—(1) For the purposes of any proceedings before the registrar under these Rules or any appeal from a decision of the registrar under the Act or these Rules, an address for service in the United Kingdom shall be filed by—

(a) every applicant for the registration of a trade mark;

(b) every person opposing an application for registration of a trade mark;

(c) every applicant applying to the registrar under section 46 for the revocation of the registration of a trade mark, under section 47 for the invalidation of the registration of a trade mark, or under section 64 for the rectification of the register;

(d) every person granted leave to intervene under rule 35 (the intervener); and

(e) every proprietor of a registered trade mark which is the subject of an application to the registrar for the revocation, invalidation or rectification of the registration of the mark.

(2) The address for service of an applicant for registration of a trade mark shall upon registration of the mark be deemed to be the address for service of the registered proprietor, subject to any filing to the contrary under paragraph (1) above or rule 44(2) below.

(3) In any case in which an address for service is filed at the same time as the filing of a form required by the registrar under rule 3 which requires the furnishing of an address for service, the address shall be filed on that form and in any other case it shall be filed on Form TM33.

(4) Anything sent to any applicant, opponent, intervener or registered proprietor at his address for service shall be deemed to be properly sent; and the registrar may, where no address for service is filed, treat as the address for service of the person concerned his trade or business address in the United Kingdom, if any.

(5) An address for service in the United Kingdom may be filed at any time by the proprietor of a registered trade mark and by any person having an interest in or charge on a registered trade mark which has been registered under rule 40.

(6) Where an address for service is not filed as required by paragraph (1) above, the registrar shall send the person concerned notice to file an address for service within two months of the date of the notice and if that person fails to do so—

(a) in the case of an applicant as is referred to in sub-paragraph (a) or (c), the application shall be treated as abandoned;

(b) in the case of a person as is referred to in sub-paragraph (b) or (d), he shall be deemed to have withdrawn from the proceedings; and

(c) in the case of the proprietor referred to in sub-paragraph (e), he shall not be permitted to take part in any proceedings.

Deficiencies in application; s.32

11. Where an application for registration of a trade mark does not satisfy the requirements of section 32(2), (3) or (4) or rule 5(1) or 8(2)(a), the registrar shall send notice thereof to the applicant to remedy the deficiencies or, in the case of section 32(4), the default of payment and if within two months of the date of the notice the applicant—

A2–014

(a) fails to remedy any deficiency notified to him in respect of section 32(2), the application shall be deemed never to have been made; or

(b) fails to remedy any deficiency notified to him in respect of section 32(3) or rule 5(1) or 8(2)(a)or fails to make payment as required by section 32(4) the application shall be treated as abandoned.

Publication, observations, oppositions and registration

Publication of application for registration; s.38(1)

12. An application which has been accepted for registration shall be published.

A2–015

Opposition proceedings: filing of notice of opposition; s38(2) (Form TM7)

13.—(1) Any person may, within three months of the date on which the application was published, give notice to the registrar of opposition to the registration on Form TM7 which shall include a statement of the grounds of opposition.

A2–016

(2) Where the opposition is based on a trade mark which has been registered, there shall be included in the statement of the grounds of opposition a representation of that mark and—

(a) the details of the authority with which the mark is registered;

(b) the registration number of that mark;

(c) the classes in respect of which that mark is registered;

(d) the goods and services in respect of which—

    (i) that mark is registered; and

    (ii) the opposition is based; and

(e) where the registration procedure for the mark was completed before the start of the period of five years ending with the date of publication, a statement detailing whether during the period referred to in section 6A(3)(a) the mark has been put to genuine use in relation to each of the goods and services in respect of which the opposition is based or whether there are proper reasons for non-use (for the purposes of rule 13C this is the "statement of use").

(3) Where the opposition is based on a trade mark in respect of which an application for registration has been made, there shall be included in the statement

of the grounds of opposition a representation of that mark and those matters set out in paragraph (2)(a) to (d), with references to registration being construed as references to the application for registration.

(4) Where the opposition is based on an unregistered trade mark or other sign which the person opposing the application claims to be protected by virtue of any rule of law (in particular, the law of passing off), there shall be included in the statement of the grounds of opposition a representation of that mark or sign and the goods and services in respect of which such protection is claimed.

(5) The registrar shall send a copy of Form TM7 to the applicant and the date upon which this is done shall, for the purposes of rule 13A, be the "notification date".

Opposition proceedings: filing of counter-statement and cooling off period (Forms TM8, TM9c & TM9t)

A2–017   13A.—(1) The applicant shall, within the relevant period, file a Form TM8, which shall include a counter-statement, otherwise his application for registration shall be deemed to be withdrawn.

(2) Unless either paragraph (3) or (4) applies, the relevant period shall begin on the notification date and end three months after that date.

(3) This paragraph applies where—

   (a) the applicant and the person opposing the registration agree to an extension of time for the filing of Form TM8;
   (b) within the period of three months beginning on the notification date, either party files Form TM9c requesting an extension of time for the filing of Form TM8; and
   (c) during the period beginning on the date Form TM9c was filed and ending twelve months after the notification date, no notice to continue on Form TM9t is filed by the person opposing the registration,

and where this paragraph applies the relevant period shall begin on the notification date and end twelve months after that date.

(4) This paragraph applies where—

   (a) a request for an extension of time for the filing of Form TM8 has been filed on Form TM9c; and
   (b) the person opposing the registration has filed a notice to continue on Form TM9t,

and where this paragraph applies the relevant period shall begin on the notification date and end one month after the date on which Form TM9t was filed or three months after the notification date, whichever is the later.

(5) The registrar shall send a copy of Form TM8 to the person opposing the registration and, unless rule 13B applies, the date upon which this is sent shall, for the purposes of rule 13C, be the "initiation date".

Opposition proceedings: preliminary indication (Form TM53)

A2–018   13B.—(1) This rule applies if—

   (a) the opposition or part of it is based on the relative grounds of refusal set out in section 5(1) or (2); and
   (b) the registrar has not indicated to the parties that she thinks that it is inappropriate for this rule to apply.

(2) After considering the statement of the grounds of opposition and the counter-statement the registrar shall notify the parties whether it appears to her that the mark should or should not be registered in respect of the goods and services listed in the application.

(3) The date upon which such notification is sent shall be the "indication date".

(4) Where it appeared to the registrar under paragraph (2) that—

    (a) the mark should be registered for all the goods and services listed in the application, the person opposing the registration shall, within one month of the indication date, file notice of intention to proceed on Form TM53, otherwise he shall be deemed to have withdrawn his opposition;

    (b) the mark should be registered for some, but not all, of the goods and services listed in the application, unless—

        (i) within the period of one month of the indication date, the applicant or the person opposing the registration files a notice of intention to proceed on Form TM53; or

        (ii) within the period of one month beginning immediately after the end of the period mentioned in paragraph (i), the applicant requests the amendment of his application so that it relates only to the goods and services which the registrar notified the parties to be goods and services for which it appeared the mark should be registered;

the applicant shall be deemed to have withdrawn his application for registration in its entirety; or

    (c) the mark should not be registered for any of the goods and services listed in the application, the applicant shall, within one month of the indication date, file notice of intention to proceed on Form TM53, otherwise he shall be deemed to have withdrawn his application for registration.

(5) The registrar need not give reasons why it appears to her that the mark should or should not be registered, nor shall her view be subject to appeal.

(6) If a notice of intention to proceed has been filed by either party then the registrar shall send a copy of that notice to all the other parties and the date upon which this is sent shall, for the purposes of rule 13C, be the "initiation date".

Opposition proceedings: evidence rounds (Form TM54)

13C.—(1) The person opposing the registration, within three months of the initiation date—   **A2–019**

    (a) shall file any evidence he considers necessary to adduce in support of his grounds of opposition; and

    (b) where—

        (i) the opposition is based on an earlier trade mark;

        (ii) the registration procedure for the earlier trade mark was completed before the start of the period of five years ending with the date of publication; and

        (iii) the truth of a matter set out in the statement of use is either denied or not admitted by the applicant,

shall file evidence supporting the statement of use.

(2) Where the person opposing the registration files no evidence under paragraph (1), he shall, unless the registrar otherwise directs, be deemed to have withdrawn his opposition.

(3) The registrar shall notify the applicant of any direction given under paragraph (2).

(4) The applicant may file any evidence he may consider necessary to adduce in support of his application—

    (a) within three months of the evidence being filed under paragraph (1); or

    (b) within three months of the registrar sending him notification that a direction has been given under paragraph (2).

(5) Where the applicant files evidence under paragraph (4), the person opposing the registration may, within three months of such evidence being filed, file any evidence in reply; such evidence shall be confined to matters strictly in reply to the applicant's evidence.

(6) The registrar may, at any time if she thinks fit, give leave to either party to file evidence upon such terms as she thinks fit.

(7) Under this rule, evidence shall only be considered filed when—

(a) it has been received by the registrar accompanied by Form TM54; and

(b) it has been sent to all other parties to the opposition.

(8) Where the periods for filing evidence under paragraphs (1) and (4) and, if relevant, paragraph (5) have expired, the registrar shall request that the parties give written notice of whether they wish to be heard.

(9) Where any party requests to be heard, the registrar shall send to the parties notice of a date for the hearing.

Decision of registrar in opposition proceedings

A2–020   14.—(1) When the registrar has made a decision on the acceptability of an application for registration following the procedure under rules 13 to 13C, she shall send the applicant and the person opposing the application written notice of it, stating the reasons for her decision.

(2) For the purpose of any appeal against the registrar's decision the date of the decision shall be the date when notice of the decision is sent under paragraph (1) above.

Observations on application to be sent to applicant; s.38(3)

A2–021   15. The registrar shall send to the applicant a copy of any documents containing observations made under section 38(3).

Publication of registration; s.40

A2–022   16. On the registration of the trade mark the registrar shall publish the registration, specifying the date upon which the trade mark was entered in the register.

Amendment of application

Amendment of application; s.39 (Form TM21)

A2–023   17. A request for an amendment of an application to correct an error or to change the name or address of the applicant or in respect of any amendment requested after publication of the application shall be made on Form TM21.

Amendment of application after publication; s.39 (Form TM7)

A2–024   18.—(1) Where, pursuant to section 39, a request is made for amendment of an application which has been published and the amendment affects the representation of the trade mark or the goods or services covered by the application, the amendment or a statement of the effect of the amendment shall also be published.

(2) Any person claiming to be affected by the amendment may, within one month of the date on which the amendment or a statement of the effect of the amendment was published under paragraph (1), give notice to the registrar of objection to the amendment on Form TM7 which shall include a statement of the grounds of objection which shall, in particular, indicate why the amendment would not fall within section 39(2).

(3) The registrar shall send a copy of Form TM7 to the applicant and the procedure in rules 13A to 14 shall apply to the proceedings relating to the objection to the amendment as they apply to proceedings relating to opposition to an application for registration, but with the following modifications—

(a) any reference to—

    (i) an application for registration shall be construed as a reference to a request for amendment of an application;

    (ii) the person opposing the registration shall be construed as a reference to the person objecting to the amendment of an application;

    (iii) the opposition shall be construed as a reference to the objection;

(b) the relevant period, referred to in rule 13A(1), shall for these purposes be the period of three months beginning on the date upon which the registrar sent a copy of Form TM7 to the applicant;

(c) rules 13A(2) to (4), rule 13B and rule 13C(1)(b) shall not apply.

Division, merger and series of marks

Division of application; s.41 (Form TM12)

19.—(1) At any time before registration an applicant may send to the registrar a request on Form TM12 for a division of his application for registration (the original application) into two or more separate applications (divisional applications), indicating for each division the specification of goods or services; each divisional application shall be treated as a separate application for registration with the same filing date as the original application.   **A2–025**

(2) Where the request to divide an application is sent after publication of the application, any objections in respect of, or opposition to, the original application shall be taken to apply to each divisional application and shall be proceeded with accordingly.

(3) Upon division of an original application in respect of which notice has been given to the registrar of particulars relating to the grant of a licence, or a security interest or any right in or under it, the notice and the particulars shall be deemed to apply in relation to each of the applications into which the original application has been divided.

Merger of separate applications or registrations; s.41 (Form TM17)

20.—(1) An applicant who has made separate applications for registration of a mark may, at any time before preparations for the publication of any of the applications have been completed by the Office, request the registrar on Form TM17 to merge the separate applications into a single application.   **A2–026**

(2) The registrar shall, if satisfied that all the applications which are the subject of the request for merger—

(a) are in respect of the same trade mark,

(b) bear the same date of application, and

(c) are, at the time of the request, in the name of the same person, merge them into a single application.

(3) The proprietor of two or more registrations of a trade mark may request the registrar on Form TM17 to merge them into a single registration; and the registrar shall, if satisfied that the registrations are in respect of the same trade mark, merge them into a single registration.

(4) Where any registration of a trade mark to be merged under paragraph (3) above is subject to a disclaimer or limitation, the merged registration shall also be restricted accordingly.

(5) Where any registration of a trade mark to be merged under paragraph (3) above has had registered in relation to it particulars relating to the grant of a licence or a security interest or any right in or under it, or of any memorandum or

statement of the effect of a memorandum, the registrar shall enter in the register the same particulars in relation to the merged registration.

(6) The date of registration of the merged registration shall, where the separate registrations bear different dates of registration, be the latest of those dates.

Registration of a series of trade marks; s.41 (Form TM12)

A2–027   **21.**—(1) The proprietor of a series of trade marks may apply to the registrar on Form TM3 for their registration as a series in a single registration and there shall be included in such application a representation of each mark claimed to be in the series; and the registrar shall, if satisfied that the marks constitute a series, accept the application.

(2) At any time before preparations of publication of the application have been completed by the Office, the applicant under paragraph (1) above may request on Form TM12 the division of the application into separate applications in respect of one or more marks in that series and the registrar shall divide the application accordingly, provided that at least one application remaining after such a division would comprise of either—

> (a) a single mark; or
> (b) two or more marks that would be a series of trade marks within the meaning of section 41(2).

(3) At any time the applicant for registration of a series of trade marks or the proprietor of a registered series of trade marks may request the deletion of a mark in that series, and the registrar shall delete the mark accordingly.

(3A) Where under paragraph (3) the registrar deletes a trade mark from an application for registration, the application, in so far as it relates to the deleted mark, shall be treated as withdrawn.

(4) The division of an application into one or more applications under paragraph (2) above shall be subject to the payment of a divisional fee and such application and class fees as are appropriate.

Collective and certification marks

Filing of regulations for collective and certification marks; Schs 1 & 2 (Form TM35)

A2–028   **22.** Within nine months of the date of the application for the registration of a collective or certification mark, the applicant shall file Form TM35 accompanied by a copy of the regulations governing the use of the mark.

Amendment of regulations of collective and certification marks; Sch.1 para.10 and Sch.2 para.11 (Forms TM36 & TM7)

A2–029   **23.**—(1) An application for the amendment of the regulations governing the use of a registered collective or certification mark shall be filed on Form TM36.

(2) Where it appears expedient to the registrar that the amended regulations should be made available to the public she shall publish a notice indicating where copies of the amended regulations may be inspected.

(3) Any person may, within three months of the date of publication of the notice under paragraph (2) above, make observations to the registrar on the amendments relating to the matters referred to in paragraph 6(1) of Schedule 1 in relation to a collective mark, or paragraph 7(1) of Schedule 2 in relation to a certification mark; the registrar shall send a copy thereof to the proprietor.

(4) Any person may, within three months of the date on which the notice was published under paragraph (2), give notice to the registrar of opposition to the

amendment on Form TM7 which shall include a statement of the grounds of opposition indicating why the amended regulations do not comply with the requirements of paragraph 6(1) of Schedule 1, or, as the case may be, paragraph 7(1) of Schedule 2.

(5) The registrar shall send a copy of Form TM7 to the proprietor and the procedure in rules 13A to 14 shall apply to the proceedings relating to the opposition to the amendment as they apply to proceedings relating to opposition to an application for registration, but with the following modifications

  (a) any reference to—
    (i) the applicant shall be construed as a reference to the proprietor;
    (ii) an application for registration shall be construed as a reference to an application for the amendment of the regulations;
    (iii) the person opposing the registration shall be construed as a reference to the person opposing the amendment of the regulations;
  (b) the relevant period, referred to in rule 13A(1), shall for these purposes be the period of three months beginning on the date upon which the registrar sent a copy of Form TM7 to the proprietor;
  (c) rules 13A(2) to (4), rule 13B and rule 13C(1)(b) shall not apply.

Disclaimers, limitations and alteration or surrender of registered trade mark

Registration subject to disclaimer or limitation; s.13
24. Where the applicant for registration of a trade mark or the proprietor by notice in writing sent to the registrar—   **A2–030**

  (a) disclaims any right to the exclusive use of any specified element of the trade mark, or
  (b) agrees that the rights conferred by the registration shall be subject to a specified territorial or other limitation,

the registrar shall make the appropriate entry in the register and publish such disclaimer or limitation.

Alteration of registered trade mark; s.44 (Forms TM25 & TM7)
25.—(1) The proprietor may request the registrar on Form TM25 for such   **A2–031**
alteration of his registered mark as is permitted under section 44; and the registrar may require such evidence by statutory declaration or otherwise as to the circumstances in which the application is made.

(2) Where, upon the request of the proprietor, the registrar proposes to allow such alteration, she shall publish the mark as altered.

(3) Any person claiming to be affected by the alteration may, within three months of the date on which the mark as altered was published under paragraph (2), give notice to the registrar of objection to the alteration on Form TM7 which shall include a statement of the grounds of objection.

(4) The registrar shall send a copy of Form TM7 to the proprietor and the procedure in rules 13A to 14 shall apply to the proceedings relating to the objection to the alteration as they apply to proceedings relating to opposition to an application for registration, but with the following modifications—

  (a) any reference to—
    (i) the applicant shall be construed as a reference to the proprietor;
    (ii) an application for registration shall be construed as a reference to a request for alteration;
    (iii) the person opposing the registration shall be construed as a reference to the person objecting to the alteration;

(iv) the opposition shall be construed as a reference to the objection;

(b) the relevant period, referred to in rule 13A(1), shall for these purposes be the period of three months beginning on the date upon which the registrar sent a copy of Form TM7 to the proprietor;

(c) rules 13A(2) to (4), rule 13B and rule 13C(1)(b) shall not apply.

Surrender of registered trade mark; s.45 (Forms TM22 & TM23)

A2–032   **26.**—(1) Subject to paragraph (2) below, the proprietor may surrender a registered trade mark, by sending notice to the registrar—

(a) on Form TM22 in respect of all the goods or services for which it is registered; or

(b) on Form TM23, in respect only of those goods or services specified by him in the notice.

(2) A notice under paragraph (1) above shall be of no effect unless the proprietor in that notice—

(a) gives the name and address of any person having a registered interest in the mark, and

(b) certifies that any such person—

(i) has been sent not less than three months' notice of the proprietor's intention to surrender the mark, or

(ii) is not affected or if affected consents thereto.

(3) The registrar shall, upon the surrender taking effect, make the appropriate entry in the register and publish the same.

Renewal and restoration

Reminder of renewal of registration; s.43

A2–033   **27.**—(1) Subject to paragraph (2) below, at any time not earlier than six months nor later than one month before the expiration of the last registration of a trade mark, the registrar shall (except where renewal has already been effected under rule 28 below) send to the registered proprietor notice of the approaching expiration and inform him at the same time that the registration may be renewed in the manner described in rule 28 below.

(2) If it appears to the registrar that a trade mark may be registered under section 40 at any time within six months before or at any time after the date on which renewal would be due (by reference to the date of application for registration), the registrar shall be taken to have complied with paragraph (1) if she sends to the applicant notice thereof within one month following the date of actual registration.

Renewal of registration; s.43 (Form TM11)

A2–034   **28.** Renewal of registration shall be effected by filing a request for renewal on Form TM11 at any time within the period of six months ending on the date of the expiration of the registration.

Delayed renewal and removal of registration; s.43 (Form TM11)

A2–035   **29.**—(1) If on the expiration of the last registration of a trade mark, the renewal fee has not been paid, the registrar shall publish that fact; and if, within six months from the date of the expiration of the last registration, the request for renewal is filed on Form TM11 accompanied by the appropriate renewal fee and additional renewal fee, the registrar shall renew the registration without removing the mark from the register.

(2) Where no request for renewal is filed as aforesaid, the registrar shall, subject to rule 30 below, remove the mark from the register.

(3) Where a mark is due to be registered after the date on which it is due for renewal (by reference to the date of application for registration), the request for renewal shall be filed together with the renewal fee and additional renewal fee within six months after the date of actual registration.

(4) The removal of the registration of a trade mark shall be published.

Restoration of registration; s.43 (Form TM13)

30.—(1) Where the registrar has removed the mark from the register for failure to renew its registration in accordance with rule 29 above, she may, upon a request filed on Form TM13 within six months of the date of the removal of the mark accompanied by the appropriate renewal fee and appropriate restoration fee, restore the mark to the register and renew its registration if, having regard to the circumstances of the failure to renew, she is satisfied that it is just to do so.

A2–036

(2) The restoration of the registration shall be published, with the date of restoration shown.

Revocation, invalidation and rectification

Application for revocation (on the grounds of non-use); s.46(1)(a) or (b) (Forms TM8 & TM26(N))

31.—(1) An application to the registrar for revocation of a trade mark under section 46, on the grounds set out in section 46(1)(a) or (b), shall be made on Form TM26(N) and be accompanied by a statement of the grounds on which the application is made.

A2–037

(2) The registrar shall send a copy of Form TM26(N) and the statement of the grounds on which the application is made to the proprietor.

(3) The proprietor shall, within three months of the date on which he was sent a copy of Form TM26(N) and the statement by the registrar, file a Form TM8, which shall include a counter-statement, and be accompanied by—

(a) two copies of evidence of use of the mark; or

(b) reasons for non-use of the mark,

otherwise the registrar may treat him as not opposing the application.

(4) The evidence of use of the mark shall—

(a) cover the period of non-use alleged by the applicant on Form TM26(N), or

(b) where the proprietor intends to rely on section 46(3), show that use of the mark commenced or resumed after the end of that period but before the application for revocation was made.

(5) The reasons for non-use of the mark shall cover the period of non-use alleged by the applicant on Form TM26(N).

(6) The registrar shall send a copy of Form TM8 and any evidence of use, or reasons for non-use, filed by the proprietor to the applicant and the date upon which this is sent shall, for the purposes of rule 31A, be the "initiation date".

Application for revocation (on the grounds of non-use): evidence rounds (Form TM54)

31A.—(1) The applicant may, within three months of the initiation date, file any evidence he may consider necessary to adduce in support of the grounds on which the application was made.

A2–038

(2) Where the applicant files no evidence under paragraph (1), the registrar shall notify the proprietor that no evidence was filed.

(3) The proprietor may, within the relevant period, file such evidence as he may consider necessary to adduce in support of his case.

(4) The relevant period—

(a) where the applicant files evidence under paragraph (1), is the period beginning on the date on which a copy of the evidence is filed and ending three months after that date; or

(b) where the applicant does not file evidence under paragraph (1), is the period beginning on the date on which the registrar sent the proprietor a notification under paragraph (2) that no evidence was filed and ending three months after that date.

(5) Where the proprietor files evidence under paragraph (3), the applicant may, within three months of such evidence being filed, file any evidence in reply; such evidence shall be confined to matters strictly in reply to the proprietor's evidence.

(6) The registrar may, at any time if she thinks fit, give leave to either party to file evidence upon such terms as she thinks fit.

(7) Under this rule, evidence shall only be considered filed when—

(a) it has been received by the registrar accompanied by Form TM54; and

(b) it has been sent to all other parties to the revocation proceedings.

(8) Where the periods for filing evidence under paragraphs (1) and (3) and, if relevant, paragraph (5) have expired, the registrar shall request that the parties give written notice of whether they wish to be heard.

(9) Where any party requests to be heard, the registrar shall send to the parties notice of a date for the hearing.

Decision of registrar in revocation (on the grounds of non-use) proceedings

A2–039   31B.—(1) When the registrar has made a decision on the application she shall send the parties to the proceedings written notice of it, stating the reasons for her decision.

(2) For the purposes of any appeal against the registrar's decision the date when the notice of the decision is sent shall be taken to be the date of the decision.

Application for revocation (on grounds other than non-use); s.46(1)(c) or (d) (Forms TM8 & TM26(O))

A2–040   32.—(1) An application to the registrar for revocation of a trade mark under section 46, on the grounds set out in section 46(1)(c) or (d), shall be made on Form TM26(O) and be accompanied by a statement of the grounds on which the application is made.

(2) The registrar shall send a copy of Form TM26(O) and the statement of the grounds on which the application is made to the proprietor.

(3) The proprietor shall, within six weeks of the date on which he was sent a copy of Form TM26(O) and the statement by the registrar, file a Form TM8 which shall include a counter-statement, otherwise the registrar may treat him as not opposing the application.

(4) The registrar shall send a copy of Form TM8 to the applicant and the date upon which this is sent shall, for the purposes of rule 32A, be the "initiation date".

Application for revocation (on grounds other than non-use): evidence rounds (Form TM54)

A2–041   32A.—(1) The applicant shall, within six weeks of the initiation date, file any evidence he may consider necessary to adduce in support of the grounds on which the application was made.

(2) Where the applicant files no evidence under paragraph (1), he shall, unless the registrar otherwise directs, be deemed to have withdrawn his application.

(3) The registrar shall notify the proprietor of any direction given under paragraph (2).

(4) The proprietor may file any evidence he may consider necessary to adduce in support of his case—

(a) within six weeks of the evidence being filed under paragraph (1); or

(b) within six weeks of the registrar sending him a notification that a direction has been given under paragraph (2).

(5) Where the proprietor files evidence under paragraph (4), the applicant may, within six weeks of such evidence being filed, file any evidence in reply; such evidence shall be confined to matters strictly in reply to the proprietor's evidence.

(6) The registrar may, at any time if she thinks fit, give leave to either party to file evidence upon such terms as she thinks fit.

(7) Under this rule, evidence shall only be considered filed when—

(a) it has been received by the registrar accompanied by Form TM54; and

(b) it has been sent to all other parties to the revocation proceedings.

(8) Where the periods for filing evidence under paragraphs (1) and (4) and, if relevant, paragraph (5) have expired, the registrar shall request that the parties give written notice of whether they wish to be heard.

(9) Where any party requests to be heard, the registrar shall send to the parties notice of a date for the hearing.

Decision of registrar in revocation (on grounds other than non-use) proceedings

32B.—(1) When the registrar has made a decision on the application she shall send the parties to the proceedings written notice of it, stating the reasons for her decision.   **A2–042**

(2) For the purposes of any appeal against the registrar's decision the date when the notice of the decision is sent shall be taken to be the date of the decision.

Application for invalidation: filing of application and counter-statement; s 47 (Forms TM8 & TM26(I))

33.—(1) An application to the registrar for a declaration of invalidity under section 47 shall be made on Form TM26(I) and be accompanied by a statement of the grounds on which the application is made.   **A2–043**

(2) Where the application is based on a trade mark which has been registered, there shall be included in the statement of the grounds on which the application is made a representation of that mark and—

(a) the details of the authority with which the mark is registered;

(b) the registration number of that mark;

(c) the classes in respect of which that mark is registered;

(d) the goods and services in respect of which—

(i) that mark is registered; and

(ii) the application is based; and

(e) where neither section 47(2A)(a) nor (b) applies to the mark, a statement detailing whether during the period referred to in section 47(2B)(a) it has been put to genuine use in relation to each of the goods and services in respect of which the application is based or whether there are proper reasons for non-use (for the purposes of rule 33A this is the "statement of use").

(3) Where the application is based on a trade mark in respect of which an ap-

plication for registration has been made, there shall be included in the statement
of the grounds on which the application is made a representation of that mark and
those matters set out in paragraph (2)(a) to (d), with references to registration being construed as references to the application for registration.

(4) Where the application is based on an unregistered trade mark or other sign
which the applicant claims to be protected by virtue of any rule of law (in particular, the law of passing off), there shall be included in the statement of the grounds
on which the application is made a representation of that mark or sign and the
goods and services in respect of which such protection is claimed.

(5) The registrar shall send a copy of Form TM26(I) and the statement of the
grounds on which the application is made to the proprietor.

(6) The proprietor shall, within six weeks of the date on which he was sent a
copy of Form TM26(I) and the statement by the registrar, file a Form TM8, which
shall include a counter-statement, otherwise the registrar may treat him as not opposing the application.

(7) The registrar shall send a copy of Form TM8 to the applicant and the date
upon which this is sent shall, for the purposes of rule 33A, be the "initiation
date".

Application for invalidation: evidence rounds (Form TM54)

A2–044   33A.—(1) The applicant, within six weeks of the initiation date—

(a) shall file any evidence he may consider necessary to adduce in support
of the grounds on which the application was made; and

(b) where—

(i)   the application is based on an earlier trade mark;
(ii) neither section 47(2A)(a) nor (b) applies to the mark; and
(iii) the truth of a matter set out in the statement of use is either denied
or not admitted by the proprietor,

shall file evidence supporting the statement of use.

(2) Where the applicant files no evidence under paragraph (1), he shall, unless
the registrar otherwise directs, be deemed to have withdrawn his application.

(3) The registrar shall notify the proprietor of any direction given under
paragraph (2).

(4) The proprietor may file any evidence he may consider necessary to adduce
in support of his case—

(a) within six weeks of the evidence being filed under paragraph (1); or
(b) within six weeks of the registrar sending him a notification that a direction has been given under paragraph (2).

(5) Where the proprietor files evidence under paragraph (4), the applicant
may, within six weeks of such evidence being filed, file any evidence in reply;
such evidence shall be confined to matters strictly in reply to the proprietor's
evidence.

(6) The registrar may, at any time if she thinks fit, give leave to either party to
file evidence upon such terms as she thinks fit.

(7) Under this rule, evidence shall only be considered filed when—

(a) it has been received by the registrar accompanied by Form TM54; and
(b) it has been sent to all other parties to the invalidation proceedings.

(8) Where the periods for filing evidence under paragraphs (1) and (4) and, if
relevant, paragraph (5) have expired, the registrar shall request that the parties
give written notice of whether they wish to be heard.

(9) Where any party requests to be heard the registrar shall send to the parties notice of a date for the hearing.

Decision of registrar in invalidation proceedings

33B.—(1) When the registrar has made a decision on the application she shall send the parties to the proceedings written notice of it, stating the reasons for her decision.

A2–045

(2) For the purposes of any appeal against the registrar's decision the date when the notice of the decision is sent shall be taken to be the date of the decision.

Procedure on application for rectification; s.64 (Form TM26(R))

34.—(1) An application for rectification of an error or omission in the register under section 64(1) shall be made on Form TM26(R) together with:

A2–046

(a) a statement of the grounds on which the application is made; and

(b) any evidence to support those grounds.

(2) Where any application is made under paragraph (1) by a person other than the proprietor of the registered trade mark the registrar—

(a) shall send a copy of the application and the statement, together with any evidence filed, to the proprietor; and

(b) may give such direction as she thinks fit with regard to the filing of subsequent evidence upon such terms as she may think fit.

(2A) A direction under paragraph (2)(b) may include a requirement that evidence shall only be considered filed when—

(a) it has been received by the registrar accompanied by Form TM54; and

(b) it has been sent to all other parties to the application.

(3) Where the periods for filing evidence specified in the directions given under paragraph 2(b) have expired, the registrar shall request the parties to state by notice to her in writing whether they wish to be heard; if any party requests to be heard the registrar shall send to the parties notice of a date for the hearing.

(4) When the registrar has made a decision on the application she shall send the parties to the proceedings written notice of it, stating the reasons for her decision; and for the purposes of any appeal against the registrar's decision the date when the notice of the decision is sent shall be taken to be the date of the decision.

Procedure for intervention

35.—(1) Any person, other than the registered proprietor, claiming to have an interest in proceedings on an application under rules 31 to 31B, rule 32, rules 32 to 32B or rules 33 to 33B may file an application to the registrar on Form TM27 for leave to intervene, stating the nature of his interest and the registrar may, after hearing the parties concerned if so required, refuse such leave or grant leave upon such terms and conditions (including any undertaking as to costs) as she thinks fit.

A2–047

(2) Any person granted leave to intervene (the intervener) shall, subject to any terms and conditions imposed in respect of the intervention, be treated as a party to the proceedings for the purposes of the application of the provisions of rule 31, rule 32, rule 33 or rule 34 (as appropriate).

Case Management Conference and Pre-Hearing Review

Case Management Conference; s.78

36. At any stage of any proceedings before her, the registrar may direct that the parties to the proceedings attend a case management conference where they shall

A2–048

have an opportunity to be heard with regard to the future conduct of the proceedings, and in particular with regard to the proposed exercise of any of the registrar's powers. The registrar shall give the parties at least fourteen days notice of the date of the case management conference.

Pre-hearing review; s.78

A2–049   37. Before hearing any party that desires to be heard in any proceedings before her, the registrar may direct that the parties to the proceedings attend a pre-hearing review at which she may give such directions as to the conduct of the hearing as she may think fit. The registrar shall give the parties at least fourteen days notice of the date of the pre-hearing review.

The register

Form of register; s.63(1)

A2–050   38. The register required to be maintained by the registrar under section 63(1) need not be kept in documentary form.

Entry in register of particulars of registered trade marks; s.63(2) (Form TM24)

A2–051   39. In addition to the entries in the register of registered trade marks required to be made by section 63(2)(a), there shall be entered in the register in respect of each trade mark registered therein the following particulars—

(a) the date of registration as determined in accordance with section 40(3) (that is to say, the date of the filing of the application for registration);

(b) the actual date of registration (that is to say, the date of the entry in the register);

(c) the priority date (if any) to be accorded pursuant to a claim to a right to priority made under section 35 or 36;

(d) the name and address of the proprietor;

(e) the address for service (if any) as furnished pursuant to rule 10 above;

(f) any disclaimer or limitation of rights under section 13(1)(a) or (b);

(g) any memorandum or statement of the effect of any memorandum relating to a trade mark of which the registrar has been notified on Form TM24;

(h) the goods or services in respect of which the mark is registered;

(i) where the mark is a collective or certification mark, that fact;

(j) where the mark is registered pursuant to section 5(5) with the consent of the proprietor of an earlier trade mark or other earlier right, that fact;

(k) where the mark is registered pursuant to a transformation application,

(a) the number of the international registration, and

(b) either:

(i) the date accorded to the international registration under Article 3(4), or

(ii) the date of recordal of the request for extension to the United Kingdom of the international registration under Article 3ter,

as the case may be, of the Madrid Protocol;

(l) where the mark arises from the conversion of a Community trade mark or an application for a Community trade mark, the number of any other registered trade mark from which the Community trade mark or the application for a Community trade mark claimed seniority and the earliest seniority date.

Entry in register of particulars of registrable transactions; s.25

A2–052   40. Upon application made to the registrar by such person as is mentioned in section 25(1)(a) or (b) there shall be entered in the register the following particulars of registrable transactions, that is to say—

(a) in the case of an assignment of a registered trade mark or any right in it—
- (i) the name and address of the assignee,
- (ii) the date of the assignment, and
- (iii) where the assignment is in respect of any right in the mark, a description of the right assigned;

(b) in the case of the grant of a licence under a registered trade mark—
- (i) the name and address of the licensee,
- (ii) where the licence is an exclusive licence, that fact,
- (iii) where the licence is limited, a description of the limitation, and
- (iv) the duration of the licence if the same is or is ascertainable as a definite period;

(c) in the case of the grant of any security interest over a registered trade mark or any right in or under it—
- (i) the name and address of the grantee,
- (ii) the nature of the interest (whether fixed or floating), and
- (iii) the extent of the security and the right in or under the mark secured;

(d) in the case of the making by personal representatives of an assent in relation to a registered trade mark or any right in or under it—
- (i) the name and address of the person in whom the mark or any right in or under it vests by virtue of the assent, and
- (ii) the date of the assent; and

(e) in the case of a court or other competent authority transferring a registered trade mark or any right in or under it—
- (i) the name and address of the transferee,
- (ii) the date of the order, and
- (iii) where the transfer is in respect of a right in the mark, a description of the right transferred;

and, in each case, there shall be entered the date on which the entry is made.

Application to register or give notice of transaction; ss.25 & 27(3) (Forms TM16, TM24, TM50 & TM51)

41.—(1) An application to register particulars of a transaction to which section 25 applies or to give notice to the registrar of particulars of a transaction to which section 27(3) applies shall be made, subject to paragraph (2) below,   **A2–053**

(a) relating to an assignment or transaction other than a transaction referred to in sub-paragraphs (b) to (d) below, on form TM16;

(b) relating to a grant of a licence, on form TM50;

(c) relating to an amendment to, or termination of a licence, on form TM51;

(d) relating to the grant, amendment or termination of any security interest, on form TM24; and

(e) relating to the making by personal representatives of an assent or to an order of a court or other competent authority, on form TM24.

(2) An application under paragraph (1) above shall—

(a) where the transaction is an assignment, be signed by or on behalf of the parties to the assignment;

(b) where the transaction falls within sub-paragraph (b), (c) or (d) of paragraph (1) above, be signed by or on behalf of the grantor of the licence or security interest;

or be accompanied by such documentary evidence as suffices to establish the transaction.

(3) Where the transaction is effected by an instrument chargeable with duty, the application shall be subject to the registrar being satisfied that the instrument has been duly stamped.

(4) Where an application to give notice to the registrar has been made of particulars relating to an application for registration of a trade mark, upon registration of the trade mark, the registrar shall enter those particulars in the register.

Public inspection of register; s.63(3)

A2–054   **42.**—(1) The register shall be open for public inspection at the Office during the hours of business of the Office as published in accordance with rule 70 below.

(2) Where any portion of the register is kept otherwise than in documentary form, the right of inspection is a right to inspect the material on the register.

Supply of certified copies etc; s.63(3) (Form TM31R)

A2–055   **43.** The registrar shall supply a certified copy or extract or uncertified copy or extract, as requested on Form TM31R, of any entry in the register.

Request for change of name or address in register; s.64(4) (Forms TM21 & TM33)

A2–056   **44.**—(1) The registrar shall, on a request made on Form TM21 by the proprietor of a registered trade mark or a licensee or any person having an interest in or charge on a registered trade mark which has been registered under rule 40, enter any change in his name or address as recorded in the register.

(2) The registrar may at any time, on a request made on Form TM33 by any person who has furnished an address for service under rule 10 above, if the address is recorded in the register, change it.

Removal of matter from register; s.64(5) (Form TM7)

A2–057   **45.**—(1) Where it appears to the registrar that any matter in the register has ceased to have effect, before removing it from the register—

(a) she may, where she considers it appropriate, publish her intention to remove that matter, and

(b) where any person appears to her to be affected by the removal, she shall send notice of her intention to that person.

(2) Within three months of the date on which her intention to remove the matter is published, or notice of her intention is sent, as the case may be—

(a) any person may file notice of opposition to the removal on form TM7; and

(b) the person to whom a notice is sent under paragraph (1)(b) above may file, in writing—

(i) his objections, if any, to the removal, or

(ii) a request to have his objections heard orally;

and where such opposition or objections are made, rule 54 shall apply.

(3) If the registrar is satisfied after considering any objections or opposition to the removal that the matter has not ceased to have effect, she shall not remove it.

(4) Where there has been no response to the registrar's notice she may remove the matter; where representations objecting to the removal of the entry have been made (whether in writing or orally) the registrar may, if she is of the view after considering the objections that the entry or any part thereof has ceased to have effect, remove it or, as appropriate, the part thereof.

Change of classification

Change of classification; ss.65(2) & 76(1)

46.—(1) Subject to section 65(3), the registrar may—   A2–058

(a) in order to reclassify the specification of a registered trade mark founded on Schedule 2 to one founded on Schedule 3, or

(b) consequent upon an amendment of the International Classification of Goods and Services referred to in rule 7(2) above,

make such amendments to entries on the register as she considers necessary for the purposes of reclassifying the specification of the registered trade mark.

(2) Before making any amendment to the register under paragraph (1) above the registrar shall give the proprietor of the mark written notice of her proposals for amendments and shall at the same time advise him that—

(a) he may make written objections to the proposals, within three months of the date of the notice, stating the grounds of his objections, and

(b) if no written objections are received within the period specified the registrar will publish the proposals and he will not be entitled to make any objections thereto upon such publication.

(3) If the proprietor makes no written objections within the period specified in paragraph (2)(a) above or at any time before the expiration of that period gives the registrar written notice of his intention not to make any objections, the registrar shall as soon as practicable after the expiration of that period or upon receipt of the notice publish the proposals.

(4) Where the proprietor makes written objections within the period specified in paragraph (2)(a) above, the registrar shall, as soon as practicable after she has considered the objections, publish the proposals or, where she has amended the proposals, publish the proposals as amended; and her decision shall be final and not subject to appeal.

Opposition to proposals; ss.65(3) & 76(1) (Form TM7)

47.—(1) Any person may, within three months of the date on which the proposals were published under rule 46, give notice to the registrar of opposition to the proposals on Form TM7 which shall include a statement of the grounds of opposition which shall, in particular, indicate why the proposed amendments would be contrary to section 65(3).   A2–059

(2) The registrar may require or admit evidence directed to the questions in issue and if so requested by any person opposing the proposal give that person the opportunity to be heard thereon before deciding the matter.

(3) If no notice of opposition under paragraph (1) above is filed within the time specified, or where any opposition has been determined, the registrar shall make the amendments as proposed and shall enter in the register the date when they were made; and her decision shall be final and not subject to appeal.

Request for information, inspection of documents and confidentiality

Request for information; s.67(1) (Form TM31C)

48. A request for information relating to an application for registration or to a registered trade mark shall be made on Form TM31C.   A2–060

Information available before publication; s.67(2)

49.—(1) Before publication of an application for registration the registrar shall make available for inspection by the public the application and any amendments made to it and any particulars contained in a notice given to the registrar under rule 41.   A2–061

(2) Nothing in section 67(2) relating to publication of information shall be construed as preventing the publication of decisions on cases relating to trade marks decided by the registrar.

Inspection of documents; ss.67 & 76(1)

A2–062   **50.**—(1) Subject to paragraphs (2) and (3) below, the registrar shall permit all documents filed or kept at the Office in relation to a registered mark or, where an application for the registration of a trade mark has been published, in relation to that application, to be inspected.

(2) The registrar shall not be obliged to permit the inspection of any such document as is mentioned in paragraph (1) above until she has completed any procedure, or the stage in the procedure which is relevant to the document in question, which she is required or permitted to carry out under the Act or these Rules.

(3) The right of inspection under paragraph (1) above does not apply to—

(a) any document until fourteen days after it has been filed at the Office;

(b) any document prepared in the Office solely for use therein;

(c) any document sent to the Office, whether at its request or otherwise, for inspection and subsequent return to the sender;

(d) any request for information under rule 48 above;

(e) any document issued by the Office which the registrar considers should be treated as confidential;

(f) any document in respect of which the registrar issues directions under rule 51 below that it be treated as confidential.

(4) Nothing in paragraph (1) shall be construed as imposing on the registrar any duty of making available for public inspection—

(a) any document or part of a document which in her opinion disparages any person in a way likely to damage him; or

(b) any document or information filed at or sent to or by the Office before 31st October 1994, or

(c) any document or information filed at or sent to or by the Office after 31st October 1994 relating to an application for registration of a trade mark under the Trade Marks Act 1938.

(5) No appeal shall lie from a decision of the registrar under paragraph (4) above not to make any document or part of a document available for public inspection.

Confidential documents

A2–063   **51.**—(1) Where a document other than a form required by the registrar and published in accordance with rule 3 above is filed at the Office and the person filing it requests, at the time of filing or within fourteen days of the filing, that it or a specified part of it be treated as confidential, giving his reasons, the registrar may direct that it or part of it, as the case may be, be treated as confidential, and the document shall not be open to public inspection while the matter is being determined by the registrar.

(2) Where such direction has been given and not withdrawn, nothing in this rule shall be taken to authorise or require any person to be allowed to inspect the document or part of it to which the direction relates except by leave of the registrar.

(3) The registrar shall not withdraw any direction given under this rule without prior consultation with the person at whose request the direction was given, unless the registrar is satisfied that such prior consultation is not reasonably practical.

(4) The registrar may where she considers that any document issued by the Office should be treated as confidential so direct, and upon such direction that document shall not be open to public inspection except by leave of the registrar.

(5) Where a direction is given under this rule for a document to be treated as confidential a record of the fact shall be filed with the document.

Agents

Proof of authorisation of agent may be required; s.82 (Form TM33)

52.—(1) Where an agent has been authorised under section 82, the registrar A2–064 may in any particular case require the personal signature or presence of the agent or the person authorising him to act as agent.

(2) Where after a person has become a party to proceedings before the registrar, he appoints an agent for the first time or appoints one agent in substitution for another, the newly appointed agent shall file Form TM33, and any act required or authorised by the Act in connection with the registration of a trade mark or any procedure relating to a trade mark may not be done by or to the newly appointed agent until on or after the date on which he files that form.

(3) The registrar may by notice in writing sent to an agent require him to produce evidence of his authority.

Registrar may refuse to deal with certain agents; s.88

53. The registrar may refuse to recognise as agent in respect of any business A2–065 under the Act—

(a) a person who has been convicted of an offence under section 84;

(b) an individual whose name has been erased from and not restored to, or who is suspended from, the register of trade mark agents on the ground of misconduct;

(c) a person who is found by the Secretary of State to have been guilty of such conduct as would, in the case of an individual registered in that register, render him liable to have his name erased from it on the ground of misconduct;

(d) a partnership or body corporate of which one of the partners or directors is a person whom the registrar could refuse to recognise under paragraph (a), (b) or (c) above.

Decision of registrar, evidence and costs

Decisions of registrar to be taken after hearing

54.—(1) Without prejudice to any provisions of the Act or these Rules requir- A2–066 ing the registrar to hear any party to proceedings under the Act or these Rules, or to give such party an opportunity to be heard, the registrar shall, before taking any decision on any matter under the Act or these Rules which is or may be adverse to any party to any proceedings before her, give that party an opportunity to be heard.

(2) The registrar shall give that party at least fourteen days' notice of the time when he may be heard unless that party consents to shorter notice.

Evidence in proceedings before the registrar; s.69

55.—(1) Where under these Rules evidence may be admitted by the registrar A2–067 in any proceedings before her, it shall be by the filing of a statutory declaration or affidavit.

(2) The registrar may in any particular case take oral evidence in lieu of or in

addition to such evidence and shall, unless she otherwise directs, allow any witness to be cross-examined on his statutory declaration, affidavit or oral evidence.

(3) Where these Rules provide for the use of an affidavit or statutory declaration, a witness statement verified by a statement of truth may be used as an alternative; the Registrar may give a direction as she thinks fit in any particular case that evidence must be given by affidavit or statutory declaration instead of or in addition to a witness statement verified by a statement of truth.

(4) The practice and procedure of the High Court with regard to witness statements and statements of truth, their form and contents and the procedure governing their use are to apply as appropriate to all proceedings under these Rules.

(5) Where in proceedings before the registrar, a party adduces evidence of a statement made by a person otherwise than while giving oral evidence in the proceedings and does not call that person as a witness, the registrar may, if she thinks fit, permit any other party to the proceedings to call that person as a witness and cross-examine him on the statement as if he had been called by the first-mentioned party and as if the statement were his evidence in chief.

Making and subscription of statutory declaration or affidavit

A2–068   **56.**—(1) Any statutory declaration or affidavit filed under the Act or these Rules shall be made and subscribed as follows—

   (a) in the United Kingdom, before any justice of the peace or any commissioner or other officer authorised by law in any part of the United Kingdom to administer an oath for the purpose of any legal proceedings;
   (b) in any other part of Her Majesty's dominions or in the Republic of Ireland, before any court, judge, justice of the peace or any officer authorised by law to administer an oath there for the purpose of any legal proceedings; and
   (c) elsewhere, before a commissioner for oaths, notary public, judge or magistrate.

(2) Any document purporting to have affixed, impressed or subscribed thereto or thereon the seal or signature of any person authorised by paragraph (1) above to take a declaration may be admitted by the registrar without proof of the genuineness of the seal or signature, or of the official character of the person or his authority to take the declaration.

Registrar's power to require documents, information or evidence

A2–069   **57.** At any stage of any proceedings before the registrar, she may direct that such documents, information or evidence as she may reasonably require shall be filed within such period as she may specify.

Registrar to have power of an official referee; s.69

A2–070   **58.**—(1) The registrar shall in relation to the examination of witnesses on oath and the disclosure and production of documents have all the powers of an official referee of the Supreme Court.

(2) The rules applicable to the attendance of witnesses before such a referee shall apply in relation to the attendance of witnesses in proceedings before the registrar.

Hearings before registrar to be in public

A2–071   **59.**—(1) The hearing before the registrar of any dispute between two or more parties relating to any matter in connection with an application for the registration of a mark or a registered mark shall be in public unless the registrar, after consultation with those parties who appear in person or are represented at the hearing, otherwise directs.

(2) Nothing in this rule shall prevent a member of the Council on Tribunals or of its Scottish Committee from attending a hearing in his capacity as such.

Costs of proceedings; s.68

60. The registrar may, in any proceedings before her under the Act or these Rules, by order award to any party such costs as she may consider reasonable, and direct how and by what parties they are to be paid.

A2–072

Security for costs; s.68

61.—(1) The registrar may require any person who is a party in any proceedings before her under the Act or these Rules to give security for costs in relation to those proceedings; and she may require security for the costs of any appeal from her decision.

A2–073

(2) In default of such security being given, the registrar, in the case of the proceedings before her, or, in the case of an appeal, the person appointed under section 76 may treat the party in default as having withdrawn his application, opposition, objection or intervention, as the case may be.

Decision of registrar (Form TM5)

62.—(1) When, in any proceedings before her, the registrar has made a decision, she shall send to each party to the proceedings written notice of it, and for the purposes of any appeal against that decision, subject to paragraph (2) below, the date on which the notice is sent shall be taken to be the date of the decision.

A2–074

(2) Where a statement of the reasons for the decision is not included in the notice sent under paragraph (1) above, any party may, within one month of the date on which the notice was sent to him, request the registrar on form TM5 to send him a statement of the reasons for the decision and upon such request the registrar shall send such a statement; and the date on which that statement is sent shall be deemed to be the date of the registrar's decision for the purpose of any appeal against it.

Appeals

Appeal to person appointed; s.76

63.—(1) Notice of appeal to the person appointed under section 76 shall be filed on Form TM55 which shall include the appellant's grounds of appeal and his case in support of the appeal.

A2–075

(1A) Such notice shall be filed with the registrar within the period of 28 days beginning on the date of the registrar's decision which is the subject of the appeal.

(2) The registrar shall send the notice and the statement to the person appointed.

(3) Where any person other than the appellant was a party to the proceedings before the registrar in which the decision appealed against was made, the registrar shall send to that person a copy of the notice and the statement.

Determination whether appeal should be referred to court; s.76(3)

64.—(1) Within 28 days of the date on which the notice of appeal is sent by the registrar under rule 63(3) above;

A2–076

  (a) the registrar, or
  (b) any person who was a party to the proceedings in which the decision appealed against was made,

may request that the person appointed refer the appeal to the court.

(2) Where the registrar requests that the appeal be referred to the court, she shall send a copy of the request to each party to the proceedings.

(3) A request under paragraph (1)(b) above shall be sent to the registrar; the registrar shall send it to the person appointed and shall send a copy of the request to any other party to the proceedings.

(4) Within 28 days of the date on which a copy of a request is sent by the registrar under paragraph (2) or (3) above, the person to whom it is sent may make representations as to whether the appeal should be referred to the court.

(5) In any case where it appears to the person appointed that a point of general legal importance is involved in the appeal, he shall send to the registrar and to every party to the proceedings in which the decision appealed against was made, notice thereof.

(6) Within 28 days of the date on which a notice is sent under paragraph (5) above, the person to whom it was sent may make representations as to whether the appeal should be referred to the court.

Hearing and determination of appeal; s.76(4)

A2–077   **65.**—(1) Where the person appointed does not refer the appeal to the court, he shall send written notice of the time and place appointed for the oral hearing of the appeal—

  (a) where no person other than the appellant was a party to the proceedings in which the decision appealed against was made, to the registrar and to the appellant; and

  (b) in any other case, to the registrar and to each person who was a party to those proceedings.

(2) The person appointed shall send the notice at least fourteen days before the time appointed for the oral hearing.

(3) If all the persons notified under paragraph (1) inform the person appointed that they do not wish to make oral representations then—

  (a) the person appointed may hear and determine the case on the basis of any written representations; and

  (b) the time and place appointed for the oral hearing may be vacated.

(4) Rules 55 to 58 and rules 60 and 61 shall apply to the person appointed and to proceedings before the person appointed as they apply to the registrar and to proceedings before the registrar.

(5) If there is an oral hearing of the appeal then rule 59 shall apply to the person appointed and to proceedings before the person appointed as it applies to the registrar and to proceedings before the registrar.

(6) The person appointed shall send a copy of his decision, with a statement of his reasons therefor, to the registrar and to each person who was a party to the appeal.

Correction of irregularities, calculation and extension of time

Correction of irregularities of procedure

A2–078   **66.** Subject to rule 68 below, any irregularity in procedure in or before the Office or the registrar, may be rectified on such terms as the registrar may direct.

Calculation of times and periods

A2–079   **67.**—(1) Where, on any day, there is—

  (a) a general interruption or subsequent dislocation in the postal services of the United Kingdom, or

  (b) an event or circumstances causing an interruption in the normal operation of the Office, the registrar may certify the day as being one on which there is an "interruption" and, where any period of time specified in the Act or these Rules for the giving, making or filing of any notice, application or other document expires on a day so certified the period shall be extended to the first day next following (not being an excluded day) which is not so certified.

(2) Any certificate of the registrar given pursuant to this rule shall be posted in the Office.

(3) If in any particular case the registrar is satisfied that the failure to give, make or file any notice, application or other document within any period of time specified in the Act or these Rules for such giving, making or filing was wholly or mainly attributable to a failure or undue delay in the postal services in the United Kingdom, the registrar may, if she thinks fit, extend the period so that it ends on the day of the receipt by the addressee of the notice, application or other document (or, if the day of such receipt is an excluded day, on the first following day which is not an excluded day), upon such notice to other parties and upon such terms as she may direct.

(4) In this rule "excluded day" means a day which is not a business day of the Office under the registrar's direction pursuant to section 80, as published in accordance with rule 70 below.

Alteration of time limits (Form TM9)

68.—(1) The time or periods—   A2–080

(a) prescribed by these Rules, other than the times or periods prescribed by the rules mentioned in paragraph (3) below, or

(b) specified by the registrar for doing any act or taking any proceedings,

subject to paragraph (2) below, may, at the written request of the person or party concerned, or on the initiative of the registrar, be extended by the registrar as she thinks fit and upon such terms as she may direct.

(2) Where a request for the extension of a time or periods prescribed by these Rules—

(a) is sought in respect of a time or periods prescribed by rules 13 to 13C, 18, 23, 25, 31, 31A, 32, 32A, 33, 33Aor 34, the party seeking the extension shall send a copy of the request to each person party to the proceedings;

(b) is filed after the application has been published under rule 12 above the request shall be on Form TM9 and shall in any other case be on that form if the registrar so directs.

(3) The rules excepted from paragraph (1) above are rule 10(6) (failure to file address for service), rule 11 (deficiencies in application), rule 13(1) (time for filing opposition), rule 13A(1) (time for filing counterstatement), rule 23(4) (time for filing opposition), rule 25(3) (time for filing opposition), rule 29 (delayed renewal), rule 30 (restoration of registration), rule 31(3) (time for filing counterstatement and evidence of use or reasons for non-use), rule 32(3) (time for filing counter-statement), rule 33(6) (time for filing counter-statement), and rule 47 (time for filing opposition).

(4) Subject to paragraph (5) below, a request for extension under paragraph (1) above shall be made before the time or period in question has expired.

(5) Where the request for extension is made after the time or period has expired, the registrar may, at her discretion, extend the period or time if she is satisfied with the explanation for the delay in requesting the extension and it appears to her to be just and equitable to do so.

(6) Where the period within which any party to any proceedings before the registrar may file evidence under these Rules is to begin upon the expiry of any period in which any other party may file evidence and that other party notifies the registrar that he does not wish to file any, or any further, evidence the registrar may direct that the period within which the first mentioned party may file evidence shall begin on such date as may be specified in the direction and shall notify all parties to the dispute of that date.

(7) without prejudice to the above, in the case of any irregularity or prospective irregularity in or before the Office or the registrar which—

  (a) consists of a failure to comply with any limitation as to times or periods specified in the Act or these Rules or the old law as that law continues to apply and which has occurred or appears to the registrar as likely to occur in the absence of a direction under this rule, and

  (b) is attributable wholly or in part to an error, default or omission on the part of the Office or the registrar and which it appears to her should be rectified,

she may direct that the time or period in question shall be altered in such manner as she may specify upon such terms as she may direct.

Filing of documents, hours of business, Trade Marks Journal and translations

Filing of documents by electronic means

A2–081   **69.** The registrar may, at her discretion, permit as an alternative to the sending by post or delivery of the application, notice or other document in legible form the filing of the application, notice or other document by electronic means subject to such terms or conditions as she may specify either generally by published notice or in any particular case by written notice to the person desiring to file any such documents by such means.

Directions on hours of business; s.80

A2–082   **70.** Any directions given by the registrar under section 80 specifying the hours of business of the Office and business days of the Office shall be published and posted in the Office.

Trade Marks Journal; s.81

A2–083   **71.** The registrar shall publish a journal, entitled "The Trade Marks Journal", containing particulars of any application for the registration of a trade mark (including a representation of the mark), such information as is required to be published under these Rules and such other information as the registrar thinks fit.

Translations

A2–084   **72.**—(1) Where any document or part thereof which is in a language other than English is filed or sent to the registrar in pursuance of the Act or these Rules, the registrar may require that there be furnished a translation into English of the document or that part, verified to the satisfaction of the registrar as corresponding to the original text.

(2) The registrar may refuse to accept any translation which is in her opinion inaccurate and thereupon another translation of the document in question verified as aforesaid shall be furnished.

Transitional provisions and revocations

Pending applications for registration; Sch.3, para.10(2)

A2–085   **73.** Where an application for registration of a mark made under the old law is advertised on or after 31st October 1994, the period within which notice of opposition may be filed shall be three months from the date of advertisement, and such period shall not be extendible.

Revocation of previous Rules

74.—(1) The Rules specified in Schedule 1 are hereby revoked.

A2–086

(2) Except as provided by rule 73 above, where—

(a) immediately before these Rules come into force, any time or period prescribed by the Rules hereby revoked has effect in relation to any act or proceeding and has not expired, and

(b) the corresponding time or period prescribed by these Rules would have expired or would expire earlier,

the time or period prescribed by those Rules and not by these Rules shall apply to that act or proceeding.

(3) Any proceeding commenced before the registrar before the entry into force of these Rules shall proceed under the Trade Mark Rules 1994 as amended or old law as appropriate; but where a new step is to be taken on or after 26th April 2000 in relation to any proceedings commenced under the Trade Mark Rules 1994 these Rules shall apply to such proceedings from that date.

Rule 74   SCHEDULE 1

REVOCATIONS

A2–087

Rules revoked	Reference
The Trade Marks Rules 1994	S.I. 1994/2583
The Trade Marks (Amendment) Rules 1998	S.I. 1998/925

Rule 7(1)   SCHEDULE 2

CLASSIFICATION OF GOODS (PRE-1938)

Schedule 2 was revoked by the Trade Marks (Amendments) Rules 2001 (SI 2001/3832).

A2–088

Rule 7(1)   SCHEDULE 3

CLASSIFICATION OF GOODS AND SERVICES

Goods

A2–089

Class 1   Chemicals used in industry, science and photography, as well as in agriculture, horticulture and forestry; unprocessed artificial resins, unprocessed plastics; manures; fire extinguishing compositions; tempering and soldering preparations; chemical substances for preserving foodstuffs; tanning substances; adhesives used in industry.

Class 2   Paints, varnishes, lacquers; preservatives against rust and against deterioration of wood; colorants; mordants; raw natural resins; metals in foil and powder form for painters, decorators, printers and artists.

Class 3   Bleaching preparations and other substances for laundry use; cleaning, polishing, scouring and abrasive preparations; soaps; perfumery, essential oils, cosmetics, hair lotions; dentifrices.

Class 4 Industrial oils and greases; lubricants; dust absorbing, wetting and binding compositions; fuels (including motor spirit) and illuminants; candles, wicks.

Class 5 Pharmaceutical, veterinary and sanitary preparations; dietetic substances adapted for medical use, food for babies; plasters, materials for dressings; material for stopping teeth, dental wax; disinfectants; preparations for destroying vermin; fungicides, herbicides.

Class 6 Common metals and their alloys; metal building materials; transportable buildings of metal; materials of metal for railway tracks; non-electric cables and wires of common metal; ironmongery, small items of metal hardware; pipes and tubes of metal; safes; goods of common metal not included in other classes; ores.

Class 7 Machines and machine tools; motors and engines (except for land vehicles); machine coupling and transmission components (except for land vehicles); agricultural implements (other than hand operated); incubators for eggs.

Class 8 Hand tools and implements (hand operated); cutlery; side arms; razors.

Class 9 Scientific, nautical, surveying, electric, photographic, cinematographic, optical, weighing, measuring, signalling, checking (supervision), life-saving and teaching apparatus and instruments; apparatus for recording, transmission or reproduction of sound or images; magnetic data carriers, recording discs; automatic vending machines and mechanisms for coin-operated apparatus; cash registers, calculating machines, data processing equipment and computers; fire-extinguishing apparatus.

Class 10 Surgical, medical, dental and veterinary apparatus and instruments, artificial limbs, eyes and teeth; orthopaedic articles; suture materials.

Class 11 Apparatus for lighting, heating, steam generating, cooking, refrigerating, drying, ventilating, water supply and sanitary purposes.

Class 12 Vehicles; apparatus for locomotion by land, air or water.

Class 13 Firearms; ammunition and projectiles; explosives; fireworks.

Class 14 Precious metals and their alloys and goods in precious metals or coated therewith, not included in other classes; jewellery, precious stones; horological and chronometric instruments.

Class 15 Musical instruments.

Class 16 Paper, cardboard and goods made from these materials, not included in other classes; printed matter; bookbinding material; photographs; stationery; adhesives for stationery or household purposes; artists' materials; paint brushes; typewriters and office requisites (except furniture); instructional and teaching material (except apparatus); plastic materials for packaging (not included in other classes); playing cards; printers' type; printing blocks.

Class 17 Rubber, gutta-percha, gum, asbestos, mica and goods made from these materials and not included in other classes; plastics in extruded form for use in manufacture; packing, stopping and insulating materials; flexible pipes, not of metal.

Class 18 Leather and imitations of leather, and goods made of these materials and not included in other classes; animal skins, hides; trunks and travelling bags; umbrellas, parasols and walking sticks; whips, harness and saddlery.

Class 19 Building materials (non-metallic); non-metallic rigid pipes for building; asphalt, pitch and bitumen; non-metallic transportable buildings; monuments, not of metal.

Class 20	Furniture, mirrors, picture frames; goods (not included in other classes) of wood, cork, reed, cane, wicker, horn, bone, ivory, whalebone, shell, amber, mother-of-pearl, meerschaum and substitutes for all these materials, or of plastics.
Class 21	Household or kitchen utensils and containers (not of precious metal or coated therewith); combs and sponges; brushes (except paint brushes); brush-making materials; articles for cleaning purposes; steelwool; unworked or semi-worked glass (except glass used in building); glassware, porcelain and earthenware not included in other classes.
Class 22	Ropes, string, nets, tents, awnings, tarpaulins, sails, sacks and bags (not included in other classes); padding and stuffing materials (except of rubber or plastics); raw fibrous textile materials.
Class 23	Yarns and threads, for textile use.
Class 24	Textiles and textile goods, not included in other classes; bed and table covers.
Class 25	Clothing, footwear, headgear.
Class 26	Lace and embroidery, ribbons and braid; buttons, hooks and eyes, pins and needles; artificial flowers.
Class 27	Carpets, rugs, mats and matting, linoleum and other materials for covering existing floors; wall hangings (non-textile).
Class 28	Games and playthings; gymnastic and sporting articles not included in other classes; decorations for Christmas trees.
Class 29	Meat, fish, poultry and game; meat extracts; preserved, dried and cooked fruits and vegetables; jellies, jams, fruit sauces; eggs, milk and milk products; edible oils and fats.
Class 30	Coffee, tea, cocoa, sugar, rice, tapioca, sago, artificial coffee; flour and preparations made from cereals, bread, pastry and confectionery, ices; honey, treacle; yeast, baking-powder; salt, mustard; vinegar, sauces (condiments); spices; ice.
Class 31	Agricultural, horticultural and forestry products and grains not included in other classes; live animals; fresh fruits and vegetables; seeds, natural plants and flowers; foodstuffs for animals, malt.
Class 32	Beers; mineral and aerated waters and other non-alcoholic drinks; fruit drinks and fruit juices; syrups and other preparations for making beverages.
Class 33	Alcoholic beverages (except beers).
Class 34	Tobacco; smokers' articles; matches.

Services

A2–090

Class 35	Advertising; business management; business administration; office functions.
Class 36	Insurance; financial affairs; monetary affairs; real estate affairs.
Class 37	Building construction; repair; installation services.
Class 38	Telecommunications.
Class 39	Transport; packaging and storage of goods; travel arrangement.
Class 40	Treatment of materials.
Class 41	Education; providing of training; entertainment; sporting and cultural activities.
Class 42	Providing of food and drink; temporary accommodation; medical, hygienic and beauty care; veterinary and agricultural services; legal services; scientific and industrial research; computer programming; services that cannot be placed in other classes.

         SCHEDULE 4

CLASSIFICATION OF GOODS AND SERVICES

Goods

A2–091

Class 1	Chemicals used in industry, science and photography, as well as in agriculture, horticulture and forestry; unprocessed artificial resins, unprocessed plastics; manures; fire extinguishing compositions; tempering and soldering preparations; chemical substances for preserving foodstuffs; tanning substances; adhesives used in industry.
Class 2	Paints, varnishes, lacquers; preservatives against rust and against deterioration of wood; colorants; mordants; raw natural resins; metals in foil and powder form for painters, decorators, printers and artists.
Class 3	Bleaching preparations and other substances for laundry use; cleaning, polishing, scouring and abrasive preparations; soaps; perfumery, essential oils, cosmetics, hair lotions; dentifrices.
Class 4	Industrial oils and greases; lubricants; dust absorbing, wetting and binding compositions; fuels (including motor spirit) and illuminants; candles and wicks for lighting.
Class 5	Pharmaceutical and veterinary preparations; sanitary preparations for medical purposes; dietetic substances adapted for medical use, food for babies; plasters, materials for dressings; material for stopping teeth, dental wax; disinfectants; preparations for destroying vermin; fungicides, herbicides.
Class 6	Common metals and their alloys; metal building materials; transportable buildings of metal; materials of metal for railway tracks; non-electric cables and wires of common metal; ironmongery, small items of metal hardware; pipes and tubes of metal; safes; goods of common metal not included in other classes; ores
Class 7	Machines and machine tools; motors and engines (except for land vehicles); machine coupling and transmission components (except for land vehicles); agricultural implements other than hand-operated; incubators for eggs.
Class 8	Hand tools and implements (hand-operated); cutlery; side arms; razors.
Class 9	Scientific, nautical, surveying, photographic, cinematographic, optical, weighing, measuring, signalling, checking (supervision), life-saving and teaching apparatus and instruments; apparatus and instruments for conducting, switching, transforming, accumulating, regulating or controlling electricity; apparatus for recording, transmission or reproduction of sound or images; magnetic data carriers, recording discs; automatic vending machines and mechanisms for coin-operated apparatus; cash registers, calculating machines, data processing equipment and computers; fire-extinguishing apparatus.
Class 10	Surgical, medical, dental and veterinary apparatus and instruments, artificial limbs, eyes and teeth; orthopedic articles; suture materials.
Class 11	Apparatus for lighting, heating, steam generating, cooking, refrigerating, drying, ventilating, water supply and sanitary purposes.
Class 12	Vehicles; apparatus for locomotion by land, air or water.
Class 13	Firearms; ammunition and projectiles; explosives; fireworks.
Class 14	Precious metals and their alloys and goods in precious metals or coated therewith, not included in other classes; jewellery, precious stones; horological and chronometric instruments.
Class 15	Musical instruments.

Class 16   Paper, cardboard and goods made from these materials, not included in other classes; printed matter; bookbinding material; photographs; stationery; adhesives for stationery or household purposes; artists' materials; paint brushes; typewriters and office requisites (except furniture); instructional and teaching material (except apparatus); plastic materials for packaging (not included in other classes); printers' type; printing blocks.

Class 17   Rubber, gutta-percha, gum, asbestos, mica and goods made from these materials and not included in other classes; plastics in extruded form for use in manufacture; packing, stopping and insulating materials; flexible pipes, not of metal.

Class 18   Leather and imitations of leather, and goods made of these materials and not included in other classes; animal skins, hides; trunks and travelling bags; umbrellas, parasols and walking sticks; whips, harness and saddlery.

Class 19   Building materials (non-metallic); non-metallic rigid pipes for building; asphalt, pitch and bitumen; non-metallic transportable buildings; monuments, not of metal.

Class 20   Furniture, mirrors, picture frames; goods (not included in other classes) of wood, cork, reed, cane, wicker, horn, bone, ivory, whalebone, shell, amber, mother-of-pearl, meerschaum and substitutes for all these materials, or of plastics.

Class 21   Household or kitchen utensils and containers (not of precious metal or coated therewith); combs and sponges; brushes (except paint brushes); brush-making materials; articles for cleaning purposes; steelwool; unworked or semi-worked glass (except glass used in building); glassware, porcelain and earthenware not included in other classes.

Class 22   Ropes, string, nets, tents, awnings, tarpaulins, sails, sacks and bags (not included in other classes); padding and stuffing materials (except of rubber or plastics); raw fibrous textile materials.

Class 23   Yarns and threads, for textile use.

Class 24   Textiles and textile goods, not included in other classes; bed and table covers.

Class 25   Clothing, footwear, headgear.

Class 26   Lace and embroidery, ribbons and braid; buttons, hooks and eyes, pins and needles; artificial flowers.

Class 27   Carpets, rugs, mats and matting, linoleum and other materials for covering existing floors; wall hangings (non-textile).

Class 28   Games and playthings; gymnastic and sporting articles not included in other classes; decorations for Christmas trees.

Class 29   Meat, fish, poultry and game; meat extracts; preserved, dried and cooked fruits and vegetables; jellies, jams, compotes; eggs, milk and milk products; edible oils and fats.

Class 30   Coffee, tea, cocoa, sugar, rice, tapioca, sago, artificial coffee; flour and preparations made from cereals, bread, pastry and confectionery, ices; honey, treacle; yeast, baking-powder; salt, mustard; vinegar, sauces (condiments); spices; ice.

Class 31   Agricultural, horticultural and forestry products and grains not included in other classes; live animals; fresh fruits and vegetables; seeds, natural plants and flowers; foodstuffs for animals; malt.

Class 32   Beers; mineral and aerated waters and other non-alcoholic drinks; fruit drinks and fruit juices; syrups and other preparations for making beverages.

Class 33   Alcoholic beverages (except beers).

Class 34   Tobacco; smokers' articles; matches.

Services

A2–092

Class 35   Advertising; business management; business administration; office functions.

Class 36   Insurance; financial affairs; monetary affairs; real estate affairs.

Class 37   Building construction; repair; installation services.

Class 38   Telecommunications.

Class 39   Transport; packaging and storage of goods; travel arrangement.

Class 40   Treatment of materials.

Class 41   Education; providing of training; entertainment; sporting and cultural activities.

Class 42   Scientific and technological services and research and design relating thereto; industrial analysis and research services; design and development of computer hardware and software; legal services.

Class 43   Services for providing food and drink; temporary accommodation.

Class 44   Medical services; veterinary services; hygienic and beauty care for human beings or animals; agriculture, horticulture and forestry services.

Class 45   Personal and social services rendered by others to meet the needs of individuals; security services for the protection of property and individuals.

Transitional Provisions of the Trade Marks (Amendment) Rules 2004

Transitional arrangements

A2–093   —20. In rules 22 to 24—

"the unamended Rules" means the Trade Marks Rules 2000 in the form they were immediately prior to these Rules coming into force;

"the amended Rules"means the Trade Marks Rules 2000 in the form they are after these Rules have come into force.

21. Rules 4, 5 and 6 shall not apply in respect of any application for the registration of a trade mark which was filed before they came into force.

22. Any proceedings commenced under rule 13, 18, 23, 25, 32 or 33 of the unamended Rules where the applicant (or, as the case may be, the proprietor) -

(a) has not filed Form TM8 before 5th May 2004—

    (i) shall proceed under the unamended Rules until the date upon which Form TM8 is filed by the applicant (or, as the case may be, the proprietor); and

    (ii) shall proceed, subject to rule 23, under the amended Rules from the point in time immediately after Form TM8 is filed;

(b) has filed TM8 before 5th May 2004 shall proceed under the unamended Rules; but where a new step is taken under such Rules on or after 5th May 2004, the amended Rules, subject to rule 23, shall apply to such proceedings from the point in time immediately after that step is taken.

23. Rules 13C(1)(b) and 33A(1)(b) of the amended Rules shall not apply to any proceedings commenced before the coming into force of these Rules.

24. Any proceedings commenced under rule 31 of the unamended Rules shall proceed under those Rules.

The Trade Marks (Fees) Rules 2000

SI 2000/137

The Secretary of State, in exercise of the powers conferred by sections 54 and 79 **A3–001**
of the Trade Marks Act 1994 ("the Act"), of the power conferred on him by
the Department of Trade and Industry (Fees) Order 1988, and of all other
powers enabling him in that behalf, hereby makes the following Rules:—

1. These Rules may be cited as the Trade Marks (Fees) Rules 2000 and shall **A3–002**
come into force on 17th February 2000.

2. These Rules shall be construed as one with the Trade Marks Rules 2000 and **A3–003**
the Trade Marks (International Registration) Order 1996.

3. The fees to be paid in respect of any matters arising under the Act, the Trade **A3–004**
Marks Rules 2000 and the Trade Marks (International Registration) Order 1996
shall be those specified in the Schedule to these Rules; and in any case where a
form specified in the Schedule as the corresponding form in relation to any matter
is specified in the Trade Marks Rules 2000 or the Trade Marks (International
Registration) Order 1996 that form shall be accompanied by the fee, if any, specified in respect of that matter (unless the Rules or the Order otherwise provide).

4. Where a fee has been paid in error, the registrar shall repay the same; and **A3–005**
where a fee is paid in excess of the amount specified hereunder, the registrar shall
remit the amount paid in excess.

5. The Trade Mark (Fees) Rules 1998 are hereby revoked. **A3–006**

Rule 3   SCHEDULE

FEES PAYABLE

(In this section references to a rule are references to that rule in the Trade Marks Rules 2000 and **A3–007**
references to an article are references to that article in the Trade Marks (International Registration)
Order 1996)

Number of corre-sponding form	Item	Amount £
TM3	Application for registration of a trade mark (rule 5) or a series of trade marks (rule 21)	200
	Class fee (rule 5), for each class over one	50
	Transformation application (articles 19–20)	—
TM3A	Application for additional classes following exami-nation of a mark (rule 8(3)), for each additional class	50
TM5	Request to the registrar for a statement of the reasons for his decision (rule 62(2))	100

Number of corresponding form	Item	Amount £
TM7	Notice of opposition to the registration of a mark (rule 13(1)), to the amendment of an application (rule 18(2)), or to the amendment of the regulations relating to a certification or collective trade mark (rule 23(4), to the alteration of a registered trade mark (rule 25(3)), to the removal of matter from the register (rule 45(2)(a)), to the reclassification of a mark from Schedule 2 to Schedule 3 (rule 47(1))	200
	Notice of opposition on the conferring of protection to the international registration (article 10)	200
TM9	Request for extension of time (rule 68(2))	50
TM9c	Request for extension to cooling off period (rule 13(4))	—
TM11	Renewal of registration (rule 28)	200
	Class fee for each class over one	50
	Delayed renewal of registration (rule 29(1)	50
TM12	Request for division of an application (rule 19(1))	100
TM13	Request for restoration and renewal of a registration removed from the register for failure to renew (rule 30(1))	100
TM16	Request to enter details of an assignment (rule 41(1)(a))	50
TM17	Request to merge either applications or registrations (rule 20(1))	—
TM23	Request by the registered proprietor for the partial surrender of a registered trade mark (rule 26(1)(b))	—
TM24	Application to record or cancel a registrable transaction other than an assignment or licence (rule 41(1)(d))	—
	Application to record or cancel a notifiable transaction (article 6)	—
TM26 (N)	Request for the revocation of a registration (on grounds of non-use) (rule 31)	200
	Request for the revocation of a protected international trade mark (UK) (on grounds of non-use) (article 13)	200
TM26(O)	Request for the revocation of a registration (on grounds other than non-use) (rule 32)	200
	Request for the revocation of a protected international trade mark (UK) (on grounds other than non-use) (article 13)	200
TM26 (I)	Request for the invalidation of a registration (rule 33)	200
	Request for the invalidation of a protected international trade mark (UK) (article 13)	200
TM26(R)	Request for the invalidation of a registration (rule 34)	—
	Request for the rectification of the supplementary register (article 15)	—
TM28	Recordal of concurrent registration (article 21)	—
TM31C	Request for information about applications and registered trade marks (rule 48)	20
TM31M	Request for information in relation to an international trade mark (UK) (article 25)	20

Number of corre-sponding form	Item	Amount £
TM31R	Request for certified copy of an entry on the register (rule 43), per certificate	20
TM35	Filing of regulations governing the use of a certification or collective mark (rule 22)	200
TM36	Request to amend regulations governing the use of a certification or collective mark (rule 23(1))	100
TM50	Application for the registration of a licence under registered trade mark (rule 41(1)(b))	—
	Submission fee for an application for international registration to the international Bureau by the Patent Office (article 22)	40
	Handling fee for the transmission by the Patent Office of monies payable to the International Bureau for renewal of an international registration (article 31)	20

APPENDIX **4**

Trade Mark Registry Forms

Please note that these new forms are valid from September 1, 2005.
Reproduced with the kind permission of the Patent Office.

Form TM3

Official fee charged

Application to register a trade mark

Please read the guidance notes about filling in this form.

The Patent Office
Trade Marks Registry
Cardiff Road, Newport
South Wales NP10 8QQ

1. Your reference

2. Illustration of your mark or marks.

3. If your mark is a three-dimensional shape or a sound or a repeating pattern, say here which it is.

4. If you have shown the mark in colour, we will assume you want the mark registered in these colours unless you tell us something different here.

5. If you have shown the mark in black and white, we will not consider these colours are a feature of the mark unless you tell us something different here.

6. If your application is for a series of marks, how many marks are in the series?

7. If your application claims priority, give these details.

Priority Date	Country	Number

8. If you are applying to transform a UK designation under an international registration into a UK application, give these details.

Transformation date	Registration number

(REV SEP05)   **Form TM3**

APPENDIX 4

9. List the goods or services which you are using, or intend to use, your mark on.

Class number	List of goods or services

List the goods or services which you are using, or intend to use, your mark on.

Class number	List of goods or services

Form TM3

10. If you are applying for a certification or collective mark, say which type you want.	
11. List any limitations or disclaimers you want to record.	
12. Full name and address (including postcode) of the person applying. Trade marks ADP number (if you know it). If you are applying in the name of a company, where is it incorporated? If incorporated in the USA, in which state is it incorporated?	
13. Name and address (including postcode) of agent (if any); or your contact address (including postcode) if not the same as in section 12 above. Trade marks ADP number (if you know it).	
14. Declaration. Signature.	The trade mark is being used by the applicant, or with his or her consent, in relation to the goods or services shown, or there is a bona fide intention that it will be used in this way.
Name in BLOCK CAPITALS.	
Date.	
15. Name and daytime phone number of the person we should contact in case of query.	
Number of sheets attached to this form.	

Fees   It costs £200 to apply to register a trade mark in one class of goods or services, and £50 for each extra class. We cannot refund this fee for any reason - it covers the cost of us examining your application and our other administrative costs. Please make cheques payable to 'The Patent Office'.

Form TM3A

Official fee £50 for each class due with this form

Application to add extra classes

The Patent Office
Trade Marks Registry
Cardiff Road, Newport
South Wales NP10 8QQ

Please read the guidance note below about filling in this form.

1. Trade mark application number.	(*Lowest*) Class
2. Full name of the applicant.	

3. List the goods or services to be added. (List on a separate sheet if there is not enough space on this form.)

Class number   List of goods or services

4. Name of agent (if any).	
5. Your signature.	
Your name in BLOCK CAPITALS.	
Date.	
6. Name and daytime phone number of the person we should contact in case of query.	
Your reference.	
Number of sheets attached to this form.	

Note   If your application covers goods or services in more than one class, list the correct classes in numerical order and list the goods or services within each class. Draw a line or leave a blank line after each class. If there is not enough space on this form, continue on separate sheets and say in section 6 how many sheets are attached.

(REV SEP05)   **Form TM3A**

A4–003

Form TM5

Official fee £100 due with this form

Request for a statement of reasons for registrar's decision

The Patent Office
Trade Marks Registry
Cardiff Road, Newport
South Wales NP10 8QQ

Please read the guidance note below about filling in this form.

1.	Trade mark application number. (Please put an 'M' in front of Madrid marks).	*(Lowest)* Class
2.	Full name of the applicant.	
3.	Name and address (including postcode) of agent (if any).	
	Trade mark ADP number (if you know it).	
4.	Signature.	
	Name in BLOCK CAPITALS.	
	Date.	
5.	Name and daytime phone number of the person we should contact in case of query.	
	Your reference.	

Note   If we refuse your application for a trade mark or protection of an international trade mark (UK), you can ask us for a statement of the reasons for the decision. However, you must do this within one month of the date when we sent you the decision.

      Form TM5

Form TM7

Official fee £200 due with this form

Notice of opposition
and statement of grounds

The Patent Office
Trade Marks Registry
Cardiff Road, Newport
South Wales NP10 8QQ

Please read the guidance notes below about filling in this form

1. Trade mark number.		*(Lowest)* Class
2. Full name of the applicant or registered proprietor.		
3. Full name and address (including postcode) of the opponent.		
4. Name and address (including postcode) of the agent (if any).		
5. Are there any related proceedings currently with the Registry or the courts? If so, give application, registration or opposition number.		
6. Under what sections of the Trade Marks Act are you opposing this application?		
7. Declaration	I believe that the facts stated in this notice and in the attached statement of grounds are true.	
Your signature.		
Your name in BLOCK CAPITALS.		
Date.		
8. Name and daytime phone number of the person we should contact in case of query.		
Your reference.		
Number of sheets attached to this form.	This is sheet 1 of	

Notes   You must attach a separate sheet for each earlier mark you rely on.

If there is not enough space for your answers to any section, you may use extra blank sheets.

Number every extra sheet and say in question 8 above how many sheets you have used.

(REV JUL04)   **Form TM7**

Form TM7   Sheet   of

Use this sheet if you are basing your opposition on section 3 of the Trade Marks Act.
Tick which section you are relying on and give your grounds.

<u>Statement of grounds for opposition based on section 3 of the Trade Marks Act 1994</u>.

☐   3 (1)(a)   signs which do not satisfy the requirements of section 1 (1) because:

☐   3 (1)(b)   trade marks which are devoid of any distinctive character because:

☐   3 (1)(c)   trade marks which consist exclusively of signs or indications which may serve, in trade, to
                       designate the kind, quality, quantity, intended purpose, value, geographical origin, the time of
                       production of goods or of rendering of services, or other characteristics of goods or services
                       because:

☐   3 (1)(d)   trade marks which consist exclusively of signs or indications which have become customary
                       in the current language or in the bona fide and established practices of the trade because:

☐   3 (6)   trade marks which shall not be registered if or to the extent that the application is made in bad
                       faith because:

☐   other   State which other part of section 3 you are relying on and give your grounds:

Form TM7

Form TM7   Sheet   of

Use this sheet if you are basing your opposition on section 5(4) of the Trade Marks Act.
Tick which section you are relying on and give details of the earlier mark.
You must use a separate sheet for each earlier mark, so copy this sheet as many times as you need.

Statement of grounds for opposition based on section 5(4) of the Trade Marks Act 1994.

☐   5(4)(a) by virtue of any rule of law (in particular, the law of passing off) protecting an unregistered trade mark
              or other sign used in the course of trade.

☐   5(4)(b) by virtue of an earlier right other than those referred to in other subsections of section 5, in particular
              by virtue of the law of copyright, design right or registered designs; and state what type of right is
              involved:

Representation of the earlier mark, sign or right.

How and where has the earlier right been used, and on what goods or services?

When was the earlier right first used on goods or services you have listed?

State which goods or services in the application you object to.

Form TM7

Form TM7   Sheet   of

Use this sheet if you are basing your opposition on section 5(3) of the Trade Marks Act and give details of the earlier mark.
You must use a separate sheet for each earlier mark, so copy this sheet as many times as you need.

Statement of grounds for opposition based on section 5(3) of the Trade Marks Act 1994.

☐   5(3)   identical with or similar to an earlier mark with a reputation.

Details of earlier trade mark

Number:

Is it a UK, Community or International mark?

Representation of the mark:

What goods or services (including their class) are covered by this mark?

State which goods or services you say this mark has a reputation for.

State which goods or services in the application you say would take unfair advantage of or be detrimental to the distinctive character or reputation of the earlier mark.

Why do you say this?

Statement of use
If the earlier mark has been registered for five years or more before the publication of the mark you are opposing, state which goods or services the earlier mark has been used on in that time, or state why the mark has not been used in that time:

Form TM7

Form TM7 Sheet of

Use this sheet if you are basing your opposition on section 5(1) or 5(2) of the Trade Marks Act.
Tick which section you are relying on and give details of the earlier mark.
You must use a separate sheet for each earlier mark, so copy this sheet as many times as you need.

Statement of grounds for opposition based on section 5(1) or (2) of the Trade Marks Act 1994.

☐   5(1)   identical with an earlier mark and for identical goods or services as the earlier mark.

☐   5(2)(a) identical with an earlier mark and for similar goods or services as the earlier mark.

☐   5(2)(b) similar to an earlier mark and for identical or similar goods or services as the earlier mark.

Details of earlier trade mark

Number:

Is it a UK, Community or International mark?

Representation of the mark:

What goods or services (including their class) are covered by this mark?

State which goods or services in the application you say are identical or similar to those covered by the earlier mark.

Statement of use
If the earlier mark has been registered for five years or more before the publication of the mark you are opposing, state which goods or services the earlier mark has been used on in that time, or state why the mark has not been used in that time:

Form TM7

Form TM7   Sheet   of

Use this sheet if you are basing your opposition on any other grounds and tick the appropriate box.

Statement of other grounds for opposition.

☐   Section 56   Protection of well-known trade marks.

☐   Section 60   Acts of agent or representative.

☐   Rule 18(2)   Application amended after publication.

☐   Rule 22   Regulations for collective or certification marks.

☐   Rule 23(4)   Amendment of regulations for collective or certification marks.

☐   Rule 25(3)   Alteration of registered mark.

☐   Rule 45(2)   Removal of matter from the register.

☐   Rule 47(1)   Reclassification of specification.

Give details to support your opposition:

Form TM7

Form TM8

Nil Fee

Notice of defence and counterstatement

The Patent Office
Trade Marks Registry
Cardiff Road, Newport
South Wales NP10 8QQ

Please read the guidance note about filling in this form.

1. Trade mark number.	*(Lowest)* Class
2. Full name of the applicant or registered proprietor.	
3. Opposition, invalidation, revocation, or rectification number.	
4. Name and address (including postcode) of the agent (if any).	
5. If a statement of use of any earlier trade marks has been given in support of the opposition or invalidation action, do you accept this statement?	
6. If you answered "No" to question 5, do you want the other side to provide proof of use of the earlier marks? If you want the other side to provide proof of use you must state in your counterstatement for which earlier marks and for which goods and services you require that proof.	

7. Counterstatement

(REV JUL04)   **Form TM8**

Counterstatement (continued from previous sheet)

8.	Declaration	I believe that the facts stated in this notice of defence and counterstatement are true.
	Your signature.	
	Your name in BLOCK CAPITALS.	
	Date.	
9.	Name and daytime phone number of the person we should contact in case of query.	
	Your reference.	
	Number of sheets attached to this form.	This is sheet 1 of

Note   If you need more space for your counterstatement you may attach separate sheets. Number each one and say in question 9 how many sheets you have used.

Form TM8

Form TM9

Fee - see note 1.

Request for an extension of time

The Patent Office
Trade Marks Registry
Cardiff Road, Newport
Please read the guidance notes below about filling in this form. South Wales NP10 8QQ

1. Trade mark number. (Please put an 'M' in front of Madrid marks.)	*(Lowest)* Class
2. Is this request for a trade mark: (a) application which has not had a hearing; (b) application which has had a hearing; or (c) which is in dispute, for example, under opposition, invalidation, revocation, or rectification.	
3. If 2(c) applies, what is the opposition, invalidation, revocation, or rectification number. (See note 2.)	
4. How many months extension do you want? (See note 3.)	
5. Why do you want more time? (Use a separate blank sheet if there is not enough space for your answer.)	
6. Full name of the person or company making this request.	
7. Your address (including postcode), or your agent's name and address, if you have one.	
8. Your signature.	
Your name in BLOCK CAPITALS.	
Date.	
9. Name and daytime phone number of the person we should contact in case of query.	
Your reference.	
Number of sheets attached to this form.	

Notes
1. There is no fee if this request is for an application which has not had a hearing. The fee is £50 in all other cases.
2. If the request is for a trade mark which is in dispute, you must send a copy of this request to everyone else involved in the case.
3. We do not normally agree requests for extensions of more than three months.

(REV SEP05) Form TM9

A4–007   FORM TM9c

Form TM9c

Nil Fee

Request for a cooling off period

The Patent Office
Trade Marks Registry
Cardiff Road, Newport
South Wales NP10 8QQ

Please read the guidance note below about filling in this form.

1. Trade mark number.	*(Lowest)* Class
2. Opposition number.	
3. Full name of person or company making this request.	
4. Is this the applicant or the opponent?	
5. Name and address (including postcode) of the agent (if any).	
6. Declaration	I confirm that the other party to these proceedings has agreed to this request for a cooling off period.
Your signature.	
Your name in BLOCK CAPITALS.	
Date.	
7. Name and daytime phone number of the person we should contact in case of query.	
Your reference.	
Number of sheets attached to this form.	

Note   You must get the other side's agreement to this request before you sign the declaration in question 6. You may attach their written agreement to this form if you wish.

We will not agree the request unless both sides want a cooling off period.
We cannot extend the twelve month cooling off period.

(REV JUL04)   **Form TM9c**

Form TM9t

Nil Fee

Request to terminate a cooling off period

	The Patent Office **Trade Marks Registry** Cardiff Road, Newport South Wales NP10 8QQ
Please read the guidance note below about filling in this form.	
1. Trade mark number.	*(Lowest)* Class
2. Opposition number.	
3. Full name of the opponent.	
4. Name and address (including postcode) of the agent (if any).	
5. Your signature.	
Your name in BLOCK CAPITALS.	
Date.	
6. Name and daytime phone number of the person we should contact in case of query.	
Your reference	

Note   Only the opponent can use this form to end a cooling off period.
The applicant may end a cooling off period by sending us their notice of defence (form TM8).

A4–009

 Form TM11

Official fee due with this form - see note

Renewal of trade mark registration

The Patent Office
Trade Marks Registry
Cardiff Road, Newport
South Wales NP10 8QQ

Please read the guidance note below about filling in this form.

1. Trade mark number.	
2. Which classes are now registered?	
3. Which classes do you want to renew, if not all?	
4. Full name of the registered proprietor.	
5. Renewal date.	
6. Fees: Amount of renewal fee.	£
Amount of late renewal fee. (You must pay this if you are renewing up to six months after the renewal date.)	£
Total fees.	£
7. Name and address (including postcode) where we should send confirmation of renewal.	
Trade marks ADP number (if you know it).	
8. Your signature.	
Your name in BLOCK CAPITALS.	
Date.	
9. Name and daytime phone number of the person we should contact in case of query.	
Your reference.	

Note   It costs £200 to renew a trade mark for the first or only class of the registration, and £50 for each extra class.

(REV SEP05)   **Form TM11**

Form TM12

Official fee £100 due with this form, but see notes

Request to divide an application

The Patent Office
Trade Marks Registry
Cardiff Road, Newport
South Wales NP10 8QQ

Please read the guidance notes below about filling in this form.

1. Trade mark application number.	*(Lowest)* Class
2. Full name of the applicant.	
3. Do you want to divide: (a) The list of goods or services; or (b) a series of marks? List the class number or numbers, or the goods or services, or the marks in the series, to be transferred. Use a separate sheet if there is not enough space on this form and say in section 7 how many sheets are attached.	
4. How many parts do you want to divide the application into?	
5. Name of agent (if any).	
6. Your signature.	
Your name in BLOCK CAPITALS.	
Date.	
7. Name and daytime phone number of the person we should contact in case of query.	
Your reference.	
Number of sheets attached to this form.	

Notes If we have objected to some of the classes in a multi-class application, you can divide the application to allow those classes which are acceptable to go forward for publication, and for objections to the remaining classes to be dealt with later in more detail. List in section 3 the class number or numbers, or the goods or services to be transferred to a divisional application. The fee for this is £100 only.

If we have objected to a series of marks, you can divide your application to allow those marks which are acceptable to go forward for publication, and for objections to the remaining marks to be dealt with later in more detail. List in section 3 the marks to be transferred to a divisional application. The fee for this is £100, plus £200 for each new application created, and £50 for each extra class if the application contains more than one class.

You cannot divide both goods or services and a series on the same form. If you want to do this, you must send us a separate form and the correct fees for each type of division.

(REV SEP05)

Form TM12

Form TM13

Official fee £100 plus renewal fee due
with this form

Request to restore and renew
a registration

The Patent Office
Trade Marks Registry
Cardiff Road, Newport
South Wales NP10 8QQ

Please read the guidance notes below about filling in this form

1. Trade mark number.	*(Lowest)* Class
2. Class or classes you want to renew, if not all.	
3. Full name of the proprietor as now shown on our records.	
4. When should the mark have been renewed?	
5. Fees: Restoration fee.	£100
Renewal fee.	
Total fees.	
6. Your name and address (including postcode), if you are not the proprietor, or your agent's name and address, if you have one.	
7. Your Signature.	
Your name in BLOCK CAPITALS.	
Date.	
8. Name and daytime phone number of the person we should contact in case of query.	
Your reference.	
Number of sheets attached to this form	This is sheet 1 of

Notes

You can apply to restore a mark up to twelve months after it should have been renewed.
You can check the renewal date by doing a case search on our website www.patent.gov.uk

You do not have to send us a renewal request (form TM11) with this form, but you must pay the correct renewal fees
(£200 for the first (or only) class and £50 for each other class you want to renew) and the restoration fee of £100 when
you send us this form. If we do not agree to restore the mark, we will refund your renewal fees.

You must attach a statement fully explaining why you did not renew the mark in time.

(REV NOV04)

Form TM13

Form TM16

Official fee £50 due with this form

Application to record a change of ownership

**The Patent Office
Trade Marks Registry**
Cardiff Road, Newport
South Wales NP10 8QQ

Please read the guidance notes on the next page about filling in this form.

1. Trade mark numbers affected. (List on a separate sheet if there is not enough space on this form).	*(Lowest)* Class
2. Full name of the applicant or proprietor as now shown on our records.	
3. Full name and address (including postcode) of the new applicant or proprietor.	
4. (a) If the new proprietor is a corporate body, in what country is it incorporated? (b) If incorporated in the USA, also give the state in which it is incorporated.	
5. Date new proprietor took over ownership, (See note 1).	
6. If only part of the ownership has been transferred, for example by partial assignment, what rights or goods or services have been transferred?	
7. Full name and address (including postcode) where we should send confirmation that we have recorded the change. Trade Marks ADP number (if you know it).	
8. We will record the address given in section 7 above as the contact address for future correspondence about these marks unless you give a different address here.	

(REV NOV04)   **Form TM16**

9. Authorisation to change the register. You must complete **(a) and (b)**. (See note 2).	
(a) Signature of the current applicant or proprietor, or their representative.	
Name in BLOCK CAPITALS.	
Status of signatory.	
Date.	
(b) Signature of the new applicant or proprietor, or their representative.	
Name in BLOCK CAPITALS.	
Status of signatory.	
Date.	
10. Name and daytime phone number of the person we should contact in case of query.	
Your reference.	
Number of sheets attached to this form.	

Notes

Use this form to ask us to record changes in the ownership of marks, including company mergers.
It is not a substitute for the assignment document or other proof of the transaction.

If the applicant or proprietor has merely changed their name, use form TM21, not this one.

We suggest you check the proprietor's name and the marks they own by doing a proprietor search on our website www.patent.gov.uk before you fill in the form.

1. If the assignment was before 28 March 2000, you will need to provide a separate declaration about whether Stamp Duty has been paid or is not payable. If you need more advice about this, contact your nearest Inland Revenue Stamp Office, or phone their Helpline on 0845 6030135.

2. Both the old and new proprietors, or their representatives, must sign this form. If you cannot do this, you may send us a copy of the deed of assignment or other written proof of the transaction.

Form TM16

Form TM17

Nil fee

Request to merge
applications or registrations

The Patent Office
Trade Marks Registry
Cardiff Road, Newport
South Wales NP10 8QQ

Please read the guidance notes below about filling in this form.

1 Trade mark numbers to be merged. (List on a separate sheet if there is not enough space on this form.)	*(Lowest)* Class
2. Full name of the applicant or proprietor as now shown on our records.	
3. Full name and address (including postcode) where we should send confirmation that we have completed the merger. Trade Marks ADP number (if you know it).	
4. We will record the address given in section 3 above as the contact address for future correspondence about these marks unless you give a different address here.	
5. Your Signature.	
Your name in BLOCK CAPITALS.	
Date.	
6. Name and daytime phone number of the person we should contact in case of query.	
Your reference.	
Number of sheets attached to this form.	

Notes

You cannot merge applications and registrations together or merge expired marks. You cannot reverse the merger process.

Applications

You can merge applications at any time before they are accepted for advertisement, as long as they have the same application date **and** are for the same marks **and** are in the same ownership.

Registrations

You can merge registrations at any time, as long as they are for the same marks **and** are in the same ownership. Registered marks do not have to have the same registration dates but, on merging, the new merged registration will take the **latest filing date.**
If you want to merge registered marks before you renew them, please send us this form at least a month before you send your renewal request (form TM11). This will help us to merge the marks before they expire.

(REV MAR05)   **Form TM17**

A4–014   FORM TM21

Form TM21

Nil Fee

Change of proprietor's name or address
or other change to an application

The Patent Office
Trade Marks Registry
Cardiff Road, Newport
South Wales NP10 8QQ

Please read the guidance notes on the next page about filling in this form.

1. Trade mark numbers to be changed or say 'ALL MARKS'. (Please put an 'M' in front of Madrid marks.) (List on a separate sheet if there is not enough space on this form.)	*(Lowest)* Class
Change of name or address 2. Full name of the applicant or proprietor as now shown on our records. Trade marks ADP number (if you know it.)	
3. New name or address (including postcode) to be recorded.	
Other change to an application 4. Details of change.	
5. Name and address (including postcode) of agent (if any), or your contact address (including postcode) if not the same as in section 3 above.	
6. Declaration. Signature.	I declare there has been no change in the ownership of the marks, and that I have the authority to request this change
Name in BLOCK CAPITALS.	
Date.	
7. Name and daytime phone number of the person we should contact in case of query.	
Your reference.	
Number of sheets attached to this form.	

(REV OCT04)   **Form TM21**

Notes

Change of name or address of the applicant or proprietor
If you want to record changes in the name or address of the applicant or proprietor, leave section 4 blank.

We suggest you check the proprietor's name and the marks they own by doing a proprietor search on our website www.patent.gov.uk before you fill in the form.

If the ownership of the marks has changed, use Form TM16, not this one.

Other changes
If you want to record any other changes in an application, such as changes to the specification after publication of the application, leave sections 2 and 3 blank.

For applications:
If you want to correct or change the name of the applicant, we may ask you to send us a witness statement explaining the reasons for your request.

For registered marks:
If you want to correct the name or address of the proprietor, for example, because of a clerical error, use form TM26(R) (for rectification), not this one.

If you want to cancel or surrender some of the goods or services, use form TM23 (partial surrender), not this one.

Please do not return these notes with your form.

Form TM21

Form TM22

Nil Fee

Notice to surrender a registration

The Patent Office
Trade Marks Registry
Cardiff Road, Newport
South Wales NP10 8QQ

Please read the guidance notes below about filling in this form.

1. Trade mark number to be surrendered.	*(Lowest)* Class
2. Full name of the registered proprietor.	
3. Does anyone else have a registered interest in the mark? (If you answer 'Yes', list their name and address on a separate sheet.)	
4. Full name and address (including postcode) where we should send confirmation that we have taken the action requested.	
5. Declaration — Cross out the statements that **do not** apply.	I declare that I have the authority to surrender this registration. I confirm that no-one else has an interest in this mark; or I confirm that I have notified everyone listed as having a registered interest in this mark three months before sending this form; or I confirm that everyone listed as having a registered interest in this mark consents to its surrender.
Signature.	
Name in BLOCK CAPITALS.	
Date.	
6. Name and daytime phone number of the person we should contact in case of query.	
Your reference.	
Number of sheets attached to this form.	

Notes

Use this form to give up all your legal rights in a trade mark registration. Once we action it, there is no way to reinstate the registration. Please use a separate form for each registration.

If you want to give up your rights in only some of the goods or services, use form TM23.

Section 3   If anyone else has a registered interest in your mark, such as a licence or security, you must tell them that you are going to give up your rights at least three months before you send us this form, or they should agree to the surrender.

(REV APR05)   **Form TM22**

Form TM23

Nil Fee

Notice to partially surrender a registration

The Patent Office
Trade Marks Registry
Cardiff Road, Newport
South Wales NP10 8QQ

Please read the guidance notes below about filling in this form.

1. Trade mark number.	*(Lowest)* Class
2. Full name of the registered proprietor.	
3. Which goods or services **do you want to surrender?** (Make sure you clearly list the goods or services, you want to give up, **not** those you want to keep registered).	
4. Does anyone else have a registered interest in the mark? (If you answer 'Yes', list their name and address on a separate sheet.)	
5. Full name and address (including postcode) where we should send confirmation that we have taken the action requested.	
6. Declaration Cross out the statements that **do not** apply.	I declare that I have the authority to partially surrender this registration. I confirm that no-one else has an interest in this mark; or I confirm that I have notified everyone listed as having a registered interest in this mark three months before sending this form; or I confirm that everyone listed as having a registered interest in this mark consents to its partial surrender.
Signature.	
Name in BLOCK CAPITALS.	
Date.	
7. Name and daytime phone number of the person we should contact in case of query.	
Your reference.	
Number of sheets attached to this form.	

Notes

Use this form to give up some of your legal rights in a trade mark registration, such as some of the goods or services. Once we action it, there is no way to reinstate those rights. Please use a separate form for each registration.

Section 4   If anyone else has a registered interest in your mark, such as a licence or security, you must tell them that you are going to give up some of your rights at least three months before you send us this form, or they should agree to the partial surrender.

(REV APR05) **Form TM23**

Form TM24

Nil Fee

Application to record or cancel a registrable transaction other than an assignment or licence

The Patent Office
Trade Marks Registry
Cardiff Road, Newport
South Wales NP10 8QQ

Please read the guidance notes on the next page about filling in this form.

1. Trade mark numbers affected. (Please put an 'M' in front of Madrid marks.) (List on a separate sheet if there is not enough space on this form.)	*(Lowest)* Class
2. Full name of the registered proprietor (that is, the grantor).	
3. Full name and address (including postcode) of the person to be recorded as having an interest in the marks listed (that is, the grantee).	
4. Say if you want to: (a) record; or (b) cancel a transaction.	
5. Details of the transaction to be recorded or cancelled.	
6. Signature of the grantor of the security interest or their representative.	
Name in BLOCK CAPITALS.	
Date.	
7. Full name and address (including postcode) where we should send confirmation that we have recorded the transaction.	
8. Name and daytime phone number of the person we should contact in case of query.	
Your reference.	
Number of sheets attached to this form.	

(REV APR05)   **Form TM24**

Form TM24

Notes

Use this form to tell us about:

The grant, amendment, or termination of any security interest over a registered trade mark, or any right in or under it.

In section 3, tell us -   the name and address of the grantee.

In section 5, tell us -   (1) the nature of the interest (whether fixed or floating); and

                         (2) the extent of the security and the right in or under the mark secured.

In section 6, the grantor of the security interest must sign this form. If you cannot do this, you may send us written proof of the transaction.

The making by personal representatives of an assent in relation to a registered trade mark, or any right in or under it.

In section 3, tell us -   the name and address of the person in whom the mark or any right in or under it vests by virtue of the assent.

In section 5, tell us -   the date of the assent.

You do not have to sign in section 6.

An order of a court or other competent authority transferring a registered trade mark, or any right in or under it.

In section 3, tell us -   the name and address of the transferee.

In section 5, tell us -   (1) the date of the order; and

                         (2) where the transfer is in respect of a right in the mark, a description of the right transferred.

You do not have to sign in section 6.

Please do not return these notes with your form.

Form TM24

Form TM25

Nil Fee

Request to alter a registered mark

The Patent Office
Trade Marks Registry
Cardiff Road, Newport
South Wales NP10 8QQ

Please read the guidance note below about filling in this form.

1. Trade mark number.	*(Lowest)* Class
2. Full name and address (including postcode) of the registered proprietor.	
3. Details of the change requested. (If the mark is pictorial, attach a copy here of how the mark will look after the changes.)	
4. Name and address (including postcode) of the agent (if any).	
Signature.	
Name in BLOCK CAPITALS.	
Date.	
5. Name and daytime phone number of the person we should contact in case of query.	
Your reference.	

Note

We may alter a registered mark **only:**
     where the mark includes the proprietor's name and address; **and**
     the alteration is limited to altering that name or address; **and**
     the alteration does not substantially affect the identity of the mark.

(REV APR05)   **Form TM25**

Form TM26(I)

Official fee £200 due with this form

Application to declare invalid a registration or a protected international trade mark (UK)

Please read the guidance note below about filling in this form.

The Patent Office
Trade Marks Registry
Cardiff Road, Newport
South Wales NP10 8QQ

1. Trade mark number.		*(Lowest)* Class
2. Full name of the registered proprietor.		
3. Full name and address (including postcode) of the applicant for invalidation.		
4. Name and address (including postcode) of the agent (if any).		
5. Declaration	I declare that to the best of my knowledge there is no action concerning this registration pending in the courts. I believe that the facts stated in the attached statement of case are true.	
Your signature.		
Your name in BLOCK CAPITALS.		
Date.		
6. Name and daytime phone number of the person we should contact in case of query.		
Your reference.		
Number of sheets attached to this form.	This is sheet 1 of	

Note   You must attach a statement of your reasons for making this application. You must give full details of the use made of any earlier trade marks registered for five years or more at the date of making this application. You must state on what goods or services the earlier marks have been used in these five years or state why the marks have not been used.

A4–020

Form TM26(N)

Official fee £200 due with this form

Application to revoke a registration or a protected international trade mark (UK) for reasons of non-use

The Patent Office
Trade Marks Registry
Cardiff Road, Newport
South Wales NP10 8QQ

Please read the guidance note below about filling in this form.

1. Trade mark number.	*(Lowest)* Class
2. Full name of the registered proprietor.	
3. Full name and address (including postcode) of the applicant for revocation.	
4. Name and address (including postcode) of the agent (if any).	
5. Are you basing your application on Section 46(1)(a), 46(1)(b), or both?	
6. If you are basing your application on Section 46(1)(b), within what 5-year period do you say the mark was not used?	
7. From what date do you want revocation to take effect?	
8. Declaration Your signature.	I declare that to the best of my knowledge there is no action concerning this registration pending in the courts. I believe that the facts stated in the attached statement of case are true.
Your name in BLOCK CAPITALS.	
Date.	
9. Name and daytime phone number of the person we should contact in case of query.	
Your reference.	
Number of sheets attached to this form.	This is sheet 1 of

Note You must attach a statement of your reasons for making this application.

(REV JUL04)   **Form TM26(N)**

Form TM26(O)

Official fee £200 due with this form

Application to revoke a registration or a protected international trade mark (UK) for reasons other than non-use

The Patent Office
Trade Marks Registry
Cardiff Road, Newport
South Wales NP10 8QQ

Please read the guidance note below about filling in this form.

1. Trade mark number.	*(Lowest)* Class
2. Full name of the registered proprietor.	
3. Full name and address (including postcode) of the applicant for revocation.	
4. Name and address (including postcode) of the agent (if any).	
5. Are you basing your application on Section 46(1)(c), 46(1)(d), or both?	
6. Declaration	I declare that to the best of my knowledge there is no action concerning this registration pending in the courts. I believe that the facts stated in the attached statement of case are true.
Your signature.	
Your name in BLOCK CAPITALS.	
Date.	
7. Name and daytime phone number of the person we should contact in case of query.	
Your reference.	
Number of sheets attached to this form.	This is sheet 1 of

Note   You must attach a statement of your reasons for making this application.

(REV JUL04)   **Form TM26(O)**

Form TM26(R)

Nil Fee

Application to rectify the register

The Patent Office
Trade Marks Registry
Cardiff Road, Newport
South Wales NP10 8QQ

Please read the guidance note below about filling in this form.

1. Trade mark number.	*(Lowest)* Class
2. Full name of the registered proprietor.	
3. Full name and address (including postcode) of the applicant for rectification (if not the registered proprietor).	
4. Details of the error or omission to be corrected. (Attach a separate sheet if necessary.)	
5. Name and address (including postcode) of the agent (if any).	
6. Declaration	I declare that to the best of my knowledge there is no action concerning this registration pending in the courts. I believe that the facts stated in the attached statement of case are true.
Your signature.	
Your name in BLOCK CAPITALS.	
Date.	
7. Name and daytime phone number of the person we should contact in case of query.	
Your reference.	
Number of sheets attached to this form.	This is sheet 1 of

Note: You must attach a statement of your reasons for making this request.

(REV JUL04)   **Form TM26(R)**

Form TM27

Nil Fee

Application to intervene in proceedings for the (a) invalidation, revocation or rectification of a UK registration, or (b) invalidation or revocation of a protected international trade mark (UK)

Please read the guidance note below about filling in this form.

The Patent Office
Trade Marks Registry
Cardiff Road, Newport
South Wales NP10 8QQ

1. Trade mark number.		*(Lowest)* Class
2. Full name of the registered proprietor.		
3. Full name and address (including postcode) of the applicant for intervention.		
4. Name and address (including postcode) of the agent (if any).		
5. Your signature.		
Your name in BLOCK CAPITALS.		
Date.		
6. Name and daytime phone number of the person we should contact in case of query.		
Your reference.		
Number of sheets attached to this form.	This is sheet 1 of	

Note You must attach a statement of your reasons for making this application.

(REV JUL04) Form TM27

Form TM28

Nil Fee

Application to record a concurrent registration

Please read the guidance notes below about filling in this form.

The Patent Office
Trade Marks Registry
Cardiff Road, Newport
South Wales NP10 8QQ

1.	UK trade mark number.	*(Lowest)* Class
2.	International (Madrid) trade mark number.	*(Lowest)* Class
3.	Full name and address of the holder of the protected international trade mark (UK).	
4.	Name and address (including postcode) of the agent (if any).	
	Trade marks ADP number (if you know it).	
5.	Your signature.	
	Your name in BLOCK CAPITALS.	
	Date.	
6.	Name and daytime phone number of the person we should contact in case of query.	
	Your reference.	

Note   You should use this form to ask us to record a protected international registration (UK) in the register against the UK registered mark.

We can do this only where:
1.   The registered trade mark is also a protected international trade mark (UK); and
2.   The proprietor of the registered trade mark is the holder of the international trade mark (UK); and
3.   All the goods or services for which the registered trade mark is registered and protected under the protected international trade mark (UK); and
4.   The date of registration of the registered trade mark is earlier than the date specified in relation to the international trade mark (UK).

(REV SEP05)   **Form TM28**

Form TM31C

Official fee £20 for each event due with this form

Request for information about events
in the progress of a trade mark

The Patent Office
Trade Marks Registry
Cardiff Road, Newport
South Wales NP10 8QQ

Please read the guidance notes below about filling in this form.

1. Trade mark number.	*(Lowest)* Class
2. Event(s) you want to be notified about:	List here the letter shown against the event.
A Application published or withdrawn, refused or abandoned before publication.	
B Opposition filed.	
C Application registered or withdrawn, refused or abandoned after publication.	
E Registration renewed or removed.	
F Registration surrendered or revoked.	
G Assignment application received.	
H Full or partial assignment actioned.	
Other - please say what you want to know.	
3. Full name and address (including postcode) where we should send the information.	
Your signature.	
Your name in BLOCK CAPITALS.	
Date.	
4. Name and daytime phone number of the person we should contact in case of query.	
Your reference.	

Notes

We charge a fee of £20 for each event that you want to be told about.
We offer a similar service, free of charge, on our website www.patent.gov.uk under Caveats
If you want a copy of a trade mark file, do not use this form - ask for 'Trade Mark sales'.
This form is not available for public inspection after we receive it.

(REV SEP05)   Form TM31C

Form TM31M

The Patent Office

Offical Fee £20 for each event due with this form

Request for information about events in the progress of an international trade mark (UK)

The Patent Office
Trade Marks Registry
Cardiff Road, Newport
South Wales NP10 8QQ

Please read the guidance notes below about filling in this form.

1. International trade mark (UK) number.	*(Lowest)* Class
2. Event you want to be notified about:	List here the letter shown against the event.
A Application published in the UK Trade Marks Journal, or withdrawn or refused before publication.	
B Opposition filed.	
C Application protected or withdrawn or refused after publication.	
D UK designation revoked or invalidated.	
3. Full name and address (including postcode) where we should send the information.	
Trade marks ADP number (if you know it).	
4. Your signature.	
Your name in BLOCK CAPITALS.	
Date.	
5. Name and daytime phone number of the person we should contact in case of query.	
Your reference.	

Note   We charge a fee of £20 for each event that you want to be told about.
This form is not available for public inspection after we receive it.

(REV SEP05)   **Form TM31M**

Form TM31R

Official fee £20 for each copy due with this form

Request for a Certified Copy

The Patent Office
Trade Marks Registry
Cardiff Road, Newport
South Wales NP10 8QQ

Please read the guidance notes below about filling in this form.

1. Trade mark number.

2. How many copies do you want?

3. Tick if certificate is for use in Guernsey.

4. Tick if certificate will later be legalised.

5. Do you want us to certify:

   a) the application as it was applied for;
   b) the application or registration as it is;
   c) anything else? (If so, give details.)

6. Full name and address (including postcode) where we should send the certificate.

7. Your signature.

   Your name in BLOCK CAPITALS.

   Date.

8. Name and daytime phone number of the person we should contact in case of query.

   Your reference.

Notes

1. We do not certify Community trade marks. You must apply to OHIM for these.
   We do not certify International (UK) trade marks. You must apply to WIPO for these.

2. We charge a fee of £20 for each copy of the certificate that you want.

3. We need to know if the certificate is for use in Guernsey, so that we can seal it.
   No other countries need special certificates.

4. We need to know if the certificate will be legalised by the Foreign & Commonwealth Office, so that we can sign it.

5. Tell us exactly what you want us to certify so that our certificate meets your needs.

(REV SEP04)

Form TM31R

Form TM33

Nil Fee

Appointment or change of agent or contact address

The Patent Office
Trade Marks Registry
Cardiff Road, Newport
South Wales NP10 8QQ

Please read the guidance note below about filling in this form.

1. Trade mark numbers affected. (Please put an 'M' in front of Madrid marks). (List on a separate sheet if there is not enough space on this form).	*(Lowest)* Class
2. Full name of the a) proprietor; or b) opponent as now shown on our records.	
3. Name and address (including postcode) of the new agent or contact address	
Trade Marks ADP number (if you know it).	
4. Declaration.	We have been appointed by the above proprietor or opponent.
Signature.	
Name in BLOCK CAPITALS.	
Date.	
5. Name and daytime phone number of the person we should contact in case of query.	
Your reference.	
Number of sheets attached to this form.	

Note We suggest you check the proprietor's name and the marks they own by doing a proprietor search on our website www.patent.gov.uk before you fill in the form.

(REV NOV04)   **Form TM33**

Form TM35

Official fee £200 due with this form

Regulations governing the use of certification or collective marks

Please read the guidance notes below about filling in this form.

The Patent Office
Trade Marks Registry
Cardiff Road, Newport
South Wales NP10 8QQ

1.	Trade mark number or numbers. (Please put an 'M' in front of Madrid marks).	*(Lowest)* Class
2.	Full name of the applicant.	
3.	Is this application for a: (a) certification mark; or (b) collective mark?	
4.	Name and address (including postcode) of agent (if any).	
	Trade marks ADP number (if you know it).	
5.	Signature.	
	Name in BLOCK CAPITALS.	
	Date.	
6.	Name and daytime phone number of the person we should contact in case of query.	
	Your reference.	
	Number of sheets attached to this form.	

Notes   You must send us this form with a copy of the regulations governing the use of the mark within nine months of the application date. Say in section 6 how many sheets are in the regulations.

The regulations can apply to a number of marks as long as they are all certification marks or all collective marks, but not a mixture of the two.

(REV SEP05)

Form TM35

Form TM36

Official fee £100 due with this form

Application to amend the regulations governing the use of certification or collective marks

Please read the guidance notes below about filling in this form.

The Patent Office
Trade Marks Registry
Cardiff Road, Newport
South Wales NP10 8QQ

1.	Trade mark number or numbers. (Please put an 'M' in front of Madrid marks.)	*(Lowest)* Class
2.	Full name of the applicant.	
3.	Is this application for a: (a) certification mark; or (b) collective mark?	
4.	Name and address (including postcode) of agent (if any).	
	Trade mark ADP number (if you know it).	
5.	Signature.	
	Name in BLOCK CAPITALS.	
	Date.	
6.	Name and daytime phone number of the person we should contact in case of query.	
	Your reference.	
	Number of sheets attached to this form.	

Notes   If you have sent us a copy of the regulations governing the use of a certification or collective mark, you must send us this form with a copy of the amendments whenever you want to change those regulations. Say in section 6 how many sheets are in the amendments.

The amendments can apply to the regulations for a number of marks as long as they are:
1.   All applications or all registered marks, but not a mixture of the two; and
2.   All certification marks or all collective marks, but not a mixture of the two.

(REV SEP05)   **Form TM36**

Form TM50

Nil fee

Application to register a licensee

The Patent Office
Trade Marks Registry
Cardiff Road, Newport
South Wales NP10 8QQ

Please read the guidance notes on the next page about filling in this form.

1. Trade mark number or numbers. (List on a separate sheet if there is not enough space on this form.)	*(Lowest)* Class
2. Full name of the proprietor as now shown on our records.	
3. Full name and address (including postcode) of the licensee.	
4. a) Date licence starts.	
b) Date licence ends (if any).	
5. Is the licence exclusive?	
6. List the goods or services within each class for which licence is to be registered (or state 'ALL').	Class Goods or services
7. Geographical area to which licence is limited (or state 'NONE').	
8. Full name and address (including postcode) where we should send confirmation that we have registered the licensee.	
9. Signature of the registered proprietor (or their representative).	
Name in BLOCK CAPITALS.	
Date.	
10. Name and daytime phone number of the person we should contact in case of query.	
Your reference.	
Number of sheets attached to this form.	

(REV SEP05)   **Form TM50**

Form TM50

Notes

Use this form to ask us to register any licences granted against the trade mark.   It is not a substitute for the licence agreement or other proof of the transaction.

If the licence is exclusive, it means that the licensee can use the trade mark in the way allowed by the licence, to the exclusion of everyone else, including the registered proprietor.

The registered proprietor (or their representative) must sign this form in section 9. If they cannot do this, you may send a copy of the licence agreement or other proof of the transaction.

Please do not return these notes with your form.

Form TM50

Form TM51

Nil fee

Application to remove or amend the registration of a licensee

Please read the guidance note below about filling in this form.

The Patent Office
Trade Marks Registry
Cardiff Road, Newport
South Wales NP10 8QQ

1. Trade mark number or numbers. (List on a separate sheet if there is not enough space on this form.)	*(Lowest)* Class
2. Full name of the proprietor as now shown on our records.	
3. Full name of the licensee.	
4. Is this request to: a) remove the licensee; or b) amend the licensee details? If so, please give full details of amendment.	
5. Full name and address (including postcode) where we should send confirmation that we have taken the action.	
6. Signature of the registered proprietor (or their representative).	
Name in BLOCK CAPITALS.	
Date.	
7. Name and daytime phone number of the person we should contact in case of query.	
Your reference.	
Number of sheets attached to this form.	

Note
The registered proprietor (or their representative) must sign this form in section 6. If they cannot do this, you may send us some other proof of the transaction.

(REV SEP05)

Form TM51

Form TM53

Nil Fee

Request to proceed to evidence rounds

The Patent Office
Trade Marks Registry
Cardiff Road, Newport
South Wales NP10 8QQ

1.	Trade mark number.	*(Lowest)* Class
2.	Opposition number.	
3.	Full name of the person or company making this request.	
4.	Is this the applicant or the opponent?	
5.	Name and address (including postcode) of the agent (if any).	
6.	Your signature.	
	Your name in BLOCK CAPITALS.	
	Date.	
7.	Name and daytime phone number of the person we should contact in case of query.	
	Your reference.	

Form TM54

Nil Fee

Notice of giving evidence

Please read the guidance note below about filling in this form.

The Patent Office
Trade Marks Registry
Cardiff Road, Newport
South Wales NP10 8QQ

1.	Trade mark number.	*(Lowest)* Class
2.	Opposition, invalidation, revocation or rectification number.	
3.	Full name of the person or company giving this evidence.	
4.	Is this the applicant, the opponent or the registered proprietor?	
5.	Name and address (including postcode) of the agent (if any).	
6.	List of evidence included. Name of the person giving the evidence.	Reference number(s) of their exhibits
7.	Is this your last evidence in this round?	
8.	Your signature.	
	Your name in BLOCK CAPITALS.	
	Date.	
9.	Name and daytime phone number of the person we should contact in case of query.	
	Your reference.	
	Number of sheets attached to this form.	This is sheet 1 of

Note   If there is not enough space for your answers to question 6, you may use separate sheets.
Number each one and say in question 9 how many sheets you have used.
Do not count the number of sheets of evidence.

(REV JUL04)   **Form TM54**

A4–035

Form TM55

Nil Fee

Notice of appeal to the Appointed Person

Please read the guidance note about filling in this form.

The Patent Office
Trade Marks Registry
Cardiff Road, Newport
South Wales NP10 8QQ

1. Trade mark number.	*(Lowest)* Class
2. Opposition, invalidation, revocation or rectification number.	
3. Full name of the person or company making this appeal.	
4. Is this the applicant, the opponent or the registered proprietor?	
5. Name and address (including postcode) of the agent (if any).	

6. Statement of grounds of appeal.

Statement of grounds of appeal (continued from previous sheet)

7.	Your signature.	
	Your name in BLOCK CAPITALS.	
	Date.	
8.	Name and daytime phone number of the person we should contact in case of query.	
	Your reference.	
	Number of sheets attached to this form.	

Note If you need more space for your grounds of appeal you may attach separate sheets. Number each one and say in question 8 how many sheets you have used.

Form TM55

APPENDIX 5

Practice Notes

Tribunal Practice Notice

(TPN 1/2000)

A5–001   PRACTICE IN PROCEEDINGS BEFORE THE COMPTROLLER

A5–002   **1.** This Practice Notice advises Patent Office customers of changes in practice in the way the Office operates as a tribunal hearing "with notice" (also known as *inter partes*) and "without notice" (also known as *ex parte*) proceedings, as well as reaffirming the continuation of certain existing practices. The changes, which are effective for all such proceedings from 26 April 2000, are among a number of measures that are being introduced following the Patent Office's review of its proceedings following Lord Woolf's report *Access to Justice*, which recommended major changes to the administration of civil justice in the courts of England and Wales. Those recommendations have since been implemented in the Civil Procedure Rules 1998. In line with the general principles set down by Lord Woolf, the Office's measures are intended to simplify and improve the speed of such proceedings before the Comptroller and thereby reduce the cost to Patent Office customers. The Standing Advisory Committee on Industrial Property and other interested parties, including the Council on Tribunals, were consulted about the proposals that emerged from the review and their views were taken into account in settling the final package of changes.

2. Some of the changes required amendment to the statutory rules. In the case of patents, registered designs and design right proceedings, these changes were respectively introduced by the Patents (Amendment) (No 2) Rules 1999, the Registered Designs (Amendment) Rules 1999, and the Design Right (Proceedings Before Comptroller) (Amendment) Rules 1999, all of which statutory instruments came into force on 22 December 1999. (Notices in the Patents & Designs Journal, Trade Marks Journal and Designs in View of 15 December 1999 gave more information about these SIs.) Changes to the trade marks rules were introduced as part of a general consolidation forming the Trade Marks Rules 2000 which came into force on 17 February 2000.

3. Many other of the changes arising from the review can, however, be introduced by altering established formal practice. This Practice Notice sets out how those changes are being made, as well as explaining how certain of the rule changes already implemented are being operated. Except as otherwise stated, this Practice Notice covers the full range of tribunal proceedings before the Comptroller, that is patents, trade marks, registered designs and design right, and references to "the rules" should accordingly be read generically.

4. The general practice with regard to the award of costs is set out in a separate notice *TPN 2/2000* entitled "Costs in Proceedings before the Comptroller".

The Overriding Objective

A5–003   **5.** In its role as a tribunal, the Office adheres to the same overriding objective as the court for dealing with cases justly, as set out in rule 1.1 of the Civil Procedure Rules 1998. This includes, so far as is practicable:

(a) ensuring that the parties are on an equal footing;

(b) saving expense;

(c) dealing with the case in ways which are proportionate—

(i) to the amount of money involved;

      (ii) to the importance of the case;
         (iii) to the complexity of the issues; and
      (iv) to the financial position of each party;
(d) ensuring that it is dealt with expeditiously and fairly; and
(e) allotting to it an appropriate share of the court's resources, while taking into account the need to allot resources to other cases.

Summary

6. The following main matters are addressed in this Practice Notice: **A5–004**

- The Office and parties should endeavour to complete *with notice* proceedings within 18 months. (paragraph 7)
- The periods for filing a counterstatement and evidence in patents, registered designs and design right proceedings has been shortened from two months to six weeks except when lodging an opposition, *e.g.* opposition to amend a patent specification under rule 40(2). (paragraph 8)
- The periods for filing a counterstatement and evidence in trade marks revocation (on grounds other than non-use), invalidation and rectification proceedings has been shortened to six weeks. However, the period will remain at three months in opposition and revocation on grounds of non-use proceedings, though an additional "cooling-off" period of three months at the start opposition proceedings will be granted when sought by both parties. (paragraph 9)
- Hearing Officers will have discretion to shorten prescribed periods, (paragraph 10)
- The Office will set a period within which a preliminary (interlocutory) hearing should take place and give parties 14 days to agree a date in that period. The Office will fix a date if after 14 days the parties do not agree a date within this period, although Hearing Officers may override the 14 days if there are genuine difficulties. (paragraph 13)
- At the commencement of the final evidence round, the Office will aim to fix a date for a substantive hearing for approximately four months later. (paragraph 14)
- The party commencing action should provide a statement of case which properly sets out the grounds on which the case against the other side is to be based. If a party fails to provide sufficient information, the Patent Office may challenge the statement. Until the statement of case is in order the proceedings will not be progressed. (paragraphs 15 to 19)
- The Office has provided broad guidelines on how to set out a statement of case. (paragraphs 20 to 25)
- A declaration of the truth of the information in claims and defences is required for trade marks proceedings and encouraged in other proceedings. (paragraph 27)
- The Office will accept a witness statement in evidence although Hearing Officers are authorised to require the filing of an affidavit or statutory declaration if they consider it necessary. (paragraph 30)
- Exceptionally the Office is prepared to accept unsigned witness statements or unsworn statutory declarations or affidavits as meeting time deadlines provided a proper version of the evidence is filed within a specified period. The Hearing Officer may impose a cost penalty if, in the event, the formal evidence is different from that originally filed. (paragraph 31)
- Where a party adduces evidence of a statement made by another person and does not call that person as a witness, the Hearing Officer may permit the other party to call that person and cross examine them. (paragraph 32)
- In deciding whether to grant specific disclosure, Hearing Officers will generally follow principles which mirror those applied by the courts. (paragraphs 33 to 37)
- The Office intends issuing questionnaires on a selective basis prior to evidence rounds. (paragraph 38)
- Hearing Officers will adopt the selective use of "case management conferences" taking into account the circumstances of the case, *e.g.* the need to clarify issues, the degree of complexity, any related actions and any wider public interest issues. (paragraph 39 and 40)

- Hearing Officers are also empowered to call a "pre-hearing review" prior to a hearing which will give them the opportunity to clarify matters and issue directions on the conduct of the hearing. (paragraph 41)
- The Office will routinely ask parties if they have considered Alternative Dispute Resolution (ADR) and Hearing Officers will be prepared to stay proceedings where ADR is being used or seriously considered. They may also take into account a party's unreasonable refusal to consider ADR when awarding costs. (paragraph 42)
- In patents revocation hearings the applicant will be invited to open proceedings while in trade marks opposition hearings the opponent will be invited to open. (paragraph 43)
- Hearing Officers will retain discretion to deal with excessively long speeches and cross examination. (paragraph 44)
- Parties will generally be expected to supply skeleton arguments and authorities at least two days before a hearing. (paragraph 45)
- Adducing new evidence during a hearing will be discouraged and will only be allowed after the other party has had sufficient time to digest it. As a rule, documents will only be allowed to be introduced in cross examination which are designed to test the honesty and reliability of a witness. (paragraph 46)
- The Office will encourage parties to hold hearings, case management conferences and pre-hearing reviews using telephone conferencing arrangements and video links in suitable cases. (paragraph 47)
- Hearing Officers will offer parties the opportunity for proceedings to be decided without the need for a hearing. (paragraph 48)

Time Related Issues

Timescale for with notice proceedings

A5–005   **7.** It has been a central aim of the Patent Office's response to the Woolf Report that proceedings before the Comptroller should be conducted expeditiously within a reasonable overall time frame whilst still ensuring that parties have a full opportunity to present their case. The Office and parties should aim to complete *with notice* proceedings within 18 months of commencement, that is to say from the date when proceedings are formally joined by the filing of a counterstatement. Faster handling will be appropriate where a matter of particular public interest arises or when the parties themselves jointly request and work towards this end.

8. A number of rule changes bear on the period for filing pleadings and evidence, and harmonise practice where possible across the range of actions handled by the Office. Hence, the relevant patents, registered designs and design right rules have been amended so that the period for filing counterstatements and evidence has been shortened from two months to six weeks except when lodging an opposition, *e.g.* opposition to amend a patent specification under rule 40(2) of the Patents Rules (as amended).

9. The Trade Marks Rules 2000 provide for the six-week period to apply to revocation (on grounds other than non-use), invalidation and rectification proceedings. The corresponding time period for opposition and revocation on grounds of non-use will remain at three months. In addition, there will be provision for a cooling off period of three months at the start of opposition proceedings which will be granted when sought by both parties. This will be extendable (again at the request of both parties) by three months.

10. The rules will continue to provide discretion to extend statutory periods in certain circumstances. However, the rules are amended to afford Hearing Officers discretion to shorten many prescribed periods where appropriate. Such circumstances might be expected to arise where both parties to an action seek accelerated processing, or where external factors demand a decision in a shorter time frame than the standard period would permit.

11. Replies to the questionnaire that the Office proposes issuing on a selected basis prior to the evidence round (see paragraph 33 below) should help Hearing Officers decide whether the circumstances in a particular case warrant extending the period for filing evidence.

12. The anticipated benefits of speedier case handling will not be achieved if parties, their professional advisers and the Office do not work within the overall 18-month objective for the completion of *with notice* proceedings.

Fixing dates for preliminary hearings

13. In the case of preliminary hearings the Office will discontinue its practice in patents, **A5–006** design right and registered designs proceedings of allowing the parties an open-ended window within which to agree a hearing date. Instead, the Office will set a window within which a preliminary hearing should take place and will give the parties 14 days (if possible) within which to notify the Office of their agreed date. Failing such notification, the Office will itself *set* a date within the window. The Office will, however, endeavour to give minimum periods of notice and Hearing Officers will have discretion to override the 14 days in those cases where a party has a genuine difficulty in agreeing a hearing date. On the other hand, the 14-day period may be abbreviated in exceptional circumstances demanding a very urgent hearing. It is the intention of the Trade Marks Directorate to adopt a similar approach in the fullness of time but in the meantime, because of the backlog of preliminary hearings involving trade mark cases, the Directorate will continue its present practice of fixing dates for such hearings.

Fixing dates for main or substantive hearings

14. At the commencement of the final evidence round, the Office will aim to arrange a **A5–007** date for main or substantive hearings for approximately four months later. The Hearing Officer will, however, have discretion to direct that an earlier date, or exceptionally a later date, be fixed. Parties will be able to offer an alternative agreed date which is no later than that fixed by the Office. In the short term, because of the backlog of substantive hearings involving trade marks cases, the Trade Marks Directorate will continue its present policy of fixing dates.

Statements of Case

Pertinent and adequate statements of case

15. In all proceedings before the Patent Office claimants are required to set out a state- **A5–008** ment of case on which the action is proceeding. The other party, for example the applicant for registration or the proprietor of the patent or trade mark, is then required to submit a counterstatement setting out the basis of the defence. Over the years a practice has built up, particularly in trade mark proceedings, whereby the statement of case has to a large extent been a recitation of the particular sections of the legislation under which the action is to proceed, with no particularisation of the case. In LIFESAVERS [1997] RPC page 567 the Hearing Officer said that in his view, "the substantive issues in this case and therefore the areas of contention between the parties have not yet been clearly defined. This is not surprising because it is only in the evidence rounds that the nature and areas of conflict are clarified." In recent judgments, the Vice-Chancellor has criticised that approach and in DEMON ALE [2000] RPC 345 Mr Geoffrey Hobbs QC acting as the Appointed Person has stated:

> "Considerations of justice, fairness, efficiency and economy combined to make it necessary for the pleadings of the parties in Registry proceedings to provide a focussed statement of the grounds upon which they intend to maintain that the Tribunal should or should not do what it has been asked to do."

16. It will be necessary, therefore, in all proceedings before the Comptroller for the party commencing the action to provide (in association with the appropriate form, *e.g.* TM7 Notice of Opposition) a statement of case upon which the case against the other side is to be based. This must include all of the grounds which the party intends to pursue and which are to be supported by evidence (where appropriate).

17. In future, the mere recitation of the section of the Act (or the provisions of a Rule) will not be sufficient to mount an action. There must be a sufficient degree of particularisation for the other side (and the Patent Office) to have a clear view of the nature of the dispute and have sufficient detail of, for example, the earlier trade marks or earlier rights and their use, on which the litigant intends to proceed.

18. As Mr Hobbs stated in the DEMON ALE decision:

"The statement should not be prolix. It should however, be full in the sense indicated by Mr Simon Thorley QC in COFFEE MIXJ [1998] RPC 717 at 722; it must be full in the sense that it must outline each of the grounds ... relied upon and state the case relied upon in support of those grounds. It should be as succinct as possible but it must be complete."

19. If a party fails to provide sufficient information in the statement of case as to the nature or extent of the grounds upon which the proceedings rely, the Patent Office may challenge the statement and seek to have it put in proper order. In those cases where there may be only some of the grounds of the action fully pleaded, the party or their representative will be asked to provide such further information as may be reasonably required to complete the statement, or to delete the deficient grounds. Until the statement of case is in order, the proceedings will not be progressed and the subsequent delay may be a factor which will be taken into account at the point at which costs are determined.

Presentation of statement of case

A5–009   **20.** With a view to fostering greater uniformity of court practice, Lord Woolf's report set out basic requirements for presenting a statement of case. Although proceedings before the Office usually commence with the lodging of an official form, there is considerable variation of practice in framing supporting state ments, particularly where private litigants are involved. The Office believes that it would be of assistance to litigants if they were given broad guidelines on how to set out their statements. This should in turn help the Office in identifying the type of action that is being launched.

21. In general the claimant (*i.e.* the person initiating the proceedings) should set out in their statement:
- the matter in issue
- the facts to be relied on, and
- the relief sought.

22. Whilst sometimes the **matter in issue** is implicit in the nature of the proceedings, generally it needs to be set out in detail. For example, the grounds on which revocation of a patent or invalidation of a trade mark is sought must be set out fully. The **facts to be relied on** (as distinct from the evidence that will later be adduced to prove those facts) should also be set out concisely but fully. Whilst in the past statements filed in proceedings before the Comptroller have sometimes been lacking in real detail as to the facts, statements must now be reasonably detailed. The **relief sought** should be clearly stated. Costs need be not specifically claimed in a statement, though they usually are.

23. In their counter-statement, the defendant must state:
- which of the allegations in the statement they deny and why (and if they intend to put forward an alternative version of events, what that version is);
- which of the allegations in the statement they are unable to admit or deny but require the claimant to prove;
- which of the allegations in the statement they admit.

24. The purpose of the counter-statement is to narrow down the field of dispute, because the claimant will not need to prove any allegations which the defendant admits. Whilst in the past counter-statements have sometimes been very sketchy, that is no longer acceptable. If a counter-statement leaves uncertainty about what is and is not in dispute, it is inadequate. Thus, the counter-statement must deal specifically with every allegation in the statement. (Indeed, any allegation not dealt with is generally deemed to be admitted by the defendant.) Again, costs need not be specifically claimed, though they usually are.

25. If the presentation of a statement or counter-statement is clearly inadequate, the Comptroller will refuse to serve it. Of course, even when a statement or counter-statement is served that does not mean the Comptroller has decided it is satisfactory, and the recipient is still entitled to object to its adequacy.

Supply of Documents with statements of case

26. The Office considered removing from the patents rules the requirement to supply documents with the statement of case, bearing in mind that the documents would have to be re-filed later as part of the evidence. However, patent practitioners did not consider it unduly burdensome to file such documents twice and to the contrary felt that it was important for the other party in proceedings to have sight of any documents referred to in the statement of case at the earliest opportunity so that they were fully aware of the case against them. It has therefore been decided to maintain present provisions in the rules that requires that copies of any documents referred to in statements of case should be supplied with the statements themselves. **A5–010**

Confirming accuracy and truth of a statement of case

27. The Office has decided to adopt Lord Woolf's recommendation that claims and defences should contain a declaration on behalf of the parties confirming the accuracy and truth of the matter contained in them. Such a declaration is required for trade marks proceedings and encouraged in other proceedings. It should be noted that such a declaration is necessary if a party wanted, in any subsequent appeal to the High Court, a statement of case to be taken into account as evidence. **A5–011**

28. Examples of a declaration that would be acceptable are:
"I/we confirm that the information contained in this statement of case is true to the best of my/our knowledge and belief."
or
"I/we believe the information contained in this statement of case to be true."

29. If, in the event, a statement or counter-statement proves to be inaccurate or untrue then, in the absence of any clear and justified explanation for the breach, the Hearing Officer will take this into account when making an award for costs.

Evidence

Witness Statements

30. The rules have been amended to permit as an alternative to sworn evidence the filing of evidence in the form of a "witness statement" verified by a statement of truth. Hearing Officers are also authorised to require the filing of an affidavit or statutory declaration instead of a witness statement if they consider such a sworn statement to be more appropriate in a particular case. A witness statement must be in writing and signed and dated and should contain the evidence which the person signing it would be allowed to give orally. It should also contain a statement by the witness that he believes the facts in it are true. **A5–012**

Filing evidence not in proper form

31. The Office intends continuing with its existing practice of requiring receipt of formally correct affidavits, statutory declarations or witness statements to trigger subsequent evidence stages. The Office will not normally accept the receipt of unsigned witness statements or unsworn affidavits or statutory declarations as meeting time deadlines, but exceptionally the Hearing Officer will be prepared to do so provided a proper version of the evidence is filed within a period the Office may specify. If, in the event, the formal evidence was shown to be inconsistent with the previously filed informal evidence, the Hearing Officer may impose a cost penalty on the party concerned when deciding on the award of costs. Parties should take care to ensure that evidence filed by facsimile transmission is received by the Office in its entirety and is legible. **A5–013**

Witness evidence

A5–014   32.   The rules have also been amended so that where a party adduces evidence of a statement made by a person otherwise than while giving oral evidence in proceedings and does not call that person as a witness, the Hearing Officer may permit any other party to call that person as a witness and cross-examine them on their statement.

Disclosure

A5–015   33.   Disclosure is not common in proceedings before the Comptroller and the Office does not expect that to change. However, parties do seek it from time to time, and the principles the Office will apply in deciding whether to grant it will mirror those applied by the courts.

34.   The principles the Office has traditionally applied reflected Order 24 of the old Rules of the Supreme Court, and this approach was endorsed by Aldous J. in *Merrell Dow Pharmaceuticals Inc's (Terfenadine) Patent* [1991] RPC 221. Thus the questions the Office has considered are whether the documents concerned relate to the matters in question in the proceedings and whether their disclosure is necessary to dispose fairly of the proceedings or to reduce costs. As in the courts, even if these tests were satisfied there was always discretion to refuse to order specific disclosure, for example if the value of the material to the applicant was outweighed by the burden it would impose on the opponent, as discussed in *Mölynlcke AB v Procter and Gamble Ltd (No.3)* [1990] RPC 498, or if the categories of documents were in such general terms as to amount to a "fishing discovery", as discussed in *British Leyland Motor Corporation v Wyatt Interpart Co Ltd* [1979] FSR 39.

35.   Under the Civil Procedure Rules 1998 the courts can order either "standard" disclosure (*i.e.* all relevant documents in a party's control) or "specific" disclosure (usually, an order to disclose specific documents or classes of documents). It is unlikely a Hearing Officer would ever order standard disclosure, but he or she may order specific disclosure. The court's Practice Direction on specific disclosure says that:

> "the court will take into account all the circumstances of the case and, in particular, the overriding objective described in Part 1."

36.   The Office will follow these principles when considering requests for disclosure in the future. It takes the view that this does not involve discarding the old tests because they are still a sensible part of considering all the circumstances of the case. However, the Office will now additionally put greater emphasis on the principle of proportionality and on the need to ensure proceedings are dealt with expeditiously.

37.   A party applying for specific discovery must explain its reasons in full and must identify the documents or classes of documents it seeks as clearly as is reasonably possible. Vague or excessively broad requests are unlikely to be granted.

Case Management

Questionnaires

A5–016   38.   The Office intends issuing questionnaires on a selective basis, prior to the evidence rounds, which should help parties and Hearing Officers gain a clearer appreciation of the issues.

Case Management Conferences

A5–017   39.   The Office has decided to adopt the selective use of case management conferences. A decision on whether or not to hold such a conference will rest with the Hearing Officer taking into account the circumstances of the case including, for instance, the need to clarify the issues, the degree of complexity, any related actions between the parties and any wider public interest issues. The rules have been amended to give the Office the necessary powers.

40. The legal and technical nature of intellectual property disputes means that they are usually conducted by professional representatives. Case management conferences should be attended by these representatives. The parties themselves will not be expected to attend but should be invited to do so if they so wish.

Pre-Hearing Reviews

41. The rules have been amended to give Hearing Officers power to call a "pre-hearing review" prior to a hearing if they consider it appropriate. Such reviews will provide Hearing Officers with an opportunity to clarify issues, particularly in complex cases, and issue directions on the conduct of hearings. This should help the parties focus on matters of most relevance.   **A5–018**

Alternative Disputes Resolution (ADR)

42. The Patent Office cannot itself provide ADR services as it would be placed in a difficult if not impossible position then to rule on the dispute if it were to return for determination by a Hearing Officer. However, except in the case of revocation action where there may be a public interest, the Office will routinely ask parties whether they have considered ADR and, where appropriate, will provide them with information about ADR. The Office will be prepared to stay proceedings in those cases where ADR is being used or seriously considered. Such stays will be closely controlled and subject to review by the Hearing Officer. Hearing Officers may also take into account a party's unreasonable refusal to consider ADR when awarding costs.   **A5–019**

Conduct of Hearing, Issuing of Decisions

Order for presenting case

43. The normal practice in *with notice* hearings is that the right to open is vested in the party who bears the initial burden of proof, *e.g.* the referrer in patent entitlement proceedings. The exception has been in applications to revoke a patent where the opponent to the application is invited to open. The Office has decided that henceforth the applicant will be invited to open proceedings at revocation hearings. Also, in trade mark opposition hearings, the opponent will now be invited to open the proceedings.   **A5–020**

Time spent on hearing and cross examination

44. The Patent Office does not, as a rule, intend imposing time limits on the length of hearings and the time spent on cross-examination. However, Hearing Officers will retain discretion to deal with excessively long speeches and cross-examinations.   **A5–021**

Supply of skeleton arguments prior to hearing

45. The Office is keen to encourage the use of skeleton arguments at hearings as they can be of considerable benefit in organising submissions and making efficient use of hearing time. Moreover, they help focus the mind and enable the Hearing Officer and the parties and their representatives to gain a better appreciation of the issues and arguments. Therefore, Hearing Officers will generally **expect** parties, particularly those that are represented by professional practitioners, to supply skeleton arguments, together with authorities, at least two days before the date of a hearing.   **A5–022**

Presentation of new evidence at a hearing

46. The practice of adducing new evidence during a hearing is to be discouraged as it can spring surprises. Even if a Hearing Officer decides to admit such evidence it will generally be allowed only after the Hearing Officer and the other party have had sufficient time to read and digest it. Hearing Officers will however, as a rule, allow documents to be introduced in cross-examination which are designed to test the honesty or reliability of a witness.   **A5–023**

Use of telephone and video conferencing for hearings

47. The Patent Office recognises that the use of telephone and video conferencing facili-   **A5–024**

ties is likely to have little application for substantive hearings. However, the scope of their use in procedural hearings can be significant by saving costs and making better use of time for both the parties and the Hearing Officer. The Office accepts that such facilities must be used with care so as not to disadvantage either party. In this respect, the Office has taken account of the firm line taken by the Patents Court on the use of telephone summonses (*e.g. Robert Hewitt v P McCann Ltd*, 30 March 1998, in which Laddie J gave the clear reminder that telephone summonses exist to save costs, that their availability must not be ignored, and that doing so could be reflected in cost orders). In view of this, and bearing this in mind Lord Woolf's encouragement of greater use of IT in legal proceedings, the Office intends encouraging parties to hold suitable hearings, case management conferences and pre-hearing reviews using telephone conferencing arrangements and video links.

Deciding cases without a hearing

A5–025   **48.**   The Office will adopt a proactive stance towards settling dispute cases without the need for hearings whilst retaining the fundamental right of parties to be heard. Parties will at least be offered the opportunity of a decision in this way.

49. Enquiries about this notice should be addressed to:

> Mike Wright
> The Patent Office
> Patents and Designs Directorate
> Room 3.Y54
> Concept House
> Cardiff Road
> Newport
> South Wales
> NP10 8QQ
> Tel 01633 814576
> Fax 01633 814347
> E-mail
> *mike.wright@patent.gov.uk*

> Ann Corbett
> The Patent Office
> Trade Marks Directorate
> Room 2.005
> Government Buildings
> Cardiff Road
> Newport
> South Wales
> NP10 8QQ
> Tel 01633 811029
> Fax 01633 811175
> E-mail
> *ann.corbett@patent.gov.uk*

Tribunal Practice Notice

(TPN 2/2000)

COSTS IN PROCEEDINGS BEFORE THE COMPTROLLER

1. As part of its response to Lord Woolf's report *Access to Justice*, the Patent Office has, in consultation with its users, reviewed the awarding of costs in proceedings before the Comptroller. This Practice Notice sets out the Comptroller's practice on costs following that review. **A5–027**

Summary

2. The following are the main points addressed in this Practice Notice: **A5–028**
- The present policy of costs awards being informed by a scale set by the Office in consultation with its users, and reviewed from time to time, will continue. (paragraph 8)
- The scale of costs has been revised: the revised scale shown in *annex A* will apply to proceedings commenced on or after 22 May 2000, while the unrevised scale shown at *annex B* will continue to apply to proceedings commenced before that date. (paragraph 11)
- Hearing Officers will be prepared to exceed the scale when circumstances warrant it, in particular but not exclusively to deal proportionately with breaches of rules, delaying tactics and other unreasonable behaviour. (paragraphs 8 and 9)
- Hearing Officers will actively consider making an award at preliminary hearings and not merely carry all costs over to the final decision. (paragraphs 12 and 13)
- A deadline for payment will be attached to a costs award. (paragraph 14)
- Security for costs will be determined on application for an amount appropriate in the case. (paragraph 16)
- In appeals to the High Court or the Registered Designs Appeal Tribunal against her without-notice decisions, the Comptroller will generally seek her costs, while being willing not to do so, for example in cases where the party is likely to suffer some form of hardship if a costs award were made against them. (paragraph 19)

The Comptroller's Power and Discretion

3. The Comptroller and hence Hearing Officers acting for her have a wide discretion to award costs under section 107 of the Patents Act 1977, section 30 of the Registered Designs Act 1949, section 68 of the Trade Marks Act 1994, section 44 of the Trade Marks Act 1938 and section 250 of the Copyright, Designs and Patents Act 1988. Factors influencing the exercise of the Comptroller's discretion in relation to the award of costs have been considered by Hearing Officers from time to time in their decisions. The leading case, however, is *Rizla Ltd's Application* [1993] RPC 365, a patents case in which judgment was given by Anthony Watson QC sitting as a Deputy Judge of the High Court. **A5–029**

4. On page 374 of *Rizla*, the Deputy Judge held that:
"The wording of section 107 could not in my view be clearer and confers on the Comptroller a very wide discretion with no fetter other than the overriding one that he must act judicially. I see no reason why the previously adopted practice could not be altered by the Comptroller in the same way as from time to time an important decision leads the courts to adopt a different attitude to what had previously been accepted practice. Thus, if the Comptroller felt it was appropriate, a form of compensatory costs could become the norm."

He went on to say:
"As a matter of jurisdiction, I entertain no doubt that if the Comptroller were of the view that a case had been brought without any *bona fide* belief that it was soundly based or if in any other way he were satisfied that his jurisdiction was being used other than for the purpose of resolving genuine disputes, he has the power to order compensatory costs."

On page 377, towards the end of his judgment he said:

"Counsel was unable to refer me to any reported case where such a strong order for costs had been made by the Comptroller and therefore there is no established yardstick to measure what might be regarded as exceptional. I believe a case such as the present can only be regarded as exceptional if it can be shown that the losing party has abused the process of the Comptroller by commencing or maintaining a case without a genuine belief that there is an issue to be tried. In my view, this is not shown to be such a case."

Significantly, the Deputy Judge added:

"There are of course a large number of other circumstances such as deliberate delay, unnecessary adjournments *etc.* where the Comptroller will be entitled to award compensatory costs, but it is unnecessary to define what is clearly a wide discretion."

5. In the light of *Rizla*, the Office considers that the existing legislation provides the power to operate a nominal cost regime or a full cost recovery regime—or anything in between—and that no legislative change is necessary to put in hand any revision of that sort.

The use of a scale

A5–030 **6.** It is the long-established practice that costs in proceedings before the Comptroller are awarded after consideration of guidance given by a standard published scale and are not intended to compensate parties for the expense to which they may have been put. Rather, an award of costs is intended to represent only a contribution to that expense.

7. In comments received from users, this existing practice was defended by some, partly on the grounds of maintaining the tribunal as a low cost one, and partly because the scale provides some certainty for businesses in budgeting for the costs they might incur. Others felt that the Office's powers in relation to costs should be significantly increased. It was also suggested that the level of costs should reflect the Office's disapproval of any breaches of the rules or unreasonable delay or complication caused by a party.

8. Users' comments taken as a whole supported the general thrust of the present policy based upon fixed reasonable costs, provided that there is the flexibility to award costs off the scale where the circumstances warrant it. The Office also believes this is the way to proceed, since it provides a low cost tribunal for all litigants, but especially unrepresented ones and SMEs, and builds in a degree of predictability as to how much proceedings before the Comptroller, if conscientiously handled by the party, may cost them. The present policy of generally awarding costs informed by guidance drawn from a scale will therefore be retained. However, the Office envisages the necessary flexibility as going beyond the criterion of "without a genuine belief that there is an issue to be tried" developed in the *Rizla* case. It is vital that the Comptroller has the ability to award costs off the scale, approaching full compensation, to deal proportionately with wider breaches of rules, delaying tactics or other unreasonable behaviour. The fact that this flexibility and the Comptroller's willingness to exercise it in suitable cases has been the subject of consultation and publicity means that there will have been "an established yardstick" underpinning a change in the previous practice.

9. It would be impossible to indicate all of the circumstances in which a Hearing Officer could or should depart from the scale of costs; indeed it would be wrong to attempt to fetter his or her discretion is such a way. The overriding factor is to act judicially in all the facts of a case. That said, it is possible to conceive of examples. A party seeking an amendment to its statement of case which, if granted, would cause the other side to have to amend its statement or would lead to the filing of further evidence, might expect to incur a costs penalty if the amendment had clearly been avoidable. In another example, the costs associated with evidence filed in respect of grounds which are in the event not pursued at the main or substantive hearing might lead to award which departs from the scale. Costs may also be affected if a losing party unreasonably rejected efforts to settle a dispute before an action was launched or a hearing held, or unreasonably declined the opportunity of an appropriate form of Alternative Dispute Resolution (ADR). A party's unnotified failure to attend a hearing would also be a relevant factor.

The numbers on the scale

10. The views of users, and the feeling of the Office itself, is that the amounts set out in the current scale, last revised in a notice published on 1 June 1994, should be adjusted to take better account of the real cost involved in litigation before the Comptroller.

A5–031

11. With the implementation of the Trade Marks Act 1994 and the need for parties to take into account decisions of OHIM and the ECJ, and decisions on Directive issues handed down by courts in other jurisdictions, the costs of litigation before the Registrar are becoming somewhat higher than in the recent past. Similar factors are also arising in patents cases. In addition, the nature of preliminary hearings is becoming more significant and time-consuming. It is therefore not unreasonable to uprate the present scale of costs to reflect more appropriately the actual costs of litigation, while still maintaining the underlying contribution-not-compensation approach. A survey of recent substantive decisions indicates that the average award of costs by Hearing Officers in patents and trade marks cases is around £700. This is an insignificant sum, even as a contribution, in the current climate. The Office has proposed, and users have not disagreed, that an average closer to £2,000 would be more suitable: this would not represent full cost recovery but would be a realistic contribution. A revised scale which should deliver an average award of that order is set out at annex A. The new scale at annex A will be applicable in respect of an award of costs in proceedings commenced on or after 22 May 2000. The scale published in the Office's journals on 1 June 1994, and reproduced at *annex B*, will continue to apply in proceedings commenced before that date.

Timing of costs awards and their payment

12. Users have remarked that the Office should be encouraged to award costs at any stage of proceedings and to order that an identified sum be paid immediately or within a limited and defined number of days. The Office agrees that in the current post-Woolf climate a regime which associates costs more closely with their cause is desirable. It is too easy when costs are, as now, generally rolled over into the final decision, for the reason they were awarded to be lost sight of, for example when an award is made to penalise the taking of a purely technical point to a preliminary hearing.

A5–032

13. The Office therefore intends, far more frequently than in the past, to make costs orders as the cause of them arises. Examples of situations in which such an award might be made are:

(a) where "blame" can be attached to one or the other party, *e.g.* a missed deadline;

(b) where amendment to the statements of case is being sought (particularly when evidence has already been filed by the other side), although that could be tempered if the statements are being amended to remove a ground and make them more focussed.

14. A deadline for payment will be attached to the award, that deadline being 7 days after the expiry of the appeal period, unless an appeal is lodged in which case payment of the costs awarded would be suspended pending the appeal. So, for example, in the case of a costs award made following a patents hearing on a procedural point, if the decision was not appealed the costs would be payable within 7 days after expiry of the 14-day appeal period, and failure to make payment would have implications for the continuation of the case.

Licence of right cases

15. It has been customary in licence of right cases for the Comptroller not to make an award of costs unless one side pursues unreasonable terms or the circumstances of the particular case are sufficiently unusual to warrant a departure from that practice. It is not intended to alter that approach, except to the extent that the flexibility to address procedural difficulties may bite.

A5–033

Security for costs

16. It has been the normal practice in patent proceedings for the Office automatically to

A5–034

require a party that is not based in a Brussels Convention state to provide security for a fixed sum of £900. This contrasts with the practice followed in trade mark proceedings and the courts where security for costs is only ordered on application and following consideration by the Hearing Officer or the judge. As there is no good reason why the practice in patents proceedings should be different, the Office has decided to bring it into line with that followed elsewhere and to consider awarding such security only on application and not on the Office's own initiative. Moreover, instead of an award of a standard amount such as £900, the award should be determined, after consideration of argument and, if necessary evidence, wholly on a case by case basis proportionate to the estimated costs likely to be awarded at its conclusion.

"Without notice" (also known as ex parte) proceedings

A5–035   **17.**   The Office has decided not to change its practice of not awarding costs in "without notice" proceedings before the Comptroller.

18.   In trade mark cases appealed to the Appointed Person, it is regarded as in keeping with the low cost of that appeal route for each side to bear its own costs. The Comptroller will continue with that approach.

19.   As for appeals to the High Court (or Court of Session in Scotland) or the Registered Designs Appeal Tribunal (RDAT), the practice has varied as between the patents, designs and some trade mark appeals which follow that route. Should the Comptroller lose on appeal, she would expect costs to be awarded against her; there is therefore an argument that the public purse should be recompensed by a similar award should the decision go in the other direction. On the other hand, it might be argued that litigants in person should be given special treatment and that the Comptroller should not seek costs in such cases. Having reviewed the situation in consultation with users, it has been decided that on balance the Comptroller should seek costs in the full range of the without-notice appeals which she defends in the High Court or RDAT, while being willing not to do so in cases where the party is likely to suffer some form of hardship if a costs award is made against them, or where a significant point of general legal interest is involved.

20.   Enquiries about this notice should be addressed to:

> Mike Wright
> The Patent Office
> Patents and Designs Directorate
> Room 3.Y54
> Concept House
> Cardiff Road
> Newport
> South Wales
> NP10 8QQ
> Tel 01633 814576
> Fax 01633 814347
> E-mail
> *mike.wright@patent.gov.uk*

> Ann Corbett
> The Patent Office
> Trade Marks Directorate
> Room 2.005
> Government Buildings
> Cardiff Road

Newport
South Wales
NP10 8QQ
Tel 01633 811029
Fax 01633 811175
E-mail
ann.corbett@patent.gov.uk

ANNEX A

SCALE OF COSTS APPLICABLE IN PROCEEDINGS COMMENCED ON OR AFTER 22 MAY 2000

(1) Application or Notice of Opposition and accompanying statement	£300 plus statutory fee (if any)	**A5–036**
(2) Considering statement of case in reply	£200	
or		
(1) Considering Application or Notice of Opposition and accompanying statement		
(2) Statement of case in reply	£300	
(3) Preparing and filing evidence	Up to £1,500	
(4) Considering evidence	One half of Item 3	
(5) Preparation for and attendance at Hearing	Up to £1,500	
(6) Where a party appears in person or where attendance of a party's witnesses is required by the opposite party, allowance will be made for general expenses and travelling, but the allowance for general expenses will not normally exceed £250 per person per day, nor an overall maximum per party of £750 per day.		

ANNEX B

SCALE OF COSTS APPLICABLE IN PROCEEDINGS COMMENCED BEFORE 22 MAY 2000

(This scale was first published in a notice in the Office's journals on 1 June 1994.)		**A5–037**
(1) Application or Notice of Opposition and accompanying Statement	£100 plus statutory fee (if any)	
(2) Perusing Counter-statement	£35	
or		
(1) Perusing Application or Notice of Opposition and accompanying statement	£35	
(2) Counter-statement	£100	
(3) Preparing and filing evidence	£200–£400	
(4) Perusing evidence	one half of Item 3	
(5) Preparation for and attendance at Hearing	£200–£900	
(6) Where the Applicant or Opponent appears in person and where attendance of witnesses is required by the opposite party, allowance will be made for general expenses and travelling, but the allowance for general expenses will not normally exceed £25 per day.		

PART III

GENERAL EUROPEAN MATERIALS

First Council Directive 89/104 of December 21, 1988—To approximate the laws of the Member States relating to trade marks
([1989] O.J. L40/1)

THE COUNCIL OF THE EUROPEAN COMMUNITIES,   A6–001

Having regard to the Treaty establishing the European Economic Community, and in particular Article 100a thereof,

Having regard to the proposal from the Commission,

In cooperation with the European Parliament,

Having regard to the opinion of the Economic and Social Committee,

Whereas the trade mark laws at present applicable in the Member States contain disparities which may impede the free movement of goods and freedom to provide services and may distort competition within the common market; whereas it is therefore necessary, in view of the establishment and functioning of the internal market, to approximate the laws of Member States;

Whereas it is important not to disregard the solutions and advantages which the Community trade mark system may afford to undertakings wishing to acquire trade marks;

Whereas it does not appear to be necessary at present to undertake full-scale approximation of the trade mark laws of the Member States and it will be sufficient if approximation is limited to those national provisions of law which most directly affect the functioning of the internal market;

Whereas the Directive does not deprive the Member States of the right to continue to protect trade marks acquired through use but takes them into account only in regard to the relationship between them and trade marks acquired by registration;

Whereas Member States also remain free to fix the provisions of procedure concerning the registration, the revocation and the invalidity of trade marks acquired by registration; whereas they can, for example, determine the form of trade mark registration and invalidity procedures, decide whether earlier rights should be invoked either in the registration procedure or in the invalidity procedure or in both and, if they allow earlier rights to be invoked in the registration procedure, have an opposition procedure or an ex officio examination procedure or both; whereas Member States remain free to determine the effects—of revocation or invalidity of trade marks;

Whereas this Directive does not exclude the application to trade marks of provisions of law of the Member States other than trade mark law, such as the provisions relating to unfair competition, civil liability or consumer protection;

Whereas attainment of the objectives at which this approximation of laws is aiming requires that the conditions for obtaining and continuing to hold a registered trade mark are, in general, identical in all Member States; whereas, to this end, it is necessary to list examples of signs which may constitute a trade mark, provided that such signs are capable of distinguishing the goods or services of one undertaking from those of other undertakings; whereas the grounds for refusal or invalidity concerning the trade mark itself, for example, the absence of any distinctive character, or concerning conflicts between the trade mark and earlier rights, are to be listed in an exhaustive manner, even if some of these grounds are listed as an option for the Member States which will therefore be able to maintain or introduce those grounds in their legislation; whereas Member States will be able to maintain or introduce into their legislation grounds of refusal or invalidity linked to conditions for obtaining and continuing to hold a trade mark for which there is no provision of approximation, concerning, for example, the eligibility for the grant of a trade mark, the renewal of the trade mark or rules on fees, or related to the non-compliance with procedural rules;

Whereas in order to reduce the total number of trade marks registered and protected in the Community and, consequently, the number of conflicts which arise between them, it is essential to require that registered trade marks must actually be used or, if not used, be subject to revocation; whereas it is necessary to provide that a trade mark cannot be invalidated on the basis of the existence of a non-used earlier trade mark, while the Member States remain free to apply the same principle in respect of the registration of a trade mark or to provide that a trade mark may not be successfully invoked in infringement proceedings if it is established as a result of a plea that the trade mark could be revoked; whereas in all these cases it is up to the Member States to establish the applicable rules of procedure;

Whereas it is fundamental, in order to facilitate the free circulation of goods and services, to ensure that henceforth registered trade marks enjoy the same protection under the legal systems of all the Member States; whereas this should however not prevent the Member States from granting at their option extensive protection to those trade marks which have a reputation;

Whereas the protection afforded by the registered trade mark, the function of which is in particular to guarantee the trade mark as an indication of origin, is absolute in the case of identity between the mark and the sign and goods or services; whereas the protection applies also in case of similarity between the mark and the sign and the goods or services; whereas it is indispensable to give an interpretation of the concept of similarity in relation to the likelihood of confusion; whereas the likelihood of confusion, the appreciation of which depends on numerous elements and, in particular, on the recognition of the trade mark on the market, of the association which can be made with the used or registered sign, of the degree of similarity between the trade mark and the sign and between the goods or services identified, constitutes the specific condition for such protection; whereas the ways in which likelihood of confusion may be established, and in particular the onus of proof, are a matter for national procedural rules which are not prejudiced by the Directive;

Whereas it is important, for reasons of legal certainty and without inequitably prejudicing the interests of a proprietor of an earlier trade mark, to provide that the latter may no longer request a declaration of invalidity nor may he oppose the use of a trade mark subsequent to his own of which he has knowingly tolerated the use for a substantial length of time, unless the application for the subsequent trade mark was made in bad faith;

Whereas all Member States of the Community are bound by the Paris Convention for the Protection of Industrial Property; whereas it is necessary that the provisions of this Directive are entirely consistent with those of the Paris Convention; whereas the obligations of the Member States resulting from this Convention are not affected by this Directive; whereas, where appropriate, the second subparagraph of Article 234 of the Treaty is applicable,

HAS ADOPTED THIS DIRECTIVE:

Article 1

Scope

This Directive shall apply to every trade mark in respect of goods or services   **A6–002**
which is the subject of registration or of an application in a Member State for registration as an individual trade mark, a collective mark or a guarantee or certi-fication mark, or which is the subject of a registration or an application for registration in the Benelux Trade Mark Office or of an international registration having effect in a Member State.

Article 2

Signs of which a trade mark may consist

A trade mark may consist of any sign capable of being represented graphically,   **A6–003**
particularly words, including personal names, designs, letters, numerals, the shape of goods or of their packaging, provided that such signs are capable of distinguishing the goods or services of one undertaking from those of other undertakings.

Article 3

Grounds for refusal or invalidity

1. The following shall not be registered or if registered shall be liable to be   **A6–004**
declared invalid:

(a) signs which cannot constitute a trade mark;
(b) trade marks which are devoid of any distinctive character;
(c) trade marks which consist exclusively of signs or indications which may serve, in trade, to designate the kind, quality, quantity, intended purpose, value, geographical origin, or the time of production of the goods or of rendering of the service, or other characteristics of the goods or service;
(d) trade marks which consist exclusively of signs or indications which have become customary in the current language or in the *bona fide* and estab-lished practices of the trade;
(e) signs which consist exclusively of:
— the shape which results from the nature of the goods themselves, or
— the shape of goods which is necessary to obtain a technical result, or
— the shape which gives substantial value to the goods;
(f) trade marks which are contrary to public policy or to accepted principles of morality;
(g) trade marks which are of such a nature as to deceive the public, for instance as to the nature, quality or geographical origin of the goods or service;

(h) trade marks which have not been authorized by the competent authorities and are to be refused or invalidated pursuant to Article 6 ter of the Paris Convention for the Protection of Industrial Property, hereinafter referred to as the "Paris Convention".

2. Any Member State may provide that a trade mark shall not be registered or, if registered, shall be liable to be declared invalid where and to the extent that:

(a) the use of that trade mark may be prohibited pursuant to provisions of law other than trade mark law of the Member State concerned or of the Community;

(b) the trade mark covers a sign of high symbolic value, in particular a religious symbol;

(c) the trade mark includes badges, emblems and escutcheons other than those covered by Article 6 ter of the Paris Convention and which are of public interest, unless the consent of the appropriate authorities to its registration has been given in conformity with the legislation of the Member State;

(d) the application for registration of the trade mark was made in bad faith by the applicant.

3. A trade mark shall not be refused registration or be declared invalid in accordance with paragraph 1 (b),(c) or (d) if, before the date of application for registration and following the use which has been made of it, it has acquired a distinctive character. Any Member State may in addition provide that this provision shall also apply where the distinctive character was acquired after the date of application for registration or after the date of registration.

4. Any Member State may provide that, by derogation from the preceding paragraphs, the grounds of refusal of registration or invalidity in force in that State prior to the date on which the provisions necessary to comply with this Directive enter into force, shall apply to trade marks for which application has been made prior to that date.

Article 4

Further grounds for refusal or invalidity concerning conflicts with earlier rights

A6–005   1. A trade mark shall not be registered or, if registered, shall be liable to be declared invalid:

(a) if it is identical with an earlier trade mark, and the goods or services for which the trade mark is applied for or is registered are identical with the goods or services for which the earlier trade mark is protected;

(b) if because of its identity with, or similarity to, the earlier trade mark and the identity or similarity of the goods or services covered by the trade marks, there exists a likelihood of confusion on the part of the public, which includes the likelihood of association with the earlier trade mark.

2. "Earlier trade marks" within the meaning of paragraph 1 means:

(a) trade marks of the following kinds with a date of application for registration which is earlier than the date of application for registration of the trade mark, taking account, where appropriate, of the priorities claimed in respect of those trade marks:

(i) Community trade marks;

(ii) trade marks registered in the Member State or, in the case of Belgium, Luxembourg or the Netherlands, at the Benelux Trade Mark Office;

(iii) trade marks registered under international arrangements which have effect in the Member State;

(b) Community trade marks which validly claim seniority, in accordance with the Regulation on the Community trade mark, from a trade mark referred to in (a) (ii) and (iii), even when the latter trade mark has been surrendered or allowed to lapse;

(c) applications for the trade marks referred to in (a) and (b), subject to their registration;

(d) trade marks which, on the date of application for registration of the trade mark, or, where appropriate, of the priority claimed in respect of the application for registration of the trade mark, are well known in a Member State, in the sense in which the words "well known" are used in Article 6 bis Paris Convention;

3. A trade mark shall furthermore not be registered or, if registered, shall be liable to be declared invalid if it is identical with, or similar to, an earlier Community trade mark within the meaning of paragraph 2 and is to be, or has been, registered for goods or services which are not similar to those for which the earlier Community trade mark is registered, where the earlier Community trade mark has a reputation in the Community and where the use of the later trade mark without due cause would take unfair advantage of, or be detrimental to, the distinctive character or the repute of the earlier Community trade mark.

4. Any Member State may furthermore provide that a trade mark shall not be registered or, if registered, shall be liable to be declared invalid where, and to the extent that:

(a) the trade mark is identical with, or similar to, an earlier national trade mark within the meaning of paragraph 2 and is to be, or has been, registered for goods or services which are not similar to those for which the earlier trade mark is registered, where the earlier trade mark has a reputation in the Member State concerned and where the use of the later trade mark without due cause would take unfair advantage of, or be detrimental to, the distinctive character or the repute of the earlier trade mark;

(b) rights to a non-registered trade mark or to another sign used in the course of trade were acquired prior to the date of application for registration of the subsequent trade mark, or the date of the priority claimed for the application for registration of the subsequent trade mark and that non-registered trade mark or other sign confers on its proprietor the right to prohibit the use of a subsequent trade mark;

(c) the use of the trade mark may be prohibited by virtue of an earlier right other than the rights referred to in paragraphs 2 and 4 (b) and in particular:

(i) a right to a name;

(ii) a right of personal portrayal;

(iii) a copyright;

(iv) an industrial property right;

(d) the trade mark is identical with, or similar to, an earlier collective trade mark conferring a right which expired within a period of a maximum of three years preceding application;

(e) the trade mark is identical with, or similar to, an earlier guarantee or certification mark conferring a right which expired within a period preceding application the length of which is fixed by the Member State;

(f) the trade mark is identical with, or similar to, an earlier trade mark which was registered for identical or similar goods or services and conferred on them a right which has expired for failure to renew within a period of a maximum of two years preceding application, unless the proprietor of the earlier trade mark gave his agreement for the registration of the later mark or did not use his trade mark;

(g) the trade mark is liable to be confused with a mark which was in use abroad on the filing date of the application and which is still in use there, provided that at the date of the application the applicant was acting in bad faith.

5. The Member States may permit that in appropriate circumstances registration need not be refused or the trade mark need not be declared invalid where the proprietor of the earlier trade mark or other earlier right consents to the registration of the later trade mark.

6. Any Member State may provide that, by derogation from paragraphs 1 to 5, the grounds for refusal of registration or invalidity in force in that State prior to the date on which the provisions necessary to comply with this Directive enter into force, shall apply to trade marks for which application has been made prior to that date.

Article 5

Rights conferred by a trade mark

A6–006   1. The registered trade mark shall confer on the proprietor exclusive rights therein. The proprietor shall be entitled to prevent all third parties not having his consent from using in the course of trade:

(a) any sign which is identical with the trade mark in relation to goods or services which are identical with those for which the trade mark is registered;

(b) any sign where, because of its identity with, or similarity to, the trade mark and the identity or similarity of the goods or services covered by the trade mark and the sign, there exists a likelihood of confusion on the part of the public, which includes the likelihood of association between the sign and the trade mark.

2. Any Member State may also provide that the proprietor shall be entitled to prevent all third parties not having his consent from using in the course of trade any sign which is identical with, or similar to, the trade mark in relation to goods or services which are not similar to those for which the trade mark is registered, where the latter has a reputation in the Member State and where use of that sign without due cause takes unfair advantage of, or is detrimental to, the distinctive character of the repute of the trade mark.

3. The following, *inter alia*, may be prohibited under paragraphs 1 and 2:

(a) affixing the sign to the goods or to the packaging thereof;

(b) offering the goods, or putting them on the market or stocking them for these purposes under that sign, or offering or supplying services thereunder;

(c) importing or exporting the goods under the sign;

(d) using the sign on business papers and in advertising.

4. Where, under the law of the Member State, the use of a sign under the conditions referred to in 1 (b) or 2 could not be prohibited before the date on which the provisions necessary to comply with this Directive entered into force in the Member State concerned, the rights conferred by the trade mark may not be relied on to prevent the continued use of the sign.

5. Paragraphs 1 to 4 shall not affect provisions in any Member State relating to the protection against the use of a sign other than for the purposes of distinguish-

ing goods or services, where use of that sign without due cause takes unfair advantage of, or is detrimental to, the distinctive character or the repute of the trade mark.

Article 6

Limitation of the effects of a trade mark

1. The trade mark shall not entitle the proprietor to prohibit a third party from using, in the course of trade,   **A6–007**

(a) his own name or address;

(b) indications concerning the kind, quality, quantity, intended purpose, value, geographical origin, the time of production of goods or of rendering of the service, or other characteristics of goods or services;

(c) the trade mark where it is necessary to indicate the intended purpose of a product or service, in particular as accessories or spare parts;

provided he uses them in accordance with honest practices in industrial or commercial matters.

2. The trade mark shall not entitle the proprietor to prohibit a third party from using, in the course of trade, an earlier right which only applies in a particular locality if that right is recognized by the laws of the Member State in question and within the limits of the territory in which it is recognized.

Article 7

Exhaustion of the rights conferred by a trade mark

1. The trade mark shall not entitle the proprietor to prohibit its use in relation to goods which have been put on the market in the Community under that trade mark by the proprietor or with his consent.   **A6–008**

2. Paragraph 1 shall not apply where there exist legitimate reasons for the proprietor to oppose further commercialization of the goods, especially where the condition of the goods is changed or impaired after they have been put on the market.

Article 8

Licensing

1. A trade mark may be licensed for some or all of the goods or services for which it is registered and for the whole or part of the Member State concerned. A licence may be exclusive or non-exclusive.   **A6–009**

2. The proprietor of a trade mark may invoke the rights conferred by that trade mark against a licensee who contravenes any provision in his licensing contract with regard to its duration, the form covered by the registration in which the trade mark may be used, the scope of the goods or services for which the licence is granted, the territory in which the trade mark may be affixed, or the quality of the goods manufactured or of the services provided by the licensee.

Article 9

Limitation in consequence of acquiescence

1. Where, in a Member State, the proprietor of an earlier trade mark as referred to in Article 4(2) has acquiesced, for a period of five successive years, in the use   **A6–010**

of a later trade mark registered in that Member State while being aware of such use, he shall no longer be entitled on the basis of the earlier trade mark either to apply for a declaration that the later trade mark is invalid or to oppose the use of the later trade mark in respect of the goods or services for which the later trade mark has been used, unless registration of the later trade mark was applied for in bad faith.

2. Any Member State may provide that paragraph 1 shall apply *mutatis mutandis* to the proprietor of an earlier trade mark referred to in Article 4 (4) (a) or an other earlier right referred to in Article 4 (4) (b) or (c).

3. In the cases referred to in paragraphs 1 and 2, the proprietor of a later registered trade mark shall not be entitled to oppose the use of the earlier right, even though that right may no longer be invoked against the later trade mark.

Article 10
Use of trade marks

A6–011   1. If, within a period of five years following the date of the completion of the registration procedure, the proprietor has not put the trade mark to genuine use in the Member State in connection with the goods or services in respect of which it is registered, or if such use has been suspended during an uninterrupted period of five years, the trade mark shall be subject to the sanctions provided for in this Directive, unless there are proper reasons for non-use.

2. The following shall also constitute use within the meaning of paragraph 1:
   (a) use of the trade mark in a form differing in elements which do not alter the distinctive character of the mark in the form in which it was registered;
   (b) affixing of the trade mark to goods or to the packaging thereof in the Member State concerned solely for export purposes.

3. Use of the trade mark with the consent of the proprietor or by any person who has authority to use a collective mark or a guarantee or certification mark shall be deemed to constitute use by the proprietor.

4. In relation to trade marks registered before the date on which the provisions necessary to comply with this Directive enter into force in the Member State concerned:
   (a) where a provision in force prior to that date attaches sanctions to non-use of a trade mark during an uninterrupted period, the relevant period of five years mentioned in paragraph 1 shall be deemed to have begun to run at the same time as any period of non-use which is already running at that date;
   (b) where there is no use provision in force prior to that date, the periods of five years mentioned in paragraph 1 shall be deemed to run from that date at the earliest.

Article 11
Sanctions for non-use of a trade mark in legal or administrative proceedings

A6–012   1. A trade mark may not be declared invalid on the ground that there is an earlier conflicting trade mark if the latter does not fulfil the requirements of use set out in Article 10(1), (2) and (3) or in Article 10(4), as the case may be.

2. Any Member State may provide that registration of a trade mark may not be refused on the ground that there is an earlier conflicting trade mark if the latter does not fulfil the requirements of use set out in Article 10(1), (2) and (3) or in Article 10 (4), as the case may be.

3. Without prejudice to the application of Article 12, where a counter-claim for revocation is made, any Member State may provide that a trade mark may not be successfully invoked in infringement proceedings if it is established as a result of a plea that the trade mark could be revoked pursuant to Article 12 (1).

4. If the earlier trade mark has been used in relation to part only of the goods or services for which it is registered, it shall, for purposes of applying paragraphs 1, 2 and 3, be deemed to be registered in respect only of that part of the goods or services.

Article 12

Grounds for revocation

1. A trade mark shall be liable to revocation if, within a continuous period of five years, it has not been put to genuine use in the Member State in connection with the goods or services in respect of which it is registered, and there are no proper reasons for non-use; however, no person may claim that the proprietor's rights in a trade mark should be revoked where, during the interval between expiry of the five-year period and filing of the application for revocation, genuine use of the trade mark has been started or resumed; the commencement or resumption of use within a period of three months preceding the filing of the application for revocation which began at the earliest on expiry of the continuous period of five years of non-use, shall, however, be disregarded where preparations for the commencement or resumption occur only after the proprietor becomes aware that the application for revocation may be filed.   **A6–013**

2. A trade mark shall also be liable to revocation if, after the date on which it was registered,

  (a) in consequence of acts or inactivity of the proprietor, it has become the common name in the trade for a product or service in respect of which it is registered;
  (b) in consequence of the use made of it by the proprietor of the trade mark or with his consent in respect of the goods or services for which it is registered, it is liable to mislead the public, particularly as to the nature, quality or geographical origin of those goods or services.

Article 13

Grounds for refusal or revocation or invalidity relating to only some of the goods or services

Where grounds for refusal of registration or for revocation or invalidity of a trade mark exist in respect of only some of the goods or services for which that trade mark has been applied for or registered, refusal of registration or revocation or invalidity shall cover those goods or services only.   **A6–014**

Article 14

Establishment a posteriori of invalidity or revocation of a trade mark

Where the seniority of an earlier trade mark which has been surrendered or allowed to lapse, is claimed for a Community trade mark, the invalidity or revocation of the earlier trade mark may be established *a posteriori*.   **A6–015**

Article 15

Special provisions in respect of collective marks, guarantee marks and certification marks

1. Without prejudice to Article 4, Member States whose laws authorize the   **A6–016**

registration of collective marks or of guarantee or certification marks may provide that such marks shall not be registered, or shall be revoked or declared invalid, on grounds additional to those specified in Articles 3 and 12 where the function of those marks so requires.

2. By way of derogation from Article 3 (1) (c), Member States may provide that signs or indications which may serve, in trade, to designate the geographical origin of the goods or services may constitute collective, guarantee or certification marks. Such a mark does not entitle the proprietor to prohibit a third party from using in the course of trade such signs or indications, provided he uses them in accordance with honest practices in industrial or commercial matters; in particular, such a mark may not be invoked against a third party who is entitled to use a geographical name.

Article 16

National provisions to be adopted pursuant to this Directive

A6–017
1. The Member States shall bring into force the laws, regulations and administrative provisions necessary to comply with this Directive not later than 28 December 1991. They shall immediately inform the Commission thereof.

2. Acting on a proposal from the Commission, the Council, acting by qualified majority, may defer the date referred to in paragraph 1 until 31 December 1992 at the latest.

3. Member States shall communicate to the Commission the text of the main provisions of national law which they adopt in the field governed by this Directive.

Article 17

Addressees

A6–018
This Directive is addressed to the Member States.
Done at Brussels, December 21, 1988.

APPENDIX 7

EC Treaty Extracts

Article 28

Quantitative restrictions on imports and all measures having equivalent effect **A7–001**
shall be prohibited between Member States.

Article 30

The provisions of Articles 28 and 29 shall not preclude prohibitions or restric- **A7–002**
tions on imports, exports or goods in transit justified on grounds of public morality, public policy or public security; the protection of health and life of humans,
animals or plants; the protection of national treasures possessing artistic, historic
or archaeological value; or the protection of industrial and commercial property.
Such prohibitions or restrictions shall not, however, constitute a means of
arbitrary discrimination or a disguised restriction on trade between Member
States.

Article 81

1. The following shall be prohibited as incompatible with the common market: **A7–003**
all agreements between undertakings, decisions by associations of undertakings
and concerted practices which may affect trade between Member States and
which have as their object or effect the prevention, restriction or distortion of
competition within the common market, and in particular those which:

(a) directly or indirectly fix purchase or selling prices or any other trading
    conditions;
(b) limit or control production, markets, technical development, or investment;
(c) share markets or sources of supply;
(d) apply dissimilar conditions to equivalent transactions with other trading
    parties, thereby placing them at a competitive disadvantage;
(e) make the conclusion of contracts subject to acceptance by the other parties
    of supplementary obligations which, by their nature or according to com-
    mercial usage, have no connection with the subject of such contracts.

2. Any agreements or decisions prohibited pursuant to this Article shall be
automatically void.

3. The provisions of paragraph 1 may, however, be declared inapplicable in the
case of:

— any agreement or category of agreements between undertakings;
— any decision or category of decisions by associations of undertakings;
— any concerted practice or category of concerted practices;

which contributes to improving the production or distribution of goods or to
promoting technical or economic progress, while allowing consumers a fair share
of the resulting benefit, and which does not:

(a) impose on the undertakings concerned restrictions which are not indispens-
    able to the attainment of these objectives;
(b) afford such undertakings the possibility of eliminating competition in re-
    spect of a substantial part of the products in question.

Article 82

A7–004   Any abuse by one or more undertakings of a dominant position within the common market or in a substantial part of it shall be prohibited as incompatible with the common market in so far as it may affect trade between Member States.

Such abuse may, in particular, consist in:

(a) directly or indirectly imposing unfair purchase or selling prices or other unfair trading conditions;

(b) limiting production, markets or technical development to the prejudice of consumers;

(c) applying dissimilar conditions to equivalent transactions with other trading parties, thereby placing them at a competitive disadvantage;

(d) making the conclusion of contracts subject to acceptance by the other parties of supplementary obligations which, by their nature or according to commercial usage, have no connection with the subject of such contracts.

PART IV

CTM MATERIALS

Council Regulation 40/94 of December 20, 1993—On the Community trade mark

THE COUNCIL OF THE EUROPEAN UNION,   **A8–001**

Having regard to the Treaty establishing the European Community, and in particular Article 235 thereof,

Having regard to the proposal from the Commission,

Having regard to the opinion of the European Parliament,

Having regard to the opinion of the Economic and Social Committee,

Whereas it is desirable to promote throughout the Community a harmonious development of economic activities and a continuous and balanced expansion by completing an internal market which functions properly and offers conditions which are similar to those obtaining in a national market; whereas in order to create a market of this kind and make it increasingly a single market, not only must be barriers to free movement of goods and services be removed and arrangements be instituted which ensure that competition is not distorted, but, in addition, legal conditions must be created which enable undertakings to adapt their activities to the scale of the Community, whether in manufacturing and distributing goods or in providing services; whereas for those purposes, trade marks enabling the products and services of undertakings to be distinguished by identical means throughout the entire Community, regardless of frontiers, should feature amongst the legal instruments which undertakings have at their disposal;

Whereas action by the Community would appear to be necessary for the purpose of attaining the Community's said objectives; whereas such action involves the creation of Community arrangements for trade marks whereby undertakings can by means of one procedural system obtain Community trade marks to which uniform protection is given and which produce their effects throughout the entire area of the Community; whereas the principle of the unitary character of the Community trade mark thus stated will apply unless otherwise provided for in this Regulation;

Whereas the barrier of territoriality of the rights conferred on proprietors of trade marks by the laws of the Member States cannot be removed by approximation of laws; whereas in order to open up unrestricted economic activity in the whole of the common market for the benefit of undertakings, trade marks need to be created which are governed by a uniform Community law directly applicable in all Member States;

Whereas since the Treaty has not provided the specific powers to establish such a legal instrument, Article 235 of the Treaty should be applied;

Whereas the Community law relating to trade marks nevertheless does not replace the laws of the Member States on trade marks; whereas it would not in fact appear to be justified to require undertakings to apply for registration of their trade marks as Community trade marks; whereas national trade marks continue to be necessary for those undertakings which do not want protection of their trade marks at Community level;

Whereas the rights in a Community trade mark may not be obtained otherwise than by registration, and registration is to be refused in particular if the trade mark is not distinctive, if it is unlawful or if it conflicts with earlier rights;

Whereas the protection afforded by a Community trade mark, the function of which is in particular to guarantee the trade mark as an indication of origin, is absolute in the case of identity between the mark and the sign and the goods or services; whereas the protection applies also in cases of similarity between the mark and the sign and the goods or services; whereas an interpretation should be given of the concept of similarity in relation to the likelihood of confusion; whereas the likelihood of confusion, the appreciation of which depends on numerous elements and, in particular, on the recognition of the trade mark on the market, the association which can be made with the used or registered sign, the degree of similarity between the trade mark and the sign and between the goods or services identified, constitutes the specific condition for such protection;

Whereas it follows from the principle of free flow of goods that the proprietor of a Community trade mark must not be entitled to prohibit its use by a third party in relation to goods which have been put into circulation in the Community, under the trade mark, by him or with his consent, save where there exist legitimate reasons for the proprietor to oppose further commercialization of the goods;

Whereas there is no justification for protecting Community trade marks or, as against them, any trade mark which has been registered before them, except where the trade marks are actually used;

Whereas a Community trade mark is to be regarded as an object of property which exists separately from the undertakings whose goods or services are designated by it; whereas accordingly, it must be capable of being transferred, subject to the overriding need to prevent the public being misled as a result of the transfer. It must also be capable of being charged as security in favour of a third party and of being the subject matter of licences;

Whereas administrative measures are necessary at Community level for implementing in relation to every trade mark the trade mark law created by this Regulation; whereas it is therefore essential, while retaining the Community's existing institutional structure and balance of powers, to establish an Office for Harmonization in the Internal Market (trade marks and designs) which is independent in relation to technical matters and has legal, administrative and financial autonomy; whereas to this end it is necessary and appropriate that it should be a body of the Community having legal personality and exercising the implementing powers which are conferred on it by this Regulation, and that it should operate within the framework of Community law without detracting from the competencies exercised by the Community institutions;

Whereas it is necessary to ensure that parties who are affected by decisions made by the Office are protected by the law in a manner which is suited to the special character of trade mark law; whereas to that end provision is made for an appeal to lie from decisions of the examiners and of the various divisions of the Office; whereas if the department whose decision is contested does not rectify its decision it is to remit the appeal to a Board of Appeal of the Office, which is to decide on it; Whereas decisions of the Boards of Appeal are, in turn, amenable to actions before the Court of Justice of the European Communities, which has jurisdiction to annul or to alter the contested decision;

Whereas under Council Decision 88/591/ECSC, EEC, Euratom of 24 October 1988 establishing a Court of First Instance of the European Communities, as amended by Decision 93/350/Euratom, ECSC, EEC of 8 June 1993, that Court shall exercise at the first instance the jurisdiction conferred on the Court of Justice by the Treaties establishing the Communities—with particular regard to appeals lodged under the second subparagraph of Article 173 of the EC Treaty— and by the acts adopted in implementation thereof, save as otherwise provided in an act setting up a body governed by Community law; whereas the jurisdiction which this Regulation confers on the Court of Justice to cancel and reform decisions of the appeal courts shall accordingly be exercised at the first instance by the Court in accordance with the above Decision;

Whereas in order to strengthen the protection of Community trade marks the Member States should designate, having regard to their own national system, as limited a number as possible of national courts of first and second instance having jurisdiction in matters of infringement and validity of Community trade marks;

Whereas decisions regarding the validity and infringement of Community trade marks must have effect and cover the entire area of the Community, as this is the only way of preventing inconsistent decisions on the part of the courts and the Office and of ensuring that the unitary character of Community trade marks is not undermined; whereas the rules contained in the Brussels Convention of Jurisdiction and the Enforcement of Judgments in Civil and Commercial Matters will apply to all actions at law relating to Community trade marks, save where this Regulation derogates from those rules;

Whereas contradictory judgments should be avoided in actions which involve the same acts and the same parties and which are brought on the basis of a Community trade mark and parallel national trade marks; whereas for this purpose, when the actions are brought in the same Member State, the way in which this is to be achieved is a matter for national procedural rules, which are not prejudiced by this Regulation, whilst when the actions are brought in different Member States, provisions modelled on the rules on lis pendens and related actions of the abovementioned Brussels Convention appear appropriate;

Whereas in order to guarantee the full autonomy and independence of the Office, it is considered necessary to grant it an autonomous budget whose revenue comes principally from fees paid by the users of the system; whereas however, the Community budgetary procedure remains applicable as far as any subsidies chargeable to general budget of the European Communities are concerned; whereas moreover, the auditing of accounts should be undertaken by the Court of Auditors;

Whereas implementing measures are required for the Regulation's application, particularly as regards the adoption and amendment of fees regulations and an Implementing Regulation; Whereas such measures should be adopted by the Commission, assisted by a Committee composed of representatives of the Member States, in accordance with the procedural rules laid down in Article 2, procedure III(b), of Council Decisions 87/373/EEC of 13 July 1987 laying down the procedures for the exercise of implementing powers conferred on the Commission,

HAS ADOPTED THIS REGULATION:

TITLE I

GENERAL PROVISIONS

Article 1

Community Trade Mark

A8–002   1. A trade mark for goods or services which is registered in accordance with the conditions contained in this Regulation and in the manner herein provided is hereinafter referred to as a "Community trade mark".

2. A Community trade mark shall have a unitary character. It shall have equal effect throughout the Community: it shall not be registered, transferred or surrendered or be the subject of a decision revoking the rights of the proprietor or declaring it invalid, nor shall its use be prohibited, save in respect of the whole Community. This principle shall apply unless otherwise provided in this Regulation.

Article 2

Office

A8–003   An Office for Harmonization in the Internal Market (trade marks and designs), hereinafter referred to as "the Office", is hereby established.

Article 3

Capacity to Act

A8–004   For the purpose of implementing this Regulation, companies or firms and other legal bodies shall be regarded as legal persons if, under the terms of the law governing them, they have the capacity in their own name to have rights and obligations of all kinds, to make contracts or accomplish other legal acts and to sue and be sued.

TITLE II

THE LAW RELATING TO TRADE MARKS

Section 1 —Definition of a Community Trade Mark Obtaining a Community Trade Mark

Article 4

Signs of which a Community Trade Mark may Consist

A8–005   A Community trade mark may consist of any signs capable of being represented graphically, particularly words, including personal names, designs, letters, numerals, the shape of goods or of their packaging, provided that such signs are capable of distinguishing the goods or services of one undertaking from those of other undertakings.

[Article 5

Persons who can be Proprietors of Community Trade Marks

1. The following natural or legal persons, including authorities established under public law, may be proprietors of Community trade marks: **A8–006**

  (a) nationals of the Member States; or

[(b) nationals of other States which are parties to the Paris Convention for the protection of industrial property, hereinafter referred to as "the Paris Convention"; or]

  (b) nationals of other States which are parties to the Paris Convention for the protection of industrial property, hereinafter referred to as "the Paris Convention", or to the Agreement establishing the World Trade Organization;

  (c) nationals of States which are not parties to the Paris Convention who are domiciled or have their seat or who have real and effective industrial or commercial establishments within the territory of the Community or of a State which is party to the Paris Convention; or

[(d) nationals, other than those referred to under subparagraph (c), of any State which is not party to the Paris Convention and which, according to published findings, accords to nationals of all the Member States the same protection for trade marks as it accords to its own nationals and, if nationals of the Member States are required to prove registration in the country of origin, recognizes the registration of Community trade marks as such proof.]

  (d) nationals, other than those referred to under subparagraph (c), of any State which is not party to the Paris Convention or to the Agreement establishing the World Trade Organization and which, according to published findings, accords to nationals of all the Member States the same protection for trade marks as it accords to its own nationals and, if nationals of the Member States are required to prove registration in the country of origin, recognizes the registration of Community trade marks as such proof.

2. With respect to the application of paragraph 1, stateless persons as defined by Article 1 of the Convention relating to the Status of Stateless Persons signed at New York on 28 September 1954, and refugees as defined by Article 1 of the Convention relating to the Status of Refugees signed at Geneva on 28 July 1951 and modified by the Protocol relating to the Status of Refugees signed at New York on 31 January 1967, shall be regarded as nationals of the country in which they have their habitual residence.

3. Persons who are nationals of a State covered by paragraph 1(d) must prove that the trade mark for which an application for a Community trade mark has been submitted is registered in the State of origin, unless, according to published findings, the trade marks of nationals of the Member States are registered in the State of origin in question without proof of prior registration as a Community trade mark or as a national trade mark in a Member State.]

Article 5

Persons who can be Proprietors of Community Trade Marks

Any natural or legal person, including authorities established under public law, may be the proprietor of a Community trade mark.

Amendment

Article 5 in bold replaced the words in italics as amended by Regulation 422/2004.

Article 6

Means whereby a Community Trade Mark is Obtained

A8–007   A Community trade mark shall be obtained by registration.

Article 7

Absolute Grounds for Refusal

A8–008   1. The following shall not be registered:

(a) signs which do not conform to the requirements of Article 4;

(b) trade marks which are devoid of any distinctive character;

(c) trade marks which consist exclusively of signs or indications which may serve, in trade, to designate the kind, quality, quantity, intended purpose, value, geographical origin or the time of production of the goods or of rendering of the service, or other characteristics of the goods or service;

(d) trade marks which consist exclusively of signs or indications which have become customary in the current language or in the bona fide and established practices of the trade;

(e) signs which consist exclusively of:

   (i) the shape which results from the nature of the goods themselves; or

   (ii) the shape of goods which is necessary to obtain a technical result; or

   (iii) the shape which gives substantial value to the goods;

(f) trade marks which are contrary to public policy or to accepted principles of morality;

(g) trade marks which are of such a nature as to deceive the public, for instance as to the nature, quality or geographical origin of the goods or service;

(h) trade marks which have not been authorized by the competent authorities and are to be refused pursuant to Article 6ter of the Paris Convention;

(i) trade marks which include badges, emblems or escutcheons other than those covered by Article 6ter of the Paris Convention and which are of particular public interest, unless the consent of the appropriate authorities to their registration has been given.

(j) trade marks for wines which contain or consist of a geographical indication identifying wines or for spirits which contain or consist of a geographical indication identifying spirits with respect to such wines or spirits not having that origin.

(k) trade marks which contain or consist of a designation of origin or a geographical indication registered in accordance withRegulation (EEC) No. 2081/92 when they correspond to one of the situations covered by Article 13of the said Regulation and regarding the same type of product, on condition that the application for registration of the trade mark has been submitted after the date of filing with the Commission of the application for registration of the designation of origin or geographical indication.

2. Paragraph 1 shall apply notwithstanding that the grounds of non-registrability obtain in only part of the Community.

3. Paragraph 1(b), (c) and (d) shall not apply if the trade mark has become

distinctive in relation to the goods or services for which registration is requested in consequence of the use which has been made of it.

Amendments

The words in bold were inserted by Regulation 3288/94, amending the CTM Regulation to take account of the effect of the Uruguay Round.

The words in bold in para.(k) were added by Regulation 422/2004.

Article 8

Relative Grounds for Refusal

1. Upon opposition by the proprietor of an earlier trade mark, the trade mark applied for shall not be registered: **A8–009**

(a) if it is identical with the earlier trade mark and the goods or services for which registration is applied for are identical with the goods or services for which the earlier trade mark is protected;

(b) if because of its identity with or similarity to the earlier trade mark and the identity or similarity of the goods or services covered by the trade marks there exists a likelihood of confusion on the part of the public in the territory in which the earlier trade mark is protected; the likelihood of confusion includes the likelihood of association with the earlier trade mark.

2. for the purposes of paragraph 1, "Earlier trade marks" means:

(a) trade marks of the following kinds with a date of application for registration which is earlier than the date of application for registration of the Community trade mark, taking account, where appropriate, of the priorities claimed in respect of those trade marks:

   (i) Community trade marks;

   (ii) trade marks registered in a Member State, or, in the case of Belgium, the Netherlands or Luxembourg, at the Benelux Trade Mark Office;

   (iii) trade marks registered under international arrangements which have effect in a Member State;

   (iv) trade marks registered under international arrangements which have effect in the Community;

(b) applications for the trade marks referred to in subparagraph (a), subject to their registration;

(c) trade marks which, on the date of application for registration of the Community trade mark, or, where appropriate, of the priority claimed in respect of the application for registration of the Community trade mark, are well known in a Member State, in the sense in which the words "well known" are used in Article 6bis of the Paris Convention.

3. Upon opposition by the proprietor of the trade mark, a trade mark shall not be registered where an agent or representative of the proprietor of the trade mark applies for registration thereof in his own name without the proprietor's consent, unless the agent or representative justifies his action.

[4. Upon opposition by the proprietor of a non-registered trade mark or of another sign used in the course of trade of more than mere local significance, the trade mark applied for shall not be registered where and to the extent that, pursuant to the law of the Member State governing that sign,]

4. Upon opposition by the proprietor of a non-registered trade mark or of another sign used in the course of trade of more than mere local significance, the trade mark applied for shall not be registered where and to the extent

that, pursuant to the Community legislation or the law of the Member State governing that sign:

    (a) rights to that sign were acquired prior to the date of application for registration of the Community trade mark, or the date of the priority claimed for the application for registration of the Community trade mark;

    (b) that sign confers on its proprietor the right to prohibit the use of a subsequent trade mark.

    5. Furthermore, upon opposition by the proprietor of an earlier trade mark within the meaning of paragraph 2, the trade mark applied for shall not be registered where it is identical with or similar to the earlier trade mark and is to be registered for goods or services which are not similar to those for which the earlier trade mark is registered, where in the case of an earlier Community trade mark the trade mark has a reputation in the Community and, in the case of an earlier national trade mark, the trade mark has a reputation in the Member State concerned and where the use without due cause of the trade mark applied for would take unfair advantage of, or be detrimental to, the distinctive character or the repute of the earlier trade mark.

Amendments

    The words in bold in para.(2) were added by Regulation 1992/2003. This amendment shall enter into force on the date on which the Madrid Protocol enters into force with respect to the European Community, which will be on October 1, 2004.

    The words in bold in the introductory sub-para.(4) were replaced by Regulation 422/2004.

Section 2 —Effects of Community Trade Marks

Article 9

Rights Conferred by a Community Trade Mark

A8–010   1. A Community trade mark shall confer on the proprietor exclusive rights therein. The proprietor shall be entitled to prevent all third parties not having his consent from using in the course of trade:

    (a) any sign which is identical with the Community trade mark in relation to goods or services which are identical with those for which the Community trade mark is registered;

    (b) any sign where, because of its identity with or similarity to the Community trade mark and the identity or similarity of the goods or services covered by the Community trade mark and the sign, there exists a likelihood of confusion on the part of the public; the likelihood of confusion includes the likelihood of association between the sign and the trade mark;

    (c) any sign which is identical with or similar to the Community trade mark in relation to goods or services which are not similar to those for which the Community trade mark is registered, where the latter has a reputation in the Community and where use of that sign without due cause takes unfair advantage of, or is detrimental to, the distinctive character or the repute of the Community trade mark.

    2. The following, *inter alia*, may be prohibited under paragraph 1:

    (a) affixing the sign to the goods or to the packaging thereof;

    (b) offering the goods, putting them on the market or stocking them for these purposes under that sign, or offering or supplying services thereunder;

(c) importing or exporting the goods under that sign;

(d) using the sign on business papers and in advertising.

3. The rights conferred by a Community trade mark shall prevail against third parties from the date of publication of registration of the trade mark. Reasonable compensation may, however, be claimed in respect of matters arising after the date of publication of a Community trade mark application, which matters would, after publication of the registration of the trade mark, be prohibited by virtue of that publication. The court seized of the case may not decide upon the merits of the case until the registration has been published.

Article 10

Reproduction of Community Trade Marks in Dictionaries

If the reproduction of a Community trade mark in a dictionary, encyclopaedia or similar reference work gives the impression that it constitutes the generic name of the goods or services for which the trade mark is registered, the publisher of the work shall, at the request of the proprietor of the Community trade mark, ensure that the reproduction of the trade mark at the latest in the next edition of the publication is accompanied by an indication that it is a registered trade mark.

A8–011

Article 11

Prohibition on the Use of a Community Trade Mark Registered in the Name of an Agent or Representative

Where a Community trade mark is registered in the name of the agent or representative of a person who is the proprietor of that trade mark, without the proprietor's authorization, the latter shall be entitled to oppose the use of his mark by his agent or representative if he has not authorized such use, unless the agent or representative justifies his action.

A8–012

Article 12

Limitation of the Effects of a Community Trade Mark

A Community trade mark shall not entitle the proprietor to prohibit a third party from using in the course of trade:

A8–013

(a) his own name or address;

(b) indications concerning the kind, quality, quantity, intended purpose, value, geographical origin, the time of production of the goods or of rendering of the service, or other characteristics of the goods or service;

(c) the trade mark where it is necessary to indicate the intended purpose of a product or service, in particular as accessories or spare parts,

provided he uses them in accordance with honest practices in industrial or commercial matters.

Article 13

Exhaustion of the Rights Conferred by a Community Trade Mark

1. A Community trade mark shall not entitle the proprietor to prohibit its use in relation to goods which have been put on the market in the Community under that trade mark by the proprietor or with his consent.

A8–014

2. Paragraph 1 shall not apply where there exist legitimate reasons for the pro-

prietor to oppose further commercialization of the goods, especially where the condition of the goods is changed or impaired after they have been put on the market.

Article 14

Complementary Application of National Law Relating to Infringement

A8–015   1. The effects of Community trade marks shall be governed solely by the provisions of this Regulation. In other respects, infringement of a Community trade mark shall be governed by the national law relating to infringement of a national trade mark in accordance with the provisions of Title X.

2. This Regulation shall not prevent actions concerning a Community trade mark being brought under the law of Member States relating in particular to civil liability and unfair competition.

3. The rules of procedure to be applied shall be determined in accordance with the provisions of Title X.

Section 3 —Use of Community Trade Marks

Article 15

Use of Community Trade Marks

A8–016   1. If, within a period of five years following registration, the proprietor has not put the Community trade mark to genuine use in the Community in connection with the goods or services in respect of which it is registered, or if such use has been suspended during an uninterrupted period of five years, the Community trade mark shall be subject to the sanctions provided for in this Regulation, unless there are proper reasons for non-use.

2. The following shall also constitute use within the meaning of paragraph 1:
  (a) use of the Community trade mark in a form differing in elements which do not alter the distinctive character of the mark in the form in which it was registered;
  (b) affixing of the Community trade mark to goods or to the packaging thereof in the Community solely for export purposes.

3. Use of the Community trade mark with the consent of the proprietor shall be deemed to constitute use by the proprietor.

Section 4 —Community Trade Marks as Objects of Property

Article 16

Dealing with Community Trade Marks as National Trade Marks

A8–017   1. Unless Articles 17 to 24 provide otherwise, a Community trade mark as an object of property shall be dealt with in its entirety, and for the whole area of the Community, as a national trade mark registered in the Member State in which, according to the Register of Community trade marks,
  (a) the proprietor has his seat or his domicile on the relevant date; or
  (b) where subparagraph (a) does not apply, the proprietor has an establishment on the relevant date.

2. In cases which are not provided for by paragraph 1, the Member State referred to in that paragraph shall be the Member State in which the seat of the Office is situated.

3. If two or more persons are mentioned in the Register of Community trade marks as joint proprietors, paragraph 1 shall apply to the joint proprietor first mentioned; failing this, it shall apply to the subsequent joint proprietors in the order in which they are mentioned. Where paragraph 1 does not apply to any of the joint proprietors, paragraph 2 shall apply.

Article 17
Transfer

1. A Community trade mark may be transferred, separately from any transfer   **A8–018**
of the undertaking, in respect of some or all of the goods or services for which it is registered.

2. A transfer of the whole of the undertaking shall include the transfer of the Community trade mark except where, in accordance with the law governing the transfer, there is agreement to the contrary or circumstances clearly dictate otherwise. This provision shall apply to the contractual obligation to transfer the undertaking.

3. Without prejudice to paragraph 2, an assignment of the Community trade mark shall be made in writing and shall require the signature of the parties to the contract, except when it is a result of a judgment; otherwise it shall be void.

4. Where it is clear from the transfer documents that because of the transfer the Community trade mark is likely to mislead the public concerning the nature, quality or geographical origin of the goods or services in respect of which it is registered, the Office shall not register the transfer unless the successor agrees to limit registration of the Community trade mark to goods or services in respect of which it is not likely to mislead.

5. On request of one of the parties a transfer shall be entered in the Register and published.

6. As long as the transfer has not been entered in the Register, the successor in title may not invoke the rights arising from the registration of the Community trade mark.

7. Where there are time limits to be observed *vis-à-vis* the Office, the successor in title may make the corresponding statements to the Office once the request for registration of the transfer has been received by the Office.

8. All documents which require notification to the proprietor of the Community trade mark in accordance with Article 77 shall be addressed to the person registered as proprietor.

Article 18
Transfer of a Trade Mark Registered in the Name of an Agent

Where a Community trade mark is registered in the name of the agent or repre-   **A8–019**
sentative of a person who is the proprietor of that trade mark, without the proprietor's authorization, the latter shall be entitled to demand the assignment in his favour of the said registration, unless such agent or representative justifies his action.

Article 19
Rights in Rem

1. A Community trade mark may, independently of the undertaking, be given   **A8–020**
as security or be the subject of rights in rem.

2. On request of one of the parties, rights mentioned in paragraph 1 shall be entered in the Register and published.

Article 20

Levy of Execution

A8–021 1. A Community trade mark may be levied in execution.

2. As regards the procedure for levy of execution in respect of a Community trade mark, the courts and authorities of the Member States determined in accordance with Article 16 shall have exclusive jurisdiction.

3. On request of one the parties, levy of execution shall be entered in the Register and published.

[Article 21

Bankruptcy or Like Proceedings

A8–022 *1. Until such time as common rules for the Member States in this field enter into force, the only Member State in which a Community trade mark may be involved in bankruptcy or like proceedings shall be that in which such proceedings are first brought within the meaning of national law or of conventions applicable in this field.*

2. Where a Community trade mark is involved in bankruptcy or like proceedings, on request of the competent national authority an entry to this effect shall be made in the Register and published.]

Article 21

Insolvency Proceedings

1. The only insolvency proceedings in which a Community trade mark may be involved are those opened in the Member State in the territory of which the debtor has his centre of main interests.

However, where the debtor is an insurance undertaking or a credit institution as defined inDirectives 2001/17/EC and 2001/24/EC, respectively, the only insolvency proceedings in which a Community trademark may be involved are those opened in the Member State where that undertaking or institution has been authorised.

2. In the case of joint proprietorship of a Community trade mark, paragraph 1 shall apply to the share of the joint proprietor.

3. Where a Community trade mark is involved in insolvency proceedings, on request of the competent national authority an entry to this effect shall be made in the Register and published in the Community Trade Marks Bulletin referred to in Article 85.

Amendment

Article 21 in bold replaced the words in italics as amended by Regulation 422/2004.

Article 22

Licensing

A8–023 1. A Community trade mark may be licensed for some or all of the goods or services for which it is registered and for the whole or part of the Community. A licence may be exclusive or non-exclusive.

2. The proprietor of a Community trade mark may invoke the rights conferred by that trade mark against a licensee who contravenes any provision in his licensing contract with regard to its duration, the form covered by the registration in which the trade mark may be used, the scope of the goods or services for which the licence is granted, the territory in which the trade mark may be affixed, or the quality of the goods manufactured or of the services provided by the licensee.

3. Without prejudice to the provisions of the licensing contract, the licensee may bring proceedings for infringement of a Community trade mark only if its proprietor consents thereto. However, the holder of an exclusive licence may bring such proceedings if the proprietor of the trade mark, after formal notice, does not himself bring infringement proceedings within an appropriate period.

4. A licensee shall, for the purpose of obtaining compensation for damage suffered by him, be entitled to intervene in infringement proceedings brought by the proprietor of the Community trade mark.

5. On request of one of the parties the grant or transfer of a licence in respect of a Community trade mark shall be entered in the Register and published.

Article 23
Effects Vis-À-Vis Third Parties

1. Legal acts referred to in Article 17, 19 and 22 concerning a Community trade mark shall only have effects *vis-à-vis* third parties in all the Member States after entry in the Register. Nevertheless, such an act, before it is so entered, shall have effect *vis-à-vis* third parties who have acquired rights in the trade mark after the date of that act but who knew of the act at the date on which the rights were acquired. **A8–024**

2. Paragraph 1 shall not apply in the case of a person who acquires the Community trade mark or a right concerning the Community trade mark by way of transfer of the whole of the undertaking or by any other universal succession.

3. The effects *vis-à-vis* third parties of the legal acts referred to in Article 20 shall be governed by the law of the Member State determined in accordance with Article 16.

4. Until such time as common rules for the Member States in the field of bankruptcy enter into force, the effects *vis-à-vis* third parties of bankruptcy or like proceedings shall be governed by the law of the Member State in which such proceedings are first brought within the meaning of national law or of conventions applicable in this field.

Article 24
The Application for a Community Trade Mark as an Object of Property

Articles 16 to 23 shall apply to applications for Community trade marks. **A8–025**

TITLE III

APPLICATION FOR COMMUNITY TRADE MARKS

Section 1 —Filing of Applications and the Conditions Which Govern Them

Article 25
Filing of Applications

1. An application for a Community trade mark shall be filed, at the choice of the applicant, **A8–026**

(a) at the Office; or

(b) at the central industrial property office of a Member State or at the Benelux Trade Mark Office. An application filed in this way shall have the same effect as if it had been filed on the same date at the Office.

2. Where the application is filed at the central industrial property office of a Member State or at the Benelux Trade Mark Office, that office shall take all steps to forward the application to the Office within two weeks after filing. It may charge the applicant a fee which shall not exceed the administrative costs of receiving and forwarding the application.

[3. Applications referred to in paragraph 2 which reach the Office more than one month after filing shall be deemed withdrawn.]

3. Applications referred to in paragraph 2 which reach the Office more than two months after filing shall be deemed to have been filed on the date on which the application reached the Office.

4. Ten years after the entry into force of this Regulation, the Commission shall draw up a report on the operation of the system of filing applications for Community trade marks, together with any proposals for modifying this system.

Amendment

The words in bold replaced the words in italics as amended by Regulation 422/ 2004.

Article 26

Conditions with which Applications must Comply

A8–027   1. An application for a Community trade mark shall contain:

(a) a request for the registration of a Community trade mark;

(b) information identifying the applicant;

(c) a list of the goods or services in respect of which the registration is requested;

(d) a representation of the trade mark.

2. The application for a Community trade mark shall be subject to the payment of the application fee and, when appropriate, of one or more class fees.

3. An application for a Community trade mark must comply with the conditions laid down in the implementing Regulation referred to in Article *[140]* **157**.

Amendment

The figure in bold replaced the figure in italics as amended by Regulation 422/ 2004.

Article 27

Date of Filing

A8–028   The date of filing of a Community trade mark application shall be the date on which documents containing the information specified in Article 26(1) are filed with the Office by the applicant or, if the application has been filed with the central office of a Member State or with the Benelux Trade Mark Office, with that office, subject to payment of the application fee within a period of one month of filing the above-mentioned documents.

Article 28

Classification

A8–029   Goods and services in respect of which Community trade marks are applied for shall be classified in conformity with the system of classification specified in the Implementing Regulation.

Section 2 —Priority

Article 29

Right of Priority

[*1. A person who has duly filed an application for a trade mark in or for any State party to the Paris Convention, or his successors in title, shall enjoy, for the purpose of filing a Community trade mark application for the same trade mark in respect of goods or services which are identical with or contained within those for which the application has been filed, a right of priority during a period of six months from the date of filing of the first application.*]   **A8–030**

1. A person who has duly filed an application for a trade mark in or for any State party to the Paris Convention or to the Agreement establishing the World Trade Organization, or his successors in title, shall enjoy, for the purpose of filing a Community trade mark application for the same trade mark in respect of goods or services which are identical with or contained within those for which the application has been filed, a right or priority during a period of six months from the date of filing of the first application.

2. Every filing that is equivalent to a regular national filing under the national law of the State where it was made or under bilateral or multilateral agreements shall be recognized as giving rise to a right of priority.

3. By a regular national filing is meant any filing that is sufficient to establish the date on which the application was filed, whatever may be the outcome of the application.

4. A subsequent application for a trade mark which was the subject of a previous first application in respect of the same goods or services, and which is filed in or in respect of the same State shall be considered as the first application for the purposes of determining priority, provided that, at the date of filing of the subsequent application, the previous application has been withdrawn, abandoned or refused, without being open to public inspection and without leaving any rights outstanding, and has not served as a basis for claiming a right of priority. The previous application may not thereafter serve as a basis for claiming a right of priority.

[*5. If the first filing has been made in a State which is not a party to the Paris Convention, paragraphs 1 to 4 shall apply only in so far as that State, according to published findings, grants, on the basis of a first filing made at the Office and subject to conditions equivalent to those laid down in this Regulation, a right of priority having equivalent effect.*]

5. If the first filing has been made in a State which is not a party to the Paris Convention or to the Agreement establishing the World Trade Organization, paragraphs 1 to 4 shall apply only in so far as that State, according to published findings, grants, on the basis of a first filing made at the Office and subject to conditions equivalent to those laid down in this Regulation, a right of priority having equivalent effect.

Amendment

The words in bold replaced the words in italics as a result of Regulation 3288/94, amending the CTM Regulation to take account of the effect of the Uruguay Round.

Article 30

Claiming Priority

A8–031   An applicant desiring to take advantage of the priority of a previous application shall file a declaration of priority and a copy of the previous application. If
the language of the latter is not one of the languages of the Office, the applicant
shall file a translation of the previous application in one of those languages.

Article 31

Effect of Priority Right

A8–032   The right of priority shall have the effect that the date of priority shall count as
the date of filing of the Community trade mark application for the purposes of
establishing which rights take precedence.

Article 32

Equivalence of Community Filing with National Filing

A8–033   A Community trade mark application which has been accorded a date of filing
shall, in the Member States, be equivalent to a regular national filing, where appropriate with the priority claimed for the Community trade mark application.

Section 3 —Exhibition Priority

Article 33

Exhibition Priority

A8–034   1. If an applicant for a Community trade mark has displayed goods or services
under the mark applied for, at an official or officially recognized international exhibition falling within the terms of the Convention on International Exhibitions
signed at Paris on 22 November 1928 and last revised on 30 November 1972, he
may, if he files the application within a period of six months from the date of the
first display of the goods or services under the mark applied for, claim a right of
priority from that date within the meaning of Article 31.

2. An applicant who wishes to claim priority pursuant to paragraph 1 must file
evidence of the display of goods or services under the mark applied for under the
conditions laid down in the Implementing Regulation.

3. An exhibition priority granted in a Member State or in a third country does
not extend the period of priority laid down in Article 29.

Section 4 —Claiming the Seniority of a National Trade Mark

Article 34

Claiming the Seniority of a National Trade Mark

A8–035   1. The proprietor of an earlier trade mark registered in a Member State, including a trade mark registered in the Benelux countries, or registered under
international arrangements having effect in a Member State, who applies for an
identical trade mark for registration as a Community trade mark for goods or services which are identical with or contained within those for which the earlier
trade mark has been registered, may claim for the Community trade mark the seniority of the earlier trade mark in respect of the Member State in or for which it
is registered.

2. Seniority shall have the sole effect under this Regulation that, where the proprietor of the Community trade mark surrenders the earlier trade mark or allows it to lapse, he shall be deemed to continue to have the same rights as he would have had if the earlier trade mark had continued to be registered.

3. The seniority claimed for the Community trade mark shall lapse if the earlier trade mark the seniority of which is claimed is declared to have been revoked or to be invalid or if it is surrendered prior to the registration of the Community trade mark.

Article 35

Claiming Seniority after Registration of the Community Trade Mark

[1. The proprietor of a Community trade mark who is the proprietor of an   **A8–036**
earlier identical trade mark registered in a Member State, including a trade mark registered in the Benelux countries, or of a trade mark registered under international arrangements having effect in a Member State, for identical goods or services, may claim the seniority of the earlier trade mark in respect of the Member State in or for which it is registered.]

1. The proprietor of a Community trade mark who is the proprietor of an earlier identical trade mark registered in a Member State, including a trade mark registered in the Benelux countries or of an earlier identical trade mark, with an international registration effective in a Member State, for goods or services which are identical to those for which the earlier trade mark has been registered, or contained within them, may claim the seniority of the earlier trade mark in respect of the Member State in or for which it was registered.

2. Article 34(2) and (3) shall apply.

Amendment

The words in bold replaced the words in italics as amended by Regulation 422/2004.

TITLE IV

REGISTRATION PROCEDURE

Section 1 —Examination of Applications

Article 36

Examination of the Conditions of Filing

1. The Office shall examine whether: **A8–037**

(a) the Community trade mark application satisfies the requirements for the accordance of a date of filing in accordance with Article 27;

[(b) the Community trade mark application complies with the conditions laid down in the Implementing Regulation;]

(b) the Community trade mark application complies with the conditions laid down in this Regulation and with the conditions laid down in the Implementing Regulation.

(c) where appropriate, the class fees have been paid within the prescribed period.

2. Where the Community trade mark application does not satisfy the require-

ments referred to in paragraph 1, the Office shall request the applicant to remedy the deficiencies or the default on payment within the prescribed period.

3. If the deficiencies or the default on payment established pursuant to paragraph 1(a) are not remedied within this period, the application shall not be dealt with as a Community trade mark application. If the applicant complies with the Office's request, the Office shall accord as the date of filing of the application the date on which the deficiencies or the default on payment established are remedied.

4. If the deficiencies established pursuant to paragraph 1(b) are not remedied within the prescribed period, the Office shall refuse the application.

5. If the default on payment established pursuant to paragraph 1(c) is not remedied within the prescribed period, the application shall be deemed to be withdrawn unless it is clear which categories of goods or services the amount paid is intended to cover.

6. Failure to satisfy the requirements concerning the claim to priority shall result in loss of the right of priority for the application.

7. Failure to satisfy the requirements concerning the claiming of seniority of a national trade mark shall result in loss of that right for the application.

Amendment

The words in bold replaced the words in italics as amended by Regulation 422/ 2004.

[Article 37

Examination of the Conditions Relating to the Entitlement of the Proprietor

A8–038   *1. Where, pursuant to Article 5, the applicant may not be the proprietor of a Community trade mark, the application shall be refused.*

2. The application may not be refused before the applicant has been given the opportunity to withdraw his application or submit his observations.]

Amendment

The words in italics are deleted for the purposes of Regulation 422/2004.

Article 38

Examination as to Absolute Grounds for Refusal

A8–039   1. Where, under Article 7, a trade mark is ineligible for registration in respect of some or all of the goods or services covered by the Community trade mark application, the application shall be refused as regards those goods or services.

2. Where the trade mark contains an element which is not distinctive, and where the inclusion of said element in the trade mark could give rise to doubts as to the scope of protection of the trade mark, the Office may request, as a condition for registration of said trade mark, that the applicant state that he disclaims any exclusive right to such element. Any disclaimer shall be published together with the application or the registration of the Community trade mark, as the case may be.

3. The application shall not be refused before the applicant has been allowed the opportunity of withdrawing or amending the application or of submitting his observations.

Section 2 —Search

[Article 39

Search

1. Once the Office has accorded a date of filing to a Community trade mark   **A8–040**
application and has established that the applicant satisfies the conditions referred
to in Article 5, it shall draw up a Community search report citing those earlier
Community trade marks or Community trade mark applications discovered which
may be invoked under Article 8 against the registration of the Community trade
mark applied for.

2. As soon as a Community trade mark application has been accorded a date
of filing, the Office shall transmit a copy thereof to the central industrial property
office of each Member State which has informed the Office of its decision to
operate a search in its own register of trade marks in respect of Community trade
mark applications.

3. Each of the central industrial property offices referred to in paragraph 2
shall communicate to the Office within three months as from the date on which it
received the Community trade mark application a search report which shall ei-
ther cite those earlier national trade marks or trade mark applications discovered
which may be invoked under Article 8 against the registration of the Community
trade mark applied for, or state that the search has revealed no such rights.

4. An amount shall be paid by the Office to each central industrial property of-
fice for each search report provided by that office in accordance with paragraph
3. The amount, which shall be the same for each office, shall be fixed by the
Budget Committee by means of a decision adopted by a majority of three-quarters
of the representatives of the Member States.

5. The Office shall transmit without delay to the applicant for the Community
trade mark the Community search report and the national search reports received
within the time limit laid down in paragraph 3.

6. Upon publication of the Community trade mark application, which may not
take place before the expiry of a period of one month as from the date on which
the Office transmits the search reports to the applicant, the Office shall inform
the proprietors of any earlier Community trade marks or Community trade mark
applications cited in the Community search report of the publication of the Com-
munity trade mark application.

7. The Commission shall, five years after the opening of the Office for the fil-
ing of applications, submit to the Council a report on the operation of the system
of searching resulting from this Article, including the payments made to Member
States under paragraph 4, and, if necessary, appropriate proposals for amending
this Regulation with a view to adapting the system of searching on the basis of
the experience gained and bearing in mind developments in searching
techniques.]

Article 39

Search

**1. Once the Office has accorded a date of filing, it shall draw up a Com-
munity search report citing those earlier Community trade marks or Community trade mark applications discovered which may be invoked under
Article 8 against the registration of the Community trade mark applied for.**

2. Where, at the time of filing a Community trade mark application, the applicant requests that a search report also be prepared by the central industrial property offices of the Member States and where the appropriate search fee has been paid within the time-limit for the payment of the filing fee, the Office shall, as soon as a Community trade mark application has been accorded a date of filing, transmit a copy thereof to the central industrial property office of each Member State which has informed the Office of its decision to operate a search in its own register of trade marks in respect of Community trade mark applications.

3. Each of the central industrial property offices referred to in paragraph 2 shall communicate to the Office within two months as from the date on which it received the Community trade mark application a search report which shall either cite those earlier national trade marks or trade mark applications discovered which may be invoked under Article 8 against the registration of the Community trade mark applied for, or state that the search has revealed no such rights.

4. The search reports referred to in paragraph 3 shall be prepared on a standard form drawn up by the Office, after consulting the Administrative Board. The essential contents of this form shall be set out in the Implementing Regulation provided for in Article 157(1).

5. An amount shall be paid by the Office to each central industrial property office for each search report provided by that office in accordance with paragraph 3. The amount, which shall be the same for each office, shall be fixed by the Budget Committee by means of a decision adopted by a majority of three-quarters of the representatives of the Member States.

6. The Office shall transmit without delay to the applicant for the Community trade mark the Community search report and any requested national search reports received within the time limit laid down in paragraph 3.

7. Upon publication of the Community trade mark application, which may not take place before the expiry of a period of one month as from the date on which the Office transmits the search reports to the applicant, the Office shall inform the proprietors of any earlier Community trade marks or Community trade mark applications cited in the Community search report of the publication of the Community trade mark application.

Amendment

The words in bold replaced the words in italics as amended by Regulation 422/2004, which will enter into force on March 10, 2008.

Section 3 —Publication of the Application

[Article 40

Publication of the Application

A8–041   *1. If the conditions which the application for a Community trade mark must satisfy have been fulfilled and if the period referred to in Article 39(6) has expired, the application shall be published to the extent that it has not been refused pursuant to Articles 37 and 38.*

2. Where, after publication, the application is refused under Articles 37 and 38, the decision that it has been refused shall be published upon becoming final.]

Article 40

Publication of the Application

1. If the conditions which the application for a Community trade mark

must satisfy have been fulfilled and if the period referred to in Article 39(7) has expired, the application shall be published to the extent that it has not been refused pursuant to Article 38.

2. Where, after publication, the application is refused under Article 38, the decision that it has been refused shall be published upon becoming final.

Amendment

The words in bold replaced the words in italics as amended by Regulation 422/2004. This amendment has already entered into force. However 39(7) refers to the new Article 39, which comes into force on March 10, 2008. Until this date it should be read as 39(6).

Section 4 —Observations by Third Parties and Opposition

Article 41

Observations by Third Parties

1. Following the publication of the Community trade mark application, any natural or legal person and any group or body representing manufacturers, producers, suppliers of services, traders or consumers may submit to the Office written observations, explaining on which grounds under Article 7, in particular, the trade mark shall not be registered *ex officio*. They shall not be parties to the proceedings before the Office.

2. The observations referred to in paragraph 1 shall be communicated to the applicant who may comment on them.

A8–042

Article 42

Opposition

1. Within a period of three months following the publication of a Community trade mark application, notice of opposition to registration of the trade mark may be given on the grounds that it may not be registered under Article 8:

(a) by the proprietors of earlier trade marks referred to in Article 8(2) as well as licensees authorized by the proprietors of those trade marks, in respect of Article 8(1) and (5);

(b) by the proprietors of trade marks referred to in Article 8(3);

(c) by the proprietors of earlier marks or signs referred to in Article 8(4) and by persons authorized under the relevant national law to exercise these rights.

2. Notice of opposition to registration of the trade mark may also be given, subject to the conditions laid down in paragraph 1, in the event of the publication of an amended application in accordance with the second sentence of Article 44(2).

3. Opposition must be expressed in writing and must specify the grounds on which it is made. It shall not be treated as duly entered until the opposition fee has been paid. Within a period fixed by the Office, the opponent may submit in support of his case facts, evidence and arguments.

A8–043

Article 43

Examination of Opposition

1. In the examination of the opposition the Office shall invite the parties, as often as necessary, to file observations, within a period set them by the Office, on communications from the other parties or issued by itself.

A8–044

2. If the applicant so requests, the proprietor of an earlier Community trade mark who has given notice of opposition shall furnish proof that, during the period of five years preceding the date of publication of the Community trade mark application, the earlier Community trade mark has been put to genuine use in the Community in connection with the goods or services in respect of which it is registered and which he cites as justification for his opposition, or that there are proper reasons for non-use, provided the earlier Community trade mark has at that date been registered for not less than five years. In the absence of proof to this effect, the opposition shall be rejected. If the earlier Community trade mark has been used in relation to part only of the goods or services for which it is registered it shall, for the purposes of the examination of the opposition, be deemed to be registered in respect only of that part of the goods or services.

3. paragraph 2 shall apply to earlier national trade marks referred to in Article 8(2)(a), by substituting use in the Member State in which the earlier national trade mark is protected for use in the Community.

4. The Office may, if it thinks fit, invite the parties to make a friendly settlement.

5. If examination of the opposition reveals that the trade mark may not be registered in respect of some or all of the goods or services for which the Community trade mark application has been made, the application shall be refused in respect of those goods or services. Otherwise the opposition shall be rejected.

6. The decision refusing the application shall be published upon becoming final.

Section 5 —Withdrawal, Restriction [and], Amendment **and Division** of the Application

Article 44

Withdrawal, Restriction and Amendment of the Application

A8–045   1. The applicant may at any time withdraw his Community trade mark application or restrict the list of goods or services contained therein. Where the application has already been published, the withdrawal or restriction shall also be published.

2. In other respects, a Community trade mark application may be amended, upon request of the applicant, only by correcting the name and address of the applicant, errors of wording or of copying, or obvious mistakes, provided that such correction does not substantially change the trade mark or extend the list of goods or services. Where the amendments affect the representation of the trade mark or the list of goods or services and are made after publication of the application, the trade mark application shall be published as amended.

Amendment

The words in bold in the heading preceding article 44 were added by Regulation 422/2004.This amendment shall apply when the necessary implementing measures have been adopted.

Article 44a

Division of the Application

A8–046   **1. The applicant may divide the application by declaring that some of the** goods or services included in the original application will be the subject of one or more divisional applications. The goods or services in the divisional application shall not overlap with the goods or services which remain in the original application or those which are included in other divisional applications.

2. The declaration of division shall not be admissible:

(a) if, where an opposition has been entered against the original application, such a divisional application has the effect of introducing a division amongst the goods or services against which the opposition has been directed, until the decision of the Opposition Division has become final or the opposition proceedings are finally terminated otherwise;

(b) during the periods laid down in the Implementing Regulation.

3. The declaration of division must comply with the provisions set out in the Implementing Regulation.

4. The declaration of division shall be subject to a fee. The application shall be deemed not to have been made until the fee has been paid.

5. The division shall take effect on the date on which it is recorded in the files kept by the Office concerning the original application.

6. All requests and applications submitted and all fees paid with regard to the original application prior to the date on which the Office receives the declaration of division are deemed also to have been submitted or paid with regard to the divisional application or applications. The fees for the original application which have been duly paid prior to the date on which the declaration of division is received shall not be refunded.

7. The divisional application shall preserve the filing date and any priority date and seniority date of the original application.

Amendment

Article 44a was inserted by Regulation 422/2004. This amendment shall apply when the necessary implementing measures have been adopted.

Section 6 — Registration

Article 45

Registration

Where an application meets the requirements of this Regulation and where no notice of opposition has been given within the period referred to in Article 42(1) or where opposition has been rejected by a definitive decision, the trade mark shall be registered as a Community trade mark, provided that the registration fee has been paid within the period prescribed. If the fee is not paid within this period the application shall be deemed to be withdrawn.   **A8–047**

TITLE V

DURATION, RENEWAL [*AND*], ALTERATION AND DIVISION OF COMMUNITY TRADE MARKS

Article 46

Duration of Registration

Community trade marks shall be registered for a period of ten years from the date of filing of the application. Registration may be renewed in accordance with Article 47 for further periods of ten years.   **A8–048**

Amendment

The words in bold were inserted by Regulation 422/2004, and shall apply when the necessary implementing measures have been adopted.

Article 47

Renewal

A8–049   1. Registration of the Community trade mark shall be renewed at the request of the proprietor of the trade mark or any person expressly authorized by him, provided that the fees have been paid.

2. The Office shall inform the proprietor of the Community trade mark, and any person having a registered right in respect of the Community trade mark, of the expiry of the registration in good time before the said expiry. Failure to give such information shall not involve the responsibility of the Office.

3. The request for renewal shall be submitted within a period of six months ending on the last day of the month in which protection ends. The fees shall also be paid within this period. Failing this, the request may be submitted and the fees paid within a further period of six months following the day referred to in the first sentence, provided that an additional fee is paid within this further period.

4. Where the request is submitted or the fees paid in respect of only some of the goods or services for which the Community trade mark is registered, registration shall be renewed for those goods or services only.

5. Renewal shall take effect from the day following the date on which the existing registration expires. The renewal shall be registered.

Article 48

Alteration

A8–050   1. The Community trade mark shall not be altered in the register during the period of registration or on renewal thereof.

2. Nevertheless, where the Community trade mark includes the name and address of the proprietor, any alteration thereof not substantially affecting the identity of the trade mark as originally registered may be registered at the request of the proprietor.

3. The publication of the registration of the alteration shall contain a representation of the Community trade mark as altered. Third parties whose rights may be affected by the alteration may challenge the registration thereof within a period of three months following publication.

Article 48a

Division of the Registration

A8–051   **1. The proprietor of the Community trade mark may divide the registration by declaring that some of the goods or services included in the original registration will be the subject of one or more divisional registrations. The goods or services in the divisional registration shall not overlap with the goods or services which remain in the original registration or those which are included in other divisional registrations.**

2. The declaration of division shall not be admissible:

(a) if, where an application for revocation of rights or for a declaration of invalidity has been entered against the original registration, such a

divisional declaration has the effect of introducing a division amongst the goods or services against which the application for revocation of rights or for a declaration of invalidity is directed, until the decision of the Cancellation Division has become final or the proceedings are finally terminated otherwise;

(b) if, where a counterclaim for revocation or for a declaration of invalidity has been entered in a case before a Community trade mark court, such a divisional declaration has the effect of introducing a division amongst the goods or services against which the counterclaim is directed, until the mention of the Community trade mark court's judgement is recorded in the Register pursuant to Article 96(6).

3. The declaration of division must comply with the provisions set out in the Implementing Regulation.

4. The declaration of division shall be subject to a fee. The declaration shall be deemed not to have been made until the fee has been paid.

5. The division shall take effect on the date on which it is entered in the Register.

6. All requests and applications submitted and all fees paid with regard to the original registration prior to the date on which the Office receives the declaration of division shall be deemed also to have been submitted or paid with regard to the divisional registration or registrations. The fees for the original registration which have been duly paid prior to the date on which the declaration of division is received shall not be refunded.

7. The divisional registration shall preserve the filing date and any priority date and seniority date of the original registration.

Amendment

Article 48a was inserted by Regulation 422/2004. This amendment shall apply when the necessary measures have been adopted.

TITLE VI

SURRENDER, REVOCATION AND INVALIDITY

Section 1 —Surrender

Article 49

Surrender

1. A Community trade mark may be surrendered in respect of some or all of   **A8–052**
the goods or services for which it is registered.

2. The surrender shall be declared to the Office in writing by the proprietor of the trade mark. It shall not have effect until it has been entered in the Register.

3. Surrender shall be entered only with the agreement of the proprietor of a right entered in the Register. If a licence has been registered, surrender shall only be entered in the Register if the proprietor of the trade mark proves that he has informed the licensee of his intention to surrender; this entry shall be made on expiry of the period prescribed by the Implementing Regulation.

Section 2 —Grounds for Revocation

Article 50

Grounds for Revocation

1. The rights of the proprietor of the Community trade mark shall be declared   **A8–053**

to be revoked on application to the Office or on the basis of a counterclaim in infringement proceedings:

  (a) if, within a continuous period of five years, the trade mark has not been put
      to genuine use in the Community in connection with the goods or services
      in respect of which it is registered, and there are no proper reasons for non-
      use; however, no person may claim that the proprietor's rights in a Com-
      munity trade mark should be revoked where, during the interval between
      expiry of the five-year period and filing of the application or counterclaim,
      genuine use of the trade mark has been started or resumed; the commence-
      ment or resumption of use within a period of three months preceding the
      filing of the application or counterclaim which began at the earliest on
      expiry of the continuous period of five years of non-use shall, however, be
      disregarded where preparations for the commencement or resumption oc-
      cur only after the proprietor becomes aware that the application or
      counterclaim may be filed;

  (b) if, in consequence of acts or inactivity of the proprietor, the trade mark has
      become the common name in the trade for a product or service in respect of
      which it is registered;

  (c) if, in consequence of the use made of it by the proprietor of the trade mark
      or with his consent in respect of the goods or services for which it is
      registered, the trade mark is liable to mislead the public, particularly as to
      the nature, quality or geographical origin of those goods or services;

  *[(d) if the proprietor of the trade mark no longer satisfies the conditions laid
      down by Article 5.]*

  2. Where the grounds for revocation of rights exist in respect of only some of
the goods or services for which the Community trade mark is registered, the
rights of the proprietor shall be declared to be revoked in respect of those goods
or services only.

Amendment

  The words in italics are deleted for the purposes of Regulation 422/2004.

Section 3 —Grounds for Invalidity

Article 51

Absolute Grounds for Invalidity

A8–054   1. A Community trade mark shall be declared invalid on application to the Office or on the basis of a counterclaim in infringement proceedings,

  *[(a) where the Community trade mark has been registered in breach of the pro-
      visions of Article 5 or of Article 7;]*

  **(a) where the Community trade mark has been registered contrary to the
      provisions of Article 7;**

  (b) where the applicant was acting in bad faith when he filed the application for
      the trade mark.

  2. Where te Community trade mark has been registered in breach of the provisions of Article 7(1)(b), (c) or (d), it may nevertheless not be declared invalid if,
in consequence of the use which has been made of it, it has after registration
acquired a distinctive character in relation to the goods or services for which it is
registered.

  3. Where the ground for invalidity exists in respect of only some of the goods
or services for which the Community trade mark is registered, the trade mark
shall be declared invalid as regards those goods or services only.

Amendment

The words in bold replaced the words in italics as amended by Regulation 422/2004.

Article 52

Relative Grounds for Invalidity

1. A Community trade mark shall be declared invalid on application to the Office or on the basis of a counterclaim in infringement proceedings: **A8–055**

(a) where there is an earlier trade mark as referred to in Article 8(2) and the conditions set out in paragraph 1 or paragraph 5 of that Article are fulfilled;

(b) where there is a trade mark as referred to in Article 8(3) and the conditions set out in that paragraph are fulfilled;

(c) where there is an earlier right as referred to in Article 8(4) and the conditions set out in that paragraph are fulfilled.

[2. A Community trade mark shall also be declared invalid on application to the Office or on the basis of a counterclaim in infringement proceedings where the use of such trade mark may be prohibited pursuant to the national law governing the protection of any other earlier right an in particular:

(a) a right to a name;

(b) a right of personal portrayal;

(c) a copyright;

(d) an industrial property right.]

2. A Community trade mark shall also be declared invalid on application to the Office or on the basis of a counterclaim in infringement proceedings where the use of such trade mark may be prohibited pursuant to another earlier right, and in particular:

(a) a right to a name;

(b) a right of personal portrayal;

(c) a copyright;

(d) an industrial property right;

under the Community legislation or national law governing the protection.

3. A Community trade mark may not be declared invalid where the proprietor of a right referred to in paragraphs 1 or 2 consents expressly to the registration of the Community trade mark before submission of the application for a declaration of invalidity or the counterclaim.

4. Where the proprietor of one of the rights referred to in paragraphs 1 or 2 has previously applied for a declaration that a Community trade mark is invalid or made a counterclaim in infringement proceedings, he may not submit a new application for a declaration of invalidity or lodge a counterclaim on the basis of another of the said rights which he could have invoked in support of his first application or counterclaim.

5. Article 51(3) shall apply.

Amendment

The words in bold replaced the words in italics as amended by Regulation 422/2004.

Article 53

Limitation in Consequence of Acquiescence

1. Where the proprietor of a Community trade mark has acquiesced, for a pe-   **A8–056**

riod of five successive years, in the use of a later Community trade mark in the Community while being aware of such use, he shall no longer be entitled on the basis of the earlier trade mark either to apply for a declaration that the later trade mark is invalid or to oppose the use of the later trade mark in respect of the goods or services for which the later trade mark has been used, unless registration of the later Community trade mark was applied for in bad faith.

2. Where the proprietor of an earlier national trade mark as referred to in Article 8(2) or of another earlier sign referred to in Article 8(4) has acquiesced, for a period of five successive years, in the use of a later Community trade mark in the Member State in which the earlier trade mark or the other earlier sign is protected while being aware of such use, he shall no longer be entitled on the basis of the earlier trade mark or of the other earlier sign either to apply for a declaration that the later trade mark is invalid or to oppose the use of the later trade mark in respect of the goods or services for which the later trade mark has been used, unless registration of the later Community trade mark was applied for in bad faith.

3. In the cases referred to in paragraphs 1 and 2, the proprietor of a later Community trade mark shall not be entitled to oppose the use of the earlier right, even though that right may no longer be invoked against the later Community trade mark.

Section 4 —Consequences of Revocation and Invalidity

Article 54

Consequences of Revocation and Invalidity

A8–057   1. The Community trade mark shall be deemed not to have had, as from the date of the application for revocation or of the counterclaim, the effects specified in this Regulation, to the extent that the rights of the proprietor have been revoked. An earlier date, on which one of the grounds for revocation occurred, may be fixed in the decision at the request of one of the parties.

2. The Community trade mark shall be deemed not to have had, as from the outset, the effects specified in this Regulation, to the extent that the trade mark has been declared invalid.

3. Subject to the national provisions relating either to claims for compensation for damage caused by negligence or lack of good faith on the part of the proprietor of the trade mark, or to unjust enrichment, the retroactive effect of revocation or invalidity of the trade mark shall not affect:

(a) any decision on infringement which has acquired the authority of a final decision and been enforced prior to the revocation or invalidity decision;

(b) any contract concluded prior to the revocation or invalidity decision, in so far as it has been performed before that decision; however, repayment, to an extent justified by the circumstances, of sums paid under the relevant contract, may be claimed on grounds of equity.

Section 5 —Proceedings in the Office in Relation to Revocation or Invalidity

Article 55

Application for Revocation or for a Declaration of Invalidity

A8–058   1. An application for revocation of the rights of the proprietor of a Community trade mark or for a declaration that the trade mark is invalid may be submitted to the Office:

(a) where Articles 50 and 51 apply, by any natural or legal person and any group or body set up for the purpose of representing the interests of manufacturers, producers, suppliers of services, traders or consumers, which under the terms of the law governing it has the capacity in its own name to sue and be sued;

(b) where Article 52(1) applies, by the persons referred to in Article 42(1);

(c) where Article 52(2) applies, by the owners of the earlier rights referred to in that provision or by the persons who are entitled under the law of the Member State concerned to exercise the rights in question.

2. The application shall be filed in a written reasoned statement. It shall not be deemed to have been filed until the fee has been paid.

3. An application for revocation or for a declaration of invalidity shall be inadmissible if an application relating to the same subject matter and cause of action, and involving the same parties, has been adjudicated on by a court in a Member State and has acquired the authority of a final decision.

Article 56

Examination of the Application

1. In the examination of the application for revocation of rights or for a declaration of invalidity, the Office shall invite the parties, as often as necessary, to file observations, within a period to be fixed by the Office, on communications from the other parties or issued by itself.   **A8–059**

2. If the proprietor of the Community trade mark so requests, the proprietor of an earlier Community trade mark, being a party to the invalidity proceedings, shall furnish proof that, during the period of five years preceding the date of the application for a declaration of invalidity, the earlier Community trade mark has been put to genuine use in the Community in connection with the goods or services in respect of which it is registered and which he cites as justification for his application, or that there are proper reasons for non-use, provided the earlier Community trade mark has at that date been registered for non-use, provided the earlier Community trade mark has at that date been registered for not less than five years. If, at the date on which the Community trade mark application was published, the earlier Community trade mark had been registered for not less than five years, the proprietor of the earlier Community trade mark shall furnish proof that, in addition, the conditions contained in Article 43(2) were satisfied at that date. In the absence of proof to this effect the application for a declaration of invalidity shall be rejected. If the earlier Community trade mark has been used in relation to part only of the goods or services for which it is registered it shall, for the purpose of the examination of the application for a declaration of invalidity, be deemed to be registered in respect only of that part of the goods or services.

3. paragraph 2 shall apply to earlier national trade marks referred to in Article 8(2)(a), by substituting use in the Member State in which the earlier national trade mark is protected for use in the Community.

4. The Office may, if it thinks fit, invite the parties to make a friendly settlement.

5. If the examination of the application for revocation of rights or for a declaration of invalidity reveals that the trade mark should not have been registered in respect of some or all of the goods or services for which it is registered, the rights of the proprietor of the Community trade mark shall be revoked or it shall be

declared invalid in respect of those goods or services. Otherwise the application for revocation of rights or for a declaration of invalidity shall be rejected.

[6. The decision revoking the rights of the proprietor of the Community trade mark or declaring it invalid shall be entered in the Register upon becoming final.]

6. A record of the Office's decision on the application for revocation of rights or for a declaration of invalidity shall be entered in the Register once it has become final.

Amendment

The words in bold replaced the words in italics as amended by Regulation 422/ 2004.

TITLE VII

APPEALS

Article 57

Decisions Subject to Appeal

A8–060   1. An appeal shall lie from decisions of the examiners, Opposition Divisions, Administration of Trade Marks and Legal Divisions and Cancellation Divisions. It shall have suspensive effect.

2. A decision which does not terminate proceedings as regards one of the parties can only be appealed together with the final decision, unless the decision allows separate appeal.

Article 58

Persons Entitled to Appeal and to be Parties to Appeal Proceedings

A8–061   Any party to proceedings adversely affected by a decision may appeal. Any other parties to the proceedings shall be parties to the appeal proceedings as of right.

Article 59

Time Limit and Form of Appeal

A8–062   Notice of appeal must be filed in writing at the Office within two months after the date of notification of the decision appealed from. The notice shall be deemed to have been filed only when the fee for appeal has been paid. Within four months after the date of notification of the decision, a written statement setting out the grounds of appeal must be filed.

[Article 60

Interlocutory Revision

A8–063   *1. If the department whose decision is contested considers the appeal to be admissible and well founded, it shall rectify its decision. This shall not apply where the appellant is opposed by another party to the proceedings.*

2. If the decision is not rectified within one month after receipt of the statement of grounds, the appeal shall be remitted to the Board of Appeal without delay, and without comment as to its merit.]

Article 60

Revision of Decisions in Ex Parte Cases

1. If the party which has lodged the appeal is the sole party to the proce-

dure, and if the department whose decision is contested considers the appeal to be admissible and well founded, the department shall rectify its decision.

2. If the decision is not rectified within one month after receipt of the statement of grounds, the appeal shall be remitted to the Board of Appeal without delay, and without comment as to its merit.

Amendment

The words in bold replaced the words in italics as amended by Regulation 422/2004.

Article 60a

Revision of Decisions in Inter Partes Cases

1. Where the party which has lodged the appeal is opposed by another party and if the department whose decision is contested considers the appeal to be admissible and well founded, it shall rectify its decision.   A8–064

2. The decision may only be rectified if the department whose decision is contested notifies the other party of its intention to rectify it, and that party accepts it within two months of the date on which it received the notification.

3. If, within two months of receiving the notification referred to in paragraph 2, the other party does not accept that the contested decision is to be rectified and makes a declaration to that effect or does not make any declaration within the period laid down, the appeal shall be remitted to the Board of Appeal without delay, and without comment as to its merit.

4. However, if the department whose decision is contested does not consider the appeal to be admissible and well founded within one month after receipt of the statement of grounds, it shall, instead of taking the measures provided for in paragraphs 2 and 3, remit the appeal to the Board of Appeal without delay, and without comment as to its merit.

Amendment

Article 60a was inserted by Regulation 422/2004.

Article 61

Examination of Appeals

1. If the appeal is admissible, the Board of Appeal shall examine whether the appeal is allowable.   A8–065

2. In the examination of the appeal, the Board of Appeal shall invite the parties, as often as necessary, to file observations, within a period to be fixed by the Board of Appeal, on communications from the other parties or issued by itself.

Article 62

Decisions in Respect of Appeals

1. Following the examination as to the allowability of the appeal, the Board of Appeal shall decide on the appeal. The Board of Appeal may either exercise any power within the competence of the department which was responsible for the decision appealed or remit the case to that department for further prosecution.   A8–066

2. If the Board of Appeal remits the case for further prosecution to the department whose decision was appealed, that department shall be bound by the *ratio decidendi* of the Board of Appeal, in so far as the facts are the same.

3. The decisions of the Boards of Appeal shall take effect only as from the date

of expiration of the period referred to in Article 63(5) or, if an action has been brought before the Court of Justice within that period, as from the date of rejection of such action.

Article 63

Actions Before the Court of Justice

A8–067   1. Actions may be brought before the Court of Justice against decisions of the Boards of Appeal on appeals.

2. The action may be brought on grounds of lack of competence, infringement of an essential procedural requirement, infringement of the Treaty, of this Regulation or of any rule of law relating to their application or misuse of power.

3. The Court of Justice has jurisdiction to annul or to alter the contested decision.

4. The action shall be open to any party to proceedings before the Board of Appeal adversely affected by its decision.

5. The action shall be brought before the Court of Justice within two months of the date of notification of the decision of the Board of Appeal.

6. The Office shall be required to take the necessary measures to comply with the judgment of the Court of Justice.

TITLE VIII

COMMUNITY COLLECTIVE MARKS

Article 64

Community Collective Marks

A8–068   1. A Community collective mark shall be a Community trade mark which is described as such when the mark is applied for and is capable of distinguishing the goods or services of the members of the association which is the proprietor of the mark from those of other undertakings. Associations of manufacturers, producers, suppliers of services, or traders which, under the terms of the law governing them, have the capacity in their own name to have rights and obligations of all kinds, to make contracts or accomplish other legal acts and to sue and be sued, as well as legal persons governed by public law, may apply for Community collective marks.

2. In derogation from Article 7(1)(c), signs or indications which may serve, in trade, to designate the geographical origin of the goods or services may constitute Community collective marks within the meaning of paragraph 1. A collective mark shall not entitle the proprietor to prohibit a third party from using in the course of trade such signs or indications, provided he uses them in accordance with honest practices in industrial or commercial matters; in particular, such a mark may not be invoked against a third party who is entitled to use a geographical name.

3. The provisions of this Regulation shall apply to Community collective marks, unless Articles 65 to 72 provide otherwise.

Article 65

Regulations Governing Use of the Mark

A8–069   1. An applicant for a Community collective mark must submit regulations governing its use within the period prescribed.

2. The regulations governing use shall specify the persons authorized to use the mark, the conditions of membership of the association and, where they exist, the conditions of use of the mark including sanctions. The regulations governing use of a mark referred to in Article 64(2) must authorize any person whose goods or services originate in the geographical area concerned to become a member of the association which is the proprietor of the mark.

Article 66

Refusal of the Application

1. In addition to the grounds for refusal of a Community trade mark application provided for in Articles 36 and 38, an application for a Community collective mark shall be refused where the provisions of Article 64 or 65 are not satisfied, or where the regulations governing use are contrary to public policy or to accepted principles of morality.   A8–070

2. An application for a Community collective mark shall also be refused if the public is liable to be misled as regards the character or the significance of the mark, in particular if it is likely to be taken to be something other than a collective mark.

3. An application shall not be refused if the applicant, as a result of amendment of the regulations governing use, meets the requirements of paragraphs 1 and 2.

Article 67

Observations by Third Parties

Apart from the cases mentioned in Article 41, any person, group or body referred to in that Article may submit to the Office written observations based on the particular grounds on which the application for a Community collective mark should be refused under the terms of Article 66.   A8–071

Article 68

Use of Marks

Use of a Community collective mark by any person who has authority to use it shall satisfy the requirements of this Regulation, provided that the other conditions which this Regulation imposes with regard to the use of Community trade marks are fulfilled.   A8–072

Article 69

Amendment of the Regulations Governing Use of the Mark

1. The proprietor of a Community collective mark must submit to the Office any amended regulations governing use.   A8–073

2. The amendment shall not be mentioned in the Register if the amended regulations do not satisfy the requirements of Article 65 or involve one of the grounds for refusal referred to in Article 66.

3. Article 67 shall apply to amended regulations governing use.

4. For the purposes of applying this Regulation, amendments to the regulations governing use shall take effect only from the date of entry of the mention of the amendment in the Register.

Article 70

Persons who are Entitled to Bring an Action for Infringement

1. The provisions of Article 22(3) and (4) concerning the rights of licensees   A8–074

shall apply to every person who has authority to use a Community collective mark.

2. The proprietor of a Community collective mark shall be entitled to claim compensation on behalf of persons who have authority to use the mark where they have sustained damage in consequence of unauthorized use of the mark.

Article 71

Grounds for Revocation

A8–075   Apart from the grounds for revocation provided for in Article 50, the rights of the proprietor of a Community collective mark shall be revoked on application to the Office or on the basis of a counterclaim in infringement proceedings, if:

(a) the proprietor does not take reasonable steps to prevent the mark being used in a manner incompatible with the conditions of use, where these exist, laid down in the regulations governing use, amendments to which have, where appropriate, been mentioned in the Register;

(b) the manner in which the mark has been used by the proprietor has caused it to become liable to mislead the public in the manner referred to in Article 66(2);

(c) an amendment to the regulations governing use of the mark has been mentioned in the Register in breach of the provisions of Article 69(2), unless the proprietor of the mark, by further amending the regulations governing use, complies with the requirements of those provisions.

Article 72

Grounds for Invalidity

A8–076   Apart from the grounds for invalidity provided for in Articles 51 and 52, a Community collective mark which is registered in breach of the provisions of Article 66 shall be declared invalid on application to the Office or on the basis of a counterclaim in infringement proceedings, unless the proprietor of the mark, by amending the regulations governing use, complies with the requirements of those provisions.

TITLE IX

PROCEDURE

Section 1 —General Provisions

Article 73

Statement of Reasons on which Decisions are Based

A8–077   Decisions of the Office shall state the reasons on which they are based. They shall be based only on reasons or evidence on which the parties concerned have had on opportunity to present their comments.

Article 74

Examination of the Facts by the Office of its Own Motion

A8–078   1. In proceedings before it the Office shall examine the facts of its own motion; however, in proceedings relating to relative grounds for refusal of registration, the Office shall be restricted in this examination to the facts, evidence and arguments provided by the parties and the relief sought.

2. The Office may disregard facts or evidence which are not submitted in due time by the parties concerned.

Article 75

Oral Proceedings

1. If the Office considers that oral proceedings would be expedient they shall be held either at the instance of the Office or at the request of any party to the proceedings.　　**A8–079**

2. Oral proceedings before the examiners, the Opposition Division and the Administration of Trade Marks and Legal Division shall not be public.

3. Oral proceedings, including delivery of the decision, shall be public before the Cancellation Division and the Boards of Appeal, in so far as the department before which the proceedings are taking place does not decide otherwise in cases where admission of the public could have serious and unjustified disadvantages, in particular for a party to the proceedings.

Article 76

Taking of Evidence

1. In any proceedings before the Office, the means of giving or obtaining evidence shall include the following:　　**A8–080**
   (a) hearing the parties;
   (b) requests for information;
   (c) the production of documents and items of evidence;
   (d) hearing witnesses;
   (e) opinions by experts;
   (f) statements in writing sworn or affirmed or having a similar effect under the law of the State in which the statement is drawn up.

2. The relevant department may commission one of its members to examine the evidence adduced.

3. If the Office considers it necessary for a party, witness or expert to give evidence orally, it shall issue a summons to the person concerned to appear before it.

4. The parties shall be informed of the hearing of a witness or expert before the Office. They shall have the right to be present and to put questions to the witness or expert.

Article 77

Notification

The Office shall, as a matter of course, notify those concerned of decisions and summonses and of any notice or other communication from which a time limit is reckoned, or of which those concerned must be notified under other provisions of this Regulation or of the Implementing Regulation, or of which notification has been ordered by the President of the Office.　　**A8–081**

Article 77a

Revocation of Decisions

1. Where the Office has made an entry in the Register or taken a decision　　**A8–082**

which contains an obvious procedural error attributable to the Office, it shall ensure that the entry is cancelled or the decision is revoked. Where there is only one party to the proceedings and the entry or the act affects its rights, cancellation or revocation shall be determined even if the error was not evident to the party.

2. Cancellation or revocation as referred to in paragraph 1 shall be determined, ex officio or at the request of one of the parties to the proceedings, by the department which made the entry or took the decision. Cancellation or revocation shall be determined within six months from the date on which the entry was made in the Register or the decision was taken, after consultation with the parties to the proceedings and any proprietor of rights to the Community trade mark in question that are entered in the Register.

3. This Article shall be without prejudice to the right of the parties to submit an appeal under Articles 57 and 63, or to the possibility, under the procedures and conditions laid down by the Implementing Regulation referred to in Article 157(1), of correcting any linguistic errors or errors of transcription and obvious errors in the Office's decisions or errors attributable to the Office in registering the trade mark or in publishing its registration.

Amendment

Article 77a was inserted by Regulation 422/2004. This amendment shall apply when the necessary implementing measures have been adopted.

Article 78
Restitutio in Integrum

A8–083   1. The applicant for or proprietor of a Community trade mark or any other party to proceedings before the Office who, in spite of all due care required by the circumstances having been taken, was unable to observe a time limit *vis-à-vis* the Office shall, upon application, have his rights re-established if the non-observance in question has the direct consequence, by virtue of the provisions of this Regulation, of causing the loss of any right or means of redress.

2. The application must be filed in writing within two months from the removal of the cause of non-compliance with the time limit. The omitted act must be completed within this period. The application shall only be admissible within the year immediately following the expiry of the unobserved time limit. In the case of non-submission of the request for renewal of registration or of non-payment of a renewal fee, the further period of six months provided in Article 47(3), third sentence, shall be deducted from the period of one year.

3. The application must state the grounds on which it is based and must set out the facts on which it relies. It shall not be deemed to be filed until the fee for re-establishment of rights has been paid.

4. The department competent to decide on the omitted act shall decide upon the application.

[5. The provisions of this Article shall not be applicable to the time limits referred to in paragraph 2 of this Article, Articles 29(1) and 42(1).]

5. This Article shall not be applicable to the time limits referred to in paragraph 2 of this Article, Article 42(1) and (3) and Article 78a.

6. Where the applicant for or proprietor of a Community trade mark has his rights re-established, he may not invoke his rights vis-à-vis a third party who, in good faith, has put goods on the market or supplied services under a sign which is

identical with or similar to the Community trade mark in the course of the period between the loss of rights in the application or in the Community trade mark and publication of the mention of re-establishment of those rights.

7. A third party who may avail himself of the provisions of paragraph 6 may bring third party proceedings against the decision re-establishing the rights of the applicant for or proprietor of a Community trade mark within a period of two months as from the date of publication of the mention of re-establishment of those rights.

8. Nothing in this Article shall limit the right of a Member State to grant *restitutio in integrum* in respect of time limits provided for in this Regulation and to be observed *vis-à-vis* the authorities of such State.

Amendment

The words in bold replaced the words in italics as amended by Regulation 422/2004.

Article 78a

Continuation of Proceedings

1. An applicant for or proprietor of a Community trade mark or any other party to proceedings before the Office who has omitted to observe a time limit vis-a-vis the Office may, upon request, obtain the continuation of proceedings, provided that at the time the request is made the omitted act has been carried out. The request for continuation of proceedings shall be admissible only if it is presented within two months following the expiry of the unobserved time limit. The request shall not be deemed to have been filed until the fee for continuation of the proceedings has been paid.   A8–084

2. This Article shall not be applicable to the time limits laid down in Article 25(3), Article 27, Article 29(1), Article 33(1), Article 36(2), Article 42, Article 43, Article 47(3), Article 59, Article 60a, Article 63(5), Article 78, Article 108, or to the time limits laid down in this Article or the time limits laid down by the Implementing Regulation referred to in Article 157(1) for claiming priority within the meaning of Article 30, exhibition priority within the meaning of Article 33 or seniority within the meaning of Article 34 after the application has been filed.

3. The department competent to decide on the omitted act shall decide upon the application.

4. If the Office accepts the application, the consequences of having failed to observe the time limit shall be deemed not to have occurred.

5. If the Office rejects the application, the fee shall be refunded.

Amendment

Article 78a was inserted by Regulation 422/2004. This amendment shall apply when the necessary implementing measures have been adopted.

Article 79

Reference to General Principles

In the absence of procedural provisions in this Regulation, the Implementing Regulation, the fees regulations or the rules of procedure of the Boards of Appeal, the Office shall take into account the principles of procedural law generally recognized in the Member States.   A8–085

Article 80

Termination of Financial Obligations

A8–086   1. Rights of the Office to the payment of a fee shall be extinguished after four years from the end of the calendar year in which the fee fell due.

2. Rights against the Office for the refunding of fees or sums of money paid in excess of a fee shall be extinguished after four years from the end of the calendar year in which the right arose.

3. The period laid down in paragraphs 1 and 2 shall be interrupted in the case covered by paragraph 1 by a request for payment of the fee and in the case covered by paragraph 2 by a reasoned claim in writing. On interruption it shall begin again immediately and shall end at the latest six years after the end of the year in which it originally began, unless, in the meantime, judicial proceedings to enforce the right have begun; in this case the period shall end at the earliest one year after the judgement has acquired the authority of a final decision.

Section 2 —Costs

Article 81

Costs

A8–087   1. The losing party in opposition proceedings, proceedings for revocation, proceedings for a declaration of invalidity or appeal proceedings shall bear the fees incurred by the other party as well as all costs, without prejudice to Article 115(6), incurred by him essential to the proceedings, including travel and subsistence and the remuneration of an agent, adviser or advocate, within the limits of the scales set for each category of costs under the conditions laid down in the Implementing Regulation.

2. However, where each party succeeds on some and fails on other heads, or if reasons of equity so dictate, the Opposition Division, Cancellation Division or Board of Appeal shall decide a different apportionment of costs.

3. The party who terminates the proceedings by withdrawing the Community trade mark application, the opposition, the application for revocation of rights, the application for a declaration of invalidity or the appeal, or by not renewing registration of the Community trade mark or by surrendering the Community trade mark, shall bear the fees and the costs incurred by the other party as stipulated in paragraphs 1 and 2.

4. Where a case does not proceed to judgment the costs shall be at the discretion of the Opposition Division, Cancellation Division or Board of Appeal.

5. Where the parties conclude before the Opposition Division, Cancellation Division or Board of Appeal a settlement of costs differing from that provided for in the preceding paragraphs, the department concerned shall take note of that agreement.

[6. On request the registry of the Opposition Division or Cancellation Division or Board of Appeal shall fix the amount of the costs to be paid pursuant to the preceding paragraphs. The amount so determined may be reviewed by a decision of the Opposition Division or Cancellation Division or Board of Appeal on a request filed within the prescribed period.]

6. The Opposition Division or Cancellation Division or Board of Appeal shall fix the amount of the costs to be paid pursuant to the preceding

paragraphs when the costs to be paid are limited to the fees paid to the Office and the representation costs. In all other cases, the registry of the Board of Appeal or a member of the staff of the Opposition Division or Cancellation Division shall fix the amount of the costs to be reimbursed on request. The request is admissible only within two months of the date on which the decision for which an application was made for the costs to be fixed became final. The amount so determined may be reviewed by a decision of the Opposition Division or Cancellation Division or Board of Appeal on a request filed within the prescribed period.

Amendment

The words in bold replaced the words in italics as amended by Regulation 422/2004. This amendment shall apply when the necessary implementing measures have been adopted.

Article 82

Enforcement of Decisions Fixing the Amount of Costs

1. Any final decision of the Office fixing the amount of costs shall be   **A8–088** enforceable.

2. Enforcement shall be governed by the rules of civil procedure in force in the State in the territory of which it is carried out. The order for its enforcement shall be appended to the decision, without other formality than verification of the authenticity of the decision, by the national authority which the Government of each Member State shall designate for this purpose and shall make known to the Office and to the Court of Justice.

3. When these formalities have been completed on application by the party concerned, the latter may proceed to enforcement in accordance with the national law, by bringing the matter directly before the competent authority.

4. Enforcement may be suspended only by a decision of the Court of Justice. However, the courts of the country concerned shall have jurisdiction over complaints that enforcement is being carried out in an irregular manner.

Section 3 —Information of the Public and of the Official Authorities of the Member States

Article 83

Register of Community Trade Marks

The Office shall keep a register to be known as the Register of Community   **A8–089** trade marks, which shall contain those particulars the registration or inclusion of which is provided for by this Regulation or by the Implementing Regulation. The Register shall be open to public inspection.

Article 84

Inspection of Files

1. The files relating to Community trade mark applications which have not yet   **A8–090** been published shall not be made available for inspection without the consent of the applicant.

2. Any person who can prove that the applicant for a Community trade mark has stated that after the trade mark has been registered he will invoke the rights

under it against him may obtain inspection of the files prior to the publication of that application and without the consent of the applicant.

3. Subsequent to the publication of the Community trade mark application, the files relating to such application and the resulting trade mark may be inspected on request.

4. However, where the files are inspected pursuant to paragraphs 2 or 3, certain documents in the file may be withheld from inspection in accordance with the provisions of the Implementing Regulation.

Article 85

Periodical Publications

A8–091   The Office shall periodically publish:
   (a) a Community Trade Marks Bulletin containing entries made in the Register of Community trade marks as well as other particulars the publication of which is prescribed by this Regulation or by the Implementing Regulation;
   (b) an Official Journal containing notices and information of a general character issued by the President of the Office, as well as any other information relevant to this Regulation or its implementation.

Article 86

Administrative Cooperation

A8–092   Unless otherwise provided in this Regulation or in national laws, the Office and the courts or authorities of the Member States shall on request give assistance to each other by communicating information or opening files for inspection. Where the Office lays files open to inspection by courts, Public Prosecutors' Offices or central industrial property offices, the inspection shall not be subject to the restrictions laid down in Article 84.

Article 87

Exchange of Publications

A8–093   1. The Office and the central industrial property offices of the Member States shall despatch to each other on request and for their own use one or more copies of their respective publications free of charge.

2. The Office may conclude agreements relating to the exchange or supply of publications.

Section 4 —Representation

Article 88

General Principles of Representation

A8–094   1. Subject to the provisions of paragraph 2, no person shall be compelled to be represented before the Office.

2. Without prejudice to paragraph 3, second sentence, natural or legal persons not having either their domicile or their principal place of business or a real and effective industrial or commercial establishment in the Community must be represented before the Office in accordance with Article 89(1) in all proceedings established by this Regulation, other than in filing an application for a Community trade mark; the Implementing Regulation may permit other exceptions.

[3. *Natural or legal persons having their domicile or principal place of business or a real and effective industrial or commercial establishment in the Community may be represented before the Office by an employee, who must file with it a signed authorization for insertion on the files, the details of which are set out in the Implementing Regulation.*] **3. Natural or legal persons having their domicile or principal place of business or a real and effective industrial or commercial establishment in the Community may be represented before the Office by an employee.** An employee of a legal person to which this paragraph applies may also represent other legal persons which have economic connections with the first legal person, even if those other legal persons have neither their domicile nor their principal place of business nor a real and effective industrial or commercial establishment within the Community.

4. The Implementing Regulation shall specify whether and under what conditions an employee must file with the Office a signed authorisation for insertion on the file.

Amendment

The words in bold replaced the words in italics as amended by Regulation 422/2004. This amendment shall apply when the necessary implementing measures have been adopted.

Article 89

Professional Representatives

1. Representation of natural or legal persons before the Office may only be undertaken by;   **A8–095**

(a) any legal practitioner qualified in one of the Member States and having his place of business within the Community, to the extent that he is entitled, within the said State, to act as a representative in trade mark matters; or

[(b) professional representatives whose names appear on the list maintained for this purpose by the Office.]

(b) professional representatives whose names appear on the list maintained for this purpose by the Office. The Implementing Regulation shall specify whether and under what conditions the representatives before the Office must file with the Office a signed authorisation for insertion on the file.

Representatives acting before the Office must file with it a signed authorization for insertion on the files, the details of which are set out in the Implementing Regulation.

2. Any natural person who fulfils the following conditions may be entered on the list of professional representatives:

(a) he must be a national of one of the Member States;

(b) he must have his place of business or employment in the Community;

(c) [*he must be entitled to represent natural or legal persons in trade mark matters before the central industrial property office of the Member State in which he has his place of business or employment.*] **he must be entitled to represent natural or legal persons in trade mark matters before the central industrial property office of a Member State.** Where, in that State, the entitlement is not conditional upon the requirement of special professional qualifications, persons applying to be entered on the list who act in trade mark matters before the central industrial property office of the said State must have habitually so acted for at least five years. However, persons whose professional qualification to represent natural or legal persons in trade mark matters before the central industrial property office of one of the Member States is officially recognized in accordance with the regulations laid down by such State shall not be subject to the condition of having exercised the profession.

3. Entry shall be effected upon request, accompanied by a certificate furnished by the central industrial property office of the Member State concerned, which must indicate that the conditions laid down in paragraph 2 are fulfilled.

4. The President of the Office may grant exemption from:

(a) the requirement of paragraph 2(c), second sentence, if the applicant furnishes proof that he has acquired the requisite qualification in another way;

(b) the requirement of paragraph 2(a) in special circumstances.

5. The conditions under which a person may be removed from the list of professional representatives shall be laid down in the Implementing Regulation.

Amendment

The words in bold replaced the words in italics as amended by Regulation 422/2004. This amendment shall apply when the necessary implementing measures have been adopted.

TITLE X

JURISDICTION AND PROCEDURE IN LEGAL ACTIONS RELATING TO COMMUNITY TRADE MARKS

Section 1 — Application of the Convention on Jurisdiction and Enforcement

Article 90

Application of the Convention on Jurisdiction and Enforcement

A8–096   1. Unless otherwise specified in this Regulation, the Convention on Jurisdiction and the Enforcement of Judgments in Civil and Commercial Matters, signed in Brussels on 27 September 1968, as amended by the Conventions on the Accession to that Convention of the States acceding to the European Communities, the whole of which Convention and of which Conventions of Accession are hereinafter referred to as the "Convention on Jurisdiction and Enforcement", shall apply to proceedings relating to Community trade marks and applications for Community trade marks, as well as to proceedings relating to simultaneous and successive actions on the basis of Community trade marks and national trade marks.

2. In the case of proceedings in respect of the actions and claims referred to in Article 92:

(a) Articles 2, 4, 5(1), (3), (4) and (5) and Article 24 of the Convention on Jurisdiction and Enforcement shall not apply;

(b) Articles 17 and 18 of that Convention shall apply subject to the limitations in Article 93(4) of this Regulation;

(c) the provisions of Title II of that Convention which are applicable to persons domiciled in a Member State shall also be applicable to persons who do not have a domicile in any Member State but have an establishment therein.

Section 2 —Disputes Concerning the Infringement and Validity of Community Trade Marks

Article 91

Community Trade Mark Courts

1. The Member States shall designate in their territories as limited a number as possible of national courts and tribunals of first and second instance, hereinafter referred to as "Community trade mark courts", which shall perform the functions assigned to them by this Regulation.

A8–097

2. Each Member State shall communicate to the Commission within three years of the entry into force of this Regulation a list of Community trade mark courts indicating their names and their territorial jurisdiction.

3. Any change made after communication of the list referred to in paragraph 2 in the number, names or territorial jurisdiction of the courts shall be notified without delay by the Member State concerned to the Commission.

4. The information referred to in paragraphs 2 and 3 shall be notified by the Commission to the Member States and published in the Official Journal of the European Communities.

5. As long as a Member State has not communicated the list as stipulated in paragraph 2, jurisdiction for any proceedings resulting from an action or application covered by Article 92, and for which the courts of that State have jurisdiction under Article 93, shall lie with that court of the State in question which would have jurisdiction *ratione loci* and *ratione materiae* in the case of proceedings relating to a national trade mark registered in that State.

Article 92

Jurisdiction Over Infringement and Validity

The Community trade mark courts shall have exclusive jurisdiction:

A8–098

(a) for all infringement actions and—if they are permitted under national law—actions in respect of threatened infringement relating to Community trade marks;

(b) for actions for declaration of non-infringement, if they are permitted under national law;

(c) for all actions brought as a result of acts referred to in Article 9(3), second sentence;

(d) for counterclaims for revocation or for a declaration of invalidity of the Community trade mark pursuant to Article 96.

Article 93

International Jurisdiction

1. Subject to the provisions of this Regulations as well as to any provisions of the Convention on Jurisdiction and Enforcement applicable by virtue of Article 90, proceedings in respect of the actions and claims referred to in Article 92 shall be brought in the courts of the Member State in which the defendant is domiciled or, if he is not domiciled in any of the Member States, in which he has an establishment.

A8–099

2. If the defendant is neither domiciled nor has an establishment in any of the Member States, such proceedings shall be brought in the courts of the Member

State in which the plaintiff is domiciled or, if he is not domiciled in any of the Member States, in which he has an establishment.

3. If neither the defendant nor the plaintiff is so domiciled or has such an establishment, such proceedings shall be brought in the courts of the Member State where the Office has its seat.

4. Notwithstanding the provisions of paragraphs 1, 2 and 3:

(a) Article 17 of the Convention on Jurisdiction and Enforcement shall apply if the parties agree that a different Community trade mark court shall have jurisdiction;

(b) Article 18 of that Convention shall apply if the defendant enters an appearance before a different Community trade mark court.

5. Proceedings in respect of the actions and claims referred to in Article 92, with the exception of actions for a declaration of non-infringement of a Community trade mark, may also be brought in the courts of the Member State in which the act of infringement has been committed or threatened, or in which an act within the meaning of Article 9(3), second sentence, has been committed.

Article 94

Extent of Jurisdiction

A8–100   1. A Community trade mark court whose jurisdiction is based on Article 93(1) to (4) shall have jurisdiction in respect of:

— acts of infringement committed or threatened within the territory of any of the Member States,

— acts within the meaning of Article 9(3), second sentence, committed within the territory of any of the Member States.

2. A Community trade mark court whose jurisdiction is based on Article 93(5) shall have jurisdiction only in respect of acts committed or threatened within the territory of the Member State in which that court is situated.

Article 95

Presumption of Validity—Defence as to the Merits

A8–101   1. The Community trade mark courts shall treat the Community trade mark as valid unless its validity is put in issue by the defendant with a counterclaim for revocation or for a declaration of invalidity.

2. The validity of a Community trade mark may not be put in issue in an action for a declaration of non-infringement.

3. In the actions referred to in Article 92(a) and (c) a plea relating to revocation or invalidity of the Community trade mark submitted otherwise than by way of a counterclaim shall be admissible in so far as the defendant claims that the rights of the proprietor of the Community trade mark could be revoked for lack of use or that Community trade mark could be declared invalid on account of an earlier right of the defendant.

Article 96

Counterclaims

A8–102   1. A counterclaim for revocation or for a declaration of invalidity may only be based on the grounds for revocation or invalidity mentioned in this Regulation.

2. A Community trade mark court shall reject a counterclaim for revocation or

for a declaration of invalidity if a decision taken by the Office relating to the same subject matter and cause of action and involving the same parties has already become final.

3. If the counterclaim is brought in a legal action to which the proprietor of the trade mark is not already a party, he shall be informed thereof and may be joined as a party to the action in accordance with the conditions set out in national law.

4. The Community trade mark court with which a counterclaim for revocation or for a declaration of invalidity of the Community trade mark has been filed shall inform the Office of the date on which the counterclaim was filed. The latter shall record this fact in the Register of Community trade marks.

[5. Article 56(3), (4), (5) and (6) shall apply.]

5. Article 56(2) to (5) shall apply.

6. Where a Community trade mark court has given a judgment which has become final on a counterclaim for revocation or for invalidity of a Community trade mark, a copy of the judgment shall be sent to the Office. Any party may request information about such transmission. The Office shall mention the judgment in the Register of Community trade marks in accordance with the provisions of the Implementing Regulation.

7. The Community trade mark court hearing a counterclaim for revocation or for a declaration of invalidity may stay the proceedings on application by the proprietor of the Community trade mark and after hearing the other parties and may request the defendant to submit an application for revocation or for a declaration of invalidity to the Office within a time limit which it shall determine. If the application is not made within the time limit, the proceedings shall continue; the counterclaim shall be deemed withdrawn. Article 100(3) shall apply.

Amendment

The words in bold replaced the words in italics as amended by Regulation 422/2004.

Article 97

Applicable Law

1. The Community trade mark courts shall apply the provisions of this Regulation.   **A8–103**

2. On all matters not covered by this Regulation a Community trade mark court shall apply its national law, including its private international law.

3. Unless otherwise provided in this Regulation, a Community trade mark court shall apply the rules of procedure governing the same type of action relating to a national trade mark in the Member State where it has its seat.

Article 98

Sanctions

1. Where a Community trade mark court finds that the defendant has infringed   **A8–104**
or threatened to infringe a Community trade mark, it shall, unless there are special reasons for not doing so, issue an order prohibiting the defendant from proceeding with the acts which infringed or would infringe the Community trade mark. It shall also take such measures in accordance with its national law as are aimed at ensuring that this prohibition is complied with.

2. In all other respects the Community trade mark court shall apply the law of

the Member State to which the acts of infringement or threatened infringement were committed, including the private international law.

Article 99
Provisional and Protective Measures

A8–105   1. Application may be made to the courts of a Member State, including Community trade mark courts, for such provisional, including protective, measures in respect of a Community trade mark or Community trade mark application as may be available under the law of that State in respect of a national trade mark, even if, under this Regulation, a Community trade mark court of another Member State has jurisdiction as to the substance of the matter.

2. A Community trade mark court whose jurisdiction is based on Article 93(1), (2), (3) or (4) shall have jurisdiction to grant provisional and protective measures which, subject to any necessary procedure for recognition and enforcement pursuant to Title III of the Convention on Jurisdiction and Enforcement, are applicable in the territory of any Member State. No other court shall have such jurisdiction.

Article 100
Specific Rules on Related Actions

A8–106   1. A Community trade mark court hearing an action referred to in Article 92, other than an action for a declaration of non-infringement shall, unless there are special grounds for continuing the hearing, of its own motion after hearing the parties or at the request of one of the parties and after hearing the other parties, stay the proceedings where the validity of the Community trade mark is already in issue before another Community trade mark court on account of a counterclaim or where an application for revocation or for a declaration of invalidity has already been filed at the Office.

2. The Office, when hearing an application for revocation or for a declaration of invalidity shall, unless there are special grounds for continuing the hearing, of its own motion after hearing the parties or at the request of one of the parties and after hearing the other parties, stay the proceedings where the validity of the Community trade mark is already in issue on account of a counterclaim before a Community trade mark court. However, if one of the parties to the proceedings before the Community trade mark court so requests, the court may, after hearing the other parties to these proceedings, stay the proceedings. The Office shall in this instance continue the proceedings pending before it.

3. Where the Community trade mark court stays the proceedings it may order provisional and protective measures for the duration of the stay.

Article 101
Jurisdiction of Community Trade Mark Courts of Second
Instance—Further Appeal

A8–107   1. An appeal to the Community trade mark courts of second instance shall lie from judgments of the Community trade mark courts of first instance in respect of proceedings arising from the actions and claims referred to in Article 92.

2. The conditions under which an appeal may be lodged with a Community trade mark court of second instance shall be determined by the national law of the Member State in which that court is located.

3. The national rules concerning further appeal shall be applicable in respect of judgments of Community trade mark courts of second instance.

Section 3 —Other Disputes Concerning Community Trade Marks

Article 102

Supplementary Provisions on the Jurisdiction of National Courts other than Community Trade Mark Courts

1. Within the Member State whose courts have jurisdiction under Article 90(1)   **A8–108** those courts shall have jurisdiction for actions other than those referred to in Article 92, which would have jurisdiction *ratione loci* and *ratione materiae* in the case of actions relating to a national trade mark registered in that State.

2. Actions relating to a Community trade mark, other than those referred to in Article 92, for which no court has jurisdiction under Article 90(1) and paragraph 1 of this Article may be heard before the courts of the Member State in which the Office has its seat.

Article 103

Obligation of the National Court

A national court which is dealing with an action relating to a Community trade   **A8–109** mark, other than the action referred to in Article 92, shall treat the trade mark as valid.

Section 4 —Transitional Provision

Article 104

Transitional Provision Relating to the Application of the Convention on Jurisdiction and Enforcement

The provisions of the Convention on Jurisdiction and Enforcement which are   **A8–110** rendered applicable by the preceding Article shall have effect in respect of any Member State solely in the text of the Convention which is in force in respect of that State at any given time.

TITLE XI

EFFECTS ON THE LAWS OF THE MEMBER STATES

Section 1 —Civil Actions on the Basis of More Than one Trade Mark

Article 105

Simultaneous and Successive Civil Actions on the Basis of Community Trade Marks and National Trade Marks

1. Where actions for infringement involving the same cause of action and be-   **A8–111** tween the same parties are brought in the courts of different Member States, one seized on the basis of a Community trade mark and the other seized on the basis of a national trade mark:

(a) the court other than the court first seized shall of its own motion decline jurisdiction in favour of that court where the trade marks concerned are identical and valid for identical goods or services. The court which would be required to decline jurisdiction may stay its proceedings if the jurisdiction of the other court is contested;

(b) the court other than the court first seized may stay its proceedings where the trade marks concerned are identical and valid for similar goods or services and where the trade marks concerned are similar and valid for identical or similar goods or services.

2. The court hearing an action for infringement on the basis of a Community trade mark shall reject the action if a final judgment on the merits has been given on the same cause of action and between the same parties on the basis of an identical national trade mark valid for identical goods or services.

3. The court hearing an action for infringement on the basis of a national trade mark shall reject the action if a final judgment on the merits has been given on the same cause of action and between the same parties on the basis of an identical Community trade mark valid for identical goods or services.

4. Paragraphs 1, 2 and 3 shall not apply in respect of provisional, including protective, measures.

Section 2 —Application of National Laws for the Purpose of Prohibiting the use of Community Trade Marks

Article 106

Prohibition of Use of Community Trade Marks

A8–112 1. This Regulation shall, unless otherwise provided for, not affect the right existing under the laws of the Member States to invoke claims for infringement of earlier rights within the meaning of Article 8 or Article 52(2) in relation to the use of a later Community trade mark. Claims for infringement of earlier rights within the meaning of Article 8(2) and (4) may, however, no longer be invoked if the proprietor of the earlier right may no longer apply for a declaration that the Community trade mark is invalid in accordance with Article 53(2).

2. This Regulation shall, unless otherwise provided for, not affect the right to bring proceedings under the civil, administrative or criminal law of a Member Sate or under provisions of Community law for the purpose of prohibiting the use of a Community trade mark to the extent that the use of a national trade mark may be prohibited under the law of that Member State or under Community law.

Article 107

Prior Rights Applicable to Particular Localities

A8–113 1. The proprietor of an earlier right which only applies to a particular locality may oppose the use of the Community trade mark in the territory where his right is protected in so far as the law of the Member State concerned so permits.

2. Paragraph 1 shall cease to apply if the proprietor of the earlier right has acquiesced in the use of the Community trade mark in the territory where his right is protected for a period of five successive years, being aware of such use, unless the Community trade mark was applied for in bad faith.

3. The proprietor of the Community trade mark shall not be entitled to oppose use of the right referred to in paragraph 1 even though that right may no longer be invoked against the Community trade mark.

Section 3 —Conversion into a National Trade Mark Application

Article 108

Request for the Application of National Procedure

1. The applicant for or proprietor of a Community trade mark may request the conversion of his Community trade mark application or Community trade mark into a national trade mark application:

    (a) to the extent that the Community trade mark application is refused, withdrawn, or deemed to be withdrawn;

    (b) to the extent that the Community trade mark ceases to have effect.

2. Conversion shall not take place:

    (a) where the rights of the proprietor of the Community trade mark have been revoked on the grounds of non-use, unless in the Member State for which conversion is requested the Community trade mark has been put to use which would be considered to be genuine use under the laws of that Member State;

    (b) for the purpose of protection in a Member State in which, in accordance with the decision of the Office or of the national court, grounds for refusal of registration or grounds for revocation or invalidity apply to the Community trade mark application or Community trade mark.

3. The national trade mark application resulting from the conversion of a Community trade mark application or a Community trade mark shall enjoy in respect of the Member State concerned the date of filing or the date of priority of that application or trade mark and, where appropriate, the seniority of a trade mark of that State claimed under Article 34 or 35.

[4. Where:

    — *the Community trade mark application is deemed to be withdrawn or is refused by a decision of the Office which has become final,*

    — *the Community trade mark ceases to have effect as a result of a decision of the Office which has become final or as a result of registration of surrender of the Community trade mark,*

the Office shall notify to the applicant or proprietor a communication fixing a period of three months from the date of that communication in which a request for conversion may be filed.

5. Where the Community trade mark application is withdrawn or the Community trade mark ceases to have effect as a result of failure to renew the registration, the request for conversion shall be filed within three months after the date on which the Community trade mark application is withdrawn or on which the registration of the Community trade mark expires.

6. Where the Community trade mark ceases to have effect as a result of a decision of a national court, the request for conversion shall be filed within three months after the date on which that decision acquired the authority of a final decision.]

4. In cases where a Community trade mark application is deemed to be withdrawn, the Office shall send to the applicant a communication fixing a period of three months from the date of that communication in which a request for conversion may be filed.

5. Where the Community trade mark application is withdrawn or the Community trade mark ceases to have effect as a result of a surrender being recorded or of failure to renew the registration, the request for conversion

A8–114

shall be filed within three months after the date on which the Community trade mark application has been withdrawn or on which the Community trade mark ceases to have effect.

6. Where the Community trade mark application is refused by decision of the Office or where the Community trade mark ceases to have effect as a result of a decision of the Office or of a Community trade mark court, the request for conversion shall be filed within three months after the date on which that decision acquired the authority of a final decision.

7. The effect referred to in Article 32 shall lapse if the request is not filed in due time.

Amendment

The words in bold replaced the words in italics as amended by Regulation 422/2004.

Article 109

Submission, Publication and Transmission of the Request for Conversion

A8–115   1. A request for conversion shall be filed with the Office and shall specify the Member States in which application of the procedure for registration of a national trade mark is desired. The request shall not be deemed to be filed until the conversion fee has been paid.

2. If the Community trade mark application has been published, receipt of any such request shall be recorded in the Register of Community trade marks and the request for conversion shall be published.

[3. The Office shall check whether conversion may be requested in accordance with Article 108(1), whether the request has been filed within the period laid down in Article 108(4), (5) or (6), as the case may be, and whether the conversion fee has been paid. If these conditions are fulfilled, the Office shall transmit the request to the central industrial property offices of the States specified therein. At the request of the central industrial property office of a State concerned, the Office shall give it any information enabling that office to decide as to the admissibility of the request.]

3. The Office shall check whether the conversion requested fulfils the conditions set out in this Regulation, in particular Article 108(1), (2), (4), (5) and (6), and paragraph 1 of this Article, together with the formal conditions laid down in the Implementing Regulation. If these conditions are fulfilled, the Office shall transmit the request for conversion to the industrial property offices of the Member States specified therein.

Amendment

The words in bold replaced the words in italics as amended by Regulation 422/2004.

Article 110

Formal Requirements for Conversion

A8–116   *[1. Any central industrial property office to which the request is transmitted shall decide as to its admissibility.]*

1. Any central industrial property office to which the request for conversion is transmitted may obtain from the Office any additional information concerning the request enabling that office to make a decision regarding the national trade mark resulting from the conversion.

2. A Community trade mark application or a Community trade mark transmitted in accordance with Article 109 shall not be subjected to formal requirements of national law which are different from or additional to those provided for in this Regulation or in the Implementing Regulation.

3. Any central industrial property office to which the request is transmitted may require that the applicant shall, within not less than two months:

(a) pay the national application fee;
(b) file a translation in one of the official languages of the State in question of the request and of the documents accompanying it;
(c) indicate an address for service in the State in question;
(d) supply a representation of the trade mark in the number of copies specified by the State in question.

Amendment

The words in bold replaced the words in italics as amended by Regulation 422/2004.

Title XII

The Office

Section 1 —General Provisions

Article 111

Legal Status

1. The Office shall be a body of the Community. It shall have legal personality.   **A8–117**

2. In each of the Member States the Office shall enjoy the most extensive legal capacity accorded to legal persons under their laws; it may, in particular, acquire or dispose of movable and immovable property and may be a party to legal proceedings.

3. The Office shall be represented by its President.

Article 112

Staff

1. The Staff Regulations of officials of the European Communities, the Conditions of Employment of other servants of the European Communities, and the   **A8–118**
rules adopted by agreement between the Institutions of the European Communities for giving effect to those Staff Regulations and Conditions of Employment shall apply to the staff of the Office, without prejudice to the application of Article 131 to the members of the Boards of Appeal.

2. Without prejudice to Article 120, the powers conferred on each Institution by the Staff Regulations and by the Conditions of Employment of other servants shall be exercised by the Office in respect of its staff.

Article 113

Privileges and Immunities

The Protocol on the Privileges and Immunities of the European Communities   **A8–119**
shall apply to the Office.

Article 114
Liability

A8–120   1. The contractual liability of the Office shall be governed by the law applicable to the contract in question.

2. The Court of Justice shall be competent to give judgment pursuant to any arbitration clause contained in a contract concluded by the Office.

3. In the case of non-contractual liability, the Office shall, in accordance with the general principles common to the laws of the Member States, make good any damage caused by its departments or by its servants in the performance of their duties.

4. The Court of Justice shall have jurisdiction in disputes relating to compensation for the damage referred to in paragraph 3.

5. The personal liability of its servants towards the Office shall be governed by the provisions laid down in their Staff Regulations or in the Conditions of Employment applicable to them.

Article 115
Languages

A8–121   1. The application for a Community trade mark shall be filed in one of the official languages of the European Community.

2. The languages of the Office shall be English, French, German, Italian and Spanish.

3. The applicant must indicate a second language which shall be a language of the Office the use of which he accepts as a possible language of proceedings for opposition, revocation or invalidity proceedings.

If the application was filed in a language which is not one of the languages of the Office, the Office shall arrange to have the application, as described in Article 26(1), translated into the language indicated by the applicant.

4. Where the applicant for a Community trade mark is the sole party to proceedings before the Office, the language of proceedings shall be the language used for filing the application for a Community trade mark. If the application was made in a language other than the languages of the Office, the Office may send written communications to the applicant in the second language indicated by the applicant in his application.

5. The notice of opposition and an application for revocation or invalidity shall be filed in one of the language of the Office.

6. If the language chosen, in accordance with paragraph 5, for the notice of opposition or the application for revocation or invalidity is the language of the application for a trade mark or the second language indicated when the application was filed, that language shall be the language of the proceedings.

If the language chosen, in accordance with paragraph 5, for the notice of opposition or the application for revocation or invalidity is neither the language of the application for a trade mark not the second language indicated when the application was filed, the opposing party or the party seeking revocation or invalidity shall be required to produce, at his own expense, a translation of his application either into the language of the application for a trade mark, provided that it is a language of the Office, or into the second language indicated when the application was filed. The translation shall be produced within the period prescribed in the implementing regulation. The language into which the application has been translated shall then become the language of the proceedings.

7. Parties to opposition, revocation, invalidity or appeal proceedings may agree that a different official language of the European Community is to be the language of the proceedings.

Article 116

Publication; Entries in the Register

1. An application for a Community trade mark, as described in Article 26(1), and all other information the publication of which is prescribed by this Regulation or the implementing regulation, shall be published in all the official languages of the European Community. **A8–122**

2. All entries in the Register of Community trade marks shall be made in all the official languages of the European Community.

3. In cases of doubt, the text in the language of the Office in which the application for the Community trade mark was filed shall be authentic. If the application was filed in an official language of the European Community other than one of the languages of the Office, the text in the second language indicated by the applicant shall be authentic.

Article 117

The translation services required for the functioning of the office shall be provided by the translation centre of the bodies of the union once this begins operation. **A8–123**

Article 118

Control of Legality

1. The Commission shall check the legality of those acts of the President of the Office in respect of which Community law does not provide for any check on legality by another body and of acts of the Budget Committee attached to the Office pursuant to Article 133. **A8–124**

2. It shall require that any unlawful acts as referred to in paragraph 1 be altered or annulled.

3. Member States and any person directly and personally involved may refer to the Commission any act as referred to in paragraph 1, whether express or implied, for the Commission to examine the legality of that act. Referral shall be made to the Commission [*within 15 days*] **within one month** of the day on which the party concerned first became aware of the act in question. The Commission shall take a decision [*within one month*] **within three months**. If no decision has been taken within this period, the case shall be deemed to have been dismissed.

Amendment

The words in bold replaced the words in italics as amended by Regulation 422/2004.

Article 118a

Access to Documents

1. Regulation (EC) No. 1049/2001 of the European Parliament and of the **A8–125**

Council of 30 May 2001 regarding access to European Parliament, Council and Commission documents shall apply to documents held by the Office.

2. The Administrative Board shall adopt the practical arrangements for implementing Regulation (EC) No. 1049/2001 within six months of entry into force of Regulation (EC) No. 1653/2003 of 18 June 2003 amending Regulation (EC) No. 40/94 on the Community trade mark.

3. Decisions taken by the Office pursuant to Article 8 of Regulation (EC) No. 1049/2001 may give rise to the lodging of a complaint to the Ombudsman or form the subject of an action before the Court of Justice of the European Communities, under the conditions laid down in Articles 195 and 230 of the Treaty respectively.

Amendment

Article 118a added by Regulation 1653/2003.

Section 2 —Management of the Office

Article 119

Powers of the President

A8–126   1. The Office shall be managed by the President.

2. To this end the President shall have in particular the following functions and powers:

(a) he shall take all necessary steps, including the adoption of internal administrative instructions and the publication of notices, to ensure the functioning of the Office;

(b) he may place before the Commission any proposal to amend this Regulation, the Implementing Regulation, the rules of procedure of the Boards of Appeal, the fees regulations and any other rules applying to Community trade marks after consulting the Administrative Board and, in the case of the fees regulations and the budgetary provisions of this Regulation, the Budget Committee;

(c) he shall draw up the estimates of the revenue and expenditure of the Office and shall implement the budget;

(d) he shall submit a management report to the Commission, the European Parliament and the Administrative Board each year;

(e) he shall exercise in respect of the staff the powers laid down in Article 112(2);

(f) he may delegate his powers.

3. The President shall be assisted by one or more Vice-Presidents. If the President is absent or indisposed, the Vice-President or one of the Vice-Presidents shall take his place in accordance with the procedure laid down by the Administrative Board.

Article 120

Appointment of Senior Officials

A8–127   1. The President of the Office shall be appointed by the Council from a list of at most three candidates, which shall be prepared by the Administrative Board. Power to dismiss the President shall lie with the Council, acting on a proposal from the Administrative Board.

2. The term of office of the President shall not exceed five years. This term of office shall be renewable.

3. The Vice-President or Vice-Presidents of the Office shall be appointed or dismissed as in paragraph 1, after consultation of the President.

4. The Council shall exercise disciplinary authority over the officials referred to in paragraphs 1 and 3 of this Article.

Section 3 —Administrative Board

Article 121

Creation and Powers

1. An Administrative Board is hereby set up, attached to the Office. Without prejudice to the powers attributed to the Budget Committee in Section 5—budget and financial control—the Administrative Board shall have the powers defined below.

A8–128

2. The Administrative Board shall draw up the lists of candidates provided for in Article 120.

3. It shall fix the date for the first filing of Community trade mark applications, pursuant to Article 143(3).

4. It shall advise the President on matters for which the Office is responsible.

5. It shall be consulted before adoption of the guidelines for examination in the Office and in the other cases provided for in this Regulation.

6. It may deliver opinions and requests for information to the President and to the Commission where it considers that this is necessary.

Article 122

Composition

1. The Administrative Board shall be composed of one representative of each Member State and one representative of the Commission and their alternates.

A8–129

2. The members of the Administrative Board may, subject to the provisions of its rules of procedure, be assisted by advisers or experts.

Article 123

Chairmanship

1. The Administrative Board shall elect a chairman and a deputy chairman from among its members. The deputy chairman shall *ex officio* replace the chairman in the event of his being prevented from attending to his duties.

A8–130

2. The duration of the terms of office of the chairman and the deputy chairman shall be three years. The terms of office shall be renewable.

Article 124

Meetings

1. Meetings of the Administrative Board shall be convened by its chairman.

A8–131

2. The President of the Office shall take part in the deliberations, unless the Administrative Board decides otherwise.

3. The Administrative Board shall hold an ordinary meeting once a year; in addition, it shall meet on the initiative of its chairman or at the request of the Commission or of one-third of the Member States.

4. The Administrative Board shall adopt rules of procedure.

5. The Administrative Board shall take its decisions by a simple majority of the representatives of the Member States. However, a majority of three-quarters of the representatives of the Member States shall be required for the decisions which the Administrative Board is empowered to take under Article 120(1) and (3). In both cases each Member State shall have one vote.

6. The Administrative Board may invite observers to attend its meetings.

7. The Secretariat for the Administrative Board shall be provided by the Office.

Section 4 —Implementation of Procedures

Article 125

Competence

A8–132   For taking decisions in connection with the procedures laid down in this Regulation, the following shall be competent:

(a) Examiners;

(b) Opposition Divisions;

(c) an Administration of Trade Marks and Legal Division;

(d) Cancellation Divisions;

(e) Boards of Appeal.

Article 126

Examiners

A8–133   An examiner shall be responsible for taking decisions on behalf of the Office in relation to an application for registration of a Community trade mark, including the matters referred to in Articles 36, 37, 38 and 66, except in so far as an Opposition Division is responsible.

Article 127

Opposition Divisions

A8–134   1. An Opposition Division shall be responsible for taking decisions on an opposition to an application to register a Community trade mark.

[2. An Opposition Division shall consist of three members. At least one of the members must be legally qualified.]

2. The decisions of the Opposition Divisions shall be taken by three-member groups. At least one member shall be legally qualified. In certain specific cases provided for in the Implementing Regulation, the decisions shall be taken by a single member.

Amendment

The words in bold replaced the words in italics as amended by Regulation 422/ 2004. This amendment shall apply when the necessary implementing measures have been adopted.

Article 128

Administration of Trade Marks and Legal Division

A8–135   1. The Administration of Trade Marks and Legal Division shall be responsible for those decisions required by this Regulation which do not fall within the competence of an examiner, an Opposition Division or a Cancellation Division. It shall in particular be responsible for decisions in respect of entries in the Register of Community trade marks.

2. It shall also be responsible for keeping the list of professional representatives which is referred to in Article 89.

3. A decision of the Division shall be taken by one member.

Article 129
Cancellation Divisions

1. A Cancellation Division shall be responsible for taking decisions in relation to an application for the revocation or declaration of invalidity of a Community trade mark.

[2. A Cancellation Division shall consist of three members. At least one of the members must be legally qualified.]

2. The decisions of the Cancellation Divisions shall be taken by three-member groups. At least one member shall be legally qualified. In certain specific cases provided for in the Implementing Regulation, the decisions shall be taken by a single member.

Amendment

The words in bold replaced the words in italics as amended by Regulation 422/2004. This amendment shall apply when the necessary implementing measures have been adopted.

Article 130
Boards of Appeal

1. The Boards of Appeal shall be responsible for deciding on appeals from decisions of the examiners, Opposition Divisions, Administration of Trade Marks and Legal Division and Cancellation Divisions.

[2. A Board of Appeal shall consist of three members. At least two of the members must be legally qualified.]

2. The decisions of the Boards of Appeal shall be taken by three members, at least two of whom are legally qualified. In certain specific cases, decisions shall be taken by an enlarged Board chaired by the President of the Boards of Appeal or by a single member, who must be legally qualified.

3. In order to determine the special cases which fall under the jurisdiction of the enlarged Board, account should be taken of the legal difficulty or the importance of the case or of special circumstances which justify it. Such cases may be referred to the enlarged Board:

(a) by the authority of the Boards of Appeal set up in accordance with the rules of procedure of the Boards referred to in Article 157(3), or

(b) by the Board handling the case.

4. The composition of the enlarged Board and the rules on referrals to it shall be laid down pursuant to the rules of procedure of the Boards referred to in Article 157(3).

5. To determine which specific cases fall under the authority of a single member, account should be taken of the lack of difficulty of the legal or factual matters raised, the limited importance of the individual case or the absence of other specific circumstances. The decision to confer a case on one member in the cases referred to shall be adopted by the Board handling the case. Further details shall be laid down in the rules of procedure of the Boards referred to in Article 157(3).

A8–136

A8–137

Amendment

The words in bold replaced the words in italics as amended by Regulation 422/2004. This amendment shall apply when the necessary implementing measures have been adopted.

[Article 131

Independence of the Members of the Boards of Appeal

A8–138   *1. The members, including the chairmen, of the Boards of Appeal shall be appointed, in accordance with the procedure laid down in Article 120, for the appointment of the President of the Office, for a term of five years. They may not be removed from office during this term, unless there are serious grounds for such removal and the Court of Justice, on application by the body which appointed them, takes a decision to this effect. Their term of office shall be renewable.*

2. The members of the Boards of Appeal shall be independent. In their decisions they shall not be bound by any instructions.

3. The members of the Boards of Appeal may not be examiners or members of the Opposition Divisions, Administration of Trade Marks and Legal Division or Cancellation Divisions.]

Article 131

Independence of the Members of the Boards of Appeal

1. The President of the Boards of Appeal and the chairmen of the Boards shall be appointed, in accordance with the procedure laid down in Article 120 for the appointment of the President of the Office, for a term of five years. They may not be removed from office during this term, unless there are serious grounds for such removal and the Court of Justice, on application by the institution which appointed them, takes a decision to this effect. The term of office of the President of Boards of Appeal and the chairmen of the Boards may be renewed for additional five-year periods, or until retirement age if this age is reached during the new term of office.

The President of the Boards of Appeal shall, inter alia, have managerial and organisational powers, principally to:

(a) chair the authority of the Boards of Appeal responsible for laying down the rules and organising the work of the Boards, which authority is provided for in the rules of procedure of the Boards referred to in Article 157(3);

(b) ensure the implementation of the authority's decisions;

(c) allocate cases to a Board on the basis of objective criteria determined by the authority of the Boards of Appeal;

(d) forward to the President of the Office the Boards' expenditure requirements, with a view to drawing up the expenditure estimates.

The President of the Boards of Appeal shall chair the enlarged Board.

Further details shall be laid down in the rules of procedure of the Boards referred to in Article 157(3).

2. The members of the Boards of Appeal shall be appointed by the Administrative Board for a term of five years. Their term of office may be renewed for additional five-year periods, or until retirement age if that age is reached during the new term of office.

3. The members of the Boards of Appeal may not be removed from office unless there are serious grounds for such removal and the Court of Justice,

after the case has been referred to it by the Administrative Board on the recommendation of the President of the Boards of Appeal, after consulting the chairman of the Board to which the member concerned belongs, takes a decision to this effect.

4. The President of the Boards of Appeal and the chairmen and members of the Boards of Appeal shall be independent. In their decisions they shall not be bound by any instructions.

5. The President of the Boards of Appeal and the chairmen and members of the Boards of Appeal may not be examiners or members of the Opposition Divisions, Administration of Trade Marks and Designs and Legal Division or Cancellation Divisions.

Amendment

Article 131 was replaced by Regulation 422/2004. This amendment shall apply when the necessary implementing measures have been adopted.

Article 132

Exclusion and Objection

1. Examiners and members of the Divisions set up within the Office or of the Boards of Appeal may not take part in any proceedings if they have any personal interest therein, or if they have previously been involved as representatives of one of the parties. Two of the three members of an Opposition Division shall not have taken part in examining the application. Members of the Cancellation Divisions may not take part in any proceedings if they have participated in the final decision on the case in the proceedings for registration or opposition proceedings. Members of the Boards of Appeal may not take part in appeal proceedings if they participated in the decision under appeal.   **A8–139**

2. If, for one of the reasons mentioned in paragraph 1 or for any other reason, a member of a Division or of a Board of Appeal considers that he should not take part in any proceedings, he shall inform the Division or Board accordingly.

3. Examiners and members of the Divisions or of a Board of Appeal may be objected to by any party for one of the reasons mentioned in paragraph 1, or if suspected of partiality. An objection shall not be admissible if, while being aware of a reason for objection, the party has taken a procedural step. No objection may be based upon the nationality of examiners or members.

4. The Divisions and the Boards of Appeal shall decide as to the action to be taken in the cases specified in paragraphs 2 and 3 without the participation of the member concerned. For the purposes of taking this decision the member who withdraws or has been objected to shall be replaced in the Division or Board of Appeal by his alternate.

Section 5 —Budget and Financial Control

Article 133

Budget Committee

1. A Budget Committee is hereby set up, attached to the Office. The Budget Committee shall have the powers assigned to it in this Section and in Article 39(4).   **A8–140**

2. Articles 121(6), 122, 123 and 124(1) to (4), (6) and (7) shall apply to the Budget Committee *mutatis mutandis*.

3. The Budget Committee shall take its decisions by a simple majority of the representatives of the Member States. However, a majority of three-quarters of the representatives of the Member States shall be required for the decisions which the Budget Committee is empowered to take under Articles 39(4), 135(3) and 138. In both cases each Member State shall have one vote.

Article 134

Budget

A8–141   1. Estimates of all the Office's revenue and expenditure shall be prepared for each financial year and shall be shown in the Office's budget, and each financial year shall correspond with the calendar year.

2. The revenue and expenditure shown in the budget shall be in balance.

[3. Revenue shall comprise, without prejudice to other types of income, total fees payable under the fees regulations, and, to the extent necessary, a subsidy entered against a specific heading of the general budget of the European Communities, Commission Section.]

3. Revenue shall comprise, without prejudice to other types of income, total fees payable under the fees regulations, total fees payable under the Madrid Protocol referred to in Article 140 for an international registration designating the European Communities and other payments made to Contracting Parties to the Madrid Protocol, and, to the extent necessary, a subsidy entered against a specific heading of the general budget of the European Communities, Commission section 67.

Amendment

The words in bold replaced the words in italics as amended by Regulation 1992/2003. This amendment shall enter into force on the date on which the Madrid Protocol enters into force with respect to the European Community, which will be on October 1, 2004.

Article 135

Preparation of the Budget

A8–142   1. The President shall draw up each year an estimate of the Office's revenue and expenditure for the following year and shall send it to the Budget Committee not later than 31 March in each year, together with a list of posts.

2. Should the budget estimates provide for a Community subsidy, the Budget Committee shall immediately forward the estimate to the Commission, which shall forward it to the budget authority of the Communities. The Commission may attach an opinion on the estimate along with an alternative estimate.

3. The Budget Committee shall adopt the budget, which shall include the Office's list of posts. Should the budget estimates contain a subsidy from the general budget of the Communities, the Office's budget shall, if necessary, be adjusted.

[Article 136

Financial Control

A8–143   *Control of commitment and payment of all expenditure and control of the existence and recovery of all revenue of the Office shall be carried out by the Financial Controller appointed by the Budget Committee.]*

Article 136

Audit and Control

1. An internal audit function shall be set up within the Office, to be performed in compliance with the relevant international standards. The internal auditor, appointed by the President, shall be responsible to him for verifying the proper operation of budget implementation systems and procedures of the Office.

2. The internal auditor shall advise the President on dealing with risks, by issuing independent opinions on the quality of management and control systems and by issuing recommendations for improving the conditions of implementation of operations and promoting sound financial management.

3. The responsibility for putting in place internal control systems and procedures suitable for carrying out his tasks shall lie with the authorising officer.

Amendment

The words in bold replaced the words in italics as amended by Regulation 1653/2003.

Article 137

Auditing of Accounts

1. Not later than 31 March in each year the President shall transmit to the Commission, the European Parliament, the Budget Committee and the Court of Auditors accounts of the Office's total revenue and expenditure for the preceding financial year. The Court of Auditors shall examine them in accordance with Article 188c of the Treaty.   **A8–144**

2. The Budget Committee shall give a discharge to the President of the Office in respect of the implementation of the budget.

Article 138

Financial Provisions

The Budget Committee shall, after consulting the Court of Auditors of the European Communities and the Commission, adopt internal financial provisions specifying, in particular, the procedure for establishing and implementing the Office's budget. As far as is compatible with the particular nature of the Office, the financial provisions shall be based on the financial regulations adopted for other bodies set up by the Community.   **A8–145**

Article 139

Fees Regulations

1. The fees regulations shall determine in particular the amounts of the fees and the ways in which they are to be paid.   **A8–146**

2. The amounts of the fees shall be fixed at such a level as to ensure that the revenue in respect thereof is in principle sufficient for the budget of the Office to be balanced.

3. The fees regulations shall be adopted and amended in accordance with the procedure laid down in Article *141* **158**.

Amendment

The figure in bold replaced the figure in italics as amended by Regulation

1992/2003. This amendment shall enter into force on the date on which the Madrid Protocol enters into force with respect to the European Community, which will be on October 1, 2004.

TITLE XIII

INTERNATIONAL REGISTRATION OF MARKS

A8–147   New Title XIII added by Regulation 1992/2003. This amendment shall enter into force on the date on which the Madrid Protocol enters into force with respect to the European Community, which will be on October 1, 2004.

Section 1 —General Provisions

Article 140

Application of Provisions

Unless otherwise specified in this title, this Regulation and any regulations implementing this Regulation adopted pursuant to Article 158 shall apply to applications for international registrations under the Protocol relating to the Madrid Agreement concerning the international registration of marks, adopted at Madrid on 27 June 1989 (hereafter referred to as "international applications" and "the Madrid Protocol" respectively), based on an application for a Community trade mark or on a Community trade mark and to registrations of marks in the international register maintained by the International Bureau of the World Intellectual Property Organisation (hereafter referred to as "international registrations" and "the International Bureau", respectively) designating the European Community.

Section 2 —International Registration on the Basis of Applications for a Community Trade Mark and of Community Trade Marks

Article 141

Filing of an International Application Regulations

A8–148   1. International applications pursuant to Article 3 of the Madrid Protocol based on an application for a Community trade mark or on a Community trade mark shall be filed at the Office.

2. Where an international application is filed before the mark on which the international registration is to be based has been registered as a Community trade mark, the applicant for the international registration must indicate whether the international registration is to be based on a Community trade mark application or registration. Where the international registration is to be based on a Community trade mark once it is registered, the international application shall be deemed to have been received at the Office on the date of registration of the Community trade mark.

Article 142

Form and Contents of the International Application

A8–149   1. The international application shall be filed in one of the official languages of the European Community, using a form provided by the Office. Unless otherwise specified by the applicant on that form when he files the international application, the Office shall correspond with the applicant in the language of filing in a standard form.

2. If the international application is filed in a language which is not one of the languages allowed under the Madrid Protocol, the applicant must indicate a second language from among those languages. This shall be the language in which the Office submits the international application to the International Bureau.

3. Where the international application is filed in a language other than one of the languages allowed under the Madrid Protocol for the filing of international applications, the applicant may provide a translation of the list of goods or services in the language in which the international application is to be submitted to the International Bureau pursuant to paragraph 2.

4. The Office shall forward the international application to the International Bureau as soon as possible.

5. The filing of an international application shall be subject to the payment of a fee to the Office. In the cases referred to in the second sentence of Article 141(2), the fee shall be due on the date of registration of the Community trade mark. The application shall be deemed not to have been filed until the required fee has been paid.

6. The international application must fulfil the relevant conditions laid down in the Implementing Regulation referred to in Article 157.

Article 143

Recordal in the Files and in the Register

1. The date and number of an international registration based on a Community   **A8–150**
trade mark application, shall be recorded in the files of that application. When the application results in a Community trade mark, the date and number of the international registration shall be entered in the register.

2. The date and number of an international registration based on a Community trade mark shall be entered in the Register.

Article 144

Request for Territorial Extension Subsequent to the International Registration

A request for territorial extension made subsequent to the international registra-   **A8–151**
tion pursuant to Article 3ter(2) of the Madrid Protocol may be filed through the intermediary of the Office. The request must be filed in the language in which the international application was filed pursuant to Article 142.

Article 145

International Fees

Any fees payable to the International Bureau under the Madrid Protocol shall   **A8–152**
be paid direct to the International Bureau.

Section 3 —International Registrations Designating the European Community

Article 146

Effects of International Registrations Designating the European Community

1. An international registration designating the European Community shall,   **A8–153**
from the date of its registration pursuant to Article 3(4) of the Madrid Protocol or from the date of the subsequent designation of the European Community pursu-

ant to Article 3ter(2) of the Madrid Protocol, have the same effect as an application for a Community trade mark.

2. If no refusal has been notified in accordance with Article 5(1) and (2) of the Madrid Protocol or if any such refusal has been withdrawn, the international registration of a mark designating the European Community shall, from the date referred to in paragraph 1, have the same effect as the registration of a mark as a Community trade mark.

3. For the purposes of applying Article 9(3), publication of the particulars of the international registration designating the European Community pursuant to Article 147(1) shall take the place of publication of a Community trade mark application, and publication pursuant to Article 147(2) shall take the place of publication of the registration of a Community trade mark.

Article 147

Publication

A8–154 1. The Office shall publish the date of registration of a mark designating the European Community pursuant to Article 3(4) of the Madrid Protocol or the date of the subsequent designation of the European Community pursuant to Article 3ter(2) of the Madrid Protocol, the language of filing of the international application and the second language indicated by the applicant, the number of the international registration and the date of publication of such registration in the Gazette published by the International Bureau, a reproduction of the mark and the numbers of the classes of the goods or services in respect of which protection is claimed.

2. If no refusal of protection of an international registration designating the European Community has been notified in accordance with Article 5(1) and (2) of the Madrid Protocol or if any such refusal has been withdrawn, the Office shall publish this fact, together with the number of the international registration and, where applicable, the date of publication of such registration in the Gazette published by the International Bureau.

Article 148

Seniority

A8–155 1. The applicant for an international registration designating the European Community may claim, in the international application, the seniority of an earlier trade mark registered in a Member State, including a trade mark registered in the Benelux countries, or registered under international arrangements having effect in a Member State, as provided for in Article 34.

2. The holder of an international registration designating the European Community may, as from the date of publication of the effects of such registration pursuant to Article 147(2), claim at the Office the seniority of an earlier trade mark registered in a Member State, including a trade mark registered in the Benelux countries, or registered under international arrangements having effect in a Member State, as provided for in Article 35. The Office shall notify the International Bureau accordingly.

Article 149

Examination as to Absolute Grounds for Refusal

A8–156 1. International registrations designating the European Community shall be subject to examination as to absolute grounds for refusal in the same way as applications for Community trade marks.

2. Protection of an international registration shall not be refused before the holder of the international registration has been allowed the opportunity to renounce or limit the protection in respect of the European Community or of submitting his observations.

3. Refusal of protection shall take the place of refusal of a Community trade mark application.

4. Where protection of an international registration is refused by a decision under this Article which has become final or where the holder of the international registration has renounced the protection in respect of the European Community pursuant to paragraph 2, the Office shall refund the holder of the international registration a part of the individual fee to be laid down in the implementing Regulation.

Article 150

Search

1. Once the Office has received a notification of an international registration designating the European Community, it shall draw up a Community search report as provided for in Article 39(1).   **A8–157**

2. As soon as the Office has received a notification of an international registration designating the European Community, the Office shall transmit a copy thereof to the central industrial property office of each Member State which has informed the Office of its decision to operate a search in its own register of trade marks as provided for in Article 39(2).

3. Article 39(3) to (6) shall apply mutatis mutandis.

4. The Office shall inform the proprietors of any earlier Community trade marks or Community trade mark applications cited in the Community search report of the publication of the international registration designating the European Community as provided for in Article 147(1).

Amendment

The words in bold were amended by Regulation 422/2004.

Article 151

Opposition

1. International registration designating the European Community shall be subject to opposition in the same way as published Community trade mark applications.   **A8–158**

2. Notice of opposition shall be filed within a period of three months which shall begin six months following the date of the publication pursuant to Article 147(1). The opposition shall not be treated as duly entered until the opposition fee has been paid.

3. Refusal of protection shall take the place of refusal of a Community trade mark application.

4. Where protection of an international registration is refused by a decision under this Article which has become final or where the holder of the international registration has renounced the protection in respect of the European Community prior to a decision under this Article which has become final, the Office shall refund the holder of the international registration a part of the individual fee to be laid down in the implementing Regulation.

Article 152

Replacement of a Community Trade Mark by an International Registration

The Office shall, upon request, enter a notice in the Register that a Community   **A8–159** trade mark is deemed to have been replaced by an international registration in accordance with Article 4bis of the Madrid Protocol.

Article 153

Invalidation of the Effects of an International Registration

A8–160   1. The effects of an international registration designating the European Community may be declared invalid.

2. The application for invalidation of the effects of an international registration designating the European Community shall take the place of an application for a declaration of revocation as provided for in Article 50 or for invalidation as provided for in Article 51 or Article 52.

Article 154

Conversion of a Designation of the European Community through an International Registration into a National Trade Mark Application or into a Designation of Member States

A8–161   1. Where a designation of the European Community through an international registration has been refused or ceases to have effect, the holder of the international registration may request the conversion of the designation of the European Community:

(a) into a national trade mark application pursuant to Articles 108 to 110 or

(b) into a designation of a Member State party to the Madrid Protocol or the Madrid Agreement concerning the international registration of marks, adopted at Madrid on 14 April 1891, as revised and amended (hereafter referred to as the Madrid Agreement), provided that on the date when conversion was requested it was possible to have designated that Member State directly under the Madrid Protocol or the Madrid Agreement. Articles 108 to 110 shall apply.

2. The national trade mark application or the designation of a Member State party to the Madrid Protocol or the Madrid Agreement resulting from the conversion of the designation of the European Community through an international registration shall enjoy, in respect of the Member State concerned, the date of the international registration pursuant to Article 3(4) of the Madrid Protocol or the date of the extension to the European Community pursuant to Article 3ter(2) of the Madrid Protocol if the latter was made subsequently to the international registration, or the date of priority of that registration and, where appropriate, the seniority of a trade mark of that State claimed under Article 148.

3. The request for conversion shall be published.

Article 155

Use of a Mark Subject of an International Registration

A8–162   For the purposes of applying Article 15(1), Article 43(2), Article 50(1)(a) and Article 56(2), the date of publication pursuant to Article 147(2) shall take the place of the date of registration for the purpose of establishing the date as from which the mark which is the subject of an international registration designating the European Community must be put to genuine use in the Community.

Article 156

Transformation

A8–163   1. Subject to paragraph 2, the provisions applicable to Community trade mark applications shall apply mutatis mutandis to applications for transformation of an international registration into a Community trade mark application pursuant to Article 9 of the Madrid Protocol.

2. When the application for transformation relates to an international registration designating the European Community the particulars of which have been published pursuant to Article 147(2), Articles 38 to 43 shall not apply.

TITLE XIV (XIII)

FINAL PROVISIONS

Numbers of the Title and Articles changed by Regulation 1992/2003. This amendment shall enter into force on the date on which the Madrid Protocol enters into force with respect to the European Community, which will be on 01 October 2004.   **A8–164**

Article 157 (140)

Community Implementing Provisions

1. The rules implementing this Regulation shall be adopted in an Implementing Regulation.

2. In addition to the fees provided for in the preceding Articles, fees shall be charged, in accordance with the detailed rules of application laid down in the Implementing Regulation, in the cases listed below:

alteration of the representation of a Community trade mark.

  late payment of the registration fee;

  issue of a copy of the certificate of registration;

registration of the transfer of a Community trade mark.

  registration of a licence or another right in respect of a Community trade mark;

  registration of a licence or another right in respect of an application for a Community trade mark;

  cancellation of the registration of a licence or another right;

  alteration of a registered Community trade mark;

  issue of an extract from the Register;

  inspection of the files;

  issue of copies of file documents;

  issue of certified copies of the application; .

  communication of information in a file;

  review of the determination of the procedural costs to be refunded.

3. The Implementing Regulation and the rules of procedure of the Boards of Appeal shall be adopted and amended in accordance with the procedure laid down in Article 158 (former 141).

Amendment

The words in italics were deleted by Regulation 422/2004. The figures in bold changed by Regulation 1992/2003. This amendment shall enter into force on the date on which the Madrid Protocol enters into force with respect to the European Community, which will be on October 1, 2004.

Article 158 (141)

Establishment of a Committee and Procedure for the Adoption of Implementing Regulations

1. The Commission shall be assisted by a committee referred to as the Com-   **A8–165**

mittee on Fees, Implementation Rules and the Procedure of the Boards of Appeal of the Office for Harmonisation in the Internal Market (trade marks and designs).

2. Where reference is made to this Article, Articles 5 and 7 of Decision 1999/468/EC shall apply. The period laid down in Article 5(6) of Decision 1999/468/EC shall be set at three months.

3. The committee shall adopt its rules of procedure.

Amendment

Amended by Regulation 807/2003.

Article 159 (142)
Compatibility with other Community Legal Provisions

A8–166   This Regulation shall not affect Council Regulation (EEC) No. 2081/92 on the protection of geographical indications and designations of origin for agricultural products and foodstuffs of 14 July1992, and in particular Article 14 thereof.

Article 159a (142a)
Provisions Relating to the Enlargement of the Community

A8–167   1. As from the date of accession of the Czech Republic, Estonia, Cyprus, Latvia, Lithuania, Hungary, Malta, Poland, Slovenia and Slovakia (hereinafter referred to as "new Member State(s)"), a Community trade mark registered or applied for pursuant to this Regulation before the date of accession shall be extended to the territory of those Member States in order to have equal effect throughout the Community.

2. The registration of a Community trade mark which is under application at the date of accession may not be refused on the basis of any of the absolute grounds for refusal listed in Article 7(1), if these grounds became applicable merely because of the accession of a new Member State.

3. Where an application for the registration of a Community trade mark has been filed during the six months prior to the date of accession, notice of opposition may be given pursuant to Article 42 where an earlier trade mark or another earlier right within the meaning of Article 8 was acquired in a new Member State prior to accession, provided that it was acquired in good faith and that the filing date or, where applicable, the priority date or the date of acquisition in the new Member State of the earlier trade mark or other earlier right precedes the filing date or, where applicable, the priority date of the Community trade mark applied for.

4. A Community trade mark as referred to in paragraph 1 may not be declared invalid:
— pursuant to Article 51 if the grounds for invalidity became applicable merely because of the accession of a new Member State,
— pursuant to Article 52(1) and (2) if the earlier national right was registered, applied for or acquired in a new Member State prior to the date of accession.

5. The use of a Community trade mark as referred to in paragraph 1 may be prohibited pursuant to Articles 106 and 107, if the earlier trade mark or other earlier right was registered, applied for or acquired in good faith in the new Member State prior to the date of accession of that State; or, where applicable, has a priority date prior to the date of accession of that State.

Amendment

The figure in bold was changed by Regulation 422/2004. This article entered into force on May 1, 2004.

Article 160 (143)

Entry into Force

1. This Regulation shall enter into force on the 60th day following that of its   **A8–168** publication in the Official Journal of the European Communities.

2. The Member States shall within three years following entry into force of this Regulation take the necessary measures for the purpose of implementing Articles 91 and 110 hereof and shall forthwith inform the Commission of those measures.

3. Applications for Community trade marks may be filed at the Office from the date fixed by the Administrative Board on the recommendation of the President of the Office.

4. Applications for Community trade marks filed within three months before the date referred to in paragraph 3 shall be deemed to have been filed on that date.

This Regulation shall be binding in its entirety and directly applicable in all Member States.

Done at Brussels, December 20,1993.

Council Regulation 3288/94 of December 22, 1994
[1994] O.J. L349/83)

A9–001 *THE COUNCIL OF THE EUROPEAN UNION,*

Having regard to the Treaty establishing the European Community, and in particular Article 235 thereof,

Having regard to the proposal from the Commission,

Having regard to the opinion of the European Parliament (1),

Whereas the Agreement establishing the World Trade Organization (hereinafter, the ' WTO Agreement') was signed on behalf of the Community; whereas the Agreement on Trade-Related Aspects of Intellectual Property Rights (hereinafter, the 'TRIPs Agreement'), annexed to the WTO Agreement, contains detailed provisions on the protection of intellectual property rights whose purpose is the establishment of international disciplines in this area in order to promote international trade and prevent trade distortions and friction due to the lack of adequate and effective intellectual property protection;

Whereas in order to ensure that all relevant Community legislation is in full compliance with the TRIPs Agreement, the Community must take certain measures in relation to current Community acts on the protection of intellectual property rights; whereas these measures entail in some respects the amendment or modification of Community acts; whereas these measures also entail complementing current Community acts;

Whereas Regulation (EC) No 40/94 creates the Community trade mark (2); whereas Article 5 of Regulation (EC) No 40/94 defines the 'Persons who can be proprietors of Community trade marks' by referring notably to the Paris Convention for the protection of industrial property and requires reciprocal national treatment from countries which are not parties to the Paris Convention; whereas Article 29 of Regulation (EC) No 40/94, concerning the right of priority, also needs to be amended in this respect; whereas in order to comply with the national treatment obligation in Article 3 of the TRIPs Agreement, these provisions should be modified to ensure that nationals of all WTO Members, even if the Member in question is not a party to the Paris Convention, receive a treatment no less favourable than that accorded to nationals of Community Member States;

Whereas Article 23 (2) of the TRIPs Agreement provides for the refusal or invalidation of trade marks which contain or consist of false geographical indications for wines and spirits without the condition that they are of such a nature as to deceive the public, a new subparagraph (j) has to be added to Article 7 (1) of Regulation (EC) No 40/94,

HAS ADOPTED THIS REGULATION:

General Note

A9–002 Amending Regulation 40/94 on the Community trade mark for the implementation of the agreements concluded in the framework of the Uruguay Round

Article 1

Regulation (EC) No 40/94 is amended as follows:

1. Article 5 (1) (b) shall be replaced by the following:

    A9–003

    '(b) nationals of other States which are parties to the Paris Convention for the protection of industrial property, hereinafter referred to as 'the Paris Convention', or to the Agreement establishing the World Trade Organization;

2. Article 5 (1) (d) shall be replaced by the following:

    '(d) nationals, other than those referred to under subparagraph (c), of any State which is not party to the Paris Convention or to the Agreement establishing the World Trade Organization and which, according to published findings, accords to nationals of all the Member States the same protection for trade marks as it accords to its own nationals and, if nationals of the Member States are required to prove registration in the country of origin, recognizes the registration of Community trade marks as such proof.'

3. In Article 7 (1) after subparagraph (i) the following shall be added:

    '(j) trade marks for wines which contain or consist of a geographical indication identifying wines or for spirits which contain or consist of a geographical indication identifying spirits with respect to such wines or spirits not having that origin.'

4. Article 29 (1) shall be replaced by the following:

    '1. A person who has duly filed an application for a trade mark in or for any State party to the Paris Convention or to the Agreement establishing the World Trade Organization, or his successors in title, shall enjoy, for the purpose of filing a Community trade mark application for the same trade mark in respect of goods or services which are identical with or contained within those for which the application has been filed, a right or priority during a period of six months from the date of filing of the first application.'

5. Article 29 (5) shall be replaced by the following:

    '5. If the first filing has been made in a State which is not a party to the Paris Convention or to the Agreement establishing the World Trade Organization, paragraphs 1 to 4 shall apply only in so far as that State, according to published findings, grants, on the basis of the first filing made at the Office and subject to conditions equivalent to those laid down in this Regulation, a right of priority having equivalent effect.'

Article 2

This Regulation shall enter into force on January 1, 1995.

A9–004

It shall be applicable as of January 1, 1996.

This Regulation shall be binding in its entirety and directly applicable in all Member States.

Done at Brussels, December 22, 1994.

Commission Regulation 2868/95 of December 13, 1995—Implementing Council Regulation (EC) No 40/94 on the Community trade mark ([1995] O.J. L303/1)

A10–001   *THE COMMISSION OF THE EUROPEAN COMMUNITIES,*

Having regard to the Treaty establishing the European Community,

Having regard to Council Regulation (EC) No 40/94 of 20 December 1993 on the Community trade mark as amended by Regulation (EC) No 3288/94, and in particular Article 140 thereof,

Whereas Regulation (EC) No 40/94 (hereinafter 'the Regulation') creates a new trade mark system allowing a trade mark having effect throughout the Community to be obtained on the basis of an application to the Office for Harmonization in the Internal Market (trade marks and designs) ('the Office');

Whereas for this purpose, the Regulation contains the necessary provisions for a procedure leading to the registration of a Community trade mark, as well as for the administration of Community trade marks, for appeals against decisions of the Office and for proceedings for the revocation or invalidation of a Community trade mark;

Whereas Article 140 of the Regulation provides that the rules implementing the Regulation shall be adopted in an implementing regulation;

Whereas the implementing regulation is to be adopted in accordance with the procedure laid down in Article 141 of the Regulation;

Whereas this implementing regulation therefore lays down the rules necessary for implementing the provisions of the Regulation on the Community trade mark;

Whereas these rules should ensure the smooth and efficient operating of trade mark proceedings before the Office;

Whereas in accordance with Article 116 (1) of the Regulation, all the elements of the application for a Community trade mark specified in its Article 26 (1) as well as any other information the publication of which is prescribed by this implementing regulation should be published in all the official languages of the Community;

Whereas, however, it is not appropriate for the trade mark itself, names, addresses, dates and any other similar data to be translated and published in all the official languages of the Community;

Whereas the Office should make available standard forms for proceedings before the Office in all official languages of the Community;

Whereas the measures envisaged in this Regulation are in accordance with the opinion of the Committee established under Article 141 of the Regulation,

HAS ADOPTED THIS REGULATION:

Article 1

A10–002   The rules implementing the Regulation shall be as follows:

TITLE 1

APPLICATION PROCEDURE

Rule 1

Content of the Application

(1) The application for a Community trade mark shall contain: **A10–003**

(a) a request for registration of the mark as a Community trade mark;

(b) the name, address and nationality of the applicant and the State in which he is domiciled or has his seat or an establishment. Names of natural persons shall be indicated by the person's family name and given name(s). Names of legal entities, as well as bodies falling under Article 3 of the Regulation, shall be indicated by their official designation, which may be abbreviated in a customary manner; furthermore, the law of the State governing them shall be indicated. The telegraphic and teletype address, telephone as well as fax numbers and details of other data communications links may be given. Only one address shall, in principle, be indicated for each applicant; where several addresses are indicated, only the address mentioned first shall be taken into account, except where the applicant designates one of the addresses as an address for service;

(c) a list of the goods and services for which the trade mark is to be registered, in accordance with Rule 2;

(d) a representation of the mark in accordance with Rule 3;

(e) if the applicant has appointed a representative, his name and the address of his place of business in accordance with point (b); if the representative has more than one business address or if there are two or more representatives with different business addresses, the application shall indicate which address shall be used as an address for service; where such an indication is not made, only the first-mentioned address shall be taken into account as an address for service;

(f) where the priority of a previous application is claimed pursuant to Article 30 of the Regulation, a declaration to that effect, stating the date on which and the country in or for which the previous application was filed;

(g) where exhibition priority is claimed pursuant to Article 33 of the Regulation, a declaration to that effect, stating the name of the exhibition and the date of the first display of the goods or services;

(h) where the seniority of one or more earlier trade marks, registered in a Member State, including a trade mark registered in the Benelux countries or registered under international arrangements having effect in a Member State (hereinafter referred to as 'earlier registered trade marks, as referred to in Article 34 of the Regulation') is claimed pursuant to Article 34 of the Regulation, a declaration to that effect, stating the Member State or Member States in or for which the earlier mark is registered, the date from which the relevant registration was effective, the number of the relevant registration, and the goods and services for which the mark is registered;

(i) where applicable, a statement that the application is for registration of a Community collective mark pursuant to Article 64 of the Regulation;

(j) specification of the language in which the application has been filed, and of the second language pursuant to Article 115 (3) of the Regulation;

(k) the signature of the applicant or his representative.

(2) The application for a Community collective mark may include the regulations governing its use.

(3) The application may include a statement by the applicant that he disclaims any exclusive right to an element of the trade mark which is not distinctive, to be specified by the applicant.

(4) If there is more than one applicant, the application may contain the appointment of one applicant or representative as common representative.

Rule 2

List of Goods and Services

A10–004   (1) The common classification referred to in Article 1 of the Nice Agreement Concerning the International Classification of Goods and Services for the Purposes of the Registration of Marks of 15 June 1957, as revised and amended, shall be applied to the classification of the goods and services.

(2) The list of goods and services shall be worded in such a way as to indicate clearly the nature of the goods and services and to allow each item to be classified in only one class of the Nice Classification.

(3) The goods and services shall, in principle, be grouped according to the classes of the Nice classification, each group being preceded by the number of the class of that Classification to which that group of goods or services belongs and presented in the order of the classes under that Classification.

(4) The classification of goods and services shall serve exclusively administrative purposes. Therefore, goods and services may not be regarded as being similar to each other on the ground that they appear in the same class under the Nice Classification, and goods and services may not be regarded as being dissimilar from each other on the ground that they appear in different classes under the Nice Classification.

Rule 3

Representation of the Mark

A10–005   (1) If the applicant does not wish to claim any special graphic feature or colour, the mark shall be reproduced in normal script, as for example, by typing the letters, numerals and signs in the application. The use of small letters and capital letters shall be permitted and shall be followed accordingly in publications of the mark and in the registration by the Office.

(2) In cases other than those referred to in paragraph 1, the mark shall be reproduced on a sheet of paper separate from the sheet on which the text of the application appears. The sheet on which the mark is reproduced shall not exceed DIN A4 size (29,7 cm high, 21 cm wide) and the space used for the reproduction (type-area) shall not be larger than 26,2 cm $\times$; 17 cm. A margin of at least 2,5 cm shall be left on the left-hand side. Where it is not obvious, the correct position of the mark shall be indicated by adding the word 'top' to each reproduction. The reproduction of the mark shall be of such quality as to enable it to be reduced or enlarged to a size not more than 8 cm wide by 16 cm high for publication in the Community Trade Mark Bulletin. The separate sheet shall also indicate the name and address of the applicant. Four copies of the separate sheet carrying the reproduction shall be filed.

(3) In cases to which paragraph 2 applies, the application shall contain an indication to that effect. The application may contain a description of the mark.

(4) Where registration of a three-dimensional mark is applied for, the application shall contain an indication to that effect. The representation shall consist of a photographic reproduction or a graphic representation of the mark. The representation may contain up to six different perspectives of the mark.

(5) Where registration in colour is applied for, the application shall contain an

indication to that effect. The colours making up the mark shall also be indicated. The reproduction under paragraph 2 shall consist of the colour reproduction of the mark.

(6) The President of the Office may determine that, as far as the requirements of paragraph 2 are concerned, the mark may be reproduced in the text of the application itself and not on a separate sheet of paper and that the the number of copies of the reproduction of the mark may be less than four.

Rule 4

Fees for the Application

The fees payable for the application shall be:

A10–006

(a) the basic fee; and

(b) a class fee for each class exceeding three to which the goods or services belong according to Rule 2.

Rule 5

Filing of the Application

(1) The Office shall mark the documents making up the application with the date of its receipt and the file number of the application. The Office shall issue to the applicant without delay a receipt which shall include at least the file number, a representation, description or other identification of the mark, the nature and the number of the documents and the date of their receipt.

A10–007

(2) If the application is filed with the central industrial property office of a Member Sate or at the Benelux Trade Mark Office in accordance with Article 25 of the Regulation, the office of filing shall number all the pages of the application with arabic numerals. Before forwarding, the office of filing shall mark the documents making up the application with the date of receipt and the number of pages. The office of filing shall issue to the applicant without delay a receipt which shall include at least the nature and the number of the documents and the date of their receipt.

(3) If the Office receives an application forwarded by the central industrial property office of a Member State or the Benelux Trade Mark Office, it shall mark the application with the date of receipt and the file number and shall issue to the applicant without delay a receipt in accordance with the second sentence of paragraph 1, indicating the date of receipt at the Office.

Rule 6

Claiming Priority

(1) Where the priority of one or more previous applications pursuant to Article 30 of the Regulation is claimed in the application, the applicant shall indicate the file number of the previous application and file a copy of it within three months from the filing date. The copy shall be certified to be an exact copy of the previous application by the authority which received the previous application, and shall be accompanied by a certificate issued by that authority stating the date of filing of the previous application.

A10–008

(2) Where the applicant wishes to claim the priority of one or more previous applications pursuant to Article 30 of the Regulation subsequent to the filing of the application, the declaration of priority, stating the date on which and the country in or for which the previous application was made, shall be submitted within a period of two months from the filing date. The indications and evidence required under paragraph 1 shall be submitted to the Office within a period of three months from receipt of the declaration of priority.

(3) If the language of the previous application is not one of the languages of the Office, the Office shall require the applicant to file, within a period specified by the Office, which shall be not less than three months, a translation of the previous application into one of these languages.

(4) The President of the Office may determine that the evidence to be provided by the applicant may consist of less than is required under paragraph 1, provided that the information required is available to the Office from other sources.

Rule 7
Exhibition Priority

A10–009　　(1) Where the exhibition priority pursuant to Article 33 of the Regulation has been claimed in the application, the applicant shall, within three months from the filing date, file a certificate issued at the exhibition by the authority responsible for the protection of industrial property at the exhibition. This certificate shall declare that the mark was in fact used for the goods or services, and shall state the opening date of the exhibition and, where the first public use did not coincide with the opening date of the exhibition, the date of such first public use. The certificate must be accompanied by an identification of the actual use of the mark, duly certified by the abovementioned authority.

(2) Where the applicant wishes to claim an exhibition priority subsequently to the filing of the application, the declaration of priority, indicating the name of the exhibition and the date of the first display of the goods or services, shall be submitted within a period of two months from the filing date. The indications and evidence required under paragraph 1 shall be submitted to the Office within a period of three months from receipt of the declaration of priority.

Rule 8
Claiming the Seniority of a National Trade Mark

A10–010　　(1) Where the seniority of one or more earlier registered trade marks, as referred to in Article 34 of the Regulation, has been claimed in the application, the applicant shall, within three months from the filing date, submit a copy of the relevant registration. The copy must be certified by the competent authority to be an exact copy of the relevant registration.

(2) Where the applicant wishes to claim the seniority of one or more earlier registered trade marks as referred to in Article 34 of the Regulation, subsequent to the filing of the application, the declaration of seniority, indicating the Member State or Member States in or for which the mark is registered, the date from which the relevant registration was effective, the number of the relevant registration, and the goods and services for which the mark is registered, shall be submitted within a period of two months from the filing date. The evidence required under paragraph 1 shall be submitted to the Office within a period of three months from receipt of the declaration of seniority.

(3) The Office shall inform the Benelux Trade Mark Office or the central industrial property office of the Member State concerned of the effective claiming of seniority.

(4) The President of the Office may determine that the evidence to be provided by the applicant may consist of less than is required under paragraph 1, provided that the information required is available to the Office from other sources.

Rule 9
Examination of Requirements for a Filing Date and of Formal Requirements

A10–011　　(1) If the application fails to meet the requirements for according a filing date because:

(a) the application does not contain:
  (i) a request for registration of the mark as a Community trade mark;
  (ii) information identifying the applicant;
  (iii) a list of the goods and services for which the mark is to be registered;
  (iv) a representation of the trade mark; or
(b) the basic fee for the application has not been paid within one month of the filing of the application with the Office or, if the application has been filed with the central industrial property office of a Member State or with the Benelux Trade Mark Office, with that office, the Office shall notify the applicant that a date of filing cannot be accorded in view of those deficiencies.

(2) If the deficiencies referred to under paragraph 1 are remedied within two months of receipt of the notification, the date on which all the deficiencies are remedied shall determine the date of filing. If the deficiencies are not remedied before the time limit expires, the application shall not be dealt with as a Community trade mark application. Any fees paid shall be refunded.

(3) Where, although a date of filing has been accorded, the examination reveals that
(a) the requirements of Rules 1, 2 and 3 or the other formal requirements governing applications laid down in the Regulation or in these Rules are not complied with;
(b) the full amount of the class fees payable under Rule 4 (b), read in conjunction with Commission Regulation (EC) No 2869/95 (hereinafter 'the Fees Regulation') has not been received by the Office;
(c) where priority has been claimed pursuant to Rules 6 and 7, either in the application itself or within two months after the date of filing, the other requirements of the said Rules are not complied with; or
(d) where seniority has been claimed pursuant to Rule 8, either in the application itself or within two months after the date of filing, the other requirements of Rule 8 are not complied with, the Office shall invite the applicant to remedy the deficiencies noted within such period as it may specify.

(4) If the deficiencies referred to in paragraph 3 (a) are not remedied before the time limit expires, the Office shall reject the application.

(5) If the outstanding class fees are not paid before the time limit expires, the application shall be deemed to have been withdrawn, unless it is clear which class or classes the amount paid is intended to cover. In the absence of other criteria to determine which classes are intended to be covered, the Office shall take the classes in the order of the classification. The application shall be deemed to have been withdrawn with regard to those classes for which the class fees have not been paid or have not been paid in full.

(6) If the deficiencies referred to in paragraph 3 concern the claim to priority, the right of priority for the application shall be lost.

(7) If the deficiencies referred to in paragraph 3 concern the claim to seniority, the right of seniority in respect of that application shall be lost.

(8) If the deficiencies referred to in paragraph 3 concern only some of the goods and services, the Office shall refuse the application, or the right of priority or the right of seniority shall be lost, only in so far as those goods and services are concerned.

Rule 10

Examination of the Conditions Relating to the Entitlement to be Proprietor

Where, pursuant to Article 5 of the Regulation, the applicant is not entitled to be the proprietor of a Community trade mark, the Office shall notify the applicant   **A10–012** thereof. The Office shall specify a period within which the applicant may withdraw the application or submit his observations. Where the applicant fails to overcome the objections to registration, the Office shall refuse the application.

Rule 11

Examination as to Absolute Grounds for Refusal

A10–013 (1) Where, pursuant to Article 7 of the Regulation, the trade mark may not be registered for all or any part of the goods or services applied for, the office shall notify the applicant of the grounds for refusing registration. The Office shall specify a period within which the applicant may withdraw or amend the application or submit his observations.

(2) Where, pursuant to Article 38 (2) of the Regulation, registration of the Community trade mark is subject to the applicant's stating that he disclaims any exclusive right in the non-distinctive elements in the mark, the Office shall notify the applicant thereof, stating the reasons, and shall invite him to submit the relevant statement within such period as it may specify.

(3) Where the applicant fails to overcome the ground for refusing registration or to comply with the condition laid down in paragraph 2 within the time limit, the Office shall refuse the application in whole or in part.

Rule 12

Publication of the Application

A10–014 The publication of the application shall contain:

(a) the applicant's name and address;

(b) where applicable, the name and business address of the representative appointed by the applicant other than a representative falling within the first sentence of Article 88 (3) of the Regulation; if there is more than one representative with the same business address, only the name and business address of the first-named representative shall be published and it shall be followed by the words 'and others'; if there are two or more representatives with different business addresses, only the address for service determined pursuant to Rule 1 (1) (e) shall be published; where an association of representatives is appointed under Rule 76 (9), only the name and business address of the association shall be published;

(c) the reproduction of the mark, together with the indications and descriptions pursuant to Rule 3; where registration in colour is applied for, the publication shall contain the indication 'in colour' and indicate the colour or colours making up the mark;

(d) the list of goods and services, grouped according to the classes of the Nice classification, each group being preceded by the number of the class of that classification to which that group of goods or services belongs, and presented in the order of the classes of that classification;

(e) the date of filing and the file number;

(f) where applicable, particulars of the claim of priority pursuant to Article 30 of the Regulation;

(g) where applicable, particulars of the claim of exhibition priority pursuant to Article 33 of the Regulation;

(h) where applicable, particulars of the claim of seniority pursuant to Article 34 of the Regulation;

(i) where applicable, a statement that the mark has become distinctive in consequence of the use which has been made of it, pursuant to Article 7 (3) of the Regulation;

(j) where applicable, a statement that the application is for a Community collective mark;

(k) where applicable, a statement by the applicant disclaiming any exclusive right to an element of the mark pursuant to Rule 1 (3) or Rule 11 (2);

(l) the language in which the application was filed and the second language which the applicant has indicated pursuant to Article 115 (3) of the Regulation.

Rule 13

Amendment of the Application

(1) An application for amendment of the application under Article 44 of the Regulation shall contain: **A10–015**

(a) the file number of the application;

(b) the name and the address of the applicant in accordance with Rule 1 (1) (b);

(c) where the applicant has appointed a representative, the name and the business address of the representative in accordance with Rule 1 (1) (e);

(d) the indication of the element of the application to be corrected or amended, and that element in its corrected or amended version;

(e) where the amendment relates to the representation of the mark, a representation of the mark as amended, in accordance with Rule 3.

(2) Where the application for amendment is subject to the payment of a fee, the application shall not be deemed to have been filed until the required fee has been paid. If the fee has not been paid or has not been paid in full, the Office shall inform the applicant accordingly.

(3) If the requirements governing the amendment of the application are not fulfilled, the Office shall communicate the deficiency to the applicant. If the deficiency is not remedied within a period to be specified by the Office, the Office shall reject the application for amendment.

(4) Where the amendment is published pursuant to Article 44 (2) of the Regulation, Rules 15 to 22 shall apply mutatis mutandis.

(5) A single application for amendment may be made for the amendment of the same element in two or more applications of the same applicant. Where the application for amendment is subject to the payment of a fee, the required fee shall be paid in respect of each application to be amended.

(6) paragraphs 1 to 5 shall apply mutatis mutandis for applications to correct the name or the business address of a representative appointed by the applicant. Such applications shall not be subject to the payment of a fee.

Rule 14

Correction of Mistakes and Errors in Publications

(1) Where the publication of the application contains a mistake or error attributable to the Office, the Office shall correct the mistake or error acting of its own motion or at the request of the applicant.   **A10–016**

(2) Where a request as referred to in paragraph 1 is made by the applicant, Rule 13 shall apply mutatis mutandis. The request shall not be subject to the payment of a fee.

(3) The corrections effected under this Rule shall be published.

(4) Article 42 (2) of the Regulation and Rules 15 to 22 shall apply mutatis mutandis where the correction concerns the list of goods or services or the representation of the mark.

TITLE II

PROCEDURE FOR OPPOSITION AND PROOF OF USE

Rule 15

Contents of the Notice of Opposition

A10–017   (1) Opposition may be entered on the basis of one or more earlier marks within the meaning of Article 8 (2) of the Regulation ('earlier marks') or of one or more other earlier rights within the meaning of Article 8 (4) of the Regulation ('earlier rights').

(2) The notice of opposition shall contain:

(a) as concerns the application against which opposition is entered:

(i) the file number of the application against which opposition is entered;

(ii) an indication of the goods and services listed in the Community trade mark application against which opposition is entered;

(iii) the name of the applicant for the Community trade mark;

(b) as concerns the earlier mark or the earlier right on which the opposition is based:

(i) where the opposition is based on an earlier mark, a statement to that effect and an indication that the earlier mark is a Community mark or an indication of the Member State or Member States including, where applicable, the Benelux, where the earlier mark has been registered or applied for, or, where the earlier mark is an internationally registered mark, an indication of the Member State or Member States including, where applicable, the Benelux, to which protection of that earlier mark has been extended;

(ii) where available, the file number or the registration number and the filing date, including the priority date of the earlier mark;

(iii) where the opposition is based on an earlier mark which is a well-known mark within the meaning of Article 8 (2) (c) of the Regulation, an indication to that effect and an indication of the Member State or Member States in which the earlier mark is well-known;

(iv) where the opposition is based on an earlier mark having a reputation within the meaning of Article 8 (5) of the Regulation, an indication to that effect, and an indication of where that earlier mark is registered or applied for in accordance with subparagraph (i);

(v) where the opposition is based on an earlier right, an indication to that effect, and an indication of the Member State or Member States where that earlier right exists;

(vi) a representation and, where appropriate, a description of the earlier mark or earlier right;

(vii) the goods and services in respect of which the earlier mark has been registered or applied for or in respect of which the earlier mark is well-known within the meaning of Article 8 (2) (c) of the Regulation or has a reputation within the meaning of Article 8 (5) of the Regulation; the opposing party shall, when indicating all the goods and services for which the earlier mark is protected, also indicate those goods and services on which the opposition is based;

(c) as concerns the opposing party:

(i) where the opposition is entered by the proprietor of the earlier mark or of the earlier right, his name and address in accordance with Rule 1 (1) (b) and an indication that he is the proprietor of such mark or right;

(ii) where opposition is entered by a licensee, the name of the licensee and his address in accordance with Rule 1 (1) (b) and an indication that he has been authorized to enter the opposition;

(iii) where the opposition is entered by the successor in title to the registered proprietor of a Community trade mark who has not yet been registered as new proprietor, an indication to that effect, the name and address of the opposing party in accordance with Rule 1 (1) (b), and an indication of the date on which the application for registration of the new proprietor was received by the Office or, where this information is not available, was sent to the Office;

(iv) where opposition is entered on the basis of an earlier right by a person who is not the proprietor of that right, the name of the person and his address in accordance with Rule 1 (1) (b) and an indication that the is entitled under the relevant national law to exercise that right;

(v) where the opposing party has appointed a representative, the name of the representative and his business in accordance with Rule 1 (1) (e);

(d) a specification of the grounds on which the opposition is based.

(3) paragraph 1 and 2 shall apply mutatis mutandis to an opposition entered pursuant to Article 8 (3) of the Regulation.

Rule 16

Facts, Evidence and Arguments Presented in Support of the Opposition

(1) Every notice of opposition may contain particulars of the facts, evidence and arguments presented in support of the opposition, accompanied by the relevant supporting documents.   **A10–018**

(2) If the opposition is based on an earlier mark which is not a Community trade mark, the notice of opposition shall preferably be accompanied by evidence of the registration or filing of that earlier mark, such as a certificate of registration. If the opposition is based on a well-known mark as referred to in Article 8 (2) (c) of the Regulation or on a mark having a reputation as referred to in Article 8 (5) of the Regulation, the notice of opposition shall in principle be accompanied by evidence attesting that it is well-known or that it has a reputation. If the opposition is entered on the basis of any other earlier right, the notice of opposition shall in principle be accompanied by appropriate evidence on the acquisition and scope of protection of that right.

(3) The particulars of the facts, evidence and arguments and other supporting documents as referred to in paragraphs 1, and the evidence referred to in paragraph 2 may, if they are not submitted together with the notice of opposition or subsequent thereto, be submitted within such period after commencement of the opposition proceedings as the Office may specify pursuant to Rule 20 (2).

Rule 17

Use of Languages in Opposition Proceedings

(1) Where the notice of opposition is not filed in the language of the application for registration of the Community trade mark, if that language is one of the languages of the Office, or in the second language indicated when the application was filed, the opposing party shall file a translation of the notice of opposition in one of those languages within a period of one month from the expiry of the opposition period.   **A10–019**

(2) Where the evidence in support of the opposition as provided for in Rule 16 (1) and (2) is not filed in the language of the opposition proceedings, the opposing party shall file a translation of that evidence into that language within a period of one month from the expiry of the opposition period or, where applicable, within the period specified by the Office pursuant to Rule 16 (3).

(3) Where the opposing party or the applicant informs the Office, before the date on which the opposition proceedings shall be deemed to commence pursuant to Rule 19 (1), that the applicant and the opposing party have agreed on a different language for the opposition proceeding pursuant to Article 115 (7) of the Regulation, the opposing party shall, where the notice of opposition has not been filed in that language, file a translation of the notice of opposition in that language within a period of one month from the said date.

Rule 18

Rejection of Notice of Opposition as Inadmissible

A10–020   (1) If the Office finds that the notice of opposition does not comply with the provisions of Article 42 of the Regulation, or where the notice of opposition does not clearly identify the application against which opposition is entered or the earlier mark or the earlier right on the basis of which the opposition is being entered, the Office shall reject the notice of opposition as inadmissible unless those deficiencies have been remedied before expiry of the opposition period. If the opposition fee has not been paid within the opposition period, the notice of opposition shall be deemed not to have been entered. If the opposition fee has been paid after the expiry of the opposition period, it shall be refunded to the opposing p arty.

(2) If the Office finds that the notice of opposition does not comply with other provisions of the Regulation or of these Rules, it shall inform the opposing party accordingly and shall call upon him to remedy the deficiencies noted within a period of two months. If the deficiencies are not remedied before the time limit expires, the Office shall reject the notice of opposition as inadmissible.

(3) Any decision to reject a notice of opposition as inadmissible under paragraphs 1 or 2 shall be communicated to the applicant.

Rule 19

Commencement of Opposition Proceedings

A10–021   (1) If the Office does not reject the notice of opposition in accordance with Rule 18, it shall communicate the opposition to the applicant and shall invite him to file his observations within such period as it may specify. The Office shall draw the applicant's attention to the fact that the opposition proceedings shall be deemed to commence two months after receipt of the communication, unless the applicant informs the Office, before the expiry of this period, that he withdraws his application or restricts the application to goods and services against which the opposition is not directed.

(2) The Office may, pursuant to Rule 71, grant an extension of the period referred to in the second sentence of paragraph 1 where such request is presented jointly by the applicant and the opposing party.

(3) There the application is withdrawn or restricted within the period specified in the second sentence of paragraph 1 or within any extension of that period granted under paragraph 2, the Office shall inform the opposing party accordingly and shall refund the opposition fee.

Rule 20

Examination of Opposition

A10–022   (1) If the application is not withdrawn or restricted pursuant to Rule 19, the applicant shall file his observations within the period specified by the Office in its communication referred to in the first sentence of Rule 19 (1).

(2) Where the notice of opposition does not contain particulars of the facts, evidence and arguments as referred to in Rule 16 (1) and (2), the Office shall call upon the opposing party to submit such particulars within a period specified by the Office. Any submission by the opposing party shall be communicated to the applicant who shall be given an opportunity to reply within a period specified by the Office.

(3) If the applicant files no observations, the Office may give a ruling on the opposition on the basis of the evidence before it.

(4) The observations filed by the applicant shall be communicated to the opposing party who shall be called upon by the Office, if it considers it necessary to do so, to reply within a period specified by the Office.

(5) If, pursuant to Article 44 (1) of the Regulation, the applicant restricts the list of goods and services, the Office shall communicate this to the opposing party and call upon him, within such period as it may specify, to submit observations stating whether he maintains the opposition and, if so, against which of the remaining goods and services.

(6) The Office may suspend any opposition proceeding where the opposition is based on an application for registration pursuant to Article 8 (2) (b) of the Regulation until a final decision is taken in that proceeding, or where other circumstances are such that such suspension is appropriate.

Rule 21

Multiple Oppositions

(1) Where a number of oppositions have been entered in respect of the same application for a Community trade mark, the Office may deal with them in one set of proceedings. The Office may subsequently decide to no longer deal with them in this way.   **A10–023**

(2) If a preliminary examination of one or more oppositions reveals that the Community trade mark for which an application for registration has been filed is possibly not eligible for registration in respect of some or all of the goods or services for which registration is sought, the Office may suspend the other opposition proceedings. The Office shall inform the remaining opposing parties of any relevant decisions taken during those proceedings which are continued.

(3) Once a decision rejecting the application has become final, the oppositions on which a decision was deferred in accordance with paragraph 2 shall be deemed to have been disposed of and the opposing parties concerned shall be informed accordingly. Such disposition shall be considered to constitute a case which has not proceeded to judgment within the meaning of Article 81 (4) of the Regulation.

(4) The Office shall refund 500f the opposition fee paid by each opposing party whose opposition is deemed to have been disposed of in accordance with paragraphs 1, 2 and 3.

Rule 22

Proof of Use

(1) Where, pursuant to Article 43 (2) or (3) of the Regulation, the opposing party has to furnish proof of use or show that there are proper reasons for nonuse, the Office shall invite him to provide the proof required within such period as it shall specify. If the opposing party does not provide such proof before the time limit expires, the Office shall reject the opposition.   **A10–024**

(2) The indications and evidence for the furnishing of proof of use shall consist of indications concerning the place, time, extent and nature of use of the opposing trade mark for the goods and services in respect of which it is registered and

on which the opposition is based, and evidence in support of these indications in accordance with paragraph 3.

(3) The evidence shall, in principle, be confined to the submission of supporting documents and items such as packages, labels, price lists, catalogues, invoices, photographs, newspaper advertisements, and statements in writing as referred to in Article 76 (1) (f) of the Regulation.

(4) Where the evidence supplied pursuant to paragraphs 1, 2 and 3 is not in the language of the opposition proceedings, the Office may require the opposing party to submit a translation of that evidence in that language, within a period specified by the Office.

TITLE III

REGISTRATION PROCEDURE

Rule 23

Registration of the Trade Mark

A10–025   (1) The registration fee provided for in Article 45 of the Regulation shall consist of

(a) a basic fee; and

(b) a class fee for each class exceeding three in respect of which the mark is to be registered.

(2) Where no opposition has been entered or where any opposition entered has been finally disposed of by withdrawal, rejection or other disposition, the Office shall request the applicant to pay the registration fee within two months of receipt of the request.

(3) If the registration fee is not paid within due time, it may still be validly paid within two months of notification of a communication pointing out the failure to observe the time limit, provided that within this period the additional fee specified in the Fees Regulations is paid.

(4) On receipt of the registration fee the mark applied for and the particulars referred to in Rule 84 (2) shall be recorded in the Register of Community trade marks.

(5) The registration shall be published in the Community Trade Marks Bulletin.

(6) The registration fee shall be refunded if the trade mark applied for is not registered.

Rule 24

Certificate of Registration

A10–026   (1) The Office shall issue to the proprietor of the trade mark a certificate of registration which shall contain the entries in the Register provided for in Rule 84 (2) and a statement to the effect that those entries have been recorded in the Register.

(2) The proprietor of the trade mark may request that certified or uncertified copies of the certificate of registration be supplied to him upon payment of a fee.

Rule 25

Alteration of the Registration

A10–027   (1) An application for alteration of the registration pursuant to Article 48 (2) of the Regulation shall contain:

(a) the registration number,

(b) the name and the address of the proprietor of the mark in accordance with Rule 1 (1) (b);

(c) where the proprietor has appointed a representative, the name and the business address of the representative in accordance with Rule 1 (1) (e);

(d) the indication of the element in the representation of the mark to be altered and that element in its altered version;

(e) a representation of the mark as altered, in accordance with Rule 3.

(2) The application shall be deemed not to have been filed until the required fee has been paid. If the fee has not been paid or has not been paid in full, the Office shall inform the applicant accordingly.

(3) If the requirements governing the alteration of the registration are not fulfilled, the Office shall communicate the deficiency to the applicant. If the deficiency is not remedied within a period to be specified by the Office, the Office shall reject the application.

(4) Where the registration of the alteration is challenged pursuant to Article 48 (3) of the Regulation, the provisions on opposition contained in the Regulation and in these Rules shall apply mutatis mutandis.

(5) A single application may be made for the alteration of the same element in two or more registrations of the same proprietor. The required fee shall be paid in respect of each registration to be altered.

Rule 26

Change of the Name or Address of the Proprietor of the Community Trade Mark or of his Registered Representative

(1) A change of the name or address of the proprietor of the Community trade mark which is not an alteration of the Community trade mark pursuant to Article 48 (2) of the Regulation and which is not the consequence of a whole or partial transfer of the registered mark shall, at the request of the proprietor, be recorded in the register.   **A10–028**

(2) An application for the change of the name or address of the proprietor of the registered mark shall contain:

(a) the registration number of the mark;

(b) the name and the address of the proprietor of the mark as recorded in the register;

(c) the indication of the name and address of the proprietor of the mark, as amended, in accordance with Rule 1 (1) (e).

(d) where the proprietor has appointed a representative, the name and the business address of the representative, in accordance with Rule 1 (1) (e).

(3) The application shall not be subject to payment of a fee.

(4) A single application may be made for the change of the name or address in respect of two or more registrations of the same proprietor.

(5) If the requirements governing the recording of a change are not fulfilled, the Office shall communicate the deficiency to the applicant. If the deficiency is not remedied within a period to be specified by the Office, the Office shall reject the application.

(6) Paragraphs 1 to 5 shall apply mutatis mutandis to a change of the name or address of the registered representative.

(7) Paragraphs 1 to 6 shall apply mutatis mutandis to applications for Community trade marks. The change shall be recorded in the files kept by the Office on the Community trade mark application.

Rule 27

Correction of Mistakes and Errors in the Register and in the Publication of the Registration

A10–029   (1) Where the registration of the mark or the publication of the registration contains a mistake or error attributable to the Office, the Office shall correct the error or mistake of its own motion or at the request of the proprietor.

(2) Where such a request is made by the proprietor, Rule 26 shall apply mutatis mutandis. The request shall not be subject to payment of a fee.

(3) The Office shall publish the corrections made under this Rule.

Rule 28

Claiming Seniority after Registration of the Community Trade Mark

A10–030   (1) An application pursuant to Article 35 of the Regulation to obtain the seniority of one or more earlier registered trade marks as referred to in Article 34 of the Regulation, shall contain:

(a) the registration number of the Community trade mark;

(b) the name and address of the proprietor of the Community trade mark in accordance with Rule 1 (1) (b);

(c) where the proprietor has appointed a representative, the name and the business address of the representative in accordance with Rule 1 (1) (e);

(d) an indication of the Member State or Member States in or for which the earlier mark is registered, the date from which the relevant registration was effective, the number of the relevant registration, and the goods and services for which the earlier mark is registered;

(e) an indication of the goods and services in respect of which seniority is claimed;

(f) a copy of the relevant registration; the copy must be certified as an exact copy of the relevant registration by the competent authority.

(2) If the requirements governing the claiming of seniority are not fulfilled, the Office shall communicate the deficiency to the applicant. If the deficiency is not remedied within a period specified by the Office, the Office shall reject the application.

(3) The Office shall inform the Benelux Trade Mark Office or the central industrial property office of the Member State concerned of the effective claiming of seniority.

(4) The President of the Office may determine that the material to be provided by the applicant may consist of less than is required under paragraph 1 (f), provided that the information required is available to the Office from other sources.

TITLE IV

RENEWAL

Rule 29

Notification of Expiry

A10–031   At least six months before expiry of the registration the Office shall inform the proprietor of the Community trade mark, and any person having a registered right, including a licence, in respect of the Community trade mark, that the registration is approaching expiry. Failure to give such notification shall not affect the expiry of the registration.

Rule 30

Renewal of Registration

(1) An application for renewal shall contain: A10–032

(a) where the application is filed by the proprietor of the trade mark, his name and address in accordance with Rule 1 (1) (b);

(b) where the application is filed by a person expressly authorized to do so by the proprietor of the mark, the name and address of that person and evidence that he is authorized to file the application;

(c) where the applicant has appointed a representative, the name and business address of the representative in accordance with Rule 1 (1) (e);

(d) the registration number;

(e) an indication that renewal is requested for all the goods and services covered by the registration or, if the renewal is not requested for all the goods and services for which the mark is registered, an indication of those classes or those goods and services for which renewal is requested or those classes or those goods and services for which renewal is not requested, grouped according to the classes of the Nice classification, each group being preceded by the number of the class of that classification to which that group of goods or services belongs and presented in the order of the classes of that classification.

(2) The fees payable under Article 47 of the Regulation for the renewal of a Community trade mark shall consist of:

(a) a basic fee;

(b) a class fee for each class exceeding three in the list of classes in respect of which renewal is applied for as shown in paragraph 1 (e); and

(c) where applicable, the additional fee for late payment of the renewal fee or late submission of the request for renewal, pursuant to Article 47 (3) of the Regulation, as specified in the Fees Regulation.

(3) Where the application for renewal is filed within the time periods provided for in Article 47 (3) of the Regulation, but the other conditions governing renewal provided for in Article 47 of the Regulation and these Rules are not satisfied, the Office shall inform the applicant of the deficiencies found. If the application is filed by a person whom the proprietor of the trade mark has expressly authorized to do so, the proprietor of the trade mark shall receive a copy of the notification.

(4) Where an application for renewal is not submitted or is submitted after expiry of the period provided for in the third sentence of Article 47 (3) of the Regulation, or if the fees are not paid or are paid only after the period in question has expired, or if the deficiencies are not remedied within that period, the Office shall determine that the registration has expired and shall so notify the proprietor of the Community trade mark and, where appropriate, the applicant and the person recorded in the Register as having rights in the mark. Where the fees paid are insufficient to cover all the classes of goods and services for which renewal is requested, such a determination shall not be made if it is clear which class or classes are to be covered. In the absence of other criteria, the Office shall take the classes into account in the order of classification.

(5) Where the determination made pursuant to paragraph 4 has become final, the Office shall cancel the mark from the register. The cancellation shall take effect from the day following the day on which the existing registration expired.

(6) Where the renewal fees provided for in paragraph 2 have been paid but the registration is not renewed, those fees shall be refunded.

TITLE V

TRANSFER, LICENCES AND OTHER RIGHTS, CHANGES

Rule 31

Transfer

A10–033   (1) An application for registration of a transfer under Article 17 of the Regulation shall contain:

(a) the registration number of the Community trade mark;

(b) particulars of the new proprietor in accordance with Rule 1 (1) (b);

(c) where not all the registered goods or services are included in the transfer, particulars of the registered goods or services to which the transfer relates;

(d) documents duly establishing the transfer in accordance with Article 17 (2) and (3) of the Regulation;

(2) The application may contain, where applicable, the name and business address of the representative of the new proprietor, to be set out in accordance with Rule 1 (1) (e).

(3) Transfers to any natural or legal persons who cannot be proprietors of Community trade marks pursuant to Article 5 of the Regulation shall not be registered.

(4) The application shall not be deemed to have been filed until the required fee has been paid. If the fee is not paid or is not paid in full, the Office shall so notify the applicant.

(5) It shall constitute sufficient proof of transfer under paragraph 1(d):

(a) that the application for registration of the transfer is signed by the registered proprietor or his representative and by the successor in title or his representative; or,

(b) that the application, if submitted by the successor in title, is accompanied by a declaration, signed by the registered proprietor or his representative, that he agrees to the registration of the successor in title; or

(c) that the application is accompanied by a completed transfer form or document, as specified in Rule 83 (1) (d), signed by the registered proprietor or his representative and by the successor in title or his representative.

(6) Where the conditions applicable to the registration of a transfer, as laid down in Article 17 (1) to (4) of the Regulation, in paragraphs 1 to 4 above, and in other applicable Rules are not fulfilled, the Office shall notify the applicant of the deficiencies. If the deficiencies are not remedied within a period specified by the Office, it shall reject the application for registration of the transfer.

(7) A single application for registration of a transfer may be submitted for two or more marks, provided that the registered proprietor and the successor in title are the same in each case.

(8) Paragraphs 1 to 7 shall apply mutatis mutandis to applications for Community trade marks. The transfer shall be recorded in the files kept by the Office concerning the Community trade mark application.

Rule 32

Partial Transfers

A10–034   (1) Where the application for registration of a transfer relates only to some of the goods and services for which the mark is registered, the application shall contain an indication of the goods and services to which the partial transfer relates.

(2) The goods and services in the original registration shall be distributed between the remaining registration and the new registration so that the goods and services in the remaining registration and the new registration shall not overlap.

(3) Rule 31 shall apply mutatis mutandis to applications for registrations of a partial transfer.

(4) The Office shall establish a separate file for the new registration, which shall consist of a complete copy of the file of the original registration and the application for registration of the partial transfer; a copy of that application shall be included in the file of the remaining registration. The Office shall also assign a new registration number to the new registration.

(5) Any application made by the original proprietor pending with regard to the original registration shall be deemed to be pending with regard to the remaining registration and the new registration. Where such application is subject to the payment of fees and these fees have been paid by the original proprietor, the new proprietor shall not be liable to pay any additional fees with regard to such application.

Rule 33

Registration of Licences and other Rights

(1) Rule 31 (1) (a) (b) and (c), (2), (4) and (7) shall apply mutatis mutandis to the registration of the grant or transfer of a licence, to registration of the creation or transfer of a right in rem in respect of a Community trade mark, and to registration of enforcement measures. However, where a Community trade mark is involved in bankruptcy or like proceedings, the request of the competent national authority for an entry in the register to this effect shall not be subject to payment of a fee.   **A10–035**

(2) Where the Community trade mark is licensed for only part of the goods and services for which the mark is registered, or for only a part of the Community, or for a limited period of time, the application for registration shall indicate the goods and services or the part of the Community or the time period for which the licence is granted.

(3) Where the conditions applicable to registration, as laid down in Articles 19, 20 or 22 of the Regulation, in paragraphs 1 and 2 above, and the other applicable Rules are not fulfilled, the Office shall notify the applicant of the irregularity. If the irregularity is not corrected within a period specified by the Office, it shall reject the application for registration.

(4) Paragraphs 1, 2 and 3 shall apply mutatis mutandis to applications for Community trade marks. Licences, rights in rem and enforcement measures shall be recorded in the files kept by the Office concerning the Community trade mark application.

Rule 34

Special Provisions for the Registration of a Licence

(1) A licence in respect of a Community trade mark shall be recorded in the Register as an exclusive licence if the proprietor of the trade mark or the licensee so request.   **A10–036**

(2) A licence in respect of a Community trade mark shall be recorded in the Register as a sub-licence where it is granted by a licensee whose licence is recorded in the Register.

(3) A licence in respect of a Community trade mark shall be recorded in the Register as a licence limited as to the goods and services or as a territorially limited licence if it is granted for only a part of the goods or services for which the mark is registered or if it is granted only for a part of the Community.

(4) A licence in respect of a Community trade mark shall be recorded in the Register as a temporary licence if it is granted for a limited period of time.

Rule 35

Cancellation or Modification of the Registration of Licences and other Rights

A10–037   (1) A registration effected under Rule 33 (1) shall be cancelled at the request of one of the persons concerned.

(2) The application shall contain:

(a) the registration number of the Community trade mark; and

(b) particulars of the right whose registration is to be cancelled.

(3) Application for cancellation of the registration of a licence or another right shall not be deemed to have been filed until the required fee has been paid. If the fee is not paid or is not paid in full, the Office shall so notify the applicant. However, the request of the competent national authority for the cancellation of an entry where a Community trade mark is involved in bankruptcy or like proceedings shall not be subject to payment of a fee.

(4) The application shall be accompanied by documents showing that the registered right no longer exists or by a statement by the licensee or the holder of another right, to the effect that he consents to cancellation of the registration.

(5) Where the requirements for cancellation of the registration are not satisfied, the Office shall notify the applicant of the irregularity. If the irregularity is not corrected within a period specified by the Office, it shall reject the application for cancellation of the registration.

(6) Paragraphs 1, 2, 4 and 5 shall apply mutatis mutandis to a request for the modification of a registration effected under Rule 33 (1).

(7) Paragraphs 1 to 6 shall apply mutatis mutandis to entries made in the files pursuant to Rule 33 (4).

TITLE VI

SURRENDER

Rule 36

Surrender

A10–038   (1) A declaration of surrender pursuant to Article 49 of the Regulation shall contain:

(a) the registration number of the Community trade mark;

(b) the name and address of the proprietor in accordance with Rule 1 (1) (b);

(c) where a representative has been appointed, the name and business address of the representative in accordance with Rule 1 (1) (e);

(d) where surrender is declared only for some of the goods and services for which the mark is registered, the goods and services for which the surrender is declared or the goods and services for which the mark is to remain registered.

(2) Where a right of a third party relating to the Community trade mark is

entered in the register, it shall be sufficient proof of his agreement to the surrender that a declaration of consent to the surrender is signed by the proprietor of that right or his representative. Where a licence has been registered, surrender shall be registered three months after the date on which the proprietor of the Community trade mark satisfies the Office that he has informed the licensee of his intention to surrender it. If the proprietor proves to the Office before the expiry of that period that the licensee has given his consent, the surrender shall be registered forthwith.

(3) If the requirements governing surrender are not fulfilled, the Office shall communicate the deficiencies to the declarant. If the deficiencies are not remedied within a period to be specified by the Office, the Office shall reject the entry of the surrender in the Register.

TITLE VII

REVOCATION AND INVALIDITY

Rule 37

Application for Revocation or for a Declaration of Invalidity

An application to the Office for revocation or for a declaration of invalidity pursuant to Article 55 of the Regulation shall contain: **A10–039**

(a) as concerns the registration in respect of which revocation or a declaration of invalidity is sought;
  (i) the registration number of the Community trade mark in respect of which revocation or a declaration of invalidity is sought;
  (ii) the name and address of the proprietor of the Community trade mark in respect of which revocation or a declaration of invalidity is sought;
  (iii) a statement of the registered goods and services in respect of which revocation or a declaration of invalidity is sought;
(b) as regards the grounds on which the application is based,
  (i) in the case of an application pursuant to Article 50 or Article 51 of the Regulation, a statement of the grounds on which the application for revocation or a declaration of invalidity is based;
  (ii) in the case of an application pursuant to Article 52 (1) of the Regulation, particulars of the right on which the application for a declaration of invalidity is based and if necessary particulars showing that the applicant is entitled to adduce the earlier right as grounds for invalidity;
  (iii) in the case of an application pursuant to Article 52 (2) of the Regulation, particulars of the right on which the application for a declaration of invalidity is based and particulars showing that the applicant is the proprietor of an earlier right as referred to in Article 52 (2) of the Regulation or that he is entitled under the national law applicable to lay claim to that right;
  (iv) an indication of the facts, evidence and arguments presented in support of those grounds;
(c) as concerns the applicant,
  (i) his name and address in accordance with Rule 1 (1) (b);
  (ii) if the applicant has appointed a representative, the name and the business address of the representative, in accordance with Rule 1 (1)(e).

Rule 38

Languages used in Revocation or Invalidity Proceedings

(1) Where the application for revocation or for a declaration of invalidity is   **A10–040**

not filed in the language of the application for the registration of the Community trade mark, if that language is one of the languages of the Office, or in the second language indicated when the application was filed, the applicant for revocation or for a declaration of invalidity shall file a translation of his application in one of those two languages within a period of one month from the filing of his application.

(2) Where the evidence in support of the application is not filed in the language of the revocation or invalidity proceedings, the applicant shall file a translation of that evidence into that language within a period of two months after the filing of such evidence.

(3) Where the applicant for revocation or for a declaration of invalidity or the proprietor of the Community trade mark inform the Office before the expiry of a period of two months from receipt by the Community trade mark proprietor of the communication referred to in Rule 40 (1), that they have agreed on a different language of proceedings pursuant to Article 115 (7) of the Regulation, the applicant shall, where the application was not filed in that language, file a translation of the application in that language within a period of one month from the said date.

Rule 39

Rejection of the Application for Revocation or for Declaration of Invalidity as Inadmissible

A10–041   (1) If the Office finds that the application does not comply with Article 55 of the Regulation, Rule 37 or any other provision of the Regulation or these Rules, it shall inform the applicant accordingly and shall call upon him to remedy the deficiencies found within such period as it may specify. If the deficiencies are not remedied before expiry of the time limit, the Office shall reject the application as inadmissible.

(2) Where the Office finds that the required fees have not been paid, it shall inform the applicant accordingly and shall inform him that the application will be deemed not to have been filed if the required fees are not paid within a period specified by the Office. If the required fees are paid after expiry of the period specified by the Office, they shall be refunded to the applicant.

(3) Any decision to reject an application for revocation or for a declaration of invalidity under paragraph 1 shall be communicated to the applicant. Where the application is considered not to have been filed pursuant to paragraph 2, the applicant shall be informed accordingly.

Rule 40

Examination of the Application for Revocation or for a Declaration of Invalidity

A10–042   (1) If the Office does not reject the application in accordance with Rule 39, it shall communicate such application to the proprietor of the Community trade mark and shall request him to file his observations within such period as it may specify.

(2) If the proprietor of the Community trade mark files no observations, the Office may decide on the revocation or invalidity on the basis of the evidence before it.

(3) Any observations filed by the proprietor of the Community trade mark shall be communicated to the applicant, who shall be requested by the Office, if it sees fit, to reply within a period specified by the Office.

(4) All communications under Article 56 (1) of the Regulation and all observations filed in this respect shall be sent to the parties concerned.

(5) If the applicant, under Article 56 (2) or (3) of the Regulation, has to furnish proof of use or proof that there are proper reasons for non-use, Rule 22 shall apply mutatis mutandis.

Rule 41

Multiple Applications for Revocation or for a Declaration of Invalidity

(1) Where a number of applications for revocation or for a declaration of invalidity have been filed relating to the same Community trade mark, the Office may deal with them in one set of proceedings. The Office may subsequently decide no longer to deal with them in this way.

A10–043

(2) Rule 21 (2) (3) and (4) shall apply mutatis mutandis.

TITLE VIII

COMMUNITY COLLECTIVE MARKS

Rule 42

Application of Provisions

The provisions of these Rules shall apply to Community collective marks, subject to Rule 43.

A10–044

Rule 43

Regulation Governing Community Collective Marks

(1) Where the application for a Community collective trade mark does not contain the regulations governing its use pursuant to Article 65 of the Regulation, those regulations shall be submitted to the Office within a period of two months after the date of filing.

A10–045

(2) The regulations governing Community collective marks shall specify:

(a) the name of the applicant and his office address;

(b) the object of the association or the object for which the legal person governed by public law is constituted;

(c) the bodies authorized to represent the association or the said legal person;

(d) the conditions for membership;

(e) the persons authorized to use the mark;

(f) where appropriate, the conditions governing use of the mark, including sanctions;

(g) where appropriate, the authorization referred to in the second sentence of Article 65 (2) of the Regulation.

TITLE IX

CONVERSION

Rule 44

Application for Conversion

(1) An application for conversion of a Community trade mark application or a registered Community trade mark into a national trademark application pursuant to Article 108 of the Regulation shall contain:

A10–046

(a) the name and the address of the applicant for conversion in accordance with Rule 1 (1) (b);

(b) where the applicant for conversion has appointed a representative, the name and the business address of the representative in accordance with Rule 1 (1) (e);

(c) the filing number of the Community trade mark application or the registration number of the Community trade mark;

(d) the date of filing of the Community trade mark application or the Community trade mark and, where applicable, particulars of the claim to priority for the Community trade mark application or the Community trade mark pursuant to Articles 30 and 33 of the Regulation and particulars of the claim to seniority pursuant to Articles 34 and 35 of the Regulation;

(e) a representation of the mark as contained in the application or as registered;

(f) the specification of the Member State or the Member States in respect of which conversion is requested;

(g) where the request does not relate to all of the goods and services for which the application has been filed or for which the trade mark has been registered, an indication of the goods and services for which conversion is requested, and, where conversion is requested in respect of more than one Member State and the list of goods and services is not the same for all Member States, an indication of the respective goods and services for each Member State;

(h) where conversion is requested pursuant to Article 108 (4) of the Regulation, an indication to that effect;

(i) where conversion is requested pursuant to Article 108 (5) of the Regulation following a withdrawal of an application for registration, an indication to that effect, and the date on which the application for registration was withdrawn;

(j) where conversion is requested pursuant to Article 108 (5) of the Regulation following a failure to renew the registration, an indication to that effect, and the date on which the period of protection has expired, the period of three months provided for in Article 108 (5) of the Regulation shall begin to run on the day following the last day on which the request for renewal can be presented pursuant to Article 47 (3) of the Regulation;

(k) where conversion is requested pursuant to article 108 (6) of the Regulation, an indication to that effect, the date on which the decision of the national court has become final, and a copy of that decision.

(2) Where a copy of a court decision pursuant to paragraph 1 (k) is required, that copy may be submitted in the language in which the decision was given.

Rule 45

Examination of Application for Conversion

A10–047   (1) Where the application for conversion does not comply with the requirements of Article 108 (1) of the Regulation or was not filed within the relevant period of three months, the Office shall reject it.

(2) Where the conversion fee has not been paid within the relevant period of three months, the Office shall inform the applicant that the application for conversion shall be deemed not to have been filed.

(3) Where the other requirements governing conversion as provided for in Rule 44 and in other Rules governing such applications are not fulfilled, the Office shall inform the applicant accordingly and invite him to remedy the deficiency within a period specified by the Office. If the deficiencies are not remedied within that period, the Office shall reject the application for conversion.

Rule 46

Publication of Application for Conversion

(1) Where the application for conversion relates to a Community trade mark   **A10–048**
application which has already been published in the Community Trade Mark
Bulletin pursuant to Article 40 of the Regulation or where the application for
conversion relates to a Community trade mark, the application for conversion
shall be published in the Community Trade Marks Bulletin.

(2) The publication of the application for conversion shall contain:

(a) the filing number or the registration number of the trade mark in respect of
which conversion is requested;

(b) a reference to the previous publication of the application or the registration
in the Community Trade marks Bulletin;

(c) an indication of the Member State or Member States in respect of which
conversion has been requested;

(d) where the request does not relate to all of the goods and services for which
the application has been filed or for which the trade mark has been
registered, an indication of the goods and services for which conversion is
requested;

(e) where conversion is requested in respect of more than one Member State
and the list of goods and services is not the same for all Member States, an
indication of the respective goods and services for each Member State;

(f) the date of the application for conversion.

Rule 47

Transmission to Central Industrial Property Offices of the Member States

Where the application for conversion complies with the requirements of the   **A10–049**
Regulation and these Rules, the Office shall transmit without delay the application for conversion to the central industrial property offices of the Member States
specified therein, including the Benelux Trade Mark Office. The Office shall
inform the applicant of the date of transmission.

TITLE X

APPEALS

Rule 48

Content of the Notice of Appeal

(1) The notice of appeal shall contain: **A10–050**

(a) the name and address of the appellant in accordance with rule 1 (1) (b);

(b) where the appellant has appointed a representative, the name and the business address of the representative in accordance with Rule 1 (1) (e);

(c) a statement identifying the decision which is contested and the extent to
which amendment or cancellation of the decision is requested.

(2) The notice of appeal shall be filed in the language of the proceedings in
which the decision subject to the appeal was taken.

Rule 49

Rejection of the Appeal as Inadmissible

(1) If the appeal does not comply with Article 57, 58 and 59 of the Regulation   **A10–051**

and Rule 48 (1) (c) and (2), the Board of Appeal shall reject it as inadmissible, unless each deficiency has been remedied before the relevant time limit laid down in Article 59 of the Regulation has expired.

(2) If the Board of Appeal finds that the appeal does not comply with other provisions of the Regulation or other provisions of these Rules, in particular Rule 48 (1) (a) and (b), it shall inform the appellant accordingly and shall request him to remedy the deficiencies noted within such period as it may specify. If the appeal is not corrected in good time, the Board of Appeal shall reject it as inadmissible.

(3) If the fee for appeal has been paid after expiry of the period for the filing of appeal pursuant to Article 59 of the Regulation, the appeal shall be deemed not to have been filed and the appeal fee shall be refunded to the appellant.

Rule 50

Examination of Appeals

A10–052

(1) Unless otherwise provided, the provisions relating to proceedings before the department which has made the decision against which the appeal is brought shall be applicable to appeal proceedings mutatis mutandis.

(2) The Board of Appeal's decision shall contain:

(a) a statement that it is delivered by the Board;

(b) the date when the decision was taken;

(c) the names of the Chairman and of the other members of the Board of Appeal taking part;

(d) the name of the competent employee of the registry;

(e) the names of the parties and of their representatives;

(f) a statement of the issues to be decided;

(g) a summary of the facts;

(h) the reasons;

(i) the order of the Board of Appeal, including, where necessary, a decision on costs.

(3) The decision shall be signed by the Chairman and the other members of the Board of Appeal and by the employee of the registry of the Board of Appeal.

Rule 51

Reimbursement of Appeal Fees

A10–053

The reimbursement of appeal fees shall be ordered in the event of interlocutory revision or where the Board of Appeal deems an appeal to be allowable, if such reimbursement is equitable by reason of a substantial procedural violation. In the event of interlocutory revision, reimbursement shall be ordered by the department whose decision has been impugned, and in other cases by the Board of Appeal.

Title XI

General Provisions

Part A

Decisions and communications of the Office

Rule 52

Form of Decisions

A10–054

(1) Decisions of the Office shall be in writing and shall state the reasons on

which they are based. Where oral proceedings are held before the Office, the decision may be given orally. Subsequently, the decision in writing shall be notified to the parties.

(2) Decisions of the Office which are open to appeal shall be accompanied by a written communication indicating that notice of appeal must be filed in writing at the Office within two months of the date of notification of the decision from which appeal is to be made. The communications shall also draw the attention of the parties to the provisions laid down in Articles 57, 58 and 59 of the Regulation. The parties may not plead any failure to communicate the availability proceedings.

Rule 53

Correction of Errors in Decisions

In decisions of the Office, only linguistic errors, errors of transcription and obvious mistakes my be corrected. They shall be corrected by the department which took the decision, acting of its own motion or at the request of an interested party.   **A10–055**

Rule 54

Noting of Loss of Rights

(1) If the Office finds that the loss of any rights results from the Regulation or these Rules without any decision having been taken, it shall communicate this to the person concerned in accordance with Article 77 of the Regulation, and shall draw his attention to the substance of paragraph 2 of this Rule.   **A10–056**

(2) If the person concerned considers that the finding of the Office is inaccurate, he may, within two months after notification of the communication referred to in paragraph 1, apply for a decision on the matter by the Office. Such decision shall be given only if the Office disagrees with the person requesting it; otherwise the Office shall amend its finding and inform the person requesting the decision.

Rule 55

Signature, Name, Seal

(1) Any decision, communication or notice from the Office shall indicate the department or division of the Office as well as the name or the names of the official or officials responsible. They shall be signed by the official or officials, or, instead of a signature, carry a printed or stamped seal of the Office.   **A10–057**

(2) The President of the Office may determine that other means of identifying the department or division of the Office and the name of the official or officials responsible or an identification other than a seal may be used where decisions, communications or notices are transmitted by telecopier or any other technical means of communication.

PART B

ORAL PROCEEDINGS AND TAKING OF EVIDENCE

Summons to Oral Proceedings

(1) The parties shall be summoned to oral proceedings provided for in Article 75 of the Regulation and their attention shall be drawn to paragraph 3 of this Rule. At least one month's, notice of the summons shall be given unless the parties agree to a shorter period.   **A10–058**

(2) When issuing the summons, the Office shall draw attention to the points which in its opinion need to be discussed in order for the decision to be taken.

(3) If a party who has been duly summoned to oral proceedings before the Office does not appear as summoned, the proceedings may continue without him.

Rule 57

Taking of Evidence by the Office

A10–059   (1) Where the Office considers it necessary to hear the oral evidence of parties, of witnesses or of experts or to carry out an inspection, it shall take a decision to that end, stating the means by which it intends to obtain evidence, the relevant facts to be proved and the date, time and place of hearing or inspection. If oral evidence of witnesses and experts is requested by a party, the decision of the Office shall determine the period of time within which the party filing the request must make known to the Office the names and addresses of the witnesses and experts whom the party wishes to be heard.

(2) The period of notice given in the summons of a party, witness or expert to give evidence shall be at least one month, unless they agree to a shorter period. The summons shall contain:
   (a) an extract from the decision mentioned in paragraph 1, indicating in particular the date, time and place of the hearing ordered and stating the facts regarding which the parties, witnesses and experts are to be heard;
   (b) the names of the parties to proceedings and particulars of the rights which the witnesses or experts may invoke under Rule 59 (2) to (5).

Rule 58

Commissioning of Experts

A10–060   (1) The Office shall decide in what form the report made by an expert whom it appoints shall be submitted.

(2) The terms of reference of the expert shall include:
(a) a precise description of his task;
(b) the time limit laid down for the submission of the expert report;
(c) the names of the parties to the proceedings;
(d) particulars of the claims which he may invoke under Rule 59 (2), (3) and (4).

(3) A copy of any written report shall be submitted to the parties.

(4) The parties may object to an expert on grounds of incompetence or on the same grounds as those on which objection may be made to an examiner or to a member of a Division or Board of Appeal pursuant to Article 132 (1) and (3) of the Regulation. The department of the Office concerned shall rule on the objection.

Rule 59

Costs of Taking of Evidence

A10–061   (1) The taking of evidence by the Office may be made conditional upon deposit with it, by the party who has requested the evidence to be taken, of a sum which shall be fixed by reference to an estimate of the costs.

(2) Witnesses and experts who are summoned by and appear before the Office shall be entitled to reimbursement of reasonable expenses for travel and subsistence. An advance for these expenses may be granted to them by the Office. The first sentence shall apply also to witnesses and experts who appear before the Office without being summoned by it and are heard as witnesses or experts.

(3) Witnesses entitled to reimbursement under paragraph 2 shall also be entitled to appropriate compensation for loss of earnings, and experts to fees for their work. These payments shall be made to the witnesses and experts after they have fulfilled their duties or tasks, where such witnesses and experts have been summoned by the Office of its own initiative.

(4) The amounts and the advances for expenses to be paid pursuant to paragraphs 1, 2 and 3 shall be determined by the President of the Office and shall be published in the Official Journal of the Office. The amounts shall be calculated on the same basis as the compensation and salaries received by officials in grades A4 to A8 as laid down in the Staff Regulations of Officials of the European Communities and Annex VII thereto.

(5) Final liability for the amounts due or paid pursuant to paragraphs 1 to 4 shall lie with:

(a) the Office where the Office, at its own initiative, considered it necessary to hear the oral evidence of witnesses or experts; or

(b) the party concerned where that party requested the giving of oral evidence by witnesses or experts, subject to the decision on apportionment and fixing of costs pursuant to Articles 81 and 82 of the Regulation and Rule 94. Such party shall reimburse the Office for any advances duly paid.

Rule 60

Minutes of Oral Proceedings and of Evidence

(1) Minutes of oral proceedings or the taking of evidence shall be drawn up, containing the essentials of the oral proceedings or of the taking of evidence, the relevant statements made by the parties, the testimony of the parties, witnesses or experts and the result of any inspection.   **A10–062**

(2) The minutes of the testimony of a witness, expert or party shall be read out or submitted to him so that he may examine them. It shall be noted in the minutes that this formality has been carried out and that the person who gave the testimony approved the minutes. Where his approval is not given, his objections shall be noted.

(3) The minutes shall be signed by the employee who drew them up and by the employee who conducted the oral proceedings or taking of evidence.

(4) The parties shall be provided with a copy of the minutes.

(5) Upon request, the Office shall make available to the parties transcripts of recordings of the oral proceedings, in typescript or in any other machine-readable form. The release under the first sentence of the oral proceedings shall be subject to the payment of the costs incurred by the Office in making such transcript. The amount to be charged shall be determined by the President of the Office.

PART C

NOTIFICATIONS

General Provisions on Notifications

(1) In proceedings before the Office, any notifications to be made by the Office shall take the form of the original document, of a copy thereof certified by, or bearing the seal of, the Office or of a computer print-out bearing such seal. Copies of documents emanating from the parties themselves shall not require such certification.   **A10–063**

(2) Notifications shall be made

(a) by post in accordance with Rule 62;

(b) by hand delivery in accordance with Rule 63;

(c) by deposit in a post box at the Office in accordance with Rule 64;

(d) by telecopier and other technical means in accordance with Rule 65;

(e) by public notification in accordance with Rule 66.

Rule 62

Notification by Post

A10–064

(1) Decisions subject to a time limit for appeal, summonses and other documents as determined by the President of the Office shall be notified by registered letter with advice of delivery. Decisions and communications subject to some other time limit shall be notified by registered letter, unless the President of the Office determines otherwise. All other communications shall be ordinary mail.

(2) Notifications in respect of addresses having neither their domicile nor their principal place of business nor an establishment in the Community and who have not appointed a representative in accordance with Article 88 (2) of the Regulation shall be effected by posting the document requiring notification by ordinary mail to the last address of the addressee known to the Office. Notification shall be deemed to have been effected when the posting has taken place.

(3) Where notification is effected by registered letter, whether or not with advice of delivery, this shall be deemed to be delivered to the addressee on the 10th day following that of its posting, unless the letter has failed to reach the addressee or has reached him at a later date. In the event of any dispute, it shall be for the Office to establish that the letter has reached its destination or to establish the date on which it was delivered to the addressee, as the case may be.

(4) Notification by registered letter, with or without advice of delivery, shall be deemed to have been effected even if the addressee refuses to accept the letter.

(5) To the extent that notification by post is not covered by paragraphs 1 to 4, the law of the State on the territory of which notification is made shall apply.

Rule 63

Notification by Hand Delivery

A10–065

Notification may be effected on the premises of the Office by hand delivery of the document to the addressee, who shall on delivery acknowledge its receipt.

Rule 64

Notification by Deposit in a Post Box at the Office

A10–066

Notification may also be effected to addressees who have been provided with a post box at the Office, by depositing the document therein. A written notification of deposit shall be inserted in the files. The date of deposit shall be recorded on the document. Notification shall be deemed to have taken place on the fifth day following deposit of the document in the post box at the Office.

Rule 65

Notification by Telecopier and other Technical Means

A10–067

(1) Notification by telecopier shall be effected by transmitting either the original or a copy, as provided for in Rule 61 (1), of the document to be notified. The details of such transmission shall be determined by the President of the Office.

(2) Details of notification by other technical means of communication shall be determined by the President of the Office.

Rule 66

Public Notification

(1) If the address of the addressee cannot be established, or if notification in accordance with Rule 62 (1) has proved to be impossible even after a second attempt by the Office, notification shall be effected by public notice. Such notice shall be published at least in the Community Trade Marks Bulletin.

(2) The President of the Office shall determine how the public notice is to be given and shall fix the beginning of the one-month period on the expiry of which the document shall be deemed to have been notified.

A10–068

Rule 67

Notification to Representatives

(1) If a representative has been appointed or where the applicant first named in a common application is considered to be the common representative pursuant to Rule 75 (1), notifications shall be addressed to that appointed or common representative.

(2) If several representatives have been appointed for a single interested party, notification to any one of them shall be sufficient, unless a specific address for service has been indicated in accordance with Rule 1 (1) (e).

(3) If several interested parties have appointed a common representative, notification of a single document to the common representative shall be sufficient.

A10–069

Rule 68

Irregularities in Notification

Where a document has reached the addressee, if the Office is unable to prove that it has been duly notified, or if provisions relating to its notification have not been observed, the document shall be deemed to have been notified on the date established by the Office as the date of receipt.

A10–070

Rule 69

Notification of Documents in the Case of Several Parties

Documents emanating from parties which contain substantive proposals, or a declaration of withdrawal of a substantive proposal, shall be notified to the other parties as a matter of course. Notification may be dispensed with where the document contains no new pleadings and the matter is ready for decision.

A10–071

PART D

TIMELIMITS

Rule 70

Calculation of Time Limits

(1) Periods shall be laid down in terms of full years, months, weeks or days.

(2) Calculation shall start on the day following the day on which the relevant event occurred, the event being either a procedural step or the expiry of another period. Where that procedural step is a notification, the event considered shall be the receipt of the document notified, unless otherwise provided.

(3) Where a period is expressed as one year or a certain number of years, it

A10–072

shall expire in the relevant subsequent year in the month having the same name and on the day having the same number as the month and the day on which the said event occurred. Where the relevant month has no day with the same number the period shall expire on the last day of that month.

(4) Where a period is expressed as one month or a certain number of months, it shall expire in the relevant subsequent month on the day which has the same number as the day on which the said event occurred. Where the day on which the said event occurred was the last day of a month or where the relevant subsequent month has no day with the same number the period shall expire on the last day of that month.

(5) Where a period is expressed as one week or a certain number of weeks, it shall expire in the relevant subsequent week on the day having the same name as the day on which the said event occurred.

Rule 71

Duration of Time Limits

A10–073   (1) Where the Regulation or these Rules provide for a period to be specified by the Office, such period shall, when the party concerned has its domicile or its principal place of business or an establishment within the Community, be not less than one month, or, when those conditions are not fulfilled, not less than two months, and no more than six months. The Office may, when this is appropriate under the circumstances, grant an extension of a period specified if such extension is requested by the party concerned and the request is submitted before the original period expired.

(2) Where there are two or more parties, the Office may extend a period subject to the agreement of the other parties.

Rule 72

Expiry of Time Limits in Special Cases

A10–074   (1) If a time limit expires on a day on which the Office is not open for receipt of documents or on which, for reasons other than those referred to in paragraph 2, ordinary mail is not delivered in the locality in which the Office is located, the time limit shall extend until the first day thereafter on which the Office is open for receipt of documents and on which ordinary mail is delivered. The days referred to in the first sentence shall be as determined by the President of the Office before the commencement of each calendar year.

(2) If a time limit expires on a day on which there is a general interruption or subsequent dislocation in the delivery of mail in a Member State or between a Member State and the Office, the time limit shall extend until the first day following the end of the period of interruption or dislocation, for parties having their residence or registered office in the State concerned or who have appointed representatives with a place of business in that State. In the event of the Member State concerned being the State in which the Office is located, this provision shall apply to all parties. The duration of the abovementioned period shall be as determined by the President of the Office.

(3) Paragraphs 1 and 2 shall apply mutatis mutandis to the time limits provided for in the Regulation or these Rules in the case of transactions to be carried out with the competent authority within the meaning of Article 25 (1) (b) of the Regulation.

(4) If an exceptional occurrence such as natural disaster or strike interrupts or dislocates the proper functioning of the Office so that any communication from the Office to parties concerning the expiry of a time limit is delayed, acts to be

completed within such a time limit may still be validly completed within one month after the notification of the delayed communication. The date of commencement and the end of any such interruption or dislocation shall be as determined by the President of the Office.

PART E

INTERRUPTION OF PROCEEDINGS

Rule 73

Interruption of Proceedings

(1) Proceedings before the Office shall be interrupted: **A10–075**

(a) in the event of the death or legal incapacity of the applicant for or proprietor of a Community trade mark or of the person authorized by national law to act on his behalf. To the extent that the above events do not affect the authorization of a representative appointed under Article 89 of the Regulation, proceedings shall be interrupted only on application by such representative;

(b) in the event of the applicant for or proprietor of a Community trade mark, as a result of some action taken against his property, being prevented for legal reasons from continuing the proceedings before the Office;

(c) in the event of the death or legal incapacity of the representative of an applicant for or proprietor of a Community trade mark or of his being prevented for legal reasons resulting from action taken against his property from continuing the proceedings before the Office.

(2) When, in the cases referred to in paragraph 1 (a) and (b), the Office has been informed of the identity of the person authorized to continue the proceedings before the Office, the Office shall communicate to such person and to any interested third parties that the proceedings shall be resumed as from a date to be fixed by the Office.

(3) In the case referred to in paragraph 1 (c), the proceedings shall be resumed when the Office has been informed of the appointment of a new representative of the applicant or when the Office has notified to the other parties the communication of the appointment of a new representative of the proprietor of the Community trade mark. If, three months after the beginning of the interruption of the proceedings, the Office has not been informed of the appointment of a new representative, it shall inform the applicant for or proprietor of the Community trade mark:

(a) where Article 88 (2) of the Regulation is applicable, that the Community trade mark application will be deemed to be withdrawn if the information is not submitted within two months after this communication is notified; or

(b) where Article 88 (2) of the Regulation is not applicable, that the proceedings will be resumed with the applicant for or proprietor of the Community trade mark as from the date on which this communication is notified.

(4) The time limits, other than the time limit for paying the renewal fees, in force as regards the applicant for or proprietor of the Community trade mark at the date of interruption of the proceedings, shall begin again as from the day on which the proceedings are resumed.

PART F

WAIVING OF ENFORCED RECOVERY PROCEDURES

Rule 74

Waiving of Enforced Recovery Procedures

A10–076   The President of the Office may waive action for the enforced recovery of any sum due where the sum to be recovered is minimal or where such recovery is too uncertain.

PART G

REPRESENTATION

Rule 75

Appointment of a Common Representative

A10–077   (1) If there is more than one applicant and the application for a Community trade mark does not name a common representative, the applicant first named in the application shall be considered to be the common representative. However, if one of the applicants is obliged to appoint a professional representative, such representative shall be considered to be the common representative unless the applicant named first in the application has appointed a professional representative. The same shall apply mutatis mutandis to third parties acting in common in filing notice of opposition or applying for revocation or for a declaration of invalidity, and to joint proprietors of a Community trade mark.

(2) If, during the course of proceedings, transfer is made to more than one person, and such persons have not appointed a common representative, paragraph 1 shall apply. If such application is not possible, the Office shall require such persons to appoint a common representative within two months. If this request is not complied with, the Office shall appoint the common representative.

Rule 76

Authorizations

A10–078   (1) Representatives acting before the Office must file with it a signed authorization for inclusion in the files. The authorization may cover one or more applications or one or more registered trade marks.

(2) A general authorization enabling a representative to act in respect of all trade mark transactions of the party giving the authorization may be filed.

(3) The authorization may be filed in any language of the Office and in the language of the proceedings if that language is not one of the languages of the Office.

(4) Where the appointment of a representative is communicated to the Office, the necessary authorization shall be filed within a period specified by the Office. If the authorization is not filed in due time, proceedings shall be continued with the represented person. Any procedural steps other than the filing of the application taken by the representative shall be deemed not to have been taken if the represented person does not approve them. The application of Article 88 (2) of the Regulation shall remain unaffected.

(5) Paragraphs 1 to 3 shall apply mutatis mutandis to a document withdrawing an authorization.

(6) Any representative who has ceased to be authorized shall continue to be regarded as the representative until the termination of his authorization has been communicated to the Office.

(7) Subject to any provisions to the contrary contained therein, an authorization shall not terminate vis-à-vis the Office upon the death of the person who gave it.

(8) Where several representatives are appointed by the same party, they may, notwithstanding any provisions to the contrary in their authorizations, act either jointly or singly.

(9) The authorization of an association of representatives shall be deemed to be an authorization of any representative who can establish that he practises within that association.

Rule 77

Representation

Any notification or other communication addressed by the Office to the duly authorized representative shall have the same effect as if it had been addressed to the represented person. Any communication addressed to the Office by the duly authorized representative shall have the same effect as if it originated from the represented person.

A10–079

Rule 78

Amendment of the List of Professional Representatives

(1) The entry of a professional representative in the list of professional representatives, as referred to in Article 89 of the Regulation, shall be deleted at his request.

A10–080

(2) The entry of a professional representative shall be deleted automatically:

(a) in the event of the death or legal incapacity of the professional representative;

(b) where the professional representative is no longer a national of a Member State, unless the President of the Office has granted an exemption under Article 89 (4) (b) of the Regulation;

(c) where the professional representative no longer has his place of business or employment in the Community;

(d) where the professional representative no longer possesses the entitlement referred to in the first sentence of Article 89 (2) (c) of the Regulation.

(3) The entry of a professional representative shall be suspended of the Office's own motion where his entitlement to represent natural or legal persons before the central industrial property office of the Member State as referred to in the fist sentence of Article 89 (2) (c) has been suspended.

(4) A person whose entry has been deleted shall, upon request pursuant to Article 89 (3) of the Regulation, be reinstated in the list of professional representatives if the conditions for deletion no longer exist.

(5) The Benelux Trade Mark Office and the central industrial property offices of the Member States concerned shall, where they are aware thereof, promptly inform the Office of any relevant events under paragraphs 2 and 3.

(6) The amendments of the list of professional representatives shall be published in the Official Journal of the Office.

Part H

Written communications and forms

Rule 79

Communication in Writing or by Other Means

A10–081   Applications for the registration of a Community trade mark as well as any other application provided for in the Regulation and all other communications addressed to the Office shall be submitted as follows:

(a) by submitting a signed original of the document in question at the Office, such as by post, personal delivery, or by any other means; annexes to documents submitted need not be signed;

(b) by transmitting a signed original by telecopier in accordance with Rule 80;

(c) by telex or telegram in accordance with Rule 81;

(d) by transmitting the contents of the communication by electronic means in accordance with Rule 82.

Rule 80

Communication by Telecopier

A10–082   (1) Where an application for registration of a trade mark is submitted to the Office by telecopier and the application contains a reproduction of the mark pursuant to Rule 3 (2) which does not satisfy the requirements of that Rule, the required number of original reproductions shall be submitted to the Office in accordance with Rule 79 (a). Where the reproductions are received by the Office within a period of one month from the date of the receipt of the telecopy by the Office, the application shall be deemed to have been received by the Office on the date on which the telecopy was received by the Office. Where the reproductions are received by the Office after the expiry of that period and the reproduction is necessary for the obtaining of a filing date, the application shall be deemed to have been received by the Office on the date on which the reproductions were received by the Office.

(2) Where a communication received by telecopier is incomplete or illegible, or where the Office has reasonable doubts as to the accuracy of the transmission, the Office shall inform the sender accordingly and shall invite him, within a period to be specified by the Office, to retransmit the original by telecopy or to submit the original in accordance with Rule 79 (a). Where this request is complied with within the period specified, the date of the receipt of the retransmission or of the original shall be deemed to be the date of the receipt of the original communication, provided that where the deficiency concerns the granting of a filing date for an application to register a trade mark, the provisions on the filing date shall apply. Where the request is not complied with within the period specified, the communication shall be deemed not to have been received.

(3) Any communication submitted to the Office by telecopier shall be considered to be duly signed if the reproduction of the signature appears on the printout produced by the telecopier.

(4) The President of the Office may determine additional requirements of communication by telecopier, such as the equipment to be used, technical details of communication, and methods of identifying the sender.

Rule 81

Communication by Telex or Telegram

A10–083   (1) Where an application for registration of a trade mark is submitted to the

Office by telex or by telegram and the application contains a reproduction of the mark pursuant to Rule 3 (2), Rule 80 (1) shall apply mutatis mutandis.

(2) Where a communication is submitted by telex or telegram, Rule 80 (2) shall apply mutatis mutandis.

(3) Where a communication is submitted by telex or telegram, the indication of the name of the sender shall be deemed equivalent to the signature.

Rule 82

Communication by Electronic Means

(1) Where an application for registration of a trademark is submitted by electronic means and the application contains a reproduction of the mark pursuant to Rule 3 (2), Rule 80 (1) shall apply mutatis mutandis.   **A10–084**

(2) Where a communication is sent by electronic means, Rule 80 (2) shall apply mutatis mutandis.

(3) Where a communication is sent to the Office by electronic means, the indication of the name of the sender shall be deemed to be equivalent to the signature.

(4) The President of the Office shall determine the requirements as to communication by electronic means, such as the equipment to be used, technical details of communication, and methods of identifying the sender.

Rule 83

Forms

(1) The Office shall make available free of charge forms for the purpose of: **A10–085**

(a) filing an application for a Community trade mark;

(b) entering opposition to registration of a Community trade mark;

(c) applying for an amendment of an application or a registration, for correction of names and addresses and of mistakes and errors;

(d) applying for the registration of a transfer and the transfer form and transfer document provided for in Rule 31 (5);

(e) applying for the registration of a licence;

(f) applying for renewal of the registration of a Community trade mark;

(g) applying for revocation or for a declaration of invalidity of a Community trade mark;

(h) applying for restitutio in integrum;

(i) making an appeal;

(j) authorizing a representative, in the form of an individual authorization and in the form of a general authorization.

(2) The Office may make other forms available free of charge.

(3) The Office shall make available the forms referred to in paragraphs 1 and 2 in all the official languages of the Community.

(4) The Office shall place the forms at the disposal of the Benelux Trade Mark Office and the Member States' central industrial property offices free of charge.

(5) The Office may also make available the forms in machine-readable form.

(6) Parties to proceedings before the Office shall use the forms provided by the Office, or copies of these forms, or forms with the same content and format as these forms, such as forms generated by means of electronic data processing.

(7) Forms shall be completed in such a manner as to permit an automated input of the content into a computer, such as by character recognition or scanning.

PART I

INFORMATION OF THE PUBLIC

Rule 84

Register of Community Trade Marks

A10–086   (1) The Register of Community Trade Marks may be maintained in the form of an electronic database.

(2) The Register of Community Trade Marks shall contain the following entries:

(a) the date of filing the application;

(b) the file number of the application;

(c) the date of the publication of the application;

(d) the name, the address and the nationality of the applicant and the State in which he is domiciled or has his seat or establishment;

(e) the name and business address of the representative, other than a representative falling within the first sentence of Article 88 (3) of the Regulation; where there is more than one representative, only the name and business address of the first named representative, followed by the words and others, shall be recorded; where an association of representatives is appointed, only the name and address of the association shall be recorded;

(f) the reproduction of the mark, with indications as to its nature, unless it is a mark falling under Rule 3(1); where the registration of the mark is in colour, the indication 'in colour' with an indication of the colour or colours making up the mark; where applicable, a description of the mark;

(g) an indication of the goods and services by their names, grouped according to the classes of the Nice Classification; each group shall be preceded by the number of the class of that classification to which that group of goods and services belongs and shall be presented in the order of the classes of that classification;

(h) particulars of claims of priority pursuant to Article 30 of the Regulation;

(i) particulars of claims of exhibition priority pursuant to Article 33 of the Regulation;

(j) particulars of claims of seniority of an earlier registered trade mark as referred to in Article 34 of the Regulation;

(k) a statement that the mark has become distinctive in consequence of the use which has been made of it, pursuant to Article 7(3) of the Regulation;

(l) a declaration by the applicant disclaiming any exclusive right to some element of the mark pursuant to Article 38(2) of the Regulation;

(m) an indication that the mark is a collective mark;

(n) the language in which the application was filed and the second language which the applicant has indicated in his application, pursuant to Article 115(3) of the Regulation;

(o) the date of registration of the mark in the Register and the registration number.

(3) The Register of Community Trade Marks shall also contain the following entries, each accompanied by the date of recording of such entry:

(a) changes in the name, the address or the nationality of the proprietor of a Community trade mark or in the State in which he is domiciled or has his seat or establishment;

(b) changes in the name or business address of the representative, other than a representative falling within Article 88 (3), first sentence, of the Regulation;

(c) when a new representative is appointed, the name and business address of that representative;

(d) alterations of the mark pursuant to Article 48 of the Regulation and corrections of mistakes and errors;

(e) notice of amendments to the regulations governing the use of the collective mark pursuant to Article 69 of the Regulation;

(f) particulars of claims of seniority of an earlier registered trade mark as referred to in Article 34 of the Regulation, pursuant to Article 35 of the Regulation;

(g) total or partial transfers pursuant to Article 17 of the Regulation;

(h) the creation or transfer of a right in rem pursuant to Article 19 of the Regulation and the nature of the right in rem;

(i) levy of execution pursuant to Article 20 of the Regulation and bankruptcy or like proceedings pursuant to Article 21 of the regulation;

(j) the grant or transfer of a licence pursuant to Article 22 of the Regulation and, where applicable, the type of licence pursuant to Rule 34;

(k) renewal of the registration pursuant to Article 47 of the Regulation, the date from which it takes effect and any restrictions pursuant to Article 47 (4) of the Regulation;

(l) a record of the determination of the expiry of the registration pursuant to Article 47 of the Regulation;

(m) a declaration of surrender by the proprietor of the mark pursuant to Article 49 of the Regulation;

(n) the date of submission of an application pursuant to Article 55 of the Regulation or of the filing of a counterclaim pursuant to Article 96 (4) of the Regulation for revocation or for a declaration of invalidity;

(o) the date and content of the decision on the application or counterclaim pursuant to Article 56 (6) or the third sentence of Article 96 (6) of the Regulation;

(p) a record of the receipt of a request for conversion pursuant to Article 109 (2) of the Regulation;

(q) the cancellation of the representative recorded pursuant to paragraph 2 (e);

(r) the cancellation of the seniority of a national mark;

(s) the modification or cancellation from the Register of the items referred to in subparagraphs (h), (i) and (j).

(4) The President of the Office may determine that items other than those referred to in paragraphs 2 and 3 shall be entered in the Register.

(5) The proprietor of the trade mark shall be notified of any change in the Register.

(6) The Office shall provide certified or uncertified extracts from the Register on request, on payment of a fee.

PART J

Community Trade Marks Bulletin and Official Journal of the Office

Rule 85

Community Trade Marks Bulletin

(1) The Community Trade Marks Bulletin shall be published in periodic   **A10–087**

editions. The Office may make available to the public editions of the Bulletin on CD-ROM or in any other machine-readable form.

(2) The Community Trade Marks Bulletin shall contain publications of applications and of entries made in the Register as well as other particulars relating to applications or registrations of trade marks whose publication is prescribed by the Regulation or by these Rules.

(3) Where particulars whose publication is prescribed in the Regulation or in these Rules are published in the Community Trade Marks Bulletin, the date of issue shown on the Bulletin shall be taken as the date of publication of the particulars.

(4) To the extent that the entries regarding the registration of a trade mark contain no changes as compared to the publication of the application, the publication of such entries shall be made by way of a reference to the particulars contained in the publication of the application.

(5) The elements of the application for a Community trade mark, as set out in Article 26 (1) of the Regulation as well as any other information the publication of which is prescribed in Rule 12 shall, where appropriate, be published in all the official languages of the Community.

(6) The Office shall take into account any translation submitted by the applicant. If the language of the application is not one of the languages of the Office, the translation into the second language indicated by the applicant shall be communicated to the applicant. The applicant may propose changes to the translation within a period to be specified by the Office. If the applicant does not respond within this period or if the Office considers the proposed changes to be inappropriate, the translation proposed by the Office shall be published.

Rule 86
Official Journal of the Office

A10–088   (1) The Official Journal of the Office shall be published in periodic editions. The Office may make available to the public editions of the Official Journal on CD-ROM or in any other machine-readable form.

(2) The Official Journal shall be published in the languages of the Office. The President of the Office may determine that certain items shall be published in all the official languages of the Community.

Rule 87
Data Bank

A10–089   (1) The Office shall maintain an electronic data bank with the particulars of applications for registration of trade marks and entries in the Register. The Office may also make available the contents of this data bank on CD-ROM or in any other machine-readable form.

(2) The President of the Office shall determine the conditions of access to the data bank and the manner in which the contents of this data bank may be made available in machine-readable form, including the charges for these acts.

PART K

INSPECTION OF FILES AND KEEPING OF FILES

Rule 88
Parts of the File Excluded from Inspection

A10–090   The parts of the file which shall be excluded from inspection pursuant to Article 84 (4) of the Regulation shall be:

(a) documents relating to exclusion or objection pursuant to Article 132 of the Regulation;

(b) draft decisions and opinions, and all other internal documents used for the preparation of decisions and opinions;

(c) parts of the file which the party concerned showed a special interest in keeping confidential before the application for inspection of the files was made, unless inspection of such part of the file is justified by overriding legitimate interests of the party seeking inspection.

Rule 89

Procedures for the Inspection of Files

(1) Inspection of the files of Community trade mark applications and of registered Community trade marks shall either be of the original document, or of copies thereof, or of technical means of storage if the files are stored in this way. The means of inspection shall be determined by the President of the Office. The request for inspection of the files shall not be deemed to have been made until the required fee has been paid.   **A10–091**

(2) Where inspection of the files of a Community trade mark application is requested, the request shall contain an indication and evidence to the effect that the applicant

(a) has consented to the inspection; or

(b) has stated that after the trade mark has been registered he will invoke the rights under it against the party requesting the inspection.

(3) Inspection of the files shall take place on the premises of the Office.

(4) On request, inspection of the files shall be effected by means of issuing copies of file documents. Such copies shall incur fees.

(5) The office shall issue on request certified or uncertified copies of the application for a Community trade mark or of those file documents of which copies may be issued pursuant to paragraph 4 upon payment of a fee.

Rule 90

Communication of Information Contained in the Files

Subject to the restrictions provided for in Article 84 of the Regulation and Rule 88, the Office may, upon request, communicate information from any file of a Community trade mark applied for or of a registered Community trade mark, subject to payment of a fee. However, the Office may require the exercise of the option to obtain inspection of the file itself should it deem this to be appropriate in view of the quantity of information to be supplied.   **A10–092**

Rule 91

Keeping of Files

(1) The Office shall keep the files relating to Community trade mark applications and registered Community trade marks for at least five years from the end of the year in which: **A10–093**

(a) the application is rejected or withdrawn or is deemed to be withdrawn;

(b) the registration of the Community trade mark expires completely pursuant to Article 47 of the Regulation;

(c) the complete surrender of the Community trade mark is registered pursuant to Article 49 of the Regulation;

(d) the Community trade mark is completely removed from the Register pursuant to Article 56 (6) or Article 96 (6) of the Regulation.

(2) The President of the Office shall determine the form in which the files shall be kept.

PART L

ADMINISTRATIVE COOPERATION

Rule 92

Exchange of Information and Communications between the Office and the Authorities of the Member States

A10–094 (1) The Office and the central industrial property offices of the Member States shall, upon request, communicate to each other relevant information about the filing of applications for Community trade marks or national marks and about proceedings relating to such applications and the marks registered as a result thereof. Such communications shall not be subject to the restrictions provided for in Article 84 of the Regulation.

(2) Communications between the Office and the courts or authorities of the Member States which arise out of the application of the Regulation or these Rules shall be effected directly between these authorities. Such communication may also be effected through the central industrial property offices of the Member States.

(3) Expenditure in respect of communications under paragraphs 1 and 2 shall be chargeable to the authority making the communications, which shall be exempt from fees.

Rule 93

Inspection of Files by or Via Courts or Authorities of the Member States

A10–095 (1) Inspection of files relating to Community trade marks applied for or registered Community trade marks by courts or authorities of the Member States be of the original documents or of copies thereof, otherwise Rule 89 shall not apply.

(2) Courts or Public Prosecutors' Offices of the Member States may, in the course of proceedings before them, open files or copies thereof transmitted by the Office to inspection by third parties. Such inspection shall be subject to Article 84 of the Regulation. The Office shall not charge any fee for such inspection.

(3) The Office shall, at the time of transmission of the files or copies thereof to the courts or Public Prosecutors' Offices of the Member States, indicate the restrictions to which the inspection of files relating to Community trade marks applied for or registered Community trade marks is subject pursuant to Article 84 of the Regulation and Rule 88.

PART M

COSTS

Rule 94

Apportionment and Fixing of Costs

A10–096 (1) Apportionment of costs pursuant to Article 81 (1) and (2) of the Regulation shall be dealt with in the decision on the opposition, the decision on the application for revocation or for a declaration of invalidity of a Community trade mark, or the decision on the appeal.

(2) Apportionment of costs pursuant to Article 81 (3) and (4) of the Regulation shall be dealt with in a decision on costs by the Opposition Division, the Cancellation Division or the Board of Appeal.

(3) A bill of costs, with supporting evidence, shall be attached to the request for the fixing of costs provided for in the first sentence of Article 81 (6) of the Regulation. The request shall be admissible only if the decision in respect of which the fixing of costs is required has become final. Costs may be fixed once their credibility is established.

(4) The request provided for in the second sentence of Article 81 (6) of the Regulation for a review of the decision of the registry on the fixing of costs, stating the reasons on which it is based, must be filed at the Office within one month after the date of notification of the awarding of costs. It shall not be deemed to be filed until the fee for reviewing the amount of the costs has been paid.

(5) The Opposition Division, the Cancellation Division or the Board of Appeal, as the case may be, shall take a decision on the request referred to in paragraph 4 without oral proceedings.

(6) The fees to be borne by the losing party pursuant to Article 81 (1) of the Regulation shall be limited to the fees incurred by the other party for opposition, for an application for revocation or for a declaration of invalidity of the Community trade mark and for appeal.

(7) Cost essential to the proceedings and actually incurred by the successful party shall be borne by the losing party in accordance with Article 81 (1) of the Regulation on the basis of the following maximum rates:

(a) travel expenses of one party for the outward and return journey between the place of residence or the place of business and the place where oral proceedings are held or where evidence is taken, as follows:

(i) the cost of the first-class rail-fare including usual transport supplements where the total distance by rail does not exceed 800 km;

(ii) the cost of the tourist-class air-fare where the total distance by rail exceeds 800 km or the route includes a sea-crossing;

(b) subsistence expenses by one party equal to the daily subsistence allowance for officials in grades A4 to A8 as laid down in Article 13 of Annex VII to the Staff Regulations of Officials of the European Communities;

(c) travel expenses of representatives within the meaning of Article 89 (1) of the Regulation and of witnesses and of experts, at the rates provided for in subparagraph (a);

(d) subsistence expenses of representatives within the meaning of Article 89 (1) of the Regulation and of witnesses and experts, at the rates provided for in subparagraph (b);

(e) costs entailed in the taking of evidence in the form of examination of witnesses, opinions by experts or inspection up to ECU 300 per proceedings;

(f) cost of representation, within the meaning of Article 89 (1) of the Regulation,

(i) of the opposing party in opposition proceedings: up to ECU 250;

(ii) of the applicant in opposition proceedings: up to ECU 250;

(iii) of the applicant in proceedings relating to revocation or invalidity of a Community trade mark: up to ECU 400;

(iv) of the proprietor of the trade mark in proceedings relating to revocation or invalidity of a Community trade mark: up to ECU 400;

(v) of the appellant in appeal proceedings: up to ECU 500;

(vi) of the defendant in appeal proceedings: up to ECU 500;

Where the taking of evidence in any of the abovementioned proceedings involves the examination of witnesses, opinions by experts or inspection, an additional amount shall be granted for representation costs of up to ECU 600 per proceedings;

(g) where the successful party is represented by more than one representative within the meaning of Article 89 (1) of the Regulation, the losing party shall bear the costs referred to in subparagraphs (c), (d) and (f) for one such person only;

(h) the losing party shall not be obliged to reimburse the successful party for any costs, expenses and fees other than those referred to in subparagraphs (a) to (g).

PART N

LANGUAGES

Rule 95

Applications and Declarations

A10–097   Without prejudice to Article 115 (5) of the Regulation,

(a) any application or declaration relating to a Community trade mark application may be filed in the language used for filing the application for a Community trade mark or in the second language indicated by the applicant in his application;

(b) any application or declaration relating to a registered Community trade mark may be filed in one of the languages of the Office. However, when the application is filed by using any of the forms provided by the Office pursuant to Rule 83, such forms may be used in any of the official languages of the Community, provided that the form is completed in one of the languages of the Office, as far as textual elements are concerned.

Rule 96

Written Proceedings

A10–098   (1) Without prejudice to Article 115 (4) and (7) of the Regulation, and unless otherwise provided for in these Rules, in written proceedings before the Office any party may use any language of the Office. If the language chosen is not the language of the proceedings, the party shall supply a translation into that language within one month from the date of the submission of the original document. Where the applicant for a Community trade mark is the sole party to proceedings before the Office and the language used for the filing of the application for the Community trade mark is not one of the languages of the Office, the translation may also be filed in the second language indicated by the applicant in his application.

(2) Unless otherwise provided for in these Rules, documents to be used in proceedings before the Office may be filed in any official language of the Community. Where the language of such documents is not the language of the proceedings the Office may require that a translation be supplied, within a period specified by it, in that language or, at the choice of the party to the proceeding, in any language of the Office.

Rule 97

Oral Proceedings

A10–099   (1) Any party to oral proceedings before the Office may, in place of the language of proceedings, use one of the other official languages of the Community, on condition that he makes provision for interpretation into the language of proceedings. Where the oral proceedings are held in a proceeding concerning the application for registration of a trade mark, the applicant may use either the language of the application or the second language indicated by him.

(2) In oral proceedings concerning the application for registration of a trade mark, the staff of the Office may use either the language of the application or the second language indicated by the applicant. In all other oral proceedings, the staff of the Office may use, in place of the language of the proceedings, one of the other languages of the Office, on condition that the party or parties to the proceedings agree to such use.

(3) In the case of taking of evidence, any party to be heard, witness or expert who is unable to express himself adequately in the language of proceedings, may use any of the official languages of the Community. Should the taking of evidence be decided upon following a request by a party to the proceedings, parties to be heard, witnesses or experts who express themselves in languages other than the language of proceedings may be heard only if the party who made the request makes provision for interpretation into that language. In proceedings concerning the application for registration of a trade mark, in place of the language of the application, the second language indicated by the applicant may be used. In any proceedings with only one party the Office may on request of the party concerned permit derogations from the provisions in this paragraph.

(4) If the parties and Office so agree, any official language of the Community may be used in oral proceedings.

(5) The Office shall, if necessary, make provision at its own expense for interpretation into the language of proceedings, or, where appropriate, into its other languages, unless this interpretation is the responsibility of one of the parties to the proceedings.

(6) Statements by staff of the Office, by parties to the proceedings and by witnesses and experts, made in one of the languages of the Office during oral proceedings shall be entered in the minutes in the language employed. Statements made in any other language shall be entered in the language of proceedings. Amendments to the text of the application for or the registration of a Community trade mark shall be entered in the minutes in the language of proceedings.

Rule 98

Certification of Translations

(1) When a translation of any document is to be filed, the Office may require   **A10–100**
the filing, within a period to be specified by it, of a certificate that the translation corresponds to the original text. Where the certificate relates to the translation of a previous application pursuant to Article 30 of the Regulation, such period shall not be less than three months after the date of filing of the application. Where the certificate is not filed within that period, the document shall be deemed not to have been received.

(2) The President of the Office may determine the manner in which translations are certified.

Rule 99

Legal Authenticity of Translations

In the absence of evidence to the contrary, the Office may assume that a transla-   **A10–101**
tion corresponds to the relevant original text.

PART O

ORGANIZATION OF THE OFFICE

Rule 100

Allocation of Duties

A10–102   (1) The President of the Office shall determine the examiners and their number, the members of the Opposition Divisions and Cancellation Divisions, and the members of the Administration of Trade Marks and Legal Division. He shall allocate duties to the examiners and the Divisions.

(2) The President of the Office may provide that examiners may also be members of the Opposition Divisions, Cancellation Divisions, and the Administration of Trade Marks and Legal Division, and that members of these Divisions may also be examiners.

(3) In addition to the responsibilities vested in them under the Regulation, the President of the Office may allocate further duties to the examiners and the members of the Opposition Divisions, Cancellation Divisions and the Administration of Trade Marks and Legal Division.

(4) The President of the Office may entrust to other members of the staff of the Office who are not examiners or members of any of the Divisions mentioned in paragraph 1 the execution of individual duties falling to the examiners, Opposition Divisions, Cancellation Divisions or the Administration of Trade Marks and Legal Division and involving no special difficulties.

TITLE XII

RECIPROCITY

Rule 101

Publication of Reciprocity

A10–103   (1) If necessary, the President of the Office shall request the Commission to enquire whether a State which is not party to the Paris Convention or to the Agreement establishing the World Trade Organization accords reciprocal treatment within the meaning of Article 5 (1) (d), Article 5 (3) and Article 29 (5) of the Regulation.

(2) If the Commission determines that reciprocal treatment in accordance with paragraph 1 is accorded, it shall publish a communication to this effect in the Official Journal of the European Communities.

(3) Article 5 (1) (d), Article 5 (3) and Article 29 (5) of the Regulation shall take effect for the nationals of the States concerned from the date of publication in the Official Journal of the European Communities of the communication referred to in paragraph 2, unless the communications states an earlier date from which it is applicable. They shall cease to be effective from the date of publication in the Official Journal of the European Communities of a communication of the Commission to the effect that reciprocal treatment is no longer accorded, unless the communication states an earlier date from which it is applicable.

(4) Communications referred to in paragraphs 2 and 3 shall also be published in the Official Journal of the Office.

Article 2

Transitional Provisions

A10–104   (1) Any application for registration of a Community trade mark filed within three months prior to the date determined pursuant to Article 143 (3) of the Regulation shall be marked by the Office with the filing date determined pursuant to that provision and with the actual date of receipt of the application.

(2) With regard to the application, the priority period of six months provided for in Articles 29 and 33 of the Regulation shall be calculated from the date determined pursuant to Article 143 (3) of the Regulation.

(3) The Office may issue a receipt to the applicant prior to the date determined pursuant to Article 143 (3) of the Regulation.

(4) The Office may examine the applications prior to the date determined pursuant to Article 143 (3) of the Regulation and communicate with the applicant with a view to remedying any deficiencies prior to that date. Any decisions with regard to such applications may be taken only after that date.

(5) With regard to the application, the Office shall not carry out any search pursuant to Article 39 (1) of the Regulation, regardless of whether or not a priority was claimed for such application pursuant to Articles 29 or 33 of the Regulation.

(6) Where the date of receipt of an application for the registration of a Community trade mark by the Office, by the central industrial property office of a Member State or by the Benelux Trade Mark Office is before the commencement of the three months period specified in Article 143 (4) of the Regulation the application shall be deemed not to have been filed. The application shall be informed accordingly and the application shall be sent back to him.

Article 3

Entry into Force

This Regulation shall enter into force on the seventh day following that of its publication in the Official Journal of the European Communities.   **A10–105**

This Regulation shall be binding in its entirety and directly applicable in all Member States.

Done at Brussels, December 13, 1995.

Commission Regulation 2869/95 of December 13, 1995—On the fees payable to the Office for Harmonization in the Internal Market (Trade Marks and Designs)

([1995] O.J. L303/33)

A11–001   *THE COMMISSION OF THE EUROPEAN COMMUNITIES,*

Having regard to the Treaty establishing the European Community,

Having regard to Council Regulation (EC) No 40/94 of 20 December 1993 on the Community trade mark, as amended by Regulation (EC) No 3288/94, and in particular Article 139 thereof,

Having regard to Commission Regulation (EC) No 2868/95 of 13 December 1995, implementing Council Regulation (EC) No 40/94 on the Community trade mark (3),

Whereas Article 139 (3) of Regulation (EC) No 40/94 (hereinafter 'the Regulation') provides that the fees regulations shall be adopted in accordance with the procedure laid down in Article 141 of the Regulation;

Whereas Article 139 (1) of the Regulation provides that the fees regulations shall determine in particular the amount of the fees and the ways in which they are to be paid;

Whereas Article 139 (2) of the Regulation provides that the amounts of the fees shall be fixed at such a level as to ensure that the revenue in respect thereof is in principle sufficient for the budget of the Office for Harmonization in the Internal Market (trade marks and designs) ('the Office') to be balanced;

Whereas, however, in the Office's start-up phase, balance can be achieved only if there is a subsidy from the general budget of the European Communities, in accordance with Article 134 (3) of the Regulation;

Whereas the basic fee for the application for a Community trade mark shall include the amount which the Office must pay to each central industrial property office of the Member States for each search report provided by such offices in accordance with Article 39 (4) of the Regulation;

Whereas to ensure the necessary flexibility, the President of the Office ('the President') should be empowered, subject to certain conditions, to lay down the charges which may be payable to the Office in respect of services it may render, the charges for access to the Office's data bank and the making available of the contents of this data bank in machine-readable form, and to set charges for the sale of its publications;

Whereas, in order to facilitate the payment of fees and charges, the President should be empowered to authorize methods of payment which are additional to those explicitly provided for in this Regulation;

Whereas it is appropriate that the fees and charges payable to the Office should be fixed in the same currency unit as is used for the budget of the Office;

Whereas the budget of the Office is fixed in ecus;

Whereas, moreover, the fixing of these amounts in ecus avoids discrepancies that may result from exchange rate variations;

Whereas payments in cash should be made in the currency of the Member State where the Office has its seat;

Whereas the measures envisaged in this Regulation are in accordance with the opinion of the Committee established under Article 141 of the Regulation,

HAS ADOPTED THIS REGULATION:

Article 1

General

The following shall be levied in accordance with this Regulation: **A11–002**

(a) fees to be paid to the Office as provided for in the Regulation and in Regulation (EC) No 2868/95;

Article 2

Fees Provided for in the Regulation and Regulation (EC) No 2868/95

The fees to be paid to the Office under Article 1 (a) shall be as follows: **A11–003**

1.	Basic fee for the application for an individual mark (Article 26(2); Rule 4(a))	975 ecu
2.	Fee for each class of goods and services exceeding three for an individual mark (Article 26(2); Rule 4 (b))	200 ecu
3.	Basic fee for the application for a collective mark (Article 26(2) and 64(3); Rules 4(a) and 42)	1675 ecu
4.	Fee for each class of goods and services exceeding three for a collective mark (Article 26(2) and 64(3); Rules 4(b) and 42)	400 ecu
5.	Opposition fee (Article 42(3); Rule 18(1))	350 ecu
6.	Fee for the alteration of the representation of a trade mark (point 1 of Article 140(2) and Article 44(2); Rule 13(2))	200 ecu
7.	Basic fee for the registration of an individual mark (Article 45; Rule 23(1)(a))	1100 ecu
8.	Fee for each class of goods and services exceeding three for an individual mark (Article 45; Rule 23(1)(b))	200 ecu
9.	Basic fee for the registration of a collective mark (Articles 45 and 64(3); Rules 23(1)(a) and 42)	2200 ecu
10.	Fee for each class of goods and services exceeding three for a collective mark (Articles 45 and 64 (3), Rules 23(1)(b) and 42)	400 ecu
11.	Additional fee for the late payment of the registration fee (point 2 Article 140(2), Rule 23(3))	250f the belated registration fee, subject to a maximum of 750 ecu

12.	Basic fee for the renewal for an individual mark (Article 47(1), Rule 30(2)(a))	2500 ecu
13.	Fee for each class of goods and services exceeding three for an individual mark (Article 47(1), Rule 30(2)(b))	Fee for each class of goods and services exceeding three for an individual mark (Article 47(1), Rule 30(2)(b))
14.	Basic fee for the renewal for a collective mark (Articles 47(1) and 64(3), Rules 30(2)(a) and 42)	5000 ecu
15.	Fee for each class of goods and services exceeding three for a collective mark (Articles 47(1) and 64(3), Rules 30(2)(b) and 42)	1000 ecu
16.	Additional fee for the late payment of the renewal fee or the late submission of the request for renewal (Article 47(3), Rule 30(2)(c))	250f the belated renewal fee, subject to a maximum of 1500 ecu
17.	Fee for the application for revocation or for a declaration of invalidity (Article 55(2), Rule 39(2))	700 ecu
18.	Appeal fee (Article 59, Rule 49(1))	800 ecu
19.	Fee for *restitutio in intergrum* (Article 78(3))	200 ecu
20.	Fee for the conversion of a mark into a national trade mark application (Article 109(1), Rule 45(2))	200 ecu
21.	Fee for the recording of the whole or partial transfer of an application for a Community trade mark (Article 24 and point 4 of Article 140(2); Rule 31(4) and (8))	200 ecu per entry, but, where multiple requests are submitted in the same application or at the same time, not to exceed a total of 1000 ecu.
22.	Fee for the registration of the whole or partial transfer of a registered Community trade mark (point 4 of Article 140(2); Rule 31(4))	200 ecu per registration, but, where multiple requests are submitted in the same application or at the same time, not to exceed a total of 1000 ecu

23.	Fee for the registration of a licence or another right in respect of a registered Community trade mark (point 5 of Article 140(2), Rule 33(1)) or an application for a Community trade mark (point 6 of Article 140(2), Rule 33(4):
	     a. grant of a licence
	     b. transfer of a licence
	     c. creation of a right in rem
	     d. transfer of a right in rem
	     e. levy of execution
		200 ecu per registration, but, where multiple requests are submitted in the same application or at the same time, not to exceed a total of 1000 ecu

24.	Fee for the cancellation of the registration of a licence or other right (point 7 of Article 140(2), Rule 35(3))	200 ecu per cancellation, but, where multiple requests lare submitted in the same application or at the same time, not to exceed a total of 1000 ecu
25.	Fee for the alteration of a registered Community trade mark (point 8 of Article 140(2), Rule 25(2))	200 ecu

26.	Fee for the issue of a copy of the application for a Community trade mark (point 12 of Article 140(2), Rule 89(5)), a copy of the certificate of registration (point 3 of Article 140(2), Rule 24(2), or an extract from the register (point 9 of Article 140(2), Rule 84 (6))
	     (a) uncertified copy or extract
	     (b) certified copy or extract
		
		 10 ecu
		 30 ecu

27.	Fee for the inspection of the files (point 10 of Article 140 (2) No. 10, Rule 89(1))	30 ecu

28.	Fee for the issue of copies of file documents (point 11 of Article 140(2) no 11, Rule 89(5))
	     (a) uncertified copy
	     (b) certified copy
	         plus per page, exceeding 10
		
		 10 ecu
		 30 ecu
		 1 ecu

29.	Fee for the communication of information in a file (point 13 of Article 140(2), Rule 90) plus per page, exceeding 10	10 ecu 1 ecu
30.	Fee for the review of the determination of the proceral costs to be refunded (point 14 of Article 140(2), Rule 94(4))	100 ecu

Article 3

Charges Laid Down by the President

1. The President shall lay down the amount to be charged for any services rendered by the Office other than those specified in Article 2.   **A11–004**

2. The President shall lay down the amount to be charged for the Community

Trade Marks Bulletin and the Official Journal of the Office as well as any other publications issued by the Office.

3. The amounts of the charges shall be laid down in ecus.

4. The amounts of the charges laid down by the President in accordance with paragraphs 1 and 2 shall be published in the Official Journal of the Office.

Article 4

Due Date for Fees and Charges

A11–005 1. Fees and charges in respect of which the due date is not specified in the Regulation or in Regulation No 2868/95 shall be due on the date of receipt of the request for the service for which the fee or the charge is incurred.

2. The President may decide not to make services mentioned in paragraph 1 dependent upon the advance payment of the corresponding fees or charges.

Article 5

Payment of Fees and Charges

A11–006 1. Fees and charges due to the Office shall be paid

(a) by payment or transfer to a bank account held by the Office,

(b) by delivery or remittance of cheques made payable to the Office, or

(c) in cash.

2. The President may allow methods of payment other than those set out in paragraph 1, in particular by means of deposits in current accounts held with the Office.

3. Determinations made pursuant to paragraph 2 shall be published in the Official Journal of the Office.

Article 6

Currencies

A11–007 1. Payments or transfers to a bank account referred to in Article 5 (1) (a), by delivery or remittance of cheques referred to in Article 5 (1) (b) or any other method of payment allowed by the President pursuant to Article 5 (2) shall be made in ecus.

2. The payments in cash referred to in Article 5 (1) (c) shall be made in the currency of the Member State where the Office has its seat. The President shall determine the ecus equivalents in that currency on the basis of the exchange rate in force, which are fixed daily by the Commission and published in the Official Journal of the European Communities in accordance with Council Regulation (EC) No 3320/94 (4).

Article 7

Particulars Concerning Payment

A11–008 1. Every payment must indicate the name of the person making the payment and must contain the necessary information to enable the Office to establish immediately the purpose of the payment. In particular, the following information shall be provided:

(a) when the application fee is paid, the purpose of the payment, namely 'application fee';

(b) when the registration fee is paid, the file number of the application which is the basis for the registration and the purpose of the payment, namely 'registration fee';

(c) when the opposition fee is paid, the file number of the application and the name of the applicant for the Community trade mark against which opposition is entered, and the purpose of the payment, namely 'opposition fee';

(d) when the revocation fee and the invalidity fee are paid, the registration number and the name of the proprietor of the Community trade mark against which the application is directed, and the purpose of the payment, namely 'revocation fee' or 'invalidity fee'.

2. If the purpose of the payment cannot immediately be established, the Office shall require the person making the payment to notify it in writing of this purpose within such period as it may specify. If the person does not comply with this request in due time, the payment shall be considered not to have been made. The amount which has been paid shall be refunded.

Article 8

Deemed Date of Payment

1. The date on which any payment shall be considered to have been made to the Office shall be as follows: **A11–009**

(a) in the cases referred to in Article 5 (1) (a), the date on which the amount of the payment or of the transfer is actually entered in a bank account held by the Office;

(b) in the case referred to in Article 5 (1) (b), the date of the receipt of the cheque at the Office, provided that the cheque is met;

(c) in the cases referred to in Article 5 (1) (c), the date of receipt of the amount of the cash payment.

2. Where the President allows, in accordance with the provisions of Article 5 (2), other methods of paying fees than those set out in Article 5 (1), he shall also lay down the date on which such payments shall be considered to have been made.

3. Where, under the provisions of paragraphs 1 and 2, payment of a fee is not considered to have been made until after the expiry of the period in which it was due, it shall be considered that this period has been observed if evidence is provided to the Office that the person who made the payment—

(a) in a Member State, within the period within which the payment should have been made:

(i) effected the payment through a banking establishment;

(ii) duly gave an order to a banking establishment to transfer the amount of the payment; or

(iii) dispatched at a post office or otherwise a letter bearing the address of the Office and containing a cheque within the meaning of Article 5 (1) (b), provided that the cheque is met;

and—

(b) paid a surcharge of 10% on the relevant fee or fees, but not exceeding ECU 200; no surcharge is payable if a condition according to sub-paragraph (a) has been fulfilled not later than 10 days before the expiry of the period for payment.

4. The Office may request the person who made the payment to produce evidence as to the date on which a condition according to paragraph 3 (a) was

fulfilled and, where required, to pay the surcharge referred to in paragraph 3 (b), within a period to be specified by it. If the person fails to comply with this request or if the evidence is insufficient, or if the required surcharge is not paid in due time, the period for payment shall be considered not to have been observed.

Article 9

Insufficiency of the Amount Paid

A11–010   1. A time limit for payment shall, in principle, be considered to have been observed only if the full amount of the fee has been paid in due time. If the fee is not paid in full, the amount which has been paid shall be refunded after the period for payment has expired.

2. The Office may, however, in so far as this is possible within the time remaining before the end of the period, give the person making the payment the opportunity to pay the amount lacking or, where this is considered justified, overlook any small amounts lacking without prejudice to the rights of the person making the payment.

Article 10

Refund of Insignificant Amounts

A11–011   1. Where an excessive sum is paid to cover a fee or a charge, the excess shall not be refunded if the amount is insignificant and the party concerned has not expressly requested a refund. The President shall determine what constitutes an insignificant amount.

2. Determinations by the President pursuant to paragraph 1 shall be published in the Official Journal of the Office.

Article 11

Entry into Force

A11–012   This Regulation shall enter into force on the seventh day following its publication in the Official Journal of the European Communities.

This Regulation shall be binding in is entirety and directly applicable in all Member States.

Done at Brussels, December 13, 1995.

APPENDIX **12**

Commission Regulation 216/96 of February 5, 1996—Laying down the rules of procedure of the Boards of Appeal of the Office for Harmonization in the Internal Market (Trade Marks and Designs)
([1996] O.J. L28/11)

THE COMMISSION OF THE EUROPEAN COMMUNITIES,

Having regard to the Treaty establishing the European Community;

Having regard to Council Regulation (EC) No 40/94 of 20 December 1994 on the Community trade mark, as amended by Regulation (EC) No 3288/94, and in particular Article 140(3) thereof;

Whereas Regulation (EC) No 40/94 (hereinafter 'the Regulation') creates a new trade mark system allowing a trade mark having effect throughout the Community to be obtained on the basis of an application to the Office for Harmonization in the Internal Market (Trade Marks and Designs) ('the Office');

Whereas for this purpose the Regulation contains in particular the necessary provisions for a procedure leading to the registration of a Community trade marks, as well as for the administration of Community trade marks, for appeals against decisions of the Office and for proceedings in relation to revocation or invalidity of a Community trade mark;

Whereas under Article 130 of the Regulation, the Boards of Appeal are to be responsible for deciding on appeals from decisions of the examiners, the Opposition Division, the Administration of Trade Marks and Legal Division and the Cancellation Divisions;

Whereas Title VII of the Regulation contains basic principles regarding appeals against decisions of examiners, the Opposition Divisions, the Administration of Trade Marks and Legal Division and the Cancellation Divisions;

Whereas Title X of Commission Regulation (EC) No 2868/95 of 13 December 1995 implementing Council Regulation No 40/94 on the Community Trade Mark (3) contains implementing rules to Title VII of the Regulation;

Whereas this Regulation supplements those other rules, in particular as regards the organization of the Boards and the oral procedure;

Whereas before the beginning of each working year a scheme should be established for the distribution of business between the Boards of Appeal by an Authority established for that purpose; whereas to this end the said Authority should apply objective criteria such as classes of products and services or initial letters of the names of applicants;

Whereas to facilitate the handling and disposal of appeals, a rapporteur should be designated for each case, who should be responsible inter alia for preparing communications with the parties and drafting decisions;

Whereas the parties to proceedings before the Boards of Appeal may not be in a position or may not be willing to bring questions of general relevance to a pending case to the attention of the Boards of Appeal; whereas, therefore, the

Boards of Appeal should have the power, of their own motion or pursuant to a request by the President, to invite the President of the Office, to submit comments on questions of general interest in relation to a case pending before the Boards of Appeal;

Whereas the measures provided for in this Regulation are in accordance with the opinion of the Committee established under Article 141 of the Regulation;

HAS ADOPTED THIS REGULATION:

[Article 1

Allocation of Duties and Authority Competent to Allocate

A12–002   *1. Before the beginning of each working year, duties shall be allocated to the Boards of Appeal according to objective criteria, and the members of each of the Boards and their alternates shall be designated. Any member of a Board of Appeal may be designated for several Boards of Appeal as a member or an alternate. These measures may, where necessary, be amended during the working year in question.*

2. The measures referred to in paragraph 1 shall be taken by an Authority composed of the President of the Office as Chairman, the Vice-President of the Office responsible for the Boards of Appeal, the Chairman of the Boards of Appeal and three other members of the Boards of Appeal elected by the full membership of those Boards, except the Chairmen, for the working year in question. The Authority may validly deliberate only if at least five of its members are present, including the President or the Vice-President of the Office and two Chairmen of Boards of Appeal. Decisions shall be taken by majority vote. In the event of a tie, the vote of the Chairman shall be decisive. The Authority may lay down its internal rules of procedure.

3. The Authority provided for in paragraph 2 shall decide on conflicts regarding the allocation of duties among different Boards of Appeal.

4. Until more than three Boards of Appeal have been set up, the Authority referred to in paragraph 2 shall consist of the President of the Office, who shall act as Chairman, the Vice-President of the Office responsible for the Boards of Appeal, the Chairman or Chairman of the Boards of Appeal which have already been set up and one other member of the Boards of Appeal elected by their full membership of the Board, except the Chairman or Chairman, for the working year in question. The Authority may validly deliberate only if at least three of its members are present, including the President or the Vice-President of the Office.]

Article 1

Presidium of the Boards of Appeal

A12–003   **1. The authority referred to in Articles 130 and 131 of the Regulation shall be the Presidium of the Boards of Appeal (referred to hereinafter as "the Presidium").**

2. The Presidium shall comprise the President of the Boards of Appeal, who shall chair it, the chairmen of the Board and Board members elected for each calendar year by and from among all the members of the Boards other than the President of the Boards of Appeal and the chairmen of the Boards. The number of Board members so elected shall be a quarter of the number of Board members, other than the President of the Boards of Appeal and the chairmen of the Boards, rounded up if necessary.

3. If the President of the Boards of Appeal is unable to act or if the post of President is vacant, the Presidium shall be chaired by:

(a) the chairman of the Board having the longest service on the Boards of Appeal; or

(b) where chairmen have the same length of service, by the eldest of those qualifying under the preceding subparagraph.

4. The Presidium may validly deliberate only if at least two-thirds of its members are present, including its chairman and two Board chairmen. Decisions of the Presidium shall be taken by a majority vote. In the event of a tie, the vote of the chairman shall be decisive.

5. Before the beginning of each calendar year, and without prejudice to Article 1(b), the Presidium shall decide on objective criteria for allocating cases among the Boards for the calendar year in question and shall designate the full and alternate members of each of the Boards for that year. Each member of the Boards of Appeal may be assigned to several Boards as a full or alternate member. These measures may be modified, as necessary, in the course of the calendar year in question. Decisions adopted by the Presidium pursuant to this paragraph shall be published in the Official Journal of the Office.

6. The Presidium shall also be competent to:

(a) lay down such rules of a procedural nature as are necessary for the processing of cases brought before the Boards and such rules as are necessary on the organisation of the Boards' work;

(b) rule on any conflict concerning the allocation of cases among the Boards of Appeal;

(c) lay down its internal rules;

(d) lay down practical instructions of a procedural nature for parties involved in proceedings before the Boards of Appeal, for example, with regard to the submission of written statements and to oral proceedings;

(e) exercise any other powers as are conferred to it by the present Regulation.

7. The President of the Boards of Appeal shall consult the Presidium on the expenditure requirements of the Boards, which he shall communicate to the President of the Office with a view to drawing up the expenditure estimates and where he considers it appropriate, on any other question relating to the management of the Boards of Appeal.

Amendment

The words in bold replaced the words in italics as a result of Regulation 2082/2004 [2004] O.J. L360/8.

Article 1(a)

Grand Board

1. The enlarged Board set up by Article 130(3) of the Regulation shall be the Grand Board. on a point of law raised by that case.   A12–004

2. The Grand Board shall comprise nine members, including the President of the Boards of Appeal, who shall chair it, the chairmen of the Boards, the rapporteur designated prior to referral to the Grand Board, if applicable, and members drawn in rotation from a list comprising the names of all members of the Boards of Appeal other than the President of the Boards of Appeal and the chairmen of the Boards.

The Presidium shall draw up the list referred to in the first paragraph and establish the rules according to which members are drawn from that list on the basis of objective criteria. The list and such rules shall be published in the Official Journal of the Office. If a rapporteur has not been designated prior to referral to the Grand Board, the chairman of the Grand Board shall designate a rapporteur from among the members of the Grand Board.

3. If the President of the Boards of Appeal is unable to act or if the post of President is vacant, or in the event of exclusion or objection within the meaning of Article 132 of the Regulation, the Grand Board shall be chaired by:

(a) the chairman having the longest service on the Boards of Appeal; or

(b) where chairmen have the same length of service, by the eldest of those qualifying under the preceding subparagraph 4.

4. If another member of the Grand Board is unable to act or in the event of exclusion or objection within the meaning of Article 132 of the Regulation, he or she shall be replaced by the person highest on the list referred to in paragraph 2 of this Article.

5. The Grand Board may not hear cases and oral proceedings may not take place before it unless seven of its members are present, including its chairman and the rapporteur.

If the Grand Board hears a case in the presence of only eight of its members, the member with the least seniority in the Boards of Appeal shall not take part in the vote, unless that member is the chairman or the rapporteur, in which case the member with the next highest seniority to that of the chairman or rapporteur shall not vote.

Article 1(b)

Referral to the Grand Board

A12–005   1. A Board may refer a case allocated to it to the Grand Board if it believes that this is justified by the legal difficulty or importance of the case or by special circumstances, for example, if Boards of Appeal have issued diverging decisions on a point of law raised by that case.

2. A Board shall refer a case allocated to it to the Grand Board if it believes that it must deviate from an interpretation of the relevant legislation given in an earlier decision of the Grand Board.

3. The Presidium may, on a proposal made by the President of the Boards of Appeal on his or her own initiative or at the request of a member of the Presidium, refer to the Grand Board a case allocated to a Board if it believes that this is justified by the legal difficulty or importance of the case or by special circumstances, for example, if Boards of Appeal have issued diverging decisions on a point of law raised by that case.

4. The Grand Board shall, without delay, refer the case back to the Board to which it was originally allocated if it believes that the conditions for the original referral are not met.

5. All decisions relating to referral to the Grand Board shall be reasoned and shall be communicated to the parties to the case.

Article 1(c)

Decisions by a single member

A12–006   1. The Presidium shall draw up an indicative list of the types of cases which the Boards may, unless special circumstances apply, devolve to a single member, such as decisions closing the proceedings following agreement between the parties, and decisions on the award of costs and the admissibility of the appeal.

The Presidium may also draw up a list of the types of cases which may not be devolved to a single member.

2. A Board may delegate to its chairman the decision to allocate to a single member cases falling within the types of cases defined by the Presidium in accordance with paragraph 1.

3. The decision to devolve the case upon a single member shall be communicated to the parties.

The member to whom the case has been devolved shall refer it to the Board if he finds that the conditions for devolution are no longer met.

Article 1(d)

Referral of a case following a ruling of the Court of Justice

1. If, pursuant to Article 63(6) of the Regulation, the measures necessary   A12–007
to comply with a judgment of the Court of Justice annulling all or part of a decision of a Board of Appeal or of the Grand Board include re-examination by the Boards of Appeal of the case which was the subject of that decision, the Presidium shall decide if the case shall be referred to the Board which adopted that decision, or to another Board, or to the Grand Board.

2. If the case is referred to another Board, that Board shall not comprise members who were party to the contested decision. This provision shall not apply if the case is referred to the Grand Board.

Amendment

Articles 1(a) to 1(d) were inserted by Regulation 2082/2004 [2004] O.J. L360/8.

Article 2

Replacement of Members

1. Reasons for replacement by alternates shall in particular include leave, sick-   A12–008
ness, inescapable commitments and the grounds of exclusion set out in Article 132 of the Regulation.

2. Any member asking to be replaced by an alternate shall without delay inform the Chairman of the Board concerned of his unavailability.

Article 3

Exclusion and Objection

1. If a Board has knowledge of a possible reason for exclusion or objection   A12–009
under Article 132 (3) of the Regulation which does not originate from a member himself or from any party to the proceedings, the procedure of Article 132 (4) of the Regulation shall be applied.

2. The member concerned shall be invited to present his comments as to whether there is a reason for exclusion or objection.

3. Before a decision is taken on the action to be taken pursuant to Article 132 (4) of the Regulation, there shall be no further proceedings in the case.

Article 4

Rapporteurs

A12–010   1. The Chairman of each Board shall for each appeal designate a member of his Board, or himself, as rapporteur.

2. The rapporteur shall carry out a preliminary study of the appeal. He may prepare communications to the parties subject to the direction of the Chairman of the Board. Communications shall be signed by the rapporteur on behalf of the Board.

[*3. The rapporteur shall prepare internal meetings of the Board and the oral proceedings.*]

[*4.*] **3.** The rapporteur shall draft decisions.

Amendment

Article 4(3) was deleted, and Article 4(4) was renumbered as Article 4(3), by Regulation 2082/2004 [2004] O.J. L360/8.

[Article 5

Registries

A12–011   *1. Registries shall be established for the Boards of Appeal. Registrars shall be responsible for the discharge of the functions of the Registries. One of the Registrars may be designated Senior Registrar.*

2. The Authority provided for in Article 1 (2) may entrust to the Registrars the performance of functions which involve no legal or technical difficulties, particularly with regard to representation, the submission of translations, inspection of files and notifications.

3. The Registrar shall submit to the Chairman of the Board concerned a report on the admissibility of each newly-filed appeal.

4. Minutes of oral proceedings and of the taking of evidence shall be drawn up by the Registrar or, if the President of the Office has agreed thereto, such other officer of the Office as the Chairman of the Board may designate.]

Article 5

Registry

A12–012   **1.A Registry shall be set up at the Boards of Appeal, and shall, inter alia, be responsible, under the authority of the President of the Boards of Appeal, for the receipt, dispatch, safekeeping and notification of all documents relating to the proceedings before the Boards of Appeal, and for compilation of the relevant files.**

2. The Registry shall be headed by a Registrar. The President of the Boards of Appeal shall appoint a Registry agent who shall perform the tasks of the Registrar when the latter is absent or unable to act or if the post of Registrar is vacant.

3. The Registrar shall, in particular, ensure that the deadlines and other formal conditions relating to the presentation of the appeal and of the statement of grounds are respected.

If an irregularity is detected which is liable to make the appeal inadmissible, the Registrar shall, without delay, send a reasoned opinion to the chairman of the Board concerned.

4. The minutes of oral proceedings and of the taking of evidence shall be drawn up by the Registrar or, if the President of the Boards of Appeal agrees, by such agent of the Boards of Appeal as the chairman of the Board concerned may designate.

5. The President of the Boards of Appeal may delegate to the Registrar the task of allocating cases to the Boards of Appeal in accordance with allocation criteria laid down by the Presidium.

The Presidium may, upon a proposal by the President of the Boards of Appeal, delegate to the Registry other tasks relating to the conduct of proceedings before the Boards of Appeal.

Amendment

The words in bold replaced the words in italics as a result of Regulation 2082/2004 [2004] O.J. L360/8.

Article 6

Change in the Composition of a Board

1. If the composition of a Board is changed after oral proceedings, the parties to the proceedings shall be informed that, at the request of any party, fresh oral proceedings shall be held before the Board in its new composition. Fresh oral proceedings shall also be held if so requested by the new member and if the other members of the Board have given their agreement.   A12–013

2. The new member shall be bound to the same extent as the other members by an interim decision which has already been taken.

3. If, when a Board has already reached a final decision, a member is unable to act, he shall not be replaced by an alternate. If the Chairman is unable to act, then the member of the Board concerned having the longer service on the Board, or where members have the same length of service, the older member, shall sign the decision on behalf of the Chairman.

Article 7

Joinder of Appeal Proceedings

1. If several appeals are filed against a decision, those appeals shall be considered in the same proceedings.   A12–014

2. If appeals are filed against separate decisions and all the appeals are designated to be examined by one Board having the same composition, that Board may deal with those appeals in joined proceedings with the consent of the parties.

[Article 8

Remission to the Department of First Instance

Where the proceedings of the department of first instance whose decision is the subject of an appeal are vitiated by fundamental deficiencies, the Board shall set aside the decision and, unless there are reasons for not doing so, remit the case to that instance or decide the matter itself.]   A12–015

Article 8

Procedure

1. If the Registrar sends the chairman of a Board of Appeal an opinion on the admissibility of an appeal in accordance with Article 5(3), second   A12–016 paragraph, the chairman of the Board in question may either suspend the proceedings and request the Board to rule on the admissibility of the appeal, or reserve judgement on the admissibility of the appeal for the decision to end the proceedings before the Board of Appeal.

2. In *inter partes* proceedings, and without prejudice to Article 61(2) of the Regulation, the statement setting out the grounds of appeal and the response to it may be supplemented by a reply from the appellant, lodged within two months of the notification of the response, and a rejoinder by the defendant, lodged within two months of notification of the reply.

3. In *inter partes* proceedings, the defendant may, in his or her response, seek a decision annulling or altering the contested decision on a point not raised in the appeal.

Amendment

The words in bold replaced the words in italics as a result of Regulation 2082/2004 [2004] O.J. L360/8. The provisions of Article 8(2) and (3) of this Regulations (as amended) shall only apply to proceedings in respect of which the appeal was lodged after the entry into force of this Regulation.

Article 9

Oral Proceedings

A12–017   1. If oral proceedings are to take place, the Board shall ensure that the parties have provided all relevant information and documents before the hearing.

2. The Board may, when issuing the summons to attend oral proceedings, add a communication drawing attention to matters which seem to be of special significance, or to the fact that certain questions appear no longer to be contentious, or containing other observations that may help to concentrate on essentials during the oral proceedings.

3. The Board shall ensure that the case is ready for decision at the conclusion of the oral proceedings, unless there are special reasons to the contrary.

Article 10

Communications to the Parties

A12–018   If a Board deems it expedient to communicate with the parties regarding a possible appraisal of substantive or legal matters, such communication shall be made in such a way as not to imply that the Board is in any way bound by it.

Article 11

Comments on Questions of General Interest

A12–019   The Board may, on its own initiative or at the written, reasoned request of the President of the Office, invite him to comment in writing or orally on questions of general interest which arise in the course of proceedings pending before it. The parties shall be entitled to submit their observations on the President's comments.

Article 12

Deliberations Preceding Decisions

A12–020   The rapporteur shall submit to the other members of the Board a draft of the decision to be taken and shall set a reasonable time-limit within which to oppose it or to ask for changes. The Board shall meet to deliberate on the decision to be taken if it appears that the members of a Board are not all of the same opinion. Only members of the Board shall participate in the deliberations; the Chairman of the Board concerned may, however, authorize other officers such as registrars or interpreters to attend. Deliberations shall be secret.

Article 13

Order of Voting

1. During the deliberations between members of a Board, the opinion of the rapporteur shall be heard first, and, if the rapporteur is not the Chairman, the Chairman last.   **A12–021**

2. If voting is necessary, votes shall be taken in the same sequence, save that if the Chairman is also the rapporteur, be shall vote last. Abstentions shall not be permitted.

Article 14

Entry into Force

This Regulation shall enter into force the third day following its publication in the Official Journal of the European Communities.   **A12–022**

This Regulation shall be binding in its entirety and directly applicable in all Member States.

Done at Brussels, February 5, 1996.

The Community Trade Mark Regulations 1996

SI 1996/1908

A13–001   *The Secretary of State, in exercise of powers confected by section 52 of the Trade Marks Act 1994 hereby makes the following Regulations:—*

A13–002   **1.**—(1) These Regulations may be cited as the Community Trade Mark Regulations 1996 and come into force on 14th August 1996.

(2) These Regulations extend to England and Wales, Scotland and Northern Ireland.

Interpretation

A13–003   **2.** In these Regulations—

"the Act" means the Trade Marks Act 1994, and references to a section are, unless the context otherwise requires, to sections of that Act;

"the Community Trade Mark Regulation" means Council Regulation (EC) No. 40/94 of 20th December 1993 on the Community trade mark;

"the Rules" means the Trade Marks Rules 1994 and references to a rule shall, unless the context otherwise requires, be construed accordingly.

Determination a posteriori of invalidity and liability to revocation

A13–004   **3.**—(1) Where the proprietor of a Community trade mark claims the seniority of a registered trade mark which has been removed from the register under section 43 or has been surrendered under section 45, application may be made to the registrar or to the court by any person for a declaration that, if the registered trade mark had not been so removed or surrendered, it would have been liable to be revoked under section 46 or declared invalid under section 47.

(2) Where a registered trade mark has been surrendered in respect of some only of the goods or services for which it is registered, paragraph (1) above shall apply in relation to those goods or services.

(3) The provisions of section 46 or 47 (as the case may be), sections 72, 74 and 76, with necessary modifications, apply in relation to an application under paragraph (1) above.

(4) The provisions of rule 31, with necessary modifications, apply in relation to the procedure on applications made under paragraph (1) above.

Groundless threats of infringement proceedings

A13–005   **4.** The provisions of section 21 apply in relation to a Community trade mark as in relation to a registered trade mark.

Privilege for communications with professional representatives

A13–006   **5.** The provisions of section 87 (privilege for communications between a person and his registered trade mark agent) apply in relation to persons on the list of professional representatives maintained in pursuance of Article 89 of the Community Trade Mark Regulation ("professional representatives") and for this purpose the definition of "trade mark agent" in subsection (3) of that section includes professional representatives.

Importation of infringing goods, material or articles

6. The provisions of section 89 (infringing goods, material or articles may be treated as prohibited goods) section 90 and section 91 of the Act (power of Commissioners of Customs and Excise to disclose information) apply in relation to goods which are, in relation to a Community trade mark, infringing goods, material or articles, and for the purposes of those provisions— **A13–007**

    (a) references to a registered trade mark shall include a Community trade mark;

    (b) the Trade Marks (Customs) Regulations 1994 shall apply in relation to notices given under the provisions of section 89.

Offences and forfeiture

7. The provisions of section 92 (unauthorised use of trade mark, etc., in relation to goods), section 93 (enforcement function of local weights and measures authority), section 97 (forfeiture: England and Wales) and section 98 (forfeiture: Scotland) apply in relation to a Community trade mark and for the purposes of those provisions— **A13–008**

    (a) references to a registered trade mark shall include a Community trade mark;

    (b) references to goods in respect of which a trade mark is registered shall include goods in respect of which a Community trade mark is registered.

Falsely representing trade mark as a Community trade mark

8.—(1) It is an offence for a person— **A13–009**

    (a) falsely to represent that a mark is a Community trade mark, or

    (b) to make a false representation as to the goods or services for which a Community trade mark is registered,

knowing or having reason to believe that the representation is false.

(2) A person guilty of an offence under this regulation is liable on summary conviction to a fine not exceeding level 3 on the standard scale.

Designation of Community Trade Mark courts

9. For the purposes of Article 91 of the Community Trade Mark Regulation, the following courts are designated as Community trade mark courts— **A13–010**

    (a) in England and Wales and Northern Ireland, the High Court, and

    (b) in Scotland, the Court of Session.

Conversion

10.—(1) The provisions of this Regulation apply where the applicant for or the proprietor of a Community trade mark requests the conversion of his Community trade mark application or Community trade mark into an application for registration of a trade mark under the Act ("conversion application") pursuant to Article 108 of the Community Trade Mark Regulation. **A13–011**

(2) Where the registrar decides that a request for a conversion application is admissible pursuant to Article 108, it shall be treated as an application for registration of a trade mark under the Act.

(3) A decision of the registrar in relation to a conversion application shall be treated as a decision of the registrar under the Act.

Application of Trade Marks Rules 1994

11. Except as otherwise provided, or where their application would be incon- **A13–012**

sistent with the provisions of these Regulations, the Rules shall apply, with the necessary modifications, to these Regulations.

PART V

OTHER EUROPEAN MATERIALS

Council Regulation 2081/92 of July 14, 1992—On the protection of geographical indications and designations of origin for agricultural products and foodstuffs

([1992] O.J. L208/1)

THE COUNCIL OF THE EUROPEAN COMMUNITIES,
A14–001

Having regard to the Treaty establishing the European Economic Community, and in particular Article 43,

Having regard to the proposal from the Commission,

Having regard to the opinion of the European Parliament,

Having regard to the opinion of the Economic and Social Committee,

Whereas the production, manufacture and distribution of agricultural products and foodstuffs play an important role in the Community economy;

Whereas, as part of the adjustment of the common agricultural policy the diversification of agricultural production should be encouraged so as to achieve a better balance between supply and demand on the markets; whereas the promotion of products having certain characteristics could be of considerable benefit to the rural economy, in particular to less-favoured or remote areas, by improving the incomes of farmers and by retaining the rural population in these areas;

Whereas, moreover, it has been observed in recent years that consumers are tending to attach greater importance to the quality of foodstuffs rather than to quantity; whereas this quest for specific products generates a growing demand for agricultural products or foodstuffs with an identifiable geographical origin;

Whereas in view of the wide variety of products marketed and of the abundance of information concerning them provided, consumers must, in order to be able to make the best choice, be given clear and succinct information regarding the origin of the product;

Whereas the labelling of agricultural products and foodstuffs is subject to the general rules laid down in Council Directive 79/112/EEC of 18 December 1978 on the approximation of the laws of the Member States relating to the labelling, presentation and advertising of foodstuffs; whereas, in view of their specific nature, additional special provisions should be adopted for agricultural products and foodstuffs from a specified geographical area;

Whereas the desire to protect agricultural products or foodstuffs which have an identifiable geographical origin has led certain Member States to introduce "registered designations of origin"; whereas these have proved successful with producers, who have secured higher incomes in return for a genuine effort to improve quality, and with consumers, who can purchase high quality products with guarantees as to the method of production and origin;

Whereas, however, there is diversity in the national practices for implementing registered designations or origin and geographical indications; whereas a

Community approach should be envisaged; whereas a framework of Community rules on protection will permit the development of geographical indica tions and designations of origin since, by providing a more uniform approach, such a framework will ensure fair competition between the producers of products bearing such indications and enchance the credibility of the products in the consumers' eyes;

Whereas the planned rules should take account of existing Community legislation on wines and spirit drinks, which provide for a higher level of protection;

Whereas the scope of this Regulation is limited to certain agricultural products and foodstuffs for which a link between product or foodstuff characteristics and geographical origin exists; whereas, however, this scope could be enlarged to encompass other products or foodstuffs;

Whereas existing practices make it appropriate to define two different types of geographical description, namely protected geographical indications and protected designations of origin;

Whereas an agricultural product or foodstuff bearing such an indication must meet certain conditions set out in a specification;

Whereas to enjoy protection in every Member State geographical indications and designations of origin must be registered at Community level; whereas entry in a register should also provide information to those involved in trade and to consumers;

Whereas the registration procedure should enable any person individually and directly concerned in a Member State to exercise his rights by notifying the Commission of his opposition;

Whereas there should be procedures to permit amendment of the specification, after registration, in the light of technological progress or withdrawal from the register of the geographical indication or designation of origin of an agricultural product or foodstuff if that product or foodstuff ceases to conform to the specification on the basis of which the geographical indication or designation of origin was granted;

Whereas provision should be made for trade with third countries offering equivalent guarantees for the issue and inspection of geographical indications or designations of origin granted on their territory;

Whereas provision should be made for a procedure establishing close cooperation between the Member States and the Commission through a Regulatory Committee set up for that purpose,

HAS ADOPTED THIS REGULATION:

Article 1

A14–002 1. This Regulation lays down rules on the protection of designations of origin and geographical indications of agricultural products intended for human consumption referred to in Annex II to the Treaty and of the foodstuffs referred to in Annex I to this Regulation and agricultural products listed in Annex II to this Regulation.

However, this Regulation shall not apply to wine products or to spirit drinks.

Annex I may be amended in accordance with the procedure set out in Article 15.

2. This Regulation shall apply without prejudice to other specific Community provisions.

3. Council Directive 83/189/EEC of 28 March 1983 laying down a procedure for the provision of information in the field of technical standards and regulations shall not apply to the designations of origin and geographical indications covered by this Regulation.

Article 2

1. Community protection of designations of origin and of geographical indica- **A14–003** tions of agricultural products and foodstuffs shall be obtained in accordance with this Regulation.

2. For the purposes of this Regulation:

(a) designation of origin: means the name of a region, a specific place or, in exceptional cases, a country, used to describe an agricultural product or a foodstuff:
— originating in that region, specific place or country, and
— the quality or characteristics of which are essentially or exclusively due to a particular geographical environment with its inherent natural and human factors, and the production, processing and preparation of which take place in the defined geographical area;

(b) geographical indication: means the name of a region, a specific place or, in exceptional cases, a country, used to describe an agricultural product or a foodstuff:
— originating in that region, specific place or country, and
— which possesses a specific quality, reputation or other characteristics attributable to that geographical origin and the production and/or processing and/or preparation of which take place in the defined geographical area.

3. Certain traditional geographical or non-geographical names designating an agricultural product or a foodstuff originating in a region or a specific place, which fulfil the conditions referred to in the second indent of paragraph 2 (a) shall also be considered as designations of origin.

4. By way of derogation from Article 2(a), certain geographical designations shall be treated as designations of origin where the raw materials of the products concerned come from a geographical area larger than or different from the processing area, provided that:
— the production area of the raw materials is limited,
— special conditions for the production of the raw materials exist, and
— there are inspection arrangements to ensure that those conditions are adhered to.

5. For the purposes of paragraph 4, only live animals, meat and milk may be considered as raw materials. Use of other raw materials may be authorized in accordance with the procedure laid down in Article 15.

6. In order to be eligible for the derogation provided for in paragraph 4, the designations in question may be or have already been recognized as designations of origin with national protection by the Member State concerned, or, if no such scheme exists, have a proven, traditional character and an exceptional reputation and renown.

7. In order to be eligible for the derogation provided for in paragraph 4, applications for registration must be lodged within two years of the entry into force of this Regulation.

Article 3

A14–004   1. Names that have become generic may not be registered.

For the purposes of this Regulation, a "name that has become generic" means the name of an agricultural product or a foodstuff which, although it relates to the place or the region where this product or foodstuff was originally produced or marketed, has become the common name of an agricultural product or a foodstuff.

To establish whether or not a name has become generic, account shall be taken of all factors, in particular:

— the existing situation in the Member State in which the name originates and in areas of consumption,
— the existing situation in other Member States,
— the relevant national or Community laws.

Where, following the procedure laid down in Articles 6 and 7, an application of registration is rejected because a name has become generic, the Commission shall publish that decision in the Official Journal of the European Communities.

2. A name may not be registered as a designation of origin or a geographical indication where it conflicts with the name of a plant variety or an animal breed and as a result is likely to mislead the public as to the true origin of the product.

3. Before the entry into force of this Regulation, the Council, acting by a qualified majority on a proposal from the Commission, shall draw up and publish in the Official Journal of the European Communities a non-exhaustive, indicative list of the names of agricultural products or foodstuffs which are within the scope of this Regulation and are regarded under the terms of paragraph 1 as being generic and thus not able to be registered under this Regulation.

Article 4

A14–005   1. To be eligible to use a protected designation of origin (PDO) or a protected geographical indication (PGI) an agricultural product or foodstuff must comply with a specification.

2. The product specification shall include at least:

(a) the name of the agricultural product or foodstuffs, including the designation of origin or the geographical indication;
(b) a description of the agricultural product or foodstuff including the raw materials, if appropriate, and principal physical, chemical, microbiological and/or organoleptic characteristics of the product or the foodstuff;
(c) the definition of the geographical area and, if appropriate, details indicating compliance with the requirements in Article 2 (4);
(d) evidence that the agricultural product or the foodstuff originates in the geographical area, within the meaning of Article 2 (2) (a) or (b), whichever is applicable;
(e) a description of the method of obtaining the agricultural product or foodstuff and, if appropriate, the authentic and unvarying local methods;
(f) the details bearing out the link with the geographical environment or the geographical origin within the meaning of Article 2 (2) (a) or (b), whichever is applicable;
(g) details of the inspection structures provided for in Article 10;
(h) the specific labelling details relating to the indication PDO or PGI, whichever is applicable, or the equivalent traditional national indications;
(i) any requirements laid down by Community and/or national provisions.

Article 5

A14–006   1. Only a group or, subject to certain conditions to be laid down in accordance with the procedure provided for in Article 15, a natural or legal person, shall be entitled to apply for registration.

For the purposes of this Article, "Group" means any association, irrespective of its legal form or composition, of producers and/or processors working with the same agricultural product or foodstuff. Other interested parties may participate in the group.

2. A group or a natural or legal person may apply for registration only in respect of agricultural products or foodstuffs which it produces or obtains within the meaning of Article 2(2)(a) or (b).

3. The application for registration shall include the product specification referred to in Article 4.

4. The application shall be sent to the Member State in which the geographical area is located.

5. The Member State shall check that the application is justified and shall forward the application, including the product specification referred to in Article 4 and other documents on which it has based its decision, to the Commission, if it considers that it satisfies the requirements of this Regulation.

If the application concerns a name indicating a geographical area situated in another Member State also, that Member State shall be consulted before any decision is taken.

6. Member States shall introduce the laws, regulations and administrative provisions necessary to comply with this Article.

Article 6

1. Within a period of six months the Commission shall verify, by means of a formal investigation, whether the registration application includes all the particulars provided for in Article 4.   **A14–007**

The Commission shall inform the Member State concerned of its findings.

2. If, after taking account of paragraph 1, the Commission concludes that the name qualifies for protection, it shall publish in the Official Journal of the European Communities the name and address of the applicant, the name of the product, the main points of the application, the references to national provisions governing the preparation, production or manufacture of the product and, if necessary, the grounds for its conclusions.

3. If no statement of objections is notified to the Commission in accordance with Article 7, the name shall be entered in a register kept by the Commission entitled "Register of protected designations of origin and protected geographical indications", which shall contain the names of the groups and the inspection bodies concerned.

4. The Commission shall publish in the Official Journal of the European Communities:

— the names entered in the Register,
— amendments to the Register made in accordance with Article 9 and 11.

5. If, in the light of the investigation provided for in paragraph 1, the Commission concludes that the name does not qualify for protection, it shall decide, in accordance with the procedure provided for in Article 15, not to proceed with the publication provided for in paragraph 2 of this Article.

Before publication as provided for in paragraph 2 and 4 and registration as provided for in paragraph 3, the Commission may request the opinion of the Committee provided for in Article 15.

Article 7

A14–008   1. Within six months of the date of publication in the Official Journal of the European Communities referred to in Article 6 (2), any Member State may object to the registration.

2. The competent authorities of the Member States shall ensure that all persons who can demonstrate a legitimate economic interest are authorized to consult the application. In addition and in accordance with the existing situation in the Member States, the Member States may provide access to other parties with a legitimate interest.

3. Any legitimately concerned natural or legal person may object to the proposed registration by sending a duly substantiated statement to the competent authority of the Member State in which he resides or is established. The competent authority shall take the necessary measures to consider these comments or objection within the deadlines laid down.

4. A statement of objection shall be admissible only if it:

— either shows non-compliance with the conditions referred to in Article 2,
— or shows that the proposed registration of a name would jeopardize the existence of an entirely or partly identical name or trade mark or the existence of products which are legally on the market at the time of publication of this regulation in the Official Journal of the European Communities,
— or indicates the features which demonstrate that the name whose registration is applied for is generic in nature.

5. Where an objection is admissible within the meaning of paragraph 4, the Commission shall ask the Member States concerned to seek agreement among themselves in accordance with their internal procedures within three months. If:

(a) agreement is reached, the Member States in question shall communicate to the Commission all the factors which made agreement possible together with the applicant's opinion and that of the objector. Where there has been no change to the information received under Article 5, the Commission shall proceed in accordance with Article 6 (4). If there has been a change, it shall again initiate the procedure laid down in Article 7;

(b) no agreement is reached, the Commission shall take a decision in accordance with the procedure laid down in Article 15, having regard to traditional fair practice and of the actual likelihood of confusion. Should it decide to proceed with registration, the Commission shall carry out publication in accordance with Article 6 (4).

Article 8

A14–009   The indications PDO, PGI or equivalent traditional national indications may appear only on agricultural products and foodstuffs that comply with this Regulation.

Article 9

A14–010   The Member State concerned may request the amendment of a specification, in particular to take account of developments in scientific and technical knowledge or to redefine the geographical area.

The Article 6 procedure shall apply *mutatis mutandis*.

The Commission may, however, decide, under the procedure laid down in Article 15, not to apply the Article 6 procedure in the case of a minor amendment.

Article 10

A14–011   1. Member States shall ensure that not later than six months after the entry into force of this Regulation inspection structures are in place, the function of which shall be to ensure that agricultural products and foodstuffs bearing a protected name meet the requirements laid down in the specifications.

2. An inspection structure may comprise one or more designated inspection authorities and/or private bodies approved for that purpose by the Member State. Member States shall send the Commission lists of the authorities and/or bodies approved and their respective powers. The Commission shall publish those particulars in the Official Journal of the European Communities.

3. Designated inspection authorities and/or approved private bodies must offer adequate guarantees of objectivity and impartiality with regard to all producers or processors subject to their control and have permanently at their disposal the qualified staff and resources necessary to carry out inspection of agricultural products and foodstuffs bearing a protected name.

If an inspection structure uses the services of another body for some inspections, that body must offer the same guarantees. In that event the designated inspection authorities and/or approved private bodies shall, however, continue to be responsible *vis-à-vis* the Member State for all inspections.

As from 1 January 1998, in order to be approved by the Member States for the purpose of this Regulation, private bodies must fulfil the requirements laid down in standard EN 45011 of 26 June 1989.

4. If a designated inspection authority and/or private body in a Member State establishes that an agricultural product or a foodstuff bearing a protected name of origin in that Member State does not meet the criteria of the specification, they shall take the steps necessary to ensure that this Regulation is complied with. They shall inform the Member State of the measures taken in carrying out their inspections. The parties concerned must be notified of all decisions taken.

5. A Member State must withdraw approval from an inspection body where the criteria referred to in paragraphs 2 and 3 are no longer fulfilled. It shall inform the Commission, which shall publish in the Official Journal of the European Communities a revised list of approved bodies.

6. The Member States shall adopt the measures necessary to ensure that a producer who complies with this Regulation has access to the inspection system.

7. The costs of inspections provided for under this Regulation shall be borne by the producers using the protected name.

Article 11

1. Any Member State may submit that a condition laid down in the product **A14–012** specification of an agricultural product or foodstuff covered by a protected name has not been met.

2. The Member State referred to in paragraph 1 shall make its submission to the Member State concerned. The Member State concerned shall examine the complaint and inform the other Member State of its findings and of any measures taken.

3. In the event of repeated irregularities and the failure of the Member States concerned to come to an agreement, a duly substantiated application must be sent to the Commission.

4. The Commission shall examine the application by consulting the Member States concerned. Where appropriate, having consulted the committee referred to in Article 15, the Commission shall take the necessary steps. These may include cancellation of the registration.

Article 12

A14–013   1. Without prejudice to international agreements, this Regulation may apply to an agricultural product or foodstuff from a third country provided that:

— the third country is able to give guarantees identical or equivalent to those referred to in Article 4,

— the third country concerned has inspection arrangements equivalent to those laid down in Article 10,

— the third country concerned is prepared to provide protection equivalent to that available in the Community to corresponding agricultural products for foodstuffs coming from the Community.

2. If a protected name of a third country is identical to a Community protected name, registration shall be granted with due regard for local and traditional usage and the practical risks of confusion.

Use of such names shall be authorized only if the country of origin of the product is clearly and visibly indicated on the label.

Article 13

A14–014   1. Registered names shall be protected against:

(a) any direct or indirect commercial use of a name registered in respect of products not covered by the registration in so far as those products are comparable to the products registered under that name or insofar as using the name exploits the reputation of the protected name;

(b) any misuse, imitation or evocation, even if the true origin of the product is indicated or if the protected name is translated or accompanied by an expression such as "style", "type", "method", "as produced in", "imitation" or similar;

(c) any other false or misleading indication as to the provenance, origin, nature or essential qualities of the product, on the inner or outer packaging, advertising material or documents relating to the product concerned, and the packing of the product in a container liable to convey a false impression as to its origin;

(d) any other practice liable to mislead the public as to the true origin of the product.

Where a registered name contains within it the name of an agricultural product or foodstuff which is considered generic, the use of that generic name on the appropriate agricultural product or foodstuff shall not be considered to be contrary to (a) or (b) in the first subparagraph.

2. However, Member States may maintain national measures authorizing the use of the expressions referred to in paragraph 1 (b) for a period of not more than five years after the date of publication of this Regulation, provided that:

— the products have been marketed legally using such expressions for at least five years before the date of publication of this Regulation,

— the labelling clearly indicates the true origin of the product.

However, this exception may not lead to the marketing of products freely on the territory of a Member State where such expressions are prohibited.

3. Protected names may not become generic.

Article 14

A14–015   1. Where a designation of origin or geographical indication is registered in accordance with this Regulation, the application for registration of a trade mark corresponding to one of the situations referred to in Article 13 and relating to the same type of product shall be refused, provided that the application for registration of the trade mark was submitted after the date of the publication provided for in Article 6 (2).

Trade marks registered in breach of the first subparagraph shall be declared invalid.

This paragraph shall also apply where the application for registration of a trade mark was lodged before the date of publication of the application for registration provided for in Article 6 (2), provided that that publication occurred before the trade mark was registered.

2. With due regard for Community law, use of a trade mark corresponding to one of the situations referred to in Article 13 which was registered in good faith before the date on which application for registration of a designation of origin or geographical indication was lodged may continue notwithstanding the registration of a designation of origin or geographical indication, where there are no grounds for invalidity or revocation of the trade mark as provided respectively by Article 3 (1) (c) and (g) and Article 12 (2) (b) of First Council Directive 89/104/EEC of 21 December 1988 to approximate the laws of the Member States relating to trade marks.

3. A designation of origin or geographical indication shall not be registered where, in the light of a trade mark's reputation and renown and the length of time it has been used, registration is liable to mislead the consumer as to the true identity of the product.

Article 15

The Commission shall be assisted by a committee composed of the representatives of the Member States and chaired by the representative of the Commission.   **A14–016**

The representative of the Commission shall submit to the committee a draft of the measures to be taken. The committee shall deliver its opinion on the draft within a time limit which the chairman may lay down according to the urgency of the matter. The opinion shall be delivered by the majority laid down in Article 148 (2) of the Treaty in the case of decisions which the Council is required to adopt on a proposal from the Commission. The votes of the representatives of the Member States within the committee shall be weighted in the manner set out in that Article. The chairman shall not vote.

The Commission shall adopt the measures envisaged if they are in accordance with the opinion of the committee.

If the measures envisaged are not in accordance with the opinion of the committee, or if no opinion is delivered, the Commission shall, without delay, submit to the Council a proposal relating to the measures to be taken. The Council shall act by a qualified majority.

If, on the expiry of a period of three months from the date of referral to the Council, the Council has not acted, the proposed measures shall be adopted by the Commission.

Article 16

Detailed rules for applying this Regulation shall be adopted in accordance with   **A14–017**
the procedure laid down in Article 15.

Article 17

1. Within six months of the entry into force of the Regulation, Member States   **A14–018**

shall inform the Commission which of their legally protected names or, in those Member States where there is no protection system, which of their names established by usage they wish to register pursuant to this Regulation.

2. In accordance with the procedure laid down in Article 15, the Commission shall register the names referred to in paragraph 1 which comply with Articles 2 and 4. Article 7 shall not apply. However, generic names shall not be added.

3. Member States may maintain national protection of the names communicated in accordance with paragraph 1 until such time as a decision on registration has been taken.

Article 18

A14–019   This Regulation shall enter into force twelve months after the date of its publication in the Official Journal of the European Communities.

This Regulation shall be binding in its entirety and directly applicable in all Member States.

Done at Brussels, July 14, 1992.

ANNEX I

A14–020   Foodstuffs referred to in Article 1 (1)
— Beer,
— Natural mineral waters and spring waters,
— Beverages made from plant extracts,
— Bread, pastry, cakes, confectionery, biscuits and other baker's wares,
— Natural gums and resins.

ANNEX II

A14–021   Agricultural products referred to in Article 1 (1)
— Hay
— Essential oils.

Council Directive 84/450 of September 10, 1984—Relating to the approximation of the laws, regulations and administrative provisions of the Member States concerning misleading advertising

Concerning misleading and comparative advertising   A15–001

([1984] O.J. L250/17)

THE COUNCIL OF THE EUROPEAN COMMUNITIES,

Having regard to the Treaty establishing the European Economic Community, and in particular Article 100 thereof,

Having regard to the proposal from the Commission,

Having regard to the opinion of the European Parliament,

Having regard to the opinion of the Economic and Social Committee,

Whereas the laws against misleading advertising now in force in the Member States differ widely; whereas, since advertising reaches beyond the frontiers of individual Member States, it has a direct effect on the establishment and the functioning of the common market;

Whereas misleading advertising can lead to distortion of competition within the common market;

Whereas advertising, whether or not it induces a contract, affects the economic welfare of consumers;

Whereas misleading advertising may cause a consumer to take decisions prejudicial to him when acquiring goods or other property, or using services, and the differences between the laws of the Member States not only lead, in many cases, to inadequate levels of consumer protection, but also hinder the execution of advertising campaigns beyond national boundaries and thus affect the free circulation of goods and provision of services;

Whereas the second programme of the European Economic Community for a consumer protection and information policy provides for appropriate action for the protection of consumers against misleading and unfair advertising;

Whereas it is in the interest of the public in general, as well as that of consumers and all those who, in competition with one another, carry on a trade, business, craft or profession, in the common market, to harmonize in the first instance national provisions against misleading advertising and that, at a second stage, unfair advertising and, as far as necessary, comparative advertising should be dealt with, on the basis of appropriate Commission proposals;

Whereas minimum and objective criteria for determining whether advertising is misleading should be established for this purpose;

Whereas the laws to be adopted by Member States against misleading advertising must be adequate and effective;

Whereas persons or organizations regarded under national law as having a legitimate interest in the matter must have facilities for initiating proceedings against misleading advertising, either before a court or before an administrative authority which is competent to decide upon complaints or to initiate appropriate legal proceedings;

Whereas it should be for each Member State to decide whether to enable the courts or administrative authorities to require prior recourse to other established means of dealing with the complaint;

Whereas the courts or administrative authorities must have powers enabling them to order or obtain the cessation of misleading advertising;

Whereas in certain cases it may be desirable to prohibit misleading advertising even before it is published; whereas, however, this in no way implies that Member States are under an obligation to introduce rules requiring the systematic prior vetting of advertising;

Whereas provision should be made for accelerated procedures under which measures with interim or definitive effect can be taken;

Whereas it may be desirable to order the publication of decisions made by courts or administrative authorities or of corrective statements in order to eliminate any continuing effects of misleading advertising;

Whereas administrative authorities must be impartial and the exercise of their powers must be subject to judicial review;

Whereas the voluntary control exercised by self-regulatory bodies to eliminate misleading advertising may avoid recourse to administrative or judicial action and ought therefore to be encouraged;

Whereas the advertiser should be able to prove, by appropriate means, the material accuracy of the factual claims he makes in his advertising, and may in appropriate cases be required to do so by the court or administrative authority;

Whereas this Directive must not preclude Member States from retaining or adopting provisions with a view to ensuring more extensive protection of consumers, persons carrying on a trade, business, craft or profession, and the general public,

HAS ADOPTED THIS DIRECTIVE:

General Note

A15–002   The amendments shown in bold type (insertions) and italics (deletions) were made by the 1997 amending Directive 97/55, to be found in App.16, *below*.

Article 1

A15–003   The purpose of this Directive is to protect consumers, persons carrying on a trade or business or practising a craft or profession and the interests of the public in general against misleading advertising and the unfair consequences thereof.

The purpose of this Directive is to protect consumers, persons carrying on a trade or business or practising a craft or profession and the interests of the public in general against misleading advertising and the unfair consequences thereof **and to lay down the conditions under which comparative advertising is permitted;**

Article 2

A15–004   For the purposes of this Directive:

1. "advertising" means the making of a representation in any form in connection with a trade, business, craft or profession in order to promote the supply of goods or services, including immovable property, rights and obligations;

2. "misleading advertising" means any advertising which in any way, including its presentation, deceives or is likely to deceive the persons to whom it is addressed or whom it reaches and which, by reason of its deceptive nature, is likely to affect their economic behaviour or which, for those reasons, injures or is likely to injure a competitor;

2a "comparative advertising" means any advertising which explicitly or by implication identifies a competitor or goods or services offered by a competitor;

3. "person" means any natural or legal person

Article 3

In determining whether advertising is misleading, account shall be taken of all its features, and in particular of any information it contains concerning: **A15–005**

(a) the characteristics of goods or services, such as their availability, nature, execution, composition, method and date of manufacture or provision, fitness for purpose, uses, quantity, specification, geographical or commercial origin or the results to be expected from their use, or the results and material features of tests or checks carried out on the goods or services;

(b) the price or the manner in which the price is calculated, and the conditions on which the goods are supplied or the services provided;

(c) the nature, attributes and rights of the advertiser, such as his identity and assets, his qualifications and ownership of industrial, commercial or intellectual property rights or his awards and distinctions.

Article 3a

1. Comparative advertising shall, as far as the comparison is concerned, be permitted when the following conditions are met: **A15–006**

(a) it is not misleading according to Articles 2 (2), 3 and 7 (1);

(b) it compares goods or services meeting the same needs or intended for the same purpose;

(c) it objectively compares one or more material, relevant, verifiable and representative features of those goods and services, which may include price;

(d) it does not create confusion in the market place between the advertiser and a competitor or between the advertiser's trade marks, trade names, other distinguishing marks, goods or services and those of a competitor;

(e) it does not discredit or denigrate the trade marks, trade names, other distinguishing marks, goods, services, activities, or circumstances of a competitor;

(f) for products with designation of origin, it relates in each case to products with the same designation;

(g) it does not take unfair advantage of the reputation of a trade mark, trade name or other distinguishing marks of a competitor or of the designation of origin of competing products;

(h) it does not present goods or services as imitations or replicas of goods or services bearing a protected trade mark or trade name.

2. Any comparison referring to a special offer shall indicate in a clear and unequivocal way the date on which the offer ends or, where appropriate, that the special offer is subject to the availability of the goods and services, and, where

the special offer has not yet begun, the date of the start of the period during which the special price or other specific conditions shall apply.

Article 4

A15–007   1. Member States shall ensure that adequate and effective means exist for the control of misleading advertising in the interests of consumers as well as competitors and the general public. Such means shall include legal provisions under which persons or organizations regarded under national law as having a legitimate interest in prohibiting misleading advertising may:

(a) take legal action against such advertising; and/or
(b) bring such advertising before an administrative authority competent either to decide on complaints or to initiate appropriate legal proceedings.

It shall be for each Member State to decide which of these facilities shall be available and whether to enable the courts or administrative authorities to require prior recourse to other established means of dealing with complaints, including those referred to in Article 5.

1. Member States shall ensure that adequate and effective means exist to combat misleading advertising and for the compliance with the provisions on comparative advertising in the interests of consumers as well as competitors and the general public.

Such means shall include legal provisions under which persons or organizations regarded under national law as having a legitimate interest in prohibiting misleading advertising or regulating comparative advertising may:

(a) take legal action against such advertising; and/or
(b) bring such advertising before an administrative authority competent either to decide on complaints or to initiate appropriate legal proceedings;

2. Under the legal provisions referred to in paragraph 1, Member States shall confer upon the courts or administrative authorities powers enabling them, in cases where they deem such measures to be necessary taking into account all the interests involved and in particular the public interest:

to order the cessation of, or to institute appropriate legal proceedings for an order for the cessation of, misleading advertising, or

if misleading advertising has not yet been published but publication is imminent, to order the prohibition of, or to institute appropriate legal proceedings for an order for the prohibition of, such publication,

to order the cessation of, or to institute appropriate legal proceedings for an order for the cessation of, misleading advertising or unpermitted comparative advertising, or

if the misleading advertising or unpermitted comparative advertising has not yet been published but publication is imminent, to order the prohibition of, or to institute appropriate legal proceedings for an order for the prohibition of, such publication,

even without proof of actual loss or damage or of intention or negligence on the part of the advertiser.

Member States shall also make provision for the measures referred to in the first subparagraph to be taken under an accelerated procedure:

— either with interim effect, or
— with definitive effect,

on the understanding that it is for each Member State to decide which of the two options to select.

Furthermore, Member States may confer upon the courts or administrative authorities powers enabling them, with a view to eliminating the continuing effects of misleading advertising the cessation of which has been ordered by a final decision:

Furthermore, Member States may confer upon the courts or administrative authorities powers enabling them, with a view to eliminating the continuing effects of misleading advertising or unpermitted comparative advertising, the cessation of which has been ordered by a final decision:

— to require publication of that decision in full or in part and in such form as they deem adequate,
— to require in addition the publication of a corrective statement.

3. The administrative authorities referred to in paragraph 1 must:

(a) be composed so as not to cast doubt on their impartiality;
(b) have adequate powers, where they decide on complaints, to monitor and enforce the observance of their decisions effectively;
(c) normally give reasons for their decisions.

Where the powers referred to in paragraph 2 are exercised exclusively by an administrative authority, reasons for its decisions shall always be given. Furthermore in this case, provision must be made for procedures whereby improper or unreasonable exercise of its powers by the administrative authority or improper or unreasonable failure to exercise the said powers can be the subject of judicial review.

Articles 5

This Directive does not exclude the voluntary control of misleading advertising by self-regulatory bodies and recourse to such bodies by the persons or organizations referred to in Article 4 if proceedings before such bodies are in addition to the court or administrative proceedings referred to in that Article.   **A15–008**

This Directive does not exclude the voluntary control, which Member States may encourage, of misleading or comparative advertising by self-regulatory bodies and recourse to such bodies by the persons or organizations referred to in Article 4 if proceedings before such bodies are in addition to the court or administrative proceedings referred to in that Article.

Article 6

Member States shall confer upon the courts or administrative authorities powers enabling them in the civil or administrative proceedings provided for in Article 4:   **A15–009**

(a) to require the advertiser to furnish evidence as to the accuracy of factual claims in advertising if, taking into account the legitimate interests of the advertiser and any other party to the proceedings, such a requirement appears appropriate on the basis of the circumstances of the particular case; and

(a) to require the advertiser to furnish evidence as to the accuracy of factual claims in advertising if, taking into account the legitimate interest of the advertiser and any other party to the proceedings, such a requirement appears appropriate on the basis of the circumstances of the particular case and in the case of comparative advertising to require the advertiser to furnish such evidence in a short period of time; and

(b) to consider factual claims as inaccurate if the evidence demanded in accordance with (a) is not furnished or is deemed insufficient by the court or administrative authority.

Article 7

A15–010 This Directive shall not preclude Member States from retaining or adopting provisions with a view to ensuring more extensive protection for consumers, persons carrying on a trade, business, craft or profession, and the general public.

1. This Directive shall not preclude Member States from retaining or adopting provisions with a view to ensuring more extensive protection, with regard to misleading advertising, for consumers, persons carrying on a trade, business, craft or profession, and the general public.

2. paragraph 1 shall not apply to comparative advertising as far as the comparison is concerned.

3. The provisions of this Directive shall apply without prejudice to Community provisions on advertising for specific products and/or services or to restrictions or prohibitions on advertising in particular media.

4. The provisions of this Directive concerning comparative advertising shall not oblige Member States which, in compliance with the provisions of the Treaty, maintain or introduce advertising bans regarding certain goods or services, whether imposed directly or by a body or organization responsible, under the law of the Member States, for regulating the exercise of a commercial, industrial, craft or professional activity, to permit comparative advertising regarding those goods or services. Where these bans are limited to particular media, the Directive shall apply to the media not covered by these bans.

5. Nothing in this Directive shall prevent Member States from, in compliance with the provisions of the Treaty, maintaining or introducing bans or limitations on the use of comparisons in the advertising of professional services, whether imposed directly or by a body or organization responsible, under the law of the Member States, for regulating the exercise of a professional activity.

Article 8

A15–011 Member States shall bring into force the measures necessary to comply with this Directive by 1 October 1986 at the latest. They shall forthwith inform the Commission thereof.

Member States shall communicate to the Commission the text of all provisions of national law which they adopt in the field covered by this Directive.

Article 9

A15–012 This Directive is addressed to the Member States.

Done at Brussels, September 10, 1984.

Directive 97/55 of European Parliament and of the Council of October 1997—Amending Directive 84/450 concerning misleading advertising so as to include comparative advertising
([1997] O.J. L290/18)

THE EUROPEAN PARLIAMENT AND THE COUNCIL OF THE EUROPEAN UNION,   A16–001

Having regard to the Treaty establishing the European Community, and in particular Article 100a thereof,

Having regard to the proposal from the Commission,

Having regard to the opinion of the Economic and Social Committee,

Acting in accordance with the procedure laid down in Article 189b of the Treaty, in the light of the joint text approved by the Conciliation Committee on 25 June 1997,

(1) Whereas one of the Community's main aims is to complete the internal market; whereas measures must be adopted to ensure the smooth running of the said market; whereas the internal market comprises an area which has no internal frontiers and in which goods, persons, services and capital can move freely;

(2) Whereas the completion of the internal market will mean an ever wider range of choice; whereas, given that consumers can and must make the best possible use of the internal market, and that advertising is a very important means of creating genuine outlets for all goods and services throughout the Community, the basic provisions governing the form and content of comparative advertising should be uniform and the conditions of the use of comparative advertising in the Member States should be harmonized; whereas if these conditions are met, this will help demonstrate objectively the merits of the various comparable products; whereas comparative advertising can also stimulate competition between suppliers of goods and services to the consumer's advantage;

(3) Whereas the laws, regulations and administrative provisions of the individual Member States concerning comparative advertising differ widely; whereas advertising reaches beyond the frontiers and is received on the territory of other Member States; whereas the acceptance or non-acceptance of comparative advertising according to the various national laws may constitute an obstacle to the free movement of goods and services and create distortions of competition; whereas, in particular, firms may be exposed to forms of advertising developed by competitors to which they cannot reply in equal measure; whereas the freedom to provide services relating to comparative advertising should be assured; whereas the Community is called on to remedy the situation;

(4) Whereas the sixth recital of Council Directive 84/450/EEC of 10 September 1984 relating to the approximation of laws, regulations and administrative provisions of the Member States concerning misleading advertising states that, after the harmonization of national provisions against misleading advertising, "at a second stage…, as far as necessary, comparative advertising should be dealt with, on the basis of appropriate Commission proposals";

(5) Whereas point 3 (d) of the Annex to the Council Resolution of 14 April 1975 on a preliminary programme of the European Economic Community for a consumer protection and information policy includes the right to information among the basic rights of consumers; whereas this right is confirmed by the Council Resolution of 19 May 1981 on a second programme of the European Economic Community for a consumer protection and information policy, point 40 of the Annex, which deals specifically with consumer information; whereas comparative advertising, when it compares material, relevant, verifiable and representative features and is not misleading, may be a legitimate means of informing consumers of their advantage;

(6) Whereas it is desirable to provide a broad concept of comparative advertising to cover all modes of comparative advertising;

(7) Whereas conditions of permitted comparative advertising, as far as the comparison is concerned, should be established in order to determine which practices relating to comparative advertising may distort competition, be detrimental to competitors and have an adverse effect on consumer choice; whereas such conditions of permitted advertising should include criteria of objective comparison of the features of goods and services;

(8) Whereas the comparison of the price only of goods and services should be possible if this comparison respects certain conditions, in particular that it shall not be misleading;

(9) Whereas, in order to prevent comparative advertising being used in an anti-competitive and unfair manner, only comparisons between competing goods and services meeting the same needs or intended for the same purpose should be permitted;

(10) Whereas the international conventions on copyright as well as the national provisions on contractual and non-contractual liability shall apply when the results of comparative tests carried out by third parties are referred to or reproduced in comparative advertising;

(11) Whereas the conditions of comparative advertising should be cumulative and respected in their entirety; whereas, in accordance with the Treaty, the choice of forms and methods for the implementation of these conditions shall be left to the Member States, insofar as those forms and methods are not already determined by this Directive;

(12) Whereas these conditions should include, in particular, consideration of the provisions resulting from Council Regulation (EEC) No 2081/92 of 14 July 1992 on the protection of geographical indications and designations of origin for agricultural products and foodstuffs, and in particular Article 13 thereof, and of the other Community provisions adopted in the agricultural sphere;

(13) Whereas Article 5 of First Council Directive 89/104/EEC of 21 December 1988 to approximate the laws of the Member States relating to trade marks confers exclusive rights on the proprietor of a registered trade mark, including the right to prevent all third parties from using, in the course of trade, any sign which is identical with, or similar to, the trade mark in relation to identical goods or services or even, where appropriate, other goods;

(14) Whereas it may, however, be indispensable, in order to make comparative advertising effective, to identify the goods or services of a competitor, making reference to a trade mark or trade name of which the latter is the proprietor;

(15) Whereas such use of another's trade mark, trade name or other distinguishing marks does not breach this exclusive right in cases where it complies

with the conditions laid down by this Directive, the intended target being solely to distinguish between them and thus to highlight differences objectively;

(16) Whereas provisions should be made for the legal and/or administrative means of redress mentioned in Articles 4 and 5 of Directive 84/450/EEC to be available to control comparative advertising which fails to meet the conditions laid down by this Directive; whereas according to the 16th recital of the Directive, voluntary control by self-regulatory bodies to eliminate misleading advertising may avoid recourse to administrative or juridical action and ought therefore to be encouraged; whereas Article 6 applies to unpermitted comparative advertising in the same way;

(17) Whereas national self-regulatory bodies may coordinate their work through associations or organizations established at Community level and *inter alia* deal with cross-border complaints;

(18) Whereas Article 7 of Directive 84/450/EEC allowing Member States to retain or adopt provisions with a view to ensuring more extensive protection for consumers, persons carrying on a trade, business, craft or profession, and the general public, should not apply to comparative advertising, given that the objective of amending the said Directive is to establish conditions under which comparative advertising is permitted;

(19) Whereas a comparison which presents goods or services as an imitation or a replica of goods or services bearing a protected trade mark or trade name shall not be considered to fulfil the conditions to be met by permitted comparative advertising;

(20) Whereas this Directive in no way affects Community provisions on advertising for specific products and/or services or restrictions or prohibitions on advertising in particular media;

(21) Whereas, if a Member State, in compliance with the provisions of the Treaty, prohibits advertising regarding certain goods or services, this ban may, whether it is imposed directly or by a body or organization responsible under the law of that Member State for regulating the exercise of a commercial, industrial, craft or professional activity, be extended to comparative advertising;

(22) Whereas Member States shall not be obliged to permit comparative advertising for goods or services on which they, in compliance with the provisions of the Treaty, maintain or introduce bans, including bans as regards marketing methods or advertising which targets vulnerable consumer groups; whereas Member States may, in compliance with the provisions of the Treaty, maintain or introduce bans or limitations on the use of comparisons in the advertising of professional services, whether imposed directly or by a body or organization responsible under the law of the Member States for regulating the exercise of a professional activity;

(23) Whereas regulating comparative advertising is, under the conditions set out in this Directive, necessary for the smooth running of the internal market and whereas action at Community level is therefore required; whereas the adoption of a Directive is the appropriate instrument because it lays down uniform general principles while allowing the Member States to choose the form and appropriate method by which to attain these objectives; whereas it is in accordance with the principle of subsidiarity,

HAVE ADOPTED THIS DIRECTIVE:

Article 1

Directive 94/450/EEC is hereby amended as follows: **A16–002**

(1) The title shall be replaced by the following:

"Council Directive of 10 September 1984 concerning misleading and comparative advertising";

(2) Article 1 shall be replaced by the following:

"Article 1

The purpose of this Directive is to protect consumers, persons carrying on a trade or business or practising a craft or profession and the interests of the public in general against misleading advertising and the unfair consequences thereof and to lay down the conditions under which comparative advertising is permitted."

(3) The following point shall be inserted in Article 2:

"2a 'comparative advertising' means any advertising which explicitly or by implication identifies a competitor or goods or services offered by a competitor;"

(4) The following Article shall be added:

"Article 3a

1. Comparative advertising shall, as far as the comparison is concerned, be permitted when the following conditions are met:

(a) it is not misleading according to Articles 2 (2), 3 and 7 (1);

(b) it compares goods or services meeting the same needs or intended for the same purpose;

(c) it objectively compares one or more material, relevant, verifiable and representative features of those goods and services, which may include price;

(d) it does not create confusion in the market place between the advertiser and a competitor or between the advertiser's trade marks, trade names, other distinguishing marks, goods or services and those of a competitor;

(e) it does not discredit or denigrate the trade marks, trade names, other distinguishing marks, goods, services, activities, or circumstances of a competitor;

(f) for products with designation of origin, it relates in each case to products with the same designation;

(g) it does not take unfair advantage of the reputation of a trade mark, trade name or other distinguishing marks of a competitor or of the designation of origin of competing products;

(h) it does not present goods or services as imitations or replicas of goods or services bearing a protected trade mark or trade name.

2. Any comparison referring to a special offer shall indicate in a clear and unequivocal way the date on which the offer ends or, where appropriate, that the special offer is subject to the availability of the goods and services, and, where the special offer has not yet begun, the date of the start of the period during which the special price or other specific conditions shall apply.";

(5) The first and second subparagraphs of Article 4 (1) shall be replaced by the following:

"1. Member States shall ensure that adequate and effective means exist to combat misleading advertising and for the compliance with the provisions on comparative advertising in the interests of consumers as well as competitors and the general public.

Such means shall include legal provisions under which persons or organizations regarded under national law as having a legitimate interest in prohibiting misleading advertising or regulating comparative advertising may:

(a) take legal action against such advertising; and/or

(b) bring such advertising before an administrative authority competent either to decide on complaints or to initiate appropriate legal proceedings.";

(6) Article 4 (2) is hereby amended as follows:

(a) the indents in the first subparagraph shall be replaced by the following:

— "to order the cessation of, or to institute appropriate legal proceedings for an order for the cessation of, misleading advertising or unpermitted comparative advertising, or

— if the misleading advertising or unpermitted comparative advertising has not yet been published but publication is imminent, to order the prohibition of, or to institute appropriate legal proceedings for an order for the prohibition of, such publication,";

(b) the introductory wording to the third subparagraph shall be replaced by the following:

"Furthermore, Member States may confer upon the courts or administrative authorities powers enabling them, with a view to eliminating the continuing effects of misleading advertising or unpermitted comparative advertising, the cessation of which has been ordered by a final decision:";

(7) Article 5 shall be replaced by the following:

"Article 5

This Directive does not exclude the voluntary control, which Member States may encourage, of misleading or comparative advertising by self-regulatory bodies and recourse to such bodies by the persons or organisations referred to in Article 4 if proceedings before such bodies are in addition to the court or administrative proceedings referred to in that Article."

(8) Article 6 (a) shall be replaced by the following:

"(a) to require the advertiser to furnish evidence as to the accuracy of factual claims in advertising if, taking into account the legitimate interest of the advertiser and any other party to the proceedings, such a requirement appears appropriate on the basis of the circumstances of the particular case and in the case of comparative advertising to require the advertiser to furnish such evidence in a short period of time; and";

(9) Article 7 shall be replaced by the following:

"Article 7

1. This Directive shall not preclude Member States from retaining or adopting provisions with a view to ensuring more extensive protection, with regard to misleading advertising, for consumers, persons carrying on a trade, business, craft or profession, and the general public.

2. Paragraph 1 shall not apply to comparative advertising as far as the comparison is concerned.

3. The provisions of this Directive shall apply without prejudice to Community provisions on advertising for specific products and/or services or to restrictions or prohibitions on advertising in particular media.

4. The provisions of this Directive concerning comparative advertising shall not oblige Member States which, in compliance with the provisions of the Treaty, maintain or introduce advertising bans regarding certain goods or services, whether imposed directly or by a body or organization responsible, under the law of the Member States, for regulating the exercise of a commercial, industrial, craft or professional activity, to permit comparative advertising regarding those goods or services. Where these bans are limited to particular media, the Directive shall apply to the media not covered by these bans.

5. Nothing in this Directive shall prevent Member States from, in compliance with the provisions of the Treaty, maintaining or introducing bans or limitations on the use of comparisons in the advertising of professional services, whether imposed directly or by a body or organization responsible, under the law of the Member States, for regulating the exercise of a professional activity."

Article 2

Complaints systems

A16–003   The Commission shall study the feasibility of establishing effective means to deal with cross-border complaints in respect of comparative advertising. Within two years after the entry into force of this Directive the Commission shall submit a report to the European Parliament and the Council on the results of the studies, accompanied if appropriate by proposals.

Article 3

A16–004   1. Member States shall bring into force the laws, regulations and administrative provisions necessary to comply with this Directive at the latest 30 months after its publication in the Official Journal of the European Communities. They shall forthwith inform the Commission thereof.

2. When Member States adopt these measures, they shall contain a reference to this Directive or shall be accompanied by such reference on the occasion of their official publication. The methods of making such reference shall be laid down by Member States.

3. Member States shall communicate to the Commission the text of the main provisions of domestic law which they adopt in the field governed by this Directive.

Article 4

A16–005   This Directive is addressed to the Member States.

Done at Brussels, October 6, 1997.

C 136, 19. 5. 1994, p. 4.

C 49, 24. 2. 1992, p. 35.

Commission declaration

The Commission declares that it intends to submit the report referred to in Article 2 as far as possible at the same time as the report on complaints systems provided for in Article 17 of Directive 97/7/EC on the protection of consumers in respect of distance contracts.

APPENDIX **17**

Regulations under the Comparative Advertising Directive (SI 1998/915 as amended by SI 2000/914 and SI 2003/3183)

SI 1988/915

Whereas the Secretary of State is a Minister designated for the purposes of section 2(2) of the European Communities Act 1972 in relation to measures relating to the control of advertising;   **A17–001**

And whereas a draft of these Regulations has been approved by a resolution of each House of Parliament pursuant to section 2(2) of and paragraph 2(2) of Schedule 2 to that Act;

Now, therefore, the Secretary of State in exercise of the powers conferred on him by section 2(2) of that Act and of all other powers enabling him in that behalf hereby makes the following Regulations:

General Note

(As amended by the Broadcasting Act 1990 (c.42), the Control of Misleading Advertisements (Amendment) Regulations 2000 (SI 2000/914) and the Control of Misleading Advertisements (Amendment) Regulations 2003 (SI 2003/3183).)   **A17–002**

Citation and commencement

1.—(1) These Regulations may be cited as the Control of Misleading Advertisements Regulations 1988 and shall come into force on 20th June 1988.   **A17–003**

Interpretation

2.—(1) In these Regulations—   **A17–004**

"advertisement" means any form of representation which is made in connection with a trade, business, craft or profession in order to promote the supply or transfer of goods or services, immovable property, rights or obligations;

[*"broadcast advertisement" means any advertisement included or proposed to be included in any programme or teletext transmission broadcast by the IBA and includes any advertisement included or proposed to be included in a licensed service by the reception and immediate re-transmission of broadcasts made by the IBA;*]

[*"Cable Authority" means the authority mentioned in section 1(1) of the Cable and Broadcasting Act 1984;*]

[**"the Commission" means the Independent Television Commission;**]

"court", in relation to England and Wales and Northern Ireland, means the High Court, and, in relation to Scotland, the Court of Session;

"Director" means the Director General of Fair Trading;

[*"IBA" means the Independent Broadcasting Authority mentioned in section 1(1) of the Broadcasting Act 1981;*]

[*"licensable service" has the meaning given by Section 2(2) of the Cable and Broadcasting Act 1984;*]

"licensed service" means [*a licensable service in respect of which the Cable Authority has granted a licence pursuant to section 4 of the Cable and Broadcasting Act 1984*] **a service in respect of which a licence has been granted under Part I or III of the Broadcasting Act 1990 or under Part I or II of the Broadcasting Act 1996** [(a) *in relation to a complaint made to the Commission, a service in respect of which the Commission have granted a licence under Part I or II of the Broadcasting Act 1990; and*

(b) *in relation to a complaint made to the Radio Authority, a service in respect of which the Radio Authority have granted a licence under Part III of that Act;*

and "licensed local delivery service" means a service in respect of which the Commission have granted a licence under Part II of that Act];

"OFCOM" means the Office of Communications established by section 1(1) of the Office of Communications Act 2002;

"products with designation of origin" are those products to which Council Regulation (EEC) No. 2081/92 of 14 July 1992 applies;

"publication" in relation to an advertisement means the dissemination of that advertisement whether to an individual person or a number of persons and whether orally or in writing or in any other way whatsoever, and "publish" shall be construed accordingly;

"S4C" and "S4C Digital" have the same meaning as in Part 3 of the Communications Act 2003;

[*"relevant body" means the Commission or the Radio Authority;*]

[*"on S4C" has the same meaning as in Part I of the Broadcasting Act 1990;*]

[*"the Welsh Authority" has the same meaning as in that Act;*]

(2) For the purposes of these Regulations an advertisement is misleading if in any way, including its presentation, it deceives or is likely to deceive the persons to whom it is addressed or whom it reaches and if, by reason of its deceptive nature, it is likely to affect their economic behaviour or, for those reasons, injures or is likely to injure a competitor of the person whose interests the advertisement seeks to promote.

(2A) For the purposes of these Regulations an advertisement is comparative if in any way, either explicitly or by implication, it identifies a competitor or goods or services offered by a competitor.

(3) In the application of these Regulations to Scotland for references to an injunction or an [*interlocutory*] interim injunction there shall be substituted references to an interdict or an interim interdict respectively.

Amendment

The words in italics were deleted, and the words in bold inserted, by the Broadcasting Act 1990 (c.42), Sch.20, para.51(1), the Control of Misleading Advertisements (Amendment) Regulations 2000 (SI 2000/914), reg.3 or the Control of Misleading Advertisements (Amendment) Regulations 2003 (SI 2003/3183), Sch.1, para.1.

Application

A17–005   3.—[(1) *These Regulations do not apply to—*

(a) *the following advertisements issued or caused to be issued by or on behalf of an authorised person or appointed representative, that is to say—*

(i) *investment advertisements; and*

(ii) *any other advertisements in respect of investment business, except where any such advertisements relate exclusively to any matter in relation to which the authorised person in question is an exempted person; and*

(b) *advertisements of a description referred to in section 58(1)(d) of the*

Financial Services Act 1986, except where any such advertisements consist of or any part of the matters referred to in section 58(1)(d)(ii) of that Act as being required of permitted to be published by an approved exchange under Part V of that Act.

(2) *In this regulation "appointed representative", "approved exchange", "authorised person", "exempted person", "investment advertisement" and "investment business" have the same meanings as in the Financial Services Act 1986.*]

Amendment

This regulation was amended by the Public Offers of Securities Regulations 1995 (SI 1995/1537) and was then repealed by the Financial Services and Markets Act 2000 (Consequential Amendments and Repeals) Order 2001 (SI 2001/3649), Pt 9, art.390.

Complaints to the Director

4.—(1) Subject to paragraphs (2) and (3) below, it shall be the duty of the Director to consider any complaint made to him that an advertisement is misleading, **or is a comparative advertisement and is not permitted under regulation 4A below,** unless the complaint appears to the Director to be frivolous or vexatious.

A17–006

(2) The Director shall not consider any complaint which these Regulations require or would require, leaving aside any question as to the frivolous or vexatious nature of the complaint, [*the IBA or the Cable Authority,*] [*the Commission, the Radio Authority or the Welsh Authority*] **OFCOM** to consider.

(3) Before considering any complaint under paragraph (1) above the Director may require the person making the complaint to satisfy him that—

(a) there have been invoked in relation to the same or substantially the same complaint about the advertisement in question such established means of dealing with such complaints as the Director may consider appropriate, having regard to all the circumstances of the particular case;

(b) a reasonable opportunity has been allowed for those means to deal with the complaint in question; and

(c) those means have not dealt with the complaint adequately.

(4) In exercising the powers conferred on him by these Regulations the Director shall have regard to—

(a) all the interests involved and in particular the public interest; and

(b) the desirability of encouraging the control, by self-regulatory bodies, of advertisements.

Amendment

The words in italics were deleted, and the words in bold inserted, by the Broadcasting Act 1990 (c.42), Sch.20, para.51(2), the Control of Misleading Advertisements (Amendment) Regulations 2000 (SI 2000/914), reg.4 or the Control of Misleading Advertisements (Amendment) Regulations 2003 (SI 2003/3183), Sch.1, para.2.

Comparative Advertisements

4A—**(1) A comparative advertisement shall, as far as the comparison is concerned, be permitted only when the following conditions are met:—**

A17–007

(a) it is not misleading;

(b) it compares goods or services meeting the same needs or intended for the same purpose;

(c) it objectively compares one or more material, relevant, verifiable and representative features of those goods and services, which may include price;

(d) it does not create confusion in the market place between the advertiser and a competitor or between the advertiser's trade marks, trade names, other distinguishing marks, goods or services and those of a competitor;

(e) it does not discredit or denigrate the trade marks, trade names, other distinguishing marks, goods, services, activities, or circumstances of a competitor;

(f) for products with designation of origin, it relates in each case to products with the same designation;

(g) it does not take unfair advantage of the reputation of a trade mark, trade name or other distinguishing marks of a competitor or of the designation of origin of competing products;

(h) it does not present goods or services as imitations or replicas of goods or services bearing a protected trade mark or trade name.

(2) In the case of a comparative advertisement referring to a special offer, such an advertisement is not permitted unless it indicates in a clear and unequivocal way the date on which the offer ends or, where appropriate, that the special offer is subject to the availability of the goods and services, and, where the special offer has not yet begun, the date of the start of the period during which the special price or other specific conditions shall apply.

(3) The provisions of this regulation shall not be construed as—

(a) conferring a right of action in any civil proceedings in respect of any contravention of this regulation (save as provided for in these Regulations); or

(b) derogating from any right of action or other remedy (whether civil or criminal) in proceedings instituted otherwise than by virtue of these Regulations.

Amendment

This regulation was added by the Control of Misleading Advertisements (Amendment) Regulations 2000 (SI 2000/914), reg.5.

Applications to the Court by the Director

A17–008   **5.**—(1) If, having considered a complaint about an advertisement pursuant to regulation 4(1) above, he considers that the advertisement is misleading **or is a comparative advertisement and is not permitted under regulation 4A,** the Director may, if he thinks it appropriate to do so, bring proceedings for an injunction (in which proceedings he may also apply for an [*interlocutory*] **interim** injunction) against any person appearing to him to be concerned or likely to be concerned with the publication of the advertisement.

(2) The Director shall give reasons for his decision to apply or not to apply, as the case may be, for an injunction in relation to any complaint which these Regulations require him to consider.

Amendment

The word in italics was deleted, and the words in bold inserted, by the Control of Misleading Advertisements (Amendment) Regulations 2000 (SI 2000/914), regs 3 and 6.

Functions of the Court

A17–009   **6.**—(1) The court on an application by the Director may grant an injunction on such terms as it may think fit but (except where it grants an [*interlocutory*] **interim** injunction) only if the court is satisfied that the advertisement to which the application relates is misleading **or is a comparative advertisement and is not permitted under regulation 4A**. Before granting an injunction the court shall have regard to all the interests involved and in particular the public interest.

(2) An injunction may relate not only to a particular advertisement but to any advertisement in similar terms or likely to convey a similar impression.

(3) In considering an application for an injunction the court may, whether or not on the application of any party to the proceedings, require any person appearing to the court to be responsible for the publication of the advertisement to which the application relates to furnish the court with evidence of the accuracy of any factual claim made in the advertisement. The court shall not make such a requirement unless it appears to the court to be appropriate in the circumstances of the particular case, having regard to the legitimate interests of the person who would be the subject of or affected by the requirement and of any other person concerned with the advertisement.

(4) If such evidence is not furnished to it following a requirement made by it under paragraph (3) above or if it considers such evidence inadequate, the court may decline to consider the factual claim mentioned in that paragraph accurate.

(5) The court shall not refuse to grant an injunction for lack of evidence that—
- (a) the publication of the advertisement in question has given rise to loss or damage to any person; or
- (b) the person responsible for the advertisement intended it to be misleading or failed to exercise proper care to prevent its being misleading; **or**
- (c) **the person responsible for the comparative advertisement intended to breach the conditions in regulation 4A(1) and (2) or failed to exercise proper care to meet the conditions in regulation 4A(1) and (2).**

(6) An injunction may prohibit the publication or the continued or further publication of an advertisement.

Amendment

The word in italics was deleted, and the words in bold inserted, by the Control of Misleading Advertisements (Amendment) Regulations 2000 (SI 2000/914), regs 3 and 7.

Powers of the Director to obtain and disclose information and disclosure of information generally

7.—(1) For the purpose of facilitating the exercise by him of any functions conferred on him by these Regulations, the Director may, by notice in writing signed by him or on his behalf, require any person to furnish to him such information as may be specified or described in the notice or to produce to him any documents so specified or described.   **A17–010**

(2) A notice under paragraph (1) above may—
- (a) specify the way in which and the time within which it is to be complied with; and
- (b) be varied or revoked by a subsequent notice.

(3) Nothing in this regulation compels the production or furnishing by any person of a document or of information which he would in an action in a court be entitled to refuse to produce or furnish on grounds of legal professional privilege or, in Scotland, on the grounds of confidentiality as between client and professional legal adviser.

(4) If a person makes default in complying with a notice under paragraph (1) above the court may, on the application of the Director, make such order as the court thinks fit for requiring the default to be made good, and any such order may provide that all the costs or expenses of and incidental to the application shall be borne by the person in default or by any officers of a company or other association who are responsible for its default.

(5) Subject to any provision to the contrary made by or under any enactment, where the Director considers it appropriate to do so for the purpose of controlling misleading advertisements **or comparative advertisements which do not comply with regulation 4A**, he may refer to any person any complaint (including any related documentation about an advertisement or disclose to any person any information (whether or not obtained by means of the exercise of the power conferred by paragraph (1) above).

(6) For the purpose of enabling information obtained under certain enactments to be used for facilitating the performance of functions under these Regulations, the following amendments shall be made in provisions respecting disclosure of information, that is to say—

[(a) *in section 133 of the Fair Trading Act 1973 there shall be inserted—*
   (i) *at the end of paragraph (a) of subsection (2) the words "the Control of Misleading Advertisements Regulations 1988 or";*
   (ii) *at the end of subsection (3) the words "or the Control of Misleading Advertisements Regulations 1988";*

(b) *in section 174 of the Consumer Credit Act 1974 there shall be inserted—*
   (i) *after the words "Consumer Protection Act 1987" in paragraph (a) of subsection (3) the words "or the Control of Misleading Advertisements Regulations 1988";*
   (ii) *after the words "Fair Trading Act 1973" in paragraph (c) of subsection (3) the words "or under the Control of Misleading Advertisements Regulations 1988";*]

(c) in section 41 of the Restrictive Trade Practices Act 1976 there shall be inserted—
   (i) at the end of paragraph (a) of subsection (1) the words "or the Control of Misleading Advertisements Regulations 1988";
   (ii) after the words "Fair Trading Act 1973" in paragraph (c) of subsection (1) the words "or the Control of Misleading Advertisements Regulations 1988";

[(d) *in section 10 of the Estate Agents Act 1979 there shall be inserted—*
   (i) *after the words "Consumer Protection Act 1987" in paragraph (a) of subsection (3) the words "or the Control of Misleading Advertisements Regulations 1988";*
   (ii) *after the words "other enactments" in paragraph (c) of subsection (3) the words "or subordinate legislation";*

(e) *in section 19 of the Competition Act 1980 there shall be inserted—*
   (i) *after the words "the enactments" in paragraphs (a) and (c) of subsection (2) the words "or subordinate legislation";*
   (ii) *after the words "the enactments" in subsection (3) the words "and subordinate legislation" and after the words "Consumer Protection Act 1987" in that subsection the words "(k) the Control of Misleading Advertisements Regulations 1988";*]

(f) in section 101 of the Telecommunications Act 1984 there shall be inserted—

    (i) after the words "the enactments" in paragraphs (b) and (d) of subsection (2) the words "or subordinate legislation";

    (ii) after the words "the enactments" in subsection (3) the words "and subordinate legislation" and after the words "Consumer Protection Act 1987" in that subsection the words "(i) the Control of Misleading Advertisements Regulations 1988";

(g) in section 74 of the Airports Act 1986 there shall be inserted—

    (i) after the words "the enactments" in paragraphs (a) and (c) of subsection (2) the words "or subordinate legislation";

    (ii) after the words "the enactment" in subsection (3) the words "and subordinate legislation" and after the words "Consumer Protection Act 1987" in that subsection the words "(j) the Control of Misleading Advertisements Regulations 1988";

(h) in section 42 of the Gas Act 1986 there shall be inserted—

    (i) after the words "the enactments" in paragraphs (b) and (e) of subsection (2) he words "or subordinate legislation";

    (ii) after the words "the enactments" in subsection (3) the words "and subordinate legislation" and after the words "Consumer Protection Act 1987" in that subsection the words "(k) the Control of Misleading Advertisements Regulations 1988".

[(7) Subject to paragraph (5) above, any person who knowingly discloses, otherwise than for the purposes of any legal proceedings or of a report of such proceedings or the investigation of any criminal offence, any information obtained by means of the exercise of the power conferred by paragraph (1) above without the consent either of the person to whom the information relates, or, if the information relates to a business, the consent of the person for the time being carrying on that business, shall be guilty of an offence and liable on summary conviction to imprisonment for a term not exceeding 3 months or to a fine not exceeding £2,000 or to both.]

(8) The Director may arrange for the dissemination in such form and manner as he considers appropriate of such information and advice concerning the operation of these Regulations as may appear to him to be expedient to give to the public and to all persons likely to be affected by these Regulations.

Amendment

The words in bold were inserted by the Control of Misleading Advertisements (Amendment) Regulations 2000 (SI 2000/914), reg.8. The words in italics were deleted by the Enterprise Act 2002 (c.40), Sch.26, para.1 and the Enterprise Act 2002 (Part 9 Restrictions on Disclosure of Information) (Amendment and Specification) Order 2003 (SI 2003/1400), Sch.5, para.1.

Complaints to the IBA

[8.—(1) It shall be the duty of the IBA to consider any complaint made to it that a broadcast advertisement is misleading, unless the complaint appears to the IBA to be frivolous or vexatious.

(2) The IBA shall give reasons for its decisions.

(3) In exercising the powers conferred on it by these Regulations the IBA shall have regard to all the interests involved and in particular the public interest.]

A17–011

Complaints to [the Commission and the Radio Authority] OFCOM

8.—[(1) Subject to paragraph (2) below, it shall be the duty of a relevant body to consider any complaint made to it that any advertisement included or

A17–012

proposed to be included in a licensed service is misleading or is a comparative advertisement and is not permitted under regulation 4A, unless the complaint appears to the body to be frivolous or vexatious.]

(1) It shall be the duty of OFCOM to consider any complaint made to them that any advertisement included or proposed to be included in a licensed service is misleading or is a comparative advertisement and is not permitted under regulation 4A, unless the complaint appears to OFCOM to be frivolous or vexatious.

[(2) The Commission shall not consider any complaint about an advertisement included or proposed to be included in a licensed local delivery service by the reception and immediate re-transmission of broadcasts made by the British Broadcasting Corporation.]

[(3) A relevant body shall give reasons for its decisions.]

(3) OFCOM shall give reasons for their decisions.

(4) In exercising the powers conferred on [*it*] them by these Regulations [*a relevant body*] OFCOM shall have regard to all the interests involved and in particular the public interest.

Amendment

New regulation 8 (in bold) was substituted for the previous regulation 8 (in italics) by the Broadcasting Act 1990 (c.42), Sch.20, para.51(3), and was then amended by the Control of Misleading Advertisements (Amendment) Regulation 2000 (SI 2000/914), reg.9 and the Control of Misleading Advertisements (Amendment) Regulation 2003 (SI 2003/3183), reg.3.

Control by the IBA of misleading advertisements

A17–013 *[9.—(1) If, having considered a complaint about a broadcast advertisement pursuant to regulation 8(1) above, it considers that the advertisement is misleading, the IBA may, if it thinks it appropriate to do so, refuse to broadcast the advertisement.*

(2) The IBA may require any person appearing to it to be responsible for a broadcast advertisement which the IBA believes may be misleading to furnish it with evidence as to the accuracy of any factual claim made in the advertisement. In deciding whether or not to make such a requirement the IBA shall have regard to the legitimate interests of any person who would be the subject of or affected by the requirement.

(3) If such evidence is not furnished to it following a requirement made by it under paragraph (2) above or if it considers such evidence inadequate, the IBA may consider the factual claim inaccurate.]

Control by [the Commission and the Radio Authority] OFCOM of misleading advertisements and comparative [advertisements] advertising

A17–014 9.—[*(1) If, having considered a complaint about an advertisement pursuant to regulation 8(1) above, it considers that the advertisement is misleading or is a comparative advertisement and is not permitted under regulation 4A, a relevant body may, if it thinks it appropriate to do so, exercise in relation to the advertisement the power conferred on it—*

(a) *where the relevant body is the Commission, by section 9(6) of the Broadcasting Act 1990 (power of Commission to give directions about advertisements), or*

(b) where the relevant body is the Radio Authority, by section 93(6) of that Act (power of Radio Authority to give directions about advertisements).]

(1) If, having considered a complaint about an advertisement pursuant to regulation 8(1) above, they consider that the advertisement is misleading, or is a comparative advertisement and is not permitted under regulation 4A, OFCOM may, if they think it appropriate to do so, exercise in relation to the advertisement any power conferred on them by virtue of a condition included in a licence in accordance with section 325(4) of the Communications Act 2003.

(2) [*A relevant body*] OFCOM may require any person appearing to [*it*] them to be responsible for an advertisement which [*the body believes*] OFCOM believe may be misleading, or may be a comparative advertisement which is not permitted under regulation 4A, to furnish [*it*] them with evidence as to the accuracy of any factual claim made in the advertisement. In deciding whether or not to make such a requirement [*the body*] OFCOM shall have regard to the legitimate interests of any person who would be the subject of or affected by the requirement.

(3) If such evidence is not furnished to [*it*] them following a requirement made by [*it*] them under paragraph (2) above within a time specified by [*the relevant body*] OFCOM or if [*it considers*] they consider such evidence inadequate, [*a relevant body*] OFCOM may consider the factual claim inaccurate.

Amendment

New regulation 9 (in bold) was substituted for the previous regulation 9 (in italics) by the Broadcasting Act 1990 (c.42), Sch.20, para.51(3), and was then amended by the Control of Misleading Advertisements (Amendment) Regulation 2000 (SI 2000/914), reg.10 and the Control of Misleading Advertisements (Amendment) Regulation 2003 (SI 2003/3183), reg.4.

Complaints to the Cable Authority

[10.—(1) Subject to paragraph (2) below, it shall be the duty of the Cable   A17–015
Authority to consider any complaint made to it that any advertisement included or proposed to be included in a licensed service is misleading, unless the complaint appears to the Authority to be frivolous or vexatious.

(2) The Cable Authority shall not consider any complaint about an advertisement included or proposed to be included in a licensed service by the reception and immediate re-transmission of broadcasts made by the IBA or the British Broadcasting Corporation.

(3) In exercising the powers conferred on it by these Regulations the Cable Authority shall have regard to all the interests involved and in particular the public interest.]

Complaints [to the Welsh Authority] about advertisements on S4C and S4C Digital

10.—[*(1) Subject to paragraph (2) below, it shall be the duty of the Welsh*   A17–016
Authority to consider any complaint made to them that any advertisement broadcast or proposed to be broadcast on S4C is misleading or is a comparative advertisement and is not permitted under regulation 4A, unless the complaint appears to the Authority to be frivolous or vexatious.]

(1) It shall be the duty of OFCOM to consider any complaint made to

them that any advertisement broadcast or proposed to be broadcast on S4C or S4C Digital is misleading, or is a comparative advertisement and is not permitted under regulation 4A, unless the complaint appears to OFCOM to be frivolous or vexatious.

[*(2) The Welsh Authority shall not consider any complaint about an advertisement broadcast or proposed to be broadcast on S4C by the reception and immediate re-transmission of broadcasts made by the British Broadcasting Corporation.*]

[*(3) The Welsh Authority shall give reasons for their decisions.*]

(3) OFCOM shall give reasons for their decisions.

(4) In exercising the powers conferred on them by these Regulations [*the Welsh Authority*] OFCOM shall have regard to all the interests involved and in particular the public interest.

Amendment

New regulation 10 (in bold) was substituted for the previous regulation 10 (in italics) by the Broadcasting Act 1990 (c.42), Sch.20, para.51(3), and was then amended by the Control of Misleading Advertisements (Amendment) Regulation 2000 (SI 2000/914), reg.11 and the Control of Misleading Advertisements (Amendment) Regulation 2003 (SI 2003/3183), reg.5.

Control by the Cable Authority of misleading advertisements

A17–017
[*11.—(1) If, having considered a complaint about an advertisement pursuant to regulation 10(1) above, it considers that the advertisement is misleading, the Authority may, if it thinks it appropriate to do so, exercise the power conferred on it by section 15(1) of the Cable and Broadcasting Act 1984 (power to give directions) in relation to the advertisement.*

(2) The Authority shall give reasons for its decision to give or not to give, as the case may be, a direction in accordance with paragraph (1) above in any particular case.

(3) The Authority may require any person appearing to it to be responsible for an advertisement which the Authority believes may be misleading to furnish it with evidence as to the accuracy of any factual claim made in the advertisement. In deciding whether or not to make such a requirement the Authority shall have regard to the legitimate interests of any person who would be the subject of or affected by the requirement.

(4) If such evidence is not furnished to it following a requirement made by it under paragraph (3) above or if it considers such evidence inadequate, the Authority may consider the factual claim inaccurate.]

Control [by the Welsh Authority] of misleading advertisements and comparative advertisements on S4C and S4C Digital

A17–018
11.—[*(1) If, having considered a complaint about an advertisement pursuant to regulation 10(1) above, they consider that the advertisement is misleading or is a comparative advertisement and is not permitted under regulation 4A, the Welsh Authority may, if they think it appropriate to do so, refuse to broadcast the advertisement.*]

(1) If, having considered a complaint about an advertisement pursuant to regulation 10(1) above, they consider that the advertisement is misleading, or is a comparative advertisement and is not permitted under regulation 4A,

OFCOM may, if they think it appropriate to do so, exercise in relation to the advertisement, the power conferred by paragraph 14 of Schedule 12 to the Communications Act 2003.

(2) [*The Welsh Authority*] OFCOM may require any person appearing to them to be responsible for an advertisement which [*the Authority*] OFCOM believe may be misleading, or may be a comparative advertisement which is not permitted under regulation 4A, to furnish them with evidence as to the accuracy of any factual claim made in the advertisement. In deciding whether or not to make such a requirement [*the Authority*] OFCOM shall have regard to the legitimate interests of any person who would be the subject of or affected by the requirement.

(3) If such evidence is not furnished to them following a requirement made by them under paragraph (2) above within a time specified by [*the Welsh Authority*] OFCOM or if they consider such evidence inadequate, [*the Welsh Authority*] OFCOM may consider the factual claim inaccurate.

Amendment

New regulation 11 (in bold) was substituted for the previous regulation 11 (in italics) by the Broadcasting Act 1990 (c.42), Sch.20, para.51(3), and was then amended by the Control of Misleading Advertisements (Amendment) Regulation 2000 (SI 2000/914), reg.12 and the Control of Misleading Advertisements (Amendment) Regulation 2003 (SI 2003/3183), reg.6.

PART VI

MADRID INTERNATIONAL MATERIALS

Protocol Relating to the Madrid Agreement Concerning the International Registration of Marks

A18–001

(Adopted in Madrid on June 27, 1989)   *27th June 1989*

Article 1

Membership in the Madrid Union

The States party to this Protocol (hereinafter referred to as "the Contracting States"), even where they are not party to the Madrid Agreement Concerning the International Registration of Marks as revised at Stockholm 1967 and as amended in 1979 (hereinafter referred to as "the Madrid (Stockholm) Agreement"), and the organizations referred to in Article 14(1)(b) which are party to this Protocol (hereinafter referred to as "the Contracting Organizations") shall be members of the same Union of which countries party to the Madrid (Stockholm) Agreement are members. Any reference in this Protocol to "Contracting Parties" shall be construed as a reference to both Contracting States and Contracting Organizations.

A18–002

Article 2

Securing Protection Through International Registration

(1) Where an application for the registration of a mark has been filed with the Office of a Contracting Party, or where a mark has been registered in the register of the Office of a Contracting Party, the person in whose name that application (hereinafter referred to as "the basic application") or that registration (hereinafter referred to as "the basic registration") stands may, subject to the provisions of this Protocol, secure protection for his mark in the territory of the Contracting Parties, by obtaining the registration of that mark in the register of the International Bureau of the World Intellectual Property Organization (hereinafter referred to as "the international registration," "the International Register," "the International Bureau" and "the Organization," respectively), provided that,

A18–003

  (i) where the basic application has been filed with the Office of a Contracting State or where the basic registration has been made by such an Office, the person in whose name that application or registration stands is a national of that Contracting State, or is domiciled, or has a real and effective industrial or commercial establishment, in the said Contracting State,

  (ii) where the basic application has been filed with the Office of a Contracting Organization or where the basic registration has been made by such an Office, the person in whose name that application or registration stands is a national of a State member of that Contracting Organization, or is domiciled, or has a real and effective industrial or commercial establishment, in the territory of the said Contracting Organization.

(2) The application for international registration (hereinafter referred to as "the international application") shall be filed with the International Bureau through the intermediary of the Office with which the basic application was filed or by which the basic registration was made (hereinafter referred to as "the Office of origin"), as the case may be.

(3) Any reference in this Protocol to an "Office" or an "Office of a Contracting Party" shall be construed as a reference to the office that is in charge, on behalf of

a Contracting Party, of the registration of marks, and any reference in this Protocol to "marks" shall be construed as a reference to trademarks and service marks.

(4) For the purposes of this Protocol, "territory of a Contracting Party" means, where the Contracting Party is a State, the territory of that State and, where the Contracting Party is an intergovernmental organization, the territory in which the constituting treaty of that intergovernmental organization applies.

Article 3
International Application

A18–004   (1) Every international application under this Protocol shall be presented on the form prescribed by the Regulations. The Office of origin shall certify that the particulars appearing in the international application correspond to the particulars appearing, at the time of the certification, in the basic application or basic registration, as the case may be. Furthermore, the said Office shall indicate,

(i) in the case of a basic application, the date and number of that application,

(ii) in the case of a basic registration, the date and number of that registration as well as the date and number of the application from which the basic registration resulted.

The Office of origin shall also indicate the date of the international application.

(2) The applicant must indicate the goods and services in respect of which protection of the mark is claimed and also, if possible, the corresponding class or classes according to the classification established by the Nice Agreement Concerning the International Classification of Goods and Services for the Purposes of the Registration of Marks. If the applicant does not give such indication, the International Bureau shall classify the goods and services in the appropriate classes of the said classification. The indication of classes given by the applicant shall be subject to control by the International Bureau, which shall exercise the said control in association with the Office of origin. In the event of disagreement between the said Office and the International Bureau, the opinion of the latter shall prevail.

(3) If the applicant claims colour as a distinctive feature of his mark, he shall be required—

(i) to state the fact, and to file with his international application a notice specifying the colour or the combination of colours claimed;

(ii) to append to his international application copies in colour of the said mark, which shall be attached to the notifications given by the International Bureau; the number of such copies shall be fixed by the Regulations.

(4) The International Bureau shall register immediately the marks filed in accordance with Article 2. The international registration shall bear the date on which the international application was received in the Office of origin, provided that the international application has been received by the International Bureau within a period of two months from that date. If the international application has not been received within that period, the international registration shall bear the date on which the said international application was received by the International Bureau. The International Bureau shall notify the international registration without delay to the Offices concerned. Marks registered in the International Register shall be published in a periodical gazette issued by the International Bureau, on the basis of the particulars contained in the international application.

(5) With a view to the publicity to be given to marks registered in the International Register, each Office shall receive from the International Bureau a number of copies of the said gazette free of charge and a number of copies at a reduced price, under the conditions fixed by the Assembly referred to in Article

10 (hereinafter referred to as "the Assembly"). Such publicity shall be deemed to be sufficient for the purposes of all the Contracting Parties, and no other publicity may be required of the holder of the international registration.

Article 3Bis
Territorial Effect

The protection resulting from the international registration shall extend to any Contracting Party only at the request of the person who files the international application or who is the holder of the international registration. However, no such request can be made with respect to the Contracting Party whose Office is the Office of origin.

A18–005

Article 3Ter
Request for "Territorial Extension"

(1) Any request for extension of the protection resulting from the international registration to any Contracting Party shall be specially mentioned in the international application.

A18–006

(2) A request for territorial extension may also be made subsequently to the international registration. Any such request shall be presented on the form prescribed by the Regulations. It shall be immediately recorded by the International Bureau, which shall notify such recordal without delay to the Office or Offices concerned. Such recordal shall be published in the periodical gazette of the International Bureau. Such territorial extension shall be effective from the date on which it has been recorded in the International Register; it shall cease to be valid on the expiry of the international registration to which it relates.

Article 4
Effects of International Registration

(1)(a) From the date of the registration or recordal effected in accordance with the provisions of Articles 3 and 3ter, the protection of the mark in each of the Contracting Parties concerned shall be the same as if the mark had been deposited direct with the Office of that Contracting Party. If no refusal has been notified to the International Bureau in accordance with Article 5(1) and (2) or if a refusal notified in accordance with the said Article has been withdrawn subsequently, the protection of the mark in the Contracting Party concerned shall, as from the said date, be the same as if the mark had been registered by the Office of that Contracting Party.

A18–007

(b) The indication of classes of goods and services provided for in Article 3 shall not bind the Contracting Parties with regard to the determination of the scope of the protection of the mark.

(2) Every international registration shall enjoy the right of priority provided for by Article 4 of the Paris Convention for the Protection of Industrial Property, without it being necessary to comply with the formalities prescribed in Section D of that Article.

Articles 4Bis
Replacement of a National or Regional Registration by an International Registration

(1) Where a mark that is the subject of a national or regional registration in the Office of a Contracting Party is also the subject of an international registration

A18–008

and both registrations stand in the name of the same person, the international registration is deemed to replace the national or regional registration, without prejudice to any rights acquired by virtue of the latter, provided that

  (i) the protection resulting from the international registration extends to the said Contracting Party under Article 3Ter (1) or (2),

  (ii) all the goods and services listed in the national or regional registration are also listed in the international registration in respect of the said Contracting Party,

  (iii) such extension takes effect after the date of the national or regional registration.

(2) The Office referred to in paragraph (1) shall, upon request, be required to take note in its register of the international registration.

Article 5

Refusal and Invalidation of Effects of International Registration in Respect of Certain Contracting Parties

A18–009   (1) Where the applicable legislation so authorizes, any Office of a Contracting Party which has been notified by the International Bureau of an extension to that Contracting Party, under Article 3Ter (1) or (2), of the protection resulting from the international registration shall have the right to declare in a notification of refusal that protection cannot be granted in the said Contracting Party to the mark which is the subject of such extension. Any such refusal can be based only on the grounds which would apply, under the Paris Convention for the Protection of Industrial Property, in the case of a mark deposited direct with the Office which notifies the refusal. However, protection may not be refused, even partially, by reason only that the applicable legislation would permit registration only in a limited number of classes or for a limited number of goods or services.

(2)(a) Any Office wishing to exercise such right shall notify its refusal to the International Bureau, together with a statement of all grounds, within the period prescribed by the law applicable to that Office and at the latest, subject to subparagraphs (b) and (c), before the expiry of one year from the date on which the notification of the extension referred to in paragraph (1) has been sent to that Office by the International Bureau.

  (b) Notwithstanding subparagraph (a), any Contracting Party may declare that, for international registrations made under this Protocol, the time limit of one year referred to in subparagraph (a) is replaced by 18 months.

  (c) Such declaration may also specify that, when a refusal of protection may result from an opposition to the granting of protection, such refusal may be notified by the Office of the said Contracting Party to the International Bureau after the expiry of the 18-month time limit. Such an Office may, with respect to any given international registration, notify a refusal of protection after the expiry of the 18-month time limit, but only if—

    (i) it has, before the expiry of the 18-month time limit, informed the International Bureau of the possibility that oppositions may be filed after the expiry of the 18-month time limit, and

    (ii) the notification of the refusal based on an opposition is made within a time limit of not more than seven months from the date on which the opposition period begins; if the opposition period expires before this time limit of seven months, the notification must be made within a time limit of one month from the expiry of the opposition period.

  (d) Any declaration under subparagraphs (b) or (c) may be made in the instruments referred to in Article 14(2), and the effective date of the declaration shall be the same as the date of entry into force of this Protocol with respect to the State or intergovernmental organization having made the declaration. Any such declaration may also be made later, in which case the declaration shall have effect three months after its receipt by the Director General of the Organization (hereinafter referred to as "the Director General"), or at any later date indicated in the declaration, in respect of any international registration whose date is the same as or is later than the effective date of the declaration.

(e) Upon the expiry of a period of ten years from the entry into force of this Protocol, the Assembly shall examine the operation of the system established by subparagraphs (a) to (d). Thereafter, the provisions of the said subparagraphs may be modified by a unanimous decision of the Assembly.

(3) The International Bureau shall, without delay, transmit one of the copies of the notification of refusal to the holder of the international registration. The said holder shall have the same remedies as if the mark had been deposited by him direct with the Office which has notified its refusal. Where the International Bureau has received information under paragraph (2)(c)(i), it shall, without delay, transmit the said information to the holder of the international registration.

(4) The grounds for refusing a mark shall be communicated by the International Bureau to any interested party who may so request.

(5) Any Office which has not notified, with respect to a given international registration, any provisional or final refusal to the International Bureau in accordance with paragraphs (1) and (2) shall, with respect to that international registration, lose the benefit of the right provided for in paragraph (1).

(6) Invalidation, by the competent authorities of a Contracting Party, of the effects, in the territory of that Contracting Party, of an international registration may not be pronounced without the holder of such international registration having, in good time, been afforded the opportunity of defending his rights. Invalidation shall be notified to the International Bureau.

Article 5Bis

Documentary Evidence of Legitimacy of Use of Certain Elements of the Mark

Documentary evidence of the legitimacy of the use of certain elements incorporated in a mark, such as armorial bearings, escutcheons, portraits, honorary distinctions, titles, trade names, names of persons other than the name of the applicant, or other like inscriptions, which might be required by the Offices of the Contracting Parties shall be exempt from any legalization as well as from any certification other than that of the Office of origin.   **A18–010**

Article 5Ter

Copies of Entries in International Register; Searches for Anticipations; Extracts from International Register

(1) The International Bureau shall issue to any person applying therefor, upon the payment of a fee fixed by the Regulations, a copy of the entries in the International Register concerning a specific mark.   **A18–011**

(2) The International Bureau may also, upon payment, undertake searches for anticipations among marks that are the subject of international registrations.

(3) Extracts from the International Register requested with a view to their production in one of the Contracting Parties shall be exempt from any legalization.

Article 6

Period of Validity of International Registration; Dependence and Independence of International Registration

A18–012　　(1)　Registration of a mark at the International Bureau is effected for ten years, with the possibility of renewal under the conditions specified in Article 7.

(2)　Upon expiry of a period of five years from the date of the international registration, such registration shall become independent of the basic application or the registration resulting therefrom, or of the basic registration, as the case may be, subject to the following provisions.

(3)　The protection resulting from the international registration, whether or not it has been the subject of a transfer, may no longer be invoked if, before the expiry of five years from the date of the international registration, the basic application or the registration resulting therefrom, or the basic registration, as the case may be, has been withdrawn, has lapsed, has been renounced or has been the subject of a final decision of rejection, revocation, cancellation or invalidation, in respect of all or some of the goods and services listed in the international registration. The same applies if—

(i)　an appeal against a decision refusing the effects of the basic application,

(ii)　an action requesting the withdrawal of the basic application or the revocation, cancellation or invalidation of the registration resulting from the basic application or of the basic registration, or

(iii)　an opposition to the basic application results, after the expiry of the five-year period, in a final decision of rejection, revocation, cancellation or invalidation, or ordering the withdrawal, of the basic application, or the registration resulting therefrom, or the basic registration, as the case may be, provided that such appeal, action or opposition had begun before the expiry of the said period. The same also applies if the basic application is withdrawn, or the registration resulting from the basic application or the basic registration is renounced, after the expiry of the five-year period, provided that, at the time of the withdrawal or renunciation, the said application or registration was the subject of a proceeding referred to in item (i), (ii) or (iii) and that such proceeding had begun before the expiry of the said period.

(4)　The Office of origin shall, as prescribed in the Regulations, notify the International Bureau of the facts and decisions relevant under paragraph (3), and the International Bureau shall, as prescribed in the Regulations, notify the interested parties and effect any publication accordingly. The Office of origin shall, where applicable, request the International Bureau to cancel, to the extent applicable, the international registration, and the International Bureau shall proceed accordingly.

Article 7

Renewal of International Registration

A18–013　　(1)　Any international registration may be renewed for a period of ten years from the expiry of the preceding period, by the mere payment of the basic fee and, subject to Article 8(7), of the supplementary and complementary fees provided for in Article 8(2).

(2)　Renewal may not bring about any change in the international registration in its latest form.

(3)　Six months before the expiry of the term of protection, the International Bureau shall, by sending an unofficial notice, remind the holder of the international registration and his representative, if any, of the exact date of expiry.

(4) Subject to the payment of a surcharge fixed by the Regulations, a period of grace of six months shall be allowed for renewal of the international registration.

Article 8

Fees for International Application and Registration

(1) The Office of origin may fix, at its own discretion, and collect, for its own benefit, a fee which it may require from the applicant for international registration or from the holder of the international registration in connection with the filing of the international application or the renewal of the international registration.   **A18–014**

(2) Registration of a mark at the International Bureau shall be subject to the advance payment of an international fee which shall, subject to the provisions of paragraph (7)(a), include,

(i) a basic fee;

(ii) a supplementary fee for each class of the International Classification, beyond three, into which the goods or services to which the mark is applied will fall;

(iii) a complementary fee for any request for extension of protection under Article 3ter.

(3) However, the supplementary fee specified in paragraph (2)(ii) may, without prejudice to the date of the international registration, be paid within the period fixed by the Regulations if the number of classes of goods or services has been fixed or disputed by the International Bureau. If, upon expiry of the said period, the supplementary fee has not been paid or the list of goods or services has not been reduced to the required extent by the applicant, the international application shall be deemed to have been abandoned.

(4) The annual product of the various receipts from international registration, with the exception of the receipts derived from the fees mentioned in paragraph (2)(ii) and (iii), shall be divided equally among the Contracting Parties by the International Bureau, after deduction of the expenses and charges necessitated by the implementation of this Protocol.

(5) The amounts derived from the supplementary fees provided for in paragraph (2)(ii) shall be divided, at the expiry of each year, among the interested Contracting Parties in proportion to the number of marks for which protection has been applied for in each of them during that year, this number being multiplied, in the case of Contracting Parties which make an examination, by a coefficient which shall be determined by the Regulations.

(6) The amounts derived from the complementary fees provided for in paragraph (2)(iii) shall be divided according to the same rules as those provided for in paragraph (5).

(7)(a) Any Contracting Party may declare that, in connection with each international registration in which it is mentioned under Article 3ter, and in connection with the renewal of any such international registration, it wants to receive, instead of a share in the revenue produced by the supplementary and complementary fees, a fee (hereinafter referred to as "the individual fee") whose amount shall be indicated in the declaration, and can be changed in further declarations, but may not be higher than the equivalent of the amount which the said Contracting Party's Office would be entitled to receive from an applicant for a ten-year registration, or from the holder of a registration for a ten-year renewal of that registration, of the mark in the register of the said Office, the said amount being diminished by the savings resulting from the international procedure. Where such an individual fee is payable,

(i) no supplementary fees referred to in paragraph (2)(ii) shall be payable if only Contracting Parties which have made a declaration under this subparagraph are mentioned under Article 3ter, and

(ii) no complementary fee referred to in paragraph (2)(iii) shall be payable in respect of any Contracting Party which has made a declaration under this subparagraph.

(b) Any declaration under subparagraph (a) may be made in the instruments referred to in Article 14(2), and the effective date of the declaration shall be the same as the date of entry into force of this Protocol with respect to the State or intergovernmental organization having made the declaration. Any such declaration may also be made later, in which case the declaration shall have effect three months after its receipt by the Director General, or at any later date indicated in the declaration, in respect of any international registration whose date is the same as or is later than the effective date of the declaration.

Article 9

Recordal of Change in the Ownership of an International Registration

A18–015   At the request of the person in whose name the international registration stands, or at the request of an interested Office made *ex officio* or at the request of an interested person, the International Bureau shall record in the International Register any change in the ownership of that registration, in respect of all or some of the Contracting Parties in whose territories the said registration has effect and in respect of all or some of the goods and services listed in the registration, provided that the new holder is a person who, under Article 2(1), is entitled to file international applications.

Article 9Bis

Recordal of Certain Matters Concerning an International Registration

A18–016   The International Bureau shall record in the International Register

(i) any change in the name or address of the holder of the international registration,

(ii) the appointment of a representative of the holder of the international registration and any other relevant fact concerning such representative,

(iii) any limitation, in respect of all or some of the Contracting Parties, of the goods and services listed in the international registration,

(iv) any renunciation, cancellation or invalidation of the international registration in respect of all or some of the Contracting Parties,

(v) any other relevant fact, identified in the Regulations, concerning the rights in a mark that is the subject of an international registration.

Article 9Ter

Fees for Certain Recordals

A18–017   Any recordal under Article 9 or under Article 9Bis may be subject to the payment of a fee.

Article 9Quarter

Common Office of Several Contracting States

A18–018   (1) If several Contracting States agree to effect the unification of their domestic legislations on marks, they may notify the Director General—

(i) that a common Office shall be substituted for the national Office of each of them, and

(ii) that the whole of their respective territories shall be deemed to be a single State for the purposes of the application of all or part of the provisions preceding this Article as well as the provisions of Articles 9Quinquies and 9Sexies.

(2) Such notification shall not take effect until three months after the date of the communication thereof by the Director General to the other Contracting Parties.

Article 9Quinquies

Transformation of an International Registration into National or Regional Applications

Where, in the event that the international registration is cancelled at the request **A18–019** of the Office of origin under Article 6(4), in respect of all or some of the goods and services listed in the said registration, the person who was the holder of the international registration files an application for the registration of the same mark with the Office of any of the Contracting Parties in the territory of which the international registration had effect, that application shall be treated as if it had been filed on the date of the international registration according to Article 3(4) or on the date of recordal of the territorial extension according to Article 3ter(2) and, if the international registration enjoyed priority, shall enjoy the same priority, provided that—

(i) such application is filed within three months from the date on which the international registration was cancelled,

(ii) the goods and services listed in the application are in fact covered by the list of goods and services contained in the international registration in respect of the Contracting Party concerned, and

(iii) such application complies with all the requirements of the applicable law, including the requirements concerning fees.

Article 9Sexies

Safeguard of the Madrid (Stockholm) Agreement

(1) Where, with regard to a given international application or a given **A18–020** international registration, the Office of origin is the Office of a State that is party to both this Protocol and the Madrid (Stockholm) Agreement, the provisions of this Protocol shall have no effect in the territory of any other State that is also party to both this Protocol and the Madrid (Stockholm) Agreement.

(2) The Assembly may, by a three-fourths majority, repeal paragraph (1), or restrict the scope of paragraph (1), after the expiry of a period of ten years from the entry into force of this Protocol, but not before the expiry of a period of five years from the date on which the majority of the countries party to the Madrid (Stockholm) Agreement have become party to this Protocol. In the vote of the Assembly, only those States which are party to both the said Agreement and this Protocol shall have the right to participate.

Article 10

Assembly

(1)(a) The Contracting Parties shall be members of the same Assembly as the **A18–021** countries party to the Madrid (Stockholm) Agreement.

(b) Each Contracting Party shall be represented in that Assembly by one delegate, who may be assisted by alternate delegates, advisors, and experts.

(c) The expenses of each delegation shall be borne by the Contracting Party which has appointed it, except for the travel expenses and the subsistence allowance of one delegate for each Contracting Party, which shall be paid from the funds of the Union.

(2) The Assembly shall, in addition to the functions which it has under the Madrid (Stockholm) Agreement, also—

(i) deal with all matters concerning the implementation of this Protocol;

(ii) give directions to the International Bureau concerning the preparation for conferences of revision of this Protocol, due account being taken of any comments made by those countries of the Union which are not party to this Protocol;

(iii) adopt and modify the provisions of the Regulations concerning the implementation of this Protocol;

(iv) perform such other functions as are appropriate under this Protocol.

(3)(a) Each Contracting Party shall have one vote in the Assembly. On matters concerning only countries that are party to the Madrid (Stockholm) Agreement, Contracting Parties are not party to the said Agreement shall not have the right to vote, whereas, on matters concerning only Contracting Parties, only the latter shall have the right to vote.

(b) One-half of the members of the Assembly which have the right to vote on a given matter shall constitute the quorum for the purposes of the vote on that matter.

(c) Notwithstanding the provisions of subparagraph (b), if, in any session, the number of the members of the Assembly having the right to vote on a given matter which are represented is less than one-half but equal to or more than one-third of the members of the Assembly having the right to vote on that matter, the Assembly may make decisions but, with the exception of decisions concerning its own procedure, all such decisions shall take effect only if the conditions set forth hereinafter are fulfilled. The International Bureau shall communicate the said decisions to the members of the Assembly having the right to vote on the said matter which were not represented and shall invite them to express in writing their vote or abstention within a period of three months from the date of the communication. If, at the expiry of this period, the number of such members having thus expressed their vote or abstention attains the number of the members which was lacking for attaining the quorum in the session itself, such decisions shall take effect provided that at the same time the required majority still obtains.

(d) Subject to the provisions of Articles 5(2)(e), 9sexies (2), 12 and 13(2), the decisions of the Assembly shall require two-thirds of the votes cast.

(e) Abstentions shall not be considered as votes.

(f) A delegate may represent, and vote in the name of, one member of the Assembly only.

(4) In addition to meeting in ordinary sessions and extraordinary sessions as provided for by the Madrid (Stockholm) Agreement, the Assembly shall meet in extraordinary session upon convocation by the Director General, at the request of one-fourth of the members of the Assembly having the right to vote on the matters proposed to be included in the agenda of the session. The agenda of such an extraordinary session shall be prepared by the Director General.

Article 11

International Bureau

A18–022   (1) International registration and related duties, as well as all other administrative tasks, under or concerning this Protocol, shall be performed by the International Bureau.

(2)(a)The International Bureau shall, in accordance with the directions of the Assembly, make preparations for the conferences of revision of this Protocol.

(b) The International Bureau may consult with intergovernmental and international non-governmental organizations concerning preparations for such conferences of revision.

(c) The Director General and persons designated by him shall take part, without the right to vote, in the discussions at such conferences of revision.

(3) The International Bureau shall carry out any other tasks assigned to it in relation to this Protocol.

Article 12

Finances

As far as Contracting Parties are concerned, the finances of the Union shall be governed by the same provisions as those contained in Article 12 of the Madrid (Stockholm) Agreement, provided that any reference to Article 8 of the said Agreement shall be deemed to be a reference to Article 8 of this Protocol. Furthermore, for the purposes of Article 12(6)(b) of the said Agreement, Contracting Organizations shall, subject to a unanimous decision to the contrary by the Assembly, be considered to belong to contribution class I (one) under the Paris Convention for the Protection of Industrial Property.

A18–023

Article 13

Amendment of Certain Articles of the Protocol

(1) Proposals for the amendment of Articles 10, 11, 12, and the present Article, may be initiated by any Contracting Party, or by the Director General. Such proposals shall be communicated by the Director General to the Contracting Parties at least six months in advance of their consideration by the Assembly.

A18–024

(2) Amendments to the Articles referred to in paragraph (1) shall be adopted by the Assembly. Adoption shall require three-fourths of the votes cast, provided that any amendment to Article 10, and to the present paragraph, shall require four-fifths of the votes cast.

(3) Any amendment to the Articles referred to in paragraph (1) shall enter into force one month after written notification of acceptance, effected in accordance with their respective constitutional processes, have been received by the Director General from three-fourths of those States and intergovernmental organizations which, at the time the amendment was adopted, were members of the Assembly and had the right to vote on the amendment. Any amendment to the said Articles thus accepted shall bind all the States and intergovernmental organizations which are Contracting Parties at the time the amendment enters into force, or which become Contracting Parties at a subsequent date.

Article 14

Becoming Party to the Protocol; Entry into Force

(1)(a)Any State that is a party to the Paris Convention for the Protection of Industrial Property may become party to this Protocol.

A18–025

(b) Furthermore, any intergovernmental organization may also become party to this Protocol where the following conditions are fulfilled:

(i) at least one of the member States of that organization is a party to the Paris Convention for the Protection of Industrial Property;

(ii) that organization has a regional Office for the purposes of registering marks with effect in the territory of the organization, provided that such Office is not the subject of a notification under Article 9Quarter.

(2) Any State or organization referred to in paragraph (1) may sign this Protocol. Any such State or organization may, if it has signed this Protocol, deposit an instrument of ratification, acceptance or approval of this Protocol or, if it has not signed this Protocol, deposit an instrument of accession to this Protocol.

(3) The instruments referred to in paragraph (2) shall be deposited with the Director General.

(4)(a) This Protocol shall enter into force three months after four instruments of ratification, acceptance, approval or accession have been deposited, provided that at least one of those instruments has been deposited by a country party to the Madrid (Stockholm) Agreement and at least one other of those instruments has been deposited by a State not party to the Madrid (Stockholm) Agreement or by any of the organizations referred to in paragraph (1)(b).

(b) with respect to any other State or organization referred to in paragraph (1), this Protocol shall enter into force three months after the date on which its ratification, acceptance, approval or accession has been notified by the Director General.

(5) Any State or organization referred to in paragraph (1) may, when depositing its instrument of ratification, acceptance or approval of, or accession to, this Protocol, declare that the protection resulting from any international registration effected under this Protocol before the date of entry into force of this Protocol with respect to it cannot be extended to it.

Article 15

Denunciation

A18–026

(1) This Protocol shall remain in force without limitation as to time.

(2) Any Contracting Party may denounce this Protocol by notification addressed to the Director General.

(3) Denunciation shall take effect one year after the day on which the Director General has received the notification.

(4) The right of denunciation provided for by this Article shall not be exercised by any Contracting Party before the expiry of five years from the date upon which this Protocol entered into force with respect to that Contracting Party.

(5)(a) Where a mark is the subject of an international registration having effect in the denouncing State or intergovernmental organization at the date on which the denunciation becomes effective, the holder of such registration may file an application for the registration of the same mark with the Office of the denouncing State or intergovernmental organization, which shall be treated as if it had been filed on the date of the international registration according to Article 3(4) or on the date of recordal of the territorial extension according to Article 3ter(2) and, if the international registration enjoyed priority, enjoy the same priority, provided that—

(i) such application is filed within two years from the date on which the denunciation became effective,

(ii) the goods and services listed in the application are in fact covered by the list of goods and services contained in the international registration in respect of the denouncing State or intergovernmental organization, and

(iii) such application complies with all the requirements of the applicable law, including the requirements concerning fees.

(b) The provisions of subparagraph (a) shall also apply in respect of any mark that is the subject of an international registration having effect in Contracting Parties other than the denouncing State or intergovernmental organization at the date on which denunciation becomes effective and whose holder, because of the denunciation, is no longer entitled to file international applications under Article 2(1).

Article 16

Signature; Languages; Depositary Functions

(1)(a) This Protocol shall be signed in a single copy in the English, French and Spanish languages, and shall be deposited with the Director General when it ceases to be open for signature at Madrid. The texts in the three languages shall be equally authentic.   **A18–027**

(b) Official texts of this Protocol shall be established by the Director General, after consultation with the interested governments and organizations, in the Arabic, Chinese, German, Italian, Japanese, Portuguese and Russian languages, and in such other languages as the Assembly may designate.

(2) This Protocol shall remain open for signature at Madrid until December 31 1989.

(3) The Director General shall transmit two copies, certified by the Government of Spain, of the signed texts of this Protocol to all States and intergovernmental organizations that may become party to this Protocol.

(4) The Director General shall register this Protocol with the Secretariat of the United Nations.

(5) The Director General shall notify all States and international organizations that may become or are party to this Protocol of signatures, deposits of instruments of ratification, acceptance, approval or accession, the entry into force of this Protocol and any amendment thereto, any notification of denunciation and any declaration provided for in this Protocol.

APPENDIX 19

The Trade Marks (International Registration) Order 1996

SI 1996/714

The Secretary of State, in exercise of the powers conferred on him by section 54   **A19–001**
of the Trade Marks Act 1994 thereby makes the following Order:—

General Note

(As amended by the Trade Marks (International Registration) (Amendment) Order 2000   **A19–002**
(SI 2000/138), the Trade Marks (International Registration) (Amendment) Order 2002 (SI
2002/692) and the Trade Marks (International Registration) (Amendment) Order 2004 (SI
2004/948).)

PRELIMINARY

Citation commencement and extent

1.—(1) This Order may be cited as the Trade Marks (International Registra-   **A19–003**
tion) Order 1996 and comes into force on 1st April 1996.

(2) This Order extends to England and Wales, Scotland, Northern Ireland and
the Isle of Man.

Interpretation

2. In this Order—   **A19–004**

"the Act" means the Trade Marks Act 1994, and references to a section are,
unless the context otherwise requires, to sections of that Act;

"basic application" and "basic registration" have the respective meanings given
by article 22

"Common Regulations" means the regulations adopted under article 10 of the
Madrid Protocol with effect from 1 April 1996 **as amended with effect from 1st
April 2002**;

"international application" means an application to the International Bureau
for registration of a trade mark in the International Register;

"International Bureau" means the International Bureau of the World Intellectual Property Organisation;

"International Register" means the register of trade marks maintained by the
International Bureau for the purposes of the Madrid Protocol;

"International registration" means the registration of a trade mark in the
International Register;

"international registration designating the United Kingdom" means an
international registration in relation to which a request has been made (either in
the relevant international application or subsequently) for extension of protection
to the United Kingdom under Article 3ter (1) or (2) of the Madrid Protocol;

"notifiable transaction" has the meaning given by article 6;

"protected international trade mark (UK)" has the meaning given by article 12,
and references to "protection" and "protected" shall be construed accordingly;

*"the Rules" means the Trade Marks Rules 1994, and references to a rule shall
unless the context otherwise requires, be construed accordingly;*

"**the Rules**" **means the Trade Marks Rules 2000 and references to a rule shall, unless the context otherwise requires, be construed accordingly;**
"supplementary register" has the meaning given by article 24;
"transformation application" has the meaning given by article 19;
"United Kingdom" includes the Isle of Man.

Amendment

The words in italics were deleted, and the words in bold inserted, by the Trade Marks (International Registration) (Amendment) Order 2000 (SI 2000/138), art.3 and the Trade Marks (International Registration) (Amendment) Order 2002 (SI 2002/692), art 3.

INTERNATIONAL REGISTRATIONS DESIGNATING THE UNITED KINGDOM

Entitlement to protection

A19–005   3.—(1) An international registration designating the United Kingdom shall be entitled to become protected subject to the provisions of articles 9 to 12 where, if the particulars of the international registration were comprised in an application for registration of a trade mark under the Act, such an application would satisfy the requirements for registration (including any imposed by the Rules).

(2) For that purpose, sections 32 to 34, rules [*5 to 8*] **5 to 8A** and rules 10 and 11 shall be disregarded.

Amendment

The words in italics were deleted, and the words in bold inserted, by the Trade Marks (International Registration) (Amendment) Order 2004 (SI 2004/948), art.3.

Effects of Protected International Trade Mark (UK)

A19–006   4.—(1) The proprietor of a protected international trade mark (UK) has, subject to the provisions of this Order, the same rights and remedies as are given by or under sections 9 to 12 and 14 to 20 to the proprietor of a registered trade mark, subject to the limits on effect and to the provisions relating to exhaustion which are applicable to a registered trade mark by virtue of section 11 and section 12 respectively.

(2) For the purposes of section 9 (rights conferred by registered trade mark)—

(a) the rights of the proprietor shall have effect as of the date on which it is to be treated as registered pursuant to article 12 or article 21;

(b) a protected international trade mark (UK) shall be treated as being in fact registered when it becomes protected pursuant to article 12.

(3) References in sections 10 and 11 to goods or services in respect of which a trade mark is registered are to goods or services in respect of which a protected international trade mark (UK) confers protection in the United Kingdom.

(4) Where the holder of an international registration designating the United Kingdom by notice in writing sent to the registrar—

(a) disclaims any right to the exclusive use of any specified element of the trade mark **in the United Kingdom,** or

(b) agrees that the rights conferred in the United Kingdom by the international registration shall be subject to a specified territorial or other limitation.

the registrar shall enter the disclaimer or limitation in the supplementary register and shall publish the disclaimer or limitation.

[(5) *Where a protected international trade mark (UK) is subject to a disclaimer or limitation, the rights conferred in relation to it by the application of section 9 are restricted accordingly.*]

(5) Where an international registration contains a disclaimer of any right to the exclusive us of any specified element of the trade mark or where a protected international trade mark (UK) is subject to a disclaimer or limitation by virtue of a notice sent to the registrar under paragraph (4) above, the rights conferred in relation to it by the application of section 9 are restricted accordingly.

(6) The remedy for groundless threats of infringement proceedings given by section 21 applies in relation to a protected international trade mark (UK) as in relation to a registered trade mark; and for this purpose—

(a) the reference in section 21(3) to the registration of the trade mark shall be treated as a reference to protection of a protected international trade mark (UK); and

(b) the reference in section 21(4) to notification that a trade mark is registered, or that an application for registration has been made, shall be treated as a reference to notification that a trade mark is a protected international trade mark (UK) or is the subject of an international application or international registration designating the United Kingdom.

Amendment

The words in italics were deleted, and the words in bold inserted, by the Trade Marks (International Registration) (Amendment) Order 2002 (SI 2002/692), art.4.

International Trade mark (UK) as an object of property

5. The provisions of sections 22, 23, 24 (except subsection (2)(b)) and 26 (which relate to a registered trade mark as an object of property) apply, with the necessary modifications, in relation to an international trade mark (UK) as in relation to a registered trade mark.   **A19–007**

Notification of transactions

6.—[(1) *The following are notifiable transactions for the purposes of this article—*   **A19–008**

(a) *the grant of a licence under a protected international trade mark (UK);*

(b) *the granting of any security interest (whether fixed or floating) over an international trade mark (UK) or any right in or under it.*]

(1) The granting of any security interest (whether fixed or floating) over an international trade mark (UK) or any right in or under it is a notifiable transaction for the purposes of this article.

(2) On application being made to the registrar by—

(a) a person claiming to be entitled to an interest in or under an international trade mark (UK) by virtue of a notifiable transaction, or

(b) any other person claiming to be affected by such a transaction.

the prescribed particulars of the transaction shall be entered in the supplementary register.

(3) The following are relevant transactions for the purposes of this article—

(a) a notifiable transaction;

(b) an assignment of an international trade mark (UK) or any right in it;

(bb) the grant of a licence under an international trade mark (UK);

    (c) the making by personal representatives of an assent in relation to an international trade mark (UK) or any right in or under it;

    (d) an order of a court or other competent authority transferring an international trade mark (UK) or any right in or under it.

(4) Until (in the case of a notifiable transaction) an application has been made for registration of the prescribed particulars or (in the case of any other relevant transaction) the transaction has been recorded in the International Register—

    (a) the transaction is ineffective as against a person acquiring an interest in or under the international trade mark (UK) in ignorance of it, and

    (b) a person claiming to be a licensee by virtue of the transaction does not have the protection of section 30 or 31 (rights and remedies of licensee in relation to infringement).

[(5) *Where a person becomes the proprietor or a licensee of an international trade mark (UK) by virtue of a relevant transaction, then unless—*

    (a) *an application for registration of the transaction (in the case of a notifiable transaction) is made, or (in the case of any other relevant transaction) a request for recordal in the International Register is made, before the end of a period of six months beginning with its date, or*

    (b) *the court is satisfied that it was not practicable for such an application or request for recordal to be made before the end of that period and that an application or request for recordal (as the case may be) was made as soon as practicable thereafter.*

he is not entitled to damages or an account of profits in respect of any infringement of the international trade mark (UK) occurring after the date of the transaction and before (in the case of a notifiable transaction) the prescribed particulars of the transaction are registered or (in the case of any other relevant transaction) the transaction is recorded in the International Register.]

(5) Where a person becomes the proprietor or licensee of an international trade mark (UK) by virtue of a relevant transaction, then unless—

    (a) a request for recordal in the International Register is made before the end of a period of six months beginning with its date, or

    (b) the court is satisfied that it was not practicable for such a request for recordal to be made before the end of that period and that a request for recordal was made as soon as practicable thereafter,

he is not entitled to damages or an account of profits in respect of any infringement of the international trade mark (UK) occurring after the date of the transaction and before the transaction is recorded in the International Register.

[(6) *"Prescribed particulars" means the particulars prescribed by rule 34.*]

(6) "Prescribed particulars" means the particulars prescribed by rule 40.

Amendment

The words in italics were deleted, and the words in bold inserted, by the Trade Marks (International Registration) (Amendment) Order 2000 (SI 2000/138), art.4 and by the Trade Marks (International Registration) (Amendment) Order 2002 (SI 2002/692), art.5 with effect from April 2, 2002 subject to transitional provisions contained in art.12 of that Order.

Licensing

A19–009   **7.**—(1) The provisions of sections 28 to 31 apply, with the necessary modifications, in relation to licences to use a protected international trade mark (UK).

(2) The reference in section 28(1) to goods or services for which a trade mark

is registered shall be treated as a reference to goods or services in respect of which the trade mark is protected in the United Kingdom.

Priority

8.—(1) The provisions of section 35 (claim to priority of Convention application) apply, subject as mentioned below, so as to confer a right to priority in relation to protection of an international registration designating the United Kingdom as they apply in relation to registering a trade mark under the Act.

(2) Subsection (5) of that section does not apply and the manner of claiming priority shall be determined in accordance with the Madrid Protocol and the Common Regulations.

A19–010

Examination

9.—(1) Upon receiving from the International Bureau notification of an international registration designating the United Kingdom, the registrar shall examine whether it satisfies the requirements of article 3.

(2) For that purpose, he shall carry out a search, to such extent as he considers necessary, of earlier trade marks.

(3) If it appears to the registrar that the requirements referred to in paragraph (1) above are not met, or are met only in relation to some of the goods or services in respect of which protection in the United Kingdom has been requested, he shall give [*notice of refusal*] **notice of provisional refusal** to the International Bureau.

(4) [*Notice of refusal*] **Notice of provisional refusal** shall specify a period within which the holder may make representations.

(5) A holder making representations shall file an address for service in the United Kingdom on Form TM33.

A19–011

Amendment

The words in italics were deleted, and the words in bold inserted, by the Trade Marks (International Registration) (Amendment) Order 2002 (SI 2002/692), art.6 with effect from April 2, 2002 subject to transitional provisions contained in art.13 of that Order.

Notifications by the International Bureau of vague, incomprehensible or linguistically incorrect terms

9A.—(1) Where the International Bureau notifies the registrar, under Rule 13(2)(b) of the Common Regulations, that a particular term used to indicate any of the goods and services included in the international registration is too vague for the purposes of classification or is incomprehensible or is linguistically incorrect then the registrar may give notice of provisional refusal to the International Bureau in respect of that term.

(2) Notice of provisional refusal shall specify a period within which the holder may make representations.

(3) A holder making representations shall file an address for service in the United Kingdom on Form TM33.

A19–012

Amendment

Article 9A was inserted, by the Trade Marks (International Registration) (Amendment) Order 2004 (SI 2004/948), art.4.

Publication, opposition proceedings and observations

A19–013   *[10.—(1) Where following examination pursuant to article 9 it appears to the registrar that the requirements of article 3 are met in relation to all or some of the goods or services comprised in the international registration, the registrar shall publish a notice specifying particulars of the international registration and specifying the goods or services for which protection will be conferred.*

(2) Any person may, within three months of the date of publication pursuant to paragraph (1) above, give notice to the registrar of opposition to the conferring of protection.

The notice shall be given in writing in the manner prescribed by rule 13, shall include a statement of the grounds of opposition and shall where opposition is based on an earlier trade mark indicate the goods or services on which the opposition is based.

*(3) The registrar shall, upon notice of opposition being given, and in any event within four months of publication pursuant to paragraph (1) above, give [notice of refusal]**notice of provisional refusal** to the International Bureau stating the matters relating to the opposition referred to in paragraph (2) above.*

[(4) Within three months of the date on which notice of refusal based on opposition is given to the International Bureau, the holder may file a counter-statement, in conjunction with notice of the same on Form TM8 and an address for service in the United Kingdom.]

(4) **Subject to paragraphs (4A) and (4B) below, within three months of the date on which [notice of refusal] notice of provisional refusal based on opposition is given to the International Bureau, the holder may file a counter-statement, in conjunction with notice of the same on Form TM8 and an address for service in the United Kingdom.**

(4A) **Subject to paragraph (4B), at any time before the expiry of the period prescribed by paragraph (4) above for filing of Form TM8 by the holder the registrar may, on request, grant an extension of three months to that period where such request is filed on Form TM9c and with the agreement of both the holder and the opposing party (the "cooling off period"); the registrar may, on request, extend the cooling off period for a further three months where such request is filed on Form TM9c and with the agreement of both the holder and the opposing party.**

(4B) **Within one month after the expiry of the cooling off period the holder may file a counter-statement, in conjunction with notice of the same on Form TM8 and an address for service in the United Kingdom.**

(5) Subject to the provisions of this article, rules 13 and 14 shall apply in relation to opposition proceedings, with the substitution of the holder for the applicant.

(5A) **The provisions of rule 36 (case management) and rule 37 (pre-hearing review) shall apply in relation to opposition proceedings.**

(6) Where a notice has been published pursuant to paragraph (1) above, any person may, at any time before the trade mark has become protected in accordance with article 12, make observations in writing to the registrar as to whether the trade mark should be protected.

A person who makes observations does not thereby become a party to proceedings in relation to the request for protection.

Publication, notice of opposition and observations

A19–014   **10.—(1) Where following examination under article 9 it appears to the**

registrar that the requirements of article 3 (entitlement to protection) are met in relation to all or some of the goods or services included in the international registration, the registrar shall publish a notice specifying particulars of the international registration and specifying the goods and services for which protection ought to be conferred.

(2) Any person may, within three months of the date on which the notice was published under paragraph (1), give notice to the registrar of opposition to the conferring of protection.

(3) Where a notice has been published under paragraph (1), any person may, at any time before protection has been conferred on the trade mark in accordance with article 12, make observations in writing to the registrar as to whether the trade mark should be protected; and the registrar shall inform the holder of any such observations.

A person who makes observations does not thereby become a party to proceedings in relation to the request for protection.

Amendment

The words in italics were deleted, and the words in bold inserted, by the Trade Marks (International Registration) (Amendment) Order 2004 (SI 2004/948), art.5 with effect from May 5, 2004 subject to transitional provisions contained in art.8 of that Order.

Opposition proceedings: filing of notice of opposition

10A.—(1) Notice of opposition to the conferring of protection given under article 10(2) shall be on Form TM7 which shall include—   A19–015

(a) a statement of the grounds of opposition; and

(b) an address for service in the United Kingdom.

(2) Where the opposition is based on a trade mark which has been registered, there shall be included in the statement of the grounds of opposition a representation of that mark and—

(a) the details of the authority with which the mark is registered;

(b) the registration number of that mark;

(c) the classes in respect of which that mark is registered;

(d) the goods and services in respect of which—

(i) that mark is registered; and

(ii) the opposition is based; and

(e) where the registration procedure for the mark was completed before the start of the period of five years ending with the date the notice was published under article 10(1), a statement detailing whether during the period referred to in section 6A(3)(a) it has been put to genuine use in relation to each of the goods and services in respect of which the opposition is based or whether there are proper reasons for non-use (for the purposes of rule 13C (which has effect by virtue of article 10C(2)) this is the "statement of use").

(3) Where the opposition is based on a trade mark in respect of which an application for registration has been made, there shall be included in the statement of the grounds of opposition a representation of that mark and those matters set out in paragraph (2)(a) to (d), with references to registration being construed as references to the application for registration.

(4) Where the opposition is based on an unregistered trade mark or other sign which the person opposing the application claims to be protected by

virtue of any rule of law (in particular, the law of passing off), there shall be included in the statement of the grounds of opposition a representation of that mark or sign and the goods and services in respect of which such protection is claimed.

(5) Where notice of opposition has been given, the registrar shall, within four months of the notice being published under article 10(1), give notice of provisional refusal to the International Bureau stating the grounds on which the opposition to the conferring of protection is based.

(6) The registrar shall send a copy of Form TM7 to the holder and the date upon which this is done shall, for the purpose of article 10B, be the "notification date".

Opposition proceedings: filing of counter-statement and cooling off period

A19–016   10B.—(1) The holder shall, within the relevant period, file a Form TM8 which shall include—

(a) a counter-statement; and

(b) an address for service in the United Kingdom,

otherwise the registrar shall notify the International Bureau that the provisional refusal has been upheld.

(2) Unless either paragraph (3) or (4) applies, the relevant period shall begin on the notification date and end three months after that date.

(3) This paragraph applies where—

(a) the holder and the person opposing the conferring of protection agree to an extension of time for the filing of Form TM8;

(b) within the period of three months beginning on the notification date, either party files Form TM9c requesting an extension of time for the filing of Form TM8; and

(c) during the period beginning on the date Form TM9c was filed and ending twelve months after the notification date, no notice to continue is filed on Form TM9t by the person opposing the conferring of protection,

and where this paragraph applies the relevant period shall begin on the notification date and end twelve months after that date.

(4) This paragraph applies where—

(a) a request for an extension of time for the filing of Form TM8 has been filed on Form TM9c; and

(b) the person opposing the conferring of protection has filed a notice to continue on Form TM9t,

and where this paragraph applies the relevant period shall begin on the notification date and end one month after the date on which Form TM9t was filed or three months after the notification date, whichever is the later.

Opposition proceedings: application of the Trade Marks Rules 2000

A19–017   10C.—(1) The registrar shall send a copy of Form TM8 to the person opposing the conferring of protection and, unless rule 13B (preliminary indication) applies (by virtue of paragraph (2)), the date upon which this is sent shall, for the purposes of rule 13C (evidence rounds) (which applies by virtue of paragraph (2)), be the "initiation date".

(2) Section 6A (raising of relative grounds in opposition proceedings in case of non-use) and rules 13B, 13C, 14 (decision of registrar in opposition proceedings), 36 (case management conference) and 37 (pre-hearing review)

shall apply to the proceedings relating to the opposition to the conferring of protection as they apply to proceedings relating to opposition to an application for registration, but with the following modifications—

(a) any reference to the applicant shall be construed as a reference to the holder;

(b) any reference to the person opposing the registration shall be construed as a reference to the person opposing the conferring of protection;

(c) any references to registration shall be construed as a reference to the conferring of protection;

(d) any reference to the publication of the application shall be construed as a reference to publication of the notice under article 10(1);

(e) any reference to an application for registration being deemed or treated as withdrawn shall be construed as meaning that the registrar shall notify the International Bureau that the provisional refusal has been upheld.

Amendment

Articles 10A, 10B and 10C were inserted by the Trade Marks (International Registration) (Amendment) Order 2004 (SI 2004/948), art.5 with effect from May 5, 2004 subject to transitional provisions contained in art.8 of that Order.

Notices of refusal

[11.—(1) Except where refusal is based on an opposition, notice of refusal shall not be given after the expiry of 18 months from the date on which the notification of the request for extension was sent to the United Kingdom.

A19–018

(2) The registrar shall inform the International Bureau that oppositions may be filed after the expiry of the period of 18 months referred to in paragraph (1) above unless, at least four months before the expiry of the said period, he has published the notice referred to in article 10(1).

(3) Notices of refusal shall set out the matters required by Article 5 of the Madrid Protocol and Rule 17 of the Common Regulations.

(4) Where—

(a) notice of refusal has been given pursuant to article 9(3), and

(i) the holder makes representations within the period specified under article 9(4), or

(ii) the holder makes no representations within the period, or informs the registrar that he does not intend to make any representations, or

(b) notice of refusal based on an opposition has been given pursuant to article 10(3) and

[(i) the holder files a counter-statement within the period specified in article 10(4), or]

(i) **the holder files a counter-statement within the period specified in article 10(4) or 10(4B), or**

(ii) the holder files no counter-statement within that period or informs the registrar that he does not intend to file a counter-statement,

the registrar shall inform the International Bureau of that fact.

(5) Where—

(a) after notice of refusal has been given pursuant to article 9(3), the holder makes representations within the period specified under article 9(4); or

[*(b) after notice of refusal based on an opposition, the holder files a counter-statement within the period specified in article 10(4),*]

(b) **after notice of refusal based on an opposition, the holder files a counter-statement within the period specified in article 10(4) or 10(4B),**

the registrar shall, upon a final decision being made in relation to the refusal, notify the International Bureau of that decision.

(6) For the purposes of paragraph (5) above, a final decision shall be regarded as being made where—

(a) the registrar, or the appointed person or the court on appeal or further appeal from the registrar, decides whether the refusal shall be upheld, in whole or in relation to some only of the goods or services in relation to which protection in the United Kingdom is requested, and any right of appeal against that decision expires or is exhausted;

(b) the representations or counter-statement are withdrawn; or

(c) the proceedings relating to the refusal are discontinued or abandoned.]

Notices of provisional refusal

A19–019   **11.—(1) Except where provisional refusal is based on an opposition, notice of provisional refusal shall not be given after the expiry of 18 months from the date on which the notification of the request for extension was sent to the United Kingdom.**

(2) The registrar shall inform the International Bureau that oppositions may be filed after the expiry of the period of 18 months referred to in paragraph (1) above unless, at least four months before the expiry of the said period, he has published the notice referred to in article 10(1).

(3) Notices of provisional refusal shall set out the matters required by Article 5 of the Madrid Protocol and Rule 17 of the Common Regulations.

(4) Where the registrar has given notice of provisional refusal to the International Bureau pursuant to article 9(3) [*or 10(3)*], 9A(1) or 10A(5), the registrar shall, upon deciding whether the provisional refusal shall be upheld, in whole or in relation to some only of the goods or services in relation to which protection in the United Kingdom is requested, notify the International Bureau of that decision.

(5) Where, after a decision of the registrar has been notified to the International Bureau pursuant to paragraph (4) the decision is referred to an appointed person or the court on appeal or further appeal from the registrar, the registrar shall notify the International Bureau of the decision of that person or court.

Amendment

The words in italics were deleted, and the words in bold inserted, by the Trade Marks (International Registration) (Amendment) Order 2002 (SI 2002/692), art.8 and the Trade Marks (International Registration) (Amendment) Order 2004 (SI 2004/948), art.6.

Protection

A19–020   *12.—[(1) Where—*

(a) following examination and publication pursuant to articles 9 and 10—

(i) the period of 18 months from the date on which the notification of the request for extension was sent to the United Kingdom has not expired, but the period for giving notice of refusal based on

an opposition in accordance with article 10(3) expires without notice of refusal (whether based on opposition or otherwise) having been given.

(ii) the period of 18 months from the date on which the notification of the request for extension was sent to the United Kingdom has expired, and the period for giving notice of opposition in accordance with article 10(2) expires without notice of opposition having been given,

([iii) notice of refusal has been given in respect of some only of the goods or services in respect of which protection in the United Kingdom has been requested and the registrar informs the International Bureau in accordance with article 11(4) that the holder has made no representations within the period specified in article 9(4) or has filed no counter-statement within the period specified in article 10(4) (as the case may be) or that the holder has informed the registrar that he does not intend to make such representations or file such a counter-statement, or]

(iii) **notice of refusal has been given in respect of some only of the goods or services in respect of which protection in the United Kingdom has been requested and the registrar informs the International Bureau in accordance with article 11(4) that the holder has made no representations within the period specified in article 9(4) or has filed no counter-statement within the period specified in article 10(4) or 10 (4B) (as the case may be) or that the holder has informed the registrar that he does not intend to make such representations or file such a counter-statement, or**

(iv) notice of refusal has been given in respect of all or some of the goods or services in respect of which protection in the United Kingdom has been requested and the registrar notifies the International Bureau in accordance with article 11(5) that a final decision has been made that the refusal is withdrawn, or is withdrawn in respect of some of the goods or services in respect of which protection in the United Kingdom has been requested; or

(b) the period of 18 months from the date on which the notification of the request for extension was sent to the United Kingdom expires without any notice of refusal having been given and without the International Bureau having been informed that oppositions may be filed after the expiry of that period,

the trade mark which is the subject of the request for protection shall thereupon be protected as a protected international trade mark (UK); and in a case where a refusal subsists in respect of some of the goods or services in respect of which protection in the United Kingdom has been requested, protection shall apply only as regards the remaining goods or services.

(1) Where the period of 18 months from the date on which the notification of the request for extension was sent to the United Kingdom expires without any notice of provisional refusal having been given and without the International Bureau having been informed that oppositions may be filed after the expiry of that period, the trade mark which is the subject of the request for protection shall thereupon be protected as a protected international trade mark (UK).

(1A) Subject to paragraph (1), where particulars of an international

registration have been published pursuant to article 10(1) in respect of all or some of the goods or services comprised in the international registration and the period for giving notice of opposition in accordance with article 10(2) expires without notice of opposition having been given in respect of any of the goods or services specified in the notice published pursuant to article 10(1) and without notice of refusal not based on an opposition having been given and not withdrawn, the trade mark which is the subject of the international registration in question shall thereupon be protected as a protected international trade mark (UK) in respect of those goods or services.

(1B) Subject to paragraph (1), where particulars of an international registration have been published pursuant to article 10(1) in respect of all or some of the goods or services comprised in the international registration and on expiry of the period for giving notice of opposition in accordance with article 10(2) notice of opposition has been given in respect of some only of the goods or services specified in the notice published pursuant to article 10(1) and no notice of refusal not based on an opposition has been given and not withdrawn in respect of the remaining goods or services specified in that notice, the trade mark which is the subject of the international registration in question shall thereupon be protected as a protected international trade mark (UK) in respect of those remaining goods or services.

(1C) Subject to paragraph (1), where particulars of an international registration have been published pursuant to article 10(1) in respect of all or some of the goods or services comprised in the international registration and within the period for giving notice of opposition in accordance with article 10(2) notice of opposition has been given in respect of all or some of the goods or services specified in the notice published pursuant to article 10(1) but subsequently a final decision is made that the notice of provisional refusal given as a result of that opposition is withdrawn, or is withdrawn in respect of some of the goods or services in respect of which protection in the United Kingdom has been requested, the trade mark which is the subject of the international registration in question shall thereupon be protected as a protected international trade mark (UK) in respect of the goods or services specified in the notice published pursuant to article 10(1) other than those in respect of which a notice of refusal (whether based on an opposition or otherwise) continues to subsist.

(1D) For the purposes of paragraph (1C) a final decision shall be regarded as being made where the registrar, or the appointed person or the court on appeal or further appeal from the registrar, decides whether the refusal shall be upheld, in whole or in relation to some only of the goods or services in relation to which protection in the United Kingdom is requested, and any right of appeal against that decision expires or is exhausted.

(2) For the purposes of application by this Order of provisions of the Act, subject to article 21, a trade mark so protected shall be treated as being registered under the Act as of the following date:—

(a) where the request for extension of protection to the United Kingdom is mentioned in the international application, or is made subsequently, but on or before the date of the international registration, the date of that international registration;

(b) where the request for such extension is made subsequently to the international registration, the date on which the request is recorded in the International Register.

[(3) *When a trade mark becomes protected pursuant to this article, the registrar shall publish particulars of the international registration specifying the date on which, and the goods or services in respect of which, protection is conferred.*]

(3) **When a trade mark becomes protected pursuant to this article, the registrar shall publish a notice specifying the number of the international registration in respect of that trade mark, the date on which protection is conferred and the date and place of publication of the notice published under article 10(1) in relation to that trade mark.**

Amendment

The words in italics were deleted, and the words in bold inserted, by the Trade Marks (International Registration) (Amendment) Order 2002 (SI 2002/692), art.9.

Correction of international registration

12A.—(1) **This article applies where the International Bureau notifies the registrar pursuant to Rule 28 of the Common Regulations that it has corrected an international registration designating the United Kingdom and the correction—**   A19–021

   (a) **substantially affects the identity of the trade mark; or**
   (b) **reduces or extends the goods or services comprised in the international registration.**

(2) **The registrar may treat a notification of correction to which this article applies as a new notification of an international registration designating the United Kingdom and where a notification of correction is so treated—**

   (a) **if the correction substantially affects the identity of the trade mark, paragraph (3) below shall apply; or**
   (b) **if the correction reduces or extends the goods or services comprised in the international registration, paragraph (4) below shall apply.**

(3) **Where this paragraph applies in accordance with paragraph (2), articles 9 to 12 shall apply to the notification of correction as if it were a new notification of an international registration designating the United Kingdom and—**

   (a) **if the trade mark which is the subject of the international registration has not become a protected international trade mark (UK) before receipt of the notification of correction in relation to it, the original notification of that international registration to the registrar shall be treated as having been withdrawn;**
   (b) **if the trade mark which is the subject of the international registration has become a protected international trade mark (UK) before receipt of the notification of correction in relation to it, the protection conferred by article 12 in respect of that trade mark shall cease on receipt of the notification of correction but this shall not affect transactions past and closed as at that date.**

(4) **Where this paragraph applies in accordance with paragraph (2)—**

   (a) **articles 9 to 12 shall apply to the notification of correction as if it were a new notification of an international registration designating the United Kingdom so far as it relates to goods or services not previously comprised in the international registration; and**
   (b) **if the trade mark which is the subject of the international registration has become a protected international trade mark (UK) before**

receipt of the notification of correction in relation to it, the protection conferred by article 12 in respect of that trade mark so far as it relates to goods or services which are no longer comprised in the international registration shall cease on receipt of the notification of correction but this shall not affect transactions past and closed as at that date.

Amendment

Article 12A inserted by the Trade Marks (International Registration) (Amendment) Order 2002 (SI 2002/692), art.10.

Revocation and Invalidity

A19–022   **13.**—(1) The provisions of section 46 (revocation of registration) and section 47 (grounds for invalidity of registration) shall apply, subject to the adaptations set out below, so as to permit the protection of a protected international trade mark (UK) to be revoked, or declared invalid.

(1A) An address for service in the United Kingdom shall be filed by—

(a) every applicant applying to the registrar for an international trade mark (UK) to be revoked or to be declared invalid; and

(b) the holder of a protected international trade mark (UK) which is subject to such proceedings.

(2) The reference in section 46(1) to the date of completion of the registration procedure shall be construed as a reference to the date of the protected international trade mark (UK) becoming protected; the reference in section 46(2) to the form in which a trade mark was registered shall be construed as reference to the form in which it is protected; and the references in section 46(5) and section 47(5) to goods or services for which the trade mark is registered shall be construed as references to those in respect of which it is protected.

(3) The references in section 46 to the registration of a trade mark being revoked and the references in section 47 to the registration of a trade mark being declared invalid shall be construed as references to the protection of a protected international trade mark (UK) being revoked or declared invalid, as the case may be.

[(4) *The provisions of rule 31, with necessary modifications, apply in relation to the procedure on application for revocation and declaration of invalidity of protection of a protected international trade mark (UK).*]

[(4) *The provisions of rules 31, 32 and 33, with necessary modifications, apply respectively in relation to the procedure on application for revocation (on grounds of non-use), revocation (on grounds other than non-use) and declaration of invalidity of protection of a protected international trade mark (UK).*]

(4) The provisions of—

(a) rules 31 to 31B apply in relation to the procedure on application for revocation on grounds of non-use;

(b) rules 32 to 32B apply in relation to the procedure on application for revocation on grounds other than non-use; and

(c) rules 33 to 33B apply in relation to the procedure on application for a declaration of invalidity;

save that any reference to the proprietor shall be construed to be a reference to the holder.

(4A) The provisions of rule 35 (intervention), rule 36 (case management) and rule 37 (pre-hearing review) apply in relation to a procedure on applica-

tion for revocation (on grounds of non-use), revocation (on grounds other than non-use) and declaration of invalidity of protection of a protected international trade mark (UK).

(5) Where the protection of a protected international trade mark (UK) is revoked or declared invalid to any extent, the registrar shall notify the International Bureau, and

(a) in the case of a revocation, the rights of the proprietor shall be deemed to have ceased to exist to that extent as from the date on which the revocation is recorded in the International Register;

(b) in the case of a declaration of invalidity, the trade mark shall to that extent be deemed never to have been a protected international trade mark (UK):

Provided that this shall not affect transactions past and closed as at the date when the invalidity is recorded in the International Register.

Amendment

The words in italics were deleted, and the words in bold inserted, by the Trade Marks (International Registration) (Amendment) Order 2000 (SI 2000/138), art.8 and the Trade Marks (International Registration) (Amendment) Order 2004 (SI 2004/948), art.7.

Effect of acquiescence

14. Section 48 (effect of acquiescence) applies where the proprietor of an earlier trade mark has acquiesced for a continuous period of five years in the use of a protected international trade mark (UK); and for that purpose—   **A19–023**

(a) the reference to a registered trade mark shall be construed as including a protected international trade mark (UK);

(b) the references to registration shall include references to protection of a protected international trade mark (UK).

Proceedings relating to invalidity and revocation of protection

15.—(1) The provisions of section 73 (certificate of validity of contested registration) apply, with the necessary modifications, in relation to proceedings before the court in which the validity of the protection of a protected international trade mark (UK) is contested.   **A19–024**

(2) The provisions of section 74 (registrar's appearance in proceedings involving the registrar) apply, with the necessary modifications, in relation to proceedings before the court involving an application for—

(a) the revocation of the protection of a protected international trade mark (UK);

(b) a declaration of the invalidity of the protection of a protected international trade mark (UK);

(c) the rectification of the supplementary register.

Importation of infringing goods, materials or articles

16. The provisions of section 89 (infringing goods, material or articles may be treated as prohibited goods) section 90 and section 91 of the Act (power of Commissioners of Customs and Excise to disclose information) apply in relation to goods which are, in relation to a protected international trade mark (UK), infringing goods, materials or articles, and for the purposes of those provisions—   **A19–025**

(a) references to a registered trade mark shall be to a protected international trade mark (UK);

(b) the Trade Marks (Customs) Regulations 1994 shall apply in relation to notices given under the provisions of section 89.

Offences and forfeiture

A19–026   17.—(1) The provisions of section 92 (unauthorised use of trade mark, etc, in relation to goods), section 93 (enforcement function of local weights and measures authority), section 97 (forfeiture: England and Wales) and section 98 (forfeiture: Scotland) apply in relation to a protected international trade mark (UK).

(2) For the purposes of the provisions referred to in paragraph (1) above—

(a) references to a registered trade mark shall be treated as references to a protected international trade mark (UK);

(b) references to goods in respect of which a trade mark is registered shall be treated as references to goods in respect of which a protected international trade mark (UK) confers protection in the United Kingdom.

(3) No offence under section 92 in relation to a protected international trade mark is committed by anything done before the date of publication pursuant to article 12(3).

Falsely representing trade mark as a protected international trade mark (UK)

A19–027   18.—(1) It is an offence for a person—

(a) falsely to represent that a mark is a protected international trade mark (UK), or

(b) to make a false representation as to the goods or services for which a protected international trade mark (UK) confers protection in the United Kingdom

knowing or having reason to believe that the representation is false.

(2) A person guilty of an offence under this article is liable on summary conviction to a fine not exceeding level 3 on the standard scale.

TRANSFORMATION OF AN INTERNATIONAL REGISTRATION INTO A NATIONAL
APPLICATION

Transformation applications

A19–028   19.—(1) The provisions of this article apply where—

(a) an international registration designating the United Kingdom is cancelled at the request of the Office of origin under Article 6(4) of the Madrid Protocol in respect of all or some of the goods or services listed in the registration;

(b) an applicant (a "transformation application") is made to the registrar, within three months of the date on which the international registration was cancelled, for registration in the United Kingdom of a trade mark identical to that comprised in the international registration in respect of some or all of the goods or services in respect of which the international registration was cancelled; and

(c) the application is made by the person who was the holder of the international registration immediately before its cancellation.

(2) A transformation application shall be made on Form TM3 and shall state that it is made by way of transformation.

(3) A trade mark registered pursuant to a transformation application shall be

treated as if it were registered as of the date of the international registration according to Article 3(4) of the Madrid Protocol or, where the request for extension to the United Kingdom was made subsequently to the international registration, on the date of recordal of that request according to Article 3ter of the Madrid Protocol, and that date shall be deemed for the purposes of the Act to be the date of registration.

Procedure on transformation application

20.—(1) Where the international trade mark (UK) has become protected pursuant to article 12 on or before the actual date on which the transformation application is made ("the transformation date") the trade mark shall be registered under the Act.

A19–029

(2) Where the international registration designating the United Kingdom has not become protected under article 12 at the transformation date and a notice has been published pursuant to article 10(1) in respect of the trade mark, the registrar shall treat the publication of such notice as being the publication of the transformation application under section 38(1) and shall publish a notice that it is being so treated. Any opposition shall be treated as opposition under section 38(2).

(3) Where a notice has not yet been published pursuant to article 10(1) at the transformation date and the registrar has issued a notice of refusal pursuant to article 9(3), the registrar shall for the purposes of the transformation application treat the notice of refusal as if it had been issued under section 37(3).

The registrar shall in that event inform the applicant of the nature of the response required of him in respect of his transformation application and shall further specify the period within which the applicant must respond to the registrar.

CONCURRENT REGISTRATIONS

Effects of international registration where trade mark is also registered under the Act

21.—(1) The provisions of this article apply, without prejudice to the rights and remedies conferred in respect of a trade mark registered under the Act, where—

A19–030

(a) the registered trade mark is also a protected international trade mark (UK);

(b) the proprietor of the registered trade mark is the holder of the international trade mark (UK);

(c) all the goods or services in respect of which the registered trade mark is registered are protected under the protected international trade mark (UK);

(d) the date of registration of the registered trade mark is earlier than the date specified in article 12(2) in relation to the international trade mark (UK).

(2) For the purposes of application by this Order of the provisions of the Act, the protected international trade mark (UK) shall be treated, notwithstanding the provisions of article 12(2), as being registered under the Act as of the date of registration of the registered trade mark as regards all the goods or services in respect of which the registered trade mark was registered.

(3) For the purpose of determining whether the international trade mark (UK) is an earlier trade mark, it shall be treated as having the date of application of the

registered trade mark as regards all the goods or services in respect of which the registered trade mark was registered, taking account (where appropriate) of the priorities claimed in respect of the registered trade mark.

(4) Where the conditions specified in paragraph (1) above are satisfied in relation to a trade mark, the provisions of paragraphs (2) and (3) above shall continue to apply in respect of the relevant international trade mark (UK) notwithstanding that the relevant registered trade mark lapses or is surrendered, but shall cease to apply if it is revoked or declared invalid.

(5) On the application of the holder of the protected international trade mark (UK), the registrar shall note the international registration in the register against the registered trade mark.

(6) For the purposes of paragraph (5) above, the holder of the protected international trade mark (UK) shall make an application to the registrar using Form TM28.

INTERNATIONAL APPLICATIONS ORIGINATING IN THE UNITED KINGDOM

Applications for international registration

A19–031   **22.**—(1) An applicant for the registration of a trade mark, or the proprietor of a registered trade mark, may, subject to the provisions of this article, apply through the registrar for the international registration of the trade mark.

(2) An application for international registration may be made only where the applicant for such registration is—

(a) a British citizen, a British dependent territories citizen, a British overseas citizen, a British subject or a British protected person;

(b) a body or a corporation sole incorporated or constituted under the law of any part of the United Kingdom;

(c) a person domiciled in the United Kingdom: or

(d) a person who has a real and effective industrial or commercial establishment in the United Kingdom.

(3) The particulars appearing in the application shall correspond with the particulars appearing at that time in the basic application or basic registration as the case may be.

(4) The applicant for international registration shall provide at the request of the registrar such evidence as may be necessary to satisfy him that the applicant is eligible to make the application in accordance with paragraph (2) above.

(5) If an international application complies with the requirements set out in this article, the registrar shall submit the international application to the International Bureau.

(6) In this Order—

(a) "basic application" means an application for registration of a trade mark in the United Kingdom in respect of which application is made for international registration:

(b) "basic registration" means a trade mark registered in the United Kingdom in respect of which application is made for international registration.

Notification to International Bureau

A19–032   **23.**—(1) Where the registrar has submitted an application for international registration, he shall notify the International Bureau of the occurrence of any of the events specified in paragraph (2) below and shall request the International

Bureau to cancel the international registration as regards those goods or services covered by the international application in respect of which the basic application or basic registration has ceased to subsist by reason of that event.

(2) The following events are specified for the purposes of paragraph (1) above:

(a) before the expiry of five years from the date of the international registration, the registrar refuses to accept the basic application as regards some or all of the goods or services covered by the international registration or, after accepting the application refuses to register the trade mark as regards some or all of those goods or services, having regard to matters coming to his notice since he accepted the application, and in either case that decision becomes a final decision, whether before or after the expiry of that period of five years;

(b) opposition proceedings begun before the expiry of five years from the date of the international registration result in a final decision not to register the trade mark as regards some or all of the goods or services covered by the international registration;

(c) the basic application is withdrawn, or is restricted as regards goods or services covered by the international registration, as a result of a request by the applicant made before the expiry of five years from the date of the international registration, or made subsequently when the basic application was at the time of the request subject to an appeal against refusal of registration or to opposition proceedings begun in either case before the expiry of that five year period;

(d) the registration resulting from the basic application or the basic registration expires without renewal and is removed from the register before the expiry of five years from the date of the international registration and no request for its restoration is made within the time specified in rule 30 or such a request is made and a final decision is made to refuse the request;

(e) a final decision is made to revoke or declare invalid the registration resulting from the basic application or the basic registration, as a result of proceedings begun before the expiry of five years from the date of the international registration:

(f) the registration resulting from the basic application, or the basic registration, is surrendered as a result of a request by the proprietor made before the expiry of five years from the date of the international registration, or made subsequently where at the time of the request—

(i) the basic application was subject to an appeal against refusal of registration or to opposition proceedings; or

(ii) the registration resulting from the basic application, or the basic registration, was subject to proceedings for revocation or invalidation;

and such appeal or proceedings were begun before the expiry of five years from the date of the international registration.

(3) For the purposes of this article:—

(a) a final decision shall be regarded as made where—

(i) any right of appeal against the decision expires or is exhausted, or

(ii) proceedings relating to an application or registration are discontinued or abandoned;

(b) reference to an application being withdrawn includes its being deemed to be withdrawn, or abandoned, or deemed never to have been made.

MISCELLANEOUS AND GENERAL PROVISIONS

Supplementary Register

A19–033   **24.**—(1) The registrar shall maintain a register ("the supplementary register") for the purpose of recording, in relation to international trade marks (UK)—

    (a) disclaimers and limitations **made under article 4(4)**;

    (b) notifiable transactions.

    (2) The supplementary register need not be kept in documentary form.

    [(3) *Rules 34 to 39 apply, with the necessary modifications, in relation to the supplementary register.*]

    (3) Rules 40 to 45 apply, with the necessary modifications, in relation to the supplementary register.

Amendment

    The words in italics were deleted, and the words in bold inserted, by the Trade Marks (International Registration) (Amendment) Order 2000 (SI 2000/138), art.9 and the Trade Marks (International Registration) (Amendment) Order 2002 (SI 2002/692), art.11.

Disclosure of Information

A19–034   **25.**—(1) Before publication of notice under article 10(1) in relation to an international registration designating the United Kingdom, the registrar shall not publish or communicate to any person documents or information relating to the international registration other than as provided in paragraph (2) below.

    (2) In relation to an international registration designating the United Kingdom, the registrar shall on request make available for inspection by the public all information in his possession which is recorded in the International Register concerning that registration, the particulars contained in any application for registration of a notifiable transaction and any entry in the supplementary register resulting from such an application.

    (3) Subject to paragraph (5) below, after publiation of notice under article 10(1) in relation to an international registration designating the United Kingdom, the registrar shall on request provide a person with such information and permit him to inspect such document, relating to the international registration as may be specified in the request.

    (4) A request for information relating to an international registration designating the United Kingdom shall be made on Form TM31M.

    [(5) *Paragraphs (2) to (5) of rule 44, and rule 45, apply in relation to the right of inspection conferred by paragraph (3) above.*]

    (5) Paragraph (2) to (5) of rule 50, and rule 51, apply in relation to the right of inspection conferred by paragraph (3) above.

    (6) Where a person has been notified that an international registration designates the United Kingdom and that the proprietor will, if the registration becomes a protected international trade mark (UK), bring proceedings against him in respect of acts done after publication of notice under article 10(1), the registrar shall on request permit inspection under paragraph (3) above notwithstanding that such notice has not been published and that paragraph shall apply accordingly.

Amendment

    The words in italics were deleted, and the words in bold inserted, by the Trade

Marks (International Registration) (Amendment) Order 2000 (SI 2000/138), art.10.

Exclusion of Liability

26.—(1) The registrar is not subject to any liability by reason of, or in connection with, any examination required or authorised by this Order, or in any report or other proceedings consequent on such examination.

(2) No proceedings lie against an officer of the registrar in respect of any matter for which, by virtue of this article, the registrar is not liable.

A19–035

Evidence of certain matters relating to an international registration

27.—(1) In all legal proceedings relating to an international trade mark (UK), the registration of a person as holder of an international trade mark (UK) shall be prima facie evidence of the validity of the original international registration and of any subsequent assignment or other transmission of it.

A19–036

(2) Judicial notice shall be taken of the following—
  (a) the Madrid Protocol and the Common Regulations;
  (b) copies issued by the International Bureau of entries in the International Register;
  (c) copies of the periodical gazette published by the International Bureau.

(3) Any document mentioned in paragraph (2)(b) or (c) above shall be admissible as evidence of any instrument or other act thereby communicated of the International Bureau.

(4) Evidence of any instrument issued by the International Bureau or any entry in or extract from such a document may be given in any legal proceedings by production of a copy; and any document purporting to be such a copy shall be received in evidence.

(5) In any legal proceedings in Scotland, evidence of any matter given in any manner authorised by this article shall be sufficient evidence of it.

(6) In this article, "legal proceedings" includes proceedings before the registrar.

Agents

28. Any act required or authorised by this Order to be done by or to a person in connection with a request for protection of an international registration as a protected international trade mark (UK) or any procedure relating to a protected international trade mark (UK) may be done by or to an agent authorised by that person orally or in writing.

A19–037

Burden of proving use of international trade mark (UK)

29. If in any civil proceedings pursuant to this Order a question arises as to the use to which an international trade mark (UK) has been put, it is for the holder to show what use has been made of it.

A19–038

Communication of information to the International Bureau

30. Notwithstanding section 67(2) or any other enactment or rule of law, the registrar may communicate to the International Bureau any information which the United Kingdom is required to communicate by virtue of this Order or pursuant to the Madrid Protocol or the Common Regulations.

A19–039

Transmission of fees to the International Bureau

31. The registrar may accept for transmission to the International Bureau fees

A19–040

payable to the International Bureau in respect of an application for international registration originating in the United Kingdom or a renewal of such an international registration, subject to such terms and conditions as he may specify, either generally by published notice, or in any particular case by written notice to the applicant desiring to make payment by such means.

Application of Trade Marks Rules [1994] 2000

A19–041   **32.**—(1) Except as otherwise provided, or where their application would be inconsistent with the provisions of this Order, the Rules shall apply, with the necessary modifications, in relation to an international registration designating the United Kingdom, (including a protected international trade mark (UK)) as in relation to a registered trade mark or application.

(2) In their application to an international registration designating the United Kingdom, the Rules shall be treated in all respects as rules made under the Act and, in particular, rules relating to costs and security for costs and to evidence before the registrar shall be enforceable in relation to proceedings under this Order in the same manner as in relation to proceedings relating to a registered trade mark or application.

Amendment

The heading to article 32 was substituted by the Trade Marks (International Registration) (Amendment) Order 2000 (SI 2000/138), art.11.

PART VII

OTHER INTERNATIONAL MATERIALS

APPENDIX 20

Paris Convention for the Protection of Industrial Property of March 20, 1883,[77] as revised at Brussels on December 14, 1900,[78] at Washington on June 2, 1911,[79] at the Hague on November 6, 1925,[80] at London on June 2, 1934,[81] at Lisbon on October 31, 1958,[82] at Stockholm on July 14, 1967 and as amended on September 28, 1979

A20–001

Article 1

[Establishment of the Union; Scope of Industrial Property][83]

(1) The countries to which this Convention applies constitute a Union for the protection of industrial property.

A20–002

(2) The protection of industrial property has as its object patents, utility models, industrial designs, trademarks, service marks, trade names, indications of source or appellations of origin, and the repression of unfair competition.

(3) Industrial property shall be understood in the broadest sense and shall apply not only to industry and commerce proper, but likewise to agricultural and extractive industries and to all manufactured or natural products, for example, wines, grain, tobacco leaf, fruit, cattle, minerals, mineral waters, beer, flowers, and flour.

(4) Patents shall include the various kinds of industrial patents recognized by the laws of the countries of the Union, such as patents of importation, patents of improvement, patents and certificates of addition, etc.

Article 2

[National Treatment for Nationals of Countries of the Union]

(1) Nationals of any country of the Union shall, as regards the protection of industrial property, enjoy in all the other countries of the Union the advantages that their respective laws now grant, or may hereafter grant, to nationals; all without prejudice to the rights specially provided for by this Convention. Consequently, they shall have the same protection as the latter, and the same legal remedy against any infringement of their rights, provided that the conditions and formalities imposed upon nationals are complied with.

A20–003

(2) However, no requirement as to domicile or establishment in the country where protection is claimed may be imposed upon nationals of countries of the Union for the enjoyment of any industrial property rights.

(3) The provisions of the laws of each of the countries of the Union relating to judicial and administrative procedure and to jurisdiction, and to the designation of an address for service or the appointment of an agent, which may be required by the laws on industrial property are expressly reserved.

---

[77] Commercial No.28 (1884), C 4043.
[78] Treaty Series No. 15 (1902), Cd. 1084.
[79] Treaty Series No. 8 (1913), Cd. 6805.
[80] Treaty Series No. 16 (1928), Cmd. 3167.
[81] Treaty Series No. 55 (1938), Cmd. 5833.
[82] Treaty Series No. 38 (1962), Cmnd. 1715.
[83] Articles have been given titles to facilitate their identification. There are no titles in the signed (French) text.

Article 3

[Same Treatment for Certain Categories of Persons as for Nationals of Countries of the Union]

A20–004   Nationals of countries outside the Union who are domiciled or who have real and effective industrial or commercial establishments in the territory of one of the countries of the Union shall be treated in the same manner as nationals of the countries of the Union.

Article 4

[A to I. Patents, Utility Models, Industrial Designs, Marks, Inventors' Certificates: Right of Priority.—G. Patents: Division of the Application]

A20–005   A.—

(1) Any person who has duly filed an application for a patent, or for the registration of a utility model, or of an industrial design, or of a trademark, in one of the countries of the Union, or his successor in title, shall enjoy, for the purpose of filing in the other countries, a right of priority during the periods hereinafter fixed.

(2) Any filing that is equivalent to a regular national filing under the domestic legislation of any country of the Union or under bilateral or multilateral treaties concluded between countries of the Union shall be recognized as giving rise to the right of priority.

(3) By a regular national filing is meant any filing that is adequate to establish the date on which the application was filed in the country concerned, whatever may be the subsequent fate of the application.

B.—Consequently, any subsequent filing in any of the other countries of the Union before the expiration of the periods referred to above shall not be invalidated by reason of any acts accomplished in the interval, in particular, another filing, the publication or exploitation of the invention, the putting on sale of copies of the design, or the use of the mark, and such acts cannot give rise to any third-party right or any right of personal possession. Rights acquired by third parties before the date of the first application that serves as the basis for the right of priority are reserved in accordance with the domestic legislation of each country of the Union.

C.—

(1) The periods of priority referred to above shall be twelve months for patents and utility models, and six months for industrial designs and trademarks.

(2) These periods shall start from the date of filing of the first application; the day of filing shall not be included in the period.

(3) If the last day of the period is an official holiday, or a day when the Office is not open for the filing of applications in the country where protection is claimed, the period shall be extended until the first following working day.

(4) A subsequent application concerning the same subject as a previous first application within the meaning of paragraph (2), above, filed in the same country of the Union, shall be considered as the first application, of which the filing date shall be the starting point of the period of priority, if, at the time of filing the subsequent application, the said previous application has been withdrawn, abandoned, or refused, without having been laid open to public inspection and without leaving any rights outstanding, and if it has not yet served as a basis for claiming a right of priority. The previous application may not thereafter serve as a basis for claiming a right of priority.

D.—

(1) Any person desiring to take advantage of the priority of a previous filing shall be required to make a declaration indicating the date of such filing and the country in which it was made. Each country shall determine the latest date on which such declaration must be made.

(2) These particulars shall be mentioned in the publications issued by the competent authority, and in particular in the patents and the specifications relating thereto.

(3) The countries of the Union may require any person making a declaration of priority to produce a copy of the application (description, drawings, etc.) previously filed. The copy, certified as correct by the authority which received such application, shall not require any authentication, and may in any case be filed, without fee, at any time within three months of the filing of the subsequent application. They may require it to be accompanied by a certificate from the same authority showing the date of filing, and by a translation.

(4) No other formalities may be required for the declaration of priority at the time of filing the application. Each country of the Union shall determine the consequences of failure to comply with the formalities prescribed by this Article, but such consequences shall in no case go beyond the loss of the right of priority.

(5) Subsequently, further proof may be required.

Any person who avails himself of the priority of a previous application shall be required to specify the number of that application; this number shall be published as provided for by paragraph (2), above.

E.—

(1) Where an industrial design is filed in a country by virtue of a right of priority based on the filing of a utility model, the period of priority shall be the same as that fixed for industrial designs.

(2) Furthermore, it is permissible to file a utility model in a country by virtue of a right of priority based on the filing of a patent application, and vice versa.

F.—No country of the Union may refuse a priority or a patent application on the ground that the applicant claims multiple priorities, even if they originate in different countries, or on the ground that an application claiming one or more priorities contains one or more elements that were not included in the application or applications whose priority is claimed, provided that, in both cases, there is unity of invention within the meaning of the law of the country.

With respect to the elements not included in the application or applications whose priority is claimed, the filing of the subsequent application shall give rise to a right of priority under ordinary conditions.

G.—

(1) If the examination reveals that an application for a patent contains more than one invention, the applicant may divide the application into a certain number of divisional applications and preserve as the date of each the date of the initial application and the benefit of the right of priority, if any.

(2) The applicant may also, on his own initiative, divide a patent application and preserve as the date of each divisional application the date of the initial application and the benefit of the right of priority, if any. Each country of the Union shall have the right to determine the conditions under which such division shall be authorized.

H.—Priority may not be refused on the ground that certain elements of the invention for which priority is claimed do not appear among the claims formulated in the application in the country of origin, provided that the application documents as a whole specifically disclose such elements.

I.

(1) Applications for inventors' certificates filed in a country in which applicants have the right to apply at their own option either for a patent or for an inventor's certificate shall give rise to the right of priority provided for by this Article, under the same conditions and with the same effects as applications for patents.

(2) In a country in which applicants have the right to apply at their own option either for a patent or for an inventor's certificate, an applicant for an inventor's certificate shall, in accordance with the provisions of this Article relating to patent applications, enjoy a right of priority based on an application for a patent, a utility model, or an inventor's certificate.

Article 4Bis

[Patents: Independence of Patents Obtained for the Same Invention in Different Countries]

A20–006   (1) Patents applied for in the various countries of the Union by nationals of countries of the Union shall be independent of patents obtained for the same invention in other countries, whether members of the Union or not.

(2) The foregoing provision is to be understood in an unrestricted sense, in particular, in the sense that patents applied for during the period of priority are independent, both as regards the grounds for nullity and forfeiture, and as regards their normal duration.

(3) The provision shall apply to all patents existing at the time when it comes into effect.

(4) Similarly, it shall apply, in the case of the accession of new countries, to patents in existence on either side at the time of accession.

(5) Patents obtained with the benefit of priority shall, in the various countries of the Union, have a duration equal to that which they would have, had they been applied for or granted without the benefit of priority.

Article 4Ter

[Patents: Mention of the Inventor in the Patent]

A20–007   The inventor shall have the right to be mentioned as such in the patent.

Article 4Quater

[Patents: Patentability in Case of Restrictions of Sale by Law]

A20–008   The grant of a patent shall not be refused and a patent shall not be invalidated on the ground that the sale of the patented product or of a product obtained by means of a patented process is subject to restrictions or limitations resulting from the domestic law.

Article 5

[A. Patents: Importation of Articles; Failure to Work or Insufficient Working; Compulsory Licenses.—B. Industrial Designs: Failure to Work; Importation of Articles.—C. Marks: Failure to Use; Different Forms; Use by Co-proprietors.—D. Patents, Utility Models, Marks, Industrial Designs: Marking]

A20–009   A.—

(1) Importation by the patentee into the country where the patent has been granted of articles manufactured in any of the countries of the Union shall not entail forfeiture of the patent.

(2) Each country of the Union shall have the right to take legislative measures providing for the grant of compulsory licenses to prevent the abuses which might result from the exercise of the exclusive rights conferred by the patent, for example, failure to work.

(3) Forfeiture of the patent shall not be provided for except in cases where the grant of compulsory licenses would not have been sufficient to prevent the said abuses. No proceedings for the forfeiture or revocation of a patent may be instituted before the expiration of two years from the grant of the first compulsory license.

(4) A compulsory license may not be applied for on the ground of failure to work or insufficient working before the expiration of a period of four years from the date of filing of the patent application or three years from the date of the grant of the patent, whichever period expires last; it shall be refused if the patentee justifies his inaction by legitimate reasons. Such a compulsory license shall be non-exclusive and shall not be transferable, even in the form of a grant of a sub-license, except with that part of the enterprise or goodwill which exploits such license.

(5) The foregoing provisions shall be applicable, mutatis mutandis, to utility models.

B.—The protection of industrial designs shall not, under any circumstance, be subject to any forfeiture, either by reason of failure to work or by reason of the importation of articles corresponding to those which are protected.

C.—

(1) If, in any country, use of the registered mark is compulsory, the registration may be cancelled only after a reasonable period, and then only if the person concerned does not justify his inaction.

(2) Use of a trademark by the proprietor in a form differing in elements which do not alter the distinctive character of the mark in the form in which it was registered in one of the countries of the Union shall not entail invalidation of the registration and shall not diminish the protection granted to the mark.

(3) Concurrent use of the same mark on identical or similar goods by industrial or commercial establishments considered as co-proprietors of the mark according to the provisions of the domestic law of the country where protection is claimed shall not prevent registration or diminish in any way the protection granted to the said mark in any country of the Union, provided that such use does not result in misleading the public and is not contrary to the public interest.

D.—No indication or mention of the patent, of the utility model, of the registration of the trademark, or of the deposit of the industrial design, shall be required upon the goods as a condition of recognition of the right to protection.

Article 5Bis

[All Industrial Property Rights: Period of Grace for the Payment of Fees for the Maintenance of Rights; Patents: Restoration]

(1) A period of grace of not less than six months shall be allowed for the payment of the fees prescribed for the maintenance of industrial property rights, subject, if the domestic legislation so provides, to the payment of a surcharge.

A20–010

(2) The countries of the Union shall have the right to provide for the restoration of patents which have lapsed by reason of non-payment of fees.

Article 5Ter

[Patents: Patented Devices Forming Part of Vessels, Aircraft, or Land Vehicles]

A20–011   In any country of the Union the following shall not be considered as infringements of the rights of a patentee:

1. the use on board vessels of other countries of the Union of devices forming the subject of his patent in the body of the vessel, in the machinery, tackle, gear and other accessories, when such vessels temporarily or accidentally enter the waters of the said country, provided that such devices are used there exclusively for the needs of the vessel;
2. the use of devices forming the subject of the patent in the construction or operation of aircraft or land vehicles of other countries of the Union, or of accessories of such aircraft or land vehicles of other countries of the Union, or of accessories of such aircraft or land vehicles, when those aircraft or land vehicles temporarily or accidentally enter the said country.

Article 5Quater

[Patents: Importation of Products Manufactured by a Process Patented in the Importing Country]

A20–012   When a product is imported into a country of the Union where there exists a patent protecting a process of manufacture of the said product, the patentee shall have all the rights, with regard to the imported product, that are accorded to him by the legislation of the country of importation, on the basis of the process patent, with respect to products manufactured in that country.

Article 5Quinquies

[Industrial Designs]

A20–013   Industrial designs shall be protected in all the countries of the Union.

Article 6

[Marks: Conditions of Registration; Independence of Protection of Same Mark in Different Countries]

A20–014   (1) The conditions for the filing and registration of trademarks shall be determined in each country of the Union by its domestic legislation.

(2) However, an application for the registration of a mark filed by a national of a country of the Union in any country of the Union may not be refused, nor may a registration be invalidated, on the ground that filing, registration, or renewal, has not been effected in the country of origin.

(3) A mark duly registered in a country of the Union shall be regarded as independent of marks registered in the other countries of the Union, including the country of origin.

Article 6Bis

[Marks: Well-Known Marks]

A20–015   (1) The countries of the Union undertake, ex officio if their legislation so permits, or at the request of an interested party, to refuse or to cancel the registration, and to prohibit the use, of a trademark which constitutes a reproduction, an imitation, or a translation, liable to create confusion, of a mark considered by the competent authority of the country of registration or use to be well known in that country as being already the mark of a person entitled to the benefits of this Convention and used for identical or similar goods. These provisions shall also apply when the essential part of the mark constitutes a reproduction of any such well-known mark or an imitation liable to create confusion therewith.

(2) A period of at least five years from the date of registration shall be allowed for requesting the cancellation of such a mark. The countries of the Union may provide for a period within which the prohibition of use must be requested.

(3) No time limit shall be fixed for requesting the cancellation or the prohibition of the use of marks registered or used in bad faith.

Article 6Ter

[Marks: Prohibitions concerning State Emblems, Official Hallmarks, and Emblems of Intergovernmental Organizations]

(1)(a) The countries of the Union agree to refuse or to invalidate the registration, **A20–016** and to prohibit by appropriate measures the use, without authorization by the competent authorities, either as trademarks or as elements of trademarks, of armorial bearings, flags, and other State emblems, of the countries of the Union, official signs and hallmarks indicating control and warranty adopted by them, and any imitation from a heraldic point of view.

(b) The provisions of subparagraph (a), above, shall apply equally to armorial bearings, flags, other emblems, abbreviations, and names, of international intergovernmental organizations of which one or more countries of the Union are members, with the exception of armorial bearings, flags, other emblems, abbreviations, and names, that are already the subject of international agreements in force, intended to ensure their protection.

(c) No country of the Union shall be required to apply the provisions of subparagraph (b), above, to the prejudice of the owners of rights acquired in good faith before the entry into force, in that country, of this Convention. The countries of the Union shall not be required to apply the said provisions when the use or registration referred to in subparagraph (a), above, is not of such a nature as to suggest to the public that a connection exists between the organization concerned and the armorial bearings, flags, emblems, abbreviations, and names, or if such use or registration is probably not of such a nature as to mislead the public as to the existence of a connection between the user and the organization.

(2) Prohibition of the use of official signs and hallmarks indicating control and warranty shall apply solely in cases where the marks in which they are incorporated are intended to be used on goods of the same or a similar kind.

(3)(a) For the application of these provisions, the countries of the Union agree to communicate reciprocally, through the intermediary of the International Bureau, the list of State emblems, and official signs and hallmarks indicating control and warranty, which they desire, or may hereafter desire, to place wholly or within certain limits under the protection of this Article, and all subsequent modifications of such list. Each country of the Union shall in due course make available to the public the lists so communicated.

Nevertheless such communication is not obligatory in respect of flags of States.

(b) The provisions of subparagraph (b) of paragraph (1) of this Article shall apply only to such armorial bearings, flags, other emblems, abbreviations, and names, of international intergovernmental organizations as the latter have communicated to the countries of the Union through the intermediary of the International Bureau.

(4) Any country of the Union may, within a period of twelve months from the receipt of the notification, transmit its objections, if any, through the intermediary of the International Bureau, to the country or international intergovernmental organization concerned.

(5) In the case of State flags, the measures prescribed by paragraph (1), above, shall apply solely to marks registered after November 6, 1925.

(6) In the case of State emblems other than flags, and of official signs and hallmarks of the countries of the Union, and in the case of armorial bearings, flags, other emblems, abbreviations, and names, of international intergovernmental organizations, these provisions shall apply only to marks registered more than two months after receipt of the communication provided for in paragraph (3), above.

(7) In cases of bad faith, the countries shall have the right to cancel even those marks incorporating State emblems, signs, and hallmarks, which were registered before November 6, 1925.

(8) Nationals of any country who are authorized to make use of the State emblems, signs, and hallmarks, of their country may use them even if they are similar to those of another country.

(9) The countries of the Union undertake to prohibit the unauthorized use in trade of the State armorial bearings of the other countries of the Union, when the use is of such a nature as to be misleading as to the origin of the goods.

(10) The above provisions shall not prevent the countries from exercising the right given in paragraph (3) of Article 6quinquies, Section B, to refuse or to invalidate the registration of marks incorporating, without authorization, armorial bearings, flags, other State emblems, or official signs and hallmarks adopted by a country of the Union, as well as the distinctive signs of international intergovernmental organizations referred to in paragraph (1), above.

Article 6Quater

[Marks: Assignment of Marks]

A20–017 (1) When, in accordance with the law of a country of the Union, the assignment of a mark is valid only if it takes place at the same time as the transfer of the business or goodwill to which the mark belongs, it shall suffice for the recognition of such validity that the portion of the business or goodwill located in that country be transferred to the assignee, together with the exclusive right to manufacture in the said country, or to sell therein, the goods bearing the mark assigned.

(2) The foregoing provision does not impose upon the countries of the Union any obligation to regard as valid the assignment of any mark the use of which by the assignee would, in fact, be of such a nature as to mislead the public, particularly as regards the origin, nature, or essential qualities, of the goods to which the mark is applied.

Article 6Quinquies

[Marks: Protection of Marks Registered in One Country of the Union in the Other Countries of the Union]

A20–018 A.—

(1) Every trademark duly registered in the country of origin shall be accepted for filing and protected as in the other countries of the Union, subject to the reservations indicated in this Article. Such countries may, before proceeding to final registration, require the production of a certificate of registration in the country of origin, issued by the competent authority. No authentication shall be required for this certificate.

(2) Shall be considered the country of origin the country of the Union where the applicant has a real and effective industrial or commercial establishment, or, if he has no such establishment within the Union, the country of the Union where he has his domicile, or, if he has no domicile within the Union but is a national of a country of the Union, the country of which he is a national.

B.—Trademarks covered by this Article may be neither denied registration nor invalidated except in the following cases:

1. when they are of such a nature as to infringe rights acquired by third parties in the country where protection is claimed;
2. when they are devoid of any distinctive character, or consist exclusively of signs or indications which may serve, in trade, to designate the kind, quality, quantity, intended purpose, value, place of origin, of the goods, or the time of production, or have become customary in the current language or in the bona fide and established practices of the trade of the country where protection is claimed;
3. when they are contrary to morality or public order and, in particular, of such a nature as to deceive the public. It is understood that a mark may not be considered contrary to public order for the sole reason that it does not conform to a provision of the legislation on marks, except if such provision itself relates to public order.

This provision is subject, however, to the application of Article 10Bis.

C.—

(1) In determining whether a mark is eligible for protection, all the factual circumstances must be taken into consideration, particularly the length of time the mark has been in use.

(2) No trademark shall be refused in the other countries of the Union for the sole reason that it differs from the mark protected in the country of origin only in respect of elements that do not alter its distinctive character and do not affect its identity in the form in which it has been registered in the said country of origin.

D.—No person may benefit from the provisions of this Article if the mark for which he claims protection is not registered in the country of origin.

F.—However, in no case shall the renewal of the registration of the mark in the country of origin involve an obligation to renew the registration in the other countries of the Union in which the mark has been registered.

F.—The benefit of priority shall remain unaffected for applications for the registration of marks filed within the period fixed by Article 4, even if registration in the country of origin is effected after the expiration of such period.

Article 6Sexies

[Marks: Service Marks]

The countries of the Union undertake to protect service marks. They shall not be required to provide for the registration of such marks.   A20–019

Article 6Septies

[Marks: Registration in the Name of the Agent or Representative of the Proprietor Without the Latter's Authorization]

(1) If the agent or representative of the person who is the proprietor of a mark in one of the countries of the Union applies, without such proprietor's authorization, for the registration of the mark in his own name, in one or more countries of the Union, the proprietor shall be entitled to oppose the registration applied for or   A20–020

demand its cancellation or, if the law of the country so allows, the assignment in his favor of the said registration, unless such agent or representative justifies his action.

(2) The proprietor of the mark shall, subject to the provisions of paragraph (1), above, be entitled to oppose the use of his mark by his agent or representative if he has not authorized such use.

(3) Domestic legislation may provide an equitable time limit within which the proprietor of a mark must exercise the rights provided for in this Article.

Article 7

[Marks: Nature of the Goods to which the Mark is Applied]

A20–021   The nature of the goods to which a trade mark is to be applied shall in no case form an obstacle to the registration of the mark.

Article 7Bis

[Marks: Collective Marks]

A20–022   (1) The countries of the Union undertake to accept for filing and to protect collective marks belonging to associations the existence of which is not contrary to the law of the country of origin, even if such associations do not possess an industrial or commercial establishment.

(2) Each country shall be the judge of the particular conditions under which a collective mark shall be protected and may refuse protection if the mark is contrary to the public interest.

(3) Nevertheless, the protection of these marks shall not be refused to any association the existence of which is not contrary to the law of the country of origin, on the ground that such association is not established in the country where protection is sought or is not constituted according to the law of the latter country.

Article 8

[Trade Names]

A20–023   A trade name shall be protected in all the countries of the Union without the obligation of filing or registration, whether or not it forms part of a trademark.

Article 9

[Marks, Trade Names: Seizure, on Importation, etc., of Goods Unlawfully Bearing a Mark or Trade Name]

A20–024   (1) All goods unlawfully bearing a trademark or trade name shall be seized on importation into those countries of the Union where such mark or trade name is entitled to legal protection.

(2) Seizure shall likewise be effected in the country where the unlawful affixation occurred or in the country into which the goods were imported.

(3) Seizure shall take place at the request of the public prosecutor, or any other competent authority, or any interested party, whether a natural person or a legal entity, in conformity with the domestic legislation of each country.

(4) The authorities shall not be bound to effect seizure of goods in transit.

(5) If the legislation of a country does not permit seizure on importation, seizure shall be replaced by prohibition of importation or by seizure inside the country.

(6) If the legislation of a country permits neither seizure on importation nor

prohibition of importation nor seizure inside the country, then, until such time as the legislation is modified accordingly, these measures shall be replaced by the actions and remedies available in such cases to nationals under the law of such country.

Article 10

[False Indications: Seizure, on Importation, etc., of Goods Bearing False Indications as to their Source or the Identity of the Producer]

(1) The provisions of the preceding Article shall apply in cases of direct or indirect use of a false indication of the source of the goods or the identity of the producer, manufacturer, or merchant.

A20–025

(2) Any producer, manufacturer, or merchant, whether a natural person or a legal entity, engaged in the production or manufacture of or trade in such goods and established either in the locality falsely indicated as the source, or in the region where such locality is situated, or in the country falsely indicated, or in the country where the false indication of source is used, shall in any case be deemed an interested party.

Article 10Bis

[Unfair Competition]

(1) The countries of the Union are bound to assure to nationals of such countries effective protection against unfair competition.

A20–026

(2) Any act of competition contrary to honest practices in industrial or commercial matters constitutes an act of unfair competition.

(3) The following in particular shall be prohibited:
1. all acts of such a nature as to create confusion by any means whatever with the establishment, the goods, or the industrial or commercial activities, of a competitor;
2. false allegations in the course of trade of such a nature as to discredit the establishment, the goods, or the industrial or commercial activities, of a competitor;
3. indications or allegations the use of which in the course of trade is liable to mislead the public as to the nature, the manufacturing process, the characteristics, the suitability for their purpose, or the quantity, of the goods.

Article 10Ter

[Marks, Trade Names, False Indications, Unfair Competition: Remedies, Right to Sue]

(1) The countries of the Union undertake to assure to nationals of the other countries of the Union appropriate legal remedies effectively to repress all the acts referred to in Articles 9, 10, and 10Bis.

A20–027

(2) They undertake, further, to provide measures to permit federations and associations representing interested industrialists, producers, or merchants, provided that the existence of such federations and associations is not contrary to the laws of their countries, to take action in the courts or before the administrative authorities, with a view to the repression of the acts referred to in Articles 9, 10, and 10Bis, in so far as the law of the country in which protection is claimed allows such action by federations and associations of that country.

Article 11

[Inventions, Utility Models, Industrial Designs, Marks: Temporary Protection at Certain International Exhibitions]

A20–028 (1) The countries of the Union shall, in conformity with their domestic legislation, grant temporary protection to patentable inventions, utility models, industrial designs, and trademarks, in respect of goods exhibited at official or officially recognized international exhibitions held in the territory of any of them.

(2) Such temporary protection shall not extend the periods provided by Article 4. If, later, the right of priority is invoked, the authorities of any country may provide that the period shall start from the date of introduction of the goods into the exhibition.

(3) Each country may require, as proof of the identity of the article exhibited and of the date of its introduction, such documentary evidence as it considers necessary.

Article 12

[Special National Industrial Property Services]

A20–029 (1) Each country of the Union undertakes to establish a special industrial property service and a central office for the communication to the public of patents, utility models, industrial designs, and trademarks.

(2) This service shall publish an official periodical journal. It shall publish regularly:

- (a) the names of the proprietors of patents granted, with a brief designation of the inventions patented;
- (b) the reproductions of registered trademarks.

Article 13

[Assembly of the Union]

A20–030 (1)(a)The Union shall have an Assembly consisting of those countries of the Union which are bound by Articles 13 to 17.

- (b) The Government of each country shall be represented by one delegate, who may be assisted by alternate delegates, advisors, and experts.
- (c) The expenses of each delegation shall be borne by the Government which has appointed it.

(2)(a)The Assembly shall:

- (i) deal with all matters concerning the maintenance and development of the Union and the implementation of this Convention;
- (ii) give directions concerning the preparation for conferences of revision to the International Bureau of Intellectual Property (hereinafter designated as "the International Bureau") referred to in the Convention establishing the World Intellectual Property Organization[84] (hereinafter designated as "the Organization"), due account being taken of any comments made by those countries of the Union which are not bound by Articles 13 to 17;
- (iii) review and approve the reports and activities of the Director-General of the Organization concerning the Union, and give him all necessary instructions concerning matters within the competence of the Union;
- (iv) elect the members of the Executive Committee of the Assembly;
- (v) review and approve the reports and activities of its Executive Committee, and give instructions to such Committee;

---

[84] Treaty Series No. 52 (1970), Cmnd. 4408.

(vi) determine the program and adopt the triennial budget of the Union, and approve its final accounts;

(vii) adopt the financial regulations of the Union;

(viii) establish such committees of experts and working groups as it deems appropriate to achieve the objectives of the Union;

(ix) determine which countries not members of the Union and which intergovernmental and international nongovernmental organizations shall be admitted to its meetings as observers;

(x) adopt amendments to Articles 13 to 17;

(xi) take any other appropriate action designed to further the objectives of the Union;

(xii) perform such other functions as are appropriate under this Convention;

(xiii) subject to its acceptance, exercise such rights as are given to it in the Convention establishing the Organization.

(b) With respect to matters which are of interest also to other Unions administered by the Organization, the Assembly shall make its decisions after having heard the advice of the Coordination Committee of the Organization.

(3)(a) Subject to the provisions of subparagraph (b), a delegate may represent one country only.

(b) Countries of the Union grouped under the terms of a special agreement in a common office possessing for each of them the character of a special national service of industrial property as referred to in Article 12 may be jointly represented during discussions by one of their number.

(4)(a) Each country member of the Assembly shall have one vote.

(b) One-half of the countries members of the Assembly shall constitute a quorum.

(c) Notwithstanding the provisions of subparagraph (b), if, in any session, the number of countries represented is less than one-half but equal to or more than one-third of the countries members of the Assembly, the Assembly may make decisions but, with the exception of decisions concerning its own procedure, all such decisions shall take effect only if the conditions set forth hereinafter are fulfilled. The International Bureau shall communicate the said decisions to the countries members of the Assembly which were not represented and shall invite them to express in writing their vote or abstention within a period of three months from the date of the communication. If, at the expiration of this period, the number of countries having thus expressed their vote or abstention attains the number of countries which was lacking for attaining the quorum in the session itself, such decisions shall take effect provided that at the same time the required majority still obtains.

(d) Subject to the provisions of Article 17 (2), the decisions of the Assembly shall require two-thirds of the votes cast.

(e) Abstentions shall not be considered as votes.

(5)(a) Subject to the provisions of subparagraph (b), a delegate may vote in the name of one country only.

(b) The countries of the Union referred to in paragraph (3)(b) shall, as a general rule, endeavor to send their own delegations to the sessions of the Assembly. If, however, for exceptional reasons, any such country cannot send its own delegation, it may give to the delegation of another such country the power to vote in its name, provided that each delegation may vote by proxy for one country only. Such power to vote shall be granted in a document signed by the Head of State or the competent Minister.

(6) Countries of the Union not members of the Assembly shall be admitted to the meetings of the latter as observers.

(7)(a) The Assembly shall meet once in every third calendar year in ordinary session upon convocation by the Director-General and, in the absence of exceptional circumstances, during the same period and at the same place as the General Assembly of the Organization.

(b) The Assembly shall meet in extraordinary session upon convocation by the Director-General, at the request of the Executive Committee or at the request of one-fourth of the countries members of the Assembly.

(8) The Assembly shall adopt its own rules of procedure.

Article 14

[Executive Committee]

A20–031

(1) The Assembly shall have an Executive Committee.

(2)(a) The Executive Committee shall consist of countries elected by the Assembly from among countries members of the Assembly. Furthermore, the country on whose territory the Organization has its headquarters shall, subject to the provisions of Article 16(7)(b), have an *ex officio* seat on the Committee.

(b) The Government of each country member of the Executive Committee shall be represented by one delegate, who may be assisted by alternate delegates, advisors, and experts.

(c) The expenses of each delegation shall be borne by the Government which has appointed it.

(3) The number of countries members of the Executive Committee shall correspond to one-fourth of the number of countries members of the Assembly. In establishing the number of seats to be filled, remainders after division by four shall be disregarded.

(4) In electing the members of the Executive Committee, the Assembly shall have due regard to an equitable geographical distribution and to the need for countries party to the Special Agreements established in relation with the Union to be among the countries constituting the Executive Committee.

(5)(a) Each member of the Executive Committee shall serve from the close of the session of the Assembly which elected it to the close of the next ordinary session of the Assembly.

(b) Members of the Executive Committee may be re-elected, but only up to a maximum of two-thirds of such members.

(c) The Assembly shall establish the details of the rules governing the election and possible re-election of the members of the Executive Committee.

(6)(a) The Executive Committee shall:

(i) prepare the draft agenda of the Assembly;

(ii) submit proposals to the Assembly in respect of the draft program and triennial budget of the Union prepared by the Director-General;

(iii) *[deleted]*

(iv) submit, with appropriate comments, to the Assembly the periodical reports of the Director-General and the yearly audit reports on the accounts;

(v) take all necessary measures to ensure the execution of the program of the Union by the Director-General, in accordance with the decisions of the Assembly and having regard to circumstances arising between two ordinary sessions of the Assembly;

(vi) perform such other functions as are allocated to it under this Convention.

(b) With respect to matters which are of interest also to other Unions administered by the Organization, the Executive Committee shall make its decisions after having heard the advice of the Coordination Committee of the Organization.

(7)(a) The Executive Committee shall meet once a year in ordinary session upon convocation by the Director-General, preferably during the same period and at the same place as the Coordination Committee of the Organization.

(b) The Executive Committee shall meet in extraordinary session upon convocation by the Director-General, either on his own initiative, or at the request of its Chairman or one-fourth of its members.

(8)(a) Each country member of the Executive Committee shall have one vote.

(b) One-half of the members of the Executive Committee shall constitute a quorum.

(c) Decisions shall be made by a simple majority of the votes cast.

(d) Abstentions shall not be considered as votes.

(e) A delegate may represent, and vote in the name of, one country only.

(9) Countries of the Union not members of the Executive Committee shall be admitted to its meetings as observers.

(10) The Executive Committee shall adopt its own rules of procedure.

Article 15

[International Bureau]

(1)(a) Administrative tasks concerning the Union shall be performed by the International Bureau, which is a continuation of the Bureau of the Union united with the Bureau of the Union established by the International Convention for the Protection of Literary and Artistic Works.[85] **A20–032**

(b) In particular, the International Bureau shall provide the secretariat of the various organs of the Union.

(c) The Director-General of the Organization shall be the chief executive of the Union and shall represent the Union.

(2) The International Bureau shall assemble and publish information concerning the protection of industrial property. Each country of the Union shall promptly communicate to the International Bureau all new laws and official texts concerning the protection of industrial property. Furthermore, it shall furnish the International Bureau with all the publications of its industrial property service of direct concern to the protection of industrial property which the International Bureau may find useful in its work.

(3) The International Bureau shall publish a monthly periodical.

(4) The International Bureau shall, on request, furnish any country of the Union with information on matters concerning the protection of industrial property.

(5) The International Bureau shall conduct studies, and shall provide services, designed to facilitate the protection of industrial property.

(6) The Director-General and any staff member designated by him shall participate, without the right to vote, in all meetings of the Assembly, the Executive Committee, and any other committee of experts or working group. The Director-General, or a staff member designated by him, shall be *ex officio* secretary of these bodies.

(7)(a) The International Bureau shall, in accordance with the directions of the As-

---

[85] Treaty Series No. 53 (1970), Cmnd. 4412.

sembly and in cooperation with the Executive Committee, make the preparations for the conferences of revision of the provisions of the Convention other than Articles 13 to 17.

(b) The International Bureau may consult with intergovernmental and international non-governmental organizations concerning preparations for conferences of revision.

(c) The Director-General and persons designated by him shall take part, without the right to vote, in the discussions at these conferences.

(8) The International Bureau shall carry out any other tasks assigned to it.

Article 16

[Finances]

A20–033   (1)(a)The Union shall have a budget.

(b) The budget of the Union shall include the income and expenses proper to the Union, its contribution to the budget of expenses common to the Unions, and, where applicable, the sum made available to the budget of the Conference of the Organization.

(c) Expenses not attributable exclusively to the Union but also to one or more other Unions administered by the Organization shall be considered as expenses common to the Unions. The share of the Union in such common expenses shall be in proportion to the interest the Union has in them.

(2) The budget of the Union shall be established with due regard to the requirements of coordination with the budgets of the other Unions administered by the Organization.

(3) The budget of the Union shall be financed from the following sources:

(i) contributions of the countries of the Union;

(ii) fees and charges due for services rendered by the International Bureau in relation to the Union;

(iii) sale of, or royalties on, the publications of the International Bureau concerning the Union;

(iv) gifts, bequests, and subventions;

(v) rents, interests, and other miscellaneous income.

(4)(a)For the purpose of establishing its contribution towards the budget each country of the Union shall belong to a class, and shall pay its annual contributions on the basis of a number of units fixed as follows:

Class I	25
Class II	20
Class III	15
Class IV	10
Class V	5
Class VI	3
Class VII	1

(b) Unless it has already done so, each country shall indicate, concurrently with depositing its instrument of ratification or accession, the class to which it wishes to belong. Any country may change class. If it chooses a lower class, the country must announce such change to the Assembly at one of its ordinary sessions. Any such change shall take effect at the beginning of the calendar year following the said session.

(c) The annual contribution of each country shall be an amount in the same proportion to the total sum to be contributed to the budget of the Union by all countries as the number of its units is to the total of the units of all contributing countries.

(d) Contributions shall become due on the first of January of each year.

(e) A country which is in arrears in the payment of its contributions may not exercise its right to vote in any of the organs of the Union of which it is a member if the amount of its arrears equals or exceeds the amount of the contributions due from it for the preceding two full years. However, any organ of the Union may allow such a country to continue to exercise its right to vote in that organ if, and as long as, it is satisfied that the delay in payment is due to exceptional and unavoidable circumstances.

(f) If the budget is not adopted before the beginning of a new financial period, it shall be at the same level as the budget of the previous year, as provided in the financial regulations.

(5) The amount of the fees and charges due for services rendered by the International Bureau in relation to the Union shall be established, and shall be reported to the Assembly and the Executive Committee, by the Director-General.

(6)(a) The Union shall have a working capital fund which shall be constituted by a single payment made by each country of the Union. If the fund becomes insufficient, the Assembly shall decide to increase it.

(b) The amount of the initial payment of each country to the said fund or of its participation in the increase thereof shall be a proportion of the contribution of that country for the year in which the fund is established or the decision to increase it is made.

(c) The proportion and the terms of payment shall be fixed by the Assembly on the proposal of the Director-General and after it has heard the advice of the Coordination Committee of the Organization.

(7)(a) In the headquarters agreement concluded with the country on the territory of which the Organization has its headquarters, it shall be provided that, whenever the working capital fund is insufficient, such country shall grant advances. The amount of these advances and the conditions on which they are granted shall be the subject of separate agreements, in each case, between such country and the Organization. As long as it remains under the obligation to grant advances, such country shall have an *ex officio* seat on the Executive Committee.

(b) The country referred to in subparagraph (a) and the Organization shall each have the right to denounce the obligation to grant advances, by written notification. Denunciation shall take effect three years after the end of the year in which it has been notified.

(8) The auditing of the accounts shall be effected by one or more of the countries of the Union or by external auditors, as provided in the financial regulations. They shall be designated, with their agreement, by the Assembly.

Article 17

[Amendment of Articles 13 to 17]

(1) Proposals for the amendment of Articles 13, 14, 15, 16, and the present **A20–034** Article, may be initiated by any country member of the Assembly, by the Executive Committee, or by the Director-General. Such proposals shall be communicated by the Director-General to the member countries of the Assembly at least six months in advance of their consideration by the Assembly.

(2) Amendments to the Articles referred to in paragraph (1) shall be adopted by the Assembly. Adoption shall require three-fourths of the votes cast, provided that any amendment to Article 13, and to the present paragraph, shall require four-fifths of the votes cast.

(3) Any amendment to the Articles referred to in paragraph (1) shall enter into

force one month after written notifications of acceptance, effected in accordance with their respective constitutional processes, have been received by the Director-General from three-fourths of the countries members of the Assembly at the time it adopted the amendment. Any amendment to the said Articles thus accepted shall bind all the countries which are members of the Assembly at the time the amendment enters into force, or which become members thereof at a subsequent date, provided that any amendment increasing the financial obligations of countries of the Union shall bind only those countries which have notified their acceptance of such amendment.

Article 18

[Revision of Articles 1 to 12 and 18 to 30]

A20–035   (1) This Convention shall be submitted to revision with a view to the introduction of amendments designed to improve the system of the Union.

(2) For that purpose, conferences shall be held successively in one of the countries of the Union among the delegates of the said countries.

(3) Amendments to Articles 13 to 17 are governed by the provisions of Article 17.

Article 19

[Special Agreements]

A20–036   It is understood that the countries of the Union reserve the right to make separately between themselves special agreements for the protection of industrial property, in so far as these agreements do not contravene the provisions of this Convention.

Article 20

[Ratification or Accession by Countries of the Union; Entry Into Force]

A20–037   (1)(a)Any country of the Union which has signed this Act may ratify it, and if it has not signed it, may accede to it. Instruments of ratification and accession shall be deposited with the Director-General.

(b) Any country of the Union may declare in its instrument of ratification or accession that its ratification or accession shall not apply:

(a) to Articles 1 to 12, or

(ii) to Articles 13 to 17.

(c) Any country of the Union which, in accordance with subparagraph (b), has excluded from the effects of its ratification or accession one of the two groups of Articles referred to in that subparagraph may at any later time declare that it extends the effects of its ratification or accession to that group of Articles. Such declaration shall be deposited with the Director-General.

(2)(a)Articles 1 to 12 shall enter into force, with respect to the first ten countries of the Union which have deposited instruments of ratification or accession without making the declaration permitted under paragraph (1) (b) (i), three months after the deposit of the tenth such instrument of ratification or accession.[86]

(b) Articles 13 to 17 shall enter into force, with respect to the first ten countries of the Union which have deposited instruments of ratification or accession without making the declaration permitted under paragraph (1) (b) (ii), three

---

[86] Articles 1–12 entered into force on May 19, 1970.

months after the deposit of the tenth such instrument of ratification or accession.[87]

(c) Subject to the initial entry into force, pursuant to the provisions of subparagraphs (a) and (b), of each of the two groups of Articles referred to in paragraph (1) (b) (i) and (ii), and subject to the provisions of paragraph (1) (b), Articles 1 to 17 shall, with respect to any country of the Union, other than those referred to in subparagraphs (a) and (b), which deposits an instrument of ratification or accession or any country of the Union which deposits a declaration pursuant to paragraph (1) (c), enter into force three months after the date of notification by the Director-General of such deposit, unless a subsequent date has been indicated in the instrument or declaration deposited. In the latter case, this Act shall enter into force with respect to that country on the date thus indicated.

(3) With respect to any country of the Union which deposits an instrument of ratification or accession, Articles 18 to 30 shall enter into force on the earlier of the dates on which any of the groups of Articles referred to in paragraph (1) (b) enters into force with respect to that country pursuant to paragraph (2) (a), (b), or (c).[88]

Article 21

[Accession by Countries Outside the Union; Entry Into Force]

(1) Any country outside the Union may accede to this Act and thereby become a member of the Union. Instruments of accession shall be deposited with the Director-General.

A20–038

(2)(a) With respect to any country outside the Union which deposits its instrument of accession one month or more before the date of entry into force of any provisions of the present Act, this Act shall enter into force, unless a subsequent date has been indicated in the instrument of accession, on the date upon which provisions first enter into force pursuant to Article 20 (2) (a) or (b); provided that:

(a) if Articles 1 to 12 do not enter into force on that date, such country shall, during the interim period before the entry into force of such provisions, and in substitution therefor, be bound by Articles 1 to 12 of the Lisbon Act,

(ii) if Articles 13 to 17 do not enter into force on that date, such country shall, during the interim period before the entry into force of such provisions, and in substitution therefor, be bound by Articles 13 and 14 (3), (4), and (5) of the Lisbon Act.

If a country indicates a subsequent date in its instrument of accession, this Act shall enter into force with respect to that country on the date thus indicated.

(b) With respect to any country outside the Union which deposits its instrument of accession on a date which is subsequent to, or precedes by less than one month, the entry into force of one group of Articles of the present Act, this Act shall, subject to the proviso of subparagraph (a), enter into force three months after the date on which its accession has been notified by the Director-General, unless a subsequent date has been indicated in the instrument of accession. In the latter case, this Act shall enter into force with respect to that country on the date thus indicated.

---

[87] Articles 13–17 entered into force on April 26, 1970.
[88] Articles 18–30 entered into force on April 26, 1970.

(3) With respect to any country outside the Union which deposits its instrument of accession after the date of entry into force of the present Act in its entirety, or less than one month before such date, this Act shall enter into force three months after the date on which its accession has been notified by the Director-General, unless a subsequent date has been indicated in the instrument of accession. In the latter case, this Act shall enter into force with respect to that country on the date thus indicated.

Article 22

[Consequences of Ratification or Accession]

A20–039   Subject to the possibilities of exceptions provided for in Articles 20 (1) (b) and 28 (2), ratification or accession shall automatically entail acceptance of all the clauses and admission to all the advantages of this Act.

Article 23

[Accession to Earlier Acts]

A20–040   After the entry into force of this Act in its entirety, a country may not accede to earlier Acts of this Convention.

Article 24

[Territories]

A20–041   (1) Any country may declare in its instrument of ratification or accession, or may inform the Director-General by written notification any time thereafter, that this Convention shall be applicable to all or part of those territories, designated in the declaration or notification, for the external relations of which it is responsible.

(2) Any country which has made such a declaration or given such a notification may, at any time, notify the Director-General that this Convention shall cease to be applicable to all or part of such territories.

(3)(a) Any declaration made under paragraph (1) shall take effect on the same date as the ratification or accession in the instrument of which it was included, and any notification given under such paragraph shall take effect three months after its notification by the Director-General.

(b) Any notification given under paragraph (2) shall take effect twelve months after its receipt by the Director-General.

Article 25

[Implementation of the Convention on the Domestic Level]

A20–042   (1) Any country party to this Convention undertakes to adopt, in accordance with its constitution, the measures necessary to ensure the application of this Convention.

(2) It is understood that, at the time a country deposits its instrument of ratification or accession, it will be in a position under its domestic law to give effect to the provisions of this Convention.

Article 26

[Denunciation]

A20–043   (1) This Convention shall remain in force without limitation as to time.

(2) Any country may denounce this Act by notification addressed to the Director-General. Such denunciation shall constitute also denunciation of all

earlier Acts and shall affect only the country making it, the Convention remaining in full force and effect as regards the other countries of the Union.

(3) Denunciation shall take effect one year after the day on which the Director-General has received the notification.

(4) The right of denunciation provided by this Article shall not be exercised by any country before the expiration of five years from the date upon which it becomes a member of the Union.

Article 27

[Application of Earlier Acts]

(1) The present Act shall, as regards the relations between the countries to which it applies, and to the extent that it applies, replace the Convention of Paris of March 20, 1883, and the subsequent Acts of revision.   **A20–044**

(2)(a)As regards the countries to which the present Act does not apply, or does not apply in its entirety, but to which the Lisbon Act of October 31, 1958, applies, the latter shall remain in force in its entirety or to the extent that the present Act does not replace it by virtue of paragraph (1).

(b) Similarly, as regards the countries to which neither the present Act, nor portions thereof, nor the Lisbon Act applies, the London Act of June 2, 1934, shall remain in force in its entirety or to the extent that the present Act does not replace it by virtue of paragraph (1).

(c) Similarly, as regards the countries to which neither the present Act, nor portions thereof, nor the Lisbon Act, nor the London Act applies, the Hague Act of November 6, 1925, shall remain in force in its entirety or to the extent that the present Act does not replace it by virtue of paragraph (1).

(3) Countries outside the Union which become party to this Act shall apply it with respect to any country of the Union not party to this Act or which, although party to this Act, has made a declaration pursuant to Article 20(1)(b)(i). Such countries recognize that the said country of the Union may apply, in its relations with them, the provisions of the most recent Act to which it is party.

Article 28

[Disputes]

(1) Any dispute between two or more countries of the Union concerning the interpretation or application of this Convention, not settled by negotiation, may, by any one of the countries concerned, be brought before the International Court of Justice by application in conformity with the Statute of the Court,[89] unless the countries concerned agree on some other method of settlement. The country bringing the dispute before the Court shall inform the International Bureau; the International Bureau shall bring the matter to the attention of the other countries of the Union.   **A20–045**

(2) Each country may, at the time it signs this Act or deposits its instrument of ratification or accession, declare that it does not consider itself bound by the provisions of paragraph (1). With regard to any dispute between such country and any other country of the Union, the provisions of paragraph (1) shall not apply.

(3) Any country having made a declaration in accordance with the provisions of paragraph (2) may, at any time, withdraw its declaration by notification addressed to the Director-General.

---

[89] Treaty Series No. 67 (1946), Cmd. 7015.

Article 29

[Signatures, Languages, Depositary Functions]

A20–046   (1)(a)This Act shall be signed in a single copy in the French language and shall be deposited with the Government of Sweden.

(b) Official texts shall be established by the Director-General, after consultation with the interested Governments, in the English, German, Italian, Portuguese, Russian and Spanish languages, and such other languages as the Assembly may designate.

(c) In case of differences of opinion on the interpretation of the various texts, the French text shall prevail.

(2) This Act shall remain open for signature at Stockholm until January 13, 1968.

(3) The Director-General shall transmit two copies, certified by the Government of Sweden, of the signed text of this Act to the Governments of all countries of the Union and, on request, to the Government of any other country.

(4) The Director-General shall register this Act with the Secretariat of the United Nations.

(5) The Director-General shall notify the Governments of all countries of the Union of signatures, deposits of instruments of ratification or accession and any declarations included in such instruments or made pursuant to Article 20(1)(c), entry into force of any provisions of this Act, notifications of denunciation, and notifications pursuant to Article 24.

Article 30

[Transitional Provisions]

A20–047   (1) Until the first Director-General assumes office, references in this Act to the International Bureau of the Organization or to the Director-General shall be deemed to be references to the Bureau of the Union or its Director, respectively.

(2) Countries of the Union not bound byArticles 13 to 17 may, until five years after the entry into force of the Convention establishing the Organization, exercise, if they so desire, the rights provided underArticles 13 to 17 of this Act as if they were bound by those Articles. Any country desiring to exercise such rights shall give written notification to that effect to the Director General; such notification shall be effective from the date of its receipt. Such countries shall be deemed to be members of the Assembly until the expiration of the said period.

(3) As long as all the countries of the Union have not become Members of the Organization, the International Bureau of the Organization shall also function as the Bureau of the Union, and the Director General as the Director of the said Bureau.

(4) Once all the countries of the Union have become Members of the Organization, the rights, obligations, and property, of the Bureau of the Union shall devolve on the International Bureau of the Organization.

Agreement on Trade-Related Aspects of Intellectual Property Rights

MEMBERS   A21–001

Desiring to reduce distortions and impediments to international trade, and taking into account the need to promote effective and adequate protection of intellectual property rights, and to ensure that measures and procedures to enforce intellectual property rights do not themselves become barriers to legitimate trade;

Recognizing, to this end, the need for new rules and disciplines concerning:

(a) The applicability of the basic principles of GATT 1994 and of relevant international intellectual property agreements or conventions;

(b) the provision of adequate standards and principles concerning the availability, scope and use of trade-related intellectual property rights;

(c) the provision of effective and appropriate means for the enforcement of trade-related intellectual property rights, taking into account differences in national legal systems;

(d) the provision of effective and expeditious procedures for the multilateral prevention and settlement of disputes between governments; and

(e) transitional arrangements aiming at the fullest participation in the results of the negotiations;

Recognizing the need for a multilateral framework of principles, rules and disciplines dealing with international trade in counterfeit goods;

Recognizing that intellectual property rights are private rights;

Recognizing the underlying public policy objectives of national systems for the protection of intellectual property, including developmental and technological objectives;

Recognizing also the special needs of the least-developed country Members in respect of maximum flexibility in the domestic implementation of laws and regulations in order to enable them to create a sound and viable technological base;

Emphasizing the importance of reducing tensions by reaching strengthened commitments to resolve disputes on trade-related intellectual property issues through multilateral procedures;

Desiring to establish a mutually supportive relationship between the WTO and the World Intellectual Property Organization (referred to in this Agreement as "WIPO") as well as other relevant international organizations;

HEREBY AGREE AS FOLLOWS:

PART I.

GENERAL PROVISIONS AND BASIC PRINCIPLES

Article 1

Nature and scope of obligations

1. Members shall give effect to the provisions of this Agreement. Members   A21–002

may, but shall not be obliged to, implement in their law more extensive protection than is required by this Agreement, provided that such protection does not contravene the provisions of this Agreement. Members shall be free to determine the appropriate method of implementing the provisions of this Agreement within their own legal system and practice.

2. For the purposes of this Agreement, the term "intellectual property" refers to all categories of intellectual property that are the subject of Sections 1 through 7 of Part II.

3. Members shall accord the treatment provided for in this Agreement to the nationals of other Members.[90] In respect of the intellectual property right, the nationals of other Members shall be understood as those natural or legal persons that would meet the criteria for eligibility for protection provided for in the Paris Convention (1967), the Berne Convention (1971), the Rome Convention and the Treaty on Intellectual Property in Respect of Integrated Circuits, were all Members of the WTO members of those conventions.[91] Any Member availing itself of the possibilities provided in paragraph 3 of Article 5 or paragraph 2 of Article 6 of the Rome Convention shall make a notification as foreseen in those provisions to the Council for Trade-Related Aspects of Intellectual Property Rights (the "Council for TRIPs")

Article 2

Intellectual property conventions

A21–003   1. In respect of Parts II, III and IV of this Agreement, Members shall comply with Articles 1 through 12, and Article 19, of the Paris Convention (1967).

2. Nothing in Parts I to IV of this Agreement shall derogate from existing obligations that Members may have to each other under the Paris Convention, the Berne Convention, the Rome Convention and the Treaty on Intellectual Property in Respect of Integrated Circuits.

Article 3

National treatment

A21–004   1. Each Member shall accord to the nationals of other Members treatment no less favourable than that it accords to its own nationals with regard to the protection[92] of intellectual property, subject to the exceptions already provided in, respectively, the Paris Convention (1967), the Berne Convention (1971), the Rome Convention or the Treaty on Intellectual Property in Respect of Integrated

---

[90] When "nationals" are referred to in this Agreement, they shall be deemed, in the case of a separate customs territory Member of the WTO, to mean persons, natural or legal, who are domiciled or who have a real and effective industrial or commercial establishment in that customs territory.

[91] In this Agreement, " Paris Convention" refers to the Paris Convention for the Projection of Industrial Property; " Paris Convention (1967)" refers to the Stockholm Act of this Convention of 14 July 1967. " Berne Convention" refers to the Berne Convention for the Protection of Literary and Artistic Works; " Berne Convention (1971)" refers to the Paris Act of this Convention of 24 July 1971. " Rome Convention" refers to the International Convention for the Protection of Performers, Producers of Phonograms and Broadcasting Organizations, adopted at Rome on 26 October 1961. "Treaty on Intellectual Property in Respect of Integrated Circuits" (IPIC Treaty) refers to the Treaty on Intellectual Property in Respect of Integrated Circuits, adopted at Washington on 26 May 1989 " WTO Agreement" refers to the Agreement Establishing the WTO.

[92] For the purposes of Article 3 and 4, "protection" shall include matters affecting the availability, acquisition, scope, maintenance and enforcement of intellectual property rights as well as those matters affecting the use of intellectual property rights specifically addressed in this Agreement.

Circuits. In respect of performers, producers of phonograms and broadcasting organizations, this obligation only applies in respect of the rights provided under this Agreement. Any Member availing itself of the possibilities provided in Article 6 of the Berne Convention (1971) or paragraph 1(b) of Article 16 of the Rome Convention shall make a notification as foreseen in those provisions to the Council for TRIPs.

2. Members may avail themselves of the exceptions permitted under paragraph 1 in relation to judicial and administrative procedures, including the designation of an address for service or the appointment of an agent within the jurisdiction of a Member, only where such exceptions are necessary to secure compliance with laws and regulations which are not inconsistent with the provisions of this Agreement and where such practices are not applied in a manner which would constitute a disguised restriction on trade.

Article 4
Most-favoured-nation treatment

With regard to the protection of intellectual property, any advantage, favour, privilege or immunity granted by a Member to the nationals of any other country shall be accorded immediately and unconditionally to the nationals of all other Members. Exempted from this obligation are any advantage, favour, privilege or immunity accorded by a Member:

A21–005

(a) deriving from international agreements on judicial assistance or law enforcement of a general nature and not particularly confined to the protection of intellectual property;
(b) granted in accordance with the provisions of the Berne Convention (1971) or the Rome Convention authorizing that the treatment accorded be a function not of national treatment but of the treatment accorded in another country;
(c) in respect of the rights of performers, producers of phonograms and broadcasting organizations not provided under this Agreement;
(d) deriving from international agreements related to the protection of intellectual property which entered into force prior to the entry into force of the WTO Agreement, provided that such agreements are notified to the Council for TRIPs and do not constitute an arbitrary or unjustifiable discrimination against nationals of other Members.

Article 5
Multilateral agreements on acquisition or maintenance of protection

The obligations under Articles 3 and 4 do not apply to procedures provided in multilateral agreements concluded under the auspices of WIPO relating to the acquisition or maintenance of intellectual property rights.

A21–006

Article 6
Exhaustion

For the purposes of dispute settlement under this Agreement, subject to the provisions of Articles 3 and 4 nothing in this Agreement shall be used to address the issue of the exhaustion of intellectual property rights.

A21–007

Article 7
Objectives

The protection and enforcement of intellectual property rights should contrib-

A21–008

ute to the promotion of technological innovation and to the transfer and dissemination of technology, to the mutual advantage of producers and users of technological knowledge and in a manner conducive to social and economic welfare, and to a balance of rights and obligations.

Article 8

Principles

A21–009   Members may, in formulating or amending their laws and regulations, adopt measures necessary to protect public health and nutrition, and to promote the public interest in sectors of vital importance to their socio-economic and technological development, provided that such measures are consistent with the provisions of this Agreement.

2. Appropriate measures, provided that they are consistent with the provisions of this Agreement, may be needed to prevent the abuse of intellectual property rights by right holders or the resort to practices which unreasonably restrain trade or adversely affect the international transfer of technology.

Part II.

Standards Concerning the Availability, Scope and Use of Intellectual Property Rights

Section 1. —Copyright and related rights

Article 9

Relation to the Berne Convention

A21–010   1. Members shall comply with Articles 1 through 21 of the Berne Convention (1971) and the Appendix thereto. However, Members shall not have rights or obligations under this Agreement in respect of the rights conferred under Article 6Bis of that Convention or of the rights derived therefrom.

2. Copyright protection shall extend to expressions and not to ideas, procedures, methods of operation or mathematical concepts as such.

Article 10

Computer programs and compilations of data

A21–011   1. Computer programs, whether in source or object code, shall be protected as literary works under the Berne Convention (1971).

2. Compilations of data or other material, whether in machine readable or other form, which by reason of the selection or arrangement of their contents constitute intellectual creations shall be protected as such. Such protection, which shall not extend to the data or material itself, shall be without prejudice to any copyright subsisting in the data or material itself.

Article 11

Rental rights

A21–012   In respect of at least computer programs and cinematographic works, a Member shall provide authors and their successors in title the right to authorize or to prohibit the commercial rental to the public of originals or copies of their copyright works. A Member shall be excepted from this obligation in respect of cinematographic works unless such rental has led to widespread copying of such works which is materially impairing the exclusive right of reproduction conferred in that Member on authors and their successors in title. In respect of computer programs, this obligation does not apply to rentals where the program itself is not the essential object of the rental.

Article 12

Term of protection

Whenever the term of protection of a work, other than a photographic work or a work of applied art, is calculated on a basis other than the life of a natural person, such term shall be no less than 50 years from the end of the calendar year of authorized publication, or, failing such authorized publication within 50 years from the making of the work, 50 years from the end of the calendar year of making.   **A21–013**

Article 13

Limitations and exceptions

Members shall confine limitations or exceptions to exclusive rights to certain special cases which do not conflict with a normal exploitation of the work and do not unreasonably prejudice the legitimate interests of the right holder.   **A21–014**

Article 14

Protection of performers, producers of phonograms (sound recordings) and broadcasting organizations

1. In respect of a fixation of their performance on a phonogram, performers shall have the possibility of preventing the following acts when undertaken without their authorization: the fixation of their unfixed performance and the reproduction of such fixation. Performers shall also have the possibility of preventing the following acts when undertaken without their authorization: the broadcasting by wireless means and the communication to the public of their live performance.   **A21–015**

2. Producers of phonograms shall enjoy the right to authorize or prohibit the direct or indirect reproduction of their phonograms.

3. Broadcasting organizations shall have the right to prohibit the following acts when undertaken without their authorization: the fixation, the reproduction of fixations, and the rebroadcasting by wireless means of broadcasts, as well as the communication to the public of television broadcasts of the same. Where Members do not grant such rights to broadcasting organizations, they shall provide owners of copyright in the subject matter of broadcasts with the possibility of preventing the above acts, subject to the provisions of the Berne Convention (1971).

4. The provisions of Article 11 in respect of computer programs shall apply *mutatis mutandis* to producers of phonograms and any other right holders in phonograms as determined in a Member's law. If on 15 April 1994 a Member has in force a system of equitable remuneration of right holders in respect of the rental of phonograms, it may maintain such system provided that the commercial rental

of phonograms is not giving rise to the material impairment of the exclusive rights of reproduction of right holders.

5. The term of the protection available under this Agreement to performers and producers of phonograms shall last at least until the end of a period of 50 years computed from the end of the calendar year in which the fixation was made or the performance took place. The term of protection granted pursuant to paragraph 3 shall last for at least 20 years from the end of the calendar year in which the broadcast took place.

6. Any Member may, in relation to the rights conferred under paragraphs 1, 2 and 3, provide for conditions, limitations, exceptions and reservations to the extent permitted by the Rome Convention. However, the provisions of Article 18 of the Berne Convention (1971) shall also apply, *mutatis mutandis*, to the rights of performers and producers of phonograms in phonograms.

Section 2. —Trademarks

Article 15

Protectable subject matter

A21–016   1. Any sign, or any combination of signs, capable of distinguishing the goods or services of one undertaking from those of other undertakings, shall be capable of constituting a trademark. Such signs, in particular words including personal names, letters, numerals, figurative elements and combinations of colours as well as any combination of such signs, shall be eligible for registration as trademarks. Where signs are not inherently capable of distinguishing the relevant goods or services, Members may make registrability depend on distinctiveness acquired through use. Members may require, as a condition of registration, that signs be visually perceptible.

2. Paragraph 1 shall not be understood to prevent a Member from denying registration of a trademark on other grounds, provided that they do not derogate from the provisions of the Paris Convention (1967).

3. Members may make registrability depend on use. However, actual use of a trademark shall not be a condition for filing an application for registration. An application shall not be refused solely on the ground that intended use has not taken place before the expiry of a period of three years from the date of application.

4. The nature of the goods or services to which a trademark is to be applied shall in no case form an obstacle to registration of the trademark.

5. Members shall publish each trademark either before it is registered or promptly after it is registered and shall afford a reasonable opportunity for petitions to cancel the registration. In addition, Members may afford an opportunity for the registration of a trademark to be opposed.

Article 16

Rights conferred

A21–017   1. The owner of a registered trademark shall have the exclusive right to prevent all third parties not having the owner's consent from using in the course of trade identical or similar signs for goods or services which are identical or similar to those in respect of which the trademark is registered where such use would result in a likelihood of confusion. In case of the use of an identical sign for identical goods or services, a likelihood of confusion shall be presumed. The rights described above shall not prejudice any existing prior rights, nor shall they affect the possibility of Members making rights available on the basis of use.

2. Article 6Bis of the Paris Convention (1967) shall apply, *mutatis mutandis*, to services. In determining whether a trademark is well-known, Members shall take account of the knowledge of the trademark in the relevant sector of the public, including knowledge in the Member concerned which has been obtained as a result of the promotion of the trademark.

3. Article 6Bis of the Paris Convention (1967) shall apply, *mutatis mutandis*, to goods or services which are not similar to those in respect of which a trademark is registered, provided that use of that trademark in relation to those goods or services would indicate a connection between those goods or services and the owner of the registered trademark and provided that the interests of the owner of the registered trademark are likely to be damaged by such use.

Article 17

Exceptions

Members may provide limited exceptions to the rights conferred by a trademark, such as fair use of descriptive terms, provided that such exceptions take account of the legitimate interests of the owner of the trademark and of third parties.   **A21–018**

Article 18

Term of protection

Initial registration, and each renewal of registration, of a trademark shall be for a term of no less than seven years. The registration of a trademark shall be renewable indefinitely.   **A21–019**

Article 19

Requirement of use

1. If use is required to maintain a registration, the registration may be cancelled only after an uninterrupted period of at least three years of non-use, unless valid reasons based on the existence of obstacles to such use are shown by the trademark owner. Circumstances arising independently of the will of the owner of the trademark which constitute an obstacle to the use of the trademark, such as import restrictions on or other government requirements for goods or services protected by the trademark, shall be recognized as valid reasons for non-use.   **A21–020**

2. When subject to the control of its owner, use of a trademark by another person shall be recognized as use of the trademark for the purpose of maintaining the registration.

Article 20

Other requirements

The use of a trademark in the course of trade shall not be unjustifiably encumbered by special requirements, such as use with another trademark, use in a special form or use in a manner detrimental to its capability to distinguish the goods or services of one undertaking from those of other undertakings. This will not preclude a requirement prescribing the use of the trademark identifying the   **A21–021** undertaking producing the goods or services along with, but without linking it to, the trademark distinguishing the specific goods or services in question of that undertaking.

Article 21

Licensing and assignment

A21–022   Members may determine conditions on the licensing and assignment of trademarks, it being understood that the compulsory licensing of trademarks shall not be permitted and that the owner of a registered trademark shall have the right to assign the trademark with or without the transfer of the business to which the trademark belongs.

Section 3. —Geographical indications

Article 22

Protection of geographical indications

A21–023   1. Geographical indications are, for the purposes of this Agreement, indications which identify a good as originating in the territory of a Member, or a region or locality in that territory, where a given quality, reputation or other characteristic of the good is essentially attributable to its geographical origin.

2. In respect of geographical indications, Members shall provide the legal means for interested parties to prevent:

(a) the use of any means in the designation or presentation of a good that indicates or suggests that the good in question originates in a geographical area other than the true place of origin in a manner which misleads the public as to the geographical origin of the good;

(b) any use which constitutes an act of unfair competition within the meaning of Article 10Bis of the Paris Convention (1967).

3. A Member shall, *ex officio* if its legislation so permits or at the request of an interested party, refuse or invalidate the registration of a trademark which contains or consists of a geographical indication with respect to goods not originating in the territory indicated, if use of the indication in the trademark for such goods in that Member is of such a nature as to mislead the public as to the true place of origin.

4. The protection under paragraphs 1, 2 and shall be applicable against a geographical indication which, although literally true as to the territory, region or locality in which the goods originate, falsely represents to the public that the goods originate in another territory.

Article 23

Additional protection for geographical indications for wines and spirits

A21–024   1. Each Member shall provide the legal means for interested parties to prevent use of a geographical indication identifying wines for wines not originating in the place indicated by the geographical indication in question or identifying spirits for spirits not originating in the place indicated by the geographical indication in question, even where the true origin of the goods is indicated or the geographical indication is used in translation or accompanied by expressions such as "kind", "style", "imitation" or the like.[93]

2. The registration of a trademark for wines which contains or consists of a geographical indication identifying wines or for spirits which contains or consists of a geographical indication identifying spirits shall be refused or invalidated, *ex officio* if a Member's legislation so permits or at the request of an interested party, with respect to such wines or spirits not having this origin.

3. In the case of homonymous geographical indications for wines, protection shall be accorded to each indication, subject to the provisions of paragraph 4 of Article 22. Each Member shall determine the practical conditions under which the homonymous indications in question will be differentiated from each other, taking into account the need to ensure equitable treatment of the producers concerned and that consumers are not misled.

4. In order to facilitate the protection of geographical indications for wines, negotiations shall be undertaken in the Council for TRIPs concerning the establishment of a multilateral system of notification and registration of geographical indications for wines eligible for protection in those Members participating in the system.

Article 24
International negotiations; exceptions

1. Members agree to enter into negotiations aimed at increasing the protection of individual geographical indications under Article 23. The provisions of paragraphs 4 through 8 below shall not be used by a Member to refuse to conduct negotiations or to conclude bilateral or multilateral agreements. In the context of such negotiations, Members shall be willing to consider the continued applicability of these provisions to individual geographical indications whose use was the subject of such negotiations.

A21–025

2. The Council for TRIPs shall keep under review the application of the provisions of this Section; the first such review shall take place within two years of the entry into force of the WTO Agreement. Any matter affecting the compliance with the obligations under these provisions may be drawn to the attention of the Council, which, at the request of a Member, shall consult with any Member or Members in respect of such matter in respect of which it has not been possible to find a satisfactory solution through bilateral or plurilateral consultations between the Members concerned. The Council shall take such action as may be agreed to facilitate the operation and further the objectives of this Section.

3. In implementing this Section, a Member shall not diminish the protection of geographical indications that existed in that Member immediately prior to the date of entry into force of the WTO Agreement.

4. Nothing in this Section shall require a Member to prevent continued and similar use of a particular geographical indication of another Member identifying wines or spirits in connection with goods or services by any of its nationals or domiciliaries who have used that geographical indication in a continuous manner with regard to the same or related goods or services in the territory of that Member either (a) for at least 10 years preceding 15 April 1994 or (b) in good faith preceding that date.

---

[93] Notwithstanding the first sentence of Article 42, Members may with respect to these obligations, instead provide for enforcement by administrative action.

5. Where a trademark has been applied for or registered in good faith, or where rights to a trademark have been acquired through use in good faith either:

(a) before the date of application of these provisions in that Member as defined in Part VI; or

(b) before the geographical indication is protected in its country of origin;

measures adopted to implement this Section shall not prejudice eligibility for or the validity of the registration of a trademark, or the right to use a trademark, on the basis that such a trademark is identical with, or similar to, a geographical indication.

6. Nothing in this Section shall require a Member to apply its provisions in respect of a geographical indication of any other Member with respect to goods or services for which the relevant indication is identical with the term customary in common language as the common name for such goods or services in the territory of that Member. Nothing in this Section shall require a Member to apply its provisions in respect of a geographical indication of any other Member with respect to products of the vine for which the relevant indication is identical with the customary name of a grape variety existing in the territory of that Member as of the date of entry into force of the WTO Agreement.

7. A Member may provide that any request made under this Section in connection with the use or registration of a trademark must be presented within five years after the adverse use of the protected indication has become generally known in that Member or after the date of registration of the trademark in that Member provided that the trademark has been published by that date, if such date is earlier than the date on which the adverse use became generally known in that Member, provided that the geographical indication is not used or registered in bad faith.

8. The provisions of this Section shall in no way prejudice the right of any person to use, in the course of trade, that person's name or the name of that person's predecessor in business, except where such name is used in such a manner as to mislead the public.

9. There shall be no obligation under this Agreement to protect geographical indications which are not or cease to be protected in their country of origin, or which have fallen into disuse in that country.

Section 4. —Industrial designs

Article 25

Requirements for protection

A21–026   1. Members shall provide for the protection of independently created industrial designs that are new or original. Members may provide that designs are not new or original if they do not significantly differ from known designs or combinations of known design features. Members may provide that such protection shall not extend to designs dictated essentially by technical or functional considerations.

2. Each Member shall ensure that requirements for securing protection for textile designs, in particular in regard to any cost, examination or publication, do not unreasonably impair the opportunity to seek and obtain such protection. Members shall be free to meet this obligation through industrial design law or through copyright law.

Article 26

Protection

1. The owner of a protected industrial design shall have the right to prevent third parties not having the owner's consent from making, selling or importing articles bearing or embodying a design which is a copy, or substantially a copy, of the protected design, when such acts are undertaken for commercial purposes.   **A21–027**

2. Members may provide limited exceptions to the protection of industrial designs, provided that such exceptions do not unreasonably conflict with the normal exploitation of protected industrial designs and do not unreasonably prejudice the legitimate interests of the owner of the protected design, taking account of the legitimate interests of third parties.

3. The duration of protection available shall amount to at least 10 years.

Section 5. —Patents

Article 27

Patentable subject matter

1. Subject to the provisions of paragraphs 2 and 3, patents shall be available for any inventions, whether products or processes, in all fields of technology, provided that they are new, involve an inventive step and are capable of industrial application.[94] Subject to paragraph 4 of Article 65, paragraph 8 of Article 70 and paragraph 3 of this Article, patents shall be available and patent rights enjoyable without discrimination as to the place of invention, the field of technology and whether products are imported or locally produced.   **A21–028**

2. Members may exclude from patentability inventions, the prevention within their territory of the commercial exploitation of which is necessary to protect *ordre public* or morality, including to protect human, animal or plant life or health or to avoid serious prejudice to the environment, provided that such exclusion is not made merely because the exploitation is prohibited by their law.

3. Members may also exclude from patentability:

(a) diagnostic, therapeutic and surgical methods for the treatment of humans or animals;

(b) plants and animals other than micro-organisms, and essentially biological processes for the production of plants or animals other than non-biological and microbiological processes. However, Members shall provide for the protection of plant varieties either by patents or by an effective *sui generis* system or by any combination thereof. The provisions of this subparagraph shall be reviewed four years after the date of entry into force of the WTO Agreement.

Article 28

Rights conferred

1. A patent shall confer on its owner the following exclusive rights: **A21–029**

(a) where the subject matter of a patent is a product, to prevent third parties not

---

[94] For the purposes of this Article, the terms "inventive step" and "capable of industrial application" may be deemed by a Member to be synonymous with the terms "non-obvious" and "useful" respectively.

having the owner's consent from the acts of: making, using, offering for sale, selling, or importing[95] for these purposes that product;

(b) where the subject matter of a patent is a process, to prevent third parties not having the owner's consent from the act of using the process, and from the acts of: using, offering for sale, selling, or importing for these purposes at least the product obtained directly by that process.

2. Patent owners shall also have the right to assign, or transfer by succession, the patent and to conclude licensing contracts.

Article 29

Conditions on patent applicants

A21–030   1. Members shall require that an applicant for a patent shall disclose the invention in a manner sufficiently clear and complete for the invention to be carried out by a person skilled in the art and may require the applicant to indicate the best mode for carrying out the invention known to the inventor at the filing date or, where priority is claimed, at the priority date of the application.

2. Members may require an applicant for a patent to provide information concerning the applicant's corresponding foreign applications and grants.

Article 30

Exceptions to rights conferred

A21–031   Members may provide limited exceptions to the exclusive rights conferred by a patent, provided that such exceptions do not unreasonably conflict with a normal exploitation of the patent and do not unreasonably prejudice the legitimate interests of the patent owner, taking account of the legitimate interests of third parties.

Article 31

Other use without authorization of the right holder

A21–032   Where the law of a Member allows for other use[96] of the subject matter of a patent without the authorization of the right holder, including use by the government or third parties authorized by the government, the following provision shall be respected:

(a) authorization of such use shall be considered on its individual merits;

(b) such use may only be permitted if, prior to such use, the proposed user has made efforts to obtain authorization from the right holder on reasonable commercial terms and conditions and that such efforts have not been successful within a reasonable period of time. This requirement may be waived by a Member in the case of a national emergency or other circumstances of extreme urgency or in cases of public non-commercial use. In situations of national emergency or other circumstances of extreme urgency, the right holder shall, nevertheless, be notified as soon as reasonably practicable. In the case of public non-commercial use, where the government or contractor, without making a patent search, knows or has demonstrable grounds to know that a valid patent is or will be used by or for the government, the right holder shall be informed promptly;

---

[95] This right, like all other rights conferred under this Agreement in respect of the use, sale, importation or other distribution of goods, is subject to the provisions of Article 6.

[96] "Other use" refers to use other than that allowed under Article 30.

(c) the scope and duration of such use shall be limited to the purpose for which it was authorized, and in the case of semi-conductor technology shall only be for public non-commercial use or to remedy a practice determined after judicial or administrative process to be anti-competitive;

(d) such use shall be non-exclusive;

(e) such use shall be non-assignable, except with that part of the enterprise or goodwill which enjoys such use;

(f) any such use shall be authorized predominantly for the supply of the domestic market of the Member authorizing such use;

(g) authorization for such use shall be liable, subject to adequate protection of the legitimate interests of the persons so authorized, to be terminated if and when the circumstances which led to it cease to exist and are unlikely to recur. The competent authority shall have the authority to review, upon motivated request, the continued existence of these circumstances;

(h) the right holder shall be paid adequate remuneration in the circumstances of each case, taking into account the economic value of the authorization;

(i) the legal validity of any decision relating to the authorization of such use shall be subject to judicial review or other independent review by a distinct higher authority in that Member;

(j) any decision relating to the remuneration provided in respect of such use shall be subject to judicial review or other independent review by a distinct higher authority in that Member;

(k) Members are not obliged to apply the conditions set forth in subparagraphs (b) and (f) where such use is permitted to remedy a practice determined after judicial or administrative process to be anti- competitive. The need to correct anti-competitive practices may be taken into account in determining the amount of remuneration in such cases. Competent authorities shall have the authority to refuse termination of authorization if and when the conditions which led to such authorization are likely to recur;

(l) where such use is authorized to permit the exploitation of a patent ("the second patent") which cannot be exploited without infringing another patent ("the first patent"), the following additional conditions shall apply:

(i) the invention claimed in the second patent shall involve an important technical advance of considerable economic significance in relation to the invention claimed in the first patent;

(ii) the owner of the first patent shall be entitled to a cross-licence on reasonable terms to use the invention claimed in the second patent; and

(iii) the use authorized in respect of the first patent shall be non-assignable except with the assignment of the second patent.

Article 32

Revocation/forfeiture

An opportunity for judicial review of any decision to revoke or forfeit a patent shall be available.   **A21–033**

Article 33

Term of protection

A21–034   The term of protection available shall not end before the expiration of a period of twenty years counted from the filing date.[97]

Article 34

Process patents: burden of proof

A21–035   1. For the purposes of civil proceedings in respect of the infringement of the rights of the owner referred to in paragraph 1(b) of Article 28, if the subject matter of a patent is a process for obtaining a product, the judicial authorities shall have the authority to order the defendant to prove that the process to obtain an identical product is different from the patented process. Therefore, Members shall provide, in at least one of the following circumstances, that any identical product when produced without the consent of the patent owner shall, in the absence of proof to the contrary, be deemed to have been obtained by the patented process:

(a) if the product obtained by the patented process is new;

(b) if there is a substantial likelihood that the identical product was made by the process and the owner of the patent has been unable through reasonable efforts to determine the process actually used.

2. Any Member shall be free to provide that the burden of proof indicated in paragraph 1 shall be on the alleged infringer only if the condition referred to in subparagraph (a) is fulfilled or only if the condition referred to in subparagraph (b) is fulfilled.

3. In the adduction of proof to the contrary, the legitimate interests of defendants in protecting their manufacturing and business secrets shall be taken into account.

Section 6. —Layout-designs (topographies) of integrated circuits

Article 35

Relation to the IPIC Treaty

A21–036   Members agree to provide protection to the layout-designs (topographies) of integrated circuits (referred to int his Agreement as "layout-designs") in accordance with Articles 2 through 7 (other than paragraph 3 of Article 6). Article 12 and paragraph 3 of Article 16 of the Treaty on Intellectual Property in Respect of Integrated Circuits and, in addition, to comply with the following provisions.

Article 36

Scope of the protection

A21–037   Subject to the provisions of paragraph 1 of Article 37, Members shall consider unlawful the following acts if performed without the authorization of the right holder[98]: importing, selling, or otherwise distributing for commercial purposes a

---

[97] It is understood that those Members which do not have a system of original grant may provide that the term of protection shall be computed from the filing date in the system of original grant.

[98] The term "right holder" in this Section shall be understood as having the same meaning as the term "holder of the right" in the IPIC Treaty.

protected layout-design, an integrated circuit in which a protected layout-design is incorporated, or an article incorporating such an integrated circuit only in so far as it continues to contain an unlawfully reproduced layout-design.

Article 37

Acts not requiring the authorization of the right holder

1. Notwithstanding Article 36, no Member shall consider unlawful the performance of any of the acts referred to in that Article in respect of an integrated circuit incorporating an unlawfully reproduced layout-design or any article incorporating such an integrated circuit where the person performing or ordering such acts did not know and had no reasonable ground to know, when acquiring the integrated circuit or article incorporating such an integrated circuit, that it incorporated an unlawfully reproduced layout-design. Members shall provide that, after the time that such person has received sufficient notice that the layout-design was unlawfully reproduced, that person may perform any of the acts with respect to the stock on hand or ordered before such time, but shall be liable to pay to the right holder a sum equivalent to a reasonable royalty such as would be payable under a freely negotiated licence in respect of such a layout-design.

A21–038

2. The conditions set out in subparagraphs (a) through (k) of Article 31 shall apply *mutatis mutandis* in the event of any non-voluntary licensing of a layout-design or of its use by or for the government without the authorization of the right holder.

Article 38

Term of protection

1. In Members requiring registration as a condition of protection, the term of protection of layout-designs shall not end before the expiration of a period of 10 years counted from the date of filing an application for registration or from the first commercial exploitation wherever in the world it occurs.

A21–039

2. In Members not requiring registration as a condition for protection, layout-designs shall be protected for a term of no less than 10 years from the date of the first commercial exploitation wherever in the world it occurs.

3. Notwithstanding paragraphs 1 and 2, a Member may provide that protection shall lapse 15 years after the creation of the layout-design.

Section 7. —protection of undisclosed information

Article 39

1. In the course of ensuring effective protection against unfair competition as provided in Article 10Bis of the Paris Convention (1967), Members shall protect undisclosed information in accordance with paragraph 2 and data submitted to governments or governmental agencies in accordance with paragraph 3.

A21–040

2. Natural and legal persons shall have the possibility of preventing information lawfully within their control from being disclosed to, acquired by, or used by others without their consent in a manner contrary to honest commercial practices[99] so long as such information:

---

[99] For the purpose of this provision, "a manner contrary to honest commercial practices" shall mean

(a) is secret in the sense that it is not, as a body or in the precise configuration and assembly of its components, generally known among or readily accessible to persons within the circles that normally deal with the kind of information in question;

(b) has commercial value because it is secret; and

(c) has been subject to reasonable steps under the circumstances, by the person lawfully in control of the information, to keep it secret.

3. Members, when requiring, as a condition of approving the marketing of pharmaceutical or of agricultural chemical products which utilize new chemical entities, the submission of undisclosed test or other data, the origination of which involves a considerable effort, shall protect such data against unfair commercial use. In addition, Members shall protect such data against disclosure, except where necessary to protect the public, or unless steps are taken to ensure that the data are protected against unfair commercial use.

Section 8. —control of anti-competitive practices in contractual licences

Article 40

A21–041   1. Members agree that some licensing practices or conditions pertaining to intellectual property rights which restrain competition may have adverse effects on trade and may impede the transfer and dissemination of technology.

2. Nothing in this Agreement shall prevent Members from specifying in their legislation licensing practices or conditions that may in particular cases constitute an abuse of intellectual property rights having an adverse effect on competition in the relevant market. As provided above, a Member may adopt, consistently with the other provisions of this Agreement, appropriate measures to prevent or control such practices, which may include for example exclusive grant-back conditions, conditions preventing challenges to validity and coercive package licensing, in the light of the relevant laws and regulations of that Member.

3. Each Member shall enter, upon request, into consultations with any other Member which has cause to believe that an intellectual property right owner that is a national or domiciliary of the Member to which the request for consultations has been addressed is undertaking practices in violation of the requesting Member's laws and regulations on the subject matter of this Section, and which wishes to secure compliance with such legislation, without prejudice to any action under the law and to the full freedom of an ultimate decision of either Member. The Member addressed shall accord full and sympathetic consideration to, and shall afford adequate opportunity for, consultations with the requesting Member, and shall cooperate through supply of publicly available non-confidential information of relevance to the matter in question and of other information available to the Member, subject to domestic law and to the conclusion of mutually satisfactory agreements concerning the safeguarding of its confidentiality by the requesting Member.

4. A Member whose nationals or domiciliaries are subject to proceedings in another Member concerning alleged violation of that other Member's laws and regulations on the subject matter of this Section shall, upon request, be granted

---

at least practices such as breach of contract, breach of confidence and inducement to breach, and includes the acquisition of undisclosed information by third parties who knew, or were grossly negligent in failing to know, that such practices were involved in the acquisition.

an opportunity for consultations by the other Member under the same conditions as those foreseen in paragraph 3.

PART III.

ENFORCEMENT OF INTELLECTUAL PROPERTY RIGHTS

Section 1. —general obligations

Article 41

1. Members shall ensure that enforcement procedures as specified in this Part **A21–042** are available under their law so as to permit effective action against any act of infringement of intellectual property rights covered by this Agreement, including expeditious remedies to prevent infringements and remedies which constitute a deterrent to further infringements. These procedures shall be applied in such a manner as to avoid the creation of barriers to legitimate trade and to provide for safeguards against their abuse.

2. Procedures concerning the enforcement of intellectual property rights shall be fair and equitable. They shall not be unnecessarily complicated or costly, or entail unreasonable time-limits or unwarranted delays.

3. Decisions on the merits of a case shall preferably be in writing and reasoned. They shall be made available at least to the parties to the proceeding without undue delay. Decisions on the merits of a case shall be based only on evidence in respect of which parties were offered the opportunity to be heard.

4. Parties to a proceeding shall have an opportunity for review by a judicial authority of final administrative decisions and, subject to jurisdictional provisions in a Member's law concerning the importance of a case, of at least the legal aspects of initial judicial decisions on the merits of a case. However, there shall be no obligation to provide an opportunity for review of acquittals in criminal cases.

5. It is understood that this Part does not create any obligation to put in place a judicial system for the enforcement of intellectual property rights distinct from that for the enforcement of law in general, nor does it affect the capacity of Members to enforce their law in general. Nothing in this Part creates any obligation with respect to the distribution of resources as between enforcement of intellectual property rights and the enforcement of law in general.

Section 2. —civil and administrative procedures and remedies

Article 42

Fair and equitable procedures

Members shall make available to right holders[1] civil judicial procedures **A21–043** concerning the enforcement of any intellectual property right covered by this Agreement. Defendants shall have the right to written notice which is timely and contains sufficient detail, including the basis of the claims. Parties shall be allowed to be represented by independent legal counsel, and procedures shall not

---

[1] For the purpose of this Part, the term "right holder" includes federations and associations having legal standing to assert such rights.

impose overly burdensome requirements concerning mandatory personal appearances. All parties to such procedures shall be duly entitled to substantiate their claims and to present all relevant evidence. The procedure shall provide a means to identify and protect confidential information, unless this would be contrary to existing constitutional requirements.

Article 43

Evidence

A21–044   1. The judicial authorities shall have the authority, where a party has presented reasonably available evidence sufficient to support its claims and has specified evidence relevant to substantiation of its claims which lies in the control of the opposing party, to order that this evidence be produced by the opposing party, subject in appropriate cases to conditions which ensure the protection of confidential information.

2. In cases in which a party to a proceeding voluntarily and without good reason refuses access to, or otherwise does not provide necessary information within a reasonable period, or significantly impedes a procedure relating to an enforcement action, a Member may accord judicial authorities the authority to make preliminary and final determinations, affirmative or negative, on the basis of the information presented to them, including the complaint or the allegation presented by the party adversely affected by the denial of access to information, subject to providing the parties an opportunity to be heard on the allegations or evidence.

Article 44

Injunctions

A21–045   1. The judicial authorities shall have the authority to order a party to desist from an infringement, *inter alia* to prevent the entry into the channels of commerce in their jurisdiction of imported goods that involve the infringement of an intellectual property right, immediately after customs clearance of such goods. Members are not obliged to accord such authority in respect of protected subject matter acquired or ordered by a person prior to knowing or having reasonable grounds to know that dealing in such subject matter would entail the infringement of an intellectual property right.

2. Notwithstanding the other provisions of this Part and provided that the provisions of Part II specifically addressing use by governments, or by third parties authorized by a government, without the authorization of the right holder are complied with, Members may limit the remedies available against such use to payment of remuneration in accordance with subparagraph (h) of Article 31. In other cases, the remedies under this Part shall apply or, where these remedies are inconsistent with a Member's law, declaratory judgments and adequate compensation shall be available.

Article 45

Damages

A21–046   1. The judicial authorities shall have the authority to order the infringer to pay the right holder damages adequate to compensate for the injury the right holder has suffered because of an infringement of that person's intellectual property right by an infringer who knowingly, or with reasonable grounds to know, engaged in infringing activity.

2. The judicial authorities shall also have the authority to order the infringer to pay the right holder expenses, which may include appropriate attorney's fees. In appropriate cases, Members may authorize the judicial authorities to order recovery of profits and/or payment of pre-established damages even where the infringer did not knowingly, or with reasonable grounds to know, engage in infringing activity.

Article 46
Other remedies

In order to create an effective deterrent to infringement, the judicial authorities shall have the authority to order that goods that they have found to be infringing be, without compensation of any sort, disposed of outside the channels of commerce in such a manner as to avoid any harm caused to the right holder, or, unless this would be contrary to existing constitutional requirements, destroyed. The judicial authorities shall also have the authority to order that materials and implements the predominant use of which has been in the creation of the infringing goods be, without compensation of any sort, disposed of outside the channels of commerce in such a manner as to minimize the risks of further infringements. In considering such requests, the need for proportionality between the seriousness of the infringement and the remedies ordered as well as the interests of third parties shall be taken into account. In regard to counterfeit trademark goods, the simple removal of the trademark unlawfully affixed shall not be sufficient, other than in exceptional cases, to permit release of the goods into the channels of commerce.

A21–047

Article 47
Right of information

Members may provide that the judicial authorities shall have the authority, unless this would be out of proportion to the seriousness of the infringement, to order the infringer to inform the right holder of the identity of third person involved in the production and distribution of the infringing goods or services and of their channels of distribution.

A21–048

Article 48
Indemnification of the defendant

1. The judicial authorities shall have the authority to order a party at whose request measures were taken and who has abused enforcement procedures to provide to a party wrongfully enjoined or restrained adequate compensation for the injury suffered because of such abuse. The judicial authorities shall also have the authority to order the applicant to pay the defendant expenses, which may include appropriate attorney's fees.

A21–049

2. In respect of the administration of any law pertaining to the protection or enforcement of intellectual property rights, Members shall only exempt both public authorities and officials from liability to appropriate remedial measures where actions are taken or intended in good faith in the course of the administration of that law.

Article 49
Administrative procedures

To the extent that any civil remedy can be ordered as a result of administrative

A21–050

procedures on the merits of a case, such procedures shall conform to principles equivalent in substance to those set forth in this Section.

Section 3. —provisional measures

Article 50

A21–051   1. The judicial authorities shall have the authority to order prompt and effective provisional measures:

(a) to prevent an infringement of any intellectual property right from occurring, and in particular to prevent the entry into the channels of commerce in their jurisdiction of goods, including imported goods immediately after customs clearance;

(b) to preserve relevant evidence in regard to the alleged infringement.

2. The judicial authorities shall have the authority to adopt provisional measures *inaudita altera parte* where appropriate, in particular where any delay is likely to cause irreparable harm to the right holder, or where there is a demonstrable risk of evidence being destroyed.

3. The judicial authorities shall have the authority to require the applicant to provide any reasonably available evidence in order to satisfy themselves with a sufficient degree of certainty that the applicant is the right holder and that the applicant's right is being infringed or that such infringement is imminent, and to order the applicant to provide a security or equivalent assurance sufficient to protect the defendant and to prevent abuse.

4. Where provisional measures have been adopted *inaudita altera parte*, the parties affected shall be given notice, without delay after the execution of the measures at the latest. A review, including a right to be heard, shall take place upon request of the defendant with a view to deciding, within a reasonable period after the notification of the measures, whether these measures shall be modified, revoked or confirmed.

5. The applicant may be required to supply other information necessary for the identification of the goods concerned by the authority that will execute the provisional measures.

6. Without prejudice to paragraph 4, provisional measures taken on the basis of paragraphs 1 and 2 shall, upon request by the defendant, be revoked or otherwise cease to have effect, if proceedings leading to a decision on the merits of the case are not initiated within a reasonable period, to be determined by the judicial authority ordering the measures where a Member's law so permits or, in the absence of such a determination, not to exceed 20 working days or 31 calendar days, whichever is the longer.

7. Where the provisional measures are revoked or where they lapse due to any act or omission by the applicant, or where it is subsequently found that there has been no infringement or threat of infringement of an intellectual property right, the judicial authorities shall have the authority to order the applicant, upon request of the defendant, to provide the defendant appropriate compensation for any injury caused by these measures.

8. To the extent that any provisional measure can be ordered as a result of administrative procedures, such procedures shall conform to principles equivalent in substance to those set forth in this Section.

Section 4. —special requirements related to border measures

Article 51

Suspension of release by customs authorities

[2] Members shall, in conformity with the provisions set out below, adopt procedures[3] to enable a right holder, who has valid grounds for suspecting that the importation of counterfeit trademark or pirated copyright goods[4] may take place, to lodge an application in writing with competent authorities, administrative or judicial, for the suspension by the customs authorities of the release into free circulation of such goods. Members may enable such an application to be made in respect of goods which involve other infringements of intellectual property rights, provided that the requirements of this Section are met. Members may also provide for corresponding procedures concerning the suspension by the customs authorities of the release of infringing goods destined for exportation from their territories.

A21–052

Article 52

Application

Any right holder initiating the procedures under Article 51 shall be required to provide adequate evidence to satisfy the competent authorities that, under the laws of the country of importation, there is *prima facie* an infringement of the right holder's intellectual property right and to supply a sufficiently detailed description of the goods to make them readily recognizable by the customs authorities. The competent authorities shall inform the applicant within a reasonable period whether they have accepted the application and, where determined by the competent authorities, the period for which the customs authorities will take action.

A21–053

Article 53

Security or equivalent assurance

1. The competent authorities shall have the authority to require an applicant to provide a security or equivalent assurance sufficient to protect the defendant and the competent authorities and to prevent abuse. Such security or equivalent assurance shall not unreasonably deter recourse to these procedures.

2. Where pursuant to an application under this Section the release of goods involving industrial designs, patents, layout-designs or undisclosed information into free circulation has been suspended by customs authorities on the basis of a

A21–054

---

[2] Where a Member has dismantled substantially all controls over movement of goods across its border with another Member with which it forms part of a customs union, it shall not be required to apply the provisions of this Section at that border.

[3] It is understood that there shall be no obligation to apply such procedures to imports of goods put on the market in another country by or with the consent of the right holder, or to goods in transit.

[4] For the purposes of this Agreement: "counterfeit trademark goods" shall mean any goods, including packaging, bearing without authorization a trademark which is identical to the trademark validly registered in respect of such goods, or which cannot be distinguished in its essential aspects from such a trademark, and which thereby infringes the rights of the owner of the trademark in question under the law of the country of importation; "pirated copyright goods" shall mean any goods which are copies made without the consent of the right holder or person duly authorized by the right holder in the country of production and which are made directly or indirectly from an article where the making of that copy would have constituted an infringement of a copyright or a related right under the law of the country of importation.

decision other than by a judicial or other independent authority, and the period provided for in Article 55 has expired without the granting of provisional relief by the duly empowered authority, and provided that all other conditions for importation have been complied with, the owner, importer, or consignee of such goods shall be entitled to their release on the posting of a security in an amount sufficient to protect the right holder for any infringement. Payment of such security shall not prejudice any other remedy available to the right holder, it being understood that the security shall be released if the right holder fails to pursue the right of action within a reasonable period of time.

Article 54

Notice of suspension

A21–055   The importer and the applicant shall be promptly notified of the suspension of the release of goods according to Article 51.

Article 55

Duration of suspension

A21–056   If, within a period not exceeding 10 working days after the applicant has been served notice of the suspension, the customs authorities have not been informed that proceedings leading to a decision on the merits of the case have been initiated by a party other than the defendant, or that the duly empowered authority has taken provisional measures prolonging the suspension of the release of the goods, the goods shall be released, provided that all other conditions for importation or exportation have been complied with; in appropriate cases, this time-limit may be extended by another 10 working days. If proceedings leading to a decision on the merits of the case have been initiated, a review, including a right to be heard, shall take place upon request of the defendant with a view to deciding, within a reasonable period, whether these measures shall be modified, revoked or confirmed. Notwithstanding the above, where the suspension of the release of goods is carried out or continued in accordance with a provisional judicial measure, the provisions of paragraph 6 of Article 50 shall apply.

Article 56

Indemnification of the importer and of the owner of the goods

A21–057   Relevant authorities shall have the authority to order the applicant to pay the importer, the consignee and the owner of the goods appropriate compensation for any injury caused to them through the wrongful detention of goods or through the detention of goods released pursuant to Article 55.

Article 57

Right of inspection and information

A21–058   Without prejudice to the protection of confidential information, Members shall provide the competent authorities the authority to give the right holder sufficient opportunity to have any goods detained by the customs authorities inspected in order to substantiate the right holder's claims. The competent authorities shall also have authority to give the importer an equivalent opportunity to have any such goods inspected. Where a positive determination has been made on the merits of a case, Members may provide the competent authorities the authority to inform the right holder of the names and addresses of the consignor, the importer and the consignee and of the quantity of the goods in question.

Article 58

Ex officio action

Where Members require competent authorities to act upon their own initiative   **A21–059**
and to suspend the release of goods in respect of which they have acquired *prima facie* evidence that an intellectual property right is being infringed:

(a) the competent authorities may at any time seek from the right holder any information that may assist them to exercise these powers;

(b) the importer and the right holder shall be promptly notified of the suspension. Where the importer has lodged an appeal against the suspension with the competent authorities, the suspension shall be subject to the conditions, *mutatis mutandis*, set out at Article 55;

(c) Members shall only exempt both public authorities and officials from liability to appropriate remedial measures where actions are taken or intended in good faith.

Article 59

Remedies

Without prejudice to other rights of action open to the right holder and subject   **A21–060**
to the right of the defendant to seek review by a judicial authority, competent authorities shall have the authority to order the destruction or disposal of infringing goods in accordance with the principles set out in Article 46. In regard to counterfeit trademark goods, the authorities shall not allow the re-exportation of the infringing goods in an unaltered state or subject them to a different customs procedure, other than in exceptional circumstances.

Article 60

De minimis imports

Members may exclude from the application of the above provisions small   **A21–061**
quantities of goods of a non-commerical nature contained in travellers' personal luggage or sent in small consignments.

Section 5. —criminal procedures

Article 61

Members shall provide for criminal procedures and penalties to be applied at   **A21–062**
least in cases of wilful trademark counterfeiting or copyright piracy on a commercial scale. Remedies available shall include imprisonment and/or monetary fines sufficient to provide a deterrent, consistently with the level of penalties applied for crimes of a corresponding gravity. In appropriate cases, remedies available shall also include the seizure, forfeiture and destruction of the infringing goods and of any materials and implements the predominant use of which has been in the commission of the offence. Members may provide for criminal procedures and penalties to be applied in other cases of infringement of intellectual property rights, in particular where they are committed wilfully and on a commercial scale.

PART IV.

ACQUISITION AND MAINTENANCE OF INTELLECTUAL PROPERTY RIGHTS AND
RELATED INTER-PARTES PROCEDURES

Article 62

A21–063   1. Members may require, as a condition of the acquisition or maintenance of the intellectual property rights provided for under Sections 2 through 6 of Part II, compliance with reasonable procedures and formalities. Such procedures and formalities shall be consistent with the provisions of this Agreement.

2. Where the acquisition of an intellectual property right is subject to the right being granted or registered, Members shall ensure that the procedures for grant or registration, subject to compliance with the substantive conditions for acquisition of the right, permit the granting or registration of the right within a reasonable period of time so as to avoid unwarranted curtailment of the period of protection.

3. Article 4of the Paris Convention (1967) shall apply *mutatis mutandis* to service marks.

4. Procedures concerning the acquisition or maintenance of intellectual property rights and, where a Member's law provides for such procedures, administrative revocation and *inter partes* procedures such as opposition, revocation and cancellation, shall be governed by the general principles set out in paragraphs 2 and 3 of Article 41.

5. Final administrative decisions in any of the procedures referred to under paragraph 4 shall be subject to review by a judicial or quasi-judicial authority. However, there shall be no obligation to provide an opportunity for such review of decisions in cases of unsuccessful opposition or administrative revocation, provided that the grounds for such procedures can be the subject of invalidation procedures.

PART V.

DISPUTE PREVENTION AND SETTLEMENT

Article 63

Transparency

A21–064   1. Laws and regulations, and final judicial decisions and administrative rulings of general application, made effective by a Member pertaining to the subject matter of this Agreement (the availability, scope, acquisition, enforcement and prevention of the abuse of intellectual property rights) shall be published, or where such publication is not practicable made publicly available, in a national language, in such a manner as to enable governments and right holders to become acquainted with them. Agreements concerning the subject matter of this Agreement which are in force between the government or a governmental agency of a Member and the government or a governmental agency of another Member shall also be published.

2. Members shall notify the laws and regulations referred to in paragraph 1 to the Council for TRIPs in order to assist that Council in its review of the operation of the Agreement. The Council shall attempt to minimize the burden on Members in carrying out this obligation and may decide to waive the obligation to notify

such laws and regulations directly to the Council if consultations with WIPO on the establishment of a common register containing these laws and regulations are successful. The Council shall also consider in this connection any action required regarding notifications pursuant to the obligations under this Agreement stemming from the provisions of Article 6Ter of the Paris Convention (1967).

3. Each Member shall be prepared to supply, in response to a written request from another Member, information of the sort referred to in paragraph 1. A Member, having reason to believe that a specific judicial decision or administrative ruling or bilateral agreement in the area of intellectual property rights affects its rights under this Agreement, may also request in writing to be given access to or be informed in sufficient detail of such specific judicial decisions or administrative rulings or bilateral agreements.

4. Nothing in paragraphs 1, 2 and 3 shall require Members to disclose confidential information which would impede law enforcement or otherwise be contrary to the public interest or would prejudice the legitimate commercial interests of particular enterprises, public or private.

Article 64

Dispute settlement

1. The provisions of Article XXII and XXIII of GATT 1994 as elaborated and applied by the Dispute Settlement Understanding shall apply to consultations and the settlement of disputes under this Agreement except as otherwise specifically provided herein.   **A21–065**

2. Subparagraphs 1(b) and 1(c) of Article XXIII of GATT 1994 shall not apply to the settlement of disputes under this Agreement for a period of five years from the date of entry into force of the WTO Agreement.

3. During the time period referred to in paragraph 2, the Council for TRIPs shall examine the scope and modalities for complaints of the type provided for under subparagraphs 1(b) and 1(c) of Article XXIII of GATT 1994 made pursuant to this Agreement, and submit its recommendations to the Ministerial Conference for approval. Any decision of the Ministerial Conference to approve such recommendations or to extend the period in paragraph 2 shall be made only by consensus, and approved recommendations shall be effective for all Members without further formal acceptance process.

PART VI.

TRANSITIONAL ARRANGEMENTS

Article 65

Transitional arrangements

1. Subject to the provisions of paragraphs 2, 3 and 4, no Member shall be obliged to apply the provisions of this Agreement before the expiry of a general period of one year following the date of entry into force of the WTO Agreement.   **A21–066**

2. A developing country Member is entitled to delay for a further period of four years the date of application, as defined in paragraph 1, of the provisions of this Agreement other than Articles 3, 4 and 5.

3. Any other Member which is in the process of transformation from a

centrally-planned into a market, free-enterprise economy and which is undertaking structural reform of its intellectual property system and facing special problems in the preparation and implementation of intellectual property laws and regulations, may also benefit from a period of delay as foreseen in paragraph 2.

4. To the extent that a developing country Member is obliged by this Agreement to extend product patent protection to areas of technology not so protectable in its territory on the general date of application of this Agreement for that Member, as defined in paragraph 2, it may delay the application of the provisions on product patents of Section 5 of Part II to such areas of technology for an additional period of five years.

5. A Member availing itself of a transitional period under paragraphs 1, 2, 3 or 4 shall ensure that any changes in its laws, regulations and practice made during that period do not result in a lesser degree of consistency with the provisions of this Agreement.

Article 66

Least-developed country Members

A21–067   1. In view of the special needs and requirements of least-developed country Members, their economic, financial and administrative constraints, and their need for flexibility to create a viable technological base, such Members shall not be required to apply the provisions of this Agreement, other than Articles 3, 4 and 5, for a period of 10 years from the date of application as defined under paragraph 1 of Article 65. The Council for TRIPs shall, upon duly motivated request by a least-developed country Member, accord extensions of this period.

2. Developed country Members shall provide incentives to enterprises and institutions in their territories for the purpose of promoting and encouraging technology transfer to least-developed country Members in order to enable them to create a sound and viable technological base.

Article 67

Technical cooperation

A21–068   In order to facilitate the implementation of this Agreement, developed country Members shall provide, on request and on mutually agreed terms and conditions, technical and financial cooperation in favour of developing and least- developed country Members. Such cooperation shall include assistance in the preparation of laws and regulations on the protection and enforcement of intellectual property rights as well as on the prevention of their abuse, and shall include support regarding the establishment or reinforcement of domestic offices and agencies relevant to these matters, including the training of personnel.

PART VII.

INSTITUTIONAL ARRANGEMENTS: FINAL PROVISIONS

Article 68

Council for Trade-Related Aspects of Intellectual Property Rights

A21–069   The Council for TRIPs shall monitor the operation of this Agreement and, in particular, Members' compliance with their obligations hereunder, and shall afford Members the opportunity of consulting on matters relating to the trade-related aspects of intellectual property rights. It shall carry out such other responsibilities as assigned to it by the Members, and it shall, in particular, provide any assistance requested by them in the context of dispute settlement procedures. In carrying out its functions, the Council for TRIPs may consult with and seek information from any source it deems appropriate. In consultation with WIPO, the Council shall seek to establish, within one year of its first meeting, appropriate arrangements for cooperation with bodies of that Organization.

Article 69
International cooperation

Members agree to cooperate with each other with a view to eliminating international trade in goods infringing intellectual property rights. For this purpose, they shall establish and notify contact points in their administrations and be ready to exchange information on trade in infringing goods. They shall, in particular, promote the exchange of information and cooperation between customs authorities with regard to trade in counterfeit trademark goods and pirated copyright goods.

A21–070

Article 70
Protection of existing subject matter

1. This Agreement does not give rise to obligations in respect of acts which occurred before the date of application of the Agreement for the Member in question.

A21–071

2. Except as otherwise provided for in this Agreement, this Agreement gives rise to obligations in respect of all subject matter existing at the date of application of this Agreement for the Member in question, and which is protected in that Member on the said date, or which meets or comes subsequently to meet the criteria for protection under the terms of this Agreement. In respect of this paragraph and paragraphs 3 and 4, copyright obligations with respect to existing works shall be solely determined under Article 18 of the Berne Convention (1971), and obligations with respect to the rights of producers of phonograms and performers in existing phonograms shall be determined solely under Article 18 of the Berne Convention (1971) as made applicable under paragraph 6 of Article 14 of this Agreement.

3. There shall be no obligation to restore protection to subject matter which on the date of application of this Agreement for the Member in question has fallen into the public domain.

4. In respect of any acts in respect of specific objects embodying protected subject matter which become infringing under the terms of legislation in conformity with this Agreement, and which were commenced, or in respect of which a significant investment was made, before the date of acceptance of the WTO Agreement by that Member, any Member may provide for a limitation of the remedies available to the right holder as to the continued performance of such acts after the date of application of this Agreement for that Member. In such cases the Member shall, however, at least provide for the payment of equitable remuneration.

5. A Member is not obliged to apply the provisions of Article 11 and of paragraph 4 of Article 14 with respect to originals or copies purchased prior to the date of application of this Agreement for that Member.

6. Members shall not be required to apply Article 31, or the requirement in paragraph 1 of Article 27 that patent rights shall be enjoyable without discrimination as to the field of technology, to use without the authorization of the right holder where authorization for such use was granted by the government before the date this Agreement became known.

7. In the case of intellectual property rights for which protection is conditional upon registration, applications for protection which are pending on the date of application of this Agreement for the Member in question shall be permitted to be amended to claim any enhanced protection provided under the provisions of this Agreement. Such amendments shall not include new matter.

8. Where a Member does not make available as of the date of entry into force of the WTO Agreement patent protection for pharmaceutical and agricultural chemical products commensurate with its obligations under Article 27, that Member shall:

(a) notwithstanding the provisions of Part VI, provide as from the date of entry into force of the WTO Agreement a means by which applications for patents for such inventions can be filed;

(b) apply to these applications, as of the date of application of this Agreement, the criteria for patentability as laid down in this Agreement as if those criteria were being applied on the date of filing in that Member or, where priority is available and claimed, the priority date of the application; and

(c) provide patent protection in accordance with this Agreement as from the grant of the patent and for the remainder of the patent term, counted from the filing date in accordance with Article 33 of this Agreement, for those of these applications that meet the criteria for protection referred to in subparagraph (b).

9. Where a product is the subject of a patent application in a Member in accordance with paragraph 8(a), exclusive marketing rights shall be granted, notwithstanding the provisions of Part VI, for a period of five years after obtaining marketing approval in that Member or until a product patent is granted or rejected in that Member, whichever period is shorter, provided that, subsequent to the entry into force of the WTO Agreement, a patent application has been filed and a patent granted for that product in another Member and marketing approval obtained in such other Member.

Article 71

Review and amendment

A21–072   1. The Council for TRIPs shall review the implementation of this Agreement after the expiration of the transitional period referred to in paragraph 2 of Article 65. The Council shall, having regard to the experience gained in its implementa tion, review it two years after that date, and at identical intervals thereafter. The Council may also undertake reviews in the light of any relevant new developments which might warrant modification or amendment of this Agreement.

2. Amendments merely serving the purpose of adjusting to higher levels of protection of intellectual property rights achieved, and in force, in other multilateral agreements and accepted under those agreements by all Members of the WTO may be referred to the Ministerial Conference for action in accordance with paragraph 6 of Article X of the WTO Agreement of the basis of a consensus proposal from the Council for TRIPs.

Article 72

Reservations

Reservations may not be entered in respect of any of the provisions of this Agreement without the consent of the other Members.

A21–073

Article 73

Security exceptions

Nothing in this Agreement shall be construed:

A21–074

(a) to require a Member to furnish any information the disclosure of which it considers contrary to its essential security interests; or

(b) to prevent a Member from taking any action which it considers necessary for the protection of its essential security interests;

   (i) relating to fissionable materials or the materials from which they are derived;

   (ii) relating to the traffic in arms, ammunition and implements of war and to such traffic in other goods and materials as is carried on directly or indirectly for the purpose of supplying a military establishment;

   (iii) taken in time of war or other emergency in international relations; or

(c) to prevent a Member from taking any action in pursuance of its obligations under the United Nations Charter for the maintenance of international peace and security.

The Trade Marks (Claims to Priority from Relevant Countries) Order 1994

SI 1994/2803

A22–001 *Her Majesty, in exercise of the powers conferred upon Her by section 36(1) and (2) of the Trade Marks Act 1994, is pleased, by and with the advice of Her Privy Council, to order, and it is hereby ordered, as follows:—*

A22–002 **1.** This Order may be cited as the Trade Marks (Claims to Priority from Relevant Countries) Order 1994 and shall come into force on 5th December 1994.

A22–003 **2.** In this Order—

"the Act" means the Trade Marks Act 1994;

"duly filed" means a filing which is adequate to establish the date on which the application was filed in the relevant country in question, whatever may be the subsequent fate of the application; and

"relevant country" means any country or territory specified in the Schedule to this Order.

A22–004 **3.** A person who has duly filed an application for the protection of a trade mark in a relevant country shall have a right to priority, for the purpose of registering the same trade mark under the Act for some or all of the same goods or services, for a period of six months from the date of filing of the application in that country.

A22–005 **4.** Where the application for registration under the Act is made within the aforesaid period of six months—

(a) the relevant date for the purpose of establishing which rights take precedence shall be the date of the filing of the application in the relevant country, and

(b) the registrability of the trade mark shall not be affected by any use of the mark in the United Kingdom in the period between that date and the date of the application under the Act.

A22–006 **5.** A subsequent application concerning the same subject as the first application, duly filed in the same relevant country, shall be considered the first application to be filed in that country (of which the filing date shall be the starting date of the period of priority) if at the time of the subsequent application—

(a) the previous application has been withdrawn, abandoned or refused, without having been laid open to public inspection and without leaving any rights outstanding, and

(b) it has not yet served as a basis for claiming a right of priority.

A22–007 **6.** A previous application may not serve as a basis for claiming a right of priority where a subsequent application is considered, in accordance with article 5 above, as the first application to be duly filed.

A22–008 **7.** A right to priority conferred by this Order—

(a) shall (unless otherwise stated in the application) vest in the person filing the application or his successor in title; and

(b) may be assigned or otherwise transmitted, either with the application or independently.

A22–009 **8.**—(1) Where a right to priority is claimed by reason of an application to which this Order relates, particulars of that claim shall be included in the application for registration filed under the Act and, unless a certificate as is referred to in paragraph (2) below is filed with the application, such particulars shall include the relevant country and the date of filing.

(2) There shall be filed within three months of the filing of the application for registration under the Act a certificate by the registering or other competent authority of the relevant country certifying, or verifying to the satisfaction of the registrar—

(a) the date of the filing of the application,
(b) the relevant country or registering or competent authority,
(c) the representation of the mark, and
(d) the goods or services covered by the application.

Article 2   SCHEDULE

RELEVANT COUNTRIES

Ecuador   **A22–010**
Hong Kong

The Trade Marks (Claims to Priority from Relevant Countries) (Amendment) Order 1995

SI 1995/2997

A23–001 *Her Majesty, in exercise of the powers conferred upon Her by section 36(1) and (2) of the Trade Marks Act 1994, is pleased, by and with the advice of Her Privy Council, to order, and it is hereby ordered, as follows:*

A23–002 **1.** This Order may be cited as the Trade Marks (Claims to Priority from Relevant Countries) (Amendment) Order 1995 and shall come into force on 1st January 1996.

A23–003 **2.** For the Schedule to the Trade Marks (Claims to Priority from Relevant Countries) Order 1994, there shall be substituted the Schedule to this Order.

Article 2   SCHEDULE

RELEVANT COUNTRIES

A23–004   Antigua and Barbuda
Bahrain
Belize
Bolivia
Botswana
Brunei Darussalam
Colombia
Djibouti
Dominica
Ecuador
Guatemala
Hong Kong
India
Jamaica
Kuwait
Macau
Maldives
Mozambique
Myanmar
Namibia
Nicaragua
Pakistan
Sierra Leone
Thailand

The Patents and Trade Marks (World Trade Organisation) Regulations 1999

SI 1999/1899

The Secretary of State, being a Minister designated for the purposes of section 2(2) of the European Communities Act 1972 in relation to measures relating to patents and trade marks, in exercise of powers conferred by section 2 (2) of the said Act of 1972, hereby makes the following Regulations:—   **A24–001**

PART I

INTRODUCTORY PROVISIONS

Citation and commencement

1.—(1) These Regulations may be cited as the Patents and Trade Marks (World Trade Organisation) Regulations 1999.   **A24–002**

(2) These Regulations come into force on 29th July 1999.

Interpretation

2. In these Regulations—   **A24–003**
 "the 1977 Act" means the Patents Act 1977;
 "the 1994 Act" means the Trade Marks Act 1994;
 "the 1995 rules" means the Patent Rules 1995.

PART II

AMENDMENTS OF THE PATENTS ACT 1977

Compulsory licences: general

3. For section 48 of the 1977 Act substitute—   **A24–004**

Compulsory licences: general

"**48.**—(1) At any time after the expiration of three years, or of such other period as may be prescribed, from the date of the grant of a patent, any person may apply to the comptroller on one or more of the relevant grounds—

 (a) for a licence under the patent;

 (b) for an entry to be made in the register to the effect that licences under the patent are to be available as of right; or

 (c) where the applicant is a government department, for the grant to any person specified in the application of a licence under the patent.

(2) Subject to sections 48A and 48B below, if he is satisfied that any of the relevant grounds are established, the comptroller may—

 (a) where the application is under subsection (1)(a) above, order the grant of a licence to the applicant on such terms as the comptroller thinks fit;

(b) where the application is under subsection (1)(b) above, make such an entry as is there mentioned;

(c) where the application is under subsection (1)(c) above, order the grant of a licence to the person specified in the application on such terms as the comptroller thinks fit.

(3) An application may be made under this section in respect of a patent even though the applicant is already the holder of a licence under the patent; and no person shall be estopped or barred from alleging any of the matters specified in the relevant grounds by reason of any admission made by him, whether in such a licence or otherwise, or by reason of his having accepted a licence.

(4) In this section "the relevant grounds" means—

(a) in the case of an application made in respect of a patent whose proprietor is a WTO proprietor, the grounds set out in section 48A (1) below;

(b) in any other case, the grounds set out in section 48B(1) below.

(5) A proprietor is a WTO proprietor for the purposes of this section and sections 48A, 48B, 50 and 52 below if—

(a) he is a national of, or is domiciled in, a country which is a member of the World Trade Organisation; or

(b) he has a real and effective industrial or commercial establishment in such a country.

(6) A rule prescribing any such other period under subsection (1) above shall not be made unless a draft of the rule has been laid before, and approved by resolution of, each House of Parliament."

Compulsory licences: WTO proprietors

A24–005   **4.** After section 48 of the 1977 Act insert—

Compulsory licences: WTO proprietors.

"**48A.**—(1) In the case of an application made under section 48 above in respect of a patent whose proprietor is a WTO proprietor, the relevant grounds are—

(a) where the patented invention is a product, that a demand in the United Kingdom for that product is not being met on reasonable terms;

(b) that by reason of the refusal of the proprietor of the patent concerned to grant a licence or licences on reasonable terms—

(i) the exploitation in the United Kingdom of any other patented invention which involves an important technical advance of considerable economic significance in relation to the invention for which the patent concerned was granted is prevented or hindered, or

(ii) the establishment or development of commercial or industrial activities in the United Kingdom is unfairly prejudiced;

(c) that by reason of conditions imposed by the proprietor of the patent concerned on the grant of licences under the patent, or on the disposal or use of the patented product or on the use of the patented process, the manufacture, use or disposal of materials not protected by the patent, or the establishment or development of commercial or industrial activities in the United Kingdom, is unfairly prejudiced.

(2) No order or entry shall be made under section 48 above in respect of a patent whose proprietor is a WTO proprietor unless—

    (a) the applicant has made efforts to obtain a licence from the proprietor on reasonable commercial terms and conditions; and

    (b) his efforts have not been successful within a reasonable period.

(3) No order or entry shall be so made if the patented invention is in the field of semi-conductor technology.

(4) No order or entry shall be made under section 48 above in respect of a patent on the ground mentioned in subsection (1)(b)(i) above unless the comptroller is satisfied that the proprietor of the patent for the other invention is able and willing to grant the proprietor of the patent concerned and his licensees a licence under the patent for the other invention on reasonable terms.

(5) A licence granted in pursuance of an order or entry so made shall not be assigned except to a person to whom the patent for the other invention is also assigned.

(6) A licence granted in pursuance of an order or entry made under section 48 above in respect of a patent whose proprietor is a WTO proprietor—

    (a) shall not be exclusive;

    (b) shall not be assigned except to a person to whom there is also assigned the part of the enterprise that enjoys the use of the patented invention, or the part of the goodwill that belongs to that part;

    (c) shall be predominantly for the supply of the market in the United Kingdom;

    (d) shall include conditions entitling the proprietor of the patent concerned to remuneration adequate in the circumstances of the case, taking into account the economic value of the licence; and

    (e) shall be limited in scope and in duration to the purpose for which the licence was granted."

Compulsory licences: other cases

5. After section 48A of the 1977 Act insert—   A24–006

Compulsory licences: other cases

"48B.—(1) In the case of an application made under section 48 above in respect of a patent whose proprietor is not a WTO proprietor, the relevant grounds are—

    (a) where the patented invention is capable of being commercially worked in the United Kingdom, that it is not being so worked or is not being so worked to the fullest extent that is reasonably practicable;

    (b) where the patented invention is a product, that a demand for the product in the United Kingdom—

        (i) is not being met on reasonable terms, or

        (ii) is being met to a substantial extent by importation from a country which is not a member State;

    (c) where the patented invention is capable of being commercially worked in the United Kingdom, that it is being prevented or hindered from being so worked—

(i) where the invention is a product, by the importation of the product from a country which is not a member State,

(ii) where the invention is a process, by the importation from such a country of a product obtained directly by means of the process or to which the process has been applied;

(d) that by reason of the refusal of the proprietor of the patent to grant a licence or licences on reasonable terms—

(i) a market for the export of any patented product made in the United Kingdom is not being supplied, or

(ii) the working or efficient working in the United Kingdom of any other patented invention which makes a substantial contribution to the art is prevented or hindered, or

(iii) the establishment or development of commercial or industrial activities in the United Kingdom is unfairly prejudiced;

(e) that by reason of conditions imposed by the proprietor of the patent on the grant of licences under the patent, or on the disposal or use of the patented product or on the use of the patented process, the manufacture, use or disposal of materials not protected by the patent, or the establishment or development of commercial or industrial activities in the United Kingdom, is unfairly prejudiced.

(2) Where—

(a) an application is made on the ground that the patented invention is not being commercially worked in the United Kingdom or is not being so worked to the fullest extent that is reasonably practicable; and

(b) it appears to the comptroller that the time which has elapsed since the publication in the journal of a notice of the grant of the patent has for any reason been insufficient to enable the invention to be so worked, he may by order adjourn the application for such period as will in his opinion give sufficient time for the invention to be so worked.

(3) No order or entry shall be made under section 48 above in respect of a patent on the ground mentioned in subsection (1)(a) above if—

(a) the patented invention is being commercially worked in a country which is a member State; and

(b) demand in the United Kingdom is being met by importation from that country.

(4) No entry shall be made in the register under section 48 above on the ground mentioned in subsection (1)(d)(i) above, and any licence granted under section 48 above on that ground shall contain such provisions as appear to the comptroller to be expedient for restricting the countries in which any product concerned may be disposed of or used by the licensee.

(5) No order or entry shall be made under section 48 above in respect of a patent on the ground mentioned in subsection (1)(d)(ii) above unless the comptroller is satisfied that the proprietor of the patent for the other invention is able and willing to grant to the proprietor of the patent concerned and his licensees a licence under the patent for the other invention on reasonable terms."

Opposition, appeal and arbitration

A24–007   **6.** For section 52 of the 1977 Act substitute—

Opposition, appeal and arbitration

"**52.**—(1) The proprietor of the patent concerned or any other person wishing to oppose an application under sections 48 to 51 above may, in accordance with rules, give to the comptroller notice of opposition; and the comptroller shall consider any opposition in deciding whether to grant the application.

(2) Where an order or entry has been made under section 48 above in respect of a patent whose proprietor is a WTO proprietor—

    (a) the proprietor or any other person may, in accordance with rules, apply to the comptroller to have the order revoked or the entry cancelled on the grounds that the circumstances which led to the making of the order or entry have ceased to exist and are unlikely to recur;

    (b) any person wishing to oppose an application under paragraph (a) above may, in accordance with rules, give to the comptroller notice of opposition; and

    (c) the comptroller shall consider any opposition in deciding whether to grant the application.

(3) If it appears to the comptroller on an application under subsection (2)(a) above that the circumstances which led to the making of the order or entry have ceased to exist and are unlikely to recur, he may—

    (a) revoke the order or cancel the entry; and

    (b) terminate any licence granted to a person in pursuance of the order or entry subject to such terms and conditions as he thinks necessary for the protection of the legitimate interests of that person.

(4) Where an appeal is brought—

    (a) from an order made by the comptroller in pursuance of an application under sections 48 to 51 above;

    (b) from a decision of his to make an entry in the register in pursuance of such an application;

    (c) from a revocation or cancellation made by him under subsection (3) above; or

    (d) from a refusal of his to make such an order, entry, revocation or cancellation,

the Attorney General, the appropriate Law Officer within the meaning of section 4A of the Crown Suits (Scotland) Act 1857 or the Attorney General for Northern Ireland, or such other counsel as any of them may appoint, shall be entitled to appear and be heard.

(5) Where an application under sections 48 to 51 above or subsection (2) above is opposed, and either—

    (a) the parties consent, or

    (b) the proceedings require a prolonged examination of documents or any scientific or local investigation which cannot in the opinion of the comptroller conveniently be made before him,

the comptroller may at any time order the whole proceedings, or any question or issue of fact arising in them, to be referred to an arbitrator or arbiter agreed on by the parties or, in default of agreement, appointed by the comptroller.

(6) Where the whole proceedings are so referred, unless the parties otherwise agree before the award of the arbitrator or arbiter is made, an appeal shall lie from the award to the court.

(7) Where a question or issue of fact is so referred, the arbitrator or arbiter shall report his findings to the comptroller."

Minor amendments of 1977 Act

A24–008 7.—(1) After subsection (5) of section 5 of the 1977 Act (priority date) insert—

"(6) References in subsection (5) above to a convention country include references to a country, other than the United Kingdom, which is a member of the World Trade Organisation."

(2) In subsection (1) of section 50 of that Act (exercise of powers on applications), after the words "in respect of a patent" insert the words "whose proprietor is not a WTO proprietor".

(3) In subsection (2) of that section, for the words "such an application" substitute the words "any application under section 48 above".

(4) In subsection (2) of section 54 of that Act (special provisions), after the words "means a country other than a member state" insert the words "or a member of the World Trade Organisation".

(5) In subsection (7) of section 60 of that Act (meaning of infringement), in the definitions of "relevant ship" and "relevant aircraft, hovercraft or vehicle", after the words "1983" insert the words "or which is a member of the World Trade Organisation".

Part II: transitional provisions

A24–009 8.—(1) A WTO proprietor of a patent in respect of which an order or entry has been made under section 48 of the 1977 Act before the relevant date may apply to the comptroller—

(a) to have the order revoked or the entry cancelled on the grounds that the grounds on which the order or entry was made are not set out in subsection (1) of section 48A of that Act; or

(b) to have the conditions subject to which any licence was granted before that date in pursuance of the order or entry modified on the grounds that the licence does not satisfy the requirements set out in subsection (6) of that section.

(2) If it appears to the comptroller on an application under paragraph (1)(a) that the grounds on which the order or entry was made are not set out in section 48A(1) of the 1977 Act, he may—

(a) revoke the order or cancel the entry; or

(b) terminate any licence granted to a person in pursuance of the order or entry subject to such terms and conditions as he thinks necessary for the protection of the legitimate interests of that person.

(3) If it appears to the comptroller on an application under paragraph (1)(b) that the conditions of the licence should be modified, he may modify the conditions accordingly; but in doing so he shall have regard to the need to protect the legitimate interests of the holder of the licence.

(4) Subsections (1), (4) and (5) of section 52 of the 1977 Act shall apply to an application under paragraph (1) as they apply to an application under sections 48 to 51 of that Act, but as if the reference in subsection (1) to the proprietor of the patent or any other person were a reference to any person.

(5) Section 48A(5) of the 1977 Act shall apply to a licence granted on or after the relevant date in pursuance of an entry made before that date in relation to a patent whose proprietor is a WTO proprietor, if the entry was made—

(a) before the commencement date and on the ground mentioned in section 48(3)(d)(ii) of that Act; or

(b) on or after that date and on the ground mentioned in section 48B(1)(d)(ii) of that Act.

(6) Section 48A(6) of the 1977 Act shall apply to a licence granted on or after the relevant date in pursuance of an entry made before that date in relation to a patent whose proprietor is a WTO proprietor.

(7) A proprietor is a WTO proprietor for the purposes of this regulation if—

(a) he is a national of, or is domiciled in, a country which is a member of the World Trade Organisation; or

(b) he has a real and effective industrial or commercial establishment in such a country.

(8) In this regulation—

"the commencement date" means the date of the coming into force of these Regulations;

"the relevant date" means the commencement date or, if later, the date on which the proprietor of the patent became a WTO proprietor.

PART III

AMENDMENTS OF THE PATENTS RULES 1995

Application for: compulsory licence under section 48(1), or revocation or cancellation under section 52(2)(a), of the 1977 Act

9. For rule 68 of the 1995 rules substitute—   A24–010

"**68.** An application under section 48(1) or 52(2)(a) shall be made on Patents Form 2/77 and shall be accompanied by a statement in duplicate of the facts upon which the applicant relies and evidence in duplicate verifying the statement.".

Procedure on receipt of application under section 48, 51 or 52 of the 1977 Act

10. For rule 70 of the 1995 rules substitute—   A24–011

"**70.**—(1) If upon consideration of the evidence submitted under rule 68 (application for: compulsory licence under section 48(1) or revocation or cancellation under section 52(2)(a)) or rule 69 (application by Minister under section 51), the comptroller is not satisfied that a prima facie case is made out for—

(a) the making of an order or an entry, or

(b) the revocation of an order or cancellation of an entry,

as the case may be, he shall notify the applicant accordingly, and unless, within one month of making such notification, the applicant requests to be heard in the matter, the comptroller shall refuse the application.

(2) Where the applicant requests a hearing within the time allowed, the comptroller, after giving the applicant the opportunity of being heard, shall determine whether the application may proceed or whether it shall be refused.

(3) If upon consideration of the evidence the comptroller is satisfied that a prima facie case has been made out for—

(a) the making of an order or an entry, or

(b) the revocation of an order or cancellation of an entry,

as the case may be, or if, after hearing the applicant, he so determines, he shall direct that the application shall be advertised in the Journal, and shall send a copy of the application, the statement and the evidence filed in support thereof—

(c) where the application is under subparagraph (a), to the proprietor of the patent and to any other person shown on the register as having any right in or under the patent; or

(d) where the application is under subparagraph (b), to any person shown on the register as having any right in or under the patent.".

Opposition under section 52 of the 1977 Act

A24–012   11. For paragraph (1) of rule 71 of the 1995 rules substitute—

"**71.**—(1) Within two months of the date of the advertisement in the Journal of an application under rule 70(3), any person may give notice to the comptroller of opposition under section 52(1) or 52(2)(b), as the case may be, to the application on Patents Form 15/77.".

Part III: transitional provisions

A24–013   12. Rules 68, 70 and 71 of the 1995 rules shall apply to an application, or opposition to an application, under regulation 8(1) as they apply to an application or opposition under section 48, or section 52, of the 1977 Act.

PART IV

AMENDMENTS OF THE TRADE MARKS ACT 1994

Amendments of 1994 Act

A24–014   13.—(1) In subsection (1)(c) of section 6 of the 1994 Act (meaning of "earlier trade mark"), after the words "protection under the Paris Convention" insert the words "or the WTO agreement".

(2) In subsection (1) of section 55 of the 1994 Act (Paris Convention: supplementary provisions), omit the word "and" at the end of paragraph (a) and after that paragraph insert—

"(aa) 'the WTO agreement' means the Agreement establishing the World Trade Organisation signed at Marrakesh on 15th April 1994, and".

(3) In subsection (2) of that section, after the words "the Paris Convention" there shall be inserted the words "or the WTO agreement".

(4) In subsections (1) and (2) of section 56 of that Act (protection of well-known trade marks), after the words "the Paris Convention" insert the words "or the WTO agreement".

(5) In subsections (2) and (3) of section 57 of that Act (national emblems etc. of Convention countries), after the words "the Paris Convention" insert the words "or the WTO agreement".

(6) In subsection (2) of section 58 of that Act (emblems etc. of certain international organisations), after the words "the Paris Convention" insert the words "or the WTO agreement".

(7) After subsection (4) of section 59 of that Act (notification under Article 6Ter of Convention) insert—

"(5) Any reference in this section to Article 6Ter of the Paris Convention shall be construed as including a reference to that Article as applied by the WTO agreement".

Part IV: transitional provisions

A24–015   14.—(1) The amendment of section 56(2) of the 1994 Act made by regulation 13(4) shall not affect the continuation of any bona fide use of a trade mark begun before the 1st January 1996.

(2) The amendment made by regulation 13(6) shall not affect the rights of a person whose bona fide use of the trade mark in question began before that date.

PART VIII

CUSTOMS MATERIALS

APPENDIX 25

Council Regulation (EC) No 1383/2003 of 22 July 2003 concerning customs action against goods suspected of infringing certain intellectual property rights and the measures to be taken against goods found to have infringed such rights

2003 1383

THE COUNCIL OF THE EUROPEAN UNION,   A25–001

Having regard to the Treaty establishing the European Community, and in particular Article 133 thereof,

Having regard to the proposal from the Commission,

Whereas:

(1) To improve the working of the system concerning the entry into the Community and the export and re-export from the Community of goods infringing certain intellectual property rights introduced by Council Regulation (EC) No 3295/94 of 22 December 1994 laying down measures to prohibit the release for free circulation, export, re-export or entry for a suspensive procedure of counterfeit and pirated goods[5], conclusions should be drawn from experience of its application. In the interests of clarity, Regulation (EC) No 3295/94 should be repealed and replaced.

(2) The marketing of counterfeit and pirated goods, and indeed all goods infringing intellectual property rights, does considerable damage to law-abiding manufacturers and traders and to right-holders, as well as deceiving and in some cases endangering the health and safety of consumers. Such goods should, in so far as is possible, be kept off the market and measures adopted to deal effectively with this unlawful activity without impeding the freedom of legitimate trade. This objective is consistent with efforts under way at international level.

(3) In cases where counterfeit goods, pirated goods and, more generally, goods infringing an intellectual property right originate in or come from third countries, their introduction into the Community customs territory, including their transhipment, release for free circulation in the Community, placing under a suspensive procedure and placing in a free zone or warehouse, should be prohibited and a procedure set up to enable the customs authorities to enforce this prohibition as effectively as possible.

(4) Customs authorities should also be able to take action against counterfeit goods, pirated goods and goods infringing certain intellectual property rights which are in the process of being exported, re-exported or leaving the Community customs territory.

(5) Action by the customs authorities should involve, for the period necessary to determine whether suspect goods are indeed counterfeit goods, pirated goods

---

[5] OJ L 341, 30.12.1994, p. 8. Regulation as last amended by Regulation (EC) No 806/2003 (OJ L 122, 16.5.2003, p. 1).

or goods infringing certain intellectual property rights, suspending release for free circulation, export and re-export or, in the case of goods placed under a suspensive procedure, placed in a free zone or a free warehouse, in the process of being re-exported with notification, introduced into the customs territory or leaving that territory, detaining those goods.

(6) The particulars of the application for action, such as its period of validity and form, need to be defined and harmonised in all Member States. The same applies to the conditions governing the acceptance of applications by the customs authorities and the service designated to receive, process and register them.

(7) Even where no application has yet been lodged or approved, the Member States should be authorised to detain the goods for a certain period to allow rightholders to lodge an application for action with the customs authorities.

(8) Proceedings initiated to determine whether an intellectual property right has been infringed under national law will be conducted with reference to the criteria used to establish whether goods produced in that Member State infringe intellectual property rights. This Regulation does not affect the Member States' provisions on the competence of the courts or judicial procedures.

(9) To make the Regulation easier to apply for customs administrations and right-holders alike, provision should also be made for a more flexible procedure allowing goods infringing certain intellectual property rights to be destroyed without there being any obligation to initiate proceedings to establish whether an intellectual property right has been infringed under national law.

(10) It is necessary to lay down the measures applicable to goods which have been found to be counterfeit, pirated or generally to infringe certain intellectual property rights. Those measures should not only deprive those responsible for trading in such goods of the economic benefits of the transaction and penalise them but should also constitute an effective deterrent to further transactions of the same kind.

(11) To avoid disrupting the clearance of goods carried in travellers' personal baggage, it is appropriate, except where certain material indications suggest commercial traffic is involved, to exclude from the scope of this Regulation goods that may be counterfeit, pirated or infringe certain intellectual property rights when imported from third countries within the limits of the duty-free allowance accorded by Community rules.

(12) In the interests of this Regulations effectiveness, it is important to ensure the uniform application of the common rules it lays down and to reinforce mutual assistance between the Member States and between the Member States and the Commission, in particular by recourse to Council Regulation (EC) No 515/97 of 13 March 1997 on mutual assistance between the administrative authorities of the Member States and cooperation between the latter and the

Commission to ensure the correct application of the law on customs and agricultural matters[6].

(13) In the light of the experience gained in the implementation of this Regulation, inter alia, consideration should be given to the possibility of increasing the number of intellectual property rights covered.

(14) The measures necessary for the implementation of this Regulation should be adopted in accordance with Council Decision 1999/468/EC of 28 June 1999 laying down the procedures for the exercise of implementing powers conferred on the Commission[7].

(15) Regulation (EC) No 3295/94 should be repealed,

HAS ADOPTED THIS REGULATION:

CHAPTER I

SUBJECT MATTER AND SCOPE

Article 1

1. This Regulation sets out the conditions for action by the customs authorities when goods are suspected of infringing an intellectual property right in the following situations: **A25–002**
  (a) when they are entered for release for free circulation, export or re-export in accordance with Article 61 of Council Regulation (EC) No 2913/92 of 12 October 1992 establishing the Community Customs Code[8];
  (b) when they are found during checks on goods entering or leaving the Community customs territory in accordance with Articles 37 and 183 of Regulation (EEC) No 2913/92, placed under a suspensive procedure within the meaning of Article 84(1)(a) of that Regulation, in the process of being re-exported subject to notification under Article 182(2) of that Regulation or placed in a free zone or free warehouse within the meaning of Article 166 of that Regulation.

2. This Regulation also fixes the measures to be taken by the competent authorities when the goods referred to in paragraph 1 are found to infringe intellectual property rights.

Article 2

1. For the purposes of this Regulation, 'goods infringing an intellectual property right' means: **A25–003**
  (a) 'counterfeit goods', namely:
    (i) goods, including packaging, bearing without authorisation a trademark identical to the trademark validly registered in respect of the same type of goods, or which cannot be distinguished in its essential aspects from such a trademark, and which thereby infringes the trademark-holder's rights under Community law, as provided for by Council Regulation (EC) No 40/94 of 20 December 1993 on the Com-

---

[6] OJ L 82, 22.3.1997, p. 1. Regulation as last amended by Regulation (EC) No 807/2003 (OJ L 122, 16.5.2003, p. 36).

[7] OJ L 184, 17.7.1999, p. 23.

[8] OJ L 302, 19.10.1992, p. 1. Regulation as last amended by Regulation (EC) No 2700/2000, of the European Parliament and of the Council (OJ L 311, 12.12.2000, p. 17).

munity Trademark[9] or the law of the Member State in which the application for action by the customs authorities is made;

    (ii) any trademark symbol (including a logo, label, sticker, brochure, instructions for use or guarantee document bearing such a symbol), even if presented separately, on the same conditions as the goods referred to in point (i);

    (iii) packaging materials bearing the trademarks of counterfeit goods, presented separately, on the same conditions as the goods referred to in point (i);

(b) 'pirated goods', namely goods which are or contain copies made without the consent of the holder of a copyright or related right or design right, regardless of whether it is registered in national law, or of a person authorised by the right-holder in the country of production in cases where the making of those copies would constitute an infringement of that right under Council Regulation (EC) No 6/ 2002 of 12 December 2001 on Community Designs[10] or the law of the Member State in which the application for customs action is made;

(c) goods which, in the Member State in which the application for customs action is made, infringe:

    (i) a patent under that Member State's law;

    (ii) a supplementary protection certificate of the kind provided for in Council Regulation (EEC) No 1768/ 92[11] or Regulation (EC) No 1610/96 of the European Parliament and of the Council[12];

    (iii) a national plant variety right under the law of that Member State or a Community plant variety right of the kind provided for in Council Regulation (EC) No 2100/94[13];

    (iv) designations of origin or geographical indications under the law of that Member State or Council Regulations (EEC) No 2081/92[14] and (EC) No 1493/1999[15];

    (v) geographical designations of the kind provided for in Council Regulation (EEC) No 1576/89[16].

2. For the purposes of this Regulation, 'right-holder' means:

(a) the holder of a trademark, copyright or related right, design right, patent, supplementary protection certificate, plant variety right, protected designation of origin, protected geographical indication and, more generally, any right referred to in paragraph 1; or

(b) any other person authorised to use any of the intellectual property rights mentioned in point (a), or a representative of the right-holder or authorised user.

3. Any mould or matrix which is specifically designed or adapted for the manufacture of goods infringing an intellectual property right shall be treated as

---

[9] OJ L 11, 14.01.1994, p. 1. Regulation as last amended by Regulation (EC) No 807/2003.

[10] OJ L 3, 5.1.2002, p. 1.

[11] OJ L 182, 2.7.1992, p. 1.

[12] OJ L 198, 8.8.1996, p. 30.

[13] OJ L 227, 1.9.1994, p. 1. Regulation as last amended by Regulation (EC) No 807/2003.

[14] OJ L 208, 24.7.1992, p. 1. Regulation as last amended by Regulation (EC) No 806/2003.

[15] OJ L 179, 14.7.1999, p. 1. Regulation as last amended by Regulation (EC) No 806/2003.

[16] OJ L 160, 12.6.1989, p. 1. Regulation as last amended by Regulation (EC) No 3378/94 of the European Parliament and of the Council (OJ L 366, 31.12.1994, p. 1).

goods of that kind if the use of such moulds or matrices infringes the right-holder's rights under Community law or the law of the Member State in which the application for action by the customs authorities is made.

Article 3

1. This Regulation shall not apply to goods bearing a trademark with the consent of the holder of that trademark or to goods bearing a protected designation of origin or a protected geographical indication or which are protected by a patent or a supplementary protection certificate, by a copyright or related right or by a design right or a plant variety right and which have been manufactured with the consent of the right-holder but are placed in one of the situations referred to in Article 1(1) without the latter's consent.   **A25–004**

It shall similarly not apply to goods referred to in the first subparagraph and which have been manufactured or are protected by another intellectual property right referred to in Article 2(1) under conditions other than those agreed with the right-holder.

2. Where a traveller's personal baggage contains goods of a non-commercial nature within the limits of the duty-free allowance and there are no material indications to suggest the goods are part of commercial traffic, Member States shall consider such goods to be outside the scope of this Regulation.

CHAPTER II

APPLICATIONS FOR ACTION BY THE CUSTOMS AUTHORITIES

SECTION 1

MEASURES PRIOR TO AN APPLICATION FOR ACTION BY THE CUSTOMS AUTHORITIES

Article 4

1. Where the customs authorities, in the course of action in one of the situations referred to in Article 1(1) and before an application has been lodged by a right-holder or granted, have sufficient grounds for suspecting that goods infringe an intellectual property right, they may suspend the release of the goods or detain them for a period of three working days from the moment of receipt of the notification by the right-holder and by the declarant or holder of the goods, if the latter are known, in order to enable the right-holder to submit an application for action in accordance with Article 5.   **A25–005**

2. In accordance with the rules in force in the Member State concerned, the customs authorities may, without divulging any information other than the actual or supposed number of items and their nature and before informing the right-holder of the possible infringement, ask the right-holder to provide them with any information they may need to confirm their suspicions.

SECTION 2

THE LODGING AND PROCESSING OF APPLICATIONS FOR CUSTOMS ACTION

Article 5

1. In each Member State a right-holder may apply in writing to the competent customs department for action by the customs authorities when goods are found in one of the situations referred to in Article 1(1) (application for action).   **A25–006**

2. Each Member State shall designate the customs department competent to receive and process applications for action.

3. Where electronic data interchange systems exist, the Member States shall encourage right-holders to lodge applications electronically.

4. Where the applicant is the right-holder of a Community trademark or a Community design right, a Community plant variety right or a designation of origin or geographical indication or a geographical designation protected by the Community, an application may, in addition to requesting action by the customs authorities of the Member State in which it is lodged, request action by the customs authorities of one or more other Member States.

5. The application for action shall be made out on a form established in accordance with the procedure referred to in Article 21(2); it must contain all the information needed to enable the goods in question to be readily recognised by the customs authorities, and in particular:

  (i) an accurate and detailed technical description of the goods;
  (ii) any specific information the right-holder may have concerning the type or pattern of fraud;
  (iii) the name and address of the contact person appointed by the right-holder.

The application for action must also contain the declaration required of the applicant by Article 6 and proof that the applicant holds the right for the goods in question.

In the situation described in paragraph 4 the application for action shall indicate the Member State or States in which customs action is requested as well as the names and addresses of the right-holder in each of the Member States concerned. By way of indication and where known, right-holders should also forward any other information they may have, such as:

  (a) the pre-tax value of the original goods on the legitimate market in the country in which the application for action is lodged;
  (b) the location of the goods or their intended destination;
  (c) particulars identifying the consignment or packages;
  (d) the scheduled arrival or departure date of the goods;
  (e) the means of transport used;
  (f) the identity of the importer, exporter or holder of the goods;
  (g) the country or countries of production and the routes used by traffickers;
  (h) the technical differences, if known, between the authentic and suspect goods.

6. Details may also be required which are specific to the type of intellectual property right referred to in the application for action.

7. On receiving an application for action, the competent customs department shall process that application and notify the applicant in writing of its decision within 30 working days of its receipt.

The right-holder shall not be charged a fee to cover the administrative costs occasioned by the processing of the application.

8. Where the application does not contain the mandatory information listed in paragraph 5, the competent customs department may decide not to process the application for action; in that event it shall provide reasons for its decision and include information on the appeal procedure. The application can only be resubmitted when duly completed.

Article 6

A25–007 1. Applications for action shall be accompanied by a declaration from the right-holder, which may be submitted either in writing or electronically, in accordance with national legislation, accepting liability towards the persons involved in a situation referred to in Article 1(1) in the event that a procedure initiated pursuant to Article 9(1) is discontinued owing to an act or omission by the right-holder or in the event that the goods in question are subsequently found not to infringe an intellectual property right.

In that declaration the right-holder shall also agree to bear all costs incurred under this Regulation in keeping goods under customs control pursuant to Article 9 and, where applicable, Article 11.

2. Where an application is submitted under Article 5(4), the right-holder shall agree in the declaration to provide and pay for any translation necessary; this declaration shall be valid in every Member State in which the decision granting the application applies.

Article 7

Articles 5 and 6 shall apply *mutatis mutandis* to requests for an extension.   **A25–008**

Section 3

Acceptance of the application for action

Article 8

1. When granting an application for action, the competent customs depart-   **A25–009** ment shall specify the period during which the customs authorities are to take action. That period shall not exceed one year. On expiry of the period in question, and subject to the prior discharge of any debt owed by the rightholder under this Regulation, the department which took the initial decision may, at the right-holder's request, extend that period.

The right-holder shall notify the competent customs department referred to in Article 5(2), if his right ceases to be validly registered or expires.

2. The decision granting the right-holder's application for action shall immediately be forwarded to those customs offices of the Member State or States likely to be concerned by the goods alleged in the application to infringe an intellectual property right.

When an application for action submitted in accordance with Article 5(4) is granted, the period during which the customs authorities are to take action shall be set at one year; on expiry of the period in question, the department which processed the initial application shall, on the right-holder's written application, extend that period. The first indent of Article 250 of Regulation (EEC) No 2913/92 shall apply *mutatis mutandis* to the decision granting that application and to decisions extending or repealing it.

Where an application for action is granted, it is for the applicant to forward that decision, with any other information and any translations that may be necessary, to the competent customs department of the Member State or States in which the applicant has requested customs action. However, with the applicant's consent, the decision may be forwarded directly by the customs department which has taken the decision.

At the request of the customs authorities of the Member States concerned, the applicant shall provide any additional information necessary for the implementation of the decision.

3. The period referred to in the second subparagraph of paragraph 2 shall run from the date of adoption of the decision granting the application. The decision will not enter into force in the recipient Member State or States until it has been forwarded in accordance with the third subparagraph of paragraph 2 and the right-holder has fulfilled the formalities referred to in Article 6.

The decision shall then be sent immediately to the national customs offices likely to have to deal with the goods suspected of infringing intellectual property rights. This paragraph shall apply *mutatis mutandis* to a decision extending the initial decision.

CHAPTER III

CONDITIONS GOVERNING ACTION BY THE CUSTOMS AUTHORITIES AND BY THE AUTHORITY COMPETENT TO DECIDE ON THE CASE

Article 9

A25–010   1. Where a customs office to which the decision granting an application by the right-holder has been forwarded pursuant to Article 8 is satisfied, after consulting the applicant where necessary, that goods in one of the situations referred to in Article 1(1) are suspected of infringing an intellectual property right covered by that decision, it shall suspend release of the goods or detain them.

The customs office shall immediately inform the competent customs department which processed the application.

2. The competent customs department or customs office referred to in paragraph 1 shall inform the right-holder and the declarant or holder of the goods within the meaning of Article 38 of Regulation (EEC) No 2913/92 of its action and is authorised to inform them of the actual or estimated quantity and the actual or supposed nature of the goods whose release has been suspended or which have been detained, without being bound by the communication of that information to notify the authority competent to take a substantive decision.

3. With a view to establishing whether an intellectual property right has been infringed under national law, and in accordance with national provisions on the protection of personal data, commercial and industrial secrecy and professional and administrative confidentiality, the customs office or department which processed the application shall inform the right-holder, at his request and if known, of the names and addresses of the consignee, the consignor, the declarant or the holder of the goods and the origin and provenance of goods suspected of infringing an intellectual property right.

The customs office shall give the applicant and the persons involved in any of the situations referred to in Article 1(1) the opportunity to inspect goods whose release has been suspended or which have been detained.

When examining goods, the customs office may take samples and, according to the rules in force in the Member State concerned, hand them over or send them to the right-holder, at his express request, strictly for the purposes of analysis and to facilitate the subsequent procedure. Where circumstances allow, subject to the requirements of Article 11(1) second indent where applicable, samples must be returned on completion of the technical analysis and, where applicable, before goods are released or their detention is ended. Any analysis of these samples shall be carried out under the sole responsibility of the right-holder.

Article 10

A25–011   The law in force in the Member State within the territory of which the goods are placed in one of the situations referred to in Article 1(1) shall apply when deciding whether an intellectual property right has been infringed under national law.

That law shall also apply to the immediate notification of the customs department or office referred to in Article 9(1) that the procedure provided for in Article

13 has been initiated, unless the procedure was initiated by that department or office.

Article 11

1. Where customs authorities have detained or suspended the release of goods **A25–012** which are suspected of infringing an intellectual property right in one of the situations covered by Article 1(1), the Member States may provide, in accordance with their national legislation, for a simplified procedure, to be used with the right-holder's agreement, which enables customs authorities to have such goods abandoned for destruction under customs control, without there being any need to determine whether an intellectual property right has been infringed under national law. To this end, Member States shall, in accordance with their national legislation, apply the following conditions:

— that the right-holder inform the customs authorities in writing within 10 working days, or three working days in the case of perishable goods, of receipt of the notification provided for in Article 9, that the goods concerned by the procedure infringe an intellectual property right referred to in Article 2(1) and provide those authorities with the written agreement of the declarant, the holder or the owner of the goods to abandon the goods for destruction. With the agreement of the customs authorities, this information may be provided directly to customs by the declarant, the holder or the owner of the goods. This agreement shall be presumed to be accepted when the declarant, the holder or the owner of the goods has not specifically opposed destruction within the prescribed period. This period may be extended by a further ten working days where circumstances warrant it;

— that destruction be carried out, unless otherwise specified in national legislation, at the expense and under the responsibility of the right-holder, and be systematically preceded by the taking of samples for keeping by the customs authorities in such conditions that they constitute evidence admissible in legal proceedings in the Member State in which they might be needed.

2. In all other cases, for example where the declarant, holder or owner objects to or contests the destruction of the goods, the procedure laid down in Article 13 shall apply.

Article 12

A right-holder receiving the particulars cited in the first subparagraph of Article **A25–013** 9(3) shall use that information only for the purposes specified in Articles 10, 11 and 13(1).

Any other use, not permitted by the national legislation of the Member State where the situation arose, may, on the basis of the law of the Member State in which the goods in question are located, cause the right-holder to incur civil liability and lead to the suspension of the application for action, for the period of validity remaining before renewal, in the Member State in which the events have taken place.

In the event of a further breach of this rule, the competent customs department may refuse to renew the application. In the case of an application of the kind provided for in Article 5(4), it must also notify the other Member States indicated on the form.

Article 13

1. If, within 10 working days of receipt of the notification of suspension of **A25–014**

release or of detention, the customs office referred to in Article 9(1) has not been notified that proceedings have been initiated to determine whether an intellectual property right has been infringed under national law in accordance with Article 10 or has not received the right-holder's agreement provided for in Article 11(1) where applicable, release of the goods shall be granted, or their detention shall be ended, as appropriate, subject to completion of all customs formalities.

This period may be extended by a maximum of 10 working days in appropriate cases.

2. In the case of perishable goods suspected of infringing an intellectual property right, the period referred to in paragraph 1 shall be three working days. That period may not be extended.

Article 14

A25–015   1. In the case of goods suspected of infringing design rights, patents, supplementary protection certificates or plant variety rights, the declarant, owner, importer, holder or consignee of the goods shall be able to obtain the release of the goods or an end to their detention on provision of a security, provided that:

(a) the customs office or department referred to in Article 9(1) has been notified, in accordance with Article 13(1), that a procedure has been initiated within the period provided for in Article 13(1) to establish whether an intellectual property right has been infringed under national law;

(b) the authority empowered for this purpose has not authorised precautionary measures before the expiry of the time limit laid down in Article 13(1);

(c) all customs formalities have been completed.

2. The security provided for in paragraph 1 must be sufficient to protect the interests of the right-holder.

Payment of the security shall not affect the other legal remedies available to the right-holder.

Where the procedure to determine whether an intellectual property right has been infringed under national law has been initiated other than on the initiative of the holder of a design right, patent, supplementary protection certificate or plant variety right, the security shall be released if the person initiating the said procedure does not exercise his right to institute legal proceedings within 20 working days of the date on which he receives notification of the suspension of release or detention.

Where the second subparagraph of Article 13(1) applies, this period may be extended to a maximum of 30 working days.

Article 15

A25–016   The conditions of storage of the goods during the period of suspension of release or detention shall be determined by each Member State but shall not give rise to costs for the customs administrations.

CHAPTER IV

PROVISIONS APPLICABLE TO GOODS FOUND TO INFRINGE AN INTELLECTUAL PROPERTY RIGHT

Article 16

A25–017   Goods found to infringe an intellectual property right at the end of the procedure provided for in Article 9 shall not be:

— allowed to enter into the Community customs territory,

— released for free circulation,
— removed from the Community customs territory,
— exported,
— re-exported,
— placed under a suspensive procedure or
— placed in a free zone or free warehouse.

Article 17

1. Without prejudice to the other legal remedies open to the right-holder, Member States shall adopt the measures necessary to allow the competent authorities:

   (a) in accordance with the relevant provisions of national law, to destroy goods found to infringe an intellectual property right or dispose of them outside commercial channels in such a way as to preclude injury to the right-holder, without compensation of any sort and, unless otherwise specified in national legislation, at no cost to the exchequer;

   (b) to take, in respect of such goods, any other measures effectively depriving the persons concerned of any economic gains from the transaction.

      Save in exceptional cases, simply removing the trademarks which have been affixed to counterfeit goods without authorisation shall not be regarded as effectively depriving the persons concerned of any economic gains from the transaction.

2. Goods found to infringe an intellectual property right may be forfeited to the exchequer. In that event, paragraph 1(a) shall apply.

A25–018

CHAPTER V

PENALTIES

Article 18

Each Member State shall introduce penalties to apply in cases of violation of this Regulation. Such penalties must be effective, proportionate and dissuasive.

A25–019

CHAPTER VI

LIABILITY OF THE CUSTOMS AUTHORITIES AND THE RIGHT-HOLDER

Article 19

1. Save as provided by the law of the Member State in which an application is lodged or, in the case of an application under Article 5(4), by the law of the Member State in which goods infringing an intellectual property right are not detected by a customs office, the acceptance of an application shall not entitle the right-holder to compensation in the event that such goods are not detected by a customs office and are released or no action is taken to detain them in accordance with Article 9(1).

2. The exercise by a customs office or by another duly empowered authority of the powers conferred on them in order to fight against goods infringing an intellectual property right shall not render them liable towards the persons involved in the situations referred to in Article 1(1) or the persons affected by the measures provided for in Article 4 for damages suffered by them as a result of the authority's intervention, except where provided for by the law of the Member State in which the application is made or, in the case of an application under Article 5(4), by the law of the Member State in which loss or damage is incurred.

A25–020

3. A right-holder's civil liability shall be governed by the law of the Member State in which the goods in question were placed in one of the situations referred to in Article 1(1).

CHAPTER VII

FINAL PROVISIONS

Article 20

A25–021 The measures necessary for the application of this Regulation shall be adopted in accordance with the procedure referred to in Article 21(2).

Article 21

A25–022 1. The Commission shall be assisted by the Customs Code Committee.

2. Where reference is made to this paragraphArticles 4 and 7 of Decision 1999/468/EC shall apply.

The period laid down in Article 4(3) of Decision 1999/468/EC shall be set at three months.

Article 22

A25–023 Member States shall communicate all relevant information on the application of this Regulation to the Commission.

The Commission shall forward this information to the other Member States.

The provisions of Regulation (EC) No 515/97 shall apply *mutatis mutandis*.

The details of the information procedure shall be drawn up under the implementing provisions in accordance with the procedure referred to in Article 21(2).

Article 23

A25–024 On the basis of the information referred to in Article 22, the Commission shall report annually to the Council on the application of this Regulation. This report may, where appropriate, be accompanied by a proposal to amend the Regulation.

Article 24

A25–025 Regulation (EC) No 3295/94 is repealed with effect from 1 July 2004.

References to the repealed Regulation shall be construed as references to this Regulation.

Article 25

A25–026 This Regulation shall enter into force on the seventh day following that of its publication in the *Official Journal of the European Union*.

It shall apply with effect from 1 July 2004.

This Regulation shall be binding in its entirety and directly applicable in all Member States.

Done at Brussels, 22 July 2003.

For the Council
The President
G. ALEMANNO

SI

CUSTOMS AND EXCISE
The Goods Infringing Intellectual Property Rights (Customs) Regulations 2004

2004/1473

Made 4th June 2004	*4th June 2004*
Laid before Parliament 7th June 2004	*7th June 2004*
Coming into force 1st July 2004	*1st July 2004* **A26–001**

The Commissioners of Customs and Excise, in exercise of the powers conferred on them by section 2(2) of the European Communities Act 1972, being a Department designated¹⁷ for the purposes of that subsection in relation to counterfeit and pirated goods, goods infringing a patent, goods infringing a supplementary protection certificate, goods infringing Community plant variety rights and goods infringing plant breeders' rights, designations of origin, geographical indications and geographical designations, hereby make the following Regulations:

Citation and commencement

1. These Regulations may be cited as the Goods Infringing Intellectual Prop-   **A26–002**
erty Rights (Customs) Regulations 2004 and shall come into force on 1st July 2004.

Interpretation

2.—(1) In these Regulations—   **A26–003**
    "the 1979 Act" means the Customs and Excise Management Act 1979;
    "application" means an application under Article 5 of the Council Regulation;
    "the Commissioners" means the Commissioners of Customs and Excise;
    "Community design"has the meaning given in Article 1(1) of Council Regulation (EC) No 6/2002 on Community designs;
    "Community plant variety right" means a right of the kind provided for in Council Regulation (EC) No 2100/1994 on Community plant variety rights;
    "the Council Regulation" means Council Regulation (EC) No 1383/2003 concerning customs action against goods suspected of infringing certain intellectual property rights and the measures to be taken against goods found to have infringed such rights;
    "the customs and excise Acts"has the meaning given in section 1(1) of the 1979 Act;
    "database rights"has the meaning given in regulation 13 of the Copyright and Rights in Databases Regulations 1997;

---

¹⁷ S.I. 1995/751 (in relation to counterfeit and pirated goods), S.I. 1999/654 (in relation to goods infringing a patent and goods infringing a supplementary protection certificate) and S.I. 2004/706 (in relation to goods infringing Community plant variety rights and goods infringing plant breeders' rights, designations of origin, geographical indications and geographical designations).

"decision" means a decision granting an application in accordance with Article 8 of the Council Regulation;

"declarant"has the meaning given in Article 4(18) of Council Regulation (EEC) No 2913/1992 establishing the Community Customs Code;

"design right"has the meaning given in section 213(1) of the Copyright, Designs and Patents Act 1988;

"designation of origin"has the same meaning as in Article 2(1)(c)(iv) of the Council Regulation;

"European patent (UK)"has the meaning given in section 130(1) of the Patents Act 1977;

"geographical designation"has the same meaning as in Article 2(1)(c)(v) of the Council Regulation;

"geographical indication"has the same meaning as in Article 2(1)(c)(iv) of the Council Regulation;

"goods infringing an intellectual property right"has the meaning given in Article 2(1) of the Council Regulation and related expressions shall be construed accordingly;

"patent" means a patent under the Patents Act 1977, or a European patent (UK) which is treated for the purposes of Parts 1 and 3 of the Patents Act 1977 as if it were a patent under that Act;

"plant breeders' right" means a right of the kind provided for in the Plant Varieties Act 1997;

"publication rights"has the meaning given in regulation 16 of the Copyright and Related Rights Regulations 1996[18];

"registered design"shall be construed in accordance with the Registered Designs Act 1949;

"right-holder"has the meaning given in Article 2(2) of the Council Regulation;

"supplementary protection certificate"has the same meaning as in Article 2(1)(c)(ii) of the Council Regulation;

"working days"has the meaning given in Article 3(1) of Council Regulation (EEC, Euratom) No 1182/1971 determining the rules applicable to periods, dates and time limits.

(2) For the purposes of these Regulations, any reference in the Council Regulation to "copyright or related right"is to be construed as a reference to "copyright, rights in performances, publication rights or database rights".

(3) These Regulations shall apply to goods which fall to be treated by virtue of Article 2(3) of the Council Regulation as being goods infringing an intellectual property right; but these Regulations shall not apply to any goods in relation to which the Council Regulation does not apply by virtue of Article 3(1) thereof.

Infringing goods liable to forfeiture

A26–004   **3.** Subject to paragraph (2) of regulation 4, goods infringing an intellectual property right which correspond to the description of goods contained in a decision shall, during the period specified in the decision, be liable to forfeiture in any of the situations mentioned in Article 1(1) of the Council Regulation.

Application for action

A26–005   **4.**—(1) If, in the course of checks carried out in relation to goods in one of the

---

[18] Amended by S.I. 2003/2498.

situations referred to in Article 1(1) of the Council Regulation, and before an application has been lodged by a right-holder or, if lodged, before it has been granted, the Commissioners have sufficient grounds for suspecting that goods infringe an intellectual property right, the Commissioners may, in accordance with Article 4 of the Council Regulation—

(a) notify a right-holder of the nature of the items and of the actual or supposed number of items and ask a right-holder to provide any information they may need to confirm their suspicions;

(b) notify a right-holder and a declarant of the possible infringement of the right;

(c) suspend the release of, or detain, those goods; and

(d) if they do so suspend or detain, invite the right-holder, in the absence of an existing application, to make an application within three working days of the notification of the suspension or detention.

(2) If at any time during the period of suspension or detention under paragraph (1) an application is granted covering the goods, the decision shall, for the purposes of regulation 3, be taken to have applied at the time the goods entered any of the situations mentioned in Article 1(1) of the Council Regulation.

Decision to cease to have effect

5. A decision shall have no further effect where—   A26–006

(a) any change, following the making of the application, which takes place in the ownership or authorised use of the intellectual property right specified in the application, is not communicated in writing to the Commissioners; or

(b) the intellectual property right specified in the application expires.

Samples of goods

6. When examining goods in accordance with Article 9(3) of the Council   A26–007
Regulation the Commissioners may make samples of the goods available to the right-holder at his request for the purposes of analysis and of facilitating subsequent procedures under the Council Regulation or these Regulations.

Detention, seizure, condemnation and forfeiture

7.—(1) Subject to regulation 8section 139[19] of, and Schedule 3 the 1979 Act   A26–008
(provisions as to detention, seizure and condemnation of goods, etc; forfeiture) shall apply in respect of any goods liable to forfeiture by virtue of regulation 3 as they apply in respect of goods liable to forfeiture under the customs and excise Acts; and, accordingly—

(a) section 144 of the 1979 Act (protection of officers, etc in relation to seizure and detention of goods, etc) shall apply in respect of seizure or detention effected by virtue of this regulation; and

(b) sections 145, 146 and 152 to 155 of the 1979 Act[20] (general provisions as to legal proceedings) shall apply in respect of condemnation proceedings brought by virtue of this regulation.

[19] Section 139(4)(c) was amended, in relation to Northern Ireland, by the Police (Northern Ireland) Act 1998 (c. 32), Schedule 4, paragraph 14.

[20] Section 153(4) was added by paragraph 9 of Part I of Schedule 8 to the Finance Act 1981 (c. 35); section 155(1) had been amended by paragraph 29(3) of Part 2 of Schedule 4 to the Criminal Justice and Public Order Act 1994 (c. 33) from a date to be appointed but, by virtue of section 44 of the Criminal Procedure and Investigations Act 1996 (c. 25), that amendment, *inter alia*, is treated as never having been enacted.

(2) Where in any condemnation proceedings brought by virtue of paragraph (1) any question arises as to whether or not any goods are or were liable to forfeiture under regulation 3, the burden of proof shall lie upon the party alleging that they are not, or were not, so liable.

Detention and seizure of goods infringing specified intellectual property rights

A26–009   **8.**—(1) Regulation 7 shall not apply in relation to goods as regards which the decision specifies as subsisting in those goods any one or more of the following intellectual property rights (whether or not they also appear to infringe any other intellectual property right)—

(a) a patent;
(b) a supplementary protection certificate;
(c) a registered design;
(d) a design right;
(e) a Community design;
(f) a plant breeders' right;
(g) a Community plant variety right;
(h) a designation of origin;
(i) a geographical indication; or
(j) a geographical designation.

(2) A right-holder may, within 10 working days of his having been notified by the Commissioners of the suspension of release of such goods, or of such goods being detained, give notice in writing to the Commissioners waiving, for the purpose of both the Council Regulation and these Regulations, any intellectual property right of his in the goods, being a right mentioned in sub-paragraphs (a) to (j) in paragraph (1).

(3) The period referred to in paragraph (2) shall be 3 working days in cases where the Commissioners have suspended the release of, or detained, perishable goods.

(4) Where notice has been given in accordance with paragraph (2)—

(a) any right so waived shall be disregarded, as regards that right-holder, in determining whether the goods fall within paragraph (1); and
(b) the goods shall be treated for the purposes of these Regulations as if that person did not have the right concerned in those goods.

(5) The following provisions of the 1979 Act shall apply to any goods falling within paragraph (1) as they apply in respect of goods liable to forfeiture under the customs and excise Acts—

(a) section 139, except subsections (5) and (6) (things seized or detained to be dealt with or disposed of as Commissioners direct; Schedule 3 to have effect); and
(b) section 144.

(6) Any thing seized or detained by virtue of this regulation shall be dealt with in such manner as the Commissioners may direct; but this paragraph shall apply subject to section 139(3) and (4) of the 1979 Act (detention or seizure by a constable; things retained in the custody of the police) in the cases there mentioned.

Initiation of proceedings

A26–010   **9.**—(1) In the case of goods falling within paragraph (1) of regulation 8, the commencement of the proceedings described in paragraph (2) below, and only such proceedings, shall constitute the initiation of proceedings to determine whether an intellectual property right has been infringed for the purposes of the Council Regulation.

(2) The proceedings mentioned in paragraph (1) above are proceedings commenced in the relevant court by a right-holder alleging that the goods infringe an intellectual property right of his and seeking relief which that court has the power to grant after a finding of such infringement.

(3) Without prejudice to any provision of the Council Regulation, the suspension of the release of the goods, or their detention, shall cease if at any time the Commissioners—

(a) are not satisfied, or cease to be satisfied, that the proceedings described in paragraph (2) have been commenced; or

(b) are satisfied that such proceedings have been withdrawn or otherwise terminated without other such proceedings having been commenced.

(4) For the purposes of this regulation proceedings shall not be taken to have been commenced before—

(a) an originating process has been issued or, in the case of the Court of Session, signeted by the relevant court; and

(b) that process has been served on the other party or, if more than one, all the other parties to the proceedings, in accordance with the rules of the court concerned.

(5) In paragraph (4), the reference to an originating process is a reference to—

(a) in England and Wales, a claim form;

(b) in Scotland, a summons; or

(c) in Northern Ireland, a writ.

(6) For the purposes of this regulation the relevant court is—

(a) in England and Wales, the High Court or any patents county court having jurisdiction by virtue of an order under section 287 of the Copyright, Designs and Patents Act 1988;

(b) in Scotland, the Court of Session; or

(c) in Northern Ireland, the High Court.

Relationship with other powers

10. Nothing in these Regulations shall be taken to affect—

A26–011

(a) any power of the Commissioners conferred otherwise than by any provision of these Regulations to suspend the release of, or detain, any goods; or

(b) the power of any court to grant any relief, including any power to make an order by way of interim relief.

Misuse of information by a right-holder

11.—(1) Where the Commissioners have reasonable grounds for believing that there has been a misuse of information by a right-holder the Commissioners may suspend the decision in force at the time of the misuse of information, in relation to a relevant intellectual property right, for the remainder of its period of validity.

A26–012

(2) Where the Commissioners have reasonable grounds for believing that there has been a further misuse of information within three years of a previous misuse of information by that right-holder the Commissioners may—

(a) suspend the decision in force at the time of the further misuse of information, in relation to a relevant intellectual property right, for the remainder of its period of validity; and

(b) for a period of up to one year from its expiry, refuse to renew the decision in force at the time of the further misuse of information, or to accept a new application, in relation to a relevant intellectual property right.

(3) In this regulation—

(a) "misuse of information" means the use of information supplied to a right-holder pursuant to the first sub-paragraph of Article 9(3) of the Council Regulation other than for the purposes specified in Articles 10, 11 and 13(1) of the Council Regulation, or pursuant to an enactment or order of a court, and related expressions shall be construed accordingly;

(b) "relevant intellectual property right" means any intellectual property right in relation to a suspected infringement of which information was supplied to a right-holder pursuant to the first sub-paragraph of Article 9(3) of the Council Regulation, and in relation to which the Commissioners have reasonable grounds for believing that there has been a misuse of that information.

Amendment of the Copyright, Designs and Patents Act 1988

A26–013   **12.** For subsection (3B) of section 111 of the Copyright, Designs and Patents Act 1988[21] there shall be substituted—

"(3B) This section does not apply to goods placed in, or expected to be placed in, one of the situations referred to in Article 1(1), in respect of which an application may be made under Article 5(1), of Council Regulation (EC) No 1383/2003 concerning customs action against goods suspected of infringing certain intellectual property rights and the measures to be taken against goods found to have infringed such rights.".

Amendment of the Trade Marks Act 1994

A26–014   **13.** For subsection (3) of section 89 of the Trade Marks Act 1994[22] there shall be substituted—

"(3) This section does not apply to goods placed in, or expected to be placed in, one of the situations referred to in Article 1(1), in respect of which an application may be made under Article 5(1), of Council Regulation (EC) No 1383/2003 concerning customs action against goods suspected of infringing certain intellectual property rights and the measures to be taken against goods found to have infringed such rights.".

Revocations

A26–015   **14.** The Regulations listed in the Schedule are hereby revoked.

M J Hanson

Commissioner of Customs and Excise

New King's Beam House, 22 Upper Ground, London, SE1 9PJ

4th June 2004

---

[21] Subsection (3B) was inserted by S.I. 1995/1445.
[22] Subsection (3) was substituted by S.I. 1995/1444.

Regulation 14   SCHEDULE

REVOCATIONS

Regulations *revoked*	*References*
The Trade Marks (EC Measures Relating to Counterfeit Goods) Regulations 1995.	S.I. 1995/1444
The Goods Infringing Intellectual Property Rights (Customs) Regulations 1999.	S.I. 1999/1601
The Goods Infringing Intellectual Property Rights (Consequential Provisions) Regulations 1999.	S.I. 1999/1618
The Goods Infringing Intellectual Property Rights (Customs) Regulations 2003.	S.I. 2003/2316

A26–016

Explanatory Note

(This note is not part of the Order)   A26–017

These Regulations, which come into force on 1st July 2004, revoke and replace the Goods Infringing Intellectual Property Rights (Customs) Regulations 1999 (SI 1999/1601, amended by SI 2003/2316) and the Goods Infringing Intellectual Property Rights (Consequential Provisions) Regulations 1999 (SI 1999/1618). Those Regulations made provisions consequential upon Council Regulation (EC) No. 3295/1994 (OJ No. L 341, December 30, 1994, p.8), as amended by Council Regulation (EC) No. 241/1999 (OJ No L 27, Febraury 2, 1999, p.1), which laid down measures concerning the entry into the Community, and the export and re-export from the Community, of goods infringing certain intellectual property rights.

Council Regulation (EC) No. 1383/2003 (OJ No. L 196, August 2, 2003, p.7), which replaces Regulation 3295/1994 with effect from July 1, 2004, introduces the following principal changes:

(a) the use of a standard application form, containing a declaration by the right-holder;

(b) the abolition of application fees;

(c) the provision of additional information to the right-holder at an earlier stage;

(d) the introduction of sanctions if a right-holder misuses information supplied to him; and

(e) the extension to goods infringing a national plant variety right, a Community plant variety right, a designation of origin, a geographical indication, or a geographical designation.

These Regulations re-enact regs 2 to 8 of SI 1999/1618 amended to reflect Regulation 1383/2003, make new provisions consequential upon Regulation 1383/2003 and re-enact paras 8(b) and (c) of SI 1999/1601. The other provisions of SI 1999/1601, relating to the application form, the provision of security by the applicant and the application fee, are rendered otiose by the changes introduced by Regulation 1383/2003.

These Regulations revoke and replace the Trade Marks (EC Measures Relating to Counterfeit Goods) Regulations 1995 (SI 1995/1444) which excluded goods covered by Reg.3295/1994 from the operation of s.89 of the Trade Marks Act 1994. These Regulations also amend s.111(3B) of the Copyright, Designs and Patents Act 1988.

These Regulations revoke the Goods Infringing Intellectual Property Rights (Customs) Regulations 2003 (SI 2003/2316), which abolished fees for applications to the Commissioners with effect from October 1, 2003 and which are now otiose.

Regulations 2, 3, 7, 9 and 10 re-enact regs 2, 3, 5, 7 and 8 of SI 1999/1618, amended to reflect the provisions of Reg.1383/2003.

Regulation 4 re-enacts reg.4 of SI 1999/1618, with the addition of para.(1)(a) and of the reference to the declarant in para.(1)(b).

Regulation 5 re-enacts paras 8(b) and (c) of SI 1999/1601.

Regulation 6 is a new provision setting out circumstances in which samples of suspected infringing goods may be provided to the right-holder.

Regulation 8 re-enacts reg.6 of SI 1999/1618, amended to reflect the extended scope of Reg.1383/2003 and to provide for a 3 day period where perishable goods are involved.

Regulation 11 is a new provision setting out the sanctions which the Commissioners may impose if there has been a misuse of information by a right-holder. In all cases the Commissioners may suspend the decision in relation to a relevant intellectual property right for the remainder of its period of validity (the maximum period of validity is one year). If the right-holder has misused information within the previous three years the Commissioners may also refuse to renew the decision, or to accept an application, in relation to a relevant intellectual property right for a period of up to one year from the date of its expiry.

Regulations 12 and 13 amend s.111(3B) of the Copyright, Designs and Patents Act 1988 and s.89(3) of the Trade Marks Act 1994 to refer to Reg.1383/2003.

Regulation 14 revokes the four Regulations referred to above and listed in the Schedule.

A full regulatory impact assessment has not been produced for this instrument as it has no impact on the costs of business, charities or voluntary bodies.

Customs and Excise Management Act 1979

1979 CHAPTER 2

An Act to consolidate the enactments relating to the collection and management   A27–001
of the revenues of customs and excise and in some cases to other matters in
relation to which the Commissioners of Customs and Excise for the time being
perform functions, with amendments to give effect to recommendations of the
Law Commission and the Scottish Law Commission.

[22nd February 1979]

Be it enacted by the Queen's most Excellent Majesty, by and with the advice and
consent of the Lords Spiritual and Temporal, and Commons, in this present
Parliament assembled, and by the authority of the same, as follows:—

PART I

PRELIMINARY

Interpretation

1.—(1) In this Act, unless the context otherwise requires—   A27–002

...

"armed forces means the Royal Navy, the Royal Marines, the regular army
and the regular air force, and any reserve or auxiliary force of any of
those services which has been called out on permanent service, or
called into actual service, or embodied;

"assigned matter" means any matter in relation to which the Commissioners are for the time being required in pursuance of any enactment to
perform any duties;

...

"boundary" means the land boundary of Northern Ireland;

"British ship" means a British ship within the meaning of the Merchant
Shipping Act 1894, so, however, as not to include a ship registered in
any country other than the United Kingdom, the Channel Islands, the
Isle of Man or a colony within the meaning of the British Nationality
Act 1948;

"claimant", in relation to proceedings for the condemnation of any thing as
being forfeited, means a person claiming that the thing is not liable to
forfeiture;

...

"commander", in relation to an aircraft, includes any person having or taking the charge or command of the aircraft;

"the Commissioners" means the Commissioners of Customs and Excise;

...

"container" includes any bundle or package and any box, cask or other
receptacle whatsoever;

"the customs and excise Acts" means the Customs and Excise Acts 1979
and any other enactment for the time being in force relating to
customs or excise;

"the Customs and Excise Acts 1979" means— this Act, the Customs and Excise Duties (General Reliefs) Act 1979, the Alcoholic Liquor Duties Act 1979, the Hydrocarbon Oil Duties Act 1979, the Matches and Mechanical Lighters Duties Act 1979, and the Tobacco Products Duty Act 1979;

"customs warehouse" means a place of security approved by the Commissioners under subsection (2) (whether or not it is also approved under subsection (1)) of section 92 below;

. . .

"customs and excise station" has the meaning given by " section 26 below;

"excise warehouse" means a place of security approved by the Commissioners under subsection (1) (whether or not it is also approved under subsection (2)) of section 92 below, and, except in that section, also includes a distiller's warehouse;

"exporter", in relation to goods for exportation or for use as stores, includes the shipper of the goods and any person performing in relation to an aircraft functions corresponding with those of a shipper;

"goods" includes stores and baggage;

"holiday", in relation to any part of the United Kingdom, means any day that is a bank holiday in that part of the United Kingdom under the Banking and Financial Dealings Act 1971, Christmas Day, Good Friday and the day appointed for the purposes of customs and excise for the celebration of Her Majesty's birthday;

. . .

"importer", in relation to any goods at any time between their importation and the time when they are delivered out of charge, includes any owner or other person for the time being possessed of or beneficially interested in the goods and, in relation to goods imported by means of a pipe-line, includes the owner of the pipe-line;

"justice" and "justice of the peace" in Scotland includes a sheriff and in Northern Ireland, in relation to any powers and duties which can under any enactment for the time being in force be exercised and performed only by a resident magistrate, means a resident magistrate;

"land" and "landing" in relation to aircraft, include alighting on water;

"law officer of the Crown" means the Attorney General or in Scotland the Lord Advocate or in Northern Ireland the Attorney General for Northern Ireland;

. . .

"master", in relation to a ship, includes any person having or taking the charge or command of the ship;

. . .

"occupier", in relation to any bonded premises, means the person who has given security to the Crown inrespect of those premises;

"officer" means, subject to section 8(2) below, a person commissioned by the Commissioners;

"owner", in relation to an aircraft, includes the operator of the aircraft;

. . .

"prescribed sum", in relation to the penalty provided for an offence, has the meaning given by section 171(2) below;

"prohibited or restricted goods" means goods of a class or description of which the importation, exportation or carriage coastwise is for the time being prohibited or restricted under or by virtue of any enactment;

"proper", in relation to the person by, with or to whom, or the place at which, anything is to be done, means the person or place appointed or authorised in that behalf by the Commissioners;

"proprietor", in relation to any goods, includes any owner, importer, exporter, shipper or other person for the time being possessed of or beneficially interested in those goods;

"Queen's warehouse" means any place provided by the Crown or appointed by the Commissioners for the deposit of goods for security thereof and of the duties chargeable thereon;

...

"ship" and "vessel" include any boat or other vessel whatsoever (and, to the extent provided in section 2 below, any hovercraft);

"shipment" includes loading into an aircraft, and "shipped" and cognate expressions shall be construed accordingly;

"stores" means, subject to subsection (4) below, goods for use in a ship or aircraft and includes fuel and spare parts and other articles of equipment, whether or not for immediate fitting;

...

"transit or transhipment", in relation to the entry of goods, means transit through the United Kingdom or transhipment with a view to the re-exportation of the goods in question;

...

"vehicle" includes a railway vehicle;

"warehouse", except in the expressions "Queen's warehouse" and "distiller's warehouse", means a place of security approved by the Commissioners under subsection (1) or (2) or subsections (1) and (2) of section 92 below and, except in that section, also includes a distiller's warehouse; and "warehoused" and cognate expressions shall, subject to subsection (4) of that section, be construed accordingly;

...

Forfeiture, offences, etc. in connection with importation

Forfeiture of goods improperly imported

49.—(1) Where—

A27–003

(a) except as provided by or under the Customs and Excise Acts 1979, any imported goods, being goods chargeable on their importation with customs or excise duty, are, without payment of that duty—

    (i) unshipped in any port,

    (ii) unloaded from any aircraft in the United Kingdom,

    (iii) unloaded from any vehicle in, or otherwise brought across the boundary into, Northern Ireland, or

    (iv) removed from their place of importation or from any approved wharf, examination station or transit shed; or

(b) any goods are imported, landed or unloaded contrary to any prohibition or restriction for the time being in force with respect thereto under or by virtue of any enactment; or

(c) any goods, being goods chargeable with any duty or goods the importation of which is for the time being prohibited or restricted by or under any enactment, are found, whether before or after the unloading thereof, to have been concealed in any manner on board any ship or aircraft or, while in Northern Ireland, in any vehicle; or

(d) any goods are imported concealed in a container holding goods of a different description; or

(e) any imported goods are found, whether before or after delivery, not to correspond with the entry made thereof, or

(f) any imported goods are concealed or packed in any manner appearing to be intended to deceive an officer,

those goods shall, subject to subsection (2) below, be liable to forfeiture.

(2) Where any goods, the importation of which is for the time being prohibited or restricted by or under any enactment, are on their importation either—

(a) reported as intended for exportation in the same ship, aircraft or vehicle; or

(b) entered for transit or transhipment; or

(c) entered to be warehoused for exportation or for use as stores,

the Commissioners may, if they see fit, permit the goods to be dealt with accordingly.

...

Forfeiture

Provisions as to detention seizure and condemnation of goods, etc.

A27–004   **139.**—(1) Any thing liable to forfeiture under the customs and excise Acts may be seized or detained by any officer or constable or any member of Her Majesty's armed forces or coastguard.

(2) Where any thing is seized or detained as liable to forfeiture under the customs and excise Acts by a person other than an officer, that person shall, subject to subsection (3) below, either—

(a) deliver that thing to the nearest convenient office of customs and excise; or

(b) if such delivery is not practicable, give to the Commissioners at the nearest convenient office of customs and excise notice in writing of the seizure or detention with full particulars of the thing seized or detained.

(3) Where the person seizing or detaining any thing as liable to forfeiture under the customs and excise Acts is a constable and that thing is or may be required for use in connection with any proceedings to be brought otherwise than under those Acts it may, subject to subsection (4) below, be retained in the custody of the police until either those proceedings are completed or it is decided that no such proceedings shall be brought.

(4) The following provisions apply in relation to things retained in the custody of the police by virtue of subsection (3) above that is to say—

(a) Notice in writing of the seizure or detention and of the intention to retain the thing in question in the custody of the police, together with full particulars as to that thing, shall be given to the Commissioners at the nearest convenient office of customs and excise;

(b) any officer shall be permitted to examine that thing and take account thereof at any time while it remains in the custody of the police;

(c) nothing in the Police (Property) Act 1897 shall apply in relation to that thing.

(5) Subject to subsections (3) and (4) above and to Schedule 3 to this Act, any thing seized or detained under the customs and excise Acts shall, pending the determination as to its forfeiture or disposal, be dealt with, and, if condemned or

deemed to have been condemned or forfeited, shall be disposed of in such manner as the Commissioners may direct.

(6) Schedule 3 to this Act shall have effect for the purpose of forfeitures, and of proceedings for the condemnation of any thing as being forfeited, under the customs and excise Acts.

(7) If any person, not being an officer, by whom any thing is seized or detained or who has custody thereof after its seizure or detention, fails to comply with any requirement of this section or with any direction of the commissioners given there-under, he shall be liable on summary conviction to a penalty of £50.

(8) Subsections (2) to (7) above shall apply in relation to any dutiable goods seized or detained by any person other than an officer notwithstanding that they were not so seized as liable to forfeiture under the customs and excise Acts.

Sections 139, 143 and 145   SCHEDULE 3

PROVISIONS RELATING TO FORFEITURE

Notice of seizure

1.—(1) The Commissioners shall, except as provided in sub-paragraph (2) below, give notice of the seizure of any thing as liable to forfeiture and of the grounds therefor to any person who to their knowledge was at the time of the seizure the owner or one of the owners thereof.   **A27–005**

(2) Notice need not be given under this paragraph if the seizure was made in the presence of—

(a) the person whose offence or suspected offence occasioned the seizure; or

(b) the owner or any of the owners of the thing seized or any servant or agent of his; or

(c) in the case of any thing seized in any ship or aircraft, the master or commander.

2. Notice under paragraph 1 above shall be given in writing and shall be deemed to have been duly served on the person concerned—

(a) if delivered to him personally; or

(b) if addressed to him and left or forwarded by post to him at his usual or last known place of abode or business or, in the case of a body corporate, at their registered or principal office; or

(c) where he has no address within the United Kingdom, or his address is unknown, by publication of notice of the seizure in the London, Edinburgh or Belfast Gazette.

Notice of claim

3. Any person claiming that any thing seized as liable to forfeiture is not so liable shall, within one month of the date of the notice of seizure or, where no such notice has been served on him within one month of the date of the seizure, give notice of his right in writing to the Commissioners at any office of customs and exercise.

4.—(1) Any notice under paragraph 3 above shall specify the name and address of the claimant and, in the case of a claimant who is outside the United Kingdom, shall specify the name and address of a solicitor in the United Kingdom who is authorised to accept service of process and to act on behalf of the claimant.

(2) Service of process upon a solicitor so specified shall be deemed to be proper service upon the claimant.

Condemnation

5. If on the expiration of the relevant period under paragraph 3 above for the giving of notice of claim in respect of any thing no such notice has been given to the Commissioners, or if, in the case of any such notice given, any requirement of paragraph 4 above is not complied with, the thing in question shall be deemed to have been duly condemned as forfeited.   **A27–006**

6. Where notice of claim in respect of any thing is duly given in accordance with paragraphs 3 and 4 above, the Commissioners shall take proceedings for the condemnation of that thing by the court, and if the court finds that the thing was at the time of seizure liable to forfeiture the court shall condemn it as forfeited.

7. Where any thing is in accordance with either of paragraphs 5 or 6 above condemned or deemed to have been condemned as forfeited, then, without prejudice to any delivery up or sale of the thing by the Commissioners under paragraph 16 below, the forfeiture shall have effect as from the date when the liability to forfeiture arose.

Proceedings for condemnation by court

8. Proceedings for condemnation shall be civil proceedings and may be instituted—

(a) in England or Wales either in the High Court or in a magistrates' court;

(b) in Scotland either in the Court of Session or in the sheriff court;

(c) in Northern Ireland either in the High Court or in a court of summary jurisdiction.

9. Proceedings for the condemnation of any thing instituted in a magistrates' court in England or Wales, in the sheriff court in Scotland or in a court of summary jurisdiction in Northern Ireland may be so instituted—

(a) in any such court having jurisdiction in the place where any offence in connection with that thing was committed or where any proceedings for such an offence are instituted; or

(b) in any such court having jurisdiction in the place where the claimant resides or, if the claimant has specified a solicitor under paragraph 4 above, in the place where that solicitor has his office; or

(c) in any such court having jurisdiction in the place where that thing was found, detained or seized or to which it is first brought after being found, detained or seized.

10.—(1) In any proceedings for condemnation instituted in England, Wales or Northern Ireland, the claimant or his solicitor shall make oath that the thing seized was, or was to the best of his knowledge and belief, the property of the claimant at the time of the seizure.

(2) In any such proceedings instituted in the High Court, the claimant shall give such security for the costs of the proceedings as may be determined by the Court.

(3) If any requirement of this paragraph is not complied with, the court shall give judgment for the Commissioners.

11.—(1) In the case of any proceedings for condemnation instituted in a magistrates' court in England or Wales, without prejudice to any right to require the statement of a case for the opinion of the High Court, either party may appeal against the decision of that court to the Crown Court.

(2) In the case of any proceedings for condemnation instituted in a court of summary jurisdiction in Northern Ireland, without prejudice to any right to require the statement of a case for the opinion of the High Court, either party may appeal against the decision of that court to the county court.

12. Where an appeal, including an appeal by way of case stated, has been made against the decision of the court in any proceedings for the condemnation of any thing, that thing shall, pending the final determination of the matter, be left with the Commissioners or at any convenient office of customs and excise.

Provisions as to proof

A27–007   **13.** In any proceedings arising out of the seizure of any thing, the fact, form and manner of the seizure shall be taken to have been as set forth in the process without any further evidence thereof, unless the contrary is proved.

14. In any proceedings, the condemnation by a court of any thing as forfeited may be proved by the production either of the order or certificate of condemnation or of a certified copy thereof purporting to be signed by an officer of the court by which the order or certificate was made or granted.

Special provisions as to certain claimants

A27–008   **15.** For the purposes of any claim to, or proceedings for the condemnation of, any thing, where that thing is at the time of seizure the property of a body corporate, of two or more partners or of any number of persons exceeding five, the oath required by paragraph 10 above to be taken and any other thing required by this Schedule or by any rules of the court to be done by, or by any person authorised by, the claimant or owner may be taken or done by, or by any other person authorised by, the following persons respectively that is to say—

    (a) where the owner is a body corporate, the secretary or some duly authorised officer of that body;

    (b) where the owners are in partnership, any one of those owners;

    (c) where the owners are any number of persons exceeding five not being in partnership, any two of those persons on behalf of themselves and their coowners.

Power to deal with seizures before condemnation, etc.

16. Where any thing has been seized as liable to forfeiture the Commissioners may at any time if they see fit and notwithstanding that the thing has not yet been condemned, or is not yet deemed to have been condemned, as forfeited—

    (a) deliver it up to any claimant upon his paying to the Commissioners such sum as they think proper, being a sum not exceeding that which in their opinion represents the value of the thing, including any duty or tax chargeable thereon which has not been paid;

    (b) if the thing seized is a living creature or is in the opinion of the Commissioners of a perishable nature, sell or destroy it.

17.—(1) If, where any thing is delivered up, sold or destroyed under paragraph 16 above, it is held in proceedings taken under this Schedule that the thing was not liable to forfeiture at the time of its seizure, the Commissioners shall, subject to any deduction allowed under sub-paragraph (2) below, on demand by the claimant tender to him—   **A27–009**

    (a) an amount equal to any sum paid by him under sub-paragraph (a) of that paragraph; or

    (b) where they have sold the thing, an amount equal to the proceeds of sale; or

    (c) where they have destroyed the thing, an amount equal to the market value of the thing at the time of its seizure.

(2) Where the amount to be tendered under sub-paragraph (1)(a), (b) or (c) above includes any sum on account of any duty or tax chargeable on the thing which had not been paid before its seizure the Commissioners may deduct so much of that amount as represents that duty or tax.

(3) If the claimant accepts any amount tendered to him under sub-paragraph (1) above, he shall not be entitled to maintain any action on account of the seizure, detention, sale or destruction of the thing.

(4) For the purposes of sub-paragraph (1)(c) above, the market value of any thing at the time of its seizure shall be taken to be such amount as the Commissioners and the claimant may agree or, in default of agreement, as may be determined by a referee appointed by the Lord Chancellor (not being an official of any government a department), whose decision shall be final and conclusive; and the procedure on any reference to a referee shall be such as may be determined by the referee.

PART IX

INTELLECTUAL PROPERTY PROCEEDINGS

Part 63—Patents and other Intellectual Property Claims and the Practice Direction—Patents and Intellectual Property Claims

Contents

IV. Appeals

         Practice Direction—Patents and other Intellectual   para. A29–001
         Property Claims

Scope of this Part and interpretation

A28-001   **63.1**—(1) This Part applies to all intellectual property claims including—

(a) registered intellectual property rights such as—
   (i) patents;
   (ii) registered designs; and
   (iii) registered trade marks; and
(b) unregistered intellectual property rights such as—
   (i) copyright;
   (ii) design right;
   (iii) the right to prevent passing off; and
   (iv) the other rights set out in the practice direction.

(2) In this Part—

(a) "the 1977 Act" means the Patents Act 1977[23];
(b) "the 1988 Act" means the Copyright, Designs and Patents Act 1988[24];
(c) "the 1994 Act" means the Trade Marks Act 1994[25];
(d) "the Comptroller" means the Comptroller General of Patents, Designs and Trade Marks;
(e) "patent" means a patent under the 1977 Act and includes any application for a patent or supplementary protection certificate granted under—

   (i) the Patents (Supplementary Protection Certificates) Rules 1997[26];

   (ii) the Patents (Supplementary Protection Certificate for Medicinal Products) Regulations 1992[27]; and

   (iii) the Patents (Supplementary Protection Certificate for Plant Protection Products) Regulations 1996[28];

(f) "Patents Court" means the Patents Court of the High Court constituted as part of the Chancery Division by section 6(1) of the Supreme Court Act 1981[29];
(g) "Patents County Court" means a county court designated as a Patents County Court under section 287(1) of the 1988 Act;
(h) "the register" means whichever of the following registers is appropriate—

   (i) patents maintained by the Comptroller under section 32 of the 1977 Act

---

[23] 1977 c.37.
[24] 1988 c.48.
[25] 1994 c.26.
[26] SI 1997/ 64.
[27] SI 1992/3091.
[28] SI 1996/3120.
[29] 1981 c.54.

(ii) designs maintained by the registrar under section 17 of the Registered Designs Act 1949[30] ;

(iii) trade marks maintained by the registrar under section 63 of the 1994 Act;

(iv) Community trade marks maintained by the Office for Harmonisation in the Internal Market under Article 83 of Council Regulation (EC) 40/94[31]; and

(v) Community designs maintained by the Office for Harmonisation in the Internal Market under Article 72 of Council Regulation (EC) 6/2002[32] ; **and**

(i) "the registrar" means—

(i) the registrar of trade marks; or

(ii) the registrar of registered designs,

whichever is appropriate.

Application of the Civil Procedure Rules

63.2 These Rules and their practice directions apply to intellectual property claims unless this Part or a practice direction provides otherwise. **A28-002**

I. PATENTS AND REGISTERED DESIGNS

Scope of Section I

63.3—(1) This Section of this Part applies to claims in— **A28-003**

(a) the Patents Court; and

(b) a Patents County Court.

(2) Claims in the court include any claim relating to matters arising out of—

(a) the 1977 Act;

(b) the Registered Designs Act 1949; and

(c) the Defence Contracts Act 19581958, c.38..

Specialist list

63.4 Claims in the Patents Court and a Patents County Court form specialist lists for the purpose of rule 30.5. **A28-004**

Starting the claim

63.5 Claims to which this Section of this Part applies must be started— **A28-005**

(a) by issuing a Part 7 claim form; or

(b) in existing proceedings under Part 20.

Defence and reply

63.6 Part 15 applies with the modification— **A28-006**

(a) to rule 15.4 that in a claim for infringement under rule 63.9, the defence must be filed within 42 days of service of the claim form; and

(b) to rule 15.8 that the claimant must—

(i) file any reply to a defence; and

(ii) serve it on all other parties,

within 21 days of service of the defence.

---

[30] 1949 c.88.
[31] [1994]O.J. L11/1.
[32] [2002] O.J. L3/1.

Case management[33]

A28-007   **63.7**—(1) Claims under this Section of this Part are allocated to the multi-track.

(2) Part 26 and any other rule that requires a party to file an allocation questionnaire do not apply.

(3) The following provisions only of Part 29 apply—

(a) rule 29.3(2) (legal representatives to attend case management conferences);

(b) rule 29.4 (the court's approval of agreed proposals for the management of proceedings); and

(c) rule 29.5 (variation of case management timetable) with the exception of paragraph (1)(b) and (c).

(4) As soon as practicable the court will hold a case management conference which must be fixed in accordance with the practice direction.

Disclosure and inspection

A28-008   **63.8** Part 31 is modified to the extent set out in the practice direction.

Claim for infringement and challenge to validity[34]

A28-009   **63.9**—(1) In a claim for infringement or an application in which the validity of a patent or registered design is challenged, the statement of case must contain particulars as set out in the practice direction.

(2) In a claim for infringement, the period for service of the defence or Part 20 claim is 42 days after service of the claim form.

Application to amend a patent specification in existing proceedings

A28-010   **63.10**—(1) An application under section 75 of the 1977 Act for permission to amend the specification of a patent by the proprietor of the patent must be made by application notice.

(2) The application notice must—

(a) give particulars of—

(i) the proposed amendment sought; and

(ii) the grounds upon which the amendment is sought;

(b) state whether the applicant will contend that the claims prior to amendment are valid; and

(c) be served by the applicant on all parties and the Comptroller within 7 days of its issue.

(3) The application notice must, if it is reasonably possible, be served on the Comptroller electronically.

(4) Unless the court otherwise orders, the Comptroller will forthwith advertise the application to amend in the journal.

(5) The advertisement will state that any person may apply to the Comptroller for a copy of the application notice.

(6) Within 14 days of the first appearance of the advertisement any person who wishes to oppose the application must file and serve on all parties and the Comptroller a notice opposing the application which must include the grounds relied on.

(7) Within 28 days of the first appearance of the advertisement the applicant must apply to the court for directions.

---

[33] Amended by Civil Procedure (Amendment No. 5) Rules 2003 (SI 2003/3361).
[34] Amended by Civil Procedure (Amendment No. 5) Rules 2003 (SI 2003/3361).

(8) Unless the court otherwise orders, the applicant must within 7 days serve on the Comptroller any order of the court on the application.

(9) In this rule, "the journal" means the journal published pursuant to rules made under section 123(6) of the 1977 Act.

Court's determination of question or application

63.11 Where the Comptroller—

A28-011

(a) declines to deal with a question under section 8(7), 12(2), 37(8) or 61(5) of the 1977 Act;

(b) declines to deal with an application under section 40(5) of the 1977 Act; or

(c) certifies under section 72(7)(b) of the 1977 Act that the court should determine the question whether a patent should be revoked,

any person seeking the court's determination of that question or application must issue a claim form within 14 days of the Comptroller's decision.

Application by employee for compensation

63.12—(1) An application by an employee for compensation under section 40(1) or (2) of the 1977 Act must be made—

A28-012

(a) in a claim form; and

(b) within the period prescribed by paragraphs (2) and (3).

(2) The prescribed period begins on the date of the grant of the patent and ends one year after the patent has ceased to have effect.

(3) Where a patent has ceased to have effect as a result of failure to pay the renewal fees within the period prescribed under rule 39 of the Patents Rules 1995([35]), and an application for restoration is made to the Comptroller under section 28 of the 1977 Act, the period prescribed under paragraph (2)—

(a) if restoration is ordered, continues as if the patent had remained continuously in effect; or

(b) if restoration is refused, is treated as expiring one year after the patent ceased to have effect, or six months after the refusal, whichever is the later.

II. REGISTERED TRADE MARKS AND OTHER INTELLECTUAL PROPERTY RIGHTS

Allocation

63.13—(1) This Section of this Part applies to—

A28-013

(a) claims relating to matters arising out of the 1994 Act; and

(b) other intellectual property rights as set out in the practice direction.

(2) [...]

(3) Claims to which this Section of this Part applies must be brought in—

(a) the Chancery Division;

(b) a Patents County Court; or

(c) a county court where there is also a Chancery district registry.

Claims under the 1994 Act

63.14 In a claim under the 1994 Act, the claim form or application notice must be served on the registrar where the relief sought would, if granted, affect an entry in the United Kingdom register.

A28-014

---

[35] SI 1995/2093.

Claim for infringement of registered trade mark

A28-015   **63.15**—(1) In a claim for infringement of a registered trade mark the defendant may—

    (a) in his defence, challenge the validity of the registration of the trade mark; and

    (b) apply by Part 20 claim for—

        (i) revocation of the registration;

        (ii) a declaration that the registration is invalid; or

        (iii) rectification of the register.

(2) Where a defendant applies under paragraph (1)(b) and the relief sought would, if granted, affect an entry in the United Kingdom register, he must serve on the registrar a copy of his claim form.

III. SERVICE

Service[36]

A28-016   **63.16**—(1) Subject to paragraph (2), Part 6 applies to service of a claim form and any document under this Part.

(2) A claim form relating to a registered right may be served—

    (a) on a party who has registered the right at the address for service given for that right in the United Kingdom Patent Office register, provided the address is within the jurisdiction; or

    (b) in accordance with rule 6.19(1) or (1A) on a party who has registered the right at the address for service given for that right in the appropriate register at—

        (i) the United Kingdom Patent Office; or

        (ii) the Office for Harmonisation in the Internal Market.

IV. APPEALS

Appeals from the Comptroller

A28-017   **63.17**—(1) Part 52 applies to appeals from the Comptroller.

(2) Patent appeals are to be made to the Patents Court, and other appeals to the Chancery Division.

(3) Where Part 52 requires a document to be served, it must also be served on the Comptroller or registrar, as appropriate.

---

[36] Amended by Civil Procedure (Amendment No. 5) Rules 2003 (SI 2003/3361).

Practice Direction—Patents and Other Intellectual Property Claims

PRACTICE DIRECTION—PATENTS AND OTHER INTELLECTUAL PROPERTY CLAIMS

Practice Direction—Patents and Other Intellectual Property Claims
This Practice Direction supplements CPR Part 63

A29-001

Contents of this Practice Direction

1.1 This practice direction is divided into three sections—

- Section I—Provisions about patents and registered designs;
- Section II—Provisions about registered trade marks and other intellectual property rights;
- Section III—Provisions about appeals.

I. PROVISIONS ABOUT PATENTS AND REGISTERED DESIGNS

2.1 This Section of this practice direction applies to claims in the Patents Court and a Patents County Court.

A29-002

2.2 The following claims must be dealt with in the court—

(1) any matter arising out of the 1977 Act, including—

(a) infringement actions;

(b) revocation actions;

(c) threats under section 70 of the 1977 Act; and

(d) disputes as to ownership;

(2) registered designs;

(3) Community registered designs; and

(4) semiconductor topography rights.

Starting the claim (rule 63.5)

3.1 A claim form to which this Section of this Part applies must be marked in the top right hand corner "Patents Court" below the title of the court in which it is issued.

A29-003

Case management (rule 63.7)

4.1 The following parts only of the practice direction supplementing Part 29 apply—

A29-004

(1) paragraph 5 (case management conferences)—

(a) excluding paragraph 5.9; and

(b) modified so far as is made necessary by other specific provisions of this practice direction; and

(2) paragraph 7 (failure to comply with case management directions).

4.2 Case management shall be dealt with by—

(1) a judge of the court; or

(2) a Master or district judge where a judge of the court so directs.

4.3 The claimant must apply for a case management conference within 14 days of the date when all defendants who intend to file and serve a defence have done so.

4.4 Where the claim has been transferred, the claimant must apply for a case management conference within 14 days of the date of the order transferring the claim, unless the court—

(1) held; or

(2) gave directions for

a case management conference, when it made the order transferring the claim.

4.5 Any party may, at a time earlier than that provided in paragraphs 4.3 and 4.4, apply in writing to the court to fix a case management conference.

4.6 If the claimant does not make an application in accordance with paragraphs 4.3 and 4.4, any other party may apply for a case management conference.

4.7 The court may fix a case management conference at any time on its own initiative.

4.8 Not less than 4 days before a case management conference, each party must file and serve an application notice for any order which that party intends to seek at the case management conference.

4.9 Unless the court orders otherwise, the claimant, or the party who makes an application under paragraph 4.6, in consultation with the other parties, must prepare a case management bundle containing—

(1) the claim form;

(2) all statements of case (excluding schedules), except that, if a summary of a statement of case has been filed, the bundle should contain the summary, and not the full statement of case;

(3) a pre-trial timetable, if one has been agreed or ordered;

(4) the principal orders of the court; and

(5) any agreement in writing made by the parties as to disclosure,

and provide copies of the case management bundle for the court and the other parties at least 4 days before the first case management conference or any earlier hearing at which the court may give case management directions.

4.10 At the case management conference the court may direct that—

(1) a scientific adviser under section 70(3) of the Supreme Court Act 1981 be appointed; and

(2) a document setting out basic undisputed technology should be prepared.

(Rule 35.15 applies to scientific advisers).

4.11 Where a trial date has not been fixed by the court, a party may apply for a trial date by filing a certificate which must—

(1) state the estimated length of the trial, agreed if possible by all parties;

(2) detail the time required for the judge to consider the documents;

(3) identify the area of technology; and

(4) assess the complexity of the technical issues involved by indicating the complexity on a scale of 1 to 5 (with 1 being the least and 5 the most complex).

4.12 The claimant, in consultation with the other parties, must revise and update the documents referred to in paragraph 4.9 appropriately as the case proceeds. This must include making all necessary revisions and additions at least 7 days before any subsequent hearing at which the court may give case management directions.

Disclosure and inspection (rule 63.8)

5.1 Standard disclosure does not require the disclosure of documents where the documents relate to—   **A29-005**

(1) the infringement of a patent by a product or process if, before or at the same time as serving a list of documents, the defendant has served on the claimant and any other party—

(a) full particulars of the product or process alleged to infringe; and

(b) drawings or other illustrations, if necessary;

(2) any ground on which the validity of a patent is put in issue, except documents which came into existence within the period—

(a) beginning two years before the earliest claimed priority date; and

(b) ending two years after that date; and

(3) the issue of commercial success.

5.2 Where the issue of commercial success arises, the patentee must, within such time limit as the court may direct, serve a schedule containing—

(1) where the commercial success relates to an article or product—

(a) an identification of the article or product (for example by product code number) which the patentee asserts has been made in accordance with the claims of the patent;

(b) a summary by convenient periods of sales of any such article or product;

(c) a summary for the equivalent periods of sales, if any, of any equivalent prior article or product marketed before the article or product in sub-paragraph (a); and

(d) a summary by convenient periods of any expenditure on advertising and promotion which supported the marketing of the articles or products in sub-paragraphs (a) and (c); or

(2) where the commercial success relates to the use of a process—

(a) an identification of the process which the patentee asserts has been used in accordance with the claims of the patent;

(b) a summary by convenient periods of the revenue received from the use of such process;

(c) a summary for the equivalent periods of the revenues, if any, received from the use of any equivalent prior art process; and

(d) a summary by convenient periods of any expenditure which supported the use of the process in sub-paragraphs (a) and (c).

Short applications

6.1 Where any application is listed for a short hearing, the parties must file all necessary documents, skeleton arguments and drafts of any orders sought, by no later than 3.00 p.m. on the preceding working day.   **A29-006**

6.2 A short hearing is any hearing which is listed for no more than 1 hour.

Timetable for trial

7.1 Not less than one week before the beginning of the trial, each party must inform the court in writing of the estimated length of its—   **A29-007**

(1) oral submissions;

(2) examination in chief, if any, of its own witnesses; and

(3) cross-examination of witnesses of any other party.

7.2 At least four days before the date fixed for the trial, the claimant must file—

(1) the trial bundle; and

(2) a Reading Guide for the judge.

    7.3 The Reading Guide filed under paragraph 7.2 must—

(1) be short and if possible, agreed;

(2) set out the issues, the parts of the documents that need to be read on each issue and the most convenient order that they should be read;

(3) identify the relevant passages in text books and cases, if appropriate; and

(4) not contain argument.

Jurisdiction of Masters

A29-008   **8.1** A Master may only deal with—

(1) orders by way of settlement, except settlement of procedural disputes;

(2) orders on applications for extension of time;

(3) applications for leave to serve out of the jurisdiction;

(4) applications for security for costs;

(5) other matters as directed by a judge of the court; and.

(6) enforcement of money judgments.

Experiments

A29-009   **9.1** Where a party seeks to establish any fact by experimental proof conducted for the purpose of litigation he must, at least 21 days before service of the application notice for directions under paragraph 9.3, or within such other time as the court may direct, serve on all parties a notice—

(1) stating the facts which he seeks to establish; and

(2) giving full particulars of the experiments proposed to establish them.

    9.2 A party served with notice under paragraph 9.1—

(1) must within 21 days after such service, serve on the other party a notice stating whether or not he admits each fact; and

(2) may request the opportunity to inspect a repetition of all or a number of the experiments identified in the notice served under paragraph 9.1.

    9.3 Where any fact which a party seeks to establish by experimental proof is not admitted, he must apply to the court for permission and directions by application notice.

Use of models or apparatus

A29-010   **10.1** Where a party intends to rely on any model or apparatus, he must apply to the court for directions at the first case management conference.

Claim for infringement and challenge to validity (rule 63.9)

A29-011   **11.1** In a claim for infringement of a patent—

(1) the statement of case must—

  (a) show which of the claims in the specification of the patent are alleged to be infringed; and

  (b) give at least one example of each type of infringement alleged; and

(2) a copy of each document referred to in the statement of case, and where necessary a translation of the document, must be served with the statement of case.

    11.2 Where the validity of a patent or registered design is challenged—

(1) the statement of case must contain particulars of—

(a) the relief sought; and

(b) the issues except those relating to validity of the patent or registered design;

(2) the statement of case must have a separate document annexed to it headed "Grounds of Invalidity" specifying the grounds on which validity of the patent is challenged;

(3) a copy of each document referred to in the Grounds of Invalidity, and where necessary a translation of the document, must be served with the Grounds of Invalidity; and

(4) the Comptroller must be sent a copy of the Grounds of Invalidity and where any such Grounds of Invalidity are amended, a copy of the amended document, at the same time as the Grounds of Invalidity are served or amended.

11.3 Where, in an application in which validity of a patent or a registered design is challenged, the Grounds of Invalidity include an allegation—

(1) that the invention is not a patentable invention because it is not new or does not involve an inventive step, the particulars must specify such details of the matter in the state of art relied on, as set out in paragraph 11.4;

(2) that the specification of the patent does not disclose the invention clearly enough and completely enough for it to be performed by a person skilled in the art, the particulars must state, if appropriate, which examples of the invention cannot be made to work and in which respects they do not work or do not work as described in the specification; or

(3) that the registered design is not new, the particulars must specify such details of the matter in the state of art relied on, as set out in paragraph 11.4.

11.4 The details required under paragraphs 11.3(1) and 11.3(3) are—

(1) in the case of matter or a design made available to the public by written description the date on which and the means by which it was so made available, unless this is clear from the face of the matter; and

(2) in the case of matter or a design made available to the public by use—

(a) the date or dates of such use;

(b) the name of all persons making such use;

(c) any written material which identifies such use;

(d) the existence and location of any apparatus employed in such use; and

(e) all facts and matters relied on to establish that such matter was made available to the public.

11.5 In any proceedings in which the validity of a patent is challenged—

(1) on the ground that the invention did not involve an inventive step, a party who wishes to rely on the commercial success of the patent must state the grounds on which he so relies in his statement of case; and

(2) the court may order inspection of machinery or apparatus where a party alleges such machinery or apparatus was used before the priority date of the claim.

Application to amend a patent specification in existing proceedings (rule 63.10)

12.1 Not later than two days before the first hearing date the applicant, the   A29-012
Comptroller if he wishes to be heard, the parties to the proceedings and any other opponent, must file and serve a document stating the directions sought.

12.2 Where the application notice is served on the Comptroller electronically under rule 63.10(3), it must comply with any requirements for the sending of electronic communications to the Comptroller.

Application by employee for compensation (rule 63.12)

A29-013   **13.1** Where an employee applies for compensation under section 40(1) or (2) of the 1977 Act, the court must at the case management conference give directions as to—

(1) the manner in which the evidence, including any accounts of expenditure and receipts relating to the claim, is to be given at the hearing of the claim and if written evidence is to be given, specify the period within which witness statements or affidavits must be filed; and

(2) the provision to the claimant by the defendant or a person deputed by him, of reasonable facilities for inspecting and taking extracts from the accounts by which the defendant proposes to verify the accounts in sub-paragraph (1) or from which those accounts have been derived.

Communication of information to the European Patent Office

A29-014   **14.1** The court may authorise the communication of any such information in the court files as the court thinks fit to—

(1) the European Patent Office; or

(2) the competent authority of any country which is a party to the European Patent convention.

14.2 Before authorising the disclosure of information under paragraph 14.1, the court shall permit any party who may be affected by the disclosure to make representations, in writing or otherwise, on the question of whether the information should be disclosed.

Order affecting entry in the register of patents or designs

A29-015   **15.1** Where any order of the court affects the validity of an entry in the register, the court and the party in whose favour the order is made, must serve a copy of such order on the Comptroller within 14 days.

15.2 Where the order is in favour of more than one party, a copy of the order must be served by such party as the court directs.

Claim for rectification of the register of patents or designs

A29-016   **16.1** Where a claim is made for the rectification of the register of patents or designs, the claimant must at the same time as serving the other parties, serve a copy of—

(1) the claim form; and

(2) accompanying documents

on the Comptroller or registrar, as appropriate.

16.2 Where documents under paragraph 16.1 are served on the Comptroller or registrar, he shall be entitled to take part in the proceedings.

European Community designs

A29-017   **17.1** The Patents Court and the Central London County Court are the designated Community design courts under Article 80(5) of Council Regulation (EC) 6/2002.

17.2 Where a counterclaim is filed at the Community design court, for a declaration of invalidity of a registered Community design, the Community design court shall inform the Office for Harmonisation in the Internal Market of the date on which the counterclaim was filed, in accordance with Article 86(2) of Council Regulation (EC) 6/2002.

17.3 On filing a counterclaim under paragraph 17.2, the party filing it must inform the court in writing that it is a counterclaim to which paragraph 17.2 applies and that the Office for Harmonisation in the Internal Market needs to be informed of the date on which the counterclaim was filed.

17.4 Where a Community design court has given a judgment which has become final on a counterclaim for a declaration of invalidity of a registered Community design, the Community design court shall send a copy of the judgment to the Office for Harmonisation in the Internal Market, in accordance with Article 86(4) of Council Regulation (EC) 6/2002.

17.5 The party in whose favour judgment is given under paragraph 17.4 must inform the Community design court at the time of judgment that paragraph 17.4 applies and that the Office for Harmonisation in the Internal Market needs to be sent a copy of the judgment.

II. PROVISIONS ABOUT REGISTERED TRADE MARKS AND OTHER INTELLECTUAL PROPERTY RIGHTS

Allocation (rule 63.13)

18.1 Any of the following claims must be brought in the Chancery Division, a   A29-018
Patents County Court or a county court where there is also a Chancery district
registry—

(1) copyright;

(2) rights in performances;

(3) rights conferred under Part VII of the 1988 Act;

(4) design right;

(5) Community design right;

(6) Olympic symbols;

(7) plant varieties;

(8) moral rights;

(9) database rights;

(10) unauthorised decryption rights;

(11) hallmarks;

(12) technical trade secrets litigation;

(13) passing off;

(14) geographical indications.

(15) registered trade marks; and

(16) Community registered trade marks.

18.2 There are Chancery district registries at Birmingham, Bristol, Cardiff, Leeds, Liverpool, Manchester and Newcastle upon Tyne.

Starting the claim

19.1 A claim form to which this Section of this Part applies must be marked in   A29-019
the top right hand corner "Chancery Division, Intellectual Property" below the
title of the court in which it is issued.

Claims under the 1994 Act (rule 63.14)

20.1 Where the registrar refers to the court an application made to him under   A29-020
the 1994 Act, then unless within one month of receiving notification of the decision to refer, the applicant makes the application to the High Court, he shall be deemed to have abandoned it.

20.2 The period prescribed under paragraph 20.1 may be extended by—

(1) the registrar; or

(2) the court

where a party so applies, even if such application is not made until after the expiration of the period prescribed.

20.3 Where an application is made under section 19 of the 1994 Act, the applicant must serve his claim form or application notice on all identifiable persons having an interest in the goods, materials or articles within the meaning of section 19 of the 1994 Act.

Claim for infringement of registered trade mark (rule 63.15)

A29-021   **21.1** Where a document under rule 63.15(2) is served on the registrar, he—

(1) may take part in the proceedings; and

(2) need not serve a defence or other statement of case, unless the court otherwise orders.

Order affecting entry in the register of trade marks

A29-022   **22.1** Where any order of the court affects the validity of an entry in the register, the provisions of paragraphs 15.1 and 15.2 shall apply.

Claim for rectification of the register of trade marks

A29-023   **23.1** Where a claim is made for the rectification of the register of trade marks, the provisions of paragraphs 16.1 and 16.2 shall apply.

European Community trade marks

A29-024   **24.1** The Chancery Division of the High Court, a Patents County Court or a county court where there is also a Chancery district registry are designated Community trade mark courts under Article 91(1) of Council Regulation (EC) 40/94.

24.2 Where a counterclaim is filed at the Community trade mark court, for revocation or for a declaration of invalidity of a Community trade mark, the Community trade mark court shall inform the Office for Harmonisation in the Internal Market of the date on which the counterclaim was filed, in accordance with Article 96(4) of Council Regulation (EC) 40/94.

24.3 On filing a counterclaim under paragraph 24.2, the party filing it must inform the court in writing that it is a counterclaim to which paragraph 24.2 applies and that the Office for Harmonisation in the Internal Market needs to be informed of the date on which the counterclaim was filed.

24.4 Where the Community trade mark court has given a judgment which has become final on a counterclaim for revocation or for a declaration of invalidity of a Community trade mark, the Community trade mark court shall send a copy of the judgment to the Office for Harmonisation in the Internal Market, in accordance with Article 96(6) of Council Regulation (EC) 40/94.

24.5 The party in whose favour judgment is given under paragraph 24.4 must inform the Community trade mark court at the time of judgment that paragraph 24.4 applies and that the Office for Harmonisation in the Internal Market needs to be sent a copy of the judgment.

Claim for additional damages under section 97(2) or section 229(3) of the 1988 Act

A29-025   **25.1** Where a claimant seeks to recover additional damages under section 97(2) or section 229(3) of the 1988 Act, the particulars of claim must include—

(1) a statement to that effect; and

(2) the grounds for claiming them.

Application for delivery up or forfeiture under the 1988 Act

26.1 Where a claimant applies under sections 99, 114, 195, 204, 230 or 231 of   **A29-026**
the 1988 Act for delivery up or forfeiture he must serve—

(1) the claim form; or

(2) application notice, where appropriate,

on all identifiable persons who have an interest in the goods, material or articles
within the meaning of sections 114 or 204 of the 1988 Act.

Olympic symbols

27.1 In this practice direction "the Olympic Symbol Regulations" means the   **A29-027**
Olympic Association Right (Infringement Proceedings) Regulations 1995.

27.2 Where an application is made under regulation 5 of the Olympic Symbol
Regulations, the applicant must serve his claim form or application notice on all
identifiable persons having an interest in the goods, materials or articles within
the meaning of regulation 5 of the Olympic Symbol Regulations.

III. PROVISIONS ABOUT APPEALS

Appeals and references from the Comptroller (rule 63.17)

28.1 Where—   **A29-028**

(1) a person appointed by the Lord Chancellor to hear and decide appeals under
   section 77 of the 1994 Act, refers an appeal to the Chancery Division of the
   High Court under section 76(3) of the 1994 Act; or

(2) the Comptroller refers the whole proceedings or a question or issue to the
   Chancery Division of the High Court under section 251(1) of the 1988 Act,

   the appeal or reference must be brought within 14 days of the reference.

PART X

OTHER

The "Heraldic Convention" for representation of colours

According to this convention, which is used to enable coloured marks to be   A30–001
represented in the black-and-white of the Trade Marks Journal, colours are
represented by shading as follows:

Red (gules): Vertical lines.

Green (vert): diagonal lines descending left to right.

Blue (azure): Horizontal lines.

Purple (purpure): Diagonal lines descending right to left.

Yellow or gold (or): Dotted ground.

Chestnut or deep orange (Tennè): Diagonal lines descending right to left
and horizontal lines, crossing.

Black (sable): Horizontal and vertical lines crossing.

White (argent): Plain ground.

This convention should be used when preparing blocks for printing representations of marks. The Registry's explanation of the convention adds: "Intermediate
colours should, as far as possible be shown by increasing or diminishing the
intensity of the lines."

APPENDIX **31**

List of contrasted marks and names

A31–001   "How can observations of judges upon other and quite different facts bear upon the present case, in which the only question is what is the result of the evidence?" Lord Watson asked in *Johnston v Orr-Ewing*[37]; but the habit of referring to reported cases at the hearing of such questions invetererate and lists of cases are given below.

1. Trade Marks
(1) CONTRASTED DEVICES

A pointer eating out of a pot, too near for registration to a similar dog standing by pail with "Stanch" beneath it.[38] A twisted curved horn with a twig bearing two roses, too near a similar untwisted horn with a cord having two loops in the same place as the roses in the twig.[39] A triangular frame with words upon it and a church inside, too near Bass's solid triangle;[40] so also a white diamond within a red diamond.[41] A half-length figure of a milkmaid, with the word "Dairymaid", too near a full-length figure of a milkmaid carrying two pails.[42] A woman's head wearing as helmet with "Athena" beneath, not too near a man's head with "Way" beneath.[43] A tower in an oval border, with a dog and harp, too near a tower, dog and harp without any border.[44] An oval label containing interlaced triangular frames with a stag's head within them, too near an oval label with three superimposed solid triangles; although the lettering on the marks was conspicuously different.[45] A suspended sheep, with the words "Golden Fleece", too near sheep with the same words.[46] A pig in outline, and H.B. & Co, not too near shaded pointer dog and "Stanch",[47] A tobacco pipe and dart, not too near a tobacco pipe alone.[48] A charging buffalo, too near a bull's head, both silver rings on yellow wrappers.[49] Lion bearing a sheaf, too near a lion with a crown.[50] An elephant in a border, with lettering round it, an infringement of a somewhat different elephant alone.[51] Winged cross surrounded by two circles, not an infringement of a lighthouse similarly surrounded.[52] Two red medals and a balloon, an infringement of a lable with two red medals only, being used for polish known in India as red metal polish.[53] A cock in the centre, with a piece of plaid with the words "Prince Charlie, King o' the Hieland Hearts", too near a label baring the words "The Cock o' the North" with a cock over a coat of arms, with a Highlander and a

---

[37] (1882) 7 App.Cas. 219.
[38] *Jelley's Application* (1878) 51 L.J.Ch. 639n.
[39] *Rosing's Application* (1878) 54 L.J.Ch. 975n.
[40] *Worthington's Trade Mark* (1880) L.J.14 Ch.D. 8.
[41] *Turney & Sons' Trade Mark* (1894) 11 R.P.C. 37.
[42] *Anglo-Swiss Condensed Milk v Metcalf* (1886) 31 Ch.D. 454; 3 R.P.C. 28.
[43] *Lyndon's Trade Mark* (1886) 32 Ch.D. 109; 3 R.P.C. 102.
[44] *Speer's Trade Mark* (1887) 4 R.P.C. 521.
[45] *Biegel's Trade Mark* (1887) 4 R.P.C. 525; 57 L.T. 247.
[46] *Australian Wine Importers* (1889) 41 Ch.D. 278; (1889) 6 R.P.C. 311.
[47] *Haines, Batchelor & Co's Trade Mark* (1888) 5 R.P.C. 669.
[48] *Lambert's Trade Mark.* (1888) 5 R.P.C. 542; (1889) 6 R.P.C. 344; 61 L.T. 138.
[49] *Farrlow's Trade Mark* (1890) 7 R.P.C. 260; 63 L.T. 233.
[50] *Murphy's Trade Mark* (1890) R.P.C. 163.
[51] *Upper Assam Tea v Herbert* (1890) 7 R.P.C. 183.
[52] *Baker v Rawson* (1890) 45 Ch.D. 519; 8 R.P.C. 89.
[53] *Wilkinson v Griffith* (1891) 8 R.P.C. 370.

horse.[54] Representation of the Royal Exchange, Glasgow, and the words "Royal Exchange Whisky" below, refused registration because it would give the right to restrain a label bearing the same representation with the words "Bodega Special Whisky" below.[55] C.B. & Co and also C.B.D. held to infringe device of a corset and the letters C.B. within a star, and of C.B. corsets.[56] The device of a red deer's head, not an infringement of a device of a moose's head.[57] The device of the cut of half an apple cut vertically with the word "Pomril" across it, too near a mark containing a representation of an apple and the words "Apple Brand", both marks being for cider.[58] J. B. D. in an oval ring, an infringement of G. B. D. in an oval ring.[59] A showcard with a device having some of the features and lines of a diamond and the word "famous" on it, not an infringement of a plain diamond.[60] A sphinx in combination with Egyptian scenery not an infringement of a sphinx in a different position.[61] A rampant cat on a horizontal barrel, known as the "Cat Brand" or "Cat and Barrel Brand", held to be infringed by a cat's head and forequarters out of the top of a barrel on end, with the words "Cat Brand".[62] The same trade mark held to be infringed by a cat sitting on the top of a barrel place on end.[63] A labael with a signature, not infringed by a label similar in structure, but having the defendant's name prominently upon it.[64] An ace of spades with the word "Hub" on it held to be an infringement of an ace of clubs with the word "Club" on it.[65] A shamrock with a stalk twisted so as to form "& Co.", not too near a compound mark of a crown and a shamrock in a different position with the letters M. V.[66] A diamond divided into two triangles, and bearing upon it a device and monogram, refused registration on the ground, *inter alia*, of similarity to other diamond marks.[67] A representation of the head of a Red Indian allowed notwithstanding representation of a Red Indian on horseback with the words "Red Indian" underneath.[68] Mark consisting of a swan within an oval and the words "Swann & Co." not too near the device of a swan with a small boy sitting on its back.[69] View of Blackfriars Bridge with St. Paul's Cathedral in the background, infringed by a view of the bridge with a supposed town containing a similar building in the background, the labels being of similar shape and having a device within a circle.[70] Although the plaintiffs' and defendants' names were on their respective labels, an injunction against passing off granted.[71] A representation of Eastern Dye Works held to be too near a different representation of the same subject.[72] Circular cake of dental composition with a raised edge and engine-turned with a band across it with the name. "Stent's", the letter "G" above, and a picture of a plate below the bank, held not to infringe and not liable to be

---

[54] *Currie's Application* (1896) 13 R.P.C. 681.

[55] *Roger's Trade Mark* (1895) 12 R.P.C. 149.

[56] *Bayer v Connell Bros* (1899) 16 R.P.C. 157. In Ireland before Porter M.R. See also *Bayer v Baird* (1898) 15 R.P.C. 615 (S. Ct of Sess).

[57] *Alaska Packers' Association v Crooks & Co* (1899) 16 R.P.C. 503; (1901) 18 R.P.C. 129.

[58] *Pomril Ltd's Application* (1901) 18 R.P.C. 181.

[59] *Maréchal and Ruchon v McColgan* (1901) 18 R.P.C. 262 (Ireland).

[60] *Bass, Ratcliff & Gretton Ltd v Davenport & Sons' Brewery Ltd* (1902) 19 R.P.C. 129 and 529.

[61] *Lambert & Butler v Goodbody* (1902) 19 R.P.C. 377.

[62] *Boord & Son v Huddart* (1904) 21 R.P.C. 149.

[63] *Boord & Son v Thom & Cameron Ltd* (1907) 24 R.P.C. 697.

[64] *Dawson v Stewart* (1905) 22 R.P.C. 250.

[65] *Munday v Carey* (1905) 22 R.P.C. 273.

[66] *Shamrock & Co's Application* (1907) 24 R.P.C. 569.

[67] *La Union Agricola's Trade Marks* (1908) 25 R.P.C. 295.

[68] *Carborundum Co's Application* (1909) 26 R.P.C. 504.

[69] *Holbrooks' Application* (1909) 26 R.P.C. 791.

[70] *Price's Patent Candle v Ogston & Tennant* (1909) 26 R.P.C. 797.

[71] *Wright, Crossley & Co v Blezard* (1910) 27 R.P.C. 299.

[72] *Greisheim Electron*, 27 R.P.C. 201.

passed off as a circular cake of dental composition with a raised edge and engine-turned in a different pattern with the name "Stents" across it in a panel and an impression plate above and below the panel, the plaintiffs not having a monopoly of the name "Stent", and the defendants' mark having been used for thirteen years, there being evidence that the limited class of purchasers for the goods would not be deceived.[73] Heart-shaped design with the initials "E.A.S.", not infringed by a more conventionally shaped heart with a letter and number, the initials being the characteristic of the plaintiffs' trade mark.[74] Letters A, B and C, and A, B, each within a diamond, held not to be infringed by a mark consisting of the letters A, B, C, in a device representing interlocked pieces of steel, and, although the plaintiffs' steel of particular qualities was known as "A Steel", "B Steel", etc., an injunction restraining the defendant from passing off by describing his steel as "A, B, C Steel" dissolved; also in an application by the plaintiffs to register a mark consisting of the letters A, B, C, in interlocked diamonds, that this mark was too near the defendant's unregistered mark.[75] The get-up of motor cabs consisting of a colouring of the cabs which was common, with the letters W. & G. in a peculiar script form, held to have been imitated by a get-up of similar colouring with the letters M. G.[76] Letter "S" twined round the body of a female, and within a wreath, too near a mark consisting of the letter "S" twined round a bird and within an oval.[77] "White Standard Table Jelly Crystals" ("White Standard" being the registered trade mark), with a single fruit denoting the flavour not a passing off of the defendant's goods as "White's Jelly Crystals" with a representation of the particular fruit, being goods sold by the plaintiffs.[78] Label containing prominently a picture of a cat lying down and a bottle of tonic wine and the words "Dubonnet Wine", not too near (1) a rampant cat on a barrel; or (2) a lable containing a sitting cat between the words "Gato Brand" ("gato" being Spanish and Portuguese for cat) and the words "Port Wine",[79] Five-pointed star in red with the letter "T" in green and "Texco" in black, not too near other star marks on the Register, not used in red, there being no evidence that any of the goods were known as star goods.[80] A label with a cat shown prominently, not to near a cat in a different attitude and in a widely different label, the cat being held to be common for the goods (gin).[81] Trade mark consisting of a skeleton map of Ireland with the proprietor's name across it, held not infringed by advertisements consisting of trays and tablets decorated with the map of Ireland and bearing the defendant's name.[82] Word "Bravo" in English and Russian charac ters within a triangle on its base not too near the letters "J.A.S." within an inverted triangle, a triangle being common to the trade.[83] Black cat on a globe not infringed by a device of a black cat standing behind a circular device.[84] Lable with the word "Victor" as its most prominent feature too near a trade mark consisting of the word

---

[73] *Claudius Ash v Invicta* (1911) 28 R.P.C. 252, 597; (1912) 29 R.P.C. 465.

[74] *Schwerdtfeger v Hart* (1912) 29 R.P.C. 236.

[75] *Andrew v Kuehnrich* (1913) 30 R.P.C. 677.

[76] *W. & G. Du Cros v Gold* (1913) 30 R.P.C. 117.

[77] *Sandow's Application* (1914) 31 R.P.C. 196.

[78] *White, Tomkins & Courage v United Confectionery* (1914) 31 R.P.C. 430.

[79] *Dubonnet's Application* (1914) 31 R.P.C. 453; (1915) 32 R.P.C. 241.

[80] *Texas Co's Application* (1914) 31 R.P.C. 53; (1915) 32 R.P.C. 442. Before the Registrar's appeal was heard one of the marks cited was removed from the Register, and by consent no order was made on the appeal.

[81] *Bagots Hutton* (1915) 32 R.P.C. 333; [1916] 2 A.C. 382; (1916) R.P.C. 357.

[82] *Dunan Alerdice v Burke* (1916) 33 R.P.C. 341.

[83] *Crispin's Application* (1917) 34 R.P.C. 249.

[84] *Tatem v Gaumont* (1918) 34 R.P.C. 181.

"Victory" and a laurel wreath.[85] Mark consisting of four panels, one of which contained a representation of a ship, too near a trade mark of a warship, the opponents' goods being known as "Ship Brand".[86] Ace of spades with device of superimposed aces (for playing cards) not an infringement of plaintiffs' similar but more artistic device.[87] Device of an oxcart not an infringement being common in the trade and device not used as a trade mark.[88] "99" and words "double nine" not in infringement of "999" or calculated to deceive.[89] Picture of a girl with the words "cabaret girl" too near pictures of dancing girls with the words "carnival" and "columbine".[90] Lighthouse for illuminating oils not infringed by the use of a petrol pump in the form of lighthouse and no passing off.[91] Head and shoulders with the word "Gardener", too near a similar picture of a younger man.[92] Labels having a generally similar appearance.[93] Sow and three little pigs, too near "Three Pigs Brand" and another picture.[94] Sun and moon trade marks not infringed by word "Permacola" with part of sun against the letter P.[95] Labels having figures of elephants.[96] Similarity of "portrait marks."[97] Design of superimposed aces together with the word "Ace" not allowed in view of use of word "Ace" by opponents for over forty years.[98] Word "Arrow" an infringement of 3 intersecting arrows plus words "Arrow Brand."[99] Corkscrew in form of lady's head sold under name "Lulu" not infringed by screw in form of clown's head sold under the name "Clown".[1] Figure of guardsman, with name "Guards", for cigarettes, too close to "Guardsman" for tobacco to be registered; but "Guardsman" for pipes not restrained in view of "Guards" cigarette mark unless with similar figure of guardsman.[2] Symbols used by scientists to indicate sex, conjoined with a heart, descriptive of business of arranging introductions and not distinctive of plaintiffs' (new) business.[3] Shamrock device within a shield surmounted by the word "Grundig" and a crown not confusingly similar to a shamrock device alone for registration.[4] "Philips" in a shield device too close to signature "Chas. H. Phillips" for registration.[5] Two horse-drawn 2-wheeled vehicles not too close.[6] Three-leafed cloverleaf with long stem, confusingly similar to stylised three leafed clover mark.[7] An oval device containing the word "Coloroll" and a botanical sprig, not too near an oval device containing the words "Laura Ashley" and a botanical sprig.[8] The use of pink paper for financial news in the Evening Standard, not confusingly similar to the use of pink paper in the

[85] *Massachusetts Saw Works* (1918) 35 R.P.C. 137.
[86] *Huxley's Application* (1924) 41 R.P.C. 423.
[87] *Goodall v Waddington* (1924) 41 R.P.C. 465 and 658.
[88] *Young v Grierson, Oldham* (1924) 41 R.P.C. 548.
[89] *Ardath v W. Sandorides* (1925) 42 R.P.C. 50.
[90] *Distributing Corporation* (1927) 44 R.P.C. 225.
[91] *Carless, Capel & Leonard v Pilmore-Bedford* (1928) 45 R.P.C. 205.
[92] *Morris & Jones* (1934) 51 R.P.C. 199.
[93] *Bryant & May v United Match* (1933) 50 R.P.C. 12.
[94] *Danish Bacon's Application* (1934) 51 R.P.C. 148.
[95] *Hollins v Cotella* (1937) 54 R.P.C. 81.
[96] *Bear v Prayag Narain* (1941) 58 R.P.C. 25.
[97] *Subbiah Nadar v Kumaraval Nadar* (1946) 63 R.P.C. 187.
[98] *Mellor's Application* (1948) 65 R.P.C. 238.
[99] *Cluett, Peabody v McIntyre Hogg, Marsh* [1958] R.P.C. 335.
[1] *Universal Agencies v Swolf* [1959] R.P.C. 247.
[2] *"Guards" Trade Mark* [1964] R.P.C. 9; *Carreras v Frankau* [1964] R.P.C. 210.
[3] *Compatibility Research v Computer Psyche* [1967] R.P.C. 201 (interlocutory injunction refused).
[4] *"Grundig" Trade Mark* [1968] R.P.C. 89.
[5] *"Philips" Trade Mark* [1969] R.P.C. 8.
[6] *Celine SA's Trade Mark Application* [1985] R.P.C. 381.
[7] *SHAMROCK Trade Mark* [1986] F.S.R. 271.
[8] *Laura Ashley Ltd v Coloroll Ltd* [1987] R.P.C. 1.

Financial Times.[9] A stylised device of the sun rising over a valley above the words "Waterford Foods", not confusingly similar to a stylised device of the sun rising over a valley leading to the sea above the words "Food Ireland".[10] An apple with about one-quarter bitten out, not likely to be associated with a whole apple device.[11] Coloured tabs on the right rear pocket of denim trousers, confusingly similar to coloured tabs on the left rear pocket of denim trousers.[12] Newspaper banner comprising "The European", not confusingly similar to a banner for "European Voice".[13] A device of two ovals, one contained within the other, the inner oval encompassing the word "Barilla", infringed by a device consisting of two ovals, one contained within the other, the inner one encompassing the word "Danis".[14] A device comprising three concentric "C's", likely to be confused with a device consisting of five concentric "C's".[15] Shape of a champagne bottle engraved with a motif and the words "Demoiselle de Champagne", infringed by a similarly shaped and engraved bottle carrying the words "Belle de Champagne".[16] Trade marked bottle shape infringed.[17] The use of three parallel stripes on sportswear, confusingly similar to a trade mark incorporating three parallel stripes applied to clothing.[18] The cursive signature "Elvis Presley", confusingly similar to "Elvisly Yours" in a similar cursive script.[19] A device consisting of the word "Naturelle" with the verticals of the letter N extended to form an oval enclosing both the word itself and three flowers, too close to the word mark "Natrel".[20] Three headed electric razor, admitted to be too close to a trade marked depiction of a three headed electric razor (but trade mark invalid).[21] Device of the word "Telecom" with red and grey dots between the letters, not infringed in a satirical newspaper article by the word "Teurer" with red and grey dots between the letters.[22] Stylised brush stroke and the word "Masters", too similar to registered stylised brush stroke.[23] A device of crossed arrows, not too similar to a device of crossed arrows and the words "Unidad De Farmacovigilancia Glaxo".[24] A black square containing the word "Booknet" in white, confusingly similar to a black square containing the words "Le Book" in white.[25] Three dimensional mark for a cylindrical device with recessed ends, not infringed by a similar cylindrical device.[26] "Dinokids" not confusingly similar to a device of a young dinosaur above the word "Dino".[27] A three-dimensional mark for a blue bottle, not infringed by a similarly shaped blue bottle.[28] "Coq D'Or" (and cockerel device), not confusingly similar to "Victoria" (and cockerel device).[29] Circular device enclosing a spanner head shape and the word "React", distinguishable from the

[9] The Financial Times Ltd v Evening Standard Co Ltd [1991] F.S.R. 7.
[10] An Bord Trachtala v Waterford Foods plc [1994] F.S.R. 316.
[11] Ciba-Geigy plc v Parke Davis & Co Ltd [1994] F.S.R. 8.
[12] Levi Strauss v Kimbyr Investments Ltd [1994] F.S.R. 335.
[13] The European Ltd v The Economist Newspapers Ltd [1996] F.S.R. 431.
[14] Barilla Alimentare SPA v Danis SRL [1996] E.T.M.R. 43 (Italy) (also [1999] E.T.M.R. 677).
[15] C (Device Trade Mark) [1998] R.P.C. 439.
[16] Vranken SA v Champagne H. Germain et Fils SA [1998] E.T.M.R. 390 (France).
[17] Kabushiki Kaisha Yakult Honsha v Danone Nederland BV [1998] E.T.M.R. 465 (Benelux).
[18] Adidas A.G. v N. v Famco [1998] E.T.M.R. 616 (Commercial Court, Belgium).
[19] ELVIS PRESLEY Trade Marks [1999] R.P.C. 567.
[20] NATURELLE Trade Mark [1999] R.P.C. 567.
[21] Philips Electronics NV v Remington Consumer Products Ltd [1999] R.P.C. 809.
[22] "Alles Wird Teurer" [1999] E.T.M.R. 49 (Germany).
[23] Reufach Marketing GmbH's Application [1999] E.T.M.R. 412.
[24] Grupo Grifols SA's Application [1999] E.T.M.R. 507 (OHIM).
[25] Sarl Le Book Editions v Ste EPC Edition Presse Communications [1999] E.T.M.R. 554 (France).
[26] Mars BV v Société Des Produits Nestle SA [1999] E.T.M.R. 862 (Benelux).
[27] Herbalife International Inc's Application [1999] E.T.M.R. 882 (OHIM).
[28] Ty Nant Spring Water Ltd v Lemon & Co SRL [1999] E.T.M.R. 969 (Italy).
[29] Fromex SA's Application [1999] E.T.M.R. 989 (OHIM).

word mark "Reactor".[30] An oval device with decorative border containing the words "Nathalies Gobelins", confusingly similar to an oval device with a decorative border containing the words "Gobelins Art".[31] The letter "K" enclosed in a rhombus, not confusingly similar to a letter "V" (or "L") in a circle, surrounded by a square border.[32] Stylised, modern looking, letter "L", not confusingly similar to a differently stylised, old fashioned looking, letter "L".[33] "Nike" in white on a black square, detrimental to the reputation of a prior mark consisting of "Nike" in white italics on a red square.[34] A proposed three-dimensional mark for a bottle in the shape of a football boot with three stripes on the outside upper, took advantage of and was detrimental to a mark for three stripes on the outside upper of footwear.[35]

(2) CONTRASTED WORDS

A31–002

"White Rose", too near "Rosaline."[36] "Condi-Sanitas", infringements of "Sanitas."[37] "Boyd's Universal Harness Composition", in a label with the Arms of the City of Dublin, not an infringement of "Propert's Improved Harness Composition" in a label with a fox's head, the labels being similarly got up.[38] "Apollinis", an infringement of "Apollinaris".[39] "Steinberg", and infringement of "Steinway", used with similar devices.[40] "Emollio", too near "Emolline".[41] "Emolliolorum", not too near "Molliscorium."[42] "Swift's Specific" not calculated to deceive merely because the words were descriptive of the opponent's drug.[43] "Oomoo", not to near "Emu".[44] "Kokoko", too near the common word "Coco".[45] "Demotic", an infringement of "Demon".[46] "Dunn's Fruit Salt Baking Powder", too near "Eno's Fruit Salt";[47] subsequently held to be an infringement.[48] "El Devino", an infringement of "El Destino".[49] Label with "El Destinacion", an infringement of a similar label with "El Destino".[50] Label with "London Pickles", an infringement of a similar label with "London Pickle Co."[51] "Stafford", an infringement of "Trafford"; "Fort" of "Fortress"; "New Mistress"; but not "New Matron", "New Master", of "Master", or "Mistress"; but "South African" not an infringement of a mark consisting of a negro's head and the word "African".[52] "Vincalis", not too near "Wincarnis", the goods being different in appearance and use.[53] "Triticumina", not infringed by "Triticine".[54] Signature "Robert Craw-

---

[30] REACT AND DEVICE Trade Mark [2000] R.P.C. 285.
[31] Rose's Lace Boutique v BVBA Parcles [2000] E.T.M.R. 1 (Benelux).
[32] Stillwater Designs and Audio Inc's Application [2000] E.T.M.R. 35 (OHIM).
[33] Loewe SA's Application [2000] E.T.M.R. 40 (OHIM).
[34] Campomar SL's Application [2000] E.T.M.R. 50 (OHIM).
[35] Inlima SL's Application [2000] E.T.M.R. 325.
[36] White Rose Trade Mark (1885) 30 Ch.D. 505.
[37] Sanitas v Condy (1886) 4 R.P.C. 195 and 530; 56 L.T. 621.
[38] Beddow v Boyd (1887) 4 R.P.C. 310.
[39] Apollinaris Co v Herfeldt (1887) 4 R.P.C. 478.
[40] Steinway v Henshaw (1888) 5 R.P.C. 77.
[41] Grossmith's Trade Mark (1889) 6 R.P.C. 180; 60 L.T. 612.
[42] Talbot's Trade Mark (1894) 11 R.P.C. 77.
[43] Swift's Trade Mark (1889) 6 R.P.C. 352.
[44] Burgoyne's Trade Mark (1889) 6 R.P.C. 227; 61 L.T. 39.
[45] Jackson & Co's Trade Mark (1889) 6 R.P.C. 80.
[46] Slazenger v Feltham (1889) 6 R.P.C. 531.
[47] Eno v Dunn (1889) 41 Ch.D. 439; (1890) 15 App.Cas. 252; (1890) 7 R.P.C. 311.
[48] (1893) 10 R.P.C. 261.
[49] Pinto v Trott (1891) 8 R.P.C. 173.
[50] Pinto v Badman (1891) 8 R.P.C. 181.
[51] Hammond v Malcolm, Brunker (1892) 9 R.P.C. 301.
[52] Smith and Wellstood v Carron (1896) 13 R.P.C. 108.
[53] Coleman v Brown (1899) 16 R.P.C. 619 (passing off).
[54] Meaby v Triticine (1898) 15 R.P.C. 1.

ford", not infringement of signature "Daniel Crawford".[55] "Margarita", an infringement of "La Flor de Margaretta".[56] "Savoline", an infringement of "Savonol".[57] "Ivory", for soap, not necessarily calculated to cause the goods to be confused with "Ivy" soap.[58] "Night Cap", not too near "Red Cap" or "Mother Red Cap".[59] "Valtine", too near "Valentine".[60] "S. Griffiths", three stars and I.X.L., not infringed by "E. Griffiths" and three stars, the stars being common marks of quality.[61] "St. Ives" cheese held too similar to "St. Ivel", registered for cheese.[62] "Neostyle", not to near "Cyclostyle".[63] "Securine", an infringement of "Seccotine".[64] "Cocosoline", not an infringement of "Cottolene".[65] Mark including the words "Jock Scott", too near "Scotch Jock".[66] "Tablones", to near "Tabloids".[67] "Neola", not to near "Pianola".[68] "Lanco", not too near "Lancashire".[69] "B.A.S.", too near "B.S.A."[70] "Midland Star", not too near "Star",[71] alleged passing off, there being several names in use in the trade which included the word "star". "Glen Thorne" for whisky, too near "Thorne's" whisky.[72] "Aquatite", not too near "Aquascutum", there being other names in the trade (water-proof garments) also beginning with "Aqua".[73] "Osowoolo", too near "Orlwoola".[74] "Murrilo", too near "Muralo".[75] "Colonial", not an infringement of or liable to be passed off as "Colonel".[76] "Sailor" beneath a picture of a sailor not too near "Skipper", although the picture was associated with the word "Skipper" in respect of other goods.[77] "Murad", too near "Muratti".[78] "Pick Them Out", preceded by work "Bargains", too near device of a pick and the word "Pick".[79] "Carvino", not to neawr "Wincarnis".[80] "Aqua-Repela", too near "Repellus", owing to the probability of abbreviation to "Repela".[81] "Schicht" held to be calculated to deceive by reason of the resemblance to "Sunlight".[82] "Stateroom", too near "State Express", the latter often abbreviated to "State".[83] "Limit", not too near "Summit".[84] "Herogen", not too near "Ceregen", the goods being

[55] *Crawford v Bernard* (1894) 11 R.P.C. 580.
[56] *Benedictus v Sullivan, Powell* (1895) 12 R.P.C. 25.
[57] *Field v Wagel* (1900) 17 R.P.C. 266.
[58] *Goodwin v Ivory Soap* (1901) 18 R.P.C. 389.
[59] *Hedley's Trade Marks* (1900) 17 R.P.C. 719.
[60] *Valentine Meat Juice v Valentine Extract* (1900) 17 R.P.C. 673 (passing off) (and see (1901) 18 R.P.C. 175).
[61] *Marshall v Sidebotham* (1901) 18 R.P.C. 43.
[62] *Aplin and Barrett v Richards* (1903) 20 R.P.C. 799.
[63] *Neostyle's Trade Mark* (1903) 20 R.P.C. 329 and 803.
[64] *McCaw, Stevenson & Orr v Nickols* (1903) 21 R.P.C. 15.
[65] *Fairbank v Cocos Butter* (1904) 21 R.P.C. 23.
[66] *Booth's Application* (1904) 21 R.P.C. 18.
[67] *Capsuloid's Application* (1906) 23 R.P.C. 782.
[68] *Pianotist's Application* (1906) 23 R.P.C. 774.
[69] *Reddaway v Irwell and Eastern* (1906) 23 R.P.C. 621; (1907) 24 R.P.C. 203.
[70] *Birmingham Small Arms v Webb* (1907) 24 R.P.C. 27, passing off.
[71] *Star Cycle v Frankenburgs* (1907) 24 R.P.C. 46 and 405.
[72] *Thorne v Pimms* (1909) 26 R.P.C. 221, rectification and passing off.
[73] *Aquascutum v Cohen and Wilks* (1909) 26 R.P.C. 651.
[74] *Brock* (1909) 26 R.P.C. 683.
[75] *Muralo v Taylor* (1910) 27 R.P.C. 261, passing off.
[76] *St. Mungo v Viper* (1910) 27 R.P.C. 420.
[77] *Angus Watson* (1911) 28 R.P.C. 313.
[78] *Muratti v Murad* (1911) 28 R.P.C. 497.
[79] *Briggs v Dunn* (1911) 28 R.P.C. 704, infringement and passing off.
[80] *Coleman v Smith* [1911] 2 Ch. 572; (1911) 28 R.P.C. 645; (1912) 29 R.P.C. 81.
[81] *Wilks' Application* (1912) 29 R.P.C. 21.
[82] *Schicht's Application* (1912) 29 R.P.C. 483.
[83] *United Kingdom Tobacco* (1912) 29 R.P.C. 489.
[84] *Smith's Application* (1913 30 R.P.C. 363.

different.[85] "Mendit" not an infringement of "Mendine", the right to the exclusive use of "Mend" being disclaimed.[86] "Onsoria", held on interloctury motion to be an infringement of "Anzora".[87] "Swankie", not too near a mark consisting of the word "Swan" with a picture of a swan.[88] "Lavroma", not an infringement of "Lavona" or "Lavona".[89] "British Dominion Bond", with distinctive lettering and a monogram, too near0"British Bond", with similar lettering and a monogram, in a passing off action.[90] "Ca Radium", an infringement of "Radium".[91] "Malagole", for pens, too near a mark bearing the name "J. B. Mallat", "Mallet" pens being well known.[92] "Anchola", not too near "Anchovette", which was registered with a disclaimer of "Anchov".[93] "Gnidroc" too near the name "Cording", which was part of the name of the opponent company, J. C. Cording & Co Ltd; as well as that of the applicant company.[94] "Oxot", an infringement of "Oxo".[95] "The Regiment", for cigarettes, not an infringement of "Regimental" or "Regimental Cigarettes".[96] "Victor" too near "Victory" and a laurel wreath.[97] "Rito", not an infringement of "Lito" or of a trade mark consisting of "Y-To" and a device.[98] "Motrate" not too near "Filtrate".[99] "Vino" and "Vyno", too near "Harvino".[1] "Molivar" and "La Molivar" too near "Bolivar".[2] "Zykol", too near "Zeekol".[3] "Egall", too near "Egrol".[4] "Pan-pep", not too near "Peps".[5] "Galaxy", with "The Milky Way", too near "Glaxo".[6] "Germocea", too near "Germolene".[7] "Cream of the North", not too near "Royal Northern Cream", in a label quite dissimilar, "Cream" being common in the trade (Whisky).[8] "Sterling" across a coin, too near a word. the symbol of a pound and the world "Lockstitch".[9] "Freia", too near "Fry".[10] "Hemvo", too near "Harvo".[11] "Amata", and infringement of "Amami".[12] "Tripcastroid", not too near "Castrol".[13] "Muralol", an infringement of "Mirabol".[14] "Faris Cycle", not too near "Fairycycle".[15] "Nuvol", too near "Nujol".[16] "Nuvola", too near "Nujol".[17] "Justikon", an infringement of

---

[85] *British Drug Houses* (1913) 30 R.P.C. 74.
[86] *Coombe v Mendit* (1913) 30 R.P.C. 709.
[87] *Lewis v Vine* (1914) 31 R.P.C. 12.
[88] *Crook's Trade Mark* (1914) 31 R.P.C. 79.
[89] *Tokalon v Davidson* (1914) 31 R.P.C. 74; (1915) 32 R.P.C. 133.
[90] *Spicer v Spalding & Hodge* (1915) 32 R.P.C. 52.
[91] *Brighten v Cavendish* (1915) 32 R.P.C. 229.
[92] *Hinks, Wells* (1916) 33 R.P.C. 281.
[93] *Waide's Application* (1916) 33 R.P.C. 320.
[94] *Cording's Application* (1916) 33 R.P.C. 83 and 325.
[95] *Oxo v King* (1917) 34 R.P.C. 165.
[96] *Imperial Tobacco v De Pasquali* (1918) 35 R.P.C. 185.
[97] *Massachusetts Saw Works* (1918) 35 R.P.C. 137.
[98] *Fitchetts v Loubet* (1919) 36 R.P.C. 296.
[99] *Fox's Application* (1920) 37 R.P.C. 37.
[1] *Wheatley, Akeroyd* (1920) 37 R.P.C. 137.
[2] *Middlemas & Wood v Moliver* (1921) 38 R.P.C. 97.
[3] *J. Brown's Application* (1921) 38 R.P.C. 15.
[4] *Egg Products* (1922) 39 R.P.C. 155.
[5] *United Chemists* (1923) 40 R.P.C. 219.
[6] *Smiths' Application* (1923) 40 R.P.C. 77.
[7] *Taylor's Application* (1923) 40 R.P.C. 193.
[8] *Hutchinson's Application* (1924) 41 R.P.C. 538.
[9] *Connor's Application* (1924) 41 R.P.C. 458.
[10] *Freia Chocolate* (1924) 41 R.P.C. 653.
[11] *Hemmings's Application* (1924) 41 R.P.C. 672.
[12] *Prichard & Constance v Amata* (1925) 42 R.P.C. 63.
[13] *London Lubricants* (1925) 42 R.P.C. 264.
[14] *Walpamur v Sanderson* (1926) 43 R.P.C. 385.
[15] *Lines Bros v Farris* (1925) 43 R.P.C. 64 (a passing-off case).
[16] *McDowell's Application* (1927) R.P.C. 335, HL.

"Ustikon".[18] "Red Knight", an infringement of "Silent Knight".[19] "Camay", too near "Cameo".[20] "Ernalde", not an infringement of "Nilde".[21] "Sunshine Snow" and picture not an infringement of "Snowfire" and picture.[22] "Ucolite" too near "Coalite".[23] "Brick", too near "Brico".[24] not too near "Lektrik", the goods being different.[25] "Abermill Bond, made in Great Britain", not too near "Hammermill".[26] "Pup", not too near (for gramphones, etc.) to a representation of a dog listening to a gramophone.[27] "Pine-exx", an infringement of "Pinette".[28] "Kleenup", an infringement of "Kleenoff".[29] "Hyde Park", allowed notwithstanding registered marks including "Park" or "Park Drive", subject to a limitation as to goods.[30] "Erectiko", too near to "Erector".[31] "Maria Lisette", an infringement of "Marie Elizabeth".[32] "Arlette", allowed notwithstanding "Ardenette" subject to limitation as to goods.[33] "Sanrus", in infringement of "Rus".[34] "Pepsi Cola", not an infringement of Coca Cola".[35] "Geoff Ray", an infringement of both "Gor-Ray" and "Kone Ray".

A31–003   "Stayco"[36], not too near "Gayco".[37] "Honomol", too near "Honyol".[38] "Rysta", too near "Aristoc".[39] "Supavite", too near "Supervita".[40] "Morex", allowed notwithstanding "Rex" and "Morrisflex".[41] "Jardex", too near "Jardox".[42] "Ovax", allowed notwithstanding "Hovis" and "Ovi".[43] "Plyopher", not allowed in view of Pliobond". "Pliowax" and 12 other marks commencing with "Plio".[44] "Vivicyllin", allowed notwithstanding "Cyllin".[45] "Diasil", allowed notwithstanding "Alasil", subject to limitation as to goods.[46] "Eastex", allowed notwithstanding "Lastex".[47] "Solibrisa", allowed notwithstanding "Summer Breeze".[48] "Burwear", too near unregistered mark "Bairnswear".[49] "Seda-Seltzer" allowed notwithstanding "Alka-Seltzer".[50] "Sunfleck", too near "Sunflex".[51] "Sunniwite",

[17] *Savage's Application* (1927) 44 R.P.C. 1.
[18] *Davis v Sussex Rubber* (1927) 44 R.P.C. 412.
[19] *Forth and Clyde v Sugg* 1928 45 R.P.C. 382.
[20] *Procter and Gamble v Pugsley Dingman* (1929) 46 R.P.C. (application for registration).
[21] *Soc. Nildé v Ernaidé* (1929) 46 R.P.C. 453.
[22] *Hampshire v General Kaputine* (1930) R.P.C. 437.
[23] *Magdalena Securities* (1931) 48 R.P.C. 477.
[24] *Lauritzen's Application* (1931) 48 R.P.C. 392.
[25] *Lundberg* (1932) 49 R.P.C. 15.
[26] *Pirie's Application* (1932) 49 R.P.C. 195; (1933) 50 R.P.C. 147.
[27] *"Pup"* (1933) 50 R.P.C. 198.
[28] *Dixon v Taylor and Cowells* (1933) 50 R.P.C. 405.
[29] *Bale and Church v Sutton, Parsons* (1934) 51 R.P.C. 129.
[30] *Harrods Application* (1935) 52 R.P.C. 65.
[31] *Bailey* (1935) 52 R.P.C. 136.
[32] *Fialho v Simond* (1937) 54 R.P.C. 193.
[33] *City Chemical's Application* (1937) 54 R.P.C. 182.
[34] *Ravenhead Brick v Ruabon* (1937) 54 R.P.C. 341.
[35] *Coca Cola of Canada v Pepsi Cola of Canada* (1942) 59 R.P.C. 127.
[36] *Stillitz v Jones & Higgins* (1943) 60 R.P.C. 15.
[37] *Angus's Application* (1943) 60 R.P.C. 29.
[38] *Marshall's Application* (1943) 60 R.P.C. 147.
[39] (1943) 60 R.P.C. 87 and (1945) 62 R.P.C. 65, HL.
[40] (1944) 61 R.P.C. 31.
[41] *Darwin's Application* (1946) R.P.C. 1.
[42] *Edward's Application* (1946) 63 R.P.C. 19.
[43] *Smith Hayden* (1946) 63 R.P.C. 97.
[44] *Beck, Koller* (1947) 64 R.P.C. 76.
[45] *Enoch's Application* (1947) 64 R.P.C. 119.
[46] *Bayer's Application* (1947) 64 R.P.C. 125.
[47] *"Eastex"* (1947) 64 R.P.C. 142: case decided under the special rules relating to defensive marks.
[48] *Baléy's Application* (1948) 65 R.P.C. 17.
[49] *Burcombe's Application* (1948) 65 R.P.C. 179.
[50] *Demuth's Application* (1948) 65 R.P.C. 342.

an infringement of "Sunlight".[52] "Chemico", not allowed in view of "Chemia".[53] "Alka-Vescent", not allowed in view of "Alka-Seltzer".[54] "Karsote Vapour Rub", an infringement of "Vapo Rub".[55] "Gilray", not too near "Gor-Ray".[56] "Gala", not too near "Goya".[57] "Star Dust", too near "Starmist".[58] "Dreamland", not allowed, in view of "Slumberland".[59] "Vanildene", not allowed, in view of "Vaseline".[60] "Micronic", allowed notwithstanding "Microvee".[61] "Sprattykat" might be confused with "Kit-e-Kat", but interlocutory relief refused.[62] "Algelox", allowed notwithstanding "Aludrox".[63] "Electrix" an infringement of "Electrux".[64] "vivos", allowed notwithstanding "Hovis".[65] Dustic", allowed notwithstanding "Bostik".[66] "White Ship", not allowed in view of "Old Ship".[67] "Pretty Kitty", not too near "Kit-e-Kat".[68] "Chamlet", too near "Babycham".[69] "Kokola", too near "Coco Cola".[70] "Pem Books", too near "Pan Books".[71] "Red Shield", etc., not allowed, in view of "Red Seal"etc.[72] "Welloy", refused registration, in view of "Walloy".[73] "Ikf Koyo", not allowed, in view of "S.K.F." and "Skefko".[74] "Watermatic", too near "Aquamatic".[75] "Naturalizet", too near "Naturalizer".[76] "Kidax" allowed notwithstanding "Daks".[77] "Velva-Glo" too close to "Vel-Glo".[78] "Knoll International" too close to "Parker-Knoll".[79] "Palexa" too close to "Plix".[80] "Galvalloy" not too close to "Galvafroid".[81] "Wells Whip" too close to "Walls Whip".[82] "Guards" with figure too close to "Guardsman" for registration but (the goods being different) "Guardsman" not necessarily deceptively close to "Guards" unless accompanied by device.[83] "Merrie Jane" a borderline case as

[51] *Crowther's Application* (1948) 65 R.P.C. 369.
[52] *Lever Bros v Sunniwite* (1949) 66 R.P.C. 84.
[53] *County Chemical's Application* (1949) 66 R.P.C. 268.
[54] *Broadhead's Application* (1950) 67 R.P.C. 113, 209.
[55] *De Cordova v Vick* (1951) 68 R.P.C. 103, 226, 270.
[56] *Gor-Ray v Gilray* (1952) 69 R.P.C. 99, 199.
[57] *Goya v Gala* (1952) 69 R.P.C. 188.
[58] *Steiner v Raymond* (1951) 69 R.P.C. 40.
[59] *Whitling's Application* (1952) 69 R.P.C. 219.
[60] *Ana Laboratories* (1951) 69 R.P.C. 146.
[61] *Automotive Products* (1953) 70 R.P.C. 224.
[62] *Chappie v Spratts* (1954) 71 R.P.C. 455.
[63] *Harker Stagg's Trade Mark* (1954) 71 R.P.C. 136.
[64] *Electrolux v Electrix* (1953) 70 R.P.C. 127, 155; (1954) 71 R.P.C. 23, CA.
[65] *Spillers' Application* (1952) 69 R.P.C. 327; 70 R.P.C. 51; (1954) 71 R.P.C. 234, HL.
[66] *Dundas' (R. K.) Application* (1955) 72 R.P.C. 151.
[67] *Mellor's Application* (1955) 72 R.P.C. 82.
[68] *Chappie v Warrington Canners* (1955) 72 R.P.C. 73.
[69] *Showerings v Bulmer* [1956] R.P.C. 307.
[70] *Coca Cola v Highlande* [1957] R.P.C. 313.
[71] *Pan Books v Word Distributors* [1957] R.P.C. 366.
[72] *Warwick Upholstery* [1958] R.P.C. 488.
[73] *British Lead Mills* [1958] R.P.C. 425.
[74] *Koyo Seiko Kabushiki Kaisha* [1957] R.P.C. 297; [1958] R.P.C. 112, CA.
[75] *Reynolds v Laffeaty's* [1957] R.P.C. 311; [1958] R.P.C. 387, CA.
[76] *Brown Shoe* [1958] R.P.C. 406; [1959] R.P.C. 29 (rectification).
[77] *"Kiddax"* [1960] R.P.C. 117, CA.
[78] *"Velva-Glo" Trade Mark* [1961] R.P.C. 225 (fluorescent paints). Registration refused.
[79] *"Parker-Knoll" case* [1962] R.P.C. 265; held that "Knoll" was a distinctive feature of "Parker-Knoll" and that "Knoll International" was bound to get shortened to "Knoll". Injunctions granted (HL).
[80] Hair-setting compositions; there were suggestions of dishonesty: *L'Oréal v Coiffeur Supplies* [1961] R.P.C. 219. Interlocutory injunctions granted.
[81] *"Galva—"* being common: *"Galvalloy"* [1963] R.P.C. 34. Registration allowed.
[82] Ice Cream: *Walls v Wells Whip* [1964] R.P.C. 197. Interlocutory injunction granted.
[83] "Guards" with figure of guardsman refused registration for cigarettes in face of "Guardsman" for tobacco, *"Guards"* [1964] R.P.C. 9; interlocutory injunction granted against "Guardsman" with figure of guardsman for pipes, in view of similar figure on plaintiffs' "Guards" cigarettes; but no

against "Mary Jane".[84] "Merrimacs" too close to "Macs".[85] "Accutron" too close to "Accurist".[86] "Buler" too close to "Bulova".[87] "Acec" not too close to "Ace" for registration.[88] "V-CIL-K" infringed by "econoCIL-VK".[89] "Butazolidin" not infringed by "Butazone".[90] "Rheinliebling" too close to "Liebling" for registration.[91] "Transfermatic" too close to "Cross Transfermatic" and "Transfer-matic" (rectification).[92] "Picot" not infringed by "Piquant".[93] "B.P." not infringed by "E.P."[94] "Coca-Cola" not infringed by "Koalo Kola".[95] "Pristacin" infringed by "Bristacyn".[96] "Bulova Accutron" too close to "Accurist" for registration".[97] "Bali" too close to "Berlei" (rectification).[98] "Cal-U-Test" not too close to marks with suffix "Test" (common to trade).[99] "Handy Andies" infringed by "Handi Hanki".[1] "Kennomeat" (for dog food) infringed by "Ken-L" (for cat food).[2] "Pick of the Pops" too close to "Top of the Pops"[3] "Frigiking" allowed in Part B against "Thermo-King".[4] "English Leather" too close to "Imperial Leather".[5] "Skins" too close to "Skinners".[6] "Phildar" not too close to "Sirdar".[7] "Predenema" too close to "Predsol Enema".[8] "Happi-Nappi" not too close to "Napp".[9] "Kojack Lollies" too close to "Kojapops".[10] "Titch" not too close to "Botstitch".[11] "Solavoid"[12] and "Pol Rama"[13] not too close to "Polaroid" (sunglasses). "Zing" too near "Ping".[14] "Rheumaton" not too close to "Rheumanosticon".[15] "Tingate" too near

---

injunction against "Guardsman" for the pipes in itself: *Carreras v Fanrkau & Co* [1964] R.P.C. 210.

[84] Dresses: distinct possibility of confusion but confusion not inevitable, so interlocutory injunction refused on balance of convenience: *"Mary Jane"* case [1961] R.P.C. 389.

[85] Medicated sweet: *Macleans v Lightbrown* (1937) 54 R.P.C. 230. Injunction granted.

[86] *"Accutron" Trade Mark* [1966] R.P.C. 152 (watches).

[87] *"Buler" Trade Mark* [1966] R.P.C. 141 (watches). There was some evidence of confusion abroad. The marks were treated as pronounced "Booler" and "Boo Lova".

[88] *ACEC Trade Mark* [1965] R.P.C. 369.

[89] *Lilly (Eli) v Chelsea Drug* [1966] R.P.C. 14. The letters "econo" were four times smaller than the capitals.

[90] *Geigy v Chelsea Drug* [1966] R.P.C. 65. Special circumstances of pharmaceutical trade taken into account (interlocutory motion in Vacation Court).

[91] *Rheinliebling* [1966] R.P.C. 68 (Rhein wines).

[92] *"Transfermatic"* [1966] R.P.C. 568. (Certain dicta, but not decision, disapproved in *"Bali"* [1969] R.P.C. 472).

[93] *Picot v Goya* [1967] R.P.C. 573 (perfumes).

[94] *British Petroleum v European Petroleum* [1968] R.P.C. 54 (petrol).

[95] *Coca-Cola v Struthers* [1968] R.P.C. 231 (Scots) (soft drinks).

[96] *Bristol-Myers v Bristol Pharmaceutical* [1968] R.P.C. 259 (pharmaceuticals).

[97] *"Bulova Accutron"* [1969] R.P.C. 102. The Court of Appeal had already held "Accutron" too close, *"Accutron"* [1966] R.P.C. 152.

[98] *"Bali"* [1969] R.P.C. 472 (brassières).

[99] *"Cal-U-Test"* [1967] F.S.R. 39 (Registry).

[1] *Bowater-Scott v Modo* [1969] F.S.R. 330.

[2] *Spillers v Quaker Oats* [1969] F.S.R. 510, compromised on appeal, [1970] F.S.R. 11.

[3] *Pickwick v Multiple Sound* [1972] R.P.C. 786, CA (passing off).

[4] [1973] R.P.C. 739.

[5] *Mem v Cussons* [1974] R.P.C. 7 (Bermuda, where "Imperial Leather" was the only "Leather" mark).

[6] *In Things v Leather Garments* [1974] F.S.R. (passing off of jeans).

[7] *Sirdar v Mulliez* [1975] F.S.R. 309 (Eire).

[8] *Glaxo v Pharmax* [1976] F.S.R. 278 (passing off; *prima facie* case of likely confusion but no injunction since pharmacists check).

[9] [1976] R.P.C. 611 (Registry).

[10] *Tavener Rutledge v Trexapalm* [1977] R.P.C. 275 ("Kojak" a TV character; passing off).

[11] *Textron v Stephens* [1977] R.P.C. 283.

[12] [1977] R.P.C. 1, PC(N.Z.).

[13] [1977] R.P.C. 581 (Registry).

[14] [1978] R.P.C. 47 (Registry).

[15] [1978] R.P.C. 406 (Registry).

"Colgate" in Trinidad.[16] "Torbogaz" too near "Turbotorch".[17] "Tornado" not too near "Torna".[18] "Fif" not too near "Jif".[19] "Unimax" too near "Univac".[20] "Sorbislo" too near "Sorbitrate".[21] "Country Fair Oven Chips" not too near "McCain Oven Chips".[22] "Merit" not too near "Nerit".[23] "Da Vinci" too close to "Vincci".[24] "Keebler" too near "Keiller".[25] "Vedonis Thermawarm" (sometimes mis-written by customers and dealers as "Vedonis Thermawear") too close to "Thermawear".[26] "Pruriderm" too close to "Prioderm".[27] "Kodiak" not allowed because of "Kodak".[28] "Lancer" allowed despite "Lancia".[29] "Benji" confusingly similar to "Bendy".[30] "Mother Care/Other Care" not confusingly similar to "Mothercare".[31] "Charles of the Ritz" and "Ritz" not confusingly similar to "Ritz".[32] "Chelsea Man" confusingly similar to "Chelsea Girl".[33] "Furniture City" distinguishable from "Furnitureland".[34] "Lifeguard" not an infringement of "Lifebuoy".[35] "Portablast" infringed "Porta".[36]

"Star" too close to "Spar".[37] "Terbuline" too close to "Terbolan" and "Terbalin".[38] "Thermos Prima" not confusingly similar to "Primark".[39] "Torre Nova" distinguishable from "Torres".[40] "Security Management Today" not similar to "Management Today", but there was a risk of association.[41] "Tamworth Herald and Post" (and disclaimer) not confusing despite "Tamworth Herald".[42] "Bensyl" confusingly similar to "Bentasil" and "Benvil".[43] "Inadin" too close to "Anadin" and "Anadin Extra".[44] "What's New In Training" magazine confusingly similar to the "What's New In ..." stable of magazines.[45] "Primasport" allowed notwithstanding "Primark".[46] "Univer" confusingly similar to "Univet".[47] "BBC Gourmet GoodFood" sufficiently different from "Gourmet".[48] "E. Quadra" too similar to "Quattro".[49] "Waterford Foods" (and device) distinguishable from

A31–004

[16] *Colgate v Pattron* [1978] R.P.C. 635, PC (infringement and passing off).
[17] [1978] R.P.C. 206 (Registry).
[18] [1979] R.P.C. 155 (Registry).
[19] [1979] R.P.C. 355.
[20] [1979] R.P.C. 469 (Registry).
[21] *Stuart v Rona* [1981]. F.S.R. 20 ("high probability" of confusion).
[22] *McCain v Country Fair* [1981] R.P.C. 69, CA (passing off).
[23] *"Nerit"* [1982] F.S.R. 72, CA. A remarkable decision.
[24] [1908] R.P.C. 237 (Registry).
[25] [1980] R.P.C. 243 (Registry).
[26] *Thermawear v Vedonis* [1982] R.P.C. 44 (infringement and passing off).
[27] [1985] R.P.C. 187 (Registry).
[28] *KODIAK Trade Mark* [1987] R.P.C. 269.
[29] *LANCER Trade Mark* [1987] R.P.C. 303.
[30] *BENJI Trade Mark* [1988] R.P.C. 251.
[31] *Mothercare U.K. Ltd v Penguin Books Ltd* [1988] R.P.C. 133.
[32] *The Ritz Hotel Ltd v Charles of the Ritz Ltd* [1989] R.P.C. 333 (Australia).
[33] *CHELSEA MAN Trade Mark* [1989] R.P.C. 111.
[34] *Furnitureland Ltd v Harris* [1989] 1 F.S.R. 536.
[35] *Unilever plc v Johnson Wax* [1989] 1 F.S.R. 145.
[36] *Portakabin Ltd v Powerblast Ltd* [1990] R.P.C. 471.
[37] *STAR Trade Mark* [1990] R.P.C. 522.
[38] *TERBULINE Trade Mark* [1990] R.P.C. 21.
[39] *THERMOS PRIMA Trade Mark* [1991] R.P.C. 120.
[40] *TORRE NOVA Trade Mark* [1991] R.P.C. 109.
[41] *Management Publications Ltd v Blenheim Exhibitions Group plc* [1991] F.S.R. 348.
[42] *Tamworth Herald Co Ltd v Thomson Free Newspapers Ltd* [1991] F.S.R. 337.
[43] *BENSYL Trade Mark* [1992] R.P.C. 529.
[44] *INADINE Trade Mark* [1992] R.P.C. 421.
[45] *Morgan-Grampian v Training Personnel Ltd* [1992] F.S.R. 267.
[46] *PRIMASPORT Trade Mark* [1992] F.S.R. 515.
[47] *UNIVER Trade Mark* [1993] R.P.C. 239.
[48] *Advance Magazine Publishing v Redwood Publishing Ltd* [1993] F.S.R. 449.
[49] *QUATTRO Trade Mark* [1993] F.S.R. 759 (Germany).

"Food Ireland" (and device).[50] "Diclomax Retard" (and device) not confusingly similar to "Voltarol Retard" (and device).[51] "Stellacream" too close to "Brylcreem".[52] "Jockey" allowed notwithstanding "Joker".[53] "Eye-Crom" confusingly similar to "Vicrom".[54] "Mini-Lift (serum)" confusingly similar to "Lift Serum" but not with "Crown Lift".[55] "Rose Cardin" refused in the light of "The Rose Garden".[56] "Origin" too similar to "Origins".[57] "Rajamama" confusingly similar to "Wagamama".[58] "International Telesis Group" too close to "Pacific Telesis International".[59] "Harrodian School" not too similar to Harrods".[60] "Neutralia" confusingly similar to "Neutrogena".[61] "Paton Calvert Cordon Bleu" distinguishable from "Constance Spry Cordon Blue" and from "Le Cordon Bleu, Paris, 1895".[62] "Opus" not infringed by "Farming Opus".[63] "Streetball" allowed despite "Setball".[64] "Eternity" not allowed in the face of "'Eternity' (used in conjunction with 'Calvin Klein')".[65] "Puffin (and get up)" confusingly similar to "Penguin (and get up)".[66] "Babewatch" not confusingly similar to "Baywatch".[67] "Zinc" infringed by "Zn" and "Zincbar", and would be infringed by "ZN", "Sinc" and "Sync".[68] "Green Peace" too close to "Green-peace".[69] "Vibradox" not confusingly similar to "Vibramycin".[70] "McAllan" confusingly similar to "McDonald's".[71] "Brava" infringed "Bravo".[72] "Stephanskreuz" (St Stephan's cross) allowed notwithstanding "Stephanskrone" (St Stephan's crown).[73] "Queen's Club" too similar to "Queen's Garden".[74] "Izod Lacoste" (and crocodile device) confusingly similar to "Lacoste" (and crocodile device).[75] "Le Lido" not confusingly similar to "Lido".[76] "UK Used" refused in the light of "Used".[77] "Comfort and Joy" not confusingly similar to "Joy".[78] "Audi-Med" allowed notwithstanding "Audi".[79] "Neutritive" likely to be confused with "Bionutritive a La Germastine".[80] "Eveready" allowed notwithstanding "Ever Ready".[81]

[50] *An Bord Trachtala v Waterford Foods plc* [1994] F.S.R. 316.
[51] *Ciba-Geigy plc v Parke Davis & Co Ltd* [1994] F.S.R. 8.
[52] *Beecham Group v Mohammed Ahmed Banafi* [1994] F.S.R. 685 (Saudi Arabia).
[53] *JOCKEY Trade Mark* [1994] F.S.R. 269.
[54] *Fisons plc v Norton Healthcare Ltd* [1994] F.S.R. 745.
[55] *MINI-LIFT Trade Mark* [1995] R.P.C. 128.
[56] *ROSE GARDEN Trade Mark* [1995] R.P.C. 246.
[57] *Origins Natural Resources v Origin Clothing Ltd* [1995] F.S.R. 280.
[58] *Wagamama Ltd v City Centre Restaurants plc* [1995] F.S.R. 713.
[59] *INTERNATIONAL TELESIS GROUP Service Mark* [1996] R.P.C. 45.
[60] *Harrods Ltd v Harrodian School Ltd* [1996] R.P.C. 697.
[61] *Neutrogena Corporation v Golden Ltd* [1996] R.P.C. 473.
[62] *PATON CALVERT CORDON BLEU Trade Mark* [1996] R.P.C. 94.
[63] *BASF plc v CEP (UK) plc* [1996] E.T.M.R. 51.
[64] *Adidas AG's Application* [1996] E.T.M.R. 66 (Portugal).
[65] *ETERNITY Trade Mark* [1997] R.P.C. 155.
[66] *United Biscuits v Asda* [1997] R.P.C. 513.
[67] *Baywatch Production Co Inc v The Home Video Channel* [1997] F.S.R. 22.
[68] *Sir Terence Orby Conran v Mean Fiddler Holdings Ltd* [1997] F.S.R. 856.
[69] *Stichting Greenpeace Council v Income Team Ltd* [1997] F.S.R. 149 (Hong Kong).
[70] *Pfizer International Inc v Durascan Medical Products A/S* [1997] E.T.M.R. 86 (Netherlands).
[71] *McDonald's Corporation USA v Allen Bjerrum Pedersen* [1997] E.T.M.R. 151 (Denmark).
[72] *Bravo Industry of Coffees SA v Fiat Auto SpA* [1997] E.T.M.R. 167 (Greece).
[73] *STEPHANSKREUZ Trade Mark Application* [1997] E.T.M.R. 182 (Germany).
[74] *QUEEN'S CLUB Trade Mark Application* [1997] E.T.M.R. 345 (Germany).
[75] *La Chemise Lacoste SA v Centro Tessile SrL* [1997] E.T.M.R. 520 (Italy).
[76] *Le Lido SA v Nationale Stichting Tot Exploitatie Van Casinospelen in Nederland* [1997] E.T.M.R. 537 (Netherlands).
[77] *Application of Union Mills SrL* [1997] E.T.M.R. 568.
[78] *Application of Merri Mayers-Head* [1997] E.T.M.R. 577.
[79] *AUDI-MED Trade Mark* [1998] R.P.C. 863.
[80] *NUTRITIVE Trade Mark* [1998] R.P.C. 621.
[81] *Oasis Stores Ltd's Trade Mark Application* [1998] R.P.C. 631.

"Open Country" distinguishable from "Openair".[82] "SWC Super Farm Fluid" too close to "Antec Farm Fluid S".[83] "Millennium" too close to "Millenia".[84] "The European" not confusingly similar to "European Voice".[85] "Jarvard" not confusingly similar to "Harvard".[86] Use of "Ca m'interesse" in the title of a radio program, confusingly similar to "Ca M'Interesse" registered for magazines.[87] "Visa" not infringed by "Visa Pour Le Muscle".[88] "Balmoral" too close to "Balmoral" and "Balmoral International".[89] "Elvis" and "Elvis Presley" not too close to "Elvisly Yours".[90] "Ener-Cap" registrable despite "EnerRing" and "EnerSeal".[91] "Fountain" confusingly similar to "Font Fountain".[92] "Lifesystem" distinguishable from "Lifestream".[93] "Naturelle" too close to "Natrel".[94] "Polaclip" allowed despite "Polaroid".[95] "QS by S. Oliver" too similar to "QS".[96] "Stopcar" confusingly similar to "Stopcard".[97] "Beauty Free Shop" too close to "Beauty Free".[98] "Humica, S.A." confusingly similar to "Humica".[99] "Horizon" (and device) distinguishable from "Ariston".[1] "La Sirena" registrable despite "Siena".[2] "Joy One Year" an infringement of "Joy".[3] "Jois & Jo" not confusingly similar to "Joy".[4] "Saint John's" not confusingly similar to "Saint-James".[5] "Isenbeck" not too close to "Beck's".[6] "Bill Baker Remembering The Glenn Miller Army Air Force Orchestra" not an infringement of "Glenn Miller".[7] "Pandau" not confusingly similar to "Up and Down".[8] "Andak" too close to "Zantac".[9] "Halloween" infringed by "Haribo-Halloween".[10] "Felix Le Souriceau" confusingly similar to "Felix the Cat".[11] "Sodeco" confusingly similar to "Sodexho".[12] "Technocite" infringed by "Techno Cite", but not confusingly similar to "Cite Des Sciences et De L'Industrie".[13] "Geo Poche" too close to "Geo".[14] "Fashion

---

[82] OPEN COUNTRY Trade Mark [1998] R.P.C. 408.

[83] Antec International Ltd v South-Western Chicks (Warren) Ltd [1998] F.S.R. 738.

[84] Pontiac Marina Pte Ltd v CDL Hotels International Ltd [1998] F.S.R. 839 (Singapore).

[85] The European Ltd v The Economist Newspapers Ltd [1998] F.S.R. 283.

[86] Kundry SA's Application [1998] E.T.M.R. 178.

[87] Prisma Presse SNC v Europe 1 Telecompagne SA [1998] E.T.M.R. 515 (France).

[88] Visa International (U.S.) v Editions Jibena [1998] E.T.M.R. 580 (France).

[89] BALMORAL Trade Mark [1999] R.P.C. 297.

[90] ELVIS PRESLEY Trade Marks [1999] R.P.C. 567.

[91] ENER-CAP Trade Mark [1999] R.P.C. 362.

[92] FOUNTAIN Trade Mark [1999] R.P.C. 490.

[93] LIFESYSTEMS Trade Mark [1999] R.P.C. 851.

[94] NATURELLE Trade Mark [1999] R.P.C. 326.

[95] POLACLIP Trade Mark [1999] R.P.C. 282.

[96] QS BY S. OLIVER Trade Mark [1999] R.P.C. 520.

[97] Electro Cad Australia Pty Ltd v Mejati RCS Sdn Bhd [1999] F.S.R. 291 (Malaysia).

[98] Beauty Free Shop BVBA's Application [1999] E.T.M.R. 20 (OHIM).

[99] Humic SA's Application [1999] E.T.M.R. 26 (OHIM).

[1] BAT Ltd's Application [1999] E.T.M.R. 32 (OHIM).

[2] Lutz Quasdorf v Les Sirenes SA [1999] 152 E.T.M.R. (OHIM).

[3] Jean Patou SA v Ste Zag Zeitschriften Verlag AG [1999] E.T.M.R. 157 (France).

[4] GTR Group's Application [1999] E.T.M.R. 164.

[5] Lyon v SA Rhums Martiniquais Saint-James [1999] E.T.M.R. 188 (France).

[6] Warsteiner Brauerei Haus GmbH & Co's Application [1999] E.T.M.R. 225 (OHIM).

[7] Glenn Miller Productions Inc v Stichting Bill Bakers Big Band Corporation [1999] E.T.M.R. 247 (Netherlands).

[8] Re PANDAU [1999] E.T.M.R. 267 (Spain).

[9] Glaxo Group Ltd v Knoll Aktiengesellschaft [1999] E.T.M.R. 358 (Denmark).

[10] Optos-Opus (SARL) v SA Haribo Ricqles Zan. [1999] E.T.M.R. 362 (France).

[11] Ste Felix The Cat Productions Inc v Ste Polygram [1999] E.T.M.R. 370 (France).

[12] Mars GB's Application [1999] E.T.M.R. 402 (OHIM).

[13] Cargo Communication Sarl v La Cité Des Sciences et De L'Industrie [1999] E.T.M.R. 545 (France).

[14] Prisma Presse Ste v SA Editions Economica [1999] E.T.M.R. 549 (France).

for You by NL" confusingly similar to "You" and "4 You".[15] "J'M" (incorporating the famous McDonalds arched 'M') not too close to "J'M Bien".[16] "21st Century Film" not confusingly similar to "XXIeme Siecle".[17] "Benecol" distinguishable from "Becel".[18] "First Lady" distinguishable from "Lady".[19] "Coq D'Or" (and cockerel device) not confusingly similar to "Victoria" (and cockerel device).[20] "Stitches" too close to "Broken Stitches".[21] "React" (and device) sufficiently different from "Reactor".[22] "Club Europe" not confusingly similar to "Club World".[23] "Amaze Collection" not confusingly similar to "Ama Zing".[24] "Jack and Danny's Rock Café" confusingly similar to "Hard Rock Café".[25] "Tahtimerkki Kauris" (in English, 'Sign of the Zodiac Capricorn') distinguishable from "Horoscope".[26] "Eudermin" confusingly similar to "Eucerin".[27] "Viagrene" too close to "Viagra".[28] "Nike" (and 'tick' device) deceptive in the light of "Nike" (and statue device).[29] "Dynalink" registrable despite "Dynanet".[30] "Principles" unregistrable in the light of "Principe".[31] "Super Mega" not an infringement of "Super Power" or "Mega Force".[32] "Cool and Slim" not too similar to "Slim".[33] "Trex" an infringement of "Trox" and "Tocillin" an infringement of "Celin" on the basis that customers might ask for "two Celin".[34] "Galaxia" not too similar to "Gala" for coffee.[35] "NLSPORT", "NLJEANS", "NLACTIVE" and "NLCollection" too similar to NL in fancy script.[36] Figurative "New Man" not too similar to figurative "New Look" and "New Girl".[37] "Kingsley" not too similar to "King Li".[38]

A31–005

2. Trade Names

(1) Injunctions granted

Hoby (carrying on The Grosvenor Library) v The Grosvenor Library Co;[39]; *Hendricks (on behalf of the Universal Life Assurance Society) v Montagu (promoter of the Universe Life Assurance Association;*[40] *The Accident Insurance Co Ltd v The Accident, Disease and General Insurance Co Ltd;*[41] *Madame Tussaud & Son Ltd v Louis Tussaud Ltd;*[42] *Wolmershausen v G. S. Wolmershausen & Co*

---

[15] *Hij Mannenmode BV v Nienhaus & Lotz GmbH* [1999] E.T.M.R. 730 (Benelux).
[16] *Norbert Robert Bertucci v McDonald's Corporation* [1999] E.T.M.R. 742 (France).
[17] *Casaubon v 21st Century Film France* [1999] E.T.M.R. 787 (France).
[18] *Unilever NV v Raisio Yhtyma Oy* [1999] E.T.M.R. 847 (Benelux).
[19] *Succès De Paris Sarl v SA Parfums Van Cleef et Arpels* [1999] E.T.M.R. 869 (France).
[20] *Fromex SA's Application* [1999] E.T.M.R. 989 (OHIM).
[21] *The House of Stitches Pty Ltd's Application* [1999] E.T.M.R. 994 (OHIM).
[22] *REACT AND DEVICE Trade Mark* [2000] R.P.C. 285.
[23] *CLUB EUROPE Trade Mark* [2000] R.P.C. 329.
[24] *AMAZE COLLECTION Trade Mark* [2000] R.P.C. 725.
[25] *Neil King's Application* [2000] E.T.M.R. 22.
[26] *Aaro Forsman OY's Application* [2000] E.T.M.R. 142 (Finland).
[27] *Icart SA's Application* [2000] E.T.M.R. 180 (France).
[28] *Pfizer Ltd v Eurofood Link (UK) Ltd* [2000] E.T.M.R. 187.
[29] *Comercial Iberica de Exclusivas Deportivas v Nike International Ltd* [2000] E.T.M.R. 189 (Spain).
[30] *Askey Computer Corporation's Application* [2000] E.T.M.R. 214 (Finland).
[31] *Principles Retail Ltd's Application* [2000] E.T.M.R. 240 (OHIM).
[32] *Sarl Mega Press v Pressimage* [2000] E.T.M.R. 403 (France).
[33] *Slim International v Delta Protypos Milk industry* [2000] E.T.M.R. 409 (Greece).
[34] *Glaxo Group v Neon Laboratories* [2004] F.S.R. 46, (HC of India).
[35] *Koffiebranderij en Theehandel v OHIM* [2005] ETMR 33 (CFI).
[36] *New Look Ltd v OHIM* [2005] ETMR 35 (CFI).
[37] *New Look Ltd v Newman* [2005] ETMR 36 (CFI).
[38] *Lidl v Kingsley* [2005] ETMR 38, (CFI).
[39] 28 W.R. 386.
[40] (1881) 17 Ch.D. 638.
[41] (1884) 54 Ch.D. 104.
[42] (1890) 44 Ch.D. 678.

Ltd;[43] *Premier Cycle Co Ltd v Premier Tube Co Ltd;*[44] *John Brinsmead & Co v Thomas Edward Brinsmead & Sons Ltd;*[45] *Pinet et Cie v Maison Pinet Ltd;*[46] *Pinet et Cie v Maison Louis Pinet Ltd.;*[47] *Eastman (whose trade name was* "Kodak") *v Griffiths* (promoters of the *Kodak Cycle Co Ltd*)[48] *Manchester Brewery Co Ltd v North Cheshire and Manchester Brewery Co Ltd;*[49] *Valentine Meat Juice Co v Valentine Extract Co Ltd;*[50] *Pearks, Gunston Tee Ltd (carrying on business as Tamley & Co) v Thompson, Talmey & Co;*[51] *Panhard et Levassor v Panhard-Levassor Motor Co Ltd;*[52] *Randall (trading as American Shoe Co) v British and American Shoe Co;*[53] *Fine Cotton Spinners, and John Cash & Sons Ltd v Harwood, Cash & Co Ltd;*[54] *International Plasmon v Plasmonade Ltd;*[55] *Standard Bank of South Africa Ltd v Standard Bank Ltd;*[56] *Dunlop Pneumatic Tyre Co Ltd v Dunlop Lubricant Co;*[57] *Ouvah Ceylon Estates Ltd v Uva Ceylon Rubber Estates Ltd;*[58] *Muratti & Sons Ltd v Murad Ltd;*[59] *Kingston, Miller & Co Ltd v Thomas Kingston & Co Ltd;*[60] *Lloyd's v Lloyd's (Southampton) Ltd;*[61] *Lloyd's Bank v Lloyd's Investment Trust Co Ltd;*[62] *Facsimile Letter Printing Co Ltd v Facsimile Typewriting Co;*[63] *Daimler Motor Co (1904) Ltd v London Daimler Co Ltd;*[64] *Teofani & Company Ltd v A. Teofani;*[65] *Ewing (trading as the Buttercup Dairy Company) v Buttercup Magarine Company Ltd;*[66] *Albion Motor Company Ltd v Albion Carriage and Motor Body Works Ltd;*[67] *R. & J. Pullman Ltd v Pullman;*[68] *Poiret v Jules Poiret Ltd and A.S. Nash;*[69] *M.P. Guimaraens & Son v Fonseca and Vasconcellos;*[70] *Dutton, Massey & Co (Liverpool) Ltd v Dut-*

---

[43] [1892] W.N. 87.

[44] (1896) 12 T.L.R. 481, interlocutory injunction granted, the defendant company's works had for six years been known as Premier Mills.

[45] (1896) 12 T.L.R. 631; 13 T.L.R. 3. *cf.* the second *Brinsmead* case (1913) 30 R.P.C. 493, CA.

[46] (1897) 14 R.P.C. 933.

[47] (1898) 15 R.P.C. 65.

[48] (1898) 15 R.P.C. 105.

[49] [1899] A.C. 83.

[50] (1900) 17 R.P.C. 673.

[51] (1901) 18 R.P.C. 185.

[52] [1901] 2 Ch. 513; 18 R.P.C. 405.

[53] (1902) 19 R.P.C. 393.

[54] [1907] 2 Ch. 184; 24 R.P.C. 533.

[55] (1905) 22 R.P.C. 543, interlocutory injunction granted.

[56] (1909) 26 R.P.C. 310.

[57] (1899) 16 R.P.C. 12.

[58] (1910) 27 R.P.C. 753. Ouvah and Uva were alternative spellings of the name of the same province in Ceylon, and both companies were rubber companies.

[59] (1911) 28 R.P.C. 497.

[60] [1912] 1 Ch. 575; .

[61] (1912) 29 R.P.C. 433.

[62] (1912) 29 R.P.C. 545.

[63] (1912) 29 R.P.C. 557.

[64] (1907) 24 R.P.C. 379. In *Army and Navy Co-operative Society Ltd v Army, Navy and Civil Service Co-operative Society of South Africa Ltd* (1902) R.P.C. 574, on appeal from an interlocutory injunction, the defendants agreed to change their name to "Naval, Military and Civil Service Co-operative Society of South Africa Ltd". In *Hopton Wood Stone Firms Ltd v Gething (trading as Hoptin Stone and Marble Quarrying Co)* (1910) 27 R.P.C. 605, the defendant undertook to prefix the word "New" to that style.

[65] (1913) 30 R.P.C. 446.

[66] [1917] 2 Ch. 1; 34 R.P.C. 232.

[67] (1917) 34 R.P.C. 257.

[68] (1919) 36 R.P.C. 240. This case was exceptional nature because the allegation was that people who *supplied* goods (skins for manufacture into leather) would be deceived, and probability of confusion was held to be established. *Held* that the plaintiff was entitled to a declaration with liberty to apply for an injunction.

[69] (1920) 37 R.P.C. 177.

[70] (1921) 38 R.P.C. 388.

ton, Massey & Co Ltd;[71] *Joseph Rodgers & Sons Ltd v W. N. Rodgers & Co*;[72] *Harrods Ltd v R. Harrod Ltd*;[73] *Reliance Rubber Company Ltd v Reliance Tyre Company Ltd*;[74] *Heels v Stafford Heels Ltd* (the plaintiffs being commonly known as Heels of Stafford);[75] *Heppels Ltd v Eppels Ltd*;[76] *Edison Accumulator Ltd v Edison Storage Batteries Ltd*;[77] *Mills v Chapman*;[78] *F. W. Woolworth & Co Ltd v Woolworths (Australasia) Ltd*;[79] *Madeira House Co Ltd v Madeira House (London) Ltd*;[80] *British Legion v British Legion Club (Street) Ltd*;[81] *British Medical Association v Marsh*;[82] *Crystalate Gramaphone Record Manufacturing Co Ltd v British Crystalite Co Ltd*;[83] *Radio Rentals Ltd v Rentals Ltd*;[84] *Hesketh Estates (Southport) Ltd v Droitwich Brine Banks Ltd*;[85] *The Clock Ltd v The Clock House Hotel*;[86] *Sturtevant Engineering Co Ltd v Sturtevant Mill Co Ltd of U.S.A.*;[87] *John Dickinson Ltd v Apsley Press Ltd*;[88] *Saville Perfumery Ltd v June Perfect Ltd and F. W. Woolworth & Co Ltd*;[89] *Plomien Fuel Economiser v National School of Salesmanship Ltd*;[90] *Delavelle (G.B.) Ltd v Harry Stanley*;[91] *Hines v Winnick*;[92] *Sales Affiliates Ltd v Le Jean Ltd*;[93] *C.C. Wakefield & Co Ltd v Sydney N. Laurence*;[94] *British Bata Shoe Company Ltd v Czechoslovakia Bata Co Ltd*;[95] *Music Corporation of America and another v Music Corporation (Great Britian) Ltd*;[96] *Midland Counties Dairy Ltd v Midland Dairies Ltd*;[97] *Marengo v Daily Sketch (Kem & Kim)*;[98] *Wright, Layman & Umney Ltd v Wright*;[99] *Dr. Barnado's Homes: National Incorporated Association v Barnado Amalga mated Industries Ltd and Jack Benardout*;[1] *Brestian v Try* restraining use of *"Charles of London"*;[2] *Parker Knoll Ltd v Knoll International Ltd*;[3] *Southern Music Publish-*

[71] (1922) 40 R.P.C. 413; (1924) 41 R.P.C. 67, CA.
[72] (1924) 41 R.P.C. 277.
[73] (1924) 41 R.P.C. 74.
[74] (1924) 42 R.P.C. 91.
[75] (1927) 44 R.P.C. 299.
[76] (1929) 46 R.P.C. 96.
[77] (1929) 46 R.P.C. 432.
[78] (1930) 47 R.P.C. 115; the plaintiff's circus was known as "London Olympia Circus" and the defendant was restrained from using the words London Olympia" in connection with a circus.
[79] (1930) 47 R.P.C. 337.
[80] (1930) 47 R.P.C. 481.
[81] (1931) 48 R.P.C. 555. Street was the name of a place in Somerset. The Club had no authority from the British Legion.
[82] (1931) 48 R.P.C. 565, the defendant was restrained from using the initials B.M.A., by which the plaintiffs were known.
[83] (1934) 51 R.P.C. 315.
[84] (1934) 51 R.P.C. 407.
[85] (1935) 52 R.P.C. 39, the plaintiffs being the owners of brine baths at Droitwich and carrying on business as "Brine Baths"; the hotels being only five miles apart.
[86] (1936) 53 R.P.C. 269.
[87] (1936) 53 R.P.C. 430.
[88] (1937) 54 R.P.C. 219, the plaintiffs being known as "Apsley."
[89] (1941) 58 R.P.C. 147.
[90] (1943) 60 R.P.C. 219.
[91] (1946) 63 R.P.C. 103 ("Blue Orchid" for brilliance).
[92] (1947) 64 R.P.C. 113 ("Dr Crock and his Crackpots").
[93] (1947) 64 R.P.C. 103 ("Jamal and Vapet").
[94] (1947) 64 R.P.C. 95.
[95] (1947) 64 R.P.C. 72 (interim injunction).
[96] (1947) 64 R.P.C. 41.
[97] (1948) 65 R.P.C. 429.
[98] (1948) 65 R.P.C. 242.
[99] (1948) 65 R.P.C. 186; 66 R.P.C. 149.
[1] (1949) 66 R.P.C. 103 (interlocutory injunction).
[2] [1958] R.P.C. 161; [1957] R.P.C. 443.
[3] [1958] R.P.C. 317.

ing Co Ltd v Southern Songs Ltd;[4] *John Letters & Co Ltd v Letters (Craigton) Ltd*;[5] *Suhner & Co A.G. v Suhner Ltd*;[6] *Legal & General Assurance Society v Daniel (trading as Legal & General Enquiry Bureau)*;[7] *Cavendish House (Cheltenham) Ltd v Cavendish-Woodhouse Ltd*;[8] "Pembridge Hotel" too close to "Pembridge Gardens Hotel.";[9] *Effluent Disposal Ltd v Midlands Effluent Disposal Ltd*;[10] *Laurie Mansfield Ltd (makers of Gay Girl ladies' clothing) v Gaygirl Ltd*;[11] *Hammond & Champness (known as "H & C" or "H + C") v H.A.C. Lifts Ltd.*[12]

"Nationwide Estate Agents" likely to be confusingly similar to "Nationwide".[13] "Chelsea Man" confusingly similar to "Chelsea Girl" (but no injunction as prior use established)[14] "2020 Communications" confusingly similar to "20/20 Telecom".[15] "Rajamama" confusingly similar to "Wagamama".[16] "International Telesis Group" too close to "Pacific Telesis International".[17] "Diabetic Society" confusingly similar to "British Diabetic Association".[18] "NAD Computer Systems" confusingly similar to "NAD Electronics".[19] "Compagnie Generale Des Eaux Sdn Bhd" confusingly similar to "Compagnie Generale Des Eaux".[20] "Zinc" infringed by "Zn" and "Zincbar", and would be infringed by "ZN", "Sinc" and "Sync".[21] "McAllan" confusingly similar to "McDonald's".[22] "Millennium Hotels" too close to "Ritz-Carlton, Millenia Singapore".[23] "RWS Translations" too similar to "Translations".[24] "Kilkenny Brewing Company Ltd" confusingly similar to "Kilkenny Irish Beer".[25]

(2) Injunctions refused A31–006

London and Provincial Law Assurance Society v London and Provincial Joint Stock Life Assurance Co;[26] Although there was evidence that the former company was usually called the London and Provincial Insurance Co; *London Assurance v London and Westminster Assurance Corporation*;[27] *Colonial Life Assurance Co v Home and Colonial Assurance Co Ltd*;[28] *London and County Banking Co v Capital and Counties Bank* (1878) Ch. D. 960 (cited in the next case); *Merchant Banking Co of London v Merchants', Joint Stock Bank*;[29] *The Army and Navy Co-*

---

[4] [1966] R.P.C. 137 (interlocutory injunction).

[5] [1967] R.P.C. 209 (Scots) (interim interdict).

[6] [1967] R.P.C. 336 (interim injunction to subscribers of defendants' memorandum of association to restrain them from "allowing the defendants to remain registered under its present name").

[7] [1968] R.P.C. 253 (interlocutory injunction).

[8] [1970] R.P.C. 234 (interlocutory injunction granted despite delay of eight months because of very strong *prima facie* case).

[9] *Bach & Jackson Ltd v Cowan* [1969] R.P.C. 156. (interlocutory injunction. Name not descriptive despite location of both hotels in "Pembridge" area).

[10] [1970] R.P.C. 238 (interlocutory injunction).

[11] [1968] F.S.R. 144 (interlocutory injunction).

[12] [1975] F.S.R. 131.

[13] *Nationwide Building Society v Nationwide Estate Agents Ltd* [1987] F.S.R. 579.

[14] *CHELSEA MAN Trade Mark* [1989] R.P.C. 111.

[15] *Stacey v 20/20 Communications plc* [1991] F.S.R. 49.

[16] *Wagamama Ltd v City Centre Restaurants plc* [1995] F.S.R. 713.

[17] *INTERNATIONAL TELESIS GROUP Service Mark* [1996] R.P.C. 45.

[18] *The British Diabetic Association v The Diabetic Society* [1996] F.S.R. 1.

[19] *NAD Electronics Inc v NAD Computer Systems Ltd* [1997] F.S.R. 380.

[20] *Compagnie Générale Des Eaux v Compagnie Generale Des Eaux Sdn Bhd* [1997] F.S.R. 610.

[21] *Sir Terence Orby Conran v Mean Fiddler Holdings Ltd* [1997] F.S.R. 856.

[22] *McDonald's Corporation USA v Allen Bjerrum Pedersen* [1997] E.T.M.R. 151 (Denmark).

[23] *Pontiac Marina Pte Ltd v CDL Hotels International Ltd* [1998] F.S.R. 839 (Singapore).

[24] *RWS Translations Ltd Sarl v Getten* [1999] E.T.M.R. 258 (France).

[25] *Guinness Ireland Group v Kilkenny Brewing Company Ltd* [1999] E.T.M.R. 807 (Eire).

[26] (1847) 17 L.J.Ch. 37.

[27] (1863) 32 L.J.Ch. 664.

[28] 33 Beav. 548; 33 L.J.Ch. 741.

[29] (1879) 9 Ch.D. 560.

operative Society Ltd v The Junior Army and Navy Stores Ltd;[30] *Australian Mortgage Land and Finance Co v Australian and New Zealand Mortgage Co;*[31] *National Cash Register Co Ltd v Theeman* (who was trading as the *Cash Register Co*)[32] *Saunders* (on behalf of the *Sun Life Assurance Society) v The Sun Life Assurance Co of Canada;*[33] *Scottish Union and National Insurance Co v Scottish National Insurance Co Ltd;*[34] *Daimler Motor Car Co Ltd v British Motor Traction Co (who were about to register the Daimler Wagon Co Ltd);*[35] *Aerators Ltd v Tollit* (the defendants being about to register Automatic Aerator Patents Ltd;[36] *Electromobile Co Ltd v British Electromobile Co Ltd;*[37] *British Vacuum Cleaner Co Ltd v New Vacuum Cleaner Co Ltd;*[38] *H. E. Randall Ltd (trading as American Shoe Co) v Bradley (trading as Anglo-American Shoe Co);*[39] *Dunlop Pneumatic Tyre Co Ltd v Dunlop Motor Co Ltd;*[40] *Meikle (trading as Kelvindale Chemical Co) v Williamson (trading as Kelvinside Chemical Co);*[41] *Royal Insurance Co Ltd v Midland Insurance Co;*[42] *Elliott (trading as the Trade Extension Co) v Expansion of Trade Ltd;*[43] *Standard Ideal Co v Standard Sanitary Manufacturing Co;*[44] *John Brinsmead & Sons Ltd v Brinsmead;*[45] *Bowden Brake Ltd v Bowden Wire Co Ltd;*[46] *Waring and Gillow Ltd. v Gillow and Gillow Ltd;*[47] *Society of Motor Manufacturers and Traders Ltd v Motor Manufacturers' and Traders' Mutual Insurance Co Ltd.*[48] In *Bumstead v the General Revesionary Co Ltd,* an interlocutory injunction was refused, because although the defendant company had adopted a name resembling that of the company of which the plaintiff was secretary, the General Reversionary and Investment Co, yet there was no probabililty of deception because the former was a small Liverpool concern, and the latter a very large London one.[49] *Tigon Mining and Finance Corporation Ltd v South Tigon Mining Co Ltd;*[50] *Jay's Ltd v Jacobi and Limburg;*[51] *Rolls Razor Ltd v Rolls (Lighters) Ltd and Others;*[52] *Natural Chemicals Ltd v Veno's Drug Co Ltd* and *Irving's Yeast-Vite (Consolidated) v Amblins Chemists Ltd;*[53] *John Jacques*

---

[30] (1879) Seb.Dig. at 393.

[31] [1880] W.N. 6, CA.

[32] (1907) 24 R.P.C. 211.

[33] [1894] 1 Ch. 537 (injunction against the use of the defendants' full name was refused, but the defendants gave an undertaking substantially not to use the name of "The Sun" or "The Sun Life" without adding the words "of Canada").

[34] (1908) 25 R.P.C. 560 (Scotland). The classes of business were quite distinct.

[35] (1901) 18 R.P.C. 465. *cf. Daimler Motor Car (1904) Ltd v London Daimler Motor Co Ltd* (1907) 24 R.P.C. 379.

[36] [1902] 2 Ch. 319; 19 R.P.C. 418.

[37] (1908) 25 R.P.C. 149.

[38] [1907] 2 Ch. 312; 24 R.P.C. 641.

[39] (1907) 24 R.P.C. 657, 773.

[40] [1907] A.C. 430; 24 R.P.C. 572.

[41] (1909) 26 R.P.C. 775, Ct of Sess (Scotland).

[42] (1909) 25 R.P.C. 728; 26 R.P.C. 95. The plaintiffs became successors in business in the year 1892, of the Midland Counties Insurance Co.

[43] (1909) 27 R.P.C. 54.

[44] (1910) 27 R.P.C. 789.

[45] (1913) 30 R.P.C. 493.

[46] (1913) 30 R.P.C. 580.

[47] (1916) 33 R.P.C. 173.

[48] (1925) 42 R.P.C. 307.

[49] (1888) 4 T.L.R. 621.

[50] (1931) 48 R.P.C. 526, the word "Tigon" was held to have acquired a geographical signification, and there was no passing off of any goods.

[51] (1933) 50 R.P.C. 132; the defendants were using the name "Jays", but the first defendant had previously been known in business as "Miss Jay".

[52] (1949) 66 R.P.C. 137 and 299.

[53] (1940) 57 R.P.C. 323.

and Sons Ltd v Chess (a firm);[54] *Bear (Thomas) and Sons (India) Ltd v Prayag Narain and Jagernath;*[55] *Stillitz v Jones and Higgins Ltd;*[56] *v S. Subbiah Nadar v E.P. Kumaraval and Others;*[57] *Office Cleaning Services Ltd v Westminster Window and General Cleaners;*[58] *Harold Lee (Mantles) Ltd v Harold Harley (Fashions) Ltd;*[59] *Drive Yourself Hire Co (London) Ltd v Parish (trading as Self Drive Cars);*[60] *Dorothy Perkins Ltd v Polly Perkins of Picadilly Ltd;*[61] *Green Arrow Rentaflower Ltd v Renta Flower Ltd;*[62] *Salaried Persons Postal Loans Ltd v Postal & Salaried Loans of Glasgow Ltd;*[63] *Morecambe & Heysham (Promoters of "Miss Great Britain" beauty contest) v Mecca Ltd (Promoters of "Miss Britain");*[64] *Bristol-Myers Co v Bristol Pharmaceutical Co Ltd;*[65] *Marathon Oil Co v Marathon Shipping Co Ltd;*[66] *Coral Index Ltd v Regent Index Ltd;*[67] *The Pet Library (London) Ltd v Walter Ellson & Son Ltd ("Ellson's Pet Library");*[68] *Park Court Hotel Ltd ("Hotel International") v Trans-World Hotels Ltd ("London International Hotel");*[69] *Industrial Furnaces Ltd v Reaves Industrial Furnaces Ltd;*[70] *Banbury Buildings Ltd v Sectional Concrete Buildings Ltd ("Banbury Mail Order");*[71] *Sterling-Winthrop Inc. v Farbenfabriken Bayer A.G.*[72] "Furniture City" distinguishable from "Furnitureland".[73] "Kem" not confusingly similar to "Kim".[74]

---

[54] (1939) 56 R.P.C. 415 and 57 R.P.C. 77, CA, reversing Crossman J. (use of "Staunton" for chessmen).

[55] (1941) 58 R.P.C. 25.

[56] (1943) 60 R.P.C. 15.

[57] (1946) 63 R.P.C. 187 (Photo Mark Beedies).

[58] (1944) 61 R.P.C. 21, 133, CA, (reversing Morton J.); 63 R.P.C. 39, HL.

[59] (1954) 71 R.P.C. 57.

[60] [1957] R.P.C. 307.

[61] [1962] R.P.C. 153; dress shops, the plaintiffs had none in the town where the defendants' was, interlocutory injunction refused on the balance of convenience.

[62] [1966] R.P.C. 19 (Scots). (Interim interdict recalled because delay had prejudiced defendants' position).

[63] [1966] R.P.C. 24 (Scots). (Interim interdict recalled because names were descriptive and balance of convenience was in defendants' favour).

[64] [1962] R.P.C. 145 (interlocutory relief refused); [1966] R.P.C. 423 (final relief refused). The case turned on the limited sorts of confusion held relevant.

[65] [1968] R.P.C. 259 (interlocutory injunction).

[66] [1968] R.P.C. 443 (interlocutory injunction). Case turned on balance of convenience, particularly the fact that the business were in different fields.

[67] [1970] R.P.C. 147 (interlocutory injunction). Businesses were gambling on performance of Share Index.

[68] [1968] F.S.R. 359 (interlocutory injunction).

[69] [1970] F.S.R. 89 (interlocutory injunction). Court accepted small differences.

[70] [1970] R.P.C. 605.

[71] [1970] R.P.C. 463.

[72] [1966] R.P.C. 477 ("Bayer" distinctive of plaintiffs, but interlocutory injunction refused against "Bayer, Germany).

[73] *Furnitureland Ltd. v Harris* [1989] 1 F.S.R. 536.

[74] *Marengo v Daily Sketch* [1992] F.S.R. 1.

Olympic Symbol etc. (Protection) Act 1995

1995 CHAPTER 32

A32–001   *An Act to make provision about the use for commercial purposes of the Olympic symbol and certain words associated with the Olympic games; and for connected purposes.*

[19th July 1995]

The Olympics association right

Creation

A32–002   **1.**—(1) There shall be a right, to be known as the Olympics association right.

(2) The right shall carry with it the rights and remedies provided by this Act, which shall be exercisable by such person as the Secretary of State may be order made by statutory instrument appoint for the purposes of this subsection.

(3) An order under subsection (2) above which revokes a previous order under that subsection may contain such supplementary and transitional provision as the Secretary of State thinks fit.

(4) A statutory instrument containing an order under subsection (2) above shall be subject to annulment in pursuance of a resolution of either House of Parliament.

Rights conferred

A32–003   **2.**—(1) The Olympics association right shall confer exclusive rights in relation to the use of the Olympic symbol, the Olympic motto and the protected words.

(2) Subject to sections 4 and 5 below, the rights conferred by subsection (1) above shall be infringed by any act done in the United Kingdom which—

    (a) constitutes infringement under section 3 below, and

    (b) is done without the consent of the person for the time being appointed under section 1 (2) above (in the Act referred to as "the proprietor").

(3) The proprietor may exploit the rights conferred by subsection (1) above for gain, but may not make any disposition of, or of any interest in or over, them.

(4) This section shall not have effect to permit the doing of anything which would otherwise be liable to be prevented by virtue of a right—

    (a) subsisting immediately before the day on which this Act comes into force, or

    (b) created by—

        (i) the registration of a design under the Registered Designs Act 1949 on or after the date on which this Act comes into force, or

        (ii) the registration of a trade mark under the Trade Marks Act 1994 on or after that day.

(5) Consent given for the purposes of subsection (2) (b) above by a person appointed under section 1(2) above shall, subject to its terms, be binding on any person subsequently appointed under that provision; and references in this Act to

doing anything with, or without, the consent of the proprietor shall be construed accordingly.

Infringement

3.—(1) A person infringes the Olympics association right if in the course of trade he uses—   **A32–004**

    (a) a representation of the Olympic symbol, the Olympic motto or a protected word, or

    (b) a representation of something so similar to the Olympic symbol or the Olympic motto as to be likely to create in the public mind an association with it,

(in this Act referred to as "a controlled representation").

(2) For the purposes of this section, a person uses a controlled representation if, in particular, he—

    (a) affixes it to goods or the packaging thereof,

    (b) incorporates it in a flag or banner,

    (c) offers or exposes for sale, puts on the market or stocks for those purposes goods which bear it or whose packaging bears it,

    (d) imports or exports goods which bear it or whose packaging bears it,

    (e) offers or supplies services under a sign which consists of or contains it, or

    (f) uses it on business papers or in advertising.

Limits on effect

4.—(1) The Olympics association right is not infringed by use of a controlled representation where—   **A32–005**

    (a) the use consists of use in a work of any of the descriptions mentioned in subsection (3) below, and

    (b) the person using the representation does not intend the work to be used in relation to goods or services in circumstances which would involve an infringement of the Olympics association right,

provided the use is in accordance with honest practices in industrial or commercial matters.

(2) The Olympics association right is not infringed by use of a controlled representation where—

    (a) the use consists of use of a work of any of the descriptions mentioned in subsection (3) below, and

    (b) the use of the work is not in relation to goods or services,

provided the use of the representation is in accordance with honest practices in industrial or commercial matters.

(3) The descriptions of work referred to in subsections (1)(a) and (2)(a) above are a literary work, a dramatic work, a musical work, an artistic work, a sound recording, a film, a broadcast and a cable programme, in each case within the meaning of Part I of the Copyright, Designs and Patents Act 1988.

(4) For the purposes of subsection (2)(b) above, there shall be disregarded any use in relation to a work which—

    (a) is of any of the descriptions mentioned in subsection (3) above, and

    (b) is to any extent about the Olympic games or the Olympic movement.

(5) For the purposes of subsection (2)(b) above, use of a work in relation to goods shall be disregarded where—

(a) the work is to any extent about the Olympic games or the Olympic movement, and

(b) the person using the work does not do so with a view to gain for himself or another or with the intent to cause loss to another.

(6) In the case of a representation of a protected word, the Olympics association right is not infringed by use which is not such as ordinarily to create an association with—

(a) the Olympic games or the Olympic movement, or

(b) a quality ordinarily associated with the Olympic games or the Olympic movement.

(7) In the case of a representation of a protected word, the Olympics association right is not infringed by use which creates an association between the Olympic games or the Olympic movement and any person or thing where the association fairly represents a connection between the two, provided the use is in accordance with honest practices in industrial or commercial matters.

(8) The Olympics association right is not infringed by use of a controlled representation where—

(a) the use is in relation to goods which bear, or whose packaging bears, the representation,

(b) the goods are not infringing goods by virtue of paragraph (a) or (b) of section 7(2) below, and

(c) the use involves doing any of the things mentioned in section 3(2)(c) or (d) above.

(9) The Olympics association right is not infringed by use of a controlled representation where—

(a) the use is in relation to goods,

(b) the goods have been put on the market in the European Economic Area by the proprietor or with his consent, and

(c) the representation was used in relation to the goods when they were so put on the market.

(10) Subsection (9) above shall not apply where there exist legitimate reasons for the proprietor to oppose further dealings in the goods (in particular, where the condition of the goods has been changed or impaired after they have been put on the market).

(11) The Olympics association right is not infringed by use of a controlled representation where—

(a) the use is for the purposes of an undertaking, and

(b) the way in which the representation is used for the purposes of the undertaking is a way in which it has been continuously used for those purposes since a date prior to the commencement of this Act.

(12) In the case of a representation of a protected word, the Olympics association right is not infringed by use as part of—

(a) the name of a company, being a name which was the company's corporate name immediately before the day on which this Act comes into force, or

(b) the name under which a business is carried on, being a business which was carried on under that name immediately before the day on which this Act comes into force.

(13) The Olympics association right is not infringed by use of a controlled representation where the use—

(a) takes place under a right subsisting immediately before the day on which this Act comes into force, or

(b) is liable to be prevented by virtue of such a right.

(14) The Olympics association right is not infringed by use of a controlled representation where the use—

(a) takes place under a right created by—

  (i) the registration of a design under the Registered Designs Act 1949 on or after the day on which this Act comes into force, or

  (ii) the registration of a trade mark under the Trade Marks Act 1994 on or after that day, or

(b) is liable to be prevented by virtue of such a right.

(15) The Olympics association right is not infringed by use of a controlled representation for the purposes of—

(a) judicial or parliamentary proceedings, or

(b) a Royal Commission or statutory inquiry.

(16) In subsection (15) above—

"judicial proceedings" includes proceedings before any court, tribunal or person having authority to decide any matter affecting a person's legal rights or liabilities;

"parliamentary proceedings" includes proceedings of the Northern Ireland Assembly or of the European Parliament;

"Royal Commission" includes a Commission appointed for Northern Ireland by the Secretary of State in pursuance of the prerogative powers of Her Majesty delegated to him under section 7(2) of the Northern Ireland Constitution Act 1973; and

"statutory inquiry" means an inquiry held or investigation conducted in pursuance of a duty imposed or power conferred by or under an enactment.

(17) In this section, references to use of a work in relation to goods include use of a work on goods.

Power to prescribe further limits on effect

5.—(1) The Secretary of State may by order made by statutory instrument specify additional cases in which the Olympics association right is not infringed.   **A32–006**

(2) Without prejudice to the generality of subsection (1) above, the matters by reference to which a case may be specified under that subsection include—

(a) the description of controlled representation used, and

(b) the description of persons by whom a controlled representation is used.

(3) An order under this section may contain such supplementary and transitional provision and savings as the Secretary of State thinks fit.

Remedies in relation to infringement

Action for infringement

6.—(1) An infringement of the Olympic association right shall be actionable by the proprietor.   **A32–007**

(2) In an action for infringement, all such relief by way of damages, injunctions, accounts or otherwise shall be available to the proprietor as is available in respect of the infringement of a property right.

Orders in relation to infringing goods material or articles

7.—(1) The Secretary of State may by regulations make, in relation to infring-   **A32–008**

ing goods, material and articles, provision corresponding to that made by the following provisions of the Trade Marks Act 1994 in relation to goods, material and articles which are infringing goods, material and articles for the purposes of that Act—

> Section 15 (order for erasure etc. of offending sign),
> section 16 (order for delivery up of infringing goods, material or articles),
> section 18 (period after which remedy of delivery up not available),
> section 19 (order as to disposal of infringing goods, material or articles), and
> section 20 (jurisdiction in Scotland and Northern Ireland in relation to proceedings for an order under section 16 or 19).

(2) Goods are "infringing goods" for the purposes of this Act if they or their packaging bear a controlled representation and—

(a) the application of the representation to the goods or their packaging was an infringement of the Olympics association right,

(b) the goods are proposed to be imported into the United Kingdom and the application of the representation in the United Kingdom to them or their packaging would be an infringement of that right, or

(c) the representation has otherwise been used in relation to the goods in such a way as to infringe that right.

(3) Material is "infringing material" for the purposes of this Act if it bears a controlled representation and either—

(a) it is used for labelling or packaging goods, as a business paper, or for advertising goods or services, in such a way as to infringe the Olympics association right, or

(b) it is intended to be so used and such use would infringe that right.

(4) Articles are "infringing articles" for the purposes of this Act if they are articles—

(a) which are specifically designed or adapted for making copies of a controlled representation, and

(b) which a person has in his possession, custody or control, knowing or having reason to believe that they have been or are to be used to produce infringing goods or material.

(5) The power conferred by subsection (1) above shall be exercisable by statutory instrument which shall be subject to annulment in pursuance of a resolution of either House of Parliament.

(6) Nothing in subsection (2) above shall be construed as affecting the importation of goods which may lawfully be imported into the United Kingdom by virtue of an enforceable Community right.

Criminal sanctions

Offences in relation to goods

A32–009   **8.**—(1) A person shall be guilty of an offence if with a view to gain for himself or another, or with intent to cause loss to another, and without the consent of the proprietor, he—

(a) applies a controlled representation to goods or their packaging,

(b) sells or lets for hire, offers or exposes for sale or hire or distributes goods which bear, or the packaging of which bears, such a representation, or

(c) has in his possession, custody or control in the course of a business any such goods with a view to the doing of anything, by himself or another, which would be an offence under paragraph (b) above.

(2) A person shall be guilty of an offence if with a view to gain for himself or another, or with intent to cause loss to another, and without the consent of the proprietor, he—

    (a) applies a controlled representation to material intended to be used—
        (i) for labelling or packaging goods,
        (ii) as a business paper in relation to goods, or
        (iii) for advertising goods,

    (b) uses in the course of a business material bearing such a representation for labelling or packaging goods, as a business paper in relation to goods, or for advertising goods, or

    (c) has in his possession, custody or control in the course of a business any such material with a view to the doing of anything, by himself or another, which would be an offence under paragraph (b) above.

(3) A person shall be guilty of an offence if with a view to gain for himself or another, or with intent to cause loss to another, and without the consent of the proprietor, he—

    (a) makes an article specifically designed or adapted for making copies of a controlled representation, or

    (b) has such an article in his possession, custody or control in the course of a business,

knowing or having reason to believe that it has been, or is to be, used to produce goods, or material for labelling or packaging goods, as a business paper in relation to goods, or for advertising goods.

(4) It shall be a defence for a person charged with an offence under this section to show that he believed on reasonable grounds that the use of the representation in the manner in which it was used, or was to be used, was not an infringement of the Olympics association right.

(5) A person guilty of an offence under this section shall be liable—

    (a) on summary conviction, to a fine not exceeding the statutory maximum, and

    (b) on conviction on indictment, to a fine.

Supplemental provisions to summary proceedings Scotland

9.—(1) Notwithstanding anything in section 331 of the Criminal Procedure (Scotland) Act 1975, summary proceedings in Scotland for an offence under this Act may be begun at any time within six months after the date on which evidence sufficient in the Lord Advocate's opinion to justify the proceedings came to his knowledge.   **A32–010**

(2) For the purposes of subsection (1) above—

    (a) a certificate of the Lord Advocate as to the date mentioned in that subsection shall be conclusive evidence, and

    (b) proceedings in Scotland shall be deemed to be begun on the date on which a warrant to apprehend or to cite the accused is granted, if such warrant is executed without undue delay.

Partnership and bodies corporate

10. Section 101 of the Trade Marks Act 1994 (offences committed by partnerships and bodies corporate) shall apply in relation to an offence under this Act as it applies in relation to an offence under that Act.   **A32–011**

Forfeiture of counterfeit goods, etc.

Forfeiture: England and Wales or Northern Ireland

A32–012   **11.**—(1) Section 97 of the Trade Marks Act 1994 (which makes provision about the forfeiture of certain goods, material or articles which come into the possession of any person in connection with the investigation or prosecution of a relevant offence) shall also have effect with the following modifications.

(2) In subsection (1) (which describes the goods, material or articles concerned)—

(a) in paragraph (a), for "sign identical to or likely to be mistaken for a registered trade mark" there shall be substituted "representation within paragraph (a) or (b) of section 3(1) of the Olympic Symbol etc. (Protection) Act 1995", and

(b) in paragraphs (b) and (c), for "sign" there shall be substituted "representation".

(3) In subsection (7)(a) (power of court to direct release instead of destruction on condition that offending sign erased etc.) for "sign" there shall be substituted "representation".

(4) In subsection (8) (which defines "relevant offence") for "section 92 above (unauthorised use of trade mark etc. in relation to goods)" there shall be substituted "section 8 of the Olympic Symbol etc. (Protection) Act 1995".

Forfeiture: Scotland

A32–013   **12.**—(1) Section 98 of the Trade Marks Act 1994 (which makes provision about the forfeiture of certain goods, material or articles on application by the procurator-fiscal or where a person is convicted of a relevant offence) shall also have effect with the following modifications.

(2) In subsection (1) (which describes the goods, material or articles concerned)—

(a) in paragraph (a), for "sign identical to or likely to be mistaken for a registered trade mark" there shall be substituted "representation within paragraph (a) or (b) of section 3(1) of the Olympic Symbol etc. (Protection) Act 1995", and

(b) in paragraphs (b) and (c), for "sign" there shall be substituted "representation".

(3) In subsection (13) (power of court to direct release instead of destruction on condition that offending sign erased etc.) for "sign" there shall be substituted "representation".

(4) In subsection (14), in the definition of "relevant offence", for "section 92 (unauthorised use of trade mark, &c. in relation to goods)" there shall be substituted "section 8 of the Olympic Symbol etc. (Protection) Act 1995".

Restrictions on acquisition of competing rights

Registration designs and trade marks

A32–014   **13.**—(1) [...]

(2) In section 4 of the Trade Marks Act 1994 (which specifies cases where a trade mark shall not be registered) there shall be inserted at the end—

"(5) A trade mark which consists of or contains a controlled representation within the meaning of the Olympic Symbol etc. (Protection) Act 1995 shall not be registered unless it appears to the registrar—

(a) that the application is made by the person for the time being appointed under section 1(2) of the Olympic Symbol etc. (Protection) Act 1995 (power of Secretary of State to appoint a person as the proprietor of the Olympics association right), or

(b) that consent has been given by or on behalf of the person mentioned in paragraph (a) above."

(3) This section has effect in relation to applications for registration made on or after the day on which this Act comes into force.

Amendment

Subsection (1) deleted by SI 2001/3949 (Registered Design Regulations), Sch.2, para.1.

Acquisition of design right

14.—(1) In section 213 of the Copyright, Designs and Patents Act 1988 (design right in original designs) after subsection (5) there shall be inserted—   **A32–015**

"(5A) Design right does not subsist in a design which consists of or contains a controlled representation within the meaning of the Olympic Symbol etc. (Protection) Act 1995."

(2) Subsection (1) above has effect in relation to designs created on or after the day on which this Act comes into force.

(3) For the purposes of subsection (2) above, a design is created on the first day on which—

(a) it is recorded in a design document, or

(b) an article is made to it.

Miscellaneous

Power to give directions to proprietor

15.—(1) The proprietor shall comply with any directions given by the Secretary of State with respect to the exercise of the rights conferred by section 2(1) above.   **A32–016**

(2) Directions under this section may be of a general or particular character and may be varied or revoked by subsequent directions.

(3) A transaction between any person and the proprietor in his capacity as such shall not be void by reason only that the transaction was carried out in contravention of a direction given under this section; and a person dealing with the proprietor shall not be concerned to see or enquire whether a direction under this section has been given or complied with.

Remedy for groundless threats of infringement proceedings

16.—(1) Where the proprietor threatens another with proceedings for infringement of the Olympics association right other than—   **A32–017**

(a) the application to goods or their packaging of a controlled representation,

(b) the importation of goods to which, or to the packaging of which, such a representation has been applied, or

(c) the supply of services under a sign which consists of or contains such a representation,

any person aggrieved may being proceedings for relief under this section.

(2) The relief which may be applied for is any of the following—

    (a) a declaration that the threats are unjustifiable,

    (b) an injunction against the continuance of the threats, and

    (c) damages in respect of any loss he has sustained by the threats;

(3) A plaintiff under this section shall be entitled to the relief applied for unless the defendant shows that the acts in respect of which proceedings were threatened constitute (or if done would constitute) an infringement of the Olympics association right.

(4) The mere notification of the rights conferred by this Act shall not constitute a threat of proceedings for the purposes of this section.

Burden of proof

A32–018   **17.**—(1) Subject to subsection (2) below, if in any civil proceedings under this Act a question arises as to the use to which a controlled representation has been put, it shall be for the proprietor to show what use was made of it.

(2) If in any civil proceedings under this Act a question arises as to the application of any of subsections (1), (2) and (6) to (15) of section 4 above or any case specified under section 5 above, it shall be for the person who alleges that the subsection or case applies to show that it does.

General

Interpretation

A32–019   **18.**—(1) In this Act—

    "business" includes a trade or profession;

    "controlled representation" has the meaning given by section 3(1) above;

    "infringing articles" has the meaning given by section 7(4) above;

    "infringing goods" has the meaning given by section 7(2) above;

    "infringing material" has the meaning given by section 7(3) above;

    "Olympic motto" means the motto of the International Olympic Committee, "Citius, altius, fortius";

    "Olympic symbol" means the symbol of the International Olympic Committee, consisting of five interlocking rings;

    "proprietor" has the meaning given by section 2(2) above; and

    "trade" includes a business or profession.

(2) For the purposes of this Act each of the following is a protected word, namely, "Olympiad", "Olympiads", "Olympian", "Olympians", "Olympic" and "Olympics".

(3) In this Act, references to the Olympic motto or a protected word include the motto or word in translation into any language.

(4) In the application of this Act to Scotland—

    "accounts" means count, reckoning and payment;

    "declaration" means declarator;

    "defendant" means defender;

    "injunction" means interdict; and

    "plaintiff" means pursuer.

Short title, commencement and extent

19.—(1) This Act may be cited as the Olympic Symbol etc. (Protection) Act   **A32–020**
1995.

(2) This Act shall come into force on such day as the Secretary of State may
by order made by statutory instrument appoint.

(3) This Act extends to Northern Ireland.

APPENDIX 33

ECJ Cases on Absolute Grounds

A33–001

	Mark (*Party*/Translation of Mark)	Case No.	AG	Judg-ment or Order	Date	Grounds (Dir/Reg)	Outcome re distinctive character
1	CHIEMSEE (*Windsurfing*)	C–108/97	Cosmas	Jmt	04.05.99	3.1.c 3.3	For National Court
2	BABY-DRY	C–383/99	Jacobs	Jmt	20.09.01	7.1.c 6.1.a	Registrable
3	BRAVO (*Merz & Krell*)	C–517/99	Co-lomer	Jmt	04.10.01	3.1.d	Not
4	Shape of 3-headed shaver (*Philips*)	C–299/99	Co-lomer	Jmt	18.06.02	3.1.e 3.3 3.1.a 2	Not
5	COMPANYLINE	C–104/00	Co-lomer	Jmt	19.09.02	7.1.b	Not
6	Smell mark (*Sieckmann*)	C–273/00	Co-lomer	Jmt	12.12.02	2	—
7	Shapes—forklift truck, torch, watch (*Linde, Winward, Rado*)	C–53/01 C–54/01 C–55/01	Co-lomer	Jmt	08.04.03	3.1.b 3.1.c	Not
8	Colour Orange (*Libertel*)	C–104/01	Leger		06.05.03	2 3.1.b 3.3	—
9	DOUBLEMINT (*Wrigley*)	C–191/01	Jacobs	Jmt	23.10.03	7.1.c	Not

	Mark (*Party*/Translation of Mark)	Case No.	AG	Judg-ment or Order	Date	Grounds (Dir/Reg)	Outcome re distinctive character
10	Sound Marks (*Shield Mark*)	C–283/01	Co-lomer	Jmt	27.11.03	2	—
11	UNIVERSAL TELEFONBUCH (Universal Telephone Book/Directory) UNIVERSALKOMMUNIKATIONS-VERZEICHNIS (Universal Communications Directory)	C–326/01	Co-lomer	Order	05.02.04	7.1.c 7.1.b	Not
12	STREAMSERVE	C–150/02P	Jacobs	Order	05.02.04	7.1.c	Not
13	POSTKANTOOR (Post Office)	C–363/99	Co-lomer	Jmt	12.02.04	3.1.c 3.1.b 2	Not
14	BIOMILD (*Campina Melkunie*)	C–265/00	Co-lomer	Jmt	12.02.04	3.1.c	Not
15	Shape of detergent bottle (*Henkel*)	C–218/01	Co-lomer	Jmt	12.02.04	3.1.b, 3.1.e	Not

	Mark (*Party*/Translation of Mark)	Case No.	AG	Judg-ment or Order	Date	Grounds (Dir/Reg)	Outcome re distinctive character
16	Detergent Tablets—square—black and white—rectangular—black and white—square—white—pale green—square—white with green speckles—pale green—square—white with yellow and blue speckles—square—white with blue speckles—square—white with green and blue speckles—rectangular—red/white—rectangular—green/white (*Procter & Gamble, Henkel*)	C–456/01 C–457/01 C–468/01 C–469/01 C–470/01 C–471/01 C–472/01 C–473–01 C–474/01	Co-lomer	Jmt	29.04.04	7.1.b	Not
17	Colours Blue and Yellow (*Heidelberger Bauchemie*)	C–49/02	Leger	Jmt	24.06.04	2	—
18	Glass pattern (*Glaverbel*)	C–445/02	Jacobs	Order	28.06.04	7.1.b	Not
19	NICHOLS	C–404/02	Co-lomer	Jmt	16.09.04	3.1.b 6.1.a	For national court
20	SAT.2	C–329/02	Jacobs	Jmt	16.09.04	7.1.b, 7.1.c	Registrable
21	Shape of waisted soap bar (*Procter & Gamble*)	C–107/03	Co-lomer	Jmt	23.09.04	7.1.b	Not
22	BSS (*Alcon*)	C–192/03P	Maduro	Order	05.10.04	7.1.d	Not
23	Shape of a torch (*Mag Instrument*)	C–136/02	Co-lomer	Jmt	07.10.04	7.1.b	Not
24	DAS PRINZIP DER BEQUEMLICHKEIT (The Comfort Principle)	C–64/02	Maduro	Jmt	21.10.04	7.1.b	Registrable

	Mark (*Party*/Translation of Mark)	Case No.	AG	Judg-ment or Order	Date	Grounds (Dir/Reg)	Outcome re distinctive character
25	Orange (*KWS Saat*)	C–447/02	Leger	Jmt	21.10.04	7.1.b	Not
26	NEW BORN BABY	C–498/01	Jacobs	Order	01.12.04	7.1.b 7.1.c	Appln Withdrawn
27	HAVE A BREAK	C–353/03	Kokott 27.01.05	Jmt	07.07.05	3.3	For national court
	BioID	C–37/03P		Pending			
	TDI (*Audi*)	C–82/04P		Pending			
	Shape of Corona bottle (*Eurocermex*)	C–286/04		Pending			

Index